W9-ARN-219

26 November 2020

Chris,

I wanted to get this book for you and your siblings to give you a little better idea of what the life was like. In particular this explains why I didn't tell you all about what I did, and also why I chose to do so at a particular time. The author and I had different jobs, but were involved in similar activities but from different perspectives. The very beginning of the book will give you an idea of what Rob's Dad was doing. I hope you find it interesting. I keep giving you all books so you can see now things I could not tell you when you

NOV 2020

The Craft We Chose

CHRIS,

Best wishes down the road,

Dick Holm

were growing up.

Love, Dad

The Craft We Chose

My Life in the CIA

Richard L. Holm

Mountain Lake Press

Mountain Lake Park, Maryland

The Craft We Chose: My Life in the CIA

Published in the United States of America
by Mountain Lake Press
www.mountainlakepress.com

Library of Congress Control Number: 2011928134
ISBN 978-0-9814773-7-4

Design by Michael Hentges

Printed in the United States of America
10 9 8 7 6 5 4 3 2

To Judy, my inspiration

AUTHOR'S NOTE

In this text I have identified some people only by their first names or sometimes with just an initial for their surnames. For others I've changed their true names. In these cases I did so to preserve their privacy or security.

I submitted the draft manuscript of this book to the agency's Publications Review Board. I freely accept this requirement, including the disclaimer displayed below.

The board functions solely to identify any information that might remain classified. Otherwise it cannot censor or alter the text in any way.

This is my story—my life in the CIA.

Richard L. Holm
Virginia, May 2011

Contents

The Craft We Chose

Foreword

APRIL 20, 2011

You can learn a lot about a person when you become the instrument of their pain. That's how it began with me and Richard L. Holm.

I met Dick when I was a U.S. Army physician at the Burn Center of Brooke Army Hospital in San Antonio, Texas. He had just been brought there in an aircraft showing not a single marking of any kind. My superiors informed me that he was a "missionary" who had suffered extensive burns in Africa.

His first words to me were, "I got out of there," spoken in a very weak voice. And then, "I have a briefcase, please take custody of it."

Custody? What the hell could be in it?

"Someone will ask you for it," he said next. "Give it to them if they show you proper identification."

I wondered what kind of church asks for identification. But the answer would have to wait; I had a job to do.

I spent that night and at least another day with Dick—I really don't recall how long. I reversed his dehydration and administered nutrition intravenously, and I balanced the two. I also began cleaning his wounds and talked with him during the brief periods when he was awake. Our friendship started then. We discovered our mutual passion for sports, particularly basketball. We found we had similar senses of humor and like-minded political views.

But no matter how friendly you become with a patient, no matter how compassionate a physician you may be, you cannot avoid hurting a burn victim on a daily basis. Most often it's when you're cutting away the dead skin and cleaning the wounds in "the tub"—as we refer to it. Most patients regard it, despite having substantial sedation, by various names that could be summarized as a brand of torture chamber.

Not so with Dick Holm. He was remarkably tough and used humor to cope. He dealt with pain by making jokes. And though he sometimes said things that hinted at who he really was, he never revealed then what he did for a living. But early on I had figured it out—and now, with this book, you can read about it.

Dick's autobiography describes a man who served his country almost entirely in secret in many places in the world we will never go and perhaps we never heard of. It is Dick's inside view of that life, that craft.

Though Dick keeps to himself much of what he accomplished—and much of it for security reasons we may never know—his story is filled with unexpected information. He helps you begin to understand the time and attention to detail required to train an agent in another country and be sure the information supplied by that agent is meaningful and reliable.

He shows you how, in the spy business, people are the currency; you must know and understand people because your job and your life depend on that judgment. He describes the deceptions and intrigue involved in uncovering a double agent as well as the cumbersome roadblocks of agency bureaucracy. He challenges today's difficult political environment, which raises the possibility that if you're wrong, or even perceived to be wrong, you can face prosecution.

This is not just a window into a life of secrets but a wide-open door. Employing the frankly spoken opinions that are his style, Dick reveals himself to be a dedicated, straightforward and ultimately honest man. That disarming honesty gives a unique but not always favorable view of the personalities he encountered over the years, from colleagues to guerrilla fighters and from politicians to diplomats—and even CIA directors.

But that's only part of it. Dick had to deal with something even worse than his burns—his blindness. In the process of sustaining his injuries, Dick's eyelids were singed shut and his eyes were so swollen we couldn't open them. When we did we discovered that his left eye was damaged beyond repair. We had to remove it to prevent the damage from spreading to his right eye. We salvaged it, but it was injured as well, to the point that during his months in the Burn Center he never saw me.

A year later, Dick received a corneal transplant at Walter Reed Army Hospital in Washington. I had flown to D.C. around that time to visit a friend and attend a party. He was there, and for the first time we saw each other.

Now, after 45 years, the friendship remains. It expanded to his late wife Judy, one of the most amazing people I have ever known, and to his wonderful daughters.

Over the years I've read and heard a great deal of criticism of the CIA. If you agree with that criticism, perhaps Dick Holm's disarmingly blunt description of his career, which spanned over three decades, will motivate you to reexamine your position. You might find reassurance that there are others like Dick Holm serving this country, people who are dedicated to protecting the United States and willing to face danger routinely as part of their job. We all owe a great debt to him, and to these men and women.

Dick writes convincingly about a host of other subjects, such as geopolitics, the Vietnam War, Bill Clinton's shameful treatment of the clandestine service, the aftermath of 9/11, the operational compromise in Paris, and the distressing incompetence of a few of the CIA directors he served. But I'll leave them for him to reveal and you to discover. Just be assured that within these pages there's a comprehensive narrative about how the craft of intelligence has evolved over the past 50 years.

Oh, and that briefcase? Soon after Dick arrived at Brooke, a nice-looking man approached me. He smiled, turned discreetly, and showed me his identification card. "I understand you might have a briefcase," he said. "May I please have it?"

Even in pain and clinging to life, Dick Holm couldn't be anything but a dedicated professional.

Timothy Miller M.D.
Professor of Surgery, Chief of Plastic Surgery, UCLA School of Medicine
Executive Director, Operation Mend

Prologue

FEBRUARY 27, 1965

The Boeing 707 jetliner streaked across the Atlantic. In my mostly unconscious state I had no idea where the plane was headed or that it belonged to the U.S. Air Force. I didn't know that in its large, open compartment it carried, along with me, only a burn specialist, two nurses and a corpsman. I didn't know that Secretary of Defense Robert McNamara had dispatched the flight at the behest of John McCone, the Director of Central Intelligence.

I also didn't know that around my neck hung a crucifix on a silver chain, a parting gift of faith by a Belgian priest whose name I would learn later.

All I knew, vaguely, was that I was still alive. Four men had walked and ridden bicycles a hundred miles across enemy-held territory to reach help for me. A nameless Azande witch doctor had treated my wounds, protecting them from infection, dehydration and those relentless insects. Another Belgian—a doctor in Leopoldville—had refused to accept that my condition was fatal.

And somehow, some way, by my own stubbornness I had refused to die.

PART I: TRAINING

1. An Intangible Difference

WASHINGTON, D.C. 1961

My career with the Central Intelligence Agency began unofficially just before Thanksgiving 1960 when I drove my black Volkswagen convertible from Fort Dix, New Jersey, to the recruiting office on 16th Street, Northwest, in Washington, D.C. I had purchased the VW during my stint of nearly two years at Camp Bussac, north of Bordeaux, France, where I had worked in the Army's Counter Intelligence Corps.

During that time, for reasons I'll explain, I became interested in joining the CIA after my discharge. But when I mailed in an application they responded by informing me that I could not apply from overseas. So when I arrived at Fort Dix, I resolved to drive down to Washington and apply in person, which I did, on an overcast morning in late November.

After I filled out the forms and took the requisite tests the interviewing officer said I could start work immediately—in the file rooms on the night shift. He added that if I performed satisfactorily I could begin advancing through the ranks. But I found the prospect of night work and a long, slow climb to a meaningful assignment disappointing. So I pushed a little, mentioning that I was a college graduate with military experience.

"Oh, this is standard," he responded.

"But it isn't what I was hoping for. Aren't there any other possibilities?"

"There's Junior Officer Training—the JOT program—but I'm not sure there are openings just now."

"What's that program like?"

He explained that JOT prepared promising young candidates for operational assignments abroad.

That sounded more like it and I filled out another application.

The interviewer cautioned me that JOT's standards were high. Suddenly I regretted the hours I had spent back in college playing basketball and bridge instead of studying in the library, and I wished my grade point average had been higher. On the other hand I had done well on my Graduate Record Examination, enough to earn a slot in the master's program in economics at Washington University in St. Louis. But given my draft status it was also something I hadn't pursued. Still I thought it might help my chances.

JOT acceptance or not I decided to wait out the verdict by visiting my family in Kansas City where my parents had moved the summer after I graduated from high school.

I was born on June 20, 1935, in Chicago in the middle of the Great Depression. My parents were both children of immigrants. My father, Carl Willard Holm, was the eldest of three sons in a Swedish family. My mother, Constance Cecilia Laux Holm, was one of eleven children descended from a Prussian grandfather who had made his way to America at the turn of the 20th century.

Both families had modest means and my parents married in 1934 with minimal fanfare. Dad graduated at the top of his class at Lane Technical High School, one of Chicago's best. He was offered and happily accepted a job with the Illinois Bell Telephone Company, where he was one of about 20,000 employees at the time. In the mid-1950s Dad transferred to AT&T where he helped in the early effort to develop area codes.

When I was about 7 years old, in what was considered at the time a bold move, Dad signed a mortgage and bought our house, a brick bungalow in Elmhurst, a small, quiet, middle-class town about 25 miles west of Chicago. No one on either side of the family had ever left the city but each workday Dad commuted to Illinois Bell's office by train.

My parents were splendid role models for me and my two brothers, Bob and Greg, and my sister Diann. My childhood in Elmhurst was idyllic and I retain fond memories of my life there, of my friends, of Boy Scouting, and then as now, of sports.

Sports were my passion. We played football in the autumn, baseball in spring and summer, and basketball almost year-round. In the process, as all children do who participate, I learned about winning, losing and playing on a team—I preferred winning.

I resumed my basketball passion a bit when I returned home on that pre-CIA visit. Along with reading as much as I could about the world of intelligence, I played in a lot of pickup games at the local YMCA in between enjoying Mom's home cooking again.

In February my parents introduced me to a neighbor who had recently fallen into a decent inheritance. When he learned that I had just returned from France he asked me to guide him on a trip to Europe, in return for which he promised to cover all of my expenses. I accepted but told him that I wouldn't be able to leave until I had heard about the job in Washington.

That news arrived in early April when the agency's interviewing officer called to tell me I had been accepted. A separate letter arrived a week later instructing me about where and when to report. I would start my training in June along with 25 other JOTs.

My immediate future assured, I took off with my neighbor for Europe. First stop, England, where I bought myself a present: a brand-new, Triumph TR3 convertible in British racing green. We broke the car in over the next six weeks driving through France, Spain, Italy and Switzerland, and then I shipped it home duty-free.

The first time I had traveled the European continent was on a slow train from Hamburg, Germany, carrying myself and other troops through Holland, Belgium and France. I had been fascinated by just about everything and spent most of the time standing between the rail cars gazing at the passing sights: the signs in foreign languages, the posters, the clothes and automobiles, and the stations. I remember watching some French railroad workers talking with cigarettes dangling from their mouths. The cigarettes would move with their lips but never fall out.

My assignment at Camp Bussac afforded me many pleasant opportunities to live and travel beyond the base. The on-site work quickly became tedious, but my occasional forays into the surrounding area or the region were interesting and enjoyable. From time to time I met with liaison officers in Toulouse and Perigueux to discuss, for example, the activities of the Russian and Polish consulates or the movement of Soviet bloc ships into the port of Bordeaux.

Most fascinating to me were the reports I obtained from my sources on and off the base. I had been given the names of several longtime contacts when I arrived. I saw them regularly and developed links of my own. I hesitate to call these people "agents," because the CIC's efforts were not very sophisticated. But they were carefully selected, unpaid individuals who knew what was going on in circles of interest to us. They also were pro-American enough to take the time to talk discreetly.

Gathering this information and compiling reports was useful in two ways. First, it enabled me to move around and use my French, because official liaison contacts were part of the effort. Second, it was clearly a learning process. In my discussions with French contacts and by reading the French press I gained a better understanding of the country and its culture.

All of it established a direction for my future. I became interested in the craft of intelligence and in living abroad. Both would become integral parts of my 35-year career in the CIA.

Before I left for Washington my parents told me they felt uneasy about the choice I had made. Dad asked me if I really knew anything about the agency. I told him I had read a lot about it and learned a little more during my time in France. That didn't seem to satisfy him, but he eventually dropped the subject and apparently accepted my decision.

In any event I was elated as I headed east in the TR3. I loved that little car, particularly then. It fit my mood. My prospects were looking good, I had been accepted into the program I wanted, and I eagerly anticipated training for the start of my professional life.

Back in D.C., I stopped by the JOT office. The receptionist gave me some leads on housing, and soon I settled into an old place along MacArthur Boulevard across from the reservoir in the western part of the city. I lived with five other men, three of whom were also JOTs. Of the two others, one served in the Air Force at the Pentagon, and the other already worked as an analyst in the agency's Directorate of Intelligence. That made many things easier. We often commuted together in town and subsequently to the Farm, the CIA's training facility in southeast Virginia. With so many things in common we bonded easily, and our friendships have lasted through the decades.

We spent the first six weeks in one of the "temps," rows of low office buildings that had been erected in haste during World War I to house the War Department—the Pentagon's precursor—and weren't removed until the 1970s. Located along Constitution Avenue near the Lincoln Memorial and its reflecting pool, the uniformly dingy buildings ruined the otherwise beautiful setting.

My fellow JOTs impressed me. Twenty-two young men and three young women—plus me—we represented the 10 percent of agency applicants who had achieved the highest standards. Almost all had served in the military, though at the time that distinction was fairly common because of the draft. Many had earned graduate degrees and the group had pursued a broad range of college majors.

Except for four of us from the Midwest and a couple from the West Coast, all were graduates of eastern schools. I felt lucky to be among them. My own service background, plus my bachelor's degree from Blackburn College in Carlinville, Illinois, had landed me a spot I never could have imagined while in school.

Our instructors began by giving us the history of World War II intelligence. Then they moved on to the origins of the agency and its four directorates: Plans, Intelligence, Science and Technology, and Administration. We all were destined for Plans, which eventually became Operations and then the National Clandestine Service.

Next they presented a detailed look at the intelligence community and how it served policymakers. A review of postwar events followed, including the beginnings of the Cold War, which would continue to dominate the world scene for three more decades. The confrontation between the

Free World, led by the United States, and the communist-inspired totalitarianism practiced by the Soviet Union, China and their satellites, would drive all of our efforts.

This wasn't the first time I had been presented with a clear picture of the communist world. Back in France at Bussac, I had met Tim Lawson, a civilian who periodically sold cars on the base. I bought the VW convertible from him.

Tim was the kind of guy you instinctively didn't trust too much. At the time I had no doubt he was making money in other ways—some probably illegal. He had served in the Army and was stationed at Bussac from 1955 until 1957, the year before I arrived. He decided to stay in France after his discharge and found the car-sales job after bumming around a bit. He was living with a French woman, appeared to have lots of local friends, and knew quite a bit about happenings in the little towns around the base. I often had trouble sorting out his rumors from facts, but I joined Tim for a cup of coffee once in a while.

I can't remember how we had raised the subject, but on one such occasion he suddenly launched into a long tirade about the 1956 Hungarian uprising. I was in college at the time, and though I had heard about it from news reports I was far from well-versed.

Tim told me that shortly after the uprising began, he and some of the other soldiers in the motor pool—where he was serving as a truck driver—heard via shortwave radio the Hungarian freedom fighters calling for help from the United States and Western Europe. Send them weapons and they would do the rest, they said. As the situation grew worse and Soviet intervention seemed imminent, the freedom fighters continued to plead for assistance from the West.

Tim said he became so agitated and frustrated that he actually had considered stealing a motor-pool truck and driving it to Hungary to fight at the side of the rebels. He insisted that others, including some young Frenchmen he knew, would have gone with him. But in the end no one went. The Russians invaded and crushed the uprising, and the freedom-fighter broadcasts stopped abruptly.

What struck me at the time was Tim's outrage, which seemed entirely heartfelt. Although he had no understanding of the international politics involved—nor did I—he still felt angry, three years later, at the Western governments for not responding.

Tim's anger had sprung from several questions—obvious ones:

Why would President Eisenhower, a military man, refuse to act?

Why would he allow the freedom fighters to be slaughtered, particularly because he knew the Europeans would follow his lead if he decided to counter the crackdown?

And how could the Russians be so brazen? How could they openly smash a rebellion in another country when the Hungarian people clearly opposed their government?

I was no expert, but given the Cold War and the geopolitical situation that prevailed, the answers seemed self-evident. The Reds had shown no restraint in brutalizing their own people, so they couldn't be expected to do so in Hungary. And the West, still war-weary in the mid-1950s, had forsaken a military response, which might have escalated into another global conflict.

Tim would have none of that, which was why he said he still felt pained that the Free World had allowed Soviet tanks to shred the Hungarian revolt.

Listening to Tim's rants forced me to think, more than I ever had before, about the Cold War, communism and the international situation in general. Sure, I had grown up with a sense of patriotism and a belief that the American position was right—whatever it was. Communism was bad, the Soviets were bad, and what happened in Hungary was just awful. It reinforced my negative feelings about communism and the efforts by its practitioners to spread their ideology so forcibly around the world.

Though I didn't realize it then, that conversation laid the groundwork for my decision to spend a career in intelligence, working to counter the communist ideology. It had made me think differently about why I was in Europe and why a U.S. base like Bussac was essential. If the Russians ever did attack Western Europe we would need every military asset we had there.

We attended several weeks of classes on international communism, presented from scholarly and historical perspectives as well as from intelligence-gathering and operational viewpoints. I had studied communist and socialist economics in college but I knew little about the politics.

Learning about the organization and inner workings of a communist cell gave us much food for thought, and we discussed it at length during breaks. Communism was a lousy system that needed to be resisted. Despite our varied backgrounds we agreed that communism had no merits.

We also began learning how to write intelligence reports and how to master the prevailing style. It was a little like newspaper writing: straightforward prose that emphasized precision and detail, and no opinion unless clearly labeled.

Some of the nuances about writing, evaluating and disseminating reports we learned from someone who would later figure prominently in my life: Wallace R. Deuel. Wally had started his career in the late 1920s after graduating from the University of Illinois. He accepted a teaching post at the American University of Beirut, in Lebanon. He met his wife Mary there as well.

Wally later joined the *St. Louis Post-Dispatch* and worked as a foreign correspondent. The paper assigned him to Rome during the early and mid-1930s, and then to Berlin during the latter part of the decade. But he grew so intensely opposed to Hitler that he left Germany in 1939.

Based on his experiences Wally wrote a book titled *People under Hitler*, which he first published in 1942. He also worked for the Office of Strategic Services, the OSS, our wartime intelligence agency and the CIA's predecessor. He later helped to write a history of the organization. When the Cold War began he recognized the need to resist another totalitarian movement, so he joined the newly established CIA to help stop communism from taking over Europe.

Along with his impressive background Wally was an articulate and entertaining public speaker with a wry sense of humor. An expert on the subject—he had developed many of our rules for writing reports—he influenced some in the class to pursue careers as reports officers and analysts.

Wally's son Mike was one of our classmates, so with his dad at the lectern we maintained our interest. I'm sure Mike was quite proud.

Wally also focused on what was called the requirements process and its impact on collecting information in the field, something we all would be doing someday.

Any part of the executive or legislative branch of the federal government may request information from the agency, and the agency is required to respond. Over the years the requirements process has been continually refined and restructured, but even back in the early 1960s many government entities were using it.

In theory, federal officials would pose their question in a neutral manner and the agency would respond objectively. In practice, some officials tended to structure their questions to elicit answers that supported their views.

On our end, the requirements staff passed along the requests to the appropriate people in the intelligence community and returned the answers to the requesters. Despite the obvious potential for politics it was a reasonable system that helped members of the federal government to develop U.S. foreign policy.

On Sundays during those early weeks in Washington, groups of us, mostly the bachelors, would congregate on the National Mall or on the Ellipse, the large oval lawn just south of the White House grounds, to play touch football. Other young men would join us as well.

I mention this because I noticed a distinction in those games early on. Whenever we would choose sides, almost invariably the outcome would be an agency team versus a foreign-service team. Granted, we tended to choose our friends and fellow trainees, but there was more to it than that.

There seemed to be an intangible difference. We were all bright, well-educated, personable men, but our respective choices for career paths revealed contrasting viewpoints and approaches. Agency trainees, particularly those aiming for the Directorate of Plans, in general were more action oriented, while our foreign-service counterparts tended to be more reflective and analytical.

This distinction would mark all of us throughout our professional lives. In my experience, agency officers and foreign-service officers rarely saw eye to eye. Those differences spawned a mutual lack of trust and confidence that consistently marred our exchanges.

The conflict persisted all the way up the ladder. The two arms of the executive branch constantly competed for the president's ear. Based on my encounters at those casual football games, each side suffered from a lack of real understanding of the other's role. We were different kinds of people, something for which there is no easy solution.

Moreover, the problem wasn't unique to us. Throughout my career, working with various allied services—particularly the French and the British—I noticed the same difficulty afflicting the bureaucracies.

In July 1961, we got to meet Allen Dulles, the DCI, Director of Central Intelligence. He enjoyed a solid reputation because of his war record with the OSS and his long history in the community. He had been DCI for eight years—longer than anyone else—and he was highly respected in Washington. His brother, John Foster Dulles, was President Eisenhower's secretary of state. His welcoming remarks included telling us war stories and emphasizing the need for good intelligence during the Cold War.

Neither Dulles nor any of us mentioned the disaster the agency had suffered in the Bay of Pigs covert operation just three months earlier, back when I was savoring my acceptance as a JOT. The operation, conceived under the previous administration but approved by President John F. Kennedy, involved the invasion of southern Cuba at a location called Playa Girón, the Bay of Pigs. It failed and many men were killed, partly because Kennedy at the last minute had withheld air cover—another case of a U.S. president refusing to order the military to resist a communist takeover of a nation.

At the time our intelligence indicated a good chance of sparking a general uprising against Castro as soon as a beachhead was established. But the point was rendered moot by the unsuccessful invasion. To this day Kennedy's hesitation remains a sore point among some agency veterans.

Speaking of whom, after about 20 minutes Dulles's secretary entered the office and announced that the president wanted to see him at the White House. The message impressed us youngsters. That his secretary may have done the same thing each time a group of JOTs met him did not occur to us—and it probably wouldn't have bothered us if true. I instantly liked Dulles and considered him sincere in his efforts to sustain a strong intelligence community and an active clandestine service.

I cannot say the same for some of my other twelve directors.

Six weeks later and the groundwork laid, the agency dispatched us to its training facility in southeast Virginia. The Farm, as it is known, is about a three-hour drive from Washington. The facility would become our home away from home until Christmas. Located on a former military base, the Farm boasted few amenities. We lived in Quonset huts, Spartan style, in rooms with shared lavatories and tabletop fans, but we stayed too busy to complain about accommodations that we used mostly for sleeping.

We dressed in military fatigues and combat boots and ate in a mess hall that served copious amounts of food. We had no complaints there, either. Each morning we walked a short distance from our quarters to a gym for physical training. Some took the PT in stride; others did not. I didn't mind. Excluding my two years in France, I had always tried to stay in good physical condition. When time permitted some of us played basketball in the gym before dinner.

The PT and occasional basketball games constituted our only distractions. Security people patrolled the fenced perimeter, keeping unauthorized individuals away. We trained in isolation and purposefully so. The instructors expected us to concentrate on our training, which we did. As a result time passed swiftly. The range and depth of subjects we covered kept us busy up to 18 hours a day throughout our five-month stay.

We began learning the art of tradecraft, the methods employed to manage an intelligence operation. It is an art because of the nuances involved and it is not easy to learn. Some, lacking the required personality traits, can never master it. The rest of us, in our limited time at the Farm, received only an introduction. We needed actual experience to perfect the techniques needed to engage, say, a Swiss banker or a Jordanian camel driver, because in a given situation both can provide vital information.

Eventually the training, new and different from anything we had experienced, took on a life of its own. The people running the Farm allotted blocks of time to cover specific subjects, and we plowed through each one:

agent recruiting, agent handling, clandestine communications, surveillance and countersurveillance, report writing (good writers, we continued to learn, enjoyed a distinct advantage), cover, security, liaison operations, covert operations, counterintelligence, debriefing and eliciting, and the art—it is likewise an art—of asking probing but non-threatening questions to obtain information.

The lectures covered the philosophical, ethical, psychological and academic aspects of every subject. But training was always hands-on. Practical exercises followed the lectures. They required us to perform, at least several times, everything they had taught us. To each class member they assigned a mentor, an experienced operations officer who monitored his or her charge's progress, observing strengths and promptly addressing any weakness that surfaced. If a trainee's skills fell short in any area, the mentor arranged remedial exercises.

The program's standards were preset and high, and every trainee had to meet or exceed them. We regarded even the training sessions with utmost seriousness. We had to. Agents' lives and diplomatic incidents detrimental to our country's best interests were at stake.

This isn't to say that our time at the Farm was devoid of lighter moments, at least for the single guys. On weekends the husbands usually returned home to D.C., but the rest of us sometimes sought companionship.

Once, four of us drove to the College of William and Mary, in Williamsburg, where we entered a girls' dormitory and tried to ingratiate ourselves with the housemother. It wasn't exactly our Bay of Pigs, but our invasion failed. She ejected us, and as we were leaving we heard one of the male students ask, "Who the hell were those guys?"

While we labored through the fall trying to master the principles of tradecraft, the agency changed leadership. A respectful seven months after the Cuban invasion disaster, Allen Dulles resigned. He had dutifully taken the rap. Following an intensive search to find "the right man," President Kennedy named John McCone, chairman of the Atomic Energy Commission, to succeed Dulles as DCI.

It was said that Kennedy had chosen McCone, a staunch Republican, to emphasize his conviction that CIA director was not a political position.

Like Kennedy, McCone was a Roman Catholic and an intense cold warrior who regarded communism as evil.

When we heard about the switch, some lamented Dulles's role as scapegoat, but the event minimally impacted our busy lives. Like frogs looking up from the bottom of a well, we had a limited view.

Our trainers staged the final three-day exercise in Baltimore. There we attempted to employ the full range of clandestine techniques we had learned. Acting as intelligence collectors we were pitted against FBI trainees in counterintelligence mode.

Stressful at times it was also fun and challenging, because it involved trying to evade and outwit our FBI counterparts. They were supposed to keep us under surveillance while we tried to meet with a designated contact.

Our collective inexperience showed. In my case, working with one colleague, we couldn't quite shake the FBI guys entirely, and they couldn't be discreet enough to avoid our detection. The exercise ended in a stalemate.

With one exception the entire class completed the course, our individual strengths and weaknesses duly recorded in our files. The exception was a trainee who dropped out shortly after we started. We learned that he had departed the agency to become an Episcopalian minister, a decision that puzzled the rest of us because of the vast differences between the two career paths.

Our joint training with the FBI had helped to underscore how important it would be for us to acquire sound tradecraft—something most of us would pursue in much greater detail in the field.

2. Waist Deep in the Big Muddy

SOUTHEASTERN VIRGINIA 1962

My JOT training marked the first of two stints at the Farm. Before they sent us back to headquarters they also gave us a glimpse of covert and paramilitary operations and how those activities fit into the range of options the agency could provide the president.

The field intrigued me, especially the paramilitary aspects. Young and single, I thought it would be exciting. So when we received the opportunity to take an intensive, four-month course, including parachute training, I volunteered, as did eight others in my class.

The agency also offered us the chance, following our training, to volunteer for a six-month temporary duty—called a TDY—serving as paramilitary advisers in Laos. Four of us—André Le Gallo, Mike Deuel, Ralph McLean and I—accepted.

After a week's leave over Christmas to visit my family, and several weeks at headquarters beginning to familiarize myself with our Laos efforts, I reported back to the Farm to begin paramilitary instruction in early February 1962.

The group included two of my MacArthur Boulevard housemates, and in preparation the three of us had been running each morning before work. It wasn't much fun, but part of the incentive was the opportunity to visit a group of young women in a neighboring house. We had struck up a friendly relationship with them, something destined to go nowhere because of our impending departure. But no matter; for young men interest in a member of the opposite sex dies hard.

Each morning the women would invite us in for coffee after our run. We liked them, particularly the two who were really attractive, and they were a welcome sight, even at "oh dark hundred" on those January mornings.

The exchanges over coffee also served a purpose. They gave us an opportunity to live our cover assignments as Department of the Army civilians. It wasn't easy, and we could tell they weren't really buying our story.

The daily runs paid off in another way. They gave us a leg up in the PT we would be taking for the duration of the paramilitary course. Our instructor, Burt Courage, also lectured on other subjects.

A big, strong guy, Burt impressed us with his one-arm pull-ups and push-ups. We may have been in good shape, but he outclassed us. We liked and respected his quiet and unassuming manner. It helped get us through the strenuous calisthenics that always ended with a several-mile run.

Like Burt, all of our instructors were highly skilled. Each man had accumulated several years of military experience, and many had served the agency in the field. Each taught a specialty, the collective goal of which was to familiarize us with a wide range of military abilities we could use later in our careers.

Military officers controlled governments in many parts of the world. Or, they were deeply involved in politics. So learning military terms and concepts could be vital in helping to recruit these men as intelligence assets.

The training also helped prepare us for the paramilitary programs the agency was running in several countries, such as Laos, where qualified officers were needed. But the sessions were blunter than tradecraft; paramilitary operations are not an art.

Another important training component covered the use of weapons. Over the course of four months we used a wide range of firearms manufactured in the United States. We tried out rifles, pistols, machine guns, rocket launchers and mortars. We also examined and fired weapons made in Russia, China and Czechoslovakia.

I had won a Marksman medal in the Army with my Ml rifle. Even so, I didn't feel particularly comfortable with this block of instruction, because I never liked guns. But I tolerated it, because learning how to hold a weapon and fire it in training surely beats having to learn about it in the midst of a life-or-death situation—something I would discover later in Laos and the Congo.

We spent a lot of time studying small-unit tactics. Our instructors presented theory and described the actions of guerrilla fighters and revolutionaries such as Che Guevara and Mao Tse-tung—as it was spelled using the Wade-Giles method at the time, instead of Mao Zedong, under the *pinyin* system followed today. We used standard U.S. tactics as our guide and spent many days in the woods and swamps on the base practicing what we had learned.

One simple but standard exercise involved following compass courses. The trainers would give us a list of moves—150 yards northwest, 60 yards south-southwest, 200 yards west, and so on—with the objective of reaching a designated target. To this day I question the value of what we derived, not from the efforts but from the idea of wading waist-deep through cold, muddy water in February and March.

When we inevitably complained the instructors' standard response was, "It builds character."

Maybe it did help us to get tougher, and the program encouraged leadership. They rotated us as platoon leaders in the practical exercises. Everyone did well, because we helped one another plan and execute the assignments—and we knew that each of us would be taking a turn.

Even with the best of intentions, though, things can go wrong.

One day we conducted a simulated raid on an enemy camp. We had held two planning sessions to work out the timing, deployment, weapons and personnel for the operation.

We thought we had prepared for everything. We would hit the camp at noon while the enemy fighters were eating lunch. At 11 a.m., the instructors dropped us off about a half-mile from the target site. From there we approached, carefully. We had studied the coordinates and terrain on our maps that morning. Up and down a couple of ridgelines and we would be there.

We moved up and down a couple of ridgelines. Then up and down a couple more. Then we retraced our steps. Then we sent out small patrols.

We never did find that damned camp.

We couldn't have missed it by much, but we missed it. In retrospect we had allowed the terrain to fool us. Everything looked the same, so in taking our bearings it was easy for us to veer off course little by little over each ridgeline. Whatever the reason we felt embarrassed as hell and the instructors wouldn't let us forget it for the rest of the course.

We spent our next block in parachute training. The lecture period was short, because there isn't much to say about throwing yourself out the door of an airplane at 2,500 feet.

Again the instructors were excellent. All had logged hundreds of jumps. They intensified our physical training, including more running along with sessions teaching us the PLF, the parachute-landing fall. We spent hours jumping into a sawdust pit from a 6-foot platform.

Next we jumped from a 60-foot tower, a standard exercise intended to instill confidence and condition us to obey the jumpmaster's commands. It was no fun and few of us liked it, but we knew it was necessary.

We descended a cable attached to the tower just inside the jump door. Each man strapped on a parachute harness and latched it to the cable. Once out the door the jumper slid down to a soft landing about 50 yards from the tower.

It sounded simple, but it wasn't.

The first tower jump was the worst. We jumped in sticks—the military term for parachuters in a line—just as we would from a plane. Four men to a stick, I was second, and I remember thinking that I'd rather have been first and gotten it over with. I climbed the tower unenthusiastically, resigned to the idea that it had to be done. At the top we waited in a small room with corrugated sheet-metal walls.

The jumpmaster stood there waiting for us, understanding our reluctance. He also knew the exercise previewed what we'd be doing on the plane, so he used the same commands. We strapped on the parachute harnesses and stood in line.

"Hook up," the instructor called out.

We complied, hitching our chute-release lines onto the cable leading out the door.

"Get in the doorway," he ordered, and the first man shifted to the opening, putting a hand on each side of the doorframe. Knees bent in ready position, the jumper waited for the next command. It always seemed as though minutes passed.

"Go!"

Out the door he went. I watched as he took the initial shock of the cable then slid down to the landing point without a problem. In a real jump the four-man stick would go in quick succession, but in the tower we went out one at a time.

Next it was my turn. Almost robot-like, I shifted to the doorway and grabbed each side of the frame. Then I did start thinking, because I could plainly see the ground 60 feet below and realized I did not want to do this. I tried looking at the horizon, as I had been instructed, but my gaze kept returning to the ground.

Stop it!

My self-coaching didn't help. As if waiting for the pilot's signal that we were over the drop zone, the jumpmaster hesitated for eight or 10 seconds, which seemed like forever. I crouched, frozen, in the doorway.

"Go!" he yelled in my ear, pretending to shout over the noise of airplane engines.

I guess I was startled, because I hesitated for a split second before I jumped. Then I went. The harness tightened as the cable caught my weight, and I slid down.

I landed without incident. That one and the two other tower jumps were no question the least-enjoyable experiences of my paramilitary training.

Soon, with the PLF technique mastered and the tower behind us, the day for our first real jump arrived, sunny and warm with few clouds in the sky. This prospect had weighed on us for months. We rode a truck to the airfield, where a two-engine, World War II-era, C-47 transport waited.

We strapped on our parachutes, military T-10 models. We assembled next to the plane, chatting nervously among ourselves. After a briefing we boarded. The cable to which we would fasten our static lines looked ominous along the ceiling. My stick was second this time. We sat on benches stretched along each side of the aisle. The main parachute and reserve chute felt bulky and uncomfortable, but no one complained. Each man held the hook attached to his static line in his right hand. Everyone tried to act casual, but the tension was readily apparent.

We took off and the pilot flew a large spiral around the field, gaining altitude with each pass. Then he leveled off and straightened out.

"We're on final," the copilot shouted back.

We all waited for the next command, the one we had practiced on the ground, first in the tower and then inside a mock-up plane. Everyone knew exactly what to do.

"Stand up!" the jumpmaster shouted, followed soon by, "Hook Up!"

On command, the four men in the first stick shuffled forward. Mike Deuel, the lead jumper, swung into position at the door, his hands gripping each side of the frame. I could see he was gripping it hard as I sat waiting in anticipation. I wasn't afraid, just intrigued by the prospect of leaping out of an airplane.

I could hear the assistant instructor speaking to the men in the first stick: "Your first jump will be the best one ever—enjoy it!"

The jumpmaster leaned out the door looking for the drop zone. When he stood up straight, and the jump light flashed on, we knew it was close.

"Go!" he shouted at Mike, swatting him on the butt.

Mike jumped. The rest of the stick quickly shuffled forward, swung into position, and at the jumpmaster's command headed out the door, each receiving the standard butt swat. All four men jumped within about eight seconds.

The rest of us sat transfixed. With the first stick gone, all we saw was sky. The jumpmaster hauled in the four static lines.

The pilot circled for another run over the drop zone. When he straightened out we heard the cries again.

"We're on final!"

"Stand up!"

Now my stick stood, hooks in hand, with me third in line. We wore serious, intent expressions—because we were serious and intent.

"First jump will be great," the assistant repeated.

I barely heard him, as I strained to hear the next command.

"Hook up!"

We snapped onto the cable. I gave my hook a hard jerk to confirm it. We also checked one another. I stared at the door.

Soon I'm going to jump. Imagine that!

"Move to the door!"

We shuffled forward. The first jumper swung into position. I wasn't even thinking at that point, just reacting.

"Go!"

The first man leaped out, receiving the swat as he left. The rest of us followed, just like in the tower and the mock-up. I moved forward quickly, planted my left foot, pivoted on it, and swung my right foot to the edge of the door. Just as I grabbed the doorframe, I got the command and the swat—and I jumped. No thinking, just discipline and practice. That part was over in an instant.

The slipstream caught me immediately and swung me sideways. I felt no sensation of falling. I saw the tail of the plane go by and disappear. The chute deployed behind me and I fell gently under it like a pendulum.

It was quiet. I looked around, realizing that everything had gone properly. I felt good, watching the base spread out below me and the river off to the side. I also saw the drop zone and happily concluded I was headed right for it.

Great!

As I drifted slowly downward it seemed clear that the jumpmaster and pilot had done their jobs well. We all would be landing in the middle of the large field that was our target.

I relaxed. It was a splendid day, no wind at all. Then I heard the instructors yelling from below.

"Loosen up, bend your knees, relax!"

Apparently my legs were locked stiff as a board, but I didn't realize it. As my stick neared the ground, the instructors became more insistent. Nothing penetrated. I was staring straight ahead waiting for my toes to touch the ground so I could smoothly roll into my perfect PLF.

But it wasn't perfect. In fact it was terrible, exactly wrong. I landed backward because I hadn't used the shrouds to control my direction.

So my heels hit first—wrong!

Butt next—wrong!

Then with a thud the back of my head banged onto the ground. Thank goodness for the helmet, which no doubt prevented a concussion given the force of the impact.

I was down, albeit with a ringing in my head, but I had made it; nothing broken.

I stood up, gingerly.

One of the instructors immediately got in my face.

"Dammit, Holm, don't you listen?"

"To what?"

"To me, when I give you instructions!"

"Sorry, I didn't hear you."

"Well, next time listen up, goddam it!"

The instructors had been talking to me all the way down via loudspeakers. So intent was I on making a good PLF that I didn't hear them at all—I didn't connect that I was the "number three man in the stick," as they had kept repeating.

I started thinking about how my first operational landing might go.

About half of our group made similar mistakes, though mine was probably the worst, and nobody did it perfectly. On the other hand, nobody got hurt on landing.

The only injury was to Bob Manning, a well-liked guy with great potential as an operations officer. Despite the checks and double-checks, Bob's static line had gotten under his arm as he hooked up. When he jumped the line immediately deployed his chute, jerking his arm upward. Fortunately the line did no serious damage; it just gave him a nasty bruise. But that didn't stop Bob from making the rest of his jumps and completing the program.

We did four more jumps, including one at dusk. Again no one got seriously hurt, our techniques got progressively better, and our confidence grew with each jump. I listened to the instructors and actually made some passable PLFs.

After parachute training they flew us to a secluded base near the Atlantic coast for explosives and small-boat operations.

As usual the sessions included PT but with several new twists. In response to questions, our instructor explained that he had developed the exercises based on his training as a frogman. He said he had designed them to strengthen our upper-arm and chest muscles, which we'd need to place magnetic limpet mines on the hull of a ship.

That explanation brought no more questions.

Each day after breakfast, which followed PT, we moved out to a practice range, where our instructors demonstrated the use of explosives. One of them, John Ward, was also quite entertaining. He could have worked as a stand-up comic. He delivered his stories and jokes with ease and good timing that captivated our group. He continued his routines in the officers' club in the evenings, but he also knew when to get serious. In the field and dealing with explosives, he was always dead serious.

In both classroom sessions and field demonstrations our instructors emphasized how powerful and efficient relatively small amounts of plastic explosives could be. I wasn't sure whether I would ever want to mess with the stuff, but I resolved to keep an open mind.

The secret of using explosives properly, they told us, was to shape the charges. That is, mold the plastic and place the charges where they could best attack the structure of the target. A small amount could drop a large tree right across a road or trail, or bring down a bridge.

Safety was the highest priority, and the instructors gave precise briefings on what to do—and what not to do. They started with primer cord, an explosive itself, which is used to detonate the plastic. During our drills it was mandatory after we lit the primer cord to yell, "Fire in the hole!" to alert everyone else to move to safe areas or bunkers.

It took a lot of practice to gauge just how much time we had before the charge would detonate after we lit the cord. It wasn't too difficult with small lengths that would explode in seconds, but figuring out how much time was needed to move away safely from, say, a bridge before it blew up proved much more of a challenge.

After several days we all grew fairly skilled at getting charges to explode just about when they should. From countdowns of ten to boom, we could get within just a few seconds of boom.

When in doubt we gave ourselves more time.

We practiced on various targets, such as trees, pieces of steel, buildings and vehicles. The instructors also taught us the basics of structural engineering, which would help us place the charges more effectively.

We also learned how to operate and maneuver small boats, in this case small, black rubber rafts propelled by powerful but silenced outboard motors. Even carrying three men plus equipment the little boats could really move.

The SEALs, the Navy's sea, air and land commandos, used the same craft to infiltrate target areas at night. After we learned the basics about the boats and their motors we also spent a lot of time training at night.

We quickly found that in darkness it's easy to lose your sense of direction on the water, and our drills concentrated on techniques to gain our bearings and stay on course. Sometimes they towed us out to a certain point and dropped us off. Other times we moved along the coast on our own. After a while we got the idea.

Our final exercise involved a night raid to destroy a simulated enemy command post that was supposedly unguarded.

We planned the operation as a group. We would bring three small boats to a designated cove. Each boat would carry explosives and three armed men, their faces blackened. After rendezvousing at a dock, six of us would move to the target, while the others would guard the boats. At the target two men would set up watch posts, and four would infiltrate and set the charges, with everything observed by our instructors.

After the team lit the primer cords everyone would move back to the boats and beat a hasty retreat. I drew the detail to guard the boats.

It seemed to take much longer than it should for the attack team to get their job done and return. It always does. Finally we heard an explosion and saw fire in the direction of the target.

Done! They should be back in a couple of minutes.

"Let's get the engines started," I whispered to the other two guards.

"What if someone hears them?" one responded.

"There's no one here," the third retorted.

"At least we will be ready and can get the hell out of here," I said, pulling the start cord. The engine sprang to life and purred softly.

The returning team needed only spot the dock and slip onto the boats, and we would pull away into the darkness. I heard a second engine start and idle quietly.

"Shit, mine won't start," was the next sound that penetrated the night.

Christ! That can't help anything.

"Keep trying," I said.

"I am, I am," he shot back, just as the attack team appeared out of the tree line and moved quickly toward us. Two jumped into each boat—and waited.

"Let's move," one of them said.

"Engine won't start."

I don't know if the instructors had built this into the exercise or not, but clearly we had to react to it.

"We can't stay here. We'll tow you. Pass us a line," I said quietly to the men in the disabled boat.

They did, and we pulled slowly but steadily away from the dock and out into the blackness of the estuary. We followed the lone boat, and everyone tried to keep a low profile. No other problems developed, and our field improvisation had worked. The instructors made no complaints. They may or may not have realized that one of the boats had been towed; so much the better.

The exercise was realistic enough to show how difficult and dangerous such a raid could be. We imagined being on an enemy coast and having to limp out with failed equipment, possibly under hostile gunfire.

Small-boat and explosives training turned out to be useful. We didn't gain expertise in either area, but we learned and practiced enough to become effective later in our careers, where certain situations would demand paramilitary skills.

3. Bats and *Bohios*

PANAMA 1962

We finished our instruction with two weeks at the Army's Jungle Operations Training School at Fort Sherman, at Toro Point in the Canal Zone. We had heard about how demanding the sessions would be down there, but we looked forward to the challenge.

By then we had really improved our physical conditioning and honed our abilities in the areas I've mentioned.

We felt ready.

Fifteen of us landed in Panama late in the morning on a pleasant, sunny day in May 1962. It had been a long flight from Washington aboard Director McCone's private plane, with one refueling stop in Tampa, Florida. Happy to touch down we practically tumbled out of the plane, stretching our legs and waiting for the base bus to pick us up.

"What's that?" Bob Manning asked, gesturing at a sleek, black jet aircraft taxiing to the end of the runway where we had just landed.

"Don't know," I answered. "Never seen anything like that. What are those things under the wings?" I asked, referring to the droppable skids that supported the wingtips when the plane was fully fueled.

"I think it's a U-2," Ralph McLean said.

Ralph was an officer in the Marines assigned to the agency in a special program, as was Mike Deuel. I figured he had seen one before at some military base.

"Yeah, I think you're right, Ralph," someone else said. By now we all watched intently as the plane prepared for takeoff. We whipped out our cameras, everyone wanting a photo. The U-2 had gained international notoriety in the spring of 1960, when an agency pilot, Francis Gary Powers, had been shot down flying a high-altitude reconnaissance mission over Russia.

Powers, who remained in Soviet custody for two years, had been sent home in February 1962 as part of a prisoner exchange. The incident caused increased tensions between the United States and the Union of Soviet Socialist Republics. It also caused worries within the agency, because Powers had failed to autodestruct his aircraft before ejecting, and so the Reds were probably able to recover or reconstruct some of the plane's secret equipment.

As JOTs we didn't know any of this at the time. We only knew the U-2 was an amazing-looking airplane, and we watched, fascinated, as the pilot started his takeoff and accelerated down the runway. As the plane gained speed, its wings, which could only be described as droopy, visibly lifted, and the wheel struts attached beneath the tips dropped away. Designed by the technicians at the famed Lockheed Skunk Works in Palmdale, California, the U-2 needed its extra-long wings for efficient cruising at high altitudes. But on takeoffs, when the fuel tanks were full and the wings sagged, the struts kept the tips from dragging on the runway, and when those wings lifted in takeoff they almost seemed to flap like a bird's.

As soon as he had the wheels up the pilot must have given the engines full throttle, because the U-2 mounted an angle of ascent steeper than I had ever seen. It shot up into the air and soon disappeared from sight, mightily impressing us observers on the ground.

At Fort Sherman we settled into a small section of a large, concrete barracks, nothing fancy but adequate. Just like at the Farm we would not be spending much time there. We joined a group of about a hundred military officers sent to Panama from all over the United States to take this course, which was given only twice a year.

Except for our group and a platoon of SEALs, all of the men were young Army officers. Such a large class embarking on the two-week course surprised us, but we felt no less eager to get started.

I'm not sure why, but we also sensed the others were looking askance at us unlabelled civilians intruding into a military training program. Maybe they suspected who we were, or they wondered whether we'd be able to keep up. Either way, that perception piqued our competitive spirit, and we resolved to make a good showing.

After dinner the first evening our instructors assembled us behind the barracks for what they billed as an administrative briefing. Instead they gave us an introductory exercise in the nearby jungle. It was nearly dark. Just a walk through the jungle to a nearby clearing, they told us. We milled around before they lined up our groups, one behind the other.

"Okay, let's move out," one instructor announced, leading the first group into the thick vegetation. Soon we could barely see, as is the case near the equator when night falls quickly. Other instructors positioned themselves along the path while we moved forward into the darkness, which had become almost total.

"Hold hands," another instructor ordered. No one argued.

"I can't see a damn thing," said Bill Watkins, a former Marine helicopter pilot.

"It's like walking in a bottle of ink," I heard another man say.

"I hope all the snakes are asleep," someone else muttered, and everyone chuckled.

We half-stumbled through thick undergrowth up and down small knolls, holding on dearly to the hands in front of and behind us. The trees had sharp needles. I didn't hear much conversation, just a few curses as people tripped or encountered the needles, but otherwise we stayed quiet. Soon we arrived at another clearing, relieved to be out of the ink bottle.

The instructors had set us up, but it was an effective learning experience. They knew that our inability to see while trying to move amid unfamiliar jungle surroundings would unnerve us. When they led us from the well-lit clearing behind the barracks into the darkness, the sudden change gave our eyes no chance to adjust to night vision, and the brief walk didn't allow time to adjust, either.

The experience created a memorably negative first impression about nighttime movement in the jungle. But we learned later that the impression was false. Our instructors would correct it over the two-week program, which would start the next morning.

"Be sure to keep a firm grip just behind his head," the instructor told me, as the 2-foot boa constrictor threw a couple of coils around my arm and started to hug.

The snake wasn't big enough to hurt anyone, particularly during a controlled demonstration. The point was to show the spot just behind the head that would cause the reptile to go limp if you squeezed. I was getting my hands-on shot at seeing how it worked.

"Can I squeeze now?"

"Go ahead."

As I did I could feel the coils loosen and fall off my arm. I handed the snake to the instructor and was pleased to do so, wondering if I'd ever need that bit of information for real.

How the hell would I get hold of the head of a big one?

The constrictor demonstration marked just one part of a first morning of useful briefings about jungle animals, birds, snakes, trees, plants—edible and inedible. All were interesting, informative and of practical use over the next two weeks, as well as to those of us headed to Africa or Southeast Asia.

Not so the course on repelling. In a jungle setting the prospect surprised our little group, though not many of the military officers. They had obtained advance knowledge of what to expect during the two weeks and knew what was coming, while we JOTs mostly had to wait and see what each day would produce.

We had become fairly competent at repelling back at the Farm, where we practiced it regularly. Here it was included not as a jungle skill but a confidence builder.

We loaded onto trucks and drove inland. After dismounting, we walked for half an hour up to the top of a precipice overlooking the Chagres River. It wasn't exactly a waterfall, but here and there the footing was slippery, because water lightly flowed across the rocks and fell about 150 feet to the river. We couldn't see all the way down until we got to the edge, where the repelling ropes had been secured. What we could see, about two-thirds of the way, was a rock shelf where we would change ropes.

At the Farm we had practiced on a 20-foot tower, and some of us had gotten good enough to make it to the ground in one or two pushes. This looked considerably more challenging.

The tropical sun beat down on us, as we waited to repel.

"Looks neat; should be fun," Bob Manning announced, moving to the edge. He would be first in our group.

"I never did like heights," Mike L., another member, responded from farther back.

We watched Bob prepare.

"Throw the rope over your shoulder and between your legs," the instructor explained.

"Yeah, I know," Bob answered, as he took the rope. He had been a pole vaulter at Princeton and had done some rock climbing in New Jersey. He also had practiced repelling a lot back at the Farm. He knew what to do.

"No, the other shoulder," the instructor said, sounding alarmed, not knowing Bob was left-handed.

"Okay, thanks," Bob responded.

Without further ado he went over the edge, and we watched as he more or less swooped down the cliff. We weren't surprised, but the instructor was. I was tempted to quip that it was his first try, but I didn't. My turn was coming.

"Throw the rope over your shoulder and between your legs," the instructor repeated for the umpteenth time that morning. I stepped into position with my back to the edge of the cliff. He looked me over, approved, and I pushed off, but less forcefully or boldly than during our tower drills.

I watched the rock below me, looking for my first touch. As soon as I connected I bounded outward again, feeling pretty comfortable. My foot slipped once and I bumped against the rocks, but I swung clear and continued down. When I reached the shelf I moved right away to the second rope, where another instructor waited. He had been watching me, as he did everyone coming down. He saw that I could repel, so he just handed me the rope and said, "Move on."

I took a moment to look up to the top of the cliff, admiring the rugged natural beauty and enjoying the pleasure of the day. Bob was right, this was fun.

More confident now, I started the shorter leg.

Shove off, facing back and down.

Let the rope run freely over your shoulder and between your legs, making sure you place it on one side or the other.

Squeeze the rope a bit to control your speed, and catch yourself with your feet as you swing into the rocks.

Pay attention.

Try to touch on flat, solid spots to avoid slipping.

I got more aggressive as I neared the bottom and covered a longer vertical distance with the last several bounds. No mishaps. I slipped off the rope and handed it to a waiting sergeant.

Maybe they thought we needed more confidence building, because the next exercise of the day involved a river crossing under a zip wire. The terrain on our side of the river was higher than on the other side, and the gorge was about 200 feet wide. They had built a crude platform in a tree about 30 feet up from the ground.

I watched those in front of me cross using the wire stretched from the tree on our side to another tree on the opposite bank. Hanging just below the wire, fixed with a roller, was a 2-foot metal bar. The idea was to reach up and grasp that bar from the platform while standing well over 40 feet above the water.

"Just hold on tight," the sergeant told Bob Manning, who stood on the platform. "And drop into the water when you get to the other side," he added.

Bob let out a yell, leaped off, slid down the wire—much as we had done from the tower during our parachute training—and dropped into the waist-deep water. He waded ashore, all grins.

By the time it was my turn, several of our group had already made the crossing. This exercise differed from the tower, because from there we had jumped with a parachute harness securing us to the wire and just slid down. Here we had to hang on as we slid and dropped off at the right time. The instructors on the other side yelled when it was time to let go.

I felt confident I could handle it.

"You got the bar?" the sergeant asked.

I nodded and gripped it firmly.

"So fly away, man!"

I jumped off the platform and started down the wire. I quickly gained speed and felt like I was rocketing toward the opposite bank. It happened quickly and there was no time to worry. I dropped off just as I heard the instructor tell me to let go. Relieved, I waded ashore and climbed up the bank.

It wasn't as much fun as the repelling.

Fourth or so behind me was Don Farley. The oldest man in our group, he had served in the Office of Medical Services. After receiving an assignment to South Vietnam, he had volunteered to take the paramilitary course. A pleasant, likeable guy we all admired for his grit, Don wasn't as physically fit as the rest of us, but he hung in there on our field exercises.

As Don made his descent, something didn't look right.

Watch out!

He froze, holding onto the bar too long; he crashed into the bank.

We rushed to him, but two of the instructors beat us there.

"Relax," one ordered.

Don was lying half in the water.

"I think I broke something," he said, in obvious pain.

"Don't try to stand," the other instructor said.

Don was right; one of his legs was clearly broken. A third instructor was already on his radio calling for a helicopter evacuation. Carefully and with considerable effort, because Don was a big man, they helped him onto the bank and tried to comfort him until help arrived.

"I suppose this means you're going to poop out on us," Bill Watkins joked.

"Nah, I'll be back after lunch," Don kidded right back.

"Tough break," Bill said. "But heck, one week in this steamy jungle is probably enough anyway."

We all knew Don would be sent home. That would be hard for him, but he had a much harder moment coming. Because of the broken leg his impending assignment to Vietnam was postponed. Eventually he went and was in the U.S. Embassy in Saigon on March 30, 1965, the day it was bombed. Like many others Don caught glass splinters in his face and eyes. The incident cost him his sight and forced his medical retirement. But his grit came through then, too, and he made a terribly difficult adjustment look easy. He continued to pursue life vigorously despite his blindness.

That afternoon we returned to the Chagres for a second river crossing. This time we would use a rope hanging about 8 feet above the water and tied to trees on either bank. We considered this drill more practical because it was the way to cross a river during a real operation.

First you stretch out atop the rope, grasping it with both hands in front of you, letting one leg dangle for balance, and hooking the other ankle over the top. To move forward you pull with your arms and push with the leg hooked over the rope.

The key is keeping your balance. If you lose it you find yourself hanging under the rope and fighting rapidly building fatigue. To cross in that position means pulling hand over hand with your legs wrapped around the rope. It's so difficult that the strong incentive is to keep your balance and stay on top.

To make the exercise seem realistic, the instructors told us that the current was forceful enough to carry us away and there were crocodiles in the water.

When my turn came I just followed the instructions. By then I had watched about a dozen others make the crossing, and I could see the advantages and pitfalls.

Don't get the rope swaying sideways.

Push with the hooked-over leg more, and pull with your arms less.

I started slowly and finished slowly, but I stayed focused and didn't fall off.

This wasn't the case for André Le Gallo, who was two behind me. In the middle of his crossing the rope started swaying sideways, and André fell under.

"You can't get back up," one instructor shouted, as André hung in the middle letting the swaying stop.

"Just come on ahead, hand over hand," another instructor yelled.

Born in France just before World War II, André had been raised in Paris, where his family, originally from Brittany, spent the war years. They had immigrated to the United States in the late 1940s and settled in northern New Jersey, where André's father, an excellent chef, ran a restaurant. André, a varsity wrestler, had very strong arms and upper body. Either he hadn't heard the instructors or he elected to ignore their counsel. With our shouts of encouragement from both banks, André calmly hoisted himself back up, a feat requiring both strength and balance, and finished his crossing.

Bravo, André!

He had impressed the instructors, but he would achieve true notoriety in another way. One night early in our second week we made camp in a clearing near the river. As usual it had been a physically demanding day, with the heat and humidity taking a lot out of us. We had been hauling packs and web belts containing personal items—underwear, socks, Dopp kits—and some field gear including a shelter half, which is essentially half a pup tent, plus a poncho, a shovel-like entrenching tool, and a machete for clearing the way through the jungle.

We paired up, using two shelter halves to set up rows of tents, with our ponchos doubling as mats to sleep on. We carried no sleeping bags. We weren't comfortable, but no one complained. We were too tired. Besides we were in the middle of the jungle, so we expected hardship.

As dusk descended we ate C-rations—small cans and boxes of prepared but cold food. We carried a couple of flashlights among us, but once it was dark there wasn't much to do except try to get some sleep. The camp quieted quickly as fatigue took its toll.

Suddenly there was a loud cry.

"What the hell is that?" Bob Manning shouted.

Bob and André were sharing a pup tent. Both were over 6 feet tall and didn't quite fit into it. André, seeking some fresh air, had been lying with his head just outside of the tent.

"I don't know. Is that blood?" André asked.

Somebody produced one of the flashlights. It was blood. We were all awake now.

"There are two small holes on the top of your forehead," Bob told

André.

"A bat?"

"A vampire bat!" Bob exclaimed, grabbing everyone's attention.

The bleeding stopped quickly. André's forehead contained two small punctures where the thing had bitten him. He had been attacked by a real vampire, *Desmodus rotundus,* whose range extends from Argentina all the way to Arizona and New Mexico and has been known to avail itself of the blood of humans sleeping outdoors.

The question foremost in our minds was, would it come back? The return to our tents caused a lot of shuffling around, as everyone tried to keep his head inside and his booted feet outside.

No one slept well that night.

Someone mentioned the possibility of an infection, but I don't think André even put a Band-Aid on the wounds. Before we departed for Panama we had received all of the required shots, so that might have helped André ward off any problem.

The story spread quickly, and André became famous among trainees and instructors alike.

The next day's theme was "Living off the Land." It was particularly tough, and many of us dragged through it for lack of sleep—though they did feed us a field-kitchen hot breakfast at dawn.

They divided us into a dozen groups to conduct compass-reading exercises, meaning lots of walking through the jungle. The point man would lead each group by wielding a machete to clear a path. Two men would follow with compasses to keep him on course.

Maps in hand we started out at about 7:30 a.m. We found one checkpoint after another and moved quickly along our assigned route. Our practice at the Farm came in handy. The exercise wasn't difficult, but it was physically tiring. We rotated point men regularly, because that was the toughest role.

By noon we had finished the course and arrived at a large clearing, where the field kitchen had set up for lunch. Hungry and tired we looked forward to a good meal, but our anticipation quickly turned to disappointment, as we noticed that lunch would be C-rations again. Usually it was a type of meat dish, some fruit, cookies or crackers, and maybe some chocolate.

"What's your fruit?" Mike Deuel asked me. "I got peaches."

"Fruit cocktail," I responded. "Want to trade?"

"Nope," he said. "I'm looking for pears."

"I got apple sauce," Bob Manning chimed in. "And beef stew. Anyone want this beef stuff?"

"Got to be better than ham," Ralph McLean said, handing Manning his meat dish. "I hate this ham."

"I don't like it much either," Bob said, "but I'm sure tired of beef stew."

It was always the same, no matter the group, location or conditions on the ground. No one liked what he got. Still it was fuel for the engine, so we always ate it all.

After lunch we gathered for a briefing on the afternoon's effort. Each group would have to build a *bohio* (bo-HEE-oh), Panamanian Spanish for a small hut constructed from trees and thatch. The instructor explained that a *bohio* is nothing more than a platform several feet off the ground—and away from snakes, bigger animals and vermin—enclosed by walls and a roof overhead. The walls and roof would be palm branches—no corrugated tin available—spread over a wood frame.

"One more thing," he added loudly. "Pass by the trucks on your way into the jungle and pick up dinner. See you here in the morning for breakfast at 6:30. Now go ye forth and build tonight's dwelling."

We moved to the trucks and formed lines. Looking ahead we could see what they were handing out for dinner.

"They're giving 'em chickens, live chickens!" Bill half-shouted in disbelief.

"And yucca roots and rice," André added.

"So that's dinner?" Bob asked, not really wanting an answer.

Each group got the same thing: two live chickens, a handful of rice and some yucca roots to boil. We collected ours and headed off to construct our *bohio*.

"Anybody ever kill a chicken?" Ward Warren asked of no one in particular. No one responded.

"We'll draw straws for the honor tonight," he said with a laugh. Ward, a graduate of the University of Michigan, had studied Chinese affairs and spoke Mandarin fluently. He was an internal, meaning that he had joined the JOT program from a position elsewhere within the agency.

We picked a site under some shade and started planning the structure. To sleep seven we figured the *bohio* platform would have to be at least 12 feet by 24 feet. Thank goodness there was no shortage of trees.

None of us had studied engineering of any sort, and we had only machetes and entrenching tools, so this would be no mean feat. The soil was soft, however, so digging the holes for logs to support the platform's frame would not be too difficult.

Three men got started with that. The rest, machetes in hand, set out to bring back suitable trees. The jungle was full of softwood varieties, and we were able to chop down trees with waist-sized-diameter trunks after about 15 minutes of hacking. Then we trimmed off the branches before carrying them back to the site.

Where possible we selected trees with a sturdy V shape in the trunk somewhere, so we could lay other trees onto them to build up the platform. We lashed some into place with vines we had stripped down with our bayonet knives.

As the afternoon wore on, the *bohio* gradually took shape. It wasn't going to win any prizes, but it would serve our purposes for one night. By dusk we were spreading the roof of palm branches, and the bloody thing was done. Ill-proportioned and uneven, lacking stairs to get in, and with a roof that likely wouldn't stop much rain, at least it was sturdy. We felt satisfied that we had completed it, and we wondered how many other groups had actually finished theirs.

Exhausted, we turned our thoughts to dinner and eyed the two poultry specimens tethered to the ground nearby.

"So who wants the honor?" Ward asked.

None of us city kids felt eager to kill and clean chickens, so Bill stepped into the breach.

"I'll kill the damn birds," he growled.

"I'll help," Ralph announced to Bill's satisfaction, and they approached our still-walking dinner.

"Do it somewhere else," Bob offered. "Blood might attract snakes."

Bill glared at him, but he and Ralph grabbed the squawking birds and headed off into the jungle.

"Let's get a fire started," I suggested. "We also have to boil the rice and yucca."

"Easier said than done," André commented. "It's hard to find dry wood."

He was right. It rained frequently in the jungle and sunlight didn't penetrate the canopy in many places, so dry kindling was scarce. But it had to be done, and we spread out looking for anything that would burn. Eventually we got a fire started, not a very hot one but a fire.

"Anyone ever boil rice?" Ward asked. "Do you put it into the water before or after the water boils?"

"After," Bob said. "I think that's how my mom always did it."

"It doesn't matter," André interjected. "It's not Minute Rice from Uncle Ben. We'll just cook it until it's soft enough to eat."

We agreed that was a good idea.

It had grown dark—very dark—and quiet; no squawking from the chickens. We used our metal canteen cups to boil the rice and the yucca roots, neither of which looked appetizing. We rigged up a crude spit to roast the chickens—nobody thought about boiling them in pieces—and set the canteen cups on rocks as close to the fire as we could. Lord only knew how long it would take for the water to start boiling.

"Here they are," Bill announced, as he and Ralph returned with the hacked-up chickens.

"We threw the insides as far away as we could," Ralph added.

"Many thanks, you guys," I said. "Couldn't have been much fun."

"Wasn't," Bill mumbled.

We skewered the chickens and put them on the makeshift spit over the fire. We waited and waited—and waited. Nothing happened. The fire wasn't hot enough to cook them. We waited some more. At least the water boiled, barely, and the rice cooked a little. Same with the yucca, but it remained hard.

Hungry as we were, in the end the fatigue won out. We managed to eat a few mouthfuls of half-cooked rice, chucked the yucca, and threw the still-raw chickens as far into the jungle as we could. Nobody wanted to wait for what might have been hours to finish cooking the food. Sleep seemed a much better choice.

We climbed onto the *bohio,* which I am pleased to report did not collapse under our weight. We settled ourselves on its hopelessly uneven floor and tried to get some rest. It really was uncomfortable, but I fell quickly into a deep sleep. The others did as well, and nothing bothered us until dawn. We had dug holes, felled trees and labored to construct our *bohio* for over seven hours, so we felt the effect.

Along with the slogging through the mud back in paramilitary training, I often wondered about the value of this effort as well. Did building a *bohio* also build character?

Next morning the field kitchen produced a hot breakfast that we thought was delicious—mainly because we were famished. I noticed everyone attacking their meals with gusto and suspected that not many of those chickens had actually been eaten.

"Wonder what this fine day has in store for us," André said.

Now in the middle of our second week we sat in the back of the truck, as it headed again into the jungle on another bright and sunny morning.

"Who knows?" I answered. "We'll find out soon. The trucks are slowing down."

We poured out of the back and found ourselves next to Gatun Lake, actually a part of the Panama Canal. The shore was sandy and the water looked inviting. About 30 large, black rubber boats floated in the shallow water, a stack of paddles on the shore. The head instructor faced the lake, and we faced him.

"Each group should get a boat and paddles," he announced. "We're going to do some work on the water today. This exercise is going to familiarize you with how to handle a small boat. No big thing, you just coordinate your paddling."

He hoisted a paddle and demonstrated where to place your hands and how to pull forward.

"Across the lake and back," he continued. "Just go around the orange buoy over there on the other side."

He seemed to be taking a lot longer than necessary to explain something that was pretty simple.

"Two more things," he continued. "First, this is going to be a race."

Everybody perked up.

"The first boat back wins. And second, it starts right now!"

We bolted to our feet and ran. As we did we could see that the boats and paddles had been shoved out onto the lake.

"Devious bastards!" someone said.

Now the boats were floating about 25 yards from shore, and the paddles were floating around them. As we got to the water, there was some momentary confusion and hesitation, but then we jumped in and it felt great. We all dashed toward the boats—over 100 men headed for 30 of them. Lots of yelling, pushing and shoving, but our small group managed to get out in front.

"Shove him in," André ordered, as he and I pushed Bob up and over the side.

"Grab some paddles," Bill said, "and throw them in the boat with Manning."

What a circus. Everyone was thrashing around. Bob pulled me and Monty Rogers, another Midwesterner, into the boat and André scrambled in as well. Then we shoved the others away as they tried to get in. Some weren't too happy. It was pandemonium. We spotted Ward and Mike Deuel and hauled them aboard.

"Grab another paddle," someone yelled, "and get lined up on either side." It was Bill, and he became our coxswain of the day, more by default than anything else; we didn't have time for an election.

We started for the other side of the lake, noting with pleasure that we had gotten under way first.

"Great!" Bill yelled. "We're far ahead. Most of them are still in the water."

We lined up, paddles in hand, on both sides of the boat. We started chanting in unison and pulling as hard as we could. We had been training together for a while now, so it hadn't taken us long to get organized. That wasn't the case for any of the other groups, and soon we enjoyed a big lead.

"Where are the SEALs?" Monty asked.

Over the whole training course the only group we ever worried about was the SEALs. They were in great shape, they were obviously accustomed to using the rubber boats, and they had lots and lots of stamina. We greatly respected their ability.

"They're coming," Bill answered. "Paddle hard."

He wasn't a great coxswain, but he kept us headed in the right direction and we made good progress.

"Right side paddle, left side hold," he yelled.

Our forward motion slowed a little while we righted our course by pulling less on one side or the other. Bob's left-handed strength helped us on that side, plus he had experience paddling a canoe.

"Pull," we all shouted. We were humming along and we felt confident as we neared the orange buoy.

"SEALs are coming," said Bill, the only one who could sneak a glance behind us. "They are clear of the mêlée and paddling hard."

No one doubted it. We knew the Navy guys wanted to win this race for the sake of their pride and they wouldn't be deterred by our big lead. But we, the unlabelled civilians, also wanted to win. We pulled even harder.

We rounded the buoy and for the first time we got a clear view of our position in the race. The SEALs were about 30 yards behind but closing. The rest were strung out behind them, looking like a band of marauding pirates. Men were shouting, standing in the boats, waving paddles.

The SEALs went right by us, headed for the buoy. They weren't wasting any breath or strength with emotional outbursts. They looked serious and determined. We tried to keep pulling hard while maintaining our rhythm.

Then some in the oncoming horde, realizing they had no chance of winning the race, decided to become spoilers. Several of the boats altered course to block us. We viewed their actions in a most unfavorable light.

"Never mind, we got 'em," Bill shouted.

We cleared the offending boats about halfway back to the beach. Now the SEALs had rounded the buoy and were bearing down on us. None of the other boats bothered them. We were running out of breath and had given up the chant, but we kept to the paddling rhythm.

"Pull harder!" Bill implored, sounding less confident. The SEALs had narrowed the gap. We were nearing the beach. We urged each other on with whatever breath we could spare.

Our strength held out and we won. In fact when we hit the beach we were able to get out of the boat and haul it ashore before the SEALs arrived. They had cut into our lead but not enough. Our great start and physical condition had carried the day.

We savored our victory, inwardly. We said nothing to the SEALs or anyone else. Now that I think about it, maybe we were so out of breath and tired that we couldn't gloat. Likewise, no one mentioned the victory to us.

"Okay, into the trucks, we're headed back," the senior instructor said impassively after the last boat had been beached. Maybe we surprised them.

The next day dawned like all the rest—clear, sunny and hot. Word had gotten around that the last training exercise would be really tough. Possibly, but we would be flying back to Virginia the following evening, so how bad could it be?

As usual we finished breakfast and took off in the trucks around 7:30. The ride seemed longer than usual. They had started out from the headquarters and barracks area, which was located at the end of a peninsula, and followed a red-clay road along the shoreline. When we reached our destination we were in a large clearing halfway up a hill.

We felt an uneasy anticipation.

An instructor, standing on a small platform in the middle of the clearing, began.

"Today will feature an escape and evasion exercise, and I'm going to give you the ground rules. Listen carefully, because I don't want any screw-ups. Here's the scenario. You're in an enemy area and have just pulled off a successful raid on their headquarters compound. They are pissed off and have alerted all their forces to apprehend or kill you. The plan calls for you to be exfiltrated by submarine from the point on the map you are now being given. A reception team will meet you, and that will signal the end of the exercise. The exercise will start soon."

His description intensified our uneasiness.

"There are more ground rules," he continued. "We—my friends and I—will function as the pissed-off enemy. All roads will be patrolled and guarded. Road crossings will be risky and must be accomplished with care. If you are caught, you lose points. If you are caught more than once, you don't pass the exercise. If you try blatantly to escape capture, you will be considered killed, which also means you don't pass the exercise. Is all that clear?"

There were no questions. It was straightforward. We had to travel 18 miles through the jungle, avoiding enemy patrols and returning approximately to where we had started out, to the exfiltration point on the beach.

"There's more," said the instructor. "The submarine can't wait past noon tomorrow, so unless you get there by then you won't be exfiltrated. That also means you don't pass the exercise."

We were carrying light packs and M1 rifles. Even though we were now much more accustomed to the jungle than we had been that first night, covering that distance was going to be no picnic. Still, we had almost 27 hours to do it.

The instructor continued.

"The exercise gives you a grace period of 15 minutes, during which you will, if you're smart, get the hell out of here and make tracks for the rendezvous point. After the 15 minutes, the enemy will react on sight. Clear? The exercise starts when I drop my hat."

He dropped his hat and all hell broke loose.

Just like the previous day at the lake, men ran in every direction trying to put distance between themselves and the clearing. They knew the enemy patrols would start soon, and the patrols would know where we'd be heading.

Try to get across the first road as soon as possible, we were thinking. "We," in this instance, included André, Mike Deuel, Monty, Mike L. and me. We hadn't planned it that way, but that's how it worked out. We were standing together listening to the instructor's briefing, and we had taken off in the same direction when he dropped his hat.

Nobody had set off alone, as far as I could see. The groups ranged from two to six men. I have no idea what the optimum number would have been. We ran along the road for almost 10 minutes then cut into the jungle along the spine of the peninsula. We saw a couple of other groups, but soon we were alone. It was still early morning, but the heat was rising and we had worked up a heavy sweat from the run.

We stopped to gather our thoughts and figure out where we were. They had given us good maps, so it didn't take long to pinpoint our location. Our sprint along the road had gained us about a mile, so we had 17 to go to reach exfiltration.

"If we can make 2 miles an hour, we could be on the beach just after dark," Mike Deuel said.

"Yeah," I responded, "but hacking our way will slow us down."

"Whatever," André said. "We need to start walking if we're going to get there."

"I'll start on the point," Monty said.

We picked up our gear and fell in line behind him. Monty handed me his rifle—he couldn't carry it and use his machete at the same time—and led us into the jungle. Within a couple of hours we reached the first road we'd have to cross. We heard a truck pass and assumed it was an enemy patrol.

How often do they pass?

We approached the road carefully after locating our position on the map. Our progress had been slow despite a steady pace and few breaks.

"Likely there will be foot patrols or outposts along the roads," Monty said.

"You're probably right," Mike Deuel added. "Let's get a good look at things before we try to cross."

Our caution was rewarded after only about five minutes. Hiding in the brush we had fanned out along the road, another red-clay ribbon about 15 feet wide running through dense jungle. We tried to spot a good place to cross while watching for patrols or guard posts.

As André and I scanned a straight stretch we saw another group crossing about 50 yards away. Whistles blew and an enemy patrol suddenly appeared.

"Busted," I heard one of them yell, probably to others still hiding on our side of the road.

We moved silently in the opposite direction and regrouped. Nobody else had seen anything, but we all had heard the shouts and whistles. Getting across the damned road was going to be trickier than anticipated.

We distanced ourselves from the patrol until we reached a curve. The patrol couldn't see us there, but we knew they were taking the names of the men they had stopped, and soon they would be on the lookout again.

We couldn't wait until dark; we had to cross right away. We decided to go one at a time, regrouping on the other side about 20 yards into the jungle. Everything seemed quiet. We'd just have to chance it. Mike L. would go first, and we'd each follow if all went well.

Our luck held. Mike dashed across and dove into the jungle. Nothing but quiet. We sighed in relief then followed one by one. As I crossed, keeping as low to the ground as I could, I saw a ditch that ran along the road on the opposite side. The others had probably seen it but couldn't warn me. As they had probably done I half-slid into the ditch—it was too wide to jump over—and scrambled up the other side.

Back together we regrouped and set off again. According to our map only two crossings remained between us and the beach.

"If the other crossings take that long, we'll never make it to the beach today," said Monty.

True. It had taken us quite a while to scout out a site and finally get across that road. We lost time.

"Doesn't really matter," Mike Deuel said. "We have to just push ahead."

We did, crossing the second road without incident by mid-afternoon. Afterward we reached a small stream and stopped to fill our canteens. The water was clear and cool, and I was tempted to avoid adding the mandatory purification tablets. I splashed some onto my head and face. It felt good. The others did the same. All were perspiring heavily, and our fatigues were drenched with sweat. We took 10 minutes to eat some C-rations. It was a welcome break.

Back on the trek under the quiet and pretty jungle canopy we reached an area that was higher in elevation with much less undergrowth. The point man had less hacking to do and the rest of us just watched our compasses. Go east, young men.

When we took our bearings again we found out we had covered about half the distance to the beach, and nobody was showing signs of fatigue yet.

Good thing we're all in shape. Things could be worse.

They were about to be.

We approached the last crossing point around 5 p.m. and sensed signs of activity. We assumed some of the other groups had made about the same progress we had and were moving in our vicinity. We also assumed the instructors knew we'd be passing by here, and acting in the role of our enemy they would try to make things as tough as possible.

We decided to play it cautious again. We found a good vantage point and just watched. Sure enough there was more road traffic than we had seen on either of the previous crossings. The noose was tightening, as our side funneled into a smaller and smaller area. It was built into the exercise. As intended, the enemy activity increased our stress level.

We talked quietly about our next moves.

"Hell, I think that curve will give us enough time to get across," Monty said, gesturing to our right. "I say we move out. We're losing time again."

"Monty's right," Mike Deuel said. "Unless they're right across the road, we'll have time to make it. We can hear jeeps or trucks well before they get here."

"Agreed," I said. "The only difference this time is more traffic, but Mike's right, we can hear them coming."

André and Mike L. nodded. We would make the crossing now.

We approached the road carefully, listening for any sign of a presence on the other side. We heard nothing. Monty was first to cross this time and Mike Deuel was last. At Mike's signal, Monty jumped out of the covering jungle and took off across the road. I began just as he disappeared on the other side.

I saw them just as I finished the crossing: an eight-man patrol. They nabbed Monty and then me. I yelled a warning, but André was already coming. Bad luck for sure. They got us all, and we had to give them our names before we could continue.

We had stumbled right into them. We cursed our bad luck, but there was nothing to do except make it to the beach within the time limit and try not to get caught again.

Soon we had moved well away from the last crossing and noticed the terrain was getting rougher: small hills, ravines and thick undergrowth. Another map check showed we had about 7 miles left and only a couple of hours of daylight. What to do?

"If we push on, we can be on the beach sometime after midnight," said Mike Deuel. "But covering this terrain in the dark won't be much fun."

I worried about someone slipping into a ravine.

"I'd love to get in tonight," I said, "but I guess discretion may be the better part of valor."

"Yeah, we don't want any injuries," Monty added.

"Well, let's at least make it as far as we can before dark," André said, "and we can see what it would be like to continue."

"So we move out briskly," Mike Deuel concluded with a grin. We did, but the terrain didn't get any better.

Dusk came and went. Mike L. had taken the lead. At one point he almost walked into a tree. We took it as a sign to call it a night. We could move through the jungle in darkness, but there were limits. This terrain was difficult enough in daylight. At night it just didn't seem smart to keep moving. We decided to get some rest and finish the last miles starting at dawn.

I leaned my rifle against a tree, took off my pack and sat down. It had been a long, stressful, demanding day. I was dead tired.

We spread out the ponchos to sleep on and got out more C-rations. Suddenly we heard noises behind us. Was it a patrol looking for us? Another bunch headed for the beach? We didn't know. There wasn't time to do much. I reached for my unloaded rifle, just because it seemed a sensible thing to do.

Just then three men we thought were from the SEAL group ran—yes, ran—right by us. We watched, amazed.

What the hell are they doing? How long have they been behind us? Was this just for effect?

Whatever the answer, the SEALs just kept going. We later learned they had arrived first on the beach, well before midnight. However imprudent they might have been, watching those men run by raised our already high regard for them.

Despite the conditions—hard ground, bugs and intermittent rain—I slept well. Fatigue will do that. Someone shook me lightly just before dawn and I rolled out and put my boots on—we had all slept in our fatigues. Much to the concern of the rest of us, Mike L. had not taken off his boots. He said he was having trouble with his feet and didn't want to look at them until we got to the beach. We had all argued that some air and dry socks would be a good thing, but he wouldn't listen.

We were already walking as dawn broke, and our spirits were high. This would be the last day of the course and the end of a tough two weeks in Panama. The sleep, fitful for some, had done us all good, and there was a spring again in our steps.

Mike Deuel took the point and set a good pace. We all wanted to get this over with. A pretty blue sky appeared over the jungle canopy, and it looked like yet another sunny day. The terrain grew less difficult as we approached the rendezvous point. It took only a couple of hours to cover the rest of the way. We reached the beach and checked in by 8:30.

I looked forward to a long hot shower and some hot food.

The military had watched and graded everyone during those two weeks. Even though we were civilians they included us in the evaluations, which turned out to be advantageous. We had done very well both individually and as a group. They awarded us points for our performance in each exercise, and total points determined how we finished. Above certain levels they awarded badges of distinction.

I left with a Jungle Expert badge, meaning I had performed at the highest level. So did all but five in our group.

The badge aside, I also left with a much greater respect for the jungle environment and how to deal with it. That turned out to be very important. What I had learned and experienced in Panama would serve me well and soon.

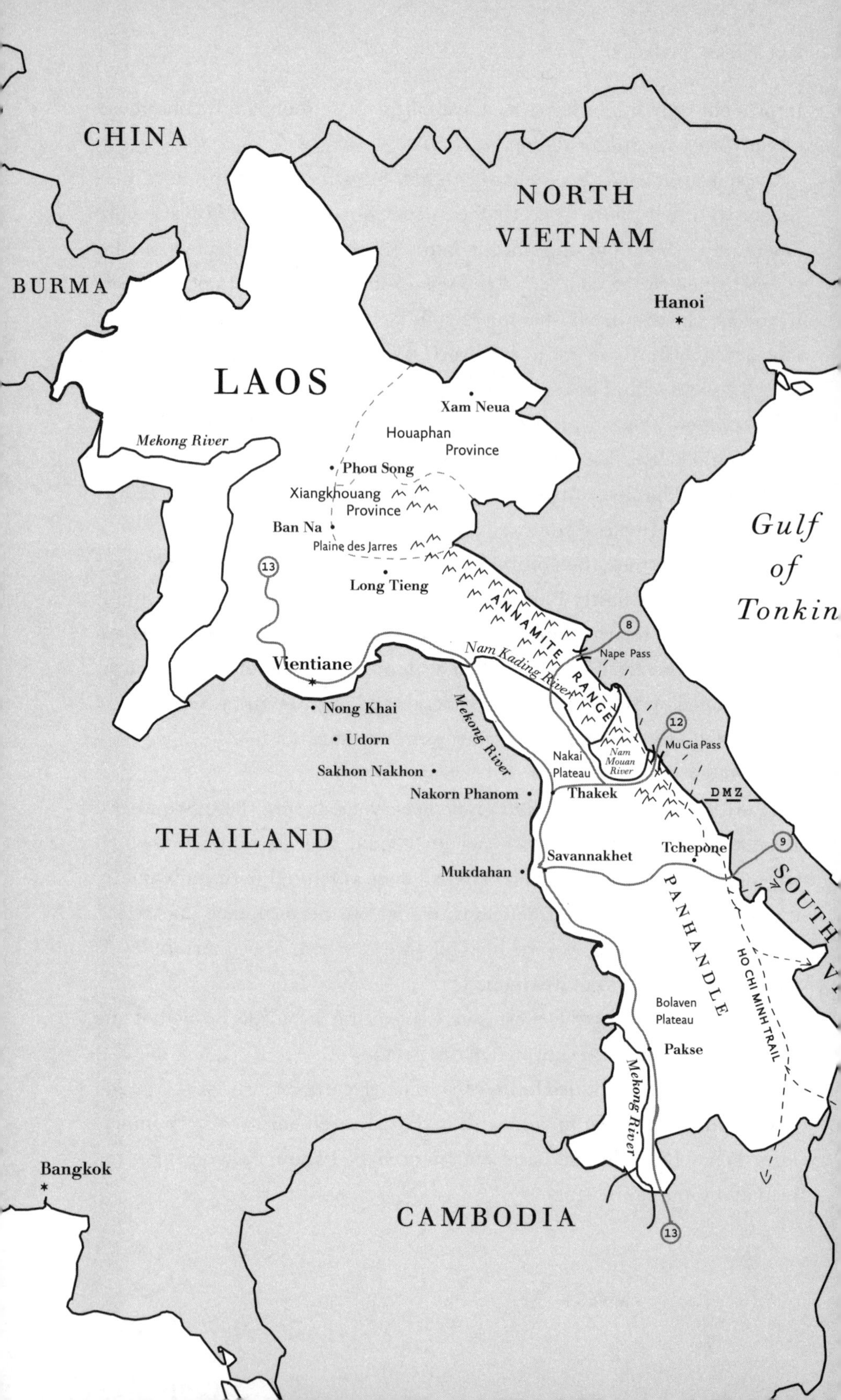
CHINA
BURMA
NORTH VIETNAM
Hanoi
LAOS
Xam Neua
Houaphan Province
Mekong River
Phou Song
Xiangkhouang Province
Ban Na
Plaine des Jarres
13
Long Tieng
ANNAMITE RANGE
Gulf of Tonkin
8
Nape Pass
Vientiane
Nam Kading River
Nong Khai
Udorn
Mekong River
12
Mu Gia Pass
Nakai Plateau
Nam Mouan River
Sakhon Nakhon
Nakorn Phanom
Thakek
DMZ
THAILAND
Tchepone
9
Savannakhet
Mukdahan
PANHANDLE
SOUTH V
HO CHI MINH TRAIL
Bolaven Plateau
Pakse
Mekong River
Bangkok
CAMBODIA
13

PART II: THE SECRET WAR

4. Going Upcountry

BAN NA, LAOS 1962

Laos would be my first of seven overseas assignments. On a muggy evening in July 1962 I was winging there, as our plane descended to refuel at one of the most challenging landings on Earth: Kai Tak Airport in Hong Kong.

Flanked on both sides by mountains that look pretty in daylight but menacing at dusk—and which can funnel crosswinds so fierce that even the biggest jets sometimes can't handle them—we dropped in smoothly, just over the dense flotilla of sampans in the harbor. All in all it was quite an experience.

Our touchdown capped the better part of two days of traveling and accumulated jet lag, which not even a first-class passage could forestall—the trip was starting to wear us down. All the good food and wine we had enjoyed couldn't overcome it. Still we felt excited to be nearing our initial destination: Bangkok, Thailand.

By now André Le Gallo, Mike Deuel, Ralph McLean and I had been training together for just over a year, and we all had volunteered for a six-month TDY in Laos. There the agency, in support of President Kennedy's decision to hold the line against communist expansion, was trying to help the Laotians maintain territorial integrity and an independent government.

We deplaned for an hour during the refueling. Hoping for a quick look at the city we moved to the door just as the flight attendant opened it.

The heavy, humid, foul air hit us like the proverbial brick wall. Whatever breeze was stirring carried the stench of rotting fish and garbage from the harbor. The combination of our travel fatigue and those odors created an unpleasant first glimpse of Southeast Asia.

Even so, when I looked at the lights shining from the windows of the houses and buildings covering the hillsides, Hong Kong appeared intriguing and even inviting. I resolved to return someday.

We arrived at Don Muang Airport in Bangkok after midnight. We were even more tired by then but also excited and curious. Agency officers met us at the gate, so it didn't take long to clear customs and get our luggage loaded into their van.

I carried a large duffel bag, a suitcase and a wooden Jack Kramer tennis racket—all of my worldly possessions at the time except for the TR3, which I had left with Dad back in Kansas City. The officers took us straight to a rest house not far from the American Embassy, where we each enjoyed the temporary luxury of a single room.

Bangkok made a good first impression. I found the Thai people attractive and friendly; I liked them right away. Many of the girls looked especially pretty. I enjoyed the Buddhist temples and the *klongs*—the city's canals, similar to those in Venice but with only the occasional small boat. Even the death-trap, three-wheeled taxis and frenetic traffic represented an exotic new world for me.

The next day we headed for Vientiane, the Laotian capital. Our days of enjoying first class were over for a while. My colleagues and I boarded a vintage, twin-engine DC-3 and lumbered north.

We landed in Vientiane a little before noon and taxied to the area reserved for Air America, an adjunct operation of the agency that traced its roots back to General Claire Chennault, the former commander of the famed Flying Tigers in China during World War II. As we climbed down the deplaning ladder and stood in a group on the tarmac, three men approached us and we realized we were about to meet our bosses: Bill Lair, Tony Poe and Pat Landry.

Each of these men had developed a reputation for courage and toughness, and we all had heard the impressive stories. Bill, Tony and Pat were men's men, willing to take on challenges anywhere, anytime. They spearheaded the heart of the agency's paramilitary efforts in Laos.

James William Lair, in his late 30s, stood about 6 feet tall and radiated strength. A graduate of Texas A&M University, he had been assigned to Southeast Asia since the early 1950s. He spent that time in Thailand running an agency project that organized and trained an elite group called the Police Aerial Reinforcement Unit, the PARU, which could parachute in to aid Thai military forces quickly in remote areas. Wearing khaki trousers, a sport shirt and glasses, Bill was now the highly respected chief of our special, independent unit housed at Vientiane's airport. His unassuming, almost shy demeanor masked a mental and physical self-discipline we would come to know well.

Anthony Alexander Poshepny, a bull of a man, looked to be about 35. Dressed in fatigues and combat boots he was balding prematurely, but at 6 feet he looked as strong and tough as his reputation. He wasn't smiling.

Tony, according to the stories we heard and later confirmed, had almost taken up professional golf, which seemed a real anomaly. He had landed on Iwo Jima in 1945 with the Marine Corps when he was still a teenager and later served in Korea. He also had worked to train groups of Tibetans to aid their resistance against the Red Chinese. He and Pat, serving in Indonesia during the late 1950s' communist rebellion, had been cut off and almost captured but eventually were exfiltrated by submarine.

Lloyd "Pat" Landry was also a graduate of Texas A&M. With his stocky build he could have played guard on the football team. He wore cotton slacks and a sport shirt and carried a swagger stick. It wasn't hard to picture him handling difficult and dangerous situations.

Not knowing what to anticipate but eager to try something new and different, we had grown more excited as we neared Vientiane and the end of our long journey. We eagerly awaited their first words of welcome.

"Jesus Christ, we asked 'em to send us more men and they sent us a bunch of kids," Tony growled. "They look green as grass."

"Damn, they must not be reading our cables," Pat added in a loud voice. "We said we wanted experienced officers. How the hell do they expect us to run this operation?"

"Well, we're just going to have to make 'em into something worthwhile," Bill sighed.

Now they were all smiling.

To say they deflated our enthusiasm and burst our bubble would be putting it mildly. Yet none of us reacted. No one pointed out that we all had military experience and had earned high praise in the agency's paramilitary course—run by men who were their cohorts. They would have known that anyway from our files. We just grinned back at them, shook hands all around, and said how happy we were to be there.

I suspected this was an oft-repeated scene with new arrivals, but they made their point. We were indeed the greenest of the green, but we would need to learn in a hurry because our responsibilities would grow quickly.

"No sense messing around," Bill told us. "I want you four to go up to Sam Thong in the morning to take a look at what we're doing. Meantime we'll sort out where each of you is going to be assigned."

He was referring to an operational site in Xiangkhouang Province, not far from the Plaine des Jarres, northeast of the capital. At the time the name meant nothing to me.

"I guess I can take one of 'em up to Sam Neua, on the border with North Vietnam," Tony said in a gentler tone, meaning Xam Neua, the capital of Houaphan, a province farther north.

"About time for some lunch," Pat announced. "Any of you guys old enough to drink beer?"

That comment confirmed that we truly were being needled, so we responded with loud shouts of feigned outrage. We headed to a small French restaurant where we enjoyed a nice meal complete with baguettes and red wine—not beer—and quickly established rapport with the trio. We definitely liked what we saw in these men, and they seemed favorably impressed with us. We began forming bonds that in some cases would last a lifetime. I felt confident our work would become challenging and rewarding.

That it would—but as I learned as my career proceeded, not necessarily in the ways I expected.

The agency had divided its paramilitary efforts in Laos—headed by Bill with Pat as his active deputy—into three geographical regions. We operated programs in the north where I would initially be assigned; in the central region, also known as the panhandle, where I would later be assigned, and in the south. We worked each region with a different group of local people—for example with mountain tribal groups such as the Hmong in the north, and with the lowland Lao who lived mostly along the Mekong River.

This arrangement typified our efforts at the time—deploying a small number of men to assist the locals at their behest.

Though the agency ran each program separately the objective was the same: monitoring and impeding—or at least harassing—efforts by the North Vietnamese to support the Pathet Lao, the communist party, in its attempt to overthrow King Savang Vatthana and the government in Vientiane headed by General Phoumi Nosavan, who headed the Lao military. A strong leader but not a politician, he was the main U.S. ally in the country at the time because he resisted the communists and he had asked for our assistance.

For geopolitical reasons—and reasons of his own, I'm sure—President Kennedy had drawn a line in Southeast Asia. He declared that U.S. policy in the region would resist communist expansionism there. Kennedy, with former President Eisenhower's blessing—indeed, Eisenhower had so advised him—stood firm on this decision.

No "dominoes" would fall, a concept that had originated with Eisenhower. In other words the United States would fight the communist insurgency in Laos and South Vietnam to keep the Red Menace from spreading across the region. But rather than deploy U.S. military forces to Laos, the Kennedy administration in its wisdom had opted for aid programs, advisers and covert action.

Vietnam was quickly becoming a different story.

The decision had triggered the planning that put Bill Lair into Laos to establish its programs. Hundreds of other agency and non-agency Americans eventually would participate in what would become known as The

Secret War in Laos. In fact, as will become clear, very little remains secret about what we did.

The biggest and most active of the programs was the one in the north supporting the Hmong tribe—though in 1962 we knew them as the Meo. It was simple ignorance on our part. In later years I discovered that Meo was a pejorative term that meant "barbarian" in Chinese. Ultimately we figured that out, but the Meo/Hmong knew we were not malicious, just dumb. They didn't make an issue of it.

My colleagues and I had arrived at the early stages of the program during an expansion effort. The Hmong (pronounced MONG) were—and still are—a tough and proud mountain people who had been pushed into Laos long ago from southern China. They rarely lived below 2,000 feet in the mountains that cover the northern part of the country. They were not afraid to fight for the right to be left alone to pursue their traditional existence. Theirs was an agricultural economy employing slash-and-burn clearing to grow mountain rice and vegetables—and poppies for opium whenever possible. We knew about the opium so we did our best to monitor everything loaded onto our aircraft to ensure that none was being transported.

Ideology was not an issue. The average Hmong could not distinguish between communism and capitalism and could not have cared less about either. They did feel threatened, however, by the Pathet Lao and their North Vietnamese supporters. The Hmong had decided to fight to preserve their autonomy, and all they asked of us was financial and materiel support.

Bill had struck the first agreement with Vang Pao, the Hmong leader, in December 1960. Vang Pao had made his position clear. Lao communists would push the Hmong off their lands if they didn't fight. But if the Americans provided weapons and other aid they could resist. This was a brave decision. For the Hmong, it would come to mean more than a decade of fighting and tens of thousands of them dying.

For purposes of managing the program the agency had divided Hmong country into regions. Each region was numbered, but often it became better known by the name of the province it occupied or by one of its main villages.

The protagonists in the north, and elsewhere in Laos, were the Royal Lao Army—also known in French as the Forces Armées Royales, the FAR—to which we were allied, and the Pathet Lao, aka the Lao People's Army. The latter force, ill-organized and poorly trained and equipped, was supported by North Vietnam, whose units were known as the Viet Cong, or VC.

The North Vietnamese, commanded by Ho Chi Minh, enjoyed a fearsome reputation because of their 1954 victory over French forces in Dien Bien Phu at the end of the colonial period. They were known as smart and aggressive fighters.

The Hmong units we would be arming and organizing opposed the PL and by extension the VC. They accepted or rather tolerated the FAR, but only for a practical purpose: both faced a common enemy. Actually the Hmong didn't like the Lao, and the feeling was mutual.

More letters in the alphabet soup of the conflict: the KL formed by Kong Le, an obstinate Lao captain who commanded a battalion of parachutists. Kong Le, angry at politics and politicians in Vientiane, had staged a coup and broken away from the FAR to form his group, which he described as "neutralists." His men fought the FAR but not the PL or the VC, so the neutralists were far from neutral.

The day after our arrival, and newly clad in field clothes and jungle boots, we climbed into a helicopter for a trip upcountry to Sam Thong. Everything north of Vientiane was considered upcountry. Whatever it was called it was a different world. There were no—and I mean no—amenities. That didn't bother us in the least; we had been looking forward to this for months.

The mountains of North Laos, ranging from 2,000 to 8,000 feet, displayed an unusual beauty and we drank it in from the copter. Enormous karsts, or limestone outcrops, rose straight up out of the ground at random.

Soon we descended to Sam Thong's dirt strip, joining a couple of small planes on the ground. After landing we learned that an Army Special Forces unit had just completed training a Hmong battalion. The men were going to graduate that morning and we were invited to watch the ceremony.

The Special Forces units, known locally as White Star, had been sent to Sam Thong to help prepare the Hmong to fight. Normally the CIA would have handled the task, but Washington had decided to use White Star, so the agency would have been hard-pressed to contest it. Still, most agency people thought the military shouldn't be conducting such a program.

The whole expansive camp seemed out of place here with its tents, latrines, drinking water purification systems, mess facilities, movies at night, mail deliveries—and peanut butter. It required logistics and daily flights from Vientiane to keep the complex supplied. This didn't seem to be a proper domain for snake-eating, live-off-the-land warriors. To me the Hmong needed training as hit-and-run guerrilla forces. They needed someone who could teach them small-unit tactics.

What they didn't need was what we saw that day. The graduation ceremony turned out to be a parade reviewed by the White Star commanding officer, who had flown in from Vientiane that morning. I still remember thinking how inappropriate it seemed to have guerrilla fighters parading in front of an American officer.

The Hmong were not much as marchers. They did their best, but their ranks were rarely straight. Unfortunately the White Star brass likewise did not do their best. They all but ignored Vang Pao and acknowledged him only as the march concluded—a serious faux pas.

Despite the clumsy ceremony the Hmong unit received, for completing their training, uniforms, boots and weapons—including machine guns, recoilless rifles and mortars. Clearly the Hmong had tolerated the marching and parading in order to obtain the equipment. When we trained them it was in groups of three or four—and we taught them how to use those weapons.

Later that day we roamed around the village to size up where we would be living for the next several months—minus the White Star amenities. The Hmong clearly were a people unlike any of the lowland Lao we had encountered in Vientiane. With sharper features similar to the Chinese, they were small in stature but strong and energetic.

The village, like other Hmong villages I would see, was almost primitive, with thatched huts, dirt floors and a latrine area in the forest. The villagers obtained their water from streams that, if they were lucky, were only a short walk away. The women and girls hauled water, cooked, sewed, and washed clothes. The men farmed, hunted, and lolled around. I saw these characteristics in every Hmong village I visited.

The village leader, the *nai ban*, introduced us to Vang Pao, or VP, as he came to be known. He looked upon each of us sternly and seriously. His English was weak, although it would improve greatly over the next decade, so we spoke French—something I had learned during my two years at Camp Bussac.

Vang Pao had learned the language as a non-commissioned officer in a French army unit several years earlier. When he heard that we would be assigned separately to Hmong regions he thanked us for coming to help his people.

I thought he was an impressive man. What struck me was how VP's conversation consisted almost entirely of small talk, but it was clear he was using it to assess each of us, as if asking himself, "Who are these guys?"

He did not share his conclusions with us. What we shared with him was lunch, Hmong style, with sticky rice, chicken, some kind of green vegetable, and lychee nuts and bananas. Because Sam Thong was well supplied we also could offer VP some Japanese beer that had been cooled in the nearby stream. It tasted pretty good.

It had been an interesting first exposure upcountry, and as we rode the helicopter back to Vientiane I was eager to know where and when I would be assigned.

I didn't have long to wait. We touched down at dusk and headed straight to what we loosely described as "the motel," the only such accommodation in Laos. It even featured a swimming pool. Bill and Pat lived there and we met them in the bar. After a couple of drinks they took each of us aside for a private chat.

Pat spoke with me and typically eschewing chit-chat got directly to the point.

"We want you to go up to Ban (the Lao word for village) Na," he announced. He frequently seemed to announce things—no debate or even discussion.

"That's great. Where's Ban Na?"

He smiled. "What if I said just outside Dien Bien Phu?"

"You wouldn't send me unless you thought I could handle it."

"Right you are, lad." He smiled. "Ban Na is just west of the Plaine des Jarres and it needs a longer landing strip. We can only land single-engine planes or choppers up there and we need a capability for larger twin-engine planes. You run the region, which is established and is quiet for the moment, but concentrate on getting that landing strip lengthened. Any questions?"

"People with shovels are the earth movers, right?"

"Right again. I could send up some cratering charges if you know how to use them."

I hesitated a moment, thinking about my basic explosives training.

"Yeah, send them up. When do I go?"

"In the morning," Pat said, looking me straight in the eye. "I know you didn't come all the way out here just to hang around Vientiane. Be at the airport at 0700."

"I'll be there. What about some field gear and a weapon?"

"You can pick up what you want at our airport warehouse in the morning. Don't take too much. You have to carry whatever you take."

Pat said nothing about the enemy or danger—that would come soon enough.

About a week earlier I had said goodbye to my parents in Kansas City and boarded the plane for San Francisco. Now I was standing next to a dirt landing strip in a Hmong village just west of the Plaine des Jarres in Laos, half a world away.

Incredible!

I watched the Helio Courier disappear over the ridgeline. The Helio, as we called it, was a single-engine aircraft built for STOL, Short Takeoff and Landing operations. It performed yeoman service for Air America and the agency during all the years we operated in Laos, such as the morning it conveyed me to Ban Na.

Before my flight, as Pat had directed, I sought out the logistics officer at our warehouse at the airport in Vientiane. Air America and another contract airline shared a large compound at one end. It included hangars, parts shops and maintenance facilities. They had a big operation that was getting bigger all the time. The agency maintained a small office and warehouse next to the compound.

"What do you think you'll need?" the logistics officer asked.

"I really don't know," I told him. "What are the guys upcountry carrying?"

"Well, they all start out with too much and end up turning in excess gear. First choice I guess is what kind of weapon you want. Nobody carries a sidearm upcountry, so the choice is really a carbine or an M1. The carbine is lighter but less reliable and has less range. What's your pleasure?"

I tried to weigh the pros and cons of each weapon.

"I'll take an M1," I said, finally. Later, after walking around in the mountains upcountry, I would exchange the rifle for the carbine.

"You want a backpack?"

"Guess I'll need something for extra clothes, but only a small one."

"That's all I have. This isn't L.L. Bean. What's more, the Hmong are all little guys so most of the gear we have is small."

"Okay, give me a small backpack."

"Most guys carry a web belt," he added. "Makes it easy to carry your emergency radio."

"My what?"

"Nobody flies around upcountry without an emergency radio," he explained. "Here's yours."

He handed me a small transmitter/receiver. Soon, just like all others working upcountry, I would take the thing everywhere I went. It fit into a pouch attached to the web belt, and it became my most important piece of gear.

"You should have a couple of extra clips of ammo and a small first aid kit, too."

I also picked up a bayonet and attached it to the web belt. It seemed a good idea but wasn't, and later I returned it in favor of a multi-blade jackknife, which was much more practical.

"That should do it, unless you have an extra pair of 9 1/2 jungle boots," I said.

"Not likely, but I can order them up from Bangkok. I'll let you know when they come in."

"Many thanks," I told him. I meant it; he had been a pleasure to deal with. No forms, no signatures, no bureaucracy, just good advice and generosity with whatever he had. In my further dealings with him I learned if I needed something to get a job done he'd give it to me, and if he didn't have it he'd get it. His attitude summed up our whole support system during the time I was in Laos and it reassured all of us living and working upcountry.

I felt as though I had come to the end of the world, and it was a lonely place. But I had begun my first real assignment, one I had worked and trained very hard to win. In Ban Na, I would operate as one of the few agency men in Laos, working quietly in a remote village and accompanied by a Thai man named Panit and his three-man team.

Panit and his colleagues belonged to the PARU, the elite group that Bill Lair had spent the last decade organizing and training in Thailand. Bill and a couple of Thai police officers had hand-picked them from hundreds of applicants. They led a 300-strong force of men who were all at least high school graduates and who spoke a language from a neighboring country in addition to Thai.

Bill had trained them at a jungle camp in central Thailand that Allen Dulles once visited, and he organized them somewhat like the Army's Special Forces, with counterinsurgency tactics one of their specialties.

In addition to general training, PARU personnel learned specific capabilities designed to enhance small-unit operations. Panit was our weapons man. He could employ, assemble, and repair the entire range of weapons the agency provided to the Hmong. The other three men included a medic, a radio operator—who was very important because he kept us linked to Vientiane—and an explosives expert. All four could train the others in the basics, and all PARU were jump qualified.

We were specifically ordered to "stay the hell out of combat." If I was ever captured by VC, when we weren't even supposed to be there, it would have caused a major incident and more trouble for Averell Harriman. He was our ambassador at large and chief representative to the talks in Geneva, Switzerland, where the United States and 13 other nations were attempting to establish Laotian neutrality in the growing war in Southeast Asia.

That was our guidance: Under no circumstances get involved in combat or risk being captured. My orders were to aid and advise the Hmong—period. They operated under their own system of leadership. Panit also advised the Hmong, and although all four men had much more experience than I did they cooperated with me because I represented their link to the supply line.

By the time I began my stay at Ban Na, workers were already lengthening the landing strip, which was situated just above the cluster of bamboo-and-thatch huts that made up the village. Earlier as the Helio was landing I could see a bunch of the residents out there digging.

"How are things going?" I asked Panit. "That's one of the things Pat Landry has asked me to focus on."

"I know it's important," he said, "and we are working on it. It's hard work, sir. We could use some explosives."

"Landry is sending up some cratering charges."

"That's good news, sir," he told me, smiling. "The Hmong will be happy."

Panit led me farther up the mountain toward a couple of huts away from the village. It was where we would be staying. The other three PARU waited there. The men quickly impressed me. Clean, strong and bright, they all exuded confidence and a willingness to get things done.

Those first impressions turned out to be accurate.

The two huts stood more or less side by side. I would share one with Panit. Each housed two bed-sized bamboo platforms about 18 inches off the dirt floor. An old parachute provided the sheets and blankets. The thatched walls would keep out the wind and rain, and with any luck the ceiling wouldn't leak. Panit put my backpack next to the bed I would use and said he hoped I'd be comfortable.

The PARU had hung a bright-orange parachute over the area between the two huts and constructed a wooden table under it—our dining room.

It also doubled as the living room where we sat to discuss things and read at night. A lantern hung over the table.

Bathing was a challenge. To wash I had to walk to a cold—really cold—mountain stream, which I eventually got used to, and stand in it about waist-deep. To shave I carried water back to the hut and heated it, though I was the only one who did so every day.

The latrine, not quite as far but thankfully in the other direction, was a little hut built over a hole in the ground. It did not feature a board to sit on, so it required a balancing act. I got used to that, too.

Early on I found myself often repeating that I had come a long way from Kansas City.

The residence tour complete, Panit took me down to the village. Forty-plus huts perched on a flat outcrop of the mountain. No streets, just lanes between the huts, with an open area in the middle that served as a gathering place. The views out over the valley below were incredible.

As we arrived, a Hmong pony, obviously male, was doing his best to mount a less-interested female, and a group of Hmong kids giggled and pointed.

We kept on walking and soon I became the object of interest and smiles. Attired in traditional garb—black dresses with multicolored bands on their heads and waists—the Hmong women looked strong and hardy. Like the men they were small in stature.

Pigs and chickens made their presence known; the ponies were the largest animals I saw. The Hmong didn't keep water buffalo as did the Lao living at lower altitudes. The big animals weren't agile enough to move around the narrow and precarious mountain trails. They also weren't required for plowing because the Hmong didn't grow rice in paddies.

After lunch Panit and I headed to the landing strip. The work required removing a large hump in the middle of a sloping area. Without the hump the strip could accommodate larger aircraft.

The villagers worked with crude hoes and shovels. They carried away the dirt in wicker baskets slung on poles. What we really needed was a bulldozer, but explosives would help.

"If we get some cratering charges we'll be done in two weeks," Panit boldly predicted. "Just moving the dirt after the charge goes off is a lot easier than having to dig it out."

The next day we visited the five outposts the Hmong were manning around Ban Na, all forming a semi-circle facing the Plaine des Jarres, from where any enemy patrols would originate. Each featured a good view of the western plain, a prominent and unusual area in North Laos. Nestled among the mountains, it is actually a plateau covering about 30 square miles. Located midway between Vientiane and the border with North Vietnam, its rolling grasslands are dotted with woods and streams.

Roads ran from it to Vietnam to the east and Vientiane to the southwest. In July 1962 the Plaine des Jarres, literally the Plain of Jars—so named by the French colonialists because of the thousands of enormous, ancient, earthen burial jars strewn across the plateau—was in the hands of the PL and the KL, who had taken it two years earlier. The VC maintained a presence there as well, running truck convoys that arrived regularly during the dry season to supply the PL units.

In truth we didn't worry much about the PL or KL, because they lacked training, equipment and courage—they weren't interested in fighting. But we did respect the toughness and tenacity of the VC, who were highly motivated to reunite their country and were using Laos to help achieve that goal.

The VC moved their supplies and reinforcements in from North Vietnam and apportioned the bulk of it to the PL, whom they wanted to take over Vientiane. Whenever I looked out over the plain from one of our outposts I would wonder if any VC units were operating down there.

The Hmong had placed the outposts to observe any approaches to Ban Na from the plain. The choices were easy because of the terrain—only a few trails and difficult ground to cover if you weren't using the trails. Each contained mortar and machine gun emplacements plus a small, low shelter, where a platoon or so of fighters ate and slept.

Panit and I and one of his men inspected each outpost. They must have been expecting us, because by the time we arrived the men were "standing tall" by their weapons. Panit introduced me and I chatted with any Hmong who spoke French. I would ask about the rationale for placing the outpost, mostly to let them know I was interested. I also would ask about their length of posting, just for my own information.

One genuinely useful item the inspections revealed was that the headspace on the .50-caliber machine guns was frequently neglected and almost always needed adjustment. Headspace is the small gap between the gun's bolt, which moves each cartridge into the firing chamber, and the base of the cartridge. The Hmong didn't really understand that it was a serious problem. Because of barrel blowback, or recoil, you had to adjust the headspace on the gun using a special tool. Without that regular maintenance, expended shells might not be properly ejected; the weapon could jam or even explode.

A .50-caliber machine gun is a no-kidding, serious weapon used in Laos and Vietnam primarily for perimeter defense. It was not easily portable and if it jammed during an attack the outpost could be easily overrun.

Whenever I spotted the problem Panit or one of the other PARU would make the adjustment.

After each brief visit we moved on, eventually returning to our huts just before sunset. It was a long day, but because I hadn't needed to walk more than about an hour between the outposts I wasn't exhausted.

My stay at Ban Na featured few highlights. I spent my days working on the hump in the airstrip, training the Hmong, and visiting the outposts and nearby villages. The weekends passed unnoticed and often we even forgot what day of the week it was.

Dinners were more of an adventure, as the others tried to prepare dishes they thought I would like. We didn't have much choice, mostly chicken or pork, and sometimes beef or horsemeat, along with boiled rice—because the Thai weren't too fond of sticky rice—and green vegetables boiled or stir-fried over a wood fire. Whatever they served was spicy hot because the Thai and the Hmong loved red peppers. Initially the food was so spicy I could hardly eat it, but just like bathing in the stream I got used to it.

After dinner we'd sit around and talk, though real communication was difficult. Only Panit spoke decent English and none of the PARU spoke French. We usually retired early because of fatigue from our active days outdoors. The village grew quiet when the sun went down. I would usually read for a while or study maps, but it never lasted long.

At least I always slept well.

Our objective was straightforward. We were there to help the Hmong defend their territory in any way we could. For me it meant helping to defend Ban Na and the sector immediately around it, just off the western end of the Plaine des Jarres. Ban Na wasn't really a region, I came to find out, but an important spot for watching what the enemy was doing on the plain. I also learned why Pat had assigned me there: It was quiet enough to send a new kid to see how he would do.

My responsibility was to manage the operations of my PARU team; not a difficult task because Panit's team knew much more about what was going on than I did. I served as the link with our logistics base, with Pat and Bill in Vientiane. Whatever the village or my team needed to get the job done, I made sure they got it. It made me a key person, and they all knew it.

I met regularly with the *nai ban*—in this case he was also a *nai khong*, chief of a group of villages—to discuss needs. Most of the men had become fighters, so agricultural activity had almost shut down. Therefore the village needed supplies regularly to augment the meager amounts of food they produced. That meant sending a radio message to Pat periodically via a transmitter that was powered by a hand generator and mounted on a bench. Our PARU communications specialist would tap out the code, while one of the other men cranked the generator.

Our system was amazingly efficient. I could always count on prompt responses to my messages—"cables," I called them. Within a day or two, sometimes within hours, the delivery would arrive. A DC-3 or C-123 transport would drop as many as 200 sacks of rice from low altitude onto the field near the landing strip, along with three or four sacks of salt.

I heard that early in the program one poor Hmong had tried to catch a sack of rice plummeting down from the sky. It crushed him. But I never saw anything like that happen. By then the villagers had learned to stay away from the drop zone until the sacks were on the ground. The drops also included uniforms, boots, hand-tools and other items we needed. Weapons, ammo and anything fragile would arrive by Helio, chopper or parachute. Occasionally Vientiane would treat us to a tasty baguette and some peanut butter. The French must have trained the city's bakers well.

We needed the longer strip at Ban Na so we could land bigger supply loads to fortify the Hmong defenses on the western end of the plain. For the length of my stay, one of my top duties was getting those supplies to the outposts, so I regularly dispatched patrols from Ban Na to hand-carry food, ammunition and other supplies.

I also kept Vientiane aware of enemy activities in my sector. We sent out patrols and individual villagers to detect and observe anything going on around us. The effort slowed in July, the rainy season, which created impassable roads and greatly decreased enemy mobility. That left us, with great off-road mobility in the mountains, in the driver's seat until the next dry season started in October or November.

We enjoyed another advantage: The enemy didn't want to engage the Hmong in Hmong territory. That allowed us to conduct guerrilla-style, hit-and-run attacks on their roads and supply points. In 1962 we were still building our capabilities, but our offensive actions were increasing. We worked to retake the plain, thereby relieving pressure on the Hmong territory around it. It was a cat-and-mouse game that grew more deadly as the decade unfolded.

The scenario became standard. The VC would push us in the dry season, and we would attack and push back in the rainy season. Later on, working with the Air Force, the agency employed extensive air support for offensives in Laos—among the most intense in all of history—but that didn't begin while I was there.

True to his word, just over two weeks after we received the cratering charges Panit's crew removed the hump and nearly doubled the length of the landing strip. The charges had simplified the task, and the workers, mostly women, labored steadily to complete the job early. We didn't pay them but their efforts earned additional food, medicine and other supplies for the village.

The middle of the strip still showed a bit of roll, and the whole thing sloped uphill, but the Air America pilot who checked it out gave his okay. Rolling uphill after touchdown would help planes stop, he said, and going downhill on takeoff was also a plus.

"We planned it that way," I lied, smiling.

Ban Na's strip could now handle a Caribou. A workhorse, Canadian-made STOL aircraft with great stability at low speeds, it could land on strips not much longer than those used by the Helio. But with twin engines and a rear-opening ramp it could handle a much larger payload. Bringing it into Ban Na meant getting more supplies closer to the plain, a strategic step forward.

A few days after the strip extension was finished, the first Caribou landed with room to spare, as the pilot told me. It had been less than three weeks since I arrived in Ban Na, and I adapted quickly to the routine. I learned the sector well by walking all over it. I totally enjoyed and felt absorbed by my work, and I knew I was contributing something tangible.

Then a cable from Pat advised me to return to Vientiane for reassignment. I thought about asking them to reconsider, but I concluded that my first assignment had gone well. I was going to be moved and that was that.

By then I had heard that Mike Deuel was working with Tony Poe in Sam Neua. Ralph was on the plain's eastern edge, and André had been given a region north and east of the plain to handle.

We were all gainfully employed. I wondered what would come next.

I headed straight to Pat's office on my return to Vientiane. He was reading cable traffic from headquarters that he must have found uninteresting, because he welcomed my interruption.

"So, kid, how was Ban Na?"

"Great. We got the strip lengthened, and I got a good look at the whole sector."

"I know," he noted drily. "That's why you were up there."

"Panit's team is really first rate."

"I know that as well, and Panit likes you, too. That's good."

I instantly understood. Panit had been assessing me for Pat while I was advising Panit and the PARU.

"Well, I'm pleased to hear that, but I have to tell you those guys are not hard to get along with. They know what the hell they are doing."

"But you came out with high marks, and that's excellent. Makes it easier for me, and I like that."

"How about some lunch?" I asked. "I need to grill you about what I'm going to do next."

"Never eat lunch. Makes me fat and sleepy. Not sure yet where you are headed. I have an idea, but I want to confirm it with Bill."

He abruptly changed the subject.

"How long would it take to walk down to the Plaine des Jarres from Ban Na?"

"That I didn't do, but the Hmong say about six hours—less than a day. It would probably take a full day coming up from the plain. Why?"

"Because I'm just thinking about us walking down there and taking over some day, that's why. We're getting stronger all the time."

"I'd like to be back up there if we're going to do that."

"Not for a while, kid, not for a while."

He always called me that.

I sensed that our conversation was over, so I got up to leave.

"Okay, I'll see you later. When might you get a chance to talk with Bill?"

"Stop by about eight tonight. We'll have a couple of drinks and eat somewhere close by. I'll have some word by then. Now go relax somewhere and get a hot shower."

Vientiane, especially after nearly three weeks in Ban Na, seemed like quite a change. It was at the time an open city. Sprawled along the Mekong River—back then the longest unbridged river in the world—with Thailand on the opposite bank, even with only 70,000 inhabitants it was the largest city in Laos.

Vientiane's architecture, street names, certain stores and restaurants, bars and cafes, plus a partially built arc de triomphe, stood as reminders of its colonial past. In better days it could have passed for a city in the south of France. Now it was decaying, with littered streets that neither the residents nor the government showed much interest in cleaning up. Still it was an intriguing and enjoyable place, and I spent some pleasant afternoons walking around there.

A few miles to the south and east was Nong Khai, the official crossing point with Thailand. On the opposite bank of the Mekong, travelers from Bangkok and elsewhere cleared the border formalities and crossed into Laos by boat. Actually people could, and routinely did, cross the Mekong anywhere and anytime—something that caused considerable angst within Thai officialdom.

The Lao, lowlanders who lived in valleys and along the rivers, comprised the majority of the city's residents. But a large number of foreigners also lived in Vientiane. Engaged mostly in commercial endeavors, they included merchants from China, India, Thailand, Vietnam and France.

The foreigners created the activity and the hustle and bustle evident in some parts of the city, such as the nightclubs, which enjoyed a flourishing business. That activity stemmed from exploiting the aid pouring into Laos to help withstand the threat from Vietnam and from its own communist insurgents. Graft and corruption of all sorts thrived. Working discreetly—and sometimes openly—with Lao politicians and military officers, the merchants siphoned off huge sums.

The scene would have made grist for Shakespeare's mill. He could have written about the daily machinations and intrigue that plagued Vientiane in particular and the country in general: a king without power, royal princes working toward opposing goals, corrupt politicians selling influence and position, and graft-seeking military officers manipulating the system relentlessly. All could have featured in a drama that surely would have been subtitled "A Tragedy in Asia."

I didn't know many details about what was transpiring, nor did any of my colleagues. In truth I didn't care. We were there for the noblest of intentions: to push back the Red Menace and save Laos—not only Laos, if one believed the Domino Theory, but also the whole of Southeast Asia. I saw our efforts as something apart from the mess in Vientiane.

Freedom and liberty were not just abstract words to me. I was strongly anticommunist, anti any authoritarian system, and I was more than willing to fight them whenever and however I could. Helping the Hmong to resist and secure the north was a step in the right direction, and it deserved all the support we were providing.

Looking back, though, arrogance and ignorance were widespread among the Americans serving in Laos. "Just do what we tell you and stay out of the way" was a common approach. It was not a malicious arrogance but one that, in the end, served us poorly. It seems obvious now that a greater understanding of what was going on in Laos would have helped us work more effectively, and perhaps it could have spared some of the pain and suffering the country eventually experienced.

After my conversation with Pat, I took a taxi back to the compound. I sometimes wondered what the cabbies thought whenever I headed up-country with my pack, web belt and weapon. I had read several books on rice growing in Southeast Asia, the paddy and mountain varieties, to be able to support my cover, but no one ever asked me what I was doing in Laos.

Starved for news about what was going on in the world I stopped to pick up a paper and some magazines. I was particularly interested in the talks about Laos under way. In fact the first thing I read was that the Geneva Agreement was about to be signed. I knew it would signal a significant change in our efforts.

Ambassador Harriman was prepared to agree that Laos would become a neutral country, requiring the United States to pull out all but diplomatic and specified aid personnel. The communists—Russia, China and North Vietnam—agreed to follow suit. All parties would have until October 7 to comply.

Things didn't turn out that way, but at the time the agreement had us wondering what would happen. Would we be sent back to Washington? I hoped not, and I had no idea what to expect, but I assumed that Pat and Bill did know. Surely they had received a cable from headquarters. Maybe that was why Pat had pulled me out of Ban Na but hadn't yet told me what I would be doing next.

Back in my room I cleaned up and wrote a letter to my parents, who by then probably thought Asia had swallowed up their eldest son. I took care to phrase my situation as benignly as possible, not wanting to cause Mom more concerns than necessary. I generally described what I had seen so far in Laos—the people, the food, the tourist sites—trying to make it all sound non-threatening.

I also got the maid to launder my clothes, which hadn't had a proper wash since I left for Ban Na.

Our group of JOTs was the second to be stationed in Laos. Four months earlier a quartet of young officers had arrived from the paramilitary class before us. They were now considered veterans, and all had been assigned upcountry.

Vint Lawrence, a member of the first group, happened to be in Vientiane that evening. It was standard practice that anyone stationed upcountry who returned to Vientiane or Bangkok would spend time with his colleagues, sharing information and swapping stories.

Vint joined Pat, Bill and me at dinner. As I had hoped the conversation quickly turned to the Geneva Agreement and Bill was able to give us quite a bit of information. Unfortunately the policy decisions hadn't been made, so no one knew what the future of our program would be. But we had until fall at least before anyone had to leave.

As always I enjoyed the evening with my two superiors. Bill was soft-spoken and quiet, but I sensed he was a man who reflected deeply on issues. When he reached a conclusion you knew it had been well considered.

Despite Pat's gruff exterior I found him to be a considerate and caring man. He worried about his subordinates, especially the "kids" like me he was sending upcountry. Both in their own ways were great guys and splendid to work for.

Before we broke up, Pat told me to come see him in the morning.

"And bring your gear. I don't want you just lolling around Vientiane."

To me that meant he'd be sending me back upcountry, which was good news.

After dinner Vint and I went to a nightclub for a couple of hours and drank a few beers, while we shared experiences and other thoughts. Like me, he was immensely pleased with what we were doing.

"Ever heard of Phou Song?" Pat asked when I walked into his office.

"I know that *phou* means mountain, but that's about all. Is it in Hmong country?"

"Yes, it is," he said, seeming more serious than usual. "It's north of Ban Na. We're expanding the program into that area and I need you up there to keep things organized. Panit can handle Ban Na now that the strip is finished and we're more established. Phou Song has a PARU team and I want you to work with them to expand the whole program up there. Phou Song also has a difficult *nai ban* but I think you can deal with him. Remember to listen."

"Just two questions," I said. "What are the bad guys doing around Phou Song and when do I go?"

"You go this morning. Not that much action yet, but I am worried about what the PL units nearby have on their minds. Best keep on eye on them."

"What's the problem with the *nai ban*?" I asked.

"Ornery and greedy" was all Pat said.

5. The Eleventh Man

PHOU SONG, LAOS 1962

It was a bigger village than Ban Na, occupying a plateau halfway up the mountain for which it was named, near the edge of a precipitous drop into the valley. You could find a truly spectacular view from anywhere in the village. Because of the large, open space nearby, Phou Song boasted a nice landing strip that easily handled twin-engine STOL aircraft. The clearing also accommodated a large drop zone.

My first landing there was quite an experience. Approaching the valley we descended to about 3,000 feet, well below Phou Song's 7,000-foot peak. Then the pilot banked left, quickly cranked down the wing flaps, which is done manually on a Helio, and landed on the strip—the end of which jutted out from the mountainside at that altitude.

The takeoffs could be equally interesting because some of the pilots delighted in scaring the bejesus out of selected passengers. They'd taxi down the runway heading toward the precipice, keeping their airspeed down enough to fall off the edge. The aircraft, seen from the starting end of the strip, would drop out of sight. Then as it dived toward the valley floor the pilot would rev up the engines and gain altitude.

It wasn't really dangerous, but it sure did grab the attention of anyone aboard.

Phou Song's location kept it safer than Ban Na. The village sat so high up the mountain its only approaches were relatively easy to monitor and block. The nearest enemy camps, in this case the PL, sat at the far end of the valley.

Courtesy of the Agency for International Development the airstrip mainly served a tin-roofed, planked-floor warehouse packed with rice, clothing and other material regularly distributed to nearby villages. But because we had enlisted most of the local men to fight the PL and the VC, Phou Song also functioned as the focal point for our operations in the area.

Prasert, the PARU team leader, appeared friendly, and I thought the other team members would be easy to work with.

After I got settled, Prasert and I took a walk around the village. Built on flatter ground than Ban Na, it also seemed to have been laid out more symmetrically. The *nai ban's* house was the biggest and featured signs of wealth, comparatively speaking: more animals, and tools and materials obviously brought in from Vientiane.

I made no comment to Prasert, but I suspected the *nai ban* had been prospering from the tough times. In the several weeks I spent at Phou Song, as I observed the *nai ban*, I confirmed what he was doing. Indeed he was, as Pat had said, greedy—more so than ornery—a man heavily engaged in feathering his own nest.

While I was there I worked to curb the nest-feathering. I kept careful counts of the bags of rice and quantities of medicine we stored in the warehouse, and I verified where it was being distributed. For a time I was able to control the poaching.

Phou Song kept me busier than Ban Na because I needed to move around more. That required me to cable regularly for air transport. Initially Prasert often accompanied me, but as I grew to know the region I often went alone, depending on the availability of French speakers.

In the villages I visited we mostly discussed what the nearby enemy units were doing and what the locals needed. The agency supplied everything from weapons and ammunition to schoolbooks, medicine, rice and salt, uniforms, building materials and money.

I acted as middleman for some of the items, arranging to ship supplies to a given village, while others actually supervised the delivery.

The villages constantly made food requests, but every so often a *nai ban* wouldn't be able to furnish the report on enemy activity I had wanted. Or sometimes I couldn't obtain a plane, or a destination had no landing strip nearby.

In such cases I would walk, taking along a Hmong patrol with a couple of the PARU. We limited these missions to the distances we could cover in under two days. Any longer used up too much of my time.

The walks were demanding. From Phou Song few of the trails we covered followed ridgelines. The bulk of them ran up and down. Worse, it was the middle of the rainy season when I arrived, and the frequent downpours made the mountain trails muddy and slippery. Plus, everyone was watching the *farang*—the foreigner—to see how he handled the trails, though my companions always made the journeys as easy as possible for me.

After the first couple of those walks I traded my M1 for the lighter carbine. I didn't need the M1's long-range capability on the trails, where you could never see farther than the next turn or rise.

The Hmong fighters, all smaller men than I, carried heavy packs of weapons, food and water. Though I was bigger and stronger they were used to lugging loads across this terrain. I strained to keep up with them—but I made sure I never slowed them down.

One morning Prasert and I left early with six young Hmong for a small village that didn't have an airstrip. The rain had relented for a couple of days, but the air still felt humid and heavy, even at altitude.

We had been making steady progress along a difficult trail and were just about to stop for lunch when we arrived at a narrow stream feeding a couple of small pools. The scene looked inviting and everyone thought a brief dip would be refreshing. We were still in a safe area so there was little concern about enemy patrols. Just in case, we posted one of the Hmong to keep watch.

Prasert and the rest of the team jumped right in and sat neck-deep in the cool water while I was still looking for a place to put down my weapon and take off the jungle boots I had worn. When I took my first step into the stream and tried to move toward the pool an unexpected visitor appeared: a snake, swirling downstream.

It was thin, green and maybe 18 inches long. What kind of snake it was or how dangerous I had no idea, but before I knew it the thing had coiled around my left leg. I don't like snakes and it scared the hell out of me. I shouted and tried to kick it away. Fortunately the reptile's skin was slippery from the water and it couldn't hold on. With all eyes focused on me after my shout, everyone got to see the snake go flying in one direction and me losing my balance and falling backwards. The snake landed in the fast-moving water and got carried downstream.

The Hmong and Prasert must have found the scene quite amusing because they howled with laughter. I stood up, bowed deeply to my audience, and jumped into the pool.

A few hours after a lunch of strips of dried meat and sticky rice we arrived at our destination. As usual the *nai ban* welcomed us, and as the honored guest I received slices of fruit and a drink of *Lao khao*, the Hmong's homemade rice whiskey. Awful stuff but there was no choice—good manners demanded that I drink it.

Over the next hour the *nai ban* explained what his village needed and how willing the people were to fight to protect Hmong country from the communists. I refrained from asking him what he thought a communist was.

We were too far from Phou Song to return that day so we ate dinner with the villagers and spent the night.

We used the same trail for our return, passing the stream a couple of hours after leaving the village. No one suggested another dip but I saw lots of smiling and laughing, and one of the Hmong imitated the "great leg kick" I had demonstrated the day before.

We continued downhill and were crossing the level ground when it started to rain, not heavily but steadily. It rained the rest of the day, which made the ascent back up to Phou Song all the more tedious. I was happy to have worn the jungle boots, because their cleats gave me added traction, but climbing up the steep mountain trail in the rain was exhausting.

We stopped a couple of times to rest but only for short periods. We also didn't eat lunch, hoping to get back to the village sooner. We arrived in the early afternoon, soaked to the skin, tired and hungry. I also felt a chill but thought nothing of it. I dried off, changed clothes, and stood by the fire sipping tea.

I woke up the next morning feeling sick. It turned out to be more than just a cold. As the day wore on I felt worse and worse. By mid-afternoon I had developed serious chills and a fever, and I couldn't eat without vomiting. I didn't stray from my hut and Prasert brought me soup and hot tea.

By evening I felt so weak I could barely get up to go to the latrine area. Prasert and I discussed my condition and we decided to call for a plane the next day to take me back to Vientiane, where I could see a doctor and get some medicine. Meanwhile the PARU medic gave me aspirin—he didn't know what else to do.

I got very little sleep that night and felt even worse the second morning.

The bad weather persisted, too, with heavy clouds and periodic rain. Prasert had cabled Pat about my condition. Pat replied that everyone at the base was concerned about me. He would send a plane as soon as possible but bad weather all over northern Laos had grounded flights for the time being. The cable ended:

WILL COME WHEN WE CAN

Word had filtered around the village that I was sick. No one could do anything about it but they all expressed concern, and even the *nai ban* stopped by to see me. I tried to put on a brave face.

"I'll be fine tomorrow," I told him.

He didn't respond but studied me carefully and a little while later the village shaman showed up. His presence seemed to worry Prasert, which in turn worried me.

"Send him away," I told him.

"It's not that easy," he responded.

"What do you mean? Tell him I'm going to see my own doctor as soon as a plane can get in here. There really isn't anything he can do. And I'm tired."

I could see that Prasert was having trouble explaining my words to the shaman.

"The *nai ban* sent him. We can't be so rude as to refuse to let him ward off the evil spirits that are troubling you. He won't leave."

"Evil spirits? Don't be silly, I've got a fever."

I realized even as I said it that we were obliged to accept the *nai ban's* gesture.

"Okay, okay," I said, "but I'm not taking any potion from him."

Prasert told the shaman, who nodded.

Then for some reason Prasert left.

The man was dressed in traditional Hmong garb: black trousers, black shirt with a leather belt, long hair and a colored scarf around his neck. He carried a leather pack on his shoulder, which he removed and set on the floor. From it he produced two gourds with rice grains or dry beans inside.

The shaman mumbled softly as he pulled other items from his pack—I couldn't see what. He stood at the end of my bed platform, leaving his pack on the ground. He never looked directly at me and his eyes seemed a little wild. Maybe it was the fever or my fatigue and weakness but I felt wary about this guy messing around.

Suddenly he began chanting loudly, swaying and shaking the two gourds. His antics startled me and I sat up a little, but he paid no attention and continued.

I recalled reading about shamans in a book at headquarters while I was preparing for Laos. Then it came back to me, vividly. He was chanting to rid me and the hut of the evil spirits that were causing my illness. The book mentioned that Lao mountain people followed no organized religion. Most were animistic, with spirits representing a large part of their beliefs. When treating the sick the shamans would attempt to ward off those spirits. But if the effort did not seem to be working they were known to leap upon patients and stab them repeatedly, making holes for the evil spirits to escape their bodies.

Can this be happening? What can I do? Where the hell is Prasert?

I don't know how long this went on—me barely conscious but watching him carefully, and him chanting and waving his gourds.

Will he actually try to stab me? Weak or not I'll have to fight him. But how? My carbine's leaning against the wall. I can't reach it quickly enough to shoot him.

That was as far as my thoughts carried. I must have passed out several times because portions of the episode remain a blank, but each time I regained consciousness he was still chanting.

When the medic returned to give me more aspirin I told him to send Prasert, who arrived shortly thereafter.

"How long must this go on?" I asked.

He said he thought the shaman would be leaving soon, because it was getting dark. Obviously I had been drifting in and out of oblivion all day.

"Don't leave me until he's gone," I instructed him.

"Okay, sir, I'll stay."

Soon thereafter the shaman began the grand finale. He became very excited, chanting faster and louder. Instead of just swaying he moved around the bed—which scared me at first. Then he abruptly stopped, half-bowed in my direction, and left.

I felt greatly relieved. If nothing else he had distracted me from my illness, which hadn't eased.

Calm returned to the hut and Prasert insisted that I try to eat some soup and boiled rice. I still felt weak and tired but suddenly my appetite returned and I managed to keep the food down.

On the third morning I discovered the fever had broken. My weakness persisted but I managed to dress and go outside. When the villagers saw me I'm sure they gave the shaman full credit for my recovery.

I cabled Pat to allay his concerns and spent the day resting. The *nai ban* stopped by in the afternoon. He didn't say anything but I guessed he felt pleased that the shaman had visited me and I seemed to be recovering.

The following night the bad weather eased and early in the morning I heard a Helio approaching. I was getting better but I welcomed the sound. It meant I could fly to Vientiane to see an American doctor—and I wouldn't have to endure a follow-up visit from the shaman.

I never could have imagined it at the time but only a few years later another medicine man's intervention really would save my life.

A few days in Vientiane and I felt like new, eager to get back upcountry. The doctor told me I probably had picked up a type of dengue fever from God knows where.

When I returned to Phou Song things were busy. Prasert had been drilling the PARU team to keep their skills sharp with weapons and explosives, and he had sent out several patrols to scout the area to our east.

Sometimes we would parachute supplies to those patrols, something that required a lot of coordination. We had to be sure we were dropping to the right guys, and we had to pick a drop point that would leave avenues for the men to get to safety after retrieving the supplies—because a drop would signal their position to enemy patrols.

I could see that the PARU were doing good work and I did my best to help them.

One day in late summer I was flying into one of the villages in our region when I spotted a plane already on the ground. That was nothing unusual. Our assignments sometimes overlapped and it was always good to meet a colleague upcountry.

When I landed I found Vint Lawrence waiting for me. Vint was coordinating all efforts under Vang Pao's command—in effect the whole Hmong program. By all accounts Vint was doing a great job, and I always looked forward to seeing him because he stayed well informed. But as I walked toward him I noticed a look of concern on his face.

"Hey, Vint, how are things?"

"Not good, we've got a problem."

"What's up? Can I help?"

"There's a Helio down. Pilot may be hurt. I think it's Tom Dieffenbach, a good guy. He was alone in the plane and we don't have much to go on. A Hmong patrol thinks they saw where he hit the side of the mountain."

"You get a message to Pat yet?"

"Tried, but he wasn't in his office. Don't know when we'll hear from Vientiane."

This was serious. Even as the new kid I knew the unwritten code we all followed. It hadn't taken long to figure it out: If a plane or chopper went down, for whatever reason, we would make every possible effort to rescue those aboard.

It reassured everyone. If something happened to me, my colleagues would move heaven and earth to find me. The same for all of us—agency officers, Air America pilots, anyone. Rescue became the highest priority and all other activities stopped if necessary to free up men or aircraft to carry out the mission.

I would learn about this practice firsthand soon enough.

"Can't we do something?" I said.

"I was standing here trying to decide when I heard you coming," Vint answered. "I was thinking that I could take a patrol and get up there."

"No question. He may be hurt. I'll come along and I say we go right now. We can send Pat a message and tell him what we're doing."

"He won't be happy. We're supposed to stay out of sticky spots."

"But this is an emergency."

I could see that Vint wanted to go; he was just talking himself into it. I was prepared to defer to Vint, because he had more experience. But I also thought we should try, even if discretion at that point turned out to be the better part of valor.

"You're right," he said. "Pat will understand."

He took out a pad and scratched out a message:

WE, DICK AND I, ARE WITH A PATROL AND HOPE TO RESCUE THE PILOT. WILL EXPLAIN LATER

Shortlythereafter we sent both Helios back to Vientiane. One of the pilots carried the note for Pat. Call it gung-ho spirit or chalk it up to our lack of experience, but we set off walking toward the crash site with little more than our determination to find the downed pilot before anyone or anything else did.

Eight Hmong accompanied us, all wearing fatigues. I had no idea how good or experienced they were but they seemed confident and they knew where they were going. Each carried a small pack with a length of bamboo hanging next to it containing boiled sticky rice. They would cut off a section of bamboo as needed and split it to provide part of a meal. It was a very efficient way to carry food.

I also wore fatigues along with my jungle boots and a wide-brimmed, Australian bush hat. Vint, taller and heavier, wore his boots as well, but he went hatless and dressed in a short-sleeved shirt. We brought our weapons but no food or extra clothing. I carried matches in a pouch on my web belt and my jackknife.

That was it.

Technically it didn't seem that far—across the valley below us and up the next mountainside. It would be a quick, in-and-out effort, I thought.

But distances are difficult to judge in the mountains.

We headed downhill toward the valley for the first couple of hours. We maintained a fast pace and took few rests. We felt a sense of urgency because we knew the pilot might be in dire need.

The Hmong thought the plane had gone down on the far side of the mountain ahead of us. They told us the PL had staked out positions on the other side of the valley, so a chopper rescue wouldn't be feasible and in between was no-man's-land.

Vint and I stayed silent. As we approached the valley floor I could sense the altitude was lower than at any other place I'd been in Hmong country. The jungle air grew thick. We followed a little-used trail almost closed in by the undergrowth. A Hmong with a machete took the lead and we all followed close behind.

I had read about leeches in the Laotian jungle but had never seen one. Vint had, and he carefully briefed me. Each man watched his own front and the back of the man ahead of him. The last two men rotated positions often. It was simple enough but important, because leech bites could lead to serious infections, which didn't take much in these steamy conditions.

We had an easier time navigating the trail than we first thought, but the many vines and branches jutting out meant making lots of twists and turns, and they brushed against us as we passed. I felt more vulnerable down in the valley than higher up where the Hmong lived and ruled.

Everyone felt that way but we pushed ahead. No one talked. The heat was oppressive and I could feel the sweat running down my back and stomach. The jungle density also made it difficult to tell how far we had traveled toward the mountain.

We reached a stream and took long drinks of the cool, clear water. Vint and I hadn't brought canteens, so we depended on water from streams and what little the Hmong carried. Fortunately, the streams flowing down from the mountains were clean and drinkable. Waterborne disease was the least of our worries at the moment.

As we waded across the stream I felt happy again to be wearing the boots. Whoever designed the small holes in the instep, and the padded insole that caused air to circulate—or in this case water to be pumped out—should have gotten a medal.

By mid-afternoon the ground began to slope upward and the jungle soon fell away from the trail. The lead Hmong sheathed his machete. The air became less heavy and humid and I felt more at ease, but my sense of urgency stayed.

We stopped for a short rest. Vint and I were both in good shape and had no trouble keeping up with the Hmong. We hoped to find the plane and the pilot before nightfall, but we couldn't be certain. We continued to have difficulty estimating distances, plus we didn't know the exact location of the crash.

After 10 minutes we resumed the climb. We couldn't hurry exactly but we maintained a steady pace. With few respites we climbed for about three more hours until almost nightfall. By then it became clear we weren't going to find the pilot that day so we looked for a place to camp. We were high above the valley by then and as the sun went down the air felt much cooler, particularly against our sweat-soaked clothing.

We reached a clearing with a hut at the far end and decided to stay there. Four Hmong moved ahead cautiously to see if other people were around. They didn't find anyone. The hut was not in good shape—not surprising, because it probably had been abandoned for some time—but its roof and walls were intact. It was apparently all that remained of a Hmong village. The view from the site, looking out over the valley, was pretty and it must have been a pleasant place to live.

We entered the hut but no one sat down. Our first priority was to check carefully for leeches. I stripped and inspected each piece of clothing before hanging it on an old rack. I pulled off my T-shirt and checked my torso: clear. Then I raised my arm to look under my right armpit and was shocked and disgusted to see a leech fastened there. I had felt nothing.

A leech inserts two hollow fangs under the skin and starts to extract blood. A protein oozes from the mouth to deaden the skin's sensitivity, making it all but impossible to feel. This ugly bloodsucker had evidently fallen on my shoulder or neck, escaping detection by the Hmong behind me and making its way to my armpit.

In Laos the accepted way to rid oneself of a leech is to apply heat—either a match or a hot coal from a fire. The leech, feeling the heat, literally rolls up into a ball, extracts its fangs, and falls off. That technique prevents the fangs from breaking off in the skin and increasing the risk of infection.

You never just grab the ugly thing and rip it off your body.

So naturally the moment I saw the leech I ripped it out and threw it on the dirt floor. Then I stomped on it. Gorged on blood, my blood, the leech squished into a small red puddle.

Soon as I did it I realized it was dumb. I glanced at Vint.

"Aw, you probably won't get infected," he said. "Let me look at it."

"Ugly goddamned thing. I didn't even think."

"Looks like you might have got the fangs out," he said, looking under my arm. "Still, it wouldn't be a bad idea to take a couple of tetracycline when we get back to Vientiane."

Tetracycline was the antibiotic of choice for everyone in Laos at the time. The doctors prescribed it for almost anything.

"Did you find any?" I asked Vint.

"Nope, I was clean," he responded.

So was everyone else, but the young Hmong who had been walking behind me took some good-natured ribbing for missing the leech.

"Too bad we didn't make it to the crash site," I said, changing the subject. We were standing away from the others as we put our clothes and boots back on.

"Yeah, I'm sorry, too," Vint said. "But we'll probably find him first thing tomorrow. Meantime, this is home for tonight. Got anything to eat?"

"Not a thing. Maybe the Hmong will take pity on us."

"We'll get something, I'm sure."

What we ended up with was a lump of sticky rice each from the Hmong patrol leader. We had nothing to drink, though, and I thought about retracing our steps to the last stream we had passed. But night had fallen so that would have been folly.

Then a Hmong came in and handed us each a cucumber. He had found them growing in a patch that the long-gone villagers had probably cultivated. I never liked cucumbers but that one was delicious and full of moisture. I've enjoyed them ever since.

The hut was stuffy so we decided to sleep outside. From where we lay we could look out over the valley. The night was clear and so full of stars I could make out the nearby mountains.

Despite my exhaustion from the tension and the walk I didn't fall asleep right away. As I lay there looking at nothing in particular, I thought a while about where I was and what I was doing. I felt more isolated and vulnerable than ever before—so far away from home. But I was confident, I harbored no regrets about the decisions I had made, and I felt lucky to have a chance to make a difference.

I also was confident, I admit without good reason, that I could handle whatever would befall me, and I felt sure that our patrol would succeed. The ten of us were going to find and save the eleventh man, the pilot. We had to. I tried not to think about the alternative or what the enemy might do to thwart us.

I slept soundly that night, lying on the ground next to an abandoned hut on a mountainside in northern Laos.

By the time I awoke, just at sunrise, the Hmong were already moving around. I nudged Vint, still sleeping alongside me, and we both got up. All things considered I felt good, though thirsty and hungry.

Ever resourceful and considerate, the Hmong had done some early foraging. It had been too risky to start a fire the night before but now they lit a small one behind the hut. Someone had discovered a slight stream above the abandoned village and returned with water, which he was heating in an old crock found in the hut. Another Hmong produced some tea leaves from his pack and served hot tea. Up to then I'd never been a tea lover, but like the cucumber that tea tasted great—that and another wad of sticky rice.

We resumed the climb. The slope eased a little and we seemed to be moving around the mountain as much as up the side, as if along a ridgeline.

Two Hmong had left at daybreak to reconnoiter above us. As we pushed ahead it struck me how much Vint and I depended on these men and how much they depended on us. We had no idea where the plane might be and no landmarks to use to get there—or back. The Hmong knew it, too, but they counted on us for the support we could call in.

Beyond dependence the two sides felt mutual trust and respect, particularly in dangerous situations like this one. I knew the Hmong would do their job and I was sure Vint and I would do ours.

An hour or so after we started, the two members of our patrol appeared. I could tell by their faces the news was bad. They talked excitedly with the patrol leader and he relayed it to us in French: The pilot was dead, probably killed on impact, because the front of the plane was smashed in. There had been no fire, but the eleventh man—Tom Dieffenbach or someone else—wouldn't make it after all.

There was more bad news. The Hmong scouts had seen activity in the valley, which meant a PL unit might be moving up the mountain to check out the crash site.

We had no idea how many might be coming, but with the pilot dead—our two Hmong had hidden away the body—prudence seemed to dictate a retreat. We could always return with more force and more knowledge about what the enemy was doing.

The Hmong deferred to us, so Vint and I talked it over.

"Rotten news," he said, "all of it. There isn't much we can do up there now except maybe get in trouble."

"I agree," I said, "and hell to pay if we get ourselves into a firefight. We can't help the pilot. Probably better to come back with more strength."

"We don't really know that the PL are moving in. Don't know that they're not, either, and we don't know how many there might be."

"True, but with our guy already dead is it worth the risk to find out?"

"We might as well haul ass."

"Makes sense to me. Back the same way we came?"

"Yep, at least we know the route. We should be back there by mid-afternoon."

We explained our decision to the Hmong patrol leader, who seemed relieved. We started back down and around the mountain. We passed the clearing where we had spent the night.

Then we heard a Helio, a most welcome sound. Vint pulled out his emergency radio and tried to make contact. The radios were line of sight, meaning there can't be any obstacles between the person transmitting and the one receiving.

At first the Helio seemed to be just out of sight behind the mountain but suddenly it appeared and the pilot must have had his radio on, because he responded to Vint right away. Someone else was riding in the plane, most likely one of our colleagues, and he sounded relieved to have reached us—though he brought another dose of unwelcome news.

Intelligence reporting had reached Vientiane that PL units had indeed moved into the valley. Therefore we might be cut off. Nobody knew for sure, but Vientiane was taking no chances. Pat meant to get us out—the sooner the better. He had sent up a chopper at first light that morning and had positioned it at a nearby landing strip.

"Same reporting says the PL has heavy weapons on the mountain opposite the crash site, so we can't fly through the valley," our Helio link concluded. "That's why we've been hanging around where we are."

"So we need to get around to the other side to get picked up?" Vint asked.

"Not enough time. We don't want you down there that long."

"Hang on," Vint said. "We've got to think."

He turned to me.

"The clearing with the hut is right behind us. The chopper could certainly get in there."

He looked across the valley. "But would he come in with the possible PL guns over there?"

Vint saw, as I did, that we weren't far enough around the mountain for it to be safe for a chopper landing. Then we saw another possibility. The other side of the valley was just coming back into view after a large cloud had passed by. Here, between 4,000 feet and 5,000 feet of elevation, each time a cloud rolled by it obscured visibility from one side of the valley to the other, something that happened all the time in the mountains during the rainy season.

"Yeah," Vint said, mulling over the same thought that had occurred to me. "If we can't see over there, then they can't see over here."

"Right," I said, with obvious pleasure. "If the chopper came in while a cloud was out in the valley the bloody PL wouldn't see a damn thing. They would hear it but have no idea where it was."

"Great!" Vint said, snapping on the radio again. Quickly and succinctly he outlined our plan for a pickup. We would retrace our steps to the clearing above us and put out a marker the patrol leader kept in his pack for parachute drops. Pilots making any kind of drop would do so only if they could see that prearranged signal spread out on the ground.

We would talk the chopper pilot in by radio and let him know when a cloud had cut off the PL's view of this side of the valley. The Helio guys understood and bought our plan. The risk would be acceptable and they were eager to get us off that mountain.

"Sounds good. You get back up to the clearing you're talking about, and we'll get in touch with the chopper and get it over here right away. With any luck he'll be in the air behind the mountain in 15 or 20 minutes."

"We're on our way," Vint responded, turning off the radio.

We briefed the patrol leader who passed the word to the others, and we started back up the mountain. We felt a renewed sense of urgency. We knew it wouldn't be difficult physically but the uncertainty about where the PL units might or might not be was troubling. For all we knew the patrol our two Hmong thought they saw could be heading down the trail toward us.

It took only about 10 minutes to reach the clearing. We looked around first then stepped out of the jungle to lay out the marker in the middle. We posted one of the Hmong on the trail just above the clearing with instructions to come running when he saw the helicopter approach. We didn't want the chopper on the ground for more than a minute or two.

We called the Helio again and they told us the copter pilot was en route. He'd be in position in five or 10 minutes. We waited—anxiously.

"This got pretty complicated," Vint said. "I wonder if Pat and Bill are pissed."

"Just a guess," I said, smiling. "I don't suppose they're happy to be having to drag us out of here by chopper. Too bad we didn't have that intelligence reporting before we took off."

"We had to make a call, and we did—I'd do it again."

"Me, too."

The Helio radioed that the chopper was in position.

"Hold on," Vint told them, "till the gods smile on us and send a big cloud through the valley."

The Helio, circling at a high altitude and out of range of any PL weapons, had already spotted the clearing and seen our marker. From their vantage point they could also see the chopper.

A few minutes later a large cloud filled the valley and obscured visibility. Vint called the Helio and they relayed the message to the chopper, which was still out of our line of sight. It worked.

I never liked helicopters, and I still don't, but I readily concede that under certain circumstances—such as this one—they're uniquely valuable.

We carefully briefed the Hmong leader and insisted that he make our instructions clear to his men. The noise and the rushing air from the rotating blades always add stress and tension for those not used to choppers—and none of us was. People get confused. They can't hear. They do stupid things.

In this instance we were better versed so we were in charge. We lined up single file behind the trees at the edge of the clearing, Vint first and me last on the side closest to the direction where we'd see our lookout emerge. Then we'd board the chopper in order, moving to the rear and away from the door.

We heard it before we saw it. The pilot hugged the side of the mountain, swung around, and touched down right in the middle of the clearing. He'd even faced the door toward us.

The Air America pilot was truly outstanding. He had plenty of skill and guts. This would not be your run-of-the-mill flight and he knew it. He could have declined but he didn't. His colleagues were the same—they rarely refused a dangerous mission. They also knew what we were doing and they fully supported it. When we needed them we could count on them. They never let us down.

I still hold great respect for Air America. I would fly with those guys anywhere, anytime.

Vint sprinted toward the chopper, followed by the Hmong and then me. Our lookout had reappeared—he wasn't about to get left behind. I pushed him ahead but held his arm until it was his turn. Then he took off for the chopper. I followed not far behind. He clambered aboard and Vint lent me a hand as I climbed on just as the pilot lifted off, never stopping the rotors.

The noise was loud, as expected, but we had gotten out without incident. There hadn't been a sound from the PL across the valley. The pilot swung back around the mountain and headed for Vientiane, carrying the ten of us. We had left the eleventh man behind, but only because we could no longer save him.

Pat and Bill waited on the tarmac as we touched down in Vientiane. We weren't sure what to expect, having taken off on what turned out to be a risky, dangerous—and unapproved—mission. We had violated specific guidelines not to place ourselves in combat or other dangerous situations. If an agency officer had somehow fallen into enemy hands we all knew the potential ramifications in Washington. They would be widespread and in our ranks there would be ample grief.

As we got off the chopper and headed toward Pat and Bill, I could see that they both looked relieved and happy to see us. But I knew we had made a lot of people nervous and concerned for our safety.

"It was worth a try," Pat growled. "Never mind all the shit I would have had to deal with if something went wrong."

"Thanks, Pat. That's what we thought," Vint told him.

"Sorry to worry everyone," I added. "We didn't think we had time to wait for a message."

"Next time it wouldn't be a bad idea to wait," Bill said.

His typically low-key comment belied the concern and strong sense of responsibility he felt. Vint and I were two of eight young officers for whom he was accountable. At the time a small number of other agency people ran the upcountry aspects of the covert paramilitary program in Laos. And Bill, with Pat's able assistance, commanded the whole show. It was a daunting task.

It also was an impressive achievement. They had put together an effective resistance force with less than a couple of dozen men. We were spread thin and we worked hard, but we wouldn't have had it any other way. We took our losses even in those early days—among agency officers and the pilots who supported us—but we got the job done.

Friends who worked directly with Pat in the office later told me he had been genuinely concerned and torn as the situation developed. On the one hand he felt frustrated and irritated that we had made the decision on our own to set out with the Hmong patrol. He knew it would be dangerous. On the other hand he was proud of us. That we hadn't hesitated to attempt to rescue a pilot in need pleased him. In the end he felt so relieved that we had returned safely he didn't chastise us. I don't even know if he ever cabled the episode to headquarters.

Eventually another team recovered Tom Dieffenbach's body.

I spent a couple of days in Vientiane reading at our compound. The Laos program was expanding and we needed to emphasize intelligence reporting along with the harassment operations, which were increasing. One needed to complement the other.

The break proved useful because it helped me develop a better picture of the operations in Vientiane. I got to meet several of the officers working at the compound with Pat and Bill. I liked them all and respected what they were doing to support all of us upcountry.

For example I observed how they managed the daily message traffic. It was no mean feat and we all knew the flow was going to get heavier as the program expanded. To keep Washington up to date they maintained an impressive map room giving the constant location of friendly and enemy units. I also met the air-operations officer who provided liaison among our office at the compound, Air America and the embassy.

I also met the support, logistics and finance people. I witnessed an extremely complex and comprehensive operation that functioned very efficiently—a tribute to the organizational and managerial skills of Pat and Bill.

I never thought of either of them as a manager but the proof was in the pudding. They had put together a solid team and been able to absorb a variety of additional officers, including the JOTs, and still made the operation hum. Despite the major changes pending due to the Geneva Agreement on Laos, the program was strong and getting stronger.

Pat asked me to stop on my way back to Phou Song to attend a ceremony at a village near Sam Thong. The ceremony, a traditional one to welcome friends, was called a *bossi* and the guest of honor was none other than Vang Pao.

Pat had also decided to send Mike Nolan, an older and experienced paramilitary officer assigned routinely to northwestern Laos. We flew to Sam Thong together. A couple of young Hmong met us at the landing strip and guided us to the village, called Long Tieng, located on the other side of a mountain ridge but within walking distance.

As we crested the ridgeline I saw Long Tieng cradled in the valley, a panorama of impressive natural beauty. From my vantage point the valley ran at least several miles, with steep karsts on both sides, a small stream flowing through it, and cultivated patches dotting its floor. Some people have called it the most secret place on Earth.

Long Tieng was small but it looked more permanent than other Hmong villages, and I could understand why. Who would want to leave this pretty valley for a place perched on the side of a mountain?

We did not fully understand the politics of the situation but some things seemed obvious. Vang Pao's arrival as leader of the Hmong required that he be welcomed in the traditional way. Meanwhile he had to demonstrate the power and influence he was about to bestow on Long Tieng, which he would do by summoning representatives from the American government—the two of us.

The evening began with a dinner of a quality and quantity I had not seen before in a Hmong village. The locals had filled a large, clay urn with locally made rice wine and provided long straws for the guests. It wasn't bad but it wasn't exactly lemonade and we needed to drink enough to make it acceptable. So we drank a lot with dinner and afterward, when the village girls performed traditional dances. Then came toasts followed by the *bossi* itself.

The villagers chanted to persuade the good spirits to protect our souls and give us good fortune. Then the local shaman, himself honored by our presence and Vang Pao's, tied strands of white cotton yarn around our wrists.

Each piece of yarn carried a specific meaning and collectively the strands assured the wearer of good luck. The yarn was supposed to tie the soul to good fortune and the wearer must never cut off the strings, which would bring bad luck. Instead the strings stayed on until they fell off naturally.

Villagers honored me in this way three or four times during my stint in Laos and each time the strings remained on my wrist a couple of weeks. I gained prestige whenever a Hmong or lowland Lao noticed I was wearing them.

We slept well that night and awoke to a beautiful day of blue sky and crisp air. A chopper was due to pick us up but we had time to walk around the valley and enjoy the pleasant surroundings.

Scenery aside, Long Tieng's location south and west of the Plaine des Jarres and within a long, flat valley made it an ideal site for a large airstrip. Eventually the military built one capable of handling cargo planes and even the stubby-winged, high-powered T-28 trainers—which in this instance had been armed—to support Hmong operations against the VC and PL.

That would be just the beginning. The valley and the villagers would witness dramatic changes over the next decade. Along with building the airstrip the Agency for International Development funded the construction of vast warehouses for food, clothing, ammunition and medicine; frame houses for senior officers and the agency's advisers, and housing for Hmong families dislocated by the heavy fighting to come—with everything delivered by a near-constant stream of air traffic. For a while Long Tieng's airport became one of the busiest in the world.

The effort would change this valley and Long Tieng forever—and exact a terrible cost after the fall of Saigon in April 1975 when the United States pulled out and cast the Hmong adrift.

But none of us foresaw this on that pretty day in 1962.

As the Geneva Agreement's October 7 deadline approached I spent my last weeks in Phou Song working to bring in as many supplies of weapons and munitions as possible, because none of us had any idea when—or if—we might be allowed to return to Laos.

It was a bitter pill to swallow. Our observations showed that the North Vietnamese had no intention of pulling their units away. On the contrary, their activities were increasing in eastern Laos, particularly in the panhandle. Our road-watch teams had documented a steady stream of VC truck convoys continuing to roll into the country.

If they weren't leaving, why should we?

The Hmong were none too happy about this development. Vang Pao routinely registered his complaints with Vint and Tony, but they could do nothing.

We tried to make all of these concerns known in our exchanges with headquarters, to no avail. The State Department ruled the day and they were determined to live by the agreement Ambassador Harriman had signed. Despite the evidence we collected of a continuing North Vietnamese presence in Laos, Washington could not be swayed. For the time being at least we had no choice but to pull out.

Our one small victory had been to persuade headquarters that we couldn't just leave the Hmong completely high and dry. So they authorized two advisers to remain discreetly at Long Tieng—now Vang Pao's headquarters. Vint, because he could speak French and had developed a good relationship with Vang Pao, and Tony, because of his paramilitary experience, would monitor the ongoing situation.

Theirs would be a tough assignment. Travel into and out of Long Tieng, as well as our other areas of operation in Laos, was now prohibited. Vint and Tony would end up spending several months there under virtual house arrest.

At first, Bill and Pat moved their headquarters from the house near Vientiane's airport to Nong Khai, just across the Mekong in Thailand. The move, bringing with it a gaggle of *farangs,* was a jolt to what had been a quiet and sleepy little river town. But the local population adjusted quickly and welcomed the boost it gave to their economy. Sales of, among other things, Thailand's Singha beer jumped noticeably.

At the airport in Udorn, a much larger town about 30 miles south, the AID had built a concrete runway. So equipped, Udorn would become a major U.S. air base and staging area for combat and supply flights into Laos.

Its facilities eventually would include a large compound, including numerous permanent buildings, one of which would house Pat and Bill's headquarters. First dozens and later hundreds of military and agency personnel would move there, with predictable results for the town. As had been the case in Vientiane the sudden influx of money caused vices of all sorts to flourish and prosper.

I can't recall where I went on my last trip upcountry, but I do remember looking down from the Helio at the Plaine des Jarres and wondering if the Hmong would ever retake it.

We all wondered what would become of us. I had covered only three months of my six-month assignment and wanted very much to fulfill it. I finally found out, as did everyone else, by late September. During a quick visit to Vientiane, Pat called me into his office.

"Lots of changes, kid, and you will be moving. We want you to take over the project in the panhandle. It's in its early stages, like the Hmong effort, and they will be moving from Thakhek, a small town on the Mekong, to Nakorn Phanom, which is right across the river in Thailand."

I was surprised. I hadn't expected to get a whole project, particularly one working with ethnic Lao instead of the Hmong. Nevertheless I felt sure I could manage it and running the show certainly appealed to me.

"I think I should say thanks, Pat, but I don't know enough about it to say anything. Mind telling me what they are doing and why you selected me?"

"They're just getting going. Tom Ahern has got the teams started and now we need to get some intelligence about what the VC are doing. His tour is up and he's going to Saigon. I need a replacement and I think you can handle it. Got it?"

Once again Pat didn't waste words.

"Ahern leaves next week, so you might as well get the hell over there. Bring in all your gear and luggage in the morning and I'll have a plane for you later in the day. They know you're coming. You should probably read a bit before you go. You can start that right now."

I had dinner that night with Mike Deuel, who would be moving to Nong Khai along with André and Ralph to work at program headquarters. He wouldn't be spending that much time in the field so he wasn't thrilled, but at least he would still be working with the Hmong, for whom we all had great respect as fighters and as individuals.

6. That's Good, That's Damn Good

NAKORN PHANOM, THAILAND 1962–1963

South Laos, if saved, can be the keystone connecting the pillars of Thailand and South Vietnam, and sealing off Cambodia from further infiltration. South Laos is the key to preventing Southeast Asia from being cut in two.

—Special Report by the Task Force on Vietnam, June 19, 1961

As we circled before landing the pilot swooped down low over the agency house to alert Tom Ahern we had arrived. The buzzing took us out over the Mekong River, wide and muddy at that time of year.

A quiet, pretty little town of several thousand in northeastern Thailand, Nakorn Phanom was clean—cleaner than Udorn and certainly cleaner than Vientiane. It featured several paved streets and a sort of commons. With few exceptions, Tom's house being one of them, the dwellings were built in typical Thai style: tin roofs over wood frames, sitting on platforms anywhere from 4 feet to 6 feet above ground. They looked Spartan but sturdy.

"Welcome to Nakorn Phanom," Tom greeted me at the landing strip. "We've only been here a short time so I don't know many people, but the ones I know are all friendly and I'm sure you'll do fine."

"Happy to be here, Tom," I replied. "How long do we have before you're out of here?"

"Four days and counting. I need to bring you up to speed so we better get back to the house and get started."

Tall and slender, Tom was a few years older than I. He walked with a distinctive, lanky gait that reminded me of Gary Cooper. His personality displayed a decidedly cynical approach to life.

"Nice little town," he continued as we drove, "but quiet so we tend to stand out. Everyone wonders what the *farang* is doing here. Many know that I moved from Thakhek and that I have contacts across the river. They also know about the Geneva Agreement. Word flows, even across rivers. If they don't already know, two and two will soon make four. Not much we can do about it, nor does anyone ever ask."

Discretion—the operative concept.

I would spend almost 20 months operating out of Nakorn Phanom, and during that period if anyone ever did wonder about me they asked no questions. The agency had backstopped my cover but only minimally. I had without fanfare moved from Laos into Thailand carrying the necessary paperwork to keep me looking legal but the rationale was pretty thin.

Still it never became an issue.

The VC violations of the Geneva Agreement had been verified by photography and SIGINT, or signals intelligence—an all-encompassing term for intercepts of transmissions from target countries, installations and units.

Today's efforts are much more sophisticated and involve many "INTs" from which to collect information. But back then the SIGINT proved enough for even Ambassador Harriman to concede that the VC were not abiding by the rules. As a result and over time we felt less and less constrained.

For example, early during my stay at Nakorn Phanom I had to meet with my team leaders on the Thai side of the Mekong. Later I would make trips into Laos at night, and eventually I began crossing over regularly and in broad daylight. Though I never carried identification or a passport, no one, least of all the border officials—Thai or Lao—ever questioned what I was doing.

At the house Tom introduced me to the PARU team and his two assistants, Jimmie and Mr. Ambrose—neither used their Thai names. Both men worked for the Thai Ministry of Defense in some capacity but their ties were never clear, and as I came to learn and appreciate, both were very good in their work.

Thais, including the government, the military, the police and the vast majority of the people, feared the communist threat though they didn't really understand it. They welcomed our support and resources and seemed more than eager to help in any way they could. Thus the PARU team and others—all of whom we paid well—proved of great assistance.

The six men on the PARU team looked just like those I had worked with upcountry in Laos. Strong and clean-cut, they responded well to our guidance. We also employed a local young man named Whet to do our cooking, cleaning and laundry—better a young man than a young woman in a house with nine men. Whet worked hard for us, and anytime I called his name he seemed to leap through the door in response.

We spent the rest of that first day checking equipment, signing the required forms about gear, administration matters and finance, and walking around the town. The latter didn't take up much time. We stopped by the Officials' Club, comprising members from the Thai government and selected private citizens. It featured a cinderblock building and three concrete tennis courts. Inside there was a bar and a big room with a snooker table. Snooker, for reasons unknown to me, was very popular in the club and in Thailand generally.

We ate that night in the only restaurant in town, the Mekong River Garden, owned and managed by a Sino-Thai man who also cooked the meals. He stood almost 6 feet, which was quite tall by local standards. Bald with a protruding stomach he always wore a tank top.

When we entered the restaurant we passed by what served as the kitchen: some shelves above a rack holding a large wok being heated over a wood fire. Following the local custom we scanned the ingredients as if looking at a menu, chatted with the owner, and selected our entrees. Everything was fresh from around the town including the fish.

Then we took seats on the small, wooden stools that encircled our table. The restaurant, located on the river bank, featured a porch extending out toward the water, which at some times of the year rushed by as you ate.

The waitresses, Lek and Deng, were both in their teens. Shamelessly overworked and underpaid they were nonetheless cheerful and pleasant. During my stay in Nakorn Phanom I would eat many meals at the Mekong River Garden. Along with the fresh food I relished the very cold bottles of Singha they kept on hand.

Everyone there grew to know me and the rest of the PARU team well, and they were always happy to see us—if for no other reason than we always tipped.

"Where should we start?" Tom asked the next morning, referring to the operational aspects of his turnover to me.

"I've read the files," I replied, "but more detail would help. Let's start with the current location of each team and your thoughts about the team leader. Where do these guys come from?"

"It's a mixed bag."

Tom and Mr. Ambrose laid out maps on a large desk in the office. Behind on the wall was a big map board showing the entire Laotian panhandle, from just north of the Nape Pass, through the Annamite Range between Laos and Vietnam, and down to the Bolaven Plateau in the south.

I soon familiarized myself with the map coordinates of places in central Laos. Within months I could cite from memory the locations of specific towns and road junctions.

Tom briefed me on each team he more or less had organized and was now supporting. He had started from scratch and been obliged to work closely with Lao military officers. All seemed corrupt by our standards but to varying degrees.

Team leaders, often nominated by the military commander of a given area, were usually former military officers who had supposedly retired, though we never really knew. Some were refugees who once had been *nai bans* in key villages, or even *nai khongs*—the heads of whole districts—in the areas where we had assigned them.

The team members were a varied lot. All were local villagers but some had been displaced by the communist takeover of the areas near the border with North Vietnam, while others were from areas along the Mekong. Some had been members of the FAR.

The seven teams ranged in size from 15 men to more than 100, but none was currently located in a useful position for intelligence observations. They provided some intelligence but it was irregular and of minimal use. It came primarily from sporadic patrols or interviewing villagers.

Each team's level of competence also varied, widely. This, I would find out, was largely a function of the leader. The teams had radios and were in daily contact with us. Two of the PARU were radio operators and maintained the base station for our project.

All of the men had received at least rudimentary weapons training and each was equipped with a firearm, a uniform and boots. We paid them well by Lao standards—more than military personnel—according to their rank or position. We paid each leader in cash and he, we hoped, distributed the wages to his men.

Tom briefed me about the strengths and weaknesses of each leader. Mr. Ambrose, who would interpret for me when I met the leaders, also knew them. He would become a great help in the coming months.

Tom's briefing took the whole day. "Mixed bag" was an understatement.

The next day an unexpected visitor arrived: a finance officer from Vientiane. He had flown to Nakorn Phanom to determine why Tom's accounts were out of balance. Tom knew the problem and so did I, but resolving it to the officer's satisfaction would be difficult.

In the confusion that prevailed when we were all pulling out of Laos, Tom had made some payments to the teams for which he couldn't account, because he hadn't obtained receipts from the leaders. Likewise on two occasions he had air-dropped payments to teams in isolated areas and hadn't gotten receipts. He had also misplaced papers and hadn't recorded the amounts of some payments.

They worked all day. Mr. Ambrose, who knew which payments had been made and to whom, helped to clarify some of the outstanding problems. But in the end the officer concluded that Tom would have to replace the missing money.

I thought the whole affair was awful, but it presented two clear lessons I never forgot and reminded myself about on numerous occasions:

This is the government's money so take good care of it.

We don't lie to one another.

Even a scrap of paper or a note would have saved Tom his anguish; none existed. The finance officer wanted to be helpful but his hands were tied.

Based on that episode I made it a rule never to open my cash box without recording what I had taken out.

Because Tom needed to occupy himself during the next two days with preparations to leave, we didn't talk much. As a result I didn't learn what he thought about the future of the project. Bill and Pat were seized with the Hmong program and its future so I received little or no guidance from them, either.

"We need some intelligence," was all Pat had said. This was going to be whatever I could make of it. The project, still in its infancy, had generated little attention at headquarters and some people didn't even know it was proceeding. It had no cryptonym; it was just there.

Nevertheless I was pleased to be in this position. I faced challenges but could see room for growth and increased reporting. I was eager to get started—my six-month tour would be ending in January.

But where to start? My day-to-day activities would keep things going but what were the long-term goals? Just how would we improve our reporting capability? How much time would I have?

A lot occupied my mind as I bid Tom goodbye.

To develop a plan I went back to the map. As Tom had laid out for me, my operations would cover much of the Laotian panhandle, ranging from just north of Thakhek to midway between Savannakhet and Pakse in the south, bordered on the west by the Mekong and by the Annamites on the east—which also constituted the border with North Vietnam.

Immediately to the east of my bailiwick, along the 17th parallel, ran the Demilitarized Zone, or DMZ, the demarcation line between North and South Vietnam. Established by the Geneva Accords of 1954, the DMZ was meant to separate the communist North from the democratic South. In theory the border, stretching only about 35 miles, was relatively easy to defend—assuming the VC honored Laotian neutrality. In practice the North Vietnamese were clandestinely using my chunk of territory to support their efforts to subvert the South. We quickly learned the importance of monitoring and disrupting their activities.

Washington and Vientiane had considered a number of ideas, including one by the military to build a road straight across from the demarcation line to the Mekong then fortify and defend that road. The brass had argued that a well-defended, east-west road would preclude any VC effort to move men or supplies south through Laos along what had come to be known as the Ho Chi Minh Trail. So named in honor of the North Vietnamese communist leader on his birthday in 1959, the trail actually comprised a network of dirt roads and footpaths running along the eastern side of the panhandle from north to south. The military's proposal was rejected.

Whatever the plan, the Ho Chi Minh Trail would be my problem. My immediate challenge was not cutting the trail or stopping the flow. I simply needed to monitor the traffic, confirm it as the problem we all knew it to be, and calculate how many men and how much materiel were moving into South Vietnam.

Later my successors would deploy teams to harass and disrupt the traffic. For now I was essentially starting from scratch.

I learned from the maps that the road network in the panhandle, which had been carved out over many decades by the colonial French, was sparse. In the north, Route 8 ran southwest through the Nape Pass in the Annamites then south, following the western edge of the Nakai Plateau, to join Route 12 just east of Thakhek. Route 12 worked its way in from the Vietnamese border via the Mu Gia Pass, ran through the Annamites, and skirted the southern edge of the Nakai before ending up in Thakhek.

Route 9 headed east out of Savannakhet across the panhandle into South Vietnam at a point south of the demarcation line. Route 13, the only north-south road in the panhandle, ran on the Lao side of the Mekong all the way from Vientiane to Pakse.

Drawing on a millennium-old tradition, the French had used a surface of crushed laterite, a reddish, iron-rich rock. It gave the roads an all-weather capacity but they still often flooded out during the rainy season.

We initially thought the VC trucks would be limited to these roads. We would come to know better.

Even as early as 1962 the North Vietnamese were building and improving roads running between routes 12 and 9 that could handle truck convoys. Meanwhile during the dry season the VC moved jeeps and sometimes trucks into areas a little farther west, such as in and around Tchepone. But in the rainy season the bulk of their movement took place on foot.

Roughly speaking, the Royal Lao Army—the FAR—controlled the western portion of the panhandle, while the Pathet Lao and Kong Le's breakaway militia ruled the east. The VC enjoyed and fully exploited free access and movement in the eastern portion.

My task was to position clandestine teams at key points to watch all traffic along the roads and trails being used by the VC after they entered Laos via one of the two passes through the Annamites. From a relatively passive and organizational stage we would be moving into a much more active and risky effort. It meant I would have to train, motivate, and support the villager-soldier members of my teams to take the risks necessary to move into enemy-controlled areas and radio reports back to our base of operations.

Choosing the locations of the watch points would be easy. Obviously we would need to monitor the Nape and Mu Gia passes. More difficult would be getting teams to those sites, partly because I would be working from across the Mekong, and partly because the teams weren't particularly motivated to move into VC-controlled areas.

During my first month in Nakorn Phanom, I met all but one of the team leaders. Each had made the journey to Thakhek and then crossed the Mekong. After that they rarely missed having monthly contact with me, but not because of any wisdom I imparted—I dispensed the payroll. The routine gave me control and leverage, and gradually I developed a personal relationship with each man.

I spent a lot of time in the first few meetings briefing team leaders on our collective mission. As expected, and as Tom had made clear, some reacted more favorably than others. Those who hesitated tended to be located comfortably near the Mekong and inside Lao-controlled areas, or they simply feared moving clandestinely into enemy territory to the east. The others either didn't want to admit they were afraid or were actually ready to take the risks involved. I read the split as about 50-50.

Getting the reluctant ones in gear required much cajoling and motivating—or changing team leaders. I knew that several would report promptly to their Lao military contacts and I could expect questions. Why did I want to make waves? Because we urgently needed to know what the VC were doing.

Soon we made progress. A team in the northern sector settled into a spot from which, with minimal effort and risk, they could send out small units to watch Route 8—but only from inside Laos near the Nape Pass. This was good but not good enough.

Another team managed to move to the Nakai Plateau and put watchers on the bluffs overlooking Route 12. Good again but too far west of the Mu Gia Pass. Traffic passing those two sites would be carrying only supplies for the KL and PL units in the area.

It wasn't the Ho Chi Minh Trail but it was a start. Farther south, along Route 9 and in the area between routes 9 and 12, it was going to take more work.

In early December, Pat cabled that my assignment had been extended by six months and he wanted to know if I had a problem with that. I promptly responded that I was happy with the extension and would use the extra months to get things going.

GET WHAT THINGS GOING? he cabled back.

By that time Bill and Pat, with staff in tow, had moved to a building at the airport in Udorn. I requested a plane and flew back to brief him in detail.

"Here's what I think we should do," I said to Pat as I spread out my maps. "If we're going to get some useful intelligence we need teams a lot farther east than we have them now. Risky yes, but they should be able to stay out of trouble, and they sure want to do that."

I pointed to the sites I had selected.

"If we can put teams at these sites with radios we can get daily reports on what is moving into Laos via the Nape and Mu Gia passes. We're not there yet but things are moving. It's going to take some time. These aren't the bravest guys in the world."

Pat had been studying the map as I talked. It looked like I had piqued his interest.

"That's good, that's damn good," he said. "Think you can do it?"

"Yeah, I think so, and it's certainly worth a try."

Pat had been reading the cable traffic from Washington and from our Saigon office, so he was more aware of the growing interest in the VC's use of eastern Laos than I was. He also knew that both Saigon and the Pentagon had proposed ways to start dealing with the problem. Each had made tentative moves into the area without success.

I didn't know it at the time, but my brother Bob was involved in some of those moves. A Force Recon officer in the Marines, he was serving in I Corps in the northernmost area of South Vietnam—probably within 30 miles of some of my teams. He likewise had no idea that while he and his men were monitoring VC activities along the Ho Chi Minh Trail from the east, my men were watching from the west.

Pat knew that we could make a major contribution if we could produce regular reports about the traffic along the main roads and the trail. He also knew that all we had at this point was a plan. If we were successful our efforts would be well received back at headquarters.

We spent a couple of hours going over specifics. I outlined what we had done team by team, showing him each planned monitoring position. Based on the depth of the questions he posed I knew Pat was interested and impressed with what we had accomplished so far—and I felt pleased.

"Okay," he said, finally, "I want a cable for headquarters outlining this whole thing."

That surprised me. I had authored almost nothing going to headquarters and frankly dreaded the prospect. I had all but forgotten the format and style requirements since my training ended.

"Why don't you write it, Pat?" I asked. "You know the whole thing now. You'll write it so headquarters will like it."

"They'll like it—and you are going to write it. And as soon as you do, I want you to go up to Vientiane to brief Whitey (Charlie Whitehurst, our chief in Laos) before we release the cable."

I wrote the thing after laboring several hours and finally producing a draft that Pat liked. He did some editing but I had supplied the guts, and he was happy.

I stayed in Udorn that night and joined several of my colleagues for dinner and war stories. Collectively our experiences were sometimes funny, sometimes harrowing and always interesting.

On the harrowing side we'd heard that one of our colleagues in northwestern Laos had developed a bad foot infection. In a shocking display of carelessness he had delayed treatment and eventually required an emergency evacuation. By the time he reached Vientiane the infection had spread. He died in hospital.

On the amusing side we played Liar's Dice, a variation on the card game called I Doubt It. You rolled the dice, hid them from view, and passed them to the next player claiming a certain score. That player believed you or called you a liar. If he believed you he rolled. If he didn't and caught you lying you paid the food bill. In the second round the loser paid for drinks. It was better by far to pay the food bill if you lost. Drinks were as cheap as the food but the quantities consumed made the difference.

Early next morning I flew to Vientiane to see Whitey. He had arrived during summer to replace Bill Jorgensen. Whitey lived with his wife Dottie and their two sons next door to Souvanna Phouma, a prince of the Lao royal family who had been designated the country's neutralist premier by the Geneva Agreement. I had never met Whitey but heard the stories about him.

Despite his relatively young age—he was about 40 when I met him—Whitey had compiled an interesting personal history. Born in the south—Florida, I think—he had played first base in semi-pro baseball in his youth. Somehow, drafted into the military perhaps, he had ended up in the Office of Strategic Services and parachuted into North Vietnam with a team of commandos intending to blow up a key bridge between Vietnam and China during World War II. He never completed the mission. Before his team could reach the objective they received word by radio that the war had ended

After the war the OSS moved him to Shanghai, where he met and married Dottie. He served there until the communist victory in 1949 forced him to move to Taipei, Formosa—now Taiwan.

Whitey had already served several times as a chief, including Singapore, before arriving in Vientiane. Given his history and experience we all expected good things from him. We weren't disappointed. Pragmatic, smart and unpretentious, Whitey handled the job with aplomb.

I visited Whitey only briefly in his office. Some crisis had erupted that required his immediate attention so he invited me to his home for dinner that evening. I was surprised he would invite such a junior officer but I accepted with pleasure, and Charles and Dorothy Whitehurst turned out to be gracious and welcoming hosts.

"Good to see you," Whitey said at the door. "It'll be a lot easier to talk here. There will be no phones, no meetings and no flaps to deal with. Come on in. How about a martini before we eat?"

"Sounds good to me."

I sort of lied; I'd never had a martini before.

Tall with thinning hair, Whitey showed the beginnings of what would become a larger-than-he-wanted stomach to lug around. In time it would cause him back problems.

Sitting in the living room while Dottie supervised dinner preparations in the kitchen, Whitey and I first talked in general terms about my background and the project in the panhandle. He had an affable and easy manner, with an unerring sense of what was important and what wasn't. He made me feel comfortable right away and he impressed me with the questions he asked. He had obviously developed a good idea of what the problems were and an understanding for dealing with Laotians.

He focused on what should be emphasized in my cable to headquarters and told me that, with a couple of changes, he wanted it sent soonest. No surprise I was delighted.

After dinner Whitey and I retired to the living room again. Coffee and cognac in hand, and maps spread out on the rug, we got into the specifics of what I foresaw for the panhandle and how much of the plan I thought I could accomplish. It was important, Whitey assured me, because the whole question of the Ho Chi Minh Trail and what to do about it was heating up considerably in Washington.

He again posed some penetrating questions:

Where are the KL units?

What about the PL?

How far west do the VC operate?

What kind of bridge is that?

How high are those bluffs? Can they walk there in a day?

I answered in detail and my responses prompted more questions.

"Are you guys having fun?" Dottie asked entering the room, coffee pot in hand.

"Yes, we are," Whitey said, asking for more coffee.

As we wrapped up the evening Whitey commented that he had no idea this concept existed.

"This could really work, Dick. We've got to get things cracking."

It was late when I left but I felt elated.

"What did you tell Whitey?" Pat asked me as I entered his office the next morning.

"Same thing I told you," I joked, "that the sun doesn't just rise and set on the Hmong project and we've got things happening in the panhandle, too."

"Don't get smart, kid," he retorted. "Well whatever it was he liked it. We're going to get the cable out of here today."

My flight back to Nakorn Phanom was a straight shot east-southeast over the town of Sakon Nakhon with its large, shallow lake, which from the air looks like a big puddle. For Jim, my pilot for the day, who was used to flying in the northern mountains of Hmong country, this was tame stuff. He gave me the controls of the Helio for a while after we reached cruising altitude. As we neared the Mekong he took over again and decided to add a little spice to our otherwise routine flight. We were well into the dry season and the river's level had dropped significantly. Indeed in some places one could actually wade across.

Jim descended within 5 feet of the water. The river was so low that the banks on either side seemed to tower over us. It was like flying in a canyon. As we buzzed some startled fishermen in their long, narrow boats a few actually jumped into the water. That, I now sheepishly admit, caused us great amusement.

Really feeling his oats by this time Jim mentioned that it might be fun to bounce his landing gear off the river surface, but perhaps noticing the nervous look on my face he thought better of the idea.

Soon we approached Nakorn Phanom. Jim flew a little farther east toward Thakhek on the Laotian side until we got just abreast of the clock tower in what passed for the town square. Still flying very low he made a sharp right turn and headed straight for the river bank, which loomed above us.

I was growing a bit concerned.

At the last moment Jim pulled the Helio sharply up and passed over, barely, the Mekong River Garden. As we roared by I could see the waitresses, who must have heard us coming, rush out onto the porch and stare in amazement.

The flight path also took us right over our house, which alerted Jimmie to come pick me up at the airstrip. Jim, sporting a small grin, cranked down the flaps and we landed in one of my more memorable arrivals.

A few days later, Pat cabled me to say that headquarters had bought the whole thing—the concept, the goals, the plan itself, everything.

Pat sounded pleased and I sure was. It hadn't really occurred to me that my plan was a perfectly logical extension of the project I had taken over, or that it would have been difficult to oppose what I wanted to do. Who could quibble about trying to collect intelligence about the Ho Chi Minh Trail? No doubt I didn't understand some of the politics involved but it didn't really matter to me; they had approved.

With the approval came a request for a budget and some reporting requirements—possible ominous signs. Was this bureaucracy rearing its head? I eventually found out that Udorn—Pat, actually—had shielded me from the bulk of the onerous reporting burden.

Headquarters had given my newly born panhandle project an official cryptonym for use in cable traffic. Henceforth it would be known as Hardnose, and the next time I was in Udorn, Pat greeted me with, "So, how are the Hardnosers doing? That's got a nice ring to it."

He went on. "I love working with hardnosed people."

"Who thought up that crypt?" I asked.

"I don't know," he said, "but I like it."

My discussions with Whitey and some reading I did while in Vientiane had provided me with useful background about the politics of the situation in the panhandle and in South Laos. The VC's use of the Ho Chi Minh Trail, and Washington's concerns about that use, had been increasing steadily since the supply route emerged in 1959.

The Pentagon had voiced alarm in no uncertain terms and proposed several different plans to address the problem—including building and defending an east-west road to bisect and block the trail. None was approved, and it seemed to me the reluctance had to do with political timidity in Washington, Vientiane and Saigon.

Despite the lack of action there clearly was a high interest in and a glaring need for intelligence on VC activities. I now understood why both Pat and Whitey had been so favorably disposed to my plan.

Let me jump ahead temporarily. Media reports from Hanoi in the mid-1990s, soon after the United States had established diplomatic relations with Vietnam during the Clinton administration, recounted details of a conversation between a visiting group of American military officers and historians, and senior members of the Vietnamese military.

That conversation included comments by the Vietnamese regarding the paramount importance they had attached to the Ho Chi Minh Trail. In unequivocal terms, the officers made clear that their unimpeded use of the trail was critical to moving troops, cadre and war materiel through eastern Laos to destinations in South Vietnam and eastern Cambodia.

"Without it," their delegation leader emphasized, "we could not have won the war."

In other words, more than three decades later, we could only lament the fact that the United States did not focus more attention on the 1961 task force report on Vietnam, an excerpt of which I quoted at the beginning of this chapter. I wonder how many senior officials, during those early months of the Kennedy administration, had even read that report.

The weeks after my meeting with Whitey seemed like a blur. Several months into 1963 my activities still were limited by the constraints imposed by the Geneva Agreement. Forced to operate from outside Laos, I couldn't meet often enough with my team leaders and I could only cross the Mekong at night. Even so, those meetings, coupled with message traffic, started to produce some results.

I began traveling to Mukdahan, a Thai town across the Mekong from Savannakhet, for meetings with two team leaders operating in the southern area of the panhandle. Later on, as headquarters eased our operational constraints, I began slipping into Laos more frequently. We discussed logistics, training, reporting, communications and above all team location—all of which except location we discussed with no problem. Getting the teams to move into enemy-controlled areas to the east, however, was always touchy.

Once I needed to take a quick trip to Mukdahan. Road travel in a Land Rover over poor, rutted roads would have taken several hours each way, and I didn't want to spend that much time. I elected to fly despite the fact that Mukdahan had no official landing strip.

I figured that a Helio flown by a skilled pilot could land on the large soccer field I had seen on the edge of town. I talked it over with Jim.

"No problem, Dick. If you think I can land there, I can land there."

So, off we went.

Mukdahan's claim to fame is its beautiful and ancient *wat*, or temple, which tradition has it houses a small vessel containing some of Buddha's ashes. For that reason the King and Queen of Thailand would visit the river town in the spring of 1964 to pay their respects—the first visit ever by Thai monarchy to the northeastern part of the country.

In what seemed like mere minutes we were over the town. Jim spotted the soccer field right away but then saw people and water buffalo milling around on it. Many of the people were gesturing at the plane, which they must have regarded as an unusual sight. So Jim swung in low across the field to signal our intent to land. It worked. Soon the space had been cleared and Jim easily put us down with plenty of room to spare.

"Many thanks," I said, as we rolled to a stop.

"At your service, sir," he grinned,

I returned about two hours later. By then the plane was surrounded by a crowd of locals who probably had never been so close to an airplane before. Kids were running around everywhere, while young people and old people gawked. It seemed as though half the town had congregated on that field.

I gestured to the crowd that they should move away from the plane because we were going to leave. As soon as they did we taxied out to the far end of the field. Jim had plenty of room to take off. The wind was blowing right at us as Jim prepared to give it full throttle.

"You want to make the takeoff?" he asked. "It'll be an easy one—good practice."

Though I had made several takeoffs out of Udorn with Jim, I was sure he was pulling my leg.

"It's very thoughtful of you," I responded, "but why don't you just go ahead?"

He did and we left to many cheers and much waving from the locals.

My problems with moving teams into the eastern part of the country continued. I recall a memorable exchange with one team leader who had crossed over from Thakhek to see me. The man was about 35 and slender like most Lao but tall, and for some reason he avoided making direct eye contact.

I never liked using an interpreter, but I had no choice at this stage of my assignment, and in any event Mr. Ambrose was always available. Later when headquarters extended my mission I started studying Thai and eventually grew conversant. Thai is similar to Lao, especially along the Mekong, where people speak what they call Lao Thai, so learning Thai meant I could begin to understand Lao.

The team leader and I discussed routine matters easily, such as logistics and training. He told me that their radio was down and he needed some spare parts to get it working again. He briefed me about FAR activities in his area, which extended south and east from Thakhek. He also provided some intelligence collected from a local who had visited a village near the Vietnamese border to see relatives. Low-level stuff but of interest; we knew next to nothing about the area.

"That's good," I exaggerated, "but we really need to have steady reporting about traffic on the network running south from Route 12 toward Tchepone."

"I know, but that's very difficult," he responded.

Because he performed this little dance each time I saw him, I decided to up the ante.

"Tell me again why your team can't move farther east?"

Mr. Ambrose knew the dance well and he smiled before he translated the question.

"Because it's too hard, sir."

"But I know that you are well-trained and brave, and I don't understand why you can't move east."

"Maybe we can move soon," he said, hoping that I'd drop the subject.

"But we really want you to move now so that you can report regularly. Where is your team located?"

I walked over to the map of the panhandle on the wall.

"Our base camp is right here," he said, pointing to a spot in the southeast, "but I send out patrols regularly to try to get information."

"I need you to be here," I said, pointing to a location much farther east. "We talked about this last month and we agreed that this location would be safe, because you would remain hidden in the jungle."

"You don't understand. That location has bad *pi*!"

I knew the term and I remembered the village shaman who had attended me in Hmong country when I was down with fever. Bloody evil spirits again. A couple of other team leaders had voiced the same excuse and I admit it perplexed me. But if they really believed in bad *pi* (pronounced PEE), I would somehow have to work through it. I would have to find other spots for them to watch the roads in the east.

The problem, as Mr. Ambrose and I came to realize, was that almost all locations in the eastern panhandle were deemed to have bad *pi*. This was not the case nearer the Mekong—areas controlled by the FAR and not the VC. Bad *pi* was the best excuse they could think of for not moving into VC-dominated areas.

I understood their dilemma but this just wouldn't do. Other teams were moving east, albeit slowly, and his team needed to move as well.

"Okay," I said, "let's pick another spot nearby that doesn't have bad *pi*. How about here?"

I pointed to a location farther east.

"It's on a hill and *pi* don't like high places," I noted authoritatively.

He blanched, hesitated, and pointed to a spot between his team's present location and my suggested alternative.

"We could move out to here. Would that be all right?"

"That will be a good first step," I told him, adding that he was not working out as a team leader. That's exactly what happened; I was obliged to replace him.

One spring day in 1963 a member of another team arrived in Thakhek and made contact with us. He told one of my PARU that his team leader had been falsely reporting their position.

Based on their information we thought they had twice moved east and were having trouble collecting intelligence about VC traffic. But the team member told us they actually had stayed not far from Thakhek.

The disclosure irritated me. I asked if he would lead us to the team and he agreed. I thought my credibility and reputation would be strengthened by a straightforward move, so I decided to confront the deceitful team leader—someone, I found out later, our informant disliked intensely.

It took some planning.

First we used the boat we kept nearby in a boathouse we had built atop 10 empty, 50-gallon gasoline cans. Purchased by the agency in Bangkok for our use, the boat had a fiberglass hull and a powerful Evinrude outboard motor with an automatic starter. It could cruise at high speeds and was the only boat of its kind in Nakorn Phanom and Thakhek.

Not exactly low profile, we used it to cross over to Laos to deliver various supplies—always without customs formalities.

We motored across at night. Jimmie drove the boat, accompanied by a PARU, the team member and me. It wasn't too challenging. We were still in the dry season so the water level was down and the current relatively gentle. Navigating the Mekong during the rainy season was altogether different. The high water and surging currents carried debris quickly downstream, including large trees, and the complete darkness presented a real danger. Eventually as our operational restrictions eased I could begin using the boat in daylight.

Next we stopped at a house we kept in Thakhek for meetings, supplies and contacts. Via those contacts we had rented a jeep—courtesy, I was sure, of some corrupt FAR officer.

Early the following morning we drove south along Route 13. The KL held the Mahaxay district, directly east of Thakhek, but our intelligence reported no active patrols so we weren't worried. "Don't rock the boat" was the KL's motto.

About 15 miles out we stopped, hid the jeep in some bushes, and started hiking east. The team member led the way while the rest of us stayed watchful, and knowing how isolated and vulnerable we were we felt a little tense. Within two hours of easy walking across the relatively flat terrain we arrived at a stream. We could see the camp on the opposite bank—quite a bit west of the location they had recently reported by radio.

I instructed the team member to wait for us. I saw no reason for a confrontation between him and the team leader.

We used the team's long and narrow pirogue to cross the stream and the men on the other side quickly saw us coming. Disembarking we walked directly into camp and summoned the team leader by name. None of the men knew who I was but my PARU quickly and sharply educated them.

The team leader appeared, looking dumbfounded and sheepish. When he saw me I'm sure his first thought was, "How could *you* be here?"

"Where is your command post?" I asked sternly.

"I'll show you," he replied, walking toward a tent with an awning covering its entrance and a table under the awning.

"Show me your maps," I demanded.

He spread a map of the sector on the table.

"Please show me on the map the location of this camp."

"It's right here," he said, indicating the camp's position along the stream.

Pulling his most recent cable from my pocket I read out the coordinates he had given and identified them on the map.

"We cannot tolerate false reporting," I snapped. "It's impossible to work with people you cannot trust."

Only the team leader and his radio operator were within earshot as Jimmie translated. That was good. I couldn't be sure how many team members knew of the deception. Not too many, I guessed. I also didn't know whether the team could be saved but I was certain that the two men standing before me had lied. I would have them dismissed, but discreetly.

"I want to see you both in Thakhek in three days," I told them, "and bring all of your gear."

Caught red-handed there was nothing they could say and they presented no defense. I later discovered that only a few of the men knew about the false reporting. I dismissed the culpable, reconstituted most of the remaining men, and transferred several members to another team.

Had I been older and wiser I probably wouldn't have acted so bluntly. Perhaps I should have assessed the risks involved more carefully. Heading into that camp I had no idea how the team leader would react. Fortunately he didn't turn hostile or violent. Maybe the element of surprise had worked in my favor.

During my entire stint in Laos it was the only time I had to take such action. But I continued to experience difficulties trying to confirm team locations, as did my colleagues. Most of the time we simply had to take the word of the team leaders but we also did what we could to verify their reports. I made surprise visits periodically, hoping word got around that I could turn up at any time.

Sometimes we used collateral reports to double-check our teams. If we had overhead coverage of the Mu Gia Pass, for example, we could check it with reporting from a team along Route 12. Udorn often did this for us. For example, it always pleased me to hear that one of our teams had reported a truck convoy on some route that air coverage had likewise spotted. Occasionally we used reports from villagers to confirm our road watchers' intelligence.

But the best verification came from our air drops of rice and other supplies. We'd make no drop unless someone displayed the proper signal at the drop zone, meaning the team had to be where they reported they were.

We also changed signals periodically just to keep the teams on their toes. Because they definitely wanted those drops they grew quite careful about the coordinates they supplied and the signals they used.

Team location remained a thorny problem but I knew we had handled it as well as we could. After my departure we began inserting teams by chopper, meaning we knew exactly where they were.

By mid-1963 the VC became increasingly aware that our teams were watching them and they began employing countermeasures. For instance, the VC actively patrolled the roads they were using and planted sources in local villages. That proved dangerous for our teams, which sometimes discreetly purchased food from some of the villages, usually from trusted friends or relatives. Once discovered by a VC patrol and lacking the firepower to stand and fight, a team could only run.

That outcome began to change later in the 1960s when we began inserting bigger teams with heavy firepower, but until then evasive action remained the only option.

Sometimes the VC would use dogs in their efforts to discover our teams. That also caused us problems, which we dutifully reported back to Udorn and headquarters.

Then one team noted that the VC dogs would retreat if they detected the presence of tigers. Reportedly anytime the dogs caught the scent of tiger excrement or urine, off they'd go—though we had no way of knowing if this was true.

On the other hand we had no reason to doubt it so we passed along the report. Apparently it perplexed the people at headquarters to the point where they held several meetings on the subject. Eventually an office in the Directorate of Science and Technology decided to investigate a possible countermeasure.

The plan was to spread a substance around our base camps that smelled like tiger excrement. The reasoning was that the decoy scent would render the dogs ineffective and keep our teams safer. It seemed a good idea but would it work? In the end it didn't but we did appreciate their effort—just one among many examples of headquarters colleagues attempting to find an innovative solution to a problem in the field.

Coincidentally, when I retired in 1996, I was talking with another senior officer, also retiring, about Laos. It turned out that he'd been a young analyst in the office that tried to help us. He remembered sending some colleagues to the National Zoo in Washington to collect samples of tiger urine and excrement for analysis.

They managed to produce a substance that closely resembled it—but it couldn't fool the dogs in Laos.

7. Forgetting Christmas

NAKORN PHANOM 1963–1964

While I continued the good fight upcountry, my colleagues and buddies Mike Deuel, André Le Gallo and Ralph McLean found themselves more or less stuck doing routine office work in Nong Khai. Understandably they weren't happy and they took no consolation in the fact that the Geneva Agreement allowed them little choice.

Pat and Bill sympathized but headquarters had tied their hands. From time to time, as a way to break the boredom, they conjured up assignments for the guys that required short trips. For Mike it meant working frequently in Chiang Khong, a town just across the Mekong from Laos, in the far north of Thailand near the border with Burma. There he served under Bill Young, the son of a missionary, who had grown up in the area and spoke several of the local dialects.

Mike had graduated from Cornell University and spent two years as an officer in the Marine Corps under a joint program that immediately assigned him to the agency. The agency in turn had assigned him to Far East Division, working in the field under Pat and Bill. After leaving us he would spend eight months at headquarters and then join the CIA officially. He would return to Laos in early 1964 as a case officer serving in Pakse, in the southern part of the panhandle.

Working with Bill Young, Mike helped to support tribal groups such as the Yao of northwest Laos who, like the Hmong, fiercely fought the communists. He supervised mule trains carrying weapons, ammunition and other supplies to the guerrillas. Such undertakings could be risky. The Nationalist Chinese operated in the area, some of whom had gotten involved in the opium trade and aggressively guarded their territory against all intruders. To my knowledge he never encountered them.

André, a former Army officer, felt equally unhappy stuck at a desk. He grabbed every opportunity to get into the field and dropped in on me for a couple of weeks during January 1963. He helped me organize Hardnose. Accompanied by my PARU he met with some of my team leaders to assess their progress.

The visit was doubly beneficial. André not only aided the project but also gave me a much-needed outlet for conversation—he let me bounce ideas off him. My Thai was still weak, which severely limited my interactions with the locals, so it was great to have him with me.

Like Mike, André would also eventually work near Pakse. Fluent in French he collected low-level but useful intelligence from a plantation owner with whom we maintained contact. Not nearly as exciting as running regions in Hmong country, André said, but it sure beat the hell out of office work.

André experienced an interesting incident on a train to Bangkok while traveling there for some R&R. None of us had paid much attention to our actual cover status when we moved out of Laos into Thailand because the Bangkok office had taken care of everything. About all we knew was that we were advisers. Because no one ever asked questions we didn't worry much.

On the train André had befriended a Thai family, mainly because he had become interested in their attractive daughter. Like him they had boarded in Nong Khai and he must have figured they lived there, so maybe he could visit the daughter sometime. The father turned out to be a general in the Thai army and he spoke English. Asked by the general what he was doing in Thailand, André said he was an adviser.

The father didn't pursue the subject and engaged in small talk—until a Thai immigration officer checking identity cards entered their compartment. The officer gave the Thai family a cursory look then turned to André, obviously a foreigner, and requested his passport. André handed it over, assuming that the agency administrative people had supplied the proper stamp, and in any case whatever information the passport contained was written in Thai. He felt no concern.

The immigration officer leafed through the passport, found the stamped page, and read it. Then he looked sharply at André, suddenly snapped to attention, and saluted. André, somewhat taken aback, nodded in recognition.

The official handed back André's passport and left—and after a moment of awkward silence the general asked if he could see the document. Hoping for some explanation André handed it over. The general found the stamped page, nodded, and handed it back, saying nothing.

André told me he never did understand what happened, but he surmised the stamp somehow identified him as an official of note or a special envoy.

In February, André returned to headquarters to work in Africa Division. Like me he had been assigned there after he completed training and lent to Far East Division, because he had volunteered for TDY in Laos. Africa Division eventually sent him to the former Belgian Congo.

Ralph also worked with me at Nakorn Phanom for a while and likewise welcomed a chance to get out of Nong Khai's office routine. A Harvard graduate, he had joined the Marines and been commissioned along with Mike before being assigned to the agency for two years.

Ralph produced and followed all reporting by various units on their positions and the positions of the enemy—a process called order of battle. He helped to map every friendly or enemy location in North and Central Laos and quickly became quite an expert. He returned to headquarters in the summer of 1963 to out-process, as it was called, from the Marines to the agency. Eventually he returned to Southeast Asia for postings in Indonesia and Burma.

Months passed. Our Hardnosers became more aggressive and more effective. We weren't stopping the Red Menace, but we had taken up positions to watch it go by.

My constant message to the teams: Stay away from the enemy.

None of them had a problem with that concept.

It was a straightforward task. Find a spot away from the road with an unobstructed view, if possible on a hill or bluff, and remain hidden. Rotate small teams from a base camp every couple of days, always stay out of sight, and move at night.

I can't say my directives were particularly brilliant—just common sense—but they worked. We handed out cameras and trained team members to photograph passing traffic. We also gave them laminated plastic cards identifying various kinds of trucks and other vehicles, and we standardized the reporting procedures.

Soon we were getting written reports along with daily radio transmissions:

"Four trucks carrying rice sacks passed grid WE 1467 at 10:30 a.m. on July 7 heading west on Route 12."

We also started getting film cassettes, which we promptly sent along to Udorn. Our photo coverage got good enough to confirm the VC's presence in Laos—important, because it helped ease the constraints on our operations. The teams photographed VC patrols, trucks, bicycles and even elephants laden with sacks and cans.

From the spring of 1963 onward our coverage of the Ho Chi Minh Trail network in the eastern panhandle increased steadily in quantity and quality. Also, following my directive the teams avoided firefights during my tenure—easy to do, because they weren't looking for trouble.

In those days we didn't deploy teams by helicopter, nor did we attempt to stop the VC traffic. The North Vietnamese, increasingly aware of and interested in the activities of our teams, judged us to be a minimal threat. They took their time initiating countermeasures. As we became more aggressive they reacted in kind.

Near the end of my extended assignment, in late spring 1964, Pat summoned me to Udorn. He was expecting a senior visitor from headquarters and needed a briefing on Hardnose, which I gladly provided. At that point I was very knowledgeable about how things were going. We still had problems but we recorded steady progress.

We went over everything with the headquarters guy including the budget—a topic I didn't know much about. On my end whenever I asked for something it appeared. Pat took care of finance and administration. The visitor seemed satisfied, even pleased. That pleased Pat, which in turn pleased me.

I spent the evening with Pat along with Vint, Mike and Ralph at a restaurant much like the Mekong River Garden. We enjoyed a splendid dinner with plentiful food and Scotch.

Next morning I stopped in to see Pat before returning to Nakorn Phanom.

"Sounds like things are okay with your Hardnosers," he said.

"Hope so," I responded. "It ain't easy but we're doing everything we can think of."

"The reporting is improving and I like that."

"We have to do more between Route 12 and Route 9 around Tchepone. We're working on it."

"Well keep at it and by the way we want headquarters to extend you till summer and just make this a full two-year tour. That okay with you?"

It was typical Pat—out of the blue. I had to think a moment before responding. I knew Africa Division was expecting me back soon but I was enjoying my work and thought I was making a useful contribution. I accepted.

My life in Nakorn Phanom settled into a routine: periods of intense activity, some punctuated by clandestine visits to Laos, coupled with lengthy stretches of calm verging on boredom. Now that I knew I would be staying for two years I had to find ways to fill those downtimes. During a short visit to Bangkok I bought a book on elementary Thai and started taking language lessons from, literally, the girl next door.

Our neighbor, a man of Vietnamese-Thai origin, had an attractive daughter in her early 20s who taught at the local school. But tradition made my attempts to get to know her difficult. I got around this by introducing myself to her little brother, who introduced me to her. So far, so good, but her family remained wary of her contacts with me. Lessons at our house were out of the question. Instead we met in the library at her school during free periods.

My first visit caused quite a sensation. I was the only *farang* in Nakorn

Phanom, and my appearance at the middle school to see Dara (meaning "little star" in Thai) attracted special notice. The students were all atwitter, though as the lessons proceeded I became less of a novelty.

Dara turned out to be a no-nonsense taskmaster who taught me well. She helped me understand the four tones—rising, falling, high and low—in the Thai language. The sound "ma," for example, can carry four separate meanings. If I needed to convey an order or a piece of intelligence precisely—or understand someone conveying a message to me—I had to differentiate those tones.

The process was tricky. In Thai, the same word means "water buffalo" and "penis," for example, except with different tones. I had to be careful with pronunciation to avoid awkward situations.

Becoming conversant in Thai would be of great help later when I learned Mandarin Chinese, which uses those same four tones. I also started reading Thai, which is based on the ancient Sanskrit language.

I spent an hour with Dara twice a week, interrupted only if a plane buzzed my house, which I could hear from the school, announcing the arrival of someone or a delivery from Udorn.

I tried to stay fit by exercising each day. My PARU team members jogged and lifted weights but I didn't join them, though I did follow a regimen in my room in the mornings.

One day on the way home from lunch I saw some guys playing basketball on a local court. I stopped to watch, ended up in a pickup game, and promptly noticed two things: 1) The players were small, very quick and knew the game, and 2) I was the "big man" on the court. Back at Blackburn College, where I had played during my four years there, I was almost always the smallest man on the team. But here when I went up for rebounds I usually got them. I also made tip-ins and posted up to the basket—I loved it.

The other players noticed something, too. The big *farang* would make a great addition to the town team; not exactly Wilt Chamberlain but for northeastern Thailand in 1963 a real find. They urged me to join and though I felt pleased at their interest and gratified by their praise I couldn't commit to regular practices and games. I did agree to coach them as time permitted. I enjoyed my interactions with those nice young men.

I also played tennis a couple of times a week in the late afternoon and I joined the Officials' Club, where out of politesse the members would open a place for me whenever I showed up. Indeed, Nakorn Phanom's residents always did whatever they could to make me feel welcome.

I particularly enjoyed my matches with a wiry little Vietnamese tailor who had moved to the town after World War II. He played well and was a fine person.

I'd often stop in the club bar after a match for a Singha and, as my Thai improved, chats with Thai officials. Sometimes I'd play snooker at their invitation. With smaller pockets and greater distances on the table I found snooker more difficult than pool. Unlike my basketball and tennis I never got good at snooker, but true to form my Thai hosts tolerated my marginal play and always loudly applauded my few successes.

Often during my periodic flights to Udorn I would take the controls from Jim for a while, though as soon as I saw our destination approaching I'd nudge him. He usually took the opportunity to grab a nap.

I logged quite a few hours in the Helio that way, and I began to feel fairly comfortable in the air. We all did this unofficially because it could be important to know something about flying, "just in case." It remained unspoken. We all knew that enemy ground fire could disable the pilot. It made sense for us frequent flyers to gain some ability at the controls.

Emerging from his slumber Jim said, "It's about time you took a try at landing this thing. You up for that?"

"Yeah, I think I can get it down," I responded cautiously.

"Just listen and do what I tell you."

I reduced the power and started down, heading for the *very* long runway. As I lined up for final approach Jim told me to lower the flaps, which I did with a hand crank in the middle of the ceiling just behind the pilot's seat. Because I was sitting on the passenger side I had to crank with my left arm—a little difficult but I got the flaps down.

I felt the plane slowing but couldn't judge its airspeed.

Jim started talking me in.

"Little lower. Little lower. Keep it steady. That's good."

I listened and tried to comply but my depth perception let me down. Or was I just impatient? I dropped the last 20 feet or so in one quick chunk and we bounced back into the air.

I could tell that Jim had gotten a little excited.

"Still plenty of runway left. Just ease her in."

I must have rushed it because we bounced again.

"Why don't I help? We can do this."

I certainly hoped *we* could. On my third try I brought the Helio in—on the second longest runway in Southeast Asia. Landing an airplane is harder than it looks.

By mid-1963 we started thinking about moving our operations back into Laos. That didn't happen while I was there but in early 1964 we rented another small house in Thakhek, and I sometimes stayed there overnight for meetings. After I left in July my successor moved the whole base station across the river to Savannakhet.

Even the previous year as the restrictions eased we could cross more frequently and travel in daylight. I increased my contacts with Lao army officers, mostly for reasons of courtesy. We didn't discuss what our teams were doing but they had a good idea anyway. Only a few times did they raise objections and then only indirectly.

I traveled a few times to their camps and strongpoints on the road leading into Thakhek from the east. My relations with the FAR were good and on a few occasions I was able to help them with communications support or logistics. In turn they provided transport, approval to land at their airstrips for resupply and refueling purposes, and selected men for our teams.

In late fall I traveled by jeep—we used Land Rovers on the Thai side—with the intention of visiting one of our teams positioned north and east of Thakhek near Route 8. In addition to checking on the team, which had been doing a fine job for us, I wanted to get a firsthand look at the terrain. The area was not fully secured and we rarely got a chance to overfly it.

Along with two of my PARU, and the team leader who helped to guide us in, I drove north along Route 13 to the point where it crossed the Nam

Kading River. There we left our vehicle and got into a waiting boat. Typical of the area it was long and narrow with a long-shaft outboard engine. The boat accommodated us all with plenty of room to spare. We carried small packs and weapons.

Heading upstream and passing by increasingly rugged hills and rocks, soon we could see a line of high karsts far ahead rising abruptly, almost vertically. Starting just north of Thakhek the line stretched for miles and formed an obstacle to east-west travel. Climbing would have been all but impossible without proper equipment, and going around meant walking a hefty extra distance. The terrain featured a couple of passes that became strategic choke points during hostilities.

Our mission aside, the scenery was truly astounding. Natural beauty abounded as we pushed upstream on what turned out to be a pretty day. We passed no villages for a long period and the river was calm—giving me time to think. I reviewed the decisions I had taken to get there, feeling satisfied I had made the right ones.

After about four hours we arrived at a large village near the karsts. Evidently the team leader had alerted the *nai ban* to my arrival because he and several others awaited us on the shore. I wasn't happy about that but I hadn't thought to tell the team leader not to advertise my visit. Given all of the lectures he had heard about the need to travel discreetly, I didn't think he would mention we were coming. He did, and now I would receive a special welcome.

The village rarely received visitors of any sort, let alone a *farang*. I would have preferred pressing on but the *nai ban*'s plans to serve us a special lunch could not be ignored. We stayed and ate, and in truth we had a pleasant time; the villagers treated us most graciously.

"Could you send us some tools?" the *nai ban* asked as we finished lunch.

I thought a moment about what to say.

"I really don't have any tools," I responded finally, "but I can certainly check with the AID office and see if they can help."

Not satisfied, the *nai ban* pressed me.

"We need them badly to complete the fish farm we have constructed."

"Well, that's the kind of thing AID likes," I told him. "I'll certainly pass along your request. How should they send the tools to you, by boat?"

"By boat would be easiest but we can come to Thakhek to get them if necessary. Or maybe you could drop them from a plane."

I ignored the last comment, noting that the *nai ban* of this isolated village understood that he could ask for all forms of help from the Americans. I was the wrong one to ask in this case, though he didn't know it. He also didn't care. Over time I imagine it only got worse.

"We don't have enough so give us more," was the mentality we had created with our well-intentioned efforts and largesse.

But what good did that do? Not much if anything, primarily because of the waste and corruption I encountered, not only in Laos but also in the Congo, in West Africa in general, and in several countries in Southeast Asia. I never did support large aid programs because I saw enormous sums of money expended with minimal if any results, and with the intended benefactors gaining the least.

I'm convinced that you will always appreciate more what you work for and earn yourself.

After lunch we got word from a patrol that enemy units had moved into the area where we were headed. The patrol members advised me to return to Thakhek and I accepted that advice, agreeing that it was too dangerous to proceed.

One night while I sat in the small house we had rented in Thakhek, working on some reports to send to Udorn the next day, I suddenly heard the sound of gunfire break out all around me. I could even hear machine guns.

What the hell's going on? Is this a raid by PL or VC units right here in Thakhek?

I killed the lights and grabbed my weapon. Crouching in the darkness I moved to the front of the house and peered out the screen door.

To my surprise I saw people shooting their firearms into the air and others making noise with whatever was at hand—pans, pails, drums. I didn't see anyone I knew so I was left to puzzle it out. I watched for a few minutes, sensed no immediate danger, and went back to my reports. Eventually things quieted down and I went to bed.

The next day I asked Mr. Ambrose about the previous night's celebration.

"The eclipse of the moon," he explained. "The Lao believe that an eclipse is actually caused by a giant frog jumping on the moon. Loud noises will frighten the frog and then it jumps off the moon making it visible again. It works every time."

"You're not serious," was my only reply.

Late in November we received a message from our team operating south of Route 12.

WE ARE SORRY TO HEAR ABOUT YOUR PRESIDENT AND WE SEND OUR CONDOLENCES

I had no idea what they meant. I had a shortwave radio in my room and sometimes I listened to the BBC for news, but I had been out of touch. Apparently the team members had heard via their shortwave set that President Kennedy had been assassinated. It turned out to be the first word of it in Nakorn Phanom.

By December reports from the teams were steadily streaming in. We had positioned most of them well, and all were maintaining the low profile I advocated. I grew busier and busier managing the project. Logistics, planning, finance, training and meetings, now frequently held in Laos, kept me occupied.

I also stayed in touch regularly with Udorn to order supplies, discuss intelligence reports and requirements, and request air transport. Although Jimmie and especially Mr. Ambrose were a big help I still had my hands full.

One day I cabled Pat with a request for planes on four consecutive days. His response:

PLANE 23 DEC OK. PLANE 24 DEC OK. PLANE 26 DEC OK. FYI 25 DEC IS CHRISTMAS DAY. WE ARE NOT FLYING ON CHRISTMAS DAY EXCEPT IN CASE OF EMERGENCY. COOL IT KID

I read his message standing up then read it again sitting down. I had to smile. I had been so focused on what I was doing in this tropical Buddhist village that I had completely forgotten about Christmas. I thought of my parents and immediately wrote a letter home. Then I declared Christmas Day a holiday in our house and altered my plans accordingly.

Early in 1964 Dick Kinsman arrived in Nakorn Phanom. Pat and Bill had sent him to support my efforts. Maybe my pre-Christmas message had caused Pat to conclude that I was losing my grip and needed help, but whatever the rationale I welcomed Dick's arrival.

A native of upstate New York, Dick had graduated from Syracuse University and had been with the agency a few years. Like the rest of us he volunteered and had arrived at Udorn the previous fall. He was a low-key guy and I could see right away we would get along well.

Dick immediately sat in on all meetings with team leaders and frequently traveled with me when I crossed into Laos. He caught on quickly. Much of our success depended on building personal relationships and he established rapport easily. Persuading, even cajoling team leaders and members about the wisdom of our suggestions was important, and Dick seemed to possess a knack for listening and for explaining without appearing arrogant.

Most of all I appreciated Dick's presence because I could discuss operational ideas with him. We talked through several possibilities for the future of the project, including one that would move us into a more aggressive mode in the eastern panhandle.

Word was coming out of Saigon that Vietnam was heating up. The VC were moving more men and materiel south via the Ho Chi Minh Trail, crossing into Laos on Route 12 via the Mu Gia Pass almost directly east of Thakhek. We knew all that because of our monitoring, but given the increasing concerns in Washington we now needed to consider ways to disrupt that traffic.

If we were going to get more aggressive we would need bigger teams packing lots of firepower. The units should be company size at least—100 men or more—to begin mining the roads the VC were using and to ambush and attack the truck convoys. This would represent a significant step, much more dangerous than counting trucks and troop traffic from a respectful distance. We tried to plan carefully.

First we would need to recruit and train more men, and we would require more resources, including PARU support for the training—something we estimated would take up to six months. We sent an outline of our thinking to Udorn; they approved it, as did headquarters.

GO SLOW, Pat cautioned in his reply.

We also needed a site to conduct our training. Dick and I crossed the Mekong to visit the military commander in Thakhek and explain our needs. Corrupt and ineffective he nevertheless agreed to let us take over a former Lao army training facility northeast of the town, at the spot where the Nam Mouan River crossed Route 12. We'd have to fix the place up a little but otherwise we could start anytime we wanted.

Next step: Evaluate the new recruits. We didn't want just anybody. We made it clear to the PARU that just being a cousin, brother or friend of a team leader would not cut it. We also wanted people who would respond quickly to training. The PARU handled both tasks well, putting the preselected recruits through a training regimen that weeded out the weak links.

Our first newly reinforced team ready, we decided in our youthful zeal—and throwing caution to the wind—to use them in what we thought was a bold shot. In hindsight it was ambitious but dangerous. We would hit the Mu Gia Pass, thereby blocking Route 12.

Our plan was to run boats up the Nam Mouan, through the karsts in that area, to a point near the team's location. It was the dry season so the boats would have no trouble dealing with swift currents or waterborne debris. Good thing, too, because they would carry 12 powerful cratering charges, which we'd transfer to a truck for the 10-mile haul to the encampment. Then a 15-man patrol would carry the explosives on foot for another 25 miles across the Nakai Plateau to the Vietnamese border, where Route 12 entered Laos via the pass.

We chose boats because we thought the base was close enough to enemy territory that an airdrop might expose its position. There weren't many villages along the route, but still the patrol would have to avoid contact with locals who might be in touch with PL units. As they approached the pass they should move only at night to reduce any chance of bumping into the enemy.

At the pass the patrol would pick a spot along a ravine or other vulnerable place and then plant the charges and detonate them under cover of darkness. The explosions would trigger a landslide and, we hoped, block the road for weeks.

We thought our audacity would shock the VC; as it turned out the only shock we delivered was to our team leader.

By this time I had developed moderate Thai language skills but never tried to discuss serious subjects on my own. I brought along Mr. Ambrose to do the translating. My comprehension had improved to the point where I could understand much of the conversation between him and the other party, so even before he relayed the necessary information I could begin considering my response. I never let on that I understood and Mr. Ambrose never disclosed my facility.

As I laid out this proposed operation to the team leader, however, I needed neither my own comprehension of Thai nor Mr. Ambrose's translation. I could see it in his eyes and facial expression—he was stunned.

He struggled to speak at first then spewed out one reason after another why such an effort would not be possible. He had so many reasons he didn't even include bad *pi*, but we got the picture.

Having a patrol walk across Laos carrying 40-pound cratering charges to the Mu Gia Pass—the enemy's lair—to blow up a vital transport link that was probably guarded at key spots would be asking a great deal of his men, he said. Then if they were successful, asking them to retreat back across Laos while eluding the VC, who would no doubt act like angry hornets whose nest had been disturbed, was more than we could expect.

I had considered going with them, but I feared Pat's ire if he found out. In a state of shock the team leader pleaded with us to reconsider. In the end we did and we never mounted the mission.

Years later, as I followed the war via newspapers and news reports, I learned that our B-52 bombers had dropped thousands of tons of bombs along the trail and in the strategic passes, including Mu Gia. The raids never managed to block the roads for more than a few days at a time. The North Vietnamese did an incredible job of repairing and/or rerouting in order to keep supplies flowing south. Our dozen cratering charges, even at that early stage, would not have made much of a statement.

In the spring the same Lao officer who had given us the training site outside of Thakhek invited us to a local celebration of *Pi Mai*, the lunar New Year, to be held at a military base about 10 miles southeast of the town. The gala affair started in late afternoon.

We crossed the river in our boat, grabbed a waiting jeep, and drove to the base. The guests were performing the *lamvong*, a traditional dance, when we arrived.

As honored guests we were offered drinks. As I soon discovered, the Lao delighted in getting their guests drunk. From the first moment someone was always putting a drink in our hands. We joined in the *lamvong*, which is for couples, even though we didn't know the steps. But it didn't matter because no one ever touched anyone else and we all just moved around in a circle.

We drank. We chatted with the Lao officers in English, French and Thai.

We drank. We participated in a *bossi*.

We drank Mekhong whiskey, a Thai concoction often mixed with Coca-Cola or soda.

We drank rice wine.

No surprise we drank too much, but so did everyone else. It was quite a party.

It had gotten dark by the time the celebration ended. Although we knew we weren't exactly ourselves we thought we could make it back to Thakhek. None of our hosts had heard the "friends don't let friends drive drunk" line.

We found our jeep and got in. It was pitch black around the perimeter of the base and I had trouble finding the knob for the headlights.

The unpaved, two-lane track in front of us looked like a tunnel through the dense jungle and overhanging trees. We both carried weapons. Dick held his M1 rifle on his lap. Within minutes he was yelling at me to stop.

"I dropped my M1," he said.

"How the hell could you do that?"

"You drove off the road and the bushes grabbed it!"

"The bushes grabbed it?"

"Yes, they did! The barrel was sticking out and when you veered off the road back there it was pulled out of the jeep. We have to go back and find it!"

"Can't see a damn thing!"

"We have to try. Turn the jeep around."

I managed to reverse course without hitting anything or going into the roadside ditch. Leaving the headlights on, we got out and started looking for the missing rifle. Somehow Dick found it, I reversed the jeep again, and we reached Thakhek without further incident. We got into the boat and cruised across to Nakorn Phanom.

It was a memorable party and a memorable night—but I'm glad to say it was a rare event.

Our abortive assault on Mu Gia notwithstanding, we felt proud of our work and sometimes one of us would actually get to take on the VC—Tony Poe, for instance.

Tony was an exceptional guy. Intensely patriotic, he reportedly kept an American flag over his bed. He also loathed the communists and fought them for most of his adult life.

We heard he had single-handedly carried out an air raid against a VC column in early 1963, something unheard of during that period. Vexed at communist advances on one of the villages in Sam Neua, he decided to retaliate. Along with a colleague, whose identity never surfaced, Tony stuffed several dozen empty peanut-butter jars with hand grenades and pulled the pins so all of the grenades were live.

The jars kept the grenade handles from springing up, so they couldn't explode. Tony sealed the jars with their lids and carefully packed them in several cardboard boxes. Then he persuaded an Air America pilot to help him.

Acting on current intelligence he and the pilot caught a VC column completely by surprise. The pilot flew in from behind the convoy at treetop level. Those in the convoy, which consisted of a few trucks and a couple of companies of foot soldiers, could only watch in disbelief as the small plane roared overhead. No one reacted quickly enough to mount any effective defense.

As they passed the length of the column, Tony rained the glass jars down onto the VC as fast as he could. As the jars hit the ground and broke, the grenades exploded, sending the troops diving into the jungle.

Apparently Tony hung halfway out the door cheering as the pilot banked away to safety. Gutsy but not crazy, they made only one pass.

Tony also had his flaws—as do we all. Sometimes he drank too much, perhaps as a way to deal with the ever-present stress and danger, and it had predictable effects on his judgment. I met him once in Bangkok while we both were enjoying a couple of days of rest.

"Tony, how the hell are you?"

"Not bad, I thought I needed a break."

"How long have you been here?"

"Eight hundred dollars!"

I was a little puzzled. "So how long are you staying?"

"Fifteen hundred!"

That was Tony. Never concerned with formalities he had decided he needed some time off or some companionship—or both. He informed Pat that he was going to Bangkok, and he did, taking $1,500 with him. He didn't mess with requesting leave or filling out any forms. With a voracious appetite for Thai girls—*any* girls, actually—and whiskey, he would consume the pleasures of Bangkok and return to work when his money was gone.

Tony also possessed a wicked sense of humor. In summer 1964, soon after I had left Thailand to return to headquarters, Dick told me that I'd just missed the arrival of a small box that Tony had sent from Long Tieng. Inside there were what appeared at first glance to be dried apricots. They were actually dried ears.

The Hmong for traditional reasons and in lieu of a body count sometimes cut off the ears of dead enemy soldiers and brought them back as proof of their prowess and courage. In the box with the ears Tony had included a short note:

MY MEN UP HERE ARE REAL FIGHTERS

He meant this, we knew, to be a slam at the lowland Lao with whom we worked. One of our newly arrived officers figured out a retort. He sent one of the PARU to the local abattoir, where the man obtained the long penis and imposing testicles of a just-slaughtered male water buffalo. The group at Nakorn Phanom custom-made a long narrow box, placed the water buffalo's genitals in it, and included a note:

WE ARE FIGHTING REAL MEN DOWN HERE

They addressed the box to Tony in Long Tieng, but inexplicably someone in Udorn, instead of waiting for the next Helio flight there, had sent the box via Vientiane.

The people who handle agency mail are required by regulation to determine what each package or envelope contains. This particular package created a commotion and the story flashed around like wildfire. No one seemed upset by the prank except Leonard Unger, our ambassador. He was not amused and ordered the box destroyed.

Tony never received his gift.

Shortly after Dick arrived in Nakorn Phanom, a U.S. Navy construction battalion—affectionately known as the Seabees—began working on a new air base about 10 miles west of us.

It must have been quite a spectacle. We learned that the Seabees had shown up in a long convoy of heavy machinery—all sorts of trucks, jeeps and earthmovers. The brass had selected the site strategically to serve two purposes.

First, the Thai military would gain a first-class air base in their sparsely populated northeastern provinces, which were deemed vulnerable to communist activity.

Second, the U.S. Air Force could use the location to support its beginning air war against North Vietnam, as well as against VC operations in northern Laos and the panhandle. Base operations would also include search-and-rescue missions for downed U.S. pilots. It was as close to the critical danger zones as our Air Force could get.

Efforts were also under way at Udorn's air base to build new facilities and improve the existing ones, to give the military the capability to support a U.S. air war—a capability that would be employed increasingly over the coming decade.

We visited the nearby site about three weeks after the Seabees had arrived to meet and welcome them. Dense jungle covered the location so their first task had been to set up camp. They had already pitched rows of large tents with plank flooring to serve as barracks, and they had put up an office building, a mess hall and a motor pool. Clearly these guys weren't messing around.

We met the commanding officer and his deputy, both of whom were surprised to learn that two Americans had been living in Nakorn Phanom. We explained that we were advising the Thai military. Whether or not they understood what we were doing they didn't pursue the subject further.

The mission was to build a 10,000-foot, pierced-steel-planking runway as quickly as possible—meaning that the base was going to handle heavy transports. The project also involved taxiways, parking areas, hangars, maintenance facilities and a security perimeter. This, we could tell, would not be some sleepy outpost—it was a major undertaking. The commander proudly assured us that it wouldn't take long, and it didn't.

We watched the construction activity for while. It was impressive. The Navy engineers had stretched an enormous steel chain between two heavy Caterpillar bulldozers. Midway across the chain was a huge steel ball that rolled forward. The two bulldozers dragged the chain, and a third Cat pushed the ball. Using this method they could level a swath of jungle about 100 feet wide in one pass. We were fascinated.

Each bulldozer's cab was enclosed in a steel cage that protected the driver from falling trees, and things falling from the trees such as snakes, several of which they killed every day. They told us that most of the reptiles were large and poisonous, but the cages kept them out and the bulldozers just crushed them. At the rate they were going, 10,000 feet didn't seem much of a challenge, and we could see why they were optimistic about finishing quickly.

The agency had expansion and modernization efforts going on at Udorn as well, including a new building to house a headquarters for Bill and Pat; they had outgrown the rented house in Nong Khai. The increased levels of activity in northwestern and southern Laos and the panhandle were part of the reason.

The new building, located in a restricted-access portion on the air base, would meet their needs though it made little difference to me. We kept in regular contact with Bill and Pat via radio messages, so all we needed to do was change the address line.

The move marked the start of a new phase for paramilitary operations in Laos. Centralized out of Udorn, with a large and efficient headquarters staff and well-established air and logistics capabilities, the momentum grew palpably.

Souvanna Phouma, the Laotian neutralist premier, had no problem with our efforts. In fact he practiced realpolitik by requesting increased levels of covert support for his government's struggle to exist. As it had been directed by President Kennedy, the agency executed that part of the U.S. response. Publicly all still paid lip service to the Geneva Agreement of 1962 but on the ground everyone ignored it.

For the remainder of the year we recorded significant progress, including my project, and we saw bright prospects ahead. Just let us get back into Laos, we told one another, and we'll really get things on track. Our attitudes were positive and our confidence high. To a man we were pleased with where we were, what we were doing, and what we had accomplished. The original game plan—assembling small, well-trained, mobile units for hit-and-run operations designed to harass and tie up the VC units—was beginning to shift incrementally toward tactics aimed at actually seizing and holding ground.

At this point none of us saw the dangers that such an approach portended. Our level of confidence may have bred excessive optimism about the future of our projects. We would definitely give the VC fits. Of that we had no doubt.

Back in Washington, President Lyndon Johnson, JFK's vice president, who was sworn in only hours after the assassination, was equally convinced that the United States would prevail, so he increased our support for South Vietnam. In truth, whether in Washington or Southeast Asia and despite some disturbing political machinations in Saigon and Vientiane, we Americans were looking at the situation through rose-colored glasses. That a world superpower could be tied down and ultimately rendered impotent in a conflict with a country the size of North Vietnam seemed inconceivable.

The harsh lessons had not yet been learned.

During a visit to Udorn in May, Bill called me in for a chat. This was unusual; he mainly concerned himself with the Hmong program and let Pat handle Hardnose and the others. I was curious as I walked into his office.

"What are you going to do when you get back to headquarters?" he asked.

"Go to Africa Division I guess," I replied. "I was supposed to go there before I volunteered to come out here."

"Happy out here?"

"Love it," I told him quite honestly.

Like Pat, Bill didn't waste words.

"If you'd like a home leave and a return to Laos, we would like to have you back here."

I didn't expect the offer so I tried to gather my thoughts. Certainly I was flattered, and such a proposal from Bill meant a lot. I knew he wouldn't have made it if he wasn't completely happy with what I'd done. I also knew that Pat must have agreed and might even have been the instigator. I felt gratified that these two men, whom I greatly respected, looked favorably on me and my efforts.

Coincidentally I had been thinking about my next move in recent months but hadn't yet reached a conclusion. I was sure if Far East Division wanted me—and now it was clear they did—they could win the bureaucratic battle.

The question was did I want them? I wasn't sure.

Bill's offer was tempting, and I truly enjoyed what I was doing, but this would be a major career decision. It would mean running paramilitary operations instead of conducting the classical intelligence collection I had envisioned before volunteering for TDY in Laos.

Single and still relatively young, I wondered if I could have it both ways. Not likely, I concluded.

"Thanks very much, Bill," I responded eventually. "Coming from you, that's a real compliment. I've been breaking my head about this exact question and I don't have an answer yet."

"I could have guessed as much," he said. "So now you know we're happy and we'd like you back to keep running Hardnose."

"It's very tempting, Bill, but I don't feel right committing myself until I've talked to headquarters. Let's just say that I'd like to come back but I don't know if I can."

I knew it sounded wishy-washy but it was the best I could do at that moment.

"It's your call, Dick," Bill continued. "You don't want to go to Africa. Those people are uncivilized. They'll eat you!"

We both laughed, neither suspecting how prescient his comment would be.

Just then the phone rang and he waved me out of the office.

Pat knew about my conversation with Bill.

"You won't come back," he predicted.

I started to protest but thought better of it. In the end Pat was right. I left Nakon Phanom for good in July, traveling to Bangkok via Udorn. Dick Kinsman, by then thoroughly familiar with our panhandle operations, took over for me.

Before flying to New Jersey, where my parents had recently moved, I met my brother Bob at Orly Airport, outside Paris.

Bob, a year younger than I, had just finished his tour with the Marines in South Vietnam. He had served a tough and dangerous duty.

Bob had no idea that my assignment had taken me so close to his location and I couldn't disclose my whereabouts or what I was doing. Through our letters to and from home our parents arranged the rendezvous. We spent three weeks together driving through France, Italy and Switzerland, and our time unwinding together helped us regroup and get ready for our next assignments.

I arrived home happy—happy with the previous two years, about my prospects for the future, and about seeing my family after such a long absence. Mom and Dad were likewise delighted to see us.

Mom responded with plenty of the cooking we both remembered and enjoyed. Dad, to his chagrin, allowed me to repossess—temporarily—the TR3, the purchase of which he had originally protested.

"You just paid a thousand dollars a seat," he had told me back then.

But while I was away he drove it quite a bit, and he had even bought himself a pair of leather driving gloves and an English golf cap.

I felt confident that my work in Laos had been worthwhile and that we all had been productive and successful. I met many officers that I had grown to like and respect—and none that I didn't like—and I thought my career had gotten off to a good start.

Now, nearly 50 years later, as I reflect on what we did and on what happened after I left, I lament many of the unintended results of our efforts, particularly what befell the Hmong and how our actions ultimately delivered Laos into the hands of a communist government.

"Too soon old and too late smart" applied to our efforts from 1961 until 1973, when we recalled all of our military personnel from Southeast Asia. So many Americans harbored ignorance and displayed arrogance without malice during that period—especially in Laos, from my perspective, and likely in Vietnam as well.

We had gone there to help those nations resist communism; of that there should be no doubt. But we possessed only minimal understanding of the history, culture and politics of the people we wanted to help. Our diplomacy in Geneva involved Cold War issues rather than the welfare of Laos or Vietnam. We imposed our own interests on the region. President Kennedy had decided to "draw the line" against the spread of communism in Southeast Asia and we would draw that line our way. For over a decade we rained down manpower and resources on the region, unable to see or maybe accept that such an approach was not working.

One example: our flawed deployment of air power. I wrote about this issue in 1995 as part of a review of *Shadow War: The CIA's Secret War in Laos*, a book by Kenneth Conboy and James Morrison about the agency's efforts:

> An interesting aspect of the book that readers may want to consider as an issue in its own right is that of the use of air support. The author carefully describes the extensive role played by U.S. airpower. From cargo planes delivering troops, war materiel and food to reconnaissance planes, helicopters, ground support fighters and even B-52

> carpet-bombing runs, virtually every U.S. airplane in Southeast Asia was deployed in support of the war effort against the communist forces. It is probably not an overstatement to say that never before and never since has an irregular "guerrilla" force been so intensely supported by the full range of a superpower air force. Dealing with their vulnerability to attack from the air presented the North Vietnamese with an enormous challenge. They responded with nighttime attacks and major offensives launched during periods of bad weather that curtailed the effectiveness of total U.S. air superiority. In the end, that air supremacy did not carry the day in Laos or in Vietnam. While airpower can tilt the playing field and postpone the inevitable, it will not win wars. The foot soldiers, who seize and hold territory, are ultimately the victors, a point clearly made during the 1960s and 1970s.

The fact is we didn't learn, we didn't adapt, and we lost. We only began to get it right in the Gulf War in 1991, in Afghanistan in 2001, and at the beginning of the Iraq War in 2003. In all three cases we broke new ground in terms of projecting air power massively at the beginning of a conflict—"shock and awe" in the military's parlance. Our ability to fuse real-time intelligence gained from multiple sources with air attacks and ground assaults quickly destroyed the enemy—including those in Afghanistan who showed themselves only rarely.

The three campaigns, and to a lesser extent the aerial bombing of the Serbs in the spring of 1999, showed potential adversaries across the world how U.S. technological superiority, and our ability to employ that superior technology anywhere and anytime, made confronting us militarily an extremely risky proposition.

Back in the early 1960s, however, the Pentagon's ability to project air superiority was limited to brute force, the literal showering of the landscape with thousands of tons of bombs, an approach which hadn't been updated since World War II. The effort was extremely destructive and costly, in terms of the effort itself, the landscape, and innocent civilians unlucky enough to find themselves in the wrong place at the wrong time.

In this instance the war planners needed a more effective tactic—and they devised a good one. They presented a proposal to build a defensive barrier on the ground between North and South Vietnam. They considered the Laotian panhandle a key area because of the VC's movements along the Ho Chi Minh Trail. Those movements represented threats not only to South Vietnam but also to Cambodia and even Thailand, according to the Domino Theory, to which the Kennedy administration adhered. If any one of those nations fell to communism the others would follow.

The Pentagon's proposed barrier took the form of constructing and defending a road running all the way from the Gulf of Tonkin across to the Mekong River. Roughly following the 17th parallel in Vietnam and Route 9 in Laos, the road would have ended at Savannakhet.

The proposal died because Ambassador Harriman remained determined to respect Laotian neutrality and not force on the country what I'm sure he regarded as a monster project, something that would have effectively cut Laos in two along with Vietnam. At the time nobody focused much on the trail, and as a result they failed to realize how much of a threat it represented.

Unaware of the deliberations taking place some 9,000 miles away, Dick Kinsman and I reached the same conclusion one night in early 1964 while working in Nakorn Phanom. We could kill the trail by building and defending a road across the 17th parallel. We sent our idea to Udorn, but it died as well—for the same reasons.

Too bad no one in Washington knew at the time that the Communist Party's politburo in Hanoi had declared the Ho Chi Minh Trail critically important to its war effort. They therefore tasked the North Vietnamese army to refine, expand, exploit, and protect the trail at any cost.

Even without that knowledge the Pentagon should have built the road, the result of a careful study of the situation by an Army task force. It made good sense. It would have precluded further North Vietnamese support of the insurgency in the south by blocking the flow of supplies, men—everything.

Moreover, we could have defended the road effectively with a deployment of tanks, artillery, air cover and troops holding fortified positions. Our naval power would have controlled the Gulf of Tonkin, and in the west we could have patrolled the Mekong to prevent attempts to outflank the barrier. We could have expanded the existing air base at Seno, near

Savannakhet, to facilitate resupply. As of early 1964, the newly constructed airport at Nakorn Phanom could have provided all kinds of support.

The advantages continued. Lacking the trail, the North Vietnamese could not easily support or resupply their operations in the south. To try to breach the barrier meant they had to come to us, instead of us chasing them in the jungles.

Had we built the road we might have been able to leave the problems of South Vietnam to the South Vietnamese. And the South Vietnamese, defended by us at their northern border, recipients of our aid, and fighting only home-grown insurgents, might well have prevailed.

As history has recorded, however, we never built the road. Political decisions, taken without vision and without a clear understanding of what was actually happening on the ground, foiled an effort that would have struck at the core of the problem in Southeast Asia at the time. It was a sin of omission.

Here is perhaps the most tragic part. The planners estimated that the barrier would have required approximately 200,000 troops to defend it. Under the strategy the Pentagon and the Johnson administration eventually adopted, a total of over 2.5 million military personnel served in the Vietnam War, including a maximum troop strength exceeding 500,000. Of those, more than 58,000 died and more than 150,000 were wounded. Deaths among South and North Vietnamese totaled an estimated 250,000 and 1.1 million, respectively.

Who knows how many of those lives would have been saved if that barrier road had been built.

Our policy failures and bad decisions during the Vietnam War extended across all of Southeast Asia, encompassing among others many thousands of the Hmong. Vang Pao's discussion in late 1960 with Bill Lair unknowingly began more than a decade of war and hardship for his people. Neither man could have foreseen what happened.

We had attempted to organize and train the Hmong to resist communist encroachment via guerrilla—I repeat, guerrilla—tactics. But the program grew incrementally into a full-frontal challenge, not only to the PL forces in Laos but also to North Vietnam itself. It was a terrible mismatch. Despite our best efforts and despite the employment of the full range of our air support, the communists decimated the Hmong.

No one wanted it to happen but it happened, the result of one faulty decision after another from the mid-1960s onward, each decision upping the ante and pushing the Hmong farther toward the point of the spear.

We introduced more training, larger units, increased firepower and enormous air support in Laos, all little by little, and all driven by our policies for South Vietnam. In fact we ended up bombing Laos nearly as much as we bombed Vietnam. Our B-52s, headed for the North from Thailand, often dumped their loads in the general area of the Ho Chi Minh Trail if bad weather forced them to abort their original missions.

The Hmong surely saw all of this happening but they courageously carried on. Vang Pao not only agreed to the decisions but also pushed for many of the offensive actions taken as the conflict wore on. By his own admission those actions cost him nearly half his force of 35,000 men.

I think his vision became clouded by the stars around him—those on his own shoulders from his promotion to lieutenant general, those on the shoulders of the American generals, and figuratively the ambassadors with whom he interacted as an equal.

Vang Pao assumed that U.S. power would save him and the Hmong. It did not. The VC launched an attack on Long Tieng that began on December 31, 1971. They could not take it, but the assault required us to transport Vang Pao and his family to the United States. He died in Fresno, California, in January 2011. Thousands of Hmong who had settled in this country attended his funeral and the associated events, which lasted six days.

Bill Lair spoke at the funeral and praised the Hmong for their skill and courage, both during the war and afterward.

We abandoned Long Tieng entirely, as well as all of Laos, when we vacated South Vietnam in April 1975. We had accepted a political agreement that allowed the communists to seize power.

That was a sin of commission, for which the Hmong, our staunch allies for more than a decade, are still suffering.

PART III: THE CHESSBOARD

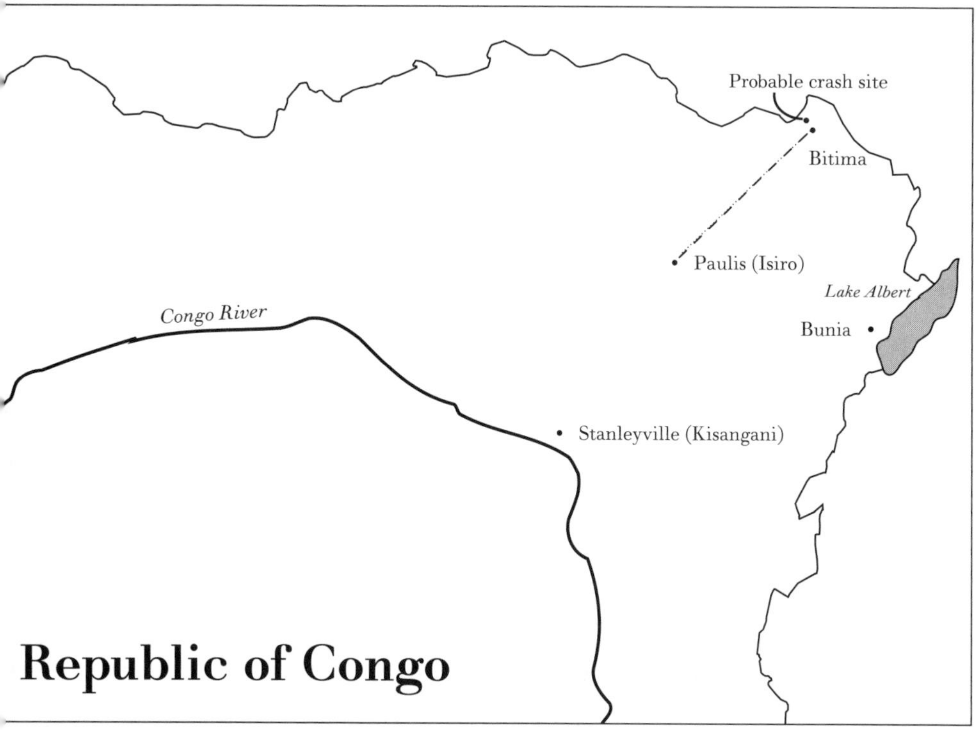

Probable crash site
Bitima
Paulis (Isiro)
Lake Albert
Bunia
Congo River
Stanleyville (Kisangani)
Republic of Congo

Probable crash site
Bitima
Paulis (Isiro)
Lake Albert
Bunia
Congo River
Stanleyville (Kisangani)
Republic of Congo
Leopoldville (Kinshasa)

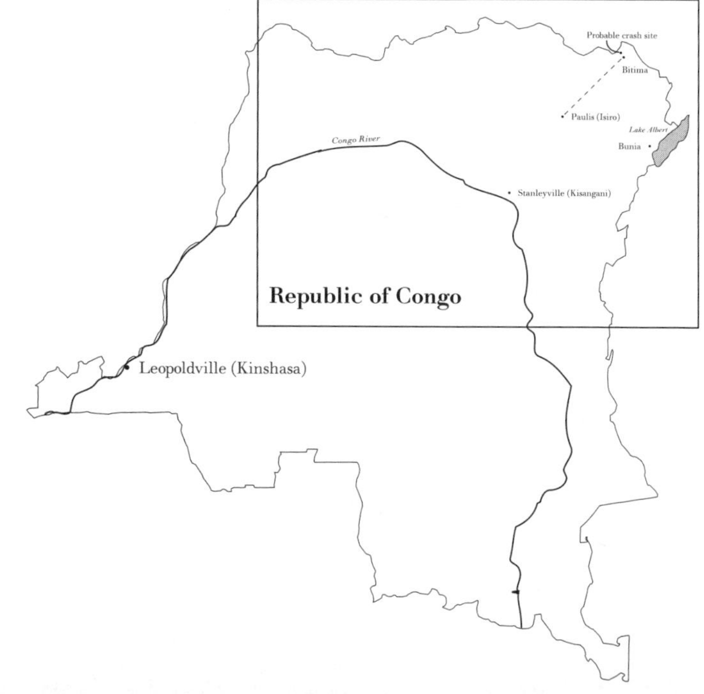

8. Standout in Stanleyville

REPUBLIC OF CONGO 1964

"You just got back from Laos?" asked the pretty admin clerk who was checking me in while I was checking her out.

"That's right."

"How long were you there?"

"I went out in July 1962," I explained, "and I was initially on six-month TDY but was extended twice, so it ended up being a two-year tour."

In mid-September 1964, after spending a couple of weeks' leave with my parents—and retrieving the TR3 from Dad—I reported back to agency headquarters, which had moved to its present location in Langley, Virginia, just across the Potomac River from Washington, in the fall of 1961. There I would join Africa Division, my original choice before I had volunteered for paramilitary duty in Laos.

I rented an apartment on MacArthur Boulevard, near the house I had shared during my JOT days, and I drove the short daily commute across Chain Bridge and up Dolley Madison Boulevard to the office.

The Southeast Asian detour had turned out to be productive. Soon after I began work at Langley the agency presented me with a medal for my service. Headquarters even authorized me to invite my father to the ceremony. Lyman Kirkpatrick, the agency's wheelchair-bound executive director, presented the award, reading a citation that made it sound as though I had fought the communist horde single-handedly. Dad was impressed and proud.

I spent what seemed like an inordinate amount of time on paperwork but the clerk assured me it was all necessary. When we finished I tried to think of something to keep our conversation going. I had noticed that she wore no ring on the third finger of her left hand, and my two years upcountry in Laos and Thailand had heightened my interest in many of the unattached young women back home.

As a single man deprived of female company for all those many months, I would make good use of the short time I spent back at Langley. I quickly reached the point where I was dating several times a week. But for the moment I had to conduct some official business. I asked about my assignment to Africa Division.

"You should act surprised when you find out," she said. "They are going to put you in North Africa Section."

I was delighted. In 1958 and 1959, during my time in France with the Army's Counter Intelligence Corps, I had learned some things about Algeria, Tunisia and Morocco. The colonial war in northwestern Africa had just ended with France ultimately granting independence to Algeria. But many French and Algerian citizens continued to harbor resentments, and in dealing with them I gained an understanding of the culture and conflict that had driven the struggle for Algerian independence.

Despite my fascination with the attractive clerk I redirected my thoughts to North Africa and to meeting Glen Fields, Africa Division's chief. Instead I met John Waller, the deputy. A gracious man, he pleased me by showing that he knew who I was and something about me. It soon became clear, however, that he had decided I needed some breaking in at headquarters. With a challenging field tour already under my belt I preferred to think of myself as an experienced officer, but I didn't contest the point.

Waller extolled my upcoming headquarters assignment, assuring me that I would gain long-term career benefits from it. Then as the clerk had predicted he told me I would be working on North Africa matters and supporting our Algiers office in particular. I feigned surprise but didn't have to pretend excitement.

The branch chief, whose name I've forgotten, arrived to walk me through the branch area, where I met everyone at the Algeria, Tunisia and Morocco desks. I was happy to see Monty Rogers, one of my JOT classmates. He had also been assigned to North Africa.

I didn't find headquarters intimidating exactly, but it sure felt different from Laos. Here I would be operating literally at the opposite end of the information flow—receiving instead of gathering. Plus I'd be double-checking facts, doing research, monitoring expenses, and in general supporting the field officers. Essential work no doubt, but considerably less interesting.

Monty was a big help getting me settled in. As the new guy I naturally received the least-exciting assignments and chores—checking names, confirming travel plans, and occasionally commenting on operational details—part of the mundane but important task of supporting an overseas office. Compartmentation, the bedrock agency policy of Need to Know, kept me unaware of the more sensitive activities, but this was a great job for starters.

I understood that I had to learn the ropes at headquarters and doing so would prepare me for heading overseas again. Toward that end I immediately started studying for what I hoped would be an assignment in the Maghreb—in Arabic, the "Place of Sunset," the Pan-Saharan region of North Africa comprising Libya, Tunisia, Algeria, Morocco and Mauritania.

Little did I know where my Africa assignment would actually lead.

I picked up several books from the branch library about the history, culture and politics of the Maghreb countries and read them in my spare time. I practiced this unofficial research throughout my career, a task greatly facilitated by the fact that I could always find dozens of good books at headquarters about any country. Our Soviet-Eastern Europe Division and our Chinese operations component of Far East Division in particular offered great arrays of books. In this instance I read mostly about Algeria but also about Morocco.

I considered taking Arabic language training, a two-year program, but decided against it. I didn't want to risk delaying my assignment by that amount of time. Also, based on what I had already learned about the differences between classical and Maghreb Arabic, it just wouldn't be that useful for an Africa Division officer.

On the other hand my French needed work. My grammar, weak

in France and weaker still in Laos, cried out for after-hours study and drills—not the most enticing prospect for a young bachelor in Washington but important from a career perspective. So I signed up for part-time French language training.

Colette, my instructor, had been inducted into the French Ordre National de la Légion d'Honneur, the Legion of Honor, for her service as an ambulance driver during World War II. She was married to Larry Devlin, one of the division's most senior officers. He headed another Africa branch and was former chief in Leopoldville in the Congo. They had met in Algiers back during World War II when they were both doing intelligence work.

A native French speaker, Colette was pleasant and a good teacher. Two nights a week I would stop by their house for an hour's lesson. We would often finish about the time Larry arrived home. A couple of evenings we all had drinks before I left.

I got to know Larry, who would eventually head the Congo office again, and we often talked about that country, at the time beset by Simbas, the Swahili word for lions, a group of fighters who believed they had been inoculated by their witch doctors to be bulletproof.

We also discussed the situation in Stanleyville, where David G., our chief there, and his two communications officers had been captured on August 5, when Nicholas Olenga and his Simba rebels overran the city.

One morning in mid-October I arrived at work to find a note on my desk directing me to call Glen Fields. I thought it was highly unusual. Fields must have known who I was because I worked in his division, but why would he want to talk to me?

I called right away and was instructed to be at Fields's office at 10 a.m. I stopped in beforehand to ask my branch chief if he knew what was going on but he had no clue. Worse, whatever it was Fields hadn't discussed it with him, so I could tell that his nose was a bit out of joint. I resolved to be more careful about such things in the future—if a division chief wants to see you, just go.

Another surprise: When I walked in Larry was there chatting with the secretary, who promptly showed us in to see the chief.

What's going on?

It didn't take long to find out. Fields welcomed me, briefly congratulated me on the medal I had recently received for my work in Laos, and got to the point: the Congo, then the highest priority for Africa Division.

He briefly reviewed the situation involving David G. and the communications officers being held by the Simbas, who now controlled the city. They also were holding—and threatening the lives of—several other Americans including the consul general and a number of missionaries, as well as several hundred Belgians and other Europeans.

"The Simba rebellion poses a grave threat to the government in Leopoldville," Glen went on. "Our policymakers are extremely concerned."

"We are in dire need of current intelligence about what is going on in the northeast Congo," Larry interjected.

I listened carefully, still wondering what the point was going to be.

"A military operation to liberate Stanleyville and free the hostages is being planned," Glen continued. "U.S. planes are going to transport Belgian paratroopers to Stanleyville probably sometime next month. The first wave will parachute onto the airport and secure it. Then planeloads of troopers will land and assault the city. We are hoping, of course, that the element of surprise will cause the Simbas to panic and keep casualties to a minimum. We haven't got a lot of choice."

"And after the operation is concluded," Larry added, "we are going to need someone on the ground in Stanleyville to provide intelligence."

Then Glen dropped the bombshell.

"I'd like you to replace David G. as chief in Stanleyville on a temporary basis."

He was looking directly into my eyes and I am sure he could see how surprised I was. Being offered chief in such a high-profile and important place for the division had been the farthest thing from my mind.

"I'm pleased to accept," I promptly responded. I couldn't have imagined saying no.

"You're my best candidate," Glen went on. "You're young, you aren't married, you speak decent French, and you've had paramilitary experience."

He clearly had received an assessment from Colette via Larry. And

Larry, who later acknowledged he had suggested me for the job, nodded sagely.

"But this won't be a walk in the park," Glen warned. "This is going to be a tough job and it may well be dangerous at times. You never know what to expect out there. But I don't think it will be any worse than Laos and you handled that."

Within months I would discover how right he had been to warn me about the Congo.

"When will I be leaving?" I asked.

"Take it easy," Glen responded. "I'm not going to send you out there until the Belgians have secured Stanleyville. Think in terms of December. For now get yourself transferred to Central Africa Branch because you've got a lot to learn in the next few weeks."

With that comment he stood to signal the meeting was over.

"I'll see you before you go," he said.

Larry shook my hand and stayed to talk with Glen.

My mission in Stanleyville would be straightforward. Before the Simba takeover, David G. had built and managed a network of agents reporting the overall and selected situations in the city and the region. Then the Simbas had arrived, totally disrupting operations and leaving our network in shambles. Fields was sending me to reassemble it and reestablish the flow of intelligence. I needed to steep myself quickly in both the conditions on the ground and the network's members.

That made for a busy several weeks. The branch chief, for whom I had worked only about a month, was none too happy but he couldn't change anything. My new assignment would be TDY for "about eight weeks, just to get things going again," I told him, meaning I'd be back before he knew it. But given my TDY in Laos, I wasn't taking any bets on how long I'd be gone.

Even on reflection I was pleased with the assignment. I liked it that division management apparently had gained so much confidence in me. I was mildly concerned about my own safety but I didn't dwell on the risks and figured I could handle whatever came up.

Cocky? Naive? You bet.

Division reaction was mixed, as it was among my friends. You must be crazy, some said. The place has been overrun, what can you do? Knowledge of the operation to liberate Stanleyville was strictly compartmented, so I just responded that I wouldn't be going until it was safe. That brought comments such as "never."

Other colleagues, case officers mostly, viewed it as I did, as a good assignment that ought to be damned interesting. Word got around. The support staffers were mostly in the "you must be crazy" camp. When I went to get my booster injections the nurses couldn't believe that I was going to Stanleyville.

"Don't you read the papers?" one of them asked.

"Of course I do," I said. "I won't be going until it's safe."

"Yeah, and you'll be going with a shot of everything we have," said another nurse, consulting her global chart.

They both laughed knowingly. Stanleyville, almost directly on the equator and with practically no medical facilities, sat in the middle of a red zone, which meant anyone going there needed injections for just about every known disease. It took me three visits to accumulate the required inoculations.

By mid-November I had accomplished a lot. I had read and sometimes reread all of the relevant files, and following my routine of doing unofficial research I finished a couple of interesting books about tribal conflicts in central Africa. I thought I was up to speed about the Simbas and their rebellion against the government of President Moise Tshombe.

I also continued working with Colette on my French vocabulary, with Belgian and African nuances, right up to departure. I settled all the admin matters. I even had my plane ticket in hand with an open travel date. I was ready and following closely the plans for the Belgian assault on Stanleyville. I noted, as did many others in my section, the added urgency caused by the sporadic but ominous reporting we were able to obtain from the beleaguered city. The Simbas were increasingly maltreating hostages and threatening their execution as an example of rebel resolve.

The policymakers met with more and more urgency, and the agency positioned the paratroopers at our Air Force base on Ascension—the tiny island in the South Atlantic located midway between Brazil and Angola—poised to act at a moment's notice. It couldn't come soon enough. As the day neared the atmosphere in the section became tense, and our workload spiked with the heavy flow of cable traffic related to our planning.

This would not be like a present-day SWAT-team assault, in which the commandos would exercise every precaution to minimize casualties. That concept didn't exist in 1964. Instead, Belgian paratroopers would jump at dawn to secure the airport, after which the rest of the battalion would land. Flying in on C-130 transports they would bring along a limited number of armored vehicles and heavy machine guns. As quickly as possible the force would move into the city to locate and liberate the hostages and rid the area of Simba forces.

That was the plan and no one doubted the Simbas would break and run. But what would they do before fleeing? It would take the Belgians at least an hour, we calculated, to get to the hostages. That meant a savage and bloody slaughter was possible. It could not be discounted. We knew that Simba violence, including wanton murder and rape, had occurred in the Congo's eastern provinces.

Back at headquarters we tried to concentrate on our work but we spent a lot of time worrying.

On November 24 the operation code-named Dragon Rouge (Red Dragon) launched at dawn. It went as planned. Within a few hours 350 Belgian commandos liberated the entire city from Simba control. The rebels killed more than 20 hostages, lashing out violently while fleeing. But David G., the consul general and our two communications officers escaped harm. In fact losses were minimal and the Belgians quickly reestablished authority. Within hours the troops withdrew in favor of a Tshombe government-sponsored mercenary force that arrived in the ransacked city. Congolese Army troops were also ferried in to help secure the area.

The operation succeeded and we all celebrated. I saw it as a step toward my departure and the start of my efforts to reestablish intelligence capability out of Stanleyville.

David returned to headquarters the first week of December. A bachelor and an absolute bear for work he was so intensely involved with the situation in the eastern Congo and the assets he had been handling that he couldn't stay away. He desperately wanted to know what was going on and therefore spent only a few days with his parents before reporting back to work. It was clear that his 111 days in Simba captivity, during which he was threatened with death several times, hadn't slowed him at all.

I met David, remarkably composed considering his harrowing experience, for the first time a couple of hours after he arrived. Glen had welcomed him back and taken him to meet with Director McCone. Then he returned to the division to see friends and well-wishers. Last, I think to his relief, he visited the Congo desk, where I met him as the temporary chief who was headed to Stanleyville to pick up the pieces.

"Good. When are you leaving?" he asked.

"As soon as Glen gives the okay."

I followed with many questions regarding the whereabouts and status of assets and acquaintances of his in Stanleyville and the eastern Congo. He answered everything and shot back questions of his own. I thought he must have been running on fumes and adrenaline. He looked thin and almost frail but the force of his personality and the strength of his desire to know what was going on at "his" office overwhelmed any frailty with intensity.

From my background reading, my review of his reporting on individual assets, and my time on the desk, I was able to fire back answers on most points. But many of my responses consisted of, "We don't know." Nevertheless he seemed pleased that someone was standing in the wings ready to go to Stanleyville and satisfied that his replacement was well prepared.

I was glad to meet David and we grew to be close friends. I liked his strong work ethic, his great loyalty, and the willingness and patience he demonstrated while fielding my questions. Over the next several weeks I learned a great deal from him.

Together we launched a not-too-subtle campaign to get me to Stanleyville as soon as possible. The city, though still surrounded by the Simbas, was more or less secure with a safe and steady air link to Leopoldville.

For a while Glen appeared unmoved. Then I learned David would be going with me. I wasn't sure why and privately questioned the wisdom of the decision, but I said nothing. I later found out it had been David's idea. So be it. A personal introduction is always better than a cold turnover. Maybe it would even end up being therapeutic for him. It sure would make things easier for me because David knew volumes about the Congo and central Africa. By mid-December we had our travel date.

"Have Christmas at home," Glen insisted, "and then go see what you can do." David and I made arrangements to meet at Newark airport the day after Christmas.

Before my departure things at home were delicate. My mother knew little about my work in Laos but she instinctively sensed it had been dangerous, even though my letters talked only about mundane activities, never mentioning things that could worry her.

It didn't matter; Mom's stress level had stayed high while I was away, and it rose even higher when Bob was shipped to Vietnam in 1963. Two sons in Southeast Asia fighting a little-known enemy would be tough on any mother. I didn't want to trigger the stress again by telling her about my assignment to Stanleyville. I told her I was going to Morocco.

I did confide in Dad, suggesting that if he really thought Mom should know he should tell her. I felt bad being untruthful to her—and worse later when it came back with a vengeance to haunt me.

On December 26, David and I took a helicopter from Newark to what was then Idlewild Airport (now John F. Kennedy International) on Long Island. From there we flew to Brussels, which was cold, damp, gray and considerably less pleasant than the only other time I had been there.

In 1959 I had driven the VW convertible from Camp Bussac to Stockholm, Sweden, to meet Dad and my grandfather. They had gone there with the Viking Club of Chicago to visit the old homeland. Then Grandpa stayed in Sweden, while Dad accompanied me to Brussels.

We spent a beautiful, clear night—something rare in Belgium—in the Grand-Place, the city's central square. Spotlights gleamed off the gold leaf on the 15th century and 16th century buildings that bordered the area. Wonderful classical music played from loudspeakers. It happened to be the Fourth of July, and the U.S. Marine Corps Band marched for Independence Day. Resplendent in their dress uniforms they boomed out a medley of John Philip Sousa marches ending with "The Stars and Stripes Forever."

Little more than five years had gone by, but that memory felt distant as our airport taxi cruised across a deserted and rainy Grand-Place and deposited us at the Hotel Amigo, only about 50 yards from the square. It was early morning and I hadn't slept much on the plane so I was looking forward to some rest. It was not to be.

David suggested we grab a quick shower and a cup of coffee and walk to the agency office to check cable traffic from Leopoldville.

"Sounds fine," was about all I could muster.

We saw no traffic of interest but it was useful to talk with some of the staff about the local reaction to the Stanleyville operation. Not surprising, the Belgians were delighted with what had happened and the cooperation between their government and ours had really boosted relations.

What did surprise us was how many questioned the wisdom of David's return to the Congo and my going so soon to try to reopen our Stanleyville office. Despite their doubts everyone was cordial and supportive, and they all wished us good luck. Our flight via SABENA—at the time the Belgian national airline—was leaving late the next afternoon and I was feeling eager to get there and get started.

I was awake and alert as we landed the following morning at Ndjili Airport in Leopoldville—now called Kinshasa. It reminded me of my arrival in Vientiane; this former colonial capital likewise had seen better days. No doubt I had just reentered the Third World. One of the support officers met us with car and driver, and we moved through customs without delay carrying our diplomatic passports. Those not so fortunate stood in a long line.

The officer took us to a motel-like guesthouse near the embassy. We were due at the office around 4 p.m., giving us several hours to kill. I didn't feel tired so I asked David if he wanted to walk around the city.

"Nope," he said, "I think I'll grab a shower and get some rest."

Our roles reversed from the previous day, I showered quickly, felt even better, and set off to explore central Leopoldville on my own.

All cities have distinct sounds and smells but Leopoldville's were different from any I had known in America, Europe or Asia. I couldn't recognize anything in particular but the air felt heavy and humid, its odors pungent and strong.

The city reminded me of Hong Kong in July but without the spectacular skyline and harbor. Sounds were muffled, the pace very slow. Nothing was neat or clean and nobody seemed to care. The streets and buildings looked poorly maintained or in some cases not maintained at all.

It was only a first impression but not a good one. The city lacked charm and personality. It was old, dirty and rundown.

We visited the office that afternoon and I was disappointed there, too. The chief, Ben Cushing, whom I had never heard of, was a New Englander and a man of few words. He had served mostly in Eastern Europe before being assigned to Leopoldville. His office featured models of old ships and pictures of the Maine coast. They hinted where his heart was.

Preparing for this assignment Cushing had learned Lingala, the most common of the Bantu languages spoken in the country. In late 1965 he would use it to introduce himself to President Joseph Mobutu, who with U.S. help had ascended to power and forced Moise Tshombe into exile.

Mobutu immediately scolded him.

"Do you think I'm some uneducated native?" he said. "I speak French!"

Cushing ran into problems with local officials as well. The rap was that he was insensitive, asking only prepared questions before quickly saying goodbye and leaving. I was told later that although Cushing was bright and experienced he didn't really like paramilitary operations.

On this particular occasion I may have caught him on a busy day and gotten a false impression. He met with us only briefly and demonstrated no real interest in what I was trying to do. After only enough conversation to be polite he showed us out and turned us over to Chuck Cogan, his deputy, who seemed considerably more interested and questioned me about my assignment.

To this day I can't figure out what Cushing's problem was or why he seemed displeased about my going to Stanleyville. Maybe, like some of the headquarters staff, he thought it was too dangerous and too soon to restart our activities there. Whatever the reason he gave precious little guidance, and we had no further contact, so I never had reason to change my assessment of him.

If anyone back at headquarters was opposing the decision no one had communicated it to me, directly or indirectly. Even if everyone else was giving only grudging support I still had a job to do. I was determined to pursue Glen's tasking. Ever enthusiastic, David ignored the office's coolness to us and arranged to get us to Stanleyville, which meant contacting our air proprietary for the Congo.

Control of all flights to Stanleyville, which delivered supplies to the mercenaries and Congolese Army units holding the still-besieged city, fell to our military attaché's office and the prop. Given the close contact we maintained with both offices David had no difficulty making the arrangements.

One problem did arise. Suddenly headquarters ordered David not to accompany me. Needless to say he wasn't pleased but there was nothing he could do unless the powers that be could be persuaded to change their minds. They could not.

For the moment only my name was added to the (very short) passenger list for the next flight to Stanleyville. In two days I would be arriving along with a shipment of hops for the local brewery, which was about the only business functioning in the city—the Congolese soldiers refused to stay if they didn't get beer.

I felt relieved to see that along with the hops on the manifest ammunition was considered a strategic materiel for the war effort. Whatever the soldiers might be doing I felt better knowing they were well supplied with ammo.

Those few days in Leopoldville left me a little perplexed. Nothing was as we had expected—not the city and certainly not my reception at the office.

Leopoldville, named for the Belgian king who had established the Congo as a colony in the late 19th century, was the capital of a vast country rich in resources. It had been independent only since 1960. One would think the city's residents would be keenly interested in what was happening out in the countryside. Yet there was no hint that the Congo's northeastern quadrant was immersed in a terribly bloody and destructive civil war.

Even at the American Embassy no one had demonstrated much concern about what was happening in Stanleyville. This contrasted starkly with the reaction at headquarters and my past three months of preparation. For weeks I had been steeped in matters concerning the conflict. But here, close to the scene, nobody appeared to care.

True, I was a young man far away from home who knew precious little about politics in Africa, only what I had recently read. Perhaps I just didn't understand the culture.

It was also true that Leopoldville, the government and the Congolese in general had witnessed a similar upheaval a few years previously, soon after the country won its independence from Belgium. The political intrigue, rebellion and conflict that followed had become all too familiar. Perhaps the people had grown inured to the Congo's seemingly endless problems.

Some might even have thought the Simba lions had been tamed and life in the northeast would return to something approaching normality.

Then there was the question of what we were doing in the Congo. What interest did the agency have in this large but poor country in the middle of Africa? It wasn't serving a strategic interest, like Laos. And though the land yielded valuable minerals—copper, cobalt and diamonds, among others—it wasn't deemed a critical source of anything.

The answer was the country represented a square on the Cold War chessboard. We were watching the Congo mainly because we wanted to know what the communists were doing as the Congolese tried to establish an independent nation. No doubt they were watching us for the same reason.

For two decades it had become standard practice. In virtually every country on the planet both sides attempted to influence events to strengthen their interests. But in the case of the Congo neither side seemed to realize this essentially tribal conflict was particularly resistant to outside pressures.

The Simbas, a ragtag bunch of illiterate dissidents, certainly weren't communists. But they posed a threat to the pro-Western Tshombe government; therefore they gained the support of the Soviet Union, China and their minions. That in turn prompted the West to support Tshombe regardless of his fitness to govern.

It was that simple, and the scenario played out elsewhere in the world many times during the Cold War and afterward with predictable results.

I took off for Stanleyville very early one morning in a C-130. The military always starts its days early. The ride to the airport was quick and easy; there was almost no traffic at that time of day. It turned out I was the only passenger—just the crew and me and the ammo and the hops.

The day was partly sunny—or partly cloudy, take your pick—and clear enough to see the terrain through the cloud openings. Our northeasterly route took us over the heart of the Congo River basin, which covers over 1.5 million square miles. Its great tropical rain forest is the second-biggest in the world, eclipsed only by the Amazon's. Except for an occasional glimpse of a dirt road or a collection of crude huts the landscape below consisted of endless jungle—the dense double- and triple-canopy type, I was told.

I was happy to be traveling well above it.

Stanleyville, now called Kisangani but originally named for British journalist Henry Morton Stanley—who famously said, "Dr. Livingston, I presume"—is nearly 800 miles from the capital and the flight seemed to take forever. With equal doses of apprehension and expectation I mulled things over as the hours passed. I think I spotted the Congo River first and then saw the city, which from the air looked unremarkable.

As I was soon to discover it was quite remarkable.

No formalities when we landed. A crew of Congolese and a couple of trucks arrived to unload the plane, but not much else happened. I had planned to stay at the Immoquator, an eight-story, relatively modern apartment block with two wings, and I bummed a ride there from one of the plane's crew. It was about the only place to stay in Stanleyville at the time.

Before the rebellion several members of the consulate staff lived in apartments at the Immoquator and, as it turned out, I was assigned to one of those apartments.

The ride into the city revealed how misleading the view had been from the air. I saw few people and little activity or traffic. After the Red Dragon operation by the Belgian paratroopers virtually every European had been evacuated and almost none had returned. The vast majority had either remained in Leopoldville or gone back to Europe.

Moreover, many of the Congolese, especially the rich and educated, had fled into the bush during the Simba occupation and were not yet convinced it was safe enough to return. The city's population, which before the occupation neared 150,000, had fallen dramatically.

It felt strange to be in a city with so few people around. Garbage and debris were piled everywhere. Broken doors and windows on virtually every house attested to the fact that all had been looted and vandalized. Abandoned vehicles, which had been stolen or appropriated by the Simbas, now littered the streets. Many were smashed against trees or walls—because most Simbas had no idea how to drive. They simply pushed pedals until disaster struck. Or they tried to drive after smoking hashish, with similar results.

I felt truly sad for Stanleyville. Once the city had been attractive and well tended but now it looked as if Attila the Hun and his pillaging horde had passed through.

The Immoquator had been spared some of the destruction so evident elsewhere in Stanleyville. Only one block had been badly damaged by heavy weapons fire during a strange incident.

In a confused night battle, as the Simbas were consolidating their control, communications between some of their forces broke down. Mistakenly thinking the opposition had taken up positions within the complex, the rebels fired on it from across the river for most of the night, devastating a block of apartments.

The other block remained mostly intact and appeared at that point to be serving as part guesthouse and part apartment building. I was assigned a small unit by a surly Greek and went up to leave my bag. It was close to noon by this time and I was getting hungry. I asked about food facilities at the lobby desk and was directed to the dining room. I still hadn't seen many people.

The dining room had probably served as a cocktail lounge in better times and featured a view of the river. The furnishings likewise had been nice in their day; they weren't anymore. The tiled floor needed sweeping and no lights were on, although the natural light was adequate.

Now the room seemed to be a place where the few occupants of the Immoquator could gather to eat, drink, talk—and even fight, from the look of the clientele. Seated at the few tables and chairs and standing at the bar lurked the roughest, toughest, nastiest bunch of men I had ever seen. No women at all—probably a fortunate thing.

There were some bad guys in Vientiane, too, but nothing like this crew. They wore an assortment of military and civilian apparel with no hesitation about mixing the two. Most sported beards or ample stubble. They had strewn their variety of weapons on the tables or the floor.

Their low murmur of conversation stopped at my arrival. Not the most comforting feeling I've ever had—standing in the doorway looking at what I knew was a group of mercenaries. I couldn't possibly have contrasted more in my slacks, short-sleeved white shirt, tie and loafers—not combat boots like the others. Clean-shaven with crew-cut hair I also carried my briefcase, which I hadn't wanted to leave in my room. The attention was unwelcome indeed.

I walked to the nearest empty table, placed my briefcase on it, and opened it. I knew that many eyes were watching me but I ignored them. I just took off my tie and put it in my briefcase. Then I took out a Walther 9mm pistol I had been issued in Leopoldville and stuffed it into my waistband. It felt uncomfortable, because I wasn't used to it, but I did it for effect.

I caught a waiter's attention, ordered a beer, and sat down. To my relief the playacting seemed work; the murmur started up again. They probably guessed that I was an American, I might have something to do with the regular flights arriving from Leopoldville, and I posed no threat.

The waiter brought my beer—horrible stuff it turned out, most likely brewed the day before—and I asked him what they had to eat.

"Rice and beans with chicken," he said.

"I'll take it," was my quick response.

The meal was as bad as the beer but eating it gave me time to get a better look at the motley group. They were even worse than my first impression had suggested. I knew from my preparatory reading that former French Foreign Legionnaires, ex-German SS troopers, various soldiers of fortune, and criminals on the run had mingled among the mercenary ranks, as well as former—or even current—South African military.

I heard snatches of conversations in English, French, German and I guessed Afrikaans, and I tried to sort out who was who. I don't know why. None seemed the slightest bit approachable, nor would I have had any reason to try to start a conversation. What I heard seemed to concern recent firefights and how many blacks they had killed—not necessarily Simbas, just blacks. Some wore strange-looking medals and many carried knives.

They really were the dregs.

After my meal I ordered coffee and while I was sipping it I spotted a familiar face approaching my table, a man called Koenraad whom I'd met two days earlier.

Before my flight to Stanleyville I had met privately with Mike Hoare, a legendary South African who led the mercenary group hired to support Moise Tshombe. "Mad Mike," as he was known, was part of a column that had raced to Stanleyville in mid-November with the goal of liberating the city. They had planned to arrive in time to support the Belgian paratroopers.

Some doubted they would make it, but to almost everyone's great surprise Mike's troops covered over 60 miles on some days.

"Periodic skirmishes with Simba groups slowed us down a bit," he told me.

They arrived a few hours after the Belgians and helped to stabilize the city.

Such exploits eventually caught the eye of Hollywood. Over a decade later Mike would serve as a technical adviser for the film *The Wild Geese*, and the writers based the character Colonel Alan Faulkner, played by Richard Burton, on Mike.

Following the Belgian withdrawal an element of Mike's mercenaries, supported by troops of the ANC, the Armeé Nationale Congolaise remained in Stanleyville to hold the city while the Belgians and the rest of the mercenaries fanned out in the eastern Congo to fight the Simba reign of terror.

My meeting with Mike had been a liaison contact. Because I would be working in the northeast it had seemed prudent to introduce myself and let him know what we were up to. He wasn't a particularly likeable guy but he briefed me in detail on the grim situation in and around Stanleyville.

Before I left Mike called in Koenraad, his number two, who would be in Stanleyville when I arrived. Mike would remain in Leopoldville to work on personnel and logistics matters.

Koenraad, also South African, was polite and reserved at that first meeting. Now he smiled as he sat down and said, "Well, what do you think of Stanleyville?"

"Looks a mess and there aren't many people."

"Every city and town we came through looked like this. It's really pretty sad."

I was surprised at such a comment from a mercenary but later I learned that Koenraad was a military man—on extended leave, he claimed—assigned to the Congo to gain experience. The South African government anticipated similar rebellions in the future and he had been sent here to learn.

"We need to get you some clothes," he commented. "You really stand out."

"I'm supposed to be a businessman," I responded, "but I know what you mean. I'm going back to Leopoldville the day after tomorrow and I'll pick up some field clothes and boots."

Koenraad was making an effort to be friendly and I appreciated that. We talked about the current situation, which seemed to be getting better. Simba control in rural areas had been weakening and more of the Congolese who had fled were returning to the city. Their soldiers were hopeless but the mercenaries had developed ways to work around that problem. The food was awful—I already knew that—and there was no hard liquor and no women.

"Sounds like a wonderful place," I joked, and Koenraad laughed.

In Leopoldville I had been careful to meet contacts discreetly, if not clandestinely, to avoid curious eyes and the journalists who were always in quest of a story. In Stanleyville there was no reason for that; I was one of the few Westerners in town.

It felt eerie that afternoon walking around the deserted and devastated city. The occasional car or truck passed by, and a few people stood off to the side of the street, but for the most part I was alone. I was glad to be carrying the Walther.

I thought about tradecraft—the mechanics of running intelligence operations—but given this situation such efforts seemed silly.

I found the U.S. Consulate empty and ransacked. Almost nothing remained. I also found David's house and went inside. No problem getting in; the doors were either gone or hanging open on their hinges. I had promised him I would look around but there wasn't much to see and I didn't stay long.

As I continued my walk I felt increasingly uneasy and couldn't decide why. I concluded it probably wasn't very smart for me to be moving around alone in this recently liberated but still semi-deserted city. I headed back toward the Immoquator, wondering again what good I could possibly do in this violated, God-forsaken place.

9. No Walk in the Park

STANLEYVILLE, THE CONGO 1965

I woke up bright and early one morning to an inviting aroma. Somewhere a bakery must have been functioning because I enjoyed fresh rolls and coffee for breakfast.

Afterward I met a small mercenary patrol heading out to the city's defense perimeter. We drove in a convoy of three jeeps and a truck to a checkpoint along a main road approaching the city from the southwest. I saw an ANC detachment and a couple of free agents standing around when we got there.

They call this a defense perimeter?

Shortly after our arrival one of the mercenaries said, matter-of-factly, "Here they come."

I looked down the road and saw a line of men—Simbas I was told—walking single file toward us. The Congolese soldiers became clearly agitated and started taking cover, but the mercenaries remained unconcerned. The Simbas were still a couple of hundred yards away, moving slowly but steadily toward us. As they grew closer I could see the guy in the lead. Waving a palm branch and muttering, he wore some type of animal skin on his head.

"He's the head medicine man," Koenraad informed me. "They still do this most days."

Then the Congolese soldiers started shooting.

"But they aren't aiming at the Simbas," I pointed out as calmly as I could, though I was obviously alarmed.

"Don't worry about it," Koenraad muttered.

With that he gave a couple of the mercenaries a signal. The men then stepped into the road and leveled a couple of bursts of machine gun fire at the approaching Simbas. Several were hit and fell. Behind them the column—if you could call it a column—stopped, and the guy with the skin on his head waved his arms. Then the whole bunch turned and started retracing their steps. It was quite bizarre.

The Congolese soldiers stopped shooting and looked down the road with happy smiles.

"What the hell is going on?" I asked Koenraad.

"Our magic is stronger than theirs."

Apparently the Simbas often approached the defense perimeter this way, led by the witch doctor with the skin on his head. It never took much to discourage them for the day.

Magic for the Simbas originated with Mama Bangala, the head witch doctor, reputed to have only one breast in the middle of her chest. Apparently she had persuaded somebody high up the Simba command, if such a structure existed, that her magic would turn bullets into water. Simbas who believed and practiced this magic could not be hurt, and all were indoctrinated in this way. To the Simbas the men who were killed or wounded had failed to believe.

On the ride back to the Immoquator I saw Africans on the street—many more than the previous day.

"Some of the locals stayed through the occupation," Koenraad said, "and of those that fled some have returned. But they all keep a pretty low profile. You wouldn't have seen many at all on the airport road or in the area where you walked. That's the European quarter and it really is deserted. That's what I think is sad. All the people that make this city work are gone."

I spent the rest of the morning and all afternoon roaming on foot. Just as Koenraad had said, I found more people in the mixed neighborhoods or in areas where only Africans lived. I didn't talk to anyone and no one approached me. I won't say I was discouraged but I wasn't happy, either. In such an environment I would have trouble making contacts and getting people to resume their intelligence gathering.

I began to understand Koenraad's observations on the city. Though far from normal Stanleyville was starting to revive and the Simba threat was receding. I sensed that as I became more familiar with the situation it would be easier to assess my chances of re-contacting our agents—our assets. Then I could review my findings with David and our other officers and we could develop a plan of action to reestablish the network. This was our first on-the-ground look since the occupation and I was the one doing the looking. Beyond my feelings of pride and excitement I was conscious of my great responsibility.

Mail remained unreliable but the phone system had worked throughout the Simba occupation and was available if I needed it. That wasn't necessarily an advantage. Before I could initiate a call I needed to know that the person I was trying to reach would be there to answer. I didn't want to have to explain to anyone else who I was or why I was calling.

Reconnecting with our agents was going to be more difficult than I had anticipated.

I returned to Leopoldville the next day to meet with David. We dined together and talked well into the night. I filled him in on what I had seen and heard. He listened carefully and quickly agreed that given the current situation we would have to alter our approach.

Our guess was that most of our agents were either dead or had left Stanleyville and not yet returned. We certainly didn't want to endanger any of the survivors. We decided to wait and see, as word circulated about my being in Stanleyville and having replaced David, if our remaining agents would find ways to contact me. Meanwhile I'd assess the evolving situation and try to reach the agents if and when it seemed prudent to do so.

Back in Stanleyville I found that nothing had changed at the Immoquator except the increasingly bored mercenaries had grown even more sullen and hostile. I had no need to interact with that crowd; avoidance seemed the best plan.

I concentrated my efforts on meeting David's friends and social contacts just to make my presence known. I had been able to scrounge up a consulate car. For reasons I never understood, the Simbas hadn't commandeered many vehicles with diplomatic plates. Now I could get around the city more easily. I met a few more people but they failed to produce any word from our agents.

Despite my best efforts the situation remained the same through January and into early February. Security in the city was improving, as was the populace's confidence in that security, but it wasn't enough to help me reconnect with anyone.

Then headquarters changed its position and permitted David to join me in Stanleyville. We hoped he would be recognized, which might prompt some of his former contacts to resurface. Meanwhile we'd both gather information about the state of the city. We started with Alexander Barlovatz, an expatriate Yugoslav doctor who had become a Belgian citizen.

Lacking reliable ways to announce our arrival we simply drove over to his house and knocked on the door. Barlovatz and his wife, whose name I can't recall, answered. David introduced me and they immediately invited us in. It was late afternoon so they asked if we could stay for dinner. We joked that our social schedule was completely clear and they laughed.

Barlovatz, who was nearly 70 at the time, and his wife, a former concert pianist, had lived in Stanleyville since the early 1920s. He had established a clinic for the local population as well as a private practice that served Europeans but the majority of his patients were Africans. Most could pay him no money and many offered food and services instead.

An intelligent and engaging man, Barlovatz had devoted his life to helping the city's poor. It had not made him rich but he and his wife enjoyed a comfortable living. Both had stayed in the city voluntarily during the Simba occupation. Like hundreds of other Europeans they felt inextricably tied to Stanleyville and to the Congo but unlike most of the others who stayed behind they were not held hostage. Barlovatz's devotion to his patients, and their mutual love and respect for him, had prevented the imprisonment and mistreatment suffered by so many others.

Something else protected Barlovatz and his wife—though they did endure occasional harassment and threats from their unpredictable occupiers. Because he was a leftist and sympathetic to the nationalist dreams of the Simba leadership they allowed him freedom of movement. He had used that freedom to bring food almost daily to David and the other American hostages during those 111 days.

David had developed a bronchial infection at one point and Barlovatz brought him medicine and a shot. He was a virtual lifesaver and our visit gave David an opportunity to thank the doctor and his wife again for all they had done for the hostages.

Barlovatz was about to conduct his afternoon rounds and asked if I wanted to accompany him. We walked the short distance behind his house to the clinic. He left me alone to inspect it while he visited his patients.

With a corrugated tin roof, thatch walls hung on a frame of wooden posts, few windows, no doors and openings at both ends, this was a no-frills facility. Inside the building was a long and narrow room with rows of beds, bare light bulbs hanging from the ceiling every 20 feet or so, and sinks with running water serving each end. Toilets must have been in the back because I didn't see them.

Patients occupied almost every bed—about 30 of them. Family members surrounded the patients and provided much of the basic care, including feeding.

It became immediately clear that everyone in the clinic, patients and staff alike, held Barlovatz in great esteem. I watched him conducting his rounds and to say he showed genuine concern would have been an understatement. He obviously cared deeply about every one of his charges and they just as obviously felt it.

Dinner with the Barlovatzes was a joy in all respects. The bad food and rotten company at the Immoquator notwithstanding, it would have been a great pleasure to dine with these two delightful and sophisticated people under any circumstances. Their home was like an island of calm and civilization in a sea of tension and turmoil.

The large living room where we had drinks was simply but tastefully appointed, with proper attention given to Stanleyville's equatorial heat and humidity. A fan whirled slowly above us and the rattan furniture was cool to the touch.

I noticed a beautiful grand piano sitting in one corner, strangely out of place. Barlovatz told me that once during the Simba period he and his wife were entertaining guests for dinner, and as was her habit she performed for them afterward. Suddenly several armed Simbas burst into the room, despite the efforts of two servants to keep them out, and shouted at Madame Barlovatz. Though she and her husband understood the local dialect neither could ascertain what was making the soldiers so agitated.

Following a determined effort to comprehend the increasingly dangerous situation they discovered that the Simba patrol had heard the piano and became convinced that Madame Barlovatz was using it somehow to communicate with government forces in Leopoldville. Barlovatz was stunned speechless when he realized what they were saying.

"How could you respond to something so absurd?" he asked, rhetorically.

He said he attempted to reason with the rebels, explaining that a piano could not transmit messages. But the Simbas remained unconvinced and threatened to arrest his wife and take away the piano. Barlovatz protested and demanded that they summon their commanding officer; otherwise he would immediately report them to Gbenye, their political leader.

The threat seemed to work. Two more Simbas arrived and the rebels discussed the situation. One of the new arrivals said he wanted to inspect the piano and Barlovatz, sensing a compromise, agreed. The new arrival, clearly the patrol leader, made a great show of carefully looking under and inside the piano.

"No transmitter," he declared, "and no antenna."

The Simbas left as abruptly as they had arrived.

With fresh meat and vegetables still in short supply dinner was not a gourmet delight. But we hardly noticed. It tasted good and was elegantly presented, and our conversation was free flowing and wide ranging. We provided news from abroad and the Barlovatzes commented about life in Stanleyville before and during the Simba occupation.

They also made clear how much respect and affection they held for David. They thanked him for his help as a supporter of their causes and for his compassion for the people of Stanleyville. After dinner Madame

Barlovatz played some classical compositions beautifully while we three gentlemen listened and sipped cognac.

David and I felt honored by their hospitality. It would have been a splendid evening in Paris or Washington. In Stanleyville in February 1965 it was incredible.

It was just too soon, we discovered, to expect to meet with our former agents or with many of David's other contacts. Time after time we came up empty trying to locate someone. Usually the house or apartment we visited was unoccupied, or someone was there but not the individual we were seeking. Our northeastern Congo network remained in shambles so we resolved to collect whatever intelligence we could, from our agents whenever possible, about the presence, activities and supply lines of the Simba units.

We discussed the prospect of expanding my area of operations. I suggested spending a couple of weeks in Bunia, located on a high plateau on the Congo's far northeastern border with Uganda.

I had two reasons. First, a couple of our agents were originally from Bunia and still had family there, and one of them had been a top asset. When fear drove them from Stanleyville perhaps they had retreated to Bunia or Uganda. Second, I might be able to collect information from people in the area that might satisfy some of the requirements that headquarters had requested.

I left for Bunia on February 12. David had concluded he could do little more in the Congo so he prepared to return to Langley.

A mercenary column had liberated Bunia the previous November 30—just six days after the Belgians carried out Red Dragon and freed Stanleyville. The Simbas had slain about a dozen whites in Bunia as well as an undetermined number of Congolese. Mad Mike's mercenaries had rescued more than 30 whites and nearly 50 ANC soldiers.

This had been a familiar story all over the northeastern Congo during December and January. Now in February the cleanup effort continued. Mercenary and occasional ANC columns moved systematically from town to town, securing central government control and sending the Simbas fleeing into the countryside. But the rebels carried out frequent reprisals, killing more than 300 whites, often viciously.

Though the exact number remains unknown the rebels also murdered thousands of Congolese. In Paulis alone—now Isiro—a small city about 225 miles northeast of Stanleyville the Simbas killed as many as 4,000. Many others, some innocent bystanders, died in the battles between the Simbas and the mercenaries or the ANC.

By the time of my arrival in Bunia most towns in the northeast were in government hands and relatively safe but an undetermined number of Simbas still roamed the countryside wreaking havoc. The pro-government forces lacked the manpower or resources to chase down the rebel units. Their highest priorities were rescuing the whites held hostage by the Simbas and liberating—which often turned into looting—the banks they encountered in the towns they secured.

The northeastern Congo, an area the size of France, was experiencing great turmoil in early 1965.

I landed at the airport, a few miles southeast of town, in a twin-engine C-46 transport. The aircraft made a couple of these flights per week and also carried supplies for our small operation there. That effort consisted of a chief of the unit, a couple of Cuban pilots, two mechanics, a radio operator, and a logistics officer who met me at the plane.

We drove into town in a Land Rover and found Bunia virtually deserted—very few people and almost no traffic. I grew apprehensive again as we approached the one small hotel still open. Bunia had not been sacked as badly as Stanleyville but fear and uncertainty had driven most of the population into the bush and back to rural villages. The Simbas had indiscriminately raped, murdered, and looted to such an extent that the few holdouts were in a state of real terror.

Our contingent, all men, worked, ate, and slept in the hotel compound. The Belgian couple who owned it said the Simba forces had not permanently occupied Bunia, so when they saw rebel units in town or passing through they stayed out of sight. They explained that they had resolved to take their chances because if they had left they would have lost everything. I admired their determination but thought they had been very lucky.

Despite food shortages, and the lack of staff and electricity, the place was tolerable—better than the thatched huts in Laos. The couple did what they could to ease the hardships and for the most part they were a congenial pair.

The wife, who appeared to run everything, was a good cook and made the most of what was available, including fresh fish from time to time. The men at the hotel told me the dinners were best the day after a C-46 had landed.

The frail husband followed his wife's orders and seemed happy to do so. A few Africans cleaned the rooms and did the laundry—both poorly. One of them emptied the gin from a bottle in my room that I brought from Leopoldville. As things turned out it didn't matter; my stay in Bunia lasted only five days.

We knew or at least sensed that the Simbas were out there but we knew nothing about their real strength or intentions. Maybe the Simbas felt the same way. They must have been aware of our presence but they did nothing about it, even though they had reasons to resent us. Our aerial patrols, flying out of Bunia in heavily armed T-28s, regularly attacked their columns and convoys, breaking off from reconnaissance missions to strafe them.

Was the lack of a Simba response a sign of weakness? No one knew.

No mercenary or ANC elements occupied Bunia, either, but some were operating nearby. We sometimes joked about the situation but only to disguise our uneasiness. We were armed with pistols and a few UZI submachine guns. If the Simbas attacked we were in deep trouble, standing little chance against a determined assault.

With little to do but worry I kept trying to find my agents. I couldn't find a map of Bunia but the hotel couple pointed me to the right area of town. I had what passed for addresses—the numbers of four houses on ill-defined streets—and I was determined to check them out.

Strolling alone through Bunia at that time was, as Glen Fields had put it, no walk in the park. I moved quickly, seeing no one and hearing nothing but the echo of my footsteps.

I reached the first house and knocked on the door. No response. As I approached the second house I thought I saw movement inside but couldn't be sure. Again I knocked. A woman appeared—I think we were both surprised. She spoke passable French with a funny accent and told me her husband was the man I was seeking.

"Where is he?" I asked.

Responding warily she said he wasn't there but would return the following day.

"Tell him I'll be back tomorrow at 5 p.m."

She nodded and I left. The other two houses were empty and still.

After dinner at the hotel several of us gathered on the terrace for coffee, beer or whatever was available. I noticed the two Cuban pilots who flew the T-28s, both of whom spoke passable English. They told me they were members of the air prop organized by the agency for the Congo. They had left Cuba after Castro took power.

We all retired after an hour or so of casual conversation. That night I felt, for the first time in my life, tremors from a mild earthquake. Although I hadn't remembered it at the time, Bunia is located on a fault line of Africa's Great Rift Valley, the 3,700-mile geological border that marks where East Africa is slowly separating from the rest of the continent.

The next night I met the agent who lived in that second house. He was educated, fairly well to do and happy to see me. I had frightened his wife, he told me, but she passed along my message. It gratified me to have finally made a contact.

David and I had been right. Fearful for his life the agent had fled Stanleyville as the Simba forces arrived. Originally from Bunia he had returned to a house owned by his relatives.

He said he and many others now felt more confident about their safety because Simba influence was clearly on the wane. The mercenaries' magic was much stronger, he commented, and everyone knew it. As a result he planned to return to Stanleyville within the week and we arranged to meet there later in the month.

We talked for over an hour. As I debriefed him I asked what he knew about the fate of Congolese government officials and prominent citizens in Stanleyville. Among those names were a few of our agents but I kept that information to myself. Several had been executed, he told me, but about most he knew nothing. I felt reassured when he said the area around Bunia was safe and that Simba control in general was falling apart.

The next morning I wrote three reports about what I had learned and radioed them to Leopoldville. I was pleased to have them out of the way. A special flight was arriving in the afternoon and I needed to meet it.

I drove out to the airport after lunch to meet an incoming C-130 heavy transport with Wes Kingsley, a communications officer who had just been transferred to the Congo from Ethiopia, and "Big Bill" Wyrozemski, the chief of the local air unit. We didn't know who or what would be arriving. It turned out to be Russ Lefevre, a colleague.

Russ, about my age or a little younger, had been a Navy officer. He had accumulated lots of experience with small boats. Now he was charged with patrolling Lake Albert, just east of Bunia on the country's border with Uganda, and blocking a channel we suspected the Simbas were using to run arms.

Russ and I had much in common and we hit it off right away. We have been friends ever since.

Headquarters had approved a plan for Russ to test one of his boats on the lake. Twenty feet long, sleek and powerful, the boat, which the C-130 crew had off-loaded before departing, sported a V-shaped hull that enhanced its speed and maneuverability. It boasted twin 350-horsepower inboard/outboard engines and looked like it could run down anything on the water. Its .30-caliber machine guns mounted fore and aft said "don't mess with me."

Russ called the boat his V-20.

After dinner we discussed what he would be doing over the next several days. In Leopoldville, Russ and another officer had met with Mike Hoare to assess mercenary operations in the northeastern Congo. Lots had been accomplished but much remained to be done. They agreed to combine forces in an effort to rid an area just west of Lake Albert of the Simba presence.

According to the plan the mercenaries would sweep in from Bunia and move along the lake forcing the Simbas east. Russ would wait for them in the V-20 and "take appropriate action" if the rebels tried to flee by boat.

The details weren't firm but the outline fit in with the tests Russ wanted to run, so it seemed reasonable. Mike Hoare was due in Bunia the next day to discuss which areas the mercenaries would attack before starting the operation.

Unforeseen events would cut short Russ's efforts on the lake. My next meeting with him would be under most unpleasant circumstances, and Mike would lead his mercenaries out of Bunia soon after Russ had left.

10. This Would Screw Things Up

BUNIA, THE CONGO 1965

On February 17, the day after Russ's departure to Lake Albert, Wes drove me out to the airport after lunch. I was to hitch a ride aboard a T-28, a two-seat, propeller-driven trainer the agency had armed and adapted for counterinsurgency duty both in Southeast Asia and now here in the Congo.

Wes had never seen a T-28 and he wanted to get a look at one. I had seen them in Laos but had never flown in one. In discussions with Big Bill the day before we had agreed this would be a good time for me to survey the terrain, road network and level of activity visible from the air in the area north of Bunia. We suspected the Simbas were smuggling in arms and ammo across the border from Sudan.

We sent two T-28s daily out of Bunia, effectively on search-and-destroy missions. The flights looked for "military targets"—in reality almost anything suspicious moving on the roads. That particular day they had been scheduled to cover an area near the border.

The T-28s could range several hundred miles on a typical mission but the vastness of the northeastern Congo swallowed up that distance quickly. The planes reconnoitered as much territory as they could in the areas north, west and south of the airport. They didn't fly east into Uganda, however, because the Simbas weren't operating there.

I had done a lot of this type of flying in Laos and was confident I'd get a good idea of what if anything was going on along the Sudanese border. The Simbas' strategy made sense to me. If I were one of their commanders I would bring the arms and ammo in at night. Security was an issue, too, but as far as we knew the Simbas didn't have any weaponry that could bring down a plane. I felt good about that. That had not been the case in Laos, where we did occasionally lose aircraft to ground fire.

Nevertheless as a precaution I took along my Walther 9mm pistol and grabbed a holster from the supply room.

The weather was good and it looked as if an easy and productive afternoon awaited me.

I formally met the two Cuban pilots, Juan Peron and Juan Tunon, just before we were to take off. They were young but experienced and each was a good flier, Big Bill had told me. I went over some maps with them and explained the areas I wanted to cover.

I understood that my objective would be secondary; military targets, if we found any, would take top priority. I could always go again if necessary. The T-28's two seats were tandem, one behind the other under the same canopy. I would fly behind Juan Peron.

Born in Havana in 1940, Juan had learned to fly light planes and became a crop duster for a small rice-growing company. In 1960, about a year after Fidel Castro overthrew the government of President Fulgencio Batista, the Cuban authorities sent Juan to Miami to pick up a new plane. He had a three-day visa.

Fearing how Castro would change Cuba, Juan's father instructed him to stay in the United States, and he did so. At age 20 he found himself in a new and strange country. Under programs for Cuban immigrants established by President Kennedy, Juan served first in the Air Force, though he did not fly, and then the Army.

In 1963 he accepted employment with one of the air proprietary companies organized by the agency and was sent to the Congo. Beforehand he received training in a World War II-vintage T-6 fighter. After arriving in the Congo he trained in the T-28 and in the twin-engine C-46. By age 25 he had become a skilled pilot.

Close up the T-28 looked bigger and in a way more menacing than I remembered. I climbed onto the wing and then into the back seat of the narrow cockpit. Wes had taken some photos and was standing about 50 yards away waiting for us to take off. I donned my flight helmet, with its push-to-talk intercom, while Juan climbed into the pilot's seat. We both wore parachutes.

As I strapped on the harness I was thinking how different this was from anything I'd ever flown in Laos. The Helio and the copters seemed positively flimsy compared to the T-28.

Juan started the powerful engine and closed the canopy. I waved to Wes and the others as we taxied out to the runway. Our takeoff confirmed what I had been sensing.

This thing is hot!

It needed speed to fly, lots of speed. This was particularly noticeable because Bunia sits about 4,000 feet above sea level and in the slightly thinner air we needed more runway to get airborne.

After takeoff and in tandem with Juan Tunon, who followed us, we circled and flew back down the runway about 10 feet off the deck. The Cubans were showing off but I didn't mind. They ended the flyby with a sharp ascent—which my stomach did mind.

As planned we headed generally north along the Sudanese border. It was unremarkable high plateau terrain covered with what Juan called rivers of trees, although not dense jungle. I saw nothing of interest. Then after maybe half an hour we spotted three trucks gathered near a junction of two unpaved roads. Evidently the drivers had heard us and were pulling under some trees. As flight commander, Juan decided to attack and destroy the vehicles. It wasn't clear to me that these were military targets but it didn't matter; I had no vote so I accepted his decision.

We circled around and with us in the lead started a strafing run. The dive was steep and again my stomach took immediate notice. Coming out we were pulling a few g's, as airmen say. It was no big deal for Juan but I had never felt it before, so it was quite uncomfortable. I had trouble seeing and couldn't tell what if anything we were hitting. Nothing on the ground moved. Tunon had been flying right behind us but I didn't see him, either.

Two more runs. Still nothing moved and no one returned fire. Juan said we were done.

Fine, let's get out of here.

I don't know how long our attack took but after we leveled off and resumed cruising it became immediately obvious that the weather had changed. A front had appeared behind us. Heavy clouds and rain were moving in our direction.

The two Juans exchanged chatter in Spanish so I couldn't make out what they were saying. Juan Peron said we'd better return to Bunia and he'd try to get around the storm but it wasn't going to be that easy.

Flying in the middle of Africa in the 1960s presented many challenges. Weather forecasting help was almost nonexistent—you knew a storm was coming when you saw it. Likewise, navigational aids were few and far between. There were no radio beacons. The landscape spanned great distances with nothing in it except the occasional plantation or small village. The few roads and large rivers meant very little to key on. Visual flight rules prevailed—you had to see it and know what it was.

We knew there were lakes to the south that could have helped us fix our location. But we couldn't see them and only Bunia and Paulis had airports that could handle a T-28.

We tried to skirt the storm. It was nasty and threw us around. The two pilots managed to stay together and took the path of least resistance. When we got out of it the Juans talked again. Peron told me we had been knocked off course. I wasn't surprised. He wasn't sure where we were but thought it best if we headed for Paulis and spent the night there.

I asked whether gaining altitude would help us spot the lakes. Neither of them thought so. I had to rely on their experience. I had confidence in them both. We flew on hoping to find Paulis. But we saw nothing familiar and soon Juan gave me the rotten news.

"We are going to have to go down," he said. "The storm screwed us up bad. We don't know where we are and fuel is getting low. I'd rather take it in while I can choose a clearing—and it will be dark soon."

Shit!

"Let's jump," I said into the intercom. "We all have chutes."

"No way," he responded. "We're better off to crash land."

Shit! A pilot's mentality!

Unless the plane is on fire or the wings fall off they won't jump. Years later Juan confirmed that mentality by telling me that he "never had any confidence in parachutes."

I was not at all happy at the prospect of crash landing in a T-28. As I had observed it needed lots and lots of space and I could see no clearings below that looked big enough. Again, I had no real choice. I couldn't open the canopy and I couldn't just leap out of the plane.

It was all happening so fast.

Tunon decided to stay up a while longer. I heard him and Peron wish each other luck.

Bloody hell, I'm wishing us all good luck!

Juan picked out a clearing. It didn't look long enough but choices were few.

Shit!

Juan made his last turn and we started losing altitude. He wanted a long approach with time to cut off the switches, touch down with full flaps, and slow our airspeed as much as possible.

"You have a weapon?" Juan asked as we glided, still going a good clip but just above the T-28's stall speed.

I reached down and touched the Walther in its holster on my hip. I was glad I had brought it along.

"Yeah," I responded, "and I'll keep it with me."

His question highlighted the fact that we were going down in unknown territory likely to be controlled by the Simbas. Odd perhaps, but I felt no fear, just frustration and irritation at our predicament. I was confident that we would make our landing somehow. Then we would lose ourselves in the bush and make our way out to safety, however long that might take.

If I had thought about it more I might have started worrying. I had never come close to crashing in Laos and I never had to go on foot so lightly armed, unaccompanied by a patrol, and lacking an escape-and-evasion kit with a radio.

Juan opened the canopy and I felt a rush of air. The approach seemed endless as he kept trying to maneuver the aircraft for the longest possible slide before we hit the trees. In order to get a better look at the clearing I lifted the sun visor on my flight helmet.

I would live to regret it.

We were still moving fast—too fast, really—but now there was nothing Juan could do about it. Our first touch caused us to bounce. We touched again and started skidding along the rough clearing, which had looked better from 3,000 feet up.

Juan told me that he spotted flames under the left wing. I didn't. I was hunched over, my seatbelt and harness as tight as I could pull them, bracing myself.

We must have slid for several hundred yards but it seemed even longer. Then we slammed into a tree.

The force caused me to lurch forward and then spring back, my head jerking up. At the same instant a splash of flaming aviation fuel spewed across the rear cockpit from the left wing.

I caught the flames in the face, left front mostly, plus my left shoulder and both hands, as well as a bit on the tops of both legs.

The splash missed the front cockpit and spared Juan. Not immediately realizing what had happened to me, and eager to get the hell out of the now-burning aircraft, he leaped out of the cockpit onto the right wing, jumped down to the ground, and ran.

Stunned and in considerable pain I had no idea how seriously I had been burned. Worse, I couldn't see—my eyelids had been singed shut and I couldn't open them.

From that point on, until early 1966, I would be essentially blind.

This would certainly screw things up!

I could hear and smell the burning fuel and knew I had to get away from the plane.

I also heard Peron shouting at me to get out.

I'm sure trying.

But my seat harness remained snugly fastened and my hands hurt a lot—I couldn't use either one.

Somehow and in great pain I managed to push open the release with one of my elbows.

With considerably more effort I started to climb out—hindered severely by my hands and the damned parachute hanging behind me.

The fire was a great motivator. I half-climbed, half-stumbled out of the cockpit and fell off the wing on the right-rear side.

Instinctively I had moved away from the fire.

Just then Juan rushed in to help me away from the burning plane, which promptly exploded into high-intensity flames. I felt that intensity and was thankful to have escaped it.

Juan said, and I agreed, that we needed to cover as much distance as possible before nightfall. If any Simbas had seen the plane come down they surely would be coming to check things out.

The problem was I could barely walk, even after Juan had unfastened the parachute harness and gotten it off me. The pain remained intense and I had almost no strength. Juan couldn't carry me very far, either, because I outweighed him by 20 pounds or so.

We stopped and I tried to think. I saw memory flashes from my earlier training: the Army, the Farm, Panama—even the Boy Scouts.

Burns mean infection and dehydration. Also, bad burns mean swelling.

I pulled my college ring from my left hand. It hurt like hell and skin came with it but I knew I had to get it off or suffer worse consequences.

I was wearing contact lenses and knew they should come out as well. I asked Juan to help because my fingers wouldn't work. It was impossible. I couldn't get my eyes open. The lenses would simply have to stay where they were until we could find help.

Another fateful development.

I could sense that Juan was very upset—who wouldn't be? Clearly my being hurt had shifted the playing field and not to our advantage.

"We'll make it out of here," I told him. "I don't know how but we will."

Of that I was certain and determined.

It started raining. I don't know how far from the plane we had moved, but it couldn't have been very far. Juan told me we had walked for only 30 minutes or so.

We stopped under some trees next to a small stream. It rained most of the night. We just sat there. Juan made me move periodically, fearing an adverse impact on my circulation. The pain grew even worse and I must have passed out for short intervals. We saw or heard no sign of patrols moving in the area. We had absolutely no idea where we were. That night seemed to last forever.

When daylight came Juan used his knife to cut the charred skin hanging from several of my fingers. Bugs had already begun feeding on some of my burns. I could hear them buzzing and thought they were some kind of bees but I wasn't sure.

We talked. We decided that since I was in no condition to walk—I could barely move by this point—Juan should leave me by the small stream so I could drink water regularly and he could go find help.

Although unstated we both knew that our chances would be far better if Juan moved out alone. So off he went, taking my Walther with him. By that time I was in left field anyway—the pain taking me into and out of consciousness.

As Juan told me later he started out by partially retracing our steps. Because we hadn't covered much ground after the crash landing he soon returned to the wreckage. He said he felt relieved to find no one—particularly the Simbas—in the area. At the same time he worried about not knowing where we were. He also saw that nothing—not his flight maps and not the UZI he had placed behind his seat—would be salvageable. He had only his pistol and mine.

In ever-increasing circles Juan started to explore the area around the crash site, looking for anything—a village, a road—that would help to identify our location. He moved cautiously for fear of running into a Simba group.

Sometime around midday he spotted some natives and tried to approach them but they fled. He followed them to a small cluster of huts, which for the northeastern Congo qualified as a village.

He saw an old man talking excitedly to a group of women. He walked up to them. None spoke French, English or Spanish, so Juan had trouble making himself understood. The women seemed hesitant and wary. Then a group of men appeared and Juan saw they were unarmed. He realized they were likely the males of the village returning from the fields.

The men neared him cautiously. Juan began addressing them in English and felt greatly relieved to hear a response. Many questions and answers later he learned that the village chief, named Faustino, had been educated by British missionaries. The villagers were Azande, a tribal group scattered across central Africa in the Congo, Sudan and the Central African Republic. They had little use for governments or borders. They also knew little and probably cared less about Moise Tshombe and his Congolese central government.

Of great importance to them, however—and of paramount importance to us—was that the Simbas, for reasons never made clear, had killed Faustino's brother, another Azande leader.

As a result Faustino hated the Simbas.

Thank God, what a stroke of good luck for us!

Juan explained our situation but told Faustino we had been hunting elephants. From a T-28? Juan didn't think Faustino believed him. I didn't think so, either. I have no idea what prompted him to fabricate such an implausible story. In my racing thoughts before the crash I had planned to pose as a French journalist.

Whatever Faustino might have thought of Juan's tale he agreed to help us get to safety.

"Where is that?" Juan asked.

"We are near the Sudan border," Faustino replied, "and the nearest government post is Paulis," over a hundred miles away.

"*Dios mio*," Juan murmured. "We will walk?"

Faustino didn't reply.

Juan thought that Faustino, in his mid-30s, had a strong build and a ruggedly handsome appearance. He looked like a warrior and displayed the aura of a leader. Juan sensed right away that the people in the village respected him and would obey him.

Faustino's authority stemmed mostly from his family ties, a tradition among the Azande, but the villagers appeared to genuinely like Faustino and respect him. The Azande were a strong and proud people, much like the Hmong. They had been powerful and independent in their lands even through the slave-trader raiding periods.

Someone in the village had reported another plane down nearby—Tunon's, no doubt—and Juan and Faustino checked out the site on the way to get me. Tunon was nowhere to be found.

Based on its location and the condition of the plane—and no evidence of fire—Juan suspected that Tunon had stalled out on his final approach. Lacking sufficient airspeed the plane must have dropped like a rock. The trees, some over a hundred feet tall, served to cushion its drop to the ground. Tunon had received training in jungle warfare and escape and evasion before his assignment in the Congo. He had taken his weapon but left his maps, which Juan was able to retrieve.

Not knowing our present location, however, the maps weren't of much use—and Faustino couldn't read them.

Tunon was never seen again. Several months later, missionary reports confirmed that while trying to make his way to safety he had been captured by a Simba patrol. The Simbas killed him and subsequently, believing that if you eat the flesh and vital organs of your enemy you will gain strength, devoured him.

May God rest his soul.

I can't remember much about the time I spent lying on the ground and waiting for Juan—mostly just stumbling into and out of the stream several times.

I have to drink a lot.

The water also gave some relief from the bees that seemed to be all over me, though if they were stinging me in my condition I wouldn't have felt it.

Juan said he was shocked when they found me the next day lying about 60 feet from the stream bank.

"You were covered with bees and you looked like a monster," he said.

In continuous pain and barely conscious I didn't even realize at first that he had returned. It had been almost 24 hours since we crashed. Knowing I would be unable to walk, Juan and the villagers fashioned a crude stretcher from branches and carried me to the village. It was an excruciating journey. Each movement of the stretcher was agony and whatever scabbing had begun on my burned skin broke open again.

This must have been a most unusual event for the inhabitants because I could hear the women and children clustering excitedly around the stretcher to look at me.

I was in bad shape. Plainly I would need help but the village had absolutely none to offer. There was no doctor and no medicines but they would do their best, Faustino promised Juan.

Faustino met with the village men and as chief proposed a plan. They would help but they had to protect themselves from the Simbas as well. They would hide me in the bush outside the village and someone would stay with me at all times. Faustino and two others would guide Juan to Paulis to seek help and return for me.

I was in such poor condition that I wasn't thinking clearly. I do remember saying that if they helped us my government would aid and protect them.

I have no idea whether I got that across. I remember giving Faustino my Walther—though Peron said he did—and giving his son my Omega wristwatch. I would have offered them the Brooklyn Bridge if I could have.

I strained to understand and participate in the planning but I couldn't stay lucid. I remember only snatches of the discussion. Juan made the decisions for us and he was right on all counts. Trying to take me along, to carry me over a hundred miles to Paulis, would have been folly. I would not have survived.

True to the plan the villagers moved me somewhere into the bush—I don't know how far. They laid me on the ground inside a crude hut. It wasn't much but it really didn't need to be—I wasn't a particularly demanding patient. It would protect me from the rain, and a small fire seemed to keep the bugs and vermin away.

Faustino's men had selected the site not for its patient comforts but because it was out of the way. No one wanted a Simba patrol to discover me anywhere near, much less in, the village. Everyone would suffer if that happened.

Also according to plan someone cared for me though I have only fleeting memories of it. My periods of consciousness became fewer and fewer.

I vaguely remember being washed with warm water and someone cleaning my burns with a knife. The bees had gone but smaller, worm-like bugs had taken over while I lay on the ground before Juan and the villagers returned for me.

Mostly the bugs were easily removed. Just scratch them off or out of the wounds. Detaching them from my hands was much more painful but my caregiver systematically dug out every one he or she could see.

The effort had predictable results, my hand surgeons told me later. Many of the extensor tendons of my fingers were cut and could no longer function. Lest that sound like criticism it definitely isn't. I survived and my fingers still work. The injuries played hell with my jump shot, but I can still hold a tennis racket. So I will always be grateful to my personal pest exterminator.

Eventually someone judged that my wounds had been sufficiently cleaned. Then the village witch doctor applied a grease- or salve-like substance onto all of my burns. I am vague in describing it because to this day I don't really know what it was. I just know it turned bluish-black, hardened, and formed a protective coating over my burned flesh. In doing so it prevented dehydration and infection—always the greatest dangers for someone who had been severely burned.

In due course doctors at the National Burn Center in San Antonio, Texas, would discover how effective this primitive tribal treatment had been. No question it saved my life. But time was the key factor. Was I strong enough, physically and mentally, to hang on until Juan got to Paulis and returned? Some, looking at my condition, may have had doubts. I had none. I simply would not die in this rotten Congo, I decided. I was determined to hold on against any odds.

But I was to be tested—severely.

The party departed the morning of February 19, two days after we had crashed. Juan left my parachute with the villagers with instructions to spread it out on the ground when the helicopter arrived for me.

Juan was optimistic. Faustino had requisitioned three bicycles. Two other villagers, Balde and Christie, would be making the trip with them. It could be dangerous, they all knew. They would avoid encountering a Simba patrol or outpost at all costs.

That meant the group would have to exercise great care when passing near towns or villages. They would have to move at night through suspect areas. They would gather water from the streams and wells they passed and either forage food from the bush or purchase it from villagers they could trust—other Azande.

Though he lacked formal education Faustino was intelligent and resourceful. Juan knew nothing about the area so he deferred to Faustino's judgment. In the end we both would owe our lives to him.

The group began and ended their trip using the same tactic. Balde, sharp-eyed and alert, rode ahead to spot any danger, avoid it, and warn those behind him to take care. He periodically left signals on the trail or road for the others to follow.

Juan said he was amazed the signals could even be recognized because they consisted of such things as a rock, a broken twig or branch, leaves arranged just so, or some other subtle indicator. Peron almost never saw one but Faustino always did—according to Faustino.

Juan carried a .45 automatic pistol, and Faustino had my Walther. Balde and Christie weren't armed. Juan and Faustino didn't talk much but they shared good rapport—despite the continually high level of stress. When a given situation required a decision Faustino made it. No one questioned his authority or leadership. Christie followed behind making sure that nothing could surprise them from the rear. Nothing did but they never changed their tactic.

Back in Bunia, Big Bill had sounded the alert when our two planes didn't return. No one knew what had happened but some feared the worst.

Early on February 18 he sent planes out to look for us. Juan remembers seeing one of them but without a survival kit or radio he could not contact it or signal his position.

Russ had no radio but Big Bill sent an airdropped message to him on the shore of Lake Albert. Russ immediately broke off his lake patrols, drove back to Bunia, and helped with the search.

Runners were sent into the bush to visit distant villages to see if anyone had received any word. No one had.

Big Bill knew the areas we had hoped to reconnoiter but he didn't know that a storm had blown us off course. Moreover, portions of the area were fairly mountainous and therefore difficult to search. That both planes were missing was odd and even more worrisome.

The search continued for several days without result—a needle-in-a-haystack situation. Hope dimmed.

As far as Juan could determine, the crash site and village were not far from the Sudanese border—no more than 15 or 20 miles. As they made their way south-southwest toward Paulis and the Congo River Basin the altitude decreased and the rainforest thickened, making progress more difficult. They covered as much distance as they could each day, riding the bicycles as much as possible and carrying or pushing them whenever the pedaling became difficult or impossible.

Juan said he didn't know how they found their way. They carried Tunon's maps even though they were of no use. Had any of them made the trip to Paulis before? Were they questioning villagers when they infrequently purchased food? Were there road signs that he didn't see? He never knew.

They never hesitated though some days were better than others. Twice they were able to use canoes to cover substantial distances with minimal physical effort. Loading the bicycles on the back they floated or paddled easily for hours at a time. The changed venue allowed them rest but it also seemed to increase the stress.

Juan said he felt more vulnerable on the rivers, because the open water exposed their presence for long distances and they had no idea what was lurking on the shores or around the next bend. Nevertheless, drifting downstream was a welcome respite for his body—his legs in particular. He was young and strong but not used to constant physical exertion. He never lagged, though, and maintained the pace Faustino had set.

A few times they rode through enormous plantations, beautiful but almost deserted. There they could find food and water without much fear for their safety. The few natives they found living on the plantations hated and feared the Simbas and were willing to help Faustino. Juan was struck by the effort that must have been required to clear and plant the fields.

The four of them usually slept in the bush though occasionally they found empty huts they could use. Fatigue caused them to sleep easily despite constant concern for their safety. But they knew the Simbas did nothing at night or in the rain because they thought their magic wouldn't work. According to Juan the intrepid travelers often reminded themselves of that particular quirk and felt reassured.

They limited their few contacts with local villagers along the way almost exclusively to other Azande. Faustino would speak with elders or chiefs and let them know who he was—brother to a Simba-slain chieftain—and help was always forthcoming. The villagers gave the group food and guided them to safe areas to sleep.

Three, four, five days passed as they made good progress covering chunks of territory without incident. Only a few times did Balde warn of something approaching they wished to avoid. They never wanted to be seen on the road so anytime Balde signaled them they would melt into the bush and wait for the traffic to pass.

Juan guessed they had been covering up to 25 miles per day but he had no idea how far they were from Paulis. Faustino's response to his questions was always, "Not too far."

During all this time they hadn't seen any sign of the Simbas. So much the better. They worried about possible sightings a few times and twice they rode for a few hours at night to move beyond an area of concern. By the end of the fifth day Juan began to feel hopeful.

Late in the afternoon on February 25, the seventh day of travel, they reached an outpost manned by Belgians and mercenaries about 20 miles east of Paulis. Balde spotted it first and rode back to Juan and Faustino with the good news. They were very happy and greatly relieved they had made it.

They rode together toward the outpost and, to be safe, Faustino approached it by himself. Soon he waved joyfully and all four entered the compound.

As soon as the garrison understood who these men were they became excited. Word of the missing planes and men reached there days ago but by the time of the group's arrival hope for our survival had grown dim.

Juan explained that I was still in the bush. The Belgians offered help but explained they could do nothing until morning. It was almost sunset and darkness falls very abruptly year-round near the equator. Juan felt disappointed but confident he would be able to rescue me soon.

Though the outpost offered no comforts to speak of, just knowing they were safe allowed the party to sleep well that night.

The morning of February 26 brought lots of activity. Immediately after breakfast, including hot coffee, a truck carried Juan, Faustino and their two companions into Paulis. The ride took about an hour. Word of their arrival had preceded them via single-sideband radio.

They went directly to the airfield where the agency ran a small contingent similar to the one at Bunia and shared the facility with a Belgian air operation. We had positioned several planes there and stationed the support crews and pilots in Paulis. Our group kept direct radio contact with Leopoldville. The Belgians maintained helicopters and aircraft, along with support crews and pilots, to aid their nationals who had remained in the former colony.

The Cuban pilots in Paulis greeted Juan, warmly expressing their delight that he had survived the ordeal. They asked about Tunon and Juan told them what he knew.

By this time the air-operations officers began firing questions at Juan about my condition and whereabouts and Juan carefully explained everything that had happened. He included high praise for Faustino, Balde and Christie, who at that point were standing off to one side.

One of the air officers thanked the three villagers, telling them, "We will be helping you as well."

Juan emphasized that my condition was extremely poor and urged that a helicopter lift off immediately for the village to pick me up. But the only choppers were Belgian, which required the rescue to be authorized. There followed a flurry of cables back and forth to Leopoldville where in turn the Belgian authorities made phone calls to their air command.

"Yes, of course, immediately," was the response.

The office also flashed cables to Washington stating that I was alive and my whereabouts had been identified but I had been badly hurt. No one knew how badly.

Paulis received the necessary approvals within a few hours. Preparations for the chopper rescue mission were already under way. Juan and Faustino crouched over maps with the Belgian pilots and agency officers trying to locate Faustino's village. This was not an easy task but they were able to narrow it down and felt confident they would find it.

They decided that Faustino, Balde and Christie would ride—for all three their first flight—in one of the helicopters and Juan would sit in the back of an accompanying T-28. The rescue effort would also include a backup copter and a C-47 transport carrying the Belgian commander. I learned all this decades later when I met Paul Van Casteren, the pilot of the lead copter.

The original plan had put Juan in one of the copters as well but the Cuban pilots persuaded him to fly escort with one of them. None had any confidence in the "bananas," as they called them, that the Belgians were flying.

Juan's description of my condition so concerned the Paulis base chief that he requested a C-130 be dispatched immediately from Leopoldville to await my arrival.

All preparations made and approvals from Leopoldville in hand the four aircraft took off mid-afternoon on February 26—nine days after we had crashed and seven days after Juan had left me with the villagers.

Heading north-northeast the rescue mission flew for almost an hour while Juan and Faustino separately strained to spot any landmark that would put them on course. They passed over the small towns they had encountered riding their bicycles so they knew they were heading in the right direction.

Finally Faustino spotted a village then an intersection of two roads and a river bridge, familiar sights that would lead him home. Overhead, Juan had heard the good news and was cheering and shouting into his headset. Soon everyone could see the villagers spreading out the parachute in the designated clearing.

Paul's copter hovered over the landing zone. As he slowly lowered it to touch down its engine suddenly failed. The craft hit the ground like a rock, rolling on its side and bending the rotor and landing gear.

No one was hurt but the copter was badly damaged. While the pilot of the backup copter looked for an alternative landing site, the villagers led Paul and the doctor to my hut where they confirmed that I was still alive.

With the daylight beginning to fade there wasn't time to carry me out. So the two men hurried to the second landing site and climbed aboard the other helicopter, which immediately lifted off and headed back to Paulis.

They had stretched their mission to the limit, time wise. With its greater airspeed the T-28 arrived in Paulis at dusk. The C-47 accompanied the slower chopper and darkness fell on them along the way. In order to help land the two aircraft the Belgians positioned vehicles to shine their lights on the runway, again demonstrating the courage and resourcefulness they had displayed during the whole operation.

Back in the little hut my condition steadily deteriorated. Someone might well have been watching over me all the time but I didn't know it. I experienced only fleeting moments of consciousness and each seemed to hurt more than the last. There was no relief.

I had learned the Swahili word for water, *maji*, and I asked for it frequently. My caretakers also tried to feed me—eggs and pineapple, I think—but whatever it was I couldn't eat it. Anything I managed to swallow I retched up almost immediately. My will to live was being challenged and my body didn't like it at all.

For years afterward I couldn't even touch a piece of pineapple, though my appetite for eggs didn't seem to be affected.

In my distressed state I experienced strange, even bizarre, delusions. I imagined myself on a giant roller coaster careening up and down a track. Going down was awful because there were intense flames at the bottom and the pain was excruciating, until the coaster emerged from the flames and climbed again. A tall, menacing African stood by the tracks, jabbing at me with his spear each time I passed and causing more pain. This went on and on and on.

I must have thrashed around a lot; I recall hands restraining and attempting to calm me.

I had no sense of time. I felt myself slipping away but I was determined to hang on. My body was closing down to its last cells and I clung to them as I clung to life itself.

At some point I experienced a different delusion. The cells I had lost floated by me and I grabbed at them. Subconsciously I was fighting to make myself whole again.

My periods of any sort of wakefulness were diminishing. I knew days were passing but I remained mostly unaware of what was going on around me. I didn't even know that the Belgian helicopter had arrived and crashed.

The people in Paulis—and Leopoldville and Washington—were well aware of the chopper crash, however, and the accident prompted much concern, frustration and disappointment. Juan, who had gotten so close to getting me out, told me he felt truly saddened by this unexpected turn of events. I can only imagine that Faustino, Balde and Christie must have thought it a rather unbecoming way to return to their village—rolling and scrambling out of a damaged helicopter.

The Belgian air command immediately authorized a second flight to pick me up. Too late to return that day they prepared to take off the following morning.

Meanwhile the C-130 had arrived from Leopoldville with a doctor aboard.

Now that my location had been established everyone felt confident that the second effort would be successful. And it was.

Early on February 27 a second Belgian helicopter, carrying armed personnel and accompanied by the T-28, landed at the village.

I was in terrible shape, one of the crewmembers told me later. Whatever the village witch doctor had applied to my burns hardened into a foul-smelling, tough coating on my skin. That was a good thing, though no one understood it at the time. All they knew was that the bluish-black color looked ominous. My face was a mess as were my hands.

But I was alive.

They quickly carried me aboard the copter and we left for Paulis where they immediately transferred me to the C-130 for the long flight to Leopoldville and hospital. Russ helped to carry my stretcher. How he managed to be there at that time I don't know. He later told me that while they were moving me from the chopper to the transport a Belgian priest named Father Josef—with the kindest of intentions, I'm sure—approached the stretcher. The bearers stopped briefly as he looked me over and concluded that the smelly blue-black paste was likely gangrene. If so it was highly doubtful I would make it to Leopoldville.

Without further ado, Russ said, the priest proceeded right there on the tarmac to give me the last rites. At that point, Russ told me later, I raised my head and said, "I am not one of your guys and I'm not ready to say any last words."

I have no recollection of that incident, which would have passed unnoticed but for the crucifix on a silver chain that Father Josef draped around my neck.

More about that shortly.

At Louvanium Hospital in Leopoldville, doctors assessed my condition and likewise concluded it was very poor. So poor in fact that an American doctor took one look, saw no hope, and left the room.

Out in the hall the good doctor reported his prognosis to a senior embassy officer. Russ, who had accompanied me all the way to the hospital, was standing nearby and overheard the doctor's comments. He refused to accept the verdict and was about to voice a strong protest when a second doctor arrived. An older Belgian with much experience in the Congo he realized that after 10 days in the bush without care my body desperately needed intervention.

Even that was an understatement but Russ was delighted. The Belgian doctor inserted IVs into both my ankles though which he supplied me with everything he could think of—antibiotics and nutrients galore. All flowed into my body, which apparently welcomed it with open arms. I sorely needed that boost and it no doubt helped prepare me for what lay ahead.

On February 26 news had reached headquarters of my rescue. Dick Helms, then the deputy director for plans and Glen Fields's immediate superior, went straight to Director McCone.

"The officer missing in the Congo has been found," Dick told him, "but his condition is very poor. The only real hope is to get him to the National Burn Center in Texas as soon as possible. We'll need an Air Force plane to pick him up in Leopoldville."

McCone called Secretary of Defense Robert McNamara, who asked only one question: "Is he still alive?"

"He is," McCone replied, "and he'll make it if we can get him to Texas."

"Then we go," said McNamara, who immediately dispatched a Boeing 707 jetliner from McGuire Air Force Base in New Jersey. It carried the burn specialist, nurses and corpsman who would care for me.

Less than 24 hours later the plane arrived in Leopoldville. The team took my vital signs and carefully assessed my condition, and the pilot prepared for the Atlantic crossing, which would include a stop in northeastern Brazil for refueling.

About midway in the flight, according to the pilot—who later related this to my father—my condition and vital signs improved slightly. No one knew why but I believe it was the result of all the medicines and fluids the Belgian doctor had pumped into me during my short stay in Leopoldville. The changes had caused the prognosis to shift from "really lousy" to "he might just make it."

The burn team leader, a Dr. Wilson, reported the changes to the pilot, who decided to skip the refueling and fly straight through to San Antonio. We arrived late on Saturday evening, February 27, 1965.

About two weeks later, as I was about to be moved to a ward from intensive care, a nurse asked me what she should do with the crucifix that had been hanging at the foot of my bed.

Somewhat puzzled I replied, "I'm not Catholic and I don't have a crucifix."

"That's strange," she said, "it's the only thing you had on you when you got here."

It remained a mystery until weeks later when Russ visited from Washington. I happened to mention the crucifix and he told me the story of Father Josef. That raised the question of what to do with it, which the nurse had told me was quite beautiful. The next time I spoke with her she said one of her daughters was in a convent so I offered the crucifix to her. She seemed touched by the gesture and accepted.

I have since regretted parting with the gift Father Josef had given me in such a sensitive and kind gesture. I also regret not being able to thank the Belgian doctor, whose basic treatment gave the airborne burn team cause for optimism about my condition. Likewise, I've never had a chance to meet or thank Faustino, Balde, Christie and the villagers, all of whom risked their lives to save me.

In 2006, when I reconnected with the Belgian aviators who had evacuated me, they sent maps pinpointing the crash site. One of the maps even listed the name of the village: Bitima.

I also learned from other sources that Faustino gained much stature from his adventure. He returned several times to Paulis where the agency gave him weapons and ammunition to defend himself and his village.

Whether the Simbas became aware of what had happened no one knows, but Faustino was taking no chances. He soon joined a group of Spanish mercenaries operating in the area of Bitima. They gave him training, a weapon and a uniform. Juan later sent me a photo of Faustino in that uniform, looking every inch an imposing figure.

The agency also arranged to airdrop a planeload of medicine, tools and clothing for Bitima. I'm told it was well received. The villagers understood it was a gesture of our gratitude for what they had done to save my life.

I add my thanks to the U.S. taxpayers who funded that effort.

Juan Peron rested for a while in Leopoldville and then resumed flying until the agency terminated operations against the Simbas several months later. Many thought he would hang it up after his narrow escape but he never considered stopping. With a lust for flying he piloted for companies in the Canary Islands, Puerto Rico, Aruba and Miami over the next three decades.

Several months after the crash, Big Bill Wyrozemski was transferred to Albertville—now Kalemie—on the shore of Lake Tanganyika. Shortly after his arrival he learned about a possible rebel force moving toward

Albertville from the west. Bill radioed Leopoldville and was authorized to make a short reconnaissance of the area.

He had been instructed not to go alone but no one was readily available so he ignored the instruction. Driving in his Land Rover, Bill rounded a blind turn and a Congolese army truck, speeding on the wrong side of the road, hit him head-on. The impact killed him instantly.

It was an ironic ending for a man, an ex-Polish army officer, who had sought out and survived many dangerous situations during his life. He had flown a Spitfire for the Royal Air Force in the Battle of Britain. It was also rumored he had piloted a B-26 during the Bay of Pigs invasion in 1961.

Juan Peron flew the transport plane that brought Bill Wyrozemski's body back to Leopoldville.

Ban Na and its newly leveled airstrip

One of our indispensable Helios

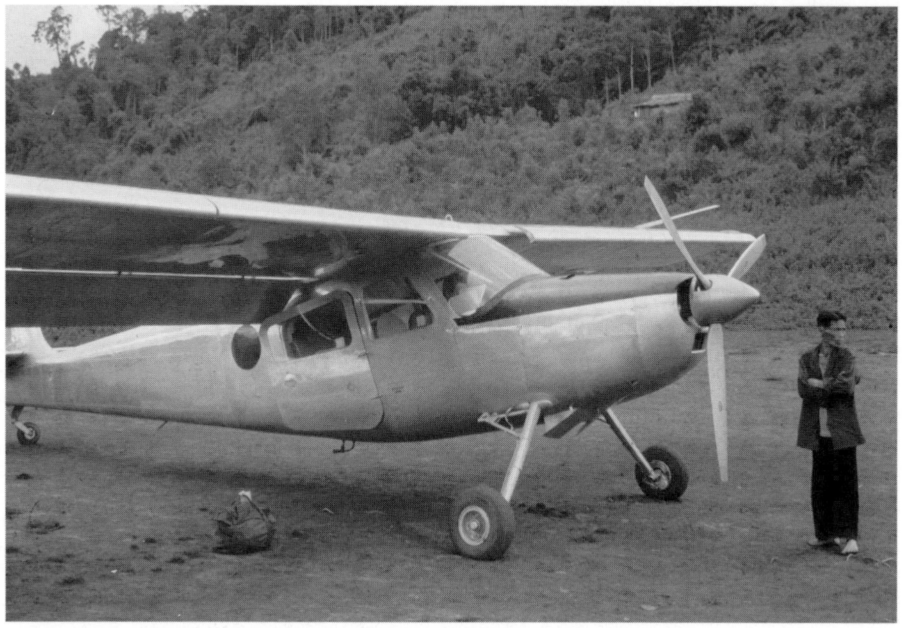

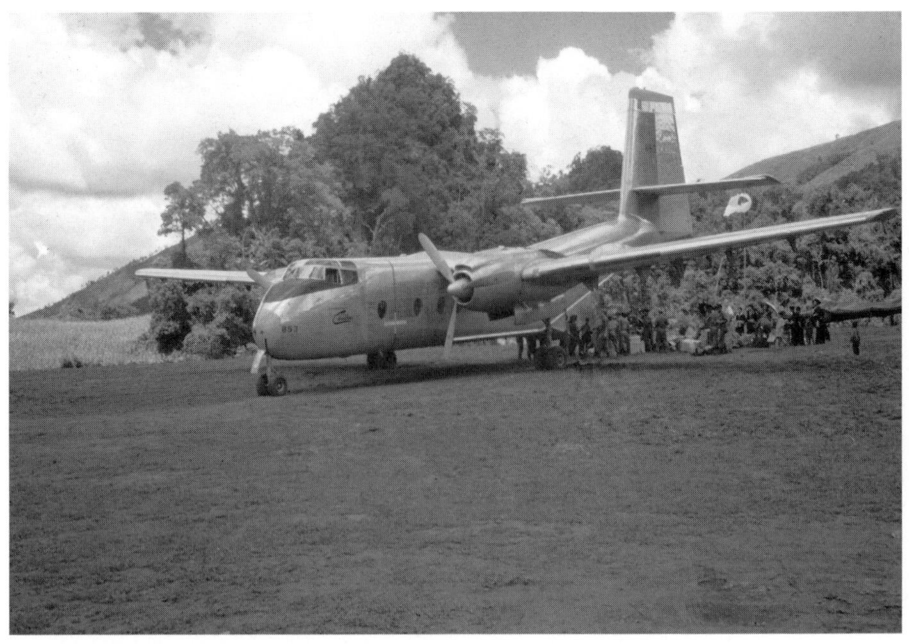

The first Caribou on the ground at Ban Na

Panit (left) with an outpost defender

Nakorn Phanom with Thakhek on the other side of the Mekong

My PARU team in Nakorn Phanom with Jimmie (right)

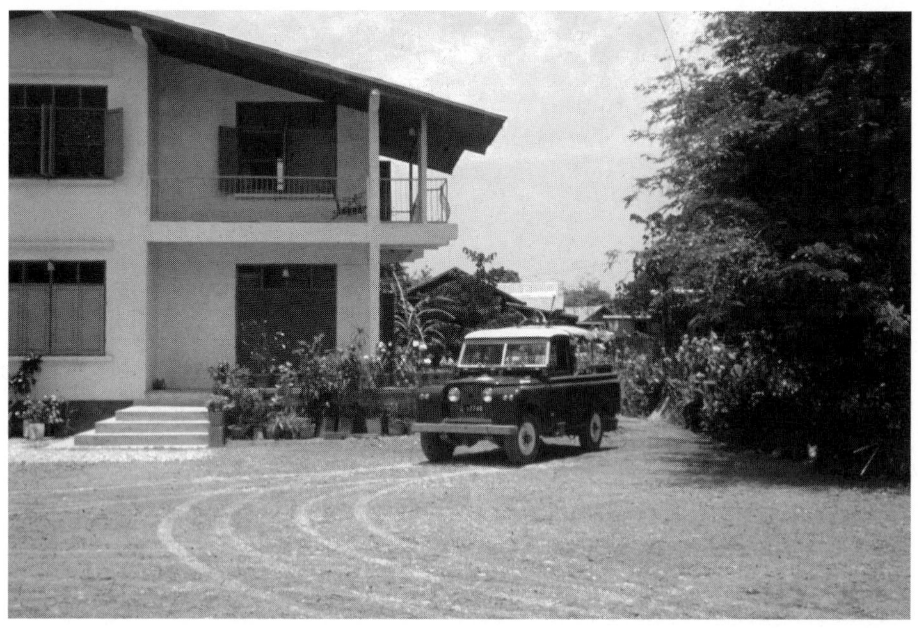

Our house and Land Rover in Nakorn Phanom

Our boathouse on the Mekong at Nakorn Phanom

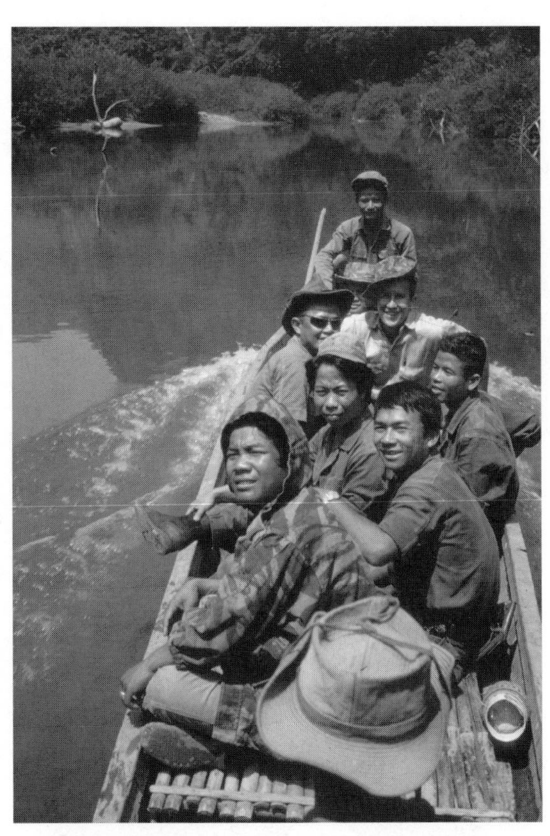

Members of one of my roadwatch teams and me (upper center) heading up the Nam Kading River

A Helio landing near Thakhek with karsts in the distance

Arriving in Stanleyville

Juan Peron (left)
with "Big Bill" Wyrozemski
in Bunia

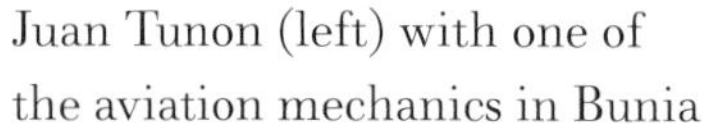

Juan Tunon (left) with one of
the aviation mechanics in Bunia

Our squadron of T-28s in Bunia

Faustino, chief of the village of Bitima

The Belgians' H-21
"banana" rescue copter

The first copter
wrecked on the ground near Bitima

The second copter delivering the rescue party

Hauling me to the plane bound for Leopoldville

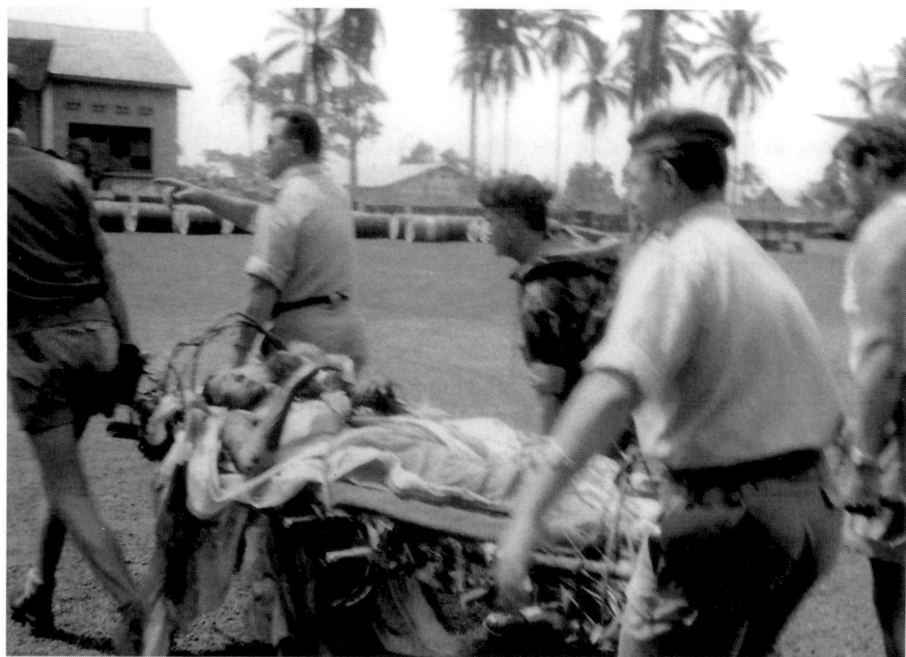

PART IV: REHAB

11. Ninety-Eight Pound Weakling

SAN ANTONIO, TEXAS 1965

Tim Miller had just downed a can of beer and was relaxing with some teammates after a basketball game late one Saturday afternoon in February. A young Army doctor putting in his military service and just out of his internship at Vanderbilt, he had been assigned to the Army's Surgical Research Unit at Fort Sam Houston's Brooke Army Hospital.

The Burn Center at the SRU at the time was considered the best in the United States, if not the world, and the staff there treated civilian patients as well as military.

Although he had attained the rank of captain Tim was not a military man even though he later served a tour with Special Forces in Vietnam. As a doctor and a surgeon he had already demonstrated to his superiors that he was going to be one of the best. Soft-spoken but tough, he was willing to put his principles on the line.

Normally, enjoying a beer was not a problem. That afternoon Tim was on what was known as flight call. If he was needed elsewhere in the country by a physician with a bad burn patient the SRU would schedule a flight out of Lackland Air Force Base, on the other side of San Antonio, usually one or two days later.

It wasn't going to be that way this time; the patient was coming to him—and soon.

Answering a page, Tim called an Air Force colonel who informed him crisply that the helicopter for transporting the SRU's burn specialists would be at the helipad at Brooke in "15 minutes."

"But sir," Tim protested, "I'm not even in uniform."

"Captain, that's your problem," the colonel snarled. He said the helicopter would be meeting an incoming flight carrying a "missionary" who had suffered burns somewhere in Africa. Then he abruptly hung up.

"Something's going on but I don't know what," Tim told his friends as he grabbed his stuff and headed for his car.

The hospital was nearby and Tim made it there within the requisite 15 minutes. He could see the chopper already on the pad, red landing lights blinking, its rotors turning.

Master Sergeant "Hawk" Hawkins, a medical corpsman, arrived at almost the same time. They both jumped aboard and the chopper lifted off.

"What the hell's going on?" Tim shouted over the noise of the rotors.

"Sure don't know, sir," Hawk responded. "But I have your medical kit for you and some hospital scrubs."

Tim changed en route. He asked the pilot where they were going. The pilot said the only information he had was they were headed for Lackland Air Force Base. Hawk looked at Tim and shrugged his shoulders.

As soon as they landed an Air Force major hurried up to Tim. Taking him aside he confirmed that the patient was a badly burned "missionary."

Within minutes a gray 707, showing no markings of any kind, landed and taxied up next to the helicopter. Tim immediately boarded the plane, which was gutted. Inside there were maybe eight seats with two stretchers attached to the wall.

I was lying on one of them.

Dr. Wilson, utterly fatigued from the long flight, began briefing Tim on my condition. Tim listened intently then introduced himself to me. Later he told me my first words were, "I made it out of there." He had no idea where "there" was but he could see I was in extremely poor shape.

He wondered just how coherent I was so he identified himself again. Apparently my briefcase had accompanied me and I seemed concerned about it. Lord knows why, because I'm sure there was nothing important inside—maybe my passport and some personal letters. I never carried classified material in the Congo.

When Tim first saw me in the dark interior of the plane he thought I was black because of that concoction the witch doctor had pasted on my burns. Maybe he half-expected a missionary from Africa to be a black man—though he told me later that he immediately became suspicious about my cover story.

The briefing went on. Dr. Wilson estimated my survival chances at 30 percent and Tim agreed with those odds. "But he seems strong," he said.

Bloody right!

That's what I would have chimed in with had I been lucid. I wasn't, and I don't even remember that first encounter, but it marked the beginning of a relationship that's alive and well nearly five decades later.

Hawk and Tim lifted me into the helicopter. As Tim recalls he tried to reassure me and let me know what was happening but I gave no response. He told me later that when we landed in front of Brooke's main entrance the place was all lit up—unusual for a Saturday night. Major General Snyder, commander of Fort Sam Houston, was waiting for us, as well as Colonel Jack Moncrief, chief of the SRU, and another man in civilian clothes who was not introduced.

They admitted to Tim that I was not really a missionary but they didn't provide any further explanation and made clear that for the moment I would be considered a missionary for identification purposes. Someone also told Tim that the 707 flight had been authorized by Secretary McNamara.

Within a few hours several other people arrived, among them Phil DeCaro, an officer I knew from my tour in Laos. Phil had crashed and been burned while serving there although his wounds weren't nearly as serious as mine. He wanted to see how I was doing.

Tim also told me that Phil and the others all seemed to have been dressed by the same fashion consultant: bland suits, ties—with an occasional paisley—and shined shoes, mostly wingtips. They all smiled but somehow not sincerely. Their expressions were analytical, as though they were sizing Tim up, trying to figure out who this guy was and whether he had ever taken care of a burn patient before.

Tim read their message clearly: "Fuck up and you are in it, boy, well above your knees."

News of the crash had reached my parents in New Jersey on February 18, the day after it happened. An agency officer drove to their home and arrived around 7 p.m. He knocked and my mother opened the door.

The officer introduced himself, showed his credentials, and asked to speak with my father. Mom sensed right away that something was wrong.

"Mr. Holm has gone bowling," she told him. "May I help?"

He insisted on speaking to Dad and asked Mom to please direct him to the bowling alley. She did and he left.

Half an hour later, and unable to find the alley, he returned.

"May I wait here until Mr. Holm returns?" he asked.

Mom agreed. The visitor sat down in our living room and she went back to the family room. Diann and Greg were also home and by this time quite worried something was wrong. When Dad arrived soon after, the officer gave them the news.

"Dick is missing in the Congo as of yesterday," he told them. "His plane did not return from a routine mission and we do not know where he is. We are making every effort to find him and the two pilots he was with."

Understandably the news hit hard. Mom asserted there must have been some mistake; I had told her I was in Morocco. Dad then explained that this wasn't true because we hadn't wanted her to worry.

It didn't help. My decision to mislead her—to lie to her—had backfired. It was a foolish action on my part. It made things worse because the news angered as well as shocked her. She cried—they all did. The officer assured my father that he would receive periodic reports on the progress of the search.

Time passed with painful slowness for them. Every two or three days someone called to report no success. My family suffered but kept their hopes alive. Finally the news arrived that I had been found but seriously injured and was en route to a hospital in Texas.

The agency flew my parents there the next day—a truly sensitive and generous gesture. Yes, I had been asked to take on a tough job. But when the chips were down the CIA spared no expense to support and help me in any way possible.

I have never forgotten.

An agency representative met Mom and Dad in San Antonio and drove them directly to Brooke Hospital where I had arrived the evening before. It was Sunday afternoon, February 28.

First they met with Colonel Moncrief. He briefed them carefully about my condition, trying to prepare them for seeing me. He made a special point of mentioning the black substance on my burns.

"We don't know what it is," he explained, "but I'm starting to think it helped him a lot."

Moncrief brought them to my bed in the intensive-care ward. I looked bad—so bad in fact that Mom was overcome with emotion. Dad remained calm and began speaking softly to me, and the effect was noticeable. The nurse and the doctor were pleased to see that I was mentally alert enough to recognize his voice. I knew Dad was talking to me. It was as if he had jerked me back into consciousness. According to him I even asked a few questions:

Where am I? How did I get here? What day is it?

Dad reassured me and said everything was going to be all right. Mom began speaking to me as well but I don't remember her being there at first.

In my mind suddenly I felt safe. I knew I had made it. If Dad was talking to me then I must be somewhere with help at hand. I could relax, rest, and sleep. I was exhausted from fighting for my life and had been straining to hang on. Now that struggle was over and I gave in to the fatigue that had hung so heavily on my entire body.

As a result I had a relapse. My vital signs wavered dangerously and my condition weakened ominously soon after my parents' visit. The hospital staff reacted to fight my decline but from that point on it would be a very long, uphill struggle.

Tim still didn't know who I was or anything about me except that I had crashed in the Congo nearly two weeks earlier and had received minimal medical treatment. But he understood his first priority: Improve those 30-percent odds.

He supervised a variety of steps designed to strengthen my condition, the most important of which was to reverse my dehydration with large volumes of IV fluid, including a battery of antibiotics to fight infection and supply nourishment to my body.

By that time my reserves were almost gone. It's hard to say how much longer I could have lasted in the Congo village—probably not more than a few days. I was young and strong and in good physical condition. Given the assignment I had accepted I felt I had to be, but I was lucky. I had limits and I wouldn't have wanted to push them much more.

Tim stayed with me almost continuously for over 24 hours. He did everything he could and gradually the odds shifted in my favor. Even the plunge in my condition didn't change what would turn out to be a steady trend of improvement. I was going to make it. Tim had done it. He became yet another individual to whom I owed very much. The list grew longer and longer.

Also during my parents' first visit one of the doctors in the room took Dad by the arm and led him out into the hallway. The doctor introduced himself as an eye surgeon.

He made no small talk but just said, "My colleagues and I have concluded that it will be necessary to remove your son's left eye."

It was another terrible shock for my poor father.

"Why?" he countered. "How could you know so soon? Can't they treat it?"

"That won't be possible," the surgeon explained. "Either the trauma or the lack of treatment for such a long time has caused a perforation and an infection of the eyeball. There's a danger that the other eye could be affected if we don't act now."

The doctors had found the contact lenses when they surgically opened my singed eyelids. They realized right away what had happened, and they debated whether one of the lenses had been the cause of the damage to my left eye, or whether my right eye had survived the splash of burning gasoline because of the other lens. I understand that some people even wrote research papers on the case, but that's academic to me.

The doctor emphasized how every minute counted and he strongly recommended immediate surgery to remove any risk to my right eye. My father had no choice; he signed the papers but with great regret. He knew what a loss I would suffer. He told my mother and she cried—again.

I have always regretted the pain my crash caused them, especially her.

They removed my left eye that day, but I didn't learn about it until the next morning when Dad and the eye doctor told me about the operation and why it had been necessary.

Outwardly I reacted with resignation. How could I question the eye surgeon's decision, particularly after the fact? But inside it hurt me terribly. I thought of the contact lens I had been unable to remove. I thought about how I had lifted the sun visor on my flight helmet during our final approach.

Lifting that visor gave me my last clear look at the world.

Dad felt nearly as awful, I could tell. Mom emphasized that there had been no choice and I agreed with her. I questioned the doctor about my remaining eye. I tried to brace myself for his response.

"It's in good shape," he said, "except the cornea has been scarred. Once the trauma has subsided we will be able to do a corneal transplant and you'll regain your vision."

It wasn't going to be that easy but in retrospect it was awfully good news.

My condition improved and stabilized, and Tim had to clean my wounds in order to start treatment. That meant carefully removing the blue-black paste the Congo witch doctor had applied to my burns. Burn patients at the time—and to this day for all I know—routinely faced a process called debridement, the surgical removal of all damaged skin.

The idea was to cleanse the affected areas and thereby reduce or eliminate the possibility of infection. It was also the required first step in preparation for skin grafts. In my case, because of the paste, debriding the wounds was exceedingly tough and most unpleasant.

Although still sedated to some extent, by this time I was lucid. Mom—bless her for the love she demonstrated—had elected to stay with me during my early period of recovery while Dad returned to New Jersey. She stayed at a base guest house and visited me for most of every day.

Mom dreaded the debridement sessions as much as I did.

My first one prompted a rather shocking revelation. A corpsman rolled a gurney next to my bed and said he would be taking me to the tub. Tim performed my debridement in a large tub of warm water, which apparently made it easier to remove the dead skin. This was particularly true of all serious cases, and because I had suffered burns over about 35 percent of my body I qualified as a serious case—lucky me.

The corpsman lifted me easily and put me on the gurney. I still could not see much so I said, "You must be a pretty big man."

"What makes you say that?" he asked.

"You picked me up like I was a little doll."

"Well fella, you only weigh 98 pounds."

I was dumbfounded. I had weighed 165 pounds at the time of the crash just a couple of weeks earlier. How could that be?

"Is that true, Mom?" I asked, as she sat beside me.

"Yes, it is, and now that you are better we just have to get you to eat a lot."

"Don't worry about that," I told her.

I could hardly believe I had lost so much weight so quickly. No wonder my parents had been shocked when they first saw me. I resolved then and there to regain my weight and strength as quickly as possible.

The corpsman wheeled me off, picked me up again, and lowered me into the debriding tub. The warm water felt good.

Tim arrived after I had been soaking for about 10 minutes. He explained what had to be done and why. Then he started the debridement, using a pair of tweezers to pull off small bits of the dead and charred skin. But the paste on my burns wouldn't budge, even after the soaking. It seemed to stick tenaciously. Instead of picking, Tim tried pulling it off. It hurt, and I told him that it hurt.

Now Tim was torn. He knew I was suffering but he also knew it was imperative to remove the burned skin. He ordered a pain shot for me and the corpsman lifted me out of the tub enough so Tim could deliver the shot into my butt—because my arms were burned and very thin. It helped but only until he started pulling off dead skin again. Nasty pain!

"It isn't working. It still hurts," I told him.

"But I gave you a painkiller," he said.

"What I'm telling you, Doctor, is that it still hurts."

"I'm sorry," he said. "I'll try to be careful."

Though he felt frustrated he had to continue. In all, Tim performed seven or eight debridement sessions and each one seemed to last forever.

As the premier burn treatment facility in the world Brooke welcomed on any given day a steady stream of visiting medical personnel and doctors interested in learning about the treatments the staff employed. Many of the visitors were from abroad.

One afternoon, awaiting another debridement, I was resting in bed and chatting with Mom when a couple of foreign doctors entered the ward accompanied by Tim and a few colleagues. He briefly summarized my situation.

One of the visiting doctors, an Ethiopian, said, "Oh, I see you use the same thing for bad burns that is sometimes used in Africa."

"Pardon me?" Tim responded.

"I mean the black substance on his burns," the Ethiopian said.

"Do you know what it is?" Tim asked.

"Not really. It's used mainly in rural areas. It's a tribal remedy that has been handed down for years and years—maybe centuries."

"Do you know what's in it?"

"No idea. I've heard that part of it comes from a boiled snake."

At least that was a lead. Tim told the Ethiopian that doctors at the Burn Center credited it with saving my life by preventing infection and dehydration. He thanked the doctor for the piece of the puzzle he had provided even though the makeup of the substance remained a mystery.

Several months later the Air Force dispatched two doctors to the Congo to investigate my strange poultice. They obtained some samples. Apparently the paste did include snake fat, as well as tree bark and some herbs that could not be identified.

Whatever the stuff was it had done wonders for me.

We would labor through several more debridement sessions before Tim announced that he had finished. It goes without saying I felt relieved; I could relax a bit. Tim likewise felt relief because the burns looked so clean—no infection at all, a clear indication that the witch doctor's potion had done its job.

Next step: skin grafts.

My first wasn't all that much fun, either. For one thing nobody had really explained to me what the procedure involved. Probably just as well.

They rolled my gurney into the operating room at about 7 a.m., and for five or 10 minutes I just lay there waiting for whatever was next. I felt apprehensive and still couldn't see but I was listening carefully, and I could sense activity in the room.

I heard several people chatting and I was appalled that they were talking about a picnic the previous day.

What the hell is this? Who cares about the bloody picnic? This is going to be a delicate operation. Who's in charge here anyway?

They must have thought I had already been given a sedative and was in la-la land but I couldn't refrain from speaking.

"If the picnic talk is finished are we gonna get serious about this operation?"

No one responded and someone put a rubber mask over my mouth and nose. The anesthetic flowed in—awful stuff—and after a couple of breaths I was out. Later I learned that operating room personnel often relieve tension by engaging in seemingly inane chatter. Apparently what I had heard was not unusual.

I woke to find myself in intensive care again. I felt groggy and somehow my chest felt constrained. I tried to assess what had happened but I couldn't figure it out. When I started to sit up a nurse gently restrained me and asked me to relax. I did until my head cleared and I could urinate.

Then three corpsmen wheeled me back to the ward, where Mom was waiting. She tried to conceal it but I could sense the distress in her demeanor. The corpsmen very carefully moved me from the gurney into my bed. They kept me flat for a reason that soon became obvious.

When Tim arrived he explained that he had taken skin from my upper torso, which had been untouched by the flaming gasoline. He then grafted it onto my burned areas. He had bandaged the grafts and covered the donor sites, as he called them, with a gauze-like material. Blood was seeping through it and I literally was a bloody mess. No wonder Mom was shocked.

Everything had gone well, Tim said, but I would be experiencing some discomfort. He was right on both counts especially the second. "Discomfort" meant real pain.

As the anesthetic wore off, my chest hurt a lot. When the bleeding stopped and the drying started I felt pain when I tried to move. For several days I tried like hell to avoid deep breaths, sneezes, coughs and laughter. Then the pain eased as the donor site dried up and the gauze fell off.

An unpleasant ordeal but it was all for a good cause. Without the skin from my chest Tim would not have been able to graft my burns.

Not long after my arrival at Brooke a psychiatrist visited me and I immediately knew why. The nightmares I had experienced in the Congo were continuing. Every night, and sometimes two or three times a night, I was chased by the same spear-carrying African who jabbed at me while I passed by him in the roller coaster.

Now in my dream I was able to run but only fast enough to avoid being killed. He stabbed at me, often repeatedly, and I just couldn't get away. I would groan—making awful sounds, I was told—and shout and thrash around in my bed. A nurse, a corpsman, sometimes both and sometimes Mom, would attempt to calm me. My sleeping was fitful at best and the nurses dutifully recorded the incidents. A few times I even dreaded going to sleep.

I knew perfectly well that these ugly visions were the result of my trauma. Still they seemed real and were causing me much distress. They also weren't helping my healing process. Mom, who had witnessed a couple of these scenes, became very concerned.

I tried to describe the nightmare to the psychiatrist as best I could, roller-coaster ride and all. He listened carefully, as did Mom, who grew frightened at what I had been enduring. I had been close to death, we agreed.

Then it was the doctor's turn. He explained that I had been feeling quite insecure.

No shit!

He went on. These were just dreams and their frequency would gradually lessen. One day they would stop.

The sooner the better.

He was right. As I got stronger, and the interval between operations lengthened, the nightmares grew less and less frequent.

About three years later I finally fought it out with the spear-carrying man. I was married, living in Hong Kong, and still periodically experiencing the nightmares, during which I would shout and roll around until my wife awakened me. I explained what the psychiatrist at Brooke had told me and she understood; it bothered her nonetheless.

Then one night in my dream the man came for me again—but this time I had a pistol. When I saw him I fired. He was far away but I saw him fall. It was over. The nightmares ended.

I stayed at Brooke until early May, during which time I had lots of visitors. The agency wanted to help me work through the ordeal so headquarters sent at least one person per week to San Antonio to visit me. It provided a link to reality. I enjoyed all of the visits immensely; they took my mind off the rehab sessions.

My old JOT buddy Ward Warren showed up and chided me about messing up the intramural basketball team we had talked about forming.

"Now you've done it," he joked. "How are we going to get our team organized?"

Ward had played college ball at the University of Michigan and we had considered ourselves the nucleus of a formidable group.

David G., a real hero to be sure, considering all that he had suffered while a hostage of the Simbas, visited and brought me up to date on events in the Congo—the Simba revolt had been all but crushed. Like all the others David voiced his distress at my condition.

My brother Bob visited, too. Back when I was healthy we used to arm-wrestle and he joked that we should continue the practice so he challenged me. Mom protested. We laughed and I begged off saying I wasn't ready yet.

The truth was that I couldn't even hold a pencil at the time and was still being fed. My hands were incredibly weak. But Bob's visit proved beneficial in a different way. For about 10 days the Brooke staff had been helping me to exercise my legs in the rehab pool. Now they wanted me to start walking again and Bob could help me try.

A corpsman carefully wrapped my legs in ACE bandages to protect my veins from rupturing. Then he helped me to my feet and Bob took over. I held his arm and he guided me around obstacles and corners.

He helped me for a couple of days. We marched up and down the hall for as long as I could stand it. The walks soon became a daily ritual as I struggled to regain my strength.

Dad returned for a visit along with an aunt and uncle from Houston, and his mother. After I told her the whole story she said, "I've always known that Vikings are tough, but this proves it."

My grandmother had married my grandfather in 1910 in Chicago. Both of them were Swedish immigrants. My grandfather had left Ljungby, in central Sweden, and sailed to the United States in June 1898. He was tough. A tailor's apprentice in Stockholm, he started his own tailoring business in Chicago. My grandparents spoke Swedish to each other and my grandfather made it clear to me that the Vikings—not Columbus—had discovered our country.

I said as much to my fourth-grade teacher, who was gracious and understanding when I explained that she'd gotten it all wrong.

Like a saint, Mom spent from early March until early May at Brooke with me. She became well known and very popular in the Burn Center. Whenever I was sleeping, receiving treatment, or having surgery, she would help other patients. Kind and sensitive, she was a godsend to many—as she was to me.

I worried about her neglecting Dad and my siblings but she wouldn't leave. "When you get better" was always her response.

When would that be?

I knew it had been a close call but at the time I couldn't believe or accept that I'd be staying in the hospital more than a couple of months. I was eager to get done with this problem but decided it was best to take things a day at a time.

After many, many days I learned the wisdom of that approach.

One morning, sitting next to my bed as usual, my mother gasped. That was not like her.

"What's wrong, Mom?"

"We got a bill."

"What for?"

"Twenty-three thousand, four-hundred dollars!"

"What's the bill for?"

She could hardly speak.

"We'll be in debt for the rest of our lives!"

No doubt. In 1965, for just about any working family, that was a lot of money. It turned out that the United States Air Force had billed me for the cost of my transport from the Congo to Texas. Actually it was for the whole trip made by the 707, from McGuire Air Force Base in New Jersey to Leopoldville to Texas and back to McGuire.

At several hundred dollars per hour—I can't remember the exact figure—I owed the Air Force the grand total of $23,400. I couldn't help laughing; Mom didn't find it funny at all.

The problem was that the rescue mission had been so unusual. The Air Force administrative staff knew only that the Secretary of Defense had ordered a plane to Africa to get me. But very few people knew that the CIA was involved or that I was a CIA officer. My arrival had been shrouded in secrecy and unanswered questions.

"James Bond has been hurt," the hospital staff joked.

When the bookkeepers had processed the paperwork the only name they had for the bill was mine so they sent it to me. In their own way they were being perfectly logical.

Mom wanted to know what to do. I told her to call the agency's representative in San Antonio and he would forward the bill to headquarters. That's what she did and I never heard anything more about it.

You might ask how many countries in the world possessed, or would so willingly expend, the resources needed to make such a flight to rescue one wounded junior officer.

The answer: one.

My two months at the Burn Center stabilized my condition and completed the initial grafting of my burns but much remained to be done. Tim and I talked it over and decided that I should be transferred to Walter Reed

Army Hospital in Washington for reconstructive surgery.

With that decision Mom reluctantly left me and returned to New Jersey and the family. I knew I would still see her often—Walter Reed was only a four-hour drive away.

It might seem odd but to this day I remain ambivalent about the Burn Center. On the one hand the people there clearly saved my life and started me on the road to recovery. On the other hand I could never see it in my mind once I had left and was unable to develop any real feelings toward the place. My ward, the debridement tubs, the hallways I trudged up and down, all remain vague memories. There is no sharpness to them and I have never been back there.

My one strong connection with Brooke is Tim Miller. We developed a close friendship for reasons not entirely clear to either of us. We shared some commonalities, such as loving sports our whole lives, and of course he saved my life. But there is something else. I can't really articulate it but it has lasted. To this day I know I can count on him and I'm sure he feels the same way.

He now lives in Los Angeles, where he has worked since the early 1970s. He is chief of plastic and reconstructive surgery at UCLA Medical Center. Until recently our contacts were infrequent, but that never diminished the bond—it's still there.

12. Three Dozen Times

WALTER REED ARMY HOSPITAL 1965

Still blind as a bat I left Brooke and the SRU in late May, three months after my arrival. The trip to Walter Reed was tedious. I was in no pain but most of the time I had no one to talk to.

They loaded me into an ambulance and drove me to the airport. They loaded me onto the plane, a military transport, where I lay by myself for hours. Then they unloaded me from the plane and drove me to the hospital. Located at the corner of Alaska Avenue and 16th Street Northwest the complex is near the northernmost point of the District of Columbia.

I had made my farewells at Brooke, except for Tim, who was on TDY somewhere, so I didn't get to thank him or say goodbye. That would come later.

I arrived at my destination, Ward 9, wheeled by two corpsmen to the nurses' station.

"Patient from Brooke in Texas."

"Yep, we've been expecting him," I heard one of them reply. "Just follow me."

My ears also detected that unlike the ward at the burn center this one was quiet. And despite the ward designation they placed me in a private room normally reserved for military brass. After the corpsmen settled me into the bed the nurse showed me where to find the call button. She instructed me use it anytime I needed to go to the toilet and not to try to get up by myself.

A private room! The agency must have worked its magic again.

Thus began what medical professionals call the reconstruction period.

Mom, Dad, Diann and Greg drove down from New Jersey to visit me that first weekend. My siblings had not seen me at Brooke so they were shocked. I could sense that Greg in particular was distressed.

Because it was a nice day they got permission to take me for a walk in the small park just across the street. As usual I had to be led and Mom and Dad asked Greg to help me. He held my arm, just like Bob had done back at Brooke, but because he had never done this sort of thing it wasn't long before I fell. Nothing serious and I didn't get hurt, only a couple of scratches, but now Greg felt even worse. Though I sympathized with his distress there wasn't much I could do or say.

Waiting for time to pass was my biggest frustration. I felt sidetracked. I wanted very much to recover as quickly as possible yet I was still in denial about how serious my injuries were. In fact I never did accept how badly I had been hurt and how much time it was going to take to get better.

I continually assured myself that soon I'd be out of the hospital and back to work. No one ever disabused me of that thought.

I tried to make a bit of progress each day so recovery would be that much nearer. I don't know whether that approach shortened my hospitalization but it did help me through some tough periods.

"So you crashed a plane in the Congo," said Dr. Michael Duffy, my reconstructive surgeon, as he examined each of my hands carefully.

"That's right. I don't recommend it," I responded.

"I can't imagine that you would. How much can you see?"

"Not much—just light versus dark."

"That's got to be a bitch but it won't slow us down," he said bullishly. "We need to get your hands in shape and a few other things need fixing, too."

"Will I ever have a jump shot again?"

I was halfway serious.

"That I don't know but I doubt you'll be a concert pianist when we get finished."

His remark caught just the right tone. He knew what I was trying to ask, obliquely.

What are my prospects?

"I am going to do a series of operations, I don't know now just how many. We'll start Monday morning and schedule subsequent operations as often as seems feasible."

"What makes them feasible?" I asked. "No sense in dragging this out."

"We need to have skin donor sites heal and you feeling okay."

"The faster we go the better I'll feel."

"I understand," he said quietly.

Duffy told me that in the first operation he would remove scar tissue from the webs of my fingers. He explained that Tim Miller had done the initial grafting to place skin over all of the open burn wounds. The grafts had prevented dehydration and infection but my hands didn't look normal. Now it would be Duffy's job to make my fingers look like fingers again and the process started with an operation to begin removing the scar tissue.

Many more would follow. Counting big and small, local anesthesia and general, the Walter Reed doctors operated on me some three dozen times.

I was first on the day's list. I always liked that because I wouldn't have to lie around all morning waiting. It was the same routine as at Brooke. First they wheeled me into a waiting room outside the OR. There the anesthesiologist would stop by to ask a few routine questions. The anesthetist would either give me a shot or infuse my IV with something to relax me. Then they'd wheel me in.

Sometimes I'd hear Dr. Duffy talking, sometimes not. Early on they put me out with a mask and ether, which I never liked. Later they used an IV and at the appointed time injected Sodium Pentothal, also known as the truth drug, which as an anesthetic can knock you out in the middle of a word.

As usual I woke up in the post-op room. The nurse checked my vital signs every quarter hour or so and I had to remain there until everything seemed normal and I could urinate.

I really don't know why but I always felt anxious to get out of recovery and back to my room. Soon I figured out the system. I would concentrate on becoming lucid enough to ask for the urine bottle. As soon as I peed they wheeled me out. I endured enough repetitions that it became automatic.

After the first operation I quickly realized something was unusual. It took me a moment to figure it out. My right arm was suspended from a mobile pole next to the bed, my right hand encased in a great ball of bandage. Nothing hurt because I was still groggy from the anesthesia. The pain would come later. I felt awkward lying in bed with one arm suspended but there was no choice. My arm had to remain raised at all times to keep blood pressure low on the hand.

By the time they returned me to the room it was just about lunch but I didn't feel like eating. The nurse tried to arrange some pillows to make me comfortable though with my arm still hanging from the pole it wasn't easy.

Then came the pain, gradually at first but then in a rush. My hand started hurting—a lot.

Despite my wife's insistence to the contrary I have always possessed a fairly high tolerance for pain. But that agonizing pain exceeded every threshold, so much that I pushed the button for the nurse, who arrived promptly.

"Problem, Mr. Holm?"

"My hand hurts like hell!"

"Yeah, hand surgery is rough. I can give you a shot for the pain if you like."

"Sooner the better; it's actually throbbing."

She left the room and returned within a couple of minutes.

"Okay, it'll be in the left hip," she instructed.

I rolled onto my side and she stuck me with the painkiller.

"Many thanks," I said. "How long does it take?"

"You'll feel better real soon."

I did. The throbbing subsided within about 10 minutes and I drifted off to sleep.

I learned that hand surgery hurts a great deal. To put it bluntly it's the pits. Because of the density of nerves in the hands the sensation of pain is amplified and intense. Unfortunately I would relive this scenario with one hand or the other for the next two years.

Within a couple of hours the pain was back. I tried to ignore it for a while after I was fully awake but that didn't work for long. I buzzed for the nurse again.

"Are you okay?"

"No, my hand is hurting again."

Then the bad news.

"I'm sorry, the pain shots are prescribed for every four hours, and it's only been three and half."

I was perplexed and I didn't understand.

"But my hand hurts now!"

"I'm sorry, that's what the doctor ordered. I'll be back in half an hour—promise!"

She walked out of the room.

It was hospital policy—silly but unchangeable. Nowadays they supply self-administered dispensers to patients with pain issues. A few pushes on a button and relief trickles down the IV tube and into your bloodstream. But back in 1965 this became a continuing problem for me, especially in the first couple of days after surgery.

I waited for what seemed a very long time and pushed the buzzer again. There was an intercom system so sometimes the nurses would just respond over the speaker.

"My hand is still hurting. Is it time yet?"

"Fifteen more minutes, Mr. Holm, I'll be in as soon as I can."

It was enormously frustrating but they wouldn't budge, so I lived with it—day and night as it turned out.

During the day three or four nurses and several corpsmen staffed Ward 9 but in the evening and overnight only one nurse worked each of those shifts. From 4 p.m. to midnight it was Mrs. Lee, a delightful, petite Chinese woman from Georgia. From midnight to 8 a.m. it was Mrs.

Moore, an older and very experienced nurse who was always cheerful and sympathetic. Both were civilians and highly competent.

The night of that first hand operation every painkilling shot would eventually wear off but neither woman breached the four-hour policy.

In all I spent about 48 hours getting those shots at four-hour intervals. It took that long for the pain to subside. By then my backside had gotten sore, too, but I never complained about it.

After that I could start going five or six hours between shots and gradually that period lengthened until I could stop taking the syringes altogether. I had a lingering fear of addiction and always tried to err on the side of avoiding medication as soon as I could handle it. Usually that would be around the third or fourth day.

Those periods also gave me trouble sleeping. I would doze off after a shot though only for a couple of hours because the pain would return to awaken me.

The arm-hanging-from-the pole bit was almost as tedious. You can only lie in a few positions with your arm suspended off the side of the bed. I tried them all and never found a comfortable one.

Then there was the ever-present donor site, the location on my body—in this case the left thigh—from which Dr. Duffy had elected to remove a piece of my skin to graft onto one of my burned areas.

After every graft the donor site would be raw and bloody. It was as if someone had just ripped off a chunk of my skin. Actually that's what they did but in a sophisticated way, using a device that resembled an electric razor.

I knew Dr. Duffy had a plan for taking skin from a particular spot but I never figured it out and I never asked him about it. Whatever the reason it always seemed to be the spot my visitors would invariably touch the moment they walked into my room. It may have been unwitting but it hurt like hell just the same.

To help the site heal the nurses set up an electric lamp with an extendible, flexible neck next to my bed. It warmed the donor site continuously until the skin dried up and stopped oozing and the gauze covering it would fall off. That usually took about four days unless it was a particularly large site.

I had trouble sleeping through the lamp sessions, too.

During the post-op periods just getting out of bed to go to the toilet was an ordeal. Getting me there required a corpsman and sometimes the nurse would change the bed while I was in the bathroom. I always did it, though, because I hated using a bedpan.

The nurses and corpsmen were wonderfully sympathetic and helpful but it was always a relief when they could take down my bandage bundle and just lay it on a pillow next to me.

It took me nearly five days to recover from that first operation, after which I experienced my first physical therapy session. The Walter Reed facility seemed impressive indeed. I couldn't actually see it but I sensed it was large and full of activity.

Dr. Duffy prescribed work for the therapy staff to perform on me every day: push and pull on my fingers, for example, or straighten my left elbow, which had ended up in a bent position. The therapists were great and they carefully explained what they were doing and why. I learned a lot about hands during my time with them.

Boiled down, I had to gain mobility in all of my finger joints and wrists, including more rotation and extension of my stiff left elbow.

Early on they just did the best they could, considering the restrictions caused by the graft and donor sites and the scarring. My hands were a royal mess and to this day I have major limitations in manual dexterity. But I still have my hands and for that I thank my unknown African witch doctor.

The therapists did a lot of basic work on my left elbow. I hadn't needed an operation at first although I had one later on to remove heavy scar tissue. It turned out I had caused much of the problem myself.

I had spent all of the time in Texas trying to protect my hands, which hurt anytime I bumped something. As a result I tended to keep my arms resting across my chest. This was particularly true of the left arm, which hurt more, and I did this even when I started to walk.

During that time, the therapists told me, calcium deposits had developed on the elbow joint. To treat the problem they would simply grab my left arm at the wrist and pull to straighten it. They explained that little by little the deposits would break up and in time I would regain the elbow's full range of motion.

Fine, but this turned out to be an exceedingly unpleasant activity. It took the therapists about six months of pulling and ultimately an operation on the scar tissue to restore the nearly complete flexibility I have today.

Despite the discomfort I quickly concluded that one daily therapy session wasn't enough. So I proposed two a day to speed up the whole process and get me out faster.

Dr. Duffy agreed. Despite the pain and soreness that followed those sessions I looked forward to them for the progress I felt I was making.

I never failed to thank the therapists for what they did each time. I developed close relationships with several of them and admired their dedication. They readily agreed to work with me twice a day and they complied with my requests for strength-building exercises.

I also started doing sit-ups, leg exercises and stretching. The effort paid off. Within a year the therapy had restored my weight and general strength to what they were before the crash.

With the hand operations proceeding I asked Dr. Duffy for an update on my eye. He fully understood my concerns and told me I would soon be meeting the head of Walter Reed's eye clinic. I learned later that one of the reasons the doctors at Brooke had selected Walter Reed for me was the strength and reputation of their ophthalmology department.

When I met with Colonel Jack Passmore, the head of the clinic and a noted ophthalmologist, he assured me he had been following my case ever since I had arrived. He said he understood my concerns and was confident that an operation would restore my sight. Then Dr. Passmore and a colleague carefully examined my right eye using a variety of machines and instruments, all of which were new to me.

"There is less trauma," he told me, "but it is certainly too soon to consider the transplant."

"How long might it be?" I persisted.

"I don't really know. It is not something we will want to rush. You'll just have to be patient and trust me. I know it's difficult."

A corpsman led me back to my room. I decided that I liked Dr. Passmore and was impressed with how well he had familiarized himself with my case. But I also resigned myself to the fact that I couldn't influence the healing process. When the trauma in my eye was gone the corneal transplant could go ahead—not before.

My transfer to Walter Reed produced a parade of visits by friends and colleagues that gratified me immensely. It never stopped. The nurses and staff on Ward 9 could hardly believe it. Rarely did an evening—and virtually never a weekend—go by when I didn't have a visitor and often several. It continued for the entire two years I spent there. It would be impossible to overstate how much it did for my morale.

Dede, one of the young women at the agency I had been dating before I went to the Congo, visited me several times a week. Pretty, sensitive and shy, she was very supportive and faithful. She lived in Georgetown so the bus ride sometimes took an hour to get to Walter Reed.

Over the first few months, some of the other girls I had dated dropped in on me as well. Sometimes they'd show up when Dede was there but she was never deterred; nor were they.

Mrs. Lee, the evening nurse, used to tease me after my female visitors had left. I told her they were just being nice and I appreciated it. Personally I had mixed feelings. I was flattered at the attention but embarrassed at the awkwardness that sometimes passed between Dede and the others.

Peter Connell, an agency colleague who later became general counsel for a large insurance company, visited often with his wife Ann. Both were wonderful to me. Ann, a charming, cheerful, understanding and altogether special person, was particularly kind. She regularly read to me from magazines or newspapers for an hour or so. I will always be grateful to her for the sense of inclusion I felt in being able to follow current events. Her generous gift of time meant a lot.

Starting with my first month at Walter Reed I could also regularly count on a Sunday morning visit from Ray Barkley, whom I had first met in Laos where he worked as a case officer in the Vientiane office. Back then I didn't get to see much of him because he worked in the capital city and I worked upcountry. But I liked him and we became friends. Still I didn't expect the thoughtfulness he displayed during my sightless year.

Barring an out-of-town trip Ray would show up after breakfast with the Sunday editions of *The New York Times* and *The Washington Post* under his arm. Over the next hour or two he would read me selected articles from the papers. We had similar tastes so he always spotted items of particular interest.

Ray also passed on bits of information from the office about what was going on in Southeast Asia. In that way his visits helped keep me abreast of things, allowing me to feel involved, albeit from a distance.

I don't know how someone could be so consistently generous with his time but I still feel grateful to Ray for those many hours he spent with me.

Because of my close friendship with Mike Deuel, I had met and enjoyed the company of his parents, Wally and Mary, back during my JOT days. Wally, whose lectures I had admired, was even more articulate and entertaining in an informal setting. Along with Mike and a couple of the other trainees I had dined with Wally and Mary at their home. They were most gracious. Wally would relate stories about their life in Beirut, Rome, Berlin or elsewhere. Mary, no doubt having heard the stories countless times, interjected pertinent comments—probably her way of keeping Wally on track.

When Wally learned I had been transferred to Walter Reed he promptly called and asked if he could see me. He turned out to be a great visitor. He made me forget my problems. Full of enthusiasm he related tale after tale and spoke glowingly of what we would do after I healed. He also brought news about Mike, who had returned to Laos.

Before we both left Laos in the summer of 1964 Mike had been dating a young woman—to the extent such activities were possible given our jobs upcountry—who worked in Bangkok. Judy Dougherty was pretty, talented and vivacious. They had gotten married in late October and had moved to Pakse, in the far southwestern part of the panhandle. Mike was running a major agency effort out of there aimed at disrupting traffic on the Ho Chi Minh Trail.

By the fall of 1965 Mike Duffy and I had developed a very friendly relationship. Of Irish descent, he had been born in Boston during the Great Depression, and he made it through medical school after a long, tough climb out of poverty.

Mike would tell me how the family would eat lobster night after night while he would crave a hamburger. During the Depression, lobster in Boston was plentiful and cheap. Indeed it was standard fare for servants, who complained about getting too much of it. Imagine that.

One day just before another operation he asked me a question.

"Really, overall, Dick, how are things going?"

I could sense he sincerely wanted to know.

"I'm hanging in there, Mike. I don't need a shrink if that's what you mean."

"I know that for sure," he replied. "Just wanted to give you a chance to voice your thoughts."

I considered the possibilities.

"Well, I wouldn't mind having a martini once in a while," I said, half-jokingly.

He was quiet for a moment.

"Why not? Why not indeed! I think it would be good for you psychologically."

He was speaking in a mock professional tone now.

"I'll prescribe it so the nurses won't rebel. But you'll have to get the booze."

"It's a deal," I responded, pleased that I'd raised the idea in the first place. "Mrs. Lee will be no problem, but Major Axeman will probably be appalled."

"Not to worry," Mike assured me. "I'll take care of everything."

At that time Major Axeman was head nurse on Ward 9. I never knew her first name, nor did I ever get to see her before she transferred out of Walter Reed prior to my eye operation. But I harbored a vivid mental image of her: a career army nurse who had served in combat zones. A strong woman both mentally and physically she probably pulled her hair back tightly into a bun. I figured she didn't smile much but maintained a facial expression as though she had just eaten something sour.

Actually I found her to be a nice enough person, just hopelessly uptight, rule-bound and fastidious. Even so, my unusual status as a civilian—and a junior one, although she didn't know that—in the VIP senior officers' ward caused her to treat me with care. As a result we got along fine—until she found out that I was being permitted to consume alcohol on her ward.

"And just what is that in your closet, Mr. Holm?" she asked accusingly one day.

"I can't really see, Major, but you must be talking about the half-gallon bottles of gin, vermouth, scotch and bourbon on the shelf."

She knew what the bottles were. She just wanted to make it clear that she wasn't pleased about it.

"Yes, I am talking about those bottles. I certainly hope you are happy."

"Well, it does help me relax after a stressful day lying here in bed."

No response. I don't know if she was glaring at me or not but she left.

The martini idea had been the brainstorm of Charlie Whitehurst, my former chief in Vientiane. He had been promoted to chief of China operations within Far East Division and had transferred back to headquarters. He was responsible for our worldwide effort aimed at collecting intelligence about China.

Whitey visited me one evening in late summer carrying a small sack. We chatted for a while about what had happened in Laos after I left, and about what was happening with mutual friends. Then he asked if I would like to have a martini.

"Sure would, but this place doesn't have a bar."

"I was afraid of that," he said; "so I brought my own."

I heard him reach into the sack, unscrew a lid, and pour liquid into two glasses—martinis for each of us! Mine tasted great.

Whitey asked what I planned to do when I got back to work. I told him I didn't really know, except that it would be as far away from Africa as I could get.

"Come to Far East Division," he urged me. "You have a lot of friends there. Think about China Operations. It's a first-class effort."

His offer pleased me and I promised I would think about it seriously.

In fact I did and a couple of months later Whitey arranged to send a tutor twice a week to get me started learning Mandarin, preparing me for a new position as soon as I could leave Walter Reed.

Cocktail time became a ritual. Friends would bring bottles—people were always asking me if I wanted anything—and I was pleased to share. Major Axeman was gone in the evenings and Mrs. Lee was most understanding.

"What do you want, some ice?" she would ask over the intercom when I buzzed her and she knew I had visitors.

It just evolved. Almost every evening my guests and I enjoyed martinis—on the rocks thanks to Mrs. Lee—or a bourbon and water or scotch and water. It was a small thing but it really helped dim the fact that we were in a hospital. Although recovering, I was still badly hurt. I looked forward to those evening visits and they greatly boosted my spirits.

Other routines developed during those months. Mike Duffy decided to give first priority to my hands. Early on he had told me, "The more they look like hands the better they will function so that's our goal."

He set the pattern: hand operation, painful recovery period, physical therapy, a brief respite—as brief as possible, because I constantly pushed him to get on with it—followed by another hand operation.

The model persisted for much of that first year and the visitors kept coming and coming. My parents visited at least monthly and Dad showed up even more often if he had a business trip to Washington.

Even though there was no end in sight I tried not to dwell on that thought.

My hands presented the physical therapists with a real challenge: how best to strengthen each tendon and gain flexibility in each joint and how to avoid damaging the newly grafted skin.

An added complication: the damage to the tendons in my hands caused by whoever had cleaned the bugs off of them in the Congo village. That damage, coupled with the heavier scarring, had impaired the ability of the extensor tendons to lift my fingers. My ability to pull my fingers down and grip something, albeit weakly, was far greater than my ability to lift them up and spread them out.

Working closely with Mike, who recognized the problem and wanted to solve it, the physical therapists fashioned a device, literally, from a coat hanger that would strengthen my extensor tendons.

He built a partial cast on my arm between the wrist and elbow. The bent coat hanger protruded from the end of the cast and loomed out over my hand. Then he attached strong rubber bands to leather loops that he hooked onto each finger. The idea was that I would strengthen my tendons by pulling on the leather loops.

It worked. When I had it on my hand looked almost normal and I was pleased with the whole idea. On the other side of the coin, after about half an hour it hurt like hell. Nevertheless I wore it almost constantly for the rest of my time at Walter Reed, encouraged—and sometimes ordered—by Mike and the physical therapists.

I knew they were right. The contraption did my hands a lot of good. I never got to the point where I could handle a diaper pin but I can still hold a tennis racket.

Dede arrived one evening in mid-October and I could sense right away that something was wrong. After a few amenities she said she had to tell me something.

"Mike Deuel crashed in a helicopter," she blurted.

She knew that Mike and I were close friends.

"Was he hurt?"

I couldn't see her face but I knew she was very upset.

"He died in the crash," she said softly. "Oh Dick, I'm so sorry."

I couldn't believe it. I was shocked and couldn't speak. Lots of thoughts immediately flooded my mind.

It's not fair! Why him? Why Mike? We always seem to lose our best men.

I remembered our time together in training and in Laos. It hit me very hard.

"Are you, sure?" I was finally able to say.

"Yes, it's confirmed. I don't know any details."

"What about his wife?"

"She's on her way home."

Judy, who was three months pregnant, had left Pakse immediately and returned via Bangkok to her home in the little village of Bulpitt, Illinois. Her tragedy was compounded because her father was terminally ill. He died in January 1966, just three months after she arrived. It took great inner strength for her to cope.

I wanted to call Wally and Mary but at that moment I didn't know what to say. I decided to wait until the next day. I tried to talk for a while to Dede but I couldn't concentrate on anything except the awful news she had just brought me. She understood and left.

I lay there for along time. Ultimately I fell asleep.

When I called Wally I could tell he was deeply wounded. Mary wouldn't, or couldn't, talk to anyone. Judy, accompanied by her two sisters and brother, traveled to Washington for the funeral and showed much courage in the face of a terrible ordeal.

Mike was buried at Arlington National Cemetery with full military honors in accordance with his status as a Marine Corps officer. A friend drove me to the cemetery so I could attend the ceremony along with many of our agency colleagues.

Late that fall, fearful of what was still an unknown future, and worried that Dede was too committed while I could make no commitment at all, I told her to stop coming to see me and to get on with her life. It was a difficult conversation. She cried but she ultimately agreed it would be best to break off our relationship.

In December the hospital asked me to speak to some of the other patients about their injuries. By that time I had become fairly well known at Walter Reed because of my lengthy tenure and because of my attitude: Deal with the problem and get on with the healing process.

Everyone knew I was in a rush to recover and they thought I might be able to help patients who weren't coping well. I agreed but wasn't sure what I was supposed to do.

Someone led me into a lounge attached to an enlisted man's ward and sat me down near a young soldier just back from Vietnam. I had met some returning Vietnam veterans back at Brooke and I was familiar with the war in Southeast Asia so there was an initial rapport. As we talked, though, it became clear this young man was despondent and lacked any will to fight for his recovery. We talked more and I asked him what wounds he had suffered.

"I lost my left foot on a land mine."

"And?"

"That's all."

"That's all?" I echoed. "So what the hell is your problem?"

My question took him by surprise and set the scene for the rest of our conversation. I was blunt, and because he could see that I was blind, my face was scarred, one of my hands was encased in a giant bandage, and the other was a mess, he sat there and took it.

My message: Things could be worse, fella.

"You just gonna give up on life?" I asked him. "Don't be stupid. This hospital can fix you up in short order and you'll hardly know the difference. Enough with the self-pity just get on with life, which means get the hell out of here."

I believed what I was telling him and that no doubt added to its impact. In truth it was foolish for this young man to sit around feeling sorry for himself when he should have been healing. I made that as clear as I could.

At the hospital's request I talked with patients about a dozen times over the next few months. Often close family or friends sat with them. I knew they agreed with me and loved the direct message I was sending. Often I heard "Right on!" or "Amen, brother!" while I spoke my piece. I was told that it helped. I hope it did.

I visited Dr. Passmore at Ophthalmology monthly so he could monitor progress in my right eye. He scheduled my visits to coincide with a monthly seminar he hosted for Washington area colleagues.

My case always generated lots of interest—not only because of the story about the crash in Africa but also because of the circumstances surrounding my injuries.

In particular they wanted to determine whether the contact lens saved my right eye or caused the loss of sight in it. I cared only about regaining my sight but doctors examining me for the first time seemed always intrigued with that question.

After a while I grew tired of being the subject of their debates though I viewed it as an opportunity to have my eye checked by the best doctors around. Also I sensed that the trauma was lessening because my vision was becoming marginally better.

"That's because the windshield is muddy, so to speak, but the eye is healing well," Dr. Passmore told me in late fall.

"So where do we go from here?" I asked.

"We're ready. We're going to do a partial-thickness corneal graft. It's called a lamellar graft. What we need now is the right donor."

I had been waiting for this day with both elation and fear. From then until after the operation, doubts and hopes almost constantly filled my mind.

I have to see again or I don't know what I'll do.

Christmas 1965 came and went. The operations kept coming and so did my visitors. Mike Duffy scheduled his work to give me some respite over the holidays but my vision and hand problems were ever-present limitations.

My family visited me and we enjoyed the time together. It had been very tough on my mother to see me still immobile but she bore up well. They stayed in my apartment on MacArthur Boulevard, the one I had rented after my return from Laos. I kept it when I went to the Congo, reasoning that I would only be gone for a couple of months.

During my recovery various friends lived there, subletting from me. I even started spending evenings or the odd weekend at the apartment because that's where I would go when my reconstruction period was over.

It would be the shore at the end of a long and difficult voyage.

13. Some Version of James Bond

WALTER REED 1965–1967

One afternoon in December, Dick Helms paid me a visit. At the time he was the agency's deputy director. Senior management had undergone several changes while I had been lounging in hospital beds.

The previous April, just weeks after my crash and while I was still at Brooke, John McCone resigned as director. He had grown deeply frustrated at President Johnson's reluctance to accept the thrust of the agency's negative and pessimistic reporting and analysis about Vietnam. He also resisted the administration's efforts to draw the CIA more deeply into the war effort.

McCone had simply had enough and decided to return to the private sector. He wasn't alone. I was told that many agency people likewise felt frustrated and deeply concerned about the conduct of the war. McCone, an outsider who had not been particularly beloved by the career officers, nonetheless commanded great respect for his intellect and for the way he had handled himself as director. He wasn't Allen Dulles, friends said, but he was a "good guy."

Remembering his decision to call Defense Secretary McNamara and request a plane to drag me out of the Congo, I heartily concurred with that assessment.

The loss of John McCone, a dedicated standard bearer for the agency, was exacerbated when Johnson named fellow Texan William Raborn, a retired naval vice admiral and submarine-launched missile specialist, to replace him. All of this was beyond my ken at the time but comments made by visiting friends conveyed that Raborn wasn't up to the job. A decent but unsophisticated man, they told me, he seemed to lack the intellectual capabilities and presence needed to cope with the demands of his office.

Dick Helms, who had been deputy director for plans, was appointed Raborn's deputy, the number-two spot in the agency. His promotion helped because of the great respect he enjoyed but it didn't save the day. After just over a year it would become painfully clear to all involved that Raborn had to go. In June 1966, in the most polite term I can put it, he re-retired to no one's great surprise. Then to the agency community's considerable delight, Johnson named Helms to replace him.

Helms would face the same problems McCone had been dealing with. Indeed they were worse because Raborn had acceded to every request from the administration, and the agency by then had become much more involved in the Vietnam War effort. But Helms would be able to walk a fine line until Johnson's departure after the 1968 election. Whatever the outcome, at my lowly status in the Directorate of Plans—well below the level at which the brass were dancing—the promotion of one of us to director came as welcome news.

When Helms showed up on Ward 9 to see me, security detail in tow, we chatted for about 15 minutes. He inquired about my condition and about what I planned to do when I got back to work.

I didn't offer him a drink—it seemed inappropriate and at 5 p.m. it was too early. He gave me the impression, and I believe it was accurate, that he cared. His sincerity was apparent. I was impressed, touched even, by the visit. That someone at his level would pay a call on a junior officer like me spoke volumes about his character.

Many other senior officers visited me at Walter Reed and when I mentioned Helms had been there few expressed surprise. "That's the kind of man he is" was the general reaction, a widespread sentiment throughout the agency.

I thought then and still think today that the CIA in general, and the clandestine service, which I know best, in particular, are populated by some of the most outstanding individuals in the whole government.

Helms's visit more or less did away with any remaining bit of cover. The Deputy Director of the Central Intelligence Agency doesn't visit just anybody. Explaining it to the nurses, doctors and staff wasn't easy, but it was a small price to pay and it added to the mystique. They figured I must be some version of James Bond.

What happened next might have confirmed their suspicions. On a Monday morning in early February 1966, Dr. Passmore called me in for an unscheduled meeting. I felt expectant and hopeful. After some brief amenities he gave me the news.

"We've got the right donor cornea. We want to operate late this week. Does that give you any problem?"

Even half expecting it I was taken aback.

At last!

"No problem at all," I responded. "I'm more than ready."

"We should talk about Dr. King," he said, "and I'll want you to meet him before the operation."

"Who is Dr. King?"

I hadn't heard that name before.

"He is the nation's leading surgeon for corneal transplants. Since they realized how important this operation is your agency insisted that we get the best surgeon to do it. Happily, Dr. King practices here in Washington and he agreed to do this operation. I am pleased that I will be his assistant, but he will be in charge."

I tried to digest it all. As it sunk in I felt elated that headquarters had again left no stone unturned in its efforts to help me recover from my injuries and regain my sight.

"Do you know Dr. King?"

"I certainly do," Dr. Passmore responded. "He's tops in our field. I'll be delighted to work with him."

"So all I have to do is show up?"

The joke was all I could muster. My mind was a jumble of emotions and I couldn't put a serious thought together. I think Dr. Passmore understood.

"That's right, Dick. Dr. King and I will take care of the rest."

He scheduled the operation for that Thursday morning. I called my parents and the Deuels but not many other people. Just then I didn't want to deal with well-wishers or questions. I was nervous—scared to death in fact—but trying as hard as I could to be optimistic.

My apprehension grew worse as the week wore on. Mike Duffy must have known it because he stopped by to wish me luck.

"Now you'll be able to see what I've been doing," he laughed.

The nurses on the ward knew it, too. On Wednesday afternoon they moved me to a post-op ward specially fitted for eye patients. Mrs. Lee and Mrs. Moore in particular were kind and optimistic.

I spent several hours just lying in bed thinking about my life—nothing in particular and everything in general: family, sports, girlfriends, my agency training, Laos, the Congo, the day of the crash, the ordeal in the hut.

About 8 p.m., Dr. Passmore visited me accompanied by Dr. King. After introductions Dr. King examined my eye and made positive comments. Then they both sat down by my bedside. Dr. King had read my file carefully, he assured me, and had studied photos of my eye. He asked a few general questions and tried to put me at ease.

Apparently everyone sensed I was nervous. I liked Dr. King, whose full name was John Harry King, Jr., but who went by his middle name.

"This is a two-step effort," he said. "I'll take off half your cornea, the scarred part."

"The muddy windshield," Dr. Passmore interjected.

"That's right," Dr. King continued, "and then replace it with the clear donor cornea. Dr. Passmore confirms what I've just seen. The trauma is completely gone, and your eye is in good condition for this procedure. I'm very optimistic. We're gonna do just fine."

As I took it all in I felt much better.

"What's the second step?" I asked.

"We can never be sure how your eye will react. Often the grafted cornea clears up nicely so that looking through your clear bottom half and clear grafted half your vision will be fine. In that case no need for step two. Sometimes though, the grafted portion doesn't clear up enough to make us happy with the results. In that case this step will have served to prepare your cornea for a full-thickness graft. That would be somewhere down the road."

I listened carefully, trying to understand everything he was saying.

"So in fact we have two shots to put your vision back to normal."

"Does a bad first graft compromise anything for the second step?"

"Not at all, it just gets the cornea ready. We wouldn't want to do a full thickness now with all that scarring."

"We agree completely," Dr. Passmore said, adding that he had scheduled the procedure for first thing the next morning.

The two men stood up and I assumed they were getting ready to leave, but then Dr. King moved closer to me.

"We can do this with a local anesthesia," he said.

"What do you mean?"

I didn't understand at first.

"You can be awake the whole time. We will have your eye anesthetized and will immobilize your head so you can't move it. No problem for us."

I couldn't believe what he was saying.

Stay awake? I'd be afraid to breathe for fear of messing something up. No way!

"Absolutely not," I blurted out. "I want a general anesthesia and I want to be totally out. I'll wake up back here and I want to hear you say the graft looks great."

They both laughed.

"As you wish, Mr. Holm," Dr. Passmore said soothingly. Then he patted my arm.

"I know you are concerned and I have ordered a sleeping pill for you. Don't argue with the nurse, just take it."

Exactly as I had requested I woke up after the operation back in the eye-patient ward. But I awoke slowly, sensing that I was in a different place—

and afraid to open my eyelids. I didn't know what I would see, if anything.

Finally I did and what I saw was muddy, not clear. I wasn't sure what to do so I did nothing. Soon Drs. King and Passmore walked in. I noticed I could distinguish their forms, though the curtains were drawn and the room was dimly lit.

"Everything went just great," Dr. King told me. "I'm really pleased with how the graft fitted in and your eye is fine."

It was precisely what I had wanted to hear and I was greatly relieved.

"It's not clear," I said.

"Don't worry about that," he replied. "It will take time. The graft will get clearer and clearer for about eight weeks. It will be hard for you but progress will be steady. You'll just have to be patient."

"You'll be on this ward for a few days," Dr. Passmore added, "and we'll keep the light level down. You just lie here quietly—no quick movements with your head. Soon we'll send you back to Ward 9."

Later, after Dr. King had departed, Dr. Passmore examined my eye and told me how impressed he had been with the surgeon's skill and knowledge. He might have said part of it to reassure me but I sensed he was sincere, and I felt grateful all over again that the agency had arranged for Dr. King to perform this important operation.

Several weeks passed. I tried to be as patient as I could. Just as Dr. King had predicted, my vision got better almost day by day.

One morning I woke up and could see the ceiling. I was elated. I stared at it for a while, thinking perhaps it might go away.

Soon I could make out things in my room, including people, and if they were close enough the features on their faces. My elation grew. Suddenly I was having a wonderful time and everyone around me helped in my celebration and, in many ways, my liberation.

Even now, so many years later, I still lack the words to convey the sensation of having my sight slowly return. It just amazed me.

My vision improved even more over the next several months. I got to the point where with a contact lens I could see at 20/40 plus. That is, I could read a couple of the letters on the 20/30 line of an eye chart. The doctors explained to me I wasn't ever going to make it back to 20/20 but with the restored vision I could drive, play tennis, ski, and even read. I would have fairly normal vision in my right eye, in other words.

Depth perception gave me fits at first, and it still gives me trouble when I'm playing tennis or skiing, but for the most part I've adjusted.

My life changed a lot for the better after my sight was restored. I really did feel liberated. I could resume many of the day-to-day activities that had been so difficult before the operation. I could eat easily from a plate, choose my clothes, step directly into the bathroom or around the hospital, go outside for walks and, after some months, even watch television.

On the down side I could see how I looked. My face and hands were—and remain—heavily scarred. That was a jolt. I wasn't prepared for what I saw. Mike said the redness and scarring would mitigate over time and he could do a lot more to help in the reconstruction. I had to take his word for it and in any event there was nothing I could do. I decided I wasn't going to worry about how I looked. Good thing, too, because it would have been a heavy burden to carry all these years.

I remained at Walter Reed through that spring, over a year after the crash. The hand operations continued but with a new twist. Now Mike worked on individual fingers. To make sure the grafts healed correctly he immobilized each finger after the operation by inserting a thin metal pin through its core. The most he ever did at one time was three.

As uncomfortable as it sounds it really didn't hurt much. Mike knocked me out when he inserted them and as a bonus of sorts I didn't have to wear that coat-hanger monster while any of my fingers was pinned.

Removing them was a different story. The technique was rather unsophisticated. Mike would take a medical version of a pair of pliers and pull them out. That hurt, a lot—a shock wave.

I had started by taking a local anesthetic before each removal but that always made me feel drowsy or queasy for a couple of hours. Before long I just took a couple of aspirin after he pulled one out. My hands were healing and the discomfort seemed to be lessening, so I reasoned that an instant of pain was better than several hours of grogginess.

Still more operations. My nose needed repair, and with the kind assistance of some cartilage from my left little toe, Mike did the job. My ears had gotten messed up, too, so to rebuild them, which was an extensive process that required two different operations, Mike took cartilage from my rib cage.

I also needed eyebrows, which required a chunk of my scalp. He gave me a local anesthetic for that one. I was awake and alert, and I could hear the good doctor and his assistant talking as they worked. By that time we all had become friends, so they decided to pull my chain a bit.

"You okay, Dick?" Mike asked.

"I'm fine," I answered.

"Okay, Jerry," he said to Dr. Quinn, who was assisting. "Let's get to work. Give me that big knife."

"You gonna use the big one, Mike?"

"Well, we need a lot of scalp."

It was quiet for a while.

"Wipe away all that blood, Jerry; I can't see what I'm cutting."

"I am. I am. Sure is a lot of blood up here."

"Oops, damn!"

"What happened?"

"No problem. It'll make a nice eyebrow."

"Yeah, but we want it to look like the other one, don't we?"

Jerry could barely conceal his amusement.

"It'll be close," Mike said, "but with all that blood it's hard to see. You just keep wiping."

I was smiling because I knew their banter was all for my consumption.

"You guys having a good time?" I asked.

"Don't you worry, Dick, we are," Mike said. "And we'll be finished in just a while, right, Jerry?"

"I can't tell," Jerry persisted, "too much blood."

I ended up with two narrow slits in my scalp. Mike and Jerry stitched one over each eye and *voilà*! I had eyebrows again. Mrs. Lee said she hadn't even noticed that I had none before the operation. The only drawback was they grew just like the hair on my head, requiring me to trim them regularly. Then somewhere along the line they stopped.

Hijinks aside, in all those surgeries there was only one mishap. After about six months of work on my hands Mike concluded that my left little finger wasn't going to make it. It had scarred so badly that he couldn't release the muscles enough to give me the flexibility I needed. That pinky was even hindering his efforts with the rest of my left hand—it had to be removed.

Mike explained how he would amputate the little finger and use a graft to close the wound; nothing particularly unusual. I agreed and he scheduled the operation.

When I awoke in the recovery room I had three problems, only one of which was normal: the big bundle of bandage around my left hand. It wasn't hurting yet but I knew the pain would come.

Then I discovered that my left side was also heavily bandaged and felt strange. Mike had never bandaged one of my donor sites before. Also, I could still feel pain in my left pinky, which caused me to wonder if something had gone wrong. Had they been unable to take it off?

Soon my left hand started hurting more than usual. The nurse assured me it was because of the amputation and she started the four-hour cycle of pain medication. Problem number one resolved.

Late that afternoon Jerry Quinn stopped in. He had screwed up, he admitted, and he wanted to explain and apologize. Must have something to do with my left side, I thought.

"Here's the story, Dick," he said. "I was assisting Dr. Duffy, as you know. He wanted me to get the experience so he had me do much of the work. The amputation went just fine."

"I was going to ask about that," I told him. "My left little finger hurts."

"I'll get to that," he said. "When I was taking skin from the donor site on your left side my hand slipped. The device I was using, like an electric shaver, operates at very high speed and there is not much margin for error. My slip took a large gouge out of your side, for which I am very sorry.

"Mike understood—he wasn't happy, but he understood. I hope you do, too. We got the skin we needed and we repaired your side, but it will hurt for a while and you'll have a scar."

I listened carefully. I knew he was sincere and I appreciated that he had apologized personally.

"So I'm gonna have a scar?"

"Yeah, I'm afraid so."

"Will it blend with all my other ones?"

"It sure will and thanks for understanding. I did get that little finger off. You are experiencing what is called 'ghost pain.' It will last for several months but believe me the little finger is gone."

With my sight restored in one eye and my condition steadily improving, they transferred me out of my private room to a semi-private, also on Ward 9. For the rest of my stay at Walter Reed I usually had a roommate—two of whom were of some note.

One was an old Navy officer who had checked into the hospital to have an aneurysm repaired. I cannot recall his name but I do remember his background.

He had been a young ensign when in 1916 he went ashore near Vera Cruz, Mexico, as part of an American effort intended to capture the Mexican bandit Pancho Villa. I sat spellbound as he related the story. Unfortunately his memory was failing and he didn't get the some of the details straight—such as when, where, how and whether they got him—but I enjoyed the story and admired the courage.

He also told me about his experience in England shortly after the end of World War I. He must have been serving somewhere in Europe and either been assigned or volunteered—probably the latter—to an experimental project somewhere south of London.

The project involved some of the first parachute jumps ever made. He told me he jumped from the basket of a balloon with his parachute over his arm.

I couldn't believe he was serious, recalling my own first jumps with a static line.

He said when he got clear of the basket he would throw the parachute above him like it was a large fishing net. It caught the wind and he landed roughly but safely. He did it several times and got better and better at it.

I was awed by his courage in doing such a dangerous thing. He was a pleasant, friendly guy and I enjoyed his company. He accepted the need for his operation but was fearful of the possible outcome. Everything went fine, however, and we said our goodbyes about a week later.

The other memorable roommate was a young Laotian military officer. He couldn't speak English but I spoke Thai, which is very close to the Lao language, plus some French. With one language or the other I became his buddy and his translator.

As we talked I developed a picture of this young man and it wasn't a nice one. He whined a lot and had a weak character. I had come to know the Lao people fairly well, and I wondered how this man managed to rise to the rank of officer. The answer was obvious: His father was a senior member of the FAR.

Then I learned he was at Walter Reed to have cosmetic surgery on a large scar on his neck. It started low on his cheek and ran downward. It didn't look that bad, actually, but he seemed quite upset about it.

It wasn't a bayonet wound gained in combat with the Viet Cong. He told me he had gotten it in a fight in a nightclub over a girl. He was a bit ashamed to admit it and I don't know how many people at the hospital were aware of the circumstances.

One of our military attachés knew his father and had offered—probably in exchange for greater influence—to have the scar fixed at the U.S. Army's finest hospital. The attaché had arranged for this young man's operation.

The more I learned about his story the less I respected him because he had never seen combat and probably never would. He was a Vientiane-based non-combatant who had not been injured in the line of duty. He was a bar crawler who had gotten stabbed fighting over a hooker. Despite my feelings I tried to be civil.

Before his operation he confided to me that he was worried about bad *pi*—that common Lao complaint about mischief by spirits and ghosts. I told him Walter Reed had no *pi* at all but he didn't seem convinced.

Maybe he was right. The morning of his operation they wheeled him back a few hours later still unconscious and looking awful. There were no bandages and his scar was untouched. Something was amiss.

The doctors briefed me so I could explain what happened when he woke up. I didn't get the full story, because I know they were very embarrassed, but I got a version thereof.

After the young officer had been put under with ether there was an interlude before the surgeon arrived. Somehow the tubes and valves had gotten mixed up and he was getting only the gas, no oxygen. By the time the surgeon took his first look the patient was turning blue or green, requiring the operating team to take emergency steps to stabilize his condition. They also had to abort the operation.

It would be rescheduled as soon as he felt better, they said, but he would feel bad for a couple of days.

"I'll bet he will," I said, laughing now that the danger was passed.

I tried explaining to him in French and Thai but was never able to persuade him that it had just been an unfortunate accident. Bad *pi* was all he could think of.

He left the hospital the next afternoon still looking a little green under the gills and wobbly, and accompanied by a couple of officers from the Laotian Embassy. Our military attaché's plan for increased influence had backfired.

Wally Deuel visited me much less often after Mike's crash but when I regained my sight I visited the Deuels from time to time. I felt torn about going there because I knew I would remind them of Mike. So I phoned them periodically as well and Wally kept me apprised of Judy's situation in Illinois. We were all concerned about her. In April 1966 she had her baby, Suzanne Michelle.

I can't remember who first thought of a trust fund but we all embraced it immediately. Ralph McLean and I organized it and we received checks from many of Mike's old classmates and agency friends. The fund would finance Suzanne's college education, and after due deliberation we invested the several thousand dollars that had been amassed into a growth mutual fund. Then we told Judy and the Deuels.

After Suzanne's birth Judy became more and more restless living in rural Illinois. She did not want to spend the rest of her life there. We all encouraged her to come to Washington. The agency guaranteed that whenever she wanted she could immediately resume her employment. That fall, Judy moved to Washington with Suzanne and everyone welcomed her warmly, Wally and Mary in particular. They supported her decision, a difficult one for a young widow to make.

The only drawback from her point of view was that after she started working again she would have to put Suzanne in day care. She didn't like the idea. So eventually and after a few detours she decided to stop working and get married again—to me.

I'll try to explain.

When Judy moved to the city she settled into an apartment that was near mine on MacArthur Boulevard. The location made the commute to headquarters quite easy.

At first she enrolled at American University—also nearby—to finish her B.A. degree. She had completed two years at the University of Illinois but stopped to join the agency and go overseas. Now she decided to major in music—she always was an excellent pianist. But because of Suzanne she decided not to enroll full time and just take a few courses, which she did for two semesters before deciding in mid-1967 to go back to work at the agency.

Soon after her move to Washington, Judy visited me at Walter Reed. She knew I was a good friend of Mike's and of the Deuels. Also, we had met in Bangkok and we had many friends in common in Southeast Asia and Washington. Plus she was just a nice person who wanted to see how I was doing.

I told her how sorry I was about Mike's crash. It wasn't easy to express my feelings but she understood. We didn't talk much about Mike after that. There simply wasn't much either of us could say.

I was delighted that she had come to see me and I enjoyed her company. She told me she felt the same way. Later she said I somehow seemed nicer than when I was in Thailand. Back in Bangkok, she had found me to be a bit (and I use the word here because she did) "cocky."

I have no idea why she got such an impression and I was shocked to hear it. But at Walter Reed, she said, I seemed more patient, subdued and overall just nicer. I hadn't noticed any change in my demeanor. Maybe that's what clinging to life for days in the jungle does to you.

I invited Judy to come back often. By then I was able to leave the hospital evenings and weekends. I began visiting her and Suzanne at her apartment and she would have me and several of her friends for dinner.

After my operations, and whenever I was confined to my hospital bed, Judy would come to see me. I always looked for ways to extend the length of her visits and I found that I liked being with her more and more. In fact I came to love our time together. She was just as she was when I first met her: pretty, charming, thoughtful and intelligent.

I still looked terrible, and sometimes I worried what she thought about it, but that didn't seem to faze her at all.

The Deuels, possibly sensing something that had not yet occurred to me, began inviting us to dinner at their house. During those pleasant evenings Wally seemed more like his old self. He and Mary adored Suzanne and she responded with great affection toward them.

Judy and I saw each other more frequently for the first half of 1967 and by fall we were dating as steadily as my situation would permit. I had fallen deeply in love with her, though I didn't quite know how she felt. We went to dinner, movies and plays, and we took Suzanne on picnics with our friends. That autumn I took Judy and Suzanne to New Jersey to meet my parents—which should have been a strong indication that I was getting serious.

Then the following January, with our relationship blooming, she invited me to dinner one night. We had a great time, as usual, though she seemed a bit pensive. She drove me home and as we were standing in front of my apartment building she dropped a blockbuster.

"I've been offered a position in Taiwan this summer."

I was shocked. My mind raced. I tried to think of something to say.

"That's ... a terrible idea and I don't want you to go."

"Why?" she asked calmly.

I was anything but calm. It had been so sudden. No warning—just awful news. I was hesitant but I figured it was now or never.

"Because I want you to marry me," I blurted out in a rush, "soon!"

She seemed genuinely surprised—yet one more example among the millions of how men do not understand women.

Now *she* was hesitant. "I'm not sure," she replied. "Do you think you're ready?"

I can't remember what I said during the next 10 minutes, which is how long it took me to persuade her that I was indeed ready to marry. I also don't know what arguments I used but whatever I told her, to my great delight and joy she said yes, she would marry me. I couldn't have been happier and we promptly called her mother and my parents to announce the glad tidings.

When I told the Deuels that Judy and I were going to get married they were absolutely thrilled. Wally couldn't stop saying how pleased he was and that made us both even happier about our plans. I still wonder if Wally and Mary had seen that day coming long before we did—or maybe hoped for it—and tried to encourage it.

Judy's arrival on the scene had changed a lot of things but it didn't get me out of the hospital any sooner. I remained there during the early months of our courtship while the surgical routine continued. With my vision restored and my hands getting better and more functional I grew increasingly impatient to be done with Walter Reed.

Mike Duffy's friendship with me kept him well-informed about my frustration. He also knew about Judy and how I felt about her, so he and his wife Caroline invited us to their home for dinner many times. At one of those evenings they also invited my brother Bob and his new wife Carol. After they married he had been assigned to Washington by the Marines for one year to study Thai.

The three women got along well and after dinner we three guys left them for the back porch to fire a .22-caliber rifle. Mike liked to use the woods behind his house for target practice. He said because he owned the woods and there were acres of them there was no danger of hitting anyone.

It was dark when Mike set up a lit candle about 50 yards away and into the trees.

"Just put out the candle," he said, handing me the rifle.

I took three shots and missed, likely by a large margin. Mike fired a few rounds next, and on one shot we thought we saw the flame waver a bit, but the candle kept burning.

"Let's see what the Marines can do," he said, handing the gun to Bob.

From a kneeling position my brother took one shot and the flame disappeared. I don't know if he just knocked down the candle or actually snuffed the flame with the bullet but it was definitely out. Lucky shot or not we were duly impressed.

"Nobody's ever done that," Mike said.

In mid-April 1967 my long-awaited liberation arrived.

"This one will be just about it, Dick," Mike told me.

"You mean I'm out of here?" I asked, almost not believing what I'd heard.

"There are a couple more small things I'll want to do," he responded, "but they can be handled on an outpatient basis. Yeah, get the hell out of here!"

I knew it had to come but after such a long time it almost stunned me. I would be leaving Walter Reed.

Lots of questions and doubts filled my mind.

How will I do? Will people react badly to how I look? Can I just pick up where I left off?

I was experiencing a sudden and unexpected crisis of confidence. I had never lacked for confidence before so this was unusual. Why would it be so hard for me to leave the hospital? The answer finally came to me: I had grown accustomed to and comfortable with my protected life there. Now I had to break that link, get on with things, and become self-reliant again.

To start I would have to prove to myself that I could function independently in the outside world. True to my cockiness I planned a trip to Casablanca, Morocco, to visit André Le Gallo and his wife Cathy.

André was one of my oldest agency friends. Our relationship went back to the house we had shared on MacArthur Boulevard. Also, André had gone on that first flight to Laos with me along with Mike Deuel and Ralph McLean.

I decided I would travel alone via Madrid, Spain, where I would see a few of the local sights. It seemed a good plan to me—though nobody else thought so.

Too much, too fast, my parents chided me.

Judy didn't like it, either, nor did many of my friends.

But I was determined. I flew out of Dulles in early May. Results of my effort to "start off right," as I had termed it, were mixed at best.

The first hint occurred on the plane.

The attendants had served dinner and a stewardess noticed me wrestling with my steak. She volunteered to cut it for me and though I was embarrassed I let her.

Next, in Madrid, I checked into a hotel and took a brief nap during the siesta period followed by a walk in late afternoon out into the city, which was bustling with shoppers and traffic. While crossing a narrow side street I got knocked down by a passing taxi. He didn't even stop. An old woman cursed him and rushed over to help me up—another embarrassing moment. I still had not adapted to my reduced peripheral vision and I hadn't seen the taxi in time to avoid it.

I thanked the lady for her concern and headed back to the hotel. Nothing was broken, I knew, but I had some scratches and would probably be sore the next day. I cleaned up as best I could and lay down on the bed.

I didn't get up again for two days. Inexplicably I had grown terribly weak and tired. I ate no dinner and just stayed in bed. During the night I developed a fever and started sweating heavily. I sent the maid away in the morning when she came to change the bed and clean the room. I remained in bed all day, still not eating and taking no medicine, and I still felt sore from my bout with the taxi.

By evening the fever broke and I felt much better, though still weak. Even so, I decided to rest until morning. I slept badly but woke the next day feeling better and very hungry.

I left Madrid that afternoon for Casablanca where André and Cathy met me and drove me to their apartment in the middle of the city. I spent several pleasant days with them.

André took some time off and we toured around Morocco a bit. Then we headed up to Tangiers and took a ferry to Gibraltar where we spent a day shopping. I bought a Rolex watch there, finally replacing the Omega I had given to Faustino, the chief of the Congo village. I still wear that watch.

A third unfortunate episode resulted from another bad idea of mine. A couple of days before heading for home I asked André to hit some tennis balls with me. He and Cathy were hesitant.

"Just so I can see what I can do," I told them.

I borrowed Cathy's racket and we went to their club. It was a nice place but the experience was terrible. I couldn't even meet the ball with the racket—my lack of depth perception again.

Worse, when I did happen to connect with the ball my hand was so weak I couldn't hold onto the racket. It only took about 10 minutes to convince me I wasn't yet ready to play. I felt really depressed. Cathy and André tried to put a positive spin on it, suggesting that I probably had been too ambitious to try tennis so soon after my lengthy hospitalization. It didn't help much.

I returned to Washington via Madrid again. Things went better on the return trip. I did some sightseeing and bought several pieces of Spanish furniture made of oak—nice pieces that I still have.

The trip did have some positive results. I got away on my own and managed to survive traveling abroad. On the other hand I couldn't deny the low points caused by limitations I would be dealing with as long as I lived.

I didn't like that aspect at all but I consoled myself by thinking that at least I hadn't perished somewhere in the northeastern Congo.

In late May I finally returned to work. Just as Charlie Whitehurst had discussed with me, I joined China Operations in Far East Division and began applying the Mandarin I had been studying since the previous summer. Then, nearly two years later, the division would transfer me to Hong Kong, where Whitey had become chief.

As Whitey must have known, studying Mandarin while I was still in the hospital did wonders for my spirits. It helped me to feel as though I was moving toward normal life again. More than colleagues we were friends; I had great respect for him.

My respect for the agency grew as well. Not only did headquarters approve my Mandarin tutoring, they also promoted me while I was at Walter Reed—something that amazed me when I heard the news. Apparently headquarters did not want me to fall behind my peers. Frankly it seemed like an act of charity to me but I was grateful nevertheless.

Over two years after the Congo crash, after all those surgeries on my hands, face and eyes, after months and months of often painful recovery and physical therapy, I was finally ready to resume my career. I had also fallen in love with Judy and won her heart, and I had been given back the rest of my life to live.

PART V: THE BAMBOO CURTAIN

14. Nuts and Bolts

HONG KONG 1969–1971

It was the same landing approach the plane had made in 1962 at the end of one leg on our trip to Laos. We flew in from the southeast and the South China Sea, glided over Tung Lung Island and the corridor formed by Hong Kong Island and the mainland, and touched down at the end of Kai Tak Airport's long main runway, which juts far out into the harbor.

But now it was March 1969, and instead of André, Mike and Ralph, I had made this flight with Judy, who was six months pregnant, and with Suzanne, delightfully approaching age 3.

We had been married the previous September 1 in Judy's hometown of Bulpitt, about 20 miles southeast of Springfield, Illinois. One of Mike Duffy's last outpatient surgeries had left me with a large bandage on my right hand. It appeared in our wedding photos and went with us on our honeymoon. It had even required me to play ping-pong left-handed with Judy. To her chagrin I still won.

The other big change: Hong Kong, not Bangkok, was our destination. I was joining Charlie Whitehurst's staff as a case officer. The Congo crash had kept me out of the game for over four years and now I was eager to get back in.

Our dominant focus was China. The same was true for the State

Department's officers in the Consulate General building on Garden Road. The U.S. Consulate—technically a consulate of our embassy in London—functioned as an embassy, but the entire community acted as China watchers and China watching was an all-consuming task, greatly complicated by the so-called Bamboo Curtain the People's Republic had erected along its border.

This was the beginning of the third decade of the Cold War. China's communist ruler, Mao Tse-tung—now Mao Zedong—had cut off his country completely from the rest of the world. Worse, China was in the midst of its Great Cultural Revolution, an extremely chaotic and brutal time, which ultimately took a terrible toll on its people as well as its priceless treasures of antiquity.

The British Crown Colony of Hong Kong, wrested from China during the Opium Wars in the mid-19th century, served as both listening post and observation tower for the West. Yet the Chinese seemed to tolerate it because Hong Kong also provided them a window on the West.

Our Hong Kong office had been tasked with gathering intelligence on political, military and economic developments—a difficult job under the circumstances. China in our parlance was a denied area. That is, the country was totally under the hostile control of its police and security services, constraints that made it extremely difficult for us to operate within its borders.

Before I left for Hong Kong I either had worked at headquarters or was attending language school for 22 months, beginning just after I was discharged from Walter Reed and that brief but disastrous trip to Spain and Morocco.

My job on the Hong Kong desk at Langley had been to provide basic support for operations. It was headquarters at its worst—day after day of nothing but administrivia in support of the real action, our activities in the field. But I was a junior case officer and could expect nothing different. I was there to do the nitty-gritty and no more, and sometimes I found it difficult to keep myself motivated.

Despite the minimal challenge I still had to labor thoroughly and carefully. Many of the safeguards built into the clandestine service depended on the quality of work accomplished at the desk level. My daily effort included confirming the identities of contacts and agents, reviewing operational plans, collecting data, providing counterintelligence guidance, and preparing budgets. Tedium aside, I knew I was helping our case officers by providing the full range of support they needed.

On the other hand, deskwork turned out to be the main reason why so many of the case officers sought field assignments. Landing a frontline position meant joining the action and excitement—though I served as a reminder of where those assignments sometimes led.

By January 1968 I figured I had gained about as much desk experience as I could stand. I likewise wanted to get back into the field. Having done my turn at paramilitary work I decided that I needed to run a clandestine operation.

Just like our efforts aimed at the Soviet Union—also a denied area—our China operations were global, meaning many prospective assignments. As I considered what to request as a field tour I determined that I wanted to work as close to the target country as I could; Hong Kong became my first choice.

There I could run agents within the colony itself as well as across the border using individuals who could enter China legally. Almost everywhere else the assignment would have been limited to contacting and recruiting people working in or for the Chinese embassies.

I lobbied my superiors for the assignment, and they supported the decision, but China Operations preferred case officers with solid language skills. It meant the ability to speak and understand Mandarin Chinese colloquially, something that would give them a clear leg up in terms of establishing contacts and developing relationships with potential agents.

I felt impatient to go abroad again but I knew the language training made sense. That spring I signed up for the agency's two-year Mandarin course. The program would begin in July and comprise one year in Washington plus another year in Taiwan.

I had mulled it over for a couple of weeks. I knew it would prolong the preparations phase but sooner or later I would need to speak Chinese fluently.

After Judy and I married we had moved into an apartment in Rosslyn, Virginia, just across the Potomac from Georgetown. The apartment was convenient to the language school and it would serve us until the new house we had purchased in McLean was completed that fall.

For reasons I can't fully explain, learning languages has never been difficult for me. French, Thai, Spanish, all came quickly. For Mandarin my grounding in Thai, also a tonal language, made it easy as well. But Chinese grammar is not particularly challenging and the effort boils down to memorization and hard work. It also takes a good ear for languages so my ability to speak French and Spanish probably helped. In any event I progressed rapidly and tested high for the first period of our training.

Then I found out that a suitable position had opened in Hong Kong. It forced us to decide whether I should continue the Chinese training, moving on to the second year in Taiwan, or take the Hong Kong assignment.

I quickly knew what I wanted to do and Judy sensed it right away. I wanted to go to Hong Kong and start working. I had a good jump on my Chinese and could continue my studies with a tutor.

"Let's go," I said, and Judy agreed.

We immediately told Wally and Mary Deuel. They had been enjoying Suzanne, their granddaughter, those past months and they delighted in seeing each new phase she entered. But they understood our decision, though we knew they were saddened at the prospect of separation. Neither of them was in good health so even the near future would be uncertain. We enjoyed a farewell dinner with them and then visited our families before our departure.

The Hong Kong staff gave us an especially warm welcome. Their thoughtfulness kept our settling-in problems to a minimum.

From the selections open to us we picked an apartment in Repulse Bay on the South China Sea side of Hong Kong Island. The massive civil unrest and rioting associated with the Cultural Revolution had spilled across the border during 1967 and 1968, and as a result headquarters and the State Department had required all staff to move to the island to preclude being cut off during a time of crisis.

An often-repeated story about that decision is worth telling. In earlier years many consulate personnel, particularly those with families and small children, enjoyed living on the scenic Kowloon peninsula. The U.S. government had purchased dozens of pleasant little houses not too far up the peninsula from the harbor. Those houses provided a welcome alternative to life in the high-rise apartments on Hong Kong Island.

The disruptions and unrest of the riots caused shaken State Department officials to reassess their housing policy and they opted to move all personnel onto the island. That raised the question of what to do with the government-owned houses. Keep them and rent them out until things settled down? No.

Instead, someone overheard a consulate officer brag that he had just "unloaded" 43 houses. In the depressed real estate market following the unrest the government lost money on the sales, but in fulfilling Washington's orders he considered it a successful effort.

Just a couple of years later the market rebounded and the houses were suddenly worth a fortune. Many staff members would have loved the option of living on the Kowloon side of the harbor. Today, with apartments commonly renting for $6,000 a month or more, those bungalows would have been a godsend.

I met with Whitey at 9 a.m. the day after we arrived. I was eager to begin my assignment, but he'd given me no hint of what it was in his cables. After briefly welcoming me, he got down to business.

"I have some problems," he said, "and I'd like you to sort things out."

That puzzled me. I still had another year to go with my Mandarin, I had no field experience with classical intelligence operations, and as far as I knew Whitey wasn't running any paramilitary efforts. What kind of problems could I help with?

"Our operational support structure is way out of whack, Dick, and it needs some careful attention."

I'm sure he saw the instant look of disappointment on my face.

"But what could I do with that?"

Ops support, as we call it, is the nuts and bolts of running clandestine programs. It wasn't at all what I had hoped for. I wanted to get into the operations themselves.

"Don't fool yourself, Dick. Ops support is the backbone of our effort and it's also where we get tripped up from time to time. It demands close scrutiny and I want you to take it over. It won't be forever; just get things squared away. We're bloated as a result of the last two years and the turmoil Hong Kong has experienced."

There wasn't a lot of choice. When your chief speaks you listen and you comply.

"I'll give it my best shot, Whitey," I said, with as much enthusiasm as I could muster.

"Good, I'll appreciate it."

He got up to shake hands and showed me out of his office.

I met next with Jim Lilley, the deputy chief, someone I also knew from earlier times. Jim knew what Whitey had told me and that I would be less than pleased with the assignment. He tried to remove some of the sting.

"Whitey's right, you know. We need to trim down and restructure our ops-support capabilities. He remembers what you put together in Laos and he thinks you're the right man to get the job done."

"I'm a little worried that I don't know enough about Hong Kong yet," I offered, hoping he might pick up on that point. "It's a pretty complex place."

"Initially you'll have to understand the problems and that will be done inside the office. You'll have time to figure things out. You're a fast learner."

Clearly I faced a united front.

"I'll do the best I can," I told him.

"Down the road you'll appreciate this experience," he replied, "and we appreciate the obvious delight with which you take on this chore."

Jim was poking me a little but he turned out to be absolutely right. All too often the chief would relegate this kind of task to the least senior officer—as Whitey had done with me. But as I would learn in subsequent tours my two years of ops-support work in Hong Kong formed a strong foundation for my tradecraft skills. When I ran offices of my own I always paid special attention to the nuts and bolts.

The man I was replacing, a mid-level officer nearing retirement, was getting ready to transfer back to headquarters so he showed me no animosity. I didn't know if he knew how his chief and deputy viewed the job he had been doing but I wasn't about to raise the subject. No sense rocking the boat on this particular occasion.

His secretary, Margie Grainer, became my secretary. She was wonderfully efficient, and I felt blessed to inherit her. Some years later she would become secretary to the Deputy Director of Operations back at headquarters, the highest level secretarial position in the directorate. Along with Margie and me, one other junior officer worked in the section.

As I listened to the briefings my predecessor provided a couple of thoughts crossed my mind. First, I could tell he had burned out and consequently had no enthusiasm for—no interest even—in his job. I had no idea why he felt that way but at the time I kept my assessment of him to myself.

Second, I thought his briefings lacked organization and structure. I soon learned that the program itself lacked those qualities and I discovered the source. For reasons difficult to trace it had grown too fast.

I suspected the problem had arisen because of the frenetic activity associated with the riots. The turmoil had prompted a rapid increase in the number of safe houses and expansion of the ops-support structure, both of which were poorly managed. We ended up with many more assets than we needed.

No wonder Whitey had been worried about it. Reshaping the entire program presented a challenge I hadn't expected. Now that I grasped the problem, maybe trying to fix it would be tolerable.

The broad nature of the program quickly exposed me to the entire range of our China operations. I had been impressed by Hong Kong's efforts while I was working at headquarters. Now on the scene my respect grew even more.

I was soon working closely with all of the branch chiefs and I admired the professional approach they took—their attention to detail, their comprehensive planning, and their efforts to expand our asset base. I actually started to enjoy my assignment. It probably helped that I knew several officers—I had done my early training with David Griese, for example—so I felt comfortable.

Word of my marching orders became widespread and everyone agreed that I should get on with the effort. Back at headquarters I had wondered what it would be like to serve in a non-paramilitary field job and I harbored some concerns. But the acceptance I received eased my reservations.

Ops support, as any John le Carré novel will reveal, comprises all adjunct activities required to run an ongoing clandestine effort, whether for intelligence gathering, covert action or counterintelligence. Just like operations, support efforts must be clandestine. Mistakes cause compromises—exposures—the worst nightmare of any field station.

Incidentally, many CIA people like to read novels about espionage and other intelligence subjects. Tradecraft is an art—a combination of common sense and imagination. Tradecraft is also pragmatic; sometimes we read the genre to glean ideas we can use in the field.

For example, a common device in spy fiction and spy fact is the safe house, a discreet, secure site for face-to-face meetings. It can be a house, an apartment or a hotel room. We choose them at random to reduce the chances that opposition intelligence services can detect patterns in our moves and start to anticipate them. We also choose them to be compatible with operations so the cover stories we create will work for the case officer and agent alike—if someone else discovers the meeting our reason for being there seems plausible.

Once the local police interrupted my meeting with an agent. Apparently they were working on a drug bust and hit the wrong apartment. Lucky for us our cover stories held, and my being a Caucasian might have had something to do with it. But it was distressing to experience the problem firsthand. The lesson: No safe house is entirely safe, so we must constantly work to improve the odds.

In operations we commonly use what we called accommodation addresses—mailing addresses secretly provided by an agent who usually has no other task or tie to us. The addresses can be apartments, post-office boxes or some variant. Our agents use them to pass messages and documents to the case officer running the operation.

We apply the cover-story principal to accommodation addresses as well. We develop a rationale for why an agent would send mail to a particular address and why the keeper of that address would be receiving it.

We also use listening posts, surveillance teams and other tactics depending on the operation being supported.

Running these components takes time, personnel and funding so it's important that each one is worth the expenditure. When I took over I could plainly see we had too many safe houses, too few reliable accommodation addresses, and a weak surveillance capability—at least, according to the incomplete records at my disposal. I identified the problems, a good first step, but solving them was another matter.

I needed to reduce our safe-house holdings by half. That was the easy part. But which ones should go and which ones continued to be operationally useful? That required careful analysis. I needed to be sure our safe-house inventory blended as closely as possible with our operational needs.

An example: Caucasians rarely ventured into certain parts of Hong Kong so except for our ethnic Chinese officers we avoided such areas, because doing so could arouse unwanted interest and trigger a security problem.

Also, the colony was much more complex than it appeared on the map. It resembled an enormous onion and you had to keep peeling away the layers to get to know it. Especially for a non-Chinese there were always more layers. That meant whatever the challenges and difficulties I had to get out on the streets to learn what was going on. Like any good operations officer I needed to understand my territory thoroughly.

I began by systematically scouring the colony, both the island and peninsula sides, for locations we might use as operational venues. I rode every bus, every trolley, every ferry line. I also used taxis and minibuses.

Then I began walking through neighborhoods. I would stop for tea, lunch, shopping or some other reason just to get a sense for a particular place. I would observe each area carefully.

Which Chinese dialect did the residents speak? Usually it was Cantonese but people used other dialects in certain neighborhoods.

Were there any English speakers?

Was a neighborhood blue collar, working class, upper class or mixed?

Was there any evidence of criminal elements or gangs?

Were any Caucasians living in the neighborhood?

For months I allocated several days or half-days per week to familiarizing myself with Hong Kong's districts. It paid off. Eventually there were few questions about the city's inner workings I couldn't answer on the spot or find the answer to. In discussions with case officers, branch chiefs and even Whitey and Jim, I could present solid reasons for keeping, acquiring, or dropping a particular safe house or accommodation address.

Along with my reconnoitering I built a database to help me deal with cables and dispatches that arrived from headquarters. Not that headquarters gave me many problems. They were pleased with Whitey's decision to pare down our ops-support holdings. But given the number of related issues involved—length of lease, cover, life of a given operation and so forth—it took me the better part of that first year in Hong Kong to feel comfortable with the safe-house picture.

By then we were operating fewer than half of the safe houses we had when I arrived. That pleased Whitey, as well as his new deputy, Bob M., who had replaced Jim Lilley over the summer.

M. and Lilley would figure prominently in our global operations for some time. Both were towers of strength and highly respected within the community.

Family life became even more of a priority for me on July 1, 1969, just over three months after our arrival in Hong Kong, when Judy gave birth to a beautiful baby girl. We were elated.

She was born at Canossa Hospital, located just above the U.S. Consulate in the city's Mid-Levels district below Victoria Peak. The hospital, founded in 1929 by the Canossian Daughters of Charity, a Catholic order, had been destroyed in a Japanese air raid during World War II and was rebuilt in 1960.

Inexperienced at such things even in my early 30s it shook me the morning Judy announced we'd best go to the hospital. But the good sisters took over as soon as we arrived and directed me into a waiting room. Soon thereafter the doctor walked in. He was Portuguese, recommended to us by colleagues on our arrival in Hong Kong, and Judy found him competent and experienced.

"Would you like to assist at the birth?" he asked me.

Today it's common for husbands to join their wives in the delivery room, but in 1969 the practice was just emerging so the idea took me aback. I had never thought of such a thing. I had never even *heard* of such a thing and I wasn't sure what he meant by "assisting."

"You mean be in the same room when Judy has the baby?"

I resisted the idea. What earthly good could I be in there? It never occurred to me that Judy might be pleased to have me share the experience with her.

Me? In the delivery room? No!

My mind couldn't fathom it.

"Yes, that's right," the doctor replied.

"No thanks. I think I'll just wait out here," I muttered.

I spent the next hour or so browsing the latest issue of *TIME* magazine, until the doctor returned to tell me that our baby—a girl—had just been born and mother and daughter were doing fine. I felt relieved and proud.

The next morning I returned to the hospital. Judy and I needed to name our new child. I had been playing tennis earlier with a Scandinavian friend and accidentally fell onto the gritty clay court. I sustained scratches on my elbow and knee. Because it was July and hot I walked into Judy's room wearing a short-sleeved shirt and Bermuda shorts so the scratches were exposed.

One of the nuns—all of whom were conscientious nurses and delightful individuals—was with Judy and she spotted my wounds.

"It's nothing," I told her.

"But it looks terrible," she gushed.

She left and promptly returned with another nun in tow. Both began fussing over me and insisting that they clean and bandage my knee and elbow. The attention embarrassed me. Judy watched the spectacle sympathetically for a while then feigned insult.

"Who's in the hospital anyway? How about some attention over here?"

We named our baby Danika Marie. Danika means "morning star" in many Eastern European languages. We had discovered it in a book of baby names and we really liked it.

As for assisting with the birth I never really discussed the doctor's invitation with Judy. But let the record show that Danika and her two subsequent sisters were born and did just fine without my assistance in the delivery room.

While I was trimming our safe houses I wrestled with the opposite problem regarding accommodation addresses: We had too few effective locations. I had weeded out the overused or inappropriate contact points but we needed more assets in our stable as soon as possible.

In the fall of 1969 I voiced that concern at one of Whitey's regular staff meetings, attended by Bob, the branch chiefs, the reports chief and me. I also proposed making it a priority to bring in some new agents.

Routine stuff on both counts but the general response was only grudgingly positive. I knew what they were thinking: Like we don't have enough to do already? But Whitey deemed my proposal worthwhile, meaning the others had to fall in line.

Part of my argument was that we also supported other field offices in Asia and even Europe, and I knew that Whitey took the responsibility seriously. My work had helped to improve that support but even after 20 months, when I stopped running ops support for Hong Kong, I remained unsatisfied with our holdings. I thought we still needed agents of narrowly defined ethnic types to perform precise tasks, for example.

I faced other challenges. Hong Kong was full of enterprising individuals, some of whom we called fabricators. Well aware of the thirst for information by China watchers of all stripes, many in Hong Kong were more than willing to provide information, either covertly or overtly. But some would fabricate documents, photos or audiotapes and present them as authentic.

Given the difficulties caused by China's closed borders and total censorship these fabricators posed a constant worry. Among other things we needed a stronger surveillance team to help us vet and test agents and prospective agents. I took steps to build such a capability—a far tougher task than I had anticipated.

It turned out that creating a first-rate surveillance team was just as hard as screening out the fabricators. I had to sift through a wide range of candidates—men and women of different ages and ethnic backgrounds. I also had to evaluate each one's ability not only to blend in with the others but also to supply a specific capability when needed. Sometimes the task was simple, such as entering a ladies' or men's restroom to survey the place after a target had stopped there.

Despite these challenges, before I left ops support I had recruited a team of young men and women that we could deploy on demand. All of the weeks of vetting, on-the-street training, and photo and communications training ultimately paid off.

For example, the team supplied us with clear, unmistakable photos that unmasked a would-be fabricator, allowing us to break off contact before being hoodwinked. It was seldom that easy but the team's photos were invaluable.

The more time I spent in our Hong Kong office the more positive my impressions grew. I found my colleagues, peers and senior officers alike, to be almost uniformly competent, well motivated and professional. We all took very seriously our responsibility to provide solid intelligence to Washington. Despite our varied backgrounds we had no problems working together. We competed but in a healthy and positive way.

The entire staff had a high competency in Chinese. Everyone, even the branch chiefs, spoke the language well. My own ability to speak the Mandarin dialect, which I pursued with the help of a tutor in the consulate, continued to improve. I came to realize, however, that it had been a mistake to avoid that additional year in Taiwan. Without it I would not attain the fluency routinely reached at that school. Our ethnic Chinese officers spoke more than one dialect, which made them particularly effective.

One aspect of operations that troubled me was supporting our covert-action programs. The agency had employed such efforts in post-World War II Europe, and during my training the instructors had described many successful examples of using media outlets to influence political attitudes. But I harbored doubts about the effectiveness of influence or media operations in Hong Kong.

The Chinese that I knew focused almost entirely on making a living and saving enough money to get out of Hong Kong if necessary. Politics in general, including the conflict between capitalism and communism and the merits of one or the other, ran far behind. I doubted that articles about those subjects would find many readers, and therefore I didn't think they were worth the resources expended.

Likewise, a program intended to foment a rebellion by lighting "prairie fires of discontent across the plains of south China," as a headquarters colleague put it, was unrealistic—hopelessly unrealistic—and represented ill-spent resources. Some of my colleagues agreed but Langley remained unmoved by the few sounds of dissent that reached there.

Despite my doubts about covert action I fully supported our efforts. Directing the bulk of our Hong Kong resources at China was a perfectly logical strategy and we pursued it vigorously. But it was a hard slog, particularly when it involved developing relationships with individuals who enjoyed direct access to the mainland. They were a wary group and I had to work arduously to identify, meet, and try to establish a rapport with them.

The Chinese maintained meticulous security procedures at Lowu, the border crossing point for the colony. Border officials alerted anyone entering the country that they would risk severe penalties by running afoul of security services—a certainty for anyone found to be cooperating with us.

The dangers notwithstanding, we constantly sought contacts with Chinese, other Asians and Europeans, and our efforts produced regular successes. We gathered a steady flow of intelligence covering economic, political and military developments within the People's Republic.

I spent a lot of time attempting to collect that intelligence. As things turned out I succeeded mainly with the Chinese in my ops-support activities and with Europeans in other areas. I was able to develop several close relationships that produced economic information about what China was buying and what little they were exporting. I focused particularly on diplomats and businessmen working on the mainland. Many of them visited Hong Kong regularly so I could meet them for discussions or debriefings.

As with so much of our work, however, such efforts were hit and miss. In late 1969, I discovered that a French diplomat was due for a posting in China during the following summer. The University of Hong Kong had invited him to teach a course, in French, on contemporary French history.

That information piqued my interest right away. Maybe I could learn some useful things from the course. Plus, I might get to know him personally, which would facilitate discussions about China whenever he visited Hong Kong. And it represented an opportunity to refresh my rusty French-language skills.

I enrolled—a once-weekly, evening class.

The lecturer started with the Franco-Prussian War in 1870. Lucky for me his French was clear and moderately paced so I had little trouble understanding him. I made a point of engaging him after each class to ask some question or compliment him on the lecture. He was pleasant and approachable, partly I think because he learned that I had lived in France and was interested in his country's history. On top of that the experience was improving my French—so far, so good.

His topics progressed chronologically and he began covering World War I, emphasizing the French role in the combined effort to defeat the Germans. He surprised me by exaggerating what the French did and downplaying the contribution of the American and British forces. I chalked it up to French pride. I thought it was skewed but I said nothing to him about it.

His lecture about the 1920s and early 1930s in France was mostly new and informative to me and it seemed designed to set the scene for what was to follow.

Then he did two lectures on World War II. Compared to what I had learned and read previously both lectures startled me. At the same time, however, I found it useful to listen to someone articulate a different version of history than American textbooks presented.

For him, it was *Vive la France!* ever glorious, ever triumphant, extolling the heroism of Charles de Gaulle, the Resistance movement, the liberation of Paris. Oh yes, there was that landing at Normandy, and the Americans and British did help some, but in essence he made clear that the French had whipped Hitler's butt.

Glossed over or unmentioned were issues such as the Vichy government's cooperation with the Germans, the questionable record of the Resistance and its penetration by communist elements that later posed problems in post-war France. He also neglected the deportation of thousands of Jews and France's total reliance on the Allies for war materiel.

This was too much for me. I knew it ran against my own best interests but I couldn't resist approaching him after that second lecture to pose some pointed questions. Predictably he became defensive. He explained his version and interpretation of what I thought was factual. The issues I had raised emphasized the wrong things, he asserted.

Sensing that I had harmed our relationship I didn't press my points. Two weeks later I called to invite him to lunch and discovered that his assignment had been cancelled for budgetary reasons and he was returning to France—so much for sitting through 12 lectures on contemporary French history. I lost out on what might have been interesting discussions about China whenever he visited Hong Kong, but I did learn a lot about France and that made the effort personally worthwhile.

As I said, hit and miss.

15. We'll Be Okay

HONG KONG 1971–1973

Scenes of domesticity were precious but rare to me during those years in Hong Kong. My work was often all-consuming as it was throughout much of my career. I labored long hours collecting research and writing reports. I endlessly walked or drove through the streets as part of my ops-support efforts. I spent many evenings in meetings with agents or work-related social activity. Even weekends weren't immune.

Despite the long hours I always managed to find time for Judy and the children, and through it all Judy understood and was unfailingly tolerant and helpful.

Aware of my desire to further a particular relationship she often deftly managed to give me time alone with that individual for in-depth discussions. If we invited a prospect and his wife for dinner Judy would manage to get the wife involved in the kitchen or with the kids. That cleared the way for me to have a conversation with the husband.

Judy also worked her magic elsewhere. If we were on someone's boat, for example, or hiking with another couple in the New Territories, the goal was always to give me time with the prospect so I could establish better rapport.

During the days when I wasn't immersed in work or entertaining for professional reasons we managed to enjoy living in and getting to know Hong Kong. We took the kids to the beaches. We rode ferries to the outer islands for picnics and hikes. We drove up to the New Territories—the area between Boundary Street and the Sham Chun River on the peninsula—to visit its floating restaurants in Sha Tin or stroll along the coastline. And we explored the intricacies of the city's numerous shopping districts.

As we grew into our marriage Judy and I discovered we had a mutual fondness for Oriental rugs and art. During our time in Hong Kong we browsed many shops featuring those items as well as jade and other precious stones, and we cherished some of our purchases for years.

I developed the habit of buying unset, precious and semiprecious stones wherever I was posted or during my travels. Over the years I bought pearls in Japan, sapphires in Bangkok, diamonds in Israel, and jade and lapis lazuli in Hong Kong. As each of our daughters turned 18 I would give her an assortment of the stones, which she could have set as she pleased.

When you live in a foreign culture for an extended period you can learn a lot about that culture. It helps to be able to read and speak the local language. For me that process had started six years earlier at Walter Reed when I began studying Mandarin, courtesy of the tutor Whitey had provided. But even if you don't immerse yourself, many destinations can enrich your experience and the experience of your family.

Hong Kong was such an international city that it was easy for us to enjoy local celebrations such as the Chinese New Year. We also attended the *Tuen Ng*—better known as the Dragon Boat Festival—which each year commemorates the rebellious Qu Yuan drowning himself in protest in the Mi Lo River two millennia ago. And we watched tandems of costumed street performers do the traditional lion dance.

Other cultural events required a bit more effort. In February 1971 some Chinese colleagues invited Judy and me to a snake dinner in Wanchai, a district that stretches along the harbor in the middle of Hong Kong Island.

February, according to Cantonese custom, is the best time of year to eat snake because it raises the body temperature and keeps you warm in cold weather. It was indeed a cold day in Hong Kong with temperatures in the 40s.

Our hosts had preplanned the meal to feature several snake species from southern China prepared in various ways and served in a large dining room on the second floor of a Cantonese restaurant. Judy and I were the only non-Chinese—a distinction noticed by most who passed by our table.

We started with a hot soup accompanied by a drink made from snake bile with chrysanthemum petals floating on top. The soup wasn't bad. The drink tasted just like you'd think something prepared from snake bile would taste—awful!

Then followed a series of dishes featuring snake that was grilled, boiled, chopped, ground, filleted, fried and I can't remember what else—after a while I lost track. Most weren't bad and I'll give the standard answer that its taste and texture resembled chicken. Still the idea of eating a snake was tough to forget. We both found it tolerable if not really tasty to our Western palates.

That dinner tested the limits of our capacity for cultural immersion.

We had driven to the snake banquet, as well as most of our destinations, in our beloved Morgan. I'd be hard-pressed to explain why but in the summer of 1970, after Danika's first birthday, we had bought a royal-blue version of the classic sports car. We waited several months for it to arrive by ship from the factory in the U.K., during which time we continued driving our white Triumph Spitfire convertible.

The Morgan sported a leather top that required two men and a boy to attach; hence we left it off for months at a stretch and could sometimes be seen driving with an umbrella covering the opening between the tonneau and the windshield. It featured a wood frame bonded to aluminum to save weight, a sheepskin strap over the bonnet—which is what the Brits call the hood—a Triumph gearbox and engine, and that famous, handmade Morgan craftsmanship. It was a great little car.

Judy had indulged me in the purchase but she liked driving the Morgan, too. She'd often drop me off at the office and spend some time tooling around town. We found it quite practical—except for the removable top and the side curtains, which grew tedious—for navigating Hong Kong's narrow and curvy roads where one rarely exceeded 45 miles an hour.

When the four of us needed to go out we'd place Suzanne and Danika in the back seat, which was actually a leather bench, and secure them in place with a long, black-leather strap attached to the frame. They couldn't move much after we'd strapped them in but the trips we took were usually short so they never complained—much. The arrangement worked fine even after Alison, our third daughter, was born in 1971 in Springfield, Illinois, while we were on home leave.

When Pia was born at the end of our fourth year we knew we had outgrown the Morgan. So we purchased a golden-hued, Ford-built station wagon. Reluctantly—and perhaps foolishly, in retrospect—we sold the Morgan before we left Hong Kong. We later regretted leaving it behind and wished we'd taken it with us.

The station wagon was another story. When we started preparing to leave Hong Kong in 1973 we tried and tried but just couldn't sell it. Finally we had to give up and I asked a colleague, Chip Schofield, to sell it for me. He experienced the same lack of buyers but figured out the problem.

In Hong Kong, just like in the U.K., a license number stays with the vehicle throughout its lifetime. The wagon's plate number was 4404. Numbers have a special significance for the Chinese and the numeral four is bad—particularly bad.

Chip discovered that 4404 pronounced in Cantonese sounds very much like "Death, death, nothing but death." Naturally no Chinese person would want a car with that plate.

Chip finally sold the wagon to an unwitting Australian. What happened to it after that, heaven knows.

With so much work and our rich family life those first two years in Hong Kong passed quickly. Then with Whitey's blessing headquarters offered me the option of a second tour after a home leave. I accepted and early in 1971 I left ops-support and moved over to a branch headed by Bill Doyle to serve as his deputy.

Bill, who spoke solid Mandarin, had been handpicked to take over the branch and strengthen our legal traveler program, involving agents with direct access to China. We were responsible for recruiting, training, and running those agents. All of our officers, except me, had acquired exceptional Chinese-language skills and an extensive knowledge of the political, military and economic situation on the mainland.

I was pleased to make the move and eager to get into the fray, but the first couple of months sped by and soon it was time for Judy and me and the kids to go home for a while.

At a party just before we left, Bob M. took me aside to compliment me on the results of my first tour. He and Whitey were both pleased, he told me, with our restructured ops-support capability. He also praised my recruitment efforts, one of the best in the office.

It gratified me to hear it. I had been fortunate to serve in Hong Kong. Whitey was an outstanding leader and Bob was both motivator and teacher to me. I thought the same about my colleagues and peers. Years later I would realize how correct my assessments had been. We had an exceptional group in Hong Kong. Two ultimately led the clandestine service. At least a dozen others rose to our senior ranks and headed major divisions, staffs and stations.

I confess I remain somewhat puzzled about the group's exceptional nature. The only parallel I can recall was with our Berlin base during the 1950s. Hong Kong and Berlin alike required intense efforts against the agency's most difficult targets. Perhaps the people who accepted those challenges were a different breed and destined to be rewarded. A willingness to take on the toughest jobs can signify outstanding ability.

Home leave—eight weeks of rushing around visiting our respective families and many friends—was a whirlwind of activity. Judy, pregnant again, had to depart early because of airline regulations. Not permitted to fly after her seventh month and wanting to have the baby at home she flew out of Hong Kong in early April 1971, the earliest she could leave and the latest she could fly. She headed for Chicago via Seattle en route to her mother's home in Bulpitt. She took Suzanne and Danika with her—20 hours in the air, a grueling trip for an expectant mother, particularly one with two small children in tow.

I followed in May and shortly after my arrival Judy gave birth to our beautiful Alison Lee.

A couple of weeks later we headed to Washington where I went back to Langley for consultations on a variety of matters both administrative and operational. The desk officers sought to gain a better understanding of how I had improved ops support in Hong Kong. The chief of the desk agreed with my actions and said he admired how I had revamped our structure.

I told him Whitey made me do it.

I also received some briefings about agent communications in anticipation of my new tasking in Hong Kong. I didn't have many spare minutes while at headquarters but I did manage to spend a little time with old friends comparing notes about our respective careers.

What I found out was that I had fallen behind the curve, largely because of the Congo incident and its long aftermath, during which I had gained no experience until the spring of 1967 when I started preparing for the Hong Kong tour. In contrast most of my peers had completed two or three assignments managing clandestine operations.

So be it—I'll just have to catch up.

Before heading back to Hong Kong we stopped to visit my parents. They had moved back to Kansas City and were living in the suburb of Shawnee, Kansas. There we managed a few days of pure relaxation—as much as is possible when traveling with three young children including a newborn. Diann lived in the neighborhood and Bob and Carol had flown in. So did Greg, bringing us back together for the first time in several years.

All in all it was an eventful and satisfying—but also hectic and tiring—home leave for us and we actually felt relieved to land once again at Kai Tak.

Events in 1971 and 1972 dramatically changed Sino-American relations—at least on the surface. It all began with the visit to Beijing of an American table-tennis team, followed by a secret trip to China by Secretary of State Henry Kissinger, who set the stage for a face-to-face meeting the following year between President Richard M. Nixon and Communist Party Chairman Mao.

Each of these events signaled a thaw in the mutual suspicion and hostility that had prevailed between the United States of America and the People's Republic of China since 1949 when Mao's communist forces had pushed the Nationalist army of Chang Kai-shek off the mainland and onto the island of Formosa—now Taiwan. Those unprecedented interactions helped usher in a period of face-to-face discussions and debate about differences.

Despite the inroads China's Cultural Revolution raged on, controlled by hard-line communists who attempted to dominate all aspects of life. Much to our regret the Bamboo Curtain remained firmly in place, keeping our two countries adversarial. The stringent security controls persisted.

Still we felt somehow encouraged by President Nixon's visit and as a result we became more than willing to redouble our efforts. Now that Washington was talking with Beijing, our policymakers needed the best possible information more than ever.

That said, running agents into China from Hong Kong would be no less difficult and perhaps harder than it had been before our table-tennis team arrived in Beijing. We remained vulnerable to fabrication and deception by the local con men. Identifying individuals who could obtain genuine firsthand information required constant, laborious sifting through our wide range of contacts and agents.

Hong Kong had many Chinese communist officials and sympathizers. Some worked in companies associated with the government of the People's Republic; some were journalists, intelligence officers and bankers. These individuals were well aware of our presence in Hong Kong and extremely wary of any approach.

Another branch had been tasked with identifying individuals with knowledge and access to information about the Chinese government, people who represented potential targets for recruitment as agents. In fact as we moved around Hong Kong we all kept a lookout for men and women of possible interest to our programs. We used various methods such as club memberships, newspaper ads and what we called access agents.

These were people who might be able to facilitate contacts with potential agents, because they either were acquainted or worked with them. Access agents also might be people working inside a Chinese installation who could provide firsthand information about activities or personnel.

Sorting out which branch would handle a prospect could be done in due course but the priority was to establish the initial contact.

We employed as much operational testing as possible to confirm a potential agent's identity, background and intentions. At best we might be able to confirm that a prospect had entered China. But beyond that we could only employ analysis and research to verify the information we received.

Whenever we identified a prospect we initiated contact through a variety of different ploys. Then we worked painstakingly to develop understanding and trust. Each time we established someone as an agent and satisfied ourselves about his or her reliability we ensured that our new recruit received essential training in tradecraft.

In all cases we were responsible for the security of our agents. We would ask or permit no one to enter China without testing that person fully for reliability and providing all of the necessary training and equipment. We needed to protect whoever would be going inside China and acting alone.

We started right in Hong Kong where we knew the Chinese security and intelligence services operated aggressively. We constantly compartmented our operations from scrutiny by any other services, friendly or not. We taught tradecraft methods with great care, often requiring an agent to repeat, multiple times, the execution of a certain technique such as retrieving a microdot. We used no shortcuts. We did, day in and day out, everything we could to penetrate a denied area clandestinely.

We had no choice. Such difficult and complex activities carried life-and-death consequences. The high risks served as a great motivator. We never lost sight of the fact that imprisonment or execution faced any agent who entered China ill-prepared or who made a stupid mistake. Whatever reason an agent had for undertaking one of our assignments—ideological, monetary or personal—we left it to him or her to assess the risk.

As carefully as we operated we did sometimes lose agents; not often, but each one caused sadness and much reflection. After a loss we made every effort to discover and understand what had gone wrong.

Usually we would learn of the arrest of one of our people via a mainland newspaper. The Public Security Bureau, China's internal security organization, often would post an announcement describing how their brave policemen had captured a Western spy.

However we acquired the information it would be terrible news—

especially for the officer who had dispatched the agent. Each time we would send a cable to headquarters detailing our best analysis of what had gone wrong. The analysis was usually thin. We knew only that a compromise and arrest had taken place on the mainland, behind the Bamboo Curtain, and further information was almost impossible to obtain.

Our conclusions were predictable. We must ensure, we wrote, that the training provided and the technology employed is of the highest level so that each agent becomes capable of defeating the PSB's comprehensive security network.

Put simply, we'd have to do better.

Recruiting and training agents was only half of the clandestine task. Counterintelligence—ruling out that a prospect was acting as a double agent, or that someone else's clandestine service had become aware of our efforts—constituted the other half.

No matter which branch handled an initial contact we had to determine how much access that person actually enjoyed and whether he or she was a fabricator or being controlled by another service hoping to penetrate our program. We'd start by checking our existing files to vet the prospect but sooner or later we'd have to initiate contact, which was often done via telephone.

We designed the initial conversations merely to break the ice and assess a candidate's willingness to move the relationship forward. Would they talk with us at all? Were they cordial, indifferent or hostile?

If we succeeded over the phone we'd next propose a meeting—often for coffee somewhere or lunch.

I recall my first effort.

I felt daunted by the prospect. For one thing my countersurveillance training was eight years old. For another, even the training I received was less than sophisticated. Our methods had advanced significantly in the intervening years and what I knew was like the difference between a high-school graduate and a Ph.D. I'm not trying to be critical; my instructors did the best they could, given the tools at their disposal.

Before venturing forth I sought advice from some of my colleagues but none was particularly enlightening. My one advantage was the knowledge of Hong Kong's streets and transportation networks I had gained during my first year and reinforced while training my team. Nevertheless when a potential contact is on the line you can't be too careful.

I quickly discovered that anytime I left the office and proceeded into the city's Central District, with the goal of eluding anyone who might be following me, the odds were against me. My colleagues faced the same problem. Central, as it's known, was densely crowded most any time of day—and 95 percent of the people were Chinese.

Everywhere I looked nearly every individual I saw was the same height with the same straight, black hair and essentially the same clothing. In such an environment there was no way I could single out a suspected surveillant. The narrow streets, heavy traffic and numerous alleyways compounded the challenge.

My solution? I moved around a lot, riding ferries, taxis and trams. Or, I shopped, but always watchful and sometimes taking hours to get to a meeting site. I always tried to arrive as clean as could be.

Standard practice today is to abort a meeting anytime you suspect you're under surveillance.

Strange as it may sound, during my time in Hong Kong we never uncovered evidence that any other intelligence service was monitoring our activities. That fact continually amazed me. It didn't seem logical. Obviously the Chinese maintained agents in Hong Kong and obviously they were working hard to uncover our activities. But we detected nary a whiff of what they were doing. Either they were extremely good at keeping tabs on us or extremely bad. Whichever, we practiced our tradecraft at all times.

One of the difficulties in running counterintelligence in areas teeming with Chinese is distinguishing among individuals. At the beginning they all looked the same to me but over time I became much more discerning. When I scanned crowds of Asians I could—and still can—differentiate between northern and southern Chinese. I could also tell with relative confidence that someone was Japanese, Korean, Thai, Cambodian, Laotian, Vietnamese—even Indonesian.

The most useful characteristics for distinguishing differences are facial features: noses, cheekbones, eyes, et cetera. Cambodians, for example, usually have flatter faces, broader lips and bigger noses than other Asians, stemming from their Polynesian origins. The features differentiate them from Vietnamese, Lao and Thai people, whose ancestors pushed down from China.

For Judy and me the second half of our Hong Kong tour was every bit as busy as the first half—with her spending much of the time having two more babies and caring for our other two daughters. We had brought Suzanne with us, Judy delivered Danika soon after we arrived, she had Pia before we left, and in between she had given birth to Alison back in the States on our home leave.

Shortly before we embarked on that leave we received an invitation to join the Ladies' Recreation Club, a pleasant tennis facility located in the Mid-Levels. Actually the invitation was an acceptance. We had applied when we first arrived in 1969 and waited two years for the response. Knowing we'd be in Hong Kong for two more years we jumped at the chance—and in what would turn out to be a stroke of excellent foresight we bought a lifetime membership.

The club featured nine courts and two swimming pools plus assorted dining rooms, a bar, a reading room and other first-class facilities. It quickly became a great place for us to spend weekends. The kids loved the pools and when we had the time Judy and I played tennis.

By then we had moved from our apartment at Repulse Bay to a place also in the Mid-Levels less than five minutes from the club. The apartment provided a wonderful view of Hong Kong harbor.

Our socializing extended beyond the club. Judy and I knew many people who owned boats and we often accepted invitations to spend a day on the waters of the Crown Colony. We had developed a wide circle of friends, including Chinese and other Asians as well as Europeans and Americans, many of whom also had young children, so our kids were often a part of the weekend social activities. It was a good life.

As I've described it was also a practical extension of my work. Gathering intelligence in a foreign post has many facets, some of which include getting to know the local people—what they're like, how they think, what their goals are. It can be extremely useful to be able to talk with a friend or acquaintance about the issues or concerns of the day.

From my tennis playing I met M.W. Lo, a fixture in Hong Kong social circles. He was educated in England and subsequently enjoyed a successful law career. He had retired in the late 1950s but remained physically and mentally active, allowing his son to carry on the family business. M.W. loved tennis and had reportedly played doubles at Wimbledon in the 1920s. He was in his late 70s when I met him but he still played an acceptable game.

M.W. lived in a large house overlooking Stanley, a small fishing village on the south side of Hong Kong Island. The house was built halfway up the island's mountainous spine and terraced next to and below it were three grass courts. All offered a view of Stanley Bay, which on weekends was usually filled with fishing and pleasure boats. It was a beautiful setting and I became part of a group that played there on Sunday afternoons.

Through M.W.'s social network I met many interesting people and developed some productive relationships. It was the best of both worlds. M.W. always chose as his doubles partner the best player there that day. Whoever played those matches would find them enjoyable but tame, given M.W.'s age. He could usually play only two sets. Then he would sit out while others took over the court.

One Sunday, Ken Rosewall, the world-class Australian player, was in town for the Hong Kong Open tournament. He had dropped in to partner with M.W., who was honorary head of the Hong Kong Tennis Association and enjoyed lots of clout in the colony's tennis world.

M.W. played one good set with Rosewall and sat out. To my great delight Rosewall then became my partner. As we walked onto the court he asked if I wanted the forehand or backhand side to receive service. I usually played backhand, but I told him I'd gladly defer to his legendary prowess. He laughed and agreed.

"How shall we play this?" he asked me.

"Well, if I don't win with you as a partner I'll never get invited back here," I responded without hesitation, "so we better win."

We did, with Ken playing a decidedly polite game, trying not to intimidate anyone and making the shots only as necessary. I felt thrilled to play with someone of his caliber who was also a true gentleman.

Tennis would become a valuable icebreaker for me through the rest of my career. For example, through it I met Jean Ingles, a private secretary to Hong Kong's governor. Jean, a typical British civil servant, had lived in the colony for years and worked for several governors.

A delightful person whom Judy and I grew to like very much, Jean invited us to play mixed doubles regularly on the three clay courts at the governor's mansion. The governor didn't play and she had access at any time she wanted.

Again tennis proved useful, both for its own enjoyment and for the people we met. The doubles matches we played weren't too demanding but the acquaintances, usually Europeans, and the conversations we had with them at teatime, were always interesting and informative.

It might sound strange but neither Judy nor I could understand more than about half of the teatime conversations when we began accepting Jean's invitations. We couldn't quite make out the accent of the Brits or their nuances of word usage—and we seemed to amuse them with our American dialect. George Bernard Shaw had it right; we truly are two peoples separated by a common language.

Eventually we all managed to tune in to one another.

One reason Judy took up tennis—in between having our children—was to accompany me to matches rather than stay at home. As with most of the things she tried she picked it up quickly and within a year she developed a very respectable game. She was strong, athletic and had good hand-eye coordination—no doubt a benefit of her tomboy, softball-playing youth.

When she started tennis in 1970 she used a Butterfly bamboo racket made in Shanghai. She took weekly lessons from a guy named, believe it or not, Charlie Chan, a freelance instructor at a local public court. By late 1971 she was playing regularly at the club and elsewhere. Those qualities of hers always impressed me.

What I came to appreciate even more was her ability to maintain a cheerful attitude despite the burden of raising our four young daughters—two of them attending different schools—and supporting my efforts at building social relationships. Nevertheless by the time we departed Hong Kong I knew she was ready to leave.

In February 1973 the agency's fortunes took a sudden and definite downturn. Although we didn't know it at the time the change marked the beginning of several years of upheaval.

Actually things started to fall apart in late November 1972 after President Nixon's reelection in what politicians and pundits like to call a "landslide." In one of his first post-election acts Nixon fired Dick Helms, our director.

I now know that their relationship had been strained for a long time. Dick had been reluctant to involve the agency more deeply in Vietnam. More pertinent, he refused to cooperate when the president asked him to cite national security as part of the White House's efforts to block the congressional investigation into the Watergate burglary. That refusal was apparently the last straw.

The firing stunned me. I'm sure my reaction was due to the role he had played in my Congo evacuation as well as his taking the time to visit me at Walter Reed. But there was more to it. I genuinely respected Dick's ability and his leadership and I liked Dick Helms personally, as did my peers and, I think, most of the agency community. He was one of us. Whatever had prompted Nixon's decision—Vietnam, Watergate or something else entirely—we all felt uneasy and the president's next decision in this matter deepened our concerns.

As our new director, the fifth to occupy the position since I joined the agency, Nixon named James R. Schlesinger. Like John McCone had been, he was chairman of the Atomic Energy Commission.

Who the hell is this guy? That's what we all asked one another. What does he know about intelligence?

We found out that Schlesinger indeed lacked practical experience in national security. He had researched the subject for several years at the Rand Corporation, a think tank. But before heading the AEC in the Nixon administration he had worked in the Bureau of the Budget as a defense specialist.

As word of his background reached us reactions included doubt, dismay and worry. A career bureaucrat would be heading the CIA. On February 2, 1973, Schlesinger took over.

It didn't take long for our fears to be confirmed. Even as far from

Washington as we were, and even from my distant view of the reins of power, I could see what I regarded as Schlesinger's misguided efforts. First he decreed that the Directorate of Plans, the clandestine service, would henceforth be known as the Directorate of Operations, to recognize the true nature of its activities. A relatively minor point, perhaps, but none of us liked the new name. Maybe it was because Schlesinger had ordered the change. If Helms had done it I doubt that many would have complained.

Far worse, he fired more than 1,500 people or forced them to resign or retire. The total included over 1,000 from the clandestine service. Again dismay set in. As panels started determining who would go and who would stay tensions mounted—though we assumed or hoped none would be let go from field positions.

Those hopes were soon dashed. Headquarters sent word that two of our officers would have to leave the service. With the announcement morale fell to the lowest point I had seen in my 12 years at the agency. Whitey appealed the decisions regarding the officers but headquarters rejected the attempt, and within a couple of months both officers departed.

More word reached us via the grapevine: Schlesinger planned to shift priority to technical operations. He regarded satellite reconnaissance, sensor arrays, communications intercepts and the like as more productive than human operations. That meant fewer resources for what we were doing.

Morale sank even lower. We had no doubt Schlesinger was flat wrong but we were powerless, as was our directorate. The fact it was Schlesinger calling the shots made it particularly hard to take. Many realized our involvement in Vietnam and Laos had left us with more officers than we needed. Had it been Helms mandating the cuts they would have been more readily accepted. But coming from Schlesinger, given his stated intention of reducing the size and importance of the clandestine service, it was hard to swallow.

Then, more change: Schlesinger moved to reorganize the entire agency. The Contact Division, an overt, intelligence-collection operation responsible for debriefing Americans who had traveled abroad, would lose its separate status. Schlesinger had moved it into Operations.

Mix an overt office with the clandestine service? What sense did that make? The consensus within the intelligence community quickly congealed that this man was a disaster.

Still more moves followed, none to our liking. To say that Schlesinger was unpopular, particularly within the Directorate of Operations, would have been a considerable understatement.

From our perspective he didn't understand the agency, didn't like the agency, and didn't give a damn about the agency's future. That he was able to make such a negative impression in such a short period of time is actually quite remarkable. Rumor had it that Schlesinger ordered a security camera installed to monitor his official portrait at Langley, apparently fearing that someone would try to vandalize it.

In addition to our continuing woes with Schlesinger, 1973 dealt several other body blows to the agency in general and the clandestine service in particular. In January *The New York Times* published a profile about Cord Meyer, one of our stalwarts, and its thrust was negative.

Also in January, the trial of Daniel Ellsberg—he of the infamous Pentagon Papers—began. Ellsberg, a Defense Department analyst, strongly disagreed with U.S. policy in Vietnam. He decided on his own to make public a batch of classified Pentagon policy papers. The *Times* had published those papers in 1971 and the government attempted to prosecute Ellsberg. For reasons too complex to describe here, the trial judge dismissed all charges against him.

The point was the Pentagon Papers controversy spilled over onto the CIA. For one thing, evidence presented by the defense at the trial revealed that E. Howard Hunt, a retired agency employee, was involved in a break-in at Ellsberg's psychiatrist's office in an attempt to discredit Ellsberg. Also involved were former agency people Eugenio Martinez, Felipe de Diego and James McCord. The disclosures fueled speculation in the press that the CIA was conducting illegal domestic spying operations.

April saw the release of a book titled *The Politics of Lying* by David Wise, an agency critic. It added to the cascade of negative press and public sentiment about the CIA. There were other instances but suffice it to say we were experiencing a miserable period. I was happy to be in the field but I knew that come summer I would be returning to headquarters.

In April 1973, just three months before we were scheduled to leave Hong Kong, Judy returned to Canossa Hospital to give birth to Pia Kristina, another beautiful baby girl. We were delighted, as were her sisters.

Not so the waiters at the Chinese restaurant in Happy Valley where we regularly dined on Sunday evenings. They had watched as we arrived in Hong Kong with one daughter and soon a second one. Then we returned from home leave in 1971 with a third girl.

The waiters always treated us politely but they often looked distressed and felt sorry—for me. When they saw us walk in with yet another daughter they could no longer conceal their disappointment. How awful it wasn't a boy, they told me.

Often during our years in Hong Kong we would encounter other reflections of the cultural differences between East and West. We had a perfect baby and couldn't be happier. But they couldn't bear to see me without a son.

"Never mind," one of them finally consoled me, "now you have the four legs of the table. Next time you will get the top."

I nodded sagely and ordered dinner.

Judy and I would again visit Hong Kong in the fall of 1997 and we stopped to eat in the same restaurant. The waiter who had consoled me still worked there and he recognized me. Again he was polite and friendly but this time he said nothing about my four daughters.

During that same visit, at the Spring Deer—another favorite restaurant, on the Kowloon side of the harbor—the maître d' approached me.

"Oh, Mr. Holm," he said, "I not see you for a long time."

By then it had been 16 years so he had quite a memory. And of course, thanks to my Congo experience and the scars it left, people don't easily forget me.

In May 1973, General Vernon Walters, the CIA's deputy director, and William Colby, the executive officer—the agency's number three—visited Hong Kong. Whitey invited a group of us to meet them for cocktails at his house one evening.

I found Colby most congenial and willing to answer the pointed questions we posed—such as what the hell was going on at headquarters. Walters was likewise friendly and he lived up to his reputation as a raconteur. He possessed an exceptional fluency in several languages, something that had allowed him to conduct discreet, important and direct interactions with various foreign leaders. He also seemed fascinated with the subway systems of the world's major cities and liked to relate personal anecdotes about them.

During that evening word arrived via cable that President Nixon had chosen Schlesinger to be his new secretary of defense, replacing Elliot Richardson, whom Nixon had nominated as attorney general in the midst of the growing Watergate scandal.

Schlesinger would be leaving the agency within days. We literally cheered the news but there was more. Nixon had nominated Colby to replace Schlesinger—a most welcome development. One of us would be in charge again. I truly hoped that Colby, who would be my sixth director, could repair the damage Schlesinger had inflicted.

Odd, but in the course of that trip to the Far East, Colby had arrived as subordinate to Walters but left as his superior. Such are the ways of Washington, I remember thinking. At least Nixon had finally gotten it right—though I had no idea that Watergate likely prompted his decision.

Whatever the reason, we were delighted to see Schlesinger's brief tenure come to an end. It had been a nightmare—but our problems were far from over.

Judy and the girls and I left Hong Kong that July. The challenge of traveling almost halfway around the world with four young children taxed us but we managed—and the girls were great. They stayed close to us during the entire trip and thankfully they slept during a large portion of it.

At the time I thought my career had finally gotten back on track. I had been promoted to a GS-13 in 1970, meaning I was keeping abreast of my peers. The extended tour in Hong Kong had gone well and I felt comfortable with all aspects of my assignment there. I liked working as a field case officer—my original intent. We had steadily improved the quality and quantity of our intelligence. To a certain extent President Nixon's diplomacy had increased our access to China, but we also helped ourselves by steadily honing our skills at vetting, recruiting, and communicating with agents. And based on the incoming messages from home we felt confident we were keeping headquarters and policymakers happy.

Soon I'd be starting a new tour, this one at headquarters. From ignorance or naiveté—or some combination thereof—I harbored no fears about the future of the clandestine service. I held this conviction despite the almost incessant bad news since Helms's firing. But I had kept my head down, proceeding with my work and assuming that headquarters would sort out its problems. My colleagues and I tended to share a decidedly wishful phrase: This too shall pass.

Even now, nearly 40 years later, I am hard-pressed to remember, let alone explain, my optimism about the issues the agency was confronting. Maybe it speaks to how highly motivated we all were.

We'll be okay, I told myself, and Bill Colby—assuming he survives what looks to be a hostile confirmation process—will run the agency well.

16. Definitely Not Happenstance

LANGLEY, VIRGINIA 1973–1976

Nothing much had changed at headquarters since I left four years earlier. Many of the same people were still around—the headquarters cadre. Quite a few friends, including colleagues with whom I had started my career, were also working at Langley.

As I entered the building in late August 1973 I read again the biblical passage carved into the marble wall of the main entrance.

And ye shall know the truth, and the truth shall make you free.

–John 8:32

I remembered how impressed I had been when I read it back in January 1962. I was full of the spirit of adventure then but now the quote underscored a far deeper sense of responsibility. Laos and the Congo had provided about as much adventure as I needed. I had grown to regard the business of providing high-quality intelligence to our policymakers as more important. Plus I had a wife and four children.

One obvious change at headquarters was that the hallways were more colorful. Somebody had the bright idea of painting doorways in pastels and hanging pictures and posters on the walls, apparently to make things cheerier.

Parking was still a pain. Even though I was a mid-level officer, instead of a junior one, I had to park in the hinterlands and walk a long way to the office. But in many respects I felt lucky. I heard horror stories from friends who worked for the FBI or the Department of State and had to face the Washington area's massive daily traffic gridlock, scrounge out parking places, and contend with the federal bureaucracy in close quarters.

I felt blessed to be working at Langley's wooded compound in the suburbs. The location offered some insulation from the dreaded transportation, parking and political problems of the city. Whatever else had befallen Allen Dulles, the agency had moved to Langley under his tenure and for that we were all grateful.

We moved back into our house in McLean, which we had occupied from November 1968 until we left for Hong Kong in March 1969, and which we had rented out during our absence. We filled all five bedrooms. My commute lasted about 10 minutes—down Old Dominion Drive then one turn onto Dolley Madison Boulevard to the main entrance.

Our other adjustments were relatively painless. We joined a country club in Vienna, a nearby suburb, and started using its tennis and swimming facilities. Over the next several years we would spend a lot of time there watching the girls' matches as they advanced through the age categories.

In the first few months back at headquarters I renewed old acquaintances and established new ones. As I moved around the building, which housed not only the clandestine service but also major portions of the three other directorates, I heard only tidbits of the trials and tribulations the agency had been and was still suffering.

The issues arose in conversations but few people expressed any real concern for the future. Most thought the storm was temporary. William Colby had suffered nasty allegations in the press about his background, stemming primarily from programs he had conceived of and run while in Vietnam, and from the ongoing debate about U.S. policy there.

Most of us were united in frustration and irritation that members of Congress had aggressively questioned Colby's fitness to lead the agency during his confirmation hearings over the summer. But by all accounts he had handled the grilling with aplomb. He was no stranger to difficult and challenging situations. During World War II Colby had served with distinction in the OSS. In late 1944 he had led a small group on one particularly perilous mission, a mid-winter parachute jump far north into German-occupied Norway.

Trained to operate behind enemy lines Colby's team linked up with Norwegian partisans and skied, mostly at night, to a key railway line the Nazis were using to transfer crack troops back through Finland to Germany.

In an account Colby himself wrote for the agency he described the mission this way:

> At about this time, the Battle of the Bulge had been liquidated, but there was fear on our side that another last gasp by the great beast was in the making. These 150,000 undefeated and still-haughty soldiers were streaming toward the Fatherland. The sea route was well taken care of by the British fleet. The roads were clogged by the wondrous snow that falls nine months of the year around the Arctic Circle. That left the railroad—the Nordland—a single-track affair between Narvik and Trondheim carrying thousands of troops Reichward each day and daily gaining in capacity. Like Carthage, this had to be destroyed.

The team blew up the line in several places and they successfully interrupted the troop trains. The mission required courage, stamina and determination, and William Colby possessed those characteristics in abundance.

In the end Congress resolved all of the issues and confirmed him as our director. Still it was painful for us to read the articles and books attacking the agency at the time and to hear criticisms of men like Colby and Cord Meyer, another World War II combat veteran whose 26 years at the agency included a steadfast devotion to defeating communism. We believed strongly that the CIA was innocent of the charges leveled against it and that our motives in following—or refusing, as Dick Helms had done—presidential orders were beyond reproach.

The truth will win out one day, we hoped, and if not at least we knew better.

In 1973—and I'm sure it's true today—the CIA was full of highly motivated people. We all thought we had a job to do for the country and we would, by damn, do it.

When I first worked at headquarters I had longed for an overseas assignment. This time around as a China Operations officer within Far East Division—now East Asia—my job promised to be more interesting. Instead of working as a desk officer supporting a station I now served in the branch responsible for supporting our entire operations targeted against China. The branch was divided geographically, in line with divisions in the directorate. I suppose because I could speak French the powers that be assigned me to the European section.

In fact I *was* the European section. I received—with copies to the relevant desks—all cable and dispatch traffic about cases being run in Europe against China. I was responsible for assessing the traffic, doing whatever research was required, and preparing a response to the field.

My branch was designed to encourage and support our actions against the target anywhere in the world. The task proved just as difficult elsewhere as it had been in Hong Kong, largely because of the wariness of Chinese officials to make or sustain contact with us.

The branch assigned what we called referents—officers responsible for monitoring China-related traffic from stations and bases worldwide—to each division, including Far East Division, and we held regular staff meetings to discuss trends and operational ideas we might want to suggest to the field.

We regularly prepared what were called book cables. These were lengthy memos containing background information on various aspects of China and suggestions on how to approach a given topic. The book cables were general in nature, unlike the tailored guidance we would transmit for a specific operation.

We also met regularly with our reports officers to discuss and evaluate incoming intelligence. I always found these meetings interesting because they were substantive. We were getting some excellent reporting from the field, which in turn encouraged us to sustain our efforts at headquarters.

All this meant busy, busy days for me. I found myself working long hours, frequently including Saturdays until noon. I didn't mind because almost all of it focused on ops with very little involving the more tedious aspects of headquarters support. In short, my new assignment differed greatly from the previous one but that was fine with me.

A typical day would begin with a look at the overnight cable traffic—a ritual. Just like a dairy farmer who begins each day milking his herd, a desk officer starts off by reading incoming traffic promptly. It was a critical part of supporting a station or operation in the field and it had to be done religiously. Often I couldn't answer every cable on the same day it arrived so I spent part of my time dealing with unresolved issues.

For example I often met with European desk officers to explain or justify a cable I wanted to send out. I also met frequently with colleagues to mull over the progress of an op. And I had mountains of material to read and digest.

As a result my knowledge of the military, geographic, economic, political and social affairs of China grew significantly—in addition to what I had amassed while in Hong Kong. I had developed a much broader picture of what China was doing and, to the extent I could understand it, why. China's policies were dead wrong, I concluded. They caused only suffering for the Chinese people. My anticommunist feelings, already strong, were being reinforced by what I was learning.

I became aware of an ongoing competition between our shop and the Soviet-ops people. The agency considered both global targets but at the time the Soviet threats were more tangible and the consensus was the Russians merited the higher priority.

But that mindset never sat well with us. We thought China was equally serious—and present-day developments have borne out this conclusion. Debate within the directorate about apportioning resources was low-key but persistent—and it grew more intense whenever budgets were discussed.

We found our Soviet-ops colleagues condescending and lacking in understanding. We argued for supporting our stations to the tune of an equally strong China-ops program. I can't say whether or not the directorate noticed our efforts, but at least it made us feel better.

As had been the case in Hong Kong, I liked and respected my peers and superiors. Jim K., chief of China Operations, had flown as tail gunner in a B-24 over Europe and served in our Berlin base during the late 1950s.

Gruff but likeable and dedicated to his work, he spent long days in the office and was adept at managing the headquarters bureaucracy.

His deputy, Harry S., a University of Michigan graduate, had served in Europe and the Far East and brought much experience to the job. Calm, patient and competent, he was widely liked and respected. He later would head Far East Division. I carpooled with him for a while and grew to know him well—and the better I knew him the better I liked him.

My fellow referents, all at about the same grade level, were mostly China-ops officers on headquarters tours. We all worked hard, considered ourselves productive, and looked forward to our next field tours, wherever they might be.

Our optimism aside, the agency was about to endure some very hard times and Director Colby would suffer enough grief to make his tenure frustrating indeed.

On August 9, 1974, President Nixon resigned in disgrace because of the Watergate scandal and his vice president, Gerald R. Ford, took office. On December 22, *The New York Times* published a front-page story by Seymour Hersh carrying the headline "Huge CIA Operation Reported in U.S. Against Anti-War Forces." The shocking revelation prompted Ford to order Nelson Rockefeller, his newly appointed vice president, to head a commission reviewing accusations of agency wrongdoing.

Ford muddied the waters even more by hinting that the agency had been involved in attempted assassinations of foreign leaders. True or not, such allegations came as a complete surprise to me, the result of the agency's pervasive practice of compartmentation—I had no Need to Know.

Soon thereafter Congress likewise took up the issue. On January 27, 1975, the Senate established the Select Committee to Study Government Operations With Respect to Intelligence Activities. It was chaired by Senator Frank Church, a Democrat from Idaho. On February 19, the House created the Select Committee on Intelligence, headed by Representative Lucien Nedzi, Democrat of Michigan.

Hoping to minimize publicity and avoid distortions, Colby presented what became popularly known as the "family jewels"—secret, unpublished and supposedly undisclosed-to-Congress details about politically sensitive operations. Much of it actually had been compiled under the direction of Schlesinger, who had sworn to "find out if there were questionable or illegal activities hidden in the secret recesses of our clandestine past that we didn't know about and that might explode at any time under our feet."

Schlesinger never had a chance to present the results of the investigation because of his shift to the Pentagon. But as Colby reported to the Rockefeller commission and Congress, the CIA had briefly conducted domestic covert actions involving student groups opposing the Vietnam War. My understanding was that we had information from abroad linking those groups to communist-front organizations that were funding and influencing them. Colby also reported that the agency had attempted to assassinate Patrice Lumumba in the Congo and Fidel Castro in Cuba.

Then Hersh struck again. On June 5, the *Times* published an article under his byline revealing that Colby had briefed Nedzi about the family jewels in 1973—two years earlier. Nedzi, who also chaired the powerful Armed Services Committee and was known as a strong agency supporter, resigned June 12. He was replaced by Otis Pike, Democrat of New York.

Congress howled about the revelation. Senator Church famously called the CIA a "rogue elephant out of control." But I suspect the reaction had more to do with the fact that so few individuals on Capitol Hill had been briefed by the agency and that the executive branch had held the information so closely.

Within the ranks of the clandestine service the turmoil had minimal effect on our work. We knew that Colby and some of our senior—division level and above—officers were intensely engaged with the Rockefeller and congressional investigators, but our superiors had compartmented themselves from the rest of us. We did our jobs while struggling with the substance of some of the revelations.

Because only a small number of officers had actually been involved in the efforts under attack, most of us knew little or nothing about the accusations. I either didn't believe them or suspected they were being distorted by the agency's opponents.

Yes, I rationalized, but that rationalization was fortified by a decade of working with these men and witnessing their devotion to duty firsthand.

The difficulties the agency and Colby suffered during this period have been extensively documented and I don't want to belabor the subject. What I can attest to is that despite the revelations about our operations and the negative publicity, the men and women of the service carried on steadfastly, not knowing how or whether the agency's image had been damaged or diminished.

As a result of the investigations Congress made the Senate and House intelligence oversight committees permanent. For the first time in its 28-year history the CIA's very existence had been questioned and legislators would be keeping close tabs on our operations from then on. None of us liked the idea but we would have to learn to live with it.

I took several trips to Europe during my three years back at headquarters, each designed to support China operations under way there. We always regarded face-to-face discussions as better than reading a cable—body language, nuances, words chosen and direct responses all supplied much more information and often brought issues to a quicker resolution.

I usually scheduled a visit whenever I determined that an op had progressed to a particularly promising point. I would stop at three or four of our offices just to multiply the value of the trip.

I typically traveled alone, contacting each office only after my arrival in the city. Nothing sinister here; I tried to keep the administrative and logistic tasks to a minimum. I was fully capable of making all of the arrangements necessary to visit our overseas offices. They were typically busy places so they didn't need the added strain of preparing at length to host me.

During my visits I usually met with the case officer running the operation and discussed its progress in detail. Often when the chief learned via cable traffic of my impending arrival he would ask me to host an informal seminar about the status of our China ops. I was always pleased to do so. With my solid background on China and my four years in Hong Kong I was able to pass along lots of useful information. I enjoyed those sessions.

Judy joined me on one of my trips through North Africa, which I took in the temporary absence of the Middle East referent. We visited Morocco, Algeria and Tunisia.

Judy's life was full and she had almost no time off from running the household and raising our "platoon" of daughters, as I began calling them. So this break seemed like a good idea. Her mother flew in from Illinois to take over the household. It would be the only time during my career that she went along on a business trip.

Case officers did not ordinarily bring their wives overseas on business, partly because of the hazard of inadvertently revealing an operational procedure and partly because of the extra personal expenses involved. Because it wasn't done much I took some good-natured ribbing from my colleagues about it.

Our first stop was Rabat, Morocco, where André and Cathy Le Gallo were living. Judy visited with them while I worked, and one weekend the two of us traveled to the city of Fez in the Atlas Mountains, a few hours' drive away. Then Judy flew to Tunis for a few days and stayed at the Hilton Hotel. Meanwhile I headed to Algiers on business.

Her trip was much more enjoyable than mine. Algiers, once the bejeweled capital of the French colony, had become, in the wake of the civil war in the 1950s and Algerian independence in 1962, a dirty and hostile place. Worse, many Algerians carried strong anti-American sentiments and their security people routinely monitored all U.S. Embassy personnel.

I met with my colleagues at our office and they briefed me on the progress of their programs. I marveled at how they could accomplish anything in such an environment. Still they all seemed enthusiastic and they welcomed my visit.

They had no active contact with the Chinese but assured me they would give it a try. Nevertheless I left Algiers with little optimism about the prospects for a strong China program there.

I also left with an unpleasant memory. Despite—or perhaps because of—my U.S. passport the customs officers hassled me at the airport. They subjected me to questioning that was inappropriate for my status. Fortunately it didn't last long and nothing came of it.

On my short flight to Tunis I thought about the beautiful Algiers that the Frenchmen I had known in Bordeaux in 1959 described to me. I wondered what they would have made of the decaying and hostile city it became. They probably would have been just as happy as I was to leave.

As planned I met Judy at the Hilton. She was lying in the sun beside the pool. The day was warm and bright but the wind was very strong, blowing steadily at about 40 miles per hour and gusting even stronger. As Judy sat up to greet me the wind blew her sunglasses into the pool. Tunis was experiencing a sirocco, a fierce, strong wind pattern out of the Sahara Desert that can continue for days.

That evening, with the sirocco still blowing, we took a taxi to the chief's residence where we had been invited for dinner. A pleasant and interesting man with considerable experience in North Africa, he and his charming wife were the perfect hosts. Despite my lack of seniority they went out of their way to make us feel welcome and he and I talked very little shop.

After drinks and hors d'oeuvres we enjoyed a delicious meal of North African specialties including roast lamb. The conversation continued through dinner and our hosts' strongest recommendation was that we visit the nearby site of the ancient city of Carthage. They even offered to take us there on the weekend.

It was and still is common in the field to welcome and entertain visitors from headquarters. It's a tradition I've always liked and something I regard as an indication of the high caliber of people who work for the agency. When I rose to station chief I always took steps to see that visitors felt welcome. It was more difficult in the larger stations because of the volume of visitors, but I always tried to keep up.

The sirocco blew on. The next day, a Friday, Judy browsed the *suq*—the city's market—while I conducted another meeting with my colleagues. Despite their small number and limited resources they had developed some interesting contacts with Chinese officials. I briefed them on general subjects about China and spent several hours with two officers who were in touch with potential agents. They posed good questions and presented useful ideas about how to proceed.

I had prepared for the meetings before I left headquarters so I was able to put some good thoughts on the table in response. I was impressed at how they were attempting to deepen their relationships with the targets. They were proceeding well and the discussions reconfirmed the value of face-to-face meetings.

I spent an informal hour or so with the chief and his deputy discussing general ops topics. I brought them up to date about what was going on at headquarters. This was standard. Anytime someone from Langley visited the field his or her job was to fill in colleagues about developments back home. Promotions, assignments, budgets, reporting and many other subjects are fair game and visitors answer questions as best as they can. In this case it was a long but thoroughly satisfying day.

The sirocco finally extinguished itself that evening and the weekend weather turned beautiful. We got our chance to see the ruins of Carthage and an artists' colony at the port of Tunis. We found the ruins unremarkable—there just wasn't much left—but the colony consisted of striking, pastel-colored buildings that had been built a long time ago. We browsed the work of Arab artists pleasantly but didn't buy anything.

I had taken leave for the next week so Judy and I could enjoy a short vacation in Spain and France. We flew to Madrid, rented a small car, and spent a couple of days sightseeing and shopping, and one evening we watched flamenco dancers perform at a theater featuring mostly Romani culture.

Then we drove down to Toledo to visit some of the ruins left by the Spanish Civil War in the 1930s. We browsed shops offering beautiful steel knives and swords produced by local artisans. We also visited La Valle de los Caídos, the Valley of the Fallen, near Madrid, a spectacular memorial to the dead of both sides of the Civil War. We never forgot the beautiful cathedral carved into solid rock.

Next we drove north to San Sebastian where I took Judy to places I had gone in the late 1950s during my stint in the Army. One highlight was the Aita-Mari, a small Basque restaurant that overlooks the city's beautiful and picturesque harbor filled with fishing boats and sailboats. They served wonderful seafood and Spanish wine.

I recalled that in July 1959 the wine had not been so sweet. That's when two friends and I danced the *jota*, a Basque folk dance, the night before we ran with the bulls in Pamplona.

Lawrence P. Jepson III—an Army friend and the only man I've ever known who was a "third"—and Olav, a Norwegian college schoolmate, had driven south from France to join La Fiesta de San Fermin. The festival starts every year on the seventh hour of the seventh day of the seventh month and lasts for seven days.

We had packed sleeping bags into my little VW convertible and planned to camp out on the ground near the car. We found space under a large tree, locked the doors, and sauntered into town. After we supplied ourselves with the red San Fermin scarves all the men were wearing we sat in a small café and began to drink the local red wine. At 7 cents a bottle it didn't taste good at all, but after a few glasses, that fact dimmed. To say the least it was a strong brew.

I was the only one who spoke Spanish, unfortunately not enough to get very far with the attractive girls strolling by. We managed to eat a little but that and the after-dinner coffee didn't inhibit us from dancing the *jota*. For one thing you didn't need a partner. Dancers stood in a circle, raised their arms with elbows bent, and alternately raised each leg—in time with the music if possible—bending it at the knee and pointing the foot forward.

After midnight things began to liven up even more. Strangers frequently offered us drinks. They would simply hand us their *boda* and invite us to take a drink. The *boda* is a leather pouch with a spout on the end. They were all filled with wine, the 7-cent variety. To take a drink you hold the *boda* above your head and squirt the wine into your mouth. All three of us missed our mouths, causing great amusement for onlookers. The wine flowed, literally. And flowed.

Dancing erupted spontaneously almost everywhere we turned and lasted into the wee hours of the morning. Larry, Olav and I loved every minute of it. The crowd was mostly young men, drunken young men, engaged in a ritual of preparation.

Around 4 a.m. the almost frenzied level of activity dwindled noticeably. Now there were quiet conversations focused on the bulls. For a moment I reflected on the wisdom of what we were about to attempt. I had seen those animals lift and toss horse and rider picadors with the strength of their necks and I knew they were bred to fight and die. The courage of the *boda* quickly blotted out any doubts, however, and I felt more than ready.

Hell that's why we're here. Let's get on with it!

When the sun rose we stopped at a public fountain in a small plaza and splashed cold water over our faces and aching eyes. We found a café and ordered coffee. Feeling the excitement building we moved to a long, narrow plaza on the edge of Pamplona that was filling rapidly, receiving a steady influx of young men. Several strong policemen held a rope that blocked access to the street leading to the bullring. No one would start, they made clear, before 7 a.m. All other streets leading into the plaza were barricaded with heavy timbers. Crowds gathered, waving flowers and red scarves.

After 7 o'clock no one was allowed out over the barriers. At that point, like it or not, we were all committed to run; our excitement was tinged with anxiety.

Then cannon thundered. Let the fiesta begin! The crowd roared.

The mass of men headed for the bullring. Some ran, some jogged, and some made a show of not moving much at all—the experienced guys who had planned to run among the bulls.

The cannon had scared the hell out of me but also sharpened my senses. I raised my arm to Larry and Olav and shouted, "See you in the ring!"

At first we jogged along together. A runner tried to climb over the barricade but the crowd wouldn't let him get out. No way, *hombre!*

Then we all heard the second cannon volley, signaling that the bulls had been released and were running through the plaza and into the street behind us.

My mind comprehended two things: 1) whatever alcohol left in my bloodstream was now being overcome by a surge of adrenaline; and 2) I must get into the arena and behind the fence that would protect me from the charging bulls. My pace increased.

I lost track of Larry and Olav. The crush on the narrow street made it impossible to keep together. I glanced back to see if any bulls were closing in but saw none. Still I began looking for a doorway to seek just in case—any port in a storm. But the narrow alcoves I passed weren't tempting. I ran even faster.

A Spaniard next to me tried to hand me a rolled-up newspaper. I didn't understand and refused. I was getting tired but kept moving.

A shout from a barricade roused me to look back. Two bulls were lumbering about 50 yards behind me. They appeared enormous, their horns almost as wide as the narrow street. They were moving really fast, closing the gap between us. As I gaped at the two strong, beautiful, dangerous animals a young man darted out of a doorway. He ran alongside one of the bulls and swatted the side of its head with a rolled-up newspaper.

Now I understood the earlier gesture but I thought the guy was crazy!

A sudden problem: I kept looking behind me, not where I was going. Naturally I stumbled into another runner and we both fell down. He cursed me in Spanish. I jumped up and took off down the street as if the race was a 50-yard dash or a fast break in basketball. To my great relief I spotted the entrance to the bullring—though I didn't know about another tradition that was playing out there.

The entrance was wide enough only for a horse-drawn wagon to pass through. A bunch of men were lying on the ground, forming a big pile of bodies. The idea was that the bulls approaching the entrance would stop at this pile and mill around for a minute. At that point the pile of men would spring to life, shout at the confused bulls, and run into the arena. This was considered a really cool thing to do and it was my fortune—or misfortune—to arrive at the entrance just as the pile was forming.

Unaware of the tradition, all I saw was a group of guys blocking access to safety. Without ceremony I put a foot on a visible butt for leverage and sprang over the pile, dashing the last few yards into the ring. What relief!

The sun was still low but bright in a clear blue sky. A small band was blaring out bullfighting songs. The mood was warm and friendly and festive.

Tradition has it that after the bulls have passed a young bull with padded horns is set loose in the ring. Unaware of this as well, I was taken by surprise when the throng near me parted to reveal a young bull bearing down on me. He may have been young but he was still a big animal. Eyes wide open, legs churning, enormous horns even if padded, he gave me only an instant to react before I dived out of the way.

Then I spotted Olav. We watched the half-frightened, half-furious bull charge around the ring. Like a motorboat on a still pond he created a wave of men jumping out of his path. The spectators enjoyed it all, most of them singing and dancing.

Next they led in a cow to calm the exhausted bull, which dutifully and meekly followed her out of the ring. That departure seemed to signal the end of the morning's activities. We found Larry and decided we'd done enough for now, having been up up all night expending lots of physical and nervous energy.

We wandered back to the car, stopping to buy juice and rolls at a bakery. The VW sat under its tree near an inviting stream. A fresh, clean, country smell with a hint of clover pleased us. We spread our sleeping bags near the car for maximum shade and dropped to the ground.

Five hours later we returned to La Plaza des Toros for the start of the day's bullfights. The matadors were all first class and they put on quite a spectacle.

Later we repeated the previous night's scene: strolling, drinking, and dancing the *jota*. At one small café's outdoor table we spied a large, strangely familiar man sipping coffee. A waiter whispered to us that he was Ernest Hemingway. Later I learned that 1959 was his ninth and last visit to the running of the bulls. He killed himself in Idaho two years later.

Once again we stayed up all night and once again we ran the next morning, all making it safely into the ring. But fatigue and dissipation began to take their toll. It had been great fun but it was time to head back to France.

Judy and I left Spain and proceeded to Bordeaux and Saint-André-de-Cubzac, where I had lived while I was stationed at Camp Bussac. Back then I loved exploring the town and the pleasant area around there remains my favorite part of France.

One thing I learned during my time in Bordeaux was that eating could be an enjoyable part of each day. Previously I had been a meat and potatoes kind of guy but found that I easily adapted to new tastes and eating one course after another.

I grew to know Jacques, the chef at the little restaurant at Hôtel de la Poste in Saint-André-de-Cubzac. Jacques took it upon himself to try to educate *l'Américain barbare* in the finer points of French cuisine and wine. Prior to arriving in Europe, I had only tasted communion wine at the Lutheran church I attended with my parents. Now I enjoyed wine every day—with lunch as well as dinner.

Jacques thought it important to teach me *why* I should be drinking a particular wine with a particular dish. He made it clear that wine was actually good for my health.

Le vin rouge tue les microbes.

"Red wine kills germs," he told me.

I have never forgotten his certitude.

Jacques also expanded my diet. My idea of a sophisticated dinner had been steak and fries with a green salad. At the time my French was so weak that I couldn't have ordered much else or selected from a menu. But soon Jacques had me enjoying French-style chicken, pork and fish, as well as vegetables, fruit and cheeses.

I learned other finer points of a French meal from Jacques. At first, when a waiter or waitress would furnish vinegar and oil for my salad dressing, I really had no idea what to do with it except to imitate what other restaurant patrons were doing. The best I could say about my technique was that it was hit and miss.

Apparently Jacques had noticed my clumsiness so on a slow night he instructed me on how to prepare a consistently good salad dressing.

Il faut regarder les bulles.

"Look at the bubbles."

The number and size of oil bubbles in the vinegar dictates the quality and taste of the dressing.

After his demonstration, and after I could actually see the bubbles, I got the point. Ever since that little lesson I've been able to produce a decent oil-and-vinegar dressing. As a young man on my first trip abroad, all sensations and experiences seemed new and fresh, and I wanted to learn as much as I could about everything. Many of those episodes served me well in my travels and interactions in later years.

Our vacation ended in Paris with Judy visiting the city for the first time. We took in all of the main tourist attractions—the Louvre, the Eiffel Tower, Notre Dame and the Arc de Triomphe. One evening we dined at a restaurant that featured cheese with every course. We both liked cheese but thought the place had carried the idea a bit too far.

We returned home, having had our first real vacation and Judy's first break from the kids in five years. We also learned the very sad news that my mother was dying from breast cancer. We had known about her declining health but the revelation still came as a shock. The disease took her two months later.

Judy and I talked it over and decided not to try to take the girls to Mom's funeral. She stayed home with them and I flew to Kansas City alone to join Dad, Bob, Diann and Greg. It was a small funeral with just our family and the friends Mom and Dad had acquired since their arrival in the Kansas City area. Two of Mom's sisters also attended, which pleased us all.

I felt a great loss and remember cursing breast cancer—she was too young to die.

Another overseas trip, this one to Rome and Athens in late November 1975, turned out to be tragically memorable.

On the last day of my visit to Athens, Richard Welch, the chief, called me into his office to discuss my views on their China program. Earlier in the day he had asked me to conduct one of my seminars on the topic.

My presentation had gone well. Everyone who attended was receptive and eager to exchange opinions. They welcomed the ideas I presented and I complimented their program.

Dick and I talked briefly about China. He mentioned that he regretted never having served in Hong Kong. Then he moved on to an unrelated subject.

"Have you seen the tourist spots here in Athens?" he asked.

"Actually no," I responded. "I've been too busy; maybe another time."

"Well, you must at least see the Acropolis. There is time right now. You don't leave till tomorrow morning, right?"

"That's right but I have some cables to write."

"You can write them at home. This is something you shouldn't miss. My driver can take you up there now. I'd go with you except I have to see the ambassador."

I could see he wasn't going to take no for an answer and in truth I did want to see the city's archaeological masterpiece. Dick's secretary made the arrangements and his car soon took me to the site. When the driver dropped me off I thanked him and waved him back to the office. I joined the tourists strolling up the path to the ancient ruins. It was a pleasant day and I felt relaxed. It had been a good trip and it was almost finished.

I was relaxed—but I wasn't asleep. My years in Hong Kong had made me instinctively aware of anything even slightly out of the ordinary going on around me. Most clandestine service officers are the same.

I didn't quite believe it at first but I picked up that I was under surveillance. It didn't seem likely but there it was. Not knowing who the hell it could be I tried as unobtrusively as I could to confirm what I thought I was seeing.

In the James Bond novel *Goldfinger*, Ian Fleming wrote, "Once is happenstance. Twice is coincidence. The third time it's enemy action." Spotting a person repeatedly is just such an indicator and I noticed the same, middle-aged Greek man in my vicinity three times within 10 minutes. Then I detected two other men, probably his colleagues, who also seemed to be interested in me.

All kept their distance but it became apparent what they were doing and it made me uneasy.

I started wondering why I had been targeted. I didn't know anyone in Athens except the people in our office and nobody knew me. But during the next half-hour as I wandered among the crowd I grew certain that at least three men were watching my movements, not aggressively but persistently.

The question was how to get rid of them. I needed to exercise a quality we constantly seek in our officers and agents—I needed to think on my feet.

I had told Dick's driver that I would catch a taxi back. Did these guys see me arrive in his car—was that the connection? Did they expect me to return to the parking lot to get picked up?

As I mulled things over, trying to decide what to do, I asked an attendant if there was another way down to the city apart from the walkway taken by the tourists. He directed me to a narrow path next to the public restrooms that also led down the hill. It was worth a try.

So I ambled toward the men's room and was pleased to see that none of the surveillants followed. They must have expected me to return to the parking lot so they kept their distance and they couldn't see the entrance of the men's room from their vantage points. I figured they'd just wait for me to reappear.

As soon as I disappeared from their sight I headed straight for the small path. I half jogged most of the way down and entered a tourist shop at the bottom. From inside I could see the end of the path. None of the three appeared and after 15 minutes of browsing I bought some blue-and-white porcelain coasters and left.

Back at the office I went directly to see Dick Welch. He could tell I was agitated and tried to ease my concerns.

"I'll bet it was Greek police," he said. "Whenever they see a new face in town with any tie to our office they just check things out. Not to worry. How was the Acropolis?"

"Maybe it was the ride in your car that fingered me," I noted and let the subject drop.

On December 23, 1975, less than a month later, Dick Welch was murdered on his doorstep by unknown assailants. News of the murder hit heavily at headquarters and I felt particularly shocked and saddened. I thought immediately of my visit to Athens and the surveillance I had reported to him. It was definitely not happenstance.

Now there was good reason to believe it wasn't Greek police I had spotted but members of Revolutionary Organization 17 November, also known as 17N, the gang that had murdered him. I immediately notified the Europe Division officers handling the Greek desk and the people who would conduct the investigation.

At the time I did not tell Judy about the people watching me.

I later found out that on November 25, just before my Athens visit, Dick's name and address had been published in the English-language *Athens News*. The report was the result of information printed in the anti-CIA newsletter *Counter Spy*. Philip Agee, who formerly worked for the agency, had provided the information to the newsletter and contributed to the exposure of many agency people worldwide. Agee denied it but many—including me—hold him responsible for Welch's death.

Agee died in Cuba in 2008 but it remains painful to know he was never punished for his treachery.

In January 1976, President Ford asked for William Colby's resignation as Director of Central Intelligence. Political realities dictated the decision. Ford was looking ahead to his reelection campaign and he regarded Colby, who had been the subject of much controversy, as a liability.

It didn't matter that the operations in question hadn't happened on Colby's watch or that Colby had gone to great lengths to cooperate with the Rockefeller and congressional committee investigations. Ford apparently decided that Bill had to go.

Agency people met the news with mixed feelings. As I mentioned, some senior officers regarded Colby's strategy of documenting and reporting the agency's alleged sins as overly solicitous—they thought he had exacerbated our problems by revealing too much. The people holding that viewpoint were not sorry to see him leave. But many others felt saddened by his departure.

Also in January, Dick and Sheila Kinsman invited Judy and me to dinner. Dick, who had replaced me in Laos in 1964 and subsequently returned to headquarters, had joined Latin America Division.

A graduate of Syracuse University and subsequently the masters program at the Thunderbird School of Global Management in Glendale, Arizona, Dick spoke fluent Spanish. All of the other agency people at the dinner were Latin America officers.

Soon I was taking a bit of good-natured kidding about why I hadn't been smart enough to join LA Division instead of Far East. I responded in kind and the conversation drifted into a discussion of language skills. They were so good, they told me, that they could sing Spanish songs with no problem. Then one of them challenged me.

"Can you sing Chinese songs? Can you sing the Chinese national anthem?"

By that time I'd had a drink—maybe two.

"Of course I can," I shot back.

"So sing it," he said, smiling at me like a Cheshire cat.

Judy, who wasn't at all sure I could sing anything in Chinese, let alone the national anthem, looked a bit uneasy.

I can pull this off. None of these guys speaks a word of Chinese so it'll be a piece of cake.

I launched into a spirited, Chinese-sounding song. I was using words randomly, and what I was saying made no sense at all, but as I had suspected no one questioned me. Oh, some cast suspicious looks but mostly they just listened.

As I was finishing I started running out of words and grew a little concerned about completing the ruse. I glanced around the room and noticed a bowl of nuts on a small table. With gusto—because by then I was sure no one understood a thing I was singing—I concluded with *yao guo ji ding*, which means "chicken and cashew nuts" in Mandarin.

I had pulled it off. There was silence.

Just then Judy, who spoke very little Chinese but had eaten so often in Chinese restaurants that she knew the Chinese names for many dishes, blurted out, "Chicken and cashew nuts?"

It blew the whole thing. The LA officers knew immediately I had been bluffing. They heaped lots of abuse on me for that one.

On January 30, George H.W. Bush took over as our director—my seventh. Most thought his nomination was politically motivated, something designed to symbolize a new beginning for the agency. A former Republican congressman from Texas, our ambassador to the United Nations, chairman of the Republican National Committee, and our first—though at the time unofficial—envoy to China, Bush was nevertheless unknown to most of us because he was an outsider. As such we received him with feelings ranging from neutral to cautious. All of that would soon change, however, and our assessments would turn positive.

Along with his extensive political experience Bush, like Colby, was a World War II combat veteran, serving as a naval aviator in the Pacific Theater.

A couple of months after he took office Bush sought to gain a better understanding of the agency's culture. He arranged a series of meetings with randomly selected mid-grade officers, inviting them to his office. I happened to be one of them.

I can't remember much about our conversation but I do remember being impressed, partly because he wanted to get to know officers of my grade and partly because he seemed to be genuinely interested in the agency. I left the meeting as a fan. If we had to have an outsider as director this man was a good choice for the job.

I wasn't alone in that conclusion. The agency as a whole came to like and respect Bush, perhaps regarding him as a harbinger of better times to come.

In February, with my headquarters tour well into its third year, and Judy and I starting to think about my doing another field tour, Harry S. invited me up to his office.

Because of our frequent carpooling I had grown to know him well and considered him a good friend.

After some small talk Harry told me that Far East Division thought it was time for me to get back to the field. He knew I was more than ready to go out again but China Operations, acting in the interests of my career, wanted to be sure it was to a good job.

I had been promoted to GS-14 in 1974 and career-wise things had gone well for me since. I knew I was in line for a better assignment. Harry said he could only tell me I had been approved for reposting that summer and I should start thinking about the move. I tried to pump him for more information but he resisted, saying only that I would hear the announcement soon.

Indeed it was soon. The next week the agency named me deputy chief in Kuala Lumpur, Malaysia. The news delighted me—it was more than I had hoped for. The appointment pleased Judy as well. She looked forward to it, having visited Kuala Lumpur while she worked in Bangkok.

More good news: The agency promoted me to GS-15 that spring. I was elated and threw myself energetically into preparing for the tour. The weeks and months flew by, and soon we were packing to leave.

17. Losing in Fascinating Ways

KUALA LUMPUR, MALAYSIA 1976–1977

One Thursday afternoon in early October I pulled into the underground parking area of one of the few shopping malls in Kuala Lumpur at the time. I browsed the mall for about 20 minutes and bought several birthday cards to mail back home. Ostensibly I was there to do some personal shopping on my lunch hour. My real purpose was to receive the first pass from my key agent.

The turnover process had gone well a few weeks earlier—part of the duties I inherited as the new deputy for our Kuala Lumpur office—and the agent and I had agreed to continue the operation as it was. He was comfortable with the structure initiated by my predecessor and we both judged the risks to be acceptable.

I even liked this particular agent and thought our relationship had started off well. That was good; every case officer/agent relationship requires mutual confidence.

In arranging drop-offs the simplest plan is often the best. That way no one forgets his role or the routine. We would set up a date, location and time. I would drive to that location, park my car, and embark on some ordinary task such as walking into a mall to buy birthday cards. The idea was to make it difficult for a rival service to tell whether I was working or just shopping. But if I had picked up a tail I would have aborted the rendezvous.

Meanwhile my agent knew where I had parked my car and what my license plate number was. I also had given him a key to the trunk. Risky items all, but this was a fully vetted agent who had been providing valuable information for a long time. I was willing to accept the risk.

According to the plan he would pass by the car about 10 minutes after I arrived and if he felt in the clear he would take the next step. In the space of a few seconds he would open the trunk, place a small package on the floor, shut the lid, and leave. After another quarter-hour or so—we always built in that much time out of respect for Murphy's Law—I would return from my mundane outing, get in the car, and drive away.

The package, which usually contained rolls of undeveloped film and short, handwritten notes, remained vulnerable only from when he had placed it in the trunk until I returned.

For other agents in other places this kind of routine wouldn't have worked nearly as well. In a hostile environment in a denied area, for example, the country's intense surveillance would have precluded leaving a roll of film alone in a car for a minute, let alone a quarter of an hour or more. In China and Russia the security forces were always watching.

On this particular occasion, involving a first pass in an unfamiliar operational environment, I was trying to act casual but I felt stressed and nervous. On my return I backed carefully out of the parking place—an accident wouldn't be helpful—and headed for the exit.

I noticed nothing unusual. This was a free lot beneath the mall so I wouldn't have to interact with an attendant. I pulled out into the heavy noontime traffic and headed back to the office, parking outside next to the building. Still noticing nothing out of the ordinary I breathed more easily, assuming that all had gone according to plan.

When I opened the trunk I saw his small package sitting next to my briefcase, which I always stored there. I did that deliberately, both to avoid tempting petty thieves and to reinforce a routine that would seem normal to surveillants. I quickly stashed the birthday cards and the small package in the briefcase, closed the trunk, and headed inside.

Using the film, which we developed that afternoon, and the short note my agent had included, I was able to write several intelligence reports. That system of passes, with periodic variations, served the op well for the entire time I ran it and it produced a consistent stream of intelligence.

As already mentioned, face-to-face meetings between case officers can be invaluable but with agents we kept such encounters to a minimum—though we could never eliminate them. Even a veteran agent needs encouragement and he shouldn't go too long without it. He needs to hear once in a while that we appreciate the risks he is taking. About three times a year I'd work out the details, including a cover story, to bolster the relationship. I'd goose the agent's morale by praising his courage and the value of his information. More important, I'd maintain the human contact.

I'm sure the meetings helped but I knew the agent also felt comfortable with our arrangements because he could always decide whether or not to take a pass. Our overall plan included alternate dates in case something prevented him from appearing or dropping off the package or he spotted something at the rendezvous point and aborted. By making an innocuous phone call he could always trigger an unscheduled meeting if necessary.

The plan was tailor-made for that agent and that environment. Although it consistently worked well I greatly respected his taking a considerable personal risk largely for ideological reasons.

We had arrived in Malaysia three months earlier in late July with our daughters in tow and me keeping track of six passports, six tickets and 14 pieces of luggage. We had transited Hong Kong before landing at Kuala Lumpur International, which lies due west of the city.

Ed Brubaker, our chief; Paul S., the deputy I was replacing, and both of their wives met us at the airport. A support officer also arrived, driving a large passenger van. They made us feel welcome and the officer whisked us to one of the city's four-star hotels. There we stayed until we found a suitable house to rent.

It had been a long trip but once again the kids—now accustomed to long-distance travel—handled it well. They all seemed excited to be in a new place.

How can we make friends? Where will we go to school? Is it always this hot? Can we go to the hotel pool?

Clearly they were none the worse for wear and Judy and I were happy to have arrived after what had been two very hectic weeks.

First thing the next morning I drove to our office, located on the top couple of floors of a tall building in the City Centre district. I learned that Ed was attending a country team meeting chaired by Francis Underhill, our ambassador. Paul was away as well, meeting an asset. So I introduced myself to the two front-office secretaries, both of whom I came to appreciate as outstanding employees, and settled in with the support officer to take care of admin matters.

After Ed returned he invited me into his office to deliver my initial marching orders. Ed was an experienced and competent senior officer with tours in Paris and elsewhere in Asia under his belt. Born and raised in West Virginia he was an enthusiastic outdoorsman; a big man, strong looking and tanned. I later found out that the Brubakers were avid golfers—and she played better than he did.

Ed briefed me about our operations in Malaysia and I could see that his welcome was genuine. As time went by I found him easy to work with. As usual I had read a lot of background before I left headquarters and I understood what he was describing and could pose some pertinent questions. My briefings at Langley had made clear that our top priority in Malaysia was recruiting third-country agents and there was a wide range of potential candidates.

Next, regarding the office itself, Ed covered personnel, logistics, finance and reporting. We discussed everything, not in much detail but enough to give me a clear idea of how he viewed our programs and staff.

I was impressed not only by his grasp of our activities and his plans for the future but also by the position I was about to assume. This would be my first management job and I looked forward to functioning as a senior officer.

I was happy to be back in the field, back where the action was, though my mood would not last long.

With plenty of food for thought and lots to digest I left Ed and stepped into the adjoining deputy's office, which would soon be mine. Paul had just returned from his meeting.

I liked him right away. A former Marine officer he was still physically imposing, with a square chin, erect stance, firm handshake and direct eye contact. As we spoke I quickly perceived something more. Apart from his looks he didn't talk or act like a Marine. He was quiet and reflective—almost visibly formulating his comments. He sounded academic but was obviously experienced in our mission and tradecraft.

Years later someone told me that after Paul retired from the agency he became a librarian.

We discussed details, including the cases I would be taking over from him. One demanded special attention: my shopping-mall agent. He was providing us with high-level intelligence, Paul told me, but I had to be careful because we would endure political and diplomatic fallout if the operation was compromised.

I had already reviewed this case back at headquarters but discussing it face-to-face with the man who had handled it for the past three years was of great value. I peppered him with questions about the agent's motivation, personality, family origins and plans for the future. Paul's responses were clear and concise, and the session did us both good.

You always feel better about handing over an agent if the receiving officer is knowledgeable and positive, and you always feel better receiving an agent if you've had the opportunity to discuss his case in person. My talk with Paul produced both results.

We also reviewed two other agents I would be taking over and again I found the direct conversation a big help. The cases were not as sensitive, with less production required and less "flap" potential—CIA slang for a diplomatic tizzy.

Paul also filled me in about our other case officers. He considered them a mixed bag and eventually I would reach the same conclusion. Each handled about a half-dozen agents but there was a definite paucity of developmental activity—not enough effort on the streets.

I asked him what we could do about it and he just shook his head. It wasn't a good answer and I resolved to address the issue as soon as possible. We broke for lunch in a nearby Malaysian restaurant where our conversation shifted to more personal matters.

Life in Kuala Lumpur was good, Paul had told me. The climate was pleasant and the pace of life was tolerable. He and his family had enjoyed their three years and been able to travel to Singapore and Thailand. He said the International School of Kuala Lumpur, where our daughters would be going, had an excellent reputation.

The school was located in the northeastern part of the city, in an area called Ukay Heights, so that's where we looked for a house. Paul's was not available for us to rent because the embassy had assigned it to another officer, but we found plenty of nice alternatives on the market.

After looking for several days Judy and I settled on a house located halfway up a hill. It featured a nice veranda around back with fruit trees all over the property. It had five bedrooms at the top of an open stairway plus a large dining and living room area with sliding doors that we kept closed only at night.

Paul highly recommended Lai and Azma, his two servants. They had been good workers, he assured me, and we would like them both. I thanked him and said we would like to meet them soon.

We did hire the women, both of whom were delightful and everything Paul said they would be. Lai, who was Chinese, could do almost anything. She was a willing worker and a fine cook of Western, Chinese and Malay cuisine. Azma, a Malay, was less capable and productive but she cheerfully completed all of the tasks we assigned her.

Both were also very good with our children. They consistently reinforced Judy's admonition to the girls that they clean their own rooms, behave themselves, and treat the servants with respect.

Our housing, school and domestic-help requirements resolved, and my work off to a seemingly promising start, Malaysia looked to be a very good tour. It wasn't exactly the center of the Cold War world or a hot spot of any sort but we had plenty to do, focusing on that wide assortment of officials serving with foreign governments as recruiting targets. The ground was fertile.

I soon discovered that Kuala Lumpur's easygoing façade concealed a dark underbelly. Unspoken except in private was the ethnic tension in Malaysia. Government census data—which many ethnic Chinese disputed—

showed that the population was about 45 percent Malay, 40 percent Chinese and the rest a mix of Indian, Aborigine and others. But the main fault line existed between the Malay and the Chinese.

The tensions had erupted in bloody riots in Singapore in 1964—before the city-state withdrew from Malaysia—and in Kuala Lumpur during spring and summer 1969 after the national elections. The riots resulted in widespread property damage, beatings and hundreds of deaths. In the aftermath the government hammered out a tenuous compromise that seemed to be holding. In effect the politicians carved up Malaysia's resource pie—enough to give almost everyone a large piece.

The country exports a significant share of the world's palm oil, tropical hardwoods, rubber and petroleum, the latter of which culminated in 1974 in the establishment of Petroliam Nasional Berhad, PETRONAS, Malaysia's national oil company.

In general the Malay controlled the government, military and police while the Chinese dominated the economy and business sector. The Malay, often none too subtly, tried to use their political control to gain economic advantage but the Chinese usually stayed one step ahead of them.

For example, the government periodically attempted to pass laws called *Bumiputra*—meaning "sons of the earth" in Malay—which gave preference to Malay-owned concerns. In response the Chinese often used lures of large salaries and perks to persuade Malays to front their companies, thereby gaining the necessary licenses to conduct business.

Over time, however, the *Bumiputra* laws took their toll. On a visit to Kuala Lumpur in 2010 a Chinese friend told me that Malaysia's population, which had reached 27 million, consisted of about 57 percent Malay and only 24 percent Chinese. Many of the expatriates have resettled in Singapore, he said, with Singapore's blessing.

That exodus can only harm Malay society and the country's economy. My personal observations suggested that the average Malay was less motivated, had a weaker work ethic, and often gave the impression of being more short-sighted than the ethnic Chinese. I reached those impressions early on but they have persisted. I have tried to follow Malaysia's progress over the ensuing years; little has happened to change my views and my recent visit confirmed them once more.

Religion provided another source of conflict. The Malays are Muslim and the Chinese, if religious at all, are Christian. Usually the difference was manageable because neither group seemed willing to use religion as an issue. The only exceptions were whenever Malays tried to use Islam to justify an action or policy with economic implications. But such instances were rare and they never really worked.

Language presented yet another dilemma. The Malays absolutely refused to learn Chinese and the Chinese refused to speak Malay. Call it stubbornness. According to our agency language school, where I studied part-time for six weeks and gained a rudimentary understanding, Malay, an offshoot of Indonesian, is the easiest language in the world to learn.

Actually the unofficial language of Malaysia is English, a holdover from nearly 170 years of British colonial rule. This is true everywhere in the country except for the remote rural areas, which are populated almost entirely by ethnic Malays. I used what little Malay I had learned now and again but English was so widespread that I rarely needed the native tongue.

When I needed to speak Chinese—in ethnic enclaves in some of the cities or in Chinese restaurants—I had Mandarin or basic Cantonese at my disposal. But English usually carried the day—a blessing for me and many other foreigners. More to the point it greatly simplified our communications with agents and potential recruits.

Because Malaysia is a charter member of the Association of Southeast Asian Nations, an organization born in 1967 to promote economic growth in the region, U.S. policymakers took a keen interest in the country. Along with the other four ASEAN members—Indonesia, the Philippines, Singapore and Thailand—Malaysia sat firmly in the Western camp as a bulwark against the People's Republic.

ASEAN's predecessor, the Southeast Asia Treaty Organization, was founded in 1954 to fight the infiltration of communism into the region from China.

Like Malaysia the other ASEAN members enjoyed plentiful natural resources that promised growth and prosperity. Both our office and the embassy's economic section monitored how ASEAN handled its economic policies and trade agreements. We also forwarded reports involving national politics to Washington if they were related to economics or internal security.

All five nations were fighting acts of internal subversion carried out by communist sympathizers or insurgents. Such groups posed little threat in Malaysia but we still kept our eyes on them, including a small group of rebels operating in the far north near the Thai border.

Not much of this reporting was earthshaking. Rather it served as grist for the mills of analysts trying to follow or discern trends of importance to U.S. interests in the region. Our Kuala Lumpur shop disseminated considerably less intelligence than Hong Kong—something I would have to get used to.

Nevertheless as deputy I was also the de facto reports officer and I quickly found out how ill-prepared I was for that responsibility. Ed continually followed my progress but he deferred to me for much of the editing and many of the decisions about whether or not to disseminate a particular report.

I worked very hard during those first weeks to get myself up to speed. I read backgrounder after backgrounder on the topics we were following as well as guidance from headquarters about reporting requirements.

It wasn't unusual. Case officers spend a sizable portion of each week reading. It's helpful—essential, really. For one thing it can help you write more complete and insightful intelligence reports. For another, reading can be invaluable when you're talking with a person of interest for the first time.

Say you're scheduled to attend a function where you might meet a Chinese official. If so you should carry in your head the latest developments in his particular field—politics, the economy or even military. Sure, it's a long shot whether you will get beyond an introduction and polite small talk, but being prepared can be valuable.

For example, that first autumn I met a Chinese diplomat at an embassy function. Based on my background reading I was able to mention the names of and details about the Gang of Four, the notorious Communist Party members who had abetted the Cultural Revolution and tried to take over the country after Mao Tse-tung's death on September 9. The Chinese diplomat—a "hard target," in our parlance—reacted with wariness and caution but I was sure I had impressed him.

We never met again but if I had engaged him sometime later our introductory exchange might have made the difference between further conversation, and possibly more, or his terse dismissal of an ignorant Westerner.

What I do know is that reading fortified my conversations, helping me to sustain interesting—and sometimes fruitful—discussions on the cocktail and liaison circuits. Based on those exchanges I sent many reports back to headquarters containing information that was useful if not necessarily essential.

I wasn't kidding anyone, least of all myself. At most I'd rate my performance as a reports officer as adequate. I longed for the expert and competent people I had encountered in Hong Kong and at headquarters. They represented a critical part of our intelligence operations in Asia—and everywhere else for that matter—and my respect for them persisted throughout my career.

One thing I learned from my posting in Kuala Lumpur was that the staffs at our small offices usually didn't include reports officers. Instead the chiefs and their deputies wrote the reports, which usually displayed a lack of professionalism. Only our larger operations featured reports officers, people I considered worth their weight in gold.

Here's one reason why: The best could take what we had collected from an agent and discern the depth of that person's access to and knowledge about the subject he or she was tracking.

They could tell, for example, how much a secretary really knew about her boss's activities—whether her information was valuable, routine or widely known.

Whether it's inborn or something you develop, whether it's an art or a skill, I came to respect that ability greatly, particularly when it was my responsibility to do likewise. Often I had to rely on the people at headquarters to pick up the slack but I learned much from the process. It turned out to be a good experience for me—albeit a humbling one.

In November, four months after our arrival in Kuala Lumpur, President Ford lost his re-election bid to Jimmy Carter, the former governor of

Georgia and an unknown to me. Carter promptly signaled his intent to change agency directors, and following his inauguration in January 1977 we lost George H.W. Bush, who had served for only a year less a week.

Bush's departure distressed me. As I said, I had liked him and held high expectations for where his leadership would take us. Many of my colleagues felt the same way and we all disliked the political nature of decisions being taken about "our" agency. We wished the White House and Congress would leave us out of their political machinations but Watergate, which in the end had dashed Ford's hopes of reelection, changed that forever.

To replace Bush, Carter named Stansfield Turner, an admiral and former colleague of Carter's at the Naval Academy. The switch generated apprehension within the service. No one knew anything about Turner and the grapevine immediately buzzed with talk about what our Navy contacts were saying about him. Apparently they portrayed him as inflexible and mean-spirited. Some of our people quipped that the only thing worse than an inexperienced politician heading the agency was an inexperienced military man.

Our misgivings meant nothing to Congress, which quickly confirmed Turner, and he took over as the eighth director of my 16-year career. Word filtering out to the field indicated that he walked in with several staff officers in tow and said he wanted to make things "shipshape"—an ominous beginning.

The cocktail circuit in Kuala Lumpur was an incessant merry-go-round, which you could jump on or exit as you liked. Some were better or more comfortable with it than others. A couple of our officers seemed to thrive on it while others were less adept and less productive.

Over the years I never developed a strong desire to attend those events. I experienced some that were enjoyable and useful and others that were a bust. But I confirmed the value of socializing because few activities could expand your circle of contacts as well or as quickly.

There's a Chinese proverb that says, approximately, you can stand atop a mountain forever but it's no guarantee a Peking duck will fly into your mouth. For our purposes if you wanted to gather useful information you needed to get out there and socialize. That was proven to me many times over. As in most endeavors you win some, you lose some—though sometimes you can lose in fascinating ways.

Judy and I were attending a party at the French Embassy on July 14, *le quatorze Juillet*, their Fête Nationale, or National Celebration. We were mingling as usual, sipping drinks, noshing on snacks, and sharing toasts. We turned to greet an acquaintance who was talking to an Asian man wearing a lapel a pin bearing the likeness of Kim II Sung, North Korea's leader.

Following protocol for these affairs our acquaintance dutifully introduced us but did not mention to the North Korean that I was a U.S. official.

"How do you do?" Judy said, smiling. I followed suit, adding his name, Mr. Lee, as I shook his hand.

He had a slight build, with close-cut, thick black hair and the inscrutable look we often ascribe to Asians. He avoided direct eye contact but shook hands firmly. He had the cheekbones and face of a North Asian and I might have picked him out as Korean even without the pin on his lapel.

"Who is that?" Judy asked, gesturing at the pin.

He seemed surprised, or at least feigned it.

"That is our Great Leader," he replied.

"What is his name?" she persisted.

I stayed silent, not knowing what she was up to.

Now looking a little flustered he quickly answered, "Kim II Sung."

Who was this woman, he might have been thinking. Could she be serious? Does she not know about our president?

"So what country are you from?" Judy continued.

Now he looked really perplexed. You could almost see the wheels turning in his head. Was she taunting him? She looked innocent enough.

After a moment's hesitation he apparently made his decision.

"I am from North Korea," he declared.

"That's nice," she said. "I've never been there."

He nodded and glanced nervously at me, wondering, I suppose, what I had made of the exchange. I just smiled, partly in awe of my wife and partly in amusement. With the exception of the Chinese and the Russians the majority of foreign diplomats at the time found North Koreans notoriously difficult to approach. Innocently or deviously, I didn't know which, Judy had disarmed him beautifully.

"We are Americans. I am a U.S. official," I told him.

It was a calculated move on my part. In other circumstances I might have withheld those comments for a while as I tried to probe a little and establish some rapport. As difficult as they were for everybody else North Koreans were by far our hardest target. They flatly refused contact with Americans of any stripe.

The story was the same worldwide. As soon as they were told they were talking with an American, North Korean diplomats would abruptly, often rudely, turn and walk away. But given how nonplussed Judy's remarks had left Mr. Lee I decided to strike while the iron was hot and he was still off balance.

What did I have to lose?

"I don't know many Americans," he said cautiously.

That was probably a gross understatement.

There followed a five-minute conversation on totally innocuous subjects: the weather, how we each liked Malaysia, where we each had been posted previously. I was delighted. Just to engage a North Korean diplomat—any North Korean, actually—represented a coup and even this brief contact got me thinking he was different. In hindsight it was wishful thinking.

Mr. Lee indicated he was about to break off the conversation so I decided to push on.

"Well, it's been nice talking with you," I said, handing him my calling card. "Do you have a card?"

Acting as if he was accepting a piece of rotten fish he took the card, muttering, "I don't have a card," and exited toward a couple of Russians.

I don't know why he stayed to talk but I concluded that Judy's innocent interrogation must have had something to do with it. It wouldn't be a stretch for me to think she even charmed him a little.

Whatever the reason nothing ever came of the contact. None of the few other North Koreans assigned to Kuala Lumpur regularly attended the diplomatic social circuit. As for Mr. Lee, I saw him once more, at a

Russian Embassy function. We made brief eye contact as I walked by but he quickly moved away.

I've always found that tennis is another good way to meet people. Not everyone plays but enough do to make it useful, for business as well as pleasure.

Soon after we arrived in Kuala Lumpur we joined the Lake Club, a well-known local establishment that featured several tennis courts, a large swimming pool, a luncheonette and a nice dining room. There was also a bar and a small gambling room with slot machines. As a diplomat I was able to join immediately.

This would not have been the case with the Royal Selangor Club, which had a splendid golf course along with tennis courts, a swimming pool and many other amenities. I enjoyed several business-related lunches in the club's first-class dining room.

The Royal Selangor, founded over a century ago by the British during the colonial period, had a long waiting list that effectively ruled out diplomats because of the relatively short periods of time they lived in Malaysia. It was an exclusive enclave whose membership was heavily weighted toward ethnic Malays.

The Lake Club served our purposes very well. With fine weather year-round Judy used it almost daily with the girls and she became active on the tennis circuit. The atmosphere was warm and friendly. Many of the members were diplomats so I derived professional benefits as well by cultivating some of them as sources of information, especially the few from the Soviet bloc countries. A couple of them would become advanced developmental contacts.

Judy and I also met a wide range of people, including from other clubs, by playing mixed doubles for the club team. Within about six months we had quite an active tennis and social circle of friends.

The club's Malaysian members were predominately ethnic Chinese, because most of the Malays preferred the Royal Selangor Club. We enjoyed their company and spent many evenings at social gatherings or dinner with them. In moments of candor they would discuss the country's cultural conflicts, more in sadness than anger.

The Europeans we met, including a number of French businessmen and diplomats, were also an entertaining lot. The few other Americans in the club viewed us first with interest and then warmth and friendliness.

I ran into a Lake Club contact the same evening we met Mr. Lee. At one point Judy and I had gotten separated and I found myself standing alone in the garden—though not for long. As I glanced around, trying to see where Judy had gone and searching for someone to chat with, Vlatko Cosic, the Yugoslavian ambassador, called out my name and approached me.

Standing 5 feet 10 and weighing about 180, Vlatko looked a little round. He wasn't fat, really, just wide around the middle. That and his balding pate made him look older than he actually was. That surprised me because a while back I had run a trace on him and discovered that we shared the same birthday, June 20, 1935. He was born in Sarajevo, Yugoslavia.

Vlatko wasn't much of a tennis player, but he was a friendly guy who got along with everyone. He rarely discussed politics. Not a communist ideologically, he had simply adjusted to realities in his country and done quite well for himself—and he wasn't about to cloud his social relationships by talking provocatively with anyone.

After meeting them at the club Judy and I maintained good chemistry with Vlatko and his wife and our interactions were always enjoyable. Whether he admitted it to himself or not—and whether he did it purposefully or not—Vlatko had been a big help. He regularly included Judy and me in the events he hosted at his residence, in local restaurants, or at the club. We tried to reciprocate but it was difficult for me to invite an ambassador, particularly one from a communist country.

Vlatko's parties routinely allowed me to meet people of interest because his circle of friends was concentrated in the bloc countries. I met a number of Russian and Eastern European diplomats and even a few Chinese nationals. A couple of them became promising developmental contacts.

I often pointedly thanked Vlatko, telling him how much I appreciated being able to meet people normally beyond my own circle. He brushed off my thanks but I think he knew what he was doing—acting, albeit informally, as a social broker for me.

One brief story about Vlatko is worth telling. He and I created tennis lore one day at the club. I was playing with Igor—about whom I'll have more to say shortly—against Vlatko and a Malaysian-Chinese club member.

I hit an aggressive return against Vlatko, who promptly smacked the ball straight up into the air. Vlatko was already known for his very high lobs and because his game featured nothing else of note he tended to nurture his notoriety.

About two counts later a dead bird fell at his feet. We all stood there for a moment in stunned silence before erupting in shouts and laughter. Vlatko smiled broadly and bowed. Soon the whole club heard the story and "Vlatko's lob" became even more famous. I have no idea where the ball ended up.

18. That Infernal Weinbach

KUALA LUMPUR 1978

Vlatko Cosic wasn't my only interesting tennis contact at the club. I'll call him Igor but that wasn't his real name. We knew he was a member of a Soviet-bloc intelligence service but as I grew to know him I discovered he was a pretty nice guy—just working the wrong side of things.

In the polite company of the club we were more or less obliged to be nice to each other. For one thing two other club members had arranged the doubles game where we met. In any event I didn't mind the cordiality because I considered Igor an attractive contact.

He played tennis with strength and enthusiasm but inconsistently, and he lacked knowledge of tactics. After the game we had drinks on the veranda where we cautiously probed each other's background. He knew or suspected I was also an intelligence officer but that didn't seem to bother him. He seemed surprisingly intrigued and forthcoming.

Cold War rhetoric often put a damper on conversations with diplomats from bloc countries but things had gone well with Igor. As we prepared to leave I suggested we have lunch together. To my surprise he accepted immediately and we set a date for the following week. We exchanged cards—and unlike the North Korean he readily accepted mine. I told him I would call to remind him but he said it wouldn't be necessary.

Maybe he didn't want me to call his office; I didn't know and didn't care.

I next met Igor at a restaurant called the Anchor Inn. Located in the City Centre it was a popular and busy place with good Western food, especially steak.

Igor had an engaging sense of humor and the chemistry seemed good—possibly because we avoided politics, which might have led to conflicts. It was a promising beginning.

Over the next 10 months I saw Igor regularly, at the club at first but later, after he had gotten to know Judy, for dinner at local restaurants with his wife and groups of friends. I grew increasingly interested in recruiting him as an agent. Igor liked to spend time in the club's gambling room playing the slot machines. That and certain other traits made me think he might not be the ideal communist of Vladimir Lenin's dreams.

Using a tennis film I had requested from headquarters, which included a player from his country, I invited Igor and his wife for dinner at our home. I could tell he was tempted but hesitant. He said he "would check" and I didn't press him.

Check? With whom? With his office? Will they permit him to come?

Whatever, he called the next day and accepted. It was a very successful evening, during which our daughters utterly captivated him and his wife. Dinner, the film and the girls combined to put them both at ease.

Eventually the conversation drifted to music. We had heard Igor play the piano several times at the club. Lacking formal training but able to pick up virtually any song by ear Igor turned out to be an accomplished pianist. Judy accompanied him vocally one evening by singing a couple of tunes popularized by Ella Fitzgerald.

There must have been an artistic gene in his family because his sister danced with the famed Bolshoi Ballet.

Seeing that we lacked a piano Igor suggested we should have one so the girls could learn. Judy, who played beautifully, exclaimed that getting a piano was a great idea. The platoon likewise expressed enthusiasm and suddenly I found myself under strong pressure. Judy smiled and the girls cheered as I—who hadn't considered the hours of practice involved—said, "Okay, okay, we'll look for a piano to rent next week."

Igor smiled as well. At that point I thought the subject had arisen innocently. Maybe it did but there's more to the story.

Kuala Lumpur had only one store that sold or rented pianos. Judy met me there the following Tuesday at lunchtime. We looked through the entire selection—though after scanning the price tags my enthusiasm was far less than Judy's. She argued that we should buy a piano, not rent one, so we could keep it as the girls grew up and take it with us when we moved back to the States. It also became clear that only a grand or baby grand would suffice. On all counts I realized this was a battle I would lose.

We settled on a Weinbach, a beautiful baby grand made in Czechoslovakia, and approached the counter to talk with the owner.

"We would like to buy a piano," I said.

"Very good, sir," he replied. "Which one?"

"The Weinbach baby grand that costs the same as a Volkswagen Golf."

He smiled. Judy frowned.

"Fine, I'll need some information for customs papers so that we can deliver it. Your name, sir?"

"Mr. Holm."

"Ah yes! Richard L., is that right?"

I nodded silently, but alarm bells suddenly went off loudly in my head.

How could he know my name?

"And your address?" he went on without a blink.

"Here's my card," I said. "My address and phone number are listed."

He took it and examined it.

"You are a diplomat, Mr. Holm?"

"That's right."

"That should make things much easier. No taxes."

My mind was working overtime as we left the store. I needed to know how the owner was able to rattle off my first name and middle initial like that. I could hardly wait to get Judy's input but said nothing until we were in the car with the motor running and the radio on.

Am I overreacting?

Before I could open my mouth Judy asked, "How did he know your first name?"

"I've been trying to figure that out."

"Seems very strange," she muttered.

"Who knew we would be in that store?"

"Only us and the girls ... and Igor."

Igor. He knew we would be looking for a piano. Maybe he also knew Kuala Lumpur had only one piano store. Maybe he had gone there before us and bribed or recruited the owner. His goal would be to gain access and plant a bug in whichever piano we chose before they delivered it to our house. That way his colleagues could listen to all conversations in the room where we placed it.

Moreover, given the open configuration of our house—which Igor had seen—they could listen to conversations on much of the ground level.

This is the nature of intelligence. It's a double-edged sword. Given the same set of circumstances in reverse I would have at least considered doing likewise.

Back at the office I checked what we had on both the shop owner, who had also given me his business card, and the shop itself. No traces; nothing suspicious.

I cabled headquarters asking for what they had, explaining what happened. The response two days later—by then the store had delivered the piano—was that they likewise had nothing on the retailer or the company. They shared my concern but seemed less agitated than I was.

Next I discussed the incident with Ed Brubaker, the chief. We concluded that to be safe we should have the piano checked out by our technicians. We asked headquarters to concur. They did and we scheduled the visit for early the next month—they couldn't make it any sooner.

The piano had been delivered while I was at work and the girls were in school. When they got home they asked, almost in unison, "Why is the piano way over in the corner?"

"I like it over there," Judy responded, "it's nice near the windows."

Judy knew how concerned I was so she had the movers place the piano at the far end of the living room, as far away as possible from where we normally had our conversations. That pleased me.

Because of the city's damp climate the piano had a built-in heating coil to reduce the possibility of humidity damage. That worried me.

We didn't plug the heater in, just in case the unit also contained a transmitter.

That was only the beginning. Increasingly I fretted that I'd been had and was determined to avoid the snare. Even without power supplied via the heating-coil cord maybe there was a battery-powered transmitter somewhere inside. I was convinced we had to remain vigilant until the technicians arrived. As soon as they could confirm what I suspected we'd consider our next steps.

Where, I wondered, could the Russians have set up their listening post? It had to be a low-powered transmitter with a range of a few hundred feet. That might put it in one of the apartments in the building just above us on the hill. It was impossible to tell. Maybe they had a more sophisticated transmitter. There was no way to know that, either.

I thought about my colleagues posted in the Soviet Union, or other opposition-controlled places, where they just assumed that their homes or apartments contained implanted audio devices and their telephones were tapped.

That was expected but it would have been unusual in Kuala Lumpur, even though we took the same precautions and never discussed sensitive subjects outside of secure areas. If Igor had managed to bug our piano I viewed it as part of the business and an occupational hazard. Still I admit I was pissed off that he had outflanked me.

We spent a couple of weeks carefully keeping our chatter away from the piano, venturing near it only for playing and listening. What we also did, though inadvertently, was create an annoying diversion for anyone who might have been eavesdropping.

We had an indoor fishpond in the entryway near where we had placed the piano. Such a pond was not unusual for houses in Malaysia, which are designed to be open to allow air to circulate.

The fishpond was dry when we moved in, showing only its decorative rocks and plants. Soon one of us got the bright idea of refilling it. After all wouldn't it be nice to have fish swimming around in it? So we went ahead and stocked it with tropical varieties.

Within a couple of weeks we learned why the previous tenant had drained the thing: it was invaded by frogs that serenaded us at night—all night. No one could sleep and we soon evicted the frogs as well as the fish. It amused me, though, that someone could have been trying to monitor our conversations and instead heard only the sound of croaking frogs.

At last our technicians arrived. I briefed them carefully and invited them over to the house for dinner that night. It had to seem normal. We didn't want to alert anyone that we were on to the device.

They arrived for dinner as planned. Afterward we chatted casually while they carefully and silently checked out the piano. After about an hour they shrugged their shoulders and indicated they had found nothing. I escorted them outside and we agreed they should come back the following afternoon with special equipment for an even more thorough study. I remained perplexed.

They returned next day and almost disassembled and rebuilt that infernal Weinbach and found ... nothing, nothing at all. I was even more perplexed. Judy laughed.

In my mind the pieces had all fit and I was sure Igor had tried to exploit a target of opportunity. But it just hadn't happened. We might as well have been the Simba rebels who invaded the home of Dr. and Madame Barlovatz in Stanleyville. They thought the Barlovatz's piano had a hidden transmitter, too.

How had that piano retailer known my first name and middle initial? I never found out. Was it that the Russians just couldn't put the operation together? That's also something I'd never know. Whatever the reality I regarded the incident as a head-scratcher as I tried to outguess ... nobody.

Had I started seeing bad guys behind every tree? Maybe so. It's part of the business but it's something you must avoid.

The piano? We still have it. The girls learned to play on it, Judy regularly produced beautiful music from it, and sometimes we'd joke that the Russian bug was still hidden somewhere inside.

Some months later on Thai National Day we were attending a cocktail party. As usual I was keeping an eye out for possible new contacts and watching for my regulars—including Igor. I saw some friends in the crowd but not him. A group of us had planned to go out for dinner after cocktails and I was hoping to use the occasion to begin asking, gently but unambiguously, about his country's political system.

After we had all dutifully toasted the King of Thailand and people started to leave I still hadn't seen Igor. Something must have happened because he had confirmed that he and his wife would be there. We left with our other friends for dinner, hoping they might join us there. They didn't.

To our considerable disappointment we learned several days later that Igor had been abruptly reassigned back to his country. The news came from a brief conversation I had in a grocery store with a Lake Club member who was one of Igor's friends. Using other local sources we were able to confirm the information.

Why the unusual move? We had no idea. Was it because of his routine of gambling and too much drinking at the club, which would have been known to other bloc diplomats? Or could it have been his relationship with me?

Eventually we heard that Igor's wife had blown the whistle on his "behavioral" problems. True or not they were gone, and their abrupt departure ended a promising opportunity.

The record of my efforts with Igor and the information I had compiled about him from then on would rest in a file for use in the future—if one of our people ever made contact with him. Of all the bloc officers I met during my career Igor was the most fascinating. I still wonder sometimes why he was reassigned and how he fared after that.

About midway through our tour in Malaysia, Dad visited us for about a week. I took some vacation time for the visit. Leaving the kids with Lai and Azma we rode the train up to the Cameron Highlands, about a hundred miles and several hours north of Kuala Lumpur, for a brief getaway. The area lies at the Malay Peninsula's highest point. The weather there is almost always cooler and less humid than anywhere else in the country, which makes it is a favorite vacation spot.

Our rustic old hotel with a British ambience faced a large, clear plateau featuring a nine-hole golf course. Dad suggested a game the afternoon of our arrival but my post-Congo lack of manual dexterity continued to rule out golf. I demurred but Judy, though a bit rusty from lack of practice, promptly volunteered. She and Dad played the nine holes, twice.

That night at dinner Judy confessed that the two rounds of golf had raised a severe blister on her right hand. It had broken and seemed to be infected. We thought little of it initially. I told her to be sure to clean it thoroughly that night, which she did, but it didn't stop the infection.

By morning she had angry red streaks shooting up her arm and a lump in her armpit. It looked serious and I became alarmed. Checking with the hotel I got directions to a nearby clinic. We walked there immediately after breakfast.

We registered with the nurse and sat down to wait. We were the only foreigners and thus the focus of some attention, though we had grown accustomed to that.

Then the next patient arrived and he caused *us* to take notice. He was an Aborigine, standing only about 4 feet tall, wearing a loin cloth, and carrying a long, bamboo blowpipe, through which he used poison darts to bring down small game. He slung a quiver full of darts over his shoulder. When he sat down the blowpipe was taller than he was.

Seeming oblivious to the rest of us he just stared straight ahead. His presence at the clinic was probably an ordinary occurrence but we had never seen an Aborigine before and couldn't help looking at him. Now, over three decades later, I wonder how the Malaysian Aborigines are faring. As they have elsewhere in Southeast Asia and Australia, Malaysia's tribes—called Orang Asli, or "original people" in the Malay language—have often locked horns with the government over control of their ancestral lands, which go back untold thousands of years.

When the nurse called our name we broke off our discreet focus on the little man and walked into the doctor's office. He asked Judy a few questions then recommended a shot of penicillin.

"I can give you some penicillin tablets to take for a few days," he went on, "but I think we should get on this right away with a shot."

"I guess there isn't much choice," she responded.

"I have to tell you," the doctor added, "that I have no American penicillin; I have only Polish penicillin. It's equally effective but it goes in harder."

Neither of us picked up on what he meant.

"Let's just go ahead," Judy replied.

He prepared a syringe that he injected into Judy's upper thigh. Soon we understood what he had tried to tell us. The Polish penicillin was visibly viscous and it took some effort for him to inject it. I could see that it hurt.

By the next morning, however, the infection was visibly less serious and by the time we returned home it was gone. We only stayed two more days in the Camerons, during which we hiked the various trails around the resort. Dad, always an eager traveler, seemed to enjoy seeing this part of Malaysia and we all spent a brief but pleasant time with him back in the city.

I was feeling increasingly frustrated at work—something new for me. Until that point, and as I've said, I had regarded my posting as a positive experience. But I came to realize that Kuala Lumpur was too far off the mainstream to function at the level of our office in Hong Kong, for example. Despite our best efforts I didn't think the quality or quantity of our reporting was up to the standards I wanted to see.

Our recruitment record wasn't strong, either. We had a few promising individuals in development but not enough had really jelled. I couldn't articulate anything specific but I had the impression of a lot of wheel-spinning without much forward motion. In retrospect I can see how naive I was. We weren't providing enough intelligence about priority targets such as China or the Soviet Union because the people we were using didn't have access to much useful information.

Maybe I was judging Kuala Lumpur too harshly. It wasn't Hong Kong and it wasn't headquarters so how could I have expected it to offer the same type of priority or activity level? Efforts here had to proceed incrementally; they depended on a lot of factors we couldn't control.

You win some and you lose some—as I've also said—and often your success depends on being in the right place at the right time. If an opportunity arises you have to act quickly to exploit it but you can't lose your edge in the meantime.

Another source of frustration: I was spending more and more time in the office instead of on the street. It wasn't something I particularly liked but I accepted it as part of my management responsibilities. I prepared monthly and annual reports. I planned budgets. I rated personnel and intelligence—none of which I had to do in my Hong Kong tour. It also hadn't occurred to me yet that I might spend the rest of my career in management.

I found it ironic that we ops officers started out in the field recruiting and running agents and as soon as we proved ourselves we got promoted, and from then on we mostly sat behind a desk. It was a well-known dynamic within the clandestine service but it didn't make much sense. To this day we haven't figured out a better alternative.

The one bright light of my office routine was the first-class performance of our two secretaries. I can no longer remember their names but I recall that one was from Pennsylvania and the other from the Midwest.

My lousy manual dexterity made me a poor typist and with so much paperwork to prepare it took me a long time to get things done. In Kuala Lumpur, for the first time in my career, I had my own secretary. I could dictate reports and memos to my heart's content.

Both women were highly skilled but their value went beyond that. They always seemed to stay one step ahead of us in the work that needed to be done. They had plenty of initiative. They were pleasant, helpful and liked by everyone. Willing and able they accomplished a wide range of secretarial, administrative and financial tasks for us all. No question without them our efficiency level would have decreased sharply. We were blessed to have them.

I basically had the same experience no matter which overseas office I worked in, headed, or visited. Our directorate was served unusually well by a competent and dedicated secretarial corps. Whether by design or good fortune their contributions merited much more praise and recognition than they ever received.

Judy and the girls and I enjoyed our life in Kuala Lumpur, which fit its reputation as a good posting for families. Just as Paul had told me soon after we arrived, the pace of life was tolerable, the climate was pleasant, and our living conditions were very comfortable.

We also enjoyed the benefits of Lai and Azma, plus a gardener and a watchman—he could not have been described as a guard—all of whom allowed us more time to spend with the girls, who were doing just fine. As we also had been told, the elementary school was good enough to challenge Suzanne and Danika appropriately.

Alison was starting kindergarten and we had put Pia in a Malaysian preschool. After school during the week Judy and the girls would go to the Lake Club. All the girls—even Pia at age 3—were strong swimmers. That made the pool sessions much less stressful than had been the case in Hong Kong, where one of us had to watch them at all times.

Judy played tennis almost daily and soon Suzanne and then Danika started hitting balls. Both seemed to like tennis—we tried not to press them—and both quickly developed promising games.

On weekends we often visited nearby tourist sites and the girls gazed wide-eyed at the beautiful beaches, lush jungles and neatly manicured plantations.

We all grew fond of the variety of cuisine available in Malaysia. The restaurants featured excellent Malay, Chinese—our favorite—and Indian fare. Plus, Lai prepared wonderful meals on a daily basis. She also provided an assortment of fresh fruit for our table. In fact we could pick bananas from our veranda, which overlooked a hillside, and other fruits grew in our yard.

I might be painting a rosy picture but that's just how we saw it. We spent two happy years in Kuala Lumpur and were reluctant to see our time end.

Just to balance things a little, here is an incident that wasn't so rosy. It occurred one day as we returned home from a visit to the Lake Club. We pulled into the driveway and as usual everyone grabbed their bags full of swimming suits, towels, tennis rackets and balls from the car. We went into the house, each daughter heading for her room on the second floor to put things away. It was a ritual.

Suddenly Suzy bolted out of her room, slammed the door, and ran down the stairs shouting about a snake. We tried to calm her 11-year-old nerves to get a clear story. Quickly regaining her composure she explained that wrapped around the wires of the blade shield on the large, post-mounted fan at the foot of her bed was a thin, bright-green snake.

I instantly recalled an adage I had heard in Thailand: The brighter the color the more poisonous the snake.

Suzy had noticed the reptile when she threw her racket on the bed and it started slithering down the post. She screamed in fright, ran out of the room, and with luck or good sense had slammed the door.

In theory at least the snake was trapped in Suzy's bedroom. What to do?

Lai had heard the commotion, understood what was happening, and told us to do nothing while she got her husband, Louie. I had no better ideas so I waited with everyone until he arrived.

"No problem," he told us when he showed up a few minutes later. "We'll just kill the snake."

"How?" Suzy blurted out. "We don't know where it is."

"I've killed snakes before," he explained. "You just wait down here."

He had walked in carrying a tree branch no thicker than his finger, about 3 feet long and flexible. He snapped the floor with it at the top of the stairs before he opened the bedroom door, and I could see the utility of his weapon. It would deliver a sharp blow across a broad area. Lai, and now Azma as well, also armed with switches, stationed themselves in the hallway in front of the bedroom as Louie prepared to open the door.

For no good reason I thought I should be involved so I grabbed a tennis racket, climbed the stairs, and stood with the two women in the hallway.

"The snake can move quickly," Louie told me, "so watch out."

Then he opened the door cautiously. Seeing nothing he slowly entered the room. Still nothing—the snake had vacated the fan. Louie carefully scanned the surroundings. He bent down and tried to see under the bed. He couldn't and decided, wisely, against getting all the way down on the floor. Positioning himself carefully he jerked the bed away from the wall.

Without warning a thin, bright-green snake—Suzy had been accurate—darted out from behind the bed and headed for the door. In rapid succession Louie delivered three quick hits just behind its head and the thing stopped moving. Two more hits for good measure and we were all convinced it was dead.

The incident wasn't unusual for Lai and Louie or for Azma but it left the rest of us somewhat shaken. Glad it had been resolved I expressed my sincere appreciation to Louie.

That wasn't the end of the story. I came home from work one day several weeks later to find the household in a tizzy. The girls told me excitedly how Azma, who had discovered a snake behind the washing machine, first lured it out and then killed it—a call for more of my sincere appreciation.

Then there was the "Komodo dragon" that regularly lounged in the sun on the brick wall behind our house. No one ever got close to him—no one *wanted* to get close to him.

It probably wasn't a Komodo dragon. For one thing it was only 2 feet long, while the real dragons can reach 10 feet. For another, they're found only on several islands in Indonesia over 2,000 miles away. But to us it was an ugly, nasty-looking lizard that made regular appearances on the wall. At least he didn't bother us and we certainly didn't bother him.

After our departure we heard from friends that because of what they called "nests of cobras" found beneath our house the embassy did not renew the lease.

Early in January 1978 Bill Graver, our division chief, arrived for an unscheduled visit. This was unusual. Division chiefs and other senior officers from headquarters rarely visited small—by Far East Division standards—offices like ours. We were pleased but couldn't help thinking something was up.

We had been hearing vague rumors about management problems in Hong Kong; other than that we knew nothing. Ed speculated about a possible connection but had no specific information.

After a private conversation with Ed, Graver walked into my office, closed the door, and announced that he wanted to talk with me about an assignment.

"I know you have asked for a third year here in Kuala Lumpur," he began, "but I need you elsewhere. I'd like to move you to Hong Kong this summer."

He caught me off guard. Ed had speculated that if Hong Kong was having problems he might be transferred to take over the office. After all, he was in his third year in Kuala Lumpur so a move for him wouldn't be unusual. That would leave me in charge, he said.

Also, Ed was a super-grade officer while I had moved up to a GS-15. He reasoned that our operations in Kuala Lumpur were top-heavy because an office this size normally would rate only one of us. It wasn't a glitch, just a coincidence. I had been promoted between the time I received the posting and my departure from Langley.

It had sounded logical to me but Graver's statement shifted the ground.

"Hong Kong?"

It was all I could think of to say.

"You would be deputy," he said.

That completed the surprise.

"I'd love it," I quickly replied, "but I'm going to have to talk with Judy."

He knew Judy and posed the question cautiously.

"Any problem there?"

"I don't know. I honestly don't know," I told him. "Her memories of Hong Kong are not as positive as mine. She had three babies during our four years there and was busy as hell. It didn't sit all that well. She was cheering when we took off."

"I'll talk with her," he said immediately. "We're talking about the needs of the service here and I'm sure she'll understand."

I smiled.

"I'm glad *you* are," I said. "You'll have your shot tonight at dinner. By the way, does Ed know about this?"

"Yes he does. I just told him before coming in here. He seemed disappointed. I guess he just doesn't want to lose a good deputy."

I said nothing.

I gave Judy the news when I got home from work. She was surprised and initially not pleased—reluctant, even.

"Don't make a hasty decision," I told her. "Bill wants to talk to you about it tonight. It would be great for my career."

She knew that.

In the end, as I had hoped—and in fact knew—she bought the plan, although she made clear she would regret leaving Kuala Lumpur after only two years.

Thinking back, at least two and maybe three factors probably influenced her decision not to protest the return to Hong Kong. First, she knew I was delighted and more than ready to help run our office there. It would be a real step up for me.

Second, she knew we weren't going to have any more babies.

Last, our lifetime membership in the Ladies' Recreation Club meant we could walk right back in the door when we got there. I was very glad I had the foresight to acquire it.

Life in Hong Kong this time would be great, I assured her. She smiled. What a honey!

I did my best to stay focused on our activities and operations but my impending summer transfer changed things for me. From that point on I harbored what is commonly known as the short-timer's mentality. I continued to follow all of our ongoing efforts—we had made contact with Igor's replacement—but inevitably I began planning for our departure.

As soon as Bill Graver named my successor, whose name I can no longer recall, Judy and I began corresponding with him and his wife. I also began preparing to turn over the sensitive asset I was handling—my shopping-mall agent.

That case had been running smoothly and productively since I had taken it over. I kept the number of personal meetings to a minimum for security reasons, but given his longtime status as one of our best agents the infrequent contact had no adverse impact on our relationship. At one point I had been able to slip down to Singapore to spend two days with him. We both enjoyed the experience because we were able to get a better understanding of each other.

The office took the news calmly. Everyone seemed to see the move as a good step and many offered congratulations. Ed had more or less shrugged his shoulders. He said he knew we were top-heavy and it didn't surprise him that Bill had decided to pull one of us out.

Suddenly our routine of school and leisure had been interrupted by moving plans and more frequent social events. We had been expecting to stay a third year in Kuala Lumpur so the Hong Kong reassignment required new thinking. Housing in Hong Kong would be no problem, nor would movement of our household effects—including the infamous piano. But now that the girls were older we would have to think more about schools and make some choices. Even Pia would be ready to start kindergarten in September.

As usual in foreign postings many of our friends and acquaintances hosted cocktail and dinner parties to mark our departure. In only two years we had cut a wide swath through Kuala Lumpur's social circles and the number of events attested to the associations we had made. Within the diplomatic corps, including Vlatko, and the local Malaysian community alike, many people were kind enough to honor us.

We attended a most pleasant and large dinner at the Lake Club, at which I was asked to give a short speech. I did so, expressing how we truly regretted leaving Malaysia. I didn't mention how much I was looking forward to getting back to Hong Kong and the mainstream but I did add how pleased Judy and I had been to meet the King of Malaysia—though technically we didn't meet the real king

The previous summer Judy and I had been selected to play a friendly, mixed doubles match with a team from the Royal Selangor Club. Yahya Petra, the king, had sponsored the tournament and he was supposed to present each player with a pewter plate as a memento of the occasion.

We later found out that Petra—who had been sultan of the state of Kelantan and was chosen king in 1975 by Malaysia's other sultans—had gone on vacation and designated one of his colleagues as king in his absence. At the tournament the organizers referred to him as the "acting king." The concept amused me. How could someone be an acting king? You're either king or you're not.

We managed to complete all of the parties and events and when my replacement arrived from headquarters I introduced him to the full range of my official and unofficial contacts.

The reassignment also entitled us to another home leave and it promised to be as hectic and stress-filled as the last one. No way could we avoid seeing both families and I'd have to stop in at Langley for some briefings and introductions.

Those last months in Malaysia stayed busy but they passed quickly and uneventfully. To keep ourselves positive, every so often Judy or I would exclaim, "But happily there's the Ladies' Recreation Club!"

Our pack-out reminded me how much one family can accumulate in just two years. I remember at one point declaring to the girls, "We are not shipping those rocks!"

It had been a good if unspectacular tour for me; lots of learning and honing of skills under a new set of responsibilities. Now I was ready to take on anew the problems and challenges in Hong Kong.

19. Hard Realities

HONG KONG 1978–1979

We made the familiar approach and touchdown at Kai Tak in July 1978. Hong Kong hadn't changed all that much during our five-year absence. Some new office and apartment buildings had sprung up and the harbor tunnel had changed traffic patterns, but the people and hectic pace of life seemed the same. It remained a vibrant, dynamic city—and it was still stifling in the summer.

We arrived early evening after a 15-hour flight from Los Angeles. As usual, agency people met us after we cleared immigration and took us to our hotel. We had just completed several busy months, including the swirl of parties in Kuala Lumpur, our home leave, and my quick stop-in at Langley. We were relieved to be at the end of our travels for a while and settling in once again.

Home leave had been a series of enjoyable but tiring trips around the country visiting family and friends. Relatives promised they would visit us, and we welcomed them, but we doubted that prospect.

Once again the girls had handled the trip splendidly. Suzanne and Danika were old enough to remember Hong Kong and they seemed excited about returning.

We blended back into life in the Crown Colony quite easily, in some ways as if we hadn't been away at all. Others seemed to have the same impression. As I had promised Judy we quickly reactivated our membership in the Ladies' Recreation Club. There I ran into a member who had been a casual acquaintance back in 1973.

"My goodness," he said, "I was just thinking that your home leave had been a long one!"

We discovered that many of our old friends still lived in Hong Kong and we resumed our contacts with ease. Judy moved back into some regular tennis games and at her vastly improved level she was promptly invited to play on the club team.

In contrast to our first arrival we knew where to go for various household purchases, and having spent the last two years in Malaysia we needed no adjustment to drive on the left side of the road.

We moved into a nice apartment on Bowen Road in the Mid-Levels. It was located at the end of the road and offered immediate access to Bowen Path where I jogged most mornings. The apartment wasn't as spacious as the house in Kuala Lumpur so Alison and Pia had to share a bedroom, but the living room was big enough to accommodate the Weinbach—and there didn't seem to be a snake in sight. Soon we all felt right at home again.

My return to the Hong Kong office at first was anything but pleasant. Bill Graver had been quite circumspect about the reason for my transfer; he wouldn't elaborate on the rumors we'd been hearing about a personnel issue. I had picked up some scuttlebutt at headquarters along similar lines.

It became immediately obvious that something was wrong because both Jack G., the chief, and Charlie K., the deputy, were gone.

It also turned out that I wasn't the only new arrival at the office. Bob Grealy had flown in from Seoul the same day. He had been chief there and Bill had chosen him to replace Jack in Hong Kong.

I hadn't met him before, despite his long record of service in Far East Division. Our paths just never crossed. But I knew of him and looked forward to getting to know him. Bob was from Boston and of Irish descent; by coincidence so was a sizable percentage of his generation of directorate officers. He was reputed to be energetic, hard-working and fair.

Bob and I were staying at the same hotel so we agreed to meet in his room the next morning. He was still half-dressed and in the middle of shaving when I knocked. In his early 50s, standing 5 feet 8 and weighing about 160 he looked in fairly good shape.

"I've heard lots of good things. Glad to finally meet you," Bob said, waving me into the room with a warm smile.

"Sit down," he continued. "Sorry I'm late. I'll be finished in a minute, then we can have some breakfast. We've got lots to talk about."

I sat in a chair by the window looking out across the harbor toward Kowloon.

"What do you know about why headquarters sent us here?" he asked from his stance in front of the bathroom mirror.

"Not much at all," I replied, "mostly rumor. It seems to be personal and they're holding it pretty close. I was in headquarters two weeks ago and got almost nothing, just briefings on what we're doing work-wise. I didn't press anybody."

He stepped out of the bathroom and finished dressing.

"Well, I've heard that Jack was messing around where he shouldn't have been and headquarters found out. They had to recall him. Charlie just got screwed by the situation. And I've also heard that one reason it's you and me is that we both have reputations as family men."

I knew Bob had friends among the senior officers so I figured he had pretty good information. He confirmed my suspicions. The "issue" everyone was tiptoeing around involved Jack having an affair with one of the office's female employees.

In the clandestine service such fraternization was and still is completely unacceptable, and headquarters withdrew Jack as soon as they became aware of the situation. Along with the damage he did to himself and his marriage, the terrible example he set and the poor leadership and judgment he demonstrated had seriously harmed morale.

Now I understood why Bill had been so tight-lipped. Although this wasn't a matter of Need to Know, no one above me at the agency ever briefed me about the details. Our unofficial rules protected personal privacy. But it wasn't difficult to piece together at least the outline of what had provoked the management change.

"I feel sorry for Charlie," I told Bob. "I know he wouldn't have done anything wrong. I'd hoped to talk with him but I'm told he's already gone."

"Yep, I think he left two days ago. Jack's gone, too. We need to get in there and raise the comfort level."

The woman involved in the affair had also been transferred out of Hong Kong. I don't know where she went from there.

One of the unfortunate casualties of this mess was Charlie, the man Bill had chosen me to replace. He had been unfairly caught up in the turmoil caused by Jack's actions. A Korean-American with a long record of loyal and exemplary service in the directorate he had been my branch chief when I worked at headquarters. He was always conscientious and hard-working and his assignment as deputy in Hong Kong had recognized his abilities and contributions.

I felt then and now that Charlie's difficulties were cultural in origin. As is often the case among Asians he was more supportive and loyal to Jack than the circumstances warranted. He hadn't known about the stories or didn't believe them, but in either case he found himself isolated and in an untenable position.

I don't know who made the decision to withdraw him short of tour or why they made it, but no one could have questioned Charlie's integrity. He had become a victim and I'm certain the shame of what had happened hurt him deeply.

I liked and greatly respected Charlie and wished I could have talked to him about the situation. But it was not to be. He returned to headquarters and retired not long thereafter. I never saw him again.

Bob studied me carefully for a moment.

"You know Hong Kong," he said. "That's going to be a big help."

Our officers had known the changes were coming and many of them were acquainted with one or the other of us, so they seemed to welcome our arrival. Many expressed confidence that Bob and I could stabilize things.

I hoped to do just that. The sooner we put the disruption behind us and focused on the work, the better. I knew Bob felt the same way.

It was important. Hong Kong had experienced little change in the years since our departure in 1973 but the situation in mainland China had shifted dramatically. January 8, 1976, had seen the death of Chou—now Zhou—En-lai, China's respected and revered prime minister. Then on

July 28 of that year a powerful earthquake had hit in the city of Tangshan in northeast China, leaving more than a quarter-million people dead. The quake reduced the coal-mining center about 200 miles northeast of Beijing to rubble. It has never been rebuilt.

On September 9, with Tangshan still feeling aftershocks from the quake, Mao Tse-tung died after a long illness. Almost immediately the Gang of Four, comprising Mao's widow and three other opportunistic, hard-line communists, seized control of the party and with it political control of the country. The turmoil continued until the arrest of the Gang of Four and the ascent to power by Hua Guofeng, though his reign lasted only until early 1978.

At that point Deng Xiaoping, who had been disgraced and removed from power during the Cultural Revolution—for among other things being a bridge player—maneuvered his way back to the top and gained full control of the party and the country.

These momentous events caused many in China to fear that Jung Gwo, the Middle Kingdom, had lost *tianming*, the mandate of heaven.

Beguiling as that thought might have been the practical result was that Mao's death signaled the end of the Cultural Revolution, which must have been a great relief to China's masses. Given the different political climate that was emerging on the mainland, we needed to change our approach to intelligence gathering.

We didn't know it at the time, and I doubt that Deng himself could have predicted what was coming, but the reforms he introduced would have profound and lasting effects on China and its relations with the rest of the world.

Those same reforms would affect our efforts as well. For many reasons, particularly trade and the economy, China under Deng became a more open society.

We could see the changes coming—we just didn't see them going as far as they eventually would. But we welcomed what we did see because it promised an easing of the security environment.

Deng's reforms, which started in the countryside as the systematic dismantlement of collective farms in favor of private plots, prompted resurgent interest in China among our government's policymakers. Those policymakers, in turn, loosed a surge of requirements on us. Much of the pressure for increased intelligence fell heavily on our office.

Clearly we were going to have to augment and fine-tune our programs.

Despite the new openness China hadn't yet lifted the Bamboo Curtain. But the People's Republic did begin to allow more businessmen and diplomats to enter its borders—including Americans. That development expanded the pool of people who could report what was going on inside the country.

The change also brought new challenges because it raised the bar for measuring the value of intelligence we were collecting. Now certain information, once obtainable only via carefully planned, clandestine operations, was available from open sources. At the same time the demands from Washington pushed us to seek intelligence that was increasingly difficult to collect.

With all of this in mind Bob and I started working to improve our operations across the board.

We began on strong footing. Our Hong Kong office, a large one, comprised a capable complement of officers and support personnel. I had learned quite a bit about the group while I was at headquarters and my respect for them was confirmed as I met them individually. All but a few spoke solid Chinese and several were Chinese Americans who spoke at least two dialects.

The management upheaval notwithstanding, each of our branches was well staffed and functioning smoothly. For several reasons, including my recent experience in Kuala Lumpur, I was particularly happy to see that we had two excellent reports officers. One, a former case officer, would be replaced the next year by an even more experienced and competent individual. The other had accumulated only headquarters experience and was on her first tour but together they ran an exceptional section.

Our support officers likewise performed admirably. They deftly handled personnel, administrative and budget matters as well as many other items that often arose unexpectedly. As I mentioned earlier—and was the norm in my experience—we had excellent secretaries, some of whom were wives of officers, who met every demand we placed on them.

Bob and I met separately with each member of the staff to gauge the effect of recent events. I found a consistent attitude and it matched our own: Let's put this whole sordid thing behind us and get on with our work.

Bob reinforced that point at our first all-hands meeting and in the separate staff powwows that followed. No one objected. Within weeks the shake-up was history and other than depressing everyone for a while the incident had little lasting impact.

I had reviewed our ops program while at headquarters and it seemed strong. Now on the scene my discussions with each of the branch chiefs reinforced my optimism. We had promising developmental efforts under way and the ongoing agent ops were producing solid intelligence. Even more heartening, we had streamlined our covert activities and made their objectives more sensible.

I did find a couple of areas that demanded my attention. One branch, which focused on Southeast Asia and to some extent Europe, was holding its own but lacked Chinese speakers. No matter the target, an inability to speak Chinese in Hong Kong was an inhibiting factor.

Also, we had established a presence inside the mainland but it was laboring under persistently severe security constraints and was just getting started. That said, the timing couldn't have been better. The table-tennis team's visit back in 1971 had kicked off considerable social and political turmoil and change, much of it working in our favor.

China and the United States had established diplomatic relations and we now had an official embassy in Beijing, replacing the U.S. Liaison Office that George H.W. Bush had run earlier in the decade. Large numbers of people were entering China, stretching thin the country's internal security network.

Our ops climate, still by no means favorable, had grown less unfavorable and we were shifting our approaches to exploit the new environment. I made a point of complimenting the branch chiefs and reported my impressions to Bob. I also made note of those impressions in a long cable to headquarters.

Jack and Charlie clearly had adjusted our Hong Kong efforts well in response to the changes inside China. Now Bob and I could build on their solid foundation.

This in no way excused Jack's behavior, the details of which to this day remain unknown to me. His transgressions couldn't have been ignored even if someone had wanted to ignore them. But our top priority was China watching as a matter of national security and Hong Kong remained, as it had for more than two decades, the agency's flagship post for those efforts.

After some discussions with friends Judy and I decided to enroll the girls in the Hong Kong International School, located on the other side of the island in Repulse Bay. Run by a Lutheran missionary group the school did not impose religion on the students, the majority of whom were from the American community, with Chinese and Europeans as well.

In fact one reason we chose the school was that it used American techniques and standards, much like the International School in Kuala Lumpur. We thought it would be easier for the girls to adjust when we eventually returned to the States.

Within months we began to doubt the wisdom of our decision. It started with Suzanne, then 12, making disquieting remarks about how things were going in her classroom. We grew similarly worried by reports from Danika and Alison.

The problems centered on what educators at the time called the open-classroom method. The last straw occurred while I was escorting a visitor from Washington on a tour of the school. We walked into one of the large classrooms where about a hundred students were milling around everywhere. It was noisy—in fact it was bedlam.

I greeted the teacher and introduced my visitor.

"It's too bad we got here during the recess period," my guest said. "I was hoping to watch some classroom sessions."

"Oh, it's not recess period," she told him. "It's just that the children have more freedom and choice in our system.

"This is the classroom. There are no smaller rooms. That teacher," she said, gesturing toward a woman sitting in a cluster of children, "is teaching now."

My visitor looked surprised and I was shocked, probably visibly so.

How the hell could anyone learn anything in a place like this?

We looked around for a few more minutes then left.

"I'm not that impressed with the open-classroom system," he said when we got outside.

Neither was I.

We decided to withdraw our girls from the school as soon as possible but we learned that only Suzanne could transfer at the end of the semester. Her sisters would have to wait until the following September for openings.

When he heard of Suzanne's withdrawal the principal asked to see me. After some initial sparring I leveled some strong criticisms of the open-classroom approach. He tried to explain and I rebutted his explanations.

Finally, exasperated, he said, "You just don't understand."

He was right. But for the record many schools soon scrapped open classrooms as unworkable and bad for students.

In contrast to this chaos the girls eventually thrived at the German Swiss International School, which used the European system stressing discipline, structure and homework, and which kept class sizes to no more than 20.

The school demanded more of them but the girls fondly remember their time there.

Our director, Stansfield Turner, did not like the agency. He was particularly suspicious of the Directorate of Operations and for some misguided reason took it upon himself to try to upgrade the morals of those serving abroad.

For reasons I never clearly understood, Turner dispatched a crony, Robert "Rusty" Williams, to investigate numerous overseas stations and report on family life. Apparently he had gained the impression that many of our officers abroad had been behaving badly. The whole idea offended us, particularly the accusatory approach taken by Turner.

No doubt the episode with Jack had added fuel to Turner's fire. It might even have been what prompted him to deploy Williams. From our vantage point it was impossible to tell but it was the kind of situation the admiral had dispatched his crony to investigate.

If Turner had wanted to root out miscreants, maybe he should have started closer to home. Overseas officers don't own the exclusive rights to human weakness. Neither do domestic personnel or public servants in general. Such failings are endemic to human beings.

Indeed we would have a President of the United States who committed adultery and engaged in sexual misbehavior in the White House. Then he stood up in front of the whole nation, wagged his finger, and lied about it. Though roundly criticized, even by members of his own political party, he escaped removal from office for reasons of political expediency.

Human beings are full of urges—wandering eyes and seductive glances can become the sources of big problems. More problematic for us, those urges can be exploited in the pursuit of intelligence. The Soviet bloc services were constantly trying to tempt or blackmail our people.

As carefully selected, tested and vetted, and high caliber as our cadre of officers was we couldn't completely screen out individuals who violated trust. It was silly to think otherwise.

Turner apparently applied his own optic. It appalled him and Williams to learn that our operations officers in Europe—as is the case globally—sometimes left their wives and families in the evening to meet agents.

It was one of the hard realities of our craft. Often the only times we could meet with agents were evenings and weekends, when they weren't working. Wives of our officers around the world accepted it as a demand of the service—an occupational necessity. Most didn't like it—Judy certainly didn't—but they understood why it had to be done. Apparently Williams and Turner could not.

Their moral crusade garnered the two men neither respect nor popularity. Turner had already alienated quite a few people when he insisted on being called "Admiral." The common reaction: If you're the director, call yourself Director. If you want to be Admiral, go back to the Navy.

Turner seemed too military, too bureaucratic, and as mentioned he particularly distrusted the clandestine service. It might have been an overly harsh judgment on my part—I never did meet the man because I remained overseas during his entire tenure—but I thought Turner was one of the worst directors the agency ever had. He and Schlesinger were running neck and neck for that distinction.

The months passed quickly and soon it was spring 1979. I stood in front of the window in my office and looked down on the traffic flowing along Garden Road toward Central District. It was late afternoon and the streets were bustling but I was looking without seeing; I was thinking.

One of our branch chiefs was in my office along with our senior reports officer. We had been discussing how we intended to respond to the latest cable from headquarters, which had raised questions about one of our operations. Langley thought we were getting flawed information.

I felt perplexed and maybe even irritated so I stood in front of the window to weigh what I would and would not condone in our response, which the reports officer would write.

"So, headquarters is still convinced that our guy is giving us bum skinny," I said, turning to sit at my desk.

"That's right," the branch chief responded, "and I'm dammed if I know why."

The incoming cable had frustrated us all.

"What do you think, Mary?" I asked the reports officer, who was experienced and excellent.

"You know what I think, Dick," she quickly replied. "I wouldn't have recommended dissemination of the intelligence if I had any questions about the agent's access or reliability."

"I think they are way off base on this one," the branch chief interjected. "Matt (the officer handling the case) has done all his homework. We've got independent confirmation of the agent's activity. Plus we saw him get on the train to Lowu. He makes the trips."

He slapped his knee.

"I think that much is clear even to headquarters," I said, "but the reporting is what they are questioning. Is this a stalemate or is there some way we can convince them that it's good stuff?"

"I'm not sure, but we have to try," Mary volunteered. "Let me draft a reply for you to look at and we can meet again before we send something back."

It wasn't an unusual meeting. We had been dealing with the case for several months. We had recruited the agent, vetted him carefully, trained him thoroughly, and dispatched him to the Chinese mainland.

We used first missions as much for testing purposes as intelligence collection. To us he looked good. We had also tested him in Hong Kong and he passed there as well. Matt had elicited a lot of background information about him and his family in China, and it all hung together.

Part of his motivation was abuse suffered by family members during the Cultural Revolution. Another part was financial; he wanted to send his children abroad for an education. Mary assessed the access he claimed and it squared with the information he was reporting. Again, we thought we were on solid ground.

Headquarters remained unconvinced. Some questioned the access he claimed and the information he reported, and they were reluctant to see it disseminated to the intelligence community until their doubts were resolved.

As the exchanges continued flashes of frustration began appearing in some of the cables despite efforts on both ends to keep things civil and substantive. I held the major portion of that responsibility at our end and I was determined to avoid letting emotions rule our presentations.

Mary wrote an excellent draft cable that struck just the right tone. Bob agreed and we fired it off to headquarters. I knew that the leader of the Doubting Thomases at Langley was a senior reports officer who had served previously in Hong Kong. I respected her professional competence and I knew she could draw on her deep experience in this type of operation and reporting. But I disagreed with her assessments and thought she had developed a bias against this particular asset.

The case illustrates why the human element can't be wrung out of the system. I see it even more clearly now than I did back then. We were clinging to our judgments and the senior reports officer was clinging to hers. Both sides were convinced they were right and neither would budge.

In the end headquarters rejected our arguments, the exchanges ground to a halt, and we dropped the asset—but we weren't happy about it.

The episode was far from unique. Reports officers at headquarters reviewed field intelligence to assure reliability and accuracy. And the field officers had to generate reports and authenticate them to Langley's satisfaction. When each side did its job the system worked well but the final say always rested at headquarters. We in the field could only press our points and try to persuade our stateside colleagues that the case in question was a good one.

The problems compounded at stations running agents into a denied area such as China. We possessed minimal ability to verify what an agent was doing or what happened after he or she crossed the border. That left many questions unanswered, not the least of which was whether they had duped us and were exposing our identities and techniques to a hostile service. We could only make informed decisions and we always risked developing biases in favor of our ops.

We were aware of that and we strove to make solid, balanced calls. Headquarters almost always accepted our judgments and disseminated the intelligence. Sometimes they did not—another unpleasant reality of our craft.

Sometimes making the calls wasn't so difficult. On another occasion Mary, the senior reports officer, Mike, the case officer and the branch chief were briefing me about a troublesome case.

"The meeting was in our safe house in Wanchai," the branch chief explained.

"Which one?" I asked.

"It's in the building right on the corner of Hennessey and Fleet, on the fourth floor. You can see the whole intersection from the window in the living room."

"Harbor side of the intersection?" I asked.

"That's right."

I could picture the building in my mind. We had set up a safe house in the same building back when I had taken over our ops-support section in 1969. But that one had been terminated; this was new. It was a good building for our purposes. It had entrances—and therefore exits—on two different streets and there was no caretaker on the premises to monitor who was coming and going.

It was easy for our Chinese support agents to rent apartments for us and we enjoyed clear access to the places all day while the agents were at work. In this case Europeans lived in the building and most of the apartments offered a good look at traffic in the intersection down in front.

Hennessey Road, named after a former Hong Kong governor, was a major thoroughfare running east-west along the north side of the island. It carried heavy traffic most of the time—cars, buses, minibuses, taxis and trucks in abundance. It offered easy, quick access for agents and case officers alike.

"Why don't you review what happened?" I asked.

"I scheduled the meeting for 11 o'clock this morning," Mike reported, "and Lynx (the cryptonym we used for the agent) arrived just a couple of minutes late. I saw him get off the minibus coming from Central. The meeting went about as planned. He didn't have much intelligence from his cousin but said he'd have more after his cousin's trip to Shanghai next week. As you know we've had some questions about his reporting."

Mary nodded.

"We set up surveillance to see what he would do after the meeting," Mike concluded.

"So what did he do?" I asked.

"He came out on the Fleet Street side, looked around quickly, and headed down Fleet for the harbor. He made a short phone call then turned east on Lockhart Road. Three blocks down Lockhart he met Au Sap Chung, who was waiting on the corner. Brazen little shit! I think our guys got a good photo of the two walking together."

"I knew it!" Mary exclaimed, almost jumping out of her chair. "He's nailed!"

Au Sap Chung was a known fabricator and catching Lynx with him immediately after a meeting with us was all we needed to resolve our doubts about his intelligence credibility. It was a coup and solid tradecraft by Mike.

"Bloody well done as the Brits would say," I told them. "It's like dodging a bullet when we dig one of these creeps out of the woodwork. We've had to do it before and we'll no doubt have to do it again."

Mary and Mike had worked closely together to set up the test that Lynx had failed so miserably—although he didn't know it yet.

This was how teamwork should turn out and I was proud of them both. In the near future we would cut off contact with Lynx, citing some plausible reason. We also would not reveal to him what had happened or that we knew about his contact with Au Sap Chung. That pained Mike, who wanted to confront Lynx with the photograph. But there were other fabricators out there and Lynx or Au might lead us to them.

That July I was sitting in the American Club in the St. George's Building, a newly built skyscraper in Central District, an easy walk from the office. I was enjoying a rare respite from the mountain of work piled on my desk.

I saw Stig approach before he spotted me at our reserved table. He was often late because lunchtime was a busy period for him. Our relationship was entirely personal. Stig was a Scandinavian friend I'd known since the early 1970s so I had no need to ferret out possible surveillance.

Despite its name the American Club hosted a mixed membership, more than half Chinese and European. It was a prestigious place, offering excellent meals and serving as a popular midday rendezvous spot for businessmen working downtown. I often used it as a place to meet and develop contacts of interest.

My friend worked in the transportation sector and had lots of dealings with Chinese officials.

"Stig, over here," I called out.

I stood up to shake hands.

"How are you?" I asked.

We exchanged pleasantries for a couple of minutes until our waiter arrived.

"What do you think? Should we have the usual?" I asked.

Without hesitation he replied enthusiastically, "The usual."

Over our years of lunching together at the American Club we had fallen into a gastronomical habit that we both liked: two Bloody Marys to start, followed by avocadoes stuffed with baby shrimp and covered with Thousand Island dressing, and steak tartare as the main course.

"Let me guess," I said, "you were late because you had a call from Europe."

He smiled.

"No, not this time. I had a meeting with a visitor from Beijing and he wouldn't stop talking."

"Well, is Deng still in charge up there?" I asked with a smile.

"Yeah, I think so, and according to this guy everyone is happy as the reforms crank along."

"I'm going up there next month. I hope they are so busy with the reforms that they don't bother a poor China watcher from Hong Kong."

"Ah, but for you there will be a special welcome," he grinned.

I had never disclosed anything to Stig and he had never pushed the point, but I knew he didn't buy my "China watcher" cover. No matter; it never affected our relationship.

"Seriously though, Dick, are you going up there? That would be an interesting trip. Can you believe that I've lived in Hong Kong for over 20 years and I've never set foot on the mainland?"

"Sure, I can believe it. There are lots of people in Hong Kong who have never been into China. But things are changing and for someone with your contacts it would be easy to set up a trip. You ought to think about it."

We had been sipping our Bloody Marys and were finishing the avocado cocktail when the waiter returned to prepare our steak tartare, which he always did with flair.

"How would we like it today?" he would ask.

"Like you always make it," was our standard response.

He started by breaking a couple of raw eggs into a large bowl on the small table he was using. He added some condiments, followed by the raw, ground steak. Then he mixed things up for a while and added salt and pepper and a few other spices.

When he finished the ceremonial preparation he presented us each a small taste of the final product.

"Does that meet with your satisfaction?" he would always ask.

"Just right," we would always respond.

I don't know what all he used but I would not have disputed the club's claim that they served the best steak tartare in Hong Kong.

As we ate, Stig and I discussed the wide range of subjects we both followed, particularly investments and finance, because he had money in the stock market and precious metals. We also hit international affairs, usually region by region.

Sooner or later we would touch on politics and his deeply held, conservative views. President Carter always caused him great pain.

Stig was intensely anticommunist and had left his home country because of the increasingly socialist and leftist policies pushed by the government there. The United States, he often told me, was the world's best hope—even with a president as naive as Jimmy Carter.

Our political and anticommunist sentiments coincided so the chemistry between us was good and our conversations always congenial.

After we finished the steak tartare, and after rationalizing the decision, we altered our routine by ordering apple pie à la mode, another club specialty. We followed the pie with our usual coffee. By this time, after many of the lunchtime patrons had left, we fell onto the subject of his dealings with the mainland Chinese.

Sometimes Stig would respond to my inquiry by saying he hadn't heard anything new. Other times he would raise the subject. He knew what was of interest to our analysts. Speaking quietly but clearly he would fill me in on recent developments. From time to time I would pose additional questions and sometimes I'd take a few notes.

Stig was always interesting. Intelligent, observant and articulate, he consistently provided me with valuable insights into what China was doing in the shipping sector. The intelligence reports I prepared from our conversations were well received at headquarters. They even singled out one of them for special praise because of the history and insights it contained. I had based it on Stig's analysis of Hong Kong's shipping industry.

My lunches with Stig were welcome respites from days of meetings, decisions, cable writing and other mundane management chores.

Basically I didn't get out much. As deputy chief my profile was too high so I could not become directly involved with agents. China's abilities inside Hong Kong, which remained unknown to us, made it too risky for me and we observed tradecraft at all times.

That's what made this kind of meeting, an innocuous lunch with an old Viking friend, as close as I could get to being on the street. Otherwise I had to be content, in an operational sense, with vicarious rewards.

Cathy and André Le Gallo in Casablanca, Morocco

Suzi on our balcony overlooking Repulse Bay

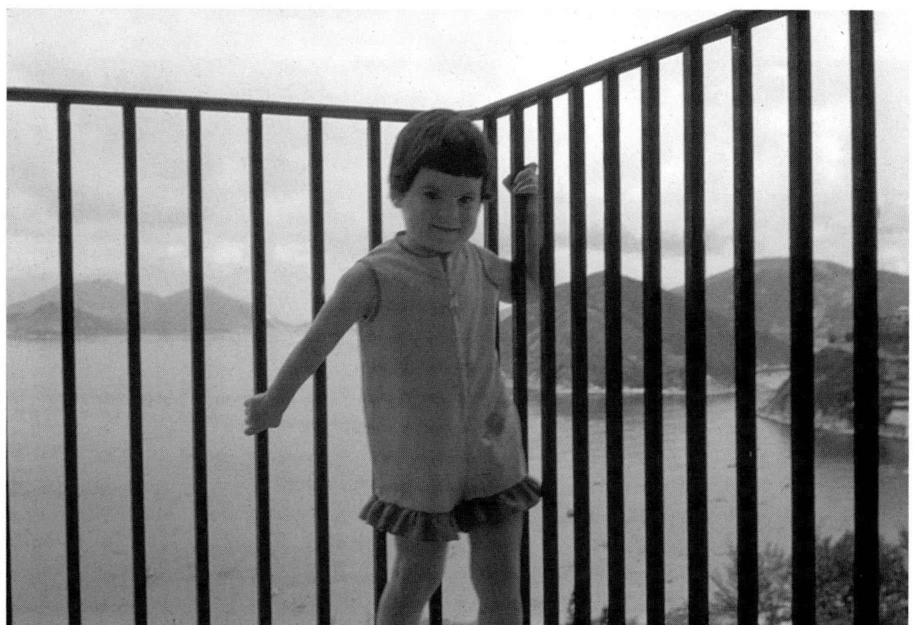

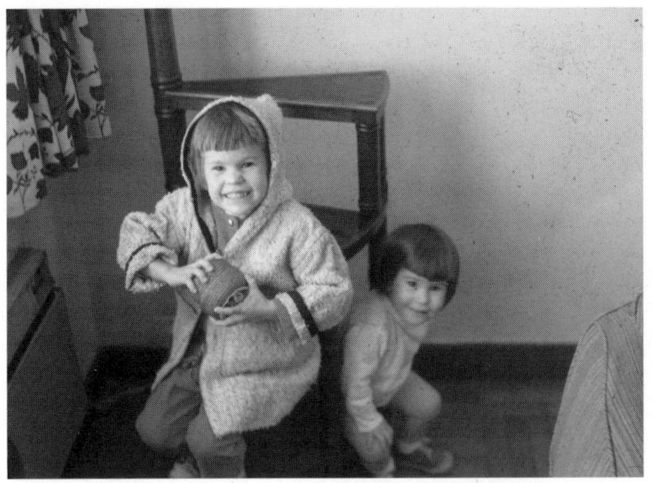

Danika and Alison
in Hong Kong

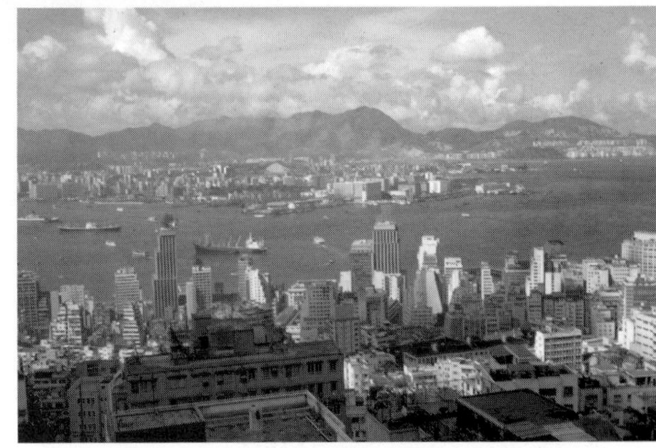

Hong Kong harbor
from our apartment on
Bowen Road

Judy, the girls,
and the Morgan

Looking across the border into China at Lowu

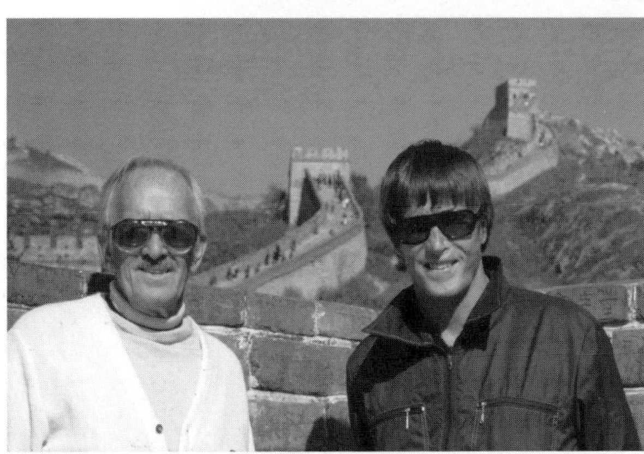

With Dad at the Great Wall

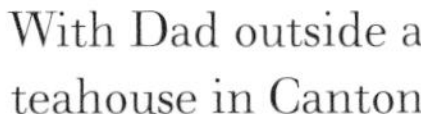

With Dad outside a teahouse in Canton

One of my favorites of Judy, on vacation in France

3/4 of the "platoon"
with me

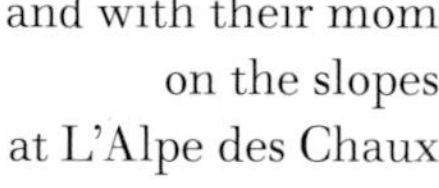

and with their mom
on the slopes
at L'Alpe des Chaux

Our house
in Waterloo

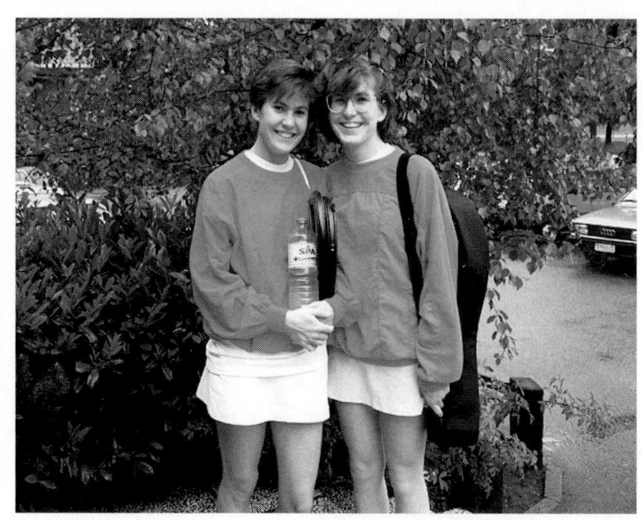

Alison and Danika
off for tennis
at St. John's

Pia

Suzi and Pia

Suzi in our "Belgian Morgan"

Suzanne, Pia, Alison and Danika visiting for Christmas in Paris

Dancing with Judy at one of our daughters' weddings

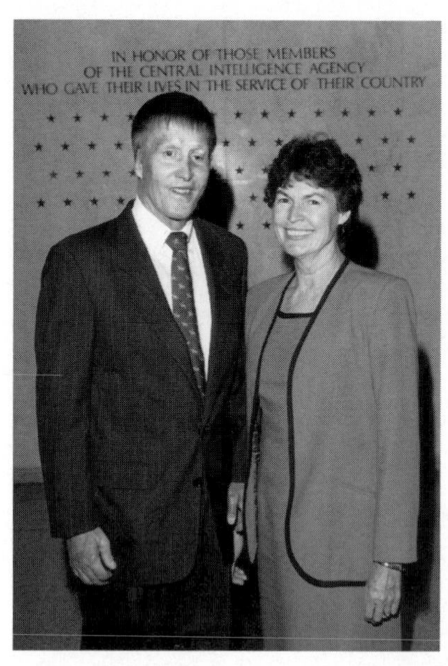

With Judy at the
Wall of Honor at Langley

With Dr. Tim Miller
at the statue of
"Wild Bill" Donovan

20. Damn *Yang Gwei-dze*

HONG KONG 1980–1981

"And what is the reason for your trip?" the immigration official at the train station in Kowloon asked.

"Tourism," I responded.

It was true. I wouldn't be undertaking anything that smacked of intelligence gathering or any other operational activity. Instead I was embarking on a familiarization trip to develop some sense of reality about the target country to which I had devoted most of my waking hours over the previous decade.

I had hoped Judy would accompany me but she declined, not wanting to leave the girls under servant care for two weeks. So Dad, who for years had wanted to see Shanghai, jumped into the breach and volunteered, and I accepted with pleasure. It would be our first trip together since 1959 when we had traveled with my grandfather to Stockholm and then Dad and I had visited Belgium.

My discretion on this visit was grounded in practicality. We had made our arrangements with China Travel Service, the official government organization responsible for dealing with tourism. CTS guides—we knew they were watchdogs—would accompany us for much of the time. We were among the first wave of tourists into the People's Republic since the reforms initiated by Deng Xiaoping in 1978 had opened the floodgates.

I wouldn't be abandoning my tradecraft altogether. I particularly wanted to experience the customs and immigration checks at Lowu—now Luohu—as we crossed into the mainland. Years earlier I had tried to prepare agents for this moment without actually knowing how it worked. Since then I had read numerous reports about what could happen. Now I could get a sense of it myself.

At Lowu we disembarked from the train and walked across the border to enter the customs hall. There we received cursory inspections. The customs officer glanced at our luggage and waved us through. They raised no questions and made no comment when they scanned our travel documents.

Frankly I hadn't been sure what to expect. I assumed that as an American diplomat on vacation I would draw some attention but I didn't know how much. As it happened these guys couldn't have cared less.

I also assumed that the Public Security Bureau, China's internal security service, at some point had pegged me as a China watcher in Hong Kong and perhaps even a suspect intelligence officer. Would they put me under surveillance or harass me in some way? That remained to be seen and it might even have been an interesting or useful experience if they had.

Alas there was no hint of any special attention to me at Lowu as we crossed into China. Was the PSB extremely good or extremely bad at detecting penetration? We always seemed to have trouble answering that question.

We left the customs hall at the opposite end from where we had entered and boarded the train waiting on the Chinese side of the border. There followed an uneventful trip to Canton, now Guangzhou. Few non-Asians rode the train so it must have been easy for the CTS guide to spot us as we exited.

The woman assigned to us approached with a big smile.

"Are you Mr. Holm?" she asked in clear English.

"Yes, I am," I smiled back and introduced my father.

"Welcome to Canton," she said. "Please follow me."

We picked up our luggage, which had been off-loaded into the station, then boarded a minibus and drove to the airport about 15 miles northwest of the city. We would be visiting Canton on our return trip, but first we were headed to Shanghai by plane.

Our next CTS guide met us on the tarmac and drove us straight to the hotel. It was decent, not deluxe, located just outside the center of the city in what used to be the German quarter before World War II.

To my surprise the guide left us on our own with nothing but a schedule of travel arrangements: three days in Shanghai as we wished, plus daytrips to Hangchow (now Hangzhou) and Soochow (Suzhou), then back to the airport for a flight to Beijing.

That unexpected freedom allowed us to wander at will around Shanghai, visiting tourist sights and cruising the Huangpu River. Dad and I both enjoyed it and I marveled at so much of what I saw.

I was delighted to be able to use Mandarin. I couldn't understand the Shanghai dialect but many residents also spoke Mandarin so most understood me. In fact a few seemed dumbstruck to hear a *yang gwei-dze*, a crazy foreign devil, speaking the Mother Tongue of the Middle Kingdom. I might even have been the first American some of them had ever seen.

Another surprise: On the river cruise I freely photographed the scenery, including shots of Chinese warships in the background. Before Deng's reforms the PSB would never have permitted such photos. Once again the thought puzzled me—were these guys really good or really bad?

We visited the Yu Garden and the famous, centuries-old teahouse therein as well as the Friendship Store where I indulged in my practice of buying jade and other semiprecious stones for Judy and the girls.

We also strolled along the famous Bund, the riverside walkway on the bank of the Huangpu built in the 1930s by German contractors.

There a Chinese man approached us.

"Are you American?" he asked.

Until that point I had detected no particular interest in us other than some startled reactions at my ability to speak Mandarin. But this man's approach caused my guard to go up.

I just nodded.

He was trim, well dressed and wearing a suit and tie. He looked about Dad's age: late 60s.

"I used to be in the United States Navy," he announced proudly. "I almost became an American citizen but the war changed everything here. My name is Wang."

"In our Navy?" I asked. "Where did you serve?"

Dad looked intrigued but said nothing.

"I worked on a Yangtze River gunboat in the '30s," he replied. "I did some training in the Philippines and I had almost 10 years of service. When the Japanese attacked I couldn't get out of China."

It sounded plausible enough so my concern ebbed a little.

He walked with us along the Bund and we chatted about some of his experiences—though he never really explained how he had gotten to Shanghai from his birthplace in central China or how he had ended up in our Navy. He did say he was recently retired and had been able to save enough to support himself.

Dad and I began to feel at ease and when Mr. Wang suggested that we have some tea we agreed. We had been walking for quite a while and I knew Dad would enjoy a break. We stopped at a nearby teahouse and sat on stools around a tall wooden table.

As we sipped tea and continued chatting Mr. Wang declared that he wanted his family to meet two real Americans. He invited us to his home for dinner that evening. At that point I hesitated even though we had no plans.

Is this offer legitimate? Or, is it a provocation engineered by the PSB? But to what end? We're doing nothing wrong.

Despite my reservations I accepted. Dad was delighted, seeing this as an exciting experience.

The taxi driver registered incredulity when I handed him the slip of paper on which Mr. Wang had written his address. I'm sure he was wondering why these two *yang gwei-dze* would be going there.

We drove for about 25 minutes through the center of the city and then out to the northeast. My tourist map wasn't detailed enough to show the street where the cabbie dropped us off, on a dark corner. He pointed us toward a small lane.

We hesitated to get out because of the lack of light but by this time there was little choice. The driver answered my question in Mandarin that the building up the lane was our destination.

I knew now that if we ran into trouble we'd have little chance of escaping. We were completely unfamiliar with this part of Shanghai, and if the PSB was behind this they had set the trap cleverly.

Even in the quiet darkness we sensed that the neighborhood was old and decrepit. We saw no one as we walked slowly up the lane. I began to have second thoughts about the wisdom of this situation but I didn't let on to Dad and I didn't start whistling in the dark.

"I can't see anything, Dick," Dad said. "You sure we're in the right place?"

"I'm pretty sure we are. The taxi driver said it was this building."

We walked along a wall that separated the lane from the buildings until we came to an opening. There had been a gate but it was broken and hanging open on rusty hinges. A small, dim light on a nearby pole illuminated the number on the front of the building.

"That's the right number," I said.

"He said fourth floor, right?" Dad asked.

"Right," I replied as we entered the front door.

Still we saw no one. We were alone in what passed for the lobby of what once must have been a nice apartment house. Now it was literally falling apart. There was no elevator so we headed for the stairwell. I continued to feel uneasy but tried not to let on.

"Do you feel like walking up four flights of stairs?" I said. "I don't see any elevator."

"No problem," Dad replied.

He started up and I followed.

Even if we find Mr. Wang how the hell are we going to get out of here?

The fourth-floor landing had doors on either side. Fortunately a readable sign on one bore the number we were looking for. We knocked and to my relief the door opened to reveal Mr. Wang smiling broadly. He ushered us in and introduced us to his two sons, who stood waiting in the living room.

One spoke a little English and the other spoke Mandarin. Two women were also present but they stayed in the background. Mr. Wang invited us to sit in the adjoining dining room and the women began serving our dinner.

After several courses, accompanied by good Chinese beer, it was clear our host wanted to impress us with his hospitality. He did. I could see that the meal was costly and I felt embarrassed about their spending so much to entertain a couple of complete strangers. The apartment offered few amenities so we concluded the family had limited means.

The pièce de résistance of the meal was a course of hairy-legged Shanghai crabs, a specialty in the city. They were delicious and I'm sure they were very expensive. Mr. Wang's family treated us as honored guests and made our evening most enjoyable. My fears of surveillance, interrogation and possible repercussions for Mr. Wang and his family evaporated after the first course and the first beer.

As we prepared to leave and said goodbye to his family I asked him for directions back to the hotel. He waved my question aside. He and a son insisted on accompanying us downstairs where we found a taxi waiting in front of the building.

Obviously he had made prior arrangements. I could make out Mr. Wang, in the Shanghai dialect, telling the driver where we were staying. We shook hands, I thanked him, and Dad and I got into the cab. Soon we were back at the hotel safe and sound.

Why did Mr. Wang insist on hosting such an affair? Perhaps he held fond memories of his days in our Navy. We had exchanged addresses and he said he would write to Dad but he never did. Not knowing his situation, and fearing a possible security problem for someone receiving mail from an American, I never wrote to him, either.

If he still lives, and wherever he is, I wish him and his family well.

After Shanghai we went on to Beijing and Nanking (Nanjing), and then back to Canton. We found those places likewise interesting and delightful.

From Canton we returned to Hong Kong one evening via hydrofoil down the Pearl River and into the South China Sea. It was a remarkable ride, during which I thought about James Clavell's character Tai-Pan in his book of the same name.

In a particularly exciting passage Tai-Pan makes the same voyage, also at night, but sailing alone on a battered junk so laden with gold that it threatens to sink at any moment, all the while being pursued by several thugs. Our ferry ride, although exciting, was not at all hair-raising.

The trip admirably accomplished its goal of letting me gain a better picture of the country that was beginning to play a larger role in our international relations. A subject of indifference for most of America's history, an ally against Japan during World War II, and then an emerging threat and economic rival during the second half of the 20th century, no doubt China would occupy our increasing attention as the new millennium unfolded. But of immediate concern, much of what I saw and experienced greatly enhanced my understanding and sense of China.

The girls just blossomed during the three years of our second tour in Hong Kong. They adjusted quickly because of the earlier tour and they enjoyed almost universally positive experiences.

They played lots of tennis, which they seemed to like, and each one did well, especially Suzanne. Her success in tournaments led to her invitation to the Hong Kong junior Davis Cup team.

Danika likewise thrived on the junior circuit though she was still too young to make the same team. Alison and Pia kept busy developing their basic skills. To this day they still play—and they can all beat their dad regularly.

Alison, while in the third grade at the German Swiss International School, had entered a colony-wide forensics competition—this after overcoming the objections of her British teacher, who criticized Ali's American accent. We all felt very proud of her when she won in her district and placed high in the colony finals. To her credit Ali's teacher graciously acknowledged her success, though she made clear that her instruction had helped Ali carry the day.

As our youngest, Pia's constant competition with her sisters helped her gain academically and athletically and she developed a sense of independence that exceeded her years. Once while Judy and I were in Switzerland to purchase a vacation apartment Pia walked all the way home alone from elementary school. She'd had a tiff with one of her schoolmates and refused to ride with the girl and her driver.

All four girls also played in piano competitions, practicing on the Weinbach.

In January 1980, about 18 months after our joint arrival, headquarters summoned Bob Grealy to become chief of East Asia Division. The change surprised us all. That made me acting chief in Hong Kong until Bob's replacement could be named and take over. Still holding a GS-15 pay grade I didn't yet rate the top spot.

Bob left in February and his replacement didn't arrive until summer. In the intervening months I held down the fort, Harry Truman style, with all the bucks stopping at my desk. My days overflowed with decisions, the ones necessary to keep everything functioning. As usual I devoted the highest priority to operations but personnel, budget and administrative matters often intruded.

For example every chief must prepare an annual Personnel Appraisal Report for each officer and other staff members carefully and thoughtfully, and I spent many hours writing or reviewing them. We had very capable officers so the task wasn't difficult, only time consuming.

Others weren't so straightforward.

On one occasion Ron, our administration officer, presented me with a draft administrative cable the office would be sending to the State Department. It had to do with budget matters and shared costs. The State people functioned as the federal government's overseas managers—the "innkeepers," we used to call them—and the other departments and agencies, including ours, contributed to the operating costs on an annual basis.

Ron needed my signature but I refused to give it.

"But Dick," he said, "we've been signing it for years. What will I tell the administrative officer?"

The cable would have committed us to provide funds for, among other things, office equipment and furniture.

"Ron," I explained, "I first arrived in 1969. I was here for four years and I knew all the offices. Today our premises are exactly the same and so is everything else. There's no new furniture, desks or typewriters. We have nothing new at all. Everything in this office and our other offices is the same as it was. So why the hell should we pay anything when we get nothing?"

"I didn't know," Ron replied. "They aren't going to be happy. This is pretty standard stuff."

"That's just tough," I declared. "We're taking it off standard. Just say we won't pay for what we don't get and tell them I'm writing headquarters and laying out the problem. They can hash it out in Washington but I'm not signing till I hear from home."

"Okay, okay," he said. "You have a point. I'll explain to the admin officer."

I knew I was making Ron's life difficult but it wasn't a fair deal for us. I didn't know how long we had been doing this but I meant to stop it—or at least express some displeasure.

Apparently Langley discussed the matter with Foggy Bottom and reached a compromise of sorts. The agency would contribute but at a reduced level. In return we would receive some new typewriters and office furniture. About time, I thought. I also enjoyed seeing my cable sent to all East Asia stations alerting them to the issue of goods not received for contributions made.

That May I learned that John McMahon, our deputy director for operations, would be visiting Hong Kong. I met him at Kai Tak and took him to his hotel—standard politesse for a visiting senior officer.

I recall being impressed at how informal he was and yet at the same time how professional. He walked out of customs carrying his own bag. He had no entourage. Next morning he arrived at the office and we provided extensive briefings about our activity.

John was already well informed and posed lots of questions. The morning passed quickly and at noon he and I attended a lunch hosted by some local officials. We discussed issues ranging from our global operations targeting China to the agency's relations with Congress and its oversight committees. We found the committees' demands intrusive and doubted Congress could keep the lid on any secrets but we agreed it was a train no one could stop. McMahon's counsel was we to learn to live with it.

At 9 a.m. the next day John and I reported to the small Royal Air Force facility in Kowloon for a helicopter ride around the colony. The copter was waiting and we were airborne within minutes.

For whatever reason, this particular aircraft had no doors. Nothing prevented pilot and passengers alike from taking a long, long fall. Not used to such contraptions I felt a bit vulnerable; John did, too. As we ascended and made our first turn I questioned the wisdom of whoever had removed the doors. Better visibility, I was told.

I pulled my seat belt with shoulder straps even tighter and noticed that John was doing the same. But soon, as we took in the sights from our aerial perch, we relaxed.

Most interesting was the border area where we spotted Chinese guard posts and military positions. I knew they were there to keep people in, not out. We flew at low altitude most of the time so we could view the landscape in detail.

Also notable was the container port in western Hong Kong harbor on the Kowloon side. Large already, it was the scene of extensive new construction. No doubt it was becoming enormous and today it is one of the largest such facilities in the world.

John left Hong Kong that afternoon to continue his Far East trip but we shared a few private moments before he departed.

"How long will you be here?" he asked.

"My tour is due to end this summer," I replied. "By then it will be four years overseas and Judy is anxious to get back to the States for a while."

"What will you do when you get back?"

"Hard to tell. I guess East Asia Division will want me to take over a branch or something like that."

"Typical narrow ops officer response," he quipped. "There are other things to do back there, you know. Would do you good to get out of the line for a while and see something new. Have you ever thought about that?"

"Not really. What kinds of things do you mean?"

"There are staffs, there are seventh-floor jobs (meaning our most senior officers), and in the intelligence community a guy like you with overseas ops experience would be a great find. What about congressional relations?"

"I've never really considered jobs outside the DO," I admitted.

"Well, open up your mind a little and think about it."

I did think about it and realized that my head had been stuck deeply in the sand. I knew very little about most of the rest of the intelligence community.

I resolved to do something different when I forwarded my reassignment request to headquarters. Ultimately I would take a job in congressional liaison, a major career decision.

I saw John a few times over the years but neither of us mentioned his pep talk to me. So I hereby thank John for dragging me out of the sand—though there's considerably more to the story.

Meanwhile, because of Bob's departure, East Asia Division asked me to extend my tour a third year. I had little choice. The new chief would need some time to fit in and the office would need some continuity, unlike the chaos created when Jack and Charlie had departed so abruptly. Their case was exceptional. The agency rarely moved a chief and deputy at the same time.

As I told John, Judy and I had been planning to return home in 1980. But now the needs of the service had intervened and I prepared to salute. Judy agreed. Life had been good for both of us in Hong Kong this time and we thought we could easily handle one more year.

The new chief and his wife arrived in July. Like Bob, John G. was another Irishman from Massachusetts but his personality was quite different. I had met him briefly once before when I passed through Brussels on the way to the Congo for my ill-fated airplane ride.

Stocky and red-faced he seemed an unhappy man. He smiled only rarely and kept his own counsel. He was much less outgoing than Bob and harder to talk with. I never could quite put my finger on it but John seemed to harbor a quirk somewhere inside that affected his personal relationships.

He was intelligent, with experience in Europe and Asia, and I did my best to make our professional relationship tolerable, but we did not become friends. That was unusual for me. Our social contact was limited to functions where we both had been invited. I didn't dislike him but he was one of the few colleagues over my entire career that seemed perpetually to strike all the wrong chords.

For example in the fall of 1980 headquarters promoted me to the Senior Intelligence Service, the highest level in the directorate. As chief, John saw the cable first—cables about personnel matters were marked as sensitive.

He called me into his office. The front office secretary, Peggy, a very experienced woman who had been an enormous help to me while I was acting chief, also had seen the cable and knew what was coming. She said nothing to spoil the surprise but I sensed her excitement.

John handed me the cable almost grudgingly and said, "They have made you an SIS officer."

He didn't stand up or shake my hand.

"Maybe it's your reward for being acting chief out here," he continued. "Seems a bit early but I'm glad for you."

That was it. He started reading other cables.

His glumness aside I was tickled to death. I bounded out of his office and hugged Peggy and Judy, the other front-office secretary. Word spread quickly and many of the staff dropped into my office to congratulate me.

A month after John G. arrived, Graham Fuller flew in from Afghanistan to take over as one of the branch chiefs. He had been running a one-man office in Kabul. An officer of the Middle East Division, Graham spoke Russian and Turkish, and he had compiled several tours in small Middle Eastern posts.

What was he doing in Hong Kong? What experience did he have and how would he fit in? The cables before his arrival informed us that he also spoke Chinese. Apparently he had learned it on his own while developing a contact with a New China News Agency journalist. Our other officers, who had spent two years working full-time to achieve fluency in Chinese, viewed this claim with skepticism.

It turned out that Graham lived up to his billing. He did an outstanding job and he moved up to replace me when I left in the summer of 1981. He took over a valuable and sensitive agent who spoke only Chinese and he soon dispelled any lingering doubts about his ability with the language.

Graham also displayed a deft touch operationally. He quickly sensed openings and cleverly orchestrated the recruitment of several fine agents during his first year. A small, wiry man, he was intelligent and academically oriented in some respects but also pragmatic and realistic. No ivory tower for him. The blend of his talents produced an exceptional ops officer.

Thinking back I realize that we often denied our complement of ethnic Chinese officers the full measure of credit they deserved. This had been true during my earlier tour in Hong Kong as well. It wasn't that they weren't appreciated and respected—they certainly were. In many ways the backbone of our operational cadre they constituted an enormous asset to our programs. Fluent in spoken and written Chinese they could move freely and inconspicuously within the colony, handling any kind of operation. The same was true when they served in other posts in Asia.

I now realize this lack of credit emanated from their weaknesses in written English, which was usually their second or even third language. That meant their reports and cables almost always required editing before going to headquarters. Candid but probably unfair mentions of their deficiencies in English routinely appeared in their appraisals.

Though unintentional this tendency diminished how much we valued their contribution. It was a flaw in our system that inhibited the ability of our Chinese officers to obtain promotions and assignments despite their successes and strengths.

Eventually we recognized the problem and worked to resolve it. It took a while but several of our Chinese American colleagues rose into the SIS ranks. One returned as deputy chief in Hong Kong, and another became chief of China ops.

I completed all of my appraisals before I left Hong Kong and as deputy I needed to write more than a dozen. It wasn't something I particularly liked but they required conscientious effort. I wrote each one with care and submitted it to John for review—the standard procedure.

One was for Mary, our chief reports officer, whom I considered highly competent, admirable even. I gave her high marks across the board, and because she would soon be ending her tour as well I wrote the appraisal to cover her entire time in Hong Kong. I noted her growth and solid contributions the whole way through.

Then I sent the draft to John G., who stunned me the next morning by returning it with his comments attached and a note to me. He had judged Mary's work to be "acceptable" and in some areas only marginally so. His note said I should consider revising my draft.

I didn't know what to think. After a few minutes and with no intention of changing anything I went to see him. Surely he must have been confused about Mary, I said. He had only been in charge for eight months so I offered to clear things up.

No dice. John laid criticisms on Mary that came out of the blue. I disputed them. We both had dealt with her every day, I said. We had discussed her work regularly. Headquarters had also assessed her reports and consistently given them high marks.

"Mary is doing a fine job," I declared.

"You don't see things that I do," he responded curtly.

For a chief and his deputy to differ so profoundly on anything, let alone the performance of a key member of the office, was unheard of.

In the end, we transmitted Mary's appraisal to headquarters with obvious and serious disagreement between the rating and the reviewing officers—a highly unusual submission. I had never been involved in such a divide before, nor would it ever happen again.

No surprise, Mary was shocked when she read John's comments. She brought them to me and asked the obvious question: Why? I told her what had happened and confessed I didn't understand his action.

"What shall I do?" she asked.

"Nothing," I counseled her. "I'm sure headquarters will focus on what I wrote. They know what you have done and you won't suffer."

We waited but heard nothing from headquarters about Mary's report and its disagreements—another unusual development. But the next year headquarters promoted her, which indicated they had indeed discounted John's dissent—also unusual.

The incident served to put even more distance between John and me.

"Does she think he would take money for making the deal?" I asked.

"I haven't specifically asked that yet," Jan replied.

Jan, one of our Chinese American officers, was handling a female agent, the mistress of a senior official heading an office in Hong Kong of a country of high interest to us. He enjoyed direct access to Communist Party policymakers and if ultimately recruited could provide top-level intelligence.

We had discovered his relationship with the woman via a couple of access agents and when we approached her she agreed to help us.

The official was in his early 50s and married but his wife was not with him. The woman, who was Chinese, was in her mid-30s and attractive. She had previously worked in a bar as a prostitute. Obviously pragmatic and tough-minded she was a retired hooker still willing to ply her trade for sufficient compensation.

The money we provided in return for her secret cooperation effectively doubled what she had been receiving from the official for services rendered. Economics motivated her; politics did not.

The discussion in my office involved our next steps in a promising operation. Jan's branch chief Don also sat in.

"We need to ask her that at the next meeting," Don interjected. "If he will take money for doing nothing in a deal we have rigged up we'll know that greed moves him. It would be a good step forward."

"Agreed," I said. "Can she influence him to look the other way and accept the deal? Does he listen to her or is the relationship just sexual?"

"Again, I'm not sure," Jan replied. "She claims she has influence over him but we don't have any way to confirm it."

"This ought to be a good test," Don asserted.

"I'll certainly press her on it when I see her next week," Jan said.

"Can we get audio into his apartment?" I asked. "Then we'd have independent confirmation of what they talk about and whether she has any influence or not."

"We're looking at that," Don said. "Not easy, though. We don't have any access to get in without her. We're checking apartments next to his that might have a common wall."

An audio operation would also give us transcripts of his conversations with other visitors. That alone might produce some intelligence.

"We're on it," Don continued. "I'll keep you posted."

Our efforts against that official were ongoing as I departed Hong Kong. We discovered that the woman was quite savvy and she managed to manipulate the official into accepting the first deal—a bribe.

That gave us optimism about our chances. Bribes are a way of life in Asian business and politics, and many individuals will accept one if they think they can do so without consequence.

That would become the critical point for us. When the target realized that we'd been the source of his funds we might be able to exploit him for better information. He represented a prime target of opportunity.

In late fall 1980 I submitted my request for reassignment, outlining what I would like to do if something appropriate opened and if East Asia Division would let me take a rotational tour—an assignment with another division.

I had thought long and hard about John McMahon's advice and concluded it would indeed be smart to broaden my knowledge of the agency and the intelligence community. With that in mind I asked for jobs I never would have considered in earlier years.

In some respects my request broke the mold at the time. Most DO officers tended to stay with the DO. On the other hand when headquarters promoted me to the SIS level, I no longer belonged to a specific directorate.

The strategy paid off. The following spring, just months before my departure, I received word I would be assigned to our Congressional Affairs office, part of the Office of Legislative Liaison, when I returned to Langley. I promptly accepted and thanked headquarters for the move.

By that time Ronald Reagan had been elected president and had named William J. Casey as DCI to replace Admiral Turner. Casey would be my ninth director, and I was fine with the switch. Few at the agency shed tears over Turner's departure but the community did welcome Casey, whose intelligence experience extended back to the OSS.

One of the people Casey brought in was J. William "Billy" Doswell of Richmond, Virginia. Casey had named Doswell, a former Marine and businessman, to run Congressional Affairs.

Many in the agency shared my initial concern that Doswell, with no experience in intelligence matters, would have difficulty representing the agency's best interests on Capitol Hill. Whatever Doswell's background and capabilities I would meet him that September and judge for myself.

For the first and only time in my career I used six weeks of accumulated home leave, plus two weeks of annual leave, to take an extended vacation between our departure from Hong Kong and my return to headquarters.

Judy and I planned a trip through Europe to expose the girls—now ages 8, 10, 12 and 15—to the historical sites and their ancestral ties in Sweden and Italy. We ordered a Volkswagen van that we picked up in Frankfurt, Germany, our first destination on the flight west from Hong Kong.

We drove first through northern Germany. By that time Suzy was proficient enough in German to be a big help in hotels and restaurants. Then we headed up through the three Scandinavian countries.

Next stop, in Sweden, we visited the small church in Ljungby, a town in the southern part of the country where my great-grandparents were buried in the adjoining cemetery. When we signed the visitors' book in the church we discovered that by sheer chance my father's cousin, who lived in California, had visited two days earlier with his immediate family. I would have loved to see them but had no idea where they went.

We drove farther north to Stockholm then west to Oslo and down the Norwegian coast where we stopped to visit a friend who had a beautiful home on an island. From there we took a ferry down to the Jutland peninsula in Denmark. We stopped at Legoland, in Billund, where the girls had a wonderful time exploring what creations could emerge from 33 million Lego blocks.

We proceeded south through Germany to L'Alpe des Chaux, a ski community just a couple of miles east of Villars-Sur-Ollon, Switzerland, to visit the chalet apartment we had purchased. We stayed there almost a week, hiking and playing tennis. Judy and Suzy faced each other in the women's finals of a local tournament we entered—Suzy won.

Back in the van we drove down to Italy where we visited the small village near Turin, in the Piedmont, where Judy's grandparents once lived. We continued south to Rome for several days of sightseeing. Then on to Florence, Venice and Switzerland, and ultimately back to Frankfurt to present the van—now technically used and therefore exempt from U.S. import fees—for shipment home.

We boarded a flight to the States the next afternoon. It had been a great time. Every day had been an adventure and I think none of us will ever forget that trip—though the girls commented that they had seen enough cathedrals and churches to last them the rest of their lives. They exaggerated.

PART VI: COUNTERTERRORISM

21. We're Running Out of Days

LANGLEY, VIRGINIA 1981–1982

Back at headquarters for the first time in five years I met with Billy Doswell in September. By then he had held his position as head of the Office of Congressional Affairs for about eight months. We quickly covered the amenities and got down to specifics.

"Are you a lawyer?" he asked.

He hasn't read my file and knows little or nothing about me—a bad start.

"No, I'm not. I'm an operations officer on a rotational tour."

"But if you're not a lawyer what can you do in this section?"

His question betrayed a serious lack of understanding of the CIA's relationship with Congress. This was understandable considering his short time at the agency but a red flag nonetheless.

We needed lawyers to deal with specific issues such as reviewing legislation and writing proposed bills for Congress to consider. But our contacts went far beyond that. Hadn't anyone explained to him that Capitol Hill, especially the intelligence oversight committees, thirsted for knowledge about overseas operations?

"The Deputy Director for Operations assigned me here to answer questions that regularly arise in the oversight committees about what we're doing overseas," I told him. "I understand that Pete (a DO officer who had just left the staff for an overseas assignment) did just that while he was here and the Hill staffs loved him."

Billy seemed unsure of himself.

"Well, we can certainly give that a try. We'll put you in the House branch."

It wasn't how I had expected to be welcomed into my new assignment. I remembered John McMahon's prodding about accepting rotational tours but I forced it out of my mind and concluded that this work would broaden my experience—and I hoped it would be interesting as well.

Along with its core and support staff our office maintained a branch dealing regularly with the Senate Select Committee on Intelligence and another one serving the House Permanent Select Committee on Intelligence.

My introductions to the HPSCI people went smoothly and their reception heartened me. It seemed to confirm what a DO officer's job on the Hill should be. Essentially he provides detailed information as someone who has been there, done that.

I spent the ensuing weeks learning the topics on which the agency regularly briefed the oversight committees. Officers from the Directorate of Intelligence conducted most of the sessions and focused on what we call finished intelligence—all-source analyses written or presented as the final product of the entire community.

My office usually stepped in whenever House committees other than the HPSCI requested briefings. I would arrange to send the appropriate people to the Hill.

I quickly became fascinated by the range of topics we covered, particularly scientific and technical. For example, briefers from the DI or the Science and Technology Directorate might discuss missile research, satellite developments, telecommunications or the economic impact of a drought. We would usually relate the substance—which sometimes was limited to a specific country—to policy issues.

From day one I fielded lots of questions from committee staffs: How do you pay agents? How do you task media agents? What do you tell liaison? Why do you tell liaison anything at all? How do you function inside the United States? Why do you need so many safe houses?

What struck me from those sessions was the degree of ignorance their questions exposed—ignorance that was laced, unfortunately, with a tendency to suspect, attack, and blame the DO.

William Casey was making his presence known as our director. First and foremost, with President Reagan's support, he had swiftly increased our budget. Agency people, including those in the clandestine service, greeted what he was doing with enthusiasm.

I got to meet Casey a couple of times, assisting him in delivering briefings to the HPSCI. The members gave Casey a hard time. Part of it stemmed from his tendency to mumble, which made him difficult to understand. But it was also because the committee sensed, accurately, that Casey disliked appearing before them. He constantly communicated that he would say no more than absolutely necessary.

I viewed him differently. He was a tough-minded individual, determined to rebuild the agency after four years of neglect by the Carter administration and focused particularly on the clandestine service.

Casey also seemed to view the congressional oversight committees, which had been spawned by the Church and Pike investigations of the mid-1970s, as ushering in a dark period for the agency. They had followed on the heels of the Watergate scandal, in which the CIA had been falsely implicated—despite Dick Helms's best efforts to keep us out of the line of fire—thanks to Richard Nixon's attempt to cloak his political misdeeds in national security.

Casey had concluded that the Church committee in particular had tarnished the agency's reputation and weakened its ability to serve the nation. The years under Carter, with Stansfield Turner as director, had done little or nothing to help clear the air or rekindle the can-do spirit we once enjoyed.

Now President Reagan had decided to face down the "Evil Empire," as he described the Soviet Union. To do that he wanted to employ every tool at his disposal, including the agency, so the nation's intelligence capabilities needed to be strengthened and Casey was determined to do it. He initiated efforts to rebuild at all levels and my DO colleagues and I agreed completely.

I managed to derive some satisfaction during my first three months at Congressional Affairs largely because I was able to defuse problems by providing honest, candid and informed responses.

I did so by briefing committee and staff members straightforwardly about operations, regardless of whether they were proceeding successfully or had been compromised or thwarted. In other words I came clean about our failures and thereby softened the flap potential. In the process I built up trust—the Hill people gained confidence in the veracity of our information.

I also felt increasingly frustrated. I knew I could do more if the section would use me more effectively. As an SIS officer I had gained enough experience to manage the branch myself and preempt some of the problems we had been facing with Congress.

Instead, as a mere staffer, I was tasked the same way as our less-senior employees. I spent many hours doing things that just about any of our officers could do, such as arranging briefings, accompanying our people to the Hill, and sitting and listening to their presentations. These routine duties took time away from dealing with more important issues

It all seemed to boil down to Billy Doswell. That red flag had returned to haunt me. Billy, who knew nothing about intelligence community matters, let alone espionage abroad, was essentially clueless. He ran Congressional Affairs as though he was still back in Richmond, where he had gained some experience in the executive branch dealing with the legislative branch—but only at the state level. Here at Langley he was completely overmatched.

I voiced my concerns to Billy but could see that he was drawing a blank. Still he promised to see what he could do so I kept my head down and waited.

By mid-December I had waited long enough. I sought support from my superiors on the seventh floor where word of my plight as an underemployed SIS officer had become widespread. Everyone I consulted acknowledged the problem but no one proposed a solution or offered to intervene.

More weeks passed. Then in January 1982, John Stein, the deputy director of operations, called me into his office.

"Well, I haven't noticed that Congress has gotten any friendlier since September, have you, Bob?" John joked, as I walked in and shook hands.

"Nope, same problems and same static," Bob M. replied.

Bob's presence surprised me. The deputy in Hong Kong for the better part of my first tour there, and a good friend, he currently served as chief of International Affairs Division.

IAD was a large organization, responsible for global issues ranging from covert action to paramilitary efforts and, as it was designated at the time, terrorism. It was a big job fraught with hazards such as drawing hostile reactions from the media or Congress for some of the operations its officers had been tasked to run.

Bright and outgoing with lots of ideas Bob handled everything well. The word at Langley was that he was doing a great job, including his frequent contacts with Casey and the oversight committees.

But he wouldn't miss a chance to pull my leg a little.

"Come on," I threw back, "it's only been four months. Rome wasn't built in a day."

"That's true, Dick," John said, "but we're running out of days. In fact they're all gone."

I glanced at Bob.

"What's that supposed to mean?"

John suddenly became serious.

"We've been following the situation in Congressional Affairs and we don't like it at all. We can't afford to have one of our SIS officers with solid operational experience working up there as a staffer."

"It is a pain," I admitted. "I've been complaining and trying to get things changed. No luck."

"Frankly the problem is Billy Doswell," John confided, "and there is little we can do about it. As soon as Casey realizes that his old buddy is miscast Billy will be out of here. But we aren't going to wait."

"What are *we* going to do?" I asked.

"Bring your rotational tour to a screeching halt. I've already told them that we are pulling you back to the DO. We have an important job for you to take over."

"Aren't they going to be pissed off?"

"No, because everybody but Casey knows that Billy is way off base."

They had made their decision and were inviting no comment from me—not that I would have protested.

"Not much of a rotation," I kidded. "John McMahon will be on my case. He's the one who told me to take this tour."

"He knows the story," John said.

The remark *really* surprised me.

What's going on?

"So what's this important job?"

With that question Bob piped up. He hadn't said much thus far and came directly to the point.

"I want you to take over the Terrorist Group in my division. I knew this was coming and I got here first. I have a crying need for a good operations officer to take over what's going to be a tough job. I know you—congratulations on the promotion by the way—and I asked John to let me make this proposal."

This was yet another time when it never occurred to me to say no. If Bob had specifically asked for me, and if the DDO was on board, then I wasn't going to be coy. But I could at least be honest. I had no idea what the Terrorist Group was or what it did, so I asked.

"It's the only element in the directorate that follows and works against global terrorism," Bob explained. "It's not big now but that's what I want you to do—build it up. Terrorism is a serious problem and it's going to get a lot worse before it gets better, if ever. The Hill is asking what we're doing about it. So far *you* are what we're doing about it."

"But I don't know a bloody thing about terrorism except what I read in the papers."

"I'm confident you'll learn quickly," Bob said, smiling. "That's what operations officers do."

"The quicker the better," John added, signaling the meeting was over.

I went back to Congressional Affairs to announce my departure. Nobody seemed to care; they had their own problems. I thought the change would be quick and painless but it didn't turn out that way. Another issue would intervene and delay the move.

HPSCI's chief budget staffer would be touring North Africa and Europe in January 1982 before Congress reconvened. He would be inspecting and visiting several of our stations and military bases. The trip would last two weeks and he asked that I accompany him to provide entrée to our stations.

Apparently my successful liaison efforts on the Hill were now working to my detriment.

With the change in my status I saw no reason to go. I asked that someone else from Congressional Affairs step in and replace me. The office gingerly raised the question with the committee's budget chief but he rejected it. Heavyset, balding and pleasant he was a savvy retired Army colonel. He had been given the choice between me and others in our office, none of whom had ever been overseas. He chose me, period. No one argued.

The outcome was typical. Almost seven years after the oversight committees had been established, and almost five years since they had been made permanent, the agency's people worried about displeasing them. Those worries applied to the committee staff as well as members, and it was true especially of this man who generated our budget and could add or delete millions of dollars with the stroke of his pen.

Even John Stein agreed I should go, so I went.

We flew to Madrid—first class, of course, as befits servants of the people. After an overnight we boarded what was technically a military aircraft and headed for North Africa.

By "technically" I mean it was an executive jet with a crew of four put at our disposal to fly us to all of our destinations. The jet, a small, sleek plane with every amenity, was perfect for the short hops we would be making.

The crew attended to all of our needs, including handling our luggage through every formality. I packed my bag before we departed each destination and left it in my hotel room. I saw it again at the next hotel room, military base or bachelor officers' quarters untouched by me in the interim. Our schedule was their schedule—they spoiled us outrageously.

The experience was educational as well as luxurious. I could see that the Pentagon was miles ahead of the DO in terms of currying favor on

Capitol Hill. No effort or expense was too great to keep our legislators and their key staffers happy, and this particular staffer seemed to feel entitled to the preferential treatment.

I found it interesting. The CIA obsessed over ways to avoid displeasing the Hill. The Pentagon, however, spared no effort, always going farther and doing everything possible to please the legislative branch.

As we visited several of our stations in North Africa each chief provided a complete briefing that always elicited the same questions from the colonel. It gratified me that our people fielded his questions well and because I knew what he was after—specifics about our operations and budgets—I could often elaborate.

I also realized that whenever this man made this type of visit—though I privately doubted the need for such visits—a DO officer like me with field ops experience should be with him. I know he gained a much better understanding of how the field DO offices worked than would have been possible without me.

Next we visited bases in Germany and Italy where I received my first dose of military briefings. They proceeded more formally than ours, led by officers tasked solely with briefing visiting dignitaries. They used lecterns, microphones, slides and overhead projectors to present so much information that listeners sometimes described the experience as like drinking water from a fire hose.

The format was always the same. First they would tell you what they were going to tell you. Then they would tell you. Then they would tell you what they had just told you. I suspected that the overload and repetition were intentional so when the briefing ended you felt so overwhelmed you couldn't formulate any questions.

Not always, however. At one unit, a military intelligence battalion, the briefer covered their cross-border efforts into Eastern Europe, a denied area. Based on what I knew the efforts weren't impressive. I said nothing—until asked.

At one point the budget chief wanted to know what I thought of a certain component of the efforts, which were meant to provide early warning of any attack by the Soviet bloc.

"Did I understand you to say that your communications link with these agents is via secret writing on postcards and letters?" I asked the briefer.

"Yes, sir, that's right."

"I may just be splitting hairs," I said, "but maybe these operations should be ones that provide early indications of an attack, like stockpiling of ammo and fuel for example. Warning of an actual attack is probably another thing. If they attack, and if your agent sends a postcard warning of that attack, there would be a question of which would get here first, the Russian tanks or the postcard."

"I understand your concern," the briefer said.

I'm not sure he did but I wasn't going to press the point.

"Maybe you should try to get some radios in there," I suggested.

We also stopped at one of our large air bases in Germany where a young Air Force captain named Holm was stationed—Greg, my youngest brother, who had been stationed there since 1980.

The commanding general of the base, with several of his deputies, hosted a marvelous luncheon in one of the Air Force's splendid officers' clubs after the morning briefing. Before we arrived I had told the budget chief that my brother was assigned to the base. He told the general, who immediately sent for him.

I had wanted to surprise Greg and his fiancée, Becky, also a captain and an Army nurse, because I wasn't sure until the last minute whether I'd be taking this trip. I did indeed surprise him. Ten minutes later, as we were finishing coffee and cognac, they ushered Greg in ostensibly to see the commander. When he spotted me his jaw dropped.

That evening he and Becky and I went out to dinner. Greg told me he was due to rotate back to the States in about another year. At that point they would marry but meanwhile they would be able to make occasional use of our apartment in Switzerland.

I began my new assignment the Monday morning after my return from Europe. I entered the offices of the Terrorist Group, identified by the sign TERRORIST GROUP on the door.

I don't know how long the thing had hung there, and I knew that no one had intended any harm by it but the name grated on me—it seemed inappropriate and misleading.

Even more basic, I didn't want to go home and tell Judy that I now ran the CIA's Terrorist Group. I had to rename it and with Bob M.'s approval we became the Counter Terrorist Group.

The effort couldn't have been timelier. Terrorism was beginning to spread globally. Individual groups were popping up all over the place like a skin infection. The Shining Path was causing havoc in Peru, the FARC guerrillas besieged Colombia, Action Directe was operating in France along with Red Army factions in Germany and Japan, and most of them imitated the usual suspects in the Middle East. A whole slate of incidents had heightened concerns in Washington and the European capitals.

For example, on December 17, 1981, a little over a month before I began the new job, four members of the Red Brigades, yet another terror group, kidnapped Brigadier General James L. Dozier from his apartment in Verona, Italy. They held him for 42 days. Dozier was NATO's deputy chief of staff. The Red Brigades were Marxists that routinely employed violence, including assassination. Eventually an Italian antiterrorist team freed him.

Libya's dictator, Colonel Muammar Gaddafi—who never could stay out of trouble—was backing several terror organizations, including the Palestinian Liberation Organization and Black September, the group that had orchestrated the murders of Israeli athletes at the 1972 Olympics in Munich, Germany. He was also cultivating ties with the Soviet Union and had even threatened to assassinate President Reagan.

Along with Libya, Iran had joined the list of state sponsors of terror, particularly attacks directed against Israel and the United States. On November 4, 1979, a supposed group of students had overrun the American Embassy in Tehran. They had taken 66 hostages—including some of our people—and held them for 444 days until January 20, 1981, the date of Ronald Reagan's inauguration.

Also in 1981 there were terror incidents in Germany, Latin America and elsewhere. On October 6 in Cairo a group of fanatics called Tanzim al-Jihad—who were associated with Egyptian Islamic Jihad and the Muslim Brotherhood—assassinated President Anwar Sadat while he reviewed a military parade.

As the incidents mounted, Washington reacted in typical fashion: Throw more resources at the problem. The entire executive branch, including cabinet departments, independent agencies and the military, either established or augmented counterterrorism offices. Now we were also gearing up to do more—and soon.

The way life unfolds has never ceased to amaze me. There I was, 20 years into my career, after spending a few months languishing away in Congressional Affairs, now heading the directorate's effort against a rising and direct threat to our nation.

I was eager to sink my teeth into the task.

We started out as a group of 17, only a few of whom had operational and overseas experience. The rest were intelligence analysts who had served mostly at headquarters. A mixed bag really, but all seemed eager to work on this problem. Still the roster concerned me. I had hoped, perhaps naively, that we would be supporting or running agents against specific terror groups. But at that point we seemed ill-equipped for such a dangerous task.

The good news was that Bob had given me great leeway in terms of what I could do, though I had to learn my new territory before I could contemplate any major changes.

I turned to my old standby, reading. I studied as many reports as I could get my hands on. I also attended briefings by members of my group and by the DI's terrorism analysts. A couple of them seemed highly capable and I planned to make use of them as the CTG expanded in size.

One of my ops officers, Chris Frederick, had been a member of our platoon during paramilitary training back in 1962. When I was sent to Laos he joined Latin America Division and went to Florida to train Cubans for boat infiltration operations.

Chris had worked in counterterrorism for a couple of years and he knew about all of the known terrorists that concerned us. At the time he was our resident expert. Bright and hard-working, I knew I could count on Chris to help me get started.

I learned what we were doing to track assorted terror groups in the Middle East, including Palestinians and other Arabs, and how we watched the organizations operating in Latin America, Europe and Asia.

Until then tracking was about all that CTG could do because we hadn't yet infiltrated any group and we hadn't made many third-party contacts. Our program was essentially moribund.

In some ways it was understandable. The agency still had the Cold War and China to contend with and terrorism had not been considered a front-burner issue. Now that was rapidly changing, and along with the FBI, Department of State, military intelligence, Department of Energy, Immigration and Naturalization Service and Secret Service, among others, the CIA had become energized by the recent events. No question we needed a much stronger national capability to fight terrorism.

As events unfolded in 1982 Bob's words, "Terrorism is a serious problem and it's going to get a lot worse before it gets better, if ever," continued to echo in my mind.

The year's incidents had begun on January 18 when our military attaché in Paris, Lieutenant Colonel Charles R. Ray, was assassinated by a member of the Lebanese Armed Revolutionary Faction. The killer shot him as he walked from his apartment to his car.

We worked closely with the Direction de la Surveillance du Territoire, the DST, France's internal service, in an effort to gather details about the incident.

Worldwide we would see 794 acts of terror in 1982, second only to the 838 in 1978—though that year had included fewer attacks against American interests.

Two deadly attacks by the LARF against Israeli diplomats—one in Paris in April and a second in London in June—prompted an incursion by the Israeli Army into Lebanon. Despite our lingering questions about whether the Palestinians had been involved, Israel decided to act. Their forces moved all the way to Beirut, ultimately forcing the Palestinians to flee to Tunisia.

For the Israelis the assassinations had functioned like waving a red flag in front of a bull.

In early spring I was in London, the last stop in my first tour as CTG chief to brief local counterterrorism officials on our operations. I had already visited France, Germany and Belgium.

It had been a successful trip. I had explained our expanded efforts to combat terrorism globally, and I had secured promises of increased levels of cooperation from each agency I visited. The Europeans made it clear they would like to have us more actively engaged.

I wasn't espousing any new initiatives—we had been cooperating with these governments for some time—but I was trying to instill a sense of renewed priority.

"The director wants you to go to Saudi Arabia to brief Prince Turki," Allen Wolfe told me.

Allen, our London chief, had read a cable that had arrived that morning.

"What the hell am I going to tell the Saudis that they don't already know?"

"That will certainly be your call, Dick. As the cable says, you are our counterterrorist expert and that's who the director wants to send to see the Saudis."

He smiled. He knew this was totally unexpected and would be a tough assignment. He also knew, as I did, that there was no option. As Director Casey had instructed. I would go to Jeddah as soon as possible.

It was—and still is—highly unusual for the DCI to issue such an order. I assumed that Bob had tried to talk with him but to no avail.

"Could I see that cable?"

"We'll make the plane reservations and get your ticket," Allen said, handing it to me. "Will you want to fly directly home from Jeddah? You'll need some money too. I'll approve an advance."

I read the cable carefully. Headquarters had done their best to give me some background about the trip. Apparently Casey had just met with the Saudis in Washington. They talked about terrorism, particularly Arab terrorism, and he was seeking increased levels of cooperation.

Also apparently—and as usual—the Saudi response was non-committal. They agreed only that we should start exchanging information. Toward this end Casey had promised to dispatch his man—me.

That was it; those were my marching orders. Headquarters knew what a difficult position this put me in. Normally I would have prepared at least several days for such a task, including a briefing from the Saudi Desk. I needed to know about the people I would be meeting and about the current internal politics of Saudi Arabia. As it was, Langley had sent only an outline of the topics I should cover and they suggested some background studies I might want to review quickly.

At least I felt confident about what I did know. During my first months running counterterrorism I had worked hard to master our intelligence holdings on Arab terror groups, the highest-priority threat.

The analysts' briefings had done much to help me put things in perspective. Also I had discussed Arab terrorism frequently during my recent stops so I was as ready as I could be for my exchange with the Saudi prince.

That evening I called Judy to tell her of my delayed return. I couldn't say much over an open phone line so I just told her I'd explain when I got home. She didn't sound too happy.

The London office had booked me on a direct flight to Jeddah the next day. Before I got off the ground, however, I suffered a minor but exasperating incident.

I had obtained my visa and the Saudi Embassy had stamped it into the passport I was carrying. Wishing to be as helpful as possible Allen had instructed his driver to pick me up at my hotel and take me to Heathrow Airport.

I appreciated this kindness because I was feeling stressed—the nature of the task at hand, I guess.

The driver did his job well. He delivered me at the airport in plenty of time because I wanted to be sure nothing went wrong. He helped me pull my bags out of the trunk. I thanked him and headed for check-in.

Then it hit me: My shoulder bag, the one I would carry onto the plane—the one holding my tickets and passport—was still sitting on the back seat of the car. I could picture it in my mind.

Shit! I won't lose the bag but I'll surely miss the plane!

I dashed for a phone to call Allen's office.

Just then the driver appeared, right in front of me, my shoulder bag in hand.

"I figured you'd probably need this one, too," he said with a big smile.

What a relief! I could have hugged the guy—maybe I did; I can't remember. He had spotted it on the back seat, parked the car, and set off to find me, and in doing so he made my day.

We landed in Jeddah just before midnight. Located on the Red Sea coast along the Kingdom of Saudi Arabia's western border, the city was both the gateway to the Muslim holy cities of Mecca and Medina and at the time the closest thing the Saudis had to a cosmopolitan playground.

The customs formalities were routine and no one from the agency arrived to meet me. I caught a taxi outside the reception hall and headed for my hotel. The driver, a large, strong-looking man who spoke decent English, seemed eager to talk. But I was tired and had little to say. He gave up after about five minutes.

The next morning I checked in at the office. The chief knew I was coming and he welcomed me. Then he told me he didn't know when Prince Turki might be available, even though the prince did know I had arrived.

"When do you think we'll get to see him?" I asked.

"No idea," he responded. "Sometimes it takes days to get in there."

"Days? But I thought this was all laid on. The director specifically sent me to brief him. Wasn't it set up at a high level?"

"Yes it was but that doesn't mean much out here. The Saudi Royal family operates on its own schedule. You'll see him. I just don't know when."

I reacted with something between frustration and irritation.

"So what the hell am I supposed to do in the meantime?"

"Just cool your heels. Sorry, but there's nothing I can do."

I sat around for three days. Once I borrowed a racket and shoes and played tennis in the 90-degree heat—but only once. I figured there must be better things to do. I stayed in my air-conditioned hotel room, caught up on more reading, and grew increasingly annoyed.

Finally, at about 10 p.m. on the third evening, the chief called to announce we could see the prince at midnight at his residence. He would pick me up, he continued, at 11:30. I didn't really understand but figured this must be a cultural thing. I didn't complain and I didn't argue.

The royal compound was dark as we approached in the chief's car, except for a lone light above the gate at the entrance. Not surprising, I thought, at this time of night. Then as we passed through the guard post and entered the interior courtyard suddenly there were lots of lights.

I saw groups of armed men loitering around several Mercedes limousines. Dressed in civilian clothes many carried UZI machineguns. The prince was in charge of internal security for the kingdom so the civilian clothes were no surprise. Nor were the weapons for that matter.

After we parked an aide who knew the chief welcomed us and led us into the prince's reception area, a large and dimly lit room with several low sofas scattered around. Each had three or four big pillows.

The aide directed us to one of the sofas where we sat down. A servant appeared with cups of thick, sweet mint tea. The chief sipped at his. I did, too, and guessed it must be an acquired taste—I didn't like it.

Soon the prince walked in and sat across from us. Three or four security men appeared at the same time and lurked in the background; apparently he was taking no chances.

Prince Turki bin Faisal Al Saud, the head of Saudi intelligence, had been educated in England and his English was quite good. He graciously welcomed us to his home—if the compound could be called a home. After some preliminaries I started briefing him.

It quickly became clear to me that this was a case of taking coals to Newcastle. I had to limit what I disclosed about certain topics so much of what I laid out was generic information about the various terror groups we were following. But I could see that the prince already knew just about everything I was telling him and I assumed that from his own sources he probably knew even more.

Per Casey's guidance I focused on the Arab terrorists, all of whom were well known to the prince. I also posed questions several times, which he deflected with polite put-offs.

"I'll have my staff look into it."

He was pleasant. He asked simple, non-contentious questions. We were equally pleasant. It all went smoothly and in the end I rated it as worth just about nothing. I told the chief as much after we had departed the compound.

"I'm sorry, Dick, but I'm not surprised," he said. "To be honest this was not a good idea from the beginning but I could hardly argue with headquarters. He was nice but you're certainly right. Not much got done."

Casey had wanted to make a gesture to the Saudis that would prompt closer, high-level cooperation. My visit with Prince Turki probably wasn't the best way to go about it.

I doubt it made the slightest difference.

22. Little Bastard

LANGLEY 1982

"Have you seen the cable from Rome?" Chris Frederick asked, signaling that it was not just an average cable.

"Not yet," I replied. "I just got back from the staff meeting."

"Take a look," he said, handing it to me.

The cable described a recent meeting between one of our officers in the Italian capital and a person they had encrypted as Spider-1, or S-1, wherein he alleged he was a member of Libyan intelligence. Furthermore he was under non-official cover; that is, he was not a member of the Libyan Embassy in Rome. It raised many questions that would have to be answered but if the guy was real he would represent a big breakthrough.

S-1 claimed to know the modus operandi employed by the Libyan service, something that would naturally be of great interest to us. He also had provided a sketchy outline of a plot to assassinate President Reagan—so perhaps Colonel Gaddafi was serious about his threat.

S-1 also had hinted that he held information about the movements of the infamous international terrorist Carlos, nicknamed the Jackal.

Born Ilich Ramírez Sánchez in 1949 in Venezuela and a lifelong communist, Carlos, his so-called professional name, had allied himself with the Popular Front for the Liberation of Palestine, a group that specialized in airline hijackings. He also participated in an attack on the Vienna headquarters of the Organization of Petroleum Exporting Countries in

1975 and he was suspected of assassinating two French security officers.

"Who has seen this?" I asked.

"Near East Division got their copy," Chris replied. "So did Europe Division. For here, just you and me so far."

"I'm not sure where this might go," I said, "but for now let's hold this pretty tight—just you, me and Gary."

I immediately assigned Gary, one of my best operations officers, to begin following the case and he immediately smelled a scam. The cable indicated that S-1 could be in contact with a group that had access to fissionable materials. Gary found the claim highly unlikely and resolved to investigate this individual as thoroughly as he could.

It was the fall of 1982. The president had long since recovered from the failed attempt on his life on March 30, 1981, and the cable from Rome hit headquarters like a ton of bricks.

Knowledge of it was tightly compartmented but those in the loop were keenly interested in follow-up information. The chief of our Libyan desk called while Chris was still in my office and we arranged to meet in an hour. There we agreed that our priority in handling this individual should be to verify S-1's bona fides—to carefully check out his documentation and every bit of information he had provided.

Our response, written by the Italian desk and coordinated by the CTG and Near East Division, told Rome how pleased we were to be in touch with S-1, a potentially valuable agent. At the same time, we added, much remains to be done to confirm his identity and the veracity of his access.

The meetings with S-1 in Rome that followed produced information that was tantalizing but difficult if not impossible to verify.

We didn't wait for confirmation. Given the possibility of an assassination plot we promptly informed the FBI, the Secret Service and the White House Security Office, all of which showed high-level interest.

Along with the chief of NE Division I began attending weekly meetings chaired by the head of White House security. The FBI and Secret Service also participated. Each time we all carefully reported the information we had collected, we coordinated what the federal government's response would be, and we decided who would take what steps.

S-1 kept providing information and it continually knocked headquarters off balance because of the cast of players involved. For example he reported that Carlos would be transiting Paris by air the last weekend in November. But we had serious doubts Carlos would be so bold—reckless, even—as to pass through Paris where the French services were so eager to get their hands on him.

The doubts sparked a debate at headquarters. Should we discount the information because we couldn't prove it? Or should we scramble to set a trap for the notorious Jackal?

We decided we couldn't risk not acting on the information so without giving specifics we informed our contacts in Paris. We asked the French to cover both Charles de Gaulle and Orly international airports for three days. The French expended considerable resources but Carlos never appeared.

S-1 explained that the Jackal had changed his plans at the last minute. Those of us who were suspicious grew more so.

Despite stronger and stronger urging from headquarters, Rome had not yet obtained the individual's basic documentation. He provided one excuse after another for not producing his ID card and his passport.

I kept thinking about the fabricators we had encountered in Hong Kong. Now, like Gary, I also smelled a rat and I learned that Chris shared our concerns as well.

As the weeks passed the FBI and Secret Service joined our wariness. But S-1 kept providing just enough checkable information to keep the operation going. For example he furnished the names of three Americans who he said were involved in the plot against the president.

We checked the names; they existed. Indeed two of them lived in the Washington area so the bureau and the service started digging into their backgrounds. They found that neither had a criminal record and both seemed ill-suited to any terror operation.

Rome eventually conducted a polygraph test on S-1 but the results were ambiguous. That frustrated everyone even more. Then Rome obtained and forwarded photos they had taken of S-1. Now at least we had something our analysts could work with.

Uncertainty about S-1 created a split between the CTG and the Libyan branch.

"Something is wrong," I insisted to the branch chief. "Step one is to check bona fides and documents, and here we are, months into this operation, and we haven't seen anything."

"You just don't understand Libyans," he responded. "They do things differently. He doesn't have a diplomatic passport."

"But we haven't seen anything at all. He has to have some kind of documentation to be in Italy."

The FBI and Secret Service people sensed the dispute we were having. My meetings at the White House had resulted in close relationships with many of them. I liked and respected them and those feelings seemed to be mutual. As a result I had been consistently open about my increasing doubts. All they could do was urge me to keep digging.

Just before one of the weekly White House meetings I bumped into Stan Klein, my FBI counterpart, emerging from his car outside the gate.

I greeted Stan, with whom I had become quite friendly, as we headed for the guard post.

"This damn case," he said. "It's driving me nuts. We have to pin him down soon."

"I agree," I told him. "Believe me we're doing everything we can."

We approached the uniformed Secret Service officer and showed our passes. He recognized us from previous meetings but still followed procedures.

"You carrying?" the guard asked Stan.

Odd question, I thought, not making any connection.

Stan didn't blink or hesitate.

"Nah," he said, "I'm just a headquarters hump."

"You're not, are you?" the guard said, now looking at me.

"Not what?"

"Not carrying a weapon."

My answer amused Stan, who related the exchange to our colleagues at the meeting. But the thought hadn't occurred to me because except for Laos and the Congo I never carried while working.

One afternoon Chris and Gary burst into my office.

"We got the little bastard!" Chris almost shouted. "Look at these."

He laid two photos on my desk. I examined them, puzzled. Both seemed to be of the same man and I assumed they were both of S-1.

"So that's him, isn't it?" I asked.

"One is," Gary said with a triumphant smile. "The other is a Lebanese fabricator named Jabril. I had some suspicions—we all did—so I've been scouring a pile of files I got from Near East Division and I found him. Near East should have done their homework, but never mind, this does it."

I was elated but still cautious.

"Let me see the files."

Gary had anticipated my reaction and had brought the files with him. I looked at the photos of S-1 that Rome had sent us.

"Great work, Gary. They are sure as hell the same guy."

"Can we tell NE right away?" Chris asked.

"Bloody right you can," I responded. "They should know soonest, and start working on a cable to Rome, too."

We had been butting our heads against the wall for several months and now Gary had found the needle in the haystack. Superb work on his part and we all owed him.

"Mary, get Stan Klein on the phone," I called out to my secretary.

We had more than bragging rights at stake. Stan had told me the FBI was just about to ask a federal judge to approve phone taps on the two U.S. citizens as a result of the information we had provided. It was a risky step but they couldn't avoid taking it as long as a potential threat existed against the president.

"Stan, do you have the court order yet?"

"Not yet. I just got all the paperwork together."

"Well, cancel the whole thing."

"You sure, Dick? For us this is serious stuff."

"I know. It's serious for us, too. I'll explain in detail when I see you but for now just be aware that the subject is phony, a fraud, and we've got proof."

"Great news, Dick. When can we get together?"

"First thing tomorrow, Stan."

I felt relieved that we had broken the case before the bureau had approached the courts. I wouldn't give Stan any details over an open phone line but I knew he'd be pleased we all hadn't been lured any farther into Jabril's trap.

Jabril had been very clever but Gary's patience and persistence had exposed him. Now we might be able to trace his connections and determine whether he was working with others. Meanwhile I nominated Gary and he received a special achievement award for his work.

I always found it fascinating to learn how our people authenticated or discredited agents and operations so I asked Gary how he had proceeded.

Early in his career, he told me, he was working on Cuba and had been deceived by a team that falsely reported the details of their mission. They had been afraid to proceed and wouldn't admit it.

It reminded me of the time in 1963 when I had to confront one of my Lao team leaders at his camp just east of Thakhek because he had been lying about his team's actual location.

Likewise once burned and twice shy, Gary had developed a career-long interest in counterintelligence. On his own initiative he began ordering files of old operations involving Libya and scouring them carefully. He had the Arabic-language portions translated, he checked all passport data, he examined all references to other operations, and he reviewed each photo.

Working carefully and methodically he found the single piece of damning information that broke the case. After months of being led down the garden path by a clever fabricator we were able to end the ordeal.

"This would mean giving the DI guys access to our raw cable traffic," I told John Stein.

"What's wrong with that?" demanded John McMahon, who had just walked in.

One of Stein's predecessors as deputy director of operations, McMahon was now William Casey's deputy.

"What are you talking about?" McMahon continued. "Why can't DI officers read that stuff? Typical DO bias is what it sounds like."

"Settle down, John," Stein said soothingly. "We're just talking about bringing Directorate of Intelligence officers into the Counter Terrorist Group and we both think it's a good idea. In fact, Dick proposed it. But we have to smooth the way so the bureaucracy can handle it. It hasn't been done before, you know."

McMahon relaxed.

"Oh," he shrugged. "Well, for the record I think it's a good idea."

The move had been gaining support for several months. As we worked more closely with the DI's terror analysts most of us had become convinced that joining forces made sense. Often their analysis of operational developments or the aftermath of a terror incident strongly affected what we did next.

It wasn't a step to be taken lightly. Ever since the agency was established in 1947 the operational and analytical directorates had steadfastly remained separate. The rationale was that each directorate would risk what was called pollution of their product by collaborating too closely.

DO officers in particular had a developed a deeply ingrained bias against sharing their traffic with DI officers—or anybody else. If we were now breaking with that 35-year-old practice it spoke more about the high priority we accorded to combating terrorism than to any real change in sentiment. Eventually that change would occur as well, though years later and only by fiat.

The bureaucratic necessities fell into place—though the process was much more complicated than I had imagined—and we absorbed the DI people who worked on terror analysis. The move made us stronger; it allowed us to couple analysis with our operational reporting, greatly compressing the time normally required to produce finished intelligence. It also augmented our operational activities by providing leads.

The size of our group grew steadily as we expanded our capabilities across the board. The increase included about a dozen of the aforementioned DI officers but many others joined our efforts as well.

At one point Bob asked if he could shift the 15-member VIP protection unit from our paramilitary Special Operations Group to my shop.

"It just seems a better fit," he reasoned, and it made sense to me as well.

Soon thereafter we hired on contract two retired Secret Service officers to upgrade our skills base and strengthen the VIP protection course we had begun offering to foreign services.

More operations officers, DO intelligence analysts and technical specialists also joined us, and we brought in specialists from our Office of Technical Services and from the National Security Agency to strengthen our responses to terror incidents.

We established an Incident Response Team, which we subsequently dispatched on request to stations dealing with attacks or incidents. It was a big step and it turned out to be a great success. Updated versions of the IRT exist today. They allow us to bolster a given station swiftly and significantly to react to a wide range of threats.

As our numbers grew we expanded the services we provided. We produced a small, classified publication for the whole community about terror groups in general. It summarized the status of ongoing investigations and provided general background.

I established and chaired a counterterrorism committee that included representatives from more than a dozen agencies, departments and military services. We used the committee to coordinate bureaucratic and operational efforts.

We also began a years-long effort to organize, coordinate, and disseminate the existing classified database on terrorists and terror groups.

Whatever the activity, we operated under the rationale that if resources could help fight terrorism none would be spared.

Much of my job as CTG chief involved maintaining close contact with foreign intelligence and security services. That meant traveling much more than I had expected or wanted. Rarely did a month go by without a liaison trip somewhere.

I had no choice. At the time most terror incidents, and therefore demand for our attention, were occurring in Europe and the Middle East. I spent a lot of time going back and forth from those areas.

Our European intelligence colleagues were dealing with internally generated terror groups, most of which maintained ties with militant organizations in the Middle East. Many—myself included—also suspected that the Soviet Union and its minions in Eastern Europe were training and providing logistical support to terrorists.

In her 1981 book *The Terror Network: The Secret War of International*

Terrorism, Italy-based author Claire Sterling wrote:

> It was never part of the Soviet design to create and watch over native terrorist movements, still less to direct the day-to-day activities. The phantom mastermind coordinating worldwide terror from some subterranean map room is a comic book concept. The whole point of the plan was to let the other fellow do it, contributing to continental terror by proxy.

Politics as much as intelligence requirements dictated that we give top priority to discovering just how much support the communist countries were providing to terror groups targeting Western interests.

President Reagan, Secretary of State Alexander Haig and Director Casey all expressed keen interest in finding the answer. But despite our efforts we found no smoking gun.

Yes, the Soviet Union and its allies seemed more than willing to help what they called nationalist fighters by providing weapons, training and money, and by allowing them unmolested travel through their countries. But no, the Russians weren't orchestrating or directing a global network of anti-Western terror groups.

Instead they took a simple approach: If the terrorists could cause problems for Western and pro-Western governments then that would be just fine with the Soviets and their cronies.

During my frequent travels other CTG officers, sometimes including our DI officers, would accompany me to offer expertise about specific terror groups.

On a typical trip we'd visit three or four countries over the course of a week or two weeks. At each stop we'd brief that country's services dealing with terror matters. We shared as much as we could, reasoning that the more each friendly service could learn about the tactics of a given terror group the more effectively it could defend against and combat that group.

The sessions were almost always mutually beneficial; we often obtained as much useful information as we provided.

Another purpose for our visits was to train security services. We willingly shared some of the course material we had developed for VIP protection, crisis management, hostage rescue and other disciplines.

The work was hard, the hours were long, and the time away from family was wearying but the effort seemed to be worth the sacrifice. Our foreign counterparts welcomed us warmly at virtually every stop and we established and maintained deep professional relationships. Our station people also seemed grateful for the visits, the information and the support. The menace had pushed us all closer together.

Where we weren't making much progress was on the unilateral side—placing our people or agents within a country without notifying its government. Our stations were trying but penetrating terror groups by recruiting their members to proved extremely difficult. To this day it still does.

Terrorists are fanatics of one type or another driven by politics, religion or ethnic hatred. Finding ways to motivate one of them to renounce his cause and work for us presented all-but-insurmountable obstacles. Even identifying a member and establishing contact represented a huge challenge. As a result our stable of unilateral agents remained small during those years and we constantly strove to expand it.

To make things worse our own regulations restricted how we could use an asset. Say, for example, one of our potential recruits was asked to participate in a terror attack—an obvious and standard test for members of militant groups, especially new members. In such a case our rules, determined by executive order, required us to veto his involvement. But pulling a recruit out of a planned attack meant putting him at risk of exposure—and probable execution.

As I mentioned, sometimes we had to resort to placing an agent inside a friendly country without notifying that country's government. As we learned, sometimes painfully, one man's terrorist is another man's freedom fighter. That reality created a steady stream of awkward, even untenable problems with liaison, constantly forcing us to seek alternatives such as recruiting agents who lurked on the fringes of the terrorist movements.

Along with those assets our technical collection activities enabled us to prevent many attacks. Perhaps even more essential, we often accomplished this without the terrorists knowing what had gone wrong with their plan.

"The dog that didn't bark," as Bob M. put it, borrowing a line from a Sherlock Holmes mystery.

Bill Buckley had joined our group in the spring of 1982 along with other members of the Protective Security Branch from Special Operations Group. I made him my deputy. A former Army officer he had compiled an excellent record of service and achievement since joining the agency. Like me, Bill had served as a paramilitary officer in Laos—in his case in the late 1960s.

Serious and intelligent, Bill had a military bearing and insisted at first on calling me "sir." It was just the normal thing to do for him but we got past it after I persuaded him that we were colleagues. Also, being called "sir" made me feel uneasy.

Our skills complemented each other. I was better at management while Bill excelled at the block-and-tackle aspects of paramilitary activities. I gave him lots of responsibility in that area: VIP protection, crisis response and hostage situations.

We quickly developed a mutual trust. Bill was professional, dependable, loyal, fair and easy to work with. He quickly won support and respect from members of the group. I sought and valued his judgments and listened to his views on operational and personnel matters.

I thought Bill was destined for top leadership. Alas, fate would intervene with him in a most tragic way.

23. The Green Line

BEIRUT, LEBANON 1982

One morning in early October I was gazing down from a helicopter at the deep blue Mediterranean. The day was sunny and clear, and we were flying east at low altitude—so low that I thought I spotted a school of dolphins or sharks swimming in the opposite direction.

We had taken off in two helicopters from Larnaca on the southern coast of Cyprus headed for Beirut, Lebanon's embattled capital. I was traveling with André Le Gallo and we were headed to Beirut for a series of meetings with Lebanese authorities.

Each copter included a crew of four, two of whom carried AK-47s. It was not a pleasant flight. My aircraft was old and noisy and I found myself planning what I might do if we had to go down. I saw no life jackets in the cabin so the plan would have involved a lot of swimming—and I suddenly hoped those were dolphins I had seen.

Lebanon had been in turmoil for seven years but the crisis only attracted international attention in 1978, when the Israel Defense Forces invaded in response to an attack by Palestinian terrorists in northern Israel that killed 37 people and wounded 76 others. The Palestinians, in the form of the Palestine Liberation Organization, were headquartered in Lebanon's Muslim areas.

At the urging of the United Nations the Israelis had pulled back to a 12-mile-wide corridor in the southernmost part of Lebanon. An international peacekeeping force moved in to separate the two combating parties.

It didn't work. For the next four years the PLO and IDF continued to clash frequently, with the former hurling rockets into Israel and the latter retaliating by shelling Palestinian positions in Lebanon, or calling on the Israeli Air Force to bomb them. One raid in 1981, on several Beirut apartment buildings, had resulted in heavy civilian casualties.

On June 6, 1982, after hundreds of PLO attacks—both in Israel and against Israeli interests abroad—the IDF pushed north again. They quickly reached the outskirts of Beirut and began a siege of Palestinian strongholds in the western part of the city.

As casualties mounted, President Reagan personally called Israeli Prime Minister Menachem Begin and asked him end the assault; Begin complied. In return the president dispatched special envoy Philip Habib to Lebanon. A Brooklyn-born Lebanese Catholic and retired career diplomat, Habib managed to broker a truce that involved withdrawal of both Israeli and PLO forces. Reagan also dispatched U.S. Marines to Beirut to help keep the peace. The Marines had landed in August.

Also in that month Bachir Gemayel was elected Lebanese president. His term lasted all of three weeks. He was assassinated on September 14. Apparently his willingness to work with Israel had made him suspect.

Gemayal's murder typified the extreme difficulty of the situation. He was caught between a bold and powerful contingent of Palestinians in the north—which had acted with impunity before the invasion—and the Israeli forces, the Middle East's strongest, in the south. The government continually proved ineffective because it could not control its territory. Neither could it subdue the PLO—or for that matter the Syrians. Along with several infamous terrorist groups they all ran roughshod over Lebanese forces.

Religion added to the difficulties. Fierce clashes persisted between the Muslim forces and the Christian militias, fighting which literally divided the country and its capital.

In the wake of the latest truce, along with Marines our government had provided aid in the form of advice and materiel. The goal was to organize and strengthen Lebanon's ability to police and control its own territory and to establish and maintain law and order. The agency's job was to train police, security and intelligence organizations—which meant sending someone to Lebanon quickly to get started.

André would initiate the training programs and I would hold discussions aimed at building a strong counterterrorist capability. Our goals were complementary but as the point men for a security program in the middle of a civil war our prospects for success were mixed at best.

Beirut's airport had been forced to close during the Israeli invasion and had not yet reopened. The politics surrounding the conflict ruled out our flying in from Damascus or Tel Aviv so we had settled on Larnaca. We flew there via commercial air and were picked up by the two Christian militia helicopters.

The militias controlled the eastern part of Beirut and portions of northern Lebanon. We maintained contact with them as well as elements of the mostly Muslim Lebanese government.

We flew along the coast and got a good look at Beirut before landing at a nearby military compound a little after 8 o'clock that morning. Jim, one of our officers, whom André knew, was waiting for us next to the landing pad with two black sedans.

After a short ride we reached our hotel in West Beirut, overlooking the Corniche—the city's seaside promenade—and just above the American Embassy. So far it showed few signs of the recent conflict. To get there we crossed the so-called Green Line, which divided the city. They called it "Green" ironically. It became a zone of weeds and bushes after the buildings along it had been mostly destroyed.

As we drove I saw burned-out or badly damaged buildings everywhere. Houses were knocked down or bombed out. Front doors were often gone. Walls were riddled with machine-gun fire. Nearly all of the shops were closed.

I saw few people on the streets but it was the opposite of Stanleyville, in the Congo. There the Simba fighters had forced out most of the city's population but had left most of the buildings untouched. Here the damage was everywhere.

Our hotel was located on a street that ran along a ridge above the coast. It offered a beautiful view of the Mediterranean and the Corniche. Though the hotel was operating—the phones worked and we had hot water sporadically—the staff was limited, as were services. On the other hand we wouldn't be spending much time there so it didn't bother us. We'd be working in our Beirut operation's no-frills, unattractive, three-story office building nearby.

Before we started our meetings with government officials we checked in with Ken Haas, the Beirut chief, and his staff to exchange information and views on a number of issues. It was a courtesy in this case, but we felt particularly compelled to extend it in such troubled and difficult times.

We had expected stress and frustration but not to the extent we found. From Ken on down there was clear evidence of fraying of nerves as our colleagues struggled in an extremely hostile environment. Ken lamented and cursed, recounting what had clearly been a harrowing period. He described it as a "bugfuck."

Just moving around the city was difficult, dangerous and sometimes impossible, Ken said. Curfews and confusion abounded and no one knew who was actually in charge, all of which made scheduling meetings with or contacting agents extremely challenging—sometimes you couldn't even tell who controlled a given intersection. The operations officers voiced similar sentiments.

We listened sympathetically to everyone and offered expressions of support but we were both struck by the severity of the situation. We could see that Ken and his officers deserved much credit for what they had been able to accomplish.

André, who had become chief of operations for Near East Division, immediately cabled back to headquarters that everyone in the Beirut office needed an R&R break as soon as possible.

After concluding our discussions, and after lunch at a nearby Lebanese restaurant, André and I visited the embassy's security officer. A career State Department employee, he had been stationed in Beirut for only six months.

We reviewed the physical and personnel security issues with him.

Based on what we saw, which we shared with Ken, we concluded that embassy security needed fortifying—urgently. Part of our concern was the highway that ran right by the building.

"Couldn't something, even 50-gallon fuel drums filled with sand, be placed in front of the building?" we had asked the security officer.

At the time we touched the subject lightly because we had no authority over embassy security matters. We could only ask pointed questions and make suggestions but we both harbored uneasy feelings about it when we left.

If we had known what was coming we would have pounded away on the topic until we saw results.

The next day was bright and sunny. I had worked my way into the eastern, Christian part of the city and was standing on the balcony of an apartment looking down at a playground full of children. A basketball game was in progress at one end and younger kids were playing soccer at the other.

You would never have guessed what turmoil had befallen the western half of the city and much of the country. Here everything seemed pleasant and normal. One of our counterparts had dropped me off a few minutes earlier and I was waiting for the man who would take me to the agent I hoped to debrief.

I wasn't sure why he couldn't have taken me directly to the agent but we didn't control such arrangements in war-torn Beirut. I had to accept their terms—trust the Christian service or not see the agent.

Soon there was a knock on the door and I met the intermediary. I had been given a name and a description, and both seemed to fit. I doubted it was his true name but that didn't matter.

We left immediately and went down to his car, which was parked out front. We headed toward Beirut's outskirts. He kept glancing in the rearview mirror to reassure himself that we weren't being followed.

"See anything?" I asked.

He smiled.

"Nothing, there won't be any problems." His English was good.

Before long we had reached the foothills northeast of the city. We stopped in front of a well-tended, two-story house built into the hillside.

Could this be the agent's home?

We went inside and the agent met us in the living room. He was elderly and looked Middle Eastern but I couldn't tell much beyond that. My ability to differentiate Asians was no help here, and I never learned whether he was Armenian, Lebanese or something else.

The subject of our discussion—he also spoke English well—would be the Armenian Secret Army for the Liberation of Armenia, known as ASALA.

Though some Armenians sympathized with and supported ASALA the group employed violence—including assassinations and bombings—against Turks and Turkish interests worldwide. They had staged attacks in Europe, the United States, Canada, Latin America and elsewhere, and those attacks had killed and injured innocent bystanders. To us ASALA was a terrorist group that needed to be stopped.

Why meet an agent in Beirut, a city awash with Arab terrorists, to discuss ASALA? Because East Beirut housed a large community of the Armenian Diaspora, at least one of whom was willing to talk to us about them.

The conflict with the Turks went back to World War I, when the Ottoman Empire had attempted to exterminate Armenians in the first of the 20th century's episodes of genocide. History records that the Turks killed more than a half-million of them during that period, and at least that number managed to flee Turkish territories to settle all over the world.

Today a sizeable Armenian community lives in Los Angeles. As a result one of the worst jobs in the Turkish Foreign Service is consul general in that city. Many of their people had been attacked and several killed.

Our FBI watched ASALA closely, as did most of our European liaison counterparts, so an opportunity to collect information about its organization or members was not to be passed up.

The agent was wary but polite and forthcoming. My companion sat and listened silently, refilling our teacups from time to time. For three hours we covered subjects such as factional infighting within ASALA, organizational history and structure, background and whereabouts of key individuals, and how the group conducted weapons and explosives training. We touched on ASALA's links with other terrorists groups as well.

As our conversation proceeded the agent seemed to relax and warm to the task. But I found myself wondering why he was doing this. What motivated him to give us this information?

I tried to probe this subject but he deflected my questions. I could only thank him sincerely for the information he had provided and offer to reimburse him for the time he had spent with me. I didn't really expect him to accept any payment, and he didn't. I reiterated how much we appreciated his cooperation and walked outside to join my companion who was already waiting for me.

After the meeting the intermediary took me directly to the headquarters of our Christian counterparts. I met André there and we spent the remainder of the day discussing training programs. We talked about schedules, logistics, curriculum, personnel and funding.

I learned that the militias were eager to obtain whatever help we could provide. They discussed our mutual concerns openly and amicably and they furnished interesting information about the Palestinians and other Arab groups operating and training in Lebanon. Time passed quickly and soon it was early evening.

The session completed, we prepared to take our leave and drive back to West Beirut but our hosts wouldn't hear of it. Their insistence on "some drinks and food" at a local restaurant took until nearly midnight. I'm not complaining. They had been gracious and relaxed throughout and we felt at ease as well—though André and I probably had more drinks than we needed.

I can't remember what we said as we left the restaurant and started back to our hotel but I was glad that I had topped off my quaffing with two cups of strong coffee.

Our colleagues knew we had to cross the Green Line, and they knew what time it was, but they didn't seem to think there was any problem. They just gave us some last-minute directions and waved us on our way.

It was a cool evening with no moonlight. André was driving. The city was strange to us both. We headed west along the coast road for about 10 minutes. Then we spotted a roadblock so we turned south, still winding in a generally westward direction.

André drove cautiously because we didn't know exactly when the demarcating Green Line would appear or what would be there. Few streetlights illuminated the streetscape and it became difficult to see very far ahead. Suddenly there were no lights at all and we reached another makeshift barricade.

"Must be the Green Line," André muttered, staring intently in front us.

"I'm sure you're right," I said. "Who mans it now, the Lebanese government?"

"Don't know," he replied as we stopped and mulled our choices.

We didn't know what would come next and we felt most uncomfortable. I found myself wishing the Israelis were still in control—at least they were predictable. We doubted the multinational forces were manning the checkpoint and probably not Christian militia, either.

Maybe no one was around.

No such luck. Without warning a couple of men appeared out of the darkness and stood in front of André's side of the car. Behind them, about 30 yards away, a small fire burned next to a shell of a building. Several men stood around it and all, including the two in front of the car, carried weapons.

Bad news.

Who the hell are these guys?

As the two nearest us stepped closer so they could get a better look at us, I became even more uncomfortable. They were not wearing complete uniforms and they didn't appear to be part of any government unit.

Short and stocky, both had scraggly, dirty beards and unkempt black hair. Their clothing was tattered and hadn't been washed for a long time. They wore black combat boots. One had a scarf wrapped around his head.

They approached André's open window.

"Where are you going?" one of them asked in French, after he noticed we were both foreigners. His tone was gruff, almost as if he was irritated because we had bothered them so late at night.

Fortunately André spoke fluent French and he thought quickly.

Désolé de vous emmerder. Nous nous sommes perdus dans la nuit.

"Sorry to bother you, we got a little lost in the dark."

Nous voulons retourner à l'hôtel, qui es tun peu plus haut que l'ambassade Américaine. Est-ce que nous sommes sur le bon chemin?

"We're trying to get back to our hotel just above American Embassy. Does this road go through?"

The gruff one paused and exchanged a quick Arabic phrase with his companion then looked back at André.

Qui êtes-vous?

"Who are you?"

There was no option.

"We are American diplomats," André said, in English.

Another pause. Someone by the fire shouted something in Arabic and the gruff one responded. By now we could tell they all had been drinking.

"We must see your passports," he said.

André and I exchanged glances.

"They look like goddamn thugs," I muttered under my breath. "And they are drunk."

"We can't tell them to bugger off," André said. "There isn't much choice. It's their barricade and they are armed."

He was right. We handed him our passports.

The gruff one took them and walked over to the group at the fire where he showed them to their presumed leader. His partner waited about 15 feet to the left front of our car.

We were perplexed and not just a little nervous. We discussed the situation briefly. We concluded that as American diplomats we probably wouldn't be bothered by these guys so we would talk our way through.

I thought of telling André to just drive around the barricade but I knew it was too late for that. We both wondered exactly who these guys were and what they represented.

The three or four minutes we waited seemed much longer. Finally we saw Mr. Gruff start back to us, the passports in hand.

"*Allez*," was all he said to André as he handed them back. His partner pulled the barricade from the street and with considerable relief we crossed the Green Line into West Beirut. At that point we were not far from our hotel and we arrived without further incident.

Most frustrating and ominous was the fact that we had no control over the circumstances. Without warning we had stumbled onto the roadblock and found ourselves in a decidedly dicey situation, a frequent reality in a city where only the slimmest thread of law and order prevailed and where deep-seated hatred lurked everywhere.

Months later, Islamic terror groups in Beirut began taking Western diplomats and senior officials hostage. Armed terrorists broke into homes and offices, or they ambushed cars to kidnap their victims.

They held many of those unfortunates for several years before releasing them. Some were executed or, as I was soon to learn, died in captivity. When the outrages began it was hard for André and me to escape the thought that we had flirted with disaster.

Beirut's airport reopened that day. The embassy managed to get us seats on one of the first flights out—happily so because it precluded another ride in one of those damned militia helicopters. The negotiations required to reopen the airport had been contentious and the situation there remained tense as we arrived. The Lebanese government's control, though tenuous, had prevailed and after several delays our Air France flight took off for Paris.

André and I shared mixed emotions. We were delighted to be getting the hell out of Beirut. But we also felt a genuine and urgent concern for our colleagues and for the other foreigners required to stay there. We took a last look at the forlorn and war-torn city as the plane took off.

Back at headquarters and using my extensive notes I wrote two lengthy intelligence reports about ASALA. Both were well received and we shared large portions with several European services.

I had many unanswered questions about the agent—I still do—but his information was good.

24. A Fine Chief

LANGLEY 1983–1985

In late spring 1983, I was asked up to William Casey's office on the seventh floor. That was unusual. I gave Bob M. a quick call to see if he could shed any light on the reason for the summons. He couldn't.

"Let me know what he wanted," he told me.

Soon after my arrival Chuck Cogan, chief of our Near East Division, joined me, and Casey's secretary showed us in to see the director.

"Hi, Dick," he said. "Have a seat. Hello, Chuck."

A man I didn't recognize was sitting in an easy chair near Casey's desk.

"Let me introduce you to Bob Woodward."

Casey recited our true names to Woodward then turned back to us.

"He works for *The Washington Post*."

We both made the connection instantly. Woodward's role in the Watergate scandal that brought down the Nixon White House was well known.

"He is going to do a three-part series for the *Post* on terrorism and he would love to talk with us about groups operating in the Middle East."

What the hell? We don't usually deal with media at all, let alone divulge our true names so casually.

"Terrorism is a key issue," Casey asserted, "and I wanted to be as helpful as possible. You two are the best guys I could think of to talk with Bob so I told him we could give him a briefing. He's going to Beirut next week."

"This is just for background and will be off the record," Woodward said, probably sensing our uneasiness.

Little did I know how bogus his assurance would be. But it was Casey's order so we had no choice. We spent the next hour answering Woodward's questions as best we could while striving to protect our sources and equities.

I have to admit it, Woodward was good. He understood our position but that didn't stop him from exploiting this occasion. It all went fairly well and we were able to satisfy many of his queries. We also alerted him to some potential problems in and around Beirut, such as in the Bekaa Valley, a hotbed of terrorist activity, in which several groups resided and trained.

The session ended when Woodward signaled that he had posed all of his questions and with gracious thanks he left.

Casey also thanked us for providing the briefing and we left as well. I considered it inappropriate to complain about his giving Woodward my true name so I remained silent.

Casey never seemed to sense the discomfort both Chuck and I felt.

On April 18, a member of Hezbollah—in Arabic, "Party of God"—a fanatical Muslim terror group, drove a delivery van filled with a ton of explosives into the ground floor lobby of the U.S. Embassy in Beirut. The explosion was detonated by either the impact of the van as it hit the building or a remotely controlled signaling device—something no more complicated than a garage-door opener.

The blast collapsed much of the building, causing numerous injuries and 67 deaths. Fifty of the dead were local embassy employees and 17 were Americans. Among them were Ken Haas, our chief; Jim, who had met André and me at the military base, Jim's wife and a senior DI analyst who happened to be visiting.

These losses were hard to accept. I thought immediately of the concerns André and I had expressed about embassy security, in particular the unimpeded access from the road just in front of the entrance.

Hindsight is always 20/20.

The worst was yet to come. On October 24, I was completing a visit to

Madrid and preparing to fly home. Bill Daugherty, one of our operations officers, traveled with me; so did John, a DI analyst. We had just finished breakfast at our hotel. As we began the short walk to the U.S. Embassy, Bill stopped to buy an *International Herald Tribune*. The front-page, headlined article described a devastating terrorist attack in Beirut the previous day. We had also heard a reference to the attack on the morning news but it gave a few details.

Our feelings of grief, sadness and frustration mounted as Bill read the article about the attack. A suicide bomber, driving a truck carrying 6 tons of explosives, had destroyed the U.S. Marine barracks. The blast had claimed 296 lives, including 220 Marines and 21 other members of the military; 60 more had been injured.

A second blast a short time later killed 58 French paratroopers at their barracks. Ironic but most of the victims were standing out on their balconies watching the aftermath of the previous blast when the suicide bomber struck.

We began assessing what details were available and tried to figure out which group was responsible for this senseless carnage. We got nowhere. To learn more we would have to wait until we got back to headquarters and obtained the most detailed information. For the moment the news underscored just how dangerous terrorism had become.

The two Beirut attacks made 1983 one of the deadliest years on record. A total of 387 Americans, 267 in Beirut alone, died at the hands of terrorists.

For the Counter Terrorist Group, as the threat continued to spread the challenge intensified. The militants were targeting Western nations on many fronts. We redoubled our efforts to combat the attacks directed at us and we enhanced our cooperation with allied services facing threats of their own.

Bill Daugherty joined our group in the fall of 1982 after gaining some first-hand experience about how terrorism works.

A former Marine aviator with combat experience in Vietnam, Bill had left the military to seek a graduate degree. He joined the agency after earning a Ph.D. in American government. He had handled our training program well and in due course the agency dispatched him to Tehran for his first field tour. The timing turned out to be lousy.

Bill arrived just weeks before rampaging Iranian students, with full support from their Islamic government, invaded and ransacked the U.S. Embassy on November 4, 1979. They initially took 66 Americans hostage. Six others managed to escape from Iran due to risky—and heroic—actions taken by the Canadian and Swiss governments.

According to newspaper accounts the hostage-takers had pieced together shredded documents, a tedious task at best, enabling them to discover that Bill was one of our officers. His captors treated him particularly harshly and kept him in solitary confinement for nearly the entire 444 days of the hostages' captivity.

After prolonged and painstaking negotiations the Iranian government released Bill and the others on January 20, 1981, only minutes after Ronald Reagan took the presidential oath of office in Washington.

It had been a dreadful experience but Bill handled it with great inner strength. He credited his military training for much of his success but there was more to it than that. Generously endowed with determination and common sense, Bill coped pragmatically with what each day dealt him. He was not overly fond of Iran but he carried few scars from of his ordeal.

We welcomed him to the group and considered him a highly productive member. In particular I admired how quickly he put his captivity behind him and got on with his life. He truly was a stout fellow and we needed all the top-flight help we could get.

Now retired from the agency, Bill teaches government and foreign policy at Armstrong Atlantic State University in Savannah, Georgia.

Among the other terror incidents of 1983, ASALA conducted a series of attacks against Turkish interests and citizens. They struck in North America and Europe, killing a score or more, including innocent bystanders. We committed major efforts and resources to neutralize them.

Arab terror groups continued actions against Israeli and Western interests. North Korea attempted to assassinate South Korean officials in Rangoon, Burma. On December 12, members of a Shi'a group called

Islamic Dawa, which derived support from Tehran, staged a coordinated assault against several facilities in Kuwait, including our embassy.

But in a stroke of good fortune, when the driver smashed his explosives-laden truck into an almost-empty annex, instead of the main building, most of the material failed to detonate. The blast caused a lot of damage but killed only five people: two Palestinians, two Kuwaitis and one Syrian.

We did achieve some successes in 1983. On June 5, militants attacked and kidnapped international aid workers near Boma, in southern Sudan. They killed several workers and took two Americans among the hostages. At the time it was an unknown group, and it might not have even met the standard definition of a terror organization, but its actions prompted our response.

When we received word of the attack we alerted the entire intelligence community. Following close consultations with several sister agencies and some liaison services we dispatched an Incident Response Team to organize and execute a rescue effort.

Within a couple of days we had everything in place to send in the rescuers. From excellent overhead reconnaissance we knew where the kidnappers' base camp was located and where they were holding the hostages. I felt confident that the group had no idea they had incurred the wrath of several Western governments, who were more than willing to respond in kind—and quickly.

Arriving by helicopter at dawn less than a week after the catalyzing incident, the highly trained rescue team routed the captors and freed all of the hostages. Losses: good guys none, bad guys many. The operation was one of the first to demonstrate the value and efficacy of the IRT concept and needless to say the results pleased us greatly.

There was more. Part of our coordinated effort employed every available resource to support the IRT and its rescue effort, including priority coverage from overhead assets—satellite surveillance. We got it in spades. The technology allowed us to watch the rescue team's dawn attack in real time—as though we were sitting in an airplane circling above. We could plainly see rocket blasts, choppers approaching and landing, individuals running on the ground, and vehicles trying to escape.

That was a lucky break, because the timing had to be just right, but we were all blown away by the capability.

Bill Buckley prepared and delivered an excellent briefing for Director Casey about the successful rescue that featured real-time photography. His briefing was well received and no doubt it raised the profile of our group up on the seventh floor.

We weren't just angling for praise. Operations such as the Sudan rescue helped us to continue expanding our staff—and it sure didn't hurt at budget time.

It's painful sometimes to consider just how fateful a decision can be in this line of work. In my own case I needed never look any farther than my flipping up the sun visor on my helmet before we crashed in the Congo. But there were others.

"Bill would make a fine chief, especially in that stress-filled environment."

That was my answer to the question: What did I think about naming my deputy, Bill Buckley, to head our office in Beirut?

Chuck Cogan had posed it. The position had been filled on a temporary basis since the April bombing when we lost Ken Haas.

"It is, as you well know, a damn tough and dangerous job. There aren't many people I would consider sending, but Bill is tough and I think he could do it," Chuck went on.

"I'm confident he can do it and I know he'll say yes if you ask him," I said.

Soon thereafter Chuck named Bill our chief in Beirut. After several weeks of various types of training, Bill reported there in early fall. As predicted the job was tough and required hard work for long hours, often seven days a week.

Bill had voiced some concerns about his lack of experience in certain areas. We all knew it was dangerous but he managed to thrive. The station's intelligence reporting stayed strong under his leadership and his management skills turned out to be a lot better that he thought.

Then on the morning of March 16, 1984, about six months after Bill had arrived, Hezbollah captured him as he was leaving for work. Two cars carrying heavily armed men blocked his vehicle. He had no way to escape. The attack had been carefully planned and within a few short moments Bill's captors forced him into a waiting car and drove away.

We received few details about his captivity. From debriefings of other hostages who were released we learned that Bill had probably developed pneumonia but received little or no medical attention. We also learned that ill treatment had contributed to his failing health.

On or about June 3, 1985, Bill died in captivity after nearly 15 months of suffering in solitary confinement—and enduring terrible periods of torture. His killers remain unpunished. I was serving in Brussels when I heard of Bill's death. I was deeply saddened at losing such an outstanding colleague and patriot.

We weren't able to recover his remains until 1991, after which William Francis Buckley was buried at Arlington National Cemetery with full military honors. Four years earlier, in August 1987, the agency had held a memorial service for him. Our DCI at the time, William Webster, delivered the eulogy. "Bill's success in collecting information in situations of incredible danger was exceptional, even remarkable," Webster said.

The agency added a star for Bill on its Wall of Honor at Langley, the wall that also honors Mike Deuel, Ken Haas and Dick Welch. For me those stars represent painful personal memories of losses suffered for the causes and beliefs we shared.

"Who the hell are all these people?" I asked Wayne Gilbert, as we arrived together in Los Angeles in the fall of 1983 for our first meeting.

"They all represent police and security organizations that will be involved when the games begin," he responded. "State police, county police, city police, park police, hostage rescue units, crisis management experts, and maybe beach police for all I know—lots of people with a finger in the pie."

"I'm glad they are going to be your problem and not mine," I said with a smile.

"Thanks, Dick, I'll remember you for that," he grinned back.

My meeting concerned the Summer Olympics, which the City of the Angels would be hosting in July and August 1984. Given the surge in terrorism over the previous two years, concerns about security for the games had prompted high-level attention in Washington. President Reagan had ordered all federal entities dealing with terror issues, many of which had been created only recently, to focus all available resources on security measures for the games.

That directive quickly translated into more than two dozen police and security organizations becoming involved. And the FBI, Wayne's agency, would lead the effort—on which, I was told later, the federal government would spend over $95 million.

My group's role, an important one, was to collect and disseminate relevant intelligence. We had alerted our stations and bases worldwide to report immediately anything related to security for the games, and we expended substantial resources of our own to support the effort.

The meetings had actually begun in Washington in the fall of 1982, the purpose being to organize the procedures and communications channels we would need nearly two years later. Eventually all of the senior representatives from the participating agencies began meeting in Los Angeles and I had flown out there with Wayne.

First we heard about all of the potential threats to security at the games. The briefers went on and on, commenting about virtually every known terror group. Then they described the Olympic Village and the event sites and what else surrounded them.

I was surprised to learn that the Iranian and Armenian communities in Los Angeles were the largest outside of their home countries. That meant any plans for protecting the Turkish athletes and officials, for example, would have to take into account the Armenians and among them possible ASALA operatives.

What the large number of resident Iranians meant from the perspective of security for visiting Iranians was less clear.

As I listened I realized what a complex effort this was going to be and why we had begun planning and organization so early.

It pleased me to see a spirit of cooperation eventually emerging. Obviously Wayne and the other FBI officers had handled the interagency disputes carefully and sensitively. My group never had a problem with the FBI's leadership, but with so many other organizations participating, internecine squabbles were inevitable.

Maybe all of the other agencies fell in line with the FBI because of its forthright guidance: Get in line and shut up.

We also enjoyed high levels of cooperation within the agency. My group worked closely with the DI and with the various geographic divisions.

The only problem I can recall concerned the dissemination of raw intelligence—the material we received directly from agents. Usually we shared the material only after we had put it together with other information—technical, open-source, research—and prepared it as finished intelligence. Then we used a long-standing mechanism for sharing it. But an internal debate erupted over the raw version, involving what could be sent directly to FBI units operating on the scene in Los Angeles and what had to be restricted to our standard dissemination channels.

By then I had been working with the bureau for more than a year and had developed great respect for their professionalism. I advocated direct dissemination but some of my colleagues objected, mainly those who acted as watchdogs for the dissemination channels. They insisted there should be no exceptions.

Fortunately the debate was short-lived. Logic and pragmatism eventually won out, and I received authority to transmit relevant intelligence directly to our people in Los Angeles, who would then alert the FBI and other security elements.

The enormously complex and costly effort paid off. Thousands of security and intelligence officers worked tirelessly to monitor and investigate threats and not a single incident occurred. The combined effort provided total safety for all of the events, athletes and spectators.

I have no doubt, however, that the FBI's reputation of competence and efficiency was a primary factor in deterring foreign groups from challenging the bureau on U.S. soil.

Our preparations for the Olympics paid dividends as well. During that time I had worked to develop strong ties with our sister agencies, such as the Secret Service and FBI, and I established close contacts with several European liaison services. That was the gratifying part.

We also experienced frustration, much of which arose from our continuing difficulties in penetrating the inner core of the terror groups. Lacking enough agents on the inside we rarely could prevent an attack or smash a terror cell. Instead we had to concentrate on training our people and implementing security measures—on playing defense. We did all we could but back then the initiative remained with the terrorists—the PLO, Hezbollah, Abu Nidal's Fatah, Abu Jibril's Darul Islam, Carlos the Jackal and a host of others.

In addition we continually had to deal with shifting sands. Once we had faced isolated groups of fanatics. Now state sponsors of terrorism were emerging as formidable threats. Whether for religious or political reasons, or some combination of the two, governments such as Tehran began showing their hands in the terror mix.

This development posed a double problem. First it required a whole new line of intelligence gathering. Second and more challenging, we had much less latitude in pursuing the bad guys. State Department policies dictated what actions we could and could not take in specific cases.

My job had included a wide range of tasks and disciplines as well as contacts with many agencies. It ranged from delivering testimony to Congress as the agency's terrorism representative, and briefing individual members and their staffs, to visiting my counterparts in Europe, Asia and the Middle East.

As usual the work was hard and the hours long but given the importance of the task I accepted the burden and didn't mind. On a personal level I had completed a watershed assignment that would put me firmly in the agency's management camp. It made my operational activity on the street a thing of the past.

My role as chief of the Counter Terrorist Group was an exciting time but often stressful. Our workload and our size grew steadily during my tenure, especially during the period from 1982 through 1983, which was marked by high levels of terrorist activity directed against U.S. interests and those of our allies.

By the time I left our staff had swelled from the original 17 to nearly 80, including analysts, communicators, paramilitary officers, operations officers and reports officers. Instead of our misnamed, vaguely defined and orphaned status at the beginning, we had achieved a stand-alone capability. We worked tirelessly to monitor or respond to terrorists and their organizations and to penetrate them whenever possible.

That effort continued. Within two years of my departure the agency had re-designated the group the Counter Terrorism Center, increased its staff to more than 200, and expanded its service to the entire intelligence community. I had been able to add lots of flesh to the skeleton I inherited. I'm also proud to say that most of the concepts we developed back then remain vital parts of the CTC to this day.

PART VII: SOVIETS AND SPYCRAFT

25. Red Side Down

BRUSSELS, BELGIUM 1985–1986

In January 1984, Chuck Cogan, chief of Near East Division, called me into his office and offered to nominate me as chief of one of our offices in that part of the world. At the time it was a frontline posting. Our people there were supporting a large effort to arm and direct Afghanistan's Mujahideen fighters against the Soviet Union's occupation of their country.

Few assignments provided more of a challenge or excitement.

Initially I was flattered by Chuck's offer but in the ensuing discussion I learned this would be an unaccompanied tour, meaning Judy and the girls could not go with me. Instead the best we could do was to move the family to Switzerland where Danika, Alison and Pia—Suzanne was already attending college at Swarthmore—could continue their schooling and I could visit them more easily.

In the past my response to virtually every assignment offer had been to accept. This one, however, with the prospect of a long period away from my family, was unsatisfactory. I turned Chuck down. He was disappointed but he understood.

I waited nearly six months to hear the alternative. That July, via the directorate's assignment process, I was named chief in Brussels and the tour would begin the following summer.

In the intervening 12 months I represented the agency, along with one of my colleagues, in the Department of State Senior Seminar, a prestigious academic year of exposure to a wide range of foreign and domestic policy issues.

The senior seminar turned out to be an enjoyable and informative experience, a definite and welcome change of pace from my pressure-cooker existence as head of the CTG and dealing with emerging terror threats. I briefly joined the rarified world of academia.

Each week we attended a slate of lectures giving us a close look at a particular domestic or foreign policy issue. The organizers timed the morning sessions so we could read the daily newspaper—a real luxury—and review related articles or studies before the first speaker began. Then we'd take a relaxed lunch break, do some more reading and reflecting, and then hear the next lecture.

After each session the presenter would open the floor for questions, giving us the opportunity to probe any issue even more deeply. Week by week we examined topics such as immigration, education, welfare, agriculture, national labor policies, drugs and the environment.

We also spent one week a month traveling within the United States for a firsthand look at the subjects we were studying. For example we went to Texas to examine immigration problems, to the northwest to see forestry programs at work, and to Minnesota to stay on dairy farms and talk with the farmers about their experiences with government policies.

For someone like me who had spent so much time abroad in recent years it was especially interesting to reexamine domestic policy questions. I hadn't thought much about these topics for a long time.

The program carried only three requirements. First, we had to show up every day and for the trips—not too taxing. Second, each of us had to choose and invite the speakers for one of the blocks of study. That meant reviewing the subject, deciding whom to invite, and then making the requisite calls and writing the letters. We could choose among journalists, academics, businessmen and government officials as possible speakers, depending on the subject. Most of those invited happily accepted.

Third, we had to write a lengthy paper on any subject we chose—though the organizers had to approve the topic. I selected the European Union. My research included visits to various embassies of the EU members plus a trip to Brussels in March 1985 to visit the organization's headquarters. There I also got a look at the office I had been chosen to lead.

The State Department program capped off what had been a productive four years in Washington but now I was more than ready to get back to the field. Judy and the girls were ready, too, and we all looked forward to life in Europe.

As mentioned, the new wrinkle was we would be leaving Suzanne behind in college, something Judy and I had been dreading. Suzi felt confident she could handle the separation but I wasn't sure that Judy could.

Suzi had grown up in what seemed like too few years since we had returned from Hong Kong. To our considerable distress her siblings would soon follow suit.

Brussels would be my first posting as chief, though I had served in an acting capacity in Hong Kong for six months. I had read over the personnel files of the office staff to gain some idea about the strengths and weaknesses of the people I had inherited. They seemed solid overall, though we didn't have enough case officers with operationally useful language skills—a common failing across the entire clandestine service at the time. We had several good French speakers but only one officer who could speak Dutch. None had any capability in Flemish, though the language differed only slightly from Dutch.

My deputy, Jack Ahrens, was a respected, skilled officer with lots of experience in dealing with headquarters and the bureaucratic problems inextricably tied to our jobs. I liked him from the start. Jack was rough around the edges, a little jaded and frustrated with his career, but none of it affected the quality of his work.

My arrival in Brussels was slightly clouded by a non-standard turnover of leadership. During my previous trip to the city, researching the paper I was writing about the EU, I had met my predecessor, who shall remain nameless.

I found myself truly disliking the man. He had worked mostly in

Middle East Division and he had openly criticized how Europe Division did some things. He also declared himself the only really competent case officer on the premises—a claim that won him few friends.

Whether or not his opinions had merit he would have been smarter to tone down the bad-mouthing. It didn't take me long to observe that most of his colleagues disliked him.

He did no better outside the office. He wore a cape instead of an overcoat, something many staffers thought was a bit of an affectation. Some of the Belgians likewise seemed upset and irritated at his attitude. I heard that after his departure his household belongings were "mistakenly" sent to Cape Town, South Africa, instead of back to the States. The locals stuck to the story that it was a snafu rather than payback.

I decided to arrive after he had exited. It meant I'd have no transition and would have to arrange to meet people on my own—a less-desirable start but I didn't want my predecessor's reputation to tarnish me.

I talked it over with Judy, who had also met him, and she agreed with my decision. I have always trusted her assessment of people and her reaction confirmed my own thinking. I skipped the normal round of cocktails and introductions.

Most of all I wanted to start out on the right foot. As diplomatically as possible—I saw no reason to alienate him—I pleaded personal and family problems that would delay my arrival until after his scheduled departure.

I began my tenure working with Ambassador Geoffrey Swaebe, a political appointee. Well-heeled from running the May Company department-store chain in California, he had been an original member of President Reagan's kitchen cabinet—a group of about a dozen friends and supporters who advised him unofficially during his presidency. Swaebe was also a major contributor to the Republican Party.

In his mid-60s, Swaebe was a shrewd and likeable man. My initial dealings with him went well, to my great relief. A chief's relationship with the ambassador often determines overall relations with the embassy staff. Ours turned out to be positive.

At first my interactions with Ron Ward, Swaebe's number two and the deputy chief of mission, were less positive. The problems started soon after we arrived in Brussels, each of us occupying his respective slot for the first time.

One day Ward called me to his office and asked me to brief him on various activities—including covert action.

He knows I can't and won't do that. So what's the angle this time? Testing, I suppose, to see just how far he can push.

I told him I couldn't brief him and pointed out that I had already briefed the ambassador.

"Did you give him specific details?" he asked

"No, I did not," I replied, "nor can I."

"We'll just see about that."

Ward explained that he needed to know about everything that was happening so he could properly manage the embassy's affairs. He would cable Washington, he said, to clear up this problem.

Was that supposed to be a threat?

I didn't bite.

"First of all it is not a problem," I told him. "It's simply that I have no options. The law forbids me to reveal our sources and methods to anyone. Cabling your superiors is a good idea."

We seemed to part amicably after agreeing to disagree, but just in case Ward decided to up the ante I cabled headquarters to explain what had happened and give them a heads-up about a possible query from the State Department. They responded promptly, asserting that I had taken the appropriate position and thanking me for alerting them.

A couple of days later Swaebe called me to his office.

"I understand you and Ron are having a problem," he said, after some initial small talk.

"Nothing serious, Ambassador," I said. "We'll get it ironed out."

I wasn't sure if Ward had explained the issue or not.

"There are limits to what I can tell him. I can brief you but no one else in the embassy."

"Well, I want to be sure that you two are getting along and working together."

I assumed he had told Ward that he was going to call me.

"I can assure you that I'm trying hard."

"It'll come, Dick," he said. "You know how some of these State guys are."

That was music to my ears.

Neither Swaebe nor Ward ever raised the issue again and I never did brief Ward on the forbidden topics. I suspect the ambassador had explained the ground rules to him. Or, perhaps Ward knew them full well and never actually cabled Washington. Maybe he was just probing for a reaction from me. If so, he got one.

Later on I realized that part of what was driving Ward was frustration about his own status. Brussels was a unique posting. The city hosted three American embassies—one for Belgium, one for the Common Market (soon to be the European Union), and one for NATO—and most diplomatic personnel agreed that the Belgian post was the least important.

That made Ward number two at the third-ranked embassy, though I doubt he would have admitted that openly. A strike in the coal mines around Liège would have been a typical concern for him, not an earth-shaking development about the Soviets or NATO.

My office, in contrast, supported all three embassies in Brussels plus the Supreme Headquarters Allied Powers Europe (SHAPE) about 30 miles away in Mons. Consequently we had a bigger staff than Ward's State Department complement—one of the few places in the world where that happened. That probably gnawed at him, as did my regular dealings with all three ambassadors and the commanding general at Mons.

I wouldn't have mentioned this to Ward but sometimes I joked that I worked for three ambassadors, as well as a lord (Lord Carrington, the head of NATO) and a four-star general (the commander at Mons). I briefed each of them periodically about various subjects, including counterintelligence. Looking back I probably would have felt just as frustrated if I had been in his place.

I did work to improve things between us, however. I briefed him whenever I could about locally germane issues, for example, and I think he appreciated my efforts. Then I discovered that Ward played tennis. I suggested a game, he accepted, and we played a few days later at a nearby club.

Thus began a thaw in our relationship as well as a healthy rivalry. I considered myself the better player but our matches were invariably close. He won as many sets as I did. I found him a fierce competitor and tenacious as hell. I've never been accused of lacking a competitive spirit, either, and I rose to the occasion.

We would often skip lunch and play for an hour or so at noon and our matches were always tough battles. I don't remember ever telling him but I admired the tenacity and guts Ron displayed every time we stepped on the court.

Suzanne, now 19, had moved to the University of California, Santa Cruz, for her second year of college to study English literature. She visited Brussels a couple of times a year during our stay and one summer she worked in the embassy's mailroom. As I recall she wasn't thrilled about the job but she did like joining us in Europe. She enjoyed speaking French and rapidly became a fluent speaker.

After considerable thought we had selected St. John's International School for the three other girls. Located in Waterloo, the small suburb of Brussels where in 1815 the Duke of Wellington ended Napoleon's domination of Europe, St. John's was reputed to be an excellent school.

We rented a big, comfortable home on the Rue des Chasseurs in Waterloo, only about five minutes from the campus. It included bedrooms for all of the girls plus a servant's quarters above the three-car garage. We soon filled one of those bays with another Morgan, a red one, which we bought used from a wealthy Belgian whose wife told him she had grown bored with the vehicle. We heard a different reaction later on from one of Alison's schoolmates, who said she thought it was a "bitchin' car."

My commute took about 25 minutes and ran through the beautiful Forêt de Soignes, the Sonian Forest, which stretched across nearly 11,000 acres just southeast of Brussels.

The girls' first day of school was memorable but not pleasantly so. They had boarded the wrong bus and ended up at a military high school northeast of Brussels near NATO headquarters. They discovered their mistake en route but could do nothing about it, and they were embarrassed by the looks they got from the other students departing the bus.

When they finally arrived at St. John's they were quite late for the opening assembly. They had to parade down the length of the aisle looking for empty seats, prompting the speaker to stop while they settled in.

At ages 12, 14 and 16 they found the experience mortifying, particularly the stares and unwanted attention that followed them. But they recovered quickly from the trials of that first day and soon became fixtures in the student body. That came as no surprise to me, their proud but objective father. How could they not be, as beautiful, talented and intelligent as they were?

St. John's, smaller than the other schools they had attended, offered an environment in which they could blossom, and blossom they did. They excelled in academics and sports alike. They played volleyball, basketball and tennis, and the fortunes of St. John's in those sports rose noticeably during the years of their attendance.

As usual they were particularly strong in tennis. In fact my stellar trio led St. John's to the European girl's championship in the International Schools League for two years in a row.

We had joined the Tennis Club de Waterloo and Judy quickly resumed her play, but more about that shortly.

As my job crystallized I found that our office in Brussels actually had zero requirements concerning Belgium. There was simply nothing going on in the small country with a population of 10 million that generated any interest among our policymakers.

That conclusion didn't apply to all Belgians, however. Some of them attracted a great deal of our attention. The country harbored its share of terrorists, underground arms merchants and exporters of computers and technology to countries not permitted to receive them. Belgium also hosted diplomats and other individuals who worked for target nations, particularly the Soviet Union.

Belgium's history is complex. For a brief time during the 17th century the northern, Flemish area of the country was part of Spain under Charles II. The town of Charleroi was named for him and it changed hands several times among the Spanish, the French and the Dutch. Other invasions occurred during the wars that are a part of Europe's past, resulting in a patchwork of ethnicities, cultures and languages. Even the Royal Belgian Tennis Federation, the sport's governing body for the country, is divided into French-speaking and Flemish-speaking leagues. The divisions run surprisingly deep and tensions can run high.

For example little love is lost between the French-speaking Walloons in the south and the Dutch-oriented, Flemish-speaking northern half. Our landlords in Waterloo practiced a kind of diplomacy that reflected this reality. In the lower level of the house they had hung a framed print above the bar. One side featured Napoleon, which they displayed when entertaining Walloons. The reverse side contained an image of the Duke of Wellington, just in case their visitors were Flemish. I have no idea what they did in mixed company.

Belgium's politics follow its geography. The Walloon-Flemish split also runs through its political parties. Disagreements are constant within the government. We never became directly involved with these issues but we always tried to stay mindful of the differences that were part of daily life for most Belgians.

What we did follow closely was the activity of the various Soviet bloc intelligence services known to be operating in Brussels. Our efforts to support the NATO and Common Market embassies were heavily focused on counterintelligence.

Working closely with the security offices of both organizations, along with the Belgian and various European services with representatives in Brussels, we constantly tracked what the bloc operatives were doing—and they were busy little beavers.

We had detected a surprisingly large number of operations being run against NATO and were sure there were others. We kept the NATO security office apprised of all hostile activities, including Russian—by both the civilian KGB and the military GRU—Czech, Polish, Romanian, Bulgarian and even Chinese. Their operatives also targeted the Common Market headquarters in central Brussels.

A favorite tactic used by most of the hostile services was to compromise members of NATO's secretarial staff. For example, access agents would help the GRU to identify a candidate—usually an unmarried, unattractive secretary with confirmed access to highly sensitive documents. Then the GRU would select another access agent—invariably handsome, suave and available.

Using a variety of ploys the service would essentially play matchmaker. From there nature would or would not take its course. Their objective was to manipulate the secretary so they could either exploit her affection for the access agent or blackmail her about the relationship. Either way they would push her to provide copies of sensitive documents.

Despite briefings and warnings out the wazoo to the secretaries and other NATO employees, the tactic worked several times during my three years in Brussels—and no doubt before I arrived and after I left as well.

The Russians also successfully recruited men working for NATO. We discovered one such case as a spin-off of another operation. It caused great concern because the person involved had classified access.

Our involvement began in autumn 1986 when I opened a pouch marked "Eyes Only Chief." It contained photographs of two individuals taken by a surveillance team working for a sister station in Europe. It included a memo outlining what they had uncovered. Our colleagues had done excellent work.

The photos clearly showed a senior Belgian Air Force officer and a known GRU general together—clear and indisputable. We were confident that neither the Russian nor the Belgian knew we had uncovered their relationship.

It was a coup but it created serious and difficult questions, several of which headquarters had posed, while others occurred to me as I read the memo. Foremost was what to do with our operational intelligence.

Certainly we wanted to expose and terminate the GRU penetration because no doubt it was providing them with sensitive NATO information. But lots of equities were at stake. We had to protect our own operations and assets while exposing and arresting the Belgian agent.

This would be extremely difficult and I knew we didn't have enough resources to succeed on our own. We would need lots of manpower and access to the agent's offices—one at NATO headquarters and another on a Belgian military compound.

That meant working with a Belgian service but which one? Also, whom should we involve at NATO headquarters? How much could we tell them? Should the NATO security office become involved?

I had my own answers and they would carry considerable weight because I was the chief on the scene, but it was a headquarters call. I sent a cable in response to the memo and I opened a dialogue about the questions.

We decided to inform Belgian military intelligence and I contacted their commanding general, who was Flemish. He was likeable and competent, a no-nonsense army officer.

The possibility of a Russian or Soviet bloc agent roaming free among the Belgian armed services weighed heavily on our minds. Every option would be risky but two points argued for our using their military intelligence service: We thought it less likely that a bloc agent had been recruited among their ranks, and they offered the major advantage of access and flexibility in investigating a fellow officer.

Headquarters considered the situation so important that they dispatched a senior member of Soviet Bloc Division to Brussels. He accompanied me when I briefed Lord Carrington, NATO's secretary general. For Carrington the session was sparse and generic, my report blunt and concise.

"You have a Soviet penetration of your organization."

The news distressed him but he agreed to our plan. He also clearly understood how many assets were involved, something which precluded us from sharing specific details and necessitated strict compartmentation.

Carrington gave us carte blanche and asked that we keep him informed. We did.

Next we briefed General Raymond Van Calster, chief of the General Intelligence and Security Service, the GSIS—Belgian military intelligence—and his deputy. This time our presentation was in depth, including the photos. They both listened carefully as we outlined our case.

After hearing it all, Van Calster glanced at the photos, which I had laid out on his desk.

"This is serious, Dick. It's awful. But I'm sure you know that we'll need more than these pictures to get this guy."

Then he asked the obvious question.

"How did you get the photos?"

We knew he would pose it and we had discussed how much we could say in response. It would be tricky. To assure that the GRU agent was arrested we wanted to provide as much detail as we could, but we also had to protect how we had obtained portions of our information. Where to draw the Need to Know line was critical.

"I can't tell you everything, Ray," I responded, "but I can tell you the city in which the photos were taken and the dates the agent was there. You'll need to check travel records to confirm that the agent was gone within that timeframe."

"You sure about this, Dick? We'll need special court approvals. Serious business."

"We're sure, Ray. That's your man on the left, and that's the GRU general, Boris Konstantin, on the right. I can't think of any innocent reason for them to meet clandestinely in another European city. It's agent and case officer."

"Okay, we'll do some checking and I'll get back to you." Van Calster said. "I'm not sure if I should say thank you or not."

"Sometimes things get nasty," I told him as we got up to leave.

Our initial traces had revealed that the Belgian agent, by virtue of his NATO position, traveled periodically to the United States for meetings with his American counterparts—a wrinkle that might require involvement by our domestic security services. He attended conferences at Air Force bases and thereby had access to our classified information. No doubt he was passing some of it along to the GRU so Van Calster had been right—this was serious business and the agent had to be stopped.

I thought of Greg, my Air Force officer brother, and other officers working with the agent and sharing information with him unaware of the fact that what they provided would find its way to the Russians.

We needed to seal the breach—soon.

Van Calster invited me over for a briefing about a week later. He didn't specify a subject, but I knew what we would be talking about.

The Belgian service had started to flesh out the picture of the agent.

He was divorced and lived alone. He had no blemishes on his record and he was on track to make general in the not-too-distant future.

It was difficult to accept that the man was a traitor, Van Calster told me, but he would reserve judgment. Because of the agent's military rank and reputation there would be hell to pay if we were wrong.

The officer in question, handsome and smooth talking, was reputed to be a ladies' man. That, as it turned out, would cast some early doubts about investigating his activities.

Because of the sensitivities involved, Van Calster held the information about the GRU penetration of NATO as tightly within his service as we were holding it in ours. Still the requirements of an effort like this—the surveillance team, the analysts, the technical support—required the participation of about a dozen officers.

Someone else sat in on Van Calster's briefing: Claude Van Miert, the Belgians' top counterintelligence officer. Van Miert, Flemish like Van Calster and in his late 50s, was a stocky man with a full head of gray hair. I had never met him before, but given the brief portrait Van Calster provided when introducing him it wasn't surprising he would be running their show. I could also see why Van Calster considered him Belgium's premier spy catcher. Events would prove that his confidence was well placed.

Van Miert had begun by thoroughly checking the suspect's files and travel records. He found that the agent had indeed been out of Belgium within the time period in question and without the permission required by military regulations. He initiated round-the-clock, discreet surveillance, a costly and politically risky effort. And he obtained special court approvals to put the agent's phone and mail under scrutiny.

Van Miert was operating precisely as we would be in a similar situation. It justified the confidence in and respect for the Belgian military that had led us to choose them to help us catch this spy.

Early in their coverage the Belgian surveillance team detected awareness on the part of their quarry. Teams are trained to be particularly attuned to the possibility that targeted individuals might be on to them, and they were excited to see it so soon in the game. The colonel had driven out of

Brussels then doubled back and parked at a roadside rest stop, obviously scanning traffic behind him.

The fact that he was on the lookout for surveillance suggested he was guilty of something. The team also felt confident he hadn't picked up their activity, because they had reacted to his maneuver by instantly co-ordinating the movement of their multiple vehicles to disguise the tail. They probably had even questioned the poor tradecraft training displayed by the GRU.

Back on the road the agent returned to his home. What had he been up to? On its face the action indicated suspicion of being followed.

Within a couple of weeks the surveillance coverage, coupled with the phone taps, revealed the reason for the colonel's cautious behavior: He was having an affair with a married woman, the wife of a fellow Air Force officer, and he thought her husband might be following him. Apparently he considered the husband a jealous and violent man—so violent that he had dubbed the husband "Rambo," after the movie character.

He may have feared the husband, but he continued the affair. It reminded me of the adage that God gave men a brain and a penis but only enough blood to run one of them at a time.

We were amused but the story had a downside. The agent's concerns about Rambo the Husband explained some of his behavior, which we had taken to be a sign of involvement in clandestine activities—the kind that interested us. But the discovery of his extramarital affair raised doubts among the Belgians. Nothing else had surfaced during several weeks of close, discreet surveillance that consumed big chunks of manpower.

To his credit and despite those doubts, Van Miert continued the coverage. Then small signs appeared. The suspected agent began requesting documents to which he would not normally have had access or on subjects for which he had no Need to Know. The team also spotted him making copies of sensitive materials.

This new information, plus the previous confirmation that the man had traveled to another city to meet with the GRU general, prompted Van Miert to order a search of the colonel's house. He lived alone so the team could complete the task easily, leaving no trace of their activity.

The search yielded the best evidence yet of espionage: spy gear, including a miniature camera and a communications plan. The team found both concealed behind a bookcase.

Van Miert then shifted to full chase mode. He knew the agent was spying for the Russians but he had to build a case that would stand up in court if necessary. Many FBI officers who have handled similar situations will tell you that compromising an agent working for a hostile intelligence service is an arduous, often boring ordeal. Such was the case for Van Miert's officers but now they were confident they would crack it.

Finally they did. Just as Gary, my operations officer in the Counter Terrorist Group, had painstakingly unmasked the Lebanese fabricator Jabril posing as a member of Libyan intelligence, one of Van Miert's team noticed a seemingly insignificant detail about our Belgian colonel: a red poster that appeared routinely on the shelf behind the back seat of his car. Most of the time the red side was up, but occasionally the colonel would turn it over or put it down on the back seat, out of view.

In surveillance activities, even the most ordinary actions can matter, and that observation led to a breakthrough. We discovered that the agent was using the poster to signal his GRU case officer about an impending drop. Soon thereafter the team photographed the agent in the act.

Then we discovered that the colonel was scheduled to attend a conference at an Air Force base in the United States, something we had worried about. Before he headed west we would have to alert the FBI, and probably Air Force Intelligence, that a GRU agent would be attempting to operate on U.S. soil—in their jurisdiction. Protocol aside we did not want the colonel gathering intelligence and sharing it with his Soviet contacts.

To check on the status of the Belgian investigation I went to see Van Calster and Van Miert.

"Is there a way to prevent the trip without alerting the agent?" I asked.

"Not to worry, Dick," Van Miert said. "We're ready to move."

"You've got your case?"

"We do. The colonel and I are going to have a talk tomorrow," he said with a broad smile.

The colonel confessed early on. The information and photos that Van Miert carefully amassed had left him no option. His motive, he disclosed, was money; the GRU had been paying him well. Belgium expelled the

GRU's case officer and sent the colonel to prison.

I don't know whether Van Calster and Van Miert tried to double the colonel or whether they considered him too much of a risk. By "double" I mean taking an agent whom you've uncovered and then persuading—or forcing—that individual to continue to work with his or her handlers. Those handlers would then be unaware of the deception, and the doubled agent would have access to valuable information about the hostile service.

For example you can learn a lot from the questions the handlers are asking the agent; among other things it reveals what they don't know.

In 2007, I was back in Brussels hosting a luncheon to thank the Belgians who had rescued me in the Congo. While there a friend told me that the colonel/Russian agent had served a 10-year term. Then, only two days after his release, he was killed in an automobile accident under mysterious circumstances. We never learned anything more about the accident but to me the traitorous colonel had received his just desserts—though he never did have to confront "Rambo."

Military, intelligence or law enforcement, whoever you are your first duty is to serve your country. To betray your country, particularly for money, is despicable.

The GSIS had done an excellent job. I congratulated Van Calster, passing on kudos received from headquarters. Van Miert had been patient, meticulous and professional in all aspects of what had been a highly sensitive and difficult case.

It's true that our information got the ball rolling but the Belgians picked up that ball and ran with it. Cooperation and mutual trust were key factors and I was pleased that we played a role.

Right from the beginning of my career at the CIA, I believed that the primary objective of our presence abroad was to produce intelligence for policymakers. Counterintelligence and covert action are also important—sometimes vital—but running collection operations is paramount. A cardinal sin is to run operations just to run them; in effect to take risks without achieving gains.

So it was in January 1986, when my patience with a particular technical operation had run out, that I dictated a cable to headquarters that ended with the phrase:

I REGRET THEN THAT WE WILL BE FORCED TO TERMINATE THE OPERATION

I didn't take this action lightly. The operation was extremely sensitive and I had been carefully briefed about it before I left for Brussels. But even back then I had raised questions about how the product of this effort would be disseminated and exploited by analysts and policymakers.

The answers had been disquieting. Basically they said the logistics were still being put together. Really? Then why take such a high risk when we didn't even know where the intelligence would be going?

There were practical questions as well. This particular operation would be producing roomfuls of information. All well and good, and it was interesting information. But information is not finished intelligence, no matter how voluminous. Unless we could collate it, analyze it, categorize it, and disseminate it to fulfill a serious purpose, it made no sense to do it at all.

I won't belabor the details of my continuing dialogue with headquarters about the operation, which had already been running for over a year by the time I got to Brussels. Suffice it to say that they never did satisfy my concerns; as soon as I sent the cable I killed it.

As I suspected, headquarters reacted with barely a ripple. Few questioned my decision—and no one strenuously. The people who had supported the operation let the whole thing drop, as though they were saying, "If you'll keep taking the risk, that's fine with us."

Not fine. The intelligence community often requires a particular type of information, which is too sensitive to be disclosed here. When the need arises the DO is tasked and our Brussels office had been running, flawlessly, a delicate, politically risky effort to fulfill that task.

So far so good, but the big picture had gotten cloudy. Basically we had collected so much raw data that we were overwhelming the system; it was unable to process the data into usable intelligence.

This kind of situation represents an ever-present danger. Chiefs need to watch out for it and resist it, not only for their own protection but also for the good of the entire community. It is the essential part of the CIA—the care we take with intelligence.

In February 1986, Judy and I and the three girls drove to our apartment in L'Alpes des Chaux, Switzerland. Suzanne had returned to the States to finish her last two years at Swarthmore. She seemed happy to be back there—especially after she met Steve, her husband-to-be.

The chalet housing the apartment sat only a few yards from a slope and each day we would put on our skis as we walked out the door and shush down to the lift.

My skiing had improved considerably since the time in February 1959 when my colleague Pete Wilson invited me to go to the Pyrenees. Back then I was serving in the Army in France and had never been on skis. But I went along with a mixed group of acquaintances and friends, eager and confident I could master the sport.

The very top of the mountain, bathed in morning sunshine with a clear blue sky and pleasant temperature, was truly a beautiful sight, one of those days that all skiers long for. I was lucky to have it for my first outing.

As soon as we lifted to the top the others in our group strapped on their skis and disappeared over what looked like a cliff. I hung around a bit; as an untutored novice I had no idea how to get down that mountain.

I began by traversing and promptly fell and slid about 60 feet downhill. Skiers streamed past me. I got to my feet but continued to slide and fall. I started to tire and slow down.

Then I realized I could use a technique I had learned playing ice hockey as a kid in Elmhurst, Illinois. To my delight I discovered I could quick-stop on snow the same way hockey players did on ice.

By that time I was about halfway down. There followed a lengthy period of further descent during which I practiced turns and stops. When the bottom finally appeared in the distance I had grown confident I could make it in one piece. Soon I saw the little restaurant where we all had agreed to meet for lunch.

Originally I had planned to meet my friends after the fourth or fifth run. But here it was lunchtime and I was just finishing my first and only attempt down the mountain. I had done it mostly by sheer determination.

I spotted Pete, who had just taken off his skis. The slope had moderated and I glided easily to him, shouting a greeting as I slid to a stop. He was surprised and impressed.

"Are you sure you've never skied before?" he asked.

"Never," I replied, acting casual but inwardly marveling at my good fortune. I didn't bother explaining it had taken me *three* hours to make one run and I had spent a significant portion of that time on my butt. He didn't ask.

On the second morning of our trip, Danika announced she was going to take Judy and me to the "top of the world." We oldsters were less adventurous and competent as skiers; we tended to stick close to home on familiar slopes and had never ventured to the area Danika was proposing.

"You'll love it," she told us confidently.

Ali and Pia had also been to the site and they sided with their sister. So we took the nearby T-bar lift to the top of the mountain. From there we could descend and climb again via numerous different slopes.

With Danika in the lead, followed closely by Ali and Pia, we descended toward a valley lying between us and an adjoining complex of ski trails. Instead of ascending back our way again, as we usually did, we traversed the valley and started up the mountain on the other side.

Several different lifts thereafter we arrived at the top and stopped for some hot chocolate. Danika assured us that we weren't there yet and pushed us onto a chair lift, which carried us to a point higher still. There we took in a truly spectacular scene: bright sunshine in a clear sky reflected on the snowy mountains, all of which seemed to be below us.

"This is the top of the world," Danika announced with certainty. None of us disagreed.

26. Not Your 'Average Diplomat'

BRUSSELS 1987–1988

St. John's leased the nearby indoor courts at our tennis club and hosted the International Schools League tournament during our second year in Belgium. To our great delight, and to the surprise of many, our girls' team swept the tournament and took all honors.

Danika and Alison won the doubles competition without a loss. Moreover they didn't lose during the two years they played together in Europe, before Danika returned home to attend Mary Washington College in Fredericksburg, Virginia.

Another St. John's girl, displaying considerable intestinal fortitude—guts—lost her first singles match, but because it was a double-elimination tournament she fought her way through the losers' bracket and won the championship. And Pia, still in middle school but drafted by the high school team, contributed a couple of wins before being beaten.

The coach's decision to play Danika and Alison in doubles instead of singles—one or the other was the rule—had paid off. I tried to be as modest and gracious as I could but it was hard to conceal my pride.

The girls enjoyed similar success in basketball. Pia starred in her last year in middle school and the team went undefeated. The boys' varsity coach, who became a good friend of our family, would even harangue his players with stories about Pia's scoring.

I had played basketball in high school and college and thought I knew something about the game. I tried to understand why Pia made almost every shot. I never did. She dribbled with either hand, so that didn't explain it, and she scored from all over the court. The high school coach could hardly wait for her to play the next year.

Then inexplicably Pia stopped shooting with two hands and began one-handed jump shots, apparently because she thought it was a much cooler style. She did well in high school, playing guard along with Alison, but her prolific scoring dropped off considerably.

St. John's maintained high academic standards and the girls continually met the challenge. They grew in many ways during those three years. We watched as they matured socially and gained more confidence. St. John's had been Judy's top choice—and I had agreed. It provided just the right social and scholastic environment for our platoon of now-teenaged daughters and they took advantage of the opportunity.

Every now and then, however, life can throw parents curveballs, and one of them got pitched while we lived in Brussels. It's something that affects every CIA family with a parent who works under cover.

Each family tends to deal with the problem differently. Some explain it to their children early on, though doing so risks an errant remark to a relative, friend or acquaintance. We had decided to wait, planning to disclose my affiliation to each daughter as she left home for college.

For example we had told Suzanne before she left for Swarthmore when we were living in McLean. As I recall her first reaction was to say, "I wondered how you could get home so fast after I had talked with you on the phone and you were at work in Washington."

She was right; driving home from the agency usually only took me about 10 minutes.

I told Danika when she left for Mary Washington after our second year in Brussels. She likewise took it in stride, asking a few innocuous questions.

Then that curveball swept toward the plate.

In 1987 I received a cable from headquarters alerting me that my true name had appeared in *Veil: The Secret Wars of the CIA 1981-1987*, the book Bob Woodward had written about Casey's tenure as agency director. According to the cable Woodward named both me and Chuck Cogan as CIA officers who had briefed him about terrorism before he traveled to Beirut to do some firsthand research on the subject.

That briefing was supposed to have been off the record and Woodward knew it. He also knew that Chuck and I were DO officers who worked clandestinely overseas.

What the hell could he have been thinking?

The disclosure ticked me off royally and I shot a cable back to headquarters voicing my concern. Langley's unsatisfying response: Nothing can be done. Woodward reportedly had pleaded ignorance about Chuck's and my status, and in any event the book had already hit the shelves.

I didn't accept his explanation. Woodward could have easily checked with the agency. I found his action highly irresponsible, especially given the sensitivity of the subject. I hadn't seen the book yet so I had no idea how many others he had exposed in this way.

This wasn't just a matter of embarrassment. I wasn't out on the street or dealing directly with agents, but I was conducting operations against the Soviet bloc and the Russians played hardball. I'm sure they would have loved to get their hands on me, a senior officer—for that matter so would the terror groups operating in Belgium and elsewhere in Europe and the Middle East.

Where did that leave Chuck and me? We had to hope that Woodward's brief reference to us would go unnoticed—particularly by the wrong people.

That slender thread snapped quickly. I played tennis a couple of times a month with Ray Jenkins, another St. John's parent. An American businessman, he supervised the sale and distribution of Levi's jeans in Europe. Ray traveled frequently, as did I, but in between trips we managed to get in a tennis game or two, usually followed by a cold drink of some sort.

One day during said cold drink he asked if he could pose a question.

"I've been reading a book written by Bob Woodward," he said. "It's called *Veil*."

Uh-oh.

"I know the book," I replied, buying a little time. "I've read it. What prompts you to read about terrorists?"

"Nothing special," he responded. "I picked it up at the airport because

I'd heard of Woodward. Are you the Dick Holm mentioned in the book? You never have seemed much like the average diplomat. I'm not trying to be difficult, just curious."

I had been quickly mulling over what to tell him.

"There are two answers to that question, Ray. One is that there must be somebody else named Dick Holm. The other is, yes, I briefed Woodward. Obviously I'd rather go with the first answer and leave it at that. Woodward had agreed not to reveal our names and should not have done so. But that can't be changed at this point."

Ray studied me for a moment.

"No problem, Dick. It must have been another Dick Holm," he said with a sympathetic smile.

I thought about the incident on the way home and then, as usual, talked it over with Judy. If Ray of all people could pick the book off a newsstand and connect me with the agency, anyone could.

Apart from the issue we didn't want to talk about—some fanatic seeking me out—the question was what, if anything, should I tell Alison and Pia? No way did I want one of them to be blindsided by a classmate or a teacher.

We decided that I needed to tell them ahead of schedule so they wouldn't be surprised and embarrassed. We also decided that I should take them to my office to tell them—to impress upon them the seriousness of the subject.

The following Saturday morning I invited them to accompany me to the office. Right away they perked up.

"I want to talk with you about something,"

"Is Mom coming?"

"She doesn't need to. She already knows."

"Is this going to be a lecture?" Ali asked.

"No, no lecture," I replied. "Let's go."

We drove into Brussels and although they had been to my office before this time they seemed expectant.

I wasn't sure how to start, maybe because I wasn't sure how they'd react. I decided to mince no words.

"I have to bring you two up to speed. Suzy and Nika already know what I'm going to tell you. I wouldn't be doing this now except that some problems have developed. It's a serious subject."

That definitely got their attention.

"It's about my job. I work for the Central Intelligence Agency. I am the chief of its office here in Brussels. I can't tell people that. I tell people that I am a special adviser to the ambassador."

Both girls were wide-eyed and digesting. Obviously neither had ever harbored any suspicions. That somehow reassured me.

"So you'll never be an ambassador?" Ali finally asked.

"You do all that James Bond stuff?" Pia blurted.

"No, Pia, I don't. That stuff is greatly exaggerated. Most of my work is pretty normal."

Both were still digesting.

"And we shouldn't tell anybody, right?" Ali asked.

"Right," I replied. "You two just say what you have always said, that your dad is a special adviser. Don't be worried; I know you both can handle it or I wouldn't have told you."

"There won't be any problem, Dad," Ali said. "Right, Pia?"

"Right," she responded promptly. "Boy, Dad, this is exciting! We can talk to Mom, right?"

"Yeah, you can talk to Mom. My name is mentioned in a recent book called *Veil*. I didn't want you to be surprised by a question from someone who might have read it. Otherwise I would have waited until you were older. But you two will deal with it just fine, I'm sure."

I felt proud of the girls and was relieved at how well they had reacted.

Judy and I liked the Belgians and during our stay we made many local friends. Once again tennis, excuse the pun, served us well. Though we were both active members at the Tennis Club de Waterloo, Judy was more active because of my lack of free time. I attended dinners once in a while, and lunches on the weekend, but I never could seem to break away for tennis as much as I would have liked.

Judy enjoyed great success on the senior ladies' team. Playing both singles and doubles she led her teammates to the finals of the Belgian national club championship. They lost, though Judy won her match, and Waterloo's team had never before advanced beyond the district level. Making it to the national finals was a triumph.

Judy received full credit for the team's success and deservedly so. She became widely known in the club and in Waterloo. After a while I was introduced as "Judy's husband."

Among the Belgian couples we counted as our friends were Jackie and Jean Paul, whom we had met on the diplomatic circuit. Walloons living east of Brussels, their home became known in our family as "the pink château." A grand villa with an aged stone facade that had turned light pink, the house was situated on a large tract of land owned by Jean Paul's family for many years.

Jackie and Jean Paul were linked to Belgium's royal family, and he even held a noble title of some sort, but they were both delightfully unpretentious. We enjoyed many visits with them but I particularly remember one Christmas Day.

It was our first visit to their home. Judy was reading me the directions as we headed out of Waterloo. All four girls accompanied us because Suzanne had flown in for the holidays so we had to use the company car, a Saab, not the Morgan. They seemed excited at the prospect of visiting a country estate and sharing Christmas dinner with some Belgians.

Within half an hour we had found—and missed—the driveway to the château. Doubling back I entered a long lane lined with tall poplars, running past a pond with geese and ducks, and ending at a wall near the front gate. It was an elegant structure, at least a hundred years old, and we were all struck by its beauty.

Introductions took a while. Their three sons, all older than the girls, seemed bemused, I thought, to meet these four young Americans. But they were extremely polite and attentive.

A little shy at first, the girls warmed up to the occasion as we settled in the drawing room and started to chat. Soon the conversation flowed smoothly. Jackie was quite gracious and pleasant and I could tell the girls were starting to like her.

The oldest son entered with a tray full of glasses and served everyone champagne. Jean Paul toasted the occasion and Jackie announced dinner would be forthcoming. With that the three young men left to help serve—impressing the girls, I'm sure.

Soon thereafter we trooped into the cavernous dining room. One of the pretty murals covering the walls had recently been cleaned and restored. I assumed that the others, also in dire need, would receive the same, expensive treatment.

The large and elegant table easily seated us all. One of the sons served wine while another served pieces of a baguette.

The girls were taking it all in, each glancing at the first course: a generous portion of rich pâté on a small plate that had been laid in front of them. After another brief toast, Jackie, for reasons I never did figure out, gave a lengthy and graphic description of how the pâté had been made.

"One must be sure to stuff as much corn as possible down the throat of the goose," she said. "Usually you have to hold the neck and just shove the corn in."

Jean Loup, their youngest son, graphically demonstrated as the girls watched silently.

"That's so you can make the goose liver as large as possible," she continued. "Then when you cut out the liver to make this delicious pâté you get the best taste."

I began to sense that the girls didn't want the details. They told me later that although they weren't happy with the demonstration they finished the bulk of the first course—partly at Judy's discreet urging. Nevertheless I was proud of them.

That hurdle cleared we went on to enjoy a delicious roast turkey dinner. We vividly remember our meal at the pink château and when we do someone always mentions the pâté.

If you've followed my narrative this far you've seen how dangerous this line of work can be. And if you've studied the history of the Cold War you know how potentially dangerous a period it was for the whole world, and why the U.S. and allied intelligence services worked so hard to track Soviet and Chinese activity in Europe and Asia.

Likewise the communist agencies worked to infiltrate us, to identify our agents, to steal our secrets, and to compromise our defenses, such as in the case of the turncoat Belgian colonel. That's why one of our highest priorities in Belgium was counterespionage.

We knew that the Belgians and the other European services also focused on the problem, but many lacked the manpower, funding and expertise to counter the hostile activities of the Russian services and their Eastern European allies. We worked closely with them, as well as our counterparts in NATO and the European Union, sharing information, cooperating on ops—tagging and bagging the bad guys.

For these reasons it disturbed me tremendously to encounter an individual working for a sister service who seemed blithely unconcerned about the need to shoulder the burden, to share the load—to do his job.

Slightly built with gray hair, Alfred was always well dressed and very dapper. An intelligent man whose English and French were excellent, he also spoke Dutch, Spanish and Italian, and I'm sure his fluency in the other languages was strong. He had been active in security matters since the late 1970s.

Outwardly my relationship with Alfred was always positive and friendly, but he maintained a wall between us that prevented me from completely trusting him. I also never knew what to expect from him. I had heard about his terrible temper but never saw it displayed, and in any event if that was his only problem I could have lived with it. Always helpful and even gracious, Alfred was consistently the picture of willingness to work together.

It's just that he never really did anything.

Alfred took the late train from his home every morning and was met by his chauffeur. He would arrive in his office at about 10:30 and start with a cup of coffee. His desk was constantly stacked with files and memos that begged for—but only rarely received—his attention. His young, attractive, able secretary literally rejoiced whenever Alfred signed a memo, enabling her to move it along. He usually left the office early for a "working lunch."

I have vivid memories of my lunches with Alfred.

I always prepared carefully and was ever ready to raise and discuss issues of mutual interest and concern. We met for lunch about every six weeks; Alfred always hosted. His secretary would call, propose two dates, and based on my response would tell me where and when to meet her boss.

Alfred always lunched at excellent restaurants, and Brussels boasted dozens in that category. One of his favorites was La Maison du Cygne on the city's Grand-Place. A superb restaurant specializing in French cuisine, it became one of my favorites as well.

Despite every tactic I tried the scenario never changed. I would arrive prepared to discuss current issues and problems but Alfred would not respond to any subject I proposed, and he raised only innocuous ones. For three years we discussed subjects such as our respective daughters, the wine and the food.

Basically our conversations never advanced beyond examining the menu, listening to the waiter recite the special dishes of the day, and making our selections. As soon as the waiter took our orders Alfred would study the wine list to ensure that he selected just the right variety for what we were going to eat. He often chose a white for the oysters, which we always had in the season, and something else for the main course.

Then he'd lecture me further on wines, on various special dishes such as game, eels or fish, or he would expound on some historic place or event. I learned a great deal about wine, oysters, fine cuisine, and local history and culture. What I got precious little of was information that aided our mutual effort to thwart the Reds.

After about two hours of this Alfred would bid me goodbye and return to his office. He'd once again touch little of the stacks on his desk. He might have a quick meeting or two, but seemingly oblivious to the fact that he had arrived late to work he would depart early to catch the train home.

This was Alfred's standard day and he got away with it for years. To my knowledge he maintained his position for some time. He was probably the most extraordinary character in Brussels—and I liked him. I even came to accept my meetings with him as merely one of my formal responsibilities as chief.

But it was not what I wanted, and given the amount of time and money wasted I found the whole experience distressing.

The three years I spent in Belgium were hectic ones for my colleagues back at Langley. They witnessed the end of an era at the CIA on January 29, 1987, when William Casey resigned as director because of a brain tumor. He died on May 6 at age 74. Casey had been a stalwart as our director. Much good came from his efforts.

As I've mentioned, Casey won significant increases in our budget—backed by President Reagan—enabling us to rebuild both operational capabilities and our personnel strength. He also expanded our covert activities against the Soviet Union and its bloc countries, something that had been restricted under the Carter administration and Stansfield Turner.

But Casey's relationship with Capitol Hill, and the intelligence oversight committees in particular, had never improved, and the agency paid dearly for it in the years after his death. Subsequent directors faced closer congressional scrutiny across the board.

The situation grew even worse when the Iran-Contra affair surfaced the year before Casey died. In the early '80s the Reagan administration had been aiding the Contras in Nicaragua, rebels who were fighting the leftist Sandinista government. But the Democrats, who controlled the House of Representatives, opposed the policy. Congressman Edward Boland of Massachusetts authored a series of amendments to Department of Defense appropriations that specifically prohibited military aid to the Contras.

To outflank the Democrats the administration conjured a complex maneuver. Someone—who it was remains unclear to this day—dispatched Marine Lieutenant Colonel Oliver North, a staffer on the National Security Council, and others to the Middle East to make contact with Iran. Their purpose was to negotiate a secret sale of surface-to-air and antitank missiles, delivered by a third party, to help the regime in its ongoing war with Saddam Hussein's Iraq.

Though everyone involved denied a direct connection it was hoped that Iran would respond to the missile deal by expediting the release of six American hostages held in Lebanon by Hezbollah. Meanwhile the administration would quietly reroute monies from the sale to provide weapons to the Contras—thereby circumventing the Boland amendments.

Which brings us back to William Casey. When the details of this operation surfaced the Democrats uncovered evidence that suggested Casey knew about and was involved in the missiles-for-Contra-arms deal.

Woodward's book *Veil* included some extremely controversial passages about Casey, whom he had interviewed 43 times. In one of them Woodward claimed to have spoken to Casey on his deathbed. There he reportedly asked Casey if he knew about taking money from Iran to divert to the Contras. Casey, he wrote, after a moment's hesitation, nodded his head affirmatively.

President Reagan in his posthumously published diaries wrote that he thought Woodward was "a liar, and he lied about what Casey is supposed to have thought of me."

William Webster—or "Judge," as he liked to be called—took over as Director of Central Intelligence on May 26. He was my tenth. Although some people in the media had compared and generally equated the two jobs, many others, including me, knew that heading the CIA was very different from running the FBI.

Webster never really fit in at the agency but he was nonetheless a good choice for the job at the time. Iran-Contra had roiled the waters—even President Reagan's staunchest supporters, such as Senator Barry Goldwater of Arizona, were furious about the affair—and we needed a stabilizing presence at the top, which meant Judge Webster would have to do some housecleaning.

For example, Clair George, Casey's deputy director of operations, was up to his eyeballs in Iran-Contra. He would have to go and Webster made it one of his first tough decisions. In January 1988, he surprised us all by selecting Dick Stolz to replace George.

I thought it was an excellent choice. Stolz had actually retired seven years earlier after a long and distinguished career. Just as Casey had done with Billy Doswell he chose Max Hugel, an obscure businessman friend, to be DDO, and Stolz left the agency in frustration. At least in the case of the Operations Directorate, Casey apparently had realized his mistake and quickly replaced Hugel with John Stein, an experienced officer.

Stein served the agency well for three years, until Casey named George as John's replacement. During his tenure as DDO, Clair George had been an aggressive and occasionally cantankerous operations officer, and little love was lost between him and the congressional oversight committees. He was generally well-respected and liked within the directorate but many worried about some of the initiatives he undertook.

George, with higher-level coordination, had authorized the mining of several Nicaraguan harbors in an attempt to prevent arms shipments to the Sandinistas. The mines damaged several ships and apparently outraged enough members of Congress to win approval for the Boland amendments.

Stolz carried none of the baggage that George had accumulated during the Casey years. And his arrival reassured the DO, which had been staggering under the criticisms and accusations generated by the Iran-Contra affair. Dick's reputation as a professional, intelligent and fair operations officer gave us confidence in his leadership and our collective future.

I would grow to know Dick well and I have great respect and admiration for him to this day. He ably led us through a hazard-filled period that included the enormous changes that came with the end of the Cold War in 1989.

I had met Webster in 1987 while he still headed the FBI. He visited Brussels to attend a meeting of the NATO Security Committee, which comprised the heads of the internal services of the member nations. The FBI represented the United States. The agency also sent an officer but strictly as an observer.

I didn't attend the meeting but was invited to one of the social functions associated with the event. I also received an invitation to play tennis with Webster and his top aide early one morning. Webster was—and though now in his late 80s possibly remains—an avid tennis player. He always tried to get in a game whenever possible.

I partnered with the NATO security chief. Webster and his deputy were better-than-average players, so the four of us split two good sets.

The experience gained me some personal impressions of Webster, which helped to color my reaction when I learned he would be heading the agency. I found him a pleasant and friendly man, and I liked him, but he was a different sort from his predecessor.

A tough, New York City kid growing up in Queens, Bill Casey had joined the OSS during World War II and ended up heading its Secret Intelligence Branch in Europe. After a corporate legal career he had served in several positions during the Nixon administration before managing Ronald Reagan's 1980 campaign.

Also a WWII veteran with a legal background, Webster hailed from St. Louis. He had spent most of his professional life prior to the FBI as a federal judge.

But these were surface distinctions. At his core Webster seemed to lack Casey's toughness and shrewdness—something that worried me as I watched him take the agency's reins.

Shortly after Webster recalled Dick Stolz from retirement to become the DDO, Dick made a European trip to visit major liaison partners—the traditional first trip for a new occupant of his office.

Dick cabled me to ask if he could stop by Brussels to see me. I promptly responded that I'd be delighted. I had never met him but was eager to do so, particularly because in less than six months I would be finishing my tour in Belgium and returning to headquarters. I rightly assumed that we would talk about my next job. I had been promoted to an SIS-3 in 1987 and felt ready to take on a senior position.

I knew it would be an interesting meeting. I had been thinking about possible headquarters positions and decided I would be open to any proposal the DDO would make.

As it turned out I was unprepared for Dick's particular proposal.

"I want you to oversee the Career Management Staff."

"What? Why me?"

Suddenly I wasn't so open.

"Think about it, Dick," he said calmly, "I consider it one of the most important jobs in the directorate. There aren't too many people who could do it and I want you to take it on. I want a senior officer with an operations background. I think one needs operations and overseas experience to do the job. You've got both. You on board?"

Of the positions I had been considering that one wasn't even on the list. I wasn't at all sure I'd like it. Running CMS was about as far off the streets as I could get.

I knew I could have said no and held out for a line job, but once again and despite my misgivings I accepted. If that's what Dick Stolz wanted me to do, I'd do it.

The remaining months in our tour passed quickly and uneventfully. Danika, who had graduated from St. John's the previous year, was awaiting our return. She had just finished her first year at Mary Washington, where she played varsity volleyball instead of tennis.

Suzanne graduated from Swarthmore in May and Judy and I returned home for her commencement. The school held the ceremony in its amphitheater and it was a beautiful setting. Suzy, to the delight of her parents, graduated with honors.

She had recently and belatedly announced that she would be starting a master's program at Bryn Mawr College, just a few miles away from Swarthmore, where Steve would be finishing his degree. How much that had to do with her decision was unclear to us, living as we were an ocean away. A lot, I suspected.

Alison, with only one year left in high school, was troubled at the prospect of doing her last year elsewhere, but everything would work out well for her back in McLean. She made friends quickly and joined the Langley High School girls' tennis team that won the state championship that year.

Pia seemed happy to return home where she would have three years of high school remaining.

Brussels had been splendid in all respects. We bade our farewells in July 1988 and left in high spirits. We looked forward to being closer to Suzanne and Danika. At age 53 and with 27 years of experience in the directorate, I viewed my upcoming headquarters job with little foreboding. I would be returning in a key, senior position and I eagerly awaited working with Dick Stolz, who was already demonstrating a strong and steady leadership style.

27. In the Engine Room

LANGLEY, VIRGINIA 1988–1992

Most movies and the media in general portray agency personnel as either cloak-and-dagger types, sometimes with superhuman abilities, or ruthless bureaucrats who would rather sacrifice one of their own than give up power. The fact is we do sometimes train people extensively before we dispatch them on dangerous missions. It's also true that once in a while a rogue wave washes its way into our sea of personnel.

But the overwhelming truth is that most of what we do parallels government work in general and much of the private sector. Some of it is downright ordinary, involving mountains of paperwork. Someone has to supervise that ordinary but important work. For a while, and for a part of it, that someone had to be me.

It didn't take long to confirm that I was taking on a very different kind of job, though I had suspected as much. Still I was surprised by what I found. Managing the broad spectrum of issues that fell to the Career Management Staff—which has since been renamed the Human Resources Staff—would be a heavy-duty challenge for me. I had a lot to learn but fortunately I inherited two terrific deputies.

I had heard of Mike McBride when we both worked as China ops officers earlier in our careers. Mike started with the agency a few years after I did. Unlike me, he accepted a job laboring nights in the file room and worked his way into the CTs, the Career Trainee Program, which succeeded the JOTs.

He obviously had done well and earned a fine reputation in the clandestine service. He managed about half of our 40-person staff and handled our promotion system—all levels except the Senior Intelligence Service, which was my responsibility. He supervised field and headquarters assignments and guided the recruitment of new officers.

Mike also supervised some peripheral issues, so his plate was full, but he never missed a step. Imbued with uncommon levels of good sense and integrity, Mike excelled in his dealings with people and inspired great confidence and trust.

I hardly knew Peggy Donnelly, my other deputy, before I took over the CMS, but I soon found her to be equally talented and competent. She ran budget and administrative matters, training programs, the grievance system, the manning table—from which we derived how many people we could hire or promote—and our formal ties to the directorate's staffs and its geographic divisions.

Peggy was affectionately known as an agency brat. She also had started her career as a junior employee in our file rooms and over the years she learned Langley's ins and outs intimately. She was exceptionally well-qualified for her job and was already handling it beautifully when I walked in the door.

I admit that Peggy knew her responsibilities far better than I did but she never pressed the point. She also seemed to have done her homework about me because she knew quite a bit about my background. Apparently she had concluded I was okay.

We quickly developed a positive and friendly relationship. I greatly respected Peggy's abilities and it took me only a few weeks to realize how lucky I was to have her in that job.

Meetings, meetings and more meetings soon became the bane of my existence. I had convened and attended lots of them when I ran the Counter Terrorist Group, but at CMS they constituted a different scale altogether.

I represented the directorate on a host of agency-wide committees, groups that determined recipients of medals, scholarships, disciplinary actions and nominations to prestigious schools and seminars, such as the State Department's Senior Seminar—which I had attended in 1984—and the National War College. I also chaired committees for the Language Incentive Program and the Family Liaison Office. There were others but this is a representative sample.

Most days I needed to carry a schedule to get me from one meeting to the next. My secretary Ginger, like Mike and Peggy, was competent, professional and an enormous help keeping me on time and on track.

Many of my meetings were with Dick Stolz. Indeed because of the myriad of issues that arose regularly I met with him far more often than just about anybody else. I also met frequently with the division chiefs to discuss assignments, promotions, disciplinary issues and other matters. The same for the chiefs of our major staffs—especially Operations Resources Management, which handled money for the directorate the same way I handled personnel.

Despite my growing aversion to this routine I took my responsibilities seriously and did my best to represent the interests and people of the DO. I wasn't immune to headquarters or inter-directorate politics but I always strove to reach what everyone would consider fair-minded decisions and results.

I grew to admire and respect my committee counterparts—representatives from the Intelligence, Administrative, and Science and Technology directorates. With few exceptions they likewise worked for the best interests of the agency. We didn't lack for disagreements, most of them provoked by loyalties to particular employees or goals, or ignorance about another directorate's mission.

It wasn't easy, say, to compare the work of a scientist with that of an ops officer or an analyst to determine who should receive an agency medal. But we worked out solutions, accepted one another's explanations, and performed our roles. Truth be told, things had always worked this way on the committees and my particular group of representatives was no exception. The job's novelty for me was how vastly different it seemed from running a station or managing street ops.

Here's an example:

Peggy announced one morning that the DO lacked candidates for the board of directors of the agency's government-subsidized health insurance program.

"Is that something a DO officer would think much about?" I asked. "Most are either overseas or want to go overseas so it's not something they would react to. Should we be surprised?"

"You're right but that's wrong," she replied tactfully. "DO officers and staff have the same interest in health insurance as anybody else, so why shouldn't we have some say in how it's run? We ought to have a DO officer sitting on the board."

"I can't argue with that but what can we do? I can't really order someone to be a candidate and even if I could who would it be?"

"What about you?" Peggy said with a smile, revealing the real reason she had told me.

"I don't know a thing about insurance programs or how they're run."

"Doesn't matter," she said. "Nobody does when they first get on the board. You could learn."

I thought about just refusing but how bad could it be? Peggy was right; health insurance wasn't trivial—not even back then.

"All right," I sighed. "Put me down as a candidate."

"You'll probably win in a landslide," she quipped as she walked out.

"Spare me," I replied to an empty doorway.

Three weeks later and despite no campaigning on my part I received a pile of votes, enough to elect me to the agency's health-insurance board. Soon I received several volumes of books to study before the next meeting—just what I needed.

For the next two years I pored over all of the necessary material and never missed a meeting or debate. I represented our many employees serving overseas and I took special interest in matters that affected them. I managed to streamline the claims process and upgrade benefits for our people abroad, and the other board members welcomed my efforts.

I learned a lot during my tenure and in retrospect I valued the experience, though it required me to become something I had never imagined before: a headquarters bureaucrat.

I spent a lot of time on training issues, which was fine with me. I had always favored strong instructional programs and I was pleased to be able to support them. At CMS, however, training was a broad subject. It covered the directorate's new employees, periodically honing and upgrading various skills, and mastering languages. I developed a close working relationship with Paul Erikson, chief of the Directorate of Administration's Office of Training and Education.

The DO and the OTE sparred regularly over the curriculum at the Farm, our training installation in southern Virginia. The DO for decades had regarded the Farm as its exclusive domain. Other agency components might use it from time to time but the place's primary function was to train DO officers—it was ours.

More recently others in the agency, including Erikson, thought the DO should share the Farm a bit more. That didn't sit well with the directorate, though some of the problems were personality driven. That could be expected given the divergent cultures of the operations and education people—like the differences I had detected early on at those Sunday touch-football games between the JOTs and the foreign-service candidates. Paul and I recognized and acknowledged it but it was hard for us to smooth the conflict enough to make the DO happy.

One reason: The OTE people had outraged the DO's experienced officers when they dared suggest how and what to teach in the basic ops training course. Eventually Paul and I managed to find the middle ground. We got the two sides to sit down and discuss their points of contention. Surprise of surprises the DOs discovered that the OTEs had suggested changes that made good sense. After that things calmed down considerably, though not entirely.

In any deeply rooted professional culture such as among DO officers—and especially those assigned to the Farm as instructors—the tendency is to resist any intervention in their business. Few in the DO regarded ideas from the DI or DA as of much use.

Sometimes sensitive issues were involved, and sometimes they became topics of discussion on the seventh floor, but top management left much of the negotiating and problem-solving to Paul and me. When they did, the two of us could usually apply enough horse sense and pragmatism to work out a practical solution.

During my first two years, and through the early 1990s, we witnessed substantial improvements in our training programs. To my knowledge, that trend has continued, and our new operations officers receive excellent initial and periodic instruction. There's always room for debate but I think most would agree with my assessment.

Language skills represented an equally important training issue and differences of opinion persisted there as well. My goal was to produce what we called operationally fluent speakers and readers, but nuances lurked within the goal that prompted debate:

How does one define "operationally fluent?"

The quick answer: good enough to recruit agents.

How important is good grammar?

Isn't speaking more important than reading?

What kind of vocabulary should be taught—political, military, economic or all three?

Should we include background on cultural and historical affairs?

You get the picture. To wrestle with those issues I needed to attend more meetings, frequently with the head of the language school, and often with groups of instructors.

How we taught languages affected assignments. We favored sending a given officer to a given country only if he or she spoke the local language. In practice we didn't always succeed and that was a constant frustration, so I worked hard to press the geographic divisions to make sure their officers already spoke or would be fully trained in the language of their destination.

Most of the divisions agreed and they boosted the percentage of language-qualified officers being assigned abroad. But there was a practical issue and I was personally aware of it. I had begun my first stint in Hong Kong without spending the standard year in Taiwan to complete my training in Mandarin. Instead I continued the instruction during my assignment.

In my case the shortfall never interfered with promotions or the overall progress of my career. That's because officers can make use of languages such as Mandarin, Russian and Arabic at many postings so there's an incentive to continue to study and gain more proficiency—there's a need for fluent speakers at many stations.

Other languages, such as Finnish or Korean, apply to a narrow geographic area. Consequently specializing in one of them can drastically limit one's usefulness and flexibility. Moreover the global languages enjoyed a higher priority in the training programs and overseas assignments.

To encourage the study of all languages, including the less-widespread tongues, the DO established the Language Incentive Program. The idea, a sound one, was to give cash awards to officers who attained proficiency and bestow additional rewards for using a language in the field.

The LIP also dispensed cash incentives, determined via testing, to off-duty officers who maintained their language skills; the same for people serving at headquarters. But it wasn't an easy program to administer and it inevitably resulted in complaints to the committee I chaired.

One issue concerned fairness; people claimed the grading was flawed. Some said their instructor, usually a native speaker, had somehow misunderstood or been too subjective, or demanded unreasonable standards. Others charged that a colleague didn't speak as well as they did but received a higher grade. Trainees also groused if they hadn't attained the level required to receive their payment.

All of this meant frequent interaction with the LIP people. I persuaded them to modify the program in several ways to make the testing more objective, such as employing panels of instructors and taping the tests. But human nature dictates that someone will always complain, and the award generated other questions that bubbled up to the committee:

Does someone at headquarters merit an award if, say, he or she travels once a month to meet and debrief an agent and exercises languages skills in the process?

If that person deserves the award should it be the whole award or only a percentage—and if so what percentage?

Does someone stationed in Stockholm who is using Spanish to develop a Latin American diplomat deserve the award because of the unique specialization?

What about officers—the vast majority of whom are native speakers—hired because of their language skills to translate documents or transcribe tapes?

We hashed out these thorny issues one at a time. I wasn't always comfortable with the outcomes but I refrained from showing my pro-DO bias. Besides, committee members representing the other directorates often presented persuasive arguments of their own.

More troubling to me was the maintenance award. In my view language fluency was supposed to be a critical work skill—something everyone should be motivated enough to display. I had no problem with awards for learning and using a language, but awards for maintaining skills that were an integral part of the job seemed too much to me.

I didn't win many hearts and minds on that issue, and my problem with it grew over time, particularly because of some egregious cases. For example a DI officer of Polish extraction was doing solid analytical work on Southeast Asia. The officer had learned Polish as a child and still spoke it well enough to pass the language exam, but he was ineligible for an attainment award. Likewise he was ineligible for a use award because he never employed it in an official task. The question was whether that officer should receive a maintenance award.

I said no and I won. True it was an unusual case but it illustrates the point—anytime you introduce cash awards the nuances flourish.

One Monday morning Peggy and a colleague, Betty, walked into my office with a proposal to make a major change in the directorate's personnel structure. They had been mulling the idea and modifying it even before I had taken over CMS.

DO procedures were structured to ensure fair competition for a limited number of promotions. To do that my predecessors had developed categories covering employees doing the same or similar work. Then the promotion panels, comprising DO officers more senior than those being reviewed, could rank the candidates but avoid comparing apples and oranges.

For example Category B covered operations officers. Each year a panel met to evaluate candidates for the next-highest grade and they approved promotions of eligible officers depending on the headroom—the number of slots available.

Straightforward? Not exactly. The panels faced tricky questions:

Who deserves a promotion more, a case officer in the field who has recruited several agents or written numerous intelligence reports, or one serving at headquarters who works at a desk but has contributed critical support?

What about a case officer who has just finished a year of language training and been out of the game? And so on.

That was just for the relatively homogenous Category B. The evaluators faced even dicier issues in other categories, some of which covered people with such varied skills—reports officers for instance—that making comparisons was extremely difficult.

I discovered that reports officers were receiving short shrift—the value of their contribution had been routinely diluted and they seemed to get fewer promotions.

Peggy and Betty were right. Change was overdue and they were advocating something to address that need. They proposed a new Category O that would contain much sharper distinctions. In other words they were pushing to level the playing field.

I briefed Dick Stolz about the proposal and obtained his approval. As CMS chief I would have to introduce the change, which I did on January 11, 1990, at a general meeting in the agency's auditorium—known as the Bubble.

Peggy, Betty and I would find out quickly if Category O would fly. The majority of those who would be affected by it had spent most of their careers at headquarters. Many of them attended my noontime presentation.

I started with what I regarded as a bit of wit. I noted that on January 11, in the year 49 B.C., Julius Caesar had crossed the Rubicon River with his army, defying Roman law and plunging the empire into civil war. I said I hoped our own point of no return would be less contentious.

Nobody even smiled.

I pushed on, detailing the change and its rationale. We had hoped those assembled would recognize the plan as an earnest effort to improve the promotions process. We also hoped they would be happier and more motivated. But as in all large, entrenched bureaucracies, even one as unusual as ours, change of any kind can be a tough sell. Some considered it a bold but unnecessary move. The system wasn't actually broken, they argued, so why fix it?

Objections noted, Category O was born on that day and became the first of several personnel restructurings. A few months later and after much discussion we introduced Category I for reports officers—who for reasons I could never quite fathom wanted to call themselves intelligence officers. After that we created Category L for the language specialists, mostly translators and transcribers. Other distinctions followed, each one helping our panels to make sharper comparisons among people doing similar work.

We also began apportioning the number of promotion slots based on the number of officers in each category. If Category X constituted 20 percent of the directorate's roster then we allotted it 20 percent of the headroom.

The agency's bureaucracy had indeed grown entrenched. The management changes we effected were the first in many years. But they weren't the last. Many others followed throughout the decade.

By summer 1990 I had been heading CMS for two years and I longed for reassignment. It was not to be. Dick Stolz asked me stay on and I reluctantly agreed. The agency was undergoing yet another hectic period and this was no time to change horses.

On the previous November 9 the Berlin Wall had fallen, some four decades after it was built and two-and-a-half years after President Reagan had stood at the Brandenburg Gate, famously calling for Soviet Premier Mikhail Gorbachev to "tear down this wall."

It was the beginning of the reunification of Germany and of the end of the Soviet Union. The Free World rejoiced but for us in the Directorate of Operations it meant seeking to understand the ramifications of the historic changes, developing new strategies to accommodate those ramifications, and setting those strategies in motion.

Dick ordered me and a half-dozen other senior ops officers to tackle those tasks. We met frequently and wrestled with alternative solutions to the problems we had identified. We quickly recognized that our proposed solutions would bring about a degree of change never before experienced by the DO.

Up to then we had targeted our main mission and its related operations at Cold War issues—the threat that communism posed to the Free World. But suddenly that threat—or the great bulk of it—had evaporated into history and things would surely be different. Ronald Reagan's admittedly simplistic—his word, not mine—but straightforward goal, "we win and they lose," had been fulfilled.

Few of us envisioned the amount of change in prospect.

After weeks of meetings and debate we assembled a strategic five-year plan. Our consensus achieved, we gained Dick's approval.

First and foremost we would shift our operational priorities to reflect the new requirements of the policymakers—though the policymakers seemed quite slow out of the blocks. They clearly wanted what they called a "peace dividend." Translation: The Cold War's over so we need to slash your spending. Beyond that they didn't provide much guidance.

In hindsight no one could have foreseen the massive resources we would need to counter the threat of global terrorism—just as few comprehended the emergence of the Soviet threat when the Russians were still our allies at the end of World War II. True, we were already actively engaging terror groups as well as the growing reach of narcotraffickers. The grim prospect of terrorists acquiring, in today's parlance, weapons of mass destruction was also becoming a priority. But none of those activities matched our anti-Soviet efforts.

Our team's assessment concluded that economic intelligence—identifying which countries were playing fair, which were quietly subsidizing their exports, and which were trying to steal our trade secrets—would become an increasingly important activity. Likewise, we would have to cover terrorism, narcotrafficking and WMD. In turn the new priorities would drive changes in recruitment, training, assignments, promotions and budgets.

Next we'd have to sell our conclusions to the agency as a whole. Dick accomplished much of that effort. He had developed a close relationship with Judge Webster and we helped him by doing our homework well.

Dick briefed the other deputy directors, mostly out of politesse, but the exchanges encouraged the directorates to prepare strategic plans of their own. Because we had done it first we were well ahead of the curve, so we could nudge the others in the directions we had taken. Given the changes we all were facing the cooperation proved valuable.

Last the agency needed to inform the members of the oversight committees. Our briefings were well received. On both the Senate and House sides the legislators understood the need for major shifts in agency objectives. Most seemed to welcome the vision our plan presented.

Inevitably some of the committee members disagreed, influenced by their staffs, which were populated by would-be ops officers who had changes of their own in mind. But we prevailed in the end and we assured members and staff alike that we would promptly implement the plan.

That effort turned out to be no cakewalk. It was a time of great challenge for our directorate and the agency. We began installing our strategic plan but it was tearing at the very fabric of our culture—everything that we had so carefully constructed through the decades of the Cold War.

One by one we were dismantling the timbers of our infrastructure and replacing them, from overall ops directives for our stations to the training courses at the Farm and the priority languages at our schools. We would chase the Soviet Bear no more—though Russia remained an area of interest and China a priority target. Instead, implausible as it might have seemed just a few years earlier, economic intelligence would take on a new importance and we began programs to collect such intelligence, even about certain "allied" countries.

CMS was experiencing its own version of the upheaval. People were pushing for changes in almost every area of our personnel structure. They wanted faster promotions, an end to our long-cherished but resource-demanding panel system, more ethnic diversity, modernizing our training structure, and smashing the glass ceiling where female officers and employees were concerned.

The list went on. People demanded a more open assignment process, a revised category system to rein in the elitism of Category B, recruiting policies that better reflected the needs outlined in our strategic plan and greater accountability. And by the way please have those changes ready by next Monday morning.

Worthwhile goals all, plus the most vocal demand, because it seemed to be a great irritant, that we produce more honest and insightful Personnel Appraisal Reports.

We heard all the cries, and more, and in each case we tried our best. But as I said, entrenched cultures resist change and many within the agency were downright fearful. My frustrations mounted as one seemingly intractable issue after another wended my way.

Thinking back now I suspect that the flood of requests, coupled with the mundane nature of many of the issues, took their toll on me. Judy noticed it. I grew irritable, because I couldn't resolve many of the issues I faced at work. I tried not to let my feelings show but it became obvious that I wanted this assignment to end.

It wasn't so unusual. Three-plus years as CMS chief could test anyone's limits, particularly someone used to working in the field—no longer on the street but still on the front lines. The obvious solution was to get myself overseas again. I had been promoted to an SIS-4 during this rotation, which made me one of the most senior officers in the directorate. My options had widened.

To give me a light at the end of the tunnel and reward my labors, in the summer of 1991 Dick offered to nominate me as chief of either London or Paris. My first inclination was Paris and when I discussed it with Judy she agreed. Dick approved my request. When the DDO speaks the directorate listens and I got Paris—but I would still have to run CMS for what turned out to be another half-year.

One of my great consolations through all of those months was the exceptional quality of my two sets of deputies. Almost by definition the managers of a large personnel office must be people-oriented individuals who can generate trust and confidence. Assignments and promotions, as well as the related activities that support our personnel structure, touch sensitive and sometimes rubbed-raw nerves of individual employees. Any officers facing such jobs need a special set of skills, and these four men and women personified them.

Mike McBride had been promoted to chief in Hong Kong during the summer of 1990, and that fall Peggy Donnelly moved on to another important slot at headquarters.

Mike's replacement, Glen Adams, returned to Langley after heading one of our overseas offices. He brought seniority, experience—mostly in Europe Division jobs—and an exceptionally high level of energy. With a University of Virginia law degree he also brought a disciplined approach to his work and a level of integrity that was beyond reproach.

Glen understood the directorate and he judged issues fairly and with compassion. Mike had suggested Glen as his replacement and when I reviewed Glen's file I could see he was an excellent choice. I was pleased when he accepted the job and more than pleased with the tasks he accomplished. I quickly grew to respect his straightforwardness in dealing with people above and below him in the hierarchy.

Peggy's replacement, Nancy, was a highly respected senior DO reports officer. Like Glen she never hesitated to put in long, hard hours researching a particular issue to make sure no point eluded her.

I developed complete confidence in her judgments and her objectivity in approaching contentious issues—which, as I've described, were many. Nancy's proposals reflected lots of common sense and a spirit of compromise when necessary. The changes required by the strategic plan affected Nancy's side of the office more than Glen's—covering budget, training, manning-table and hiring issues, among others—but she met the challenges with considerable skill.

Even my capable deputies couldn't always help me, such as with disciplinary actions, which was one of my committee assignments. In those instances the buck landed on my desk with a thud.

Most of the cases involved sexual misconduct or excessive drinking. At one point I remarked that if we could just control bottles and zippers we'd solve most of our personnel problems before they got started. More straight-faced I asked why these episodes kept cropping up when we took such pains to select and hire the highest-caliber people. No one responded.

I can only think back to that effort by Rusty Williams, whom Stansfield Turner had dispatched overseas to investigate misconduct at the stations, which uncovered the shocking revelation that agency personnel displayed the same weaknesses as the rest of the human race.

Sometimes, though, the new era brought unprecedented dilemmas, such as the emerging concept of political correctness. One particularly frustrating case concerned an operations officer whose work and comportment fell far below the standards we expected.

Serving in a European post he had produced questionable accountings, demonstrated bad judgment, and practiced exceptionally poor tradecraft. He was a relatively senior officer so we had every right to expect much more from him than he was delivering.

The trouble began when complaints from other officers generated an investigation by our Inspector General. I became involved at the conclusion when the IG briefed me and the Europe Division chief on the results.

The investigation painted a portrait of an officer clearly failing in his responsibilities, his duty. The IG doesn't mete out punishment; the directorate would have to decide what to do next. The division chief and I separately studied the IG report to determine what we would recommend to the DDO. We met several days later to discuss our conclusions.

We agreed that the report was damning, that the officer's performance had been unacceptable in all respects. The IG had compiled solid evidence, much of it irrefutable and some of which the officer himself had admitted. We discussed dismissal, which he deserved, but his appraisal reports, as was often the case, had not adequately reflected the poor quality of his work and would not support such a strong step.

We drafted a memo for his file, signed by the DDO, which would preclude future assignments in the field or in any management position. We stated that the directorate had lost confidence in his judgment and integrity and he could either retire now or spend the remainder of his career at headquarters under close scrutiny.

By this time Dick Stolz had left as DDO and Tom Twetten, who was Dick's handpicked replacement, accepted our conclusion and signed the memo.

My friendship with Tom went back to our JOT days. Given the far-reaching changes under way within the directorate and the agency he stepped in at a particularly difficult time. Tom also shared my Viking heritage and Midwestern roots. His competence and years of experience in the clandestine service served him well in the job—but his signature on the memo was not the end of the story.

The case's outcome would seem ordinary to anyone managing a federal office today. The offending officer, of Hispanic origin, challenged the IG report. He claimed discrimination because of his minority background. People didn't like him, he alleged, because he was a Latino and everyone had lied about his performance.

No one ever contacted me or the Europe Division chief about the challenge, which ended up in court. There the officer won the case and received a cash award. Had we been contacted we would have produced overwhelming evidence of his failings that had nothing to do with his allegations.

This was a revolting development. The settlement saddled the directorate with an officer who had violated the trust that is the foundation of our system. Bluntly stated, if you can't trust an ops officer to report truthfully what transpires at an agent meeting then you can't trust the entire reporting cycle.

Apparently the man's lawyer had exploited flaws in the IG report, enough to make the officer seem vindicated. Yet the DO was not involved in the court case. Instead it was handled by the IG and the Office of Legal Affairs. The dispute had been taken from our hands and my efforts and those of the Europe Division chief were for naught. No, this wasn't a notorious case *à la* Aldrich Ames, which I'll describe later. But it wasn't a trivial matter, either. Our bureaucracy had dropped the ball and produced an embarrassing, unjust outcome.

The case also exposed a set of painful alternatives: Was this guy always so aggressively incompetent? If so it meant no one had the guts to mention it in his Personnel Appraisal Reports. Or, was he a competent officer whose performance had tailed off or plummeted? Ditto about the guts and either way the directorate fared the same as many other agency and federal-government offices would in similar circumstances in ensuing years.

I could see this situation developing for quite a while. The fact was that PARs were seldom if ever candid when dealing with professional or personal deficiencies. Hoping to find a solution I visited military and private-sector personnel offices alike to discuss the issue and found it was a universal problem—nobody wanted to cast on-the-record aspersions, however justified, on colleagues or subordinates.

Finally I mandated that all PARs would contain an "Areas for Improvement" section. It was a way to address deficiencies in a positive and non-threatening way—and to begin building a paper trail for potentially troublesome personnel.

I maintained the practice for the rest of my tenure. But soon after I departed CMS my successor, bowing to complaints, rescinded it. As far as I know the lack-of-candor problem in PARs continues to this day.

Times were a-changin' on the home front as well as at the office. The hardest for Dad to accept: My girls weren't girls any more. Without my consent they had grown into young women.

Eventually Pia was the only one still living at home. Given her superb experience at St. John's in Brussels we thought a parochial school in McLean would be a good idea. After a year, though, Pia could see this particular school wasn't her cup of tea so she transferred to Langley High School. There, once again, she excelled at tennis, basketball and softball and she earned a 3.4 grade point average, all in a highly competitive environment. She seemed free of teen angst and we were very proud of her.

Alison had earned an early admission to the College of William and Mary in Williamsburg, Virginia. She spent part of her junior year in Aix-en-Provence in the south of France studying French and European affairs. She had met Tom, her husband-to-be, during her freshman year and he—astutely, in my view—had tenaciously pursued a courtship of her.

Danika, already at Mary Washington College when we returned from Brussels, continued there until her graduation in 1991. She played volleyball and majored in geography, something which I learned encompasses "more than state capitals." She then lived in California for a year before returning east to begin graduate school at the University of South Carolina in Columbia.

Suzanne finished her master's degree in social work at Bryn Mawr and to no one's surprise announced that she and Steve were engaged.

They married in August 1990 and spent a portion of their honeymoon at our apartment in Switzerland. Immediately thereafter they moved into a—really—small apartment in Paris, not far from Notre Dame Cathedral. They lived there for an academic year teaching English at two high schools. They had a great time and were able to see much of France and tour other parts of Europe.

As for Judy and me, we were beginning the empty-nest state of our lives. We didn't much like the idea of the girls moving away. But as Pia approached graduation from Langley and her eventual start at Mary Washington, following in Danika's footsteps, we began adjusting to the idea of going back overseas platoonless.

Someone higher up also moved along after four years. In August 1991 Judge Webster had retired as director. In November, George H.W. Bush, who had been elected president in 1988, named Robert Gates, a career intelligence officer, to succeed Webster.

Gates would be my eleventh DCI. His understanding of intelligence and his agency background put him in good standing with the community, but he was from the DI side and that worried us a little in the DO. Intelligent, professional and well connected to the inner circles in the capital, Gates seemed uncomfortable with the clandestine service. But we hoped his familiarity with Washington's ways and his ability to maneuver through its ever-present minefields would work to our benefit.

By early 1992, Tom Twetten had identified my replacement and I felt more eager about preparing for my Paris tour than I had since awaiting my release from Walter Reed. This was true even though my latest stint at Langley ended on a bright note.

Tom presented me with the Donovan Award, the DO's highest honor for service rendered. It meant my colleagues had recognized how hard I had worked in the job. Now someone else would have to take up those chores.

In all honesty I derived little pleasure or satisfaction from performing my tasks at CMS. I regarded the experience as though I was chief of the engine room in a battleship—or maybe more precisely a submarine.

I labored in a windowless enclosure, directing the resources—the energy—needed to keep the ship moving while Dick Stolz and Tom Twetten either steered from topside or at least kept watch on the horizon through a periscope.

I knew I would face administrivia in Paris as well—reading personnel and operational files, writing appraisals, returning to Washington to visit various departments and agencies with ties to Paris, and resuming work on my French to improve my fluency. At that point I didn't care. I had just spent nearly four years away from operations managing nuts and bolts again. Whatever challenges Paris would present I was eager to meet them.

Or so I thought.

28. At the End of the Day

PARIS 1992–1993

Sans daughters, Judy and I arrived at Charles de Gaulle Airport on a sunny morning in late August 1992. We had decided to finish our language training with two weeks of total immersion at a school in Provence so we picked up a car and headed south. I hoped also to take the pulse of political realities in the provinces; thus we planned to drive south via the west coast to Bordeaux and the foothills of the Pyrenees.

Charlie, our administrative officer, met us as we passed through customs and welcomed us to France. An outstanding and experienced professional who was also a very likeable person, Charlie had introduced himself back at headquarters when he stopped by my office before heading to Paris for his assignment. Here he handed me the keys to the car we would use for our trip to the language school, wished us good luck, and left to return to Paris.

We hadn't slept much on the plane; Judy never slept well on flights. Because we had no particular itinerary in mind we headed out of Paris until fatigue overtook us after a couple of hours. We decided to spend the bulk of our first day resting. By then we had reached Chartres, a delightful city with a magnificent Gothic cathedral that is visible for miles around and is known for its incredibly beautiful stained-glass windows.

After Chartres and for the next week we made our way through La Rochelle, Bordeaux and Toulouse en route to the school in Provence. We made frequent stops along the way and I used every occasion to engage the locals in conversations about a wide range of subjects. The encounters helped me exercise my language skill and flesh out the impressions I had gained from my extensive background reading. I wanted to deepen my understanding of what made the French tick—I still don't know.

An important subject at the time was the impending national referendum on participation in the European Union. My conversations, plus reading newspaper editorials in the towns we visited, helped me understand the contentious issues being debated. In the end the government's argument for greater EU involvement prevailed by a slim majority.

The school, located in Pont-Saint-Esprit, about 30 miles north of Avignon, occupied a former monastery on a rural site just outside of town. Everything had been restored and modernized so our accommodations were modest but comfortable.

The classrooms and dining room were on an upper level and easily accessible. The dining room served non-gourmet but acceptable family-style meals. A French instructor sat at each table. They used a large, open room on the lower level for breaks and for cultural programs in the evenings.

The grounds featured two tennis courts near the main building. Though in poor condition, they afforded the only distraction available. We used them a few times between afternoon classes and dinner.

The no-nonsense setting emphasized improving French proficiency. That was why we were there and we had no problem with the focus. Agency students had studied at the school before, as well as at its branch in Spa, Belgium.

We spoke French 24 hours a day, Monday through Friday. Weekends were free. They placed Judy and me in different classes because of our respective levels of fluency. She had actually studied more French than I, including courses at the Alliance Française in Hong Kong years earlier and in Belgium during our tour there. She was clearly stronger in vocabulary and grammar.

The school served both of us well over the course of those two weeks. It was an excellent jump-start to our arrival in Paris—though our second week included a bizarre incident.

I was asked to give a talk as part of one of the evening sessions, which included a speech or lecture. The school often invited local politicians or teachers to present their views on a variety of subjects, after which we would ask questions—practical exercises all.

Attending in my cover capacity I had been asked to speak about the life of a diplomat. At first, I was reluctant; the thought of giving a talk of any kind in French was daunting. But finally I agreed and spent a couple of hours preparing some remarks, which wasn't difficult because I knew how embassy officers spent their days.

As we entered the dining room the next morning Judy spotted a handmade sign someone had posted on a bulletin board:

VENEZ POUR ENTENDRE JAMES BOND PARLER

"Come to hear James Bond talk," it announced in bold letters, complete with a drawing of a pistol with an American flag protruding from the barrel.

My first reaction was irritation.

Who would have done this? Why?

I wondered if Woodward's *Veil* was haunting me again. I took the thing down and crumpled it into a nearby wastebasket.

Feeling less irritated after breakfast, I asked Judy what I should do next. She counseled restraint and I followed her advice. I gave my talk and it went uneventfully—nothing untoward, no questions about anything except diplomacy. I never discovered who had posted the sign, why it was done, or what had prompted someone to suspect I was not a diplomat.

Just before Thanksgiving we moved into a 1920s' vintage townhouse in Neuilly-sur-Seine, a western Parisian suburb. With newly refinished parquet floors, modernized bathrooms and a complete repainting it was good as new; completely comfortable yet with the character and ambiance you would expect in a European home. It even had a nice first-floor terrace with a stairway down to a flower-filled back yard. Best of all perhaps, because of the constant parking problem in Paris, our house had a connected ‑-car garage with a remote-controlled steel door.

commute took me along the Bois de Boulogne, the enormous

wooded park on the western edge of Paris, through a large circle above a Metro station near the Bois called the Porte Maillot, and then down Avenue Charles de Gaulle and around the Place de l'Etoile with the Arc de Triomphe in the middle.

It must be said, and I think most Parisians would agree, that l'Etoile presented traffic planners with a real challenge. With twelve major streets and avenues feeding in and out, negotiating it is a formidable task until you figure out the system. Then it flows rather well. I was always amazed at how efficiently the whole thing worked during rush hour.

From l'Etoile my commute took me straight down the Champs Elysées. It was broad and strikingly beautiful and led to the almost equally famous Place de la Concorde. There, on January 21, 1793, the revolutionary government guillotined King Louis XVI, Marie Antoinette, Charlotte Corday and other members of the aristocracy.

My daily destination stood just off the same corner where the guillotine once fell with regularity. A few months after we settled in Paris, on January 21, 1993, a group of Royalists staged a memorial at the site to mark the event's bicentennial. I watched them from my office window.

Yes, some mornings I had meetings and would go elsewhere, and yes in deference to security concerns I did vary my route and use other streets, but that was my most frequent itinerary and it never got old. I drank in beauty and history at every turn.

Our house sat 50 meters from the Bois. Its lakes adorned with ducks and swans, its beautiful flowerbeds and its well-tended paths all made for pleasant scenes year round and we took full advantage of the proximity. I jogged there most mornings and Judy took long, daily power walks. The park had a stable within earshot of the house and we often awoke to the sound of horses clattering by with riders on their early outings.

Our lush surroundings aside, we chose where we would live because of security concerns. With my experience in counterterrorism, and the knowledge of what had happened to Dick Welch in Athens and Bill Buckley in Beirut, plus the lingering uncertainty about what kind of mischief the Woodward book might have incited, we felt it best to err on the side of caution.

Granted I could have solved the problem by forgoing overseas assignments but I discarded that option. I had spent three decades serving the agency and gaining the necessary experience to run an office and I wasn't about to let security concerns restrict me.

On the other hand I wasn't going to ignore the risks. For our residence in Paris we selected a house and location where we would feel safe, one that featured an armed French policeman constantly standing guard at a post not 10 feet from our garage. Our two neighbors were considered possible terrorist targets by the French and therefore they warranted protection. Frequent vehicle patrols augmented the guard post.

No guarantees, but the police presence and activity comforted us.

Our office in Paris had always been an active and important facility and my tour would be no different. I was delighted to be there and I eagerly met with my staff to gain a sense of what was going on.

As in Hong Kong, Kuala Lumpur and Brussels, I began focusing my attention on our ops-support structure. Right away I could see the need for some changes. I didn't want to ruffle feathers, however, so I made it clear that the adjustments reflected my own management style and I meant no criticism of my predecessors.

The core of the changes concerned counterintelligence. Often left in the hands of the most junior and inexperienced officers and only rarely reviewed, these operations had caused compromises—exposures—in the past.

The problems were obvious. We needed to treat the keepers of safe houses and the people who provided accommodation addresses with the same care that we applied to all other ops involving agents.

I gave our counterintelligence officer two weeks to compile a review of our ops-support structure. As a result of her efforts we terminated our relationships with certain agents and we shut down a number of safe houses. In both cases we found the assets to be outdated or unnecessary, or their longevity had increased their vulnerability to compromise.

Next I turned to the subjects that interested the policymakers back home. As one of Europe's primary cultural crossroads, Paris offered a lth of information about many international issues, including those ng to the Middle East and Africa. My job was to construct and manage ops that would yield the information we sought.

Given my experience, and the fact that I was assuming command of an active and productive office, the task should have been a cinch. Then, as if on cue, the Congress of the United States threw a monkey wrench into my plans.

Just after Thanksgiving, following Bill Clinton's election as president, headquarters sent a cable announcing that our budget for the current fiscal year—the one that had already started on October 1—had been cut in half.

The news stunned us. No one had seen this coming. Congress had decided to cash in the peace dividend.

The action gave us two options: live with it—or live with it. I had two reactions. The first was a sense of betrayal. All of the reviews, discussions and plans we had assembled at headquarters in 1990 and 1991 were for naught. Congress, being Congress, had accepted our presentations and agreed with our proposals about rebuilding the agency's mission to reflect the post-Cold War world. Now, a year later, our distinguished representatives had chosen political expediency by unceremoniously slashing our funding.

My second reaction was that Congress was dead wrong. Yes, the United States was reducing its military presence in the world, but doing so meant we would need a stronger—not weaker—global intelligence capability.

Just because the Soviet Union had fallen did not mean the threats to our country were ending. For all of our improved relations, China remained an adversary and potential enemy; likewise the mullahs in Iran, Saddam Hussein in Iraq and Gaddafi in Libya. All harbored hostility toward the United States, as did Hezbollah and a dozen or more Islamic terror groups growing in strength and numbers. Even tiny, impoverished North Korea, headed by Kim Il-sung, could cause serious trouble on the Korean Peninsula and elsewhere in Asia.

Then there was the greatest danger of all: the threats we didn't yet know existed. Being unprepared had caused our country enormous pain at the beginning of World War II. Was Congress so sure we could accomplish our mission on half of our previous budget? I wasn't, not by a long shot.

This wasn't a case of penny-pinching legislators looking to save money for the taxpayers. I saw it as a symptom of alarming uncertainty at the national level about how the United States, now the world's lone superpower, should conduct itself. It was an unacceptable risk for us to tie our own hands.

I could understand why Congress would want to use the Soviet downfall as an opportunity to cut the military and intelligence budgets and focus on domestic issues. I even agreed that reductions were warranted. But they were wielding the ax indiscriminately. In the DO's case the cuts would hit excessively and arbitrarily at our overseas operations.

Charlie and his assistants briefed me on the consequences of the budget cuts for our office and they weren't pretty. We were already into the second quarter of the fiscal year so we had spent one-fourth of our original budget—half of the revised budget. That meant getting through the rest of the year not with a 50-percent decrease but more like a 67-percent cut. Charlie said we would have to make heavy reductions across the board.

Seeking some clarification and hoping for some wiggle room, I asked him to send an immediate cable to headquarters. He drafted the cable and included a dig along the lines of, "If we don't get some relief the last guy out will turn off the lights."

Apparently that bit of levity was lost on Joe DeTrani, the Europe Division chief at the time. The grapevine reported back that Joe had complained about the quip and admonished us to be more serious. In fact, we were quite serious.

Headquarters made it clear: I was going to have to make do with half of the original budget. Worse, the comptroller had convinced Director Gates to hit the four directorates equally, with no attempt to determine the impact such cuts would have on individual programs. Gates's order likewise gave no consideration to whether our overseas operations would suffer potentially crippling problems.

In a time of such uncertainty, as the nation struggled to find its way in a dramatically different world, the clandestine service was being not just reduced but slashed. Many of us had recognized early on that in the absence of the Cold War we would lose funding and we had begun planning with that reality in mind. But none of us had anticipated this tactic, as our British colleagues would say, "at the end the day."

I asked Charlie and his staff to draft a new budget that included the now-unavoidable cuts. With a real sense of dread I reviewed what they had produced before meeting with my deputy Charlie D. and our branch chiefs. I wasn't happy with the revised budget, but I knew it was realistic and I thought Charlie's administrative team had done a good job.

At the meeting we discussed budget issues in general terms. Then I gave everyone a copy of the draft and asked them to reconvene three days later when we would have to make the tough decisions. They should all be prepared to argue their respective cases, I told them, as we focused on reducing the scope of our activities—not a pleasant prospect.

We spent much of that long, subsequent meeting debating. We scrutinized everything and emotions ran high, but we eventually agreed what should suffer the cuts. The pain would be considerable but I was pleased to see everyone maintaining a spirit of cooperation. We were all in this together, even though the process had hammered morale and it took several months to right the ship, so to speak.

We deeply cut our administrative and support areas but considered the actions merely a nuisance we could live with. In contrast, the drastic operational reductions hit squarely at our raison d'être, causing us to question why we were there, what we would be doing in the future, and what the hell we would do if we faced even more cuts.

I could also see staff reductions on the horizon—we were going to lose people.

There was a specific, practical risk involving cuts in our counterintelligence and operational security. When you tell an asset that his or her services are no longer needed you can't be sure of the reaction. We had to proceed with extreme care to ensure soft landings for these people. Easier said than done, but my able staff merited praise for weathering the storm without permitting a known incident or breach of security.

Much of our storm-weathering ability rested with Charlie D. Just as Mike McBride and Peggy Donnelly did at CMS, Charlie commanded great respect among the Paris staff. Fair and objective, he possessed an unusually strong grasp of tradecraft. His counsel on ops matters was widely sought, including by me, and his judgments were consistently solid and accurate.

Charlie D.'s reputation was so good that Langley sometimes seconded him to handle particularly sensitive operational activities elsewhere. Quiet and plainspoken, he quickly made the easy decisions but took the hard ones head on; no procrastination allowed. I felt lucky to have him for the first two years of my tour. I wish he had been there at the end.

I had started with three branch chiefs but as I expected the budget cuts forced me to pare down to two, a woman and a man, both hard-working, fully committed and broadly experienced. They were also personable and well liked by their subordinates.

The woman was one of the most competent officers, male or female, with whom I have ever worked. In addition to her strong management skills she handled some particularly sensitive operational activities extremely well. For example her management enabled the production of high-quality reports from her branch despite an unusually disparate group of case officers.

The man, fluent in several languages, had extensive denied-area experience and acted as a talented mentor for several of our younger officers. He handled one of the cases, a unilateral effort involving an unusual degree of sensitivity, so well that he enabled me to sleep better at night.

Paris turned out to be every bit as fascinating as Hong Kong, though in different ways, and enjoyable in virtually all respects. The tendency of the working populace to call frequent strikes was a drag, I must admit, but the walk-offs didn't seem to bother the Parisians very much and we got used to them.

As I mentioned, parking was an ever-present problem but I became quite creative in finding places to leave our car. The museums, the restaurants, the parks and just exploring some new part of the city occupied our leisure time.

Our first Christmas in Paris was, despite the logistics required, a family affair. All of the girls flew in and United Airlines must have loved it. So did the girls. They were delighted to spend 10 days in the City of Light.

Our spacious, four-bedroom house easily accommodated everyone for what turned out to be a memorable family get-together. We spent much of the holiday visiting the tourist sights and the museums, and even taking in the weekend flea market. And of course we enjoyed some wonderful meals en masse. The girls visited us several other times while we lived in Paris but we enjoyed the first one particularly.

In January 1993 and shortly after he took office as president, Bill Clinton relieved Robert Gates as Director of Central Intelligence. As Gates's replacement Clinton named R. James Woolsey, Jr., of Tulsa, Oklahoma. He was an experienced Washington bureaucrat and self-styled "Scoop Jackson Democrat" who had served in the Carter, Reagan and H.W. Bush administrations. As he started the job he admonished that although the Soviet Bear was gone, "now we must live in a jungle filled with a bewildering variety of poisonous snakes."

The twelfth man to serve as director during my career took command in early February. Few of us knew much about him and the community's reaction seemed fairly neutral coupled with a wait-and-see attitude.

One morning that winter, as our budget turmoil continued, I arrived at my office to find a large manila envelope sitting on my desk. Addressed to Walter Curley, our ambassador, whose office had forwarded it to me, the envelope contained a stack of documents ostensibly purloined from the files of the Direction Générale de la Sécurité Extérieure, the DGSE, France's equivalent of the CIA.

The documents, which had been altered to make them appear current, outlined a DGSE plan to collect technical and economic information clandestinely in the United States, the United Kingdom and Switzerland. From other information included in the envelope we learned that the same documents, or at least a portion thereof, had been sent to newspapers in the three countries.

Left unclear was whether or not other intelligence services were in possession of the packet—though as soon as the media reports surfaced the services would no doubt be acting on the information. For us the material was old news but that didn't mean it wasn't a potential tar baby—

once entangled it would be difficult to extricate ourselves. We were wary of addressing the problem though we knew we had to do something. We would have to seek the answers to a host of questions as we focused on what steps to take and how to react.

We continued to puzzle over who might have sent the packet and why. Some answers were obvious, some less so. Surely it was a person who disliked the DGSE and wanted to stir up problems for them—a most angry and vindictive individual. The obvious candidate: a member or former member of the French service.

Only from the inside could someone have gained access to documents as sensitive as these. Or, perhaps it was someone who cooperated with a second party to acquire the packet. Exactly what they hoped to accomplish remained unclear.

Our initial cable exchanges with headquarters offered opinions and hypotheses but no conclusions—from either side of the Atlantic. Frankly the stuff puzzled us. Based on the contents of the package we could reconstruct a recent history of DGSE activities in the United States and in Paris itself. But the documents also revealed subtle changes to make them appear current, plus details linking the papers to a specific earlier period.

The reason it was old news was those operations had been compromised and the French agency had already explained and clarified its actions to one of my predecessors. That involved some sensitive and delicate conversations, after which an understanding had been reached.

In short, the earlier issue had been resolved. So why leak to us now in Paris as well as to the British, the Swiss and the media? The obvious answer was someone wanted to reopen an old wound for the DGSE and pour salt into it.

It worked. We expended a lot of energy in the form of consternation and fretting about exactly what to do. No doubt our British and Swiss counterparts were in the same pickle, though we never discussed the issue with them.

The one thing we couldn't do was ignore it; newspaper articles about the documents had appeared in all three countries. The DGSE, the articles claimed, had engaged in practices such as planting listening devices on Air France flights to pick up conversations between businessmen. The media reports didn't generate much follow-up but they must have pleased the perpetrator or perpetrators to see the embarrassment and problems they had caused French intelligence officials.

Soon after we had received the packet I briefed Ambassador Curley; we didn't want him blindsided by the newspaper articles and in any event he needed to know immediately about the disclosures.

Curley deferred to me to decide what action to take with the DGSE and said he would support whatever action I took. Meanwhile our exchanges with headquarters produced an agreement about what to do. I would take a copy of the packet to my French counterparts and dutifully ask for an explanation—the straightforward approach.

The chief of the DGSE was away so I met with his deputy. Putting on the best face possible the deputy told me the documents were way out of date. No such programs were ongoing, he assured me.

I used my game face as well, politely accepting his explanation. Without simply calling him a liar there was little more I could say. We were confident that the French got our message—you've been busted so back off.

The DGSE packet affair and its aftermath raised some interesting points about the nuances emerging in the relationships among Cold War allies and their intelligence services.

On the one hand some of the activities of each service would remain compatible with those of its allies. During the Cold War we had all worked together against the Soviets and their minions. For example such cooperation had driven our joint operation with the GSIS, Belgian military intelligence, to expose a Russian spy in NATO's midst.

On the other hand, absent a common foe, some activities grew decidedly incompatible—even occasionally adversarial—as was the case outlined in the DGSE documents. For many reasons, especially political ones, such incompatibility can cause serious problems between intelligence services that require delicate handling. In these cases discreet discussions became the preferred course of action—hence the chat with my French colleague—to contain the damage and avoid potentially corrosive publicity.

These were the evolving, unwritten rules of the game. But absent the Soviet bloc as the common enemy, some of our allies were putting more emphasis on self-interest as their primary policy driver.

As a result the concept of "friendly" relationships was taking a new tack. Gone was the good guys/bad guys theme that had ruled the Cold War. The new environment demanded a more difficult assessment of which activities should be considered compatible.

If anyone had harbored doubts before, the DGSE episode had driven home the value that many of the Western nations now placed on economic intelligence. Yet the issue wasn't clear cut. We wrestled quite a bit with definitions. What's the difference, for example, between economic intelligence and outright industrial espionage? The answer seemed to be: It depends on who's doing it and who's trying to detect it.

The DGSE documents caused us some aggravation but they contained no real surprises. Information shared by the FBI and our own counterintelligence reporting, much of which had been published in the media, made us well aware of French efforts to conduct industrial spying in the United States.

The French weren't alone in this endeavor. Any nation, friend or foe, is bound to be seeking cutting-edge technology the easy way: by stealing it. The obvious place to look is the United States, the world's leader in research and development. Many countries continue to do just that.

29. Blood on the Floor

PARIS 1993–1995

In late spring 1993 the embassy staff was preparing to receive the new ambassador. Bill Clinton had formally requested Walter Curley's resignation. In his place—for a post widely considered to be one of the plums of Europe—he named Pamela Harriman, the world-famous socialite, Democrat fundraiser, former wife of Winston Churchill's son and widow of Averell Harriman.

I really never knew what to expect from Clinton but this choice took me by surprise. I had heard her name mentioned during the speculation period but I didn't take it seriously. I doubted she could handle the diplomatic chores in a country as important as France.

When I learned about the choice I fretted about Harriman's ability to absorb sensitive briefings and render sound judgments. But fortunately my doubts and concerns soon evaporated.

Along with Avis Bohlen, the deputy chief of mission, and several embassy counselors, I met Ambassador Harriman at Charles de Gaulle Airport. I remember marveling at the time at how bright and attractive she looked, at age 72, after an overnight flight from Washington.

After some brief introductions her new subordinates whisked her away to the ambassador's residence on Rue St. Honoré, just behind the embassy.

Our first professional meeting occurred a few days later when she invited me to her office to discuss my section's activities and programs.

That conversation involved just the two of us because some of the material was "Ambassador Only."

I was comprehensive and candid, and she surprised me with the depth of her understanding. But at the time I concluded that she had been well briefed at headquarters. I wasn't ready to credit her for being an unusually smart and savvy individual—that would come soon enough.

The session went well despite my nagging concerns. I was impressed by her easy manner and seemingly sincere interest in intelligence matters. I later told Charlie D. that I liked her, but he continued to harbor doubts.

Before I left I suggested that I brief her periodically on selected intelligence that, from my understanding of current priorities, would be of interest. She liked the idea and accepted, asking that Bohlen be included in the briefings.

That posed no problem for me. I had developed a high regard for Avis's deep knowledge of France and for her professionalism. We decided on twice-weekly sessions and Harriman proceeded to build them into her schedule. That pleased me for several reasons.

The briefings gave me regular contact with the ambassador. That allowed me to deepen her understanding of the reports we were receiving from outside of France. I briefed her on our own reporting as well as sensitive communications from other places. The exchanges worked well. I kept her regularly informed about our efforts and she conveyed the issues she considered most important.

As the briefings became routine I enlisted some help. One of our staffers, a senior analyst from the Directorate of Intelligence, each day systematically reviewed all clandestinely acquired intelligence and certain items for the ambassador's attention. He began accompanying me and eventually gave the briefings. The whole situation became advantageous. The analyst provided raw intelligence but because of his background Ambassador Harriman also received the benefit of his insights.

I benefited as well. Although I tried to keep my schedule clear for these briefings sometimes I couldn't attend. But the briefings continued regularly because our senior analyst could ably carry on. When I could attend I consistently enjoyed them because they gave me the opportunity to get to know Pamela Harriman, whom I came to regard as a talented and charming woman.

I never got to the "Hi Pamela" stage, which would have been unacceptably informal, but we did become good friends and we each appreciated the other's abilities. I particularly enjoyed the occasions when she would let her hair down, so to speak, and render candid views about individuals or problems. She pulled no punches.

"[So and so] is a lightweight jerk," she would say. Or, "That guy (usually a politician) simply has no balls."

I almost always agreed with her assessments and noted that she didn't spare members of the administration. I never asked her about it—another unacceptable informality—but I couldn't understand her prominence as a Democrat or her support for President Clinton. Reams have been written about him so there's no point airing my own criticism.

During her tenure as ambassador, Pamela Harriman was liked and respected by the staff; the same was true among the French. They enjoyed her spicy and intriguing background—her romantic experience was legendary. She spoke the language fluently. She was attractive, intelligent and charming. As a result France accepted her with open arms, and despite my initial misgivings I found her to be effective.

Harriman once referred to the dominance of senior female officers in the embassy's State Department contingent as her "all-girl band." But I was never sure whether she liked or disliked the situation. With few exceptions senior State officers in the embassy and each of the three consulates general, in Bordeaux, Marseilles and Strasbourg, were women. Most thought this was the result of a class action suit against the department in the early 1980s.

As I understood it, female employees had launched the suit to protest the glass ceiling. The settlement afforded females preferential treatment in assignments and rank, such as the highly sought-after slots in France.

As had been the case in previous tours—and indeed as it continues to this day—terror groups seemed to be simmering all over. But back then terrorist activity tended to spike in response to some political event or issue.

For example the Algerian military annulled the country's parliamentary elections in 1991 after the Islamic Salvation Front won a majority. In response, militant Islamic groups launched a deadly wave of assassinations and terror attacks, which under Al-Qaeda in the Islamic Maghreb continues to this day.

The trouble in Algeria quickly spread to French soil. Because U.S. policy opposed the terrorism in Algeria the agency found itself in the position of supporting, in any way we could, the French efforts to combat Algerian militants.

Part of that effort required, and continues to require, immense patience. For each terror incident the allied intelligence and security services collect and share disparate bits of information, sometimes obtained via an outside party. Often one of those bits has provided the key to bringing a given terrorist to justice. But the files stay open until all those responsible for a specific attack have been hunted down.

Now, even decades later, we have not forgotten Dick Welch's or Bill Buckley's murderers. One day we will find them.

Case in point: The Direction de la Surveillance du Territoire, the DST, France's equivalent of the FBI, had obtained from a friendly service a piece of information concerning the whereabouts of Carlos the Jackal, the infamous international terrorist who had been on the run for many years.

Among many other murderous attacks Carlos had killed three members of the DST. Naturally my French compatriots were determined to bring Carlos to justice. Given my position as Paris chief I was able to monitor closely the effort to apprehend the Jackal.

Despite doubts by the French, the friendly service remained confident of its information. Digging even deeper, within weeks it provided the French information pinpointing where Carlos had gone into hiding: Khartoum, Sudan. Having been forced out of several other Arab countries the Jackal had sought Khartoum's relative oblivion. This time the data really rang the French bell and they eagerly set up what had become an extremely promising operation.

Close cooperation ensued, including frequent meetings and exchanges of information.

Rémy Philippe—not his true name—a highly respected and

professional DST senior officer, led the effort. France would spare no resources to capture the murderer of the French officers, he made clear. A quiet, unflappable man who exuded confidence and competence, as a young military officer Philippe had served with reconnaissance units in Algeria during the latter stages of the French-Algerian War.

I clearly detected his inner toughness. He had accumulated decades of experience dealing with Middle Eastern affairs and he was a walking encyclopedia on terrorists, their supporters and their collaborators.

During the operation Philippe worked constantly to sift through the minutiae within the intelligence stream. He enjoyed high points when the effort seemed poised to snatch Carlos, and he suffered deep lows when the chase encountered false leads and dead ends. But he never gave up and he urged colleagues and allies to persist as well.

For example three months into the investigation the noose appeared to be tightening around Carlos. Philippe's team had obtained information that their quarry would be traveling to a North African city in two days. He notified cooperative authorities in that city immediately and they devised a plan to intercept the Jackal at the airport. A determined effort turned up nothing; the report had been based on inaccurate information.

Two weeks later Philippe received a similar tip. Despite some questions about the source's access he decided that couldn't afford *not* to act. Again colleagues were mobilized and again they waited at the designated city's airport.

The result: another no-show.

The disappointments seemed to make Philippe even more determined. He instinctively knew he was on the verge of capturing Carlos and he wasn't about to give up. He convened more planning sessions, each carefully evaluating possible actions and bearing in mind the political and operational realities.

Would political and diplomatic pressure carry the day?

Should they attempt a covert, paramilitary operation to snatch Carlos from his hiding place?

In the end, behind-the-scenes diplomatic pressure made the difference. Buttressed by the information they had amassed, the French made a strong case that the Sudanese government finally accepted. They decided they were willing to turn over a has-been terrorist, an infidel who drank excessively and womanized constantly. The two nations arranged a clever and surprisingly simple plan.

It turned out that Carlos was due to undergo a minor surgical procedure to reverse a vasectomy to assuage his new, young Arab wife. After the surgery, while Carlos was still under sedation, he was strapped to a gurney, transported to the airport, and turned over to the French.

Reportedly Carlos at first was terrified that his captors were Israelis—if so his punishment would have been swift and severe. But after a long flight, during which not a word was spoken, he finally heard the pilot communicating with the control tower in French. He must have heaved a sigh of relief to realize he wasn't in Israeli hands.

France does not allow the death penalty, and it took almost five years to bring Carlos to trial. But the court sentenced him to life in prison. That is where he remains and I fervently hope that is where he will stay.

In these chapters I've tried to illustrate the dual-sided nature of being a senior operations officer. We move between two worlds, one filled with the dangers and challenges of protecting our country and the other composed of the same tasks and problems besetting any large bureaucracy.

But sometimes those two worlds can collide, particularly when they pertain to personnel matters. I'll explain shortly but first I want to mention three troublesome cases our office experienced during my tenure in Paris.

Shortly after my arrival headquarters assigned a highly regarded minority woman to our office. A former Marine Corps officer and an attorney, she had amassed impressive credentials back at Langley. As a result she bagged Paris as her first field tour. I assessed her record and based on discussions about her with my deputy and both branch chiefs we agreed that in deference to her relative inexperience we would assign her a lighter workload.

About six months later her branch chief began expressing concerns about the quality and quantity of her performance. After more discussion we decided to give her extra time to grow accustomed to the job. The branch chief also began counseling her and working more closely with her.

Another six months went by and the problem grew worse. For

example her French remained weak and she had done nothing to improve it; likewise her writing skills, which resulted in poor reports. Yet we hadn't increased her workload and her number of hours of work per day stayed far below the norm. We then moved her to another branch hoping for a spurt of interest and product.

Her new branch chief, also a woman, talked heart-to-heart with her and encouraged her to show her stuff—get out into the city and make contacts—and demonstrate some interest in and ability to be an operations officer. The deputy also talked with her; so did I.

More time passed and still she showed no improvement. She took umbrage at comments in her Personnel Appraisal Report that cited inadequacies in her work. She also alleged that her branch chief was showing favoritism and discrimination. Increasingly she carped and complained about management in general. Our standards were too high, she contended at one point.

We never succeeded in our efforts to change her and things went from bad to worse. Everyone knew about the problem—and if they didn't she told them—because her relationship with management had veered so far from the norm. The situation was sad and frustrating because we had expended considerable effort trying to help her.

In the end we couldn't escape the conclusion that for whatever reason this person remained unwilling to work through her situation. She was producing a woefully inadequate return for the position she occupied. We sent her home.

The second case, also involving a female officer, had been simmering for several years before I arrived in Paris. Experienced in field operations she was intelligent and competent. She also was highly regarded for the excellent work she did in her cover capacity.

For reasons that never became clear to me, however, she had grown increasingly critical of the agency and the tasks we were asking her to perform. Her husband, also an operations officer specializing in Central Asia—but in fact a closet academic—likewise was a frequent critic of the agency. He resigned about a year after my arrival when he found other employment. We learned that our officer was also seeking employment elsewhere but she never admitted it.

Needless to say, neither side of this couple added much to morale. They were endlessly critical of headquarters and field decisions alike, and they expressed jealousy of officers who had moved ahead of them in grade. She alleged favoritism within her branch, even though her appraisal reports consistently reflected the high quality of her work and reporting.

I concluded that she would have been far happier, and probably even more productive, if she had worked for the State Department instead of the agency. Finally she resigned but not without having been a real burr under our collective saddle.

The third instance involved a male officer in his early 30s who was married and had several children. He'd served a previous tour in the Soviet Union and considered himself an exceptional operations officer.

The problem was that his strengths lay in the technical field, not in operational tradecraft where he was no better than average. Above all an ops officer must develop and recruit sources of information that can satisfy the requirements of the intelligence community. He had done none of that at his previous post.

Moreover this individual didn't even realize how much he disliked the whole idea of recruiting agents. He had decided that his evenings and weekends must be his own and essentially never worked during those times no matter what. That conceit made him useless for many of our most important activities, meaning one of our key ops slots was entirely unproductive.

No amount of explanation, cajoling or even direct orders could dissuade him; he would handle only established cases. He was good at that but it was only half of his job. He was likeable and pleasant enough but his duties were simply more than he chose to handle.

After he finished his tour he resigned from the agency and began a 9-to-5 job in the Washington area—involving technical matters.

There's a lesson from these cases for station and headquarters chiefs alike. It's analogous to the way our bomber pilots used to train in World War II. They strove to fly in tight formations, as tight as the pilots could manage them. That way the bomber gun crews could concentrate their fire on enemy aircraft, greatly improving their defenses and discouraging fighter pilots from venturing too close.

The tactic worked—as long as everyone stayed with it. But if a pilot drifted out of position he weakened the formation and endangered his aircraft and everyone else's. In our tradecraft, when an individual officer isn't pulling his or her weight, the quality of the whole effort suffers.

There can be many reasons for personnel problems such as the three I've mentioned. One I can think of is weakness in our rating system. We become unwilling to provide absolutely candid assessments. Officers responsible for rating a colleague or staff member become reluctant to render honest evaluations of performance.

It was why, when I ran the CMS, I had instituted the "Areas for Improvement" category in the Personnel Appraisal Reports.

It's human nature. Fearing a face-to-face confrontation, an officer fails to note problems or shortcomings. But in doing so, unintentionally or not the officer ends up hiding a colleague's or an employee's flaws and weaknesses from the rest of us, and we remain unaware that someone among us can't hold up his or her position in formation.

Performance isn't always the issue. Sometimes an individual just doesn't belong in a field position or perhaps in the agency at all. In such instances our screening mechanisms have failed.

I wish I could offer simple and quick solutions to these problems but I can't. They've been with us since the beginning and no doubt they'll remain to vex future chiefs. But in our business it's imperative to identify and deal with personnel problems as soon as possible and never to consider them trivial matters. As you will see, so much of what we do depends on judging our people correctly and dealing with problems as soon as they arise.

On February 22, 1994, we received a cable from headquarters that verified the newspaper headlines popping up all over Europe. The FBI had arrested Aldrich Ames, one of our officers, on charges of espionage and treason.

The revelation hit us all with great force. A traitor in our midst, inside the clandestine service, had been all but unthinkable. Now it was a reality and it involved someone not only born and raised in the United States but also the son of a career CIA officer. The grim truth was that Ames had cost us dearly, in terms of both intelligence treasure and, more tragically, the lives of some of our agents.

As our internal investigation unfolded it turned out that Ames had been showing disturbing signs for a long time. After a less-than-satisfactory first assignment overseas—he showed a reluctance to contact and recruit agents—Ames returned to headquarters in the early 1970s. There his appraisals improved greatly and he seemed to settle down, but he was cited for excessive drinking and for a couple of careless security breaches. Then on his next assignment, to Mexico City, Ames raised more red flags, including extramarital affairs and one very public display of drunkenness.

The real trouble began in the mid-1980s when Ames conducted a sanctioned effort to sell bogus information to the Soviets at their embassy in Washington. He succeeded. But instead of continuing in that vein, Ames began selling, for large sums, genuine information. He provided details about our counterintelligence activities and he began identifying important Soviet assets.

When some of our operations became compromised, and when our assets started drying up—or disappearing—the clandestine service began suspecting it had suffered a serious penetration. I was in Brussels at the time and we likewise had developed growing concerns about Soviet ops.

Those suspicions resulted in several years of tenacious counterintelligence work, much of it in cooperation with the FBI. Ultimately Ames was uncovered. Convicted in a federal court he was sentenced to life in prison. Many of us thought the death penalty, which his treachery had caused for several of our agents, would have been more just.

It turned out that Ames's drinking problem had continued unabated through his career. So did the womanizing. Soon after the first Soviet caper, Ames began spending far above his means, on his home in Arlington, on his cars, and on his own and his second wife's clothing.

That behavior jumped out at investigators as the clandestine service began looking at the losses we were encountering in our Soviet program. They identified Ames as a prime suspect but privacy laws limited how deeply the investigators could probe the source of his finances. By the time he was arrested and questioned, and by his own admission, Ames had exposed every agency asset and operation he knew about.

Director Woolsey received the results of the investigation report in mid-summer. Though he reprimanded 11 people, including Ted Price, his DDO, he fired no one. "Sorry, that's not my way," Woolsey said in a headline-making statement in September.

Predictably, his words made Congress furious. Legislators had wanted to see "blood on the floor" and there were even some within the agency who agreed. I did not.

Knowing the extent of the efforts that had been undertaken, and aware of the limitations that had to be overcome, I was satisfied with Woolsey's "punishment" within the agency. Still, in December, buckling under the prevailing view that he had badly mishandled the Ames affair, Woolsey resigned.

Fortunately, 1994 also contained a major highlight. That year France prepared to commemorate the 50th anniversary of the D-Day landings at Normandy on June 6. Part of the commemoration would include a visit by President Clinton. My office helped with the security arrangements.

The staff and I had begun meeting with the Secret Service early in the year to discuss security concerns, which would eventually involve more than a dozen of our officers. The meetings went well and so did Clinton's visit—so well, in fact, that after the event the embassy threw a "wheels up" party celebrating the success.

More commemorations followed. The embassy's military attaché office, which also had been heavily involved in the president's visit, began attending events in many of the cities and towns liberated by the Allies as they had swept across France after the Normandy landings. For months the office's personnel attended event after event, giving speeches and presenting our colors. As prickly as our relations with the French could be from time to time, on these occasions they showed genuine gratitude for the sacrifices made by American GIs to free their country from the Nazis.

I became involved in one such event with a slightly different twist. It commemorated an operation in southwestern France in March 1944 that had been supported by the Office of Strategic Services, the CIA's predecessor. It involved an effort aimed at support for French Resistance units to gather intelligence about German defenses, and it centered on a man named Alain Griotteray.

I first met Griotteray at his office at *Le Figaro,* where he ran and wrote columns for *Le Figaro Magazine*, a weekly supplement to the French daily newspaper. Then in his mid-70s, he was a dynamic and impressive man who had been involved in the national political scene for decades and was well known for his insightful commentaries. I liked him right away and my favorable impressions grew to great respect as I learned the details of his exploits.

Griotteray had been a part of the Resistance in the early years of the war. Then he had worked his way out of occupied France and joined the forces headed by General Charles de Gaulle in North Africa. Based in Algeria in 1944, he was picked to return to France for an important mission. He was to contact agent networks and report via radio on German transport and logistics activities in northwestern France—information that would ultimately be of great value to the D-Day planners.

On March 16, a U.S. Army Air Forces B-24 carrying only its crew and Griotteray took off from Algiers headed for a drop zone just west of the town of Pau in the foothills of the Pyrenees. On instructions from the pilot Griotteray positioned himself above a small, open round hole in the plane's belly, ready to drop on command. But overcast skies prevented the pilot from seeing the ground signals from the waiting group of Resistance fighters. He aborted the mission and flew back to Algiers.

The next day they tried again. This time the pilot saw the signals and gave the command. Griotteray dropped through the belly hole into the dark night sky. His main parachute deployed, and the pilot had skillfully positioned the path of his descent, so that he dropped right into the arms of the Resistance team.

The reception group immediately moved Griotteray to a safe house and kept him in seclusion for two days. Then, supplied with forged papers, he made his way north. Eventually, he established the contacts he needed to provide the intelligence the Allies were seeking about German defenses.

As I digested the details of what Griotteray had done, I reflected on the amount of courage, determination and patriotism required for success in such an undertaking—he could've been one of us.

I introduced Griotteray to Ambassador Harriman, and her reaction to him paralleled mine. We discussed plans for a ceremony that would take place at the site near Pau where Griotteray had landed. In recognition and appreciation of the role the OSS had played in training him and transporting him to the drop zone, he invited me and a member of the military attaché's office to attend the ceremony. I accepted with pleasure. The event would be sponsored, we learned, by an organization of Resistance veterans called Orion Reseau, the Orion Network.

The invitations included spouses so Judy accompanied me and we flew to Pau, where we rented a small car. After I figured out how to put the bloody transmission into reverse, which took about 10 minutes, we drove into town. We stayed at a beautiful old hotel in Pau's central district and we met the officer from the military attaché's office and his wife shortly after we checked in.

The next morning we drove for about 30 minutes to the small village near the field where Griotteray had landed. Again I was touched by the warmth of the welcome. One French official after another expressed genuine appreciation for what the United States had done during the war.

The opening ceremony took place at the village church, filled to overflowing with local residents and visitors from Paris. Many people wore vintage uniforms. The local band played badly but loudly and enthusiastically. The organizers had held seats for us and soon after we sat down the event began. Short but emotionally moving, it provoked many memories among those gathered in the church—especially, I'm sure, for Alain Griotteray.

Afterward we were invited to the military base in Pau for a luncheon. It seemed fitting that Pau was and remains the home of France's Ecole des Troupes Aéroportées, which trains its military parachutists. It was a splendid affair and after a great meal the guests assembled by the drop zone next to the dining hall to watch a group of recent recruits demonstrate a combat-training jump.

It had been an exhilarating experience for us and I told Griotteray so as we said our goodbyes. He thanked me for attending and presented me with a medal issued by Orion for the occasion—a memento of an experience I won't forget.

In the aftermath of the Ames affair and Woolsey's resignation the agency essentially remained leaderless—and cowed—for five months. No question the clandestine service had been chastened.

During that time Admiral William Studeman—another one who insisted on being called "Admiral"—the deputy director, did his best to run the agency while President Clinton worked his way through a list of potential Woolsey replacements.

Studeman couldn't hold back the tide. Attacks on the agency multiplied in Congress and the media, creating an increasingly hostile climate. Finally Clinton turned to John Deutch, the deputy secretary of defense and a chemist by trade, to replace Woolsey. Deutch took over on May 10, 1995, clearly a reluctant dragon, and many thought he had accepted the post because he saw it as a stepping stone to bigger and better things.

Who could blame him? For all his shortcomings, on July 14 Clinton presented Studeman with the President's National Security Medal, the highest honor anyone in the intelligence community can receive. About a month later, at Studeman's retirement ceremony—the most elaborate the agency had seen up to then—Deutch gave him the Distinguished Intelligence Medal, the agency's own highest honor.

As had become standard over the years Deutch brought in new senior staff officers with him. As one of his top priorities Deutch made clear he would "rein in" the clandestine service, dismantle the "old-boy network," and change the culture of elitism that had prevailed within the DO.

Across the Atlantic I shuddered at the thought of what was to come.

30. Blown

PARIS AND LANGLEY 1995–1996

As I explained much earlier, what any CIA chief in the field dreads, almost more than anything else, is an operational compromise. Simply defined, a compromise is the discovery of an "incompatible" op—as in incompatible with a diplomatic mission—by the internal service in the country in which you are working. Other than being captured or killed it ranks right up there with the worst things that can happen in an intelligence career.

However it happens, a compromise represents a failure of every effort we make to keep our ops clandestine—unknown to anyone except those with Need to Know. And however hard you try, as chief you can never track it all. You must trust your officers, knowing that the fallout from any compromise tends to collect on the chief's lapels.

As I also explained previously, a unilateral operation is conducted inside a host nation without that nation's knowledge. Sometimes it's a matter of top national security, such as infiltrating a terror group within a country that might be ignoring or tolerating the group's activities. Other times it can be something that serves the needs of policymakers, whether in the executive branch—at the direction of the president or his cabinet—or within the agency itself.

Either way, whenever we're ordered to conduct a unilateral operation, we conduct it expressly at the behest of our superiors and our government—headquarters has sanctioned it.

Naturally such activity entails risk, though intelligence professionals regard it as an occupational hazard. The risk is obvious: Even a friendly host government can react most unpleasantly if it detects such an operation.

In Paris, the last overseas posting of my career, I learned firsthand and most painfully the consequences of a compromise.

The trouble began in January 1995 when the French Minister of Interior met with Ambassador Harriman and informed her that the activities of several U.S. diplomats were "unacceptable" and had to stop. The minister, Charles Pasqua, produced photographs—none of which he would relinquish—to support his contention. He also presented a list of three of our officers whose activities he deemed objectionable.

Pasqua said he would not declare the officers persona non grata, meaning they would not be formally expelled from the country. Nevertheless, he told Harriman, the French government wanted them to leave—voluntarily and soon.

It wasn't a long meeting and Harriman, who had been taken by surprise, found herself in a rare and awkward position. She had never dealt with such a situation, and she wasn't sure what to do or what would happen next. But she did know who could tell her.

When the proverbial stuff hit the fan I was in Rome on agency business.

My new deputy, Ed, called me with a blunt message.

"You'd better come home right now."

It was evening and all I could do was catch the first flight after I got to Fiumicino Airport. It was the only time in my life that I paid a million of anything for anything. I could not get a seat in coach so I had to fly first class—at 1.2 million lira.

As soon as I arrived in Paris I met with the staff to determine what the hell had happened. Based on the information we could piece together, one of our agents had been doubled. The Direction de la Surveillance du Territoire had discovered a French citizen working for us. They then clandestinely recruited the individual to work for them to expose the agency officer or officers handling the case. They also photographed the interactions—the pictures Pasqua had displayed to Ambassador Harriman.

Here's the rub: This was a dormant operation. Several of our officers indeed had been working with the French agent on matters the French government considered sensitive. But the meetings had occurred over a year earlier. We might have upgraded the agent's activity, but we hadn't heard from or seen him over that one-year period, so we considered the case terminated. It turned out that as soon as the DST had collected all of the necessary information about our activities with the agent they ordered him to break off contact. He complied.

At some point—we never learned when or why—Pasqua's office had gotten wind of the matter and chose that January meeting to confront Ambassador Harriman with the evidence, including the names of the three agency individuals involved.

I briefed the ambassador on what we knew. I explained the history of the operation and assured her that the activity had long been ended. She fully understood.

"We will simply have to weather the storm," she told me.

Next I cabled headquarters to bring them up to speed. Someone would need to go to Capitol Hill and inform the oversight committees that one of our ops had been compromised—"blown" in our jargon.

At first, legislators and their staffs alike took the news in stride, more or less indicating that they accepted the need for such efforts. They made comments such as, "Go get those French," "No problem," "We're backing you up," and "Don't worry, it will pass."

There was the question of how to deal with the DST, but the DST resolved it. In effect they informed me that I could no longer act in an official capacity with them—that they were ending all interactions and communications with me.

The DST's action fell within the ballpark. It was maybe a little harsher than our response to the earlier episode under Walter Curley's tenure, in which we learned about the Direction Générale de la Sécurité Extérieure's similarly defunct operation to obtain economic intelligence about the United States.

At the time I had informed my French counterparts that we knew about the operation, and we needed to be reassured they had pulled the plug. That's what I expected from the DST, and I regarded their decision as a formality that would eventually be rescinded.

I grew a little more worried, however, when Pasqua summoned Ambassador Harriman to a second meeting, at which he added two names to the list of our people who should promptly depart the country: one other officer—and me. Though it was an irregular move it was still essentially logical that as Paris chief I would be added to the list. We never did understand why they named the other officer.

Would the interior minister now leave it to the services to sort things out?

No such luck. The situation took a sudden and dramatic turn for the worse. Pasqua's office, in an unprecedented move, leaked the DST dossiers on the case to the French press. That precipitated a media firestorm lasting several weeks with details—including my name—emblazoned in newsprint. *Le Monde*, *Le Figaro* and *Aujourd'hui en France*, the largest French dailies, all published sensational articles.

I was basically defenseless. Reporters would contact me and politely ask for comment. I would politely respond that I could not discuss anything about the subject. It was all civilized, but it didn't stop the distortions, conjectures, inaccuracies and outright falsehoods that followed.

All through it the most sympathetic entity was the DGSE. I even dined with two DGSE officers one night and they expressed dismay about the whole matter. They regarded it as a minor infraction—particularly because we knew they were engaging in the same type of economic intelligence gathering against us.

"We didn't do this, Dick," one of the officers assured me. "We think this is a bad way to do things. We're embarrassed by it."

In effect they told me they were frustrated about the way the incident had been handled, particularly in light of the help my office had given France not very long ago in the capture of Carlos the Jackal.

We could only guess why the interior minister had chosen this particular time to confront us.

Pasqua, whose sometimes scurrilous political activities had earned him the nickname "Old Fox," was engaged with his Gaullist party in an intense primary election campaign. His history of alleged misdeeds was lengthy even then—enough to make our own worst politicians look like choirboys. As was often the case he was under investigation, this time for illegal wiretap operations against his opponents. He faced fierce criticism for it in the national media.

We suspected, as did his opponents, that he had exploited a weak link in our security chain as a diversionary tactic—he wanted to redirect the heat away from himself.

It made sense. If the French had wanted to make more than political hay with the case, Alain Juppe—the foreign minister and a political rival of Pasqua's—would have been the one to meet with Ambassador Harriman. We were all accredited through the Foreign Ministry and they had the authority to declare us persona non grata.

Pasqua's involvement had to be purely political.

Given the exposure of our operation against an allied country, either the agency or the Hill, or both—dealing with this from overseas I was never sure which—concluded that the matter needed to be investigated. Suddenly concerns arose about possible agency misconduct. What had been considered understandable at the beginning somehow changed in the light of media coverage.

The Inspector General at the time, who had worked briefly and much earlier as an operations officer, appointed a team to carry out the investigation instead of deferring on the matter. This was unheard of. An operational compromise is by definition a DO concern. If it does not involve fraud, malfeasance or corruption, aspects which would throw it into the IG's bailiwick, then it should be and always had been handled within the directorate.

Another worrisome aspect: Only one member of the IG team had any ops experience at all and it was minimal. None of the others, including the team leader, had worked overseas. It was akin to sending a team of coal miners to investigate a plane crash.

Then Ted Price, the DDO, decided to convene what he called an accountability team, essentially to match the IG's effort. The idea appalled me. I returned briefly to headquarters to argue the point with Price. I made clear to him that as chief I was already accountable. I said we were conducting our internal review in the field, that we would present it to headquarters as soon as we completed it, and that we didn't need another board of inquiry to tell us what we could determine for ourselves.

He overruled me, saying he feared allegations of a cover-up.

A third inquiry added to what would quickly become a circus atmosphere. Convened by the Counterintelligence staff it would investigate exactly the same material as the other two groups. Comprising from five to eight individuals—the number kept changing—the CI team, like their IG counterparts, had few members with ops experience.

For the next several months I spent a great deal of time accommodating the various investigators, who dutifully winged across the Atlantic to interview me and everyone else in the office. All three teams had the same mission and all three teams reached the same conclusion: They could not pinpoint the exact cause of the compromise.

There the similarities ended.

Several of the CI investigators seemed determined to cast a negative spin on us. Whatever they wrote, they demonstrated near-zero objectivity.

It went further than that. Both the team leader and his deputy had professional-oversight ties to the handling officer who was directly involved in the compromise. Yet they seemed oblivious to this flagrant conflict of interest.

Their incompetence astounded me.

The IG team wasn't much better. Like the CI investigators they strayed far afield from the matter under investigation and posed totally unrelated questions. As an example they interviewed every single member of the Paris staff.

They asked a finance officer what he thought about the countersurveillance practices of a particular operations officer—a feckless and inappropriate question.

Another instance: On two occasions I had to explain to the IG team leader what types of cover we employed because she could not understand the concept. I doubt that she ever did. She seemed to be saying that she needed to understand what I was doing so that she could make judgments about how well I was doing it.

What was this individual, who had no clue what went on in an overseas operational situation, doing on a team investigating a compromise?

Eventually the IG and CI teams broadened the scope of their inquiries to include every aspect of our day-to-day activities. This went far beyond their mandate. Worse, it precipitated an unnecessary and severe blow to morale.

Only the three-member accountability team, which included an ops officer with overseas experience, conducted a rational effort. Within a few months they produced a solid and well-reasoned report. They did so by interviewing only the officers involved in the compromise and focusing exclusively on relevant issues. I could quibble with a few of their conclusions but the end product was entirely professional. It would be useful—valuable even—to our senior management and the director.

Meanwhile we had carefully scrutinized the compromise and returned our own results to headquarters. We also examined all of our related operational activities. Media and political frenzy aside it was essential to do so. The case in question involved a relatively minor effort, but we needed to find the flaw that had exposed us because it could endanger other ops.

We arrived at a well-educated guess. The officer who had originally handled the doubled agent had practiced poor tradecraft—poor enough to have compromised herself to any French intelligence officer worth his salt.

At least it wasn't bad *pi.*

I stayed in Paris until May 1995, dealing with the investigation and still trying to run the office. But my days were numbered. With my identity made public and my name still on the Ministry of Interior's list I realized that my effectiveness had likewise been blown.

I stepped down voluntarily, leaving Ed as acting chief and returning to Langley. The office would have to press on in its wounded state.

Soon thereafter I met with the Inspector General. I had few illusions about how the encounter would go but I was determined to raise my concerns. It was not a pleasant experience.

I began by registering dismay at the composition of the team he had assembled. They lacked the competence to do the job, I argued, citing specific examples such as the ones I mentioned. I asked why they had expanded their inquiry to include issues completely unrelated to the compromise.

"We didn't find enough related [information to expose] the compromise," he responded, "So I decided to do a complete investigation of the office."

Excuse me?

"Then you must send a team with the competence to do so," I retorted.

"They are smart people," he said, "and they can do the work."

I thought of contesting both ideas but I kept silent.

Raising an issue I haven't yet mentioned, I told the IG that his team had been colluding with the CI team on the investigation. Both were meeting and sharing the results of their queries, creating the prospect of contaminated and biased conclusions.

That was inappropriate, I asserted.

He agreed on that point and said he would look into it. I don't know if he did but in any event the damage had been done.

Last I asked when the team would complete its investigation and issue its report—they had already been at it for several months.

"Soon," the IG responded. But it was not soon.

I hadn't yet sensed just how politicized the matter had become in the Clinton administration and under Director of Central Intelligence John Deutch. Our new director—my unlucky thirteenth—had already made clear that he wanted to "bring to heel" the old-boy, elitist ethic of the clandestine service.

Also during that period Deutch named David Cohen as DDO. The new arrival had spent most of his career as an intelligence analyst. He had almost no ops experience and had never served overseas.

I thought he lacked the requisite talents and that his appointment was a mistake. Coupled with Deutch's stated intentions, many of us in the DO took Cohen's appointment as an ominous development—the beginning of a "dark age" for the clandestine service.

Driven by that attitude the investigations proceeded in a climate that can only be described as hostile. The office had already completed its inquiry. All the IG and CI teams needed to do at that point was collect our interviews, compare them with their own and with the accountability team's results, and with the DO's standard procedures. Then they could issue their conclusions.

Not even close.

Over the months after my meeting with the Inspector General—and long after the accountability team had concluded its work—the IG and CI team members labored on in fits and starts. They wrote and rewrote drafts, and they interviewed and re-interviewed people, including some at headquarters.

I finally saw the IG report in late February 1996. It was so replete with distortions and inaccuracies I could hardly believe it was about the office I had headed. All of my suspicions about their incompetence had proven true.

Astounding, but the lengthy document covered the compromise in passing—mentioning only once the name of the officer who handled the case and the approximate time period when it had occurred. Instead the report focused on alleged tradecraft weaknesses of selected officers—incredibly, not that of the handling officer.

Then there was the allegation that the office lacked concern for counterintelligence. That one arrived out of the blue. Neither the IG nor the CI team had raised the subject with me at all during my interviews—and it was utterly, demonstrably untrue. As described earlier I initiated over a dozen specific steps in Paris aimed at shoring up our counterintelligence posture.

Moreover, everyone involved in ops at the office knew about the steps we had taken. All the investigators had to do was ask about counterintelligence during the interviews. Yet neither report mentioned a single one of those measures.

Far from deserving criticism my officers should have been commended for their effective tradecraft and counterintelligence measures. Instead the teams made only general allegations against me, such as "he managed his office poorly." Allegations against several other officers were more specific but just as inaccurate.

This was no investigation. I could see clearly that the writers had intended beforehand to heap criticism on the clandestine service—to break "the barons," as they called its senior officers.

More personally it represented an unjustified slam against my professionalism. It hurt deeply.

The distortions and inaccuracies were so egregious that three other officers, equally frustrated by the report, said they wanted to join me in crafting a rebuttal. We all wondered the same thing: After so much time and labor, how could they possibly have gotten so much wrong?

The IG, who had waited over a year for his team to complete its effort, gave us one week to review it and respond.

He was eager to report the results, he told me, though he relented and gave us an additional week. Within that time we prepared a response that refuted item-for-item the IG team's charges and conclusions.

The Inspector General's report, a classified document, reached the seventh floor on March 12, 1996, absent both our rebuttal and the accountability team's conclusions.

It turned out the IG had earlier insisted to Deutch that his report should take precedence over the CI and accountability team inquiries and therefore must be the first one published within the agency. That meant the straightforward and professional effort by the accountability team would not see the light of day until after the skewed and damaging result of the IG investigation.

Damaging it was. The next day an article in *The New York Times* described our "blunders" in attempting to gather economic intelligence and essentially placed me at the top of the story. The writer declared that the "career of one legendary spy is over."

The article didn't quote from the report directly, citing only unnamed "officials familiar with" the document.

Among its many inaccuracies, reflecting the poor quality of the report, the article asserted that I had kept Ambassador Harriman "in the dark about important aspects" of my work. Number one, that's standard procedure in every chief-ambassador relationship. Number two, I had never improperly omitted details about our ops.

Harriman actually wrote Deutch voicing strong support for my handling of "a difficult and sensitive situation." She specifically advised him not to seek a scapegoat for this, by now, highly publicized contretemps.

Deutch disregarded Harriman's advice.

What had I been doing between the time I left Paris and the release of the report? From June 1995 through the rest of the year, and lacking a formal assignment, other than fighting this good fight I helped out as best I could, ending up in of all places the Human Resources Staff, the renamed version of my old shop, the Career Management Staff.

To say the least this period was extremely difficult for me. Emotionally it was almost as bad as my worst days at Walter Reed.

My own directorate treated me like a pariah. I had no real job, and I more or less languished while the Office of the Inspector General and the top brass fiddled with my fate.

I'm not exaggerating about being a pariah. Cohen kept rejecting my requests to see him, claiming he was "too busy" and in any case there was nothing he could do.

From the man who was chief of our entire overseas effort, that was an extraordinary response. It meant he was not even willing to listen. It meant he didn't want to hear what I thought had caused the compromise. He also apparently did not care about how one of his chiefs was being treated. Nor did he care about morale—because what was happening to me did not go unnoticed within the directorate.

By this time I had no doubt Cohen had been miscast, like his boss. I also thought he quickly became cowed by Deutch, who had voiced his intention to "lay one on" the clandestine service. Whatever the cause he displayed precious little backbone.

Another target for criticism was Paul Redmond, the deputy director for counterintelligence, who should have known better. But he also resisted meeting me to discuss the compromise, deferring to the investigators.

After I read the IG report, and its allegations about my lack of concern for CI issues, I insisted on a meeting with Redmond and showed him the list of steps I had taken—a list that clearly refuted the allegations.

"I didn't know that," he said, after reading the list.

This was a comment from the man directly responsible for such matters—it was his *job* to know. He and other senior officers had been shockingly obtuse while their colleagues were being pilloried.

Worst of all was the leader of the CI's investigation team. To be blunt he behaved reprehensibly. He held longstanding, professional-oversight ties to the officer who had been directly linked to the compromise. He should have let someone else handle the matter. Instead he led the investigation and it veered sharply away from anything involving that officer.

The CI staff's report even downplayed the officer's role in the compromise. Like the IG's report the CI document highlighted the erroneous contention that we all lacked sufficient CI awareness—an issue the team leader never discussed with me.

By knowingly acting as he did, he not only skewed the conclusions of his own report but he also tainted those of the IG.

Awful as this affair had become it no longer affected me directly. In January 1996, reaching the end of my patience, I had formally retired from the agency.

My decision presented a problem for Deutch. Not long after the IG report appeared—evidently he hadn't read the accountability team's effort or our rebuttal—he sent me a letter reprimanding me for "poor management standards."

I wrote him a response, making clear that I did not accept the IG's conclusions. I considered the report to be hopelessly flawed, I asserted, and I could not accept his reprimand.

I enclosed his original in the envelope.

In retrospect I can understand how the media frenzy would have incited political responses during a particularly bad period for the agency.

We had endured the Aldrich Ames affair. The media had picked up and run with another controversial revelation about a delicate operation in Latin America. There was the continuing push to pare back the entire intelligence community in the wake of the collapse of the Soviet Union. Many stations worldwide were working to comply with the new directive to collect economic intelligence. And for six months the agency had been operating essentially leaderless, between James Woolsey's resignation and John Deutch's installation.

It was like a perfect storm.

In each circumstance we had made our best case and we took our lumps. What I couldn't and still don't understand or accept was how shabbily my colleagues and I were treated by the Inspector General and by my directorate's most senior officers. These people should have known that when they sent us overseas to do this kind of work the compromise hazard remained ever present and many things could trigger it.

Poor tradecraft employed by the handling officer, a brief but a careless moment, a missed clue, an offhanded remark to the wrong person—all can expose and thereby sink an entire operation.

In the most sensitive cases lives are at stake. In the incident I described, the headlines notwithstanding, our pride took more of a beating than anything else. This was not the first compromise nor would it be the last. But in every such security breach our most important task is to find the source of the problem and prevent it from reoccurring.

When headquarters approved our operation and it was ultimately compromised, instead of accomplishing that task they left us hanging in the wind. More shameful, some of our own helped to hang us out there. Our self-correction process ran amok.

One of my colleagues summed up the episode and our collective feelings perfectly when she wrote:

> With the clarity of retrospection, we would like to offer our thoughts on the lessons learned from the operational compromise now being investigated. Central to our reflection on the topic is the premise that *preventing all future compromises is impossible.* No amount of process, oversight, or structural reconfiguration will result in risk-free operations, especially those directed at a sophisticated host country target. By their very nature, clandestine operations are a continual process of compromise between risk and gain. The officer and the station conducting those operations are called upon daily to take calculated risks based on imperfect knowledge. At best, these are judgments, and while guidance from headquarters or more senior officers is necessary and welcome, it is not possible to establish "rules" to cover every contingency. And while no stint of effort to mitigate those risks can be tolerated, it must be expected that occasionally the officer/

> station will misjudge. However, for any operation to have a chance of success, the case officer and the station must be encouraged to make those risk-versus-gain judgments—with the possibility of getting it wrong—and know that *absent malfeasance or incompetence, the Directorate of Operations and the agency will support their efforts when a compromise occurs.* (Emphases mine.)

In September 1996 headquarters and Director Deutch presented me with the Distinguished Intelligence Medal, the agency's highest award. Apparently and within the confines of Langley my former superiors had decided to bestow on me what they could not bring themselves to state publicly: recognition of my service and an apology for their extreme mismanagement of the Paris case.

Among those in the audience was Dr. Tim Miller, the dedicated reconstructive surgeon who had defied the odds and saved my life after the Congo experience, allowing me to continue and ultimately complete my career. I was blind during the time he had so skillfully worked on me at Brooke but he was a most welcome sight here.

To a packed house Director Deutch spoke in glowing terms about my contributions to the agency, making only scant, backhanded and non-critical references to the compromise.

In my speech I expressed gratitude for the honor. I made some other remarks but I was affected by the emotions I was feeling and could only convey a portion of them. The audience's response was warm and strongly supportive and I was deeply moved.

I didn't understand it then but I do now. I suffered two traumatic ordeals in the service of my country, one physical and the other emotional. Both symbolized the risk I had accepted when I first walked through the doors of the old headquarters building as a new hire and JOT candidate 35 years earlier.

I crashed in the Congo but I survived. I could have just as easily been flying in the other T-28 with Juan Tunon, whose remains were never found. I also could have been flying with Tom Dieffenbach, the "eleventh man," whose body we had to abandon on a mountaintop in Laos. I could have been riding with Big Bill Wyrozemski when his Land Rover collided with the Congolese Army truck. I could have died in a helicopter instead of Mike Deuel, Judy's first husband. I could have been appointed chief in Beirut instead of Bill Buckley, whom Hezbollah kidnapped, held hostage, and tortured until he died. And I could have been assassinated in Athens instead of Dick Welch.

Like these brave and good men I took risks to do my job. My ordeals, though painful, were less severe. But even if the worst had happened I would have understood, because this was the craft we chose.

I am proud to have served with them.

EPILOGUE

A Half Century Later

2011

It has now been 50 years since I joined the Central Intelligence Agency and 15 years since I retired. I have learned many things during that time, but two of them stand above all. One is that the job I performed for most of my career—as the man on the street, the one who identifies, develops, and where possible recruits agents in the service of the United States government—remains the most crucial task the agency performs.

The other is how much the world in which we operate has changed.

Back in 1961, I never suspected that anyone—government, media or citizen—would question the need for the agency or criticize its work. After all, I served with colleagues who dedicated themselves to our craft in the service of the country. They worked tirelessly, sometimes in mortal peril, to preserve democracy and defeat America's enemies. Who could object to such a mission?

Experience taught me just how naïve that assumption was.

The reason is politics. As I have described, even the most serious endeavors of our government cannot be removed from political influence. Through the Vietnam War, Watergate and its aftermath, the Iran-Contra affair, and the quest to cash in the peace dividend provided by the end of the Cold War, politics continually pulled the agency in one direction or another.

Our elected and appointed officials weren't the only ones doing the yanking. The news media aided and abetted them in exploiting those momentous events. The media often treated the agency—particularly the clandestine service—with suspicion and outright hostility. They published or produced so many biased and distorted reports about CIA activities conducted under presidential order that I lost count.

I also can't remember how many times I saw the phrase "intelligence failure" associated with a news report or analysis—and how many times it was applied erroneously.

It isn't my purpose to dredge up those unfortunate instances. What I do want to do, here in May 2011, nearly a decade after the horrendous attacks of 9/11 and only a couple of weeks after the United States finally tracked down and killed Osama bin Laden, is to make a few, brief points concerning matters that are vital for our country and our future.

First and most urgent, amid much of the controversy surrounding the operation to get bin Laden, including debate over the methods used to gather intelligence about his hiding place, there has been unprecedented media exposure of the agency's sources and methods. Unnamed officials have been leaking classified details, which even within the CIA would normally be closely guarded under the Need to Know concept.

Let me be blunt. This kind of irresponsible disclosure is appalling. It can jeopardize the effective functioning of the agency, the security of future operations and the lives of intelligence officers. It needs to be stopped and if necessary the leakers prosecuted.

Second, involving ongoing policy, the position of Director of National Intelligence, which blanketed the agency under an extra layer of bureaucracy, has only complicated its efforts to run operations abroad.

Clearly the DNI has emerged as a superfluous entity—the position adds nothing of real value to our counterterrorism or intelligence-gathering efforts. Five different men have served in the position's first six years, and not one of them has been able to take the reins with a firm, steady hand. We should eliminate the job.

I harbor similar thoughts about the Department of Homeland Security. This huge and growing mass of bureaucrats—well-intentioned though they may be—is weighing down the agencies it has absorbed and inhibiting the effectiveness they used to demonstrate individually.

Third—and this is good news—the Federal Bureau of Investigation has risen to the challenge of fighting international terror in the post-9/11 world. Reactive and ill-equipped no more, the FBI has developed a formidable intelligence arm and has reformed its culture in many important respects.

Yes, the bureau still chases bank robbers, the mob and many other versions of domestic criminals, collecting evidence and making arrests. Essential tasks all, but today's FBI also displays a fearsome counterterrorism capability that has foiled many plots against our citizens.

The FBI's new strength should please every American. The bureau and the clandestine service cooperate extensively, and the roots of that cooperation go back to when I was building the agency's Counter Terrorism Group. We provided much of their initial training, and the bureau people proved to be very quick learners.

Personally I'm gratified to see that the grumbling has evaporated about establishing a new federal agency equivalent to Britain's MI5, which handles that country's internal security. The FBI has shown it can do the job.

Fourth, the Patriot Act, which Congress passed and President George W. Bush signed within three months of 9/11, has greatly strengthened all of our intelligence and security agencies. I was very glad to see Congress and President Barack Obama agree to a four-year extension, and I hope that in the future the law will be extended indefinitely.

The country needs it. We live in a period that future historians might describe as an intercontinental religious conflict. Bin Laden may be dead but radical Islamists continue to lash out at the rest of the world—particularly the West—as well as their fellow Muslims. They seek a return to the time when Islam was spreading across the Middle East, the Asian subcontinent, Africa and eventually Europe, attracting believers, vanquishing nonbelievers, and attempting to establish a global caliphate.

The militants have set their sights on the United States as well. They have launched many attacks against us over the past two decades, but 9/11 was by far the worst. Dealing with the continuing jihad—using their word—means more tumultuous times ahead. I fear that a renewed peaceable age for America lies far in the future.

Ironic, but attaining that coveted status will depend largely on the intelligence community's ability to accurately report on the struggle *within* Islam, where a desperate fight for dominance is under way. On one side, groups such as al-Qaeda, Hamas, Hezbollah and other murderous extremists are plotting to take over every Muslim country. On the other side stand the moderates—to the extent such a term can be used—those brave souls who risk death at every turn to coexist with democracy and secularism.

We must support and cooperate with those moderate Muslim leaders and governments willing to seek common ground. If they fail, the world's prospects for peace in the 21st century will be dim indeed.

Winning this fight is essential, no less so than was winning World War II and the Cold War. It won't be easy and it could take many more years. Anger toward and distrust of the United States abound despite our repeated efforts—in Kuwait, Kosovo, Afghanistan and Iraq—to liberate Muslims from tyranny. Millions of them hate us even though we have spilled our blood for them.

Yet we have no choice but to persevere.

We could argue the pros and cons of President George H.W. Bush's decision to force Saddam Hussein's army out of Kuwait in 1991. We could question George W. Bush's military operations to rout al-Qaeda and the Taliban from Afghanistan in 2001 and his invasion of Iraq in 2003. Likewise we could cast doubts about the wisdom of Barack Obama's continuing campaign in Afghanistan and his strike at Muammar Gaddafi in Libya in 2011. But make no mistake; the targets of those military actions were men whose capacity for brutality and desire to expand their own power knew no bounds.

They are the true enemies of Muslims.

I hope that in the wake of bin Laden's demise we can make progress using diplomacy, compromise and reason, but I know we almost certainly will need more covert and military actions to combat the threat. Whatever the challenge, however, the Central Intelligence Agency, particularly the National Clandestine Service, will be directly involved, and they will need top-notch men and women more than ever. The NCS is our first line of defense—the tip of the spear—in the age of Islamic terrorism.

We saw no clearer evidence of this than in the recent culmination of our 10-year effort to find bin Laden and bring him to quick justice. Our perennial but friendly rivals, those magnificent Navy SEALs, penetrated his compound in Abbottabad, Pakistan, and summarily ended his reign of terror. The media focused on the near-flawless efforts of the SEALs but it was the NCS that obtained and provided the essential pieces of intelligence.

Which brings me to my two parting points; bear with me.

Nearly 20 years ago the White House, under President Bill Clinton, and Congress eagerly pursued the peace dividend as an opportunity to cut appropriations for the military and the intelligence community in the wake of the Soviet Union's collapse.

That occasion of great relief also ushered in a critical miscalculation.

In their zeal to cut spending, Congress and the executive branch forgot that during the previous four decades the CIA had been the go-to organization for the country's most sensitive and dangerous tasks. When the chips were down the government called on the agency, the agency called on the clandestine service, and the clandestine service did its utmost to fulfill the mission.

Fortunately the CIA was full of professionals with that kind of ability—time after time they did what had to be done. But even the most capable people can't do the impossible if their hands are tied.

I wrote this book to help readers understand what we in the clandestine service did and what role we served for the federal government and the American people. We performed many functions, but in all cases we did *only* what the President of the United States ordered us to do.

Now the bulk of those orders consists of preventing and defeating attacks against this country, something that will depend to a huge degree on the quality of intelligence we can gather, on exposing the plans and intentions of our enemies, and when necessary pinpointing their locations.

What happened in America on 9/11 illustrates the consequences when the agency is inhibited from pursuing its primary mission; when it is denied the funding—and consequently the tools—needed to function at peak effectiveness.

In the mid-1990s we as a nation allowed the CIA's core resources to languish. Budget and personnel cuts rendered the Directorate of Operations far below its previous strength. We lacked the capabilities in language and other skills required to monitor and penetrate al-Qaeda. Regulations compounded the weaknesses by preventing us from cooperating with the FBI and the other security services.

Today, facing unprecedented budget deficits, Congress and the administration once again may be tempted to trim funding for clandestine activities. After all, they might argue, getting bin Laden essentially cut the head off the snake.

I strongly advise against it. If we repeat those mistakes we will risk another 9/11-like disaster, possibly something even greater in damage and scope.

Point two concerns a limitation in intelligence gathering that figures to be with us for a long time. Back when the Soviet Union and Communist China constituted our primary targets, it was, relatively speaking, easy to penetrate them both. The U.S.S.R. was a vast country with a large population of subjugated people, many of whom were willing to help bring down the Evil Empire for patriotic reasons. Many others were at least open to supplementing their meager incomes in exchange for useful information. The same with China. In both cases we had developed a large contingent of excellent Russian and Chinese speakers to locate, contact, and recruit agents.

Not so the terror groups. In the early years of fighting them we hadn't cultivated nearly enough people fluent in Arabic, Farsi, Urdu and other languages. But even that was secondary. The main stumbling block—and it was formidable—was that the terrorists existed in tightly knit networks whose members were well known to one another. Recruiting an individual from within one of those cabals was and continues to be extremely difficult.

Nevertheless we managed during the '90s to score some victories, particularly against al-Qaeda. On more than one occasion we accumulated enough intelligence to capture or kill the group's leaders. Had the president done so then we might have been able to prevent much of what followed—and bin Laden's rendezvous with destiny might have occurred more than a decade earlier.

It wasn't an intelligence failure; our leaders didn't act, and their lack of political courage and determination not only tied our hands but also cost the lives of God knows how many victims.

This painful reality persists. We may be living in a brand new millennium but the dilemma is the same. On the one hand we have no option. Although some of our methods will continue to evolve, the bedrock premise of clandestine intelligence-gathering remains: We must employ the techniques we used during the Cold War, and we will need just as much patience and persistence now as we needed then. We must continue to recruit agents and potential agents. They are out there and we can find them.

On the other hand, when we do obtain what is called actionable intelligence, our leaders must not flinch at taking decisive action. Killing bin Laden marked a good step in that direction. The agency provided the necessary intelligence and analysis, the SEALs provided the lightning-fast boots on the ground, and the president used them both effectively.

But textbook operations like that are rare. Often our leaders face choices that aren't so clear-cut. I've written about some of the risks and their associated consequences. Injury, death, compromise, all can occur at any time in just about any operation. There's one more choice. It is different from the others but no less an integral part of using people to collect intelligence: We sometimes need to deal with individuals who aren't much better than those we're battling.

This is a difficult and admittedly controversial issue—with no comfortable solutions for a democracy and a free people. We simply can't infiltrate the worst of the worst using only instruments that are pure as the driven snow. Anyone—politician, jurist, journalist or activist—who tells you otherwise either doesn't know about or cannot deal with the type of enemies we face.

Based on my own experiences I'm extremely sympathetic to the challenges confronting my successors—particularly the political challenges. But just as my generation repeatedly rose to the occasion and recovered from every setback to engage our country's enemies anew, I know the men and women of today's clandestine service will continue that tradition.

I have every confidence in them.

Acknowledgments

This is the second time I have written about my life in the CIA. My first effort, *The American Agent*, was published nearly a decade ago. Now, for several reasons, I decided to visit my past again and add the perspectives the additional years have furnished me.

Within these pages I have described not only the work I did in my various postings but also the reasons for those assignments and for my decisions and actions in fulfilling them. I've provided some background about what led me to join the agency and what I learned during my training days. I included a few brief passages about my earlier years. And because they gave me such joy and inspiration I wrote about Judy and our "platoon" of wonderful daughters who accompanied me on five of my seven overseas tours.

For a long time the idea of chronicling my career never would have occurred to me. I agreed with many of my colleagues who objected to operations officers writing books, particularly memoirs. They considered the risks greater than the rewards.

Then someone persuaded me to change my mind.

As you've read, over the years I had the great privilege of interacting with Richard Helms, a towering figure in the U.S. intelligence community and a highly respected, outstanding Director of Central Intelligence.

On one of those occasions, in the 1990s, Dick invited me to lunch at his club. There he urged me to record my experiences with the agency. As usual I balked at the idea. But then he told me, "If we don't write about the Cold War period it will be written by journalists and academics, and they will get it wrong."

I couldn't disagree with him, and this book represents the product of Dick's sage counsel. For that and for the many things he did for me—and for our country's clandestine service—he has my eternal gratitude.

Dick was absolutely right. The United States continues to defend itself against enemies who are hell-bent on destroying us. The National Clandestine Service is playing a vital part in that seemingly unending fight because electronic intelligence gathering can take us only so far. The human element is indispensible and must endure.

Dick Helms knew it is imperative for Americans to understand and support what the CIA does. To put it plainly, the agency needs a constituency. He believed, and I concur wholeheartedly, that the more the public appreciates what we do the stronger their support will be.

In a nutshell, that is why I wrote *The American Agent* in 2002 and now *The Craft We Chose*. I labored to the best of my recollection, with the help of friends and colleagues who shared the experience—I kept no diary. That meant I needed help to dredge up from my dimming memory the necessary details about specific events, people and places. To refresh and confirm my recollections I called on many of those who served with me at various times in my career. A lunch, a phone call or an e-mail often served to put a given subject into better perspective. They were all generous with their time and willingly responded to my questions aimed at making the manuscript as accurate as possible.

In fact, so many friends and colleagues participated that I won't attempt to list each name here—but you know who you are and I very much appreciate the help you gave me.

Three individuals, who will remain nameless, deserve special note. They suffered along with me during the trials and tribulations of the "Great Inspector General Investigation Debacle," as we called it. I will always remember the wisdom, patience and support they offered during what became the most difficult period of my career.

Several others also went above and beyond the call to assist me.

Members of the Belgian Air Force who were stationed unofficially at Paulis in February 1965 generously supplied the photos of their aircraft and their heroic efforts to rescue and evacuate me from the Congo.

Dr. Tim Miller, whose surgical skills saved my life that same month, helped me to recollect and describe the beginning of my rehabilitation. He also wrote the book's Foreword, which affectionately exaggerates the achievements that his efforts enabled me to pursue.

André Le Gallo, my longtime friend, helped me to exhume several important memories, including the name of Alain Griotteray. André found it by calling Le Musée des Parachutists, the paratrooper museum in Pau, and employing his enduring French fluency. He remains as grateful as I am that we managed to cross the Green Line safely that night so long ago in Beirut.

My compatriots Jim Campbell and Richard Sheres took the time to read and review the entire manuscript. Each contributed important comments and suggestions that I adopted.

Jessie Thorpe likewise read the manuscript and provided essential help with the text.

Phil Berardelli of Mountain Lake Press, my editor, whom I call my "resident wordsmith," gave me invaluable assistance in making the book more readable and complete.

Last, heartfelt thanks to my good friend and former colleague Jon Monett. Now the chairman of Quality of Life Plus (http://www.qlplus.org), an organization that uses engineering and technology to help disabled veterans, Jon is continuing his lifetime of service to his country. He championed this project from the start and lent his unwavering support at every turn.

Index

NOTE: The abbreviation "RLH" is used for Richard L. Holm.

THE TEMPEST

Contents

◂◂ BRAČ, CROATIA ◂ OLD TOWN SQUARE, PRAGUE PAGE 16 LOFOTEN ISLANDS, NORWAY

0
500 km
0
250 miles
Metres
4000
2000
1000
400
200
0
below
sea level
Arctic Circle
REYKJAVÍK
ICELAND
Faroes
Shetland
Bergen
ATLANTIC
OCEAN
NORTH
SEA
Edinburgh
Belfast
IRELAND
DUBLIN
York
UNITED
KINGDOM
Cardiff
LONDON
NETHER-
LANDS
AMSTERDAM
BRUSSELS
BELGIUM
Cologne
LUX.
LUXEMBOURG
CITY
PARIS
FRANCE
BERN
Zürich
SWITZERLAND
Lyon
Milan
Bordeaux
Santiago de
Compostela
Bilbao
Porto
PORTUGAL
ANDORRA
Marseille
MONACO
MADRID
LISBON
SPAIN
Barcelona
Corsica
(Fr.)
Valencia
Ibiza
Mallorca
Seville
MEDITERRANE
Tangier
Casablanca
RABAT
Fes
ALGIERS
TUNIS
MOROCCO
Essaouira
Marrakesh
ALGERIA
TUNISIA

NORWAY
SWEDEN
FINLAND
HELSINKI
St Petersburg
RUSSIA
STOCKHOLM
TALLINN
ESTONIA
Gothenburg
BALTIC SEA
RĪGA
LATVIA
MOSCOW
COPENHAGEN
LITHUANIA
RUSSIA
VILNIUS
MINSK
BELARUS
LIN
WARSAW
POLAND
KIEV
PRAGUE
Kraków
CZECH REPUBLIC
UKRAINE
SLOVAKIA
BRATISLAVA
VIENNA
MOLDOVA
CHIŞINĂU
STRIA
BUDAPEST
HUNGARY
LJUBLJANA
ROMANIA
VENIA
ZAGREB
CROATIA
GEORGIA
BELGRADE
BOSNIA-HERZEGOVINA
BUCHAREST
T'BILISI
BLACK SEA
SARAJEVO
SERBIA
tic Sea
BULGARIA
PODGORICA
SOFIA
MONTENEGRO
SKOPJE
ALBANIA
MACEDONIA
İstanbul
Naples
TIRANA
Thessaloniki
ANKARA
TURKEY
GREECE
Aegean Sea
İzmir
ATHENS
Sicily
SYRIA
EA
ALTA
Crete
CYPRUS
LEBANON
IRAQ

Introduction to

Europe

No continent on Earth packs a punch like Europe. Not only is it rich in beauty, history and romantic appeal, it's also astonishingly diverse. One day you might be strolling down a grand boulevard, absorbing centuries of civilization, and the next you could be skiing headlong down a black run surrounded by snow-capped, saw-toothed mountains. There are ancient forests to explore, super-strong espressos to sup, and incredible architectural wonders that will have you relentlessly grabbing for your camera.

Virtually wherever you end up, however – on a baking-hot beach in Portugal or in the wintry snows of Finland – you'll find some surprising common ground that will ease your path. There's the shared currency, for starters (the euro is already used in sixteen EU states), and a unique "open borders" policy that allows hassle-free travel between countries that were once fierce enemies. Back in those days, exploring Europe was only for the wealthy. Not anymore.

In fact, armed with the right know-how, it's possible to see Europe's best sights on a budget, party till you can't party any more, and still have enough cash left for a decent breakfast. You could grab a croissant in Paris, where speed and convenience are increasingly *de rigueur*, or go slow in Copenhagen with a stomach-stretching platter of open sandwiches. Then, check into your hostel (Europe has one of the world's best networks of budget accommodation) and head out in search of fun with the vast student populations that make cities like Rome and Barcelona stand out from the crowd. If culture's more your bag, it's possible to get a free fix in almost every European capital. In London, for example, you can spend days getting lost in stupendous collections of international treasures and it won't cost you a penny.

Free history lessons are everywhere, too. You can wander through sacred grottos on the sun-scorched islands of Greece, or imagine yourself com-

GELATERIA, SAN GIMIGNANO, ITALY

ing face to face with a vampire at "Dracula's" medieval castle in Romania. It seems nowhere is without a story. But for a collection of countries with such rich heritage, Europe doesn't spend much time looking backwards. It's home to some spectacularly futuristic modern architecture; some of the world's best nightclubs; and fresh, cutting-edge restaurants that set the senses alight.

The key to experiencing all of this on a budget is knowing where to look, and we've packed this book with expert tips to help you make the most of your trip for less. We've covered all of the must-see attractions – from the Vatican to the Brandenburg Gate – plus diverse cities on Europe's outer fringes, like İstanbul and Marrakesh. Away from the beaten track, there's advice on getting to grips with Norway's majestic fjords, soaring Alpine peaks and the glittering Balkan coastline.

Hostels with the X factor

Once synonymous with creaking bunk beds, dodgy plumbing and 10pm curfews, Europe's hostels have smartened up their act. You'll now find en-suite double rooms, flat-screen TVs and words like "boutique" and "designer" used to describe them. What's more, a number of ingenious conversion projects have seen everything from jumbo jets to prisons reborn as budget-friendly accommodation. Here are five of our favourites:

▸▸ **Celica Youth Hostel, Slovenia** Try a night behind bars at this artfully refurbished prison in Ljubljana (see p.1052).

▸▸ **Jumbo Hostel, Stockholm** Wake up on board a 1970s Pan-Am jumbo jet, either in a dorm room or the cockpit suite (see p.1165).

▸▸ **Ostel, Berlin** Experience Iron Curtain retro chic at this GDR-themed hostel (see p.470).

▸▸ **Shoestring Cave Hostel, Turkey** If sleeping in a cave sounds extreme, note that this one comes with a pool and en-suite rooms (see p.1252).

▸▸ **Villa St-Éxupéry, Nice** Former monastery beautifully converted into a buzzing hostel close to the beaches of the French Riviera (see p.441).

SECOND-HAND SHOP, AMSTERDAM

So how do you get from one place to the next? Well, with myriad budget airlines you could fly, but it's hardly the greenest option. And when you think of all the sights and smells you'd miss out on by jumping on a plane (not to mention the hassle of hanging around in airports) travelling overland takes on a whole new appeal. High-speed train lines and spectacular stations are popping up across Europe, and just looking at an arrivals board whirring its way through destinations should be enough to whet your appetite – Paris, Rome, Warsaw and Moscow are all just a platform away. And thankfully, if you take the train you won't have to spend much either. A range of cheap, convenient rail passes are available for pan-European travel: there's the InterRail pass – now a byword for criss-crossing continents by train – and Eurail, its sister pass for non-Europeans. Both can be tailored to your trip, whether you're staying in one country for a few months or hotfooting your way round the entire continent.

NYHAVN, COPENHAGEN

GLASTONBURY FESTIVAL, ENGLAND

When to go

Europe is a year-round destination, so don't worry too much about what the weather will be doing; good conditions for snowboarding aren't ever going to be ideal for sunbathing. In terms of budget, however, it makes sense to travel in the off season (basically October through to May). Cheaper menus appear on restaurant tables, hotels drop their rates, and haggling over prices becomes a realistic option. This is especially true of tourist hotspots like Paris, Barcelona and Rome, which attract far bigger crowds in July and August.

If you do decide to travel during the peak **summer** season, try heading east – the Balkan coastline, the Slovenian mountains and Baltic cities are all fantastic places for making the most of your money. When tourist traffic dies down towards the **autumn**, head to the Med. The famous coastlines and islands of southern Europe are quieter at this time of year, and the cities of Spain and Italy begin to look their best. **Wintertime** brings world-class skiing and snowboarding to European mountainsides (though not always) and countless festive markets pop up in the towns and cities below. There are epic New Years' parties everywhere from Moscow to Lisbon and, despite the cold weather elsewhere at this time of year, there's still the possibility of sunshine in Turkey and Morocco. While it's no secret that **spring** is the time to hit the French capital, it's also worth heading north to the Netherlands, Scandinavia and the British Isles where you'll find beautifully long days and relatively affordable prices before the summer season kicks in around July.

While **weather** extremes are not the issue they are in say, Asia or Africa, you should still bear them in mind when planning your trip. The Arctic winter in Scandinavia and Russia can bring temperatures as low as -35°C, with the sun barely rising above the horizon for months at a time. Conversely, summer days in central, southern and eastern parts of continental Europe can be sweltering – temperatures of around 40°C are not unheard of.

Ideas Art and culture

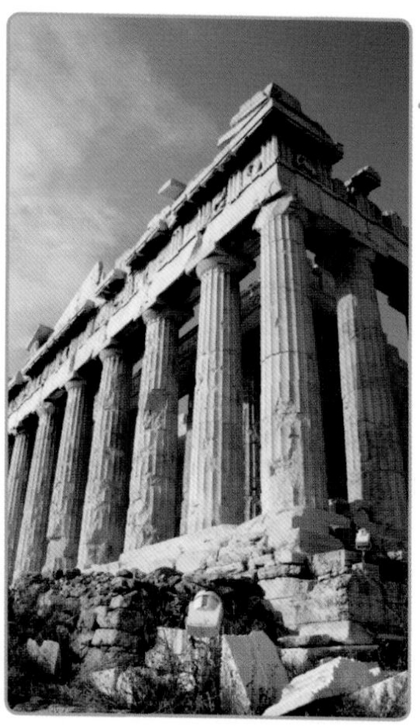

THE PARTHENON, ATHENS The iconic image of Western civilization and template for buildings the world over. **See p.536**

SISTINE CHAPEL, THE VATICAN Michelangelo's stupendous ceiling is worth craning your neck for. **See p.662**

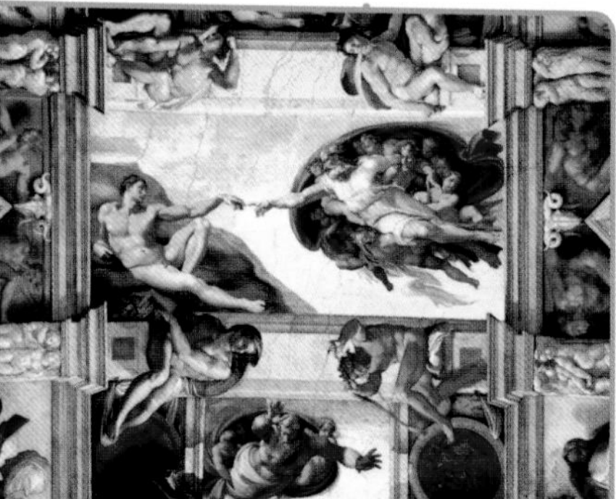

COMIC ART, BRUSSELS Alongside its Flemish treasures, the Belgian capital is a magnet for fans of *la bande dessinée*. **See p.107**

SHAKESPEARE'S GLOBE, LONDON Shakespeare the way it was meant to be seen – up close, raw and rowdy. **See pp.153 & 163**

MUSEO GUGGENHEIM, BILBAO Europe's most spectacular museum houses work by some of the biggest names in modern art. **See p.1146**

AYA SOFYA, İSTANBUL Christianity and Islam meet at this sixth-century architectural marvel. **See p.1222**

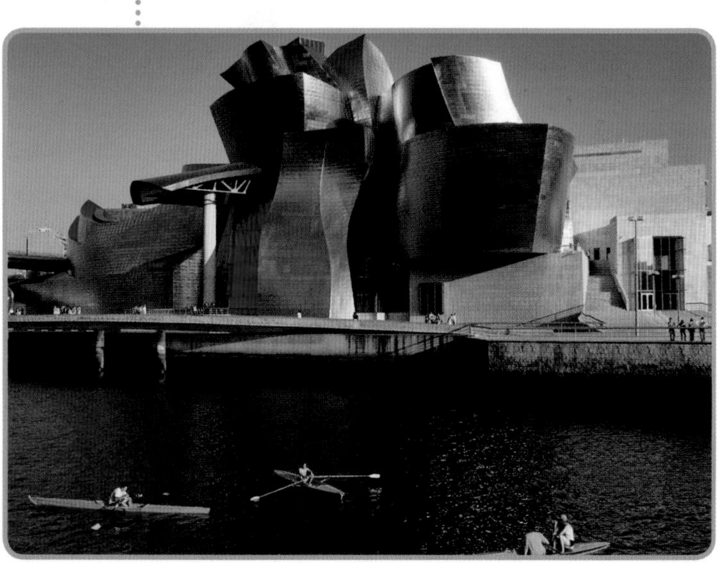

Ideas Outdoor activities

TAKING A SAUNA, FINLAND Heat yourself to boiling point then take a bone-chilling plunge. **See p.376**

SKIING AND SNOWBOARDING, FRANCE The French Alps offer the gnarliest and liveliest skiing and boarding on the continent. **See p.448**

SURFING, PORTUGAL Join the surf bums riding the Atlantic breakers off Portugal's coast. **See p.925**

ISLAND-HOPPING, GREECE Create your own odyssey on board a yacht in the Aegean. **See p.556**

HIKING THE TATRAS, POLAND/SLOVAKIA World-class hiking in summer and some of Europe's best-value skiing in winter. **See pp.916 & 1038**

WHITE-WATER RAFTING, MONTENEGRO The foaming waters of the Tara River are perfect for rafting and kayaking. **See p.796**

Ideas Festivals and events

EDINBURGH FESTIVAL
Comedy, drama, juggling, bag-pipes – you'll find them all at this unparalleled arts festival.
See p.207

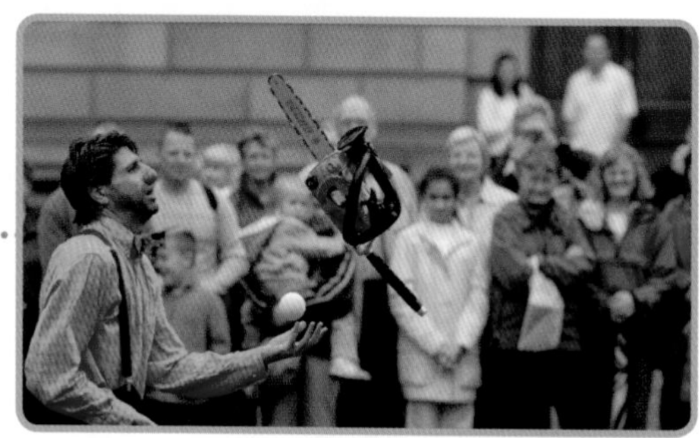

OKTOBERFEST, MUNICH
Sheer unadulterated beer guzzling at the world's largest public festival.
See p.517

THE PALIO, SIENA See the dust fly and the passions rise at the most exciting horse race on earth.
See p.698

LA TOMATINA, SPAIN Indulge your inner naughty child at this enormous food fight. **See p.1113**

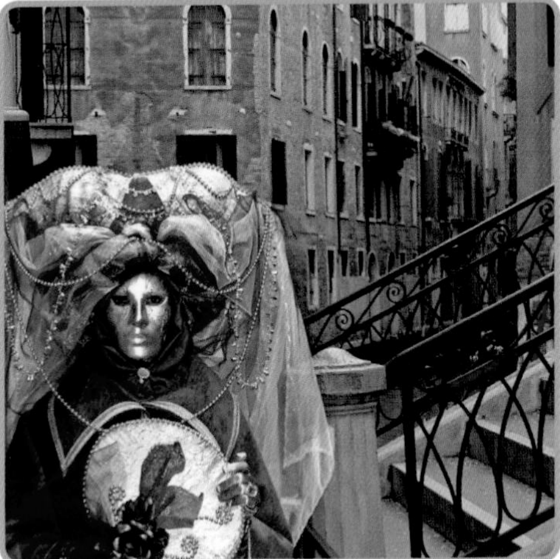

CARNIVAL, VENICE Ten days of masks, costumes and frenetic partying in the run-up to Lent. **See p.686**

EXIT FESTIVAL, SERBIA A beautiful fortress setting, a thumping sound system and top-name acts – what's not to like? **See p.1018**

ITINERARIES

ITINERARIES

Europe itineraries

You can't expect to fit everything Europe has to offer into one trip and we don't suggest you try. On the following pages are a selection of itineraries that guide you through the different regions of the continent, taking you from the misty Scottish Highlands to the bazaars of İstanbul. Each itinerary could be done in two to three weeks if followed to the letter but don't knock yourself out – with so much to see and do you're going to get waylaid somewhere you love or head off the suggested route.

BRITAIN AND IRELAND

Home to four proud nations, these two small islands pack in a huge amount from stately castles and windswept moors to theatre, Premiership football and Europe's best music festivals. Don't forget your brolly, drinking hat and sense of humour.

❶ **LONDON** As the saying goes, when a man is tired of London, he is tired of life. One of the world's greatest cities is also one of the most expensive, but follow our tips to emerge with your wallet intact. **See p.148**

❷ **OXFORD** The famous university town offers the chance to punt along the river, admire the college architecture or down a few in a student pub. **See p.178**

❸ **SNOWDONIA** Despite the notoriously unpredictable weather, the misty Welsh mountains offer excellent hiking and some of Britain's best hostels. **See p.203**

❹ **YORK** From a Viking museum and medieval streets to the soaring Gothic Minster, if you want to soak up some British history, York is the place to do it. **See p.193**

❺ **EDINBURGH** With its stunning cityscape, lively bars and – if you time it right – international festival, the Scottish capital has something for everyone. **See p.205**

❻ **THE HIGHLANDS** Find your inner Braveheart, knock back some whisky and hike, climb or ski surrounded by Britain's most stunning scenery. **See p.220**

❼ **BELFAST** A fascinating if troubled history, friendly if unintelligible locals and access point to one of Europe's natural wonders, the Giant's Causeway. **See p.640**

❽ **DUBLIN** Yep, Guinness really does taste better here though there's a lot more to see and do in Ireland's sophisticated capital. **See p.614**

❾ **IRELAND'S WEST COAST** From Galway to Cork, Ireland's west coast is studded with buzzing towns and beautiful, windswept beaches. **See p.629**

FRANCE AND SWITZERLAND

Still the world's number-one tourist destination, France can smugly claim to have it all from mountains and sun-kissed beaches to unrivalled food and fashion. Pricey it may be, but nearby Switzerland is worth the expense for its attractive, appealingly relaxed cities and the jaw-dropping mountain views.

❶ **PARIS** Laze over a coffee in a Left Bank café, arrange a romantic rendezvous or tick off the many museums in Europe's most elegant capital. **See p.387**

❷ **THE LOIRE VALLEY** Bucolic valley that's filled with some of the most impressive chateaux you'll see in the country. **See p.406**

❸ **BORDEAUX** An elegant, bustling city, world-famous wine-growing region and, a short drive away, some of Europe's finest surf beaches. **See p.415**

❹ **THE PYRENEES** Clear your head after all that wine with the fresh air and fine walks of this mountain range bordering Spain. **See p.423**

❺ **THE CÔTE D'AZUR** Nice, Cannes, Monaco – the names alone ooze glamour so get your glad rags on and show the world your fabulous side. **See p.439**

❻ **CORSICA** France's adventure playground, Corsica is home to one of Europe's toughest and most rewarding treks, the GR20. **See p.449**

❼ **LYON** There's no better city in which to indulge your passion for French cuisine than here in the country's gastronomic capital. **See p.443**

❽ **THE ALPS** Try your luck scaling Europe's highest mountains, or spend a season as a ski instructor or chalet monkey. **See pp.448 & 1202**

❾ **ZÜRICH** Laid-back Zürich is now one of Europe's clubbing hotspots and benefits from a wonderful riverside setting. **See p.1206**

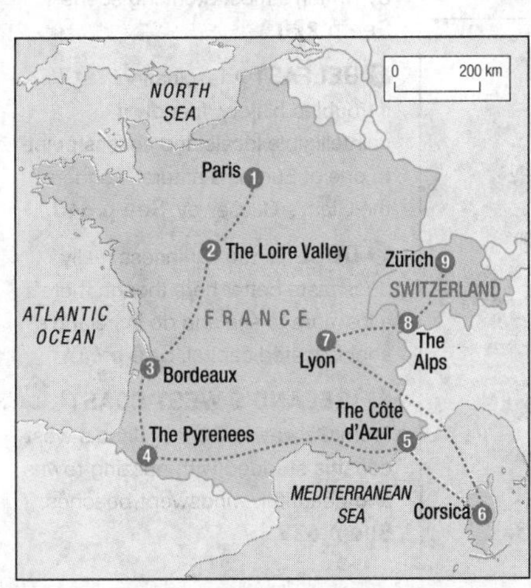

BENELUX, GERMANY AND AUSTRIA

From fine chocolates and champion beers to fairy tale castles, dark forests and clinking cowbells, this region has something for most people. The cities can pass in a blur of late nights but try and make time for the scenery too.

❶ **AMSTERDAM** Whatever you're looking for – cannabis, clubs, high culture or cuisine – the Netherlands' largest city will provide it. **See p.840**

❷ **BRUGES** It may be brazenly touristy but this gem of Flemish architecture is still worth a visit for its atmospheric canals and beautiful buildings. **See p.118**

❸ **COLOGNE** Linked to Brussels and beyond by super-fast trains, Cologne makes a perfect first stop in Germany with its spectacular old town and lively festivals. **See p.492**

❹ **HAMBURG** Germany's northern gateway boasts a vast port, magnificent red-brick warehouses and a riotous bar and live music scene. **See p.484**

SPAIN, PORTUGAL AND MOROCCO

Penélope Cruz, Cristiano Ronaldo, tapas, port and Rioja – it's hard not to warm to the Iberian peninsula. To the south, Morocco is just a short hop across the sea but a different planet in many respects.

❶ **BILBAO** Capital of the Basque country, Bilbao is Spain's friendliest city and home to one of Europe's most spectacular buildings: the Guggenheim. **See p.1145**

❷ **BARCELONA** Innovative architecture, city beaches, late-night bars and an atmospheric old town – you'll find it hard to leave the Catalan capital. **See p.1121**

❸ **IBIZA** Europe's clubbing capital packs in more sunburnt skin per square inch of dance floor than anywhere on earth, but you can also find a secluded beach if you look hard enough. **See p.1116**

❺ **BERLIN** Twenty years since the fall of the Wall, Berlin still has a raw, youthful energy that belies its history of division and destruction. **See p.462**

❻ **DRESDEN** Bombed to bits in World War II, Dresden is the classic Phoenix from the flames story and now one of Europe's favourite backpacker hangouts. **See p.474**

❼ **MUNICH** From beer-fuelled thigh-slapping to modern art and mountain scenery, you'll find it all in Bavaria's capital. **See p.513**

❽ **SALZBURG** Hit the Mozart trail, pose Julie Andrews-style in homage to *The Sound of Music* or pull on some skis and head for the mountains. **See p.87**

❾ **VIENNA** Austria's capital is chock full of palaces, museums and grand boulevards – with coffee and cake in a grand café never too far away. **See p.76**

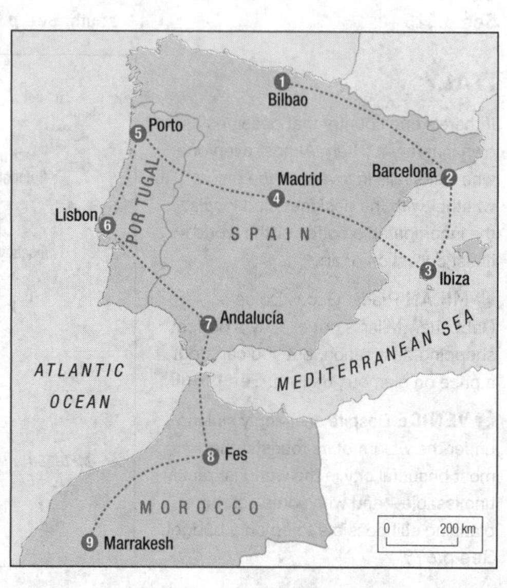

❹ **MADRID** Take your cue from the locals in the Spanish capital – if you're dining before 10pm, dancing before midnight and asleep before dawn, you haven't experienced a truly Madrileño night out. **See p.1071**

❺ **PORTO** Wander the atmospheric cobbled streets of Portugal's second city – and sample a drop at one (or more) of the countless port lodges. **See p.944**

❻ **LISBON** Portugal's immediately likeable capital has a great setting, delicious food and a huge amount of historic interest. **See p.929**

❼ **ANDALUCÍA** Spain in a nutshell – flamenco, fine wines, bullfighting and heat. If you're pushed for time stick to the unmissable cities of Seville and Granada. **See p.1092**

❽ **FES** Once across the Straits of Gibraltar, dive head first into Morocco with a stay in this medieval city of labyrinthine alleys, souks and mosques. **See p.814**

❾ **MARRAKESH** Stunning, atmospheric city with the Atlas Mountains as a backdrop and the live circus that is the Djemaa el Fna square at its heart. **See p.825**

ITALY

If there's one country that deserves its own itinerary it's Italy. Almost everyone who visits falls in love with the place, whether with the designer-clad locals, the incomparable coffee or the world's finest collection of art.

❶ **MILAN** Prada, Gucci, Dolce & Gabbana…Milan's not exactly a budget shopping destination, but you can't put a price on glamour, dahling. **See p.668**

❷ **VENICE** Despite seemingly sinking under the weight of its tourists, the most beautiful city in the world is frankly unmissable – and with some careful planning still possible to do on a budget. **See p.679**

❸ **BOLOGNA** Capital of the foodie nirvana Emilia-Romagna (think Parma ham, Parmesan, balsamic vinegar), Bologna is an essential pit stop for anyone with a digestive system. **See p.687**

❹ **TUSCANY** Birthplace of the Renaissance, Florence rightly pulls in the masses; nearby Siena is just as beautiful, full of fun-loving students and an excellent base to explore the region's hill towns. **See p.691 & p.698**

❺ **ROME** You can hardly "do" Europe and not "do" Rome. Whether you're queuing for St Peter's, the Sistine Chapel or the Colosseum you can at least rest assured that it'll be worth every minute. **See p.657**

❻ **NAPLES** The home of pizza – and the best place to eat it – Naples is also a frenetic, crumblingly attractive city with an intriguing dark side. **See p.706**

❼ **POMPEII** Seeing a Roman town frozen in time is an experience you won't forget. **See p.712**

❽ **MATERA** Try sleeping in a cave in this hand-carved stone city – the perfect introduction to Italy's captivating far south. **See p.716**

❾ **SICILY** Beaches, volcanoes and, in Palermo, one of Italy's most in-your-face cities – Sicilians simply do it better. **See p.717**

CENTRAL AND EASTERN EUROPE

Having long shrugged off the Iron Curtain, the region we used to regard as Eastern Europe is now firmly at the beating heart of the continent. With elegant cities and vast tracts of unspoiled countryside, these countries provide a remarkable set of riches.

❶ **PRAGUE** The Czech capital would probably win a pan-European beauty contest for its architecture. As for the beer…well, let's just say you won't be disappointed. **See p.288**

❷ **WARSAW** Beyond the Polish capital's immaculately reconstructed old town there are beautiful palaces and parks – and a restaurant, club and vodka-soaked bar scene – to explore. **See p.900**

❸ **KRAKÓW** Arty and atmospheric, picture-postcard-pretty Kraków should not be missed, though neither should a sobering trip to nearby Auschwitz. **See p.910**

❹ **TATRAS MOUNTAINS** Stretching between Poland and Slovakia the Tatras are that rare thing – majestic wilderness without hordes of Gore-Tex-clad tourists. **See p.915 & p.1036**

❺ **BUDAPEST** Two cities for the price of one: stately, museum-packed Buda and across the not-so-blue Danube, nightlife and restaurant hotspot Pest. **See p.588**

❻ **GREAT PLAIN, HUNGARY** Once you've got over the fact that you're still in Europe rather than Outer Mongolia, it's time to saddle up and explore the wide-open space. **See p.604**

❼ **TRANSYLVANIA** No, you probably won't see any vampires, but this history-steeped region holds myriad other attractions, from fairytale villages and colourful festivals to tracking wolves in the spectacular Carpathians. **See p.972**

SCANDINAVIA

While it can hit your finances, Scandinavia's worth persevering with. Apart from resembling Europe's answer to Middle Earth it's also full of stylish cities, ingenious design, and friendly if hard to fathom locals.

❶ **COPENHAGEN** Picturesque and user-friendly, the Danish capital is a lively, welcoming introduction to the region. **See p.316**

❷ **GOTHENBURG** Sweden's second city boasts elegant architecture, a debauched nightlife scene and a fully functioning rainforest among its standout attractions. **See p.1169**

❸ **OSLO** Paying €7 for a beer can put people off the Norwegian capital. If you

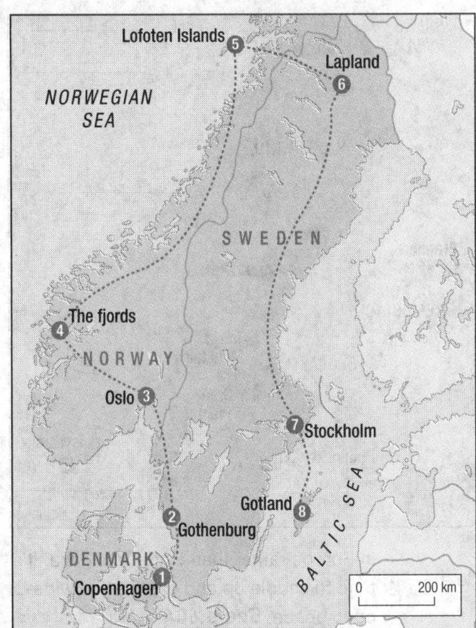

can get over the prices, though, you'll understand why it frequently tops "best places to live" lists. **See p.870**

❹ **THE FJORDS** No trip to Norway would be complete without a visit to the country's western coastline and its magnificent fjords. **See p.883**

❺ **LOFOTEN ISLANDS** A mild climate, wild scenery and cute, laid-back fishing villages pull in the crowds to this remote archipelago in Norway's far north. **See p.889**

❻ **LAPLAND** Synonymous with Santa, Lapland (whether Swedish or Finnish) fits the winter fantasy perfectly with reindeer, yapping huskies and the staggering Northern Lights. **See p.377 & p.1180**

❼ **STOCKHOLM** Scandinavia's best-looking capital offers up an unspoilt medieval core, über-hip nightlife and, incongruously enough, some fine beaches. **See p.1160**

❽ **GOTLAND** Sweden's party island buzzes in summer when the DJs hit the decks in Visby and the beaches fill with bronzed bodies. **See p.1177**

RUSSIA AND THE BALTIC COAST

Big scary bear it may be, but ever-changing Russia should not be missed, even if it's just to dip into its most "European" city, St Petersburg. Its compact Baltic neighbours, meanwhile, provide some of the beautiful – and most fun – cityscapes in Eastern Europe.

❶ **MOSCOW** Big, brash, expensive, surreal and exciting, twenty-first-century Moscow is almost a nation in itself and well worth the effort to get to. **See p.988**

❷ **ST PETERSBURG** With jaw-dropping architecture and priceless art collections, Russia's second city is at its best during the midsummer White Nights festival. **See p.996**

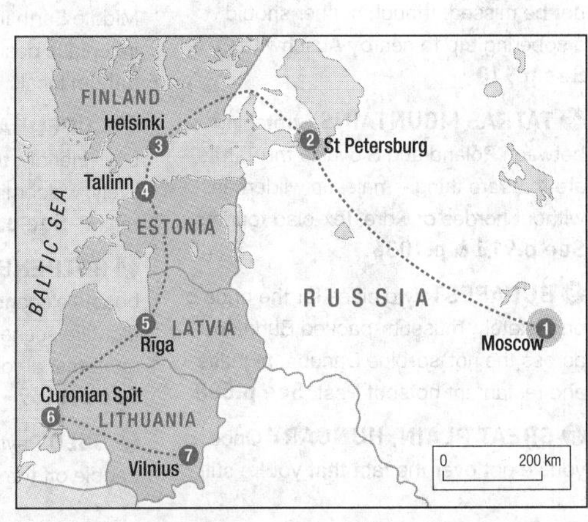

❸ **HELSINKI** The love child of the Russian and Swedish empires, since brought up to be proudly Finnish, Helsinki is a fascinatingly schizophrenic capital. **See p.366**

❹ **TALLINN** Having survived its tenure as a cheap stag- and hen-party venue par excellence, the beautifully preserved Estonian capital still retains a huge amount of charm. **See p.345**

❺ **RĪGA** Larger and more cosmopolitan that its neighbours, Latvia's atmospheric capital is full of architectural treasures and is the gateway to some wonderful coastal scenery. **See p.735**

❻ **CURONIAN SPIT** This narrow strip of lofty sand dunes and dense pine forest is the place to get your hiking boots on and strike out on the numerous walking trails. **See p.766**

❼ **VILNIUS** The friendliest and perhaps prettiest of the Baltic capitals, Vilnius's largely undiscovered status means you can get a break from the crowds. **See p.753**

THE BALKAN PENINSULA

A fascinating cultural meeting-point, the Balkans today are an exciting, safe (mostly) and mercifully cheap place to travel. While Croatia, Slovenia and Bulgaria have been on the scene for a while, send a postcard from Bosnia-Herzegovina or Macedonia and you're bound to have someone at home reaching for an atlas.

❶ **LJUBLJANA** Repeat after me: "Lyoo-bly-AH-nah". It may be hard to pronounce but the Slovenian capital is a small, perfectly formed pit-stop between central Europe and the Adriatic. **See p.1049**

❷ **DALMATIAN COAST** Croatia's dramatic Dalmatian coast and islands are the perfect place to drop out for the summer with watersports, cheap wine and Vitamin D on unlimited offer. **See p.265**

❸ **MOSTAR** Engineering feat, symbol of Bosnian regeneration and a ridiculously high diving board, Mostar's old bridge is the iconic sight of the region. **See p.136**

❹ **DUBROVNIK** Rivalling Venice in its day, the "pearl of the Adriatic" has survived centuries of conquest and intrigue, not to mention being on an easyJet flight route. **See p.276**

❺ **BUDVA** Montenegro's star resort boasts the requisite pretty old town but it's the unspoilt beaches and throbbing open-air bars that pull in the party set. **See p.791**

❻ **OHRID** Impossibly picturesque, set on the shimmering shores of the eponymous mountain-backed lake, Ohrid is the jewel in Macedonia's crown. **See p.780**

❼ **SOFIA** While no beauty, Bulgaria's laid-back capital is on absorbing mix of cultural influences and boasts some of Eastern Europe's best hostels. **See p.231**

❽ **BELGRADE** Hectic and hedonistic, the Serbian capital is fast attracting the hip crowd thanks to its adrenalin-charged nightlife. **See p.1011**

GREECE AND TURKEY

Whether you're interested in classical antiquity and the founding of Western civilization or just sparkling blue seas and sandy beaches, Greece and Turkey are essential destinations.

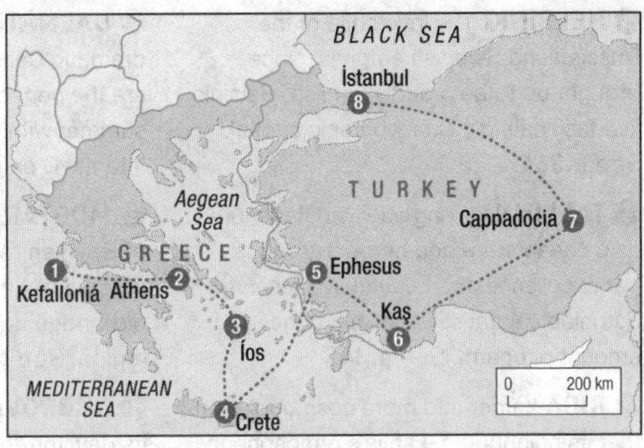

❶ **KEFALLONIÁ** The least developed of the Ionian islands, Kefalloniá is the perfect place to hop on a moped and find that perfect beach. **See p.573**

❷ **ATHENS** Crowded, noisy and polluted the Greek capital may be, but once you've seen the sun set over the Parthenon you'll be hooked. **See p.533**

❸ **ÍOS** A favourite among hard-partying backpackers, Íos maintains a bohemian, hippie-era charm and is the best stop on the Cyclades island-hopping trail. **See p.561**

❹ **CRETE** Home to the Minotaur and a fair few trashy resorts, Crete also boasts the dramatic Samarian Gorge, Europe's answer to the Grand Canyon. **See p.574**

❺ **EPHESUS** Turkey's best-preserved archeological site is a treasure-trove of ruined temples, mosaics, baths and some spectacular public conveniences. **See p.1240**

❻ **KAŞ** Fill your days mountain biking, paragliding or diving then relive it all in some of the Med's liveliest bars. **See p.1244**

❼ **CAPPADOCIA** It's a long trip east but Cappadocia's unique volcanic landscape has an irresistible allure – stay in a cave hotel and visit a subterranean city. **See p.1251**

❽ **İSTANBUL** Squeeze every kuruş out of your Turkish Lira shopping in the bazaars, having a rub down in a hamam and enjoying the surprisingly hectic nightlife. **See p.1222**

BASICS

BASICS

Getting there

Airfares will always depend on the season: they're usually highest in the summer and over the Christmas period, as well as over public holidays. Note also that flying on weekends or requiring a non-stop journey sometimes adds quite a bit to the round-trip fare; price ranges quoted below assume budget-friendly midweek travel.

Barring special offers, the cheapest of the **airlines' published fares** usually require advance purchase of two to three weeks, and impose certain restrictions, such as heavy penalties if you change your schedule. Most cheap return fares will only give a percentage refund, if any, should you need to cancel or alter your journey, so check the restrictions carefully before buying.

You can often cut costs by going through a **discount agent**, which in addition to dealing with discounted flights may also offer special student and youth fares and a range of other travel-related services such as travel insurance, rail passes and tours.

If Europe is only one stop on a longer journey, and especially if you are based in Australia or New Zealand, you might want to consider buying a **Round-the-World (RTW) ticket**. Prices vary based on the number of stops you make – the more stops allowed, the pricier the ticket. Figure on around US$1500–2000/Aus$2500/NZ$3350 for a RTW ticket including one or two European stopovers.

FROM BRITAIN AND IRELAND

Heading **from Britain** to destinations in northwestern Europe, it's not just cheaper and greener to go by train, long-distance bus or ferry – it can be quicker too. However, it's normally cheaper to fly than take the train to most parts of southern Europe, **From Ireland**, you may save a little money travelling by land, sea or even air to London and buying your flight there, but the difference isn't much. Budget airlines often have special deals and sales on, so it's always a good idea to check.

By plane

London is predictably **Britain**'s main hub for air travel, offering the highest frequency of flights and widest choice of destinations from its five airports (Heathrow, Gatwick, Stansted, Luton and City). Manchester also has flights to most parts of Europe, and there are regular services to the Continent from Birmingham, Bristol, Cardiff, Glasgow, Edinburgh, Leeds/Bradford and Newcastle. From the **Republic of Ireland**, you can fly direct to most major cities in mainland Europe from Dublin, Shannon and Cork. **From Belfast**, there are direct flights with easyJet to a handful of destinations; otherwise, you'll need to change in London or Manchester.

Budget airlines such as easyJet, bmibaby and Ryanair offer low-cost tickets to airports around Europe (though not always at the most convenient airports), and they often have some seriously cheap special offers in winter; see p.30 for a list of some of the more established operators, though be aware that

> **ROUGH GUIDES ONLINE**
>
> Find everything you need to plan your next trip at ⓦwww.roughguides.com. Read Rough Guides content on destinations worldwide, make use of our unique trip-planner tool, book transport and accommodation, check out other travellers' recommendations and share your own experiences.

the budget air travel industry is in a permanent state of flux, and airlines go in and out of business all the time. If you only want to go one-way, choose a budget airline as they charge for each leg of the journey separately. It's also worth checking with flight agents who specialize in low-cost, discounted flights (charter and scheduled), some of them – like STA Travel and Trailfinders – concentrating on deals for young people and students. In addition, there are agents specializing in offers to a specific country or group of countries on both charters and regular scheduled departures.

European budget airlines

At the time of writing there were 44 budget airlines serving countries in or near Europe. We've listed the more established operators below but for full details of routes visit ⓦwww.flycheapo.com, while ⓦwww.skyscanner.net is an invaluable price comparison resource.

Air Berlin ⓦwww.airberlin.com
Atlas Blue ⓦwww.atlas-blue.com
Blue Air ⓦwww.blueair-web.com
bmibaby ⓦwww.bmibaby.com
easyJet ⓦwww.easyjet.com
Flybe ⓦwww.flybe.com
FlyGlobespan ⓦwww.flyglobespan.com
Fly Niki ⓦwww.flyniki.com
Germanwings ⓦwww.germanwings.com
Jet2 ⓦwww.jet2.com
MyAir ⓦwww.myair.com
Norwegian Air Shuttle ⓦwww.norwegian.no
Ryanair ⓦwww.ryanair.com
Transavia ⓦwww.transavia.com
TUIfly ⓦwww.tuifly.com
Vueling ⓦwww.vueling.com
Wizzair ⓦwww.wizzair.com

By train

Direct **trains** through the Channel Tunnel from London to Paris (20 daily, 2hr 15min) and Brussels (11 daily, 1hr 51min) are

SIX STEPS TO A BETTER KIND OF TRAVEL

At Rough Guides we are passionately committed to travel. We feel strongly that only through travelling do we truly come to understand the world we live in and the people we share it with – plus tourism has brought a great deal of **benefit** to developing economies around the world over the last few decades. But the extraordinary growth in tourism has also damaged some places irreparably, and of course **climate change** is exacerbated by most forms of transport, especially flying. This means that now more than ever it's important to **travel thoughtfully** and **responsibly**, with respect for the cultures you're visiting – not only to derive the most benefit from your trip but also to preserve the best bits of the planet for everyone to enjoy. At Rough Guides we feel there are six main areas in which you can make a difference:

- Consider what you're contributing to the **local economy**, and how much the services you use do the same, whether it's through employing local workers and guides or sourcing locally grown produce and local services.
- Consider the **environment** on holiday as well as at home. Water is scarce in many developing destinations, and the biodiversity of local flora and fauna can be adversely affected by tourism. Try to patronize businesses that take account of this.
- Travel with a purpose, not just to tick off experiences. Consider **spending longer** in a place, and getting to know it and its people.
- Give thought to how often you **fly**. Try to avoid short hops by air and more harmful night flights.
- Consider **alternatives to flying**, travelling instead by bus, train, boat and even by bike or on foot where possible.
- Make your trips "**climate neutral**" via a reputable carbon-offset scheme. All Rough Guide flights are offset, and every year we donate money to a variety of charities devoted to combating the effects of climate change.

YOU AND THE EU

After a tricky birth in the aftermath of World War II, the **EU** (European Union) is now reaching maturity. A recent growth spurt has increased the number of member states to 27 and it now stretches from the beaches of Portugal in the west, across the former Iron Curtain, to the shores of the Black Sea in Bulgaria. So what does this self-styled "family of democratic nations" mean to the average traveller? Well, a key part of it is likely to be in your pocket – the **euro** (see p.50) is the currency of sixteen EU countries, and the remainder (apart from the notable exceptions of Britain, Denmark and Sweden) are likely to adopt it once their economies are ready. You'll also find your passport gathering dust as there are no internal **border controls** among the countries using the euro (although you should carry ID for random checks), and if you run into trouble dial ⓣ**112** – the universal EU emergency number. If you're lucky enough to hold an EU passport, the continent really begins to open up: you can work, study, shop, receive free healthcare and even take your pet wherever you like across the member states.

operated by **Eurostar**. Tickets for under 26s start at £40 one-way, £49 return. For over 26s, the cheapest return ticket, at £59, costs far less than a single fare (£178) – in theory, the cheaper ticket involves a "compulsory return". Through-ticket combinations with onward connections from Brussels and Paris can be booked through International Rail and Rail Europe (see p.35 & p.38).

Other rail journeys from Britain involve a **sea crossing** by ferry or, sometimes, catamaran. Tickets can be bought from International Rail, and from most major rail stations or from Dutchflyer (ⓦdutchflyer.co.uk) if routed via the Hook of Holland. For some destinations, there are cheaper SuperApex fares requiring advance booking and subject to greater restrictions. Otherwise, international tickets are valid for two months and allow for stopovers on the way, providing you stick to the prescribed route (there may be a choice, with different fares applicable). One-way fares are generally around two-thirds the price of a return fare. If you're **under 26** you're entitled to all sorts of special deals, not least cut-price youth fares.

From Ireland, direct rail tickets to Europe via Britain generally include both boat connections, and are available from Irish Railways offices in the Republic (ⓣ01/703 1884, ⓦwww.irishrail.ie), or Northern Ireland Railways in the North (ⓣ028/9066 6630, ⓦwww.translink.co.uk).

For **rail passes**, contacts and other types of discounted rail travel, see "Getting around", p.34.

By bus

If you're really watching your pennies, a long-distance **bus** is probably the very cheapest option, although much less comfortable than the train. The main operator is **Eurolines** (ⓦwww.eurolines.co.uk; ⓦwww.eurolines.ie), which has a network of routes spanning the continent. **Prices** can be up to a third less than the equivalent train fare, and there are marginally cheaper fares on most services for those under 26, which undercut youth rail rates for the same journey. There's usually a discount if you buy your ticket at least four days in advance, and bigger discounts for return journeys booked two weeks or a month in advance: as an example, current Eurolines fares from London's Victoria Coach Station to Paris or Amsterdam start at £25 for a one-way ticket booked four days in advance, or for a return booked fifteen days in advance (with special offer £15 one-way fares on some services). Connecting services from elsewhere in Great Britain add around £15–20 each way to the price of the ticket.

Eurolines also has **Minipass** return tickets from London to two or more European cities, valid for ninety days. Alternatively, you might consider their fifteen-, thirty- and forty-day passes, or one of the various passes offered by **Busabout** for their

services around the continent (see "Getting around", p.38).

By ferry

There are numerous **ferry services** between Britain and Ireland, and between the British Isles and the European mainland. Ferries from the southeast of Ireland and the south coast of England connect with northern France and Spain; those from Kent in southeast England reach northern France and Belgium; those from Scotland and the east coast and northeast of England cross the North Sea to Belgium, the Netherlands, Germany and Scandinavia.

Ferry operators

Brittany Ferries UK ⓣ0871/244 0744, ⓦwww.brittany-ferries.co.uk; Ireland ⓣ021/427 7801, ⓦwww.brittanyferries.ie. Cork to Roscoff (April–Oct); Portsmouth to Caen, Cherbourg, St Malo and Santander; Poole to Cherbourg; Plymouth to Roscoff and Santander.

Condor Ferries UK ⓣ0845/609 1024, ⓦwww.condorferries.co.uk. Portsmouth to Cherbourg; Portsmouth, Poole, and Weymouth to St Malo via Jersey and Guernsey.

DFDS Seaways UK ⓣ0871/522 9955, ⓦwww.dfdsseaways.co.uk. Harwich to Esbjerg (Denmark); Newcastle to Amsterdam.

Irish Ferries UK ⓣ0870/517 1717, ⓦwww.irishferries.com; Ireland ⓣ0818/300 400, ⓦwww.directferries.ie. Dublin to Holyhead; Rosslare to Pembroke, Cherbourg (March–Dec) and Roscoff (May–Sept).

LD Lines UK ⓣ0844/576 8836, ⓦwww.ldlines.co.uk. Dover to Boulogne; Portsmouth to Le Havre.

Norfolkline UK ⓣ0844/847 5042 (Dover–Dunkerque), ⓣ0844/499 0007 (Irish Sea), Ireland ⓣ01/819 2999; ⓦwww.norfolkline.com. Dover to Dunkerque; Belfast and Dublin to Birkenhead.

P&O Ferries UK ⓣ0871/664 5645, ⓦwww.poferries.com. Hull to Zeebrugge and Rotterdam; Dover to Calais; Portsmouth to Bilbao.

P&O Irish Sea UK ⓣ0871/664 4999, Ireland ⓣ01/407 3434; ⓦwww.poirishsea.com. Larne to Cairnryan and Troon (March–Oct); Dublin to Liverpool.

SeaFrance UK ⓣ0870/423 7119, ⓦwww.seafrance.com. Dover to Calais.

Stena Line UK ⓣ0870/570 7070, ⓦwww.stenaline.co.uk; Ireland ⓣ01/204 7777, ⓦwww.stenaline.ie. Harwich to Hook of Holland; Rosslare to Fishguard; Dun Laoghaire and Dublin to Holyhead; Belfast to Stranraer; Larne to Fleetwood.

Superfast Ferries UK ⓣ0870/420 1267, ⓦwww.superfast.ferries.org. Rosyth to Zeebrugge.

Transmanche Ferries ⓣ0800/917 1201, ⓦwww.transmancheferries.com. Newhaven to Dieppe.

FROM THE US AND CANADA

From the US the best deals are generally from the main hubs such as **New York**, **Washington DC** and **Chicago** to London. Fixed-date advance-purchase tickets for mid-week travel to London cost around US$500 in low season (roughly speaking, winter), US$750 in high season (summer, Christmas and Easter) from New York and Washington DC, US$650/950 from Chicago. A more flexible ticket will set you back around US$1600 out of New York, US$1750 out of Chicago. Fixed-date advance-purchase alternatives include New York to Paris for US$500/900, US$600/750 to Frankfurt, US$550/900 to Madrid, or US$600/1100 to Athens; flying from Chicago, discounted tickets can be had at US$500/1000 to Paris, US$500/900 to Frankfurt, US$600/1000 to Madrid, or US$650/1100 to Athens. There are promotional offers from time to time, especially in the off-peak seasons; Virgin Atlantic, for example, sometimes has very cheap New York–London fares in late winter with no advance purchase necessary.

From the **west coast** the major airlines fly at least three times a week and up to twice daily from Los Angeles, San Francisco and Seattle to the main European cities. Flexible economy-class tickets from LA to London will set you back at least US$2000 in high season. If you can buy your tickets in advance and don't need flexibility, you can get to London for US$550/950 (low/high season), to Paris for US$650/1100, to Frankfurt for US$600/1100, to Madrid for US$650/1000, or to Athens for US$750/1150.

From Canada

Most of the big airlines fly to the major European hubs from **Montreal** and **Toronto** at least once daily (three times a week for smaller airlines). From Toronto, London is your cheapest option, with the lowest direct round-trip fare around Can$650/900. For a

flexible economy-class ticket on the same route, you're looking at around Can$3000. Fares from Montreal to Paris start at Can$900/1100. Vancouver and Calgary have daily flights to several European cities, with round-trip fares to London from around Can$780/1000, depending on the season.

FROM AUSTRALIA AND NEW ZEALAND

There are flights from **Melbourne**, **Sydney**, **Adelaide**, **Brisbane** and **Perth** to most European capitals, with not a great deal of difference in the fares to the busiest destinations: a scheduled return from Sydney to London, Paris, Rome, Madrid, Athens or Frankfurt should be available through travel agents for around Aus1900 in low season (Australia's summer, Europe's winter) and slightly higher in high season (though you can sometimes get great deals). A one-way ticket costs slightly more than half that, while a return flight from **Auckland, Wellington or Christchurch** to Europe is approximately NZ$2000 in low season and from around NZ$2500 in high season. Asian airlines often work out cheapest, and may throw in a stopover. Some agents may also offer "open jaw" tickets, flying you into one city and out from another, which needn't necessarily even be in the same country. For **RTW** deals and other low-price tickets, the most reliable operator is STA Travel (see "Agents and operators" below), which also supply packages with companies such as Contiki and Busabout, can issue rail passes, and advise on visa regulations – for a fee they'll even do all the paperwork for you.

FROM SOUTH AFRICA

Many major airlines fly **from Johannesburg and Cape Town** to a number of European capitals, sometimes via a hub airport. Flying to Frankfurt with Lufthansa is about ZAR6000 from Johannesburg; Air France fly direct to Paris from Johannesburg for around ZAR7000, and from Cape Town for slightly more; and BA fly direct to London from Johannesburg or Cape Town for a similar price. You might also try flying with Emirates via Dubai.

AGENTS AND OPERATORS

ebookers UK ⓣ 020/3320 3320, ⓦ www.ebookers.com; Republic of Ireland ⓣ 01/4311 311, ⓦ www.ebookers.ie. Low fares on an extensive selection of scheduled flights to Europe.

North South Travel UK ⓣ 01245/608 291, ⓦ www.northsouthtravel.co.uk. Discounted fares worldwide. Profits are used to support projects in the developing world, especially the promotion of sustainable tourism.

STA Travel UK ⓣ 0871/230 0040, US ⓣ 1-800/781-4040, Australia ⓣ 134 STA, New Zealand ⓣ 0800/474 400, South Africa ⓣ 0861/781781; ⓦ www.statravel.com. Worldwide specialists in independent and student travel; also student IDs, travel insurance, car rental, rail passes, and more.

Trailfinders UK ⓣ 0845/058 5858, Republic of Ireland ⓣ 01/677 7888, Australia ⓣ 1300/780 212; ⓦ www.trailfinders.com. One of the best-informed and most efficient agents for independent travellers.

USIT ⓣ 01/602 1906, Northern Ireland ⓣ 028/9032 7111, ⓦ www.usit.ie. Ireland's main student and youth travel specialists.

Getting around

It's easy enough to travel in Europe, and a number of special deals and passes can make it fairly economical too, especially for students and travellers under 26. Air links are extensive and, thanks to the growing number of budget airlines, flights are often cheaper than taking the train, but you'll appreciate the diversity of Europe best at ground level, by way of its enormous and generally efficient web of rail, road and ferry connections.

BY TRAIN

Trains are generally the best way to tour Europe. The rail network in most countries is comprehensive and the continent boasts some of the most scenic rail journeys in the world. **Costs** are relatively low, too – apart from Britain, where prices can be absurdly steep – as trains are heavily subsidized, and prices are brought down further by passes and discount cards. We've covered the various passes here, as well as the most important international routes and most useful addresses; frequencies and journey times are given throughout the guide.

During the summer, especially if you're travelling at night or a long distance, it's best to make **reservations** whenever you can; on some trains (TGV services, for example) it's compulsory. See our "Extra rail charges" box for more on supplements.

If you intend to do a lot of rail travel, the **Thomas Cook European Timetable** (Ⓦwww.thomascookpublishing.com) is an essential investment, detailing the main lines throughout Europe, as well as ferry connections, and is updated monthly. **Online**, Ⓦwww.bahn.de is the best resource, with comprehensive domestic and international rail listings across Europe, while Ⓦwww.seat61.com is another excellent source of information.

Finally, whenever you board an international train in Europe, check the route of the car you are in, since trains frequently split, with different carriages going to different destinations.

Europe-wide rail passes

InterRail

InterRail passes have long been synonymous with young European backpackers travelling across the continent on the cheap. There are two types of pass available: the **Global Pass** and **One Country Pass**. Both can be bought direct from Ⓦwww.interrailnet.com and from main stations and international rail agents in all thirty countries covered by the scheme. To qualify, you need to have been **resident** in one of the participating countries for six months or

EXTRA RAIL CHARGES

Note that even if you've bought an InterRail or Eurail pass, you will still need to pay **extra charges** or **supplements** to travel on most express trains (such as Eurostar, TGV and ICE), night trains and those on special scenic routes. Even where there is in theory no supplement, there's often a compulsory reservation fee, which may cost you double if you only find out about it once you're on the train. For details of charges check the InterRail website under "special trains" or "supplements". You can often avoid these charges if you plan your journey within domestic networks.

more. The only countries in this book which are not covered by the scheme are Albania, Andorra, Estonia, Latvia, Lithuania, Morocco, Northern Ireland and Russia.

InterRail Global Pass The daddy of all rail passes, offering access to almost the entire European rail network. You can choose between four different time periods – continuous blocks of 22 days or one month – or set amounts of travel – either five days within ten days or ten days within 22 days. Youth (under-26) passes valid for second-class travel start from €159/£145 for five days up to €399/£369 for a month. Note that you cannot use the pass in the country in which you bought it although discounts of up to fifty percent are usually available.

InterRail One Country Pass Same principle as the Global Pass but valid for just one country (or the Benelux zone of Belgium, the Netherlands and Luxembourg). Time periods and prices vary depending on the country. A three-day second-class youth pass will set you back €32/£29 in Bulgaria, €71/£65 in Spain and €125/£115 in France.

Eurail

Non-European residents aren't eligible for InterRail passes. For them the **Eurail** scheme (ⓦwww.eurail.com) offers a range of passes giving unlimited travel in twenty-five European countries. There are four types of pass – the **Global Pass**, **Select Pass**, **Regional Pass** and **One Country Pass**, all of which should be bought outside Europe. Apart from some One Country Passes, all are available at discounted youth (25 or younger) rates for second-class travel and saver rates for adults travelling in groups.

Eurail Global Pass A single pass valid for travel in 21 countries: Austria, Belgium, Croatia, Czech Republic, Denmark, Finland, France, Germany, Greece, Hungary, Ireland, Italy, Luxembourg, the Netherlands, Norway, Portugal, Romania, Slovenia, Spain, Sweden and Switzerland. There are seven different time periods available from ten days' travel within two months, up to three months' continuous travel. Prices start at €332/US$449 for a youth pass valid for fifteen days.

Eurail Select Pass Allows you to select a pass covering three, four or five bordering countries out of the 21 countries above plus three "bonus" countries. Prices start at €211/US$285 for a three-country youth pass valid for five days' travel within two months.

Eurail Regional Pass Similar to the Select Pass but offering 25 predetermined combinations of countries. Prices depend on the country combination; for example an Austria–Czech Republic youth pass valid for five days' travel in two months will cost you €134/US$179 whereas the same period for Germany–Switzerland costs €215/US$289.

Eurail One Country Pass Offers travel within one of the following seventeen countries (or the Benelux zone of Belgium, the Netherlands and Luxembourg): Austria, Croatia, Czech Republic, Denmark, Finland, Greece, Hungary, Ireland, Italy, the Netherlands, Norway, Poland, Portugal, Romania, Slovenia, Spain and Sweden. Prices vary depending on the size of the country and whether youth passes are available: for example a youth pass in Denmark valid for three days' travel costs €48/US$65; the same time period costs €153/US$209 in Spain where special youth passes are not available.

Regional rail passes

In addition to the InterRail and Eurail schemes there are a few **regional rail passes** which can be good value if you're doing a lot of travelling within one area; we've listed some of the main ones below. **National rail passes** (apart from InterRail and Eurail) are covered in the relevant chapter of the Guide.

Balkan Flexipass Offers unlimited first-class-only travel through Bulgaria, Greece, Macedonia, Serbia, Montenegro, Romania and Turkey. Prices start at US$256 for five days' travel in one month.

Britrail pass + Ireland ⓦwww.britrail.com. Allows unlimited travel in Britain, Northern Ireland and the Republic of Ireland. Prices start from US$454 for five days' standard-class travel in one month.

European East Pass Gives five days' travel in a month in Austria, the Czech Republic, Hungary, Poland and Slovakia for US$209, plus up to five additional days at US$28 each.

Rail contacts

UK

European Rail ⓣ020/7619 1083, ⓦwww.europeanrail.com. Independent specialists for continental rail travel.

Eurostar ⓣ0870/518 6186, ⓦwww.eurostar.com. UK to France and Belgium.

International Rail ⓣ0870/084 1410, ⓦwww.international-rail.com. Global rail specialist.

InterRail ⓦwww.interrailnet.com. Official site for InterRailing.

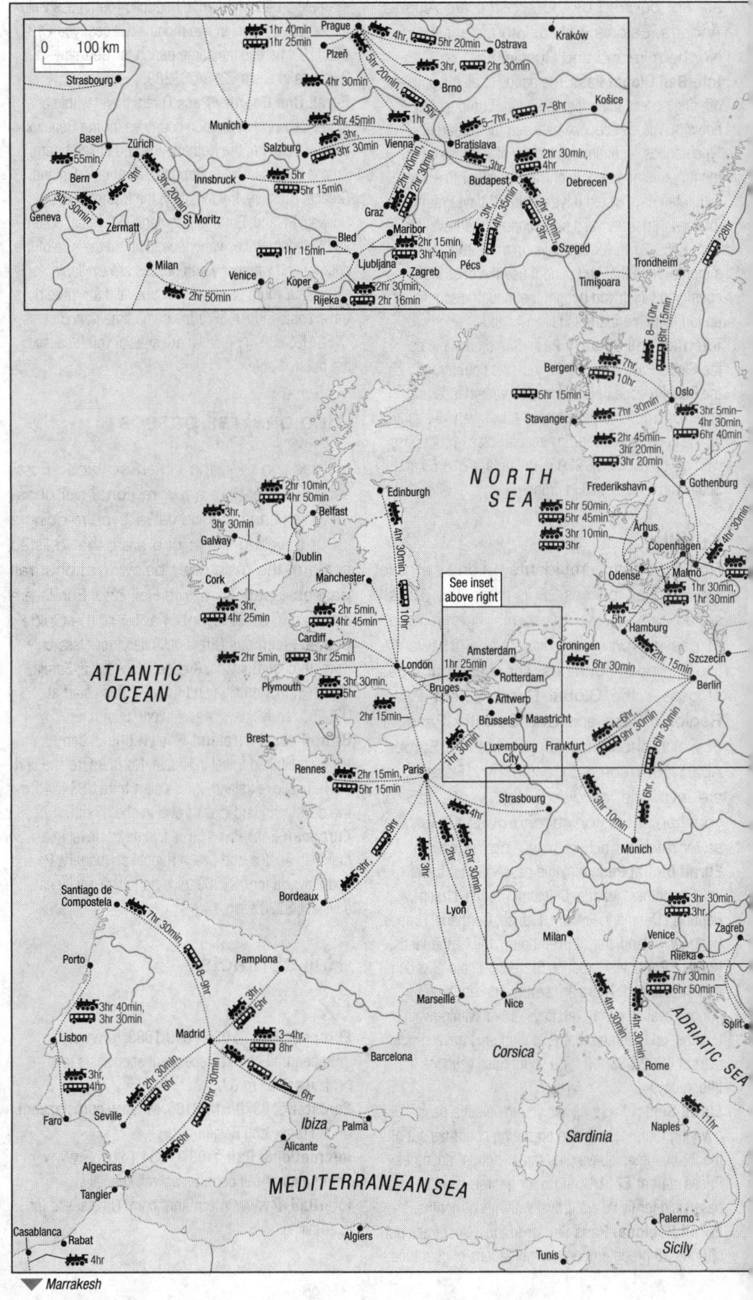
0 100 km
Strasbourg
Prague
1hr 40min
1hr 25min
Plzeň
4hr, 5hr 20min
Ostrava
Kraków
3hr, 2hr 30min
5hr 20min, 5hr
Brno
4hr 30min
Munich
5hr 45min
1hr
5–7hr, 7–8hr
Košice
Basel
Zürich
55min
Bern
3hr
3hr 20min
Salzburg
3hr, 3hr 30min
Vienna
Bratislava
2hr 30min, 4hr
3hr
Innsbruck
5hr
5hr 15min
2hr 40min, 2hr 30min
Budapest
Debrecen
Geneva
3hr 30min
Zermatt
St Moritz
Graz
3hr, 4hr 35min
2hr 30min, 3hr
Bled
Maribor
2hr 15min, 3hr 4min
Szeged
1hr 15min
Ljubljana
Pécs
Milan
Venice
Koper
Zagreb
2hr 50min
2hr 30min, 2hr 16min
Rijeka
Timişoara
Trondheim
28hr
8–10hr, 8hr 15min
Bergen
7hr, 10hr
5hr 15min
Oslo
Stavanger
7hr 30min
3hr 5min–4hr 30min, 6hr 40min
2hr 45min–3hr 20min, 3hr 20min
Gothenburg
NORTH SEA
Frederikshavn
Edinburgh
2hr 10min, 4hr 50min
Belfast
3hr, 3hr 30min
Galway
Dublin
5hr 50min, 5hr 45min
3hr 10min, 3hr
Århus
Copenhagen
4hr 30min
Odense
Malmö
1hr 30min, 1hr 30min
4hr 30min, 10hr
Manchester
Cork
3hr, 4hr 25min
2hr 5min, 4hr 45min
See inset above right
5hr
Hamburg
Cardiff
Groningen
Amsterdam
2hr 15min
Szczecin
2hr 5min, 3hr 25min
London
1hr 25min
Rotterdam
6hr 30min
Berlin
ATLANTIC OCEAN
Plymouth
3hr 30min, 5hr
Bruges
Antwerp
2hr 15min
Brussels
Maastricht
4–6hr, 9hr 30min
6hr 30min
Brest
1hr 30min
Luxembourg City
Frankfurt
Rennes
2hr 15min, 5hr 15min
Paris
Strasbourg
4hr
3hr 10min
6hr, 6hr
Munich
3hr, 9hr
2hr
5hr 30min
3hr
Santiago de Compostela
Bordeaux
Lyon
3hr 30min, 3hr
Zagreb
7hr 30min, 8–9hr
Milan
Venice
Rijeka
Porto
Pamplona
7hr 30min, 6hr 50min
3hr 40min, 3hr 30min
3hr, 5hr
4hr 30min
4hr 30min
Marseille
Nice
ADRIATIC SEA
Split
Lisbon
Madrid
3–4hr, 8hr
Barcelona
Corsica
Rome
3hr, 4hr
2hr 30min, 6hr
8hr 30min
6hr
11hr
Faro
Seville
Ibiza
Palma
Naples
6hr
Alicante
Sardinia
Algeciras
Tangier
MEDITERRANEAN SEA
Palermo
Casablanca
Rabat
Algiers
4hr
Tunis
Sicily
Marrakesh

JOURNEY TIMES
BY TRAIN & BUS
HIGH-SPEED TRAIN TIMES
Rome–Naples 1hr 30min
Paris–Brest 2hr 15min
Paris–London 2hr 15min
London–Brussels 1hr 25min
Paris–Bordeaux 3hr
Paris–Brussels 1hr 30min
Brussels–Amsterdam 2hr 40min
Amsterdam–Frankfurt 3hr 45 min
Copenhagen–Stockholm 5hr
Barcelona–Alicante 4hr 40min
Berlin–Hamburg 1hr 30min
Geneva–Zürich 2hr 43min
Milan–Zürich 3hr 40min
0 100 km
Groningen
Amsterdam
1hr,
2–3hr
Rotterdam
2hr 40min
2hr 35min
2hr 20min,
4hr 12min
Bruges
Antwerp
Brussels
45min
Maastricht
1hr
3hr
Luxembourg City
Nordkapp
Tromsø
14hr
Rovaniemi
10hr
13hr 25min
Joensuu
5hr 30min
7hr 10min
2hr,
2hr 30min
Turku
Helsinki
7hr, 3hr from 2011
9hr
St Petersburg
Stockholm
8hr 30min
BALTIC SEA
Tallinn
7–9hr
12–14hr
7–9hr
15hr
12hr
4hr 30min
8hr 30min
16hr,
17hr
Moscow
Riga
7hr
5hr
22min
1hr
Vilnius
Gdánsk
Minsk
5hr
5hr
6hr
Warsaw
3hr
6hr
Kiev
Kraków
See inset
above left
Suceava
6hr 30min
6hr 30min
Timişoara
7hr
6hr 30min,
7–10hr
3hr,
2hr 50min
Banja Luka
5hr
5–6 hr
Belgrade
7hr
Bucharest
Constanţa
BLACK SEA
T'bilisi
Sarajevo
8hr 30min
3hr 30min
8hr 30min
8hr, 30min
7hr
Varna
Yerevan
Mostar
Podgorica
Sofia
6hr 30min
5hr 30min
Burgas
Dubrovnik
Shkodra
2hr 30min
2hr
Plovdiv
5hr
Skopje
Istanbul
5–9hr,
5hr 30min
Tirana
3–4hr
3hr
6hr 40min
Bitola
Ankara
Pogradeci
Thessaloniki
6hr 30min
2hr
5hr
0 500 km
Corfu
4–8hr
6hr
AEGEAN
SEA
7hr
11hr
Izmir
Athens
7hr
Antalya

The Man in Seat 61 Ⓦ www.seat61.com. Comprehensive informational site set up by a rail enthusiast.
Rail Europe Ⓣ 0844/848 4064, Ⓦ **www.raileurope.co.uk.** European rail experts.

US and Canada

ACP Rail International US & Canada Ⓣ 1-866-9-EURAIL, Ⓦ www.eurail-acprail.com. Eurail agent.
BritRail Travel US & Canada Ⓣ 1-866/BRITRAIL, Ⓦ www.britrail.com. British passes.
Europrail International Canada Ⓣ 1-888/667-9734, Ⓦ www.europrail.net. European and many individual country passes.
Eurail US & Canada Ⓦ www.eurail.com.
Rail Europe US & Canada Ⓣ 1-800/622-8600, Ⓦ www.raileurope.com. Official Eurail agent, with the widest range of regional and one-country passes.

Australia and New Zealand

CIT World Travel Australia Ⓣ 1300/361 500, Ⓦ www.cittravel.com.au. Eurail and Italian rail passes.
Octopus Travel Australia Ⓣ 1300/727 072, NZ 0800 450 485; Ⓦ www.octopustravel.com/au;.
Rail Plus Australia Ⓣ 03/9642 8644, Ⓦ www.railplus.com.au; NZ Ⓣ 09/377 5415, Ⓦ www.railplus.co.nz. Eurail and BritRail passes.

South Africa

Rail Europe Ⓣ 011/628 2319, Ⓦ www.raileurope.co.za. Official distributor for European rail in South Africa.

BY BUS

Long-distance journeys by bus between major European cities are generally slower and less comfortable than by train and – if you have a rail pass – not necessarily cheaper. If you're only travelling to a few places, however, a **bus pass** or **circular bus ticket** can undercut a rail pass, especially for over 26s. There's also the option of a bus tour if you're on a tight schedule or simply want everything planned for you.

Eurolines Ⓦ www.eurolines-pass.com. Offers the Eurolines pass, valid for travel between 35 cities in sixteen countries. It costs £189/€250 (£229/€270 for over 26s) for fifteen days in high season (late June to mid-Sept as well as Christmas/New Year) and £249/€295 (£299/€355) for 30 days. Prices are around a third lower in low season.
Busabout Ⓦ **www.busabout.com.** Offers a hop-on, hop-off service throughout Western Europe operating May–Oct. There are three "loops" on offer as well as a Flexitrip Pass where you design your own route. Prices start from £315/€375 for a one-loop pass or £279/€330 for the Flexitrip Pass.
Contiki Ⓦ **www.contiki.com.** Long-established operator offering bus tours throughout Europe for 18–35-year-olds from three to 46 days. An eleven-day tour from Amsterdam to Barcelona costs £999/€1200 including hotel accommodation and meals.

BY FERRY

Travelling by **ferry** is sometimes the most practical way to get around, the obvious routes being from the mainland to the Mediterranean islands, and between the countries bordering the Baltic and Adriatic seas. There are countless routes serving a huge range of destinations, too numerous to outline here; we've given the details of the most useful routes within each chapter. For further details of schedules and operators, see the *Thomas Cook European Timetable*.

BY PLANE

Most European countries now have at least one budget airline selling **low-cost flights** online, and invariably undercutting train and bus fares on longer international routes. Apart from its environmental impact, travelling by air means you miss the scenery and "feel" for a country that ground-level transport can provide; there's also the inconvenience of getting between airports and the cities they serve, often quite a haul in itself. But, if you're pressed for time, and especially if you want to get from one end of Europe to another, flying is definitely an option. See p.30 for a selective list of budget airlines.

Accommodation

Although accommodation is one of the key costs to consider when planning your trip, it needn't be a stumbling block to a budget-conscious tour of Europe. Indeed, even in Europe's pricier destinations the hostel system means there is always an affordable place to stay. If you're prepared to camp, you can get by on very little while staying at some excellently equipped sites.

The one rule of thumb is that in the most popular cities and resorts – Venice, Amsterdam, Prague, Paris, Barcelona, the Algarve, and so on – things can get very busy during the peak summer months. Be sure to book in advance regardless of your budget.

HOSTELS

The cheapest places to stay around Europe are the innumerable **hostels** that cover the continent. Recent years, particularly in popular cities, have seen a blossoming in the number of good-quality **independent hostels**, though the majority of hostels remain members of **Hostelling International** (HI), which incorporates the national youth hostel associations of every country in the world. Most are clean, well-run places, always offering dormitory accommodation, and often a range of private single and double rooms, or rooms with four to six beds. Many hostels also either have self-catering facilities or provide low-cost meals, and the larger ones have a range of other facilities – a swimming pool and a games room for example. There is usually no age limit, but where there is limited space priority is given to those under 26. The best rates are usually available online, on the hostel website or through booking engines such as Hostelworld (ⓦwww.hostelworld.com) or Hostelbookers (ⓦwww.hostelbookers.com).

Strictly speaking, to use an HI hostel you have to have **membership**, although if there's room you can stay at most hostels by simply paying a bit extra. If you do intend to do a lot of hostelling, however, it's certainly worth joining, which you can do through your home country's hostelling association (we've given the name and website of the relevant national hostelling organization in each chapter). HI hostels can usually be booked through their country's hostelling association website, almost always over-the-counter at other hostels in the same country, and often through the international HI website, ⓦwww.hihostels.com. Alternatively try ⓦwww.hostels.com or www.hostelz.com, which also offer non HI-affiliated hostels.

Youth hostel associations

US and Canada

Hostelling International-American Youth Hostels ⓦwww.hiayh.org.
Hostelling International Canada ⓣ1-800/663-5777, ⓦwww.hihostels.ca.

ACCOMMODATION PRICES

All accommodation prices listed are for high season. The prices we list for **hotels**, guesthouses, B&Bs, *pensions* and private rooms are for the cheapest double room. For **hostels**, it is the price of the cheapest dorm bed, and for **campsites** the cost of a night's stay per person, except where noted.

UK and Ireland

Youth Hostels Association (YHA) England and Wales ⓣ01629/592700, ⓦwww.yha.org.uk.
Scottish Youth Hostels Association ⓣ01786/891400, ⓦwww.syha.org.uk.
Irish Youth Hostel Association Republic of Ireland ⓣ01/830 4555, ⓦwww.anoige.ie.
Hostelling International Northern Ireland ⓣ028/9032 4733, ⓦwww.hini.org.uk.

Australia, New Zealand and South Africa

Australia Youth Hostels Association ⓦwww.yha.com.au.
Youth Hostelling Association New Zealand ⓣ0800/278 29, ⓦwww.yha.co.nz.
Hostelling International South Africa ⓦwww.hihostels.com.

HOTELS AND PENSIONS

With **hotels** you can really spend as much or as little as you like. Most hotels in Europe are graded on some kind of star system. One- and two-star category hotels are plain and simple on the whole, usually family-run, and rooms often lack private facilities; sometimes breakfast won't be included. In three-star hotels rooms will nearly always be en suite, prices will normally include breakfast and there may well be a phone or TV in the room; while four- and five-star places will certainly have all these, plus swimming pool, and other such niceties. In the really top-level places breakfast, oddly enough, isn't always included.

Obviously prices vary greatly, but you're rarely going to be paying less than £25/US$35 for a basic double room even in southern Europe, while in the Netherlands the average price is around £50/US$70, and in Scandinavia and the British Isles somewhat higher than that. In some countries a **pension** or B&B (also variously known as a guesthouse, *pensão*, *Gasthaus* or numerous other names) is a cheaper alternative, offering just a few rooms of simple accommodation. In some countries these advertise with a sign in the window; in others they can be booked through the tourist office, which may demand a small fee. There are various other kinds of accommodation – apartments, farmhouses, cottages, *gîtes* in France, and more – but most are geared to longer-term stays and we have detailed them only where relevant.

CAMPING

The cheapest form of accommodation is, of course, a **campsite**, either pitching your own tent or parking your caravan or camper van. Most sites charge per person, with additional charges per plot and/or per vehicle. Facilities can be excellent, especially in countries such as France where camping is very popular, though of course the better the facilities, the pricier the site. If you don't have a vehicle you should add in the cost and inconvenience of getting to the site, since most are on the outskirts of towns, sometimes further. Some sites also have **cabins**, which you can stay in for a little extra, although these are usually fairly basic affairs, only really worth considering in regions like Scandinavia where budget options are thin on the ground. **Tourist offices** can often recommend well-equipped and conveniently located sites.

As for **camping rough**, it's a fine idea if you can get away with it – though perhaps an entire trip of rough camping is in reality too gruelling to be truly enjoyable. In some countries it's easy – in parts of Scandinavia

COUCHSURFING

Couchsurfing (ⓦwww.couchsurfing.com) is an internet-based hospitality service offering travellers the chance to stay for free with local people. Hosts are verified through references and a vouching system but you should obviously think carefully about who you are prepared to stay with and have a back-up plan if things don't work out (there are plenty of **safety tips** detailed on their website). There are now more than a million couchsurfer members. Many sites have tried to piggyback on this trend, but few are as popular – one worth checking out though is Room FT (ⓦwww.roomft.com).

it's a legal right, and in Greece and other southern European countries you can usually find a bit of beach to pitch down on – but in others it can get you into trouble with the law.

Camping carnets

If you're planning to do a lot of camping, an **international camping carnet**, which gives discounts on member sites, is a good investment. In **the US and Canada** the carnet is available from home motoring organizations, or from Family Campers and RVers (FCRV; ⓣ1-800/245-9755, ⓦwww.fcrv.org). In **the UK and Ireland**, the carnet costs £4.95, and is available to members of the AA in Ireland or the RAC in the UK, or for members only from the Camping and Caravanning Club (ⓣ084/5130 7632, ⓦwww.campingandcaravanningclub.co.uk; annual membership £35).

Festivals and annual events

There's always some event or other happening in Europe, and the bigger shindigs can be reason enough for visiting a place. Be warned, though, that if you're intending to visit a place during its annual festival you need to plan well in advance; accommodation can be booked up months beforehand, especially for the most famous events. For a complete guide to world festivals check out ⓦworldparty.roughguides.com.

FESTIVAL CALENDAR

Many of the **festivals** and **annual events** you'll come across in Europe have their origin in – and in many cases still represent – religious celebrations, commemorating a local miracle or saint's day. Others are decidedly more secular – from film and music festivals to street carnivals. The following are some of the biggest celebrations, further information on which can be found online or at local tourist offices.

January

Twelfth Night (Jan 6) Rather than Christmas Day, in Spain this is the time for present-giving, while in Orthodox Eastern Europe, Jan 6 is Christmas Day.
La Tamborrada, San Sebastián, Spain (Jan 20) Probably the loudest festival you will encounter as scores of drummers take to the streets of San Sebastián.

February

Berlin Film Festival, Germany (early to mid-Feb) Home of the Golden Bear award, this film bash is geared towards the general public.
Carnival/Mardi Gras (mid-Feb) Celebrated most famously in Venice, but there are smaller events across Europe, notably in Viareggio (Italy), Luzern and Basel (Switzerland), Cologne (Germany), Maastricht (Netherlands) and tiny Binche (Belgium).

March

Las Fallas, Valencia, Spain (March 15–19) The passing of winter is celebrated in explosive fashion with enormous bonfires, burning effigies and plenty of all-night partying.

St Patrick's Day (March 17) Celebrated wherever there's an Irish community, in Dublin it's a five-day festival with music, parades and a lot of drinking.

April

Easter Celebrated with most verve and ceremony in Catholic and Orthodox Europe, where Easter Sunday or Monday is usually marked with some sort of procession; note that the Orthodox Church's Easter can fall a week or two either side of the Western festival.

Feria de Abril, Seville, Spain (mid-April) A week of flamenco music and dancing, parades and bullfights, in a frenzied and enthusiastic atmosphere.

Queen's Day, Amsterdam, Netherlands (April 30) Queen Beatrix's official birthday is the excuse for this anarchic 24-hour drinking and dressing-up binge – remember your orange attire.

May

Cannes Film Festival, France The world's most famous cinema festival is really more of an industry affair than anything else.

PinkPop Festival, Landgraaf, Netherlands (late May/early June) Holland's biggest pop music festival.

June

Festa do São João, Porto, Portugal (June 23–24) Portugal's second city puts on the mother of all street parties, culminating in revellers hitting each other with plastic hammers.

Glastonbury Festival, England (mid/late June) Despite being one of Europe's largest (most expensive) music festivals, Glastonbury is a surprisingly intimate affair thanks to its beautiful setting and hippie vibe.

Roskilde Festival, Denmark (late June/early July) An eclectic range of music (rock, dance, folk) and performance arts, with profits going to worthy causes.

July

The Palio, Siena, Italy (July 2 & Aug 16) Italy's most spectacular annual event: a bareback horse race between representatives of the different quarters of the city around the main square.

Exit Festival, Novi Sad, Serbia (early July) Europe's hippest music festival held in a beautiful fortress and attracting top DJs and artists from around the world.

Montreux Jazz Festival, Switzerland (early July) These days only loosely committed to jazz, this festival takes in everything from folk to breakbeats.

Fiesta de San Fermín, Pamplona, Spain (July 6–14) Anarchic fun, centred on the running of the bulls through the streets of the city, plus music, dancing and of course a lot of drinking.

Avignon Festival, France Slanted towards drama but hosts plenty of other events too.

Dubrovnik Summer Festival, Croatia (July & Aug) A host of musical events and theatre performances against the backdrop of the town's beautiful Renaissance centre.

The Proms, London (July–Sept) World-famous concert series that maintains high standards of classical music at egalitarian prices.

August

Edinburgh Festival, Scotland A mass of top-notch and fringe events in every performing medium, from rock to cabaret to modern experimental music, dance and drama.

Locarno Film Festival, Switzerland (early Aug) Movies from around the world compete on the banks of Lake Maggiore.

La Tomatina, Buñol, Spain The last Wednesday in August sees the streets of Buñol packed for a one-hour food fight disposing of 130,000 kilos of tomatoes.

Notting Hill Carnival, London (last weekend of Aug) Predominantly Black British and Caribbean celebration that's become the world's second biggest street carnival after Rio.

Ramadan (Aug/Sept in 2010 & 2011) Commemorating the revelation of the Koran to the Prophet Mohammed, the month of fasting from sunrise until sunset ends with a huge celebration called Eid el-Fitr. Morocco, Turkey, Kosovo, Albania, Bosnia-Herzegovina, plus Muslim areas of Bulgaria and Greece.

September

Ibiza Closing Parties, Spain (first week in Sept) The summer dance music Mecca goes out with a bang in September with all the main clubs holding closing parties.

Venice Film Festival, Italy (first 2 weeks in Sept) First held in 1932, this is the world's oldest film festival.

Regata Storica, Venice, Italy (early Sept) A trial of skill for the city's gondoliers.

Oktoberfest, Munich, Germany (final 2 weeks of Sept) A huge beer festival and fair, attracting vast numbers of people to consume gluttonous quantities of beer and food.

Galway International Oyster Festival, Ireland (last weekend in Sept) The arrival of the oyster season is celebrated with a three-day seafood, Guinness and dancing shindig.

October

Combat des Reines, Switzerland (mid-Oct) Quirky cow-fighting contest held to decide the queen of the herd in the Valais region of Switzerland. The main event is the copious drinking and betting on the sidelines (and no, the cows don't get hurt).

Mondial du Snowboard, Les Deux Alpes, France (last weekend in Oct) World-class boarders and plenty of hangers-on kick off the snow season at this beautiful Alpine resort.

November

Bonfire Night, Lewes, England (Nov 5) Huge processions and tremendous fireworks light up this sleepy town every year.

Madonna della Salute Festival, Venice, Italy (Nov 21) Annual candle-lit procession across the Grand Canal to the church of the Santa Maria della Salute.

December

Christmas Festive markets sprout up across the continent in the run-up to Christmas. One of the best is found in Cologne, Germany.

New Year's Eve Celebrated with fireworks and parties across Europe, it's probably best experienced in Edinburgh where over a hundred thousand cram the streets for Hogmanay.

Work and study

The best way of getting to know a country properly is to work there and learn the language. Study opportunities are also a good way of absorbing yourself in the local culture, though they invariably need to be fixed up in advance; check newspapers for ads or contact one of the organizations listed on p.44.

WORKING IN EUROPE

There are any number of jobs you can pick up on the road to supplement your spending money. It's normally not hard to find **bar** or **restaurant work**, especially in large resort areas during the summer, and your chances will be greater if you speak the local language – although being able to speak English may be your greatest asset in more touristy areas. Cleaning jobs, nannying and **au pair** work are also common, if not spectacularly well paid, often just providing room and board plus pocket money. Some of them can be organized on the spot, while others need to be arranged before you leave home.

The other big casual earner is **farm work**, particularly grape-picking, an option from August to October when the vines are being harvested. The best country for this is France, but there's sometimes work in Germany too, and you're unlikely to be asked for documentation. Also in France, along the Côte d'Azur, and in other yacht-havens such as Greece and parts of southern Spain, there is sometimes **crewing work** available, though you'll obviously need the appropriate experience.

Rather better paid, and equally widespread, if only during the September to June period, is **teaching English** as a foreign language (TEFL), though it's sometimes hard to find English-teaching jobs without a TEFL qualification. You'll normally be paid a liveable local salary, sometimes with somewhere to live thrown in, and you can often supplement your income with more lucrative private lessons. The TEFL teaching season

is reversed in Britain and to a lesser extent Ireland, with plenty of work available during the summer in London and on the English south coast (but again, some kind of TEFL qualification is usually required).

A final tip for those hoping to work abroad: buy a book dedicated to the subject. We recommend those published in the UK by Vacation Work; visit Ⓦwww.crimsonpublishing.co.uk for their catalogue. Travel magazines like *Wanderlust* (Ⓦwww.wanderlust.co.uk) have a Job Shop section which often advertises job opportunities with tour companies, while Ⓦwww.studyabroad.com is a useful website with listings and links to study and work programmes worldwide.

STUDYING IN EUROPE

Studying abroad invariably means learning a language, doing an intensive course that lasts between two weeks and three months and staying with a local family. There are plenty of places you can do this, and you should reckon on paying around £200/US$300 a week, including room and board. If you know a language well, you could also apply to do a short course in another subject at a local university; scan the classified sections of the newspapers back home, and keep an eye out when you're on the spot. The EU runs a programme called **Erasmus** in which university students from Britain and Ireland can obtain mobility grants to study in one of 31 European countries for between three months and a full academic year if their university participates in the programme. Check with your university's international relations office, or see Ⓦwww.britishcouncil.org/erasmus.

Work and study contacts

AFS Intercultural Programs US Ⓣ1-800/AFS-INFO, international enquiries Ⓣ+1-212/352-9810; Ⓦwww.afs.org. Global UN-recognized organization running summer programmes to foster international understanding.

American Institute for Foreign Study UK Ⓣ020/7581 7300, US Ⓣ1-866/906-2437; Ⓦwww.aifs.com. Language study and cultural immersion for the summer or school year.

ASSE International UK Ⓣ01952/460 733, US Ⓣ1-800/677-2773, Canada Ⓣ1-800/361-3214, Australia Ⓣ03/9775 4711; Ⓦwww.asse.com. International student exchanges and summer language programmes across most of Europe.

Association for International Practical Training US Ⓣ410/997-2200, Ⓦwww.aipt.org. Summer internships in various European countries for students who have completed at least two years of college in science, agriculture, engineering or architecture.

British Council UK Ⓣ0161/957 7775, Ⓦwww.britishcouncil.org. The Council's Recruitment Group recruits TEFL teachers with degrees and TEFL qualifications for posts, while its Education and Training Group runs teacher exchange programmes and enables those who already work as educators to find out about teacher development programmes abroad.

Council on International Educational Exchange (CIEE) US Ⓣ1-800/40-STUDY, Ⓦwww.ciee.org/study. An international organization worth contacting for advice on studying, working and volunteering in Europe. They run summer-semester and one-year study programmes, and volunteer projects.

International House UK Ⓣ020/7611 2400, Ⓦwww.ihlondon.com. Head office for reputable English-teaching organization that offers TEFL training leading to the award of a Certificate in English Language Teaching to Adults (CELTA), and recruits for teaching positions in Britain and abroad.

World Learning US Ⓣ1-800/257-7751, Ⓦwww.worldlearning.org. The Experiment in International Living (Ⓦwww.experimentinternational.org) has summer programmes for high-school students, while the School for International Training (Ⓦwww.sit.edu/studyabroad) offers accredited college semesters abroad, with language and cultural studies, homestay and other academic work.

Travel essentials

COSTS

It's hard to generalize about what you're likely to spend travelling around Europe, but it's generally not cheap. Some countries – Norway, Switzerland, the UK – are among the most expensive in the world, while in others (Turkey, for example) you can live quite well on a fairly modest budget. Remember however that all of Europe is modern and well touristed which means higher prices than in the developing world. In general, countries in the north and west of Europe are more expensive than those in the south and east, though keep an eye on exchange rates.

Accommodation will be your largest single expense, and can really determine where you decide to travel. **Food and drink** costs also vary wildly, although again in most parts of Europe you can assume that a cheap restaurant meal will cost £8–15/US$15–25 a head, with prices nearer the top end of the scale in Scandinavia, at the bottom end in eastern and southern Europe, and below that in Turkey and Morocco. **Transport** costs are something you can pin down more exactly if you have a rail pass. Nowhere, though, are transport costs a major burden, except perhaps in Britain where public transport is less heavily subsidized than elsewhere.

The bottom line for an **average daily budget** touring the continent – camping, self-catering, hitching, etc – might be around £25/US$35 a day per person. Adding on a rail pass, staying in hostels and eating out occasionally would bring this up to perhaps £40/US$60 a day, while staying in private

> At the beginning of each chapter you'll find a guide to "rough costs" including food, accommodation and travel. Prices are quoted in euros for ease of comparison. Within the chapter itself prices are quoted in local currency.

GETTING BY ON A BUDGET

Buy a rail pass. Whether you're planning to take in all of Europe or just a few countries, a rail pass will save you a bundle (see p.34).

Find a roommate. Accommodation in hotels, *pensions* and private rooms is cheaper if you share, so buddy up.

Student/youth discounts. If you're a student or under 26, make sure you bring your student or youth card (see p.52) and always ask about discounts.

Head for the countryside. Don't spend more time than you need to in the city – prices will always be highest.

Shun tourist traps. Eat and drink with the locals and try regional food as it'll usually be cheaper.

Self-cater. Markets in Europe are full of fresh, seasonal picnic fare which makes self-catering a treat.

Take a water bottle. Water's free to refill, after all.

Drink at home. Have a few drinks before you go out – you can usually pick up beer and wine from local shops at a fraction of the price that you'll pay in bars.

Be flexible. Transport is often cheaper in off-peak hours.

Sleep on the train. Make your longest journeys overnight – you'll forego accommodation costs for the night.

Bargain, bargain, bargain. Don't be afraid to haggle (especially in places like Morocco where it's expected), but know when to stop.

rooms or hotels and eating out once a day would mean a personal daily budget of at least £60/US$90. See the box on p.45 for tips on keeping your costs down.

CRIME AND PERSONAL SAFETY

Travelling around Europe should be relatively trouble-free, but, as in any part of the world, there is always the chance of petty theft. Conditions vary greatly depending on the country: in Scandinavia, for example, you're unlikely to encounter much trouble of any kind, whereas in the inner-city areas of metropolises such as London, Paris or Barcelona, the crime rate is significantly higher. Finally, in poorer regions such as Morocco, Turkey and southern Italy, street crime tends to be low, but tourists are an obvious target.

Safety tips

In order to minimize the risks, you should take some basic **precautions**. First and perhaps most important, you should try not to look too much like a tourist. Appearing lost, even if you are, is to be avoided, and it's not a good idea – especially in southern Europe – to walk around flashing an obviously expensive camera: the professional bag-snatchers who tour train stations can have your valuables off you in seconds.

Be discreet about using a **mobile phone**, and be sure to put it back into a secure pocket as soon as you've finished; be similarly protective of your iPod. If you're waiting for a train, keep your eyes (and hands if necessary) on your bags at all times; if you want to sleep, put everything valuable under whatever you use as a pillow. Exercise caution when choosing a train compartment and avoid any situation that makes you feel uncomfortable. **Padlocking** your bags to the luggage rack if you're on an overnight train increases the likelihood that they'll still be there in the morning. It's also a good Idea to wear a money belt.

If you're staying in a hostel, take your valuables out with you unless there's a very secure store for them on the premises. Having **photocopies** of your passport and ID is a good idea, as is storing a copy of your address book with friends or family. If you're driving, don't leave anything valuable in your parked car.

If the worst happens and you do have something stolen, inform the **police** immediately (we've included details of the main city police stations – and where relevant dedicated tourist police – in the Guide); the priority is to get a statement from them detailing exactly what has been lost, which you'll need for your insurance claim back home. Generally you'll find the police sympathetic enough, sometimes able to speak English, but often unwilling to do much more than make out a report for you.

Drugs

It's hardly necessary to state that **drugs** such as amphetamines, cocaine, heroin, LSD and ecstasy are illegal all over Europe, and although use of cannabis is widespread in most countries, and legally tolerated in some (famously in the Netherlands, for example), you are never allowed to possess more than a tiny amount for personal use, and unlicensed sale remains illegal. Penalties can be severe (in certain countries, such as Turkey, even possession of cannabis can result in a hefty prison sentence) and your consulate is unlikely to be sympathetic.

ELECTRICITY

The supply in Europe is 220v (240v in the British Isles), which means that anything on North American **voltage** (110v) normally needs a transformer – or at least a plug adapter if the power cord has a built-in transformer. Some countries (notably Spain and Morocco) still have a few places on 110v or 120v, so check before plugging in or you could fry your electronics. Continental, Moroccan and Turkish **sockets** take two round pins, British and Irish ones take three rectangular pins. A travel plug which adapts to all these systems is useful to carry. See Ⓦwww.kropla.com for more.

ENTRY REQUIREMENTS

Citizens of the UK (but not other British passport holders), Ireland, Australia, New Zealand, Canada and the US do not need a visa to enter most European countries (current exceptions are listed in the box below), and can usually stay for between one and three months, depending on nationality; for some countries, passports must be valid for at least six months beyond the end of stay. EU countries never require visas from British or Irish citizens. Always check **visa requirements** before travelling, as they can and do change; this especially applies to Canadian, Australian and New Zealand citizens intending to visit Eastern European countries.

> **VISA ALERT!**
>
> Everyone needs a visa to visit **Russia**, which must be obtained in advance, and if you're passing through **Belarus** to get there, you'll need a transit visa for that country as well. Citizens of most countries also need a visa for **Turkey**, which is available at the border (see p.1216). **South Africans** need a visa to enter most European countries so be sure to check with the appropriate embassy before travelling.

Twenty-five countries (Austria, Belgium, Czech Republic, Denmark, Estonia, Finland, France, Germany, Greece, Hungary, Iceland, Italy, Latvia, Lithuania, Luxembourg, Malta, Monaco, the Netherlands, Norway, Poland, Portugal, Slovakia, Slovenia, Spain and Sweden), known as the **Schengen group**, now have joint visas which are valid for travel in all of them; in theory, there are also no immigration controls between these countries, but, in practice, there are often more ID spot-checks within their borders.

Customs

Customs and duty-free restrictions vary throughout Europe, but are standard for travellers arriving in the EU at one litre of spirits, four litres of table wine, plus 200 cigarettes (or 250g tobacco, or fifty cigars). There is no duty-free allowance for travel within the EU: in principle you can carry as much in the way of duty-paid goods as you want, so long as it is for personal use. Note that Andorra, Gibraltar, the Canary Islands and Ceuta are outside the EU for customs purposes. Remember that if you are carrying prescribed drugs of any kind, it might be a good idea to have a copy

of the prescription to show to suspicious customs officers. Note also that many countries, including all EU members, restrict the importation of meat, fish, eggs, vegetables and honey, even for personal consumption.

GAY AND LESBIAN TRAVELLERS

Gay men and lesbians will find most of Europe a tolerant place in which to travel, the west rather more so than the east. Gay sex is no longer a criminal offence in any country covered by this book except Morocco, but some still have measures that discriminate against gay men (a higher age of consent for example). Lesbianism would seem not to officially exist, so it is not generally subject to such laws. For further information, check the International Lesbian and Gay Association's European region website at Ⓦwww.ilga-europe.org.

HEALTH

There aren't many particular health problems you'll encounter travelling in Europe. You don't need to have **inoculations** for any of the countries covered in this book, although for Morocco and Turkey typhoid jabs are advised, and in southeastern Turkey malaria pills are a good idea for much of the year – check Ⓦwww.cdc.gov/travel/regionalmalaria for full details. When travelling, remember to be up-to-date with your polio and tetanus boosters.

EU citizens are covered by reciprocal health agreements for free or reduced-cost emergency treatment in many of the countries in this book (main exceptions are Albania, Morocco and Turkey). To claim this, you will often be asked for your proof of residence or European Health Insurance Card (EHIC), which you can apply for in Britain at Ⓦwww.dh.gov.uk, and in Ireland at Ⓦwww.ehic.ie. Without an EHIC, you won't be turned away from hospitals but you will almost certainly have to pay for any treatment or medicines. Also, in practice, some countries' doctors and hospitals charge anyway and it's up to you to claim reimbursement when you return home. Make sure you are insured for potential medical expenses, and keep copies of receipts and prescriptions.

Doctors, hospitals and pharmacies

For minor health problems it's easiest to go to a **pharmacy**, found pretty much everywhere. There will always be at least one local pharmacy open 24 hour – check any pharmacy window, which will have a rota indicating the branch currently open through the night.

In cases of serious injury or illness contact your nearest consulate, which will have a list of English-speaking **doctors**, as will the local tourist office. In the accounts of larger cities we've listed the most convenient **hospital** casualty units/emergency rooms.

Contraceptives

Condoms are available everywhere, and are normally reliable international brands such as Durex, at least in northwestern Europe; the condoms in eastern European countries, Morocco and Turkey are of uncertain quality, however, so it's best to stock up in advance.

AIDS is of course as much of a problem in Europe as in the rest of the world, and it hardly needs saying that unprotected casual sex is extremely dangerous; members of both sexes should carry condoms.

The pill is available everywhere, too, though often only on prescription; again, bring a sufficient supply with you. In case of emergency, the morning-after pill is available from pharmacies without a prescription in Belgium, Denmark, Finland, France, Greece, Holland, Morocco, Norway, Poland, Portugal, Sweden, Switzerland and the UK.

Drinking water

Tap water in most countries is drinkable, and only needs to be avoided in Morocco and parts of Turkey. **Unfamiliar food** may well give you a small dose of the runs, but this is usually nothing to worry about, and is normally over in a couple of days.

INSURANCE

Wherever you're travelling from, it's a very good idea to have some kind of **travel insurance**. Before paying for a new policy,

ROUGH GUIDES TRAVEL INSURANCE

Rough Guides has teamed up with WorldNomads.com to offer great **travel insurance** deals. Policies are available to residents of over 150 countries, with cover for a wide range of **adventure sports**, 24hr emergency assistance, high levels of medical and evacuation cover and a stream of **travel safety information**. Roughguides.com users can take advantage of their policies online 24/7, from anywhere in the world – even if you're already travelling. And since plans often change when you're on the road, you can extend your policy and even claim online. Roughguides.com users who buy travel insurance with WorldNomads.com can also leave a positive footprint and donate to a community development project. For more information go to **www.roughguides.com/shop**.

however, it's worth checking whether you're already covered: students will often find that their student health coverage extends into the vacations and for one term beyond the date of last enrolment; and some credit cards include travel insurance.

Otherwise you should contact a specialist **travel insurance company**. A typical policy usually provides cover for the loss of baggage, tickets and – up to a certain limit – cash or cheques, as well as cancellation or curtailment of your journey. Most of them exclude so-called **dangerous sports** unless an extra premium is paid: in Europe this can mean anything from scuba-diving to mountaineering, skiing and even bungee-jumping. With **medical coverage**, you should ascertain whether benefits will be paid as treatment proceeds or only after you return home, and whether there is a 24-hour medical emergency number. When securing baggage cover, make sure that the per-article limit will cover your most valuable possession. If you need to make a claim, you should keep receipts for medicines and medical treatment, and in the event you have anything stolen, you must obtain an official statement from the police.

INTERNET AND EMAIL

More and more **internet cafés** are opening up across Europe and in major capitals you're likely to find many hotels and cafés offer **wireless access** (wi-fi) for those with their own laptops or iPhones. Obviously the further you get off the beaten track, the slower connection speeds will become and you may even have to resort to somewhat expensive dial-up access.

LEFT LUGGAGE

Almost every train station of any size has facilities for depositing **luggage** – either lockers or a desk that's open long hours every day. We've given details in the accounts of the major capitals.

MAIL

We've listed the **central post offices** in major cities and given an idea of opening hours. Bear in mind, though, that throughout much of Europe you can avoid long waits in post offices by buying stamps from newsagents, tobacconists and street kiosks. If you know in advance where you're going to be and when, it is possible to receive mail through the **poste restante** system, whereby letters addressed to you, marked "poste restante" and sent to the main post office in any town or city will be kept under your name – for at least two weeks and usually

NEWSPAPERS

British and American newspapers and magazines are widely available in Europe, sometimes on the day of publication, more often the day after. They do, however, cost around three times as much as they do at home. In addition, there are often locally produced English-language papers available in major European capitals, usually on a weekly or monthly basis. These are often a much more engaging way to get your news fix and learn more about local issues and events.

for a month. When collecting mail, make sure you take your passport for identification, and be aware that there's a possibility of letters being misfiled by someone unfamiliar with your language; try looking under your first name as well as your surname.

MAPS

Though you can often buy **maps** on the spot, you may want to get them in advance to plan your trip – if you know what you want, the best advice is to contact a firm such as Stanfords in the UK (ⓦwww.stanfords.co.uk) or Rand McNally in the US (ⓦwww.randmcnally.com); both sell maps online or by mail order. In addition, Rough Guides produce a range of regional and country maps printed on rip-proof, waterproof paper (see ⓦwww.roughguides.com for the full range).

We've recommended the best maps of individual countries throughout the book. If you intend to travel mainly by rail, it might be worth getting the *Thomas Cook Rail Map of Europe*. For extensive motoring, it's better to get a large-page road atlas such as Michelin's Tourist and Motoring Atlas.

MONEY

The easiest way to carry your money is in the form of plastic. Hotels, shops and restaurants across the continent accept major **credit and debit cards**, although cheaper places may not. More importantly, you can use them 24/7 to get cash out of ATMs throughout the region, including Morocco and Turkey, as long as they are affiliated to an international network (such as Visa, MasterCard or Cirrus). As well as carrying a **cash back-up**, you may also want to consider **traveller's cheques**, in either US dollars, euros or UK pounds.

In some countries **banks** are the only places where you can legally change money, and they often offer the best exchange rates and lowest commission. Local banking hours are given throughout this book. Outside normal hours you can use **bureaux de change**, often located at train stations and airports, though their rates and/or commissions may well be less favourable.

THE EURO (€)

The euro is the currency of 21 EU countries. Coins come as 1c, 2c, 5c, 10c, 20c, 50c, €1 and €2, with one side of the coin stating the denomination while the other side has a design unique to the issuing country. Euro notes come as €5, €10, €20, €50, €100, €200 and €500. At the time of writing, £1 was worth €1.18, US$1 got you 69c, Can$1 was 64c, Aus$1 equalled 58c, NZ$1 was 47c and ZAR1 was 9c.

PHONES

It is nearly always possible, especially in Western Europe, to make **international calls** from a public call box. Otherwise, you can go to a **post office**, or a special **phone bureau**, where you can make a call from a private booth and pay afterwards. Most countries have these in one form or another, and the local tourist office will point you in the right direction. Avoid using the phone in your **hotel room** – unless you have money to burn.

To **call any country** in this book from Britain, Ireland, South Africa or New Zealand, dial ⓣ00, then the country code, then the city/area code (if there is one) without the initial zero – except for Russia, Latvia and Lithuania, where an initial 8 is omitted; Italy, where the initial zero must be dialled; and Spain, where the initial 9 must be dialled – then the local number. From the US and most of Canada, the international access code is ⓣ011, from Australia it's ⓣ0011; otherwise the procedure is the same.

To **call home** from almost all European countries, including Morocco and Turkey, dial ⓣ00, then the country code, then the city/area code (without the initial zero if there is one), then the local number. The exception is Russia, where you dial ⓣ8, wait for a continuous dialling tone and then dial ⓣ10, followed by the country code, area code and number.

For **collect calls**, "Home Country Direct" services are available in most of the places covered in this book. In the UK and some other countries, international calling cards

available from newsagents enable you to call North America, Australia and New Zealand very cheaply. Most North American, British, Irish and Australasian phone companies either allow you to call home from abroad on a credit card, or billed to your home number (contact your company's customer services before you leave to find out their toll-free access codes from the countries you'll be visiting), or else will issue an international calling card which can be used worldwide, and for which you will be billed on your return. If you want a calling card and do not already have one, leave yourself a few weeks to arrange it before leaving.

Mobile/cell phones

Cell phones from the US and Canada may not work in Europe – for details contact your provider. **Mobiles** from the UK, Ireland, Australia and New Zealand and South Africa can be used in most parts of Europe, and a lot of countries – certainly in Western Europe – have nearly universal coverage, but you may have to inform your provider before leaving home to get international access switched on, and you will be charged for receiving calls and even voicemail. Also note that it will not always be possible to charge up or replace your pre-paid cards, so again check beforehand and, if necessary, top up your credit before you leave.

The most useful resource for information on phone codes and electrical systems around the world is ⓦwww.kropla.com.

SHOPPING

Europe is a great place to **shop** – with outlets running the gamut from high fashion houses in Paris and Milan to the souks of Morocco you'll be spoilt for choice. We've included country-specific information on shopping in each individual chapter, especially in capital cities. See the chart below for size conversions.

CLOTHING AND SHOE SIZES

Women's dresses and skirts

American	4	6	8	10	12	14	16	18
British	8	10	12	14	16	18	20	22
Continental	38	40	42	44	46	48	50	52

Women's blouses and sweaters

American	6	8	10	12	14	16	18
British	30	32	34	36	38	40	42
Continental	40	42	44	46	48	50	52

Women's shoes

American	5	6	7	8	9	10	11
British	3	4	5	6	7	8	9
Continental	36	37	38	39	40	41	42

Men's suits

American	34	36	38	40	42	44	46	48
British	34	36	38	40	42	44	46	48
Continental	44	46	48	50	52	54	56	58

Men's shirts

American	14	15	15.5	16	16.5	17	17.5	18
British	14	15	15.5	16	16.5	17	17.5	18
Continental	36	38	39	41	42	43	44	45

Men's shoes

American	7	7.5	8	8.5	9.5	10	10.5	11	11.5
British	6	7	7.5	8	9	9.5	10	11	12
Continental	39	40	41	42	43	44	44	45	46

STUDENT AND YOUTH DISCOUNTS

It's worth flashing whichever discount card you've got at every opportunity – you never know what you might get. If you're a student, an **International Student Identity Card** (ISIC for short) is well worth the investment. It can get you reduced (usually half-price, sometimes free) entry to museums and other sights – costs which can eat their way into your budget alarmingly if you're doing a lot of sightseeing – as well as qualifying you for other discounts in certain cities. It can also save you money on some transport costs, notably ferries. The card costs £9 in the UK, E13 in Ireland, US$22 in the US, Can$16 in Canada, Aus$25 in Australia, NZ$25 in New Zealand and ZAR110 in South Africa. If you're not a student but under 26, get an **International Youth Travel Card**, which costs the same and can in some countries give much the same sort of reductions. Both cards are available direct from Ⓦwww.isiccard.com or from youth travel specialists such as STA.

As well as the above options, the **EURO<26 youth card** (Ⓦwww.euro26.org) entitles anyone under 26 (or up to 30 in some countries) to a wide range of discounts on transport services, tourist attractions, activities and accommodation for up to a year. It is available online for people living outside Europe and at designated outlets throughout the continent (apart from France) for residents – you'll need proof of age and a passport-sized photo. Although the card is valid across the region, prices vary across individual countries (from around €5 to €14), as do the relevant discounts (see website for full details).

TIME

This book covers four **time zones** (see map below). GMT (Greenwich Mean Time), aka UTC, or Universal Time, is five hours ahead

of Eastern Standard Time, eight hours ahead of Pacific Standard Time, eight hours behind Western Australia, ten hours behind eastern Australia, twelve hours behind New Zealand and two hours behind South Africa. Note that all countries in this book (except Morocco) have daylight saving time from March to October; thankfully, they usually all manage to change over at the same time. This change, along with daylight saving in North America, Australia and New Zealand, can affect the time difference by an hour either way.

TOURIST INFORMATION

Before you leave, it's worth contacting the **tourist offices** of the countries you're intending to visit for free leaflets, maps and brochures. This is especially true in parts of central and eastern Europe, where up-to-date maps can be harder to find within the country, though note that a few countries do not have any official tourist offices abroad.

Once you're in Europe, on-the-spot information is easy enough to pick up. Most countries have a network of tourist offices that answer queries, dole out a range of (sometimes free) maps and brochures, and can often book accommodation, or at least advise you on it. They're better organized in northern Europe – the UK, Scandinavia, the Netherlands, France, Switzerland – with branches in all but the smallest village, and mounds of information; in Greece, Turkey and eastern Europe you'll find fewer tourist offices and they'll be less helpful on the whole, sometimes offering no more than a couple of dog-eared brochures and a photocopied map. We've given further details, including a broad idea of opening hours, in the introduction for each country.

Tourist information websites

If there is no office in your home country, apply to the embassy instead.

Albania Ⓦwww.albaniantourism.com.
Andorra Ⓦwww.andorra.ad.
Austria Ⓦwww.austria.info.
Belgium Ⓦwww.visitbelgium.com.
Bosnia-Hercegovina Ⓦwww.bhtourism.ba.
Britain Ⓦwww.visitbritain.com.
Bulgaria Ⓦwww.bulgariatravel.org.
Croatia Ⓦwww.croatia.hr.
Czech Republic Ⓦwww.czechtourism.com.
Denmark Ⓦwww.visitdenmark.com.
Estonia Ⓦwww.visitestonia.com.
Finland Ⓦwww.visitfinland.com.
France Ⓦwww.franceguide.com.
Germany Ⓦwww.germany-tourism.de.
Greece Ⓦwww.gnto.gr.
Hungary Ⓦwww.hungary.com.
Ireland Ⓦwww.tourismireland.com.
Italy Ⓦwww.enit.it.
Latvia Ⓦwww.latviatourism.lv.
Lithuania Ⓦwww.tourism.lt.
Luxembourg Ⓦwww.ont.lu.
Macedonia Ⓦwww.exploringmacedonia.com.
Montenegro Ⓦwww.montenegro.travel.
Morocco Ⓦwww.visitmorocco.org.
Netherlands Ⓦwww.holland.com.
Norway Ⓦwww.visitnorway.com.
Poland Ⓦwww.polandtour.org.
Portugal Ⓦwww.visitportugal.com.
Romania Ⓦwww.romaniatourism.com.
Russia UK Ⓦwww.visitrussia.org.uk; US Ⓦwww.russia-travel.com.
Serbia Ⓦwww.serbia-tourism.org.
Slovenia Ⓦwww.slovenia.info.
Spain Ⓦwww.tourspain.es.
Sweden Ⓦwww.visit-sweden.com.
Switzerland Ⓦwww.myswitzerland.com.
Turkey Ⓦwww.tourismturkey.org.

TRAVELLERS WITH DISABILITIES

Prosperous northern Europe is easier for **disabled travellers** than the south and east, but the gradual enforcement of EU accessibility regulations is making life easier throughout the European Union at least. **Wheelchair access** to public buildings nonetheless remains far from common in many countries, as is wheelchair accessibility to public transport. Most buses are still inaccessible to wheelchair users, but airport facilities are improving, as are those on cross-Channel ferries. As for rail services, these vary greatly: France, for example, has very good facilities for disabled passengers, as have Belgium, Denmark, Switzerland and Austria, but many other countries make little if any provision. For comprehensive info on disabled travel, check out Ⓦwww.disabledtravelers.com.

WOMEN TRAVELLERS

One of the major irritants for women travelling through Europe is **sexual harassment**, which in Italy, Greece, Turkey, Spain and Morocco especially can be almost constant for women travelling alone. By far the most common kind of harassment you'll come across simply consists of street whistles and catcalls; occasionally it's more sinister and very occasionally it can be dangerous. Indifference is often the best policy, avoiding eye contact with men and at the same time appearing as confident and purposeful as possible. If this doesn't make you feel any more comfortable, shouting a few choice phrases in the local language is a good idea; don't, however, shout in English, which often seems to encourage them. You may also come across gropers on crowded buses and trains, in which case you should complain as loudly as possible in any language – the ensuing scene should be enough to deter your assailant.

Albania

HIGHLIGHTS

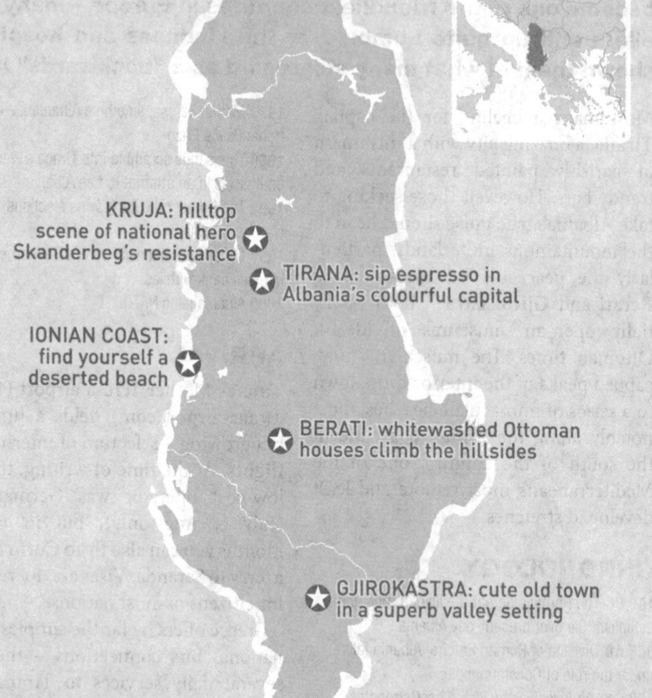

KRUJA: hilltop scene of national hero Skanderbeg's resistance
TIRANA: sip espresso in Albania's colourful capital
IONIAN COAST: find yourself a deserted beach
BERATI: whitewashed Ottoman houses climb the hillsides
GJIROKASTRA: cute old town in a superb valley setting

ROUGH COSTS

DAILY BUDGET Basic €20/occasional treat €35

DRINK Raki €0.75

FOOD Qoftë (lamb rissoles) €2

HOSTEL/BUDGET HOTEL €10/€25

TRAVEL Tirana–Berati (120km) €3.50 by bus; Tirana–Pogradeci (135km) €1.80 by train.

FACT FILE

POPULATION 3.5 million

AREA 28,748 sq km

LANGUAGE Albanian (Shqip)

CURRENCY Lekë

CAPITAL Tirana (population 850,000)

INTERNATIONAL PHONE CODE ⓣ355

Introduction

Albania is something of an oddity within Europe: mosques abound, roads are occasionally wretched and the language bears no relation to that of its neighbouring countries. Idiosyncrasies such as these serve to attract intrepid travellers like moths to a flame. While still a little rough around the edges, Albania has largely shrugged off its years of isolation to become one of the friendliest countries in Europe – many travellers end up quite humbled by the kindness and hospitality shown them in what many still regard as a "backwards" land.

Most make a beeline for the capital, **Tirana**, a buzzing city with a mishmash of garishly painted restaurants and trendy bars. However, those seeking to take Albania's true pulse should head to the mountainous hinterlands, particularly the peaceable hillside towns of **Berati** and **Gjirokastra** – both essentially open-air museums of life in Ottoman times. The muscular, snow-capped peaks of the interior drop down to a series of immaculate beaches, most notably along the **Ionian coastline** in the south of the country, one of the Mediterranean's most remote and least developed stretches.

CHRONOLOGY

168 BC The Romans defeat the Illyrian tribe and establish rule over present-day Albania.
395 AD Division of Roman Empire; Albania falls under the rule of Constantinople.
300s–500s Invasions by Visigoths, Ostrogoths and Huns.
1343 Serbian invasions.
1443–1479 Resistance against Ottoman rule, most of it led by national hero Skanderbeg.
1614 Founding of Tirana.
1912 Albania gains independence.
1922 Ahmet Zogu becomes prime minister, president, then finally crowns himself King Zog in 1928.
1939 Mussolini annexes Albania; King Zog retreats to the *Ritz* in London.
1946 Proclamation of People's Republic of Albania, led by Enver Hoxha.
1967 "Cultural Revolution" sees agriculture collectivized, religious buildings destroyed and cadres purged.
1979 Mother Teresa, an ethnic Albanian, wins the Nobel Peace Prize.
1990 Thousands scramble into Tirana's Western embassies in an attempt to flee Albania.
1992 The Democratic Party wins elections, ending communist rule.
1997 Collapse of financial pyramid schemes results in mass bankruptcies.
2009 Albania joins NATO.

ARRIVAL

Tirana's Mother Teresa airport (Ⓦwww.tirana-airport.com) fields a limited – but growing – selection of international **flights**. At the time of writing, the only low-cost operator was Germanwings (July & Aug only), but in warmer months you can also fly to Corfu and get a ferry to Saranda. Visas are not required for citizens of most nations.

Greece offers by far the simplest international **bus** connections – there are several daily services to Tirana from both Athens and Thessaloniki (from €25), and it's also possible to get direct buses to a number of other Albanian cities. From Macedonia there are direct buses from Skopje (via Struga). Getting there from Montenegro is still a pain, though it's now possible to take an early morning *furgon* to Shkodra from Ulcinj.

The most interesting form of arrival is by **ferry** from Italy – Venezia Lines (Ⓦwww.venezialines.com) runs daily services to Durrësi from Bari from €62, while Agemar (Ⓦwww.agemar.it) has thrice-weekly ferries from both Trieste

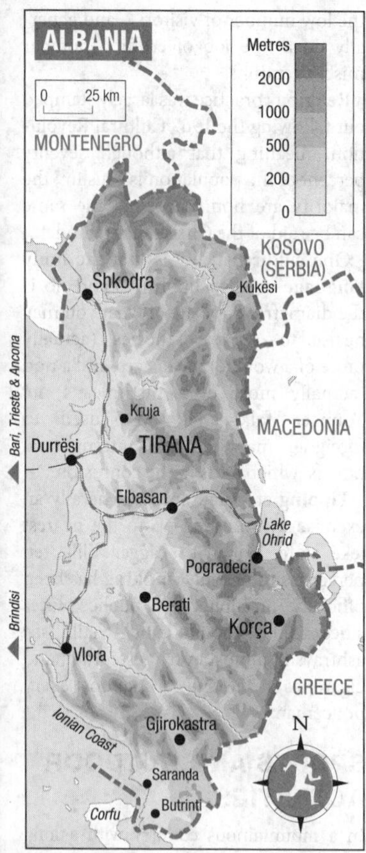

and Ancona. There are also services from Brindisi to Vlora with Skenderbeg Lines (Ⓦwww.skenderbeglines.com). It's also possible to get to Saranda by ferry from Corfu (€15), with at least one ferry per day making the short hop.

GETTING AROUND

Albania's transport infrastructure is a bit of a mess, though don't let this put you off – you simply need a little time and a little patience, and to treat travel information as guideline rather than gospel.

Travel is usually by **bus**; most of the vehicles are fine, fares are cheap, and the roads are continually being improved. However, the authorities have steadfastly refused to build any bus stations – fine in smaller towns, but a nightmare in a city as large as Tirana where matters are utterly confusing. Buses are supplemented by minibuses known as **furgons**, which are more numerous but run to no fixed schedule, and with no obligation to depart until full, drivers tend to roam around town until they have the required number of passengers. Note that most buses and *furgons* depart in the morning, and tend to dry up by mid-afternoon.

Albania also boasts a limited **train** network. The main line runs from Tirana to Durrësi, then heads south before splitting off to Vlora and Pogradeci; there's also a route heading north to Shkodra. The trains are slow and sport cracked windows, but are worth trying at least once; tickets can be bought on board. Note that InterRail passes are not valid in Albania.

ACCOMMODATION

Accommodation is surprisingly plentiful for a country with such low tourist numbers, and while state-owned monstrosities were once the norm, a recent building boom has unleashed a whole generation of clean, good-value **hotels**. You should be able to find a double room for under €25 (prices are almost always quoted in euros), and breakfast is usually included. During summer, **private rooms** come into play at beach resorts, and there are now **hostels** in Tirana, Saranda and Berati, all charging around €10 for a dorm bed. There are almost no dedicated **campsites**, though the secluded beaches

ALBANIAN ADDRESSES

Note that outside Tirana, postal addresses are almost non-existent, since few streets have official names. This can make it tricky to track down a particular hotel or restaurant, but locals are always willing to help.

of the Ionian coast are great for those who don't need facilities.

FOOD AND DRINK

Albania's largely meat-based cuisine brings together elements of Slavic, Turkish and Italian fare. Spit-roasted lamb is the traditional dish of choice, though today it's *qebab* (kebabs) and *qoftë* (grilled lamb rissoles) that dominate menus, often served with a bowl of *kos* (yoghurt). Another interesting dish is *fergesë*, a mix of egg, onions and tomatoes (and meat in some regions) cooked in a clay pot. Seafood is also plentiful around the coast, but for all this choice the modern Albanian youth – and many a tourist – subsists almost entirely on snack food, particularly *burek*, a pastry filled with cheese, meat or spinach; and *sufllaqë*, sliced kebab meat and french fries stuffed in a roll of flatbread. There are some excellent **desserts** on offer, including spongy *shendetlije*, cream-saturated *trilece*, and the usual Turkish pastries.

As for drinks, **coffee** is king in Albania. Consumed throughout the day, it's traditionally served Turkish-style, with grounds at the bottom (*kafe turke*), though there has recently been a marked shift towards espresso. There are cafés everywhere you look, and it's worth noting that cafés and bars generally melt into the same grey area – what's one by day will usually morph into the other by night.

The alcoholic drink of choice is **raki** – like coffee, this spirit is something of a way of life in Albania, and usually consumed with meals. The country also pumps out some good **wine**, mostly red; though most locals will own to a preference for Macedonian fare, Rilindja is a good, easy-to-find local label. **Beer** is easy to find, and it's also worth noting the delicious Skënderbeg **cognac**.

CULTURE AND ETIQUETTE

Albanians tend to go out of their way to welcome foreign guests – partly due to the low number of visitors – and generally do a fine job of eroding popular misconceptions.

Religious practice was largely stamped out following the 1967 Cultural Revolution, meaning that although seventy percent of the population is Muslim, the majority are non-practising; the same can be said of the Christian remainder.

One cultural nicety is that the **body language** used to imply yes and no is the diametric opposite of what you may be used to – a shake of the head (actually more of a wobble) means yes, and a nod (actually more of a tilt) means no. Younger folk and those used to foreigners may well follow international norms, which adds to the confusion.

Tipping at restaurants is generally an exercise in rounding up to the nearest lekë note, but with bigger bills ten percent is the norm. **Smoking** has been officially prohibited in public places since 2007, though you'll still see ashtrays in almost every restaurant, and cigarettes in the fingers of almost every policeman.

SPORTS AND OUTDOOR ACTIVITIES

In a mountainous country with a long coastline, the main attractions are pretty obvious – there are some delightful places to **swim** along the Ionian coast, while the most accessible **hiking** is in the national park area of Mount Dajti. More adventurous activities are thin on the ground, with a monopoly of sorts held by Outdoor Albania (Ⓣ04/227 2075, Ⓦwww.outdooralbania.com), an adventurous young team that can organize treks and **ski-shoeing** trips, or more high-octane fun such as **kayaking** and **paragliding**.

COMMUNICATIONS

Albania's network of **post offices** continues to grow, and most are open Monday to Friday from 9am to 5pm. While their quality of distribution is also improving – from a pretty low base

Albanian

Note that the dual nature of Albanian nouns – all have definite and indefinite forms – can cause some confusion with place names. Tirana is alternately referred to as Tiranë, Durrësi as Durrës, Berati as Berat, Saranda as Sarandë and Gjirokastra as Gjirokaster.

	Albanian	Pronunciation
Yes	*Po*	Paw
No	*Jo*	Yaw
Please	*Ju lutem*	Yoo lootem
Thank you	*Faleminderit*	Falemin-derit
Hello/Good day	*Tungjatjeta*	Toongya-tyeta
Goodbye	*Mirupafshim*	Meeropafshim
Excuse me	*Më falni*	Muh falni
Where?	*Ku?*	Koo?
Good	*Mirë*	Mir
Bad	*Keq*	Kek
Near	*Afër*	Afur
Far	*Larg*	Larg
Cheap	*I lirë*	Ee lir
Expensive	*I shtrenjtë*	Ee shtrenyt
Open	*I hapur*	Ee hapoor
Closed	*Mbyllur*	Mbeeloor
Today	*Sot*	Sawt
Yesterday	*Dje*	Dye
Tomorrow	*Nesër*	Nesur
How much is...?	*Sa kushton…?*	Sa kushton…?
What time is it?	*Sa është ora?*	Sa ushtu awra?
I don't understand	*Unë nuk kuptoj*	Oonuh nook koop-toy
Do you speak English?	*A flisni anglisht?*	Ah fleesnee anglisht?
One	*Një*	Nyuh
Two	*Dy*	Deeh
Three	*Tre*	Treh
Four	*Katër*	Katur
Five	*Pesë*	Pes
Six	*Gjashtë*	Gyasht
Seven	*Shtatë*	Shtat
Eight	*Tetë*	Tet
Nine	*Nëntë*	Nuhnt
Ten	*Dhjetë*	Dyet

– it's still prudent to hang onto any valuable parcels until you're out of the country. Public **phones** are hard to track down, and almost all use cards; you may be offered these on the street but it's safer – and cheaper – to buy from a post office, many of which will also have public phones of their own. **Internet** cafés are surprisingly widespread in urban areas; expect to pay anything from 50 to 200 lekë per hour.

EMERGENCIES

Despite its bad rap, the **crime rate** in Albania is actually quite low by European standards, and it's as good as impossible to find yourself stumbling

EMERGENCY NUMBERS

Police ☎129; Ambulance ☎127; Fire ☎128.

ALBANIA ON THE NET

Ⓦ **www.albaniantourism.com** Official site of the tourist board.

Ⓦ **www.albania-hotel.com** Good for booking rooms online.

Ⓦ **www.albanianhistory.net** Collection of historical articles.

Ⓦ **www.enverhoxha.info** Detailing the greatness of former dictator Enver Hoxha.

into one of the famed blood feuds, some of which still bubble away up north. It is, however, worth mentioning a high **road accident** rate made vividly clear by the alarming number of memorial stones by the roadside.

Albania's **hospitals** are in very poor shape – most locals go abroad for treatment if they can afford it, and you should do likewise if possible. There are very few ambulances, so should you or a friend come across an accident it's usually best to hunt down a cab. **Pharmacies** exist in all urban areas, and are usually open 9am to 7pm.

INFORMATION

Most of the popular tourist spots now have a **tourist information office**, though hours can be somewhat irregular, especially outside the summer months.

MONEY AND BANKS

Albania uses the **lekë**, which is also often used in its singular form, lek. Coins of 1, 5, 10, 20, 50 and 100 lekë are in circulation, as are notes of 100, 200, 500, 1000, 2000 and 5000 lekë. Exchange **rates** are currently around 130 lekë to the euro, 150 lekë to the pound, and 100 lekë to the US dollar. Note that many Albanians haven't yet caught up with the **chopping off of a zero** in the 1970s – you may be quoted 100 lekë when they mean 1000. Accommodation prices are quoted in euros at all but the cheapest places, and some of the more upmarket restaurants do likewise; in these you can pay with either currency, though will usually save a little paying in lekë. **Banks** are the best places to exchange money, and are usually open on weekdays 9am–3pm. **ATMs** are everywhere in Tirana and easy to find in any town, while **credit cards** are increasingly accepted in hotels.

OPENING HOURS AND HOLIDAYS

Few **shops** and restaurants in Albania have set **working hours**, though you can expect restaurants to be open from breakfast to supper, and shops from 9am to 5pm. **Museums** are usually closed on Mondays.

Most shops and all banks and post offices are closed on **public holidays**: January 1 & 2, January 6, March 14, March 22, May 1, October 19, November 28 & 29 and December 25, as well 95 Eastertime, both Catholic and Orthodox.

Tirana

There's a real sense of purpose about **TIRANA**. A ruined regime bequeathed unto it potholes, overlarge boulevards and grey buildings galore, but its increasingly switched-on young populace is, step by tiny step, fulfilling its city's apparent dream of becoming a "regular" European capital. The central **Blloku** area was off-limits to all but party members during communist times, but you'll now find a warren of stylish, fun-loving youngsters, supping espresso before hunting down the latest trendy bar.

Tirana has been a major city since the Ottoman era, though events of the twentieth century eroded much of its legacy. Instead, you'll continually find yourself amongst buildings that expose influences from Italian to communist to post-modern. In the 1920s, Italian planners used fascistic templates to create **Skanderbeg Square** and its surrounding area, before dictator Enver Hoxha added his own frills. More recently, charismatic mayor Edi Rama attempted to paint his city into the modern day; the resulting kaleidoscope of **colourful buildings** performs a continuous palette shift from lemon to lime, saffron to cinnamon and burgundy to baby blue, making it appear the beneficiary – some locals say victim – of a made-for-television makeover.

What to see and do

Tirana is more apt for strolling than sightseeing, but there's plenty to keep you occupied in the southbound stretch from **Skanderbeg Square** to the **Grand Park**, which narrowly bypasses the trendy **Blloku** district on the way.

Skanderbeg Square

All roads in Tirana lead to **Skanderbeg Square**, centrepoint of the city and, therefore, the nation as a whole. The equestrian statue of national hero Skanderbeg, who led the ultimately unsuccessful resistance to fifteenth-century Ottoman invasions, observes proceedings at the southern end of the square; you can do likewise from a number of cafés to the north. Most imposing is the **National History Museum** (daily except Mon 9am–1pm & 5–7pm, closes 3pm Sun; 300 lekë), whose exterior features a fascinating mosaic mural – try to count the number of weapons. On the inside, a seemingly never-ending gamut of treasures spreads across several floors, laid out in chronological order from prehistoric to post-Hoxha.

Heading clockwise around the square you'll find the **Palace of Culture**, which houses a gallery and the Theatre of Opera and Ballet. Then comes the pretty **Et'hem Bey Mosque**, which was closed off during communist rule; one sunny day in 1991, thousands flocked here to make use of their newfound religious freedom. Right next door is the tall **clock-tower**, which can be climbed for views of the square (Mon 9am–1pm, Thurs 9am–1pm & 4–6pm; 100 lekë).

Bulevard Dëshmorët e Kombit and Blloku

Heading south from Skanderbeg Square is the "Boulevard of National Martyrs". The first major sight is the **National Art Gallery** (9am–1pm & 5–8pm, closed Mon; 100 lekë), which is well worth some of your time; the most notable exhibitions are Onufri's renowned icons, and a collection of Socialist Realist paintings. Continuing south, the pleasant green verges of the **Lana** are a good place to get a handle on some of Tirana's **colourful buildings**. South of the river, any road on the right will take you to the **Blloku** district, while on the left is the distinctive **Pyramid**; once a museum dedicated to the life and times of Enver Hoxha, said to be designed by

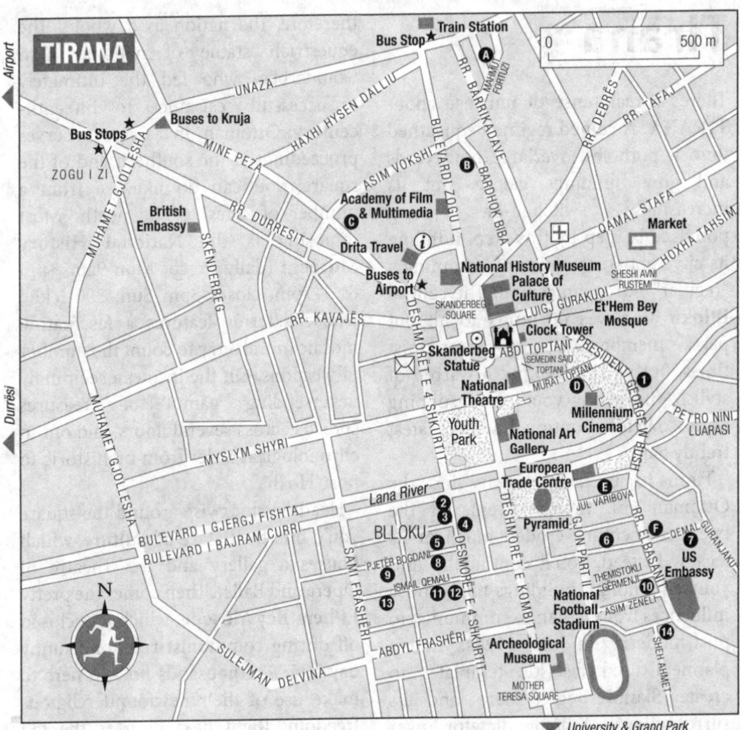

ACCOMMODATION				EATING						DRINKING & NIGHTLIFE			
Areela	A	Tirana Backpackers	F	Artist Lounge	6	Embelaza Franceze	3	Lulishte 1 Maji	1	Buda Bar	11	Raum	9
Freddy's	B	Vila Tafaj	C	Asiana	14	Era	13	Quo Vadis	12	Charl's	5	Sky Club	4
Green House	E			Dani	7			Vila Ambasador Chocolat	10	Flex	2		
Kalaja	D									Lollipop	8		

his daughter (though many dispute this), it's now a conference centre. Grandiose buildings line the road until you emerge in Mother Teresa Square, home to a passable **Archeological Museum** (Mon–Fri 10.30am–2.30pm; free). Further back, though not terribly easy to access, is the splendid **Grand Park**, whose main feature is an artificial lake around which Tiranese of all sorts come for a spot of relaxation.

Arrival

Air Mother Teresa International Airport (also known as Rinas Airport) is located 20km northwest of Tirana. Taxis usually charge around 2000 lekë for the 30min trip into town – haggle in euros and you'll likely pay more – though it's far cheaper to take the hourly Rinas Express bus (7am–7pm; 250 lekë), which drops off at the north end of Skanderbeg Square.

Bus Arriving in Tirana by bus is something of a Kafkaesque adventure – amazingly, the city has not yet seen the need to build a bus station, so you may be dropped at any one of a dozen places, depending upon your point of embarkation; in addition, legal wrangles between bus companies and *furgon* drivers mean that the latter often have to shift their bases. The most common drop-off point is the Zogu i Zi junction northwest of town, though arrivals from the north often use the train station as a base. In general, if leaving Tirana it's best to ask locals – more than one, preferably, since you're likely to get a few different answers.

Train The station is north of the centre, at the top of Bulevardi Zogu I, though allow a good 10min to find the station entrance if leaving Tirana by train.

Information

Tourist office Behind the National History Museum on Ded Gjo Luli (Ⓣ04/222 3313). Handing out maps and leaflets is their forte, though some staff are adept at answering questions.
Listings Event listings are found in the *Tirana Times*, an English-language weekly, while the biannual *Tirana In Your Pocket* is also a good source of information.
Tickets Drita Travel (Ⓣ04/225 1777, Ⓦwww.dritatravel.com), on Ded Gjo Luli, can organize international bus tickets, as well as ferries from Durrësi to Italy.

City transport

Buses run every 15–30min on a few main routes 6am–10pm; it's just 30 lekë a ride.
Taxis should cost 300–500 lekë for a trip within the city centre (none have meters), though the centre is just about small enough to cover on foot.

Accommodation

Hostels

Freddy's Bardhok Biba Ⓣ04/226 6077, Ⓔalfredsalku@yahoo.com. Family home in a peaceful neighbourhood. Some dorms have just two beds, making this a cheap option for couples. €12.

Tirana Backpackers Elbasanit Ⓣ04/373 407, Ⓦwww.tiranahostel.com. Hammocks and greenery give this friendly place a vague hippie feel quite at odds with its central location. €12.

Hotels

Areela Mahmut Fortuzi Ⓣ04/222 6579, Ⓔhotelareela@hotmail.it. Good-value place in a quiet location, which seems to be over its previous rodent problems. Basement rooms are cheapest but it's worth shelling out extra for one with a view. €25.

TREAT YOURSELF

Green House Jul Varibova Ⓣ04/225 1015, Ⓦwww.greenhouse.al. Boutique hotel with a range of arty, immaculate rooms from €130; those on the ground floor get you more space at no extra cost. There's also a superb restaurant whose prices are within budget reach; think 1100 lekë for a veal fillet with truffle sauce.

Kalaja Murat Toptani Ⓣ04/225 0000. Collection of comfy rooms – those downstairs are best – set into a wonderful niche in the old castle walls. There's also a small but pleasant courtyard area for relaxing over morning coffee. €30.
Vila Tafaj Mine Peza Ⓣ04/222 7581, Ⓦwww.tafaj.com. Fresh, spacious rooms set within a graceful old building; they're justifiably proud of their interior courtyard. €65.

Eating

Cafés

Artist Lounge Ismael Qemali. This sophisticated den may be a little pricey, but the sumptuous shakes and cakes have many a traveller coming back for more. One of the only places in Tirana to project a trendy vibe without soaking it in deafening music.
Embelaza Franceze Dëshmorët e 4 Shkurtit. Cakes and coffees served up in a lavish interior. Savoury dishes are available but somewhat overpriced.
Quo Vadis Ismael Qemali. Multi-section café-bar that's hugely popular with preening locals. Sit in the front section to soak up views of Hoxha's old house while throwing down your espresso.

Restaurants

Asiana Sheh Ahmet Pazari. Good-looking Indian restaurant that scores high marks for authenticity, fair for speed of service, and poor for dish size. Curries 700 lekë.
Dani Qemal Guranjaku. Working-man's den with a menu full of cheap-but-tasty Albanian staples. Bolognese-topped *pilaf* with a side serving of *kos* will only cost 200 lekë.

Era Ismael Qemali. Often jam-packed with hungry locals thanks to a large and varied menu of uniformly well-prepared dishes, such as lamb with artichoke, stuffed eggplant or goose fillet with mushroom. Cheap wine rounds out the picture. Mains 350–700 lekë.
Lulishte 1 Maji Presidenti George W Bush. Sprawling family restaurant that serves Italian, Albanian and Mexican meals on the ground floor, and Chinese food upstairs.

Vila Ambasador Chocolate Asim Zeneli. Still awaiting UN recognition, the Chocolate Republic's minions dish out excellent Italian and Albanian fare at reasonable prices (mains 300–1000 lekë), as well as mouthwatering desserts.

Drinking and nightlife

Tirana's nightlife scene moves up a notch with each passing year. Almost everything of note is concentrated in the fashionable Blloku area.

Buda Bar Ismael Qemali. The Buddha-meets-alcohol concept is not yet passé in Tirana, meaning that weekends regularly see this elegantly illuminated bar packed to the walls.
Charl's Pjetër Bogdani. Student-heavy lounge bar throwing regular live events, with the music usually more conducive to nodding than rocking.
Flex Dëshmorët e 4 Shkurtit. Funky bar staff, funky lamps, funky outdoor seating, funky mirror shards on the walls. And funky mojitos: 300 lekë.
Lollipop Pjetër Bogdani. One of those clubs that nobody intends to go to, but everybody ends up at. Bring your dancing shoes.
Raum Pjetër Bogdani. Two upper floors frequented by a young and arty set, who make a sundown shift from coffee to cocktails. Also stages occasional art exhibitions.
Sky Club Dëshmorët e 4 Shkurtit. Okay, so you're basically paying extra for height, but this lofty bar's revolving floor means that you can see the whole of Tirana in one drinking session. There's also a good restaurant one level down.

Entertainment

Usually held in December, and improving by the year, the Tirana Film Festival (Ⓦ www.tiranafilmfest.com) has screenings at the Millennium Cinema and National Theatre.
Academy of Film and Multimedia Alexsandër Moisiu Ⓣ 04/236 5188, Ⓦ www.afmm.edu.al. Occasional free screenings of foreign movies (usually Thurs at 7pm).
Millennium Cinema Murat Toptani Ⓦ www.ida-millennium.com. Season-old Hollywood films shown in a wonderful old theatre whose outdoor café is a delight on sunny days. Tickets from 300 lekë.
National Theatre Sermedin Said Toptani Ⓣ 04/222 8933. Grand old building hosting a variety of Albanian-language performances.
Theatre of Opera and Ballet Palace of Culture, Skanderbeg Square Ⓣ 04/222 4753. Another grand old building, though one where performances are more apt to transcend linguistic barriers. Tickets 300 lekë, performances usually 7pm.

Shopping

Tirana isn't exactly a shopper's paradise, though if you've a shopping mall itch to scratch the Galleria, in the European Trade Centre on Bajram Curri (daily 9am–8pm), provides a handy remedy. As well as shops and cafés, it houses Conad, a well-stocked supermarket selling Italian goods; the more downmarket Kedi is inside the Sheraton Mall, south of the stadium. Tirana also has a fascinating daily market, which sprawls over several blocks north of the Sheshi Avni Rustemi roundabout; Sundays are best. Adrion, on Skanderbeg Square, has English-language books, newspapers and magazines.

Directory

Embassies and consulates UK, Skënderbeg Ⓣ 04/223 4973; US, Elbasanit Ⓣ 04/224 7285.
Exchange It's hard to find yourself outside visible range of an ATM in Tirana. All of the attached banks will be able to exchange cash during banking hours.
Hospital Civilian Hospital, Dibrës.
Internet There are plenty of internet cafés around, usually charging 50–80 lekë/hr.
Pharmacies Bulevardi Zogu I (8am–8pm; Ⓣ 04/222 2241; closed Sun); Dëshmorët e 4 Shkurtit (Ⓣ 04/222 6759, staff on duty 24hr).
Post office Çameria. Mon–Fri 8am–8pm.

Moving on

Train Durrësi (7 daily; 1hr); Pogradeci (2 daily; 6hr 40min).
Bus Athens (daily; 12hr); Berati (hourly; 3hr); Durrësi (hourly; 40min); Gjirokastra (6 daily; 4hr 30min); Saranda (6 daily; 6hr); Skopje (daily; 10hr).

Around Tirana

Local landmarks from which you can peer down on Tirana include the slopes of **Mount Dajti** and the hilltop town of **Kruja**, while also within range is the laid-back port of **Durrësi**. All can be visited on a day-trip from the capital.

MOUNT DAJTI

The dark, looming shape of **Mount Dajti** is easily visible from Tirana, a temptation that can prove too much for city-dwellers, who head to the forested slopes in droves on sunny weekends. The mountain's network of paths can engender a surprising sense of remoteness, even though you're only 25km from the capital. There's no public transport to the mountain, but by taxi

it should be no more than 500 lekë to the base of the cable car (8am–10pm; 500 lekë return) that whisks passengers to within a slog of the summit. It's a good place to enjoy spit-roasted lamb: try the *Panorama* – also a hotel – or *Gurra e Përrisë*.

KRUJA

Lofty **KRUJA**, 35km from Tirana, was the focal point of national hero Skanderbeg's resistance to the Ottoman invasions of the fifteenth century, and you'll see his likeness all over town. Most people make a bee-line straight to the **castle**, which houses a number of restaurants and an excellent **History Museum** (9am–1pm & 3–6pm, closed Mon; 200 lekë), whose diverting collection of weaponry, icons and the like is augmented by impressive modern flourishes. Also within the castle walls is the **Ethnographic Museum** (same times; 300 lekë), housed in a gorgeous building with a serene outdoor courtyard. Souvenir salesmen have taken over the town, and the best place to buy your Albania-flag t-shirt, Skanderbeg statuette or Mother Teresa lighter is the restored **Ottoman bazaar**, just below the castle access road. *Furgons* from Tirana (200 lekë) leave regularly from the end of Mine Peza.

DURRËSI

Sitting atop a 10km stretch of Adriatic beach, the port city of **DURRËSI** is the easiest escape route for sea-seeking Tiranese, and on summer weekends there are few better places to party. There may be far better beaches down south, but the city's historical pedigree makes it worth a stop. Known as Dyrrhachium, it was already an important port in Roman times, and was used as a launchpad for fifth-century Visigoth attacks on Italy; it also served as Albania's capital for a short time after independence. It's now a major transport hub – most buses and trains pass through on their way to Tirana, and daily ferries arrive from Italy.

A Roman **forum** and **amphitheatre** sit just off opposite ends of the main square, Sheshi i Lirisë; the latter (8am–8pm; 200 lekë) is the largest such construction in the Balkans, while in between stands an elegant **mosque**. You can then either follow the old **castle wall** or cobblestoned Tregëtare downhill to the seafront **promenade**; a ten-minute stroll will bring you to the enjoyable **Archeological Museum** (daily except Mon 9am–3pm; 200 lekë).

The **train and bus stations** sit almost side-by-side within an easy walk of the main square. You'll find the best culinary and **sleeping** options around the bottom of Tregëtare. The lofty *Mediterran* (Ⓣ052/227074, Ⓔmediterran_hotel.dr@hotmail.com; €20) is both the best value and easiest to find, while the *Arvi* (Ⓣ052/230403, Ⓦwww.hotelarvi.com; €60) is halfway to the museum. The pizza-serving *Piazza* is the best **restaurant** in these parts, while unmissable across the way is the *Fly Bar*, a good-looking café-bar boasting fifteen-storey views.

ALBANIA'S BUNKERS

Cross into Albania by land or sea, and you'll soon notice clutches of grey, dome-like structures dotting the countryside. Under Hoxha's rule, these were scattered around the country in tremendous numbers – estimates run as high as 750,000, which would have meant that there was more than one for every four Albanians. These were no family shelters, as might be expected, but strategic positions to which every able-bodied man was expected to head, weapon in hand, at the onset of war. Though Western spies did indeed make attempts to infiltrate the country, the bunkers were never really put to the test; almost impossible to shift, they're now a semi-permanent part of Albanian life.

Southern Albania

With its jumble of rugged mountains fringed by pristine curls of beach, Albania's south is the most appealing part of the country. Most head for **Saranda**, using it as a jump-off point for exploration of the **Ionian Coast** and the ruins of **Butrinti**, while clutches of wonderful Ottoman buildings make Berati and **Gjirokastra** perhaps the most visually rewarding towns in the land.

BERATI

A well-preserved relic of Ottoman times, **BERATI** is one of Albania's must-sees. Fishscaling the slopes of an ancient **citadel** are huddles of **Ottoman houses**, their dark, rectangular windows staring from whitewashed walls like a thousand eyes. While modern-day Berati spreads out for quite some way down the Osumi valley, most of the old buildings come in three central clusters – **Kalasa** is inside the citadel, **Mangalemi** lurks beneath, and sleepy **Gorica** sits across the river.

What to see and do

You'll have great views of Berati from the fourteenth-century **Kalasa**, a citadel (daily 9am–9pm; 100 lekë; other times free) towering above town, which is accessed via a steep, cobbled road. Unlike other such places in Albania this is still a functioning part of town and home to hundreds, yet almost nothing dilutes its centuries-old vibe. There were once over thirty **churches** here but just a handful remain; oldest and most beautiful is the thirteenth-century **Church of the Holy Trinity**, sitting on the slope below the inner fortifications. Churches remain locked for most of the year, but you can ask around to find the key-keepers. Also within the grounds is the **Onufri Museum** (daily except Mon 9am–4pm; 200 lekë), dedicated to the country's foremost icon painter, famed for his use of a particularly vivid red; there are some wonderful examples inside. Heading back down the access road you'll come across the diverting **Ethnographic Museum** (Oct–April 9am–4pm, Sun to 2pm; May–Sept 9am–1pm & 4–7pm, Sun 9am–2pm; 200 lekë) and the first of the centre's three main **mosques**.

Arrival and information

Bus The central square acts as a bus station of sorts, though it's also possible to pick up or be dropped off at various locations on the main road.

Tours Trips around nearby Mount Tomorri can be organized through Outdoor Albania (Ⓦwww.outdooralbania.com), while the *Castle Park* can organize rafting in small groups from around €50 per person.

Internet East of the bus station on Skraparit, just before the *Hotel Gega*; (100 lekë/hr).

Accommodation

Berat Backpackers Ⓣ069/306 4429, Ⓦberatbackpackers.com. English-owned hostel, located over the river in the delightful district of Gorica. Has a chill-out room with free internet, and a garden patio for summer evening drinks. Dorms €10.

Berati Ⓣ032/36953. Cheap rooms, some with balconies, in a central location just west of the bus station square – look for the sign. A/c and breakfast can be forgone for a small discount. Also has a very reasonable in-house restaurant. €15.

Castle Park Ⓣ069/209 2154, Ⓦwww.castle-park.com. Good-looking hotel in a delightfully secluded forest setting 2km from town – cross the bridge into Gorica, turn left and keep going. €40.

Mangalemi Ⓣ032/32093, Ⓔhotel_mangalemi_tomi@yahoo.it. Traditional-styled guesthouse whose rooms offer excellent value; all are en suite with comfy beds and powerful showers. Near the centre of town, on the road to the citadel. €25.

Eating and drinking

The King Trendy café-bar which would be quite at home in Tirana. The only place in town to attract a female clientele for evening drinks.

Mangalemi Professional service, large portions and reasonable prices – 500 lekë can get you

nicely full. The *qoftë* is particularly good. Inside the guesthouse of the same name.

Nova Slightly pricey menu (mains 700–1000 lekë) centred on steaks and kebabs, though a romantic hilltop setting near the citadel entrance more than compensates.

Onufri Simple restaurant inside the citadel walls.

White House ⓣ032/234570. Upmarket riverside restaurant serving the best pizzas in town (delivery service available) as well as seafood dishes and traditional Albanian fare.

Moving on

Bus Durrësi (hourly; 2hr); Gjirokastra (2 daily; 4hr); Tirana (hourly; 3hr).

THE IONIAN COAST

Albania's stretch of **Ionian Coast** is one of Europe's only unspoilt sections of Mediterranean shore, a near-permanently sunny spot where the twin blues of sea and sky are ripped asunder by a ribbon of grey mountains. However, since there are rarely more than a couple of bus services a day, you'll likely have to hitchhike or rent some wheels to get the most out of the area.

The route starts in the port town of **Vlora**, which is likeable enough but lacks any specific attractions. Once you're out of town the snake-like **Karaburuni peninsula** swings into view, the start of a mountain chain that the now zigzagging road finally meets at the 1027m-high **Llogaraja Pass**; there are places to stay and eat in the area, which is high enough to afford views of Italy on a clear day. From here it's downhill to the coast's best beaches, notably those at **Palasa** and **Dhërmiu**; the latter has plenty of places to sleep. **Himara** is the next major town, but though still a pleasant place to stay it's rapidly falling victim to overdevelopment. From here it's south to **Saranda**, and the nearby ruins of **Butrinti**.

SARANDA AND BUTRINTI

Staring straight at the Greek island of Corfu, and even within day-trip territory, sunny **SARANDA** is perhaps Albania's most appealing entry-point. A recent building boom has eroded some of the town's original genteel atmosphere, but it's still a great place to kick back, stroll along the promenade and watch the sun-set over cocktails. There are beaches in town, but better are those near the village of Ksamili, which lies next to the archeological treasure-trove of Butrinti.

Butrinti and the Blue Eye

Splendidly sited on an exposed nub of land, the isolated ruins of **Butrinti** (daylight hours; 700 lekë) offer a peek into over 2500 years of history, and are a delight to explore on its eucalyptus-lined trails. The area was first developed by the Greeks in the fourth century BC, and the expansive **theatre** and nearby **public baths** were built soon after. Butrinti then reached its zenith during Roman times – Julius Caesar stopped by in 44 AD – though most of the statues unearthed from this period are now in the museums of Tirana. You can see most of Butrinti's sights on a looped footpath, though do head up to the **Acropolis** for wonderful views. If travelling by taxi you may also care to loop around to the wonderful **Blue Eye** on the way back to Saranda. This underwater spring forms a pool of deepest blue, and its setting in a cool, remote grove is quite spectacular. *Furgons* **to Butrinti** (six daily; 40min; 100 lekë) leave from a bus stop outside Saranda's tourist office, but given the paucity of public transport many opt to shell out for a taxi (around €20 including waiting time, double that if including the Blue Eye).

Arrival and information

Boat A small terminal sits on the west side of town, and hosts services to Corfu (1–6 daily). Tickets can be bought from a shack on the access road, and sometimes on the vessels themselves.

Bus The bus "station" (you'll see…) is just north of the centre on Vangjel Pando. The harbour is a 5min walk downhill.

Tourist office In a handy location on Skënderbeu (daily 8am–8pm), just uphill from the harbour, but

good for little bar maps. Useful listings and local information are found on Ⓦ www.saranda-guide.com.
Internet A couple of cafés in the side streets around the tourist office charge 100 lekë/hr.

Accommodation

Saranda witnesses dramatic price-swings across the year.
Aulona Ⓣ 085/23155, Ⓕ 26677. A hard-to-find location makes this one of the cheapest places in town, though rooms are perfectly adequate. Head east from the bus station. €30.
Hairy Lemon Ⓣ 069/355 9317, Ⓦ www.hairylemonhostel.com. Clean and friendly, this is one of Albania's only hostels; beds are highly comfy and the chill-out area is a great place to meet travel buddies. A 10min walk west of the centre, past the ferries. Dorms €13.
Kaonia Ⓣ 085/22600. Perhaps the best value of the hotels around the harbour. All rooms have balconies, but not all offer sea views so look before you pay. €50.
Livia Ⓣ 069/205 1263, Ⓦ www.liviahotel.com. Good-value hotel sitting next to the ruins in Butrinti. Rooms are large and modern, and the setting ideal. €35.
Palma Ⓣ 085/22929. Spick-and-span hotel next to the ferry terminal – ask for a balcony room, if you don't mind the noise. Room prices can drop as low as €15 off-season – a steal. €40.

Eating and drinking

Café Del Mar Stylish café-bar on the promenade whose palm-shaded outdoor seats are a drinker's delight. Draught beer and cocktails from 200 lekë.
Limani The most popular place in town by some margin, good for coffee in the day and ouzo in the evening. Also serves pizzas (from 400 lekë) in warmer months. On the harbour.
Paradise A winning blend of style, service and reasonable prices at this seafront restaurant. Simple spaghetti or rice meals go from 380 lekë, though you'll pay at least double that for their renowned seafood dishes. East of town off the Butrinti road.
Restorant Statha Cheap option with meat dishes from 300 lekë; real penny-pinchers will appreciate the 70 lekë *pilaf*. On Flamurit though you'll miss the tiny sign; look for a larger one saying "Insig".

Moving on

Bus Gjirokastra (6 daily; 1hr 20min); Tirana (6 daily; 6hr).

GJIROKASTRA

Sitting proudly above the sparsely inhabited Drinos valley, **GJIROKASTRA** is one of Albania's most attractive towns, and home to some of its friendliest people – a real must-see, and something of a step back in time. Its days as an Ottoman trading hub have bequeathed it a wealth of sparkling **Ottoman houses**, which line a grey-white-pink tricolore of steep, cobbled streets. Gjiro is also etched into the nation's conscience as the birthplace of former dictator **Enver Hoxha**, and more recently the world-renowned author Ismail Kadare.

What to see and do

The Old Town's centrepiece is its imposing **citadel** (May–Sept 9am–7pm; 200 lekë), which is clearly visible from any point in town. Built in the sixth century and enlarged in 1811 by Ali Pasha Tepelna, it was used as a prison by King Zog, the Nazis and Hoxha's cadres; the interior remains suitably spooky, but now contains a bar and restaurant. There are also tanks and weaponry to peruse, but most curious is the shell of an **American jet** which was forced down in 1957 after being suspected of espionage by the communist regime. Other than the castle, Gjiro's most appealing sight is its collection of mainly nineteenth-century **Ottoman houses**; there are some prime examples in Partizani, a steep residential area just west of the castle.

Arrival and information

Bus Buses and *furgons* stop on the highway intersection below the New Town. From here it's a steep, half-hour walk to the Old Town, or a 300-lekë taxi ride.
Tourist office On the entrance road to the castle; theoretically open daily 9am–5pm, but far less often in practice. Some useful information can be found at Ⓦ www.gjirokastra.org.
Tours The *Kotoni* can organise a variety of interesting tours, including horseriding and picnics on the nearby hills.

Accommodation

None of these establishments have addresses, but they're easy to find. The *Gjirokastra* is next to the theatre on the road running under the castle wall, where you'll also find signs to the *Kotoni*; the *Kalemi* is further up the same road.

Gjirokastra ⓣ084/265 982. Small but modern guesthouse with an excellent location; small discounts are available outside peak season. €25.

Kalemi ⓣ084/263 724, ⓦhotelkalemi.tripod.com. Lofty old building with a variety of pleasant rooms on offer, some with commanding valley views and chunky wooden floors. €35.

Kotoni ⓣ084/263 526, ⓦwww.bb-kotoni.com. Cosy Ottoman-era building whose owners may well be the most amiable couple in Gjirokastra. Homely touches include excellent breakfasts and handmade trimmings in the bedrooms. €25.

Eating and drinking

All of the establishments listed above serve excellent food.

Fantazia Uphill from Qafa e Pazarit. Stylish and extremely popular café offering splendid valley views, and a variety of teas, coffees and alcoholic drinks. Espresso 70 lekë.

Festivali Qafa e Pazarit. Cheap Albanian meals dished out under a cloak of faded opulence. Mains (300–750 lekë) run the gamut from frogs' legs to *pasha qoftë.*

Kërculla Lagjia Palorto. Gjiro's best restaurant sits in an Ottoman house way up on the hill opposite the castle – look for the red-and-white mast – and serves traditional local specialities.

Moving on

Bus Berati (2 daily; 4hr); Saranda (6 daily; 1hr 20min); Tirana (6 daily; 4hr 30min).

Austria

HIGHLIGHTS

COFFEE AND CAKE, VIENNA: indulge in mouthwatering treats in one of Vienna's ornate coffeehouses

VIENNESE ART: feast your eyes on stunning paintings by Gustav Klimt and Egon Schiele

THE SOUND OF MUSIC TOUR, SALZBURG: cheesy, but a firm favourite

HALLSTATT: visit this picture-postcard village in the lovely Salzkammergut region

ADVENTURE SPORTS, INNSBRUCK: hiking, mountain-biking, canyoning and more, in the stunning setting of the Austrian Alps

ROUGH COSTS

DAILY BUDGET Basic €55/occasional treat €75

DRINK Beer, wine or coffee €3

FOOD Schnitzel €8.50

HOSTEL/BUDGET HOTEL €20/€60

TRAVEL Graz–Vienna (2hr 40min) €31.40; Vienna–Salzburg (3hr) €44.20

FACT FILE

POPULATION 8.3 million

AREA 83,872 sq km

LANGUAGE German

CURRENCY Euro (€)

CAPITAL Vienna (population: 1.7 million)

INTERNATIONAL PHONE CODE Ⓣ43

Introduction

Glorious Alpine scenery, monumental Habsburg architecture, and the world's favourite musical – Austria's tourist industry certainly plays up to the clichés. However, it's not all bewigged Mozart ensembles and schnitzel; modern Austria boasts some of Europe's most varied museums and contemporary architecture, not to mention a plethora of trendy bars and clubs.

Long the powerhouse of the Habsburg Empire, **Austria** underwent decades of change and uncertainty in the early twentieth century. Shorn of her empire and racked by economic difficulties, the state fell prey to the promises of Nazi Germany. Only with the end of the Cold War did Austria return to the heart of Europe, joining the EU in 1995.

Politics aside, Austria is primarily known for two contrasting attractions – the fading imperial glories of the capital, and the stunning beauty of its Alpine hinterland. **Vienna** is the gateway to much of central Europe and a good place to soak up the culture of *Mitteleuropa*. Less renowned provincial capitals such as **Graz** and **Linz** provide a similar level of culture and vitality. The most dramatic of Austria's Alpine scenery is west of here, in and around **Tyrol**, whose capital, **Innsbruck**, provides the best base for exploration. **Salzburg**, between **Innsbruck** and Vienna, represents urban Austria at its most picturesque, an intoxicating Baroque city within easy striking distance of the mountains and lakes of the **Salzkammergut**.

CHRONOLOGY

1st century BC Romans take over Celtic settlements in present-day Austria.

788 AD Charlemagne conquers Austrian land.

1156 The "Privilegium Minus" gives Austria the status of Duchy.

1278 The Habsburgs seize control of the area, and retain it until WWI.

1773 Wolfgang Amadeus Mozart becomes Court Musician in Salzburg.

1797 Napoleon defeats Austrian forces, taking Austrian land.

1814 An Austrian coalition force defeats Napoleon.

1866 Austrian territory is lost as a result of the Austro-Prussian war.

1899 Sigmund Freud publishes *The Interpretation of Dreams*, introducing the concept of the ego.

1914 The assassination of the Austrian Archduke, Franz Ferdinand, begins the events that lead to World War I.

1920 A new constitution creates the Republic of Austria.

1938 Hitler incorporates Austria into Germany through "Anschluss".

1945 Austria is occupied by Allied forces as World War II ends.

1965 *The Sound of Music* draws attention to Austria on the big screen.

1967 Austrian Arnold Schwarzenegger becomes the youngest ever Mr Universe at the age of 20.

1980s Protests at election of President Kurt Waldheim, due to rumours implicating him in Nazi war crimes.

1995 Austria joins the EU.

1999 The far-right Freedom Party led by Joerg Haider wins 27 percent of the vote in national elections.

2004 Social Democrat Heinz Fischer is announced as President.

2007 Rioting teenagers in Krems, Lower Austria, are played music by Mozart and Beethoven in an attempt to calm them down.

2008 The world is enthralled by the case of Josef Fritzl – who imprisoned his daughter in a cellar for twenty-four years, fathering seven children with her.

ARRIVAL

Austria's major international **airport** lies less than thirty minutes outside of Vienna by S-Bahn or the City Airport Train. You can also fly to Salzburg, Innsbruck, Graz and Linz in Austria and even to the Slovak capital Bratislava: only a 1hr 15min bus journey

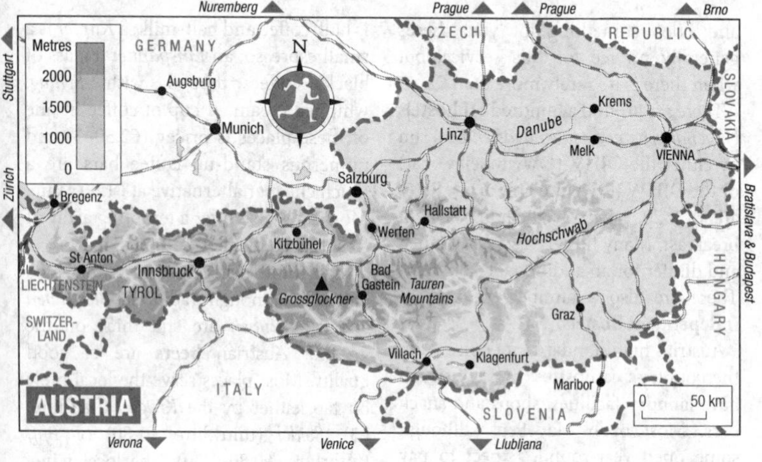

from Vienna, which is also one of central Europe's major rail-hubs. **Trains** from Budapest and the west terminate at the Westbahnhof, whilst those from Bratislava, Prague and occasionally Berlin arrive into the Südbahnhof. Trains from Croatia and Slovenia stop in the south of Austria at Graz, before also terminating here. Both stations are short, easy hops from central Vienna by tram or U-Bahn. Arriving from northern Italy (Verona and Venice, for example), it's likely you'll arrive in Innsbruck, which also has good rail connections with Munich and southern Germany.

GETTING AROUND

Austria's **public transport** is fast, efficient and comprehensive. Austrian Federal Railways, or **ÖBB** (ⓦwww.oebb.at), runs a punctual, clean and comfortable network, which includes most towns of any size. **Trains** marked EC or EN (EuroCity and EuroNight international expresses), ICE or IC (Austrian InterCity expresses) are the fastest. Those designated D (*Schnellzug*) or E (*Eilzug*) are next, stopping at most intermediate points, while the *Regionalzug* is the slowest, stopping at all stations. All stations in cities and larger towns have left-luggage lockers.

The **Bahnbus** and **Postbus** system serves remoter villages and Alpine valleys; fares are around €10 per 100km. As a general rule, Bahnbus services, operated by ÖBB, depart from outside train stations; the Postbus tends to stop outside the post office. Daily and weekly regional travelcards (*Netzkarte*), covering both trains and buses, are available in many regions.

Austria is bike-friendly, with **cycle lanes** in all major towns. Many train stations rent **bikes** for around €15 per day (€10 with a valid rail ticket). You can return them to any station for an extra fee of €10/€5.

ACCOMMODATION

Outside popular tourist spots such as Vienna and Salzburg, **accommodation** need not be too expensive. Good-value **B&B** is usually available in the many small family-run hotels known as *Gasthöfe* and *Gasthaüser*, with prices from €50 per double. In the larger towns and cities a **pension** or *Frühstuckspension* will offer similar prices. Most places also have a stock of **private rooms** or *Privatzimmer*, although in well-travelled rural areas, roadside signs offering *Zimmer Frei* are common (double room €30–45). Local tourist offices will have lists of these and will often ring around

and book something for you; there's generally no fee for this service, but when there is it's rarely more than €2.

There are around a hundred **HI hostels** (*Jugendherberge* or *Jugendgästehaus*), run by either the ÖJHV (Ⓦwww.oejhv.or.at) or the ÖJHW (Ⓦwww.oejhw.or.at). Rates are €13–20, normally including a light breakfast. Many hostels also serve lunch and dinner for an additional €3.50–5.50. There are also a number of excellent **independent hostels**.

Austria's high standards are reflected in the country's **campsites**, most of which have laundry facilities, shops and snack bars. Most open May–Sept, although some open year-round. Expect to pay €5–8 per person and €3–9 per pitch.

FOOD AND DRINK

Eating out in Austria is often cheaper than self-catering, but both form a large chunk of your daily expenses. For ready-made snacks, try a bakery (*Bäckerei*) or confectioner's (*Konditorei*). **Fast food** centres on the *Würstelstand*, which sells hot dogs, *Bratwurst* (grilled sausage), *Käsekrainer* (spicy sausage with cheese), *Bosna* (spicy, thin Balkan sausage) and *Currywurst*. In town-centre *Kaffeehäuser* or cafés and bars you can get light meals and **snacks** starting at about €5; most restaurant and café menus have filling stand-bys for less than €6. Main dishes (*Hauptspeisen*) are dominated by **Schnitzel** (tenderized veal) often accompanied by potatoes and a vegetable or salad: *Wienerschnitzel* is fried in breadcrumbs, *Pariser* in batter, *Natur* served on its own or with a creamy sauce. Expect to pay €6–10 for a standard main course.

Drink

For urban Austrians, daytime drinking traditionally centres on the **Kaffeehaus**, relaxed places serving alcoholic and soft drinks, snacks and cakes, alongside a wide range of different coffees: a *Schwarzer* is small and black, a *Brauner* comes with a little milk, while a *Melange* is half-coffee and half-milk; a *Kurzer* is a small espresso; an *Einspänner* a glass of black coffee topped with *Schlag*: whipped cream. A cup of coffee in one of these places is pricey (€2.50–3) and numerous stand-up coffee bars are a much cheaper alternative at €1.50 a cup. Most cafés also offer a tempting array of freshly baked **cakes and pastries**.

Night-time drinking centres on **bars** and cafés, although traditional *Bierstuben* and *Weinstuben* are still thick on the ground. Austrian **beers** are of good quality. Most places serve the local brew on tap, either by the *Krügerl* (half-litre, €3), *Seidel* (third-litre, €1.80) or *Pfiff* (fifth-litre, €0.80–1.30). The local **wine**, drunk by the *Viertel* (25cl mug) or the *Achterl* (12.5cl glass), is widely consumed. The *Weinkeller* is the place to go for this or, in the wine-producing areas, a *Heuriger* or *Buschenshenk* – a traditional tavern, customarily serving cold food as well.

CULTURE AND ETIQUETTE

Austrian culture and etiquette is much like the rest of Western Europe, with leisurely café culture a central fixture. In restaurants, bars and cafés modest tipping – around ten percent or rounding up to the nearest euro – is expected.

AUSTRIA ON THE NET

Ⓦ**www.austria.info** Austrian Tourist Board website.
Ⓦ**www.oebb.at** Train site, including excellent English-language journey planner.
Ⓦ**www.austrosearch.at** Search engine, news and chat for all things Austrian.
Ⓦ**www.tiscover.com** Detailed information on all regions of the country.
Ⓦ**www.wienerzeitung.at** Website of the official Vienna city authorities' newspaper, with an English version packed with news and tourist information.

SPORTS AND ACTIVITIES

With stunning mountain scenery and beautiful lakes, Austria is an ideal destination for all sorts of outdoor sports. **Skiing** and snowboarding are major national pastimes (see box, p.96) and **hiking** and biking trails clearly marked and graded. Tourist offices will usually have a surfeit of details on local routes and every other possible local activity.

COMMUNICATIONS

Most **post offices** are open Monday to Friday 8am to noon and 2 to 6pm; in larger cities they do without the lunch break and also open Saturday 8 to 10am. **Stamps** can also be bought at tobacconists (*Tabak-Trafik*). The smallest coin accepted in **public phones** is €0.20; two should suffice for a local call. Insert €0.50 and upwards if calling long distance, or buy a phone card (*Telefonkarte*), available from tobacconists. You can make international calls from all public phones, but it's easier to do so from booths at larger post offices. The operator and directory enquiries number is ⓣ118 11. **Internet access** is widespread in cities, but not in rural areas; expect to pay €2–5/hr.

EMERGENCIES

Austria is law-abiding and reasonably safe. **Police** (*Polizei*) are armed and not known for their friendliness. As for **health**, hospital casualty departments will treat you and ask questions later. **Pharmacies** (*Apotheke*) follow shopping hours. A rota system covers night-time and weekend opening; Pharmacies have details posted in the window.

INFORMATION

Tourist offices (usually *Information*, *Tourismusverband*, *Verkehrsamt* or *Fremdenverkehrsverein*) are plentiful, often hand out free maps and almost always book accommodation.

EMERGENCY NUMBERS

Police ⓣ133; Ambulance ⓣ144; Fire ⓣ122.

STUDENT AND YOUTH DISCOUNTS

It is definitely worth carrying an **ISIC card** in Austria; entry to museums and art galleries is costly, particularly in Vienna, and proving your student status will reap substantial savings (often up to fifty percent).

MONEY AND BANKS

Austria's currency is the **euro** (€). Banking hours tend to be Monday to Friday 8am to 12.30pm and 1.30 to 3pm, Thursday until 5.30pm. Post offices charge slightly less commission on exchange than banks, and in larger cities, have longer hours.

OPENING HOURS AND PUBLIC HOLIDAYS

Traditionally, **opening hours** for **shops** are Monday to Friday 9am to noon and 2 to 6pm, with late opening on Thursday till 7 or 8pm and Saturday 8am to noon. It's increasingly common for shops to open all day Saturday and in big cities most don't close for lunch. Many **cafés and restaurants** also have a weekly *Ruhetag* (closing day). Shops and **banks** close, and most museums have reduced hours, on **public holidays**: January 1, January 6, Easter Monday, May 1, Ascension Day, Whit Monday, Corpus Christi, August 15, October 26, November 1, December 8, December 25 and 26.

LANGUAGE

A high proportion of Austrians speak English, though any attempt at a few phrases of **German** (see p.461) will be heartily appreciated – the standard greeting throughout Austria is *Grüss Gott*.

Vienna

Most people visit **VIENNA** (Wien) with a vivid image in their minds: a romantic place, full of imperial nostalgia, opera houses and exquisite cakes. Even so, the city can overwhelm with its eclectic feast of architectural styles, from High Baroque, through the monumental imperial projects of the late nineteenth century, to Modernist experiments and enlightened municipal planning.

Vienna became an important centre in the tenth century, then in 1278 the city fell to **Rudolf of Habsburg**, but didn't become the imperial residence until 1683 due to threats from the Ottoman Empire. The great aristocratic families, grown fat on profits from Turkish wars, flooded in to build palaces and summer residences in a frenzy of construction that gave Vienna its **Baroque character**. By the end of the Habsburg era the city had become a breeding ground for the ideological passions of the age: nationalism, socialism, Zionism and anti-Semitism. This turbulence was reflected in the **cultural sphere**, and the ghosts of Freud, Klimt, Schiele, Mahler and Schönberg are nowadays bigger tourist draws than old stand-bys such as the Lipizzaner horses and the Vienna Boys' Choir.

What to see and do

Central Vienna may well bowl you over with its grandiosity, but for all that, it's surprisingly compact: the historical centre, or **Innere Stadt**, is just 1km wide at its broadest point. The most important sights are concentrated here and along Ringstrasse – the series of boulevards that form a ring road around the inner city – including Museumsstrasse, Museumsplatz, Getreidemarkt and Am Heumarkt. The best way to grasp its grand sweep is to board tram #1 or #2 from outside the Staatsoper (Opera House), both of which circle the boulevard. Efficient public transport allows you to cross the city in less than thirty minutes, making even peripheral sights, such as the monumental imperial palace at **Schönbrunn**, easily accessible.

Stephansdom

The obvious place to begin exploring is **Stephansplatz**, the lively pedestrianized central square dominated by the hoary Gothic **Stephansdom** (Mon–Sat 6am–10pm, Sun 7am–10pm; free). The highlight in the nave is the early sixteenth-century carved stone. To get a good look at the Wiener Neustädter Altar, a late Gothic masterpiece, and the tomb of the Holy Roman Emperor Friedrich III, you must sign up for a guided tour (English tours April–Oct daily 3.45pm; €4.50). The **catacombs** (Mon–Sat 10–11.30am & 1.30–4.30pm, Sun 1.30–4.30pm; €4.50) contain the entrails of illustrious Habsburgs housed in bronze caskets. Stellar views reward those climbing the 137m-high spire (daily 9am–5.30pm; €3.50).

The Jesuitenkirche and MAK

The warren of alleyways north and east of **Stephansdom** preserve something of the medieval character of the city, although the architecture reflects centuries of continuous rebuilding. The seventeenth-century **Jesuitenkirche** (Mon–Sat 6am–10pm, Sun 7am–10pm; free) is easily Vienna's most awesome High Baroque church. Particularly striking are its red and green barley-sugar spiral columns, exquisitely carved pews and clever trompe-l'oeil dome. Nearby, beyond Stubenring, is the enjoyable **MAK** (Tues 10am–midnight, Wed–Sun 10am–6pm; €9.90, free Sat; ⓦwww.mak.at), a museum whose eclectic collection spans from the Romanesque period to the twentieth century and includes Klimt's *Stoclet Frieze* and an unrivalled Wiener Werkstätte collection.

Judenplatz

Though one of Vienna's prettiest little squares, **Judenplatz**, is dominated by a bleak concrete **Holocaust Memorial** by British sculptor Rachel Whiteread. The square marks the site of the medieval Jewish ghetto and you can view the foundations of an old synagogue at the excellent **Museum Judenplatz** at no. 8 (Sun–Thurs 10am–6pm, Fri 10am–2pm; €4), which brings something of medieval Jewish Vienna to life. Buy a joint ticket (€10) to also visit the intriguing **Jüdisches Museum**, Dorotheergasse 11 (Sun–Fri 10am–6pm; €6.50; Ⓦwww.jmw.at), a more general museum of Jewish tradition and culture.

Kärntnerstrasse and around

From Stephansplatz, pedestrianized Kärntnerstrasse runs south past street entertainers and elegant shops to the illustrious **Staatsoper** (Ⓦwww.wiener-staatsoper.at), opened in 1869 in the first phase of the Ringstrasse's development. A more unusual tribute to the city's musical genius can be found at the state-of-the-art **Haus der Musik**, Seilerstätte 30 (daily 10am–10pm; €10, €5 Tues from 5pm; Ⓦwww.hausdermusik.com), a hugely enjoyable museum of sound. For art of a different kind, head west to the **Albertina** (Wed 10am–9pm, Thurs–Tues 10am–6pm; €9.50; Ⓦwww.albertina.at), one of the world's largest graphic art collections, with works by Raphael, Rembrandt, Dürer and Michelangelo.

The Hofburg and around

The immense, highly ornate **Hofburg** palace (Ⓦwww.hofburg-wien.at) houses many of Vienna's key imperial sights. Skip the rather dull **Kaiserappartements** in favour of the more impressive **Schatzkammer** (daily: Mon & Wed–Sun 10am–6pm; €10). Here you can see some of the finest medieval craftsmanship and jewellery in Europe, including relics of the Holy Roman Empire and the Habsburg crown jewels. Steps beside the Schatzkammer lead up to the **Hofmusik Kapelle** (Mon–Thurs 11am–3pm, Fri 11am–1pm; €1.50), primarily known as the venue for Mass with the **Vienna Boys' Choir** (mid-Sept to June Sun 9.15am; Ⓣ01/533 9927, Ⓦwww.wsk.at), for which you can obtain free, standing-room-only tickets from 8.15am.

The Spanish Riding School and Lipizzaner Museum

On the north side of the Hofburg, the imperial stables are home to the white horses of the **Spanish Riding School** (performances: Feb–June & mid-Aug–Dec; standing from €23, seats from €47. Training sessions: same months Tues–Sat 10am–noon; €12; Ⓦwww.srs.at). Tickets for performances are hard to come by, but training-session tickets are sold at the entrance to the **Lipizzaner Museum** (daily 9am–6pm; €5). You can also buy tickets on the day at the Josefsplatz entrance box office – the queue is at its worst early on, but by 11am it's usually easy enough to get in.

The Ring and Rathausplatz

The Ring, the large boulevard just south of the Hofburg, along with its

VIENNA'S HEURIGEN

If you fancy sampling some Austrian wines and a scenic excursion out of the city, take a trip to one of the rustic wine-producing villages situated on Vienna's outskirts. To the north of the Danube, Stammersdorf (tram #31 from Schottenring; 40 min) is surrounded by vineyards and filled with traditional, family-run *Heurigen* (wine taverns). A great place to start is **Wienhof Wieninger**, 21 Stammersdorferstrasse 78 (Wed–Fri 3pm–midnight, Sat & Sun noon–midnight; Ⓦwww.wieninger.at), which has a pleasant garden, an excellent, inexpensive buffet and a good selection of own-label whites available by the glass.

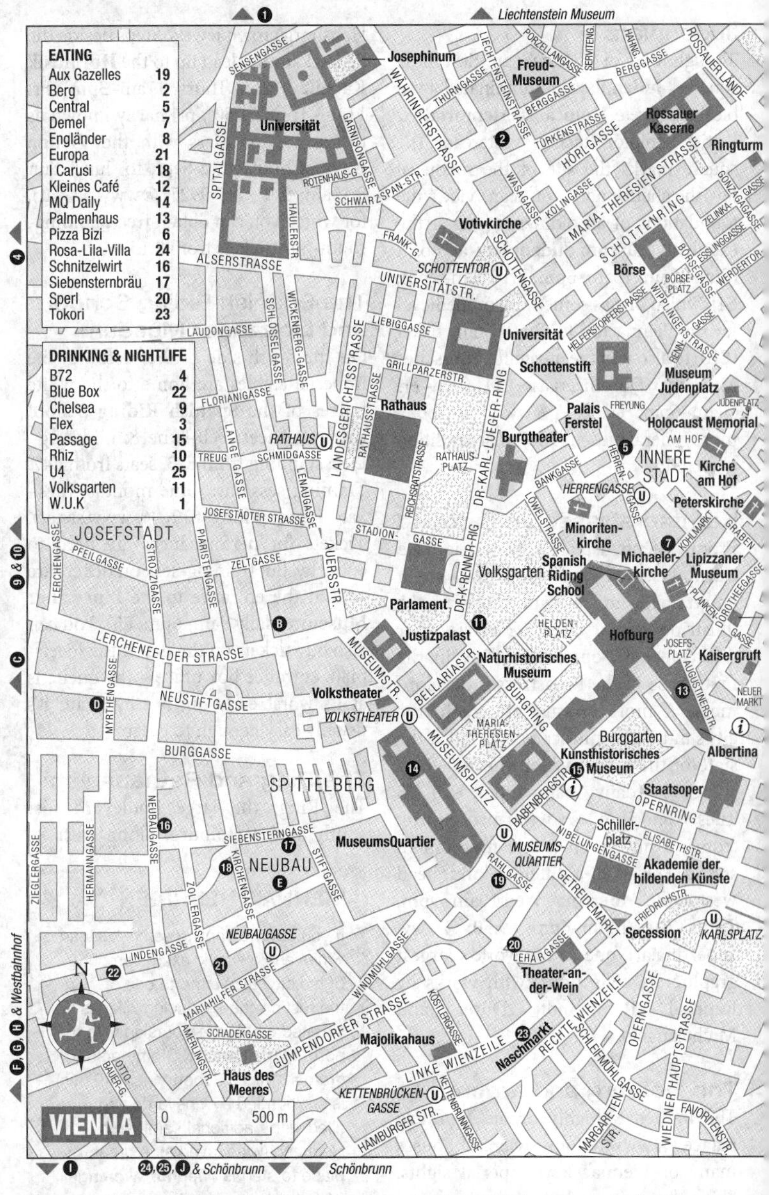

attendant monumental civic buildings, was created to replace the town's fortifications, demolished in 1857. Many of these buildings now house museums, including the outstanding **Kunsthistorisches Museum** (Tues, Wed & Fri–Sun 10am–6pm, Thurs 10am–9pm; €10; Ⓦwww.khm.at), one of the world's greatest collections of Old Masters – comparable with the Hermitage or Louvre. An unrivalled collection of sixteenth-century paintings by Bruegel

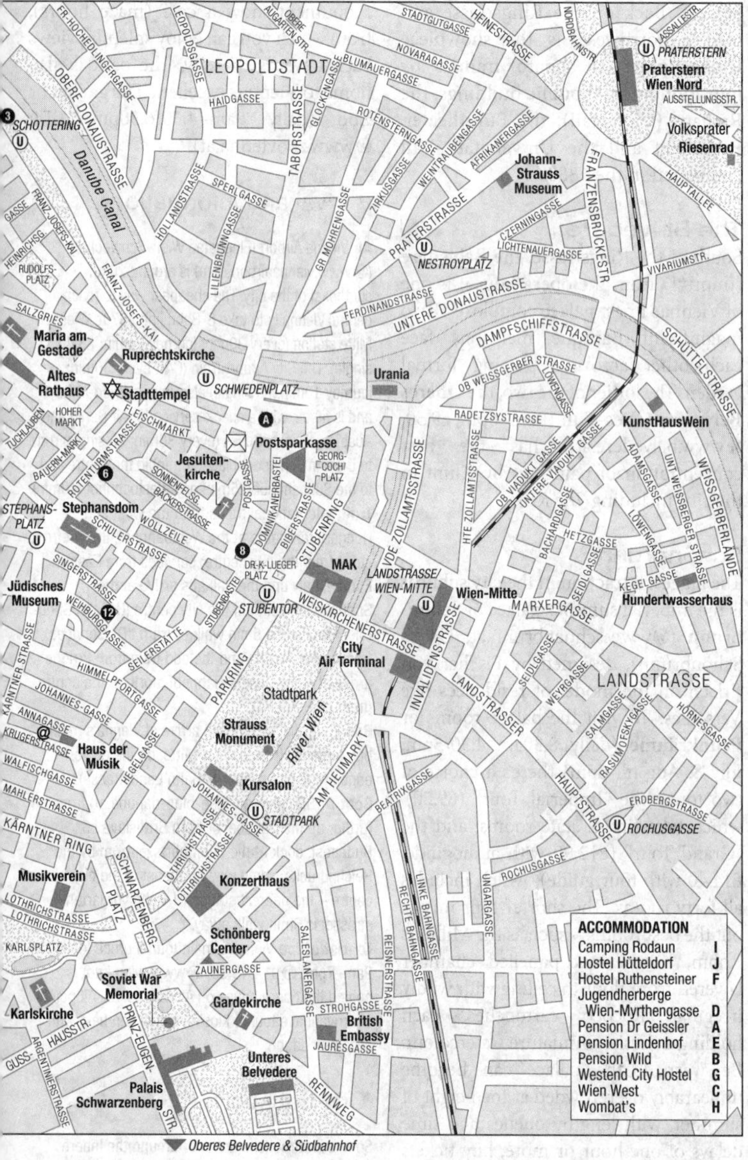

the Elder particularly draws the crowds. The Peter Paul Rubens collection is also very strong, while a number of Greek and Roman antiquities add breadth and variety. Just to the southwest is Vienna's **MuseumsQuartier** (MQ; ⓦwww.mqw.at), a whole host of new museums and galleries in the old imperial stables. The best is the **Leopold Museum** (Wed & Fri–Mon 10am–6pm, Thurs 10am–9pm; €10), with fine work by both Klimt and

Schiele. Back on the Ringstrasse and to the northwest, is the showpiece **Rathausplatz**, a square framed by four monumental public buildings: the Rathaus (City Hall), the Burgtheater, Parlament and the Universität – all completed in the 1880s.

The Belvedere

South of the Ringstrasse, the **Belvedere** (tram #D from the opera house) is one of Vienna's finest palace complexes. Two magnificent Baroque mansions face each other across a sloping formal garden. The loftier of the two, the **Oberes Belvedere** (Tues–Sun 10am–6pm; €9.50; Ⓦwww.belvedere.at), has the best concentration of paintings by Klimt in the city, including *The Kiss*.

Schönbrunn

The biggest attraction in the city suburbs is the imperial summer palace of **Schönbrunn** (Ⓦwww.schoenbrunn.at; U4 to Schönbrunn), designed by Fischer von Erlach on the model of residences like Versailles. To visit the palace rooms or **Prunkräume** (daily 8.30am–4.30/5pm; July & Aug till 6pm) there's a choice of two tours: the "Imperial Tour" (€9.50), which takes in 22 state rooms; and the "Grand Tour" (€12.90 with audioguide, €14.40 with tour guide), which includes all forty rooms. The shorter tour misses out the best rooms – such as the Millions Room, a rosewood-panelled chamber covered from floor to ceiling with wildly irregular Rococo cartouches, each holding a Persian miniature watercolour. Be warned, the palace can become unbearably overcrowded at the height of summer, with lengthy queues and time delays of one hour or more; buy tickets online to avoid all this. There are also coaches and carriages in the **Wagenburg** (April–Oct daily 9am–6pm; Nov–March 10am–4pm; €4.50), a maze and labyrinth in the **Schlosspark** (daily: April–Sept 9am–6/7pm; Oct 10am–5pm; €2.90) and the **Gloriette** – a hilltop colonnaded monument, now a café (maze hours), from which you can enjoy splendid views back towards the city. The park is also home to Vienna's excellent **Tiergarten** or Zoo (daily 9am–4.30/6.30pm; €14; Ⓦwww.zoovienna.at).

Arrival and information

Air Vienna Airport (Flughafen Wien-Schwechat) (Ⓦwww.viennaairport.com) is around 20km southeast of the city. The cheapest way to reach central Vienna is to take S-Bahn line #S7 to Wien-Mitte station (every 30min; journey 24min; €3.40 single). The City Airport Train (CAT; every 30min; journey 10min; €9 single) also runs to Wien-Mitte and is faster, with a check-service for Air Berlin and Austrian Airlines. Buses (every 30min; €6 single) run to U-Bahn Schwedenplatz (20min) in the centre and to the Südbahnhof (25min) and Westbahnhof (40min).

Train International trains from the west and Hungary terminate at the Westbahnhof, five metro stops from the city centre; services from Eastern Europe, Italy and the Balkans arrive at the Südbahnhof, south of the city centre (U-Bahn Südtiroler Platz and a 5min walk or tram #D); services from Lower Austria and the odd train from Prague arrive at Franz-Josefs-Bahnhof, north of the centre (tram #D).

Bus Long-distance buses arrive at Vienna's main bus terminal, beside Wien-Mitte, on the eastern edge of the city centre (U-Bahn Landstrasse).

Boat DDSG (Ⓦwww.ddsg-blue-danube.at) from further up the Danube, or from Bratislava or Budapest, dock at the Schiffahrtszentrum by the Reichsbrücke, some way northeast of the city centre – the nearest station (U-Bahn Vorgartenstrasse) is 5min walk away.

Tourist office Vienna's main tourist office (daily 9am–7pm; Ⓣ01/245 55, Ⓦwww.wien.info) is behind the opera house on Albertinaplatz. All points of arrival have tourist kiosks, which can help with accommodation.

City transport

So many attractions are in or around the Innere Stadt that you can do a great deal on foot.

Public transport runs 5am–midnight (outside these times night buses called NightLine run from Schwedenplatz). The network consists of trams (Strassenbahn or Bim), buses, the U-Bahn (metro) and the S-Bahn (fast commuter trains).

Tickets Buy your ticket from the ticket booths or machines at U-Bahn stations and from tobacconists,

and punch it on-board buses and trams or before entering the U- or S-Bahn. Fares are calculated on a zonal basis: tickets for the central zone (covering all of Vienna) cost €1.70 and allow unlimited changes on any mode of transport. Much better value is a day-pass (24hr/48hr/72hr Stundenticket; €5.70/10/13.60) and the much-touted Wien-Karte or Vienna Card (€18.50). This acts as a 72-hour travel pass and also gives small discounts at attractions. If you have an ISIC card, simply buying a travel pass is a better bet.

Bike rental Pedal Power, 2, Ausstellungstr. 3 (Ⓣ01/729 72 34, Ⓦwww.pedalpower.at; €24 for 5hr).

Taxis run from the ranks around town; to book, call Ⓣ01/313 00 or 01/601 60.

Accommodation

There's no shortage of expensive accommodation, but extreme pressure on the cheaper end of the market means booking ahead is essential in summer and advisable during the rest of the year.

Hostels

Hostel Hütteldorf 13, Schlossberggasse 8 Ⓣ01/877 15 01, Ⓦwww.hostel.at. A 300-bed hostel out in the sticks, but convenient for Schönbrunn. Light breakfast included. Free wi-fi. Bike hire available. S- and U-Bahn Hütteldorf. Dorms €17.50, doubles €55.

Hostel Ruthensteiner 15, Robert Hamerlinggasse 24 Ⓣ01/893 42 02, Ⓦwww.hostelruthensteiner.com. Excellent, friendly and relaxed hostel an easy walk from the Westbahnhof. There's a spacious leafy courtyard, plus bar, musical instruments, kitchen, barbecue, internet, laundry and free wi-fi. U-Bahn Westbahnhof. Dorms €17, doubles €60.

Jugendherberge Wien-Myrthengasse 7, Myrthengasse 7 & Neustiftgasse 85 Ⓣ01/523 63 16, Ⓦwww.oejhv.or.at. Central HI hostel a short walk up Neustiftgasse from U-Bahn Volkstheater. Book well in advance. Dorms €17.50, twins €35.

Westend City Hostel 6, Fügergasse 3 Ⓣ01/597 67 29, Ⓦwww.westendhostel.at. A few minutes' walk from the Westbahnhof, a refurbished 211-bed former hotel with friendly staff, patio, left-luggage and laundry. Dorms €22.50, en-suite rooms €68.

Wombat's 15, Grangasse 6 and Mariahilferstr. 137 Ⓣ01/897 23 36, Ⓦwww.wombats.at. One of a pair of party-orientated *Wombat's* hostels near the Westbahnhof. With guest kitchen, laundry and free wi-fi. Dorms €21, doubles €58.

> **VIENNESE ADDRESSES**
>
> Vienna is divided into **numbered districts** (*Bezirke*). District 1 is the Innere Stadt, the area enclosed by the Ringstrasse; districts 2–9 are arranged clockwise around it; beyond here, districts 10–23 are a fair way out. All Viennese addresses begin with the number of the district, followed by the street name, then the house number followed, where relevant, by the number of the apartment separated by a forward slash.

Hotels and pensions

Pension Dr Geissler 1, Postgasse 14 Ⓣ01/533 28 03, Ⓦwww.hotelpension.at. Anonymous, modern *pension*; all rooms have cable/satellite TV, and those with shared facilities are among the cheapest in the Innere Stadt. U-Bahn Schwedenplatz. Doubles €65.

Pension Lindenhof 7, Lindengasse 4 Ⓣ01/523 04 98, Ⓔpensionlindenhof@yahoo.com. Quirky *pension* in a great location just off Mariahilferstrasse. The hallway is filled with plants and rooms have creaky parquet flooring. Breakfast is included, but you pay €2 extra per shower in rooms with shared facilities. U-Bahn Neubaugasse. Doubles €67.

Pension Wild 8, Lange Gasse 10 Ⓣ01/406 51 74, Ⓦwww.pension-wild.com. Friendly, laid-back *pension*, a short walk from the Ring in a student district behind the university. Especially popular with gay travellers; booking is essential. U-Bahn Rathaus/Volkstheater. Doubles €53.

Campsites

Camping Rodaun 23, An der Au 2 Ⓣ01/888 41 54. Nice streamside location 9km southwest of the centre. Tram #60 from U-Bahn Hietzing to terminus, then a 5min walk. Mid-June–Oct. Tents €12.

Wien West 14, Hüttelbergstr. 80 Ⓣ01/914 2314, Ⓦwww.wiencamping.at. In the plush far-western suburbs of Vienna, with two- and four-bed bungalows to rent. Bus #151 from U-Bahn Hütteldorf or a 15min walk from tram #49 terminus. Tents €12.70, dorms €16, bungalows €35.

Eating

Cafés

Berg 9, Berggasse 8. Adjoined to a gay bookshop, *Berg* is trendy, modern and relaxed, attracting a mixed gay/straight clientele. Good food, often with an Asian twist. Mains €10. Open till 1am. U-Bahn Schottentor.

Central 1, Herrengasse 14. Traditional meeting-place of Vienna's intelligentsia, and Trotsky's

favourite *Kaffeehaus* – of all Vienna's cafés, perhaps the most ornate. Snacks and mains for under €10. Closes 6pm. U-Bahn Herrengasse.

Demel 1, Kohlmarkt 14. Elaborately displayed, *Demel*'s patisseries and cakes are highly prestigious and correspondingly pricey. Closes 7pm. U-Bahn Herrengasse.

Engländer 1, Postgasse 2; Great *Kaffeehaus* with a long pedigree and food that has a touch of *nouvelle cuisine*. Snacks €3–7, mains €9–15. Open till 1am. U-Bahn Stubentor.

Europa 7, Zollergasse 8. Lively, modern café hosting a young, trendy crowd. Good breakfast menu. Open till 5am. U-Bahn Neubaugasse.

Kleines Café 1, Franziskanerplatz 3. Tiny café with outside seating, tucked away in a tranquil cobbled square, serving delicious open sandwiches (€3.50). U-Bahn Stephansplatz.

MQ Daily 7, Museumsplatz 1; Best of the MuseumsQuartier cafés, with vaulted, floral ceramic ceiling, imaginative menu and a friendly vibe. Open till midnight; closed Sun eve. U-Bahn Museums Quartier.

Palmenhaus 1, Burggarten. Stylish café in a lofty greenhouse filled with lush palms and foliage in the Burggarten behind the Hofburg. Salads €5–10, mains €12.50–22. Open till 2am. U-Bahn Karlsplatz.

Rosa-Lila-Villa 6, Linke Wienzeile 102 ⓦ www.villa.at. Gay and lesbian centre housing a café/restaurant with a nice leafy courtyard. A good place to pick up information about events. Open till 2am. U-Bahn Pilgramgasse.

Sperl 6, Gumpendorferstr. 11. The fin-de-siècle interior is among the finest of the city's coffee houses, with reasonably priced food (€6.50). July & Aug closed Sun. Open till 11pm. U-Bahn Karlsplatz/Babenbergerstr.

Restaurants

Aux Gazelles 6, Rahlgasse 5. Vast North African enterprise with café, brasserie, oyster bar, *salon de thé* and even a small *hammam*. *Tagines* €16.50. Closed Sunday. U-Bahn MuseumsQuartier.

I Carusi 7, Kirchengasse 21. Modern, stylish trattoria with high ceilings, serving excellent thin-crust pizzas (€9.50). U-Bahn Neubaugasse.

Pizza Bizi 1, Rotenturmstrasse 4 and other locations. Cheap, central, self-service stomach-filler chain serving pizzas for €7 (€2.40 per slice). U-Bahn Stephansplatz.

Schnitzelwirt 7, Neubaugasse 52. Great place for *Wienerschnitzel* – a bargain at €6. Closed Sun. Tram #49.

Siebensternbräu 7, Siebensterngasse 19. Popular modern *Bierkeller* that brews its own beer and serves solid Viennese food from €6. U-Bahn Volkstheater/Neubaugasse.

Tokori Naschmarkt 177–178. Simple Japanese place in the market, with generous portions of sushi and noodles for €7. U-Bahn Karlsplatz.

Markets

Naschmarkt The city's main fruit and veg market is held off Karlsplatz (Mon–Fri 6am–7.30pm, Sat 6am–5pm). It's a great place to assemble a picnic or grab a quick lunch: there's a plethora of stalls and snack joints, serving everything from falafel to sushi.

Drinking and nightlife

B72 8, Stadtbahnbögen 72, Hernalser Gürtel ⓦ www.b72.at. Dark, designer club featuring a mixture of DJs and live indie bands; one of several beneath the U-Bahn arches. Open till 4am. U-Bahn Alserstr.

Blue Box 7, Richtergasse 8 ⓦ www.bluebox.at. Musikcafé with resident DJs and a good snack menu. Open till 2am or later. U-Bahn Neubaugasse.

Chelsea 8, Gürtelbögen 29–30, Lerchenfelder Gürtel ⓦ www.chelsea.co.at. Popular, grungy rock venue with up-and-coming guitar bands. Situated underneath the railway arches. U-Bahn Thaliastr.

Flex 1, Am Donaukanal ⓦ www.flex.at. Serious dance-music club by the canal, attracting some of the city's best DJs. Open till 4am. U-Bahn Schottenring.

Passage 1, Babenberger Passage, Burgring/Babenbergerstrasse ⓦ www.sunshine.at. Funky futuristic club, in a converted pedestrian underpass. Open till 4am. U-Bahn MuseumsQuartier/Volkstheater.

Rhiz 8, Gürtelbögen 37–38, Lerchenfelder Gürtel ⓦ www.rhiz.org. Bar/café/club under the U-Bahn arches, with DJs spinning dance, trance and the like. Open till 4am. U-Bahn Josefstädterstr.

U4 12, Schönbrunnerstr. 222 ⓦ www.u-4.at. A dark, cavernous club, popular with an alternative crowd, different musical theme every night: from 80s to 90s and punk to disco. Open till 5am. U-Bahn Meidling-Hauptstr.

Volksgarten 1, Burgring 1 ⓦ www.volksgarten.at. Vienna's longest-running club in the park of the same name. Open till 5am. U-Bahn Volkstheater.

W.U.K. 9, Währingerstr. 59 ⓦ www.wuk.at. Big old school turned arts venue with a relaxed café and a wide programme of events, including live music and DJ nights. Open till 2am. Tram #40, #41 or #42.

Entertainment

The local listings magazine *Falter* (ⓦ www.falter.at) has comprehensive details of the week's

cultural programme. The tourist office also publishes the free monthly *Programm*. Bookings for classical venues can usually be made at Bundestheaterkassen, 1, Hanuschgasse 3 (Ⓦwww.bundestheater.at). Cheap standing-room tickets are often available by queuing up an hour before a performance.

Konzerthaus 3, Lothringerstr. 20 Ⓦwww.konzerthaus.at. Major classical venue, which also has performances of jazz and world music.

Musikverein 1, Karlsplatz 6 Ⓦwww.musikverein-wien.at. Ornate concert hall, home of the Vienna Philharmonic.

Porgy & Bess 1, Riemergasse 11 Ⓣ01/512 88 12, Ⓦwww.porgy.at. A converted porn cinema, now the home for Vienna's top jazz venue, attracting acts from all over the world. U-Bahn Stubentor.

Staatsoper 1, Opernring 2 Ⓣ01/513 15 13, Ⓦwww.wiener-staatsoper.at. One of Europe's most prestigious opera houses. The season runs from September to June and tickets range from a mere €8 to over €240. Tickets often sell out weeks in advance, but the ticket office also sells hundreds of standing-place tickets (*Stehplätze*) each night 1hr 20min before a performance (from €3/4).

Shopping

Mariahilferstrasse is one of the most popular shopping streets in the city, and best for high-street clothes shops and the big chains. Neubaugasse, nearby, is more eclectic. On Saturday mornings a flea market extends south of the Naschmarkt (U-Bahn Kettenbrückengasse).

Aida 1, Stock-im-Eisen-Platz 2. The distinctive pink neon signs of this ubiquitous Viennese coffee chain announces the presence of great cakes and sweets to take home. U-Bahn Stephansplatz.

Shakespeare & Co 1, Sterngasse 2, Ⓦwww.shakespeare.co.at. Friendly English-language bookshop; also sells translations of Austrian authors. U-Bahn Schwedenplatz.

Directory

Embassies Australia, 4, Mattiellistr. 2–4 Ⓣ01/506 74; Canada, 1, Laurenzerbergg. 2 Ⓣ01/531 38 30 00; Ireland, 1, Rotenturmstr. 16–18 Ⓣ01/715 42 46; UK Consulate, 3, Jaurèsgasse 10 Ⓣ01/71 61 30; US, 9, Boltzmanngasse 16 Ⓣ01/31 33 90.

Exchange Outside banking hours try bureaus at the Westbahnhof or the Südbahnhof.

Hospital Allegemeines Krankenhaus, 9, Währinger Gürtel 18–20; U-Bahn Michelbeuern-AKH.

Internet Surfland Internet Café, 1, Krugerstrasse 10; daily 10am–11pm; 30min €3.90.

Laundry Waschcenter TOP, Ottakringer Str. 52; €5; 6am–10pm; U-Bahn Josefstädter Str.

Pharmacy Alte Feldapotheke, opposite the Stephansdom.

Post offices 1, Fleischmarkt 19; Westbahnhof; Südbahnhof; all 7am–10pm.

Moving on

Trains Bratislava (every 30min; 1hr); Budapest (every 30min; 3hr); Graz (hourly; 2hr 40min); Innsbruck (10 daily; 5hr); Krems (every 30min; 1hr 30min); Linz (hourly; 1hr 30min); Melk (2 hourly; 1hr 15min); Prague (8 daily; 4hr 30min); Salzburg (every 30min; 3hr).

Boats DDSG (Ⓦwww.ddsg-blue-danube.at) operates boats at weekends between Vienna and Bratislava (6 daily; 1hr 15min).

Central Austria

Some 70km west of Vienna, the Danube snakes through the Wachau, one of its most scenic stretches, where castles and vineyards cling to steep slopes above quaint villages. The western end of this 40km stretch is marked by a stunning Baroque monastery in the town of **Melk**. Further west the river steadily loses charm, though it's still a focus for several towns and cities, including workaday but attractive **Linz**, whose high-tech Ars Electronic Museum is particularly enjoyable. South of the Danube region, the land slowly climbs and rolls into the hills of Stryia, with its attractive and bustling capital **Graz**. Northwest of here, the land rises again up to the Salzkammergut, a region of fine Alpine scenery and pretty lakes within easy reach of the dignified and attractive city of **Salzburg**. Among the most appealing Salzkammergut settlements are **St Wolfgang** and **Hallstatt**, but even these are sleepy and quiet save for the influx of summer visitors. South of the Salzkammergut the peaks really start to soar and resorts like

Bad Gastein take full advantage of the landscape, clean air and healthy spring waters to offer great skiing, all sorts of outdoor activities and first-rate spa facilities. Note too, that **Berchtesgaden** (see p.520), Hitler's favoured Alpine retreat, lies just over the German border from Salzburg and is easily accessible using its public transport.

MELK

For real High Baroque excess, head for the early eighteenth-century **Benedictine monastery** at **MELK** – a pilgrimage centre associated with the Irish missionary St Koloman. The monumental coffee-cake monastery, perched on a bluff over the river, dominates the town. Highlights of the interior (daily: April & Oct 9am–4.30pm; May–Sept 9am–5.30pm; tours in English 11am & 2pm; Nov–March guided tours only: in English 11am & 2pm; €7.70, €9.50 with guided tour; Ⓦwww.stiftmelk.at) are the exquisite library, with a cherub-infested ceiling by Troger, and the rather lavish monastery church, with similarly impressive work by Rottmayr.

Melk's river station is about ten minutes' walk north of town; the train station is at the head of Bahnhofstrasse, which leads directly into the old quarter. The **tourist office**, at Babenbergstr. 1, (April Mon–Fri 9am–noon & 2–6pm Sat 10am–noon; May, June & Sept Mon–Fri 9am–noon & 2–6pm, Sat & Sun 10am–noon & 4–6pm; July & Aug 9am–7pm, Sun 10am–noon & 5–7pm; Oct Mon–Fri 9am–noon & 2–5pm, Sat 10am–noon; Ⓣ02752/52 30 74 10), has a substantial stock of private rooms, though few are central. The **HI hostel** is ten minutes' walk from the tourist office, at Abt Karl-Str. 42 (Ⓣ02752/526 81, Ⓦmelk.noejhw.at; mid-March–Oct; dorms €17.90, doubles €46, breakfast included). The town **campsite** is a similar distance in the opposite direction, *Melker Camping* (Ⓣ02752/532 91; March–Nov; €11), by the river.

LINZ

Away from its industrial suburbs, **LINZ** is a pleasant Baroque city straddling the Danube, even though its greatest claim to fame is as the childhood home of Adolf Hitler, something about which the local tourist board is understandably coy.

What to see and do

The heart of the city is the expansive rectangular main square, **Hauptplatz**, with its pastel-coloured facades and central Trinity Column, crowned by a gilded sunburst. In the nearby **Pfarrkirche**, a gargantuan marble slab contains Emperor Friedrich III's heart (the rest of him is in Vienna's Stephansdom). A modern addition to the city's cultural scene nestles beside the Danube: the shimmering, hangar-like steel-and-glass **Lentos** (10am–6pm, Thurs daily till 9pm; €6.50; Ⓦwww.lentos.at), which houses contemporary and modern art, including Klimt, Kokoschka, and Schiele. Just across the river is Linz's other major attraction, the unusual **Ars Electronica Center**, Hauptstrasse 2 (Tues, Wed & Fri 9am–5pm, Thurs 9am–9pm, Sat & Sun 10am–6pm; €7; Ⓦwww.aec.at), which is dedicated to new technology with a

LINZ ORIENTATION

Linz straddles the Danube. To the north of the river lies the suburb of Urfahr; to the south is the city's compact old town, the hub of which is the Hauptplatz. Many of the city's liveliest bars are clustered just a short walk to the west of here, around the triangle formed by Hoffgasse, Altstadt and Hahnengasse. Heading south from the Hauptplatz, the busy shopping street Landstrasse leads south towards the train station, whilst parallel Herrengasse brings you to the cathedral.

range of interactive high-tech exhibits. The main highlight is the "CAVE", a virtual-reality room with 3D projections on the walls and floor – get there early to book for it.

Arrival and information

Train station Linz's train station is 2km south of the centre, at the end of the city's main artery, Landstrasse; tram #3 runs to Hauptplatz.
Tourist office Alte Rathaus, Hauptplatz 1 (Nov–April Mon–Fri 9am–6pm, Sat & Sun 10am–6pm; May–Oct Mon–Fri 9am–7pm, Sat & Sun 10am–7pm; ⓣ0732/70 70 20 09, ⓦwww.linz.at).

Accommodation

Campsite Seeweg 11 ⓣ0732/24 78 70; mid-March to Oct; bus #33 or #33a from Rudolfstrasse in Urfahr. On the Pleschinger See, 3km northeast of the centre on the Danube. Tents only, €6.
Jugendherberge Stanglhofweg 3 ⓣ0732/66 44 34, ⓦwww.jugendherbergsverband.at; March–Sept. Friendly youth hostel 2km from Hauptbahnhof; bus # 17, #19, #45 to "Leondingerstrasse". All bedrooms are en suite, breakfast included. Dorms €15, doubles €35.
Wilder Mann Goethestr. 14 ⓣ0732/65 60 78, ⓦwww.wildermann.cc. Family-run place, down near the station; rooms available with shared facilities or with en-suite showers but hallway WCs. Doubles €44.

Eating, drinking and nightlife

Alte Welt Hauptplatz 4. Unpretentious bar and wine cellar in a cosy courtyard just off the Hauptplatz. Austrian/Italian-influenced mains; €6.50–15. Open till 2am.
Klosterhof Landstr. 30. Former monastery with large beer garden serving solid Austrian fare. *Schnitzel* €9.60.
Smaragd Altstadt 2. One of several bar-clubs lining Altstadt, with cocktails and a dancefloor. Open till 6am. Live music Tues–Thurs, including a popular Latino night (Thurs).
Traxlmayr Promenade 16. Traditional coffee house; a good place to treat yourself to a slice of *Linzer Torte*, the town's ubiquitous almond-and-jam *torte* (€2.60). Closed Sun.

GRAZ

Austria's second-largest city, **GRAZ**, owes its importance to the defence of central Europe against the Turks. From the fifteenth century, it was constantly under arms, rendering it more secure than Vienna and leading to a modest seventeenth-century flowering of the arts (Baroque appeared first in Graz). The city's former reputation as a conservative place has been superseded, thanks to a clutch of modern glass-and-steel architectural adventures and a large student population, and it's a fun place to spend a few days without the tourist traffic of Innsbruck or Salzburg.

What to see and do

Graz is compact and easy to explore, with most sights within easy walking distance of its central **Hauptplatz**.

Schlossberg

To get your bearings take a trip up the wooded hill that overlooks the town: either walk up the zigzagging stone stairs from Schlossbergplatz or take the lift (Oct–April daily 8am–12.30am; May–Sept Mon–Wed & Sun 8am–12.30am, Thurs–Sat 8am–2.30am; €0.60 each way) or funicular (daily: April–Sept 9am–2am; Oct–March 10am–10pm; €1.80), from Sackstrasse. The **Schloss**, or fortress, was destroyed by Napoleon in 1809; only a few prominent features survive – most noticeably the huge sixteenth-century **Uhrturm** (clock tower), and more distant **Glockenturm** (bell tower), whose bell, "Liesl", is said to be cast from 101 Turkish cannonballs.

The Altstadt

From Hauptplatz, it's a few steps to the River Mur and two examples of Graz's architectural renaissance: the **Murinsel** is an ultra modern floating bridge-cum-meeting-place linking the two banks, inspired by an open mussel, while the giant submarine-like **Kunsthaus Graz** (Tues–Sun 10am–6pm; €7; ⓦwww.kunsthausgraz.at), a museum of

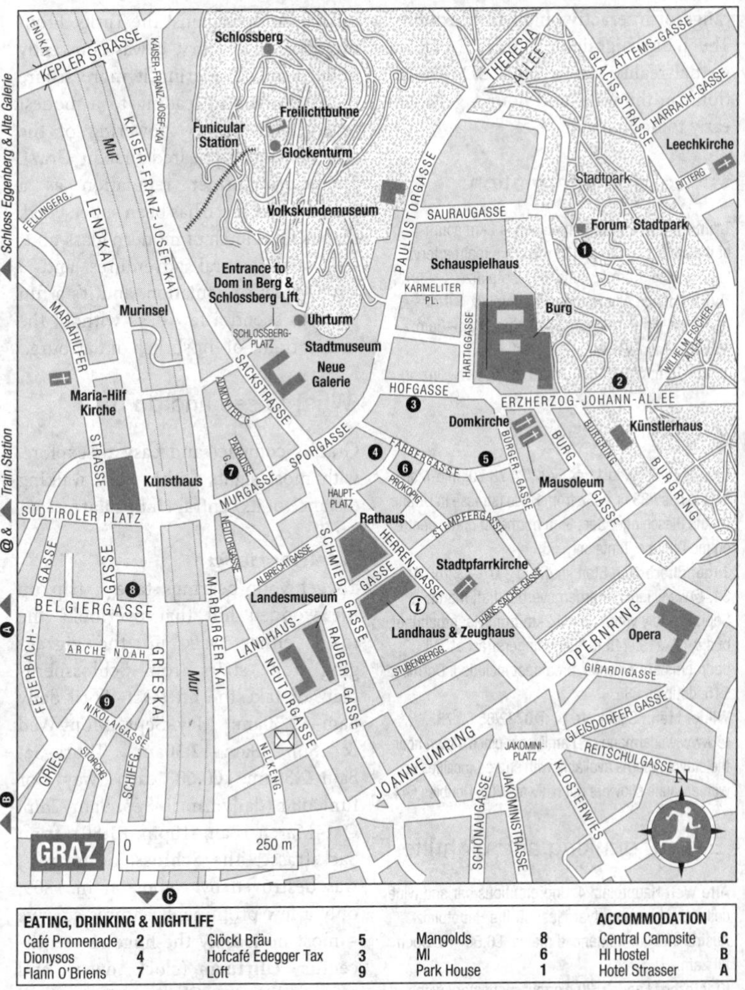

contemporary design, video installation and photography. Entrance tickets to the Kunsthaus function as a day-pass for several city museums that form part of the Landesmuseum Joanneum (ⓦwww.museum-joanneum.at), a city-wide institution.

Among them is the **Zeughaus** (April–Oct daily 10am–6pm; Nov–March Mon–Sat 10am–3pm, Sun 10am–4pm; €7), the city armoury on Herrengasse just south of the Hauptplatz **Landhaus**, which bristles with sixteenth-century weapons used to keep the Turks at bay.

Schloss Eggenberg

Another part of the Landesmuseum Joanneum is the **Baroque Schloss Eggenberg**, 4km west of the city centre, (tram #1 from the Hauptplatz). Designed in imitation of Escorial for Hans Ulrich von Eggenberg (1568–1634), chief minister to Ferdinand II, the Schloss houses the Alte Galerie (April–Oct

Tues–Sun 10am–6pm; Nov–March 10am–5pm; €7), whose Gothic devotional paintings include a macabre *Triumph of Death* by Jan Bruegel. English-language tours of the palace rooms (Prunkräume; hourly: Tues–Sun 10am–4pm, except 1pm), explore a house designed as an allegory of the universe (24 rooms, 365 windows, four towers and so on); the highlight is the "Room of the Planets" a great hall with an elaborate ceiling depicting the zodiac.

Arrival and information

Trains Graz's train station is on the western edge of town, a 15min walk or short tram ride (#1, #3, #6 or #7) from Hauptplatz.
Tourist office Herrengasse 16 (Jan–March & Nov Mon–Fri 10am–5pm, Sat & Sun 10am–6pm; April–June, Sept, Oct & Dec; July & Aug 10am–7pm, 10am–6pm; ⓣ0316/807 50, ⓦwww.graztourismus); also at the station (daily: Mon–Fri 9am–5pm).
City transport Central Graz has an effective bus and tram network. Both branches of the tourist office can sell you a 24hr transport pass for €3.80 (valid on both), which is worthwhile if you plan on making more than a couple of journeys (singles cost €1.80). Simply validate the pass the first time you travel.
Internet Internet Tele Discount, Annenstrasse 10 (Mon–Sat 10am–10pm).

Accommodation

Central Campsite Martinhofstr. 3 ⓣ0316/378 51 02, ⓦwww.tiscover.at/campingcentral; April–Oct; bus #32 from Jakominiplatz. Well-equipped campsite south of Graz, with a large swimming pool. Doubles €25.
HI Hostel Idlhofgasse 74 ⓣ05/708 32 10, ⓦwww.jgh.at. Friendly, modern hostel an easy walk from both the train station and centre. In addition to dorms and budget doubles, the complex offers more expensive hotel-style rooms with TV and en suite. There's also a climbing wall on site. Dorms €20, doubles €60.
Hotel Strasser Eggenburger Gürtel 11 ⓣ0316/71 39 77, ⓦwww.hotelstrasser.at. Don't let the shabby exterior put you off; inside are comfortable, if garish, doubles with TV and massage showers. Close to the station and 15min walk from the centre. Doubles €64.

Eating

Cafés

Café Promenade Erzherzog-Johann-Allee 1. Attractive, Neo classical pavilion, with stylish modern décor and a terrace overlooking the Stadtpark. Open till midnight, serving soups (€3.20), salads and mains (€6–12.50).
Hofcafé Edegger Tax Hofgasse 8. Sedate, genteel little café, adjoined to a long-established city-centre cake shop. Coffee €2. Closed Sun.

Restaurants

Dionysos Farbergasse 6–8. Central Greek restaurant serving up *souvlaki*, *mezze* and grills. Daily specials €7; *moussaka* €10.90.
Glöckl Bräu Glockenspielplatz 2–3. Traditional place, with busy beer terrace serving hearty Austrian fare for under €10.
Mangolds Griesgasse 11. Popular self-service place and excellent veggie option, with fresh juices and a large salad bar (pay according to weight: €1.15/100gm). Closed Sun.

Drinking and nightlife

Flann O'Briens Paradiesgasse. Lively Irish pub, with plenty of outside seating. Guinness €4.60/pint; nachos €4.40.
Loft Griesgasse 25 ⓦwww.loftgraz.at. Regular live music nights and guest DJs spinning eclectic sounds; equally popular with both a gay and straight crowd. Open daily until 4am and all night on Fri and Sat.
MI Färberplatz. Stylish, split level third-floor café-bar, with a designer interior and an attractive roof-terrace. Cappuccino and cake €4.80. Closed Sun.
Park House Stadtpark. Buzzing pavilion, tucked away in the park, with regular DJ nights. Open till 4am.

Moving on

Train Innsbruck (4 daily; 6hr); Linz (6 daily; 6hr); Salzburg (9 daily; 4hr).

SALZBURG

For many visitors, **SALZBURG** represents the quintessential Austria, offering ornate architecture, mountain air, and the musical heritage of the city's most famous son, Wolfgang Amadeus **Mozart**, whose bright-eyed visage peers from every box of *Mozartkugeln,* the city's ubiquitous chocolate delicacy.

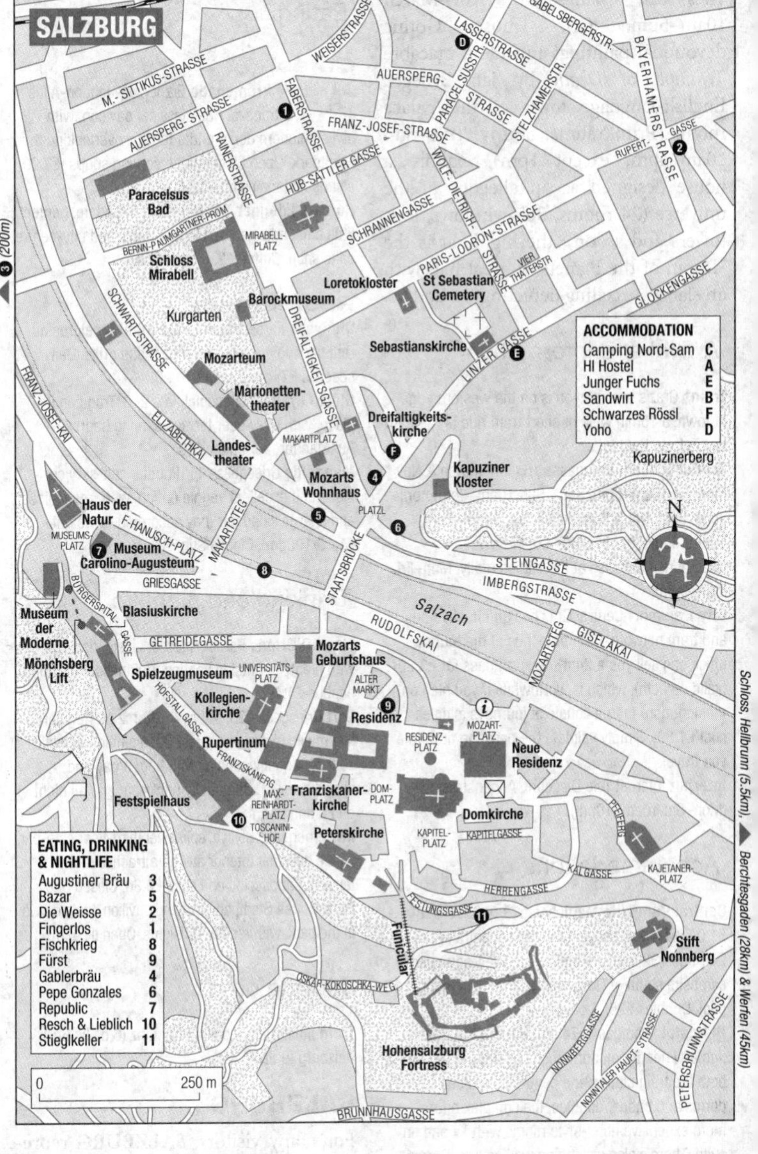

What to see and do

Salzburg's compact centre straddles the River Salzach. The city and surrounding area used to be ruled by a series of prince-archbishops and the resulting collection of episcopal buildings on the **west bank** forms a tight-knit network of alleys and squares, overlooked by the medieval **Hohensalzburg fortress**. From here it's a short hop over the river to a narrow ribbon of essential sights on the **east bank**.

Mozartplatz and around

From the Staatsbrücke, the main bridge, Judengasse, funnels you to **Mozartplatz**, home to a statue of the composer and overlooked by the **Glockenspiel**, a seventeenth-century musical clock whose chimes attract crowds at 7am, 11am and 6pm. The complex of Baroque buildings on the right exude the ecclesiastical and temporal power of Salzburg's archbishops, whose erstwhile living quarters – the **Residenz** – dominate the west side of Residenzplatz. You can take a self-guided audio-tour of the lavish **state rooms** (daily 10am–5pm; combined ticket with Residenzgalerie €8.50), and then visit the **Residenzgalerie** (closed Mon), one floor above, which includes works by Rembrandt and Caravaggio.

Domplatz and Franziskanerkirche

The pale marble facade of the **Dom** dominates **Domplatz**, while inside, the impressively cavernous Renaissance structure dazzles with its ceiling frescoes. Across Domplatz, an archway leads through to the Gothic **Franziskanerkirche**, which houses a fine Baroque altar around an earlier *Madonna and Child*. The altar is enclosed by an arc of nine chapels, and a frenzy of stucco. Look out for the twelfth-century marble lion that guards the stairway to the pulpit.

Mozarts Geburtshaus and Mozarts Wohnhaus

Getreidegasse, the main street in Salzburg's old town, is lined with opulent boutiques, painted facades and wrought-iron shop signs. At no. 9 is the canary yellow **Mozarts Geburtshaus** (daily: July & Aug 9am–8pm; Sept–June 9am–5.30pm; €6.50; joint ticket with Wohnhaus €10 Ⓦwww.mozarteum.at), where the musical prodigy was born (in 1756) and lived until age 17. Between the waves of tour parties it can be an evocative place, housing some fascinating period instruments, including a baby-sized violin used by Wolfgang Amadeus as a child. Heading north over the Salzach river via the Staatsbrücke, then two blocks northwest to Makartplatz, is **Mozarts Wohnhaus**, the family home from 1773–87 (same hours; €6.50), containing an engrossing multimedia history of the composer and his times.

Hohensalzburg

Overlooking the city from the rocky Mönchsberg, the fortified **Hohensalzburg** (daily: Jan–April 9.30am–5pm; May–Sept 9.30am–7pm; Ⓦwww.salzburg-burgen.at) is Salzburg's key landmark. You can get up here using the oldest funicular in Austria (daily: May–Sept 9am–9.30pm; Oct–April 9am–5pm; every 10min) from Fesstungsgasse behind the Dom and Kapitelplatz, although the walk up isn't as hard as it looks. Begun around 1070, the fortress gradually became a more salubrious courtly seat. The "fortress card" (€10.50) covers the funicular journey, entrance to the museum, and an audioguide for the state rooms. If you walk up and down to the fortress, the museum and audioguide cost €8.50. In summer, between 7–9.30pm, entrance to the fortress's ramparts and passageways is free, providing a good feel for the place, and fine evening views over Salzburg.

Schloss Mirabell

Dreifaltigkeitsgasse leads north to **Schloss Mirabell**, Mirabellplatz, on the site of a previous palace built by Archbishop Wolf Dietrich for his mistress Salome, with whom the energetic prelate was rumoured to have sired a dozen children. Rebuilt in the early eighteenth century, and reconstructed after a fire in the nineteenth, it features a Baroque, cherub-lined staircase and ornate gardens – the rose-filled high ground of the adjoining Kurgarten,

which offers a much-photographed view back across the city.

Schloss Hellbrunn and the Untersberg

The Italianate palace Schloss Hellbrunn on Salzburg's southern fringe – 5km from the city centre – was built in the early seventeenth century by Salzburg's decadent archbishop Marus Sitticus. Built in part as a hunting lodge, its mustard buildings (late March, April & Oct 9am–4.30pm; May, June & Sept 9am–5.30pm; July & Aug 9am–10pm; €8.50; Ⓦwww.hellbrunn.at) are chock full of trophies, but also memorabilia of Sitticus's wider animal collection – which included albino farm animals and an eight-legged horse. But the main attraction here is the ornamental gardens in which an impressive array of fountains, *Wasserspiele*, form the centrepiece.

To get to Schloss Hellbrunn you can take frequent bus #25 from Salzburg's train station. This bus also continues to the village of St Leonhard, 7km further south, where the 1853-metre **Untersberg** is climbed by a cable car (March–June & Oct 8.30am–5pm; July–Sept 8.30am–5.30pm; Dec–Feb 9am–4pm; return €18), for impressive views of Salzburg to the north and the Alps to the south, making it a hit with summer hikers and skiers in winter.

THE SOUND OF MUSIC

Salzburg certainly wastes no time cashing in on its connection with the legendary singing Von Trapp family, immortalized in the movie *The Sound of Music*. From its kiosk on Mirabellplatz, Panorama Tours (Ⓣ0662/883 21 10, Ⓦwww.panoramatours.com) runs what they dub **"The Original Sound of Music Tour"** (daily 9.30am & 2pm; 4 hours; €37) on which you're bussed to the key film locations, such as Hellsbrun Palace and Mondsee Cathedral, played the soundtrack and sent away with a free edelweiss souvenir.

Arrival and information

Trains The main station is 2km north of Mozartplatz, reachable using buses #3, #6, #170: a single costs €1.30, a 24-hour pass costs €3.20.

Tourist office There's a tourist kiosk at the train station (platform 2a; daily: June–Sept 8.30am–8pm; Oct–May 9am–6pm), and a larger office at Mozartplatz 5 (daily: June–Sept 9am–7pm; Oct–May 9am–6pm; Ⓣ0662/88 98 73 30, Ⓦwww.salzburginfo.at). Both offices book rooms for a small fee; they also sell the **Salzburg Card** (€24/32 for 24/48hr), which grants unlimited use of public transport and free admission to all of the sights.

Accommodation

Hostels and camping

Camping Nord-Sam Samstr. 22a Ⓣ0662/64 04 94, Ⓦwww.camping-nord-sam.com. The most central campsite with a heated outdoor pool. April–Sept; bus #23. Tents €14.

HI Hostel Haunspergstr. 27 Ⓣ0662/87 50 30, Ⓦwww.lbsh-haunspergstrasse.at. Mid-July & Aug only. HI-affiliated hostel three blocks west of the train station. Dorms €22, doubles €56.

Yoho Paracelsusstr. 9 Ⓣ0662/87 96 49, Ⓦwww.yoho.at. Very popular and often fully-booked hostel near the train station. With sociable bar, internet café and laundry facilities. Dorms €18, doubles €46.

Hotels and pensions

Junger Fuchs Linzergasse 54 Ⓣ0662/87 54 96. Spartan and clean *pension* up a dingy stairwell but, given the location, a bargain. Doubles €48.

Sandwirt Lastenstr. 6a Ⓣ0662/87 43 51. Cheap, clean and friendly *pension* in the rather dreary, but handy, neighbourhood just east of the Hauptbahnhof. Rooms are cramped, but there's a guest kitchen and free parking. Doubles €66.

Schwarzes Rössl Priesterhausgasse 6 Ⓣ0662/87 44 26, Ⓦwww.academia-hotels.co.at. Wonderful, creaky old place, in a central location. Great value for money. Rooms available with shared or private facilities. July–Sept. Doubles €66.

Eating

Cafés

Bazar Schwarzstr. 3. Elegant coffeehouse with a pleasant river-view terrace. Breakfast €4.50–11.

Fingerlos Franz Josef Str. 9. Stylish and relaxed café, serving cakes as fine as you'll find in Salzburg. Cappuccino €3; cake €2.50.
Fürst Brod Gasse 13. Up market coffeehouse that claims to have invented the ubiquitous marzipan "Mozart Ball". Coffee €3.40.

Restaurants

Fischkrieg Hanusch-Platz 4. Self-service riverside place serving fish and seafood in every form: fishburgers or grilled squid €6.60. Closes at 6.30pm and Sun.
Gablerbräu Linzergasse 9. Cheerful Austrian restaurant (mains from €6.50), also serving sandwiches and lighter snacks. Fantastic salad/ *antipasti* buffet for €4.70/8.
Resch & Lieblich Toscaninihof 1. Tucked away near the Festspielhaus, offering good-value Austrian cuisine in dining rooms carved out of the Hohensalzburg cliffs. Daily specials €7.20. Closed Sun.
Stieglkeller Festungsgasse 10. Enormous brewery with a beer terrace overlooking the town. Solid traditional food €8–17.

Drinking and nightlife

Augustiner Bräu Augustinerstr. 4–6. Fifteen minutes northwest of the centre, this vast beer hall has a raucous open-air terrace. Own-brewed beer is served in huge glasses. Open from 3pm daily.
Die Weisse 10 Rupertgasse. Lively micro-brewery, well off the tourist track, with nice little beer garden and great pub food. Goulash and dumplings €11.
Pepe Gonzales Steingasse 3. Intimate cocktail bar near the river. Open till 3am.
Republic Anton-Neumayr-Platz 2. Trendy restaurant-club, serving food until 11pm. The wide-ranging DJ and live music programme (anything from salsa to blues or electro) attracts a young, trendy crowd. Open till 4am Friday and Saturday.

Entertainment

The city hosts dozens of concerts – many of them Mozart-related – all year round; check with Salzburg Ticket Service (W www.salzburgticket.com), inside the tourist office on Mozartplatz.
Salzburg Festival (late July to late-Aug; T 0662/804 55 00, W www.salzburgfestival.at) is one of Europe's premier festivals of classical music, opera and theatre. The city is at its most vibrant during the festival, with outdoor concerts and open-air cinemas.

Directory

Emergency doctor Hausärzte-Bereitschaftsdienst, Dr.-Karl-Renner-Str. 7 T 0662/814 40.
Consulates UK, Alter Markt 4 T 0662/84 81 33; US, Alter Markt 1 T 0662/84 87 76.
Exchange Outside banking hours try at the Hauptbahnhof.
Internet Isis in train station (€3/hr).
Laundry Bubble Point, Karl-Wurmb-Str. 2 (daily 7am–11pm).
Left luggage 24hr lockers at the main station.
Pharmacy Elisabeth Apotheke, Elisabethstr. 1a. Closed Saturday afternoon and Sunday.
Post office Postamt 1010, Residenzplatz 9.

Moving on

Trains Bad Gastein (9 daily; 1hr 30min); Innsbruck (9 daily; 2hr); Linz (every 30min; 1hr 15min); Werfen (hourly; 50min).
Bus Strobl (for St Wolfgang; hourly; 1hr 10min); Hallstatt (12 daily; 2hr 20min).

WERFEN

With its impressive fortification and spectacular ice caves, **WERFEN**, 40km south of Salzburg, offers a great day of sightseeing from Salzburg, but arrive early to comfortably see both. The moody castle **Festung Hohenwerften** (April, Oct & Nov 9.30am–4pm; May, June & Sept 9am–5pm; July & Aug 9am–6pm; €10.50), on an outcrop above town, lies a twenty-minute signed walk from Werfen's train station. Though much modified over the years, it has eleventh-century origins and all the usual components – ornate chapel and torture chamber included – are neatly gathered around a courtyard. Daily falconry displays (11am & 3pm) are included in the entrance price.

Werfen's castle may tower over the town, but up the road at the **Eisriesenwelt ice caves**, it's a mere pimple on the valley floor. The caves are more than two hours' walk from the entrance building, so most visitors take a cable car, cutting 90 minutes off the journey. Tours (at least hourly: daily July & Aug 9.30am–4.30pm, May–June & Sept–Oct 9.30am–3.30pm;

€19 with cable car, €8.50 without) explore the first kilometre of a 40km network and last around 75 minutes. Inside, gaudy illumination of the spectacular ice formations has been resisted (contrary to what postcards suggest) to allow you to navigate the ice mass, using the sort of oil lamps that the original nineteenth-century explorers used. It's cold enough to require a jumper.

Both S-Bahns and trains from Salzburg frequently arrive at Werfen's station, from where buses to the caves depart daily at 8.20am, 10.20am, 12.20pm & 2.20pm, with more departures from an official departure point across the river. Bus drivers sell a combined ticket for the ride up, the cable car and the cave (€22.60). If you're hungry, try the inns on the main street – both *Goldener Hirsch* and *Alte Post* on Markt dish up a good square Austrian meal for about €8.

ST WOLFGANG

Hourly buses between Salzburg and Bad Ischl run east along the southern shore of the Wolfgangersee, bypassing the lake's main attraction, the village of **ST WOLFGANG**, on the opposite shore: so get off at Strobl, at the lake's eastern end, and pick up a connecting bus, or a boat across the lake (hourly; €4.70). St Wolfgang can be crowded in summer, but is worth visiting, if only to see the **Pfarrkirche**, just above the lake shore; its high altar, an extravagantly pinnacled structure 12m high, was completed between 1471 and 1481, and features brightly gilded scenes of the *Coronation of the Virgin* in the centrepiece flanked by scenes from the life of St Wolfgang. Little trains climb the local **Schafberg** peak (May–Oct; €27.80 return; to avoid queuing, reserve a seat on ⓣ06138/223 20, ⓦwww.schafbergbahn.at) from a station on the western edge of town. The **tourist office** (Mon–Fri 9am–6pm, Sat 9am–noon; ⓣ06138/80 03, ⓦwww.wolfgangsee.at) is at the eastern entrance to the road tunnel.

HALLSTATT

The jewel of the Salzkammergut is **HALLSTATT**, which clings to the base of precipitous cliffs on the shores of the Hallstättersee, 20km south of Bad Ischl. With towering peaks and a pristine lake, this is a stunning setting in which to hike, swim or rent a boat. Arriving **by train** is an atmospheric and evocative experience; the station is on the opposite side of the lake, and the ferry, which meets all incoming trains, gives truly dramatic views. (Note that after 6.30pm, trains don't stop here and instead continue to Obertraun, 5km away on the lakeshore.) **Buses** stop in the suburb of Lahn, a ten-minute lakeside walk away.

What to see and do

Hallstatt gave its name to a distinct period of Iron Age culture after Celtic remains were discovered in the salt mines above the town. Many of the finds date back to the ninth century BC, and can now be seen in the **Museum Hallstatt** (April & Oct daily 10am–4pm; May–Sept 10am–6pm; Nov–March Tues–Sun 11am–3pm; €7.50; ⓦwww.museum-hallstatt.at).

The **Pfarrkirche** has a south portal adorned with sixteenth-century Calvary scenes and, inside, a Gothic winged altar on the right with heavily gilded statuettes of the Madonna and Child flanked by St Catherine (the patron of woodcutters, on the left) and St Barbara (the patron of miners). In the graveyard outside is a small stone structure known as the **Beinhaus** (daily 10am–5pm; €1.50), traditionally the repository for the skulls of villagers. The skulls, some quite recent, are inscribed with the names of the deceased and dates of their death, and are often decorated.

The steep Gainswand-Weg starts behind the graveyard to lead up to the **Salzachtal** (1hr 30min of hard hiking), the highland valley where **salt mines** once

ensured the area's prosperity, and can still be viewed (guided tour only: late April–late Oct daily 9.30am–3/4.30pm; €16). You can also take the **funicular** (late-April–late Oct daily 9am–4.30pm/6pm; €10 return) from the nearby suburb of Lahn. A combined ticket for tour and funicular is €22.

Arrival and information

Trains Hallstatt's station is across the lake and free ferries are timed to coincide with trains.

Tourist office Located in the centre of town (July & Aug Mon–Fri 9am–5pm; Sept–June Mon–Fri 9am–noon & 2–5pm; ⓣ06134/82 08, ⓦwww.hallstatt.net).

Accommodation

Camping Klausner-Höll Lahnstrasse ⓣ06134/83 22, ⓦwww.camping.hallstatt.net. A short walk from the landing stage at Lahn, on the outskirts of the village. Quiet and well equipped. Open mid-April to mid-Oct. Tents €11.

Gasthaus zur Mühle Kirchenweg 36 ⓣ06134/83 18. Cosy guesthouse set back from the landing stage. Dorms €14.

Pension Hallberg Seestr. 113 ⓣ06134/87 09, ⓦwww.pension-hallberg.at.tf. Pleasant lake-side guesthouse, handily opposite the tourist office. All the simple, pine-furnished rooms are sparklingly clean, most have lake views. Doubles €58.

Eating and drinking

Bräugasthof Seestr. 120. Excellent Austrian food, with a popular lakeside terrace and competitively priced fresh fish, caught from Hallstatt's lake, from €12.50. Daily set menu €11.50.

Gasthaus zur Mühle Kirchenweg 36. Welcoming, small bar in the friendly guesthouse, with a good line in pizzas (€7).

OUTDOOR ACTIVITIES

Canoes and other **boats** can be rented from the boatshed beside the landing stage (€8.50 for 30min). The tourist office can advise on a route for the four-hour **hike** up to the Wiesberghaus mountain hut (ⓣ06134/206 20; Jan–Oct; €18) – which can be reduced to 90min using the Krippenstein cable car – and sell you hiking guides for other local trails. The lake at the southern end of town has a beach, and is a good spot for a **swim**.

BAD GASTEIN

Combining the quiet elegance of an old nineteenth-century spa destination with modern trappings and reasonably modest price-tags, the resort of **BAD GASTEIN**, 94 km south of Salzburg, is one of Austria's best budget mountain getaways.

What to see and do

The town fills the head of the Gastein valley with most hotels arranged in tiers leading up to the centre of the resort – location of the cable cars, spa and most shops. The mountains are the chief attraction, served year-round by two gondolas, and are a big draw for winter skiers. The four **ski areas** (ⓦen.winter.skigastein.com) offer plenty for every standard; day-passes cost €41. In summer, the gondolas serve a web of **hiking trails**, with the 2246-metre Stunerkogel mountain trail (June–mid-Oct 8.30am–4pm; €18 return) offering particularly fine views. However, it is Bad Gastein's radon-rich waters (a radioactive gas thought to stimulate cell growth) that have made it a destination since medieval times. To sample them today head to the Felsentherme, Bahnhofplatz (daily 9am–9pm; ⓦwww.felsentherme.com; 3hr €17.50), a spa with a collection of stylish pools and saunas, many with splendid views, and a full menu of therapeutic and beauty treatments.

Arrival and information

Buses and trains The station is in the centre, within walking distance of most central accommodation.

Tourist office Kaiser-Franz-Josef-Str. 1, a short walk downhill from the bus and train station (June–mid-July Mon–Fri 8am–6pm, Sat 9am–noon;

mid-July–Sept Mon–Fri 8am–6pm, Sat 9am–3pm, Sun 9am–noon; Oct–May Mon–Fri 8am–6pm; ⓣ06432/339 35 60, ⓦwww.gastein.com/en-gastein-bad_gastein.htm). Can book private rooms (from €36).

Accommodation

Euro Youth Hotel Krone Bahnhofsplatz 8 ⓣ06434/23 300, ⓦwww.euro-youth-hotel.at. Large, sociable and in the thick of things close to the station. Offers ski or spa packages. Dorms €17, doubles €54.

Junge Hotel Bad Gastein Ederplatz 2 ⓣ06434/20 80, ⓦwww.hostel-badgastein.at. Slick HI hostel, a 5min walk south of the centre. Dorms €16, doubles €52.

Eating and drinking

Jägerhäusl Kaiser-Franz-Josef-Str. 9 ⓣ06434/202 54. A lively place to eat with a big outdoor terrace and *Schnitzels* for €9.

Silver Bullet Bar Meyerbeerweg 1. Western themed place that stays open until 2am. The place to be in winter for aprés-ski.

Western Austria

West towards the mountain province of **Tyrol**, Austria's grandiose Alpine scenery begins to emerge. Most trains from Vienna and Salzburg travel through a corner of Bavaria in Germany before joining the Inn valley and climbing back into Austria towards **Innsbruck**. A less direct but more scenic route (more likely if you're coming from Graz) cuts by the majestic **Hoher Tauern** – site of Austria's highest peak, the Grossglockner – before joining the Inn valley at Wörgl. As Tyrol's main town and focal point, Innsbruck offers the most convenient mix of urban sights and Alpine splendour.

INNSBRUCK

High in the Alps and encircled by ski resorts, **INNSBRUCK** is a compact city cradled by towering mountains. It has a rich history: Maximilian I based his imperial court here in the 1490s, placing this provincial Alpine town at the heart of European politics and culture for a century and a half. This combination of historical pedigree and proximity to the mountains has put Innsbruck firmly on the tourist trail.

What to see and do

Most attractions are confined to the central Altstadt, bounded by the river and the Graben, a road that follows the course of the moat that once surrounded the medieval town.

Maria-Theresien-Strasse

Innsbruck's main artery is **Maria-Theresien-Strasse**, famed for the view north towards the great Nordkette, the mountain range that dominates the city. At its southern end the triumphal arch, **Triumphpforte**, was built for the marriage of Maria Theresa's son Leopold in 1756. Halfway along, the **Annasäule**, a column supporting a statue of the Virgin, commemorates the retreat of the Bavarians, who had been menacing the Tyrol in 1703. Herzog-Friedrich-Strasse leads on into the centre, opening out into a plaza lined with arcaded medieval buildings. At the plaza's southern end is the **Goldenes Dachl**, or "Golden Roof" (though the tiles are really copper), built in the 1490s to cover an oriel window from which the court of Emperor Maximilian could observe the square below. The **Goldenes Dachl Museum** (May–Sept daily 10am–5pm; Oct–April Tues–Sun 10am–5pm; €4), is flashy but disappointing. Aside from a brief glimpse of the balcony, the main attraction is an entertaining documentary about the Emperor Maximilian.

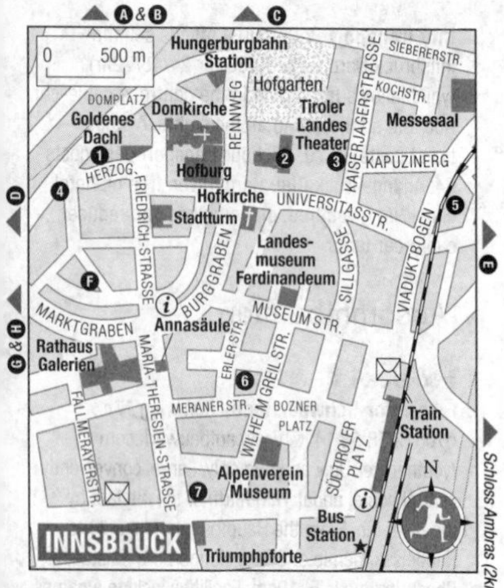

ACCOMMODATION		EATING & DRINKING	
Camping Kranebitten	G	Café Central	6
Fritz-Prior-Schwedenhaus	C	Café Konditorei	
Glockenhaus	B	Munding	F
HI Jugendherberge Innsbruck	E	Das Stadtcafé	2
Innbrücke	D	Elferhaus	1
Innrain	H	Magic Pizza Kebab	4
Nepomuk's	F	No. 1	3
Pension Paula	A	Theresienbräu	7
		Weli	5

Domplatz

An alley to the right leads down to Domplatz and the ostentatious **Domkirche St Jakob**, home to a valuable *Madonna and Child* by German master Lucas Cranach the Elder, although it's buried in the fussy Baroque detail of the altar. The adjacent **Hofburg**, entered around the corner, has late-medieval roots but was remodelled in the eighteenth century, its Rococo state Kaiserapartments crammed with opulent furniture (daily 9am–5pm; €5.50). At the head of Rennweg, entered through the Tiroler Volkskunstmuseum (see below), is the **Hofkirche** (Mon–Sat 9am–6pm, Sun 12.30–6pm; €4; Ⓦwww.hofkirche.at), which contains the imposing **Cenotaph of Emperor Maximilian**. This extraordinary project was originally envisaged as a series of 40 larger-than-life statues, 100 statuettes and 32 busts of Roman emperors, representing both the real and the spiritual ancestors of Maximilian, but in the end only 32 of the statuettes and 20 of the busts were completed. Upstairs is the Silberkapelle or Silver Chapel, named after the silver Madonna that adorns the far wall.

Museums and galleries

Housed in the same complex as the Hofkirche (see above), the **Tiroler Volkskunstmuseum** (daily: 9am–6pm; €6; combined ticket with Hofkirche €8), features recreations of traditional wood-panelled Tyrolean peasant interiors. A short walk south, the **Tiroler Landesmuseum Ferdinandeum**, Museumstr. 15 (Tues–Sun 9am–6pm; €8), contains one of the best collections of Gothic paintings in Austria; most originate from the churches of the South Tyrol (now in Italy). Also worth a visit is **Schloss Ambras** (daily: Aug–Oct 10am–5pm; Nov closed; Dec–July 10am–7pm; April–Oct €8, Dec–March €4.50), 2km southeast on tram #6. Alternatively take tram #3 to Amras and then walk for ten minutes on the path leading beneath the motorway and up the hill. Set in attractive grounds, this was the home of Archduke Ferdinand of Tyrol and still houses a collection of Habsburg portraits and an intriguing selection of curios amassed from around the globe, including giant playing cards, fossils and musical instruments.

Hungerburg plateau

A good starting point for hikes is the **Nordpark**, the northern slopes of the Nordkette range, accessible from the centre of town via a swish **cable railway** from opposite the Hofgarten to Hungerburg; then by taking a two-stage sequence of cable cars to just below the summit (€25 return; Ⓦwww.nordpark.com). The rewards are stupendous views of the high Alps and the possibility of all sorts of hikes including heading back into town via various *Hütten*, where you can stop for food.

Outdoor activities

As befits its stunning setting, Innsbruck's great for all sorts of outdoor activities; the tourist office has a wide range of comprehensive brochures.

Biking Many cycling and mountain-bike routes are accessible from central Innsbruck, though some of the trails are experts only. For rentals try Sport Neuner, Salurnerstrasse 5 (Ⓣ0512/56 15 01; from €20/day).

Hiking As well as having free maps, Innsbruck's tourist office runs an extensive programme of free guided walks – including sunrise and night-time hikes – from June to September.

Bobsleigh Shoot down a 1000-metre bobsleigh run in just over a minute in summer in Igls, 13km southwest of Innsbruck (Aug–Oct Wed–Fri 4pm & 6pm; Ⓣ05275/53 86, Ⓦwww.knauseder-event.at; €25) and in winter at Olympiaworld (Ⓣ0512/33 83 82 21, Ⓦwww.olympiaworld.at; €30).

Arrival and information

Train Trains arrive at Innsbruck's main station on the Südtirolerplatz, just to the east of the old town. It's an easy walk from here into the centre.

Bus Buses arrive immediately to the south of the train station.

Tourist office Innsbruck's train station has a tourist kiosk (daily 9am–7pm), while the main office is at Burggraben 3 (daily 9am–6pm; Ⓣ0512/598 50, Ⓦwww.innsbruck.info).

City transport Both tourist offices sell the Innsbruck Card (€25/30/35 for 24/48/72hr), which allows free travel in the centre, a cable-car ride and admission to all the sights. A single ticket costs €1.70; 24-hour transport pass costs €4. An Innsbruck Club Card (given free on hotel check-in) gives free, guided hikes and reduced cable-car fares.

Accommodation

Hostels

Fritz-Prior-Schwedenhaus Rennweg 17b Ⓣ0512/58 58 14, Ⓦwww.aufbauwerk.com/youthhostel. July and Aug only. Large, conveniently central hostel about 1km north of the Altstadt by the River Inn. From the Hauptbahnhof take #4 to Handelsakademie or D/E to Hungerburg-Talstation. Check-in time is 5–10pm. Facilities include a games room, internet and laundry. Dorms €13, doubles €38.

Glockenhaus Weiherburggasse 3 Ⓣ0512/28 65 15, Ⓦwww.hostelnikolaus.at. Ramshacle hostel, uphill of the River Inn's west bank, an easy walk from the centre. Suffers from the absence of communal facilities, and unpleasant bathrooms. Bus #W to bus stop Schloss Büchsenhausen, from the train station. Dorms €17, doubles €54.

HI Jugendherberge Innsbruck Reichenauerstr. 147 Ⓣ0512/34 61 79, Ⓦwww.youth-hostel-innsbruck.at. Large, functional HI hostel on the outskirts of the city. Bus #O stops outside and runs every 5–10min during the day. Dorms €18, doubles €52.

SKIING

Of Innsbruck's nine **ski areas** (Ⓦwww.ski-innsbruck.at) the closest to the city is **Nordpark** (Ⓦwww.nordpark.com), accessible via the Hungerburgbahn, with its fabulous panoramas, impressive half-pipe and taxing expert-level runs. The other eight ski areas – including the Patscherkofel, Axamer Lizum, Glungezer, Mutereralm, Schlick 2000, Kühtai and Rangger Köpfl. – are all on the opposite, southern, side of the valley and tend to offer much mellower terrain ideal for relaxed, wide-turn skiing. The most exceptional is the **Stubai Gletscher** (Ⓦwww.stubaier-gletscher.com), where glacier skiing is possible year-round.

Innsbruck's tourist offices offer summer packages for around €50 per person – which include transport, equipment and a pass. In winter, **lift passes** cover all these ski regions individually or in combination for one or more days. The Nordpark, for example, offers day-passes for €27, less if you arrive later in the day (reductions offered at hourly intervals until 2pm when passes cost only €15). The **Innsbruck Gletcher Skipass** covers the whole of the Innsbruck area, includes ski shuttles from the town centre, and costs Innsbruck Club Card holders (see above) €99 for three days, €170 for six. The **Innsbruck Super Skipass** combines three days' skiing in the Innsbruck region with a day each at St Anton and Kitzbühel, for €213, including transfers. Passes are available from all lift stations or from the Innsbruck tourist office.

Nepomuk's Kiebachgasse 16 ⓣ0512/58 41 18, ⓦwww.nepomuks.at. Slightly ramshackle one-dorm hostel above *Café Munding*, whose owners also run the hostel and serve its good breakfasts. Also has a couple of doubles, though one is windowless and noisy. Dorms €20, doubles €50.

Hotels and pensions

Innbrücke Innstr. 1 ⓣ0512/28 19 34, ⓦwww.gasthofinnbruecke.at. Plain but comfortable *Gasthof* on the west bank of the Inn, just over the bridge from the Altstadt. More expensive rooms have en-suite facilities, although most are without. Doubles €75.

Innrain Innrain 38 ⓣ0512/58 89 81, ⓦwww.gasthof-innrain.com. Pleasant family-run place, above a café near the old town. Doubles €50.

Pension Paula Weiherburggasse 15 ⓣ0512/29 22 62, ⓦwww.pensionpaula.at. Friendly, good-value *pension* in a chalet on a hillside north of the river – some rooms have balconies and mountain views. Doubles €52.

Camping

Camping Kranebitten Kranebittner Allee 214 ⓣ0512/28 41 80, ⓦwww.campinginnsbruck.com May–Oct. Well-equipped campsite 5km west of town. Bus #LK from Boznerplatz, a block west of the station, to Klammstrasse. Tents €8.60.

Eating and drinking

Café Central Gilmstr. 5. Venerable coffeehouse serving up excellent cakes and decent breakfasts (from €6). Good spot to linger over a coffee and slice of cake (€2.80).

Café-Konditorei Munding Kiebachgasse 16. Renowned for its sweets and pastries.

Das Stadtcafé Universitätsstr. 1. Magnificent lounge club with enormous designer café and bars, mainstream DJs and often live music playing to a busy dancefloor until 4am on weekend nights. Closed Mon.

Elferhaus Herzog-Friedrich-Strasse 11. Popular old-town beer bar, with a lively atmosphere, serving good basic Austrian food. Daily specials €7.80.

Magic Pizza Kebab Innrain 1. Very central pizza and kebab joint with a vague American-diner feel and delicious giant pizza slices (from €2.50) that always ensure the place bustles until midnight.

No. 1 Kaserjägerstrasse. Excellent, cheap Thai restaurant around the corner from the Hofkirche with tasty *Tagesmenüs* from €7.

Theresienbräu Maria-Theresien-Strasse 51–53. Animated fun-pub serving ales brewed on the premises to a young, hedonistic crowd. It also does cheap lunchtime menus.

Weli Viaduktbogen. 26. Informal, unpretentious café/bar with snacks. Good starting point for exploring the various late-opening bars under the railway arches. Open from 7pm.

Directory

Consulates UK, Kaiser Jägerstr. 1 ⓣ0512/58 83 20.

Hospital Universitätklinik, Anichstr. 35 ⓣ0512/50 40.

Internet access Internet Café, Rathaus-Galerien, free during shopping hours.

Laundry Bubble Point, Andreas-Hoferstr. 37 & Brixnerstr. 1 (Mon–Fri 8am–10pm, Sat & Sun 8am–8pm; €4).

Pharmacy Apotheke Bahnhof, by the train station (Mon–Fri 8am–6pm, Sat 8am–noon).

Post office Maximilianstr. 2.

Moving on

Trains Munich (hourly; 2hr); Venice (6 daily; 5hr 30min).

Belgium and Luxembourg

HIGHLIGHTS

BRUGES: discover why everyone raves about this perfect medieval town

GHENT: marvel at the town's castle and lively bars

BRUSSELS: see the most well-preserved square in the country, the Grand-Place

ARDENNES: cycle, kayak or hike through the Ardennes woods

LUXEMBOURG CITY: visit Europe's most dramatically sited capital

ROUGH COSTS

DAILY BUDGET Basic €35/ occasional treat €50

DRINK Jupiler beer €1.60

FOOD Mussels with chips €10–15

HOSTEL/BUDGET HOTEL €15–20/€55–65

TRAVEL Train: Brussels–Antwerp (46km) €7; Brussels–Namur (63 km) €8

CURRENCY Euro (€)

FACT FILE

POPULATION Belgium: 10.5 million; Luxembourg: 480,000

AREA Belgium: 30,582 sq km; Luxembourg: 2586 sq km

LANGUAGE Belgium: Flemish, French, German; Luxembourg: Letzebuergesch, French, German

CAPITAL Belgium: Brussels; Luxembourg: Luxembourg City

INTERNATIONAL PHONE CODE Belgium: ⓣ32; Luxembourg: ⓣ352

Introduction

A federal country, with three official languages and an intense rivalry between its two main groups – Dutch-speaking Flemish and French-speaking Walloons – Belgium has a cultural diversity that belies its rather dull reputation. Lively, cultured cities in the predominantly urban north give way to beautiful forests and rugged hills in the south; and regular and affordable trains and an impressive range of good-value accommodation make the country a pleasure to travel, as does the Belgians' enthusiasm for fine cuisine and almost endless varieties of beer.

Roughly in the middle of Belgium lies the capital, Brussels, the heart of the EU and a genuinely vibrant and multicultural city. North of here stretch the flat landscapes of Flemish Belgium, whose main city, Antwerp, is a bustling old port with doses of high art, high fashion, and twice as many bars as Amsterdam. Further west, also in the Flemish zone, are the charismatic cities of **Bruges** and **Ghent**, each with a stunning concentration of medieval architecture. Belgium's most scenic region, the Ardennes, is, however, in Wallonia, its deep, wooded valleys, high elevations and dark caverns sprawling away to the south, with the town of Namur the obvious gateway.

The Ardennes reach across the border into the northern part of the Grand Duchy of Luxembourg, a dramatic landscape of rushing rivers and high hills topped with crumbling castles. The best base for rural expeditions is Luxembourg City, an exceptionally picturesque place with a rugged setting.

CHRONOLOGY

Belgium

54 BC Julius Caesar defeats the Belgae tribes.
496 AD The King of the Franks, Clovis, founds a kingdom which includes Belgium.
1400–1500 The Belgian cities of Bruges, Brussels and Antwerp become the European centres of commerce and industry.
1477 Following the marriage of Austrian King Maximilian I and Mary of Burgundy, Belgium becomes part of Austria.
1713 Treaty of Utrecht transfers Belgian territory from French to Austrian rule.
1790 The Belgians form an independent state from Austria, though it does not last long. They are subsequently invaded by Austria, France and the Netherlands in quick succession.
1830 Belgium gains independence from the Netherlands.
1885 King Leopold II establishes a personal colony in the African Congo.
1908 The Belgian government takes over the Congo Free State after reports of Leopold's brutal regime are circulated.
1914–1918 Belgium is invaded by Germany, and is the site of heavy fighting, before it is liberated.
1929 *Tintin in the Land of the Soviets*, the first Tintin comic produced by Georges Prosper Remi (better known as "Hergé"), is published.
1940–1944 Nazi invasion, and ultimately liberation by Allied forces.
1957 Belgium is a founder member of the European Economic Community (EEC).
1960 Independence granted to Congo.
1967 René Magritte, one of the great Surrealist artists, dies.
1992 Belgium ratifies the Maastricht Treaty on the European Union.
2007 Following the resignation of Prime Minister Guy Verhofstadt, Belgium is without a government for 100 days.

Luxembourg

963 AD Count Siegfried of Ardenne founds the capital of Luxembourg.
1354 Luxembourg's status is raised from fief to duchy by Emperor Charles IV.

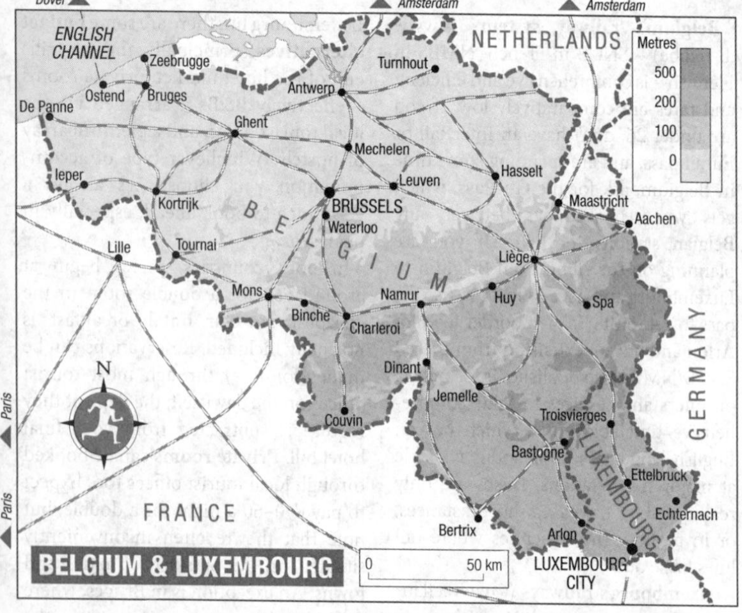

1477 The Habsburgs take control of Luxembourg.
1715 Luxembourg integrated into the Austrian Netherlands.
1867 Second Treaty of London ensures Luxembourg's independence and neutrality.
1890 Luxembourg announces its own ruling monarchy, relinquishing its ties to the Netherlands.
1914–1918 German occupation.
1920 Joins the League of Nations.
1939–1945 German occupation.
1957 Luxembourg is a founder member of the EEC.
2000 Grand Duke Jean abdicates, handing responsibility over to his son Henri.
2008 Constitutional crisis is provoked by Grand Duke Henri threatening to block a bill legalizing euthanasia. As a result, Parliament approves a reform which restricts the monarch to a purely ceremonial role.

ARRIVAL

Most airborne travel is into Brussels, which has two **airports**: the closer one is Zaventem (also known as Brussels International), while Charleroi (which serves most budget airlines including Flybe and Ryanair) lies about 55km from the centre. There are frequent **rail** connections from London, Paris, Amsterdam and Luxembourg, with almost all international trains getting in to Bruxelles-Midi (Brussel-Zuid), and frequently also stopping in Ghent or Antwerp. Eurostar tickets are valid to any station in Belgium. Eurolines **buses** from Paris, Amsterdam, London and other destinations get into Brussels' Gare du Nord, as well as Antwerp, Ghent and Bruges. Numerous **ferry** services ply between the UK and Belgian ports, including Ramsgate–Ostend (4hr), Rosyth–Zeebrugge (20hr) and Hull–Zeebrugge (15hr).

GETTING AROUND

Travelling around Flanders is rarely a problem. Distances are short, and an efficient train network links all the major and many minor towns and villages. The Ardennes and Luxembourg, on the other hand, can be a little more problematic: the train network is not extensive and bus timetables can demand careful study for longer journeys.

Belgium's railway system (Ⓦwww.b-rail.be) – SNCB in French, NMBS in Flemish – is comprehensive and efficient, and fares are comparatively low. If you are under 26, don't have an InterRail or Eurail pass, and are spending some time in Belgium, ask for the **Go-Pass**, which gets you ten journeys between any Belgian stations for €50. (If you are planning on travelling from Belgium to Luxembourg and have a Go-Pass, use the pass to get to the Belgian border town of Arlon and buy an extension from there.) SNCB/NMBS also publishes information on offers and services in their comprehensive timetable book, which has an English-language section and is available at major train stations. **Buses** are only really used for travelling short distances, or in parts of the Ardennes where rail lines fizzle out.

Luxembourg's railways (Ⓦwww.cfl.lu) comprise one main north–south route down the middle of the country, with a handful of branch lines fanning out from the capital, but most of the country can only be reached by **bus**. Fares are comparable with those in Belgium, and there are a number of passes available, giving unlimited train and bus travel.

The modest distances and flat terrain make **cycling** in Belgium an attractive proposition, though only in the countryside is there a decent network of signposted cycle routes. You can take your own bike on a train for a small fee or rent one from any of around thirty train stations during the summer at about €10 per day; note also that some train excursion tickets include the cost of bike rental. In Luxembourg you can rent bikes for around €10 a day, and take your own bike on trains (not buses) for a minimal fee per journey. The Luxembourg Tourist Office has leaflets showing cycle routes and also sells cycling guides.

ACCOMMODATION

Accommodation is one of the major expenses on a trip to Belgium or Luxembourg but there are some **budget alternatives**, principally the no-frills end of the hotel market, private rooms – effectively B&Bs – arranged via the local tourist office, and a plentiful array of hostels. Whichever type of accommodation you choose, it's always a good idea to book ahead, especially in peak season.

In both countries, prices begin at around €60 for a double room in the cheapest one-star **hotel**; breakfast is normally included. Reservations can be made (for free) through most tourist offices on the day itself; the deposit they require is subtracted from your final hotel bill. **Private rooms** can be booked through local tourist offices too. Expect to pay €40–60 a night for a double, but note that they're often inconveniently situated on the outskirts of cities and towns. An exception is in Bruges, where private rooms – many of them in the centre – can be booked direct.

Belgium has around thirty **HI hostels**, run by two separate organizations: Vlaamse Jeugdherbergcentrale in Flanders (Ⓣ032 32 72 18, Ⓦwww.vjh.be), and Jeunesse de Wallonie in Wallonia (Ⓣ022 19 56 76, Ⓦwww.laj.be). Most charge a flat rate per person of €15–20 for a bed in a dormitory or €42–48 for a double room, with breakfast included. Many also offer lunch and dinner for €5–15. Some of the more touristy cities such as Bruges, Antwerp and Brussels also have **privately run hostels**, which normally charge about €20 for a dorm bed. There are ten HI hostels in Luxembourg, all of which are members of the Centrale des Auberges de Jeunesse Luxembourgeoises (Ⓣ26 27 66 40, Ⓦwww.youthhostels.lu). Dorm-bed rates for HI members are around €15, with non members paying an extra €3. Breakfast is always included; lunch or dinner is €6–8.

In Belgium, there are literally hundreds of **campsites**, anything from a field with a few tent pitches through to

extensive complexes. The vast majority are simpler one- and two-star establishments, for which two adults with a tent can expect to pay €10–20 per night, though surprisingly, most four-star sites don't cost much more – add about €5. All of Luxembourg's campsites are detailed in the Duchy's free tourist office booklet. Prices vary considerably, but are usually €3–5 per person, plus €3–5 for a pitch. In both countries, campsite phone numbers are listed in free camping booklets, and in Luxembourg the national tourist board (Ⓣ42 82 82 10, Ⓦwww.ont.lu) will make a reservation on your behalf.

FOOD AND DRINK

One of the great pleasures of a trip to Belgium is the cuisine, and if you stay away from tourist spots, it's hard to go wrong. Southern Belgian (or Wallonian) cuisine is similar to traditional French, retaining its neighbour's fondness for rich sauces and ingredients. The Ardennes region is renowned for its smoked ham and pâté. **Luxembourg**'s food is less varied and more Germanic, but you can still eat out extremely well. In Flanders the food is more akin to that of the Netherlands, with mussels and French fries the most common dish. Throughout the country, pork, beef, game, fish and seafood are staple items, often cooked with butter, cream and herbs, or sometimes in beer; hearty soups are also common. *Hesprolletjes* (chicory and ham baked in a cheese sauce) and *stoemp* (puréed meat and vegetables) are two traditional dishes worth seeking out. Traditional Flemish dishes such as *waterzooi*, or "watery mess" (fish or chicken stew), and *Carbonnade* (beef casserole) are also widely available. There are plenty of good **vegetarian** options too, such as quiche and salad, and you can find vegetarian restaurants in all of the larger cities.

In both countries, bars and **cafés** are a good source of inexpensive meals, at least at lunchtime, serving simple dishes – omelettes, steak, mussels, plus a dish of the day for around €10. **Restaurants** are usually pricier, but the food is generally excellent. **Frituurs** (stands serving chips) are ubiquitous, cheap and usually offer a bewildering variety of sauces.

Belgium is also renowned for its chocolate. The big *chocolatiers*, Godiva and Leonidas, have shops in all the main towns and cities, but high-quality chocolate is also available in supermarkets at a much lower price – try Jacques or Côte d'Or.

Drink

Beer in Belgium is a real treat. Beyond the common lager brands – Stella Artois, Jupiler and Maes – there are about seven hundred speciality beers, from dark stouts to fruit beers, wheat beers and brown ales – something to suit any palate and enough to overwhelm the hardiest of livers. The most famous are the strong ales brewed by the country's six **Trappist monasteries**; Chimay is the most widely available. **Luxembourg** doesn't really compete, but its three most popular brews – Diekirch, Mousel and Bofferding – are pleasant enough lagers.

French **wines** are universally sold, but Luxembourg's wines, produced along the north bank of the Moselle, are very drinkable. You'll also find Dutch-style **jenever** (similar to gin) in most bars in the north of Belgium, and in Luxembourg home-produced **eau-de-vie**, distilled from various fruits.

STUDENT AND YOUTH DISCOUNTS

Most museums and galleries offer substantial discounts to those under 26, even if you don't have an ISIC card. Train travel is also cheaper for travellers aged under 26 if you buy a Go-Pass (see "Getting around", opposite).

CULTURE AND ETIQUETTE

The Belgians' relaxed attitude extends to the service – it's not unusual to be left waiting at the bar while the barman methodically polishes all the glasses. Don't worry about politely drawing some attention to yourself, as they're usually very helpful once they've noticed you. Leaving a ten percent **tip** is common in restaurants, but elsewhere is expected only when service has been exceptional.

SPORTS AND OUTDOOR ACTIVITIES

The Ardennes are ideal for hiking, kayaking, cycling and horseriding (see p.122 for operators); cross-country skiing is also an option. La Roche-en-Ardenne and Bouillon make excellent bases in Belgium, while in Luxembourg the towns of Vianden and Echternach (each about an hour from Luxembourg City) are popular destinations for hikers and cyclists. See p.102 & p.110 for more on cycling.

COMMUNICATIONS

Post offices are usually open Mon–Fri 9am–noon & 2–5pm. Some urban post offices also open on Saturday mornings. Many public **phones** take only phonecards, which are available from news-agents and post offices. **Internet** access is widespread, with at least one or two cybercafés in all the larger cities and some cafés with free wi-fi; libraries are often a good bet where all else fails.

EMERGENCIES

You shouldn't have much cause to come into contact with the **police** in either country. If you're unlucky enough to have something **stolen**, report it immediately to the nearest police station and get a report number, or better still a copy of the statement itself, for your insurance claim when you get home. With regard to **medical emergencies**, if you're reliant on free treatment within the EU health scheme, try to remember to make this clear to the ambulance staff and any medics you subsequently encounter. Outside working hours, all **pharmacies** should display a list of open alternatives. Weekend rotas are also listed in local newspapers.

EMERGENCY NUMBERS

Belgium Police ⓣ101; fire and ambulance ⓣ100.
Luxembourg Police ⓣ113; fire and ambulance ⓣ112.

INFORMATION

In both Belgium and Luxembourg, there are **tourist offices** in all but the smallest of villages. They usually provide free local maps, and in the larger towns offer a free accommodation booking service too.

MONEY AND BANKS

Belgium and Luxembourg both use the **euro** (€). **Banks** are the best places to change money and are generally open Monday to Friday 9am to 4/4.30pm in both countries, though some have a one-hour lunch break between noon and 2pm, and some close after lunch on Friday. **ATMs** are commonplace.

BELGIUM AND LUXEMBOURG ON THE NET

ⓦ**www.belgiumtheplaceto.be** Information on Brussels and southern Belgium.
ⓦ**www.visitluxembourg.lu** The Luxembourg tourist board's official site.
ⓦ**www.use-it.be** Excellent online guide for young travellers on Brussels and the Flanders region.
ⓦ**www.visitflanders.com** Information on Brussels and the Flanders region.

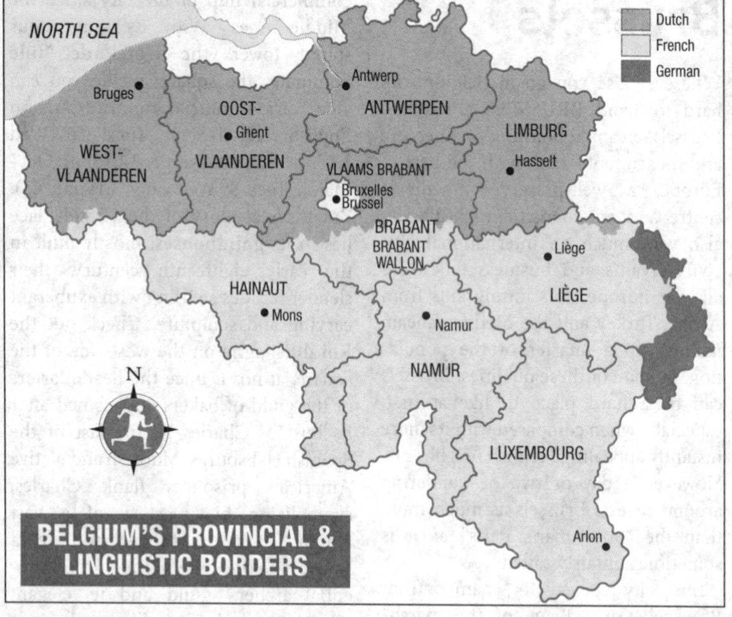

BELGIUM'S PROVINCIAL & LINGUISTIC BORDERS

OPENING HOURS AND HOLIDAYS

In both countries, most shops are closed on Sunday with some only re opening on Monday afternoon, even in major cities. Nonetheless, normal **shopping hours** are Monday to Saturday 9/10am to 6/7pm with many urban supermarkets staying open until 8/9pm on Fridays and smaller places shutting early on Saturday. In the big cities, a smattering of convenience stores (*magasins de nuit/avondwinkels*) stay open either all night or until around 1/2am daily, and some souvenir shops open late and on Sundays too. Most **museums** are closed on Mondays, though look out for occasional late-night openings, especially in Brussels. Restaurants also often close on Mondays. Many **bars** have relaxed closing times, claiming to stay open until the last customer leaves. Less usefully, many restaurants and bars close for at least a couple of weeks in July or August.

Shops, banks and many museums are closed on the following **public holidays**: New Year's Day, Easter Sunday, Easter Monday, May 1, Ascension Day (forty days after Easter), Whit Sunday, Whit Monday, June 23 (Luxembourg only), July 21 (Belgium only), Assumption (mid-Aug), November 1, November 11 (Belgium only), Christmas Day.

LANGUAGE

There are three official languages in **Belgium** (Flemish, which is effectively Dutch, plus French and German), though speaking French in the Flemish north is likely to make you extremely unpopular. Most Belgians in both parts of the country speak English. Natives of **Luxembourg** speak Letzebuergesch, a dialect of German, but most people also speak French and German and many speak English too. See p.335, p.441 and p.838 for some basic French, German and Dutch language tips.

Brussels

Wherever else you go in Belgium, it's hard to avoid **BRUSSELS** (Bruxelles, Brussel), a capital boasting architecture and museums to rank with the best in Europe, a well-preserved medieval centre and an energetic nightlife. It's also very much an international city, civil servants and business folk from all over Europe, plus immigrants from Africa, Turkey and the Mediterranean, making up a quarter of the population. In spite of these qualities, Brussels can be a hard place to like at first, especially when compared with its more instantly appealing Flemish neighbours. However, a day or two of wandering around reveals Brussels as much more than the "poor man's Paris", as it is sometimes unfairly called.

The city takes its name from Broekzele, or "village of the marsh", which grew up in the sixth century on the trade route between Cologne and the towns of Bruges and Ghent. In the nineteenth century it became the capital of the newly independent Belgium, and was kitted out with all the attributes of a modern European capital. Since World War II, the city's appointment as headquarters of both NATO and the EU has brought major developments, including a métro.

What to see and do

Central Brussels is enclosed within a rough pentagon of boulevards – the **petit ring** – which follows the course of the medieval city walls. The centre is also divided between the Ville Haute and Ville Basse, the former being the traditional home of the city's upper classes who kept a beady eye on the workers down below.

The Grand-Place

The obvious place to begin any tour of the **Ville Basse** is the **Grand-Place**, the commercial hub of the city since the Middle Ages. With its stupendous spired tower, the **Hôtel de Ville** dominates the square; inside you can view various official rooms (tours in English: April–Sept Tues & Wed 3.15pm, Sun 10.45am & 12.15pm; Oct–March Tues & Wed only 3.15pm; €3). But the real glory of the Grand-Place lies in its **guildhouses**, mostly built in the early eighteenth century, their slender facades swirling with exuberant carving and sculpture. Check out the **Roi d'Espagne** on the west side of the square, at no. 1, once the headquarters of the guild of bakers and named after its bust of Charles II, the last of the Spanish Habsburgs. Moorish and Native American prisoners flank Charles, symbolizing his mastery of a vast empire. At no. 5, the **Maison de la Louve** was once the home of the influential archers' guild and its elegant pilastered facade is studded with pious representations of concepts like Peace and Discord. Adjoining it, at no. 6, the **Maison du Cornet** was the headquarters of the boatsmen's guild, a fanciful creation of 1697 whose top storey resembles the stern of a ship.

The Manneken Pis

Rue de l'Etuve leads south from the Grand-Place down to the **Manneken Pis**, a diminutive statue of a little boy pissing that's supposed to embody the city's irreverent spirit, and is today one of Brussels' biggest tourist draws. The original statue was cast in the 1600s, but was stolen several times – the current one is a copy.

Notre Dame de la Chapelle and the Quartier Marolles

Across boulevard de l'Empereur, a busy carriageway that scars this part of the centre, you'll spy the crumbling brickwork of **La Tour Anneessens**, a chunky remnant of the medieval city wall, while to the south gleams the immaculately

restored **Notre Dame de la Chapelle** (June–Sept Mon–Sat 9am–5pm, Sun 11.30am–4.30pm; Oct–May daily 12.30–4.30pm; free), a sprawling Gothic structure founded in 1134 that is the city's oldest church. Running south from the church, rue Haute and parallel rue Blaes form the spine of the **Quartier Marolles**, traditionally a working-class neighbourhood which today gentrification has almost overwhelmed. **Place du Jeu de Balle**, the heart of Marolles, has retained its earthy character and is the site of the city's best **flea market** (daily 7am–2pm; busiest on Sun). You can get back to the Ville Haute using the free glass-walled lift from the rue Haute, which drops you off in place Poelaert and offers fantastic views of the city.

The Cathédrale

The steep slope that marks the start of the **Ville Haute** rises just a couple of minutes' walk to the east of the Grand-Place. Here, at the east end of rue d'Arenberg, you'll find the **Cathédrale** (Mon–Fri 7am–6pm, Sat 8.30am–3.30pm, Sun 2–6pm; €1), a splendid Brabantine-Gothic building begun in 1220 and sporting a striking twin-towered, white stone facade. Look out also for the gorgeous sixteenth-century **stained-glass windows** in the transepts and above the main doors.

Place Royale

In the middle of the museum quarter, known as the Mont des Arts, a wide stairway climbs up towards **place Royale** and **rue Royale**, the dead-straight backbone of the Ville Haute. Ahead to the left of the top of the stairway is the Old England Building, one of the finest examples of Art Nouveau in the city. Once a department store, it now holds the **Musée des Instruments de Musique**, at rue Montagne de la Cour 2 (MIM; Tues–Fri 9.30am–5pm, Sat & Sun 10am–5pm; €5/4), which contains an impressive collection of musical instruments. The rooftop café has great views of the city. Back on place Royale, at the start of rue de la Régence, the **Musées Royaux des Beaux-Arts** (Tues–Sun 10am–5pm; €5/3.50 for both museums) comprise two museums: the Musée d'Art Moderne and the Musée d'Art Ancien, which together make up Belgium's most satisfying all-round collection of fine art, including works by Bruegel, Rubens and the Surrealists. Nearby at rue Baron Horta 9 is the **Cinematek** (Ⓦwww.cinematek.be), which screens silent movies every evening, sometimes with piano accompaniment. And in an impressive site on the place Royale, the new **Musée Magritte** (daily except Mon 9.30am–5pm, Wed till 8pm; Ⓦwww.musee-magritte-museum.be) contains two hundred of the Surrealist artist's works, the largest collection in the world.

Outside the petit ring

Brussels by no means ends with the petit ring. To the east of the ring road, the **Quartier Leopold** has been

COMICS IN BRUSSELS

Brussels is a city made for comic book-fans. The **Centre Belge de la Bande Dessinée** (Comic Strip Museum; daily except Mon 10am–6pm; €7.50) at 20 rue des Sables focuses on Belgian comics (Tintin, Smurfs and so on) but also contains an interesting permanent exhibition about the creation of a comic strip. The shopping focus for comics is **boulevard Lemonnier**, between La Bourse and place Anneessens, which boasts ten comic-book shops. Rather endearingly, various walls around the city have been decorated with building-sized scenes from comic strips, and tourist information can supply you with a trail following the major ones. And if you're around in early October, you might be able to catch the city's annual **Comics Festival** (Ⓦwww.comicsfestivalbelgium.com).

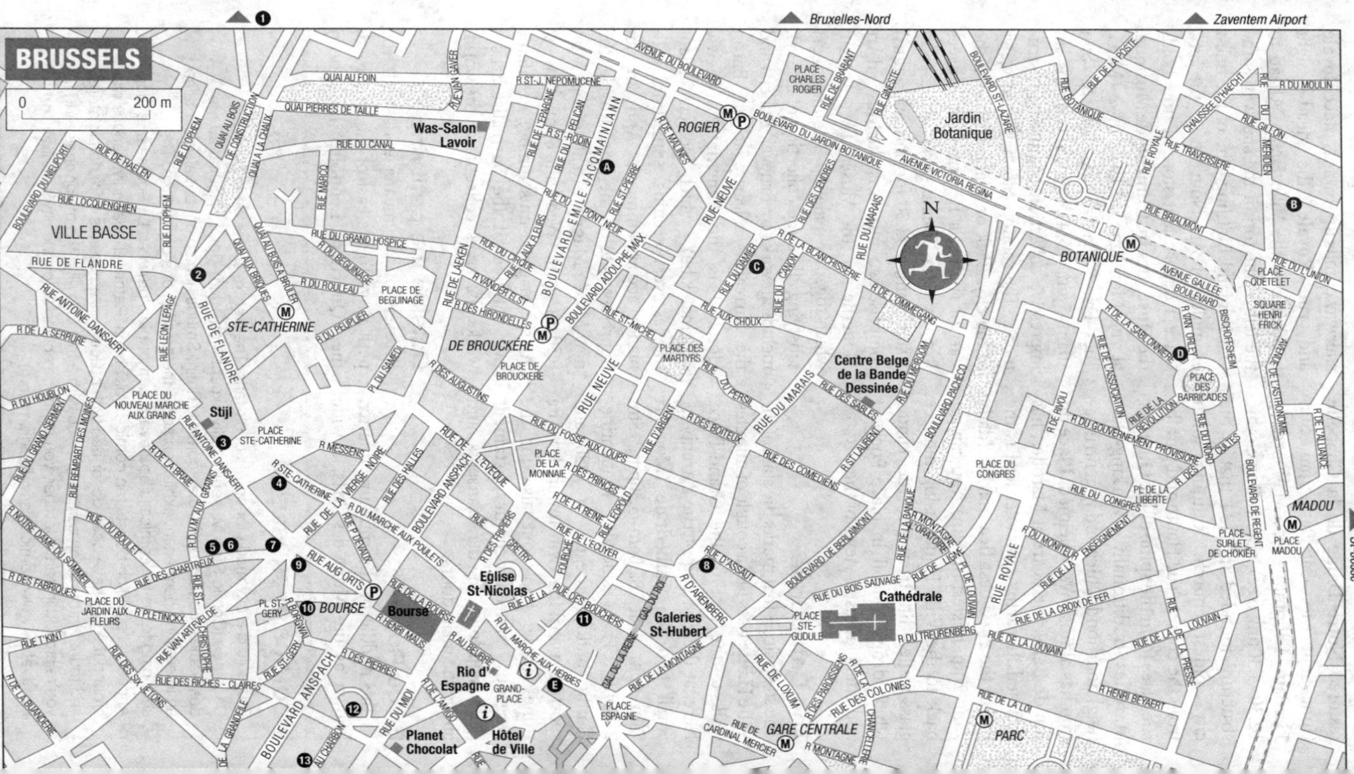
BRUSSELS
0 200 m
1
Bruxelles-Nord
Zaventem Airport
St-Josse
N
Jardin Botanique
VILLE BASSE
Was-Salon Lavoir
ROGIER
BOTANIQUE
STE-CATHERINE
DE BROUCKERE
Centre Belge de la Bande Dessinée
Stijl
PLACE STE-CATHERINE
PLACE DU NOUVEAU MARCHE AUX GRAINS
PLACE DE BEGUINAGE
PLACE DE BROUCKERE
PLACE DES MARTYRS
PLACE DE LA MONNAIE
PLACE DU CONGRES
PLACE CHARLES ROGIER
PLACE QUETELET
SQUARE HENRI FRICK
PLACE DES BARRICADES
PLACE SURLET DE CHOKIER
PLACE MADOU
MADOU
PL DE LA LIBERTE
Eglise St-Nicolas
BOURSE
Bourse
PL ST-GERY
PLACE DU JARDIN AUX FLEURS
Galeries St-Hubert
Cathédrale
PLACE STE-GUDULE
Rio d' Espagne
GRAND-PLACE
Hôtel de Ville
Planet Chocolat
PLACE ESPAGNE
GARE CENTRALE
PARC
BOULEVARD ANSPACH
BOULEVARD EMILE JACQMAINLANN
BOULEVARD ADOLPHE MAX
BOULEVARD DU JARDIN BOTANIQUE
AVENUE VICTORIA REGINA
BOULEVARD ST-LAZARE
BOULEVARD DE REGENT
BOULEVARD BISCHOFFSHEIM
BOULEVARD PACHECO
BOULEVARD DE BERLAIMONT
BOULEVARD DU NIEUPORT
AVENUE DU BOULEVARD
AVENUE GALILEE
AVENUE DE L'ASTRONOMIE
RUE NEUVE
RUE DU MARAIS
RUE ROYALE
RUE DE FLANDRE
RUE ANTOINE DANSAERT
RUE DE LAEKEN
RUE DU CANAL
QUAI AU FOIN
QUAI PIERRES DE TAILLE
QUAI AU BOIS DE CONSTRUCTION
QUAI A LA CHAUX
QUAI AU BOIS A BRULER
QUAI AUX BRIQUES
RUE DES CHARTREUX
RUE DU MARCHE AUX POULETS
RUE DU MARCHE AUX HERBES
RUE DES BOUCHERS
RUE DE LA MONTAGNE
RUE DES COLONIES
RUE DE LOXUM
RUE DE LA LOI
RUE DE LA CROIX DE FER
RUE DE LOUVAIN
RUE DES COMEDIENS
RUE DES SABLES
RUE AUX CHOUX
RUE DU FOSSE AUX LOUPS
RUE DES RICHES - CLAIRES
RUE DU MIDI
RUE DES PIERRES
RUE AUG ORTS
RUE DE LA VIERGE NOIRE
RUE DU GRAND HOSPICE
RUE DU BOIS SAUVAGE
RUE DU CONGRES
R DU GOUVERNEMENT PROVISOIRE
A B C D E 2 3 4 5 6 7 8 9 10 11 12 13

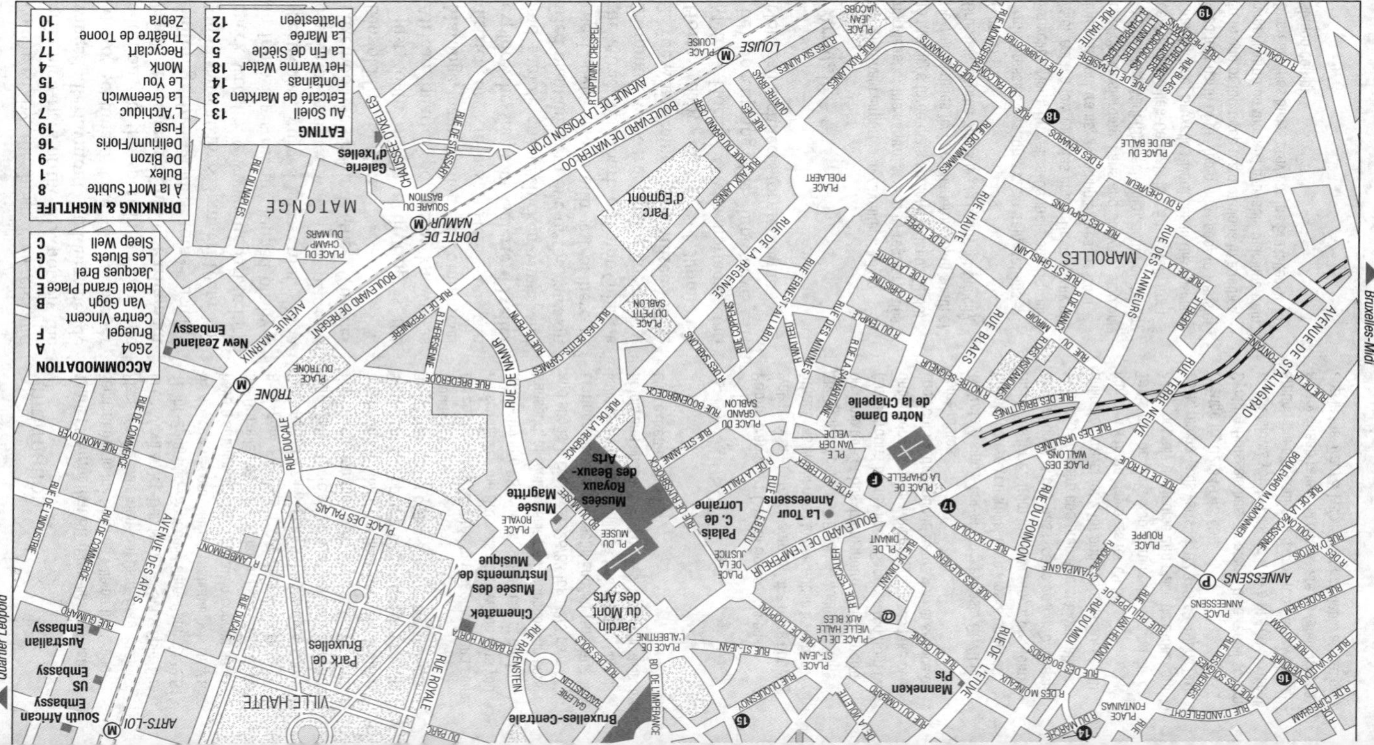
ACCOMMODATION
2Go4 A
Bruegel F
Centre Vincent Van Gogh B
Hotel Grand Place E
Jacques Brel D
Les Bluets G
Sleep Well C
DRINKING & NIGHTLIFE
À la Mort Subite 8
Bulex 1
De Bizon 9
Delirium/Floris 16
Fuse 19
L'Archiduc 7
La Greenwich 6
Le You 15
Monk 4
Recyclart 17
Théâtre de Toone 11
Zebra 10
EATING
Au Soleil 13
Eetcafé de Markten 3
Fontainas 14
Het Warme Water 18
La Fin de Siècle 5
La Marée 2
Plattesteen 12
Quartier Leopold
Musée Victor Horta
Porte de Hal & G
Bruxelles-Midi
VILLE HAUTE
Park de Bruxelles
MATONGÉ
MAROLLES
Parc d'Egmont
Musées Royaux des Beaux-Arts
Musée Magritte
Musée des Instruments de Musique
Cinematek
Jardin du Mont des Arts
Palais C. de Lorraine
La Tour Anneessens
Notre Dame de la Chapelle
Manneken Pis
Bruxelles-Centrale
Galerie d'Ixelles
South African Embassy
US Embassy
Australian Embassy
New Zealand Embassy
ARTS-LOI
TRÔNE
PORTE DE NAMUR
LOUISE
ANNEESSENS

colonized by the huge concrete and glass high-rises of the **EU**, notably the winged **Berlaymont** building beside Métro Schuman. One of the newer additions to the sprawling EU is the lavish **European Union Parliament building** (free guided tours: usually Mon–Thurs 10am & 3pm, Fri 10am, but check website; Ⓦwww.europarl.eu.int), an imposing structure topped off by a spectacular, curved glass roof. It's a couple of minutes' walk from place du Luxembourg, behind the Quartier Léopold train station.

Just south of the petit ring is the African quarter popularly known as **Matongé**, named after the commercial district of Kinshasa. Here you can explore the shops of **Galerie d'Ixelles** and sample cheap chicken wings and fried plantain from one of the cafés on rue Longue Vie. Southwest of here in the attractive suburb of Saint-Gilles, a 25-minute walk from place Poelaert at 25 rue Américaine, is the **Musée Victor Horta** (daily except 2–5.30pm; €7; Métro Horta; Ⓦwww.hortamuseum.be), occupying the innovative Art Nouveau architect's former home.

Arrival

Air The main airport is in Zaventem, 13km northeast of the centre, served by regular trains to the city's three main stations (30min; €2.80). No-frills airlines fly into Charleroi, 55km south of Brussels; shuttle buses leave hourly for the city (1hr; €11).
Train Brussels has three main train stations – Bruxelles-Nord, Bruxelles-Centrale and Bruxelles-Midi, each a few minutes apart. The majority of international trains, including expresses from London, Amsterdam, Paris and Cologne, stop only at Bruxelles-Midi (Brussel-Zuid), south of the city centre. Bruxelles-Centrale is a 5min walk from Grand-Place; Bruxelles-Nord lies in the business area just north of the main ring-road. To transfer from one of the three main stations to another, simply jump on the next available mainline train.
Bus Eurolines buses arrive at the Bruxelles-Nord station complex.

Information

Tourist information BIT (Bruxelles International Tourisme) is in the Hôtel de Ville on the Grand-Place (Jan–Easter Mon–Sat 9am–6pm; Easter to end April & Oct–Dec Mon–Sat 9am–6pm, Sun 10am–2pm; May–Sept daily 9am–6pm; Ⓣ02 513 89 40, Ⓦwww.brusselsinternational.be). They also have a smaller office on the main concourse of the Bruxelles-Midi train station (May–Sept daily 8am–8pm, Fri till 9pm; Oct–April Mon–Thurs 8am–5pm, Fri 8am–8pm, Sat 9am–6pm, Sun 9am–2pm). There's also a Belgian tourist information centre near the Grand-Place at rue du Marché aux Herbes 63 (Mon–Fri 9am–6pm, Sat & Sun 9am–1pm & 2–6pm; Ⓣ02 504 03 90). Maps for an Art Nouveau or comic-strip trail are available around the city.
Discount cards All three tourist offices and some museums sell the Brussels Card, which gets you free entry into 23 museums, free use of public transport, as well as selected reductions in bars and shops. It costs €20/28/33 for 1/2/3 days.
Listings *Agenda* is a useful English-language listings magazine, available free in many hostels, hotels and shops. *Use-It* guides, free in hostels, are also extremely helpful.

City transport

Public transport Central Brussels is easily walkable, but to reach some of the more outlying attractions you'll need to use public transport. The system, called STIB (Ⓦwww.stib.be), runs on a mixture of bus, tram, métro and prémétro (underground trams) lines. Services run from 6am until midnight, after which night buses take over. Look out for the antique trams now in service on some routes.
Tickets A single flat-fare ticket costs €1.70 if bought before you travel from kiosks or ticket machines, or €2 from the driver (bus, prémétro or tram only). A day-pass (*carte de jour*/*dagpas*), available at métro and prémétro stations, allows unlimited travel for 24hr and costs €4.50, or you can buy a three-day pass for €9.50.
Taxis can be picked up from ranks around the city – notably on Bourse and place de Brouckère; to book, phone Taxis Verts (Ⓣ02 349 49 49) or Taxis Orange (Ⓣ02 349 43 43).
Cycling Brussels has adopted a bike rental scheme which allows you to pick up a bike at 180 locations around the city centre and drop it off elsewhere at a very cheap rate. Full details are on Ⓦen.villo.be and in the *Train & Vélo* leaflet (available at stations).

Accommodation

Belgium's central reservation agency, Resotel (T 02 779 39 39, W www.belgium-hospitality.com), operates an efficient hotel reservation service, seeking out the best deals and discounts. Alternatively, if you arrive in the city with nowhere to stay, both BIT offices operate a free same-night hotel booking service.

Hostels

2Go4 bd Emile Jacmainlaan 99 T 02 219 30 19, W www.2go4.be. Excellent hostel with designer lounge and extremely helpful staff. Large groups (of over six) aren't admitted, which gives the place a cosy atmosphere, as does the fireplace in the lounge. Some rooms have baths – ask for the penthouse (which is the same price as the other rooms). A new branch is due to open soon off the Grand-Place, with private rooms only. Free wi-fi access; breakfast not included; reception closed 1–4pm. Métro De Brouckère. Dorms €20, double €60.

Bruegel rue du Saint-Esprit 2 T 02 511 04 36, W www.vjh.be. Huge official HI hostel in a fun area towards the Marolles. A basic breakfast – as well as the hire of sheets – is included in the overnight fee, and dinner costs €9. Check-in 10am–1pm & 2–4pm; curfew at 1am. Métro Gare Centrale. Dorms €19, double €46.

Centre Vincent Van Gogh rue Traversière 8 T 02 217 01 58, W www.chab.be. A rambling, spacious, 228-bed hostel just out of the petit ring with friendly staff, though it can all seem a bit chaotic. Laundry and kitchen facilities available and no curfew; bedsheets and breakfast included. 18–35-year-olds only. Métro Botanique. Dorms €18, double €52.

Jacques Brel rue de la Sablonnière 30 T 02 218 01 87, W www.laj.be. Modern and comfortable HI hostel. Breakfast and bedding are included in the price, there's no curfew and cheap meals can be bought on the premises. Métro Madou. Dorms €16, double €46.

Sleep Well rue du Damier 23 T 02 218 50 50, W www.sleepwell.be. Bright but bland hostel beloved of school groups and situated close to the city centre, with bar (often empty), restaurant and lounge areas. Métro Rogier. Dorms €20, double €56.

Hotels

Hostel Grand Place Haringstraat 6–8 T 02 219 30 19, W www.2go4.be. The best-located budget option in the city, right next to the Grand-Place. Pleasant rooms (no dorms), though check-in is inconveniently located at the *2Go4* hostel (see above). €59.

Les Bluets rue Berckmans 124 T 02 534 39 83, W www.bluets.be. Charming, family-run hotel in St-Gilles with just ten en-suite rooms in a large, handsome old stone terrace house. Immaculate decor in rich fin-de-siècle style. No lift. One block south of the petit ring and Métro Hôtel des Monnaies. €68.

Eating

Brussels has an international reputation for the quality of its food, and even at the dowdiest snack bar you'll find well-prepared Bruxellois dishes featuring amalgamations of Walloon and Flemish cuisine. The city is also among Europe's best for sampling a wide range of different cuisines, from Turkish (make for St-Josse, east of the centre) to Congolese (in Matongé), Vietnamese and Japanese. Rue de Flandre, near the bustling place Ste-Catherine, has a wide choice of good restaurants, though many of its best spots are closed on Mondays.

Cafés

Au Soleil rue du Marché au Charbon 86. Unfussy, bohemian bar serving *croque monsieurs* and pasta dishes at very reasonable prices. Métro Bourse.

Eetcafé de Markten place du Vieux Marché aux Grains. Vibrant café offering no-nonsense, good-quality salads (€8), lasagnes and quiches at very reasonable prices. Métro Ste-Catherine.

Fontainas rue du Marché au Charbon 91. Just down the road from *Au Soleil*, *Fontainas* changes from chilled-out café in the day to lively gay cocktail bar at night-time. Free wi-fi. Métro Bourse.

Het Warme Water rue des Renards 25. Very cosy café in the Marolles, serving simple Belgian food. Quiche €5. Métro Hotel des Monnaies.

Restaurants

La Fin de Siècle rue de Chartreux 9. Excellent Belgian food in buzzing street full of cafés and art galleries. The kitchen usually stays open till midnight. Mains around €12. Prémétro Bourse.

La Marée rue de Flandre 99 T 02 511 00 40. Pocket-sized bistro specializing in fish and mussels (and not to be confused with its namesake on rue au Beurre). The decor is pretty basic, but the food is always creative. Mains €12. Closed Sun & Mon. Métro Ste-Catherine.

Plattesteen rue du Marché au Charbon 41 T 02 512 82 03. Delicious Bruxellois dishes served at this traditional family restaurant, set in the middle of the gay district. Open every day for lunch and dinner. Mains €10. Métro Bourse.

Drinking and nightlife

Brussels' bars are a joy. The best area for evening drinking is place St-Géry, especially in the summer

where bars spill out into the square. Most places stay open until 1am. Rue du Marché au Charbon is the hub of gay nightlife.

Bars

À la Mort Subite rue Montagne aux Herbes Potagères 7. Infamous 1920s bar that loaned its name to a popular bottled beer. It occupies a long, narrow room with nicotine-stained walls, long tables and lots of mirrors, and on a good night is inhabited by a dissolute arty clientele. Métro Gare Centrale.

Delirium/Floris impasse de la Fidelité 87. The home of Delirium Tremens has long been a backpacker favourite and boasts over two thousand types of beer. *Floris*, its sister café opposite, serves fifty kinds of Absinthe. Métro Gare Centrale.

L'Archiduc rue Antoine Dansaert 6. Art Deco bar with jazz sessions, including "Jazz after Shopping" on weekend afternoons. Ring the doorbell to get in. Prémétro Bourse.

Le Greenwich rue des Chartreux 7. Very quiet bar patronized by chess and backgammon enthusiasts and selling beer at rock-bottom prices. Prémétro Bourse.

Monk rue Ste-Catherine 42. Large and popular bar named after the jazz musician Thelonious Monk – appropriately a grand piano has pride of place. Métro Ste-Catherine.

Théâtre de Toone impasse Schuddeveld 6. Ancient bar decorated with puppets belonging to resident theatre. Métro Gare Centrale.

Zebra place St-Géry 33–35. Small, upbeat bar on a lively square, attracting a young crowd. Prémétro Bourse.

Clubs

Bulex Ecole de Batellerie, rue Claessens 10 Ⓦwww.bulexasbl.be. This monthly all-night party (first Sat of the month), in an abandoned school, is one of Brussels' biggest and most popular nights; arrive around 3am, when the queue has dissipated but the party's just getting started. Entry €10, free drink included. Métro Pannenhuis, or taxi.

De Bizon rue du Pont de la Carpe 7. Fun bar with free blues jam sessions every Monday. Prémétro Bourse.

Fuse rue Blaes 208 Ⓦwww.fuse.be. One of Brussels' institutions, with big-name DJs usually lined up for its Sat techno nights. Entry €5 before midnight, €10 after. Usually Wed–Sat, with monthly gay nights. Métro Porte de Hal.

Le You rue Duquesnoy 6 Ⓦwww.leyou.be. Club hosting a variety of gay and straight nights including "Gay and Friendly Tea Dance" on Sun. Thurs–Sun. €10, free drink included. Métro Bruxelles-Centrale.

Recyclart rue des Ursulines 25 Ⓦwww.recyclart.be. "Artistic laboratory" in a disused station that holds irregular but reliably interesting club nights. Métro Bruxelles-Chapelle.

Shopping

Aside from the Marolles flea market (see p.107) and the vintage shops nearby such as Foxhole on rue des Renards, rue Antoine Dansaert is a good spot for window-shopping – check out Stijl at no. 74. More reasonable clothes shops can be found on and around rue du Marché au Charbon. For chocolate to take home, try Planète Chocolat at rue du Lombard 24, which holds demonstrations every Sat at 4pm (€7).

Directory

Embassies Australia, rue Guimard 6 Ⓣ02 286 05 00; Canada, av de Tervuren 2 Ⓣ02 741 06 11; Great Britain, rue d'Arlon 85 Ⓣ02 287 62 11; Ireland, rue Wiertz 89–93 Ⓣ02 235 66 76; New Zealand, 7th Floor, square de Meeus 1 Ⓣ02 512 10 40; South Africa, rue de la Loi 26 Ⓣ02 285 44 00; USA, bd du Régent 27 Ⓣ02 508 21 11.

Hospital Hôpital St Pierre, rue Haute 322 Ⓣ322 535 3111.

Internet BXL, place de la Vieille Halle aux Blés 46.

Laundry Was-Salon Lavoir, rue de Laeken 145, 7am–10pm.

Left luggage At all three main train stations.

Pharmacies Agora, rue du Marché aux Herbes 109; Multipharma, rue du Marché aux Poulets 37.

Post office First floor, Centre Monnaie, place de la Monnaie.

Moving on

Train to: Amsterdam (hourly; 2hr 40min); Antwerp (every 30min; 40min); Bruges (every 30min; 1hr); Ghent (every 30min; 40min); London (every 2hr; 2hr); Luxembourg City (hourly; 2hr 50min); Marloie (for La Roche-en-Ardennes; hourly; 1hr 50min); Namur (every 30min; 1hr 15min); Ostend (hourly; 1hr 20min); Paris (hourly; 1hr 30min).

Northern Belgium

Almost entirely **Flemish**-speaking, the region to the north of Brussels possesses a distinctive and vibrant cultural identity, its pancake-flat landscapes punctuated by a string of fine historic cities. These begin with **Antwerp**, a large old port dotted with many reminders of its sixteenth-century golden age. To the west lie two more fascinating cities, **Ghent** and **Bruges**, which became prosperous during the Middle Ages on the back of the cloth trade. All three cities have great restaurants and a lively bar scene.

ANTWERP

ANTWERP, Belgium's second city, and the de facto capital of Flemish Belgium, fans out from the east bank of the Scheldt River about 50km north of Brussels. Many people prefer it to the capital, and indeed it is an immediately attractive place, famous for Rubens, fashion, food and diamonds. Antwerp also boasts a breathtakingly beautiful station, one of the world's oldest zoos, the second largest docks in Europe – and the best nightlife in Belgium.

What to see and do

At the centre of Antwerp is the spacious **Grote Markt**, where the conspicuous **Brabo fountain** comprises a haphazard pile of rocks surmounted by a bronze of Silvius Brabo, the city's first hero, depicted flinging the hand of the giant Antigonus – who terrorized passing ships – into the Scheldt. The north side of Grote Markt is lined with daintily restored sixteenth-century **guild-houses**, while the west is hogged by the handsome **Stadhuis** (tours Mon–Thurs at 2pm; €1).

The underground canals

One of the city's more unusual sights – its network of **underground canals**, which date back to the twelfth century – can be accessed from Suikerrui 21, just south of the Grote Markt. Visitors can choose between pricey, three-hour tour with a guide (€18; book on ⓣ03 232 01 03), or a much shorter look at the sewers (€2.50).

Onze Lieve Vrouwe Cathedral

Southeast of Grote Markt, the **Onze Lieve Vrouwe Cathedral** (Mon–Fri 10am–5pm, Sat 10am–3pm, Sun 1–4pm; €4) is one of the finest Gothic churches in Europe, dating from the middle of the fifteenth century. Inside, the seven-aisled nave is breathtaking. Four early paintings by Rubens are displayed here.

Plantin-Moretus Museum

It's a five-minute walk southwest from the cathedral to the **Plantin-Moretus Museum** on Vrijdagmarkt (Tues–Sun 10am–5pm; €6), which occupies the grand old mansion of Rubens' father-in-law, the printer Christopher Plantin. It provides a beautiful, richly decorated setting for two of the oldest printing presses in the world.

ModeNatie and Museum voor Schone Kunsten

In the heart of the city's fashion quarter along Nationalestraat, the **ModeNatie** (ⓦwww.modenatie.com) is an ambitious

> **FERRIES TO BRITAIN**
>
> Belgium's main international ferry port is **Zeebrugge**, just outside Bruges, with ferries from Hull and Rosyth in Britain. Ferry companies provide bus connections from the port to the train station. Transeuropa ferries run from Ramsgate to the resort town of **Ostend**, from where trains to Bruges take fifteen minutes.

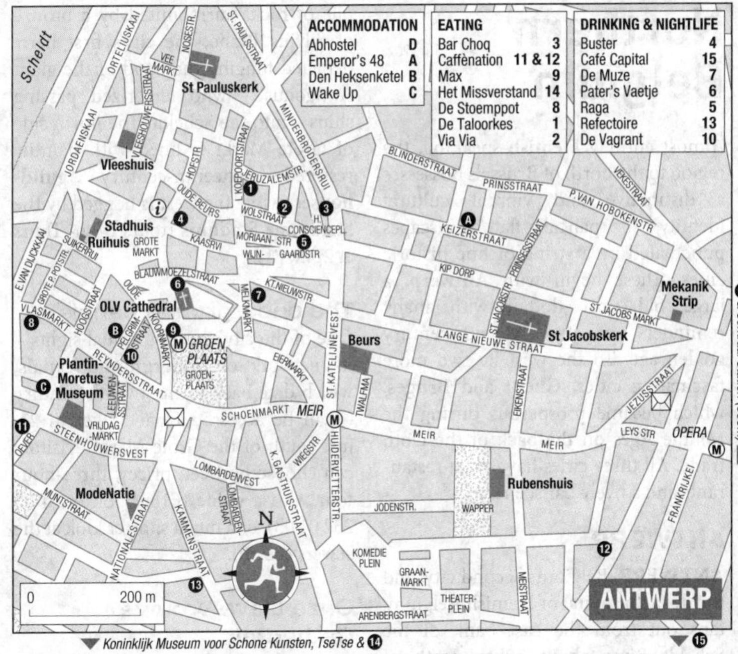

complex spread over several floors that showcases some of the avant-garde fashion for which the city is famous. Part of the building contains **MoMu** (Mode Museum; daily 10am–6pm; €4; ⓦwww.momu.be), which has some great contemporary fashion displays.

About fifteen minutes' walk further south at Leopold De Waelplaats, the **Koninklijk Museum voor Schone Kunsten** (Tues–Sun 10am–5pm, €6; ⓦwww.kmska.be) has one of the country's best fine-art collections. Its early Flemish section features paintings by Jan van Eyck and Quentin Matsys, while Rubens has two large rooms to himself. The museum is a fifteen-minute walk from the ModeNatie, or take tram #8 from Groenplaats towards Bolivarplaats, and ask for the museum stop.

North of the Grote Markt

It's a short walk north of the Grote Markt to the impressively gabled **Vleeshuis** (Tues–Sun 10am–5pm; €5), built for the guild of butchers in 1503 and distinguished by its striped brickwork; it now holds temporary exhibitions. Just north of here, along Vleeshouwersstraat, the airy and elegant nave at the sixteenth-century **St Pauluskerk** (May–Sept daily 2–5pm; free) is decorated by a series of paintings depicting the Fifteen Mysteries of the Rosary, including Rubens' exquisite *Scourging at the Pillar* of 1617.

Rubenshuis and St Jacobskerk

Ten minutes' walk east of the Grote Markt is the **Rubenshuis**, at Wapper 9 (Tues–Sun 10am–5pm; €6); the former home and studio of Rubens, it's now restored as a very popular museum. On his death in 1640, Rubens was buried in the chapel behind the high altar at **St Jacobskerk**, just to the north at Lange Nieuwstraat 73. It includes one of his last works, *Our Lady Surrounded by Saints*, featuring himself as St George,

his two wives as Martha and Mary, and his father as St Jerome.

Arrival, information and city transport

Train Antwerp has two mainline train stations, Berchem and Centraal. The latter is the one you want for the city centre. Centraal Station is located about 2km east of the Grote Markt; trams #2 and #15 (direction Linkeroever) run from the Diamant underground tram station beside Centraal Station to the centre; get off at Groenplaats.
Tourist information Grote Markt 13 (Mon–Sat 9am–5.45pm, Sun 9am–4.45pm; ⓣ03 232 01 03, ⓦwww.visitantwerp.be).
City transport The centre is easily traversed on foot, and there are very good bus, métro and tram services covering the rest of the city. Franklin Rooseveltplaats and Groenplaats are two of the main transport hubs. A flat-rate single-fare ticket on any part of the city's transport system costs €1.60; a 24hr pass (*dagpas*) €3.80.

Accommodation

Finding accommodation is rarely difficult, although there are surprisingly few places in the centre. Many mid-priced and budget establishments are around Centraal Station, where you should exercise caution at night.

Abhostel Kattenberg 110 ⓣ03 473 57 01 66, ⓦwww.abhostel.com. Very comfortable and cosy family-run hostel 15min walk from the centre. Call ahead for check-in times. Dorms €19, double €50.
Den Heksenketel Pelgrimstraat 22 ⓣ03 226 71 64, ⓦwww.heksenketel.org/hostel. Cheap, central accommodation: not the cleanest or most efficient, but very relaxed. Downstairs there's a folk-music bar with regular jam sessions. Tram to Groenplaats. Dorms €17.
Emperor's 48 Keizerstraat 48 ⓣ04 8603 3397, ⓦwww.emperors48.com. Comfortable and well-designed B&B on a quiet street. Tram #11 to Kipdorp. €80.

TREAT YOURSELF

Wake Up Hoogstraat 68 ⓣ03 225 16 06, ⓦwww.wake-up.be. Bright, well-located hotel with breakfast in the lovely café downstairs included. The rooms accommodating four are an especially good deal. Book in advance in the summer. Double €85, quadruple €120.

Eating

Antwerp is an enjoyable and inexpensive place to eat, full of informal café-restaurants. Several of the best are clustered on Suikerrui and Grote Pieter Potstraat near the Grote Markt, and there's another concentration in the vicinity of Hendrik Conscienceplein, a gorgeous piazza containing an impressive Baroque church. For fast food, try the kebab and falafel places on Oude Koornmarkt, or of course any of the *frituurs*.

Cafés and snacks

Bar Choq Minderbroedersrui 64. Cosy café where coffee and hot chocolate are taken very seriously by the friendly owner. Closed Sun.
Caffènation Hopland 46. Great coffee, including some adventurous recipes, and a nice garden at this café close to Rubenshuis. There's another one at Oever 18 which also serves fresh smoothies.
Max Groenplaats 12. Handily located *frituur* known as the best in town, with room to sit upstairs.
Via Via Wolstraat 43. Popular traveller's café serving dishes from around the world. Opposite unpretentious student bar *'t Plantsje*. Mains €10.

Restaurants

De Stoemppot Vlasmarkt 12.This cosy little restaurant is the best place to eat classic *stoemp*. Mains €10. Closed Wed.
De Taloorkes Lange Koepoorstraat 61. Five minutes' walk from Grote Markt but a world away from its touristy offerings, this lively yet laid-back locals' restaurant serves mouthwatering stews and mussels dishes. Mains €15.
Het Missverstand St Andriesplaats 17. Situated on a quiet square close to ModeNatie, this friendly bar serves daily specials in a beautifully decorated setting. Closed Sun & Mon.

Drinking and nightlife

Antwerp is an excellent place to drink, the narrow lanes of its centre dotted with small and atmospheric bars serving an overwhelming variety of beers. Be sure to try the local brew, Bolleke Koninck.

Bars

Buster Kaasrui 1. Straightforward bar featuring a wide range of live music most nights. Closed Sun & Mon.
De Vagant Reyndersstraat 21. Specialist gin bar serving an extravagant range of Belgian and Dutch *jenevers* in comfortable, laid-back surroundings.

Pater's Vaetje Blauwmoezelstraat 1. There's a great range of beers at this central old-fashioned pub, popular with tourists and locals alike.

Raga H. Conscienceplein 18. Wine bar with a friendly owner and jazz soundtrack – good for the lone traveller, with lots of books to read.

Refectoire Kleinemarkt 6. Former cheese shop converted into a very bohemian bar with eclectic decor and cheap drinks, near the shops of Kammenstraat and MoMu. Open 6pm to midnight.

Clubs

Café Capital Rubenslei 37 Ⓦ www.cafecapital.be. Popular club which attracts world-famous DJs, set in the middle of the Stadspark, a 15min walk from the Groenplaats. Fri & Sat only; best on Sat after 1am. €9.

De Muze Melkmarkt 15 Ⓣ 03 226 01 26. Renowned jazz bar, with free live performances Mon–Sat at 10pm and Sun at 3pm.

Shopping

Kammenstraat is good for vintage clothes shops, while Lange Koepoortstraat has plenty of second-hand record shops including FatKat at no. 57 and Record Collector at no. 70. Everything from pricey antique shops to cavernous junk shops can be found along Kloosterstraat.

Mekanik Strip Sint-Jacobsmarkt 73. The biggest comic-book shop in Belgium, stocking a huge range of underground graphic novels as well as the famous Belgian publications such as *Tintin* and *The Smurfs*. There's an English-language section at the back.

TseTse Kronenburgstraat 72. Another store stocking a good selection of graphic novels and comics. Closed Sun & Mon.

Moving on

Train Bruges (hourly; 1hr 20min); Brussels (every 30min; 40min); Ghent (every 30min; 50min); Ostend (hourly; 1hr 40min).

GHENT

The largest town in Western Europe during the thirteenth and fourteenth centuries, **GHENT (Gent)** was once at the heart of the medieval Flemish cloth trade. It's now the third largest city in Belgium, with – for many – the attractions of Bruges (beautiful canals,

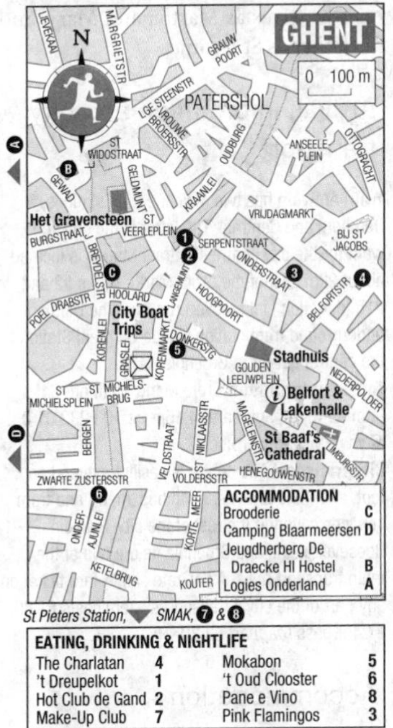

well-preserved medieval architecture), without the stifling tourism.

What to see and do

A captivating university town with a spirited nightlife and its own **castle**, Het Gravensteen, Ghent's main appeal lies in wandering the cobbled streets which line the canalside and sampling the city's many bars.

St Baafsplein

The best place to start exploring is at the mainly Gothic **St Baaf's Cathedral**, squeezed into the corner of St Baafsplein (Mon–Sat 8.30am–5.30pm, Sun noon–5pm; free). Inside, a small chapel (April–Oct Mon–Sat 9.30am–5pm, Sun 1–4.30pm; Nov–March Mon–Sat 10.30am–4pm, Sun 1–4pm; €3) holds Ghent's greatest treasure, the altarpiece of the *Adoration of the Mystic Lamb*, a wonderful, early fifteenth-century painting by Jan van Eyck.

On the west side of St Baafsplein lurks the medieval **Lakenhalle** (Cloth Hall), a gloomy hunk of a building. One of its entrances leads to the adjoining **Belfort** (Belfry; mid-March to mid-Nov daily 10am–6pm; €3), a much-amended edifice dating from the fourteenth century. A lift climbs up to the roof for excellent views over the city centre.

The Graslei and Patershol

A five-minute walk along Catalonie-straat, the **Graslei** forms the eastern side of the old city harbour and is home to a splendid series of medieval guild-houses. On warm days it's packed with students sunning themselves. From here you can catch boat tours, the most relaxing way to explore Ghent. Nearby just to the north are the narrow cobbled lanes and alleys of the **Patershol**, a pocket-sized district that was formerly home to the city's weavers, but is now Ghent's main restaurant quarter. To the west, on Sint-Veerleplein, stands **Het Gravensteen** (April–Sept 9am–6pm; Oct–March 9am–5pm, €8), a spectacular twelfth-century castle, now a chilling torture museum.

SMAK

Strolling south from the centre along Ghent's main shopping street, Veldstraat, it takes about twenty minutes to reach the old casino, parts of which have been turned into **SMAK** (Citadelpark; Tues–Sun 10am–6pm; €5; ⓦwwwsmak.be), a museum of contemporary art that is well known for its adventurous programme of temporary exhibitions.

Arrival, information and city transport

Arrival Of Ghent's two train stations, St Pieters is the handiest one for town, about 2km to the south of the city centre; trams run up to the Korenmarkt, plumb in the centre of town, every few minutes, or you can rent a bike.

Tourist information In the crypt of the Lakenhalle, on the Botermarkt (daily: April–Oct 9.30am–6.30pm; Nov–March 9.30am–4.30pm; ⓣ09 266 52 32, ⓦwww.visitgent.be).

City transport Ghent's centre is very compact, so you probably won't need to buy a day-pass. The flat-rate fare for trams is €1.20 per journey; you need to validate the ticket at the machine once you get on.

GHENT FESTIVAL

For ten days during the second half of July, Ghent transforms into a 24-hour city of drinking and dancing as it pulsates with the **Gentse Feesten** (ⓦwww.gentsefeesten.be). Stages are set up in all the town's main squares and blast out every kind of music from reggae to folk and jazz. Accommodation can get booked up months before the festival, so be sure to make a reservation, and try to avoid the city just afterwards – everything is shut for the next two weeks or so as the city takes a rest.

Accommodation

The tourist office publishes a free and comprehensive brochure detailing local accommodation, and operates a free hotel booking service.

Brooderie Jan Breydelstraat 8 ⓣ09 225 06 23, ⓦwww.brooderie.be. Three neat and trim little rooms above an appealing little café, handily located in the city centre. The included breatkfast is excellent. €50.

Camping Blaarmeersen Zuiderlaan 12 ⓣ09 266 81 60. Popular campsite to the west of the town centre, with excellent sports facilities including a lake. March to mid-Oct. €15 per person.

Jeugdherberg De Draecke HI Hostel St Widostraat 11 ⓣ09 233 70 50, ⓦwww.vjh.be. Well equipped and central, Ghent's only hostel has over a hundred beds and facilities including lockers, bike rental and a bar. Advance reservations advised. Trams #1, #10 or #11 to Gravensteen. Dorms €17.50, double €44.

Logies Onderland Rabotstraat 62 ⓣ09 228 85 38, ⓦwww.onderland.be. Restored coachhouse with a large garden that feels quiet despite its location near the Gravensteen. It's a 10min walk from the Groetenmarkt, or hop on tram #1 or #10 from the station. Garden and kitchen facilities. Three nights' minimum stay. Doubles €72, quadruples €95.

Eating, drinking and nightlife

Fancier restaurants are concentrated in and around the Patershol, while less-expensive spots, including a number of fast-food joints, cluster the Korenmarkt. Sleepstraat is lined with good Turkish restaurants and snack bars. Thanks to its student population, Ghent boasts a much more energetic drinking and live music scene than you might expect of a town of its size, though there's only one bona fide nightclub.

Cafés and restaurants

Mokabon Donkersteeg 35. The best coffee in town is served at this unpretentious locals' café, located on a street full of restaurants and delis.
Pane e Vino Savaanstraat 5. Cheap and delicious pizzas in a simple setting. Margharita pizza €5. Closed Sun.

Bars

The Charlatan Vlasmarkt 6. Studenty bar with at least three concerts a week. Free gigs every Thurs. Closed Mon.
Pink Flamingos Onderstraat 55. Weird and wacky little place stuffed with everything kitsch, from plastic statues to tacky religious icons. Attracts a hip crowd, and is a great place for an aperitif or cocktails. Open till 3am Thurs–Sat; food served until 11pm.
't Dreupelkot Groentenmarkt 12. Old-fashioned, cosy bar specializing in *jenever*, of which it stocks more than 215 brands, all kept at icy temperatures.

Clubs and live music

Hot Club de Gand Schuddevisstraatje Groentenmarkt 15b Ⓦwww.hotclubdegand.be. Best jazz spot in town, with jam sessions on Wed evenings.
Make-Up Club Ketelvest 51b Ⓦwww.make-up-club.be. The only club in central Ghent; take tram #1 to Ketelvest. Entry €5. Open Fri & Sat.

Moving on

Train Antwerp (every 30min; 50min); Bruges (every 20min; 25min); Brussels (every 30min; 40min); Ostend (every 30min; 50min).

TREAT YOURSELF

't Oud Clooster Zwarte Zusterstraat 5 Ⓣ09 233 78 02. Hidden away in a side street, this lively restaurant in an old monastery serves delicious traditional Belgian dishes at reasonable prices, and has a wide range of beers. Mains €12. Closed Mon.

BRUGES

The reputation of **BRUGES (Brugge)** as one of the most perfectly preserved medieval cities in Europe has made it the most popular tourist destination in Belgium. Inevitably, the crowds tend to overwhelm the city's charms, but you would be mad to come to Belgium and miss the place. Bruges boomed throughout the Middle Ages, sharing control of the Flemish cloth trade with its two great rivals, Ghent and Ieper (Ypres), its weavers turning English wool into items of clothing that were exported all over the world. By the end of the fifteenth century, however, Bruges had begun its decline. Frozen in time, the city escaped damage in both world wars to emerge as the perfect tourist attraction, with its student population also providing a decent nightlife.

What to see and do

The older sections of Bruges fan out from two central squares, Markt and Burg.

Markt, Belfort and Hallen

Markt, edged on three sides by nineteenth-century gabled buildings, is the larger of the two squares, an impressive open space flanked on its south side by the mighty **Belfort** (Belfry; daily 9.30am–5pm; €5), built in the thirteenth century when the town was at its richest and most extravagant. The belfry is attached to the rectangular **Hallen**, a much-restored edifice also dating from the thirteenth century. Entry to the Belfry is via the Hallen; inside, a tapering staircase leads up to the roof from where there are wonderful views over the city centre.

The Burg and the Heilig Bloed Basilek

From the Markt, Breidelstraat leads through to the **Burg**, whose southern

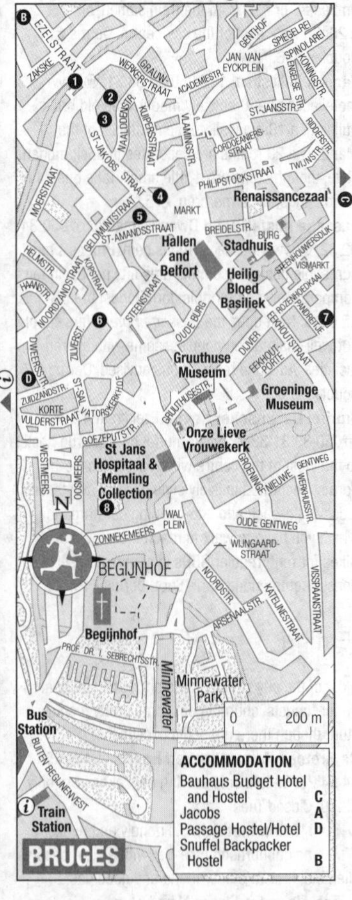

EATING		DRINKING & NIGHTLIFE	
De Bretoen Pannenkoeken	1	B-in	8
L'Estaminet	7	't Brugs Beertje	6
Médard	5	De Kleine Nachtmuziek	2
Pickles	4	De Republiek	3

half is fringed by the city's finest group of buildings. One of the best is the **Heilig Bloed Basiliek** (Basilica of the Holy Blood; daily: April–Sept 9.30am–noon & 2–6pm; Oct–March Mon, Tues & Thurs–Sun 10am–noon & 2–4pm, Wed 10am–noon; free), which holds a phial of the blood of Christ brought back from Jerusalem by the Crusaders. The basilica divides into a shadowy Lower Chapel, built to house another relic, that of St Basil, and an Upper Chapel where the phial is stored in a grandiose silver tabernacle. The Holy Blood is still venerated on Ascension Day, when it is carried through the town in a colourful but solemn procession.

The Stadhuis

To the left of the basilica, the **Stadhuis** has a beautiful, turreted sandstone facade, behind which is a magnificent **Gothic Hall** (daily 9.30am–5pm; €2.50). The price of admission covers entry to the former alderman's mansion, the nearby **Renaissancezaal 't Brugse Vrije** (Tues–Sun 9.30am–12.30pm & 1.30–5pm), which has just one exhibit: an enormous sixteenth-century chimneypiece carved in honour of the ruling Habsburgs, who are flattered by their enormous codpieces.

The Groeninge and Gruuthuse museums

From the arch beside the Stadhuis, Blinde Ezelstraat ("Blind Donkey Street") leads south across the canal to the huddle of picturesque houses crimping the **Huidenvettersplein**, the old tanners' quarter that now holds some of the busiest places to eat and drink in town. Nearby, the Dijver follows the canal to the **Groeninge Museum**, at Dijver 12 (Tues–Sun 9.30am–5pm; €8), which houses a superb sample of Flemish paintings from the fourteenth to twentieth centuries. The best section is the early Flemish work, including several canvases by Jan van Eyck. Further along the Dijver, at no. 17, the **Gruuthuse Museum** (same times; €6) is sited in a rambling fifteenth-century mansion and holds a varied collection of fine and applied art, including intricately carved altarpieces, locally made tapestries and many different types of antique furniture.

Onze Lieve Vrouwekerk

The **Onze Lieve Vrouwekerk** (Tues–Sat 9.30am–5pm, Sun 1.30–5pm; €2.50), on

Mariastraat, is a rambling shambles of a building, but among its assorted treasures is a delicate marble *Madonna and Child* by Michelangelo and, in the chancel (same hours; €2.50) the exquisite Renaissance mausoleums of Charles the Bold and his daughter Mary of Burgundy.

St Jans Hospitaal and Begijnhof

Opposite the church, the large medieval ward of **St Jans Hospitaal** (Tues–Sun 9.30am–5pm; €8) has been turned into a lavish museum celebrating the city's history in general and St John's Hospital in particular. In addition, the old Hospital chapel displays a small but exquisite collection of paintings by **Hans Memling**. Born near Frankfurt in 1433, Memling spent most of his working life in Bruges, producing serene but warmly coloured and stunningly beautiful paintings. From St Jans, it's a quick stroll down to the **Begijnhof** (daily 9am–6pm or sunset if earlier; free), a circle of whitewashed houses around a tidy green. Nearby is the romantic **Minnewater**, often known as the "Lake of Love".

Arrival and information

Arrival Bruges's train station adjoins the bus station about 2km southwest of the centre. Local buses leave from outside the train station for the main square, the Markt; tickets cost €1.20.

Tourist information The main office is in the city concert hall, the Concertgebouw, a 10min walk west of the Markt at 't Zand 34 (daily 10am–6pm, Thurs till 8pm; ⓣ050 44 86 86, ⓦwww.brugge.be). There is a smaller branch inside the train station (Tues–Sat: April–Sept 10am–1pm & 2–6pm; Oct–March 9.30am–12.30pm & 1–5pm; ⓣ050 44 86 86).

Accommodation

Bauhaus Budget Hotel and Hostel Langestraat 133 ⓣ050 34 10 93, ⓦwww.bauhaus.be. Cheap and cheerful hotel/hostel comprising twenty private rooms, dorms and apartments. An excellent bar lends the place some atmosphere. It's a short ride on bus #6 or #16 from the train station, or a 20min walk east of the city centre. Dorms €14, doubles €36.

Jacobs Baliestraat 1 ⓣ050 33 98 31, ⓦwww.hoteljacobs.be. Creatively modernized old brick building, a 10min walk to the northeast of the Markt. The 23 rooms are decorated in brisk modern style, though some are a little small. Take bus #4 or #8 to Langerei/Carmerbrug. €75.

Passage Hostel/Hotel Dweersstraat 26 ⓣ050 34 02 32, ⓦwww.passagebruges.com. Bruges's most agreeable hostel accommodates fifty people in ten comparatively comfortable dormitories; breakfast is €5 extra. Next door, the *Passage Hotel* offers simple but well-maintained doubles, some with shared facilities. Advance reservations advised. Dorms €15, doubles €50.

Snuffel Backpacker Hostel Ezelstraat 47–49 ⓣ050 33 31 33, ⓦwww.snuffel.be. Well-run hostel to the west of the centre with four- to twelve-bed dorms, decorated in lively style by local artists, and a cosy, laid-back and late-opening bar (through which you have to walk to reach the showers). Bikes for rent; regular BBQs in summer. Reservations recommended April–Sept. Dorms €15.

Eating

Most of the city's restaurants and cafés are geared up for tourists, churning out some pretty mediocre stuff, though there are some exceptions.

De Bretoen Pannenkoeken Ezelstraat 4 ⓣ050 34 54 25. Simple café serving pancakes from only €2.70. Closed Tues.

L'Estaminet Park 5. Friendly and relaxed neighbourhood café-bar with a cosmopolitan clientele, first-rate beer menu and good pasta dishes. Mains €8. Closed Mon & Thurs.

Médard Sint-Amandsstraat 18. Family-run Italian restaurant very close to the Markt dishing up generous portions of pasta – just €3 for a huge bowl. Closed Thurs.

Pickles *Frituur* just off the Markt; one of the best options for fries. Open till 4am on the weekend.

Drinking and nightlife

B-in Zonnekemeers ⓦwww.b-in.be. Hip bar/club kitted out with eye-catching coloured fluorescent tubes. Guest DJs play house on the weekends, and there are reasonably priced drinks and cocktails. Gets going about 11pm. Free entry. Tues–Sat 11am till late.

De Kleine Nachtmuziek St Jakobsstraat 60. Peaceful whisky bar with a jazz and blues soundtrack. Closed Tues & Wed.

 **De Republiek** St Jakobsstraat 36. Trendy bar with a lovely terrace and DJs at weekends. Also serves food. Open every day.

't Brugs Beertje Kemelstraat 5 Ⓦ www.brugsbeertje.be. This small and friendly speciality bar claims a stock of three hundred beers. Popular with backpackers as well as locals. Closed Wed.

Moving on

Train Antwerp (hourly; 1hr 20min); Brussels (every 30min; 1hr); Ghent (every 20min; 25min); Ostend (every 20min; 15min); Zeebrugge (hourly; 15min).

Southern Belgium

South of Brussels lies **Wallonia**, French-speaking Belgium, where a belt of heavy industry interrupts the rolling farmland that precedes the high wooded hills of the **Ardennes**. The latter spreads over three provinces – **Namur** in the west, **Luxembourg** in the south and Liège in the east – and is a great place for hiking and canoeing.

NAMUR

NAMUR is a pleasant, medium-sized town, whose antique centre is dotted with elegant, eighteenth-century mansions. It also possesses a number of first-rate restaurants and a lively bar scene, lent vigour by its university students – although you wouldn't know it during late July and August, when many of its best cafés and bars are shut. Namur's main attraction, however, is as a jumping-off point to get to the Ardennes forest.

What to see and do

The town occupies an important strategic location, straddling the confluence of the rivers Sambre and Meuse, the main result being the massive, rambling **citadel**, which rolls along the top of the steep bluff overlooking the south bank of the Sambre. Its nooks and crannies can take a couple of days to explore, though you can speed things up by using the tourist **mini-train** (April–Oct; €5), which runs every half-hour.

Cutting through the old town centre is rue de l'Ange and its continuation rue de Fer, which together comprise the main shopping street. A few metres east of here, the **Trésor du Prieuré d'Oignies**, at rue Julie Billiart 17 (Treasury of the Oignies Priory; Tues–Sat 10am–noon & 2–5pm, Sun 2–5pm; €2), is Namur's best – and smallest – museum. Located in a nunnery, it holds a spellbinding collection of reliquaries and devotional pieces created by local craftsman Hugo d'Oignies in the first half of the thirteenth century; the nuns give the guided tour in English.

Arrival and information

Arrival Namur's train and bus stations are on the northern edge of the city centre on place de la Station.

Tourist information The tourist office is just a few steps away on square Léopold, at the north end of rue de Fer (daily 9.30am–6pm; Ⓣ 081 24 64 49, Ⓦ www.ville.namur.be). They give advice on cycling, walking and canoeing in the Ardennes and will also arrange accommodation. There's also a seasonal tourist information chalet (April–Oct daily 9.30am–6pm), 10min walk away, over the Sambre bridge on the other side of the centre.

Accommodation

Auberge de Jeunesse av Félicien Rops 8, 3km from the train station Ⓣ 081 22 36 88, Ⓦ www.laj.be. Friendly hundred-bed hostel occupying a big

TREAT YOURSELF

Les Tanneurs rue des Tanneries 13 Ⓣ 081 24 00 24, Ⓦ www.tanneurs.com. Comfortable four-star hotel in a lavishly and imaginatively renovated old brick mansion, located down a quiet alley close to the town centre. The cheap rooms are fine, but if you're prepared to pay a lot more you can get a room with its own sauna, jacuzzi or hammam. Rooms €40.

old house on the banks of the Meuse at the southern edge of town. There's a kitchen, laundry and self-service restaurant, and no lockout. Take bus #3 or #4 from the centre. Dorms €16, double €31.

Eating and drinking

Restaurants are clustered in the quaint, pedestrianized squares just west of rue de l'Ange, on and around place Marché-aux-Légumes and neighbouring place Chanoine Descamps.

Le Monde à L'Envers rue Lelièvre 28. Lively, fashionable bar just up from the cathedral. A favourite spot for university students.

Le Moulin à Poivre rue Bas de la Place 19. Cosy little restaurant offering tasty French food from premises just off place d'Armes. Main courses around €15.

Piano Bar place Marché-aux-Légumes. One of Namur's most popular bars. Live jazz Fri & Sat from 10pm.

Moving on

Train to: Brussels (every 30min; 1hr 15min); Luxembourg City (hourly; 1hr 40min); Marloie (for La Roche-en-Ardenne; hourly; 35min); Melreux (for La Roche-en-Ardenne; hourly; 1hr).

LA ROCHE-EN-ARDENNE

If you've had enough of Belgian cities or flat landscape, head to the **Ardennes** for a change of scene. **La Roche-en-Ardenne** is one of the area's best bases for outdoor activities; it's a small town and gets packed in the summer (mostly with young families), but it's easy to escape into the gorgeous woods that surround it. The only downside is that, aside from the town's fairly impressive **castle ruins** (daily 10/11am–4/5pm; €4), there's not too much to amuse you if the weather's bad.

Arrival and information

Train and bus The nearest stations to La Roche are Marloie and Melreux, both around half an hour away; buses leave every 2hr. Catch bus #3 from Melreux or #15 from Marloie (2hr 35min). Buses drop passengers off in the centre of town.

Tourist information place du Marché 15 (daily 9.30am–5pm, till 6pm July & Aug; ⓣ084 36 77 36, ⓦwww.la-roche-tourisme.com). Offers internet access, hiking information, plus hiking maps for a few euros.

Activities

There's no shortage of companies offering excursions and bike rental. Kayaking, hiking, mountain biking and rafting are the most popular activities; horseriding, archery and paragliding are also available.

Ardenne Aventures rue du Hadja 1 ⓣ084 41 19 00, ⓦwww.ardenne-aventures.be. Long (25km; €20) and short (10km; €15) kayak trips all year round, leaving hourly in high season; bike rental (3hr for €15); guided quad-bike outings (€45 for 45min); rafting (Nov–April; €18 for 1hr 30min). You can get good rates if you combine two activities on one day.

Brandsport *Auberge La Laiterie*, Mierchamps 15 ⓣ084 41 10 84, ⓦwww.brandsport.be. Orienteering (€15 for a half-day); forest rope adventures (€30); archery (€25 for a half-day). Horseriding, abseiling and caving can also be organized.

Laroch'ailes ⓦwww.larochailes.be. Local paragliding club which runs frequent events.

Les Kayaks de L'Ourthe rue de l'Eglise 35 ⓣ084 36 87 12, ⓦwww.kayaksdelourthe.be. Kayaking (10km €12; 25km €17); mountain bikes (€12 for 3hr).

Accommodation

Camping Le Vieux Moulin Petite Strument 62, about 800m to the south of the town centre along the Val du Bronze ⓣ084 41 15 07, ⓦwww.strument.com. Huge campsite with a picturesque setting beside a stream. Open Easter–Oct. €12 per person.

Domaine des Olivettes chemin de Soeret 12 ⓣ084 41 16 52, ⓦwww.lesolivettes.be. Fifteen minutes out of town, this relaxed place combines hostel, hotel, restaurant, bar and equestrian centre. Dorms €12, double €35 pp.

Eating and drinking

La Roche's restaurants are generally overpriced and underwhelming. Aside from *Le Clos René*, your best bet is to buy delicious local ham and pâté or an *assiette* of local produce from the butcher, Maison Bouillon et Fils, at place du Marché 9.

Le Clos René rue Chamont 30. Delightful pancake house that also serves delicious *cidre de poire*. Pancakes start at €6.

Luxembourg

Famous as a tax haven, financial centre and headquarters for various European institutions, the **Grand Duchy of Luxembourg**, one of Europe's smallest sovereign states, unsurprisingly gets written off by many travellers. However, this is a mistake: **Luxembourg City** is well worth a night or two.

LUXEMBOURG CITY

LUXEMBOURG CITY is one of the most spectacularly sited capitals in Europe. The valleys of the rivers Alzette and Pétrusse, which meet here, cut a green swathe through the city, their deep canyons formerly key to the city's defences.

What to see and do

Luxembourg City divides into four distinct sections. The tight grid of streets in the old town (northern side of the Pétrusse valley) holds most of the city's sights and is the most appealing quarter. Across the river, the modern city is less attractive but is home to the train station and cheap hotels. The atmospheric valleys of the **Grund** area (east) provide a great panorama from the massive bastions that secure the old town. The **Kirchberg** section (northeast) with its banks and striking modern buildings, provides a complete contrast to the old town.

The old town

The old town focuses on two squares, the more important of which is **place d'Armes**, fringed with cafés and restaurants. To the north lie the city's principal shops, mainly along **Grande Rue**, while on the southern side a small alley cuts through to the larger **place Guillaume**, the venue of Luxembourg's main general market (Wed & Sat am). Nearby, on rue du St-Esprit, the **Musée d'Histoire de la Ville de Luxembourg** (Tues–Sun 10am–6pm, Thurs till 8pm; €5; ⓦwww.musee-hist.lu) includes a permanent exhibition explaining Luxembourg's history, unusual temporary exhibitions and a glass-walled lift offering dramatic views of the Grund.

Just a few minutes' walk east of the museum on the montée de Clausen lie the **Casements du Bock** (March–Oct daily 10am–5pm; €1.75), underground fortifications built by the Spaniards in the eighteenth century.

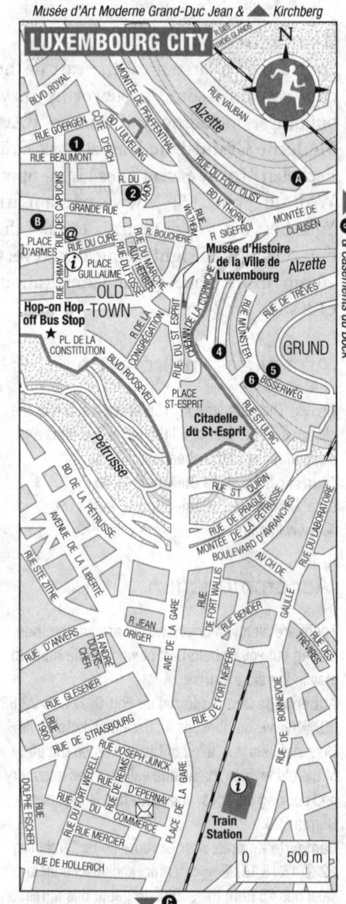

ACCOMMODATION	
Auberge de Jeunesse	A
Campsite Kockelscheuer	C
Français	B

EATING, DRINKING & NIGHTLIFE	
Art Café	1
Brasserie Bosso	5
Café des Artistes	4
Chiggeri	2
Rives de Clausen	3
Scott's Pub	6

The Grund

The dramatic **chemin de la Corniche** tracks the side of the cliff with great views of the slate-roofed houses of the quaint and leafy **Grund** down below. It leads to the gigantic **Citadelle du St-Esprit**, whose top has been levelled off and partly turned into a leafy park. The Grund is especially worth visiting on Wednesday and Friday nights when its bars kick into action.

Kirchberg

Spread over a large area, the east of the city contains some noteworthy new buildings, including the **Musée d'Art Moderne Grand-Duc Jean** at Park Dräi Eechelen 3 (daily except Tues 11am–6pm, Wed till 8pm; €5; Ⓦwww.mudam.lu). Your best bet to see them is to take the hop-on hop-off **sightseeing bus** (every 20min from place de la Constitution; €12; valid for 24hr).

Arrival and information

Arrival The train station, 15min walk south of the old town, is the hub of all the city's bus lines and close to many of the cheapest hotels.
Tourist office place Guillaume (Mon–Sat 9am–6/7pm, Sun 10am–6pm; Ⓣ22 28 09, Ⓦwww.lcto.lu).

Accommodation

There are plenty of cheap hotels around the train station but you're better off paying a little more to stay in the old town.
Auberge de Jeunesse rue du Fort Olisy 2 Ⓣ22 68 89, Ⓦwww.youthhostels.lu. Excellent, hotel-style HI hostel 3km northeast of the station on the edge of the old town in the Alzette valley. It has a laundry and cooking facilities, and breakfast is included. Dorms €20.
Campsite Kockelscheuer route de Bettembourg 22 Ⓣ47 18 15, Ⓦwww.camp-kockelscheuer.lu. Take bus #5 from the station to get to this agreeably located campsite three miles out of the city. Closed Nov–April. €8.50.
Français places d'Armes 14 Ⓣ47 45 34, Ⓦwww.hotelfrancais.lu. This attractive, if pricey, place has smart and spotless rooms furnished in crisp modern style. Great location, too, on the old town's main square, though light sleepers might do well to avoid the rooms at the front. €140.

Eating

The old town is crowded with inexpensive cafés and restaurants. French cuisine is popular here, but traditional Luxembourgish dishes are found on many menus too, mostly meaty affairs such as neck of pork with broad beans (*judd mat gaardebounen*) or black sausage (*blutwurst*). Keep an eye out also for *gromperenkichelchen* (potato cakes usually served with apple sauce) and, in winter, stalls and cafés selling *glühwein* (mulled wine).
Art Café rue Beaumont 1a. Beautiful café decorated in the style of a plush theatre. Mains €10.
Brasserie Bosso rue Bisserweg 7. In the Grund part of town, this friendly restaurant has a lovely terrace and an extensive menu including many Luxembourgish options. Mains €12.

Drinking and nightlife

There's a lively bar scene in the old town and Grund, and the new development of pubs and restaurants at Rives de Clausen (10min walk from the HI hostel) gets especially busy on Fri evenings.
Café des Artistes Montée du Grund 22. Edith Piaf would feel at home in this very atmospheric little piano bar with frequent singalongs. Live music Wed–Sat. Closed Mon.
Chiggeri rue du Nord 15. Popular bar in the old town that has a great atmosphere, funky decor and a mixed straight and gay clientele. Wi-fi available.
Scott's Pub rue Bisserweg 4. Loud pub in the Grund with a young, expat crowd: the most backpacker-friendly hang-out in Luxembourg.

Directory

Bike rental Vélo en Ville, rue Bisserweg 8, Grund Ⓣ496 23 83 (Mon–Fri 10am–noon & 1–8pm, plus Sat & Sun Easter–Oct). Advance booking advised.
Internet Cyber-Beach, rue du Curé 3.
Laundry Quick-Wash, rue de Strasbourg 31.
Left luggage At the train station.
Pharmacies Goedert, place d'Armes 5; Mortier, av de la Gare 11.
Post office rue Aldringen 25 (Mon–Fri 7am–7pm, Sat 7am–5pm).

Moving on

Train to: Brussels (hourly; 2hr 40min); Cologne (hourly; 5hr); Namur (hourly; 1hr 40min); Nancy (every 40min; 1hr 30min); Strasbourg (hourly; 2hr).

Bosnia-Herzegovina

HIGHLIGHTS

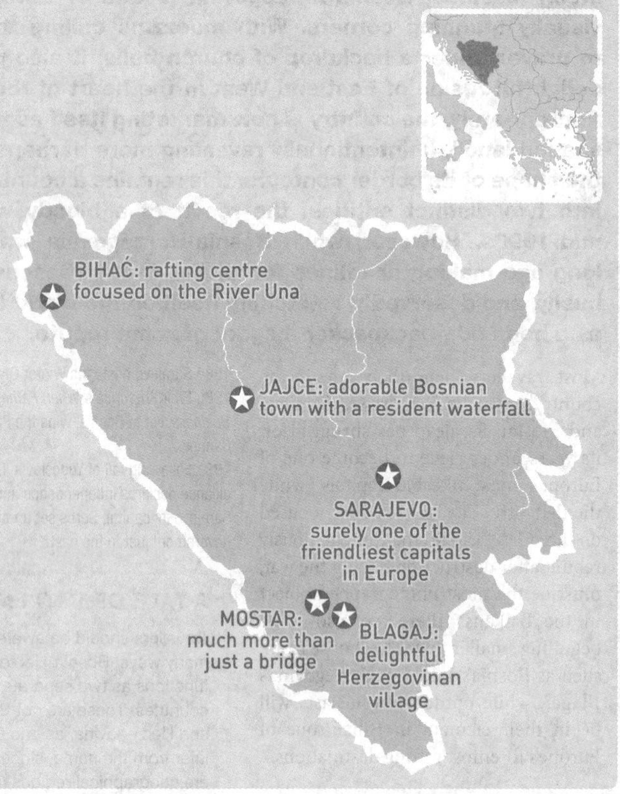

BIHAĆ: rafting centre focused on the River Una
JAJCE: adorable Bosnian town with a resident waterfall
SARAJEVO: surely one of the friendliest capitals in Europe
MOSTAR: much more than just a bridge
BLAGAJ: delightful Herzegovinan village

ROUGH COSTS

DAILY BUDGET Basic €25/occasional treat €40

DRINK Bosnian coffee €0.50–1

FOOD čevapčići (meat rissoles) €2–4

HOSTEL/BUDGET HOTEL €12/€25

TRAVEL Sarajevo–Bihać (341km) €25 by bus; Sarajevo–Mostar (135km) €5 by train.

FACT FILE

POPULATION 4 million

AREA 51,197 sq km

LANGUAGES Bosnian, Croatian, Serbian

CURRENCY Convertible Mark (KM)

CAPITAL Sarajevo (population 400,000)

INTERNATIONAL PHONE CODE ☎387

Introduction

A land where turquoise rivers run swift and sheep huddle on steep hillsides, Bosnia-Herzegovina is one of Europe's most visually stunning corners. With muezzins calling the faithful to prayer under a backdrop of church bells, it also provides a delightful fusion of East and West in the heart of the Balkans. Appropriately, the country is now marketing itself as the "heart-shaped land", unintentionally revealing more perhaps than just the shape of its border contours: this remains a country cleaved into two distinct entities, the result of a bloody war in the mid-1990s. However, while Bosnia-Herzegovina was not too long ago making headlines for all the wrong reasons, it's now busily, and deservedly, re-etching itself on the world travel map as a bona fide backpacker magnet of some repute.

Most travellers spend their time in the country's two major draws: Sarajevo and Mostar. Sarajevo has shrugged off its years under siege to become one of Europe's most likeable capitals, while the delightful city of **Mostar** is focused on an Old Bridge that, meticulously rebuilt after destruction during the war, must be the most photographed object in the Balkans. There are also some beguiling smaller towns to choose from, such as Bosnia's **Jajce**, or Herzegovina's **Blagaj**, while outdoor enthusiasts will be in their element in **Bihać**, one of Europe's foremost rafting destinations.

CHRONOLOGY

9 AD Annexed by Rome.
395 Division of Roman Empire; the area that comprises today's Bosnia-Herzegovina stays under rule of Rome.
553 Emperor Justinian I conquers the area for the Byzantine Empire.
1463 Bosnia falls to the Ottoman Empire.
1482 Herzegovina falls to the Ottoman Empire.
1878 Russian defeat of Turkey sees Bosnia-Herzegovina transferred to Austria-Hungary.
1914 Franz Ferdinand shot in Sarajevo by a Bosnian Serb, eventually leading to World War I.
1918 Bosnia-Herzegovina becomes part of the Kingdom of Serbs, Croats and Slovenes.
1961 Ivo Andrić, born near Travnik, wins the Nobel Prize for Literature.
1984 Sarajevo hosts the Winter Olympics.
1985 Emir Kusturica's *When Father Was Away on Business*, set in Bosnia, wins the Palme d'Or at Cannes.
1991 Following fall of Yugoslavia, Croat-Muslim alliance declares independence and makes Sarajevo its capital; Serbs set up their own government just to the east.

A TALE OF TWO ENTITIES

Travellers should be aware that, in many ways, Bosnia-Herzegovina functions as two separate countries. These are not Bosnia and Herzegovina, as one might infer from the name, since these are geographical regions (Bosnia makes up around 80 percent of the country, with Herzegovina a small triangle south of Sarajevo). Rather, the country is split along ethnic lines. To the west, and including Sarajevo, is the **Federation of Bosnia and Herzegovina**, a Muslim-Croat alliance; while to the east and north is the **Republika Srpska**, an ethnic-Serb territory of almost equal size, centred on its capital Banja Luka. To add to the confusion, there are three official languages – all essentially the same – and three presidents. "Most countries just have one idiot in charge", says a local, "but we've got three."

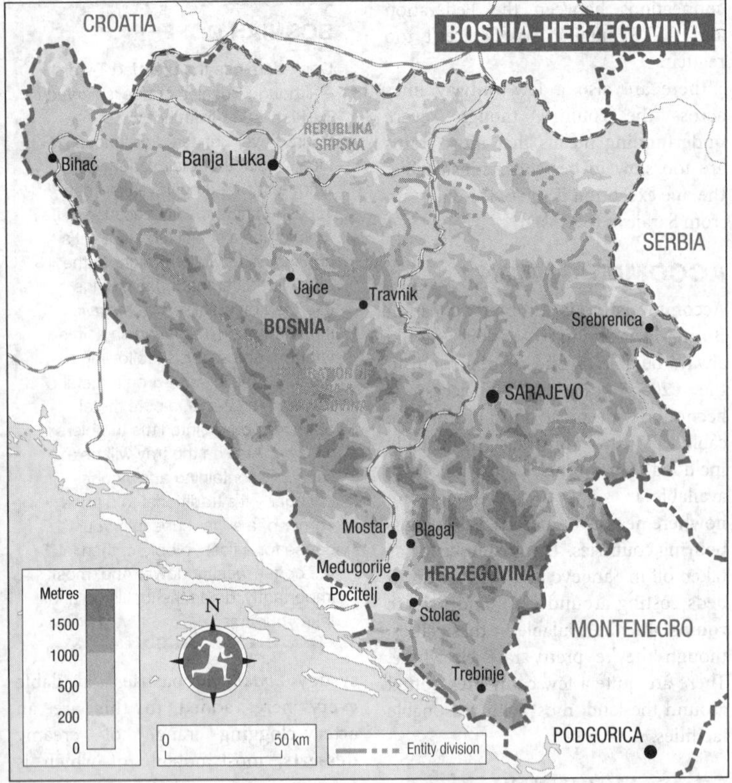

1992 Led by Radovan Karadžić, Bosnian Serbs start campaign of "ethnic cleansing".
1993 Fighting breaks out between Croats and Muslims.
1995 NATO shelling ends siege of Sarajevo; peace terms set out by Dayton Agreement.
2001 *No Man's Land* becomes the first Bosnian movie to win an Academy Award.
2008 Radovan Karadžić arrested on charges of war crimes.

ARRIVAL

As close to landlocked as it's possible to get, Bosnia-Herzegovina is fairly easy to enter from all sides. Sarajevo serves **trains** from Belgrade and Budapest, while a daily service between the Croatian cities of Ploče and Zagreb runs through Mostar and Sarajevo on the way. **Bus** connections are more numerous and points of origin include Podgorica, Split and a number of German cities. There are a smattering of international **flights** from Western Europe, but those seeking budget carriers must fly in to Zagreb or Dubrovnik.

GETTING AROUND

Bosnia-Herzegovina isn't the easiest country to get around, since much of its transport infrastructure – particularly the rail network – was damaged during the war. Things are improving, however, and decent **bus** services will almost always be able to get you where you want to go; it'll just take a little longer than you might expect, and perhaps cost a little more too. Also note that

connections between the Federation and the Republika Srpska aren't too regular.

There are also a few **railway** lines across the country, though severe underfunding means that most trains are too slow to be worth considering; the one exception is the twice-daily run from Sarajevo to Mostar.

ACCOMMODATION

Accommodation is still pretty cheap in Bosnia-Herzegovina – you should always be able to find a **hotel** room in the €20–35 range. Wi-fi access is becoming widespread, most rooms have cable TV, and breakfast is usually included. **Guesthouses** (*pansiona*) are available in some towns, though are nowhere near as numerous as in neighbouring countries. The **hostel** scene has taken off in Sarajevo and Mostar (dorm beds costing around €12), and **private rooms** are still available in these cities, though they're pretty rare elsewhere. There are quite a few **campsites** dotted around the land, most with reasonable facilities.

FOOD AND DRINK

Centuries of Ottoman rule have left Turkish fingerprints on the nation's **cuisine**. You'll find *ćevapčići* joints everywhere, selling grilled meat rissoles that are usually served up with *somun* (spongy bread) and chopped onion. Similarly hard to avoid are stands selling *burek*, greasy pastries filled with meat, spinach, cheese and sometimes pumpkin or potato; many travellers rate Sarajevo the best *burek* city in the Balkans. Soups (*čorba*) and vegetables pop up all over the place on the country's menus, though more often than not the latter are stuffed with mincemeat; **vegetarians** will often have to content themselves with salads, or certain selections from the ubiquitous pizzerias. Sweeties also have a Turkish ring to them, with syrupy *baklava* pastries available everywhere; added to this are an artery-clogging range of creamy **desserts**, most notable of which is *tufahije*, a marinaded apple topped with walnut and cream.

The consumption of **coffee** (*kafa*) has been elevated to something approaching an art form (see box above). For alcohol, there are a few good domestic **beers** (*pivo*), and Herzegovina produces a lot of **wine** – try Blatina, a local variety of red. Locals are also fond of telling guests that Bosnian tap water is safe to drink – evidently a major source of pride.

BOSNIAN COFFEE

Don't dare use the dreaded T-word – although Bosnian coffee is served **Turkish-style**, with hot water poured over unfiltered grounds, locals insist that their variety is unique. It's markedly weaker than Turkish coffee, mainly because of its function as a social lubricant – it's consumed fervidly throughout the day, with different coffee sittings ascribed different terms: *razgalica* in the morning, *razgovoruša* a little later on, and *sikteruša* following a meal. Coffee is **served** on a metal tray from a *džezva*, a cute metal pot, and poured into little tumblers (*fildžan*). Also on the tray will be a *šečerluk*, containing a few cubes of sugar – it's traditional to dip the corner of a sugar cube into your coffee for a flash, nibble it, then let the coffee wash it down. And, most importantly, do as the locals do and take your time.

CULTURE AND ETIQUETTE

It's imperative to note that there are three distinct **ethnicities** in Bosnia-Herzegovina – **Bosnian Serb**, mostly Orthodox; **Bosnian Croat**, mostly Catholic; and Muslims known as **Bosniaks**. Of course, they had

something of a coming together in the mid-1990s; the **war** affected every single person in the country, and reverberations can still be felt today – it's never too far away from people's minds. Some locals are more than willing to talk about their experiences, particularly in Sarajevo, but of course it's best to let them make the first move.

Also worth noting is the **geographical split** evident in the country's name – you'll find yourself using "Bosnian" as an adjective most of the time, and this is accepted, though in Herzegovina it's a bit of a faux pas to tell locals how much you're "enjoying Bosnia".

As for the more regular facets of travel etiquette, you should **dress** conservatively around religious buildings, leave small change or a little more as **tips** in a restaurant, and be aware that for all the ethnic rivalry, **smoking** is perhaps the country's dominant religion.

SPORTS AND OUTDOOR ACTIVITIES

Bosnia-Herzegovina is pretty good for outdoor pursuits. Beefy mountains mean that **hiking** is popular, though the continued presence of landmines means that you should seek local confirmation that an area is safe before setting off. During winter, a few **ski** slopes around Sarajevo come to life, while there's year-round **rafting** to be had on several of the country's rushing rivers – best is the Una, near Bihać.

COMMUNICATIONS

Most **post offices** (*pošta*) are open weekdays from 9am–5pm, and often on Saturday mornings too. Public **phones** use cards, which can be bought at post offices and kiosks, but it's usually cheaper to make international calls at a post office. **Internet** access is fairly widespread, even in small towns, and you should expect to pay 1–2KM/hr.

BOSNIA-HERZEGOVINA ON THE NET

www.bhtourism.ba Official tourist board site.
www.bhmac.org Contains some useful info about landmine dangers.
www.sonar.ba Excellent event listings, mainly focused on Sarajevo.

EMERGENCIES

With the war still fresh in many minds, travellers often arrive expecting Bosnia-Herzegovina to be a dangerous place; it will quickly become clear that this is not the case, and that the **crime rate** is very low by European standards. The country's two **police** forces are usually easy to deal with, but keep your passport or a copy handy in case of a spot check. One very important danger to note is the presence of **landmines**. Strewn liberally during the war, the vast majority have now been cleared, and there's no danger in any urban area. In the countryside, however, it's advisable to stick to clear paths.

Pharmacies usually follow shop hours, though in larger cities you'll likely find ones that stay open until late, sometimes even 24 hours.

INFORMATION

Larger cities have **tourist information offices** with English-speaking staff; some can make accommodation bookings. Free city **maps** are handed out at most hotels and all tourist offices.

MONEY AND BANKS

The currency of Bosnia-Herzegovina is the **convertible mark**, usually abbreviated to KM. Notes of 5, 10, 20, 50, 100

EMERGENCY NUMBERS

Police ☎122; Ambulance ☎124; Fire ☎123.

Bosnian

The Bosnian language is essentially the same as Serbian, which is essentially the same as Croatian (see p.257), and all three are listed as official languages in Bosnia-Herzegovina. Note that the Republika Srpska uses the **Cyrillic alphabet**, which may cause some problems with street signs, menus and timetables.

and 200 KM are in circulation, as are coins of 10, 20 and 50 feninga, and 1, 2 and 5 KM. Exchange **rates** are currently around 1.96KM to the euro, 2.28KM to the pound, and 1.39KM to the US dollar. One interesting little quirk of Bosno-Herzegovinan society is an apparent allergy to **large notes** – even paying for a 2KM coffee with a 5KM bill may result in a ten-minute hunt for change, while whipping out a 50KM bill for a small purchase will see you laughed down the road.

Accommodation prices are almost always quoted in euros, as are meals at some upmarket restaurants. In urban areas you won't have to look too far for an **ATM**, and **exchange offices** are plentiful in places used to tourists. **Banks** are usually open weekdays from 9am to 4pm, and often on Saturday mornings too.

OPENING HOURS AND HOLIDAYS

Times are less rigid here than in most countries – **shops** usually open when they want to open, which in most cases is after 10am, and in larger cities there's little difference on weekends. All banks and post offices will be closed on **public holidays** – January 1, March 1, May 1 and November 25 – though these dates are far from the end of the story as the Catholic and Orthodox churches celebrate Easter and Christmas at different times, and Muslims celebrate a biannual holiday known as Bajram.

Sarajevo

With their imaginations and travel memories fired by spiky minarets, grilled kebabs and the all-pervasive aroma of ground coffee, many travellers see in **SARAJEVO** a Slavic mini-Istanbul. The Ottoman notes in the air are most prominent in Baščaršija, the city's delightful Old Town, which is home to umpteen mosques, bazaars, kebab restaurants and cafés. Further afield, burnt-out buildings evoke the catastrophic war of the mid-1990s, though the fun-loving, easy-going Sarajevans do a great job of painting over the scars of those tumultuous years – it's hard to walk around without being offered coffee, and it's hard to be invited for coffee without making friends.

Sarajevo gained importance during **Roman** times, and after a short slumber was reinvigorated as a trading hub during the **Ottoman** period, but sadly its recent history is far more pertinent. The international spotlight fell on the city as the host of the **1984 Winter Olympics**, but less than a decade later the world's eyes were retrained on it during a **siege** that lasted for almost four years – by some estimates, the longest in military history. Bosnian Serb forces made a near-unbroken ring around the city, shelling major buildings and shooting civilians dead on their way to work, while years of litter lay rotting in the streets. When the ceasefire was announced in 1996, around ten thousand people had been killed; on the ground you may notice some of the many **Sarajevo Roses** – flower-like scars of mortar shell explosions, poignantly filled in with red resin.

What to see and do

The central district of **Baščaršija** is Sarajevo's prettiest and contains most of its sights. Heading west from here, the city's history unravels like a tapestry – Ottoman-era mosques slowly give way to the churches and elaborate buildings of the Austro-Hungarian period, before communist behemoths herald your arrival into "Sniper Alley" and its shells of war.

Baščaršija

The pedestrianized streets of **Baščaršija** are a delight to wander around, and the area is filled to the brim with cafés, snack stands and trinket stalls. It's most logical to approach this district from the east, where you'll find the once-glorious **National Library**, a pink-and-yellow cream cake of faded beauty that's still begging for restoration – in 1992, a single day's shelling destroyed over three million books. A little way along is the central square, home to **Sebilj**, a small fountain, and **Baščaršija Mosque**. Far more beautiful is the **Gazi Husrev Beg Mosque** just down the way, which is worth a peep inside. Further west, you'll come across the **Bezistan**, an Ottoman-era bazaar now sadly filled with football shirts, racks of sunglasses and other goods unsuited to such an elegant structure.

Baščaršija is also home to the six buildings that make up the **Museum of Sarajevo** – by far the largest is located inside the old Bursa Bezistan bazaar (Mon–Sat 10am–4pm; 2KM), just off the main square.

The Latin Bridge and around

Heading through the Bezistan will bring you close to the **Latin Bridge**, scene of the assassination of Archduke Franz Ferdinand and, by extension, the start of World War I; off the northern end, a small **museum** commemorates the incident (Mon–Sat 10am–4pm; 2KM). Across the Miljacka River you'll see the fascinating **Papagajka**, a decaying yellow-and-green residential block apparently designed with hovercars in

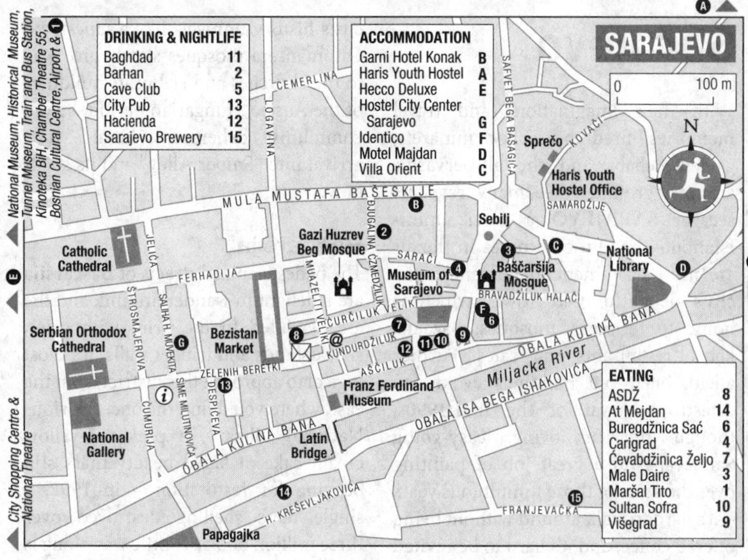

mind – this is how the Jetsons may have lived under Communism. Back in the centre are the **Catholic cathedral** and a **Serbian Orthodox church** – both rather beautiful – and the **City Shopping Centre**, which was the only place to buy and exchange goods during the siege. Also in the area is the National Gallery (Mon–Fri 10am–6pm; free), whose rolling exhibitions can feature anything from kids' paintings to black-and-white wartime photography.

"Sniper Alley" museums

Within walking distance west of Baščaršija are a pair of museums that count as the city's best. First is the elegant **National Museum** (Tues–Fri & Sun 10am–3pm; 5KM), which has an interesting and varied collection of artefacts amongst its pillars and domes, and puts on good rolling exhibitions. A stone's throw away is the **Historical Museum** (Mon–Fri 9am–4pm, Sat & Sun 9am–1pm; 4KM). Don't be put off by the somewhat brutal exterior and shabby entrance, as there's plenty to see; the permanent exhibition details how Sarajevo functioned during the siege. On the other side of the main road it's worth peeking inside the **Holiday Inn**, a distinctive yellow building that was the city's only functioning hotel during the siege, and as home to foreign journalists was also one of its safest places.

Accessible on tours laid on by the tourist office is the interesting **Tunnel Museum** (tours 9am & 2pm; €12). During the siege, the only way in or out of Sarajevo was via the NATO-held airport, the only break in the city's surrounding ring of Serb forces; an 800m-long tunnel dug underneath the runways provided access. At the museum, you'll be played a home-movie-style DVD that describes the tunnel's creation, and the reasoning behind it, before being led through a small section of the now-collapsed route.

Arrival and information

Air Sarajevo's airport is just 7km from the city centre, a trip that will cost 17–20KM by cab.

Train and bus The stations are located almost alongside each other west of Baščaršija. It's a half-hour walk into the centre, a short trip on tram #1, or a 7KM cab ride.

Tourist office Zelenih Beretki 22. Pretty useful place, able to advise on accommodation and sightseeing (Mon–Fri 9am–5.30pm, Sat & Sun 9am–3pm).
Tours Both the *Haris* and *City Center* hostels organize popular day-long tours of surrounding sights for about €15. The tourist office also puts on a slightly overpriced "Tunnel Tour" (see opposite).
Listings Try to pick up a copy of the useful *Sarajevo Navigator*, a monthly booklet available at the tourist office and most hotels, and check out Ⓦwww.sonar.ba.

City transport

Public transport An efficient system of buses, trams and trolleybuses operates throughout the city from 5am to 1am. Tickets can be bought from a kiosk for 1.60KM, or for 1.80KM from the driver; be sure to validate your ticket on board, as fines are steep and ticket inspectors strict.
Taxis are pretty cheap with flagfall at 2KM, though a ride in the centre is more likely to cost around 5KM.

Accommodation

Hotels have always been a bit pricey in Sarajevo, but the city now has a fair few hostels. If you get stuck, agencies around Baščaršija will be able to set you up with a private room.

Hostels

Haris Youth Hostel Vratnik Mejdan 29 ⓣ033/232563, Ⓦwww.hyh.ba. Friendly hostel a 15min walk uphill from the centre. Check in at their office, near the Baščaršija tram stop, and they'll give you and your bag a free ride up. Can sometimes collect from the station too. €12.
Hostel City Center Sarajevo Muvekita 2/3 ⓣ033/203213, Ⓦwww.hcc.ba. Central location, stylish fittings, friendly owners, free coffee, cereal and internet, comfy common areas, low price. Could this be the perfect hostel? €12.

Hotels

Garni Hotel Konak Mula Mustafe Bašeskije 48 ⓣ033/476900, Ⓦwww.hotel-konak.com. Amiable business hotel. In addition to their somewhat pricey rooms, they are able to organize private accommodation from €15 per bed. €100.
Identico Halači 3 ⓣ033/233310, Ⓔidentiko@bih.net.ba. Super-cheap guesthouse in the city centre, though paper-thin walls mean that it can get noisy. €30.

TREAT YOURSELF

Hecco Deluxe Ferhadija 2 ⓣ033/559995, Ⓦwww.hotel-hecco.net. Hovering over the city centre this immaculate boutique hotel occupies the top three floors of a tall block, and its luxurious rooms are a steal. The restaurant is good for coffee (3KM) or a light meal (from 10KM) whether you're staying here or not. €90.

Motel Mejdan Mustaj-Pašin Mejdan 11 ⓣ033/233 563, Ⓦwww.motelmejdan.com. Tucked into the hillside near the river, this motel feels quite secluded despite its proximity to the centre. €45.
Villa Orient Oprkanj 6 ⓣ033/232 754, Ⓔorient@bih.net.ba. Comfortable rooms in an attractive, central hotel. €70.

Eating

It's hard to walk for five metres in Baščaršija without coming across yet another *kebapči* joint. *Burek* is similarly easy to hunt down, and many travellers rate it the best in the Balkans.

Cafés

At Mejdan Obala Isa Bega Ishakovića. Set in and around a park-centre pavilion near the Latin Bridge, this is a great place for coffee on a summer's day. Also has occasional jazz or orchestral music shows in the evening.
Carigrad Trgovke. Mouthwatering selection of rich cakes, syrupy *baklava* and other sweet sins from just 1.50KM.
Male Daire Luleđina. Peace-out café just behind the Baščaršija Mosque, where you can throw down good Bosnian coffee for 1.50KM, and suck on a *nargileh* for just 5KM. Across the way, *Dibek* is similar and prettier, but usually pumps out awful music.
Maršal Tito Bihaćka. Military-themed café-bar tucked under a wing of the Historical Museum. With socialist realist pictures on the inside and a gunship sitting outside, it's an interesting place to drink and chat.

Restaurants

ASDŽ Ćurčiluk Mali 3. Curiously named canteen-style restaurant with rows of simple, tasty local staples to choose from, usually costing 6KM a plate. Service can be gruff.

Buregdžnica Sać Bravadžiluk Halači. With something as simple as *burek*, there should be very little to choose between purveyors, but the ones on offer here are simply a cut above the rest. Try the pumpkin (*tykva*) variety, with lashings of yoghurt. 2–3KM per portion.
Ćevabdžinica Željo Kućna Dostava. Other Baščaršija kebab joints may be a little more polished, but this pair – close by each other – are always packed with locals, who know that they provide the most bang for their buck. 6KM for ten *kebapči*.
Sultan Sofra Kundurdžiluk. Turkish fast-food joint. A *pide* (funny-shaped pizza) will cost from 7KM, though penny-pinchers will appreciate the *lahmacun* (small, normal-shaped pizza) which will fill a hole for just 2KM.
Višegrad Halači 14. Pleasantly old-fashioned two-level restaurant, whose menu is packed with stuffed vegetables. Figure on 10KM for a decent feed, a little more if you fancy a drink.

Drinking and nightlife

Baghdad Bazerdžani 6. Elaborate, dimly lit cocktail bar that may well be the best looking in Sarajevo. Drinks are a little pricey, though.
Barhana Đjugalina 8. Set in a tucked-away courtyard and good for a quiet drink, particularly on one of the candlelit outdoor tables.
Cave Club South bank of the Miljacka. Taking the word "cavernous" to at least one literal extremity, this booming club is popular with locals who fancy a dance and a cocktail. On warm evenings they throw beanbags onto the river bridge – a great chill-out area.
City Pub Despićeva. An English-style pub may not sound that interesting, but this is usually the busiest place in town on weekday evenings. Thursday is music night.
Hacienda Bazerdžani 3. Mexican-themed bar that throws parties most nights; most raucous are the weekend DJ sets.
Sarajevo Brewery Franjevačka. If you like Sarajevsko Pivo, why not head straight for the source? Their city-centre factory has a large, ornate bar out back, where it costs 5KM for a large glass of the good stuff.

Entertainment

Bosnian Cultural Centre Branilaca Sarajeva 24 ⓦwww.bkc.ba. Large venue used for concerts and suchlike.
Chamber Theatre 55 Maršala Tita 54 ⓦwww .kamerniteatar55.ba. Homely place used by the more experimental elements of Sarajevo's theatre.
Kinoteka BiH Alipašina 19 ⓦwww.kinotekabih .ba. Interesting mix of subtitled movies shown weekdays at 7pm.
National Theatre Obala Kilina Bala. The largest such place in the country, and home to Sarajevo's opera and ballet academies.
Sarajevo War Theatre Gabelina 16. Hosts a fascinating clutch of performances from home and abroad.

FESTIVALS IN SARAJEVO

Baščaršija Nights ⓦwww .bascarsijskenoci.ba. An array of ballet, theatre, music and art exhibitions spread across the month of July.
Sarajevo Film Festival ⓦwww.sff .ba. One of the most important film festivals in the Balkans, and largely focused on the region's own output. Held in August.
MESS ⓦwww.mess.ba. International, English-centred festival of theatre. October.
Jazz Fest ⓦwww.jazzfest.ba. Decent jazz festival, usually held in November.
Saravejo Winter ⓦwww .sarajevskazima.ba. Artistic festival taking place each November.

Shopping

Most useful to the traveller is a small area around Mula Mustafa Bašeskije, where you'll find a couple of appealing markets – indoor and outdoor – and a few second-hand clothing stores. The most appealing souvenir purchase is a Bosnian coffee set: while whole teams of Baščaršija stands sell cheap ones, Sprečo on Kovači 15 sells beautiful hand-made copper-and-tin sets for €30.

Directory

Embassies and consulates Canada, Grbavička 4 ⓣ033/222033; UK, Tina Ujevića 8 ⓣ033/282200; US, Alipašina 43 ⓣ033/445700.
Money Banks and ATMs are everywhere, and currency can be exchanged in the train station.
Hospital Kranjčevićeva 12 ⓣ033/208100.
Internet Kundurdžiluk 1, and in the same alcove as *Sultan Sofra*.

SKIING AROUND SARAJEVO

The slopes around Sarajevo are great for skiing: **Jahorina** is the closest resort to town (Ⓦwww.oc-jahorina.com), and has over 30km of ski runs; day-passes start at 25MK, equipment can be rented, and there are a fair few hotels and **pansions** around. There is usually one very early bus a day from Sarajevo.

Pharmacy Obala Kulina 7 (Ⓣ033/272300; daily 8am–8pm) and Zelenih Beretki 28 (Ⓣ033/626200; Mon–Sat 9am–8pm).
Post office Zmaja od Bosne 88 (Mon–Sat 7am–8pm).

Moving on

Train Belgrade (daily; 9hr); Budapest (daily; 11hr); Mostar (2 daily; 3hr 30min). Zagreb (2 daily; 9hr).
Bus Belgrade (daily; 7hr); Bihać (3 daily; 7hr); Dubrovnik (daily; 6hr); Jajce (3 daily; 3hr 30min); Mostar (12 daily; 2hr 30min); Travnik (5 daily; 2hr); Zagreb (3 daily; 8hr).

Bosnia

Occupying roughly four-fifths of the country, mountainous Bosnia contains some of the country's most appealing towns, and helpfully all can be visited on a fairly straight route linking Sarajevo and Zagreb. First up, get a sense of medieval history in **Travnik**, Bosnia's former capital, then head to **Jajce**, a tiny town with a waterfall crashing through its centre. Lastly there's laid-back **Bihać**, one of Europe's best rafting hotspots.

TRAVNIK

Just a couple of hours out of Sarajevo, **TRAVNIK** is a good day-trip target, though its position on a main transport route detracts slightly from a delightful setting. This was the **Bosnian capital** during the latter part of Ottoman rule, and the residence of high-ranking officials known as viziers – you'll see their tombs (*turbe*) dotted around town. More recently, Travnik also gained fame as the birthplace of Ivo Andrić, a Nobel Prize-winning novelist whose *Bosnian Chronicle* was set in his hometown.

The best place to soak up Travnik's history is its majestic fifteenth-century **castle** (10am–6pm; 1.5KM), built to hold off Ottoman forces but completed a few years too late. It's now great for a clamber around, and provides spectacular views of the surrounding mountains. Just under the castle is **Plavna Voda**, a quiet huddle of streamside **restaurants** where you can eat trout caught further upstream.

JAJCE

Whereas Travnik has grown a little too busy for its size, little **JAJCE** is simply adorable – even its name is cute, a diminutive form of the word "egg", and therefore translating as something like "egglet". The name is said to derive from the shape of a hill jutting up in the Old Town, ringed with walls and topped with an impressive **citadel**. In the Middle Ages, Bosnian kings were crowned just down the hill in the **Church of St Mary**; the last coronation, of Stjepan Tomašević, took place here in 1461, but two years later the king had his head lopped off during the Ottoman invasion. Opposite the church are the **catacombs** (1KM), essentially an underground church, complete with a narthex, nave, presbytery and baptistry; you'll find the keyholder in the restaurant opposite. Further downhill, the 21-metre-high **waterfalls** are a splendid sight, despite the pounding they took during the Bosnian conflict.

Jajce's **bus station** is a short walk from all the main sights, but there are

very few **places to stay**, so book ahead to get a room at the excellent *Stari Grad* (Ⓣ030/654006; €42) in the Old Town. Failing that, rooms at the *Hotel Turist* (Ⓣ030/654144, Ⓦwww.hotel-turist98.com; €42) are far nicer than its horrid exterior might suggest. There are a few **restaurants** dug into the cliffside just over the bridge from the bus station, but most notable is *Vodopad*, just inside the gates, which doles out colossal double-scoop ice creams for just 1KM – don't expect to finish one if the weather's hot.

BIHAĆ

Herzegovina has no shortage of great **rafting** locales, but Bosnia's **BIHAĆ** beats them all. The crystal-clear **River Una** rushes through town, though it's a little further upstream that you'll find the best rafting; the river is highest in the spring and autumn. Adventure sports aside, Bihać is a pleasant, compact town with a cheerful pedestrianized zone in the centre. Here you'll find the **Church of Zvonik** and **Fathija Mosque**, but most interesting is the **Captain's Tower**, once a prison, now a museum (9am–4pm, to 2pm Sat, closed Sun; 1KM).

Central Bihać is small enough to walk around, and the **bus station** is conveniently located at the north of town. The best **accommodation** for budget travellers is just down the road at the switched-on *Villa Una* (Ⓣ037/311393; €35), who can help to organize rafting trips; otherwise the area is great for **campsites**, particularly the *Aduna* (Ⓣ037/221431, Ⓦwww.aduna.ba), a riverside site 5km from town. For **food**, try fresh fish at the *River Una*, so close to the water that you can bathe your feet, or good pizza across the bridge in the attractive *Belvedere*.

RAFTING IN NORTHWEST BOSNIA

Rafting in the Bihać area is possible year-round – the continuous flow of tourist traffic means that you'll usually be able to join a group (6–10 per boat) in any month, though the main season runs from March to October. Six kilometres from town, **Una Kiro** (Ⓣ037/361110, Ⓦwww.una-kiro-rafting.com) is the best set up company for foreigners, and has a camping ground next to their base. There are three main routes to choose from; listed per-person prices include equipment and transport, but not meals.

Kostela-Bosanska Krupa An easy 24km, 5hr stretch that's best for novices. €37.

Kostela-Grmuša Short, but packs in a few meaty rapids on a 13km, 3hr course. €27.

Štrbački Buk-Lohovo An absolutely terrifying 15km, 4hr route featuring a 25m rapid. €42.

Herzegovina

Wedged into the far south of the country, little Herzegovina is less known than its big brother, Bosnia, but this land of muscular peaks and rushing rivers arguably has more to see. Pride of place goes to **Mostar** and its famed Old Bridge, but it's worth venturing outside the city to see little **Blagaj**, or absorb the religious curiosities of **Međugorije**. Those on their way to Dubrovnik or Montenegro should also call in at **Trebinje**, by far the most pleasant town in the Republika Srpska.

MOSTAR

On arrival at the train or bus station, you may be forgiven for thinking that the beauty of **MOSTAR** has been somewhat exaggerated. There then begins a slow descent to the Old Town, during which it becomes more and

more apparent that it really is something very special indeed. Attentive ears will pick out rushing streams, salesmen crying their wares, as well as church bells and muezzins competing for attention, while steep, cobblestoned streets slowly wind their way down to the fast-flowing, turquoise-blue Neretva River and its Old Bridge, incredibly photogenic even when the Speedo-clad *mostari* – the brave gents who dive from the apex – aren't tumbling into the waters below.

Mostar's history is irrevocably entwined with that of its bridge. Like hundreds of locals, this was to fall victim in 1993 when the Croats and Muslims of the town, previously united against the Serbs, turned on each other: the **conflict** rumbled on for two long years, each side sniping at the other from opposing hills. Locals claim that prior to the war, more than half of the city's marriages were mixed, but the figure has since dwindled to nothing; while relations have started to improve, bitterness remains in the air, and messages of hate still graffitied onto the walls.

What to see and do

The **Old Town**, spanning both sides of the Neretva, contains most things of interest in Mostar, and in its centre is the **Old Bridge**, focal point of the city and the obvious place to kick off your sightseeing. On the eastern bank is the more interesting Muslim part of town, while the west is mainly home to Catholic Croats.

The Old Bridge

Transit point, dungeon, tourist attraction, war victim and macho launchpad, Mostar's small, hump-backed **Stari Most** has led an interesting life. With tradesmen terrified by the rickety nature of its wooden predecessor and the fast-flowing Neretva below, it was built in the 1560s at the instigation of Suleyman the Magnificent. Those employed to guard the bridge were called the **mostari**, a term later borrowed when naming the city, and then used to describe the brave gents who dive from the apex, 21m down into the Neretva. After 427 years in service, the bridge was strategically destroyed by Croat forces in November 1993, symbolizing the ethnic division of the city. There then began the arduous process of rebuilding it piece by piece, following the same techniques used in its initial construction, and it only fully reopened in 2004. The *mostari* are still there, day after day; they'll try to work the crowd into shelling out an acceptable fee – officially a secret, but sneaky investigations have found the precise figure to be €50 – before taking the plunge. Join them if you dare, especially in July, when the annual **diving festival** marks the highlight of Mostar's year.

The east bank

Off the eastern end of the bridge is **Helebija**, a tower that now accommodates the enlightening **Old Bridge Museum** (daily except Mon 10am–6pm; 5KM), spread over four levels, and topped with a viewing point; you'll be able to see pictures of the bridge's destruction, and footage of its rebirth. Lined with trinket stores, cobblestoned Kujundžiluk then climbs uphill, soon leading to the **Koski Mehmed Paša Mosque**. For all its beauty, the panoply of souvenir sellers shows that tourism, rather than religious endeavour, is the current priority, but it's still worth paying the 8KM to climb the minaret. Passing another mosque, the road segues quickly into modern Mostar, though pay attention to signs pointing out the **Turkish House** (irregular hours; 2KM) on your left, a fascinating peek into the Ottoman traditions of yesteryear.

Above Kujundžiluk you'll see the **Cejvan Cehaj Mosque**, Mostar's oldest, on the way to the **Museum of Herzegovina** (Mon–Fri 9am–2pm, Sat 10am–noon; 2KM). Between the two lies a Muslim **graveyard**, and it's hard not to be moved when you notice that almost everybody laid to rest here died the same year, 1993.

The west bank

Tara, the bridge's western tower, was once a dungeon into which prisoners were thrown to die, either from injury, starvation or – in rafting season – drowning. It's now a café and the base of the diving club, who for a rip-off 2KM will allow you to see the dungeon (just ask to use the toilet and you'll see the same thing for free). A little zigzagging will bring you to the **Crooked Bridge** – apparently built as a warm-up for the big boy, and almost as pleasing – and the **Tabhana**, a former bathhouse now filled with bars and restaurants. Up the hill you'll see the overlarge **Catholic Church**, with its even more oversized bell tower, evidently raised to such heights in a fit of religious pride. To reach the church you'll have to cross a main road that, during the war, served as the **front line** – walking along to the north reveals a succession of battered buildings.

Arrival and information

Bus and train The stations are located side-by-side in an ugly area to the east of town, a 20min walk from the Old Bridge.
Tourist office ⓣ033/580833. Behind the Tabhana, just west of the Old Bridge, and good at arranging accommodation or city tours (May–Sept 8am–8pm; open irregular hours in other months).
Tours *Hostel Majdas* runs jam-packed full-day tours for €20 per person, including hiking and diving in areas unreachable on public transport.

Accommodation

The tourist office can help to organize private rooms, which cost €10–25 per person depending upon the season, room size and proximity to the Old Town.
Emen Onešćukova 32 ⓣ036/581120, ⓦwww.motel-emen.com. Rooms in this motel are simply gorgeous, and the Old Town location ideal. €60.
Hostel Majdas Franje Miličevića 39 ⓣ061/382940, ⓔmajdasofra@yahoo.com. Friendly, cosy and within a short walk of the Old Town, this is Mostar's best hostel by a long way. Their day-long tours usually see guests come back covered in sweat and mud, yet happy as Larry. €12.
Kriva Cuprija Kriva Cuprija 2 ⓣ036/550953, ⓦwww.motel-mostar.ba. Decent rooms next to the rushing waters that surge beneath the Crooked Bridge. Excellent restaurant attached. €65.
Pansion Oscar Onešćukova 33 ⓣ036/580237. Rooms at this guesthouse are a little musty, but perfectly adequate for the price. Take a look around as there are several styles available. €30.

Eating and drinking

Perhaps the best place to head for food is the Tabhana, just west of the Old Bridge, which has a number of restaurants and bars. For drinking, there are also plenty of bars around the Rondo, a roundabout 10min further west by foot.
Bella Vista Old Bridge. The outdoor balcony is about as close as you can get to the bridge, with good meals including pizzas or schnitzels for 7KM, and trout for 12KM.
Divers' Club Old Bridge. Café in the tower at the western end of the bridge, and home to the diving society. Espresso 2KM.
Jami Braće Fejića 15. Take-away joint claiming to make the best *burek* in town... if they're not right, they're not far off.
Kriva Cuprija Kriva Cuprija 2. Excellent value, considering the quality of the food,

TREAT YOURSELF

Muslibegović House Osman Dikića 32 ⓣ036/551379, ⓦwww.muslibegovichouse.com. A rare and surprisingly affordable chance to stay in a national monument – this home has been in the hands of the noble Muslibegović family for over 300 years. Rooms have been renovated with tasteful, individual designs, and cost €85 in peak season; it's worth the extra €10 for the suites.

and an excellent location under the Crooked Bridge. Fresh trout with salad and a berry sauce will only cost 10KM, a little more for the "Hercegovinan Plate" of rice, lamb and potatoes.

Restorant Balkan Braće Fejića. Almost next door to the Cejvan Cehaj Mosque, here you can throw back pre-made staples for around 6KM a plate.

Moving on

Train Sarajevo (2 daily; 3hr 30min).

Bus Dubrovnik (5 daily; 4hr); Sarajevo (12 daily; 2hr 30min); Trebinje (3 daily; 3hr 30min).

EXCURSIONS FROM MOSTAR

Using Mostar as a base, you have a whole slew of opportunities to choose from. Unfortunately, the paucity of public transport means that it's tough to crack more than one off in a day, and some places aren't accessible at all, so it may be best to organize a **tour** in Mostar.

Blagaj

Closest to Mostar is the village of **BLAGAJ**, just 12km to the east and accessible by local buses #10, #11 and #12. Once you disembark, carry straight ahead through the town to the **Tekija** (daily 8am–8pm; 4MK). Huddled into a niche in the cliff-face, this wonky wooden building was once the residence of dervishes, and the interior is suitably Spartan. Right next to it, a never-ending torrent of water gushes out of the cliff, apparently reaching levels of 43,000 litres per second; some of this is skimmed off to make tea and coffee, which you can order at a waterside table for just 1.5KM, including a free chunk of *lokum* (Turkish delight).

Međugorije

Twenty-six kilometres south of Mostar is the curious village of **MEĐUGORIJE**, a mere non-entity until June 1981, when a group of teenagers claimed to have been spoken to by the **Virgin Mary**. Unlike Lourdes and Fatima, this has not been officially recognized by the Vatican, but that doesn't stop pilgrims arriving in such numbers that there are now thousands of rooms available to accommodate them. The main sights here are the **Church of St James** and the nearby "Weeping Knee" statue, so named as it apparently flouts the laws of thermodynamics by dribbling out a constant flow of fluid. You can get here on local bus #48 from Mostar, though – get this – they don't run on Sundays.

Počitelj and the Kravice Waterfalls

A few kilometres south of Međugorije is the hillside village of **POČITELJ**, one of the most traditional in Herzegovina. The place is quite stunning, and dotted with remnants from the fifteenth century, most notably a citadel and a terrific mosque. Unfortunately there are no direct buses here, so it's best to join a tour. Groups heading here will likely swing through to see the nearby **Kravice Waterfalls**, which are similarly tough to get to on public transport. High, wide and handsome, the pool below is a great place for a dip.

TREBINJE

The Republika Srpska's most appealing town by a country mile, **TREBINJE** is tucked into Herzegovina's southern extremity, and its proximity to Dubrovnik and the Montenegrin border make it the ideal start or finish line to a race through the country. It's most famed for the Arslanagić Bridge – a longer version of the one in Mostar – which sits a ten-minute walk from the town centre, and a couple of **hilltop monasteries**, which are worth the climb.

Back in the centre is the **Old Town**, a pretty warren of streets now largely filled with cafés; better yet for coffee-slurping is elegant **Jovan Dučić Square**, home

to a daily market and almost totally cloaked with maple leaves (*platani*). These have given their name to the adjacent *Hotel Platani* (☎059/270420; €50), by far the best **place to stay** in town and fair value for the price; staff may also be able to advise on finding private rooms in the area. It also has a good **restaurant** attached to it, though more elegant is *Porto Bello* in the Old Town, which doles out good steaks for 15KM, and cheaper is *Market 99*, a food court on top of the city supermarket.

Britain

HIGHLIGHTS

OVER THE SEA TO SKYE: craggy peaks, sparkling water and Celtic mystery in the Scottish islands
EDINBURGH FESTIVAL: the world's biggest arts festival
MANCHESTER: find your own next big thing in Manchester, home to Britain's most cutting-edge music scene
STRATFORD-UPON-AVON: Shakespeare's home town and host to the world-renowned Royal Shakespeare Company
THE BRITISH MUSEUM: an unrivalled collection of arts and antiquities in the centre of London
SURFING, NEWQUAY: test the Atlantic rollers

ROUGH COSTS

DAILY BUDGET basic €45/occasional treat €75

DRINK Lager €4 per pint

FOOD Fish and chips €6

HOSTEL/BUDGET HOTEL €20/€60–90

TRAVEL train: London–Brighton (53 miles) €25; bus London–Manchester (201 miles) €30

FACT FILE

POPULATION 61 million (includes Northern Ireland)

AREA 244,820 sq km

LANGUAGE English

CURRENCY Pound sterling (£)

CAPITAL London (population: 7.5 million)

INTERNATIONAL PHONE CODE: ⓣ44

Introduction

A famous British newspaper headline in the 1950s declared: "Fog in Channel, Continent Cut Off". Britain's outlook on the world has always been unique, born of its status as an island nation on the western edge of Europe. And yet within this compact territory you'll find not just one country but three – England, Wales and Scotland – and a multitude of cultural identities: God forbid you should call a Scot or a Welshman English.

The capital, **London** is a ceaselessly entertaining city, and the one place that features on everyone's itinerary. **Brighton** and **Canterbury** offer contrasting diversions – the former a lively seaside resort, the latter one of Britain's finest medieval cities. The southwest of England has the rugged moorlands of **Devon**, the rocky coastline of **Cornwall**, and the historic spa city of **Bath**, while the chief attractions of central England are the university cities of **Oxford** and **Cambridge**, and Shakespeare's hometown, **Stratford-upon-Avon**. Further north, the former industrial cities of **Manchester**, **Liverpool** and **Newcastle** are lively, rejuvenated places, and **York** has splendid historical treasures, but the landscape, especially the uplands of the Lake District, is the biggest magnet. For true wilderness, head to the **Welsh mountains** or **Scottish Highlands**. The finest of Scotland's lochs, glens and peaks, and the magnificent scenery of the West Coast islands, can be reached easily from the contrasting cities of **Glasgow** and **Edinburgh** – the latter perhaps Britain's most attractive urban landscape.

CHRONOLOGY

54 BC The Romans attack Britannia but are forced back until a successful invasion in 43 AD.

1066 AD Duke William II of Normandy defeats the last Anglo-Saxon ruler, King Harold II, at the Battle of Hastings.

1215 The Magna Carta forms the basis upon which English law is built.

1301 Edward I conquers Wales, giving his heir the title Prince of Wales.

1534 Henry VIII breaks with the Catholic Church. The Head of State becomes Head of the Church of England.

1603 King James VI of Scotland also becomes James I of England in the Union of the Crowns.

1653–1658 A brief period of republicanism under Oliver Cromwell, following the English Civil War.

1707 The Act of Union unites the parliaments of Scotland and England, with the addition of Ireland in 1800.

1800s The Industrial Revolution helps Britain to expand her Empire and become a dominant world force.

1914–1918 Britain fights in World War I.

1928 Women attain full suffrage after a hard-fought campaign.

1939–1945 Britain fights in World War II. London and other major centres are heavily bombed during the Blitz.

1947 Indian independence from British rule heralds the gradual demise of the British Empire.

1960s The Beatles sing their way through the swinging sixties.

1979 Margaret Thatcher becomes Britain's first female Prime Minister.

1998 Devolution in Scotland and Wales.

2005 On July 7, London is rocked by terrorist bombings, leaving 52 dead.

2012 London to host the Olympics.

ARRIVAL

If you're travelling from outside mainland Europe or Ireland, clearly the only direct route to Britain is by **air**. Long-haul flights now land at a range of destinations throughout the UK, including Manchester, Edinburgh and Glasgow, though most air passengers still find themselves passing through London's airports – Gatwick, Heathrow,

"**Great Britain**", or just "Britain", is a geographical term encompassing England, Scotland and Wales, including their islands. However, it can also be used politically, in the context of central government, "British" nationals, or for national teams at sporting events such as the Olympics, in which case it includes Northern Ireland. "**United Kingdom**" is a political term, referring to the sovereign state of England, Scotland, Wales and Northern Ireland. In this guide Northern Ireland is covered with the rest of the island in the Ireland chapter.

Stansted and Luton are the capital's main airports, the latter two the principal hubs of no-frills carriers like Ryanair and easyJet, which also operate out of smaller regional airports around the country. Greener alternatives for getting to Britain from mainland Europe include the **Eurostar** (ⓦwww.eurostar.com) high-speed train from Paris or Brussels to St Pancras International in London, Eurolines **bus**, or **ferry**: boats from Ireland, France, Belgium, the Netherlands, Denmark and Spain dock at ports across the UK.

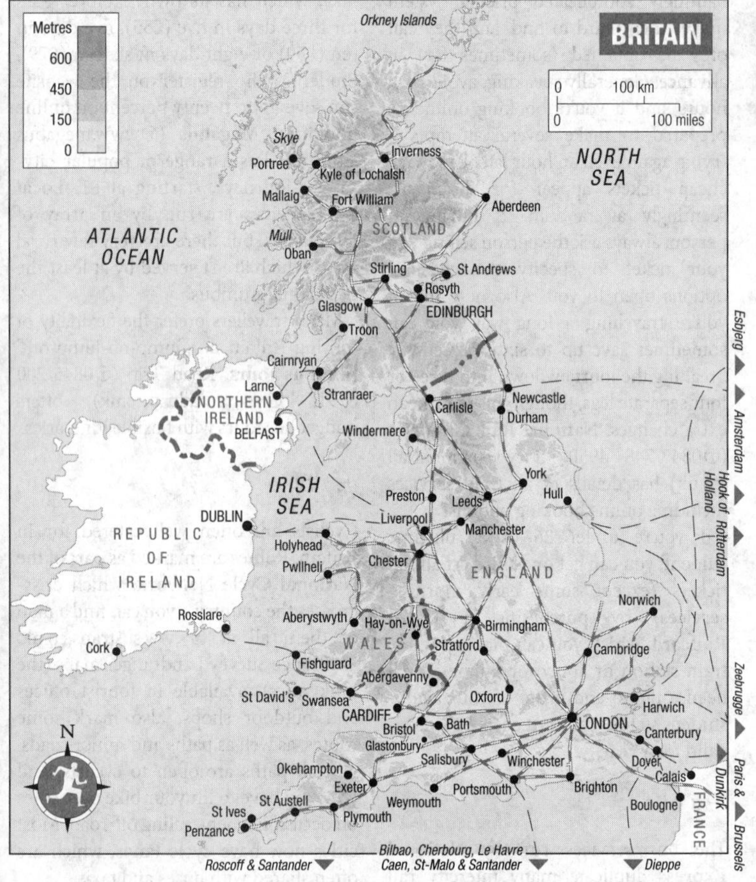

GETTING AROUND

Most places are accessible by train and/or coach (as long-distance buses are known), though costs are among the highest in Europe. **Traveline** (daily 8am–8pm; ⓣ0871/200 2233, ⓦwww.traveline.org.uk) is a national service that can advise on trains, coaches, ferries and, most usefully, local buses.

By train

Having suffered decades of chronic under-investment, the British **train** network is slowly beginning to improve, though **fares** remain some of the highest in Europe. Cheap tickets do exist, but the bafflingly complicated pricing system makes them hard to find, and they can only be obtained (sometimes far) in advance. Generally speaking, avoid rush hours, and if you're booking online be prepared to make several attempts – trying again even an hour later can make cheap tickets appear (or disappear) seemingly at random. If buying in person, always ask the person selling you your ticket to specify the cheapest options open to you. Also note that if you're travelling a long way you can sometimes save up to sixty percent by breaking the journey down into three or four separate legs, though this may mean extra changes. **National Rail Enquiries** (ⓣ0845/748 4950, ⓦwww.nationalrail.co.uk) has details of all train services including online booking options.

If you're under 26 or a full-time student, you can get one-third off all rail tickets (except some early morning services) by purchasing a **16–25 Railcard**, which you can pick up at any train station or apply for online. You'll need a photo and proof of your age or student status. The card costs £24 and is valid for a year.

By bus

The bus services run by **National Express** duplicate many intercity rail (ⓣ08717/818181, ⓦwww.nationalexpress.com) routes, very often at half the price or less, though for long distances in particular they're usually much slower than trains. If you're a student or under 26 you can buy a National Express Coachcard (£10), which gives up to thirty percent off standard fares. Their BritXplorer Pass offers unlimited travel for £79 for seven days, £139 for two weeks and £219 for a month. Both the Coachcard and Pass are valid on National Express through-routes to Scotland, but not on services within Scotland itself. These are provided by the sister company **Scottish Citylink** (ⓣ0870/550 5050, ⓦwww.citylink.co.uk), which has its own Explorer Pass for three days in five (£35), five days in ten (£59) or eight days in sixteen (£79). Students who register on the website can save up to twenty percent on online bookings. **Megabus** (ⓦwww.megabus.com/uk) has a range of popular city-to-city journeys, starting at £1. **Local bus services** are run by an array of companies, but there are very few rural areas which aren't served by at least the occasional minibus.

Many travellers prefer the flexibility of touring Britain on "jump-on-jump-off" **minibus tours**. Road Trip (ⓣ0845/200 6791, ⓦwww.roadtrip.co.uk) offers budget bus tours with flexible itineraries.

By bike

Cyclists are often well catered for in Britain. Routes are marked as part of the **National Cycle Network**, which criss-crosses the country – you can find a map of them all at ⓦwww.sustrans.co.uk. Ordnance Survey Landranger maps (the pink ones), available in tourist offices and outdoor shops, also mark some routes, as well as paths and minor roads. Not all paths are open to cyclists, and you may have to lift your bike over stiles on occasion when cycling off-road. Most cities now have **cycle lanes**, which are often shared with buses and taxis.

Bikes can generally be taken on **trains**, though some companies may charge you and/or require you to book in advance. National Express **coaches** only take bikes if they can fold and are bagged.

ACCOMMODATION

Accommodation in Britain is expensive and it's a good idea to reserve in advance. Many tourist offices will book rooms for you, although expect to pay a small fee for this, as well as putting down a deposit.

Britain has an extensive network of **HI hostels** operated by the Youth Hostel Association (Ⓦwww.yha.org.uk). In Scotland (Ⓦwww.syha.org.uk), a bed for the night can cost as little as £5, except in the cities, where you might pay twice that or more. In England and Wales charges start at around £12, but can easily rise to twice that in peak times. Most places of interest will also have at least one **independent hostel**, which will generally be of a comparable standard and can be several pounds cheaper.

In tourist cities it's hard to find a double in a **hotel** for less than £60 a night; hotel chains such as Travelodge (Ⓦwww.travelodge.co.uk) periodically run special offers, offering rooms for as low as £20, though they're frequently in out-of-the-way locations. A more pleasant option for budget accommodation, and often cheaper (particularly if you're on your own), are **guesthouses** and **B&Bs** – usually a comfortable room in a family home, plus a substantial breakfast – starting at around £25 a head (more in London).

There are more than 750 official **campsites** in Britain, charging from around £5 per person per night. In the countryside, farmers will often let you camp in a field if you ask, sometimes charging a couple of pounds. Camping rough in England and Wales technically requires the landowner's permission, while in Scotland it is mostly legal as long as you're unobtrusive and leave the site as you found it.

FOOD AND DRINK

Long lampooned as a culinary wasteland, Britain has seen a transformation in both the quality and variety of its restaurants over the past two decades. "Modern British" cuisine – in effect anything inventive – has been at the core of this change, though wherever you go you'll find places serving Indian, Italian and Chinese food, and often plenty of other international cuisines. If you're on a tight budget, the temptation is still to head for the nearest fast-food joint, but with a little effort, alternatives can easily be found, with even higher-end establishments often offering reasonably priced lunchtime or early evening deals.

Wherever you stay you'll almost certainly be offered an **"English breakfast"** – basically eggs, bacon, sausage, though other ingredients such as tomatoes and mushrooms are also usually added; you'll also be given the option of cereal, toast and fruit as well. Every major town will have upmarket restaurants and so-called **gastropubs** serving daintily presented cuisine, but traditional British cooking – the mainstay of pub food – is hearty and filling. Typical dishes include the quintessential fish and chips, steak and kidney pie, shepherd's pie (minced lamb topped with mashed potato), and – particularly on Sundays – roast dinners, served with roast potatoes, veg and (particularly with beef) Yorkshire pudding, made from savoury batter. Britain is one of Europe's better set up countries for **vegetarians**, and wherever you eat there'll always be at least one veggie choice, though it may not be anything more exciting than pasta.

Drink

Drinking traditionally takes place in the **pub**, where beer – sold by the pint or

half-pint – generates most of the business, although wine, bottled beer and spirits are also popular. Despite the popularity of cold, fizzy lager, traditional British beer, known as real ale or bitter, is undergoing something of a renaissance; richer and usually darker than lager, and served at cellar temperature rather than chilled, it comes in thousands of varieties. In England pubs are generally open Monday to Saturday from 11am to 11pm, and on Sunday from noon to 10.30pm; hours are often longer in Scotland, while Sunday closing is common in Wales.

In Scotland, the national drink is of course **whisky**. The best – and most expensive – are single malts, best drunk neat or with a splash of water to release the flavour.

CULTURE AND ETIQUETTE

Famed for their "stiff upper lip" and polite reticence, the British do tend to be more reserved than their continental counterparts, though you wouldn't think so on a weekend night after they've had a few drinks. Possibly the most cosmopolitan place in Europe – in the larger cities anyway – Britain has developed a reputation for liberal tolerance and benefits from a diverse range of faiths, creeds and colours.

Tipping is expected (if not mandatory) in restaurants; ten percent of the total is the norm, though some places, particularly the more upmarket ones, may add up to 12.5 percent service charge on your bill. Technically this is optional, though you will be frowned at if you ask for it to be removed. It's also customary to tip taxi drivers and hairdressers a similar amount, though it is not necessary to tip bartenders at bars and pubs.

SPORTS AND OUTDOOR ACTIVITIES

Football (soccer) is a British obsession. "The beautiful game" was codified here in 1863, and seeing a match is a must for any sports fan, though for top games it can be extremely difficult and costly to acquire tickets. The best option to guarantee seeing a Premier League match is to choose a lesser-known club: in London, Fulham (ⓦwww.fulhamfc.com) is a good bet. **Rugby** and **cricket**, though popular, do not generally inspire the same fervent tribalism as football, and consequently can offer a more relaxed spectator experience. You can turn up and buy tickets on the day for domestic matches at Lord's cricket ground in London (ⓦwww.lords.org) during the season (April–Sept).

Britain's diverse geography and geology, with access to large bodies of fresh and salt water, mean that venues for **outdoor pursuits** are easily accessible. **Walking** is one of the finest ways to see the country, and an excellent infrastructure of long-distance footpaths crisscrosses Britain (ⓦwww.walkingbritain.co.uk). The uplands of Wales (ⓦwww.visitwales.co.uk/active), Scotland (ⓦwww.adventure.visitscotland.com) and the English Lake District (ⓦwww.lakedistrictoutdoors.co.uk) are particularly good for hiking, climbing and watersports, while Devon and Cornwall (ⓦwww.southwestsurf.info) have the best **surfing** in the UK.

COMMUNICATIONS

Internet cafés and wi-fi are common, and you'll also find access at most hostels and some public phones. Prices vary, but £1 should be enough for you to reply to your email. **Post offices** open Monday to Friday 9am to 5.30pm, and some open on Saturday 9am to 12.30/1pm. Phonecards for **public phones** (operated mainly by BT) can be bought from post offices and newsagents; most booths also accept credit cards. Newsagents can sell you good-value cards from other phone companies for making international calls.

BRITAIN ON THE NET

Ⓦ **www.visitbritain.com** Tourist board site with links to regional sites.
Ⓦ **www.rail.co.uk** Information on public transport.
Ⓦ **www.backpackers.co.uk** The low-down on independent hostels.
Ⓦ **www.knowhere.co.uk** Irreverent local knowledge.
Ⓦ **www.streetmap.co.uk** Town plans and area maps.

For the operator, call Ⓣ100 (domestic) or 155 (international).

EMERGENCIES

Police are approachable and helpful. Tourists aren't a particular target for criminals except in the crowds of the big cities, where you should be on your guard against **pickpockets**. Britain's bigger conurbations all contain inner-city areas where you may feel uneasy after dark, but these are usually away from tourist sights.

For complaints that require immediate attention, go to the **A&E** (accident and emergency) department of the local hospital. For minor injuries you can also use NHS walk-in clinics. **Pharmacists** dispense only a limited range of drugs without a doctor's prescription. Most are open standard shop hours, though in large towns some may stay open as late as 10pm; local newspapers carry lists of late-opening pharmacies.

INFORMATION

Tourist offices exist in virtually every British town, offering information and a basic range of maps. **National parks** (Ⓦwww.nationalparks.gov.uk) also have their own information centres, which are better for guidance on outdoor pursuits. The most comprehensive series of maps is produced by the **Ordnance Survey** (Ⓦwww.ordnancesurvey.co.uk) – essential if you're planning walking or serious hiking.

EMERGENCY NUMBERS

Police, fire and ambulance Ⓣ999 or 112.

MONEY AND BANKS

The **pound** (£) sterling, divided into 100 pence, remains the national currency. There are coins of 1p, 2p, 5p, 10p, 20p, 50p, £1 and £2; and notes of £5, £10, £20 and £50; notes issued by Scottish banks are legal tender but sometimes not accepted south of the border. At the time of writing, £1 was worth €1.18 and $1.70. Normal **banking hours** are Monday to Friday 9.30am to 5pm, branches are increasingly open on Saturday. **ATMs** accept a wide range of debit and credit cards. Shops, hotels, restaurants and most other places readily accept **credit cards** for payment.

OPENING HOURS AND HOLIDAYS

General **shop hours** are Monday to Saturday 9am to 5.30/6pm, although many places in big towns are also open Sunday (usually 10am–4pm in England and Wales, longer in Scotland) and till 7/8pm – or later – at least once a week. **Public holidays** ("bank holidays") are: January 1, Jan January 2 (Scotland only), Good Friday, Easter Monday (not Scotland), first Monday and last Monday in May, last Monday in August, St Andrew's Day (Nov 30, or nearest Mon if weekend; Scotland only), Christmas Day and Boxing Day (Dec 25 & 26) – though in practice it's only on January 1, January 2 (Scotland only) and Christmas Day that everything shuts down; on other holidays, many shops in larger towns and cities – as well as nearly all sights – remain open.

England

Politically and financially, **England** has always dominated the United Kingdom, much to the resentment of her smaller neighbours. Football matches aside – when the red St George's Cross flies proud – English national identity is less easily defined than that of the Welsh and the Scots. In part, this reflects distinctive regional variations. From frenetic, cosmopolitan London to the stark wilds of rural Northumberland, intersected by Hadrian's Wall, England's regions are as diverse in culture as they are in landscape.

While the tourist industry thrives on clichéd images of pomp and tradition, most visitors quickly discover that there's much more to England than the monarchy and a predilection for tea. The country's quainter, more historic corners still feature heavily on most people's itineraries. In the major urban centres, though, the history sits alongside a resolutely modern outlook. Centuries of colonial expansion, superseded by close relations with the Commonwealth, have left a unique legacy of multiculturalism. Add to this a decade of urban regeneration, culminating in London's successful bid for the 2012 Olympics, and you'll find England's big cities more dynamic and multi-ethnic but also more socially segregated than you might expect. London, in particular, accommodates a bewildering yet exciting hotchpotch of different cultures, languages and neighbourhoods.

LONDON

With a population of around 7.5 million, **LONDON** is Europe's biggest city, sprawling over an area of more than 600 square miles from its core on the River Thames. Like most cities this large, the capital is really a messy conglomeration of "villages", and often changes dramatically within the space of a short walk. Central London is where the country's news, art and money are made and the city exudes an undeniable buzz of success. The pace of life is fast (just watch commuters bolting down the escalators) – but high-octane excitement comes at a price, with accommodation and transport costs among the most expensive in the world.

London's world-class museums and **galleries** have been reinvented in recent years and many of the best, such as the Tate, the National Gallery and the British Museum, are **free of charge**. Skip exorbitantly priced palaces in favour of them, and the city's excellent parks. Alternatively, London's famous department stores and offbeat weekend **markets** offer limitless **shopping**, while its cultural scene caters for all tastes, churning out everything from naff tribute musicals to experimental live music. With arts sector doyens desperate to lower the average audience age, there's plenty of cheap theatre and opera tickets up for grabs, nor is it hard to eat reasonably cheaply, either, with **pubs** and restaurants offering an array of world cuisine suited to any pocket.

What to see and do

The majority of sights are north of the **River Thames**, but there's no single focus of interest. Most people head, at one time or another, to the area around Whitehall, with **Trafalgar Square** at one end and Parliament Square at the other. All are just a ten-minute stroll east of **Buckingham Palace**. The busiest, most popular area for visitors and locals alike is the **West End**, centred on Leicester Square and Piccadilly Circus, and home to the majority of the city's theatres. The financial district lies a mile or so to the east, and is known, confusingly, as the **City of London**, at once the most ancient and most modern part of London. Over on the other side of the river, the **South**

Bank is now a prime tourist destination thanks to the London Eye, Tate Modern and Shakespeare's Globe. Further afield, **Greenwich** makes for a great day out, as do the Royal Botanic Gardens at **Kew**, and the outlying royal palace at **Hampton Court**.

Trafalgar Square and the National Gallery

Trafalgar Square's focal point is **Nelson's Column**, featuring the one-eyed admiral who died defeating the French at the 1805 Battle of Trafalgar. Four lions guard the column's base, while the fountains are a magnet for overheating sightseers during the summer. Extending across the north side of the square is the **National Gallery** (daily 10am–6pm, Wed till 9pm; free; Ⓦwww.nationalgallery.org.uk), one of the world's great art collections. Masterpieces include paintings by Raphael, Michelangelo, Leonardo da Vinci and Rembrandt, along with Impressionist works by the likes of Van Gogh and Monet. Tickets for the major exhibitions cost around £12 and should be booked in advance. Round the side of the National Gallery, in St Martin's Place, is the fascinating **National Portrait Gallery** (daily 10am–6pm, Thurs & Fri till 9pm; free; Ⓦwww.npg.org.uk), which houses images of the great and good from Hans Holbein's larger-than-life drawing of Henry VIII to Sam Taylor-Wood's video portrait of David Beckham.

The Mall and Buckingham Palace

The tree-lined sweep of **The Mall** runs from Trafalgar Square through the imposing Admiralty Arch, and on to **Buckingham Palace** (Aug & Sept daily 9.45am–6.00pm; £16.50; Ⓦwww.royal.gov.uk), which has served as the monarch's permanent residence since the accession of Queen Victoria in 1837. The building's exterior, last remodelled in 1913, is pretty bland, but inside it's suitably lavish. There's more high-class art on display in the **Queen's Gallery** (daily 10am–5.30pm; £8.50), on the south side of the palace. When Buckingham Palace is closed, most folk mill about outside the gates to catch the **Changing of the Guard** (May–July daily 11.30am; Aug–April alternate days; no ceremony if it rains). However, you're better off heading for the **Horse Guards** building on Whitehall, where a more elaborate equestrian ceremony takes place (Mon–Sat 11am, Sun 10am). Wherever you watch the Changing of the Guard, you can unwind afterwards in the immaculately laid-out **St James's Park.**

Whitehall

Heading south from Trafalgar Square, **Whitehall** is lined with government buildings. The original Whitehall was a palace built for King Henry VIII, but virtually the only bit to survive a fire in 1698 is the supremely elegant **Banqueting House** (Mon–Sat 10am–5pm; £4.80; Ⓦwww.hrp.org.uk), home to some vast ceiling paintings by Rubens, glorifying the Stuart dynasty. Further down the west side of Whitehall is **Downing Street**, where no. 10 has been the residence of the Prime Minister since 1732. During World War II, the Cabinet was forced to vacate Downing Street in favour of a bunker in nearby King Charles Street. The **Churchill Museum and Cabinet War Rooms** (daily 9.30am–6pm; £12.95; Ⓦwww.iwm.org.uk) – left more or less as they were in 1945 – provide a glimpse of the claustrophobic suites from which Winston Churchill directed wartime operations and a fascinating insight into the life of the man himself.

The Houses of Parliament

Clearly visible at the south end of Whitehall is London's finest Gothic Revival building, the Palace of

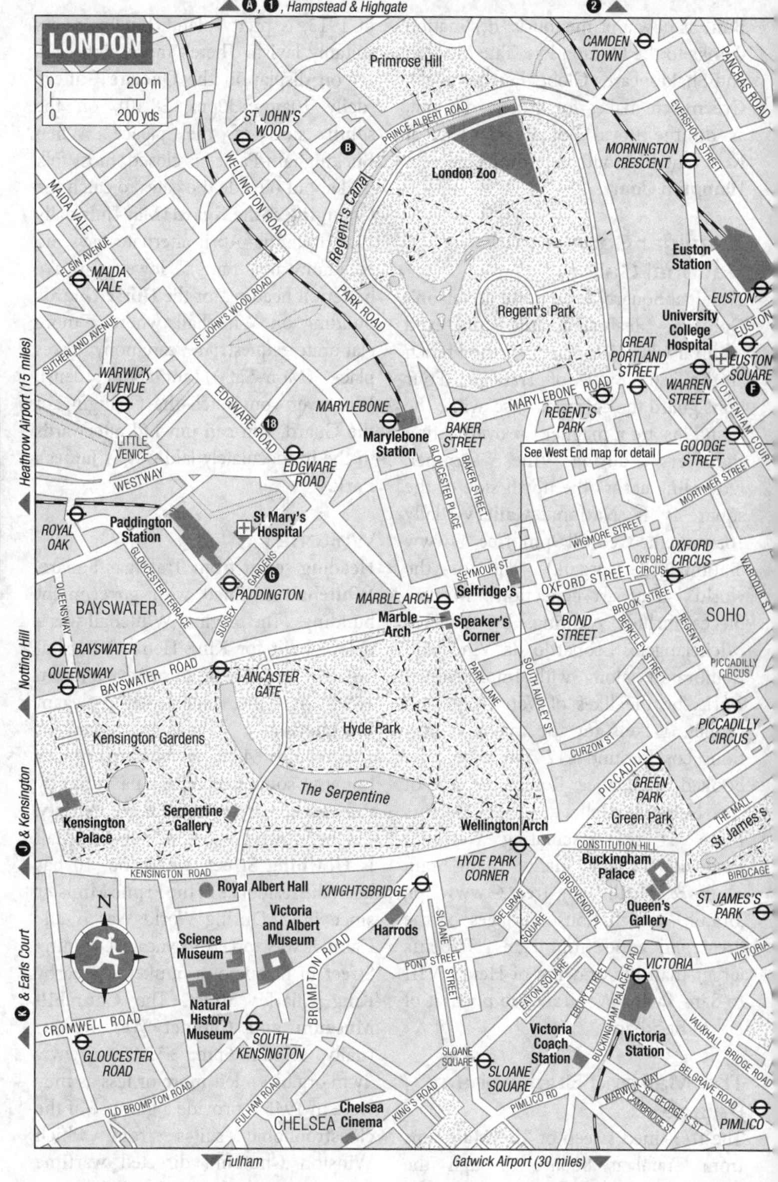

Westminster, better known as the **Houses of Parliament**. It is distinguished above all by the ornate, gilded clock tower popularly known as **Big Ben**, after the thirteen-ton bell that it houses. The original royal palace, built by Edward the Confessor in the eleventh century, burnt down in 1834. The only part to survive is the magnificent Westminster Hall, which can be glimpsed en route to the **public galleries** from which you can watch

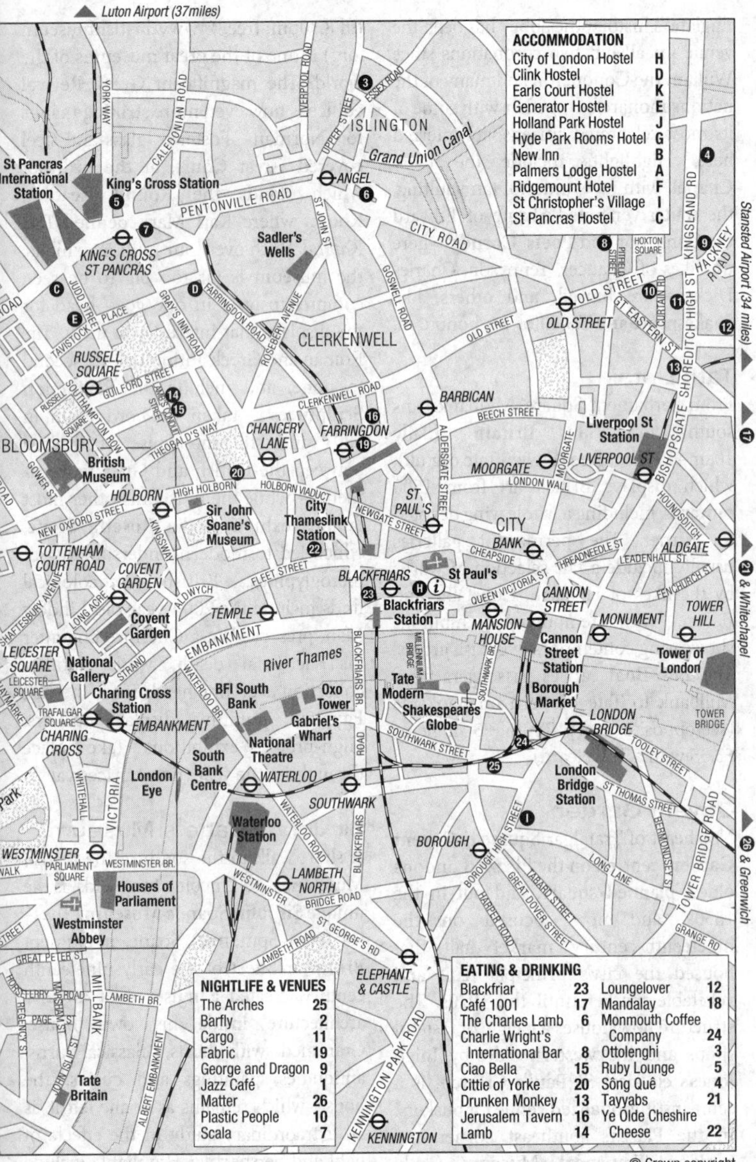

parliament's proceedings – Friday is the easiest day to get tickets (free; ⓦ www.parliament.uk; check parliament is in session), when sittings commence at 9.30am: turn up early to avoid queues.

Westminster Abbey

The Houses of Parliament dwarf their much older neighbour, **Westminster Abbey** (Mon–Fri 9.30am–4.30pm, Wed until 6pm, Sat 9.30am–2.30pm; £15). Encompassing the grand sweep of

England's history, the abbey has been the venue for all but two coronations since William the Conqueror, and many of the nation's monarchs, together with some of its most celebrated citizens, are interred here. Highlights include the **Lady Chapel**, with its wonderful fan vaulting, the much venerated Shrine of Edward the Confessor and **Poets' Corner**, where the likes of Chaucer, Tennyson, Charles Dickens are buried, and others, like Shakespeare and T.S. Eliot, are honoured.

Tate Britain

From Parliament Square, Millbank runs south to **Tate Britain** (daily 10am–5.50pm; free; Ⓦwww.tate.org.uk), which displays British art from 1500 onwards, including a whole wing devoted to Turner. The permanent galleries usually include a fair selection of works by the likes of Hogarth, Constable and Bacon, with temporary exhibitions showcasing contemporary British artists. The **Tate Boat** carries passengers from Millbank to Tate Modern on Bankside (see opposite; every 40min; £5 single or £3.35 with a Travelcard).

Covent Garden

Northeast of Trafalgar Square is **Covent Garden**, centred on the Piazza, London's oldest planned square, laid out in the 1630s, and now focused on the nineteenth-century market hall that housed the city's principal fruit and vegetable market until the 1970s. The structure now houses a gaggle of tasteful shops and the western side, by Inigo Jones's classical **St Paul's Church**, is a semi-institutionalized venue for buskers. In the Piazza's southeast corner, the **London Transport Museum** (daily 10am–6pm, Fri 11am–9pm; £10 Ⓦwww.ltmuseum.co.uk) offers a fun scamper through the history of public transport.

The British Museum

The **British Museum** on Great Russell Street (daily 10am–5.30pm, Thurs & Fri till 8.30pm; free; Ⓦwww.britishmuseum.org) is one of the great museums of the world. The magnificent Greek Revival edifice is now even more striking thanks to Norman Foster's glass-and-steel covered Great Court, at the heart of which stands the **Round Reading Room**, where Karl Marx penned *Das Kapital*. With over four million exhibits, the museum is far too big to be seen comprehensively in one go – head for the displays that interest you most. The Roman and Greek antiquities are second to none, and include the **Parthenon Sculptures** – taken by Lord Elgin in 1801 and still the cause of discord between the British and Greek governments – while the museum's other most famous exhibit is the **Rosetta Stone**, which led to modern understanding of hieroglyphics. British archeological finds include the 2000-year-old Lindow Man, preserved in a Cheshire bog after his sacrificial death, while another collection everyone heads for is the vast Egyptian mummy display upstairs. High-profile exhibitions take place throughout the year (ticket prices vary).

Sir John Soane's Museum

A short walk to the south of the British Museum, at 13 Lincoln's Inn Fields, is the unique **Sir John Soane's Museum** (Tues–Sat 10am–5pm; free). Soane, an eminent British architect of the early nineteenth century, created a museum of art and architecture inside his own house. Crammed with busts, classical urns, antiquities, paintings and curios, the house, which remains as Soane left it, is an extraordinary study in the effects of light and perspective. Highlights include the atmospheric Monk's Parlour, poking fun at the nineteenth-century penchant for the Gothic, and the seemingly diminutive Picture Room, which in fact contains more than one hundred pictures, including Hogarth's *A Rake's Progress*, hung on a series of secret hinged screens.

The London Eye and South Bank

The South Bank of the Thames is home to one of London's most prominent landmarks, the **London Eye** (daily: May, June & Sept 10am–9pm, July & Aug 10am–9.30pm, Oct–April 10am–8pm; £17; ⓣ0870/500 0600, ⓦwww.londoneye.com; booking advised), a 135m-tall observation wheel that revolves above the Thames. From the Eye, a riverside footpath heads east past the ugly concrete edifices of the **South Bank Centre** (see p.163), taking in the craft shops and restaurants in Gabriel's Wharf and the OXO Tower, for a mile or so before reaching Bankside, the old entertainment district of Tudor and Stuart London.

Bankside and the Tate Modern

Contemporary Bankside is dominated by the austere-looking **Tate Modern** (daily 10am–6pm, Fri & Sat till 10pm; free; ⓦwww.tate.org.uk), formerly a power station. The collection is arranged thematically and revisions take place every six months or so, but you're pretty much guaranteed to see works by Monet, Bonnard, Matisse, Picasso, Dalí, Mondrian, Warhol and Rothko. Major exhibitions run for about three months and tend to be very popular, so it's worth booking ahead.

Directly outside Tate Modern is Norman Foster's **Millennium Bridge**, which wobbled so worryingly when it first opened in 2000 that it was closed for repairs for almost two years. The crossing, with spectacular views, will take you across the river to St Paul's Cathedral.

Globe Theatre

Dwarfed by Tate Modern is **Shakespeare's Globe Theatre**, a reconstruction of the polygonal playhouse where most of the Bard's later works were first performed. The Globe's pricey but stylish exhibition (daily: May–Sept 9am–5pm; Oct–April 10am–5pm; £10.50) is worth a visit, and includes a guided tour of the theatre, except during summer afternoon – when you're better off watching a show.

St Paul's Cathedral

The finest building in the area of London now known as the City is St Paul's Cathedral (Mon–Sat 8.30am–4pm; £11), designed by Sir Christopher Wren. The most distinctive feature of this Baroque edifice is the vast dome, one of the largest in the world. The interior of the church, recently restored to its former glory, is mostly filled with dull funerary monuments, but a staircase in the south transept leads up to a series of galleries in the dome. The internal **Whispering Gallery** is the first, so called because of its acoustic properties – words whispered to the wall on one side are clearly audible on the other. The broad exterior Stone Gallery and the uppermost Golden Gallery both offer good panoramas over London. The **crypt** is the resting place of Wren, along with Turner, Reynolds and other artists, but the most imposing sarcophagi are the twin black monstrosities occupied by the Duke of Wellington and Lord Nelson.

Tower of London

Despite all the hype, the **Tower of London** (March–Oct 9/10am–5.30pm, Nov–Feb 9/10am–4.30pm; £16.50; ⓦwww.hrp.org.uk), on the river a mile southeast of St Paul's, remains one of London's most remarkable buildings. Begun by William the Conqueror, and pretty much completed by the end of the thirteenth century, the Tower is the most perfectly preserved (albeit heavily restored) medieval fortress in the country. The central **White Tower** holds part of the Royal Armouries collection, and, on the second floor, the Norman Chapel of St John, London's oldest church. Close by is Tower Green, where

Lady Jane Grey, Anne Boleyn and Catherine Howard were beheaded. The Waterloo Barracks house the **Crown Jewels**, amongst which are the three largest cut diamonds in the world.

Tower Bridge

River views from the Tower of London are dominated by the twin towers of **Tower Bridge**, completed in 1894 and one of London's most famous landmarks. The raising of the bridge to allow tall ships through remains an impressive sight. Sadly, though, you can only visit the walkways linking the summits of the towers by joining a guided tour dubbed the "Tower Bridge Experience" (April–Sept 10am–6.30pm; Oct–March 9.30am–6pm; £7; ⓦwww.towerbridge.org.uk).

Hyde Park

The best way to approach **Hyde Park**, central London's largest green space, is from the southeastern corner known as Hyde Park Corner. Here, in the middle of the traffic interchange, **Wellington Arch** (Wed–Sun 10am–4/5pm; £3.50), commemorates Wellington's victories in the Napoleonic Wars. In the middle of Hyde Park is **The Serpentine**, a lake with a popular lido towards its centre; the nearby **Serpentine Gallery** (daily 10am–6pm; free; ⓦwww.serpentinegallery.org) hosts excellent contemporary art exhibitions. In the northeast corner of the park, towards Marble Arch, **Speakers' Corner** has long been associated with public free speech. Anyone can turn up to pour forth on whatever subject they chose; Sunday is the best day to hear impassioned oratory.

Kensington Palace

To the west of Hyde Park are Kensington Gardens, leading to **Kensington Palace** (daily 10am–5/6pm; £12.50; ⓦwww.hrp.org.uk), a modestly proportioned Jacobean brick mansion that was Princess Diana's London residence following her separation from Prince Charles. The highlights of the sparsely furnished state apartments are the *trompe-l'oeil* ceiling paintings by William Kent, and the oil paintings in the King's Gallery.

Victoria and Albert Museum

London's richest concentration of free museums lies to the south of Hyde Park. In terms of sheer variety and scale, the **Victoria and Albert Museum** (daily 10am–5.45pm, Fri until 10pm; free; ⓦwww.vam.ac.uk), on Cromwell Road, is the greatest museum of applied arts in the world. In addition to its displays on fashion through the ages, the most celebrated of the V&A's exhibits are the Raphael Cartoons, seven vast biblical paintings that served as templates for a set of tapestries destined for the Sistine Chapel, and the refurbished Jameel gallery, housing the enormous Ardabil carpet, the oldest in the world.

Science Museum and the Natural History Museum

The impressive **Science Museum** on Exhibition Road (daily 10am–6pm; free; ⓦwww.sciencemuseum.org.uk) is the scientific counterpart to the V&A, displaying inventions ranging from Crick and Watson's DNA model to Puffing Billy, the world's oldest surviving steam train. Back on Cromwell Road, the nearby **Natural History Museum** (Mon–Sat 10am–5.50pm; free; ⓦwww.nhm.ac.uk) is most famous for its dinosaur gallery, while the more modern "Red Zone" offers a visually exciting romp through the earth's evolution, including the slightly tasteless Kobe earthquake simulator. The site is currently undergoing major expansion; the state-of-the-art Darwin Centre should have opened by the time you read this.

London Zoo

As with almost all of London's royal parks, Londoners have Henry VIII to

thank for **Regent's Park**, which he confiscated from the Church for yet more hunting grounds – though its present layout dates from the early nineteenth century. Flanked by some of the city's most elegant residential buildings, the park is home to **London Zoo** (daily 10am–4/6pm; £16.80; ⓦwww.zsl.org), one of the world's oldest and most varied collections of animals.

Hampstead Heath and Highgate Cemetery

North of Regent's Park, the affluent suburb of Hampstead gives access to **Hampstead Heath**, one of the few genuinely wild areas left in London. East of Hampstead is **Highgate Cemetery**, ranged on both sides of Swains Lane (Highgate or Archway tube). Karl Marx lies here in the East Cemetery (daily 10/11am–4/5pm; £3; ⓦwww.highgate-cemetery.org); more atmospheric is the overgrown West Cemetery (guided tours only: March–Nov Mon–Fri 2pm, Sat & Sun hourly 11am–4pm; Dec–Feb Sat & Sun hourly 11am–3pm; £5), with its spooky Egyptian Avenue and terraced catacombs.

Greenwich

Some seven miles southeast of central London, **Greenwich** (pronounced "gren-itch") is one of London's most beguiling spots, a haven of water and sky looking northwards to the virile skyscrapers of Canary Wharf. Transport links are good: boats run regularly from Westminster Pier, trains from London Bridge, and the Docklands Light Railway scoots east from Bank via the redeveloped Docklands south to the *Cutty Sark*, the famous tea clipper (sadly closed for restoration until at least spring 2011 after a devastating fire). Hugging the riverfront to the east is Christopher Wren's beautifully symmetrical Baroque ensemble of the **Old Royal Naval College** (daily 10am–5pm; free). Across the road the **National Maritime Museum** (same hours; free; ⓦwww.nmm.ac.uk) exhibits model ships, charts and globes. From here Greenwich Park stretches up the hill, crowned by the Wren-inspired **Royal Observatory** (same hours; free), home of Greenwich Mean Time and Zero Longitude.

Kew Gardens and Hampton Court

Boats ply westwards from Westminster Pier upstream to **Kew** where you'll find the **Royal Botanic Gardens** (daily 9.30am–dusk; £13; Kew Gardens tube; ⓦwww.kew.org), established in 1759, and now home to over forty thousand species. Thirteen miles southwest of the centre and also served by riverboat is **Hampton Court Palace** (Daily: April–Oct 10am–6pm; Nov–March 10am–4.30pm; £14; ⓦwww.hrp.org.uk). Built in 1516 by the upwardly mobile Cardinal Wolsey, it was enlarged and improved by Henry VIII, and later rebuilt by William III who hired Wren to remodel the buildings. The most rewarding sections are Henry VIII's State Apartments, the King's Apartments and the Tudor Kitchens. In the grounds, lying just north of the palace, is the famous **maze**, laid out in 1714.

Arrival by air

Flying into London, you'll arrive at one of the capital's five international airports: Heathrow, Gatwick or Stansted (ⓦwww.baa.com), Luton (ⓦwww.london-luton.co.uk) or City (ⓦwww.londoncityairport.com).

Heathrow, fifteen miles west, is served by Piccadilly Line underground trains, which run to central London in about an hour (£4), or there are Heathrow Express trains to Paddington Station (every 15min; 15–20min; £16.50). National Express also runs coach services to Victoria Coach Station (every 30min; 55min; £5). After midnight, night bus #N9 runs to Trafalgar Square (every 20min; 1hr; £2).

Gatwick, thirty miles south, is connected by several train companies: the Gatwick Express speeds to Victoria Station (every 15min; 30min; £16.90), although Southern trains on the same

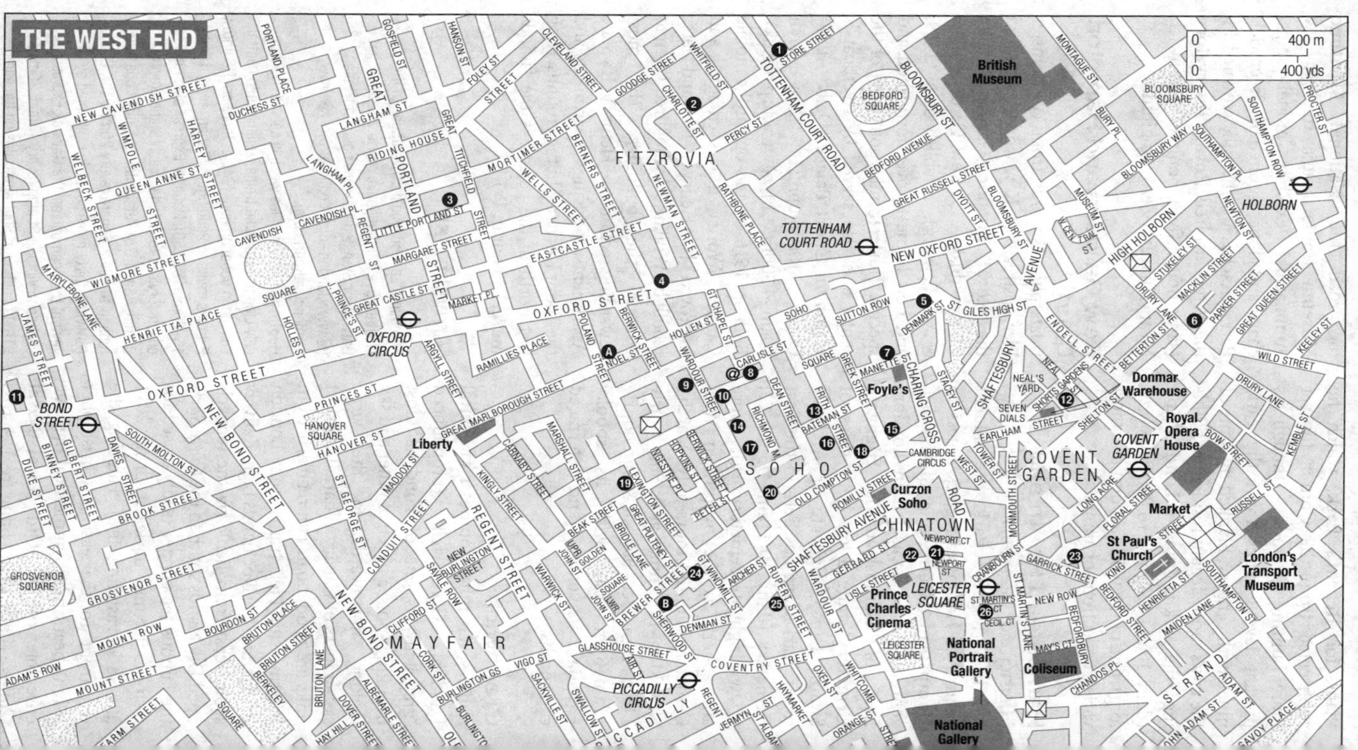
THE WEST END
0 400 m
0 400 yds
British Museum
BEDFORD SQUARE
BLOOMSBURY SQUARE
FITZROVIA
TOTTENHAM COURT ROAD
HOLBORN
OXFORD CIRCUS
BOND STREET
SOHO
COVENT GARDEN
CHINATOWN
MAYFAIR
PICCADILLY CIRCUS
LEICESTER SQUARE
COVENT GARDEN
Liberty
Foyle's
Donmar Warehouse
Royal Opera House
Market
St Paul's Church
London's Transport Museum
Curzon Soho
Prince Charles Cinema
National Portrait Gallery
National Gallery
Coliseum
SEVEN DIALS
NEAL'S YARD
CAMBRIDGE CIRCUS
HANOVER SQUARE
GROSVENOR SQUARE
LEICESTER SQUARE
SOHO SQUARE
CAVENDISH SQUARE
OXFORD STREET
NEW OXFORD STREET
TOTTENHAM COURT ROAD
CHARING CROSS ROAD
SHAFTESBURY AVENUE
REGENT STREET
NEW BOND STREET
HIGH HOLBORN
STRAND
PICCADILLY

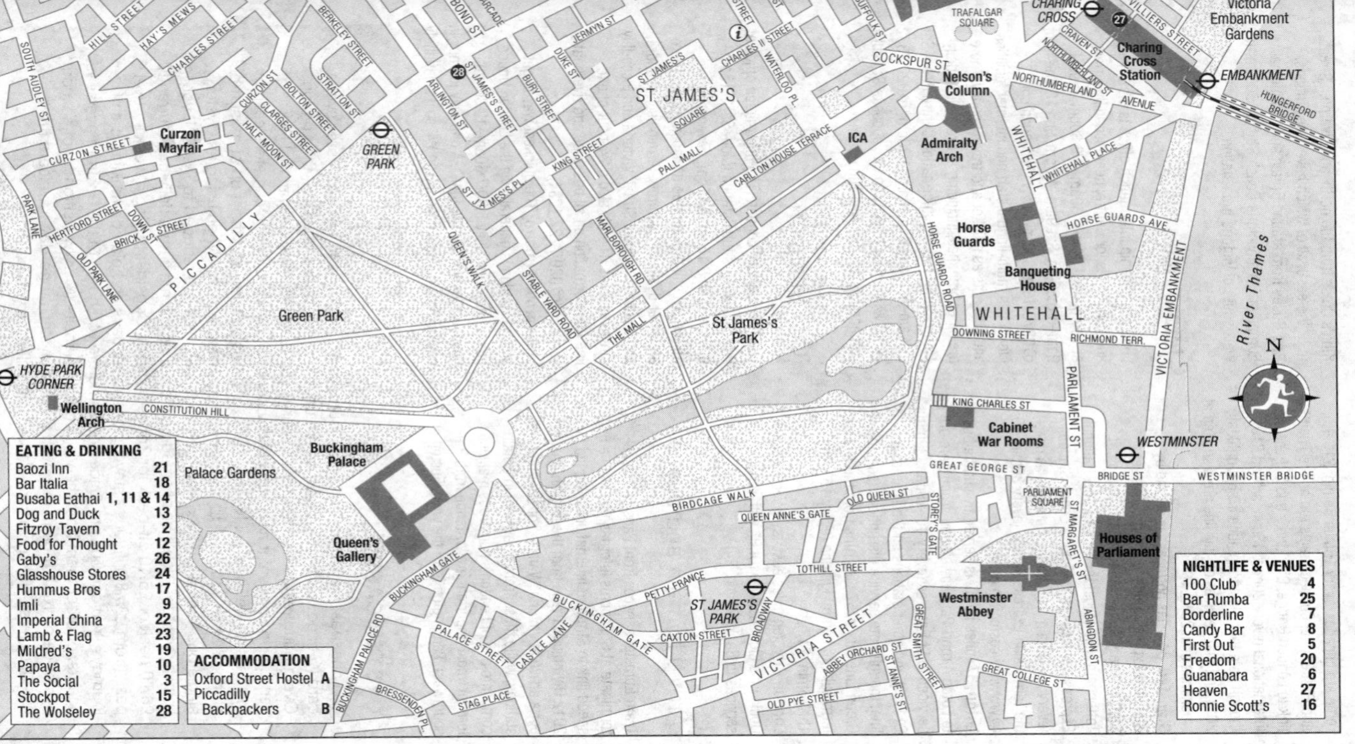
EATING & DRINKING
Baozi Inn 21
Bar Italia 18
Busaba Eathai 1, 11 & 14
Dog and Duck 13
Fitzroy Tavern 2
Food for Thought 12
Gaby's 26
Glasshouse Stores 24
Hummus Bros 17
Imli 9
Imperial China 22
Lamb & Flag 23
Mildred's 19
Papaya 10
The Social 3
Stockpot 15
The Wolseley 28
ACCOMMODATION
Oxford Street Hostel A
Piccadilly Backpackers B
NIGHTLIFE & VENUES
100 Club 4
Bar Rumba 25
Borderline 7
Candy Bar 8
First Out 5
Freedom 20
Guanabara 6
Heaven 27
Ronnie Scott's 16
Green Park
St James's Park
Buckingham Palace
Palace Gardens
Queen's Gallery
Wellington Arch
HYDE PARK CORNER
GREEN PARK
ST JAMES'S PARK
WESTMINSTER
EMBANKMENT
CHARING CROSS
Charing Cross Station
Victoria Embankment Gardens
Nelson's Column
Admiralty Arch
Horse Guards
Banqueting House
Cabinet War Rooms
Houses of Parliament
Westminster Abbey
ICA
Curzon Mayfair
ST JAMES'S
WHITEHALL
River Thames
N
PICCADILLY
CONSTITUTION HILL
BIRDCAGE WALK
THE MALL
HORSE GUARDS ROAD
PARLIAMENT ST
VICTORIA EMBANKMENT
WESTMINSTER BRIDGE
VICTORIA STREET
BUCKINGHAM GATE
TRAFALGAR SQUARE
PALL MALL
COCKSPUR ST
HUNGERFORD BRIDGE
© Crown copyright

route are cheaper (every 15min; 35min; £10.90), and First Capital Connect trains run on the Thameslink to London Bridge, Blackfriars and St Pancras International (every 20min; 45min; around £10), though note that Blackfriars tube is shut until late 2011 and that services on this line are disrupted at weekends until 2012.

Stansted, 34 miles northeast, is served by Stansted Express trains to Liverpool Street Station (every 15min; 45min; £18); hop off at Tottenham Hale to join the Victoria line. National Express services run to Victoria Coach Station (every 20–30min; 1hr 30min; from £8), as does the Terravision Express Shuttle (every 30min; £9; ⓦwww.lowcostcoach.com).

Luton, 37 miles north, is served by shuttle buses to Luton Airport Parkway station, from there are services to St Pancras (every 10–15min; 30min; £11.50) and other stations on the Thameslink line, though note service disruptions (see above). Green Line bus #757 also runs from the airport terminal into central London (every 15–20min; 1hr 15min; £13).

London City, ten miles east, is served by the Docklands Light Railway (DLR), with regular services to Bank (22min; £4).

Arrival by train and bus

Train Eurostar services from Paris or Brussels terminate at St Pancras International (with a high-speed link to Stratford International planned for the 2012 Olympics). Trains from the English Channel ports arrive at Victoria, Waterloo or Charing Cross stations, while those from elsewhere in Britain come into one of London's numerous mainline termini (most important are Waterloo from the southwest, Paddington from the west, Euston or King's Cross from the north, and Liverpool Street from the east), all of which have tube stations.

Bus Buses from around Britain and continental Europe arrive at Victoria Coach Station, 500 yards walk south of Victoria train station.

Information

London's flagship information office is the Britain and London Visitor Centre, near Piccadilly Circus at 1 Regent St (Mon 9.30am–6/6.30pm, Tues–Fri 9am–6/6.30pm, Sat 9am–4/5pm, Sun 10am–4pm; ⓣ0870/1566 366, ⓦwww.visitlondon.com), which has multi-lingual staff and internet facilities, and also acts as a ticket and travel agency. There are other branches, including at Greenwich (daily 10am–5pm). The City Information Centre (Mon–Sat 9.30am–5.30pm, Sun 10am–4.30pm; ⓣ020/7332 1456, ⓦwww.visitthecity.co.uk), opposite St Paul's Cathedral, is another well-run option.

City transport

The Transport for London (TfL) information office at Piccadilly Circus tube station (Mon–Sat 7.15am–9.15pm, Sun 8.15am–8.15pm; ⓦwww.tfl.gov.uk) will provide free transport maps. There are other desks at Heathrow Terminals 1, 2 and 3, and Euston, Liverpool Street, Victoria and Piccadilly Circus stations. There's also a 24-hour phone line for information on all bus, tube and riverboat services (ⓣ020/7222 1234).

Underground (metro) The quickest way to get around London is generally via the London Underground network (daily 5.30/7.30am–12.30am), popularly known as "the tube". A one-way journey in central Zone 1 costs a whopping £4, so it's definitely

OYSTER CARDS

The cheapest way to pay for single journeys in London is to use an **Oyster** swipe card (ⓦtfl.gov.uk/oyster), valid on the underground, buses, the DLR, the London Overground rail network and, by the time you read this, also on National Rail services in London; it also attracts discounts on riverboats. You can store cash on the card as well as weekly travel cards and bus passes, and top it up at most tube stations when you need to, as well as many newsagents. When using an Oyster, single bus fares are halved and tube fares in Zone 1 are reduced to £1.60. If you "pay as you go", you'll be charged no more than the maximum daily cap (currently £6.70 peak or £5.10 off-peak for Zones 1 and 2). Consider buying a week's travel pass (from £25.80) if you're staying for several days and plan on making lots of journeys. You can buy pre-loaded cards before you come to the UK from overseas agents, or order them from the Visit London website (ⓦwww.visitlondonoffers.com/oyster-card). Note though that even without Oyster, a one-day travelcard (from £5.60) or three-day travelcard (£18.40) will still save you pounds.

worth getting an Oyster card (see opposite). Tickets must be bought in advance from the machines or booths in station entrance halls and need to be kept until the end of your journey so that you can leave the station. If you use Oyster, be sure to always touch the card reader on the way in and out of each station. If you cannot produce a valid ticket or Oyster card on demand, you'll be charged an on-the-spot penalty fare of £50. Bear in mind that during rush hour the tube is packed with commuters and best avoided if you are laden with baggage.

Buses are a great way to see the city, especially from the top of London's famous red double deckers. If you don't have an Oyster card, you will need to buy a single ticket (£2) from the machine at the bus stop before boarding. Show the ticket to the driver on entering. After midnight, night buses prefixed with the letter "N" take over; fares remain the same. Note that many bus stops are request stops.

Boats Riverboat trips on the Thames are a pleasant way to travel. Westminster Pier, Embankment Pier and Waterloo Pier are the main central embarkation points and there are regular sailings to Bankside, London Bridge, Tower Bridge, Greenwich, Kew and Hampton Court. Timings and services alter frequently so pick up the Thames River Services Booklet from a TfL travel information office, phone ⓣ020/7222 1234 or visit ⓦwww.thamesclippers.com. Tickets are pricey but Travelcards get you a third off your fare. By the time you read this, Oyster should be compatible with boats, too.

Taxis If you're in a group, London's metered black cabs (taxis) can be a viable way of riding across the centre. There's a minimum £2.20 fare, and a two-mile journey costs around £7, but after 8pm fares go sky high and you're best off using the tube. A yellow light on the roof above the windscreen indicates that cab is available – just wave to hail it. To book in advance, call ⓣ020/7272 0272. Minicabs look just like regular cars and are considerably cheaper than black cabs, but need to be booked by phone in advance.

Bikes Cycling, although not for the faint-hearted, is popular in London. A good central option for bike hire is London Bicycle Tour Co (£4/hr, £19/day; ⓣ020/7928 6838, ⓦwww.londonbicycle.com) in Gabriel's Wharf on the South Bank; otherwise you can find hire shops through the London Cycling Campaign website (ⓦwww.lcc.org.uk). Pick out cycle-friendly routes using the free guides available from transport information offices, or check the TfL website.

Accommodation

The Visit London hotel booking service (ⓣ0845/644 3010, ⓦwww.visitlondon.com) will get you the best available prices with no additional charge. Student rooms are also available over the summer vacation from July to Sept; try Imperial College (ⓣ020/7594 9507, ⓦwww.imperial.ac.uk) or the LSE (ⓣ020/7955 7575, ⓦwww.lsevacations.co.uk). Places are shown on the map on pp.150–151 except where noted.

Hostels

To book a hostel bed, contact the individual hostels, or for HI hostels, the YHA (ⓣ01629/597700, ⓦwww.yha.org.uk). A good website for booking independent hostels is ⓦwww.hostellondon.com.

City of London 36 Carter Lane ⓣ0845/371 9012, ⓦwww.yha.org.uk. 200-bed hostel right by St Paul's Cathedral. The area is very quiet at night but it's close to the centre. St Paul's or Blackfriars tube. Dorms £24.50, doubles £66.95.

Clink 78 King's Cross Rd ⓣ020/7183 9400, ⓦwww.clinkhostel.com. Quirky, well-designed new hostel housed in a Victorian courthouse, with trendy pod-bed dorms. For added authenticity, sleep in the claustrophobic confines of a former police cell. King's Cross tube. Dorms £15, cells £63, doubles £73.

Earls Court 38 Bolton Gardens ⓣ0845/371 9114, ⓦwww.yha.org.uk. Attractive, comfortable period property, newly refurbished with a modern café. Earls Court tube. Dorms £24.50, doubles £60.95.

Generator Compton Place ⓣ020/7388 7666, ⓦwww.generatorhostels.com. Raucous, 837-bed hostel with neon-lit post-industrial decor and a youthful clientele. Twin rooms have bunks. Russell Square or Euston tube. Dorms £22.50, twins £60.

Holland Park Holland Walk ⓣ0845 371 9122, ⓦwww.yha.org.uk. Fairly convenient for the centre, in tranquil location overlooking the park. Self-catering kitchen and garden. Holland Park or High St Kensington tube. Dorms £24.50.

Oxford Street 14 Noel St ⓣ0845/3719133, ⓦwww.yha.org.uk. In the heart of the West End, but with only 75 beds, it fills up fast. Oxford Circus or Tottenham Court Rd tube; see map, pp.156–157. Dorms £24.50, doubles £60.95.

Palmers Lodge 40 College Crescent ⓣ020/7483 8470, ⓦwww.palmerslodge.co.uk. Superb hostel in a converted Victorian mansion, retaining much of its period character. Double-bed dorms are available for couples. Swiss Cottage tube. Dorms £18, doubles £70.

Piccadilly Backpackers 12 Sherwood St ⓣ020/7434 9009, ⓦwww.piccadillybackpackers.com. Incredibly central (practically on Piccadilly Circus), but you'll have to put up with noise. Piccadilly Circus tube; see map, pp.156–157. Dorms £12, doubles £60.

St Christopher's Village 121 Borough High St ⓣ020/7407 1856, ⓦwww.st-christophers.co.uk. (other branches in Camden, Hammersmith, Shepherd's Bush and Greenwich). Cheerful party hostel in a series of buildings near London Bridge, with a café and late bar on site. London Bridge tube. Dorm £18, twins £56.
St Pancras 79 Euston Rd ⓣ0845/371 9344, ⓦwww.yha.org.uk. Modern hostel opposite St Pancras International station and within walking distance of both the West End and Camden Town. King's Cross tube. Dorms £24.50, doubles £60.95.

Hotels and B&Bs

Hyde Park Rooms Hotel 136 Sussex Gardens ⓣ020/7723 0225, ⓦwww.hydeparkrooms.com. Welcoming, immaculately clean B&B near Paddington station. Paddington tube. Doubles £55–65.
New Inn 2 Allitsen Rd ⓣ020/77220726 ⓦwww.newinnlondon.co.uk. Five clean, cosy en-suite rooms above a pub in leafy St John's Wood, close to Regent's Park. St John's Wood tube. Breakfast not included. Doubles £75.
Ridgemount Hotel 65–67 Gower St ⓣ020/7636 1141, ⓦwww.ridgemounthotel.co.uk. Old-fashioned, family-run hotel with a garden and a laundry service. Excellent location. Goodge St tube. Doubles £60–78.

Campsites

Abbey Wood Federation Rd ⓣ020/8311 7708, ⓦwww.caravanclub.co.uk. Leafy, well-equipped site east of Greenwich. Open all year. Train from Charing Cross to Abbey Wood. £18.50.
Crystal Palace Crystal Palace Parade ⓣ020/8778 7155, ⓦwww.caravanclub.co.uk. All-year site, handily situated on the #3 bus route from Piccadilly. £18.50.

Eating

Few cities can match London for the sheer diversity of eating experiences on offer. You'll find restaurants of every nationality, with pubs just as likely to offer Thai green curry as steak and ale pie. With so much choice, it's not hard to eat well on a budget, provided you're happy with "ethnic" food. In addition to the places below, there are a handful of good London-specific chains with several branches around the city, including *Leon* (ⓦwww.leonrestaurants.co.uk), which offers inventive, health-conscious fast food, and the *S&M Café* (ⓦwww.sandmcafe.co.uk), specializing in an old English classic – sausage and mashed potato.

Cafés

Bar Italia 22 Frith St. A great place to people-watch, this tiny, buzzing, late-night café is a Soho institution. Open 24hr except Sun. Leicester Square tube.
Food For Thought 31 Neal St. Subterranean vegetarian café serving wholesome salads, soups and mains from £4.50. Covent Garden tube.
Gaby's 30 Charing Cross Rd. Jewish café serving a wide range of home-cooked Mediterranean specialities. Hard to beat for value, choice and location. Mains £3.80–9. Leicester Square tube.
Hummus Bros 88 Wardour St. The prices at this slick café are as attractive as their bowls of filling, velvety hummus. Eat in or takeaway from £2.80. Tottenham Court Rd tube.
Monmouth Coffee Company 2 Park St. Opposite Borough Market, you can't miss the irresistible aroma of freshly ground beans emanating from this bustling coffee shop. Closed Sun. London Bridge tube.
Ottolenghi 287 Upper St. With a tantalizing array of meringues, tarts and cupcakes, this Islington café is a great choice for coffee and cake. At lunch, stop by for delicious, if rather pricey, Mediterranean and Middle Eastern salads (£9). Angel tube.
Papaya 14 St Anne's Court. The limited menu and fresh flavours make this small Thai café a must. Mains £3.90. Closed Sat & Sun. Tottenham Court Rd tube.

Restaurants

Baozi Inn 25 Newport Court. Authentic and fresh Beijing and Chengdu street snacks served at simple wooden tables. Mains £6. Leicester Square tube.
Busaba Eathai 8–13 Bird St (other branches at Wardour St and Store St). Stylish surroundings complement stylish, well-presented food in this sleek Thai restaurant. Mains £8.50. Bond St tube.
Ciao Bella 86–90 Lamb's Conduit St. Jolly, old-style Italian, serving huge plates of pasta for £7.50. Russell Square tube.
Imli 167–169 Wardour St. A contemporary take on Indian food, serving curry tapas-style. Dishes start at around £4. Tottenham Court Rd tube.

TREAT YOURSELF

Tea at the Wolseley Traditional British afternoon tea doesn't come much more special than this: exquisite cream teas from £9.75 in the beautiful Art Deco surroundings of the opulent *Wolseley* restaurant at 160 Piccadilly. Don't worry about dressing up though; the experience is surprisingly relaxed.

DRINKING ON A BUDGET

For a break from London's sky-high drink prices check out the sensitively restored Victorian pubs owned by the **Samuel Smith's** brewery. Prices are kept staggeringly low by the omission of large-corporation spirits and soft drinks, and a pint of lager starts at just £2.15. For atmosphere and history, try the *Cittie of York*, 22 High Holborn or *Ye Olde Cheshire Cheese* at 145 Fleet St. Other central Sam Smith's pubs include the *Glasshouse Stores*, 55 Brewer St and the *Fitzroy Tavern* on Charlotte Street.

Imperial China White Bear Yard, 25 Lisle St. Large restaurant with excellent *dim sum* and service that is Chinatown brusque. Dim sum from £2.30. Leicester Square tube.

Mandalay 444 Edgware Rd. A real gem, serving pure, freshly cooked, unreconstructed Burmese cuisine. Closed Sun. Mains £3.90–£7.90. Edgware Rd tube.

Mildred's 45 Lexington St. Intimate veggie restaurant and bar with an imaginative menu, featuring burritos, tagines and stir fries. Light meals £5.50, mains £7.50. Closed Sun. Oxford Circus or Piccadilly Circus tube.

Sông Quê 134 Kingsland Rd. Crispy spring rolls and fragrant noodle soup are among the favourites at this East London Vietnamese. Mains under £10. Liverpool St or Old St tube.

Stockpot 18 Old Compton St. There's a touch of the school dinners about the menu here, but the *Stockpot* won't be beaten on price. Honest, reliable dishes. £7 set menu. Leicester Square or Tottenham Court Rd tube.

Tayyabs 83–89 Fieldgate St (off Whitechapel Rd). Close to, but not on, Brick Lane (home to pushy curry touts), this Pakistani/Punjabi restaurant is popular for its spicy kebabs, bold flavours and bring your own alcohol policy. Be prepared to queue. Aldgate East tube.

Drinking and nightlife

From Victorian pubs serving ale to old gents, to hip bars and clubs frequented by an eternally young, edgy clientele, London has it all. To the east, a thriving bar and club scene has spouted around Shoreditch, Hoxton and Old Street. Leggings and vintage specs predominate here, though the coolest of the cool are increasingly shifting their parties elsewhere. The most fashionable places seem to change as often as their patrons' haircuts, so pick up a copy of *Time Out*, the weekly listings magazine, to check what's on.

Pubs and bars

Blackfriar 174 Queen Victoria St. One of the capital's most unusual pubs, with marble walls, stained-glass windows and carved or illustrated monks in every nook and cranny. Blackfriars tube.

Café 1001 91 Brick Lane. Sprawling, grungy bar above a heaving café. Squishy vintage sofas and live music from jazz to deep house draw a youthful, laid-back crowd. Liverpool St tube.

The Charles Lamb 16 Elia St. Appealing Islington local tucked away on a side street close to Angel; calming mint-green interior, real ales and interesting wines. Angel tube.

Charlie Wright's International Bar 45 Pitfield St. Shoreditch trendiness has completely passed this place by; it's the buzzing late-night jazz and fusion gigs that attract a crowd. Arrive late and try not to look too hard at your surroundings. Old St tube.

Dog & Duck 18 Bateman St. Minuscule pub that's retained its character and a loyal clientele of Soho post-work drinkers. Leicester Square tube.

Drunken Monkey 222 Shoreditch High St. A warm, but lively ambience waits in this haven for cocktail and *dim sum* lovers. Old St or Liverpool Street tube.

Jerusalem Tavern 55 Britton St. Cool Clerkenwell's the setting for this packed pub, serving some of the best ales in London.

Lamb 94 Lamb's Conduit St. You can feel the history in this atmospheric boozer decorated with portraits of music hall stars. Holborn tube.

Lamb & Flag Rose St. A respite from hectic Covent Garden, this compact pub was once known as the *Bucket of Blood* – after the prize fights held here. Covent Garden or Leicester Square tube.

Ruby Lounge 33 Caledonian Rd. Great pre-club bar with deep red walls and boudoir-like lighting. DJs spin some decent groove and funk tunes. King's Cross tube.

The Social 5 Little Portland St. Buzzing, industrial club/bar, with great DJs playing everything from rock to rap for a truly hedonistic crowd. Closed Sun. Oxford Circus tube.

Clubs

The Arches 51–53 Southwark St Ⓦwww.the-arches.com. Versatile, large-capacity club playing a range of sounds, including house, techno

TREAT YOURSELF

A cocktail at **Loungelover**, 1 Whitby St (Ⓣ 020/7012 1234), may not come cheap, but even if you just have the one, it's worth the trip to see the fabulously camp decor of this lavish, bejewelled bar tucked incongruously off Bethnal Green Rd. You'll need to dress well if you don't want to feel intimidated. It's advisable to book a table at weekends; otherwise just walk in and stand at the bar. Liverpool St tube.

and dubstep on Fri, with gay nights Wed and Sat. London Bridge tube.

Bar Rumba 36 Shaftesbury Ave Ⓦ www.barrumbadisco.co.uk. Small West End venue with a programme of Latin, drum and bass and funk. Piccadilly Circus tube.

Cargo 83 Rivington St Ⓦ www.cargo-london.com. Live music bar/club with globally influenced music, trendy crowds and a laid-back vibe. Old Street tube.

Fabric 77a Charterhouse St Ⓦ www.fabriclondon.com. If you're seriously into dance music, head for *Fabric* at the weekends and get there early. Farringdon tube.

Guanabara Parker St Ⓦ www.guanabara.co.uk. Nightly samba, bossa-nova and Latin beats keep the punters on the dancefloor at this fun Brazilian club. Holborn or Covent Garden tube.

Matter The 02 Ⓦ www.matterlondon.com. London's latest superclub has given the ill-fated Millennium Dome (now The 02 Arena) a new lease of life. Run by the folk behind *Fabric*, cutting-edge audio and visuals attract the likes of Armand Van Helden and DJ Yoda. North Greenwich tube or boat from Waterloo/London Bridge.

Plastic People 147 Curtain Rd Ⓦ www.plasticpeople.co.uk. An intimate venue playing a mix of house, hip-hop, funk and jazz. Old St or Liverpool St tube.

Scala 278 Pentonville Rd Ⓦ www.scala-london.co.uk. Multi-faceted nights take in film, live bands and music from hip-hop to deep house. King's Cross tube.

Gay and lesbian nightlife

Candy Bar 4 Carlisle St. Britain's first seven-day all-girl bar offers a retro-style cocktail bar-cum-pool room upstairs, and a noisy, beery ground level cruising area. Tottenham Court Rd tube.

First Out 52 St Giles High St. The West End's original gay café/bar, and still permanently packed, serving good veggie food at reasonable prices (mains from £6.75). At weekends, there's music and DJ acts in the downstairs bar. Closes 11pm. Tottenham Court Rd tube.

Freedom 66 Wardour St, Soho. Hip, busy café/bar attracting a gay and straight crowd. Leicester Square tube.

George and Dragon 2–4 Hackney Rd. Behind the shabby exterior lurks one of Shoreditch's most popular gay bars.

Heaven under The Arches, Villiers St. Britain's most popular gay club, this legendary, 2000-capacity club continues to reign supreme. It now hosts G.A.Y's Friday "Camp Attack" night. Charing Cross or Embankment tube.

Entertainment

Cinemas

BFI South Bank Ⓦ www.bfi.org.uk. Serious arts cinema showing up to ten different films each day and screening the London Film Festival (Oct) and London Lesbian and Gay Film Festival (late March). Waterloo tube.

Prince Charles 2–7 Leicester Place Ⓦ www.princecharlescinema.com. The bargain basement of London's cinemas, with a programme of newish movies and cult favourites. Leicester Square tube.

Curzon Cinemas Various locations including Soho, Mayfair and Chelsea Ⓦ www.curzoncinemas.com. Arthouse chain specializing in European cinema.

Live music venues

100 Club 100 Oxford St Ⓦ www.the100club.co.uk. Historically important venue – the Sex Pistols played here – in a very central location hosting quality new talent. Tottenham Court Rd tube.

Barfly 49 Chalk Farm Road Ⓦ www.barflyclub.com. Where a large array of punk, rock and indie bands make their debut. Camden Town or Chalk Farm tube.

Borderline Orange Yard, Manette St Ⓦ www.mamagroup.co.uk/borderline. Intimate venue best known for Indie and ska. Good place to catch new bands. Also has club nights. Tottenham Court Rd tube.

Jazz Café 5 Parkway Ⓦ www.jazzcafe.co.uk. Futuristic, white-walled venue with an adventurous booking policy including Latin, rap, funk, hip-hop and fusion. Camden Town tube.

Ronnie Scott's 47 Frith St Ⓦ www.ronniescotts.co.uk. London's most famous jazz club; big name acts play in the dimly lit, red-velvet downstairs club. Less pricey and great fun is Wed's late-night jam session (from 10.30pm) in the upstairs bar. Tottenham Court Rd tube.

CULTURE ON THE CHEAP

With a little bit of effort, it's possible to bag tickets to some of the best plays and classical music in London at bargain-basement prices. Under 26s can currently apply for free tickets at theatres throughout London (see ⓦ www.anightlessordinary.org.uk for details of how to register). Many theatres offer student discounts, and have standing or cut-price standby tickets available last minute (see individual listings). Another option is to head to the large booth in Leicester Square selling half-price tickets (Mon–Sat 10am–7pm, Sun noon–3pm) for that day's performances at West End theatres. Finally, between July and September, standing tickets go on sale for around £5 for the **Proms**, the annual classical music festival held at the Royal Albert Hall.

South Bank Centre ⓦ www.southbankcentre.co.uk. Vast arts complex, showcasing high-quality music of all genres; it includes the Royal Festival Hall and the Purcell Room, both top classical music venues.

Theatres

London's West End theatre scene is dominated by big musicals, but there's no shortage of other performances on offer, many of which are world class.

Donmar Warehouse Earlham St ⓦ www.donmarwarehouse.com. Formerly the spiritual home of director Sam Mendes, and the best bet for a central off-West End show. Covent Garden tube.

English National Opera Coliseum, St Martin's Lane ⓦ www.eno.org. More radical and democratic than the Royal Opera House, with opera (in English) and ballet. Leicester Square tube.

Institute of Contemporary Arts (ICA) Nash House, The Mall ⓦ www.ica.org.uk. Contemporary theatre, dance, films and art at this enduringly cutting-edge venue. Charing Cross tube.

National Theatre South Bank Centre, South Bank ⓦ www.nationaltheatre.org.uk. The NT has three separate theatres and consistently good productions. With almost half of all tickets for certain plays going on sale at £10, it's no wonder that some performances sell out months in advance. If you haven't booked, ask about discounted day seats or £5 standing tickets. Waterloo tube.

Sadler's Wells Rosebery Ave ⓦ www.sadlerswells.com. London's biggest dance venue puts on a mix of the best contemporary dance and ballet. Angel tube.

Shakespeare's Globe New Globe Walk ⓦ www.shakespeares-globe.org. Replica open-air Elizabethan theatre that puts on shows from May to early Oct, with standing tickets for £5. London Bridge, Blackfriars or Southwark tube.

Shopping

London's up there with Paris and New York for the sheer variety of its shopping, and there are many stores and boutiques you simply won't find anywhere else. If you're on a budget, window-shopping is still a great way of spending time; better still, visit one of the capital's many markets.

Shopping streets

Charing Cross Road Great place to pick up reading material. Rummage in one of the many secondhand bookshops, or browse new titles in Foyles.

Covent Garden (ⓦ www.coventgardenlife.com) Plenty of high street stores, plus independent fashion outlets around the Neal St area, Floral St and Long Acre.

Oxford Street London's most famous and frequented shopping strip, home to gargantuan branches of high street shops including Topshop, Primark and Niketown.

Soho and Carnaby Street Seedy Soho is crammed with quirky fashion shops, independent record stores and erotica to suit all tastes. At its western boundary, Carnaby Street (ⓦ www.carnaby.co.uk) trades heavily on its association with the swinging sixties, but is still a good bet for cool trainers and young fashion.

Markets

Borough Market Off Borough High St. A foodie's paradise, with stalls selling quality organic produce and gourmet foods ranging from quail and fudge to English wine. It's pricey, but a whole range of free tasters is on offer. Open Thurs 11am–5pm, Fri noon–6pm, Sat 9am–4pm. London Bridge tube.

Camden Market Camden Lock, Chalk Farm Rd. A magnet for teens, goths and indie kids, selling everything from bizarre clothes to ethnic throws and assorted bric-à-brac. Daily 10am–6pm. Camden Town tube.

Columbia Road Market Columbia Rd. London's most colourful market – cockney traders peddle a riot of fabulous flowers and plants, surrounded by quirky jewellery shops and galleries. Sun 8am–2pm. Bethnal Green or Old St tube.

Portobello Road Market Portobello and Golborne rds. The antiques, bric-à-brac and assorted

QUINTESSENTIAL LONDON SHOPS

Harrods on Brompton Rd is London's grandest department store and a major tourist attraction in its own right; check out the incredible food hall with its Arts and Crafts tiling. A better bet for clothes is **Selfridges** on Oxford Street. Famous for its creative window displays, it sells pretty much everything from sushi, via stationery to astronomically expensive designer handbags. Just off Regent Street is the elegant mock-Tudor department store **Liberty** on Great Marlborough Street, with jewellery, scarves, bags and fabrics in rich, and peculiarly calming surroundings.

paraphernalia are still a draw, but the local fashionistas come for the vintage clothes and young designers' stalls under the Westway. Antiques market Sat 8am–5pm; general market Mon–Wed, Fri & Sat 8am–6.30pm, Thurs 9am–1pm. Ladbroke Grove or Notting Hill Gate tube.

Directory

Embassies Australia, Australia House, Strand ⓣ020/7379 4334 (Holborn or Temple tube); Canada, 38 Grosvenor St ⓣ020/7258 6600 (Bond St tube); Ireland, 17 Grosvenor Place ⓣ020/7235 2171 (Hyde Park Corner tube); New Zealand, 80 Haymarket ⓣ020/7930 8422 (Piccadilly Circus tube); South Africa, South Africa House, Trafalgar Square ⓣ020/7451 7299 (Charing Cross tube); United States, 24 Grosvenor Square ⓣ020/7499 9000 (Bond St tube).
Exchange Shopping areas such as Oxford St and Covent Garden are littered with private exchange offices, but their rates are usually worse than the banks. You'll find branches of major banks all around the centre.
Hospitals St Mary's Hospital, Praed St ⓣ020/7886 6666 (Paddington tube); University College Hospital, 235 Euston Rd ⓣ0845/1555 000 (Euston Square tube).
Internet Netstream in St Anne's Court (off Wardour St) is open 24hr. Tottenham Court Rd tube.
Left luggage At all airport terminals and major train stations.
Pharmacy Bliss, 5 Marble Arch, W1 (daily 9am–midnight). Marble Arch tube.
Post office 24–28 William IV St (Leicester Square or Charing Cross tube). Mon–Fri 8.30/9.15am–6.30pm, Sat 9am–5.30pm.

Moving on

Train Bath (every 30min; 1hr 30min); Brighton (every 15min; 1hr–1hr 20min); Bristol (every 30min; 1hr 45min); Brussels (12 daily; 2hr 5min); Cambridge (every 15min; 45min–1hr 15min); Cardiff (every 30min; 2hr 10min); Dover (every 30min; 1hr 45min); Durham (hourly; 2hr 45min); Edinburgh (hourly; 4hr 30min–7hr 30min); Glasgow (hourly; 4hr 30min–5hr 30min); Lille (8 daily; 1hr 45 min); Liverpool (hourly; 2hr 10min); Manchester (every 20min; 2hr 10min); Newcastle (every 30min; 3hr); Oxford (every 20–30min; 1hr–1hr 45min); Paris (1–2 hourly; 2hr 15min); Penzance (10 daily; 5hr 15min–7hr); Stratford-upon-Avon (6 daily; 2hr 20min); Winchester (every 15–20min; 1hr); York (every 30min; 2hr).
Bus Amsterdam (3–5 daily; 12hr); Bath (hourly; 2hr 30min–4hr 20min); Berlin (1 daily; 19hr); Brighton (hourly; 2hr 10min); Bristol (hourly; 2hr 30min); Cambridge (hourly; 2hr 30min); Cardiff (hourly; 3–4hr); Dover (1–2 hourly; 2hr 30min–3hr); Dublin (3–5 daily; 12–16hr); Durham (4 daily; 6hr–7hr 25min); Edinburgh (6 daily; 8hr 40min–12hr 30min); Glasgow (7 daily; 8hr–10hr 30min); Inverness (2 daily; 12hr 35min–13hr 30min); Liverpool (1–2 hourly; 5hr 10min–6hr 40min); Manchester (1–2 hourly; 4hr 45min–6hr 35min); Newcastle (5 daily; 6hr 40min–7hr 45min); Oxford (every 15min; 1hr 40min); Paris (5 daily; 8hr 15min–9hr 45min); Penzance (6 daily; 8hr 20min–9hr 55min); Stratford-upon-Avon (4 daily; 3hr 25min); York (5 daily; 4hr 55min–6hr 15min).

Southeast England

Nestling in self-satisfied prosperity, **southeast England** is the richest part of Britain. Swift, frequent rail and coach services make it ideal for **day-trips** from London. Medieval ecclesiastical power-bases such as **Canterbury** and **Winchester** are full of history, while, on the coast the upbeat, hedonistic resort of **Brighton** is London's summer playground by the sea.

DOVER

DOVER is the main port of entry along this stretch of coast, and the country's busiest. It's not exactly an inspiring town, and its famous White Cliffs are best enjoyed from a boat several miles out. If you have time to kill though, visit **Dover Castle** (Feb & March daily 10am–4pm, April–Oct daily 9.30/10am–5/6pm, Nov–Jan Thurs–Mon 10am–4pm; £10), an imposing medieval fortress, from whose secret war tunnels Vice-Admiral Ramsey orchestrated the Allied evacuation of Dunkerque in 1940. **Ferries** sail to Calais and Dunkerque from the Eastern Docks, which is also the starting point for LD Lines's service to Boulogne. The main **train station**, for services to Canterbury and London (last one around 11pm), is Dover Priory, ten minutes' walk west of the centre and served by shuttle buses from the Eastern Docks. **Coaches** to London (last one around 8pm) pick up from both the docks and the town-centre bus station on Pencester Road. The **tourist office** is on Biggin Street (daily 9/10am–4/5.30pm; Oct–March closed Sun; ⓣ01304/205108, ⓦwww.whitecliffscountry.org.uk).

CANTERBURY

CANTERBURY, still home to England's pre-eminent Archbishop, was one of medieval Europe's hottest pilgrimage destinations. As Chaucer's *Canterbury Tales* attest, pilgrims flocked to the shrine of Archbishop Thomas à Becket, who was brutally murdered in the cathedral nave in 1170, victim of an unseemly spat between Church and State. Becket's shrine continued to attract crowds until its demolition in 1538, during Henry VIII's Reformation. Enclosed on three sides by medieval walls, quaint Canterbury now hosts a sizeable student population, but the main draw for visitors is still the towering edifice of the cathedral.

What to see and do

Built in stages from 1070 onwards, **Canterbury Cathedral** (Mon–Sat 9am–5/6.30pm, Sun 12.30–2.30pm; £7.50) derives its distinctive presence from the perpendicular thrust of its late Gothic towers, dominated by the central, sixteenth-century Bell Harry tower. In the northwest transept, a modern sculpture, portraying ragged swords, is suspended over the place where Becket met his violent end. You'll also want to see the Romanesque arches of the crypt, one of the few remaining visible relics of the Norman cathedral.

East of the cathedral, across the ring road, are the evocative ruins of **St Augustine's Abbey** (April–June Wed–Sun 10am–5pm, July & Aug daily 10am–6pm, Sept–March Sat & Sun 10am–4/5pm; £4.30), on the site of a church founded by St Augustine, who began the conversion of the English in 597. The best exposition of local history is provided by the interactive **Museum of Canterbury**, on Stour Street (Mon–Sat 10.30am–4pm, plus June–Sept Sun 1.30–4pm; £3.60).

Arrival and Information

Train Canterbury has two train stations: Canterbury East for most services from London Victoria and Dover Priory, and Canterbury West for services from London Charing Cross – the stations are 10min south and northwest of the centre respectively.

Bus St George's Lane, below the High St.

Tourist office 13 Sun St, opposite the entrance to the cathedral ⓣ01227/378100, ⓦwww.canterbury.co.uk (March–Aug daily 9.30/10am–5/6pm, Sun 10am–4pm; Sept–Feb daily 9.30/10am–4/5pm; closed Sun Dec–Feb).

Accommodation

Ann's House 63 London Rd ⓣ01227/768767, ⓦwww.annshousecanterbury.co.uk. Traditional Victorian villa, a short walk from West Station. Some rooms have four-poster beds. Doubles £55.

Canterbury Camping & Caravanning Bekesbourne Lane ⓣ01227/463216, ⓦwww.campingandcaravanningclub.co.uk. A mile outside the city and served by regular buses. £22.
Canterbury YHA 54 New Dover Rd ⓣ0845/371 9010, ⓦwww.yha.org.uk. Gothic Victorian house a mile southeast of the centre, with a self-catering kitchen and internet. Dorms £15.95.
Kipps Hostel 40 Nunnery Fields ⓣ01227/786121, ⓦwww.kipps-hostel.com. Homely independent hostel, within walking distance of the centre. There's a communal kitchen, free wi-fi and a garden with space for a couple of tents. Dorms £16, doubles from £36.

Eating and drinking

Café des Amis 95 St Dunstan's St. This jolly Mexican place has been around for years and still has a loyal following. Mains from £7.95. Student discounts.
Café Belge 89 St Dunstan's St. Excellent Belgian restaurant, serving up moules frites (from £12.95) and a vast range of beers. Check out the £10 lunch menu.
Coffee & Corks 13 Palace St. Delicious coffee in a bohemian sanctuary away from the crowds; this place has an almost horizontally relaxed vibe.
Goods Shed Canterbury West station. Atmospheric café and farmers' market (daily except Mon 9am–7pm; Sun until 4pm). Source top-notch local picnic ingredients here.
Osteria Posillipo 16 The Borough. Neapolitan restaurant serving perfectly charred pizza from its wood-fired oven, plus home-made pastas. Mains from £5.95.
Thomas Becket 21 Best Lane. Lively independent pub, tucked down a back street, with guest ales and a ceiling adorned with hops.

Moving on

Train Brighton (change at Ashford International; hourly; 2hr 15min); Dover (every 20min; 20–30min); London (every 20min; 1hr 30min).
Bus Dover (hourly; 40min); London (hourly; 1hr 50min).

BRIGHTON

BRIGHTON has been a magnet for day-tripping Londoners since the Prince Regent (later George IV) started holidaying here in the 1770s with his mistress, launching a trend for the "dirty weekend". One of Britain's most entertaining seaside resorts, the city has emerged from seediness to embrace a new, fashionable hedonism, becoming one of the country's premier gay centres. This factor – along with a large student presence – has endowed Brighton with a buzzing nightlife scene, and there's a colourful music and arts festival (ⓦwww.brightonfestival.org), which runs for three weeks in May.

What to see and do

From the train station on Queen's Road it's a ten-minute stroll straight down to the seafront, a four-mile-long pebble beach bordered by a balustered promenade.

The seafront

The wonderfully tacky **Palace Pier** is an obligatory call; it's basically a half-mile amusement arcade lined with booths selling fish and chips, candyfloss and assorted tat. If you are feeling brave, hop on the hair-raising "Super Booster" ride. A more sedate option is the nearby **Volk's Electric Railway** (Easter to mid-Sept daily 10am–5/6pm; £2.70 return), whose antiquated locomotives run eastward towards the marina and the nudist beach. On the western seafront you can see – but not enter – the brooding wreckage of the **West Pier**, damaged in World War II, severed from the mainland following a hurricane in 1987, and gutted by fire in 2003.

The Royal Pavilion and around

Inland, overlooking the traffic-heavy Old Steine, is the flamboyant **Royal Pavilion** (daily: Oct–March 10am–5.15pm, April–Sept 9.30am–5.45pm; £8.80), a wedding-cake confection of pagodas, minarets and domes built in 1817 as a pleasure palace for the Prince Regent. Do pay to enter: the pavilion's interior, decorated with

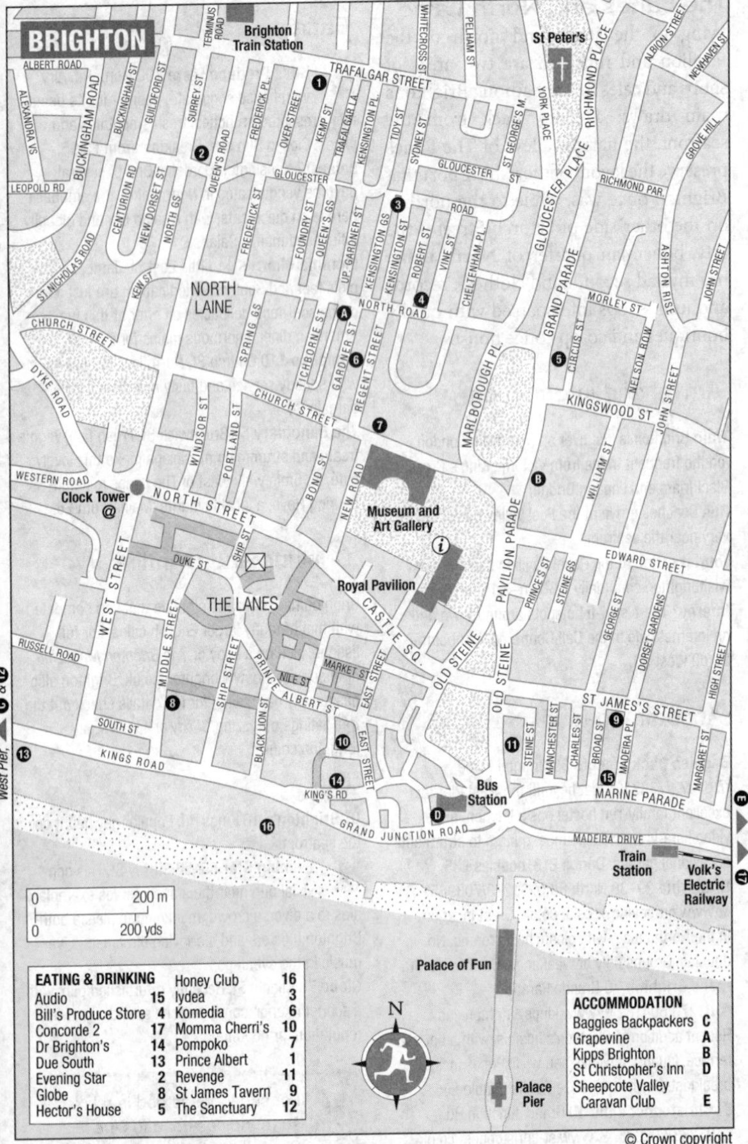

ostentatious chandeliers and exotic chinoiserie, is even more impressive than the exterior. Just across the lawns from the pavilion is Brighton's **Museum and Art Gallery** (Tues 10am–7pm, Wed–Sat 10am–5pm, Sun 2–5pm; free; Ⓦ www.brighton.virtualmuseum.info), with displays of Art Nouveau and a pair of the corpulent Prince Regent's enormous trousers.

The Lanes and North Laine

Lying to the south and north of the Pavilion and museum are two areas of shops and cafés that are among Brighton's main draws: a block back from the seafront, the narrow alleys of **The Lanes** preserve the layout of the fishing port that Brighton once was, while to the north – on the other side of Church Street – the arty, bohemian quarter of **North Laine** has myriad secondhand clothes-, record- and junk-shops interspersed with quirky boutiques and co-op coffee houses.

Arrival and information

Train Brighton is just over an hour from London (on the frequent trains from Victoria, King's Cross, Blackfriars and London Bridge).

Bus Coaches arrive at the Pool Valley bus station, very near the seafront.

Tourist office At the Royal Pavilion shop ⓦwww.visitbrighton.com (daily 9.30am–5.15pm).

Internet There's wi-fi hotspots around town and an internet café in the Call Centre on Cranbourne St (off West St).

Accommodation

Baggies Backpackers 33 Oriental Place ⓣ01273/733740. Just beyond the West Pier this excellent family-run hostel has a kitchen, huge video library, spacious lounge, guitars to strum and occasional parties. Dorms £13, doubles £35.

Grapevine 29–30 North Rd ⓣ01273/703985, ⓦwww.grapevinewebsite.co.uk. Great location in the North Laine, with clean, basic rooms. No doubles. Groups only at weekends. Dorms £12.50.

Kipps Brighton 76 Grande Parade ⓣ01273/604182 ⓦwww.kipps-brighton.com. Recent addition to Brighton's hostels, with a bar, roof terrace, laundry facilities and wi-fi. Prices include breakfast. Dorms £17.95, en-suite double £65.

St Christopher's Inn 10 Grand Junction Rd ⓣ01273/202035, ⓦwww.st-christophers.co.uk. Party hostel with a lively bar (ten percent discount for guests), close to the seafront. Dorms £17, doubles £50.

Sheepcote Valley Caravan Club East Brighton Park ⓣ01273/626546, ⓦwww.caravanclub.co.uk. Two miles east of town, this family-friendly campsite is easily reached by bus or the Volks railway. £18.50.

Eating

Bill's Produce Store 100 North Rd. Airy warehouse shop/café, popular for its beautifully presented brunches, fresh smoothies and juices. Closed Sun eve. Breakfast from £3.95.

Iydea 17 Kensington Gardens. One of several daytime veggie cafés in North Laine, the emphasis here is on quick eats, with a salad bar and globally influenced mains. Salads £4.

Momma Cherri's 11 Little East St. Jambalaya, pig's feet and Southern-fried catfish are just some of the soul-food delicacies on offer at this fun American diner. Enormous mains for £11.50.

Pompoko 110 Church St. No-frills Japanese with speedy service and tasty rice dishes for a bargain £4.

The Sanctuary 51 Brunswick St. Fresh fish, veggie treats and strumming musicians make this lovely café, a 15min walk west of The Lanes in neighbouring Hove, a local favourite. Mains from £6.

Drinking and nightlife

Brighton has a frenetic nightlife that can compete with that of many larger English cities. For full listings, pick up a copy of *The Brighton Magazine* or check out ⓦwww.brighton.co.uk. Brighton also has a lively gay scene; for full details check out the free listings magazine *3Sixty* or ⓦwww.gay.brighton.co.uk.

Pubs

Dr Brighton's 16 Kings Rd. Popular gay haunt on the seafront.

Evening Star 55–56 Surrey St. This convivial pub near the station serves exemplary ales to a diverse crowd, managing to please both Brighton hipsters and ale-loving old timers. Live music in the evenings.

Globe 78 Middle St. Recently refurbished pub, with a scarlet interior, comfy armchairs and a growing reputation for good food.

TREAT YOURSELF

For superior seafood in relaxed surroundings head to **Due South** at 139 Kings Rd Arches, which brings a classier touch to the sometimes tatty seafront. With an uninterrupted sea view and scrumptious seasonal produce, it's worth missing breakfast and lunch for. Mains from £12.50.

Hector's House Grand Parade. A favourite student hangout with pre-club music and cheap drinks.
Prince Albert 48 Trafalgar St. Near the station, this pub has live rock and real ales, though the grubby interior might deter some.
St James Tavern 16 Madeira Place. Lively pub in the gay district (but with a mixed clientele), offering an enormous selection of rums and other tipples.

Clubs and live music

Audio 10 Marine Parade ⓦwww.audiobrighton.com. Brighton's trendiest club, specializing in funk and house.
Concorde 2 Madeira Drive ⓦwww.concorde2.co.uk. Live music venue with club nights at weekends; it's around a mile east of the centre along Madeira Drive.
Honey Club 214 Kings Rd Arches, ⓦwww.thehoneyclub.co.uk. By the seafront near the bottom of Ship St, this attracts a youngish crowd, dancing to garage, house and hip-hop.
Komedia 44 Gardner St ⓦwww.komedia.co.uk. Cool venue offering everything from cabaret to rock gigs.
Revenge 32 Old Steine ⓦwww.revenge.co.uk. Two-floor, predominantly gay venue also featuring cabaret.

Moving on

Train Canterbury (change at Ashford International hourly; 2hr 20min); London (every 15min; 1hr–1hr 15min); Southampton (hourly; 1hr 50min).
Bus London (hourly; 1hr 50min–2hr 35min).

WINCHESTER

Nowadays it's hard to imagine that tranquil **WINCHESTER** was once the chief political and ecclesiastical power-base of southern England. Fifty miles southwest of London, the city rose to prominence in the ninth century as King Alfred the Great's capital. Alfred's statue now stands at the eastern end of the Broadway, the town's hilly main thoroughfare, which becomes the High Street as it progresses west towards the train station.

South of the High Street is the main attraction: the vast, mostly twelfth-century **cathedral** (daily 8.30am–6pm; £6). Mortuary chests above the high altar hold the remains of the pre-Conquest kings of England, whilst immediately outside you can see traces of the original Saxon cathedral, built in the seventh century. Look out, too, for the grave of the novelist Jane Austen, buried on the north side of the nave. A short stroll west along the High Street brings you to the thirteenth-century **Great Hall** (daily 10am–5pm; free), renowned for what is alleged to be King Arthur's Round Table. South of Winchester Cathedral is the fourteenth-century Pilgrims Hall, from where a signposted route leads through a medieval quarter to **Winchester College**, the oldest of Britain's public schools. It's then a half-hour stroll across the Water Meadow to the hospital of **St Cross** (April–Oct Mon–Sat 9.30am–5pm, Sun 1–5pm; Nov–March Mon–Sat 10.30am–3.30pm; £3), founded in 1132.

Trains from London Waterloo arrive at the train station on Stockbridge Road, about a mile northwest of the cathedral. **Buses** terminate on Broadway. There's no hostel; if you want to stay, contact the tourist office in the Guildhall (Mon–Sat 10am–5pm, plus May–Sept Sun 11am–4pm; ⓣ01962/840500, ⓦwww.visitwinchester.co.uk) for details of local B&Bs. For lunch, *Blues*, a friendly sandwich bar at 1A Southgate St, is a good budget option. Alternatively, The *Wykeham Arms*, 75 Kingsgate St, has cosy nooks and crannies and tasty, though not cheap, food.

The West Country

England's **West Country** is not a precise geographical term, but as a broad generalization, the cosmopolitan feel of the southeast begins to fade into a slower, rural pace of life from **Salisbury**

onwards, becoming more pronounced the further west you travel. In Neolithic times a rich and powerful culture evolved here, as shown by monuments such as **Stonehenge** and **Avebury**. Urban attractions include studenty **Bristol** and the elegant Regency spa town of **Bath**, while those in search of rural peace and quiet should head for the compelling bleakness of **Dartmoor**. The southwestern extremities of Britain include some of the most beautiful stretches of coastline: with rugged, rocky shores battered by the Atlantic and excellent sandy beaches, **Cornwall** is one of the country's busiest corners over the summer.

All of the region's major centres can be reached fairly easily by train or coach from London. Local bus services cover most areas, although in the rural depths of Dartmoor they can be very sparse indeed. Check the tourist office website ⓦwww.westcountrynow.com.

SALISBURY

SALISBURY's central feature is the elegant spire of its **cathedral** (daily 7.15am–6.15/7.15pm; £5 donation; ⓦwww.salisburycathedral.org.uk), the tallest in the country, rising over 400ft. Spire aside, the cathedral was almost entirely completed in the thirteenth century, and is one of the few great English churches that is not a hotchpotch of different styles. A lofty octagonal chapter house, approached via the cloisters (Mon–Sat 9.30/10am–5.15/6.45pm, Sun noon–5.30pm; free), holds one of the four extant copies of the 1215 **Magna Carta**, England's most famous constitutional document.

Most of Salisbury's remaining sights are grouped in a sequence of historic houses around The Close, the old walled inner town around the cathedral. The **Salisbury and South Wiltshire Museum** on West Walk (Mon–Sat 10am–5pm; July & Aug also Sun noon–5pm; £6 ⓦwww.salisburymuseum.org.uk), is a good place to bone up on the Neolithic history of the region before heading out to Stonehenge. **Mompesson House** on The Close's North Walk (April–Oct Sat–Wed 11am–5pm; £5.20) is a fine eighteenth-century house complete with Georgian furniture.

Arrival and information

Train It's a short walk east from Salisbury's train station (services from London Waterloo) across the River Avon into town.

Bus Buses from Winchester and elsewhere terminate behind Endless St, a short walk northeast of the cathedral.

Tourist office Just off Market Square, a block south of the bus station ⓣ01722/334956, ⓦwww.visitsalisbury.com (daily 9.30/10.30am–4.30/6pm; closed Sun in winter).

Accommodation

Salisbury Caravan Club Castle Rd ⓣ01722/320713, ⓦwww.campingandcaravanningclub.co.uk. A peaceful, family site a mile north of town. April–Oct. £22.

Salisbury YHA Milford Hill House, Milford Hill ⓣ0845/371 9537, ⓦwww.yha.org.uk. Excellent secluded hostel 5min walk east of the city centre. Dorms £15.95, twins £38.95.

Eating and drinking

Haunch of Venison 1 Minster St. Tiny, atmospheric, old pub supposedly home to two ghosts, the "Grey Lady" and the "Demented Whist Player". The food's good, but expensive. Mains from £10.

Polly Tea Rooms 8 St Thomas's Square. Time-warped tearoom, serving a tempting assortment of sticky buns and home-made cakes.

Moloko 5 Bridge St. Anomalously cool, this vodka bar opens till late.

Moving on

Train Bath (hourly; 55min); Bristol (hourly; 1hr 10min); Exeter (for Dartmoor; every 1–2hr; 2hr); London (every 25–35min; 1hr 30min); Winchester (change at Southampton or Basingstoke; every 15–30min; 1hr–1hr 20min).

Bus Bath (1 daily; 1hr 20min); Bristol (1 daily; 2hr 10min); London (3 daily; 2hr 45min); Southampton (hourly; 1hr); Winchester (1 daily; 1hr 30min).

STONEHENGE AND AVEBURY

The uplands northwest of Salisbury were a thriving centre of Neolithic civilization, the greatest legacy of which is **Stonehenge** (daily 9/9.30am–4/7pm; £6.60). A tour bus runs daily from Salisbury's train and bus stations (£11, or £17.50 including admission to Stonehenge), travelling via the remains of the prehistoric and Norman forts at **Old Sarum**. Stonehenge was built in several distinct stages and adapted to the needs of successive cultures, the first stones being raised within earthworks about 3500 BC. During the next six hundred years, the incomplete bluestone circle was transformed into the familiar formation observed today. At its centre are the five local Wiltshire sarsen stones up to 21ft in height and topped by horizontal slabs. The way in which the sun's rays penetrate the central enclosure at dawn on midsummer's day has led to speculation about Stonehenge's role as either an astronomical observatory or a place of sun worship. The only way to enter the circle itself is to **pre-book** for entry outside standard visiting hours (apply on ⓣ01722/343830 or at ⓦwww.english-heritage.org.uk; £13.70).

Salisbury also serves as a base for visiting the Neolithic site around thirty miles north at **Avebury** (bus #5 to Pewsey, then bus #95 or #96; 1hr 40min). The Avebury monoliths were probably erected soon after 2500 BC, and the main circle – with a diameter of some 1300ft – easily beats Stonehenge in terms of scale, though it's not as impressive in its architectural sophistication. Visit Avebury's **Alexander Keiller Museum** (daily April–Oct 10am–6pm, Nov–March 10am–4pm; £4.20) for more on the monoliths.

BATH

Of all the south's cities, **BATH** is surely a contender for the prettiest. An ancient Roman spa town, revived and reconstructed in the eighteenth century as a retreat for the wealthy and fashionable, the city is an elegant confection of harmonious terraces constructed from the local honey-coloured sandstone. Jane Austen satirized Bath society in her novel *Northanger Abbey* and the city retains a genteel air of refinement even today. Bath hosts an **International Music Festival** (ⓦwww.bathmusicfest.org.uk) in May and June each year. Accommodation at this – or indeed any – time can be hard to find, so book early.

What to see and do

Bounded on three sides by the River Avon, Bath's core is relatively compact. From Bath Spa railway station, head north along Manvers Street, then Pierrepoint Street in the direction of Pulteney Bridge and turn off left to reach the Abbey.

The Roman Baths and Bath Abbey

The hot spring that gave the city its name was dedicated to Sulis, the Celtic goddess of the waters, and provided the centrepiece of an extensive **Roman Baths** complex, now restored and holding a fascinating museum (daily 9/9.30am–5.30/6pm, July & Aug till 9pm; ⓦwww.romanbaths.co.uk; £11). The pools, pipes and underfloor heating are remarkable demonstrations of the ingenuity of Roman engineering. The **Pump Room**, built above the Roman site in the eighteenth century, is now a restaurant and tearoom; the Roman Baths entrance ticket entitles you to a free glass of the unpleasantly tepid spa water. Next to the Roman Baths, **Bath Abbey** (Mon–Sat 9am–4.30/6pm, Sun 1–2.30pm & 4.30–5.30pm; £2.50 donation) is renowned for the lofty fifteenth-century vault of its choir and the dense carpet of gravestones and memorials that cover the floor.

TREAT YOURSELF

Follow in the footsteps of the Romans and pamper yourself in stylish, contemporary surroundings at **Thermae Bath Spa** (daily 9am–10pm; www.thermaebathspa.com), Britain's only natural hot spa. A two-hour session, with access to the spectacular open-air rooftop pool, costs £22.

The Royal Crescent and Assembly Rooms

The best of Bath's eighteenth-century architecture is on the high ground to the north of the town centre, where the well-proportioned Georgian urban planning is showcased by the elegant **Circus** and the adjacent **Royal Crescent**. The house at **1 Royal Crescent** is now a museum (Tues–Sun 10.30am–5pm; closed Jan to early Feb; £5), showing how the Crescent's houses would have looked in the Regency period. The social calendar of Bath's elite centred on the **Assembly Rooms** (daily: March–Oct 10.30am–6pm, Nov–Feb 10.30am–5pm, £7, includes Fashion Museum), just east of the Circus; it includes the fascinating **Fashion Museum** (closes 1hr before Assembly Rooms; www.fashionmuseum.co.uk; joint ticket with Roman Baths £14.50).

Arrival and information

Train and bus The train and bus stations are both on Manvers Street, 5min south of the centre.

Tourist office Just off the Abbey churchyard www.visitbath.co.uk (Mon–Sat 9.30am–5/6pm, Sun 10am–4pm).

Internet Try the *Green Park Brasserie* at Old Green Park Station, off James St.

Accommodation

Backpackers' Hostel 13 Pierrepoint St ⓣ01225/446787, www.hostels.co.uk. Relaxed hostel, just 5min walk from the train and bus stations. No doubles. Dorms £15.

Bath YHA Bathwick Hill ⓣ0845/371 9303, www.yha.org.uk. Hillside villa a mile east of town; bus #18 or #418. Dorms £15.95.

Bath YMCA Broad St Place ⓣ01255/325900, www.ymca.co.uk. Institutional hostel in the centre of town, serving cheap meals. Dorms £15, twins £42.

Belmont 7 Belmont, Lansdowne Rd ⓣ01225/423082, www.belmontbath.co.uk. Spacious rooms in an attractive Georgian house near the Assembly Rooms. Doubles £45/£60 en-suite.

St Christopher's Inn 9 Green St ⓣ01225/481444, www.st-christophers.co.uk. Basic but central party hostel. Guests benefit from discounted drinks at the bar below. Dorms £12, doubles £58

Eating and drinking

Cafés and restaurants

Café Retro 18 York St. Café and bistro with an inventive international menu and a relaxed atmosphere. Great breakfasts too. Closed Sun & Mon. Evening mains £3.50–£10.

Chandos Deli 12 George St. Local deli chain serving exemplary sarnies to eat in or take out to the park (£3).

Walrus and Carpenter 28 Barton St. Friendly place behind the theatre, offering steaks and burgers as well as veggie dishes. Mains from £8.75.

Yum Yum 17 Kingsmead Square. An antidote to countless genteel tea rooms, this Thai place has a bargain £5.95 lunch special.

Pubs

The Bell 103 Walcot St. Everything you could want from a neighbourhood pub with a great range of beers, a mixed and lively crowd, garden and live music Mon and Wed eve, plus Sun lunch.

The Porter 15 George St. Something of a Bath institution, with decent vegetarian food, live music during the week and DJ sets at weekends. Next door is *Moles* club, the best place to see live music in Bath.

The Salamander 3 John St. This small, characterful pub gets packed with knowledgeable drinkers lapping up the locally brewed ales.

Moving on

Train Bristol (every 20min; 11–20min); London (every 30min; 1hr 30min); Oxford (change at Didcot Parkway; every 30min–1hr; 1hr 10min–1hr 30min); Salisbury (hourly; 55min).

Bus Bristol (10 daily; 1hr); Glastonbury (1 direct daily; 1hr), London (every 30min; 2hr 55min–4hr).

BRISTOL

Situated on a succession of lumpy hills twelve miles west of Bath and just inland from the mouth of the River Avon, **BRISTOL** grew rich on transatlantic trade – the slave trade, in particular – in the early part of the nineteenth century. It has moved on since then, while remaining a wealthy, commercial centre, and is home to a major university, a thriving music scene that produced some of the most significant bands (Portishead, Tricky, Massive Attack) of the Nineties, and Banksy – guerrilla artist and agent provocateur whose subversive stencils adorn neglected city walls throughout the country. More ethnically diverse than other cities in the Southwest, in part because of its dubious heritage, Bristol manages to combine clued-up urban culture with enticing green spaces and striking industrial architecture. In August, the city hosts Europe's largest hot-air balloon fiesta.

What to see and do

The city centre – in so far as there is one – is an elongated traffic interchange. Walking from the station, detour via the **church of St Mary Redcliffe**, a glorious Gothic confection begun in the thirteenth century, before continuing across the river, through elegant Queen's Square. The southern end of the centre gives way to the city's **Floating Harbour**, an area of waterways that formed the hub of the old port. It is now the location of numerous bars and restaurants as well as two of Bristol's best contemporary arts venues: the **Arnolfini**, a cool, white gallery space, and the **Watershed Arts Centre**, which has an excellent café. Behind the Watershed lies **at-Bristol** (daily 10am–5/6pm; £11.90; Ⓦ www.at-bristol.org.uk), a hands-on science centre geared towards kids. Just to the north, **College Green** is overlooked by the city's nineteenth-century cathedral and the curvaceous red-brick Council House. From here, Park Street ascends steeply to the main university buildings and Clifton. A short walk west along the southern side of the harbour, or a brief ride on the ferry, brings you to Isambard Kingdom Brunel's **SS Great Britain** (daily 10am–4/6pm; £10.95) the world's first propeller-driven iron ship, launched from this dock in 1843, and to a replica of the *Matthew*, which carried John Cabot to North America in 1497.

Clifton

Genteel **Clifton Village** (bus #8 from the centre) is a great place to wander with airy terraces reminiscent of the Georgian splendours of nearby Bath, enticing pubs and upmarket antiques shops. Overhanging the limestone abyss of the Avon gorge is the **Clifton Suspension Bridge**, another creation of the indefatigable engineer Brunel. On a height above the bridge, a Victorian camera obscura (Easter–Oct daily 10.30am–5pm, Nov–Easter weekends only; closed when cloudy; £2) encompasses views of the gorge and bridge, and provides access to a steep tunnel ending at Giant's Cave, a ledge on the side of the gorge (same hours; £1.50). From the Clifton side of the Suspension Bridge, the Downs, the city's largest green space, stretches north for a couple of miles.

Arrival and information

Air Bristol's airport is eight miles south of town. Regular buses run to the stations and the city centre.

Train The main station, Bristol Temple Meads, is a 5min bus ride southeast of the centre (bus #8 or # 9), or a 15min walk.

Bus Close to the Broadmead shopping centre on Marlborough St.

Tourist office In at-Bristol on the Harbourside Ⓣ 0333/321 0101, Ⓦ www.visitbristol.co.uk (daily 10am–5/6pm).

Accommodation

Bristol Backpackers 17 St Stephen's St ⓣ0117/9257900, ⓦwww.bristolbackpackers.co.uk. Loud, convivial place in the heart of the centre, with late bar and internet access. Dorms £15, twin £36.

Bristol YHA 14 Narrow Quay ⓣ0845/371 9726, ⓦwww.yha.org.uk. Splendidly situated hostel in an old wharfside building next to the Arnolfini, extensively refurbished in 2009. Dorms £15.95, twins £38.95.

Full Moon 1 North St ⓣ0117/9245007, ⓦwww.fmbristol.co.uk. Spacious hostel near the bus station, with chunky wooden bunk-beds, wi-fi and a late bar. Dorms £16.50, twin £39.

Eating and drinking

Boston Tea Party 75 Park St. Relaxed café over two floors of a Georgian townhouse, with great coffee and cakes, locally sourced food and sunny garden.

Coronation Tap 8 Sion Place. A Clifton institution, famous for its Exhibition Cider, a lethal brew restricted to half-pint measures. A must if you want to sample the West Country's regional tipple.

Mud Dock 40 The Grove. Bike shed café-restaurant on the quayside, with a bargain £5 weekday lunch.

Olive Shed Floating Harbour, Princes Wharf. Located on the waterside amid ramshackle wharfs, this place serves delicious Mediterranean-style cuisine in charming surroundings. Closed Mon. Tapas dishes from £2.50.

Planet Pizza 83 Whiteladies Rd. Good-value pizzeria with a mellow feel and some outside tables. Buy-one-get-one-free Sun–Wed 5–7pm. A quarter pizza £3.95.

Entertainment and nightlife

For nightlife and music listings galore check out the magazine *Venue* (ⓦwww.venue.co.uk) available at any newsagent. The Arnolfini (ⓦwww.arnolfini.org.uk) and Watershed (ⓦwww.watershed.co.uk) both have superb arts cinemas, and there's a renowned theatre company at the Old Vic on King St (ⓦwww.bristololdvic.org.uk).

Blue Mountain Stokes Croft. Non-mainstream club spinning funk, hip-hop and drum'n'bass.

The Croft 117–119 Stokes Croft ⓦwww.the-croft.com. Showcases progressive homegrown bands and DJs.

The Old Duke 45 King St. Lively central pub with nightly jazz and open mic sessions.

Thekla The Grove ⓦwww.theklabristol.co.uk. Legendary riverboat venue staging eclectic events, gigs and Bristol's best club nights (Thurs–Sat until 3am or later).

Moving on

Train Bath (every 20min; 11–20min); Cardiff (every 20min; 35–50min); Salisbury (hourly; 1hr 10min); York (hourly; 4hr).

Bus Bath (10 daily; 1hr); Cardiff (every 1–2hr; 1hr 10min); Glastonbury (some via Wells; every 30min; 1hr 20min); Oxford (1 daily; 2hr 50min); Salisbury (1 daily; 2hr 10 min).

GLASTONBURY

GLASTONBURY is a small rural town whose associations with the Holy Grail and King Arthur have made it a magnet for those with a taste for the mystical – the **Tor**, a natural mound overlooking the town, is identified with the Isle of Avalon and the young Jesus Christ was a supposed visitor.

The impressive ruins of the **abbey** are approached from nearby Magdalene Street (daily 9/10am–4.30/6pm; £5; ⓦwww.glastonburyabbey.com); the choir is alleged to hold the tomb of King Arthur and Guinevere. A mile to the east is the Tor, at the base of which stands the natural spring known as **Chalice Well** (daily: April–Oct 10am–5.30pm; Nov–March 10am–4pm;

GLASTONBURY FESTIVAL

Glastonbury is synonymous with the world-famous **Glastonbury Festival** (ⓦwww.glastonburyfestivals.co.uk) held by avuncular farmer, Michael Eavis, at Worthy Farm over the last weekend in June. When first hosted in 1970, this small-scale event cost £1, including free milk from the farm. Nowadays, it draws 175,000-plus people to its binge of music and all-round hedonism and the £175 tickets sell out in hours. The cost may be exorbitant, but there's still nothing else quite like it.

£3.25). The ferrous waters that flow from the hillside here were popularly thought to have gained their colour from the blood of Christ, supposedly flowing from the Holy Grail, buried here by Joseph of Arimathea.

The easiest way to access Glastonbury is by **bus** (#376; every 30min) from Bristol bus station or just outside Bristol Temple Meads train station, which stops at Glastonbury Town Hall. The **tourist office** is housed in the Tribunal on the High Street (daily 10am–4/5.30pm; ⓣ01458/832954, ⓦwww.glastonburytic.co.uk). There's a friendly crowd at the Glastonbury Backpackers **hostel** on Market Place (ⓣ01458/833353, ⓦwww.glastonburybackpackers.com; dorms £14, doubles £40), while the Isle of Avalon **campsite** is a short walk up Northload Street from the centre (ⓣ01458/833618; £15).

DARTMOOR

Dartmoor (ⓦwww.dartmoor.npa.gov.uk), an expanse of uplands some 75 miles southwest of Bristol, is one of England's most beautiful wilderness areas. It's home to an indigenous breed of **wild pony** and dotted with **tors**, characteristic wind-eroded pillars of granite.

Postbridge

One focus for visitors in the middle of the park is **POSTBRIDGE**, reached by local bus from Exeter (#82 Transmoor service, Sun only) and from Plymouth (via Tavistock, bus #98 twice daily). Famous for its medieval bridge over the East Dart river, this is a good starting point for walks in the woodlands surrounding **Bellever Tor** to the south. Postbridge's **tourist office** is on the main road through the village (Easter–Oct daily 10am–5pm, Nov & Dec weekends 10am–4pm, closed Jan–Easter; ⓣ01822/880272). The nearest **hostel** is at Bellever, one mile south (ⓣ0845/371 9622, ⓦwww.yha.org.uk; dorms £11.95, small discount for arrival on foot/bike).

> **CAMPING ON DARTMOOR**
>
> Camping wild on certain common land in Dartmoor is permitted for one or two nights, though you shouldn't pitch on farmland, within 100m of a road or on an archeological site; check out ⓦwww.dartmoor-npa.gov.uk/vi-wildcamping for a helpful map. Always obtain consent from the landowner if pitching on private land.

Okehampton

The wildest parts of the moor, around its highest points of High Willhays and Yes Tor, are a few miles south of the market town of **OKEHAMPTON**, served by regular buses from Plymouth and Exeter. This starkly beautiful terrain is used by the Ministry of Defence as a firing range: details of times when it's safe to walk the moor are available from the **tourist office** on Fore Street (Mon–Sat 10am–5pm; ⓣ01837/53020, ⓦwww.okehampton.co.uk). Surrounded by woods one mile southwest of town is the now crumbling Norman keep of **Okehampton Castle** (April–Sept daily 10am–5/6pm; £3.30). There's a **hostel/activity centre** in a converted goods shed at the station (ⓣ0845/371 9651, ⓦwww.yha.org.uk; dorms £13.95).

THE EDEN PROJECT

Occupying a 160-foot-deep disused clay pit in the heart of Cornwall, the **Eden Project** (April–Oct daily 9am–6pm; Nov–March Mon–Fri 10am–4pm, Sat & Sun 10am–6pm; £16; ⓦwww.edenproject.com) showcases the diversity of the planet's plant life in a stunningly landscaped site. The centrepiece is two vast geodesic "biomes", or conservatories, one holding plants more usually found in warm, temperate zones, and the larger of the two recreating a tropical environment. The Eden

Project lies four miles northeast of St Austell (bus #T9 from St Austell train station or #T10 from Newquay). Arrive early and allow at least half a day for a full exploration.

PENZANCE AND AROUND

The busy port of **PENZANCE** forms the natural gateway to the westernmost extremity of Cornwall, the Penwith Peninsula. All the major sights of the region can be reached on day-trips from here.

What to see and do

From the train station, at the northern end of town, Market Jew Street threads its way through the compact town centre, culminating in the Neoclassical facade of Market House. West of here, a series of pleasant parks and gardens punctuate the quiet residential streets overlooking the promenade. The **Penlee House Gallery and Museum**, off Morrab Road (Mon–Sat 10/10.30am–4.30/5pm; £3, free on Sat), features works by members of the Newlyn School, late nineteenth-century painters of local land- and seascapes.

St Michael's Mount

The view east across the bay is dominated by **St Michael's Mount**, site of a fortified medieval monastery perched on an offshore pinnacle of rock. At low tide, the Mount is joined by a cobbled causeway to the mainland village of Marazion (regular buses from Penzance); at high tide, a boat can ferry you over (£1.50). You can amble part way along the Mount's shoreline, but most of the rock lies within the grounds of the **castle**, now a stately home (April–Oct daily except Sat 10.30am–5pm; £6.60).

Land's End

The other obvious excursion is to **LAND'S END**, the extremity of the Penwith Peninsula, accessible on bus #1/1A or #504 (1hr). Despite the hold it exerts over the popular imagination, the site may fail to live up to expectations – especially now that a particularly grim theme park has been built here – so it's worthwhile using the coastal path to explore some of the less frequented spots of the peninsula. A mile and a half south of Land's End you'll find rugged beauty at **Mill Bay**, while there are acres of beaches at **Whitesand Bay** to the north, and more spectacular headlands around **Cape Cornwall**, four miles north of Land's End.

Arrival and information

Train and bus Both stations are at the north-eastern end of town, a step away from Market Jew St.

Tourist office By the bus station ⓣ01736/362207, ⓦwww.go-cornwall.com (Mon–Fri 9am–5pm, plus Easter–Sept Sat and hols 10am–4pm).

Accommodation

Penzance Backpackers Alexandra Rd ⓣ01736/363836, ⓦwww.pzbackpack.com. Good independent hostel on a quiet tree-lined road, with kitchen and wi-fi. Dorms £15, twins £32.

Penzance YHA Castle Horneck, Alverton ⓣ0845/371 9653, ⓦwww.yha.org.uk. Converted and refurbished Georgian manor house about a mile from the centre off the Land's End Rd. Dorms £17.95, doubles £43.95.

Whitesands Hotel Sennen, near Whitesand Bay ⓣ01736/871776, ⓦwww.whitesandslodge.co.uk. Excellent hotel with a cheaper surf lodge and tipis for groups. Tipis accommodate six at a squeeze (£16 per person, discounts for each extra day you stay).

Eating and drinking

The Admiral Benbow 46 Chapel St. Friendly seventeenth-century pub crammed with maritime fittings.

Archie Browns Bread St. Welcoming veggie café and health food shop using locally sourced ingredients. Lunches from £5. Daytime only; closed Sun.

The Turk's Head Chapel St. Ancient inn with a piratical heritage that includes a smugglers' tunnel. Touristy but fun.

Moving on

Train Bristol (4 daily; 4hr 15min), London (5 direct daily; 5hr 15min–8hr); Par (for Newquay; every 45min–1hr; 1hr); St Ives (change at St Erth; every 45min–1hr; 45–55min).
Bus Bristol (2 daily; 6hr 55min); London (5 daily; 8hr 35min–10hr); Newquay (2 daily; 1hr 35min–1hr 45min); St Ives (every 25–30min; 30min).

ST IVES

Across the peninsula from Penzance, the fishing village of **ST IVES** is the quintessential Cornish resort, featuring a maze of narrow streets lined with whitewashed cottages, sandy beaches, lush subtropical flora and squawking seagulls. The village's erstwhile tranquillity attracted several major artists throughout the twentieth century, including Ben Nicholson and Barbara Hepworth, whose work – amongst others – can be viewed at **Tate St Ives**, overlooking Porthmeor Beach (daily 10am–4.20/5.20pm; Nov–Feb closed Mon; £5.65; Ⓦwww.tate.org.uk/stives). A combined ticket (£8.55) also admits you to the much more charming **Barbara Hepworth Museum and Garden** on Barnoon Hill (same hours; £4.65), which preserves the studio of the modernist sculptor. Of the town's three beaches, the largest, north-facing Porthmeor occasionally has good surf; boards can be rented here. Alternatively, ramble along the costal path south towards Zennor for beautiful views of craggy coves and wild flowers.

The train **station** is at Porthminster Beach. The **tourist office**, in the Guildhall (June–Sept Mon–Fri 9am–5pm, Sat 10am–4pm, Sun 10am–2pm; Oct–May Mon–Fri 9am–5pm, Sat 10am–1pm; Ⓣ01736/796297, Ⓦwww.go-cornwall.com), is a couple of minutes from both stations. Nearby, the *St Ives Backpackers* **hostel** occupies a restored Wesleyan chapel on The Stennack, opposite the cinema (Ⓣ01736/799444, Ⓦwww.backpackers.co.uk/st-ives; dorms £17.95, doubles £38); it has a large kitchen and courtyard area.

NEWQUAY

Buffeted by Atlantic currents, Cornwall's north coast has a harsh grandeur, and is the area of the West Country most favoured by the **surfing** set. King of the surf resorts is **NEWQUAY**, whose tacky centre is surrounded by seven miles of golden sands, including Fistral Beach, the venue for surfing championships. Equipment can be hired on most beaches or from one of the surf shops around town, and the town is an excellent place to ride the waves for the first time: several surf schools are based here, including the British Surfing Association's National Surfing Centre (Ⓦwww.nationalsurfingcentre.com).

Newquay's **airport** is three miles north of the town; bus #556 runs to the centre. The **train station** (change in Par or Plymouth) is just east of the centre; buses terminate on Manor Road. There's a **tourist office** at Marcus Hill (Easter to mid-Sept; Ⓣ01637/854020, Ⓦwww.visitnewquay.org) and numerous campsites and **hostels**, including the hospitable if rather cramped *Newquay International Backpackers*, 69 Tower Rd (Ⓣ01637/879366, Ⓦwww.backpackers.co.uk/newquay; dorms £19.95, doubles £46), and *Matt's Surf Lodge* at 110 Mount Wise (Ⓣ01637/874651, Ⓦwww.matts-surf-lodge.co.uk; dorms £15, doubles £40).

PADSTOW

Ten miles north of Newquay (take bus #556), **PADSTOW** makes a more appealing base for some first-class beaches, such as Constantine Bay, four miles west, and Polzeath, on the eastern side of the Camel estuary. Primarily a fishing port, Padstow is renowned for its fish restaurants, not least those belonging to celebrity chef Rick Stein; dodge the expensive *Seafood Restaurant* and *St Petroc's Bistro* in favour of *Stein's Fish & Chips* (from £5.85 take-away) on South Quay. There's a YHA **hostel** just off the beach at Treyarnon Bay

(Ⓣ0845/371 9664, Ⓦwww.yha.org.uk; call for winter opening; dorms £17.95, twin £43.95).

Central England

Encompassing both the old industrial towns and cities of the Midlands and some postcard-pretty countryside, alongside some of the England's major cultural landmarks, Central England defies easy categorization. With close on a million residents, Birmingham is by far the Midlands' largest city, but despite boasting one of the best concert halls in the country, is still unlikely to feature on a whistle-stop national tour. More appealing for a quick-fix of history and culture are **Stratford-upon-Avon**, the birthplace of William Shakespeare, and the rival university cities of **Oxford** and **Cambridge**.

OXFORD

Thoughts of **OXFORD** inevitably conjure up the university, revered as one of the world's great academic institutions. The city's skyline is dominated by its "dreaming spires", while its streets form a dense maze of historic honeystone buildings, containing the university's 38 colleges. Although in term time you're never far from the university or its thousands of students, Oxford is a sizeable city in its own right, and the combination of workaday vitality with sleepy academic tradition is a distinct part of its appeal. Note that access to colleges may be restricted during examinations – especially in May and June – conferences and functions.

What to see and do

The main point of reference is **Carfax**, a central crossroads overlooked by the chunky **Carfax Tower**. Better panoramic views, however, are to be had from the spire of the University Church, **St Mary the Virgin**, on the High Street (Mon–Sat 9am–5/6pm, Sun 11.30am–5/6pm; £3).

Christ Church College and the cathedral

From Carfax, head south down St Aldates to **Christ Church**, one of the wealthiest and most ostentatious of Oxford's colleges (Mon–Sat 9am–5pm, Sun 2–5pm; £6), whose grand dining hall featured as that of Hogwarts in the Harry Potter films. The main entrance – though visitors are usually ushered in further south – is overlooked by the imposing Tom Tower, built in 1681 by Wren, and opens onto the vast expanse of Tom Quad, mostly dating from the college's foundation in the sixteenth century. The city's late Norman **cathedral** serves as the college chapel. Christ Church's Picture Gallery (May–Sept Mon–Sat 10.30am–5pm, Sun 2–5pm; Oct–April Mon–Sat 10.30am–1pm & 2–4.30pm, Sun 2–4.30pm; £3) is also worth a peek for its prestigious old master drawings.

PUNTING IN OXBRIDGE

Hiring a punt – essentially a flat-bottomed Venetian-style gondola powered by a brave soul brandishing a pole – is one of the finest ways to experience both Oxford and Cambridge. In **Oxford**, Cherwell Boathouse (Ⓦwww.cherwellboathouse.co.uk) rents punts for £12/hr for exploration of the tranquil, less touristy upstream stretch of the River Cherwell, north of the University Parks. For a more central option, try the Magdalen Bridge Boathouse. In **Cambridge**, Scudamore's (Ⓦwww.scudamores.co.uk) rents out punts from £16/hr for a cruise downstream past the architectural splendours of the college Backs or, for the adventurous, a trip upstream to rural Grantchester.

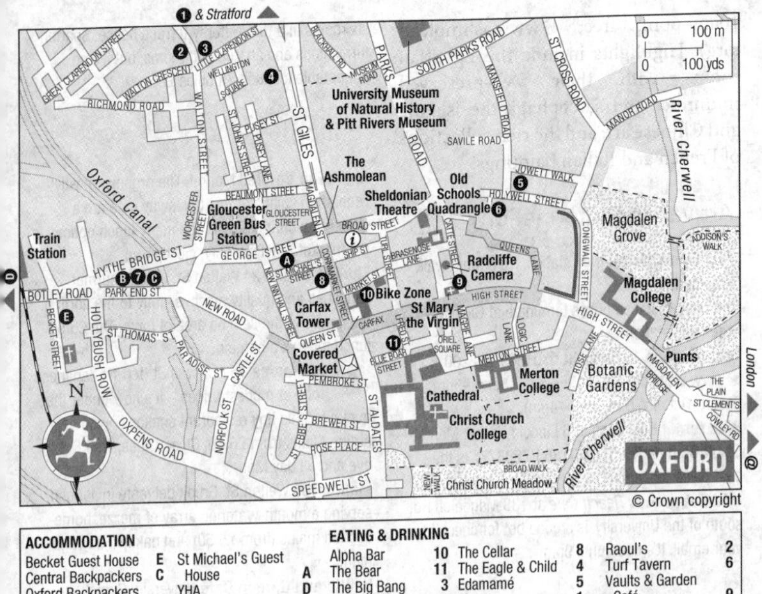

ACCOMMODATION				EATING & DRINKING					
Becket Guest House	E	St Michael's Guest House	A	Alpha Bar	10	The Cellar	8	Raoul's	2
Central Backpackers	C	YHA	D	The Bear	11	The Eagle & Child	4	Turf Tavern	6
Oxford Backpackers Hostel	B			The Big Bang	3	Edamamé	5	Vaults & Garden Café	9
				The Bridge	7	Manos	1		

Christ Church Meadow, Merton and Magdalen

South of Christ Church, **Christ Church Meadow** offers scenic views and gentle walks – either east along Broad Walk to the River Cherwell or south along New Walk to the Thames (referred to hereabouts as the Isis). From the Broad Walk, paths lead to **Merton** (Sat & Sun 10am–4pm; free), amongst the oldest and prettiest of Oxford's colleges. Nearby Rose Lane emerges at the eastern end of the High Street opposite **Magdalen College** (pronounced "maudlin"; daily noon/1–6pm; £4), which boasts its own deer park and a prestigious college choir.

The Radcliffe Camera and around

Many of the university's most imposing buildings lie just north of the High Street. The most dramatic is the Italianate **Radcliffe Camera**. Built in the 1730s by James Gibbs, it is now one of the **Bodleian Library**'s many reading rooms. The Bodleian's main building, housing the beautiful fifteenth-century Duke Humphrey's Library, is immediately to the north in the Old Schools Quadrangle. Most of the Bodleian is closed to the public, but you can see parts of it on an hour-long guided tour (Mon–Sat 10.30am, 11.30am, 2 & 4pm; £6). The adjacent **Sheldonian Theatre** (Mon–Sat 10am–12.30pm & 2–3.30/4.30pm; £2), a copy of the Theatre of Marcellus in Rome, was designed by Christopher Wren and is now a venue for concerts and graduation ceremonies.

University museums

A couple of hundred yards north along Parks Road lies the **Pitt Rivers Museum** (Mon noon–4.30pm, Tues–Sun 10am–4.30pm; free), a fascinating anthropological hoard, while five minutes west of the Sheldonian is the mammoth Neoclassical edifice containing the recently refurbished **Ashmolean Museum** (Tues–Sun

10am–6pm; free; Ⓦwww.ashmolean.org). Highlights include the Egyptian rooms with their well-preserved mummies and sarcophagi, the Islamic and Chinese art; and the rich collections of French and Italian paintings.

Arrival and information

Train From Oxford's train station, it's a 5min walk to the centre.

Bus Long-distance buses terminate at Gloucester Green bus station.

Tourist office 15 Broad St Ⓣ01865/252200, Ⓦwww.visitoxford.org (Mon–Sat 9.30am–5pm, Easter–Oct also Sun 10am–4pm).

Bike rental Bike Zone at 6 Lincoln House, Market St, off Cornmarket St (Ⓣ01865/728877), is the best place for rental.

Internet access *Reach Café* at 138 Magdalen Rd, south of the University, is a good bet for checking your email. It's open until 9pm.

Accommodation

Oxford has a good choice of hostels, and out of term time, some colleges also make student rooms available to tourists (Ⓦwww.oxfordrooms.co.uk). Wherever you stay, it's advisable to book in advance.

Becket Guest House 5 Becket St Ⓣ01865/724675, Ⓔbecketguesthouse@yahoo.co.uk. Simple, homely B&B in a plain terrace, very close to the train station. Doubles £55 or £65 en-suite.

Central Backpackers 13 Park End St Ⓣ01865/242288, Ⓦwww.centralbackpackers.co.uk. Near to the train station, with free wi-fi and internet, roof terrace, laundry and sports equipment. Breakfast included. No doubles. Dorms £16.

Oxford Backpackers Hostel 9a Hythe Bridge St Ⓣ01865/721761, Ⓦwww.hostels.co.uk. Independent hostel with fully-equipped kitchen, laundry, bar and internet facilities. Handy location, between the train station and the centre. Dorms £15.

Oxford YHA 2a Botley Rd Ⓣ0845/371 9131, Ⓦwww.yha.org.uk. Next door to the train station, this clean, modern HI hostel has 184 beds, inexpensive meals, self-catering facilities, internet access and laundry. Dorms £15.95, twins £45.95.

St Michael's Guest House 26 St Michael's St Ⓣ01865/242101. Often full, this basic B&B has six rooms in a three-storey terrace house. Spartan furnishings and shared bathrooms, but it's an unbeatable location. Doubles £65.

Eating

Alpha Bar Covered Market. The organic, mostly vegetarian salads at this takeaway café are a student favourite. Best of the many lunch options in the market. Daytime only; closed Sun.

The Big Bang 124 Walton St. Local, gourmet sausages and quality mash, slightly to the north of the centre in the Jericho area of town. The £5.50 lunch menu's a bargain.

Edamamé 15 Holywell St. Terrific Japanese food at modest prices – it's no wonder the queue for this tiny restaurant snakes down the street. Mains from £6.50. Closed Tues, Wed & Sun eve and all day Mon.

Manos 105 Walton St. Greek deli/café in Jericho, serving a mouth-watering array of mezze, home-cooked mains (from £5.50) and baklava day and night.

Vaults and Garden Café University Church. Atmospheric vaulted café on Radcliffe Square, open in the daytime, with good organic food, including soups, salads and cakes.

Drinking and nightlife

For listings of gigs and other events, consult *Daily Info*, a poster put up in colleges and all around town (daily term time, otherwise weekly; Ⓦwww.dailyinfo.co.uk).

The Bear 6 Alfred St. Ancient inn with low ceilings, real ales and snippets from interesting neck ties – proffered by their owners in exchange for a pint.

The Bridge 6 Hythe Bridge St. Mainstream club plying drunken punters with commercial dance, r'n'b and pop.

The Cellar Frewin Court, off Cornmarket St. Probably the closest you get to a serious club in Oxford. Nightly music, often drum'n'bass, attracts a more discerning breed of student.

The Eagle & Child 49 St Giles. This pub was once the haunt of J.R.R. Tolkien, C.S. Lewis and other literary types, and still attracts an engaging mix of professionals and academics.

Raoul's 32 Walton St. The place to head if you can't stomach another historical tavern. Clean lines, retro decor and the best cocktails in Oxford.

Turf Tavern Off Holywell St. Famous old pub, tucked down a winding alleyway (which also connects with New College Lane), beloved by tourists and students alike, with fine ales and plenty of outdoor seating.

Moving on

Train Bath (change at Didcot Parkway; every 30min–1hr; 1hr 10min–1hr 30min); London (every 20–30min; 1hr); Manchester (every 30min; 3hr); Stratford-upon-Avon (change at Banbury; every 2hr; 1hr 30min).
Bus Cambridge (every 30min; 3hr 20min); Heathrow Airport (every 30min; 1hr 20min); London (every 15min; 1hr 45min); Stratford-upon-Avon (2 daily; 1hr).

STRATFORD-UPON-AVON

STRATFORD-UPON-AVON plays up the "merrie old England" image, making the most of its association with William Shakespeare, who was born here on April 23, 1564. There are five restored properties celebrating Shakespeare, three in the town itself and two on the outskirts. To access these sites you have to purchase a **combined ticket** (£12 for the three town properties, £17 for all five) valid for one year; alternatively, save your money, meander along the river and go and watch the excellent Royal Shakespeare Company instead.

What to see and do

Top of everyone's Bardic itinerary is **Shakespeare's Birthplace Museum** (April–Oct daily 9am–5pm; Nov–March daily 10am–4pm) on Henley Street, an ugly modern visitor centre attached to the heavily restored half-timbered building where the great man was born. A short walk away on Chapel Street is the engaging **Nash's House** (April–Oct daily 11am–5pm; Nov–March daily 11am–4pm), once the property of Thomas Nash, first husband of Shakespeare's granddaughter, Elizabeth Hall. The house is kitted out with period furnishings and has a display on the history of Stratford.

Old Town Street is home to the impressive medieval **Hall's Croft** (opening hours as Nash's House), former home of Shakespeare's elder daughter, Susanna, and her doctor husband, John Hall. Immaculately maintained and more atmospheric than Nash's House, it holds a fascinating display on Jacobean medicine. Beyond, Old Town Street steers right to reach the handsome **Holy Trinity Church** (March & Oct Mon–Sat 9am–5pm, Sun 12.30–5pm; April–Sept Mon–Sat 8.30am–6pm, Sun 12.30–5pm; Nov–Feb Mon–Sat 9am–4pm, Sun 12.30–5pm; free), whose mellow, honey-coloured stonework is enhanced by its riverside setting. Shakespeare lies buried here in the chancel (£1.50).

About a mile west of the town centre in Shottery is the thatched, wood-beamed **Anne Hathaway's Cottage** (opening hours as the Birthplace Museum; £6.50), home to Anne before she married Shakespeare.

Arrival and information

Train Stratford's train station is on the northwestern edge of town, 10min walk from the centre.
Bus Long-distance buses pull into the Riverside Station on the east side of the town centre, off Bridgeway.

THE ROYAL SHAKESPEARE COMPANY

The **Royal Shakespeare Company**, or RSC (box office Mon–Sat 9am–8pm; ⓣ0844/800 1110, ⓦwww.rsc.org.uk), works on a repertory system, which means you could see four or five different plays in a visit of a few days (though not all by The Bard himself). Tickets start at around £5 for standing room and a restricted view, rising to £40 for the best seats in the house, though note that the most popular shows get booked up months in advance. At the time of writing, the main RSC performance spaces were being overhauled in an ambitious plan due for completion in 2010, when performances will be held in the redeveloped Royal Shakespeare Theatre.

Tourist office At the junction of Bridgeway and Bridgefoot, a couple of minutes' walk from the bus station by the bridge ⓣ0870/160 7930, ⓦwww.shakespeare-country.co.uk (Mon–Sat 9am–5/5.30pm, Sun 10am–3/4pm); it operates an efficient accommodation booking hotline.
Bike rental Clarke's Cycles, 3 Guild St ⓣ01789/205057.
Internet Cyber@Junction at 28 Greenhill St is central.

Accommodation

Hamlet House 52 Grove Rd ⓣ01789/204386 ⓦwww.hamlethouse.com. Friendly B&B 5min walk from the centre, with quirky themed rooms and a resident parrot named Dolly. Free internet, bike hire and jumbo breakfasts. Doubles £52.
Stratford YHA Hemmingford House, Alveston ⓣ0870/770 6052, ⓦwww.yha.org.uk. Rambling Georgian mansion with its own café-bar on the edge of the pretty village of Alveston, two miles east of town. Regular buses from Stratford's Riverside bus station. Dorms £19.95, doubles £55.95.

Eating and drinking

Deli Café 13–14 Meer St. Popular family-run café with all-day breakfasts, sandwiches and mains (from £5). Licensed.
The Dirty Duck (aka *The Black Swan*) 53 Waterside. The archetypal actors' pub, stuffed to the gunwales every night with a vocal entourage of RSC employees and hangers-on. Essential viewing, plus good food.
The Garrick Inn 25 High St. Arguably the town's most photogenic and best-preserved old ale house: exposed beams, real ales and decent food.

Moving on

Train London (5 daily; 2hr 15min); Oxford (change at Banbury; every 2hr; 1hr 30min);
Bus London (4 daily; 3hr 35min–4hr 5min); Oxford (2 daily; 1hr).

CAMBRIDGE

Tradition has it that the University of **CAMBRIDGE** was founded by refugees from Oxford, who fled that town after one of their number was lynched by hostile townsfolk in the 1220s; there's been rivalry between the two institutions ever since, though nowdays it's manifested, less violently, in the annual boat race. What distinguishes Cambridge is **"the Backs"**, the green swath of land straddling the River Cam, which overlooks the backs of the old colleges, and provides the town's most enduring image of grand academic architecture. As in Oxford, access to the colleges may be restricted during examinations, conferences and functions. For four days in late July, the town hosts the popular **Cambridge Folk Festival** (ⓦwww.cambridgefolkfestival.co.uk).

What to see and do

Cambridge city centre is bounded to the west by the Cam and is dominated by historic university buildings. The logical place to start a tour of the colleges is King's Parade, originally the medieval High Street.

King's College

Flanking King's Parade, **King's College** has a much-celebrated, extraordinarily beautiful **chapel** (term time Mon–Fri 9.30am–3.30pm, Sat 9.30am–3.15pm, Sun 1.15–2.15pm; rest of year Mon–Sat 9.30am–4.30pm, Sun 10am–5pm; £5) and is home to an almost equally vaunted choir (term time Evensong Mon–Sat 5.30pm). At the northern end of King's Parade, the **Senate House** is the scene of graduation ceremonies.

Gonville and Caius College and Clare College

Adjacent Trinity Street holds the main entrance to **Gonville and Caius College**, known simply as Caius (pronounced "keys"), whose two adjoining courts boast three fancy gates representing different stages on the path to academic enlightenment. On the south side, the "Gate of Honour" leads into Senate House Passage, which heads west to **Clare College** (daily

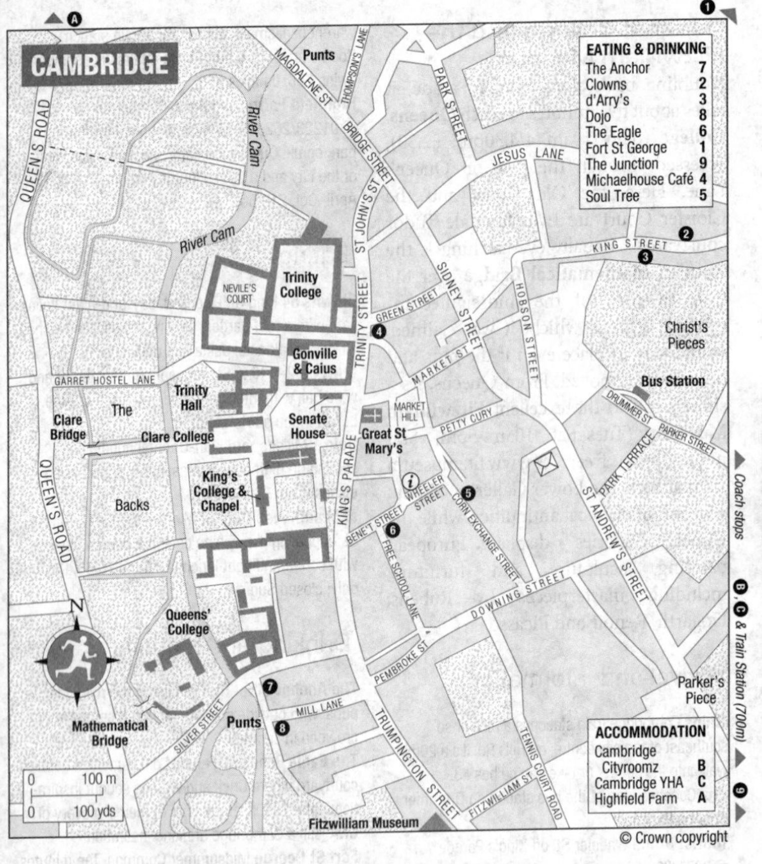

10.30am–4.30pm; £2.50). One of seven colleges founded by women, Clare's plain period-piece courtyard leads to one of the most picturesque of all the bridges over the Cam, **Clare Bridge**. Beyond lies the Fellows' Garden, open to the public (times as college).

Trinity College

Just north of Caius, **Trinity College** (daily 10am–5pm; £3) is the largest of the Cambridge colleges. A statue of Henry VIII, who founded it in 1546, sits in majesty over Trinity's Great Gate, his sceptre replaced with a chair leg by a student wit. Beyond lies the vast asymmetrical expanse of Great Court, which displays a fine range of Tudor buildings, the oldest of which is the fifteenth-century clock-tower – the annual race against its midnight chimes is now common currency thanks to the film *Chariots of Fire*. To get through to Nevile's Court – where Newton first calculated the speed of sound – you must pass through "the screens", a passage separating the Hall from the kitchens, a common feature of Oxbridge colleges. The west end of Nevile's Court is enclosed by the beautiful Wren Library (term time Mon–Fri noon–2pm, Sat 10.30am–12.30pm; rest of year Mon–Fri only; free). Back outside Trinity, it's a short hop to the River Cam, where you can go **punting** – the quintessential Cambridge pursuit (see p.178).

Queens' College and the Fitzwilliam Museum

Doubling back along King's Parade, it takes about five minutes to reach **Queens' College** (daily 10am–4/4.30pm; £2.50), accessed through the gate on Queen's Lane. Here, the Old Court and the Cloister Court are twin fairytale Tudor courtyards. Equally eye-catching is the wooden **Mathematical Bridge** over the Cam, a copy of the mid-eighteenth-century original which, it was claimed, would stay in place even if the nuts and bolts were removed. From Queens', it's a short stroll to the excellent **Fitzwilliam Museum** (Tues–Sat 10am–5pm, Sun noon–5pm; free; Ⓦwww.fitzmuseum.cam.ac.uk). The Lower Galleries contain a wealth of classical antiquities, while the Upper Galleries display European painting, sculpture and furniture, including masterpieces by Rubens, Hogarth, Renoir and Picasso.

Arrival and information

Trains Cambridge train station is a mile or so southeast of the city centre, off Hills Rd. It's a 20min walk into the centre, or take shuttle bus #3.
Bus Coaches stop at the bus station on Drummer St or on Parkside.
Tourist office Wheeler St, off King's Parade Ⓣ0871/226 8006, Ⓦwww.visitcambridge.org (Mon–Sat 10am–5/5.30pm, plus May–Sept Sun 11am–3pm). It operates a useful accommodation booking service (Ⓣ01223/457581).
Bike rental There are several bike hire outlets, including Station Cycles outside the train station (Ⓣ01223/307125).
Internet *Budget Internet Café* at 30 Hills Rd, close to the train station, is a good option.

Accommodation

Cambridge YHA 97 Tenison Rd Ⓣ0870/770 5742, Ⓦwww.yha.org.co.uk. This well-equipped HI hostel has dorms and twin rooms, laundry and self-catering facilities, a small courtyard garden, and serves breakfast (included) and evening meals. It's close to the train station, off Station Rd. Dorms from £19.95, doubles £51.50.
Cityroomz Station Rd Ⓣ01223/304050, Ⓦwww.cityroomz.com. Budget hotel in a converted warehouse, smack opposite the train station. Rooms are simple bunk-style affairs with showers. Twins £55, doubles £65.
Highfield Farm Long Road, Comberton Ⓣ01223/262308, Ⓦwww.highfieldfarmtouringpark.co.uk. Quiet, rural campsite, five miles west of the city and a 20min journey on bus #18 or 18A. April–Oct. £19.50.

Eating

Clowns 54 King St. Licensed, day-and-night Italian café with a roof garden, serving cakes, sandwiches, all-day breakfasts, pasta and daily specials.
d'Arry's 2–4 King St. Atmospheric restaurant and wine bar, with intelligent Modern British cuisine. Lunch menu starts at £5.50.
Dojo 1 Miller's Yard. Pan-Oriental noodle bar serving up high quality, reasonably priced Asian dishes (from £7.50).
Michaelhouse Café St Michael's Church, Trinity St. Appealing mezzanine café in a church nave, with coffee and light lunches. Mains £6.65. Daytime only; closed Sun.

Drinking and nightlife

The Anchor Silver St. The pick of the riverside pubs, with outside seating, though it can be very crowded in summer.
The Eagle Bene't St. Famous old inn with a cobbled courtyard where Crick and Watson sought inspiration in the 1950s, at the time of their discovery of DNA; still a Cambridge drinking institution.
Fort St George Midsummer Common. Ten minutes from the centre in an idyllic spot on the banks of the Cam, this pub has real ales and a large beer garden. Follow the Cam east from Magdalen St across Jesus Green or head north across the Common.
The Junction Clifton Rd Ⓦwww.junction.co.uk. Live bands, club nights, comedy, drama, dance, performance and digital art at this popular and eclectic venue. It's 5min walk south of the train station, just off Hills Rd.
Soul Tree Corn Exchange St Ⓦwww.soultree.co.uk. Welcome alternative to Cambridge's sometimes turgid nightlife, with soon-to-be-big live acts and soul, funk and disco club nights.

Moving on

Train London (every 15min; 45min).
Bus London (every 30min–1hr; 2hr–3hr); Oxford (every 30min; 3hr 20min); Stansted Airport (every 1hr 15min; 1hr).

Northern England

The biggest draw of **northern England** is the **Lake District**, a scenic region just thirty miles across, taking in stone-built villages, sixteen major lakes and the steeply pitched faces of England's highest mountains. But the region is also home to many of the country's major cities, most significant of which are **Manchester** and **Liverpool** in the northwest and **Newcastle** in the northeast. Their centres combine the ostentatious civic architecture of nineteenth-century capitalism with twenty-first-century renewal. The great ecclesiastical centres of **Durham** and **York** take you further back in time, their famous cathedrals providing a focus for extensive medieval remains.

MANCHESTER

Few cities in the world have embraced social change so heartily as **MANCHESTER**. From engine of the Industrial Revolution to cutting-edge metropolis, Manchester boasts one of the country's most vibrant social and cultural scenes. The city has a huge student population, the lively Gay Village, and a history of churning out talent for the twin glories of British culture – music and football.

What to see and do

From the main Piccadilly train station, it's a few minutes' walk northwest to **Piccadilly Gardens** (hub of the local tram and bus network), an obvious starting point for an exploration of the city.

Manchester Art Gallery

The **Manchester Art Gallery** (Tues–Sun 10am–5pm; free; ⓦwww.manchestergalleries.org) has a fine collection of Pre-Raphaelite paintings, Impressionist pictures of Manchester by Adolphe Valette and an excellent interactive gallery. It is located a quarter of a mile from the gardens, on Mosley Street.

Royal Exchange Theatre and Urbis

A short walk north is St Ann's Square, home to the wonderful **Royal Exchange Theatre** (ⓦwww.royalexchangetheatre.org.uk). If you don't have time to see a show, pop in and have a look at the building – formerly the Cotton Exchange – whose florid, pink marble columns and lofty cupolas surround the spherical performance space, an egg-like module that squats in the centre. New Cathedral Street runs down to Exchange Square, home of the **Wheel of Manchester**, a huge Ferris wheel offering views of the whole city (9/10am–11pm/midnight; £6.50). Just round the corner, in Cathedral Gardens, you'll find **Urbis** (daily 10am–6pm; free; ⓦwww.urbis.org.uk), a spectacular, wedge-shaped glass building housing displays of modern art focused on city life and culture and a stylish café bar.

Museum of Science and Industry

South down Deansgate and right onto Liverpool Road, the superb **Museum of Science and Industry** (daily 10am–5pm; free; ⓦwww.mosi.org.uk) celebrates the triumphs of industrialization. Exhibits include working steam engines, textile machinery, a hands-on science centre, atmospheric recreations of period rooms, and a glimpse of the Manchester sewer system complete with realistic smells.

Salford Quays and Old Trafford

Metrolink trams from Mosley Street and Piccadilly stop at **Salford Quays**, scene of a massive urban renewal scheme in the old dock area. Centrepiece is the spectacular waterfront **Lowry Centre** (daily 10/11am–8/6pm;

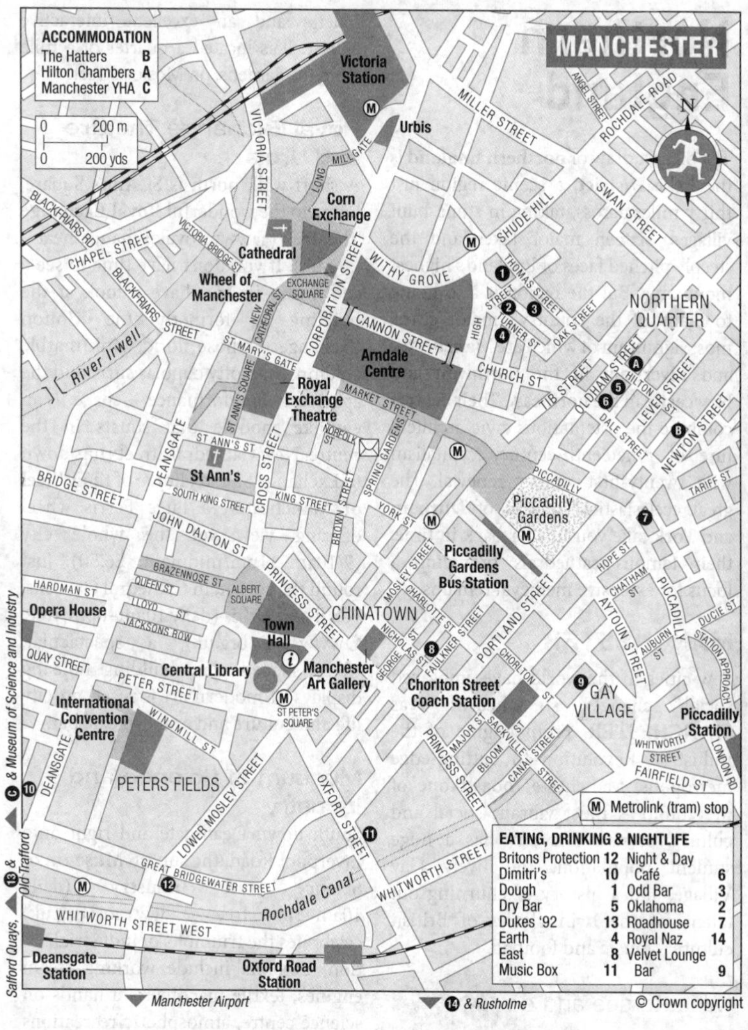

free; ⓦwww.thelowry.com), housing theatres and galleries, where room is always made for the work of the artist L.S. Lowry, best known for his "match-stick men" scenes. To get here, take the Eccles tram to Harbour City, or walk down the docks from the Salford Quays stop. A footbridge runs across the docks to the **Imperial War Museum North** (daily 10am–5/6pm; free; ⓦnorth.iwm.org.uk), a striking aluminium-clad building designed by Daniel Libeskind, where imaginative exhibits explore the effects of war since 1900. Equally resonant in its way is the other great building looming in the near distance: **Old Trafford**, home of Manchester United Football Club, whose museum, a must-see for any football fan, is sited in the North Stand (daily 9.30am–5pm; museum & tour £12, museum only £8.50; advance booking essential for tours ⓣ0870/442 1994, ⓦwww.manutd.com; Metrolink towards Altrincham to

Old Trafford, or towards Eccles to Exhange Quay).

Arrival and information

Air The airport is ten miles south, with a fast and frequent train service to Piccadilly.
Train Most trains arrive at Piccadilly station, on the city's east side.
Bus Long-distance buses stop at Chorlton St, just west of Piccadilly station.
Tourist office The Manchester Visitor Centre is in the town hall extension on Lloyd St, facing St Peter's Square (Mon–Sat 10am–5.30pm, Sun 10.30am–4.30pm; ⓣ 0871/222 8223, ⓦ www.visitmanchester.com), with branches at the airport and the Lowry too.

Accommodation

The Hatters 50 Newton St ⓣ 0161/236 9500, ⓦ www.hattersgroup.com. More cheap than cheerful, this hostel, housed in a converted listed building in the fashionable Northern Quarter, is friendly nonetheless. Staff will provide tourist information and book tours. Dorms £14.50–18.50, doubles £50–55.
Hilton Chambers 15 Hilton St ⓣ 0161/236 4414, ⓦ www.hattersgroup.com. This pleasant hostel has internet access, space for barbecues and travel information. Prices go up at weekends. Dorms £15–19, doubles £45–70.
Manchester YHA Potato Wharf, Castlefield ⓣ 0870/770 5950, ⓦ www.yha.org.uk. Opposite the Science and Industry Museum, this swanky HI hostel (all dorm rooms have en-suite bathrooms), has a great canal-side location. Dorms from £20.

Eating

For budget eating, head a couple of blocks east of the visitor centre to Chinatown. Alternatively, the scores of restaurants along Wilmslow Rd in Rusholme (buses #40–48, except #45), otherwise known as "Curry Mile", feature some of Britain's best (and least expensive) Asian cooking.
Dimitri's 1 Campfield Arcade, Deansgate. Pick and mix from the Greek/Spanish/Italian menu, or grab an arcade table and sip a drink. 3-course lunch £10.
Dough 75–77 High St. A stylish yet affordable pizza restaurant, with creations ranging from goat's cheese and chives to Moroccan lamb and mango, starting at £4.95.
Dukes '92 Castle St, Castlefield. Former stable block for canal horses, now a large, sociable pub with terrace seating, a woodfire pizza oven and a great-value range of pâtés and cheeses.
Earth 16–20 Turner St. Veggie food – curries, pies, salads and juices – in a stylish Northern Quarter café in the Manchester Buddhist Centre. Mains from £2.80. Closed Mon & Sun.
East 52 Faulkner St. Popular dim sum restaurant in Chinatown. The £4 lunch menu is superb value.
Oklahoma 74 High St. This combination of café, record store, art gallery and novelty shop defies categorization and epitomizes the creative energies of the Northern Quarter. It has to be seen to be believed.
Royal Naz IFCO Centre, Wilmslow Rd. Top-rated curry house on the Curry Mile. £5.99 for a two-course lunch.

Drinking and nightlife

Manchester has no shortage of places to drink. The two best-known areas are the Northern Quarter, around Oldham St, and the Gay Village, around Canal St. For details of nightlife, consult Friday's *Manchester Evening News.*
Britons Protection 50 Great Bridgewater St. Elegantly decorated traditional pub, with home-made food, comedy nights and other events, and a beer garden.
Dry Bar 28–30 Oldham St. A "Madchester" institution – it was owned by Factory Records – and catalyst for much of what goes on in the Northern Quarter, this cool bar has banned the likes of Liam Gallagher for bad behaviour.

MANCHESTER MUSIC

In 1978, local TV personality Tony Wilson started **Factory Records** and gave voice to a musical movement that came to define both Manchester and Britain's post-punk musical soundscape. Bands like Joy Division, New Order and the Happy Mondays emerged and embraced the new electronic music that was played at Factory's club, **The Hacienda**, the prototype for the industrial warehouse spaces ubiquitous in club design today. The Hacienda closed in 1997 but its legacy lives on, with places like the Night & Day Café (16 Oldham St ⓦ www.nightnday.org) and the Roadhouse (8 Newton St ⓦ www.theroadhouselive.co.uk) providing stages for up-and-coming talent.

Music Box 65 Oxford St ⓦwww.musicboxmanchester.com. Respected underground club hosting several popular nights and live bands during the week.

The Odd Bar 30–32 Thomas St. A funky little place, lively when the rest of the Northern Quarter hasn't kicked off yet. It boasts a huge range of beers, and a fake moose head garlanded with flowers.

Velvet Lounge Bar 2 Canal St. As the name implies, you'll find elegance and opulence at this high-class bar in the Gay Village, decorated with plush velvet curtains and zebra-striped chairs on which to sip your elegant cocktails.

Moving on

Train Liverpool (every few min; 45min–1hr); London (every 20min; 2hr 30min); Newcastle (every 30min; 2hr 40min; some change at York); Windermere (3 direct trains daily; 1hr 45min); York (every 30min; 1hr 30min).

Bus Durham (3 daily; 4hr 30min); Glasgow (9 daily; 5hr); Newcastle (10 daily; 5-6hr); York (3 daily; 3hr).

LIVERPOOL

Once Britain's main transatlantic port and the empire's second city, **LIVERPOOL** spent most of the twentieth-century postwar years struggling with poverty. Things are looking up at last, as regeneration projects have brightened the centre and the old docks on the River Mersey, while the city's role as 2008 European Capital of Culture brought renewed positive interest. Acerbic wit and loyalty to one of the city's two football teams are the linchpins of Liverpudlian or "Scouse" culture, along with an underlying pride in the local musical heritage – fair enough from the city that produced The Beatles.

What to see and do

From Lime Street train station it's a short walk to William Brown Street and the renowned **Walker Art Gallery** (daily 10am–5pm; free; ⓦwww.thewalker.org.uk), which takes you on a jaunt through British art history, with Hogarth, Gainsborough, Stubbs and Hockney all well represented.

The Waterfront

From here it's a fifteen-minute walk west to the **Pier Head** and Liverpool's waterfront, where it's worth taking a "Ferry 'cross the Mersey" (as sung by Gerry and the Pacemakers) to Birkenhead for the views back towards the city; ferries serve commuters during morning and evening rush hours (£2.30 return), but in between there are hourly cruises with commentary (£5.30). Just behind the ferry terminal, but best seen from the river itself, stands the **Liver Building**, with its enormous clock faces and local mascots – a Liver bird perched on each tower.

A short stroll south is the **Albert Dock**, showpiece of the renovated docks area, whose main focus is the **Tate Liverpool** (daily 10am–6pm; closed Mon Oct–March; free; ⓦwww.tate.org.uk/liverpool), northern home of the national collection of modern art.

THE FAB FOUR

Liverpool's most famous sons, The Beatles, account for a large number of the city's tourist attractions, with plenty of pubs and shops providing a high dose of Fab Four nostalgia. On the Albert Dock you'll find **The Beatles Story** (daily 9am–7pm; £12.25), a multimedia attempt to capture the essence of the band's rise. Buses depart from here for a two-hour **Magical Mystery Tour** (book on ⓣ0151/236 9091 or at tourist offices; £13.95) of sites associated with the band, such as Penny Lane and Strawberry Fields. Real fans will also want to visit **20 Forthlin Rd**, once home of the McCartney family, and **Mendips**, the house where John Lennon lived between 1945 and 1963. Both are preserved by the National Trust and only accessible on a pre-booked minibus tour (Feb–Nov Wed–Sun; £16; ⓣ0151/427 7231). Finish your Fab tour with a night at **The Cavern Club** (see opposite)

Occupying the other side of the dock is the **Maritime Museum** (daily 10am–5pm; free; Ⓦwww.liverpoolmuseums.org.uk/maritime), now incorporating the **International Slavery Museum**, a sobering exploration of the transatlantic slave trade and its legacy.

The cathedrals

To the east, at either end of Hope Street, stand the city's two very different but equally powerful twentieth-century cathedrals: the Roman Catholic **Metropolitan Cathedral** (daily 8am–5/6pm; donation requested), a ten-minute walk up Mount Pleasant, is a vast inverted funnel of a building, while the pale red Anglican **Liverpool Cathedral** (daily 8am–6pm; donation requested) is the largest in the country: a muscular, neo-Gothic creation, designed by Sir Giles Gilbert Scott in 1903 but not completed until 1978.

Arrival and information

Air Liverpool John Lennon airport is eight miles south of the city, with buses heading into town every 30min.
Train Trains arrive at Lime Street station, on the eastern edge of the city centre.
Bus Coaches stop on Norton St, northeast of the station.
Boat Ferries from Dublin and Belfast dock just north of Pier Head.
Tourist office Whitechapel Ⓣ0151/233 2008, Ⓦwww.visitliverpool.com. Mon–Sat 9/10am–6/7pm, Sun 11am–4pm.

Accommodation

Aachen 89–91 Mount Pleasant Ⓣ0151/709 3477, Ⓦwww.aachenhotel.co.uk. The most central and popular budget hotel, with value-for-money rooms and big "eat-as-much-as-you-like" breakfasts. £60.
International Inn 4 South Hunter St, off Hardman St Ⓣ0151/709 8135, Ⓦwww.internationalinn.co.uk. Converted Victorian warehouse with en-suite dorms for two to ten people, helpful staff, plus kitchen and laundry. Adjacent café has internet access, and cheap rooms and apartments are also available. Dorms £15, rooms £43.
Liverpool YHA Wapping Ⓣ0845/371 9527, Ⓦwww.yha.org.uk. One of the best HI hostels, just south of Albert Dock. Smart three-, four- or six-bed rooms, all with private bathroom, plus licensed café, laundry and 24hr reception. Dorms £15.95–24.50, triple £93.95.
Nightingale Lodge 1 Princes Rd Ⓣ01229/432378 Ⓦwww.thenightingalelodge.co.uk. This friendly hostel, just round the corner from the Anglican Cathedral, is housed in a lovely historic building complete with stained-glass windows. Dorm £17.

Eating

Liverpool's Chinatown, around Berry and Nelson streets, is a good place to look for cheap food.
Kimo's 38–44 Mount Pleasant. Moroccan-style cafe-restaurant serving burgers and pizzas from £3.20 and tasty Moroccan dishes from £5.50.
May Sum 180–181 Elliot St. There are some fifty-plus dishes to choose from at this hugely popular, good-value all-you-can-eat Chinese buffet (£5.95 before 5.30pm Mon–Thurs; £6.45 all day Sun).
Yuet Ben 1 Upper Duke St. The celebrated yet reasonably priced Peking cuisine here is authentic, with plenty of vegetarian options – try the set menu for £9.50. Mains from £6.50. Closed Mon.

Drinking and nightlife

The Cavern Quarter around Mathew St is home to myriad pubs, often Beatles-themed, lining pedestrianized streets. The evening paper, the *Liverpool Echo*, has what's-on listings, while annual festivals like the Summer Pops (July) and International Beatles Festival (Aug) are when the city lets its hair down.
The Baltic Fleet 33a Wapping. Restored maritime pub with its own excellent brewery in the cellar, friendly staff, pub grub (lunchtimes and weekend evenings) and a view out to the docks from the front.
The Cavern Club 10 Mathew St Ⓦwww.cavernclub.org. Rebuilt version of The Beatles' original venue, hosting live bands Thurs–Sun.
Korova 39–41 Fleet St Ⓦwww.korova-liverpool.com. Chic bar/club/diner opened by Scouse electronica outfit Ladytron. The focus is emphatically on the music, with live bands and DJs playing to a very cool crowd.
The Magnet 45 Hardman St Ⓦwww.magnetliverpool.co.uk. Blood-red decor, an abundance of history and plenty of soul – there's a funky club downstairs hosting quality live talent.
Nation Wolstenholme Square Ⓦwww.cream.co.uk and www.chibuku.com. Nightclub hosting Liverpool's most infamous nights – Cream and Chibuku.

The Philharmonic 36 Hope St. Fabulous, ornate pub boasting mosaic floors, gilded wrought-iron gates and marble decor in the gents, as well as reasonably priced food.

Entertainment

Everyman Theatre and Playhouse Hope St Ⓦwww.everymanplayhouse.com. Multi-purpose venue presenting drama, dance, poetry and music.
FACT 88 Wood St Ⓦwww.fact.co.uk. The Foundation for Art and Creative Technology shelters two galleries showing film, video and new media projects, as well as an arthouse cinema, café and bar.
Liverpool Academy 11–13 Hotham St Ⓦwww.o2academyliverpool.co.uk. The best medium-sized live music venue in town, with good club nights.
Royal Court Theatre 1 Roe St Ⓦwww.royalcourtliverpool.co.uk. Good for touring plays and stand-up comedians.

Moving on

Train Cardiff (change at Crewe; every 45min–1hr; 4hr); Manchester (every few min; 45min–1hr); York (hourly; 2hr 20min).
Bus Cardiff (4 daily; 6hr 20min); Manchester (hourly; 1hr); Newcastle (6 daily; 6hr 30min); Oxford (5 daily; 5hr 30min); York (3 daily; 3hr 50min).

THE LAKE DISTRICT

The site of England's highest peaks and its biggest concentration of lakes, the glacier-carved **Lake District National Park** is the nation's most popular walking area. The weather here in Cumbria changes quickly, but the sudden shifts of light on the bracken and moorland grasses, and on the slate of the local buildings, are part of the area's appeal. The region is informally divided into the North Lakes, which include **Keswick**, and South Lakes, including **Windermere** and **Ambleside**.

Arrival and local transport

Train Use the mainline service from London Euston to Glasgow, disembarking at Lancaster or Oxenholme. Within the Lake District only Windermere and Kendal are accessible by train, on a branch line from Oxenholme.
Bus National Express coaches run daily from London Victoria and Manchester to the Lake District. Stagecoach buses go everywhere in the region, and offer Explorer Tickets, valid on the whole network, for 1, 4 or 7 days (£9.50/21/30). Tourist offices provide a complete list of services, but the main routes are #555 from Lancaster to Kendal, Windermere, Ambleside, Grasmere, Keswick and Carlisle, and the summer-only open-top #599, from Bowness to Ambleside via Windermere and Brockhole.

Windermere

Windermere is the largest of the lakes, with its main town of **WINDERMERE** set a mile or so back from the water. Other than the short climb up to the viewpoint of **Orrest Head** (30min), it offers little to do, but it is the region's main service centre. The **tourist office** is just outside the train station (daily 9am–6/7.30pm; ⓣ01539/446499). **Bikes** can be rented from Country Lanes at the train station (ⓣ01539/444544, Ⓦwww.countrylanes.co.uk). The *Elleray* on Victoria Street offers huge portions of tasty pub **food** for significantly less money than anywhere else in town.

For trips onto Windermere itself, catch bus #618 or #599 from outside Windermere station to the prettier, but often more crowded, lakeshore town of **BOWNESS**. Lake **ferries** (ⓣ01539/43360, Ⓦwww.windermere-lakecruises.co.uk) run to Lakeside at the southern tip (£8.85

ACCOMMODATION IN THE LAKES

There are 25 YHA **youth hostels** in the region, including one in all the areas listed here, with the exception of Bowness. Go to Ⓦwww.yha.org.uk for details – be aware that hostels can get both busy and expensive in summer. **Campsites** also proliferate, some in exceptional locations. For more information visit the official site of the Cumbria Tourist Board, Ⓦwww.golakes.co.uk.

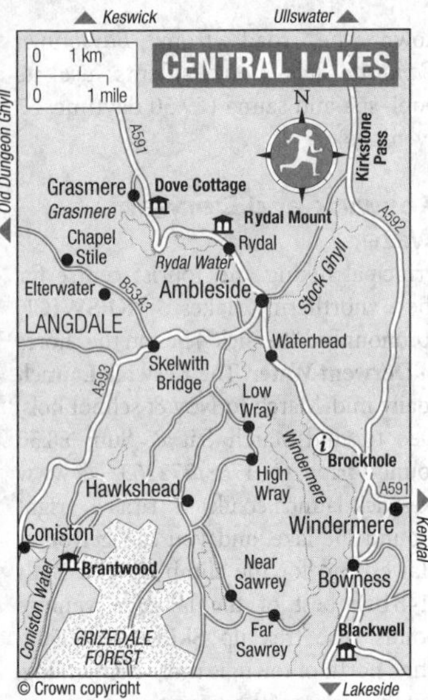

return) or to Waterhead (for Ambleside) at the northern end (£8.60 return); a 24-hour Freedom of the Lake ticket costs £11.60. There are also boats (£6.60 return) to the **Lake District National Park Visitor Centre** at Brockhole, which boasts an excellent information centre as well as exhibitions on the Lake District past, present and future (mid-Feb to Oct daily 10am–5pm; free; ⓣ01539/446601; bus #555 or #599). A mile and a half south of Bowness on foot, there's the rare chance to visit a house designed by one of the major exponents of the Arts and Crafts Movement, Mackay Hugh Baillie Scott's **Blackwell** (daily 10.30am–4/5pm; £6.30; ⓦwww.blackwell.org.uk). In Bowness, don't miss a drink or a meal in *The Hole in't Wall* **pub** behind the church, the town's oldest hostelry.

Accommodation

The accommodation listed below is in Windermere: places to stay in Bowness tend to be expensive,

Brendan Chase 1 College Rd ⓣ01539/445638, ⓦwww.placetostaywindermere.co.uk. Friendly B&B, particularly toward backpackers and hikers, with en-suite rooms. £60.

Lake District Backpackers' Lodge High St ⓣ01539/446374, ⓦwww.lakedistrictbackpackers.co.uk. This little hostel close to the station is unmanned, so don't turn up without a booking as this provides the code for you to get in. They take cash only, and don't give change. Free laundry. Dorms £14.50.

Ambleside

Pretty but touristy, **Ambleside** is a good place to stock up on outdoor gear, and makes a reasonable base between north and south lakes. The **tourist office** is in the Central Buildings by the Market Cross (daily 9am–5.30pm; ⓣ01539/432582) and the tiny **Ambleside Armitt Museum** (daily 10am–5pm; £2.50) exhibits items of local geological, archeological and literary interest. *Zeffirelli's*, a cinema on Compston Road, also offers **food**, either in the daytime café or upstairs in the dinner-only pizza restaurant.

Accommodation

Ambleside Backpackers Old Lake Rd ⓣ01539 432340, ⓦwww.englishlakesbackpackers.co.uk. Independent family-run hostel located in a quiet part of town, with immaculate rooms. Dorms £17.

Ambleside Football Club Seasonal campsite open for six weeks in summer on the pitch on the west side of town. Showers, WC and self-catering facilities.

TREAT YOURSELF

A few miles north of Ambleside in the village of Grasmere, **The Jumble Room** (ⓣ01539/435188, ⓦwww.thejumbleroom.co.uk; closed Tues) – restaurant, café, art gallery and way of life for its owners – offers excellent food made from fresh local produce, a friendly, laid-back atmosphere, outdoor seating for the brave, and above all, something a little bit different. Main courses start at around £10, but you'll need to be able to stretch to £15-plus or so for choice. Bus #599 runs from Windermere, and the #555 and X8 connect with both Windermere and Keswick.

Linda's Shirland, Compston Rd ⓣ01539/432999. B&B and bunkhouse run by the eponymous indefatigable Linda. Cheaper rates for self-caterers. £50

Elterwater and Langdale

The #516 bus from Ambleside to the *Old Dungeon Ghyll* runs four miles west to the charming hamlet of **ELTERWATER**, centred on a tiny green boasting the *Britannia Inn*, an old lakeland pub with tasty food. The valley offers dramatic scenery and plenty of good walking, including up to Stickle Tarn and the peaks of **Langdale**. *Sticklebarn Tavern*, two miles beyond Elterwater on the same bus route, is a good place to start from, though you should make sure you have good shoes, waterproofs and a map. It also has a fantastic hikers' bar and a bunkhouse with basic dorm beds (ⓣ015394/37356; dorms £12). Canny campers stay just before the *Sticklebarn* at the *Baysbrown Campsite* in Chapel Stile (ⓣ01539/437150; £3), which offers stunning views down the valley, plus showers and a breakfast roll van. If you need some luxury and relaxation after a long day's walking, the *Langdale Hotel* down the road from *Baysbrown Campsite* lets non-residents use its pool, spa and sauna (£9.50 daytime; £7 evenings).

Keswick and Derwent Water

Principal hiking and tourist centre for the northern lakes, **KESWICK** (pronounced "kez-ick") lies on the shores of **Derwent Water**. The **Keswick Launch** (daily mid-March to Nov & school hols; Dec to mid-March Sat & Sun; £8.50 round trip; ⓣ01768/772263, ⓦwww.keswick-launch.co.uk) runs right around the lake, and you can get off at Hawes End for the climb up **Cat Bells** (1481ft), best of the lakeside vantage points. The trek up **Skiddaw** (3050ft; 5hr), north of town, is more demanding, but the easiest of the many true mountain hikes around and about. Walks round the lake down **Borrowdale**, perhaps the most beautiful valley in England, take three to five hours, depending on whether you stick to the lakeside or climb up above it. There's also a bus (#17) along the lakeside road. Otherwise, stroll a mile and a half eastwards to **Castlerigg**

LAKE DISTRICT LUMINARIES

The lakeland landscape has been an inspiration to some of England's most revered literary figures. **William Wordsworth** lived at Rydal Mount (March–Oct daily 9.30am–5pm; Nov–Feb Wed–Sun 11am–4pm; £6, gardens only £4), three miles northwest of Ambleside on the #555 bus, and the more interesting Dove Cottage, which still holds many of the Wordsworth's possessions (daily 9.30am–5.30pm; closed Jan; £7.50) at Grasmere. Wordsworth and his sister Dorothy lie in simple graves in the churchyard of St Oswald's in the village.

Beatrix Potter, author, illustrator and botanist, lived at Hill Top (mid-Feb to Oct daily except Fri10.30/11am-3.30/4.30pm; £6.20; ticket numbers limited; NT), a lovely seventeenth-century house in the hamlet of Near Sawrey. You can take a ferry from Bowness and cover the steep two miles to the house on foot or by minibus. Get there early to beat the crowds.

From the village of Coniston, reached by bus #505 from Windermere or Ambleside, you can take the wooden *Coniston Launch* (£7.90 return; ⓣ01768/775753, ⓦwww.conistonlaunch.co.uk) or the steam yacht *Gondola* (April–Oct; £7 return, ⓣ01539/441288, ⓦwww.nationaltrust.org.uk/gondola) to the elegant lakeside villa, Brantwood (mid-March to mid-Nov daily 11am–5.30pm; mid-Nov to mid-March Wed–Sun 11am–4.30pm; £5.95, gardens only £4), once home of artist and critic **John Ruskin**. The house is full of Ruskin's own drawings and sketches, as well as items relating to the Pre-Raphaelite painters he inspired.

Stone Circle, a Neolithic monument commanding a spectacular view.

Arrival and information

Buses The terminal is behind Booths Foodstore, off Keswick's Main St.
Tourist office Moot Hall, Market Square ⓣ01768/772645. Daily 9.30am–4.30/5.30pm.
Bike rental Keswick Mountain Bikes, Southey Hill ⓣ01768/775202, ⓦwww.keswickmountainbikes.co.uk.

Accommodation

Bluestones 7 Southey St ⓣ01768/774237, ⓦwww.bluestonesguesthouse.co.uk. A welcoming guesthouse that offers big buffet breakfasts. £60.
Denton House Penrith Rd ⓣ01768/775351, ⓦwww.vividevents.co.uk. This very friendly, laid-back hostel focuses on the Lake District's outdoor attractions, and can organize activities or provide information on the best places to go. Dorm £13.
Keswick Camping Crow Park Rd ⓣ01768/772392, ⓦwww.campingandcaravanningclub.co.uk. Very convenient location west of town, 5min from the bus station, this well-appointed site can be crowded. Booking advised. £7.65.

Eating, drinking and entertainment

Dog and Gun Lake Rd. Keswick's best pub, with local beers and a celebrated goulash (from £4.16).
Lakeland Pedlar Henderson's Yard, off Main St. Keswick's most agreeable café, with excellent home-made cakes and scones, as well as soups and sandwiches.
Theatre by the Lake ⓦwww.theatrebythelake.com. Hosts drama, dance and music.

YORK

Modern **YORK**'s sinuous cobbled streets are filled with cafés and craft shops, surrounded by picturesque medieval ramparts and centred on the spectacular Gothic Minster. But today's prettiness hides a tumultuous past: the Romans used York as their capital in northern Britain, as did Edwin of Northumbria, whose conversion to Christianity in 627 granted it huge spiritual importance. The Vikings swept through in 866, and ruled until 954, when Eric Bloodaxe lost Jorvik – as it was then known – to King Edred, who brought it into his unified England.

What to see and do

The best introduction to York is a stroll along the **city walls** (daily till dusk), a three-mile circuit – two miles of it on the walls themselves – that takes in the various medieval "bars", or gates, with fine views of the Minster. Daily free two-hour **guided walks** (10.15am, plus 2.15pm April–Sept & 6.45pm July & Aug), led by the York Association of Voluntary Guides, depart from outside the art gallery in Exhibition Square; just turn up.

York Minster

Ever since Edwin built a wooden chapel on the site, **York Minster** (Mon–Sat 9/9.30am–5pm, Sun noon–3.45pm; £6) has been the centre of religious authority for the north of England. Most of what's visible now was built in stages between the 1220s and the 1470s, and today it ranks as the country's largest Gothic building. Inside, the scenes of the East Window, completed in 1405, and the abstract thirteenth-century Five Sisters window, represent the finest collection of stained glass in Britain. Various parts of the Minster have their own admission charges, though the full £9.50 ticket covers all the attractions – don't miss climbing the central tower, which gives views over the medieval pattern of narrow streets to the south, known as **The Shambles**.

Yorkshire Museum and National Railway Museum

Southwest of the Minster, just outside the city walls, Museum Gardens leads to the ruins of the Benedictine abbey of

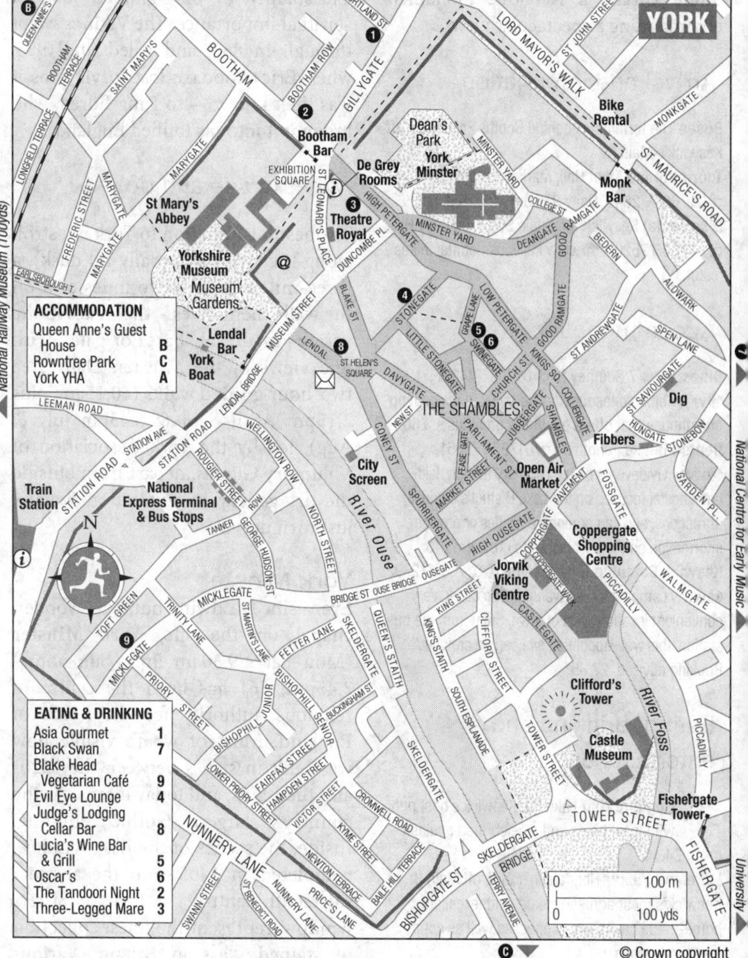

St Mary and the **Yorkshire Museum** (daily 10am–5pm; £5, or £9.50 including the Castle Museum), which contains much of the abbey's medieval sculpture, and a selection of Roman, Saxon and Viking finds. Another museum worth a call is the excellent **National Railway Museum**, ten minutes' walk from the station on Leeman Road (daily 10am–6pm; free), which includes the nation's finest collection of steam locomotives.

Jorvik, Dig and the Castle Museum

From the Minster, shopping streets spread south and east, focusing eventually on Coppergate, former site of the city's Viking settlement. The blockbuster experience that is **Jorvik Viking Centre** (daily: April–Oct 10am–5pm; Nov–March 10am–4pm; £8.50; ⓦwww.jorvik-viking-centre.co.uk) provides a taste of the period through a recreation of Viking streets, complete with appropriate

sounds and smells, accompanied by an informative commentary. It gets very busy at peak period, and you may want to book your tickets online. Just north of here, within St Saviour's Church, is **Dig** (daily 10am–5pm; £5.50; Ⓦwww.digyork.co.uk), a hands-on museum where visitors carry out their own archeological excavation, discovering artefacts and learning about the science and processes of archeology. Further south, the superb **Castle Museum** (daily 9.30am–5pm; £7.50) has full-scale recreations of life in bygone times, with evocative street scenes of the Victorian and Edwardian periods.

Arrival and information

Train York's train station lies outside the city walls.
Buses Long-distance coaches drop off and pick up at the train station, as well as on Rougier St, 200m northeast of the station, just before Lendal Bridge.
Tourist office The main tourist office (Ⓣ01904/550099, Ⓦwww.visityork.org) is in the De Grey Rooms on Exhibition Square, though there's also a branch at the train station (both Mon–Sat 9am–5/6pm, Sun 10am–4/5pm). They sell the York Pass (from £28 for one day), which includes access to nearly all the sights.

Accommodation

The University of York offers good-value rooms and self-catering flats during Easter and summer holidays (Ⓣ01904/328 431, Ⓦwww.york.ac.uk; £28 one-way).
Queen Anne's Guest House 24/26 Queen Anne's Rd Ⓣ01904/629389, Ⓦwww.queen-annes-guesthouse.co.uk. Welcoming B&B a short walk northwest of Bootham Bar. Clean, comfortable rooms, most with en-suite facilities. £60.
Rowntree Park Terry Ave Ⓣ01904/658997, Ⓦwww.caravanclub.co.uk. Conveniently placed campsite on the banks of the river Ouse, just south of town, within easy walking distance. £13.
York YHA 42 Water End, Clifton Ⓣ0870/770 6102 Ⓦwww.yha.org.uk. Twenty minutes' walk along Bootham, with dorms and some private rooms (book in advance), a licensed café, laundry, self-catering facilities, internet access, bike rental and large garden. Dorms £25, twin £53.95.

Eating

Asia Gourmet 61 Gillygate. Ignore the off-putting plastic food and suspended forks in the window, and take advantage of Japanese dishes from £5.90.
Blake Head Vegetarian Café 104 Micklegate. Bookstore/café with patio for freshly baked cakes, breakfasts, quiches, salads and soups. Lunch dishes around £6.50.
Lucia's Wine Bar and Grill 12–13 Swinegate Court East. The food at *Lucia's* would seem good value at twice the price. As it is, £6.45 will get you a fantastic risotto or pasta dish, which you can enjoy either inside or out on the heated terrace.
Oscar's 27 Swinegate. Lively wine bar and restaurant, that does a good line in snacks and larger bites. You can get a baguette for £3.30.
The Tandoori Night 21–23 Bootham. A convenient curry house just outside the walls, serving a wide range of curries from about £6.50.

Drinking and nightlife

Black Swan Peasholme Green. York's oldest (sixteenth-century) pub with some superb stone flagging and wood panelling, plus regular singer-songwriter and folk nights.
Evil Eye Lounge 42 Stonegate. Inviting bar with comfy sofas, an encyclopedic range of spirits, quaffable cocktails and great Thai food. Open until 1am at weekends.
Judge's Lodging Cellar Bar 9 Lendal. Lively drinking hole in the eighteenth-century cellars of a smart hotel, with a large outdoor terrace and DJs or live music at weekends.
The Three-Legged Mare 15 High Petergate. York Brewery's bright but unpretentious outlet for its own beers is named after the three-person gallows that stands in the garden.

Entertainment

Cinema City Screen, 13 Coney St (Ⓦwww.picturehouses.co.uk), is an art-house cinema, with a riverside café-bar and live music and DJ nights.
Music The National Centre for Early Music in St Margaret's Church, Walmgate (Ⓦwww.ncem.co.uk) hosts a prestigious early music festival in July, plus world, jazz and folk gigs. Indie and guitar-pop bands play most nights of the week at Fibbers, Stonebow House, Stonebow (Ⓦwww.fibbers.co.uk).

Moving on

Train Edinburgh (every 30min; 2hr 25min–2hr 40min); London (every 30min; 2hr–2hr 20min); Manchester (every 15–30min; 1hr 30min); Newcastle (every 30min; 1hr).
Bus Edinburgh (2 daily; 6hr 15min); Glasgow (1 daily, 7hr 30min); London (4 daily; 4hr 55min); Manchester (1 daily; 2hr 35min); Newcastle (4 daily; 2hr 20min).

DURHAM

Seen from the train, **DURHAM** presents a magnificent sight, with cathedral and castle perched atop a bluff enclosed by a loop of the River Wear (pronounced "weer"), and linked to the suburbs by a series of sturdy bridges. Once one of northern England's power bases, today it's a quiet provincial town with a strong student presence. There's no hostel, so you might be best covering the city as a day-trip from Newcastle, just a ten-minute train ride away.

What to see and do

The town was initially famed for possessing the remains of St Cuthbert, the patron saint of Northumbria, which were evacuated to Durham in the ninth century because of Viking raids. Since then, his shrine has dominated the eastern end of the spectacular **cathedral** (Mon–Sat 9.30am–6pm, Sun 12.30–5.30pm; open till 8pm daily mid-July to Aug; £4 donation requested). The cathedral itself is the finest example of Norman architecture in England, and also contains the tomb of the Venerable Bede, the country's first historian. The **Treasures of St Cuthbert** exhibition, which includes his coffin as well as items relating to the cathedral's history over the centuries, is in the undercroft (Mon–Sat 10am–4.30pm, Sun 2–4.30pm; £2.50), while the **tower** gives breathtaking views (Mon–Sat 10am–3/4pm; £3). On the opposite side of Palace Green is the **castle** (regular guided tours; £5; call ⓣ0191/334 3800 for details), a much refurbished Norman edifice that's now a university hall of residence. A half-hour stroll follows a pathway on the wooded river bank below the cathedral and castle, all the way around the peninsula, passing a succession of elegant bridges.

Arrival and information

Train Durham train station is 10min walk from the centre, via either of two river bridges.
Bus The bus station is just south of the train station on North Road.
Tourist office Millennium Place ⓣ0191/384 3720, ⓦwww.durhamtourism.co.uk (Mon–Sat 9.30am–5.30pm, Sun 11am–4pm). Also has a theatre, library, café and bar.

Accommodation

Durham University has rooms available – including within the castle – at Easter and from July to Sept (ⓣ0800/289970, ⓦwww.dur.ac.uk/conference_tourism; £80); they can be cheaper to book via the YHA (ⓦwww.yha.org.uk).

Eating, drinking and entertainment

Durham's no clubbers' paradise, but there are some nice pubs and The Gala Theatre and Cinema at Millennium Place hosts drama, music, comedy and film nights (ⓣ0191/332 4041, ⓦwww.galadurham.co.uk).
The Almshouses Palace Green. Located in a World Heritage site beside the cathedral, this café-restaurant conjures up tasty dishes for around £7 (till 8pm in summer).
Café Continental Elvet Bridge. This cheap café and restaurant offers a wide range of food including jacket potatoes, burgers, and more substantial main courses such as TexMex dishes.
Vennel's Café Saddler's Yard, off Saddler St. Café serving everything from cakes to pasta in a lovely little hidden courtyard. The upstairs bar here kicks into action after 7pm.

NEWCASTLE UPON TYNE

A tough, formerly industrial city with a proud shipbuilding heritage, **NEWCASTLE UPON TYNE** has retained its undeniable raw vigour, most conspicuously in its notoriously

high-spirited nightlife. These days, it's streets ahead of its rivals in the northeast, and has a slew of fine galleries and arts venues, as well as a handsome Neoclassical downtown area fanning out from the lofty Grecian column of **Grey's Monument**, the city's central landmark.

What to see and do

Arriving by train from the south, your first view is of the **River Tyne** and its redeveloped quaysides, along with the Norman keep of the castle itself. A series of bridges span the Tyne, linking Newcastle to the **Gateshead** side of the river – most famous is the single steel-arched **Tyne Bridge**, built in 1928. It's both echoed and revitalized by the hi-tech "winking" **Millennium Bridge**, a wonderful sweeping arc of sparkling steel channelling pedestrians over the river.

Laing Gallery and BALTIC

The northeast's main art collection is housed in the **Laing Gallery** on New Bridge Street (Mon–Sat 10am–5pm, Sun 2–5pm; free; Ⓦwww.twmuseums.org.uk/laing), but is overshadowed by the excellent **BALTIC** (Baltic Centre for Contemporary Art; daily 10/10.30am–6/6.30pm, free; Ⓦwww.balticmill.com) next to the Millennium Bridge in Gateshead. Second only in size to London's Tate Modern, this converted former flour mill accommodates exhibition galleries, artists' studios, a café-bar and two restaurants.

The Sage

On a similarly ambitious scale, the BALTIC has been joined by **The Sage Gateshead** (Ⓦwww.thesagegateshead.org), a billowing steel, aluminium and glass structure (likened by detractors to a decapitated slug) by Norman Foster that's home to the Northern Sinfonia, one of Europe's most acclaimed chamber orchestras. The programme of concerts (classical and contemporary) and activities here has transformed this side of the river.

Day-trips

An easy out-of-town trip on the Metro will take you to **Bede's World** (Mon–Sat 10am–4.30/5.30pm, Sun noon–4.30/5.30pm; £4.50; Bede station), five miles east in Jarrow, which imaginatively evokes the life and times of the great early Christian scholar, alongside the remains of Bede's monastery.

Buses #28 and 28A will take you to **Beamish Open Air Museum** (April–Oct 10am–5pm, last admission 3pm; Nov–March Tues–Thurs, Sat & Sun 10am–4pm, museums closed; £16, £6 in winter; Ⓦwww.beamish.org.uk). This fascinating place, about an hour from Newcastle, gives a real insight into the history and life of northeast England, via recreations including a colliery village, farm and tramway, as well as museums and hands-on exhibits.

Arrival and information

Air The airport is six miles north, served by the local Metro system (Day Saver for unlimited rides, £3.90, after 9am on weekdays).

Train Newcastle's Central Station is a couple of minutes' walk from the centre.

Bus The coach station, on St James's Boulevard, is a few minutes' walk west of the station.

Ferry The ferry port (for crossings from Amsterdam) is in North Shields, seven miles east, with connecting buses running to the centre.

Tourist office There are tourist offices (Ⓣ0191/277 8000, Ⓦwww.visitnewcastlegateshead.com) on Market St (Mon–Sat 9/9.30am–5.30pm) and at Guildhall, Quayside (Mon–Fri 10am–5pm, Sat 9am–5pm, Sun 9am–4pm).

Accommodation

The University of Northumbria (Ⓣ0191/227 4717) and Newcastle University (Ⓣ0191/222 6296) offer good-value, summertime B&B (mostly single rooms) in their halls of residence (£34.75). Upmarket Jesmond – a mile north of the centre, on the Metro – is the main location for budget hotels and B&Bs.

Albatross Backpackers In! 51 Grainger St Ⓣ0191/233 1330, Ⓦwww.albatrossnewcastle.co.uk. The most convenient place to stay in Newcastle, this large, friendly hostel is both cheap and central. Dorm £16.50.

George 88 Osborne Rd ⓣ0191/281 4442. Family-run B&B offering decent en-suite rooms at reasonable prices. They also rent out quad rooms Sun–Thurs for £20pp. £60.
Newcastle YHA 107 Jesmond Rd ⓣ0845/371 9335, ⓦwww.yha.org.uk. Clean, basic rooms in a peaceful, recently refurbished Georgian building north of the city centre. Dorm £17.95, twin £43.95.

Eating

City-centre restaurants, pubs and bars are clustered around the notorious Bigg Market, a block west of Grey St, and down on the more sophisticated Quayside.
Hei Hei 46 Dean St. Chic, modern Chinese that delivers on taste. Two-course lunch £7.50.
Little Saigon 6 Bigg Market. An oasis of calm amid Bigg Market's mayhem, this bamboo-ornamented Vietnamese restaurant serves huge portions of tasty food. Mains from £5.
Side Café Bistro 1–3 The Side. Arty café, gallery and cinema near the quayside serving simple food in relaxed surroundings.
Uno's Trattoria 18 Sandhill. Popular pizza place that can't be faulted for value. Happy-hour pizzas (noon–5/7pm, except Sun) are £4.75.

Drinking and nightlife

The free monthly listings magazine, *The Crack*, available in pubs and record shops, is the best way to find out about gigs, clubs and other entertainment.
Crown Posada 31 The Side. A traditional drinking den with a beautifully preserved Victorian interior and good ales.
Digital Times Square ⓦwww.yourfutureisdigital.com. The home of Shindig, Newcastle's legendary Saturday house night, and proud owner of the best sound system in the city.
Head of Steam 2 Neville St. Pub and live music space opposite the station offering real ales and local bands. Don't worry if it looks deserted inside – head upstairs for the bar and downstairs for the beat.
Powerhouse 7–19 Westmoreland Rd. The north-east's only exclusively gay club, playing something for everyone till 4am over its three floors.

Moving on

Train Durham (every few min; 10min); Edinburgh (every few min; 1hr 30min); Glasgow (via Edinburgh; 2hr 40min–3hr); London (every 30mins; 3hr–3hr 15min); Manchester (via York; 2hr 35min–3hr 20min); York (every 10–30min; 1hr).
Bus Durham (3 daily, 30min); Edinburgh (3 daily; 2hr 40min–3hr 10min); Glasgow (1 daily; 3hr 55min); Liverpool (3 daily; 5hr 25min); London (5 daily; 6hr 35min–8hr 20min); Manchester (5 daily; 5hr–6hr 10min); York (4 daily; 2hr 20min–3hr).

HADRIAN'S WALL

Hadrian's Wall, separating Roman England from barbarian Scotland, can be a wonderfully atmospheric place, especially on a rainy day, when it's not difficult to imagine Roman soldiers gloomily contemplating their bleak northern posting from atop the wall. Nowadays the **Hadrian's Wall Path**, an 84-mile waymarked trail (5–7 days) runs from coast to coast, linking the substantial remains. The start is at Segedunum at Wallsend, the "strong fort" four miles east of Newcastle that was the last outpost of Hadrian's great border defence. You can visit the excavations (daily April–Oct 10am–5pm, Nov–March 10am–3pm; £3.95; Wallsend metro station), and get your "walk passport" stamped here. Otherwise, the best jumping-off point and base for longer exploration is the abbey town of **HEXHAM**, 45 minutes west of Newcastle by train or bus. Some of the finest preserved sections of wall include **Housesteads** (daily 10am–4/6pm; £4.50), the most complete Roman fort in Britain, set in spectacular countryside, and the partly recreated fort and lively museum at **Vindolanda** (daily 10am–5/6pm; £5.20). The circular route starting and finishing at Once Brewed provides a decent walk, covering around 7.5 miles and taking in both Housesteads and Vindolanda, as well as some dramatic scenery.

Arrival and information

Bus The Hadrian's Wall #AD122 bus (Easter–Oct: 7 daily, though not all services cover the whole route; 1-day ticket £7.50, 3-day £15, 7-day £30) runs between Hexham and Carlisle via all the main sites; at least once a day it links through to Newcastle and Wallsend. Some services have guides. The year-round #685 bus runs from Carlisle

to Housesteads via Haltwhistle (on the Newcastle–Carlisle train line).

Tourist office Hexham has a tourist office in the main car park (daily 9/10am–5/6pm; Nov–Easter closed Sun; ⓣ01434/652220, ⓦwww.hexhamnet.co.uk). There's also a National Park Centre at Once Brewed (Easter–Oct daily 9.30am–5pm; Nov–Easter Sat & Sun 10am–3pm).

Accommodation and eating

Once Brewed ⓣ0845/371 9753, ⓦwww.yha.org.uk. HI hostel in a modern, purpose-built block 15 miles west of Hexham and within easy walking distance of the wall. Feb–Nov only. Dorm £17.95.

Twice Brewed Inn ⓣ01434/344534, ⓦwww.twicebrewedinn.co.uk. Friendly pub on the same site with simple rooms, food (served till 8.30pm), local beers and internet access. Closed Jan. £53.

Wales

Picturesque **WALES** has long appealed to English holidaymakers, drawn by unspoilt countryside, in which the population of sheep vastly outnumbers that of humans. The relationship between Wales and England, however, has never been entirely easy. Fed up with demarcation disputes, the eighth-century Mercian king Offa constructed a dyke to separate the two countries: the 177-mile **Offa's Dyke Path** still (roughly) marks the border to this day, though Wales passed under English rule in the late thirteenth century. The arrival, in 1999, of the National Assembly for Wales, the first all-Wales tier of government for nearly six hundred years, may well indicate that power is shifting back, though so far it's a slow trickle. Despite centuries of rule from Westminster, however, Wales has retained a strong national identity, most clearly manifested in the Welsh language (see box below).

Much of the country, particularly the **Brecon Beacons** in the south and **Snowdonia** in the north, is relentlessly mountainous and offers wonderful walking terrain, while **Pembrokeshire** to the west boasts a spectacular rugged coastline. The biggest towns, including the capital **Cardiff** in the south, **Aberystwyth** in the west, and **Caernarfon** in the north, all cling to the coastal lowlands, but even then the mountains are no more than a bus-ride away. **Holyhead**, on the island of **Anglesey**, is the main British port for ferry sailings to Dublin.

WELSH CULTURE AND LANGUAGE

Indigenous **Welsh culture** survives largely through language and song. Music, poetry and dance is celebrated at Eisteddfod festivals throughout the country; most famous are the annual Royal National Eisteddfod (ⓦwww.eisteddfod.org.uk), a very Welsh affair that breaks out in a different location during the first week of August, and the Llangollen International Musical Eisteddfod (ⓦwww.internationaleisteddfod.co.uk), held on the first full week in July.

The **Welsh language** is undergoing a revival and you'll see it on road signs all over the country, although you're most likely to hear it spoken in the north, west and mid-Wales, where for many, it's their first language. Some Welsh place names have never been anglicized, but where alternative names do exist, we've given them in the text.

Some basics

Two	*To*	Toh
Hello	*Helo*	Hello
Goodbye	*Hwyl*	huh-will
Please	*Os gwelwch chi'n da*	Oss gway-look un tha
Thank you	*Diolch*	Dee-ol'ch

CARDIFF

Though once shackled to the fortunes of the coal-mining industry, Wales's capital city, **CARDIFF** (Caerdydd), has been revitalized over the past decade, not least due to the arrival of the Welsh Assembly. The city's narrow Victorian arcades are interspersed with new shopping centres and wide pedestrian precincts.

What to see and do

Cardiff's city centre extends north of Cardiff Central train station. To the west of the centre, overlooking the River Taff, is the gleaming **Millennium Stadium** (Ⓦwww.millenniumstadium.com); Cardiff's main historical landmark, the castle, is a short stroll northeast of here.

Cardiff Castle and the National Museum

Cardiff Castle (daily 9am–5/6pm; £8.95) is the historical heart of the city. Standing on a Roman site developed by the Normans, the castle was embellished by the English architect William Burges in the 1860s, and each room is now a wonderful example of Victorian "medieval" decoration; best are the Chaucer Room, the Banqueting Hall, the Arab Room and the Fairy-tale Nursery. Five minutes' walk northeast, the **National Museum and Gallery** in Cathays Park (Tues–Sun 10am–5pm; free; Ⓦwww.museumwales.ac.uk) houses a fine collection of Impressionist paintings, together with natural history and archeological exhibits.

Cardiff Bay

A half-hour walk south of the centre is the **Cardiff Bay** area, also reached by bus #7 from Central Station, or a train from Queen Street. Once known as Tiger Bay, the long-derelict area has seen massive redevelopment since the opening of the Welsh Assembly. The area is now dominated by the **Wales Millennium Centre**, which houses a huge theatre for the performing arts (see opposite). Nearby, you can pick up tourist information in the Cardiff Bay **Visitor Centre** (see below), known as "The Tube" for its unique, award-winning design. Pleasant waterfront walks, glittering millennium architecture and an old Norwegian seamen's chapel, converted into a cosy café, add to the new air of refinement.

Around Cardiff

The Museum of Welsh Life (daily 10am–5pm; free; Ⓦwww.museumwales.ac.uk) is at St Fagans, four miles west of the centre on buses #32/320. This 100-acre open-air museum is packed with reconstructed rural and industrial heritage buildings. Fans of William Burges' elaborate interiors shouldn't miss the fairy tale **Castell Coch**, perched dramatically on a steep, forested hillside at Tongwynlais, five miles north of town on bus #26 (March & Nov Mon–Sat 9.30am–4pm, Sun 11am–4pm; April–Oct daily 9am–5pm; £3.60; closed for six weeks every Jan & Feb).

Arrival and information

Air Cardiff Airport is around 35min west of the centre; bus #X91 runs hourly to Cardiff Central.

Train/bus Long-distance coaches, and buses from the airport, arrive at the bus terminal, right beside Cardiff Central train station, south of the city centre off Penarth Rd. Local trains use Queen St station instead, east of the centre.

Tourist office The Old Library on The Hayes (Mon–Sat 9.30am–6pm, Sun 10am–4pm; Ⓣ0870/1211 258, Ⓦwww.visitcardiff.com), and Cardiff Bay Visitor Centre (daily 9.30/10.30am–5/6pm; Ⓣ029/2046 3833).

Accommodation

Big Sleep Hotel Bute Terrace, near Cardiff International Arena Ⓣ029/2063 6363, Ⓦwww.thebigsleephotel.com. Trendy, central budget hotel with clean lines and a modern interior. Doubles £65.

Cardiff YHA 2 Wedal Rd ⓣ0845/371 9311, ⓦwww.yha.org.uk. A couple of miles north of the centre, with lounge, kitchen, laundry and internet. No doubles. Dorms £15.95.

NosDa at Cardiff Backpackers 98 Neville St ⓣ029/2034 5577, ⓦwww.nosda.co.uk. Excellent hostel with a young crowd, barbecues and a bar, west of the centre across the River Taff. Dorms £17, doubles £40.

NosDa Studio Hostel 53–59 Despenser St ⓣ029/2037 8866, ⓦwww.nosda.co.uk. Sister hostel to *NosDa* on Neville St (just across the river from the centre, opposite the Millennium Stadium), this place offers superb facilities at budget prices. Dorms are bright and modern and there's a bar, terrace, internet access, gym and 24hr reception. Dorm £17.50, doubles £54.

Eating, drinking and nightlife

Barfly Kingsway ⓦwww.barflyclub.com. The best place to go for live indie music.

Madame Fromage 18 Castle Arcade. Cheese experts, serving up delicious soups, cold platters and larger bites in a pretty Victorian arcade opposite the castle.

Milgi Lounge 213 City Rd ⓦwww.milgilounge.com. Video-art gallery and cocktail bar in the student district, a mile and a half north of the centre, hosting live music and a monthly vintage clothing jumble sale.

Old Arcade 14 Church St. Traditional pub retaining some character – one of the best in the centre.

The Plan 28–29 Morgan Arcade. Busy daytime café with a delightful assortment of teas and coffees, serving salads (£6.20) and light lunches.

Zerodegrees 27 Westgate St. Sleek glass-fronted restaurant and microbrewery close to the Millennium Stadium. Stone-fired pizzas from £6.95, though it's the beers that are the real attraction.

Entertainment

Wales Millennium Centre ⓣ0870/040 2000, ⓦwww.wmc.org.uk. Wide-ranging arts programme, including opera, ballet, contemporary dance, music and comedy.

Moving on

Train Abergavenny (every 30min; 40min); Bristol (every 20min; 35–50min); Conwy (3 daily; 4hr); London (every 30min; 2hr); Manchester (hourly; 3hr 25min); Pembroke (2 daily; 3hr).

Bus Abergavenny (hourly; 2 hr 20min); Brecon (6 daily; 1hr 25min); Bristol (8 daily; 1hr 15min); London (hourly; 3hr 20min–3hr 50min).

CHEPSTOW AND TINTERN ABBEY

South Wales' main historical treasure is accessible from the market town of **CHEPSTOW** (Cas-Gwent), a sleepy spot boasting stunning views of cliff-faces soaring above the river and of the first stone **castle** in Britain, built by the Normans in 1067 (April–Oct daily 9am–5pm; Nov–March Mon–Sat 9.30am–4pm, Sun 11am–4pm; £3.60). Nothing in town, however, can match the six-mile stroll north along the Wye to the romantic ruins of **Tintern Abbey**, built in 1131 and now in a state of majestic disrepair (same hours as castle; £3.60). If you don't fancy walking, catch bus #69 (every 2hr), which runs from Chepstow to Tintern and on to Monmouth, eight miles north.

For information on Chepstow and the **Offa's Dyke Path** contact the **tourist office** on Bridge Street (daily: March–Oct 9.30am–5.30pm; Nov–March 10am–3.30pm; ⓣ01291/623772). The cheapest place to stay is someway out: the spooky *St Briavels Castle* HI **hostel** (ⓣ0845/371 9042, ⓦwww.yha.org.uk; dorms £17.95) occupies a moated Norman castle seven miles northeast of Chepstow on bus #69.

THE BRECON BEACONS

The **Brecon Beacons National Park** (ⓦwww.breconbeacons.org) occupies a vast area of rocky uplands that are perfect walking terrain. The Beacons themselves, a pair of hills 2900ft high accessed from Brecon town, share the limelight with the **Black Mountains**, in the eastern part of the park, which rise north of pretty Crickhowell.

Dedicated Beacons buses run from towns around South Wales on Sundays and Bank Holidays from late May until

September. There are regular train services from Cardiff to **Abergavenny** and Sixty Sixty's X43 bus service runs from Cardiff to Abergavenny, **Brecon** and **Crickhowell** (Ⓦwww.sixtysixty.co.uk). Buses from Hereford in England (accessible by rail) travel to **Hay-on-Wye** (#39) and Brecon.

Abergavenny and around

The market town of **ABERGAVENNY** (Y Fenni) sits in a fold between seven green hills at the eastern edge of the Brecon Beacons National Park. Before setting out for the mountains, pick up maps from the **tourist office** (daily April–Oct 9.30am–5.30pm; Nov–March 10am–4pm; Ⓣ01873/857588) on Cross Street beside the bus station – and check what sort of weather to expect, as conditions change rapidly. The most accessible walking areas are the **Sugar Loaf** (1955ft), four miles northwest, and **Holy Mountain** (Skirrid Fawr; 1595ft), three miles north. Serious hikers can attempt the 100-mile Beacon Way, traversing the entire national park from Abergavenny to Llangadog, which should take around eight days. Accommodation in Abergavenny includes the *Black Sheep Backpackers* **hostel** in the *Great Western Hotel,* opposite the train station (Ⓣ01873/859125, Ⓦwww.blacksheepbackpackers.com; dorm £15, twin £35).

Crickhowell and around

CRICKHOWELL (Crughywel), a friendly village with a fine seventeenth-century bridge five miles west of Abergavenny, is more picturesque. A great six-mile hike into the **Black Mountains** from here takes you through remote countryside to tiny **Partrishow Church**; inside, you'll find a rare carved fifteenth-century rood screen complete with dragon, and an ancient mural of the grim reaper. For more dramatic scenery, you could try the six-and-a-half mile round-trip to Table Mountain, the summit of which offers great views of the Black Mountains.

Crickhowell's **tourist office** (daily: March–Sept 9.30am–5pm, Oct–Feb 10am–4pm; Ⓣ01873/812105) is on Beaufort Street; the bus stops nearby on the square. The best value **accommodation** in town is at the *Riverside Campsite* (Ⓣ01873/810397; £10) by the bridge.

Hay-on-Wye

To the north of the Black Mountains, on the border with England, charming **HAY-ON-WYE** is famous as the second-hand book capital of the world and is home to Britain's leading literary festival (annually in late May). **Accommodation** is scarce during the festival and prices high, so book ahead: pick of the crop is *The Bridge*, 4 Bridge St (Ⓣ01497/822952, Ⓦwww.thebridgehay.co.uk; doubles £58), a small, family-run B&B serving excellent cooked breakfasts. *Kilverts* Inn on The Bullring has superior **pub** food and good cask ales.

Brecon

The largest of the central Brecon Beacons rise just south of **BRECON** (Aberhonddu), a lively little town eight miles west of Crickhowell renowned for its mid-August international jazz festival. For details of the numerous hiking routes call in at the **tourist office** in the Cattle Market car park (daily 9am–5/5.30pm; Ⓣ01874/622485). The *Brynich Caravan Park*, half an hour from town, is a good option for campers (Ⓣ01874/623325, Ⓦwww.caravanclub.co.uk; April–Oct; £19.50) and there's an HI **hostel** two miles east of Brecon at Groesfford (Ⓣ0845/371 9506, Ⓦwww.yha.org.uk; dorms £15.95, twin £38.95), a mile off the Abergavenny bus route.

PEMBROKESHIRE AND ST DAVID'S

The sleepy town of **Pembroke** (Penfro), accessible by train from Cardiff, is the jumping-off point from which to

explore **Pembrokeshire Coast National Park** (Ⓦwww.pcnpa.org.uk), covering some 258 miles of coastline. The coastal path here includes some of the country's most stunning and remote scenery and a series of dedicated coastal bus services, all of which can be hailed by walkers, makes this beautiful corner of Britain accessible to those without their own wheels.

St David's

Around thirty miles north of Pembroke, the city of **ST DAVID'S** (Tyddewi), Britain's smallest, is one of the most enchanting spots in Britain (Ⓦwww.stdavids.co.uk). Its beautiful **cathedral** (£4 donation requested), delicately tinted purple, green and yellow by a combination of lichens and geology, hosts a prestigious classical music festival in late May or early June. Across a thin trickle of river the remains of the magnificent fourteenth-century **Bishop's Palace** (Easter–Oct daily 9am–5pm; Nov–Easter Mon–Sat 9.30am–4pm, Sun 11am–4pm; £3) add to the wonderful setting.

To get to St David's, take bus #349 north to Haverfordwest, from which bus #411 runs the sixteen miles west to the city. St David's HI **hostel** is at Llaethdy, close to Whitesands Beach (Ⓣ0845/371 9141 Ⓦwww.yha.org.uk; dorms £15.95, twin £38.95). There's a national park **visitor centre** in town at the Oriel y Parc Landscape Gallery (daily: late March to Oct 9.30am–5.30pm; Nov to late March 10am–4.30pm; Ⓣ01437/720392, Ⓦwww.orielyparc.co.uk).

ABERYSTWYTH

ABERYSTWYTH, a lively, thoroughly Welsh seaside resort of neat Victorian terraces, has a thriving student culture. The flavour of the town is best appreciated from the seafront, where one of Edward I's castles bestrides a windy headland to the south. There's also a Victorian **camera obscura** further north, which can be reached via the clanking **cliff railway** (April–Oct Sun–Thurs 10am–6pm, Fri & Sat 10am–11pm; Nov–March Wed–Sun 10am–4pm; £3.20 return). For a more extended rail trip, you could take the popular **Vale of Rheidol** narrow-gauge steam train to **Devil's Bridge**, a canyon where three bridges span a dramatic waterfall (April–Oct; £13.50).

The **train station** is ten minutes south of the seafront, reached by walking up Terrace Road past the **tourist office** (Mon–Sat 10am–5pm, plus Sun in July & Aug; Ⓣ01970/612125). The town seafront is lined with genteel **guesthouses**; try *Yr Hafod*, 1 South Marine Terrace (Ⓣ01970/617579, Ⓦwww.yrhafod.co.uk; doubles £56). Out of term time, contact the University of Wales about beds in **student halls** (Ⓣ01970/621960, Ⓦwww.aber.ac.uk/visitors; single en-suite rooms £20). *The Treehouse*, on Eastgate, is a great daytime vegetarian **café** with mains from £6.40.

SNOWDONIA AND THE NORTH COAST

With some of the most dramatic mountain scenery Britain has to offer –

FERRIES TO IRELAND

Two ferries to Rosslare in Ireland (4hr) leave from **Pembroke Dock**, two miles north of Pembroke, every day. About 17 miles further north, at the end of the main train line from Cardiff and London – is **Fishguard** (Abergwaun), another embarkation point for Rosslare, with ferries and catamarans departing daily. **Holyhead (Caergybi)**, on Anglesey, is the busiest Welsh ferry port, with several daily ferry and catamaran sailings leaving for Dublin.

jagged peaks, towering waterfalls and glacial lakes – it's not surprising that walkers congregate in large numbers in **Snowdonia National Park**, with a steady stream of tourist traffic even in the bleakest months of the year. The park covers an enormous area stretching from Aberdyfi in the south to Conwy on the north coast; its highlight, though, is the glory of North Wales – **Mount Snowdon**, at 3560ft the highest mountain in England and Wales, and the blue-grey, slate towns and villages that surround the peak.

Whenever you come, make sure you're equipped with suitable shoes, warm clothing, and food and drink to see you through any unexpected hitches. There are two main access routes. From Porthmadog, a few miles north of Harlech (both on the local rail network), **buses** skirt the base of Snowdon west to Caernarfon and Llanberis; mainline **trains** from Crewe and Chester hug the north coast through Bangor to Holyhead, passing through Llandudno Junction and Conwy (the latter is a request stop).

Caernarfon

CAERNARFON is a handy springboard for trips into Snowdonia. **Caernarfon Castle** (daily: April–Oct 9am–5pm; Nov–March Mon–Sat 9.30am–4pm, Sun 11am–4pm; £5.10), built in 1283, is arguably one of the most splendid castles in Britain. It's here that heirs to the throne, the princes of Wales, are ceremonially invested. Although little of the castle's interior has survived, the atmospheric towers and rambling stone passageways are well worth exploring.

Buses stop on Penllyn, just across Castle Square from the **tourist office** on Castle Street (April–Oct daily 9.30am–4.30pm; Nov–March Mon–Sat 9.30am–3.30pm; Ⓣ01286/672232, Ⓦwww.visitcaernarfon.com). *Totters*, an independent backpacker **hostel** at 2 High St (Ⓣ01286/672963, Ⓦwww.totters.co.uk; dorms £14) is an excellent budget place to stay, while the *Black Boy Inn* on Northgate Street serves hefty portions of good **pub** food (mains from £6.95).

Llanberis and Snowdon

Regular buses run the seven miles southeast from Caernarfon to **LLANBERIS**, a lakeside village in the shadow of **Snowdon**, which offers another convenient base for an exploration of the area. The longest but easiest ascent of the mountain is the **Llanberis Path**, a signposted five-mile hike (3hr), manageable by anyone reasonably fit. Alternatively, take the generally steam-hauled **Snowdon Mountain Railway** (daily mid-March to October; £23; Ⓦwww.snowdonrailway.co.uk), which operates from Llanberis to the summit, weather permitting. The slate quarries that seared Llanberis's surroundings now lie idle, but the **Welsh Slate Museum** (Easter–Oct daily 10am–5pm; Nov–Easter daily except Sat 10am–4pm; free; Ⓦwww.museumwales.ac.uk) remains as a memorial to the workers' tough lives.

Buses stop near the **tourist office**, 41 High St (Easter–Oct daily 9.30am–4pm; Nov–Easter Fri–Mon 9.30am–3pm; Ⓣ01286/870765, Ⓔllanberis.tic@gwynedd.gov.uk). Stodgy caff classics at *Pete's Eats*, 40 High St, opposite, fuel up walkers for a Snowdn ascent. There's a good choice of accommodation for walkers. The Sherpa Bus services (£4 all day) collectively encircle Snowdon providing access to several well-equipped HI **hostels** (Ⓦwww.yha.org.uk), each at the base of a footpath up the mountain. The *Llanberis YHA* (Ⓣ0845/371 9645) is closest to amenities and to the fastest path up Snowden; *Bryn Gwynant* (Ⓣ0845/371 9108), *Pen-y-Pass* (Ⓣ0845/371 9534) and *Snowdon Ranger* (Ⓣ0845/371 9659) are more secluded. Dorms at each cost £17.95, twins £43.95.

Anglesey

The little island of **Anglesey** (Ynys Môn) is connected to North Wales by the Menai Bridge, built by Thomas Telford in 1826 and one of the island's principal sights, even though it's been superseded by a newer rival alongside. The other draw is one of Edward I's masterpieces, **Beaumaris Castle** (April–Oct daily 9am–5pm; Nov–March Mon–Sat 9.30am–4pm, Sun 11am–4pm; £3.70), reached by bus #53, #57 or #58 from Bangor. The giant castle was built in 1295 to guard the straits and has a fairy-tale moat enclosing its twelve sturdy towers. From Holyhead, at the island's western tip, you can take a ferry to Ireland (see box, p.203).

Conwy

A couple of miles west of Llandudno Junction is **CONWY**, where Edward I's magnificent **castle** (same hours as Beaumaris; £4.70) and the town walls are a UNESCO World Heritage Site; the entrance also contains the **tourist office** (Ⓣ01492/592248). The ramparts offer fine views of Thomas Telford's recently restored 1826 suspension bridge (April–Oct daily; £1) over the River Conwy. Conwy's **HI hostel**, *Lark Hill*, is just west of the centre (Ⓣ0845/371 9732, Ⓦwww.yha.org.uk; dorm £15.95, twin £38.95).

Scotland

Scotland is a prime example of how a small nation can retain its identity within the confines of a larger one. Down the centuries the Scots, unlike the Welsh, successfully repulsed the expansionist designs of England, and although the "old enemies" formed a union in 1707, Scotland retained many of its own institutions, notably distinctive legal and educational systems. However, the most significant reawakening of Scottish political nationalism since then has been in the last couple of decades, culminating in a referendum in which the Scottish people voted in favour of devolution. The Scottish Parliament held its first meeting in 1999, and the 2007 elections saw the Scottish National Party win the largest number of seats.

Most of the population clusters around the two principal cities: stately **Edinburgh**, the national capital, with its magnificent architecture and imperious natural setting, and busy **Glasgow**, a powerhouse of the Industrial Revolution, now as well known for its cultural core as for its rough edges. Outside this Central Belt, Scotland is overwhelmingly rural. In the **Highlands and Islands**, the harsh, mountainous landscape is spectacularly beautiful, its vistas enhanced by an extraordinary variety of light and colours, shifting with the weather. It's a terrific place for outdoor activities, and many of the most scenic spots – such as the famous **Loch Lomond** and **Loch Ness** – are easily accessible.

EDINBURGH

EDINBURGH, the showcase capital of Scotland, is a historic, cosmopolitan and cultured city. Its stone-built houses, historic buildings and imposing castle, perched on a rocky crag right in the heart of the city, make it visually stunning, and it is little surprise that the city is the most popular tourist draw in Scotland. The 440,000 population swells massively in high season, peaking in August during the **Edinburgh Festival**. Yet despite this annual invasion, Edinburgh is still emphatically Scottish in character and atmosphere, mixing rich history with its political role as a dynamic European capital.

What to see and do

The centre has two distinct parts. The castle rock is the core of the medieval

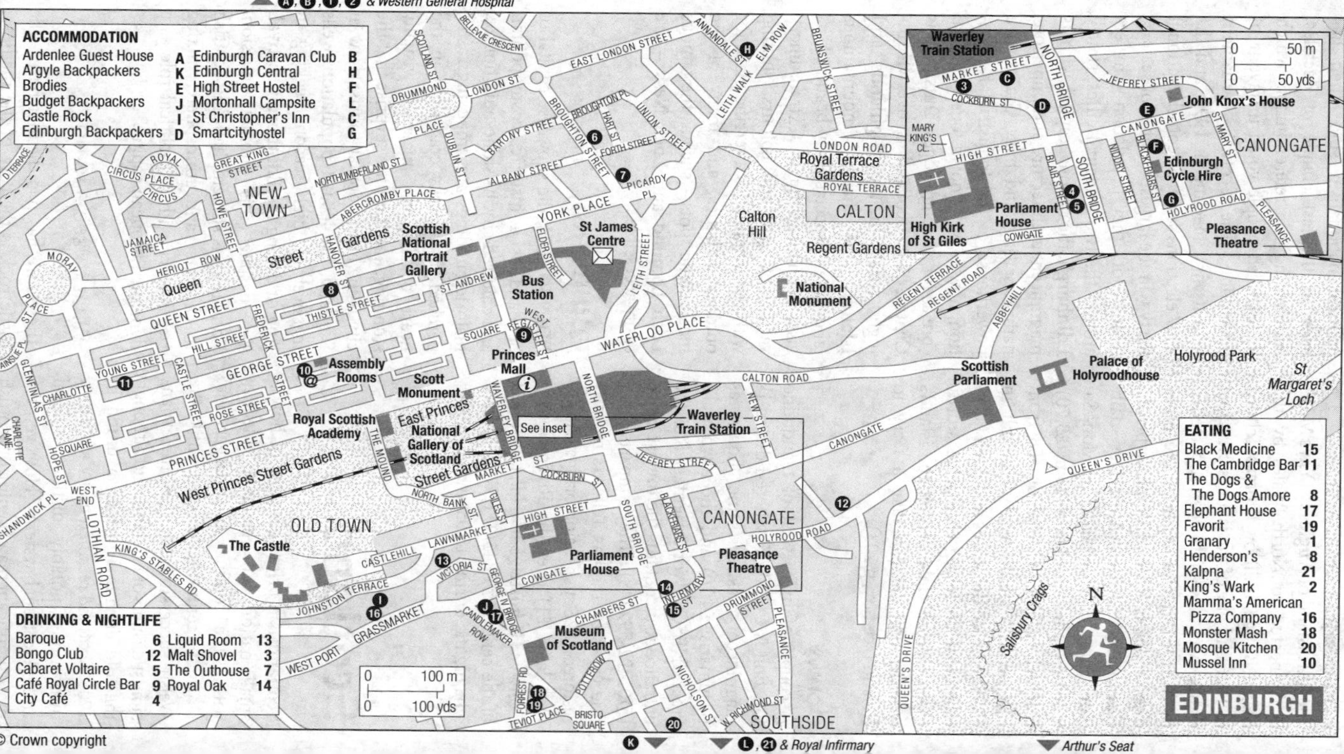
EDINBURGH
ACCOMMODATION
Ardenlee Guest House A
Argyle Backpackers K
Brodies E
Budget Backpackers J
Castle Rock I
Edinburgh Backpackers D
Edinburgh Caravan Club B
Edinburgh Central H
High Street Hostel F
Mortonhall Campsite L
St Christopher's Inn C
Smartcityhostel G
EATING
Black Medicine 15
The Cambridge Bar 11
The Dogs & The Dogs Amore 8
Elephant House 17
Favorit 19
Granary 1
Henderson's 8
Kalpna 21
King's Wark 2
Mamma's American Pizza Company 16
Monster Mash 18
Mosque Kitchen 20
Mussel Inn 10
DRINKING & NIGHTLIFE
Baroque 6
Bongo Club 12
Cabaret Voltaire 5
Café Royal Circle Bar 9
City Café 4
Liquid Room 13
Malt Shovel 3
The Outhouse 7
Royal Oak 14
A, B, 1, 2 & Western General Hospital
Scottish National Gallery of Modern Art
Airport
K
L, 21 & Royal Infirmary
Arthur's Seat
NEW TOWN
OLD TOWN
CALTON
CANONGATE
SOUTHSIDE
Calton Hill
Regent Gardens
Royal Terrace Gardens
National Monument
Holyrood Park
St Margaret's Loch
Salisbury Crags
Palace of Holyroodhouse
Scottish Parliament
St James Centre
Bus Station
Princes Mall
Waverley Train Station
See inset
Scottish National Portrait Gallery
Assembly Rooms
Scott Monument
Royal Scottish Academy
National Gallery of Scotland
East Princes Street Gardens
West Princes Street Gardens
The Castle
Parliament House
Pleasance Theatre
Museum of Scotland
Queen Street Gardens
YORK PLACE
LEITH STREET
WATERLOO PLACE
CALTON ROAD
NORTH BRIDGE
SOUTH BRIDGE
HIGH STREET
CANONGATE
HOLYROOD ROAD
QUEEN'S DRIVE
PRINCES STREET
GEORGE STREET
QUEEN STREET
ROSE STREET
THISTLE STREET
HILL STREET
YOUNG STREET
CASTLE STREET
FREDERICK STREET
HANOVER ST
ST ANDREW SQUARE
WEST REGISTER ST
LOTHIAN ROAD
GRASSMARKET
WEST PORT
COWGATE
CHAMBERS ST
NICHOLSON ST
PLEASANCE
LONDON ROAD
ROYAL TERRACE
BRUNSWICK STREET
LEITH WALK
ELM ROW
EAST LONDON STREET
BROUGHTON STREET
ALBANY STREET
PICARDY PL
ABERCROMBY PLACE
HERIOT ROW
HOWE STREET
0 100 m
0 100 yds
Waverley Train Station
MARKET STREET
COCKBURN ST
MARY KING'S CL.
High Kirk of St Giles
Parliament House
BLAIR STREET
NIDDRY STREET
BLACKFRIARS ST
ST MARY ST
JEFFREY STREET
John Knox's House
Edinburgh Cycle Hire
Pleasance Theatre
CANONGATE
0 50 m
0 50 yds

THE EDINBURGH FESTIVAL

By far the biggest arts event in Europe, August's **Edinburgh Festival** (Ⓦwww.edinburghfestivals.com) is really a multitude of festivals, mostly theatre-based, attracting artists, performers, comedians and tourists in their thousands. **The Fringe** festival, begun as a sideline to the International Theatre Festival to showcase alternative performances, is now the largest draw, mainly for its up-and-coming and big-name comedians. But with a ticket even on the Fringe often hitting £10 or more, and accommodation prices soaring, the only way to experience the Festival cheaply is often to work it. Anything and everything becomes a venue, and every venue needs box office, front of house, technical and bar staff. You won't make much money, but you'll often end up with accommodation and free passes for your venue's shows, and sometimes others. The main Fringe venues to approach are the Assembly Rooms (Ⓦwww.assemblyfestival.com), Gilded Balloon (Ⓦwww.gildedballoon.co.uk), Underbelly (Ⓦwww.underbelly.co.uk) and Pleasance (Ⓦwww.pleasance.co.uk/edinburgh). The Book Festival is also a good bet. Note that the Edinburgh Film Festival now takes place in June.

city – the **Old Town** – where nobles and servants lived side by side for centuries within tight defensive walls. Edinburgh earned its nickname "Auld Reekie" from the smog and smell generated by the cramped inhabitants of the Old Town, where the streets flowed with sewage tipped out of tenement windows and disease was rife. The **New Town**, designed by eminent architects of the day, was begun in the late 1700s: still largely intact, it's an outstanding example of Georgian town planning.

The Old Town and castle

The cobbled **Royal Mile** – composed of Castlehill, Lawnmarket, High Street and Canongate – is the central thoroughfare of the **Old Town**, running down a prominent ridge to the Palace of Holyroodhouse from the **castle** (daily 9.30am–5/6pm; £11, or £9.79 if you book online; Ⓦwww.edinburghcastle.gov.uk), a formidable edifice perched on sheer volcanic rock. Within its precincts are St Margaret's Chapel, containing the ancient Crown Jewels of Scotland and the even older Stone of Destiny, coronation stone of the kings of Scotland. There's a large military museum here, too, and the castle esplanade provides a dramatic setting for the Military Tattoo, an unashamed display of martial pomp staged during the Festival. Year round, at 1pm (not Sun) a cannon shot is fired from the battlements.

Museum of Scotland

Further down at the eastern end of Lawnmarket, George IV Bridge leads south from the Royal Mile to Chambers Street; here the **Museum of Scotland** (daily 10am–5pm; Ⓦwww.nms.ac.uk) is home to many of the nation's historical treasures, ranging from Celtic pieces to twentieth-century icons. It is undergoing an expansion programme until 2011, but its main artefacts are still on display in the sandstone modern wing.

The High Kirk of St Giles and Parliament House

Back on the Royal Mile, High Street starts at Parliament Square, dominated by the **High Kirk of St Giles** (Mon–Sat 9am–5/7pm Sun 1–5pm; £3 donation), whose beautiful crown-shaped spire is an Edinburgh landmark. Inside, the Thistle Chapel is an amazing display of mock-Gothic woodcarving. On the south side of Parliament Square are the Neoclassical law courts, incorporating the seventeenth-century **Parliament House**, under whose spectacular hammerbeam roof the Scottish parliament met until the 1707 Union.

HAUNTED EDINBURGH

From serial-killing corpse-dealers Burke and Hare to the malevolent Mackenzie Poltergeist, the winding streets and underground vaults of the Old Town shelter a multitude of spooks, and several entertaining **ghost tours** operate around the High Street. Some favour a historical approach while others lean firmly toward the high theatrical, using "jumper-ooters" – usually costumed students – to scare unsuspecting tour-goers. **The Real Mary King's Close** (ⓣ0870/243 0160, ⓦwww.realmarykingsclose.com), off the Royal Mile, is a tour of an intact old close built over after the plague and only recently reopened, offering a fine balance between the informative and the chilling.

John Knox's House and the Scottish Parliament

The final section of the Royal Mile, Canongate, starts just beyond **John Knox's House** (Mon–Sat 10am–6pm, plus July & Aug Sun noon–6pm; £3.50), atmospheric home of the city's fierce Calvinist cleric, now joined to the Scottish Storytelling Centre. The road leads to the new **Scottish Parliament** (daily 9/10am–4/6pm; free) a costly and controversial but undoubtedly striking piece of contemporary architecture.

The Palace of Holyroodhouse and Arthur's Seat

Next door is the imposing **Palace of Holyroodhouse** (daily: April–Oct 9.30am–6pm; Nov–March 9.30am–4.30pm; £10), the Royal Family's official Scottish residence, which principally dates from the seventeenth century. The public are admitted to the sumptuous state rooms unless the royals are in residence. The **Queen's Gallery** (same hours; £3) displays works of art from the royal collection. The palace looks out over Holyrood Park, from where fine walks lead along the **Salisbury Crags** and up **Arthur's Seat** beyond; a fairly stiff climb is rewarded by magnificent views over the city and out to the Firth of Forth.

The New Town

The wide grassy valley of Princes Street Gardens marks a clear divide between the Old and New Towns. Along the north side runs **Princes Street**, the main shopping area. Splitting the gardens halfway along is the **National Gallery of Scotland** (daily 10am–5pm, Thurs till 7pm; free; ⓦwww.nationalgalleries.org), an Athenian-style sandstone building. One of the best small collections of pre-twentieth-century art in Europe, it displays works by major European artists including Botticelli, Titian, Rembrandt, Degas, Gauguin and Van Gogh. Look out for the charming *Reverend Robert Walker Skating* by Henry Raeburn – a postcard favourite. The National is linked, via a splendid Neoclassical underground chamber, to the **Royal Scottish Academy** (same opening hours; free). Originally designed in 1826, the building has been sensitively refurbished and now serves as an exhibition space.

The Scott Monument and Calton Hill

East of the National Gallery stands the peculiar Gothic spire of the **Scott Monument** (daily: April–Sept 9/10am–6pm; Oct–March 9/10am–3pm; £3), a tribute to Sir Walter Scott. You can climb the tightly winding internal spiral staircase for heady views of the city below and hills beyond.

East of here, **Calton Hill** rises up above the New Town and is worth climbing, both for the views you'll get across the city, and for the odd collection of Neoclassical follies, including the unfinished **National Monument**, perched on the very top of the hill.

Scottish National Portrait Gallery

North of Princes Street is the broad avenue of Queen Street, at whose eastern end stands the **Scottish National Portrait Gallery** (daily 10am–5pm, Thurs till 7pm; free). The remarkable red sandstone building is modelled on the Doge's Palace in Venice; inside the collection of portraits offers an engaging procession through Scottish history with famous Scots such as Bonnie Prince Charlie on display alongside contemporary heroes like Sean Connery.

Scottish Modern Art Galleries

In the northwest corner of the New Town lies **Stockbridge**, a smart residential suburb with bohemian pretensions. From here Belford Road leads up to the **Scottish National Gallery of Modern Art** and the **Dean Gallery** extension opposite (both daily 10am–5pm; free); the two offer an accessible introduction to all the notable movements of twentieth-century art. The sculpted garden area by Charles Jencks is a popular work of art in itself.

Arrival

Air Edinburgh airport is seven miles west of the centre; there are bus connections around the clock to the city, and from 2011 a controversial new tram line will also run into town.

Train Edinburgh's Waverley Station is bang in the centre on Princes St.

Bus The coach terminal is on St Andrew Square, just north of Princes St. The best way to get around the city centre is on foot. There's also a good local bus service, although the extensive roadworks in preparation for the trams mean they're often diverted; day-passes are available on board (£3, but beware the two firms operating don't take each other's passes – Lothian also don't give change).

Information and tours

Tourist office 3 Princes St, above the station on the top level of Princes Mall ⓣ0845/225 5121, ⓦwww.edinburgh.org (July & Aug Mon–Sat 9am–8pm, Sun 10am–8pm; Sept–June Mon–Sat 9am–5/7pm, Sun 10am–5/7pm). There's also one at the airport.

Tickets An Edinburgh Pass secures free airport transfer, unlimited bus travel and access to 27 of the city's attractions (one-day pass £24, two-day £36, three-day £48). The pass can be obtained from the main tourist office.

Bike rental Biketrax, 11 Lochrin Place ⓣ0131/228 6333, ⓦwww.biketrax.co.uk; Edinburgh Cycle Hire, 29 Blackfriars St ⓣ0131/556 5560, ⓦwww.cyclescotland.co.uk. Edinburgh itself is hard work, but there's pleasant cycling along the canal as far as Glasgow if you fancy.

Accommodation

If you want to stay during the Festival (early Aug to early Sept), you'll need to book months in advance and be prepared to pay more than the usual high season prices. Minto St, which starts about a mile and a half south of the train station and Pilrig St, off Leith Walk, hold myriad B&Bs.

Hostels and guesthouses

Ardenlee Guest House 9 Eyre Place ⓣ0131/556 2838, ⓦwww.ardenlee.co.uk. Welcoming guest house, near the Royal Botanic Garden, with comfortable rooms. £60.

EDINBURGH OUTDOORS

Many of Scotland's outdoor features can be enjoyed – albeit on a more limited scale than in the Highlands – within striking distance of the capital. The **Pentland Hills** are ideal for moderate but scenic walking (take Lothian buses #10, 11, 15 or 16). At **Glentress** (ⓦwww.thehubintheforest.co.uk; First buses #62 or 62A), an area of forest near Peebles, about an hour south of Edinburgh, you can hire mountain bikes to enjoy the purpose-built tracks and runs, and follow it up with great cakes at the café. Edinburgh also offers some pleasant **beaches**: it's worth making the hour or so trip out along the east coast to find the best ones. First buses #124 and X5 stop at Longniddry and beautiful Gullane, each with shallow, sandy bays and surprisingly warm water.

EDINBURGH SEAFOOD

Surrounded by cold northern waters, Scotland has always been a prime producer of seafood. The best place to go in Edinburgh is **The Shore**, where the Water of Leith meets the Forth: bus #16 for Colinton will take you there. You'll have your pick of restaurants, but of particular note are the less expensive **King's Wark** at no. 36, a pub where you can get a main course for below £10, as well as excellent beers, and the smarter but pricier **Granary** opposite.

Argyle Backpackers 14 Argyle Place, Marchmont ⓣ0131/667 9991, ⓦwww.argyle-backpackers.co.uk. Quiet hostel, with small dorms and a dozen double/twin rooms. Pleasant location in studenty Marchmont, off Melville Drive, the road running through The Meadows, a pleasant park. Dorms £23, doubles £60.

Brodies 93 High St ⓣ0131/556 2223, ⓦwww.brodieshostels.co.uk. Tucked down a typical Old Town close, it's cosier than many others, but with limited communal areas. Dorms £24, doubles £62.

Budget Backpackers 37–39 Cowgate ⓣ0131/226 6351, ⓦwww.budgetbackpackers.com. Welcoming and relaxed hostel, in a handy location on the Grassmarket, with a great chill-out room, friendly staff and decent rooms. Dorms £22.

Castle Rock 15 Johnston Terrace ⓣ0131/225 9666, ⓦwww.scotlands-top-hostels.com. Friendly 200-bed hostel tucked below the castle ramparts. It comes with a comfortable lounge, "period" features and a ghost. Dorms £13, doubles £40–55.

Edinburgh Backpackers 65 Cockburn St ⓣ0131/220 2200, ⓦwww.hoppo.com. Big hostel with a great central location in a side street off the Royal Mile. Rooms are of a good standard and clean. They also have self-catering apartment-style doubles. Dorms £22, doubles £50.75.

Edinburgh Central 9 Haddington Place ⓣ0131/524 2090, ⓦwww.edinburghcentral.org. Excellent modern HI hostel off Leith Walk, though it's lacking in character compared to the Old Town options. Airy, clean rooms and a café/bistro. Dorms £15, doubles £37.

High Street Hostel 8 Blackfriars St ⓣ0131/557 3984, ⓦwww.scotlands-top-hostels.com. Large, lively hostel, in a sixteenth-century building just off the Royal Mile, with basic rooms. Dorms £13, doubles £55.

St Christopher's Inn 9–13 Market St ⓣ0131/226 1446, bookings ⓣ020/7407 1856, ⓦwww.st-christophers.co.uk. 110 beds with smallish private rooms as well as dorms and a bar downstairs. The bunks are a tad rickety. Dorms £17, doubles £58

Smartcityhostel 50 Blackfriars St ⓣ0131/524 1989, ⓦwww.smartcityhostels.com. This immaculate modern hostel is definitely flashpacker territory, offering hotel-standard accommodation, with a stylish bar, terrace and restaurant. The spotless rooms are all en-suite. Dorms £15, doubles £39.95.

Campsites

Edinburgh Caravan Club Marine Drive, Silverknowes ⓣ0131/312 6874. Pleasantly located close to the shore in the northwestern suburbs, 30min from the centre on buses #8, 27 and 42. £13.

Mortonhall Campsite Frogston Rd ⓣ0131/664 1533 ⓦwww.meadowhead.co.uk. A good site, five miles south of the centre, near Braid Hill; take bus #11 (marked Captain's Rd) or #18 from the centre of town. Closed Jan–March. £10.

Eating

Cafés

Black Medicine 2 Nicholson St. All totem poles and wooden furniture, this funky café offers cheap paninis, wi-fi and great smoothies.

Elephant House 21 George IV Bridge. Popular café with a cavernous back room, famous as the birthplace of Harry Potter. Mains from £4.

Favorit Teviot Pl. Modern café/diner open till the wee small hours. A great place for late, lazy breakfasts.

Mosque Kitchen 19a West Nicholson St. Authentic, delicious curries served from the back of the Edinburgh Central Mosque. The food's on plastic plates, but the outdoor tables and basic setting can't detract from the taste or value. £3.

Restaurants

The Cambridge Bar 20 Young St. A wide range of home-made burgers, with more toppings than you could possibly imagine, starting at £5.95.

The Dogs & **The Dogs Amore** 104 & 110 Hanover St. Two adjacent restaurants offering locally sourced meat and seafood, with an imaginative twist to many dishes. *The Dogs* has a Scottish menu, while *Amore* is Italian-biased. Mains from around £7.50.

Henderson's 94 Hanover St. Self-service restaurant with a lively atmosphere, good-value

vegetarian food and occasional live music. Mains from around £5.

Kalpna 2 St Patrick Square. Prize-winning Southside vegetarian Indian; great prices for superb food. Try the £6 lunch menu.

Mamma's American Pizza Company 30 Grassmarket. Good pizzas and a lively atmosphere that often spills out onto the Grassmarket cobbles. Pizzas for around £6.

Monster Mash 4a Forrest Rd. Hugely popular diner, serving quality renditions of British standards at small cost.

Mussel Inn 61–65 Rose St. Owned by two Scottish shellfish farmers; you can feast here on a kilo of mussels for around £10.

Drinking and nightlife

Hardcore clubbers head over to Glasgow, but Edinburgh still has a lively nightlife, and there's something going on most nights – pick up a copy of *The List* to find out what and where it is. If you're just out for a drink, you'll find traditional-style pubs on Rose St, or, better but further out, on The Shore in Leith (see box opposite). George St houses the posher wine bars, while the top of Leith Walk is the place for gay nightlife.

Pubs and bars

Baroque 39-41 Broughton St. This split-level bar with its outdoor terrace and large windows offers a great vantage point for people-watching. Also serves food.

Café Royal Circle Bar 19 West Register St. Make a point of visiting this Grade A listed pub, arguably Edinburgh's most beautiful watering-hole.

City Café 19 Blair St. A bar, club and internet café rolled into one. The food's good too.

Malt Shovel 11 Cockburn St. Good beer, plenty of local colour and a wide choice of single malt whiskies; live jazz some evenings.

The Outhouse 12a Broughton St Lane. A heated outdoor area makes this the venue for year-round alfresco drinking.

Live music and clubs

Bongo Club 37 Holyrood Rd ⓦwww.thebongoclub.co.uk. Top club, playing reggae, funk, soul, drum and bass and electro. The big nights go on until 3am.

Cabaret Voltaire 36–38 Blair St ⓦwww.thecabaretvoltaire.com. Eclectic beats and the occasional live band. You can party until 3am.

Liquid Room 9c Victoria St ⓦwww.liquidroom.com. Holds house and indie nights; also a popular live venue. Doors close at 3am.

Royal Oak Infirmary St ⓦwww.royal-oak-folk.com. The venue for Scottish folk music, you'll hear plenty of talented people playing here any night of the week, and it's definitely not all old fogies.

Directory

Embassies and consulates Australia, Capital House, 2 Festival Square ⓣ0131/228 4771; Canada, 50 Lothian Rd ⓣ0131/473 6320; New Zealand, 22 Hailes Grove ⓣ0131/222 8109; USA, 3 Regent Terrace ⓣ0131/556 8315.

Exchange Several big bank branches on and around St Andrew's Square, Hanover St and along George St.

Hospital Royal Infirmary, Old Dalkieth Rd ⓣ0131/536 1000; Western General Hospital, Crewe Rd South ⓣ0131/537 1000 for minor injuries.

Internet easyInternetcafe, 58 Rose St.

Laundry Ace Cleaning Centre, 13 Sth Clerk St; Tarvit Launderette, 7 Tarvit St.

Left luggage At Waverley Station and in lockers by St Andrew Square bus station.

Pharmacy Boots, 11 Princes St.

Post office St James' Shopping Centre, near the east end of Princes St.

Moving on

Train Aberdeen (hourly; 2hr 30min); Durham (every 30min; 2hr); Glasgow (every 15min; 50min); Inverness (10 daily; 3hr 50min); Leuchars (for St Andrews; hourly; 1hr 10min); Newcastle (every 30min; 1hr 30min); Stirling (every 30min; 50min); York (every 30min; 2hr 30min).

SCOTLAND'S MUSIC FESTIVALS

In recent years several summer festivals have sprung up in Scotland, many of them against a backdrop of stunning scenery. For mainstream acts, check out **T in the Park**, near Kinross (July; ⓦwww.tinthepark.com), and **Rock Ness**, near Inverness (June; ⓦwww.rockness.co.uk). For something more alternative, try **Outsider**, in the Cairngorms (June; ⓦwww.outsiderfestival.co.uk), or the **Wickerman Festival** (July; ⓦwww.thewickermanfestival.co.uk), near Dundrennan in the Borders, which culminates in the burning of a huge wicker effigy.

Bus Durham (1 daily; 4hr 30min); Glasgow (every 15min; 1hr 15min); Inverness (hourly; 4hr 30min); Manchester (2 direct daily; 6hr 25min–9hr 30min); Newcastle (5 daily; 3hr); St Andrews (every 30min; 2–3hr); Stirling (hourly; 1hr).

GLASGOW

Having shrugged off its post-industrial malaise, rejuvenated **GLASGOW**, Scotland's largest city, has undergone a change of image, acknowledged through the success of its application to host the 2014 Commonwealth Games. It's also home to one of the world's best art schools and a live music scene to rival that of London or Manchester. Glasgow is a more functional city than elegant Edinburgh, but is favoured by many for its down-to-earth ambience.

What to see and do

Glasgow's centre lies on the north bank of the River Clyde, around the grandiose **George Square**, a little way east of Central Station. The solid civic buildings here and in the rest of the Merchant City, and the elegant mansions of the South Side and West End, display the grandeur that led the Victorians to label Glasgow the "second city of the Empire".

The Gallery of Modern Art and The Lighthouse

Just south of George Square, down Queen Street, is the **Gallery of Modern Art** (Mon–Wed & Sat 10am–5pm, Thurs 10am–8pm, Fri & Sun 11am–5pm; free; Ⓦwww.glasgowmuseums.com). Formerly a "temple of commerce" built by one of the eighteenth-century tobacco lords, it now houses an exciting collection of contemporary Scots art, notably works by Toby Paterson and John Byrne. A short way west on Mitchell Lane, just off Buchanan Street, **The Lighthouse** (Mon–Sat 10.30/11am–5pm, Sun noon–5pm; £4; Ⓦwww.thelighthouse.co.uk) was the first commission of Glasgow's famous architect Charles Rennie Mackintosh, whose distinctively streamlined Art Nouveau designs appear in shops all over the city; inside, you'll find an exhibition devoted to the man and a panoramic view over the city.

Glasgow School of Art

Just off Sauchiehall Street (pronounced "socky-hall") is the **Glasgow School of Art** at 167 Renfrew St, a remarkable building designed by Mackintosh which fuses Scottish manor house solidity with Modernist refinement. The interior, making maximum use of natural light, was also furnished and fitted entirely by the architect, and can be seen on a guided tour (daily: April–Sept hourly 10am–4pm; Oct–March 11am & 3pm; £7.75; Ⓣ0141/353 4500, Ⓦwww.gsa.ac.uk).

Cathedral and Necropolis

Northeast of George Square is the **cathedral** on Castle Street (Mon–Sat 9.30am–4/5.30pm, Sun 1–4/5.30pm). Originally built in 1136, it's the only Scottish mainland cathedral to have escaped the country's sixteenth-century religious reformers, whose hatred of anything that smacked of idolatry wrecked many of Scotland's ancient churches. Just as interesting as the cathedral is the adjacent **Necropolis**, a hilltop cemetery for the magnates who made Glasgow rich; there are great views across the city from here.

Kelvingrove Art Gallery and the West End

The boundaries of the leafy **West End** are marked by the magnificent, baroque crenellations of **Kelvingrove Art Gallery** (daily 10/11am–5pm; free; Ⓦwww.glasgowmuseums.com), which boasts pieces by Rembrandt, Degas, Millet, Van Gogh and Monet, as well as an impressive body of Scottish painting. Don't miss Dalí's *Christ of St John of the Cross* – an arresting vision of the Crucifixion painted from above. Sitting on the banks of the River Kelvin, the museum regards

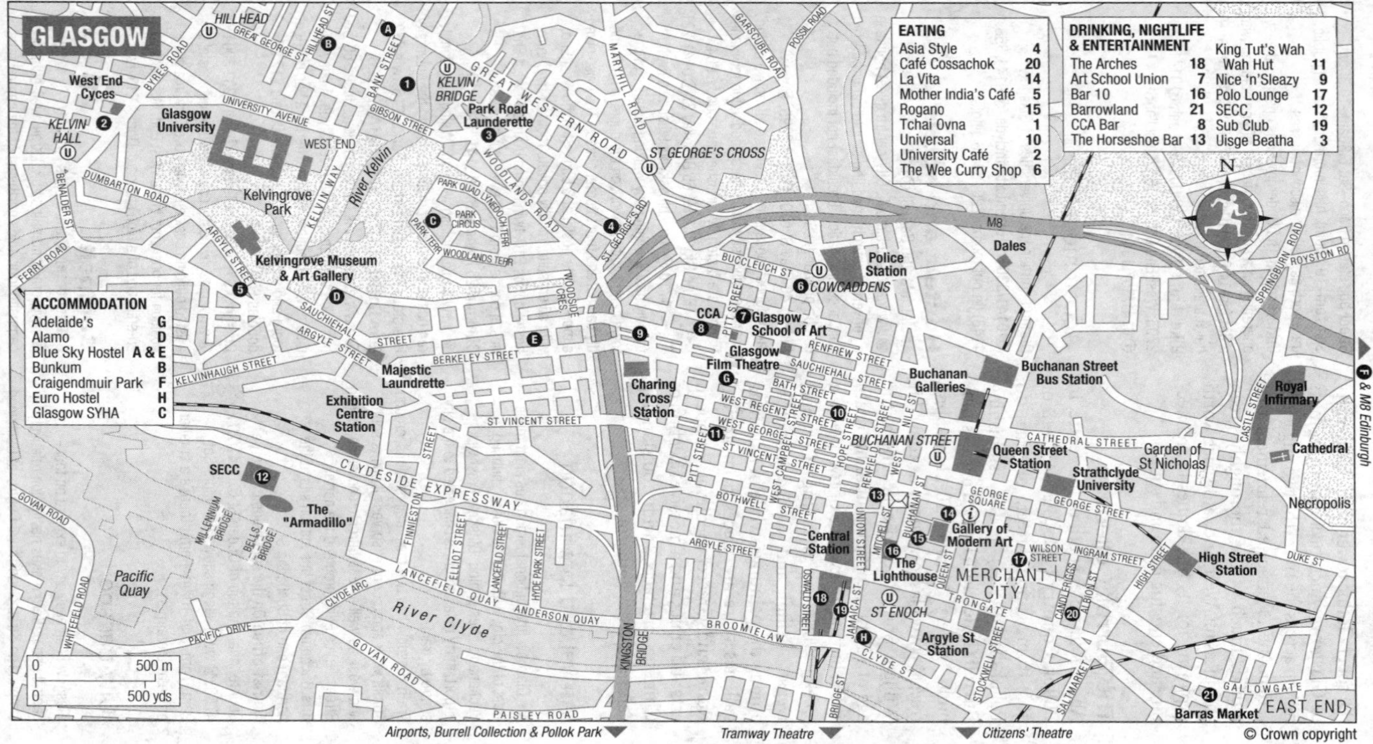
GLASGOW
EATING
Asia Style 4
Café Cossachok 20
La Vita 14
Mother India's Café 5
Rogano 15
Tchai Ovna 1
Universal 10
University Café 2
The Wee Curry Shop 6
DRINKING, NIGHTLIFE & ENTERTAINMENT
The Arches 18
Art School Union 7
Bar 10 16
Barrowland 21
CCA Bar 8
The Horseshoe Bar 13
King Tut's Wah Wah Hut 11
Nice 'n'Sleazy 9
Polo Lounge 17
SECC 12
Sub Club 19
Uisge Beatha 3
ACCOMMODATION
Adelaide's G
Alamo D
Blue Sky Hostel A & E
Bunkum B
Craigendmuir Park F
Euro Hostel H
Glasgow SYHA C
N
West End Cycces
Glasgow University
Kelvingrove Park
Kelvingrove Museum & Art Gallery
Park Road Launderette
Majestic Laundrette
Exhibition Centre Station
Charing Cross Station
SECC
The "Armadillo"
Pacific Quay
River Clyde
River Kelvin
Police Station
Dales
CCA
Glasgow School of Art
Glasgow Film Theatre
Buchanan Galleries
Buchanan Street Bus Station
Queen Street Station
Strathclyde University
Garden of St Nicholas
Royal Infirmary
Cathedral
Necropolis
Gallery of Modern Art
The Lighthouse
Central Station
Argyle St Station
High Street Station
MERCHANT CITY
Barras Market
EAST END
HILLHEAD
KELVIN BRIDGE
KELVIN HALL
ST GEORGE'S CROSS
COWCADDENS
BUCHANAN STREET
ST ENOCH
GREAT WESTERN ROAD
CLYDESIDE EXPRESSWAY
KINGSTON BRIDGE
M8
0 500 m
0 500 yds
F & M8 Edinburgh
Airports, Burrell Collection & Pollok Park
Tramway Theatre
Citizens' Theatre
© Crown copyright

the sober Gothic tower of the **University of Glasgow**, which peers down from its hilltop across the river. The two engage in a dialogue of educated refinement that typifies much of the thoroughly green and pleasant West End, a district worth exploring for its fine domestic architecture and enticing cafés and shops.

The Burrell Collection

About four miles south of the centre, in **Pollok Country Park** (bus #45, #48 or #57 from Union Street, or train to Pollokshaws West), is the astonishing **Burrell Collection**, housed in a custom-built gallery (daily 10/11am–5pm; free; ⓦwww.glasgowmuseums.com). Sir William Burrell began collecting at the age of 15 and kept going until his death at 96, buying an average of two pieces a week. Works by Memling, Cézanne, Degas, Bellini and Géricault feature among the paintings, while in adjoining galleries there are pieces from ancient Rome and Greece, medieval European arts and crafts, and a massive selection of Chinese artefacts, with outstanding ceramics, jades and bronzes.

Arrival and information

Air Glasgow International airport lies eight miles west of the city, with regular buses shuttling to Buchanan St bus station; Glasgow Prestwick airport, thirty miles south, is connected to the city centre by train.
Train Glasgow has two main train stations, around 10min walk apart: Central serves all points south and west, as well as Edinburgh on occasion; Queen Street serves Edinburgh and the north.
Bus Buchanan Street bus station sits at the northern end of Buchanan St.
Tourist office On the south side of George Square, near the top of Queen St ⓣ0141/204 4758, ⓦwww.seeglasgow.com (Mon–Sat 9am–7pm, Sun 10am–6pm); there's a smaller office at the airport.

City transport

Glasgow is an easy city to explore on foot – its central grid pattern makes navigation relatively simple. The Strathclyde Travel Centre, at Buchanan Street bus station (Mon–Sat 6.30am–10.30pm, Sun 7am–10.30pm), has information on all public transport, as well as discount passes.
Underground The Underground is cheap and easy, operating on a circular chain of fifteen stations with a flat fare of £1.20 (Discovery Ticket £3.50 for a day's unlimited travel).
Bike rental Dales, 150 Dobbies Loan ⓣ0141/332 2705; West End Cycles, 16 Chancellor St ⓣ0141/357 1344.

Accommodation

During summer, the universities of Glasgow (ⓣ0141/330 4116) and Strathclyde (ⓣ0141/553 4148) let out rooms (£20–34.26 single).

Hostels and hotels

Adelaide's 209 Bath St ⓣ0141/248 4970, ⓦwww.adelaides.co.uk. City-centre guest house in a converted church providing simple but comfortable accommodation. Breakfast not included but can be provided. £54.
Alamo 46 Gray St ⓣ0141/339 2395, ⓦwww.alamoguesthouse.com. Quiet and attractive option near the university that offers good value for money. Rooms are tastefully furnished and comfy. £64.
Blue Sky Hostel 65 Berkeley St ⓣ0141/221 1710 ⓦwww.blueskyhostel.com. A lively, friendly hostel within easy walking distance of the town centre, with artwork on the doors, a huge cuddly canine, and free internet access. They also own a more sedate hostel at 3 Bank St in the West End, with all en-suite, mostly private rooms. City Centre hostel dorms £10, twin rooms from £25; West End hostel dorms from £13, twins/doubles £38.
Bunkum 26 Hillhead St ⓣ0141/581 4481, ⓦwww.bunkumglasgow.co.uk. Welcoming, family-run hostel in a great position close to the university in a stately Victorian terrace. Dorms £16, twin £32.
Euro Hostel 318 Clyde St ⓣ0141/222 2828, ⓦwww.euro-hostels.co.uk/glasgow. Huge 360-bed hostel on the banks of the River Clyde. A convenient if somewhat soulless option. There's a bar, chill-out room and a 24hr alcohol licence. Dorms £12.95, doubles £50.
Glasgow SYHA 8 Park Terrace ⓣ0141/332 3004, ⓦwww.glasgowhostel.co.uk. Refurbished hostel in a listed building beside Kelvingrove Park in a good position for going out in the West End. All rooms are en-suite and of a high standard. Dorms £13, twin £42.

Campsite

Craigendmuir Park Stepps ⓣ0141/779 4159 ⓦwww.craigendmuir.co.uk. Large, well-equipped campsite four miles northeast of the centre; take

TREAT YOURSELF

Rogano 11 Exchange Place. *Rogano* is Glasgow's oldest and most revered restaurant. The food, though excellent, is very expensive, but you can pop into the bar for a glass of champagne and some oysters (six will cost £9) or eat affordably in the café (mains from £9.50). The 1930s Art Deco interior, which mirrors the same style as the luxury liners built on the Clyde at that time, is a must-see.

a train to Stepps, from where it's a 15min walk. £12.25.

Eating

Asia Style 185 St George's Rd. This no-frills Chinese, on an unremarkable stretch by the motorway, is the insiders' choice for authentic Asian cuisine. Mains from around £5.

Café Cossachok 38 Albion St. Russian restaurant, gallery and live venue that envelops diners in soft red light with haunting violin music. The menu includes Slavic staples like borscht.

La Vita 1–5 St Vincent Place. Italian restaurant spread over three floors on the corner of George Square. The food is excellent and the portions enormous. Pizzas from £7.95.

Mother India's Café 1355 Argyle St. Innovative, tapas-style approach to curry and great value make this bustling place, near Kelvingrove Museum, a winner. Alex "Franz Ferdinand" Kapranos is a fan. Dishes from £3.40.

Tchai Ovna 42 Otago Lane. Enchanting "magic teashop", tucked down a lane in the arty West End. Sample exotic teas in an atmosphere that's part opium den, part hippy commune. Excellent vegetarian food for under £5.

Universal 57–59 Sauchiehall Lane. Hidden on a side street behind the shops of Sauchiehall St, this unpretentious little place, with a red-brick bar, offers generous portions of pub food in cosy surroundings. Live music on Sun afternoons. Mains from £6.25.

University Café 87 Byres Rd. An original Art Deco-style café – something of an institution. The menu is of the no-frills kind – think steak pie and Knickerbocker Glory. Dishes from £3.50.

The Wee Curry Shop 7 Buccleuch St. Tiny establishment offering excellent-value Indian meals. Dishes for around £6.

Drinking and nightlife

Pubs and nightspots cluster around the city centre, the suave Merchant City to the east of Queen St, and the West End around Byres Rd and Ashton Lane, a charming cobbled street lined with bars and eateries.

Pubs and bars

Bar 10 10 Mitchell Lane. A great pre-club bar with DJs. Its industrial interior is the work of Ben Kelly, designer of Manchester's fabled, but now demolished, *Hacienda*.

CCA Bar 350 Sauchiehall St. Arty hangout within the Centre for Contemporary Arts serving continental beers to a fashionable crowd. There's a DJ on Fri and Sat.

The Horseshoe Bar 17 Drury St. Rarely a quiet moment at this city-centre pub which features the longest bar in the UK and almost perpetual karaoke.

Uisge Beatha 232–246 Woodlands Rd. Warm, candle-lit pub with kilted bar staff, stuffed animals and a friendly blend of locals and students supping a vast array of whiskies.

Clubs

The Arches 30 Midland St Ⓦ www.thearches.co.uk. Cavernous club and live venue, under Central Station, that pulls off gigs, theatre and lysergic club nights with equal aplomb. The bigger nights can go on past 4am.

Art School Union 167 Renfrew St. Ⓦ www.theartschool.co.uk. Cheap drinks, and anything from drum and bass to cabaret, make this a favourite for students and serious clubbers alike.

Polo Lounge 84 Wilson St. Popular gay club that mixes refined drinking upstairs with a packed, cruisey dancefloor in the basement.

Sub Club 22 Jamaica St Ⓦ www.subclub.co.uk. Underground club and purveyor of the finest techno and electro.

Entertainment

Live music

Barrowland 244 Gallowgate Ⓦ www.glasgow-barrowland.com. Glasgow's most famous live venue, with a medium-size capacity for soon-to-be-big bands and more established acts.

King Tut's Wah Wah Hut 272a St Vincent St Ⓦ www.kingtuts.co.uk. Famous as the place where Oasis were discovered, and still hosting excellent gigs.

Nice 'n' Sleazy 421 Sauchiehall St Ⓦ www.nicensleazy.com. Late-night bar, with the best jukebox

in town and great gigs in its sweaty basement.

SECC Exhibition Way ⓦ www.secc.co.uk. The Scottish Exhibition and Conference Centre, including the famous "Armadillo" building, hosts the big name touring bands and comedy acts.

Cinema and theatre

Centre for Contemporary Arts (CCA) 350 Sauchiehall St ⓦ www.cca-glasgow.com. Cultural centre that has a reputation for a programme of controversial performances and exhibitions.

Citizens' Theatre 119 Gorbals St ⓦ www.citz.co.uk. South Side theatre famous for sourcing top Scottish talent and producing innovative and thought-provoking work.

Glasgow Film Theatre 12 Rose St ⓦ www.gft.org.uk. Wonderful cinema showing art films and old favourites.

Tramway Theatre 25 Albert Drive ⓦ www.tramway.org. Intimate performance spaces, showing challenging theatre, in a complex that includes the tranquil Hidden Gardens.

Directory

Hospital Royal Infirmary, 84 Castle St ⓣ 0141/211 4000.

Laundry Park Road Launderette, 14 Park Rd; Majestic Launderette, 1110 Argyle St.

Pharmacy Boots, Buchanan Galleries.

Police Pitt St ⓣ 0141/532 2000.

Post office 47 St Vincent St.

Moving on

Train Balloch (every 30min; 45min), Edinburgh (every 15min; 1hr); Inverness (5 daily; 3hr 15min); Liverpool (via Wigan or Preston; 18 daily; 3hr 30min); Mallaig (for Skye; Mon–Sat 3 daily; Sun 1 daily; 5hr 15min); Manchester (2 direct, 23 daily via Preston or Carlisle; 3hr 15min–3hr 45min); Oban (for Mull; Mon–Sat 3 daily; Sun 1 daily; 3hr); Newcastle (every 30min–1hr; 2hr 40min; most change in Edinburgh); Stirling (every 30min; 30min).

Bus Edinburgh (every 10–15min; 1hr 10min–1hr 30min); Inverness (5 daily; 4hr); Liverpool (1 daily; 5hr 20min); Manchester (5 daily; 5hr 30min); Newcastle (1 daily; 4hr); Oban (for Mull; 3 daily; 3hr); St Andrews (hourly; 2hr 20min); Skye (3 daily; Kyle of Lochalsh 5hr, Portree 6hr, Uig 6hr 30min); Stirling (hourly; 45min).

STIRLING

Occupying a key strategic position between the Highlands and Lowlands at the easiest crossing of the River Forth, **STIRLING** has played a major role throughout Scottish history. With its castle and steep, cobbled streets, it can appear like a smaller version of Edinburgh.

What to see and do

Imperiously set on a rocky crag, the atmospheric **castle** (daily 9.30am–5/6pm; £8.50) combined regal and military functions. Highlights within the complex are the **Royal Palace**, dating from the late Renaissance, and the earlier **Great Hall**, with its restored hammerbeam roof. The oldest part of Stirling huddles around the streets leading up to the castle. Look out for the Gothic, timber-roofed **Church of the Holy Rude** (daily 10am–5pm), where the infant James VI – later James I of the United Kingdom – was crowned King of Scotland in 1567. From here, Broad Street slopes down to the lower town, passing the **Tolbooth**, the city's recently restored arts and cultural centre. Stirling is famous as the scene of Sir William Wallace's victory over the English in 1297, a crucial episode in the Wars of Independence. The Scottish hero was commemorated in the Victorian era with the **Wallace Monument** (daily 9/10am–5/6pm, shorter hours in winter; £6.50) a bizarre Tolkienesque tower providing stupendous views – finer even than those from the castle.

Arrival and information

Train and bus The train and bus stations are both just east of the centre in the lower part of town.

Tourist office 41 Dumbarton Rd, in the lower part of town ⓣ 01786/475 019, ⓦ www.visitscottishheartlands.com (June to mid-Sept daily 9am–6/7pm, Sun 9.30/10am–4pm; mid-Sept to May Mon–Sat 9/10am–4/5pm).

Accommodation

Willy Wallace Hostel 77 Murray Place ⊕01786/446773, ⓦwww.willywallacehostel.com. Lively, welcoming backpacker hostel with a comfortable common room. Dorms £15, doubles £36.

Witches Craig Campsite Off St Andrew's Rd ⊕01786/474947, ⓦwww.witchescraig.co.uk. Picturesque site three miles east of town; take bus #62. Closed Nov–March. £7.

YHA St John St ⊕0870/004 1149, ⓦwww.syha.org.uk. The HI hostel is a little characterless but occupies a great setting at the top of town in a converted church. Dorms £14.50, twin £32.

Eating

Barnton Bar and Bistro 3½ Barnton St. Licensed café serving staples from £5.

La Ciociara 41 Friars St. Good-value Italian in the heart of Stirling.

No. 2 Baker Street Pleasant, quiet pub serving good-value basics in huge portions from noon till 7pm.

ST ANDREWS

Polished **ST ANDREWS**, on the coast 56 miles northeast of Edinburgh and reachable as a day-trip from the capital, has a self-important air. Retaining memories of its days as medieval Scotland's metropolis, it is the country's oldest university town, with a snob-appeal to match – Prince William is a recent alumnus. St Andrews' other source of grandeur is golf, with six courses, including the oldest in the world.

What to see and do

Entering the town from the Edinburgh road, you pass no fewer than four golf links, the last of which is the **Old Course**, the most famous and – in the opinion of Jack Nicklaus – the best in the world. At the southern end of the Old Course, down towards the waterfront, is the **British Golf Museum** (March–Oct daily 9.30/10am–5/5.30pm; Nov–March daily 10am–4pm; £5.50); if you want to step onto the famous fairways, head to the **Himalayas** putting green, located right by the first hole and only £2 per round. A wonderful crescent of sandy beach sweeps north from the Old Course; immediately south of it runs North Street, one of St Andrews' two main arteries. Much of the street is taken up by university buildings, with the tower of **St Salvator's College**, dating from 1450, rising proudly above all else.

The castle and cathedral

Further east on North Castle Street is the ruined **castle** (daily: April–Sept 9.30am–5.30pm; Oct–March 9.30am–4.30pm; £5.20, combined ticket with cathedral £7.20). A short distance further along the coast is the equally ruined Gothic **cathedral** (same hours; £4.20), the mother church of medieval Scotland and the largest and grandest ever built in the country. With the cathedral entrance ticket you can get a token to ascend the austere Romanesque **St Rule's Tower** for superb views over the sea and town.

Arrival and information

Train There are no direct trains, though frequent buses connect with the train station five miles away in Leuchars.

Bus The bus station is west of town on City Rd.

Tourist office 70 Market St ⊕01334/472021, ⓦwww.visit-standrews.co.uk. Mon–Sat 9.15/9.30am–5/7pm, plus Sun April to mid-Oct 10/11am–4/5pm.

Accommodation

The tourist office will book rooms for a ten percent deposit – worth doing in the summer and during big golf tournaments, when accommodation is in short supply.

Cairnsmill Caravan Park ⊕01334/473604. A large, family campsite a mile from town with a swimming pool and games room. Bunkhouse accommodation available. £15.

St Andrews Tourist Hostel ⊕01334/479911, ⓦwww.standrewshostel.com. Nicely decorated hostel with clean, basic dorm rooms, a well-equipped kitchen and comfy lounge. Dorms £14.

Eating and drinking

Grillhouse Inchcape House, St Mary's Place. Informal Mexican restaurant with a fun atmosphere

and great food for reasonable prices. At lunch you can get a filling main for less than £5.

The Lizard *Ogstons*, 147 North St ⓦwww.ogstonsonnorthst.com. This fantastic building contains a great restaurant, pleasant bar and the cosy basement *Lizard Lounge* music venue and club, as well as a lovely hotel, all in one. Why go anywhere else?

LOCH LOMOND AND THE TROSSACHS

Lying at at the heart of the **Trossachs National Park**, **Loch Lomond** – the largest stretch of fresh water in Britain – is the epitome of Scottish scenic splendour, thanks in large part to the ballad that fondly recalls its "bonnie, bonnie banks". From the main hub at **BALLOCH**, at the loch's southwestern tip, you can take a cruise around the 33 islands nearby (ⓣ01389/752376, ⓦwww.sweeney.uk.com; from £6.50 for a one-hour cruise) – wallabies escaped from a private collection have made their home on one of them. The **western shore** is easily accessible by bus from Balloch, with the upgraded A82 zipping along its banks. The **eastern shore**, however, is much more peaceful, as large sections of it are only accessible via the footpath which forms part of the West Highland Way. The easiest access to the graceful peak of **Ben Lomond** (3192ft) is from Rowardennan, from where it's a straightforward three-hour hike to the summit; in summer you can reach Rowardennan by ferry from Inverbeg (accessible by bus from Balloch) on the western shore.

Arrival and information

Train The easiest way to get to the loch is to take one of the frequent trains from Glasgow Queen St Station to Balloch.

Tourist office The Gateway Centre at Balloch, incorporating shops, information points and cafés, also has a tourist office (daily 10am–5pm; ⓣ01389/727700, ⓦwww.lochlomond-trossachs.org).

Accommodation

The tourist office has details of the wide choice of campsites and B&Bs in all the villages. The hostels below are open only from March to October.

Loch Lomond Hostel ⓣ01389/850226, ⓦwww.syha.org.uk. A couple of miles northwest of Balloch, this is Scotland's most beautiful HI hostel, and comes complete with resident ghost. Dorm £15.75.

Rowardennan Hostel ⓣ01360/870259, ⓦwww.syha.org.uk. Another alluringly sited HI hostel – see opposite for how to get here. Dorms £13.50, twin £30.

INVERNESS

Lying 160 miles north of Edinburgh, **INVERNESS** is the capital of the Highlands. The town boasts a fine setting astride the River Ness at the head of the Beauly Firth, but has no particularly strong sense of character. The chief attraction of historical interest lies six miles east of town, on bus line #1A from the city centre. In 1746, Culloden Moor was the scene of the last pitched battle on British soil, when Bonnie Prince Charlie's Jacobite army was crushed in just forty minutes, ending Stuart ambitions of regaining the monarchy forever. The **Culloden Visitor Centre**

MIDGE ALERT

During the summer months, particularly in wetter areas, the Highlands and Islands are blighted by midges – tiny biting insects that appear in swarms. If you're camping or hiking, make sure you have insect repellent – locals swear by Avon's Skin So Soft moisturizer – or a midge hood, a net fitting over a wide-brimmed hat which, while making no concessions to fashion, should protect the face. Even a light breeze will blow the midges away though, so try and pick somewhere that isn't completely still to camp.

THE LOCH NESS MONSTER

Tales of **Nessie** date back at least as far as the seventh century, when the monster came out second best in an altercation with St Columba. However, the possibility that a mysterious prehistoric creature might be living in the loch only attracted worldwide attention in the 1930s, when sightings were reported during the construction of the road along its western shore. Numerous appearances have been reported since, but even the most hi-tech surveys of the loch have failed to come up with conclusive evidence.

here includes exhibitions as well as a rooftop viewing area of the battlefield (daily: April–Oct daily 9am–6pm; Nov–March 10am–4pm; £10).

Arrival and information

Air Inverness airport is seven miles northeast of the town. There's a bus into the city every half-hour, and the journey takes 20min.

Train and bus The train and bus stations are adjacent to each other just northeast of the centre off Academy St.

Tourist office Castle Wynd ⓣ0845/225 5121, ⓦwww.inverness-scotland.com (Mon–Sat 9am–5/6pm Sun 9.30/10am–4/5pm). Will find rooms for a small fee.

Bike Hire *Barney's*, 35 Castle St ⓣ01463/232249.

Accommodation

Bazpackers 4 Culduthel Rd ⓣ01463/717663 ⓦwww.bazpackershostel.co.uk. The smallest hostel in town, with an open fire, friendly staff and views over the River Ness. Dorms £10, doubles £26.

Eastgate Backpackers 38 Eastgate ⓣ01463/718756, ⓦwww.eastgatebackpackers.com. There's a young crowd at this well-run hostel in the centre of town, though its position on the main shopping thoroughfare's uninspiring. Dorms £14, doubles £32.

Inverness Student Hotel 8 Culduthel Rd ⓣ01463/236556, ⓦwww.invernessstudenthotel.com. The pick of the budget accommodation in town, this cosy, welcoming hostel has great views and a quiet location by the castle. Dorms £13.50.

Inverness YHA Victoria Rd ⓣ0870/004 1127, ⓦwww.syha.org.uk. Large, modern HI hostel with excellent facilities, though it's not the most central option. Dorms £17.50.

Eating and drinking

Hootananny 67 Church St. Lively pub that has live gigs and good Thai food.

The Market Bar 32 Church St. A popular place on two floors, with live music upstairs.

Moving on

Train Aviemore (10 daily; 35–45min); Edinburgh (7 daily; 3hr 15min–4hr 45min); Glasgow (3 direct daily, or change at Perth; 3hr 20min); Kyle of Lochalsh (for Skye; Mon–Fri 4 daily; Sat 2 daily; Sun 1 daily; 2hr 30min, weekend trains not direct); Stirling (some change at Perth; 10 daily; 2hr 45min).

Bus Edinburgh (12 daily; 3hr 30min–4hr 30min); Glasgow (13 daily, most change at Perth; 4hr 30min); Stirling (4 daily, change at Perth; 3hr 50min).

LOCH NESS

Loch Ness forms part of the natural fault line known as the Great Glen, which slices across the Highlands between Inverness and Fort William. Most visitors are eager to catch a glimpse of the elusive **Loch Ness Monster**: to find out the whole story, take a bus to **DRUMNADROCHIT**, fourteen miles southwest of Inverness, where the **Loch Ness Exhibition Centre** (daily: Feb–May & Oct 9.30am–5pm, June & Sept 9am–6pm, July & Aug 9am–6.30pm, Nov–Jan 10am–3.30pm; £6.50; ⓦwww.lochness.com) attempts to breathe life into the old myth. Most photographs allegedly showing the monster have been taken around the ruined **Castle Urquhart** (daily April–Sept 9.30am–6pm, Oct until 5pm, Nov–March until 4.30pm; £7), one of Scotland's most beautifully sited fortresses, a couple of miles further south.

HIGHLAND TOURS

A couple of rival companies offer lively minibus tours designed specifically for backpackers: **Haggis** (ⓣ0131/557 9393, ⓦwww.haggisadventures.com) and **Macbackpackers** (ⓣ0131/558 9900, ⓦwww.macbackpackers.com) depart from Edinburgh on trips lasting between one and seven days, covering the likes of Loch Ness, Skye and the Highlands. Three-day tours to Skye cost around £60.

THE HIGHLANDS

With its beguiling mix of bare hills, green glens and silvery lochs and rivers, the spectacular scenery of the **Highlands** (which covers most of Scotland north of the Central Belt and west of the city of Aberdeen) is a major draw. The distances involved, however, as well as scarce public transport, mean that you really need a few days to explore any one part of it properly. Coachloads of sightseers take in what they can from carefully positioned viewpoints on the main roads, but **outdoor activities** are a major reason to visit: most tourist information centres and backpacker hostels carry information on good local hiking routes, bike rental and adventure sports.

Getting around the Highlands without a car does require patience, although good-value travel passes are available on First ScotRail's train network (ⓦwww.scotrail.co.uk), which has some superbly scenic stretches.

Aviemore and the Cairngorms

AVIEMORE, at the foot of the looming **Cairngorm** range, now a national park, is a good base for challenging hiking, ancient pine forests, and winter sports. *Glenmore Lodge* (ⓣ01479/861256, ⓦwww.glenmorelodge.org.uk), which runs excellent, though expensive, outdoor courses, offers B&B **accommodation** (£25–30) and plenty of advice. In town, there's an SYHA hostel just south of the train station on Grampian Road (ⓣ01479/810345, ⓦwww.syha.org; dorm £15). For **food**, the *Cairngorm Hotel* opposite the station offers surprisingly reasonable and very tasty pub-style options – don't miss their venison stew in Yorkshire pudding.

Fort William

On the west coast, the rather ugly town of **FORT WILLIAM** is a useful base for draws such as the Nevis Range, with skiing in winter and mountain biking in summer, and **Glen Coe**, where soaring scenery and poignant history combine like nowhere else in the country. If you want to climb **Ben Nevis** (the highest peak in Britain), the easiest route (7hr return) begins just outside Fort William, but make sure you wear suitable clothing, as capricious weather conditions and poor visibility can combine to make the ill-prepared hiker extremely vulnerable. Fort William also marks one end of the West Highland Way, which runs all the way to Glasgow.

There is surprisingly little budget **accommodation** in Fort William itself, though you could try *Fort William Backpackers* just up from the train station on Alma Road (ⓣ01397/700711 ⓦwww.fortwilliambackpackers.com; dorm £13.50, twin £40). The surrounding area is full of hostels, most with stunning views. The SYHA has one in Glen Nevis, 2.5 miles out of town (ⓣ01397/702336 ⓦwww.syha.org; dorm £17.50), right at the foot of Ben Nevis – a taxi from the train station will set you back around £6.

THE ISLE OF MULL AND AROUND

The **Isle of Mull** is the most accessible of all the Hebridean islands off the west coast of Scotland: just 45 minutes by ferry from **Oban**, which is linked by

train to Glasgow. The island's chief appeal is the remarkably indented coastline – three hundred miles of it in total. Despite its proximity to the mainland, the slower pace of life is clearly apparent: most roads are single lane, with only a handful of buses linking the main settlements.

Craignure and Duart Castle

CRAIGNURE, the ferry terminal for boats from Oban (3–6 daily; 45min; £4.45 single), is little more than a smattering of cottages. It does, however, hold the island's main **tourist office** (mid-Oct to March Mon–Sat 9am–5pm, Sun 10.30am–noon & 3.30–5pm; April to mid-Oct Mon–Fri 8.30am–5.15/7pm, Sat 9am-5.15/6.30pm, Sun 10/10.30am–5.15/7pm; ⓣ01680/812377, ⓦwww.visitscottishheartlands.com), a decent pub, bike rental and a campsite. On its way into Craignure, the ferry passes the dramatic **Duart Castle** (April Mon–Thurs & Sun 11am–4pm; May to mid-Oct daily 10.30am–5.30pm; £5), two miles' walk along the bay. The stronghold of the MacLean clan from the thirteenth century, it was restored earlier last century – you can peek in the dungeons and ascend to the rooftops.

Tobermory

Mull's "capital", 22 miles northwest of Craignure, is easily the most attractive fishing port in the west of Scotland, its clusters of brightly coloured houses and boats sheltering in a bay backed by a steep bluff. For a list of the local **B&Bs** head for the **tourist office** (April–Oct daily 9/10am–5/6pm; ⓣ01688/302 182), in the CalMac ferry ticket office at the northern end of the harbour. The **HI hostel** (ⓣ01688/302481; dorms £13.25, closed Nov–Feb) is on Main Street, or you could try the *Tobermory Campsite* (ⓣ01688/302624; £6, closed Nov–Feb) twenty minutes' walk from town on the Dervaig road. Also on Main Street is the *Mishnish Hotel* pub, popular for live folk music at the weekends.

The Isle of Iona

At the opposite end of Mull, 35 miles west of Craignure, sits the **Isle of Iona**. This tiny island has been a place of pilgrimage for several centuries: it was here that St Columba fled from Ireland in 563 and established a monastery that was responsible for the conversion of more or less all of pagan Scotland. The present **abbey** (daily 9.30am– 4.30/5.30pm; £4.70) dates originally from around 1200, and Iona's oldest building, **St Oran's Chapel**, lies just south. It stands at the centre of the burial ground, Reilig Odhrain, which is said to contain the graves of sixty kings, including the two immortalized by Shakespeare – Duncan and Macbeth. Iona is a popular day-trip in summer, reached in a few minutes by ferry from **Fionnphort** at the western tip of Mull. Camping is not permitted, but the excellent *Iona Hostel* (ⓣ01681/700781, ⓦwww.ionahostel.co.uk; dorms £18.50), a mile or so from the ferry, has comfortable beds and superb views.

The Isle of Staffa

A basaltic mass rising straight from the sea, the **Isle of Staffa** marks the northern end of the Giant's Causeway (see p.645), and is the most romantic of Scotland's many uninhabited islands. On one side, its rockface has been cut into caverns of cathedral-like dimensions, notably **Fingal's Cave**, whose haunting noises

> **ISLAND-HOPPING**
>
> The sea off Scotland's west coast is dotted with islands, from tiny rocks to substantial landmasses. The main ferry company, **Caledonian MacBrayne** (CalMac; ⓦwww.calmac.co.uk), connects most of them, and offers a range of island-hopping tickets designed to let you explore at your leisure. In addition to those described here, **Arran**, **Islay** and the **Small Isles** (Rum, Muck and Eigg) are all particularly worth visiting.

SKYE TRANSPORT

By train, the two jumping-off points for Skye are **Kyle of Lochalsh**, from which buses head over the Skye Bridge to Kyleakin, where you can pick up local buses, and **Mallaig**, from where you can take the ferry to Armadale in the southeast corner of the island. The West Highland Railway from Glasgow to Mallaig is one of the most scenic routes in the UK, cutting through glens and past lochs – the Harry Potter Hogwarts Express train scenes are filmed on this line.

Rapsons coaches operate a number of bus services around the island (Ⓣ0871/200 2233, Ⓦwww.rapsons.com for timetable info).

inspired Mendelssohn's *Hebrides Overture*. To get to Staffa, jump aboard the *Iolaire* (Ⓣ01681/700358; £20), which sails out of Fionnphort and Iona.

THE ISLE OF SKYE

The deeply indented coastline, azure water, spectacular summits, and bright, clear light of the **Isle of Skye** make this one of the most captivating spots in Britain. The island's most popular destination is the **Cuillin ridge**, whose jagged peaks dominate during clear weather and offer excellent walking and climbing for the more experienced hiker; equally dramatic are the rock formations of the **Trotternish peninsula** in the north.

Elgol and the Cuillins

The best approach to the Cuillins is by #49 bus from Broadford, where there's a small **tourist office** (summer only: Mon–Fri 10am–5pm, Sat 11am–4pm; Ⓣ01471/822361), on the dramatic road to **ELGOL**, fourteen miles southwest. From here there are boat trips on the *Bella Jane* (March–Oct Mon–Sat; one-way £14, return trip £20; Ⓣ0800/731 3089, Ⓦwww.bellajane.co.uk) to the stunning scenery of Loch Coruisk, where there's a seal colony. You can walk back to Elgol from the loch, though this requires adequate preparation and gear. Serious hikers also head for **GLENBRITTLE**, west of the Cuillins, where there's an HI hostel (Ⓣ01478/640278; Ⓦwww.syha.org.uk; dorms £14, closed Oct–Feb) and a campsite not far away by the sandy beach (Ⓣ01478/640404; £5, closed Nov–March).

Portree

The only real town on Skye is **PORTREE**, an attractive fishing port in the north of the island, which has the island's main tourist office just off Bridge Road (Mon–Sat 9am–5/6pm, plus April–Oct Sun 10am–4pm; Ⓣ01478/612137). The town has several hostels, smartest of which is the *Bayfield Backpackers* (Ⓣ01478/612231; Ⓦwww.skyehostel.co.uk; dorm £13), Bayfield, though the *Portree Independent Hostel* in the old post office is larger (Ⓣ01478/613737; Ⓦwww.hostelskye.co.uk; dorms £14). Food in Portree can be pricey, but the fish and chips down by the harbour are excellent, and the cheerful *Arriba Inn* just up from the harbour does fantastic cakes.

The Old Man of Storr and Uig

Some nine miles from Portree on the **Trotternish peninsula**, at the edge of the Storr ridge, is a distinctive 165-foot sea-stack known as the **Old Man of Storr**, while a further ten miles north, rising above Staffin Bay, sits the **Quiraing** – a spectacular forest of rock formations. The straggling village of **UIG**, on the west coast, has ferries to the islands of the Outer Hebrides, including Harris and North Uist, as well as an HI hostel (Ⓣ01470/542746; dorms £14, closed Oct–March). The very friendly, year-round *Uig Bay Campsite* (Ⓣ01470/542714, Ⓦwww.uig-camping-skye.co.uk; £5) rents out bikes.

Bulgaria

HIGHLIGHTS

ALEXSANDAR NEVSKI CATHEDRAL, SOFIA: the capital's most striking building

THE BLACK SEA COAST: white sand and beach bars

RILA MONASTERY: fabulous frescoes deep in the mountains

PLOVDIV'S OLD QUARTER: get lost among the ornate houses and Roman remains

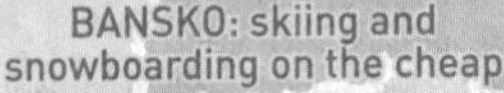

BANSKO: skiing and snowboarding on the cheap

ROUGH COSTS

DAILY BUDGET Basic €20/occasional treat €35

DRINK Beer (0.5l) €0.70

FOOD Shopska salad €2

HOSTEL/BUDGET HOTEL €10/€30

TRAVEL Train: Sofia–Plovdiv (150km) €5; bus: €5

FACT FILE

POPULATION 7.2 million

AREA 110,910 sq km

LANGUAGE Bulgarian

CURRENCY Lev (Lv)

CAPITAL Sofia (population: 1.4 million)

INTERNATIONAL PHONE CODE ⓣ359

Introduction

With several dramatic mountain ranges, superb beaches, numerous historic towns and a web of working villages with traditions straight out of the nineteenth century, Bulgaria has a wealth of attractions crammed into a relatively compact country. More than anything else, this is a land of adventures: once you step off the beaten track, road signs and bus timetables often disappear (or are only in Cyrillic), and few people speak a foreign language, but almost everyone you meet will be determined to help you on your way.

Bulgaria's image has altered dramatically in recent years, thanks largely to the modernization of the country's tourist infrastructure coupled with soaring foreign interest in inexpensive rural and coastal properties. Independent travel is increasingly common: costs are low, and for the committed there is much to take in. Romantic National Revival era architecture is a particular draw, with **Koprivshtitsa**, **Bansko** and **Plovdiv** foremost amongst examples of the genre. The monasteries are stunning, too – the finest, **Rila**, should be on every itinerary, while for city life aim for **Sofia**, Plovdiv, and the cosmopolitan coastal resorts of **Varna** and **Burgas**.

CHRONOLOGY

4000s BC Thracian tribes settle in the area of present-day Bulgaria.

600s BC Greeks settle in the area of present-day Bulgaria.

100s AD Romans invade the Balkan Peninsula.

200 A popular Roman amphitheatre draws people to Serdica (Sofia).

681 The First Bulgarian Kingdom is formed.

864 Bulgaria accepts the Orthodox Church.

1018 The country falls under Byzantine control.

1185 The Byzantines are repelled and the Second Bulgarian Kingdom is proclaimed.

1396 The Ottomans conquer Bulgaria, ushering in almost five hundred years of Turkish rule.

1876 Revolutionaries based at Koprivshtitsa carry out the ill-fated April Rising, which provokes savage Ottoman reprisals.

1877 War of Liberation sees Russia declare war on Turkey to win freedom for Bulgaria.

1886 The Treaty of Bucharest ends the Serbo–Bulgarian war begun the previous year, and Bulgaria gains territory.

1908 Bulgaria declares itself an independent kingdom.

1912 First Balkan War; Bulgaria sustains heavy losses in victory over the Ottomans.

1913 Second Balkan War; previous allies Serbia and Greece defeat Bulgaria.

1914–1918 Bulgaria sides with the Central Powers during World War I.

1945 Soviet army invades German-occupied areas of Bulgaria.

1954 Todor Zhivkov becomes head of the Bulgarian Communist Party in power.

1989 Zhivkov ousted among calls for democratization.

1991 New constitution proclaims Bulgaria a Parliamentary Republic.

2001 Former king Simeon II is elected Prime Minister.

2004 Bulgaria joins NATO.

2007 Bulgaria joins the EU.

2009 Zhivkov's former bodyguard, Boiko Borisov, is elected Prime Minister.

ARRIVAL

The majority of tourists arrive at either of Sofia's two airport terminals, although in summer many fly directly to the coastal cities of Varna and Burgas on charter flights. Frequent **low-cost flights** from London and other European cities to Sofia, Burgas and Varna are provided by Wizzair and easyJet. The national carrier Bulgaria Air (Ⓦwww.air.bg) serves most of Europe but there are no direct flights to or from North America or Australasia.

Bulgaria has land borders with five countries and reliable international **rail** links. Popular routes include from Bucharest to Veliko Tarnovo (5–6hr) or to Sofia (11hr), and from Thessaloniki to Sofia (10hr), while trains from İstanbul traverse the country, stopping at Plovdiv (11hr) and Sofia (14hr) before continuing to Belgrade. Eurolines (Ⓦwww.eurolines.bg) has offices in most major Bulgarian cities; it runs frequent **bus** services to Sofia from many major European cities, though not from Istanbul – these are run daily by Metro, who have an office in Sofia's new bus station (Ⓣ02/813 3213).

GETTING AROUND

Public transport in Bulgaria is inexpensive but often slow and not always clean or comfortable. Travelling by **bus** (*avtobus*) is usually the quickest way of getting between major towns and cities, with a growing number of faster and more comfortable privately run services. Generally, you can buy tickets (*bileti*) at the bus station (*avtogara*) at least an hour in advance when travelling between towns, but on some routes they're only sold when the bus arrives. On rural routes, tickets are often sold by the driver.

Bulgarian State Railways (BDZh; Ⓦwww.bdz.bg) can get you to most towns; trains are punctual and fares low. Express services (*ekspresen*) are restricted to main routes, but on all except the humblest branch lines you'll find so-called Rapid (*barz vlak*) trains. Where possible, use these rather than the snail-like *patnicheski* services. Long-distance or overnight trains have reasonably priced couchettes (*kushet*) and/or sleepers (*spalen vagon*). For these, on all expresses and many rapids, you need seat **reservations** (*zapazeni mesta*) as well as tickets (*bileti*). To ensure a seat in a non-smoking carriage

(*myasto nepooshachi*), you will have to specify this when booking. In large towns, it's usually easier to obtain tickets and reservations from railway booking offices (*byuro za bileti*) rather than at the station, and it's wise to book a day in advance at weekends and in summer. Tickets can only be bought on the day of travel at the station. Advance bookings are required for **international tickets** and are bought through the Rila Agency (Ⓦwww.bdz-rila.com); branches can be found in all major cities. Most stations have **left-luggage** offices (*garderob*). InterRail and Balkan Flexipass are valid, although it often works out cheaper to buy rail tickets as you go.

Cycling in Bulgaria's congested cities, where cycle lanes are few and far between, is best avoided, but the country's quiet minor roads linking towns and villages are a delight for cyclists. Of the few bike hire outfits in Bulgaria, Bikearea (Ⓦwww.bikearea.org) is one of the most reliable and also runs organized tours.

ACCOMMODATION

The number of good quality private **hostels** (*turisticheska spalnya*) is growing, and they now exist in most places of interest. Most one- and two-star **hotels** (for the most part in uninspiring high-rise blocks) rent double rooms from around 50Lv, a little more in Sofia and Plovdiv. Cosier family-run hotels are common on the coast and in village resorts such as Koprivshtitsa and Bansko. **Private rooms** (*chastni kvartiri*) are available in most large towns, and are usually administered by accommodation agencies, although in the smaller resorts you can usually find a room by asking around; expect to pay around 25–50Lv for a double, more in Sofia and Plovdiv. As a rule, private rooms in big cities will be in large residential blocks, while those in village resorts can often be in atmospheric, traditional houses.

Some towns have a **campsite** (*kamping*; usually summer only) on the outskirts, although these are few and far between, and can be unkempt affairs with poor connections to the town centre. Many also feature two-person chalets (20–30Lv per night). Camping rough is technically illegal and punishable with a fine, though authorities usually turn a blind eye.

FOOD AND DRINK

Sit-down meals are eaten in either a **restorant** (restaurant) or a **mehana** (tavern). There's little difference between the two, save that a *mehana* is likely to offer folksy decor and a wider range of traditional Bulgarian dishes. Wherever you go, you're unlikely to spend more than 20Lv for a main course, salad and drink. The best-known traditional dish is *gyuvech* (which literally means "earthenware dish"), a rich stew comprising peppers, aubergines and beans, to which is added either meat or meat stock. *Kavarma*, a spicy meat stew (either pork or chicken), is prepared in a similar fashion. **Vegetarian meals** (*yastia bez meso*) are hard to obtain, although *gyuveche* (a variety of *gyuvech* featuring baked vegetables) and *kachkaval pane* (cheese fried in breadcrumbs) are worth trying.

Foremost among **snacks** are *kebapcheta* (grilled sausages), or variations such as *shishche* (shish kebab) or *kiofteta* (meatballs). Another favourite is the *banitsa*, a flaky-pastry envelope with a filling – usually cheese – sold by street vendors in the morning and evening. Elsewhere, *sandvichi* (sandwiches) and *pitsi* (pizzas) dominate the fast-food repertoire. Bulgarians consider their **yoghurt** (*kiselo mlyako*) the world's finest, and hardly miss a day without consuming it.

Drink

The quality of Bulgarian **wines** is constantly improving. Among the best

BODY LANGUAGE

Bulgarians shake their heads when they mean "yes" and nod when they mean "no" – and sometimes reverse these gestures if they know they're speaking to foreigners, thereby complicating the issue further. Emphatic use of the words *da* (yes) and *ne* (no) should help to avoid misunderstandings.

reds are the heavy, mellow Melnik, and rich, dark Mavrud, while Dimyat is a good dry white. If you prefer the sweeter variety, try Karlovski Misket (Muscatel) or Traminer. Cheap native **spirits** are highly potent: *mastika* (like Greek *oúzo*) is drunk diluted with water; *rakiya* – brandy made from either plums (*slivova*) or grapes (*grozdova*) – is generally sipped, accompanied by salad. Bulgarian **beer** is as good as any, but brands such as Kamenitza, Zagorka, and Shumensko must now compete with the likes of Staropramen, Stella Artois and Heineken, which are brewed locally under licence.

Coffee (*kafe*) usually comes *espresso* style. **Tea** (*chai*) is nearly always herbal – ask for *cheren chai* (literally "black tea") if you want the real stuff, normally served with lemon.

CULTURE AND ETIQUETTE

Bulgarians are predominantly Orthodox Christian; Muslims of Turkish descent make up around 12 percent of the population. Social etiquette in Bulgaria is still rather formal. Shaking someone's hand is the most common form of **greeting** and you should address someone with their title and surname unless you know them well. It is appropriate to wait for the Bulgarian person to decide when to become less formal with you. When invited to someone's home it is polite to bring a small gift, and something from your own country will be particularly appreciated.

As for **tipping**, leaving a tip will definitely be well received, although it is not obligatory.

SPORTS AND OUTDOOR ACTIVITIES

Bulgaria's mountainous terrain offers plenty of adventurous options. The **ski season** lasts from December to March, and the country has several well-known resorts. Bansko (Ⓦwww.bansko.bg), in the spectacular Pirin mountain range in the southwest, is the best known, with alpine peaks and challenging runs perfect for experienced skiers and snowboarders. Other large resorts include Pamporovo (Ⓦwww.pamporovoresort.com) in the Rhodope mountains, which is the best for beginners, and Borovets (Ⓦwww.borovets-bg.com) and Malyovitsa in the Rila range; for more information see Ⓦwww.bulgariaski.com.

Of all Bulgaria's ranges, the Rila mountains (Ⓦwww.rilanationalpark.org) provide some of the country's most attractive **hiking** destinations, including the highest peak – Mount Musala (2925m) – from where a two–three-day trail leads to Rila Monastery. For the best maps, advice and organized hikes visit Odysseia-In in Sofia (see p.233). **Horseriding** is growing in popularity, and a small number of travel agencies can arrange trips of varying length (see box, p.238).

Despite the popularity of team sports such as basketball, handball and volleyball, none can compete with **football** for the passion with which it is involved. Teams in the premier division ("A" Grupa) play on Saturday or Sunday afternoons. **Tickets** are generally cheap and sold at booths outside the grounds on the day of the match. The Bulgarian Football Association maintains an informative website with English-language content (Ⓦwww.bulgarian-football.com).

COMMUNICATIONS

You'll find **internet cafés** in most towns and cities, where you'll rarely pay more than 2Lv/hr. **Post offices** (*poshta*) are usually open Mon–Sat 8.30am–5.30pm, longer in big towns. **Phonecards** (*fonkarta*) for both Bulfon's orange phones and Betcom's blue phones are available from post offices and many street kiosks and shops. Cheap SIM cards from Bulgaria's three network providers are widely available. The operator number for domestic calls is ☎121, for international calls ☎0123.

EMERGENCIES

Petty theft is a danger on the coast, and the Bulgarian **police** can be slow in filling out insurance reports unless you're insistent. Foreign tourists are no longer a novelty in much of the country, but **women** travelling alone can expect to encounter stares, comments and sometimes worse, and clubs on the coast are pretty much seen as meat markets. A firm rebuff should be enough to cope with most situations. Note that everyone is required to carry some form of **ID** at all times.

If you need a **doctor** (*lekar*) or dentist (*zabolekar*), go to the nearest health centre (*poliklinika*), whose staff might speak English or German. Emergency treatment is free of charge although you must pay for **medicines** – larger towns will have at least one 24-hour pharmacy.

BULGARIA ON THE NET

ⓦ**www.bulgariatravel.org** Comprehensive travel information.

ⓦ**www.discover-bulgaria.com** Travel information and hotel booking.

ⓦ**www.sofiaecho.com** News site.

ⓦ**www.travel-bulgaria.com** Information on history and culture, as well as travel.

ⓦ**www.programata.bg** Very good English-language listings.

ⓦ**www.inyourpocket.com** Invaluable site producing downloadable online guides on Sofia, Burgas, Bansko and other cities.

EMERGENCY NUMBERS

Police ☎166; ambulance ☎150; fire ☎160.

INFORMATION

Most major towns and cities have modern **tourist information centres** where staff speak several languages and can provide maps, brochures and leaflets although they aren't usually authorized to make hotel reservations. The best general **maps** of Bulgaria and Sofia are published by Kartografiya and Domino; both are available in Latin alphabet versions and sold at street stalls, petrol stations and bookshops.

MONEY AND BANKS

Until Bulgaria joins the Eurozone (target date: Jan 1, 2015) the currency remains the **lev** (Lv), which is divided into 100 stotinki (st). There are notes of 1Lv, 2Lv, 5Lv, 10Lv, 20Lv and 50Lv, and coins of 1st, 2st, 5st, 10st, 20st and 50st, and 1Lv. Pegged to the euro, the lev is stable and although hotels and travel agencies frequently quote prices in euros, you will be expected to pay in the local currency. At the time of writing, €1 was equal to around 2Lv, $1 to 1.45Lv, and £1 to 2.20Lv. Producing a **student ID card** at museums and galleries will often get you a discount of between a third and a half.

Banks are open Monday to Friday 9am to 4pm, and there are ATMs in every town. Private exchange bureaux, offering variable rates, are widespread – but beware of hidden commission charges. Also watch out for black market moneychangers who approach unwary foreigners with offers of better rates; if they sound too good to be true, they are. Many smaller banks and offices won't take traveller's cheques, and credit cards are generally acceptable only at the

Bulgarian

Hotel and travel agency staff in Sofia and the larger towns and coastal resorts generally speak some **English**, but knowledge of foreign languages elsewhere in the country is patchy; younger people are more likely to know a few words of English. Most street signs, menus and so on are written in the **Cyrillic** alphabet, but an increasing number have English transliterations.

	Bulgarian	**Pronunciation**
Yes	Да	Da
No	Не	Ne
Please	Моля	Molya
Thank you	Благодаря	Blagodarya
Hello/Good day	Добър ден	Dobur den
Goodbye	Довиждане	Dovizhdanye
Excuse me	Извинявайте	Izvinyavitye
Where?	Къде?	Kude?
Good	Добро	Dobro
Bad	Лошо	Losho
Near	Близо	Blizo
Far	Далече	Daleyche
Cheap	Евтино	Eftino
Expensive	Скъпо	Skupo
Open	Отворено	Otvoreno
Closed	Затворено	Zatvoreno
Today	Днес	Dnes
Yesterday	Вчера	Vechera
Tomorrow	Утре	Utre
How much is...?	Колко струва…?	Kolko stroova…?
What time is it?	Колко е часът?	Kolko ai chasu?
I don't understand	Не разбирам	Ne razbiram
Do you speak English?	Говорите ли английски?	Govorite li Angliski?
One	Един/Една	Edin/edna
Two	Две	Dve
Three	Три	Tree
Four	Четри	Chetiri
Five	Пет	Pyet
Six	Шест	Shest
Seven	Седем	Sedem
Eight	Осем	Osem
Nine	Девет	Devyet
Ten	Десет	Deset
Do you have any vegetarian dishes?	Имате ли вегетерианска храна?	Imate li vegitarianska hrana?
Cheers	Наздраве	Nazdrave
The bill, please	Може ли сметката	Mozhe li smetkata
Is this the bus for…?	Това ли е автобусът за…?	Tova li avtobusat za…?
Is this the train to…?	Това ли е влакът за…?	Tova li e vlakut za…?
Have you got a single/double	Имате ли единична двойна стая	Imate li edinichnaroom dvoyna staya
How much for the night?	Колко струва нощувката?	Kolko struva noshtuvkata?

more expensive shops, hotels, and restaurants.

OPENING HOURS AND HOLIDAYS

Big-city **shops** and **supermarkets** are generally open Monday to Friday 8.30am to 6pm or later; on Saturday they close at 2pm. The massive malls that have sprung up in recent years are usually open daily from 10am to 10pm. In rural areas and small towns, an unofficial siesta may prevail between noon and 3pm. Many shops, offices, banks and museums are closed on the following **public holidays**: January 1, March 3, Easter Sunday and Monday, May 1, May 24, September 6, September 22, December 25 & December 31. Additional public holidays may occasionally be called by the government.

Sofia

With its drab suburbs and crumbling old buildings **SOFIA** (София) can appear an uninspiring place to first-time visitors. However, much has been done in recent years to revitalize the heart of the city, and once you've settled in and begun to explore, you'll find it a surprisingly vibrant place, especially on fine spring days, when its lush public gardens and pavement cafés buzz with life. It also possesses the draw of verdant **Mount Vitosha**, just 12km to the south.

Sofia was founded by a Thracian tribe some three thousand years ago, and various **Roman ruins** attest to its zenith as a regional imperial capital in the fourth century AD. The Bulgars didn't arrive on the scene until the ninth century, and with the notable exception of the thirteenth-century Boyana Church, their cultural monuments largely disappeared during the Turkish occupation (1396–1878), whose own legacy is visible solely in a couple of stately **mosques**. The finest architecture postdates Bulgaria's liberation from the Turks: handsome public buildings and parks, and the magnificent **Aleksandar Nevski Cathedral**.

What to see and do

Most of Sofia's sights are centrally located and within easy walking distance of each other. Bulevard Vitosha forms the heart of the shopping district and leads north to the Church of Sveta Nedelya, from where bul. Tsar Osvoboditel passes the major public buildings, culminating with the grand Aleksandar Nevski Church.

Sveta Nedelya Church

At the heart of Sofia is **ploshtad Sveta Nedelya**, a pedestrianized square dominated by the distinctive **Sveta Nedelya Church** (daily 7am–7pm), whose broad dome dominates the vast interior chamber. Colourful modern frescoes adorn every square inch of its walls.

The Largo, Party House and Council of Ministers

Heading north, you'll come to the **Largo**, an elongated plaza flanked on three sides by severe monumental buildings, including the towering monolith of the former **Party House**, originally the home of the Communist hierarchy, and now serving as government offices. The plaza extends westwards to the Serdika metro station, watched over by the city's symbol, the **Sofia Monument**, representing the eponymous Goddess of Wisdom. On the northern side of the Largo is the **Council of Ministers**, Bulgaria's cabinet offices.

The Banya Bashi Mosque and the mineral baths

Just beyond, on bul. Knyaginya Mariya Luiza, you'll find the **Banya Bashi Mosque**, built in 1576 by Mimar Sinan, who also designed the great mosque at Edirne in Turkey. The mosque is not officially open to tourists but modestly dressed visitors may visit outside of prayer times. Behind stand Sofia's **mineral baths**, housed in a yellow-and-red striped *fin-de-siècle* building, closed since 1986 and still being restored. Locals gather daily to bottle the hot, sulphurous water that gushes from public taps into stone troughs outside, opposite ul. Exzarh Iosif.

The Rotunda of St George and the Presidency

Sofia's oldest church is the fourth-century **Rotunda of St George**, built upon the city's oldest Roman foundations and housing frescoes from the eighth century onwards. Next to the church is the **Presidency**, guarded by soldiers in colourful nineteenth-century garb (Changing of the Guard hourly).

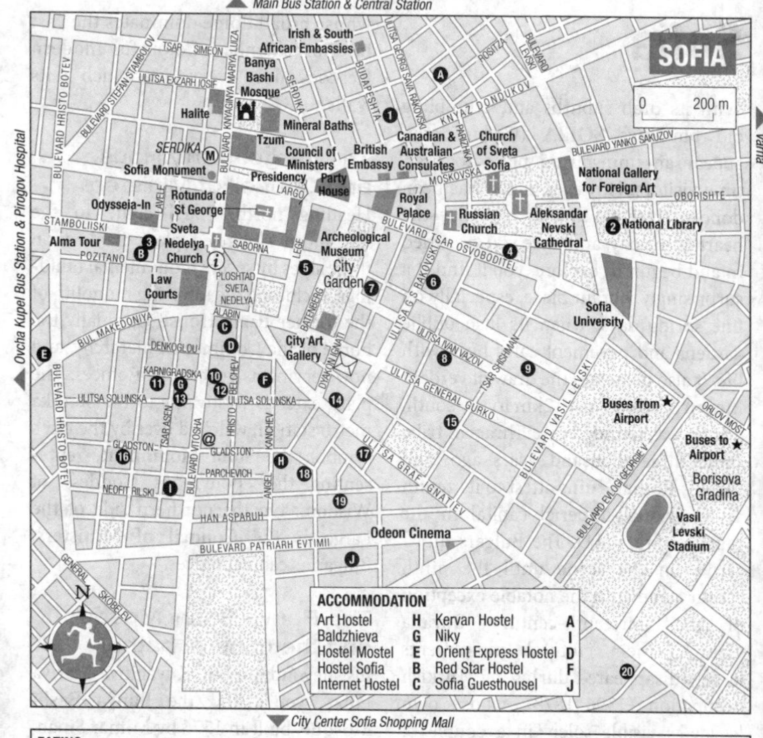

EATING

Art Club Museum Café	5	Pizza Troll	10 & 14
Baalbek	7	Pri Yafata	13
Before & After	12	Slunce Luna	16
Club Lavazza	10	Tea House (Chai vuv fabrikata)	1
Divaka	18		
Dream House	C		

DRINKING, NIGHTLIFE & ENTERTAINMENT

Alcohol	6	Exit Club	3
Apartment	19	Hambara	17
Bibliotekata	2	J.J. Murphy's	11
Bilkovata	15	My Mojito	8
Blaze	9	Swingin' Hall	20
Chervilo	4		

The Archeological Museum

Immediately to the east, a fifteenth-century mosque now holds the **Archeological Museum** (daily 10am–6pm; 10Lv), whose prize exhibit is the magnificent Valchitran Treasure, a Thracian gold cauldron plus cups. Also on show is a collection of Thracian armour, medieval church wall paintings and numerous Roman tombstones.

The City Art Gallery

The **City Art Gallery** (Tues–Sat 10am–7pm, Sun 11am–6pm; free) in the City Garden, immediately to the south of pl. Aleksandar Batenberg, stages monthly exhibitions of contemporary Bulgarian art.

The Russian Church and Aleksandar Nevski Cathedral

Follow bul. Tsar Osvoboditel east and you'll see the **Russian Church**, a stunning golden-domed building with an emerald spire and an exuberant mosaic-tiled exterior, which conceals a dark, candle-scented interior. Just beyond is a particularly busy road junction; turn left, up ul. Rakovski, for the **Aleksandar Nevski Cathedral** (daily 7am–7pm, daily liturgy usually at 8am & 5pm; free), one of the finest

pieces of architecture in the Balkans. Financed by public subscription and built between 1882 and 1924 to honour the 200,000 Russian casualties of the 1877–78 War of Liberation, it's a magnificent structure, bulging with domes and semi-domes and glittering with gold leaf. Within the gloomy interior, a beardless Christ sits enthroned above the altar, and numerous scenes from his life, painted in a humanistic style, adorn the walls. The crypt, entered from outside (Tues–Sun 10am–6pm; 6Lv), contains a superb collection of icons from all over the country.

The National Gallery for Foreign Art

On the northeastern edge of the cathedral square, an imposing white building houses the **National Gallery for Foreign Art** (daily except Tues 11am–6.30pm; 4Lv, free Mon; ⓦwww.foreignartmuseum.bg), which devotes a lot of space to Indian wood-carvings and second-division French and Russian artists, though there are a few minor works by the likes of Rodin, Chagall and Kandinsky. Heading west across the square, you'll pass two recumbent lions flanking the Tomb of the Unknown Soldier, set beside the wall of the plain, brown-brick **Church of Sveta Sofia**.

Borisova Gradina

Down bul. Tsar Osvoboditel, past Sofia University, is **Borisova Gradina**, named after Bulgaria's interwar monarch, Boris III. The park – the largest in Sofia – has a rich variety of flowers and trees, outdoor bars, two football stadiums and two huge Communist monuments.

Mount Vitosha

A wooded granite mass 20km long and 16km wide, **Mount Vitosha**, 12km south of the city, is where Sofians come for picnics and skiing. The ascent of its highest peak, the 2290-metre **Cherni Vrah**, has become a traditional test of stamina. Getting here on public transport is straightforward, although there are fewer buses on weekdays than at weekends. Take tram #5 from behind the Law Courts to Ovcha Kupel bus station, then change to bus #61, which climbs through the forests towards **Zlatni Mostove**, a beauty spot on the western shoulder of Mount Vitosha beside the so-called **Stone River**. Beneath the large boulders running down the mountainside is a rivulet which once attracted gold-panners. Trails lead up beside the stream towards the mountain's upper reaches: Cherni Vrah is about two to three hours' walk from here.

Arrival and information

Air Sofia airport (ⓦwww.sofia-airport.bg) has two terminals: budget carriers arrive at Terminal 1; Bulgaria Air and other major airlines are handled by smart new Terminal 2. The best way to get into the centre of town from Terminal 1 is to catch *marshrutka* #30, which runs until around 10pm (every 15–30min; 1.50Lv). Bus #84 leaves from Terminal 1 and #284 from Terminal 2; tickets (1Lv) can be bought from the airport newspaper kiosk – you'll need additional tickets for any oversized bags. Waiting taxis might well try to charge you an exorbitant 40Lv or more, so it's wise to book one at the booth in the arrivals hall (10–15Lv).

Train Trains arrive at Central Station (Tsentralna Gara), a concrete hangar harbouring a number of exchange bureaux and snack bars, but little else to welcome the visitor. It's a 5min ride along bul. Knyaginya Mariya Luiza (tram #1 or #7) to pl. Sveta Nedelya, within walking distance of several hotels.

Bus Most buses arrive in the new bus station, just next to the train station, although some Bansko services and Blagoevgrad buses (for connections to Rila Monastery) use the Ovcha Kupel terminal, 5km southwest of the centre along bul. Tsar Boris III.

Tourist office The National Tourist Information Centre at pl. Sveta Nedelya 1 (Mon–Fri 9am–5pm; ⓣ02/933 5845, ⓦwww.bulgariatravel.org) is a smart, modern affair offering free maps and travel advice. A nearby alternative is the friendly travel agent Odysseia-In at bul. Stamboliiski 20 (entrance on ul. Lavele; Mon–Fri 9am–7.30pm, daily in summer; ⓣ02/980 5102, ⓦwww.odysseia-in.com),

which charges a 5Lv consultation fee, although not for accommodation booking.

City transport

Public transport There's a flat fare of 1Lv on all urban routes, whether by bus (*avtobus*), trolleybus (*troleibus*), the one-line metro system, or tram (*tramvai*). Tickets (*bileti*) are sold from street kiosks and occasionally on board, and must be punched as you enter the vehicle (inspections are frequent and there are 10Lv spot fines for fare-dodgers). Kiosks at the main tram stops sell one-day tickets (*karta za edin den;* 3Lv) and a strip (*talon*) of ten tickets (7.50Lv) – the tickets are numbered and must be used in sequence. Metro tickets can only be bought from metro stations.

Taxis and minibuses The most reliable taxis are the yellow OK taxis, charging 59st per kilometre until nightfall, 70st afterwards, and 60st initial fare; make sure the driver has his meter running. Additionally, there's a fleet of private minibuses (*marshrutka*), acting like shared taxis and covering around forty different routes across the city for a flat fare of 1.50Lv. Destinations and routes are displayed on the front of the vehicles – in the Cyrillic alphabet – and passengers flag them down like normal taxis, calling out when they want them to stop.

Accommodation

Sofia has a number of good hostels, and some small, reasonably priced hotels. Private rooms (doubles 50–80Lv) can be booked by agencies such as Odysseia-In (see p.233) and Alma Tour at bul. Stamboliiski 27 (Mon–Fri 9am–6.30pm, Sat 10.30am–4pm; Ⓣ02/987 7233, Ⓦwww.almatour.net).

Hostels

Art Hostel ul. Angel Kanchev 21a Ⓣ02/987 0545, Ⓦwww.art-hostel.com. Sofia's trendiest hostel, hosting art exhibitions, live music, resident DJs and drama performances. An extensive travel library and varied activities add to the mix. Guests have access to a kitchen and tea room-cum-bar, as well as free Internet and wi-fi. Breakfast included. Dorm 20Lv, private apartment for two with kitchen facilities 72Lv.

Hostel Mostel bul. Makedoniya 2A Ⓣ0889/223296, Ⓦwww.hostelmostel.com. Superb hostel located in a historic building with free 24-hour internet access and satisfying all-you-can-eat breakfast. The ground floor has a large, comfortable and sociable lounge space, with flat screen TV, DVDs. Free bowl of pasta and a beer for every night you stay. Dorm 20Lv, double 60–70Lv.

Hostel Sofia ul. Pozitano 16 Ⓣ02/989 8582, Ⓦwww.hostelsofia.net. Clean and well-run hostel just behind the Law Courts, with around fifty beds on two floors, shared kitchen, bathroom and cable TV. Breakfast, internet and tea and coffee included. Dorms 20Lv.

Internet Hostel ul. Alabin 50a Ⓣ0889/138298, Ⓔinterhostel@yahoo.co.uk. Friendly hostel with doubles, triples and quads, as well as studio apartments. Located on the second floor of a shopping arcade, above the *Dream House* restaurant. Kitchen and free Internet and wi-fi access. Breakfast included as well as a free drink at the Irish bar downstairs. Dorm 20Lv, double 60Lv, studio apartment 80Lv.

Kervan Hostel ul. Rositza 3 Ⓣ02/983 9428, Ⓦwww.kervanhostel.com. Three-dorm, bohemian hostel in a quiet area of the centre, close to Nevski Cathedral. There's a kitchen plus free Internet and wi-fi access. The hostel also offers a range of day-trips and even bungee jumping. Breakfast included. Dorm 20Lv, double 60Lv.

Orient Express Hostel ul. Hristo Belchev 8A Ⓣ0888/384828, Ⓦwww.orientexpresshostel.com. Small and homely hostel, with modern fittings combined with traditional antique and salvaged furniture, and TVs in every room. Its fifth-floor position makes for great views from the rooms, but some arduous stair climbing as there's no lift. Very friendly and helpful staff. Breakfast and free internet access included. Dorm, doubles and triples available. Dorm 20Lv, doubles 60Lv.

Red Star Hostel ul. Angel Kanchev 6 Ⓣ02/986 3341, Ⓔredstarhostel@yahoo.com. Simple, clean hostel with doubles, triples and dorms. Breakfast included, along with free internet access. Dorm 20Lv, doubles 60Lv.

Sofia Guesthouse bul. Patriarh Evtimiy 27 Ⓣ02/403 0100, Ⓦwww.sofiaguest.com. Large new hostel in the city centre with clean, bright rooms, plus a garden and TV lounge. Free breakfast. Staff can arrange day-trips and offer a pick up/drop off service from the train/bus station or airport for 10–20Lv. Dorm 20Lv, double 60Lv.

Hotels

Baldzhieva ul. Tsar Asen 23 Ⓣ02/981 1257, Ⓦwww.baldjievahotel.net. Small hotel with a pleasant yard one block west of bul. Vitosha. Rooms are simply furnished, clean and cosy, all with phone, fridge, TV, wi-fi Internet, and bathroom. Double 40Lv.

Niky ul. Neofit Rilski 16 Ⓣ02/952 3058, Ⓦwww.hotel-niky.com. Good-value accommodation in a converted apartment block just off bul. Vitosha. Standard doubles are small but neat and tidy with modern showers and a/c; bigger apartment-style

rooms have a kitchenette and en-suite bath. Doubles 100Lv.

Eating

The cheapest places to grab a beer or a coffee are the many cafés and kiosks around bul. Vitosha or in the city's public gardens. In addition, there are plenty of pricier restaurants offering a range of international cuisine.

Cafés

Art Club Museum Café Corner of ul. Saborna & ul. Lege. Chic café with a pleasant patio, set amid Thracian tombstones next to the Archeological Museum. Live DJs in the basement Thurs, Fri & Sat nights. Serves a variety of light meals, desserts and drinks, such as cappuccino with coconut and banana (3.50Lv). Open 24hr.

Club Lavazza bul. Vitosha 13. Smart place for coffee and cakes, which also offers light meals and an excellent-value English breakfast.

Tea House (Chai vuv fabrikata) ul. Georgi Benkovski 11. Atmospheric traditional tea house with a formidable array of teas including "monks' tea", Kashmir tchai and rose priced from 2 to 5Lv.

Restaurants

Baalbek ul. Dyakon Ignati 4. Highly regarded Lebanese establishment, with sit-down restaurant upstairs and fast-food counter offering kebabs, *shawarma* and falafel on the ground floor.

Before & After ul. Hristo Belchev 12. Elegant and popular restaurant near the *Orient Express Hostel*, with a range of Bulgarian, Turkish and Continental dishes, including some fantastic traditional desserts. Also great for vegetarian options, including grilled vegetables in yoghurt and dill (4.80Lv). Hosts tango dances on Sun.

Divaka ul. Gladston 54. Bright and busy restaurant, just west of Graf Ignatiev, behind the *Art Hostel*, serving excellent, meat-heavy Bulgarian dishes. Chicken kebab 7Lv, vegetarian shish kebab 5Lv. Open 24hr.

Dream House ul. Alabin 50a ⓣ02/980 8163. Intimate, friendly and well-established vegetarian restaurant above a shopping mall. Has a good choice of meals and snacks using seasonal produce, including grilled bean croquettes with salsa (5.40Lv) and tofu and algae soup (2.80Lv). They also deliver within the city centre area.

Pizza Troll bul. Vitosha 27. One of the better pizza and pasta restaurants in the centre, with vaguely Art Nouveau decor. There's another branch on Graf Ignatiev.

Pri Yafata ul. Solunska 28. Brash but fun take on a traditional *mehana*, complete with live music, costumed staff and a great Bulgarian menu.

Slunce Luna ul. Gladston 18b. Popular vegetarian restaurant with rustic furniture and a bakery producing great wholemeal bread. Lethargic service is offset by the relaxed atmosphere. Closed Sun.

Drinking and nightlife

For evening entertainment, there's an ever-growing number of clubs, most playing a mix of pop, retro, rock or the ubiquitous local "folk pop"(*chalga*). Jazz and Latino music are also popular.

Bars

Apartment ul. Neofit Rilski 68. One of the city's most stylish and laid-back bars, occupying a pair of nineteenth-century flats and hung with an eclectic array of artwork. The pricy drinks menu keeps the riff-raff at bay. Daily noon–2am.

Bilkovata ul. Tsar Shishman 22. A buzzing, smoky cellar with decent music and a young crowd, *Bilkovata* is something of a legend in Sofia, fondly remembered by successive generations of students, arty types and young professionals, and still going strong. Packed beer garden in summer. Daily 10am–2am.

Hambara ul. 6-ti septemvri 22. Hidden behind an unmarked doorway just off the street, this dark, candle-lit, stone-floored bar is one of the most atmospheric places in the centre for a long night of drink-fuelled conversation. Live jazz several nights a week. Daily 7pm–2am.

J.J. Murphy's ul. Karnigradska 6. Sofia's top Irish bar, offering filling pub grub, big-screen sports and live music at the weekends.

Clubs

Clubs can fill up on Fri and Sat, when you may be kept waiting outside. Entrance fees range from 5Lv to 20Lv depending on the venue, more if a major DJ is manning the decks.

Bibliotekata bul. Vasil Levski 88 ⓣ02/943 3978. Glitzy nightclub beneath the National Library building, drawing in a moneyed young crowd. Daily 9pm–4am.

Blaze ul. Slavyanska 36 ⓣ0888/354004. Lively bar and club near the university, with a good sound system and trendy clientele. Daily 9pm–3am.

Chervilo bul. Tsar Osvoboditel 8 ⓦwww.chervilo.com. Stylish city-centre club offering the latest in house, techno, Latin and lounge music on two floors. The action spreads out onto the terrace in summer, when it's more like an elite, pay-to-enter pavement café than a club.

Exit Club ul. Lavele 16. This popular gay club also serves food in the daytime and early evening. Avoid confusion with the straight *Exit Club* on ul. Saborna. Daily 8pm–2am.
My Mojito ul. Ivan Vazov 12 ⓣ0895/490691. One of Sofia's trendiest clubs, with regular DJ slots and a laid-back crowd. Daily 9pm–5am.

Entertainment

Live music

Alcohol ul. Rakovski ⓣ0888/655500. Underground nightspot that looks like a huge subterranean barn and has an eclectic something-for-everybody music policy. An Oriental-style chillout room boasts cushions and hubble-bubble pipes.
Swingin' Hall ul. Dragan Tsankov 8 ⓣ02/963 0696. Cheap, cheerful and crowded bar, with live music (usually pop/rock or jazz) on two stages.

Cinema

Cineplex bul. Arsenalski 2 ⓣ02/964 3007, ⓦwww.cineplex.bg. Multi-screen cinema in the City Center Sofia shopping mall, with various snack possibilities in the vicinity.
Odeon bul. Patriarh Evtimiy 1 ⓣ02/969 2469. Shows oldies and prize-winning art films past and present. Small café in the lobby.

Shopping

The city's main shopping street, bul. Vitosha, is the place where you are most likely to come across familiar high-street shops and brands. In addition to those listed below, the City Center (bul. Arsenalski 2) and Sofia (bul. Stamboliiski 101) malls are characterless yet immensely popular malls stuffed with clothes shops, eateries and bars.

Malls

Halite bul. Knyaginy Mariya Luiza, opposite the Banya Bashi Mosque. This elegant building houses Sofia's central food hall with two floors of shops and food stalls.
Tzum Once the preserve of the party elite, Sofia's premier shopping mall stocks upmarket and luxury goods.

Markets

Aleksandar Nevski Located at the apex of the three central churches on pl. Aleksandar Nevski, this collection of stalls offers an odd mix of religious paintings, Turkish-influenced silver jewellery, traditional Bulgarian peasant clothing, lace and textiles, and antique and replica Communist items. Some may find the large array of Nazi memorabilia on some of the tables in rather bad taste.
Zhenski pazar One of the city's best outdoor markets is on ul. Stefan Stambolov where trinkets, fresh fruit, vegetables and other foodstuffs are on sale.

Directory

Embassies and consulates Australia, Trakia 37 ⓣ02/946 1334; Canada, Moskovska 9 ⓣ02/969 9710; Ireland, Bacho Kiro 26–30 ⓣ02/985 3425; South Africa, Bacho Kiro 26 (2nd floor) ⓣ02/981 6682; UK, Moskovska 9 ⓣ02/933 9222; US, Kozyak 16 ⓣ02/9375100.
Gay Sofia Bulgarian Gay Organization, bul. Vasil Levski 3, apt. 7 ⓣ02/987 6872, ⓦwww.bgogemini.org.
Hospital Pirogov hospital, bul. General Totleben 21 ⓣ02/915 4411. For an ambulance call ⓣ150.
Internet Site, bul. Vitosha 45 (4.20Lv per hour; 24hr.
Pharmacy No. 7, pl. Sveta Nedelya 5; 24hr.
Post office ul. General Gurko 6 (daily 7am–8.30pm).

Moving on

Bus Bansko (7 daily; 3hr); Burgas (hourly; 7hr); Koprivshtitsa (2 daily; 2hr); Plovdiv (hourly; 2hr); Rila village (2–3 daily; 2hr); Varna (every 30min; 7hr); Veliko Tarnovo (8 daily; 4hr).
Train Bansko (4 daily; 7hr); Belgrade (1 daily; 7hr 30min); Blagoevgrad (6 daily; 2hr 30min–3hr 30min); Bucharest (1 daily; 9hr 30min); Burgas (7 daily; 6hr 30min); Gorna Oryahovitsa (10 daily; 4hr 30min); Istanbul (1 daily; 11hr); Koprivshtitsa (5 daily; 1hr 40min); Plovdiv (16 daily; 2hr–3hr 30min); Septemvri (16 daily; 1hr 30min–2hr 15min); Thessaloniki (2 daily; 6hr); Varna (7 daily; 8hr 30min).

Southern Bulgaria

The route south from Sofia skirts the Rila and Pirin mountain ranges, swathed in forests and dotted with alpine lakes, and home to Bulgaria's highest peaks. If time is short, the place to head for is the most revered of Bulgarian monasteries, **Rila**,

around 30km east of the main southbound route. **Bansko**, on the eastern side of the Pirin range, boasts a wealth of traditional architecture, as well as being a major ski resort and a good base for hiking. Another much-travelled route heads southeast from Sofia towards Istanbul. The main road and rail lines now linking Istanbul and Sofia essentially follow the course of the Roman Serdica–Constantinople road, past towns ruled by the Ottomans for so long that foreigners used to call this part of Bulgaria "European Turkey". Of these, the most important is **Plovdiv**, Bulgaria's second city, whose old quarter is a wonderful mixture of National Revival mansions and classical remains. Some 30km south of Plovdiv is **Bachkovo Monastery**, containing Bulgaria's most vivid frescoes.

RILA MONASTERY

As the most celebrated of Bulgaria's religious sites, famed for its fine architecture and mountainous setting – and declared a World Heritage site by UNESCO – the **Rila Monastery** receives a steady stream of visitors, many of them day-trippers from Sofia. Joining one of these one-day tours from the capital (which can be arranged with Odysseia-In; see p.233) is the simplest way of getting here, but can work out expensive (most tours cost around 150Lv). It's much more economical to get there by public transport, though realistically you'll have to stay the night.

What to see and do

Ringed by mighty walls, the **monastery** (daily 6am–10pm; free) has the outward appearance of a fortress, but this impression is negated by the beauty of the interior, which even the crowds can't mar. Graceful arches above the flagstoned courtyard support tiers of monastic cells, and stairways ascend to wooden balconies. Bold red stripes and black-and-white check patterns enliven the facade, contrasting with the sombre mountains behind and creating a harmony between the cloisters and the **church**. Richly coloured frescoes shelter beneath the church porch and cover much of its interior. The iconostasis is splendid, almost 10m wide and covered by a mass of intricate carvings and gold leaf. Beside the church is **Hrelyo's Tower**, the sole remaining building from the fourteenth century. Cauldrons, which were once used to prepare food for pilgrims, occupy the soot-encrusted kitchen on the ground floor of the north wing, while on the floors above you can inspect the spartan refectory and panelled guest rooms. Beneath the east wing is the **treasury** (daily 8.30am–4.30pm; 10Lv), where, among other things, you can view a wooden cross carved with more than 1500 miniature human figures during the 1790s.

Arrival

Bus There are 2–3 daily buses from Sofia's Ovcha Kupel terminal (reached by tram #19 from the railway station, or #5 from behind the Law Courts) to Rila village, from where four buses a day make the 27km run up to the monastery. Otherwise, you'll need to catch the bus or train to Blagoevgrad in the Struma Valley, and then change to a local bus for Rila village (hourly; 35min).

Accommodation

It's possible to stay in the monastery's reasonably comfortable rooms (ⓣ07/054 2208; gates close at 11pm; 60Lv double).

Zodiac ⓣ048/772657. Pleasant campsite occupying an attractive riverside spot, with smart double bungalows and a good restaurant. Camping 10Lv per person, bungalow 35Lv.

Eating

For cheap snacks, delicious bread and doughnuts, you should head for the bakery opposite the east gate.

Drushliavitsa Built over a stream on the hillside just beyond the East Gate, this traditional-style Bulgarian restaurant offers polite service and shaded outdoor seating. The menu features Bulgarian standards and fresh local trout.

HORSERIDING IN THE RILA MOUNTAINS

A unique way to experience the spectacular terrain of the **Rila Mountains** is on horseback. Some of the trails pass through virtually untouched forest areas and alongside staggering glacial lakes; there are also some seriously rocky options for experienced or adventurous riders. The tour operator Horseriding Bulgaria at ul. Saborna 20, Plovdiv (Ⓣ02/400 3095, Ⓦwww.horseridingbulgaria.com) offers a number of tour options, including individual tours with a guide, out of their Iskar Ranch at the foot of the Rila Mountains. They can organize tours of different difficulty grades and can also offer riding instruction if you need it.

Rila Situated behind the bakery. Identical in style to the *Drushliavitsa* with a similar menu, but provides a somewhat lethargic level of service.

Moving on

There are three buses a day from Rila Monastery to Rila village from where hourly buses depart for nearby Blagoevgrad and beyond.

Bus Blagoevgrad to: Bansko (12 daily; 1hr); Sofia (hourly; 2hr).

BANSKO

Lying some 40km east of the main Struma Valley route, **BANSKO** (Банско) is the primary centre for walking and skiing on the eastern slopes of the Pirin mountains. Originally an agricultural centre, it's witnessed massive investment in ski tourism in recent years, resulting in the eyesore of half-built apartment blocks and hotels squeezed into the backyards of stone-built nineteenth-century farmhouses. Despite this overdevelopment, the central old town, with its numerous traditional pubs hidden away down labyrinthine cobbled streets, is as attractive as ever and the perfect place to wind down after a hard day on the slopes.

Though connected to Sofia and other towns by bus, Bansko can also be reached by a **narrow-gauge railway**, which leaves the main Sofia–Plovdiv line at Septemvri and forges its way across the highlands. It's one of the most scenic trips in the Balkans, but also one of the slowest, taking five hours to cover just over 100km.

What to see and do

Bansko centres on the modern pedestrianized pl. Nikola Vaptsarov, where the **Nikola Vaptsarov Museum** (daily 8am–noon and 2–5.30pm; 3Lv) relates to the local-born poet and socialist martyr. Immediately north of here, pl. Vazrazhdane is watched over by the solid stone tower of the **Church of Sveta Troitsa**, whose interior contains exquisite nineteenth-century frescoes and icons. On the opposite side of the square, the **Rilski Convent** contains an icon museum (Mon–Fri 9am–noon & 2–5pm; 3Lv) devoted to the achievements of Bansko's nineteenth-century icon painters.

From the main square, ul. Pirin leads north towards the **cable car** (Dec–March daily 8.30am–5pm; 16Lv), where there is a buzzing collection of ski-hire shops, bars and restaurants. Ski passes start at 50Lv per day, and 280Lv for six days (half-price for children), with ski and snowboard hire around 30Lv per day. The cable car doesn't operate outside the ski season so the only option for reaching the summit in the summer months is to head west – on foot or by taxi – via a steep fourteen-kilometre uphill climb to the Vihren hut, where cheap dorm accommodation (10Lv) is available. This is the main trailhead for hikes towards the 2914-metre summit of **Mount Vihren**, Bulgaria's second-highest peak, or gentler rambles around the meadows and lakes nearby.

Arrival and information

Bus and train The bus and train stations are on the northern fringes of town, 10min walk from pl. Vaptsarov.

Tourist information ul. Pirin 70a ⓣ0886/543262, ⓦwww.banskotouristinformation.com (daily 10am–8pm).

Accommodation

Durchova Kushta ul. P R Slavejkov 5 ⓣ0749/88223, ⓦwww.durchova-kashta.com. Comfortable but plain en-suite, pine-furnished rooms with TV, phone and minibar. Also has a sauna. Double 40–60Lv.

Kadiyata ul. Yane Sandanski 8 ⓣ0899/969370, Family-run place in the heart of the old town, offering smart en-suites with modern furnishings and TV. Double 40Lv.

Roshkova Kashta ul. Mozgovitsa 17 ⓣ0886/840827, ⓦwww.roshkoff-house.netfirms.com. Pleasant hotel situated on a quiet street just outside the centre of Bansko. En-suite rooms, wi-fi and breakfast included. Free daily bus to the lift station. 50Lv double.

Eating and drinking

Dedo pene ul. Aleksandar Buynov 1, just south of pl. Vazrazhdane. The whole range of traditional Bulgarian food and Bansko specialities, in a characterful dining room crammed with folksy decorations – and you can sit in the vine-shaded courtyard in summer.

Molerite ul. Glazne 41, just north of pl. Nikola Vaptsarov. Two floors of wooden benches and ethnic textiles, and superb local specialities such as roast lamb and sword-grilled shish kebabs. Turns into a folk-pop disco after about 11pm.

Oxygen ul. Stefan Karadzha 27. Basement bar in the town centre with mixed programme of DJ-driven sounds, potent cocktails and good vibes.

Moving on

Train Septemvri (4 daily; 5hr 20min).

Bus Blagoevgrad (15 daily; 1hr); Plovdiv (6 daily; 4hr); Sofia (16 daily; 3hr).

PLOVDIV

Bulgaria's second largest city, **PLOVDIV** (Пловдив) has more obvious charms than Sofia, which locals tend to look down on. The old town embodies Plovdiv's long history – Thracian fortifications subsumed by Macedonian masonry, overlaid with Roman and Byzantine walls. Great timber-framed mansions, erected during the Bulgarian renaissance, symbolically look down upon the derelict Ottoman mosques and artisans' dwellings of the lower town. But this isn't just another museum town: the city's arts festivals and trade fairs are the biggest in the country, and its restaurants and bars are equal to those of the capital.

What to see and do

Plovdiv centres on the large **ploshtad Tsentralen**, dominated by the monolithic *Hotel Trimontium Princess.*

Ploshtad Dzhumaya

Heading north from here, the pedestrianized ul. Knyaz Aleksandar I, lined with shops, cafés and bars, leads onto the attractive **ploshtad Dzhumaya**, where stallholders gather to sell a range of touristy knick-knacks, including paintings, jewellery and icons. The ruins of a **Roman stadium**, visible in a pit beneath the square, are just a fragment of the arena where up to thirty thousand spectators watched gladiatorial spectacles. Among the variously styled buildings here, the recently renovated **Dzhumaya Mosque**, with its diamond-patterned minaret and lead-sheathed domes, steals the show; it's believed that the mosque dates back to the reign of Sultan Murad II (1359–85).

The Old Quarter

Covering one of Plovdiv's three hills with its cobbled streets and colourful mansions, the **Old Quarter** is a painter's dream and a cartographer's nightmare. As good a route as any is to start from pl. Dzhumaya and head east up ul. Saborna. Blackened fortress walls dating from Byzantine times can be seen around

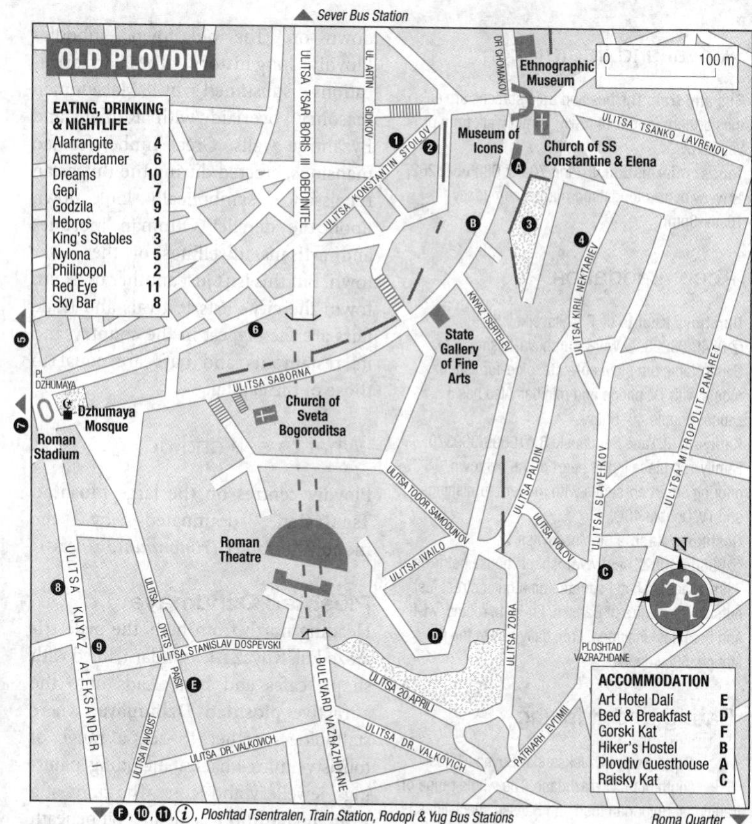

Saborna and other streets, sometimes incorporated into the dozens of timber-framed National Revival houses that are Plovdiv's speciality. Outside and within, the walls are frequently decorated with niches, floral motifs or false columns, painted in a style known as *alafranga*. Turn right, up the steps beside the Church of Sveta Bogoroditsa, and continue, along twisting cobbled lanes, to the **Roman Theatre** (daily 8am–5.30pm; 3Lv), the best preserved in the country, and still an impressive venue for regular concerts and plays (advertised around the town and in the local press).

The State Gallery of Fine Arts and around

Back on Saborna, the **State Gallery of Fine Arts** (Mon–Fri 9.30am–5.30pm, Sat & Sun 10am–5pm; 3Lv, free Thurs) holds an extensive collection of nineteenth- and twentieth-century Bulgarian paintings, including some fine portraits by renowned National Revival realist painter Stanislav Dospevski. Further along, the **Church of SS Constantine and Elena** contains a fine gilt iconostasis, partly decorated by the prolific nineteenth-century artist Zahari Zograf, whose work also appears in the adjacent **Museum of Icons** (Mon–Fri 9.30am–5.30pm, Sat & Sun 10am–5pm; 3Lv, free Thurs). A little further uphill is the richly decorated Kuyumdzhioglu House, now home to the **Ethnographic Museum** (Tues–Sun 9am–noon & 2–5pm; 4Lv). Folk costumes and crafts are on display on the ground floor, while upstairs, the elegantly furnished

rooms reflect the former owner's taste for Viennese and French Baroque.

Arrival and information

Train Plovdiv's train station is on bul. Hristo Botev, a 10min bus ride (#20 or #26) south of the centre.

Bus Two of Plovdiv's three bus stations are near the train station: Rodopi, serving the mountain resorts to the south, is just on the other side of the tracks; while Yug, serving Sofia and the rest of the country, is one block east. The third bus station, Sever, is north of the river (bus ##3 or #99; 20min) and serves destinations such as Koprivshtitsa and Veliko Tarnovo.

Tourist information pl. Tsentralen 1 ⓣ032/656 794, ⓦwww.plovdiv-tour.info (Mon–Fri 9am–6pm, Sat & Sun 10am–2pm). Can reserve hotel rooms, arrange excursions. For horse-riding tours in the Rila Mountains, see box, p.238.

Accommodation

Plovdiv's hotel prices are relatively high, but there are a few decent-value options. Private rooms (50Lv per double) can be booked through Esperansa, at Ivan Vazov 14, just south of pl. Tsentralen (daily 9am–7pm; ⓣ032/260653, ⓦwww.esperansa.hit.bg).

Hostels

Hiker's Hostel ul. Saborna 53 ⓣ0885/194553, ⓦwww.hikers-hostel.org. Small but comfortable and friendly hostel in the middle of the old town, with fantastic views and a traditional open fire during winter. Breakfast and unlimited internet use included. Also organizes day-trips in Plovdiv and the surrounding area, and guests can even pitch tents in the back yard. Dorm 20Lv, twin room 50Lv.

Plovdiv Guesthouse ul. Saborna 20 ⓣ02/400 3098, ⓦwww.plovdivguest.com. Modern hostel has ten rooms with fifty beds in total and a shower/WC in each room, as well as a large TV lounge area. Dormitories and private rooms are available. Breakfast is included. Dorm 20Lv, twin room 55Lv

Raisky Kat ul. Slaveikov 6 t032/268849, ⓦwww.raiskykat.hostel.com. Welcoming, family-run hostel offering doubles and triples in the old town. 20Lv p.p./48Lv double

Hotels

Art Hotel Dalí ul. Otets Paisii 11 ⓣ032/621530, ⓦwww.hoteldali.hit.bg. Tucked away in a back street near the old town, the surrealist-themed *Dalí* has smart, modern rooms. Doubles 90Lv.

Bed & Breakfast ul. Knyazh Tseretelev 24 ⓣ0878/434770, ⓔbedbreakfast@abv.bg. Situated high up in the old town, this cosy family-run hotel has large comfortably furnished en suites. Doubles 90–120Lv.

Campsite

Gorski Kat 4km west of Plovdiv. ⓣ032/951 360. Reached by bus #222 from outside the train station, or on buses #4, #18 or #44 from opposite the *Trimontium Princess* hotel on pl. Tsentralen. With a restaurant and bar, this campsite offers a self-contained and slightly more peaceful alternative to staying in the main town. Camping 8Lv per person; double bungalows 40Lv.

Eating

The most atmospheric restaurants are in the old town, many occupying elegant old houses and serving good, traditional Bulgarian food. In the new town, ul. Knyaz Aleksandar I is awash with cheaper fast-food outlets, though better quality can be found away from the main drag.

Alafrangite ul. Kiril Nektariev 17. Lovely National Revival-style restaurant housed in an old town mansion. Mid-range prices, plus nightly live music in the fig-shaded courtyard.

Amsterdamer ul. Konstantin Stoilov 10. Stylish reproduction of a Dutch restaurant serving reasonably priced international and Bulgarian cuisine.

Dreams ul. Knyaz Aleksandar I 42. A popular spot for coffee, cocktails and cakes.

TREAT YOURSELF

For some the best wine and food that southern Bulgaria has to offer, head to the restaurant of the **Hebros** hotel at ul. Konstantin Stoilov 51 (ⓣ032/260 180 or 625 929, ⓦwww.hebros-hotel.com). The traditional Bulgarian menu usually changes depending on what the chef has found in the market that day, although there are always vegetarian options and an array of desserts. Main courses are around 30Lv and appetizers, such as hot foie gras with apples, around 20Lv. Tempting as the food is, it is the wine that really gives *Hebros* its reputation, with recommended wines for every dish and an extensive cellar with wines from all over Bulgaria; prices range from 20Lv to 250Lv.

Godzila ul. Knyaz Aleksandar I 29a. Pizzeria on the main street that serves a reasonable selection of dishes. One of Plovdiv's few 24-hour eating places.
King's Stables ul. Saborna 9a. One of the old town's nicest and most reasonably priced restaurants. Serves large portions of traditional Bulgarian food, including some excellent grilled dishes (2–8Lv). The yoghurt with home-made blueberry jam is definitely worth trying. There's also a bar that offers equally generous measures of spirits and weekly live music performances. Summer only.
Philipopol ul. Konstantin Stoilov 56b. An excellent restaurant, serving hearty Bulgarian food and with a nice garden. The *shkembe* (tripe soup) is delicious (2.50Lv).

Drinking and nightlife

The best drinking holes are the pavement cafés of ul. Knyaz Aleksandar I. The Kapana area just north of the Dzhumaya mosque is the best place to head for late-night drinks and dancing.
Gepi ul. Lady Strangford 5. A vibrant bar-cum-club with frequent live music as well as retro, dance, jazz, and Latino nights. Located up a side street just west of pl. Dzhumaya. Open 9pm–4am.
Nylona ul. Benkovski 8. Dimly lit and unsigned rock bar in the Kapana area that attracts an alternative crowd and hosts irregular live music performances.
Red Eye ul. Gladston 8. Just off pl. Tsentralen, this tiny, but incredibly popular bar is crammed into the first floor of a rickety old building. Features a staple diet of rock and retro.
Sky Bar ul. Knyaz Alexandar I 32. Sleek, outdoor cocktail bar with white leather sofas and plasma video screens.

Directory

Hospital For 24hr emergency treatment try Medicus Alpha at ul. Veliko Tarnovo 21 (☎032/634463), alongside the park next to pl. Tsentralen.
Internet Zeon below pl. Dzhumaya is the most reliable 24hr internet.
Post office pl. Tsentralen 1 (Mon–Sat 7am–7pm, Sun 7am–11am).
Pharmacy Kamea, ul. Hristo Danov 4, close to pl. Dzhumaya is open 24hr.
Travel agents Several agencies at the Yug bus station sell tickets for international buses. Hebros Bus (daily 7.30am–7pm; ☎032/626 916), a Eurolines agent, can book seats on buses to Greece, Turkey and Western Europe.

Moving on

Train Burgas (7 daily; 4–5hr); Istanbul (1 nightly; 10hr 30min); Kopriovshtitsa (3 daily; 4–5hr); Sofia (16 daily; 2hr–3hr 30min); Varna (4 daily; 5hr).
Bus Avtogara Rodopi: Smolyan (via Bachkovo monastery) (hourly; 40min);
Avtogara Sever: Koprivshtitsa (1 daily; 2hr 30min); Veliko Tarnovo (3 daily; 4hr);
Avtogara Yug: Burgas (4 daily; 4hr); Sofia (hourly; 2hr); Varna 4 daily; 5hr).

BACHKOVO MONASTERY

The most attractive destination around Plovdiv is **Bachkovo Monastery** (daily 7am–8pm; free), around 30km away and an easy day-trip from the city (hourly buses from Rodopi station to Smolyan). Founded in 1038 by two Georgians in the service of the Byzantine Empire, this is Bulgaria's second-largest monastery. A great iron-studded door admits visitors to the cobbled courtyard, surrounded by wooden galleries and adorned with colourful frescoes. Along one wall is a pictorial narrative of the monastery's history, showing Bachkovo roughly as it appears today, and watched over by the

THE NIGHT TRAIN TO ISTANBUL

There's a nightly **train** to Istanbul, which leaves Plovdiv at 9.55pm; tickets should be bought in advance from the BDZh/Rila office opposite the train station at bul. Hristo Botev 31A (Mon–Fri 8am–6pm, Sat 8am–2pm).

Turkish **visas** (see p.1216) can be bought at the Kapikule frontier; you can use pounds, dollars or euros but have the exact sum ready in cash, as they don't always have change and won't let you in without the visa. Other nationals should contact the Turkish consulate at ul. Filip Makedonski 10 in Plovdiv (☎032/632 309) for current visa prices.

Madonna and Child. Beneath the vaulted porch of Bachkovo's principal church, **Sveta Bogoroditsa**, are frescoes depicting the horrors in store for sinners; the entrance itself is more cheery, overseen by the Holy Trinity. Just outside the main gate is the recently restored **ossuary**, which dates from the eleventh century and contains a number of early medieval frescoes, but sadly it's rarely open to visitors.

It's possible to **stay** in recently refurbished rooms in the monastery (☎03327/277; 20Lv per person with shared bathroom and cold water, 35Lv per person with hot water and en suite), and there are three **restaurants** just outside; *Vodopada*, with its mini-waterfall, is the best.

Central Bulgaria

For over a thousand years, Stara Planina – known to foreigners as the **Balkan range** – has been the cradle of the Bulgarian nation. It was here that the Khans established the First Kingdom, and here, too, after a period of Byzantine control, that the Boyars proclaimed the Second Kingdom and created a magnificent capital at **Veliko Tarnovo**. The nearby Sredna Gora (Central Mountains) were inhabited as early as the fifth millennium BC, but for Bulgarians this forested region is best known as the Land of the April Rising, the nineteenth-century rebellion for which the picturesque town of **Koprivshtitsa** will always be remembered.

Although they lie a little way off the main rail lines from Sofia, neither Veliko Tarnovo nor Koprivshtitsa is difficult to reach. The former lies just south of Gorna Oryahovitsa, a major rail junction midway between Varna and Sofia, from where you can pick up a local train or bus; the latter is served by a stop on the Sofia–Burgas line, where four daily trains in each direction are met by local buses to ferry you the 12km to the village itself.

KOPRIVSHTITSA

Seen from a distance, **KOPRIVSHTITSA** (Копривщица) looks almost too lovely to be real, its half-timbered houses lying in a valley amid wooded hills. It would be an oasis of rural calm if not for the tourists drawn by the superb architecture and Bulgarians paying homage to a landmark in their nation's history.

What to see and do

All of the town's museums are open 9.30am–5.30pm, with half of them closing on Mondays, and the other half on Tuesdays. You can buy a combined ticket for all six for 5Lv at the tourist office and at any of the museums; individual houses are priced at 2Lv each. It's also possible to hire an English-speaking guide for a two-hour tour (20Lv).

A street running off to the west of the main square leads to the **Oslekov House** (closed Mon). Its summer guest room is particularly impressive, with a vast wooden ceiling carved with geometric motifs. Cross the Freedom Bridge opposite the information centre to reach **Karavelov House** (closed Tues), the childhood home of Lyuben Karavelov, a fervent advocate of Bulgaria's liberation who spent much of his adult life in exile where he edited revolutionary publications. Near the Surlya Bridge is the birthplace of the poet **Dimcho Debelyanov** (closed Mon), who is buried in the grounds of the hilltop **Church of the Holy Virgin**. A gate at the rear of the churchyard leads to the birthplace of **Todor Kableshkov** (closed Mon), leader of the local rebels. Kableshkov's house now displays weapons used in the Rising and features a wonderful circular vestibule. Continuing south, cross the **Bridge**

KOPRIVSHTITSA AND THE APRIL RISING

From the Bridge of the First Shot to the Place of the Scimitar Charge, there's hardly a part of Koprivshtitsa that isn't named after an episode or participant in the **April Rising of 1876**, a meticulously planned grassroots revolution against Ottoman control that failed within days because the organizers had vastly overestimated their support. Neighbouring towns were burned by the *Bashibazouks* – the irregular troops recruited by the Turks to put the rebels in their place – and refugees flooded into Koprivshtitsa, spreading panic. The rebels eventually took to the hills while local traders bribed the *Bashibazouks* to spare the village – and so Koprivshtitsa survived unscathed, to be admired by subsequent generations as a symbol of heroism. Although the homegrown Bulgarian revolution failed, the barbarity of the Turkish reprisals outraged the international community and led to the 1877–88 War of Liberation which won freedom for Bulgaria from over five hundred years of Ottoman rule.

of the First Shot, which spans the Byala Reka stream, head up ul. Nikola Belodezhdov, and you'll come to the **Lyutov House** (closed Tues), once home to a wealthy yoghurt merchant and today housing some of Koprivshtitsa's most sumptuous interiors. On the opposite side of the River Topolnitsa, steps lead up to the birthplace of another major figure in the Rising, **Georgi Benkovski** (closed Tues). A tailor by profession, he made the famous silk banner embroidered with the Bulgarian lion and "Liberty or Death!".

Arrival and information

Train Buses to Koprivshtitsa usually meet trains arriving at the station 8km south of town.

Bus The small bus station is 200m south of the main square.

Tourist information The tourist office on the main square, pl. 20 April (daily 9am–5pm; ⓣ07184/2191, ⓦwww.koprivshtitza.com), and a museum centre (Wed–Sun 9.30am–5.30pm); both sell tickets for Koprivshtitsa's six house museums.

Accommodation

The tourist office can also book private rooms (40Lv) in charming village houses. Advance reservations are recommended in summer.

Bolyarka ⓣ07184/2043. Four-room B&B just uphill from the centre, offering bright, pine-furnished rooms and a lovely garden. Double 40Lv.

Panorama ⓣ07184/2035, ⓦwww.panoramata.com. A well-run complex south of the centre with smart modern rooms on the ground floor and traditional-style rooms above; most have sweeping views of the town. Double 50Lv.

Trayanova Kashta ⓣ07184/3057. Just up the street from the Oslekov House, with delightful rooms in the National Revival style. Double 45Lv.

Eating and drinking

Dyado Liben Inn A fine nineteenth-century mansion opposite the main square serving traditional dishes such as *gyuvech* (meat stew) for 5Lv.

Lomeva Kashta A folk-style restaurant just north of the square, serving grills and salads from 4Lv.

Moving on

Bus Istanbul (1 nightly; 8hr 30min); Plovdiv (1 daily; 2hr 30min); Sofia (4 daily; 2hr).

Train Plovdiv (3 daily; 3hr 20min); Sofia (3 daily; 6hr); Veliko Tarnovo (2 daily; 6hr).

VELIKO TARNOVO

With its dramatic medieval fortifications and huddles of antique houses teetering over the lovely River Yantra, **VELIKO TARNOVO** (Велико Търново) holds a uniquely important place in the minds of Bulgarians. When the National Assembly met here to draft Bulgaria's first constitution in 1879, it did so in the former capital of the Second Kingdom (1185–1396), whose civilization was snuffed out by the Turks. It was here, too, that the Communists chose to proclaim the People's Republic in 1944.

What to see and do

Modern Tarnovo centres on **ploshtad Mayka Balgariya**: from here bul. Nezavisimost (which becomes ul. Stefan Stambolov after a few hundred metres) heads northeast into a network of narrow streets that curve above the River Yantra and mark out the old town, with its photogenic houses. From ul. Stambolov, the narrow cobbled ul. Rakovski slopes up into the **Varosh Quarter**, a pretty ensemble of nineteenth-century buildings once home to bustling artisans' workshops and now occupied by clothing and souvenir boutiques.

Sarafina House

Continuing along Stefan Stambolov, you'll notice steps leading downhill to ul. General Gurko; don't miss the **Sarafina House** at no. 88 (Mon–Fri 9am–5.30pm; 4Lv), whose elegant restored interior is notable for its splendid octagonal vestibule and a panelled rosette ceiling.

Museum of the Bulgarian Renaissance and Constituent Assembly

Rejoining Stefan Stambolov and continuing downhill, you'll find the blue-and-white building where the first Bulgarian parliament assembled in 1879. It's now home to the **Museum of the Bulgarian Renaissance and Constituent Assembly** (daily except Tues 9am–6pm; 4Lv), where you can see a reconstruction of the original assembly hall, and a collection of icons.

Tsarevets

Ulitsa Ivan Vazov leads directly from the museum to the medieval fortress, **Tsarevets** (daily: April–Oct 8am–7pm, Nov–March 9am–5pm; 4Lv). A successful rebellion against Byzantium was mounted from this citadel in 1185, and Tsarevets remained the centre of Bulgarian power until 1393, when, after a three-month siege, it fell to the Turks. The partially restored fortress is entered via the **Asenova Gate** halfway along the western ramparts. To the right, paths lead round to **Baldwin's Tower**, where Baldwin of Flanders, the so-called Latin Emperor of Byzantium, was incarcerated by Tsar Kaloyan. Visitors can climb up to the parapet of the fully renovated tower for sweeping views of the town.

Arrival and information

Train All trains between Sofia and Varna stop at Gorna Oryahovitsa, from where local trains and frequent buses cover the remaining 13km to Veliko Tarnovo. From Tarnovo train station, 2km south of the city centre, buses #4 and #13 run to pl. Mayka Balgariya.

Bus Buses to and from Sofia and Varna use the main bus terminal (Avtogara Yug), a 10min walk south of the centre on bul. Hristo Botev; they also pick up and drop off just behind the tourist office. Buses to Plovdiv use the western terminal (Avtogara Zapad), 4km southwest of town, from where bus #10 and trolley buses #1 and #3 go to the centre.

Tourist office pl. Mayka Balgariya (Mon–Fri 8am–6pm, summer also Sat 8am–6pm; ⓣ062/600768, ⓦwww.velikoturnovo.info).

Internet There's a reliable 24hr internet club in the basement of the Evropa shopping centre at Nezavisimost 3.

Accommodation

Comfort ul. Paneyot Tipografov 5 ⓣ062/628728. A spotless, family-run place, with splendid views of the Tsarevets. Located just above the Varosh Quarter's bazaar. Doubles 50Lv.

Hikers Hostel ul. Rezervoarska 91 ⓣ0889/691661, ⓦwww.hikers-hostel.org. A friendly hostel tucked away in a narrow street above the Varosh Quarter which offers yet more striking views, along with excellent dorm accommodation, free internet access and kitchen. Dorm 20Lv, twin 50Lv.

Hostel Mostel ul. Iordan Indjeto 10 ⓣ0897/859359, ⓦwww.hostelmostel.com. Located in a beautifully restored 140-year-old Ottoman building south of the road leading to Tsarevets, with comfortable dorms and private rooms. Offers a free all-you-can-eat breakfast, plus a free dinner and a beer for every night of your stay, laundry and free Internet. There's also

a barbecue and tent space in the garden. Dorm 20Lv, doubles 60Lv.

Eating and drinking

Café Aqua ul. Stefan Stambolov. A relaxed café overlooking the gorge, with good coffee and cakes.
Mecha Dupka ul. Rakovski. Serves authentic Bulgarian fare (main courses 7–15Lv) in a Varosh Quarter cellar, often with accompanying music and dancing.
Pepys Bar pl. Slaveykov 1. Small, dimly lit jazz bar frequented by locals and expats.
Shastlivetsa ul. Stambolov 79. Restaurant on the main road towards Tsarevets offering local dishes, as well as a large range of pizzas and pastas. Main courses around 4Lv.
Yasna pl. Slaveykov. A good spot for coffee or cocktails.

Moving on

International trains must be booked in advance through the Rila/BDZh office behind the tourist office at ul. Kaloyan 2 (Mon–Fri 8am–noon & 1–4.30pm, Sat 8am–noon).
Bus Burgas (5 daily; 4hr 30min); Plovdiv (5 daily; 4hr 30min); Sofia (hourly; 4hr); Varna (hourly; 5hr).
Train Veliko Tarnovo to Gorna Oryahovitsa (10 daily; 30min). Gorna Oryahovitsa to Bucharest (2 daily; 5–6hr); Burgas (9 daily; 7hr); Plovdiv (7 daily; 5hr 30min); Sofia (8 daily; 4hr 30min); Varna (6 daily; 3hr 30min).

The Black Sea coast

Bulgaria's **Black Sea** resorts have been popular holiday haunts for more than a century, though it wasn't until the 1960s that the coastline was developed for mass tourism, with Communist party officials from across the former Eastern Bloc descending on the beaches each year for a spot of socialist fun in the sun. Since then, the **resorts** have mushroomed, growing increasingly sophisticated as the prototype mega-complexes have been followed by holiday villages. With fine weather practically guaranteed, the selling of the coast has been a success in economic terms, but with the exception of ancient **Sozopol** and touristy **Nesebar**, there's little to please the eye. Of the coast's two cities – **Varna** and **Burgas** – the former is by far preferable as a base for getting to the less-developed spots.

VARNA

VARNA (Варна) is a cosmopolitan place, and nice to stroll through: Baroque, nineteenth-century and contemporary architecture are pleasantly blended with shady promenades and a handsome seaside park. As a settlement it dates back almost five millennia, but it wasn't until seafaring Greeks founded a colony here in 585 BC that the town became a port. The modern city is used by both commercial freighters and the navy, as well as being a popular tourist resort in its own right.

What to see and do

Social life revolves around **ploshtad Nezavisimost**, where the opera house and theatre provide a backdrop for restaurants and cafés. The square is the starting point of Varna's evening promenade, which flows eastward from here along bul. Knyaz Boris I and towards bul. Slivnitsa and the seaside gardens. Beyond the opera house, Varna's main lateral boulevard cuts through pl. Mitropolit Simeon to the domed **Cathedral of the Assumption**. Constructed in 1886, it contains a splendid iconostasis and bishop's throne, with armrests carved in the form of magnificent winged panthers. The **Archeology Museum** on the corner of Mariya Luiza and Slivnitsa (April–Oct Tues–Sun 10am–5pm; closed Sun Nov–March; 4Lv) houses one of Bulgaria's finest collections of antiquities. Most impressive are the skeletons adorned with Thracian gold jewellery that were

unearthed in Varna in 1972 and date back almost six thousand years.

South of the centre on ul. Han Krum are the extensive remains of the third-century **Roman baths** (10am–5pm: April–Oct Tues–Sun; Nov–March Mon–Fri; 4Lv). It's still possible to discern the various bathing areas and the once huge exercise hall. At the southern edge of the Sea Gardens, the **Navy Museum** (Mon–Fri 10am–6pm; 4Lv) is worth a trip to see the boat responsible for the Bulgarian Navy's only victory; it sank the Turkish cruiser *Hamidie* off Cape Kaliakra in 1912.

Beaches

Varna's municipal beach offers a useable stretch of sand but little tranquillity as it's dominated by open-air bars and clubs. The beaches at the busy resorts of **Golden Sands** and **Albena** to the north are hardly any quieter, but are certainly wider and much more attractive. Beyond Albena the coastline turns rocky until the villages at **Krapets** and **Durankulak**, just short of the Romanian border, which boast some wonderful undeveloped sandy beaches.

Arrival and information

Air Varna airport is about a 5min ride (bus #409; every 15min 6am–11pm; 1.50Lv) northwest of the city. Taxis cost 10–15Lv.

Train The train station is 10min walk south of the centre along ul. Tsar Simeon.

Bus The bus terminal is a 10min journey (bus #1, #22 or #41) northwest of the centre on bul. Vladislav Varnenchik.

Tourist office pl. Musala (summer daily 9am–6pm; ⓣ052/654519, ⓔotic.vn@mail.bg). The staff sell city maps, reserve hotel rooms and organize excursions.

Internet access Try Doom, ul. 27 July 13, or Frag, facing pl. Nezavisimost on the first floor at ul. Zamenov 1; both are open 24hr.

Accommodation

Private rooms (doubles 30–40Lv) can be arranged by Astra Tour in the railway station (daily; summer 7am–10pm; winter 9am–6pm; ⓣ052/605 861, ⓔastratur@yahoo.com) who also sell useful city maps.

Hostels

Flag Hostel First floor, ul. Sheinovo 2 ⓣ0897/408 115, ⓦwww.varnahostel.com. Very central but hard to find; phone ahead for directions. It offers three dormitories, kitchen access, 24hr check-in and free breakfast. Friendly staff. Dorms 20Lv.

Gregory's Backpackers Hostel ul. Fenix 82, Zvezditsa ⓣ052/379909 or 0897/634186, ⓦwww.hostelvarna.com. Very friendly and busy hostel, with a tent area as well as dorms and double rooms. The licensed bar, internet café area and barbecue in the garden only add to the sociable atmosphere. Located just outside the city, they offer a free daytime pick-up and drop-off service from Varna train and bus stations, as well as a free beach shuttle. Camping 14Lv per person, Dorms 22Lv, doubles 56Lv.

Yo Ho Hostel ul. Ruse 23 ⓣ0887/933340, ⓦwww.yohohostel.com. A fun, welcoming hostel, centrally located just off pl. Nezavisimost, with a nautical theme including staff in pirate costume. Breakfast included and there are Internet and laundry facilities. Dorm 24Lv.

Eating and drinking

There are plenty of bars to choose from along bul. Knyaz Boris I, while in summer, the beach, reached by steps from the Sea Gardens, is lined with open-air bars, fish restaurants and a seemingly unending strip of nightclubs. Outside high season, though, it's pretty dismal.

Arkitekt ul. Musala 10. A traditionally furnished wooden townhouse west of the centre serving authentic Bulgarian dishes and plenty of grilled meat (5–10Lv), with a pleasant courtyard garden.

Bar Na Gorniya Etazh bul. Knyazh Boris 24. Quirky first-floor bar with chessboard ceiling lamps, bathroom mosaics, old furniture and a great selection of cocktails.

Happy Bar and Grill pl. Nezavisimost. American-style eatery with a picture menu offering a mixture of Bulgarian and international food. The *kashkaval pane* (battered cheese) is particularly good (3.50Lv).

Hotel Chernomore bul. Slivnitsa. Head to the sixteenth-floor cocktail bar for unrivalled views of the city.

Morske vulk ul. Odrin. Just south of pl. Exarch Yosef, this is one of the friendliest and cheapest restaurants in town, with a vibrant, alternative crowd and brilliant Bulgarian dishes, including vegetarian options such as pizza for around 6Lv.

Moving on

Bus Burgas (hourly; 3hr); Golden Sands (every 20–30min; 20min); Sunny Beach (hourly; 2hr 10min); Veliko Tarnovo (9 daily; 4hr).
Train Plovdiv (4 daily; 6–7 hr); Sofia (7 daily; 8–9hr).

BURGAS

The south coast's prime urban centre and transport hub, **BURGAS** (Бургас) provides easy access to the picture-postcard town of Nesebar to the north and Sozopol to the south. Bypassed by most tourists, the pedestrianized city centre, lined with smart boutiques, bars and cafés, is pleasant enough, though Burgas's best features are the well-manicured **Sea Gardens**, overlooking the beach and its rusting pier at the eastern end of town.

Arrival and information

Bus and train stations Both are located at the southern edge of town, near the port.
Tourist information Beneath bul. Hristo Botev in the underpass opposite the opera house ⓣ056/825772, ⓦwww.tic.burgas.bg. Provides maps and can make hotel reservations.

Accommodation

Burgas has long suffered from a shortage of cheap accommodation, though the establishment of a small hostel suggests that things may change. A budget alternative is to take a private room (around 25Lv per person) booked through the tourist office.
Burgas Hostel Slavyanka 14 ⓣ056/825854 or 0886/096747, ⓦwww.hostelburgas.com. Central hostel with friendly, helpful staff located 10min from the railway station. Offers clean dorms, sea views from its roof terrace, wi-fi, kitchen and laundry facilities as well as a free pick-up service from the bus and train stations. Dorms 26Lv.
Fors ul. K. Fotinov 17 ⓣ056/828852, ⓦwww.hotelfors-bg.com. Smart new central hotel with good service, air-conditioned en suites, free wi-fi and a pizza restaurant attached. Doubles 75Lv.
Fotinov ul. K. Fotinov 22 ⓣ0897 834130, ⓦwww.hotelfotinov.com. Pleasant family-run hotel near the *Fors*. Facilities include fitness equipment, wi-fi, sauna and a/c. Doubles 70Lv.

Eating and drinking

Burgas' pedestrianized central boulevards are crammed with bars, cafés, and restaurants that spill out onto the streets in summer. There are several pleasant places to eat in the Sea Gardens and plenty more bars along the beach.
Zheleznyat Svetilnik ul. K. Fotinov 28. Great traditional-style restaurant with shaded outdoor seating serving typical Bulgarian dishes with an emphasis on grilled meat. Excellent wine list.
Zlatna Kotva bul. Bogoridi 64. Popular nautical-themed place serving a broad variety of reasonably priced fish dishes along with Bulgarian and international cuisine.

Moving on

Bus Nesebar (every 40min; 50min); Sofia (hourly; 6hr 30min); Sozopol (every 30min; 50min); Varna (hourly; 3hr).
Train Plovdiv (5 daily; 4hr 30min); Sofia (7 daily; 8–9hr).

NESEBAR

Famed for its delightful medieval churches, nineteenth-century wooden architecture, and labyrinthine cobbled streets, **NESEBAR**'s (Несебър) old town, 35km northeast of Burgas, lies on a narrow isthmus connected by road to the mainland. It was founded by Greek colonists and grew into a thriving port during the Byzantine era, and ownership alternated between Bulgaria and Byzantium until the Ottomans captured it in 1453. The town remained an important centre of Greek culture and the seat of a bishop under Turkish rule, which left Nesebar's **Byzantine churches** reasonably intact. Nowadays the town depends on them for its tourist appeal, demonstrated by the often overwhelming stream of summer visitors. Outside the hectic summer season, the place seems eerily deserted, with little open other than a few sleepy cafés.

What to see and do

A man-made isthmus connects Nesebar's old town with the mainland.

Standing just inside the city gates, the **Archeological Museum** (Mon–Fri 9am–7pm, Sat & Sun 9am–1pm & 2–6pm; 4Lv) has an array of Greek tombstones and medieval icons on display. Immediately beyond the museum is **Christ Pantokrator**, the first of Nesebar's churches, currently in use as an upmarket art gallery. It features an unusual frieze of swastikas – an ancient symbol of fertility and continual change. Downhill on ul. Mitropolitska is the eleventh-century church of **St John the Baptist** (now also an art gallery), only one of whose frescoes still survives. Overhung by half-timbered houses, ul. Aheloi branches off from ul. Mitropolitska towards the **Church of Sveti Spas** (summer only: Mon–Fri 10am–5pm, Sat & Sun 10am–1.30pm; 4Lv), outwardly unremarkable but filled with seventeenth-century frescoes.

A few steps to the east lies the ruined **Old Metropolitan Church**, dominating a plaza filled with pavement cafés and street traders. The church itself dates back to the sixth century, and it was here that bishops officiated during the city's heyday. Standing in splendid isolation beside the shore, the ruined **Church of St John Aliturgetos** represents the zenith of Byzantine architecture in Bulgaria. Its exterior employs limestone, red bricks, crosses, mussel shells and ceramic plaques for decoration.

Beaches

Visitors can either head for Nesebar's handful of small beaches or hop on a shuttle bus to the unattractive neighbouring resort of **Sunny Beach** where a great expanse of golden sand studded with thousands of umbrellas stretches for several kilometres along the overdeveloped coastline.

Arrival

Bus Buses arrive at either the harbour at the western end of town, or further up Han Krum before turning around to head for the nearby Sunny Beach resort.

Accommodation

Private rooms (30–80Lv), many in fine old houses, can be booked through Messemvria, at Messembria 10 (ⓣ0554/45880, ⓦwww.messemvria.com), near the St John the Baptist church.

Rai ul. Sadala 7 ⓣ0554/46094. A small and comfortable family-run pension on the northern side of the peninsula. Open summer only. Double 40Lv.

Tony ul. Kraybrezhna 20 ⓣ0554/42403. Nearby the *Rai* hotel in the old town, this hotel's pleasant, a/c rooms have balconies with sea views. Double 50Lv.

Eating and drinking

There are plenty of places to eat, although most restaurants are aimed at the passing tourist crowd, serving predictably mediocre food. Snacks are available from summertime kiosks along the waterfront.

Kapitanska Sreshta ul. Mena 22. Atmospheric fish restaurant housed in a nineteenth-century building with a lovely shaded terrace overlooking the old town's harbour.

Neptun ul. Neptun 1. Pleasant outdoor spot on the southeastern tip of the old town with great sea views. Serves a reasonably priced selection of Bulgarian standards.

Moving on

Bus Burgas (every 40min; 50min); Sofia (8 daily; 6hr 30min); Varna (5 daily; 2hr 10min).

SOZOPOL

SOZOPOL (Созопол) is a busy fishing port and holiday resort, especially popular with East European tourists. The town's charm owes much to its **architecture**, the old wooden houses jostling for space, their upper storeys almost meeting across the town's narrow cobbled streets. The oldest settlement in Bulgaria, Sozopol was founded in the seventh century BC by Greek colonists, who called the town Apollonia and prospered by trading textiles and wine for honey and corn.

What to see and do

The **Archeological Museum** (Mon–Fri: summer 10am–5pm; winter 8am–noon;

4Lv) behind the library holds a worthwhile collection of ancient ceramics, as well as a number of artefacts uncovered in the local area. Further into the town, follow the signs to the **Southern Fortress Wall and Tower Complex** (summer only: 9.30am–7.30pm; 4Lv), which gives access to a beautifully restored tower dating from the 4th century BC.

Sozopol's two small **beaches** are predictably overcrowded in high season, so it's worth making the short trip north to the emptier beaches around the *Zlatna Ribka* campsite (see opposite).

Arrival and information

Bus Buses from Burgas arrive at pl. Han Krum on the southern edge of the old town. Those from other Bulgarian cities usually arrive and depart from pl. Cherno More in the the new town.

Tourist office In the absence of a municipal tourist office, the best source of information is Lotos tourist agency located high in the new town at ul. Musala 7 (summer daily 8am–8pm; ⓣ0550/23925, ⓦwww.aiatour.com).

Accommodation

Accommodation in Sozopol can be even harder to find during summer than in Nesebar, and most places shut down for the rest of the year. The Lotos tourist agency can arrange private rooms of varying standards (20–30Lv per person).

Art ul. Kiril I Metodii 72 ⓣ0550/24081, ⓦwww.arthotel-sbh.com. Smart modern hotel and restaurant perched on a rocky cliff at the northern end of the peninsula. Doubles 80Lv.

Rusalka ul. Milet 36 ⓣ0550/23047. On the south of the peninsula, this is the best value old-town hotel with comfortable a/c rooms overlooking the sea. Doubles 60Lv.

Zlatna Ribka ⓣ0550/22427. Popular seaside campsite 3km north of town on the Burgas bus route. 4Lv per person, 5Lv per tent; double bungalow 25Lv.

Eating and drinking

Art ul. Kiril I Metodii 72. Great restaurant with outdoor tables on the cliff's edge. Serves a mid-priced range of Bulgarian and international meals.

Chuchura ul. Ribarska 10. Situated on the western side of the old town, this is a popular traditional-style restaurant with a particularly good selection of fish dishes (around 20Lv per person).

Vyatarna Melnitsa ul. Morski Skali 27. Similar in style and price to the Chuchura, the "Windmill" perches on the northern tip of the peninsula.

Moving on

Bus Burgas (every 30min; 50min); Plovdiv (7 daily; 5hr); Sofia (8 daily; 7hr 15min).

Croatia

HIGHLIGHTS

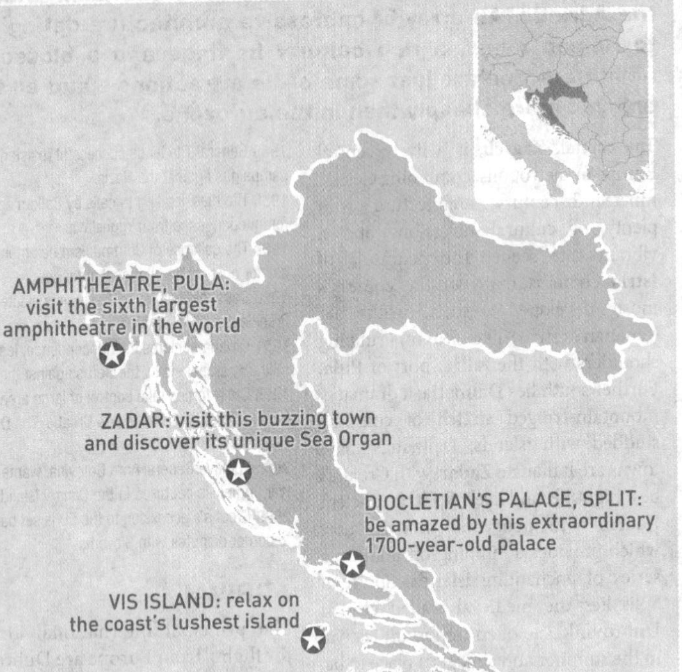

AMPHITHEATRE, PULA: visit the sixth largest amphitheatre in the world

ZADAR: visit this buzzing town and discover its unique Sea Organ

DIOCLETIAN'S PALACE, SPLIT: be amazed by this extraordinary 1700-year-old palace

VIS ISLAND: relax on the coast's lushest island

DUBROVNIK SUMMER FESTIVAL: enjoy world-class classical music at Croatia's prestigious festival

ROUGH COSTS

DAILY BUDGET Basic €28/occasional treat €35

DRINK Litre of local wine €7

FOOD Čevapčići (mini kebabs) €5

PRIVATE ACCOMMODATION/ HOSTEL/PENSION €14–27

TRAVEL Ferry travel within Dalmatian islands €3–5; Bus: Zagreb–Split €20

FACT FILE

POPULATION 4.4 million

AREA 56,594 sq km

LANGUAGE Croatian (Hrvatski)

CURRENCY Kuna (kn)

CAPITAL Zagreb (population: 800,000)

INTERNATIONAL PHONE CODE ⓣ385

Introduction

The sheer natural beauty of Croatia (Hrvatska), with some 6000km of serpentine coastline, dotted with numerous islands, has made it a must-visit European destination. But the country has far more to offer than its breathtaking views of the Adriatic. An array of impressive architecture dating back to Roman times, a rich cultural heritage and a blossoming nightlife scene are just some of its attractions – and all to be enjoyed more cheaply than in the eurozone.

The capital, **Zagreb**, is a lively central European metropolis, combining elegant nineteenth-century architecture with plenty of cultural diversions and a vibrant café scene. The peninsula of **Istria** contains many of the country's most developed resorts, with old Venetian towns like **Rovinj** rubbing shoulders with the raffish port of **Pula**. Further south lies **Dalmatia**, a dramatic, mountain-fringed stretch of coastline studded with islands. Dalmatia's main towns are Italianate **Zadar**, with Croatia's best nightlife, and lively **Split**, an ancient Roman settlement and modern port which provides a jumping-off point to a series of enchanting **islands**. South of Split lies the medieval walled city of **Dubrovnik**, site of an important festival in the summer and a magical place to be, whatever the season.

CHRONOLOGY

168 BC The Romans conquer the Illyrians in the area known as present-day Croatia.

600s AD Early Croatian Slavic forefathers settle in the region.

799 Charlemagne invades the Dalmatian area of Croatia, establishing Frankish interest in the area.

925 Tomislav is crowned the first King of Croatia.

1102 Croats are forced to accept Hungarian rule.

1214 The Statute of the Island of Korčula is the first document in Europe to abolish the slave trade.

1526 Habsburg dynasty takes control of Croatia after the Battle of Mohacs.

1918 After defeat of Habsburgs in World War I, Croatia joins the Kingdom of the Serbs, Croats and Slovenes.

1929 The kingdom becomes known as Yugoslavia.

1945 General Tito leads successful resistance campaigns against the Nazis.

1980 Tito dies, leading to calls by Balkan countries for independence from Yugoslavia.

1989 The collapse of Communism heightens the call for political and national autonomy.

1990 Conservative Franjo Tudjman is elected President.

1991 Croatia declares its independence, leading to military campaigns by the Serbs against the Croats.

1995 Croat forces take control of large areas, forcing Croatian Serbs to flee Croatia. The Dayton Peace Accords end the war.

2005 Fugitive General Ante Gotovina, wanted for war crimes, is captured in the Canary Islands.

2009 Croatia's accession to the EU is set back due to border disputes with Slovenia.

ARRIVAL

The principal international **airports** for flights from Europe are Dubrovnik, Pula, Split, Zadar and Zagreb, and low-cost flights are easy to find. Ryanair runs services to Pula from London Stansted and to Zadar from Stansted, Dublin, Edinburgh, Düsseldorf, Frankfurt, Pisa and Stockholm. EasyJet flies from London Gatwick, Berlin, Milan and Paris to Dubrovnik and from London Gatwick, Bristol and Milan to Split. Wizz Air flies from Luton to Zagreb, and Jet2 from Belfast and Leeds to Dubrovnik and from Newcastle to Split. The national carrier, Croatia Airlines (Ⓦwww.croatiaairlines.com), operates routes throughout Europe.

Ferry routes to Croatia run frequently from Italy: Split and Zadar from

Ancona, Split from Pescara, Rovinj from Trieste and Venice, Pula from Venice and Dubrovnik from Bari. See Ⓦwww.jadrolinija.hr, or Ⓦwww.venezialines.com for the ferries from Venice.

Croatia is linked by **rail** with Austria, Bosnia-Herzegovina, Hungary, Italy, Serbia, Montenegro, Slovenia, Slovakia, Switzerland, Germany, Bulgaria, Romania, the Czech Republic, Ukraine and Russia; see Ⓦwww.hznet.hr for timetables.

Eurolines (Ⓦwww.eurolines.com), partnered with AutoTrans (Ⓦwww.autotrans.hr) in Croatia, run **buses** from Vienna to Zagreb and from Sarajevo to Dubrovnik, Split and Zagreb. Several German cities are connected with Croatia too; see Ⓦwww.touring.de. For services from Trieste to Pula, Rovinj, Zadar, Split and Dubrovnik, check Ⓦwww.saf.ud.it.

GETTING AROUND

Croatia's **train** service covers the north and east pretty well, but on the coast, you're more likely to use Croatia's extensive **bus** network.

By train

Croatian Railways *(Hrvatske željeznice;* Ⓦwww.hznet.hr*)* runs a smooth and efficient service, connecting all major cities except Dubrovnik. Trains (*vlak*, plural *vlakovi*) are divided into *putnički* (slow ones, which stop at every station) and IC (intercity trains that are faster and more expensive). Tilting trains operate on the Zagreb–Split line, which take half the usual journey time. Timetables (*vozni red*) are usually displayed on boards in stations – *odlazak* means

departure, *dolazak* arrival. You may travel on all trains with an **InterRail** pass, and must pay a small reservation fee for longer journeys.

By bus

Croatia has an array of small local bus companies. The leading one is AutoTrans (Ⓦwww.autotrans.hr); services are well integrated and punctual and bus stations tend to be well organized. If you're at a big city bus station, tickets (*karta*) must be bought from ticket windows before boarding the bus. Elsewhere, buy them from the driver. You'll be charged around 7kn for items of baggage to be stored in the hold.

By ferry

Jadrolinija (Ⓦwww.jadrolinija.hr) operates **ferry** services down the coast on the Rijeka–Split–Korčula–Dubrovnik route twice a week in both directions. Rijeka to Dubrovnik is a 22-hour journey, involving one night on the boat. In addition, ferries and faster catamarans link Split with the islands of Brač, Hvar, Vis and Korčula. **Fares** are reasonable for short trips: Split to Hvar costs 27kn. For longer journeys, prices vary greatly according to the level of comfort you require. **Book** in advance for longer journeys, wherever possible, and note that ferry timetables change around the end of May and end of September.

ACCOMMODATION

Private rooms (*privatne sobe*) have long been the mainstay of Croatian tourism. Bookings are made through private travel agencies (usually open daily 8am–8/9pm in summer). High-season prices are around €23/170kn per person for a simple double sharing a toilet and bathroom, €30/220kn for an en-suite double; stays of less than three nights are often subject to a surcharge of thirty percent or more. Places fill up quickly in July and August: arrive early or book ahead. Single travellers will sometimes find it difficult to get accommodation at all at this time, unless they're prepared to pay the price of a double room; at other times, you could expect to get a thirty percent discount. It's very likely you'll be offered a place to stay by elderly ladies waiting outside train, bus and ferry stations, particularly in southern Dalmatia. Don't be afraid to take a room offered in this manner, but be sure to establish the location and agree a price before setting off: expect to pay around twenty percent less than you would with an agency. However you find a room, you can usually examine it before committing to paying for it. Official rooms establishments should have a blue plaque saying "*sobe*" or "*apartmani*" outside – if they don't, they're not legal.

Hostels are cropping up more and more – especially in the larger towns – as Croatia becomes increasingly incorporated into backpackers' itineraries. The Croatian Youth Hostel website (Ⓦwww.hfhs.hr) has details and prices of HI-affiliated hostels.

One-star **hotels** are in short supply; in most places, the cheapest are two-star, where you should expect to pay €55–75/400–550kn for a double room. There's a growing number of family-run **pensions**, offering two- or three-star comforts at a slightly cheaper price – around €40–60/300–450kn for a double.

FOOD AND DRINK

Croatia has a varied and distinctive range of **cuisine**, largely because it straddles two culinary cultures: the fish- and seafood-dominated cuisine of the Mediterranean and the hearty meat-oriented fare of Central Europe.

For **breakfasts** and **fast food**, look out for street stalls or snack-food outlets selling *burek* (about 8kn), a flaky pastry filled with cheese; or grilled meats such as *čevapčići* (rissoles of minced beef, pork or lamb sold in a bun with relish;

30kn for a dozen from street stalls). Bread (*kruh*) is bought from either a supermarket or a *pekarna* (bakery).

A **restaurant** menu (*jelovnik*) will usually include starters such as *pršut* (home-cured ham) and *paški sir* (piquant hard cheese). Typical mains include *punjene paprike* (peppers stuffed with rice and meat), *gulaš* (goulash) or some kind of *odrezak* (fillet of meat, often pan-fried), usually either *svinjski* (pork) or *teleški* (veal). On the coast, you'll be regaled with every kind of seafood. *Riba* (fish) can come either *na žaru* (grilled) or *pečnici* (baked). *Brodet* is a hot peppery fish stew. Other main menu items on the coast are *lignje* (squid), *škampi* (unpeeled prawns eaten with your fingers), *rakovica* (crab), *oštrige* (oysters), *kalamari* (squid), *školjke* (mussels) and *jastog* (lobster); *crni rizoto* is risotto with squid.

No town is without at least one **pizzeria**, serving good stone-baked pizzas from 35kn. A **konoba** is a no-frills, often family-run restaurant, usually serving local dishes at low prices.

Typical **desserts** include *palačinke* (pancakes), *voćna salata* (fruit salad) and *sladoled* (ice cream).

Drink

Croatia is laden with relaxing **cafés** (*kavanas*) for daytime drinking. Coffee (*kava*) is usually served black unless specified otherwise – ask for *mlijeko* (milk) or *šlag* (cream). Tea (*čaj*) is widely available, but is drunk without milk.

Croatian **beer** (*pivo*) is of the light lager variety; Karlovačko and Ožujsko are two good local brands. The local **wine** (*vino*) is consistently good and reasonably cheap: in Dalmatia there are some pleasant, crisp white wines such as Kastelet, Grk and Posip, as well as reds including the dark, heady Dingač and Babić; in Istria, *Semion* is a bone-dry white, and Teran a light fresh red. Local spirits include *medenica*, a honey-based slow-burning nectar; *loza*, a clear grape-based spirit; and *Maraskino*, a cherry liqueur from Dalmatia.

CULTURE AND ETIQUETTE

With an almost ninety percent Roman Catholic population, religious holidays in Croatia are celebrated with gusto – not least because outward displays of religion were discouraged by Tito, leading to what seems like a "making up for lost time" attitude. A fun-loving people generally, especially among the younger generation, Croatians are welcoming and will happily engage you in conversations about food, wine and politics over a beer or two.

A service charge is not usually added to restaurant bills and it is the norm to leave a **tip** at your discretion (ten percent is quite acceptable).

SPORTS AND OUTDOOR ACTIVITIES

The Dalmatian coast is great for **watersports**, including windsurfing, kitesurfing, wake-boarding and some less hardcore pursuits, such as banana-boating and renting a motorboat. If you're a serious watersports fan, head to Brač: in July, the week-long Vanka Regule extreme sports event (Ⓦwww.vankaregule.com) takes over Sutivan, near Supetar; there's free diving and windsurfing – and some more land-based sports, such as climbing and cycling. Brač, Hvar and Vis have plenty of well-marked **cycling and hiking** trails.

Football remains the nation's favourite diversion, Dinamo Zagreb being the best-known team internationally. The Maksimir stadium is situated to the northeast of the capital (tram #4, #7, #11 or #12; Ⓦwww.nk-dinamo.hr); tickets cost from 30kn.

COMMUNICATIONS

Post offices (*pošta* or HPT) are discernible by their bright yellow signs and open Monday to Friday 7am to 7pm, Saturday 7am to 2pm. In big towns and resorts, some are open daily and until 10pm. Stamps (*marke*) can also be bought at newsstands, and letter boxes are painted the same yellow as post office signs.

Public **phones** use cards (*telekarta*), which come in denominations of 15kn, 25kn, 50kn and 100kn; you can buy these from post offices or newspaper kiosks. You can also make international calls from the post office. You can buy a Croatian SIM card for about 50kn. **Internet** is now available even in small towns; expect to pay around 25kn per hour.

EMERGENCIES

The crime rate is low by European standards and **police** (*policija*) are generally helpful when dealing with tourists. They often make routine checks on identity cards and other documents, so always carry your passport. In an **emergency**, call ⓣ12.

Hospital treatment is free for EU members. Travel insurance comes highly recommended though, as public facilities are not always available. **Pharmacies** (*ljekarna*) tend to follow normal shopping hours (see opposite) and a rota system covers nights and weekends; details are posted in the window of each pharmacy.

INFORMATION

Most towns of any size have a **tourist office** (*turističke informacije*), which will give out brochures and local maps. Few offices book private rooms, but they will at least direct you to an agency that does.

MONEY AND BANKS

The local currency is the **kuna** (kn), which is divided into 100 lipa. There are coins of 1, 2, 5, 10, 20 and 50 lipa, and 1kn, 2kn and 5kn; and notes of 5kn, 10kn, 20kn, 50kn, 100kn, 200kn, 500kn and 1000kn. Accommodation and ferry prices are often quoted in euros, but you still pay in kuna. **Banks** (*banka*) are open Monday to Friday 9am to 5pm (sometimes with longer hours in the summer), Saturday 8am to 1pm. Money can also be changed in post offices, travel agencies and **exchange bureaux** (*mjenjačnica*). Credit cards are accepted in a large number of hotels and restaurants, and you can use them to get cash from ATMs. At the time of writing, €1 was equal to around 7kn, $1 to 5kn, and £1 to 8kn. It's relatively hard to get rid of kuna once you've left Croatia (though exchange offices in neighbouring countries often accept it); spend up or exchange before leaving.

OPENING HOURS AND HOLIDAYS

Most **shops** open Monday to Friday 8am to 8pm, Saturday 8am to 3pm, although many supermarkets, outdoor markets and the like are open daily 7am–7pm. Many **museums and galleries** are closed on Mondays. All shops and banks are closed on the following **public holidays**: January 1, January 6, Easter Monday, May 1, Corpus Christi, June 22, June 25, August 5, August 15, October 8, November 1, and December 25 & 26.

CROATIA ON THE NET

ⓦ **www.adriatica.net** Information on the Adriatic resorts, and an accommodation booking service.
ⓦ **www.croatia.hr** Official tourist board site.
ⓦ **www.istra.com** Covers the Istrian peninsula.
ⓦ **www.dalmacija.net** Covers Dalmatia.
ⓦ **www.dubrovnik-online.com** Excellent city site, including message board.

Croatian

	Croatian	Pronunciation
Yes	*Da*	Dah
No	*Ne*	Neh
Please	*Molim*	Mo-leem
Thank you	*Hvala*	Hvahlah
Hello/Good day	*Bog/Dobar dan*	Dobahr dan
Goodbye	*Bog/Dovidjenja*	Doh veedehnyah
Excuse me	*Izvinite*	Izvineet
Sorry	*Oprostite*	Auprausteete
Today	*Danas*	Danass
Good	*Dobro*	Dobroh
Bad	*Loše*	Losheh
How much is...?	*Koliko stoji…?*	Koleekoh sto-yee…?
What time is it?	*Koliko je sati?*	Koleekoh yeh satee?
I don't understand	*Ne razumijem*	Neh rahzoomeeyehm
Do you speak English?	*Govorite li engleski?*	Govoreeteh lee ehngleskee?
One	*Jedan*	Yehdan
Two	*Dva*	Dvah
Three	*Tri*	Tree
Four	*Četiri*	Cheteeree
Five	*Pet*	Pet
Six	*Šest*	Shest
Seven	*Sedam*	Sedam
Eight	*Osam*	Osam
Nine	*Devet*	Devet
Ten	*Deset*	Deset
Where is...?	*Gdje je…?*	Gdyeh ye…?
Where are...?	*Gdje su…?*	Gdyeh soo…?
entrance	*ulaz*	oolaz
exit	*izlaz*	eezlaz
Tourist office	*Turistički Ured*	Tooristichkee oored
toilet	*zahod*	zah-haud
private rooms	*sobe*	saubey
I'd like to book...	*Ja bih revervirala…*	Ya bee reserveerahla…
Cheap	*Jeftino*	Yeftinoh
Expensive	*Skupo*	Skoopoh
Open	*Otvoreno*	Otvoreenoh
Closed	*Zatvoreno*	Zatvoreenoh

Zagreb

Capital of Croatia since 1991, **ZAGREB** has served as the cultural and political focus of the state since the Middle Ages. The city grew out of two medieval communities, Kaptol, to the east, and Gradec, to the west, each sited on a hill and divided by a river long since dried up but nowadays marked by a street known as Tkalčićeva. Zagreb grew rapidly in the nineteenth century, and the majority of its buildings are relatively well-preserved, grand, peach-coloured monuments to the self-esteem of the Austro-Hungarian Empire. Nowadays, with a population reaching almost one million, Zagreb is the style-conscious, boisterous capital of a newly self-confident nation. A number of good museums and a varied and vibrant nightlife ensure that a few days here will be well spent.

What to see and do

Zagreb falls neatly into three parts. **Donji Grad**, or Lower Town, which extends north from the train station to the main square, Trg bana Jelačića, is the bustling centre of the modern city. Uphill from here, to the northeast and the northwest, are the older quarters of **Kaptol** (the Cathedral Quarter) and **Gradec** (the Upper Town), both peaceful districts of ancient mansions, quiet squares and leafy parks.

The Art Pavilion and Archeological Museum

Tomislavov Trg, opposite the train station, is the first in a series of three shaded, green squares that form the

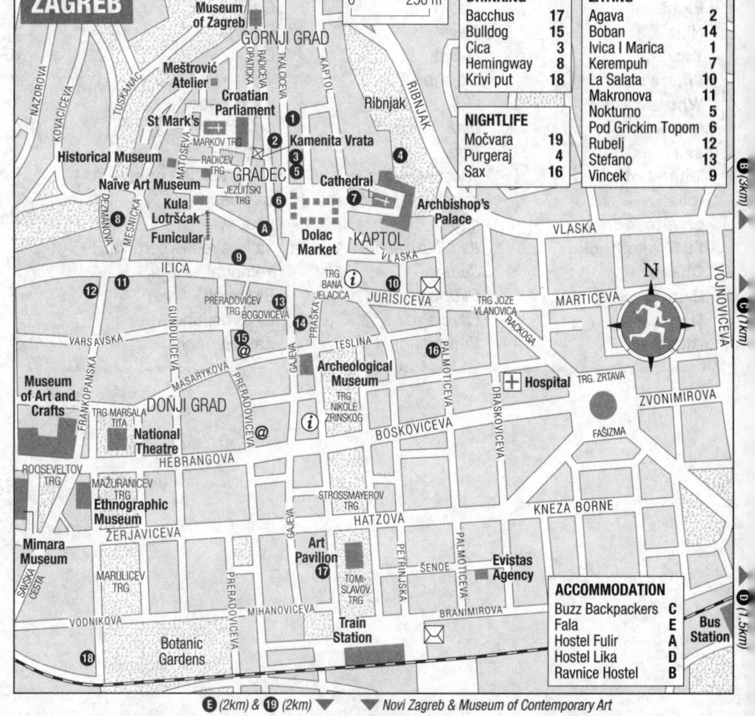

backbone of the lower town. Its main attraction is the **Art Pavilion** (Mon–Sat 11am–7pm, Sun 10am–1pm; 20kn, free Mon), built in 1898 and now hosting art exhibitions in its gilded stucco and mock-marble interior. In the last of the three squares – **Trg Nikole Zrinskog** – stands the **Archeological Museum** (Tues, Wed & Fri 10am–5pm, Thurs 10am–8pm, Sat & Sun 10am–1pm; 20kn), which houses interesting pieces from prehistoric times to the Middle Ages.

Ilica and the National Theatre

Flanked by cafés, hotels and department stores, **Trg bana Jelačića** is hectic with the whizz of trams and hurrying pedestrians; the statue in the centre is of the nineteenth-century governor of Croatia, Josip Jelačića. Running west from the square, below Gradec hill, is **Ilica**, the city's main shopping street. A little way along it and off to the right, you can take a **funicular** (daily 6.30am–9pm, every 10min; 5kn) up to the Kula Lotršćak; alternatively, head south via **Preradovićev Trg**, a small, lively square where there's a flower market, to **Trg maršala Tita**. This is a grandiose open space, centred on the late nineteenth-century **National Theatre**, a solid ochre-coloured pile behind a water sculpture by Ivan Meštrović, the *Well of Life*.

The Museum of Arts and Crafts and the Ethnographic Museum

The impressive **Museum of Arts and Crafts**, just west of the National Theatre (Tues, Wed, Fri & Sat 10am–7pm, Thurs 10am–10pm, Sun 10am–2pm; 20kn), holds pieces dating from the Renaissance to the present day, while on nearby Mažuranićev Trg, the **Ethnographic Museum** (Tues–Thurs 10am–6pm, Fri–Sun 10am–1pm; 15kn, free Thurs) has a collection of costumes from every corner of the country, as well as an array of curios brought back by Croatian explorers from all over the world.

Mimara Museum

The **Mimara Museum** at Rooseveltov Trg 5 (Tues, Wed, Fri & Sat 10am–5pm, Thurs 10am–7pm, Sun 10am–2pm; 20kn) houses one of Zagreb's most prized art collections, belonging to Zagreb-born Ante Topić Mimara. Highlights include Chinese art from the Shang through to the Song dynasty, as well as a fine collection of European paintings, including works by Rembrandt, Rubens, Renoir and Velázquez.

The cathedral and Kaptol

The filigree spires of Zagreb's **cathedral** mark the edge of the district (and street) known as **Kaptol**, ringed by the ivy-cloaked turrets of the eighteenth-century **Archbishop's Palace**. Destroyed by an earthquake in 1880, it was rebuilt in neo-Gothic style, with a high, bare interior. Behind the altar lies a shrine to Archbishop Stepinac, head of the Croat church in the 1940s, imprisoned by the communists after World War II, and beatified by the Pope in 1998.

Gradec

Gradec is the most ancient and atmospheric part of Zagreb, a leafy, tranquil quarter of tiny streets, small squares and Baroque palaces. From Trg bana Jelačića, make your way to the **Dolac market**, which occupies several tiers immediately beyond the square; this is the city's main food market, held every morning. From the far side of Dolac market, the long-since dried-up river **Tkalčićeva** spears north, dividing Kaptol and Gradec. Entry to Gradec proper from here is by way of **Krvavi Most**, which connects the street with Radićeva. On the far side of Radićeva, the **Kamenita Vrata** is a gloomy tunnel with a small shrine that formed part of Gradec's original fortifications. Close by, the **Kula Lotršćak** (May–Oct Tues–Sun 11am–8pm; 10kn)

marks the top station of the funicular (see p.259) and provides fantastic views over the rest of the city and the plains beyond.

The Naïve Art Museum and Church of St Mark

The **Naïve Art Museum**, Cirilmetodska 3 (Tues–Fri 10am–6pm, Sat & Sun 10am–1pm; 20kn), provides a captivating introduction to the world of Croatia's self-taught village painters. Just north of here, the focus of **Markov Trg** is the squat **Church of St Mark**, a much-renovated structure, whose tiled roof displays the coats of arms of the constituent parts of Croatia.

The Meštrović Atelier and Museum of Zagreb

North of St Mark's, the **Meštrović Atelier**, at Mletačka 8 (Tues–Fri 10am–6pm, Sat & Sun 10am–2pm; 20kn), is a wonderful exhibition dedicated to Croatia's most famous twentieth-century artist in the sculptor's former home and studio. The **Museum of Zagreb**, at Opatička 20 (Tues, Wed & Fri 10am–6pm, Thurs 10am–10pm, Sat 10am–7pm, Sun 10am–1pm; 20kn), tells the tale of Zagreb's development, from medieval times to the early twentieth century, as well as displaying political and religious propaganda posters.

Museum of Contemporary Art

Zagreb's newest and most stylish attraction is the **Museum of Contemporary Art** (Tues, Wed, Fri & Sat 10am–6pm, Thurs 10am–8pm, Sun 10am–2pm; 30kn), occupying a swish modern building on the south side of the river Sava on Avenija Većeslava Holjevaca – take tram #14 to the Siget stop. The museum showcases home-grown movements in abstract, conceptual and performance art, and there's a strong international collection too, including works by Picasso, Dalí and Miró. A cinema, concert space and café-restaurant are further draws.

Arrival and information

Air Zagreb airport is 10km southeast of the city; buses run to the main bus station (7am–8pm; every 30min–1hr; 30kn).
Train Zagreb's central train station is on Tomislavov Trg, on the southern edge of the city centre, a 10min walk from Trg bana Jelačića, the main square.
Bus The main bus station is a 10min walk east of the train station, at the junction of Branimirova and Držićeva – trams #2, #3 and #6 run between the two, with #6 continuing to the main square.
Tourist office Trg bana Jelačića 11 (Mon–Fri 8.30am–9pm, Sat 9am–5pm, Sun 10am–2pm; ⓣ01/48-14-051, ⓦwww.zagreb-touristinfo.hr).
Discount cards The tourist office sells the Zagreb Card (72hr; 90kn), which offers unlimited city transport and good discounts in museums and restaurants.
Listings The free monthly pamphlet *Events and Performances*, available from the tourist office, contains listings in English of all forthcoming events.

City transport

Tickets Tram journeys within two stops of the main Trg bana Jelačića are free – which means that you can get from the train station to the square for free, but journeys to or from the bus station have to be paid for. Tram and bus tickets (*karte*), valid for 1hr 30min if travelling in one direction, are sold at kiosks (8kn) or from the driver (10kn); day-tickets (*dnevne karte*) cost 24kn. Validate your ticket by punching it in the machines on board.
Bus The bus network serves the capital's peripheries, setting off from the suburban side of the train station.
Trams The easiest way to get about, with sixteen routes. Lines #2, #3 and #6 run between the bus and train stations, #6 taking you into Jelačića, the main crossing point in the city. There's also a four-line network of night services.
Taxis There are ranks at the station and the north-eastern corner of Trg bana Jelačića. The standard rate is 25kn plus 7kn per km, which goes up by twenty percent 10am–5pm, Sundays and holidays. Luggage costs 5kn per item.

Accommodation

Private rooms Arranged through the Evistas agency at Šenoe 28, midway between the train and

bus stations (Mon–Fri 9am–8pm, Sat 9.30am–5pm; ⓣ01/48-39-546, ⓔevistas@zg.htnet.hr). Rooms from 550kn.

Hostels and hotels

Buzz Backpackers Babukićeva 1b ⓣ01/24-20-267, ⓦwww.buzzbackpackers.com. Smart, comfortable hostel 2km east of the centre offering a mix of dorms and private doubles. Small kitchen and common room too. Trams #4 or #9 from the train station to Kvaternikov trg, or trams #5 or #7 from the bus station to Heinzelova. Dorms 135–155kn, rooms 400kn.

Fala II Trnjanske ledine 18 ⓣ01/61-11-062, ⓦwww.hotel-fala-zg.hr. Family-run hotel a 15min walk south of the train station. Rooms are small but come with en-suite bathroom and TV. Tram #5 from the bus station to Vatroslav Lisinski, then bus #219, #220, #221 or #268, or bus #219, #220, #221 or #268 from the train station. 550kn.

Hostel Fulir Radićeva 3a ⓣ01/48-30-882, ⓦwww.fulir-hostel.com. In a good location off Tkalčićeva, *Fulir* offers functional dorms, a well-equipped kitchen and a cosy common room. Dorms 145kn.

Hostel Lika Pašmanska 17 ⓣ098/561-041, ⓦwww.hostel-lika.com. Friendly hostel in a quiet street near the bus station. Reasonable dorms with clean facilities, plus frequent barbecues in a shady garden. Tram #6 to Slavonska, then follow the yellow feet painted on the ground. Dorms 87–170kn.

Ravnice Hostel I Ravnice 38b ⓣ01/233-23-25, ⓦwww.ravnice-youth-hostel.hr. Clean, welcoming hostel 4km east of the centre near Maksimir Park. Tram #4, #11, #12 or #7 to the Ravnice stop, by the Kraš chocolate factory, then 5min walk south along I Ravnice. Tents can be pitched in the garden for 60kn per night. Dorms 112–125kn.

Eating

Zagreb has a wealth of cafés and bars offering outdoor seating in the pedestrian area around Gajeva and Bogovićeva – particularly along trendy Tkalčićeva, just north of Trg bana Jelačića. For picnic food, head to Dolac market (see p.259).

Cafés

Ivica I Marica Tkalčićeva 70. Fantastic cakes and pastries and an outdoor terrace perfect for people-watching. Also has a fine restaurant next door.

La Salata Jurišićeva 3. French-run snack bar in an off-street courtyard, offering fresh salads, quiche and strong coffee.

Vincek Ilica 18. The very best place in town to stop for ice cream, cakes and hot chocolate.

Restaurants

Agava Tkalčićeva 39. Croatian restaurant offering a balanced menu of Central European meat dishes and Adriatic seafood. Outdoor seating provides a bird's-eye view of café life on Tkalčićeva. Mains around 110kn.

Boban Gajeva 9. Popular and central pasta place in the vaulted basement of the café of the same name, with dishes 40–60kn.

Kerempuh Kaptol 3, Dolac. Hidden away behind the Dolac market (where ingredients are sourced for the daily-changing menu); this is one of the best places in town to fill up on traditional Croatian favourites. Lunchtime special 50kn.

Makronova Ilica 72. Stylish and compact vegetarian restaurant serving imaginative and tasty dishes. Mon–Fri only. Mains 30–55kn.

Nokturno Skalinska 4, on a sloping, cobbled street off the enchanting Tkalčićeva. One of the best budget places in the area, dishing out decent pizza (from 50kn) and salads (25kn).

Pod Grickim Topom on the steps leading down from Strossmayerovo Šetalište to Trg bana Jelačića, with great views of the Lower Town from the terrace. Enjoy superb Croatian food from grilled fish to Dalmatian *pašticada* (beef stewed in prunes) and local steak. Mains 90–140kn.

Rubelj Frankopanska 2 & Dolac market. Cheapest central place for simple but tasty Balkan grilled-meat standards, at around 40kn per dish.

Stefano Bogovićeva 3. Italian place offering quality pasta dishes, pizzas and wholesome salads, with outdoor seating right in the middle of central Zagreb's busiest pavement-café strip. Mains 60–80kn.

Drinking and nightlife

Bars

Bacchus Trg kralja Tomislava. Hidden in a courtyard off the square in front of the train station, this tiny semi-submerged pub hosts jazz gigs in the winter and has a popular garden terrace in summer.

Bulldog Bogovićeva 6. A typically elegant Zagreb bar and pavement café, this is one of the most popular meeting places in the town centre. *Millennium*, diagonally opposite, is good for an evening ice cream.

Cica corner of Tkalčićeva and Skalinska. Funky café with an eccentric interior filled with washing machines and plenty of tables on the street outside. Famous for offering a big choice of potent fruit- and herb-flavoured brandies.

Hemingway Dežmanova and Trg Maršala Tita. Trendy cocktail bar, popular with Zagreb's smart set.

Krivi put Runjanina bb. Enjoyably raucous bar in a former warehouse near the railway tracks, with frequent live gigs. The spacious courtyard is packed on summer nights. Open until 2am.

Clubs

Aquarius Aleja Mira bb ⓦ www.aquarius.hr. At the eastern end of Lake Jarun, 6km southwest of the centre, this place specializes in techno and drum'n'bass. Occasional live bands too. Tram #17 from Trg bana Jelačića. Thurs–Sun.

Močvara Tvornica Jedinstvo building, Trnjanski nasip ⓦ www.mochvara.hr. The "Swamp" is an unpretentious cultural centre in an old factory on the banks of the River Sava. Live gigs, film shows and DJ sessions – there's something on every night. Take any bus heading for Novi Zagreb and get off just before the bridge – the club is on your right.

Purgeraj Ribnjak ⓦ www.purgeraj.hr. In a leafy park behind the cathedral, *Purgeraj* has a regular programme of rock, jazz and blues, with the action spreading onto a big outdoor terrace in summer. Also serves very well as a mellow daytime café.

Sax Palmotićeva 22. Large, comfortable basement club, two blocks east of Trg N. Zrinskog, with live music (with a jazz bias) most nights.

Festivals

In-music Late June ⓦ www.t-mobileinmusic festival.com. Three-day rock-and-pop festival on the shores of Lake Jarun with three stages, early-morning DJ sets and plenty of food and drink. Guests in recent years have included Sonic Youth, Franz Ferdinand and Moby. Camping available.

Rokaj Early July ⓦ www.rokajfest.com. Also on Lake Jarun, Rokaj goes for the alternative end of the rock spectrum, with a mix of local and international acts (past visitors have included Morrissey, The Fall and Primal Scream). Usually a two-day affair. Camping available.

Shopping and markets

The principal area for shopping is along Ilica, off Trg bana Jelačića, which has several independent stores as well as familiar high-street names such as Mango and Lush, punctuated by handsome coffee shops and a few tempting bakeries.

Markets The bric-a-brac market in Britanski Trg on a Sunday is a magpie's dream – jewellery, traditional Croatian embroidery, farming implements, binoculars…you name it, it's there. Worth going even just for a coffee on the sidelines. Get there before 2pm.

Directory

Embassies Australia, Nova Ves 11 ⓣ 01/48-91-200; Canada, Prilaz Gjure Deželića 4 ⓣ 01/48-81-200; UK, Ivana Lučića 4 ⓣ 01/60-09-100; US, Thomasa Jeffersona 2 ⓣ 01/66-12-200.

Exchange In the post office on Branimirova.

Hospital Heinzelova 88 ⓣ 01/63-02-911.

Internet Art Net Club, Preradovićeva 25; Sublink, Teslina 12.

Laundry Predom, Draškovićeva 31 (Mon–Fri 7am–7pm, Sat 8am–noon).

Left luggage At the train and bus stations (both 24hr).

Pharmacy Ilica 43 (24hr).

Post offices Branimirova 4 (24hr); Jurišićeva 13 (Mon–Fri 7am–9pm, Sat 7am–7pm, Sun 8am–2pm).

Moving on

Train Belgrade (3 daily; 6hr 30min); Budapest (3 daily; 6hr); Ljubljana (7 daily; 2hr 20min); Munich (2 daily; 9–10hr); Salzburg (3 daily; 7hr); Sarajevo (hourly; 1hr 15min); Split (3 daily; 5hr 30min); Venice (1 daily; 7hr 40min); Vienna (1 daily; 6hr 30min).

Bus Dubrovnik (9 daily; 9–11hr); Pula (hourly; 3hr 30min–5hr); Rijeka (hourly; 2hr 30min–3hr); Rovinj (7 daily; 5–6hr); Split (every 30min; 4–6hr); Trieste (1 daily; 5hr); Vienna (2 daily; 6hr).

Istria

A large peninsula jutting into the northern Adriatic, **Istria** is Croatian tourism at its most developed. Many of the towns here were resorts in the nineteenth century, which in recent years have attracted an annual influx of sun-seekers from Germany, Austria and the Netherlands. Yet the growth of tourism has done little to detract from the essential charm of the region. This stretch of the coast was under Venetian rule for four hundred years and there's still a fair-sized Italian community, with Italian very much the second language. Istria's largest centre is the port city of **Pula**, which, with its Roman amphitheatre and other relics of

Roman occupation, is a rewarding place to spend a couple of days. On the western side of the peninsula, the resort town of **Rovinj**, with its cobbled piazzas and shuttered houses, is almost overwhelmingly pretty.

PULA

Once the chief port of the Austro-Hungarian Empire, **PULA** is an engaging combination of working port, naval base and vibrant riviera town. The Romans put the city squarely on the map when they arrived in 177 BC, transforming it into an important commercial centre.

What to see and do

The chief reminder of Pula's Roman heritage is its impressive amphitheatre; south of here, the town centre circles a pyramidal hill, scaled by secluded streets, dotted with Roman relics and topped with a star-shaped Venetian fortress.

The amphitheatre

The first-century-BC **Roman amphitheatre** (daily: June–Sept 8am–9pm; Oct–May 9am–6pm; 40kn) is the sixth largest in the world, and once had space for over 23,000 spectators. The outer shell is fairly complete, as is one of the towers, up which a slightly hair-raising climb gives a good sense of the enormity of the structure and a view of Pula's industrious harbour. The cavernous rooms underneath are now given over to piles of dusty amphorae and reconstructed olive presses. The amphitheatre hosts the annual **Pula Film Festival** (Ⓦwww.pulafilmfestival.hr) at the end of July, as well as concerts throughout the summer.

The Triumphal Arch and the Temple of Augustus

On the eastern side of the hill, Istarska – which later becomes Giardini – leads down to the first-century-BC **Triumphal Arch of the Sergians**, through which Sergijevaca, Pula's main drag, leads in turn to a square known as **Forum** – site of the ancient Roman forum and now the centre of Pula's old quarter. On the far side of here, the slim form of the **Temple of Augustus** was built between 2 BC and 14 AD to celebrate the cult of the emperor; its imposing Corinthian columns, still intact, make it one of the best examples of a Roman temple outside Italy.

The cathedral and Archeological Museum

Heading north from Forum along Kandlerova leads to Pula's **cathedral** (June–Aug daily 10am–1pm & 5–8pm; 5kn), a broad, simple and very spacious structure that displays another mixture of periods and styles: a fifteenth-century renovation of a Romanesque basilica built on the foundations of a Roman temple. Over the road, you can follow streets up to the top of the hill, the site of the original Roman Capitol. It's now the home of a mossy seventeenth-century **fortress**, built by the Venetians, behind which are the remains of a small **Roman Theatre** (free) and the **Archeological Museum** (May–Sept Mon–Fri 9am–8pm, Sat & Sun 9am–3pm; Oct–April Mon–Fri 9am–2pm; 20kn), where pillars and toga-clad statues mingle haphazardly with ceramics, jewellery and trinkets from all over Istria, some dating back to prehistoric times.

Arrival and information

Air Pula's airport is 6km northeast of the city. The bus ride to the centre costs 29kn; taxis are around 120kn.

Train Pula's train station is a 10min walk north of the centre, at the far end of Kolodvorska.

Bus The bus station is 10min northeast of the centre, along Istarska Divizije.

Tourist office In the Forum (June–Sept Mon–Sat 8am–10pm, Sun 10am–5/6pm; Oct–May Mon–Sat 9am–6/7pm, Sun 10am–4pm; Ⓣ052/219-197, Ⓦwww.pulainfo.hr).

Accommodation

Private rooms Book through A Turizam, opposite the cathedral at Kandlerova 24 (ⓣ052/212-212, ⓦwww.a-turizam.hr), or Atlas, Starih Statuta 1 (ⓣ052/393-040). Rooms from 100kn.
Pula Youth Hostel Valsaline bay, 3km south of the centre ⓣ052/391-133, ⓔpula@hfhs.hr. Large HI-affiliated hostel in a scenic bay. Bus #2 or #3 from Giardini to Vila Idola and then bear right towards the bay. Dorms from 88kn.
Stoja 3km southeast of town ⓣ052/387-144, ⓔacstoja@arenaturist.hr. A basic campsite on a rocky wooded peninsula; take bus #1 from Giardini. Camping 89kn.

Eating and drinking

The vast market on Narodni Trg (daily till 2pm) is useful for picnics.
Augustov Hram Kapitolinski Trg 9. A pavement café offering cheap and tasty Croatian dishes such as *ćevapi* (kebabs) and stuffed peppers. Dishes from 12kn.
Jupiter Castropola 38. A pretty and tranquil pizzeria perched on a hill near the fortress with garden seating. Tasty pizzas from 28kn.
Pietas Julia Riva bb. This loungey, chilled-out bar just west of the amphitheatre attracts a fun-loving crowd at weekends.
Uljanik Dobrilina 2. Counter cultural club of many years' standing that has DJ nights at weekends and live music in summer. Open Thurs–Sat.

Moving on

Bus Dubrovnik (1 daily; 15hr); Rijeka (every 30min; 2hr 30min); Rovinj (every 30min; 1hr); Split (3 daily; 10hr); Trieste (10–14 daily; 3hr); Venice (1daily; 5hr) ; Zagreb (12–18 daily; 4–6hr).
Ferry Zadar (2–5 weekly June–Sept; 5hr); Venice (1 weekly June–Sept; 3hr 30min; book through Commodore Travel at Riva 14 ⓣ052/211-631).
Train Ljubljana (7 daily; 4hr); Zagreb (6 daily; 6hr 30min).

ROVINJ

ROVINJ lies 40km north of Pula, its harbour an attractive mix of fishing boats and swanky yachts, its quaysides a blend of sun-shaded café tables and the thick orange of fishermen's nets.

What to see and do

From the main square, **Trg maršala Tita**, the Baroque **Vrata svetog Križa** leads up to Grisia Ulica, lined with galleries selling local art. It climbs steeply through the heart of the Old Town to **St Euphemia's Church** (daily: July & Aug 10am–6pm, Sept–June 11am–3pm), dominating Rovinj from the top of its peninsula. This Baroque eighteenth-century church has the sixth-century sarcophagus of the saint inside, and you can climb its 58-metre-high tower (same times; 20kn). **Trg Valdibora** is home to a small produce market. Paths on the south side of Rovinj's busy harbour lead south towards **Zlatni rt**, a densely forested cape, crisscrossed by tracks and with numerous rock-climbing routes, many suitable for beginners. The best of the **beaches** – all rocky – are here, but you can also try the two islands just offshore: **Sveta Katarina**, the nearer of the two, and **Crveni otok**, just outside Rovinj's bay. Both are linked by boats from the harbour (every 30min; 20–30kn).

Arrival and information

Bus Rovinj's bus station is 5min walk southeast of its centre, just off Trg na lokvi, at the junction of Carrera and Carducci.

MOVING ON FROM ISTRIA: RIJEKA

Travelling on from Istria towards Zagreb or Dalmatia, most routes lead through the port city of **RIJEKA**, hardly worth a stop in its own right but an important transport hub for onward travel: regular **buses** run from here to Zagreb, Zadar, Split and Dubrovnik, and it's the starting point for the Jadrolinija coastal **ferry**, which calls in at Zadar, Split and Dubrovnik on its way south. Rijeka's train and bus stations are about 400m apart: the former at the western end of Trpimirova, the latter at the eastern end of the same street on Trg Žabica. The Jadrolinija ferry office (daily 7/8am–5/8pm; ⓣ051/666-111) is along the waterfront from the bus station at Riva 16.

Tourist office Just back from the waterfront at Obala Pina Budicina 12 (June–Sept daily 8am–10pm; Oct–May Mon–Fri 8am–3pm, Sat 8am–1pm, Sun 9am–1pm; ⓣ052/811-566, ⓦwww.tzgrovinj.hr).

Accommodation

Private rooms Natale, opposite the bus station at Carducci 4 (ⓣ052/813-365), or Globtour at Alda Rismondo 2 (ⓣ052/814-130, ⓦwww.globtour-turizam.hr), who also rent bikes for 60kn/day. Rooms from 110kn.
Porton Biondi Aleja Porton Biondi 1 ⓣ052/813-557, ⓦwww.portonbiondi.hr. A pine-shaded campsite right by the sea, 700m north of town. Mid-March to Oct. Camping 47kn.

Eating and drinking

There's a supermarket next to the bus station.
Da Sergio Grisia 11. One of the best places for pizzas at around 40kn.
Monte Carlo Svetoga Križa 23. A more rough-and-ready alternative to *Valentino* (beer, rather than cocktails) where you can intersperse afternoon drinks with refreshing dips in the sea. Bottled beer 20kn.
Trattoria Dream Joakima Rakovka 18. You can sit outdoors at this popular place, just off the harbour, and the pastas, risottos and salads (from 65kn) make a welcome change from seafood.
Valentino Svetoga Križa. A cocktail bar perched on the rocks overlooking the sea. Pricey, but an atmospheric place to watch the sun go down with a mojito (50kn).

Moving on

Bus Dubrovnik (1 daily; 15hr); Pula (hourly; 1hr); Rijeka (6 daily; 3hr); Split (3 daily; 10–11hr); Trieste (4–5 daily; 2–3hr); Zadar (1 daily; 15hr); Zagreb (8 daily; 5hr).
Ferry Trieste (summer only; 2–3 daily; 2hr 20min); Venice (1 weekly; 3hr 30min).

The Dalmatian Coast

Stretching from Zadar in the north to the Montenegrin border in the south, the **Dalmatian Coast** is one of Europe's most dramatic shorelines. All along, well-preserved medieval towns sit on tiny islands or just above the sea on slim peninsulas, beneath a grizzled karst landscape that drops precipitously into some of the clearest – and cleanest – water in the Mediterranean. For centuries, the region was ruled by Venice, spawning towns, churches and architecture that wouldn't look out of place on the other side of the water. The busy northern port city of **Zadar** provides a vivacious introduction to the region. Otherwise, the main attractions are in the south: the lively provincial capital **Split** is served by trains from Zagreb and provides onward bus connections with the walled city of **Dubrovnik**. Ferry and catamaran connections to the best of the islands – **Brač, Hvar, Vis** and **Korčula** – are also from Split.

ZADAR

A bustling town of around 100,000 people, **ZADAR** boasts a compact historic centre crowded onto a tapered peninsula jutting northwest into the Adriatic. It displays a pleasant muddle of architectural styles, with Romanesque churches competing for space with modern café-bars. In recent years, it has made a name for itself as a hub of Croatian nightlife, with a number of summer festivals taking place in nearby **Petrčane** (see box, p.267).

What to see and do

Zadar's main square – or **Forum** – is dominated by the ninth-century **St Donat's Church** (June–Aug daily 9am–10pm; 10kn), a hulking cylinder of stone with a bare interior built – according to tradition – by St Donat himself, an Irishman who was bishop here for a time. Opposite, the **Archeological Museum** (summer Mon–Sat 9am–1pm & 5–9pm; winter Mon–Fri 9am–2pm, Sat 9am–1pm; 10kn) has an

absorbing collection of Neolithic, Roman and medieval Croatian artefacts. The adjacent **Exhibition of Church Art** (Mon–Fri 10am–12.30pm & 6–7.30pm, Sat 10am–12.30pm; 20kn) is a storehouse of Zadar's finest church treasures. On the northwestern side of the Forum, the twelfth- and thirteenth-century **Cathedral of St Anastasia** has an arcaded west front reminiscent of Tuscan churches. Around the door frame stretches a frieze of twisting acanthus leaves, from which various beasts emerge – look out for the rodent and bird fighting over a bunch of grapes.

South of the Forum

Southeast of the Forum lies **Narodni Trg**, an attractive Renaissance square overlooked by the clock tower of the sixteenth-century **Guard House**. A little further southeast, on Trg Petra Zoranića, the Baroque **St Simeon's Church** houses the exuberantly decorated reliquary of St Simeon, ordered by Queen Elizabeth of Hungary in 1377 and fashioned from 250kg of silver by local artisans. Overlooking the harbour at Poljana Zemaljskog odbora 1 is the state-of-the-art **Museum of Ancient Glass** (daily 9am–9pm; 30kn), opened in 2009, which contains one of the finest collections of ancient Roman glassware outside Italy. The modern glass-and-steel structure affords wonderful views of the harbour, too.

Arrival and information

Air Zadar's airport is 12km east of town. Buses (25kn) run from here into town.
Train and bus The train and bus stations are about 1km east of the town centre, a 15min walk or a quick hop on bus #5 – tickets cost 8kn from the driver or 13kn (valid for two journeys) from kiosks.
Boat Ferries arrive on Liburnska obala, from where the town centre is a 5min walk uphill.
Tourist office Narodni Trg (May–Sept Mon–Fri 8am–9/10pm, July & Aug till midnight; Oct–April Mon–Fri 8am–8pm, Sat & Sun 8am–1/2pm; ⓣ023/316-166, ⓦwww.tzzadar.hr).

THE SEA ORGAN

Zadar's quirkiest feature, the **Sea Organ** was part of a millennium redevelopment project. It consists of wide marble steps leading into the sea, with a set of polyethylene tubes and cavities carved underneath, which enable the sea and wind to orchestrate a constant harmony. Emitting a strange sound, a bit like pan pipes crossed with whale song, the Organ has to be seen – and heard – to be believed. Next to it is Zadar's latest attraction, **A Salute to the Sun**: a huge disk which accumulates solar power during the day and radiates a hypnotic glow by night.

Accommodation

Private rooms Organized by Aquarius at Nova Vrata bb (ⓣ023/212-919, ⓦwww.juresko.hr) and Miatours, Vrata sv. Krševana (ⓣ023/254-300, ⓦwww.miatours.hr), both under the arches in the town wall near the ferry quays. Rooms from 150kn.
Borik Majstora Radovana 7 ⓣ023/332-074, ⓔkamp@hoteliborik.hr. Well-equipped campsite near the youth hostel (5km northwest at Borik; bus #5 or #8 from the bus and train stations). Camping 122kn.
Venera Šime Ljubića 4a ⓣ023/214-098, ⓦwww.hotel-venera-zd.hr. A good location in the Old Town, with neat but minuscule en suites. 450kn.
Zadar Youth Hostel Obala kneza Trpimira 76 ⓣ023/331-145, ⓔzadar@hfhs.hr. Big, friendly hostel 5km northwest at the beach resort of Borik (bus #5 or #8 from the bus and train stations). Dorms 117kn.

Eating

There's a supermarket at the corner of Široka and Dalmatinskog sabora.
Arsenal Trg Tri Bunara ⓦwww.arsenalzadar.com. Arts centre, lounge bar, restaurant and concert venue on three floors, *Arsenal* is one of the coolest spots in Zadar, if not Croatia. Pop in for a reasonably priced breakfast, lunch or dinner, or catch a concert, film or DJ set.
Malo Misto Jurja Dalmatinca 3. This simple restaurant opens a terrace serving grilled meats in the summer. Mains from 75kn.

PETRČANE FESTIVALS

Petrčane, a sleepy 900-year-old fishing village just north of Zadar, may seem an unlikely spot for dusk-to-dawn partying, but in recent years clubbers have tired of Ibiza's crowds and prices, and have been pitching up here for their dose of summertime fun instead. The first festival was set up by the people behind *The Garden* club in Zadar (see below), in 2005. It now attracts big-name international DJs, and has spawned a host of summer festivals: at the last count, seven now take place on the same idyllic peninsula just out of town. The site is based around a beachfront bar and *Barbarella's*, a club done up in retro Seventies style. There's plenty of live music, of course, but you can also join one of the Argonaut boat parties to prolong the fun offshore. **Getting there** from Zadar is easy – it's a twenty-minute taxi ride – and there's plenty of **accommodation** too, both in Petrčane and in Punta Skala, 1km away; contact the Oliva agency (ⓣ023/364-251, ⓔoliva-rms@inet.hr; private rooms from 290kn). There are several **campsites** near the site (25–50kn/night); *Camping Pineta* (ⓦwww.camp-pineta.com) is the largest.

Airbound Early Aug; €59; ⓦwww.airbound.net.

Disco 3000 Early Sept; €60; ⓦwww.disco3k.com.

Electric Elephant End Aug; €80; ⓦwww.electricelephant.co.uk.

Exodus Mid-Sept; €85; ⓦwww.exoduscroatia.com.

The Garden Festival Early and mid-July; €80; ⓦwww.thegardenfestival.eu.

Like-Minded Mid-Aug; €57; ⓦwww.likemindedfestival.co.uk.

Soundwave Mid-July; €68; ⓦwww.soundwavecroatia.com.

Stomorica Stomorica 12. Good for Dalmatian specialities such as *pašticada* (slow-cooked beef stew) and fish stew (30kn), with a tiny interior as well as a few outdoor tables.

Trattoria Canzona Stomorica 8. Great-value pizzas and mains such as grilled tuna with local greens (70kn), or pizza from 38kn; try to nab one of the tables on the atmospheric alley outside.

Drinking and nightlife

Start your night bar-hopping between the atmospheric café-bars tucked into the alleys off Narodni Trg – head down Klaiča and its continuation Varoška to find them – before heading on to *Arsenal* (see p.266), *The Garden* or *Gotham City*.

Dina Varoška 2. A tiny gallery and café with tables shaped like artists' palettes, perfectly placed for watching the world go by.

The Garden Bedemi zadarskih pobuna; ⓦwww.thegardenzadar.com. A kind of tree-house for grown-ups, this lounge-bar sits high up in the city walls: there are big beds to relax on, cocktail in hand, as well as a dancefloor that regularly boasts big-name DJs. See also box above.

Gotham City Marka Oreškovića. Just north of the Old Town, this is a quirky *Batman*-themed summer club.

Moving on

Bus Dubrovnik (8 daily; 8hr 30min); Pula (3 daily; 6hr 30min); Rijeka (11 daily; 4hr 30min); Split (every 30min; 3hr); Zagreb (18 daily; 4hr 30min).

Ferry Ancona (1 daily; 6hr); Pula (5–7 weekly; 4hr 45min; book through Miatours, see opposite).

SPLIT

The largest city in the region, and its major transit hub, **SPLIT** is a hectic place, but one of the most enticing spots on the Dalmatian Coast. At its heart lies a crumbling Old Town built within the precincts of Diocletian's Palace, some of the most outstanding classical remains in Europe.

What to see and do

Diocletian's Palace is still the hub of the city – lived in almost continuously since Roman times, it has gradually become a warren of houses, tenements and churches. Almost everything worth seeing is concentrated here, behind the waterfront Riva. The Old Town is

hemmed in by a network of narrow, atmospheric alleys, while to the west is the lush **Marjan Peninsula**.

Diocletian's Palace

Built as a retirement home by Dalmatian-born Roman Emperor Diocletian in 305 AD, **Diocletian's Palace** has been modified over the centuries, but has remained the core of Split. The best place to start a tour of the palace area is on the seaward side, through the **Bronze Gate**, a functional gateway giving access to the sea that once came right up to the palace itself. Inside, you find yourself in a vaulted hall, from which imposing steps lead through the now domeless vestibule to the **Peristyle**, which these days serves as the main town square. At the southern end, steps lead up to the **vestibule**, a round, formerly domed building that's the only part of the imperial apartments to be left anything like intact. You can get some idea of the grandeur of the old apartments by visiting the **subterranean halls** (daily: July & Aug 8am–8pm; Sept–June 9am–6pm; 25kn) beneath the houses that now stand on the site; the entrance is to the left of the Bronze Gate.

The cathedral

On the eastern side of the Peristyle stands one of two black granite Egyptian sphinxes, dating from around 15 BC, which flanked the entrance to Diocletian's mausoleum; the octagonal building, surrounded by an arcade of Corinthian columns, has since been converted into Split's **cathedral** (daily 8am–7/8pm; 15kn). On the right of the entrance is the **campanile** (same hours; 10kn), a restored Romanesque structure – from the top, the views across the city are magnificent. The cathedral's striking walnut and oak **doorway** was carved in 1214 and shows scenes from the life of Christ. Inside, the dome is ringed by two series of decorative Corinthian columns and a frieze that contains portraits of Diocletian and his wife. The church's finest feature is a cruelly realistic *Flagellation of Christ* depicted on the Altar of St Anastasius, completed by local artist Juraj Dalmatinac in 1448.

The Golden Gate and Archeological Museum

North of the cathedral, along Dioklecijanova, is the grandest and best preserved of the palace gates: the **Golden Gate**. Just outside there's a piece by Meštrović, a gigantic statue of the fourth-century Bishop **Grgur Ninski**. Fifteen minutes' walk northwest of here, the **Archeological Museum**, at Zrinsko Frankopanska 25 (June–Sept Mon–Sat 9am–2pm & 4–8pm; Oct–May Mon–Fri 9am–2pm & 4–8, Sat 9am–2pm; 20kn), contains displays of Illyrian, Greek, medieval and Roman artefacts. Outside, the arcaded courtyard is crammed with a wonderful array of Greek, Roman and early Christian gravestones, sarcophagi and decorative sculpture.

The Marjan peninsula

If you want some peace and quiet, head for the woods of the **Marjan peninsula** west of the Old Town. It's accessible from the long road, Obala hrvatskog narodnog preporoda, via Sperun and then Senjska, which cuts up through the slopes of the **Varoš** district. Most of Marjan's visitors stick to the road around the edge of the promontory with its scattering of tiny rocky **beaches**; the Bene beach, on the far northern side, is especially popular. From the road, tracks lead up into the heart of the Marjan Park, which is thickly wooded with pines.

Meštrović Gallery

The main historical highlight of the Marjan peninsula lies some fifteen minutes west of the centre (bus #12 from the seafront). The **Meštrović Gallery**, Ivana Meštrovića 46 (May–Sept Tues–Sun 9am–7pm; Oct–April

Tues–Sat 9am–4pm, Sun 10am–3pm; 30kn, includes entrance to Kaštelet), is housed in the ostentatious Neoclassical building that was built – and lived in – by Croatia's most famous twentieth-century artist, the sculptor Ivan Meštrović (1883–1962). This fabulous collection consists largely of boldly fashioned bodies curled into elegant poses. Meštrović's former workshop, **Kaštelet** (same hours), is 200m up the same road, and contains a chapel decorated with one of his most important set-piece works: a series of wood-carved reliefs showing scenes from the Stations of the Cross.

Arrival and information

Air Split airport is 16km west of town; Croatia Airlines buses connect with scheduled flights and run to the waterfront Riva (35kn); ask at their office at Riva 9 for timetables. Alternatively, the #37 Split–Trogir bus runs from the main road outside the airport to the bus station (every 20min; 15kn).
Train and bus Split's main bus and train stations are next to each other on Obala Kneza Domagoja, 5min walk round the harbour from the centre.
Boat The ferry terminal and Jadrolinija booking office are a few hundred metres south of the train and bus stations.
Discount card The Splitcard, available from the tourist office, costs 35kn (valid 72hr), but is free if you're staying three days or more. It gets you free or discounted entrance to several of the sights, plus reductions on hostels and restaurants.
Tourist office In the Peristyle of the Palace (Mon–Sat 8am–8pm, Sun 9am–1pm; ⓣ021/345-606, ⓦwww.visitsplit.com).

Accommodation

Private rooms Booked through Turist Biro at Obala narodnog preporoda 12, on the waterfront (ⓣ021/347-100, ⓔturist.biro.split@st.t-com.hr. Rooms from 380kn.
B&B Kastel Mihovilova Sirina 5 ⓣ021/343-912, ⓦwww.kastelsplit.com. In a great location within the palace walls, this newly refurbished B&B has stylish en-suite rooms. Rooms 750kn, sea-view apartment sleeping four 1170kn.
Silver Central Kralja Tomislava 1 ⓣ021/490-805, ⓦwww.silvercentralhostel.com. A modern, central hostel with a buzzy common area and airy dorms. Its sister hostel, *Silver Gate*, is nearby at Hrvojeva 6. Dorms 145kn.
Split hostel booze & snooze Narodni trg 8 ⓣ021/342-787, ⓦwww.splithostel.com. Very central and welcoming hostel run by Croatian-Australians who like boozing with their guests. A sister hostel with an on-site bar is due to open at Kruževičeva 5 in April 2010. Free internet. Dorms 180kn.

Eating

The daily market at the eastern edge of the Old Town is the place to shop for fruit, veg and local cheeses.
Bistro Black Cat Corner of Petrova and Šegvića. Midway between the Old Town and Baćvice beach, this is a popular backpackers' hangout, with soups, quiches and international dishes at fair prices.
Buffet Fife Trumbićeva obala 11. This no-frills local favourite is an excellent budget option, serving up dishes such as stuffed sweet peppers (35kn) and seafood risotto (45kn) in huge portions.
Fab Food Narodni Trg 12. Tasty fresh salads and wraps (from 20kn) to take away. It's a good breakfast stop too.
Konoba kod Jože Sredmanuška 4. Ten minutes northeast of the Old Town, this atmospheric place has an off-the-beaten-track feel and specializes in seafood dishes (from 60kn).
Konoba Marjan Senjska 1. A backstreet cheapie serving Dalmatian staples such as seafood risotto for around 50kn.
Konoba Trattoria Bajamont Bajamontićeva 3. Dalmatian staples such as *ćevapčići* (50kn) and fish soup (30kn). Eat inside and watch your dinner being prepared in front of you, or outside, where a few tables line the alleyway.
Šperun Šperun 3. Dinky pavement seating and a cosy stone-walled dining room. The mainly fishy menu includes a tasty grilled tuna with capers (70kn).

Drinking and nightlife

The beach at Bačvice, a few minutes' walk south past the train station, is a popular party place in summer.
Gaga Iza Lože 5. Candlelit outdoor seating, pumping music and cheap cocktails (35kn).
Ghetto Club Posud 10. A great spot for a beer, the arty *Ghetto Club* is a bar, café and gallery in a lovely courtyard setting.
Puls Buvinina 1. A bohemian café-bar sprawled across wide steps decorated with cushions, mini-sofas and tables and chairs. Cocktails from 35kn.

ALL ABOARD

Croatian Railways run **"disco-trains"** between Zagreb and Split in July and August, offering passengers music and drinks in a special carriage during the eight-hour trip. Trains leave Zagreb on Friday night, returning from Split on Saturday night.

Teak just off Majstora Jurja. A pleasant, popular joint, good for a coffee or a cocktail. The same goes for the nearby *Mosquito* and *Kala* café-bars. Beer from 20kn.

Directory

Internet *Internet & Games* at Obala kneza Domagoja bb, up from the bus station, has internet access (15min/5kn) and sells secondhand books in English; the internet café next door rents bikes (20kn/hr).
Laundry Šperun 1. Daily 8am–8pm; 50kn/load. Also has internet access and left-luggage facilities.
Left luggage At the bus station (daily 7am–9pm; 6.50kn for the first hour, then 2.20kn/hr).

Moving on

Bus Belgrade (2 daily; 11hr 30min); Dubrovnik (every 30min; 4hr 30min); Ljubljana (1 daily; 11hr); Pula (3 daily; 10hr); Rijeka (hourly; 8hr); Sarajevo (5 daily; 5–6hr); Trieste (4–5 daily; 9–10hr); Zadar (hourly; 3hr 30min); Zagreb (every 30min; 7–9hr).
Ferry Ancona (4 weekly; 11hr); Brač (Supetar; hourly; 50min); Brač (Bol; 1 daily in summer; 55min); Dubrovnik (3 weekly; 8hr); Hvar (Hvar Town; 2 daily; 1hr); Hvar (Stari Grad; 5–6 daily; 2hr); Korčula (Vela Luka; 2 daily; 2hr 45min); Pescara (7 weekly; 5hr 45min); Vis (4 daily; 2hr 20min).
Train Budapest (5 daily; 16hr); Frankfurt (5 daily; 12hr); Ljubljana (5 daily; 13hr); Munich (5 daily; 11hr 30min); Saravejo (5 daily; 1hr 30min); Venice (5 daily; 11hr 30min); Zagreb (9 daily; 8hr).

BRAČ

BRAČ is famous for its milk-white marble, which has been used in places as diverse as Berlin's Reichstag, the high altar of Liverpool's Metropolitan Cathedral, the White House in Washington – and, of course, Diocletian's Palace in Split. In addition to the marble, a great many islanders were once dependent on the grape harvest, though the phylloxera (vine lice) epidemics of the late nineteenth and early twentieth centuries forced many of them to emigrate. Even today, as you cross Brač's interior, the signs of this depopulation are all around in the tumbledown walls and overgrown fields. The easiest way to reach Brač is by **ferry** from Split to **Supetar**, an engaging, laid-back fishing port on the north side of the island, from where it's a hour's bus journey to **Bol**, a major windsurfing centre on the island's south coast and site of one of the Adriatic's most beautiful beaches, **Zlatni Rat** (Golden Horn).

Supetar

Though the largest town on the island, **SUPETAR** is a rather sleepy village onto which package tourism has been painlessly grafted. There's little of specific interest, save for several attractive shingle **beaches** which stretch west from the harbour, and the **Petrinović Mausoleum**, a neo-Byzantine construction on a wooded promontory 1km west of town, built by sculptor Toma Rosandić to honour a local-born shipping magnate.

Arrival and information

Tourist office Beside the ferry dock at Porat 1 (June–Sept daily 8.30am–10.30pm; Oct–May Mon–Fri 8.30am–3.30pm; ⓣ021/630-551, ⓦwww.supetar.hr).

Accommodation

Private rooms Available from Atlas (ⓣ021/631-105) on the harbourfront at Porat 10, and Start (ⓣ021/757-741), opposite the ferry dock. Rooms from 300kn.
Shangri La Backpackers Ive Jakšića ⓣ021/630-937, ⓦhttp://brachostels.com. This hostel is a 10min walk from the harbour and has four- and six-bed dorms, as well as one double. Facilities include a kitchen, free wi-fi and a DVD library. Dorms 110kn, double room 300kn.

Eating and drinking

There's a supermarket in the harbour.
Konoba Lukin Porat 32. Harbourside seating, a cosy, familial atmosphere and well-prepared local

dishes make this the best option for a meal. Mixed grill 70kn.

Palute Porat 4. The best of the places to eat on the harbourfront: serves good grilled fish (mains from 70kn).

Restaurant Punta Punta 1, near the *Supetrus* hotel complex. An extensive, fairly priced menu (starting at around 50kn for an omelette) and a lovely waterside setting – perfect for a sunset drink.

Activities

Scuba diving Fun Dive Club in the *Supetrus* hotel complex at Put Vela Luke 4 (Ⓣ0981/307-384; closed Oct–April) rents gear and arranges scuba and snorkelling courses (from 225kn).

Mountain biking ACF at bana J. Jelačića 14 rents out mountain bikes (80kn/day).

Quad biking You can rent quad bikes (180kn/3hr) and scooters (90kn/3hr) from M&B, opposite the ferry dock.

Bol

Stranded on the far side of the Vidova Gora mountains, you cannot help but be overwhelmed by the beauty of **BOL**'s setting, or the charm of its old stone houses. However, the main attraction of the village is its beach, **Zlatni Rat**, which lies to the west of the centre along the wooded shoreline. The pebbly cape juts into the sea like an extended finger, changing shape from season to season as the wind plays across it. Unsurprisingly, it does get very crowded during summer. Near here, dramatically perched on a bluff just east of central Bol, is the late fifteenth-century **Dominican Monastery** (daily 10am–noon and 5–8pm), whose main attraction is an altar painting by Tintoretto.

Arrival and information

Buses From Supetar, 12–13 daily buses make the hour-long trip to Bol's harbour.

Tourist office In the harbour (June–Aug daily 8.30am–10pm; Sept daily 8.30am–3pm & 5–9pm; Oct–May Mon–Fri 8.30am–3pm; Ⓣ021/635-638, Ⓦwww.bol.hr).

Accommodation

Private rooms Boltours at Vladimira Nazora 18 (Ⓣ021/635-693, Ⓦwww.boltours.com), 100m west of the bus stop, arrange private rooms (from 200kn) and apartments (from 415kn for two). Alternatively, try Adria at Bračka Cesta 10 (Ⓣ021/635-966, Ⓦwww.adria-bol.hr), a 10min walk west.

Kito Camping Karmelić Srećko, Ante Radića 1 Ⓣ021/635-551, Ⓔkamp_kito@inet.hr. Large, friendly campsite close to the beach and centre of Bol, with kitchens and a nearby supermarket. Camping 137kn.

Eating and drinking

There's a Konzum supermarket in the harbour.

Cocktail Bar Bolero Put Zlatnog rata. A shady spot right on the waterfront, with capacious wicker sofas and killer cocktails (around 50kn).

Konoba Mlin Ante Starčevića 11. A lovely restaurant in an old stone-mill, with live music and an outdoor grill where freshly caught fish are cooked to taste. Open June–Oct. Mains from 70kn.

Pivnica Moby Dick Porat bolskih pomoraca bb. A laid-back little bar in a great position overlooking the harbour, *Moby Dick* serves cheap meals (pizza from 45kn), has a pool table and is open till 2am.

Varadero Frane Radića. DJs, an extensive list of cocktails and a prime position in the main square – this is the place to be after dark. Open May–Oct.

Activities

Hiking The 778-metre peak of Vidova gora is within easy reach of Bol: a marked trail (2hr each way) heads uphill just beyond the *Kito* campsite.

Mountain biking The tourist office has free cycling maps. Next door, *Big Blue Café* rents out bikes (100kn/day).

Watersports Big Blue (Ⓣ021/635-614, Ⓦwww.big-blue-sport.hr; April–Nov), on the path leading to Zlatni Rat, is the best of several windsurfing centres. Board rental 250kn/day; courses for beginners around 800kn/8hr; sea-kayak rental 50kn/hr.

Moving on

Ferry Hvar (Jelsa; 1 daily; 20min); Split (1 daily; 55min).

HVAR

One of the most hyped of all the Croatian islands, **HVAR** is undeniably

beautiful – a slim, green slice of land punctured by jagged inlets and cloaked with hills of lavender. Tourist development hasn't been too crass, and the island's main centre, **Hvar Town**, retains much of its old Venetian charm.

What to see and do

The best view of **HVAR TOWN** is from the sea: a tiny town hugging the bay, grainy-white and brown with green splashes of palms and pines. At the centre, the main square is flanked to the south by the arcaded bulk of the **Venetian arsenal**, the upper storey of which was added in 1612 to house a **theatre** (closed for refurbishment at the time of writing), the oldest in Croatia. At the eastern end of the square is Hvar's **cathedral** (usually open mornings), a sixteenth-century construction with an eighteenth-century facade – a characteristic mixture of Gothic and Renaissance styles. Inside, the **Bishop's Treasury** (daily: June–Aug 9am–noon & 5–7pm; Sept–May 10am–noon; 20kn) holds a small but fine selection of chalices and reliquaries. The rest of the Old Town stretches back from the piazza in an elegant confusion of twisting lanes and alleys. Up above, the **fortress** (April–Sept daily 8am–dusk; 20kn) was built by the Venetians in the 1550s. From here, you can pick out the fifteenth-century **Franciscan Monastery** (Mon–Fri 10am–noon and 5–7pm, Nov–April mornings only; 20kn), to the left of the harbour; next door, the monastic church is pleasingly simple, with beautifully carved choir stalls.

Beaches and islands

The **beaches** nearest to town are rocky and crowded, so it's best to make your way towards the **Pakleni otoci**, just to the west. Easily reached by water taxi from the harbour (about 20kn each way), the Pakleni are a chain of eleven wooded islands, three of which cater for tourists with simple bars and restaurants: Jerolim, a naturist island, is the nearest; next is Marinkovac; then Sv Klement, the largest of the islands. Bear in mind that camping is forbidden throughout Pakleni, and that naturism is popular.

Arrival and information

Arrival At least one daily hydrofoil from Split arrives at Hvar Town itself; numerous ferries head for Stari Grad, 4km east, from where buses run into Hvar Town. There's also one daily ferry from Bol on Brač to Jelsa in the centre of the island, from where there are three to four daily buses to Hvar Town (though all leave before the ferry arrives) and five to eleven to Stari Grad.

Tourist office On the waterfront below the theatre at Trg sv. Stjepana bb (July & Aug daily 8am–2pm & 3–10pm; June & Sept Mon–Sat 8am–2pm & 3–8/9pm, Sun 10am–noon & 6–8/9pm; Oct–May Mon–Sat 8am–2pm; Ⓣ021/741-059, Ⓦwww.tzhvar.hr).

Accommodation

Private rooms Contact Atlas on the harbour at Obala bb (Ⓣ021/741-911, Ⓔinfo2atlas-hvar.hr), or Pelegrini, by the ferry dock at Riva bb (Ⓣ021/742-743, Ⓔpelegrini@inet.hr). Rooms from 400kn.

The Green Lizard Lucica (residential area) Ⓣ0981/718-729, Ⓦwww.greenlizard.hr. A clean, family-run hostel 10min walk east of the ferry port, with dorms and private rooms, some with beautiful sea views. Staff will pick you up from the ferry or bus. Dorms 150kn, rooms 320kn. Easter–Oct.

Jagoda & Ante Bracanovič House Poviše Škole 21 Ⓣ021/741-416, Ⓔvirgilye@yahoo.com. Neat rooms with balconies, shared kitchen and a pretty garden, a 10min walk from town or free pick-up from the bus station. 270kn.

Eating and drinking

There's a supermarket and a produce market next to the bus station. The best ice cream in town is at *Garip*, at the start of the Riva.

4 Palme Riva 3. Run by the same family for three generations, this is a model of honest pricing amongst the chi-chi places that line the Riva. Mains from 60kn.

Kod Matkovića Godina Tradicije 50. A huge menu with plenty of Dalmatian specialities, and fairly

> **TREAT YOURSELF**
>
> Said to be the best cocktail bar in Croatia, **Carpe Diem**, on the Riva, is the epitome of jet-set. It attracts glamorous partygoers to its pricey cocktail pitchers and thumping speakers like moths to a flame; later on, DJs spin crowd-pleasing tunes till the early hours. Cocktails cost around 70kn.

priced too. A vast plate of mussels in a wine and garlic sauce will set you back just 60kn.

Veneranda Šumica bb, east of the harbour. This monastery-turned-club is where the crowds from *Carpe Diem* come to rip up the dancefloor later on. Open till 5am.

Activities

Watersports Hvar Adventure at Obala bb, just off the Riva (T 091/154-3072, W www.hvaradventure.com), run sailing and kayaking tours; prices start at 350kn for a sunset sea-kayaking tour. Rock-climbing and hiking excursions are also organized.

Moving on

Bus Stari Grad (4–6 daily; 35min).
Ferry Korčula (Korčula Town; 1 daily; 1hr 45min); Korčula (Vela Luka; 1 daily; 1hr); Split (2–3 daily; 1hr); Vis (1 weekly; 1hr).

VIS

Compact, humpy, and at first glance a little forbidding, **VIS** is situated further offshore than any other of Croatia's inhabited Adriatic islands. Closed to foreigners for military reasons until 1989, the island has never been overrun by tourists, and even now depends much more heavily on independent tourism than its package-oriented neighbours. Croatia's bohemian youth have fallen in love with the place over the last decade, drawn by its wild mountainous scenery, two good-looking towns, **Vis Town** and **Komiža**, and great beaches and bars. Ferries and, in summer, catamarans from Split arrive at Vis Town, from where buses depart for Komiža on the western side of the island.

Vis Town

VIS TOWN is a sedate arc of grey-brown houses on a deeply indented bay, above which looms a steep escarpment covered with the remains of abandoned agricultural terraces. A five-minute walk from the harbour is the town's main sight: the **history museum** (Tues–Sat 10am–1pm & 5–9pm, Sun 10am–1pm; 20kn), which holds pottery, jewellery and sculpture from the Greek and Roman eras. East of the ferry landing is the suburb of **Kut**, an atmospheric, largely sixteenth-century tangle of narrow cobbled streets overlooked by the summer houses built by nobles from Hvar. A kilometre further on lies a small British war cemetery, and just behind it, a wonderful pebbly **beach**. Heading west around the bay soon brings you to a small peninsula, from which the campanile of the Franciscan **monastery of St Hieronymous** rises gracefully alongside a huddle of cypresses.

Information

Tourist office Just to the right of the ferry dock (June–Sept daily 8.30am–2.30pm & 5.30–7.30pm; Oct–May Mon–Sat 8.30am–2pm; T 021/717-017, W www.tz-vis.hr).

Accommodation

The tourist board have extensive private rooms listings on their website (see above).

Private rooms Ionios (Obala Sv Jurja 37 T 021/711-532, E ionios@st.hinet.hr) book private rooms (from 560kn) and also rent out scooters and cars, and organize trips to Biševo.

Eating and drinking

Kantun Biskupa Mihe Pusića. A wine bar, restaurant and art gallery, *Kantun* is worth a visit if only for a drink in their relaxing shady garden. Mains from 70kn.

Karijola Šetaliste Viskog Boha 4. June–Sept. A great pizzeria in an unbeatable position, on the peninsula on the way to Kut. The pizzas are tasty too (from 40kn).

Kod Paveta Dinko I Anka Tomić. One of the cutest joints in Croatia, opposite Vis's

open-air cinema, with delicious, well-priced fish dishes. Try the home-made gnocchi for 50kn.
Pizzeria Katerina Ivanišević Marinko, near the ferry dock. Good for a quick bite (around 50kn), with cheap beers. Next door's bar plays an eclectic mix of music until the early hours, beneath a bamboo roof.

Moving on

Bus Komiža (6–8 daily; 15min).
Ferry Hvar (1 weekly; 45min); Split (2 daily; 1hr 15min–2hr 30min).

Komiža

KOMIŽA, 10km from Vis Town, is the island's main fishing port – a compact town with a palm-fringed seafront on one side and a ring of mountains on the other. Dominating the southern end of the harbour is the **Kaštel**, a stubby sixteenth-century fortress which now holds a charming **Fishing Museum** (June–Sept Mon–Sat 10am–noon and 7–10pm, Sun 7–10pm; 10kn). Komiža's nicest **beaches** are ten minutes south of the museum, where you'll find a sequence of pebbly coves. Each morning, small boats leave Komiža harbour for the nearby island of Biševo in order to visit the **Blue Cave**, a grotto filled with eerie shimmering light; expect to pay around 110kn for a half-day trip.

Arrival and information

Buses from Vis Town terminate about 100m behind the harbour.
Tourist office A short walk south of the bus station on the Riva just beyond the Kaštel (June–Aug Mon–Sat 8am–9pm, Sun 8.30am–12.30pm; Sept–May Mon–Sat 8am–noon & 5–7pm; ⓣ021/713-455).

Accommodation

Private rooms Booked through Darlić & Darlić, on the harbourfront (ⓣ021/717-205, ⓦwww.darlic-travel.hr); Srebrnatours, Ribarska 4 (ⓣ021/713 668, ⓦwww.srebrnatours.hr), also organizes trips to the caves and diving excursions. Rooms from 250kn.

Eating and drinking

Aquarius Kamenica beach. A hugely popular summertime beach club, with projections beamed onto the sea and dancing till dawn.
Bistro Pol Rogoc Barnna Ransonnea 5. Signposted from the tiny main square, Škor. A popular little place with a wood-fired grill in the garden and lunch specials.
Caffe Bar Bejbi Šetalište Stare Isse. Škor is ringed by café-bars, or try this bar near the docks, with pool tables, a buzzy atmosphere and occasional live music.

KORČULA

Like so many islands along this coast, **KORČULA** was first settled by the Greeks, who gave it the name Korkyra Melaina or "Black Corfu" for its dark and densely wooded appearance. Even now, it's one of the greenest of the Adriatic islands, and one of the most popular. The island's main settlement is **Korčula Town**; the rest of the island, although beautifully wild, lacks any real centres.

What to see and do

KORČULA TOWN sits on a beetle-shaped hump of land, a medieval walled city ribbed with a series of narrow alleys that branch off the main street. The Venetians first arrived here in the eleventh century, and stayed, on and off, for nearly eight centuries, and their influence is particularly evident in Korčula's Old Town.

The Cathedral and Bishop's Treasury

The Old Town huddles around the **Cathedral of St Mark**, whose facade is decorated with a gorgeous fluted rose window and a bizarre cornice frilled with gargoyles. The interior is one of the loveliest in the region – a curious mixture of styles, ranging from the Gothic forms of the nave to the Renaissance northern aisle, tacked on in the sixteenth century.

The best of the cathedral's treasures have been moved to the **Bishop's Treasury** (July & Aug: daily 10am–noon and 5–7pm; at other times enquire at the tourist office; 10kn), a couple of doors down. This small collection of fine and sacral art is one of the best in the country; look out for the Leonardo da Vinci sketch of a soldier wearing a costume bearing a striking resemblance to that of the Moreška dancers (see box below).

The Town Museum and the House of Marco Polo

A former Venetian palace holds the **Town Museum** (Mon–Sat: July–Sept 10am–9pm; Oct–June 10am–2pm; 15kn), whose more modest display includes a plaster cast of a fourth-century-BC Greek tablet from Lumbarda – the earliest evidence of civilization on Korčula. Near the main square, down a turning to the right, is another remnant from Venetian times, the **House of Marco Polo** (July & Aug daily 10am–1pm and 5–7pm; Sept–June Mon–Sat 10am–1pm; 10kn). Korčula claims to be the birthplace of the explorer, although it seems unlikely that he had any connection with this seventeenth-century house, which these days is little more than an empty shell.

Beaches

Your best bet for **beaches** is to head off by water taxi from the old harbour to one of the **Skoji islands** just offshore. The largest and nearest of these is **Badija**, where there are some secluded rocky beaches, a couple of snack bars and a naturist section. There's also a sandy **beach** just beyond the village of **Lumbarda**, 8km south of Korčula (reached by hourly bus in the summer).

Arrival and information

Bus Korčula's bus station is 400m southeast of the Old Town. The bus service from Dubrovnik crosses the narrow stretch of water dividing the island from the mainland by ferry from Orebić.

Boat The main coastal ferry and the catamaran from Hvar dock in Korčula Town harbour. In addition, local ferries travel daily from Split and Stari Grad (Hvar) to Vela Luka at the western end of Korčula island, from where there's a connecting bus service to Korčula Town.

Tourist office On the northwestern side of the peninsula from the ferry port at Obala dr. Franje Tudmana 4 (June–Sept Mon–Sat 8am–3pm & 5–9pm, Sun 9am–1pm; Oct–May Mon–Sat 8am–2pm; ⓣ020/715-701, ⓦwww.korcula.net).

Accommodation

Private rooms Contact Atlas, by the fort ⓣ020/711-231, ⓔatlas-korcula@du.t-com.hr. Rooms from 300kn.

Apartments/Rooms Depolo Hrvatske bratske zajednice 62 ⓣ020/721-172, ⓔegon.depolo@du.t-com.hr. Spotless, tastefully decorated rooms midway between the bus station and the Old Town. Rooms 370kn, apartments 440kn.

Onelove Hrvatske Zajednice 6 ⓣ020/716-755, ⓦwww.korculabackpacker.com. The place to stay if you want to party with other travellers. It's near the ferry port and bus terminal, where staff come to meet you. You can rent boats, scooters and bikes here too, and there's a 24hr bar on the ground floor where films are screened. 120–140kn.

Eating and drinking

There's a small market to the right of the main steps by the harbour leading up to the Old Town, and a Konzum supermarket in the corner of the harbour.

MOREŠKA

Performances of Korčula's famous folk dance, the **Moreška**, take place outside the main gate to the Old Town throughout the summer, every Monday and Thursday evening (tickets from Atlas, see above; 100kn). This frantic, sword-based dance is the story of a conflict between the Christians (in red) and the Moors (in black): the heroine, Bula, is kidnapped by the evil foreign king and his army, and her betrothed tries to win her back in a ritualized sword fight which takes place within a shifting circle of dancers.

Buda Biline, off Plotaka, the main square. Traditional home-cooking in a cosy, wood-beamed space filled with nautical knick-knacks. The 30kn menu features dishes such as goulash and peppers stuffed with meat.
Massimo Setaliste Petra Kanavelic. This cocktail bar, ensconced in a medieval turret, may be pricey but it's one of the prime spots for admiring a Korčula sunset. You have to go up (and eventually come down) by ladder – worth keeping in mind after a couple of *Massimo*'s ultra-strong cocktails (from 45kn).
Noa Opposite the bus station. This cavernous pizzeria serves up Korčula's best pizzas (from 34kn).
Planjak Plokata 21. Cheap but tasty meals, with delicious grilled calamari for 50kn.

Moving on

Bus Dubrovnik (1 daily; 3hr 30min).
Ferry From Vela Luka: Hvar (1 catamaran daily; 45min); Split (2 ferries daily; 3hr). From Korčula Town: Split (1 catamaran daily; 1hr 45min).

DUBROVNIK

The immaculately preserved medieval city of **DUBROVNIK**, at Croatia's southern tip, is a sight to behold. Lapped by the glittering Adriatic Sea, sturdy walls encircle the city's white marble streets, lined with imposing Baroque buildings.

First settled by Roman refugees in the early seventh century and given the name Ragusa, the town soon exploited its favourable position on the Adriatic with maritime and commercial genius. By the mid-fourteenth century it had become a successful and self-contained city-state, its merchants trading far and wide. Dubrovnik continued to prosper until 1667, when an earthquake devastated the city. Though the city-state survived, it fell into decline and, in 1808, was formally dissolved by Napoleon. An eight-month siege by Yugoslav forces in the early 1990s caused much destruction, but the city swiftly recovered.

What to see and do

Within its fabulous **city walls**, Dubrovnik is a sea of roofs faded into a pastel patchwork, punctured now and then by a sculpted dome or tower. The best way to get your bearings is by making a tour of the walls (daily: May–Oct 8am–6/7.30pm; Nov–April 10am–3pm; 50kn), which are 25m high and with all five towers intact. From here, you get a spectacular view of the **Old Town**, bisected by the main street, Stradun. The main attractions, all within the walls, can easily be covered in a day and a half – although many people find the city such a beguiling place that they choose to stay longer.

Pile Gate and Minčeta fortress

The **Pile Gate**, main entrance to the Old Town, is a fifteenth-century construction complete with a statue of St Blaise, the city's protector, set in a niche above the arch. At ground level, just inside it, **Onofrio's Large Fountain**, built in 1444, is a domed affair at which visitors to this hygiene-conscious city had to wash themselves before they were allowed any further.

Of the various towers and bastions that punctuate the walls, the 1455 **Minčeta fortress**, which marks the northeastern side, is by far the most imposing.

The Franciscan monastery and Stradun

The museum of the fourteenth-century **Franciscan monastery** complex (daily

DUBROVNIK SUMMER FESTIVAL

The prestigious **Summer Festival** (☎020/326-100, Ⓦwww.dubrovnik-festival.hr) is held from July 10 to August 25 and is a good time to be around, with classical concerts and theatre performances in most of the city's courtyards, squares and bastions. Book tickets well in advance – you can try your luck with booking on the day, although you may end up without a proper seat, having to stand or sit on stairs for the performance.

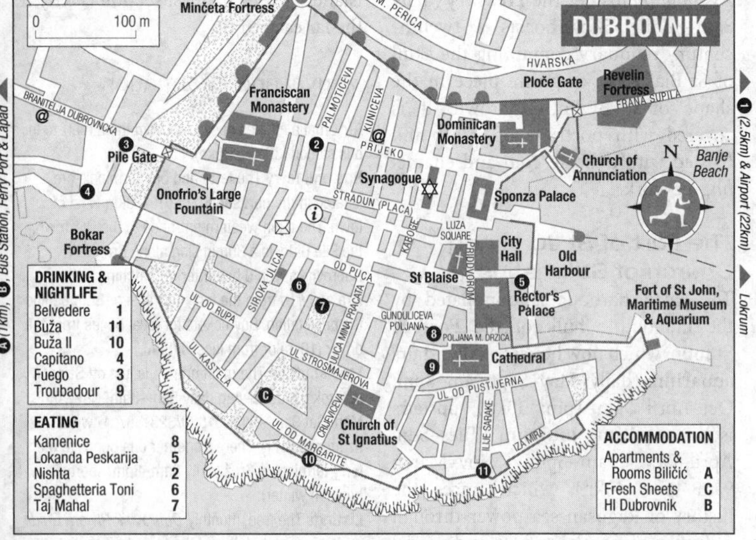

9am–6pm; 30kn) holds some fine Gothic reliquaries and manuscripts tracing the development of musical scoring, together with objects from the apothecary's shop, dating from 1317. Outside, look out for the gargoyle below knee height, on which crowds of tourists try – and fail – to keep their balance. From here, **Stradun** (also known as Placa), the city's main street, runs dead straight across the Old Town, its limestone surface polished to a slippery shine by the tramping of thousands of feet. The far end of Stradun broadens into the airy **Luža Square**, the centre of the medieval town and even today the hub of much of its activity, especially during the Summer Festival. On the left, the **Sponza Palace** was once the customs house and mint, with a facade showing off an elegant weld of florid Venetian Gothic and more sedate Renaissance forms; its majestic courtyard is given over to contemporary art exhibitions.

The Church of St Blaise and Rector's Palace

Built in 1714, the Baroque-style **Church of St Blaise** serves as a graceful counterpoint to the palace. Outside the church stands the carved figure of an armoured knight, known as **Orlando's Column** and once the focal point of the city-state.

A street leads round the back of St Blaise towards the fifteenth-century **Rector's Palace**, the seat of the Ragusan government, in which the incumbent Rector sat out his month's term of office. Today it's given over to the **City Museum** (daily: May–Sept 9am–6pm; Oct–April 9am–4pm; 40kn), though for the most part it's a rather paltry collection, with mediocre sixteenth-century paintings and dull furniture.

The Dominican monastery

The arcaded courtyard of the **Dominican monastery**, filled with palms and orange trees, leads to a small **museum** (daily 9am–6pm; 10kn), with outstanding examples of local sixteenth-century religious art.

Cathedral

The seventeenth-century **cathedral** is a rather plain building, although there's an impressive Titian polyptych of *The*

Assumption inside. The **Treasury** (daily 8am–8pm; 15kn) boasts a twelfth-century reliquary containing the skull of St Blaise; an exquisite piece in the shape of a Byzantine crown, it is covered with portraits of saints and frosted with delicate gold and enamel filigree work.

The Fort of St John and Church of St Ignatius

The small harbour is dominated by the monolithic hulk of the **Fort of St John**, which now houses a downstairs **aquarium** (daily: May–Sept 9am–8pm; Oct–April 9am–1pm; 30kn); upstairs is the **maritime museum** (Tues–Sun: April–Oct 9am–6pm; Nov–March 9am–4pm; 40kn), which traces the history of Ragusan sea power through a display of naval artefacts and model boats. Walking back west from here, you skirt one of the city's oldest quarters, **Pustijerna**, much of which predates the seventeenth-century earthquake. On the far side, the **Church of St Ignatius**, Dubrovnik's largest, is a Jesuit confection, modelled, like most Jesuit places of worship, on Rome's enormous Gesù church. Steps sweep down from here to **Gundulićeva Poljana**, the square behind the cathedral, which is the site of the city's morning produce market.

Beaches

The noisy and crowded main city beach is a short walk east of the Old Town; a better bet is to head for the less crowded, and somewhat cleaner, beach on the Lapad peninsula, 5km to the west (bus #6 from the Pile Gate), or to catch one of the taxi boats from the old city jetty (April–Oct 8am–5pm, every 30min; journey time 10min; 25kn return) to the wooded island of **Lokrum.** Crisscrossed by shady paths overhung by pines, Lokrum is home to an eleventh-century Benedictine monastery-turned-palace and has some extensive rocky beaches running along the eastern end of the island – with a naturist section (FKK) at the far eastern tip.

Arrival and information

Air Croatia Airlines buses run from the airport to the bus station (30min; 35kn).
Bus and ferry The ferry and bus terminals are located in the port suburb of Gruž, 3km west of town. The main western entrance to the Old Town, the Pile Gate, is a 30min slog along Branitelja Dubrovnika; you'd be better off catching a bus – #1a and #1b from the ferry terminal or from behind the bus station. Buy tickets for local buses from the driver (10kn) or from kiosks (8kn).
Tourist office The main branch is just off Stradun at Široka 1 (June–Aug daily 8am–8pm; Nov–April Mon–Sat 9am–3pm; ⓣ020/323-587, ⓦwww.tzdubrovnik.hr). There's another one opposite the ferry terminal in Gruž (daily 8am–8pm, shorter hours in winter).
Listings The free, monthly *Dubrovnik Riviera Guide*, available from hotels and the tourist office, lists bus and ferry timetables, as well as forthcoming events.

Accommodation

Private rooms Locals offering private rooms meet bus and ferry arrivals. Alternatively, try Gulliver, opposite the ferry terminal at Obala Stjepana Radića 32 (ⓣ020/410-888, ⓦwww.gulliver.hr), or Atlas, at Durda 1 (ⓣ020/442-585, ⓔatlas.pile@atlas.hr). Rooms 400–450kn.

Apartments & Rooms Biličić Privežna 2 ⓣ020/417-152, ⓦwww.dubrovnik-online.com/apartments_bilicic. Well-equipped rooms a 5min walk from the Old Town, with a lovely garden and terrace where guests can cook breakfast. The welcoming owner, Marija, picks guests up from the airport or ferry. Rooms 440kn, four-person apartments 880kn.

Fresh Sheets Vetraniceva 4 ⓣ091/799-2086, ⓦwww.igotfresh.com. This brand-new hostel, run by a Canadian-Croatian couple, has colourful dorms, free internet and breakfast and a communal kitchen. Dorms 188kn, double 366kn.

HI Dubrovnik Vinka Sagrestana 3; steps lead up from bana Jelačića 15–17 ⓣ020/423-241, ⓔdubrovnik@hfhs.hr. Connected to the Old Town and bus and ferry terminals by buses #1, #4, #7 and #8. Alternatively, head up Branitelja Dubrovnika from the ferry port and turn uphill to the right after 5min. Basic, well-run hostel with good showers, a leafy breakfast courtyard and friendly staff. Dorms 80kn.

Eating

There's a morning market (Mon–Sat) at Gundulićeva Poljana in the Old Town, a couple of streets from the harbour, and you'll find supermarkets outside the Pile and Ploče gates.

Kamenice Gundulićeva Poljana 8. A simple place with a limited menu, serving up cheap portions of *girice* (tiny deep-fried fish) and *kamenice* (oysters). About 45kn/portion.

Lokanda Peskarija Right on the old harbour, with terrace tables, this seafood-only restaurant serves up a small but fantastic menu including a sinister-looking but tasty black cuttlefish risotto (60kn).

Nishta Prijeko bb. A meal at this stylish vegetarian café makes a welcome change from Croatia's meat and fish staples. A healthy portion of falafel and salad will set you back 59kn.

Spaghetteria Toni Nikole Bozidarevica 14. A simple pasta place with an extensive menu and generous portions (from 42kn).

Taj Mahal Nikole Gučetića 2. Don't be fooled by the name or the exotic decor – *Taj Mahal*, tucked away off the main drag, offers traditional Bosnian dishes such as kebabs from 70kn.

Drinking and nightlife

Belvedere Frana Supila 28. This disused hotel is crammed with clubbers on occasional summer Saturdays, who get down to dance and electro, or cool off on the stretch of private beach outside.

Buža Accessed from Ilije Sarake. Reached via a hole in the city walls, this is a beautiful spot for a dip in the sea and a drink, with a clutter of tables perilously perched on rocky terraces. Its less chaotic sister bar, *Buža II*, is at Crijeviceva 9.

Capitano Između vrta 2. A raucous place to end the evening, this bar attracts a boozy crowd up for drinking and dancing the night away to pumping dance tunes.

Fuego Just outside the Pile Gate. This mainstream old-timer with cheap drinks attracts a fun-loving crowd.

Troubadour Bunićeva Poljana 2. A buzzing bar with a great view of the cathedral, plus live music – usually jazz – most nights. Beer 30kn.

Directory

Consulates UK: Vukovarska 22/1 ⓣ020/324-597.
Exchange The offices all along Stradun (Mon–Fri 8am–8pm, Sat 8am–2pm) offer similar rates.
Hospital Roka Mišetića bb ⓣ020/431-777.
Internet access Dubrovnik Internet Centar, Branitelja Dubrovnika 7 (Mon–Sat: summer 8am–7/8pm, winter 8am–3pm; 5kn/12min); *Netcafé*, Prijeko 21 (daily 9am–11pm; 10kn/20min).
Left luggage At the bus station (daily 4.30am–10.30pm; 10kn).
Pharmacy Kod Zvonika, Stradun (Mon–Fri 7am–8pm, Sat 7.30am–8pm).
Post office Široka (Mon–Fri 8am–8pm, Sat 8.30am–3pm).
Watersports Adriatic Kayak Tours organize excursions from their office at Zrinsko Frankopanska 6 (ⓣ020/312-770, ⓦwww.adriatickayaktours.com; from 255kn for a half-day tour to Lokrum island).

Moving on

Bus Korčula (1 daily; 3hr); Ljubljana (1 daily; 16hr); Montenegro (various towns; 1 daily); Pula (1 daily; 15hr); Rijeka (4 daily; 11hr 30min); Rovinj (1 daily; 16hr); Sarajevo (4 daily; 6hr); Split (17 daily; 4hr 30min – make sure you take your passport, as you pass through Bosnia on the way); Trieste (2 daily; 15hr); Zadar (7 daily; 8hr 30min); Zagreb (8 daily; 11hr).

Ferry Bari, Italy (2–4 weekly; 8–9hr); Korčula (5 weekly; 3hr); Rijeka (2 weekly; 21hr); Split (3 weekly; 8hr 30min).

Czech Republic

HIGHLIGHTS

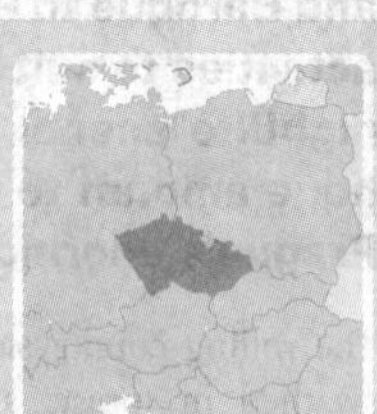

PRAGUE: lose yourself in the streets of Staré Mešto

KUTNÁ HORA: see the human bones in the subterranean ossuary at Sedlec

PLZEŇ: visit the home of Pilsner Urquell, the original lager

OLOMOUC: discover a more laid-back side to the Czech Republic in this lovely university town

ČESKÝ KRUMLOV: a trip along the Vltava River is the best way to see this fairytale town

ROUGH COSTS

DAILY BUDGET Basic €35/occasional treat €42

DRINK Pilsner Urquell €2

FOOD Pizza €4–5

HOSTEL/BUDGET HOTEL €19/€30

TRAVEL Train: Prague–Karlovy Vary (236km) €10; Bus: 2hr 15 min (€5)

FACT FILE

POPULATION 10.3 million

AREA 78,866 sq km

LANGUAGE Czech

CURRENCY Czech koruna (Kč)

CAPITAL Prague (population: 1.2 million)

INTERNATIONAL PHONE CODE ⓣ420

Introduction

Most people will have heard rave reviews about the Czech capital of Prague, and justifiably so – physically, it's a beauty, with stunning architecture ranging from Art Nouveau and Baroque to Renaissance and Gothic, and there are cultural activities to suit every taste, not to mention a buzzing café and nightlife scene. However, the rest of the country also has a huge amount to offer, and much of it benefits from not having Prague's enormous tourist quota.

The rolling countryside of **Bohemia** is swathed in forests and studded with perfectly preserved medieval towns and castles, such as the compact, picture-perfect town of Ceske Krumlov. To the west lies the peaceful spa town of **Karlovy Vary**, where you can admire stunning colonnades and try some health-boosting spa water. The country's eastern province, **Moravia**, boasts the spectacular karst region, as well as some lively, pretty little cities such as **Olomouc** and **Brno**, which arguably offer the same charms as Prague with less of the tourist tat and high price-tags.

CHRONOLOGY

Fourth century BC The Celtic "Boii" tribe inhabit the area now known as Bohemia (from the Latin Boiohaemum).

500s AD Slavic tribes arrive.

830 AD The Great Moravian Empire is Established along the Morava River.

907 Hungarians take over the Moravian empire.

1355 Charles IV, "the father of the Czech nation", is crowned Holy Roman Emperor, as Prague enjoys economic prosperity.

1415 Religious reformer Jan Hus is found guilty of heresy and executed, sparking years of fighting between his followers and Catholics.

1458 George of Podebrady is pronounced King, and maintains a peaceful rule.

1526 King Ferdinand I of the Habsburg dynasty takes the Czech throne, reintroducing Catholicism as the main religion.

1800s Rapid growth in nationalism and industrialization.

1916 Franz Kafka completes his famous work *Metamorphosis*.

1918 The independent Republic of Czechoslovakia is declared at the end of World War I.

1938 German troops enter the Sudetenland area of western Czechoslovakia.

1945 German occupation ends as the Allies move in.

1948 The Communist Party seizes control.

1968 The "Prague Spring" sees a period of political liberalization, before the Soviets invade to repress it.

1972 Martina Navratilova wins the Czech National Tennis Championships at the age of 15.

1989 The "Velvet Revolution" returns democracy to Czechoslovakia.

1993 The Czech Republic and Slovakia divide peacefully into two countries.

2004 The Czech Republic joins the EU.

2009 The US scraps plans to build a radar base near Prague.

ARRIVAL

There are direct flights from more than a dozen UK airports and from New York's JFK airport to Prague's **airport**, Ruzyně (Ⓣ220 113 314, Ⓦwww.csl.cz), 10km northwest of the city. Several international routes (including one from London Stanstead by Ryanair) serve Brno, and there are a couple of flights a week to and from Karlovy Vary (Ⓦwww.airport-k-vary.cz) to destinations such as Moscow and Rhodes.

Prague is served by direct **train** services from numerous major European cities, including Berlin, Vienna and Budapest.

Eurolines (Ⓦwww.eurolines.com) have good international **bus services** to the Czech Republic, as do Capital Express

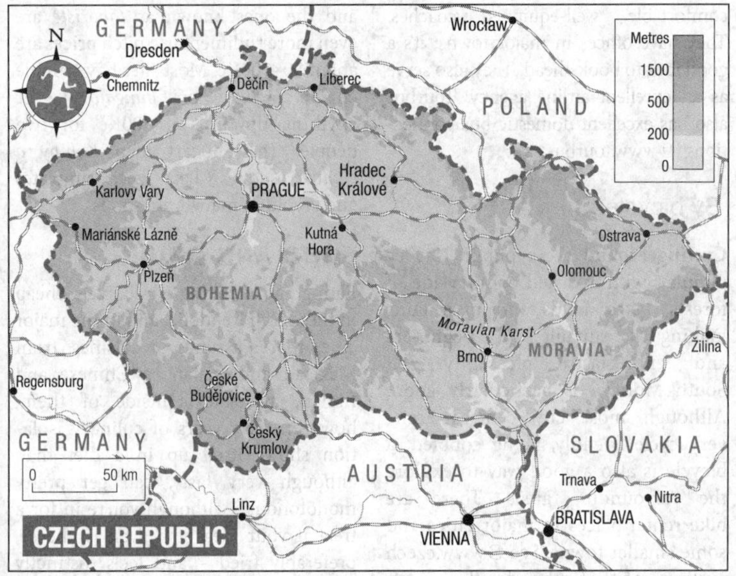

(ⓦwww.capitalexpress.cz) and Tourbus (ⓦwww.tourbus.cz) to Prague, Brno, Olomouc and other major cities.

GETTING AROUND

Both bus and train networks are generally efficient and good value in the Czech Republic. A useful **website** for train and bus times is ⓦwww.vlak.cz.

By train

The Czech Republic has one of the most comprehensive **rail** networks in Europe. Czech Railways (České dráhy or ČD; ⓦwww.cd.cz) runs two main types of train: *rychlík* (R) or *spěšný* (Sp) trains are the faster ones which stop only at major towns, while *osobní* trains stop at just about every station, averaging as little as 30km/hr. Fast trains are further divided into SuperCity (SC), which are first class only, EuroCity (EC) or InterCity (IC), for which you need to pay a supplement, and Expres (Ex), for which you don't. **Tickets** (*jízdenky*) for domestic journeys can be bought at the station (*nádraží*) before or on the day of departure. ČD runs reasonably priced **sleepers** to and from a number of cities in neighbouring countries, for which you must book as far in advance as possible. **InterRail** and Eurail passes are valid in the Czech Republic.

By bus

Regional **buses** – mostly run by the state bus company, Česká státní automobilová doprava (ČSAD; ⓦwww.csadbus.cz) – travel to most destinations, with private companies such as ČEBUS providing an alternative on popular inter-city routes. **Bus stations** are usually next to the train station, and though some have ticket offices you can usually buy your ticket from the driver. For long-distance journeys it's a good idea to book your ticket at least a day in advance.

The Student Agency (ⓣ800 100 300, ⓦwww.studentagency.cz, www.studentagencybus.com) runs an excellent, very reasonably priced bus service, with direct routes between popular destinations on

comfortable, well-equipped coaches. They have offices in major towns; it's a good idea to book ahead. They also serve as an excellent airline agency. Tourbus also has excellent domestic bus connections (Ⓦwww.tourbus.cz).

By bicycle

Cycling around the republic is very popular, with a varied countryside of forests, lakes, fields and mountains making it suitable for beginners and enthusiasts; pleasantly flat South Moravia is particularly good. Although most city centres aren't very cycle friendly, being cobbled, a bicycle is also a good way to explore the surrounding areas. There are bike rental places in major cities and some smaller towns. See Ⓦwww.czechcycling.info for further details.

ACCOMMODATION

Accommodation is the most expensive aspect of travelling in the Czech Republic. Though there is no organized hostel system, some places are affiliated with Hostelling International (HI; Ⓣ220 805 684, Ⓦwww.czechhostels.com). There are also some independent travellers' hostels in major destinations; for more information see Ⓦwww.travellers.cz.

Private rooms are available in all the towns on the tourist trail, and are usually the best bet, as you'll find the price difference between a room and a dorm bed is negligible. Keep your eyes peeled for signs saying *Zimmer Frei* or book through the local tourist office. Prices start at around 300Kč per person per night, more in Prague. Hotels are usually a little more expensive, but most of them are either recently refurbished or new, though cheaper ones tend to lack character. Continental or buffet-style breakfast is normally included.

Campsites, known as *autokemp*, are plentiful; the facilities are often basic and the ones known as *tábořiště* are even more rudimentary; pitch prices are about 50–100Kč. Most sites have simple **chalets** (*chaty* or *bungalovy*) for anything upwards of 300Kč for two people. The Shocart map *Kempy a chatové osady ČR* lists Czech campsites and is sold in many bookshops.

FOOD AND DRINK

Eating and drinking is relatively cheap in the Czech Republic, and in the major cities there's a range of cuisines, from Mexican and Italian to Chinese and Indian, available. Outside of them, however, forty years of culinary isolation shows itself up in a diet that, although very tasty, can get pretty monotonous – although you're in for a treat if your idea of heaven is cheese, preferably fried – and feels distinctly like its sole aim is to leave you needing a coronary bypass.

The whole concept of **breakfast** (*snidaně*) is alien to the Czechs. Popular **street snacks** include *bramborák*, a potato pancake with flecks of bacon; *párek*, a frankfurter dipped in mustard or ketchup and shoved in a white roll; and *smažený sýr*, a slab of melted cheese fried in breadcrumbs and served in a roll with tartare sauce. The coffee is generally delicious, and the **cake shop** (*cukrárna*) is an important part of the country's social life – another (admittedly usually very yummy) aid to the clogging of your arteries.

Restaurants (*restaurace*) serve hot meals from about 11am until 9pm. Most **pubs** (*pivnice*) also serve basic hot Czech dishes, as do **wine bars** (*vinárna*) – often the most stylish places around. Lunchtime menus start with soup (*polévka*), one of the country's culinary strong points. **Main courses** are overwhelmingly based on pork (*vepřový*) or beef (*hovězí*), but one treat is carp (*kapr*), traditional at Christmas and cheaply and widely offered just about everywhere, along with trout

(*pstruh*). Goose (*husa*), duck (*kachna*) and wild boar (*kanci maso*) dishes are also generally delicious. Main courses are served with **dumplings** (*knedlíky*) or vegetables, most commonly potatoes (*brambory*) and lots of cabbage (*zelí*). Desserts include pancakes (*palačinky*), filled with chocolate or fruit and cream, fruit dumplings (*ovocné knedlíky*) and ice cream (*zmrzlina*). If you're looking not to have a three-course sit-down meal at lunchtime, sandwich places and the like are generally few and far between – stock up at supermarkets where you can.

Drink

Even the simplest *bufet* (self-service cafeteria) almost invariably has **beer** (*pivo*) on draught. For evening drinking, **pubs** are the most traditional (and generally the most rowdy) places to drink – they mostly close around 11pm; wine bars are more upmarket and cocktail bars have opened up in larger towns.

The Czech Republic tops the world league table of **beer** consumption – hardly surprising since its beer ranks among the best in the world. The most natural starting point for any beer tour is the Bohemian city of **Plzeň** (Pilsen), whose local lager is the original Pilsner. The other big brewing town is **České Budějovice** (Budweis), home to Budvar, a mild beer by Bohemian standards but still leagues ahead of the American Budweiser. There's also a modest selection of medium-quality **wines**; the largest wine-producing region is southern Moravia. The home-production of firewater is a national pastime, resulting in some almost terminally strong concoctions, most famously a plum brandy called *slivovice*. The best-known Czech **spirit** is Becherovka, a medicinal herbal tipple from Karlovy Vary, known as a *beton* when ordered with ice and tonic. It tastes like bile and aniseed cough mixture combined.

CULTURE AND ETIQUETTE

It can be easy to mistake the Czechs' shyness for surliness, and people who actually speak pretty good English will often tell you that they don't speak it at all – it's often from lack of confidence rather than unfriendliness, and if you can get past some initial resistance, people are usually helpful and kind. Obviously, it helps if you learn some basic words – *Dobry den* (hello), *Na shledanou* (goodbye), *Prosim* (please) and *Děkuji vam* (thank you) will take you far.

Ten percent is usual for **tips**, depending on the establishment: give fifteen percent for more upmarket places.

SPORTS AND ACTIVITIES

Football is a national obsession. The most successful team is Sparta (Ⓦwww.sparta.cz). Matches are usually on Saturdays Aug–Nov and March–May.

Ice hockey is another national craze: you can watch matches in bars in most towns in the Czech Republic, or arrange to see games in stadiums during the season (book tickets through Ⓦwww.sazkaticket.cz).

There are plenty of **outdoor activities** such as cycling, hiking and rock climbing to be enjoyed in Bohemia, as well as **caving** in the Moravian karst.

THE CZECH REPUBLIC ON THE NET

Ⓦ**www.czech.cz** Basic information on the whole country.

Ⓦ**www.praguepost.com** Online version of the capital's own English-language paper.

Ⓦ**www.radio.cz/english** Updated news and cultural features.

Ⓦ**www.ticketpro.cz**, Ⓦ**www.ticketstream.cz**, Ⓦ**www.ticketsbti.cz** Three good sites for finding out what's on in Prague and for booking tickets online.

COMMUNICATIONS

Most **post offices** (*pošta*) are open Monday to Friday 8am to 5pm, Saturday 8am to noon. Look for the right sign to avoid queuing: *známky* (stamps), *dopisy* (letters) or *balky* (parcels). You can also buy stamps from newsagents, tobacconists and kiosks. The majority of **public phones** only take phonecards (*telefonní karty*), available from post offices, kiosks and some shops. You can make local and international calls from all card phones, all of which have instructions in English. You'll find **internet cafés** in almost every Czech town; charges are usually 60–100Kč/hr.

EMERGENCIES

Pickpockets are as rife in the centre of Prague as in any European capital, particularly in the Old Town Square, on Charles Bridge, on the #22 tram, in the metro and in the main train stations. You're unlikely to get much sympathy or help if you do get pickpocketed, so take care. **Theft** from cars is also a problem. By law, you should carry your **passport** with you at all times, though you're unlikely to get stopped.

Minor ailments can be easily dealt with at a **pharmacy** (*lékárna*), but language is likely to be a problem outside the capital. If it's a repeat prescription you want, take any empty bottles or remaining pills along with you. If the pharmacist can't help, they'll be able to direct you to a **hospital** (*nemocnice*).

INFORMATION

Most cities and towns have their own **tourist office** (*informační centrum*), where you should find at least one English-speaker. A comprehensive range of **maps** is usually available, often very cheaply, either from the tourist office or from bookshops, petrol stations and some hotels. Ask for a *plán města* (town plan) or *mapa okolí* (regional map).

EMERGENCY NUMBERS

Police ☎158; Fire ☎150; Ambulance ☎155.

MONEY AND BANKS

The local **currency** is the Czech *crown*, or *koruna česká* (Kč). Euros are also accepted in some places, but the euro price tends to be more expensive. **Banks** are usually open Monday to Friday 8am to 5pm. There are plenty of ATMs throughout the country. At the time of writing, €1 was equal to 25Kč, $1 to 20Kč, and £1 to 28Kč.

OPENING HOURS AND HOLIDAYS

Shops are open Monday to Friday 9am to 5pm, with some, especially in Prague, and most supermarkets, staying open till 6pm or later. Smaller shops close for lunch between noon and 2pm, while others stay open late on Thursdays. In larger towns, some shops stay open all day at weekends, and the corner shop (*večerka*) stays open daily till 11pm. Museums, galleries and churches are generally open daily; synagogues are closed on Saturdays and Jewish holidays. Many attractions are closed on Mondays.

Public holidays include January 1, Easter Monday, May 1, May 8, July 5 and 6, September 28, October 28, November 17, December 24–26.

STUDENT DISCOUNTS

Discounts can be quite substantial – often students pay just half or two-thirds of adult prices – but make sure you get an ISIC card, as many places will not accept regular university cards.

Czech

	Czech	Pronunciation
Yes	*Ano*	Uh-no
No	*Ne*	Neh
Please	*Prosím*	Ro-seem
Thank you	*Děkuji vam*	Dye-koo-yi vam
Good day/Hello	*Dobry den/Ahoj*	Dob-rie den/a-hoy
Goodbye	*Na shledanou*	Nu shle-dan-uh
Excuse me	*Promiňte*	Prom-in-teh
Where?	*Kde*	Gde
Good	*Dobrý*	Dob-rie
Bad	*Špatný*	Shput-nie
Near	*Blízko*	Blee-sko
Far	*Daleko*	Duh-lek-o
Cheap	*Levný*	Lev-nie
Expensive	*Drahý*	Dru-hie
Open	*Otevřeno*	Ot-evrsh-en-o
Closed	*Zavřeno*	Zavrsh-en-o
Today	*Dnes*	Dnes
Yesterday	*Včera*	Ftch-er-a
Tomorrow	*Zítra*	Zeet-ra
How much is…?	*Kolík stojí…?*	Kol-ik sto-yee…?
What time is it?	*Kolík je hodin?*	Kol-ik ye hod-in
I don't understand	*Nerozumím*	Ne-ro-zoom-eem
Do you speak English?	*Mluvíte Anglicky?*	Myuv-ee-te ang-lits-ky?
Where…?	*Kde…?*	Gudeh…?
Toilet	*Toaleta*	Tu-uleta
Square	*Náměstí*	Nahmnyestyee
Station	*Nádraží*	Nahdrujee
Platform	*Nástupiště*	Nahstoopish-tyeh
One	*Jeden*	Yed-en
Two	*Dva*	Dva
Three	*Tři*	Trshi
Four	*Čtyři*	Chtirsh-i
Five	*Pět*	Pyet
Six	*Šest*	Shest
Seven	*Sedm*	Sed-um
Eight	*Osum*	Oss-um
Nine	*Devět*	Dev-yet
Ten	*Deset*	Dess-et

Prague

Simply put, **PRAGUE** is stunning. No other European capital can present six hundred years of architecture so untouched by war. Walking over the Charles Bridge and through the town centre, especially at night, there's a breathtakingly beautiful sight around every corner. The only problem is that with so much incredible craftsmanship and architecture around, it's easy to overlook things that would be a feature in themselves in any other city. Alongside its heritage, Prague has a lively atmosphere, and is full of cafés, restaurants and bars humming with people.

Prince Bořivoj, the city's first Christian ruler, founded the Přemyslid dynasty and his grandson, Prince Václav, became the **Good King Wenceslas** of the Christmas carol and the country's patron saint. Prague enjoyed its golden age under Holy Roman Emperor **Charles IV**, who transformed it into one of the most important cities in fourteenth-century Europe. He founded the university and an entire new town, Nové Město, along with iconic Gothic structures such as the Charles Bridge and St Vitus' Cathedral.

MUSEUM AND BUILDING ENTRY

If you want to see the interior of historic buildings in Prague, such as castles and some churches, often the only way is to go on a **guided tour** that will last at least 45 minutes; the last tour usually leaves an hour before the advertised closing time. Ask for an *anglický* (English) text. Worth considering is the **Praguecard** (Ⓦwww.praguecard.biz): it costs €34, and gives you four days' city transport and coupons for free entry to over fifty major attractions. It can be bought online as well as at tourist offices, the airport and some hotels.

What to see and do

The River Vltava divides the capital into two unequal portions. The castle district of Hradčany and Malá Strana are on the left bank, and Staré Město, Josefov and Nové Město are on the right.

Hradčany, on the hill, contains the most obvious sights – the castle, the cathedral and the Old Royal Palace. Below Hradčany, **Malá Strana** (Little Quarter) is the city's ministerial and diplomatic quarter. Its narrow eighteenth-century streets crammed with shops and cafés down nooks and crannies are ideal for getting lost in, and the Czech senate's beautiful Baroque gardens are open daily from noon to 4pm.

Over the river, **Staré Město** (Old Town) is a web of alleys and passageways centred on the city's most beautiful square, Staroměstské náměstí. Enclosed within the boundaries of Staré Město is the old Jewish quarter, **Josefov**, whose synagogues and cemetery are reached along tree-lined avenues of designer boutiques.

Nové Město (New Town), the focus of the modern city, covers the largest area, laid out in long wide boulevards – most famously the American chain-store-lined Wenceslas Square – stretching south and east of the old town.

Prague Castle

Hradčany is wholly dominated by the city's omnipresent landmark, **Prague Castle** (daily 5/6am–11pm/midnight; most sights 9am–4/5pm; Ⓦwww.hrad.cz). You can have a good wander for free around the substantial castle courtyards and impressive cathedral. Otherwise, there are multiple kinds of entry tickets: 350Kč for all the sights, 220 Kč for a ticket covering St Vitus' Cathedral, the great tower, the Old Royal Palace and Golden Lane.

St Vitus' Cathedral

Work on the **cathedral** (daily: March–Oct Mon–Sat 9am–5pm, Sun noon–5pm; Nov–Feb Mon–Sat 9am–4pm, Sun noon–4pm) started under Charles IV, who employed the precocious 23-year-old German mason Peter Parler, although the cathedral wasn't finally completed until 1929. The grand **Chapel of sv Václav**, by the south door, was built by Parler, and its rich decoration of semi-precious stones resembles the inside of a jewel casket.

A door in the south wall, recognizable by its seven ostentatious locks, leads to the coronation chamber, which houses the Bohemian **crown jewels**, including the gold crown of St Wenceslas. At the centre of the choir, within a fine Renaissance grill, cherubs lark about on the sixteenth-century marble **Imperial Mausoleum**.

Old Royal Palace

The **Old Royal Palace** (Starý královský palác), just across the courtyard from the south door of the cathedral, was home to the princes and kings of Bohemia from the eleventh to the seventeenth centuries. The massive **Vladislav Hall** (Vladislavský sál) is where the early Bohemian kings were elected, and where every president since Masaryk has been sworn into office.

St George's Basilica (Bazilika sv Jiří)

St George's Basilica (50Kč), Prague's most beautiful Romanesque monument, on the square to the east of St Vitus, is fronted by quite a crude-looking red facade. Inside it is meticulously restored to re-create the honey-coloured basilica that replaced the original tenth-century church in 1173. Concerts are often held in its stunning interior.

Golden Lane

Golden Lane (Zlatá ulička) is a blind and crowded alley of miniature sixteenth-century cottages in dolly-mixture colours. It's apparently so called because Rudolf II installed his community of alchemists there to ensure that if they did succeed in turning anything to gold, they wouldn't be able to escape with the formula. A plaque at no. 22 commemorates Franz Kafka's brief sojourn here during World War I. There's a 50Kč entry charge during the day, but after 6pm when the guards and stallholders have shut up shop, you can wander through for free, appreciating the distinct lack of jostling crowds.

The Royal Gardens

North of the castle walls, across the peaceful, tree-lined **Powder Bridge** (Prasný most), is the entrance to the **Royal Gardens** (Královská zahrada; April–Oct daily 10am–6pm; free), founded in the early sixteenth century and still the best-kept gardens in the country, with fountains, immaculately cropped lawns and explosively bright flowerbeds in spring.

Šternberg Palace

Hradčanské náměstí fans out from the castle's main gates, surrounded by the oversized palaces of the old nobility. A passage down the side of the Archbishop's Palace leads to the early eighteenth-century **Šternberg Palace** (Tues–Sun 10am–6pm; 150Kč), housing the National Gallery's relatively modest Old European **art collection**.

Lobkowicz Palace

A new permanent exhibition (Jiřská 3, Hradčany; Tues–Sun 9am–5pm; 20Kč) is housed in the **Lobkowicz Palace**, a stunningly refurbished wing of the palace complex, and includes Old Masters, original manuscripts and fine musical instruments. The exhibits were seized from the family by the Nazis in 1939, then again by the Communists in 1945 and finally recovered in 1990.

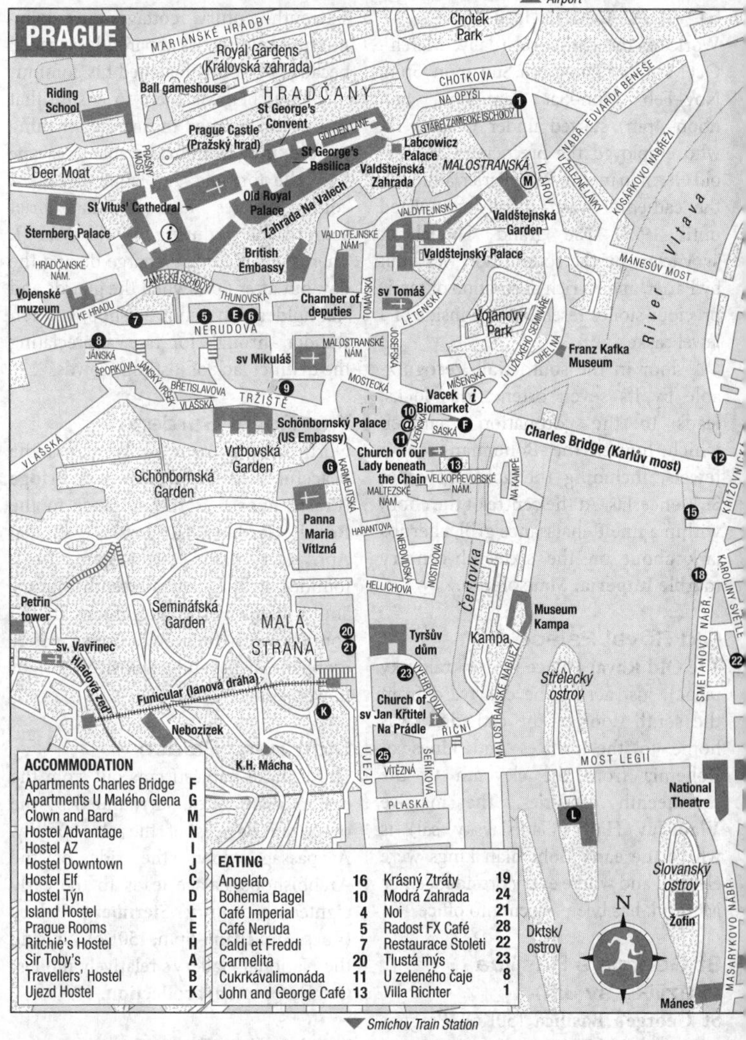

Sv Mikuláš

Malostranské náměstí is the main square in Malá Strana and houses the former Jesuit seminary and church of **sv Mikuláš** (daily 9am–4/5pm; tower: April–Oct daily 10am–6pm; Nov–March Sat & Sun 10am–5pm; free), possibly the most magnificent Baroque building in the city. The High Baroque interior is incredible – the **fresco** in the nave alone covers over 1500 square metres.

Petřín tower

Heading south of the main square, a continuation of Karmelitská brings you to the **funicular railway** up **Petřín hill** (daily 9am–11.20/11.30pm; every 10–15min; 50Kč), a lush green space perfect for a picnic.

Charles Bridge

Linking Staré Město to Malá Strana is the **Charles Bridge** (Karlův most), the

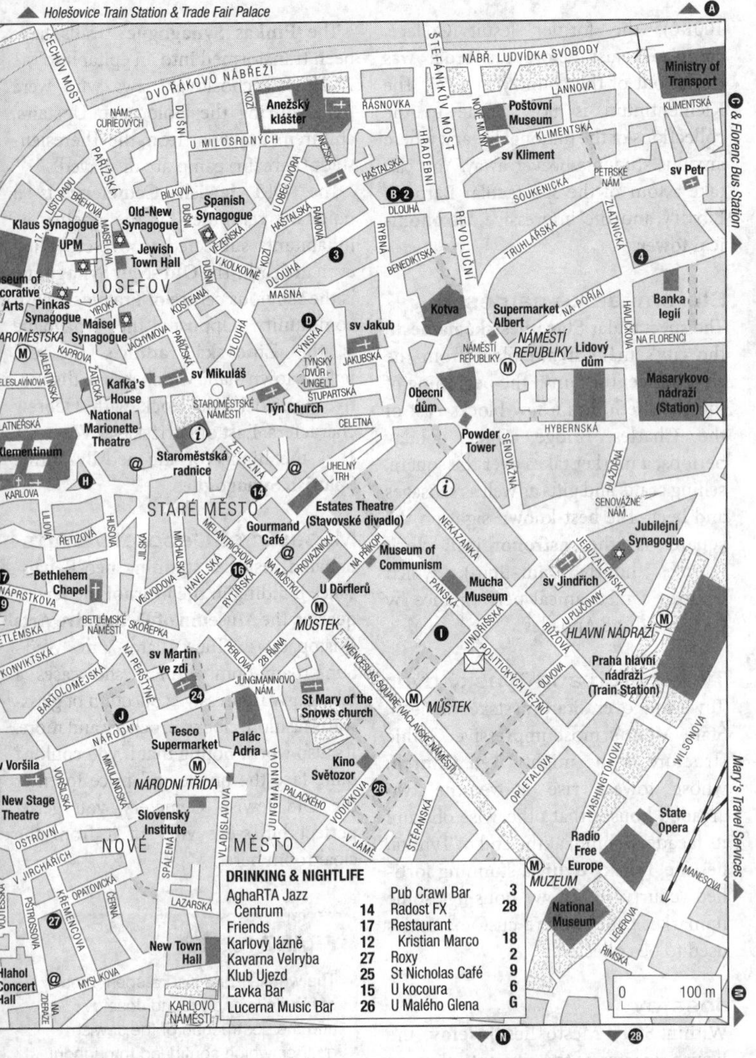

city's most famous monument, begun in 1357. The **statues** that line it – brilliant pieces of Jesuit propaganda added during the Counter-Reformation – have made it renowned throughout Europe and it is choked with tourists throughout the year. Don't forget to touch the little golden dog at the base of the statue of John of Nepomuk (the country's patron saint, who was thrown off the bridge by Wenceslas IV because he refused to divulge the queen's confessions); it shines from having been rubbed so much. You'll also meet the love of your life on Charles Bridge, apparently, so look out. Also look out for pickpockets, who are, sadly, more guaranteed.

Klementinum

On the north side of the Charles Bridge is the massive **Klementinum** (Mon–Fri 2–6/7pm, Sat & Sun 10/11am–6/7pm;

100Kč), the former Jesuit College, completed just before the order was turfed out of the country in 1773. The Klementinum is now home to the collections of the national library, where anxious students beaver away. You can take a tour of the spectacular Baroque Library and the impressive **astronomical tower**.

Staroměstské náměstí

The spectacular **Staroměstské náměstí**, the city's main marketplace from the eleventh century until the beginning of the twentieth, lies a few blocks east of the Charles Bridge. Over holiday periods, a market takes over the square, selling crafts and gifts as well as sausages and beer. The best-known sight on the square is the **astronomical clock** (chimes hourly 9am–9pm), which features a mechanical performance by Christ and the Apostles.

Týn Church and Týnský dvur

Towering over Staroměstské náměstí, Staré Město's most impressive Gothic structure is the mighty **Týn Church**, whose towers rise above the two arcaded houses that otherwise obscure its facade. Behind, at the end of Týnská, lies the **Týnský dvur**, a stunning fortified courtyard (now housing some upmarket cafés) where customs duties used to be collected.

Josefov

Within Staré Město lies **Josefov**, the Jewish quarter of the city until the end of the nineteenth century, when this ghetto area was demolished in order to create a beautiful bourgeois district on Parisian lines. Most synagogues and sights (including the cemetery) of Josefov are covered by one ticket, available from the synagogues themselves (daily except Sat & Jewish holidays 9am–4.30/6pm; 300Kč, plus 200Kč for the Old–New Synagogue; Ⓦwww.jewishmuseum.cz).

The **Pinkas Synagogue**'s walls have been transformed into an epitaph to the 77,297 Czechoslovak Jews who were killed during the Holocaust. Upstairs, children's drawings from the Theresienstadt (Terezín) camp are displayed.

The **Old Jewish Cemetery** is a poignant reminder of the ghetto, its inhabitants subjected to overcrowding even in death. The **Old–New Synagogue** is the religious centre of Prague's Jewish community. Opposite the synagogue is the **Židovská radnice**, the old Jewish town hall, which has a distinctive anticlockwise clock with Hebrew characters. East of Pařížská, at Vězenská 1, is the highly ornate neo-Byzantine **Spanish Synagogue**.

Museum of Decorative Arts

Situated inside a stunning neo-Renaissance building in the heart of the Jewish quarter, the **Museum of Decorative Arts** (Listopadu 2; Tues 10am–7pm, Wed–Sun 10am–6pm; 120Kč) showcases a fabulously impressive collection of glassware, fashion, clocks, crockery and more. It's also worth noting that if you couldn't quite face the queue and price to enter the Old Jewish Cemetery, you get a perfect bird's-eye view of it from the cloakroom here.

FRANZ KAFKA

The writer **Franz Kafka** spent most of his life in and around Josefov, and the destruction of the Jewish quarter, which continued throughout his childhood, had a profound effect on his psyche. He was born at what is now náměstí Franze Kafky 5, and there's an excellent, informative Franz Kafka **museum** on the other side of the river, at Cihelna 2b (daily 10am–6pm; 120Kč). As well as first editions and manuscripts of the majority of his works, the museum displays letters, photographs, diaries and drawings that give a fascinating insight Into Kafka's life and work.

The National Theatre

In Nové Město, at the river end of Národní, stands the gold-crested **National Theatre**, completed in 1881, a proud symbol of the Czech nation. Refused money by the Austrian state, Czechs of all classes dug deep into their pockets to raise funds for the venture themselves.

The Mucha Museum

A turning halfway along Na příkopě leads to the **Mucha Museum**, at Panská 7 (daily 10am–4/6pm; 120Kč), dedicated to the most famous Czech practitioner of Art Nouveau, Alfons Mucha.

Obecní dům

On náměstí Republiky stands the **Obecní dům**, the **Municipal House**. Begun in 1903, it was decorated inside and out with the help of almost every artist connected with the Czech Art Nouveau, or Secession, movement. You can take a guided **tour** of the interior (also in English); tickets are available from the information centre inside (daily 10am–6pm; 150Kč).

Museum of Communism

Situated on the first floor, ironically above *McDonalds* and next to the casino, the **Museum of Communism**, Na Přikopě 10 (daily 9am–9pm; 180Kč), presents a vivid account of all aspects of life under communism, including politics, daily life, history, labour camps and much more. The replicas of classrooms and barren shops are particularly memorable and the presentation of artefacts and information with music and interviews is thoughtful and interesting.

Wenceslas Square

The pivot of modern Prague and the political focus of the events of 1989 is **Wenceslas Square** (Václavské náměstí). The square's history of protest goes back to the Prague Spring of 1968: towards the top end, there's a small **memorial** to the victims of Communism, the most famous of whom, the 21-year-old student **Jan Palach**, set himself alight on this very spot in 1969 in protest against the Soviet occupation. Now it's a glut of capitalism, with big-name shops competing for space.

Trade Fair Palace: The Museum of Modern Art

One excellent reason to hop on a tram is to visit the city's modern art museum, housed in a stylish 1920s functionalist building, known as the **Trade Fair Palace** (Veletržní palác; Tues–Sun 10am–6pm; 100Kč for each floor or 250Kč for all four; tram #5 from nám. Republiky), on Dukelských hrdinů 47. The museum houses Czech art, as well as works by Klimt, Picasso and the French Impressionists.

Arrival and information

Air Prague's airport, Ruzyně (☎220 113 314, Ⓦwww.csl.cz), is 10km northwest of the city. The cheapest way of getting into town is to take local bus #119 (4am–midnight; every 7–15min; 20min) to Dejvická metro station, the start of line A, which will take you directly to the centre of town, or local bus #179 to Nove Butovice metro station on line B, if you're staying further south. Alternatively, the ČEDAZ express minibus (5.30am–9.30pm; every 30min; 20min to Dejvická, 40min–1hr to city centre) stops first at Dejvická metro station and terminates at náměstí Republiky (90Kč). "Fixed-price" taxis are expensive, at around 700Kč per taxi to the centre. There are internet terminals at the airport in *Café Mattoni* in Departure Terminal 2.

Train Arriving from the west, you're most likely to end up at Praha hlavní nádraží, the main station, where international trains terminating in Prague arrive. It's only a short walk to Wenceslas Square from here (inadvisable at night), and the station has its own metro stop on line C, a direct line to Museum on Wenceslas Square, and with connections to the main sights. International expresses that are passing through Prague usually stop only at Praha Holešovice station, north of the city centre (metro Nádraží Holešovice). Some trains from Moravia and Slovakia wind up at the central Praha Masarykovo station (metro Náměstí Republiky),

and trains from the south at Praha Smíchov station (metro Smíchovské nádraží).

Bus The main bus station is Praha-Florenc on the eastern edge of Staré Město (metro Florenc).

Bicycle rental and tours 24 Dlouhá (daily 9am–10pm; ⓣ732 388 880, ⓦwww.prahabike.cz). Organized tours around Prague and the surrounding countryside, and bike rental 440Kč/6hr.

Internet *Gourmand Café*, Rytirska. Internet terminals in the back, behind hundreds of cakes in a slightly bizarre 1970s setting; Picture gallery, Kamzíkova (daily 10am–10pm; 1.5Kč/min), and also cheap international calls; *Globe* (see p.297; daily 10am–midnight; 1.50 Kč/min) also has several fast terminals.

Tourist office The Prague Information Service, or PIS (Pražská informačni služba), has several branches around town; main office at Na příkopě 20 (Mon–Fri 9am–6/7pm, Sat 9am–3/5pm; April–Oct also Sun 9am–5pm; ⓦwww.pis.cz). The staff speak English, but their helpfulness varies; they can usually answer most enquiries, and organize accommodation, sell maps, guides and theatre tickets. There's also a good information centre on Mostecká 4 (daily 9am–10pm; ⓣ257 214 500), on the right-hand side inside the passage before Charles Bridge on Malá Strana. For events listings, pick up English-language monthly *Prague Events* or *Heart of Europe*.

City transport

Central Prague is small enough to walk around (Prague Castle to Wenceslas Square takes around 30–40min), and this is the most interesting and convenient way to get around. Having said that, the transport systems are pleasant and efficient.

Tickets There are two main tickets: the 26Kč *přestupní jízdenka* is valid for 75min (1hr 30min off-peak), and allows you to change metro lines, trams and buses as often as you like; the 15Kč *nepřestupní jízdenka* allows you to travel for up to 15min on a single tram or bus, or up to four stops on the metro. Buy tickets from a tobacconist, kiosk or the ticket machines inside metro stations and at some tram stops, then validate them on board or at the metro entrance. To take a large backpack on public transport you'll need an extra half-fare ticket.

Travel passes If you're going to be using the system a lot, it's worth getting a travel pass (*Časová jízdenka*; 100Kč/24hr, 330Kč/72hr); remember to validate it when you first use it. Plain-clothes inspectors check tickets – it's a fine of 400Kč on the spot if it's not valid.

Metro The metro (daily 5am–midnight) is the fastest and most useful form of city transport, and with only three lines, it's easy to navigate as well.

Trams Running every 10–15min, trams navigate Prague's hills and cobbles with remarkable dexterity. Tram #22, whose run includes Vinohrady and Hradčany, is a good way to sightsee, but beware of pickpockets. Night trams (numbers #51–#59; midnight–4.30am; every 30min) all pass by Lazarská in Nové Město.

Taxis To avoid being ripped off, best bet is to call the English-speaking AAA (ⓣ140 14; 34Kč plus 25Kč per 1km).

Accommodation

Prague's hotels are exorbitant for what you get; as a result, most tourists on a budget now stay in private rooms or hostels, with private rooms often best value if there's more than one of you. The hostels are often a little out of the centre. During holidays and over the summer, rooms get booked up fast so arrange accommodation in advance. The main international train stations and the airport have accommodation agencies dealing with hotels, pensions and private rooms too. A good one to try is the extremely friendly and helpful Mary's Travel Services (Italská 31, Vinohrady; daily 9am–7pm: ⓣ222 254 007, ⓦwww.marys.cz). Also worth checking out is ⓦwww.city-info.cz, which often has fantastic-value late deals on apartments and rooms. Prague's university, the Karolinum, rents out over a thousand student rooms in summer; contact the booking office at Voršilská 1, Nové Město (Mon–Fri only; ⓣ224 930 010; beds available July to mid-Sept; from around 350Kč).

Hostels

Clown and Bard Borivojova 102 ⓣ222 716 453, ⓦwww.clownandbard.com. If you don't mind being a little way out of the city and can sleep through lots of rowdy noise, this lively hostel is a good bet. Tram #5, #9 or #26 from the main train station. Dorms 250Kč, doubles 1000Kč.

Hostel Advantage Sokolská 11 ⓣ224 914 062, ⓦwww.advantagehostel.cz. Hardly prepossessing, but offering clean, functional accommodation, with kitchens and breakfast included. HI affiliated. Metro stop I.P. Pavlova (or take tram #22 to get there), and it's a 5min walk down Sokolská. Dorms 420Kč, doubles 900Kč.

Hostel AZ Jindřišská 5, Nové Město ⓣ224 241 664 or 777 206 892, ⓦwww.hostel-az.cz. Clean, new hostel with friendly staff, a smoky lounge and self-catering facilities. The entrance is through the shopping centre alleyway. Dorms 320Kč, doubles 100Kč.

Hostel Downtown Národní 19, Nové Město ⓣ224 240 570, ⓦwww.hosteldowntown.cz. Clean, basic HI-affiliated hostel. Dorms 450Kč, doubles 950Kč.

Hostel Elf Husitská 11 ⓣ222 540 963, ⓦwww.hostelelf.com. Laid-back, well-equipped hostel with cheerfully painted interior. From Florenc metro station, it's a 5min walk, or take bus #133 or #207. Dorm 320Kč, doubles 730Kč.

Hostel Týn Týnská 19, Staré Město ⓣ224 828 519, ⓦwww.hostel-tyn.web2001.cz. Excellent location, simple but clean rooms and dorms. Metro Náměstí Republiky. Dorms 400Kč, doubles 1200Kč.

Island Hostel Střelecký ostrov 36 ⓣ224 932 991, ⓦwww.travellers.cz. Great location, 10min from the central metro station of Mustek but on a quiet island in the middle of the Vltava river. Basic, clean dorms and an open-air cinema. Open June 23–Aug 29. Dorms 300Kč.

Ritchie's Hostel Karlova 13, Staré Město ⓣ222 221 229, ⓦwww.ritchieshostel.cz. A hostel-cum-hotel ideally located between the Staroměstské náměstí and the Charles Bridge. Internet access. Metro Staroměstská. Dorms 320Kč, doubles 1700Kč.

Sir Toby's Dělnická 24 ⓣ246 032 610, ⓦwww.sirtobys.com. This hostel is well worth the journey out of the centre. There's a relaxed cellar bar, a lounge with board games, free internet, rustic kitchen and clean, spacious dorms. You can walk from metro stop Nádraží Holešovice, or from Vltavská metro station, take any tram departing to the left and get off at Dělnická. Dorm 360Kč, doubles 1600Kč.

Travellers' Hostel Dlouhá 33, Staré Město ⓣ224 826 662, ⓦwww.travellers.cz. Centrally located party hostel, with a bar, laundry and internet access. Metro Náměstí Republiky. Dorms 350Kč, doubles 1300Kč.

Újezd Hostel U lanové dráhy 3 ⓣ257 216 057, ⓦwww.travellers.cz. Another branch of the travellers' hostel, centrally located at the bottom of Petřin hill. Tram #12, #20 or #22 to Újezd from metro Malostranská (or you can walk). Open June 16–Aug 29. Dorms 250Kč.

Rooms and apartments

Apartments Charles Bridge Mostecka 6 ⓣ605 229 791, ⓦwww.apartmentcharlesbridge.com. Comfortably furnished rooms with excellently equipped kitchens. Reasonably priced. Doubles 1700Kč.

Apartments U Malého Glena Karmelitská 23 ⓣ257 531 717, ⓦwww.malyglen.cz. Four comfortable self-catering flats above a popular jazz bar a few minutes' walk from Charles Bridge. Excellent value. Doubles 1350Kč.

Prague Rooms Nerudova 10 ⓣ257 532 921. Run by the friendly Skokanovas, these self-catering apartments are unbelievably central, spacious, and offer stunning views over Prague. Undoubtedly the most impressive bargain in Malá Strana. Doubles 1000Kč.

Eating

While traditional Czech food still predominates in the city's pubs, Prague now has a wide range of restaurants offering anything from French to Japanese cuisine, and a lovely variety of cafés. There's a big Tesco Supermarket at Národní Třída where you can stock up if you're planning to do your own cooking, as well as a large Supermarket Albert on Náměstí Republiky. Vacke Biomarket on Mostecka is the closest supermarket to Charles Bridge – but the other shops are cheaper.

Cafés

Angelato all natural ice cream Rytiøska. The best ice cream in Prague in a tiny, unassuming little shop.

Bohemia Bagel Lázenská 19. Bagels, croissants and coffee in a laid-back atmosphere, as well as internet (when it works). There are also branches on Masná 2 and Tylovo nám 1.

Café Imperial Na poříčí 15, Staré Město ⓣ246 011 440. Newly refurbished to its Habsburg-era splendour, this *Kaffeehaus* has a new lease of life, serving up deliciously heavy little cakes and super-strength coffee in dinky cups to students and gossiping ladies alike.

Café Neruda 18 Nerudova. Charming little café ideal for people-watching. Sandwiches 80Kč.

Caldi et Freddi Nerudova 44, Malá Strana. Though the interior is plush, the prices in this café are remarkably reasonable and the sandwiches and cakes are great. Enjoy a huge apple strudel and coffee for 99Kč.

Cukrkávalimonáda Lázenská 7. A gorgeous little café in an unassuming square, where both the interior and staff are soothingly calm. Great breakfasts. Mains 80–200Kč.

John and George Café Velkopřevorské Nám 4 ⓣ257 217 736. Great food and cool candlelit interior and tables backing onto a stunning garden boasting the oldest tree in Prague, just behind the John Lennon wall. Perfect.

Krásný Ztráty Náprstkova 10, Staré Město. A sprawling gallery, café and bar popular with Prague's arty types. The *nakládaný Hermelín*, pickled cheese stuffed with garlic and chillies, is delicious here.

U zeleného čaje Nerudova 19. Cosy little teahouse with only four tables, serving dozens of different teas.

Restaurants

Carmelita Újezd 31, Malá Strana ⓣ257 312 564. Divine Italian food in a rustic interior. If you want a break from Czech food, this is just the ticket. Risotto with squid ink 130Kč.

Modrá Zahrada Narodni 37. Tasty, cheap pizza and pasta in a cheerful low-key setting from the "Blue Garden" mini-chain. Pizza 120Kč.

Noi Újezd 19 ⓣ257 311 411. Gloriously atmospheric Thai restaurant and bar with delicious food – the *tom yum koong* is perfect. Mains from 120Kč.

Radost FX Café Bělehradská 120, Vinohrady. Superb vegetarian food attracts an ultra-fashionable crowd. Open till very late; brunch at weekends. Mains 145–285Kč.

Restaurace Stoleti Karolíny Svetle 21, Staré Město ⓣ222 220 008. Exceptionally good Czech food in a cosy setting. This place fills up quickly so book ahead or arrive early. The venison skewers are delicious. Mains 120–250Kč.

Tlustá mýs Všehrdova 19, Malá Strana. Cosy cellar bar, restaurant and gallery, offering reasonably priced, hearty Czech food washed down with Pilsner Urquell. Mains 60–250Kč.

Drinking and nightlife

For no-nonsense boozing you need to head for a pub (*pivnice*), which invariably serves excellent beer by the half-litre, but many of which close around 11pm. For late-night drinking, head for one of the clubs or all-night bars. If you fancy having your evening organized for you and meeting other travellers, give the notorious Prague Pub Crawl a go. For 390 Kč, you get an hour's unlimited boozing, followed by entry to four bars and a club. And free water and a kiss, you'll be glad to hear. Tours are on every night at 8 and 9pm. Go to the *Pub Crawl bar*, Dlouhá 24 (ⓣ731 067 775, ⓦwww.pubcrawl.cz).

TREAT YOURSELF

Villa Richter St Wenceslas' Vineyard, Staré Zámecké Schody 6, Pražský Hrad ⓣ257 219 079, ⓦwww.villarichter.cz. Stunning views over the rolling vineyards and out on to Prague accompanied by impeccable formal service and divine food. Alternatively, the terrace has a coffee and cake deal for 99Kč – perfect for soaking up the sun after a walk around Prague Castle.

Bars and pubs

Friends Náprstkova 1, Staré Město. A friendly, laid-back gay/lesbian cellar bar in the old town.

Kavárna Velryba Opatovická 24 ⓣ249 12 391. Meaning "whale", the inside of this underground pub and gallery is decorated with sea-coloured scales. It's full of Prague's young intellectuals, debating noisily and eating homely cuisine. Pork escallops with damson sauce 120Kč.

Klub Újezd Újezd 18. Smoky after-hours bar with a giant metal snake erected above the bar.

Lavka Bar Novotného Lávka 1 ⓦwww.lavka-nights.cz. True, the food is probably a little beyond budget means, but this is an awesome place to enjoy a beer (50Kč) and soak in the view from the riverside. The attached club has popular local DJs and is open until 2am.

Restaurant Kristian Marco Smetanovo Nábø. Located on a pier where you can dip your feet in the water and admire the passing swans while enjoying your beer. Live music. Beer 32Kč.

St Nicholas Café Tržiště 10 ⓣ257 530 204, ⓦwww.stnicholascafe.com. Atmospheric cellar bar serving delicious cheap pizza (around 120Kč) till late, with occasional live music and great cocktails.

U kocoura (The Cat). Nerudova. An unexpectedly genuine smoky Czech pub, with big wooden tables where everyone crowds around hearty food and lots of beer.

U Malého Glena Karmelitská 23 ⓣ257 531 717, ⓦwww.malyglen.cz. Dark, smoky place buzzing with locals. Good restaurant upstairs serving Czech staples and burgers at around 120Kč, and a tiny but very popular jazz venue downstairs.

Clubs

Karlovy lázně Novotného lávka 1, Staré Město ⓦwww.karlovylazne.cz. A staple of the Prague club scene, this is a high-tech super-cheesy mega-club by the Charles Bridge; techno on the top floor, progressively more retro as you descend to the internet café on the ground floor.

Lucerna Music Bar Vodičkova 36, Nové Město ⓦwww.musicbar.cz. Central, small dance space, with live, mainly indie, music. A staple of Prague nightlife.

Radost FX Bělehradská 120, Vinohrady ⓦwww.radostfx.cz. Still the slickest (and latest-opening – till 5am) all-round dance-club venue in Prague, with a great veggie café-restaurant attached.

Entertainment

Theatre

Theatre in Prague is thriving, though unless you know the language your scope is limited, but there's a tradition of innovative mime and puppetry.

The Black Light Theatre of Prague ⓦwww.blacktheatreprague.cz. With nine venues in all, it specializes in glow-in-the-dark non verbal performances, which make creative use of lighting and are ideal for non-Czech speakers. These performances include impressive dance, circus, puppetry and music. Tickets are available from various agencies, including Ticketpro (Rytířská 12 ⓣ296 329 999, ⓦwww.ticketpro.cz) as well as from the venues and tourist offices. The one on Mostecká 4 (ⓣ257 214 500), on the right-hand side inside the passage just after Charles Bridge on Malá Strana, often has special offers and late deals on tickets.

National Marionette Theatre Žatecká 1 ⓣ224 819 323, ⓦwww.mozart.cz. The most popular puppet theatre, which performs Mozart's *Don Giovanni* for marionettes.

Cinemas

Kino Světozor Vodičkova 41, Nové Město ⓣ224 946 824, ⓦwww.kinosvetozor.cz. One of the best cinemas, which shows English-language films with Czech subtitles, and lots of international arthouse movies.

Pop and rock music

For live music, the classical scene still has the edge in Prague, though there are also some good jazz clubs.

AghaRTA Jazz Centrum Železná 16, Staré Město ⓦwww.agharta.cz. Prague's best jazz club, with a good mix of top international names and local bands. Concerts daily from 9pm.

Roxy Dlouhá 33, Staré Město ⓦwww.roxy.cz. Once a cinema, now a live music venue with a gallery and theatre, as well as club nights.

Classical music

Throughout the year, concert halls, churches and palaces host concerts. In the summer open-air concerts and plays are organized at Hradčany. For more information and tickets, try Bohemia Ticket, Na Příkopech 16 (ⓣ224 215 031, ⓦwww.bohemiaticket.cz), or ⓣ224 224 706, ⓦwww.classicconcertstickets.com.

Estates Theatre (Stavovské divadlo). Ovocný trh 1, Staré Město ⓦwww.narodni-divadlo.cz. Theatre, ballet and opera in the venue that premiered Mozart's *Don Giovanni.*

Národní Divadlo Národní 2, Nové Město ⓦwww.narodni-divadlo.cz. Grand nineteenth-century theatre with a highly ornate interior showing theatre, ballet and opera.

Prague State Opera Wilsonova 4, Nové Město ⓦwww.opera.cz. The city's second-choice venue for opera and ballet.

Rudolfinum Alsovo nábřeží 12, Staré Město ⓦwww.rudolfinum.cz. Stunning neo-Renaissance concert hall and home to the Czech Philharmonic.

Shopping

Globe Pštrossova 6. Excellent English-language bookshop with a buzzy café.

Golden Lane Prague Castle. Craft and gift shops aplenty in the old alchemists' quarter.

Havelske Trziste Havelska. Main open-air market in the city centre, just a couple of minutes' walk from Wenceslas Square. Sells crafts, fruit and vegetables.

Nový Smíchov Mall Plzenksa 8. A huge shopping mall with high-street names and a supermarket.

Pařížská For amazing designer window-shopping, head to this lovely leafy avenue in Josefov.

Wenceslas Square and its surrounding streets are the best places to buy souvenirs and jewellery; also book and department stores.

Directory

Embassies and consulates Australia (honorary), Klimentská 10, Nové Město ⓣ296 578 350; Canada, Muchova 6, Hradčany ⓣ272 101 800; New Zealand, Dykova 19, Vinohrady ⓣ222 514 672; Ireland, Tržiště 13, Malá Strana ⓣ257 530 061; UK, Thunovská 14, Malá Strana ⓣ257 402 111; US, Tržiště 15, Malá Strana ⓣ257 530 663.

Hospital Na Františku Hospital, Na Františku 847 ⓣ222 801 111; emergencies (English spoken) ⓣ248 102 80/69.

Laundry Laundryland, Londýnska 71, Nové Město (daily 8am–10pm), has a basement bar. Several other locations around town (ⓦwww.laundryland.cz).

Left luggage There are lockers or left-luggage offices at all of the train stations.

Pharmacies Palackého 5, Nové Město (Mon–Fri 7am–7pm, Sat & Sun 8am–noon; ⓣ224 946 982); Štefánikova 6, Malá Strana (24hr; ⓣ257 320 918).

Post office Jindřišská 14, Nové Město (daily 2am–midnight).

Moving on

Train Berlin (every 2hr; 4hr 45min); Bratislava (daily; 5hr 20min); České Budějovice (up to 14

daily; 2hr 15min–3hr); Dresden (daily; 2hr 30min); Karlovy Vary (3 daily; 4hr 5min–5hr 10min); Olomouc (1–2 hourly; 3hr 10min–3hr 30min); Plzeň (hourly; 1hr 40min).

Bus Most buses depart from Florenc bus station. For Student Agency buses, book ahead (see p.283; main office in Florenc bus station; ⓣ800 100 300, ⓦwww.studentagencybus.com.
Berlin (daily; 6hr 30min); Bratislava (up to 6 daily; 3–6hr); Brno (every 30min–1hr; 2hr 20min–3hr 30min); České Budějovice (up to 8 daily; 2hr 30min–3hr 25min); Český Krumlov (2–6 daily; 2hr 40min–3hr 25min); Karlovy Vary (hourly; 2hr 10min–2hr 40min); Kutná Hora (hourly on weekdays; 1hr 15min).

Bohemia

South Bohemia, bordered by the Šumava Mountains, is the least spoilt of the Bohemian regions; its largest town by far is the brewing centre of **České Budějovice**, and its chief attraction, aside from the thickly forested countryside, is a series of pretty, Disney-esque medieval towns, whose undisputed gem is **Český Krumlov**.

Neighbouring **West Bohemia** has a similar mix of rolling woods and hills, and its capital **Plzeň** is a lively student town and the home of Pilsen beer and the Škoda empire. As you approach the German border, Bohemia's famous **spa region** unfolds, with magnificent resorts such as **Karlovy Vary** enjoying sparkling reputations.

KUTNÁ HORA

Best done as a day-trip from Prague, **KUTNÁ HORA** has a laid-back, sleepy atmosphere. Once one of the most important centres in Bohemia, today the pretty medieval lanes provide a calming respite from the teeming crowds of Prague. The ground beneath Kutná Hora is riddled with exhausted silver and gold mines – from 1308, Bohemia's royal mint at Kutná Hora converted the silver into coins called Groschen which were used all over Central Europe.

What to see and do

Kutná Hora's pretty medieval centre is focused on attractive but unassuming main square Palackého naměstí, with the massive towers of sv Jakub and sv Barbora looming over the town.

The ossuary at Sedlec

Kutná Hora's most famously macabre monument is the **ossuary** (or *kostnice*), containing over 40,000 complete sets of human bones (daily: April–Sept 8am–6pm; Oct–March 9am–noon & 1–4pm; 45Kč). The ancient Gothic chapel was scattered with holy earth from Golgotha in the twelfth century, and the ensuing vogue for being buried here, as well as the number of dead brought on by the Plague, ensured that the piles of bones mounted up until the nineteenth century, when František Rint was given leave to get creative with them. Its highlight is perhaps the chandelier, which makes use of every bone in the human body. The ossuary is a ten-minute walk from the train station. Otherwise, take bus #1 or #4 from town to the giant tobacco factory 3km northeast of the centre, and the ossuary is behind the Baroque church of the Assumption of Our Lady.

Cathedral of sv Barbora

The hill that leads to the imposing **Cathedral of sv Barbora** (Tues–Sun: April–Oct 9am–6pm; Nov–March 10am–4pm), bristling with pinnacles, finials and flying buttresses, is lined with impressive Baroque sculptures of saints similar to those on the Charles Bridge in Prague. On the right-hand side of the approach is the simple but majestic Jesuit College.

The Italian Court

From Palackého naměstí, head down 28 října to the **Italian Court** where

Florentine craftsmen once minted coins. Entrance is by thirty-minute guided tour only (daily: April–Sept 9am–6pm; March & Oct 10am–5pm; Nov–Feb 10am–4pm; 130Kč). The **park** next door runs down to the river and is a pleasant picnic spot.

The Mining Museum

In a tiny medieval fort at the junction of Barborská and Ruthardská, just north of the Jesuit College, the **Mining Museum** (April–Oct Tues–Sun 9/10am–5/6pm; 130Kč) has a collection of silver; visitors can descend into the mines wearing mad-inventor-style white coats and goggles.

Arrival and information

Bus The most straightforward way to get here is to take a bus from Florenc in Prague (4 daily; 1hr 30min); it drops you close to the city centre.
Train From Prague the train takes less than an hour, but the station is a good way out, near Sedlec (although useful for visiting the ossuary). Take the #1 or #4 bus into the town centre (where buses from Prague arrive), or one stop further to sv Barbora.
Tourist office Palackého náměstí 377 (April–Sept daily 9am–6pm; Oct–March Mon–Fri 9am–5pm, Sat & Sun 10am–4pm; ⓣ327 512 378, ⓦwww.kh.cz). Can book private rooms and has internet access.

Eating and drinking

Barborská Bar Barborská 35. Possibly the tiniest cocktail bar in the world, filled with young, friendly locals.
Restaurant Kometa Barborská 29. Enjoy a view of the church with plates of tasty traditional food.

ČESKÉ BUDĚJOVICE

ČESKÉ BUDĚJOVICE is all about beer. The town was built in 1265, and originally brewed its lager for the Holy Roman Emperor. In the seventeenth century war and fire pretty much destroyed the place but it was rebuilt by the Habsburgs in lavish style, and now its elegant arcaded squares and winding backstreets lined with cafés and bars are the perfect place to enjoy a Budvar (the original Budweiser).

What to see and do

The compact old town is only a five-minute walk from the train and bus stations, with the medieval grid plan leading to the magnificent central **náměstí Přemysla Otakara II**, one of Europe's largest market squares.

A guided tour around beer-distilling instruments and the science of brewing is of fairly limited interest, but obviously if you're here it's basically compulsory to visit the **Budvar brewery**. It's 2.5km up the road to Prague, on Karolíny Světlé (bus #2), and has a modern *pivnice* inside the nasty titanium-blue headquarters. You'll need to book ahead for the one-hour tours – don't forget to ask for them in English (daily 9am–4pm; 100Kč; ⓣ387 705 341, ⓦwww.budweiser.cz).

Arrival and information

Bus and train The town's train and bus stations are just a 5min walk from the old town: from the stations head west along the pedestrianized Lannova třída. There are several daily direct trains and buses from Prague; it's possible to make your visit a day-trip, but if you want to visit the brewery, you should consider staying overnight.
Tourist office Naměstí Přemysla Otakara 2 (May–Sept Mon–Fri 8.30am–6pm, Sat 8.30am–5pm, Sun 10am–noon & 12.30–4pm; Oct–April Mon–Fri 9am–4pm, Sat 9am–noon & 1–3pm; ⓣ386 801 413, ⓦwww.c-budejovice.cz).

Accommodation

Ask at the tourist office for accommodation in private rooms and in student halls in summer.
Penzion Centrum Biskupska 103 ⓣ387 311 801, ⓦwww.penzioncentrum.cz. Airy, comfortable rooms in a low-key pension situated just off the main square. Doubles 1200Kč.
Penzion U Výstaviště U Výstaviště 17. Student halls 30min outside the city on bus #1 from the bus station. Somewhat utilitarian, but clean and cheap. 270Kč per person.

Stromovká Autocamp ⓣ387 203 597. A pleasant campsite 2km southwest of town, with friendly owners. Bus #16 from Lidická třída. Tent 240Kč. April–Oct.

Eating and drinking

C K Solnice Česka. A pleasantly rough-around-the-edges bar with a cosy atmosphere and live jazz.
Restaurant Beran Žižkova 3. A hugely popular cellar restaurant and bar with eccentric interior decor. Czech and international food on the menu.

Moving on

Train Brno (4–5 daily; 4hr 20min); Český Krumlov (8 daily; 1hr); Plzeň (12–13 daily; 2hr–3hr 25min).
Bus Brno (3–6 daily; 3hr 30min–4hr 30min); Český Krumlov (every 15–30min; 25–50min).

ČESKÝ KRUMLOV

ČESKÝ KRUMLOV is a tiny, near-perfect medieval town with a fantastically over-the-top Renaissance castle and beautiful houses on its narrow cobbled streets, which earned UNESCO World Heritage status in 1992. Despite the crowds of trippers in high summer it's still a relaxing place to spend a couple of days.

What to see and do

The twisting River Vltava divides the town into two: the circular **Staré Město** on the right bank and the **Latrán** quarter on the hillier left. The chateau tower and the tower of sv Vitus, rising above the red rooftops of the main square, **náměsti Svornosti**, on the right bank, are good navigation landmarks.

Latrán Chateau

For centuries, the focal point of the town has been the Disney-esque **castle** in Latrán (Tues–Sun: April, May, Sept & Oct 9am–5pm; June–Aug 9am–6pm). It's possible to walk through some of the castle's grounds without a tour, but if you want to venture into the interesting bits, it's worth forking out. There's a choice of tours: tour 1 (240Kč) concentrates on the stunning Renaissance parts of the castle and tour 2 (180Kč) will take you into the eighteenth- and nineteenth-century quarters. Pricy tour 3 (380Kč) is worth joining if you can stretch to it, as it's the only way to view the impressive Rococo chateau theatre on the other side of the bridge.

The Eggenberg Brewery

The castle's former armoury on Latrán became the Eggenberg Brewery in 1630. You can have a look around it for 100Kč with no tastings (daily 11am–4pm; ⓣ380 711 225, ⓦwww.eggenberg.cz), or you can choose from tours with a range of freebies, the most extravagant being the 480Kč tour, which includes unlimited beer and food from the brewery's restaurant.

Egon Schiele Art Centrum

West of the square, on Široká, is the **Egon Schiele Art Centrum** (daily 10am–6pm; 120Kč; ⓦwww.schieleartcentrum.cz). The museum is devoted in part to the Austrian painter Egon Schiele, who lived here briefly in 1911 and caused a scandal by getting young local girls to pose naked for him. It also houses temporary exhibitions by contemporary artists.

Arrival and information

Bus and train The bus station is a 5min walk northeast of the inner town; the train station is further out, 1km from the chateau. In both cases, you will have to change at České Budějovice if coming from Prague.
Tourist office Náměstí Svornosti 2 (daily: April, May & Oct 9am–6pm; June & Sept 9am–7pm; July & Aug 9am–8pm; Nov–March 9am–5pm; ⓣ380 704 621, ⓦwww.ckrumlov.cz). Internet access is on the main square.

Accommodation

There are several campsites south of town along the road to Rožmberk but you'll need your own transport to get there.
Hostel Postel Rybářská 35 ⓣ226 201 910. Basic but thoughtfully furnished rooms arranged around a

pretty courtyard, with kitchen, internet access and laundry. Dorms 240Kč, doubles 600Kč.

Hostel Skippy Plesivecka 123 ⓣ 380 728 380, ⓦ www.skippy.wz.cz. Arty, homely hostel run by the friendly Skippy and Teresa, located right on the river. Self-catering facilities. Dorms 250Kč, doubles 600Kč.

Travellers Hostel Soukenická 43 ⓣ 380 711 345, ⓦ www.travellers.cz. Popular HI-affiliated hostel with cheerfully decorated rooms, internet, laundry, a rowdy bar and a kitchen. Dorms 300Kč, doubles 900Kč.

Eating and drinking

Cikánská Jizba Dlouhá 31. This small, unassuming "gypsy bar" has live local music and excellent simple food such as goulash (90Kč) and dumplings with sauerkraut (80Kč).

Horror Bar Nebeské Pastviny. An underground cavern covered in cobwebs and skulls, with ghouls and spiders hanging from the ceilings. Beware the absinthe cocktail, which will leave you feeling horrific for far longer than you intended.

U dwau Maryí Parkán 104. Friendly staff serve delicious traditional Bohemian cuisine. There's a lovely garden outside overlooking the river. Mains from 90Kč.

PLZEŇ

PLZEŇ is Bohemia's second city, with a population of around 175,000. With a lively student scene and an unending supply of (probably) the best beer in the world, it offers plenty to do both day and night.

What to see and do

The main square, náměstí Republiky, presents a full range of architectural styles, starting with the exalted heights of the Gothic **cathedral** of **sv Bartoloměj**, its green spire, the tallest in the country (daily 10am–6pm, 20Kč to climb the 300-odd steps to the top), reaching up almost 103m. Over the way rises the impressively sgraffitoed Renaissance old town hall. Also well worth a look is the Velká **synagogue** (April–Sept Mon–Fri & Sun 10am–6pm; Oct Mon–Fri & Sun 10am–5pm; Nov Mon–Fri 10am–4pm, Sun 10am–5pm; 50Kč adults, 35Kč students) with its unusual and flamboyant twin onion domes, and moving photographic and art exhibitions. It's the third largest synagogue in the world after those in Jerusalem and Budapest.

The Pilsner Urquell brewery

The reason most people come to Plzeň is to sample its famous 12° Plzeňský Prazdroj, better known as **Pilsner Urquell (Original Pilsner)** abroad. Beer has been brewed in the town since it was founded in 1295, but it wasn't until 1842 that the famous Bürgerliches Brauhaus was built, after a near-riot by the townsfolk over the declining quality of their brew. For a guided tour of the **brewery**, you can either book in advance or simply show up at 12.30pm or 2pm for tours in English. If you don't fancy going out to the brewery itself, check out the **Pivovarske Brewery Museum**, built in the original brewery just off Perlová instead, for explanations and a video on the art of brewing (daily: April–Dec 10am–6pm; Jan–March 10am–5pm; brewery only 120Kč, museum only 70Kč, combined ticket 200Kč; ⓣ 222 710 159, ⓦ www.prazdroj.cz/en). You could, of course, just settle for a half-litre or two at the vast **Na Spílce** pub (daily 11am–10pm), just inside the brewery's triumphal arch.

Arrival and information

Train and bus You can get to Plzeň from Prague 1hr 30min by either bus or train, making it just doable as a day-trip, although it's fun to stay a night or two. The main train station, Hlavní nádraží, is just a little east of the city centre. The bus terminal is on the west side of town. From both, the city centre is only a short walk (10min or so) . There are direct buses from Prague.

Tourist office Nám. Republiky 41 (daily: April–Sept 9am–7pm; Oct–March 9am–6pm; ⓣ 378 035 330, ⓦ www.plzen.eu).

Accommodation

Apartmaný Pod Černov Věži Lidická 112 ⓣ 608 370 011/776 370 042, ⓦ www.ubytovaniplzen.cz.

Bright, pleasant apartments located just above the Ergoline Solarium 100m from the main square. Doubles 800Kč.

Pension City Sady 5 května 52 ⓣ377 326 069, ⓦwww.pensioncityplzen.cz. Exceptionally friendly English-speaking staff in a bright, airy pension by the river. Doubles with breakfast 1400 Kč.

Pension V Solní Solní 8 ⓣ377 236 652, ⓦwww.volny.cz/pensolni. Cosy three-room pension just off the main square. Doubles with breakfast 1200Kč.

Eating and drinking

With its lively student population, Plzeň is full of unusual, fun places to eat, drink and be merry.

Anděl Vegetarian Restaurant, Café and Bar Bezručova 5–7. Delicious vegetarian food in the cosy upstairs restaurant (mains from 90 Kč), and a trendy bar two doors down with live music. Open until midnight.

Archa Veleslavinova 22. A buzzing cocktail bar that opens out on to a flowered courtyard and attracts an energetic crowd. Weekdays until 1am, weekends until 3am.

Café Corso Smetanovy Sady 6. Enjoy a cocktail topped with paper umbrellas or an iced coffee piled with cream in this popular café which plays great tunes.

Fresh Juice Bar Pražská 17. Amazing array of fresh vegetable and fruit juices at a hippy bar. Check out the unusual (legal) cannabis pharmacy round the back, where you can buy cannabis cosmetics and souvenir rolling papers.

Perlova Cajovna Perlova 10. A tiny oriental teahouse whose relaxed, incense-filled atmosphere makes it the perfect place to while away a wet afternoon.

Rango Pražská 10 ⓣ377 329 969. Divine Italian food served in the arched stone cellar which once formed part of the historical Plzeň underground. The restaurant section upstairs is non smoking. Pasta dishes 110Kč.

U Salzmannů Pražská 8. Traditional Czech dishes in a cosy, popular setting. Mains 79–499Kč.

Moving on

Train České Budějovice (3–4 daily; 1hr 30min–2hr); Prague (hourly; 1hr 40min).

Bus Karlovy Vary (8–9 daily; 1hr 30min–1hr 50min); Prague (hourly; 1hr 20min–1hr 50min).

KARLOVY VARY

KARLOVY VARY, undisputed king of the Bohemian spas, has a surprisingly continental atmosphere – you could be forgiven for thinking you were on the French Riviera or in one of Italy's affluent seaside resorts. The town is picture-perfect, though it does get over run by tourists. The area commonly referred to as the centre is in the northern part of the town, while the spa quarter is further south.

What to see and do

Unfortunately, it's almost inevitable that your first sight of Karlovy Vary will include the eye-sore communist-era *Hotel Thermal* (ⓦwww.thermal.cz). The best way to deal with this is to climb up onto its roof and enjoy the (tepid but pleasant) open-air spring water swimming pool (daily 8.30am–8pm; 80Kč). Otherwise, turn your back on the *Thermal* and wander along the river, bracing yourself to sip at the medicinal water at the **colonnades** along the way. It tastes a bit like fizzy mucus, but this can be diluted by eating the over priced *oblaten*, sweet wafers, designed specifically to take away the taste. You'll see all the visitors solemnly sipping out of teapot-like drinking cups, which apparently stop the water from staining your teeth – you can take along a plastic bottle and risk the discolouration, or buy your own drinking cup in a souvenir kiosk for an eye-watering 200Kč. The valley narrows in front of the graceful **Mlýnská kolonáda**. The most powerful of the town's twelve springs is the **Vřídlo**, which belches out over 2500 gallons every hour in 12m fountains, and is housed in the modern **Vřídelní kolonáda** (daily 6am–7pm).

For stunning views and gorgeous greenery, walk up to the forested hill, or take the **funicular** behind the *Grand Hotel Pupp* (Feb–May & Sept–Dec 9am–6pm; June–Aug 9am–7pm; every 15min; 50Kč return). You can enjoy a beer in the garden of the *Diana* restaurant at the top.

Moser glassworks and museum

The glassworks that churn out world-famous **Moser glass** are situated in the suburbs of Karlovy Vary (Kpt Jaroše 46; tours every 30min, daily 9am–2.30pm; closed July 7–Aug 27; 120 Kč; ⓣ353 449 455, ⓦwww.moser-glass.com). You can also visit the stunning Moser glass museum next door (daily 9am–5pm; closed July 7–Aug 27; 80Kč). Take bus #22 or #1 from Tržnice in the centre of town. Alternatively, you can just have a look in the Moser glass shop on the Stará louka.

Arrival and information

Train and bus Trains from Prague arrive at Horní Nádraží to the north of town while trains from Mariánské Lázně come in at Dolní nádraží close to the main bus station and the town centre. Buses run to the spa area from all stations. If you're bussing it from Prague get off one stop early at Tržnice, even closer to the spa area. There's a Student Agency bus from Prague airport and Florenc (7 daily; 1hr 45min; ⓣ800 100 300, ⓦwww.studentagencybus.com), making it just about doable as a day-trip.

Tourist office next to the Mlýnská kolonáda at Lázeňská 1 (Mon–Fri 9am–5pm, Sat & Sun 10am–5pm; ⓣ355 321 176, ⓦwww.karlovyvary.cz). There's also one in the main bus station.

Accommodation

Accommodation in the centre is pricey – for cheaper options head further out. Private rooms are good value for more than one person – ask at the tourist office.

Egerlaender Hof Tržiště 39 ⓣ353 229 332, ⓦwww.volny.cz/egerlaender. Bright, roomy doubles situated around a pleasant courtyard behind a popular pub in the spa area. Doubles with breakfast 1200Kč.

Hotel Kavalerie T.G. Masaryka 43 ⓣ353 229 613, ⓦwww.kavalerie.cz. Conveniently close to the bus and train stations, this hotel offers comfortable, quiet rooms. Doubles with breakfast. 1200Kč.

Quest Hostel and Apartments Moravská 44 ⓣ353 820 030, ⓦwww.hostel-karlovy-vary.cz. Bright, cheerfully decorated dorms, doubles and self-catering apartments in the spa centre. Take bus #2, #8, #11 or #12 from the main bus station in the direction of the *Imperial Hotel*. Breakfast included. Dorms 410Kč, doubles 1300 Kč.

INTERNATIONAL FILM FESTIVAL

Karlovy Vary hosts a renowned **film festival** (ⓦwww.kviff.com) in July, when the town buzzes with filmmakers and visitors. As well as Czech films, there are European arthouse offerings, and visitors can buy inexpensive tickets to the various screenings and activities. If you plan to visit at this time, book your accommodation even further in advance than usual.

Eating and drinking

Most visitors eat at the expensive hotel restaurants so the town is deserted and not very budget-friendly at night. For food on the go, head to the well-stocked bakery Pekařstvi Cukrářstvi at T.G. Masaryka 30, or the Billa supermarket on the opposite side of the road.

Barracuda Jaltská 7. Caribbean-themed underground cocktail bar. Mon–Thurs till 1am, Fri & Sat till 3am. Closed Sun.

Diana Café-Restaurant Observation tower *Diana*, at the top of the funicular ⓣ353 222 872. Cosy chalet-style hut offering both fire-side and terrace dining. Typical Czech dishes from 120Kč.

Egerlaender Hof Tržiště 39. Austrian-style pub and restaurant. Enjoy a beer out on the terrace in the early evening with views across the spa.

Moving on

Train Prague (3 daily; 4hr–5hr 10min).
Bus Plzeň (8–9 daily; 1hr 30min–1hr 50min); Prague (hourly; 1hr 30min– 2hr 10min).

Moravia

Wedged between Bohemia and Slovakia, **Moravia** is the smallest of the three provinces that once made up Czechoslovakia, but perhaps the prettiest, friendliest and most bucolic. Despite

industrialization and high unemployment in some areas, much of Moravia is rural, and folk roots, traditions and religion are strongly felt. The Moravian capital, **Brno**, a once-grand nineteenth-century city, is within easy striking distance of Moravia's spectacular **karst region**. In the northern half of the province, the Baroque riches of the Moravian prince-bishopric have left their mark on the old capital, **Olomouc**, now a thriving university town and one of the region's main attractions.

BRNO

Brno is similar to Prague in many respects – it boasts the same lively atmosphere, café culture and cultural charms, though it has fewer tourists, a more compact, "lived-in" town centre, and a plethora of pretty boulevards and parks. In the nineteenth century it was a major textile centre and known as "rakousky Manchestr" (Austrian Manchester). Between the wars the city enjoyed a cultural boom, heralded by the 1928 Exhibition of Contemporary Culture.

What to see and do

The triangular **náměstí Svobody** is the central point of Brno, with the streets of the old town spanning out from here. Central Brno is dominated by brooding **Špilberk castle**, situated atop Špilberk hill, to the west, and the **Cathedral of SS Peter and Paul** on top of Petrov hill to the south.

Zelný trh

Though **zelný trh** means "cabbage market", there's a notable lack of cabbages here. A wonderfully evocative vegetable market on a sloping cobbled square, south of náměstí Svobody, with a huge fountain at its centre, this is a colourful place for an amble.

Capuchin crypt

The Capuchin crypt makes for a somewhat macabre monument in the **Capuchin church** (Mon–Sat 9am–noon & 2–4.30pm, Sun 11–11.45am & 2–4.30pm; Oct–Feb closed Mon), housing a charming collection of mummified dead monks.

The Old Town Hall

In the south of the old town, on Stará Radnice, is the **Old Town Hall**. The fifteenth-century master mason, Anton Pilgram, designed its impressive Gothic doorway: the thistly pinnacle above the statue of Justice is symbolically twisted – Pilgram's revenge on the town aldermen who short-changed him for his work. Inside, the courtyard's jam-packed with tour groups, most of them here to see the so-called **Brno dragon** (a stuffed crocodile) and the *Brno Wheel*, which was carved from a tree one morning by a cartwright in Lednice, 50km from Brno, and rolled to Brno before sunset as the result of a bet. The **tower** (April–Sept daily 9am–5pm; 20Kč) offers a stunning panoramic view across the red-tiled rooftops.

The Petrov hill and Cathedral of SS Peter and Paul

Southwest of the town centre, the Petrov hill – on which the **Cathedral of SS Peter and Paul** stands – is one of the best places to escape from the streets below. The cathedral's needle-sharp Gothic spires dominate the skyline for miles around.

UPM

On the western edge of the city centre, the **UPM** Museum of Applied Arts at Husova 14 (Wed–Sun 10am–6/7pm; 50Kč) contains one of the country's best collections of decorative art.

Arrival and information

Air Brno airport (Ⓦ www.airport-brno.cz) is served by several international airlines; from the airport, take bus #76 to the main bus station.

Train and bus Brno's main train and bus stations sit close together, on the edge of the city centre; the

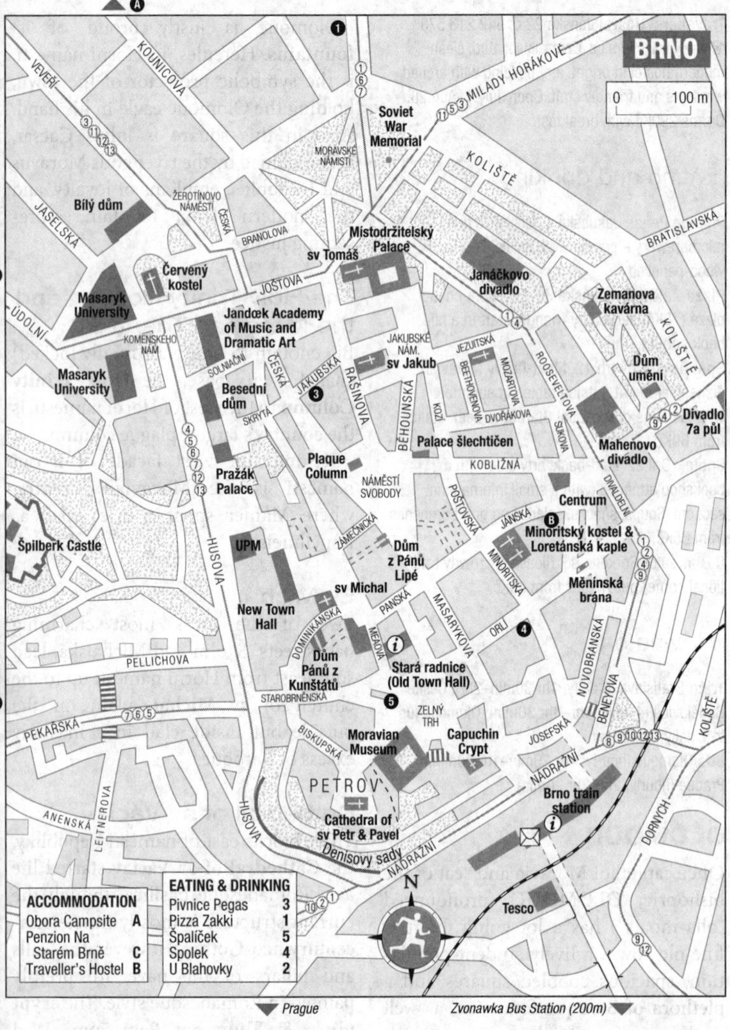

train station has lockers and a 24hr left-luggage office.

Tourist office Old Town Hall at Radnická 8 (April–Sept Mon–Fri 8.30am–6pm, Sat & Sun 9am–5.30pm; Oct–March Mon–Fri 9am–6pm, Sat 9am–5.30pm, Sun 9am–3pm; ⓣ 542 211 089, ⓦ www.ticbrno.cz).

Accommodation

Brno hosts lots of trade fairs in Feb, April and Aug–Oct, and during these times, accommodation prices can double, so book as far in advance as possible. The tourist office can help with private rooms, where prices tend not to rise quite so drastically.

Obora Campsite Rakovecká 72 ⓣ 546 223 334, ⓦ www.autocampobora.cz. Pleasant lake-side bungalows and a leafy campsite a 15min bus ride from the stations (tram #1 to the zoo, then bus #103). Bungalow 230Kč per person, tent 80 Kč.

Penzion Na Starém Brně Mendlovo nám 1 ⓣ 543 247 872, ⓦ www.pension-brno.com. Welcoming little pension in an old monastery, with a wine cellar attached. Go through Vankovka shopping centre from the train and bus stations and take tram #1. Double 1050Kč.

Travellers' Hostel Jánská 22 ⓣ542 213 573, ⓦwww.travellers.cz. Centrally located, clean, modern hostel in bright, airy building with arched windows and friendly staff. Open July 1–Aug 28. Dorms 290Kč with breakfast.

Eating and drinking

Pivnice Pegas Jakubská 4. Moravia's first microbrewery – popular with locals. Cosy and wood-panelled.
Pizza Zakki Antonínská 30. Excellent cheap pizza (70Kč) served by friendly staff in a laid-back setting.
Špalíček Zelný trh 12. Meat-heavy Moravian dishes served at outside tables in summer, with lashings of the local Starobrno beer. Mains from 69Kč.
Spolek Orli 22. Laid-back, arty café with a bookshop attached (with a small international section). Soups, snacks, salads and great brunches from 65Kč.
U Blahovky Gorkého 96. Pleasantly rowdy traditional corner pub. Mains from 89Kč.

Moving on

Train Bratislava (8 daily; 1hr 30min–2hr); České Budějovice (4 daily; 4hr–4hr 30min); Olomouc (up to 7 daily; 1hr 25min).
Bus Olomouc (hourly; 1hr 20min–1hr 50min); Prague (hourly; 2hr–3hr 20min).

OLOMOUC

Once capital of Moravia and seat of the bishopric, **OLOMOUC** (pronounced "olla-moats") has a lot going for it: a fine old town, a lively student population, spacious cobbled squares and a plethora of Baroque fountains, as well as the massive added advantage that it has a fraction of the number of tourists as Prague.

What to see and do

In the western half of the old town, all roads lead to the city's two central squares, Horní (upper) and Dolni (lower) náměstí. The irregular Horní náměstí has an astronomical clock – a modern reconstruction of the original, which was destroyed in World War II.

Olomouc is justly proud of its **fountains**. Hercules, in Horní náměstí, is the symbolic protector of the town, holding the Olomouc eagle in his hand. Also in this square is Julius Caesar, accompanied by the river gods Moravus and Danubius, emblems of loyalty, and the modern *Arion* fountain, representing justice.

The Holy Trinity Column and the Moravian Theatre

Big enough to house a (usually locked) chapel at its base, the **Holy Trinity Column** to the west of Horní náměstí, is the country's largest plague column.

Set into the west facade of Horní náměstí is the **Moravian Theatre**, where Mahler spent a brief spell as Kapellmeister.

Sv Michál

Two of the city's most charming backstreets, Školní and Michalská, lead southeast from Horní náměstí up to the church of **sv Michál**, plain on the outside but inside clad in a masterly excess of Baroque.

Cathedral of sv Václav

Three blocks east of náměstí Republiky, the **Cathedral of sv Václav** started life as a Romanesque basilica, though the current structure is mostly nineteenth-century neo-Gothic. However, the walls and pillars of the nave are prettily painted in Romanesque style. The **crypt** (Tues & Thurs–Sat 9am–5pm, Wed 9am–4pm, Sun 11am–5pm) holds a macabre display of gory reliquaries.

Arrival and information

Train station 1.5km east of the old town; on arrival take any tram heading west up Masarykova and get off after three or four stops.
Bus station Further out, and connected to the centre by tram #4.
Tourist office In the town hall (daily 9am–7pm; ⓣ585 513 385, ⓦwww.olomouc-tourism.cz); can book private rooms.

FESTIVAL FRENZY

There are mainstream and unusual festivals year-round In Olomouc. April brings a quirky documentary film festival, **Academia Film**, to town, with a particular focus on popular science films (Ⓦwww.afo.cz). There's also the **Dvorak festival** in June, which misleadingly, celebrates not only Dvorak but all Czech composers (Dvorak worked extensively in Olomouc and his *Te Deum* and *Requiem* were premiered here). The churches and squares are filled with concerts by visiting orchestras (Ⓦwww.mfo.cz). Olomouc also hosts the Czech Republic's biggest **beer festival** (Ⓦwww.beerfest.cz) in May, where local and internationally renowned bands play, and, you'll be glad to hear, the international meeting of Beer Souvenir Collectors takes place. There's also the ten-day **Olomouc City festival** in June, with plays, concerts, art exhibitions, parades and other events, often for free, and **Flora Olomouc** have flower shows In the botanical gardens throughout the year (Ⓦwww.flora-ol.cz). See Ⓦwww.olomouc-tourism.cz for more details.

Accommodation

Hostel Bétanie Wurmova 5 Ⓣ587 405 330. Simple individual rooms with shared bathrooms and a cheerful café downstairs. Doubles 750Kč.
Poets Corner Hostel Sokolská 1 Ⓣ777 570 730, Ⓦwww.hostelolomouc.com. Small, homely hostel run by Aussie backpackers, a short walk from the main square. Self-catering facilities. Dorms 300Kč, doubles 980Kč.

Eating and drinking

For picnics and snacks, there's a supermarket, Potraviny, at Horní náměstí 9.
Caesar Horní náměstí. Popular, atmospheric pizzeria in the cobbled vaults under the town hall. Mains 56–156Kč.
Café 87 Denisove 87. Something of an Olomouc institution, just next to the Museum of Art. Bright and cheerful, with great coffee and desserts.
Kaldera Kosinova 7. A creative student bar with a lovely courtyard and gallery, and small, tasty menu, hosting poetry evenings and open-mike nights.
U Andela Hrnčírska 10. Covered in potted plants and unusual antiques, this place serves generously portioned traditional food. Dinosaur steak (chicken fillet, pork cutlet and beef steak) 140Kč.

Moving on

Train Brno (5 daily; 1hr 30min); Prague (hourly; 3hr–3hr 30min).
Bus Brno (up to 15 daily; 1hr 30min).

Denmark

HIGHLIGHTS

SKAGEN: sample fantastic seafood and world-class are at this lovely seaside resort

ÅRHUS NIGHTLIFE: Denmark's second city buzzes with a mixture of live music and trendy riverside bars

TIVOLI, COPENHAGEN: a timeless pleasure park with nightly fireworks

VIKING SHIP MUSEUM, ROSKILDE: take to the seas on board a Viking longboat

ODENSE: quaint, cobbled and home to Denmark's biggest literary export – Hans Christian Andersen

ROUGH COSTS

DAILY BUDGET Basic €45/ occasional treat €75

DRINK Carlsberg (pint) €5.50

FOOD Pølser (Danish hot dog) €3.50

HOSTEL/BUDGET HOTEL €20/€65

TRAVEL Train: Copenhagen–Århus (210km) €45; bus €37.50

FACT FILE

POPULATION 5.5 million

AREA 43,094 sq km

LANGUAGE Danish; English widely spoken

CURRENCY Danish krone (kr)

CAPITAL Copenhagen (population: 1.2 million)

INTERNATIONAL PHONE CODE: ⓣ45

Introduction

Denmark is consistently ranked as the happiest place to live on the planet. And it certainly seems that way when you meet the locals – Danes are some of the most gregarious people you are likely to meet, with an instinctive sense of fun and even a special word (hygge) to describe the art of creating a cosy, convivial atmosphere. Add to that an efficient transport infrastructure, pristine environment and the fact that everything you find, from a chair to an office block, seems to be designed to perfection, and you can see why the Danes are not complaining very loudly about their woes.

Wedged between mainland Europe and the rest of Scandinavia, Denmark has preserved a distinct national identity, exemplified by the universally cherished royal family and the reluctance to fully integrate with the EU (the Danish rejection of the euro was more about sovereignty than economics). There's also a sense of a small country that has long punched above its weight: it once controlled much of northern Europe and still maintains close ties with Greenland, its former colony.

Geographically, three main landmasses make up the country – the islands of Zealand and Funen and the peninsula of Jutland, which extends northwards from Germany. Most visitors make for **Zealand** (Sjælland), and, more specifically, **Copenhagen**, an exciting focal point with a beautiful old centre, a good array of museums and a boisterous nightlife. **Funen** (Fyn) has only one real urban draw, **Odense**, once home to Hans Christian Andersen; otherwise, it's renowned for cute villages and sandy beaches. **Jutland** (Jylland) has, as well as some varied scenery, ranging from soft green hills to desolate heathlands, **Århus** and **Aalborg**, two of the liveliest Danish cities.

CHRONOLOGY

400 BC "Tollund Man", a body found preserved in a bog in 1950, provides evidence of habitation during the Iron Age.

500 AD First mention of the "Dani" tribe is made by foreign sources.

695 First Christian mission to Denmark.

825 First Danish coinage introduced.

1397 The Union of Kalmar unites Denmark, Sweden and Norway under a single Danish monarch.

1523 Sweden leaves the Kalmar Union.

1536 Religious Reformation leads to the establishment of the Danish Lutheran Church.

1629 Sweden heavily defeats Charles IV's Denmark in the Thirty Years' War, resulting in losses of Danish territory.

1814 Denmark cedes Norway to Sweden.

1836 Hans Christian Andersen writes "The Little Mermaid".

1849 Constitutional monarchy is established.

1864 Defeat by Prussia results in the loss of much territory.

1914 Neutrality is adopted during World War I.

1918 The vote is granted to all Danes.

1934 Children's playtime is transformed by the invention of Lego by Ole Kirk Christiansen.

1940 Nazi invasion meets minimal resistance.

1945 Denmark is liberated by Allied forces.

1979 Greenland is given greater autonomy by the Danish.

1989 First European country to legalize same-sex marriages.

2004 Crown Prince Frederick marries Australian Mary Donaldson in a lavish ceremony.

2006 Cartoon depictions of the Prophet Mohammed in Danish newspapers spark mass protests in the Muslim world.

ARRIVAL

The vast majority of visitors arrive in Copenhagen, either flying in to its gleaming **Kastrup Airport** or pulling

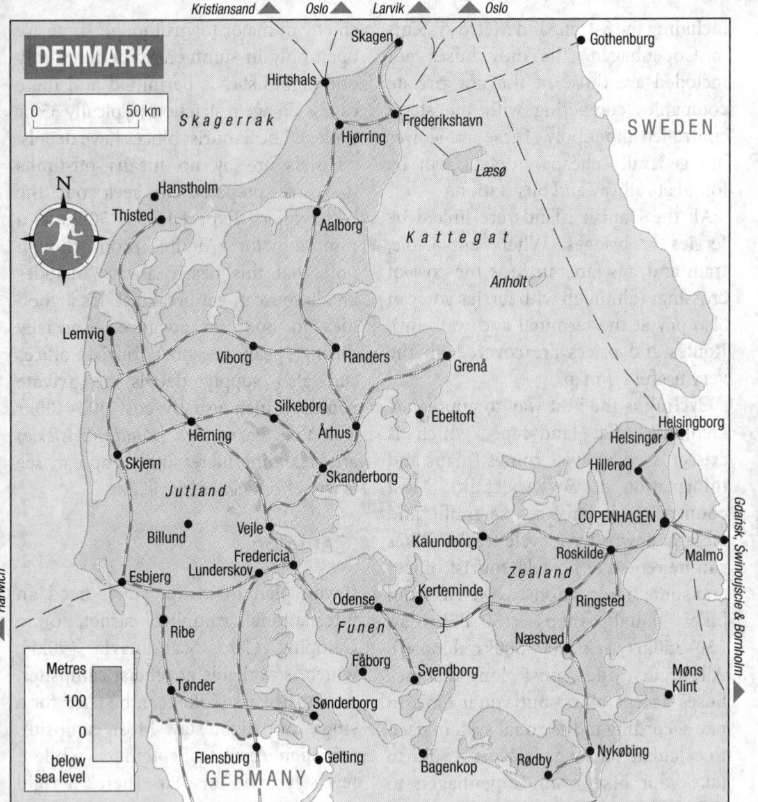

in to the city's **Central Station**, connected with the European rail network via Germany and, across the spectacular Øresund bridge, to Sweden. Most international bus routes also arrive at Central Station. In addition, the **regional airports** at Aalborg, Århus and Billund handle a growing number of budget flights, mostly operated by Ryanair. There are regular **ferry services** to and from the UK (via Esbjerg) and Sweden and Norway (both via Frederikshavn or Hirtshals).

GETTING AROUND

Denmark has a swift and easy-to-use public transport system. Danish State Railways (Danske Statsbaner or DSB; ⓦwww.dsb.dk) runs an exhaustive and reliable **rail** network supplemented by a few privately owned rail lines. Services range from the large inter-city expresses *(lyntog)* to smaller local trains *(regionaltog)*. InterRail and Eurail passes are valid on all DSB trains, with reduced rates on most privately owned lines. Ticket prices are worked out according to a countrywide zonal system and travel by local transport within the zone of departure and arrival is included in the price.

Everywhere not served by train can be easily reached via the **bus** network, which often supplements the train timetable. Some are operated privately and some by DSB itself; railcards are valid. DSB **timetables** or *Køreplan* detail train, bus and ferry services,

including the S-train and Metro systems in Copenhagen. The only buses not included are those of the few private companies competing with the state-controlled monopoly. These are slower but generally cheaper; details can be found at railway and bus stations.

All the Danish islands are linked by **ferries** or bridges. Where applicable, train and bus fares include the cost of crossings (although with ferries you can also pay at the terminal and walk on). Routes and prices are covered on the very useful HI map.

Cycling is the best way to appreciate Denmark's flat landscape, which is crisscrossed by cycle routes (maps and information at Ⓦwww.dcf.dk). Most country roads have sparse traffic and all large towns have cycle tracks. Bikes can be rented at hostels, tourist offices and some train stations, as well as from bike rental shops (50–85kr/day, 250–350kr/week; 200–500kr deposit). All trains and most long-distance buses accept bikes, but you'll have to pay according to the zonal system used to calculate passenger tickets – 50kr to take your bike from Copenhagen to Århus by train with 20kr on top if you want to reserve a space in advance, or 80kr by bus.

ACCOMMODATION

Accommodation is a major expense when travelling in Denmark, although there is a wide network of good-quality **hostels**. Most have a choice of private rooms, often with en-suite toilets and showers, as well as dorm accommodation; nearly all have cooking facilities. Rates are around 150kr per person for a dorm bed; non-HI members pay an extra 35kr a night (160kr for a one-year HI membership). Danhostel Danmarks Vandrerhjem (Ⓦwww.danhostel.dk) produces a free hostel guide. For a similar price, **sleep-ins** (smaller hostels geared towards backpackers and often run by volunteer staff) can be found chiefly in major towns though some are open only in summer. Sometimes only one night's stay is permitted and there can be an age restriction (typically 35 or under). Local tourist offices have details.

Hotels are by no means off-limits if you're prepared to seek out the better offers. Expect to pay 500kr as a minimum for a double room, though note that this nearly always includes an all-you-can-eat breakfast. It's a good idea to book in advance, especially during peak season. Tourist offices can also supply details of **private rooms**, which usually cost 300–400kr a double. **Farmstays** (*Bondegårdsferie*) are becoming increasingly popular; see Ⓦwww.bondegaardsferie.dk.

Camping

If you plan to **camp**, you'll need an international camping carnet, or a Camping Card Scandinavia (90kr), which is available at official campsites. A Transit Pass (25kr) can be used for a single overnight stay. Most campsites are open April to September, while a few stay open all year. There's a rigid **grading system**: one-star sites have toilets and at least one shower; two-stars also have basic cooking facilities and a food shop within 2km; three-stars include a laundry and a TV-room; four-stars also have a shop, while five-stars include a cafeteria. Prices are around 65–100kr per person. Many campsites also have **cabins** to rent, usually with cooking facilities, for 2000kr–4000kr per week for a six-berth place, although they are often fully booked in summer. Tourist offices offer a free leaflet listing all sites. **Camping rough** without permission is illegal, and an on-the-spot fine may be imposed.

FOOD AND DRINK

Traditional **Danish food** is characterized by rather stodgy meat or fish and two veg combos, although the quality of

ingredients is usually excellent. Specialities worth seeking out include *stegt flæsk med persille sovs* (thinly sliced fried pork with boiled potatoes and a creamy parsley sauce) and the classic *røget sild* (smoked herring). **Breakfast** (*morgenmad*) is usually a treat, with almost all hotels and hostels offering a spread of cereals, freshly made bread, cheese, ham, fruit juice, milk, coffee and tea, for around 60kr (if not included in the price of the room). **Brunch**, served in most cafés from 11am until mid-afternoon, is a popular and filling option for late starters and costs 80–100kr. A traditional **lunch** (*frokost*) is *smørrebrød* – slices of rye bread heaped with meat, fish or cheese, and assorted trimmings – sold for 30–50kr a piece and very filling. An excellent-value set lunch can usually be found at restaurants and *bodegas* (bars that sell no-frills food). *Tilbud* is the "special", *dagens ret* the "dish of the day"; expect to pay around 80kr for one of these, or 100–140kr for a three-course set lunch.

For daytime **snacks**, there are hot dog stands (*pølsevogn*) on all main streets and at train stations, serving hot dogs (*pølser*), toasted ham and cheese sandwiches (*parisertoast*) and chips (*pommes frites*). Bakeries and cafés sell Danish pastries (*wienerbrød*), tastier and much less sweet than the imitations sold abroad, and *rundstykker* (literally "round pieces"), a type of crispy bread roll. Restaurants are pretty expensive for dinner (reckon on 120–150kr) but you can usually find a Middle Eastern or Thai place offering **buffets** for around 80–100kr. Kebab shops are also very common and often serve pizza slices for around 30kr. If you plan to save money by **self-catering**, head for Netto or Fakta supermarkets, which offer good value.

Drinking

The most sociable places to **drink** are pubs (variously known as a *værtshus*, *bar* or *bodega*) and cafés, where the emphasis is on **beer**. The cheapest is bottled lager – the so-called gold beer (Guldøl or Elefantøl; 25–35kr/bottle) is the strongest. Draught lager (Fadøl) is more expensive and a touch weaker, but tastes fresher. The most common brands are Carlsberg and Tuborg, although microbreweries are increasingly visible and there are now many pubs making their own beer on the premises. Most international **wines** (from 40kr) and **spirits** (20–40kr) are widely available. There are many varieties of **schnapps**, including the potent Aalborg-made Aquavit.

CULTURE AND ETIQUETTE

Denmark is one of the most liberal and tolerant countries on earth and you are unlikely to run into cultural problems. One thing to bear in mind is that the Danish language doesn't have a specific word for "please" so don't be upset if Danes leave it out when talking to you in English (which most Danes speak very well). When wandering about make sure you don't stray into the cycle lanes alongside most roads and note that locals will wait for the green "walk" light at pedestrian crossings even when there isn't a car in sight.

Tipping is not expected as service charges are included in hotel, restaurant and bar bills; however, if you think you've had particularly good service it's not unheard of to leave a few kroner. **Smoking** is banned in most restaurants, cafés and bars.

SPORTS AND OUTDOOR ACTIVITIES

With over 1600 registered clubs, football (soccer) is far and away the most popular **sport** in Denmark. The biggest teams are FC Copenhagen and Brøndby (both from the capital) who play in the twelve-team Superliga (Ⓦwww.dbu.dk). As for **outdoor activities**, there's a series

of cycle routes and hiking paths (Ⓦwww.dvl.dk) and watersports are always an option thanks to Denmark's spotlessly clean beaches and waterways; ask at tourist offices for details of safe places to swim.

COMMUNICATIONS

Post offices are open Monday to Friday 9.30/10am to 5/6pm and Saturday 9.30/10am to noon/2pm, with reduced hours in smaller communities. You can buy stamps from most newsagents. If you're in Denmark for some time you may want to buy a **Danish SIM** for your mobile – prepaid cards from operators such as Telmore and CBB are available from petrol stations and post offices from 99kr. **Internet access** is free at most libraries and some tourist offices, and most towns have internet cafés.

EMERGENCIES

Danish **police** are generally courteous and most speak English. For **prescriptions**, doctors' consultations and dental work – but not hospital visits – you have to pay on the spot.

INFORMATION

Most places have a **tourist office** that can help with accommodation. They're open daily in the most popular spots, but have reduced hours from October to March. All airports and many train stations also offer a hotel booking service.

MONEY AND BANKS

Currency is the **krone** (plural *kroner*), made up of 100 øre. It comes in notes of 50kr, 100kr, 200kr, 500kr and 1000kr, and coins of 50øre, 1kr, 2kr, 5kr, 10kr and 20kr. **Banking hours** are Monday to Friday 9.30/10am to 4pm, Thursday until 5.30/6pm. Banks are plentiful and are the easiest place to **exchange cash** and traveller's cheques, although they usually charge around 30kr per transaction. Forex bureaux tend to charge 20kr to exchange cash and 10kr per traveller's cheques but are scarce. Most airports and ferry terminals have late-opening exchange facilities, and ATMs are widespread. At the time of writing, €1 was equal to 7.5kr, US$1 to 5.4kr and £1 to 8.6kr.

EMERGENCY NUMBERS

All emergencies Ⓣ112.

OPENING HOURS AND HOLIDAYS

Standard **shop hours** are Monday to Friday 9.30/10am to 5.30/7pm, Saturday 9/9.30am to 2/5pm. All shops and banks are closed, and public transport and

STUDENT AND YOUTH DISCOUNTS

Your **ISIC card** will get you between thirty and fifty percent off most museum and gallery admission prices, although bear in mind free entry is often available on Wednesdays and Sundays. If you're staying long-term a **DSB Wildcard** (180kr) offers fifty percent off train fares for a year (Ⓦwww.dsb.dk).

DENMARK ON THE NET

Ⓦ**www.visitdenmark.com** Excellent Danish tourist board site.

Ⓦ**www.cphpost.dk** News and reviews from the *Copenhagen Post*, the capital's English-language weekly.

Ⓦ**www.aok.dk** Listings for most of Zealand.

Ⓦ**www.rejseplanen.dk** Public transport journey planner (with English-language option).

Danish

	Danish	Pronunciation
Yes	*Ja*	Ya
No	*Nej*	Nye
Please	*Vær så venlig*	Verso venly
Thank you	*Tak*	Tagg
Hello/Good day	*Goddag*	Go-day
Goodbye	*Farvel*	Fah-vell
Excuse me	*Undskyld*	Unsgul
Good	*God*	Got
Bad	*Dårlig*	Dohli
Near	*Nær*	Neh-a
Far	*Fjern*	Fee-ann
Cheap	*Billig*	Billie
Expensive	*Dyr*	Duy-a
Open	*Åben*	Oh-ben
Closed	*Lukket*	Lohgget
Ticket	*billet*	bill-le
Today	*Idag*	Ee-day
Yesterday	*Igår*	Ee-goh
Tomorrow	*Imorgen*	Ee-mon
How much is...?	*Hvad koster...?*	Val kosta...?
I'd like...	*Jeg vil gerne ha...*	yai vay gerna ha...
What time is it?	*Hvad er klokken?*	Val eayr cloggen?
Where is...?	*Hvor er...?*	Voa eayr...?
A table for...	*et bord till...*	et boa te...
I don't understand	*Jeg forstår ikke*	Yai fusto igge
Do you speak English?	*Taler de engelsk?*	Tayla dee engellsgg?
One	*En*	Ehn
Two	*To*	Toh
Three	*Tre*	Tray
Four	*Fire*	Fee-a
Five	*Fem*	Fem
Six	*Sex*	Sex
Seven	*Syv*	Syu
Eight	*Otte*	Oddeh
Nine	*Ni*	Nee
Ten	*Ti*	Tee

many museums run to Sunday schedules on **public holidays**: January 1; Maundy Thursday to Easter Monday; Prayer Day (4th Fri after Easter); Ascension (fortieth day after Easter); Whit Sunday and Monday; Constitution Day (June 5); December 24 (pm only); December 25 and 26. On **International Workers' Day**, May 1, many offices and shops close at noon.

Copenhagen

COPENHAGEN (København) is one of Europe's most user-friendly capitals: welcoming and compact, with a centre largely given over to pedestrians. First-rate galleries, museums and summertime street entertainers fill your days, while by night the live music and intimate bar and club scene are rivalled only by those on offer in Århus.

Until the twelfth century, when **Bishop Absalon** built a castle on Christiansborg's present site, there was little more than a tiny fishing settlement to be found here. Trade and prosperity flourished with the introduction of the Sound Toll on vessels in the Øresund, and the city became the Baltic's principal harbour, earning the name **København** ("merchants' harbour"). By 1443 it had become the Danish capital. A century later, Christian IV created Rosenborg Castle, Rundetårn and the districts of Nyboder and Christianshavn, and in 1669 Frederik III graced the city with its first royal palace, Amalienborg.

What to see and do

The historic core of the city is **Slotsholmen**, originally the site of the twelfth-century castle and now home to the huge Christiansborg complex. Just over the Slotsholmen Kanal to the north is the medieval maze of **Indre By** ("inner city"), while to the south the island of **Christianshavn** is dotted with cutting-edge architecture as well as the alternative enclave of **Christiania**. Northeast of Indre By are the royal quarters of Kongens Have and **Frederiksstaden**, while to the west the expansive Rådhuspladsen leads via the Tivoli Gardens to Central Station and the hotspots of **Vesterbro** and **Nørrebro**.

Tivoli

Just off hectic Vesterbrogade outside the station is Copenhagen's most famous attraction, **Tivoli** (mid-April to mid-Sept Sun–Thurs 11am–11pm, Fri & Sat 11am–midnight; mid-Nov to end Dec closes one hour earlier; Ⓦwww.tivoli.dk; 85kr), an entertaining mixture of landscaped gardens, outdoor concerts (every Fri) and fairground rides. You'll probably hear it before you see it thanks to its high perimeter walls and the constant screams from the roller coasters (multi-ride tickets 200kr). On a summer evening when the park is illuminated by thousands of lights and lamps reflected in the lake, it's an almost magical experience.

Ny Carlsberg Glyptotek

Founded by Carlsberg tycoon Carl Jacobsen, the **Ny Carlsberg Glyptotek** (daily 11am–5pm; 60kr, Sun free; Ⓦwww.glyptoteket.dk) is Copenhagen's finest art gallery. There's a knockout selection of Greek and Roman sculpture on the first floor as well as some excellent examples of modern European art, including Degas casts, Monet's *The Lemon Grove* and works by Gauguin, Toulouse-Lautrec and Van Gogh upstairs. Wind up your visit with a slice of delicious cake in the café facing the delightful winter garden.

Thorvaldsens and the National museums

On the north side of Slotsholmen, the **Thorvaldsens Museum** (Tues–Sun 10am–5pm; 20kr, Wed free; Ⓦwww.thorvaldsensmuseum.dk) is the home of an enormous collection of work and memorabilia (not to mention the body) of Denmark's most famous sculptor, Bertel Thorvaldsen, who lived from 1770 to 1844. A short walk away over the Slotsholmen moat is the **Nationalmuseet** (National Museum; same hours, with guided tours July–Sept Tues, Thurs & Sun at 11am; free; Ⓦwww.natmus.dk), which has excellent displays on Denmark's history from the Ice Age to the present day. The prehistory section

COPENHAGEN ON A BUDGET

Copenhagen can be a tricky place to get by on a budget but with a bit of planning you can make the most of your wallet. Museums with **free admission** include the National Museum, the Museum of the Danish Resistance and the Statens Museum for Kunst (National Gallery), while many others offer free entry one day per week. You should also consider buying a CPHCARD (see p.321). As for getting around, you can walk to most places, use the free city bikes or take the harbour bus-boats.

in particular is fascinating, and includes amber animals, gold Viking horns, numerous corpses preserved in bogs and Denmark's oldest coin, struck around 995. As the museum is free, it's worth making two visits to take it all in.

Indre By and the Rundetaarn

West of Kongens Nytorv, the city's largest square and home to some of the best hot dog stalls in town, pedestrianized **Strøget** leads into the heart of **Indre By**. This is Denmark's premier shopping area, with the likes of Prada and Hermes jostling for space with the ubiquitous H&M and local giant, Illums Bolighus. There are plenty of affordable independent boutiques running off the arterial streets. One of the capital's quirkiest sights, the 35-metre-high **Rundetaarn** (Round Tower; June–Sept 10am–8pm, Oct–May 10am–5pm, 25kr) dominates the skyline northwest of Strøget in the city's university or Latin quarter. Built as an observatory and finished in 1642, the main attraction is the view from the top reached via a spiral walkway. It's still a functioning observatory and you can view the night sky through its astronomical telescope (mid-Oct to mid-March Tues & Wed 7–10pm).

Nyhavn and Frederiksstaden

Running east from Kongens Nytorv, a slender canal divides the two sides of **Nyhavn** ("new harbour"), picturesquely lined with colourful eighteenth-century houses – now bars and cafés – and thronged with tourists in summer. Just north of Nyhavn, the royal district of **Frederiksstaden** centres on cobbled Amalienborg Slotsplads, home to the four **Amalienborg** royal palaces. Two remain as royal residences, and there's a changing of the guard at noon if the monarch is at home. In the opposite direction is the great marble dome of **Frederikskirken**, also known as Marmorkirken or marble church (Mon–Thurs 10am–5pm, Fri–Sun noon–5pm; admission to dome 1pm & 3pm Sat & Sun, plus Mon–Fri June–Aug; free), which was modelled on St Peter's in Rome. Further along Bredgade, a German armoured car commandeered by the Danes to bring news of the Nazi surrender marks the entrance to the **Frihedsmuseet** (Museum of the Danish Resistance Movement; Tues–Sun 10am–3pm, May–Sept until 5pm; free; ⓦwww.frihedsmuseet.dk).

Kongens Have and Rosenborg Slot

West of Frederikskirken, **Kongens Have** is the city's oldest public park and a popular spot for picnics. Within the park is the fairytale **Rosenborg Slot** (May–Oct daily 10/11am–4/5pm; Nov–April Tues–Sun 11am–2pm; 70kr), the castle that served as the principal residence of Christian IV. The main building includes the furnished rooms used by the regal occupants, although the highlight is the downstairs treasury, where the **crown jewels** and rich accessories worn by Christian IV are on display.

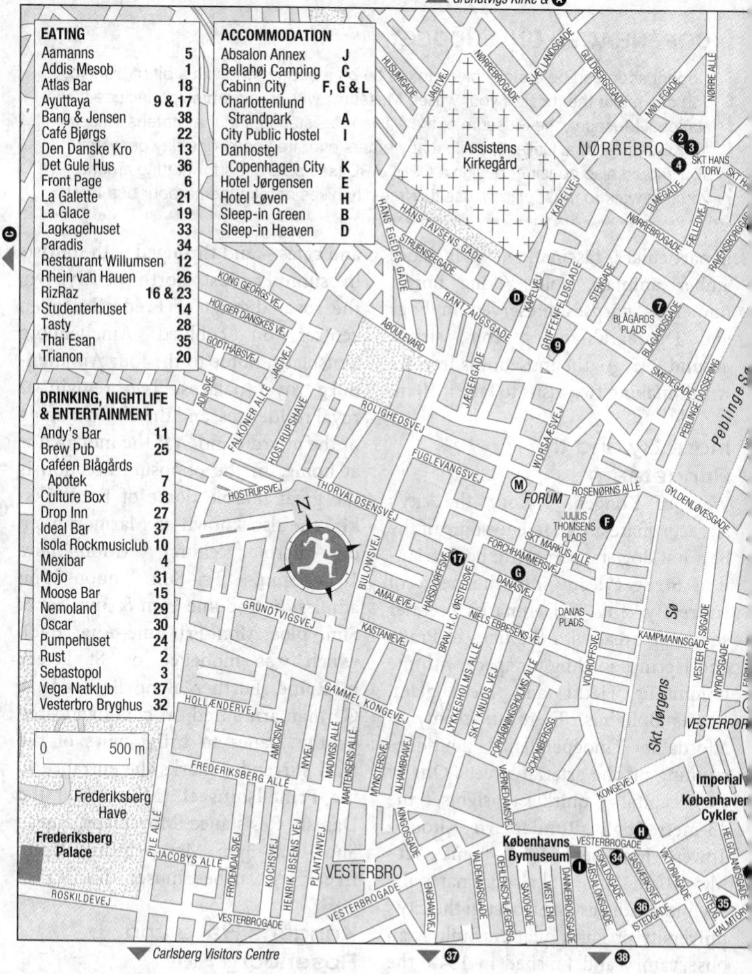

The Botanisk Have and art galleries

On the west side of Kongens Have is the **Botanisk Have** (Botanical Garden; daily 8.30am–4/6pm; winter closed Mon; free), dotted with greenhouses and rare plants. The neighbouring **Statens Museum for Kunst** (Tues–Sun 10am–5pm, Wed until 8pm; free; ⓦwww.smk.dk) holds a vast collection of art, from minor Picassos to major works by Matisse, Titian and Rubens – although it's the light and spacious architecture of its new wing that steals the show. Across the park on Stockholmsgade, **Den Hirschsprungske Samling** (The Hirschsprung Collection; daily except Tues 11am–4pm; 50kr, free on Wed; ⓦwww.hirschsprung.dk) holds a collection of twentieth-century Danish art, including work by the Skagen artists (see p.336), renowned for their interesting use of light.

The Little Mermaid

Just north of the **Kastellet**, a star-shaped fortress with five bastions on a corner overlooking the harbour, sits the diminutive **Little Mermaid**, a magnet for

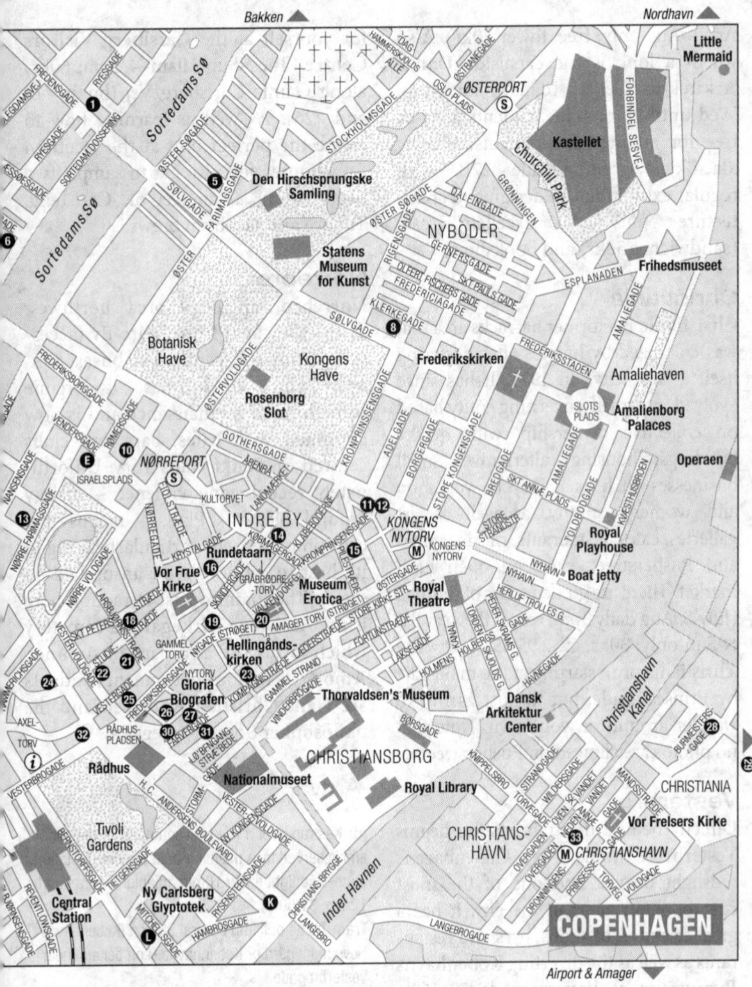

tourists since her unveiling in 1913. A bronze statue of the Hans Christian Andersen character, it was sculpted by Edvard Eriksen and paid for by the founder of the Carlsberg brewery. Over the years she's been the victim of several attacks, having her head and arms chopped off and even being blown up by a bomb in 2003, but she remains the most enduring symbol of the city. Note that from April to November 2010, the mermaid will be leaving Denmark for the first time, to be exhibited at the World's Fair in Shanghai. During that period a sculpture by a Chinese artist will take her spot on Langelinie pier.

Christianshavn

From Christiansborg, a bridge crosses to **Christianshavn**, built by Christian IV in the early sixteenth century and nicknamed "Little Amsterdam" thanks to its small canals, cute bridges and Dutch-style houses. Reaching skywards on the far side of Torvegade is one of the city's most recognizable features, the copper and golden spire of **Vor Frelsers Kirke** (daily 11am/noon–3.30pm; tower

April–Aug only; free, tower 20kr). Also worth a look is the canalside **Dansk Arkitektur Center** (daily 10am–5pm, Wed until 9pm; 40kr; students 25kr or free for architecture students, Ⓦwww.dac.dk), at Strandgade 27B, with regular exhibitions on design and architecture plus an excellent café (sandwiches 58kr) and bookshop.

Christiania

Christiania is a former barracks area that was colonized by hippies after declaring itself a "free city" in 1971. It has since evolved into a self-governing entity based on collective ownership, with quirky buildings housing alternative small businesses such as a bicycle workshop and women's smithy, as well as art galleries, cafés, restaurants, music venues and Pusherstreet, once an open hash market. There are guided tours of the area (July & Aug daily 3pm, rest of the year Sat & Sun only; 30kr; Ⓣ32.95.65.07, Ⓦwww.christiania.org), starting at the main gate by Prinsessegade, but it's just as fun to wander around on your own. Note that no photos are allowed on Pusherstreet.

Vesterbro

Directly behind the train station begins **Vesterbro**, home to Copenhagen's red-light district and one of the most cosmopolitan areas in the city. It has a great selection of shops, bars and restaurants as well as the diverting **Københavns Bymuseum** at Vesterbrogade 59 (City Museum; daily 10am–4pm, Wed until 9pm; 20kr though free on Fri), which covers the history of the city. The elaborate banquet hall upstairs, now used for classical concerts, is a highlight. While the area is perfectly safe to walk around, male travellers may want to give Istedgade a wide berth later in the evening to avoid being propositioned.

The Carlsberg Visitors Centre

"Probably the best beer in the world" goes the ad slogan. Well, you can decide for yourself at the **Carslberg Visitors Centre** (Tues–Sun 10am–4/5pm; 60kr) along Gamle Carlsberg Vej (buses #18 and #26). As well as learning how to create the perfect pint at the Jacobsen Brewhouse, you also get to sample two beers from a choice of Carlsberg, Tuborg and Jacobsen brews.

Nørrebro

Nørrebro, an edgy area northwest across the canal from Indre By (accessible from the centre via buses #3A, #4A and #5A), has undergone something of a renaissance and is now crammed with cafés, bars and clubs centred on Sankt Hans Torv. Unfortunately recent gang violence – mainly around Blågårds Plads – means that caution is advised, particularly at night: it's best to ask locals for an update on safety. The main tourist attraction here is the **Assistens Kirkegård**, a cemetery which locals use as a park in summer. Among its famous permanent residents are Hans Christian Andersen and the philosopher Søren Kirkegaard.

Arrival

Air Kastrup airport is 11km southeast of the centre, and is served by a mainline train to Central Station (5am–midnight every 10min; midnight–5am hourly; 12min; 31.50kr).

Train Trains pull into Central Station (Københavns Hovedbanegård or Københavns H on tickets) near Vesterbrogade.

Bus Long-distance buses from elsewhere in Denmark stop at or near the Central Station.

Boat Ferries dock an S-train ride away north of the centre at Nordhavn (two stops from Nørreport station).

Information

Tourist office Vesterbrogade 4a, across from Central Station Ⓣ70.22.24.42, Ⓦwww.visitcopenhagen.com (May & June Mon–Sat 9am–6pm; July & Aug Mon–Sat 9am–8pm, Sun 10am–6pm; Sept–April Mon–Fri 9am–4pm, Sat 9am–2pm). Accommodation (including private rooms) can be booked for free via their website. Note that pickpockets operate in the tourist office

COPENHAGEN TOURS

When the weather's good it's worth forking out on a **city tour** to familiarize yourself with Copenhagen; the difficulty is choosing your means of transport. Open-top **bus tours** (from 120kr; ⓦwww.sightseeing.dk) let you hop off and on at stops throughout the city. Netto Boats (March–Oct 10am–5pm; 30kr; ⓦwww.netto-baadene.dk) operates hour-long canal and harbour **boat tours** past the old stock exchange (not open to the public), the island of Holmen and the Little Mermaid, leaving regularly from Nyhavn.

For bike enthusiasts, City Safari (daily summer 1.30pm & 8pm; 250kr for 3hr including bike rental; ⓣ33.23.94.90, ⓦwww.citysafari.dk) runs themed **cycle tours** with knowledgeable guides starting from the Dansk Arkitektur Center; and Bike Copenhagen with Mike (April–Dec 10am, plus June–Sept 2pm; 165kr for 3hr, plus 85kr for bike rental; ⓣ26.39.56.88, ⓦwww.bikecopenhagenwithmike.dk) tours depart from Københavns Cykler at Reventlowsgade 11, next to the train station. City, country and individual tours are offered. See below for more on cycling in Copenhagen.

and thefts are common: be vigilant with your possessions (the same applies in the train station).

Discount cards If you're sightseeing on a tight schedule, consider the CPHCARD (225/450kr for 24/72hr), which is valid for the entire public transport network (including much of eastern Zealand) and gives entry to most museums and attractions in the area. It's available at tourist offices, hotels, travel agents and the train station.

City transport

Metro, S-tog and bus An integrated network of buses, electric S-trains (S-tog) and an expanding metro covers the city (5am–1am); night buses (*natbus*) take over after 1am, along with metro services on Thurs, Fri and Sat nights, though the latter are less frequent. Night fares are double daytime fares and if you're taking your bike you'll need to buy a special ticket. Free route maps are available from stations.

Tickets The cheapest ticket is the *billet* (21kr for two zones), valid for an hour's unlimited travel. You can also buy a *Klippekort* containing ten *billets* (130kr for two zones). Other options include the CPHCARD (see above); the *24-hour billet* (120kr), which covers the same area for 24 hours, but doesn't include admission to museums; and the *Flexicard 7 days* (205kr for two zones). Make sure you stamp *billets* when boarding buses or in machines on station platforms. Single *billets* can be bought on board buses; all other tickets can be bought at train stations and newsagents. Travelling without a ticket can get you an instant 600kr fine.

Cycling The City Bike scheme (April–Nov; ⓦwww.bycyklen.dk) allows you to borrow bikes from racks across the city for a deposit of 20kr, which is returned when the bike is locked back into any other rack. Bike rental is available from CPH Bike Rental, Turesensgade 10 (from 50kr per day); Københavns Cykelbørs, Gothersgade 157 (from 60kr per day); and Københavns Cykler, Reventlowsgade 11 (from 85kr per day).

Accommodation

Copenhagen has a good selection of hostels although most are a little way out from the centre; space is only likely to be a problem in the peak summer months, when you'll have to book in advance or turn up as early as possible to be sure of a place. Hotels can be pricey but there are often online deals available and a few cheaper options in the centre. Note that private rooms (around 400kr) booked through the tourist office are usually an S-train ride away from the centre. Breakfast is not included in the prices given, unless otherwise stated.

Hostels and sleep-ins

City Public Hostel Absalonsgade 8, Vesterbro ⓣ33.35.00.81, ⓦwww.citypublichostel.dk. Just 10min walk from the train station, with a noisy sixty-bed dorm on the lower floor, less crowded conditions on other levels. Free wi-fi; 24hr check-in; cash only; breakfast 30kr. Buses #6a and #26 stop close by. Closed Sept–April. Dorms 150kr.

Danhostel Copenhagen City H.C. Andersens Boulevard 50 ⓣ33.11.85.85, ⓦwww.dgi-byen.com/hostel_cph_city. Priding itself as Europe's largest "designer" youth hostel, this thousand-bed monster, a short walk from Central Station, is housed in a multi-storey building overlooking the harbour. Has TV room, guest kitchen and internet café (1hr for 29kr). Bikes for 100kr per day. Dorms 185kr, doubles 740kr

Hotel Jørgensen Rømersgade 11 ⓣ33.13.81.86, ⓦwww.hoteljoergensen.dk. Hostel offering 6–12-bed dorms and basic rooms, with a buffet breakfast included. Common room with TV, pool and table football. A stone's throw from Nørreport station on Israels Plads. Dorms 150kr, doubles 675kr.

Sleep-in Green Ravnsborggade 18, Nørrebro ⓣ35.37.77.77, ⓦwww.sleep-in-green.dk. Eco-friendly hostel (solar power, organic breakfasts) with eight-, twenty- and 38-bed dorms. Age limit 35; free internet; breakfast 40kr. Bus #5a/#16, night bus #81N/#84N from the centre (10min). Closed Sept to mid-June. Dorms 120kr.

Sleep-in Heaven Struenseegade 7, Nørrebro ⓣ35.35.46.48, ⓦwww.sleepinheaven.com. Popular hostel in a quiet spot next to Assistens Kirkegård. Six-, nine- or fourteen-bed dorms, plus double rooms (shared bathroom). Welcoming atmosphere, with youthful staff; age limit 35; breakfast 40kr. Open 24hr; pool table; free internet. Bus #12 or #69, nightbus #92N from the centre (10min). Dorms130kr, doubles 500kr.

Hotels

Absalon Annex Helgolandsgade 15 ⓣ33.24.22.11, ⓦwww.absalon-hotel.dk. Basic, slightly worn rooms with TV and shared bathroom in a one-star annexe of this three-star hotel. Price includes a good breakfast buffet. Doubles 600kr.

Cabinn City Mitchellsgade 14 ⓣ33.46.16.16, ⓦwww.cabinn.com. Clean cabin-style rooms close to Tivoli and the station. All are en-suite and have TV; breakfast is 60kr extra. Two other branches in Frederiksberg. Doubles 545kr.

Hotel Løven Vesterbrogade 30 ⓣ33.79.67.20, ⓦwww.loevenhotel.dk. A real bargain for such a central location, Løven looks small from the outside (ring the bell marked "1st floor Løven" for admittance), but inside has 46 airy and spacious rooms spread over five floors; most have a fridge, and some have a/c and bathroom. No breakfast but has kitchen for self-catering. Reservations essential in summer. Doubles 490kr.

Campsites

Bellahøj Camping Hvidkildevej 66 ⓣ38.10.11.50, ⓦwww.bellahoj-camping.dk. The most central site but rather grim, with long queues for the showers. Rents bikes for 65kr per day. Bus #2a, nightbus #82N. Closed Sept–May. 65kr per person.

Charlottenlund Strandpark Strandvejen 144, Charlottenlund ⓣ39.62.36.88, ⓦwww.campingcopenhagen.dk. Beautifully situated 6km from Copenhagen at Charlottenlund Beach and with good, clean facilities. Very busy in summer. S-train line A, B or C to Svanemøllen then bus #14. Closed mid-Sept to April. 135kr per person.

Eating

Copenhagen has more Michelin-starred restaurants than the rest of Scandinavia put together but there is also a decent range of budget options – heading out of the centre, towards Nørrebro and Vesterbro, is your best bet for saving a few kroner. For self-caterers, bakeries are a good option, while for take-away *smørrebrød* try the outlets at Domhusets Smørrebrød, Kattesundet 18; Centrum Smørrebrød, Vesterbrogade 6C; and Klemmen at Central Station. There are Netto supermarkets at Nørre Voldgade 94, Nørrebrogade 43, Landemærket 11 and Store Kongensgade 47. Fakta supermarket is on Nørrebrogade 14–16 and Borgergade 27.

Cafés

Bang & Jensen Istedgade 130. Popular café at the quieter end of Istedgade, offering a filling breakfast buffet (60kr), brunch (75kr) and sandwiches and light meals all day (around 75kr). Turns into a busy bar at night.

Café Bjørgs Vester Voldgade 19. Bright, central café serving excellent coffee and good-value sandwiches, salads and brunch. Brunch 99kr.

Det Gule Hus Istedgade 48. Trendy, bright-yellow café/bar offering three types of brunch (89kr) and a range of filling salads. Mains 75kr.

Front Page Sortedam Dossering 21. The food's not cheap, but with its lakeside setting, this is a perfect spot for a quiet coffee or a cool beer. Club sandwich 115kr.

La Galette Larsbjørnsstræde 9. Authentic Breton pancakes made with organic buckwheat and an array of fillings – from ham and eggs to smoked salmon and caviar. Pancakes 35–100kr.

Paradis Vesterbro Torv, Vesterbrogade. Very popular Italian-style ice-cream outlet with over thirty flavours made fresh each morning. Also branches at Sankt Hans Torv and Løngangstræde, Indre By. Two scoops 25kr.

Studenterhuset Købmagergade 52. Friendly student hangout by the Rundetaarn with table football and pinball machines. Live music Thurs–Sat and an international party every Wed for foreign exchange students. Coffee and cake 22kr; sandwich 33kr; large beer 23kr (a student card gets you a third off all prices).

Restaurants

Aamanns Øster Farimagsgade 10. Good place for cheap *smørrebrød* and other Danish dishes (from 44kr), to eat in or to take away.

COPENHAGEN'S BEST BAKERIES

The Danes take their bakeries seriously and you'll see them all around Copenhagen. The range of loaves and pastries on offer can almost be intimidating, but staff will happily advise. As well as *rundstykker* and flaky pastries, most bakeries offer sandwiches, which can make for a cheap lunch option. The following five are among the best in the city:

Emmerys Vesterbrogade 34, Nørrebrogade 8, and Østerbrogade 51, among others. Trendy bakery chain with organic bread and filling sandwiches (around 60kr).

Lagkagehuset Torvegade 45, Christianshavn. Opposite the metro station, this justifiably popular bakery offers a bewildering range of breads baked in stone ovens, as well as great pastries (from 14kr) and fruit-covered cakes. There's a smaller branch in the tourist office.

La Glace Skoubougade 3, east of Gammel Torv. Copenhagen's oldest confectioner (dating to 1870), this is an essential stop for cake and freshly made hot chocolate on a chilly day.

Rhein van Hauen Mikkelbryggersgade 8, near Rådhuspladsen, and Østergade 22. Scrumptious Danish pastries and luscious *rundstykker* (bread rolls); a great stop for breakfast or an afternoon pick-me-up.

Trianon Hyskenstræde 8, east of Nytorv. Purveyors to the queen – so the standard of breads and pastries here is top-notch.

Addis Mesob Fredensgade 11. You may not have come to Copenhagen to try Ethiopian food but this place isn't to be missed. Try their spicy stews eaten by hand with flatbread. Mains 79kr; lunchtime buffet 125kr.

Atlas Bar Larsbjørnsstræde 18. Busy basement bar/restaurant with an imaginative range of world food from ostrich and Japanese beef to Mexican vegetarian burritos (kitchen closes 10pm). Mains from 105kr.

Ayuttaya Griffenfeldsgade 39. Excellent authentic Thai soups, noodle dishes and curries to eat in or take away (mains 80–95kr). Also has a sister restaurant in Frederiksberg at H.C. Ørstedsvej 53.

Den Danske Kro Nørre Farimagsgade 13. A good choice for traditional Danish fare and *smørrebrød*. The portions are large and the fish dishes come recommended. Mains around 99kr.

Restaurant Willumsen Store Regnegade 26. Initimate restaurant with a somewhat antiquarian decor, offering a wide range of *smørrebrød*, such as sausage with onion and aspic (58kr) and various herring dishes (52kr). Has live jazz on Wed evenings.

RizRaz Kompagnistræde 20. Stylish Mediterranean chain with an excellent vegetarian buffet including spinach lasagne, pizza and feta salad for 79kr (89kr after 4pm). Another branch at Store Kannikestræde. Mains around 139kr.

Tasty Burmeistersgade 34. Aptly named Indian restaurant hidden away between Prinsessegade and Christianshavn's canal. Good selection of fish curries including a fantastic prawn biryani. Mains from 69kr.

Thai Esan Lille Istedgade 7. Good value and perennially popular Thai fare. If it's full, try *Thai Esan 2* around the corner at Halmtorvet 44. Mains 80kr.

Drinking and nightlife

Bars

Andy's Bar Gothersgade 33B. Packed late-night bar with a very jovial vibe – you'll end up leaving the place with lots of new friends. Daily 11pm–6am.

Brew Pub Vestergarde 29. Popular micobrewery bang in the centre of town with a range of ales (37/58kr for small/large) and a great beer garden. Also has an excellent (though pricey) Danish/French menu.

Caféen Blågårds Apotek Blågårds Plads 20. Unpretentious bar with a mixed crowd: students attracted by the cheap beer and an older crowd here for the regular live blues and jazz.

Ideal Bar Enghavevej 40. Part of the Vega music complex, this bar has a cool 1950s interior and a buzzing pre-club vibe.

Mexibar Elmegade 27. Small, tucked-away place with a straw-roofed bar and a friendly atmosphere. Some of the best and cheapest cocktails in town, made with fresh fruit (try the strawberry daiquiri, 44kr). You can also double up on spirits for 12kr. Understandably packed at weekends.

GAY COPENHAGEN

The Danish capital has a small but lively **gay scene** and hosts regular festivals and events including an annual Gay Pride march. Check out Ⓦ www.visitcopenhagen.com/gay for more information.

Moose Bar Sværtegade 5. Dingy pub/bar with a juke machine, an equal mix of Danes and tourists, a good vibe and cheap beer (large Carlsberg 23kr).
Nemoland Christiania. Run by Christiania residents, this is one of the city's most popular open-air bars, with picnic tables and decent café food. In winter, the crowd moves indoors to the pool tables and backgammon boards.
Oscar Rådhuspladsen 77. Café-bar in a perfect location off Rådhuspladsen; popular with a gay clientele. DJs hit the decks on Fri and Sat nights.
Sebastopol Sankt Hans Torv 2. Trendy café-bar with a retro feel on the Sankt Hans Torv square; gathers large crowds in summer. Small/large beer 28/52kr. Good brunches too.
Vesterbro Bryghus Vesterbrogade 2B. Probably the best option for a drink close to Tivoli, this micro-brewery offers a 10cl sample of each of its five home-made beers for 59kr; all beers are 2-for-1 during happy hour (4–6pm).

Clubs

Culture Box Kronprinsessegade 54A Ⓦ www.culture-box.dk. Stylish basement club by Kongens Have: the best electronica venue in town. Entry 60–120kr.
Isola Rockmusiclub Linnésgade 16A. Intimate club/bar playing mostly soul, rock and R&B. Free entry. Thurs–Sat 8pm–5am.
Rust Guldbergsgade 8 Ⓦ www.rust.dk. Popular club and concert venue playing indie, rock and hip-hop. Admission 60kr.
Vega Natklub Enghavevej 40 Ⓦ www.vega.dk. Part of the Vega live music complex in trendy Vesterbro, this club offers a good mix of underground and mainstream house and electro. Fri & Sat 11pm–5am. Free until 1am, then 60kr.

Shopping

Clothes Istegade and the parallel Vesterbrogade have the best selection of boutiques including vintage and little-known designer wear. Check out Donn Ya Doll at Istedgade 55 for a great range of gadgets and Scandinavian designer labels. Among the clothes shops off Strøget you'll find Lust, at Mikkel Bryggersgade 3A, a sleaze-free erotic gift shop aimed at women and couples.
Danish design ILLUM, hard to miss halfway down Strøget at Østergade 52, is Copenhagen's premier department store and sells a range of Danish homeware. Even if you can only afford a teaspoon, it's worth visiting just to marvel at the interior. Nearby is Bang & Olufsen's flagship store at Kongens Nytorv 26, selling top-end TVs, cordless telephones and so on. More affordably, the Bodum store at Østergade 10 offers a range of imaginative kitchenware including their classic cafetiere.
Markets The most central market is the celebrated but pricey Gammel Strand flea market (every Fri & Sat 8am–5pm), which mainly focuses on antiques. It's better to head out a bit further to Nørrebro's Assistens Cemetery for cheaper deals on everything from porcelain to clothes (every Sat May to mid-Oct 7am–2pm).

Entertainment

Cinema

Gloria Biografen Rådhuspladsen 59 Ⓣ 33.12.42 92, Ⓦ www.gloria.dk. Stylish little cinema, with a good mix of mainstream and arthouse films (around 70kr).
Imperial Ved Vesterport 4 Ⓣ 70.13.12.11, Ⓦ www.kino.dk. Copenhagen's largest cinema, with only one theatre which can fit over 1100 people and has terrific surround sound. Seats around 90kr but worth it for the experience.

Live music

As well as the options below, check out the programmes at *Vega* and *Rust* (see opposite).
Drop Inn Kompagnistræde 34 Ⓦ www.drop-inn.dk. Laid-back, unpretentious place with jazz/blues acts during the week and cover bands at weekends. Cheap beer and great range of whiskies. Open until 5am.
Mojo Løngangsstræde 21C, Indre By Ⓦ www.mojo.dk. Atmospheric, divey blues venue with live acts every night. Happy hour 8–10pm; open until 5am. Entrance free or 60/120kr depending on act.
Pumpehuset Studiestræde 52 Ⓦ www.pumpehuset.dk. A concert venue in a former salt warehouse, with bars on both floors. Hosts Danish bands and also attracts international names such as Kaiser Chiefs and Röyksopp. Entrance 70–250kr.

Opera and theatre

If you're under 25 (or if you're buying after 4pm on the day of the performance) then you may be able to get tickets at half price for any of the three

venues below: ask at the Royal Theatre box office for details.

Operaen Christianshavns Torv ⓦwww.operaen.dk. The city's spectacular opera house is as much an architectural as a musical attraction. A cheap way to see a performance is to buy a standing stalls ticket on the day of performance (from 90kr). Guided tours are also offered, though must be booked in advance (75min; 100kr).

Royal Playhouse Sankt Annæ Plads 36 ⓦwww.kgl-teater.dk. Opened in February 2008, this dramatic waterside building has three stages, one of which can be opened onto the promenade for alfresco plays or jazz performances in summer. All plays are in Danish, but it's worth stopping off in the café inside, which has a superb view over the harbour. There are also highly recommended tours of the playhouse in English for 100kr (see website for times).

Royal Theatre Kongens Nytorv ⓦwww.kgl-teater.dk. Denmark's oldest and grandest theatre hosts ballet, opera, drama and concerts.

Directory

Embassies Australia, Dampfærgevej 26 ⓣ70.26.36.76; Canada, Kristen Bernikowsgade 1 ⓣ33.48.32.00; Ireland, Østbanegade 21 ⓣ35.42.32.33; UK, Kastelsvej 40 ⓣ35.44.52.00; US, Dag Hammerskjölds Allé 24 ⓣ35.55.31.44.

Exchange Den Danske Bank at the airport (daily 6am–8.30pm); Forex and X-Change at the Central Station (daily 7/8am–9pm).

Hospital Rigshospitalet, Blegdamsvej 9 ⓣ35.45.35.45.

Internet Boomtown at Axeltorv 1–3, opposite Tivoli main entrance (30kr per hr).

Left luggage Lockers at Central Station, from 30kr for 24hr.

Pharmacies Steno Apotek, Vesterbrogade 6C; Sønderbro Apotek, Amagerbrogade 158. Both 24hr.

Police In Central Station and at Halmtorvet 20, off Lille Istedgade.

Post office Købmagergade 33 and at Central Station.

Moving on

Trains Aalborg (2 hourly; 4hr 25min–4hr 50min); Århus (2 hourly; 2hr 55min–3hr 10min); Hamburg (hourly; 5hr); Helsingør (every 20min; 50min); Malmö (every 30min; 22min); Odense (4 hourly; 1hr 30min); Roskilde (8 hourly; 25min).

Buses Aalborg (3–5 daily; 4hr 45min); Århus (6–7 daily; 3hr); Malmö (hourly; 55min).

DAY-TRIPS FROM COPENHAGEN

When the weather's good, you can top up your tan at the **Amager Strandpark beach**, just 5km from the centre (bus #12 or take the Metro to Øresund, Amager Strand or Femøren then a 5min walk). If Tivoli hasn't exhausted your appetite then make for the world's oldest amusement park at **BAKKEN** (April–Aug daily noon/2pm–10pm/midnight; 219kr), close to the Klampenborg stop at the end of lines C and F+ on the S-train. Besides slightly sinister clowns and some vintage roller coasters it offers pleasant woods to wander around.

There are two more excellent attractions on Zealand's northeastern coast. Fifteen minutes' walk from Rungsted Kyst train station, the peaceful **Karen Blixen Museum** (May–Sept Tues–Sun 10am–5pm; Oct–April Wed–Sun 11am/1pm–4pm; 50kr) presents a moving testament to this remarkable woman, best known as the author of *Out of Africa*. In **HUMLEBÆK**, 10km further north and a short walk from its train station, is **Louisiana**, an outstanding modern art gallery, at Gammel Strandvej 13 (Tues–Fri 11am–10pm, Sat–Sun 11am–6pm; 90kr; ⓦwww.louisiana.dk). The gallery's setting is worth the journey alone – a harmonious blend of art, architecture and the natural landscape.

The rest of Zealand

As home to Copenhagen, **Zealand** is Denmark's most visited region, and, with a swift metropolitan transport network covering almost half of the island, you can always make it back to the capital in time for an evening drink. North of Copenhagen, **Helsingør** (Elsinore) is the departure point for

ferries to Sweden and the site of the legendary Kronborg Castle. To the west, and on the main train route to Funen, is **Roskilde**, with an extravagant cathedral that served as the resting place for Danish monarchs, and a gorgeous location on the Roskilde fjord, from where five Viking boats were salvaged and are now restored and displayed in a specially built museum.

HELSINGØR

First impressions of **HELSINGØR** are none too enticing, but away from the bustle of its train and ferry terminals it's a quiet and likeable town. Its position on the narrow strip of water linking the North Sea and the Baltic brought the town prosperity when, in 1429, the Sound Toll was imposed on passing vessels. Today it's once again an important waterway, with ferries to Swedish Helsingborg accounting for most of Helsingør's through-traffic and innumerable cheap booze shops.

What to see and do

The town's great tourist draw is **Kronborg Castle** (May–Sept daily 10.30am–5pm; Oct–April Tues–Sun 11am–3/4pm; 65kr, 90kr joint ticket with the Maritime Museum; Ⓦwww.kronborgcastle.com), principally because of its literary associations as Elsinore Castle, the setting for Shakespeare's *Hamlet*. There's no evidence that Shakespeare ever visited Helsingør, and the tenth-century character Amleth on whom his hero was based long predates the castle. Nevertheless, the Hamlet souvenir business continues to thrive here. The present castle dates from the sixteenth century when it stood out like a raised fist into the sound, a warning to passing ships not to consider dodging the toll. Though various parts have been destroyed and rebuilt since, it remains a grand affair, enhanced immeasurably by its setting; the interior, particularly the royal chapel, is spectacularly ornate. Beneath the castle are the casemates, a gloomy network of cavernous rooms that served as soldiers' quarters during times of war.

The castle also houses the surprisingly captivating **National Maritime Museum** (50kr, 90kr joint ticket with the castle), which, apart from a motley collection of model ships and nautical knick-knacks, contains relics from Denmark's conquests in Greenland, India, the West Indies and West Africa, as well as the world's oldest surviving ship's biscuit (1852).

The medieval quarter

Helsingør's well-preserved medieval quarter is dominated by **Stengade**, the main shopping street, linked by a number of narrow alleyways to Axeltorv, the town's small market square and a nice place to enjoy a beer. Near the corner of Stengade and Skt. Annagade is Helsingør's cathedral, **Skt. Olai's Kirke** (daily: May–Aug 10am–4pm, Sept–April 10am–2pm; free), with its renovated spire. Just beyond is **Skt. Mariæ Kirke** (daily 10am–2pm, free; guided tours at Mon–Fri 2pm; 20kr), whose Karmeliterklostret, built circa 1400, is now the best-preserved medieval monastery in Scandinavia (guided tours only; arrange via the church office). Its former hospital now contains the **Town Museum** (daily noon–4pm, Sat until 2pm; 20kr), which displays an unnerving selection of surgical tools used in early brain operations.

Arrival and information

Train station On Jernbanevej, a 2min walk south of the centre.

Tourist office Havnepladsen 3, just opposite the train station (Mon–Fri 10am–4pm; ⓣ49.21.13.33, Ⓦwww.visithelsingor.dk).

Accommodation

Danhostel Helsingør Nordre Strandvej 24 ⓣ49.21.16.40, Ⓦwww.helsingorhostel.dk.

FERRIES TO SWEDEN

Three ferry companies (ⓦwww.acelink.dk, ⓦwww.hhferries.dk and ⓦwww.scandlines.dk) make the twenty-minute crossing from Helsingør to **Helsingborg** in Sweden every 20–30min (around 50kr return). All services leave from the main terminal by the train station. Eurail is valid on Scandlines and InterRail and the Copenhagen Card give a 25 percent discount.

Beautifully located hostel in a restored villa right on the beach (suitable for swimming) 2km north of town; bus #340 from the station (8min; get off at Højstrup Trinbraet stop). Rents bikes for 75kr per day. Dorms 175kr, doubles 350kr

Eating and drinking

Café Manhattan Jernbanevej 6, opposite station. Good spot to shoot some pool and meet the locals. Has free wi-fi. Happy hour Thurs–Sat 8–10pm; closed Sun.

Phonoteket Stengade 36. Cosy music store café popular with locals. Sandwiches 69kr; coffee 22kr.

Pizzeria Pakhuset Strengade 26. Great-value pizza and pasta (both from 62kr) in a trattoria-style restaurant.

Moving on

Train Copenhagen (every 20min; 50min).

ROSKILDE

Once the capital of Denmark, **ROSKILDE** is worth a visit even if you can't make it to its famous rock festival (see below). Its Viking Ship museum is a world-class attraction while the cathedral and old centre are lovely to wander around.

What to see and do

The fabulous **Roskilde Domkirke** (April–Sept Mon–Sat 9am–5pm, Sun 12.30–5pm; Oct–March Tues–Sat 10am–4pm, Sun 12.30–4pm; 25kr), was founded by Bishop Absalon in 1170 and largely completed by the fourteenth century, although bits have been added since. It's stuffed full of dead Danish monarchs including twenty-one kings and eighteen queens. The most impressive chapel is that of Christian IV, full of bronze statues, frescoes and vast paintings of scenes from his reign.

A roofed passageway, the Arch of Absalon (not open to the public) runs from the cathedral into the Roskilde Palace next door, housing the diverting **Museum of Contemporary Art** (Tues–Fri 11am–5pm, Sat & Sun noon–4pm when there are exhibitions on; 40kr, Wed free), which hosts temporary exhibitions and includes a charming sculpture garden. Just east of the cathedral, at Sankt Ols Gade 15, is the **Roskilde Museum** (daily 11am–4pm; free; ⓦwww.roskildemuseum.dk), with a curious array of miscellanea relating to Roskilde's history, from Neolithic daggers to fourteenth-century shoes and a 200-year-old toboggan.

The Viking Ship Museum

Fifteen minutes' walk north of the centre on the banks of the fjord is the modern **Viking Ship Museum** (daily 10am–5pm; 95kr May–Sept, otherwise 55kr; ⓦwww.vikingshipmuseum.dk). Inside, five superb specimens of Viking shipbuilding are displayed: a deep-sea

ROSKILDE FESTIVAL

Book well in advance if you wish to stay during the **Roskilde Festival** (ⓦwww.roskilde-festival.dk), one of the largest open-air music festivals in Europe, attracting almost 100,000 people annually. Tickets go on sale in December and tend to sell out quickly. The festival usually takes place in early July and there's a special free camping ground beside the festival site, to which shuttle buses run from the train station every few minutes.

trader, a merchant ship, a warship, a fishing vessel and a longship, each retrieved from the fjord where they were sunk to block invading forces. Two life-size models of ships are next door, which you can board after trying on traditional Viking clothes. Outside, you can watch boat-building and sail-making using only tools and materials available during the Viking era; when the weather allows you can also experience a replica ship's seaworthiness on the fjord – you'll be handed an oar when you board and be expected to pull your weight as a crew member (50min; 75kr on top of the museum ticket; minimum 12 people). It's a humbling experience when you consider that similar ships made it all the way to Greenland.

Arrival and information

Train and bus The train station is at the southern edge of town. The bus station is within the same complex.

Tourist office On the main square, Stændertorvet 1 (Mon–Fri 10am–5pm, Sat 10am–1/2pm; ⓣ46.31.65.65, ⓦwww.visitroskilde.com).

Accommodation

Roskilde Vandrerhjem Vindeboder 7 ⓣ46.35.21.84, ⓦwww.danhostel.dk/roskilde. Beautifully situated modern hostel in the harbour area near the Viking Museum. Free internet access and also rents out bikes (50kr per day or 300kr per week). Dorms 200kr, doubles 500kr.

Eating and drinking

Café Druedahls Skomagergade 40. Popular café just south of the cathedral, with a range of beers and sandwiches. Offers a good-value brunch for 79kr.

Gimle Helligkorvej 2, a 10min walk east of the tourist office. Live music venue with a café serving burgers (75kr) and sandwiches (45kr) noon–midnight. Turns into a club Fri & Sat nights (midnight–5am).

Moving on

Train Copenhagen (every 20min; 30min); Odense (every 30min; 1hr 10min).

Funen

Funen is the smaller of the two main Danish islands. The pastoral outlook of the place and the laid-back fishing villages along the coast draw many visitors, but the main attraction is **Odense**, Denmark's third city and the birthplace of writer Hans Christian Andersen and composer Carl Nielsen.

ODENSE

Named after Odin, chief of the pagan gods, **ODENSE** (pronounced Own-suh) is over a thousand years old. It's one of Denmark's most attractive cities with cobbled streets set around the River Odense Å. The inner core of the city is pedestrianized with a range of good museums to visit and the nightlife is surprisingly energetic, with a focus on live music.

What to see and do

The city's major attraction is the **Hans Christian Andersen Hus** at Bangs Boder 29 (June–Aug daily 9am–6pm; Sept–May Tues–Sun 10am–4pm; 60kr), where the writer was born in 1805. The museum includes a library of Andersen's works and headphones for listening to some of his best-known fairy tales read by the likes of Sir Laurence Olivier. There's also plenty of intriguing paraphernalia on the man, including school reports, manuscripts, paper cuttings and drawings from his travels. Check out the telling quotes on Andersen's unconventional looks and talent: "He is the most hideous man you could find but has a poetic childish mind," commented a female contemporary.

Hans Christian Andersens Barndomshjem and Skt. Knuds Kirke

There's more about Andersen at Munkemøllestræde 3–5, between Skt.

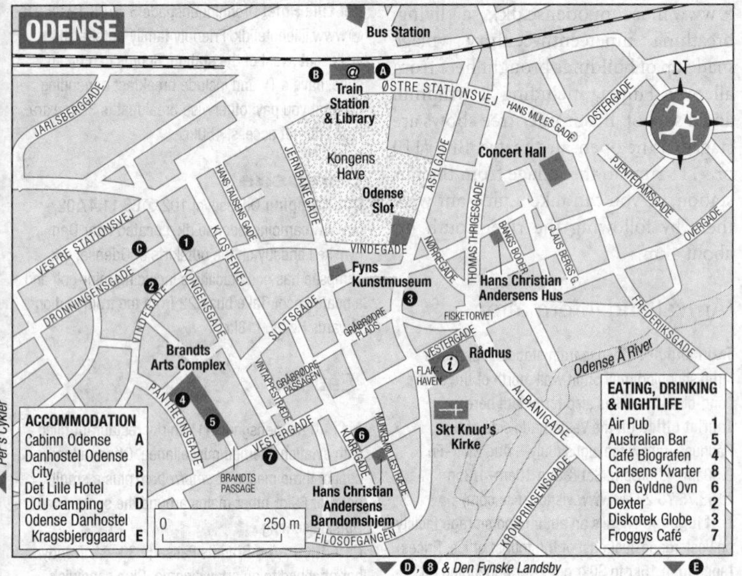

Knud Kirkestræde and Horsetorvet, in the tiny **Hans Christian Andersens Barndomshjem** (Childhood Home; daily 10/11am–3/4pm; 25kr), where the writer lived between the ages of two and fourteen. Nearby, the crypt of **Skt. Knuds Kirke** (Mon–Sat 10am–4/5pm, Sun noon–5pm; free) holds the remains of King Knud II and his brother Benedikt, both murdered in 1086 at the altar of nearby Skt. Albani Kirke. The cathedral's Gothic exterior is complemented by an elegant white interior while its main draw is the rather overwhelming wooden altarpiece, coated in twenty-three carat gold leaf; one of the greatest works of the Lübeck master, Claus Berg.

The Fyns Kunstmuseum and Brandts Arts Complex

At Jernbanegade 13, the **Fyns Kunstmuseum** (Funen Art Gallery; Tues–Sun 10am–4pm; 40kr; Ⓦwww.museum.odense.dk), just a few minutes' walk from Skt. Knuds, gives a good introduction to the Danish art world during the late nineteenth century; the collection contains some stirring works by Vilhelm Hammershøi, P.S. Krøyer, Michael and Anne Ancher, and H.A. Brendekilde's emotive *Udslidt* ("Exhaustion"). West of the centre is the **Brandts Arts Complex** on Brandts Passage, just off Vestergade. Once a large textile mill, the area has been beautifully converted and now features an art school, cinema, music library, and three museums (Tues–Sun 10am–5pm; 70kr combined ticket; Ⓦwww.brandts.dk). In the large hall that once housed the huge machinery is the **Kunsthallen**, which displays works by the cream of new talent in art and design, and the **Museet for Fotokunst**, featuring changing exhibitions of photography. On the third floor the **Danmarks Mediemuseum** chronicles the development of printing, bookbinding and illustrating from the Middle Ages to the present.

Den Fynske Landsby

South of the centre at Sejerskovvej 20 is **Den Fynske Landsby** (Funen Village; April–Oct Tues–Sun 10am–5/7pm; Nov–March Sun 11am–5pm; 60kr;

Ⓦwww.museum.odense.dk), a living, breathing nineteenth-century village made up of buildings brought here from all over Funen, including a windmill and a school. In summer free shows are staged at the open-air theatre. Bus #110 or #111 runs to the village from the bus station, or you can take a pleasant walk there by following the river south for about 4km.

Arrival and information

Train and bus Odense train station is part of a large shopping mall 5min walk north of the centre. Long-distance buses also terminate here.
Tourist office On the Vestergade side of the Rådhus – follow the signs (July & Aug Mon–Fri 9.30am–4.30/6pm, Sat & Sun 10am–1/3pm; Ⓣ63.75.75.20, Ⓦwww.visitodense.com).
Left luggage There's an automated storage facility on Vestergade, just east of the tourist office. Prices range from 15kr to 30kr per 24hr depending on size of locker.
Internet The library at the train station has free internet access.
Bike rental Per's Cykler og Knallerter, at Vesterbro 95, rents bikes for 60/350kr per day/week, with a 100kr deposit.

Accommodation

Hostels

Danhostel Odense City Østre Stationsvej 31 Ⓣ66.11.04.25, Ⓦwww.cityhostel.dk. Conveniently located in a former hotel next to the train station, this five-star hostel has clean rooms, wi-fi for 30kr per day and 24hr automated check-in. Also has a good café with buffet breakfast for 65kr. Dorms 175kr, doubles 500kr.
Odense Danhostel Kragsbjerggaard Kragsbjergvej 121 Ⓣ66.13.04.25, Ⓦwww.odense-danhostel.dk. Sister hostel to the city branch, this one is set in a manor house surrounded by woodland 2km south of the centre (bus #61 & 63 from the station). Breakfast included. Dorms 259kr, doubles 598kr.

Hotels

Cabinn Odense Østre Stationsvej 7–9 Ⓣ63.14.57.00, Ⓦwww.cabinn.com. Budget chain hotel close to the train station. All rooms are short on space but are en suite and have TV. Free internet access; buffet breakfast 60kr. 485kr.
Det Lille Hotel Dronningensgade 5 Ⓣ66.12.28.21, Ⓦwww.lillehotel.dk. Friendly family hotel a short walk southwest of the station. Rooms can be en suite, have a TV and include breakfast depending on what you pay; otherwise breakfast is 35kr extra. Free internet access. 450kr.

Campsite

DCU Camping Odensevej 102 Ⓣ66.11.47.02, Ⓦwww.camping-odense.dk. Located near Den Fynske Landsby on the outskirts of Odense, this campsite has good facilities including mini-golf and a heated pool. Take bus #22 from the train station towards Højby. 118kr.

Eating

Air Pub Kongensgade 41. Quirky restaurant filled with aviation-themed miscellanea. Offers a lunch deal of three pieces of *smørrebrød* plus a small beer for 69kr; other mains around the same price. Outside seating.
Café Biografen Brandts Passage 39–41. Trendy bar attached to an artsy cinema. Club sandwich 68kr; coffee 22kr.
Den Gyldne Ovn Klaregade 14. Reliable spot for freshly made pastries and sandwiches (48kr).
Froggys Café Vestergade 68. Cosy café/bar bang in the centre serving delicious salads (86kr) and the legendary Froggy's burger (99kr). DJs at weekends.

Drinking and nightlife

Australian Bar Brandts Passage 10. Aussie-themed sports bar by day switching to a nightclub after 10pm Thurs–Sat (40kr entrance with shots for 10kr). Popular with exchange students and teenagers.
Carlsens Kvarter Hunderupvej 19. Cosy bar in the style of a country pub, with a relaxed atmosphere and Odense's best selection of beers, including all the Belgian Trappist ales. Try the fantastic elderflower-flavoured Fynsk Forår (29kr).
Dexter Vindegade 65 Ⓣ63.11.27.28. Jazz, blues and folk venue with live music 2–3 times per week (entry 50–60kr) and a free jam night on Mon evenings. Good range of international beers too.
Diskotek Globe Asylgade 7–9 Ⓣ41.28.99.18, Ⓦwww.diskotekglobe.dk. Odense's main nightclub and the best place in town for a dance and a cocktail. Thurs–Sat 11pm–5am.

Moving on

Train Århus (every 30min; 1hr 40min); Copenhagen (3 hourly; 1hr 35min); Esbjerg (hourly; 1hr 20min).

Jutland

Long ago, the Jutes, the people of **Jutland**, were a separate tribe from the more warlike Danes who occupied the eastern islands. By the Viking era, however, the battling Danes had spread west, absorbing the Jutes, and real power gradually shifted towards Zealand, where it has largely stayed ever since. Unhurried lifestyles and rural calm are the overriding impressions of Jutland for most visitors. **Århus**, halfway up the eastern coast, is Jutland's main urban centre and Denmark's second city. Further inland, the landscape is dramatic – all stark heather-clad moors and dense forests. North of vibrant **Aalborg**, the landscape becomes increasingly wind-battered and stark until it reaches **Skagen**, on the very tip of the peninsula.

THE FERRY PORTS: ESBJERG AND FREDERIKSHAVN

There are two main international ferry ports in Jutland. **ESBJERG** has overnight ferries to and from Britain; bus #5 connects the passenger harbour with the centre (a 15min walk). The train station, with trains to and from Copenhagen (3hr 10min), is at the end of Skolegade, and, at no. 33, you'll find the tourist office (Ⓣ75.12.55.99, Ⓦwww.visitesbjerg.dk).

FREDERIKSHAVN, in the far north of the region (2hr 45min by train from Århus), has express ferries to Sweden and Norway. Its ferry terminal is near Havnepladsen, not far from the centre, while all buses and most trains terminate at the central train station, a short walk from the town centre; some trains continue to the ferry terminal itself. The tourist office is close by at Skandiatorv 1 (Ⓣ98.42.32.66, Ⓦwww.frederikshavn-tourist.dk).

ÅRHUS

Denmark's second-largest city, **ÅRHUS**, is an instantly likeable assortment of intimate cobbled streets, sleek modern architecture, brightly painted houses and student hangouts. It's small enough to get to grips with in a few hours, but lively enough to make you linger for days – an excellent music scene, interesting art, pavement cafés and energetic nightlife all earn it the unofficial title of Denmark's capital of culture.

What to see and do

Århus's main street, the pedestrianized Ryesgade/Søndergade, leads down from the train station, across the river and into the main town square, Bispetorvet. The square is dominated by the fifteenth-century **Domkirke** (Mon–Sat 9.30/10am–3/4pm) a massive Gothic church with some exquisite frescoes decorating the whitewashed interior as well as a miniature Danish warship hanging from the ceiling. The area to the north, known as the Latin Quarter, is crammed with browsable shops, galleries and enticing cafés. Across the road from the cathedral, hidden away in the basement of the Nordea Bank, is the

DENMARK'S OLDEST CITY?

Until recently it was thought that **Vikings** first settled in Århus or Aros ("river mouth" in old Nordic) around the year 900 AD. However, new excavations have revealed that they arrived as early as the mid-eighth century, causing no end of excitement for the local tourist board who are cheekily claiming Århus is "arguably" **Denmark's oldest city**. This is unlikely to go down well in Ribe, Southern Jutland, the current holder of the title with evidence of Viking settlement from the beginning of the eighth century. The rivalry is set to increase as archeologists continue to dig deeper.

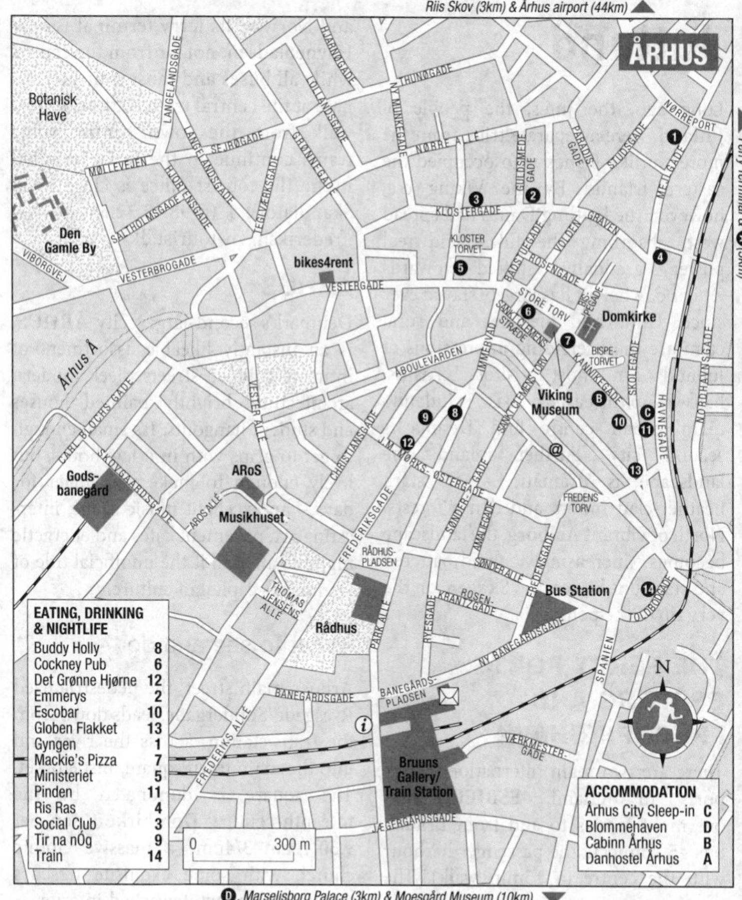

tiny **Viking Museum** (Mon–Fri 10am–4pm, Thurs until 5.30pm; free), which will fill you in on Århus's early development.

The Rådhus

One of Denmark's most divisive buildings, Århus's 1941 **Rådhus** (city hall) was designed by Arne Jacobsen and Eric Moller in a modern functionalist style. Above the entrance hangs Hagedorn Olsen's huge mural, *A Human Society*, symbolically depicting the city emerging from World War II. You can wander in and investigate this for yourself, but to enjoy a view over the city and bay from the bell tower, you'll need to take a guided tour (mid-June to Aug Tues & Thurs 2pm; 10kr).

ARoS

Opened in 2004, **ARoS** (Tues–Sun 10am–5pm, Wed until 10pm; 90kr; ⓦ www.aros.dk) is one of Europe's most beautiful contemporary buildings and a fantastic modern art museum. It contains seven floors of works from the late eighteenth century to the present day accessed from a centrepiece spiral walkway reminiscent of the Guggenheim in New York. As well as a fine collection of home-grown art, including

paintings by the Skagen artists, you'll find works by Gilbert & George, several Warhols and the staggeringly eerie *Boy*, a five-metre-high sculpture by the Australian Ron Mueck.

Den Gamle By

A short walk northwest of the centre is one of the city's best-known attractions, **Den Gamle By** ("the old town"), on Viborgvej (daily: mid-June to Aug 9am–6pm; Sept to mid-June 10/11am–3/5pm; 100kr; ⓦwww.dengamleby.dk), an open-air museum of traditional Danish life, with seventy-odd half-timbered town houses and actors in contemporary dress. A new town expansion is under construction (due to be completed in 2014), which will feature shops and homes from 1900 to 1974 and attractions such as a poster museum. Close by are the pleasant **botanical gardens**, containing a greenhouse with over five thousand foreign plant species (Mon–Sat 1–3pm, Sun 11am–3pm; free).

Beaches and parks

On Sundays Århus resembles a ghost town, most locals spending the day in the parks or beaches on the city's outskirts. The closest **beaches** are north of the city at Riis Skov, easily reached by bus #6 or #16. Otherwise, Marselisborg Skov, south of the centre, is the city's largest park, and home to **Marselisborg Palace**, summer residence of the Danish royals: its landscaped grounds can be visited when the monarch isn't staying (usually at all times outside Easter, Christmas and late Jun to early Aug).

Moesgård Museum

Ten kilometres south of Århus, the **Moesgård Museum** (daily 10am–4/5pm; Oct–March closed Mon; 60kr; ⓦwww.moesmus.dk), reached direct by bus #6, details Danish civilizations from the Stone Age onwards. Its most notable exhibit is the "Grauballe Man", an amazingly well-preserved sacrificial victim dating from around 100 BC discovered in a peat bog west of town in 1952. Also remarkable is a runic hall and the Illerup Ådal collection of Iron Age weapons, found in a lake near Skanderborg. From the museum, a scenic "prehistoric trail" runs 3km to the sea, past a scattering of reassembled dwellings, monuments and burial places. A striking redesign of the museum that will triple its area (but won't affect access) should be complete by 2013.

Arrival and information

Train and bus The train station is just south of the centre and part of the Bruuns Gallery shopping mall. Buses pull in at the terminus across the road.
Air Århus airport is 44km northeast of the centre. Frequent buses run to the train station (45min; 90kr). Note that Billund airport is also accessible from Århus by bus (80min; 180kr).
Ferry Ferries from Zealand dock around 500m east of the centre at the end of Nørreport.
Tourist office VisitAarhus, Banegårdspladsen 20 (ⓣ87.31.50.10, ⓦwww.visitaarhus.com; Mon–Fri 10am–4.30/5.30pm, Sat 10am–3pm). As well as booking rooms for a 50kr fee, they offer the Århus Card (119/149kr for 24/48hr), which, along with unlimited bus travel, covers entrance to most museums and sights.
Internet Boomtown, Åboulevarden 21 (30kr/hr).

City transport

Buses A basic ticket costs 18kr from machines in the back of the bus and is valid for any number of journeys for 2hr from the time stamped on it.
Bike rental From May to Oct you can borrow one of the 400 free city bikes (ⓦwww.aarhusbycykel.dk) dotted around the city centre (20kr coin deposit). Outside this period bikes4rent at Vestergade 41 (ⓦwww.bikes4rent.dk) rents out bikes from 75kr per day, with a 250kr deposit.

Accommodation

Århus City Sleep-In Havnegade 20 ⓣ86.19.20.55, ⓦwww.citysleep-in.dk. The most central hostel, with facilities including a guest kitchen, pool and TV rooms and a courtyard for summer barbecues. Organic breakfast is 65kr; also has free internet access. Dorms 140kr, doubles 400kr.

Blommehaven Ørneredevej 35 ⓣ86.27.02.07, ⓦwww.blommehaven.dk. Overlooking a bay 5km south of the city centre, this campsite has access to a beautiful beach. Closed mid-Oct to mid-March (bus #6 or #19). 108kr.

Cabinn Århus Kannikegade 14 ⓣ86.75.70.00, ⓦwww.cabinn.com. Good-value cabin-style rooms in a centrally located hotel by the river. All rooms are en suite and equipped with TV and telephone. 705kr.

Danhostel Århus Marienlundsvej 10 ⓣ86.21.21.20, ⓦwww.aarhus-danhostel.dk. Peaceful hostel set in woods 3km northeast of the centre and close to the popular Den Permanente beach. Regular bus connections to the Marienlund stop include #1, #6, #8, #9, #16, #56 and #58. Dorms 160kr, doubles 506kr.

Eating

There is no shortage of trendy restaurants in Århus, especially along the river on Åboulevarden. If you can't afford the somewhat inflated prices, it's a lovely spot for a picnic. For self-catering, there's a late-opening supermarket (8am–midnight) at the train station.

Cafés

Emmerys Guldsmedgade 24–26. Superb organic Danish bread and pastries; the coffee is freshly ground and the cakes (35kr) are excellent.

Globen Flakket Åboulevarden 18. Perhaps the best of the riverside cafés, this offers a good range of microbrewery beers and has a weekend brunch buffet for 98kr.

Ministeriet Kloster Torvet 5. Sit outside and enjoy brunch (55–90kr) at this stylish café-restaurant. Sandwiches 60kr.

Restaurants

Det Grønne Hjørne Frederiksgade 60. Great choice for a big feed on the cheap, as the all-you-can-eat lunch buffet (11.30am–4.30pm; 59kr) includes plenty of meat-and-potato variations, soup, salads and desserts – and it's pretty tasty too.

Gyngen Mejlgade 53. Impressive veggie burgers (110kr) and a mean chilli con carne with crème fraîche (68kr). Live music Tues–Sat (entrance 20–125kr); happy hour 9–10pm. Closed Sun.

Mackie's Pizza Sankt Clemens Torv 9. Zany pizza joint with diner-style interior full of sports and music memorabilia. Decent pizzas (80kr), with the rule that you have to eat them without cutlery.

Pinden Skolegade 29. The best place in town for traditional Danish food including a knockout *stegt flæsk med persille sovs* (pork in a creamy parsley sauce) for 92kr. All-you-can-eat lunch buffet for 125kr 12.30–3.30pm. Closed Sun.

Drinking and nightlife

Thanks to its large student population, Århus nightlife almost matches that of Copenhagen.

Bars

Cockney Pub Maren Smeds Gyde 8. Cosy little bar with an excellent range of English, Danish and Belgian ales and a sociable clientele. Smoky, so you may want to sit outside. Live jazz Sunday afternoons.

Escobar Skolegade 32. Popular student hangout with cheap beer (draught 38kr), loud music and friendly bar staff. Open until 3am.

Ris Ras Filliongongong Majlegade 24. Chilled student hangout with a vast range of beers. No food served but you're welcome to bring your own – it's that kind of place.

Tir na nÓg Frederiksgade 40. Large, lively Irish bar with big-screen football and live folk/rock music at weekends. Pint of Carlsberg 25kr noon–7pm. Open until 3am.

Clubs

Buddy Holly Frederiksgade 29 ⓦwww.buddy-aarhus.dk. Cheap and cheerful club that soaks up the late-night crowd. Plenty of drinks deals and a ladies' night on Thurs. Mon–Thurs & Sat 11pm–6am, Fri 7pm–6am.

Social Club Klostergade 34. Large warehouse-style club with a huge dancefloor and free entrance for students. Thurs–Sat 11pm–5am.

Train Toldbodgade 6 ⓦwww.train.dk. Århus's most popular nightclub is also a concert venue that pulls in some big-name DJs and international acts. Entry fees for club nights 70–100kr, or up to 225kr for concerts.

Moving on

Train Aalborg (every 30min; 1hr 20min–1hr 40min); Copenhagen (every 30min; 3hr–3hr 20min); Odense (every 30min; 1hr 40min).

AALBORG

The main city of north Jutland, **AALBORG** is renowned for its raucous nightlife and nearby Viking burial ground. It's also the main transport terminus for the region, and will be a likely stop on your way north to the beaches of Skagen.

What to see and do

Aalborg's well-preserved **old town** is worth a wander, with pleasant cobbled streets and a small but elegant Gothic cathedral, the **Budolfi Domkirke** (Mon–Fri 9am–3/4pm, Sat 9am–noon/2pm), housing a collection of religious paintings. On the other side of Østerågade, the sixteenth-century **Aalborghus Castle** is notable for its dungeon (May–Oct Mon–Fri 8am–3pm; free) and underground passages (until 9pm). Those after a further culture fix should head to the **Kunsten Museum of Modern Art** (Tues–Sun 10am–5pm; 40kr, free in December; ⓦwww.kunsten.dk), a stunning modern art gallery close to a sculpture park (take bus #15 or walk ten minutes west of the train station). Just west of here, up a staircase through the woods, is the **Aalborg Tower** (April–Oct 11am–5pm, 10am–7pm in July; 30kr; ⓦwww.aalborgtaarnet.com), a futuristic silver edifice with spectacular views of the city and a bistro restaurant.

Apart from the above, the city's main attractions are bacchanalian in nature. Leading down to the waterfront, **Jomfru Ane Gade** is Denmark's booziest street, lined with bars and packed most evenings. Aalborg is also the home of Aquavit, the potent Scandinavian spirit, and you can sample some on a guided tour of the **V&S Distillery** at Olensens Gade 1, a ten-minute walk northwest of the centre (tours July & Aug Tues & Thurs 10am and 1pm; 50kr; other times by appointment via ⓔguide.vs.aalborg@distillers.dk; minimum group size 20).

Lindholm Høje

A few kilometres north of Aalborg, the atmospheric **Lindholm Høje** (Lindholm Hills; free) is Scandinavia's largest Viking burial site with more than seven hundred graves. It's best to visit early or late in the day as the slanting sunlight glints off the burial stones, many of which are set in the outline of a Viking ship. You can learn more about the lives of those buried beneath your feet at the site's **museum** (April–Oct daily 10am–5pm; Nov–March Tues–Sun 10am–4pm; 40kr). To get to Lindholm take bus #2 (15min).

Arrival and information

Air Aalborg airport (served by budget airline Norwegian Air Shuttle from London Gatwick) is 7km northwest of the centre and connected by bus #2 (20min).

Train and bus Both terminals are on J.F. Kennedys Plads, 10min walk southwest of the centre. The train station has left-luggage lockers (20kr for 24hr).

Tourist office Centrally located in the old town at Østerågade 8 (Mon–Fri 9am–4.30/5.30pm, Sat 10am–1/4pm; ⓣ98.12.60.22, ⓦwww.visitaalborg.com). You can buy the Aalborg Card here (179/299kr for 24/72hr), which gives you free public transport, free admission to most attractions and discounts in cafés and shops.

Internet There is free access in the city library at Rendsburggade 2, about 400m east of the tourist office off Nytorv.

Accommodation

Aalborg doesn't have any affordable central options, but the tourist office can also book rooms (350kr) in the centre for a fee of 25kr.

Danhostel Aalborg ⓣ98.11.60.44, ⓦwww.danhostelnord.dk/aalborg. Large, well-equipped hostel 3km west of the town on the Limfjord bank beside the marina – take bus #13 to the Egholm ferry junction and continue on foot for 5min following the signs. Dorms 285kr, doubles 478kr.

Strandparken Skydebanevej 20 ⓣ89.12.76.29, ⓦwww.strandparken.dk. Pleasant campsite 2km west of the centre with access to an open-air swimming pool and beach. Closed mid-Sept to mid-March. 90kr.

Zleep Hotel Hadsundvej 182 ⓣ98.10.97.00, ⓦwww.zleephotels.com. Modern budget business hotel attached to a conference centre 3km southeast of town (bus #12; 10min). Rooms are spacious, en-suite and have cable TV. Book well in advance, preferably over sixty days before you stay, in order to get the best deal – rates start at 299kr.

Eating and drinking

Packed with late-opening bars, clubs and restaurants, Jomfru Ane Gade dominates Aalborg's

nightlife and keeps prices competitive with plenty of food and drink deals luring the punters in.

Café Base Lounge Vesterbro 91. Stylish café/bar with filling brunches (89kr) and Aalborg's widest choice of cocktails (59–89kr), with a 2-for-1 deal on Fri and Sat nights, when a DJ is usually in house.

Irish House Østerågade 25. Popular pub serving traditional Irish food (mains 49–69kr) and ales, with regular drinks deals. Live music Thurs–Sat, jam session on Mon and sport on TV most evenings.

Mette Vons Østerågade 16. Great little sandwich shop with a range of filled ciabatta (48kr) and home-made brownies and cookies. Also serves some hot food, such as roast chicken and potatoes. Excellent coffee too (from 15kr).

Studenterhuset Gammeltorv 11, opposite Budolfi Domkirke ⓦwww.studenterhuset.dk. Student-run music venue and café: the place to catch local Danish bands. Also has book exchange library and free internet access. Coffee 14kr; large beer 29kr. Mon–Sat 11.30am–late.

Moving on

Train Århus (2 hourly; 1hr 20min); Copenhagen (2 hourly; 4hr 30min); Frederikshavn (hourly; 1hr 10min).

Bus Århus (via Hobro; 1–2 daily; 4hr); Copenhagen (3 daily; 5hr 30min); Odense (via Hobro; 4 weekly; 4hr).

SKAGEN

About 100km north of Aalborg, **SKAGEN** perches at the very top of Denmark amid a breathtaking landscape of heather-topped sand dunes. Now a popular resort, it attracts thousands of visitors every year thanks to its artistic connections and wonderful seafood restaurants.

What to see and do

Much of Skagen's appeal lies in aimlessly wandering its marina, watching the comings and goings of the yachtie set, or cycling out to the beaches along its coastal bike paths. There is one star sight however – the **Skagen Museum** (follow the signs from the train station; daily 10am–5pm, closed Mon Sept–April; 80kr; ⓦwww.skagensmuseum.dk), displaying much of the work of the influential Skagen artists. Nearby, at Markvej 2–4, is the home of one of the group's leading lights and his wife, herself a skilful painter: the **Michael and Anna Anchers Hus** (May–Oct daily 10/11am–3/6pm; Nov–April Sat 11am–3pm; 50kr). The exhibition evokes the atmosphere of the time through an assortment of used tubes of paint, piles of canvases, paintings, sketches, books and ornaments. Around 1.5km southwest of the hostel is the **Buried Church**, which was engulfed by sand drift in 1795 and subsequently abandoned. Today the white spire is all that remains amid the dunes, a testament to nature's destructive capacity.

THE SKAGEN ARTISTS

Skagen has long been popular with artists thanks to the warm, golden sunlight that illuminates its coastal scenery. During the 1870s a group of painters inspired by naturalism settled here and began to paint the local fishermen working on the beaches as well as each other. The **Skagen artists**, among them Michael and Anna Ancher and P.S. Krøyer, stayed until the turn of the century and achieved international recognition for their work, now on display at the Skagen Museum.

Grenen

Denmark's northernmost tip is at **Grenen**, 3km from Skagen along Sct. Laurentii Vej, Fyrvej and the beach, where two seas – the Kattegat and Skagerrak – meet, often with a powerful clashing of waves. You can get to the tip by a tractor-drawn bus (April to mid-Oct; 20kr return) – although it's an enjoyable walk through some beautiful seaside scenery.

Arrival and information

Train The train station is on Sct. Laurentii Vej, the town's main thoroughfare. It is served by privately operated trains from Frederikshavn (50 percent

discount with Eurail and InterRail) roughly once an hour. There are lockers at the station for left luggage (20kr for 24hr).

Tourist office Vestre Strandvej 10, close to the marina (June–Aug Mon–Sat 9am–6pm & Sun 10am–4pm; rest of year Mon–Fri 9/10am–4/5pm, Sat 10am–1/4pm; ⓣ98.44.13.77, ⓦwww.skagen-tourist.dk). Can arrange private rooms from 75kr.

Bike rental Skagen Cykeludlegning by the train station (80kr per day with 200kr deposit).

Accommodation

Danhostel Skagen Rolighedsvej 2 ⓣ98.44.22.00, ⓦwww.danhostelnord.dk/skagen. A little way out of the centre, but the rooms are clean and good value. Linen 50kr (compulsory If you don't have your own). If you're arriving by train it's closest to the Frederikshavnsvej stop. Reservations essential in summer. Closed Dec–mid Feb. Dorms 150kr, doubles 500kr.

Grenen Camping Fyrvej ⓣ98.44.25.46, ⓦwww.grenencamping.dk. By the beach 1.5km along the road to Grenen. Closed mid-Sept to early May. 95kr.

Eating, drinking and nightlife

Skagen has fantastic "fresh-off-the-boat" seafood and you should treat yourself to a blow-out meal at one of the marina restaurants. Eating on a budget can be tricky but there are plenty of fast-food joints on Havnevej.

Buddy Holly Havnevej 16 ⓦwww.buddy-skagen.dk. Pretty cheesy but this is Skagen's liveliest club with plenty of drinks deals and friendly bar staff. 10pm–5am in summer.

Guldbagaren Skagen Sct Laurentii Vej 104. Bakery serving a great range of pastries and sandwiches, plus excellent coffee.

Jacobs Café Havnevej 4. Lively café/bar with outside seating and free internet access. Sandwiches 75–85kr.

Pakhuset Rødspættevej 6, by the marina. Grab an outside table and settle in for delicious seafood with a Danish twist – try the fish cakes with curry sauce or plaice with cranberry compote (both 80kr).

Moving on

Train Frederikshavn (hourly; 35min).

Estonia

HIGHLIGHTS

LAHEMAA NATIONAL PARK: pristine wilderness teeming with wildlife on Estonia's north coast

TALLINN'S OLD TOWN: wander this beautifully preserved corner of the city

SAAREMAA: a perfect island getaway with a beautiful castle and relaxing spa hotels

TARTU: party the night away with the student population of Tartu

PÄRNU BEACH: enjoy a bracing dip in the Baltic or take a mud bath in a local spa

ROUGH COSTS

DAILY BUDGET basic €40/occasional treat €55

DRINK A. Le Coq beer €2

FOOD Blood sausage and sauerkraut €3.50

HOSTEL/BUDGET HOTEL €20/€40

TRAVEL Bus: Tallinn–Saaremaa (5hr) €16; Tartu–Tallinn (2hr) €12

FACT FILE

POPULATION 1.4 million

AREA 45,227 sq km

LANGUAGE Estonian

CURRENCY Kroon (EEK)

CAPITAL Tallinn (population: 402,586)

INTERNATIONAL PHONE CODE ☎372

Introduction

Little remains of the stagnation suffered by Estonia under Soviet rule until 1991. Some grim apartment buildings aside, visitors encounter a mix of the medieval and the contemporary, with colourful design permeating urban landscapes. An efficient transport system makes it easy to get around, and the tech-savvy, dynamic residents welcome visitors with open arms. While friction still exists between older generations of Russians and Estonians, younger people mix freely, and those who get past the Estonians' natural reserve find them to be gregarious, uninhibited hosts.

Estonia's capital, **Tallinn**, has a magnificent medieval centre and lively nightlife, rivalled only by that of **Tartu**, an exuberant university town. **Pärnu**, a popular seaside resort, is also worth a day or so. For inexpensive spa treatments, a fine castle and unspoilt countryside head for the island of **Saaremaa**, while **Lahemaa National Park,** outside Tallinn, offers a taste of pristine wilderness.

CHRONOLOGY

100s AD Tacitus refers to the Aestii people – the forebears of the Estonians.

1154 Estonia depicted on a map of the world for the first time.

1219 Danish conquer North Estonia, ushering in over a century of Danish rule.

1227 German crusaders invade the rest of Estonia.

1346 Danish territories in Estonia sold to the German Livonian Order.

1525 First book printed in the Estonian language.

1561 Livonian Order surrender their Estonian territory to Sweden.

1625 Sweden takes control over all Estonia.

1632 Estonia's first university opens in Tartu.

1721 Russia defeats Sweden in the Northern War and takes over Estonia.

1816 Serfdom is abolished in Estonia.

Late 1800s The spread of the Estonian language in schools is instrumental in increasing Estonian nationalism.

1918 Estonia states its claim to independence but is invaded by the Red Army starting the Estonian War of Independence.

1920 The Russians are defeated giving Estonia full independence.

1934 Authoritarian rule is established by Prime Minister Konstantin Pats.

1940 Soviets invade Estonia.

1944 Soviets maintain control by end of World War II, ushering in Communist rule.

1988 The "Singing Revolution" begins with huge crowds gathering to sing national songs.

1991 The fall of the Soviet Union leads to Estonian independence.

2004 Estonia joins NATO and EU.

2007 Estonia is the first country to introduce Internet voting for national elections.

2009 Estonia's economy takes a downturn as a result of the global economic crisis.

ARRIVAL

The compact and ultra-modern **Tallinn Airport** (ⓦwww.tallinn-airport.ee) is served by fifteen European airlines, including easyJet. Estonian Air (ⓦwww.estonian-air.ee) offers direct flights from many major capitals including London, Dublin, Frankfurt, Barcelona and Stockholm. International **bus lines**, such as Eurolines (ⓦwww.eurolines.ee), Ecolines (ⓦwww.ecolines.net) and Hansabuss (ⓦwww.hansabuss.ee), connect Tallinn via Tartu or Pärnu to Russia (Kaliningrad, St Petersburg), Latvia (Riga), Lithuania (Vilnius, Kaunas), Poland (Kraków, Warsaw), and Germany (Berlin, Bonn, Cologne, Hamburg, Munich, Stuttgart), among others. The only international **rail service** from Estonia is the daily overnight train from Tallinn to Moscow – book seats for this

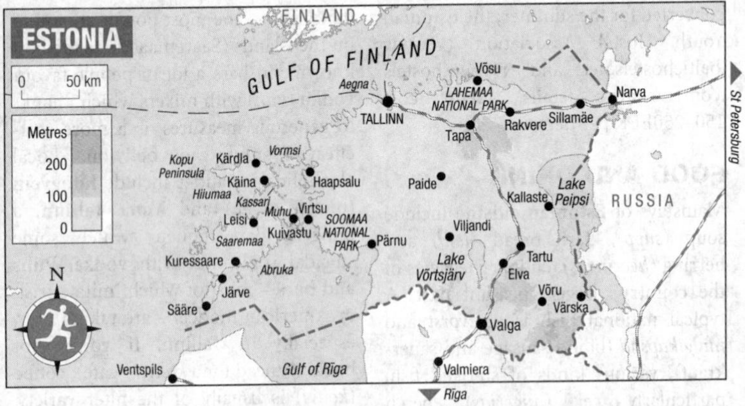

in advance. (The service to St Petersburg is not running at the time of writing.) Tallinn can also be reached by **ferry** from Helsinki, Finland and from Stockholm, Sweden.

GETTING AROUND

Places covered in this chapter are all easily reached by **bus**, and schedules are posted online with an English version (ⓦwww.bussireisid.ee). Tickets can be bought either from the bus station ticket office or directly from the driver. Buy tickets in advance if you're travelling in the height of summer or at weekends and opt for an express (*ekspress*) bus if possible. **Buses** are also the best method for travelling to neighbouring Baltic countries, with numerous daily services linking Tallinn, Vilnius and Riga via Pärnu.

The **rail network** is limited, but the domestic routes in operation are as fast as buses and slightly cheaper. Tickets can be I klass, II klass and tavaklass; check ⓦwww.edel.ee for times and prices. Ticket windows at stations are marked *linnalähedanel* for suburban lines, *piletite müük* for national services and *rahvusvaheline* for international, though they are often unmanned and you have to purchase your ticket from the conductor. Both train and bus information is available from station timetable boards – departure is *väljub*, arrival is *saabub*.

The bigger cities have efficient **public transport** systems, while smaller places, such as Saaremaa, are best explored by **bike**; inexpensive rentals are available. Due to the scarcity of public transport on the islands, many locals hitchhike; the usual precautions apply.

ACCOMMODATION

Though cheaper than in Western Europe, accommodation in Estonia will still take a large chunk out of most budgets. **Youth hostels** aside, booking a **private room** is often the cheapest option (usually 300–450EEK per person). This can be arranged through tourist offices or private agencies. You should be able to find plain but clean hotel or pension rooms for 400–550EEK per person including breakfast, though the cheapest of these are usually not centrally located. Outside of Tallinn **hostels** are often just student dorms

ESTONIA ON THE NET

ⓦ**www.visitestonia.com** Tourist board site.
ⓦ**www.ttw.ee** Entertainment listings for Tallinn.
ⓦ**www.baltictimes.com** English-language weekly newspaper.

converted for the summer; the Estonian Youth Hostel Association (Ⓦwww.baltichostels.net and Ⓦwww.hostels.com) have details. Beds cost 150–250EEK per person.

FOOD AND DRINK

Mainstays of **Estonian cuisine** include soup (*supp*), dark bread (*leib*) and herring (*heeringas*), culinary legacies of the country's largely peasant past. A typical national dish is *verevorst* and *mulgikapsad* (blood sausage and sauerkraut); various kinds of smoked fish, particularly eel (*angerjas*), perch (*ahven*) and pike (*haug*), are popular, as are **Russian dishes** such as *pelmeenid* (ravioli with meat or mushrooms). There are a few good places to try Estonian food in Tallinn, and both the capital and Tartu boast an impressive choice of ethnic **restaurants**. Outside these two cities, **vegetarians** will find their choice to be rather more limited.

When eating out, it's cheaper to head for bars and cafés, many of which serve **snacks** like pancakes (*pannkoogid*) and salads (*salatid*). In a café you should be able to have a modest meal for 70–95EEK, while in a typical restaurant two courses and a drink would come to around 180EEK. Some places going under the name of **café** (*kohvik*) are canteen-style restaurants with dishes-of-the-day (*päevapraad*) for as little as 40EEK. **Self-catering** poses no major problems, as supermarkets and fresh produce markets are plentiful.

Restaurant opening hours tend to be between 11am–midnight; cafes keep similar hours, but open 8/9am.

Drink

Estonians are enthusiastic drinkers, with **beer** (*õlu*) being the most popular tipple. The principal local brands are Saku and A. Le Coq, both of which are rather tame, lager-style brews, although both companies also produce stronger, dark beers – the most potent are found on the islands (Saaremaa õlu is the best known). In bars a lot of people favour **vodka** (*viin*) with mixers which, thanks to generous measures, is a more cost-effective route to oblivion. Local alcoholic specialities include **hõõgvein** (mulled wine) and **Vana Tallinn**, a pungent dark liqueur which some suicidal souls mix with vodka. **Pubs and bars** – most of which imitate Irish or American models – are taking over, especially in Tallinn. If you're not boozing, head for a *kohvik* (café); **coffee** (*kohvi*) is usually of the filter variety, and **tea** (*teed*) is served without milk (*piima*) or sugar (*suhkur*) – ask for both if necessary. Bars are usually open from noon until 2/4am on weekends.

CULTURE AND ETIQUETTE

Estonia has fully embraced the digital age and there is a proliferation of free wi-fi spots all over the country, in the capital and rural areas alike, and computer literacy per capita is among the highest in Europe. Estonians tend to be reserved when you first meet them, though if you are lucky enough to be invited to a local home, you will see their warm and generous side. Unused to loud displays of emotion, they are scandalized by the loutish behaviour of foreign stag parties, although they themselves enjoy sociable drinking. **Tipping** is relatively new here and ten percent is sufficient in restaurants to reward good service; otherwise just round up the bill.

SPORTS AND OUTDOOR ACTIVITIES

Football and **basketball** are the national sports; for the former, go to the A. Le Coq Arena (Asula 4c; Ⓣ627 9940) whereas Tallinn's Kalev Stadium (Juhkentali 12; Ⓣ644 5171) is the best place to see a basketball game. In the summertime, Estonia becomes a haven

for **watersports**: windsurfing, kayaking, canoeing or simply hitting the beach. **Hiking**, **biking** and **horseriding** are popular both on the Estonian mainland and on the islands off its coast, such as Saaremaa and Hiimaa. Almost twenty percent of Estonia is protected land, divided between four **national parks** and numerous **nature reserves**, which are home to many species of wild animals and birds. National parks are best visited between May and September; RMK (ⓦwww.rmk.ee) manages the protected areas and campsites.

COMMUNICATIONS

Post offices (*postkontor*) are open Monday to Friday 9am to 6pm and Saturday 9am to 3pm. Poste restante is generally held for a month. You can buy **stamps** here and at some shops, hotels and kiosks. Most **public phones** take phone cards (of 50 and 100EEK; available at kiosks and post offices) for local and long-distance calls; alternatively, you will find that using a mobile phone from another European country could be relatively inexpensive; consult your

Estonian

	Estonian	Pronunciation
Yes	*Jah*	Yah
No	*Ei*	Ey
Please	*Palun*	Palun
Thank you	*Aitäh/tänan*	Ayteh, tanan
Hello/Good day	*Tere*	Tere
Goodbye	*Head aega*	Heyad ayga
Excuse me	*Vabandage*	Vabandage
Where?	*Kus?*	Kus?
Student ticket	*Õpilase pilet*	Ypilahse pilet
Toilet	*Tualett*	Tualet
I'd like	*Ma sooviksin*	Mah sawviksin
I don't eat meat	*Ma ei söö*	Mah ay serr
The bill, please	*Palun arve*	Pahlun ahrrve
Good/Bad	*Hea/Halb*	Heya/Holb
Near/Far	*Lähedal/Kaugel*	Lahedal/Cowgal
Cheap/Expensive	*Odav/Kallis*	Odav/Kallis
Open/Closed	*Avatud/Suletud*	Avatud/Suletud
Today	*Täna*	Tana
Yesterday	*Eile*	Eyle
Tomorrow	*Homme*	Homme
How much is...?	*Kui palju maksab...?*	Kuy palyo maksab...?
What time is it?	*Mis kell praegu on?*	Mis kell prego on?
I don't understand	*Ma ei saa aru*	May saaru
Do you speak English?	*Kas te räägite inglise keelt?*	Kas te raagite inglise kelt?
One	*Uks*	Uks
Two	*Kaks*	Koks
Three	*Kolm*	Kolm
Four	*Neli*	Neli
Five	*Viis*	Vees
Six	*Kuus*	Koos
Seven	*Seitse*	Seytse
Eight	*Kaheksa*	Koheksa
Nine	*Üheksa*	Ooheksa
Ten	*Kümme*	Koome

EMERGENCY NUMBERS

Police ⓣ110; Fire & ambulance ⓣ112.

service provider about roaming charges. You'll find **internet cafés** in most towns; expect to pay 45–80EEK/hr. Free wi-fi is offered by most cafes, restaurants and hostels.

EMERGENCIES

Theft and street crime are at relatively low levels. The **police** (*politsei*) are mostly young and some speak English. **Emergency health care** is free and, at least in Tallinn, emergency operators speak English.

INFORMATION

Tourist offices can be useful for booking B&Bs and hotel rooms, as well as good-quality free **maps**; most bookstores also have good map sections. **Addresses** often include *mantee* (mnt.), meaning road; *puistee* (pst.), avenue; *tänav* (tn.), street; and *väljak*, square. The *In Your Pocket* guides (ⓦwww.inyourpocket.com) are invaluable listings guides, available from tourist offices and kiosks for 35EEK.

MONEY AND BANKS

Currency is the **Eesti kroon** (Estonian Crown, abbreviated EEK), pegged to the euro at €1 to 15.65EEK, and divided into 100 sents. Notes come as 2, 5, 10, 25, 50, 100 and 500 EEK and **coins** as 0.10, 0.20, 0.50, 1 and 5 EEK. Bank (*pank*) opening hours are Monday to Friday 9am to 4pm, many staying open in larger towns till 6pm and most also open Saturday 9am to 2/4pm. **ATMs** are widely available. **Credit cards** can be used in most hotels, restaurants and stores, but outside urban areas cash is preferred.

OPENING HOURS AND HOLIDAYS

Most **shops** open Monday to Friday 9/10am to 6/7pm and Saturday 10am to 2/3pm, but many larger ones stay open later and are also open Sun. **Public holidays**, when most shops and all banks are closed, are: January 1, February 24, Good Friday, Easter Monday, May 1, June 23 and 24, August 20, December 25 and 26.

Tallinn

TALLINN, Estonia's compact, buzzing capital, has been shaped by nearly a millennium of outside influence. However, once the staple crumbling backdrop for Soviet fairy-tale films, Tallinn has now reinvented itself as an inexpensive weekend getaway for Europeans, and these days its buzzing cafés, pubs and clubs can offer a variety of hedonistic pursuits on a night out, though be warned: the cobbled streets of the Old Town make it the worst place in the world to wear high heels.

What to see and do

The heart of Tallinn is the **Old Town**, still largely enclosed by the city's medieval walls. At its centre is the **Raekoja plats**, the historic marketplace, above which looms **Toompea**, the hilltop stronghold of the German knights who controlled the city during the Middle Ages. West of the city centre there are several places worth a visit including **Kadriorg Park**, a peaceful wooded area to the east with a cluster of historic buildings and a view of the sea, the forested island of **Aegna** and the **Lauluväljak** amphitheatre, home to many thousand-strong choirs during the all-Estonia Song Festival.

Raekoja plats

Raekoja plats, the cobbled market square at the heart of the Old Town, is as old as the city itself. On its southern side stands the fifteenth-century **Town Hall** (Tallinna Raekoda), boasting an elegant arcade of Gothic arches at ground level, and a delicate steeple at its northern end. Near the summit of the steeple, **Vana Toomas**, a sixteenth-century weathervane depicting a medieval town guard, is Tallinn's city emblem. The well-labelled and informative **museum** inside the cellar hall (May–Sept Tues–Sat 10am–4pm; rest of the year closed weekends; 15EEK) depicts Tallinn town life through the ages, and there is a good view from the belfry. For an even better view, climb the spiral staircase of the **Town Hall Tower** (*Raekoja Torn*; May–Sept daily 11am–6pm; 40EEK). Records indicate that the **Town Council Pharmacy** (Raeapteek), set in the northeastern corner with a white seventeenth-century facade, was standing in 1422 and may be even older.

Church of the Holy Ghost and St Nicholas's Church

The fourteenth-century **Church of the Holy Ghost** (daily 10am–2pm) on Pühavaimu is the city's most appealing church, a small Gothic building with stuccoed limestone walls, stepped gables, a tall, verdigris-coated spire and an ornate clock from 1680 – the oldest in Tallinn.

Contrasting sharply is the late Gothic **St Nicholas's Church**, southwest of Raekoja plats. Dating back to the 1820s and rebuilt after being mostly destroyed in a 1944 Soviet air raid, the church now serves as a museum of medieval artworks and a concert hall (daily 9.30am–5pm; museum 35EEK). It also hosts free organ recitals (Sat & Sun 4pm) as well as evening concerts (around 100EEK).

Toompea and the Aleksander Nevsky Cathedral

Toompea is the hill where the Danes built their fortress after conquering what is now Tallinn in 1219. According to legend, it is also the grave of **Kalev**, the mythical ancestor of the Estonians. Approach through the sturdy gate tower – built by the Teutonic Knights to contain the Old Town's inhabitants in times of unrest – at the foot of Pikk jalg. This is the cobbled continuation of Pikk, the Old Town's main street, that climbs up to Lossi plats, dominated by the impressive-looking **Aleksander Nevsky Cathedral** (undergoing restoration at time of writing). This imposing onion-domed structure was

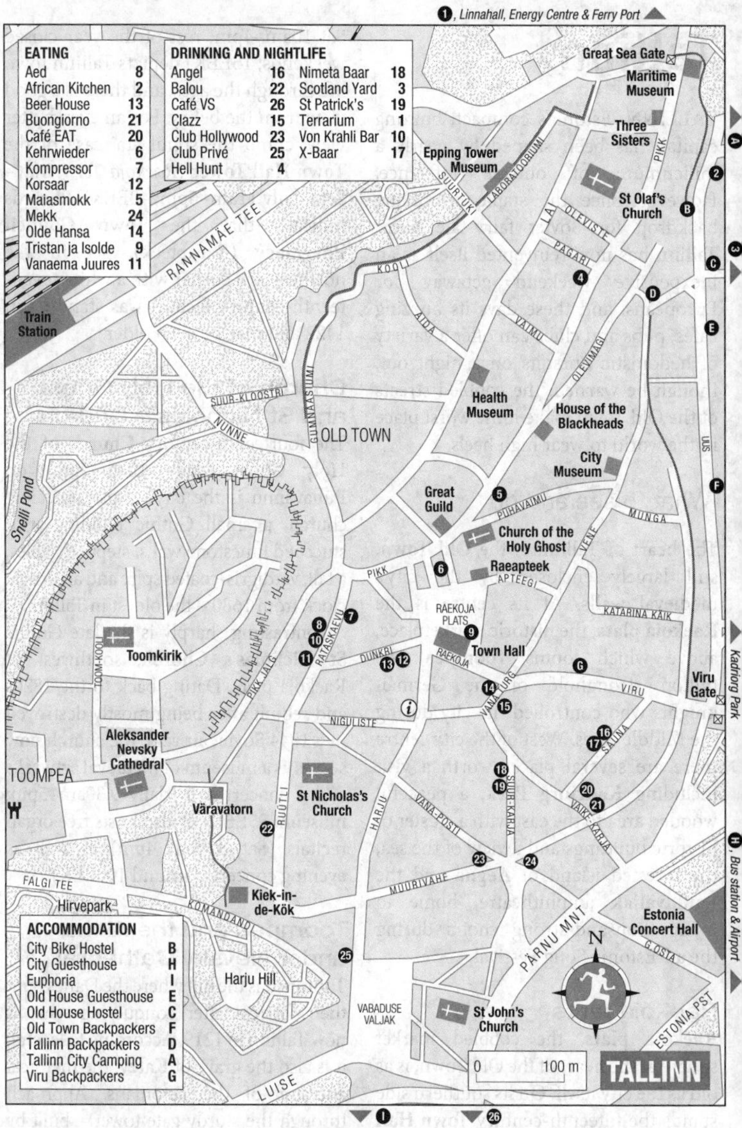

built at the end of the nineteenth century for the city's Orthodox population – an enduring reminder of the two centuries Tallinn spent under tsarist rule.

Toompea Castle

At the head of Lossi plats, the pink **Toompea Castle** stands on the original Danish fortification site. Today's castle is the descendant of a stone fortress built by the Knights of the Sword, the Germanic crusaders who kicked out the Danes in 1227 and controlled the city until 1238 (when the Danes returned). The building is now home to the **Riigikogu**, Estonia's parliament. A little south of here on Komandandi tee is the imposing **Kiek-in-de-Kök tower** dating

from 1475. It houses displays on the development of the town and its fortifications throughout its history, as well as an excellent contemporary photography display in the cellar (closed until September 2009 due to renovations). Guided tours of the passages under the bastions can be arranged (Ⓣ644 6686; Tues–Sun 11am–4pm; 50EEK).

The Toomkirik and Occupation Museum

From Lossi plats, Toom Kooli leads north to the **Toomkirik** (Tues–Sun 9am–6pm), the city's outwardly understated Lutheran cathedral, with a splendid interior. South of Lossi plats, on Toompea 8, the airy and modern **Occupation Museum** (Tues–Sun 11am–6pm; 20EEK) brings to life the personal experience of Estonians under Nazi and Soviet occupation through use of interactive exhibitions, and displays of artefacts from 1940–1991. The basement contains statues of vanquished Communist leaders, including a giant bust of Lenin.

Elsewhere in the Old Town

Pikk tänav, running northeast from Pikk jalg gate and linking Toompea with the port area, has some of the city's most elaborate examples of **merchants' houses** from the Hanseatic period, including the **Great Guild** at Pikk 17, headquarters of the German merchants who controlled the city's wealth; the **House of the Blackheads**, Pikk 26, with a lavishly decorated Renaissance façade; and the **Three Sisters**, a gabled group at Pikk 71. Supremely functional with loading hatches and winch-arms set into their facades, these would have served as combined dwelling places, warehouses and offices. Take the parallel street of Vene to the outstanding **City Museum** at no. 17 (March–Oct Wed–Mon 10.30am–5.30pm, Nov–Feb 10.30am–5pm; 35EEK), which recounts the history of Tallinn from the thirteenth century through to Soviet and Nazi occupation and beyond in imaginative multimedia style, with helpful staff at hand. On nearby Lai, you will find the quirky **Health Museum** at no. 28 (Tues–Sat 11am–6pm; 40EEK). Though primarily designed to show children how the human body works, some of the gems on display, such as the mummified man, will interest any visitor.

St Olaf's Church

At the northern end of Pikk stands the enormous Gothic **St Olaf's Church**, first mentioned in 1267 and named in honour of King Olaf II of Norway, who was canonized for battling against pagans in Scandinavia. The church is chiefly famous for its 124-metre spire, which you can climb for a spectacular view of the city (daily 10am–6pm; 30EEK; students 15EEK).

The Maritime Museum and city wall

At its far end Pikk is straddled by the sixteenth-century **Great Sea Gate**, flanked by two towers. The larger of these, Fat Margaret Tower, has walls four metres thick and now houses the **Estonian Maritime Museum** (Wed–Sun 10am–6pm; 50EEK; some English captioning), a surprisingly entertaining four floors of nautical instruments, scale models of ships and antique diving equipment. Down Suur-Kloostri, west of Lai street, is one of the longest extant sections of Tallinn's medieval **city wall**. The 4km of walls that surrounded the Old Town were mostly constructed during the fourteenth century. Today, 1.85km of it still stands, along with twenty of the original 46 towers. You can enter three of the oldest towers, Nunne, Kuldjala and Sauna, from Gümnaasiumi 3 (Mon, Tues & Fri noon–5pm, Sat & Sun 11am–4pm; 15EEK).

Kadriorg Park

Kadriorg Park, a heavily wooded area 2km east of the Old Town along Narva

mnt., was laid out according to the instructions of Russian tsar Peter the Great. The main entrance to the park is at the junction of Weizenbergi tänav and J. Poska (tram #1 or #3 from Viru väljak). Weizenbergi cuts through the park, running straight past **Kadriorg Palace**, a Baroque residence designed by the Italian architect Niccolò Michetti, which Peter had built for his wife Catherine. The palace houses the **Museum of Foreign Art** (May–Sept Tues–Sun 10am–5pm; Oct–April Wed–Sun 10am–5pm; 65EEK), with a fine collection of Dutch and Russian paintings. A short walk up Weizenbergi, the futuristic-looking **KUMU** building houses the largest collection of Estonian art (May–Sept Tues–Sun 11am–6pm; Oct–April Wed–Sun 11am–6pm; 90EEK all exhibitions), featuring paintings from the eighteenth to the twentieth centuries influenced by contemporary artistic trends, as well as innovative modern exhibitions.

Lauluväljak

Just to the northeast of Kadriorg Park, at Narva mnt. 95, is the **Lauluväljak** (Ⓣ611 2100, Ⓦwww.lauluvaljak.ee), a vast amphitheatre which is the venue for **Estonia's Song Festivals**. These gatherings, featuring choirs thousands strong, are held every two years, and have been an important form of national expression since the first all-Estonia Song Festival was held in Tartu in 1869. The grounds were filled to the 45,000-person capacity for the 1988 festival when people joined their voices in song as a significant public expression of longing for independence from Soviet rule, in what became known as the "**Singing Revolution**".

Pirita Beach and Aegna Island

To reach Tallinn's popular **Pirita Beach** and the large wooded park stretching behind it, take bus #1, #34 or #38 from the underground stop at the Viru Centre. An hour's ride on the boat from the nearby **Pirita harbour** (75EEK return), tiny peaceful **Aegna** is an excellent day-trip destination (May–Sept Mon & Wed–Fri three ferries daily; Sat & Sun four ferries daily). Its forest-covered interior and clean beaches attract locals who camp here in the summer.

Arrival and information

Air The Lennart Meri Tallinn Airport (*lennu jaam*) is 3km southeast of the city centre and linked to Viru väljak by bus #2 (every 20min between 6am and midnight). It stops behind the Viru shopping mall, 5min walk from the Old Town's Viru Gate.

Train Tallinn's train station (*balti jaam*) is at Toompuiestee 35, just northwest of the Old Town, 10min walk to the Town Square. ATMs are by the front doors.

Bus The city's bus terminal (*autobussi jaam*) is at Lastekodu 46, 2km southeast of the centre; there is an ATM and luggage storage. Trams #2 and #4 run from nearby Tartu mnt. to Viru väljak at the eastern entrance to the Old Town; alternatively, take any bus heading west along Juhkentali.

Boat Arriving by sea, the passenger port (*reisi-sadam*) is just northeast of the centre at Sadama 25. For updated schedules see Ⓦwww.portoftallinn.com.

Information The tourist office, in the Old Town at Kullasseppa 4 (May–Sept Mon–Fri 9am–7pm, Sat & Sun 10am–5pm; Oct–April Mon–Fri 9am–5pm, Sat 10am–3pm; Ⓣ645 7777, Ⓦwww.tourism.tallinn.ee), sells various maps and city guides. You can also buy the Tallinn Card here (Ⓦwww.tallinncard.ee; 185/375/435/495EEK for 6/24/48/72hr), particularly useful for those in town for a short time, as it gives free entry to numerous museums and churches, unlimited use of public transport and other discounts. The widely available free paper *Tallinn This Week* (Ⓦwww.ttw.ee), and the excellent *Tallinn In Your Pocket* (Ⓦwww.inyourpocket.com; 35EEK) city guide feature comprehensive listings.

City transport

Public transport Tallinn has an extensive tram, bus and trolleybus network. Tickets (*talongid*) for all three systems are available from kiosks near stops for 13EEK (book of 10 for 90EEK) or from the driver for 20EEK. Validate your ticket using the on-board punches.

Taxis Taxis are reasonably cheap (around 35–45EEK base rate, plus 7–10EEK/km on top, slightly more after 10pm); rates should be posted on the right rear window. Since Tallinn taxis are notorious for overcharging, it's best to call a reputable taxi company rather than grab a cab on the street. These include: Sõbra Taxo ⓣ621 5080, and Krooni Taxo ⓣ638 1111.

Accommodation

Demand for budget accommodation still outstrips supply in summer, so book in advance. You can find central and excellent-value private rooms at Mere 4 with *Bed & Breakfast Rasastra* (Mon–Sat 9.30am–6pm, Sun 9.30am–5pm; ⓣ661 6291, ⓦwww.bedbreakfast.ee), an agency offering rooms (325–700EEK) in family homes throughout the Baltics, and private apartments (800–2500EEK) for longer stays.

City Bike Hostel Uus 33 ⓣ511 1819, ⓦwww.citybike.ee. Small, friendly hostel with a dorm, a double and a loft for two, wi-fi, lounge and kitchenette. Bicycles for rent available. More dorms and doubles in a second building at Nunne 1. Dorm 200EEK; doubles 250EEK per person or 350EEK as single.

City Guesthouse Pärnu mnt. 10 ⓣ628 2236, ⓦwww.cityguesthouse.ee. Fairly spartan but clean singles, doubles, triples and quads in a large Old Town building. All but the suites share facilities; wi-fi and airport transfers available. Dorm/single/double/triple 200/360/550/600EEK.

Euphoria Roosikrantsi 4 ⓣ5837 3602, ⓔinfo@traveller.ee. A four-storey hostel with a great communal atmosphere, clean dorms and a couple of rooms, all with shared facilities. Extras include wi-fi, kitchen and a large common room where you can even paint your own mural. Dorms 220EEK; rooms 380EEK.

Old House Guesthouse Uus 22 ⓣ641 1464, ⓦwww.oldhouse.ee. Second branch of the *Old House* has five small but clean rooms with shared facilities. Single/twin/quad 490/690/1300EEK; seven-bed dorm 290EEK.

Old House Hostel Uus 26 ⓣ641 1281, ⓦwww.oldhouse.ee. Renovated Old Town house with attractive dorms and a handful of cosy twin rooms with shared bath and kitchen. Wi-fi enabled. Single/twin/quad 490/690/1300EEK.

Old Town Backpackers Uus 14 ⓣ5742 6961, ⓦwww.balticbackpackers.com. This central backpacker favourite consists of two large rooms with bunk beds and additional pull-out couches. Huge guest kitchen, breakfast and free use of sauna included. Dorms 200EEK.

Tallinn Backpackers Olevimägi 11–1 ⓣ644 0298, ⓦwww.tallinnbackpackers.com. Lively two-dorm hostel with wi-fi, video room and sauna. They offer day-trips to Lahemaa National Park, as well as occasional pub outings. Dorms 200–225 EEK; doubles 600 per person.

Tallinn City Camping Pirita tee 28 ⓣ613 7322, ⓦwww.tallinn-city-camping.ee. Large campsite near the sea with ample facilities, such as tent, mattress and grill rental, as well as internet and

WHICH TOUR?

Tallinn can be explored in many different ways. Here are some of the more innovative ones:

City Bike Tours Uus 33 ⓣ683 6383, ⓦwww.citybike.ee. Tours of the Old Town and beyond run by young, energetic guides, as well as a "Legends and Secret Tunnels" afternoon walking tour. Groups can try the weird and wonderful "Conference Bike". Guided and self-guided tours of Lahemaa National Park available.

EstAdventures ⓣ5385 5511, ⓦwww.estadventures.ee. Small group tours of Tallinn (the View With a Brew comes particularly recommended), as well as day-trips to Lahemaa National Park.

Hop-on, hop-off bus For easy access to attractions outside the Old Town, such as Kadriorg Park, complete with running commentary, hop on one of the tour buses just outside Viru Gate. Bus passes: 24/48/72hr 250/300/350EEK.

Super Segway Vene 3 ⓣ641 3888. Propel yourself around the cobbled streets on a Segway. Prices start from 300EEK/hr.

Tallinn Traveller Info Info tent opposite tourist office ⓣ5814 0442, ⓦtraveller-info.com. The excellent and inexpensive Chill-out Tour, Beautiful Bike Tour or the Funky Bike Tour present Tallinn and its environs in a novel way, led by young, knowledgeable, multilingual student guides. Daily 10am–10pm.

sauna. To get to the Old Town, catch any westbound bus along Pirita. Camping space 200EEK.

Viru Backpackers Viru 5 ⓣ644 6050. Affordable singles, doubles and triples at this sister hostel to *Tallinn Backpackers*. Clean rooms, kitchen, internet, wi-fi and cheap laundry service. Access to *Tallinn Backpackers* facilities. Rooms 450–600EEK

Eating

Although traditional food figures prominently on many restaurant menus, the choice of international cuisines around the Old Town is impressive. These are the best places for vegetarians, though conventional restaurants usually offer one or two meat-free options. Most of the cafés and bars listed below also offer inexpensive snacks and meals.

Cafés

Café EAT Sauna 2. Popular with students, this basement establishment offers different kinds of *pelmeenid* (dumplings) and doughnuts, sold by weight (7–15EEK/100g). Cheap and very filling. Pint of cider 30EEK.

Kehrwieder Saiakang 1. Comfy sofas ideal for curling up with a top-quality coffee in this dimly lit cellar café, with big windows looking out on Raekoja plats. Coffee 45EEK.

Kompressor Rataskaevu 3. Roomy café-bar popular with a youngish crowd, and famous for its wonderfully stodgy Estonian pancakes with sweet and savoury fillings (55EEK).

Maiasmokk Pikk 16. Tallinn's most venerable café – founded in 1864 – with a beautiful wood-panelled interior. Queue up for your inexpensive coffee and delicious marzipan or pastry. Coffee 40EEK.

Tristan ja Isolde Raekoja plats 1. Dark, atmospheric café in the Town Hall with a full range of drinks; famous for its pastries. Cappuccino 45EEK.

Restaurants

Aed Rataskaevu 8. The self-styled "Embassy of Pure Food" delivers delicious and imaginative fusion dishes, including many vegetarian options. Budget pastas and salads in the attached café (65EEK).

African Kitchen Uus 34. Good selection of peanut, coconut and rice dishes, some spicy and many vegetarian, prepared by a Nigerian chef and served in a jungle-themed lounge. Tasty smoothies (50EEK) and prawn mains (170EEK).

Beer House Dunkri 5. Busy, roomy beer cellar which brews its own ales and serves up generous portions of imaginative meat dishes, such as elk and wild boar (160–300EEK). Live music nightly.

Buongiorno Müürivahe 17. A genial atmosphere reigns in this casual restaurant which serves affordable and authentic pizza and pasta; popular with Tallinn's resident Italians. Mains 115EEK.

Mekk Suur-Karja 17/19. Even if you don't come for the modern Estonian cuisine in a stylish setting, you must come for the exquisite desserts. The chocolate pudding with caramelised Vana Tallinn liqueur cream (95EEK) is to die for.

Olde Hansa Vana turg 1. Extremely popular yet affordable medieval-style restaurant. Ask your serving wench for a starter plate to share and some elk/boar/bear sausages (300 EEK).

Vanaema Juures Rataskaevu 10/12. "Grandma's Place" serves quality traditional Estonian food in a cosy cellar setting. Try Grandma's Roast or lamb in blue cheese sauce (280EEK). Closes 6pm Sundays.

Drinking and nightlife

Most of Tallinn's highly popular clubs cater for a mainstream crowd. More underground, cutting-edge dance music events change location frequently and are advertised by flyposters, or try asking around in the city's hipper bars; expect to pay 50–150EEK admission.

Bars

Café VS Pärnu mnt. 28. Purple/silver industrial decor, late-night DJs, hip clientele and great Indian food make this one of the top spots in Tallinn. Bring a friend if you order the tikka biriyani – portion size is generous (185EEK).

Hell Hunt Pikk 39. Lively pub packed with expats and locals most nights. It's spacious, friendly and serves its own excellent dark Hunt beer.

Nimeta Baar (Pub Without a Name) Suur-Karja 4/6. This lively bar draws a mixture of expats, locals

TREAT YOURSELF

FEAST LIKE A PIRATE

Korsaar, an award-winning subterranean restaurant decked out like a pirate ship at Dunkri 5, is Tallinn's newest culinary attraction. The attention to detail is astounding – from the live shark tank and strategically-positioned skeletons, to the dishes, mostly with fish and seafood leanings, prepared with flair and imagination. As for the meat dishes, the lamb with jambalaya is highly recommended. Those on a budget can take advantage of the three-course business lunches on weekdays for 250EEK.

and stag parties. DJs and live music at weekends, international football matches screened live and cheap beer are all part of the draw. Age 21+.

St Patrick's Suur-Karja 8. The pick of Tallinn's Irish pubs, set in a beautifully restored medieval house and popular with expats, tourists and locals alike. Your fourth Saku Originaal beer comes free. Happy hour 4–6pm daily.

Scotland Yard Mere pst. 6e. Large, lively pub with live music nightly, a large dancefloor, and toilets shaped like electric chairs. You may wait a while to get served, though.

Von Krahli Bar Rataskaevu 10/12. Large hip hangout that's always packed with a bohemian crowd. Frequent live music – from alternative to reggae to hip-hop. Good, cheap food: huge daily specials 50EEK.

X-Baar Sauna 1. Extremely popular gay bar with bright pink decor and karaoke most nights, as well as a lively little dancefloor.

Clubs

Angel Sauna 3 Ⓦwww.clubangel.ee. Frequented by a mixed gay and straight crowd for great music and free vodka, Tallinn's premier gay club can be difficult to get into on weekends; put your name on the list online. Lively bar upstairs. Mon–Wed noon–2am, Thurs & Fri noon–5am, Sat 2pm–5am, Sun 2pm–1am. Entry 85EEK.

Balou Rüütli 18. Popular subterranean club with a young crowd. Fri & Sat 8pm–4am; 50–100EEK. Age 18+.

Club Hollywood Vana-Posti 8 Ⓦwww.clubhollywood.ee. Large Old Town dance club playing techno, R'n'B and hip-hop. Very popular with a younger crowd as well as tourists. Wed & Thurs 10pm–4am, Fri & Sat 10pm–5am; 50–100EEK; free entry for ladies on Wednesdays.

Club Privé Harju 6 Ⓦwww.clubprive.ee. Style-conscious temple to cutting-edge dance culture, often attracting big-name DJs. Free entry for ladies before midnight. Wed–Sat 10pm–4am; 75–250EEK. Age 20+.

Terrarium Sadama 6 Ⓦwww.terrarium.ee. Visiting international DJs, Russian men and beautiful young things frequent this large minimalist club by the port. Free drinks for girls before midnight. Occasional male stripper. Fri & Sat 11pm–5am; 50–100EEK. Age 18+.

Entertainment

Cinemas

Coca-Cola Plaza Hobujaama 5 Ⓦwww.forumcinemas.ee. High-tech 11-screen cinema showing the latest blockbusters. 140EEK.

Sõprus Vana-Posti 8 Ⓦwww.kino.ee (website in Estonian only). Shows a full range of independent films. 50–90EEK.

Live music

Clazz Vana Turg 2 Ⓦwww.clazz.ee. One of the most popular venues in the Old Town for nightly live music – from blues to jazz to Latin. Mon–Thurs 5pm–3am, Fri–Sun noon–3am.

Estonia Concert Hall Estonia pst. 4 Ⓣ614 7760, Ⓦwww.concert.ee. Tallinn's premier venue for classical music.

Estonian National Opera Estonia pst. 4 Ⓣ683 1201, Ⓦwww.opera.ee. Frequent opera and ballet performances; book in advance.

Linnahall Mere pst. 20 Ⓣ641 1500, Ⓦwww.linnahall.ee. Live pop concert venue by the harbour.

Saunas

Saunas (see box, p.352) are a quintessential part of Estonian life, and private saunas are common in most guesthouses and hotels. While traditionally saunas started out as an important part of health and cleanliness rituals, for many Estonians they are now places to socialise with family and friends. Estonian saunas tend to be wooden, specialising in dry heat, as opposed to steam saunas in Latvia and Lithuania.

African Kitchen Uus 34 Ⓣ644 2555, Ⓦwww.africankitchen.ee. The funky private sauna in this popular restaurant has its own sound system. You can hire it for 350EEK/hr; ask at the bar.

Club 26 (in the Reval Hotel *Olümpia*) Liivalaia 33 Ⓣ631 5585, Ⓦwww.revalhotels.com. The ultimate sauna experience – complete with a wonderful bird's-eye view of Tallinn – at the health club on the 26th floor of the *Olümpia* hotel. Private saunas hold up to 10 people. 300EEK/hr until 3pm, 600EEK/hr after. Daily 8am–11pm.

Kalma Vana-Kalamaja 9a Ⓣ627 1811, Ⓦwww.bma.ee/kalma. Kalma is Tallinn's oldest public bath (built in 1928), containing private saunas for rent as well as men's and women's general baths (complete with swimming pool). Men 115–130EEK, women 95–100EEK. Daily 10am–11pm.

Shopping

Antiik Kinga 5. Come here for all your Soviet kitsch, including a number of Lenin busts.

Apollo Raamatumaja Viru 23. Large bookstore with numerous English-language books and travel guides.

SAUNA ETIQUETTE

The first thing to do when you go to an Estonian **sauna** is get naked. Being completely naked is the norm, while in mixed saunas wrapping a towel around you is up to your discretion. Once you get used to the heat, try scooping some water onto the hot stones; it evaporates instantaneously, raising the temperature. Once everyone is sweating profusely, you might notice others gently swatting themselves or their friends with birch branches; this increases circulation and rids the body of toxins. Make sure you don't overdo it – ten minutes should be long enough, but get out immediately if you start to feel dizzy. Locals normally follow up with a plunge into a cold lake, although a cold shower will suffice.

Balti Jaama Turg Kopli 1. Sprawling market area behind the railway station where locals come for daily essentials, including the cheapest fresh fruit and vegetables in town.

Namarie Aia 3. Original clothing by young, up-and-coming Estonian fashion designers.

Directory

Embassies Canada, Toomkooli 13, 2nd floor, ⓣ627 3311; Ireland, 2nd floor, Vene 2 ⓣ681 1888; UK, Wismari 6 ⓣ667 4700; US, Kentmanni 20 ⓣ668 8100.

Exchange Outside banking hours, try Tavia at Aia 5 for good rates, though their overnight rates are not as favourable as their day rates. Beware of Monex exchange offices which offer poor rates.

Hospital Tallinn Central Hospital, Ravi 18 ⓣ620 7000. English-speaking doctors available. Or call the Tallinn First Aid hotline on ⓣ697 1145 for treatment advice in English.

Internet access *Kohvik@Grill*, Aia 3 (daily 9am–9pm; 40EEK/hr).

Laundry Washcentre, Maakri 23; *Seebimull*, Liivalaia 7.

Left luggage At the bus station (Mon–Sat 6.30am–10pm, Sun 7.45am–8pm).

Pharmacies Aia Apteek, Aia 7 (9am–9.30pm); Tõnismäe Apteek, Tõnismägi 5 (24hr).

Police Pärnu mnt. 11 ⓣ612 3523.

Post office Narva mnt. 1, opposite the *Viru Hotel*. Mon–Fri 7.30am–8pm; Sat 8am–6pm.

Moving on

Train Pärnu (2 daily; 2hr 40min); Moscow (1 daily; 15hr); Tartu (3–4 daily; 2hr 30min).

Bus Kuressaare (6–12 daily; 4hr 30min); Pärnu (every 30min 6.20am–9pm; 2hr); Rīga (11 daily; 4hr 30min); St Petersburg (6–8 daily; 7–9hr); Tartu (every 30min 5.45am–11pm; 2hr 30min); Vilnius (2 daily; 8hr–8hr 30min).

Ferry Helsinki (14–16 daily; 1hr 30min–3hr 30min); Stockholm (1 daily at 6pm; 16hr).

The rest of Estonia

There are several attractions outside Tallinn that are well worth visiting, such as the vast, beautiful expanse of **Lahemaa National Park** and the pretty island of **Saaremaa**, home to the Bishop's Castle. The seaside resort of **Pärnu** is a slightly livelier affair, outshone in vibrancy by the buzzy university town of **Tartu**.

LAHEMAA NATIONAL PARK

The largest of Estonia's national parks, 72,500-hectare **Lahemaa** lies an hour's drive from Tallinn. It stretches along the north coast, comprising lush forests, pristine lakes, ruggedly beautiful coves and wetlands, dotted with erratic rocks left over from the last Ice Age and tiny villages throughout, and home to brown bears, wild boar, moose and lynx. The park is best explored by bicycle, as the villages are all connected by good paved roads. Though parts of the park are doable as a day-trip, you will probably want to stay longer.

Exploring the park

The following route is a good introduction to the park: start in the village of **Palmse**, where you can take in the grand German manor and cycle 8.5km

northeast to **Sagadi Manor**, a well-preserved eighteenth-century aristocratic home (May–Sept daily 10am–6pm; 40EEK), before heading north for 3km to **Oandu** – the start of several nature trails. A 4.5km interpretive trail leads you through the dense forest, pointing out the marks of various animals and identifying the native plant and bird species. You can also take the 8km hiking/biking trail through the forest to the large village of **Võsu**, though you'll need a sturdy mountain bike. Just before the fishing village of Altja, 2km to the north, you'll find the short **Beaver Trail** where you can see beavers building dams. From Altja you can cycle around the coast of the **Vergi peninsula**, taking in the picturesque villages (17km), or take the shorter road to Võsu from Oandu (8km). A seaside trail heads north from Võsu for 6km before arriving at the attractive village of **Käsmu**. If you have any energy left, you can then tackle the rugged cycle trails along the western half of the Käsmu peninsula before returning to Palmse.

Park practicalities

The **Lahemaa National Park Visitor Centre** (ⓣ329 5555, ⓦwww.lahemaa.ee May–Aug 9am–7pm; Sept 9am–5pm) is located in tiny Palmse; you can take a Rakvere- or Narva-bound bus from Tallinn to Viitna (hourly; 1hr) and hike or hitchhike the 7.2km to Palmse. The helpful staff at the visitor centre can advise on accommodation, biking and hiking trails and nature tours, and provide a detailed map of the area.

Public transport is infrequent; although there are several buses daily from Tallinn to Võsu, with one going as far as Käsmu, cycling is the best way to get around. Hitchhiking is practised among locals, but the usual precautions apply.

Basic **accommodation and food** is available throughout the park; Võsu has the most choice. There are **bicycles for rent** at the *Palmse Hotel* (25EEK/hr or 180EEK/day) and Sagadi manor (170EEK/day); alternatively, make arrangements at Tallinn's *City Bike Hostel* (see p.349), which arranges transfers and day-trips to Lahemaa.

SAAREMAA

The island of **SAAREMAA**, off the west coast of Estonia, is claimed by many to be one of the most authentically Estonian parts of the country. It is yet under-exploited, leaving its forests and coastline ripe for exploration. Buses from Tallinn, Tartu and Pärnu come here via a ferry running from the mainland village of Virtsu to Muhu island, which is linked to Saaremaa by a causeway.

What to see and do

The principal attraction is Kuressaare's thirteenth-century castle, one of the finest in the Baltic region, but the rest of the island also deserves exploration, with bike rides the preferred means of seeing the sights.

Kuressaare

In **KURESSAARE**'s Kesk väljak (main square) you'll find the yellow-painted **Town Hall**, dating from 1670, its door guarded by stone lions. From the square, Lossi runs south past a monument commemorating the 1918–20 War of Independence to the magnificent **Bishop's Castle** (Piiskopilinnus), set in the middle of an attractive park and surrounded by a deep moat. The formidable structure dates largely from the fourteenth century and is protected by huge seventeenth-century ramparts. The labyrinthine keep houses the **Saaremaa Regional Museum** (May–Sept daily 10am–7pm; Oct–April Wed–Sun 11am–7pm; 50EEK; students 25EEK), a riveting collection of displays charting the history, culture and nature of the island, which you can reach by

going up and down spiral staircases and peering into numerous cellars. It's also possible to climb the watchtowers, one of which houses stunning contemporary art and photography exhibitions.

Around the island

Saaremaa is mostly flat, and cycling the 40km route from Kuressaare to **LEISI**, on the opposite side of the island, is a wonderful way of seeing rural Estonia, with alternating landscapes of pine forest, tiny villages and vast fields. Rent a bike from Bivarix Rattapood (Tallinna 26, Mon–Fri 10am–6pm, Sat 10am–4pm 120EEK/4hr, 190EEK/day). Follow Route 10 out of town and turn left onto Route 79. **KAALI** village makes a worthy detour halfway along – it is home to a giant **meteorite crater**, a round, murky green pool about 100m in diameter and 1–6 metres in depth, thought to be at least four thousand years old. Try the delicious *solyanka* (Russian meat soup) at the *Kaali Tavern* across the road. There are 3–5 buses to Kaali daily (Kuivastu direction; 15EEK).

Just short of Leisi lies **ANGLA**, with five much-photographed wooden windmills by the roadside. Take the bus back to Kuressaare (40EEK, plus 20EEK for the bicycle); the Leisi bus "station" is a brightly-graffitied shelter to the right of the main road. There are 4–6 buses to Leisi daily.

Alternatively, cycle to **JARVE**, the local beach hangout, 10km southwest of Kuressaare along Route 77. It's a long, narrow strip of sand, hidden behind the dunes, just a short walk through the pine forest. The cool, crystal-clear water is a welcome respite in the summer. Route 77 carries on down to the tip of the Torgu peninsula, ending 47km from Kuressaare in an amazing view from the jagged cliffs.

Arrival and information

Bus From the bus station on Pihtla turn left onto Tallinna to reach the main square.

Tourist office The tourist office in the Town Hall (Tallinna 2; June–Aug daily 9am–7pm, Sept–May Mon–Fri 9am–5pm; ⓣ45/33120, ⓦwww.saaremaa.ee) books private rooms across the island for around 200EEK per person (but only if you require accommodation on the day of arrival), and provides information on cycling and hiking trails around Saaremaa and bus timetables.

Internet Available at the public library, Raekoja 1 (Mon–Fri 9am–6pm, Sat 10am–4pm).

Accommodation

Kraavi Holiday Cottage 500m southeast of the castle at Kraavi 1 ⓣ45/55242, ⓦwww.kraavi.ee. Cosy, spacious doubles, with a hearty breakfast included and free wi-fi. Use of sauna and bicycle rent is extra. Single/double/triple 350/600/780 EEK.

Ovelia Majutus Suve 8 ⓣ45/55732. Friendly and clean guesthouse with basic rooms and shared bathroom and kitchen. Ten minutes' walk from bus station. Rooms 350 EEK.

Piibelehe Holiday Home Piibelehe 4 ⓣ45/36206, ⓦwww.piibelehe.ee. On the outskirts of town, this place has several airy, attractive guest rooms, some en suite and with use of a kitchen; camping also available. Tents 100EEK; rooms 35–51 euros.

Eating and drinking

Classic Lossi 9. Bustling café with an excellent selection of pasta, salads (50–75EEK), omelettes and pancakes (40–55EEK), as well as more exotic fare.

TREAT YOURSELF

SPA HOTEL RUUTLI

Pargi 12 ⓣ45/48100, ⓦwww.sanatoorium.ee. Modern, luxurious hotel with airy rooms, cable TV, wi-fi and buffet breakfast included. Numerous spa treatments on offer for guests and non-guests include "Charcot's Shower" – strip naked and be pummelled with strong jets of water (145 EEK); and "Neo-Qi energy cocoon" – infrared sauna, steam room, vibration massage and Vichy shower, followed by water massage (295EEK). Treatments take place between 8am–3pm; book in advance. Doubles 1584EEK.

La Perla Lossi 3. Good-sized portions of well-cooked, inexpensive pasta. Mains 95–135EEK.

Kodulinna Lokaal Tallinna mnt. 12. Popular café on the main square dishing up inexpensive soups and light meals. Try the Saaremaa-style potato pancake (45EEK).

Vana Konn Kauba 6. Youth-oriented drinking spot with Czech and German beers on tap, a pool table and Estonian pub grub. A. Le Coq beer 35EEK.

Veski Pärnu 19. Popular pub in an old windmill serving the most imaginative dishes in town. Wild boar in juniper berry marinade (185EEK) and pumpkin cake with lingonberry jam (35EEK) stand out.

Moving on

Bus Kaali (2–5 daily; 20min); Leisi (4–6 daily; 55min); Parnu (4 daily; 3hr); Tallinn (5–14 daily; 4hr 30min); Tartu (4 daily; 5hr 45min–6hr).

PÄRNU

PÄRNU, Estonia's main seaside resort, comes into its own in summer, when it fills up with locals and tourists and plays host to daily cultural and musical events.

What to see and do

Rüütli, cutting east-west through the centre, is the Old Town's main pedestrianised thoroughfare, lined with shops, while the parallel Kuninga boasts the largest concentration of restaurants. The worthwhile **Pärnu Museum** lies at Rüütli 53 (Mon–Sat 10am–6pm; 30EEK, students 15EEK), tracing local history up until World War II; ask for the information sheet in English. The oldest building in town is the **Red Tower** (Punane Torn, Mon–Sat 10am–5pm), a fifteenth-century remnant of the medieval city walls on Hommiku, a block north from Rüütli. At the western end of Uus is the Orthodox green-domed **Catherine Church**, dating from 1760 and named after the Russian empress Catherine the Great. Reptile and tarantula lovers should check out the Mini Zoo at Akadeemia 1, a block west (daily 10am–7pm; 50EEK). Follow Nikolai south from the centre and you'll reach the **Chaplin Centre** (daily 9am–9pm; www.chaplin.ee; 35EEK;) set in the Communist party HQ at Esplanaadi 10. It holds regular shows, film festivals and excellent temporary exhibitions of contemporary Estonian art. South of here Nikolai joins Supeluse, which leads to the beach, passing beneath the trees of the shady Rannapark. Beyond the sand dunes lies the clean sandy beach, packed during the summer months.

Arrival and information

Train The train station is about 5km east of the centre at Riia mnt. 116.

Bus The bus station is on Pikk at the northeastern edge of the Old Town (information & ticket office round the corner at Ringi 3; daily 6.30am–7.30pm). Luggage storage by platform 8 (Mon–Fri 8am–7.30pm, Sat–Sun 9am–5pm; 25EEK/day).

Tourist office The tourist office at Rüütli 16 (June–Aug Mon–Fri 9am–6pm, Sat 10am–4pm Sun 10am–3pm; Sept–May Mon–Fri 9am–4pm; 44/73000, www.parnu.ee) can book accommodation for 25EEK; extensive information available on Pärnu.

Internet head to the Chaplin Centre (see above; 30EEK/hr).

Accommodation

Hommiku Hostel Hommiku 17 445 1122, www.hommikuhostel.ee. All doubles, triples and quads in this welcoming, centrally-located budget hotel are en suite and have their own kitchenettes; singles share a bathroom. Wi-fi enabled throughout. Single/double/triple/quad 600/900/1200/1400EEK.

Hostel Lõuna Lõuna 2 443 0943, www.hot.ee/hostellouna. Centrally located, with comfortable, spacious dorms and rooms. Dorms (300EEK); single/double/triple 650/850/900EEK.

Terve Hostel Ringi 50 507 7332, www.terve.ee. Attractive guesthouse run by an effusive hostess, offering airy, clean doubles with shared facilities just south of the town centre. Doubles 700EEK.

Eating and drinking

Club Str& Tammsaare pst. 35. A seafront hotel club with quirky decor attracting a mixed crowd of locals and tourists, and some decent DJs. Fri & Sat 10pm–4am; 55–100EEK. Age 21-plus.

Onu Sam Suvituse 11. Serves inexpensive burgers, hot dogs and pizzas (25–40EEK) to beach-bound revellers. Open 24hrs June–Aug.

Ruutlihoov Ruutli 29. This lively pub has friendly service and live music on weekends. The outdoor terrace is a good spot for a cold beer (35EEK).

Sõõrikubaar Pühavaimu 15. An essential stop for caffeine addicts, this popular little café does tasty pastries and *sõõrikud* (Estonian doughnuts).

Steffani Nikolai 24. Extremely popular restaurant with a wide choice of tasty pizza and pasta dishes. Huge *calzones* 100EEK. Runs a popular café between Ranna pst. and the beach in the summer, serving similar fare. Closes 2am Fri & Sat.

Si-Si Restaurant and Lounge Supeluse 21. Excellent new Italian restaurant serving authentic dishes made from fresh ingredients to the beach crowd. Mains 140EEK.

Moving on

Bus to: Kuressaare (4–5 daily; 3hr); Tallinn (at least 1 hourly 5.10am–8.30pm; 2–3hr); Tartu (19 daily–6.45am–9pm; 2hr 30min).

Train to: Tallinn (2 daily; 2hr 30min).

TARTU

TARTU, less than three hours southeast of Tallinn, is an attractive town, liveliest during term time, with events all year round (Ⓦwww.visittartu.com).

What to see and do

The main sights lie between **Cathedral Hill**, right in the centre, and the **River Emajõgi**, and include the Art Museum, the Cathedral and the colourful Supilinn district.

Town Hall and around

The city's centre is its cobbled Raekoja plats, fronted by the Neoclassical Town Hall, a pink-and-white edifice with the Kissing Students statue in the fountain in front of it. The northeast corner features the **Leaning House**, home of the **Tartu Art Museum**. The Neoclassical theme continues in the cool white facade of the main **Tartu University** building at Ülikooli 18, just north of the square. Upstairs you can look at the Student Lock-up, where students were incarcerated in the nineteenth century for such offences as the late return of library books and duelling (weekdays 11am–5pm; 25EEK; joint ticket with the Art Museum on the ground floor). About 100m beyond the university is the red-brick Gothic **St John's Church** (Tues–Sat 10am–6pm), founded in 1330, and most famous for over one thousand pint-sized terracotta sculptures set in niches around the main entrance.

Cathedral Hill and around

Behind the Town Hall, Lossi climbs Cathedral Hill, a pleasant park with the remains of the red-brick **Cathedral** at the top, housing the University History Museum. Built by the Knights of the Sword in the thirteenth century, it boasts the best view of Tartu from the rooftop terrace (June–Aug daily 10am–5pm; May & Sept Wed–Sun 11am–5pm; Oct–Nov Sat–Sun 11am–5pm; 25EEK). Nearby is the **Sacrifice Stone** left over from Estonia's pagan past; students now burn their lecture notes on it after the exams. Behind the stone you'll find Kissing Hill, where newlywed grooms carry their brides.

Just east of Kissing Hill, you can take a path down to the Tartu Toy Museum at Lutsu 8 (Wed–Sun 11am–6pm; 25EEK), which has fascinating exhibits of toys through the ages, puppetry in different cultures and film and animation characters.

Two blocks west of Cathedral Hill, the former **KGB headquarters** at Riia 15b houses a cellar **museum** with exhibits on deportations and life in the Soviet gulags, summarised in English (Wed–Sun 11am–6pm; 20EEK).

North of the centre, a walk through the historic **Supilinn** (Soup Town) district, with streets named after fruit and vegetables, old wooden houses and a colourful bohemian population of musicians, artists and students, offers a glimpse into prewar Tartu.

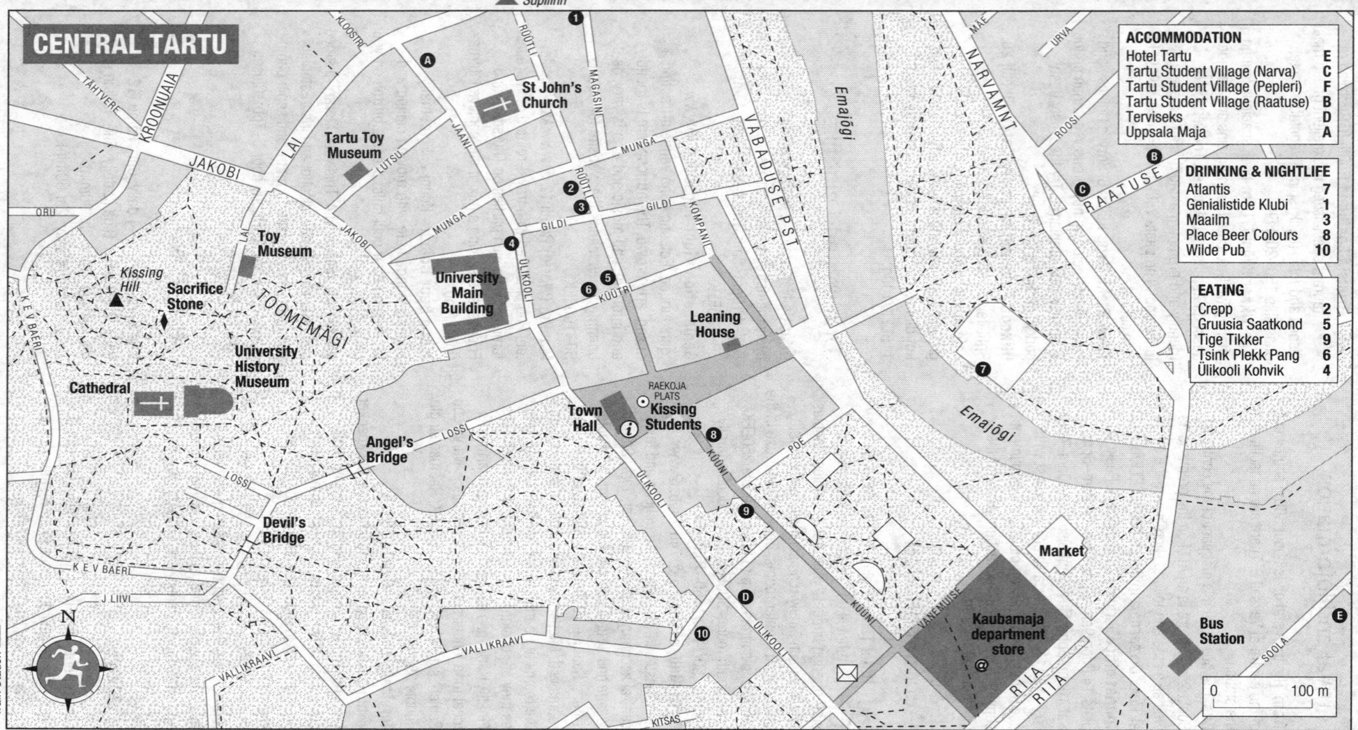
CENTRAL TARTU
ACCOMMODATION
Hotel Tartu E
Tartu Student Village (Narva) C
Tartu Student Village (Pepleri) F
Tartu Student Village (Raatuse) B
Terviseks D
Uppsala Maja A
DRINKING & NIGHTLIFE
Atlantis 7
Genialistide Klubi 1
Maailm 3
Place Beer Colours 8
Wilde Pub 10
EATING
Crepp 2
Gruusia Saatkond 5
Tige Tikker 9
Tsink Plekk Pang 6
Ülikooli Kohvik 4
Supilinn
St John's Church
Tartu Toy Museum
Toy Museum
University Main Building
Leaning House
Kissing Hill
Sacrifice Stone
TOOMEMÄGI
University History Museum
Cathedral
RAEKOJA PLATS
Kissing Students
Town Hall
Angel's Bridge
Devil's Bridge
Emajõgi
Market
Kaubamaja department store
Bus Station
Train Station
KGB Museum & F
KLOOSTRI
RÜÜTLI
MAGASINI
JAANI
MUNGA
LAI
JAKOBI
KROONUAIA
TÄHTVERE
LUTSU
ORU
GILDI
KOMPANII
KÜÜTRI
ÜLIKOOLI
VABADUSE PST
NARVA MNT
MÄE
URVA
ROOSI
RAATUSE
LOSSI
POE
KÜÜNI
VANEMUISE
RIIA
SOOLA
K E V BAERI
J LIIVI
VALLIKRAAVI
KITSAS
N
0 100 m

Arrival and information

Train The train station is about 500m southwest of the centre at Vaksali 6. There are no facilities at the station.

Bus The bus station is just east of the centre at Soola 2, and there is an ATM on the premises as well as a café and toilets. There's luggage storage at *Hotel Dorpat* next to the station (10EEK/bag).

Tourist office Tartu's tourist office at Raekoja plats 14 (Mon 9am–6pm, Tues–Fri 9am–5pm, Sat 10am–5pm; May–Sept also Sun 10am–4pm; ⓣ744 2111, ⓦwww.tartu.ee) can assist with accommodation. You can pick up a complimentary copy of *Tartu in Your Pocket* here and surf the internet free for 20min.

Accommodation

Hotel Tartu Soola 3 ⓣ731 4300, ⓦwww.tartuhotell.ee. Clean hotel with helpful staff offering budget "youth room" triples, doubles and 4-person family rooms. Fifteen percent ISIC discount on regular rooms, free computer use in the lobby, and sauna for up to fifteen people 250EEK/hour. Youth rooms 300EEK; single/double/family rooms 750/1150/1450–1650EEK.

Tartu Student Village ⓣ740 9955, ⓦwww.tartuhostel.eu. The best bet for cheap and fairly central accommodation in summer, *Tartu Student Village* has three locations: Narva mnt. 27, Pepleri 14 and Raatuse 22. Pepleri offers spartan en-suite rooms with kitchenettes and internet connection; the rooms at Raatuse share facilities but are larger as they are designed for students with disabilities. Finally, Narva has five self-contained apartments, ideal for a longer stay. Book in advance. Narva and Pepleri: single/double 450/700EEK; Raatuse single/double 350/600EEK.

Terviseks Ülikooli 1–6 ⓣ742 3324, ⓦhttp://hostelterviseks.blogspot.com. Backpacker favourite run by friendly, energetic young staff, consisting of two dorms, a guest kitchen and an ever-busy lounge. Great for meeting fellow wanderers. Dorms 225–250EEK.

Uppsala Maja Jaani 7 ⓣ736 1535, ⓦwww.uppsalamaja.ee. Friendly central guesthouse with five immaculate rooms, a large kitchen, dining room and wi-fi. Single/double 615–1035/1175–1415EEK.

Eating

Crepp Rüütli 16. Chic café with delicious salads, baguettes and filling crepes (40EEK), though the service can sometimes be leisurely.

Gruusia Saatkond Rüütli 8. Georgian restaurant specializing in excellent grilled meat dishes and *lobio* (thick, spiced vegetable paste). Shashliks 150–200EEK.

Tige Tikker Küüni 7. Ultra-cool, spacious lounge offering well-executed fusion mains and decadent desserts at reasonable prices. The service is friendly and prompt, making this an excellent lunch spot. The pasta with grilled salmon (95EEK) is excellent.

Tsink Plekk Pang Küütri 6. Serves Chinese and Indian food, including numerous vegetarian options, in an arty café ambiance. Try the "rusty busty porky" or the "angry cow".

Ülikooli Kohvik (University Café) Ulikooli 20. Split-level establishment with a plush café upstairs and a bargain buffet on the ground floor, serving a selection of salads and hot dishes to hungry students; pay by weight. 115EEK/100g.

Drinking and nightlife

Atlantis Narva mnt. 2 ⓦwww.atlantis.ee. Large, lively mainstream disco across the river. Tues & Wed 10pm–3am, Thurs–Sat 10pm–4am; 50–125EEK.

Genialistide Klubi Magasini 5 ⓦwww.genklubi.ee. Eclectic boho venue attracting a mixed, arty crowd. The atmosphere is friendly and informal, and music and events vary, as do opening times; check the website for details. 50–100EEK.

Maailm (World) Rüütli 12 ⓦwww.klubimaailm.ee. Pub plastered with travel-related memorabilia, famous for its wild parties on Thursdays and Fridays, and serving a mix of inexpensive international food.

Place Beer Colours Küüni 2. Perpetually packed lounge café with moving ceiling and interesting beer cocktails; press a button on your table to order.

Wilde Pub Vallikraavi 4. This vast, literary-themed pub offers tea, coffee, alcohol and Irish/Estonian pub grub amidst grand furniture and sepia photographs. Live music. Happy hour 5–7pm. Closes 2am Fri & Sat.

Moving on

Bus Kuressaare (3–4 daily; 6hr); Pärnu (12–17 daily; 2hr 30min); Rīga (2 daily; 5hr); Tallinn (1–2 hourly 3am–9pm; 2hr 30min).

Train Tallinn (4 daily; 2hr 30min).

Finland

HIGHLIGHTS

SÁMI CULTURE, INARI: one of Europe's last frontiers, where nomadic reindeer herders live in harmony with snowmobiles and Nokias

KUOPIO SAUNA: warm your bones at the world's biggest woodsmoke sauna

LENIN MUSEUM, TAMPERE: fascinating museum delving into the relationship between Lenin and Finland

OLAVINLINNA CASTLE, SAVONLINNA: one of the best-preserved medieval castles in northern Europe

DESIGN DISTRICT, HELSINKI: sample the shops, cafés and nightlife of this vibrant and trendy area of the capital

ROUGH COSTS

DAILY BUDGET Basic €40/occasional treat €65

DRINK Salmiakki (liquorice-flavoured vodka) €4–6 a shot

FOOD Reindeer stew with potatoes €9

HOSTEL/BUDGET HOTEL €20/€45

TRAVEL Helsinki–Tampere by bus (177km) €24; Helsinki–Rovaniemi by train (830km) €81

FACT FILE

POPULATION 5.2 million

AREA 338,145 sq km

LANGUAGE Finnish and Swedish

CURRENCY Euro (€)

CAPITAL Helsinki (population 560,000)

INTERNATIONAL PHONE CODE ⓣ358

Introduction

Drawing strong influences both from its easterly neighbour, Russia, as well as from the West, Finland remains one of Europe's least understood countries. It's a land best known for its laconic, pithy people with a penchant for kicking back in a sauna *sans* clothes, and for its quirky and bizarre annual festivals – and its strangeness is a good part of its charm. And while it's no budgeteer's paradise, there are definitely ways to save – that is, *if* you know where to drink.

The country is mostly flat and punctuated by huge forests and lakes, but has wide regional variations. The south contains the least dramatic scenery, but the capital, **Helsinki**, more than compensates, with its brilliant architecture and superb collections of national history and art, as does the former capital of **Turku**, with some great museums and nightlife. Stretching from the Russian border in the east to the industrial city of **Tampere**, the vast waters of the **Lake Region** provide a natural means of transport for the timber industry – indeed, water here is a more common sight than land with towns lying on narrow ridges between lakes. North of here, the gradually rising fells and forests of **Lapland** represent Finland's most alluring terrain and are home to the Sámi, semi-nomadic reindeer herders. For a few months on either side of midsummer, the midnight sun is visible from much of the region.

CHRONOLOGY

1800 BC Tribes from Russia settle in Lapland.
98 AD Roman historian Tacitus writes first recorded reference of the "Fenni".
1150s Sweden invades southwestern Finland.
1293 Sweden defeats Finland again, establishing dividing lines between the Catholic West and Orthodox East.
1642 First complete Finnish translation of the Bible produced.
1721 In the Treaty of Uusikaupunki, Sweden cedes Finnish land to Russia.
1809 Russians take Finland after military victory over Sweden.
1812 Helsinki is declared capital of Finland.
1858 Confusion caused as Russia forces Finns to drive on the right-hand side of the road.
1860 Finland acquires its own currency, the markka.
1906 Finland gains its own national parliament. Finnish women are the first in the world to receive full political rights.
1917 Finland declares independence from Russia.
1939–40 Soviet troops invade Finland but meet fierce resistance during the "Winter War".
1941 Under the Moscow Peace Treaty, the southeast territory of Karelia is ceded to the Russians.
1952 Helsinki holds the Olympic Games.
1987 Finnish company Nokia begins to make hand-held mobile phones.
1995 Finland joins the EU.
2000 Tarja Halonen becomes the first female president.
2002 Finland adopts the euro.
2006 National celebrations as Finnish death metal group Lordi win Eurovision song contest.
2009 Finnish government sells its share in Santa Park, signalling that the global economic crisis has reached the North Pole.

ARRIVAL

There are over twenty airports dotted around the country, but you're most likely to arrive at Helsinki Vantaa or Tampere Pirkkala, which are the main hubs for **international flights**. Ryanair flies into Tampere and easyJet into Helsinki from the UK, but the biggest low-cost airline in Finland is Blue1 (Ⓦwww.blue1.com), which offers routes to and from most major European cities. Finnair (Ⓦwww.finnair.com) is also a good bet for cheap flights. **Ferries** arrive from Tallinn in Estonia or Stockholm at Helsinki and Turku; contact

either Silja Line (ⓦwww.silja.com) or Viking Line (ⓦwww.vikingline.fi) for tickets and timetables. Another increasingly popular route into the country is overland by **train** from St Petersburg to Helsinki, which by 2011 will take less than three hours.

GETTING AROUND

For the most part trains and buses integrate well, and you'll only need to plan with care when travelling through the more remote areas of the far north and east. **Trains** are operated by Finnish State Railways (VR; ⓦwww.vr.fi). Comfortable Express and InterCity trains, plus faster, tilting Pendolino trains, serve the principal cities several times a day. If you're travelling by night train, it's better to go for the more expensive sleeper cars if you want to get any rest, as no provision is made for sleeping in the ordinary seated carriages. Elsewhere, especially on east–west hauls through sparsely populated regions, trains are often tiny or replaced by buses on which rail passes are still valid. InterRail passes are valid on all trains. The best timetable is the *Rail Pocket Guide* published by VR and available from all train stations and tourist offices. **Buses** – privately run, but with a common ticket system – cover the whole country, but are most useful in the north. Tickets can be purchased at bus stations and most travel agents; only ordinary one-way tickets can be bought on board. The timetable (*Pikavuoroaikataulut*), available at all

main bus stations, lists all bus routes, or check ⓦ www.matkahuolto.fi.

Domestic flights can be comparatively cheap as well as time-saving, especially if you're planning to visit Lapland and the far north. Finnair and Blue1 are the main operators, though cheaper tickets are generally only available if booked well in advance. One-way tickets with Blue1 can be especially good value.

Cycling can be an enjoyable way to see the country at close quarters, particularly because the only appreciable hills are in the far north and extreme east. You can take your bike along with you on an InterCity train for a €10 fee (reservations rarely necessary), and most youth hostels, campsites and some hotels and tourist offices offer bike rental from around €10 per day, or €45 per week; there may also be a deposit of around €30.

ACCOMMODATION

There's a good network of 72 official **HI hostels** (ⓦ www.srmnet.org) as well as a few independents. Most charge €5–6 for breakfast and bed linen is often extra, too (€4–7), so if you're on a tight budget it's worth bringing your own sheets. Dorms are almost always single-sex. The free *Finland: Budget Accommodation* booklet, available from any tourist office, contains a comprehensive list of hostels and campsites.

Hotels are expensive. Special offers in summer mean that you'll be able to sleep well on a budget in high season, but may have difficulty finding anything affordable out of season – the reverse of the norm. Expenses can be trimmed somewhat by using discount schemes such as Finncheques (ⓦ www.finncheque.fi) or Scandic Holiday Cheques (ⓦ www.scandichotels.com), which can be purchased from either a Finnish Tourist Board office or specialist travel agents abroad. In many towns you'll also find **tourist hotels** (*matkustajakoti*) offering fewer frills for €35–50 per person, and **summer hotels** (*kesähotelli*; June–Aug only), which offer decent accommodation in student blocks for €25–45 per person.

Official **campsites** (*leirintäalue*) are plentiful. The cost to camp is roughly €10–12 per pitch, plus €3–4 per person, depending on the site's star rating (we give the price per pitch plus for two people sharing a tent in this chapter). Most open from May or June until August or September, although some stay open longer and a few all year round. Many three-star sites also have cottages, often with TV, sauna and kitchen. To camp in Finland, you'll need a Camping Card Scandinavia , available at every site for €7 and valid for a year. Camping rough is illegal without the landowner's permission – though in practice, provided you're out of sight of local communities, there shouldn't be any problems.

FOOD

Finnish food is a mix of Western and Eastern influences, with Scandinavian-style fish specialities and exotic meats such as reindeer and elk alongside dishes that bear a Russian stamp – pastries, and casseroles strong on cabbage and pork. Also keep an eye out for *karjalan piirakka* – oval-shaped pastries containing rice and mashed potato, served hot with a mixture of finely chopped hard-boiled egg and butter. *Kalakukko* is another inexpensive delicacy, if an acquired one: a chunk of bread with pork and whitefish baked inside it; it's legendary around Kuopio but available almost everywhere. Slightly cheaper but just as filling, *lihapiirakka* are envelopes of sweet pastry filled with rice and meat – ask for them with mustard (*sinappi*) and/or ketchup (*ketsuppi*).

Breakfasts (*aamiainen*) in hotels usually consists of a buffet of herring, eggs, cereals, cheese, salami and bread,

while you can lunch on the economical **snacks** sold in market halls (*kauppa-halli*) or adjoining cafés. Most train stations and some bus stations and supermarkets also have cafeterias offering a selection of snacks, greasy nibbles and light meals, and street stands (*grillis*) turn out burgers and hot dogs for around €3. Otherwise, campus **mensas** are the cheapest places to get a hot dish (around €4); theoretically, you have to be a student, but you're only asked for ID on occasion. In regular restaurants or *ravintola*, **lunch** (*lounas*) deals are good value, with many places offering a lunchtime buffet table (*voileipäpöytä* or *seisovapöytä*) stacked with a choice of traditional goodies for a set price of around €10. Pizzerias are another good bet, serving lunch specials for €6–9. For **evening meals**, a cheap pizzeria or *ravintola* will serve up standard plates of meat and two veg, while in Helsinki and the big towns there's usually a good range of options, including Chinese and Thai.

Drink

Most restaurants are fully licensed, and many are frequented more for drinking than eating. **Bars** are usually open till midnight or 1am and service stops half an hour before closing. You have to be eighteen to buy beer and wine, twenty to buy spirits, and some places have an age limit of twenty-four. The main – and cheapest – outlets for take-out alcohol are the ubiquitous government-run **ALKO** shops (Mon–Thurs 9am–6pm, Fri 9am–8pm, Sat 9am–4pm).

Beer (*olut*) falls into three categories: "light beer" (I-Olut), like a soft drink; "medium strength beer" (*keskiolut*; III-Olut), perceptibly alcoholic, sold in supermarkets and cafés; and "strong beer" (A-Olut or IV-Olut), on a par with the stronger European beers, and only available at licensed restaurants, clubs and ALKO shops. Strong beers, such as Lapin Kulta and Koff, cost about €1.30 per 300ml bottle at a shop or kiosk. Imported beers go for €2.20–3 per can. Finlandia **vodka** is €19 for a 700ml bottle; Koskenkorva, a rougher vodka, is €15. You'll also find Finns knocking back **salmiakki**, a premixed vodka/liquorice cocktail which looks, smells and tastes like cough medicine.

CULTURE AND ETIQUETTE

To an outsider, Finns can seem almost alarmingly withdrawn: little value is put on exuberance, and you can have an entire conversation with a Finn without their making any discernible facial expression. Underneath this reserve, of course, Finnish people are as full of enthusiasm and affection as any other nation. This is all the more true when there's drink around, but alcohol abuse really has long been a noticeable problem here, and it's wise to avoid trying to keep up with the Finnish capacity for drinking.

Tipping is rare in Finland, and **buying rounds** is unheard of. Service is usually included in restaurant bills although it's common to round the bill up to the nearest convenient figure when paying in cash (the same applies for taxi fares).

SPORTS AND OUTDOOR ACTIVITIES

The winter landscape lends itself to **cross-country skiing**, the season lasting from December until January in the

FINLAND ON THE NET

Ⓦ **www.visitfinland.com** The Finnish tourist board site.
Ⓦ **www.finland.fi** A government informational site on Finnish culture and society.
Ⓦ **www.sauna.fi** The Finnish Sauna Society.
Ⓦ **www.festivals.fi** A comprehensive listing of festivals throughout Finland.

Finnish

Stress on all Finnish words always falls on the first syllable.

	Finnish	Pronunciation
Yes	*Kyllä*	Koo-leh
No	*Ei*	Ay
Thank you	*Kiitos*	Keetos
Hello/Good day	*Hyvää päivää*	Hoo-veh pai-veh
Goodbye	*Näkemiin*	Nek-er-meen
Excuse me	*Anteeksi*	Anteksi
Where?	*Missä?*	Miss-eh?
Good	*Hyvä*	Hoo-veh
Bad	*Paha*	Paha
Near	*Lähellä*	Le-hell-eh
Far	*Kaukana*	Kau-kanna
Cheap	*Halpa*	Halpa
Expensive	*Kallis*	Kallis
Open	*Avoinna*	Avoyn-na
Closed	*Suljettu*	Sul-yet-oo
Today	*Tänään*	Ten-ern
Yesterday	*Eilen*	Aylen
Tomorrow	*Huomenna*	Hoo-oh-menna
How much is...?	*Kuinka paljon maksaa...?*	Koo-inka pal-yon maksaa...?
What time is it?	*Paljonko kello on?*	Palyonko kello on?
I don't understand	*En ymmärrä*	Enn oomerreh
Do you speak English?	*Puhutteko englantia?*	Poohut-tuko englantia?
One	*Yksi*	Uksi
Two	*Kaksi*	Kaksi
Three	*Kolme*	Col-meh
Four	*Neljä*	Nel-yeh
Five	*Viisi*	Veesi
Six	*Kuusi*	Coosi
Seven	*Seitsemän*	Sayt-se-men
Eight	*Kahdeksan*	Car-deksan
Nine	*Yhdeksän*	Oo-deksan
Ten	*Kymmenen*	Kummenen

south and April in northern and central Finland. There are ski slopes, too – see ⓦwww.ski.fi for more information – and several operators offering off-piste skiing. Watery pursuits like **kayaking** (or kite-surfing on the frozen lakes in the winter) are a worthwhile option in the lake regions, especially around Lake Inari. Popular national **sports** include the distinctively Finnish *pesäpallo*, similar to baseball, and ice hockey.

COMMUNICATIONS

Communications are dependable and quick. Free **internet access** is readily available, either at the tourist office or local library (booking sometimes required), and major towns and cities have free, comprehensive wi-fi. **Post offices** are generally open 9am to 6pm, with later hours in Helsinki. Public **phones** are being phased out in favour of mobile service; if you plan to make a lot of calls in Finland, invest in a Finnish SIM card for use in your phone. €20 will get you a Finnish number with about sixty minutes of domestic calling time or several hundred domestic text messages. Directory enquiries are ⓣ118 (domestic) and ⓣ020208 (international).

EMERGENCY NUMBERS

☎112 for all emergency services.

EMERGENCIES

You hopefully won't have much cause to come into contact with the Finnish **police**, though if you do they are likely to speak English. As for **health problems**, if you're insured you'll save time by seeing a doctor at a private health centre (*lääkäriasema*) rather than waiting at a national health centre (*terveyskeskus*), though you're going to pay for the privilege. Medicines must be paid for at a **pharmacy** (*apteekki*), generally open daily 9am to 6pm; outside these times, a phone number for emergency help is displayed on every pharmacy's front door.

INFORMATION

Most towns have a **tourist office**, some of which will book accommodation for you, though in winter, their hours are much reduced and some don't open at all. You can pick up the decent map of Finland free from tourist offices.

MONEY AND BANKS

Finland's currency is the **euro** (€). Banks are open Monday to Friday 9.30am to 4.15pm. Some **banks** have exchange desks at transport terminals, and **ATMs** are widely available. You can also change money at hotels, but the rates are generally poor. **Credit cards** are widely accepted right across the country.

OPENING HOURS AND HOLIDAYS

Most **shops** generally open Monday to Friday 9am to 6pm, Saturday 9am to 4pm. Along with banks, they close on **public holidays**, when most public transport and museums run to a Sunday schedule. These are: January 1, Jan January 6 (Epiphany), Good Friday and Easter Monday, May 1, Ascension (mid-May), Whitsun (late May), Midsummer (late June), All Saints' Day (early Nov), December 6 and 24 to 26.

Helsinki

Instantly lovable, **HELSINKI** is remarkably different from the other Scandinavian capitals, and closer both in mood and appearance to the major cities of Eastern Europe. For a century an outpost of the Russian Empire, Helsinki's very shape and form derives from its more powerful neighbour. Yet during the twentieth century it became a showcase for independent Finland, much of its impressive architecture reflecting the dawning of Finnish nationalism and the rise of the republic. Today, visitors will find a youthful buzz on the streets, where the boulevards, outdoor cafés and restaurants are crowded with Finns taking full advantage of the short summer. At night the pace picks up in Helsinki's great selection of lounges, cafés, bars and clubs.

What to see and do

Following a devastating fire in 1808, and the city's designation as Finland's capital in 1812, Helsinki was totally rebuilt in a style befitting its new status: a grid of wide streets and Neoclassical brick buildings modelled on the then Russian capital, St Petersburg.

Esplanadi and Senate Square

Esplanadi, a wide tree-lined boulevard across a mishmash of tramlines from the harbour, is Helsinki at its most charming. At its eastern end, the **City Museum** at Sofiankatu 4 (Mon–Wed & Fri 9am–5pm, Thurs 9am–7pm, Sat & Sun 11am–5pm; free) offers a record of 450 years of Helsinki life in an impressive permanent exhibition called "Helsinki Horizons".

To the north is Senate Square (Senattintori), dominated by the exquisite form of the recently renovated **Tuomiokirkko** (Cathedral; June–Aug daily 9am–11pm; Sept–May Mon–Sat 9am–6pm, Sun noon–6pm; free). After the elegance of the exterior, the spartan Lutheran interior comes as a disappointment; more impressive is the gloomily atmospheric **crypt** (same times; entrance on Kirkkokatu), now often used for exhibitions.

Uspenski Cathedral

Walking east, the square at the end of Aleksanterinkatu is overlooked by the onion domes of the Russian Orthodox **Uspenski Cathedral** (Mon–Fri 9.30am–4pm, Sat 9.30am–2pm, Sun noon–3pm; Oct–April closed Mon; tram #3). Inside, there's a glitzy display of icons. Beyond is **Katajanokka**, a wedge of land extending between the harbours; with its beautiful Art Nouveau architecture it's one of the city's most atmospheric places to walk around.

Ateneum

Directly opposite the city bus terminal at Kaivokatu 2 is the **Ateneum** (Tues & Fri 10am–6pm, Wed & Thurs 10am–8pm, Sat & Sun 11am–5pm; €7/€8 during special exhibitions; ⓦwww.ateneum.fi). This art museum's stirring selection of artworks spans the period 1710 to 1980, and includes Akseli Gallén-Kallela and Albert Edelfelt's scenes from the Finnish epic, the *Kalevala*, and Juho Rissanen's moody studies of peasant life, recalling a time when the spirit of nationalism was surging through the country.

Kiasma and Lasipalatsi

Kiasma is Helsinki's museum of contemporary art (Tues 10am–5pm, Wed–Fri 10am–8.30pm, Sat & Sun 10am–6pm; €7; ⓦwww.kiasma.fi), its gleaming steel-clad exterior and hi-tech interior making it well worth a visit. Temporary exhibitions are drawn from a vast collection, displaying everything from paintings to video installations. Opposite is the **Lasipalatsi**, a multimedia complex situated in a recently renovated 1930s classic Functionalist building, now home to a number of trendy shops and cafés.

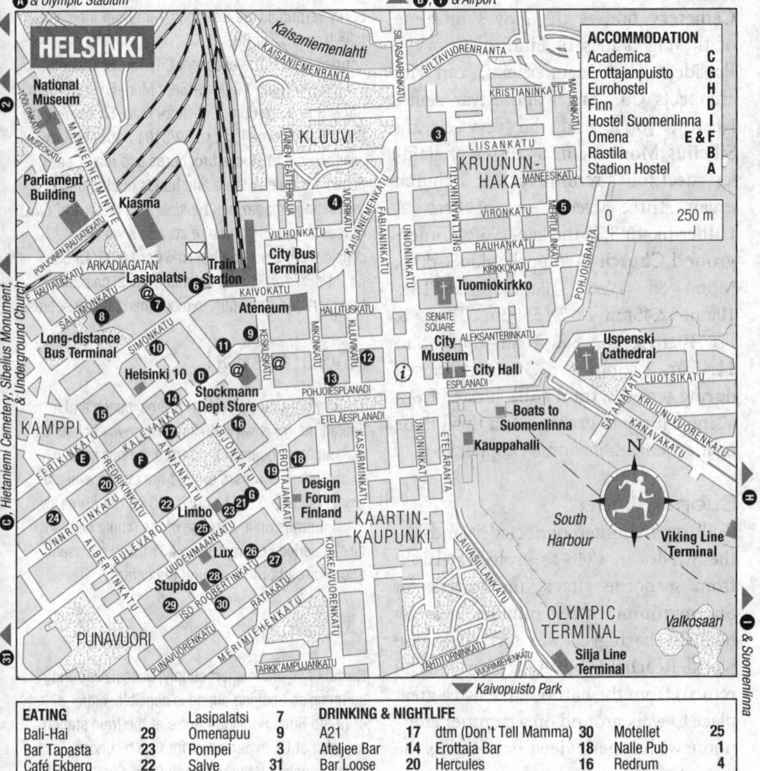

EATING				DRINKING & NIGHTLIFE					
Bali-Hai	29	Lasipalatsi	7	A21	17	dtm (Don't Tell Mamma)	30	Motellet	25
Bar Tapasta	23	Omenapuu	9	Ateljee Bar	14	Erottaja Bar	18	Nalle Pub	1
Café Ekberg	22	Pompei	3	Bar Loose	20	Hercules	16	Redrum	4
Café Fazer	12	Salve	31	Bar Nº9	21	Jenny Woo	10	Room Albert	24
Café Tin Tin Tango	2	Strindberg	13	Beatroot	27	Kafe Moskova	15	Tiger	8
Kasakka	5	Uni Café	11	Cuba!	19	Lost & Found	26	We Got Beef	28
		Vltava	6						

Parliament and National Museum

Further along Mannerheimintie on the left, the multi-columned and rather solemn **Parliament Building** (guided tours only: free) was completed in 1931. There's more information on the parliament from the attached visitor centre at Arkadiankatu 3 (July & Aug Mon–Fri 10am–4pm; rest of year Mon–Thurs 10am–6pm, Fri closes 4pm; free). North of here is the **National Museum** (Tues & Wed 11am–8pm, Thurs–Sun 11am–6pm; €7), its design drawing on the country's medieval churches and granite castles. The exhibits, from prehistory to the present, are exhaustive; it's best to concentrate on a few specific sections, such as the fascinating medieval church art and the ethnographic displays from the nation's varied regions. Look out for the world's oldest fishing net.

Olympic Stadium

A mile and a half further up Mannerheimintie, the **Olympic Stadium** is clearly visible; originally intended for the 1940 Olympics, it hosted the second postwar games in 1952. Its **tower** (Mon–Fri 9am–8pm, Sat & Sun 9am–6pm; €2) gives an unsurpassed view over the city and a chunk of the southern coast.

Hietaniemi Cemetery and Underground Church

Two kilometres southwest of here, back towards the city centre, the **Hietaniemi**

Cemetery houses the graves of some of the big names of Finnish history – President Carl Mannerheim, and city architects C.L. Engel and Alvar Aalto. Nearby, you'll find the very elegant **Sibelius Monument**, a cluster of stainless steel tubes reminiscent of a church organ. Three streets east of here, at Lutherinkatu 3, is the late-1960s **Underground Church** (Temppeliaukio kirkko; Mon & Wed 10am–5pm, Tues 10am–12.45pm & 2.15–5pm, Thurs & Fri 10am–8pm, Sat 10am–6pm, Sun 11.45am–1.45pm & 3.30–6pm; closed during services; tram #3B), blasted from a single lump of granite. It's a thrill to be inside, beneath its domed copper roof.

Suomenlinna

Built on five interconnected islands by the Swedes in 1748 to protect Helsinki from seaborne attack, the fortress of **Suomenlinna**, fifteen minutes away by boat, is the biggest sea fortress in the world. Reachable by ferry (hourly; €3.80 return) from the harbour, it's also a great place to walk around on a summer afternoon, with superb views back across the water towards the capital: you can either visit independently or take one of the hour-long summer **guided walking tours**, beginning close to the ferry stage and conducted in English (June–Aug daily 11am & 2pm, Sept–May Sat & Sun 1.30pm; €6.50). Suomenlinna has a few museums, none particularly riveting, but the best of the lot is **Suomenlinna Museum** (daily May–Sept 10am–6pm, Oct–April 10am–4pm; €5), which contains a permanent exhibition on the island.

Arrival and information

Air Vantaa airport is 20km to the north, connected by Finnair buses to the central train station (every 20min; €5.90).
Train The train station is in the heart of the city on Kaivokatu.
Bus The long-distance bus station is under the Kamppi shopping centre on Simonkatu.
Ferry Terminals are less than 1km from the centre; take tram #3T or 3B.
Tourist office The excellent City Tourist Office at Pohjoisesplanadi 19 (May–Sept Mon–Fri 9am–8pm, Sat & Sun 9am–6pm; Oct–April Mon–Fri 9am–6pm, Sat & Sun 10am–4pm; ⓣ 09/3101 3300, ⓦ www.visithelsinki.fi) stocks brochures and maps, sells tickets for guided tours and hands out the useful, free listings magazines *Helsinki This Week* and *City*.
Museum passes If you're staying a while, consider purchasing a Helsinki Card (€33/45/55 for 24/48/72hr), giving unlimited travel on public transport and free entry to more than fifty museums.

City transport

The city's transport system (trams, buses and a limited metro) is very efficient. One-way tickets can be bought on board (€2) or from the bus station, tourist office or kiosks around the centre, while a tourist ticket (€6.80/13.60/20.40 for one/three/five days) permits unlimited use of the whole network for the period covered. Tram #3T follows a useful figure-of-eight route around the centre.

Accommodation

Hostel beds are in short supply, especially during summer, so booking ahead is sensible, either direct or at the Hotel Booking Centre at the train station for a fee of €5 in person or for free by phone, email or online (Mon–Fri 9am–6pm, Sat & Sun 10am–5/6pm; closed Sun Sept–May; ⓣ 09/2288 1400, ⓦ www.helsinkiexpert.fi).

Hostels

Academica Hietaniemenkatu 14 ⓣ 09/1311 4334 ⓦ www.hostelacademica.fi. On the fringes of the city centre with single-sex dorms and double rooms. Breakfast and bed linen included in price. June–Aug only. Tram #3T (stop "Kauppakorkeakoulu"). Dorms €24, rooms €58.

Erottajanpuisto Uudenmaankatu 9 ⓣ 09/642 169, ⓦ www.erottajanpuisto.com. Atmospheric and sociable hostel (think shabby couches) in a grand old building on Helsinki's best street for bar hopping. Dorms €25, rooms €70.

Eurohostel Linnankatu 9 ⓣ 09/622 0470, ⓦ www.eurohostel.fi. The biggest hostel in Finland, close to the ferry terminals and with a free sauna. Dorms €22.40, rooms €44.80.

Hostel Suomenlinna ⓣ 09/684 7471, ⓦ www.leirikoulut.com. Easily the most idyllic place to stay, placed on the fortress island of Suomenlinna (see above). Dorms €25, Rooms €60.

Stadion Hostel Olympic Stadium ⓣ09/477 8480, ⓦwww.stadionhostel.com. Some 2km out of the centre and often crowded, but cheap and open all year. Trams #3T, #4, #7 or #10 to stadium, then follow the signs. Dorms €20, Rooms €47.

Hotels

Finn Kalevankatu 3b ⓣ09/684 4360, ⓦwww.hotellifinn.fi. A peaceful, modern option on the top floor of an office block, virtually in the city centre. €80.

Omena Eerikinkatu 24 & Lönnrotinkatu 13 ⓦwww.omenahotels.com. Helsinki's best deals can often be found at either of these two centrally located, self-service, internet-reserved hotels. Rooms are very sleek, and start from €45.

Campsite

Rastila Karavaanikatu 4 ⓣ09/3107 8517, ⓦwww.rastilacamping.fi. Great camping spot with cabins and dorms in an attached hostel. It's 13km east of the city centre, near the end of the metro line (Vuosaari) and served by night buses #90N till 1.30am during the week and 4.15am Fri & Sat. Camping €13, dorms €19, cabins €45.

Eating

Many places offer good-value lunchtime deals, and there are plenty of affordable ethnic restaurants and fast-food *grillis* for the evenings. At the end of Eteläesplanadi the *kauppahalli* (Mon–Fri 8am–7pm, Sat 8am–4pm) is good for snacks and sandwiches, as are the numerous university student cafeterias around the city.

Cafés

Café Ekberg Bulevardi 9. Nineteenth-century fixtures and a *fin-de-siècle* atmosphere, with starched waitresses bringing expensive sandwiches and pastries to marble tables. Lunch €8.40.

Café Fazer Kluuvikatu 3. Owned by Finland's biggest chocolate company, with celebrated cakes and pastries.

Café Tin Tin Tango Töölöntorinkatu 7. Oddball café/bar with laundry machines and a sauna (book a day in advance) en route to the Olympic Stadium. Slough off the travel dirt and have a beer at the same time.

Uni Café Mannerheimintie 3. Cheap, filling meals at this university cafeteria right in the centre of town.

> TREAT YOURSELF
>
> **Strindberg** Pohjoisesplanadi 33. A classic Finnish café: the upstairs restaurant serves contemporary Scandinavian cuisine, while the street level café is one of the places in town to see and be seen. Mains from €15.

Restaurants

Bali-Hai Iso Roobertinkatu 35. One of the hippest little restaurants in town with a spartan, almost Hopper-esque interior. Try the scrumptious house *rödburger*.

Bar Tapasta Uudenmaankatu 13. Bustling tapas joint with Spanish beers and wine to accompany the fairly authentic food. Open from 4.30pm, closed on Sun. Tapas from €4.60.

Kasakka Meritullinkatu 13. Great atmosphere and food in this old-style Russian restaurant. Mains from €18.

Lasipalatsi Mannerheimintie 22–24. Decent modern Finnish food served in a classic Functionalist-style building with great views of the street life below. Mains from €8.

Omenapuu Keskuskatu 2. Just opposite the train station, this great little buffet-style spot has some of the best – and cheapest – meals in town. Lunch buffet €10.90.

Pompei Snellmaninkatu 16. Excellent, down-at-heel neighbourhood Italian restaurant run by a friendly Neopolitan. Really great pizzas.

Salve Hietalahdenranta 11. Unselfconsciously old-school sailors' restaurant at the end of Bulevardi that's been serving up the same heavy Finnish fare for over a century. Well worth a visit. Mains €6–11.

Vltava Elielinaukio 2. Pronounced "Valltava," this Czech restaurant just next to the train station serves grilled sausage, steaks and a great collection of pilsners.

Drinking and nightlife

Drinking in Helsinki is about as autonomic an activity as breathing for city residents. Wed is a popular night for going out, while on Fri and Sat it's best to arrive as early as possible to get a seat. Several venues put on a steady diet of live music and there are occasional free gigs on summer Sundays in Kaivopuisto Park, south of the centre. There's also a wide range of clubs and discos, which charge a small admission fee (€5–8). For details of what's on, read the back page of the culture section of *Helsingin Sanomat*, or the free fortnightly English-language paper *City*, found in record shops, bookshops, department stores and tourist offices.

Bars

A21 Annankatu 21. This award-winning bar offers excellent if pricey cocktails, designer seating and

cliques of clientele who spend way too much time in front of the mirror.

Ateljee Bar *Hotel Torni*, Yrjönkatu 26. The best views of Helsinki from this stylish (but expensive) rooftop bar.

Bar Loose Fredrikinkatu 34. Hip, Detroit-inspired rock'n'roll bar, open till 2am every night.

Bar Nº9 Uudenmaankatu 9. A popular hangout for professionals at lunchtime and bohos in the evening, with a beer list and menu as cosmopolitan as its staff. Food is reasonably cheap and filling and there is always a vegetarian option.

Beatroot Iso Roobertinkatu 10. Intimate, beatniky bar. At weekends the downstairs club, the *Rose Garden*, is open till late.

Cuba! Erottajankatu 4. Popular bar with a decent-sized dance floor that puts on electronica, rock, pop, and house music in addition to some steamy salsa nights.

Erottaja Bar Erottajankatu 15–17. Stripped-down underground bar. Busy at weekends, when DJs play electro and the like until 3am.

Jenny Woo Simonkatu 6. Hip downstairs club that is very big among younger Finns – you'll pick up a lot of local high-school slang here. Get here early for happy-hour bargain cocktails.

Kafe Moskova Eerikinkatu 11. Like the Cold War never happened. Intimate, cool Russian-themed bar.

Motellet Annankatu 10. Laid-back bar with comfy felt sofas and sticky floors that is immensely popular with Helsinki's media set.

We Got Beef Iso Roobertinkatu 21 Ⓦwww.wegotbeef.fi. Reggae, ska and funk are the turntable mainstays at this hipster bar, with a small dancefloor out back.

Clubs

Lost & Found Annankatu 6 Ⓦwww.lostandfound.fi. Gay-friendly straight club with the latest opening hours on the block. Two bars on two floors, with a small dancefloor downstairs. Very popular at weekends. Daily 8am–4am.

Redrum Vuorikatu 2 Ⓦwww.redrum.fi. Some excellent, inventive dance nights and an unbeatable sound system at this central, youngish club. Daily 10pm–4am.

Tiger 1A Urho Kekkosenkatu. This extremely popular sprawling nightclub consists of several levels, multiple black-marble dancefloors, large terrace lounges and VIP rooms. Wed–Sat 10pm–4am.

Gay Helsinki

The gay scene in Helsinki is flourishing. For the latest details, pick up a copy of the monthly *Z* magazine – in Finnish only but with a useful listings section – widely available in larger newsagents, or drop into the state-supported gay organization SETA, Hietalahdenkatu 2b 16 (Ⓣ09/681 2580).

dtm (Don't Tell Mamma) Iso Roobertinkatu 32. The capital's legendary gay night club, with occasional drag shows and house music most nights.

Hercules Lönnrotinkatu 4b. A fairly relaxed club that plays varied music; popular with younger gay men.

Nalle Pub Kaarlenkatu 3–5. The heart of Helsinki's lesbian scene, this apartment-like spot in the Kallio district features a jukebox and a daily happy hour (3–6pm).

Room Albert Kalevankatu 36. One of Helsinki's better neighbourhood bars; attracts the young and beautiful.

Shopping

Look out for Design District stickers, marking the city's most interesting boutiques and designer shops.

Design Forum Finland Erottajankatu 7. Comprehensive shop, café and studio space devoted to Finnish design: clothes, homeware, ceramics, jewellery, you name it.

Helsinki 10 Eerikinkatu 3. Some great clothing brands from Finland and further afield at this lovingly stocked boutique.

Limbo Annankatu 13. Finnish clothing brand, which also stocks work by other Finnish designers. Some men's clothes, but mostly quirky, colourful womenswear and accessories.

Lux Uudenmaankatu 26. Clothes, books, comics and records, with a focus on up-and-coming young designers.

Stockmann Department Store Corner of Aleksanterinkatu and Mannerheimintie. Sprawling Constructivist edifice selling everything from bubble gum to Persian rugs. Next door, the Akateeminen Kirjakauppa is the city's best bookstore.

Stupido Iso Roobertinkatu 23. Independent record shop with a dedicated Finnish section featuring a lot of heavy metal and Europop. A good place to pick up flyers and listings.

Directory

Embassies Australia (honorary consulate), Museokatu 25b Ⓣ09/4777 6640; Canada, Pohjoisesplanadi 25b Ⓣ09/228 530; Ireland, Erottajankatu 7A Ⓣ09/646 006; South Africa, Rahapajankatu 1A Ⓣ09/6860 3100; UK, Itäinen Puistotie 17 Ⓣ09/2286 5100; US, Itäinen Puistotie 14a Ⓣ09/616 250.

Exchange Apart from the banks, try Travelex at the airport (5.30am–11.30pm) or Forex at the train station (daily 8am–9pm).

Hospital Marian Hospital, Lapinlahdenkatu 16 ⓣ09/4716 3339.
Internet *Cafe Aalto*, Akateeminen Kirjakauppa, Keskuskatu 1; *mbar* in the Lasipalatsi, Mannerheimintie 22–24; Netcup, Aleksanterinkatu 52.
Laundry Rööperin pesulapalvelut, Punavuorenkatu 3; *Café Tin Tin Tango*, Töölöntorinkatu 7 (ring ⓣ09/2709 0972 to reserve).
Left luggage At the train station.
Pharmacy Yliopiston Apteekki, Mannerheimintie 5 & 96 (24hr).
Post office Mannerheiminaukio 1.

Moving on

Air Ivalo (for Inari; 2–3 daily; 1hr 40min); Oulu (10–15 daily; 1hr); Rovaniemi (5–7 daily; 1hr 20min).
Train Oulu (8–10 daily; 7hr); Rovaniemi (5 daily; 9hr 45min); St Petersburg (2 daily; 6hr; 3hr from 2011); Tampere (hourly; 2hr); Turku (12 daily; 2hr).
Bus Porvoo (15 daily; 1hr); Turku (every 30min; 2hr 15min).
Ferry Stockholm (4 daily; 9hr 45min); Tallinn (15–25 daily; 1hr 40min–4hr).

AROUND HELSINKI: PORVOO

About 50km east of Helsinki, **PORVOO** is one of the oldest towns on the south coast and one of Finland's most charming. Its narrow cobbled streets, lined by small wooden buildings, give a sense of Finnish life before the capital's bold squares and Neoclassical geometry. Close to the station, the **Johan Ludwig Runeberg House**, Aleksanterinkatu 3 (Mon–Sat 10am–4pm, Sun 11am–5pm; Sept–April closed Mon & Tues; €5), is where the famed Finnish poet lived from 1852; one of his poems provided the lyrics for the Finnish national anthem. The old town is built around the hill on the other side of Mannerheimkatu, crowned by the fifteenth-century **Tuomiokirkko**, where Alexander I proclaimed Finland a Russian Grand Duchy and convened the first Finnish Diet. The cathedral survived a serious arson attack in 2006 and reopened two years later. The town's past can be explored in the **Porvoo Museum** (daily 10am/noon–4pm; Sept–April closed Mon & Tues; €5) at the foot of the hill in the main square.

Buses run daily from Helsinki to Porvoo (€9.20 one-way; 1hr), arriving opposite the **tourist office**, Rihkamakatu 4 (Mon–Fri 9am–4.30/6pm, Sat & Sun 10am–2/4pm; Sept to early June closed Sun; ⓣ019/520 2316, ⓦwww.porvoo.fi). There's a **hostel** at Linnankoskenkatu 1–3 (ⓣ019/523 0012, ⓦwww.porvoohostel.cjb.net; dorms €18, rooms €44) and a **campsite**, *Porvoo Camping Kokonniemi* (ⓣ019/581 967, ⓦwww.fontana.fi; June–Aug; €21) 1.5km from the town centre. The cheapest **place to eat** is *Rosso* at Piispankatu 21, which does a fixed-price lunch for €8.50.

The southwest

The area immediately west of Helsinki is probably the blandest section of the country – interminable forests interrupted only by modest-sized patches of water and virtually identical villages and small towns. The far southwestern corner is more interesting, with islands and inlets around a jagged shoreline and some of the country's distinctive Finnish-Swedish coastal communities.

TURKU

European Capital of Culture for 2011 (along with Tallinn), **TURKU** was once the national capital, but lost its status in 1812 and most of its buildings in a ferocious fire in 1827. These days it's a small and sociable city, bristling with history and culture and with a sparkling nightlife, thanks to the students from its two universities.

What to see and do

To get to grips with Turku and its pivotal place in Finnish history, cut through the centre to the Aura River which splits

the city. This tree-framed space was, before the great fire of 1827, the bustling heart of the community.

Tuomiokirkko

Overlooking the river, the **Tuomiokirkko** (daily 9am–7/8pm except during services) was erected in the thirteenth century and is still the centre of the Finnish Lutheran Church. Despite repeated fires, a number of features survive, and there's a small museum in the south gallery exhibiting the religious knick-knacks collected by the church over the course of its history.

Turku Art Museum

The **Turku Art Museum** (Tues–Fri 11am–7pm, Sat & Sun 11am–5pm; €7, or €8 during special exhibitions) is housed in a lovely building constructed in 1904. It contains one of the better collections of Finnish art, with works by all the great names of the country's nineteenth-century Golden Age plus a commendable stock of modern pieces.

Aboa Vetus and Ars Nova

Turku's newest and most splendid museum is the combined **Aboa Vetus and Ars Nova** (daily 11am–7pm, Sept–March closed Mon; €8; guided tours July to early Aug daily 1.30pm), along the riverbank. Digging the foundations of the modern art gallery revealed a warren of medieval lanes, now on show as part of an exhibition exploring Turku's past. The gallery comprises 350 striking works plus temporary exhibits, and there's a great café too.

Turku Castle

Crossing back over Aurajoki and down Linnankatu and then heading towards the mouth of the river will bring you to **Turku Castle** (daily 10am–6pm; late Sept to April closed Mon; €7). If you don't fancy the walk, hop on bus #1 from the market square. The featureless exterior conceals a maze of cobbled courtyards, corridors and staircases, with a bewildering array of finds and displays – a 37-room historical museum. The castle probably went up around 1280; its gradual expansion accounts for the patchwork architecture.

Arrival and information

Train and bus Both the stations are within easy walking distance of the river, just north of the centre.
Ferry From the Stockholm ferry, take the train to the terminal, 2km west, or catch bus #1 to Linnankatu.
Tourist office Aurakatu 4 ⓣ 02/262 7444, ⓦ www.turkutouring.fi (Mon–Fri 8.30am–6pm, Sat & Sun 9/10am–3/4pm).

Accommodation

Campsite Ruissalo ⓣ 02/262 5100, ⓦ www.turku.fi/ruissalocamping. On the island of Ruissalo, which has two sandy beaches and overlooks Turku harbour. June–Aug; bus #8. €14.
Hostel Turku Linnankatu 39 ⓣ 02/262 7680, ⓦ www.turku.fi/hostelturku. One of the cleanest, most efficient and best-run hostels in Finland, situated right by the river. Take bus #1 or #30. €18.
Linnasmaki Lustokatu 7 ⓣ 02/4123 500, ⓦ www.linnasmaki.fi. Basic 56-room summer hostel in the Christian Institute, 4km from town (bus #14 or 15). Mid-May to mid-Sept only. €25.
Omena Hotelli Humalistonkatu 7 ⓦ www.omenahotels.com. Alvar Aalto fans should stay in this building designed by Finland's most famous architect. The hotel is self-service, with an automated reception area. €45.
Tuure Bed and Breakfast ⓣ 02/233 0230, ⓦ www.netti.fi/~tuure2/. Clean, pleasant little guesthouse in the centre of town. €50.

Eating and drinking

Fresh produce is sold in the *kauppatori* (market square), near the tourist office every day; in summer it's full of open-air cafés; nearby, the effervescent market hall or *kauppahalli* (Mon–Fri 8am–5pm, Sat 8am–2pm) offers a slightly more upmarket choice of delis and other places to eat. A drink at one of the many floating bar-restaurants moored along Itäinen Rantakatu is a popular summer tradition.

Cafés and restaurants

Assarin Ulakko Rehtorinpellonkatu 4A. This rock bottom-priced student cafeteria offers a lively

atmosphere great for meeting local uni students. Lunch costs €5.20. Closed Sun.

Baan Thai Kauppiaskatu 17. Great Thai food at respectable prices. Mains €7.

Blanko Aurakatu 1. Popular bar/restaurant just opposite the tourist office. Good lunches, and house and electro DJs till 3am at weekends. Mains from €8.

Foija Aurakatu 10. Busy cellar restaurant with vaulted ceilings and great service opposite the market square. Great pastas, salads and pizzas from €7.50.

Herman Läntinen Rantakatu 37. A bright, airy storehouse right on the river dating from 1849, with excellent lunches from €8.60.

Bars and clubs

Baari Kärpänen Kauppiakatu 8. Excellent hard rock bar with lovely embroidered red velvet seating inside and a cobblestone terrace in front. Looks rough, but actually very sociable.

Dynamo Linnankatu 7. A rocking bar set across two floors, with red velour chairs and olive leather couches. Doesn't really get going until after around 1am.

Edison Kauppiaskatu 4. Bistro-styled bar extremely popular with young professionals as well as Erasmus students. Best before 10pm.

Klubi Humalistonkatu 8. Cavernous, studenty venue featuring live bands and DJ nights – for listings, check the posters liberally applied to lamp posts all over town.

Kuka Linnankatu 17. Furnished with an eclectic mix of classic Finnish design pieces and retro madness, this cool, arty bar attracts Turku's creative types. Live music or DJs several nights a week.

Moving on

Train Helsinki (hourly; 2hr); Tampere (8 daily; 2hr).
Bus Helsinki (every 30min; 2hr 10min–2hr 45min), Tampere (every 30min; 2hr–2hr 55min.
Ferry Stockholm (4 daily; 10–11hr).

The Lake Region

About a third of Finland is covered by the **Lake Region**, a huge area of bays, inlets and islands interspersed with dense pine forests. Despite holding much of Finland's industry, it's a tranquil, verdant area, and even **Tampere**, a major industrial city, enjoys a peaceful lakeside setting. The eastern part of the region is the most atmospheric: slender ridges furred with conifers link the few sizeable landmasses. The regional centre, **Savonlinna**, stretches gorgeously across several islands and boasts a fine medieval castle, inside which a superb opera festival is held every summer, while bustling **Kuopio** offers a good taste of the region.

TAMPERE

Scandinavia's largest inland city, **TAMPERE** is a leafy place of cobbled avenues, sculpture-filled parks and two sizeable, placid lakes. It was long a manufacturing centre, founded a century ago when the Scot James Finlayson opened a textile factory. Thanks to an impressive arts patronage, it has become one of Finland's most enjoyable cities, with free outdoor concerts, a healthy nightlife and one of the best modern art collections in Finland.

What to see and do

The main streets run off either side of Hämeenkatu. To the left, up slender Hämeenpuisto, the **Lenin Museum** at no. 28 (Mon–Fri 9am–6pm, Sat & Sun 11am–4pm; €5) commemorates the revolutionary's ties with Finland and his life in general; the absorbing exhibition has a devoted, trainspotter feel. Moomin fans shouldn't miss the adorable **Moomin Museum** (Tues–Fri 9am–5pm, Sat & Sun 10am–6pm, plus Mon 9am–5pm June–Aug; €4) in the basement of the city library at Hämeenpuisto 20, a respectful and exhaustive overview of Tove Jansson's creations. Nearby, at Puutarhakatu 34, the **Art Museum of Tampere** (Tues–Sun 10am–6pm; €6) holds temporary art exhibitions, but if you're looking for Finnish art you might be better off visiting the **Hiekka Art Gallery**, a few minutes' walk away at Pirkankatu 6

(Tues–Thurs 3–6pm, Sun noon–3pm; €5). Better still is the tremendous **Sara Hildén Art Museum** (daily 11am–6pm, closed Mon Oct–April; €4), built on the shores of Näsijärvi, a quirky collection of Finnish and foreign modern works; take bus #16 (or #4 in summer) from the centre.

Arrival and information

Air Bus #61 operates between the airport and the city centre, taking 40min.
Train The station's at Rautatienkatu 25, at the end of Hämeenkatu.
Bus The long-distance bus station is in the town centre, off Hämeenkatu.
Tourist office In the railway station ⓣ03/5656 6800, ⓦwww.gotampere.fi (Jan–May Mon–Fri 9am–5pm; June–Aug Mon–Fri 9am–8pm, Sat & Sun 9.30am–5pm; Sept Mon–Fri 9am–5pm, Sat & Sun 9.30am–5pm; Oct–Dec 9am–5pm, Sat & Sun 11am–3pm).

Accommodation

Härmälä Campsite ⓣ020/719 9777. 4km south of the city centre in gorgeous wooded environs with cabins (€34); bus #1. Mid-May to Aug only. €21.
Hostel Sofia Tuomiokirkonkatu 12a ⓣ03/254 4020, ⓦwww.hostelsofia.fi. Bright, attractive hostel with rooms that look smack onto the cathedral. €26.
Omena Hotelli Hämeenkatu 28 ⓦwww.omenahotels.com. This excellent, self-service hotel has no reception and you must book online, but it offers some of the best deals in town. A second hotel is slated to open here in 2010. €55.

Eating

Coyote Bar and Grill Hämeenkatu 3. Retro dining spot filled with young locals scarfing down burgers and finger food, then lingering on bottles of Karjala IV.
Kahvila Pulo Ojakatu 3. This bookish, high-ceilinged space is the best café in town. Try the cakes and admire the beautiful furniture.
Salud Tuomiokirkonkatu 19. A lively Spanish restaurant serving mixed tapas (plates €8.40) and an amply sized weekday lunch buffet (€9.50).

Drinking

 **Doris** Kauppakatu 16. Tues evenings are especially crowded at this boho underground bar; DJs spin until 4am every day of the week.
Tullikamari Tullikamarinaukio 2 ⓦwww.klubi.net. Busy nightclub and concert venue in an old customs house behind the train station.
Vanha Monttu Hämeenkatu 17. Cellar bar filled with ex-punk and hard-rocker kids. The lively drunken karaoke nights are a particularly good spot to see the Finnish national character up close.

Moving on

Train Helsinki (hourly; 2hr); Kuopio (8 daily; 3hr 45min); Oulu (7 daily; 5hr); Savonlinna (2 daily; 5hr); Turku (8 daily; 2hr).

SAVONLINNA AND AROUND

SAVONLINNA is one of the most relaxed towns in Finland, renowned for its **opera festival** (ⓣ015/476 750, ⓦwww.operafestival.fi) in July. It's packed throughout summer, so book well ahead if you're visiting at this time. Out of peak season, its streets and beaches are uncluttered, and the town's easy-going mood and lovely setting – amidst a confluence of forests and lakes – makes it a pleasant place to linger.

What to see and do

The best locations for soaking up the atmosphere are the **harbour** and **market square** at the end of Olavinkatu, where you can cast an eye over the grand *Seurahuone* hotel, with its Art Nouveau fripperies. Follow the harbour around picturesque Linnankatu, or better still around the sandy edge of Pihlajavesi, which brings you to atmospheric and surprisingly well-preserved **Olavinlinna Castle** (guided tours daily 10am–4/6pm; €5), perched on a small island. Founded in 1475, the castle witnessed a series of bloody conflicts until the Russians claimed possession of it in 1743 and relegated it to the status of town jail. Nearby is the **Savonlinna Provincial Museum** in Riihisaari (Tues–Sun 11am–5pm, plus Mon same times in July & Aug; €5), which occupies an old

granary and displays an intriguing account of the evolution of local life, with rock paintings and ancient amber carved with human figures.

Arrival and information

Train There are two train stations: be sure to get off at Savonlinna-Kauppatori, just across the main bridge from the tourist office.
Bus The bus station is off the main island, but within easy walking distance of the town centre.
Tourist office Puistokatu 1 ⓣ015/517 510, ⓦwww.savonlinnatravel.com (July to early Aug Mon–Sat 9am–7pm, Sun 10am–4pm; early Aug to June Mon–Fri 9am–5pm).

Accommodation

Perhehotelli Hospitz Linnankatu 20 ⓣ015/515 661, ⓦwww.hospitz.com. Attractive, central hotel. Prices go up during the opera festival. €95.
Savonlinna SKO Hostel Opistokatu 1 ⓣ015/72 910, ⓦwww.sko.fi. Likeable summer hostel (June–Aug only) in the town's Christian Institute. 6km from the city centre. Dorms €25, rooms €60.
S/S Heinävesi Savonlinna harbour ⓣ015/517 510, ⓦwww.savonlinnanlaivat.fi. In the summer, this steamship offers 34 beds in comfy on-board cabins. €66.
Vuohimäki Camping Vuohimäentie 60 ⓣ015/537 353, ⓦwww.fontana.fi. The nearest campsite, though still a good 7km from the centre. June–Aug; bus #4. €21.

Eating and drinking

Good, cheap food is available at the pizza joints along Olavinkatu and Tulliportinkatu.
Majakka Satamakatu 11. Tasty Finnish nosh, with some good deals at lunchtime.
Paviljonki Rajalahendenkatu 4. The restaurant of a local cookery school, serving great €14 lunches (11am–4.30pm) including dessert and coffee.

Moving on

Train Parikkala (for Helsinki; 2 daily; 50min); Punkaharju (3 daily; 20min);
Bus Kuopio (3–7 daily; 2hr 45min–4hr 20min)

Around Savonlinna

Savonlinna boasts beautiful scenery all around, and the place to sample it is **Punkaharju Ridge**, a narrow strip of land between the Puruvesi and Pihlajavesi lakes, 28km from town. Locals say it has the healthiest air in the world, super-oxygenated by abundant conifers: this is the Lake Region at its most breathtakingly beautiful. The ridge is traversable by road and rail, both running into the town of **Punkaharju** and passing the incredible **Retretti Arts Centre** (June–Aug daily 10am–5/6pm; €15), set in caves and with a large sculpture park. Trains and buses make the short journey between Savonlinna and Retretti.

KUOPIO

The pleasant lakeside town of **KUOPIO** is best known for its enormous smoke sauna, the biggest in the world, and makes for a worthwhile pit-stop on your way north to Lapland. One of the best times to visit is during the annual **Kuopio Dance Festival** (ⓦwww.kuopiodance festival.fi) in mid-June.

What to see and do

Built on a grid system, the centre is easy to navigate. Just south of the train station is the main square, the *kauppatori*. From here Kauppakatu leads east to the **Kuopio Museum** (Tues–Fri 10am–5pm, till 7pm on Wed; Sat & Sun 11am–5pm; €5) at no. 23 with two floors of natural and cultural history. Further up the road, at no. 35, the **Kuopio Art Museum** (same times; €3) is housed in a converted bank. The thoughtfully curated temporary exhibitions focus mainly on modern Finnish art. Around the corner on Kuninkaankatu, the **Victor Barsokevitsch Photographic Centre** (June–Aug Mon–Fri 10am–7pm, Sat & Sun 11am–4pm; Sept–May Tues–Fri 11am–5pm, till 7pm on Wed, Sat & Sun 11am–3pm; summer €5, winter €3) is a real find – one of the best photography galleries in the country, with changing exhibitions featuring the gallery's founder and other photographers.

Kuoipio's **woodsmoke sauna** (Tues year-round, plus Thurs mid-May to mid–Sept; €11; Ⓦwww.rauhalahti.fi), set at the *Jätkänkämppä Lumberjack Lodge*, is the main draw in town, and about as quintessentially Finnish an experience as you'll find: there are traditional Finnish evenings each night the sauna is open, which include dinner, music and dancing – enquire at the tourist office for details. The lodge is located 4km south of the centre in the *Rauhalahti* spa hotel complex. See the box on p.352 for advice on sauna etiquette.

Arrival and information

Train and bus Kuopio's train and bus stations are located opposite each other just north of the *kauppatori*.

Tourist office Within the City Hall at Haapaniemenkatu 17 Ⓣ017/182 584, Ⓦwww.kuopioinfo.fi (June–Aug Mon–Fri 9.30am–5pm, plus Sat 9.30am–3pm in July; rest of year Mon–Fri 9.30am–4.30pm). The Kuopio Card (€12) on sale here, offers free entry to the town's museums as well as admission to the smoke sauna.

Accommodation

Hostelli Hermanni Hermanninaukio 3e Ⓣ040/910 9083, Ⓦwww.hostellihermanni.net. Comfortable if basic hostel 1.5km out of town. Dorms €20, rooms €50.

Rauhalahti Katiskaniementie 8, 5km from the city centre Ⓣ01/747 3000, Ⓦwww.rauhalahti.com. Attractive lakeside campsite with cottages (€30), a hostel (€43) and space for tents. €20.

Youth Hostel Virkkula Asemakatu 3 Ⓣ040/418 2178. Summer hostel in a colourful converted school just by the train station. Mid-June to early Aug. Dorms €17.

Eating and drinking

Café Kaneli Pohjolankatu 2a. Charming little café cluttered with knick-knacks and pictures, serving great coffee and cake.

Kreeta Tulliportinkatu 46–48. Excellent Greek restaurant with mains from €8.40.

Sampo Kauppakatu 13. Proudly traditional fish restaurant that has been serving Finnish dishes since 1931. Mains around €12.

Wanha Satama At the harbour. Set in a former customs house, this modern Finnish restaurant is popular on sunny summer evenings, serving inexpensive sandwiches and more expensive local dishes.

Moving on

Train Helsinki (4–5 daily; 4hr–4hr 50min); Oulu (4 daily; 4hr 10min–4hr 30min); Rovaniemi (4 daily; 7hr); Savonlinna (3 daily; 3hr–3hr 50min); Tampere (4–5 daily; 3hr 30min).

The north

The northern regions take up a vast portion of Finland: one third of the country lies north of the Arctic Circle. It's sparsely populated, with small communities often separated by long distances. The coast of Ostrobothnia is affluent due to the adjacent flat and fertile farmland; busy and expanding **Oulu** is the region's major city as well as a centre of high-tech expertise, though it maintains a pleasing small-town atmosphere. Further north is the remote and wild territory of **Lapland**, its wide-open spaces home to several thousand Sámi, who have lived in harmony with this harsh environment for millennia. Up here are two good bases: the buzzing town of **Rovaniemi** and, further north, the quiet village of **Inari**, Lapland's de facto capital and a great jumping-off point for trips to the rest of the region; there is an extensive bus service and regular flights from Helsinki. Make sure you try Lappish **cuisine**, too – fresh cloudberries, smoked reindeer and wild salmon are highlights.

OULU

OULU, with its renowned university, is a leading light in Finland's burgeoning computing industry and a great place to pause on your way up north, with a good collection of restaurants and cafés and a pulsing nightlife, especially in the warmer months. On Kirkkokatu, the copper-domed and stuccoed **Tuomiokirkko** (June–Aug daily 11am–8/9pm;

Sept–May Mon–Fri noon–1pm) seems anachronistic amid the bulky blocks of modern Oulu. Across the small canal just to the north, the **Northern Ostrobothnia Museum** (Tues–Sun 10/11am–6/7pm; €3) has a large regional collection with a good Sámi section.

Arrival and information

Bus and train The adjacent stations are located a few blocks east of the *kauppatori* and *kauppahalli*.
Tourist office Torikatu 10 (Mon–Fri 9am–4pm; mid-June to Aug until 5pm, plus Sat 10am–3pm; ⓣ044/703 1330, ⓦwww.oulutourism.fi).
Internet Try the library at Kaarenväylä 3.

Accommodation

Hotel Turisti Rautatienkatu 9 ⓣ08/563 6100, ⓦwww.hotellituristi.fi. Central hotel opposite the train station with well-designed, inexpensive rooms. Good deals for singles and at weekends. €65.
Nallikari Holiday Village ⓣ08/5586 1350, ⓦwww.nallikari.fi. Campsite with cabins on Hietasaari Island, 4km from town; take bus #17 from Isokatu in the town centre. Cabins €35, pitches €21.

Eating, drinking and nightlife

45 Special Saarisonkatu 12 ⓦwww.45special.com. Legendary rock club with three floors and frequent live bands; the Sunday jams are a good bet.
Finlandia Hallituskatu 31. No-nonsense pizzeria.
Katri Antell Rotuaari Kirkkokatu 17. Traditional bakery/café justly famed for its cakes. Closed Sun.
Never Grow Old Hallituskatu 13–17 ⓦwww.ngo.fi. Quirky reggae bar perfect for late-night dancing.
Valve Café Hallituskatu 7. Oulu's youth and cultural centre has a relaxed courtyard café that's super in the afternoons. Films are screened every evening in the same building.

Moving on

Train Helsinki (5 daily; 6–9hr); Rovaniemi (5 daily; 3hr); Tampere (11 daily; 4hr 50min–7hr).

ROVANIEMI

Easily reached by train, **ROVANIEMI** is touted as the capital of Lapland, and while its fairly bland shopping streets are a far cry from the surrounding rural hinterland, they do evoke a distinct Arctic sensibility. Take a day or two here to gear up for an exploration of the Lappish hinterland and – depending on the season – catch a glimpse of the midnight sun or head out for some winter adventure.

What to see and do

The best way to prepare yourself for what lies further north is to visit the 172m-long glass tunnel of **Arktikum** at Pohjoisranta 4 (Tues–Sun 9/10am–6/7pm plus Mon mid-June to Aug; €12; ⓦwww.arktikum.fi). Subterranean galleries along one side house the **Provincial Museum of Lapland**, with genuine Sámi crafts and costumes. Across the corridor is the **Arctic Centre**, which gives a thorough treatment of all things circumpolar.

For a couple of weeks either side of midsummer, the **midnight sun** is visible from Rovaniemi. The best vantage points are either the striking bridge over the Ounaskoski or atop the forested and mosquito-infested hill, Ounasvaara, across the bridge.

Most other things of interest are outside town, not least the **Arctic Circle**, 8km north and connected by the hourly bus #8 from the railway station (€5.80 return). On the circle is the **Santa Claus Village** (daily 9/10am–5/6/7pm; free), a large log cabin where you can meet Father Christmas all year round and leave your name for a Christmas card from Santa himself.

Arrival and information

Air The airport is located 5 miles north of town, and connected by bus (€5).
Train The station is just outside the town centre, at Ratukatu 3.
Bus The bus station is just west of the centre, off Postikatu, a few minutes' walk east from the train station.
Tourist office Rovakatu 21 ⓣ016/346 270, ⓦwww.rovaniemi.fi (Mon–Fri 9am–6pm. plus June–Aug Sat & Sun 9am–1pm).

Accommodation

Guesthouse Borealis Asemieskatu 1 ⓦwww.guesthouseborealis.com. Wonderful family-run spot with colourful rooms and great service.
Hostel Rudolf Koskikatu 41, book via ⓣ016/321 321, ⓦwww.hotelsantaclaus.fi. Modern hostel with colourful rooms 10min walk from the centre. There are no staff on site; check-in and reservations are handled by the *Clarion Hotel Santa Claus*, Korkalonkatu 29. April–Nov €26.50, Dec–March €30.
Ounaskoksen Camping ⓣ016/345 304. Campsite on the far bank of Ounaskoski, facing town – a 20min walk from the station. €24.

Eating and drinking

Antinkaapo Rovakatu 13. The best café in town serves wide range of cakes and pastries.
Hydos Kansankatu 10. This great Turkish restaurant does an unbeatable €7 lunch.
Kauppayhtiö Valtakatu 24. Unexpectedly fantastic café/bar with a mishmash of retro furniture. DJs at the weekend and a gallery at the back. Free wi-fi.
Zoomit Korkalonkatu 29. Modern, if somewhat gaudy bar popular with local university students.

Moving on

Air Helsinki (3 daily; 1hr 20min).
Train Helsinki (5 daily; 9hr 45min); Oulu (5 daily; 3hr).
Bus Inari (4 daily; 5hr 30min); Nordkapp, Norway (June to late Aug 1 daily; 10hr 30min).

INARI

A half-day bus ride north of Rovaniemi, **INARI** lies along the fringes of Inarijärvi, one of Finland's largest lakes, and makes an attractive base from which to further explore this part of Lapland. In the town itself, the excellent **SIIDA** (Sámi Museum; Tues–Sun: June–Sept 9am–8pm, Oct–May 10am–5pm; €8; ⓦwww.siida.fi) has an outstanding outdoor section giving you an idea of how the Sámi survived in Arctic conditions in their tepees, or *kota*, while the indoor section has a well laid-out exhibition on all aspects of life in the Arctic. Towards the northern end of the village, summer **boat tours** (€12) depart from under the bridge to the ancient Sámi holy site on the island of **Ukonkivi**. If walking's your thing then check out the pretty **Pielpajärvi Wilderness Church**, a well-signposted 7km (2hr) hike from the village.

Arrival and information

Air Ivalo airport is a 40min bus ride from town.
Bus Buses stop outside the tourist office, in the centre of town, before continuing to Karasjok in Norway and – from June to late Aug only – Nordkapp, about the most northerly point in Europe.
Tourist office The helpful tourist office (Mon–Fri 9/10am–5/6pm; June–Sept also Sat & Sun; ⓣ016/661 666, ⓦwww.inarilapland.org) is in the SIIDA museum complex. Staff here can advise on guided snow-scooter trips in winter and fishing trips around the lake in summer – even trips across the Russian border to Murmansk.

Accommodation

Finding accommodation should not be too problematic, though Inari does get very busy during the summer.
Lomakylä Inari Inarintie 26 ⓣ016/671 108, ⓦwww.lomakyla-inari.fi. A brief walk from town, these lakeside log cabins are open year-round and most have private bath. €35.
Uruniemi Campsite 2km south of the village ⓣ016/671 331, ⓦwww.uruniemi.com. In a lovely location right by the lake, with cabins and rooms arranged around manicured grounds. Oct–May advanced booking obligatory. €20.
Villa Lanca Opposite the tourist office ⓣ040/748 0984, ⓦwww.villalanca.com. Cheery guesthouse with gorgeous rooms. €68.

Eating

Inarin Kultahovi Saarikoskentie 2. This pricey hotel's restaurant dishes up the best meals in town, including reindeer carpaccio and skewered tiger prawns.
SIIDA The museum restaurant prepares excellent Arctic dishes, including a succulent baked salmon fillet with hollandaise sauce.

Moving on

Bus Ivalo (3–6 daily; 40min); Rovaniemi (3–6 daily; 4hr 45min–7hr 50min).

France

HIGHLIGHTS

MUSÉE D'ORSAY, PARIS: the capital's most enjoyable museum, with an unparalleled collection of Impressionist art

LOIRE: marvel at fairytale châteaux in stunning riverside locations, and then visit the nearby vineyards

LYON: spend an evening devouring regional specialities in one of the city's excellent bouchons

BORDEAUX: enjoy the superb local wines in one of the many sun-drenched squares

CORSICA: explore the rugged mountains and fine sand beaches of the "island of beauty"

ROUGH COSTS

DAILY BUDGET Basic €40/occasional treat €65

DRINK Glass of wine €2.50, beer €3

FOOD Baguette/sandwich €3–5

HOSTEL/BUDGET HOTEL €16–30/€25–55

TRAVEL Paris–Nice by train (5hr 30min) €25

FACT FILE

POPULATION 63.4 million

AREA 547,030km

LANGUAGE French

CURRENCY Euro (€)

CAPITAL Paris (population: 9.6 million)

INTERNATIONAL PHONE CODE ☎33

Introduction

France is one of Europe's most stylish and dynamic countries. The largest country in Western Europe, it offers a variety of cultural and geographical experiences unmatched across the continent. Yet, despite its size, it's surprisingly easy to explore, with a fantastic high-speed train network which means that within hours of indulging in the café culture of the capital, you could be swimming in the clear waters of the Cote d'Azur.

Paris continues to captivate visitors with its world-class museums, distinctive neighbourhoods and exuberant nightlife. To the west, **Normandy** boasts some of the country's greatest Romanesque architecture, while the lush countryside and rocky coastline of neighbouring **Brittany** provide great surroundings for getting away from it all. Just south lie the grand chateaux of the **Loire valley**, and beyond that the gorgeous hills and valleys of the **Dordogne**. The Atlantic coast has a misty charm, including low-key **La Rochelle** and the surfing capital of **Biarritz**. Though most people push on south to the country's most obvious attractions, there's a lot to be said for exploring the Germanic towns of **Alsace** in the east and the high and rugged heartland of the **Massif Central**.

France's gastronomic capital, **Lyon**, acts as a gateway to the heady southern region of **Provence**, characterized by beautiful countryside, charming towns and sublime food. The **Côte d'Azur** retains something of its old glamour, while **Marseille** is more worthy of exploration than its reputation would have you believe. The very south of the country, marked by the canyons of the **Pyrenees**, hides the dream-like fortress of Carcassonne, and provides some of the country's best walking territory, alongside the **Alps.** The student cities of **Montpellier** and **Toulouse** should be stops on any budget traveller's itinerary, boasting cheap restaurants, excellent nightlife and a relaxed ambience.

CHRONOLOGY

51 BC Julius Caesar conquers Gaul.
486 AD Clovis I, leader of the Franks, establishes his rule over Gaul.
800 Charlemagne rules as King of the Franks.
1066 William, the Duke of Normandy, invades England and is crowned King of England.
1337 The Hundred Years War with England begins.
1431 After leading the French army to victory, Joan of Arc is burnt at the stake for heresy, at the age of 19.
1589 Henry IV is the first of the Bourbon dynasty to become King of France. Enforces Catholicism over the country.
1789 The French Revolution ends the rule of the monarchy and establishes the First Republic.
1804 Napoleon I declares himself Emperor of the French Empire.
1815 Napoleon I is defeated at the battle of Waterloo; the monarchy is restored.
1848 Louis-Napoleon, Napoleon I's nephew, is made President of the Second Republic before declaring himself Emperor a few years later.
1871 Defeat in the Franco-Prussian War leads to the creation of the Third Republic.
1872 Monet starts the Impressionist Movement.
1889 Eiffel Tower is built, making it the tallest building in the world.
1905 Church and State are legally separated.
1914–1918 World War I – over 1.5 million killed.
1939–1944 Nazi Germany occupies France leading to four years of fascist rule under the Vichy regime. France is liberated by Allied forces in August 1944.
1962 Algeria gains independence from French colonial rule.
1995 Jacques Chirac elected President.
2002 The euro replaces the franc.
2005 Civil unrest and riots across the country after the death of two teenagers who were running from police in one of Paris' impoverished housing estates.
2007 Nicolas Sarkozy is elected President, narrowly beating Ségolène Royal, France's first female presidential candidate.
2008 Smoking is banned in bars and cafés.

ARRIVAL

The main hub for arrivals by **air** is Paris Charles de Gaulle, which is served by both major and budget airlines. In addition, there are around 34 other airports, including Lyon, Nice, La Rochelle and Marseille. France has excellent train connections to the rest of continental Europe. The main access point by **train** from most countries is Paris: Gare du Nord links to Amsterdam, Brussels, Germany and the UK; Gare de Lyon to Italy; and Gare d'Austerlitz to Spain. There are also excellent connections from the south of France to Italy and Spain.

The Eurolines **coach service** (Ⓦwww.eurolines.com) connects most European countries to France; the main arrival point in Paris is the *gare routière* in the suburb of Bagnolet.

GETTING AROUND

France has the most extensive **rail** network in Western Europe, run by the government-owned SNCF (Ⓦwww.sncf.com). The only areas not well served are parts of the Alps and the Pyrenees, where some rail routes are replaced by SNCF buses. Private bus services tend to be uncoordinated and are best used only as a last resort.

Train fares are reasonable, especially if booked well in advance; Paris to Lyon, for example, can cost as little as €19, but four times that if booked on the day of travel. InterRail and Eurail passes are valid on normal trains at all times. The

high-speed and very efficient TGVs (*Trains à Grande Vitesse*) require reservations (€3), and there is a supplement to travel on certain other trains (from €1). All tickets (not passes) must be stamped in the orange machines in front of the platform of the train station (*gare*) on penalty of a steep fine. All but the smallest stations have an information desk but only a handful have *consignes automatiques* – coin-operated left-luggage lockers. The word *autocar* on a timetable column indicates that it's an **SNCF bus service**, on which rail tickets and passes are valid.

Should you wish to **cycle** in France, you'll find it easier to cope outside the big cities, where traffic can be overwhelming. Bikes that can be dismantled go free on all trains – if you can't collapse your bike then it can still travel free as long as the train doesn't require reservations and there's room. If you're catching a train that requires a reservation, your bike will also need a booking, and you'll have to pay a flat fee of €10 (regardless of distance). The main SNCF stations and larger tourist offices often rent bikes for around €10–15 per day.

ACCOMMODATION

Outside the summer season and school holidays, it's generally possible to turn up in any town and find accommodation. However, many hostels get booked up with school groups, so where possible it's worth reserving in advance.

All **hotels** are officially graded and are required to post their tariffs inside the entrance. If you're travelling with another person, you'll find that it's often just as economical (and often much nicer) to stay in a cheap hotel as it is to stay in a hostel.

Most **hostels** in France are operated by FUAJ, the French youth hostel association (part of the worldwide Hostelling International; Ⓦ www.hihostels.com). Many of the hostels are situated some distance away from the centre of town, and the quality varies widely – from old-fashioned institutional accommodation to bright, modern, well-situated buildings. Many FUAJ hostels close in the middle of the day so you are unable even to leave your bags, and all require that you vacate the rooms by around 10am, even if you're not checking out. There's also an increasing number of independent hostels, some of which are more like boutique hotels – these usually offer superior accommodation, facilities and a more casual atmosphere, though often at an inflated price. Almost all hostels provide bed linen, and most provide free breakfast, with the exception of a few private hostels.

Gîtes d'étape provide bunkbeds and simple kitchen facilities in rural areas for climbers, hikers, cyclists, etc – they are listed, along with mountain refuges, on Ⓦ www.gites-refuges.com.

Local **campsites** provide a good budget alternative as they are generally clean, well-equipped and often enjoy prime locations. Prices are usually for two people plus a tent – we've noted any exceptions. Ask tourist offices for lists of sites or consult Ⓦ www.campingfrance.com.

FOOD AND DRINK

Eating out in France isn't particularly cheap, but the quality of the food is often excellent and, even in the big cities, it's usually easy to find somewhere where you can enjoy a *plat* and a glass of wine for under €15.

Generally the best place to eat **breakfast** (*petit déjeuner*) is in a bar or café. Most serve *tartines* (baguette with butter and/or jam) and croissants, until around 11am. Coffee is invariably served black and strong – *un café* is an espresso, while *un café crème* is made with hot milk. Tea (*thé*) and hot chocolate (*chocolat chaud*) are also available – though the former is served without milk unless you request it on the side.

Cafés are often the best option for a light **lunch**, usually serving omelettes, sandwiches (generally half-baguettes filled with cheese or meat) and *croque-monsieur* (toasted ham and cheese sandwich; €3–6), as well as more substantial meals. Creperies are ubiquitous throughout France and are usually very reasonably priced (from €5), and Oriental restaurants are also a good choice for a cheap, filling meal (from €7). Most cafés and restaurants have a midday *formule* (set menu) of two or three courses, often including a glass of wine. With *formules* starting at around €9, it's worth making lunch your main meal to make the most of these offers, which will often allow you to enjoy high-quality restaurant food that you wouldn't otherwise be able to afford. Most restaurants serve food from noon to 2pm and 7pm to 11pm, but some cafés serve snacks throughout the day.

Though it's easier to find **vegetarian** food in France than ever before, you might still struggle to find dishes that you can eat on a lot of menus. However, vegetarian restaurants are becoming more common, especially in large cities, and if you make it clear that you're *un végétarien*, something can normally be arranged in all but the most basic of places.

Drink

Drinking is an important part of French life, with the local bar playing a central social role. It is acceptable to drink throughout the day, though drunkeness is frowned upon.

Wine (*vin*) is the national drink, and drunk at just about every meal or social occasion. Even the most basic of cafés usually offer a wide range of wines by the glass, and ordering a *pichet* or a carafe (usually ranging from a quarter bottle to a half bottle) is often great value.

Beer can be very expensive, especially if ordered by the pint. Beer on tap (*à la pression*) is the best value – ask for *une pression* or *un demi* (0.33 litre). Spirits such as **cognac** and **armagnac**, and of course the notorious **absinthe**, are widely drunk but not cheap. A pleasant, inexpensive pre-dinner drink is *un kir*, a mix of white wine and crème de cassis, and if you're in the south of France it's definitely worth sampling the local **pastis**, drunk over ice and diluted with water – very refreshing on a hot day.

CULTURE AND ETIQUETTE

Making an effort to speak French, however dreadful your accent, is always highly appreciated; a few basic words will get you a lot further than any amount of grimacing and pointing.

It's customary to **tip** porters, tour guides, taxi drivers and hairdressers, usually one to two euros. Restaurant prices almost always include a service charge, so there's no need to leave an additional cash tip unless you feel you've received service out of the ordinary.

SPORTS AND OUTDOOR ACTIVITIES

The main sport in France is undoubtedly **football**. The French football league (ⓦwww.lfp.fr) is divided into Ligue 1 (the highest), Ligue 2 and National; teams playing in the first category include Saint-Étienne, Lyon and Paris Saint-Germain. Match tickets are available from specific club websites, or in the town they are playing – ask at the local tourist office.

Rugby is another major pursuit, especially in southwestern France, and the country often puts up a good showing in the Six Nations Tournament in March and April. Further details of rugby fixtures can be found at the French-language website ⓦwww.francerugby.fr. The annual Tour de France, an epic 3000km **cycle** race across the country

every July (Ⓦwww.letour.fr), is one of the country's most popular sporting events.

The country's best **skiing** can be enjoyed in the Alps, and it's usually possible to ski from November to April. Prices can be high, however, so it's worth checking package prices in resort towns such as Chamonix (see p.448).

France also has some excellent long-distance footpaths, known as *sentiers de grande randonnée* or GRs, and facilities for **hikers** are generally very good, including mountain refuges and excellent information centres in major hiking regions. The most popular areas for hiking are the Pyrenees and the Alps, though the Massif Central has some impressive, off-the-beaten-track routes.

COMMUNICATIONS

Post offices (*la poste*) are widespread and generally open from 8.30am to 6.30pm Monday to Friday, and 8.30am to noon on Saturday. **Stamps** (*timbres*) are also sold in *tabacs* (tobacconist shops). International **phone calls** can be made from any phone box (*cabine*), using phonecards (*télécartes*), which are available from post offices, *tabacs* and train station ticket counters. For all calls within France you must dial the entire ten-digit number, including area code.

FRANCE ON THE NET

Ⓦ**www.tourisme.fr** French Tourist Board.
Ⓦ**www.franceguide.com** Excellent resource, with links to many tourist offices.
Ⓦ**www.france.com** Indispensable guide on travelling around the country and places to stay, with the opportunity to interact with other travellers.
Ⓦ**www.discoverfrance.net** Useful tourist information, with links to other sites.
Ⓦ**www.viafrance.com** Information on festivals, expos, events and concerts.

EMERGENCY NUMBERS

Police ⓣ17; Ambulance ⓣ15; Fire ⓣ18; or ⓣ112 for all three.

The number for directory enquiries is ⓣ12. **Internet access** is widespread, if not especially cheap; prices begin at around €1/hr and can go up to €6/hr.

EMERGENCIES

There are two main types of **police**, the Police Nationale and the Gendarmerie Nationale, and you can report a theft, or any other incident, to either.

To find a **doctor**, ask for an address at any *pharmacie* (chemist) or tourist information office. Consultation fees for a visit will be €20–25 and you'll be given a *Feuille de Soins* (Statement of Treatment) for any insurance claims. EU citizens are, with an EHIC, exempt from charges – see p.48.

INFORMATION

Most towns and villages have an *Office de Tourisme*, giving out local **information** and free maps. The larger ones can book accommodation anywhere in France, and most can find you a local room for the night, albeit with an added service charge.

MONEY AND BANKS

The currency of France is the **euro** (€). Standard **banking hours** are Monday to Friday 9am to noon and 2 to 4.30pm; in cities, some also open on Saturday morning. **ATMs** are found all over France and most accept foreign cards. Credit cards are generally accepted by larger shops, and most restaurants and hotels.

OPENING HOURS AND HOLIDAYS

Basic **working hours** are 9am to noon/1pm and 2/3 to 6.30pm. The traditional **closing days** for shops (and

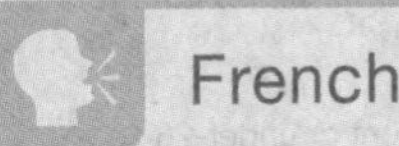

French

	French	Pronunciation
Yes	*Oui*	Whee
No	*Non*	No(n)
Please	*S'il vous plaît*	See voo play
Thank you	*Merci*	Mersee
Hello/Good day	*Bonjour*	Bo(n)joor
Goodbye	*Au revoir/à bientôt*	Orvoir/abyantoe
Excuse me	*Pardon*	pardo(n)
Today	*Aujourd'hui*	Ojoordwee
Yesterday	*Hier*	Eeyair
Tomorrow	*Demain*	Duhma(n)
What time is it?	*Quelle heure est-il?*	Kel ur et eel?
I don't understand	*Je ne comprends pas*	Je nuh compron pah
How much?	*Combien?*	combyen
Do you speak English?	*Parlez-vous anglais?*	Parlay voo onglay?
One	*Un*	Uh(n)
Two	*Deux*	Duh
Three	*Trois*	Trwah
Four	*Quatre*	Kattre
Five	*Cinq*	Sank
Six	*Six*	Seess
Seven	*Sept*	Set
Eight	*Huit*	Wheat
Nine	*Neuf*	Nurf
Ten	*Dix*	Deess
Where's the...?	*Où est...?*	Oo ay...?
Entrance	*Entrée*	Ontray
Exit	*Sortie*	Sortee
Tourist office	*Office de tourisme*	Ofees der tooreesmer
Toilet	*Toilettes*	Twalet
Hotel	*Hôtel*	Otel
Youth hostel	*Auberge de jeunesse*	obairzh der zherness
Church	*Église*	Ay-gleez
Museum	*Musée*	Mewzay
What time does the...leave?	*À quelle heure part...?*	A kel er par...?
Boat	*Le bateau*	Ler bato
Bus	*Le bus*	Ler bews
Plane	*L'avion*	Lavyon
Train	*Le train*	Ler trun
Ticket	*Billet*	Beelay
Do you have a... room?	*Avez-vous une chambre...?*	avay voo ewn shombrer...?
Double	*Avec un grand lit*	avek un grand lee
Single	*À un lit*	A un lee
Cheap	*Bon marché*	Bo(n) marchay
Expensive	*Cher*	Share
Open	*Ouvert*	Oovair
Closed	*Fermé*	Fermay

STUDENT AND YOUTH DISCOUNTS

Most of the museums and attractions listed here offer a student or under-26 discount, which can be anything up to a third off. To make the most of these, buy an **ISIC** (International Student) or **IYTC** (International Youth) card. For more information see Ⓦwww.isiccard.com.

It's also worth noting that many museums have free entry on the first Sunday of every month.

some restaurants) are Sunday and Monday, though you'll always find at least one *boulangerie* (bakery) open. **Museums** are usually closed on Mondays, with reduced opening hours outside of summer. All shops, museums and offices are closed on the following **national holidays**: January 1, Easter Sunday and Monday, Ascension Day, Whit Monday, May 1, May 8, July 14, August 15, November 1, November 11, December 25.

Paris

All the cliches about **PARIS** are true – stylish, romantic, glamorous and utterly compelling – yet it retains surprises that continue to delight even the most seasoned visitors. Undoubtedly France's jewel in the crown, it is an essential stop on any visit. The landscape of the city changes as you cross from *quartier* to *quartier*. Each area has a distinct style and atmosphere, from cosmopolitan **St-Germain** and the genteel Luxembourg Gardens to the vibrant Marais, abuzz with bars and cafés, and the steep cobbled streets of **Montmartre**. Paris is suprisingly small for a capital city, and the best way to explore it is on foot – or do as the locals do and hire a bike (see p.393). Of course, it goes without saying that the café, bar and restaurant scene here is among the best in Europe, even for travellers on a budget.

What to see and do

Paris is split into two halves by the Seine, each with its own distinct identity. On the north of the river, the **Right Bank** *(Rive droite)* is home to the *grands boulevards* and its most monumental buildings, many dating from the civic planner Baron Haussmann's nineteenth-century redevelopment. Most of the major museums are here, as well as the city's widest range of shops around rue de Rivoli and Les Halles.

The **Left Bank** (*Rive gauche*) has a noticeably different feel. A legendary Bohemian hang-out since the nineteenth century, the city's best range of bars and restaurants are based here, as well as some of its most evocative streets, such as the areas around St-Germain and St-Michel. These days much of the area has given in to commerce, with increasingly expensive and chic shops opening up, though it's not hard to discover some of its old spirit if you wander off the main roads.

PARISIAN ARRONDISSEMENTS

Paris is divided into twenty postal districts, known as *arrondissements*, which are used to denote addresses. The first, or *premier* (abbreviated as 1er), is centred on the Louvre and the Tuileries, with the rest (abbreviated as 2e, 3e, 4e etc) spiralling outwards in a clockwise direction.

Parts of Paris, of course, don't sit so easily within such definitions. **Montmartre**, rising up to the north and dominated by the great white dome of Sacré Coeur, has managed to retain a village-like atmosphere despite its tourist popularity, and the islands of the Seine (de la Cité and St-Louis), though touristy themselves, retain a charming old-fashioned atmosphere within their side streets.

The Arc de Triomphe, Champs-Élysées and around

The **Arc de Triomphe** (daily 10am–10.30/11pm; €9; M° Charles-de-Gaulle-Etoile), at the head of the Champs-Élysées, is an imposing Parisian landmark, matched only by the Eiffel Tower, and offers panoramic views from the top. The celebrated **avenue des Champs-Élysées** is now, unfortunately, home to little more than a constant stream of tourists and too many fast-food and chain shops. It leads to the vast, usually traffic-clogged **place de la Concorde**, whose centrepiece, a gold-tipped obelisk from the temple of Luxor, was presented to the city by the viceroy of Egypt in 1829. Beyond lies the formal **Jardin des Tuileries** (daily 8/9am–7/8pm; M° Concorde), the perfect place for a stroll with its grand vistas and symmetrical flowerbeds. Towards the river, the **Orangerie** (daily except Tues 9am–6pm; €7.50; M°Concorde) displays Monet's largest water-lily paintings in a specially designed room, as well as

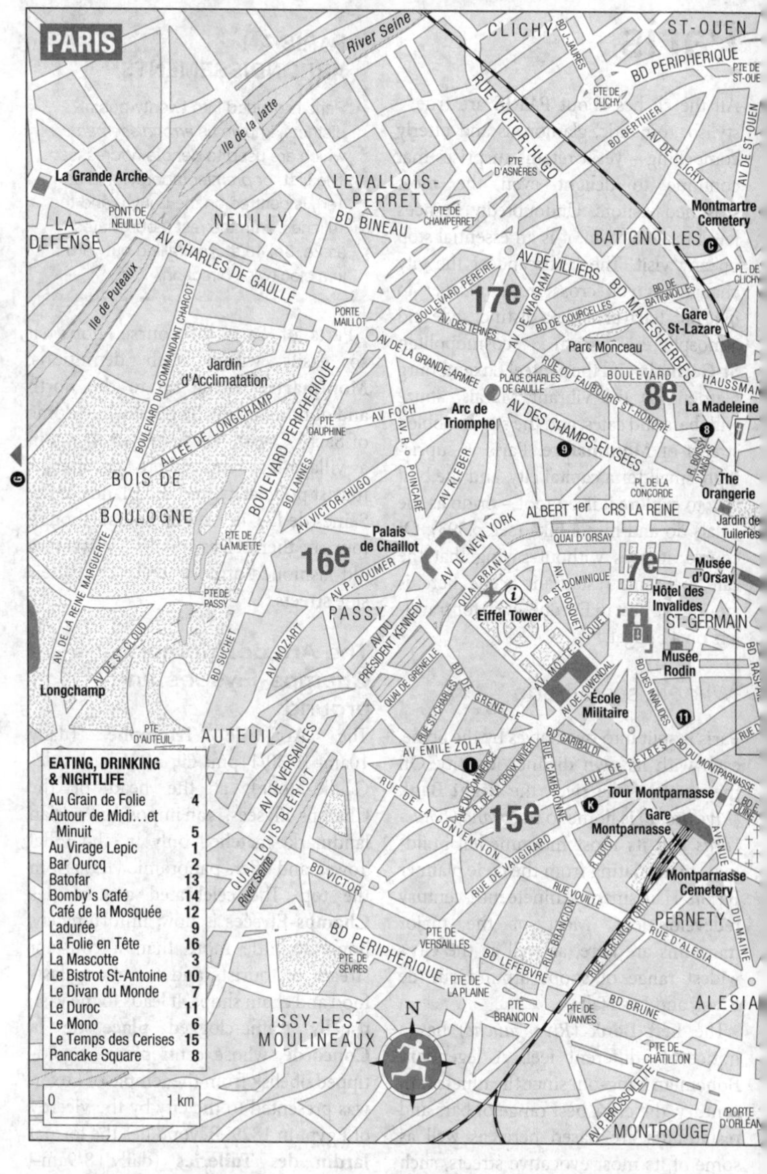

works by Cézanne, Matisse, Utrillo and Modigliani.

The Louvre

On the east side of the Jardin des Tuileries is arguably the world's most famous museum, the **Louvre** (daily except Tues 9am–6pm; Wed & Fri till 10pm; €9, €6 after 6pm; M° Palais Royal-Musée du Louvre/Louvre-Rivoli). The building was first opened to the public in 1793 and within a decade Napoleon had made it

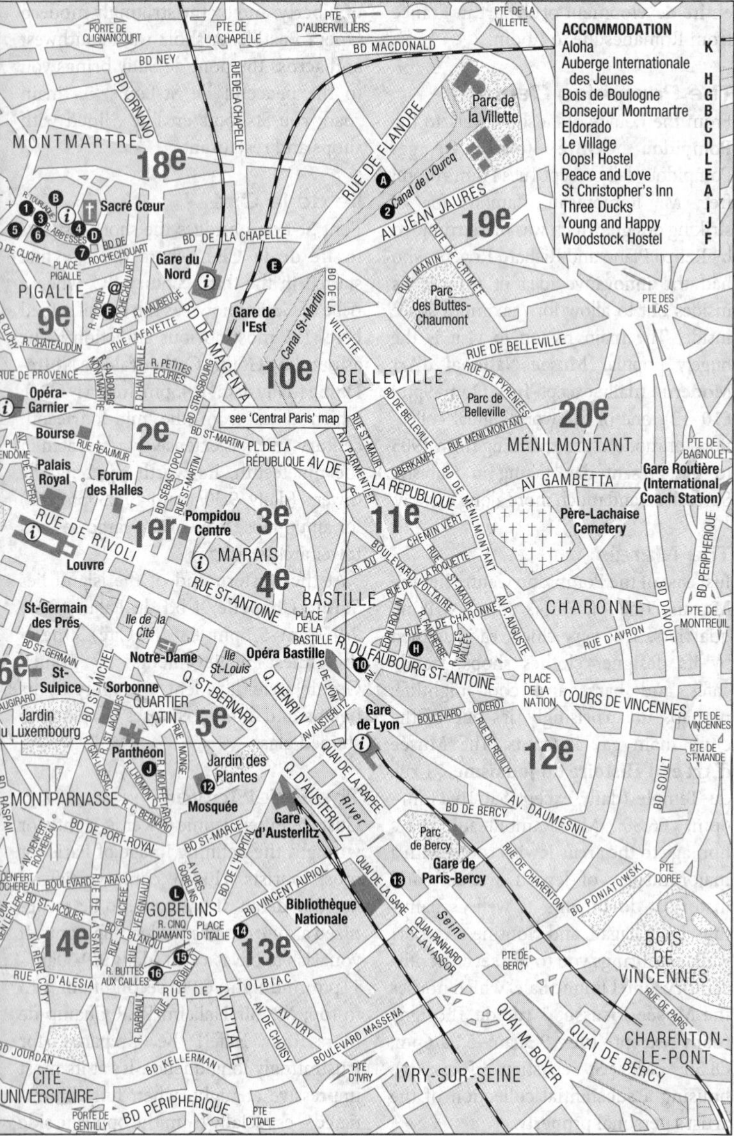

the largest art collection on earth with the takings from his empire, which explains the remarkably eclectic collection.

The main entrance is via I.M. Pei's iconic glass pyramid, but to avoid the (lengthy) queues, enter through the Louvre Rivoli Métro station or through the Louvre Carousel shopping arcade. Most people head straight for Da Vinci's *Mona Lisa*, but it's definitely worth exploring some of the other sections such as **Sculpture**, which covers the

entire development of the art in France from Romanesque to Rodin.

The Pompidou Centre

From the Louvre, it's a short walk to the **Pompidou Centre** (place Georges Pompidou; daily except Tues 11am–10pm; free; M° Rambuteau), famous for its striking design, which was masterminded by Renzo Piano and Richard Rogers, who had the innovative idea of turning its insides out to allow for maximum space inside. The main reason to visit is the hugely popular **Musée National d'Art Moderne** (daily except Tues 11am–9pm; €10–12), one of the world's great collections of modern art, spanning from 1905 to the present day, taking in Cubism, Surrealism and much more along the way.

The Marais

Just east of the Pompidou Centre lies the **Marais**, one of Paris's more striking quartiers. This very chic area is defined by its designer clothes shops, trendy cafés and bars, and cool nightlife; perhaps unsurprisingly, it's one of the city's main gay hotspots. The **Musée d'Art et d'Histoire du Judaïsme**, 71 rue du Temple (daily except Sat 10/11am–6pm; €6.80; M° Rambuteau), pays homage to the area's Jewish roots, with a major display of Jewish artefacts and historical documents as well as paintings by Chagall and Soutine. A short walk east brings you to the seventeenth-century Hôtel Juigné Salé, which houses the **Musée Picasso**, 5 rue de Thorigny (daily except Tues 9.30am–5.30/6pm; €8.50; M° St-Sébastien Froissart), housing a substantial collection of the artist's personal property.

The Bastille and Île St-Louis

Southeast of the Marais is **place de la Bastille**, the site of the Bastille prison that was famously stormed in 1789, beginning the French Revolution. Now the place is marked by the Colonne de Juillet, topped by a green bronze figure of Liberty, and by the strikingly modern Opéra Bastille. A short walk southwest and across the pont de Sully brings you to the peaceful Île St-Louis, its main road, rue St-Louis en l'Île , lined with shops and restaurants.

Île de la Cité

Pont St-Louis bridges the short distance to **Île de la Cité**, where the city first started in the third century BC, when a tribe of Gauls known as the Parisii settled here. The most obvious attraction is the astounding Gothic **Cathédrale de Notre-Dame** (daily 8am–6.45pm; free; M° Cité), which dates from the mid-fourteenth century and was extensively renovated in the nineteenth. It's worth climbing the towers (daily 9.30/10am–5/6.30pm; €8) for an up-close view of the gargoyles and tower architecture.

At the western end of the island lies **Sainte-Chapelle**, 4 bd du Palais (daily 9/9.30am–5/6pm; €8; M° Cité). One of the finest achievements of French Gothic style, it is lent a fragility by its height and huge expanses of glorious stained glass.

The Eiffel Tower

Gustave Eiffel's iconic tower is, rightly or wrongly, the defining image of Paris for most tourists. Hugely controversial on its 1889 debut, it has come to be recognized as one of the city's leading sights. If you wish to pay it a visit (daily 9/9.30am–11pm/midnight; €8 to second floor, €13 to top; M° Bir Hakeim/RER Champ de Mars-Tour Eiffel) be prepared for frustratingly long queues. It's at its most impressive at night, when fully illuminated – especially from the opposite side of the river.

Les Invalides and the Musée Rodin

A short walk from the Eiffel Tower is the Hôtel des Invalides, easily spotted by its gold dome. Built as a home for invalid soldiers on the orders of Louis XIV, it

now houses the giant **Musée de l'Armée,** 129 rue de Grenelle (daily 10am–5/6pm; €8.50; M° Varenne). Military buffs will be fascinated by the vast collection of armour, uniforms, weapons and Napoleonic relics, and the wing devoted to World War II. Immediately east, on 77 rue de Varenne, the **Musée Rodin** (Tues–Sun 9.30am–4.45/5.45pm; €6; M° Varenne) contains many of Rodin's greatest and most famous works, including *The Thinker* and *The Kiss*.

Musée d'Orsay

In a beautifully converted train station by the river, the celebrated **Musée d'Orsay**, 62 rue de Lille (Tues–Sun 9.30am–6pm, Thurs till 9.45pm; €8; RER Musée d'Orsay/M° Solférino), is much more compact and manageable than the Louvre. Covering the periods between the 1840s and 1914, the collection features legendary artists such as Renoir, Van Gogh and Monet, and famous works including Manet's *Le Déjeuner Sur L'Herbe* and Courbet's striking *The Origin Of The World*. The queues are always long, but booking tickets the day before at the advance ticket office on site will allow you priority entrance.

The Latin Quarter

The neighbourhood around the boulevards St-Michel and St-Germain has been known as the **Quartier Latin** since medieval times, when it was the home of the Latin-speaking universities. It is still a student-dominated area – its pivotal point being **place St-Michel** – and schizophrenic in its mixture of cool hangouts and tacky tourist traps. There are, however, some excellent bars and restaurants that reward a visit.

Immediately south of here stand the prestigious Sorbonne and Collège de France universities, the jewels in the crown of French education and renowned worldwide. Nearby, the elegant surroundings of the **Jardin du Luxembourg** (daily dawn–dusk; RER Luxembourg) are perfect for a leisurely picnic.

St-Germain

The northern half of the *6e arrondissement* is an upmarket and expensive part of the city, but fun to wander through. The area is steeped in history: Picasso painted *Guernica* in rue des Grands-Augustins; in rue Visconti, Delacroix painted, and Balzac's printing business went bust; and in the parallel rue des Beaux-Arts, Oscar Wilde died quipping "Either the wallpaper goes or I do." **Boulevard St-Germain** is home to the famous *Flore* and *Deux Magots* cafés, both with rich political and literary histories; however the astronomical prices mean that gawping rather than sipping is the best option.

Montparnasse

Southeast of the Luxembourg gardens is the former bohemian quarter of Montparnasse. It has somewhat lost its lustre since the erection of the hideous 59-storey skyscraper **Tour Montparnasse**, which has rightly become one of the city's most hated landmarks since its construction in 1973. Its sole redeeming feature is the view it offers if you take the lift to the 56th floor (daily 9.30am–10.30/11.30pm; €10.50; M° Montparnasse-Bienvenüe). The nearby **Montparnasse cemetery** on boulevard Edgar Quinet (daily 8/9am–5.30/6pm; free; M° Raspail) offers a little peace in this busy *quartier* and has plenty of illustrious names, including Samuel Beckett and Serge Gainsbourg.

Montmartre

In the far north of the city, in the middle of the *18e arrondissement*, is the glorious district of **Montmartre**. Though the area around Sacré-Cœur and place du Tertre can be horribly touristy, the quieter streets that surround lively rue des Abbesses are a pleasure to wander around, and still suggest a bygone age.

The nineteenth-century neo-Byzantine **Sacré-Cœur** (daily 6.45am–10.30pm; free; M° Anvers/Abbesses) crowns the Butte Montmartre – to get there, take the funicular from place Suzanne Valadon (ordinary métro tickets and passes are valid) or climb the (very) steep stairs via place des Abbesses. The views from the top of the dome (daily 9am–6/7pm; €5) can be rather disappointing, except on the clearest of days. Off nearby rue Lepic is the **Moulin de la Galette**, the last remaining windmill in Montmartre. Further down the hill, in the seedy district of Pigalle, is the famous Moulin Rouge, though it's not worth going out of your way to see.

Père-Lachaise

To the east of the city lies one of the world's most famous graveyards, the **Père-Lachaise cemetery**, boulevard de Ménilmontant, 20e (daily 8/9am–5.30/6pm; free; M° Père-Lachaise), which attracts pilgrims to the graves of Oscar Wilde (in division 89) and Jim Morrison (in division 6). There are countless other famous people buried here, among them Chopin (division 11) and Edith Piaf (division 97) – pick up a map at the entrance as it's easy to get lost.

Arrival

Air Paris has two main airports: Charles de Gaulle and Orly. A much smaller one, Beauvais, 76km north, is used primarily by the low-cost airlines Ryanair and Wizzair. Charles de Gaulle (CDG) is 23km northeast and connected to Gare du Nord train station by RER train line B (every 15min, 5am–midnight; 30min; €7.85). There's also the Roissybus, which terminates at M° Opéra (every 15min, 5.45am–11pm; 45min; €8.50) and two Air France bus lines to M° Charles-de-Gaulle-Étoile (every 15min, 5.45am–11pm; 50min; €12), or to Gare de Lyon and Gare Montparnasse (every 30min, 7am–9pm; 1 hour; €12). Orly, 14km south of Paris, connects to the centre via Orlybus, a shuttle bus direct to RER line B station Denfert-Rochereau on the Left Bank, from where you can get on the métro (6am–11.20pm; 30min; €6.10) and via Orlyval, a fast shuttle train line to RER line B station Antony with connections to M° Dénfert-Rochereau, St-Michel and Châtelet (every 4–8min, 6am–11pm; 35min; €9.30).

Train Paris has six mainline train stations, all served by the métro. You can buy national and international tickets at any of them. Gare du Nord serves northern France, while trains from nearby Gare de l'Est go to eastern France. Gare St-Lazare serves the Normandy coast; Gare de Lyon the southeast and the Alps; Gare Montparnasse serves Chartres, Brittany, the Atlantic coast and TGV lines to Tours and southwest France; and Gare d'Austerlitz serves the Loire valley and the southwest.

Bus Most international and national long-distance buses use the main *gare routière* at Bagnolet in eastern Paris (M° Gallieni).

Information

Tourist office There are tourist office branches all over the city. The most useful one is at 25 rue des Pyramides 1er (June–Oct daily 9am–7pm; Nov–May Mon–Sat 10am–7pm, Sun 11am–7pm; ⓣ08.92.68.30.00, ⓦwww.paris-info.com; M° Pyramides/RER Auber) and can help with last-minute accommodation, as can the offices at Gare de Lyon (Mon–Sat 8am–6pm) and Gare du Nord (daily 8am–6pm). You can also book tickets to museums at the tourist offices – handy for skipping the long queues.

Discount passes Many museums offer discounted entry to under-26s (with ID, see p.386), and there are reduced fees for everyone on Sundays. They're also often free on the first Sunday of every month, but they do get very busy because of it. The tourist office sells the handy Paris City Passport (€5), a booklet of discounts on various attractions and activities.

City transport

Tickets Single tickets (€1.50) are valid on buses, the métro and, within the city limits (zones 1–2), the RER rail lines. If you're going to be using a fair bit of public transport, it makes more sense to buy a carnet of ten tickets (€11.10).

Métro The métro (abbreviated as M°) is an easy way of travelling around the city. The various lines are colour-coded and numbered, and the name of the train's final destination is signposted to buy you know its direction. The métro operates from 5.20am to 1.20am.

Bus The bus network runs from 5.45am until around 12.30am Mon–Sat, with a reduced service from 7am to 8.30pm on Sun. Night buses run from 1am to 5.30am on eighteen routes from place du Châtelet near the Hôtel de Ville (every 30min–1hr).

Train Longer journeys across the city, or out to the suburbs, are best made on the underground RER express rail network, which overlaps with the métro.

Bike rental There are over 1500 locations in the city from where you can hire a bike as part of the city's Velib scheme (Ⓦwww.velib.paris.fr). You'll need a credit card for a deposit in case the bike is damaged, and passes cost €1 for one day, €5 for a week. The first half-hour is free, and charges after that start from €1 per half hour; the bikes can be deposited at any of the Velib stands in the city.

Accommodation

Accommodation is a lot more expensive in Paris than elsewhere in the country, and it's best to book in advance throughout the year. The city has a good selection of independent youth hostels, some of which are more like boutique hotels than the usual standard of hostel in France.

Hostels

The prices listed below are for a bed in a dorm. The MIJE hostels listed below all require the additional purchase of MIJE membership (€2.50; valid for a year).

Aloha 1 rue Borromée, 15e Ⓣ01.42.73.03.03, Ⓦwww.aloha.fr. Fun hostel with basic dorms and very good drink deals at the in-house bar. M° Volontaires. €25.

Auberge Internationale des Jeunes 10 rue Trousseau, 11e Ⓣ01.47.00.62.00, Ⓦwww.aijparis.com. Popular, friendly hostel for under-30s in a good location, 5min from the Bastille. The next door sister *Bastille* hostel (Ⓦwww.bastillehostel.com) offers smart single and twin rooms from €21 per person. M° Ledru-Rollin. €25.

BVJ Paris Louvre 20 rue J. J. Rousseau Ⓣ01.53.00.90.90, Ⓦwww.bvjhotel.com. The most central hostel in Paris, close to the Louvre and Les Halles. Dorms are simple and a little old-fashioned. M° Louvre Rivoli. €29.

BVJ Paris Quartier Latin 44 rue des Bernardins, 5e Ⓣ01.43.29.34.80, Ⓦwww.bvjhotel.com. In a good, quiet location in St-Germain, this clean and bright hostel has small but comfortable rooms, all with shower. M° Maubert-Mutualité. €29.

FUAJ Jules Ferry 8 bd Jules-Ferry, 11e Ⓣ01.43.57.55.60, Ⓦwww.fuaj.org. Located in the lively gay-friendly area by the Canal St Martin, this is a very popular hostel, despite being a little care-worn and basic. Dorms are on the small side. M° République. €22.50.

Le Village 20 rue d'Orsel, 18e Ⓣ01.42.64.22.02, Ⓦwww.villagehostel.fr. Though located in the least attractive area of Montmartre, this reliable hostel has good facilities and a terrace with views of Sacré-Coeur. 2am curfew. M° Anvers. €28.

MIJE Le Fauconnier 11 rue du Fauconnier, 4e Ⓣ01.42.74.23.45, Ⓦwww.mije.com. Charming and comfortable hostel in a beautiful and rather grand seventeenth-century mansion with a courtyard. M° St-Paul. €30.

MIJE Le Fourcy 6 rue de Fourcy, 4e Ⓣ01.42.74.23.45, Ⓦwww.mije.com. Large, friendly hostel in a converted mansion with small four- to eight-bed dorms. Breakfast included and there's a decent, budget restaurant on site. M° St-Paul. €30.

MIJE Maubuisson 12 rue des Barres, 4e Ⓣ01.42.74.23.45, Ⓦwww.mije.com. A stone's throw from the Seine, this impressive hostel is housed in a magnificent medieval building on a quiet street and offers comfortable dorms. M° Pont-Marie. €30.

Oops! Hostel 50 avenue des Gobelins, 13e Ⓣ01.47.07.47.00 Ⓦwww.oops-paris.com. The city's first, self-proclaimed, "design hostel" is situated south of the Latin Quarter near Place d'Italie. All rooms are en-suite and well-decorated, though a little cramped and overpriced. M° Place d'Italie. €30.

Peace and Love 245 rue La Fayette, 19e Ⓣ01.46.07.65.11, Ⓦwww.paris-hostels.com. Right opposite the Canal St Martin, this is a good choice if sleep isn't high on your priorities, with a cheap, popular onsite bar that's open till 2am. All rooms have attached shower. Maximum age 35. M° Louis-Blanc. €33.

St Christopher's Inn 159 rue de Crimée, 19e Ⓣ01.40.34.34.40, Ⓦwww.stchristophers.co.uk. Smart, modern hostel on the Canal St-Ourcq with spacious, well-equipped dorms. Facilities include internet access, a female-only floor and a "quiet room" where films are shown. Cheap meals are served in the attached *Belushi's* bar, where guests can enjoy discounted drinks. M° Laumière. €25.

Three Ducks 6 place Étienne-Pernet, 15e Ⓣ01.48.42.04.05, Ⓦwww.3ducks.fr. The dorms at this party hostel are looking a bit dated, but its inexpensive on-site bar makes it a popular choice. Sheets not included. M° Félix Faure. €24.

Woodstock Hostel 48 rue Rodier, 9e Ⓦwww.woodstock.fr. This popular hostel has a great location, just a few streets away from Montmartre and an easy walk from the city centre. Additional €2 for Fri and Sat night stays. €22.

Young and Happy 80 rue Mouffetard, 5e Ⓣ01.45.35.09.53, Ⓦwww.youngandhappy.fr. In the heart of a student enclave in the Latin Quarter,

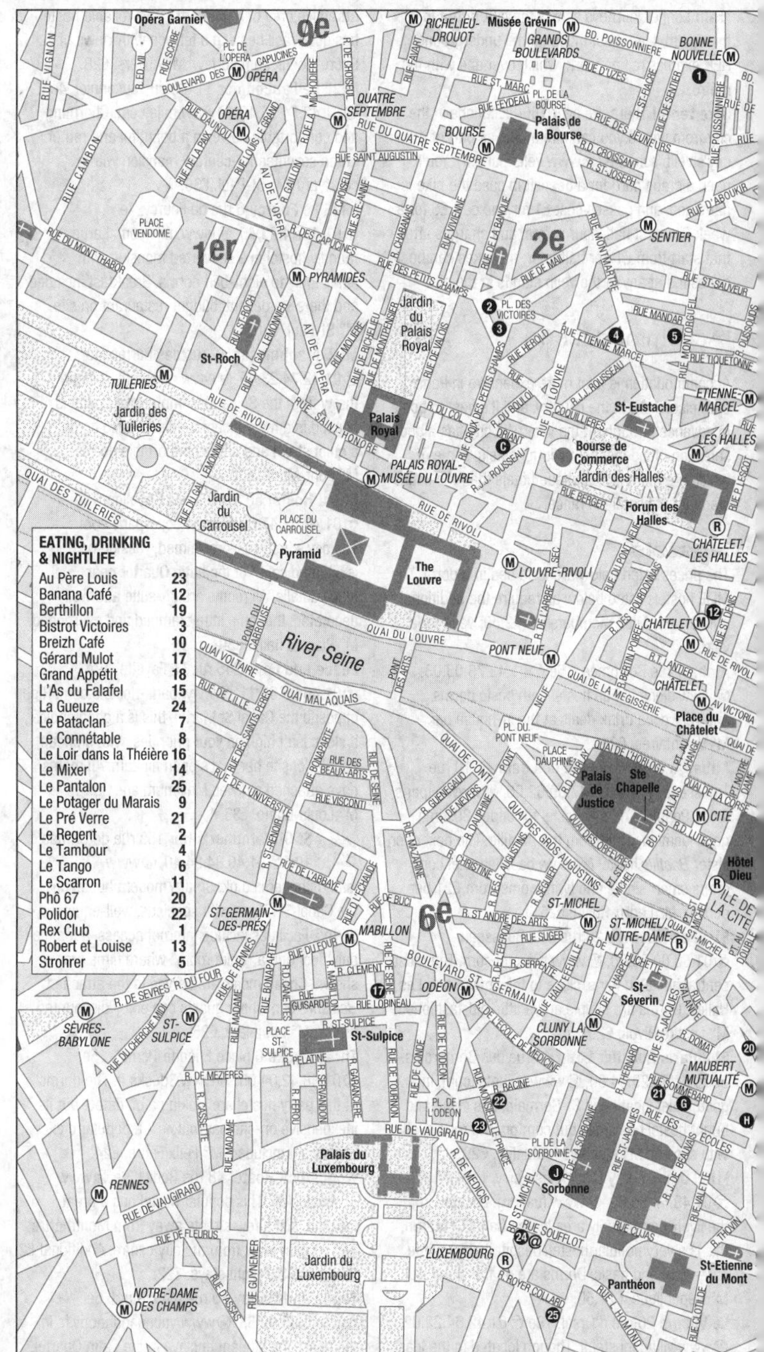
EATING, DRINKING & NIGHTLIFE
Au Père Louis 23
Banana Café 12
Berthillon 19
Bistrot Victoires 3
Breizh Café 10
Gérard Mulot 17
Grand Appétit 18
L'As du Falafel 15
La Gueuze 24
Le Bataclan 7
Le Connétable 8
Le Loir dans la Théière 16
Le Mixer 14
Le Pantalon 25
Le Potager du Marais 9
Le Pré Verre 21
Le Regent 2
Le Tambour 4
Le Tango 6
Le Scarron 11
Phô 67 20
Polidor 22
Rex Club 1
Robert et Louise 13
Strohrer 5
Opéra Garnier
9e
1er
2e
6e
Musée Grévin
Palais de la Bourse
Jardin du Palais Royal
St-Roch
Jardin des Tuileries
Palais Royal
Jardin du Carrousel
Pyramid
The Louvre
River Seine
Bourse de Commerce
Jardin des Halles
Forum des Halles
St-Eustache
Place du Châtelet
Palais de Justice
Ste Chapelle
Hôtel Dieu
ILE DE LA CITE
St-Séverin
St-Sulpice
Palais du Luxembourg
Jardin du Luxembourg
Sorbonne
Panthéon
St-Etienne du Mont
OPÉRA
QUATRE SEPTEMBRE
RICHELIEU-DROUOT
GRANDS BOULEVARDS
BONNE NOUVELLE
BOURSE
SENTIER
PYRAMIDES
TUILERIES
PALAIS ROYAL-MUSÉE DU LOUVRE
LOUVRE-RIVOLI
ETIENNE-MARCEL
LES HALLES
CHÂTELET-LES HALLES
CHÂTELET
PONT NEUF
CITÉ
ST-MICHEL
ST-MICHEL/NOTRE-DAME
ST-GERMAIN-DES-PRÉS
MABILLON
ODÉON
CLUNY LA SORBONNE
MAUBERT MUTUALITÉ
SÈVRES-BABYLONE
ST-SULPICE
RENNES
NOTRE-DAME DES CHAMPS
LUXEMBOURG

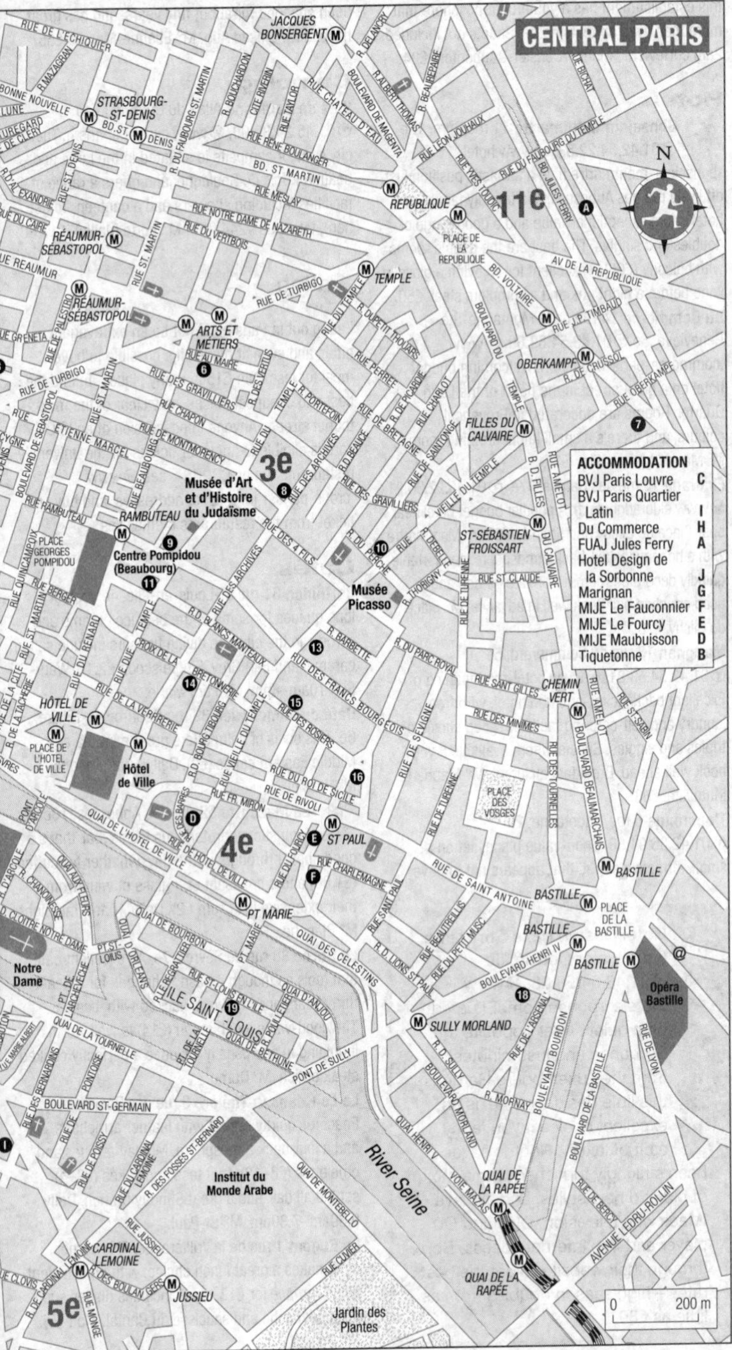

FRANCE
PARIS

www.roughguides.com

this establishment has a youthful atmosphere that more than lives up to its name. Sheets not included. 2am curfew. M° Monge/Censier-Daubenton. €24.

Hotels

Bonsejour Montmartre 11 rue Burq, 18e ⓣ01.42.54.22.53, ⓦwww.hotel-bonsejour-montmartre.fr. In a fantastic position just off lively rue des Abbesses, this friendly family-run hotel offers exceptional value and a good range of doubles and singles. The best are the double rooms with balcony (€66) – excellent for enjoying a glass of wine before a night out, and a complete steal. €50.

Du Commerce 14 rue de la Montagne-Ste-Geneviève, 5e ⓣ01.43.54.89.69, ⓦwww.commerce-paris-hotel.com. Welcoming budget hotel on a quiet street in the heart of the Latin Quarter. Rooms are decorated in Provencal colours, and there's a small kitchen/dining room. M° Maubert-Mutualité. €49.

Eldorado 18 rue des Dames, 17e ⓣ01.45.22.35.21, ⓦwww.eldoradohotel.fr. A popular budget hotel near busy Place de Clichy and 5min walk from Montmartre, with a bohemian, laid-back atmosphere, comfortable, quirkily decorated rooms, a private garden and a good attached bar. Book well in advance. M° Place de Clichy. €70.

Marignan 13 rue du Sommerard, 5e ⓣ01.43.54.63.81, ⓦwww.hotel-marignan.com. Excellent backpacker-oriented hotel, with free laundry and self-catering facilities; good choice of triples and singles. Special offers available if you book well ahead. Breakfast included. M° Maubert-Mutualité. €68.

Tiquetonne 6 rue Tiquetonne, 2e ⓣ01.42.36.94.58. Good-value place, set on a small, attractive street, that appears not to have been changed for about fifty years, and has great hospitality. Closed Aug. M° Étienne-Marcel. €55.

TREAT YOURSELF

Hotel Design de la Sorbonne 6 rue Victor Cousin, 5e ⓣ01.43.54.58.08, ⓦwww.hotelsorbonne.com. Situated on a quiet street opposite the Sorbonne and just minutes from the Luxembourg Gardens, this little designer hotel is an excellent choice if you fancy a bit of luxury. Rooms have been strikingly furnished with a mix of old and new styles, and all have IMacs with television, DVD and CD player and free internet access. Book through their website to get the best rates – high season doubles from as little as €89.

Camping

Bois de Boulogne Allée du Bord de l'Eau ⓣ01.45.24.30.00, ⓦwww.campingparis.fr. The city's major campsite is situated in the large and beautiful Bois de Boulogne, and offers a range of facilities including showers and a canteen. To get here, take bus #244 from M° Porte Maillot. €17.20.

Eating

Eating out in Paris need not be an extravagant affair, and even at dinner, it's possible to have a meal for less than €15 in many places. To find the best and cheapest places, stay clear of the main tourist streets. Anyone in possession of an ISIC card is eligible to apply for tickets for the university restaurants run by CROUS – see ⓦwww.crous-paris.fr for a list of addresses, and buy your ticket from the restaurants themselves.

Cafés

Berthillon 31 rue St-Louis-en-l'Île, 4e. Expect long queues for some of the best ice creams and sorbets in the city; the divine flavours include salted caramel and Earl Grey. Single scoop €2.10. Wed–Sun 10am–8pm. M° Pont Marie.

Café de la Mosquée 39 rue Geoffroy-St-Hilaire, 5e. This oasis of calm offers great mint tea and Middle Eastern cakes (€2). Daily 10am–midnight. M° Jussieu.

La Mascotte 52 rue des Abbesses, 18e. A fantastic, unpretentious locals' bar that's a good choice throughout the day, whether for coffee (€1.60) and a croissant or a glass of wine from their extensive list (from €2). Daily 10am–midnight. M° Blanche.

Le Duroc 88 rue de Sèvres, 7e. An excellent café that feels as though it hasn't changed for at least thirty years and is always packed with locals. The good-value lunch menu (€14) is well worth indulging in and usually includes a perfectly cooked steak option. M° Duroc.

Le Loir dans la Théière 3 rue des Rosiers, 4e. Peaceful, quirky retreat with leather armchairs and a laid-back atmosphere. Midday *tartines* and omelettes (€8–10), fruit teas and cakes (€2–4) served all day, and a great Sunday brunch. Daily 9.30am–7.30pm. M° St-Paul.

Le Regent 1 rue de la Vrillière, 2e. This corner café makes a great lunch choice, with an excellent value *formule* for €13 which includes dishes such as steak haché and saucisse du Cantal. Mon–Fri. M° Bourse.

TOP THREE PARISIAN PATISSERIES

You can't walk far in Paris without stumbling over a patisserie, many of which have been serving cakes for hundreds of years. Here are three of the best that are worth braving the queues for:

Gérard Mulot 76 rue de Seine, 6e. Expect queues at this justifiably famous patisserie, which is usually crammed with locals. The many delights include a red-fruit millefeuille and lemon meringue tart (from €4).

Ladurée 75 av des Champs-Élysées. Famous for its delectable macaroons (€2.10), which come in flavours such as violet and blackcurrent, salted caramel, and orange blossom. Indulge in one of their many treats over a cup of their delicate tea in this ornate tearoom, or head to the more intimate branch at 16 rue Royale.

Strohrer 51 rue Montorgueil. The city's oldest patisserie serves arguably its most divine selection of cakes – the Rosier (large rose macaroon filled with rose-flavoured cream and raspberries; €4.50) is particularly blissful.

Restaurants

Au Grain de Folie 24 rue de la Vieuville, 18e. This homely Montmartre restaurant specializes in unpretentious and basic vegetarian dishes such as a salad with lentils, vegetables and grilled goats cheese. *Prix fixe* €12–16. M° Abbesses.

Au Père Louis 38 rue Monsieur le Prince, 6e ☎01.43.26.54.14. Usually packed with locals, this cosy, somewhat labyrinthine restaurant is a great choice for a long, enjoyable meal. The menu is packed with classic French dishes, including an excellent *cassoulet* (€15). Save room for the *café gourmand* – espresso served alongside *Viennoiseries* (Viennese pastries) and ice cream (€7). Daily noon–2pm, 7–10.30pm. M° Odéon.

Au Virage Lepic 61 rue Lepic, 18e ☎01.42.52.46.79. Simple, good-quality food, focusing on meat and game (from €12), served in a noisy, friendly, old-fashioned bistro. Very popular so book ahead. M° Abbesses.

Bistrot Victoires 6 rue de la Vrillière, 2e. A convivial local bistro, tucked away near the Palais Royale. The fantastic old bar and big mirrors lend it a timeless appeal, and the food is surprisingly cheap (and excellent) for this part of the city (*confit de canard* €10). Daily noon–3pm, 7–11pm. M° Bourse

Breizh Café 109 rue Vieille du Temple, 3e ☎01.42.72.13.77. On one of the quieter streets in the Marais, *Breizh Café* serves excellent, authentic Breton *galettes* and crêpes in a refreshingly modern interior. The *complète champignon* (ham, cheese, egg and mushrooms; €6.80) is particularly good, as are the dessert crêpes with salted caramel (€4.50). Wed–Sun noon–11pm. M° Rambuteau.

Grand Appétit 9 rue de la Cerisaie, 4e. Vegetarian and macrobiotic meals for around €15 in this dedicated eco-vegetarian restaurant. M° Bastille.

L'As du Falafel 34 rue des Rosiers, 4e. Famous throughout the city for its delicious falafel special – pitta bread stuffed full of cabbage, aubergine, hummus, yoghurt and falafel (€5); a more extensive menu is available for eating in. Sun–Thurs. M° St-Paul.

Le Bistrot St-Antoine 58 rue Faubourg Saint-Antoine, 11e. Close to the Bastille, this popular bistro has a dark, attractive interior in which to enjoy the well-priced (if rather standard) dishes, such as *poulet rôti* (€7.50), as well as sandwiches from €4.50. M° Bastille.

Le Mono 40 rue Véron, 18e. Togolese restaurant serving delicious grilled fish and meats (from €9) in a boisterous, noisy atmosphere. Save space for the delicious banana desserts. Closed Wed. M° Abbesses.

Le Potager du Marais 22 rue Rambuteau, 3e. Chic and lively vegetarian restaurant with some great daily specials, such as a brilliant aubergine curry. Set menu €25. M° Rambuteau.

Le Pré Verre 8 rue Thénard, 6e ☎01.43.54.59.47. Informal wine bar-restaurant with an excellent lunch menu (starter, main, glass of wine and a coffee €13.50) which might include dishes such as grilled pork with sautéed potatoes or cumin and pepper soup. Tues–Sat noon–2pm, 7.30–10pm.

Le Temps des Cerises 18–20 rue de la Butte-aux-Cailles, 13e. Homely, good-value neighbourhood bistro with reassuringly traditional dishes such as steak-frites and a decent wine list. Lunch menu €15. M° Corvisart.

Pancake Square 4 rue de Surène, 8e. A nautical-themed crêperie near place de la Madeleine, with decent crêpes such as the *flibustier* (cheese, crème fraiche and mushrooms; €7) and *pichets* of Breton cider (€7.50). M° Madeleine.

Phô 67 59 rue Galande, 5e. Fantastic little Vietnamese restaurant in what is otherwise a very touristy part of town. Most people come here for the exquisite Phô (beef and noodle soup; €8), but

TREAT YOURSELF

Robert et Louise 64 rue Vieille du Temple ⓣ01.42.78.55.89. The unassuming facade of this Marais institution doesn't betray anything of the cosy restaurant's rustic, down-to-earth interior. The ground-floor dining room, where you're likely to be seated shoulder to shoulder with other diners, is permeated by the heady smell of the wood fire, over which the signature dish *côte de boeuf pour deux* (€40) is beautifully cooked. M° Rambuteau.

it's also worth leaving room for the desserts – especially the taro root in coconut milk (€4). M° Cluny – La Sorbonne.

Polidor 41 rue Monsieur-le-Prince, 6e. Historic bistro that was a favourite of James Joyce; short-tempered service but the food is good and reasonably priced (boeuf bourguignon €11). M° Odéon.

Drinking and nightlife

Drinks are charged in bars according to where you sit, with standing at the bar the cheapest option. The university quarter near St-Germain-des-Prés has some great spots, as does the Marais with its small, crowded café-bars and trendy gay bars. Most places are open all day until around 2am, and many offer an early evening "happy hour" until around 8pm. Be warned that beer is much more expensive than wine and can cost up to €8 for a pint. For listings, the best, inexpensive, weekly guide is *Pariscope*, with a small section in English, and available from newsagents. It's also worth checking out the webzine *Paris Voice* (ⓦwww.parisvoice.com) for the latest events.

Bars

Bomby's Café 9 place d'Italie, 13e. This unpretentious café is a good spot to enjoy an early evening drink (wine €3) and has more of a locals' feel than most cafés on this busy place. The food, however, leaves a lot to be desired. M° Place d'Italie.

La Folie en Tête 33 rue de la Butte-aux-Cailles, 13e. Down to earth, fun place, decorated with old musical instruments; happy-hour drinks from €1.50. Mon–Sat 5pm–2am. M° Place-d'Italie.

La Gueuze 19 rue Soufflot, 5e. Belgian beers aplenty in this somewhat themey bar near the Jardin du Luxembourg. Great happy hour from 4–7pm (two for one on *pression*), and also 11pm–2am Fri–Sun. 9am–2am daily. M° St-Michel.

Le Connétable 55 rue des Archives, 3e. This lively, cosmopolitan bar attracts a mixed crowd of all ages, especially after midnight. Wine from €4. Daily 11am–3pm, 7pm–3am. M° Rambuteau.

Le Divan du Monde 75 rue des Martyrs, 18e ⓦwww.divandumonde.com. Café-bar with an eclectic selection of live music and occasional big-name DJs. Drinks from €5. M° Pigalle.

Le Pantalon 7 rue Royer Collard, 5e. Eccentrically decorated bar with cheaper-than-average drinks and an absurd daily happy hour from 5.30–7.30pm, when pints cost from €2.50. Mon–Sat 11am–2am. M° St-Michel.

Le Tambour 41 rue Montmartre, 2e. Lovely bar on a quiet side street which has a great range of wines at reasonable prices, beginning at around €3 a glass. Tues–Sat noon–3am, Sun & Mon 6pm–3am. M° Sentier.

Clubs

Autour de Midi…et Minuit 11 rue Lepic, 18e ⓣ01.55.79.16.48, ⓦwww.autourdemidi.fr. A cosy subterranean jazz club which has an excellent and varied programme, including jam sessions on Wednesdays (free), and be-bop and hard bop on the second and third weekends of the month (€12).

Bar Ourcq 68 quai de la Loire, 19e. Pull up a deckchair and enjoy a *demi* (€2.40) at one of the hippest spots along the canal. The regular DJ creates a chilled atmosphere. M° Laumière.

Batofar quai Francois Mauriac, 13e. A quirky boat venue near the Bibliothèque Nationale, with music ranging from house and techno to hip-hop. M° Quai-de-la-Gare.

Le Bataclan 50 bd Voltaire, 11e ⓦwww.bataclan.fr. This old theatre has one of the best line-ups of any venue, covering everything from international and local dance to rock, opera, comedy and techno nights. M° Oberkampf.

Rex Club 5 bd Poissonnière, 2e. One of Paris' best-known clubs, playing electronic music and attracting big-name DJs. Entrance €10–13. 10pm–4am. M° Grands-Boulevards.

Gay and lesbian Paris

Paris has a well-established gay scene concentrated mainly in the Halles, Marais and Bastille areas. For information, check out *Têtu* (ⓦwww.tetu.com), France's biggest gay monthly magazine, or visit the main information centre, Centre Gai et Lesbien de Paris, 3 rue Keller, 11e (ⓣ01.43.57.21.47; M° Ledru-Rollin/Bastille).

Banana Café 13 rue de la Ferronnerie, 1er. Seriously hedonistic club-bar, packing in the punters with up-tempo clubby tunes. Daily

6pm–5am; happy hour 6.30–9.30pm. Free entry. M° Châtelet.

Le Mixer 23 rue Ste-Croix-de-la-Bretonnerie, 4e ⓣ01.48.87.55.44. Popular gay, lesbian and straight-friendly bar with futuristic decor, a good atmosphere and a tiny dancefloor. Entrance free before 10pm, €5 after. Daily 5pm–2am. M° Hôtel-de-Ville.

Le Scarron 3 rue Geoffroy l'Angevin, 4e. A cosy club in the heart of the Marais, which attracts a creative, mixed crowd. Wed–Sun 10pm–6am; free.

Le Tango 13 rue au Maire, 3e. This old dance-hall plays an eclectic range of music, from disco to tango, and also hosts tea dances on Sunday. 10.30pm–5am; €7.

Entertainment

Cinema tickets cost around €8 in Paris and discounted tickets are offered across the city on Wednesdays. Films are identified as either *v.o.,* which means they're shown in their original language, or *v.f.,* which means they're dubbed into French.

Many **theatres** and concert venues offer standby tickets at a reduced rate, which are generally only released around 20min before the performance, and many offer discounted tickets to students. The *Cité de la Musique,* 221 av Jean-Jaurès, 19e (M° Porte-de-Pantin; from €8; ⓦwww.cite-musique.fr) has an eclectic **music** programme that covers Baroque, contemporary works, jazz, *chansons* and world music, while the city's original **opera** house, *Palais Garnier,* place de l'Opéra, 9e (M° Opéra; from €5; ⓦwww.opera-de-paris.fr) stages operas and ballets within its lavish interior.

Shopping

Galeries Lafayette 40 blvd Haussmann, 9e ⓦwww.galerieslafayette.com. This massive department store sells everything from lingerie and designer fashion to books and DVDs. Worth a visit just to gawp at the astonishing architecture. M° Auber.

Marché aux Puces de St-Ouen rue des Rosiers,18e ⓦwww.les-puces.com. Bargain hunters congregate on this massive flea market (Europe's largest), with over 2500 stalls – be prepared to haggle. M° Porte de Clignancourt.

Réciproque 88 & 95 rue de la Pompe, 16e. Heavily reduced (up to half-price) *dépôt-vente* selling seconds and old stocks of clothing. Great for accessories and last season's hits.

TREAT YOURSELF

Hédiard 21 place de la Madeleine, 8e ⓦwww.hediard.fr. Gastronomes will be in seventh heaven in this smart shop, where the finest foods have been sold since its foundation in 1854. Fine chocolates and patisseries, great wines and some amazing delicacies are all readily available – and the budget-conscious will be able to find a few less expensive treats too. M° Madeleine.

Directory

Embassies and consulates Australia, 4 rue Jean-Rey, 15e ⓣ01.40.59.33.00; Canada, 35 av Montaigne, 8 e ⓣ01.44.43.29.00; Ireland, 4 rue Rude, 16 e ⓣ01.44.17.67.00; New Zealand, 7 rue Léonard-de-Vinci, 16 e ⓣ01.45.01.43.43; UK, 35 rue du Faubourg-St-Honoré, 8e ⓣ01.44.51.31.00; US, 2 av Gabriel, 8e ⓣ01.43.12.22.22.

Exchange A good *bureau de change* is the Comptoir des Tuileries, near the Louvre at 27 rue de l'Arbre Sec, 1er ⓣ01.42.60.17.16.

Hospital Contact SOS-Médecins ⓣ01.43.37.77.77 for 24hr medical help, or dial ⓣ15 for emergencies.

Internet World Net Com, 66 rue Rodier, 18e; Webcafé Milk, 17 rue Soufflot, 6e.

Left luggage Lockers (€3.50–9.50) are available at all train stations.

Pharmacy Dérhy, 84 av des Champs-Élysées is open 24hr.

Post office 52 rue du Louvre, 1er.

Moving on

Train Avignon (13–17 daily; 2hr 40min–3hr 30min); Bayonne (7 daily; 4hr 45min); Bordeaux (hourly; 3hr); Boulogne (hourly; 2hr 10min); Carcassonne (12 daily; 5hr 10min–8hr 40min); Dijon (hourly; 1hr 40min); Grenoble (hourly; 2hr 50min–4hr 30min); Le Havre (hourly; 2hr); Lille (hourly; 1hr); Lyon (hourly; 2hr); Marseille (hourly; 3hr); Montpellier (12–17 daily; 3hr 30min); Nancy (12 daily; 1hr 30min–2hr 30min); Nantes (11 daily; 2hr); Nice (13 daily; 5hr 30min–6hr); Nîmes (16 daily; 3hr); Poitiers (14 daily; 1hr 40min); Reims (12 daily; 45min–1hr 40 min); Rennes (hourly; 2hr 15min); Rouen (hourly; 1hr 15min); Strasbourg (17 daily; 2hr 20min); Toulouse (10 daily; 5hr–6hr 30min); Tours (hourly; 1hr–1hr 30min).

DAY-TRIPS FROM PARIS

Within easy day-trip distance from Paris are three of the country's most popular sights – stately **Versailles**, the cathedral of **Chartres** and Monet's beautiful garden at **Giverny**.

Versailles

The **Palace of Versailles** (Tues–Sun 9am–5.30/6.30pm; €20 palace and gardens, €13.50 palace only, €10 after 3pm) is the epitome of decadence and luxury, with its staggeringly lavish architectural splendour that is an homage to its founder, the "Sun King" Louis XIV. The **ornamental gardens** (7/8am–6/7pm) are particularly splendid and ostentatious, complete with canals, boating lakes and fountains. The easiest way to get to Versailles is on the half-hourly RER line C5 from Gare d'Austerlitz to Versailles-Rive Gauche (40min; €5.10 return).

Chartres

About 35km southwest of Versailles, an hour by frequent train (€12.50) from Paris-Montparnasse, is the modest market town of **CHARTRES**. It's well worth visiting to see the **Cathédrale Notre-Dame** (daily 8am–7.30pm; free), one of Europe's most impressive architectural achievements. A magnificent Gothic structure, it was built in the thirteenth century and has a number of fascinating features, including the tallest Romanesque steeple in existence and the Ste-Voile, reputedly the Holy Veil worn by the Virgin Mary.

Giverny

Less than an hour west of Paris, **GIVERNY** is famous for **Monet's house and gardens,** complete with water-lily pond (April–Oct Tues–Sun 9.30am–6pm; €6). Monet lived here from 1883 until his death in 1926 and the gardens that he laid out were considered by many – including Monet himself – to be his "greatest masterpiece"; the best months to visit are May and June, when the rhododendrons flower around the lily pond and the wisteria hangs over the Japanese bridge, but it's overwhelmingly beautiful at any time of year. To get here, take a train to nearby **Vernon** from Paris-St-Lazare (4–6 daily; 45min; €12.10), then either rent a bike from the station or take the Gisors bus from the station (not Mon).

Northern France

Northern France includes some of the most industrial and densely populated parts of the country. However, there are some curiosities hidden away in the far northeastern corner. **Lille** with its *vieux ville* is lovely to amble around and **Boulogne** is by far the prettiest port town. Further south, the *maisons* and vineyards of **Champagne** are the main draw, for which the best base is **Reims,** with its fine cathedral.

BOULOGNE

BOULOGNE is a pleasant Channel port with admirable architecture and good food and drink. Its **ville basse** (Lower Town), where the main port is located, is home to pretty *pâtisseries, salons du thé* and a range of contemporary shops and brasseries. Rising above, the **ville haute** (Upper Town) is where you'll find the medieval ramparts surrounding the twelfth-century castle, the cathedral and a range of quaint cafés and restaurants.

The main **tourist office** is in Nausicaá aquarium, boulevard St-Beauve (ⓣ03.21.10.88.10), and there's an annexe office on boulevard de la Poste (both offices: July & Aug daily 9am–7pm; Sept–June Mon–Sat 9am–12.30pm & 2–6pm, April–June also Sun 10am–1pm;

Ⓦwww.tourisme-boulognesurmer.com). The cheapest **beds** in town can be found at the friendly *FUAJ Bologne-sur-Mer* in front of Boulogne Ville Gare, 56 place Rouget de Lisle (closed 11am–5pm at weekends; Ⓣ03.21.99.15.30; Ⓦwww.fuaj.org; €18.55). On the other side of the station, *Hôtel le Menestrel*, 21 rue de Brequerecque, is a bit stark but a cheap place to lay your head (Ⓣ03.21.31.60.16, Ⓦwww.le-menestrel.com; €36), while *Hôtel des Arts*, 102 bd Gambetta (Ⓣ03.21.31.53.31; €43) is a good base just a few minutes away from the port. For fabulous home-made cakes and a range of tea (enough to sink a ship), try *L'Arbre à Thé*, 91 Grande Rue. Near the cathedral on rue de Lille, *Restaurant de la Haute Ville* offers typical cuisine (*plat du jour* €9) and *Crêperie St-Michel* (next door) serves sweet and savoury crepes.

CALAIS

CALAIS is one of the main arrival ports for ferries from the UK. Unless you have an early-morning departure there's little reason to make a special stop here, but if you need a place to lay your head for the night, *Hôtel Balladins*, opposite the **train station**, 2 quai du Danube (Ⓣ03.21.96.10.10, Ⓦwww.balladins.com; €40), offers spacious rooms. The *Centre Européen de Séjour Auberge de Jeunesse*, avenue du Maréchal de Lattre de Tassigny, (Ⓣ03.21.34.70.20; €18.10) is a fifteen-minute walk away from the station, or take bus #3 from right outside. The majority of **restaurants** are concentrated on place d'Armes – *Bollywood Bar* serves curries from €8 or next-door *Au Coq D'Or* does *plats du jour* from €8. For last-minute **ferry** bookings both Sea France (Ⓣ03.21.17.70.33) and P&O Ferries (Ⓣ0820 010 020) are on opposite sides of the square.

LILLE

LILLE has a lively atmosphere and some good cultural activities making it worth visiting for a day or two. The winding, cobbled streets of the old town are lined with traditional patisseries, brasseries and a range of upmarket shops. The **Grand-Place**, also known as place du Général de Gaulle, is a busy square dominated by the old exchange building (**Vieille Bourse**), which now houses an afternoon book market (Mon–Sat). South of the old quarter lies the modern place Rihour, beyond which is the **Musée des Beaux-Arts**, place de la République (Mon 2–6pm, Wed–Sun 10am–6pm, Fri till 7pm; €5; Ⓣ03.20.06.78.00), a notable fine arts museum that's well worth a visit to see its excellent collection of Renaissance art and varying exhibitions.

Arrival and information

Train Gare Lille-Flandres is on place de la Gare where there is a range of hotels and places to eat. Gare Lille-Europe is a couple of minutes walk further east, and serves London, Brussels, Amsterdam, Lyon and Strasbourg.
Bus All local buses stop outside Gare Lille-Flandres.
Tourist office In the old Palais Rihour on place Rihour (Mon–Sat 9.30am–6.30pm, Sun 10am–noon & 2–5pm; Ⓦwww.lilletourism.com).
Discount vouchers Pick up a free copy of *PiliPili Lille* magazine in any bar or café and make the most of the money-off vouchers. Whether you fancy a reduced-price hair cut, a new pair of shades or a hearty meal, this magazine has discounts for everything.
Internet Net-K, 13 rue de la Clef (€3/hr).

Accommodation

Faidherbe 42 place de la Gare Ⓣ03.20.06.27.93. Just opposite the station, this pleasant and well-equipped hotel is clean and welcoming. €35.
Flandre-Angleterre 13 place de la Gare Ⓣ03.20.06.04.12, Ⓔhotel-flandre-angleterre@wanadoo.fr. The clean, comfortable rooms are somewhat on the small side but it's a stone's throw from Gare Lille-Flandres. €69.
FUAJ Lille 12 rue Malpart Ⓣ03.20.57.08.94, Ⓦwww.fuaj.org. A basic, good-value FUAJ youth hostel, centrally located near the Hôtel de Ville. Breakfast included. Internet facilities. Dorms €17.70.
Premiere Classe Hotel 19 place des Reignaux Ⓣ03.28.36.51.10, Ⓦwww.premiere-classe-lille-centre.fr. This cosy, functional hotel is clean and

great value if travelling in a group: prices are per room, and each room sleeps up to three people. Free wi-fi. €50.

Eating and drinking

Aux Moules 34 rue de Béthune. A fine little restaurant that specializes in the excellent regional speciality *carbonnade* (beef braised in beer; €17).
Café Ugo place Rihour. Popular with locals, this relaxed, laid-back café is just off the main square. €3.60 for coffee and delicious croissants.
La Pate Brisée Restaurant rue de la Monnaie. Located in the old town, this restaurant serves great warming staples such as baked potatoes and an array of quiches. Open 7–10pm. Main meal plus drink from €8; cocktails from €3.
Les Trois Brasseurs 18–22 place de la Gare. A fun microbrewery (part of a small chain) with good local beers from €4.
So Good Café place de Béthune. Healthy fast-food joint that serves a range of sandwiches (from €2) and salads to eat in or takeaway, also caters for vegetarians. Open 8.30am–9pm.

Moving on

Train From Gare Lille-Flandres: Calais (hourly; 1hr 10min); Paris (2 hourly; 1hr). From Gare Lille Europe: Brussels (7 daily; 35min); London St Pancras (hourly; 1hr 30min); Lyon (10 daily; 3hr–3hr 50min); Strasbourg (12 daily; 3hr 50min),

REIMS

REIMS is located at the heart of the Champagne region, which makes it worth a stop for a tipple or two. If culture is more your thing then there's also the UNESCO-listed Gothic **Cathédrale Notre Dame** (daily 8am–7pm), one of the most beautiful in France. The interior is renowned for the stained-glass designs by Marc Chagall in the east chapel and glorifications of the champagne-making process in the south transept.

If you're in town for the **champagne**, head to place des Droits-de-l'Homme and place St-Niçaise, around which most of the champagne *maisons* are situated; cellar tours involve a small fee which includes a tasting at the end. Good houses to visit are **Mumm**, 34 rue du Champ-de-Mars (March–Oct daily 9.30–11am & 2–4.30pm; Nov–Feb Sat & Sun 2–5pm; €7.50; ⓦwww.mumm.com), which is informative but informal, while **Piper-Heidsieck**, 51 bd Henry Vasnier (daily 9.30–11.45am & 2.30–6pm; closed Jan & Feb; €6; ⓦwww.piper-heidsieck.com), is more glitzy and ostentatious. You have to book to visit the bigger name brands, Veuve Clicquot, 1 place des Droits-de-l'Homme (April–Oct Mon–Sat; Nov–March Mon–Fri; €7; ⓣ03.26.89.53.90, ⓦwww.veuve-clicquot.fr), is the least pompous. All have English language tours.

The **train station** is on the northwest edge of the town, on square Colbert, just a short walk north of the centre. The **tourist office** is located opposite the cathedral on the main square at 2 rue Guillaume de Machault (May–Aug Mon–Sat 9am–7pm, Sun 10am–6pm; Sept–April Mon–Sat 9am–6pm, Sun 10am–1pm; ⓣ08.92.70.13.51 ⓦwww.reims-tourism.com). The *Alsace Hotel* (6 rue du Général Sarrail; ⓣ03.26.47.44.08. ⓦwww.hotelalsace.com; €50) is the cheapest and least pretentious of the **hotels** in the centre. The *Centre International de Séjour* (Parc Léo Lagrange; ⓣ03.26.40.52.60, ⓦwww.cis-reims.com; €16.40) has the best dorm accommodation although it's a fifteen-minute walk from the station (take bus B, K, H or N from outside the station). For lunch try *L'Apostrophe*, (59 place Drouet d'Erlon), a stylish **brasserie** serving traditional French dishes (from €12) and a delicious assortment of cakes.

Normandy and Brittany

To the French, the essence of **Normandy** is in its food and drink: a gourmand's paradise, this is the land of butter and cream, cheese and seafood, cider

and calvados. Many of the towns also have great historic as well as architectural importance: **Rouen** is where Joan of Arc was burned at the stake, **Bayeux** is rightly celebrated for its eponymous tapestry; the 80km stretch of northern coastline was the site of the **D-Day landings**; and the granite spectacle of **Mont St-Michel** dates back to the thirteenth century. The striking coastline, sandy beaches and lush countryside of **Brittany** seem to belong to a very different part of France; it seems almost unbelievable that the verdant pastures are within easy reach of Paris. People here are both fiercely proud and defiantly isolationist; you might be forgiven for thinking at times that you had left France altogether.

ROUEN

ROUEN is a city of impressive churches, half-timbered houses and small cobbled streets. The town's focal point is place du Vieux-Marché, where Joan of Arc was burned at the stake in 1431. The main old market square leads on to rue du Gros-Horloge, which has a colourful one-handed clock arching over the street. Walking along here brings you to the impressive **Cathédrale de Notre-Dame** (Mon 2–6pm, Tues–Sun 8am–6pm; free), a Gothic masterpiece built in the twelfth and thirteenth centuries, which is now best known for Monet's series of paintings of it that explore the interaction between light and shadow.

Arrival and information

Train The main train station, Rouen Rive-Droite, is a 10min walk from the centre.

Bus The bus station is just off the southern end of the main rue Jeanne d'Arc.

Tourist office Opposite the cathedral at 25 place de la Cathédrale (Mon–Sat 9am–12.30pm & 1.30–6/7pm, Sun 9.15/10am–12.30/1pm & 2–6pm; Oct–April closed Sun afternoon; Ⓦwww.rouentourisme.com).

Internet Cyber Net, 47 place du Vieux-Marché (€4/hr).

Accommodation

Campsite Municipal rue Jules-Ferry, Déville-lès-Rouen Ⓣ02.35.74.07.59. Situated 5km out of town, this campsite has a shop, café and showers. To get here, take bus #2 from Théatre des Arts. €4.30 per person, plus €1.70 per tent.

Des Arcades 52 rue des Carmes Ⓣ02.35.70.10.30 Ⓦwww.hotel-des-arcades.fr. Centrally located, near place du Vieux-Marché, this hotel has colourful rooms. €39.

Hotel Astrid 11 place Bernard Tissot Ⓣ02.35.71.75.88, Ⓦwww.hotel-astrid.fr. Located right opposite the train station. The en-suite rooms are a little tatty but reasonably priced. €55.

Eating and drinking

Brasserie Paul 1 place de la Cathédrale. An old-fashioned and very French brasserie where you can have a good meal of calves' liver and *escargots* from €10.

La Boîte à Bières 35 rue Cauchoise. The town's best bar, with a great atmosphere and sometimes live music.

Le Maupassant 39 place du Vieux Marché. Located on the main square, this is a great place for typical French cuisine with *plats du jour* from €9.

Le Taormina 18 rue de Vieux Palais. A great selection of pizzas and large bowls of pasta from €7.50. Value meals including starter, drink and main are available from €10.

Moving on

Train Caen (hourly; 2 hr); Dieppe (12–15 daily; 45min); Le Havre (12–15 daily; 1hr); Paris (6–8 daily; 1hr 10min).

BAYEUX

BAYEUX's world-famous **tapestry** depicting the 1066 invasion of England by William the Conqueror is one of the highlights of a visit to Normandy. The 70m strip of linen, embroidered over nine centuries ago, is housed in the **Centre Guillaume le Conquérant**, rue de Nesmond (daily: 9/9.30am–6/6.30/7pm; Nov to mid-March closed 12.30–2pm; €7.70). The **cathedral**, place de la Liberté (8.30am–6/7pm), is a spectacular thirteenth century edifice, with some parts dating back to the eleventh century.

Bayeux's **train station** is on the southern side of town, on boulevard Sadi Carnot, and the **tourist office** is at Pont St-Jean (Mon–Sat 9am–7pm, Sun 9am–12.30pm & 2–6.30pm; Oct–June closed Mon–Sat 12.30–2pm & all day Sun; ⓣ02.31.51.28.28, ⓦwww.bayeux-tourism.com). Just 500m from the station is the friendly and decent HI **hostel**, *The Family Home*, 39 rue du Général de Dais (ⓣ02.31.92.15.22, ⓦwww.bayeux-familyhome.com; €17.80), which also serves three-course meals. The most affordable of the hotels in town are the *Maupassant*, 19 rue St-Martin (ⓣ02.31.92.28.53, ⓦwww.hotel-le-maupassant-bayeux.com; from €40), which has small but functional rooms, and *La Gare*, 26 place de la Gare (ⓣ02.31.92.10.70, ⓦwww.normandy-tours-hotel.com; €30), which is also home to Normandy Tours (see box, below). The nearest **campsite** (ⓣ02.31.92.08.43; closed Oct–April; €4.70 per person) is on boulevard d'Eindhoven, a fifteen-minute walk from the centre or you can catch bus #3. Most of the **restaurants** are on pedestrianized rue St-Jean, of which the best is *La Table du Terroir* at no 42, a carnivore's paradise with dishes from €12.

ST-MALO

ST-MALO is a beautiful Breton coastal town with cobbled streets surrounded by medieval ramparts. You can easily spend a lazy day or so ambling through the lanes, strolling along the beaches and taking your chances against the tide to reach some of the old fort islands. The **town museum**, in the castle to the right as you enter the main city gate, Porte St-Vincent (daily 10am–noon/12.30pm & 2–6pm; winter closed Mon; €5.40), covers the city's eventful history, which has encompassed colonialism, slave-trading and privateers, amongst other initiatives. The **Cathédrale St-Vincent** on place Jean de Châtillon was severely damaged during World War II, as was most of the old town, but has since been restored.

There's abundant opportunity for windsurfing, sailing or wakeboarding. **Surf School St-Malo** is located just off chaussée du Sillon along the bay (2 av de la Hoguette; ⓣ02.99.40.07.47, ⓦwww.surfschool.org); contact them for details of prices and availability.

Arrival and information

Train The station is a 15min walk heading south from the walled city.

Bus Buses from out of town stop at Porte St-Vincent.

Tourist office Esplanade St-Vincent (Mon–Sat 9/10am–12.30pm & 1.30/2.30–6/7.30pm; winter closed Sun; ⓦwww.saint-malo-tourisme.com).

Internet Cop Imprime, 39 bd des Talards (€4/hr); Cyber Lan, 68 Chaussée du Sillon (€4/hr).

D-DAY BEACHES

On June 6, 1944, 135,000 Allied troops stormed the beaches of Normandy in Operation Overlord. After heavy fighting, which saw thousands of casualties on both sides, the Allied forces took command of all the beaches, which was a major turning point of World War II. The 80km stretch of coastline north of Bayeux that saw the D-Day landings includes: **Omaha**, now home to the Musée Mémorial d'Omaha Beach (daily 9.30/10am–6/6.30pm; €5.80, ⓦwww.musee-memorial-omaha.com), where exhibits include uniforms and a tank; and **Arromanches**, 10km northwest of Bayeux, which was the main unloading point for cargo (some four million tonnes of it). The interesting museum at Arromanches, **Musée du Débarquement**, place du 6 juin (daily 9/10am–5/7pm; €6.50; ⓦwww.normandy1944.com), has further information on France's liberation. One of the best ways to see the beaches is on a **tour**: contact D-Day Tours (ⓣ02.31.51.70.52; €35–45) or Normandy Tours (ⓣ02.31.92.10.70; €34–39)

Accommodation

Auberge de Jeunesse Éthic Étapes 37 av du Père Umbricht ⓣ02.99.40.29.80, ⓦwww.centrevarangot.com. Spotlessly clean and relatively comfortable hostel located 1.5km from the train station (take bus #2 or #5). Book well in advance. €16.10.

Aux Vieilles Pierres 9 rue Thevenard ⓣ02.99.56.46.80. Centrally located within the ramparts, though the rooms are looking a bit tired. €33.

Camping Aleth Cité d'Aleth, Gaston Buy ⓣ02.99.81.60.91, ⓦcamping-saint-malo.fr. Perfectly positioned campsite on a peninsula by the beach that's also well located for nightlife. Amenities include a café, shop and showers. €10.50.

Port Malo Hotel 15 rue Ste-Barbe ⓣ02.99.20.52.99. Inside the walls, this quaint ageing hotel does the trick even if the rooms are showing their age, plus there's a bar right downstairs. €34.

Eating and drinking

The Marche Plus supermarket is centrally located on rue Ste Barbe.

Coquille d'Oeuf 20 rue de la Corne de Cerfs. A small, cosy café serving pizzas, baguettes and quiches from €5.

Le Semper 1 place Guy la Chambre. This place serves up great seafood; try the locally caught mussels, from €10.

La Terasse du Corps de Garde montée Notre-Dame. Tick into delicious crêpes while enjoying the fabulous view out to sea from the top of the ramparts. From €2.20.

Tam's Kaffe 5 place des Frères Lamenais. This laid-back bar has a funky vibe and resident DJs playing on the terrace. Cocktails from €6. Open till 2am.

Tanpopo place de la Poissonnerie. Good-value Japanese food, with set meals including a bento box, drink and dessert from €18.

TREAT YOURSELF

Beaufort 52 chaussée du Sillon ⓣ02.99.40.99.99, ⓦwww.hotel-beaufort.com. Right on the sea-front, this cosy boutique hotel has the softest king-size beds and massaging power showers. Enjoy sunset views from the ambient lounge bar. €79.

Moving on

Train Dinan (8 daily; 1hr); Paris (3 daily; 3hr); Rennes (hourly; 1hr).

MONT ST-MICHEL

Although officially part of Normandy, the island of **MONT ST-MICHEL** is easily reached from Brittany and just a short hop from St-Malo. It's also the site of the striking Gothic **Abbaye du Mont-Saint-Michel** (tours daily 9/9.30am–6/7pm; €8.50), whose church, known as La Merveille, is visible from all around the bay. The granite structure was sculpted to match the contours of the hill, and the overall impression is stunning. It's important to remember to keep an eye on the tide; the Mont can become entirely surrounded by the sea remarkably quickly.

The best way of **getting here** is to take the train to Pontorson, and then take one of the regular buses on to Mont St-Michel. **Accommodation** is quite pricey here; the cheapest hotel inside the walls is *Hôtel du Guesclin* (ⓣ02.33.60.14.40, ⓦwww.hoteldugueslin.com; €69). A good place for **lunch** is *Crêperie La Sirène*, serving hearty, unpretentious food from €6.

NANTES

Part of Brittany until the 1960s, **NANTES** is a pleasant riverside town. It remains closely affiliated to the region, and has a vibrant atmosphere reminiscent of other Breton towns. Lining the main road is the **Château des Ducs** (daily 9am/10am–6pm/7pm; €8), built by two of the last rulers of independent Brittany, François II and his daughter Duchess Anne, who was born here in 1477. In 1800 the castle's arsenal exploded, shattering the stained glass of the **Cathédrale de St-Pierre et St-Paul** (9am–6pm/7pm), 200m away, just one of many disasters that have befallen the church.

The **train station,** on rue de Richebourg, is a short métro ride from the

central stop of "Commerce". The **tourist office**, at 3 cours Olivier-de-Clisson (Mon-Sun 10am–1pm & 2–6pm, Tues 10.30am–6pm; ⓣ08.92.46.40.44, ⓦwww.nantes-tourisme.com) sells a "Nantes Pass" which gives you entry to the town's museums, free tram travel and also includes boat cruises up the Loire to see the many châteaux. (from €18 per day). For **accommodation**, try the charming, atmospheric and central *Hôtel Rénova*, 11 rue Beauregard (ⓣ02.40.47.57.03, ⓦwww.hotel-renova.com; €35) or *Hotel du Château*, 5 place de la Duchesse (ⓣ02.40.74.17.16; €35), just opposite the Château des Ducs. The *FUAJ Nantes Le Manu* **hostel** is at 2 place de la Manu (closed noon–4pm; ⓣ02.40.29.29.20, ⓦwww.fuaj.org; €17.40); take tram #1 or #12 to Manufacture. The place du Commerce is a largely pedestrianized area thronged with decent, inexpensive **bars** and **restaurants**. Try *Ma Saison Préférée*, 10 rue du Château, for delicious savoury tarts and quiches (from €6), or *Café Cult*, place du Change, for a cool, bohemian atmosphere and some great cheese and cured ham dishes (from €12).

The Loire Valley

With countless **châteaux** overlooking the stunning river and panoramic views over some of France's best vineyards, the Loire Valley is deservedly one of the country's most celebrated regions. Alongside the luxurious châteaux there are numerous lovely towns to be visited, including dependably enjoyable **Tours,** laid-back **Saumur**, historic **Orléans** and the fairytale town of **Amboise**.

TOURS

The elegant and compact regional capital **TOURS** makes a good base for travelling around the Loire. The city has two main areas, situated on either side of the central rue Nationale. To the east looms the extravagant towers and stained-glass windows of the **Cathédrale St-Gatien** (9am–7pm), with some handsome old streets behind. Adjacent, the **Musée des Beaux-Arts** (9am–12.45pm & 2–6pm, closed Tues; €4), on place François Sicard, has some beautiful paintings in its collection, notably Mantegna's *Christ in the Garden of Olives* and *Resurrection*. The **old town** crowds around medieval place Plumereau, on the west side of the city, its half-timbered houses imposing and neatly ordered.

Arrival and information

Train The train station is located to the south of the city, on rue Édouard Vaillant.

Tourist office 78–82 rue Bernard-Palissy, in front of the train station (Mon–Sat 8.30/9am–6/7pm, Sun 10am–12.30/1pm & 2.30–5pm; mid-Oct to mid-April closed lunch and Sun afternoon; ⓣ02.47.70.37.37, ⓦwww.ligeris.com).

Accommodation

FUAJ Tours 5 rue Bretonneau ⓣ02.47 37 81 58, ⓦwww.fuaj.org. This inexpensive, friendly hostel seems to have countless rooms. It's a well-located cheapie with optional extras such as bike rental (€10/day); breakfast is included. Closed noon–5pm Sept–June. €18.50.

Saint-Jean 13 place des Halles ⓣ02.47.38.58.77. A decent hotel with mid-sized rooms just a stone's throw from rue de la Monnaie. €39.

Terminus 7/9 rue de Nantes ⓣ02.47.05.06.24. Clean, comfortable rooms, good if you're catching an early morning train but a 15min walk from all the action. €42.

Val de Loire 33 bd Heurteloup ⓣ02.47.05.67.53, ⓔhotel.val.de.loire@club-internet.fr. A pleasant and good-value hotel in a very central location. All fourteen rooms are nicely decorated. €45.

Eating and drinking

Comme Autre Fouée 11 rue de la Monnaie. This charmingly old-fashioned place specializes in the miniature sweet and savoury dough-based snacks, *fouée*, with fillings such as goat's cheese or honey (€10).

CYCLING THE LOIRE VALLEY

There are over 300km of safe cycling routes to take you around the highlights of the Loire Valley. Cycle paths meander along the river from Tours to **Château de Villandry** (ⓦwww.loire-a-velo.fr has all the details). You can hire bikes from Detours de Loire, 35 rue Charles Gille (ⓣ02.47.61.22.23), or Velomania, 109 rue Colbert (ⓣ02.47.05.10.11).

Et tranche thé 38 rue Bernard Palissy. This café offers all kinds of fruity concoctions – smoothies and the like from €1.40.

L'Etoile rue de la Monnaie. This bar-club is open from midnight until 5am every night apart from Monday.

La Palais 15 place Jean-Jaurès. One of the best spots to hang; around €3 for a beer.

Moving on

Train Amboise (frequent; 22min); Chenonceaux (5–7 daily; 30min); Chinon (5–10 daily; 45min); Orléans (frequent; 1hr–1hr 30min); Paris (frequent; 1hr 15min); Saumur (frequent; 45min).

CHÂTEAUX NEAR TOURS

Villandry

One of the Loire's most popular châteaux, **Villandry** (daily 9am–5/6.30pm; gardens till 5.30/7.30pm; €9, €6 gardens only) boasts extraordinary ornamental Renaissance gardens set out on several terraces that have marvellous views over the river. The château dates from 1536 and has a collection of Spanish paintings and a Moorish ceiling from Toledo. There's no public transport here, but it's easy to reach by bike from Tours. Alternatively, shuttle buses operate July to August between Tours and the château (3 daily; 35min; timetables at ⓦwww.tourainefilvert.com).

Chenonceaux

Perhaps the finest Loire château is that straddling the river at **Chenonceaux** (daily 9am–4.30/7pm; €10), about 15km from Villandry and accessible by train from Tours. As with Villandry, the stunning formal gardens and beautiful river views are the highlight. The château's charming interior is preserved in pristine condition.

Chinon

The ruined château at **CHINON** (daily 9/9.30am–5/7pm; €7) is a fascinating relic of France's historic past: parts of it date from the twelfth and thirteenth centuries, and there's even evidence of graffiti carved by imprisoned and doomed Templar knights in the western **Tour Coudray**.

Wedged between the castle and the River Vienne, the ancient town of Chinon is an attractive place to stop. The **tourist office** is on place Hofheim (May–Nov daily 10am–7pm; Oct–April closed 1pm–2pm & Sun; ⓣ02.47.93.17.85, ⓦwww.tourisme.chinon.com). The *Gar Hotel*, 14 av Gambetta (ⓣ024.7.93.00.86, ⓦwww.garhotel.fr; €46) is a pleasant, central **place to stay**, while a five-minute walk from the town across the river on Île-Auger is a **campsite** (ⓣ02.47.93.08.35; €4.70 per person) that rents out kayaks in the summer to both guests and visitors. *La Treille* is a wonderfully old-fashioned **restaurant** that serves excellent game and fish dishes (lunch menu €13).

SAUMUR

SAUMUR is a peaceful, pretty riverside town, and a good place to base yourself, within easy reach of Tours and Chinon. The town is a major centre of absinthe distillation; the **Distillerie Combier**, 48 rue Beaurepaire (€3), offers bilingual tours and tastings. On a more cultural note, the immense **Abbaye de Fontevraud** (daily 9/10am–5.30/6.30pm; €8.40), 13km on bus #16 from the town centre (4–6 daily; 35min), was founded in 1099 as both a nunnery and a monastery with an abbess in charge. Its chief significance is as the burial ground of the

Plantagenet kings and queens, notably Henry II, Eleanor of Aquitaine and Richard the Lionheart; some of the tombs are extraordinarily elaborate.

Arrival and information

Train Saumur's train station is on the north bank of the river; head over two bridges to get to the south bank and the main part of the town.
Tourist office place de la Bilange (Mon–Sat 9.15am–7pm, Sun 10/10.30am–noon/12.30pm & 2.30–5.30pm; ⓣ02.41.40.20.60, ⓦwww.ot-saumur.fr) can help book accommodation.

Accommodation

Camping l'Île d'Offard rue de Verden ⓣ02.41.40.30.00, ⓦwww.cvtloisirs.com. This campsite has a swimming pool, small bar and restaurant. €25.50.
Centre International de Séjour Île d'Offard ⓣ02.41.40.30.00. Centrally located hostel, which has bright rooms ranging in size up to eight-bed dorms. €11.50.
Le Cristal 10 place de la République ⓣ02.41.51.09.54, ⓦwww.cristal-hotel.fr. A two-star delight with river views from most rooms. €55.

Eating and drinking

Auberge St-Pierre 6 place St-Pierre. Not good for vegetarians but meat eaters will love the steak (€10), frogs' legs with white wine sauce (€10.50) or rich game dishes.
Les Forges de St-Pierre 1 place St-Pierre. Serves good staple meals of lamb and chicken; *plats du jour* from €12.

AMBOISE

AMBOISE is a beautiful town based along the banks of the Loire. The main feature is the **Château Royal d'Amboise** (9am–5/6/7pm; €9.50), perched up high holding a majestic spot overlooking the river and visible from all points around town. It was built in the eleventh century and saw further additions by successive royals. Leonardo de Vinci's final residence, **Clos-Lucé**, is also located here (2 rue de Clos-Lucé; 9/10am–7/8pm; €12.50), housing a collection of some of his inventions.

Accommodation

Camping de L'Île d'Or Île d'Or ⓣ02.47.57.23.37, ⓦwww.camping-amboise.com. Campsite located just the other side of the island from the hostel with access to a big open-air swimming pool. €2.40 per person, plus €3.40 per pitch.
Centre Charles Péguy Hostel Île d'Or ⓣ02.47.30.6.90 ⓦwww.mjcamboise.fr. This large hostel has a great location right on the river and is walking distance to the château. Most rooms have fabulous views. €10.50.
Le Chaptal 13 rue Chaptal ⓣ02.47.57.14.46, ⓦwww.hotel-chaptal-amboise.fr. A good central cheapie with small and somewhat chintzy rooms. €43.

Eating

Le Parvais 3 rue Mirabeau. Popular with locals, this restaurant off the main drag serves typically French cuisine. *Plats du jour* from €12.50.
The Shaker 3 quai Francois Tissard. Funky bar that's great for late-night alfresco drinks in a picturesque spot – its riverside location is overlooked by the château. Beers from €3, cocktails from €7. Open 6pm–3am/4am weekends.

Moving on

Train Orleans (frequent; 1hr); Tours (frequent; 20min).

ORLÉANS

Due south of Paris, **ORLÉANS** became legendary when Joan of Arc delivered the city from the English in 1429. Stained-glass windows in the nave of the enormous, Gothic **Cathédrale Sainte-Croix** (daily 9.15am–noon & 2.15–5pm; free) tell the story of her life, from her childhood through to her heroic military career and her eventual martyrdom. Immediately opposite, the **Musée des Beaux-Arts** (Tues–Sat 9.30am–12.15pm & 1.30–5.45pm, Sun 2–6.30pm; €3) has an excellent collection of French paintings.

The **tourist office** is at 2 place de l'Etape (daily April–Aug 9.30am–6.30pm; Sept–March closed lunch & Sun; ⓣ02.38.24.05.05, ⓦwww.tourisme-orleans.fr). The *Auberge de Jeunesse*,

7 av de Beaumarchais (Ⓣ02.38.53.60.06, Ⓔauberge.crjs45@wanadoo.fr; €16.75) is 10km south of the city; staff are helpful and readily provide good information about the town. For somewhere central try *Hôtel de L'Abeille* (64 rue Alsace-Lorraine Ⓣ02.38.53.54.87; €45), a charming, traditionally decorated **hotel** with oak wood floors. For **food**, *La Petite Marmite*, 178 rue de Bourgogne, serves traditional dishes such as *carbonnade* and *escargots*; *plats du jour* from €9. *Le Metalic*, 119 rue de Bourgogne, is the best place for late-night drinking and dancing, open until 3am.

Burgundy

Burgundy has some charming towns and villages, as well as some of the country's finest food and drink. **Dijon**, the capital, is a slick and affluent town with great shops and lovely architecture. Heading south, **Beaune** is a good place to sample the best of the region's famous wine, and to try local specialities such as *escargots à la bourguignonne, bœuf bourguignon* and *coq au vin*.

DIJON

DIJON is a smart, modern town based around a range of shop-lined streets. Most famous for its mustard, it also has some beautiful architecture and numerous relaxed and friendly bars.

What to see and do

The Palais des Ducs, in the heart of the city, is notable both for the fifteenth-century **Tour Philippe le Bon** (daily April–Nov 9am–noon & 1.45–5.30pm; Dec–March Sat & Sun 9am–3.30pm, Wed 1.30–3.30pm; tours every 15min; €2.30) and the fourteenth-century **Tour de Bar**, which houses the magnificent **Musée des Beaux-Arts** (daily except Tues 9.30/10am–5/6pm; free) with its collection of paintings ranging from Titian and Rubens to Monet and Manet. **Place de la Libération**, a graceful semi-circular space, has beautiful fountains and is lined with a number of coffee bars. Heading up rue Rameau and following the road to the left brings you to the stunning thirteenth-century Gothic **church of Notre-Dame**, the north wall of which holds a small sculpted owl (*chouette*), which people touch for luck.

Arrival and information

Train and bus Dijon's train and bus stations sit next to each other at the end of av Maréchal-Foch, 5min from place Darcy.

Tourist office place Darcy Ⓣ 08.92.70.05.58, Ⓦwww.dijon-tourism.com (April–Sept Mon–Sat 9.30am–6.30pm, Sun 10am–6pm; Oct–March Mon–Sat 9:30am–1pm & 2–6pm, Sun 10am–4pm) and also at 11 rue des Forges (Mon–Sat 9am–noon & 2–6pm).

Internet Cyberisey, 53 rue Berbisey (€3/hr); Cyber-space, 46 rue Monge (€4/hr).

Accommodation

B&B Hotel 5 rue du Chateau Ⓣ08.92.70.75.06, Ⓦwww.hotel-bb.com. With a fabulous central location, this is a tidy and compact boutique-style hotel with comfortable beds. €48.

Camping du Lac off bd Chanoine Kir, about 3km from the centre Ⓣ03.80.43.54.72, Ⓦwww.camping-dijon.info. This pleasant campsite has the usual amenities, such as hot showers, a small café and a shop. To get here take bus #12. Closed Nov–March. €3.80 per tent.

CRISD 1 bd Champollion Ⓣ03.80.72.95.20. The local HI option is comfortable, cheap and has excellent self-catering facilities. Only drawback is that it's 2.5km from the centre – take bus #5 from place Grangier. €18.50.

Hostellerie Le Sauvage 64 rue Monge Ⓣ03.80.41.31.21, Ⓦwww.hotellesauvage.com. Beautifully restored fifteenth-century hotel in a great central location with a good restaurant. Can be noisy so light sleepers should ask for a room away from the kitchen. €45.

Le Jacquemart 32 rue Verrerie Ⓣ03.80.60.09.60, Ⓦwww.hotel-lejacquemart.fr. A basic but adequate small hotel handily located in the centre. €33.

Eating, drinking and nightlife

Au Bon Pantagruel 20 rue Quentin. Near the covered market, this inexpensive bistro serves fine, traditional French meals from €14.

Café de l'Univers 47 rue Berbisey. Head to this place for a night of serious dancing, where there's a variety of music held on different nights of the week. On Saturday and Sunday mornings, things go on until 9am.

L'O Restaurant 14 rue Quentin. Laid-back tapas and wine bar with a great range of tasty dishes, from €10 for a selection.

My Wok Big bowls of noodles with a build-your-own choice of ingredients. Also does late-night takeaway. Noodles from €4.50.

Restaurant a la Casa rue Quentin. Popular with the Sunday lunch crowd, this place serves a range of tapas, but it's worth trying their delicious pizzas with a range of toppings from €7.

Se Bar rue Monge. Late-night drinking spot, popular with a young crowd. Has outdoor seating and a good range of beers on tap.

Moving on

Train Beaune (frequent; 20min); Bern (daily; 5hr 30min); Lyon (frequent; 1hr 30min–2hr 15min); Milan (daily; 6hr 30min); Paris (frequent; 1hr 45min);

BEAUNE AND THE BURGUNDY VINEYARDS

BEAUNE is the major producer of the region's best wine, and one of the best places in France for tasting it. Its other major attraction is the fifteenth-century multi-coloured hospital, the **Hôtel-Dieu** (daily 9am–6.30pm; €6), which houses three museums, a number of courtyards and small, dingy cellars with remaining features from the hospices. On nearby rue d'Enfer is the **Musée du Vin** (daily 9.30am–5/6pm; Dec–March closed Tues; €5.50), which does an excellent job of explaining the region's wine history. The **Marché aux Vins** (daily 9.30–11.30am & 2–5.30pm; €10), the town's main wine-tasting establishment, is a rather more taster-friendly experience, allowing you to sample numerous delectable vintages.

Arrival and information

Train From Beaune train station, the town centre is 500m up av du 8 Septembre, across the boulevard and left onto rue des Tonneliers.

Bus Buses leave from rue Maufoux, beyond the walls.

Tourist office 6 bd Perpreuil (Mon–Sat 9/10am–5/7pm, Sun 10am–1pm & 2–5/6pm; ⓣ03.80.26.21.30, ⓦwww.ot-beaune.fr). Has useful information on wine tours.

Accommodation

Foch 24 bd Maréchal Foch ⓣ03.80.24.05.65, ⓦwww.hotelbeaune-lefoch.fr. This is a pleasant little hotel, run by a charming old lady who extends warm hospitality; shared bathrooms. €30.

Les Cent Vignes rue Auguste Dubois ⓣ03.80.22.03.91. Located just 1km out of Beaune, this good-value campsite has showers and a shop. Walk or take bus #2 from the tourist office. €4 per tent.

Eating and drinking

Bistrot Bourguignon 8 rue Monge. Tiny but charming restaurant that does a good-value lunch (€13), with wine from €3 a glass.

BURGUNDY VINEYARDS

The Burgundy vineyards are justly famous for their produce. The best way to explore them is on the **Route des Grand Crus** ⓦwww.route-des-grands-crus-de-bourgogne.com), which takes in such places as **Montrachet** and **Chassagne**, both famous for their high-calibre wines. The wine is cheaper if bought from source – expect to pay around €10 for a good bottle and €20 and upwards for an excellent one. If you fancy learning more about the wines, the **École des Vins de Bourgogne** in Beaune, 6 rue du 16e Chasseurs (ⓣ03.80.26.35.10, ⓦwww.ecoledesvins-bourgogne.com), offers reasonably priced (from €15) crash courses in wine appreciation, some in English.

Pickwick's Pub & Wine Bar 2 rue Notre-Dame. This hilariously tacky would-be English pub is worth a look if you're a whisky connoisseur – they have an excellent range, starting at €5.
Piqu' Boeuf Grill 2 rue du Faubourg Madeleine. Carnivores will love this place, with rich, bloody steaks (€12) and some lovely wines (from €4).

Alsace and Lorraine

Dominated by the remarkable city of **Strasbourg**, the eastern region of Alsace often bears more similarity to Germany or Switzerland than to the rest of the country. The *mélange* of cultures is at its most vivid in the string of little wine towns that punctuate the Route du Vin along the eastern margin of the wet and woody Vosges mountains. The province of Lorraine is home to the elegant eighteenth-century provincial capital of **Nancy**. Food and drink is excellent in the region: from local brew Kronenbourg to delicious white Rieslings and Gewürztraminers, the alcohol is excellent (and relatively inexpensive), and the *winstubs* (or wine rooms) that dominate towns offer inexpensive, unpretentious food based around pork, veal and beef, often in stews or casseroles.

NANCY

NANCY, capital of Lorraine, is a refined and beautiful town, dominated by opulent squares and splendid boulevards. At the centre is **place Stanislas**, a supremely elegant square at the far end of rue Stanislas, dominated by the **Hôtel de Ville**. The roofline of this UNESCO World Heritage Site is topped by florid urns and lozenge-shaped lanterns dangling from the beaks of gilded cockerels. On the west side of the square, the **Musée des Beaux-Arts** (daily except Tues 10am–6pm; €6) boasts work by Caravaggio, Dufy, Modigliani and Matisse. A little to the north is the **Musée Lorrain**, 64 Grande-Rue (daily except Tues 10am–12.30pm & 2–6pm; €5.50), devoted to Lorraine's history. It's housed in the splendid Palais Ducal, which is worth a look on its own merits.

Arrival and information

Train Nancy's train station is at the end of rue Stanislas, a 5min walk from place Stanislas.
Tourist office The wonderfully helpful tourist office is at 1 place Stanislas (Mon–Sat 9am–6/7pm, Sun 10am–1/5pm; ⓣ03.83.85.30.00, ⓦwww.ot-nancy.fr). Buy *Le Pass Nancy* (€14) – this gets you reduced museum entry, a cinema ticket, guided city tour and other goodies.
Internet e-café, 11 rue des Quatre Églises.

Accommodation

Camping de Brabois av Paul-Muller ⓣ03.83.27.18.28, ⓦwww.camping-brabois.com. The nearest campsite to town, with showers, shop and a café on-site. Around 2km out of the city; take bus #3 or #5 from the train station. Closed mid–Oct to March.
Centre d'Accueil Château de Rémicourt, 149 rue de Vandoeuvre ⓣ03.83.27.73.67. The local hostel is a 10min bus ride (bus #26, #16 or #4 from outside the station) but is a respectable and friendly option. €16.80.
De l'Académie 7bis rue des Michottes ⓣ03.83.35.52.31, ⓦacademie-hotel.com. Rooms are a little on the small side but this is a cheap, cheerful hotel in the town centre. €28.

Eating

Grand Café Foy Located in the heart of place Stanislas, this café is popular with locals and serves up typical French cuisine from €9.

TREAT YOURSELF

De Guise 18 rue de Guise ⓣ03.83.32.24.68, ⓦwww.hoteldeguise.com. A wonderfully atmospheric choice in the centre of the old town, with rooms themed according to past kings. Room rate includes a delicious breakfast of flaky pastries, fruit and fresh coffee. €67.

Gustatori 40 rue Stanislas. Lovely Italian *épicerie* which serves beautifully fresh pasta dishes. Fixed menus from €9.90.

L'Excelsior 50 rue Henri Poincaré. This stylish Art Deco place is like stepping back into the 1920s. Slightly pricey but an excellent place for a treat; great wine list and set menus from €30 per person.

Moving on

Train Lyon (frequent; 4hr 40min); Paris (10 daily; 1hr 30min); Strasbourg (8–13 daily; 1hr 30min).

STRASBOURG

STRASBOURG is a major city with the feel of a charming provincial town. It has one of the loveliest cathedrals in France, an ancient but active university and is the current seat of the Council of Europe and the European Court of Human Rights, as well as part-time base of the European Parliament. Even if you're not planning to spend much time in eastern France, Strasbourg is well worth a detour.

What to see and do

Strasbourg focuses on two main squares, the busy **place Kléber** and, to the south, **place Gutenberg**, named after the fifteenth-century pioneer of printing type.

Cathédrale de Notre-Dame

The major landmark is the nearby **Cathédrale de Notre-Dame** (daily 7–11.30am & 12.40–7pm; free) which beautifully combines ostentatious grandeur with chocolate-box fragility. Climb to the top platform for stunning views to the Black Forest (€4.40), and don't miss the tremendously complicated **astrological clock** (noon–12.20pm; €1), built in 1842. Visitors arrive in droves to witness its crowning performance – striking the hour of noon with unerring accuracy at 12.30pm.

South of the Cathedral

The **Musée de l'Oeuvre Notre-Dame**, 3 place du Château (Tues–Sun 10am–6pm; €4), houses the original sculptures from the cathedral exterior, as well as some of Europe's finest collected stained glass. A particular highlight is the *Les Amants Trépassés* in room 23, which shows two lovers being punished, and makes the average Hollywood horror film look mild in comparison.

Grand Île & Petite France

The **Grand Île** section of the city is the most striking, featuring the beautiful Petite France area, which has winding streets bordered by sixteenth- and seventeenth-century houses with carved woodwork and decked with flowers. The name Petite France was given to the area by the Alsatians in the seventeenth century, having been a quarantine area for patients of a devastating sixteenth-century venereal disease, attributed to the French. The **Musée d'Art Moderne et Contemporain**, 1 place Jean-Hans Arp (Tues, Wed, Fri & Sat 11am–7pm, Thurs noon–10pm, Sun 10am–6pm; €5), stands on the west bank of the river and houses an impressive collection featuring Monet, Klimt, Ernst and Klee. If your tastes are more alcoholic, pop into **Kronenbourg**, a short way from the centre on 68 route d'Oberhausbergen (Tues–Sat 10am–4pm; €5), which runs daily **brewery** tours.

Arrival and information

Train The train station is a 15min walk from place Kléber.

Tourist office 17 place de la Cathédrale (daily 9am–6/7pm; ⓣ03.88.52.28.28, ⓦwww.ot-strasbourg.fr). There are also branches in the underground shopping centre, in front of the train station and at the Pont de l'Europe, on the German border.

Internet Midi Minuit, 5 place du Corbeau (€3/hr). Also, plenty of internet places line rue du Maire Kuss, opposite the train station.

Accommodation

It's worth bearing in mind that hotels – never cheap at the best of times – get booked up early when

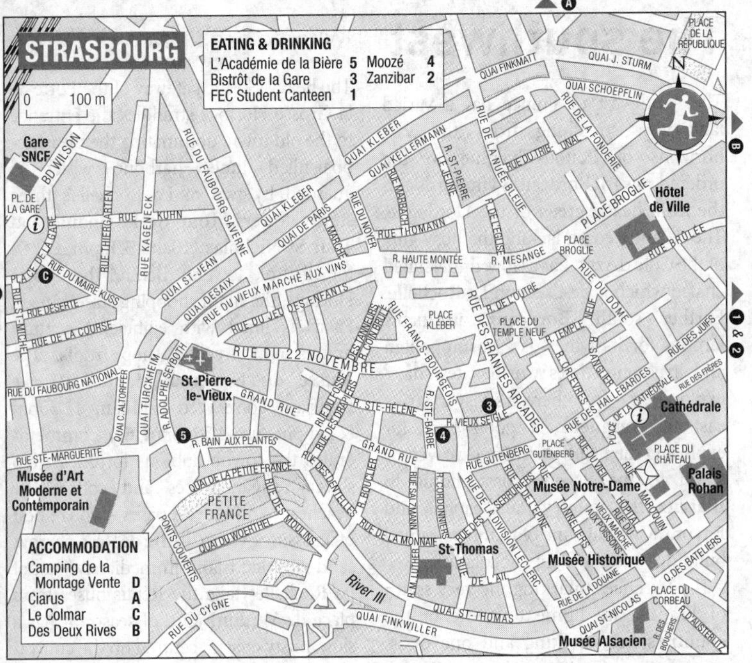

the European Parliament is in session (one week a month); visit ⓦwww.europarl.eu.int for up-to-date information.

Camping de la Montagne Verte 2 rue Robert Forrer ⓣ03.88.30.25.46 ⓦwww.camping-montagne-verte-strasbourg.com. Just 10min away from the centre (take the tram towards Petit France), this leafy campsite has an on-site shop and bike hire. €9.60 for one person and tent.

Ciarus 7 rue de Finkmatt ⓣ03.88.15.27.88, ⓦwww.ciarus.com. Pleasant and comfortable hostel, with regular social events. In the north of the city, around 25min by foot, or take bus #2, #4 or #10 from place Gutenberg. €28.50.

Des Deux Rives rue des Cavaliers by the Pont de l'Europe ⓣ03.88.45.54.20. Quiet hostel set in a large park on the banks of the Rhine with a 2am curfew; take bus #21 from place Gutenberg towards Kehl. €19.

Le Colmar 1 rue du Maire Kuss ⓣ03.88.32.16.89, ⓔhotel.le.colmar@wanadoo.fr. One of the best budget options just a short walk from the train station, *Le Colmar* is situated on the western edge of the Grande Île with en-suite rooms and a good buffet breakfast. €50.

Eating and drinking

Bistrôt de la Gare 18 rue du Vieux-Marché-aux-Grains. This homely little place serves good pasta and salads, with meals from €10.

FEC Student Canteen place St-Étienne. Good, unpretentious meals at rock-bottom prices, such as beef stew and grilled or fried fish. Expect to pay no more than €4 for a main course.

L'Académie de la Bière 17 rue Adolphe-Seyboth Frequented by locals and tourists alike, who come to appreciate the fine beer served here; pints from €3.

Moozé 1 rue de la Demi-Lune. A lovely Japanese place where a plate of sushi costs around €3.

Zanzibar 1 place St-Étienne. Cellar bar with a hip crowd thronging the sweaty dance floor; admission from €4.

Moving on

Train Basel (frequent; 1hr 15min); Frankfurt (8–9 daily; 2hr 30min); Nancy (frequent; 1hr 15min); Paris (hourly; 2hr 20min)

The southwest

The southwest of France has a varied landscape, stretching from the vast horizons of Poitou-Charente to the ordered rows of Bordeaux's vineyards and the lush, heady green of the Dordogne. The Atlantic coast, lacking the busy glitz of the Côte d'Azur, has a slow, understated charm which is best seen in **La Rochelle**. Further south, **Bordeaux**, justifiably famous for its wines, is a cosmopolitan and lively city that's worth a few days' exploration – from here, it's easy to strike east to **Périgueux**, a good base for exploring the nearby prehistoric caves, or south to the Basque coast, home to **Biarritz**, the country's surf capital, and **Bayonne**, with its fine old timber-framed buildings and excellent chocolatiers.

The Pyrenees, marking the very south of France, are home to some of the country's best walking and one of its most vibrant cities, the rose-brick university town of **Toulouse**, whose youthful energy is matched only by **Montpellier**. Medieval **Carcassonne**, between the two, is undoubtedly the biggest tourist trap of the region, but it's hard not to be wowed when you first see its fairytale spires rising above the surrounding buildings.

LA ROCHELLE

The lively port town of **LA ROCHELLE** has an exceptionally beautiful seventeenth- and eighteenth-century centre and is a very pleasant place to linger for a few days. Granted a charter by Eleanor of Aquitaine in 1199, it rapidly became a port of major importance, trading in salt and wine. Following a makeover in the 1990s, which established a university, pedestrianized the centre and moved out the fishing operation, La Rochelle has become the largest Atlantic yachting port in Europe, without the exclusivity of some of its Mediterranean counterparts.

What to see and do

The heavy Gothic gateway of the Porte de la Grosse Horloge straddles the entrance to the old town, dominating the pleasure-boat-filled inner harbour, which is guarded by two of La Rochelle's three sturdy towers, **Tour de la Chaîne** and **Tour St Nicholas** (10am–6.30pm; €6, €8 for all three towers). Behind the Grosse Horloge, the main shopping street rue du Palais is lined with eighteenth-century houses and arcaded shop fronts. The **Musée du Nouveau Monde**, 10 rue Fleuriau (Mon & Wed–Sat 10am–12.30pm & 2–6pm, Sun 2.30–6pm; €4), commemorates the town's dubious fortunes from slavery, sugar, spices and coffee. For beaches – and bicycle paths – you're best off crossing over to the **Île de Ré**, a narrow, sand-rimmed island immediately west of La Rochelle (take the Rébus buses from place de Verdun). Out of season it has a slow, misty charm, centred on the cultivation of oysters and mussels; in summer it's packed to the gills.

Arrival and information

Train From the train station, it's a 7min walk down av du Général de Gaulle to the town centre.
Tourist office Near the harbour on place de la Petite Sirène (April–June & Sept Mon–Sat 9am–6/7pm, Sun 10.30am–5.30pm; July & Aug Mon–Sat 9am–8pm, Sun 10.30am–5.30pm; Oct–March Mon–Sat 9am–6pm, Sun 10am–1pm; ⓣ05.46.41.14.68, ⓦwww.larochelle-tourisme.fr).
Internet Squat, 63 rue St-Nicolas.

Accommodation

Atlantic 23 rue Verdière ⓣ05.46.41.16.68. Simply furnished rooms sleeping one to three, some of which open onto a sweet courtyard. Those at the top of the hotel are a little more run-down. €68.
FUAJ La Rochelle 17 av des Minimes ⓣ05.46.44.43.11, ⓦwww.fuaj.org. Modern hostel in a good position by the Port des Minimes, 20min walk from the station. The bright, nicely decorated rooms are all en suite and roomy; dinner is available (from €6) and outdoor activities are often organised. To get here from the station, follow signs to Porte des Minimes. Closed noon–5.30pm & 7–9pm. €16.

Hotel de l'Océan 36 cours des Dames ⓣ05.46.41.31.97 ⓦwww.hotel-ocean-larochelle.com. This small, friendly hotel is decked out in blues and yellows that lend it a slightly nautical feel. All rooms have shower and toilet attached, and those at the front have excellent views of the port. €54.

Le Soleil av Crépeau ⓣ05.46.44.42.53. This municipal campsite has ping-pong, pétanque and hot showers, and allows barbecues. Its best asset is its location; right by the sea, just 800m from the town centre. Open mid-May to mid-Sept. €13.30.

Eating, drinking and nightlife

À Côté de Chez Fred 34 rue St-Nicolas ⓣ05.46.41.21.35. Next to a fishmonger, this is the best place in town to enjoy fresh fish; head here at lunchtime for their more affordable menus (two courses, €13).

Café Leffe 52–54 cours des Dames. Another good spot on the port, which is popular throughout the day and evening. The extensive menu includes tasty sandwiches (€3.80) and a well-priced *plat du jour* (€9.90). The eponymous Leffe beer is available in various flavours, from €3.80.

L'Oxford Prom de la Concurrence ⓣ05.46.41.51.81, ⓦwww.club-oxford.com. This fun nightclub plays techno, ragga and house, with a second room for 1980s tunes. Entry from €5 depending on day, includes one drink.

Original Pasta 19 Petite rue du Temple. Fast-food pasta in big, filling boxes and small, but adequate, boxes with a choice of sauces such as bolognese and carbonara (from €3.70). Big box and drink €7.20.

Moving on

Train Bordeaux (6 daily; 2hr 20min); Cognac (6 daily; 1hr 20min–2hr); Nantes (4 daily; 1hr 50min); Poitiers (12 daily; 1hr 45min).

BORDEAUX

Though crammed with grand, old buildings, **BORDEAUX** still has a surprisingly youthful feel. Café culture is in full swing here – indeed, one of the most pleasurable things about a visit to the city is sitting out on a sun-drenched terrace enjoying a glass or two of the region's fabulous wines. If you have time, and want to find out more about the justifiably world-famous wines of the region, it's definitely worth doing a wine tour (see box, p.417).

What to see and do

The centre of Bordeaux bends around the east bank of the **Garonne** River in the shape of *un croissant de lune* (a crescent moon) – and is colloquially known as *Porte de la Lune*.

Le Triangle d'Or and Quinconces

The "golden triangle", full of chic Parisian boutiques, runs between **place Gambetta**, with its eighteenth-century Porte Dijeaux, place de la Comédie with the classical 1780 **Grand Théâtre**, and place Tourny at the peak. In a breathtaking nineteenth-century colonial warehouse to the north of the vast Esplanade des Quinconces is the unmissable **CAPC musée**, 7 rue Ferrère (Tues–Sun 11am–6pm, Wed till 8pm; permanent collection free, temporary exhibitions €5).

COGNAC

On the La Rochelle to Bordeaux line, the little town of **Cognac** (ⓦwww.tourism-cognac.com) is shrouded in the heady scent of its famous brandy. Of the various *cognac chais* (distilleries) huddled around the end of the Grande-Rue, Otard is one of the best choices for a guided tour (April–Oct daily 11am–5pm; Nov & Dec Mon–Fri 11am–5pm; ⓦwww.otard.com), which recounts a history of the site, the principles of making cognac and, most importantly, a tasting. A good restaurant choice in town is *La Bonne Goule*, 42 allées de la Corderie, for its local Charentais plates (from €11). If you get carried away with the brandy and need to stay the night, *L'Oliveraie*, 6 place de la Gare (ⓣ05.45.82.04.15, ⓦwww.oliveraie-cognac.com; €50), has simple rooms.

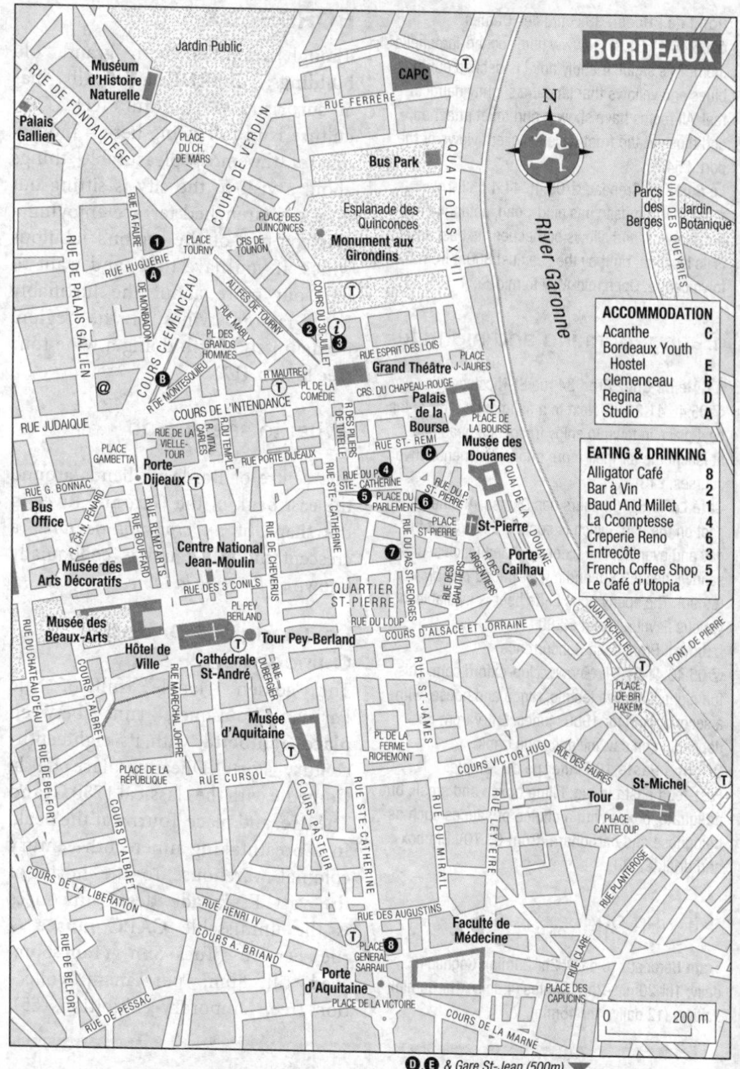

This is the finest contemporary art exhibition space in France, displaying pioneering national and international works with admirable use of space and lighting. The permanent collection includes Richard Long and Gilbert&George, but the temporary installations are often the most exciting.

Sainte-Catherine, Saint Pierre and Place de la Victoire

The central pedestrian artery, **rue Ste-Catherine**, leads down from place de la Comédie to the city's best historical museum, the **Musée d'Aquitaine**, 20 cours Pasteur (Tues–Sun 11am–6pm, Wed till 8pm; free),

WINE TASTING IN THE BORDEAUX REGION

Along with Burgundy and Champagne, the wines of Bordeaux form the Holy Trinity of French **viticulture**. Bordeaux is mostly a red-wine region, growing high-class (and more expensive) **Cabernet Sauvignon** on the Left Bank (the countryside to the west of the Garonne river and Gironde estuary), while smaller growers make predominantly Merlot and Cabernet-Franc based wines on the Right Bank. There are also some very good white wines, mainly from the Pessac and Graves regions to the south and southeast – largely based on **Sauvignon Blanc** and **Semillon**, and come in both dry and sweet forms. The easiest way to taste the wines is in the village of **St Emilion**, to the east of Bordeaux, where there are many wine shops that hold wine tastings. L'Envers du Décor, 11 rue du Clocher (Ⓣ05.57.74.48.31), is a good choice and has reasonable prices. The Bordeaux tourist office (see below) has information on châteaux visits and wine-tastings, and organizes a good variety of half and full day wine tours of the area.

which illustrates the history of the region from prehistoric times through to the 1800s. A few streets north stands the **Cathédrale St-André** (Mon–Fri 7.30–11.30am & 2–6pm; free), with its exquisite stained-glass windows and slender twin spires. Around the corner at 20 cours d'Albret, the **Musée des Beaux-Arts** (daily except Tues 11am–6pm; €5) displays works by Rubens, Matisse and Renoir, as well as Lacour's evocative 1804 Bordeaux dockside scene, *Quai des Chartrons*. To the east lies the striking **place de la Bourse**, best viewed from the river's edge, reflecting in the glassy Font du Miroir, while farther south you'll find the student-friendly **place de la Victoire**, surrounded by cafés, restaurants and late-night bars.

Arrival and information

Air Bordeaux Mérignac airport, 12km west, is connected by regular shuttle bus (daily 7am–10.45pm; 30–45min; €7) to place Gambetta, cours du 30-Juillet and Gare St Jean.

Train The station, Gare St Jean, lies 2km southeast of central Bordeaux, easily accessed by tram C from Esplanade des Quinconces (10min; €1.40).

Tourist office 12 cours du 30-Juillet (daily 9am–7pm, Sun till 6.30pm; Ⓣ05.56.00.66.00, Ⓦwww.bordeaux-tourisme.com). Organises a plethora of wine and city tours.

Internet Iphone, 24 rue du Palais Gallien.

City transport

Tram/bus The hubs of the comprehensive transport networks are place Gambetta for buses and Esplanade des Quinconces for trams. Buy tickets at the machines on the platforms before boarding and validate them on board; one hour's travel €1.40, day pass €4.80.

Bike hire Liberty Cycles, 104 cours d'Yser (Ⓣ05.56.92.77.18; €9/day).

Accommodation

Acanthe 12–14 rue St-Rémi Ⓣ05.56.81.66.58 Ⓦwww.acanthe-hotel-bordeaux.com. Centrally located, with brightly decorated, spacious rooms. €66.

Bordeaux Youth Hostel 22 cours Barbey Ⓣ05.56.33.00.70, Ⓦwww.auberge-jeunesse-bordeaux.eu. This modern hostel has a slightly impersonal feel but good facilities including free internet. Rooms are clean and large, and most have attached shower or bath. Fifteen minutes from the centre by foot. €21.50.

Clémenceau 4 cours Georges Clémenceau Ⓣ05.56.52.98.98, Ⓦwww.hotel-bordeaux-clemenceau.com Light, neutrally decorated rooms with plain but nice furnishings. Ask for one of the newly renovated rooms on the first floor. €65.

Regina 34 rue Charles Dominique Ⓣ05.56.91.32.88, Ⓦwww.hotelreginabordeaux.com. Opposite the station, this friendly hotel offers bright, good-sized rooms, all with shower or bath. Fifteen minutes' walk to the city centre. €36.

Studio 26 rue Huguerie Ⓣ05.56.48.00.14. In an excellent position, this is a big backpacker's favourite with small, clean white rooms, all en suite, and a helpful owner. €33.

Eating

Baud & Millet 19 rue Huguerie ⓣ06.70.79.24.93. This fantastic wine shop has tables set up at the back where you can enjoy a leisurely glass of wine (from €4) and a plate of cheese and charcuterie (€12.50). The friendly Monsieur Baud speaks excellent English and delights in helping you with your choice.

Crêperie Reno 34 rue du Parlement St-Pierre. A good, casual crêperie that has a nice terrace on this pedestrian street. The €9 lunch menu is excellent value.

French Coffee Shop 20 rue du Parlement St-Catherine. A good place for a quick lunch stop, with fresh smoothies (€3.50) and reasonably priced snacks such as *croque-monsieur* (€2.20). Free wi-fi.

L'Entrecôte 4 cours du 30 Juillet. Simplicity at its tastiest: two servings of beautifully tender steak, with a fabulous sauce, perfectly cooked chips and a green salad (€17). The dessert menu is extensive – try the profiteroles (€5.50). Expect to queue.

Le Café d'Utopia 5 place Camille Jullian. A lively, casual place in a beautiful old building that also houses the Utopia art-house cinema, popular throughout the day and evening. Try one of their huge hot sandwiches (from €6) or the delicious gourmet salads (from €10).

Drinking and nightlife

Alligator Café 3 place du Général-Sarrail. Popular student bar, with a great terrace, snooker table and a dancefloor downstairs.

Bar à Vin 1 cours du 30-Juillet ⓣ05.56.00.22.88. Promoters for Bordeaux wine growers and home to a wine-tasting school, the bar here is a good place to sample the region's excellent wines (from €3), best enjoyed with one of the wonderful cheese plates (€7).

La Ccomptesse 25 rue du Parlement-Ste-Pierre ⓣ05.56.51.03.07. Eclectic music, often samba or electro, to shake your *derrière* to late night; demi €3. Open 8pm–2am.

SURFING IN LACANAU

Bordeaux's nearest beach, **Lacanau-Océan** (ⓦwww.lacanau.com), is well known for its beautiful lake and famous for its world-class **surfing**. If you fancy catching some waves, take bus #702 from opposite gare St Jean (3 daily; 1hr 50min; €14) – once there, you can rent boards and learn to surf at Lacanau Sports Club (ⓣ05.56.26.38.84), located on the corner of bd Plage and bd Liberty. *La Villa Zénith*, 16 av Adjudant Guittard (ⓣ06.84.66.88.08, ⓦwww.lacanau-zenith.com; €22), is 200m from the beach and has comfy dorms, cooking facilities and equipment lockers.

Moving on

Train Bayonne and Biarritz (10–12 daily; 1hr 40min–2hr 10min); Marseille (5–6 daily; 6–7hr); Nice (4 daily; 8hr 30min–10hr 10min); Paris (19 daily; 3hr–3hr 30min); Périgueux (10–12 daily; 1hr 10min–1hr 30min); Toulouse (10–17 daily; 2hr–2hr 45min)

PÉRIGUEUX

The bustling market town of **PÉRIGUEUX**, with its beautiful Renaissance and medieval centre, makes a fine base for visiting the **Dordogne's** pre-historic caves.

What to see and do

The centre of town focuses on **place Bugeaud**, west of which is the striking **Cathédrale St-Front** (daily 8am–7pm) – its square, pineapple-capped belfry surging above the roofs of the surrounding medieval houses. During a nineteenth-century restoration, the architect Paul Abadie added five Byzantine domes to the roof, which served as a prototype for his more famous Sacré-Cœur in Paris (see p.392). Heading north along rue St-Front, you'll reach the **Musée d'Art et d'Archéologie du Périgord**, at 22 cours Tourny (Mon & Wed–Fri 10am–5.30pm, Sat & Sun 1–6pm; €4), which boasts some beautiful Gallo-Roman mosaics found locally.

Arrival and information

Train The station is a 10min walk to the west of place Bugeaud.

Tourist office 26 place Francheville (daily 9/10am–1pm & 2–6/7pm; ⓣ05.53.53.10.63, ⓦwww.tourisme-perigueux.fr).

Internet Ouratech, place du Général Leclerc.

Accommodation

Camping Barnabé 80 rue des Bains ⓣ05.53.53.41.45, ⓦwww.barnabe-perigord.com. This peaceful campsite enjoys an excellent position on the banks of the River Isle. Plots are shady, and there's a bar, ping-pong and mini-golf on site. To get there cross pont des Barris and follow the south riverbank for 20min. €4.30 per person, plus €3.50 per tent.

Des Barris 2 rue Pierre Magne ⓣ05.53.53.04.05, ⓦwww.hoteldesbarris.com. A lovely little hotel with twelve simple but attractive wood-furnished rooms. All are en suite and the best have views across the river to the cathedral. €53.

Le Midi 18 rue Denis-Papin ⓣ05.53.53.41.06, ⓦwww.hotel-midi.fr. Right opposite the station, this bar-hotel offers the cheapest rooms in town, though not the most friendly of welcomes. €43.

Eating and drinking

Cocotte 17 rue Voltaire. A popular choice, with a lovely terrace that's ideal for enjoying the reasonably priced food, such as *confit de canard* (€9)

Gouter de Charlotte 9 rue Voltaire. Hearty crêpes and galettes (from €2) are served in this charming old café overlooking the square. Lunch menu €12

La Vertu 11 rue Notre-Dame ⓣ05.53.53.20.75. A friendly, local inn with a flowery terrace serving cheap beers, cocktails and sturdy dinners (€13). Open June–Sept only.

Moving on

Train Bordeaux (13 daily; 1hr 10min–1hr 30min); Les Eyzies (2–6 daily; 35min); Paris (12 daily; via Libourne or Limoges; 4–5hr).

THE VÉZÈRE VALLEY CAVES

This lavish cliff-cut region, riddled with **caves** and subterranean streams, is half-an-hour or so by train from Périgueux. Cro-Magnon skeletons were unearthed here in 1868 and since then an incredible wealth of archeological evidence about the life of late Stone Age people has been found. The paintings that adorn the caves are remarkable not only for their age, but also for their exquisite colouring and the skill with which they were drawn.

What to see and do

The centre of the region is **LES EYZIES**, a rambling, somewhat unattractive village dominated by tourism. Worth a glance before or after visiting the caves is the **Musée National de la Préhistoire** (June & Sept daily except Tues 9.30am–6pm; July & Aug daily 9.30am–6.30pm; Oct–May daily except Tues 9am–12.30pm & 2.30–5.30pm; €5). Les Eyzies' **tourist office**, 19 rue de la Préhistoire (June–Sept Mon–Sat 9am–7pm, Sun 9/10am–noon & 2–5/6/7pm; Oct–May Mon–Sat 9am–noon & 2–6pm, closed Sun, except April & May 10am–noon & 2–5pm; ⓣ05.53.06.97.05, ⓦwww.leseyzies.com) has information on private rooms in the area, internet and rents out bikes for €14 per day. The Périgueux tourist office (see opposite) has a fact sheet detailing how to get to the caves and back in a day

Font de Gaume caves

Just outside Les Eyzies, off the road to Sarlat, the **Grotte de Font-de-Gaume** (daily except Sat: mid-May to mid-Sept 9.30am–5.30pm; mid-Sept to mid-May 9.30am–12.30pm & 2–5.30pm; ⓣ05.53.06.86.00; €7) contains dozens of polychrome paintings, the colour remarkably preserved by a protective layer of calcite. The tours last forty minutes but only two hundred people are admitted each day, so to be sure of a place you should reserve in advance by phone or arrive before 9.30am.

The Cap Blanc frieze

The **Abri du Cap Blanc** (daily: mid-May to mid-Sept 9.30am–5.30pm; mid-Sept to mid-May 9.30am–12.30pm & 2–5.30pm; ⓣ05.53.59.60.30; €8) is a steep 7km bike ride from Les Eyzies. This is not a cave but a rock shelter, containing a 15,000-year-old frieze of horses and bison, the only exhibited prehistoric sculpture in the world.

Grotte des Combarelles

The road continues to the **Grotte des Combarelles** (daily except Sat: mid-May to mid-Sept 9.30am–5.30pm; mid-Sept to mid-May 9.30am–12.30pm & 2–5.30pm; €7), whose engravings of humans, reindeer and mammoths from the Magdalanian period (about twenty thousand years ago) are the oldest in the region.

Montignac

Up the valley of the Vézère river to the northeast, **MONTIGNAC** is more attractive than Les Eyzies. Its prime interest is the cave paintings at nearby **Lascaux** – or, rather, the tantalizing replica at Lascaux II (daily April–Sept 9.30am–7pm; July & Aug 9am–8pm; Oct–March 10am–12.30pm & 2–5.30pm; closed Mon mid-Nov to March; closed Jan; forty-minute guided tour €8.20); the original has been closed since 1963 due to deterioration caused by the breath and body heat of visitors. Produced seventeen thousand years ago, the paintings are considered the finest prehistoric works in existence. The **tourist office** (Mon–Sat 10am–1pm & 3–6pm; ⓣ05.53.51.82.60, ⓦwww.bienvenue-montignac.com) is at place Bertran-de-Born. Montignac is short on moderately priced **accommodation**; the best option is the *Hôtel de la Grotte*, 63 rue du 4 Septembre (ⓣ05.53.51.80.48, ⓦwww.hoteldelagrotte.fr; €30), which has a nice restaurant (menus from €12.50). There's also a **campsite**, *Le Moulin du Bleufond* (closed mid-Oct to March; ⓣ05.53.51.83.95, ⓦwww.bleufond.com; €11.40), on the riverbank.

BIARRITZ

A former Viking whaling settlement, **BIARRITZ** became famous in the nineteenth century when Empress Eugénie started coming here with the last French Emperor, Napoleon III. He built her a seaside palace in 1855 and an impressive list of kings, queens and tsars followed, bringing *belle époque* and Art Deco grandeur to the resort. Today Biarritz is the undisputed surf capital of Europe, hosting the prestigious weeklong Surf Festival in July, which includes a longboard competition and nightly parties on the Côte des Basques beach. The town feels as though its glory days are well past, and now it's a rather traditional (and tacky) seaside resort that can't compete with the Côte d'Azur.

What to see and do

The town's beaches are the main attraction. The best surfing is found on the long competition beach, **plage de la Côte des Basques**, to the south – those less interested in surfing should try the intimate **Port-Vieux** beach for a calmer swim. The **Musée de la Mer** (July & Aug daily 9.30am–midnight; Sept & June

PELOTE BASQUE

The fastest ball game in the world, **pelote** (or *pilota* in Basque) consists, in essence, of propelling a ball (*pelote*) against a wall (*fronton*) so that your opponent cannot return it. There are over twenty versions with different courts, rackets and balls, but the three main ways to play are: bare-handed *(main nue)*, with a wooden bat *(paleta)* and, in the fastest version, slung from a wicker claw *(cesta-punta or jai alai)*, in which the pelote has reached speeds of over 300km/hr. The biggest tournaments in Biarritz – the Open in July and the Gant d'Or in August, played in the parc Mazon on av Joffre and the Plaza Berri on av Foch – are great spectacles, often with the crowd singing the score after every point. If you fancy trying it out yourself, head to the *centre sportif* El Hogar d'Anglet (ⓣ05.59.57.10.90; bus #72 to El Hogar from Hotel de Ville in Bayonne), which runs free introductory classes. The tourist office in Biarritz can provide information on matches.

daily 9.30am–7pm; Oct–March Tues–Sun 9.30am–12.30pm & 2–6pm; €7.80), opposite Rocher de la Vierge, has an interesting aquarium taken from the Bay of Biscay, and a rooftop seal pool. **Asiatica**, at 1 rue Guy Petit (Mon–Fri 10.30am–7pm, Sat & Sun 2–8pm; €7), uphill and left off avenue Foch, houses one of Europe's most important collections of oriental art.

Arrival and information

Air Aérodrome Biarritz-Bayonne-Anglet is 10min from av Foch in the town centre by bus #6.

Train The station lies 3km from the centre in La Négresse. Bus #2 and the "navette des plages" (see below) connect it to square d'Ixelles.

Tourist office 1 square d'Ixelles (Mon–Fri 9am–6pm, Sat & Sun 10am–5pm; ⓣ05.59.22.37.10, ⓦwww.biarritz.fr).

Scooters Rent a Bike, 24 rue Peyroloubilh (ⓣ05.59.24.94.47) rents scooters and beach buggies; ID and credit card required (€33/day).

Accommodation

Biarritz Camping 28 rue Harcet ⓣ05.59.23.00.12, ⓦwww.biarritz-camping.fr. A spacious and well-equipped campsite, just a short walk from the beach and 2km from the centre of town. Open mid-may to mid-Sept. €17.

Estelle Residence 13 av du Maréchal Joffre ⓣ05.59.22.08.22. Small but reasonable rooms, and rather eccentric service at this hotel just south of the centre. €49.

FUAJ Biarritz 8 rue Chiquito de Cambo ⓣ05.59.41.76.00, ⓦwww.fuaj.org. Just 1.5km from the beach and close to the station and the lake, this comfortable, modern hostel has two- to four-bed dorms, rents out bicycles and has some good deals on surf lessons. To get here, take bus #2, #9, or ligne B bus on Sun to "Bois de Boulogne". April–Sept closed 12.30–6pm; Oct–March closed 11.30am–6pm. €18.30.

Maïtagaria 34 av Carnot ⓣ05.59.24.26.65, ⓦwww.hotel-maitagaria.com. Central, family-run hotel with clean, tasteful en-suite rooms and free wi-fi. €73.

Palym 7 rue du Port-Vieux ⓣ05.59.24.25.83, ⓦwww.le-palmarium.com. One of the town's cheaper options in a good, central location with basic rooms. €40.

Eating and drinking

Bar Jean 5 rue des Halles ⓣ05.59.24.41.00. Don't miss out on this local tapas favourite (from €4.90), which also serves plates of the excellent local ham (€11.50) and sangria (€3).

Blue Cargo av d'Ilbarritz, Bidart ⓣ05.59.23.54.87. This open-air beach café, popular with young surfers, is a great place to watch the sunset. At night, the terrace and the beach become the dance floor. Open April–Sept daily 11am–2am; to get here take the beach bus to "Boulogne".

Le Caveau 4 rue Gambetta ⓣ05.59.24.16.17. This fun gay-friendly club is the best in town. Get there before midnight to avoid the €10 cover charge. 11pm–5am.

Les Halles place Sobradiel ⓣ05.59.34.52.02. Most towns have a good *halles* (covered food markets) but this one is excellent. Go for breakfast, a picnic lunch or to indulge in a *gateau Basque* (jam- or custard-filled cake).

Le Surfing 9 bd du Prince-de-Galles ⓣ05.59.24.78.72. Grills and seafood for under €10 in this laid-back restaurant, which is decorated with antique surf boards.

Sideria Hernani 29 av du Maréchal Joffre ⓣ05.59.23.01.01. Heavy wooden tables, barrels and local warmth accompany excellent Basque cuisine and cider. The *côte de boeuf* (€16) is huge but well worth it.

Moving on

Bus Bus #1 from square d'Ixelles and #2 from outside the casino both go to Bayonne; in July and August, the *navette des plages* (beach bus) covers all the beaches from Anglet to Ilbarritz, departing from outside the casino. See ⓦwww.bus-stab.com for further information. Two buses daily to Bilbao (2hr 55min; €17.20) and San Sebastian (1hr 45min; €6.30) depart from rue Joseph Petit at 12.15pm and 6.45pm.

Train Bayonne (14 daily; 15–30min); Paris (5 daily, connect in Bayonne; 5hr–6hr 15min).

BAYONNE

Capital of the French Basque country and home of the bayonet, **BAYONNE** lies 6km inland at the junction of the Nive and Adour rivers. Having escaped the worst effects of mass tourism, it remains a cheerful and pretty town, with the shutters on the older half-timbered

houses painted in the distinctive Basque tones of green and rust-red.

What to see and do

The town's two medieval quarters line the banks of the Nive, whose quays are home to many bars and restaurants. Grand Bayonne on the west bank is the administrative and commercial centre, while Petit Bayonne, to the east, has a more bohemian feel and is full of places to eat and drink.

Petit Bayonne

On **quai des Corsaires,** along the Nive's east bank, stands the **Musée Basque** (Sept–June Tues–Sun 10am–6.30pm; July & Aug daily 10am–6.30pm; €5.50), which provides a comprehensive overview of modern Basque culture. The city's second museum, **Musée Bonnat**, 5 rue Jacques Laffitte (daily except Tues: May–Oct 10am–6.30pm; Nov–April 10am–12.30pm & 2–6pm; €5.50), has an unexpected treasury of art, including works by Goya, El Greco, Rubens and Degas.

Grand Bayonne

The **Cathédrale Ste-Marie** (Mon–Sat 10–11.45am & 3–5.45pm, Sun 3.30–6pm), across the Nive, looks best from a distance, its twin spires rising with airy grace above the houses; the **cloister** (daily 9/9.30am–12.30pm & 2–5/6pm; free) rewards a visit with a good view of the stained glass and buttresses. Near here are a number of chocolateries and the small but interesting **Choco-musée de Puyodebat**, 66 rue d'Espagne (daily 10.30am–noon & 4.30–6pm; free), introduces the local relevance and techniques of chocolate-making, brought here by Jewish chocolatiers fleeing the Spanish inquisition. It was here that a devilish brew, hot chocolate, was introduced to the country, much to the distaste of the Catholic church due to its aphrodisiac qualities – the best place in town to try it is *Cazenave* (see opposite).

FÉRIA

Wear red, green and white for the **Fête de Bayonne** in the first week of August, a smaller, less tourist-dominated version of Pamplona's San Fermín (see box, p.1133). You can't run with the bulls at this festival but try to catch the waking of King Léon daily at midday, when drunken crowds gather outside the Hôtel de Ville and sing a song imploring him to get out of bed ("debout, debout, debout Léon!") until the giant puppet king comes out onto the balcony. ⓦwww.fetes.bayonne.fr.

Arrival and information

Train Bayonne's train station is in the St-Esprit quarter on the opposite bank of the Adour from the centre, 10min walk over the Pont St-Esprit.

Tourist office Take rue Bernède from the Hôtel de Ville, to place des Basques (Mon–Sat 9/10am–6/7pm; July & Aug also Sun 10am–1pm; ⓣ08.20.42.64.64, ⓦwww.bayonne-tourisme.com); it has an excellent scheme that lends bikes for free.

Internet CyberNetCafé, place de la République.

Accommodation

Best Western Le Grand 21 rue Thiers ⓣ05.59.59.62.00, ⓦwww.bw-legrandhotel.com. A good hotel in a central location, though rooms are pretty bland. €69.

Hôtel des Basques 4 rue des Lisses ⓣ05.59.59.08.02. Charmingly dilapidated hotel with basic rooms and clean facilities, right in the thick of Petit Bayonne. €40.

Monbar 24 rue Pannecau, Petit Bayonne ⓣ05.59.59.26.80. Though a bit fusty and lacking a little in character, this quiet family-run hotel has clean and bright en-suite rooms. €32.

Eating and drinking

Bistrot Ste-Cluque 9 rue Hugues, St-Esprit ⓣ05.59.55.82.43. Make sure you try the local cured ham (€7.50), flavoured with salt from nearby mines, at this jolly bistro by the station; three-course dinner menu €16.

Café Salud 63 rue Pannecau ☎05.59.59.14.49. Friendly, family-run modern café that does a good range of food and drink, including wonderful large salads (€7.80) and cocktails (from €4).

Café Victor Hugo 1 rue Victor Hugo ☎05.59.25.62.26. Basque beef and fish dishes and a good vegetarian selection in an ideal location overlooking the Nive and Adour rivers, although the service isn't great. Two-course menu €12.

Cazenave 19 Arceaux du Pont-Neuf. The pick of the chocolatiers; try the famous *chocolat mousseux* – delicious, hand-whipped hot chocolate served with chantilly cream (€5.20) – with a serving of their hot, buttered toast (€3).

Moving on

Train Bordeaux (6–12 daily; 1hr 40min–2hr 10min); Hendaye (14 daily; 35min) on the border with Spain, where the Euskotren makes the crossing to St Sébastien (every 30min; 45min); Lourdes (5–8 daily; 1hr 45min–2hr); Paris (14–16 daily, some indirect; 4hr 45min–6hr); Toulouse (7–12 daily; 3hr 10min–4hr 40min).

LOURDES

In 1858 Bernadette Soubirous, 14-year-old daughter of a poor local miller in **LOURDES**, had eighteen visions of the Virgin Mary in a spot called the Grotte de Massabielle. Miraculous cures at the grotto soon followed and Lourdes grew exponentially; it now sees six million Catholic pilgrims a year and whole streets are devoted to the sale of religious kitsch. At the **grotto** itself – a moisture-blackened overhang by the riverside with a statue of the Virgin inside – long queues of the faithful process through. Above looms the first, neo-Gothic church built here, in 1871, and nearby the massive subterranean **basilica** has a capacity of twenty thousand. Lourdes **train station** is on the northeastern edge of town. For the **tourist office** (Mon–Sat 9am–noon & 2–6/7pm; Easter–Oct also Sun 11am–6pm; ☎05.62.42.77.40, Ⓦwww.lourdes-infotourisme.com) on place Peyramale turn right outside the station, then left down Chaussée Maransin. There's an abundance of inexpensive **hotels** in Lourdes, including the simple *Hotel Croix des Nordistes*, 29 bd de la Grotte (☎05.62.94.28.57, Ⓦwww.hotelcroixdesnordistes-lourdes.com; €40), and a number of **campsites** in the area, such as *Plein Soleil*, 11 av du Monge (☎05.62.94.40.93, Ⓦwww.camping-pleinsoleil.com; €19).

TOULOUSE

TOULOUSE is one of the most vibrant provincial cities in France, thanks to its sizeable student population that is second only to that of Paris. The city has

HIKING IN THE PYRENEES

From Lourdes train station, several SNCF buses run daily to **Gavarnie** and **Barèges**, two resorts near the heart of the Parc National des Pyrénées Occidentales. From either, a few hours on the Pyrenees-spanning hiking trail, GR10, or the harder HRP (Haute Randonnée Pyrénéenne), brings you to staffed alpine refuges (rough camping is not generally allowed in the park). In summer, serious and properly equipped hikers may wish to continue on the trails, which are well-served with refuges, though the weather and terrain make them highly dangerous in winter. The Lourdes and Bayonne tourist offices have information, or check Ⓦwww.lespyrenees.net. Gavarnie is smaller and pricier than Barèges, but has an incomparable natural ampitheatre towering above, forming the border with Spain. You can stay in dorms at *Le Gypaëte* (☎05.62.92.40.61; €11), or camp at the primitive but superbly positioned *La Bergerie* (☎05.62.92.48.41, Ⓦwww.camping-gavarnie-labergerie.com; €7), towards the cirque. Barèges has more of a real village feel, with a good streamside campsite – *La Ribère* (☎05.62.92.69.01, Ⓦwww.laribere.com; €13) – and two high-quality gîtes next to each other: *L'Oasis* (☎05.62.92.69.47, Ⓦwww.gite-oasis.com; €38) and *L'Hospitalet* (☎05.62.92.68.08, Ⓦwww.hospitalet-bareges.com; €38).

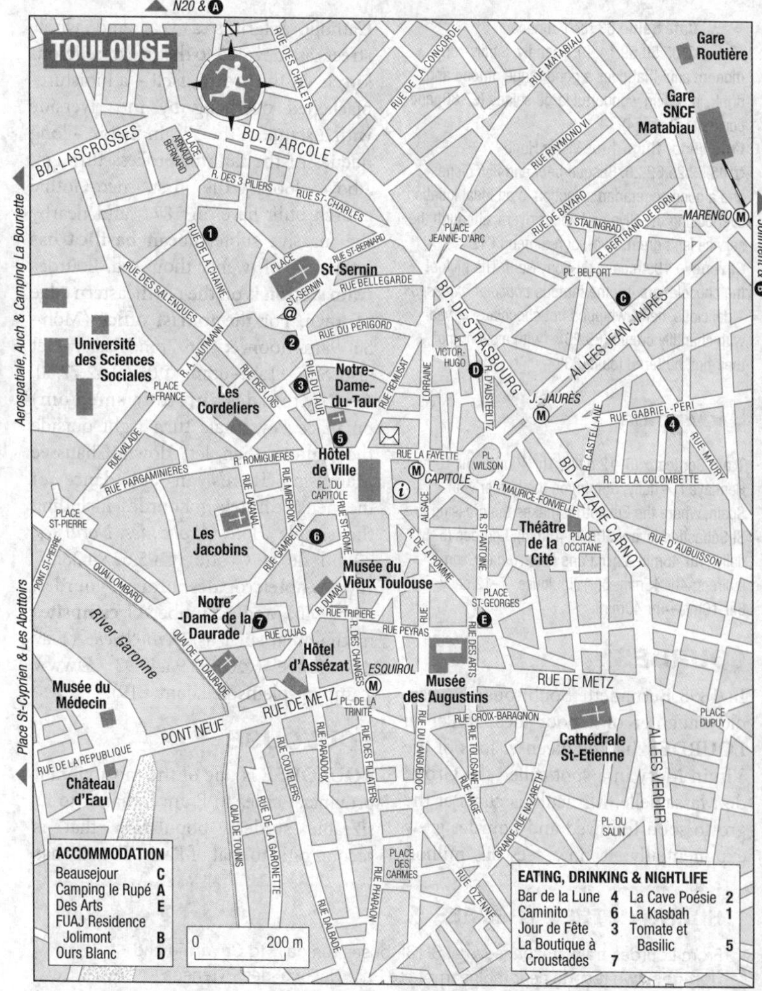

long been a centre for aviation – St-Exupéry and Mermoz flew out from here on their pioneering flights over Africa in the 1920s – and has more recently been developed as the country's centre of high-tech industry.

What to see and do

The centre of Toulouse is a rough hexagon clamped around a bend in the wide, brown Garonne river.

Place du Capitole and the old city

The **place du Capitole** is the site of Toulouse's town hall and a prime meeting-place, with numerous cafés and a weekday market. South of the square, and east of rue Alsace-Lorraine, lies the **old town**. The predominant building material here is the flat Toulousain brick, whose cheerful rosy colour gives the city its nickname of *ville rose*. Best known of these buildings is the Hôtel d' Assézat,

Most museums in Toulouse are free on the first Sunday of the month.

towards the river end of rue de Metz, which houses the marvellous private art collection of the **Fondation Bemberg** (Tues–Sun 10am–12.30pm & 1.30–6pm, Thurs till 9pm; €5), including excellent works by Bonnard.

St-Sernin

Rue du Taur leads northwards from place du Capitole to place St-Sernin and the largest Romanesque church in France, **Basilique de St-Sernin** (daily: July–Sept 8.30am–6.15pm, Sun till 7.30pm; Oct–Jun 8.30–11.45am & 2–5.45pm, Sun till 7pm). Dating back to 1080, it was built to accommodate passing hordes of Santiago pilgrims and is one of the loveliest examples of its kind.

Les Jacobins

West of place du Capitole, on rue Lakanal, the church of **Les Jacobins** (daily, 9am–7pm) is another impressive ecclesiastical building. This is a huge fortress-like rectangle of unadorned brick, with an interior divided by a central row of slender pillars from whose capitals spring a colourful splay of vaulting ribs.

Across the Garonne

Across the Pont-Neuf on the west bank of the Garonne stands the brick tower of the inspirational **Chateaux d'Eau**, (Tues–Sun 1–7pm; €2.50) the first public gallery dedicated to photography in France and holding over four thousand pieces, along with antique equipment. Continue west from the river, then north up Allées de Fitte to the vaulted nineteenth-century slaughterhouse, **Les Abattoirs** (Wed–Sun 11am–7pm; €6), whose comprehensive modern and contemporary art collections include the striking eight-metre-high Picasso theatre screen.

Arrival and information

Air Shuttle buses leave Aéroport Toulouse-Blagnac every 20min and take half an hour to reach Gare Matabiau (€4).
Bus and train Buses and trains arrive at Gare Matabiau, a 15min walk from the city centre down allées Jean-Jaurès.
Tourist office place Charles de Gaulle (Mon–Sat 9am–6/7pm, Sun 10/10.30am–5pm; Oct–May closed Sat–Sun 12.30–2pm; ⓣ05.61.11.02.22, ⓦwww.toulouse-tourisme.com).
Bikes Velo Toulouse bike stands can be found throughout the city – credit card guarantee required, first half-hour free, then from €1/30min.
Internet Nethouse, 1 rue de Trois Renards.

Accommodation

Beausejour 4 rue Caffarelli ⓣ05.61.23.36.21, ⓔhotelbeausejour@cegetel.net. The cheapest option in town, with very basic rooms, however the neighbourhood is far from salubrious. €38.
Camping le Rupé 21 chemin du Pont de Rupé ⓣ05.61.70.07.35, ⓔcampinglerupe31@wanadoo.fr. The closest campsite, just north of the city in a green park, with waterskiiing and fishing spots nearby. Take bus #59 from place Jeanne-d'Arc to Rupé. €14.40.
Des Arts 1bis rue Cantegril ⓣ05.61.62.65.84. Lovely little hotel tucked away in the old town. Rooms vary in size and are basic but nicely decorated. €40.
FUAJ Residence Jolimont 2 av Yves Brunaud ⓣ05.34.30.42.80, ⓔfoyerjolimont@wanadoo.fr. Though not very central, this hostel is only 1km from the station and offers simple but clean dorm rooms. €16.

Eating

Caminito 3 rue des Gestes ⓣ05.61.23.51.74. Great Argentinian cuisine, the highlight of which are the delicious *empanadas* (€2.90), with a range of

TREAT YOURSELF

Ours Blanc 25 place de Victor-Hugo ⓣ05.61.23.14.55, ⓦwww.hotel-ours-blanc.fr. Set in a beautiful building right in the centre, all rooms at this welcoming hotel are en-suite and have flat screen TVs and air-conditioning. €79.

fillings, including meat, fish, and cheese and onion. Closed Sun.

La Boutique à Croustades 54 rue Peyrolières ⓣ05.61.12.47.04. A lovely little café for lunch or a tea break, with a menu that features home-made quiche, soup, cakes and an extensive selection of teas (from €3).

La Kasbah 30 rue de la Chaîne ⓣ05.61.23.55.06. Excellent, authentic Algerian cuisine served around a fountain, with mains very reasonably priced at €9.

Tomate et Basilic 10 rue du Taur ⓣ05.61.12.48.21. Inexpensive yet delicious pasta dishes to eat in or take away. The pasta is handmade daily and there's a good choice of sauces (from €4.50).

Drinking and nightlife

Bar de la Lune 22 rue Palaprat ⓣ05.34.41.16.96. Relax with one of 120 types of beer (from €2 a bottle) in this friendly bar where the music allows for conversation.

Jour de Fête 43 rue du Taur. A student-filled café-bar which is busy throughout the day. Drinks from €2.50, *menu du jour* €7, including drink.

La Cave Poésie 71 rue du Taur ⓣ05.61.23.62.00, ⓦwww.cave-poesie.com. This intimate venue, which plays host to theatre, poetry, dance, music and more, has a good bar attached; glass of red wine €2.

Moving on

Bus Andorra (2 daily; 3hr 30min).

Train Barcelona (3 daily, via Narbonne; 4hr 50min–5hr 45min); Bayonne (18–22 daily; 2hr 30min–3hr 45min); Bordeaux (16 daily; 2hr–2hr 45min); Carcassonne (18 daily; 45min–1hr 15min); Lourdes (9–14 daily; 2hr); Lyon (10–14 daily; 4hr–6hr); Marseille (9–12 daily; 3hr 50min–5hr 50min); Paris (8–12 daily; 5–7hr).

CARCASSONNE

The fairy-tale aspect of **CARCASSONNE**'s old town (la Cité), was the inspiration for the castle in Walt Disney's *Sleeping Beauty*. Viollet-le-Duc rescued it from ruin in 1844, and his rather romantic restoration has been furiously debated ever since. Unsurprisingly, it's become a real tourist trap, its narrow lanes lined with innumerable souvenir shops and regularly crammed with hordes of day-trippers.

What to see and do

The **Cité** is a twenty-minute walk from the station (fifteen minutes from the new town) – well worth it to get a full view of the fortress from below. There's no charge for admission to the main part of the Cité, or the grassy *lices* (moat) between the walls. However, to see the inner fortress of the **Château Comtal** (daily 9.30am–5/6.30pm; €8), with its small museum of medieval sculpture, and to walk along the walls, you have to join one of the half-hourly guided tours from the ticket office. In addition to wandering the town's narrow streets (though they can be a bit of a squeeze in summer), don't miss the beautiful, thirteenth-century church of **St-Nazaire** (daily 9–11.45am & 1.45–5/6pm; free) at the end of rue St-Louis.

Arrival and information

Train The station is on the northern edge of the new town, at the end of ave du Maréchal Joffre, from where it's a 20min walk to the Cité (very steep for the last 5min) or catch ligne 4 from the bus stop on bd Omar Sarraut (Mon–Sat hourly 7am–7pm; €1.20).

Tourist office Located in the turret of the eastern entrance to la Cité, the Porte Narbonnaise (July–Aug daily 9am–7pm; Sept–June daily 9am–5pm; ⓣ04.68.10.24.30, ⓦwww.carcassonne-tourisme.com).

Accommodation

Astoria 53 rue Jean Bringer ⓣ04.68.25.31.38, ⓦwww.astoriacarcassonne.com. Down a quiet side street just across the river from the station, the *Astoria* offers simple, clean rooms, the more expensive of which (€54) are en suite. €34.

Campéole la Cité rte St-Hilaire ⓣ04.68.25.11.77, ⓦ www.uk.camping-carcassonne.info. This campsite has a well-shaded riverside location and good sporting facilities, and is less than 10min walk from the Cité. €22.90.

FUAJ Carcassone rue du Vicomte Trencavel ⓣ04.68.25.23.16, ⓦ www.fuaj.org. A fantastic hostel in an unsurpassable position in the heart of la Cité. Dorms are comfortable and have attached shower, and there's also table tennis,

themed nights in the bar, bike rental and organized trips to the surrounding countryside. €19.30.

Hotel de la Bastide 81 rue de la Liberte ⓣ04.68.25.24.99, ⓦwww.hotel-bastide.fr. Simple, basic rooms including some reasonably priced singles (€30), just a few streets from the station and close to the heart of the new town. €50.

Eating and drinking

Blanche de Castille 21 rue Cros-Mayrevieille. A cute little patisserie with a lovely patio at the back, though prices are steep for what's essentially pretty basic food. Omlettes from €7.50, baguettes €6.90.

Comptoir des Vins et Terroirs 3 rue du Comte Roger. Just around the corner from the youth hostel, this smart but unpretentious wine bar offers a great opportunity to try the best of the region's wines (from €2.50), accompanied by a delicious plate of local cheeses (€6).

La Taverne du Château 1 place du Château. Right in the thick of it, serving a good range of standards such as *croque-monsieur* (€5) and pizza (€11).

Le Trouvère ⓣ04.68.25.72.60. Like everywhere in la Cité, this restaurant is usually packed with tourists and offers the ubiquitous *cassoulet* (€11) and *confit de canard* (€10). However, the beamed, candlelit dining room makes it one of the more atmospheric options.

Moving on

Train Barcelona (6 daily, via Narbonne; 4hr–5hr 10min); Montpellier (14 daily, 1hr 15min–1hr 45min); Nice (6 daily, via Marseille; 4–5hr); Paris (11–16 daily; 3–6hr); Perpignan (13 daily; 1hr 30min–2hr 15min); Toulouse (18–22 daily; 45min–1hr 15min).

MONTPELLIER

MONTPELLIER is a vibrant city, renowned for its ancient university, once attended by such luminaries as Petrarch and Rabelais. Most of the central area is pedestrianized, which lends itself to unhurried exploration and many enjoyable evenings at terrace cafés.

What to see and do

At the town's hub is place de la Comédie, a grand oval square paved with cream-coloured marble and surrounded by cafés. The Opéra, an ornate nineteenth-century theatre, presides over one end, while the other end leads onto the pleasant Champs de Mars park. Nearby, the much-vaunted **Musée Fabre** (39 bd Bonne Nouvelle; Tues, Thurs, Fri & Sun 10am–6pm, Wed 1–9pm, Sat 11am–6pm; €6) has a wide art collection stretching from the Renaissance to the modern day, housed in a number of exceptionally beautiful buildings. The tangled, hilly lanes of Montpellier's old quarter lie behind the museum, and are full of seventeenth- and eighteenth-century mansions and small museums. The **Jardin des Plantes** (Tues–Sun noon–6/8pm; free), just north of the old town, with its alleys of exotic trees, is France's oldest botanical garden, founded in 1593. Opposite the gardens lies the **university quarter**, with its beautiful old buildings and lively café life.

Arrival and information

Air The airport is 8km to the west of Montpellier, by the beaches, connected to the city by *navettes* (€4.90, including one bus or tram connection in town).

Bus and train The bus and train stations are on the southern edge of town, a short walk down rue de Maguelone from the centre.

Internet Asnam, 15 rue des Ecoles-Laïques.

Tourist office The main branch, by place de la Comédie (Mon–Wed & Fri 9am–6.30pm, Thurs 10am–6.30pm, Sat 10am–6pm, Sun 10am–1pm & 2–5pm; ⓣ04.67.60.60.60, ⓦwww.ot-montpellier.fr) books accomodation and sells tickets for events; there's also a desk in the train station during July and August.

Accommodation

FUAJ Montpellier rue des Écoles-Laïques ⓣ04.67.60.32.22, ⓦwww.fuaj.org. Housed in a handsome building in the old town, this helpful hostel offers pretty standard FUAJ accommodation, and has a lounge with table football and a pool table. Closed noon–3pm. €15.90.

Les Étuves 24 rue des Étuves ⓣ04.67.60.78.19, ⓦwww.hoteldesetuves.fr. A small family run hotel, full of *belle époque* touches. The spotless, white rooms have en-suite showers or baths. €37.

Les Fauvettes 8 rue Bonnard ⓣ04.67.65.73.30, ⓔlesfauvettes4@wanadoo.fr. The cheapest hotel in town offers clean doubles with toilets,

MONTPELLIER MARKETS

"Allez-allez-allez!" is the call of Montpellier's stallholders in the many markets around the town. Here are three of the best: **Les Halles Jacques-Coeur** (Tues–Sat 8am–8pm, Sun 8am–2pm) opposite the tram on bd Antigone has quality home-made food; across the place, the **Marché Paysan** (Sun 9.30am–1.30pm) sells all local produce; **Plan-Cabanes**, at Faubourg du Courreau and Gambetta (daily 7.30am–1.30pm) is the most fun – here you can eat Arab and African cuisine for next to nothing.

situated in a peaceful little house beyond the Jardin des Plantes, 5min walk from the centre. €30.

Majestic 4 rue du Cheval Blanc ⓣ04.67.66.26.85, ⓔmajesticmontpellier@yahoo.fr. Though it hardly lives up to its name, this friendly hotel offers simple, surprisingly spacious rooms in a great position in the old town, close to the place de la Comédie. €40.

Eating and drinking

Bistrot d'Alco 4 rue Bonnier-d'Alco ⓣ04.67.63.12.89. This friendly restaurant serves rich, hearty dishes such as *confit de canard* and roast Camembert with sliced apple to dip in it; two courses €14.50, three courses €16.50.

Le Huit 8 rue de l'Aiguillerie. A retro-style bar popular with a student crowd, especially during happy hour (Mon 6pm–1am, Tues–Sun 6–9pm) when cocktails cost €5 and 50cl of beer is a bargain at €3.

Le St Roch 22 rue de St-Roch. A loud, busy little bar decorated with old advertising that's a great place to start off an evening, especially if you can get a seat on the square. Demi €2.50.

Le Wok 2 rue de l'Herberie. This little hole-in-the-wall serves up noodles and rice cooked to order, with your choice of meat, fish or veg and one of a number of sauces. From €6.90.

Tripti-Kulai 20 rue Jacques-Coeur ⓣ04.67.66.30.51. Don't be put off by the slightly hippy vibe of this casual vegetarian restaurant – the food is well prepared and very tasty. Try the fragrant cardamom and mango lassi (€3.20) and the excellent *savoyarde* (potatoes and vegetarian sausage baked in a creamy sauce with Reblochon cheese; €10).

Moving on

Train Avignon (12 daily; 1hr); Barcelona (4 daily, 2 via Port-Bou; 4hr 20min–7hr); Carcassonne (9 daily; 1hr 25min–1hr 45min); Marseille (10 daily; 1hr 30min–2hr 20min); Nîmes (frequent; 30min); Paris (12 daily; 3hr 30min); Perpignan (16 daily; 1hr 30min–2hr).

PERPIGNAN

This far south, climate and geography alone ensure a palpable Spanish influence, but **PERPIGNAN** is actually Spanish in origin and home to the descendants of refugees from the Spanish Civil War. It's a cheerful city, with Roussillon's red and yellow striped flag atop many a building, and makes an ideal stop-off en route to Spain or Andorra.

What to see and do

The centre of **Perpignan** is marked by the palm trees and smart cafés of **place Arago**. From here rue d'Alsace-Lorraine and rue de la Loge lead past the massive iron gates of the classical **Hôtel de Ville** to the tiny **place de la Loge**, the focus of the old heart of the city. Just north up rue Louis-Blanc is one of the city's few remaining fortifications, the crenellated fourteenth-century gate of **Le Castillet**, now home to the **Casa Païral**, a fascinating museum of Roussillon's Catalan folk culture (daily except Tues 10/11am–5.30/6.30pm; €4).

Arrival and information

Train The station is a 15min walk from the city centre.

Bus The bus station is by Pont Arago, on avenue du Général-Leclerc.

Tourist office In the Palais des Congrès at the end of boulevard Wilson (Mon–Sat 9am–6/7pm, Sun 9/10–1/4pm; ⓣ04.68.66.30.30, ⓦwww.perpignantourisme.com).

Accommodation

Camping Catalan rte de Bompas ⓣ04.68.63.16.92, ⓦwww.camping-catalan.com. A lively campsite 5km

COLLIOURE AND THE CÔTE VERMEILLE

The **Vermilion Coast** (Ⓦwww.collioure.com) is named for its richly coloured rocks, which attracted artists such as Picasso, Dalí and Matisse. The latter's 1905-06 paintings of Collioure saw the birth of Fauvism, the forerunner to Cubism. Aside from these colourful rocks, the coast is also home to some lovely beaches and charming fishing towns. Over ten trains a day run between Perpignan and Collioure (25min).

from the centre, with washing machines, a swimming pool and frequent pétanque competitions. Ask for shade as not all pitches have it. €18.50.

FUAJ Perpignan Parc de la Pépinière Ⓣ04.68.34.63.32, Ⓦwww.fuaj.org/perpignan. Badly situated as it backs onto a very busy major road, but convenient for the train station (5min). Dorms are bright but basic and meals are available. Closed from 10am–5pm. €15.20.

Hotel Alexander 15 bd Clemenceau Ⓣ04.68.35.41.41, Ⓦwww.hotel-alexander.fr. On the main road on the way into town from the station, this friendly hotel offers simple but cheerful rooms. €36.

Eating and drinking

Espi 43 quai Vauban. An excellent choice for breakfast or lunch, especially on sunny days when you can sit by the river. Their imaginative *plat du jour* is well-priced at €9.50 – follow it up with one or two of their delicious *macarons* (€1.20).

Le Petit Moka 9 place de la République. This popular café on a busy square is one of the more reasonable places to eat in Perpignan (*croque-monsieur* €4.80), and a good spot to while away the evening over a glass or two of sangria (€3).

Qu'on se le Dise 6 rue Grande des Fabriques. Cosy little café that specializes in sweet and savoury tarts – their well-priced lunch menu includes a savoury tart, salad and a dessert for €10.

Moving on

Train Barcelona (5 daily; 2hr 50min–5hr); Carcassonne (via Narbonne; 13–16 daily; 1hr 30min–2hr); Montpellier (16–20 daily; 1hr 30min–2hr); Paris (10–16 daily; 5hr–9hr 20min); Toulouse (16 daily; 1hr 30min–2hr).

Provence and the Côte d'Azur

Provence is held by many to be the most irresistible region in France, with attractions that range from the high mountains of the southern Alps to the wild plains of the **Camargue**. Though technically part of the neighbouring region of Languedoc, the old Roman town of **Nîmes** is a good place to start exploring, as is nearby **Arles**, most famous for van Gogh's paintings and a great place to indulge in the area's café culture. **Avignon**, home of a wonderful summer festival, is so crammed full of history that it can sometimes feel like a living museum, while just to the north lies Europe's best-preserved Roman theatre, in **Orange**. Most of the region's towns are full of cobbled streets lined with brightly coloured, shuttered buildings, which are a delight to explore, and none more so than **Aix-en-Provence.**

By contrast, **Marseille**, France's second city, still hasn't shaken off its gritty image. Yet it rewards a little exploration and is home to some of the area's finest food. It also makes a good base for exploring the stunning **Calanques**. The Côte d'Azur certainly lives up to its name – taking a train along the coast reveals sparkling turquoise sea, packed in many places with the glitzy yachts of the rich and famous. **Nice** has all the trappings of a jet-set lifestyle, yet it feels a little more down-to-earth than nearby **Cannes**, and makes a great base for exploring small villages in the hills and other seaside towns.

NÎMES

NÎMES is intrinsically linked to two things: ancient Rome – whose influence is manifest in some of the most extensive

PONT DU GARD

This stunning vestige of the 50km aqueduct built in the first century AD to carry spring water from Uzès to Nîmes is a poignant memorial to the hubris of Roman civilization. It sits peacefully in the valley of the Gardon river, and is a great place to cool off on hot summer days. Tours are run from the informative museum on the left side of the valley; to get there, take a bus from Nîmes to Uzès, where six *navettes* run to the Pont each day; bring a swimsuit, walking shoes and a picnic. ⓦwww.ot-pontdugard.com.

Roman remains in Europe – and denim, a word corrupted from *de Nîmes*. First manufactured as *serge* in the city's textile mills, denim was exported to America to clothe workers, where a certain Mr Levi Strauss made it world famous. These days, the town has a relaxed charm, and with an excellent hostel makes for a good place to relax for a few days.

What to see and do

The old centre of Nîmes spreads northwards from place des Arènes, site of the magnificent first-century **Les Arènes** (daily 9/9.30am–5/6/7pm; €7.70), one of the best-preserved Roman arenas in the world. Turned into a fortress by the Visigoths while the Roman Empire crumbled, the arena went on to became a huge medieval slum before it was fully restored. Now, with a retractable roof, it hosts opera, an international summer jazz festival and bullflights during the high-spirited Ferías on Pentecost and the third weekend of September. Another Roman survivor can be found northeast along boulevard Victor Hugo – the **Maison Carrée** (daily: April–Sept 10am–6.30/7pm; Oct–March 10am–4.30/6pm; €4.50), a compact temple built in 5 AD and celebrated for its harmony of proportion – the entrance price includes a 3D film about Roman Nîmes.

Arrival and information

Air The airport is 8km to the south, accessible by navettes leaving from av Feuchères, in front of the station.

Bus and train Nîmes' bus and train stations are at the end of av Feuchères, just a few minutes' walk southeast from the amphitheatre. Regional buses leave from bays situated out the back.

Internet Netgames, place de la Maison Carrée.

Tourist office 6 rue Auguste, by the Maison Carrée (Mon–Sat 8.30/9am–6.30/7/8pm, Sun 10am–5/6pm; ⓣ04.66.58.38.00, ⓦwww.ot-nimes.fr); buy the monument and museum pass (€9.80) here, which gives access to the town's attractions for three days.

Accommodation

Cat 22 bd Amiral-Courbet ⓣ04.66.67.22.85. A charming, friendly hotel in an excellent position. Rooms are surprisingly big and some have views of a sweet little courtyard. €32.

Central 2 place du Château ⓣ04.66.67.22.85, ⓦwww.hotel-central.org. A simple, central hotel that looks grander than it actually is. Rooms have fans and wi-fi. €45.

FUAJ Nîmes 257 chemin de l'Auberge de Jeunesse, Cigale ⓣ04.66.68.03.20, ⓦwww.fuaj.org. Set in a beautiful arboretum, in the hills 2km west of Nîmes, this friendly hostel offers modern two-, four- or six-bed dorms. There's a great bar on-site serving cheap drinks, as well as good kitchen facilities and bike hire. Take bus #I from the station to Stade. €12.60.

Eating and drinking

Café Latin 29 place de la Maison Carrée. Popular place throughout the day, with a fantastic, sunny terrace on which to sit out and enjoy a drink or leisurely lunch (*croque-monsieur* €3).

Le Pavillon de la Fontaine 9 quai Georges Clemenceau. Beautifully situated in the Jardins de la Fontaine, this is an idyllic spot for lunch, though you pay extra for the location. Lunch menu €12.50, glass of wine €2.50.

Mezzo di Pasta 38 rue de la Madeleine. A good choice for a quick, filling lunch, serving cheap, tasty pasta with a range of sauces (from €4.80).

Mogador 2 place du Marché. A cheap and friendly café, with a terrace on the square that catches the afternoon sun. Serves tasty savoury tarts and other French dishes; *plat du jour* €9.

Moving on

Train Arles (6 daily; 25min); Avignon (16 daily; 30min); Clermont-Ferrand (3 daily; 5hr); Lyon (9 daily; 1hr 20min); Marseille (14 daily; 50min–1hr 20min); Montpellier (frequent; 30min); Nice (6 daily, via Marseille; 4–5hr); Paris (11 daily; 3hr); Perpignan (13 daily; 2hr 10min–2hr 40min).

ARLES

ARLES is a lovely, relaxed little Provençal town, steeped in Roman history. In 1888, Vincent Van Gogh was drawn in by the picturesque town, where he painted *Starry Night* and *Night Café*, but also got into a drunken argument with Gauguin and cut off the lower part of his left ear. Today, Arles is the centre of French photography as home to the École Nationale de Photographie and host to the summer photographic **festival**, Les Rencontres (July to mid-Sept; ⓦwww.rencontres-arles.com).

What to see and do

Around the Amphitheatre

The focal point for tourists in Arles is the striking **amphitheatre**, at the end of rue Voltaire (daily: March–Oct 9am–6/7pm, Nov–Feb 10am–5pm; €6), built at the end of the first century. The surrounding Rond-Point des Arènes is crammed full of touristy shops, cafés and restaurants, and can get very crowded on summer days. No original Van Gogh paintings remain in Arles, but the **Fondation Van Gogh**, 24 Rond-Point des Arènes (April–Sept daily 10–7pm; Oct–March Tues–Sun 11am–5pm; €6), exhibits works based on his masterpieces by well-known contemporary artists, such as Hockney and Bacon. From here, it's a short walk down some atmospheric side streets to the place de la République and the **Cathédrale St-Trophime**, whose doorway is one of the most famous examples of twelfth-century Provençal carving, depicting a Last Judgement trumpeted by rather enthusiastic angels.

> **VAN GOGH'S ARLES**
>
> The tourist office (see below) issues a good booklet of themed **walking tours** in Arles (€1). The best of these is the Van Gogh trail which, by following various markers on the pavements, takes you to the sites of his most famous paintings – it's fascinating to see how the town has changed since he was here.

Cirque Romain

The best insight into Roman Arles can be found at the **Musée de l'Arles Antique** (daily April–Sept 9am–7pm, Oct 10am–6pm, Nov–March 11am–5pm; €5.50), west of the town centre, by the river. The fabulous mosaics, sarcophagi and sculpture illuminate Arles' early history.

Place Constantin

Housed in a splendid medieval building once used by the Knights of the Order of Malta, the **Musée Réattu** (Tues–Sun March–Sept 10am–7pm; Oct–Feb 10am–12.30pm & 2–6.30pm; €7) hosts a fine collection of modern art, including sketches and sculptures by Picasso. Opposite are the remains of the fourth-century **Roman baths** (daily: May–Sept 9am–midday & 2–7pm; Oct–April 9am–midday & 2–6pm; €3).

Arrival and information

Train The train station is 5min walk from the amphitheatre on avenue Paulin.

Tourist office Opposite rue Jean Jaurès on bd des Lices (April–Sept daily 9am–5.45/6.45pm; Oct–March Mon–Sat 9am–4.45/5.45pm, Sun 10am–2.15pm; ⓣ04.90.18.41.20, ⓦwww.tourisme.ville-arles.fr), and provides a hotel booking service. There's also a handy tourist office in the station (daily 9am–6.45pm).

Internet Cyber City, 41 rue du 4 Septembre.

Accommodation

De Paris 8 rue de la Cavalerie ⓣ04.90.96.05.88. Large, simple rooms, all with shower, just inside the city walls. Some have an additional sitting area overlooking the street. €32.

TREAT YOURSELF

Le Calendal Hotel 5 rue Porte de Laure ⓣ04.90.96.11.89, ⓦwww.lecalendal.com. Mere steps from the amphitheatre, this sunny hotel is a great choice if you feel like splashing out. Rooms are bright and decorated in traditional Provencal colours without being twee; all are en suite, with air-conditioning and satellite television. The real selling point is the gorgeous garden at the back, the perfect place to enjoy a leisurely drink at the end of a hot day. €119.

FUAJ Arles 20 av du Maréchal-Foch ⓣ04.90.96.18.25, ⓦwww.fuaj.org. The dorms are somewhat old-fashioned, but clean and airy, and there's a small bar on site. Often gets overrun with noisy school kids, but the location is good – just 5min from the centre of town and 15min walk from the train station. Closed 10am–5pm. €16.10.

Le Voltaire 1 place Voltaire ⓣ04.90.96.49.18, ⓔlevoltaire13@aol.com. Sweet, basic little rooms above a bar-restaurant, with balconies that look onto the place. €28.

Eating and drinking

Bar le Baroque 4 bd Georges Clemenceau. Sink into one of the cosy armchairs in this modern café, which serves three variations of lasagne (salmon and spinach; aubergine; bolognese; €8), best washed down with a glass of wine (€8).

Bistrot Arlésien place du Forum. One of many rather touristy cafés on this sunny place, with a good terrace to enjoy a glass of wine on (€3). They have a decently priced lunch menu (€13.50), though the food is a little uninspired and the service surly.

Chez Néné et Bébé 12 impasses du Forum. Tucked away off busy place du Forum, with a friendly, chatty owner and a constant stream of locals popping in for a drink. The pizzas (all €10) are excellent and drinks are very reasonably priced (pastis €2, wine €2) – a great place to finish the day.

Comptoir du Sud 2 rue Jean-Jaurès. A lovely little *épicerie* selling local produce and a tasty selection of sandwiches to take away or eat in (from €2.30). Mon–Sat 10am–6pm.

Moving on

Train Avignon (11–16 daily; 20min–1hr); Lyon (7–9 daily; 2hr 20min–2hr 55min); Marseille (15–20 daily; 45min–1hr); Montpellier (15–20 daily; 55min); Nîmes (8–11 daily; 25min).

THE CAMARGUE

The flat, marshy delta immediately south of Arles – **the Camargue** – is a beautiful area, used as a breeding-ground for the bulls that participate in local corridas (bullfights), and the white horses ridden by their herdsmen. The wildlife of the area also includes flamingos, marsh-birds and seabirds, and a rich flora of reeds, wild flowers and juniper trees. The only town is **SAINTES-MARIES-DE-LA-MER**, best known for the annual Gypsy Festival held each May, and which is linked by a regular bus service to Arles (5–7 daily from bd Georges Clemenceau; 1hr; €5.20). It's a pleasant, if touristy place, with some fine sandy beaches. If you're interested in birdwatching or touring the lagoons, your first port of call should be the **tourist office** on 5 av Van Gogh (daily: July & Aug 9am–8pm; Sept–June 9am–5/7pm; ⓣ04.90.97.82.55, ⓦwww.saintesmaries.com), which can tell you where to rent bicycles, horses or 4x4s, if you prefer to explore the delta alone. There's a **hostel** in the hamlet of Pioch-Badet, 10km north of Stes-Maries and on the bus route from Arles (ⓣ04.90.97.51.72, ⓦwww.auberge-de-jeunesse.camargue.fr; closed 10.30am–5pm; €29.70 half-board) – accommodation is in simple three-to ten-bed dorms, and they can arrange bike rental, horse riding and boat trips. Note that reservations are obligatory.

AVIGNON

AVIGNON, great city of the popes and for centuries one of the major artistic centres of France, is today one of the country's biggest tourist attractions and is always crowded in summer. It's worth putting up with the inevitable queues and camera-wielding hordes to enjoy the unique stock of monuments, churches and museums of this immaculately preserved medieval town. During

the **Avignon festival** in July, it's the only place to be – around 200,000 spectators come here for the show, though, so doing any normal sightseeing becomes virtually impossible.

What to see and do

Central Avignon is enclosed by thick medieval walls, built by one of the nine popes who based themselves here in the fourteenth century, away from the anarchic feuding and rival popes of Rome. Place de l'Horloge is lined with cafés and market stalls on summer evenings, beyond which towers the enormous **Palais des Papes** (daily: March–June 9.30am–7pm; July & Aug 9am–8/9pm; Sept & Oct 9am–7pm; Nov–Feb 9.30am–5.45pm; €10.50, joint ticket with Pont St-Bénézet €13). Save your money though: the denuded interior gives little indication of the richness of the papal court, although the building is impressive for sheer size alone. The nearby **Musée du Petit Palais** (daily except Tues 9.30/10am–1pm & 2–5.30/6pm; €6) houses a collection of religious art from the thirteenth to sixteenth centuries. Jutting out halfway across the river is the famous **Pont St-Bénézet** (also known as Pont d'Avignon; same hours as Palais des Papes; €4.50). The struggle to keep the bridge in good repair against the ravages of the Rhône was finally abandoned in 1660, three-and-a-half centuries after it was built, and today just four of the original 22 arches survive.

AVIGNON FESTIVAL

During Avignon's three-week July **festival** (Ⓣ04.90.27.66.50, Ⓦwww.festival-avignon.com), over one hundred venues show multiple plays every day, alongside opera, classical music and film. The most popular aspect of the festival is probably the **street performers** – musicians, magicians, dancers, jugglers, clowns, artists and mime acts – which bring great colour and noise to the city. Make sure you book your hotel early.

Arrival and information

Train Avignon's main train station is opposite the porte de la République on bd St-Roch, just 5min from the central place de l'Horloge. A regular shuttle bus runs to the separate TGV station, 3km to the southeast, from just inside porte de la République (2–4 hourly; 13min; €1.20).

Tourist office 41 cours Jean-Jaurès (April–Oct Mon–Sat 9am–6pm, Sun 10am–5pm; Nov–March Mon–Fri 9am–6pm, Sat 9am–5pm, Sun 10am–noon; Ⓣ04.32.74.32.74, Ⓦwww.avignon-tourisme.com); accommodation booking service and English language tours.

Internet Cabine, 15 rue de Florence.

Accommodation

Bagatelle 25 allée Antoine-Pinay Ⓣ04.90.86.30.39 (camping), Ⓣ04.90.86.71.31 (hostel), Ⓦwww.campingbagatelle.com. Well located on Île de la Barthelasse, just 20min walk from the station, this is the nearest campsite to town. It also has a busy hostel with clean but small dorms and a handful of private rooms. There's a bar and restaurant on site, but they have the feel of a rather old-fashioned holiday camp. Camping €10; dorm €16.50.

Innova 100 rue Joseph Vernet Ⓣ04.90.82.54.10, Ⓦwww.hotel-innova.fr. This family-run hotel offers small, clean and sound-proofed rooms. A good price for the centre. €58.

Mignon 12 rue Joseph Vernet Ⓣ04.90.82.17.30, Ⓦwww.hotel-mignon.com. This little hotel has rooms decked out in Provencal colours, all with satellite TV, a/c and wi-fi. Breakfast is included in the price and can be enjoyed in your room for no extra charge. €66.

Monclar 13–15 av Monclar Ⓣ04.90.86.20.14, Ⓦwww.hotel-monclar.com. An attractive eighteenth-century house with a pleasant garden, situated outside the town walls, close to the train station. Rooms are clean and bright and there is free internet access. €30.

Eating

Au Tout Petit 4 rue d'Amphoux Ⓣ04.90.82.38.86. This gem of a restaurant is so small that the chef is also the waiter. The truly creative fusion cuisine includes snail ravioli in a basil cream and *cassolette* of mussels, almonds

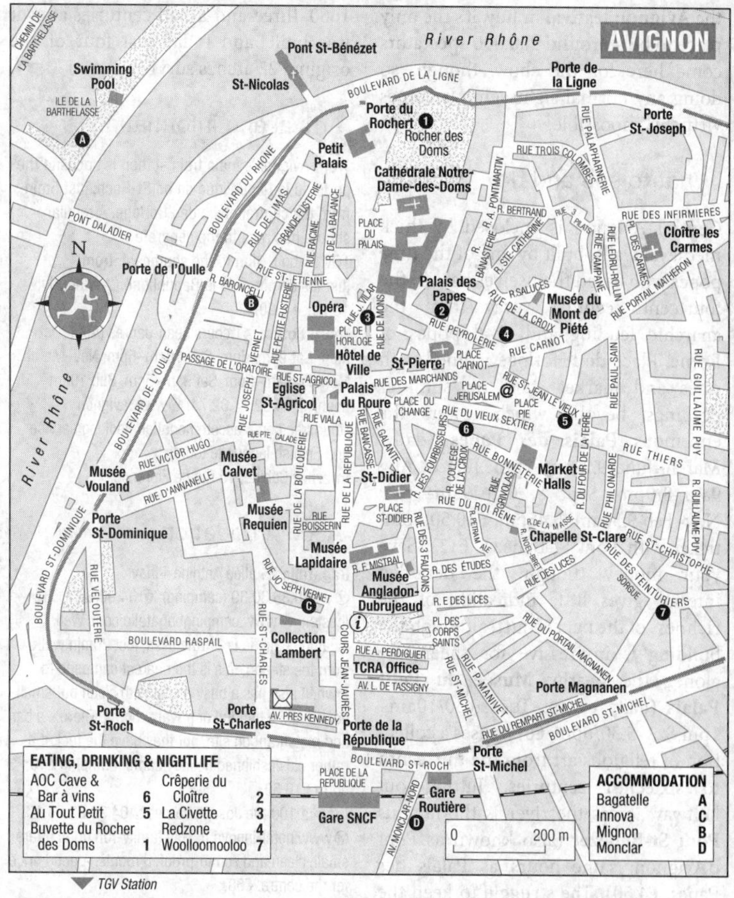

and prawns with galangal. Two-course lunch menu €11, two-course dinner €16.

Buvette du Rocher des Doms Rocher des Doms. This little café is situated beside a peaceful duck pond in the lovely park behind the Palais des Papes. The delicious sandwiches are very reasonably priced (from €4), especially considering the location, and they also do more substantial meals (from €10).

Crêperie du Cloître 9 place du Cloître Saint-Pierre. Tucked away in a peaceful square behind St-Pierre, this is a lovely spot to enjoy generously filled sweet and savoury crêpes (from €5.90).

Woolloomooloo 16bis rue des Teintures ⓣ04.90.85.28.44. World food and drink, served in atmospheric, quirky surroundings. Dishes include chicken tajine with prunes and honey, crab-stuffed Caribbean squash and a delicious gingerbread cake with cherries. Midday two-course menu €15, evening menu €23.

Drinking and nightlife

AOC Cave & Bar à vins 5 rue Trémoulet ⓣ04.90.25.21.04. Friendly, English-speaking Christophe will guide you through his selection of over 150 wines, much of which is the local Côtes du Rhône. Prices start from €2 a glass. Tues–Fri noon–2pm & 6pm–1am, Sat 6pm–1am.

La Civette place de l'Horloge. There are many touristy brasseries on the square; this one, facing the opera, is one of the best and a great place for a drink and some people-watching. Pastis €2.10, glass of wine €2.50.

Redzone 25 rue Carnot. Popular club, with a good range of theme nights, from salsa to electro and hip-hop. Open till 3am; free entry.

Moving on

Gare SNCF Arles (frequent; 20–40min); Lyon (10 daily; 2hr 20min); Nîmes (15 daily; 20–40min); Toulouse (11 daily, 8 via Nîmes or Montpellier; 3hr 10min–4hr 30min).

Gare TGV Lyon (2 hourly; 1hr 5min–1hr 30min); Nice (12 daily; 3hr–4hr 10min); Paris (15 daily; 2hr 40min–3hr 30min).

AIX-EN-PROVENCE

For many visitors, **AIX-EN-PROVENCE** is the ideal Provencal city, the cobbled streets of its old town still retaining the romance of days past, especially when lit by the sun. The city has a (not entirely unfair) reputation for snobbishness, but it is still a relaxed and enjoyable place, where the greatest pleasure is in winding through the streets and relaxing in a shady place over a *pastis*.

What to see and do

Aix's old town stretches back from the leafy expanse of cours Mirabeau, and it's easy to spend a few hours just exploring the atmospheric streets, which are dotted with interesting shops and cafés. The only museum worth heading to is the **Musée Granet** (daily 11am/noon–6/7pm; €4), whose permanent collection includes some minor works by the town's most famous painter, Paul Cézanne, and a number of archeological finds from the region; it's the interesting and often inventive temporary exhibitions, however, that make a visit worthwhile. To find out more about Cézanne, you can visit the **Atelier Cézanne** (daily: July & Aug 10am–6pm; Sept–June 10am–noon & 2–5/6pm; €5.50), his studio, which looks exactly the same as it did at the time of his death. To get there, catch bus #1 from la Rotondo to stop Paul Cézanne.

Arrival and information

Train The *gare SNCF* is located on rue Gustavo-Desplace, just 5min southwest of the old town. It's more likely that you'll arrive at the gare TGV, 13km southwest of Aix and linked by regular *navette* (every 20min; 15min; €3.80) to the *gare routière* on av de l'Europe.

Tourist office 2 place du Général de Gaulle (June–Sept daily 8.30am–8/9pm; Oct–May Mon–Sat 8.30am–7pm, Sun 10am–1pm & 2–6pm; ⓣ04.42.16.11.61, ⓦwww.aixenprovencetourism.com). Offers a hotel booking service and arranges tours to Cézanne's home (€5.50).

Internet Point Com, 6 rue Gaston de Saporta.

Accommodation

Des Arts 69 bd Carnot ⓣ04.42.38.11.77, ⓔhotelaix@yahoo.fr. Very small rooms with attached (but tiny) bathrooms, situated at the edge of the old town. Breakfast (€5) is expensive for what you get, but you can't get cheaper than this in this part of town. €42.

FUAJ Aix-en-Provence 3 av Marcel Pagnol ⓣ04.42.20.15.99, ⓦwww.fuaj.org. Situated 2km out of the city in a residential area, this hostel offers modern dorms, a bar and laundry facilties, but don't expect service with a smile. To get here, take bus #4 from the *gare routière* to Vasarely. Closed 1–5pm. €17.30.

Le Manoir 8 rue d'Entrecasteaux ⓣ04.42.26.27.20, ⓦwww.hotelmanoir.com. A charming hotel, tucked away in the old town, with lovely rooms that have an olde-worlde feel without being fusty. Some look onto a courtyard, and all have good-sized bathrooms. Breakfast is served in the fourteenth-century cloister. €62.

Eating and drinking

Brasserie de la Mairie 2 rue Vauvenargues. A great place to sit out in the sun and people watch, right by the Hotel de Ville. Especially lively in early evening. *Pastis* €2.50.

Le Crep Sautière 18 rue Bedarrides. A fantastic range of delicious crêpes (from €6) are on offer in this busy little restaurant.

Le Passage 10 rue Villars ⓣ04.42.37.09.00. An excellent restaurant which, although a bit pricey for dinner, offers a good-value lunch menu (€13) which includes the region's famous mesclun salad and chicken brochettes.

Moving on

Gare SNCF Marseille (every 30min; 30–45min).

Gare TGV Avignon TGV (17 daily; 20min); Lyon (10 daily; 1hr 30min); Marseille (frequent; 15min); Paris (8 daily; 3hr).

MARSEILLE

France's second most populous city, **MARSEILLE** has been a major centre of international maritime trade ever since it was founded by Greek colonists 2600 years ago. Like the capital, the city has suffered plagues, religious bigotry, republican and royalist terror, had its own Commune and Bastille-storming, and it was the presence of so many revolutionaries from this city marching to Paris in 1792 that gave the name Marseillaise to the national anthem. A working city with little of the glamour of its ritzy Riviera neighbours, it is nevertheless a vibrant, exciting place, with a cosmopolitan population including many Italians and North Africans.

What to see and do

The old harbour, or **Vieux Port**, is the hub of the town and a good place to indulge in the sedentary pleasure of observing the city's streetlife over a *pastis*. Two fortresses guard the entrance to the harbour and the town extends outwards alongside the harbour from its three quais.

Le Panier

On the northern side of the harbour is the original site and former old town of Marseille, known as **Le Panier**. During the occupation, large sections were dynamited by the Nazis to prevent resistance members hiding in the small, densely populated streets, which in turn prompted a mass deportation of residents from the northern docks. Rebuilt and repopulated in the 1950s, today's Le Panier is full of a young, fashionable and bohemian working-class. The quarter's main attraction is La Vieille Charité, a Baroque seventeenth-century church and hospice complex, on rue de la Charité, now home to several museums, including the **Musée d'Archéologie Méditerranéenne** (Tues–Sun 10/11am–5/6pm; €2), housing a superb collection of Egyptian mummified animals.

La Canebière

Leading east from the Vieux Port is La Canebière, Marseille's main street. Just off the lower end, in the Centre Bourse shopping mall, is a museum of finds from Roman Marseille, the **Musée d'Histoire de Marseille** (Mon–Sat noon–7pm; €2), which includes the well-preserved remains of a third-century Roman merchant vessel. South of La Canebière are Marseille's main shopping streets, rue Paradis, rue St-Ferréol and rue de Rome, and the **Musée Cantini**, 19 rue Grignan (Tues–Sun 10/11am–5/6pm; €2), which houses a fine collection of twentieth-century art with works by Dufy, Léger and Picasso.

South of the Vieux Port

A little further west is the **Abbaye St-Victor** (daily 8.30am–6.30pm; free), the city's oldest church. It looks and feels like a fortress – the walls of the choir are almost 3m thick. Dominating the skyline to the south, astride a rocky hill, is the marble and porphyry basilica of Marseille's most famous landmark, the cathedral of **Notre-Dame de la Garde** (daily 7am–7/8pm; free). Crowning the high belfry, and visible across most of the city is a 9m gilded statue of the Virgin Mary, known locally as the *Bonne Mère* (Good Mother). Inside are beautiful mosaics and shrines covered in ex-votos – trinkets, plaques, paintings and, more recently, football shirts – offered to the Saints for good luck.

LE CORBUSIER

If you're interested in architecture, it's definitely worth taking the short bus journey out to Le Corbusier's **Unité d'Habitation.** Completed in 1952, this seventeen-storey block of flats is surprisingly striking even today, and you can take the lift up to the rooftop to enjoy fantastic views of the city and the surrounding area. To get here, take bus #21 from Centre Bourse to Le Corbusier.

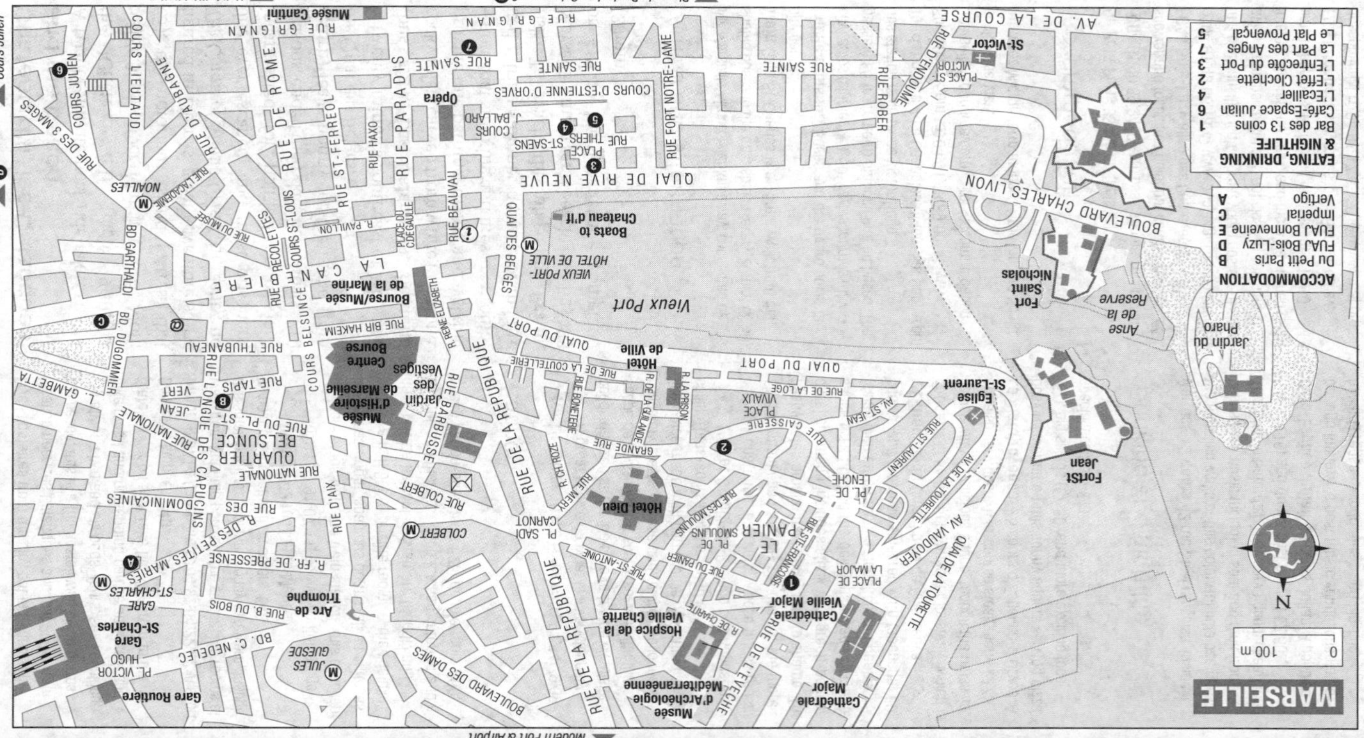
MARSEILLE
0
100 m
N
ACCOMMODATION
Du Petit Paris B
FUAJ Bois-Luzy D
FUAJ Bonneveine E
Imperial C
Vertigo A
EATING, DRINKING & NIGHTLIFE
Bar des 13 coins 1
Café-Espace Julian 6
L'Ecailler 4
L'Effet Clochette 2
L'Entrecôte du Port 3
La Part des Anges 7
Le Plat Provençal 5
Cours Julien
Unité d'Habitation
Plage du Prado, Les Calanques & E
Modern Port & Airport
Vieux Port
Boats to Chateau d'If
VIEUX PORT-HÔTEL DE VILLE
Fort Saint Nicholas
FortSt Jean
Anse de la Reserve
Jardin du Pharo
Eglise St-Laurent
Hôtel de Ville
Hôtel Dieu
Cathédrale Major
Cathédrale Vieille Major
Musée d'Archéologie Méditerranéenne
Hospice de la Vieille Charité
Arc de Triomphe
Gare St-Charles
Gare Routière
Musée d'Histoire de Marseille
Jardin des Vestiges
Centre Bourse
Bourse/Musée de la Marine
Opéra
Musée Cantini
St-Victor
LE PANIER
QUARTIER BELSUNCE
LA CANEBIERE
QUAI DU PORT
QUAI DE RIVE NEUVE
BOULEVARD CHARLES LIVON
RUE DE LA REPUBLIQUE
RUE PARADIS
RUE DE ROME
RUE ST-FERREOL
COURS BELSUNCE
COURS ST-LOUIS
RUE D'AUBAGNE
COURS JULIEN
COURS LIEUTAUD
RUE SAINTE
RUE GRIGNAN
AV. DE LA COURSE
BOULEVARD DES DAMES
QUAI DE LA TOURETTE
AV. VAUDOYER
COLBERT
NOAILLES
JULES GUESDE
GARE ST-CHARLES

Chateau d'If, les Calanques and the beach

A twenty-minute boat ride takes you to the **Château d'If** (daily 9.30am–5.30/6.30pm; Oct–March closed Mon; €5), the notorious island fortress that figured in Dumas' great adventure story, *The Count of Monte Cristo*. In reality, no one ever escaped, and most prisoners, incarcerated for political or religious reasons, ended their days here. Boats (€10 return) leave hourly for the island from the Quai des Belges.

Twenty minutes southeast of Marseille (bus #21), **Les Calanques**, beautiful rocky inlets carved from white limestone, provide fine bathing, diving and walking – note that smoking and fires are prohibited during summer because of the fire risk. To reach the **plage du Prado**, Marseille's main sand beach, take bus #83 or #19 to the Promenade Pompidou (20min).

Arrival and information

Air Marseille Airport is 25km away, connected by shuttle buses to the train station (every 20min; €8.50).
Train Gare St-Charles is a 15min walk from the city centre.
Public transport Buses and the métro cover the city: *solos* (singles) €1.50, *cartes journée* (day passes) €5 from métro stations and on buses. The bus station is on place Victor Hugo.
Tourist office 4 La Canebière (Mon–Sat 9am–7pm, Sun 10am–5pm; ⓣ04.91.13.89.00, ⓦwww.marseille-tourisme.com). Free accommodation booking service.
Internet Microinformatique, 31 rue Vincent Scotto.

Accommodation

Du Petit Paris 33 rue du Tapis Vert ⓣ04.91.90.89.94. Clean, basic rooms, most with shower and toilet, in a quiet but central location. €50.
FUAJ Bois-Luzy allée des Primevères ⓣ04.91.49.06.18, ⓦwww.fuaj.org. Though situated in a château, this isn't a great youth hostel – it's 4km away from the centre and not close to anything of interest. Rooms are basic and there's a kitchen and small shop on-site. Closed noon–5pm. €12.10.
FUAJ Bonneveine impasse Dr Bonfils, off av Joseph Vidal ⓣ04.91.17.63.30, ⓦwww.fuaj.org. Five kilometres from the city, but in a fantastic location near Les Calanques and just 200m from the beach, this is a fun hostel, with clean dorms of between two and six beds. Tours, sea kayaking, bike rental and horseriding can be arranged, and there's a bar on site. Take bus #44 from to the Bonnefon stop. €17.40.
Imperial 87 La Canebière ⓣ04.91.64.22.22. A short walk from both the port and the station, the rooms at this small hotel are looking slightly careworn, though some are a lot better than others. €42.
Vertigo 42 rue Petits Mariés ⓣ04.91.91.07.11, ⓦwww.hotelvertigo.fr. Mere steps from the train station, this excellent hostel has bright, spacious dorms, all en suite, as well as a number of private rooms – the "deluxe" have private balconies. Staff are friendly and helpful, and there's a good kitchen, internet and a cheap bar on-site. Dorm €25, double room €60.

Eating

L'Ecailler 10 rue Fortia ⓣ04.91.54.79.39. A great choice on what is a very touristy pedestrianized street. Be sure to try the exquisite *soupe de poissons* (fish soup), served with the obligatory toasts, cheese and *rouille* (mayonnaise-like sauce made with garlic, olive oil, saffron and chilli). Three-course dinner menu €15.
L'Effet Clochette 2 place des Augustins. A charming, tiny café, whose prices (*pastis* €1.80), quality and friendly service put the more flashy cafés around the nearby port to shame. The excellent menu includes steak with green-pepper sauce (€12.50) and the delicious *salade clochette* (salad with cured ham, artichokes, red pepper, cheese and croutons smeared with tapenade; €9).
L'Entrecôte du Port 6 quai de Rive Neuve ⓣ04.91.33.84.84. Renowned for its steak, which is served with a delicious sauce, though the mussels are also very good. Two-course steak menu €17.
Le Plat Provençal 26 cours d'Estienne-d'Orves. A busy restaurant on this sunny square serving pizza (€7), big salads (€7.50) and more exciting local specialities from €11.

Drinking and nightlife

Bar des 13 coins 42 rue Ste-Françoise. Inside the muralled walls of this colourful little bar, guest bands play music including soul and funk from Thursday to Saturday. They serve good, cheap food (under €10) and drinks cost around €2.50.
Café-Espace Julian 39 cours Julian. A popular bar and the town's best music venue, orientated towards reggae, world music and hip-hop.

La Part des Anges 33 rue Sainte. A cosy wine bar with a very good cellar (glass of wine €2) a relaxed atmosphere. The food is good but pricey (from €17).

Moving on

Ferry Ajaccio (10 weekly; 10–12hr); Bastia (10 weekly; 10–12hr).
Train Arles (frequent; 40min–1hr); Avignon (12–15 daily; 1hr 10min); Cannes (15 daily; 2hr); Lyon (8–12 daily; 1hr 40–3hr 30min); Montpellier (18–23 daily; 1hr 30min–3hr); Nice (15 daily; 2hr 20min–2hr 45min).

CANNES

Fishing village turned millionaires' playground, **CANNES** is best known for the International Film Festival, held in May, during which time it is overrun by the denizens of Movieland, their hangers-on, and a small army of paparazzi. The seafront promenade, **La Croisette**, and the Vieux Port form the focus of Cannes' eye-candy life, while the old town, **Le Suquet**, on the steep hill overlooking the bay from the west, with its quaint winding streets and eleventh-century castle, is a pleasant place to wander.

Arrival and information

Train The station is on rue Jean-Jaurès, a short walk north of the centre along rue des Serbes.
Tourist office The main office is in the Palais des Festivals on the waterfront and there is also a booth at the station (both Mon–Sat 9am–7pm; ⓣ04.93.39.24.53, ⓦwww.cannes.fr).
Internet Cap Cyber, 12 rue du 14 Août.

Accommodation

Albe 31 rue du Bivouac Napoléon ⓣ04.97.06.21.21, ⓦwww.albe-hotel.com. A good-value two-star with bright and clean rooms with a/c, just one street from the Palais and the beach. €60.
Parc Bellevue 67 av Maurice Chevalier ⓣ04.93.47.28.97, ⓦwww.parcbellevue.com. The nearest campsite is in the suburb of La Bocca, 3km to the west of Cannes; most plots are shaded and there is a 40m pool. Take bus #2 from the train station. €20.
PLM 3 rue Hoche ⓣ04.93.38.31.19, ⓦwww.hotel-cannes-plm.com. A comfortable little hotel in a good location close to the station and a short walk from the beachfront. Rooms are decorated in soothing, neutral colours and there's free wi-fi. €68.

Eating and drinking

Ernest 52 rue Meynadier. Indulge your sweet tooth with a delicious patisserie (éclairs €3.50), or choose from an array of savoury treats. Closed Mon.
La Crêperie 66 rue Meynadier. Cheerful little crêperie with a good-value menu that is served all day (a savoury and a sweet crêpe, plus a glass of cider or wine; €10.50).
Palais Club ⓦwww.palais-club.com. The grand venue for the film awards becomes a huge indoor and outdoor club in July and Aug, with an impressive international DJ line-up. Out of season it plays host to a variety of live bands. Entry from €10.
Zanzibar 85 rue Félix-Faure. One of the oldest gay bars in France, this wood-panelled spot is fun and also hetero-friendly.

Moving on

Train Marseille (frequent; 2hr–2hr 20min); Monaco (frequent; 1hr–1hr 10min); Nice (frequent; 25–40min).

NICE

NICE, capital of the French Riviera and France's fifth-largest city, grew into a major tourist resort in the nineteenth century, when large numbers of foreign visitors – many of them British – were drawn here by the mild Mediterranean climate. The most obvious legacy of these early holidaymakers is the famous **promenade des Anglais** stretching along the pebble beach, which was laid out by nineteenth-century English residents to facilitate their afternoon stroll by the sea. These days, Nice is a busy, bustling city, but it's still a lovely place, with a beautiful location and attractive historical centre.

What to see and do

Vieux Nice and La Plage

The old town, a rambling collection of narrow alleys lined with tall, rust-and-ochre houses, centres on place

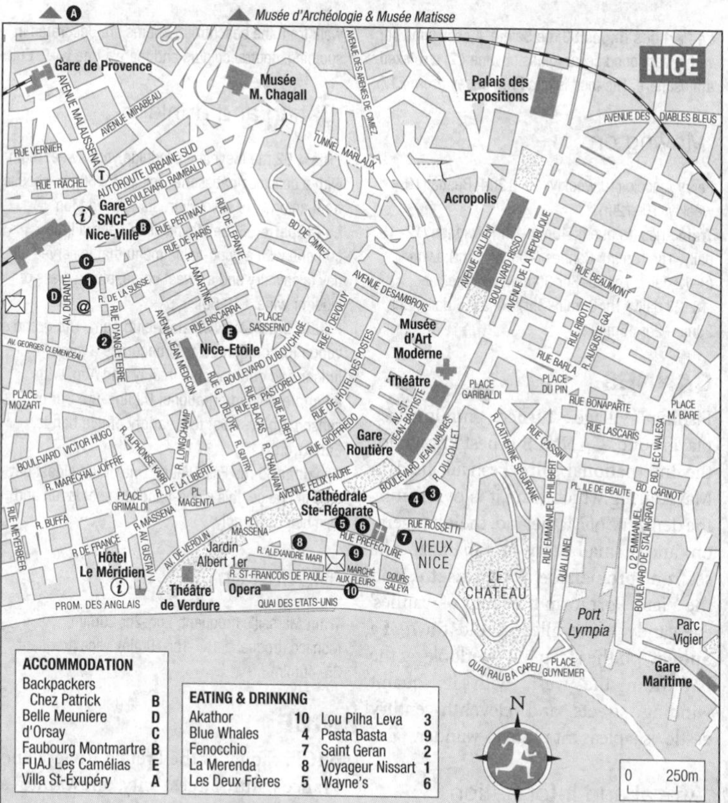

Rossetti and the Baroque **Cathédrale Ste-Réparate**. It's worth making the nearby Parc du Château one of your first stops to take in the view, which stretches across the town and west over the bay. It's a steep walk up, or there's a lift, tucked just under the stairs (€2) on the western side. A short walk north through the old town takes you to the promenade des Arts, where the **Musée d'Art Moderne et d'Art Contemporain** (daily except Tues 10am– 6pm; free) has a collection of Pop Art and neo-Realist work, including pieces by Andy Warhol and Roy Lichtenstein.

Cimiez

Up above the city centre is Cimiez, a posh suburb that was the social centre of the town's elite some seventeen centuries ago, when the city was capital of the Roman province of Alpes-Maritimae. To get here, take bus #15 from in front of the train station. The **Musée d'Archéologie,** 160 av des Arènes (daily except Tues 10am–6pm; free) houses excavations of the Roman baths, along with accompanying archeological finds. Overlooking the museum is the wonderful **Musée Matisse** (daily except Tues 10am–6pm; €4): Nice was the artist's home for much of his life and the collection covers every period. Nearby, the beautiful **Musée Chagall**, 16 av du Docteur-Ménard (daily except Tues 10am–5/6pm; €9.50), exhibits dazzlingly colourful Biblical paintings, stained glass and book illustrations.

Arrival, information and city transport

Air Nice airport is 6km southwest of the city, connected to the train station by bus #23 (every 30min; daily 6am–9pm; €1).
Train The main train station, Nice-Ville, is a 10min walk northwest from the centre, on av Thiers.
Ferry Passenger boats arrive at quai de l'Amiral Infernet, a 5min walk from the old town.
Bus and tram Single tickets for both cost €1, and one-day tickets (€4) are also available.
Tourist office The main branch is at 5 promenade des Anglais (Mon–Sat 8/9am–6/8pm; June–Sept also Sun 9am–6pm; ⓣ08.92.70.74.07, ⓦwww.nicetourism.com), with outlets at the airport and next to the station.
Internet Nice Nett, 19 rue Paganini.

Accommodation

Backpackers Chez Patrick First floor, 32 rue Pertinax ⓣ04.93.80.30.72, ⓦwww.backpackerschezpatrick.com. A friendly hostel close to the station, with no curfew. Reception closed 12.30–5pm. €24.
Belle Meunière 21 av Durante ⓣ04.93.88.66.15. Housed in a beautiful old building close to the station and a short walk from the town centre, this hotel offers simple but pleasant rooms and a number of dorms. Barbeques are occasionally organized during the summer. Dorm €17, double room €49.
D'Orsay 18 rue Alsace-Lorraine ⓣ04.93.88.45.02. Simple, plainly decorated rooms in a good location, close to the station and 10min walk from the old town. €45.
Faubourg Montmartre 32 rue Pertinax ⓣ04.93.62.55.03. A rather eccentric hostel, run by two elderly ladies who also have a restaurant downstairs. Dorms are very small and cramped, but all have attached kitchenettes. Private "studios" are also available but get booked up quickly. Dorm €17, studio €22.
FUAJ Les Camélias 3 rue Spitalieri ⓣ04.93.62.15.54, ⓦwww.fuaj.org. In an excellent, central location, not far from the old town, this is a great, friendly hostel with clean, modern dorms and a good bar on-site. €22.
Villa St-Éxupéry 22 av Gravier ⓣ0800.307.409 (free in France) or 04.93.84.42.83, ⓦwww.vsaint.com. Housed in a beautiful old monastery above town, this is a real party hostel, and deservedly popular. Most dorms are en suite and a few have terraces with views over the city. The bar, housed in the old chapel, serves beer and wine for €1 and is packed every night, and there's also free internet, cheap dinners, and an excellent breakfast spread (included). Take the tram from the station towards Las Planas and get off at "Comte de Falicon". €30.

Eating

Fenocchio 2 place Rossetti. The master ice-cream maker of Nice, with a huge variety of flavours, such as vanilla, rose and black pepper. One scoop €2.
Lou Pilha Leva 3 rue Collet. This is undoubtedly the place to go to for Niçoise specialities. Order at the counter and then sit at one of the bright-orange tables in the street – don't miss the *socca* (chickpea flatbread; €2.50), best washed down with a cold glass of rosé (€1.60).
Pasta Basta 18 rue de la Préfecture. Cosy little Italian restaurant in the old town serving an excellent range of pasta – you choose the type and then the sauce (from €6.90) – featuring local ingredients, as well as pizzas (€8).
Saint Géran 12 rue Paganini. Delicious food from the island of Mauritius, with seafood menus from €11.70. Closed Sun eve & Mon.
Voyageur Nissart 19 rue Alsace-Lorraine, ⓣ04.93.82.19.60. Near the station, this highly recommended restaurant dishes up good-value Niçoise fare; three-course menu €15.90, closed Mon.

Drinking and nightlife

Akathor 32 cours Saleya. The fifty different European beers and cheap menus on offer attract both locals and tourists in their droves. Happy hour 5–9pm (pint €3.70).
Blue Whales 1 rue Mascoïnat. A relaxed place, with regular live-music nights. Happy hour 6pm–midnight (demi €2).
Les Deux Frères 1 rue du Moulin. A very cool bar with neon lighting and park benches. They have a

TREAT YOURSELF

La Merenda 4 rue Raoul Bosio. Tucked away behind a nondescript door, an ex-chef of the grand Negresco Hotel (on the prom des Anglais) prepares faultless Niçoise cuisine such as sausage with lentils and *daube de boeuf à la provencale*, though the menu changes regularly. *Plats* start at €12.

varied, nightly line-up, but principally electro and drum 'n' bass. Tues–Sat 9pm–2.30am.

Wayne's 15 rue de la Préfecture. Live music every night at this bar, which heaves with backpackers. Dancing on the table is a nightly ritual. Daily 2.30pm–12.30am, happy hour 5–9pm.

Moving on

Train Avignon TGV (10 daily; 2hr 50min–3hr 35min); Genoa (5 daily, 4 via Ventimiglia; 3hr 5min–4hr 30min); Lyon (hourly, some via Marseille; 4hr 40min–5hr 20min; Marseille (16 daily; 2hr 20min–2hr 45min); Milan (5 daily, 4 via Ventimiglia; 4hr 50min–5hr 10min); Monaco (frequent; 40min); Paris (10 daily; 5hr 30min–6hr 10min).

MONACO

The tiny independent principality of **MONACO** rears up over the rocky Riviera coast like a Mediterranean Hong Kong. The three-kilometre-long state consists of the old town of Monaco-Ville; Fontvieille; La Condamine by the harbour; Larvotto, with its artificial beaches of imported sand; and, in the middle, **MONTE CARLO**. There are relatively few conventional sights – indeed, Monaco seems composed of little other than roads, fast cars and apartment blocks – but one worth heading to is the superb (though expensive) **Musée Océanographique** on avenue St-Martin (daily 9.30/10am–6/7.30pm; €13), which displays a living coral reef, transplanted from the Red Sea into a 40,000-litre tank. If you want to try your luck at the famous **casino** (over 18s only; open from 2pm daily), you'll have to dress smartly – no shorts or t-shirts – and show your passport.

Arrival and information

Train Monaco train station is underground, reached from av Prince-Pierre. Bus #4 (direction Larvotto) takes you from the train station to the Casino-Tourism stop, near the tourist office.

Bus The bus station is on place d'Armes.

Tourist office 2a bd des Moulins (Mon–Sat 9am–7pm, Sun 10am–noon; ⓣ92.16.61.16, ⓦwww.monaco-tourisme.com).

Accommodation

Hôtel de France 6 rue de la Turbie ⓣ04.93.30.24.64, ⓦwww.monte-carlo.mc/france. Comfortable and clean, this is as cheap as they get for a double room in the centre. €112.

RIJ Villa Thalassa ⓣ04.93.78.18.58, ⓦwww.clajsud.fr. This clean and welcoming hostel is a great choice and just 3km away from Monte Carlo along the coast near a good beach at Cap d'Ail. You can walk here in 25min from the city, or get the train to Cap d'Ail. €17.

Eating and drinking

Arlecchino 6 rue Notre Dame de Lorette. For a cheap (daytime) bite to eat, this little café does sandwiches from €3.30, among other Italian treats. To find it, take the first set of stairs up from rue Portier.

Stars 'n' Bars 1er, 6 quai Antoine. This feisty, well-known bar on the quai serves up good-value food (for Monaco). Pizzas from €9; happy hour 5.30–7.30pm.

The southeast

The southeast of France encompasses a geographically varied area, from the thick forests of the Massif Central to the dramatic peaks of the Alps. The Massif Central, not the most accessible part of the country, is worth going out of your way for, especially to see the dramatic landscape that surrounds **Le Puy-en-Velay**, which makes an excellent base for exploration. Most travel in the region will require passing through **Lyon**, a beautiful city that's worth lingering over, especially to sample some of its exquisite restaurants. From here, a few hours on a train will take you to **Grenoble**, hemmed in by snow-capped mountains, and to **Chamonix**, which really comes alive during the ski-season, and a great place for extreme sports throughout the year.

LE PUY-EN-VELAY

LE PUY sprawls across a broad basin in the mountains, a muddle of red

roofs and poles of volcanic rock; both landscape and architecture are completely theatrical. The town is a good base for explorations of the Massif Central – the tourist office (see below) is well stocked with information to help you plan your visit.

The **cathedral**, at the top of Mont Corneille, with its small, almost Byzantine cupolas and Romanesque façade, dominates the old town. The nearby **church of St-Michel** (daily: May–Sept 9am–6.30pm; Oct–April 9.30am–noon & 2–5.30pm; €2.75), at the top of Rocher d'Aiguilhe, is an eleventh-century construction that appears to have grown out of the rock.

The main **bus stop and train station** are on place du Maréchal Leclerc, a fifteen-minute walk from the **tourist office** on place du Clauzel (July & Aug daily 8.30am–7.30pm; Sept–June daily 8.30am–noon & 1.30–6.15pm, closed Sun Oct–Easter; ⓣ04.71.09.38.41, ⓦwww.ot-lepuyenvelay.fr). The *Régional*, 36 bd du Maréchal Fayolle (ⓣ04.71.09.37.74; €28) is a basic **hotel** attached to a friendly bar, with cheap and comfortable doubles; even cheaper are the old but clean dorms in the *FUAJ Centre Pierre Cardinal*, 9 rue Jules Vallès (ⓣ04.71.05.52.40; reservations compulsory for weekend stays; check in from 2–11pm only; €10.80) which has basic breakfasts (€3) and cooking facilities. The municipal **campsite**, *Bouthézard* (ⓣ04.71.09.55.09; mid-March to mid-Oct; €14), is half an hour's walk north from the station, or take bus #6 from chemin de Roderie. For inexpensive regional **food** and a good cheeseboard, sit out on the beautiful terrace of the *Âme des Poètes*, by the cathedral on rue Séguret, or *La Main à la Pâte*, a crêperie at 59 rue Chaussade.

There are three trains to Lyon daily (2hr 25min) and four to Clermont Ferrand (2hr 20min–2hr 40min), from where there are connections to Paris.

LYON

It's hardly surprising that **LYON** is France's gastronomic capital, with more restaurants per square metre here than anywhere else on earth. Lyon also has a vibrant nightlife and cultural scene, the highlight of which is the summer-long festival Les Nuits de Fourvière, celebrating theatre, music and dance.

What to see and do

The city is split into three by its two rivers – the Saône and the Rhône. The elegant city centre, **Le Presqu'Île**, is made up of grand boulevards and public squares, while across the Saône lies the beautifully preserved and atmospheric old Renaissance quarter of Vieux Lyon.

Le Presqu'Île

North from Gare de Perrache, the pedestrian rue Victor-Hugo opens out onto the vast place Bellecour, which dwarfs even its statue of Louis XIV on horseback. On rue de la Charité, the **Musée des Tissus et des Arts Decoratifs** (Tues–Sun 10am–5.30pm; €5; M° Ampère Victor-Hugo), has an interesting collection of fabrics, clothes and tapestries dating from ancient Egypt to the present, alongside a collection of period furnishings. Northwest of place Bellecour, on the east bank of the Saône, the quai St-Antoine is lined every morning with a colourful food market; a book market takes place just upriver on Sundays.

North and inland from the river, Place des Terreaux is home to the **Musée des Beaux-Arts** (daily except Tues 10/10.30am–6pm; €6; M° Hôtel de Ville). This absorbing collection includes ancient Egyptian, Greek and Roman artefacts as well as works by Rubens, Renoir and Picasso.

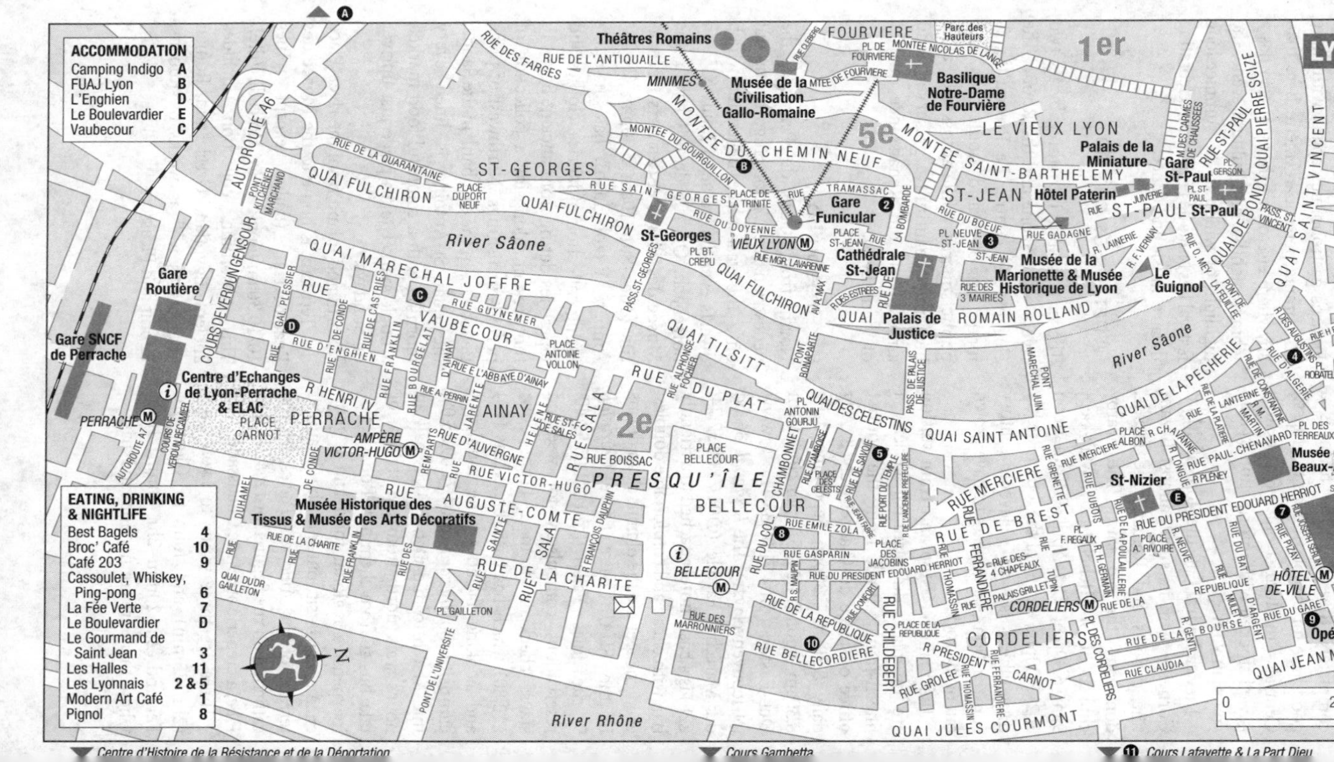
LYON
ACCOMMODATION
Camping Indigo A
FUAJ Lyon B
L'Enghien D
Le Boulevardier E
Vaubecour C
EATING, DRINKING & NIGHTLIFE
Best Bagels 4
Broc' Café 10
Café 203 9
Cassoulet, Whiskey, Ping-pong 6
La Fée Verte 7
Le Boulevardier D
Le Gourmand de Saint Jean 3
Les Halles 11
Les Lyonnais 2 & 5
Modern Art Café 1
Pignol 8
Théâtres Romains
Musée de la Civilisation Gallo-Romaine
Basilique Notre-Dame de Fourvière
Palais de la Miniature
Gare St-Paul
Hôtel Paterin
St-Paul
Gare Funicular
Cathédrale St-Jean
Palais de Justice
Musée de la Marionette & Musée Historique de Lyon
Le Guignol
St-Georges
Gare Routière
Gare SNCF de Perrache
Centre d'Echanges de Lyon-Perrache & ELAC
Musée Historique des Tissus & Musée des Arts Décoratifs
St-Nizier
Musée des Beaux-Arts
Hôtel de Ville
Opéra
LE VIEUX LYON
ST-GEORGES
ST-JEAN
ST-PAUL
FOURVIERE
PRESQU'ÎLE
BELLECOUR
CORDELIERS
AINAY
PERRACHE
River Saône
River Rhône
Centre d'Histoire de la Résistance et de la Déportation
Cours Gambetta
Cours Lafayette & La Part Dieu
& La Croix-Rousse
200 m

La Croix-Rousse

North of place des Terreaux, the old silk weavers' district of **La Croix-Rousse** has an authentic, creative feel to it. It is still a working-class area, but today only twenty or so people work on the computerized looms that are kept in business by the restoration and maintenance of tapestries within France's palaces and châteaux. The famous *traboulés*, or covered alleyways, that run between streets were originally used to transport silk safely through town, later serving as wartime escape routes and hideouts for la Résistance. Look out for small signs dotted about on walls in this area – follow the arrows to do a self-guided walking tour.

Vieux Lyon

The streets on the left bank of the Saône form an attractive muddle of cobbled lanes and Renaissance facades. The **Musée de la Marionnette**, in the **Musée Gadagne** (Wed–Sun 11am–6.30pm; €6; M° Vieux Lyon), place du Petit Collège, is well worth an hour or two of your time, containing not just Lyon's famous puppets but also a collection of puppets from around the world. At the southern end of the rue St-Jean lies the **Cathédrale St-Jean**; though damaged during World War II, its thirteenth-century stained glass is in perfect condition.

Lyon Romain

Just beyond the cathedral, at M° Vieux Lyon on avenue Adolphe-Max, is a funicular station, from which you can ascend (€2.40/rtn) to the two **Roman theatres** on rue de l'Antiquaille (daily 7am–7/9pm; free), and the excellent **Musée de la Civilisation Gallo-Romaine**, 17 rue Cléberg (Tues–Sun 10am–6pm; €4), containing mosaics and other artefacts from Roman Lyon. Crowning the hill, the **Basilique de Notre-Dame** (daily 8am–7pm) is a gaudy showcase of multi-coloured marble and mosaic, and there are fantastic views over the city from the gardens at the back of the church.

Elsewhere in the city

Reminders of the war are never far away in France and the **Centre d'Histoire de la Résistance et de la Déportation**, 14 av Berthelot (Wed–Sun 9am–5.30/6pm; €4), tells of the courage and ingenuity of the French resistance. It also serves as a poignant memorial to the city's deported Jews. To the southeast of town, the **Musée Lumière**, 25 rue du Premier-Film (Tues–Sun 11am–6.30pm; €6; M° Monplaisir-Lumière), houses the Lumière brothers' cinematograph, which in 1895 projected the world's first film.

Arrival and information

Air *Navettes* run from both Part-Dieu and Perrache stations to Lyon-St-Exupéry airport (every 20min; 5am–9.20pm; €8.90).

Train The main TGV train station, Part Dieu, is on boulevard Marius-Vivier-Merle, in the heart of the commercial district on the east bank of the Rhône, and connected to the centre by métro. Other trains arrive at the Gare de Perrache, to the southern edge of the centre on the Presqu'île.

Tourist office place Bellecour (daily 9am–6pm; ⓣ04.72.77.69.69, ⓦwww.en.lyon-france.com).

Internet Raconte-moi La Terre, 38 rue Thomassin, with a bookshop specializing in travel literature (closed Sun).

City transport

Bus-train-Métro Tickets for all city transport cost a flat €1.60, or buy the tourist office's liberté ticket for a day's unlimited travel on trams, buses and métro (€4.50).

Bikes Velo-V is a city-wide cycling scheme where you take and leave a bike from one of about a hundred sites around town for €1/2 an hour (depending on length of hire); credit card authorization required.

Accommodation

Camping Indigo Porte de Lyon ⓣ04.78.35.64.55, ⓦwww.camping-lyon.com. The closest campsite, with a bar, restaurant, internet and a summer swimming pool. Ten minutes by bus #89 from the bus station in Gare de Vaise, north of the city. €18.40.

FUAJ Lyon 41–45 montée du Chemin Neuf ⓣ04.78.15.05.50. An excellent hostel, well worth the hike up from the métro station (Vieux Lyon) for the fantastic views of the city from its terrace. Dorms are comfortable and clean, the staff are very friendly and helpful, and there's a good bar. To avoid the walk up, catch the funicular to Minimes and walk down from there. €17.30.

L'Enghien 22 rue d'Enghien ⓣ04.78.37.42.63, ⓦwww.enghien-lyon.fr. A surprisingly smart budget choice, with brightly decorated, spacious rooms, some with attached toilet and all with private showers. Very close to Gare de Perrache. €43.

Le Boulevardier 5 rue de la Fromagerie ⓣ04.78.28.48.22, ⓦwww.leboulevardier.com. In a great, central location, this peaceful and friendly hotel offers simple but comfortable rooms that are a real bargain. Worth staying for the attached bar alone (see below). €45.

Vaubecour 28 rue Vaubecour ⓣ04.78.37.44.91. Very handy for Gare de Perrache and housed in a lovely old building, though the rooms are rather basic and now looking quite dated. €42.

Eating

Best Bagels place Robatel. This café lives up to its name – try the pepper-filled "Louisiana Fire". The attached shop sells a good range of American food brands, from Oreos to Dr Pepper. Bagel, drink and accompaniment €6.95.

TREAT YOURSELF

Les Lyonnais 1 quai des Celestins ⓣ04.78.37.41.80. Everything you want from a *bouchon*: deep-red walls, decorated with black and white photos, lilting jazz on the stereo and a convivial, local, atmosphere. The refined food is influenced by that day's market produce, and the friendly owner will more than likely recommend the best wine to complement your dishes – yet it remains an unfussy, unpretentious restaurant where you'll happily lose a few hours of your day. The three-course *menu des gones* is excellent value at €19.80 and includes deliciously cooked fish of the day and the city's traditional scarlet-coloured praline tart. There's a second branch in Vieux Lyon at 19 rue de la Bombarde (ⓣ04.78.37.64.82).

Café 203 9 rue du Garet. This delightful café attracts a young crowd and has an excellent €13 *formule – plat au choix* (such as *terrine de poisson* or an oriental-inspired prawn pasta) plus one of their absolutely scrummy desserts.

Cassoulet, Whiskey, Ping-pong 4ter rue de Belfort. Apart from offering what it says on the sign – the owner's three favourite things – this little bar has good jazz, cheap beer and wine and a great atmosphere. Cassoulet €10, whiskey from €2.

Le Gourmand de Saint Jean 4 place Neuve St-Jean. One of a number of unpretentious, if touristy, *bouchons* serving the full range of Lyonnaise specialities, including *andouillette* (tripe sausage), and offering a number of good-value menus – it's worth splashing out on the €15 menu for the choice it affords you.

Les Halles 102 cours Lafayette. Lyon's covered market has enough gorgeous produce to keep a gourmand happy for weeks – a great stop on sunny days when you can pick up everything you need for a picnic. Tues–Sat 7am–noon & 3–7pm, Sun 7am–noon.

Pignol 17 rue Emile Zola. Justifiably famous Lyonnaise patisserie, serving a mouthwatering array of sweet treats to eat in or take away, and a number of savoury lunch dishes such as *croque-monsieur* (€6.80).

Drinking and nightlife

Broc' Café 2 place de l'Hôpital. The cosy, dark interior of this busy bar-café makes a great stop for a drink or two – or to watch the world go by on the place. Demi €2.50. 8am–1am.

La Fée Verte 4 rue Pizay. A small dedicated absinthe bar where DJs play accessible hip-hop and electro. Absinthe €2.70.

Le Boulevardier 5 rue de la Fromagerie. A great little bar, with a charming, relaxed feel that matches the jazz played here (both live and recorded). A good place to start or finish your night off (wine €2.50, demi €2.70). Mon & Tues 8am–4pm, Wed–Sun 8am–midnight.

Modern Art Café 65 bd de la Croix Rousse ⓦwww.modernartcafé.net. Recline on a deckchair or retro leather sofa in this unpretentious bar where the friendly owner organizes original art exhibitions and brilliant DJs. Cocktails from €7.

Moving on

Train Arles (7 daily; 2hr 40min); Avignon TGV (16 daily; 1hr 10min); Dijon (17 daily; 1hr 40min–2hr 45min); Geneva (13–15 daily; 1hr 45min–2hr 50min); Grenoble (frequent; 1hr–2hr 10min);

HIKING IN THE ALPS

There are six **national and regional parks** in the Alps – Vanoise, Écrins, Bauges, Chartreuse, Queyras (the least busy) and Vercors (the gentlest) – each of which covers ideal walking country, as does the **Route des Grandes Alpes**, which crosses all the major massifs from Lake Geneva to Menton and should only be attempted by seasoned hikers. All walking routes are clearly marked and equipped with refuge huts, known as **gîtes d'étape** (ⓦwww.gites-refuges.com). The Maisons de la Montagne in Grenoble and Chamonix (see below and p.448) provide detailed information on GR paths (an abbreviation of Grande Randonnée meaning "long ramble"), and local tourist offices often have maps of walks in their areas. Bear in mind that anywhere above 2000m will only be free of snow from early July until mid-September.

Marseille (frequent; 1hr 45min–3hr 45min); Paris (every 30min; 1hr 50min–2hr 10min); Turin (via Chambery; 4 daily, 4–5hr).

GRENOBLE

The economic and intellectual capital of the French Alps, **GRENOBLE** is a thriving city, beautifully situated on the Drac and Isère rivers and surrounded by mountains. The old centre, south of the Isère, focuses on place Grenette and place Notre-Dame, both popular with local students, who lounge around in the many outdoor cafés. The central **Musée de Grenoble**, 5 place Lavalette (daily except Tues 10am–6.30pm; €5), is considered, by dint of its twentieth-century masterpieces, to be one of the best in Europe and includes works by Matisse, Chagall and Gauguin. Grenoble's highlight, however, especially in good weather, is the trip by **téléphérique** from the riverside quai Stéphane Jay up to Fort de la Bastille on the steep slopes above the north bank of the Isère (daily 9.15/11am–6.30pm/12.15am; €5 one-way). It's a hair-raising ride to an otherwise uninteresting fort, but the views over the mountains and down onto the town are stunning, and the walk down is lovely and tranquil.

Arrival and information

Bus and train The train and bus stations are on the western edge of the city, at the end of avenue Félix Viallet, a 5min walk to the centre.

Tourist office 14 rue de la République, near place Grenette (Mon–Sat 9am–noon & 2–6pm, Sun 10am–1pm; April–Sept also Sun 2–5pm; ⓣ04.76.42.41.41, ⓦwww.grenoble-isere.info).

Internet Internet Café, 15 rue Jean-Jacques Rousseau.

Hiking information Maison de la Montagne, 3, rue Raoul Blanchard (Mon–Fri 9.30am–12.30pm & 1–6pm, Sat 10am–1pm & 2–5pm; ⓦwww.grenoble-montagne.com).

Accommodation

Alizé 1 place de la Gare ⓣ04.76.43.12.91, ⓦwww.hotelalize.com. Just across the road from the station, Grenoble's cheapest hotel offers a friendly welcome and basic but surprisingly spacious and airy rooms. €36.

FUAJ Grenoble 10 av du Gesivaudan ⓣ04.76.09.33.52. This smart, modern, eco-friendly hostel has ultra-clean dorms and a good atmosphere. There's excellent information about hiking in the area and skiing in winter; unfortunately it's 5km from the centre of town. Take bus #1 to la Quinzaine or tram A to la Rampe. €18.30.

Les Trois Pucelles ⓣ04.76.96.45.73, ⓦwww.camping-trois-pucelles.com. Four kilometres from Grenoble, in Seyssins, this campsite has sixty pitches, two swimming pools and a restaurant in an arboretum by the Drac river. Open all year; to get here take tram A to La Poya then change onto bus #51 to Mas des Îles, from here it's 400m south at the river's edge. €14.50.

Lux 6 rue Crépu ⓣ04.76.46.41.89, ⓦwww.hotel-lux.com. Simple but pleasant en-suite rooms in this quiet hotel close to the station. €52.50.

Eating and drinking

Bukana 1 quai Créqui. The flags across the ceiling reflect the diversity of the exchange student clientele in this little bar, which has cheap deals

(happy hour cocktails €3), televised sport (in English) and theme evenings such as salsa night.
Café des Arts 36 rue St-Laurent. An intimate venue with an excellent programme of live music, mainly jazz. Daily 8pm–midnight.
Mark XIII 8 rue Lakanal ⓣ04.76.86.26.94. A two-floor bar and venue that draws in an exciting depth and variety of underground electronic DJ talent (progressive house, drum'n'bass, techno, ambient).
Tarteline 6 Grande Rue. Cute little place with a country feel offering delicious savoury and sweet tarts, such as the Reblochon (potato, reblochon cheese and bacon; €6.50) as well as a good-value lunch menu for €11.50.
Tonneau de Diogène 6n place Notre Dame. Cheap and hearty food in a genuine bohemian atmosphere, among books and chess boards, make this a favourite with students. Steak-frites €9.

Moving on

Train Chamonix (1 daily via Chambéry; 4hr 35min); Lyon (frequent; 1hr 30min–2hr); Paris (8 daily; 3hr); Turin (2 daily, via Chambéry; 3hr 50min–6hr 15min).

CHAMONIX AND MONT BLANC

At 4810m, **Mont Blanc** is both Western Europe's highest mountain and the Alps' biggest draw. Nestled at its base, the town of **CHAMONIX** is lively year-round; in summer it's popular for rock climbing and hiking, while in winter its draw is the area's vast skiing possibilities. The pricey **téléphérique** (daily: April to mid-June & Sept 8.10am–4/4.30pm; mid-June to Aug 6.10/7.10am–4.30pm; early Nov & mid-Dec to March 8.30am–3.30pm; ⓣ08.92.68.00.67; €40 return) soars to the Aiguille du Midi (3842m), a terrifying granite pinnacle on which the cablecar station and a restaurant are precariously balanced. Here, the view of Mont Blanc, coupled with the altitude, will literally leave you breathless. Book the téléphérique ahead to avoid the queues and get there early, before the clouds and the crowds close up.

Arrival and information

Train Chamonix station is 3min walk from the centre, down Avenue Michel Croz. Behind it, at

TREAT YOURSELF

One of the most exhilarating experiences you can have in the Alps is not on the ground, but in the air. A number of companies operate **tandem paragliding flights**, which allow you to take in the fantastic scenery from a different perspective. Fly Chamonix (ⓣ610.28.20.77, ⓦwww.flychamonix.com) offers tandem flights from €80 – for more information, or to book a flight, head to Fall Line, 97 rue Vallot, Chamonix (daily 9am–noon & 3–7pm).

Montvers station, a mountain train serves only the glaciers.
Bus Buses leave from in front of the train station.
Tourist office 85 place du Triangle-de-l'Amitié (daily 8.30am–12.30pm & 2–7pm; ⓣ04.50.53.00.24, ⓦwww.chamonix.com); able to book accommodation, provides good information on local activities and advises on weather and snow conditions.
Hiking information The Maison de la Montagne (daily 9am–noon & 3–6pm; ⓣ04.50.53.22.08, ⓦwww.ohm-chamonix.com) on place de L'Église is the place for organizing climbing, trekking, mountain biking and parapenting. They also have good information about the Gîtes de Montagne that are situated along the major hiking trails.

Accommodation

Camping Marmottes 147 rte des Nants ⓣ04.50.53.61.24, ⓦwww.camping-lesmarmottes.com. Situated off the main road, south of Chamonix, this campsite is linked to the town via a free bus service. Facilities include a games room, use of barbeques and a laundry, and you can enjoy great views of Mont Blanc. €11.20.
Du Louvre 95 impasse Androsace ⓣ04.50.53.00.51. Right in the centre of the village, this old hotel offers simple but clean rooms. €69.
FUAJ Chamonix-Mont Blanc 127 montée J Balmat, les Pélerins d'en Haut ⓣ04.50.53.14.52, ⓦwww.fuaj.org. Situated in a traditional chalet, 2km out of the centre, this hostel has good dorms and a friendly atmosphere, but no on-site kitchen. Take bus #5 to the Pélerins-Auberge stop or the train to Les Pélerins. Closed noon–5pm & 7.30–8.30pm. €19.
Gîte Vagabond 365 av Ravanel-le-Rouge, ⓣ04.50.53.15.43 ⓦwww.gitevagabond.com. This lively and friendly hostel is a good choice year-round and invaluably cheap for the ski-season (book ahead). €14.40.

Eating and drinking

Alan Peru 199 av de l'Aiguille du Midi ⓣ04.50.53.16.04. Clever fusion cooking combining regional and Asian influences, making a nice change from the usual cheese and potato-based offerings (from €13).

Aux Petits Gourmands 168 rue du Docteur Paccard. A great stop for a warming hot chocolate (from €1.50) and a delicious patisserie (€1–3). Closed Sun.

Chambre 9 272 av Michel Croz. A renowned, loud and lively bar on the ground floor of the *Gustavia* hotel, full of young, dancing tourists. Cocktails €6.50.

Tigre, Tigre 239 av Michel Croz. Warm up with this likeable Indian restaurant's large curries (€11–15) after coming down the mountain.

Moving on

Bus Courmayeur, Italy (2–6 daily; 45min); Geneva (2–5 daily; 2hr).

Train Grenoble (daily, via St Gervais; 4hr 20min); Lyon (3 daily, via Aix-les-Bains; 4–5hr).

Corsica

Known to the French as the "île de beauté", Corsica has an amazing diversity of natural landscape. Being one-third national park, its magnificent rocky coastline is interspersed with **outstanding beaches**, while the interior mountains soar as high as 2706m. Two French *départements* divide Corsica, each with its own capital: Napoleon's birthplace, **Ajaccio** on the southwest coast; and **Bastia**, which faces Italy in the north. The old capital of **Corte** dominates the interior, backed by a formidable wall of mountains. Of the coastal resorts, **Calvi** draws tourists with its massive citadel and long sandy beach; while **Bonifacio**'s Genoan houses perch atop limestone cliffs, overseeing the clearest water in the Mediterranean, on the island's southernmost point. Still more dramatic landscapes lie around the **Golfe de Porto** in the far northwest, where the famous red cliffs of the **Calanches de Piana** rise over 400m.

AJACCIO

Set in a magnificent bay, **AJACCIO** has all the ingredients of a Riviera-style town with its palm trees, spacious squares, glamorous marina and street cafés. **Napoleon** was born here in 1769, but did little for the place except to make it the island's capital for the brief period of his empire. It is, however, a lovely place to spend time, particularly around the harbour and narrow streets inland

GETTING TO CORSICA

Air France (ⓦwww.airfrance.fr) and its partner company **Air Corsica** (CCM; ⓦwww.aircorsica.com) have regular flights to Corsica's four airports at Ajaccio, Bastia, Calvi and Figari (near Bonifacio). It's often possible to get discounts if you are under 25.

The three principal **ferry companies** serving the island are **Corsica Ferries** (ⓦwww.corsicaferries.com), **Mobylines** (ⓦwww.mobylines.it) and **SNCM** (ⓦwww.sncm.fr). Prices are between €20 and €40, with the cheapest from the Italian ports. From October to March routes are scaled back to several journeys a week; check websites for details. Routes marked * below are covered by superfast NGV hydrofoils.

Nice to: Ajaccio* (5 daily; 4hr–5hr 20min); Bastia* (1 daily; 5hr); Calvi* (3 daily; 3–6hr).

Marseille to: Ajaccio* (6 weekly; 8hr 45min–12hr); Bastia (1 daily; 5hr 30mins); Calvi (1 weekly; 11hr 30min).

Livorno to: Bastia* (April–Oct 9 weekly; 4hr); Genoa to: Bastia* (1 daily; 4hr 45min).

Savona to: Bastia (1 weekly; 3hr 30min); Calvi (1 weekly; 3hr).

Santa-Teresa-di-Gallura to: Bonifacio (2–8 daily; 1hr).

Porto Torres to: Ajaccio (1 weekly; 4hr 30min).

from the fifteenth-century **Genoese** citadel. The **Musée Fesch**, rue Cardinal-Fesch (Mon 1.30–5.15/6pm, Tues–Sun 9.15am–12.15pm & 2.15–5.15/6.30pm; €5.35) is home to the country's most important collection of Renaissance paintings outside Paris, including works by Botticelli, Titian and Poussin. The best beach to head to is **plage Trottel**, ten minutes southwest from the centre along the promenade.

Arrival and information

Air The airport, Campo dell'Oro, is 8km southeast and connected to the town by shuttle bus (*navette*; €5); taxis cost around €25.
Bus and ferry The ferry port and bus station occupy the same building off quai L'Herminier.
Train The train station is a 10min walk north along the seafront.
Tourist office 3 bd du Roi Jerome (April–June, Sept & Oct Mon–Sat 8am–7pm, Sun 9am–1pm; July & Aug Mon–Sat 8am–8.30pm, Sun 9am–1pm & 4–7pm; Nov–March, Mon–Fri 8am–12.30pm & 2–6pm, Sat 8am–midday & 2–5pm; ⓣ04.95.51.53.03, ⓦwww.ajaccio-tourisme.com).
Internet Cyber Café Agora, rue Emmanuel Arène, two blocks behind tourist office.

Accommodation

Budget accommodation in Ajaccio is hard to find and hotels get booked up quite quickly. The tourist office can provide a list of those available as well as private apartments to rent.

> **TREAT YOURSELF**
>
> **Kallisté** 51 cours Napoléon ⓣ04.95.51.34.45, ⓦwww.hotel-kalliste-ajaccio.com. The best hotel in Ajaccio, with attractive, a/c rooms in a tastefully renovated nineteenth-century building. Extras include scooter rental and free internet. €85.

Camping de Barbicaja rte des îles Sanguinaires ⓣ04.95.52.01.17. The most convenient campsite is 3km out of town, near the beach, and has a bar and hot showers. It's a short bus ride away from place Général-du-Gaulle on bus #5. Closed Oct–April. €5.50 per person plus €2.70 per tent.
Marengo 2 rue Marengo ⓣ04.95.21.43.66, ⓦwww.hotel-marengo.com. A sweet little hotel with spacious, clean rooms that boast a/c. Some rooms lead onto a floral courtyard. €61.

Eating and drinking

Ariadne route des Sanguinaires ⓣ04.95.52.09.63. Feast on Thai and Moroccan dishes (set two-course menu €15) or pizzas (€10–11) to the slow beat of salsa or reggae, live most nights, at a terrace on the beach.
Grand Café Napoléon 10 cours Napoléon. Sip a cocktail (€8), or a coffee (€1) while nibbling olives at this city centre place, which serves fabulous Corsican food. Best saved as a special treat: set menus from €28.
Le Trou dans le Mur 1 bd du Roi-Jérôme ⓣ04.95.21.49.22. A busy restaurant near the market, serving great lasagne (€14) and good Italian desserts. Open lunchtime and Friday evenings.

BASTIA: COMING AND GOING

Bastia is the island's main transport hub – while there's little of particular interest here, there's a good chance that you'll pass through the town at least once during your visit.
Air Bastia's airport, Poretta, is 16km south of town. Shuttle buses (35min; €8) meet all flights and stop outside the train station in the centre of town.
Ferry The port is in the north of town, a five-minute walk from the centre. See the box on p.449 for ferry routes and journey times. Services include Nice (5hr 30min), Toulon (8hr), Marseille (11hr 30min) and Livorno (4hr)
Train The station, west of place St-Nicolas, serves: Ajaccio (4–5 daily; 3hr 15min); Calvi (2 daily; 3hr, change Ponte Leccia); and Corte (2–4 daily; 1hr 45min).
Buses run from the train station to Calvi (daily 4.30pm except Sun; 2hr) and Corte (3 weekly, Mon, Wed & Fri 12.10pm; 1hr 25min–1hr 45min), and from rue du Nouveau Port to Ajaccio (2 daily 7.45am & 3pm; 3hr) and Porto Vecchio (2 daily June–Sept only, 8.30am & 4pm; 3hr).

ISLAND TRANSPORT

Corsica is somewhat difficult to navigate around if relying on public transport, with services slow and infrequent.

Train Corsica's narrow-gauge railway crosses the mountains to connect the island's main towns along the most scenic of lines. Lines run from Calvi-Ponte Leccia in the interior and from Ajaccio-Bastia. InterRail and other cards reduce the fare to half for all services, or you could buy a **Carte Zoom**, which gives one week's unlimited train travel for €47. The cards are available from any station.

Bus Buses are infrequent between the larger towns and rarely reach the interior villages; main routes include Bastia–Porto Vecchio, Ajaccio–Bastia and Calvi–Bastia. Services are scaled back drastically between November and May.

Scooter With little public transport and many secluded beaches to visit, the roads that undulate and meander around Corsica mean it's a great place to rent a scooter. Try Agence Corse Location, 51 cours Napoléon in Ajaccio (€50/day), Corse Moto Services on quai Nord in Bonifacio (€40/day) or Garage d'Angeli at 4 rue Villa St-Antoine in Calvi (€40–50/day).

Car This is by far the most convenient way to get around Corsica. Hertz (ⓦwww.hertz.fr), Europcar (ⓦwww.europcar.com) and Avis (ⓦwww.avis.fr) all have offices in the big towns and airports. Car hire isn't cheap though, with prices starting from €93 per day.

Marché Campinchi place César Campinchi. This market is open 8am–noon Tues–Sun, and is a great place to stock up in fresh fruit and veg, plus cheese and Corsica's famed charcuterie at its cheapest.

Moving on

Bus Bastia (2 daily; 3hr); Bonifacio (2 daily; 4hr); Corte (2 daily; 2hr).

Train Bastia (4 daily; 3hr 15min); Calvi (2 daily; 4hr 30min); Corte (2–4 daily; 2hr).

LE GOLFE DE PORTO

Corsica's most startling landscapes surround the **Golfe de Porto**, on the west coast. A deep blue bay enfolded by outlandish red cliffs, among them the famous **Calanches de Piana** rock formations, the gulf is framed by snow-topped mountains and a vast pine forest. The entire area holds endless possibilities for outdoor enthusiasts, with a superb network of marked trails (free maps available from the Ajaccio tourist office) and **canyoning** routes, perfect bays for **kayaking** and some of the finest **diving** sites in the Mediterranean.

Less adventurous visitors can explore the coast on one of the excursion boats from the village of **PORTO**, the gulf's main tourist hub, where there's a **tourist office** (ⓣ04.95.26.10.55, ⓦwww.porto-tourisme.com) and a huge range of **accommodation**. Best value among the cheap **hotels** is *Le Golfe*, 1km from the sea opposite the Genoese watch-tower (ⓣ04.95.26.13.33; ⓦwww.hotel-le-golfe-porto.com; €65). *Camping Oliviers,* situated just along from the supermarket on the main road east from the village (ⓣ04.95.26.14.49, ⓦwww.camping-oliviers-porto.com; €7 per person plus €3 per tent) is lovely, with pitches under the shade of olive trees. Amenities include a bar, swimming pool, gym, hot tub, a hammam and massages. The campsite also has wooden chalets with terrace, private bathroom and double room (€85). For an inexpensive **meal**, try one of the pizzerias lining the roadside above the marina.

CALVI

Seen from the water, the great citadel of **CALVI** resembles a floating island, defined by a hazy backdrop of snow-capped mountains. The island's third port, the town draws thousands of tourists for its 6km of sandy beach. The

ville haute, a labyrinth of cobbled lanes and stairways encased by a citadel, rises from **place Christophe Colomb**, which links it to the town and marina of the *ville basse*. The square's name derives from the local belief that the discoverer of the New World was born here, in a now ruined house on the edge of the citadel. To reach the public **beach**, keep walking south, past the boats in the marina, and – unless you want to pay for a lounger and waited service – past the private beach bars.

Arrival and information

Air Calvi's Ste-Catherine airport is 8km southeast of the town, connected only by taxis (€16–18).
Train The train station, on av de la République, is just off the marina to the south of the town centre.
Ferry The ferry port is on the opposite side of the marina, below the citadel.
Bus Buses to and from Bastia and Calenzana stop in place Porteuse d'Eau, next to the station. Porto buses stop outside the supermarket 200m south of the train station.
Tourist office Port de Plaisance (April–Oct daily 9am–5/7pm; Nov–March Mon–Sat 9am–noon & 2–5pm; Ⓣ04.95.65.16.67, Ⓦwww.balagne-corsica.com).

Accommodation

Du Centre 14 rue Alsace-Lorraine Ⓣ04.95.65.02.01. The most convenient budget accommodation, hidden away in the *ville basse*, with modest and well-kept rooms. €50.
La Pinède Ⓣ04.95.65.17.80, Ⓦwww.camping-calvi.com. One of the smartest of several campsites that are sheltered in the pine forest behind the public beach, with tennis, a bar and a good shop. It's a 2km walk along av de la République or take the hourly beach train (*ferrovière*) towards Île Rousse for two stops; open Apr–Oct. €9.50 per person plus €3.50 per tent.
U Carabellu rte de Pietra-Maggiore Ⓣ04.95.65.14.16. Hostels are a rare breed in Corsica, so book ahead for this one, whose dorms are tidy and have plenty of room. It also has a great out-of-town spot overlooking the bay; from the station, turn left down av de la République, then right at the Total garage after 500m and keep walking for 3.5km. Also offers full- (€31) and half-board (€26) options. €17.

Eating and drinking

Bar de la Tour quai Landry. A lovely spot overlooking the water, it's a great place for an early evening beer (€4).
Chez Tao rue Ste-Françoise. A famous, beautiful and expensive piano bar, set in a sixteenth-century former bishop's palace. It's a romantic place to share a bottle of wine on the terrace and enjoy impressive views of the bay. Open 8pm–5am.
Pizzeria Cappuccino quai Landry. This restaurant has a great atmosphere and serves up good-value *calzones* (€10–14) and pasta.
U Minellu Traverse à l'Eglise. Away from the tourist crowds, this restaurant has a lovely terrace area and serves Corsican specialities. Set menus from €17.

Moving on

Train All services go via Ponte Leccia; Ajaccio (4 daily; 5hr); Bastia (4 daily; 3hr 30mins); Corte (4 daily; 3hr 30min).
Bus Bastia (daily 4.30pm except Sun; 2hr 30min); Porto: (daily 3.30pm; 3hr)

CORTE

Perching on the rocky crags of the island's spine, **CORTE**, the island's only interior town, is regarded as the spiritual capital of Corsica, as this is where **Pasquale Paoli** had his seat of government during the brief period of independence in the eighteenth century. Paoli founded a university here and its student population adds some much-needed life. For outdoor enthusiasts, this is also an ideal base for **trekking** into the island's steep valleys, with two superb gorges stretching west into the heart of the mountains.

What to see and do

The main street, **cours Paoli**, runs the length of town, culminating in **place Paoli**, a pleasant market square lined with cafés. A cobbled ramp leads up to the **ville haute**, where you can still see the bullet marks made by Genoese soldiers during the War of Independence in tiny

THE GR20

The GR20 hiking trail stretches across Corsica's dramatic granite spine from Calenzana in the north to Conza in the south. Covering a breathtaking landscape, the route takes you through some lush countryside and over the snow-capped peaks of the heart of island. It is manageable for anyone in reasonable shape with basic trekking common sense, but proper hiking equipment is essential, as are nerves of steel for the ropes and vertical staircases built into the mountain side. Covering a distance of 180km, it takes around two weeks to complete, walking 2–6hr per day; red and white waymarks show the route, which is well serviced with bunked **mountain refuges**. Although the refuges cook and sell food, several days' supplies and a good stock of water are recommended. Do not attempt the route outside of the summer months; even then there is some residual snow in parts. Buses go from Calvi to Calenzana (June & Sept 4 weekly; July & Aug 2 daily; 30min; €6), where the walk begins. Accommodation and more detailed information about the route can be found at ⓦwww.calinzana.corsica-isula.com. Detailed maps can be obtained from the tourist office.

place Gaffori. Continuing north you'll soon come to the gates of the **citadelle**, whose well-preserved ramparts enclose the **Museu di a Corsica** (Tues–Sun 10am–6/8pm; June–Sept daily; Nov & Dec closed Sun; €5.30). The best views of the citadel, the town and its valley are from the **Belvédère**, a man-made look-out post on the southern end of the ramparts.

Arrival and information

Train Corte's train station is 1km east of town at the foot of the hill near the university.
Bus Buses stop at the south end of cours Paoli.
Tourist office In the *citadelle* (Mon–Fri 9am–1pm & 2–6/8pm; ⓣ04.95.46.26.70, ⓦwww.corte-tourisme.com). It also houses the Parc Naturel Régional Corse office, the best information source on the island for walkers.

Accommodation

Ferme Équestre l'Albadu Ancienne route d'Ajaccio ⓣ04.95.46.24.55. The nicest of the seven local campsites, located 15min walk from town – follow the main road south down the hill from place Paoli and take the second right after the second bridge. €4.50 per person, plus €2 per tent.
Hotel du Nord 22 cours Paoli ⓣ04.95.46.00.68, ⓦwww.hoteldunord-corte.com. The oldest hotel in town is well maintained and pleasantly decorated, a friendly place with a busy bar and internet access. €64.
HR allée du 9 Septembre ⓣ04.95.45.11.11, ⓦwww.hotel-hr.com. Cheap and cheerful rooms in an old converted police station southwest of the station and just 10min from the centre. €40.

Eating and drinking

A Merenda 3 rue Paoli. Popular café, frequented by students who come for the cheap meals, such as *steak-frites* (€7.50), paninis (€3.50) and *bruschetta* (€4).
Café du Cours 22 rue Paoli. Student nights and well-priced drinks at this busy bar which also has internet access, some live Corsican bands and daytime left-luggage facilities; *demi* €3.20.
U Museu 1 rampe Ribanelle ⓣ04.95.61.08.36. Huddled beneath the citadel walls, this place serves a superb goat's cheese salad and tasty wild-boar stew; three-course menu €15.

Moving on

Bus Ajaccio (2 daily, 9am & 4.15pm; 2hr); Bastia (2 daily, 9.30am & 4.40pm; 1hr 15min); Calvi (daily except Sun, change at Ponte Leccia; 4.40pm; 2hr 15min).
Train Ajaccio (2–4 daily; 2hr); Bastia (2–4 daily; 1hr 30min); Calvi (2 daily; 2hr 30min).

BONIFACIO

The port of **BONIFACIO** has a superb, isolated position on a narrow peninsula of dazzling white limestone at Corsica's southernmost point, only an hour away by boat from Sardinia. For hundreds of

years the town held the most powerful **fortress** in the Mediterranean and was a virtually independent republic. Nowadays, people are met with sights of precariously balanced houses edging their way into the sea. Bonifacio has become a chic holiday spot, sailing centre and deluxe day-trip.

What to see and do

The **ville haute** is connected to the marina by a steep flight of steps at the west end of the quay, at the top of which you can enjoy glorious views across the straits to Sardinia. Within the massive fortifications of the citadel is an alluring maze of cobbled streets which bring you back down to the marina, where a **boat excursion** (around €14) round the base of the cliffs gives a fantastic view of the town and the **sea caves**. Some outstanding beaches lie near Bonifacio, most notably the shell-shaped **plage de la Rondinara**, 10km north; further north still, off the main Porto-Vecchio road, the **plages de Santa Giulia** and **Palombaggia** wouldn't look out of place in the Maldives. Buses to Rondinara leave two to four times daily, from the back of the quay.

Arrival and information

Bus Buses stop in the car park at the base of the harbour.

Ferry Boats from Santa-Teresa-di-Gallura on Sardinia dock at the far end of the quay at the bottom of the hill.

Internet *Boni Boom* on quai Comparetti. A lovely waterside location that also serves tasty pasta dishes from €8.

Tourist office The seemingly indifferent tourist office is based in the *ville haute*, at the bottom of rue Fredi-Scamaroni (May–Sept daily 9am–8pm; Oct–April Mon–Fri 9am–noon & 2–6pm; ⓣ04.95.73.11.88, ⓦwww.bonifacio.fr).

Accommodation

L'Araguina av Sylver Bohn ⓣ04.95.73.02.96. The only campsite close to the town has lumpy and sandy pitches but loans out tents and sleeping bags for those unprepared. It's north from the marina, 1km out of town. €6 per person, plus €2.50 per tent.

Royal 8 rue Fred Sacramoni ⓣ04.95.73.00.51. A good option in the centre of town, only minutes away from the tourist office. Don't let slightly faded blue carpet and curtain-less showers put you off – the beds are comfy and it offers a decent night's sleep. €60.

Eating and drinking

B52 quai Camparetti. A laid-back and tasteful late-night bar, with tapas bites to accompany the house cocktails.

Cantina Doria rue Doria ⓣ04.95.73.40.59. Serving traditional, hearty, Corsican specialities; *aubergine à la bonifacienne* and fish soup being the main draw. Three-course menu for €15.

L' Archivolto 2 rue Archivolto ⓣ04.95.73.17.58. Centrally based in the *ville haute*, this friendly restaurant has a family-run feel. The seafood stew and terrines both come highly recommended. Mains €12–14.

Moving on

Bus Ajaccio (July–Sept; 2 daily, 6.30am & 2pm, Mon–Sat; 3hr 30min); Porto Vecchio, for connections to Bastia (from July–Sept 4 daily; 30min).

Ferry Santa-Teresa-di-Gallura in Sardinia (2–8 daily; 1hr).

Germany

HIGHLIGHTS

BERLIN: dramatic history and gritty modernity combine in this most untamed of European capitals

DOM, COLOGNE: Cologne's cathedral is Gothic grandeur on a massive scale

DRESDEN: glorious Baroque architecture by day; decadent bar-crawling by night

FREIBURG: mosaic streets, a majestic setting and one of Germany's most beautiful churches

OKTOBERFEST, MUNICH: the world's most famous beer festival

ROUGH COSTS

DAILY BUDGET Basic €40/occasional treat €55

DRINK Beer (half-litre €3.50)

FOOD Schnitzel €8

HOSTEL/BUDGET HOTEL €18/€40–70

TRAVEL Train: Munich–Berlin (500km) €39–113

FACT FILE

POPULATION 82.3 million

AREA 357,090 sq km

LANGUAGE German

CURRENCY Euro (€)

CAPITAL Berlin (population: 3.4 million)

INTERNATIONAL PHONE CODE ⓣ49

Introduction

With its quaint medieval villages, dynamic urban centres and beautiful landscapes, Germany is an enticing, but often underrated, destination. It also has a rich cultural diversity, a hangover from the days when the country was a patchwork of independent states. This regionalism is one of the most fascinating aspects of the country, allowing extremes of tradition and modernity to coexist – as well as scores of dialects, brewing traditions and cuisines.

Another advantage of such regional distinctiveness is the number of cities in Germany with the cosmopolitan air – and world-class museum collections – of national capitals. **Berlin** itself is electrifying – an old city bursting with youth, art and energy. **Munich** is a star attraction, with great museums and a thriving nightlife. **Cologne**'s skyline is still dominated by a spectacular cathedral begun in 1248, while its decidedly impious Carnival celebration is the biggest in Europe. **Hamburg** is a large, bustling harbour city with a nightlife that rivals many of the continent's capitals. In the east there's the Baroque splendour and thriving counterculture of **Dresden**. Then there are the smaller towns, offering another side of Germany: the pastoral, the quaint, the romantic. There's nowhere as well loved as the university town of **Heidelberg**, while smaller stars such as **Trier**, **Regensburg**, **Potsdam** and small but cultured **Weimar** all reward exploration.

Among the scenic highlights are the **Bavarian Alps** on Munich's doorstep, the **Bodensee** (Lake Constance) marking the Swiss border, the **Black Forest** and the **Rhine Valley**, whose majestic sweep has spawned a rich fund of legends and folklore.

CHRONOLOGY

57 BC Julius Caesar invades and conquers "Germania Inferior".

800 AD Charlemagne, the Frankish ruler over territory including Germany, is crowned Holy Roman Emperor.

1438 Habsburg dynasty rules over Germany with election of Albert I.

1517 Martin Luther writes his *95 Theses* against corruption in the Catholic Church, a protest that culminates in the Protestant Reformation.

1648 End of the Thirty Years' War between European Catholic and Protestant powers leads to the division of Germany into princely states.

1871 Unification of Germany under Chancellor Otto von Bismarck, after German success in the Franco-Prussian War.

1880s Bismarck establishes German colonies in Africa.

1918 Germany is defeated in WWI; the Treaty of Versailles enforces heavy reparation payments upon Germany.

1919 The Weimar Republic is established.

1923 Hyper inflation causes economic meltdown.

1933 Hitler becomes Chancellor of Germany.

1939 WWII begins as Germany invades Poland.

1939–1945 Millions die at the hands of the Nazis in concentration camps during the Holocaust.

1945 Germany is defeated, as the Allies occupy the country.

1949 Germany is divided between Communist East and Democratic West.

1961 The Berlin Wall is constructed.

1989 Following mass protests, the Berlin Wall is torn down.

1990 The two Germanys are reunited on Oct 3.

2002 The Euro replaces the Mark as Germany's currency.

2005 Angela Merkel becomes first female – and first eastern – Chancellor.

2006 Germany hosts the Football World Cup.

2009 Germany celebrates twenty years since the fall of the Wall; Angela Merkel is re-elected as chancellor.

ARRIVAL

Flying is, predictably, the cheapest and most convenient way to get to Germany

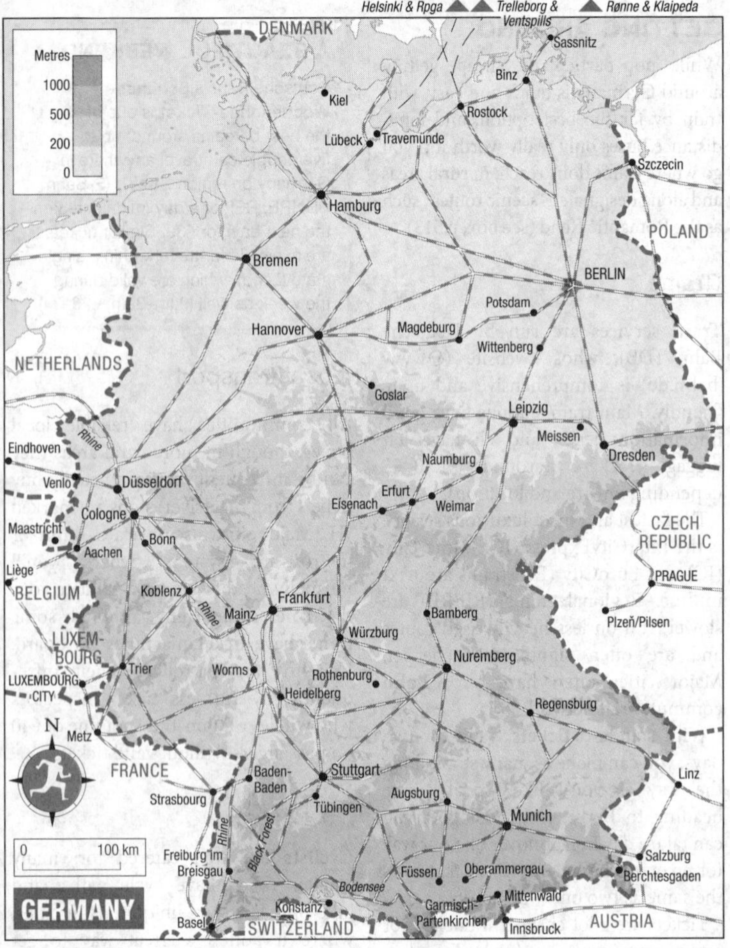

from overseas, as well as from many other European countries thanks to the proliferation of discount airlines. The largest airport is Frankfurt Airport (FRA), and there are over forty others to choose from. Germany is well connected by **bus and train** with destinations throughout continental Europe. Check Deutsche Bahn's website (ⓦwww.bahn.de) for international routes; several private bus companies, such as Berlin-LinienBus (ⓦwww.berlinlinienbus.de), Gulliver's (ⓦwww.gulliver.de), Eurolines (ⓦwww.eurolines.com) and Touring (ⓦwww.touring.de) run routes from as far afield as Barcelona and Bucharest.

Ferries operate services between the German Baltic ports of Lübeck (Travemünde), Rostock (3hr by train north of Berlin) and Sassnitz-Mukran and Denmark, Finland, Latvia, Lithuania and Sweden. The major carriers are Scandlines (ⓦwww.scandlines.de), Tallink/Silja (ⓦwww.tallinksilja.com), Lisco (ⓦwww.dfdslisco.com), Finnlines (ⓦwww.finnlines.com) and TT-Line (ⓦwww.ttline.com).

GETTING AROUND

While not particularly cheap, getting around Germany is quick and easy, with train by far the best option, and long-distance buses only really worth it if you go where trains don't reach, in rural areas and along designated "scenic routes", such as the Romantic Road (see box, p.513).

Trains

Train services are run by Deutsche Bahn (DB), whose website (Ⓦwww.bahn.de) is comprehensive and user-friendly. Main train stations have good information desks, and all have left luggage lockers (around €1.50–€5 depending on size and location).

The fastest and most luxurious service is the InterCityExpress (ICE). InterCity (IC) and EuroCity (EC) trains are next in line. Regional trains (RE/RB) are slower, run on less heavily used routes and are often significantly cheaper. Major cities often have an **S-Bahn** commuter rail network.

With standard **tickets**, valid for two days, you can make as many stops along the way as you'd like. So if you're heading to Berlin from Cologne, you can take a day in Hannover on your way for no extra charge. A return ticket costs the same as two one-way tickets.

Tickets are a lot cheaper if booked for set journeys in advance (up to three days before) – with 25 and 50 percent discounts often available – and there are numerous discount passes for groups and individuals (see box opposite). InterRail and Eurail are both valid (including on S-Bahn trains). The InterRail One Country Pass (Ⓦwww.InterRailnet.com) is available for Germany, providing three, four, six or eight days of travel in one month (€189/209/269/299). **Supplements** apply on sleepers, the Thalys (a service between Cologne and Brussels), Berlin–Warszawa Express and ICE Sprinters – a fast service between a few key places, such as Frankfurt–Berlin.

> **A BEAUTIFUL WEEKEND**
>
> Deutsche Bahn's **Schönes-Wochenende-Ticket** is one of the best bargains around: up to five people can travel anywhere in Germany on regional trains (S-Bahn, RB, IRE, RE) for a day (midnight–3am the next day) for €39. Similar tickets are available for travel within a single state (*Land*), which are valid during the week as well (9am–3am; €26–34).

Local transport

All communities have reliable local **buses**, though in more rural areas they can be infrequent. You can usually buy tickets from the driver; stops are marked "H". Major cities also have a **U-Bahn**, or metro/tram system, where you'll normally need to buy and validate your ticket before boarding, although some trams have ticket machines on board. U-Bahns are patrolled, albeit infrequently, by ruthless ticket inspectors who will levy an on-the-spot fine of €40 on passengers without valid tickets.

By bicycle

Cyclists are well catered for: many smaller roads have cycle paths, and bike-only lanes are ubiquitous in cities, where it's often a great way to get around. There are also some excellent long-distance cycle routes. Many train stations have bicycle rental outlets (around €8–12/day), including DB's Call a Bike scheme (Ⓦwww.callabike.de); hostels also often rent bikes. If you want to take your bike on a train, it'll need its own ticket: €4.50 on regional trains and €9 on IC/EC trains. Bikes are not allowed on ICE services.

ACCOMMODATION

It's often best to reserve ahead for **accommodation** in Germany, especially in the cities, where trade fairs and heavy

seasonal tourism can create high demand. Nearly all tourist offices will reserve **accommodation** for a fee.

You're never far away from a large, functional **HI hostel** (*Jugendherberge*) run by DJH (Ⓦwww.jugendherberge.de) – but they are often block-booked by school groups, so reserve in advance, and aren't particularly cheap (around €22, breakfast and sheets included). Non-HI members pay an extra €3.10 per night (until you have six stamps, which gives you membership); people aged 27 and over also pay around €3 extra. There are usually no curfews or lockouts, but reception hours may be limited. **Independent hostels** are usually a better choice in cities – friendly, relaxed and often an excellent source of local tips. Expect to pay €15–22; breakfast and sheets are not always included. The Backpacker Network Germany (Ⓦwww.backpackernetwork.de) lists many options.

Hotels are graded, clean and comfortable. In rural areas, prices start at about €30 for a double room; in cities, about €40–50. **Pensions** and B&Bs are plentiful; local tourist offices will have a list (or look for signs saying *Fremdenzimmer* or *Zimmer frei*); rates start at around €20 for a double.

Even the most basic **campsites** have toilets, washing facilities and a shop. For a complete list of campsites see Ⓦwww.bvcd.de.

FOOD AND DRINK

German **food** is both good value and high quality, and though traditionally solid and meat-heavy, at least in cities there's often a wide range of international choices. Most hotels and guesthouses include **breakfast** in the price of the room – typically including cold meats and cheeses, bread and jam.

Traditionally **lunch** tends to be treated as the main meal, with good-value daily menus on offer. A *Gaststätte*, *Gasthaus*, *Gasthof*, *Brauhaus* or *Wirtschaft* functions as a *gemütlich* (cosy) meeting-point, pub and restaurant. The cuisine here resembles hearty home cooking, with pork and sausages featuring heavily, with distinct regional variations.

The distinction between café, restaurant and bar is often blurred, with many offering good simple menus of breakfasts, salads and some mains. The easiest option for snacks however, is to head for the ubiquitous **Imbiss** stands and shops, which range from traditional Wurst sellers to popular döner kebap places.

For **vegetarians**, Germany is fairly easy. Though traditional menus are very meaty, there's usually something on offer – such as *Maultaschen* (similar to ravioli) and *Käsespätzle* (like macaroni cheese) – and anywhere more contemporary will nearly always have a veggie choice or two. A wide variety of **international cuisines** are available: Italian restaurants are the most reliable, but there are also plenty offering Balkan, Greek, Turkish and Chinese cooking.

Drink

For **beer** drinkers, Germany is paradise. Munich's beer gardens and beer halls are the most famous drinking dens in the country, offering a wide variety of premier products, from dark lagers through tart *Weizens* to powerful *Bocks*. Cologne holds the world record for the number of city breweries, all of which produce the beer called *Kölsch*, but wherever you go you can be fairly sure of getting a locally brewed beer. There are many high-quality German **wines**, especially those made from the Riesling grape. **Apfelwein** is a variant of cider beloved in and around Frankfurt.

CULTURE AND ETIQUETTE

Most Germans are friendly, hospitable and helpful, and if you stand at a corner long enough with a map in your hand, someone's bound to volunteer to help you out. **Jaywalking** is illegal in Germany; you could be fined if caught,

but are most likely to get off with disapproving looks from passers-by (less so in large cities).

Paying at a restaurant is also a little different. If you're in a group, you'll be asked if you want to pay individually (*getrennt*) or all together (*zusammen*). To **tip**, round your bill up to the next €0.50 or €1 and give the total directly to the waiter.

SPORTS AND OUTDOOR ACTIVITIES

Bundesliga football (ⓦwww.bundesliga.de/en) is the major spectator sport in Germany, with world-class clubs playing in top-notch stadiums (revamped for the 2006 World Cup). Important matches sell out well in advance; tickets can be purchased from the clubs' websites.

Germany's great outdoors has a lot to offer, with **hiking** and **cycling** featuring high on the list. The most popular regions for hiking are in the Black Forest and the Bavarian Alps, but there are well-maintained, colour-coded hiking routes all over Germany. The country is criss-crossed with long-distance cycling routes. The cycling page on Germany's tourism website (ⓦwww.germany-tourism.de/cycling) is excellent for route planning.

For **cross-country skiing**, head to the Black Forest region around Titisee (see p.509). For downhill, the Bavarian Alps, especially around Garmisch-Partenkirchen (see p.519) are your best bet.

COMMUNICATIONS

Post offices are open Monday to Friday 8am to 6pm and Saturday 8am to 1pm. Call shops are the cheapest way to phone abroad, though you can also **phone** abroad from all payphones except those marked "National"; phonecards are widely available. The operator is on ⓣ03. Internet access is widespread; expect to pay €2–4/hr.

GERMANY ON THE NET

ⓦwww.germany-tourism.de Official tourist board site.
ⓦwww.stadtplandienst.de City maps.
ⓦwww.webmuseen.de Information on the country's museums.

EMERGENCIES

The **police** (*Polizei*) usually treat foreigners with courtesy. Reporting thefts at local police stations is straightforward, but inevitably there'll be a great deal of bureaucracy to wade through. Doctors generally speak English. **Pharmacies** (*Apotheken*) can deal with many minor complaints; all display a rota of local pharmacies open 24hr.

INFORMATION

You'll find a good **tourist office** in every town, which can provide large amounts of literature and maps; the town or region's tourist website is usually also excellent. City tourist offices usually offer discount cards, which typically cover public transport and either free or discounted entry to major sights. These can be worthwhile, but check first what discounts are offered – they can be the same as a student price.

MONEY AND BANKS

German currency is the **euro** (€). **Exchange facilities** are available in most banks, post offices and commercial exchange shops called *Wechselstuben*. The Reisebank has branches in the train stations of most main cities (generally open daily, often till 10/11pm). Basic **banking hours** are Monday to Friday 9am to noon and 1.30 to 3.30pm, Thursday till 6pm. **Credit cards** are fairly widely accepted – but certainly not universally – with restaurants and cafés sometimes not taking them. There can

EMERGENCY NUMBERS

Police ⓣ110; Fire & Ambulance ⓣ112

German

Pronunciation Consonants: "w" is pronounced like the English "v"; "sch" is pronounced "sh"; "z" is "ts". The German letter "ß" is basically a double "s". Vowels: "ei" is "eye", "ie" is "ee", "eu" is "oy".

	German	Pronunciation
Yes	*Ja*	Yah
No	*Nein*	Nine
Please	*Bitte*	Bitteh
Thank you	*Danke*	Duhnkeh
Hello/Good day	*Güten Tag*	Gooten tahg
Goodbye	*Tschüss, ciao*, or *auf Wiedersehen*	Chuss, chow, or owf veederzain
Excuse me	*Entschuldigen Sie, bitte*	Entshooldigen zee bitteh
Today	*heute*	hoyteh
Yesterday	*gestern*	gestern
Tomorrow	*morgen*	morgan
I don't understand	*Ich verstehe nicht*	Ik vershtayeh nikt
How much is...?	*Wieviel kostet...?*	Vee feel costet...?
Do you speak English?	*Sprechen Sie Englisch?*	Sprecken zee aing-lish?
I'd like a beer	*Ich hätte gern ein Bier*	Ik hetteh gairn ein beer
entrance /exit	*der Eingang/der Ausgang*	dare aingahng/ dare owsgahng
Toilet	*das WC/die Toilette*	dahs vay-tsay/dee toyletteh
HI hostel	*die Jugendherberge*	dee yoogendhairbairgeh
Main train station	der *Hauptbahnhof*	howptbahnhof
Bus	*der Bus*	dare boos
Plane	*das Flugzeug*	das floog-tsoyg
Train	*der Zug*	dare tsoog
Cheap/expensive	*billig/teuer*	billig/toy-er
Open/closed	*offen/auf geschlossen/zu*	uhffen/owf gehshlossen/tsoo
One	*Eins*	Einz
Two	*Zwei*	Tsvi
Three	*Drei*	Dry
Four	*Vier*	Fear
Five	*Fünf*	Foonf
Six	*Sechs*	Zex
Seven	*Sieben*	Zeeben
Eight	*Acht*	Ahkt
Nine	*Neun*	Noyn
Ten	*Zehn*	Tsain

be a surcharge in hostels and smaller hotels. **ATMs** are widespread.

OPENING HOURS AND HOLIDAYS

Shops open at 8am and close around 6 to 8pm weekdays and 2 to 4pm Saturday, and in most places are closed all day Sunday, though regulations vary by state. Exceptions are pharmacies, petrol stations and shops in and around train stations, which stay open late and at weekends. **Museums** and **historic monuments** are, with few exceptions (mainly in Bavaria), closed on Monday. **Public holidays** are: January 1, Jan January 6 (regional), Good Friday, Easter Monday, May 1, Ascension Day, Whit Monday, Corpus Christi (regional), August 15 (regional), October 3, November 1 (regional) and December 25 and 26.

Berlin

Energetic and irreverent, **BERLIN** is a welcoming, exciting city where the speed of change in the past few years has been astounding. With a long history of decadence and cultural dynamism, the revived national capital has become a magnet for artists and musicians. Culturally, it has some of the most important archeological collections in Europe, and an impressive range of galleries and museums. Its nightlife is an exuberant, cutting-edge mix that could keep you occupied for weeks.

The city reeks of modern European history, having played a dominant role in Imperial Germany, during the Weimar Republic after 1914, and in the Nazis' Third Reich. After 1945, the city was partitioned by the victorious Allies, and as a result was the frontline of the Cold War. In 1961, its division into two hostile sectors was given a very visible expression by the construction of the notorious Berlin Wall. After the Wall fell in 1989, Berlin became the national capital once again in 1990. These days, parliament (Bundestag) sits in the renovated Reichstag building, and the city's excellent museum collections have been put back together again. The physical revival of Berlin has put it at the forefront of contemporary architecture, and there is a plethora of dramatic new buildings around the city.

What to see and do

Most of Berlin's main sights are in the central district of **Mitte**, focused on Unter den Linden between the Brandenburg Gate and Museuminsel and the area around Hackescher Markt just further northeast. To the south of the Brandenburg Gate lies Potsdamer Platz and the museums of the Kulturforum, while to the west of the Tiergarten park you'll find the central shopping area, the Ku'damm, and the famous Bahnhof Zoo. Together with **Mitte**, the districts of **Kreuzberg**, **Prenzlauer Berg** and **Friedrichshain** are the city's liveliest.

MUSEUM ENTRY

Berlin's superb **state museums and galleries** (including all Museuminsel and Kulturforum museums; ⓦ www.smb.museum) are all **free** from four hours before closing on **Thursdays**. A three-day ticket (**SchauLUST Pass**) for all Berlin's state-owned museums, as well as the Jewish Museum, is a steal at €19/students €9.50. With a **student ID card** almost all sights and museums give up to fifty percent discounts.

The Brandenburg Gate and the Reichstag

The most atmospheric place to start a tour of Berlin is the **Brandenburg Gate**, built as a city-gate-cum-triumphal-arch in 1791. To its north stands the **Reichstag**, the nineteenth-century home of the German parliament, remodelled by Norman Foster for the resumption of its historic role in 1999, when the much-photographed glass cupola was added. A trip to the top (daily 8am–midnight; free) affords stunning views over the new government quarter that has developed around the Reichstag and the vast Tiergarten to the west. The queue tends to be shorter in the late afternoon.

The Holocaust Memorial

To the south of the Brandenburg Gate lies the bold Holocaust Memorial (officially known as the **Memorial to the Murdered Jews of Europe**), a monument consisting of 2711 upright concrete slabs of varying height arranged in a dizzying grid. The exhibition in the underground information centre (Ort der Information; Tues–Sun: April–Sept 10am–8pm; Oct–March 10am–7pm; free) is carefully presented and moving.

Unter den Linden

East of the Brandenburg Gate stretches broad and stately **Unter den Linden**, once Berlin's most important thoroughfare. Post-unification renewal, including over-sized embassies and museums flanking the boulevard, only hint at its former grandeur.

Bebelplatz, at Unter den Linden's eastern end, was the site of the infamous Nazi book-burning of May 10, 1933; an unusual memorial – an underground room housing empty bookshelves visible through a glass panel set in the centre of the square – marks the event.

More than anyone, it was architect Karl Friedrich Schinkel who shaped nineteenth-century Berlin and one of his most famous creations stands opposite the Staatsoper further along Unter den Linden: the **Neue Wache**, a former royal guardhouse resembling a Roman temple and now a memorial to victims of war and tyranny. Next door the Baroque old Prussian **Zeughaus** (Arsenal) now houses the excellent **Deutsches Historisches Museum** (daily 10am–6pm; €5). It covers two thousand years of German history in imaginative displays that often focus on social history, making good use of the vast selection of artefacts in the collection: from a seventeenth-century Turkish tent taken during the siege of Vienna to parallel displays of life in 1950s East and West, complete with Trabant and VW Beetle. Behind the main building an elegant glass spiral annexe designed by I.M. Pei is used for temporary exhibitions.

The Gendarmenmarkt

Following Charlottenstrasse south from Unter den Linden, you come to the elegant **Gendarmenmarkt**, where the **Französischer Dom** and lookalike **Deutscher Dom** dominate on either side of the square. The former was built as a church for Berlin's influential Huguenot community at the beginning of the eighteenth century. Between them stands the Neoclassical **Konzerthaus** by Schinkel. A block west of here lies **Friedrichstrasse**, a high-class shopping district.

Schlossplatz and Museuminsel

At the eastern end of Unter den Linden is the **Schlossplatz**, former site of the imperial palace, then of the GDR's Palast der Republik (parliament), demolished in 2008. At the time of writing it was a vast building site, and there are plans to reconstruct the old Schloss's facade. The Platz stands at the midpoint of a city-centre island whose northern half, **Museuminsel**, is the location of five of Berlin's top museums, and the **Berliner Dom**, which overlooks the green Lustgarten. Grandest and most impressive is the **Pergamonmuseum** (daily 10am–6pm, Thurs till 10pm; €10/students €5), which boasts a treasure-trove of the ancient world, including the spectacular Pergamon Altar, which dates from 160 BC, and the huge Processional Way from sixth-century BC Babylon. The **Alte Nationalgalerie** (Tues–Sun 10am–6pm, Thurs till 10pm; €8/students €4) contains a collection of nineteenth-century European art. At the island's northern tip is the beautifully restored **Bode-Museum** (daily 10am–6pm, Thurs till 10pm; same prices), which houses Byzantine art and medieval to eighteenth-century sculpture. In the **Altes Museum** (same hours and prices) are Greek and Roman antiquities. The **Neues Museum** (Mon–Wed & Sun 10am–6pm; Thurs–Sat 10am–8pm; €10/students €5) houses the Ägyptisches Museum and parts of the Museum of Pre- and Early History.

Alexanderplatz

To reach **Alexanderplatz**, the stark commercial square that was the hub of communist East Berlin, head along Karl-Liebknecht-Strasse (the continuation of Unter den Linden), past the

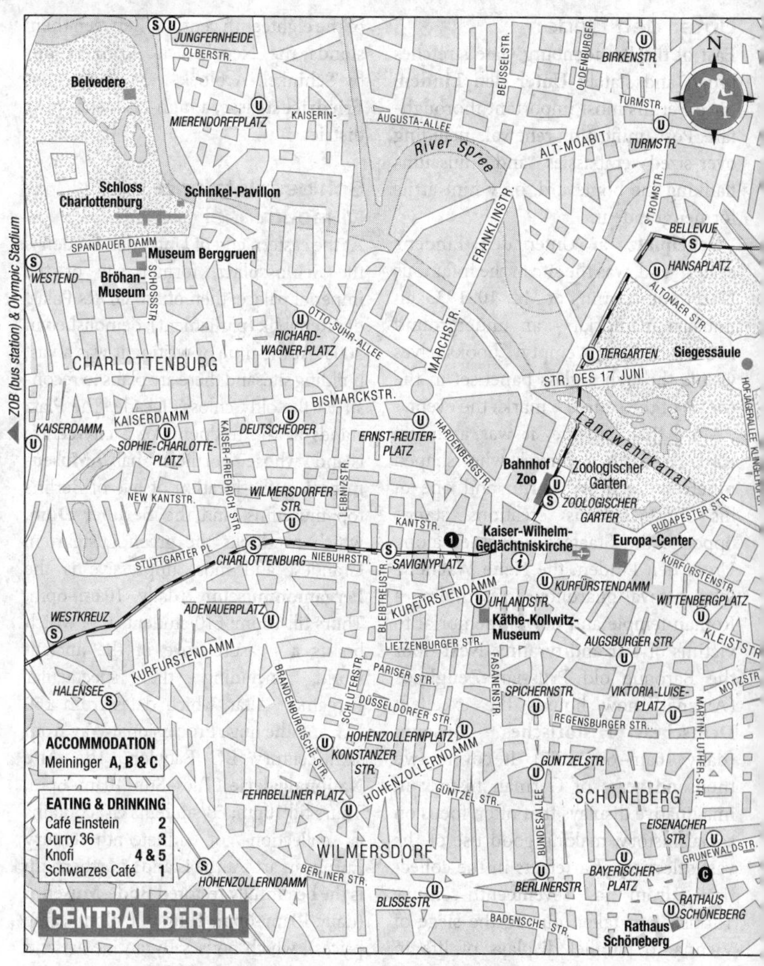

Neptunbrunnen fountain and the thirteenth-century Marienkirche. Like every other building in the vicinity, the church is overshadowed by the gigantic **Fernsehturm** (TV tower; daily: March–Oct 9am–midnight; Nov–Feb 10am–midnight; €10), whose 203-metre-high observation platform and revolving café offer unbeatable views. Southwest of here lies the **Nikolaiviertel**, a quarter of reconstructed medieval buildings and winding streets, which was razed overnight on June 16, 1944.

Hackescher Markt and around

If Unter den Linden is the formal centre of the reunified Berlin, **Hackescher Markt**, and in particular **Oranienburger Strasse**, **Augustusstrasse** and the streets around, were, immediately post-reunification, the social, cultural and artistic heart. Though now fairly touristy and upmarket, the area is still a bustling, attractive place to wander and window-shop, particularly in the quarter's distinctive *Höfe*, or series of courtyards. The elegant **Hackesche**

Höfe are the grandest of these, with eight courtyards featuring cafés, galleries and designer shops, but others – such as Heckmannhof and Kunsthof, both running between Augustusstrasse and Oranienburger Strasse – are worth exploring, as is pretty Sophienstrasse.

Historically this was the Jewish quarter, a legacy most evident in the rebuilt Moorish-style gold dome of the **Neue Synagoge** on Oranienburger Strasse (Sun–Thurs 10am–6pm; March–Oct Sun & Mon till 8pm; Fri: April–Sept 10am–5pm, Oct–March 10am–2pm; €3, students €2). Little remains of the building beyond the facade, but there are exhibitions on the history of the synagogue and on Jewish culture.

Potsdamer Platz

The heart of prewar Berlin was to the south of the Brandenburg Gate, its core formed by **Potsdamer Platz**, an area starkly cut through by the Wall. Post-reunification, huge commercial development has created Berlin's small financial district, at its core the impressive Sony Center, which includes

cinemas, shops and an attractive semi-open plaza.

The Kulturforum

West of Potsdamer Platz lies the Kulturforum, a series of museums centred on the unmissable **Gemäldegalerie** (Tues–Sun 10am–6pm, Thurs till 10pm; €8/students €4; S- & U-Bahn Potsdamer Platz). Inside is a world-class collection of Old Masters, covering all the main European schools from the Middle Ages to the late eighteenth century. The interconnected building to the north houses the **Kunstgewerbemuseum** (Tues–Fri 10am–6pm, Sat & Sun 11am–6pm; same ticket), a sparkling collection of European arts and crafts. A couple of minutes' walk to the south, the **Neue Nationalgalerie** (Tues–Sun 10am–6pm, Thurs till 10pm, Sat till 8pm; same ticket) hosts temporary modern art exhibitions and has a good permanent collection of twentieth-century German paintings, including Berlin portraits and cityscapes by George Grosz and Otto Dix.

The course of the Wall

It's now twenty years since the Berlin Wall came down, and recently an increased effort has been made to remember the impact of the Wall and those who died trying to cross it. Much of the course is marked by a row of two cobblestones, with information posts located at key points. There are also several stretches preserved as memorials. Immediately east of Potsdamer Platz, a sizeable, crumbling section of Wall runs along Niederkirchnerstrasse, behind which is the captivating open-air exhibition, **Topography of Terror** (daily: May–Sept 10am–8pm; Oct–April 10am–6pm; free), which occupies the former site of the Gestapo and SS headquarters and documents their chilling histories; a permanent documentation centre is due to open here in 2010.

Where Niederkirchnerstrasse meets Friedrichstrasse is the site of the most infamous point: **Checkpoint Charlie**. Here, along with a reconstruction of the actual checkpoint, is a fascinating open-air display on the Wall's history, preferable by far to the **Mauermuseum/Haus am Checkpoint Charlie**, nearby at Friedrichstr. 43–45 (daily 9am–10pm; €12.50/students €9.50).

At Bernauer Strasse, just north of Mitte, there's a short stretch of wall that has been preserved as the **Berlin Wall Memorial**. This is the only section where the two parallel walls plus "death strip" between remain, viewable from a lookout at the small documentation centre over the road (Tues–Sat: April–Oct 10am–6pm; Nov–March 10am–5pm; free; S-Bahn Nordbahnhof/U-Bahn Bernauer Str.).

Stretching along the River Spree, near Friedrichshain, a 1.3-kilometre-long section of the Wall known as the **East Side Gallery** (S-Bahn Ostbahnhof) is covered with paintings by international artists, which were produced in the months after the fall of the Iron Curtain.

At Bernauer Strasse, Checkpoint Charlie and the East Side Gallery there are kiosks where you can pick up a GPS audioguide to follow the course of the Wall (4hr €8, day €10, students €5/€7; Ⓦ www.mauerguide.com).

Jüdisches Museum

Daniel Libeskind's striking zinc-skinned **Jüdisches Museum**, Lindenstr. 9–14 in west Kreuzberg (Jewish Museum; Mon 10am–10pm, Tues–Sun 10am–8pm; €5/students €2.50; U-Bahn Hallesches Tor/Kochstr.), is part museum, part memorial. Its lower ground level is Libeskind's reflection on three strands of the Jewish experience in Berlin: exile, Holocaust and continuity, and is a disorientating but compelling experience. You are then directed to the upper two floors, a more conventional exhibition which documents the culture, notable achievements and history of Berlin's Jewish community.

Ku'damm and around

A short walk south of Bahnhof Zoo station, at the focus of the city's western side, is the start of the Kurfürstendamm, or **Ku'damm**, a 3.5-kilometre strip of ritzy shops, cinemas, bars and cafés. Western Berlin's most famous landmark here is the **Kaiser-Wilhelm-Gedächtniskirche**, mostly destroyed by British bombing in 1943, the broken spire left as a reminder of the horrors of war, with a modern church built alongside.

Tiergarten

Berlin zoo, beside Zoo Station, forms the beginning of the giant **Tiergarten**, a restful expanse of woodland and a good place to wander along the banks of the Landwehrkanal. Strasse des 17 Juni heads all the way through the Tiergarten to the Brandenburg Gate, with the **Siegessäule**, the iconic victory monument, at the central point.

Schloss Charlottenburg

The sumptuously restored **Schloss Charlottenburg** is on Spandauer Damm 10–22 (Old Palace; Tues–Sun: April–Oct 10am–6pm, Nov–March 10am–5pm, €10/students €7; New Wing Mon & Wed–Sun: April–Oct 10am–6pm, Nov–March 10am–5pm, €6/students €5; 10min walk from S-Bahn Westend or bus #M45 from Zoo). Commissioned by the future Queen Sophie Charlotte in 1695, it was added to throughout the eighteenth and early nineteenth centuries. Admission to the Old Palace includes a tour of the main state apartments and self-guided visits to the private chambers, while the New Wing includes an array of paintings by Watteau and other eighteenth-century French artists. South of the Schloss complex, the **Museum Berggruen** at Schlossstrasse 1 (Tues–Sun 10am–6pm; €8/students €4) presents a large Picasso collection, among others.

The Olympiastadion

Located at the west of the city is the site of the 1936 Olympics, and of the 2006 Football World Cup final, the **Olympiastadion**. If you can't make it to a Hertha BSC (Ⓦwww.herthabsc.de) match, you can visit at other times (daily: 9am–4/7/8pm; €4/students €3; various tours available €8–10; Ⓦwww.olympiastadion-berlin.de; U- or S-Bahn to Olympiastadion); check online or at the tourist office first.

Arrival

Air Both Berlin's airports (Ⓦwww.berlin-airport.de) are within Berlin public transport's zone AB, so normal single (€2.10) or day tickets apply. From Tegel airport (TXL) the frequent #TXL express bus runs to the Hauptbahnhof and Alexanderplatz, while #X9 express or local #109 buses run to Bahnhof Zoo. From Berlin's Schönefeld airport (SXF) S-Bahn line S9 runs to Alexanderplatz, the Hauptbahnhof and Bahnhof Zoo (every 30min; 30min); bus #X7 runs to nearby U-Bahn Rudow. In 2011 Tegel is due to close and Schönefeld extended into Berlin Brandenburg International airport.
Train The huge Hauptbahnhof northeast of the Brandenburg Gate is well connected to the rest of the city by S- and U-Bahn.
Bus Most international buses stop at the bus station (ZOB), linked to the centre by express buses #X34 and #X49, as well as regular buses #104, #139, #218, #349 and #M49; U-Bahn #2, from Kaiserdamm station; S-Bahn from Messe-Nord/ICC.

Information

Tourist offices At the Hauptbahnhof Ⓣ030/25 00 25, Ⓦwww.visitberlin.de (daily 8am–10pm). Also at: Brandenburg Gate (daily 10am–7pm); Kurfürstendamm 21 (Mon–Sat 10am–8pm, Sun 10am–6pm); and in the ALEXA shopping centre, Alexanderplatz (Mon–Sat 10am–8pm).
Discount passes The WelcomeCard (Berlin AB: 48hr €16.50/72hr, €22/5-day €29.50; Berlin and Potsdam ABC: 48hr €18.50/72hr, €25/5-day €34.50; Ⓦwww.berlin-welcomecard.de) provides free travel and up to fifty percent off at many of the major tourist sights, though not those on the Museuminsel, and many of the discounts are the same as student prices.

City transport

BVG (Ⓦwww.bvg.de) operate an efficient, integrated system of U- and S-Bahn train lines,

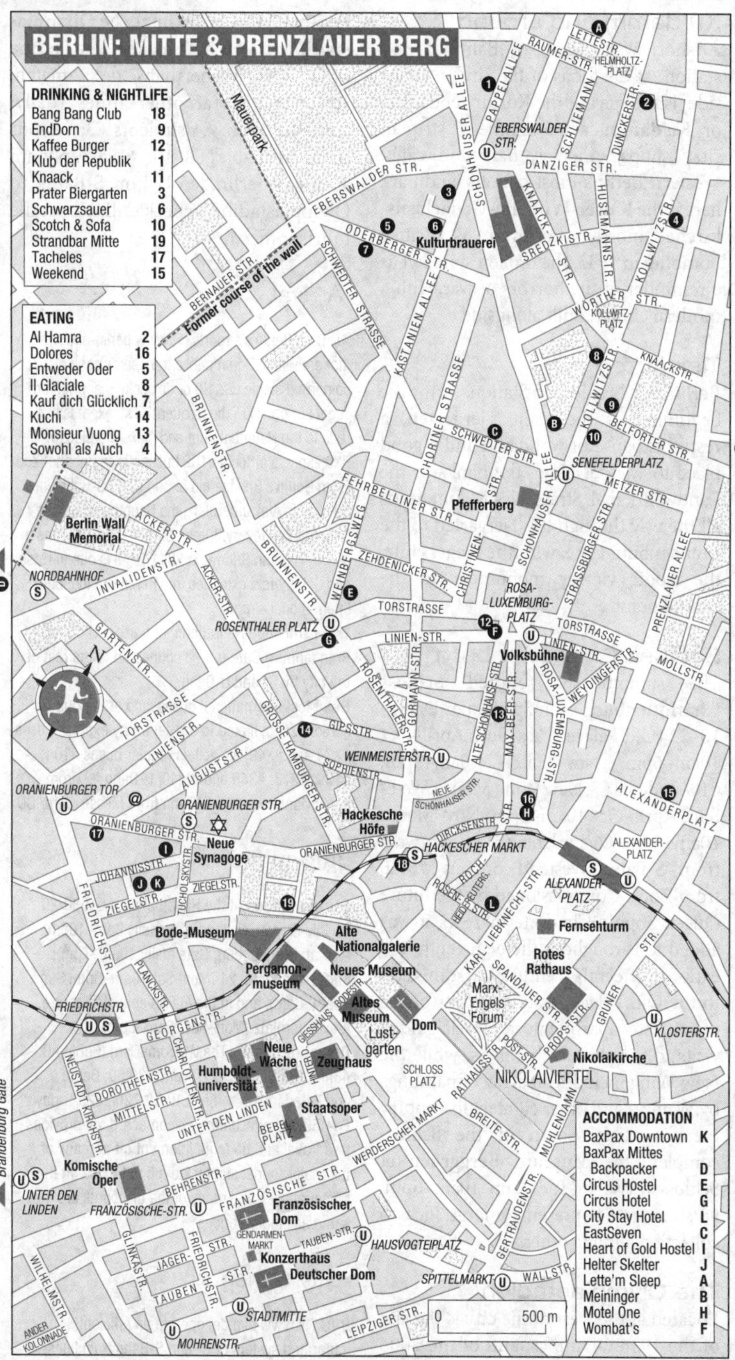
BERLIN: MITTE & PRENZLAUER BERG
DRINKING & NIGHTLIFE
Bang Bang Club 18
EndDorn 9
Kaffee Burger 12
Klub der Republik 1
Knaack 11
Prater Biergarten 3
Schwarzsauer 6
Scotch & Sofa 10
Strandbar Mitte 19
Tacheles 17
Weekend 15
EATING
Al Hamra 2
Dolores 16
Entweder Oder 5
Il Glaciale 8
Kauf dich Glücklich 7
Kuchi 14
Monsieur Vuong 13
Sowohl als Auch 4
ACCOMMODATION
BaxPax Downtown K
BaxPax Mittes Backpacker D
Circus Hostel E
Circus Hotel G
City Stay Hotel L
EastSeven C
Heart of Gold Hostel I
Helter Skelter J
Lette'm Sleep A
Meininger B
Motel One H
Wombat's F
Mauerpark
Former course of the wall
Berlin Wall Memorial
Kulturbrauerei
Pfefferberg
Volksbühne
Hackesche Höfe
Neue Synagoge
Bode-Museum
Alte Nationalgalerie
Pergamonmuseum
Neues Museum
Altes Museum
Dom
Lustgarten
Neue Wache
Zeughaus
Humboldt-universität
Staatsoper
Komische Oper
Französischer Dom
Konzerthaus
Deutscher Dom
Fernsehturm
Rotes Rathaus
Marx-Engels Forum
Nikolaikirche
NIKOLAIVIERTEL
SCHLOSS PLATZ
GENDARMENMARKT
BEBELPLATZ
ALEXANDERPLATZ
EBERSWALDER STR.
SENEFELDERPLATZ
NORDBAHNHOF
ROSENTHALER PLATZ
ROSA-LUXEMBURG-PLATZ
WEINMEISTERSTR.
ORANIENBURGER TOR
ORANIENBURGER STR.
HACKESCHER MARKT
FRIEDRICHSTR.
KLOSTERSTR.
UNTER DEN LINDEN
FRANZÖSISCHE-STR.
HAUSVOGTEIPLATZ
SPITTELMARKT
STADTMITTE
MOHRENSTR.
Brandenburg Gate
SCHÖNHAUSER ALLEE
PAPPELALLEE
KASTANIENALLEE
TORSTRASSE
INVALIDENSTR.
BERNAUER STR.
UNTER DEN LINDEN
KARL-LIEBKNECHT-STR.
FRIEDRICHSTR.
PRENZLAUER ALLEE
0 500 m

buses and trams, though cycling in Berlin is also very easy (see p.473 for bike rental outlets).

U- and S-Bahn Trains run daily 4.30am–12.30am (Fri & Sat all night).

Bus and tram The city bus network – and the tram system mainly in eastern Berlin – covers most of the gaps left by the U-Bahn; several useful tram routes centre on Hackescher Markt, including the M1 to Prenzlauer Berg. A night-time network of buses and trams operates, with buses (around every 30min) often following U-Bahn line routes; free maps are available at most stations.

Tickets Available from machines at U-Bahn stations, on trams or from bus drivers: zone AB single ticket €2.10; zone ABC single €2.80; short-trip ticket (*Kurzstreckentarif*) for three train or six bus/tram stops €1.30; zone AB day ticket €6.10; for two, three or five days the WelcomeCard (see p.467) is good value. Validate single tickets in the yellow machines on platforms before travelling.

Taxi Fares are €3 flag fall then €1.20–1.55/km; if you hail a taxi on the street – rather than at a stand or by phone – you can ask for a short-trip price (*Kurzstreckentarif*) before the trip starts and pay €3.50 for a 2km ride. Taxi firms include: Taxi Funk ⓣ030/44 33 22 and Funk Taxi ⓣ030/26 10 26.

Accommodation

Berlin has plenty of great hostels, primarily in Mitte, Prenzlauer Berg, Kreuzberg and Friedrichshain; several newer ones, somewhere between a hostel and hotel, are often the best option for private rooms as well as dorms. It's best to book at least a couple of weeks in advance in high season. A few of the larger hostels vary their prices considerably depending on demand; high-season prices are quoted.

Hostels

BaxPax ⓦwww.baxpax.de. Trio of backpacker outfits with clean, bright-as-a-button rooms. *Kreuzberg* (Skalitzer Str. 104; ⓣ030/695 183 22; U-Bahn Görlitzer Bahnhof; dorms €9–22, doubles €42–60) and *Mittes Backpacker* (Chausseestr. 102; ⓣ030/283 909 65; U-Bahn Zinnowitzer Str; dorms €14–26, doubles €50–68) are laid-back, offering cooking facilities, bike rental and (in Kreuzberg only) a rare chance to sleep in a VW Beetle. The *Downtown BaxPax* (Ziegelstr. 28; ⓣ030/278 748 80; S- & U-Bahn Friedrichstr.; dorms €13–45, rooms €54–132), in the best location, is a little more hotel-like, with most rooms en suite. Prices vary hugely depending on season; sheets €2.50.

The Circus Hostel Weinbergsweg 1a, Mitte ⓣ030/20 00 39 39, ⓦwww.circus-berlin.de. Welcoming, clean, fun and deservedly popular base in a great location between Mitte and Prenzlauer Berg, with helpful staff. U-Bahn Rosenthaler Platz. Dorms €19–25, doubles €56, en suite €70.

City Stay Hotel Rosenstr. 16, Mitte ⓣ030/23 62 40 31, ⓦwww.citystay.de. Bright and airy hostel in the bustling heart of Mitte which, thanks to its off-street location, is a peaceful and safe base for travellers. S-Bahn Hackescher Markt. Dorms €17–21, doubles €50, en suite €64.

EastSeven Schwedter Str. 7, Prenzlauer Berg ⓣ030/936 222 40, ⓦwww.eastseven.de. Cosy, small, independent hostel with kitchen and pretty garden, including a barbecue. Some nice touches, such as communal meals on Monday, discounts in local shops and good tips on nearby clubs. U-Bahn Senefelderplatz. Sheets €3. Dorms €17–21, doubles €50.

Heart of Gold Hostel Johannisstr. 11, Mitte ⓣ030/29 00 33 00, ⓦwww.heartofgold-hostel.de. Well located in the heart of downtown Mitte, this *Hitchhiker's Guide*/starship-themed place has a relaxing bar, spotless rooms and friendly pilots. Sheets included. S-Bahn Friedrichstr. Dorms €15–22, doubles €60.

Helter Skelter Kalkscheunenstr. 4–5, Mitte ⓣ030/280 44 997, ⓦwww.helterskelterhostel.com. Lively and central old-school backpackers' place with kitchen and sheets included. S-Bahn Friedrichstr. Dorms €14–22, doubles €54.

Lette'm Sleep Lettestr. 7, Prenzlauer Berg ⓣ030/44 73 36 23, ⓦwww.backpackers.de. Chilled-out hostel with free internet, a kitchen and a good location, on a particularly attractive square in Prenzlauer Berg. U-Bahn Eberswalder Str. Dorms €17–28, doubles €49.

Meininger ⓣ030/66 63 61 00, ⓦwww.meininger-hostels.de. Although not directly in the centre, all these places are modern, friendly, and include breakfast and sheets; cheaper if booked online, and prices vary significantly depending on demand. Prenzlauer Berg: Schönhauser Allee 19 (U-Bahn Senefelderplatz; dorms €19–39); Schöneberg: Meininger Str. 10 (U-Bahn Rathaus Schöneberg; dorms €12–29); Kreuzberg: Hallesches Ufer 30 and its less attractive overspill at Tempelhofer Ufer 10 (U-Bahn Möckernbrücke; dorms €14–37).

Odyssee Globetrotter Hostel Grünberger Str. 23, Friedrichshain ⓣ030/29 00 00 81, ⓦwww.globetrotterhostel.de. Young, well-organized hostel with quirky, individually designed rooms and a guest kitchen, ideally situated for the Friedrichshain nightlife scene – though a touch far from the sights. U-Bahn Frankfurter Tor. Dorms €13.50–20, doubles €47, en suite €54.

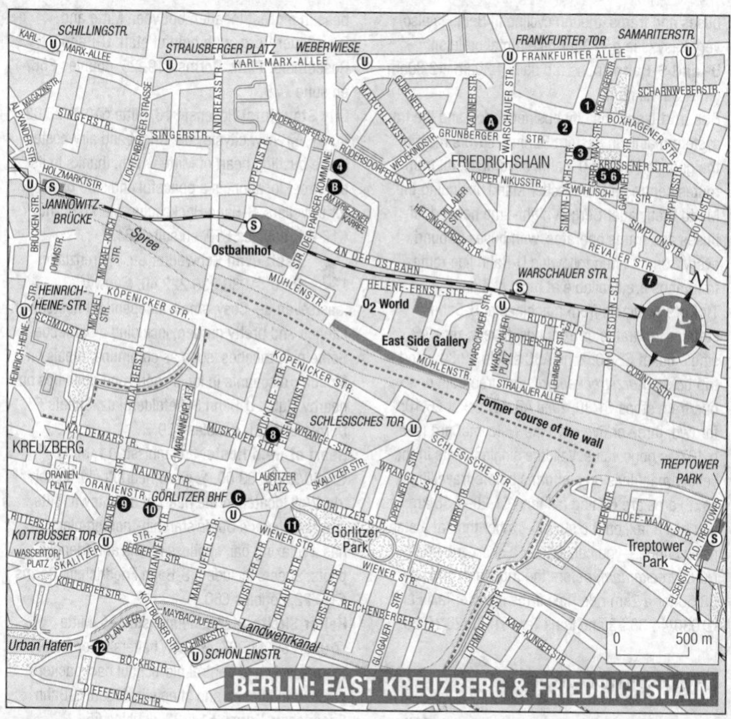

ACCOMMODATION		EATING				DRINKING & NIGHTLIFE			
BaxPax Kreuzberg	C	Burgeramt		Knofi	9	Astro	3	Morena Bar	11
Odyssee Globetrotter	A	Frühstücksklub	5	Kuchen Rausch	2	Berghain	4	Privatclub	8
Ostel	B	Il Casolare	12	Lurette	1	Feuermelder	6	Rosi's	7
								SO 36	10

Ostel Wriezener Karree 5 ⓣ030/25 76 86 60, ⓦwww.ostel.eu. Novelty *Ostalgie*-themed hostel and hotel, all authentically decked out GDR-style, though with some very modern facilities like free wi-fi. S-Bahn Ostbahnhof. Dorms advertised from €9, but more like €20 in summer, doubles from €69, breakfast €4.50.

Wombat's Alte Schönhauser Str. 2 ⓣ030/847 108 20, ⓦwww.wombats.eu. Bright, friendly and well-equipped new hostel, in a great location near some good bars. All dorms are en suite, the spacious apartments with kitchens are particularly stylish, and the roof bar has superb views over the city. U-Bahn Rosa-Luxemburg-Platz. Dorms €21, doubles €58, double room apartment €100.

Hotels

Circus Hotel Rosenthalerstr. 1 ⓣ030/20 00 39 39, ⓦwww.circus-berlin.de. Fantastic new hotel from the *Circus Hostel* people. All the rooms are stylishly decorated and with great en-suite showers. The staff are helpful, and there are some nice extras, like free wi-fi – and free loan of laptops – a good breakfast (€8), and tons of local advice on hand; the streetside rooms do get some noise. U-Bahn Rosenthaler Platz. Doubles €78 or €88.

Motel One Berlin-Alexanderplatz Dircksenstr. 36 ⓣ030/20 05 40 80, ⓦwww.motel-one.com. A ubiquitous chain hotel, but the location of this one is unbeatable and the rooms stylish. Breakfast €7.50. S-Bahn Alexanderplatz. Doubles from €84.

Eating

The difference between café, bar and restaurant is fairly indistinct, with many particularly good for a weekend brunch. The bustling Kreuzberg/Neukölln market (Tues & Fri noon–6pm) on the Maybach Ufer (U-Bahn to Schönleinstr. or Kottbusser Tor), is great for cheap breads, vegetables, meat and Turkish sweets.

Al Hamra Raumerstr. 16, Prenzlauer Berg. Relaxed, extremely popular Arabian-style café-bar. Good food and cheap drinks every day – Sunday brunch until 5pm is especially tasty (€8). U-Bahn Eberswalder Str. or S-Bahn Prenzlauer Allee.

Burgeramt Frühstücksklub Krossener Str. 22, on Boxhagener Platz. *Imbiss* place with a slightly eccentric line in burger toppings – pineapple, teriyaki and gouda appear together – but there are plenty of classic burger options, and veggie versions, making it a perfect pit-stop while bar-hopping round Friedrichshain. Open till around midnight. Burgers €2–5. U-Bahn Frankfurter Tor/S-Bahn Warschauer Str.

Café Einstein Kurfürstenstr. 58, Charlottenburg. Housed in a seemingly ancient mansion, this place exudes the formal ambience of a Viennese *Kaffeehaus*. Breakfast served daily till 2pm, though the food is a little pricey, so maybe better for its delicious *Kuchen* (€5). U-Bahn Nollendorfplatz.

Curry 36 Mehringdamm 36, west Kreuzberg. One of the best places to try Berlin *Currywurst* (€1.40) – a traditional fast-food combination of grilled sausage, hot tomato sauce and curry powder. Open until 4am every day. U-Bahn Mehringdamm.

Dolores Rosa-Luxemburg-Str. 7, Mitte. Mouthwatering California-style Mexican fast food, complete with full-on San Francisco decor and the predictable concentration of expats. Burritos from €3.90. S-/U-Bahn Alexanderplatz or Hackescher Markt.

Entweder Oder Oderberger Str. 15, Prenzlauer Berg. Friendly, typically Prenzlauer Berg café-bar, with a tasty menu of German dishes that's perfect for a hangover-beating breakfast: either a big platter for two for €12.90, or the "Italian" option – an espresso and a cigarette (€2). U-Bahn Eberwelder Str.

Il Casolare Grimmstr. 30, Kreuzberg. A wonderful, always-packed Italian restaurant offering great pizzas, in a lovely, leafy spot by the canal. Pizzas from €7. U-Bahn Schönleinstr.

Il Glaciale Kollwitzstr. 59, Prenzlauer Berg. This tiny gelateria makes all its ice cream in-house, with delectable, exciting results, with regularly changing flavours. Open April–Nov. One scoop €0.70. U-Bahn Senefelderplatz.

Kauf dich Glücklich Oderberger Str. 44, Prenzlauer Berg. Super-cute, café-bar-shop-waffle and ice cream parlour combination, all done out in Fifties-retro furniture (that you can buy). U-Bahn Eberwelder Str.

Knofi Bergmannstr. 11 & 98, west Kreuzburg (U-Bahn Mehringdamm). The *Gössies* – filled Turkish crêpes – are cheap (€3.80), huge and delicious at this lively local Mediterranean café (no. 11) and deli (no. 98); there's the same menu of soups, salads and some hot dishes at both, and a smaller choice at their other deli at Oranienstr. 179 (U-Bahn Kottbusser Tor), where you can get a plate of salads and pâtes for €6.50.

Kuchi Gipsstr. 3, Mitte. Deliciously fresh, imaginative sushi, all prepared in front of you, is the speciality at this stylish Mitte restaurant. Well worth the slightly higher prices: sushi selection from around €9, stir-fried noodles with tofu €10. U-Bahn Weinmeister Str.

Kuchen Rausch Simon-Dach-Str. 1, Friedrichshain. Stylish bar/restaurant serving decent German cuisine, and good cakes, with outdoor seating. Breakfast from €4.50, schnitzel €13.90. U-Bahn Frankfurter Tor/S-Bahn Warschauer Str.

Monsieur Vuong Alte Schönhauser Str. 46, Mitte. Small, hip and popular Vietnamese place with a high-quality, low-price menu that changes daily. Meals €7. U-Bahn Weinmeisterstr.

Sowohl als Auch Kollwitzstr. 88, Prenzlauer Berg. Excellent cake selection, with an extensive coffee and tea menu to boot; also popular for breakfast. U-Bahn Eberswalder or Senefelderplatz.

Drinking and nightlife

Berlin nightlife outstrips most other European capitals, and it's centred on several different neighbourhoods. As Mitte goes upmarket, and a little touristy, the best bars tend to be away from Oranienburger Str., with Gipastr., Augustusstr., and the areas around Rosenthaler Platz and Rosa-Luxemburg-Platz all good for bar-crawling. Continue further north to Prenzlauer Berg, such as the area around Kastanienallee, and there's a relaxed, neighbourhood feel. Further east, Friedrichshain – around Boxhagener Platz and Simon-Dach-Str. – is currently late-night Berlin at its ramshackle best, with some of the city's top clubs. Over the river in Kreuzberg, it ranges from slightly alternative to solidly hipster.

GAY BERLIN

Berlin's diverse **gay scene** is spread across the city, but with a focus of sorts in Schöneberg, around Nollendorfplatz. The magazine *Siegessäule* (ⓦ www.siegessaeule.de) has listings and can be picked up in many cafés and shops. Club nights by GMF (ⓦ www.gmf-berlin.de) at various venues, including Sundays at *Weekend*, are always worth checking out. The Christopher Street Day Gay Pride festival takes place every year in June (ⓦ www.csd-berlin.de).

Bars

Astro Simon-Dach-Str. 40, Friedrichshain. Always packed pre-club kitsch bar with different DJs nightly. U-Bahn Frankfurter Tor/S-Bahn Warschauer Str.

EndDorn Belforter Str. 27, Prenzlauer Berg. Cosy, brick-walled bar, which also does cheap food, mainly for under €5. Closed Sun, drinks only Sat. U-Bahn Senefelderplatz.

Feuermelder Krossenerstr. 24, Friedrichshain. Lively corner bar popular with scruffy artsy types on Boxhagener Platz. U-Bahn Frankfurter Tor/S-Bahn Warschauer Str.

Klub der Republik Pappelallee 81, Prenzlauer Berg. Cheap drinks and frequent live DJs in this fabulous chilled-out lounge-bar that gets the shabby-retro look just right. Fire-escape steps up to the entrance. U-Bahn Eberswalder Str.

Lurette Boxhagener Str. 105, Friedrichshain. Retro bar/club, complete with Sixties wall projections, dishing up cheap cocktails to an upbeat crowd. U-Bahn Frankfurter Tor/S-Bahn Warschauer Str.

Morena Bar Wiener Str. 60, Kreuzberg. Studenty, blue-tiled bar that opens early for good breakfasts. U-Bahn Görlitzer Bhf.

Prater Biergarten Kastanienallee 7–9. Large and relaxed Prenzlauer Berg beer garden. April–Sept daily from noon (weather permitting). The attached *Gaststätte* serves German classics year round. U-Bahn Eberswalder Str.

Schwarzes Café Kantstr. 148, Charlottenburg. Kantstrasse's best hang-out, with a bohemian atmosphere and good music. Great breakfasts, too (€7.50). Open 24/7 except Tues 3–11am. S-/U-Bahn Savignyplatz or Zoologischer Garten.

Scotch & Sofa Kollwitzstr. 18, Prenzlauer Berg. Trendy, relaxed pre-club bar with free internet and a loyal crowd. U-Bahn Senefelderplatz.

Strandbar Mitte Monbijoustr. 3, Mitte. Seasonal (April–Oct), popular city beach bar with sand and deck chairs overlooking the River Spree. S-Bahn Hackescher Markt or Oranienburger Str.

Tacheles Oranienburger Str. 54–56, Mitte. Now a bit of a counter-culture theme park, the huge squat-style arts centre is something of an institution. It includes a cinema, three bars and beer garden. Its *Café Zapata* gets some good bands in. U-Bahn Oranienburger Tor.

Clubs

Don't bother turning up before midnight or 1am to clubs in Berlin. To find out what's on, pick up one of the listings magazines, *Zitty* (ⓦ www.zitty.de), *Tip* (ⓦ www.tip-berlin.de), or the English-language *Exberliner* (ⓦ www.exberliner.com).

Bang Bang Club Mitte ⓦ www.bangbang-club.de. Studenty indie club, which is one of the locations of the excellent *Karrera Klub* (ⓦ www.karreraklub.de), and puts on good gigs. S-Bahn Hackescher Markt.

Berghain Am Wriezener Bahnhof, Friedrichshain ⓦ www.berghain.de. Legendary techno club in a huge former power station, which attracts a mixed gay-straight crowd; entrance policy can be strict. Upstairs *Panorama Bar* Fri & Sat, *Berghain* usually Sat only, until well into Sun. S-Bahn Ostbahnhof.

Kaffee Burger Torstr. 60, Mitte ⓦ www.kaffeeburger.de. Small, former GDR bar decorated in deep flushed red, with an eclectic range of live music, spoken word events and club nights, including the infamously funky Russian disco twice monthly. U-Bahn Rosenthaler Platz/Rosa-Luxemburg-Platz.

Knaack Greifswalder Str. 224, Prenzlauer Berg ⓦ www.knaack-berlin.de. Indie, rock and pop club and live music venue. Tram M4 to Am Friedrichshain.

Privatclub Pücklerstr. 34, Kreuzberg ⓦ www.privatclub-berlin.de. Intimate basement club (under *Markthalle*, a more sedate café) with an eclectic range of nights, including soul, Balkan-electronica and indie. Open Fri & Sat; other nights for the occasional live gig. U-Bahn Görlitzer Bhf.

Rosi's Revalerstr 29, about 10min walk from the junction with Simon-Dach-Str., Friedrichshain ⓦ www.rosis-berlin.de. Quirky and hugely fun club in a mis matched cluster of buildings – there's table tennis outside, and inside it's a bit like a private house, complete with small kitchen and living room, plus a couple of dancefloors. The music tends towards indie, but also features house, drum 'n'bass, and more. S-Bahn Warschauer Str.

SO 36 Oranienstr. 190, Kreuzberg ⓦ www.so36.de. Punky cult club with a large gay and lesbian following. Sunday's Café Fatal – ballroom dance class at 7pm, dancing from 8pm – is a fantastically friendly gay and mixed free-for-all. Also frequent live music. U-Bahn Görlitzer Bhf.

Weekend Alexanderplatz 7, Mitte ⓦ www.week-end-berlin.de. Floors 12, 15 and the roof of a GDR-era tower block (the one with the Sharp sign at the top) are taken over by this techno club – great views, particularly from the roof, but slightly posey. U- & S-Bahn Alexanderplatz.

Entertainment

CineStar Potsdamerstr. 4 ⓦ www.cinestar.de. Cinema in the Sony Center on Potsdamer Platz that screens films in English; €8/students €6. S-/U-Bahn Potsdamer Platz.

O2 World Mühlenstr. ⓦ www.o2world.de. Huge, new arena near the river for big-name acts. S-Bahn Ostbahnhof.

Philharmonie Herbert-von-Karajan-Str. 1 ⓣ030/25 48 80, ⓦwww.berliner-philharmoniker.de. Custom-built home of the world's most celebrated orchestra, the Berlin Philharmonic. U-/S-Bahn Potsdamer Platz.
Staatsoper Unter den Linden 7 ⓣ030/20 35 40, ⓦwww.staatsoper-berlin.org. Excellent operatic productions in one of central Berlin's most beautiful buildings. S-/U-Bahn Friedrichstr.

Shopping

Clothes Boutiques and local designers are in good supply in Berlin, though bargains can be hard to find. The part of Mitte just northeast from S-Bahn Hackescher Markt is the best place for shoe boutiques. Head to Prenzlauer Berg (from Kastanienallee to Helmholzplatz) for high-quality, high-priced local designers, and to the Boxhagener Platz area in Friedrichshain for the latest hipster apparel.
Markets Flea markets (*Flohmärkte*) abound in Berlin; head to the Mauerpark in Prenzlauer Berg on Sunday from 8am to 6pm (tram M10 to Bernauer Str./Wolliner Str.) for the best bargains.

Directory

Bike rental and tours Nearly all hostels rent bikes for around €12/day, as do numerous rental places including: Fat Tire (daily: March–Nov 9.30am–6pm; mid-April to Sept till 8pm; call or email out of season ⓣ030/24 04 79 91, ⓦfattirebiketours.com/berlin), beneath the TV tower at Alexanderplatz. Also offer half-day bike tours (4hr 30min; €20/students €18).
Embassies and consulates Australia, Wallstr. 76–79 ⓣ030/880 08 80; Canada, Leipziger Platz 17 ⓣ030/20 31 20; Ireland, Friedrichstr. 200 ⓣ030/22 07 20; New Zealand, Friedrichstr. 60 ⓣ030/20 62 10; South Africa, Tiergartenstr.18 ⓣ030/22 07 30; UK, Wilhelmstr. 70–71 ⓣ030/20 45 70; US, Pariser Platz 2 (postal address Clayallee 170) ⓣ030/830 50.
Exchange ATMs and exchange at the airports, and major stations including: Reisebank, at the Hauptbahnhof (daily 8am–10pm), Zoo station (daily 8am–9pm), Friedrichstr. station (Mon–Fri 7.30am–8pm, Sat & Sun 8am–8pm) and Ostbahnhof (Mon–Fri 7am–9pm, Sat & Sun 8am–8pm).
Hospitals There's an emergency room at Campus Charité Mitte, entrance Luisenstr. 65/66, Mitte ⓣ030/450 50.
Internet Free wi-fi at the Sony Center; internet access in all hostels (around €1.50/30min), also NetLounge, Auguststr. 89.
Laundry Schnell & Sauber, Oderberger Str. 1, Prenzlauer Berg; Eco-Express, Danziger Str. 7, Prenzlauer Berg.
Pharmacy Apotheke Haupbahnhof, at the Hauptbahnhof. Open 24/7.
Post office Dircksenstr. 2, Mitte (Mon–Sat 8am–10pm).

Moving on

Train Cologne (hourly; 4hr 20min); Dresden (every 2hr; 2hr 15min); Frankfurt (hourly; 4hr); Hamburg (hourly; 1hr 40min); Hannover (hourly; 1hr 40min); Leipzig (hourly; 1hr 15min); Munich (hourly; 5hr 45min–6hr 30min); Paris (overnight train 3–7 weekly; 13hr 30min); Prague (every 2hr; 4hr 45min); Warsaw (3 direct daily; 5hr 50min); Weimar (every 2hr; 2hr 20min).

DAY-TRIPS FROM BERLIN

There are a couple of engaging day-trips easily reachable by S-Bahn. The town of **Potsdam** to the southwest makes an excellent (and popular) excursion to explore Frederick the Great's lavish summer palaces and gardens at Sanssouci. Thirty-five kilometres north of the city lies the far more sombre sight of **Sachsenhausen** concentration camp.

Potsdam: Park Sanssouci

Stretching westwards from **POTSDAM**'s town centre is Park Sanssouci (park entry free, but €2 donation requested for which you get a useful map; day ticket for all sights €19/students €14, without Schloss Sanssouci €14/10), a dazzling collection of eighteenth- and nineteenth-century Baroque and Rococo palaces and ornamental gardens that were the fabled retreat of the Prussian kings. Dotted with follies, fountains and themed gardens, you could easily lose a day exploring the extensive park. **Schloss Sanssouci** (Tues–Sun: April–Oct 10am–6pm; Nov–March 10am–5pm; €12/students €8), the star attraction, was a pleasure palace completed in 1747, where Frederick the Great could escape the stresses of Berlin and his wife. You should head here first, as tickets are timed and sell out fast. East of the

palace is the **Bildergalerie** (May–Oct Tues–Sun 10am–6pm; €3/students €2.50), a restrained Baroque creation with paintings by Rubens, Van Dyck and Caravaggio. On the opposite side of the Schloss, the **Neue Kammern** (April Sat & Sun 10am–6pm; May–Oct Tues–Sun 10am–6pm; €3/students €2.50) was originally used as an orangerie and later converted into a guest palace in similar lavish Rococo style. West of here, the **Orangerie**, a later, Neoclassical palace built by Frederick William IV in 1826 (April Sat & Sun 10am–6pm; May–Oct Tues–Sun 10am–6pm; guided tour only hourly; €4/students €3, tower €2), features the astonishing Raphael Hall, covered with high-quality copies of many of Raphael's most famous works. At the west end of the 1.5km-long stylized gardens, stands the massive Rococo **Neues Palais** (Mon & Wed–Sun: April–Oct 10am–6pm; Nov–March 10am–5pm; €6/students €5). The interior is exquisitely opulent – the ground-floor Grotto Hall alone, decorated from floor to ceiling with shells and semiprecious stones to form images of sea monsters and dragons, merits a trip from Berlin.

Arrival and information

Arrival S-Bahn #7 (every 10min; 40min; zone C) or a regional train to Potsdam. From Potsdam train station bus #695 (every 20min) or bus #X15 on weekends go to Schloss Sanssouci (2km); #695 also stops at the Neues Palais, the Orangerie and the Dachhaus.

Information Potsdam tourist offices in the train station and Brandenburger Str. 3 (both Mon–Fri 9.30am–8pm, Sat 9am–8pm, Sun 9am–4pm). Sanssouci's main information office is by the windmill (Historische Mühle; daily: March–Oct 8.30am–5pm; Nov–Feb 9am–4pm) near the Schloss entrance.

Bike rental Potsdam per Pedales at the train station (May–Sept daily 9.30am–7pm; ⓣ0331/748 00 57, ⓦwww.pedals.de) rents bikes (€10.50/day) and Potsdam audioguides (€6/day). However, you can only cycle on a single loop within the park.

Gedenkstätte Sachsenhausen

Over 200,000 people were imprisoned at Sachsenhausen **concentration camp** between 1936 and 1945, of which many tens of thousands died at the hands of the Nazis. The original buildings have been turned into various exhibitions and a memorial (daily: mid-March to mid-Oct 8.30am–6pm; mid-Oct to mid-March 8.30am–4.30pm; free; ⓦwww.gedenkstaette-sachsenhausen.de). Take S-Bahn #1 to Oranienburg (every 10min; 50min; zone C), and then bus #804 (hourly) or a twenty-minute signposted walk.

Eastern Germany

Berlin stands apart from the rest of the East, but its dynamism finds an echo in the two other main cities: particularly in **Dresden**, the beautiful Saxon capital so ruthlessly destroyed in 1945, now rebuilt and thriving, and **Leipzig**, which provided the vanguard of the 1989 revolution. Both combine some interesting sights and excellent museums and galleries, with a fun, irreverent bar and club scene. Equally enticing are some of the smaller places, notably the beautiful, diminutive **Weimar**, the fountainhead of much of European art and culture, while small town **Meissen** retains the appearance and atmosphere of prewar Germany.

DRESDEN

Once generally regarded as Germany's most beautiful city, **DRESDEN** survived World War II largely unscathed until the night of February 13, 1945. Then, in a matter of hours, it was reduced to ruins in saturation bombing, with around 18,000 to 25,000 people killed.

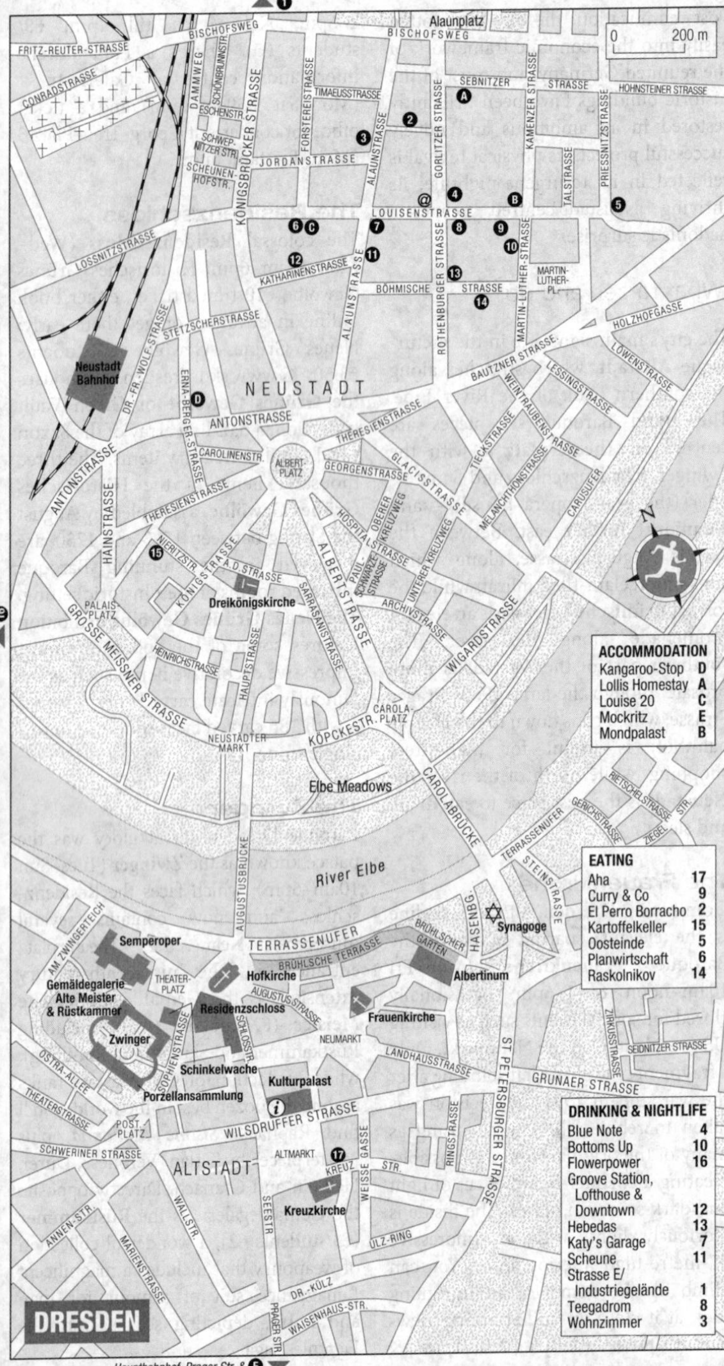
DRESDEN
ACCOMMODATION
Kangaroo-Stop D
Lollis Homestay A
Louise 20 C
Mockritz E
Mondpalast B
EATING
Aha 17
Curry & Co 9
El Perro Borracho 2
Kartoffelkeller 15
Oosteinde 5
Planwirtschaft 6
Raskolnikov 14
DRINKING & NIGHTLIFE
Blue Note 4
Bottoms Up 10
Flowerpower 16
Groove Station, Lofthouse & Downtown 12
Hebedas 13
Katy's Garage 7
Scheune 11
Strasse E/ Industriegelände 1
Teegadrom 8
Wohnzimmer 3
0 200 m
NEUSTADT
ALTSTADT
Alaunplatz
Neustadt Bahnhof
Albert-Platz
Dreikönigskirche
Elbe Meadows
River Elbe
Semperoper
Gemäldegalerie Alte Meister & Rüstkammer
Zwinger
Hofkirche
Residenzschloss
Frauenkirche
Albertinum
Synagoge
Schinkelwache
Kulturpalast
Porzellansammlung
Kreuzkirche
Neumarkt
Altmarkt
Theaterplatz
Postplatz
Carolaplatz
Palaisplatz
Neustädter Markt
Martin-Luther-Pl.
Bischofsweg
Fritz-Reuter-Strasse
Conradstrasse
Königsbrücker Strasse
Louisenstrasse
Alaunstrasse
Görlitzer Strasse
Rothenburger Strasse
Böhmische Strasse
Bautzner Strasse
Antonstrasse
Hauptstrasse
Albertstrasse
Carolabrücke
Augustusbrücke
Terrassenufer
Brühlsche Terrasse
Wilsdruffer Strasse
St Petersburger Strasse
Grunaer Strasse
Grosse Meissner Strasse
Ostra-Allee
Hauptbahnhof, Prager Str. & E

Post-reunification, the city has slotted easily into the economic framework of the reunited Germany, and most of the historic buildings have been brilliantly restored in an ambitious and hugely successful project. Its physical revival is reflected in its resurgent nightlife, its thriving Neustadt-centred scene a hedonistic surprise.

What to see and do

The city's main sights are in the picturesque **Altstadt**, which stretches along the southern bank of the River Elbe. The grand Baroque set pieces are centred on **Theaterplatz** – with the Zwinger, Residenzschloss and Semperoper (the grand opera house) – and **Neumarkt** further east. Between the two is Augustusstrasse, along which runs a porcelain-tiled mural, while the formal **Brühlsche Terrasse** is an elegant promenade along the river. The southern part of the Altstadt is more prosaic, though the large 1960s Prager Strasse, which runs down to the Hauptbahnhof, is useful for high-street shopping, while north of the river the **Neustadt** is the best place to eat, drink and sleep.

The Frauenkirche

Dominating Dresden Altstadt's skyline is the elegant, soaring dome of the Baroque **Frauenkirche** (Mon–Fri 10am–noon & 1–6pm; occasionally closed for special events such as visiting US presidents), on the **Neumarkt**. Only a fragment of wall was left standing after the war, and in 1991 the decision was taken to rebuild the church, using as many of the original stones as possible, creating a chequer-board effect of light and dark stones in places. The inside is gloriously light, with an impressive 37-metre-high interior dome. You can climb up the dome for an intriguing look at it close up and stunning views across town (daily 10am–1pm & 2–6pm; Nov–March till 4pm; €8/students €5). There's a Frauenkirche information centre at Galeriestr. 1 (Mon–Sat 9.30am–6pm) and a ticket office for concerts at Georg-Treu-Platz 3 (Mon–Fri 9am–6pm).

The Residenzschloss

The colossal **Residenzschloss** (Wed–Mon 10am–6pm; Historisches Grünes Gewölbe €10 timed ticket, either book online in advance, or get there early; Neues Grünes Gewölbe €6/students €3.50; Ⓦwww.skd-dresden.de) houses the **Grünes Gewölbe** or Green Vault collection, a dazzling array of the Saxon royal family's treasury items. The three thousand items of the **Historisches Grünes Gewölbe**, assembled by August the Strong between 1723 and 1730, are displayed in the stunning Baroque mirrored rooms of their historic setting. The **Neues Grünes Gewölbe** exhibition features some of the collection's most impressive decorative items, such as the famously intricate carved cherry stones – with 185 carved faces squeezed onto a single stone.

The Zwinger

Baroque Dresden's great glory was the palace known as the **Zwinger** (Tues–Sun 10am–6pm), which faces the Residenzschloss and now contains several museums. Near the Theaterplatz entrance, in the nineteenth-century extension, is the **Gemäldegalerie Alte Meister** (€7/students €4.50, including Rüstkammer and Skulpturensammlung), whose collection of Old Masters ranks among the dozen best in the world: you'll find Raphael's *Sistine Madonna*, plus masterpieces by Titian, Veronese, Dürer, Holbein and Cranach. Directly opposite the Gemäldegalerie is the **Rüstkammer** (€3/students €2), a wonderful collection of weaponry that includes a magnificent Renaissance suit of armour for man and horse, depicting scenes from the Hercules saga.

Beautifully displayed in the southeastern pavilion, entered from Sophienstrasse, is the **Porzellansammlung** (€6/students €3.50), featuring porcelain items from the famous Meissen factory, as well as from China and Japan. The southwestern pavilion, closed until 2010, houses the **Mathematisch-Physikalischer Salon**'s collection of globes, clocks and scientific instruments.

The **Albertinum** on Brühlischer Garten, which is closed until 2010 for renovation, houses the outstanding New Masters Gallery of nineteenth- and twentieth-century works, including a sculpture collection; until it re-opens a small selection of sculptures is displayed in the Zwinger, near the Gemäldegalerie (€2.50, students €1.50).

The Altmarkt and Kreuzkirche

At the north end of Prager Strasse is the **Altmarkt**; the only building of note here is the **Kreuzkirche**, a church that mixes a Baroque body with a Neoclassical tower. On Saturdays at 6pm, and at 9.30am Sunday services, it usually features the Kreuzchor, one of the world's leading church choirs.

The Neustadt

Across the River Elbe, the **Neustadt** was a planned Baroque town. The north bank of the Elbe features the green open space of the Elbe Meadows, with a couple of beer gardens and the best views of the Altstadt skyline. Further back is the focus of the city's gentrification, with a burgeoning art scene; wander through the bohemian **Kunsthofpassage** with its courtyards, houses and arty shops.

Arrival

Air Dresden Airport (Ⓦ www.dresden-airport.de) is connected to the Hauptbahnhof and the Neustadt Bahnhof by S-Bahn S2 (every 30min; 13–23min; €1.80).

Train Dresden has two main train stations – the Hauptbahnhof, south of the Altstadt, and Neustadt Bahnhof, at the northwestern corner of the Neustadt.

Information

Tourist office In the Kulturpalast on Altmarkt Ⓣ 0351/50 160 160, Ⓦ www.dresden-tourist.de (Mon–Fri 10am–7pm, Sat 10am–6pm, Sun 10am–3pm).

Discount passes The good-value Dresden-City-Card (€21/48hr) covers public transport, entrance to all Dresden state museums, except the Historiches Grünes Gewölbe, and sundry discounts. The Dresden Regio-Card (€32/72hr) extends to regional transport.

City transport

Public transport The network of trams, buses and S-Bahn is frequent and reliable, though the main sights are easily walkable. For getting between the Neustadt and Altstadt trams #8 (to Theaterplatz) and #7 (to Synagoge by Brühlischer Garten) are useful. Single €1.80; day ticket €4.50.

Accommodation

Kangaroo-Stop Erna-Berger-Str. 8–10, Neustadt Ⓣ 0351/314 34 55, Ⓦ www.kangaroo-stop.de. Cheap, spacious hostel with a kitchen on a quiet street 3min from the Neustadt Bahnhof. Dorms in one building and apartments and private rooms in another. Dorms €12.50–17, rooms €38, apartments €72–84.

Lollis Homestay Görlitzer Str. 34, Neustadt Ⓣ 0351/810 84 58, Ⓦ www.lollishome.de. This wonderfully cosy independent hostel is right in the centre of the lively Neustadt, with friendly staff, a kitchen and free bikes – though the central location means it can be loud at night. Tram to Alaunplatz or 20min from Neustadt Bahnhof. Sheets €2. Dorms €13–19, rooms €40.

Louise 20 Louisenstr. 20, Neustadt Ⓣ 0351/889 48 94, Ⓦ www.louise20.de. Bright, quiet, though slightly bland, hotel-quality hostel. Dorms €16–18, rooms €40–46.

Mockritz Boderitzer Str. 30 Ⓣ 0351/47 15 250, Ⓦ www.camping-dresden.de. This campsite is open year-round. Reception 8–11am & 4–9pm. Bus #76 from the Hauptbahnhof. €5.50 per person; €2.10 for a small tent.

Mondpalast Louisenstr. 77, Neustadt Ⓣ 0351/56 34 050, Ⓦ www.mondpalast.de. Another great backpackers' place with a kitchen, on one of the Neustadt's main thoroughfares. Bike rentals

€7/day. Tram to Louisenstr., Pulsnitzerstr. or a 20min walk from the Neustadt Bahnhof. Sheets €2. Dorms €14–19.50, rooms €44–52.

Eating

Aha Kreuzstr. 7, Altstadt. Slightly hippy-ish fair-trade café and shop, with a good-value menu of soups and hearty main dishes.
Curry & Co Louisenstr. 62, Neustadt. Ultra-hip, minimalist Currywurst joint. Currywurst and fries €3.50.
El Perro Borracho Kunsthof alleyway, Alaunstr. 70, Neustadt. A highly regarded, lively Spanish restaurant. Tapas from €3.50.
Kartoffelkeller Nieritzstr. 11, Neustadt. Potato served in myriad ways, in a beautiful cellar space, at good rates. Roast potatoes with herring fillets €8.80.
Oosteinde Preissnitzstr. 18, Neustadt. Delicious, good-value food served under a low vaulted roof or outside in a peaceful beer garden. Mains from €6.
Planwirtschaft Louisenstr. 20, Neustadt. Café-bar-restaurant and *Biergarten* with great breakfast buffet (Mon–Fri €9, Sat & Sun €10.80).
Raskolnikov Böhmische Str. 34, Neustadt. A large, rambling, bohemian Russian bar/café and restaurant. Great food and atmospheric beer garden.

Drinking and nightlife

With over 130 bars and clubs clustered around a handful of cobbled, narrow streets, the Neustadt provides something for everyone. For up-to-date nightlife listings, pick up a copy of *Sax* or *Dresdner*, from kiosks or backpacker hostels.

Bars

Blue Note Görlitzer Str. 2b, Neustadt Ⓦwww.bluenote-dresden.de. Dark, smoke-filled and boozy jazz bar, packed to the gills every night for its live music. Daily 8pm–5am, till the last person's standing at weekends.
Bottoms Up Martin-Luther-Str. 31, Neustadt. Down a quiet backstreet away from the main action, this large easy-going bar and beer garden is an unpretentious favourite.
Hebedas Rothenburger Str. 30, Neustadt. Atmospheric bar that epitomizes the Neustadt alternative scene.
Scheune Alaunstr. 36–40, Neustadt Ⓦwww.scheune.org. Neustadt arts centre with a welcoming bar, large beer garden, live music, theatre and gay and lesbian nights; the *Scheune Café* serves tasty Indian food (curries €10–13).
Teegadrom Louisenstr. 48, Neustadt. An alternative to the Neustadt hipster scene: calm and candlelit, with board games. 7pm–1/2am.
Wohnzimmer Alaunstr. 27/Jordanstr. 19, Neustadt. Two levels of living-room-themed bar, with comfy couches and good cocktails.

Clubs

Flowerpower Erfurterstr. 11, behind Fleigeno, Neustadt (about 15min walk west of Bahnhof Neustadt) Ⓦwww.flower-power.de. It's always the summer of love at this slightly cheesy but good fun indie and oldies student club. *Nubeatzz* upstairs in the same building is slicker, with mainstream hip-hop nights.
Groove Station, Lofthouse & Downtown Katherinenstr. 11–13, Neustadt Ⓦwww.groovestation.de, Ⓦwww.lofthouse-dresden.de & Ⓦwww.downtown-dresden.de. Set around a courtyard, this rough-and-ready rock, hip-hop and dance bar and live music complex has been a Neustadt cornerstone for years.
Katy's Garage Alaunstr. 48, Neustadt Ⓦwww.katysgarage.de. Another Neustadt institution – you'll recognize it by the car on its roof – with a chilled beer garden at the front, and club behind (from 8pm); Monday is student night.
Strasse E/Industriegelände Werner-Hartmann-Str. 2 Ⓦwww.strasse-e.de. Industrial area turned club/venue mini-city north of the Neustadt, where there's always something on; next door *Strassen-cafe* (Thurs–Sun from 6pm) with board games, pool, table football and darts, is good for a pre-club drink. Tram #7 or #8 to Industriegelände, along Hermann-Mende-Str. then right onto Werner-Hartman-Str.

Moving on

Train Berlin (every 2hr; 2hr 15min); Frankfurt (hourly; 4hr 45min); Leipzig (every 30min; 1hr 15min–1hr 40min); Meissen (every 30min; 40min); Prague (every 2hr; 2hr 10min); Weimar (hourly; 2hr 10min); Wrocław (3 daily; 3hr 30min).

DAY-TRIPS FROM DRESDEN

Around Dresden there is stunning scenery in **Saxon Switzerland** and the quaint unspoilt town of **Meissen**, making the city a good base for exploring the region. Both are within Dresden's regional transport network, and the three-day Dresden Regio-Card is good value (see p.477).

Sächsische Schweiz (Saxon Switzerland)

The **Sächsische Schweiz** (Saxon Switzerland) region southeast of Dresden is a natural wonderland of majestic sandstone mountains, offering ample opportunities for hiking, cycling and climbing. One classic route is the 115-kilometre Malerweg (Painter Route), overnighting in the tourist-friendly villages along the way. There are countless day hikes as well, such as Königstein to Rathen via Lilienstein (7km), through woods and open vistas.

It's easy to visit this region from Dresden; just take S-Bahn #1 (every 30min; 3-zone ticket €5.10) to Kurort Rathen, Königstein or Bad Schandau and follow trailheads from there; local buses also connect these towns. The tourist office in Dresden (see p.477) sells maps and gives information on the Sächsische Schweiz, or check out Ⓦwww.saechsische-schweiz.de.

Meissen

The cobbled square and photogenic rooftop vistas are reason enough to visit the porcelain-producing town of **MEISSEN,** which, unlike its neighbour Dresden, survived World War II almost unscathed.

What to see and do

Walking towards the centre from the train station, you see Meissen's commandingly sited castle almost immediately, rising just back from the Elbe's edge. The **Albrechtsburg** (daily: March–Oct 10am–6pm; Nov–Feb 10am–5pm; Jan 15–31 weekends only; €4/students €2) is a late fifteenth-century combination of military fortress and residential palace, which housed a porcelain factory in the eighteenth and nineteenth centuries. Its current interior is nineteenth century, with lavish murals celebrating Saxon history. Cocooned within the castle precinct is the Gothic **Dom** (daily: April–Oct 9am–6pm; Nov–March 10am–4pm; €2.50/students €1.50; combined ticket €6/students €3); inside, look out for the superb brass tomb-plates of the Saxon dukes.

The **Staatliche Porzellan-Manufaktur Meissen** is at Talstr. 9 (daily: May–Oct 9am–6pm; Nov–April 9am–5pm; €8.50/students €4.50), about 1.5km south of the central Markt. This is the latest factory to manufacture Dresden china, whose invention came about when Augustus the Strong imprisoned the alchemist Johann Friedrich Böttger, ordering him to produce gold. Instead, he invented the first true European porcelain. You can also view many of the factory's finest creations in the **museum**.

Arrival and information

Train station On the opposite side of the River Elbe from the centre. It's a 20min walk over the railroad bridge or the Altstadtbrücke; both are signposted.

Tourist office Markt 3 ⓣ03521/41 940, Ⓦwww.touristinfo-meissen.de (April–Oct Mon–Fri 10am–6pm, Sat & Sun 10am–4pm; Nov–March Mon–Fri 10am–5pm, Sat 10am–3pm, Jan closed weekends).

LEIPZIG

LEIPZIG has always been among the most dynamic of German cities. With its influential and respected university, and a tradition of trade fairs dating back to the Middle Ages, there was never the degree of isolation from outside influences experienced by so many cities behind the Iron Curtain. Leipzigers have embraced the challenges of reunification, and the city's imposing monuments, narrow cobbled backstreets and wide-ranging nightlife make for an inviting visit.

What to see and do

Most points of interest lie within the old centre, a compact, attractive mix of

traditional and often strikingly modern, with several *Passagen*, covered shopping arcades, often with stylish Jugendstil touches running between the main streets.

Nikolaikirche and Markt

Following Nikolaistrasse due south from the train station brings you to the **Nikolaikirche**, a rallying point during the collapse of the GDR, when its weekly peace prayers, which had been going on for several years, escalated into large protests. Although a sombre medieval structure outside, inside the church is a real eye-grabber thanks to rich decoration, works of art and pink columns with palm-tree-style capitals. A couple of blocks west is the Markt, whose eastern side is entirely occupied by the **Altes Rathaus**, built in the grandest German Renaissance style with elaborate gables and an asymmetrical tower. To the rear of the Altes Rathaus is the **Alte Handelsbörse**, a Baroque gem that was formerly the trade exchange headquarters. South of the Markt is **Mäddler Passage**, an elegant arcade famous for the restaurant *Auerbach's Keller*, which features in Goethe's *Faust*.

Museum der bildenden Künste

Immense and striking, the new building of the **Museum der bildenden Künste**, at Katharinenstrasse 10 (Tues & Thurs–Sun 10am–6pm, Wed noon–8pm; €5/students €3.50), houses a distinguished collection, from Old Masters through to twentieth-century artists, and is particularly strong on Leipzig-born Max Beckmann. Traditional galleries are interspersed with airy, two-storey spaces that feature contemporary pieces, many by local artists. The result is imaginative and playful, and showcases some of the work of a thriving local art scene. To explore it further, check out the excellent **Galerie für Zeitgenössische Kunst**, Karl-Tauchnitz-Str. 11, just outside the Ring southwest of the centre (Gallery for Contemporary Art; Tues–Sun noon–7pm; €8/students €4), and the **Spinnerei** complex of galleries in an old cotton mill west of the centre (S-Bahn Plagwitz; ⓦ www.spinnerei.de).

The Thomaskirche and Bach-Museum

Just southwest of the Markt, on Thomaskirchof, stands the **Thomaskirche**, where Johann Sebastian Bach served as cantor for the last 27 years of his life. Predominantly Gothic, the church has been altered through the centuries. The most remarkable feature is its musical tradition: the Thomanerchor choir, which Bach once directed, can usually be heard on Fridays (6pm), Saturdays (3pm) and during the Sunday service (9.30am). Directly across from the church is the **Bach-Museum**, due to reopen after renovation in spring 2010 (Tues–Sun 10am–6pm; €6/students €4).

Runde Ecke and Zeitgeschichtliches Forum

In the autumn of 1989 Leipzig was at the forefront of protests against the GDR, and one focus for this was the **Runde Ecke**, at Dittrichring 24, the city's headquarters for the Stasi, East Germany's secret police (daily 10am–6pm; free; helpful English audioguide €3). Much of it has been preserved as it was, complete with a typical Stasi official's office and examples of listening devices, making it a fascinating trawl through the methods and machinery of the Stasi.

Less atmospheric but slicker is the **Zeitgeschichtliches Forum** (Tues–Fri 9am–6pm, Sat & Sun 10am–6pm; free; ask for English notes), just south of the Markt at Grimmaische Strasse 6, a multimedia museum on the history of the GDR.

The Grassi museums

Just east of the centre is the **Grassi museum** complex, which houses a trio of impressive museums at Johannisplatz 5–11 (Tues–Sun 10am–6pm; combined ticket €12/students €9; trams #4, #7, #12 or #15 to Johannisplatz), with the **Museum für Angewandte Kunst** (Applied Arts; €5/students €3.50), the star, a huge and well-displayed collection of decorative arts. The other two are the **Museum für Völkerkunde** (Ethnology; €4/€2) and the **Museum für Musikinstrumente** (Musical instruments; €4/€2).

Arrival and information

Air Leipzig-Halle Airport (www.leipzig-halle-airport.de) is connected with the main train station by the Airport Express train (every 30min; 15min).

Train Leipzig's enormous Hauptbahnhof is at the northeastern corner of the Ring, which encircles the old part of the city.

Tourist office Opposite the station's Osthalle (East Hall) at Richard-Wagner-Str. 1 ☎0341/71 04 260, www.leipzig.de (Mon–Fri 9.30am–6pm, Sat 9.30am–4pm, Sun 9.30am–3pm; Nov–Feb opens Mon–Fri at 10am); staff can book private rooms (free service). Their Leipzig Card (1-day €8.90/3-day €18.50), which covers public transport and various discounts, is unlikely to work out as good value – particularly if you get student discounts, which are often the same.

City transport A network of trams and buses centring on the Hauptbahnhof covers places outside the city centre; trams #9 and #11 are useful for Karl-Liebknecht-Str. Single ticket €2, day ticket €5.20.

Accommodation

Auensee Gustav-Esche-Str. 5 ☎0341/46 51 600, www.camping-auensee.de. This campsite is open year-round, with bungalow rooms available (€30). Reception daily: April–Oct 7.30am–1pm & 2–9.30pm; Nov–March 8am–1pm & 2–7.30pm; tram #10 or #11 (direction Wahren/Schkeuditz) to Annaberger Str., then bus #80 to Auensee.

Central Globetrotter Kurt-Schumacher-Str. 41 ☎0341/14 98 960, www.globetrotter-leipzig.de. Popular backpacker spot 3min walk west of the station. Sheets €2.50, sleeping bags not allowed. Dorms €12.50–18, rooms €38–44.

Sleepy Lion Käthe-Kollwitz-Str. 3 ☎0341/99 39 480, www.hostel-leipzig.de. Well-run hostel just west of the centre. 15min walk from the station (around the ring) or tram to Gottschedstr. Sheets €2.50, sleeping bags not allowed. Dorms €14–€19, rooms €42.

Zur City Karl-Liebknecht-Str. 40 ☎0341/2 11 33 05, www.pension-leipzig.de. Excellent *pension* between the hip Südvorstadt neighbourhood and the centre. Quads available, breakfast not included. Tram #10 or #11 to Südplatz. Doubles €66.

Eating and drinking

Gottschedstr., just west of the Thomaskirche, is lined with attractive cafés and bars, while Karl-Liebknecht-Str. a couple of tram stops south of the centre, is lively and studenty.

Kickers in Karl-Liebknecht-Str. 82. Small, relaxed bar with free table football. Tram #10 or #11 to Südplatz.

Luise Bosestr. 4, corner of Gottschedstr. Chic café-bar with an attractive vaguely Pop Art decor, that serves excellent breakfasts (from €4.50) and pasta dishes.

Maga Pon Gottschedstr. 11. The trendiest spot in town may just be this well-located and eccentrically decorated *Waschcafé* – scrambled eggs and a load of laundry, €3 each; also has a small beer garden.

Zur Pleissenburg Ratsfreichulstr. 2, just south of Thomaskirche off Burgstr. Great-value pub/restaurant in the centre serving hearty German food daily until 4am. They still accept the old German Mark. Ribs for €5.50.

Nightlife

Ilses Erika Bernhard-Göring-Str. 152, Südvorstadt www.ilseserika.de. Indie bar, club and music venue Thurs–Sat; beer garden all summer long. Tram to Connewitz Kreuz.

Moritzbastei Universitätsstr. 9 www.moritzbastei.de. A cavernous student cellar bar and club, with lots of events on, including live music, and with beer gardens and a cheap student canteen. Tram to Leuschner-, Ross-, or Augustusplatz.

naTo Karl-Liebknecht-Str. 46, Südvorstadt www.nato-leipzig.de. Popular bar, live music venue and cinema. Trams #10 or #11 to Südplatz.

Moving on

Train Berlin (hourly; 1hr 20min); Dresden (every 30min; 1hr 15min–1hr 40min); Frankfurt (hourly; 3hr 30min); Meissen (hourly; 1hr 20min); Weimar (hourly; 1hr).

WEIMAR

Despite its modest size, **WEIMAR** has played an unmatched role in the development of German culture: Goethe, Schiller and Nietzsche all made it their home, as did the architects and designers of the Bauhaus school. The town was also chosen as the drafting place for the constitution of the democratic republic established after World War I, a regime whose failure ended with the Nazi accession. Add to all this the town's cobbled streets and laid-back, quietly highbrow atmosphere and Weimar makes an attractive stop for a day or two.

What to see and do

Weimar's main sights are concentrated in the city's walkable centre, south of the main train station and on the west side of the River Ilm. The meadow-like **Park an der Ilm** stretches 2km southwards from the **Schloss** on both sides of the river. The former concentration camp at **Buchenwald** is a bus ride to the northwest.

The Schloss and Markt

Weimar's former seat of power was the **Schloss**, set by the River Ilm at the eastern edge of the town centre, a Neoclassical complex of a size more appropriate for ruling a mighty empire. It's now a museum (Tues–Sun: April–Oct 10am–6pm; Nov–March 10am–4pm; €5/students €4), with a collection of Old Masters on the ground floor, including pieces by both Cranachs and Dürer, while the first-floor rooms are well-preserved, grand Neoclassical chambers, with lavish memorial rooms to great poets – most notably Goethe and Schiller. South of nearby Herderplatz is the spacious **Markt**, lined with an unusually disparate jumble of buildings, of which the most eye-catching is the green and white gabled Stadthaus on the eastern side, opposite the neo-Gothic Rathaus.

The Goethewohnhaus und Nationalmuseum

On Frauenplan, south of the Markt, is the **Goethewohnhaus und Nationalmuseum** (Tues–Sun: April–Sept 9am–6pm, Sat till 7pm; Oct 9am–6pm; Nov–March 9am–4pm; Wohnhaus €6.50/students €5; Nationalmuseum €3.50/students €2.50; combined €8.50/students €6.50). Goethe lived here for some fifty years until his death in 1832, and the house is atmospherically preserved as it was in his lifetime, complete with oversized Classical sculptures, his extensive collections and the chair in which he died.

Theaterplatz and around

Weimar's most photographed symbol is the large double statue of Goethe and Schiller. It stands in the centre of Theaterplatz, a spacious square west of the Markt. The **Nationaltheater** on the west side of the square was founded and directed by Goethe, though the present building is a modern copy. Directly opposite is the small but interesting **Bauhaus museum**, with a collection of artefacts from the school (daily 10am–6pm; €4.50/students €3.50).

Schillerstrasse snakes away from the southeast corner of Theaterplatz, with **Schillerhaus** at no. 12 (Tues–Sun: April–Sept 9am–6pm, Sat till 7pm; Oct 9am–6pm; Nov–March 9am–4pm; €4/students €3), the home of the poet and dramatist for the last three years of his life.

Konzentrationslager Buchenwald

The **Konzentrationslager Buchenwald** (Tues–Sun: April–Oct 10am–6pm; Nov–March 10am–4pm; free; Ⓦwww.buchenwald.de) is situated north of Weimar on the Ettersberg heights, and can be reached by bus #6 (hourly from Goetheplatz and the train station). Over 240,000 prisoners were incarcerated in this concentration camp, with 65,000

dying here. Very few original buildings remain, but an audioguide (€3) and the historical exhibition paint a vivid picture of life and death in the camp.

Arrival and information

Train Weimar's train station, on the Leipzig line, is a 20min walk north of the main sights.
Tourist office Markt 10 ⓣ03643/54 54 07, ⓦwww.weimar.de (April–Oct Mon–Fri 9.30am–6pm, Sat & Sun 9.30am–3pm; Nov–March Mon–Fri 9.30am–4pm, Sat & Sun 9.30am–2pm).

Accommodation

DJH Germania Carl-August-Allee 13 ⓣ03643/85 04 90, ⓦwww.djh-thueringen.de. Neat and tidy HI hostel between the station and the centre. There's another DJH on the other side of the centre at Humboldt Str. 17 (ⓣ03643/85 07 92). Dorms €23.50.
Labyrinth Hostel Goetheplatz 6 ⓣ03643/81 18 22, ⓦwww.weimar-hostel.com. Fantastic, central and friendly hostel with attractive, quirkily decorated, spotless rooms – each one was designed by a different local artist. There's a good kitchen, relaxed communal area and courtyard, and they're always keen to offer local tips and advice. Dorms €13–20, doubles €44.
Savina Meyerstr. 60 ⓣ03643/8 66 90, ⓦwww.pension-savina.de. Convenient *pension* where all rooms have en-suite bathrooms and kitchenettes. Doubles from €60.

Eating and drinking

There's a market on the Markt (Mon–Sat 9am–4.30pm).
ACC Burgplatz 1. A relaxed bar and restaurant with quiet candlelit tables lining a cobbled side street, free internet and an upstairs gallery. Specials €5.
Estragon Herderplatz 3. Small café that's part of an organic supermarket, with a daily changing menu of tasty, filling soups (€2.80–5.30) and a salad bar (pay by weight). Mon–Fri 10am–7pm, Sat 10am–4pm.
Giancarlo's Schillerstr. 11. Gloriously old-fashioned Italian ice-cream parlour, with a hundred home-made flavours – try the bitter chocolate. Single scoop €1, or there are extravagant sundaes and waffles, and the €1 breakfast (9–11am) of coffee and a croissant, doughnut or roll is unbeatable value.
Kasseturm Goetheplatz 10. Student club in an atmospheric brick tower, which has some good live music nights.
Roxanne/c keller/Galerie Markt Markt 21. Three small places at one address – all cheap, relaxed and studenty: *Roxanne* is a scruffy bar, but with internet terminals (30min €1) and tables out on the Markt; *Galerie Markt* is an incredibly laid-back gallery and café-bar upstairs; and *c keller* is a small club at the back downstairs (daily from 9pm).

Moving on

Train Dresden (hourly; 2hr 10min); Eisenach (every 30min; 45min–1hr 10min); Frankfurt (hourly; 2hr 30min); Leipzig (hourly; 1hr).

EISENACH: THE WARTBURG

A small town on the edge of the Thuringian Forest, **EISENACH** is home to the best-loved medieval castle in Germany, the **Wartburg**. The castle complex, first mentioned in 1080, includes one of the best-preserved Romanesque palaces this side of the Alps, as well as newer additions, including the Festsaal, a nineteenth-century interpretation of medieval grandeur so splendid that Ludwig II of Bavaria had it copied for his fairy-tale palace, Neuschwanstein. The tour takes you through the ornately decorated rooms, with murals and mosaics re-telling the history of the castle's most notable residents. Also on view is a small exhibition of paintings – including some elegant portraits by Cranach – and, the **Lutherstube**, the room in which Martin Luther translated the New Testament into the German vernacular while in hiding in 1521–22. The castle can only be viewed on **guided tours** (every 15min; daily: March–Oct 8.30am–5pm; Nov–Feb 9am–3.30pm; €8/students €5); ask for an English translation of the guide's script.

Arrival and information

Arrival Eisenach is 45min–1hr 10min from Weimar by train, and can be done as a day-trip.

The Wartburg is a good hour's walk from the train station (you can get a map from DB information at the train station or tourist office). From the station head southwest along Wartburgallee; after 20–30min at Reuter Villa there's a signposted footpath up to the Wartburg – it's a pretty steep 30min climb from here; April–Oct bus #10 runs hourly from the train station to the Eselstation (donkey station), from where it's a 15min steep climb to the castle.

Tourist information Markt 9 ⓣ03691/79 230, ⓦwww.eisenach.de (Mon–Fri 10am–6pm, Sat & Sun 10am–5pm).

Accommodation and eating

There's a traditional restaurant at the Wartburg, cheap and tasty Thuringian *Rostbratwurst* stalls near the donkey station, and a dozen or so cafés and restaurants around the Markt in the town centre.

DJH Artur Becker Mariental 24 ⓣ03691/74 32 59, ⓦwww.djh-thueringen.de. Clean and friendly hostel, a 30min walk from the station, or take bus #3 or #10; it's on the Wartburg side of town (at the bottom of the hill; about 30min walk from the top). Dorms €22.

Northern Germany

Hamburg, Germany's second city, is infamous for the sleaze and hectic nightlife of the Reeperbahn strip – but is far more than this, with a sophisticated cultural scene, handsome warehouse quarter and big city allure. Another maritime city, **Lübeck**, has a strong pull, with a similar appeal to the mercantile towns of the Low Countries. To the south lies **Hannover**, worth a visit for its museums and gardens. The province's smaller towns present a fascinating contrast – the former silver-mining town of **Goslar**, in particular, is unusually beautiful.

HAMBURG

Stylish media centre and second-largest port in Europe, **HAMBURG** is undeniably cool – more laid-back than Berlin or Frankfurt, more sophisticated than Munich, and with nightlife to rival the lot. Its skyline is dominated by the pale green of its copper spires and domes, but a few houses and the churches are all that's left from older times. Much of the subsequent rebuilding might not be especially beautiful, but the result is an intriguing mix of old and new, coupled with an appealing sense of open space – two-thirds of Hamburg is occupied by parks, lakes or tree-lined canals.

What to see and do

Much of the fun of Hamburg is in exploring different quarters, each with a distinctive feel and purpose. The centre, defined by the Binnenalster and Aussenalster lakes to its northeast, and the docks and port to the south, is focused on the oversized **Rathaus**. The streets that span north from here, particularly **Jungfernstieg** and around, are classy and commercial, with a few upmarket arcades. But the real heart of Hamburg is arguably along the water's edge around the **docks** and **warehouses** along the Elbe River. North from the port are the best neighbourhoods after dark: **St Pauli** and its infamous Reeperbahn, the studenty **Schanzenviertel** further north, and chic **Altona** off to the west.

The Rathaus

The commercial and shopping district centres on **Binnenalster** lake and the neo-Renaissance **Rathaus** (guided tours several times a day in English: Mon–Thurs 10am–3pm, Fri 10am–1pm, Sat 10am–5pm, Sun 10am–4pm; €3), a magnificently pompous demonstration of the city's power and wealth in the nineteenth century.

Nikolaikirche and St Michaelis

Hamburg's skyline is punctuated by a series of church spires – it's worth

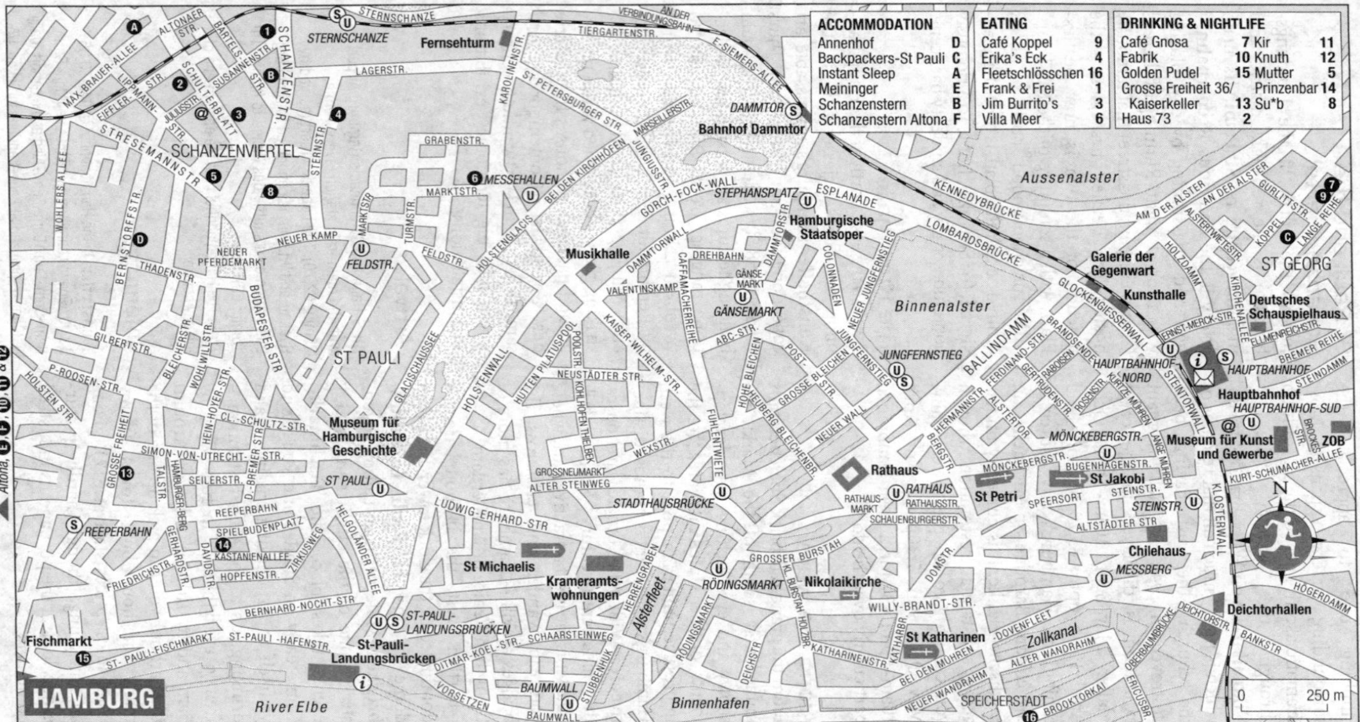
HAMBURG
ACCOMMODATION
Annenhof D
Backpackers-St Pauli C
Instant Sleep A
Meininger E
Schanzenstern B
Schanzenstern Altona F
EATING
Café Koppel 9
Erika's Eck 4
Fleetschlösschen 16
Frank & Frei 1
Jim Burrito's 3
Villa Meer 6
DRINKING & NIGHTLIFE
Café Gnosa 7
Fabrik 10
Golden Pudel 15
Grosse Freiheit 36/ Kaiserkeller 13
Haus 73 2
Kir 11
Knuth 12
Mutter 5
Prinzenbar 14
Su*b 8
Sternschanze
Fernsehturm
Schanzenviertel
Bahnhof Dammtor
Dammtor
Aussenalster
Binnenalster
Hamburgische Staatsoper
Musikhalle
Messehallen
St Georg
Galerie der Gegenwart
Kunsthalle
Deutsches Schauspielhaus
Hauptbahnhof
Hauptbahnhof-Nord
Hauptbahnhof-Sud
Museum für Kunst und Gewerbe
ZOB
St Pauli
Museum für Hamburgische Geschichte
Rathaus
St Petri
St Jakobi
Chilehaus
Deichtorhallen
St Michaelis
Krameramtswohnungen
Nikolaikirche
St Katharinen
Zollkanal
Speicherstadt
Binnenhafen
Alsterfleet
St-Pauli-Landungsbrücken
Fischmarkt
Reeperbahn
River Elbe
Jungfernstieg
Gänsemarkt
Stephansplatz
Feldstr.
Rödingsmarkt
Stadthausbrücke
Mönckebergstr.
Steinstr.
Messberg
Baumwall
Hafen City
Altona, E, F, 10, 11 & 12
0 250 m
N

climbing one to appreciate the surrounding watery expanses. Most dramatic ascent goes to the glass lift up through the skeletal spire of **Nikolaikirche** on Willy-Brandt-Strasse, which is pretty much all that remains of the church, the rest having been destroyed in 1943. A small, poignant exhibition is displayed in the crypt (daily: May–Sept 10am–8pm; Oct–April 10am–6pm; €3.70 for spire and exhibition). Hamburg's city church is the elegant Baroque **St Michaelis**, on Englische Planke. It is currently undergoing substantial restoration, though you can still go up the tower (daily: May–Oct 9am–7.30pm; Nov–April 10am–5pm; €3) for a clear panorama, particularly over the docks.

Along the water

From the grand red-brick **Speicherstadt** immediately south of the Markt, via showy and eye-catching new developments of the **HafenCity** area to the impressive utilitarian **port** to the west, Hamburg's waterfront is its most distinctive area. With its tall, ornate warehouses, the nineteenth-century Speicherstadt quarter is the most attractive part, where you can wander and crisscross the bridges at will – Hamburg has more of them than Venice or Amsterdam.

Further west, the harbour area is dominated by the clock tower and green dome of the **St Pauli Landungsbrücken**, while west again along Hafenstrasse one of the city's main weekly events takes place: the **Fischmarkt**. Come early on Sunday and you'll find yourself in an amazing trading – and drinking, it's a post-club institution – frenzy; everything is in full swing by 5am and by 10am it's all over. Around the harbour you can pick up one of the many one-hour **boat tours** (many companies; prices start at €12), giving an intriguing, though hardly picturesque, look at the port and its industrial containers.

St Pauli and the Schanzenviertel

Just to the north of the Landungsbrücken is the red-light district and nightlife centre of **St Pauli**. Its main artery is the notorious **Reeperbahn** – ugly and unassuming by day, blazing with neon at night. Running off here is Grosse Freiheit, the street that famously hosted The Beatles' first gigs – the junction of the two is now Beatles-Platz, with a sculpture of the Fab Four.

The neighbourhood north of here, centred on Schulterblatt, is the **Schanzenviertel**, (or Schanze), home to a riotously good fun, scruffy and studenty bar scene.

The Kunsthalle

Away to the east, north of the Hauptbahnhof on Glockengiesserwall, is the **Kunsthalle**, Hamburg's unmissable art collection (Tues–Sun 10am–6pm, Thurs till 9pm; €8.50/students €5). The main building features an outstanding collection, ranging from Old Masters to twentieth century, and includes works by Rembrandt, Ernst Ludwig Kirchner and Munch. A second building, a striking glass cube reached via an underground passageway, houses the **Galerie der Gegenwart** (Contemporary Art; same ticket), with late twentieth-century works plus big temporary exhibitions and installations.

Arrival

Air S-Bahn line S1 connects Hamburg Airport with the main train station (every 10min; 25min; €2.70). The Lübeck Airport (served by Ryanair and Wizzair) is connected to Hamburg bus station by a shuttle bus (timed to flights; 1hr 15min; €9).
Train The Hauptbahnhof is at the eastern end of the city centre.

Information

Tourist office In the Hauptbahnhof ⓣ040/30 05 13 00, ⓦwww.hamburg-tourismus.de (Mon–Sat 8am–9pm, Sun 10am–6pm). Also at the airport (daily 5.30am–11pm) and St Pauli–Landungsbrücken 4/5

(Mon–Wed 9.30am–6pm, Thurs–Sat 9.30am–7pm, Sun 9am–6pm).

Discount pass The Hamburg Card (single €8.50/18.90/33.90, group up to five people €12.50/31.50/54.90 for 1/3/5 days) gives reduced admission to some of the city's museums as well as free use of public transport.

City transport

Hamburg is big, so its extensive public transport network, made up of U-Bahn, S-Bahn and buses, can come in handy. A short trip costs €1.30, a single trip €2.60, a day ticket €5.10, a day ticket for up to five people €8.60, and a three-day ticket €15.

Accommodation

Annenhof Lange Reihe 23 ⓣ040/24 34 26, ⓦwww.hotelannenhof.de. Friendly, small *pension*, with bright high-ceilinged rooms on a café-lined street near the train station. Reception closes at 8pm weekdays, at 6pm weekends; no breakfast. Most with shared bathroom. Doubles €60–80, triple €100.

Backpackers-St Pauli Bernstorffstr. 98 ⓣ040/23 51 70 43, ⓦwww.backpackers-stpauli.de. Friendly, small backpacker hostel, well located for both St Pauli and the Schanze, with good communal area and bar next door. U-Bahn Feldstr. Dorms €19.50–25, rooms €60.

Instant Sleep Max-Brauer-Allee 277 ⓣ040/43 18 23 10, ⓦwww.instantsleep.de. Located in the lively Schanze area, this laid-back, basic hostel has the cheapest beds in town, and a kitchen and internet access, though on a noisy corner above a bar. S-/U-Bahn Sternschanze. Dorms €16.50–21, rooms €52.

Meininger Goetheallee 9–11 ⓣ040/414 31 40 08, ⓦwww.meininger-hostels.com. Slick, large, hotel-standard hostel from this ever-growing chain. All dorms are en suite, the communal areas are stylish, and it's 5min walk from Altona station (Max-Brauer-Allee exit). Prices vary considerably depending on demand, and are cheaper online. Dorms €15–31, rooms from €64.

Schanzenstern Bartelsstr. 12 ⓣ040/439 84 41, ⓦwww.schanzenstern.de. Eco-hostel in the Schanze area, with an attached organic restaurant. Sheets included. S-/U-Bahn Sternschanze. Second comfortable branch in Altona (Kleine Rainstr. 24–26; S-Bahn Altona; ⓣ040/3991 9191). Dorms €19, rooms from €54.

Eating

Café Koppel In Koppel 66, Lange Reihe 75, northeast of the train station in St Georg district. Relaxed but classy vegetarian café-restaurant that's part of an arts centre, with a small menu of home-made daily specials (around €7), delicious cakes and a pretty summer garden.

Erika's Eck Sternstr. 98. This is a firm student favourite, serving huge portions of traditional German dishes almost round the clock, making it popular post-clubbing. Daily from 5pm, till 2pm the next day Mon–Fri, till 9am Sat & Sun. U-/S-Bahn Sternschanze.

Fleetschlösschen Brooktorkai 17. Atmospheric little café in a small, stand-alone building right in the Speicherstadt – worth stopping at to browse through its collection of books on Hamburg and the harbour. Short menu of fairly standard pasta dishes and good coffee. U-Bahn Messberg.

Frank & Frei Schanzenstr. 93. Enormous salads, pasta and pizza-like *Flammkuchen* for €7, in this lively local pub. U-/S-Bahn Sternschanze.

Jim Burrito's Schulterblatt 12, Schanzenviertel. Laid-back Schanze take on Mexican: order at the counter, help yourself to a beer from the fridge, and your burrito will emerge sometime later. The food's tasty, cheap and filling, if not particularly spicy (ask for it hot), and there's a definite charm to the place. Burritos €3.50–7.90. U-/S-Bahn Sternschanze.

Villa Meer Marktstr. 142. Cute, bright little café with a short daytime menu and heavenly cakes – a good spot for people-watching on this street of stylish shops. Mon–Wed 11am–7pm, Thurs–Sat 11am–10pm. U-Bahn Messehallen.

Drinking and nightlife

Hamburg's nightlife is outstanding: the Schanzenviertel for studenty bar-crawling; St Pauli for clubs and live music venues; while Altona attracts an older, more relaxed crowd. For information on the gay scene check *Hinnerk* magazine, available from the tourist office, cafés and bars.

Bars

Café Gnosa Lange Reihe 93. Well-known gay bar/café northeast of the train station. Packed at weekends. Marvellous cakes for €3, and good breakfasts.

Knuth Grosse Rainstr. 21. Relaxed but stylish neighbourhood café-bar. S-Bahn Altona.

Mutter Stresemannstr. 11. Small, atmospheric (and smoky) retro-styled bar that's often the last to shut. U-/S-Bahn Sternschanze.

Su*b Schanzenstr. 18. Packed and lively shabby-chic bar. U-Bahn Feldstr.

Clubs and live music

Fabrik Barnerstr. 36 ⓦwww.fabrik.de. Major live music and club venue in Altona, with a huge range

of music and occasional mixed gay nights. Usually open nightly; entry from €7 (club nights) to €40 (major live acts). S-Bahn Altona.

Golden Pudel Am St Pauli Fischmarkt 27 Ⓦwww.pudel.com. Often packed and raucous club in what looks like a fisherman's hut on the harbour, that gets some great DJs – including electro, dub and hip-hop. S-Bahn Reeperbahn or U-/S-Bahn Landungsbrücken.

Grosse Freiheit 36/ Kaiserkeller Grosse Freiheit 36 Ⓦwww.grossefreiheit36.de. A tourist attraction in itself, *Grosse Freiheit 36* books major acts most weekends. Emphasis on goth and rock. The massive *Kaiserkeller* below plays mostly alternative music, and is famous for hosting The Beatles in the early 1960s. Closed Tues & Sun. U-Bahn St Pauli or S-Bahn Reeperbahn.

Haus 73 Schulterblatt 73 Ⓦwww.dreiundsiebzig.de There's always something going on in this ramshackle building, which feels somewhere in between a community centre and a club, complete with a small kiosk in the corner, from Sunday afternoon dance classes to film showings and reggae club nights. All very drunken and good fun. U-/S-Bahn Sternschanze.

Kir Barnerstr. 16 Ⓦwww.kir-hamburg.de. Dance club spinning indie and electro with occasional mixed gay and lesbian nights. Closed Tues and Sun. S-Bahn Altona.

Prinzenbar Kastanienallee 20, St Pauli Ⓦwww.prinzenbar.net. This wonderfully atmospheric venue, all crumbling Baroque cherubs, chandeliers and dark corners, hosts small club nights and live gigs, mainly indie. U-Bahn St Pauli or S-Bahn Reeperbahn.

Directory

Bike rental Fahrradladen St Georg, Schmilinskystr. 16, 10min from Hauptbahnhof (Mon–Fri 10am–7pm, Sat 10am–1pm); Fahrradstation, Schlüterstr. 11, S-Bahn Dammtor (Mon–Fri 9am–6pm).

Consulates New Zealand, Domstr. 19 Ⓣ040/442 55 50; US, Alsterufer 28 Ⓣ040/41 17 11 00.

Exchange Reisebank, at the train station.

Internet In the basement of the Saturn department store, southern building of the main train station (Hauptbahnhof-Süd; 30min €1.50). Also Teletime on Schultterblatt (30min €1).

Laundry Schnell & Sauber, Schanzenstr. 27, 6am–11pm.

Pharmacy At the train station.

Post office At the train station.

Shopping

Mönckebergstrasse, running from the train station to the Rathaus, is department store central, while Poststrasse and Neuer Wall (just east of the Rathaus) is the place to window-shop for exclusive designers. The areas around the Sternschanze station and around Marktstrasse (U-Bahn Feldstr.) are good places for chic boutiques.

Moving on

Train Århus (2 daily; 5hr); Berlin (hourly; 1hr 40min); Copenhagen (4 daily; 5hr); Frankfurt (hourly; 4hr); Hannover (every 30min; 1hr 35min); Lübeck (every 30min; 40min); Munich (hourly; 6hr–6hr 30min).

LÜBECK

Just an hour from Hamburg, **LÜBECK** makes a great day-trip. Set on an egg-shaped island surrounded by the water defences of the River Trave and the city moat, the pretty Altstadt is an attractive and compact place to wander, with a cluster of small lanes and courtyards to explore.

What to see and do

The city's emblem – and your first view of the Altstadt as you approach from the station – is the twin-towered and leaning **Holstentor** (daily: Jan–March 11am–5pm; April–Dec 10am–6pm; €5/students €2.50), with a small city museum inside. Straight ahead, over the bridge and up Holstenstrasse, the first church on the right is the Gothic **Petrikirche**; an elevator goes to the top of its spire (daily 9am–9pm; €3/students €2). Back across Holstenstrasse is the Markt and the elaborate **Rathaus**. Just behind, you'll find **Konditorei-café Niederegger**, renowned shop crammed with marzipan products and free museum dedicated to the sugary substance.

Behind the north wing of the town hall stands the **Marienkirche**, Germany's oldest brick-built Gothic church.

The interior makes a light and lofty backdrop for the church's treasures: a magnificent 1518 carved altar, a beautiful Gothic gilded tabernacle and an ornate astronomical clock. The church's huge bells remain embedded in the floor where they fell when the church was bombed in 1942.

Katharinenkirche, on the corner of Königstrasse and Glockengiesserstrasse, boasts three sculptures on its west facade by Ernst Barlach; he was commissioned to make a series of nine in the early 1930s, but had completed only these when his work was banned by the Nazis. To the north at Königstrasse 9–11 are the **Behnhaus** and the **Drägerhaus**, two patricians' houses now converted into a museum (Tues–Sun: Jan–March 11am–5pm; April–Dec 10am–5pm; €5/students €2.50) housing a good collection of modern and nineteenth-century paintings.

Arrival and information

Air Bus #6 goes from Lübeck airport to the train station (every 20min; 25min; €2.50).
Train station 5min west of the Altstadt: walk down Konrad-Adenauer-Str. to the Holstentor.
Ferry Lübeck's port, Travemünde, is 20min by train from Lübeck.
Tourist office Holstentorplatz 1 ⓣ01805/889 97 00, ⓦwww.luebeck.de (June–Sept Mon–Fri 9.30am–7pm, Sat 10am–3pm, Sun 10am–2pm; Oct–May Mon–Fri 9.30am–6pm, Sat 10am–3pm; Dec also Sun 10am–2pm). It has internet terminals (€3/hr), a café, arranges walking tours and has information on boat tours.
Discount passes The Happy Day Card (€6/12 24/72hr) covers public transport and up to a fifty percent discount at museums. Combined museum tickets are also available: two museums in three days €7/students €4, three in three days €10/5, all museums in one week €15/8.

Eating

Hüxstrasse, which runs east from the Markt, has several good cafés and bars.
Cole Street Beckergrube 18, west of the Markt, off Breite Str. Incongruously named after a south London street where the owner once lived, this stylish café, bar and gallery is good for a light lunch or drink.

Moving on

Train Copenhagen (4 daily; 4hr 20min); Hamburg (every 30min; 40min).
Ferry Lisco Baltic Service (ⓣ04502/88 66 90, ⓦwww.dfdslisco.com) travel to Rīga (2 weekly; 35hr; €74). Finnlines (ⓣ04502/805 43, ⓦwww.ferrycenter.fi): to Helsinki (9 weekly; 28hr) and Malmö (3 daily; 8–9hr). TT-Line (ⓣ04502/ 801 81, ⓦwww.ttline.com) to Trelleborg (4 daily; 7hr).

HANNOVER

HANNOVER is a major transport hub and trade-fair city and, unfortunately, that's primarily what it looks like. The city's showpiece – refreshingly – is not a great cathedral, palace or town hall, but a series of **gardens** and first-class **museums**. Hannover's location at the intersection of many major cross-country rail lines and its lack of budget accommodation make it a perfect candidate for a pit stop – on your way to somewhere else.

What to see and do

Hannover's commercial centre is a short walk southwest of the train station. The best **museums** are further south, on the other side of Friedrichswall, while the splendid **royal gardens** are north-west of the centre. The centre is pretty bland, but there are some attractive corners and interesting neighbourhoods if you explore a bit further out.

The Altes Rathaus and Marktkirche

A short distance southwest of the train station, a few streets of rebuilt half-timbered buildings convey some impression of the medieval town. The elaborate brickwork of the high-gabled fifteenth-century **Altes Rathaus** is impressive, despite the shop-filled, modern interior. Alongside is the fourteenth-century red-brick Gothic

Marktkirche, with some miraculously preserved stained glass.

Niedersächsisches Landesmuseum and Sprengel Museum

Southeast of the Marktkirche, across Friedrichswall on Willy-Brandt-Allee, is the **Niedersächsisches Landesmuseum** (Tues–Sun 10am–5pm, Thurs till 7pm; €4/students €3, Fri 2–5pm free; U-Bahn Aegidientorplatz), housing an excellent collection of paintings from the Middle Ages to the early twentieth century, plus archeology and ethnology collections. A bit further down the road lies the **Sprengel Museum** (Tues–Thurs & Sun 10am–8pm, Fri & Sat 10am–10pm; €7/students €4, higher during special exhibitions; Ⓦwww.sprengel-museum.de), with a first-rate collection of twentieth- and twenty-first century painting and sculpture.

The Neues Rathaus

West of the Landesmuseum on Friderichswall is the vast, green-domed **Neues Rathaus**, built at the start of the twentieth century. In the foyer are four models of Hannover in 1689, 1939, 1945 and today, illuminating the extent of wartime loss, something that is all too clear as you look over the city from the top of the town hall's **dome** (Mon–Fri 9.30am–6pm, Sat & Sun 10am–6pm; €2.50/students €2), reached via a curved lift.

The gardens

The royal gardens of **Herrenhausen**, featuring Europe's biggest fountain, stretch out northwest of the centre. Proceeding north from town along Nienburger Strasse, the **Georgengarten**, an English-style landscaped garden, is to the left, a foil to the the city's pride and joy, the magnificent formal **Grosser Garten** beyond (daily 9am till dusk May–August till 8pm; €3, €4 with Berggarten; trams #4 and #5 to Herrenhäuser Gärten, main entrance just by the stop on Herrenhäuser Str.). If possible, time your visit to coincide with the fountain displays (mid-March to mid-Oct daily 11am–noon & 2/3–5pm). Directly opposite, on Herrenhäuser Strasse, is the entrance to **Berggarten**, the botanic garden (same hours; €2).

Arrival and information

Airport S-Bahn #5 (every 30min; 20min; €2.80) runs between Hannover Airport and the train station.

Train and bus The train station is in the centre of town, just northeast of main shopping district Kröpke; behind is the bus station.

Tourist office Across from the train station, Ernst-August-Platz 8 ⓣ0511/12 34 51 11, Ⓦwww.hannover-tourism.de (Mon–Fri 9am–6pm, Sat 9am–2pm; May–Sept also Sun 9am–2pm); they'll book you into a hotel for a €2.50 fee.

Discount pass The Hannover Card (single €9/16, up to 5 people €18/31 for 1/3 days), covers public transport and provides discounts to the main museums and sights.

Internet Inside the *Burger King* in the train station (€2/hr); cheap phone and internet places around Steintor.

City transport

The best of Hannover is outside the centre, so its excellent transport network of tram/U-Bahn, S-Bahn and buses centred on the Hauptbahnhof, Kröpke and Aegidientorplatz is useful. The tram/U-Bahn network has some overground tram lines (like #17 and #10) and some hybrid tram/U-Bahn lines where central stops are underground, with lines emerging above ground to become street-level trams further out (such as #4 and #5). Singles €2.10, day tickets €4.10.

Accommodation

There are very few budget options in Hannover, and prices double or more during trade fairs.

DJH Ferdinand-Wilhelm-Fricke-Weg 1 ⓣ0511/131 76 74, Ⓦwww.jugendherberge.de. Modern HI hostel, with two- and four-bed dorms. Take U-Bahn #3 or #7 to Fischerhof, double back north, then turn right on Lodemannweg; it's a signposted 10min walk from there. Dorms from €27.60.

Flora Heinrichstr. 36 ⓣ0511/38 39 10, Ⓦwww.hotel-flora-hannover.de. Spotless hotel behind the train station, with breakfast included. Doubles €59–75.

Hostel Hannover Lenaustr. 12 ⓣ0511/131 99 19, ⓦwww.hostelhannover.de. Basic but friendly, slightly old-fashioned hostel with decent communal areas, but packed dorms. Outside the centre, but good for the Linden-Limmer nightlife; women only for now, but may go mixed in the future. Trams #10 and #17 to Goetheplatz. Check-in 8–11am & 5–8pm. Dorms €15–25 (€5 more at weekends and trade fairs). Sheets €3.

Eating and drinking

In the centre, slightly twee, touristy Kramerstr. and Knochenhauerstr. near the Markt, are your best options. More fun for nightlife is the sprawling Linden-Limmer district west of the centre, particularly around Goetheplatz and Schwarze-Bär. Lister Meile, behind the station, is also a good bet.

Blattgold In der Steinriede 9, corner of Körtingstr., one block east of Lister Meile. Cute, retro bar on an attractive corner, with deckchairs outside and good happy hours. U-Bahn Listerplatz.

Café Glocksee Glockseestr. 35 ⓦwww.cafe-glocksee.de. Great, scruffy little club and venue. Tram #10 to Goetheplatz; head along Lenaustr. and it's the graffitied building at the end (entrance round the back).

Café Safran Königsworther Str. 39, corner of Braunstr. This laid-back café-bar has some sort of cheap deal every day, such as beer and a pizza for €6. Tram #10 to Glocksee.

Markthalle Karmaschstr. 49, near the Markt. The indoor market is packed full of dozens of food stalls – German, Italian, Spanish, Turkish and Japanese, and even a cocktail bar – selling good-value meals. Mon–Wed 7am–8pm, Thurs & Fri 7am–10pm, Sat 7am–4pm.

Moving on

Train Amsterdam (every 2hr; 4hr 20min); Berlin (hourly; 1hr 40min); Cologne (hourly; 2hr 40min); Goslar (hourly; 1hr); Frankfurt (hourly; 2hr 20min); Hamburg (every 30min; 1hr 35min); Munich (hourly; 4hr 20min–4hr 40min).

GOSLAR

GOSLAR is an absurdly picturesque mining town located at the northern edge of the gentle, wooded Harz Mountains, about an hour by train from Hannover. Silver was discovered in the nearby Rammelsberg in the tenth century, and Goslar soon became the "treasure chest of the Holy Roman Empire". The presence of a POW hospital during World War II spared the town's attractive medieval architecture from bombing; it's now a UNESCO World Heritage Site.

What to see and do

The town's geographic and cultural centre is the **Marktplatz**, with an elegantly Gothic **Rathaus** and buildings with roofs of bright red tiles and contrasting grey slate. The **Huldigungssaal** in the Rathaus (April–Oct Mon–Fri 11am–3pm, Sat & Sun 10am–4pm; €3.50) is covered with dazzling medieval wall and ceiling paintings, though it's very fragile, so you can only look in from a glass bubble. Just behind the Rathaus is the **Marktkirche**, facing the sixteenth-century **Brusttuch** house, whose top storey is crammed with satirical carvings. Goslar's half-timbered beauty begins in earnest in the streets behind the church with the oldest houses lying in the Bergstrasse and Schreiberstrasse areas.

On the southern edge of the centre is the **Kaiserpfalz**, built in the early eleventh century. Much of the interior (daily 10am–5pm, Nov–March till 4pm; €4.50) is occupied by the vast Kaisersaal, decorated with Romantic depictions of the German emperors.

The real surprise in traditional Goslar is the imaginative **Mönchehaus Museum**, Mönchestr. 1, northwest of the Markt (Tues–Sun 10am–5pm; €5/students €1.50). A black-and-white half-timbered building over 450 years old is the curious home to Goslar's modern art museum, which displays striking temporary exhibitions among the beams, and has permanent sculptures and installations dotted around the garden and outbuildings.

Arrival and information

Train Head left out of the train station; it's a 5min walk into the centre.

Tourist office Markt 7 ⓣ05321/780 60, ⓦwww.goslar.de (April–Oct Mon–Fri 9.15am–6pm, Sat 9.30am–4pm, Sun 9.30am–2pm; Nov–March Mon–Fri 9.15am–5pm, Sat 9.30am–2pm). Has a good list of guesthouses.

Accommodation

DJH Rammelsberger Str. 25 ⓣ05321/222 40, ⓦwww.jugendherberge.de/jh/goslar. The quaint HI hostel is a 30min walk southwest from the centre (or bus #803 to Theresienhof). Dorms from €20.10.

Eating and drinking

Barock-Café Anders Hoher Weg 4. Join the local grannies for their afternoon *Kaffee and Kuchen*. It's chintzy and old fashioned, but the cake selection is superb.

Butterhanne Marktkirchhof 3. Traditional, good-value restaurant, with outside tables in a lovely spot by the Marktkirche. Mains €7–12.

Central Germany

Central Germany is the country's most populous region and home to its industrial heartland – the Ruhrgebiet. **Cologne** stands out here, with its many splendid reminders of long centuries as a free state, cheek-by-jowl bars and a populace that's legendary for its friendliness. Neighbouring **Bonn**, Beethoven's birthplace, is also venerable, and quite hip and happening for its size, while nearby **Aachen** is of interest as the first capital of the Roman Empire. To the south the Rhineland-Palatinate is famed for the Romantic Rhine: a vineyard-lined stretch of the river which passes through a gorge of impressive rock outcrops, studded with the sort of castles that have given rise to many a tall tale. Nowadays pleasure cruisers – and the railway line – make the attractive journey through the **Gorge**, and beyond to the state capital of **Mainz**, where the printing press was invented, as celebrated in the excellent Gutenberg Museum. Joining the Rhine at Koblenz, the Mosel has a similar combination of vineyards and ruined castles paving the way south to the aged town of **Trier**, with its extraordinarily well-preserved Roman remains – some of the best outside Italy. To the northeast, in the province of Hesse, dynamic **Frankfurt** dominates, with its banking and communications industries providing the region's economic base.

COLOGNE (KÖLN)

COLOGNE (Köln) has a population of just over a million, and its huge Gothic Dom is the country's most visited monument. The Dom is about all that was spared in World War II, putting the city at the mercy of a botched 1950s rebuild. The people here do more than enough to compensate for their city's unremarkable architecture: Cologne is one of Germany's friendliest cities. Try to catch the annual **Carnival** in early spring – when huge parties fill the streets and very little work gets done for a full five days.

Cologne has a long and glorious history – as a Roman colony (*Colonia*), then a pilgrimage centre, a major trading city, and finally as the marketer of toilet water eau de Cologne.

What to see and do

Cologne's sights are all within walking distance of the train station, in a dense centre on the west bank of the Rhine.

The Dom

One of the largest Gothic buildings ever built, Cologne's gigantic **Dom** (daily 6am–7.30pm; free) once symbolized its power – its archbishop was one of the seven Electors of the Holy Roman Empire, and the Dom remains the seat of the Primate of Germany. Begun in 1248, the extravagant project was

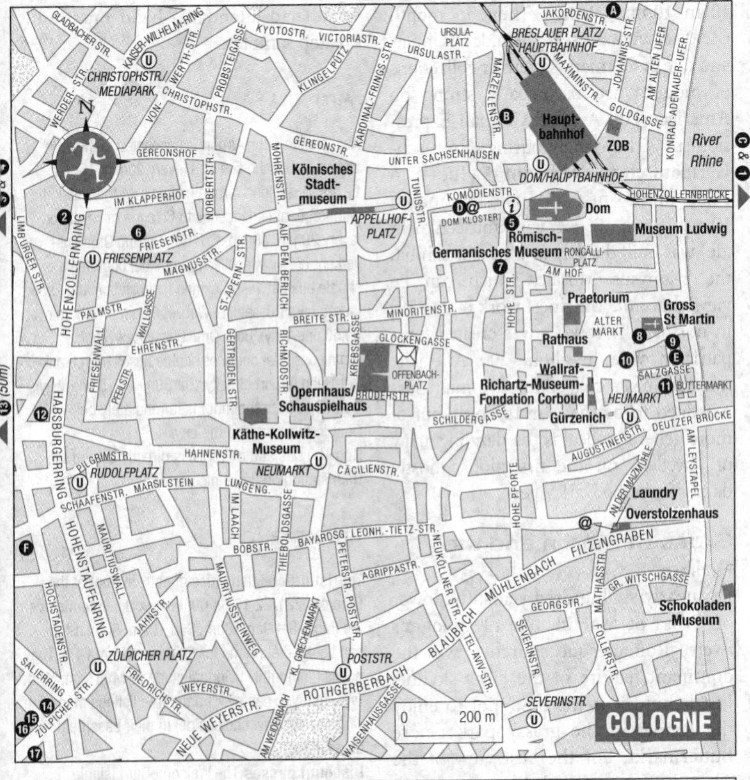

ACCOMMODATION		EATING	
Das Kleine Stapelhäuschen	E	Cafe Reichard	5
Good Sleep	D	Früh am Dom	7
Köln Deutz City Hostel	C	Gaffel Haus	8
Meininger	F	Habibi	16
Rossner	A	Im Bauturm	13
Station Backpacker's	B	Im Martinswinkel	9
		Päffgen	6
		Rendevous	15

DRINKING & NIGHTLIFE	
Biermuseum	11
Comeback	10
Filmdose	17
Gebäude 9	1
LiveMusicHall	3
Nachtflug	2
Roxy	12
Stiefel	14
Underground	4

abandoned in 1560, to be resumed only in the nineteenth century. The centrepiece of this cathedral is the spectacular golden shrine to the Magi (1181). Other masterpieces include the ninth-century Gero crucifix, the most important monumental sculpture of its period, and Stefan Lochner's *Adoration of the Magi*, the greatest work of the fifteenth-century Cologne school of painters. Climb the 509 steps to the top of the south tower for a breathtaking panorama over the city and the Rhine (daily: May–Sept 9am–6pm; March, April & Oct 9am–5pm; Nov–Feb 9am–4pm; €2.50). The **Domschatzkammer** (daily 10am–6pm; €4, joint ticket with tower €5) in the cellars, entered from the north side of the building, contains a stunning array of treasury items, the original sculptures from the medieval south portal and items excavated from Merovingian royal graves.

Museum Ludwig and the Römisch-Germanisches Museum

In a modern building next to the Dom, the outstanding **Museum Ludwig** (Tues–Sun 10am–6pm, first Thurs in month

10am–10pm; €9, first Thurs in month €4.50; Ⓦwww.museenkoeln.de) is huge, and one of Germany's premier collections of modern art, particularly strong on American Pop Art and German Expressionism. The neighbouring **Römisch-Germanisches Museum** (Tues–Sun 10am–5pm, first Thurs in month 10am–10pm; €6; Ⓦwww.museenkoeln.de) was built directly over its star exhibit, the Dionysus Mosaic, which can be viewed *in situ*. The finest work of its kind in northern Europe, it was created for a patrician villa in about 200 AD. The museum has a collection of Roman glass reckoned to be the world's finest, but of more general appeal is the dazzling array of jewellery on the first floor, mostly dating from the Dark Ages.

Gross St Martin and the Rhine

For nearly six hundred years, the tower of **Gross St Martin**, one of Cologne's twelve Romanesque churches, was the dominant feature of the city's skyline. Just behind it is the best spot to enjoy the Rhine, in the grassy park before Buttermarkt. For the best view of the Altstadt, cross the bridge and walk along the other side of the Rhine.

Wallraf-Richartz-Museum

Southwest of Gross St Martin is the strikingly angular **Wallraf-Richartz-Museum** (Tues, Wed & Fri 10am–6pm, Thurs 10am–10pm, Sat & Sun 11am–6pm; €9.50; Ⓦwww.museenkoeln.de), whose holdings centre on the fifteenth-century Cologne school as well as a fine Impressionist collection.

Schokoladenmuseum

Further south, on the banks of the Rhine, is the **Schokoladenmuseum** (Tues–Fri 10am–6pm, Sat & Sun 11am–7pm, last entry 1hr before closing; €7.50; Ⓦwww.schokoladenmuseum.de), a thoroughly enjoyable museum focusing on the history and production of chocolate. The highlight is the chocolate fountain where white-clad attendants hand out freshly created samples.

Arrival

Air Cologne/Bonn Airport is connected to the train station by S-Bahn line S13 (every 20min; 15min; €2.40). Düsseldorf Airport has its own train station, with frequent connections to Cologne main station (every 30min; 40min; €18.50). Shilling Omnibusverkehr (Ⓦwww.schillinggruppe.de) operates a shuttle bus between Cologne main station and Airport Weeze (aka Düsseldorf-Weeze; 8 daily; 1hr 30min; €9.50 one-way). Bohr Omnibus (Ⓦwww.bohr-omnibusse.de) operates shuttle buses from Frankfurt-Hahn Airport (6 daily; 2hr 30min; €15 one-way).
Train The Hauptbahnhof is immediately below the Dom in the centre of the city.
Bus The bus station (ZOB) is directly behind the train station on Johannisstrasse.

Information

Tourist office Main office directly in front of the Dom Ⓣ0221/22 13 04 00, Ⓦwww.koelntourismus.de (Mon–Sat 9am–8pm, Sun 10am–5pm). Staff can book hotel rooms for €3 (rooms from €44). They publish a monthly bilingual guide to what's on, *Köln im...*, and you can pick up the free listings magazine *Choices* (Ⓦwww.choices.de) in their basement ticket office.
Discount passes The WelcomeCard (single €9/14/19, up to three people €18/28/38 for 24hr/48hr/72hr) provides free transport and around twenty percent off most sights.

City transport

The public transport network is a mixture of buses and trams/U-Bahn. A short trip costs €1.60, a single trip €2.40, a day-pass €6.90 (€10.10 for five people) and a strip of four single trips €8.30.

Accommodation

Hostels

Köln Deutz City Hostel Siegesstr. 5 Ⓣ0221/81 47 11, Ⓦwww.jugendherberge.de/jh/koeln-deutz. Large and functional HI hostel close to Deutz station, directly across the Rhine from the Altstadt. Dorms €24.80, doubles €62.
Meininger Engelbertstr. 33–35 Ⓣ0221/92 40 90, Ⓦwww.meininger-hostels.com. This branch of the hostel chain has a great location, roughly between the student area and downtown. Wi-fi, kitchen and

bar. U-Bahn Rudolphplatz or Zülpicher Platz. Dorms €17, twins €68.

Station Backpacker's Marzellenstr. 40–48 ⓣ0221/912 53 01, ⓦwww.hostel-cologne.de. Large, privately run hostel just north of the station, with kitchen and free internet. Dorms €17, twins €48.

Hotels and guesthouses

Das Kleine Stapelhäuschen Fischmarkt 1–3 ⓣ0221/272 77 77, ⓦwww.koeln-altstadt.de /stapelhaeuschen. Characterful Altstadt hotel/restaurant rebuilt to resemble its seventeenth-century appearance, very near Gross St Martin. Rooms overlooking the river are the nicest. Rooms €64.

Good Sleep Komödienstr. 19–21 ⓣ0221/257 22 57, ⓦwww.goodsleep.de. Bare-bones but clean hotel, with good central location. Rooms €65.

Rossner Jakordenstr. 19 ⓣ0221/12 27 03. Homely and clean 1950s throwback and the pick of the cluster of hotels behind the station. Rooms €52.

Eating

Cafés

Café Reichard Unter Fettenhennen 11. Local institution for delicious cakes in elegant surroundings; fine Dom views to boot.

Im Bauturm Aachener Str. 24. Build your own breakfast at this lovely bohemian café-by-day, bar-by-night, open daily until 3am. Breakfasts from €3. U-Bahn Rudolphplatz.

Restaurants

Habibi Zülpicher Str. 28. Serving arguably the best falafel in Germany, this Lebanese restaurant in the student neighbourhood stays open for the late-night munchies. Eat in/take out. Falafel €1.90.

Im Martinswinkel Fischmarkt 9. Inexpensive and relatively non-touristy riverfront restaurant, serving salads and sausages, coffee and cake. *Bratwürst* plate €7.90.

Rendevous Zülpicher Str. 11a. One of a handful of good-value Italian restaurants in the student area. Big portions and a young, friendly crowd. Pizza from €5.50.

Beer halls

Früh am Dom Am Hof 12–14. Located opposite the Dom, this heavily touristed *Brauhaus* serves excellent food. Ribs €9.

Gaffel Haus Alter Markt 20–22. Typical, old-style restaurant, serving huge portions; much cosier than most beer halls. Schnitzel €12.

Päffgen Friesenstr. 64–66, just off Friesenplatz. Less touristy than the places near the Dom, with a younger clientele and *Kölsch* brewed on the premises. Mains €10.

Drinking and nightlife

Bars

Biermuseum Buttermarkt 39. Small Altstadt bar tucked away near the river, serving countless types of beer on tap and in bottles. The surrounding area is the main focus of nightlife for visitors.

Comeback Alter Markt 10. Very central gay bar with pleasant terrace; a good place to pick up advice about where to go in the area south of Heumarkt, a local gay stronghold.

Filmdose Zülpicher Str. 39 ⓦwww.filmdose-koeln .de. Fun pub that's packed with students enjoying a post-lecture *Kölsch*; it has a tiny cabaret stage and also shows films in English. All-day breakfasts €5. U-Bahn Dasselstr./Bhf Süd.

Stiefel Zülpicher Str. 18. Dilapidated and relaxed punk-rock bar in a student quarter that's packed with cheap restaurants and lively bars. A great place to nurse a beer or shoot pool. Closed Sun.

Clubs

Gebäude 9 Deutz-Mühlheimer-Str. 127–129 ⓦwww.gebaeude9.de. Intimate bar, club and theatre hall where events and exhibitions take place, as well as drum'n'bass/live gigs. U-Bahn Messe/Deutz.

LiveMusicHall Lischtstr. 30 ⓦwww .livemusichall.de. Don't let the name fool you: music here is primarily from DJs, with regular pop, rock and 80s nights. Fri, Sat & some Wed. U-Bahn Venloer Str.

Nachtflug Hohenzollernring 89 ⓦwww.nachtflug .com. Probably the best of several fairly mainstream clubs on the Ring between Zülpicher Platz and Christophstrasse. Best for techno and the all-day event every Sunday which runs from dawn until dusk – if you've got the legs for it. €13.

KÖLSCH

Cologne's unique beer, **Kölsch** is a light and aromatically bitter brew served in a small, thin glass (hence its rather effete image among German beer-drinkers). The best places to try it are the *Brauhäuser*, brewery-owned beer halls, which, although staffed by excruciatingly matey waiters called *Köbes*, are definitely worth exploring, not least because they serve some of the tastiest food in the city.

COLOGNE'S CARNIVAL

Though Cologne's **carnival** actually begins as early as November 11, the real business starts with Weiberfastnacht on the Thursday prior to Lent. The city goes wild for the next five days until Ash Wednesday; prepare yourself for drunken dancing in the streets and wild costumes. The best of the numerous parades are the alternative Geisterzug Saturday night, complete with fire-juggling and drumming, and the spectacular Rose Monday Parade, which features music, floats and political caricatures.

Roxy Aachener Str. 2. Open midnight until 7am, this is the place to hit at the end of the night. Two bars, one packed dancefloor and an eclectic music mix.

Underground Vogelsanger Str. 200 Ⓦ www.underground-cologne.de. Great for live gigs, especially rock and punk, the *Underground* has a beer garden and a big indie/alternative following. Free entry mid-week. U-Bahn Venloer Str.

Directory

Bike rental Rent-a-Bike, Markmannsgasse, on the banks of the Rhine before the Deutzer Brücke Ⓣ 0171/629 87 96. Three-hour tour (May–Oct daily 1.30pm, €15), bike rental (€10/day).

Cinema Metropolis, Ebertplatz 19 Ⓦ www.metropolis-koeln.de. Small cinema showing English-language films. U-Bahn Ebertplatz.

Hospital St Marien, Kunibertskloster 11 Ⓣ 0221/162 90.

Internet TelePost, Komödienstr. 19. €1.50/hr. Also next door to laundry below: €0.80/hr.

Laundry Kölns' Schneller Waschsalon, Mathiasstr. 24; €3.80.

Left luggage At the train station.

Pharmacy At the train station.

Post office Breite Str. 6 & at the train station.

Moving on

Train Aachen (every 20min; 50min); Amsterdam (6 daily; 2hr 40min); Berlin (hourly; 4hr 20min); Bonn (frequent; 20min); Brussels (hourly; 2hr 20min); Frankfurt (every 30min; 1hr 20min); Heidelberg (hourly; 2hr); Luxembourg (hourly; 3hr 30min); Mainz (frequent; 1hr 45min); Paris (hourly; 4hr); Stuttgart (hourly; 2hr 15min).

River cruise K-D Ⓦ www.k-d.com to Bonn (April–Oct 1–2 daily; 2hr 15min).

BONN

A great day-trip from Cologne, lovely, riverside **BONN** was West Germany's unlikely capital from 1949 until unification in 1990, when Berlin regained its former status. But even with its role diminished, Bonn is still worth a visit to see the birthplace of Ludwig van Beethoven, a string of top-rated museums and an attractive Old Town, and to witness the students of its forward-thinking university making sure the town punches above its weight in nightlife.

What to see and do

The small pedestrianized **Altstadt** centres on two spacious squares. That to the east is named after the huge **Münster**, whose central octagonal tower with its soaring spire is the city's most prominent landmark. Head around the back to check out the gigantic decapitated heads of the church's patrons, the martyrs SS Cassius and Florentius. The Markt square is dominated by a very different monument, the pink Rococo **Rathaus**, and hosts a market every day except Sunday.

The Beethoven-Haus and the Schloss

A couple of minutes' walk north of the Markt, at Bonngasse 20, is the **Beethoven-Haus** (April–Oct Mon–Sat 10am–6pm, Sun 11am–6pm; Nov–March Mon–Sat 10am–5pm, Sun 11am–5pm; €5; Ⓦ www.beethoven-haus-bonn.de), one of the few old buildings here that escaped wartime devastation. Beethoven left the city for good aged 22, but this hasn't deterred Bonn from building up the best collection of memorabilia of its favourite son. To the east is the enormously long Baroque **Schloss**, once the seat of the Archbishop-Electors of Cologne and now part of the university.

The Museumsmeile

The **Museumsmeile** (U-Bahn Heussallee) is home to the **Kunstmuseum** (Tues–Sun 11am–6pm, Wed till 9pm; €5; ⓦwww.kunstmuseum.bonn.de), with its fine Expressionism collection. Next door is the **Kunst- und Ausstellungshalle** (Tues & Wed 10am–9pm, Thurs–Sun 10am–7pm; €8, combined ticket with Kunstmuseum €11; ⓦwww.bundeskunsthalle.de), a monumental postmodern arts centre for important temporary exhibitions. The Kunstmuseum's other neighbour is the **Haus der Geschichte** (Tues–Sun 9am–7pm; free; ⓦwww.hdg.de), a fascinating museum exploring German contemporary history from the end of World War II to the present.

Arrival and information

Train and bus Bonn's train station lies in the middle of the city; just to the east is the bus station, whose local services, along with the trams (which become U-Bahns in the city centre), form part of a system integrated with Cologne's (see p.494).
Tourist office Windeckstr. 1, near Münsterplatz ⓣ0228/77 50 00, ⓦwww.bonn-region.de (Mon–Fri 9am–6.30pm, Sat 9am–4pm, Sun 10am–2pm).
Discount pass The WelcomeCard (single €9/14/19, up to three people €18/28/38 for 24hr/48hr/72hr) is a great deal in Bonn, providing free travel and free admission to almost all museums and sights.

Eating

Alter Zoll Brassertufer 1, at Konviktstr. Best *Biergarten* in town, with a great Rhine view and yummy snacks. There's a discount on pizza from noon to 3pm (€2.60). Summer only.
Cassius Garten Maximilianstr. 28d, across from the station. Offers mouthwatering vegetarian choices, buffet style. Daily 8am–8pm. €1.50/100g, twenty percent off between 7 and 8pm.
Zebulon Stockenstr. 19. This Altstadt bar is a big favourite with students, especially of the American-study-abroad variety. Light meals €3.20.

AACHEN

AACHEN has a laid-back atmosphere that reflects its large student population, making it a good day-trip from Cologne or a stop off between countries. Bordering both Belgium and the Netherlands, Aachen was once the hub of Charlemagne's vast European-wide eighth-century empire. The choice was partly strategic but also because of the presence of hot springs. Relaxing in these waters was one of the emperor's favourite pastimes, and their health-enriching properties remain a major draw.

What to see and do

The surviving architectural legacy of Charlemagne is small, but its crowning jewel, the former **Palace chapel**, has pride of place at the heart of the **Dom** (daily: April–Oct 7am–6pm; Nov–March 7am–7pm; ⓦwww.aachendom.de). At its end, the gilded shrine of Charlemagne, finished in 1215 after fifty years' work, contains the emperor's remains, while the gallery has the imperial throne, viewable only to those on a tour (4–5 daily; €3). Next to the Dom, the **Schatzkammer** (Mon 10am–1pm, Tues–Sun 10am–6pm, Thurs till 9pm; €4; entrance on Johannes-Paul-II-Str.) is a dazzling treasury and UNESCO World Heritage Site. Its highlights are the tenth-century Lothar Cross and a Roman sarcophagus once used as Charlemagne's coffin. The emperor's palace once extended across the Katschhof to the expansive **Markt**,

TREAT YOURSELF

To enjoy the healing waters Charlemagne once enjoyed, head to the luxurious **Carolus Thermen** (daily 9am–11pm, last entry at 9.30pm; ⓦwww.carolus-thermen.de), a spa northeast of the centre, where the accumulated grunge of weeks on the road will quickly soak away. Two and a half hours costs €11 (full day €14) or €13 including transport on bus #34 or #51, from the centre of Aachen. The driver sells the tickets.

which now boasts the finest medieval houses left in the city. Here two of the palace towers remain, incorporated into the fourteenth-century **Rathaus**, whose facade is lined with the figures of fifty Holy Roman Emperors, 31 of whom were crowned in Aachen. The glory of the interior (daily 10am–1pm & 2–5pm; €2) is the much-restored Kaisersaal, repository of the crown jewels – in reproduction.

Arrival and information

Train The centre is 10min walk from the train station – down Bahnhofstrasse, then left into Theaterstrasse.
Tourist office In the Elisenbrunnen on Friedrich-Wilhelm-Platz ⓣ0241/180 29 60, ⓦwww.aachen.de (Jan–Easter Mon–Fri 9am–6pm, Sat 9am–2pm; Easter–Dec also Sun 10am–2pm).

Eating and drinking

The student quarter centres on Pontstrasse – which leads northeast out of the Markt – and is lined with bars and cheap eateries.
Egmont Pontstr. 1. Classy, wood-panelled bistro, a popular haunt. Great cakes. Coffee and cake €4.20.
Kittel Pontstr. 37. Relaxed bohemian café with good-size portions of great inexpensive food. Tagliatelle €5. Open until 3am.
Leo van den Daele Büchel 18. Venerable wood-clad café with great cakes and particularly good *Printen*, a spiced gingerbread that's the main local speciality.
Ocean Pontstr. 164. One of a group of sports and cocktail bars, with plentiful outdoor seating and a cheerful atmosphere.

Moving on

Train Brussels (hourly; 1hr 30min); Cologne (every 20min; 50min); Liège (hourly; 50min); Maastricht (every 30min; 1hr); Paris (hourly; 3hr).

MAINZ

At the confluence of the Rhine and Main rivers, **MAINZ** is an agreeable mixture of old and new, with an attractive restored centre and a jovial populace who are responsible for Germany's second biggest carnival bash (after Cologne). Its long-standing ecclesiastical power aside, Mainz is also famous for Johannes Gutenberg, who pioneered printing here in the sixteenth century.

What to see and do

Rearing high above central Mainz, the **Dom** (March–Oct Mon–Fri 9am–6.30pm, Sat 9am–4pm, Sun 1–2.45pm & 4–6.30pm; Nov–Feb Mon–Fri & Sun till 5pm) is unusual for sharing its outer walls with rows of eighteenth-century houses. Inside, the choirs at both ends indicate it as an imperial cathedral, with one for the emperor and the other for the clergy. The bustling **market square** outside (markets: Tues, Fri & Sat mornings) adjoins Liebfrauenplatz and the fascinating **Gutenberg Museum** (Tues–Sat 9am–5pm, Sun 11am–3pm; €5; ⓦwww.gutenberg.de), paying tribute to one of the greatest inventions of all time, which enabled the mass-scale production of books. Its extension next door is the Druckladen (Printing shop; Mon–Fri 9am–5pm Sat 10am–3pm; by donation of around €3–5, ⓣ06131/12 26 86, ⓦwww.druckladen.mainz.de), where visitors are shown how to hand-set type, and produce posters, cards and the like.

Arrival and information

Train The station is a 15min walk northwest of the city centre; head down Bahnhofstrasse or take a tram or bus to Höffchen.
Tourist office At Brückenturm am Rathaus ⓣ06131/28 62 10, ⓦwww.info-mainz.de (Mon–Fri 9am–6pm, Sat 10.30am–2.30pm, Sun 11am–3pm). Tricky to find, with an isolated position: it's elevated above the street beside a pedestrian bridge. Offers a free room-booking service, with rooms from €54.

Accommodation

DJH Otto-Brunfels-Schneise 4 ⓣ06131/853 32, ⓦwww.jugendherberge.de. Standard HI hostel, with single, twin and four-bed rooms, in the wooded heights of Weisenau. Buses #62 & #63 will take you within 400m of it. Dorms €19.90, rooms €50.80.

Stadt Coblenz Rheinstr. 49 ⓣ06131/629 04 44, ⓦwww.stadtcoblenz.de. Conveniently located and comfy hotel near the Dom, though some rooms suffer from street noise. Rooms €55.

Eating and drinking

Mainz boasts more vineyards on its outskirts than any other German city; the many lovely wine bars are the best places to sample their produce.

Alt Deutsche Weinstube Liebfrauenplatz 7. The oldest wine bar in town, offering cheap daily dishes. Evenings only; local wine from €2.60.

Eisgrub-Bräu Weisslilengasse 1a. Microbrewery with an accomplished range of its own beers and a good line of inexpensive food, including breakfast, lunch and dinner buffets for €4–8.50.

Heiligeist Rentengasse 2. Attractive and inexpensive bistro in the Gothic vaults of a fifteenth-century hospital; mains (€6–15) are international and include several Italian options.

Kuz Dagobertstrasse 20b ⓣ06131/28 68 60, ⓦwww.kuz.de. Mainz's most dependably happening club with a sociable beer garden and busy events list which often involves live music, particularly world music. Usually busy until at least 4am at the weekend; cover charge around €8.

Moving on

Train Cologne (frequent; 1hr 45min); Frankfurt (frequent; 40min); Heidelberg (frequent; 1hr 20min); Koblenz (every 30min; 1hr); Stuttgart (every 30min; 1hr 30min); Trier (hourly; 2hr 30min).

River cruises K-D ⓦwww.k-d.com to Bacharach/Kaub (April–Oct 1–2 daily; 2hr 30min).

THE RHINE GORGE

North of Mainz, the Rhine snakes west to **BINGEN**, where the spectacular eighty-kilometre-long **Rhine Gorge**, a **UNESCO World Heritage region**, begins. Its most famous sight is the **Lorelei**, a rocky projection between Oberwesel and St Goar, where, legend has it, a blonde woman would lure passing mariners to their doom with her siren song. The region is best visited by boat or by bike, spending a night in Bacharach or Koblenz, but if you're pressed for time, the train will do. The railway between Koblenz and Mainz runs along the riverbank, offering wonderful gorge views from the windows on the train's eastern side. Some **river cruises** (mainly April–Oct) depart from Mainz, but more begin at Bingen. The full one-way boat fare from Bingen to Koblenz is €28.20.

Bacharach

At **BACHARACH**, 10km downstream from Bingen, the twelfth-century castle of Burg Stahleck houses the *Jugendherberge Bacharach* (ⓣ06743/12 66, ⓦwww.djh.de; dorms €18.90, rooms €48.80) – probably Germany's most atmospheric hostel. It's a steep uphill climb to get there, but the views of the Rhine Valley are worth it. The best budget hotel is the lovely half-timbered *Im Malerwinkel* (ⓣ06743/12 39, ⓦwww.im-malerwinkel.de; all rooms en suite; €62), built into the old town wall. There's also a **campsite** at Strandbadweg 9 (ⓣ06743/17 52, ⓦwww.camping-sonnenstrand.de; €8), 5min south of the station.

Koblenz

Quiet **KOBLENZ** stands where the Rhine and Mosel meet at the **Deutsches Eck** (German corner). Across the Rhine in the district of **Ehrenbreitstein** is the imposing **fortress**, one of the world's largest and now partly home to the *Jugendherberge Koblenz* (ⓣ0261/97 28 70, ⓦwww.jugendherberge.de; dorms €19.90, rooms €50.80). The fortress and hostel can be reached by chairlift in the summer: it's a five-kilometre walk from the station, or take bus #7, #8 or #9 to Ehrenbreitstein Berg Str. The central *Jan van Werth*, Van-Werth-Str. 9 (ⓣ0261/3 65 00 ⓦwww.hoteljanvanwerth.de; doubles €50, singles €24), is also a good option. The **campsite** (ⓣ0261/827 19, ⓦwww.camping-rhein-mosel.de; April to mid-Oct; €8) is across the Mosel from the Deutsches Eck.

Moving on

Train Koblenz to: Bacharach (hourly; 40min); Bingen (every 30min; 45min); Cologne (frequent;

1hr 15min); Frankfurt (every 30min; 1hr 45min); Heidelberg (every 30min; 2hr); Mainz (every 30min; 1hr); Stuttgart (every 30min; 2hr 20min); Trier (every 30min; 1hr 30min).

River cruises K-D ⓦwww.k-d.com. Koblenz to: Bacharach/Kaub (April–Oct 4 daily; 4hr 30min); Bingen (April–Oct 4 daily; 6hr); Bonn (April–Oct 1 daily; 5hr 30min); Mainz (April–Oct 1 daily; 8hr 30min).

TRIER

Birthplace of Karl Marx, and the oldest city in Germany, **TRIER** was once the capital of the Western Roman Empire. Nowadays, it has the less-exalted role of regional centre for the upper Mosel valley, its relaxed air a world away from its former status. Despite a turbulent history, an amazing amount of the city's past has been preserved, in particular the most impressive group of Roman monuments north of the Alps.

What to see and do

The centre corresponds roughly to the Roman city and can easily be covered on foot. From the train station, it's a few minutes' walk down Theodor-Heuss-Allee to the **Porta Nigra**, Roman Trier's northern gateway. From here, Simeonstrasse runs down to the **Hauptmarkt**, a busy pedestrian area, where market stalls sell groceries and flowers. At the southern end of the Hauptmarkt, a half-hidden Baroque portal leads to the exquisite Gothic **St Gangolf**, built by the burghers of Trier in an attempt to aggravate the archbishops, whose political power they resented.

The Dom and Konstantinbasilika

Up Sternstrasse from the Hauptmarkt, the magnificent Romanesque **Dom** (daily: April–Oct 6.30am–6pm; Nov–March 6.30am–5.30pm) lies on the site of the one built in the fourth century by Emperor Constantine. The present church dates from 1030, and the original facade has not changed significantly since then. From here, take Liebfrauenstrasse past the ritzy **Palais Kesselstadt** and turn left on An der Meerkatz, to the **Konstantinbasilika** (April–Oct Mon–Sat 10am–6pm Sun noon–6pm, Nov–March Tues–Sat 11am–noon & 3–4pm Sun noon–1pm). Built as Constantine's throne hall, its dimensions are awe inspiring: 30m high and 67m long, it is completely self-supporting. It became a church for the local Protestant community in the nineteenth century.

The Rheinisches Landesmuseum

Just beyond some formal gardens southwest of the Konstantinbasilika, the **Rheinisches Landesmuseum** (usually open daily, but enquire at the tourist office for opening hours and admission fee; ⓦwww.landesmuseum-trier.de) is easily the best of Trier's museums, with a collection that brings to life the sophistication and complexity of Roman civilization; prize exhibit is the *Neumagener Weinschiff*, a Roman sculpture of a wine ship. A few minutes' walk further south, the **Kaiserthermen** (daily: March & Oct

BOAT TRIPS ON THE MOSEL

The final 195km-long stretch of the Mosel between Trier and Koblenz cuts a sinuous and attractive gorge that gives Germany some of its steepest vineyards and best full-bodied wines. Boats offer an ideal way to explore the valley: the Personen-Schiffarht Gebrüder Kolb (ⓦwww.moselfahrplan.de) offer regular sailings from Trier to Bernkastel-Kues; the Mosel-Schiffs-Touristik (ⓦwww.moselpersonenschifffahrt.de) concentrate on the middle leg around Traben-Trarbach and Bernkastel-Kues; while Köln-Düsseldorfer (ⓦwww.k-d.com) cover the northern leg between Cochem and Koblenz. Pick up the latest timetables for all three companies at the tourist information office in Trier or Koblenz.

9am–5pm April–Sept 9am–6pm, Nov–Feb 9am–4pm; €2.10) was once one of the largest bath complexes in the Roman world. The extensive underground heating system has survived, and you can walk its passages.

The Karl-Marx-Haus

Southwest of the Hauptmarkt, the **Karl-Marx-Haus**, Brückenstrasse 10 (April–Oct Mon 1–6pm, Tues–Sun 10am–6pm; Nov–March Mon 2–5pm, Tues–Sun 10am–1pm & 2–5pm; €3; Ⓦwww.museum-karl-marx-haus.de), is where Karl Marx was born. It now houses a modern three-storey museum on his life and work, as well as a general history of Communism up to the present day.

Arrival and information

Tourist office At An der Porta Nigra Ⓣ0651/97 80 80, Ⓦwww.tourist-information-trier.de (May–Oct Mon–Thurs 9am–6pm, Fri & Sat 9am–7pm, Sun 9am–5pm; Nov–April Mon–Sat 9am–5pm, Sun 10am–1pm). It sells the Trier-Card (€9/3 days), which covers transport and provides discounts at the museums.

Bike rental At the train station by platform 11. Mid-April–Oct daily 9am–7pm; Nov to mid-April Mon–Fri 10am–6pm. €9/day.

Accommodation

DJH An der Jugendherberge 4 Ⓣ0651/14 66 20, Ⓦwww.djh.de. Brand-new HI hostel, with games rooms and sports facilities. Bus #12. Dorms €19.90, rooms €50.80.

Camping Treviris Luxemburger Str. 81 Ⓣ0651/820 09 11, Ⓦwww.camping-treviris.de. Campsite on the western bank of the Mosel, over the Konrad-Adenauer bridge. Open April–Oct. €10.55 per person.

Hille's Gartenfeldstr. 7 Ⓣ0651/710 27 85, Ⓦwww.hilles-hostel-trier.de. Homely, clean and sociable independent hostel a 10min walk south of the station. Reception Nov–June 4–6pm, July–Oct 2–8pm. Sheets included. Dorms €18, rooms €50.

Eating and drinking

Alt Zalawen Zurlaubener Ufer 79, north of the Kaiser-Wilhelm-Brücke. This traditional tavern, complete with outdoor seating overlooking the Mosel, makes an excellent place to try out the local cider, Viez. Meat platter €5. Daily from 3pm.

AstArix Karl-Marx-Str. 11. This relaxed student bar is your best bet for good and inexpensive food, and there's always something on at night. Pizza €3.50–5. The entrance is down an alley.

Forum Hindenburgstr. 4 Ⓦwww.forum-trier.com. An invariably packed café/bar/club spinning Latin, house and hip-hop to a younger crowd. Occasional live shows. Open Wed–Sat.

Weinstube Palais Kesselstatt Liebfrauenstr. 10. Late-opening, well-known wine bar – the pick among the many possibilities for tasting local wines. Wine from €4.

Moving on

Train Cologne (every 30min; 2hr 30min); Frankfurt (every 30min; 3hr 30min); Koblenz (every 30min; 1hr 30min); Luxembourg (hourly; 50min).

FRANKFURT

Straddling the River Main just before it meets the Rhine, **FRANKFURT AM MAIN** is known as Germany's cut-throat financial capital. Less known is the fact that Frankfurt spends more on the arts than any other European city. It has some of Germany's best museums and some excellent (if expensive) nightlife. Over half of the city, including almost all of the centre, was destroyed during the war and the rebuilders often opted for innovation over restoration, resulting in an architecturally mixed skyline – part skyscraper, part quaint, Germanic red brick.

What to see and do

Frankfurt's centre is defined by its old city walls, now a semicircular stretch of public gardens. The low hill of **Römerberg** is the historical and geographical centre and where Charlemagne built his fort to protect the original *frankonovurd* (Ford of the Franks). The whole quarter was flattened by bombing in 1944, but the most significant survivor was the thirteenth-century St Bartholomäus or **Dom**, which emerged with its main walls intact. To the right of the choir is the restored Wahlkapelle, where the

ACCOMMODATION		EATING		DRINKING & NIGHTLIFE			
Backer	A	Café Karin	11	Adolf Wagner	15	U60311	9
Frankfurt Hostel	C	Café Laumer	4	Atschel	13	Unity	8
Haus der Jugend – HI	D	Iwase	5	Batchkapp	1	Zum Eichkatzerl	12
One Twenty	B	Mirador	3	Club Voltaire	7	Zum Gemalten Haus	16
Primus	E	NYC	14	Cooky's	10		
Royal	F	Vinum	6	Harvey's	2		

seven Electors would choose the Holy Roman Emperor.

Museum für Moderne Kunst and Imperial Hall

To the north, in Domstrasse, is the **Museum für Moderne Kunst** (Tues & Thurs–Sun 10am–6pm, Wed 10am–8pm; €8, free last Sat of the month; Ⓦwww.mmk-frankfurt.de), a three-storey affair featuring major modern artists (Lichtenstein, Warhol, Flavin, Beuys) and innovative temporary exhibitions. At the opposite end of the Römerberg is the **Römer**, formerly the Rathaus. The **Imperial Hall** (Kaisersaal; daily 10am–1pm & 2–5pm; €2), with its distinctive facade of triple-stepped gables, fronts the Römerplatz market square, home to a twinkling **Christmas Market** in December.

Jewish Museum

A short distance to the west, on Untermainkai, is the interesting **Jewish Museum** (Jüdisches Museum; Tues–Sun 10am–5pm, Wed 10am–8pm; €4; Ⓦwww.juedischesmuseum.de), which examines the city's Jewish community, of whom 10,000 died in Nazi hands.

Sachsenhausen and Museumsufer

For a laid-back evening out, head for **Sachsenhausen**, the city-within-a-city on the south bank of the Main. The network of streets around Affentorplatz is home to the famous apple-wine (*Ebbelwei*) houses, while on Schaumainkai – also known as **Museumsufer** – the Saturday **flea market** is worth a browse. Museumsufer is also lined with excellent museums, pick of the bunch being the **Städel**, located at no. 63 (Tues, Fri, Sat & Sun 10am–6pm, Wed & Thurs 10am–9pm; €10; Ⓦwww.staedelmuseum.de), one of the most comprehensive art galleries in Europe. All the big names in German art are represented, including Dürer, Holbein and Cranach – as well as other European masters from Rembrandt to Picasso. The **Deutsches Filmmuseum** at no. 41 (Tues, Thurs & Fri 10am–5pm, Wed, Sat & Sun 10am–7pm; €2.50, screenings €6; Ⓦwww.deutschesfilmmuseum.de) has its own cinema and is a popular spot for foreign films and art-house screenings. If you're into architecture, check out the **Deutsches Architekturmuseum**, no. 43 (Tues & Thurs–Sun 11am–6pm, Wed 11am–8pm; €6; Ⓦwww.dam-online.de), installed in an avant-garde conversion of a nineteenth-century villa. The museum's high point is the "house within a house" which dominates the museum like an oversized dolls' house.

Arrival

Air Frankfurt Airport (Ⓦwww.airportcity-frankfurt.com) has its own long-distance train station, Frankfurt Flughafen Fernbahnhof, with regular rail links to most German cities and Frankfurt's Hauptbahnhof (frequent; 11min; €2.20), also linked to the airport by two S-Bahn lines. The deceptively named Frankfurt Hahn Airport (Ⓦwww.hahn-airport.de) actually lies mid way between Trier and Koblenz but is connected to Frankfurt by bus (hourly; 1hr 45min; €12).
Train From the Hauptbahnhof it's a 15min walk to the centre, or take U-Bahn line #4 or #5, or tram #11.

Information

Tourist office In the train station ⓣ069/21 23 88 00, Ⓦwww.frankfurt-tourismus.de (Mon–Fri 8am–9pm, Sat & Sun 9am–6pm), and also at Römerberg 27 (Mon–Fri 9.30am–5.30pm, Sat & Sun 10am–4pm). Free listings magazines, *Frizz* and *Strandgut*, are available at both.
Discount passes The Frankfurt Card (€8.70/12.50 for 1/2 days) can be bought from tourist offices and allows travel throughout the city, plus fifty percent off entry charges to most museums. The Museumsufer Ticket (€12) provides free entrance to 29 museums for two days.

City transport

Frankfurt has an integrated public transport system made up of S-Bahn, U-Bahn and trams. A short trip is €1.65, a single trip €2.20 and a day ticket €5.40.

Accommodation

Accommodation is pricey, thanks to the expense-account clientele – and rates can double during trade fairs. For a €3 fee the tourist office will book a room.

Hostels

Frankfurt Hostel Kaiserstr. 74 ⓣ069/247 51 30, Ⓦwww.frankfurt-hostel.com. Right in front of the station with internet and common room/kitchen. Sheets and breakfast included. Dorms €18, rooms €65.
Haus der Jugend–HI Deutschherrnufer 12, Sachsenhausen ⓣ069/610 01 50, Ⓦwww.jugendherberge-frankfurt.de. Around 470 places in dorms of up to twelve beds each. 2am curfew. Bus #46 to Frankensteiner Platz – in the evenings and at weekends take tram #16 to Lokalbahnhof. Dorms €17, rooms €61.

Hotels

Backer Mendelssohnstr. 92 ⓣ069/74 79 92. Clean and close to the university, although use of the showers costs €2 a time. U-Bahn #6 or #7 to Westend. Rooms €40.
One Twenty Mainzer Landstr. 120 ⓣ069/74 26 28. Pleasant budget hotel just north of the train station, away from the sleazier streets. Rooms €55.
Primus Grosse Rittergasse 19–21 ⓣ069/62 30 20. Basic, good-value hotel in Sachsenhausen. All rooms en suite, €58.
Royal Wallstr. 17 ⓣ069/62 30 26. Slightly more upscale big sister of *Primus*. In the heart of

Sachsenhausen, close to some of the well-known apple-wine taverns. Rooms €67.

Eating

Café Karin Grosser Hirschgraben 28. Frankfurt institution that's friendly, unpretentious and well worth a visit. Breakfast all day and bistro/bar in the evenings. Pasta €8, *Apfelwein* €1.55.
Café Laumer Bockenheimer Landstr. 67. Dignified old café amid a forest of skyscrapers, halfway up the Westend's main thoroughfare. Daily specials €6.70.
Iwase Vilbeler Str. 31. Tiny Japanese place, with seating at the counter and a few tables. Closed Sun. Maki from €6.
Mirador Bergerstr. 65. Trendy café-bar with gold-dusted decor on a street lined with such places. Drink specials €5. U-Bahn #4 to Merianplatz.
NYC Hans-Thoma-Str. 1, at Schweizerstr., Sachsenhausen. Funky café-bar with a young crowd, outside tables and all manner of American food, including tasty breakfast pancakes (€4). Continental breakfast €8.80; burgers €6.80.
Vinum Kleine Hochstr. 9. Rustic wine cellar with local range of wines to try (from €4). Slightly pricey food (mains €12), but in the heart of Frankfurt.

Drinking and nightlife

Apfelwein (cider) is Frankfurt's speciality. Although you'll find it everywhere, the apple-wine taverns of Haidhausen are the most atmospheric places to try it. The trendiest bars and clubs can be found around the Salzhaus in the centre and in the Ostend district, around Hanauer Landstrasse.

Apple-wine taverns

Adolf Wagner Schweizer Str. 71, Sachsenhausen. One of the best of the taverns, with a lively clientele of all ages and a cosy garden terrace. Meals €12, *Apfelwein* €1.60.
Atschel Wallstr. 7. This place offers a more extensive menu than many of its counterparts, and has bargain set lunches. Closed Mon. "Frankfurt slaughter platter" (consisting of almost every part of the slaughtered pig) €8.70.
Zum Eichkatzerl Dreieichstr. 29, Sachsenhausen. An excellent, traditional tavern with a large courtyard and some veggie options; from €8. Daily 5pm–1am.
Zum Gemalten Haus Schweizer Str. 67, Sachsenhausen. A bit kitsch with its oil-painted facade and stained-glass windows, but quite intimate and lively, with long rows of tables outside. Closed Mon. Schnitzel €10.

Bars

Club Voltaire Kleine Hochstr. 5. Tasty, good food with a Spanish bias, and an eclectic clientele. Frequent events include musical improv evenings and political debates. Open 6pm–1am. Chilli con carne €5.50.
Harvey's Bornheimer Landstr. 64. Slick, high-ceilinged, colonnaded bar in an appealing end-of-terrace building, which in the evening hosts a mainly gay and lesbian crowd. Tram #12 to Friedberger Platz.

Clubs

Batschkapp Maybachstr. 24 Ⓦ www.batschkapp.de. Grimy, sweaty venue for top-rank indie bands – avoid the school-age club nights though. S-Bahn #6 to Eschersheim or U-Bahn #1, #2 or #3 to Weisser Stein.
Cooky's Am Salzhaus 4 Ⓦ www.cookys.de. Hip-hop, house and soul club north of Berliner Strasse, hosting popular DJ nights plus occasional live acts. Cover €7.
U60311 Rossmarkt 6, at Am Salzhaus Ⓦ www.u60311.net. Long-standing favourite and one of the best techno clubs in town, in a former pedestrian underpass. It would be hard to find if it weren't for the queue. Closed Mon & Tues. Hauptwache U-Bahn.
Unity Hanauer Landstr. 2 Ⓦ www.unity1.de. Intimate, crowded and fun club, playing house music until 5am. Closed Mon. U-Bahn Zoo or Ostendstr.

Directory

Consulates Australia, Grüneburgweg 58–62 Ⓣ 069/90 55 80; UK, Bockenheimer Landstr. 42 (Triton Haus) Ⓣ 069/170 00 20; US, Siesmayerstr. 21 Ⓣ 069/753 50.
Exchange Reisebank, at the train station.
Hospital Bürgerhospital, Nibelungenallee 37–41 Ⓣ 069/15 00 00.
Internet Internet Callshop, Kaiserstr. 70. In front of the train station, €2/hr. Museum für Kommunikation, free.
Laundry Wash World, Moselstr. 17, east of the station. Closed Sun; €4.
Left luggage At the train station.
Pharmacy At the train station.
Post office At the train station and Goetheplatz 6.

Moving on

Train Berlin (every 30min; 4hr 10min); Cologne (frequent; 1hr 25min); Hamburg (hourly; 3hr 40min); Heidelberg (every 30min; 1hr); Munich (hourly; 3hr 10min); Nuremberg (hourly; 2hr 5min); Würzburg (hourly; 1hr 10min).

Baden-Württemberg

The southwestern state of **Baden-Württemberg** is Germany's most prosperous. The motor car was invented here in the late nineteenth century, and the region has stayed at the forefront of technology ever since, with **Stuttgart** still the home of Daimler (Mercedes) and Porsche. Also in the region is the famous university city of **Heidelberg**, and the elegant spa resort of **Baden-Baden**, which remains evocative of its nineteenth-century heyday as a playground for European aristocracy. **Baden-Württemberg**'s scenery is wonderful: its western and southern boundaries are defined by the Rhine and its bulge into Germany's largest lake, the **Bodensee** (Lake Constance). Within the curve of the river lies the **Black Forest**, source of another of the continent's principal waterways, the Danube.

HEIDELBERG

Home to Germany's oldest university, **HEIDELBERG** is majestically set on the banks of the swift-flowing Neckar, 70km south of Frankfurt. For two centuries, it has seduced travellers like no other German city. The centrepiece is the Schloss, a compendium of magnificent buildings, made more atmospheric by their ruined condition – making this one castle where you won't end up traipsing through over-decorated bedchambers. The rest of the city has some good museums, but the main appeal is its picturesque cobbled streets, crammed with old-style eateries and student pubs. In spring and early summer the streets hum with activity and late-night parties – by July and August, most students have left, to be replaced by swarms of visitors.

What to see and do

The dominating **Schloss** can be reached from the Kornmarkt by the *Bergbahn* funicular (€5 return), which continues to the Königstuhl viewpoint (€8 return); you can also walk up in ten minutes via the Burgweg. At the southeastern corner is the most romantic of the ruins, the Gesprengter Turm; a collapsed section lies intact in the moat, leaving a clear view into the interior. The **Schlosshof** (daily 8am–5.30pm; €5, grounds free from 6pm until dusk; Ⓦwww.schloss-heidelberg.de) is a group of Renaissance palaces that now contains the diverting Pharmacy Museum and the Grosses Fass, an eighteenth-century wine barrel capable of holding 220,000 litres.

The Altstadt

The **Altstadt**'s finest surviving buildings are grouped around the sandstone **Heiliggeistkirche** on Marktplatz. Note the tiny shopping booths between its buttresses, a feature ever since the church was built. The striking Baroque **Alte Brücke** is reached from the Marktplatz down Steingasse; dating from the 1780s, it was painstakingly rebuilt after being blown up during World War II. The **Palais Rischer** on Untere Strasse was the most famous venue for the university's *Mensur*, or fencing match; wounds were frequent and prized as badges of courage – for optimum prestige, salt was rubbed into them, leaving scars that remained for life. Universitätsplatz, the heart of the Old Town, is flanked by the eighteenth-century **Alte Universität** (April–Sept Tues–Sun 10am–6pm; Oct Tues–Sun 10am–4pm; Nov–March Tues–Sat 10am–2pm; €3) and the **Neue Universität**, erected with US funds in 1931. The oddest of Heidelberg's traditions was that its students didn't used to come under civil jurisdiction: offenders were dealt with by the university authorities, and could serve their punishment at leisure. The **Students' Prison** around the corner

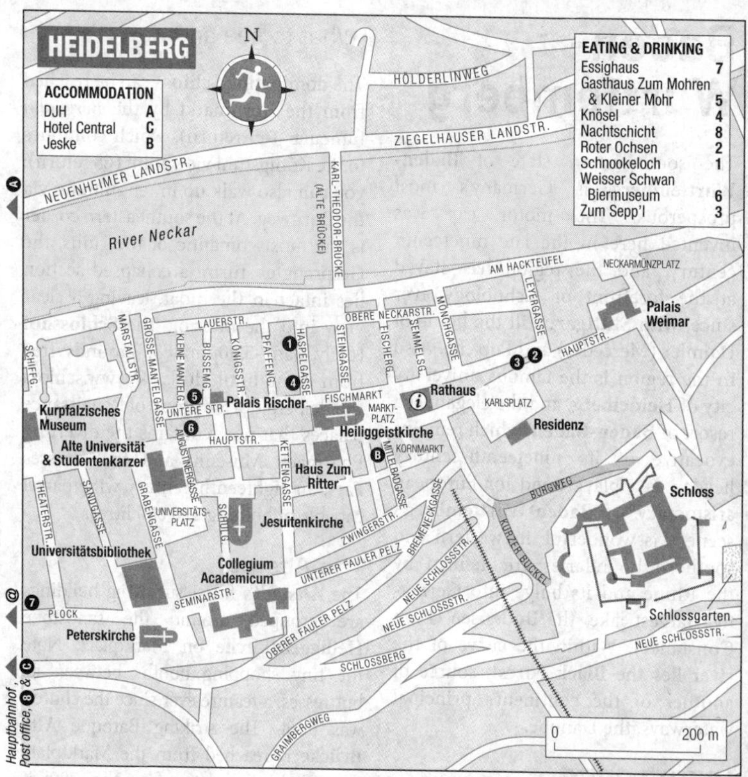

at Augustinergasse 2 (Studentenkarzer; same hours and ticket as Alte Universität) was used from 1778 to 1914; its spartan cells are covered with graffiti.

Arrival and information

Air The Baden-Airpark (Ⓦ www.badenairpark.de) is connected to Heidelberg train station by the Hahn-Express bus (1hr 30min; €18).

Train and bus Heidelberg's train and bus stations are in an anonymous quarter west of the centre a 20min walk west of the Altstadt. Tram #1 and buses #11 and #33 run into the centre.

Tourist office On the square outside the station Ⓣ 06221/194 33, Ⓦ www.cvb-heidelberg.de (April–Oct Mon–Sat 9am–7pm, Sun 10am–6pm; Nov–March Mon–Sat 10am–6pm). There's also a smaller branch (summer only, same hours) at Neckarmünzplatz and beside the Schloss Bergbahn terminus.

Discount pass The Heidelberg Card (1/2/4 days €12.50/17/22) provides free entrance to some sights, including the Schloss, and transport.

City transport Heidelberg is small, but the bus and tram system is handy. Single trip €2.10, 24hr ticket €5, 24hr ticket for up to five people €8.50.

Internet Heidelberger Internet Café, Plöck 101 (up the road from Essighaus). Daily 10am–10pm, €1/hr.

Accommodation

Hotels are often booked solid and fairly expensive; the chart outside the tourist office lists vacancies.

DJH Tiergartenstr. 5 Ⓣ 06221/65 11 90, Ⓦ www.jugendherberge-heidelberg.de. This hostel is on the north bank of the Neckar, about 4km from the centre. Take bus #33 from Hauptbahnhof or Bismarkplatz to "Jugendherberge". Dorms €23.80.

Hotel Central Kaiserstr. 75 Ⓣ 06221/206 41, Ⓦ www.hotel-central-heidelberg.de. Sparkling and airy, but rather bland, modern hotel near the train station; one of the best-value places in town that's likely to have a bed. Rooms €95.

Jeske Mittelbadgasse 2 ⓣ 06221/237 33, ⓦ www.pension-jeske-heidelberg.de. This is a good, central option, a few steps off Marktplatz. Breakfast not included. Rooms €55.

Eating and drinking

Some of the best places to eat are the city's atmospheric student taverns, known for their basic dishes at reasonable prices.

Essighaus Plöck 97. A traditional restaurant serving large set menus at low prices: soup, schnitzel and salad €11. Mon dinner only; food daily until 11.30pm.

Gasthaus Zum Mohren & Kleiner Mohr Untere Str. 5. One of several hip, young drinking spots along this alley, with various nightly events until 3am. Bar food includes two Bratwürste with fries for €8.

Knösel Haspelgasse 16. Try the famous *Heidelberger Studentenkuss*, a dark chocolate filled with praline and nougat (€2.15), at this chic café or at the shop next door. Coffee €2.

Nachtschicht Bergheimer Str 147 ⓦ www.nachtschicht.com. Popular club in a former factory with hip-hop, disco and house nights. Just north of the train station. Wed–Sat.

Roter Ochsen Hauptstr. 217. This is one of the city's most famous student taverns, so prices here are slightly above average. Mains €10.

Schnookeloch Haspelgasse 8. The oldest tavern in town and still cosy. Swabian ravioli (*Maultaschen*) €8.

Weisser Schwan Biermuseum Hauptstr. 143. Spacious establishment offering 24 types of beer with its meals. *Käsespätzle* – the traditional local equivalent to macaroni cheese – with salad €9.50.

Zum Sepp'l Hauptstr. 213. Next to *Roter Ochsen* – the other famous student tavern – and plastered with stolen street signs. Schnitzel €7.50.

Moving on

Train Frankfurt (every 30min; 1hr); Freiburg (hourly; 1hr 45min); Mainz (frequent; 1hr 20min); Stuttgart (every 30 min; 45min).

THE BLACK FOREST REGION

Home of the cuckoo clock and source of the celebrated Danube River, the **Black Forest**, stretching 170km north to south, and up to 60km east to west, is Germany's largest and most beautiful forest. Its name reflects the mountainous landscape darkened by endless pine trees and, as late as the 1920s, much of this area was eerie wilderness, a refuge for boars and bandits. Nowadays, many of its villages are geared toward tourism, brimming with tacky souvenir shops; the old forest trails have been smoothed for easier walking. Most of the Black Forest is associated with the Margravate of Baden, whose old capital, **Baden-Baden**, is at the northern fringe of the forest, in a fertile orchard and vine-growing area. **Freiburg im Breisgau**, doubtless one of Germany's most enticing cities, is surrounded by the forest.

Baden-Baden

The therapeutic value of the town's hot springs, first discovered by the Romans, is still the main draw in **BADEN-BADEN** – hardly the recipe for a party atmosphere. Nevertheless, it's a pretty town for a stroll.

What to see and do

Along the west bank of the tiny River Oos runs Baden-Baden's most famous thoroughfare, Lichtentaler Allee, landscaped with exotic trees and shrubs. It's flanked by the **Kunsthalle** (Tues &

TREAT YOURSELF

Above the Römerbad, just east on Römerplatz, is the famous **Friedrichsbad** (daily 9am–10pm, last entry 8pm; bathing is nude and on most days mixed-sex; ⓦ www.roemisch-irisches-bad.de). Begun in 1869, it's as grand as a Renaissance palace. Speciality of the house is a three-hour "Roman-Irish Bath", a series of baths, showers and steam of varying temperatures, that will set you back €21 (€29 for soap-brush massage). At the **Caracalla Therme** (daily 8am–10pm, last entry 8pm; 2/3/4hr €13/15/17; same website), just to the east in a modern complex, you're allowed to wear a swimsuit.

Thurs–Sun 11am–6pm, Wed 11am–8pm; €5; Ⓦ www.kunsthalle-baden-baden.de), an exhibition venue for international modern and contemporary art, and the **Museum Frieder Burda** (Tues–Sun 10am–6pm; €9, combined ticket with Kunsthalle €12; Ⓦ www.museum-frieder-burda.de), which contains an excellent collection including several works by Beckmann, Kirchner, Picasso and de Kooning. Just north at Kaiserallee 1 is the famously opulent **Casino**, the oldest in Europe, whose gilded frescoes and chandeliers are well worth a peek (Kurhaus; daily tours, German only, every 30min: April–Sept: 9.30–11.30am; Oct–March 10–11.30am; €4 or visit in the evening for a flutter, €3 – ID required; Ⓦ www.casino-baden-baden.de). For women, dresses or skirts are obligatory, while men need a jacket and tie (to rent €8 and €3 respectively), and while smart jeans are permitted, sports shoes aren't.

Arrival and information

Air The Baden-Airpark (Ⓦ www.badenairpark.com) is connected to the Baden-Baden train station by the Hahn-Express and bus #140 (€9).

Train Located 4km northwest in the suburb of Oos; bus #201 goes to the centre, "Leopoldplatz/Stadtmitte".

Tourist office In the Trinkhalle on Kaiserallee Ⓣ 07221/27 52 00, Ⓦ www.baden-baden.de (Mon–Sat 9am–5pm, Sun 2pm–5pm); staff can book rooms.

Accommodation

Deutscher Kaiser Hauptstr. 35 Ⓣ 07221/721 52, Ⓦ www.hoteldk.de. This pleasant, family-run hotel is 2km from the centre in the lovely suburb of Lichtental. Take bus #201 to "Eckerlestr." Rooms €52.

DJH Hardbergstr. 34 Ⓣ 07221/522 23, Ⓦ www.jugendherberge-baden-baden.de. Uninspiring HI hostel between the train station and the centre. Take bus #201 to "Grosse-Dollenstrasse"; from there it's a signposted 10min climb. Dorms €21.

Eating and drinking

The centre is full of cheap snack joints.

Leo's Luisenstr. 10. A trendy café-bar serving huge, delicious salads (€11). Open until 3am.

Löwenbräu Gernsbacher Str. 9. If you're sick of Swabian fare, head to Löwenbräu and eat like a Bavarian. Boisterous summer beer garden. Traditional breakfast (*Weisswurst, brezn* & beer) €6.

Rathausglöckel Steinstr. 7 Ⓣ 07221/906 10. Traditional favourites like venison goulash (€9.50) and winter-warmer potato soup (€7) are served in this cosy sixteenth-century house on a side street off the Marktplatz.

Moving on

Train Freiburg (hourly; 1hr 15min); Heidelberg (every 30min; 1hr 15min); Strasbourg (every 30min; 1hr 30min).

Freiburg im Breisgau

FREIBURG IM BREISGAU – midway between Strasbourg (France) and Basel (Switzerland) – basks in the laid-back atmosphere you'd expect from Germany's sunniest city. It's been a university town since 1457 and its youthful presence is maintained all year round with the help of a varied programme of festivals. It's a thoroughly enjoyable place to visit, and makes the perfect urban base for exploring the surrounding Black Forest – if you can bring yourself to leave.

What to see and do

The city's highlight is the dark-red sandstone **Münster**, whose openwork spire makes it one of the most dazzling churches in the country. Begun in about 1200, the church has a masterly Gothic nave, with flying buttresses, gargoyles and statues – the magnificent sculptures of the west porch are the most important German works of their time. From the tower (Mon–Sat 9.30am–5pm, Sun 1–5pm; €1.50) there's a fine panorama of the city and the surrounding forest-covered hills. Walking south from here on Kaiser-Josef-Strasse, Freiburg's central axis, you come to the Martinstor, one of two surviving towers of the medieval fortifications. Just southeast of here is the main channel of the Bächle; follow it along Fischerau (the old fishermen's

street) and Gerberau, to the **Schwaben Tor**, the other thirteenth-century tower.

Shauinsland

The hills of the Black Forest almost rise out of Freiburg's Altstadt, giving the town a hugely convenient outdoorsy playground for hikers and mountain bikers, and the tourist information office has an abundance of good hiking and biking maps, as well as suggestions for numerous trailheads accessible by public transport. The largest of these forested peaks, **Shauinsland**, peaks 7km south of the city and is easily ascended, thanks to the Shauinslandbahn cable car (daily: Jan–June & Oct–Dec 9am–5pm; July–Sept 9am–6pm; return €11.50; ⓣ0761/451 17 77, ⓦwww.bergwelt-schauinsland.de; tram #2 to Günterstal terminus then bus #21). From its top a five-minute walk leads to a lookout tower and the top of several well-marked trails. These offer first-class hiking and mountain biking – partly because almost the entire 14km journey back to Freiburg is downhill – with great views along the way.

Höllental and Titisee

The Black Forest rises rapidly southeast of Freiburg, becoming much wilder, and is best appreciated along the deep, dark canyon of the **Höllental**. Its raw jagged and shaded cliffs are followed by the course of the Höllentalbahn, a railway that winds through a creative network of tunnels and viaducts that was built in 1887 to be an engineering marvel of its time. All this is best appreciated along the gorge footpath, which makes for a good four-hour hike back to Freiburg from the station of the touristy lake resort of **Titisee**, 29km from Freiburg. If you fancy staying a bit longer in Titisee, you'll find plenty to do winter and summer, with many well-marked hiking, cycling and cross-country skiing routes in the area, and a peaceful lake to mess around on using rentable rowing boats. The most obvious walk is the easy 6km hike around the lake and the 1192m Hochfirst. Both need only the most basic of maps, available free from the tourist office at Strandbadstrasse 4 (May–Oct Mon–Fri 9am–6pm, Sat & Sun 10am–1pm; Nov–April Mon–Fri 9am–noon & 1.30–5pm; ⓣ07651/980 40, ⓦwww.titisee-neustadt.de) in the Kurhaus, a signed five-minute walk from the train station. Local accommodation includes the *DJH* hostel, Bruderhalde 27 (ⓣ07651/238, ⓦwww.jugendherberge-titisee-veltishof.de; dorms €19.50), a fine hostel 2km south of the tourist office – take bus #7300 or it's a thirty-minute walk – and the good-value *Gästehaus Wiesler*, Bruderhalde 8 (ⓣ07652/16 18, ⓦwww.gaestehaus-wiesler.de; €54).

Arrival and information

Train and bus The train station, with the bus station on its southern side, is about a 10min walk west from the city centre.

Internet Shake'n'Surf, Bismarckallee 5, is a cheap internet café near the station (daily 10am–10pm).

Tourist office Following Eisenbahnstrasse, you come to the tourist office in the Altes Rathaus at Rathausplatz 2–4 ⓣ0761/388 18 80, ⓦwww.freiburg.de (June–Sept Mon–Fri 8am–8pm, Sat 9.30am–5pm, Sun 10am–noon; Oct–May Mon–Fri 8am–6pm, Sat 9.30am–2.30pm, Sun 10am–noon). For €3, they'll find you a room (from €20).

Accommodation

Black Forest Hostel Kartäuserstr. 33 ⓣ0761/881 78 70, ⓦwww.blackforest-hostel.de. Buzzing backpackers' place in an old factory, and by far the best place to stay in town. Well-equipped kitchen, internet, and bikes for €5/day. Sheets €3. Tram to Schwabentorbrücke or 30min walk east from the station. Dorms €13, rooms €48.

Hirzberg Kartäuserstr. 99 ⓣ0761/35 054, ⓦwww.freiburg-camping.de. The most convenient of Freiburg's three campsites, between the two hostels to the east of the centre. Open all year round. Tram to Stadthalle, then head north across the Dreisam. €11 per person.

Schemmer Eschholzstr. 63 ⓣ0761/20 74 90, ⓦwww.hotel-schemmer.de. West of the train

station, this is the cheapest central hotel. Tram to Eschholzstr. or a 10min walk. Rooms €55.

Eating and drinking

Nightlife revolves around the junction of Universitätstrasse and Niemenstrasse; pick up a free *Freiburg Aktuell* magazine to see what's on.

Jazzhaus Schnewlinstr. ⓣ0761/349 73, ⓦwww.jazzhaus.de. Club in an old wine cellar that hosts all manner of musical events, from world music concerts to blues, jazz, rock and hip-hop, to busy, fairly mainstream weekend club nights, attracting a range of ages. Big names occasionally play here, when tickets run to around €10–30; otherwise the cover is about €6. Open until at least 3am most nights.

Karma Bertoldstr. 51–53 ⓦwww.karma-freiburg.de. The *Karma* complex has everything you need: a café-bar daily till 3am, a restaurant (closed Sun) with weekday lunch specials (€7.50) and a club in the cellar playing funk and house Fri & Sat.

Markthalle Martinsgässle 235 & Grünewalderstr. 4. Food court that bustles with locals visiting different kiosks for quality regional Swabian, Mexican, Indian, Asian, French and Italian dishes. It's standing only, but the food is excellent value and service quick. One entrance lies at the end of an alley just east of the Martinstor; the main entrance is barely more obvious and off Grünewalderstrasse.

Onkel Wok Bertoldstr. 53 ⓣ0761/767 15 67. Hectic Asian place with an open kitchen and the kind of great, freshly prepared food that keeps it busy around the clock. Fill up from as little as €4.

Weinstube Oberkirch Münsterplatz 22. Pricey but excellent restaurant, serving local specialities. Ox with *Späztle* €14.

Moving on

Train Basel (every 30min; 45min); Frankfurt (hourly; 2hr 10min); Heidelberg (hourly; 1hr 40min); Strasbourg (hourly; 1hr 10min); Stuttgart (hourly; 2hr); Zürich (hourly; 2hr).

STUTTGART

In the centre of Baden-Württemberg, 85km southeast of Heidelberg, **STUTTGART** is home to the German success stories of Bosch, Porsche and Daimler. Founded around 950 as a stud farm (Stutengarten), it became a town only in the fourteenth century. Though certainly not the comeliest of cities, it has a range of superb museums and a sophisticated cultural scene and nightlife.

What to see and do

From the train station, Königstrasse passes the dull modern Dom and enters Schlossplatz, on the south of which is the **Altes Schloss**, home to the **Württembergisches Landesmuseum** (Tues–Sun 10am–5pm; €3; ⓦwww.landesmuseum-stuttgart.de). This large and richly varied museum explores the history of the region from the Stone Age to the present through archeological exhibitions as well as arts and crafts. Northeast of Schlossplatz at Konrad-Adenauer-Strasse 30–32 is the **Staatsgalerie** (Tues, Wed & Fri–Sun 10am–6pm, Thurs 10am–9pm, 1st Sat of month 10am–midnight; €4.50; ⓦwww.staatsgalerie.de). There's an Old Masters section as well as a New Gallery focusing on various schools within twentieth-century art movements.

The Mercedes-Benz-Museum and the Porsche Museum

As much as they are collections of vintage cars, the Mercedes and Porsche museums are also temples to fine engineering, human ingenuity and thousands of hours of careful hard work. So slick are the museums – their modern architecture airy and futuristic, the displays self-confident, seamless and high-tech – that they can't fail to inspire. As corporate propaganda vehicles they are hard to beat and it's almost impossible to decide which is better. The **Mercedes-Benz-Museum** (Tues–Sun 9am–6pm; €8; S-Bahn #1 to Gottlieb-Daimler-Stadion; ⓦwww.mercedes-benz.com/museum) is strong on the early parts of motoring history, since its founders invented both the motorbike and motor car. However, the earliest examples of each are eclipsed by the rest of the museum that's chock-full of

luxury cars and the machines designed for world-record attempts. The **Porsche Museum** (Tues–Sun 9am–6pm; €8; S-Bahn #6 to Leonberg/Weil der Stadt; Ⓦ www.porsche.com/uk/aboutporsche/porschemuseum) is no less flashy. Dozens of priceless, highly polished examples of engineering at its finest are interpreted by an intelligent audio guide (free) and touch-screen monitors. Racing driver video testimonials help bring the vehicles to life as do recordings of engine noises. The success of the brand is underlined by a display of some of Porsche's 28,000 trophies.

Arrival and information

Air Stuttgart Airport is linked to the train station by S-Bahn #2 and #3 (frequent; 30min).
Train and bus Stuttgart's train and bus stations are in the centre of town. A day ticket for the extensive integrated public transport network costs €5.60, a single trip €1.90.
Tourist office Opposite the train station at Königstr. 1a Ⓣ0711/2 22 89, Ⓦwww.stuttgart-tourist.de (Mon–Fri 9am–8pm, Sat 9am–6pm, Sun 1–6pm). Another branch at the airport, in Terminal 3 (Mon–Fri 8am–7pm, Sat & Sun 9am–noon & 1–6pm).
Discount passes The StuttCard (€9.70/three days) covers admission to most museums and numerous freebies; the combination StuttCard (€20/three days) also includes use of local public transport.
Internet, youth information and bike rental You'll find internet access, bike rental, information for young people and helpful staff at the youth centre Tips'n'Trips, Lautenschlagerstr. 22 (Mon–Fri noon–7pm, Sat 10am–2pm), 200m southwest of the station. Internet €2/hr; bike rental for 24hr: €15/students €11.

Accommodation

Alex 30 Alexanderstr. 30 Ⓣ0711/838 89 50, Ⓦwww.alex30-hostel.de. Convenient independent hostel near the Bohnenviertel. Has a bar, café, kitchen and tiny terrace, and free wi-fi and sheets are included. U-Bahn to Olgaeck or 20min walk southeast from the station. Dorm €23, rooms €56.
DJH Haussmannstr. 27 Ⓣ0711/664 74 70, Ⓦwww.jugendherberge-stuttgart.de. Large, well-organized hostel, but standard DJH. Take tram #15 or bus #42 to Eugensplatz and then continue 5min uphill. Dorms €23.80, rooms €57.
Jugendgästehaus Richard-Wagner-Str. 2 Ⓣ0711/24 11 32 or 0711/248 97 30, Ⓦwww.hostel-stuttgart.de. Independent hostel without much personality, but breakfast and sheets are included. Tram #15 to Bubenbad. Dorms €19, singles €21.50.
Museum-Stube Hospitalstr. 9 Ⓣ0711/29 68 10. Spotless guesthouse above a Croatian restaurant, and one of the few central bargains. Some rooms en suite. Rooms €90.

Eating and drinking

Stuttgart is surrounded by vineyards, and its numerous *Weinstuben* are excellent places to try good-quality, traditional, noodle-based dishes and local wines at low cost. *Lift* and *Prinz Stuttgart*, available from newsagents, have complete nightlife listings.
Calwer-Eck-Bräu Calwerstr. 31. Microbrewery with good beer and food. Mains €8, beer €2.70. S-Bahn Stadtmitte.
Die Röhre Willy-Brandt-Str. 2 Ⓦwww.die-roehre.com. Legendary local club in an old tunnel with an industrial feel. Music from across the board, with everything from more mainstream alternative and drum'n'bass to death metal, played to three dancefloors. Fri & Sat 10pm–5am. Cover €6.
Dilayla Eberharstr. 49. Dimly lit basement that bustles with a broad spectrum of people dancing to Seventies and Eighties hits or lounging on couches; open until 4am week nights, 6am weekends; get there after midnight.
Palast der Republik Friedrichstr. 27. A tiny circular funk shack on the square where Bolzstrasse meets Lautenschlagerstrasse, with outdoor seating in the summer.
Weinhaus Stetter Rosenstr. 32. A lovely atmosphere, excellent service and the widest choice of wines in town await you at this family-run *Weinstube*. The lentil soup with sausages (€6) is outstanding. Wine from €3.

Moving on

Train Freiburg (hourly; 2hr); Heidelberg (hourly; 45min); Konstanz (hourly; 2hr 30min); Munich (hourly; 2hr 20min); Zürich (every 2hr; 2hr 45min).

KONSTANZ AND THE BODENSEE

In the far south, hard on the Swiss border, **KONSTANZ** lies at the tip of a tongue of land sticking out into the huge **Bodensee** (Lake Constance). The town itself is split

by the water, giving Konstanz the air of a sea town. The town's convivial atmosphere is best experienced in the summer, when street cafés invite prolonged stays and the water is a bustle of sails.

What to see and do

Konstanz's most prominent building is the **Münster** church, dating from the Romanesque period and located in the heart of the Altstadt. The regional highlights are two small Bodensee islands. The nearby **Insel Mainau** (daily: April–Oct 7am–8pm; Nov–March 9am–6pm; €11.90; Ⓦwww.mainau.de) has a royal park featuring magnificent floral displays, formal gardens, greenhouses, forests, a butterfly house and a handful of well-placed restaurants. The other island, **Reichenau**, preserves three stunning Romanesque churches. You can reach this tranquil island 8km west of Konstanz by bike, ferry (summer only; will take bikes too) or public transport: take a regional train to Reichenau station, then change to bus #7372 to "Mittelzell" (Mon–Fri only; 14 daily; 50min).

Arrival and information

Tourist office Beside the train station at Bahnhofplatz 13 Ⓣ07531/13 30 30, Ⓦwww.konstanz.de/tourismus (April–Oct Mon–Fri 9am–6.30pm, Sat 9am–4pm, Sun 10am–1pm; Nov–March Mon–Fri 9am–12.30pm & 2–6pm); staff can book private rooms (€50).

Bike rental Kultur-Rädle, Bahnhofplatz 29 Ⓦwww.kultur-raedle.de (Mon–Fri 9am–12.30pm & 2.30–6pm, Sat 10am–4pm; Easter–Oct also Sun 10am–12.30pm; €12/day).

Accommodation

Campingplatz Bruderhofer Fohrenbühlweg 45 Ⓣ07531/313 88, Ⓦwww.campingplatz-konstanz.de. One of two pleasant neighbouring campgrounds on the lakeshore 3km northeast of the centre and around 1km from the car-ferry dock. A 10min walk from bus #4 (to Tannenhof). €11.30 per person.

DJH Konstanz Zur Allmannshöhe 18 Ⓣ07531/322 60, Ⓦwww.jugendherberge-konstanz.de. Excellent hostel uniquely located in an old water tower, but a fair way out of town. Take bus #1 (to Allmannsdorf-Post) or #4 (to Jugendherberge). Dorms €22.30.

Jugendwohnheim Don Bosco Salesianerweg 5 Ⓣ07531/622 52, Ⓦwww.donbosco-kn.de. Large hostel a 20min walk from the centre. Take bus #1 or #4 to Tannenhof. Reception 4–8pm. Dorms €18.50.

Lake cruises

You can get information on cruises and ferries from the Bodensee-Schiffsbetriebe at Hafenstr. 6 (Ⓣ07531/364 03 89, Ⓦwww.bsb-online.com). Ferries run regularly around the lake, as well as on a scenic trip to the impressive Rhine falls in Switzerland (€30), covered in Chapter 34.

Moving on

Train Basel (hourly; 2hr 20min); Freiburg (hourly; 2hr 30min); Munich (hourly; 4hr); Stuttgart (hourly; 2hr 30min); Zürich (hourly; 1hr 20min).

Bavaria

Bavaria (Bayern), Germany's largest federal state, fills the southeast of the country, providing its entire border with Austria. It's also the home of almost all German clichés: beer-swilling men in *Lederhosen*, piles of sauerkraut and sausages galore. But that's only a small part of the picture, and one that's almost entirely restricted to the Bavarian Alps that lie south of the magnificent state capital, **Munich**. Eastern Bavaria – whose capital is **Regensburg** – is dominated by rolling forests where life revolves around logging and minor industries like glass production. To the north, Nuremberg is the hub of Protestant **Franconia** (Franken), a region known for its vineyards and nature parks as well as the beautifully preserved and atmospheric medieval towns – notably Rothenburg ob der Tauber, which is but a highlight among the glut of attractive places that dot Bavaria's Romantic Road.

THE ROMANTIC ROAD

The **Romantic Road** (Romantische Strasse; Ⓦwww.romantischestrasse.de) is perhaps Germany's most famous and best-loved tourist route, running from the vineyards of Würzburg in northern Bavaria over 366km of pastoral scenery and quaint medieval villages to the fairy-tale castles of Füssen in the south. Cheesy as it sounds, the Romantic Road harbours the charming, picturesque Germany promised by brochures.

Bus From April to October, Touring (Ⓣ069/790 32 30, Ⓦwww.romanticroadcoach.de) runs daily buses in each direction between Frankfurt and Füssen via Munich, up and down the Road, with short stops in many of the towns.

Train Not all points on the Road are served by the Deutsche Bahn, but going by train to one or two towns (like Rothenburg or Füssen) is a great way to avoid the bus crowds and get a feel for the route.

Bicycle Touring by bike is the most scenic way to explore the region. The well-maintained cycling route stretches 424km from the Main to Bavarian Alps – order a route map online (Ⓦwww.romantischestrasse.de) or pick one up from any of the tourist offices along the way.

MUNICH

Founded in 1158, **MUNICH** (München) has been the capital of Bavaria since 1503, and as far as the locals are concerned it's the centre of the universe. The city is impossibly energetic, bursting with a good-humoured self-importance that is difficult to dislike. After Berlin, Munich is Germany's most popular city – and with its compact and attractive old centre it's certainly far easier to digest. It also has a great setting, with the mountains and Alpine lakes just an hour's drive away. The best time of year to come here is from June to early October, when the beer gardens, street cafés and bars are in full swing – not least for the world-famous **Oktoberfest** beer festival.

What to see and do

Just ten minutes' walk east of the train station, the twin onion-domed towers of the red-brick Gothic Frauenkirche **(Dom)** form the focus of the city's skyline. The pedestrian shopping street **Kaufingerstrasse**, just below, heads east to the centre and the main square, the Marienplatz.

Marienplatz

The **Marienplatz** is the bustling heart of Munich, thronged with crowds being entertained by street musicians and artists. At 11am and noon (and 5pm March–October), the square fills with tourists as the tuneless carillon in the **Rathaus** tower jingles into action. To the right is the plain Gothic tower of the Altes Rathaus, which now houses a vast toy collection in the **Spielzeugmuseum** (daily 10am–5.30pm; €3).

Alter Peter and the Viktualienmarkt

Close by, the **Peterskirche** tower (*Alter Peter*; Mon–Fri 9am–5.30pm, Sat & Sun 10am–5.30pm; €1.50) offers the best views of the Altstadt. Directly below, you'll find the **Viktualienmarkt**, a huge open-air food market selling everything from *Weisswurst* and beer to fruit and veg. West of here, at Sendlinger Str. 62, stands the pint-sized **Asamkirche**, one of the most splendid Rococo churches in Bavaria.

The Hofbräuhaus and the Residenz

Northeast of Marienplatz is the **Hofbräuhaus**, Munich's largest and most famous drinking hall (see p.517). North of here, on Residenzstrasse, is the entrance to the palace of the Wittelsbachs, the immense **Residenz** (daily: April to mid-Oct 9am–6pm;

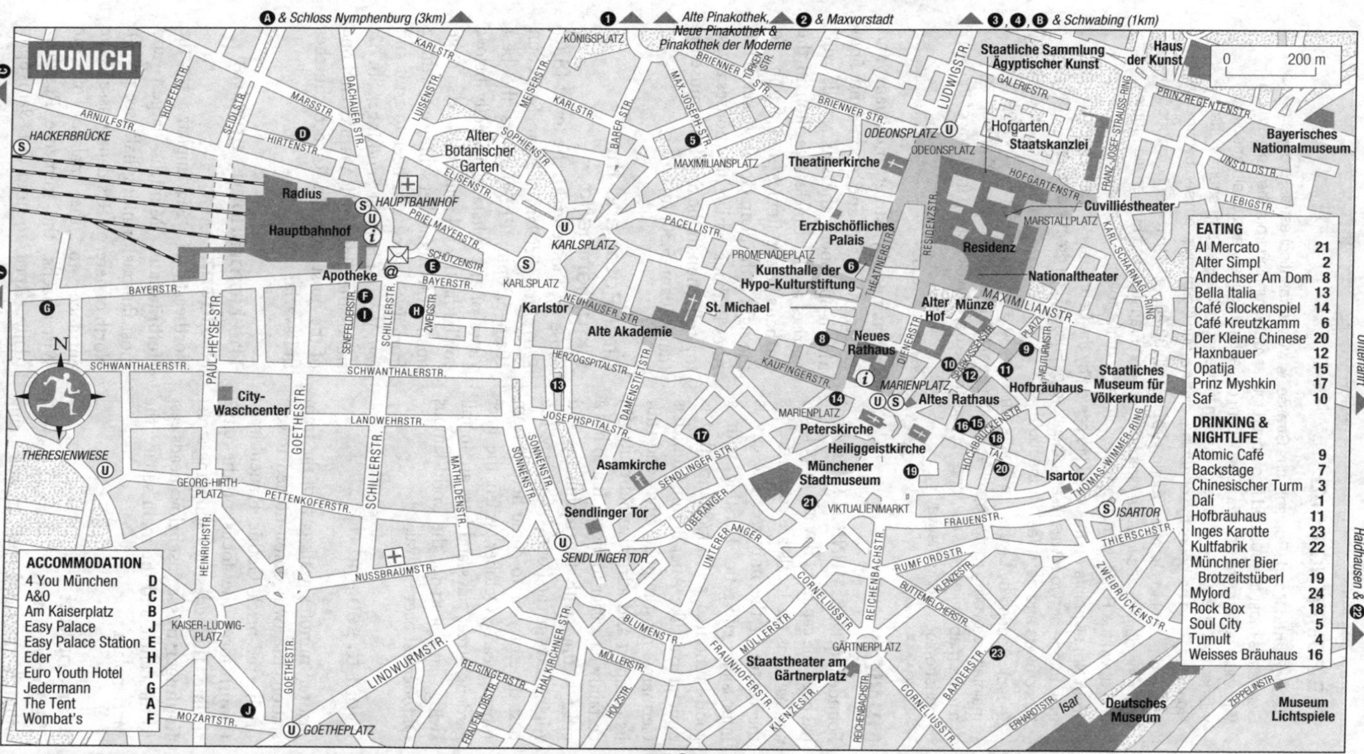

MUNICH
A & Schloss Nymphenburg (3km)
1
Alte Pinakothek, Neue Pinakothek & Pinakothek der Moderne
2 & Maxvorstadt
3, 4, B & Schwabing (1km)
Unterfahrt
Haidhausen & 22
C
7
0 200 m
ACCOMMODATION
4 You München D
A&O C
Am Kaiserplatz B
Easy Palace J
Easy Palace Station E
Eder H
Euro Youth Hotel I
Jedermann G
The Tent A
Wombat's F
EATING
Al Mercato 21
Alter Simpl 2
Andechser Am Dom 8
Bella Italia 13
Café Glockenspiel 14
Café Kreutzkamm 6
Der Kleine Chinese 20
Haxnbauer 12
Opatija 15
Prinz Myshkin 17
Saf 10
DRINKING & NIGHTLIFE
Atomic Café 9
Backstage 7
Chinesischer Turm 3
Dalí 1
Hofbräuhaus 11
Inges Karotte 23
Kultfabrik 22
Münchner Bier Brotzeitstüberl 19
Mylord 24
Rock Box 18
Soul City 5
Tumult 4
Weisses Bräuhaus 16
Hauptbahnhof
Radius
Apotheke
HAUPTBAHNHOF
HACKERBRÜCKE
Alter Botanischer Garten
KARLSPLATZ
Karlstor
St. Michael
Alte Akademie
Kunsthalle der Hypo-Kulturstiftung
Erzbischöfliches Palais
Theatinerkirche
ODEONSPLATZ
Residenz
Cuvilliéstheater
Nationaltheater
Hofgarten
Staatskanzlei
Staatliche Sammlung Ägyptischer Kunst
Haus der Kunst
Bayerisches Nationalmuseum
Alter Hof
Münze
Neues Rathaus
MARIENPLATZ
Altes Rathaus
Hofbräuhaus
Staatliches Museum für Völkerkunde
Peterskirche
Heiliggeistkirche
Münchener Stadtmuseum
VIKTUALIENMARKT
Asamkirche
Sendlinger Tor
SENDLINGER TOR
Isartor
ISARTOR
Staatstheater am Gärtnerplatz
GÄRTNERPLATZ
Deutsches Museum
Museum Lichtspiele
Isar
City-Waschcenter
THERESIENWIESE
GOETHEPLATZ
KAISER-LUDWIG-PLATZ
GEORG-HIRTH-PLATZ
KÖNIGSPLATZ
MAXIMILIANSPLATZ
PROMENADEPLATZ
MARSTALLPLATZ
ARNULFSTR.
HOFFENSTR.
SEIDLSTR.
MARSSTR.
HIRTENSTR.
DACHAUER STR.
LUISENSTR.
KARLSTR.
MEISERSTR.
SOPHIENSTR.
ELISENSTR.
PRIELMAYERSTR.
SCHÜTZENSTR.
BAYERSTR.
SENEFELDERSTR.
SCHILLERSTR.
ZWEIGSTR.
PAUL-HEYSE-STR.
SCHWANTHALERSTR.
LANDWEHRSTR.
GOETHESTR.
PETTENKOFERSTR.
MATHILDENSTR.
SONNENSTR.
HERZOGSPITALSTR.
JOSEPHSPITALSTR.
DAMENSTIFTSTR.
NEUHAUSER STR.
KAUFINGERSTR.
PACELLISTR.
BARER STR.
MAX-JOSEPH-STR.
BRIENNER STR.
TÜRKENSTR.
LUDWIGSTR.
GALERIESTR.
RESIDENZSTR.
THEATINERSTR.
HOFGARTENSTR.
FRANZ-JOSEF-STRAUSS-RING
PRINZREGENTENSTR.
UNSÖLDSTR.
LIEBIGSTR.
KARL-SCHARNAGL-RING
MAXIMILIANSTR.
DIENERSTR.
SPARKASSENSTR.
NEUTURMSTR.
PLATZL
MARIENPLATZ
HOCHBRÜCKENSTR.
TAL
THOMAS-WIMMER-RING
SENDLINGER STR.
OBERANGER
UNTERER ANGER
FRAUENSTR.
THIERSCHSTR.
RUMFORDSTR.
KLENZESTR.
BUTTERMELCHERSTR.
REICHENBACHSTR.
CORNELIUSSTR.
ZWEIBRÜCKENSTR.
BAADERSTR.
ERHARDTSTR.
ZEPPELINSTR.
MÜLLERSTR.
FRAUNHOFERSTR.
BLUMENSTR.
HOLZSTR.
THALKIRCHNER STR.
REISINGERSTR.
FRAUENLOBSTR.
LINDWURMSTR.
NUSSBRAUMSTR.
HEINRICHSTR.
MOZARTSTR.
N

mid-Oct to March 10am–5pm; €6; Ⓦwww.residenz-muenchen.de). One of Europe's finest Renaissance buildings, it was so badly damaged in the last war that it had to be almost totally rebuilt. At 1.30pm, the selection of chambers open to the public changes, so arrive before the switch if you want to see both selections. The splendid Antiquarium, the oldest part of the palace, is open all day long. A separate ticket is necessary to see the fabulous treasures of the **Schatzkammer** (same hours; €6, €9 combined ticket); the star piece is the dazzling stone-encrusted statuette of St George, made around 1590. Across Odeonsplatz from the Residenz is one of the city's most regal churches, the **Theatinerkirche**, whose golden-yellow towers and green copper dome add a splash of colour to the roofscape.

The Pinakothek museums

For art lovers, it's the Pinakothek museums (Ⓦwww.pinakothek.de) around Barerstrasse that are the city's main draw. The **Alte Pinakothek** (Tues 10am–8pm, Wed–Sun 10am–6pm; €9, Sun €5) is one of the largest galleries in Europe, housing the world's finest assembly of German art. The **Neue Pinakothek** (Mon & Thurs–Sun 10am–6pm, Wed 10am–8pm; €5.50, Sun €1) holds a fine collection of nineteenth-century art. The **Pinakothek der Moderne** (Tues 10am–8pm, Wed–Sun 10am–6pm; €9.50, Sun €1) is worth visiting for its stunning architecture alone. The stark glass-and-concrete structure presents an impressive collection, from Dalí and Picasso to German greats such as Beckmann and Polke, and features exhibitions of design, architecture and graphics.

The Deutsches Museum

Munich's most impressive museum – the **Deutsches Museum** (daily 9am–5pm; €8.50; Ⓦwww.deutsches-museum.de) – occupies a mid-stream island in the Isar, southeast of the centre. Covering every conceivable aspect of technical endeavour, from the first flint tools to the research labs of modern industry, this is the most compendious collection of its type in Germany.

Arrival

Air Munich's airport, Franz Josef Strauss Flughafen, is connected to the Hauptbahnhof by S-Bahn #1.

Train The Hauptbahnhof is in the centre, 2km west of Marienplatz.

Bus The ZOB is on Arnulfstrasse, behind the station.

Information

Tourist office There are tourist offices (Ⓣ089/23 39 65 00, Ⓦwww.muenchen.de) at Bahnhofplatz 2 (Mon–Sat 9am–8pm, Sun 10am–6pm) and in the Neuen Rathaus on Marienplatz (Mon–Fri 10am–8pm, Sat 10am–4pm, Sun 10–2pm), either of which can book rooms (from €79).

City transport

Metro, trams & buses Short trips (up to two S- or U-Bahn stops, or up to four bus or tram stops) cost €1.10, single trips €2.30. One-day/three-day passes, valid for all public transport in the central city area, are a good investment at €5 (single) and €9 (up to five people). Also available are strip cards (€11 for 10); stamp two strips for every zone crossed – the zones are shown on maps at stations and tram and bus stops. For short trips, only one strip needs to be cancelled.

Accommodation

Cheap accommodation can be hard to find, especially in summer. If you're going to be in town during Oktoberfest, it's essential to book well in advance; be warned that prices can double during this period.

Hostels

4 you München Hirtenstr. 18 Ⓣ089/552 16 60, Ⓦwww.the4you.de. Scruffy but lively eco friendly outfit very close to the main station, with some singles and doubles, as well as standard dorms. Linen and breakfast included. Dorms €13, doubles €42.

A&O Arnulfstr. 102 Ⓣ089/45 23 59 58 00, Ⓦwww.aohostels.com. This branch of the rather bland A&O chain is a 15min walk west from the station or S-Bahn Hackerbrücke. Dorms €21, rooms €42.

Easy Palace Mozartstr. 4 ⓣ089/558 79 70, ⓦwww.easypalace.de. Welcoming hostel within spitting distance of the Oktoberfest grounds; 15min walk south from the train station or U-Bahn to Goetheplatz. Sheets included. Dorms €19, doubles €69.

Euro Youth Hotel Senefelderstr. 5 ⓣ089/599 08 80 11, ⓦwww.euro-youth-hotel.de. Good atmosphere and location with late-closing bar and helpful staff. Dorms €16, twins €53.

The Tent In den Kirschen 30 ⓣ089/12 88 70 70, ⓦwww.the-tent.com. Top budget digs – bed down in a vast circus tent, located a 15min tram ride from the Hauptbahnhof (#17 – runs all night), or pitch your own tent. Beds €7.50.

Wombat's Senefelderstr. 1 ⓣ089/59 98 91 80, ⓦwww.wombats-hostels.com. The pick of the backpackers' bunch. Modern, lively and central with a great bar, winter garden and friendly staff. Sheets included. Dorms €19, rooms €70.

Hotels and guesthouses

Am Kaiserplatz Kaiserplatz 12 ⓣ089/34 91 90. Very friendly place in a good location with big rooms, each done out in a different style – from red satin to Bavarian rustic. Four-bed rooms can be arranged. U-Bahn Münchener Freiheit. Room with shared bathroom €49.

Easy Palace Station Schützenstr. 7 ⓣ089/552 52 10, ⓦwww.easypalace.de. Between the station and the centre; what this clean, basic hotel lacks in charm it makes up for in convenience. Rooms €55.

Eder Zweigstr. 8 ⓣ089/55 46 60, ⓦwww.hotel-eder.de. Cosy hotel in a quiet road near the train station, offering nicely appointed rooms for €62.

Jedermann Bayerstr. 95 ⓣ089/54 32 40, ⓦwww.hotel-jedermann.de. Classy, family-run hotel just 5min walk from the train station. The buffet breakfast is especially good and free internet is available. Rooms €67.

Eating

Gaststätten offer filling soups, salads and sandwiches. An excellent place to stock up on fresh bread, sausages and fruit is the bustling Viktualienmarkt, which offers an array of outdoor eateries in summer.

Cafés

Alter Simpl Türkenstr. 57. Famous literary café-bar and favoured student haunt named after the satirical magazine *Simplicissimus*. Lunch €5.

Café Glockenspiel Marienplatz 28 (5th floor). Classy café-bar with a fusion menu and surprisingly few tourists; it has a direct view across to its namesake. The entrance is in the passageway behind the shops. Cappuccino €4.

Café Kreutzkamm Maffeistr. 4. Airy and elegant; one of the best (and most expensive) *Kaffee-und-Kuchen* establishments. Closed Sun. Cake €6.

BREAKFAST OF CHAMPIONS

Weisswurst (white veal sausage), *Brezen* (bready pretzels eaten with sweet mustard) and *Weissbier* (wheat beer) make up a typical **Bavarian breakfast**. While touristy restaurants in Munich will serve it from dawn till dusk, traditionally the highly perishable *Weisswurst* isn't to be eaten past noon. How the traditionalists function with a half-litre of beer in them before noon is anyone's guess.

Restaurants

Al Mercato Prälat-Zistl-Str. 12. No-frills Italian serving cheap pizzas and pasta dishes, just south of the Viktualienmarkt. Closed Sun. Pizza €5.50–8.

Andechser am Dom Weinstr. 7a, behind the Dom. Traditional place serving beer from the Andechs monastic brewery and solid Bavarian fare to a cheerful crowd. Mains €11.

Bella Italia Herzog-Wilhelm-Str. 8. One of a small chain of inexpensive Italian restaurants. Open until 12.30am. Pasta €4–6.

Der Kleine Chinese Im Tal 28. Cheap, filling Chinese dishes served all day in this tiny eatery near Marienplatz. Mains €5–8.

Haxnbauer Corner of Sparkassenstr. and Ledererstr. Specializes in Germany's famous roasted pork knuckles; the lamb version is no less tasty. Knuckles €15.

Opatija Hochbrückenstr. 3. Excellent, cosy Croatian restaurant with good prices, despite its proximity to Marienplatz. Daily specials €6.50.

Prinz Myshkin Hackenstr. 2. Best vegetarian in the city, with international dishes served beneath a high vaulted ceiling. Mains €11.

Saf Ledererstr. 3. Forget the struggles, of vegetarianism in Bavaria in this stylish organic veggie canteen. Dine at long tables in a cavernous basement and enjoy soups, salads, wraps and daily specials €8.50. Mon–Sat 11am–7pm.

Drinking and nightlife

Drinking is central to social life in Munich and, apart from the *Gaststätten* and beer gardens, the

OKTOBERFEST

The huge **Oktoberfest**, held on the Theresienwiese fairground for sixteen days following the penultimate Saturday in September, is an orgy of beer drinking, spiced up by fairground rides that are so hairy they're banned in the US. The fairgrounds are divided along four main avenues, creating a boisterous city within a city, heaving from morning till night. The event began when a fair held to celebrate a Bavarian royal wedding in October 1810 proved so popular that it's been repeated ever since. For more information, check out ⓦwww.oktoberfest.de.

city has a lively café-bar culture. North of the centre, hip student bar/cafés in the Maxvorstadt fade into the glitz of Schwabing. For a good alternative head for Haidhausen, across the river to the southeast of the centre; it has a nice mix of bars, cafés and restaurants. For listings check out the English-language *MunichFound* (ⓦwww.munichfound.de).

Bars and beer halls/ gardens

Chinesischer Turm Englischer Garten 3. One of several beer gardens in the lovely Englischer Garten. Frequent live Bavarian brass band appearances. Lunch from €6.50.

Dalí Tengstr. 6, Schwabing. Chic Spanish bodega serving delicious tapas. Open 5pm–1am. Serrano ham €5. U-Bahn Josephsplatz.

Hofbräuhaus Platzl 9. The most famous and touristy of the beer halls, but beer and food prices are reasonable. Mass (1L beer) €6.60.

Münchner Bier Brotzeitstüberl Viktualienmarkt. Popular beer garden in the centre of the market, with wooden trestles set under oak trees. *Bratwurst* €3.50.

Tumult Blütenstr. 4 ⓦwww.tumult-in-muenchen.de. Packed Fifties-burlesque-themed bar in the Maxvorstadt, catering to a friendly and hip rockabilly-punk crowd. Closed Sun. U-Bahn Universität.

Weisses Bräuhaus Im Tal 7. Famous for its *Weissbier* (€3.30) and a little cosier than the *Hofbräuhaus*.

Clubs

Most of Munich's clubs are either east or west of the centre; expect to pay €5–15.

Atomic Café Neuturmstr. 5 ⓦwww.atomic.de. Retro-style bar, club and live music venue near the *Hofbräuhaus* catering to a fashionable, rock-loving crowd.

Backstage Friedenheimer Brücke 7 ⓦwww.backstage089.de. One of the best clubs in town, with nightly DJs spinning everything from hip-hop and electro to rock. Plenty of live shows as well. Tram #16 or #17 to Steubenplatz or Lautensackstr.

Kultfabrik Grafinger Str. 6, Haidhausen ⓦwww.kultfabrik.de. Along with adjacent *Optimolwerke* at Friedenstr. 10 (ⓦwww.optimolwerke.de), this mini-city of clubs and bars housed in a network of old factory buildings attracts upwards of 30,000 on any given weekend. A mix of musical genres and locales makes this Munich's premier nightspot. S- or U-Bahn Ostbahnhof.

Rock Box Im Tal 15, entrance on Hochbrückenstr. Newish lounge-club in a small tried-and-tested venue opposite *Opatija*. Open late, with DJs on Fri & Sat.

Gay Munich

Despite Bavaria's deep conservatism, Munich has an active and visible gay scene, centred primarily on Gärtnerplatz. *OurMunich* is a free gay listings mag, available in German only.

Inges Karotte Baaderstr. 13 ⓦwww.inges-karotte.de. Café-bar predominantly for lesbians, open daily from 6pm. U-Bahn Fraunhoferstr.

Mylord Ickstattstr. 2a. Nostalgic, comfy bar with an older crowd, 5min southwest from Gärtnerplatz. U-Bahn Fraunhoferstr.

Soul City Maximilianplatz 5. Popular gay disco in the heart of the city; Thursday nights heteros welcome. S-/U-Bahn Karlsplatz.

Entertainment

Munich has three first-rate symphony orchestras – the Münchener Philharmoniker, the Bayrisches Rundfunk Sinfonie Orchester and the Staatsorchester – as well as eleven major, and numerous fringe, theatres. Advance tickets for plays and concerts can be bought at the box offices or at the tourist office at Marienplatz (ⓦwww.muenchenticket.de).

Museum-Lichtspiele Lilienstr. 2, Haidhausen ⓦwww.museum-lichtspiele.de. Small cinema showing English-language films.

Olympiapark ⓦwww.olympiapark-muenchen.de. Free lakeside rock concerts at the Theatron on Sunday mornings in July and August. U-Bahn Olympiazentrum.

Unterfahrt Einsteinstr. 42, Haidhausen ⓦwww.unterfahrt.de. Showcase for avant-garde jazz,

with many big names gracing the stage. U-Bahn Max-Weber-Platz.

Directory

Bike rental Radius, at the train station near platform 32 ⓦ www.radiusmunich.com (daily: mid-April to mid-Oct 9.30am–6pm; mid-Oct to mid-April weather dependent; €14.50/day). Also offers bike and walking tours.
Consulates Canada, Tal 29 ⓣ 089/219 95 70; Ireland, Denningerstr. 15 ⓣ 089/20 80 59 90; South Africa, Sendlinger-Tor-Platz 5 ⓣ 089/231 16 30; UK, Möhlstr. 5 ⓣ 089/21 10 90; US, Königinstr. 5 ⓣ 089/288 80.
Exchange Reisebank, at the train station and airport.
Hospital Rotkreuz Krankenhaus Nymphenburger Str. 163 (ⓣ 089/12 78 97 90); Bereitschaftsdienst der Münchener Ärtze, Elisenstr. 3 (ⓣ 089/55 17 71), is a late-night clinic near the train station.
Internet easyInternetcafé, Bahnhofplatz 1. Open 24hr. €2–3/hr.
Laundry City-Waschcenter, Paul-Heyse Str. 21. Open daily 7am–11pm, €4/load.
Left luggage At the train station.
Pharmacy Bahnhof-Apotheke, Bahnhofplatz 2.
Post office Bahnhofplatz 1.

Moving on

Train Augsburg (frequent; 40min); Berchtesgaden (every 30min; 2hr 30min); Berlin (hourly; 6hr); Garmisch-Partenkirchen (hourly; 1hr 40min); Innsbruck (every 30min; 2hr 30min); Nuremberg (frequent; 1hr 10min); Regensburg (frequent; 1hr 50min); Salzburg (every 30min; 1hr 30min); Vienna (hourly; 5hr 45min).

DAY-TRIPS FROM MUNICH

Schloss Nymphenburg (daily: April to mid-Oct 9am–6pm; mid-Oct to March 10am–4pm; €5, €10 combined ticket with pavilions and Marstall), the summer residence of the Wittelsbachs, is reached by tram #17 from the train station. Its kernel is a small Italianate palace begun in 1664 for the Electress Adelaide, who dedicated it to the goddess Flora and her nymphs – hence the name. More enticing than the palace itself are the wonderful park and its four distinct pavilions (individual pavilions €2 each). Don't miss the stunning **Amalienburg**, the hunting lodge built behind the south wing of the Schloss by court architect François Cuvilliés. This supreme expression of the Rococo style marries a cunning design – which makes the little building seem like a full-scale palace – with the most extravagant decoration imaginable.

Dachau

On the northern edge of Munich, the town of **Dachau** was the site of Germany's first **concentration camp** (Tues–Sun 9am–5pm; free; ⓦ www.kz-gedenkstaette-dachau.de), and the motto that greeted arrivals at the gates has taken its chilling place in the history of Third Reich brutality: *Arbeit Macht Frei*, "Work Sets You Free". There are many original buildings still standing, and a replica hut gives an idea of the conditions under which prisoners were forced to live. There's also a thorough exhibition of photographs and text in English detailing the history of the Third Reich. Turn up at 11.30am, 2pm or 3.30pm and you can view the short, disturbing documentary *KZ-Dachau* in English. There are also **tours** in English (May–Sept Tues–Fri 1.30pm, Sat & Sun noon & 1.30pm; Oct–April Thurs, Sat & Sun 1.30pm; €3). Take the S2 to Dachau, then bus #726 to "KZ-Gedenkstätte".

THE BAVARIAN ALPS

It's among the picture-book scenery of the **Alps** that you'll find the Bavarian folklore and customs that are the subjects of so many tourist brochures. The region also encompasses some of the most famous places in the province, such as the Olympic ski resort of **Garmisch-Partenkirchen** and the fantasy castle of **Neuschwanstein**, just one of the lunatic palaces built for mad King Ludwig II of Bavaria. The western reaches are generally cheaper and less touristy, partly because they're not so

easily accessible to Munich's weekend crowds. Much of the eastern region to **Berchtesgaden** is heavily geared to the tourist trade, but outside July and August, it's considerably quieter.

King Ludwig II's fairytale palaces

Lying between the Forggensee reservoir and the Ammer mountains, around 100km by rail from Munich, **FÜSSEN** and the adjacent town of **SCHWANGAU** are the bases for visiting Bavaria's two most popular castles. **Schloss Hohenschwangau** (daily: April–Sept 8am–5.30pm; Oct–March 9am–3.30pm; Ⓦwww.hohenschwangau.de; €9), originally built in the twelfth century but heavily restored in the nineteenth, was where Ludwig II spent his youth. A mark of his individualism is left in the bedroom, where he had the ceiling painted with stars that were spotlit in the evenings. **Schloss Neuschwanstein** (daily: April–Sept 8am–5pm; Oct–March 9am–3pm; €9, €17 combination ticket for both castles), the ultimate storybook turreted castle and the inspiration for Disneyland's Sleeping Beauty Castle, was built by Ludwig a little higher up the mountain. The architectural hotchpotch includes a Byzantine throne hall and an artificial grotto. Left incomplete at Ludwig's death, it's a monument to a very sad and lonely man. The interiors of these castles can only be visited with timed tickets on guided tours; tickets can be purchased online or at the **Ticket-Service** (Alpseestr. 12, Hohenschwangau Ⓣ08362/93 08 30; daily: April–Sept 8am–5.30pm; Oct–March 9am–3.30pm). Take the train to Füssen (hourly from Munich; 2hr) and then bus #73 or #78 to Hohenschwangau. The nearest HI **hostel** is in Füssen, a ten-minute walk from the train station at Mariahilferstr. 5 (Ⓣ08362/77 54, Ⓦwww.fuessen.jugendherberge.de; dorms €19.50), otherwise the **tourist office**, Kaiser-Maximilian-Platz 1 (April–Oct Mon–Fri 9am–6pm, Sat 10am–2pm; Nov–March Mon–Fri 9am–5pm, Sat 10am–2pm; Ⓣ08362/938 50, Ⓦwww.fuessen.de) in Füssen, can book accommodation. Füssen is also the end of the much-publicized **Romantic Road** from Würzburg via Augsburg (see box, p.513), served by special tour buses in season.

Garmisch-Partenkirchen

GARMISCH-PARTENKIRCHEN is the most famous town in the German Alps, partly because it's at the foot of the highest mountain – the **Zugspitze** (2962m) – and partly because it hosted the 1936 Winter Olympics. It has excellent facilities for skiing, skating and other winter sports, as well as for hiking in the summer. The **tourist office**, Richard-Strauss-Platz 1 (Mon–Sat 8am–6pm, Sun 10am–noon; Ⓣ08821/18 07 00, Ⓦwww.garmisch-partenkirchen.de), has maps and full accommodation lists. The ascent of Zugspitze by **rack-railway** or **cable car** (both €47 return, €36 in winter) is the most memorable local excursion.

Accommodation

DJH Jochstr. 10 Ⓣ08821/96 70 50, Ⓦwww.garmisch.jugendherberge.de. In the northern suburb of Burgrain; take bus #3 or #4. Closed mid-Nov to Dec 26. Dorms €22.80.

Eierschmalz Promenadestr. 4 Ⓣ08821/24 34. Homey B&B in central Garmisch. €42.

Geyer-Ostler Mohrenplatz 5 Ⓣ08821/28 47. Friendly B&B with an excellent location just north of Marienplatz. €38.

Eating

Zur Schranne Griessstr. 4. Hearty food in a traditional Wirtshaus, off Marienplatz. Closed Tues. Ox €8.

Zum Wildschütz Bankgasse 9. Sample wild game at this kitschy restaurant southwest of Marienplatz. Lovely summer terrace. Venison €8.

Mittenwald

Cuddled up against the Austrian border and just 15km from Garmisch-Partenkirchen, tiny **MITTENWALD** makes a

lovely base for hiking and cycling. The **Karwendel mountain** towering above is a popular climb, and the view from the top is exhilarating; it's reachable by cable car (€22 return). The **tourist office**, at Dammkarstr. 3 (May–Sept Mon–Fri 8.30am–6pm, Sat 9am–noon, Sun 10am–noon; Oct–April Mon–Fri 8.30am–6pm; ⓣ08823/339 81, ⓦwww.mittenwald.de) provides free maps of the area. The hostel, *Jugendherberge Mittenwald*, Buckelwiesen 7 (ⓣ08823/17 01, ⓦwww.mittenwald.jugendherberge.de; €19.80), is 4km north of the town. There are plenty of good **guesthouses**, such as the outdoorsy *Bergzauber*, Klausnerweg 26 (ⓣ08823/939 60, ⓦwww.bergzauber.de; €52), with bike-repair facilities on the premises, and the central *Simon*, Soiernstr. 6 (ⓣ08823/13 63, ⓦwww.simon-mittenwald.de; €46). The nearest **campsite** (ⓣ08823/52 16, ⓦwww.camping-isarhorn.de; €10.50) is 3km north, on the road to Garmisch.

Berchtesgaden

Almost entirely surrounded by mountains at Bavaria's southeastern extremity – but easily reached by rail from Munich – the area around **BERCHTESGADEN** has a magical atmosphere, especially in the mornings, when mists rise from the lakes and swirl around lush valleys and rocky mountainsides.

What to see and do

A star attraction is the stunning emerald **Königssee**, Germany's highest lake, which bends around the foot of the towering **Watzmann** (2713m), 5km south of town – regular buses run out here – and has year-round **cruises** (every 30min; €15.50 return). You can also take a cable car up the **Jenner**, immediately above the lake (€20 return), used mostly by skiers in the winter months. Berchtesgaden is still indelibly associated with **Adolf Hitler**, who rented a house in the nearby village of Obersalzberg, which he later enlarged into the **Berghof**, a stately retreat where he could meet foreign dignitaries. High above the village, Hitler's Kehlsteinhaus, or "**Eagle's Nest**", survives as a restaurant, and can be reached by bus and lift from Obersalzberg once the snow has melted (April to mid-Oct; €15 return; ⓦwww.kehlsteinhaus.de). In addition to downhill skiing facilities for the winter months, Berchtesgaden has some great **mountain walks** to take you away from the crowds in summer – maps of suggested walking routes can be found at the **tourist office** (June–Sept Mon–Fri 8.30am–6pm, Sat 9am–5pm, Sun 9am–3pm; Oct–May Mon–Fri 8.30am–5pm & Sat 9am–noon; ⓣ01805/86 5200, ⓦwww.berchtesgaden.de), opposite the train station. Berchtesgaden is also home to an unexpected diversion, the **Salzbergwerk** (daily: May–Oct 9am–6pm; Nov–April 11.30am–4pm, last entry an hour before closing; ⓦwww.salzzeitreise.de; €14), a historic salt mine that's been refurbished with an hour-long amusement-park-like ride/tour through its massive underground caverns.

TREAT YOURSELF

Paragliding in the Bavarian Alps offers a truly awesome way to rise gracefully and quietly above jagged snow-crusted peaks to the distant sound of cowbells. Aerotaxi, Beim Gerber 2, Mittenwald (ⓣ08823/32 91 40 or 0171/281 91 99, ⓦwww.aerotaxi.de; €75–110), offer many different trips for which no experience is necessary.

Accommodation

Guesthouse options include the friendly *Haus am Hang*, Göllsteinbichl 3 (ⓣ08652/43 59, ⓦwww.hausamhang.de; €38), and *Haus Achental*, Ramsauer Str. 4 (ⓣ08652/45 49; €46), where all rooms have bathrooms. The tourist office can direct you to any of the five campsites in the valley.

REGENSBURG

The undisturbed medieval ensemble of central **REGENSBURG**, stunningly located on the banks of the Danube midway between Nuremberg and Munich, can easily be visited as a day-trip. Getting lost in the web of cobbled medieval lanes, nursing a drink in one of the wide, sunny squares or cycling along the Danube are the main draws here.

What to see and do

A good place to start is the twelfth-century **Steinerne Brücke**, the only secured crossing along the entire length of the Danube at the time it was built. To the left, the **Historische Wurstkuchl** (daily 8am–7pm) originally functioned as the bridge-workers' kitchen. This local institution, run by the same family for generations, serves little else but delicious Regensburg sausages (plate €6.90). Just south, the Gothic **Dom**, begun around 1250, has some beautiful fourteenth-century stained-glass windows. The cathedral's Domspatzen boys' choir is famous throughout Germany; catch them performing at Sunday services from 10am. A short way south, the Neupfarrkirche occupies the site of the old synagogue, wrecked during the 1519 Jewish expulsion. **Schloss Thurn und Taxis** (visit only possible with tour, July–Sept daily at 1.30pm; €11.50; Ⓦwww.thurnundtaxis.de), one of the largest inhabited palaces in Europe, is in the converted monastic buildings of the abbey of St Emmeram in the city's southern quarter.

Arrival and information

Train Maximilianstrasse leads straight from the train station north to the centre.

Tourist office At Rathausplatz 3 Ⓣ0941/507 44 10, Ⓦwww.regensburg.de (April–Oct Mon–Fri 9am–6pm, Sat 9am–4pm, Sun 9.30am–4pm; Nov–March same hours but Sun 9.30am–2.30pm).

Bike rental Rent a Bike Ⓣ0800/460 24 60, Ⓦfahrradverleih-regensburg.de. Branches next to and opposite the station. €9/day.

Internet Lokin, first floor of train station. Daily 6am–11pm; €4/hr.

Eating and drinking

Brauereigaststätte Kneitinger Arnulfsplatz 3. For a real *Gaststätte* experience, head for this honourable establishment to the east of the centre, with its delicious Bavarian fare. Roast ox €8.

Dicker Mann Krebsgasse 6. Vine-covered and candlelit café-restaurant on a tiny side street off Haidplatz serving delicious, good-value meals. Breakfast from €3.30, dinner specials from €5.

Goldene Ente Badstr. 32. A lovely beer garden popular with students, across the Eisener Steg (iron bridge) from the Altstadt. Baked camembert and salad €6.30.

Oma Plüsch Rote-Stern-Gasse 6 (entrance Pfarrergasse). Cosy and friendly with huge portions and cheap beer. Roast pork €6.50.

Moving on

Train Munich (hourly; 1hr 30min); Plzeň (twice daily; 2hr 40min); Vienna (every two hours; 4hr).

NUREMBERG

In many minds, the medieval town of **NUREMBERG** (Nürnberg) conjures up images of the Nazi rallies, the 1935 "Nuremberg Laws" which deprived Jews of their citizenship and forbade them relations with Gentiles, and then the war-crime trials. Yet all this infamy is a world away from the friendly, bustling town of today. Nuremberg's relaxed air makes whiling away a day amongst its half-timbered houses, fine museums and beer halls hard to beat.

What to see and do

Meticulous postwar rebuilding means you'd never guess that a storm of bombs on January 2, 1945, reduced ninety percent of Nuremberg's centre to rubble. The reconstructed medieval core is compact, surrounded by ancient city walls and neatly bisected by the River Pegnitz. The **Kaiserburg**, whose **Sinwellturm** can be climbed for great views (daily: April–Sept 9am–6pm; Oct–March 10am–4pm; €3), forms the northwest corner of the city walls.

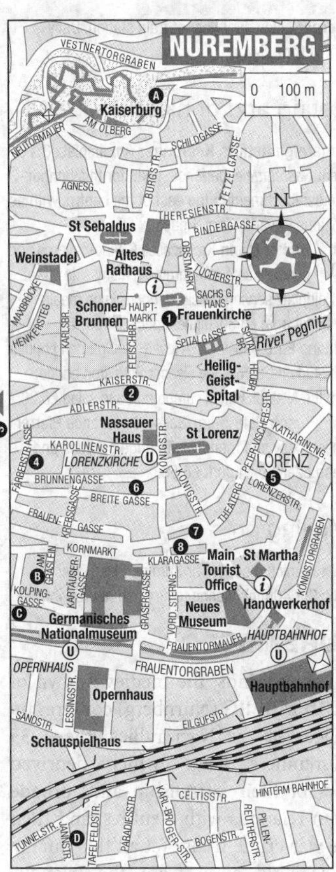

ACCOMMODATION			
DJH	A	Lebkuchen Schmidt	1
Lette'm Sleep	C	Souptopia	5
Pfälzer Hof	B	**DRINKING & NIGHTLIFE**	
Vater Jahn	D	Barfüsser 7 / Stereo	8
EATING		Mach 1 2 / Treibhaus	3
Bratwürst Herzle	6	Mohr	4

St Sebaldus and the Hauptmarkt

Heading south, you'll find the city's oldest church, the thirteenth-century **St Sebaldus**. Highlights include the impressive bronze shrine of St Sebald. The **Hauptmarkt**, further south, hosts daily markets and the famous **Christmas market.** At noon, a clockwork mechanism tinkles away on the facade of the **Frauenkirche**.

St Lorenz

On the south side of the river rises **St Lorenz**, home to a graceful, late fifteenth-century sandstone tabernacle, some 20m high. Across the plaza is the oldest house in the city, the thirteenth-century **Nassauer Haus**.

The Germanisches Nationalmuseum

The **Germanisches Nationalmuseum** (Kartäusergasse 1; Tues & Thurs–Sun 10am–6pm, Wed 10am–9pm; €6; Ⓦwww.gnm.de) presents the country's cultural history through this large, important collection of artefacts and art from German central Europe, from the Bronze Age to the present. Look out for the first globe of the earth, made by Martin Behaim in 1491 – just before Columbus "discovered" America.

The Neues Museum

The **Neues Museum** (Tues–Fri 10am–8pm, Sat & Sun 10am–6pm; €4, Sun €1; Ⓦwww.nmn.de) offers a cross-section of contemporary art and design, including works by Gerhard Richter and Verner Panton.

The Fascination and Terror exhibition

The Nazi Party rallies were held on the Zeppelin and March fields in the suburb of Luitpoldhain. Nearby, in the gargantuan but never-completed Congress Hall, the **Documentation Centre Nazi Party Rally Grounds** has an unmissable multimedia exhibition documenting the history of the rally grounds and the ruthless misuse of power under National Socialism (Mon–Fri 9am–6pm, Sat & Sun 10am–6pm; €5; tram #9 to Doku-Zentrum; Ⓦwww.museen.nuernberg.de).

Arrival and information

Air The U2 underground service connects Nürnberg airport with the train station (every 15min; 12min).

Train The Hauptbahnhof is just outside the southern edge of the city walls; follow Königstr. into the centre.
Tourist office At the entrance to the Altstadt opposite the train station ⓣ0911/233 61 32, ⓦwww.nuernberg.de (Mon–Sat 9am–7pm, Sun 10am–4pm). Smaller office at Hauptmarkt 18, in the Altstadt (Mon–Sat 9am–6pm; May–Oct & Dec Mon–Sat 9am–7pm; ⓣ0911/231 55 55).
Discount pass The Nürnberg Card (€19/two days) covers public transport plus entrance to museums.
City transport There is an U-Bahn and bus system; a single trip costs €1.90, a day ticket (or both Sat & Sun) €3.80.
Internet Flat-S, top floor of the train station's middle hall; open 24hr; €4/hr.

Accommodation

DJH Burg 2 ⓣ0911/230 93 60, ⓦwww.nuernberg.jugendherberge.de. The HI hostel has a wonderful location within the Kaiserburg, overlooking the Altstadt. U-Bahn #2 to Rathenauplatz, then bus #36 to Burgstrasse or 25min walk from the station. Dorms €21.90.
Lette'm Sleep Frauentormauer 42 ⓣ0911/992 81 28, ⓦwww.backpackers.de. This friendly and popular hostel offers free internet access. Dorms €16, rooms €49.
Pfälzer Hof Am Gräslein 10 ⓣ0911/22 14 11. This little hotel is in a calm corner of central Nuremberg, off Kornmarkt. Rooms €48.
Vater Jahn Jahnstr. 13 ⓣ0911/44 45 07. Friendly guesthouse just south of the Opernhaus on the other side of the railway tracks. Rooms €45.

Eating and drinking

There are plenty of *Imbiss*-style snack joints in the pedestrian zone around St Lorenz, while the area around Rathenauplatz U-Bahn is packed with student café-bars. To find out what's on, pick up monthly magazine *Dopplepunkt* (free) or *Plärrer* (€2) from the tourist office.
Barfüsser Hallplatz 2. This popular beer hall in cavernous cellars brews its own beer and serves good food. Schnitzel €8.
Bratwurst Herzle Brunnengasse 11. More down-to-earth than some options, *Herzle* is a great place for sampling Nuremberg's mini-sausages. Four *Bratwürstl* €4.80.
Lebkuchen Schmidt Hauptmarkt. Taste Christmas year-round at this shop selling the Nuremberg speciality: a spicy gingerbread cookie called *Lebkuchen* (€2).
Mach 1 Kaiserstr. 1–9 ⓦwww.mach1-club.de. This trendy club has four different bars and a plethora of DJs. Thurs–Sat 10pm–5am.
Mohr Färberstr. 3. Fashionable café-bar in the Altstadt, open late. Pasta specials €4.
Souptopia Lorenzerstr. 27. If you're sick of sausage, head for this little wonder, where five types of soup are on offer daily, including at least one vegan option. Bowl of soup €5.50.
Stereo Klaragasse 8. This lounge-like club is more relaxed than most and hosts indie and pop nights. Thurs–Sat 9pm–3am.
Treibhaus Karl-Grillenberger-Str. 28. Refreshingly out of the way yet still in the Altstadt (take Kaiserstrasse, then Hintere Ledergasse to their western ends, then turn right), this hip café-bar offers everything you need from 8am to 2am. South of Maxbrücke. Huge, delicious salads €6, cocktails €5.50.

Moving on

Train Augsburg (hourly; 1hr 10min); Berlin (hourly; 4hr 40min); Frankfurt (hourly; 2hr 10min); Leipzig (hourly; 3hr 10min); Munich (every 30min; 1hr 10min); Regensburg (every 30min; 1hr); Vienna (every 2hr; 5hr); Würzburg (every 30min; 1hr).

ROTHENBURG OB DER TAUBER

The **Romantic Road** (see box, p.513) winds its way along the length of western Bavaria, running through the most visited – and most beautiful – medieval town in Germany: **ROTHENBURG OB DER TAUBER.** This fairy-tale location is besieged with tour groups during the day, so spend the night – or at least an evening – to appreciate it in relative peace.

What to see and do

The views of the surrounding countryside from the fourteenth-century town walls are magnificent, but Rothenburg's true charms lie amongst its medieval half-timbered houses and cobbled streets. The sloping **Marktplatz** is dominated by the arcaded front of the Renaissance Rathaus; the sixty-metre tower of the Altes Rathaus (daily: April–Oct 9.30am–12.30pm & 1–5pm; Dec noon–3pm; Nov & Jan–March weekends only noon–3pm; €2) provides the best views.

The Ratsherrntrinkstube clocks

The other main attractions on the Marktplatz are the figures on each side of the three clocks of the **Ratsherrntrinkstube**. Seven times a day these figures re-enact an episode in which former mayor Nusch allegedly saved Protestant Rothenburg from the wrath of Catholic General Tilly during the Thirty Years' War, by downing three litres of wine. Northeast of the Marktplatz is the Gothic **St Jakob-Kirche** (Mon–Sat 9am–5.30pm, Sun 10.30am–5.30pm; €2), with its massive towers (currently undergoing restoration) and exquisitely carved altars.

The Kriminalmuseum

Of the local museums, the most interesting is the **Kriminalmuseum** at Burggasse 3 (daily: Jan, Feb & Nov 2–4pm; March & Dec 10am–4pm; April 11am–5pm; May–Oct 10am–6pm; last entry 45min before closing; €3.80; Ⓦ www.kriminalmuseum.rothenburg.de). It contains collections of medieval torture instruments and related objects, such as the beer barrels that drunks were forced to walk around in.

Arrival and information

Train Ten-minute walk east of the centre. From the station head left on Bahnhofstrasse, then right on Ansbacherstrasse, which takes you straight through Röder city gate.

Tourist office In the Ratsherrntrinkstube on Marktplatz Ⓣ 09861/40 48 00, Ⓦ www.rothenburg.de (May–Oct Mon–Fri 9am–6pm, Sat & Sun 10am–3pm; Nov–April Mon–Fri 9am–5pm, Sat 10am–1pm, Dec also Sun 10am–3pm). Organizes daily English-language tours €6/1hr.

Accommodation

DJH Mühlacker 1 Ⓣ 09861/941 60, Ⓦ www.rothenburg.jugendherberge.de. Housed in two beautifully restored houses and a modern annexe off the bottom of Spitalgasse. Dorms €20.

Pöschel Wenggasse 22 Ⓣ 09861/34 30, Ⓦ www.pensionpoeschel.de. Charming family-run *pension*, with an excellent breakfast. Rooms €40.

Raidel Wenggasse 3 Ⓣ 09861/31 15, Ⓦ www.romanticroad.com/raidel. A wonderfully creaky 600-year-old house, this guesthouse oozes character. Rooms €49.

Zur Goldenen Rose Spitalgasse 28 Ⓣ 09861/46 38, Ⓦ www.goldenerose-rothenburg.de. This *Gasthof* has pleasant rooms and serves great home-cooked food in one of the town's many fine restaurants. Rooms €85.

Moving on

Train Augsburg (hourly; 2hr 20min); Nuremberg (hourly; 1hr 15min); Würzburg (hourly; 1hr 10min).

Greece

HIGHLIGHTS ✪

✪ METEORA: awe-inspiring Byzantine monasteries in a magical setting

✪ ATHENS: roam the Acropolis and hit the capital's clubs

✪ OLYMPIA: discover where the games were born

SANTORÍNI: take in the sunset from this spectacular island ✪

✪ KNOSSOS: visit the home of the Minotaur

ROUGH COSTS

DAILY BUDGET Basics €30/ occasional treat €40

DRINK Oúzo €3

FOOD Souvláki (shish kebab) €8

HOSTEL/BUDGET HOTEL €10/€35

TRAVEL Bus: Athens–Delphi €13; ferry: Athens–Crete €32

FACT FILE

POPULATION 11.2 million

AREA 131,900 sq km (including 6000 islands)

LANGUAGE Greek

CURRENCY Euro (€)

CAPITAL Athens (population: 4 million)

INTERNATIONAL PHONE CODE ⓣ30

Introduction

With 166 inhabited islands and a landscape that ranges from Mediterranean to Balkan, Greece has enough appeal to fill months of travel. The beaches are distributed along a convoluted coastline, where cosmopolitan resorts lie surprisingly close to remote islands where boats may call only once or twice a week. The initial glimpse of sapphire water or the discovery of millennia-old ruins bordered by ancient olive groves is intoxicating, and it's the mingling of history and hedonism that ensures Greece's enduring appeal. Island-hopping is still popular, but if you're on a tight budget, consider exploring the mainland or the Peloponnese by bus, or save on multiple ferry trips by focusing on a few highlights.

The country is the sum of an extraordinary diversity of influences. Romans, Arabs, Frankish Crusaders, Venetians, Slavs, Albanians, Turks, Italians, as well as the thousand-year Byzantine Empire, have all been and gone since the time of Alexander the Great. Each has left its mark: the **Byzantines** through countless churches and monasteries; the **Venetians** in impregnable fortifications such as Monemvasiá in the Peloponnese; the **Franks** with crag-top castles, again in the Peloponnese but also in the Dodecanese and east Aegean. Most obvious, perhaps, is the heritage of four hundred years of **Ottoman Turkish** rule which exercised an inestimable influence on music, cuisine, language and way of life.

Even before the fall of Byzantium in the fifteenth century, Greek peasants, fishermen and shepherds had created one of the most vigorous and truly **popular cultures** in Europe, which found expression in song and dance, costumes, embroidery, furniture and the distinctive whitewashed houses. Though having suffered a decline under Western influence, Hellenic culture – architectural and musical heritage in particular – is undergoing a renaissance.

CHRONOLOGY

c. 800 BC Homer writes *The Iliad* and *The Odyssey*.
776 BC First Olympic Games are held in Olympia.
486 BC The building of the Parthenon is completed.
399 BC The trial and execution of Socrates, the founding father of philosophy, takes place.
380 BC Plato establishes the Athens Academy.
323 BC Alexander the Great dies heralding the beginning of the Hellenistic period.
88 BC Romans attack Athens.
330 AD Byzantine Empire established at Constantinople. Christianity becomes dominant religion.
1387 The Ionian Islands fall under Venetian rule.
1456 Ottoman Turks invade Athens and occupy the city.
1829 Greeks win their independence from Ottoman rule.
1833 Athens becomes the capital of Greece.
1924 Monarchy is abolished in favour of a Republic.
1935 The monarchy is restored.
1941 Greece is invaded and occupied by German, Italian and Bulgarian forces. Liberation comes three years later with the help of heavy resistance fighting.
1952 A new constitution is passed which retains the monarchy as head of state whilst introducing parliamentary democracy.
1967 Military coup led by Colonel George Papadopoulos.
1973 Monarchy is abolished and Papadopoulos is overthrown in a bloodless coup.
1974 Turkish invasion of Greek-held northern Cyprus.
2002 Greece adopts the euro.
2004 The Olympic Games are held in Athens.
2009 Forest fires threaten the northern suburbs of Athens, destroy ancient forest and leave hundreds homeless.

ARRIVAL

There are international **airports** on the mainland at Athens and Thessaloníki, both well connected with their respective cities. Other destinations served by budget flights include Crete, Corfu and Rhodes, as well as numerous other mainland and island destinations. By **boat**, there are regular ferries from Ancona, Bari, Brindisi, Trieste and Venice in Italy, arriving at Corfu, Kefalloniá, Igoumenítsa and Pátra. Eurail and InterRail pass holders may travel with Superfast Ferries (Ⓦwww.superfast.com) at **discounted fares** from Ancona and Bari. You can also travel by boat from Turkey to the Dodecanese and the northern Aegean islands (Rhodes, Kós, Sámos, Híos and Lésvos), and from Albania to Corfu. By **land**, crossing into Greece is possible from Albania, Macedonia, Bulgaria, Romania and Turkey either by bus or by train, arriving in Thessaloníki. There are two trains daily from Belgrade via Skopje and two trains daily from Sofia to Thessaloníki, one of which starts its journey in Budapest. From Istanbul, a daily train leaves for Thessaloníki. If you arrive overland from the north at Thessaloníki, onward travel to the rest of the country is straightforward.

GETTING AROUND

The **rail** network (Ⓦwww.osenet.gr) is limited, and trains are slower than the equivalent buses – except on the showcase IC (intercity) lines. However, most trains are cheaper than buses, and some of the routes are highlights in their own right. **Eurail** and **InterRail** are valid, though pass holders must

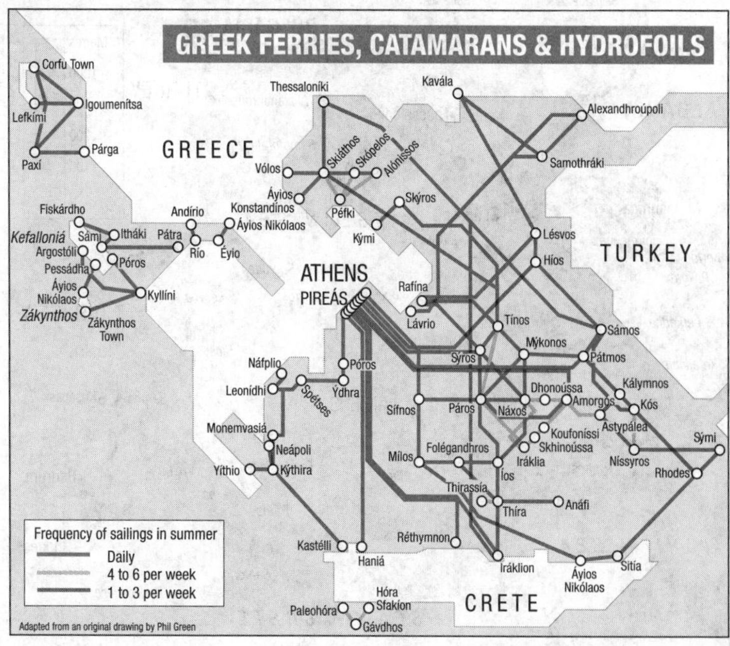

Adapted from an original drawing by Phil Green

reserve like everyone else, and there's a small supplement on the intercity services. It is essential to validate your train ticket on the platform before you board the train.

Buses form the bulk of public land transport, and service on the major routes is efficient, with companies organized nationally into a syndicate called **KTEL**. If starting a journey from a bus station, you will be issued with a one-way ticket which has a seat number. Return tickets are rare.

Schedules for **sea transport** are notoriously erratic. Regular ferry tickets are best bought on the day of departure, unless you need to reserve a cabin – although from March 23 to 25, the weeks before and after Orthodox Easter and during August it's best to book several days in advance. The cheapest ticket is "deck class". Leave plenty of time for your journey as ferries are often late, or take longer to reach their destinations than scheduled. Hydrofoils and high-speed catamarans are roughly twice as fast and twice as expensive as ordinary ferries. In season, *kaïkia* (caïques) sail to more obscure islets.

Once on the islands, almost everybody rents a **scooter** or a **bike**. Scooters cost from €12 a day, mountain bikes a bit less. To rent a motorbike (anything over 50cc) you usually need to show an appropriate licence.

ACCOMMODATION

Most of the year you can turn up pretty much anywhere and find a **room**. Only around Easter (Orthodox) and during July and August are you likely to experience problems; at these times, it's worth booking well in advance. If this isn't possible, head off the tourist routes, or arrive at each new place early in the day.

Hotels are categorized from "Luxury" down to "E-class", but these ratings have more to do with amenities and number of rooms than pricing – a budget hotel

will typically cost €30–60 for a double. Throughout Greece, you have the additional option of **privately let rooms** (*dhomátia*). These are divided into three classes (A–C), and are usually cheaper than hotels. As often as not, rooms find you: owners descend on ferry and bus arrivals to fill any space they have. On the islands, minibuses from campsites and hotels meet new arrivals for free transfers. Increasingly, rooms are being eclipsed by **self-catering facilities**, which can be equally good value; if signs or touts are not apparent, ask for studios at travel agencies which usually cluster around arrival points. There are a handful of **hostels** outside Athens, which charge around €8–12 a night. Note that hotels and hostels do not normally include breakfast in their prices; an extra charge of €5 is standard.

Bringing a tent, if you can carry one, increases your options for cheap accommodation. Official **campsites** range from basic island compounds to highly organized complexes, mostly closed in winter (Nov–April). Many sites hire tents or have more permanent accommodation in the form of lodges or caravans. Rough camping is forbidden.

FOOD AND DRINK

Eating out in Greece is popular and reasonably priced: €10–15 per person for a meal with beer or cheap wine. Typical **taverna** dishes to try include *moussakás* (aubergine and meat pie), *yígandes* (white haricot beans in red sauce), *tzatzíki* (yoghurt, garlic and cucumber dip), *melitzanosaláta* (aubergine dip), *khtapódhi* (octopus) and *kalamarákia* (fried baby squid). Quintessentially Greek **ouzerí** and **mezedhopolía** serve filling *mezédhes* (the Greek version of tapas) with drinks, adding up to a substantial meal. Note that people eat late: 2.30–4pm for lunch & 9–11.30pm for dinner, although plenty of places serve food all day.

BUDGET EATING

Head to a supermarket and stock up on Greek yoghurt and honey for breakfast and buy *tyrópites* and *spanakópites* (cheese and spinach pies respectively) from a bakery for lunch. **Snacks** are one of the pleasures of Greek eating; *souvlákia* (small kebabs) and *yíros* (doner kebabs), served in *píta* bread, are sold everywhere.

As for **drinks**, the traditional coffee shop or **kafenío** is the central pivot of rural life; like tavernas, these range from the sophisticated to the old-fashioned. Their main business is sweet Greek coffee, but they also serve spirits such as aniseed-flavoured *oúzo* and brandy, as well as beer and soft drinks. Islanders take pre-dinner *oúzo* an hour or two before sunset: you'll be served a glass of water alongside, to be tipped into your *oúzo* until it turns milky white. **Bars** are ubiquitous in the largest towns and resorts. Drinks, at €5.50–10, are invariably more expensive than at a *kafenío*.

CULTURE AND ETIQUETTE

It is important to be respectful when visiting one of Greece's many **churches** or **monasteries**, and appropriate clothing should be worn – covered arms and legs for both sexes. The more popular sites often provide such clothing, should you be without it. Photography is also banned in sacred places. Another important part of Greek life is the afternoon **siesta**, when peace and quiet are valued. In restaurants, **tipping** is not expected but usually customers round up the bill, or leave a little more for exceptional service. **Topless bathing** is now legal on virtually all Greek beaches but, especially in smaller places, be aware of local sensitivities before stripping off; full nudity is tolerated only at designated or isolated beaches.

SPORTS AND OUTDOOR ACTIVITIES

The larger islands and resorts on the mainland have countless opportunities for **watersports** – including waterskiing, windsurfing, diving and snorkelling. There are usually information kiosks at the main beaches. The country's mountainous landscape provides plenty of **walking** and **climbing** options. The most rewarding areas are in northern Greece, concentrating around Mount Olympus to the east and the Epirus region to the northwest. Always wear sturdy walking boots for long treks, and carry plenty of water. If you want to do some serious hiking, it's worth buying a specialist map.

COMMUNICATIONS

Most **post offices** operate Monday to Friday 7.30am to 2pm, and into the evening and even weekends in the largest cities and major resorts. **Stamps** can also be bought at designated postal agencies inside newsstands or stationers. **Public phones** are mainly card-operated; buy phonecards from newsagents and kiosks. It's possible to make collect (reverse-charge) or charge-card calls from these phones, but you need credit on a Greek phone card to begin. There are no area codes per se; you merely dial all ten digits of every phone number. The operator is on ⓣ132 (domestic) or ⓣ139 (international). If you're in the country for more than a week or so it's worth buying a **pay-as-you-go SIM card** available from mobile-phone shops; you can get your phone unlocked here, too. All big towns have **internet cafés**, and there's usually at least one place on the more visited islands. Expect to pay around €1–3 per hour.

GREECE ON THE NET

ⓦ**www.culture.gr** Ministry of Culture site, with information on ruins and museums.
ⓦ**www.athensnews.gr** Useful and literate English-language weekly.
ⓦ**www.gnto.gr** Greek National Tourist Organization site.
ⓦ**www.gtp.gr** Information on all ferry and hydrofoil schedules except some minor lines.

PERÍPTERO PAVEMENT KIOSKS

You can't walk far in Greece without coming across a *períptero* pavement kiosk. Selling everything from bus tickets to condoms, razors and stationery, they're often the first port of call for directions, too. Many are open 24 hours.

EMERGENCIES

The most common causes of a run-in with the **police** are drunken loutishness and camping outside an authorized site. For minor medical complaints go to the local **pharmacy**, usually open Monday to Friday 8am to 2pm. Details of pharmacies open out-of-hours are posted in all pharmacy windows. For serious medical attention you'll find English-speaking doctors in all bigger towns and resorts; consult the tourist police for names. Emergency treatment is free in state hospitals, though you'll only get the most basic level of nursing care.

INFORMATION

There are **National Tourist Organization (EOT)** offices in most larger towns and resorts; in other places, try the municipal tourist offices, which often have longer hours. The **tourist police** often have lists of rooms to let, but are mostly there to assist if you have a serious complaint about a hotel or restaurant.

EMERGENCY NUMBERS

Police ⓣ110; Ambulance ⓣ166; Fire ⓣ199

Greek

	Greek	Pronunciation
Yes	*Néh*	Ne
No	*Óhi*	Ohi
Please	*Parakaló*	Parakalo
Thank you	*Efharistó*	Efharisto
Hello/Good day	*Yás sas/Hérete*	Yas sas/*Herete*
Goodbye	*Adío*	Adio
Excuse me	*Signómi*	Siynomi
Sorry	*Lupámai*	Lipame
When?	*Póte?*	Pote?
Where?	*Pou?*	Poo?
Good	*Kaló*	Kalo
Bad	*Kakó*	Kako
Near	*Kondá*	Konda
Far	*Makriá*	Makria
Cheap	*Fthinó*	Fthino
Expensive	*Akrivó*	Akrivo
Open	*Aniktó*	Anikto
Closed	*Klistó*	Klisto
Today	*Símera*	Simera
Yesterday	*Khthés*	Khthes
Tomorrow	*Ávrio*	Avrio
How much is...?	*Póso káni...?*	Poso kani...?
What time is it?	*Ti óra íneh?*	Ti ora ine?
I don't understand	*Dhen katalavéno*	Then katalaveno
Do you speak English?	*Xérete angliká?*	Xherete anglika?
Do you have a room?	*Éhete éna eléfthero domátio?*	Ehete ena elefthero domatyo?
Where does this bus go to?	*Pou piyaínei autó to leoforeío?*	Poo piyeni afto to leoforio?
What time does it leave?	*Ti óra févyi?*	Ti ora fevyi?
A ticket to...	*Éna isitírio yiá...*	Ena isitirio yia...
I'm going to...	*Páo stó...*	Pao sto...
Can I have the bill please?	*To logariasmó, parakaló?*	To loghariazmo, parakalo?
One	*Éna/mía*	Ena/mia
Two	*Dhýo*	Thio
Three	*Trís/tría*	Tris/tria
Four	*Tésseres/Tesseris*	Téssera/Tessera
Five	*Pénde*	Pende
Six	*Éxi*	Exhi
Seven	*Eftá*	Efta
Eight	*Októ*	Okto
Nine	*Enéa*	Enea
Ten	*Dhéka*	Theka

MONEY AND BANKS

Greece's currency is the **euro** (€). **Banks** are normally open Monday to Thursday 8am to 2.30pm, Friday 8am to 2pm. They charge a flat fee (€2–3) to change money, the National Bank usually being the cheapest; travel agencies and designated exchange booths give a poorer rate, but often levy a sliding two-percent commission, which makes them better than banks for changing small amounts. Plenty of **ATMs** accept foreign cards;

STUDENTS AND YOUTH DISCOUNTS

Many state-owned **museums and sites** are free for students from EU countries (a valid card is required, but not necessarily an ISIC). Non-EU students generally pay half-price. Holders of the ISIC card may also be eligible for ferry discounts; check Ⓦwww.greekferries.gr for details.

in isolated areas, a small quantity of US dollar/sterling notes – not traveller's cheques – will prove useful. **Credit cards** are generally accepted in more upmarket hotels, restaurants and shops.

OPENING HOURS AND HOLIDAYS

Shops generally open at 8.30/9am, then take a long break at 2/2.30pm before reopening in the late afternoon (5.30/6pm–8.30/9pm) on Tuesday, Thursday and Friday only. However, tourist areas have shops and offices often staying open right through the day. On Sundays many shops remain closed and **public transport** reduces dramatically or ceases completely, so be careful not to get stranded. Opening hours for **museums** and **ancient sites** change with exasperating frequency, although many are closed on Mondays. Smaller sites generally close for a long siesta (even when they're not supposed to), as do monasteries. Most museums and archeological sites are free on the following days: Sundays November to March; 1st Sunday of April, May, June and October; 2nd Sunday of July to September; all national holidays. There's a vast range of **national holidays** and **festivals**. The most important, when almost everything will be closed, are: January 1 and 6, 1st Monday of Lent (March 7 in 2011), March 25, May 1, Orthodox Easter Sunday and Monday, Pentecost/Whit Monday (May 24 in 2010, June 13 in 2011), August 15, October 28, December 24–27.

Athens

Chaotic and exhilarating, **ATHENS** has been inhabited continuously for over seven thousand years. Vastly improved by a vigorous scrub before the Olympics in 2004, it has an efficient, user-friendly metro and its mix of contemporary culture, nightlife and heritage rivals that of almost any European city. Part of Athens' charm is the mix of retro and contemporary: cutting-edge clothes shops and designer bars stand by the remnants of the Ottoman bazaar, while brutalist 1960s apartment-blocks dwarf crumbling Neoclassical mansions.

Athens' acropolis, protected by a ring of mountains and commanding views of all seagoing approaches, was a natural choice for prehistoric settlement. Its development as a city-state reached its zenith in the fifth century BC with a flourish of art, architecture, literature and philosophy that has pervaded Western culture ever since. The **ancient sites** are the most obvious of Athens' attractions, but the attractive cafés, markets and landscaped stair-streets, the startling views from the hills of Lykavitós and Filopáppou, and, around the foot of the Acropolis, the scattered monuments of the Byzantine, medieval and nineteenth-century town all have their appeal.

What to see and do

Pláka is the best place to begin exploring the city. One of the few parts of Athens with charm and architectural merit, its narrow streets and stepped lanes are flanked by nineteenth-century Neoclassical houses. The interlocking streets provide countless opportunities for watching the world – or at least, the tourists – go by. While the Acropolis complex is an essential sight, it can be rewarding to stumble across smaller and more modest relics, such as the fourth-century Monument of Lysikratos, or the first-century Tower of the Winds. Or take a walk through the pleasant National Gardens, away from the chaos of Athens' traffic-choked streets. Save some energy for the balmy evenings, however – with fantastic restaurants and funky bars, Athens knows how to juxtapose the ancient with the modern, leaving the visitor full of the wonders of both.

ANCIENT MONUMENTS ENTRY

The **ticket** to the Acropolis (€12, non-EU students €6, EU students free) is valid for four days and allows free access to all the other ancient sites in Athens. Otherwise, minor sites charge a separate €2 admission fee if you haven't visited the Acropolis. All the sites have the same hours (April–Sept 8am–7pm, Oct–March 8am–sunset).

The Acropolis

A rugged limestone outcrop, watered by springs and rising abruptly from the plain of Attica, the **Acropolis** (April–Sept 8am–7pm; Oct–March 8am–sunset) was one of the earliest settlements in Greece, supporting a Neolithic community around 5000 BC. During the ninth century BC, it became the heart of the first Greek city-state, and in the fifth century BC, Pericles had the complex reconstructed under the direction of architect and sculptor Pheidias, producing most of the monuments visible today, including the Parthenon. Having survived more or less intact for over two millennia, the Acropolis finally fell victim to the vagaries of war. In 1801 Lord Elgin removed the frieze (the "Elgin Marbles"), which he later sold to the British Museum and which has caused much controversy ever since. While the original religious significance of the Acropolis is now non existent, it is still imbued with a sense of majesty.

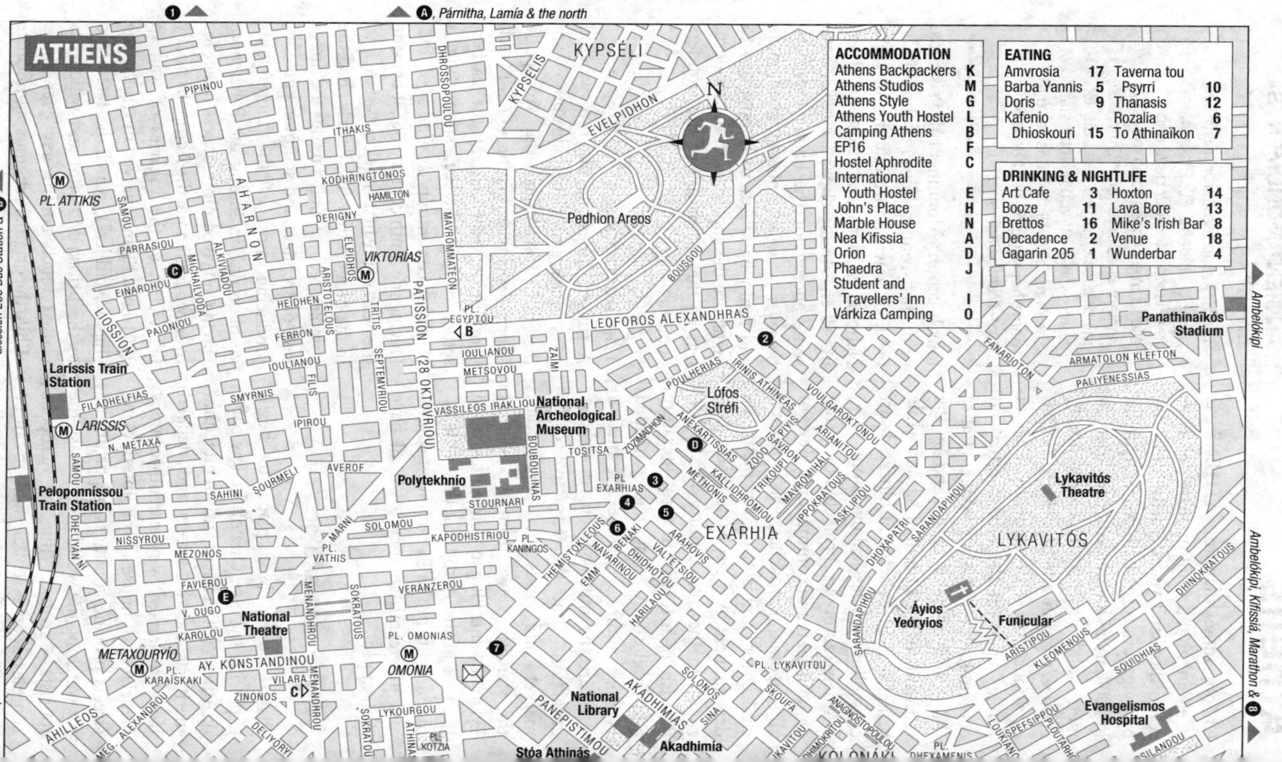
ATHENS
Párnitha, Lamía & the north
Liossion 260 Bus Station &
& the Peloponnese
Ambelókipi
Ambelókipi, Kifissiá, Marathon &
ACCOMMODATION
Athens Backpackers K
Athens Studios M
Athens Style G
Athens Youth Hostel L
Camping Athens B
EP16 F
Hostel Aphrodite C
International Youth Hostel E
John's Place H
Marble House N
Nea Kifissia A
Orion D
Phaedra J
Student and Travellers' Inn I
Várkiza Camping O
EATING
Amvrosia 17
Barba Yannis 5
Doris 9
Kafenio Dhioskouri 15
Taverna tou Psyrri 10
Thanasis 12
Rozalia 6
To Athinaïkon 7
DRINKING & NIGHTLIFE
Art Cafe 3
Booze 11
Brettos 16
Decadence 2
Gagarin 205 1
Hoxton 14
Lava Bore 13
Mike's Irish Bar 8
Venue 18
Wunderbar 4
KYPSÉLI
Pedhion Areos
LEOFOROS ALEXANDHRAS
Panathinaïkós Stadium
Lófos Stréfi
National Archeological Museum
Polytekhnío
EXÁRHIA
LYKAVITÓS
Lykavitós Theatre
Áyios Yeóryios
Funicular
Evangelismos Hospital
Larissis Train Station
Peloponnissou Train Station
PL. ATTIKIS
LARISSIS
VIKTORÍAS
METAXOURYÍO
OMONIA
National Theatre
National Library
Akadhimía
Stóa Athinás
PATISSION (28 OKTOVRIOU)
AHARNON
LIOSSION
AY. KONSTANDINOU
PL. OMONIAS
PL. LYKAVITOU
PL. EXARHIAS
PL. EGYPTOU
PL. VATHIS
PL. KANINGOS
PL. KARAÏSKAKI
PANEPISTIMIOU
AKADHIMIAS
KOLONÁKI

Kiffissoú 100 Bus Station, Kórinthos
Gázi, Pireás & 14
Ilísia
Goúva
L
N
Pireás, Néa Smýrni & Kalithéa
O, 18, Glyfádha, Vouliagméni & Soúnion
Commercial Bank
Central Market
City of Athens Mus.
National Bank
Benáki Museum
British Council
Cycladic Art Museum
National Gallery
EVANGELISMÓS
SYNDAGMA
Parliament
Presidential Palace
PSYRRÍ
Flower Market
Flea Market
Kerameikos
THISSIO
MONASTIRAKI
Cathedral
National Gardens
PANGRÁTI
Hephaisteion
Ancient Agora
Stoa
Roman Forum
Tower of the Winds
PLÁKA
Cine Paris
Záppio
Panathenaic Stadium
ACROPOLIS
Parthenon
Áyii Apóstoli
Areopagus
Hill ofthe Nymphs
Hill of the Pnyx
Herodes Atticus Theatre
Asklepion
Theatre of Dionysus
Hadrian's Arch
Temple of Olympian Zeus
Ardhittós
AKRÓPOLI
MAKRIYIANNI
METS
Ay. Dhimítrios
Prison of Socrates
ÁNO PETRÁLONA
FILOPÁPPOU HILL
Monument of Philopappos
Dora Stratou Theatre
SYNGROÚ-FIX
KOUKÁKI
First Cemetery
LOCAL BUSES
A Dháfni, Eléfsina
B Ráfina, Sounío, Lávrio, Marathón, Rhámnous
C #051 terminal
0 250 m

The vistas alone are worth the climb, as the Acropolis's height affords a rare bird's-eye view over the capital. Go early or late to beat the crowds and savour a moment alone with this icon of Western civilization.

The Parthenon

With the construction of the **Parthenon**, fifth-century Athens reached an artistic and cultural zenith. No other monument in the ancient Greek world had achieved such fame, and it stood proud as a symbol of the greatness and the power of Athens. The first and largest building constructed by Pericles' men, the temple is stunning, achieving an unequalled harmony in temple architecture. Built on the site of earlier temples, it was intended as a new sanctuary for Athena and a house for her cult image, a colossal statue decked in ivory and gold plate that was designed by Pheidias and considered one of the Seven Wonders of the Ancient World; unfortunately the sculpture was lost in ancient times.

The Erechtheion

To the north of the Parthenon stands the **Erechtheion**, the last of the great works of Pericles. The building is intentionally unlike anything else found among the remnants of ancient sites. The most bizarre and memorable feature is the Porch of the Caryatids, as the columns are replaced by six maidens (caryatids) holding the entablature gracefully on their heads. The significance of this design continues to puzzle both historians and visitors.

The Acropolis Museum

The new **Acropolis Museum** (Tues–Sun 8am–8pm; ⓦwww.theacropolismuseum.gr; €1) opened to much fanfare in 2009 in a striking, purpose-built building at the foot of the rock. It contains nearly all the portable objects removed from the Acropolis since 1834. Prize exhibits include the *Moschophoros*, a painted marble statue of a young man carrying a sacrificial calf; the graceful sculpture of Athena Nike adjusting her sandal, known as *Iy Sandalízoussa*; and four caryatids from the Erechtheion. Athens now has a suitable facility for the storage and display of the Elgin Marbles – but whether the British Museum will now return them remains to be seen.

Herodes Atticus Theatre and Theatre of Dionysus

Dominating the southern slope of the Acropolis hill is the second-century Roman **Herodes Atticus Theatre**, restored for performances of music and classical drama during the summer festival (the only time it's open). The main interest hereabouts lies in earlier Greek sites to the east, pre-eminent among them the **Theatre of Dionysus**. Masterpieces of Aeschylus, Sophocles, Euripides and Aristophanes were first performed here, at one of the most evocative locations in the city. The ruins are impressive; the theatre, rebuilt in the fourth century BC, could hold some seventeen thousand spectators.

The Agora

Northwest of the Acropolis, the **Agora** was the nexus of ancient Athenian city life, where acts of administration, commerce and public assembly competed for space. The site is a confused jumble of ruins, dating from various stages between the sixth century BC and the fifth century AD. For some idea of what you are surveying, head for the **museum** in the rebuilt Stoa of Attalos. At the far corner of the precinct sits the nearly intact but distinctly clunky Doric **Temple of Hephaistos**, otherwise known as the Thissíon from the exploits of Theseus depicted on its friezes.

The Roman Forum

The **Roman Forum**, or Roman agora, was built as an extension of the

Hellenistic Agora by Julius Caesar and Augustus. The best-preserved and most intriguing of the ruins, though, is the graceful, octagonal structure known as the **Tower of the Winds**. It was designed in the first century BC by a Syrian astronomer, and served as a compass, sundial, weather vane and water clock powered by a stream from one of the Acropolis springs. Each face of the tower is adorned with a relief of a figure floating through the air, personifying the eight winds.

Sýndagma Square and the National Gardens

All roads lead to Platía Syndágmatos – **Sýndagma Square** – with its pivotal metro station. Geared to tourism, with a main post office, banks, luxury hotels and travel agents grouped around, it has little to recommend it. Behind the parliament buildings on the square, the **National Gardens** provide the most refreshing spot in the city, a shady oasis of trees, shrubs and creepers. South of the gardens stands **Hadrian's Arch**, erected by the Roman emperor to mark the edge of the classical city and the beginning of his own. Directly behind are sixteen surviving columns of the 104 that originally comprised the **Temple of Olympian Zeus** – the largest in Greece, dedicated by Hadrian in 131 AD.

Town museums

At the northeastern corner of the National Gardens is the fascinating and much-overlooked **Benáki Museum**, Koumbári 1 (Mon, Wed, Fri & Sat 9am–5pm, Thurs 9am–midnight, Sun 9am–3pm; €6, students €3), with a well-organized collection that features Mycenaean jewellery, Greek costumes, memorabilia of the Greek War of Independence and historical documents, engravings and paintings.

Taking the second left off Vassilísis Sofías after the Benáki Museum will bring you to the **Museum of Cycladic and Ancient Greek Art**, Neofýtou Dhouká 4 (Mon & Wed–Sat 10am–5pm, Thurs 10am–8pm, Sun 11am–5pm; €7, students €2.50), impressive for both its subject and the quality of its displays.

To the northwest, beyond Omónia, the fabulous **National Archeological Museum**, Patissíon 44 (Mon 1–7.30pm, Tues–Sun 8am–7.30pm; €7, students €3), contains gold from the grave circle at Mycenae, including the so-called Mask of Agamemnon, along with an impressive classical art collection and findings from the island of Thíra, dating from around 1450 BC, contemporary with the Minoan civilization on Crete.

Arrival and information

Air The Suburban Rail line whisks you from Eleftheríos Venizélos airport to Laríssis train station (hourly; 7am–midnight; €6), involving a change at Nerantziotissa, where you can also transfer to the Line #1 metro. Although this is the quickest mode of transport, the airport is also directly connected to the Line #3 metro (every 30min; 5am–midnight; €6). The #X95 bus (every 10–15min; 24hr) from outside Arrivals goes direct to Sýndagma Square; the #X94 bus (every 15–20min; 7.30am–10pm) heads for Ethnikí Ámyna metro station; and the #X96 bus (every 15–20min; 24hr) runs to Pireás port; all cost €3.20 one way.

Train International trains arrive at the Laríssis train station to the northwest of the city centre, with its own metro station on Line #2. From here, there are trains to all parts of Greece, although for some destinations in the Peloponnese you may need to take the Suburban Rail to Corinth and change there.

Bus Buses from northern Greece and the Peloponnese arrive at Kifissoú 100 bus station, 10min from the centre by bus #051 (5am–midnight). Buses from central Greece arrive closer to the centre at Liossíon 260, north of the train station. From here bus #024 goes to Sýndagma (5am–midnight). Most international buses drop off at the train station or Kifissoú 100; a few will drop you right in the city centre.

Boat If you arrive by boat at Pireás, the easiest way to get to the centre is by metro on Line #1, with the station being a few steps from the quay.

Tourist office The city's main EOT office is at Leofóros Amálias 26 (Mon–Fri 9am–7pm, Sat & Sun 10am–6pm; ⓣ2103 310 392, ⓔinfo_desk@gnto.gr).

FERRY PORTS

The port of **Pireás**, effectively an extension of Athens, is the main terminus for international and inter-island ferries. Get there from Athens by metro: Pireás is the last stop on Line #1 heading southwest from Monastiráki. Once there, blue-and-white buses shuttle passengers around the port for free. The other ports on the east coast of the Attic peninsula, **Rafína and Lávrio**, are alternative departure points for many of the Cycladic and northeastern Aegean islands. Frequent buses connect them with central Athens.

City transport

Tickets For €3 you can buy a ticket valid on all public transport for 24hr. You can also buy a single-journey ticket valid on all forms of transport for €1. All public transport operates daily from 5am–midnight. At the weekend (Fri–Sun), trams operate 24hr.

Bus and trolley Athens' bus and trolley network is extensive but very crowded at peak times. Tickets for buses must be bought in advance from kiosks and validated once on board.

Tram A tram line built for the Olympiad runs from Sýndagma to the seaside resorts of Glyfádha and Faliro.

Metro Line #1 of the metro runs from Pireás to Kifissiá, with central stops at Thissío, Monastiráki and Omónia; Line #2 runs from Áyios Andónios to Áyios Dhimítrios via Sýndagma and a station at the foot of the Acropolis; Line #3 heads east from Monastiráki to Dhoukíssis Plakendías (with special metro cars continuing direct to the airport). Tickets (€0.80) are available at all stations from automatic coin-op dispensers or staffed windows. They must be validated before boarding.

Taxis can be surprisingly difficult to hail and fairly expensive. Taxi drivers will often pick up several passengers along the way, each paying the full fare for their journey – so if you're picked up by an already occupied taxi, memorize the meter reading; you'll pay from then on, including a €1.50 minimum charge.

Accommodation

The city can be packed to the gills in July and August but for much of the rest of the year there is good availability.

Hostels

Athens Backpackers Makri 12, Makriyiánni ⓣ2109 224 044, ⓦwww.backpackers.gr. Relaxed hostel in a prime location with clean, simple dorms, internet access, rooftop bar with Acropolis views and a buzzing atmosphere. The free walking tour and organized bar crawl make it a great place to meet fellow travellers. Dorms €24.

Athens Style Agias Theklas 10, Monastiráki ⓣ2103 225 010, ⓦwww.athenstyle.com. Newly opened hostel with roof terrace, wi-fi, free breakfast and a great location a few minutes' walk from Monastiráki metro. Private rooms and studio apartments (three beds) available. Dorms €20, rooms €60, apartments €100.

Athens Youth Hostel Dhamáreos 75, Pangráti ⓣ2107 519 530, ⓦwww.athens-yhostel.com. In a congenial (if remote) neighbourhood – trolleys #2 or #11 stop nearby – with cooking and laundry facilities. Dorms €12.

Hostel Aphrodite Inárdhou 12, Omónia ⓣ2108 810 589, ⓦwww.hostelaphrodite.com. Friendly and helpful hostel with clean rooms, a travel service, lively bar and free internet. Dorms €15, rooms €45.

International Youth Hostel Víktoros Ougó 16, Omónia ⓣ2105 232 540, ⓔinfo@aiyh-victorhugo.com. Central Athens' cheapest option, an official HI hostel with a cheerful atmosphere and well-kept facilities, though the location in noisy, down-at-heel Omónia isn't wonderful. Dorms €13, rooms €25.

Student and Travellers' Inn Kydhathinéon 16, Pláka ⓣ2103 244 808, ⓦwww.studenttravellersinn.com. Popular, clean and well-run hotel-cum-hostel in a prime location. Cheerful rooms, as well as luggage storage, free internet access and a garden bar with big screen. Dorms €21, rooms €35.

Hotels

John's Place Patróöu 5, Pláka ⓣ2103 229 719. Dark rooms with shared bath, but neat and well kept. Centrally located, it is in a peaceful backstreet off Mitropóleos, with a cheap restaurant on the ground floor. €60.

Marble House Cul-de-sac off Anastasíou Zínni 35, Koukáki ⓣ2109 228 294, ⓦwww.marblehouse.gr. Peaceful, welcoming pension south of the Acropolis. Most rooms en suite and with balcony; all rooms have fans and fridge. Closed Jan and Feb. €45.

Orion Emm. Benáki 105, corner Anexartisías, Exárhia ⓣ2103 302 387, ⓔorion-dryades@mail.com. Quiet, well-run budget hotel across from the Lófos Stréfi park – a steep final walk to get there, yet close to many attractions. Rooftop kitchen and common area with an amazing view. €45.

Phaedra Adhriánou & Herefóndos 16, Pláka ⓣ2103 238 461, ⓔinfo@hotelphaedra.com. Cheerful and clean rooms with a/c, just over half en suite. Excellent location on a pedestrianized street overlooking a Byzantine church and the Acropolis. €60.

Apartments and studios

Athens Studios Veikou 3a, Makriyiánni ⓣ2109 235 811, ⓦwww.athensstudios.gr/web. Well-priced serviced studios run by the team at *Athens Backpackers*. Simple, spacious and clean with kitchen, TV and wi-fi. Extra sleepers can be accommodated on fold-out beds. Six-bed apartment €150.

Campsites

Camping Athens Leofóros Athinón 198–200 ⓣ210 58 14 114, ⓦwww.campingathens.com.gr. 7km west of Athens, this is the closest campsite to the city. Decent facilities, mini-market and snack bar. €8 per person, €5 per tent.

Nea Kifissia Potamoú 60, Néa Kifissiá ⓣ2106 205 646, ⓦwww.camping-neakifissia.gr. In a leafy suburb, this year-round place has its own swimming pool. Metro to Kifissiá then bus #522 or #523 behind the station. €8 per person, €5 per tent.

Eating

Despite the touts and tourist hype, Pláka provides a pleasant evening's setting for a meal, but for good-value, good-quality fare, outlying neighbourhoods such as Psyrrí, Omónia and Exárhia are better bets. Note that Athens sells some of Europe's most expensive coffee, at €3 for an espresso even at an ordinary café: developing a taste for Greek coffee (*ellinikós*) will prove slightly cheaper.

Cafés and ouzerí

Kafenio Dhioskouri Dhioskoúron 13, Pláka. Popular, shady bar/café with an unbeatable view of the ancient agora, where cold drinks and coffees take precedence over slightly pricey snacks. *Mezédhes* €5–9.

To Athinaïkon Themistokléous 2, corner of Panepistimíou, Omónia. Long-established, sophisticated *ouzerí* with marble tables and old posters, popular with local workers at lunch; strong on fresh seafood. Closed Sun.

TREAT YOURSELF

Stay in considerable style at **EP16 apartments** (Epikourou 16, Psyrrí; ⓣ6976 484 135, ⓦwww.EP16.com). Cool, contemporary apartments in a refurbished 1930s block with sleek furnishings, a well-stocked beer fridge (drinks included) and a shady roof terrace with Acropolis views. One- or two-bed apartments €90–110 per night.

Restaurants

Amvrosia Dhrákou 3–5, right by Syngroú-Fix metro, Veïkoú. The best grill on this pedestrian street, always packed. Good takeaway *ghýros* (Greek kebabs), or enjoy a whole roast chicken at outdoor tables. Kebabs €6–9.

Barba Yannis Emmanouíl Benáki 94, Exárhia. Vast menu of inexpensive oven-cooked food, served both indoors – in a charmingly old-fashioned interior – and out. Food is best at lunch, but it's open until 1am Mon–Fri, until 6pm Sat. Mains €5–8.

Doris Praxitelous 30. Daytime-only restaurant with a loyal local clientele. Ignore the dodgy decor and tuck into hearty stews and cheap pasta. Greek doughnuts (*loukoumades*) are a speciality. Mains from €4.

Rozalia Valtetsíou 58, Exárhia. A great all-round *mezédhes*-and-grills taverna with an extensive menu. There's also a garden, open in summer. *Mezédhes* €4.

Taverna tou Psyrri Eskhýlou 12, Psyrrí. Straight-forward taverna that excels in grilled/fried seafood, vegetable starters and wine from basement barrels. Arrive early or wait for a table. Mains €5–8.

Thanasis Mitropóleos 69, Monastiráki. Reckoned the best *souvláki* and Middle Eastern kebabs in this district. Always packed with locals at lunchtime, but worth the wait. Take out or eat in. Kebabs €8.

Drinking and nightlife

Many bars are open as cafés during the day, serving snacks and coffees, but transform themselves in the evenings, often with live music. The bars in Exárhia are popular with local students and are relaxed and more affordable, whilst those in Kolonáki are cool and hip, although more expensive. All clubs charge admission fees, sometimes as much as €15–20, although this usually includes a free drink. Clubs do not start filling up until after midnight but stay open until dawn. In summer much of Athens' nightlife moves to larger outdoor venues on the southern coast, easily accessible by tram which operates round the clock at weekends.

Bars

Art Cafe Themistokléous & Dervenion 60, Exárhia. A small and intimate bar serving everything from

Mythos (Greek beer) and *oúzo* to fruity cocktails. Sit at the cosy downstairs bar or at outdoor tables. Open until 2am. *Oúzo* €3; cocktails €7.

Booze Kolokotroni 57 ⓣ2103 240 944, ⓦwww.boozecooperativa.com. Cavernous, dark space with a cool daytime crowd draped at long tables supping draft beer and playing board games. Stick around at night for DJs, exhibitions and the latest from the Athens avant-garde. Open from 10am until late.

Brettos Kydathinéon 41, Pláka. With colourful bottles and wooden barrels lining the walls, this is a sophisticated spot which oozes reminders of its hundred-year history. Open until 3am. *Oúzo* €3; cocktails €7.

Hoxton Voutadon 42, Gazi ⓣ2103 413 395. Hip, industrial-style bar/club playing rock, electro and pop to Gazi scenesters. Daily 9pm–3am.

Mike's Irish Bar Sinópis 6, Ambelókipi ⓣ2107 776 797. A lively watering hole which has something to suit everyone, including karaoke, live music, and big screens for sport. Guinness drinkers are especially well catered for. Daily 8pm–4am.

Wunderbar Themistokléous 80, Exárhia ⓣ2103 818 577. Handy Exárhia meeting place that's open all day – first café, then bar, and finally club with electro and techno-pop sounds.

Clubs and live music

Decadence Voulgaroktonou 69, Exárhia ⓣ2108 827 045, ⓦwww.decadence.gr. Athens' top alternative/indie venue with popular 1960s nights. Two levels with a bar on the lower floor and club upstairs. Daily 10pm–5am.

Gagarin 205 Liossíon 205, near Metro Attikís ⓣ2108 547 601, ⓦwww.gagarin205.gr. The place to catch the best international up-and-coming indie bands and more established acts.

Lava Bore Filellínon 25, Pláka ⓣ2103 245 335. Cheap and cheesy, Athens' most central option is popular with a young foreign crowd. Admission is €7 which includes a free shot. Daily 10pm–5am.

Venue Km30 on the Athens–Sounion road, Várkiza ⓣ2108 970 333. Lush setting and eclectic selection of dance music, including some Greek, attracts a young crowd. Daily 10pm–5am.

THE ATHENS FESTIVAL

The **Athens Festival** (ⓣ2109 282 900, ⓦwww.greekfestival.gr), from late May to late September, encompasses classical Greek theatre, contemporary dance, classical music, big-name jazz, traditional Greek music and a smattering of rock shows. Most performances take place at the Herodes Atticus Theatre – an atmospheric venue on a warm summer's evening. There are also bus excursions to the great ancient theatre at Epidaurus (see p.545). The main festival box office is at Hatzikhrístou 23; tickets cost from €15.

Entertainment

For up-to-the-minute listings, get yourself a copy of the English-language weekly *Athens News* (ⓦwww.athensnews.gr), which has details of clubs, galleries, concerts and films.

Dora Stratou Dance Theatre Filopáppou Hill ⓣ2103 244 395, ⓦwww.grdance.org. May–Sept: Tues–Sat 9.30pm, Sun 8.15pm. Dancers, singers and folk musicians unite to give spectators an insight into continuing local Greek traditions. Classes are also available. Tickets €15.

Shopping

Books and maps Compendium (Níkis 28, off Sýndagma) has books on Greece, travel guides, magazines and a secondhand section. Eleftheroudhakis (Panepistimíou 17 plus other branches) has the largest foreign-language stock in town, plus maps.

Clothes For high-street shopping, head to the stores along Ermoú.

Markets The Monastiráki flea market is open daily and has an interesting selection of weird and wonderful goods for sale. Sunday is the best time for a visit, as the market expands into the surrounding streets. The nearby Central Market sells local foods.

Souvenirs Tourists head to Pláka where souvenir shops abound, and where leather goods and jewellery take precedence. For gifts check out Lesvos Shop, Athinás 33, for its reasonably priced *oúzo*, wine, olive oil, baklava and honey, as well as toiletries such as olive-oil soap.

Directory

Embassies and consulates Australia, Dhimitríou Soútsou 37 ⓣ2108 704 000; Canada, Ioánni Yennadhíou 4 ⓣ2107 273 400; Ireland, Vassiléos Konstandínou 7 ⓣ2107 232 771; New Zealand, Kifissiás 268 ⓣ2106 874 700; UK, Ploutárhou 1, Kolonáki ⓣ2107 272 600; US, Vassilísis Sofías 91 ⓣ2107 212 951.

STARLIT CINEMA

Outdoor cinema is a charming Greek tradition and there are hundreds of al fresco screens throughout the country. A balmy evening watching a classic in a bougainvillea-draped courtyard with a few beers is hard to beat. Try the centrally located Cine Paris (Ⓣ2103 220 721, Ⓦwww.cineparis.gr) in Athens or the Cinema Kamari (Ⓣ2286 031 974, Ⓦwww.cinekamari.gr) on Santoríni (see p.563).

Hospitals Evangelismós, with its own metro stop, is the most central, but KAT, way out in Maroússi, is the designated Greater Athens emergency ward.
Internet Easy Internet Café, main branch over *Everest* at Pl. Syndágmatos; Museum Internet Café, Patissíon 46; Sofokleous.com Internet Café, Stadhíou 5.
Laundry Angélou Yerónda 10, off Platía Filomoússou Eterías, Pláka.
Left luggage Many hotels store luggage for free. If not, try Pacific Ltd, Níkis 26, Syndágma Ⓣ2103 241 007.
Post offices Main branch Eólou 100, just off Omónia; more convenient one on Mitropóleos, corner Sýndagma.

Moving on

Train Corinth (12/13 daily; 1hr 30min); Kalamáta (3 daily; 7–8hr); Pátra (8/9 daily; 3hr 20min–4hr); Pýrgos (5 daily; 5–6hr); Thessaloníki (11 daily; 4–7hr); Vólos (1 daily; 4hr 30min).
Bus Corfu (3 daily; 9–10hr); Corinth (half-hourly; 1hr 15min); Delphi (6 daily; 3hr); Igoumenitsa (4 daily; 7hr 30min); Ioánnina (9 daily; 6hr 30min); Kalamáta (9 daily; 3hr 30min–4hr 30min); Kefalloniá (3–4 daily; 8hr); Kými, for Skýros ferries (5 daily; 3hr 30min); Mycenae-Fíkhti (hourly; 2hr 30 min); Náfplio (hourly; 2hr 30min); Pátra (every 30min; 2hr 30 min–3hr); Pýrgos (10 daily; 5hr); Rafína (every 30min; 1hr–1hr 30min); Sounion (hourly; 2hr); Spárti (10 daily; 4hr); Thessaloníki (12 daily; 6hr 30min); Tríkala (8 daily; 4hr 30min); Tripoli (12 daily; 2hr 15min); Vólos (12 daily; 4hr 30min); Zákynthos (4 daily; 6hr).
Ferry (from Pireás) to: Crete (5–7 daily; 12hr); Híos (1–3 daily; 6–9hr); Íos (2–3 daily; 3hr 30min–10hr); Kós (2 daily; 7–12hr); Lésvos (1–2 daily; 9–13hr); Mýkonos (4 daily; 3hr 30min–5hr 30min); Náxos (5–7 daily; 5–8hr); Páros (3–4 daily; 3–7hr); Pátmos (4–5 weekly; 7–12hr); Rhodes (1–3 daily; 11–23hr); Santoríni (4–5 daily; 4–16hr); Sífnos (4–6 daily; 2–7hr); Sýros (4–6 daily; 3–5hr).

DAY-TRIPS FROM ATHENS

The 70km of shoreline south of Athens has good but highly developed beaches. At weekends the sands fill fast, as do innumerable bars, restaurants and clubs. But for most visitors, this coast's attraction is at the end of the road. **Cape Sounion** is among the most imposing spots in Greece, and on it stands the fifth-century-BC **Temple of Poseidon** (daily 9.30am–sunset; €4, students free), built in the time of Pericles as part of a sanctuary to the sea god. In summer you've faint hope of solitude unless you arrive before the tours do, but the temple is as evocative a ruin as Greece can offer. Doric in style, it preserves sixteen of its thirty-four columns, and the view is stunning. Below the promontory lie several coves, the most sheltered of which is a five-minute walk east from the car park and site entrance. The main Sounion **beach** is more crowded, but has a group of tavernas at the far end, which – considering the location – are reasonably priced. There's a single **campsite** about 5km short of the cape, the *Bacchus* (Ⓣ2292 039 572, Ⓦwww.tggr.com/camping-bacchus; €7.50 per person, €7 per tent). Buses to Sounion leave every hour from the KTEL terminal on Mavromatéon at the southwest corner of the Pédhion Áreos park in central Athens. They alternate between coastal and inland services, the latter slightly longer and more expensive (the coastal route takes around 2hr).

The Peloponnese

The appeal of the **Peloponnese** is hard to overstate. The **beaches** of this southern peninsula are among the finest and least developed in the country, while its ancient sites include the Homeric palace of Agamemnon at **Mycenae**, the Greek theatre at **Epidaurus** and the sanctuary of **Olympia**, host to the Olympic Games for a millennium. Medieval remains run from the fabulous castle at **Acrocorinth** and the strange tower-houses and frescoed churches of the **Máni**, to the extraordinary Byzantine towns of **Mystra** and **Monemvasiá**. The Peloponnese also boasts Greece's most spectacular train route, an hour-long journey on the **rack-and-pinion rail line** from Dhiakoftó to Kalávryta (see box opposite).

PÁTRA

The city of **PÁTRA** is one of the largest in the country, and connects the mainland to Italy and the Ionian Islands. Unlike many other destinations in the Peloponnese, Pátra is a thriving working city and has a life of its own which extends far beyond tourism, despite the number of travellers passing through. In 2006 the city was named the European Capital of Culture, and unsurprisingly there are enough sites and museums to fill a day's sightseeing, though most people choose to pass through rather more quickly. The city is best enjoyed in the evening, when thousands of party-going university students transform the streets. At the heart of the drinking scene is Agíou Nikoláou, a pedestrian street which is crammed with bars.

> **GETTING TO THE PELOPONNESE**
>
> The usual approach from Athens is on the frequent buses and trains that run via modern **Kórinthos** (Corinth). From Italy and the Adriatic, **Pátra** is the main port of the Peloponnese, although some ferries from the Ionian islands arrive at Kyllíni.

Arrival and information

Train The train station is located by the port on Óthonos Amalías.

Bus Buses arrive at the KTEL Achaia bus station 200m north of the train station.

Ferry Ferries from all departure points arrive at the port close to the bus and train stations.

Tourist office Óthonos Amalías 6 (daily 8am–10pm; ⓣ2610 461 740, ⓦwww.patras.gr). Friendly and well-stocked, with free bikes for hire.

Tourist police At the Italian ferry terminal ⓣ2610 452 512.

Accommodation

Pension Nicos Patréos 3 and Agíou Andhréou 121 ⓣ2610 623 757. Rooms (some en suite) are a little small but this hotel is convenient for the port, train and bus stations and there's a rooftop bar. €40.

Youth Hostel Iróön Polytekhníou 62 ⓣ2610 427 278. Located 1.5km north of the centre, but it does have the cheapest beds in town. Dorms €12.

Moving on

Train Athens (8–9 daily; 3hr 20min–4hr); Corinth (3 daily; 2hr–2hr 30min); Kalamáta (1 daily; 4–5hr); Pýrgos (4 daily; 1hr 30min–2hr).

Bus Ámfissa (4 daily; 3hr); Athens (every 30min; 2hr 30–3hr); Ioánnina (2–4 daily; 5hr); Kalamáta (2 daily; 4hr); Pýrgos (6–10 daily; 2hr).

Ferry Corfu (1 daily; 8–11hr); Igoumenítsa (1 daily; 6–11hr); Itháki (1–2 daily; 3–4hr); Kefalloniá (1–2 daily; 2hr 30min–3hr); Ancona (3 daily; 20hr); Bari (1–2 daily; 16hr); Brindisi (3–7 per week; 13hr); Venice (4–6 per week; 30hr).

ANCIENT CORINTH

Whoever possessed **CORINTH** – the ancient city that displaced Athens as capital of the Greek province in Roman times – controlled both the trade between northern Greece and the Peloponnese, and the short cut between the Ionian and Aegean seas. It's unsurprising, therefore, that the city's history

DHIAKOFTÓ TO KALÁVRYTA RAILWAY

A contender for one of Europe's quirkiest railway journeys, the **rack-and-pinion rail line** from Dhiakoftó to Kalávryta is a must for any visitor to the region. Trains grind their way up vertiginous slopes, rattle through tunnels and clank over crazily narrow bridges on their way through the dramatic Vouraikós Gorge.

is a catalogue of invasions and power struggles, until it was razed by the Romans in 146 BC. The site lay in ruins for a century before being rebuilt, on a majestic scale, by Julius Caesar in 44 BC.

What to see and do

Nowadays, the remains of the city occupy a rambling site below the acropolis hill of Acrocorinth, itself littered with medieval ruins. To explore both you need a full day, or better still, to stay close by. The modern village of **ARHÉA KÓRINTHOS** spreads around the main archeological zone, where you'll find plenty of places to eat and sleep, including a scattering of **rooms** to rent in the backstreets.

The main site

The main excavated site (daily 8am–5/7.30pm; €6) is dominated by the remains of the Roman city. You enter from the south side, which leads straight into the **Roman agora**. The real focus, however, is a survival from the classical Greek era: the fifth-century-BC **Temple of Apollo**, whose seven austere Doric columns stand slightly above the level of the forum.

Acrocorinth

Towering 575m above the lower town, **Acrocorinth** (summer: daily 8.30am–7pm; winter: Tues–Sun 8.30am–3pm; free) is an amazing mass of rock still largely encircled by 2km of wall. During the Middle Ages this ancient acropolis of Corinth became one of Greece's most powerful fortresses. It's a 4km climb up (about 1hr), but well worth it. Amid the sixty-acre site, you wander through a jumble of semi-ruined chapels, mosques, houses and battlements, erected in turn by Greeks, Romans, Byzantines, Franks, Venetians and Ottomans.

Arrival

Bus and train Frequent bus and train services run from Athens and Pátra to modern Kórinthos, from where you can catch a local bus from KTEL Kórinthos or the main square to Arhéa Kórinthos and the adjacent site (hourly; 20min; €1.20).

Accommodation

Shadow Rooms Arhéa Kórinthos ⓣ 2741 031 481. Located along the Kórinthos road heading out of the village, these en-suite rooms open out onto a veranda with beautiful views across the village. Double €50.

Tasos Rooms ⓣ 2741 031 225. A good choice, these are clean rooms with a/c and shared bathrooms. There's a popular restaurant downstairs, too. Double €35.

Moving on

Train Athens (12/13 daily; 1hr 30min); Dhiakoftó (3 daily; 1hr 15min–1hr 30min); Kalamáta (3 daily; 6hr–7hr 30min); Pátra (3 daily; 45min–1hr 30min).

Bus (KTEL bus station) Ancient Corinth (hourly; 20min); Árgos (hourly; 1hr); Kalamáta (7 daily; 3hr 15 min–4hr); Mycenae-Fíkhti (hourly; 30min); Náfplio (7 daily; 1hr 20min); Spárti (8 daily; 4hr).

MYKÍNES (MYCENAE)

Southwest of Corinth, the ancient site of **MYCENAE** is tucked into a fold of the hills just 2km northeast of the modern village of **Mykínes.** Agamemnon's citadel, "well-built Mycenae, rich in gold", as Homer wrote, was uncovered in 1874 by the German archeologist Heinrich Schliemann, who was convinced of a factual basis to Homer's epics. Brilliantly crafted gold and sophisticated architecture bore out the accuracy of Homer's words. The buildings unearthed by

Schliemann show signs of having been occupied from around 1950 BC until 1100 BC, when the town, though still prosperous, was abandoned. No coherent explanation has been found for this event, but war between rival kingdoms was probably a major factor.

What to see and do

You enter the **Citadel of Mycenae** (summer Mon 12.30–7.30pm, Tues–Sun 8am–7.30pm; winter daily 8.30am–5pm; €8, EU students free) through the mighty **Lion Gate**. Inside the walls to the right is **Grave Circle A**, the cemetery which Schliemann believed contained the bodies of Agamemnon and his followers, murdered on their triumphant return from Troy. In fact the burials date from about three centuries before the Trojan war, but they were certainly royal, and the finds are among the richest yet unearthed. Schliemann took the extensive **South House**, beyond the grave circle, to be the Palace of Agamemnon. But a much grander building was later discovered on the summit of the acropolis. Rebuilt in the thirteenth century BC, it is, like all Mycenaean palaces, centred on a **Great Court**. The small rooms to the north are believed to have been royal apartments and in one of them the remains of a red stuccoed bath have led to its fanciful identification as the place of Agamemnon's murder.

Outside the walls of the citadel lay the main part of the town, and extensive remains of **merchants' houses** have been uncovered near to the road. A few minutes' walk down the road is the astonishing **Treasury of Atreus**, a royal burial vault entered through a majestic fifteen-metre corridor.

Arrival

Orientation The village of Mykínes has one main street, where all accommodation and places to eat are located. You will need to travel onward from Fíkhti or the ancient site to get there.

Train There's a train station at Fíkhti, 2km west of Mykínes. If you don't want to walk you can catch a local bus.

Bus Most long-distance KTEL buses will drop you off at Fíkhti, while three daily buses from Náfplio stop at the site entrance.

Tours There are numerous bus tours from Athens, making this a popular day-trip destination.

Accommodation

Camping Atreus ☎2751 076 221. This shady campsite comes equipped with clean facilities, a swimming pool, and a restaurant on site. Late Feb–early Oct. €10.

Hotel Belle Hélène ☎2751 076 225. Once the home of Schliemann, these rooms are spacious and the shared bathrooms are clean. Breakfast included. €40.

Eating

Taverna O Spiros. Surrounded by flowers and foliage, enjoy traditional Greek dishes at this friendly local taverna. Mains €6.

Moving on

Bus Árgos (5 daily; 30min); Náfplio (3 daily; 1hr).

NÁFPLIO

NÁFPLIO, a lively, beautifully sited town with a faded elegance, inherited from when it was briefly modern Greece's first capital, makes an attractive base for exploring the area or for resting up by the sea.

What to see and do

The main fort, the **Palamídhi** (daily: summer 8am–7pm; winter 8am–sunset; €4), is most directly approached by 899 stone-hewn steps up from Polyzoïdhou Street. Within its walls are three self-contained castles, all built by the Venetians in the 1710s. To the west, the **Acronafplía** fortress occupies the ancient acropolis, whose walls were adapted by successive medieval occupants. The third fort, the photogenic **Boúrtzi**, occupies the islet offshore from the harbour and allowed

the Venetians to close the shallow shipping channel with a chain. In the town itself, Platía Syndágmatos, the main square, is a great place to relax over a coffee. There's also a thriving nightlife, with a string of bars along the waterfront at Bouboulínas.

Arrival and information

Train The train station is on the waterfront, 600m north of the bus station.

Bus Buses arrive on Syngroú, just south of the interlocking squares Platía Trión Navárhon and Platía Kapodhístria.

Tourist office The EOT office is at 25-Martíou 2 (daily 9am–1pm & 4–8pm; ⓣ2752 024 444).

Accommodation

Dimitris Bekas Rooms Efthimiopoúlou 26 ⓣ2752 024 594. Don't be disheartened by the stone steps leading up to this welcoming pension – the views from the roof terrace are stunning. It is located close to the centre of the old town. €25.

Hotel Economou Argonaftón 22 ⓣ2752 023 955. A 15min walk out of town and in need of modernizing, but this hotel is one of only a few budget options. Even when it's full, you'll be squeezed in somewhere. Dorms €15, rooms €30.

Eating

Old Mansion Siokóu 7. Bustling taverna serving up Greek favourites to the accompaniment of live traditional music (Fri–Sun). Mains €7–12.

Moving on

Bus Árgos (hourly; 30min); Athens (hourly; 3hr); Epidaurus (4 daily; 45min); Mycenae (3–4 daily; 1hr); Trípoli (2–4 daily; 1hr).

EPIDAURUS

From the sixth century BC to Roman times, **EPIDAURUS**, 30km east of Náfplio, was a major spa and religious centre; its **Sanctuary of Asclepius** was the most famous of all shrines dedicated to the god of healing. The magnificently preserved 14,000-seat theatre (daily 8am–5/7pm; €6, Sun free) is the venue for evening classical-theatre **performances** (June–Aug Fri & Sat; ⓦwww.greekfestival.gr) during the Athens and Epidaurus Festival. If you want to camp, *Camping Nicholas*, in Paleá Epidaurus (ⓣ2753 041 218, ⓦwww.nicolasgikas.gr; €6 per person, €5 per tent), has wonderful pitches among orange and mulberry groves, right on the beach. Elsewhere, try *Hotel Alkyon*, Asklipíou 195 (ⓣ2753 022 002; €35), 5km north of the theatre at **Lygourió**.

MYSTRA

A glorious, airy place, hugging a steep flank of the Taïyetos mountains, **MYSTRA** is an astonishingly complete Byzantine city that once sheltered a population of some twenty thousand. The castle on its summit was built in 1249 by Guillaume II de Villehardouin, fourth Frankish Prince of the Morea (as the Peloponnese was then known), and together with the fortresses of Monemvasiá and the Máni it guarded his territory. In 1262 the Byzantines drove out the Franks and established the Despotate of Mystra.

To explore the site of the **Byzantine city** (daily: summer 8am–8pm; winter 8am–2pm; €5), it makes sense to take the bus from Spárti (ten daily; €1.20) which stops at Néos Mystrás and then continues up the hill. It's best to make for the top entrance, then explore a leisurely downhill route. Following this course, the first identifiable building you come to is the fourteenth-century church of **Ayía Sofía**. The **Kástro**, reached by a path that climbs directly from the upper gate, maintains the Frankish design of its thirteenth-century construction, though modified by successive occupants. Heading down from Ayía Sofía, there are two possible routes. The right fork winds past the ruins of a Byzantine mansion, while the left fork passes the massively fortified **Náfplio Gate** and the vast, multi storey complex of the **Despots'**

Palace. At the **Monemvasiá Gate**, linking the upper and lower towns, turn right for the **Pandánassa convent**, which is perhaps the finest that survives in the town. Further down on this side of the lower town make sure you see the diminutive **Perívleptos monastery**, whose single-domed church, partly carved out of the rock, contains Mystra's most complete cycle of frescoes. The **Mitrópolis**, or cathedral, immediately beyond the gateway, ranks as the oldest of Mystra's churches, built from 1270 onward.

SPÁRTI

SPÁRTI (ancient Sparta, though there's little left to see) is a good alternative base to Mystra, with cheaper accommodation. Spárti has everything you would expect from a town of its size, including vibrant bars and cafés. If you want to see Mystra without sacrificing an evening's worth of entertainment, then make it a day-trip from Spárti.

Arrival

Bus The KTEL bus station is at the far eastern end of Lykoúrgou, a 10min walk from the centre. Buses for Mystra leave from here.
Internet Ladas Lykoúrgou 130 ⓣ2731 083 016, ⓦwww.cafe-ladas.gr. €2/hour.

Accommodation

Apollon Thermopýlon 84 ⓣ2731 022 491. This friendly hotel has plenty of clean and comfortable en-suite rooms. €55.
Castle View Néos Mystrás ⓣ2731 083 303, ⓦwww.castleview.gr. Shady and quiet, this campsite is within walking distance of the village. Buses to Néos Mystrás stop at the entrance. April–Oct. €6 per person, €4 per tent.
Hotel Cecil Paleológou 125 ⓣ2731 024 980. A warm welcome awaits at this small hotel, with clean en-suite rooms equipped with a/c and TV. €55.
Paleologio Mystras 2.5km from Spárti ⓣ2731 022 724. Well-run campsite with good facilities. Buses to Néos Mystrás stop at the entrance. Open all year. €4 per person, €7 per tent.

Eating and drinking

Diethenes Paleológou 105. The garden is an oasis of calm, especially atmospheric in the evenings. Hearty Greek favourites (around €6) are dished up to the sound of birdsong.
Ministry Paleológou 84. One of the most popular bars in town, with tables spilling onto the pavement and a sophisticated, cocktail-quaffing crowd.

Moving on

Bus Areópoli (2 daily; 2hr); Athens (10 daily; 4hr); Corinth (8 daily; 2hr); Kalamáta (2 daily; 2hr 30min); Monemvasiá (3 daily; 2hr 30min); Ýíthio (5 daily; 1hr).

MONEMVASIÁ

Set impregnably on a great eruption of rock connected to the mainland by a causeway, the Byzantine seaport of **MONEMVASIÁ** is a place of grand, haunted atmosphere. At the start of the thirteenth century it was the Byzantines' sole possession in the Morea, eventually being taken by the Franks in 1249 after three years of siege. Regained by the Byzantines as part of the ransom for the captured Guillaume de Villehardouin, it served as the chief commercial port of the Despotate of the Morea. At its peak in the Byzantine era, Monemvasiá had a population of almost sixty thousand.

What to see and do

A causeway connects mainland **Yéfira** to Monemvasiá. The twenty-minute walk provides some wonderful views, but there is also a free shuttle bus in season. The **Lower Town** once sheltered forty churches and over 800 homes, though today a single main street harbours most of the restored houses, plus cafés, tavernas and a scattering of shops. The foremost monument is the **Mitrópolis**, the cathedral built by Emperor Andronikos II Komnenos in 1293, and the largest medieval church in southern Greece. Across the square, the tenth-century domed church of **Áyios Pétros** was

transformed by the Ottomans into a mosque and is now a small **museum** of local finds (Mon noon–7.30pm, Tues–Sun 8am–7.30pm; free). Towards the sea is a third church, the **Khrysafítissa**, with its bell hanging from an old acacia tree in the courtyard. The climb to the **Upper Town** is highly worthwhile, not least for the solitude. Its fortifications, like those of the lower town, are substantially intact; within, the site is a ruin, though infinitely larger than you could imagine from below.

Arrival and information

Bus Buses arrive in the village of Yéfira on the mainland, where most accommodation is located. The bus stop is outside Malvasia Travel.
Information There is no tourist office, but Malvasia Travel (see above) is helpful. It also sells bus tickets.

Accommodation

Akrogiali Yéfira ⓣ2732 061 360. The best budget option: nine spotless rooms in the centre of town. Double €45.
Camping Paradise 3.5km south of Yéfira ⓣ2732 061 123, ⓦwww.monemvasia-online.com/camping. The closest campsite is near a decent beach, and has plenty of facilities including internet access. March–Nov. €8–10.

Eating

Matoula Monemvasiá. This restaurant has plenty of fresh fish on offer, and a shady terrace on which to enjoy the food and the views. Mains €8–12.
To Kanoni Monemvasiá. A small and friendly place with split-level seating, offering a variety of vistas. Also open for breakfast. Mains €7–10.

TREAT YOURSELF

Malvasia Monemvasiá ⓣ2732 061 323, ⓦwww.malvasia-hotel.gr. If Monemvasiá has cast its enchanting spell over you, then splash out to stay on the rock itself. *Malvasia* is a peaceful hotel full of character and charm, retaining many traditional features, and the views are breathtaking. €85.

Moving on

Bus Athens (4–6 daily; 5hr); Corinth (3 daily; 4hr 30min); Spárti (5–6 daily; 1hr 30min); Trípoli (3 daily; 2hr 30min).

YÍTHIO

YÍTHIO, Sparta's ancient port, is the gateway to the dramatic Máni peninsula and one of the south's most attractive seaside towns. Its low-key harbour, with occasional ferries, has a graceful nineteenth-century waterside, while out to sea, tethered by a long narrow causeway, is the islet of **Marathoníssi** (ancient Kranae), where Paris and Helen of Troy spent their first night after her abduction from Sparta.

Arrival

Bus Buses from Athens and Spárti drop you close to the centre of town, at the bus station which is located on Vassiléos Pávlou.

Accommodation

Meltemi On the Yíthio–Areópoli road ⓣ2733 022 833, ⓦwww.campingmeltemi.gr. Good facilities, and also hires out bungalows. April–Oct. €6 per person, €5 per tent.
Rooms Matina Vassiléos Pávlou 19 ⓣ2733 022 518. Little English is spoken but the staff are welcoming. Rooms are spacious and airy, and there's a small terrace too. €50.
Saga Pension Tzanetáki ⓣ2733 023 220, ⓦwww.sagapension.gr. Spacious and comfortable rooms, most with balconies towards the sea. There's also a popular restaurant downstairs. €50.

Eating

En Plo Vassiléos Pávlou 27. Tiled floors, wood beams and stone walls decorate the interior, or there's outdoor seating right on the waterfront. Mains €5–7.
To Korali Plateia Yíthio. This is the place to do as the locals do – order some *oúzo* and watch the world go by from the corner of the square.

Moving on

Bus to: Areópoli (4 daily; 30min); Athens (4–6 daily; 5hr); Corinth (6 daily; 2hr 45min); Spárti (6 daily; 50min); Trípoli (3 daily; 2hr 30min).

THE MÁNI PENINSULA

The southernmost peninsula of Greece, the **Máni peninsula**, stretches from Yíthio in the east and Kalamáta in the west down to Cape Ténaro, mythical entrance to the underworld. It's a wild and arid landscape with an idiosyncratic culture and history: nowhere else in Greece seems so close to its medieval past. There are numerous opportunities for outdoor activities too. The quickest way into it is to take a bus from Yíthio to **AREÓPOLI**, gateway to the so-called Inner Máni. For onward travel to the Outer Máni, a change at Ítylo is involved.

Arrival

Bus Buses from Yíthio drop you in the centre of town, by the main square. The bus station is behind the small church – look for the KTEL sign outside.

Accommodation

Hotel Kouris Main Square ⓣ 2733 051 340. All rooms are en suite and have balconies, and it's the cheapest option in town. Double €40–50.

Pyrgos Tsimova Behind the Church of Taxiárhes ⓣ 2733 051 301. A renovated tower-house in the old lower town, full of character and charm. Double €50.

Moving on

Bus Ítylo (3 daily; 20min); Yíthio (4 daily; 30min).

Outer Máni

More attractions lie to the north of Areópoli, along the eighty-kilometre road to Kalamáta, which has views as dramatic and beautiful as any in Greece. There are numerous cobbled paths for hiking and a series of **small beaches**, beginning at **ÁYIOS NIKÓLAOS**, which has fish tavernas and rooms, and extending more or less through to Kardhamýli. **STOÚPA**, which has possibly the best beaches, is now geared very much to British tourism, with several small hotels, two **campsites**, supermarkets and tavernas. **KARDHAMÝLI**, 8km north, remains a beautiful place despite its commercialization and busy road, with a long pebbly beach and a restored tower-house quarter.

Arrival

Bus Buses stop in Kardhamýli next to the main square. There is no bus station, but Wunder Travel has bus timetables.

Accommodation

Iphigenia Rooms Kardhamýli ⓣ 2721 073 648. A wonderful base for exploring the area. Rooms have small kitchenettes and balconies. €35.

Lela's Kardhamýli ⓣ 2721 073 541, or 6977 71 6017 in winter. Tucked away (look for signs from the main road), these rooms occupy prime position beside the sea. There's also a good taverna (see below). €45.

Eating and drinking

Aman Café Kardhamýli. Next to *Lela's*, this lively bar, open all day, is the perfect place to watch the sunset from the leafy terrace. Cocktails €7.50.

Lela's Kardhamýli. With an ever-changing menu, *Lela's* is ideal for a delicious, home-cooked meal. Go early to grab a table with the best views. Mains €8.

Moving on

Bus Kalamáta (4 daily; 1hr).

OLYMPIA

The historic resonance of **OLYMPIA**, which for over a millennium hosted the Panhellenic Games, is rivalled only by Delphi or Mycenae. Its site, too, ranks with this company, for although the ruins are confusing, the setting is as perfect as could be imagined: a luxuriant valley of wild olive and plane trees beside the twin rivers of Alfiós and Kladhéos, overlooked by the pine-covered hill of Krónos.

What to see and do

The entrance to the **ancient site** (May–Oct daily 8am–7pm; Nov–April

Mon–Fri 8am–5pm, Sat & Sun 8.30–3pm; €6, or €9 with museum) leads along the west side of the sacred precinct wall, past a group of public and official buildings. Here the fifth-century-BC sculptor Pheidias was responsible for creating the great gold-and-ivory cult statue in the focus of the precinct, the great Doric **Temple of Zeus**. The smaller **Temple of Hera**, behind, was the first built here; prior to its completion in the seventh century BC, the sanctuary had only open-air altars. Rebuilt in the Doric style in the sixth century BC, it's the most complete structure on the site. However, it's the 200-metre track of the **Stadium** itself that makes sense of Olympia: the start and finish lines are still there, as are the judges' thrones in the middle and seating banked to each side, which once accommodated up to thirty thousand spectators. Finally, in the **archeological museum** (May–Oct Mon 12.30pm–7.30pm, Tues–Sun 8am–7.30pm; Nov–April Mon 10.30am–5pm, Tues–Sun 8.30am–4/5pm; €6, or €9 with site), the centrepiece is the statuary from the Temple of Zeus, displayed in the vast main hall. Most famous of the individual sculptures is the **Hermes of Praxiteles**, dating from the fourth century BC; one of the best-preserved of all classical sculptures, it retains traces of its original paint.

Arrival and information

Train and bus Most people arrive at Olympia via Pýrgos, which has frequent buses and trains to the site. The train station is close to the town's centre. The bus stop is at one end of Praxitéles Kondhýli.

Tourist office On Praxitéles Kondhýli (daily 8am–3pm; ⓣ2624 023 100), with useful information in the window.

Accommodation

Camping Diana ⓣ2624 022 314. The closest campsite, 1km from the site, has a pool and good facilities. March–Dec. €7 per person, €5 per tent.

Youth Hostel Praxitéles Kondhýli 18 ⓣ2624 022 580. This dingy hostel is in the centre of town but this is its only selling point. There's hot water only in the mornings and evenings, and an 11pm curfew. Dorms €10.

Eating

Symposio Karamanli. This taverna is located away from the neon lights of the main drag, and this is reflected in the prices. Good food, welcoming atmosphere. Grills €6–8.

Moving on

Bus Pýrgos (hourly; 45min); Trípoli (1–3 daily; 3hr 30min).

The centre and north

Central and northern Greece has an indeterminate character, encompassing both ancient and modern, from the mythical home of the gods on **Mount Olympus** to the urban splendour of **Thessaloníki**, and a plethora of landscapes. The highlights lie at the fringes: site of the ancient oracle **Delphi** above all, and further northwest at the otherworldly rock-monasteries of **Metéora**. Access to these monasteries is

ONWARD TRAVEL

Igoumenítsa is Greece's third passenger port after Pireás and Pátra, with almost hourly ferries to Corfu; several daily to and from Italy (Ancona, Bari, Brindisi and Venice) make it a likely arrival point. The tourist office is next to the customs house on the old quay (daily 8am–2pm; ⓣ2665 022 227), while the bus station sits two blocks back from here in the town centre, on Kyprou. There are frequent bus and train services **from Thessaloníki** on to Bulgaria, Romania or Turkey, though you should get any necessary visas in Athens.

through **Kalambáka**, beyond which the **Katára pass** over the Píndhos mountains provides a stunning backdrop. En route lies **Métsovo**, perhaps the easiest location for a taste of mountain life, though blatantly commercialized. Nearby **Ioánnina**, once the stronghold of the notorious Ali Pasha, still retains some character. To the south, closer to Athens, is the monastery of **Ósios Loukás**, one of Greece's finest Byzantine buildings and worth a detour en-route to Delphi.

DELPHI

With its position on a high terrace overlooking a great gorge, in turn dwarfed by the ominous crags of Parnassós, it's easy to see why the ancients believed the extraordinary site of **DELPHI** to be the centre of the Earth. But what confirmed this status was the discovery of a chasm that exuded strange vapours and reduced all comers to frenzied, incoherent and obviously prophetic mutterings. For over a thousand years a steady stream of pilgrims toiled their way up the dangerous mountain paths to seek divine direction, until the oracle eventually expired with the demise of paganism in the fourth century AD.

What to see and do

You enter the **Sacred Precinct of Apollo** (daily: summer 7.30am–7.30pm; winter 8am–5pm; €6, or €9 with museum) by way of a small agora, enclosed by ruins of Roman porticoes and shops for the sale of votive offerings. The paved **Sacred Way** begins after a few stairs, zigzagging uphill between the foundations of memorials and treasuries to the **Temple of Apollo**. The theatre and stadium used for the main events of the Pythian games are on terraces above the temple. The **theatre**, built in the fourth century BC, was closely connected with Dionysus, god of drama and wine. A steep path leads up through pine groves to the stadium, which was banked with stone seats in Roman times.

The **museum** (Mon noon–6.30pm, Tues–Sun 7.30am–7.15pm) contains a collection of ancient sculpture matched only by finds on the Acropolis in Athens; the most famous exhibit is *The Charioteer*, one of the few surviving bronzes of the fifth century BC. Following the road east of the sanctuary towards Aráhova, you reach a sharp bend. To the left, the celebrated **Castalian spring** still flows from a cleft in the cliffs, where visitors to Delphi were obliged to purify themselves. Across and below the road from the spring is the **Marmaria** or Sanctuary of Athena Pronoia (same hours as main site; free), the "Guardian of the Temple". The precinct's most conspicuous building is the **Tholos**, a fourth-century BC rotunda whose purpose remains a mystery. Above the Marmaria, a **gymnasium** also dates from the fourth century BC, though it was later enlarged by the Romans.

Arrival and information

Delphi is 150km northwest of Athens – an easy day-trip by bus.

Bus The small bus station is on Pávlou & Fredheríkis, at the opposite end of the town to the archeological site.

Tourist office Above the town hall on Pávlou & Fredheríkis (Mon–Fri 7.20am–2.30pm; ⓣ 2265 082 900).

Accommodation

Apollon 1.5km west towards Ámfissa ⓣ 2265 082 750, ⓦ www.apolloncamping.gr. A good camping option, and the closest to Delphi. Open all year. €7.50 per person, €5 per tent.

Athina Pávlou & Fredheríkis 55 ⓣ 2265 082 239. Most rooms at this guesthouse face the valley for spectacular views, and all have fans. Breakfast included. April–Oct. €30.

Sibylla Pávlou & Fredheríkis 9 ⓣ 2265 082 335, ⓦ www.sibylla-hotel.gr. The recently

ÓSIOS LOUKÁS

The monastery of **Ósios Loukás** may be remote, but its Byzantine mosaics – the finest in the country – are definitely worth seeking out. From Delphi, take the bus to Livadhiá and then on to Dhistomo, from where you can take a taxi the remaining 8km.

renovated rooms are spotless and comfortable and the staff are helpful. Close to the site. €24.

Eating

Iy Skala On the stair-street opposite the *Sibylla*. A small taverna serving a good selection of set menus (€8–10).

Taverna Vakchos Apóllonos. This taverna combines a wonderful setting and mouthwatering food. The menu includes plenty of home-made fare, including wine and baklava. Mains €6–8.

Moving on

Bus Athens (6 daily; 3hr); Pátra (1 daily; 3hr); Thessaloníki (2 daily; 5hr).

KALAMBÁKA AND METÉORA

Few places are more exciting to arrive at than **KALAMBÁKA** and the neighbouring village of **Kastráki**. Your eye is immediately drawn to the weird grey cylinders of rock overhead – these are the outlying monoliths of the extraordinary valley of **Metéora**. The earliest religious communities in the valley emerged during the late tenth century, when hermits made their homes in the caves that score many of the rocks. In 1336 they were joined by two monks from Mount Áthos, one of whom established the first monastery here.

What to see and do

Today, put firmly on the map by films such as the James Bond classic *For Your Eyes Only*, the four most visited monasteries are essentially museums. Only two others, Ayías Triádhos and Ayíou Stefánou, continue to function with a primarily religious purpose. Each monastery levies an **admission charge** of €2 and operates a strict **dress code**: skirts for women (supplied at the monasteries), long trousers for men and covered arms for both sexes.

Beyond the monastery of **Ayíou Stefánou**, firmly planted on a massive pedestal, stretches a chaos of spikes, cones and stubbier, rounded cliffs. Visiting the monasteries demands a full day, which means staying two nights nearby.

Ayíou Nikoláou Anápavsa and Varlaám

From Kastráki, the fourteenth-century **Ayíou Nikoláou Anápavsa** (9am–3.30pm, closed Fri) is reached first. Some 250m past the car park and stairs to Ayíou Nikoláou, a clear path leads up a ravine between assorted monoliths; soon, at a fork, you've the option of bearing left for Megálou Meteórou or right to **Varlaám** (9am–3/4pm, closed Thurs; Nov–April also closed Fri), which ranks as one of the oldest and most beautiful monasteries in the valley.

Megálou Meteórou and Roussánou

From the fork below Varlaám the path also takes you northwest to **Megálou Meteórou** (9am–4/5pm, closed Tues; Nov–April also closed Wed), the grandest of the monasteries and also the highest. Next you follow trails until you reach the signed access path for the tiny, compact convent of **Roussánou** (April–Nov Thurs–Tues 9am–5pm; Dec–March Thurs–Tues 9am–2pm).

Ayías Triádhos and Ayíou Stefánou

It's less than a half-hour from Roussánou to the vividly frescoed **Ayías Triádhos** (April–Nov Fri–Wed

9am–5pm; Dec–March Fri–Tues 10am–3pm), approached up 130 steps carved through a tunnel in the rock. **Ayíou Stefánou** (9/9.30am–1/1.30pm & 3/3.30–5/5.30pm, closed Mon), the last of the monasteries, lies a further fifteen minutes' walk east of Ayías Triádhos; bombed in World War II, it's the one to omit if you've run out of time.

Arrival and information

Train The train station is 100m south of the bus station in Kalambáka.
Bus Buses arrive at the bus station in Kalambáka on Ikonomou. All long-distance buses from Thessaloníki or the south involve a change at Tríkala. To get to Kastráki you can either walk for 20min along the sign-posted road, or take one of the hourly buses (in season only) from Platía Dhimarhíou, at the fountain, two of which continue to Metéora (Mon–Fri 9am & 12.30pm, Sat & Sun 8.30am & 1pm).
Tourist office Next to the bus stop.
Internet *All Time Café*, on the Metéora road, Kastráki (daily 8pm–3am).

Accommodation

Hotel Meteora Ploutárhou 13 ⓣ2432 022 367, ⓦwww.meteorahotels.com. The pick of the Kalambáka hotels. En-suite rooms, delicious breakfasts and great value for the high standard. €35.
Plakias Not far from the square, Kastráki ⓣ2432 022 504, ⓦwww.meteora-plakias.gr. A homely feel accompanies these clean and crisp en-suite rooms, although the ground-floor rooms sacrifice their views of Metéora. €25.
Hotel Tsikeli Kastráki ⓣ2432 022 438, ⓦwww.tsikelihotel.gr. A wonderful, relaxing guesthouse, with simple rooms and stunning views. Breakfast is served in the lush garden. €40.
Vrachos ⓣ2432 022 293, ⓦwww.campingkastraki.gr. A well-equipped campsite with a large swimming pool and caravans to rent. Also offers rock-climbing lessons and bike hire. €6 per person, €4 per tent.

Eating

Bakalarkaia Below the square and church in Kastráki, a traditional taverna, with cheap fried hake and house wine. Mains €5–7.
Paradhissos Kastráki. This taverna offers a spacious terrace with beautiful views and a variety of Greek specialities. Mains €5–8.

Moving on

Train Athens (2 daily; 5hr).
Bus Ioánnina (2–3 daily; 3hr); Métsovo (3 daily; 1hr 30min); Tríkala (hourly; 30min).

IOÁNNINA

The fortifications of **IOÁNNINA**'s old town, former capital of the Albanian Muslim chieftain Ali Pasha, are punctuated by towers and minarets. From this base Ali, "the Lion of Ioánnina", prised from the Ottoman Empire a fiefdom encompassing much of western Greece. Disappointingly, most of the city is modern and undistinguished; however, the fortifications of Ali's citadel, the **Kástro**, survive more or less intact. Apart from this, the most enjoyable quarter is the old **bazaar** area, outside the citadel's main gate.

On the far side of the lake from Ioánnina, the island of **Nissí** is served by water-buses (every 30min; €1.70) from the quay northwest of the Froúrio. Its village, founded during the sixteenth century, is flanked by several beautiful, diminutive monasteries, with the best thirteenth-century frescoes in **Filanthropinón**.

Arrival and information

Bus The main bus station is at Zozimádhon 4, serving most points north and west; a smaller terminal at Bizaníou 19 connects villages south and east.
Tourist office Dhodhónis 39 (Mon–Fri 7.30am–2.30pm, also open evening and Sat morning in summer), south of the centre; can provide information on the whole Epirus region.
Internet The Web at Pyrsinélla 21 (24hr; €2.50/hr).

Accommodation

Dellas Rooms Nissí ⓣ2651 081 494. If you want to stay on the island, try these basic, family-run rooms. €30.
Filyra Andhroníkou Paleológou 18 ⓣ2651 083 560. Modern, bright studios with individual touches located in the historic Kástro. Small kitchenettes are ideal for self-catering. €65.

Limnpoula Kanari 10 ⓣ2651 025 265. This pleasant lakeshore campsite is 2km out of town on the Pérama/airport road. €8 per person, €4 per tent.

Eating

Fysa Roufa Avéroff 55. Open 24 hours a day, this popular restaurant serves oven-baked dishes. Mains €5–8.

To Rembetiko Platía Georgíou 14. This friendly taverna offers traditional fare at reasonable prices, with *rembétika* music playing in the background. Mains €4–6.

Moving on

Bus Athens (9 daily; 7hr 30min); Igoumenítsa (8 daily; 2hr 30min); Métsovo (4 daily; 1hr 30min); Pátra (4 daily; 3hr 30min); Thessaloníki (6 daily; 5hr); Tríkala (2–3 daily; 3–4hr).

THESSALONÍKI

Second city of Greece, **THESSALONÍKI** feels more Balkan-European and modern than Athens. The city's **nightlife** is buzzing, with many bars and clubs concentrated in the regenerated warehouse area of Ladhádhika around the port. During the Byzantine era, it was the second city after Constantinople, reaching a cultural "Golden Age" until the Ottoman conquest in 1430. As recently as the 1920s, the city's population was as mixed as any in the Balkans: besides the Ottoman Turks, who had been in occupation for close on five centuries, there were Slavs, Albanians and the largest European **Jewish** community of the period – eighty thousand at its peak.

What to see and do

Today, Thessaloníki boasts some excellent sights – including a superb Archeological Museum and some lovely frescoed Byzantine churches – but the most obvious pleasures of Greece's second city are to be found in its myriad bars, first-rate restaurants and pumping clubs.

The Archeological Museum

The renovated **Archeological Museum** (Mon 1.30–8pm, Tues–Sun 8am–8pm; €6) is a few paces from the White Tower, the last surviving bastion of the city's medieval walls. The museum contains finds from the tombs of Philip II of Macedon and others at the ancient Macedonian capital of Aegae (Vergina). They include startling amounts of gold and silver – masks, crowns, necklaces, earrings, bracelets – all of extraordinary craftsmanship, although the exhibits are now depleted following the transfer of the star items back to a purpose-built subterranean gallery at Vergína itself (see p.556).

The Museum of Byzantine Culture and Black Tower

The well-curated **Museum of Byzantine Culture** (same hours; €4), just east of the archeological museum, is also worth a look for its finely preserved tombs, splendid mosaics, icons and jewellery. Close by, on the waterfront, Thessaloníki's enduring landmark, the **White Tower** (Tues–Sun 8.30am–3pm; €4), has reopened after a sensitive refurbishment and now tells the story of the city through a high-tech multimedia exhibit.

Churches

Among the city's many **churches**, the best three are Áyios Yeóryios, originally a Roman rotunda, decorated with superb mosaics emerging from long restoration; Áyios Dhimítrios, with more seventh-century mosaics of the patron saint in various guises; and still-later Ayía Sofía, with mosaics of the *Ascension* and the *Virgin Enthroned*.

The Photography and Contemporary Art museums

If, after all the icons and alabaster you feel like something a little more contemporary, the excellent portside **Museum of Photography** (Tues–Fri 11am–7pm,

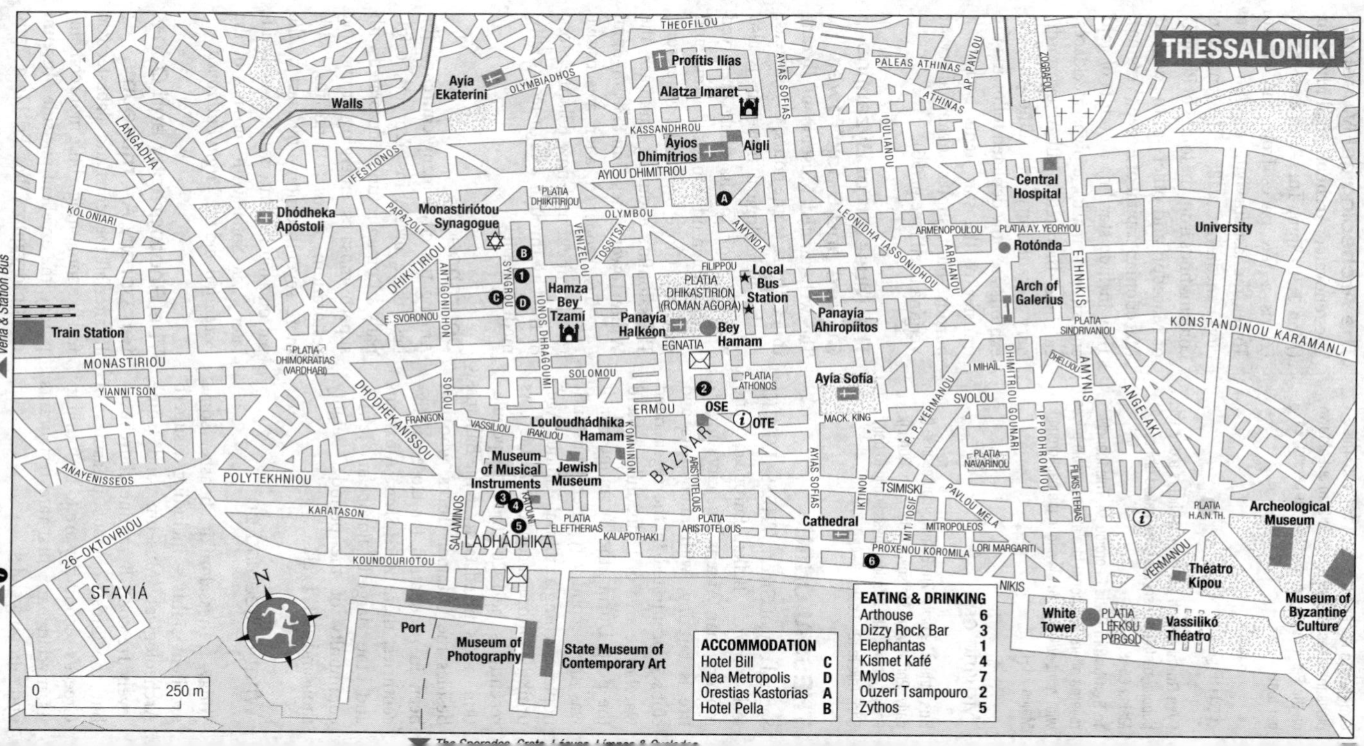
THESSALONÍKI
Profítis Ilías
Ayía Ekateríni
Walls
Alatza Imaret
Áyios Dhimítrios
Aigli
Dhódheka Apóstoli
Monastiriótou Synagogue
Hamza Bey Tzamí
Panayía Halkéon
Bey Hamam
Local Bus Station
Panayía Ahiropiítos
Central Hospital
University
Rotónda
Arch of Galerius
Train Station
Ayía Sofía
OSE
OTE
Louloudhádhika Hamam
Museum of Musical Instruments
Jewish Museum
BAZAAR
LADHÁDHIKA
Cathedral
Archeological Museum
Théatro Kípou
White Tower
Vassilikó Théatro
Museum of Byzantine Culture
Port
Museum of Photography
State Museum of Contemporary Art
SFAYIÁ
Véria & Station Bus
0
250 m
ACCOMMODATION
Hotel Bill C
Nea Metropolis D
Orestias Kastorias A
Hotel Pella B
EATING & DRINKING
Arthouse 6
Dizzy Rock Bar 3
Elephantas 1
Kismet Kafé 4
Mylos 7
Ouzerí Tsampouro 2
Zythos 5
THEOFILOU
OLYMBIADHOS
PALEAS ATHINAS
AP. PAVLOU
ATHINAS
ZOGRAFOU
AYIAS SOFIAS
KASSANDHROU
IOULIANDU
LANGADHA
IFESTIONOS
AYIOU DHIMITRIOU
PLATIA DHIKITIRIOU
OLYMBOU
KOLONIARI
PAPAZOLI
LEONIDHA IASSONIDHOU
AMYNDA
ARMENOPOULOU
PLATIA AY. YEORYIOU
ETHNIKIS
DHIKITIRIOU
ANTIGONIDHON
SYNGROU
VENIZELOU
TOSSITSA
FILIPPOU
PLATIA DHIKASTIRION (ROMAN AGORA)
ARRIANOU
IONOS DHRAGOUMI
E. SVORONOU
EGNATIA
PLATIA SINDRIVANIOU
KONSTANDINOU KARAMANLI
PLATIA DHIMOKRATIAS (VARDHARI)
MONASTIRIOU
SOLOMOU
PLATIA ATHONOS
I MIHAIL
DHIMITRIOU GOUNARI
AMYNIS
DHELLIOU
ANGELAKI
YIANNITSON
SOFOU
FRANGON
ERMOU
MACK. KING
P. P. YERMANOU
SVOLOU
DHODHEKANISSOU
VASSILIOU
IRAKLIOU
KOMNINON
PLATIA NAVARINOU
IPPODHROMIOU
ANAYENISSEOS
POLYTEKHNIOU
ARISTOTELOUS
AYIAS SOFIAS
IKTINOU
TSIMISKI
PAVLOU MELA
FILIKIS ETERIAS
KARATASON
SALAMINOS
KATOUNI
PLATIA ELEFTHERIAS
PLATIA ARISTOTELOUS
KALAPOTHAKI
MIT. IOSIF
MITROPOLEOS
PLATIA H.A.N.TH.
YERMANOU
26-OKTOVRIOU
KOUNDOURIOTOU
PROXENOU KOROMILA
LORI MARGARITI
NIKIS
PLATIA LEFKOU PYRGOU

Sat & Sun 11am–9pm; free) and the **State Museum of Contemporary Art** (daily 10am–2pm & 6–10pm; free) are both worth a few hours' exploration.

Arrival and information

Air From the airport, 16km out at Mikrá, buses #78 (every 15–20min; 5.30am–11pm) and #78N (every 30min; 11pm–5.30am) run to the train station and KTEL terminal.
Train The train station on the west side of town is a short walk from the central grid of streets and the waterfront.
Bus Buses use a KTEL terminal 3km southwest of the centre; city buses #8 & #31 go there from Egnatía (€0.60).
Ferry The port is at the southern edge of the city, close to Ladhádhika.
Tourist office A helpful tourist office is located at Tsimiskí 136 (Mon–Sat 9am–9pm & Sun 9am–3pm; ⓣ2310 221 100).

Accommodation

Hotel Bill Syngroú 29, corner Amvrossíou ⓣ2310 537 666. Rooms (some with private bathroom) are dated and drab but are the cheapest in town. €30.
Hotel Pella Íonos Dhragoúmi 63 ⓣ2310 524 221. A friendly and accommodating hotel with small but well-equipped, spotless rooms. €50.
Nea Mitropolis Syngroú 22 ⓣ2310 530 363, ⓦwww.neametropolis.gr. The beige paint job doesn't do it many favours but the sense of faded grandeur has a certain charm. Big rooms and a central location make this hotel a pleasing option. €50.
Orestias Kastorias Agnóstou Stratiótou 14 ⓣ2310 276 517, ⓦwww.okhotel.gr. Housed in a recently renovated Neoclassical building, the simple rooms have balconies with views towards the Roman Forum or Áyios Dhimítrios. €64.

Eating

Ouzerí Tsampouro Alley off Platía Áthonos. There are plenty of *ouzerís* in this area, and this is one of the most popular. Striking black-and-white photos decorate the outside walls. *Souvláki* €5.
Zythos Platía Katoúni 5. A hip bar-restaurant, with dozens of well-kept foreign beers and an innovative menu. Mains €6–8.

Drinking and nightlife

Arthouse Vogatsikou 4. An excellent, small club hosting the coolest nights in town and playing everything from reggae to techno with aplomb. Top international DJs occasionally pass through.
Dizzy Rock Bar Egiptou 5. It may look closed from the outside, but this edgy bar keeps on rocking until the early hours.
Elephantas Corner of Syngroú and Filíppou. Relaxed, welcoming bar with chilled sounds and quality cocktails. A classy but laid-back place to kick off an evening.
Kismet Kafé Platía Katoúni 11. Intimate and cosy, with mellow sounds. Outside there are candlelit tables, perfect for a relaxed drink. Closed Sun.
Mylos Andhréou Yeoryíou 56 ⓣ2310 525 968, ⓦwww.mylos.gr. The main indoor music venue is the multidisciplinary complex *Mylos*, out in an old flour mill, where you'll find more bars, a summer cinema and exhibition galleries.

Directory

Consulates Canada, Tsimiskí 17 ⓣ2310 256 350; UK, Aristotélous 21 ⓣ2310 278 006; US, Tsimiskí 43 ⓣ2310 242 905. If you need a visa for onward Balkan travel, it's best to get it in Athens.
Hospital Yenikó Kendrikó, Ethnikís Amýnis 41 ⓣ2310 211 211.
Internet Atlantic City, Venizelou; IQ Station, Ágiou Dhimítriou.
Laundry Bianca, Antoniádhou 3; Freskadha, Filíppou 105.
Post office Aristotélous 26; open all day Mon–Fri, mornings Sat & Sun.

Moving on

Train Athens (11 daily; 4–7hr); Belgrade (2 daily; 12hr); İstanbul (2 daily; 12hr); Kateríni (13 daily; 40min–1hr); Litóhoro (4 daily; 1hr); Skopje (2 daily; 4hr); Sofia (2 daily; 6 hrs); Vólos (2 daily; 3hr).
Bus Athens (hourly; 7hr); Delphi (2 daily; 6hr); Ioánnina (5 daily; 6hr); İstanbul (2 daily; 12hr); Kalambáka (7 daily; 4hr 30min); Litóhoro (6 daily; 1hr 30min); Korça (3 daily; 6hr); Métsovo (6 daily; 3hr 30min); Sofia (2–4 daily; 7hr); Tríkala (6 daily; 3hr); Véria (hourly; 1hr 15min); Vólos (4 daily; 4hr).
Ferry Híos (1–4 weekly; 18–20hr); Iráklion (2 weekly; 30–33hr); Kós (1 weekly; 24hr); Lésvos (1–2 weekly; 15hr); Mýkonos (1–4 weekly); Náxos (1 weekly; 24hr); Páros (1 weekly; 22hr); Santorini (1–4 weekly; 24hr); Skópelos (4 weekly; 7–9hr).

VERGÍNA (ANCIENT AEGAE)

In 1977, archeologists discovered the burial sanctuary of the ancient Macedonian dynasty which culminated in Alexander the Great at the hitherto insignificant village of **VERGÍNA**. The four **Royal Tombs** (summer Mon noon–7.30pm, Tues–Sun 8am–7.30pm; winter daily 8.30am–3pm; €8) constitute the focus of an unmissable underground museum, featuring delicate gold and silver funerary artefacts, the facades of the tombs, and the bones of the deceased in ornate ossuaries. It's easy to make this a day-trip from Thessaloníki: hourly buses run to Véria, from where eleven onward buses per day cover the final 20 minutes to modern Vergína village.

MOUNT OLYMPUS

Highest, most magical and most dramatic of all Greek mountains, **Mount Olympus** – the mythical seat of the gods – rears straight up nearly 3000m from the shores of the Thermaïkos gulf. Dense forests cover its lower slopes and its wild flowers are gorgeous. If you're well equipped, no special expertise is necessary to reach the top between mid-June and October, though it's a long hard pull, and its weather is notoriously fickle. You'd do well to buy a proper **map** of the range in Athens or Thessaloníki (#31 Road Editions 1:50,000 is adequate).

Litóhoro

The usual approach to Mount Olympus is via **LITÓHORO** on the eastern slopes, a pleasant village in a magnificent mountain setting. The easiest way to reach the village is to travel by bus or train to Katerini, from where hourly buses make the 25-minute journey. There is a train station at Litóhoro, but it is inconveniently located. Best-value **accommodation** is the hotel *Enipeas*, with balconied rooms and a central location (☎2352 084 328; €50). Best **eats** are at *To Pazari*, uphill on 25 Martou, or *Taverna Zeus*, at the start of the road up the mountain. There's a small **tourist office** (summer only: Mon–Fri 9am–2pm & 3–9pm, Sat & Sun 10am–2pm & 5–9pm) opposite the bus stop, which can provide information on the region.

The ascent

Four to five hours' walking along the well-marked, scenic E4 long-distance path up the Mavrólongos canyon brings you to **Priónia**, from where there's a sharper three-hour trail-climb to the *Spilios Agapitos* **refuge** (☎2352 081 800; €10 per person; €4.20 to camp; mid-May to mid-Oct). It's best to stay overnight here, as you need to make an early start for the three-hour ascent to **Mýtikas**, the highest peak (2917m), as the summit frequently clouds over towards midday. The path continues behind the refuge, reaching a signposted fork above the tree line in about an hour; straight on, then right, takes you to Mýtikas via the ridge known as Kakí Skála, while the abrupt right reaches the *Yiosos Apostolidhis* **hut** in one hour (no phone; €10 per person; mid-June to mid-Sept). From the hut there's an enjoyable loop down to the **Gortsiá** trailhead and from there back down into the Mavrólongos canyon, via the medieval monastery of Ayíou Dhionysíou.

The Cyclades

The **Cyclades** is the most satisfying Greek archipelago for island-hopping, with its vibrant capital on **Sýros**. The majority of the islands are arid and rocky, with brilliant-white, cubist architecture, making them enormously popular with tourists. **Íos**, the original hippie island, is still a backpackers'

paradise, while **Mýkonos** – with its teeming old town, nude beaches and highly sophisticated clubs and bars (many of them gay) – is by far the most visited of the group. Arriving by ferry at the partially submerged volcanic caldera of **Santoríni**, meanwhile, is one of the world's great travel adventures. **Páros**, **Náxos** and **Sífnos** are nearly as popular, while the one major ancient site worth making time for is **Délos**, the commercial and religious centre of the classical Greek world. Almost all of the Cyclades are served by boats from Pireás, but there are also ferries from Rafína.

SÝROS

Home to the capital of the Cyclades, **Sýros** is the most populous island in the archipelago. The main town and port of **ERMOÚPOLI** is a lively spot, bustling with a commercial life that extends far beyond tourism. Crowned by two imposing churches, the Catholic Capuchin **Monastery of St Jean** in the medieval quarter of Ano Sýros and the Orthodox **Anástasis**, the city is one of the most religiously and culturally diverse places in the whole of Greece.

Accommodation

Dream Off Naxou ⓣ2281 084 356, ⓦwww.dream-rooms.gr. Decent, basic rooms, some with balconies, run by a charming family and situated just back from the waterfront. €40.

Kastro Rooms Kalomenopoúlo 12 ⓣ2281 088 064. Spacious rooms in a beautiful old mansion house near the main square, with access to a communal kitchen. €40.

Eating

Stin Ithaki Stefanou 1. Tucked down a side street, this welcoming taverna has all the Greek classics and vibrant bougainvillea overhead. Mains €6–8.

Yiannena Estiatorio Platía Kanári. Popular, friendly spot by the water with a French bistro feel. Serves great seafood and other Greek standards. Mains €6–9.

Moving on

Ferry Íos (2–4 weekly; 5–8hr 30min); Mýkonos (2–4 daily; 30min–2hr); Náxos (2–3 daily; 1hr 15min–3hr); Pireás (3–4 daily; 1hr 30min–5hr 30min); Santoríni (1 daily; 4–10hr); Sífnos (1–2 daily; 3hr 30min–6hr 30min).

SÍFNOS

Although **Sífnos** – notable for its classic Cycladic architecture and pottery – often gets crowded, its modest size makes exploring the picturesque island a pleasure, whether by the excellent in-season bus service or on foot over a network of old stone pathways.

KAMÁRES, the port, is tucked at the base of high bare cliffs in the west. A steep twenty-minute bus ride takes you up to **APOLLONÍA**, a rambling collage of flagstones, belfries and flowered courtyards. The island bank, post office and tourist police are all here, while the Aegean Thesaurus agency (ⓣ2284 033 151, ⓦwww.thesaurus.gr) should be able to help with rooms. As an alternative base, head for **KÁSTRO**, a forty-minute walk or regular bus ride below Apollonía on the east coast; built on a rocky outcrop with an almost sheer drop to the sea on three sides, this medieval capital of the island retains much of its character. The island's finest walk is through the hills to **VATHÝ**, a fishing village around three hours from Apollonía's Katavatí "suburb".

Accommodation

Hotel Stavros Kamáres ⓣ2284 033 383, ⓦwww.sifnostravel.com. These crisp en-suite rooms have balconies with sea views. There's also a decent book exchange in the reception. €50.

Makis Camping Kamáres ⓣ2284 032 366, ⓦwww.makiscamping.gr. This campsite has good facilities, as well as five en-suite rooms with sea views. April–Oct; camping €7 per person, €5 per tent; rooms €50.

Moving on

Boat Íos (1 weekly; 6hr 30 min); Mýkonos (1 weekly; 5hr); Náxos (3–6 weekly; 3hr); Pireás (4–6

daily; 3–6hr); Santoríni (10 weekly; 1hr 40min–10hr); Sýros (1 daily; 3hr 30min–6hr 30min).

MÝKONOS

Mýkonos has become the most popular and expensive of the Cyclades, visited by nearly a million tourists a year. If you don't mind the crowds, the upmarket capital, **MÝKONOS TOWN** (also known as **HÓRA**), is one of the most beautiful and vibrant of all island towns. Dazzlingly white, it's the archetypal Greek island, with sugar-cube buildings stacked around a cluster of seafront fishermen's dwellings.

The closest decent **beach** is **Áyios Stéfanos**, 4km north and connected by a very regular bus service, though **Platýs Yialós**, 4km south, is marginally less crowded. A *kaïki* service from

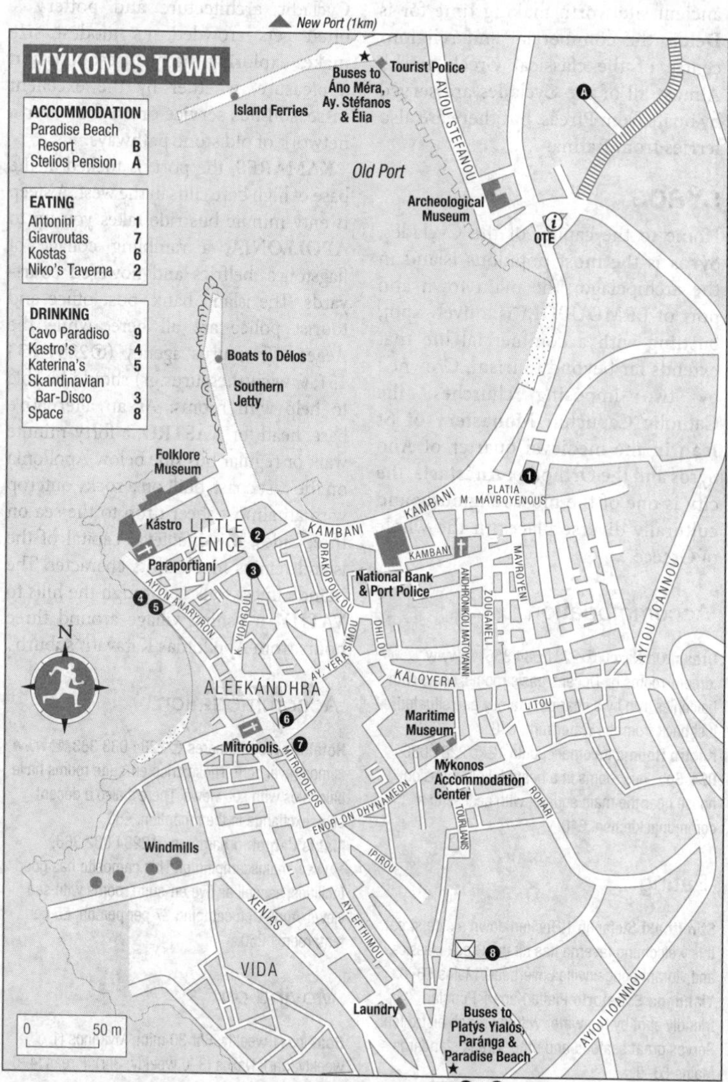

DÉLOS

Boats from the west end of Mýkonos harbour (€15 return) leave for ancient **Délos**, the sacred isle where Leto gave birth to the twins Artemis and Apollo. It's worth a day-trip for the magnificent views across to the nearby Cyclades from Mount Kýnthos, and for the archeological site (Tues–Sun 8.30am–3pm; €5) with remains of ancient temples, mosaics and an array of phallic artefacts.

Mýkonos Town connects almost all the beaches east of Platýs Yialós: gorgeous, pale-sand **Paránga** beach, popular with campers; **Paradise**, well sheltered by its headland and predominantly nudist; and **Super Paradise**, which has a friendly atmosphere and two bars. Probably the island's best beach is **Eliá** on the southeast coast: a broad sandy stretch with a verdant backdrop, split in two by a rocky area. Less busy, but harder to get to, is **Pánormos Bay** on the island's windswept northern coast, with its relatively sheltered Pánormos and Áyios Sostis beaches.

Arrival and information

Air The airport is about 3km out of town, a short taxi ride away.

Ferry Boats dock at either the "new" port (2km out of town) or the more central "old" port. Frequent local buses connect the two. *Kaïkia* to Délos (see box above) leave from the west end of Mýkonos harbour.

Information Mýkonos Accommodation (see below) have information about activities around the island.

Island buses The harbour curves around past the dull, central beach, behind which is the bus station for Áyios Stéfanos. A second bus terminus, for beaches to the south of town, is right at the other end of Hóra, beyond the windmills.

Tourist police Continue along the seafront to the southern jetty for the tourist and port police.

Accommodation

Ferries are met by a horde of hotel and room touts; you'd do better to proceed to the helpful Mýkonos Accommodation Center in town (Mon–Sat 9am–9pm & Sun 10am–9pm; ⓣ 2289 023 160, ⓦ www.mykonos-accommodation.com). In high season, prices rocket and availability plummets; try the pensions further out of town at Áyios Stéfanos.

Paradise Beach Resort ⓣ 2289 022 129, ⓦ www.paradisemykonos.com. A lively campsite, also with beach cabins and bungalows, 5km south of town. April–Oct. Camping €10 per person, €5 per tent; cabins €56; bungalows €86.

Stelios Pension ⓣ 2289 024 641or 2289 026 779. A whitewashed Mykonian-style building, with comfortable rooms which have balconies. On steps leading up from behind the OTE telecommunications office. €100.

Eating

Antonini Platía M. Mavroyénous. A reliable choice on the main square, serving Greek dishes at reasonable prices. Mains €7–9.

Giavroutas Mitropóleos 11. Open until 6am, this restaurant has a pleasant beachy feel, with white-washed walls and wooden furniture. Mains €7–10.

Kostas Mitropóleos 5. Buried deep in the town's labyrinthine centre, this restaurant serves everything from seafood to grills. Mains €8–10.

Niko's Taverna Near the port at Little Venice. Another popular option, strong on fresh fish but also serving traditional Greek cuisine. Mains €7–9.

Drinking and nightlife

Cavo Paradiso Paradise Beach ⓦ www.cavoparadiso.gr. Close to the *Paradise Beach Resort*, this usually packed after-hours club is one of the stops on the international DJ circuit.

Kastro's Little Venice. Enjoy an early-evening drink in this intimate bar on the waterfront, serving fruity and "special" cocktails. Opens at 6.30pm.

Katerina's Little Venice. Low-key decor combined with sea views from the terrace make this a relaxing place for a drink. Cocktails €10. Open all day.

Skandinavian Bar-Disco K. Georgouli. A good choice for the backpacker set, the buzzing bars are numerous and housed around a small square. Plenty of room for dancing, too.

Space Lákka Square ⓣ 2289 024 100 for table reservations. The largest dance club in town, home to a host of resident and guest DJs.

Moving on

Ferry Íos (1–2 daily; 1hr 30min–7hr); Náxos (3 daily; 1hr–3hr); Páros (5 daily; 1hr–1hr 30min);

Pireás (3–4 daily; 3hr 30min–5hr 30min); Santoríni (1–2 daily; 2hr 15min–9hr); Sýros (1–3 daily; 45min–1hr 15).

PÁROS

With its old villages, monasteries, fishing harbour and labyrinthine capital, **Páros** has everything one expects from a Greek island, including boat connections to virtually the entire Aegean.

PARIKÍA, the main town, has ranks of white houses punctuated by the occasional Venetian-style building and church domes. Just outside the centre, the town also has one of the most interesting churches in the Aegean – the sixth-century **Ekatondapylianí**, or "Church of One Hundred Gates". The town culminates in a seaward Venetian **kástro**, whose surviving east wall incorporates a fifth-century-BC round tower. The second village of Páros, **NÁOUSSA** retains much of its original character as a fishing village with winding, narrow alleys and simple Cycladic houses. Though very busy in summer, it makes a good base for exploring nearby beaches.

Arrival and information

Ferry All ferries dock at Parikía, the main town.
Tourist information Located in the windmill in the centre of the roundabout opposite the quay (Mon–Fri 9am–4pm).
Island buses The bus stop is centrally located in Parikía next to the quay. There are buses to Náoussa every 30min.

Accommodation

Hotel Arian Parikía ⓣ 2284 021 490, ⓦ http://cycladesnet.gr/arian. In the peaceful streets behind the ancient cemetery, this small, charming hotel is set around a courtyard planted with blooms. Rooms are small but immaculate with new bathrooms and a/c. €60.
Krios Camping 2km from Parikía ⓣ 2284 021 705, ⓦ www.krios-camping.gr. Good facilities, including internet and a pool. May–Sept. €8 per person, €3 per tent.
Rena Rooms Parikía ⓣ 2284 022 220, ⓦ www.cycladesnet.gr/rena. Close to the port and the beach, this excellent pension has good-value rooms, and sea views from the top floor. €50.
Young Inn Náoussa ⓣ 6976 415 232, ⓦ www.young-inn.com. Comfortable en-suite bedrooms, some with kitchenettes, with free transfers to the port. A sociable place, as there are all kinds of organized activities. Dorms €8, rooms €25.

TREAT YOURSELF

Happy Green Cows Just behind the main square in Parikía, this place serves excellent, inventive vegetarian food in kitsch, colourful surrounds. From around €10 for a main, it's not cheap, but if you fancy a break from taverna standards it's a great choice. Carnivore concessions include chicken and fish dishes.

Eating

Argonautica Platía M. Mavroyénous, Parikía. A friendly restaurant on the main square, a good spot for watching the town spring to life in the evening. Mains €7–9.
Trata Parikía. Down a side street off the road heading east out of town, this popular taverna specializes in seafood. Mains €6–8.

Moving on

Ferry Íos (1–3 daily; 1hr 10 min–3hr 10min); Mýkonos (4–5 daily; 40min–2hr 40min); Náxos (6–7 daily; 40min–1hr 20mins); Pireás (3–4 daily; 3–7hr); Santoríni (3–4 daily; 1hr 30min–8hr); Sífnos (1–2 daily; 3hr 30min–4hr 30min); Sýros (1–2 daily; 45min–2hr).

NÁXOS

Náxos is the largest and most fertile of the Cyclades with high mountains, intriguing central valleys, a spectacular north coast, sandy beaches in the south-west, and Venetian towers and fortified mansions scattered throughout.

What to see and do

A long causeway protecting the harbour connects **NÁXOS TOWN** with the islet of Palátia, where the huge stone portal of an unfinished sixth-century-BC

Temple of Apollo still stands. Most of the town's life goes on down by the port or in the streets just behind it; the quaint Old Market Street has narrow, stone paths leading to small shops and a handful of restaurants and cafés. From here, stepped lanes lead up past crumbling balconies and through low arches to the fortified medieval **kástro**, near the **Archeological Museum** (Tues–Sun 8am–7.30pm; €3), with its important early sculpture collection and a Hellenistic mosaic on the roof terrace. The town has a laid-back feel, with unashamedly long happy-hours which last for most of the day. There's a thriving nightlife, with plenty of bars scattered along the waterfront and the bigger clubs dominating either end.

Beaches

The island's best **beaches** are regularly served by buses in season. Within walking distance of Náxos Town is **Áyios Yeóryios**, a long sandy bay south of the hotel quarter, with several tavernas and the *Soula Hotel*. An hour's walk further south, however, you'll find the more inviting **Áyios Prokópios** and **Ayía Ánna** beaches, with plenty of rooms to let and a few modest tavernas. Beyond the headland stretches **Pláka** beach, a 5km-long vegetation-fringed expanse of white sand, which comfortably holds the summer crowds of nudists and campers from its two friendly campsites: *Maragas* (ⓣ2285 024 552; €10), which also has rooms (€45), and the newer *Plaka* (ⓣ2285 042 700m ⓦwww.plakacamping.gr; April–Oct; €8 per person, €3 per tent).

Arrival and information

Ferry Boats dock at the quay at the northern end of Náxos Town.

Tourist information Opposite the quay; you can pick up leaflets or leave your luggage here (daily 8.30am–midnight).

Island buses The bus stop in Náxos Town is between the quay and the tourist office. There are buses to Ayía Ánna (every 30min), Áyios Prokópios (every 30min) and Pláka (every 30min).

Accommodation

Despina's Rooms Náxos Town ⓣ2285 022 356. Hidden beneath the castle in the Kástro, the rooms are small but clean and airy, with shared bathroom and balconies with sea views. €50.

Hotel Panorama Náxos Town ⓣ2285 022 330, ⓔpanoramanaxos@in.gr. A comfortable hotel in the old town whose name gives a clue to its main attraction – a large roof terrace with stunning views. €50.

Soula Hotel Áyios Yeóryios beach ⓣ2285 023 196, ⓔhotel-soula@nax.forthnet.gr. A family-run budget hotel close to both the beach and the town, with free internet access. Dorms €10, rooms €45.

Eating and drinking

Elia Old Market Street, Náxos Town. Housed in a beautiful stone building, this smart bar has live music and an enticing atmosphere. Also serves breakfast and lunch. Open 9am–3pm & 7pm–late. Cocktails €5.

Manolis Garden Taverna Old Market Street, Náxos Town. A peaceful spot for an evening meal, with traditional Greek dishes. Open from 6pm. Mains €6–8.

Popi's Grill Paralia, Náxos Town. On the seafront, serving traditional Greek fare. It also has its own wine and cheese shop. Mains €6–8.

Moving on

Ferry Íos (1–2 daily; 2hr); Mýkonos (3 daily; 1hr); Páros (6–7 daily; 40min–1hr 30min); Pireás (5 daily; 5–8hr); Santoríni (2–3 daily; 2hr 30min); Sífnos (6 weekly; 4hr); Sýros (1–2 daily; 1hr 15min–3hr).

Íos

Once a hippie hangout, the island remains popular with a younger crowd seeking fun and sun, which **Íos**, party capital of the Aegean, provides in abundance. However, although no other island attracts more under-25s, Íos has miraculously maintained much of its traditional Cycladic charm, with picture-perfect whitewashed houses and churches. Íos's lively nights lead to lazy days, perfect for exploring the island.

What to see and do

Don't expect a quiet stay in the town of **HÓRA**, as every evening the streets throb to music with the larger **clubs** clustered near the bus stop. To get the most out of the nightlife, start around 11pm with the bars and clubs around the central square, which tend to close at 3am. Around this time the larger clubs on the main street begin to liven up, and the party continues (even if you don't) until 8am.

Mylopótas and Manganári

The most popular stop on the island's bus routes is **MYLOPÓTAS**, site of a magnificent beach and mini-resort. There are plenty of activities on offer, including quad biking (Far Out Moto Club; ⓣ2286 092 345), water sports and diving (ⓣ2286 091 622, ⓦwww.ios-sports.gr). It gets very crowded, so for a bit more space, head away from the terminus where there are dunes behind the beach. From Yialós, boats depart daily at around 10am to **MANGANÁRI** on the south coast, the beach to go to for a serious tan. You can also reach Manganári by bus, as there are two daily buses from Hóra and Mylopótas.

Arrival

Ferry Boats dock at the quay in Yialós. Regular buses connect the port to Hóra and Mylopótas (every 15min; 8am–12.30am) and many hotels and hostels offer a free transfer.

Accommodation

Camping Ios Yialós ⓣ2286 091 329. The nearest campsite to the port, and quieter than those on Mylopótas beach. €8.

Drakos Pension Mylopótas ⓣ2286 091 626. Pleasant rooms in a Cycladic-style building next to a popular Greek restaurant. €60.

Far Out Camping Mylopótas ⓣ2285 091 468, ⓦwww.faroutclub.com. By far the most popular campsite, thanks to its facilities and fun factor. Also has bungalows to hire. April–Sept. Camping €12, bungalows €20.

Francesco's Hóra ⓣ2286 091 223, ⓦwww.francescos.net. A favourite option with the backpacker set, with the only dorm beds in town as well as private rooms. Lively bar and terrace with sea views and a new pool. Dorms €15, rooms €50.

Marko's Village Hóra ⓣ2286 091 059, ⓦwww.markosvillage.com. Tastefully decorated rooms set around a pool and noisy bar, a short stumble from the nightlife. Free internet. €70.

Eating

Ali Baba's Hóra. Thai chefs dish up generous portions of authentic Thai food, served in a relaxed atmosphere. Open from 6pm. Stir-fries €9.

Harmony Mylopótas. A laid-back Mexican restaurant overlooking the beach, with hammocks and cushioned sofas. Open from noon. Enchiladas €10.

Lord Byron Hóra. An intimate restaurant with funky decor, serving generous meze plates to share (€5–7). A restaurant for those with an appetite. Open from 6pm.

Pomodoro Hóra. A wonderful roof garden with views over Íos, with an Italian and Mediterranean menu. There's a selection of unusual fusion main courses too. Open from 6.30pm. Pasta €7–11.

Porkies Hóra. Close to the main square, all-night *Porkies* serves obligatory post-party *ghýros* (kebabs with *píta*) for €2–3.

Drinking and nightlife

Kandi Main street. The most popular place to wind up, *Kandi*'s dancefloor throbs until dawn (and beyond). Entry €5 including a free cocktail.

Red Bull Bar Main square. Small bar specializing in dance music – and the well-known energy drink, mixed with large doses of spirits. Some outdoor tables.

Slammer Bar Main square. Legendary bar, although beware of saying the word "slammer" too loudly. Plays popular music from the Eighties to current tunes. Entry €5 including a free drink.

Sweet Irish Dream Main street. Satisfy your cravings for a pint of the black gold here. Entry €5 including a free drink.

Moving on

Ferry Mýkonos (1–2 daily; 2–6hr); Náxos (1–2 daily; 3hr); Páros (1–3 daily; 70min-5hr); Pireás (2–3 daily; 3hr 30min–10hr); Santoríni (3–4 daily; 1hr); Sífnos (1–2 weekly; 6hr); Sýros (2–3 weekly; 6hr).

SANTORÍNI (THÍRA)

Santoríni is the epitome of relaxation, with its sun-drenched beaches and ambling white-washed stone paths. The island (a partially submerged volcanic caldera poking above the ocean's surface in five places) is a welcome destination to those who have spent too many nights partying on Íos. As the ferry manoeuvres into the great bay, gaunt, sheer cliffs loom hundreds of feet above. Nothing grows to soften the view, and the only colours are the reddish-brown, black and grey pumice strata layering the cliff face of **THÍRA**, Santoríni's largest island. Despite a past every bit as turbulent as the geological conditions that formed it, the island is now best known for its spectacular views, dark-sand beaches and light, dry white wines.

What to see and do

Regular buses meeting the ferries at **Órmos Athiniós** make their way to the island's capital **FIRÁ**; half-rebuilt after a devastating earthquake in 1956 and lurching dementedly at the cliff's edge. Besieged by day-trippers from cruise-ships, it's somewhat tacky and commercialized, though watching the sunset from a cliff-hugging terrace of any of the overpriced restaurants you'll understand why it's so popular. There's no shortage of **rooms** in the area, though most are expensive. The town boasts a couple of **museums** (Tues–Sun 8.30am–3pm; €3 for both): the Archeological Museum, near the cable car to the north of town, and the Museum of Prehistoric Thíra, between the cathedral and the bus station.

Around the island

Near the northwestern tip of the island is one of the most dramatic towns of the Cyclades, **ÍA**, a curious mix of pristine white reconstruction and tumbledown ruins clinging to the cliff face. With a post office, travel agencies and an excellent **youth hostel** (see p.564), it makes a good base from which to explore the island. Santoríni's **beaches** are bizarre: long black stretches of volcanic sand which get blisteringly hot in the afternoon sun. There's little to choose between **KAMÁRI** and **PERÍSSA**, the two main resorts: both have long beaches and a mass of restaurants, rooms and apartments, although Períssa gets more backpackers.

At the southwestern tip of the island, evidence of a Minoan colony was found at **Akrotíri** (summer Tues–Sun 8.30am–3pm; €5; bus from Firá or Períssa), a town buried under banks of volcanic ash. Nearby is the spectacular, red-sand **Kókkini Ámmos** beach.

> **BOAT TRIPS TO THE VOLCANO**
>
> Take a **boat trip** (€10–30) from Firá or Ía to explore the magma-encrusted islets of the caldera and to swim in the sulphurous hot springs. You can book trips of varying lengths from your accommodation or a travel agent.

Arrival

Ferry Most boats arrive at the somewhat grim port of Órmos Athiniós from where buses meeting the ferries make their way to the island's capital.

Island buses Bus services are plentiful enough between Firá and other destinations around the island.

Accommodation

Anna Períssa ⓣ 2286 082 182, ⓔ annayh@otenet.gr. A basic and noisy hostel on the main road, with large dorms and helpful staff. Free transfers from the port. Dorms €12.

Caldera View Bungalows Akrotíri ⓣ 2286 082 010, ⓦ www.calderaview-santorini.com. Recently built bungalows with a/c, balconies and private bathrooms. Open early May to late Sept. €85.

Kykladonisia Firá ⓣ 2286 022 458, ⓦ www.santorinihostel.com. Sleek, upmarket hostel with a swimming pool. Try to get one of the rooms with a sunset view. Dorms €25, rooms €68.

Santorini Camping Firá ⓣ 2286 022 944, ⓦ www.santorinicamping.gr. A shady campsite with a pool, restaurant and internet access. Also has wooden tents for hire. Camping €10 per person, €5 per tent, wooden tents €15.

Youth Hostel Ía ⓣ 2286 071 465. An excellent hostel with a terrace and shady courtyard, a bar and clean dorms. Breakfast included. Dorms €15.

Moving on

Ferry Crete (1–2 daily; 1hr 50min–7hr); Íos (4–5 daily; 50min–1hr); Mýkonos (2–3 daily; 2hr 30min); Náxos (2–3 daily; 1hr 30min–2hr); Páros (2–3 daily; 1hr 45min–3hr); Pireás (4–5 daily; 4–9hr); Sífnos (1–2 daily; 1hr 30min–7hr); Sýros (1–2 daily; 4–8hr).

The Dodecanese

The **Dodecanese** islands lie so close to the Turkish coast that some are almost within hailing distance of the shore. They were only included in the modern Greek state in 1948 after centuries of occupation by Crusaders, Ottomans and Italians. Medieval **Rhodes** is the most famous, but almost every one has its classical remains, its Crusaders' castle, its traditional villages and grandiose, Italian-built Art Deco public buildings. The main islands of Rhodes, **Kós** and **Pátmos** are connected almost daily with each other, and none is hard to reach. Rhodes is the principal transport hub, with ferry services to Turkey, as well as connections with Crete, the northeastern Aegean islands, selected Cyclades and the mainland.

RHODES

It's no surprise that **Rhodes** is among the most visited of Greek islands. Not only is its east coast lined with sandy beaches, but the core of the capital is a beautiful and remarkably preserved medieval city.

What to see and do

RHODES TOWN divides into two unequal parts: the compact old walled city and the new town sprawling around it in three directions. There's plenty to explore in the rest of the island too, not least charming **Haráki** and lively **Líndhos**.

Rhodes Town

First thing to meet the eye, and dominating the northeast sector of the city's fortifications, is the **Palace of the Grand Masters** (summer Mon 1.30–7pm, Tues–Sun 8am–7.30pm; winter Mon 12.30–3pm, Tues–Sun 8am–3pm; €6, or €10 combination ticket with other museums). Two excellent **museums** occupy the ground floor: one devoted to medieval Rhodes, the other to ancient Rhodes. The heavily-restored **Street of the Knights** (Odhós Ippotón) leads due east from the front of the palace. The "Inns" lining it housed the Knights of St John for two centuries, and at the bottom of the slope the Knights' Hospital now houses the **Archeological Museum** (Tues–Sun 8.30am–7pm; €3, or €10 combination ticket), where the star exhibits are two statues of Aphrodite. Across the way is the **Byzantine Museum** (Tues–Sun 8.30am–2.40pm; €2, or €10 combination ticket), housed in the Knights' chapel and highlighting the island's icons and frescoes. Heading south, it's hard to miss the most conspicuous Ottoman monument in Rhodes, the candy-striped **Süleymaniye Mosque** (ask at tourist office for hours; free).

Arrival and information

Ferry Boats dock at the harbour in Rhodes Town outside the walls of the Old Town, south of the New Town.

Tourist office The EOT tourist office (Mon–Fri 8am–2.45pm; ⓣ 2241 023 255) is on the corner of Papágou and Makaríou; the municipal tourist office

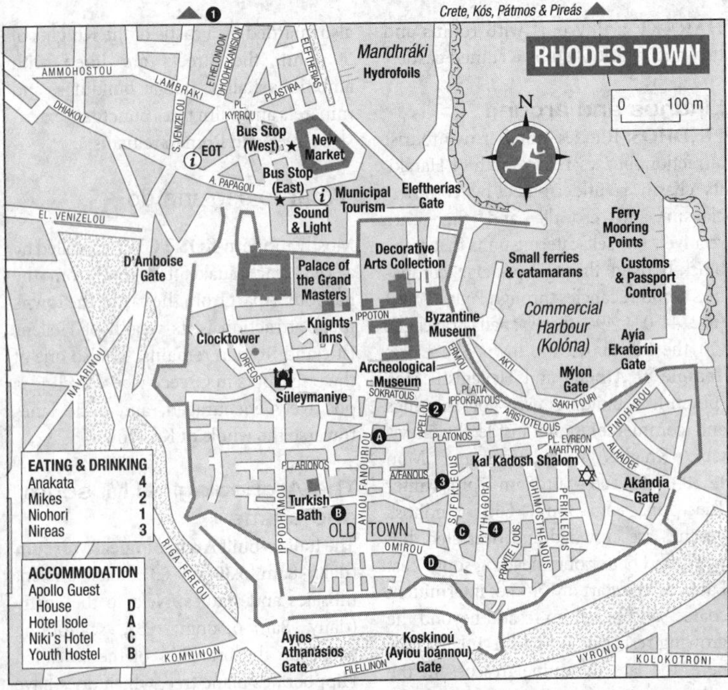

(June–Sept daily 7.30am–11pm) is next to the Italian-built New Market.

Island buses Buses for the rest of the island leave from two terminals within sight of the New Market.

Internet *Rock Style* at Dhimokratías 7, just southwest of the old town, and *Cosmonet*, at Platía Evreon Martyon 45.

Accommodation

Apollo Guest House Omírou 28c ⓣ2241 032 003, ⓦwww.apollo-touristhouse.com. Six individual en-suite rooms with large double beds. Simple yet elegant. €65.

Hotel Isole Evdhóxou 75 ⓣ2241 020 682, ⓦwww.hotelisole.com. Simple, clean hostel in a converted Ottoman house with a beautiful roof terrace. The multilingual owners are charming. €40.

Niki's Hotel Sofokléous 39 ⓣ2241 025 115, ⓦwww.nikishotel.gr. Wonderful views over the old town from the roof garden, and breakfast served outside on a lovely patio. €56.

Youth Hostel Eryíou 12 ⓣ2241 030 491. A friendly hostel with dorm beds, double rooms and studios. The dorms are basic, but the studios are carefully restored in a separate building, with original features retained. Dorms €10, studios €25.

Eating

Anakata Pythagora 79, Rhodes Town. Enjoy a light lunch or a coffee in this shady garden surrounded by vibrant pink flowers. Take a peek at the art gallery, too. Closed Sun. Sandwiches €3.

Mikes Alley off Sokrátous, Rhodes Town. This modest taverna with pavement seating has some of the cheapest fish in town (€20 per kilo).

Niohori Ioánni Kazoúli 29, Rhodes Town. This restaurant is worth the 10min walk out of the old town, as it serves Greek cuisine at reasonable prices. Mains €5–7.

Haráki

Heading down the east coast from Rhodes Town, the giant promontory of **Tsambíka**, 26km south, is the first place to seriously consider stopping – there's an excellent beach just south of the headland. The best overnight base on this stretch of coast is probably

HARÁKI, a tiny port with rooms and tavernas overlooked by a ruined castle.

Líndhos and around

LÍNDHOS, Rhodes' number-two tourist attraction, buzzes 12km south of Haráki. Its charm is undermined by commercialism and crowds, and there are relatively few self-catering units that aren't block-booked through package companies – find vacancies through Pallas Travel (ⓣ2244 031 494, ⓦwww.pallastravel.gr). On the hill above the town, the Doric **Temple of Athena** and Hellenistic stoa (porch-like building used for meetings and commerce) stand inside the inevitable Knights' Castle (summer Mon 12.30–7pm, Tues–Sun 8am–7pm; winter Tues–Sun 8am–3pm; €6). Líndhos's beaches are crowded and overrated, but you'll find better ones heading south past Lárdhos, the start of 15km of intermittent coarse-sand beach up to and beyond the growing resort of **Yennádhi**. Inland near here, the late Byzantine frescoes in the village church of **Asklipió** are among the best on Rhodes.

Moving on

Ferry Crete (1–4 weekly; 10–14hr); Kós (2–3 daily; 2hr 30min–3hr 30min); Marmaris (daily; 1hr); Pátmos (2 daily; 4–5hr); Pireás (9 weekly; 11–23hr); Samos (2 weekly; 9hr); Santoríni (1–2 weekly; 7–14hr); Sýros (2–3 weekly; 8–11hr).

KÓS

Kós is the largest and most popular island in the Dodecanese after Rhodes, and there are superficial similarities between the two. Like its rival, the harbour here is also guarded by a castle of the Knights of St John, the streets are lined with ambitious Italian public buildings, and minarets and palm trees punctuate extensive Greek and Roman remains.

> **TREAT YOURSELF**
>
> **Nireas** Sofokléous 22. Occupying a lovely, leafy courtyard in the Old Town, a world away from the tourist traps, *Nireas* serves up tasty, fresh seafood with panache. A meal will cost about €30 but the setting and the quality are worth skipping breakfast and lunch for.

What to see and do

Mostly modern **KÓS TOWN**, levelled by a 1933 earthquake, fans out from the harbour. Apart from the castle, the town's main attraction is its wealth of Hellenistic and Roman remains. It's also one of the only spots in Greece where cycling is positively encouraged, and cycle lanes traverse the whole of Kós Town.

The Archeological Museum and castle

The Italian-built **Archeological Museum** (daily 8am–6.30pm; €3) holds ancient mosaics and statues. Next to the **castle** (daily 8am–6.30pm; €3), scaffolding props up the branches of the so-called Hippocrates plane tree, which does have a fair claim to being one of the oldest trees in Europe.

The Asklepion and Platáni

Hippocrates is also honoured by the **Asklepion** (summer daily 8am–6.30pm; winter closes earlier; €3), a temple to Asklepios and renowned centre of Hippocratic teaching, 45 minutes on foot (or a short bus ride) from town. The road to the Asklepion passes through the village of **PLATÁNI**, where the island's Turkish population run the popular *Arap* (ⓣ2242 028 442) and *Sherif* (ⓣ2242 023 784) tavernas (summer only), serving excellent, affordable food.

Beaches

To get to the **beaches** you'll need to use buses or rent scooters or bikes. Around 12km west of Kós Town, **Tingáki** is easily accessible but busy. **Mastihári**, 30km from Kós Town, has a decent beach and private rooms for hire. Continuing west, buses run as far as **Kéfalos**, which covers

a bluff looking back along the length of Kós. Well before Kéfalos are **Áyios Stéfanos**, where the exquisite remains of a mosaic-floored fifth-century basilica overlook tiny Kastrí islet, and **Kamári**, the package resort just below Kéfalos. Beaches begin at Kamári and extend east past Áyios Stéfanos for 7km, almost without interruption; "Paradise" has the most facilities, but "Magic" (officially Polémi) and Langádhes are calmer and more scenic.

Arrival and information

Ferry Boats arrive at the harbour, to the north of the centre in Kós Town.
Tourist office The tourist office (Mon–Fri: May–Oct 7.30am–3pm; Nov–April 8.30am–2.30pm; ⓣ2242 024 460), 500m south of the ferry dock on the shore road, offers maps and ferry schedules.
Island buses Buses arrive 500m west of the tourist office. From the centre there are buses to Platáni (15 daily), Tingáki (12 daily), Mastihári (7 daily) and Paradise (6 daily).

Accommodation

Hotel Afendoulis Evripýlou 1, Kós Town ⓣ2242 025 321, ⓦwww.afendoulishotel.com. Homely en-suite rooms with balconies are set around a mezzanine floor, and there's a warm family welcome. €30.

Pension Alexis Irodhótou 9, Kós Town ⓣ2242 028 798, ⓦwww.pensionalexis.com. The accommodating Sonia will welcome late arrivals and provide plenty of local information. A popular budget option set around a shady garden with a veranda. €40.

Eating

Ambavris 1.5km inland in the eponymous hamlet. This taverna may be some distance out of town, but it has an excellent selection of *mezédhes* and is popular with the locals. Dinner only. Mains €6–8.
Koakon Artemisías 56. Located in a residential area, this restaurant has a varied Greek menu, including fish dishes. Mains €6–8.

Moving on

Ferry Bodrum (1–2 daily; 30–45min); Pátmos (1–3 daily; 1hr 30min–2hr 30min); Pireás (7 weekly; 9–12hr); Rhodes (1–3 daily; 2–4hr).

PÁTMOS

St John the Divine reputedly wrote the Book of Revelation in a cave on **Pátmos**, and the monastery which commemorates him, founded here in 1088, dominates the island both physically and politically. While the monks no longer run Pátmos as they did for more than six centuries, their influence has stopped most of the island going the way of Rhodes or Kós.

What to see and do

SKÁLA, the port and main town, is the only busy part of the island, crowded with day-trippers from Kós and Rhodes. **HÓRA** is a beautiful little town whose antiquated alleys conceal over forty churches and monasteries, plus dozens of shipowners' mansions dating from the seventeenth and eighteenth centuries.

Monastery of St John

The **Monastery of St John** (daily 8am–1.30pm, Tues, Thurs & Sun also 4–6pm; monastery free, treasury €5) shelters behind massive defences in the hilltop capital of **Hóra**. Buses go up, but the thirty-minute walk along a beautiful old cobbled path puts you in a more appropriate frame of mind.

Monastery of the Apocalypse

Just over halfway is the **Monastery of the Apocalypse**, built around the cave where St John heard the voice of God issuing from a cleft in the rock. This is merely a foretaste, however, of the main monastery, whose fortifications guard a dazzling array of religious treasures dating back to medieval times.

Beaches

The next bay north of the main harbour in Skála shelters **Méloï beach**, with a well-run campsite. For swimming, the second beach north, **Agriolivádhi**, is

usually less crowded. From Hóra a good road runs above the package resort of Gríkou to the isthmus of **Stavrós**, from where a thirty-minute trail leads to the excellent beach, with one seasonal taverna, at **Psilí Ámmos** (summer *kaïki* from Skála). There are more good beaches in the north of the island, particularly **Livádhi Yeránou**, shaded by tamarisk groves and with a decent taverna, and **Lámbi** with volcanic pebbles and another quality taverna, *Leonidas*.

Arrival and information

Ferry Boats arrive at the harbour, in the middle of Skála.

Tourist office Close to the police station opposite the harbour, the tourist office (summer only; hours vary) can assist with accommodation.

Island buses The bus stop is next to the harbour. There are buses to Hóra (11 daily) and Gríkou (8 daily).

Accommodation

Pension Maria Paskalides In Skála on the road to Hóra ⓣ2247 032 152. A homely feel pervades this pension, with its fragrant front garden and basic rooms. €25.

Stefanos Camping Méloï ⓣ2247 031 821. A basic campsite, but with clean facilities and a restaurant. May–Oct. €10.

Eating

Art Café Skála. Excellent bar/café with flickering candles, views to the harbour and the monastery, draft beer and a breezy roof garden. Behind the post office.

Ouzerí To Hiliomodhi Skála. As the decor suggests, this is the place for fish and seafood dishes. Open from 5pm. Mains €5–7.

Moving on

Ferry Kós (1–3 daily; 1hr 30min–2hr 30min); Pireás (4–5 weekly; 7–12hr); Sámos (1–2 daily; 1–3hr).

Northeastern Aegean

The seven scattered islands of the **northeastern Aegean** form a rather arbitrary archipelago. Local tour operators do a thriving business shuttling passengers for absurdly high tariffs between the easternmost islands and the Turkish coast. The most-visited island, Sámos, is overrun with package tours in summer; tranquil **Lésvos** has a more low-key appeal.

LÉSVOS

Lésvos, birthplace of Sappho, the ancient world's foremost woman poet, may not at first seem particularly beautiful, but the craggy volcanic landscape of pine and olive groves grows on you. Despite the inroads of tourism, this is still essentially a working island, with few large hotels outside the capital, Mytilíni, and the resorts of Skála Kallonís and Mólyvos.

What to see and do

Few people stay in **MYTILÍNI**, but do pause long enough to peek at the **Archeological Museum**, with its superb Roman mosaics (Tues–Sun 8.30am–3pm; €3). Sleepy **MÓLYVOS**, also known as Mithymna, on the north-western coast, is easily the most attractive spot on Lésvos, and much more appealing than its neighbour Petra. Tiers of sturdy, red-tiled houses mount the slopes between the picturesque harbour and the Genoese castle. Wandering through the cobbled streets is a pleasure, since the town's hillside location provides plenty of stunning vistas across the sweeping bay. If the exploration has worn you out, reward yourself with a visit to the **hot springs** of

Eftaloú (daily: old baths 6–8am & 6–10pm, new baths 9am–6pm; €3.50 for the public pool). The main lower road, past the tourist office, heads towards the picturesque harbour, where there are some good-quality seafood tavernas. Lésvos's best beach is at **SKÁLA ERESSOÚ** in the far southwest, with rooms far outnumbering hotels. Tavernas with wooden terraces line the beach – try *Eressos Palace* or *Blue Sardine*. **PLOMÁRI** in the southeast, long the *oúzo* capital of Greece, is another good base, though it lacks beaches within walking distance.

Arrival and information

Ferry Boats arrive at the quay in Mytilíni. On arrival, turn left to reach the town centre.
Tourist office The office in Mytilíni is located at Aristárhou 6 near the quay (Mon–Fri 9am–1pm; ⓣ2251 042 511). The office in Mólyvos is close to the bus stop (summer only: Mon–Sat 10am–8.30pm, Sun 10.30am–2pm & 5–8.30pm; ⓣ2253 071 347, ⓦwww.mithymna.gr) and can help with accommodation.
Island buses The bus station in Mytilíni is located at the southwestern end of the waterfront, slightly inland near Platía Konstandinopóleos. There are buses to Mólyvos (5 daily), Plomári (5 daily), and Skála Eressoú (3 daily).

Accommodation

Molivos Camping Mólyvos ⓣ2253 071 169, ⓦwww.molivos-camping.com. A shady campsite with good facilities, 800m from town. May–Oct. €10.
Nassos Guest House Mólyvos ⓣ2253 071 432, ⓦwww.nassosguesthouse.com. A charming, converted Turkish house built around 1900. There are fine views of the town from the rooms and the terrace. €35.
Pension Lida Plomári ⓣ2252 032 507. A fine restoration inn occupying adjacent old mansions, with seaview balconies. €30.

Eating

The Captain's Table Mólyvos. Set among the fishing boats in the picturesque harbour, with good fish as well as traditional dishes. Open from 5.30pm. Fish €7–8.
To Hani Mólyvos. Near the market, this restaurant serves delicious meals, complemented by a wonderful terrace with views over the town towards the sea. Mains €6–8.

Moving on

Ferry Pireás (1–2 daily; 9–13hr); Thessaloníki (1–2 weekly; 14hr); Ayvalik/Dikili, Turkey (daily; 1hr 30min).

The Sporades

The **Sporades**, scattered across the northwestern Aegean, are an easy group to island-hop. The three northern islands – package-tourist haven Skiáthos, Alónissos and **Skópelos**, the pick of the trio – have good beaches, transparent waters and thick pine forests. **Skýros**, the fourth Sporade, is isolated from the others and less scenic, but with perhaps the most character; for a relatively uncommercialized island within a day's travel of Athens it's unbeatable.

SKÓPELOS

More rugged yet better cultivated than neighbouring Skiáthos, **Skópelos** is also very much more attractive. **SKÓPELOS TOWN** slopes down one corner of a huge, almost circular bay. There are dozens of rooms to let – take up one of the offers when you land or visit the Roomowners Association (see p.570) for vacancies. Within the town, spread

GETTING TO THE SPORADES

The **Sporades** are well connected to Athens by bus and ferry via Áyios Konstandínos (for Skópelos) or Kými (for Skýros), and to Vólos (for Skópelos). Be aware that the only way to get to Skýros is from the mainland port of Kými.

below the oddly whitewashed ruins of a Venetian *kástro*, are an enormous number of churches – 123 reputedly, though some are small enough to be mistaken for houses.

Beaches

Buses run along the island's one asphalt road to Loutráki about seven times daily, stopping at the turn-offs to all the main beaches and villages. **Stáfylos** beach, 4km out of town, is the closest, but it's small, rocky and increasingly crowded; the overflow, much of it nudist, flees to **Valanió**, just east. Much more promising, if you're after relative isolation, is sandy **Limnonári**, a fifteen-minute walk or short *kaïki* ride from **AGNÓNDAS** (which has tavernas and rooms). The large resort of **Pánormos** has become overdeveloped, but slightly further on, **Miliá** offers a tremendous 1500m sweep of tiny pebbles beneath a bank of pines.

Arrival and information

Ferry Boats arrive at the quay in the middle of Skópelos Town. The island also has another port at Loutráki.

Island buses The bus stop is next to the quay, near the taxi rank. There are buses to Agnóndas (20 daily), Loutráki (8 daily), Miliá (17 daily), Pánormos (17 daily) and Stáfylos (20 daily).

Accommodation

The Roomowners Association, opposite the quay (daily 9.30am–2pm; ⓣ 2424 024 576), has lists of the island's accommodation.

Archontiko Skópelos Town ⓣ 2424 022 765. This welcoming guesthouse has traditional decor and a homely atmosphere, situated on a quiet, cobbled street. €35.

Hotel Regina Skópelos Town ⓣ 2424 022 138. Close to the waterfront, these spacious en-suite rooms have large double beds and balconies. Breakfast included. €55.

Eating

Alexander Skópelos Town. A delightful garden restaurant, serving traditional Greek food alongside more unusual local specials, such as pork with plums. Open from 7pm. Mains €7–12.

O Molos Old Harbour, Skópelos Town. A reliable taverna on the waterfront, serving typical Greek cuisine. Mains €7–8.

Moving on

Ferry Áyios Konstandínos (1 daily; 2hr 15min–3hr); Skiáthos (6 daily; 45min–1hr); Vólos (1–2 daily; 2hr 30min–4hr).

SKÝROS

Skýros remained until the 1980s a very traditional and idiosyncratic island. The older men still wear the vaguely Cretan costume of cap, vest, baggy trousers, leggings and clogs, while the women favour yellow scarves and long embroidered skirts. Skýros also has a particularly lively *Apokriátika* or pre-Lenten **carnival**, featuring the "Goat Dance", performed by masked revellers in the village streets.

What to see and do

A **bus** connects Linariá – a functional little port with a few tourist facilities – to **SKÝROS TOWN**, spread below a high rock rising precipitously from the coast. Traces of classical walls can still be made out among the ruins of the Venetian *kástro*; within the walls is the crumbling, tenth-century monastery of **Áyios Yeóryios**. Despite the town's peaceful afternoons, the narrow streets come alive in the evening, as the sun sets behind the hills, bathing the white buildings in a soft light. There are several hotels and plenty of **rooms** to let in private houses; you'll be met with offers as you descend from the bus. The campsite is down the hill at the fishing village of **MAGAZIÁ**, with rooms and tavernas fronting the island's best beach.

Arrival and information

Ferry Boats arrive at the functional port of Linariá. Buses meet the boats and connect the port to Skýros Town.

Information There is no tourist office, but Skýros Travel on the main street (Ⓣ 2222 091 123, Ⓦ www.skyrostravel.com) can help with accommodation.

Accommodation

Hotel Elena Skýros Town Ⓣ 2222 091 738. With tiled floors, white walls and wooden furniture, these rooms are clean, comfortable and centrally located. €45.

Eating

Liakos Skýros Town. Tasty local dishes are served on a rooftop terrace with a panoramic view over the town. Open Mon from 6pm, Tues–Sun from 1pm. Mains €6–11.

Nostos Café Skýros Town. On the central square above the bank, this is the perfect place for a pre-dinner drink as you watch the sunset from the terrace.

O Pappous k'Ego Skýros Town. This popular place opens for dinner only and serves Skyrian specialities with a smile. Tables spill out onto the cobbled pavement. Mains €5–9.

Moving on

Ferry Kými (1–2 daily; 2hr).

Ionian islands

The six **Ionian islands** are, both geographically and culturally, a mixture of Greece and Italy. Floating on the haze of the Adriatic, their green silhouettes come as a surprise to those more used to the stark outlines of the Aegean. The islands were the Homeric realm of Odysseus and here alone of all modern Greek territory the Ottomans never held sway. After the fall of Byzantium, possession passed to the Venetians, and the islands became a keystone in that city-state's maritime empire from 1386 until its collapse in 1797. Tourism has hit **Corfu** in a big way but none of the other islands has endured anything like the same scale of development. For a less sullied experience, head for **Kefalloniá**.

CORFU (KÉRKYRA)

A visit to **Corfu** is an intense experience, if sometimes a beleaguered one, for it has more package hotels and holiday villas than any other Greek island. The commercialism is apparent the moment you step ashore at the ferry dock, or cover the 2km from the airport. That said, **KÉRKYRA TOWN**, the capital, has a lot more going for it than first exposure to the summer crowds might indicate.

What to see and do

Although unavoidably touristy, **Kérkyra Town** has a buzzy appeal: cafés on the Esplanade and in the arcaded Listón have a civilized air, and become lively bars when the sun sets. The rest of the island is dotted with some lovely beaches and appealing villages.

Kérkyra Town and around

In Kérkyra Town, the Palace of Sts Michael and George at the north end of the Spianádha is worth visiting for its **Asiatic Museum** (Tues–Sun 8.30am–7.30pm; €3) and **Municipal Art Gallery** (daily 9am–5pm; €1.50). The **Byzantine Museum** (Tues–Sun 8am–7pm; €2) and the cathedral are both interesting, as is the **Archeological Museum**, Vraíla 3 (Tues–Sun 8.30am–3pm; €3), where the small but intriguing collection features a 2500-year-old Medusa pediment. The island's patron saint, Spyrídhon, is entombed in a silver-covered coffin in his own church on Vouthrótou, and four times a year, to the accompaniment of much celebration and feasting, the relics are paraded through the streets. Some 5km south of town lies the picturesque convent of **Vlahérna**, which is joined to the plush mainland suburb of Kanóni by a short causeway;

the tiny islet of **Pondikoníssi** in the bay is visited by frequent *kaïkia* (€1.50 return).

Kérkyra Town is just a short hop on the ferry to Albania.

Vátos and Pélekas

Much of the island's coastline has been remorselessly developed; the tiny village of **VÁTOS**, just inland from west-coast Érmones, is the one place within easy reach of Kérkyra Town that has an easy, relaxed feel to it and reasonable rooms and tavernas. Nearby **PÉLEKAS** is rather busy, but it's a good alternative base. The best option for independent travellers is to stay in the village, which has a free bus service to the beaches of Pélekas and Glyfada. Thanks to the village's hilltop location, there are some fine views over the surrounding countryside towards the coast.

Áyios Górdhis and around

Further south, **ÁYIOS GÓRDHIS** beach is more remote but that hasn't spared it from the crowds who come to admire the cliff-girt setting. Beyond Messongí stretches the flat, sandy southern tip of Corfu. **Áyios Yeóryios**, on the southwest coast, consists of a developed area just before its beautiful beach, which extends north alongside the peaceful Korissíon lagoon. **Kávos**, near the cape itself, rates with its many clubs and discos as the nightlife capital of the island; for daytime solitude and swimming, you can walk to beaches beyond the nearby hamlets of Sparterá and Dhragotiná.

Arrival and information

Air The airport is 2km from town. Local buses #2 and #3 leave from 500m north of the terminal gates. A taxi should cost €10.

Ferry Boats arrive at the new port, 1km west of town.

Tourist office There's an information booth at Platía Saróko (summer only: Mon–Sat 8am–11pm, Sun 8am–4pm).

Island transport

Local buses The bus stop is at Platía Saróko, where there's also a kiosk with timetable information. Bus #11 goes to Pélekas (7 daily).

Long-distance buses The bus station is on Avramiou, near the new fortress and the new port.

Accommodation

The Roomowners Association at D. Theotóki 2a near the Archeological Museum (daily 9am–1.30pm; Ⓣ2261 026 133, Ⓔoitkcrf@otenet.gr) is the best source of independent accommodation.

Kérkyra

Dionysus Camping Village Dhassiá, 8km north of Kérkyra Town Ⓣ2661 091 417, Ⓦwww.dionysuscamping.gr. Campsite with good facilities and sporting activities. Also has bungalows to rent for an extra €10 per person. Take bus #7. April–Oct. €6 per person, €4 per tent.

Europa Yitsiáli 10 Ⓣ2661 039 304. Close to the new port, these are the cheapest rooms in town, although hot water and cleanliness are not guaranteed. €30.

Around the island

Corfu Traveler's Inn Áyios Górdhis Ⓣ2661 053 935, Ⓔcorfutravelersinn@hotmail.com. Beachside accommodation with plenty of activities on offer. Prices include breakfast and dinner. Dorms €25, rooms €60.

Pension Martini Pélekas Ⓣ2261 094 326. Simple rooms have balconies with great views, and there's a lush garden too. €30.

The Pink Palace Áyios Górdhis Ⓣ2661 053 103, Ⓦwww.thepinkpalace.com. An enormous, youth-orientated holiday complex with jacuzzis, club, sports facilities, hairdressers, money exchange and more. Prices include breakfast and dinner. Dorms €23, rooms €40.

Vatos Camping Vátos Ⓣ2661 094 505. A small and simple campsite but close to the picturesque Myrtiótissa Beach. €10.

Eating and drinking

Kérkyra

Aleko's Beach On the jetty below the Palace of Sts Michael and George, serving typical Greek cuisine and seafood. Go later in the evening to soak up the atmosphere. Mains €7–9.

Mikro Café Theotóki & Kotárdou 42. A delightful café-bar with an inviting garden. Perfect for an evening drink. Beers €3, cocktails €6.50.

To Paradosiakon Solomoú 20. This colourful restaurant with pavement seating serves traditional dishes. Open from 10am. Mains €7–9.

Pélekas

Jimmy's Opposite a tiny, yellow church near the crossroads of the roads to Pelekas Beach and Kaiser's Throne lookout point, this friendly taverna serves excellent food all day, including vegetarian dishes and local specials. Mains €7–9.

Zanzibar By the small town square. Small, popular café-bar with an extensive cocktail menu and live music in the evenings. Beers €2, cocktails €4.50.

Moving on

Ferry Albania (1 daily; 30min); Ancona (2 weekly; 5hr); Bari (1 weekly; 9hr); Brindisi (2 daily; 8hr); Igoumenítsa (hourly; 1hr 30min); Pátra (daily; 8–11hr).

KEFALLONIÁ

Kefalloniá is the largest, and, at first glance, least glamorous, of the Ionian islands; the 1953 earthquake that rocked the archipelago was especially devastating here, with almost every town and village levelled. Already popular with Italians, the island has, in recent years, been attracting large numbers of British tourists, in no small part thanks to Louis de Bernières' novel, *Captain Corelli's Mandolin*, which was set here.

What to see and do

There's plenty of interest: beaches to compare with the best on Corfu or Zákynthos, good local wine, and the partly forested mass of Mount Énos (1628m). The island's size, skeletal bus service and shortage of summer accommodation make renting a motorbike or car a must for extensive exploration.

Argostóli

ARGOSTÓLI, with daily ferries to Kyllíni on the mainland, is the bustling, concrete, island capital. The town's **Archeological Museum** (Tues–Sun 8.30am–3pm; €3) is second only to Corfu's in the archipelago.

North of the island

Heading north, you come to the beach of **Mýrtos**, considered the best on the island, although lacking in facilities; the closest places to **stay** are nearby Dhivaráta and almost bus-less **Ássos**, a beautiful fishing port perched on a narrow isthmus linking it to a castellated headland. At the end of the line, **Fiskárdho**, with its eighteenth-century houses, is the most expensive place on the island; the main reason to come would be for the daily **ferry** to Lefkádha island, and crossings to Itháki.

The east coast

SÁMI, set against a natural backdrop of verdant, undulating hills, nestles itself into a sweeping bay. The town is the second port on the island, with boats to Itháki and Pátra. For film fanatics Sámi has an added appeal, since the region was the setting for the 2001 film *Captain Corelli's Mandolin*.

However, **AYÍA EFIMÍA**, 10km north, makes a far more attractive base. Between the two towns, 3km from Sámi, the **Melissáni cave** (daily 9am–sunset; €6), a partly submerged Capri-type "blue grotto", is well worth a stop. Southeast from Sámi are the resorts of **PÓROS**, with regular ferries to Kyllíni.

GREECE IN THE MOVIES

It's no surprise that Greece's photogenic sea, sands and dazzling light have provided the set for numerous films. Worth seeking out before your trip are **Shirley Valentine** (1989), the story of a downtrodden housewife's discovery of Mýkonos (see p.558) and al fresco love; the romantic musical comedy **Mamma Mia** (2008), filmed on Skópelos (see p.569) and the Bond film **For Your Eyes** Only (1981), set amid the spectacular cliff-top monasteries of the Metéora (see p.551).

Arrival and information

Ferry Ferries from Kyllíni mostly dock at Póros, although a daily ferry docks at Argostóli. Ferries from Pátra dock at Sámi.

Tourist offices The waterfront tourist office in Argostóli (Mon–Fri 7.30am–2.30pm; in summer also Mon–Fri 6–10pm & Sat & Sun 9am–2pm & 6–10pm; ⓣ26710 22 248) has lists of accommodation. There's also a tourist office in Sámi near the quay (ⓣ2674 022 019).

Island buses The bus station in Argostóli is just past the causeway, on I. Metaxa. There are buses to Ayía Efimía (4 daily), Fiskárdho (2 daily), Póros (2 daily) and Sámi (4 daily). There is no bus service on Sundays.

Accommodation

Hotel Melissani Sámi ⓣ2674 022. An interestingly, if wackily, decorated hotel. The fifteen en-suite rooms have balconies or verandas. May–Oct. €50.

Karavomilos Beach Sámi ⓣ2674 022 480, ⓦwww.camping-karavomilos.gr. A shady campsite near the beach, 1km from town. May–Sept. €7.50 per person, €6 per tent.

Moustakis Hotel Ayía Efimía ⓣ2674 061 030, ⓦwww.moustakishotel.com. Small but smart, this family-run hotel offers clean rooms with balconies. €70.

St Gerassimos Agíou Gerassímou 6, Argostóli ⓣ2671 028 697. Welcoming and centrally located hotel. Rooms are slightly dated but are well-equipped. €45.

Eating and drinking

Captain's Table Cnr I. Metaxa & 21 Maïou, Argostóli. A waterfront restaurant with a nautical theme serving everything from home-made pizza to fresh fish. Mains €6–9.

Mermaid Restaurant Sámi. In a wonderful location on the seafront, this friendly restaurant uses local produce to create hearty dishes. Mains €6–9.

Phoenix Vergoti 2, Argostóli. Just off the central square, this enclosed garden is a peaceful spot for a coffee by day, and a popular bar by night.

Moving on

Ferry Bari (1 weekly; 13hr 30min); Brindisi (1 weekly; 11hr); Itháki (5 daily; 30–45min); Kyllíni (11–12 daily; 1hr 15min–3hr); Pátra (1–3 daily; 2hr 30min).

Crete

CRETE is distinguished as the home of the **Minoan** civilization, Europe's earliest, which made the island the centre of a maritime trading empire as early as 2000 BC and produced artworks unsurpassed in the ancient world. The capital, **Iráklion**, is not the prettiest town on the island, although visits to its superb Archeological Museum and the Minoan palace at nearby **Knossos** are all but compulsory. There are other great Minoan sites at **Mália** on the north coast and at **Phaestos** in the south. Near the latter are the remains of the Roman capital at **Gortys**.

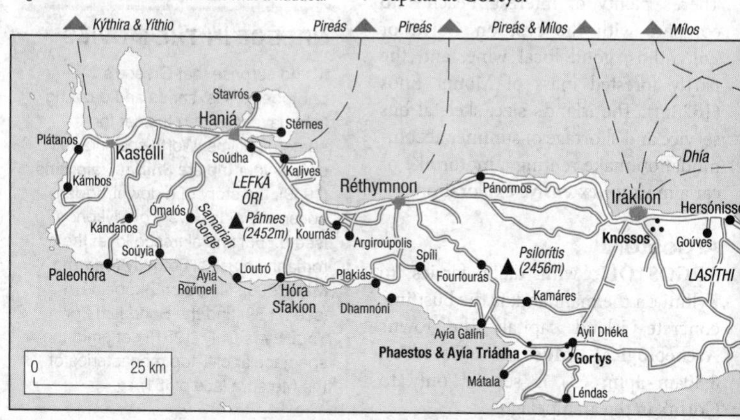

TRANSPORT AND ORIENTATION ON CRETE

Crete's **transport connections** are excellent. There are regular ferries from Pireás to Iráklion, Réthymnon, Haniá and Áyios Nikólaos, as well as regular connections to Kastélli and Sitía (all on the north coast), a constant stream of buses running between these places, and onward bus connections from these main centres to much of the rest of the island. Thanks to the tourists, there are also plenty of **day-trips** available in season, and small boats linking villages on the south coast. Rather than head for Iráklion, you're better off basing yourself initially in the beautiful city of Haniá (for the west, the mountains and the famous Samarian Gorge), in Réthymnon (only marginally less attractive, and handy for Iráklion, the major Minoan sites and the south), or Sitía to explore the far east.

Historical heritage apart, the main attractions are that inland this is still a place where traditional rural life continues, and that the island is big enough to ensure that, with a little effort, you can still get away from it all. There's also a surprisingly sophisticated club scene in the north-coast cities, and plenty of manic, beer-soaked tourist fun in the resorts in between.

IRÁKLION

The best way to approach bustling **IRÁKLION** is by sea; that way you see the city as it should be seen, with Mount Ioúktas rising behind and the Psiloritis range to the west. As you get closer, it's the fifteenth-century city walls which first stand out, still dominating and fully encircling the oldest part of town, and finally you sail in past the great Venetian fort defending the harbour entrance. With few sights to trek around, Iráklion is best enjoyed as a centre of great **café** life: the pedestrianized alleys off Dedhálou, especially Koráï, are crammed with tables and packed evenings and weekends. One thing not to miss is the excellent **Archeological Museum**, just off the north side of the main square, Platía Eleftherías (Mon 1–7.30pm, Tues–Sun 8am–7.30pm; €6). It hosts a collection that includes almost every important prehistoric and Minoan find on Crete (go early or late in the day to avoid tour groups).

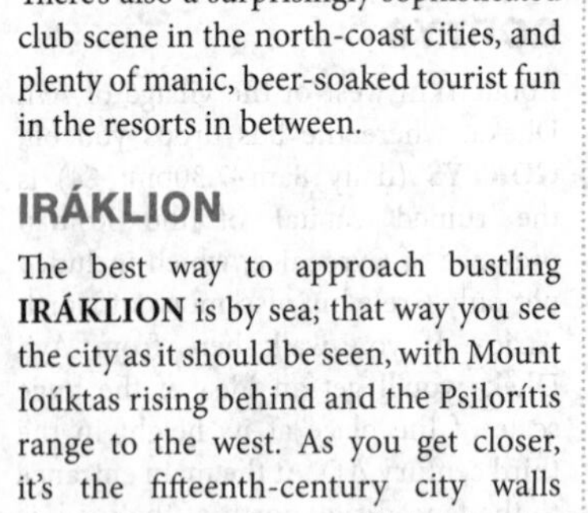

▲ Thíra
CRETE
N
Mália
Pláka
Áyios Nikólaos
Dhíkti (2148m)
Ierápetra
Mýrtos
Sitía
Vái
Zákros
Káto Zákros
Kásos, Kárpathos & Rhodes

Arrival and information

Ferry Boats dock at the quay which is at the eastern end of town. As you arrive, turn right to reach the centre.

Buses For all points along the north-coast highway and Knossos use Bus Station A close to the ferry dock; services on inland routes to the south and west (for Phaestos, for example) leave from a terminal outside the city walls at Haniá Gate.

Tourist office Close to the museum is the EOT (Mon–Sat 8.30am–8.30pm; ⓣ2810 246 106, ⓦwww.heraklion-city.gr).

Internet Gallery Games, Koráï 14, is open daily until 4am; €1.50/hr.

Accommodation

Hellas Rent Rooms Hándhakos 24 ⓣ2810 288 851. A popular option, with a roof garden, cheap breakfasts, a snack bar and panoramic views. Dorms €12, rooms €30.

Rea Kalimeráki 1 ⓣ2810 223 638, ⓦwww.hotelrea.gr. A clean and comfortable pension in a quiet location, with friendly staff. April–Oct. €32.
Youth Hostel Vírονos 5 ⓣ2810 286 281, ⓔherakliyouthhostel@yahoo.gr. Shabby and none too clean, but you won't find anything cheaper. Inexpensive meals are served in the restaurant, with home-grown ingredients. Dorms €10.

Eating

Ippokambos Sofokli Venizelou 3. The locals' choice for grilled meats and the freshest seafood. Authentic and delicious. Mains €6–9.
Peri Orexeos Koráï 10. A good choice for typical Cretan cuisine. There's a pleasant terrace too, for lazy breakfasts and snacks. Mains €6–9.

Moving on

Bus Áyios Nikólaos (every 30min until 10pm; 1hr 30min); Haniá (18 daily; 3hr); Hersónissos (every 30min; 45min); Knossos (every 10min; 20min); Mália (every 30min; 45min); Phaestos (8 daily; 1hr 30min); Réthymnon (hourly; 1hr 30min); Sitía (6 daily; 3hr).
Ferry Mýkonos (1–2 daily; 5–9hr); Iráklion to Páros & Cyclades (1–2 daily; 4–12hr); Iráklion to Pireás (5–7 daily; 12hr); Iráklion to Rhodes (2 weekly; 12–13hr); Kastélli to Yíthio (2 weekly; 7–8hr); Áyios Nikólaos and Sitía to Rhodes (3 weekly; 10hr).

KNOSSOS

The largest of the Minoan palaces, **KNOSSOS** (daily: April–Sept 8am–7.30pm, Oct–March 8.30am–5pm; €6; frequent buses from Iráklion) reached its cultural peak over 3500 years ago. Evidence of a luxurious lifestyle is plainest in the **Queen's Suite**, off the grand **Hall of the Colonnades** at the bottom of the stunningly impressive **Grand Staircase** (which visitors are no longer allowed to use but which can be viewed from above). Most extraordinary is the fact that until just over 100 years ago, Knossos was known only as a mythical place, the court of King Minos; the site was excavated by Sir Arthur Evans from 1900 onwards.

KNOSSOS AND THE MINOTAUR

Legend has it that King Minos built the labyrinth at Knossos to contain the **minotaur**. This terrifying creature with a man's body and a bull's head fed on fresh maidens and young men – until Theseus, prince of Athens, arrived to slay the monster, and, with Minos's daughter Ariadne's help, successfully escape the maze.

TREAT YOURSELF

Pagopiion is a chic and sleek bar/restaurant occupying a prime spot on Platía Ayíou Títou. A night's drinking soon adds up here, but the supercool setting in an old ice house is *the* place to experience a night out in Iráklion.

GORTYS

About 1km west of the village of Áyii Dhéka, where the bus drops you off, **GORTYS** (daily 8am–7.30pm; €4) is the ruined capital of the Roman province of Cyrenaica, which included not only Crete but also much of North Africa. If you walk here from Áyii Dhéka you'll get an idea of the huge scale of the place at its height in the third century AD. At the main entrance to the fenced site, north of the road, is the ruined but still impressive basilica of **Áyios Títos**, the island's first Christian church and burial place of the saint (Titus) who converted Crete and was also its first bishop. Beyond this is the **Odeion**, which houses the most important discovery on the site, the **Law Code** – ancient laws inscribed on stones measuring about 10m by 3m.

HERSÓNISSOS AND MÁLIA

The coast east of Iráklion was the first to be developed, and is still the domain of the package tourist. There are some good beaches, but all of them fully occupied. The heart of the development lies around **HERSÓNISSOS** and

MÁLIA, which these days form virtually a single resort. If it's the party-holiday spirit you're after, this is the place to come. Hersónissos is perhaps slightly classier, but Mália was a bigger place to start with, which means there's a real town on the south side of the main road, with more chance of reasonably priced food and accommodation. Wherever you go, you'll have no problem finding bars, clubs and English (or Irish or even Dutch) pubs. Some of the better beaches stretch east from Mália, where the atmospheric ruins of the **Palace of Mália** (Tues–Sun 8am–7pm; €4), much less visited than Knossos or Phaestos, boast a virtually intact ground plan.

SITÍA

Sleepy **SITÍA**, the port and main town of the relatively unexploited eastern edge of Crete, may be about to wake up. For the moment, though, it still offers a plethora of waterside restaurants, a long sandy beach and a lazy lifestyle little affected by the thousands of visitors in peak season. There are several cheap **rooms** around Kondhiláki, a few streets back from the harbour. At the eastern end of the island, **VÁÏ BEACH** is the most famous on Crete thanks to its ancient grove of palm trees. In season, though, its undoubted charms, now fenced off, are diluted by crowds of day-trippers. Other beaches at nearby **Ítanos** or **Pálekastro** – Crete's main windsurfing centre – are less exotic but emptier. Or head further south – at **Káto Zákros** the pebbly beach is right by another important Minoan palace.

Arrival and information

Bus The bus station is on the southern edge of town, a short walk from the town's centre.
Ferry The harbour is centrally located.
Tourist offices On the seafront (Mon–Fri 9.30am–2.30pm & 5–9pm, Sat 9.30am–2.30pm; ☎2843 028 300).

Accommodation and eating

Hotel Arhontiko Kondhiláki 16, Sitía ☎2843 028 172. This welcoming family-run guesthouse has clean and simple rooms, and a leafy garden at the front. €25.
Taverna Mihos Kornárou 117, Sitía. A traditional taverna with seating along the waterfront. There's a varied menu, including seafood and Cretan specialities. Mains €5–9.

Island transport

Bus Áyios Nikólaos (7 daily; 1hr 30min); Iráklion (7 daily; 3hr); Mália (7 daily; 2hr 15min).

RÉTHYMNON

West of Iráklion, the old town of **RÉTHYMNON** is a labyrinthine tangle of Venetian and Turkish houses set around an enclosed sixteenth-century harbour and wide sandy beach. Medieval minarets lend an exotic air to the skyline, while dominating everything from the west is the superbly preserved outline of the **Venetian fortress** (daily 8am–8pm; €3.10). Much of the pleasure is in wandering the streets of the old town once the sun has set; there's an unbroken line of tavernas, cafés and cocktail bars right around the waterside and into the area around the old port. Better-value places are found around the seventeenth-century Venetian **Rimóndi Fountain**, an easily located landmark. The heart of Réthymnon's nightlife – which, although abundant, doesn't warm up until midnight – centres on the Venetian port.

Arrival and information

Bus From the bus station, head around the inland side of the fortress to reach the beach and the centre.
Tourist office Located right on the beach (Mon–Fri 8am–2.30pm, Sat 10am–4pm; ☎2831 029 148).

Accommodation

Barbara Dokimaki Rooms Dambérgi 14 ☎2831 024 581. Pleasant en-suite rooms with kitchenettes, set around a small courtyard or terrace area. €40.

Camping Elizabeth Missiria, 4km east of Réthymnon ⓣ2831 028 694, ⓦwww.camping-elizabeth.com. This campsite is in the hotel strip along the beach, served by frequent buses from the main bus station. April–Oct. €7.20 per person, €5.20 per tent.

Olga's Pension Soulíou 57 ⓣ2831 053 206. Small but attractive rooms are individually decorated, and there's a flower-filled roof garden. A gem. €45.

Youth Hostel Tombázi 41 ⓣ2831 022 848, ⓦwww.yhrethymno.com. This friendly and relaxed hostel has clean facilities, cheap breakfasts and internet access. Dorms €10.

Eating, drinking and nightlife

Rock Club Cafe I. Petichaki 6. A long-standing favourite near the harbour, this club kicks off around midnight and plays mainstream sounds.

Metropolis Nearchou 15 ⓦwww.metropolis-crete.com. A funky bar with a scattering of themed events, karaoke and live music. Free entry.

Stella's Kitchen Soulíou 55. Popular with the locals, this café is good for breakfasts and great-value daily specials, a couple of which are always vegetarian. Open 8am–9pm. Mains €5–6.

To Pigandi Xanthoúdhidhou 31. Despite the well-dressed clientele, this unpretentious restaurant is great value. There's an atmospheric garden and excellent food with attentive service. Mains €7–12.

Moving on

Bus Haniá (hourly; 1hr); Iráklion (hourly; 1hr 30min).

PLAKIÁS

Réthymnon lies at one of the narrower parts of Crete, so it's relatively quick to cut across from here to the south coast. The obvious place to head is **PLAKIÁS**, a growing resort which has managed to retain a small-town atmosphere. There are numerous **rooms**, very busy in August, as well as a relaxed and friendly youth **hostel** (ⓣ2832 032 118, ⓦwww.yhplakias.com; dorms €9) at the back of the town, and *Camping Appollonia* (ⓣ2832 031 507; €10) on the road in from Réthymnon. Locals can point you in the direction of quieter beaches all around, with boat trips to many of them.

HANIÁ

HANIÁ is the spiritual capital of Crete; for many, it is also the island's most attractive city – especially in spring, when the snowcapped peaks of the Lefká Óri (White Mountains) seem to hover above the roofs.

What to see and do

The **port area** is the oldest and the most interesting part of town. The little hill that rises behind the landmark domes of the quayside Mosque of the Janissaries is called **Kastélli**, site of the earliest Minoan habitation and core of the Venetian and Turkish towns. Beneath the hill, on the inner harbour, the arches of sixteenth-century Venetian arsenals survive alongside remains of the outer walls. Behind the harbour lie the less picturesque but more lively sections of

HIKING THE SAMARIAN GORGE

The **Samarian Gorge** – Europe's longest – is an easy day-trip from Haniá (May–Oct only), as there are regular buses. If you do it, though, be warned that you will not be alone: dozens of coachloads set off before dawn from all over Crete for the dramatic climb into the White Mountains and the long (at least 4hr) walk down. At the bottom of the gorge is the village of Ayía Roúmeli from where boats will take you east to Hóra Sfakíon and your bus home, or west towards the pleasant resorts of Soúyia and Paleohóra. The mountains offer endless other **hiking challenges** to help you escape the crowds. Soúyia and Paleohóra are both good starting points, as is Loutró, a tiny place halfway to Hóra Sfakíon, accessible only by boat. These places also have decent beaches, and from Paleohóra you can reach more at the far west of the island where only Elafoníssi, an isolated beach with an almost tropical-lagoon feel, ever sees crowds.

the old city. Around the cathedral on Halídhon are some of the more animated shopping areas, particularly leather-dominated **Odhós Skrídhlof**.

Beaches

Haniá's **beaches** all lie to the west: the packed city beach is a ten-minute walk beyond the Maritime Museum, but for good sand you're better off taking the bus from the east side of Platía 1866 along the coast road to Kalamáki. In between you'll find emptier stretches if you're prepared to walk some of the way.

Arrival and information

Bus The bus station is on Odhós Kydhonías, within easy walking distance of the centre: turn right, then left down the side of Platía 1866, and you'll emerge at a major road junction opposite the top of Halídhon, the main street of the old quarter.

Ferry Ferries dock about 10km away at the port of Soúdha: there are frequent city buses which will drop you by the market on the fringes of the old town.

Tourist office In the *Dhimarhío* (town hall) at Kydhonías 29, four blocks east of the bus station (summer only: Mon–Fri 8am–2.30pm; ⓣ2821 036 155). They can help with accommodation.

Internet Triple W, on the corner of Balantinou & Halídhon, is open 24 hours a day.

Accommodation

Camping Hania 4km west of town ⓣ2821 031 138. A small site, but it has a pool and is close to the beaches. Get there by city bus from Platía 1866. March–Oct. €5 per adult, €4 per tent.

Earini Rooms Halídhon 27 ⓣ2821 057 666. A hospitable welcome and decent rooms are found at this well-situated guesthouse. There's also a large apartment. Rooms €50, apartment €165.

Mme Bassia Betólo 45–51 ⓣ2821 055 087, ⓦwww.mmebassia.gr. A charming pension with a homely atmosphere. Traditionally decorated rooms are a good size, and there's a tiny roof garden too. €45.

Pension Nora Theotokopoúlou 60 ⓣ2821 072 265, ⓔpensionnora@yahoo.co.uk. Charming a/c en-suite rooms in an old wooden Turkish house, with access to a shared kitchen. €40.

Eating and drinking

Ababa Tapas Café 12 Eisodion. Secreted off a side street behind the harbour, this warm, funky bar lures with twinkling lights, decent tunes and charming staff. Tapas dishes from €6.

Ellotia 1 Párodos Pórtou 6. This cosy garden taverna serves delicious traditional fare in a leafy setting. Grills €6–9.

Metropolitan Betólo 28. Food is pricey, but come to this American-style bar in the evenings for live music from 10pm. Cover charge €1.50.

Tamam Zambelíou 49. A converted Turkish bathhouse houses this restaurant which has an adventurous menu. Especially popular with vegetarians and wine-lovers. Mains €5–9.

Moving on

Bus Iráklion (hourly; 3hr); Omalos (for the Samarian Gorge; 4 daily when the gorge is open; 1hr); Réthymnon (hourly; 1hr).

Hungary

HIGHLIGHTS ✪

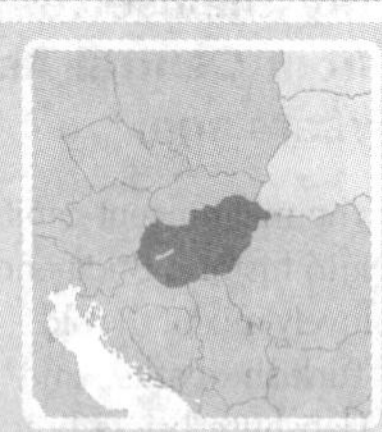

SZÉPASSZONY VALLEY: sup some outstanding wines at the valley's various cellars

THERMAL BATHS, BUDAPEST: take a plunge into the steamy, healing waters

COMMMUNIST STATUE PARK, BUDAPEST: visit the fascinating graveyard for statues of old dictators

KECSKEMÉT: enjoy fabulous horse-riding, and feast on the region's famous Mangalica pork

PÉCS: chill out in this young, lively city packed with brightly coloured buildings and great cafés

ROUGH COSTS

DAILY BUDGET Basic €25/occasional treat €45

DRINK Beer (large) €1.10

FOOD Goulash €3

HOSTEL/BUDGET HOTEL €10–30

TRAVEL Budapest–Szeged (175km); €10 by train Pécs–Keszthely (150km) €10 by bus

FACT FILE

POPULATION 10 million

AREA 93,000 sq km

LANGUAGE Hungarian

CURRENCY Forint (Ft)

CAPITAL Budapest (population 2.5 million)

INTERNATIONAL PHONE CODE ☎36

Introduction

Visitors who refer to Hungary as a Balkan country risk getting a lecture on how this small, landlocked country of ten million people differs from other Slavic nations: locals fiercely identify themselves as Magyar – a race that transplanted itself from Central Asia into the heart of Europe over a thousand years ago.

The magnificent capital, **Budapest** (split into historic Buda and vibrant Pest), is a lovely mix of the old – with coffee houses, Turkish baths and a penchant for Habsburg bric-a-brac – and the new: it has an eager modern feel, with international fashions snapped up and adapted to local tastes. Outside the capital, there's much to explore: a short way north of Budapest, on a beautiful stretch of the River Danube, is **Szentendre**, while to the west lies **Lake Balaton**, the "nation's playground", encircled with a string of brash resorts, such as **Siófok** and **Keszthely**, and the lush volcanic **Badacsony** region. The Great Plain stretches south, covering half of the country with some stunning National Parks and the culture-rich cities of **Szeged** and **Kecskemét**. Other highlights include the delightful city of **Sopron**, on the border with Austria, and Turkish-flavoured **Pécs**, in the south. The forested Northern Uplands in the far northeast towards Ukraine envelop the beautiful Baroque town of **Eger**, famed for its wine.

CHRONOLOGY

9 BC Area around the Danube is conquered by the Romans.
453 AD Attila the Hun's empire is based in Hungary.
896 Country of the Magyars founded.
1000 Kingdom of Hungary established by Saint Stephen.
1242 The Mongols attack Hungary, wreaking havoc across the country.
1526 The Hungarian army is defeated by the Ottomans in the Battle of Mohács and the country is split into three areas.
1699 The Turks are defeated and expelled from Hungary by the Austrian Habsburgs.
1867 In order to quell separatist calls, Austria accepts greater Hungarian autonomy and officially becomes Austria-Hungary.
1918 After World War I, Austria-Hungary is split into two countries.
1938 Hungarian journalist Lasislao Jose Biro invents the ballpoint pen.
1939 Hungary opts for neutrality at the beginning of World War II.
1945 Soviets invade Hungary, causing devastation.
1947 Soviets consolidate their postwar power in Hungary.
1956 National uprising against Soviet occupation is brutally repressed.
1989 Collapse of Soviet Communism.
1990 Hungary's first free elections held.
2004 Hungary joins the EU.
2006 Mass protests as it transpires the government lied about the state of the economy in order to gain re-election.
2008 The IMF grants a €20 billion package to rescue the Hungarian economy during the global financial crisis.

ARRIVAL

Flights to Budapest arrive at Ferihegy airport, 20km from the centre; bus and metro connect into Budapest or alternatively, there's an airport bus that will take you straight to your accommodation. Several budget airlines now fly to Balaton airport – the closest town is Keszthely, with a regular bus service between the two.

Most international **trains** arrive at Keleti pu in Budapest, although Nyugati pu and Déli pu also handle international arrivals (see "Arrivals" in the Budapest section). Global or One Country Interrail passes are valid on all trains.

International **buses** are generally operated by Eurolines, or Volánbusz, its

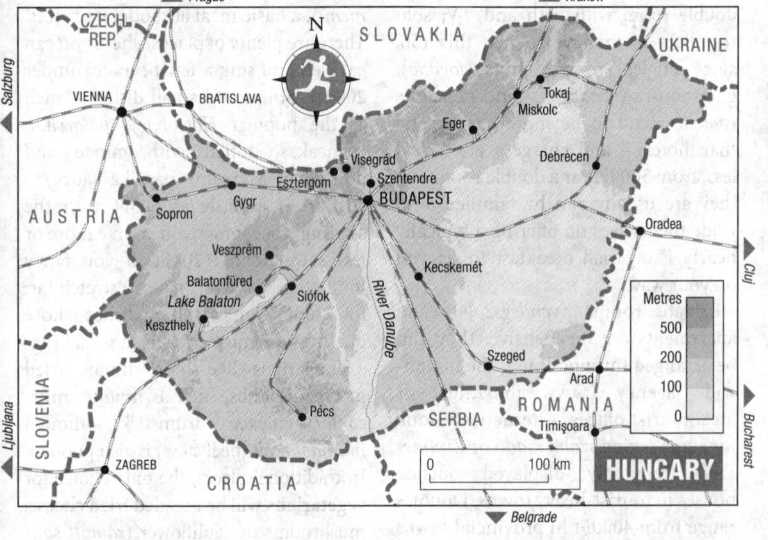

Hungarian associate, with their two main terminals in Budapest.

GETTING AROUND

Public transport in Hungary is cheap, clean and fairly reliable. The only problem is getting information – staff rarely speak anything but Hungarian, or a little German.

Intercity **trains** are the fastest way of getting to the major towns, though seat reservations, made at any MÁV office (Ⓦwww.mav-start.hu), are compulsory and cost an extra 350–480Ft; *személyvonat* trains, which stop at every hamlet en route, do not incur the reservation fee. You can buy **tickets** (*jegy*) for domestic services at the station (*pályaudvar* or *vasútállomás*) on the day of departure, but it's best to buy tickets for international trains (*nemzetközi gyorsvonat*) at least 36hr in advance. You're permitted to break your journey once. When buying your ticket, specify whether you want a one-way ticket (*egy útra*), or a return (*retur* or *oda-vissza*). For a journey of 100km, travelling second-class on an express train, expect to pay around 2000Ft.

Volán (Ⓦwww.menetrendek.hu) runs the bulk of Hungary's **buses**, which are often the quickest way to travel between the smaller towns. Arrive early to confirm times and get a seat. For **long-distance services** from Budapest and the major towns, you can book a seat up to 30min before departure; after that, you get them from the driver (and risk standing). For a journey of 100km, expect to pay around 1500Ft.

ACCOMMODATION

Accommodation tends to fill up during high season, so it's wise to **book ahead**. Well-run youth **hostels** are becoming increasingly common in the main tourist destinations, but in smaller, less-visited towns you may have to rely on characterless but extremely cheap university dorms – rooms are rented out in July and August, and are often available at weekends year-round; local tourist offices will provide information and assist with bookings.

Outside Budapest and Lake Balaton (where prices are thirty percent higher), a three-star **hotel** (*szálló* or *szálloda*) will charge from around 12,000Ft for a

double room with bath and TV; solo travellers often have to pay this too, since singles are rare. **Inns** (*fogadó*), guesthouses (*vendégház*) and **pensions** (*panzió*) tend to be more charismatic than hotels – and charge a good deal less, from 5000Ft for a double room – as they are usually run by families, who pride themselves on offering a typically hearty Hungarian breakfast to set you on your way.

Private rooms (*vendégszoba*) and apartments are inexpensive; they can be arranged through Ibusz, the nationwide agency (Ⓦwww.ibusz.hu), or local tourist offices. Alternatively, look for signs saying *szoba kiadó* or *Zimmer Frei*, frequently displayed outside houses in tourist-heavy towns. Doubles range from 4000Ft in provincial towns to around 6000Ft in Budapest and around Balaton.

Bungalows (*faház*) proliferate around resorts and on the larger campsites. First-class bungalows come with kitchens, hot water and a sitting room or terrace, and will cost a few thousand forints, while the most primitive at least have clean bedding and don't leak. **Campsites** (usually signposted *Kemping*) range from de luxe to third class. In high season, expect to pay anything up to 3500Ft, more around Lake Balaton.

FOOD AND DRINK

For foreigners, the archetypal **Hungarian dish** is goulash (*gulyásleves*) – historically a soup made of potatoes and meat, which was later flavoured with paprika. Hungarians like a calorific **breakfast** (*reggeli*) that includes cheese, eggs and salami, plus bread and jam. **Coffee houses** (*kávéház*) are increasingly trendy and you'll find many serving breakfast and a coffee with milk (*tejeskávé*) or whipped cream (*tejszínhabbal*). Most Hungarians take their coffee short and strong (*eszpresszó*).

The main meal of the day is **lunch**, when some places offer set menus (*napi menű*), a basic meal at moderate prices. There are plenty of places where you can eat well and sink a few beers for under 2000Ft. Soups and small dishes – such as the popular *Hortobágyi palacsinta* (pancakes stuffed with mince and doused in a creamy paprika sauce) – cost from as little as 600Ft with the starting price for a main course more or less standard at 1200Ft. If you fancy indulging, you won't have to stretch far: for 2500Ft, you can enjoy dishes whose quality – and quantity – is fit for a king.

Hungarians like most things fried in breadcrumbs, such as *rántott csirkecomb* (chicken drumstick), though *marhapörkölt* (beef stew) is also popular. In traditional places, the only choice for **vegetarians** will be breaded fried cheese, mushrooms or cauliflower (*rántott sajt/gomba/karfiol*). A whole range of places sell **snacks:** pancakes (*palacsinta*, from 1000Ft) with fillings are very popular, as are strudels (*rétes*; about 350Ft). On the streets you can buy, in summer, corn-on-the-cob (*kukorica*) and in winter, roasted chestnuts (*gesztenye*); while stalls selling fried fish (*sült hal*) are common in towns near rivers or lakes.

Drink

Hungary's mild climate and diversity of soils is perfect for **wine** (*bor*), which is perennially cheap, whether you buy it by the bottle (*üveg*) or the glass (*pohár*). Perhaps the most famous region is the Tokaj-Hegyalja, known predominantly for dessert wine. *Bikavér*, produced in Eger and known as "Bull's Blood", is a well-known, robust red, while the rich, sweet Médoc Noir, from the same vineyard, is worth a try. The best whites are found in the Balaton region, especially around the Badacsony.

Wine bars (*borozó*) are ubiquitous, while true grape devotees make pilgrimages to the wine cellars (*borpince*) around Pécs and Eger. The best-known types of **brandy** (*pálinka*) are distilled

from apricots (*barack*) and plums (*szilva*), the latter often available in private homes in a mouth-scorching, home-distilled version. **Beer** (*sör*) of the lager type (*világos*) predominates, although you can also find **brown ale** (*barna*): these come in draught form (*csapolt sör*) or in bottles (*üveges sör*). Local brands to look out for are Pécsi Szalon sör and Soproni Ászok.

CULTURE AND ETIQUETTE

Hungarians are not generally a reserved bunch, and almost always go out of their way to help if you need directions or assistance. The younger generation are especially welcoming and approachable, eager to show visitors a good time and share their views on their country and its history.

The expected rules apply regarding sensible clothing in churches and places of worship. **Tipping** waiters and taxi-drivers roughly ten percent is more or less expected; in restaurants it is more common to do so as part of paying the bill, rather than leaving it on the table.

SPORTS AND OUTDOOR ACTIVITIES

Hungary offers some of the best **horse-riding** in Europe, as well as fantastic horse-shows during the summer. Head for the Great Plain, especially Kecskemét and areas around the Kiskunság National Park. There are a number of tour operators but it's cheapest to go for independent ones – local tourist offices have relevant details. Visit ⓦwww.hiddentrails.com/country/Hungary.aspx for details.

The flatness of the Great Plain and beautiful landscape are great for **cycling**. Tourinform (the national tourist office, with branches in every town) can provide cycling maps with recommended routes, and bikes can be hired in almost every town at reasonable prices. There are scores of **hiking** opportunities all over the country; the Badacsony in Balaton, in particular, is very accessible, and has stunning views over the lake to reward you at the end of your trek. Tourinform can provide maps and information.

HUNGARY ON THE NET

ⓦ**www.tourinform.hu** National tourist office.
ⓦ**www.travelport.hu** Transport and accommodation info.
ⓦ**www.budapestinfo.hu** Comprehensive site with up-to-the-minute listings.
ⓦ**www.mav-start.hu** Train timetables and information.

COMMUNICATIONS

Larger **post offices** (*posta*) are usually open Monday to Friday 8am to 6pm, Saturday 8am to 1pm. Smaller branches close at 3pm and don't always open on Saturday. You can make local calls from **public phones**, where 20Ft is the minimum charge, or, better, from cardphones; cards come in 50 and 120 units and can be bought from post offices and newsstands. To make national calls, dial ⓣ06, wait for the buzzing tone, then dial the area code and number. You can make international calls from most public phones: dial ⓣ00, wait for the buzzing tone, then dial the country code and number as usual. **Internet access** is widely available (usually 400–700Ft/hr) in most towns.

EMERGENCIES

Tourists are treated with respect by the police (*rendörség*) – unless they're suspected of black-marketeering, drug

EMERGENCY NUMBERS

Police ⓣ107; Ambulance ⓣ104; Fire ⓣ105.

Hungarian

	Hungarian	Pronunciation
Yes	*Igen*	I-gen
No	*Nem*	Nem
Please	*Kérem*	Kay-rem
Thank you	*Köszönöm*	Kur-sur-nurm
Hello/Good day	*Jó napot*	Yo nopot
Goodbye	*Viszontlátásra*	Vee-sont-lar-tarsh-rar
Excuse me	*Bocsánat*	Botch-ah-not
Good	*Jó*	Yo
Bad	*Rossz*	Ross
Today	*Ma*	Ma
Yesterday	*Tegnap*	Teg-nop
Tomorrow	*Holnap*	Hall-nop
How much is...?	*Mennyibe kerül...?*	Men-yi-beh keh-rool...?
What time is it?	*Hány óra van?*	Hine-ora von?
I don't understand	*Nem értem*	Nem ear-tem
Do you speak English?	*Beszél Angolul?*	Beh-sail ong-olool?
One	*Egy*	Edge
Two	*Kettö*	Ket-tur
Three	*Három*	Hah-rom
Four	*Négy*	Naidge
Five	*Öt*	Urt
Six	*Hat*	Hot
Seven	*Hét*	Hait
Eight	*Nyolc*	Nyolts
Nine	*Kilenc*	Kee-lents
Ten	*Tíz*	Teez
Where is/are?	*Hol van/vannak?*	Hawl-von/von-nok?
Entrance	*bejárat*	beyah-ro
Exit	*kijárat*	kiyah-rot
Women's toilet	*női*	nuy
Men's toilet	*férfi mosdó*	fayr-fi maws-daw
Toilet	*WC*	vait-say
hotel	*szálloda*	sahlaw-da
Railway station	*vasútállomás*	voh-sootal-law-mass
Bus/train stop	*megalló*	meh-gall-o
Plane	*repülőgép*	repoo-lur-gepp
Near	*közel*	kur-zel
Far	*távol*	tav-oll
Single room	*egyágyas szoba*	edg-yahg-yos saw-ba
Double room	*kétágyas szoba*	kay-tadg-yas soba
Cheap	*Olcsó*	Ol-cho
Expensive	*Drága*	Drah-ga
Open	*Nyitva*	Nyeet-va
Closed	*Zárva*	Zah-rva

smuggling or driving under the influence of alcohol. Most police have some German, but rarely any other foreign language. Be sure to always carry your passport or a photocopy.

All towns and some villages have a **pharmacy** (*gyógyszertár* or *patika*), with staff – often German-speaking – authorized to issue a wide range of drugs. Opening hours are generally Monday to

Friday 9am to 6pm, Saturday 9am to noon or 1pm; signs in the window give the location of all-night pharmacies (*ügyeletes gyógyszertár*). Tourist offices can direct you to local medical centres or doctors' surgeries (*orvosi rendelő*); these will probably be in private (*magán*) practice, so be sure to carry health insurance. EU citizens have reciprocal arrangements for emergency treatment, but only at state hospitals.

INFORMATION

You'll find branches of **Tourinform**, Hungary's national tourist office, in the capital and in just about every other town across the country. They don't usually book accommodation, but do have information on where rooms and beds are available, including the *Hungarian Hotel and Camping Guide* booklet. There are also **local tourist offices** in larger towns (such as Balatontourist around Lake Balaton), where you can **book rooms**.

MONEY AND BANKS

Currency is the **forint** (Ft), which comes in notes of 200Ft, 500Ft, 1000Ft, 2000Ft, 5000Ft, 10,000Ft and 20,000Ft, and in coins of 1Ft, 2Ft, 5Ft, 10Ft, 20Ft, 50Ft and 100Ft. At the time of writing, €1=285Ft, US$1=200Ft, and £1=325Ft. Standard **banking hours** are Monday to Thursday 8am to 4pm, Friday 8am to 3pm. **ATMs** are widespread throughout the country, and you can use a **credit card** to pay in many hotels, restaurants and shops.

OPENING HOURS AND HOLIDAYS

Shops are generally open Monday top Friday 10am to 6pm, Saturday 10am to 1pm, except on the following public holidays: January 1, March 15, Easter Monday, May 1, Whit Monday, August 20, October 23, November 1, December 25 and 26. Shopping centres operate later hours and are generally open every day.

Budapest and around

The importance of **BUDAPEST** to Hungary is difficult to overestimate. Around two million people – one-fifth of the population – live in the city, and everything converges here: wealth, political power, cultural life and transport. Surveying the city from Castle Hill, it's obvious why Budapest was dubbed the "Pearl of the Danube" – its grand buildings and sweeping bridges look magnificent, especially when floodlit.

The **River Danube** (Duna) determines basic orientation, with **Pest** sprawled across the eastern plain and **Buda** reclining on the hilly west bank. Each of Budapest's 23 districts (*kerületek*) is designated on maps, street signs and at the beginning of addresses by a Roman numeral; "V" is Belváros (inner city), on the Pest side; "I" is the Castle district in Buda.

What to see and do

Castle Hill (Várhegy) is the most prominent feature of the **Buda** district, a plateau one mile long, laden with old mansions and the huge Buda Palace. **Pest**, across the river, is busy and brimming with youthful enthusiasm – quite the opposite of its fairytale "other half".

Buda: Castle Hill

Castle Hill is easily reached via the **Chain Bridge**, opened in 1849 and the first permanent bridge between Buda and Pest. From the busy Clark Ádám tér on the western side of the bridge, you can ride up Castle Hill on the nineteenth-century funicular or **Sikló** (daily 7.30am–10pm; 800Ft up or 1400Ft return), or else make the view even more satisfying by walking up the leafy path from Clark Ádám tér. Alternatively, take the red metro to Moszkva tér and the *Várbusz* from there.

Szentháromság tér

Szentháromság tér, the busy square at the heart of the district, sprawls in front of the wildly asymmetrical **Mátyás Church** (Mon–Fri 9am–5pm, Sat 9am–1pm, Sun 1–5pm; 700Ft). The church is a riotous nineteenth-century recreation grafted onto those portions of the thirteenth-century structure that survived one hundred and fifty years of Ottoman rule, during which time it became a mosque, to be turned back into a church after the siege of 1686. An equestrian statue of **King Stephen** stands outside the church, commemorating the ruler who forced Catholicism onto his subjects, thus aligning Hungary with the culture of Western Europe. Behind the church is the decorative, neo-Romanesque **Fishermen's Bastion** or Halászbástya (daily mid-March to Oct 9am–11pm; 200Ft), which offers a splendid view of Parliament across the river.

Buda Palace

To the south of Szentháromság tér the street widens as it approaches the **Buda Palace**. The fortifications and dwellings have undergone relentless invasions and reconstructions since the thirteenth century, each time rebuilt in the architectural style of the age. Today's neo-Classical style was taken on following destruction during the Second World War. The **National Gallery** (Tues–Sun 10am–6pm; 800Ft; Ⓦwww.mng.hu), occupying the central wings B, C and D, contains Hungarian art spanning the Middle Ages to the present day. On the far side of the Lion Courtyard, the fascinating and comprehensive **Budapest History Museum** in Wing E (March–Sept 10am–6pm, Oct–Feb Wed–Mon 10am–4/6pm, closed Tues; 1200Ft Ⓦwww.btm.hu) gives the turbulent history of the city, with reproductions of what it would have looked like in medieval times.

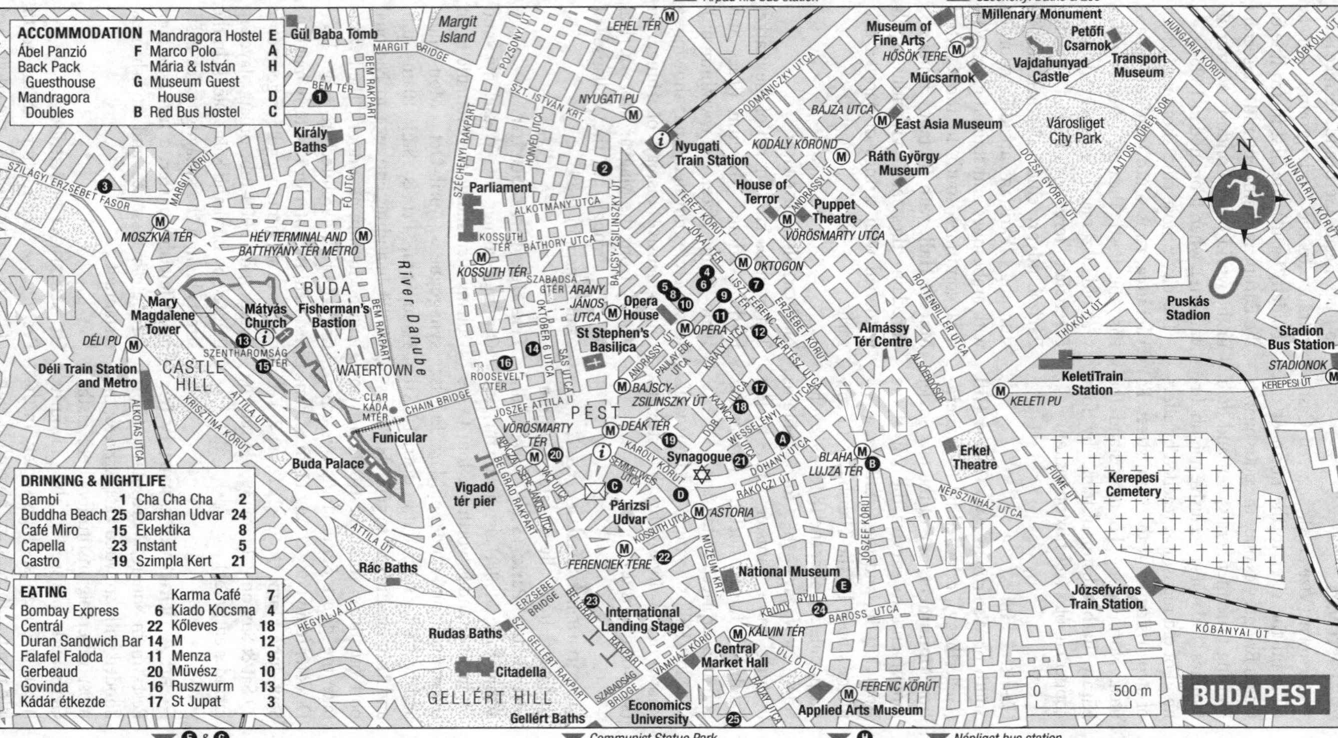
BUDAPEST
ACCOMMODATION
Ábel Panzió F
Back Pack Guesthouse G
Mandragora Doubles B
Mandragora Hostel E
Marco Polo A
Mária & István H
Museum Guest House D
Red Bus Hostel C
DRINKING & NIGHTLIFE
Bambi 1
Buddha Beach 25
Café Miro 15
Capella 23
Castro 19
Cha Cha Cha 2
Darshan Udvar 24
Eklektika 8
Instant 5
Szimpla Kert 21
EATING
Bombay Express 6
Centrál 22
Duran Sandwich Bar 14
Falafel Faloda 11
Gerbeaud 20
Govinda 16
Kádár étkezde 17
Karma Café 7
Kiado Kocsma 4
Kőleves 18
M 12
Menza 9
Müvész 10
Ruszwurm 13
St Jupat 3
Árpád híd bus station
Széchenyi Baths & Zoo
F & G
Communist Statue Park
H
Népliget bus station
Gül Baba Tomb
Margit Island
MARGIT BRIDGE
BEM TÉR
BEM RAKPART
Király Baths
FŐ UTCA
SZILÁGYI ERZSÉBET FASOR
MARGIT KÖRUT
MOSZKVA TÉR
HÉV TERMINAL AND BATTHYÁNY TÉR METRO
XII
II
I
BUDA
Mary Magdalene Tower
Mátyás Church
Fisherman's Bastion
DÉLI PU
SZENTHÁROMSÁG TÉR
CASTLE HILL
WATERTOWN
Déli Train Station and Metro
ALKOTÁS UTCA
KRISZTINA KÖRUT
ATTILA ÚT
CLARK ÁDÁM TÉR
CHAIN BRIDGE
Funicular
Buda Palace
River Danube
Rác Baths
HEGYALJA ÚT
Rudas Baths
Citadella
GELLÉRT HILL
Gellért Baths
ERZSÉBET BRIDGE
SZT. GELLÉRT RAKPART
SZABADSÁG BRIDGE
POZSONYI ÚT
SZT. ISTVÁN KRT.
HONVÉD UTCA
SZÉCHENYI RAKPART
Parliament
KOSSUTH TÉR
ALKOTMÁNY UTCA
BÁTHORY UTCA
SZABADSÁG TÉR
ARANY JÁNOS UTCA
OKTÓBER 6 UTCA
SAS UTCA
V
ROOSEVELT TÉR
JÓZSEF ATTILA U
VÖRÖSMARTY TÉR
VÁCI UTCA
APÁCZAI CSERE JÁNOS UTCA
BELGRÁD RAKPART
Vigadó tér pier
PEST
DEÁK TÉR
Párizsi Udvar
FERENCIEK TERE
KOSSUTH UTCA
International Landing Stage
LEHEL TÉR
NYUGATI PU
BAJCSY-ZSILINSZKY ÚT
Nyugati Train Station
VI
PODMANICZKY UTCA
TERÉZ KÖRUT
JÓKAI TÉR
Opera House
St Stephen's Basilica
OPERA
ANDRÁSSY ÚT
PAULAY EDE UTCA
KIRÁLY UTCA
KAZINCZY
DOB
WESSELÉNYI
Synagogue
KÁROLY KÖRUT
SEMMELWEIS UTCA
DOHÁNY UTCA
RÁKÓCZI ÚT
ASTORIA
MÚZEUM KRT.
National Museum
KÁLVIN TÉR
VÁMHÁZ KÖRUT
Central Market Hall
Economics University
IX
ÜLLŐI ÚT
RÁDAY UTCA
LISZT FERENC TÉR
OKTOGON
KODÁLY KÖRÖND
House of Terror
Puppet Theatre
VÖRÖSMARTY UTCA
ERZSÉBET KÖRUT
KERTÉSZ UTCA
Almássy Tér Centre
VII
BLAHA LUJZA TÉR
JÓZSEF KÖRUT
VIII
GYULA
KRÚDY
BAROSS UTCA
FERENC KÖRUT
Applied Arts Museum
Museum of Fine Arts
HŐSÖK TERE
Millenary Monument
Műcsarnok
BAJZA UTCA
East Asia Museum
Ráth György Museum
Vajdahunyad Castle
Petőfi Csarnok
Transport Museum
Városliget City Park
DÓZSA GYÖRGY ÚT
AJTOSI DÜRER SOR
HUNGÁRIA KÖRUT
THÖKÖLY ÚT
ROTTENBILLER UTCA
ALSÓERDŐSOR
Puskás Stadion
Stadion Bus Station
STADIONOK
KEREPESI ÚT
KeletiTrain Station
KELETI PU
Erkel Theatre
NÉPSZINHÁZ UTCA
FIUME ÚT
Kerepesi Cemetery
Józsefváros Train Station
KŐBÁNYAI ÚT
N
0
500 m

Watertown

Watertown (Víziváros), between Castle Hill and the river to the north of the Chain Bridge, was once the poor quarter housing fishermen, craftsmen and their families. Today it's a reclusive neighbourhood of old mansions, reached by alleys of steps rising from the main street, Fő utca. North along Fő utca stand the **Király baths** distinguishable by four copper cupolas (see box opposite).

Gellért Hill

South of Watertown rises **Gellért Hill** (Gellérthegy), crowned by the **Liberation Monument**, one of the few Soviet monuments to survive the fall of the Iron Curtain, and the **Citadella**, a low fortress built by the Habsburgs to cow the population after the 1848–49 revolution. Nowadays the fort contains nothing more sinister than a few exhibits, a tourist hostel, a terrace bar and an overpriced restaurant.

Gellert Hill is home to the most well-known of the city's baths, Gellert Baths (see box opposite).

Communist Statue Park

Budapest's ironically nostalgic **Communist Statue Park** (Szoborpark; daily 10am–dusk; 2450Ft) also lies on this side of the river and is worth a detour to see the monumental statues of Marx, Engels and Lenin. It's stuck out in district XXII and it's rather difficult to get public transport out there; the easiest option is to take the direct Statue Park bus from Deák tér (daily: July & Aug 11am & 3pm; Sept–June 11am; Dec 3–21 & Jan 7–Feb 29 Sat & Sun only, 11am; 3950Ft return, includes entry fee).

Pest: Around Vörösmarty tér

Pest's main square, **Vörösmarty tér** is flooded with crowded café terraces; the most venerable institution here is the **Gerbeaud** patisserie, the favourite haunt of Budapest's high society in the late nineteenth century, now filled with tourists. Beside Gerbeaud's terrace is the entrance to the Underground Railway (Földatti Vasút), the first metro line on the European continent and the second in the world (after London's Metropolitan line), when it opened in 1896.

The city's most chic shopping street, **Váci utca**, runs south from the square. Past the Pesti Theatre, where twelve-year-old Liszt made his concert debut, is **Ferenciek tere**, overlooked by the **Párizsi udvar**, chiefly known for its stunning "Parisian arcade", adorned with arabesques and stained glass. Váci utca continues south to the **Central Market Hall**, with its fancy ironwork, porcelain tiles and vivacious stalls festooned with strings of paprika and garlic.

National Museum

Ten minutes' stroll north of the market is the **National Museum** (Tues–Sun 10am–6pm; free; Ⓦwww.hnm.hu), sensitively renovated and showing a comprehensive display of Hungarian history from the Magyar tribes' arrival in 896 through to the collapse of communism in 1989.

The Jewish quarter

On the corner of Wesselényi and Dohány utca stands the dramatic main **synagogue** (April–Oct Mon–Thurs 10am–5pm, Fri & Sun 10am–2pm; 1400Ft including entrance to National Jewish Museum next door). The Byzantine-Moorish architecture has been restored; the interior is utterly magnificent with shimmering golden geometric shapes and a 5000-tube organ, played in the past by Liszt and Saint Saëns. In the streets behind the synagogue lies Pest's main **Jewish quarter**, a favourite spot for cute patisseries and stylish new restaurants.

St Stephen's Basilica

Peering over the rooftops to the north of Vörösmarty tér is the dome of

TAKING A BATH IN BUDAPEST

Budapest has some of the grandest **baths** in Europe (see Ⓦwww.spasbudapest.com), and a visit to one of them is an essential part of any trip to the city. A basic ticket covers three hours in the pools, sauna and steam rooms (*gözfürdo*), with a money-back scheme operating in the Széchenyi and Gellért baths; for example, if you stay just an hour, you get 300Ft back. Supplementary tickets are available for such delights as the mud baths (*iszapfürdo*) and massages (*masszázs*).

Built in 1913, the magnificent **Gellért baths**, with original Art Nouveau furnishings, awesome mosaics, sculptures and stained glass attracts the most visitors (daily 6am–6/7pm; 2800Ft pool and locker, 3100Ft pool and cabin). You can get cheaper tickets just for the stunning thermal baths (which close earlier at weekends; separate baths for men and women).

The Turkish **Király baths** date back to 1565; men and women must visit separately (men only Tues, Thurs & Sat 9am–8pm; women only Mon, Wed & Fri 7am–6pm; 2100Ft). The atmospheric **Rudas baths** house a charming octagonal pool under a characteristic Turkish dome (men only Mon–Fri 6am–8pm, women only Tues 6am–8pm, communal Fri & Sat 10pm–4am, Sat & Sun 6am–7pm; 1500Ft).

Finally, the lovely **Széchenyi Spa Baths** in Pest are the hottest in the capital, and boast the nicest outdoor pools (May–Sept daily 6am–10pm, Oct–April 6am–5pm; 2800Ft).

St Stephen's Basilica, from the top of which there's a fine view over the city (dome: April–Oct Mon–Sat 10am–6pm; 500Ft). On his name day, August 20, St Stephen's mummified hand – Hungary's most famous reliquary, usually on show in a side chapel – is paraded round the building.

Parliament

Dominating the banks of the Danube is the large dome of the **parliament,** a stupendous nineteenth-century creation whose impressive interior is replete with sweeping staircases and a gilded 96m-high central dome. It houses the old **Coronation Regalia,** the most prized treasure in Hungary. There are daily **tours** of the building – in English – if parliamentary business allows (10am, noon, 2pm; free for EU citizens, 2820Ft for others; tickets from Gate X, halfway along the east front; Ⓦwww.parlament.hu).

Andrássy út

To the east of St Stephen's basilica, **Andrássy út** runs dead straight for 2.5km, a parade of grand buildings laden with gold leafing, including the magnificent Opera House at no. 22. A little further along, at no. 60, is the **House of Terror** (Tues–Sun 10am–6pm; 1500Ft). Once the headquarters of the dreaded secret police, the building now houses a collection of sobering exhibits pertaining to Stalin, the Nazis and the Holocaust, as well as the Soviet "liberation" and the 1956 uprising.

Hosök tere

Hosök tere was built to mark the 1000th anniversary of the Magyar conquest; its centrepiece is the **Millenary Monument**, portraying the great Magyar leader Prince Árpád, as well as statues of Hungary's most illustrious leaders, from King Stephen to Kossuth. Also on the square is the **Museum of Fine Arts** (Tues–Sun 10am–5.30pm; 1400Ft; Ⓦwww.szepmuveszeti.hu), the jewel of which is a collection of paintings by El Greco. Behind the museum lies **Budapest Zoo** (daily 10am–6/7pm; 1850Ft), worth a visit for the architecture alone – the Palm House, the Elephant House and the Aviary in particular. Opposite the zoo are the yellow neo-Baroque walls of the **Széchenyi baths.** Watch locals play chess on floating boards while wallowing in the steam.

The Városliget and Petőfi Csarnok

The **Városliget** (City Park) starts just behind the Hosők tere and holds the romantic Vajdahunyad Castle, an imitation of a Transylvanian castle of the same name. Originally constructed in wood and cardboard in 1896, the castle was made a permanent fixture eight years later, and rebuilt in stone and brick. The mysterious statue of the hooded monk Anonymus in the castle court is worth a look – it depicts the first historian to chronicle Hungarian history in a twelfth-century court.

An artificial lake stretches out at the foot of the castle, popular with rowers in the summer and a spectacular spot for ice-skating in the winter. Heading behind Vajdahunyad will lead you to **Petőfi Csarnok**, a youth leisure centre that hosts big-name concerts (check out Ⓦwww.petoficsarnok.hu) and a fine flea market every Sunday (see "Shopping", p.595 for details)

Arrival and information

Air From Ferihegy airport (Ⓣ01/296-9696), an airport minibus will deliver to specific hotels (2900Ft single, 4900Ft return; book it in the terminal building). The journey is much cheaper and almost as quick by public transport; take the Reptérbusz (airport bus #200) to the final stop Kobánya-Kispest and from there, it's ten metro stops to the centre, Deák tér (230Ft). Alternatively, take the airport train directly to Nyugati station (see below; 300Ft). The airport taxi-drivers are notorious sharks and best avoided.

Train There are three main train stations, all of which are directly connected by metro with the central Deák tér metro station in the Belváros, in the district of Pest. Keleti station (Eastern station; Ⓣ01/313-6835) handles most international trains, including those from Vienna (Westbahnhof), Belgrade, Bucharest, Zagreb and Bratislava, as well as domestic arrivals from Sopron and Eger; Nyugati station (Western station; Ⓣ01/349-0115) receives trains from Prague and Bratislava, some from Bucharest, and domestic ones from the Danube Bend; and Déli station (Southern station Ⓣ01/355-8657) has one train a day from Vienna (Südbahnhof), the occasional train from Zagreb, and domestic services from Pécs and Lake Balaton.

Bus The central bus station is at Népliget (blue metro), serving international destinations and routes to Transdanubia. Also in Pest, Stadion bus station (red metro) serves areas east of the Danube; and Árpád híd bus station (blue metro) serves the Danube Bend.

Boat Hydrofoils from Vienna dock alongside the Danube embankment on the Pest side.

Tourist office Tourinform (daily 8am–8pm; Ⓣ01/438-8080, Ⓦwww.tourinform.hu) is just around the corner from Deák tér metro at Süţo utca 2, and also houses the Tourist Police office; other branches are on Liszt Ferenc tér (Mon–Fri 10am–6pm) and in the Castle District on Szentháromság tér (daily 9am–6/7pm). Other offices include the Vista Tourist Center, Paulay Ede utca 7 (Mon–Fri 9am–8pm, Sat & Sun 10am–6pm; Ⓣ01/267-8603, Ⓦwww.vista.hu) and Budapest Tourist, in the subway in front of Nyugati train station (Mon–Fri 9am–4pm; Ⓣ01/342-6521).

Discount passes A Budapest Card (6300/7500Ft for two/three days), available at the airport and town centre tourist offices, hotels and major metro stations, gives unlimited travel on public transport, free museum admission, reductions on the airport minibus and other discounts.

City transport

See Ⓦwww.bkv.hu for comprehensive info on Budapest city transport.

Tickets A basic 290Ft ticket is valid for a journey along one metro line, and also for a single journey on buses, trolleybuses, trams and the HÉV suburban train as far as the city limits. You can also buy 240Ft tickets for metro journeys of up to three stops. Books of 10 tickets (2600Ft) or passes (1500/3700Ft for one/three days) offer better value and convenience; buy tickets from metro stations or (quicker) from street stands or newsagents, and punch in the machines at the station entrance before the journey commences (or on board buses, trolleybuses and trams). You must use a new ticket for each connection if you are changing lines.

Metro The metro (daily 4.30am–11.15pm) has three lines intersecting at Deák tér; services run every 2–15 min.

Bus and tram Buses (*busz)* with red numbers make limited stops, while those with the red suffix "E" go nonstop between termini; all run frequently during the day – as do trams (*villamos*) and trolleybuses (*trolibusz*) – and every thirty to sixty minutes between 11pm and dawn along routes with a night service (denoted with the black suffix "E").

Taxi Taxis are a common rip-off, unless booked through a company. Go for Főtaxi (☎01/222-2222) or the English-speaking Citytaxi (☎01/211-1111): both charge a basic fee of around 300Ft plus up to 240Ft per kilometre.

Accommodation

The best places to stay are districts V, VI and VII in Pest, and the parts of Buda nearest Castle Hill. For hotel bookings, contact the Vista Visitor Center, VI, Paulay Ede utca 7 (☎01/429-9950, Ⓦwww.vista.hu). Hostels can be booked through the Hungarian Youth Hostel Association near Keleti Station (☎01/413-2065, Ⓦwww.youthhostels.hu), or by visiting the individual hostel websites. Private rooms downtown cost from 4500Ft a night, rising to 10,000Ft or more in high season.

Hostels

Back Pack Guesthouse XI, Takács Menyhért utca 33 ☎01/385-8946, Ⓦwww.backpackbudapest.hu. Colourful and homely hostel on a tree-lined residential street in Buda, with themed dormitories, a wonderfully relaxed atmosphere and a beautiful garden with hammocks strewn between fruit trees. Tram #49 or bus #7 to Tétényi út stop. Dorms 3800Ft, doubles 11,000Ft, camping 3000Ft per person.

Mandragora Hostel VIII, Krúdy Gyula 12 ☎01/789-9515, Ⓦwww.mandragorahostel.com. Gorgeous, bohemian boutique hostel, where hammocks hang amongst the leafy indoor plants, and the lofty dormitories are divided into mezzanines and partitioned with colourful cloths. Yoga and massage available. Dorms 4000Ft.

Marco Polo VII, Nyár utca 6 ☎01/413-2555, Ⓦwww.marcopolohostel.com. Giant and clean hostel in the Jewish quarter. Dorms 4500Ft, doubles 17500Ft.

Museum Guest House V, Károly Körút 10, 1st Floor ☎01/266-7774, Ⓦwww.budapesthostel.com. Conveniently located hostel with bright, spacious rooms and very helpful staff. Dorms from 3000Ft.

Red Bus Hostel V, Semmelweis utca 14 ☎01/266-0136, Ⓦwww.redbusbudapest.hu. Ideally located 2min from Deák tér, this small and friendly hostel offers modern, bright dorms and doubles/twins facing onto a quiet courtyard. Red Bus Books next door will swap all your dog-eared paperbacks. Dorms 4000Ft, doubles 9500Ft.

Hotels and pensions

Ábel Panzió XI, Ábel Jenő utca 9 ☎01/381-0553, Ⓦwww.abelpanzio.hu. Fantastic 1913 villa with beautiful Art Nouveau fittings in a quiet street a 30min walk from the Belváros. Take tram #6 to Móricz Zsigmund Körter then #61 to Szúret utca. Just ten rooms, so it's essential to book in advance. Doubles 17000Ft.

Mandragora Doubles József Körút 2 ☎01/789-9515, Ⓦwww.mandragorahostel.com. Three beautifully decorated double rooms in a spacious old apartment run by the same people as *Mandragora Hostel*, each with en-suite mosaic-tiled bathrooms. Doubles 12,000–17,000Ft.

Mária & István IX, Ferenc körút 39 ☎01/216-0768, Ⓦwww.mariaistvan.hu. Wonderfully friendly couple who rent out rooms in their tastefully decorated flat. They also have two private apartments for rent sleeping up to 5 (see website). Doubles 18,000Ft.

Campsites

Csillebérc Camping XII, Konkoly Thege M. út 21 ☎01/395-6537, Ⓦwww.datanet.hu/csill. Large, well-equipped site also offering a range of bungalows. A short walk from the last stop of bus #21 from Moszkva tér. Open all year. Camping 3000Ft, bungalows 7000Ft.

Római Camping III, Szentendrei út 189 ☎01/368-6260, Ⓔromaicamping@message.hu. Huge site beside the road to Szentendre in Rómaifürdő (25min by HEV). Rates include use of the nearby swimming pool. Open all year. 4000Ft per person.

Eating

Magyar cooking has been overtaken in Budapest's restaurants by scores of places devoted to international cuisine. Prices by Western European standards are very reasonable, and your budget should stretch to at least one binge in a top-flight place.

Patisseries

Centrál V, Károlyi Mihály utca 9. Grand old coffee house, 3min walk south from Ferenciek tere, restored to its former glory, with a broad menu ranging from cheap to very expensive.

Müvész VI, Andrássy út 29. Classic old coffee house that's less touristy and cheaper than *Gerbeaud*.

TREAT YOURSELF

Gerbeaud (V, Vörösmarty tér 7) is a popular, extremely grand patisserie in central Pest. A coffee and a *torte* will set you back around 1500Ft, but worth it for the ambience. The same rich pastries are cheaper in *Kis Gerbeaud* around the corner.

Ruszwurm I, Szentháromság utca 7. Excellent cakes, served production-line fashion to those taking a break from sightseeing on Castle Hill.

Snacks

Bombay Express VI, Andrássy út 44. Fun Indian fast-food on Oktogon with tasty wraps (650Ft) and refreshing mango lassi.

Duran Sandwich Bar V, Október 6 utca 15. A quirky joint with a wide selection of fresh mini-sandwiches for you to pick and mix. From 149Ft apiece. Closed Sun.

Falafel Faloda VI, Paulay Ede utca 53. Best of the city's falafel joints. From 400Ft. Closed Sun

Karma Café VI, Liszt Ferenc tér 11. Beautifully decorated café with excellent tapas, situated on Pest's trendiest square for eating. Dinner will set you back about 1900Ft.

Restaurants

Govinda V, Vigyázó Ferenc utca 4. An oasis of spiritual calm in a little side street, just north of Roosevelt tér, serving a good range of Indian vegetarian dishes (600Ft each) and salads.

Kádár étkezde VII, Klauzál tér 9. Jewish home-cooking in the old quarter, where friendly staff serve lunches of chicken in fruit sauces and excellent Hungarian desserts. Closed Sun & Mon. Mains 1200Ft.

Kiado Kocsma VI, Jókai tér 3. Gorgeous interior, heavenly tapas (try the aubergine paté), Moroccan teas and exhibitions all mean you can chill out in style. Tapas from 900Ft.

Kőleves Dob utca/Kazinczy utca (next to Klauzál tér). Marvellous restaurant at the heart of the Jewish quarter. Fresh, colourful, high-quality ingredients in a wide range of inventive dishes, including braised goose leg with red cabbage and warm goats cheese salad. Funky music, friendly staff and vegetarian-friendly too. Mains 2000Ft.

M Kersetz ut (off Liszt Ferenc tér). *M*'s shoe-box-sized restaurant is a delightful place; the plain walls have had all the accoutrements of a café drawn onto them – books, a hat-stand, a fish tank – with a highly animated chef to boot (he's real). The food completes the picture – fresh, beautifully prepared Franco-Hungarian delights. Menu changes weekly, from 1500Ft.

Menza VI, Liszt Ferenc tér. Stylish, retro-looking place offering excellent and moderately priced Hungarian dishes to be enjoyed alfresco. Try stuffed paprika for 1700Ft.

St Jupat Retek ut 16. Giant portions of Hungarian home-style cooking near the bustling Mammut Malls. Mains from 1200Ft.

Drinking and nightlife

Bars

Look out for *Kerts* ("gardens") – fun, makeshift bars set up for short periods of time in buildings awaiting demolition (although *Szimpla Kert* has become a permanent fixture). They are often advertised in the local press, or else ask in other bars for them.

Bambi I, Frankel Leó utca 2–4 (off Bem tér). Atmospheric old bar from the socialist era with a typical crew of old locals playing chess. Serves breakfast, snack lunches, cakes and alcohol.

Café Miro I, Úri utca 30. A trendy bar in the Castle district, which often has live music. Its sister bar in Mammut serves good food.

Castro V, Madách Imre tér 3. A lively café-bar close to Deák tér, which also serves excellent Serbian food.

Darshan Udvar VIII, Krúdy Gyula utca 7. The largest bar in a growing complex of bars, cafés and shops. Set at the back of the courtyard, with oriental/hippie decorations, good food, world music and leisurely service.

Eklektika VI, Nagymező utca 30. Arty, gay-friendly bar with 1960s furniture, art exhibitions, a pasta/salad menu and women-only evenings on the second Saturday of the month.

Instant VI, Nagymező utca 38. The city's newest *kert*, a three-storey labyrinthine venue hosting four bars, a café, contemporary art gallery, fourteen "house parties" (small rooms with different music in each) and an open courtyard complete with a pond full of fish.

Szimpla Kert VII, Kazinczy utca 14. The centre of Budapest's alternative scene, the original *kert* operates from an abandoned warehouse, with film screenings, funky tunes and a great outdoor bar, furnished with an eclectic array of old furniture. Open til 2am.

Clubs

The floating party scene (held on river boats) is growing constantly: check flyers and posters around town, or look in the "Könnyű" section of *Pesti Est*, the free listings magazine. There's also a variety of cheap student clubs. Entry costs anything from 800–4000Ft.

Buddha Beach IX, Közraktár utca 9–11. Outside bar attracting a wealthy young crowd, one of the few places you can dance outside until the early hours with an awesome view of the capital. Good bar food too so it's worth booking a table if you're eating. March–Oct.

Capella V, Belgrád rakpart 23. An eclectic mix of cross-dressing bar staff, funky house music and lots of kitsch in this gay-friendly, sweaty club; catch the drag show nightly at midnight.

Cha Cha Cha VI, Bajcsy-Zsilinszky út 63. Recently relocated and very popular hangout attracting an eclectic crowd, with comics on the walls and electro and funk DJs Thurs–Sat.

Entertainment

Tickets for most events can be bought through Ticket Express (VI, Andrássy út 18; ⓣ01/312-0000, ⓦwww.tex.hu) for classical and pop music; or Publika for rock and jazz, VII, Károly körút 9 (ⓣ01/322-2010).

Almássy tér Cultural Centre VII, Almássy tér 6. Popular venue for folk music.

Fonó XI, Sztregova utca 3, Buda ⓦwww.fono.hu. Popular music hall and CD store, specialising in Central/East European folk, ethno jazz, and some theatre and art as well.

Peţofi Csarnok Városliget ⓦwww.petoficsarnok.hu. Folk music, dance events and big acts in the City Park.

Trafó IX, Liliom utca 41 ⓦwww.trafo.hu. A revamped transformer station in Pest with its finger on the capital's cultural pulse and a café-bar that frequently hosts local young jazz giants.

Shopping

Shops There are several malls with standard high-street names, notably Mammut and Mammut II by Moskvá tér (ⓦwww.mammut.hu). Most shops open Monday to Friday 10am to 6pm, and on Saturday until 1pm, although many now stay open later at the weekend, including Sundays. The main shopping area within the capital is south of Vörösmarty tér in central Pest, with glamorous designer places located on Váci utca and Petőfi Sándor utca.

Markets The Central Market Hall in Pest is a great place for presents, and a better alternative to the pricey tourist-oriented places by the Vár. There are three flea markets in Budapest, but the best one is Petőfi Csarnok (Sat & Sun 7am–2pm) in the Városliget.

Directory

Embassies and consulates Australia, XII, Királyhágó tér 8–9 ⓣ01/457-9777; Canada, XII, Ganz u. 12-14 ⓣ01/392-3360; Ireland, V, Szabadság tér 7, 5th floor, Bank Center ⓣ01/301-4960; New Zealand, VII, Nagymező utca 47, ⓣ01/302-2484; UK, V, Harmincad utca 6 ⓣ01/266-2888; US, V, Szabadság tér 12 ⓣ01/475-4400.

Exchange Gönc Szövetkezeti Takarékpénztár at V, Rákóczi út 5; Magyar Külkereskedelmi Bank at Türr István utca at the top of Váci utca, Pest; Tribus tourist office at V, Apáczai Csere János utca 1.

Hospitals V, Hold utca 19, behind the US embassy ⓣ01/311-6816; II, Ganz utca 13–15 ⓣ01/202-1370.

Internet CEU Net, V, Október 6 utca 14 (daily 11am–10pm); Electric Café, VII, Dohány utca 37 (daily 9am–midnight); Millenarium Park C Building (free for one hour); Matávpont, V, Petőfi utca 17–19 and all large shopping malls (daily 9am–8pm).

Listings *Budapest Official Guide* provides practical info on sights and transport. The fortnightly Budapest Funzine (ⓦwww.funzine.hu) is the best publication in English for nightlife and events listings and also contains restaurant reviews and shopping info. *Pestiest* (Magyar only) contains comprehensive events, nightlife, exhibition and cinema listings. All are available from hotels, cafés and tourist information points.

Maps Tourist offices supply free maps, but far better is the wirebound 1:25,000 Budapest Atlas

FESTIVALS IN BUDAPEST

See ⓦwww.festivalcity.hu for information on all of Budapest's festivals.

Budapest Spring Festival Two weeks in March or April. An eclectic mix of jazz, folk, opera, chamber music, exhibitions, flamenco shows and theatre. The festival pulls in world-class artists and takes place in various venues over the capital. The Budapest Fringe Festival runs at the same time, usually offering fresh, underground talent.

Summer on the Chain Bridge Every weekend July–Aug. Scores of classical and popular concerts; the famous bridge is jam-packed with market stalls, food and live music.

Sziget Festival Mid-Aug ⓦwww.sziget.hu. The week-long Sziget (meaning "island") Festival attracts international rock, pop, jazz and electro acts; the headiest party on the Danube.

St Stephen's Day Aug 20. The area around the Royal Palace becomes one big folk and crafts fair, and in the evening people line the embankments to watch the fireworks.

Autumn Music Weeks Late Sept to late Oct. Features top international contemporary performances in different locations around the city.

(1700Ft), from newsstands, bookshops and Tourinform offices.
Pharmacies Alkotás utca 1B, opposite Déli station, and Teréz körút 41, near Oktogon, are both open 24hr.
Police The tourist police office is located inside the main Tourinform office, V, Sútő utca 2 ⓣ01/438-8080. Tourists can also report a crime at V, Kecskeméti út (ⓣ01/317-0711) or V, Szalay utca (ⓣ01/373-1000) police stations.
Post office V, Petőfi utca 13.
Tours The Discover Hungary agency (ⓣ01/266-8777, ⓦwww.discoverhungary.com), Sútő utca 2, offers a varied programme of citywide excursions, bike rides and pub crawls.

Moving on

Train Balatonfüred (every 1–2hr; 2hr 30min); Eger (8 daily; 1hr 50min–2hr 20min); Kecskemét (12 daily; 1hr 30min); Pécs (11 daily; 3hr); Siófok (14 daily; 2hr); Sopron (7 daily; 3hr); Szeged (12 daily; 2hr 30min); Szentendre (every 10–20min; 40min);
Bus Balatonfüred (5 daily; 2hr 15min–3hr); Eger (hourly; 2hr–3hr 20min); Hévíz (4 daily; 3hr 20min–4hr); Keszthely (4 daily; 3hr 15min–4hr 15min); Pécs (5 daily; 4hr); Siófok (7 daily; 1hr 35min–2hr 10min); Sopron (3–5 daily; 3hr 45min); Szentendre (every 30min; 30–45min).
Ferry/Hydrofoil (Usually operating April–Oct/Nov, weather permitting; ⓣ01/484-4013) Szentendre (1–3 daily; 1hr 40min); Vienna (1–2 daily; 6hr 20min).

SZENTENDRE

To escape Budapest's humid summers, many people flock north of the city to the **Danube Bend**, one of the grandest stretches of the river. The historic town of **SZENTENDRE** on the west bank is the most popular day-trip from the capital (40min by HÉV train from Batthyány tér; 1hr 30min by boat from Vigadó tér pier), a touristy but friendly maze of houses painted in autumn colours, secret gardens, and cobbled alleys leading to hilltop churches.

What to see and do

Szentendre's original character was largely shaped by Serbs seeking refuge from the Ottomans. Their townhouses – now converted into galleries, shops and cafés – form a set piece around **Fő tér**, the main square. On the north side of the square is **Blagovestenska Church** (Tues–Sun 10am–5pm; winter open for worship only; 300Ft), with a striking iconostasis painted by Mikhail Zivkovic (1776–1824). Just around the corner at Vastagh György utca 1 stands the wonderful **Margit Kovács Museum** (daily 10am-6pm; 1000Ft), displaying the lifetime work of Hungary's greatest ceramicist and sculptor, born in 1902. Above Fő tér there's a fine view over Szentendre's steeply banked rooftops and gardens from the hilltop **Templom tér**, from which the spire of the **Serbian Orthodox Cathedral** pokes above a walled garden; tourists are generally not admitted, but you can see the cathedral iconostasis and treasury in the adjacent **museum** (Tues–Sun 10am–4/6pm; 500Ft). Beyond the square at Bogdányi út 32 is the impressive contemporary arts centre, **ArtMill** (daily 10am–6pm; 100Ft), an exciting new development, housed in a large disused sawmill, displaying the works of local and visiting international artists.

Arrival and information

Bus and train stations Both located a 5min walk south of town. Local buses run in along Dunakanyar körut.
Ferry port 100m north of the town centre.
Tourist office Tourinform, Dumtsa Jenő utca 22 ⓣ26/317-965, ⓦwww.szentendreprogram.hu (June–Aug Mon–Fri 9am–7pm, Sat & Sun 9am–5.30pm; Sept–May Mon–Sat 9.30am–4.30pm, Sun 10am–2pm).
Listings There are regular pop and rock concerts in the centre of town: ask Tourinform for details.

Accommodation

The cheapest option is a private room, advertised widely throughout town.
Horváth Panzió Daru piac 2 ⓣ26/313-950, ⓦwww.everyoneweb.com/horvath.fogado. Small, quiet pension north of the centre, decorated with Hungarian folk crafts. Doubles 10,000Ft.
Ilona Panzió Rákóczi utca 11 ⓣ26/313-599. Simple rooms in a pleasant location in the heart of the old quarter. Doubles 8000Ft.

Pap-Sziget Pap Island, 1.5km north of town ⓣ26/310-697, ⓦwww.pap-sziget.hu. Take any bus heading towards Visegrád or Esztergom and get off by the *Danubius Hotel*. May–Sept only. Camping 2000Ft per person, double bungalows 9000Ft, hostel dorm 2500Ft.

Eating and drinking

Avakum Alkotmány 4. Cooling café in a cellar near the Belgrade church.

Café Dorothea Jankó Janos 4. The sloping patio is a perfect spot for a glass of excellent local wine and lunch; the menu includes wonderful salads (980Ft), toasties (600Ft) and home-made pasta (1500Ft).

Palapa Dumtsa Jenő utca 22. Mexican with good food, cocktails and sterling service. Mains from 1600Ft.

Rab Ráby Kucsera Ferenc utca 1. Traditional, filling, Magyar cuisine from 1500Ft for a hearty dish.

Western Hungary

The major tourist attraction to the west of the capital is **Lake Balaton**, over-romantically labelled the "Hungarian sea", but very much the nation's playground, with vacation resorts lining both shores. The more built-up southern shore has the livelier resorts, chief amongst which is **Siófok** – the lake's popular party place – while, on the western tip, lies the appealing university town of **Keszthely** and Europe's largest thermal lake at **Hévíz**. Also worth a visit is the seductive **Badacsony** village, located beneath a hulk of volcanic rock next to three other small villages on the northern shore.

The western region of **Transdanubia** is the most ethnically diverse in the country. Its valleys and hills, forests and mud flats have been a melting pot since Roman times: settled by Magyars, Serbs, Slovaks and Germans; torn asunder and occupied by Ottomans and Habsburgs; transformed from a state of near-feudalism into brutal collectives; and now operating under modern capitalism. All the main towns display evidence of this evolution, especially **Sopron**, with its gorgeous, well-preserved medieval centre, and **Pécs**, which boasts an Ottoman mosque and minaret.

SIÓFOK

The largest, busiest and trashiest resort on Balaton, **SIÓFOK** is *the* place for bathing, boozing and dancing. The two main waterfront resort areas are Aranypart (Gold Shore) to the east of the Sió Canal, and Ezüstpart (Silver Shore) to the west. Though the central stretch of shoreline consists of paying **beaches** (daily mid-May to mid-Sept 7am–9pm; 1000Ft), there are free *strand* beaches 1km further along at both resort areas. You can rent **windsurfing** and wakeboards from 1700Ft/hour and small **sailing** boats at most beaches. Sailing boats cost from €120 (excluding tax) for up to six people for one day.

Arrival and information

Bus and train stations Next to each other in the centre of town on Fő utca.

Tourist office Tourinform office in the water tower (Víztorony) on Szabadság tér (mid-June to mid-Sept Mon–Fri 8am–8pm, Sat & Sun 10am–noon; mid-Sept to mid-June Mon–Fri 9am–4pm; ⓣ84/315-355, ⓦwww.siofok.com). They book private rooms, as can Ibusz, inside the atrium at Fő utca 174/6 (June–Aug Mon–Fri 8am–6pm, Sat 9am–6pm, Sun 9am–1pm; Sept–May Mon–Fri 8am–4pm; ⓣ84/510-720, ⓔi081@ibusz.hu).

Accommodation

Aranypart Camping Szent László utca 183–185 ⓣ84/352-801. Five kilometres east of the centre (bus #2) is this large, well-equipped campsite. Mid-April to mid-Sept. Tent 7000Ft, chalets sleeping four 25,500Ft.

Caesar Apartments Vitorlás utca 9 ⓣ30/274-0094, ⓦwww.siofok-balaton-holiday.com. The shabby exterior hides modern apartments sleeping up to 6, each with kitchenette and private balcony. Doubles 7000Ft.

Touring Hotel Cseresznye utca 1/0 ⓣ84/310-551, ⓔtouring@siofok-hostel.com. Large hostel 2km from the centre open May–Sept. Twins 6500Ft.

Város Kollégiuma Petőfi Sétány 1 ⓣ84/312-244, ⓦwww.siofokvaroskollegiuma.sulinet.hu. Large student residence accommodating visitors in summertime and weekends all year. On the shore of Golden Beach 5 mins from Siófok. 2530Ft per person.

Eating and drinking

Amigo Fő utca 99. Varied menu including a fantastic range of pizzas for around 1800Ft.
Ételbár Főzelékfaló Fő utca 43. Healthy soups, salads and sandwiches to offset the ill-effects of too much partying. Open 11–4pm.
Flört Just off Fő utca on the east bank of the canal ⓦwww.flort.hu. High-energy techno and club anthems keep the party people occupied until it's time to hit the beach again in the morning.
Palace Dance Club West of town at Deák Ferenc utca 2 ⓦwww.palace.hu. The most famous club in Siófok has two floors of house, dance, techno and a steady stream of foam parties until dawn. Buses leave every hour from 9pm outside the Víztorony (water tower).

Moving on

Ferry Badacsony (July & Aug 4 daily; 4hr 20min).
Bus Keszthely (2 daily) 1hr 40min.

KESZTHELY

Gracefully absorbing thousands of visitors, **KESZTHELY** possesses charms to suit everyone's taste, with some good eating and drinking options, several beaches, and a university to give it a life of its own.

Keszthely's waterfront has two bays (one for swimming, the other for ferries) formed by man-made piers, an area of parkland backed by plush hotels and miniature golf courses, and dozens of fast-food joints. In the evenings, action shifts to the bars and restaurants in the centre.

What to see and do

Walking up from the train station along Martírok útja, you'll pass the **Balaton Museum** at the junction with Kossuth Lajos utca (May–Oct Tues–Sun 10am–6pm; Nov–April Tues–Sat 9am–5pm, 500Ft), holding exhibits on the region's history and wildlife. Kossuth utca is given over to cafés, vendors, buskers and strollers and leads up towards the **Festetics Palace.** Founded in 1745 by Count György Festetics (Sept–June Tues–Sun: 10am–5pm, July & Aug 9am–6pm; 1700Ft; ⓦwww.helikonkastely.hu), the palace attracted the leading lights of Magyar literature from the nineteenth century onwards. Highlights are the gilt, mirrored ballroom and the Helikon Library, a masterpiece of joinery and carving built in 1801. The palace stages regular summer concerts – check with Tourinform (see below) or the Palace Ticket Office; there are also recommended wine tasting tours conducted in the underground cellar (2500Ft).

Arrival and information

Train and bus stations Both 5min walk southwest of the cluster of lakeside hotels along Kazinczy utca. Some buses drop off on Fő tér, halfway along Kossuth utca, the main drag.
Boat dock 10min walk south of the centre, along Erzsébet királyné útja.
Tourist information Tourinform, Kossuth utca 28 ⓣ83/314-144, ⓦwww.keszthely.hu (June to mid-Sept 9am–7pm; mid-Sept to May Mon–Fri 9am–5pm, Sat 9am–12.30pm).

Accommodation

Private rooms can be booked through Keszthely Tourist, Kossuth utca 25 (June–Aug daily 9am–8/9pm, Sept–May Mon–Sat 8am–5pm; ⓣ83/312-031, ⓦwww.keszthelytourist.hu). For information on rooms in college dorms (July & Aug only), check with Tourinform (see above).
Ambient Hostel Sopron utca 10 ⓣ30/460-3536, ⓔkeszthely.szallas@citromail.hu. Clean and bright dormitories, en-suite doubles and small apartments are offered in this very modern hostel next to the Festetics Palace. Dorms 3000Ft, doubles 8000Ft.
Kiss-Maté Penzion Katona Josef utca 27. Homely pension with welcoming hosts and a kitchen for guest use. Rooms 8800Ft.
Múzeum Panzió Múzeum utca 3 ⓣ83/313-182. Friendly management in this cute pension near the station. Doubles from 9000Ft.
Sport Camping Csárda utca ⓣ83/313-777. Big,

HÉVÍZ

Half-hourly buses from Keszthely train station run to **HÉVÍZ**, a spa based around Europe's largest thermal lake, **Hévízi Gyógy-tó**. The wooden terraces surrounding the **Tófürdo** ("lake bath"; daily 8.30/9am–4/6pm; 3hr 2000Ft, all day 2900Ft) are pleasant for a beer and sunbathe in the summer. The slightly radioactive water is believed to have strong curative properties, and the baths are predominantly occupied by the elderly, injured and disabled, bobbing on the murky, egg-scented lake in rented inner-tubes.

friendly campsite close to the lake just south of the train station. Mid-May to Sept.

Eating and drinking

Close to Kossuth Lajos ut is the daily Piac Market (off Bem József utca) that sells fresh fruit, as well as traditional Hungarian foodstuffs.

512 Club Georgikon utca 1. Grungy rock bar with a pool table.

Béke Vendéglő Kossuth utca 50. Home-made Hungarian food, often accompanied by live traditional music. Mains 1500Ft.

Easy Music House Kossuth Lajos ut 79. Trendy and colourful student bar with live music. The *Kolibri* bar next door is also worth a visit.

Oázis Rákóczi tér 3, down Szalasztó utca from the palace. Superb, healthy all-vegetarian option with a packed salad bar and friendly service. A filling plate of salad costs about 700Ft. Mon–Fri 11am–4pm.

Moving on

Bus Badacsony (8 daily; 1hr); Hévíz (every 15min; 10–20min).

Ferry Badacsony (July & Aug 4 daily; 2hr).

BADACSONY

The **BADACSONY** – a hefty hunk of cooled molten magma and volcanic rock with four villages nestled at its feet – is one of Hungary's most striking features. **Badacsony village** is the most visitor-friendly of the four, and a base for some of the best hikes in the country.

What to see and do

The main attractions of Badacsony – the **Rósa Szegedy House** and **Rose Rock** – lie nestled among the vineyards, between the glassy lake south of the railway track and the tip of the village.

Róza Szegedy House and Rose Rock

For a novel way to avoid a steep 2.5km walk, take one of the open-top jeep taxis (600Ft per person) from Park utca – the main street – up through the vineyards to the **Róza Szegedy House** (Szegedy Róza Ház; May–Sept Tues–Sun 10am–6pm; 500Ft). Róza Szegedy met her future husband, the poet Sándor Kisfaludy, on the rugged slopes of Badacsony in 1795, and he wrote some of his most beautiful works from the house. Now a museum, the house contains some of his literature and Szegedy's original furniture.

Up a path a little further from Róza Szegedy House is **Rose Rock** (Rókzako), where romance lingers on; according to legend, if a man and woman sit together with their backs facing Lake Balaton and think about each other, they shall marry within a year.

Kisfaludy and the Stone Gate

The Rose Rock is a great starting point for an invigorating hike to the **Kisfaludy** lookout tower (437m) and, twenty minutes further north, the **Stone Gate** formed from two great basalt towers. Both points offer splendid views of the lake and the green patchwork of Badacsony's vineyards. For a longer hike buy a 1:80,000 scale map and ask at Tourinform for suggested routes. After a hike you'll want to jump straight into the lake – Badacsony has clean, paying beaches (400Ft), accessible just by the ferry pier.

Arrival and information

Train station In the village, just up from the ferry pier.

Bus stop On the main street, Park utca.

Tourist information Park utca 14 ⓣ87/431-046, ⓦwww.badacsony.com (May to mid-June & mid-Sept to Oct Mon–Fri 9am–5pm & Sat 9am–1pm; mid-June to mid-Sept 9am–6/7pm; Nov–April 9am–3.30pm).

Accommodation

Balatontourist (next door to Tourinform) can book private rooms (May, June & Sept Mon–Fri 8.30am–3.30pm, Sat 8am–noon; July & Aug Mon–Sat 8am–9pm, Sun 8am–noon; ⓣ87-531-021, ⓦwww.balatontourist.hu).

Badacsony Camping ⓣ97/531-041. Shady campsite 15 mins walk west of the ferry pier (mid-May to Sept).

Hotel Neptun Római ut 170 ⓣ87/531-032 ⓦwww.borbaratok.hu. Tastefully decorated rooms in a beautifully renovated old building. Includes a filling buffet breakfast. Doubles 11,000Ft.

Eating and drinking

Bacchus Kossuth utca 1. Gorgeous views over the lake from *Bacchus*'s terrace and very nice local wines. From 1100Ft.

Neptun (part of the *Hotel Neptun*), Római ut 170. Well prepared salads, soups, fish and meat dishes from 900Ft.

SOPRON

SOPRON – the nearest big Hungarian town to Vienna and consequently a popular destination – has 240 listed buildings, which allow it to claim to be "the most historic town in Hungary".

What to see and do

The horseshoe-shaped **Belváros** (inner town) is north of Széchenyi tér and the main train station. At the southern end, **Orsolya tér** features Renaissance edifices dripping with loggias and carved protrusions, and a Gothic church. Heading north towards the main square, **Új utca** (New Street – one of the town's oldest thoroughfares) is a gentle curve of arched dwellings painted in red, yellow and pink, with chunky cobblestones and pavements. At no. 22 stands one of the **medieval synagogues** (May–Sept Tues–Sun 10am–6pm; 600Ft) that flourished when the street was known as Zsidó utca (Jewish Street); Sopron's Jewish community survived the expulsion of 1526 only to be almost annihilated during World War II.

Goat Church

Fő tér is a parade of Gothic and Baroque architecture partly overshadowed by the **Goat Church** (Mon–Sat 8am–8pm) – so called, as legend has it, because its construction in the late thirteenth century was financed by a goatherd whose flock unearthed a cache of loot. The attached **Chapter House** (March–Oct 10am–noon & 2–5pm), which served as a prayer house and burial chapel, contains fine frescoes and religious statues, and is considered one of the finest examples of Gothic religious architecture in Hungary.

Storno House and Firewatch Tower

The Renaissance **Storno House**, also on the square, exhibits an enjoyable collection of Roman, Celtic and Avar relics, plus mementoes of Liszt (Tues–Sun: April–Sept 10am–6pm; Oct–March 10am–2pm; 1000Ft). North of here rises Sopron's symbol, the **Firewatch Tower** (April, Sept & Oct Tues–Sun 10am–6pm; May–Aug daily 10am–8pm; 700Ft), founded upon the stones of a fortress originally laid out by the Romans. From the top there's a stunning view of the town's narrow streets and weathered rooftops. The "**Gate of Loyalty**" at the base of the tower commemorates the townfolk's decision, when offered the choice of Austrian citizenship in 1921, to remain Magyar subjects.

Arrival and information

Train station Mátyás Király utca, 500m south of Széchenyi tér and the old town; Sopron is linked to Vienna by a fast intercity service, though it's not on the main Budapest–Vienna route.

Bus station Northwest of the old town, 5min walk along Lackner Kristóf utca from Ógabona tér.

Tourist office Tourinform is inside the Liszt Cultural Centre at Liszt utca 1 (mid-June to mid-Sept

Mon–Fri 9am–5pm, Sat & Sun 9am–12pm; mid-Sept to mid-June Mon–Fri 9am–5pm, Sat 9am–3pm; ⓣ99/517-560, ⓦwww.tourinform.sopron.hu).

Internet Free at the tourist office.

Accommodation

Vacáció Youth Hostel Ady Endre utca 31 ⓣ99/338-502, ⓦwww.vakacio-vendeghazak.hu. Large and characterless hostel next to Erzsébet Kert (Elizabeth Gardens), 15 mins walk from the centre, or take bus #1 or #10. Dorms 2800Ft.

Jégverem Panzió Jégverem utca 1 ⓣ99/510-113, ⓦwww.jegverem.hu. Pleasant *pension* with a quaint inn atmosphere and a lovely restaurant (see below). Doubles 10,000Ft.

Eating and drinking

Cézár Cellar Hátsókapu utca 2. Popular candlelit medieval cellar with fantastic wine accompanied by snackboards of cured meats and cheese.

Fórum Pizzeria Szent György utca 3. Decent pizzas, a pleasant setting and happy staff. Also does a good line in pastas, grills and salads. From 900Ft.

Jégverem Fogadó Jégverem utca 1. A wide-ranging menu with tantalizing Hungarian dishes from 1400Ft served in a rustic garden setting.

Liszt Szalon Szent György utca 12. Delicate cakes served in an intimate café dedicated to the composer, or outside in a pretty courtyard. Daily 10am–10pm.

ESTERHÁZY PALACE

Twenty-seven kilometres east of Sopron (hourly buses), in the village of Fertőd, lies a monument to one of the country's most famous dynasties: the **Esterházy Palace**. Originally minor nobility, the Esterházy family began its rise thanks to Miklós Esterházy I (1583–1645), who married two rich widows, sided with the Habsburgs, and got himself elevated to count. The palace itself was started by his grandson, Miklós the Ostentatious. Fronted by a vast horseshoe courtyard where Hussars once pranced to the music of Haydn – Esterházy's resident maestro for many years – the palace was intended to rival Versailles. **Guided tours** (every 40min; March–Oct Tues–Sun 10am–6pm; Nov–Feb Fri–Sun 10am–4pm; 1350Ft) cover 23 of the 126 rooms in the palace, including several blue-and-white chinoiserie salons and the Banqueting Hall with its superb ceiling fresco. Should you wish to stay, ask at the Tourinform office opposite the palace gates (April–Oct Mon–Sat 9am–5pm; Nov–March Tues–Sat 10am–4pm; ⓣ99/370-544, ⓔfertod@tourinform.hu), or try the *Újvári Panzio*, about 500m from the palace at Kossuth utca 57a (ⓣ99/537-097, ⓦwww.ujvaripanzio.hu; doubles 9000Ft).

PÉCS

PÉCS is one of Transdanubia's largest and most attractive towns; indeed, it lays claim to being the finest in the country, with its tiled rooftops climbing the vine-laden slopes of the Mecsek range. Besides some good museums, the fifth-oldest university in Europe (founded in 1367) and a great market, Pécs contains Hungary's best examples of **Islamic architecture**, a legacy of the long Ottoman occupation.

What to see and do

The majority of Pécs's main sites are concentrated in the **Belváros** (Old Town), radiating outwards from Széchenyi tér: it's easy to take them in, starting with the synagogue by Kossuth tér, then heading through the centre towards the leafier western side, where you'll find the magnificent cathedral. Pécs is also an excellent starting-point for heading to the nearby **wine region** of Villány to the south – ask at Tourinform for information.

Synagogue and Mosque of Gázi Kászim Pasha

Heading up Bajcsy-Zsilinszky út from the bus terminal, or by bus #30 from the train station towards the centre, you'll pass the **synagogue** (March–Oct Sun–Fri 10am–5pm; 300Ft). The beautiful nineteenth-century interior is hauntingly impressive, with romantic frescoes swirling around a space emptied by the

murder of almost 3500 Jews – ten times the number that live in Pécs today. During the Ottoman occupation (1543–1686) the principal Christian church in Pécs, located to the north on Széchenyi tér, was converted into the **Mosque of Gázi Kászim Pasha** (mid-April to mid-Oct Mon–Sat 10am–4pm, Sun 11.30am–4pm; mid-Oct to mid-April Mon–Sat 10am–noon, Sun 11.30am–2pm; donations). In a twist of history, the mosque has changed sides again and operates as the City Centre Catholic Parish Church.

Archeological Museum and cathedral

Behind the mosque, the **Archeological Museum** (Tues–Sun 10am–2/4pm; 300Ft) displays items testifying to a Roman presence between the first and fifth centuries. From here you can follow either Káptalan or Janus Pannonius utca towards the **cathedral** (April–Oct Mon–Sat 9am–5pm, Sun 1–5pm, Nov–March Mon–Sat 10am–4pm, Sun 1pm–4pm; 700Ft). Though its architects have incorporated a crypt and side-chapels from eleventh- to fourteenth-century churches, the cathedral is predominantly nineteenth-century neo-Romanesque.

Pécs Fair

Pécs Fair, held on the morning of the first Sunday of each month, sees some hard bargaining and hard drinking, and there are smaller markets on the same site every Sunday, selling everything from old antiques to household pets. Hourly bus #50 carries local shoppers from outside the Konzum store in Rákóczi utca (get a ticket from a newsstand or the train station before boarding), but it is often packed – consider cycling (15min) or taking a taxi from Széchenyi tér.

Arrival and information

Train station 20min walk south of the centre on Indoház tér.

Bus station Northeast of the train station on Zsolyom utca.

Tourist office Tourinform is at Széchenyi tér 9 (June–Sept Mon–Fri 9am–6pm, Sat 9am–2pm, closed Sun; Oct–May Mon–Fri 9am–4/6pm; ⓣ72/213-315, ⓔbaranya-m@tourinform.hu).

Internet Matrix Café, Kiraly utca 15 (9am–midnight).

Accommodation

For inexpensive, central accommodation, you can book a private room or student hostel bed through *Ibusz*, Király utca 11 (Mon–Fri 9am–5pm; ⓣ72/212-157, ⓦi077@ibusz.hu).

Familia Privát Camping 3km east at Gyöngyösi I utca ⓣ72/327-034. Reasonable campsite that's open all year. Take bus #31. 1250Ft per person.

Főnix Hotel Hunyádi út 2 ⓣ72/311-680, ⓦwww.fonixhotel.hu. Just north of Széchenyi tér, the simple rooms in this 1980s hotel offer reasonable value. Lovely staff. Doubles 12,500Ft.

Gulyás Gabriella ⓣ72/211-764 ⓔgajbla@freemail.hu. Charming old house with just two rooms sleeping up to four people each, with an eccentric array of old antique furniture and collectibles. Excellent value. Doubles 7000Ft.

Hostel Kiraly utca 23–25 ⓣ72/950-684, ⓦwww.naphostel.com. Colourful, homely hostel in the historic centre, with modern dorms, a kitchen, wonderfully friendly hosts and the most beautiful balcony in Pécs. Dorms 3500–4500Ft, doubles 12,500Ft.

Eating and drinking

For cheap pizza, pasta and burgers, head to one of the numerous student restaurants to the west of town along Hungária utca.

Az Elefántos Jokai tér 6. Simple pizza and pasta dishes served on a pleasant terrace on the square. Occasional live music. From 1500Ft.

Cellárium next to the *Főnix Hotel*. A cavernous cellar restaurant serving up high-quality Hungarian cuisine. Closed Sun. Mains 1800Ft.

Kanta Bár Irgalmasok utca 6. Laid-back little café-bar tucked away from the street in a leafy courtyard, with funky tunes, cheap beer and friendly staff.

Kino Café Hungária utca 19. Part of the Uránia Cinema, this rowdy student bar has a packed dance-floor at the weekends.

Kioszk Szent Istvan tér. Sweet café next to the cathedral with friendly staff and a range of liqueurs.

Kulturkert Quiet terraced courtyard café accessed off the western side of Szent Istvan tér, with stunning views of the surrounding countryside. Summer only.

Eastern Hungary

The hilly and forested northern region of **eastern Hungary** will not feature prominently in any hurried tour of the country, but nobody should overlook the gorgeous wine-producing town of **Eger**, and the nearby "Valley of the Beautiful Woman", famed for its wine cellars.

EGER

Its colourful architecture suffused by sunshine, **EGER** seems a fitting place of origin for *Egri Bikavér*, the famous red wine marketed abroad as "Bull's Blood", which brings hordes of visitors to the town.

What to see and do

The principal attractions in Eger stretch either side of the main square, **Dobó István tér**, extending to the compact, cobbled streets around the castle, north-east of the centre. The square itself is a vast, bustling affair, surrounded by little boutiques and cafés; nearby, on Knézich utca, is the elegant fourteen-sided minaret that has become Eger's most photographed structure.

Cathedral

The Neoclassical **cathedral**, designed by József Hild and constructed between 1831 and 1836, is five minutes' walk southwest from the main square. The florid **Lyceum** directly opposite the cathedral is worth visiting for its library (March to mid-Nov Tues–Sun 9.30am–1.30/3.30pm, mid-Nov to Feb Sat & Sun only 9.30am–1.30pm; 700Ft), whose beautiful floor and fittings are made of polished oak. The **observatory**, at the top of the tower in the east wing (same hours; 800Ft), houses a nineteenth-century camera obscura which projects a view of the entire town.

Archbishop's Palace and Minaret

Close by stands the **Archbishop's Palace** (8/9am–4/5pm; 400Ft), a U-shaped Baroque pile with fancy wrought-iron gates. Its right wing houses the treasury and a history of the bishopric of Eger. Cross the bridge and head to the left where a slender minaret extends skyward (April–Oct 10am–6pm; 200Ft), looking rather lonely without its mosque, which was demolished during a nineteenth-century building boom.

Castle

Uphill from Dobó István tér are the gates of the **castle** (exhibition times: daily March–Oct 8am–6/7/8pm, Nov–Feb 8am–5pm; 500Ft, castle times vary so check with Tourinform). From the bastion overlooking the main gate, a path leads up to the ticket office and the fifteenth-century **Bishop's Palace**: tapestries, ceramics, Turkish handicrafts and weaponry fill the museum upstairs, while downstairs are temporary exhibits and a Hall of Heroes, where a life-size marble István Dobó lies amid a bodyguard of heroes of the 1552 siege in which two thousand soldiers and Eger's women repulsed a Turkish force six times their number.

Arrival and information

Train station Állomás tér; to reach the centre, walk up the road to Deák Ferenc út, catch bus #10 or #12, and get off when you see the cupola of the cathedral.

Tourist office Tourinform office at Bajcsy-Zsilinszky utca 9 (mid-June to Aug daily 9/10am–7pm; Sept to mid-June Mon–Fri 9am–5pm, Sat 9am–1pm; Ⓣ36/517-715, Ⓦwww.eger.hu).

Bike rental Eger Jokai 6 Ⓣ70/775-0041, 500Ft per hour.

Accommodation

For student hostels and private rooms, contact Ibusz, Széchenyi utca 9 (Ⓣ36/311-451, Ⓔi047@ibusz.hu).

Hotel Minaret Knézich K. utca 4 Ⓣ36/410-233, Ⓦwww.hotelminaret.hu. Large, welcoming hotel in the centre of Eger. Doubles from 12,000Ft.

WINE-TASTING IN THE VALLEY OF THE BEAUTIFUL WOMAN

Just west of town, in the Szépasszonyvölgy – translated as "Valley of the Beautiful Woman" – local **vineyards** produce four types of wine: *Muskotály* (discreet, semi-sweet Muscatel), *Bikavér* (Bull's Blood – smooth, spicy and ruby red), *Leányka* (medium-dry white with a hint of herbs) and *Medoc Noir* (rich, dark and sweet red) – and it's possible to sample all of them in the tourist-focused cluster of cellars in the heart of the valley, a twenty-minute walk or a pleasant cycle from Eger. Finding the best cellar is a matter of luck and taste, but you could try Auntie Anci's Olaszrizling at no. 28 or the Medoc Noir in Sándor Arvai's at no. 31. Cellars close by 8pm.

Tourist Motel Mekcsey utca 2 ⓣ36/429-014. Basic place just along from the castle, with good-value rooms sleeping up to 4. Doubles from 7500Ft.

Tulipán Szépasszonyvölgy 71, Heves County ⓣ36/410-580. Campsite in the Szépasszony Valley; open all year.

Eating and drinking

Efendi Kossuth utca 19. Large portions of traditional Hungarian specialities from 1300Ft.

Egri Est Café Széchenyi utca 16. A good drinking spot on a lively street. Also serves decent food and occasionally has live music.

Palacsintavár Dobó utca 9. Terrific range of sweet and savoury pancakes and an amusing interior festooned with all manner of things: postcards, exotic cigarette packs and magazine covers.

Várkert Étterem Dózsa György ter 8. Atmospheric café-restaurant with a convivial terrace serving Hungarian specialities. The vampish blackcurrant deer stew with blood orange is wonderfully rich. 1800Ft.

The Great Plain

Encompassing half of Hungary, the **Great Plain** is romantically wild and liberating in its expansive flatness; yet punishing winters and the bleak monotony of its landscape make for harsh living conditions in its more remote villages. Between the Danube and the Tisza are two lively, culturally rich cities, **Kecskemét** and **Széged**, as well as protected national parks for superb horseriding.

KECSKEMÉT

Easily accessible as a day-trip from Budapest, **KECSKEMÉT** is the ideal place to escape the hustle and bustle of the capital. With its eclectic architecture and a pedestrianized centre, the town has a self-assured feel about it – due, in part, to Kecskemét's comparatively harmonious history: unlike neighbouring towns it was spared devastation by the Turks, who took a shine to the place instead. Not only is the town itself charming, it is also the gateway to the lovely **Kiskunság National Park**.

What to see and do

The main attraction in Kecskemét is the marvellous **Cifra Palace** – an exemplary Art Nouveau creation designed by Géza Markus in 1902, which now houses the **Kecskemét Art Gallery** (Tues–Sun 10am–5pm; 320Ft). The collection includes work by the Jewish painter, István Farkas, who died in Auschwitz. Upstairs is the magnificent peacock ballroom, once a casino, and further up a terrace offers a close-up view of the Art Nouveau chimneys and gables. South of Szabadság tér is the **Town Hall** – its elaborate decoration and musical clock seemingly fit for a toy town. The building, constructed in 1893, is well worth a look around, especially the Grand Hall, which contains murals by Bertalan Székely, who decorated the Matyás Church in Budapest. The Town Hall operates under somewhat irregular opening hours, however you should be able to have a look around if you ask at reception. In the summer, films are projected in the courtyard – ask at Tourinform

for details. The **Hungarian Photography Museum** at Katona József tér 12 (Wed–Sun 10am–4/5pm; 400Ft; ⓦwww.fotomuzeum.hu) is housed in a former dance-hall, with excellent rotating exhibitions of mostly Hungarian, and some international, photographers.

Arrival and information

Bus and train stations Next to one another north of the centre. Head down Nagykőrösi utca or Rákóczi utca from the station towards the main square, Szabadság tér.

Tourist information Tourinform is situated in the corner of the Town Hall (Sept–May Mon–Fri 8am–4/5pm, mid-June to Aug Mon–Fri 9am–6pm, Sat & Sun 9am–2pm; ⓣ76/481-065, ⓦwww.kecskemet.hu). They can give detailed information on horseriding operators and trips to the Kiskunság National Park, and also offer bike rental (350Ft per hour).

Accommodation

Private apartments can be booked with Ibusz at Korona utca 2 in the Malom shopping centre (daily Mon–Sat 10am–7pm, Sun 10am–2pm). During the summer rooms in colleges are available from Jókai tér 4 (ⓣ76/481-529) and Izsáki utca 10 (ⓣ76/506-526).

Fábián Panzió Kápolna utca 14 ⓣ76/477-677, ⓦwww.hotels.hu/Fabian. Run by a super-friendly family and the best place to stay by far in Kecskemét. Smart, spacious rooms and the wonderful breakfast includes home-made apricot jam. Doubles 11,800Ft.

Eating and drinking

The region's speciality is Mangalica pork, a rich, marbled meat reputed to have essential health benefits, made from pigs with a sheep-like fleece.

Geniusz Kisfaludy utca 5. Convivial place at the back of the Alföld Aruház shopping centre, with some adventurous dishes from a Hungarian and international menu. Great duck and red cabbage for 1800Ft.

Kis Bugaci Munka'csy Miha'ly utca. Excellent traditional restaurant just down from the *Fábián Panzió* offering simply prepared dishes at great prices. Mains 1100Ft.

Liberté Sazbadság tér 2. Attractive spot for a drink or light bite under an outsized awning, where you can hear the chimes of the town hall clock and watch people amble by.

Lordok Café Kossuth tér 7. Quality fast-food joint attached to a trendy café-bar, serving giant portions of lasagne and salad for 700Ft.

Activities

Bathing Thermal baths and outdoor pools abound in Kecskemét. The closest to the centre are Kecskeméti Élményfürdő, Csabay Géza krt. 2 (ⓣ76/417-407) and Fedett Uszoda, Izsáki utca 1 (ⓣ76/482-152).

Horseriding For information on horseriding operators, ask Tourinform, or try Somodi Tanya farm (ⓣ76/377-095, ⓦwww.somoditanya.hu) in Fülöpháza, which can accommodate all levels of riding ability (2800Ft/hr) for fantastic hacks into the countryside bordering the Kiskunság National Park. Call to arrange in advance and someone will pick you up from the bus. Lodgings also available (doubles from 7000Ft) if you want to wake up to an early morning ride.

Moving on

Train Budapest (10 daily; 1hr 30min); Szeged (12 daily; 1–2hr).

Bus Budapest (every 1hr–1hr 30min; 1hr 45min); Szeged (10 daily; 1hr 30min).

SZEGED

SZEGED, the most sophisticated city in the Great Plain, straddles the River Tisza before it enters Serbia. The present layout of the city dates from after the great flood of 1879, when the Tisza swelled and destroyed most of the city. Thanks to help from foreign capital, it was rebuilt using every architectural style possible, with strapping new buildings and squares that seem to laugh in the face of the flood with their enormous size. The place is now vibrant with music festivals and has a thriving university atmosphere.

What to see and do

The centre of activity in Szeged is **Dom tér square**, surrounded by impressive arcades and busts of celebrated Hungarians. It was created in 1920 to accommodate the enormous **Votive Church** (Mon–Sat 8am–5pm, Sun 1–5pm; 400Ft), which the townsfolk pledged to erect after the great flood. At 12.15pm, 5.45pm and,

in summer, 8.45pm, the charming **Musical Clock** on the south side of the square comes alive, as figurines from inside the clock pop out and move to the chiming of bells.

Móra Ferenc Museum

The **Móra Ferenc Museum** (Tues–Sun 10am–5/6pm; 400Ft) contains a huge painting of the great flood by Pál Vágó and an interesting section on the Avars, the people displaced by the arriving Magyars at the beginning of the eighth century. From the museum, it's a short walk to the grassy Széchenyi tér, and to the Baroque **town hall**; look out for the pretty "Bridge of Sighs", modelled on the Venetian original, which links the hall to a neighbouring house. The Klauzál tér, a charming piazza south of the hall, has some tantalizing ice-cream parlours.

Great Synagogue

The **Great Synagogue** (Új Zsinagóga) is one of the largest synagogues in Europe; the entrance is on Jósika utca, not far from Klauzál tér (Sun–Fri 10am–noon & 1–5pm). Built between 1900 and 1903 by Lipót Baumhorn, who designed twenty-two synagogues throughout the country, it is purported to be the finest example of his work, with a spectacular dome in blue stained glass.

Thermal baths

For rest and relaxation, head to the **thermal baths** on Tisza Lajos körút (6am–8pm; 1800Ft), which has indoor steam baths, ten pools and a water-park with some retro flumes.

Arrival and information

Bus station Mars tér, a 5min walk to the heart of the Belváros (old city).

Train station South of the Belváros, a short tram ride on the #1.

Tourist information Tourinform, Dugonics tér 2 (June–Aug Mon–Fri 9am–6pm, Sat 9am–1pm; Sept–May Mon–Fri 9am–5pm; ⓣ63/488-690, ⓦwww.szeged.hu). They also have an info-point in Széchenyi tér (8am–8pm).

Festivals As host of the famous Szeged Open Air Festival (ⓦwww.szegediszabadteri.hu) in July and August, the city attracts swarms of culture-hungry visitors to a steady stream of opera, theatre and classical music concerts. For two weeks in mid-May, the main square, Szechenyi tér, is host to hundreds of wine stalls for the Szeged Wine Festival, where you can sample varieties from across Hungary, accompanied by live music and tasty snacks.

Accommodation

Private rooms can be booked through Szeged Tourist located at Klauzál tér 7 (Mon–Fri 9am–5pm; ⓣ62/420-428, ⓔszegedtourist@mail.tiszanet.hu) and Ibusz on Oroszlán utca 3 (Mon–Fri 9am–6pm, Sat 9am–1pm; ⓣ62/471-177, ⓔi085@ibusz.hu). College dorms are available in the summer – ask at Tourinform.

Familia Panzió Szentharomság utca 71 ⓣ62/441-122, ⓦwww.familiapanzio.hu. Large, friendly place south of the centre and a 10min walk west of the train station. Doubles 14,000Ft.

Partfürdő Camping Középkikötő sor ⓣ62/430-843, ⓦwww.szegedkemping.hu. On the river bank in Újszeged, 5min walk from the centre, with wooden chalets (from 5500Ft) and its own thermal bath.

Eating and drinking

The fruit and veg market is just behind Mars tér, with tumbling piles of paprika and aromatic seasonal fruits aplenty.

Botond Étterem Széchenyi tér. A simple, reasonably priced choice in the centre of town with Hungarian mains at around 1700Ft.

Chaplin Bar & Grill Arany János utca 5. Fun, budget option that has student-friendly food at student prices (350Ft for a bagel or falafel, 450Ft for spaghetti). Mon–Fri 7am–4pm.

Halászcsárda Roosevelt tér 14. Welcoming restaurant with a lively band of staff, folk music and tasty fish goulash. Mains from 800Ft.

Kiskörössy Halászcárda at Felzo-Tizsa-part 336. Take bus #73 or #73Y from Mars tér and ask the driver to tell you the stop. Highly recommended restaurant on the riverbank with fish so fresh it seems to have jumped straight from the water onto your plate – delicious.

Moving on

Train Budapest (11 daily; 2hr).

Bus Budapest (7 daily; 3hr); Kecskemét (10 daily; 1hr 30min).

Ireland

HIGHLIGHTS

GIANT'S CAUSEWAY: marvel at the astonishing basalt columns

SLIEVE LEAGUE: witness astounding views from Europe's highest sea cliffs

ARAN ISLANDS: be amazed by spectacular archeological remains

DUBLIN: visit the home of world-famous Guinness

COUNTY CLARE: enjoy traditional Irish music in Clare's pubs

ROUGH COSTS

DAILY BUDGET Basic €40/occasional treat €60–70

DRINK Guinness €4.50/pint

FOOD Irish stew €10

HOSTEL/BUDGET HOTEL €15/€35–45

TRAVEL Bus: Kilkenny–Dublin €10.80

FACT FILE

POPULATION 6 million (Republic: 4.2 million, Northern Ireland: 1.8 million)

AREA 70,300 sq km

LANGUAGE English; Gaelic

CURRENCY Euro € (Republic); pound sterling £ (Northern Ireland)

CAPITALS Dublin (Republic: 1.1 million); Belfast (Northern Ireland: 300,000)

INTERNATIONAL PHONE CODE ⓣ353 (Republic); ⓣ44 (Northern Ireland)

Introduction

In both Northern Ireland and the Republic, Ireland's lures are its landscape and people – the rain-hazed loughs and wild coastlines, the talent for conversation and wealth of traditional music. While economic growth has transformed Ireland's cities, the countryside remains relatively unchanged.

Ireland's west draws most visitors; its coastline and islands – especially Aran – combine vertiginous cliffs, boulder-strewn wastes and dramatic mountains. The interior is less spectacular, though the southern pastures and low wooded hills are classic landscapes. Northern Ireland's principal highlights are the bizarre basalt formation of the **Giant's Causeway** and the alluring, island-studded **Lough Erne**.

Dublin is an extraordinary mix of youthfulness and tradition, of revitalized Georgian squares and vibrant pubs. **Belfast**, victim of perennial bad press, is undergoing a massive rejuvenation in every sense, while the cities of **Cork** and **Galway**, in particular, sparkle with energy.

No introduction can cope with the complexities of Ireland's **politics**, which still permeate most aspects of daily life in many areas in the North. However, regardless of partisan politics, Irish hospitality is as warm as the brochures say, on both sides of the border.

CHRONOLOGY

c. 3000 BC Neolithic tombs first constructed.

c. 500 BC Celts arrive in Ireland heralding the Iron Age.

c.100 BC Romans refer to Ireland as "Hibernia".

432 AD Saint Patrick arrives in Ireland, converting pagans to Christianity.

795 Viking raids on Ireland.

1167 Arrival of Anglo-Norman invaders, ushering in eight hundred years of English rule.

1558–1603 Policy of Plantation of Irish lands under Queen Elizabeth I.

1649–53 Cromwell re-conquers Ireland, after a bloody campaign against Irish Catholics and English Royalists.

1690 Battle of the Boyne marks decisive victory by the Protestant king William of Orange over Catholic James II of England, as he attempted to regain the crown.

1704 Penal Code introduced, barring Catholics from voting, education and the military.

1759 Arthur Guinness begins to brew his famous stout in Dublin.

1798 Rebellion of the United Irishmen led by Wolfe Tone and supported by French troops is suppressed.

1801 Act of Union makes Ireland officially part of Great Britain.

1803 Second United Irishmen Rebellion under Robert Emmet defeated.

1845–49 Potato famine causes widespread starvation and prompts mass migration to the United States.

1879–82 Land War increases support for the Home Rule movement led by Charles Stewart Parnell.

1916 Easter Rising by Irish nationalists is brutally repressed by the British.

1922 Irish War of Independence ends with secession of 26 Irish counties from the UK to form the Irish Free State. Six counties in the North remain part of Great Britain.

1922 James Joyce's *Ulysses* is published.

1949 The Republic of Ireland is declared.

1970s The Provisional IRA steps up violent campaigns in Northern Ireland and the UK.

1972 British troops kill thirteen civilians in Derry, Northern Ireland in an event known as Bloody Sunday.

1973 Ireland joins the European Community.

1998 Good Friday Agreement signed by the British and Irish governments heralding a new era of peace and cooperation in Northern Ireland.

2002 The euro is introduced in the Republic of Ireland.

2005 The Provisional IRA announces a full ceasefire.

2007 Agreement between rival party leaders, Ian Paisley and Gerry Adams, to share power in an elected assembly for Northern Ireland.

2008 Crisis in the Irish banking system combines with a worldwide recession, bringing an end to economic prosperity enjoyed during the "Celtic Tiger" years.

ARRIVAL

Ireland has four international **airports**: Dublin, Cork, Shannon and Knock in the Republic, and Belfast International in the North. Regional airports, which also serve the UK, are Belfast City, Derry, Donegal, Galway, Kerry and Sligo.

Ferry routes from the UK comprise Cairnryan–Larne, Fishguard–Rosslare, Fleetwood–Larne, Holyhead–Dublin, Holyhead–Dún Laoghaire, Isle of Man–Belfast, Isle of Man–Dublin, Liverpool–Belfast, Liverpool–Dublin, Pembroke–Rosslare, Stranraer–Belfast and Troon–Larne. Travelling by ferry without a vehicle is not expensive (about €60 return), and departure times are generally more civilized than most low-cost flights. Taking a car on the ferry is pricey (€200–300 in high season), but convenient if you're travelling in a group.

GETTING AROUND

You can **save money** on rail and bus services by buying multi-journey tickets in advance; the **Freedom of Northern Ireland/Irish Rover** tickets give you unlimited bus/rail travel for three, five, eight or fifteen days. See ⓦwww.translink.co.uk/exploreireland200708.asp for further information.

By train

In the Republic, Iarnród Éireann (Ⓦwww.irishrail.ie) operates **trains** to most major towns and cities. Few routes run north–south across the country, so, although you can easily get to the west coast by train, you can't use the railways to explore. The **Dublin–Belfast line** is the only cross-border service, and very frequent stops north of Dublin means it's not particularly fast, the full journey taking a little over two hours (€18). NI Railways (Ⓦwww.translink.co.uk) operates just a few routes in Northern Ireland.

The Global and One Country **InterRail** passes are valid in Ireland – though you need two separate One Country passes for the Republic and Northern Ireland.

By bus

The express **buses** of the Republic's Bus Éireann (Ⓦwww.buseireann.ie) cover most of the island, including several cross-border services. Citylink also runs a good service between Dublin, Galway, Limerick and Cork (Ⓦwww.citylink.ie) at slightly cheaper rates. Aircoach (Ⓦwww.aircoach.ie) run buses direct from Dublin airport to Cork and Belfast. Bus **fares** are generally cheaper than trains, especially midweek. Remote villages may only have a couple of buses a week, so it's essential to find out the times – major bus stations stock free timetables. Private buses operate on major routes throughout the Republic and are often cheaper than Bus Éireann: J.J. Kavanagh & Sons, for instance, provide an efficient service from Dublin airport to Shannon airport, Limerick, Galway, Kilkenny and Waterford (Ⓣ056/883 1106, Ⓦwww.jjkavanagh.ie). In the North, Ulsterbus (Ⓦwww.translink.co.uk) runs regular and reliable services.

By bike

Cycling is an enjoyable and reasonably safe way of seeing Ireland. In the Republic, bikes can be rented in most towns and Raleigh is the main operator (€20/day, €80/week; from €100 deposit, depending on the dealer; Ⓣ01/465 9659, Ⓦwww.raleigh.ie); local dealers (including some hostels) are cheaper. It costs an extra €10 to carry a bike on a bus, and €3–10 on a train, though not all buses or trains carry bikes; check in advance. In the North, bike rental (around £15/day) is more limited; tourist offices have lists of local operators. Taking a bike on a bus costs half the adult single fare (up to a maximum of £5) and, on a train, a quarter of the adult single fare (with no upper limit).

By car

Driving is the best way to see the country, and **car rental**, if shared between a few people, can also work out cheaper than public transport. Budget (Ⓣ090/662 7711, Ⓦwww.budget.ie) and Thrifty (Ⓣ01/844 1944, Ⓦwww.thrifty.ie) have the cheapest rates, around €11–20 per day depending on the season. Book online for the best deals. Note that the driver must be over 25 years of age.

ACCOMMODATION

Hostels run by **An Óige** (Irish Youth Hostel Association; Ⓦwww.anoige.ie) and **HINI** (Hostelling International Northern Ireland; Ⓦwww.hini.org.uk) are affiliated to Hostelling International. Overnight prices start at €11–17 in the Republic and £9.50–13 in the North. Most Irish hostels are **independent hostels**, which usually belong to either Independent Holiday Hostels (Ⓣ01/836 4700, Ⓦwww.hostels-ireland.com) or the Independent Hostels Owners network (Ⓣ074/973 0130, Ⓦwww.hostellingireland.com). There are a few disreputable hostels around, so it's a good idea to enquire locally before booking. In the Republic, expect to pay €10–18 for a dorm bed, €17–32 (rising

to €46 in some Dublin hostels) per person for private rooms where available; in the North, it's £7–12/£14–25.

B&Bs vary enormously, but most are welcoming, warm and clean. Expect to pay from around €32/£20 per person; en-suite facilities are usually a little more and most **hotels** are generally pricier. For an extra €4 (Republic) or £2 (Northern Ireland), you can book through tourist offices. Booking ahead is always advisable during high season and major festivals (best rates are usually online).

Camping usually costs around €10 a night in the Republic, £7 in the North. In out-of-the-way places nobody minds where you pitch, but try to ask permission first. Farmers in popular tourist areas may ask for a small fee to use their land. Some hostels also let you camp for around €8/£5 per person.

FOOD AND DRINK

Irish **food** is meat-orientated. B&Bs usually provide a "traditional" **Irish breakfast** of sausages, bacon and eggs (although many offer vegetarian alternatives). **Pub lunch** staples are usually meat or fish and two veg, with a few veggie options, while specifically vegetarian places are sparse outside major cities and popular tourist areas. All towns have fast-food outlets, but traditional fish-and-chips is a better bet, especially on the coast. For the occasional treat, there are some very good seafood restaurants, particularly along the southwest and west coasts. Most towns have daytime cafés serving a selection of affordable hot dishes, salads, soups, sandwiches and cakes.

Drink

The stereotypical view of the "Irish national pastime" has a certain element of truth; especially in rural areas, the **pub** is the social heart of the community and the focus for the proverbial **craic** (pronounced "crack"), a particular blend of Irish fun involving good company, witty conversation and laughter, frequently against a backdrop of music. The classic Irish drink is **Guinness**, best in Dublin, home of the brewery, while the Cork stouts, Beamish and Murphy's, have their devotees. For English-style keg **bitter**, try Smithwicks. Irish **whiskeys** are world famous – try Paddy's, Jameson's or Bushmills.

CULTURE AND ETIQUETTE

With the huge influx of visitors to Ireland in recent years, the country has acquired an increasingly **cosmopolitan** feel, particularly in the big cities. Ironically, this outside influence has also encouraged an increased sense of national identity and heritage. Traditional music sessions are still the primary form of evening entertainment in pubs.

Despite the decreasing influence of Catholicism in Ireland, old-school manners and family values still reign here. It's hard to miss the hospitality and friendliness that most clearly define the Irish.

Smoking is now banned in all indoor public places, including pubs, cafés and restaurants. Most pubs, however, have installed outdoor smoking areas of some description. In restaurants and cafés, a ten percent **tip** is generally expected for good service.

SPORTS AND OUTDOOR ACTIVITIES

Walking and **cycling** in Ireland are great ways of enjoying some of the country's fantastic landscapes (see ⓦwww.walking.ireland.ie for suggested routes). There are great opportunities for **horse-riding** (see ⓦwww.discoverireland.ie); a lovely ride is along the white sands of Connemara. **Watersports** are popular: Ireland is increasingly praised for its

surfing spots, such as Portrush in the north, Bundoran in Donegal, and Lahinch in Clare (see Ⓦwww.isasurf.ie).

The two great Gaelic sports, **hurling** (the oldest field game in Europe, and similar to hockey, though arguably more exciting) and **Gaelic football** (a mixture of soccer and rugby, but predating both these games), are very popular spectator sports. Croke Park Stadium in Dublin is home to the big fixtures (see Ⓦwww.gaa.ie and Ⓦwww.crokepark.ie for information and tickets).

Horse racing (Ⓦwww.goracing.ie) looms large on the sporting agenda: you'll never be far from a race in Ireland, whether it's a big racecourse like Galway or a soggy village affair in the middle of nowhere.

COMMUNICATIONS

Main **post offices** are open Monday to Friday 9am to 5.30pm, Saturday 9am to 1pm. Stamps and phonecards are also often available in newsagents. **Public phones** are everywhere, and usually take **phonecards**; coin-operated phones are rare in rural areas. **International calls** are cheaper at weekends or after 6pm (Mon–Fri). For the **operator** in the Republic call Ⓣ10 (domestic) or Ⓣ114 (international); in Northern Ireland Ⓣ100 or Ⓣ155. To call the Republic from Northern Ireland dial Ⓣ00353 followed by the area code (without the initial 0) and the local number (note cross-border calls are charged at the international rate). Call centres offer cheaper international rates than public telephones. To call the North from the Republic use the code Ⓣ048, followed by the eight-digit local number. **Internet access** is widely available and costs about €1.50 per hour; it's generally cheaper in big towns and cities.

IRELAND ON THE NET

Ⓦwww.tourismireland.com Information on getting to Ireland from all over the world.
Ⓦwww.discoverireland.ie Bord Fáilte.
Ⓦwww.discovernorthernireland.com Northern Ireland Tourist Board.
Ⓦwww.heritageireland.com Information on Ireland's main heritage sites.
Ⓦwww.ireland.com *Irish Times* site with up-to-date info on Dublin.
Ⓦwww.browseireland.com Useful site with a massive number of Irish links.
Ⓦwww.ntni.org.uk Details of the National Trust's properties in Northern Ireland.

EMERGENCIES

The Republic's police are known as the **Gardaí** (pronounced "gar-dee"), while the **PSNI** (Police Service of Northern Ireland) operates in the North. **Hospitals** and medical facilities are high quality; you'll rarely be far from a hospital, and both Northern Ireland and the Republic are within the European Health Insurance Card scheme. Most **pharmacies** open standard shop hours, though in large towns some may stay open until 10pm; they dispense only a limited range of drugs without a doctor's prescription.

INFORMATION

Tourist offices are abundant in Ireland, in the smaller as well as larger towns on the tourist trail. **Bord Fáilte** provides tourist information in the Republic; the **Northern Ireland Tourist Board** in the North. They provide free maps of the city/town and immediate vicinity, and sell a selection of more extensive and specialized maps.

MONEY AND BANKS

Currency in the Republic is the **euro** (€), in Northern Ireland the **pound**

EMERGENCY NUMBERS

In the Republic Ⓣ112 or Ⓣ999; in Northern Ireland Ⓣ999.

STUDENT DISCOUNTS

A **student card** usually gives reduced entrance charges of up to fifty percent and, if you're visiting sites run by the Heritage Service in the Republic (Ⓦwww.heritageireland.ie), it's worth buying a **Heritage Card** (€21, students €8), which provides a year's unlimited admission.

sterling (£). Standard **bank hours** are Monday to Friday 9.30am to 4.30pm (Republic and Northern Ireland). However, hours vary from branch to branch; most have a later closing time on Thursday (5pm) and some are open Saturday morning. There are **ATMs** throughout Ireland – though not in all villages – and most accept a variety of cards. The exchange rate at the time of writing was €1.15/£1.

OPENING HOURS AND HOLIDAYS

Opening hours are roughly Monday to Saturday 9am to 6pm, with some late evenings (usually Thurs), half-days and Sunday opening. In rural areas, hours are often more flexible, with later closing times. The main **museums and attractions** will normally be open regular shop hours, though outside the cities, many only open during the summer.

Public holidays in the Republic are: Jan 1, St Patrick's Day (March 17), Easter Monday, May Day (first Mon in May), June Bank Holiday (first Mon in June), August Bank Holiday (first Mon in Aug), October Bank Holiday (Halloween, last Mon in Oct), December 25 and 26. Note that some places may also close on Good Friday. In the North: January 1, St Patrick's Day (March 17), Good Friday, Easter Monday, May Day (first Mon in May), Spring Bank Holiday (last Mon in May), July 12, August Bank Holiday (last Mon in Aug), December25 & 26.

THE IRISH LANGUAGE

Though **Irish** is the first language of the Republic, you'll rarely hear it spoken outside the areas officially designated as *Gaeltacht* ("Irish-speaking"), namely West Cork, West Kerry, Connemara, some of Mayo and Donegal, and a tiny part of Meath. However, two important words you may encounter sometimes appear on the doors of pub toilets *Fir* (for men) and *Mná* (for women). You'll also find the word *Fáilte* (welcome) popping up frequently as you enter towns and tourist spots. A few other words to get your tongue round:

Sláinte	cheers, good health
Gardaí	police
An lár	city centre
Dia dhuit	hello
Slán	goodbye

More information on the Gaeltacht areas is available at Ⓦwww.gaelsaoire.ie.

Dublin and around

Set on the banks of the River Liffey, **DUBLIN** is a splendidly monumental city with an increasingly cosmopolitan feel, and a fizzing, internationally renowned nightlife. Ireland's booming economy has brought extensive urban regeneration, but sadly there's still much deprivation. Ironically, though, it's this very collision of the old and the new, the slick and the shabby, that gives Dublin such an exciting vibe.

Dublin began as the Viking trading post **Dubh Linn** (Dark Pool), which soon amalgamated with the Celtic settlement of **Baile Átha Cliath** (Town of the Hurdle Ford) – still the Irish name for the city. The city's fabric is essentially **Georgian**, hailing from when the Anglo-Irish gentry invested their income in new townhouses. After the 1801 Act of Union, Dublin entered a long economic decline, but remained the focus of much of the agitation that eventually led to independence.

Dublin city also serves as an excellent base for excursions to the picturesque mountains, lakes, forested estates and rural villages of **Wicklow** county, or to the five-thousand-year-old passage tombs at Newgrange in the Boyne Valley, County Meath.

What to see and do

Dublin's fashionable **Southside** is home to the city's trendy bars, restaurants and shops – especially in the cobbled alleys of **Temple Bar** leading down to the **River Liffey** – and most of its historic monuments, centred on **Trinity College**, **Grafton Street** and **St Stephen's Green**. But the **Northside**, with its long-standing working-class neighbourhoods and inner-city communities, vaunts itself as the real heart of the city. Across the bridges from Temple Bar are the shopping districts around **O'Connell Street**, where you'll find a flavour of the old Dublin. Here, you'll also find a fair amount of graceful – if slightly shabby – residential streets and squares, with plenty of interest in the museums and cultural hotspots around the elegant **Parnell Square**.

The Vikings sited their assembly and burial ground near what is now **College Green**, a three-sided square where Trinity College is the most famous landmark.

Trinity College

Founded in 1592, Trinity College played a major role in the development of a Protestant Anglo-Irish tradition: right up to 1966, Catholics had to obtain a special dispensation to study here, though now they make up the majority of the students. The stern grey and mellow red-brick buildings are ranged around cobbled quadrangles in a larger version of the quads at Oxford and Cambridge. **The Old Library** (Mon–Sat 9.30am–5pm, Sun 9.30am/noon–4.30pm; €9, students €8) owns numerous Irish manuscripts. Pride of place goes to the illustrated ninth-century **Book of Kells**, which contains the four Gospels written in Latin on vellum, the script adorned with patterns and fantastic animals intertwined with the text's capital letters. The first of the great Irish illuminated manuscripts, the **Book of Durrow**, which dates from between 650 and 680, is also on display.

Grafton Street and around

Just south of College Green, the streets around pedestrianized **Grafton Street** frame Dublin's quality shopping area – featuring boutiques, department stores and designer outlets, as well as some secondhand, more alternative shops. At the southern end of Grafton Street lies **St Stephen's Green**, whose pleasant gardens and pools provide a pleasant

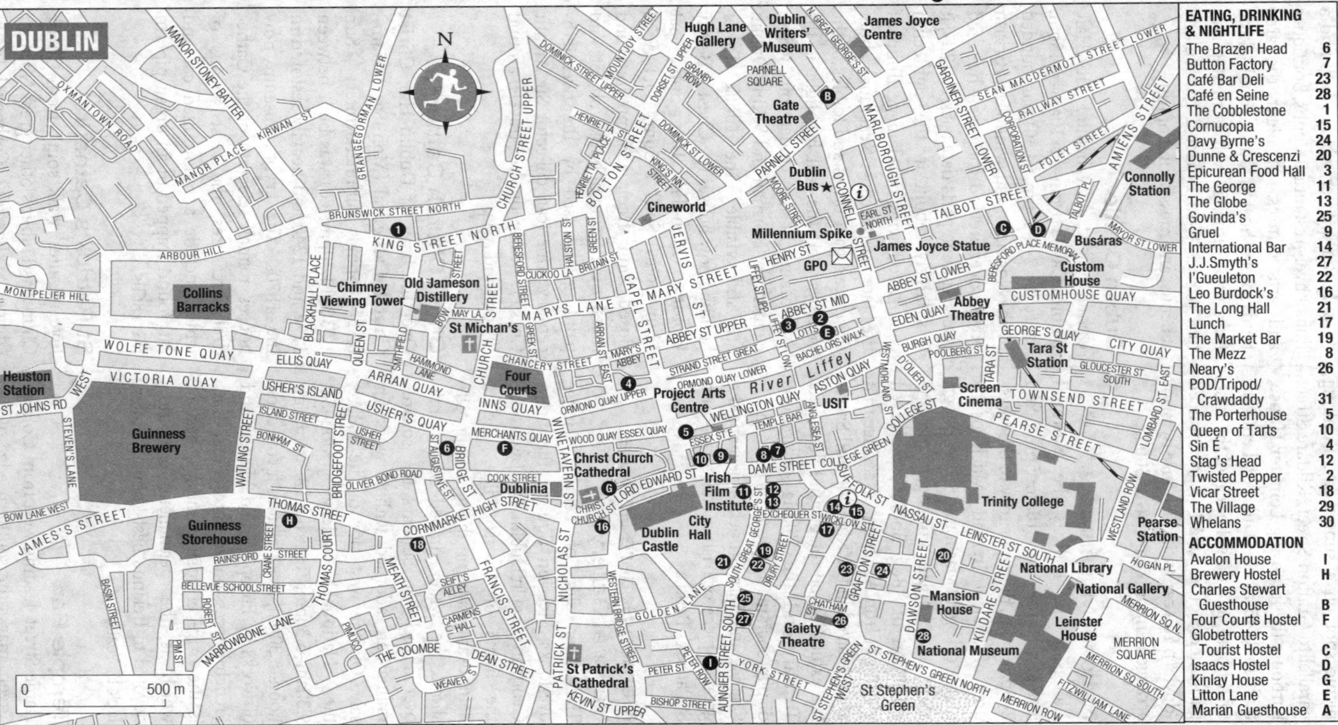

DUBLIN
EATING, DRINKING & NIGHTLIFE
The Brazen Head 6
Button Factory 7
Café Bar Deli 23
Café en Seine 28
The Cobblestone 1
Cornucopia 15
Davy Byrne's 24
Dunne & Crescenzi 20
Epicurean Food Hall 3
The George 11
The Globe 13
Govinda's 25
Gruel 9
International Bar 14
J.J.Smyth's 27
l'Gueuleton 22
Leo Burdock's 16
The Long Hall 21
Lunch 17
The Market Bar 19
The Mezz 8
Neary's 26
POD/Tripod/ Crawdaddy 31
The Porterhouse 5
Queen of Tarts 10
Sin É 4
Stag's Head 12
Twisted Pepper 2
Vicar Street 18
The Village 29
Whelans 30
ACCOMMODATION
Avalon House I
Brewery Hostel H
Charles Stewart Guesthouse B
Four Courts Hostel F
Globetrotters Tourist Hostel C
Isaacs Hostel D
Kinlay House G
Litton Lane E
Marian Guesthouse A
Phoenix Park
Irish Museum of Modern Art
Kilmainham Gaol
Hugh Lane Gallery
Dublin Writers' Museum
James Joyce Centre
Gate Theatre
Cineworld
Dublin Bus
Millennium Spike
James Joyce Statue
GPO
Busáras
Connolly Station
Custom House
Abbey Theatre
Tara St Station
Screen Cinema
USIT
Project Arts Centre
Chimney Viewing Tower
Old Jameson Distillery
St Michan's
Collins Barracks
Heuston Station
Four Courts
Guinness Brewery
Guinness Storehouse
Christ Church Cathedral
Dublinia
Irish Film Institute
City Hall
Dublin Castle
Trinity College
Pearse Station
National Library
National Gallery
Mansion House
Leinster House
National Museum
Gaiety Theatre
St Patrick's Cathedral
St Stephen's Green
Merrion Square
River Liffey
0 500 m
29 & 30
31

picnic spot on a sunny day. Running parallel to Grafton Street, Kildare Street harbours the imposing **Leinster House**, built in 1745 as the Duke of Leinster's townhouse, and now the seat of the Irish parliament, the **Dáil** (pronounced "doyle"). You can visit the house by prior arrangement only (☎01/618 3000).

National Museum

Alongside the Dáil is the **National Museum** (Tues–Sat 10am–5pm, Sun 2–5pm; free), the repository of the treasures of ancient Ireland. Much of its prehistoric gold was found in peat bogs, along the Lurgan Longboat and the collection of "Bog Bodies", preserved victims of Iron Age human sacrifice that are displayed in the Kingship and Sacrifice exhibition on the ground floor. The Treasury and the Viking exhibitions display such masterpieces as the Ardagh Chalice and Tara Brooch – perhaps the greatest piece of Irish metalwork – and St Patrick's Bell.

Merrion Square and the National Gallery

The other side of Leinster House overlooks **Merrion Square**, the finest Georgian plaza in Dublin. No. 1 was once the home of Oscar Wilde, and a flamboyant statue on the green opposite shows the writer draped insouciantly over a rock; on Sundays the square's railings are adorned with artwork for sale. On the west side of the square, the **National Gallery** (Mon–Sat 9.30am–5.30pm, Thurs until 8.30pm, Sun noon–5.30pm; free) features a collection of works by European Old Masters and French Impressionists, but the real draw is the trove of Irish paintings, best of which is the permanent exhibition devoted to Ireland's best-known painter, Jack B. Yeats.

Temple Bar

Dame Street, leading west from College Green, marks the southern edge of the **Temple Bar** quarter, where you'll find a hub of lively restaurants, pubs, boutiques and arts centres. At night the area tends to play host to tourists out looking for a good time, as well as to stag and hen parties – so expect a particularly raucous, and messy, kind of fun.

Dublin Castle

Uphill, tucked away behind City Hall, **Dublin Castle** (Mon–Fri 10am–4.45pm, Sat & Sun 2–4.45pm; €4.50) was founded by the Normans, and symbolized British power over Ireland for seven hundred years. Though parts date back to 1207, it was largely rebuilt in the eighteenth century following fire damage. Tours of the State Apartments reveal much about the extravagant tastes and foibles of the viceroys, and the real highlight is the excavations in the Undercroft, where elements of Norman and Viking Dublin are still visible. The Clock Tower building now houses the **Chester Beatty Library** (Mon–Fri 10am–5pm, Sat 11am–5pm, Sun 1–5pm; Oct–April closed Mon; free), a sumptuous and massive collection of books, objects and paintings amassed by the twentieth-century American collector Sir Arthur Chester Beatty on his travels around Europe and Asia.

Christ Church Cathedral

Over the brow of Dublin Hill, **Christ Church Cathedral** (Mon–Sat 9.45am–6.15/4.15pm summer/winter; Sun 12.30–14.30pm; €6) was built between 1172 and 1240 and heavily restored in the 1870s. The crypt museum now houses a small selection of the Cathedral's treasures, the least serious of which include a mummified cat and rat, found trapped in an organ pipe in the 1860s.

St Patrick's Cathedral

Five minutes' walk south from Christ Church is Dublin's other great Norman edifice, **St Patrick's Cathedral** (daily

9am–5.30pm; Nov–Feb Sun closes 3pm; €5.50), founded in 1191, and replete with relics of Jonathan Swift, its dean from 1713 to 1747.

Guinness Brewery

West of Christ Church, the **Guinness Brewery** covers a large area on either side of James's Street. Guinness is the world's largest single beer-exporting company, dispatching some 300 million pints a year. Set in the centre of the brewery, the **Guinness Storehouse** (daily 9.30am–5pm; July & Aug until 7pm; €15, ten percent discount if you book online; Ⓦwww.guinness-storehouse.com) serves as a kind of theme park for Guinness-lovers – and even if you're not a fan, you can't fail to be entertained by the interactive displays and activities, which include learning how to pour the perfect pint and watching some of those great Guinness TV ads again. Visits to the Storehouse end with reputedly the best pint of Guinness in Dublin, in the panoramic *Gravity Bar* at the top of the building (the head of the pint), with amazing views over the city.

Irish Museum of Modern Art

Regular buses (#26, #51, #79 and #90) run along The Quays to Heuston Station from where it's a five-minute walk to the **Royal Hospital Kilmainham**, Ireland's first Neoclassical building, dating from 1680, which now houses the **Irish Museum of Modern Art** (Tues–Sat 10am–5.30pm, Wed opens 10.30am, Sun noon–5.30pm; free). Its permanent collection of Irish and international art includes works by Gilbert and George, Damien Hirst, Sean Scully, Francesco Clemente and Peter Doig.

General Post Office and the Monument of Light

Halfway up O'Connell Street looms the **General Post Office** (Mon–Sat 8am–8pm; free), the insurgents' headquarters in the 1916 Easter Rising; only the frontage survived the fighting, and you can still see where bullets were embedded in the pillars. Across the road on the corner of Essex Street North is a **statue of James Joyce**. At the same junction, where the city's most famous landmark, Nelson's Pillar, once stood (it was blown up by the IRA on the fiftieth anniversary of the Easter Rising in 1966), stands a huge, illuminated stainless-steel spike – the **Monument of Light** – representing the city's hopes for the new millennium.

Parnell Square

At the northern end of O'Connell Street lies Parnell Square, one of the first of Dublin's Georgian squares. Its plain red-brick houses are broken by the grey-stone **Hugh Lane Gallery** (Tues–Thurs 10am–6pm, Fri & Sat until 5pm, Sun 11am–5pm; free), once the Earl of Charlemont's townhouse and the focus of fashionable Dublin. The gallery exhibits work by Irish and international masters, and features a reconstruction of Francis Bacon's working studio. Almost next door, the **Dublin Writers Museum** (Mon–Sat 10am–5pm, Sun 11am–5pm; €7.50) whisks you through Irish literary history from early Christian writings up to Samuel Beckett. Two blocks east of Parnell Square, at 35 North Great George's St, the **James Joyce Centre** (Tues–Sat 10am–5pm, Sun noon–5pm; €5; Ⓦwww.jamesjoyce.ie) runs intriguing walking tours of the novelist's haunts (summer only; €10; Ⓣ01/878 8547); combined tickets with the Dublin Writers Museum are available.

Old Jameson Distillery

Fifteen minutes west of O'Connell Street, on Bow Street, is the **Old Jameson Distillery** (daily 9am–6.30pm, last tour 5.30pm; €13.50). Tours cover the history and method of distilling what the Irish called *uisce beatha* (anglicized to whiskey and meaning "water of life") – which differs from Scotch

whisky by being thrice-distilled and lacking a peaty undertone – and end with a tasting session. The Distillery also has two **bars**, which pride themselves on their Jameson cocktails, and a **restaurant** which serves breakfast and lunch (9am–4.45pm; light lunch €7). Outside, a lift chugs you to the top of the old distillery **chimney** (Mon–Sat 10am–5pm, Sun 11am–5.30pm; €5), where an observation platform provides views of the city.

Phoenix Park

Phoenix Park is one of the world's largest urban parks, a great escape from the hustle and bustle of the centre (bus #10 from O'Connell Street or #25 from Wellington Quay); originally priory land, it's now home to the Presidential Lodge, Áras an Uachtaráin (free tours every Sat 10.30am–4.30pm) and **Dublin Zoo** (daily 9.30am–4/6pm; €15).

Arrival and information

Air The airport is 10km north of the city; Airlink buses #747 and #748 run to Busáras bus station (every 10–20 min; 30min; €6 single, €10 return), and the AerDart service #A1 (every 15min; €5.50 single) connects with the DART railway at Howth Junction, or there are regular Citybus services #16A, #41, #41B & #41C (every 10–20min; €1.80). Aircoach (Ⓦ www.aircoach.ie) run services to the city centre and South Dublin (€7 single/€12 return), and cheap, comfortable coaches all the way to Belfast and Cork (€15/22). A taxi to Dublin centre should cost €25–30.

Train Trains terminate at either Connolly Station on the Northside, or Heuston Station on the Southside.

Bus Bus Éireann coaches arrive at Busáras bus station, off Beresford Place, just behind The Custom House; private buses use a variety of central locations.

Boat Ferries dock at either Dún Laoghaire, 10km south of the city centre, from where DART railway connects to the city (every 20min; €2; 20min), or at the closer Dublin Port, where a Citybus service (€2.50; 15min) – or the local bus #53 – meets arriving ferries; through-coaches from Britain usually drop you at Busáras.

Tourist office Suffolk St, off College Green (Mon–Sat 9am–5.30/7pm; July & Aug also Sun 10.30am–3pm; Ⓦ www.visitdublin.com), with branches at 14 Upper O'Connell St, the Dún Laoghaire ferry terminal and the airport.

Travel agency USIT on Aston Quay, by O'Connell Bridge (Mon–Fri 10am–6.30pm, Thurs till 7pm, Sat 9.30am–5pm; Ⓣ 01/602 1904, Ⓦ www.usit.ie), books B&Bs during the summer and includes a travel agency offering student discounts.

City transport

Bus Dublin has an extensive route network and all buses are exact fare only. Fares are €1–1.85, a one-day bus pass is €6, or there are bus and rail passes (including DART or LUAS) for one day/three days (€10.20/€20). Free bus timetables are available from Dublin Bus, 59 Upper O'Connell St. Nitelink night buses cost €5.

Tram The LUAS tram service operates along two routes: from Connolly Station to Tallaght via Abbey St to Heuston Station, and from St Stephen's Green to Sandyford. Tickets cost €1.60–2.30 single, €2.90–4.30 return. A one-day pass is €4.50 and a combined bus/LUAS one-day pass €7.50.

Train The DART railway links Howth and Malahide to the north of the city with Bray and Greystones to the south via Pearse, Tara St and Connolly stations in the city centre (maximum fare €4). A trip on the DART is an activity in itself, affording stunning views of the Dublin suburbs and coastline. Get off at Howth, Malahide, Sandymount, Dún Laoghaire, Killiney Bray or Greysones for pleasant seaside walks.

Bike rental Cycle Ways, 185 Parnell St Ⓣ 01/873 4748.

City tours

Bus tours City Sightseeing (Ⓦ www.citysightseeingdublin.com) and Dublin Bus Tours (Ⓦ www.DublinSightseeing.ie) run similar hop-on, hop-off tours to all the major sights in the city (€15); both collect from the front of Trinity College.

Walking tours Tour Gratis (Ⓦ www.neweuropetours.eu) operate free walking tours, picking up from all of the listed hostels every morning. The highly recommended 1916 Rebellion walking tours (Mon–Sat 11.30am, Sun 1pm, meet at the *International Bar*, 23 Wicklow St; €12; Ⓦ www.1916rising.com) visit sights of interest relating to the 1916 Rising.

Organized pub crawls Dublin Literary Pub Crawl (April–Oct daily 7pm; Nov–March Thurs–Sun 7.30pm; meet at *The Duke Pub*, 9 Duke St; €12); and the more raucous Backpacker Pubcrawl (April–Sept daily 8pm, March–Oct Thurs–Sat 8pm; meet

Trinity College Front Gates; €10; Ⓦwww.backpackerpubcrawl.com).

Accommodation

Although Dublin has stacks of accommodation, anywhere central will probably be full at weekends, around St Patrick's Day (March 17), at Easter and in high summer so it's wise to book ahead (preferably online). The cheaper places are generally north of the river, especially around the bus and train stations northeast of the centre. All hostels listed provide free breakfast.

Hostels

Avalon House 55 Aungier St Ⓣ01/475 0001, Ⓦwww.avalon-house.ie. Bustling and friendly hostel with slightly cramped dorms but plenty of twin or four-bedded rooms. Performers get a free night's accommodation for an evening recital in the café. Dorms €16–28, rooms €50–75.

Brewery Hostel 22–23 Thomas St Ⓣ01/435 8600, Ⓦwww.irish-hostel.com/brewery_hostel. Housed in a fine converted library near the Guinness brewery, this small hostel has regular barbecues when the weather's good. Dorms €15–22, rooms €60–75.

Four Courts Hostel 15–17 Merchants Quay Ⓣ01/672 5839, Ⓦwww.fourcourtshostel.com. In a very central location, this hostel is housed in Georgian buildings overlooking the River Liffey. Excellent facilities and helpful staff. Dorms €17–30, rooms €30–50.

Globetrotters Tourist Hotel 46 Gardiner St Lower Ⓣ01/873 5893, Ⓦwww.globetrottersdublin.com. Upmarket hostel where security-locked dorms and individual bed lights make for a peaceful night's sleep. Also some spacious private rooms. All prices include full Irish breakfast. Dorms €18–28, rooms €80.

Isaacs Hostel 2–5 Frenchman's Lane Ⓣ01/855 6215, Ⓦwww.isaacs.ie. Housed in an eighteenth-century wine warehouse with its own restaurant on site, and a free sauna in the basement. Conveniently close to the bus station. Dorms €19–26, rooms €60–75.

Kinlay House 2–12 Lord Edward St Ⓦwww.kinlaydublin.ie. Large, friendly and popular hostel right beside Christchurch Cathedral. Dorms €12.50–30, rooms €60–80.

Litton Lane 2–4 Litton Lane Ⓣ01/872 8389, Ⓦwww.irish-hostel.com. Excellent hostel in a former recording studio, with great facilities and friendly staff. Adorned with colourful murals and posters depicting Irish rock stars. Dorms €10–20, rooms €50–80.

Guesthouses and B&Bs

Charles Stewart Guesthouse 5/6 Parnell Square Ⓣ01/878 0350, Ⓦwww.charlesstewart.ie. Very reasonably priced accommodation in elegant Georgian surroundings and with friendly staff. Virtually opposite the Gate Theatre. €60–80.

Marian Guesthouse 21 Upper Gardiner St Ⓣ01/874 4129, Ⓦwww.marianguesthouse.ie. Welcoming, good-value, family-run guesthouse, kitschly decorated with plenty of fake flowers and ornaments. 1km north of the city centre. €60–70.

Camping

Camac Valley Tourist Caravan and Camping Park Naas Rd, Clondalkin Ⓣ01/464 0644, Ⓦwww.camacvalley.com. The most convenient campsite, with excellent facilities, located on the N7, a 35min drive from the centre. Bus #69 from the centre (Aston Quay, near O'Connell Bridge; ask the driver for Camac Valley), stops right outside the campsite. The last bus is at 11.15pm, so if you're any later, a taxi (around €25) is your only option. €10 per person.

Eating

Café Bar Deli *Bewley's Café*, 78 Grafton St. Great pasta, pizza and salads in a room that sports some fabulous wallpaper and stained-glass windows. Mains from €10.50. You can also catch a lunchtime performance in its theatre upstairs.

Cornucopia 21 Wicklow St. One of the city's few vegetarian cafés and highly popular for its generous portions of home-made soups, salads, curries and gratins. Mains €8–12.

Dunne & Crescenzi 14–16 South Frederick St. Authentic Italian restaurant serving delicious bruschetta, antipasti, panini and simple pasta dishes, washed down by the cheapest (yet very palatable) house wine in Dublin. Mains €6–12.

Epicurean Food Hall Lower Liffey St. Collection of deli counters and food stands offering lunches from around the world in a communal dining area.

Govinda's 4 Aungier St. Huge helpings of dhal and rice and tasty vegetarian curries, plus daily veggie specials, served by very friendly staff. €7–10.

Gruel 68a Dame St. Quality quiches, focaccia and roast-in-a-roll lunches (€5–7), and a varied menu of well-prepared fish, meat and vegetarian dishes in the evening, like goat's cheese and roasted pepper risotto and Toulouse sausages with onion gravy. Dinner €13.

Leo Burdock's 2 Werburgh St. Dublin's best fish-and-chips – takeaway only. Fresh cod is €5.75. There's another branch on Liffey St Lower. Closed Sun.

TREAT YOURSELF

Dinner at the intimate, candlelit French bistro **L'Gueuleton** (1 Fade St; ⓣ01/675 3708) is a real treat. The food is thoughtfully prepared to the highest standards using ingredients from small, carefully selected producers in Ireland and France. The menu changes regularly but expect dishes like slow-roast belly of pork and duck confit. They don't take reservations, so prepare to queue at weekends. Mains €15–28.

Lunch 63 South William St. Vibrant Italian café serving good-value pizza, pasta and panini, with live music in the evenings. Mains €6–10.

The Market Bar 14 Fade St. Dublin's first gastro-bar serving classy tapas and Mediterranean food in a converted abattoir. Tapas €4–12.

Queen of Tarts Dame St. Tiny café offering irresistible cakes and pastries as well as savoury food.

Drinking and nightlife

Most of Dublin's eight hundred pubs serve food as well. The music scene – much of which is pub-based – is changeable, so it's always best to check the listings magazines such as the free *Event Guide* (ⓦwww.eventguide.ie), *In Dublin* (ⓦwww.indublin.ie) and *Totally Dublin* (ⓦwww.totallydublin.ie) or, for music events, *Hot Press* (€3.50). Camden St is the best place to find live traditional and rock sessions; hit Temple Bar for clubs playing pop and dance music, and touristy traditional sessions.

Bars

Café en Seine 40 Dawson St. Sip on a cocktail or two at Dublin's classiest establishment, an Art Nouveau-style café-bar with three floors and five bars.

Davy Byrne's 21 Duke St. An object of pilgrimage for *Ulysses* fans, since Leopold Bloom stopped here for a snack. Attracts a sophisticated crowd and also serves good food (traditional Irish stew €12).

The Globe 11 South Great George's St. Trendy, dimly lit bar with loud music and lots of space. Backs onto *RíRá*, an intimate but very lively club.

The Long Hall 51 South Great George's St. Victorian pub encrusted with mirrors and antique clocks.

Neary's 1 Chatham St. Plenty of bevelled glass and shiny wood, plus Liberty print curtains to show some style appropriate for the theatrical clientele in this intimate, low-key pub just off Grafton St.

Sin É 14–15 Ormond Quay Upper. Cool and popular Northside bar with a friendly crowd and splendid soundtracks.

Stag's Head 1 Dame Court, Dame St, almost opposite the Central Bank. Wonderfully intimate pub, full of mahogany, stained glass and mirrors. Very popular with local Dubliners, and does good pub lunches.

Clubs

Button Factory Curved St ⓦwww.buttonfactory.ie. Housed in the refurbished Temple Bar Music Centre, this is the place to find top Irish and international DJs in the Thurs–Sun club.

The George South Great George's St. Dublin's oldest and most popular gay bar and club.

POD/Tripod/Crawdaddy 35 Harcourt St ⓦwww.pod.ie. Multiple venues housed in an old railway station, famously photographed in 1900 with a train crashed through its walls. Great local house DJs are a regular feature, with occasional international guests.

Twisted Pepper 54 Middle Abbey St ⓦwww.bodytonicmusic.com/thetwistedpepper. Split into four main areas, the *Twisted Pepper* hosts live gigs, club nights and multimedia events.

The Village Wexford St. Popular bar, club and music venue offering chart-rock and classic funk till late Thurs–Sat.

Live music

The Brazen Head 20 Lower Bridge St. The oldest pub in Dublin, with traditional music nightly from 9.30pm.

The Cobblestone 77 King St North. Atmospheric pub on the edge of the Smithfield Plaza, famous for its nightly traditional sessions.

International Bar 23 Wicklow St. Large saloon with rock bands and a comedy club upstairs or in the cellar.

J.J. Smyth's 12 Aungier St. One of the few places to catch local jazz and blues talent.

The Mezz 23–24 Eustace St. Café-bar with live rock, jazz, blues funk, soul and reggae every night. Bar food served 2.30–9.30pm. Mains from €6.50.

The Porterhouse 16–18 Parliament St. There are live gigs every night at this popular bar, which brews its own beer. Also has a great evening menu; mains €7.50–18.50.

Vicar Street 58–59 Thomas St. One of the city's finest music venues, offering a varied programme of major music and comedy acts.

Whelans 25 Wexford St. Notorious music pub and club attracting a host of up-and-coming international stars as well as local talent.

Entertainment

Theatres

Dublin's theatres are among the finest in Europe, offering a good mix of classical and more avant-garde performances. Tickets start at around €20, with concessions offered on Mon–Thurs nights and for matinees. Check the *Event Guide* (Ⓦ www.eventguide.ie) for performances.

The Abbey Lower Abbey St Ⓦ www.abbeytheatre.ie. Ireland's most historic theatre, founded in 1899 by W.B. Yeats to promote Irish culture and drama.

The Gaiety South King St Ⓦ www.gaietytheatre.ie. Dublin's oldest and most ornate theatre, showing pantomimes and popular plays.

The Gate 1 Cavendish Row Ⓦ www.gate-theatre.ie. Showcases contemporary Irish drama, alongside European classics.

Cinemas

Cineworld Parnell St Ⓣ 1520/880 444, Ⓦ www.cineworld.ie. Seventeen-screen multiplex showing blockbusters and more alternative cinema.

Irish Film Institute 6 Eustace St, Temple Bar Ⓣ 01/679 5744, Ⓦ www.irishfilm.ie. Shows classics and new independent films, and has a shop and educational programme with a strong Irish emphasis. There's also a good bar and restaurant.

Screen D'Olier St Ⓣ 0818/300 301, Ⓦ www.screencinema.ie. Arthouse and independent films.

Shopping

Charity and secondhand Camden St has some good charity shops, while Harlequin, Castle Market, and Wild Child, Temple Bar, sell good-quality vintage gear.

High street and department stores Try Grafton St and Henry St for high-street shops, including Topshop (top of Grafton St) and Penny's (37 O'Connell St), which sells ridiculously cheap clothes, shoes and accessories. Dundrum (Mon–Fri 9am–9pm, Sat 9am–7pm & Sun 10am–7pm; Ⓦ www.dundrum.ie) is home to the biggest shopping centre in Europe; take LUAS from St Stephen's Green to Balally, or get bus #44A or #48A (about 12min).

Markets You can pick up some great bargains on retro clothes and accessories and Irish designer goods at Cow's Lane Market in Meeting House Square in Temple Bar (Sat). George's St Arcade (Mon–Sat) also has some interesting buys – books, vinyl artwork and clothes.

Directory

Embassies Australia, Fitzwilton House, Wilton Terrace Ⓣ 01/664 5300; Canada, 7–8 Wilton Terrace Ⓣ 01/234 4000; UK, 29 Merrion Rd Ⓣ 01/205 3700; US, 42 Elgin Rd, Ballsbridge Ⓣ 01/668 8777.

Exchange Thomas Cook, 118 Grafton St; General Post Office O'Connell St; most city centre banks.

Hospitals Southside: St James's, James St Ⓣ 01/410 3000; Northside: Mater Misericordiae, Eccles St Ⓣ 01/885 8888.

Internet Central Cybercafé, 6 Grafton St; Global Internet Café, 8 Lower O'Connell St; Oz Cyber Café, 39 Abbey St Upper; Planet Cyber Café, 13 St Andrew's St.

Laundry All American Launderette, Wicklow Court, South Great George's St.

Left luggage Busáras, Heuston and Connolly stations.

Pharmacy Dame Street Pharmacy, 16 Dame St; O'Connell's, 55 O'Connell St.

Post office GPO O'Connell St (Mon–Sat 8am–8pm); St Andrew's St (Mon–Fri 9am–6pm, Sat 9am–1pm).

Moving on

Train (Connolly) Belfast (7 daily, Mon–Sat, 5 on Sun; 2hr 10min); Drogheda (33 daily; 30min–1hr); Rosslare (3 daily; 3hrs); Sligo (4–5 daily; 3hr 10min–3hr 30min).

Train (Heuston) Cork (15 daily, Mon–Sat, 10 on Sun; 2hr 50min); Ennis (4 daily, via Limerick; 2hr 55min–3hr 40min); Galway (6–7 daily; 2hr 20min–2hr 50min); Kilkenny (6 daily Mon–Sat, 4 on Sun; 1hr 40min–1hr 50min); Killarney (7 daily; 3hr 30min–3hr 50min); Westport (2–3 daily; 3hr 20min–3hr 40min).

Bus Belfast (20 daily; 2hr 55min); Cashel (6 daily; 2hr 50min); Cork (6 daily; 4hr 25min); Derry (9 daily; 4hr); Donegal town (6 daily; 3hr 45min–4hr 10min); Doolin (2 daily; 6hr 15 min); Drogheda (35 daily; 1hr 20min); Ennis (12 daily; 4hr 20min–6hr 50min); Enniskillen (6 daily; 2hr 20min–3hr); Galway (15 daily; 3hr 30min); Kilkenny (6 daily; 2hr 10min–2hr 30min); Killarney (5 daily; 6hr 10min); Newgrange (3 daily; 1hr 40min–1hr 55min); Portrush (1–2 daily; 5hr 40min); Rosslare Harbour (13 daily; 3hr 20min); Sligo (6 daily; 4hr); Westport (3 daily; 5hr–5hr 40min).

WICKLOW

Referred to as the "Garden of Ireland", the picturesque mountains, lakes, forested estates and rural villages of **Wicklow County** provide a stunning

backdrop for a bracing country walk or scenic drive. Given its proximity to the capital, the region is easily visited on a day-trip from Dublin, but there are plenty of B&Bs and hostels in the area.

The wonderfully unspoilt 127km mountain trail, the **Wicklow Way**, bisects the Wicklow Mountains, looping through glacial valleys, farmland and forests. The trail passes through the villages of **Roundwood**, **Rathdrum** and **Enniskerry** (bus #44 from Townsend St in Dublin city centre), from where the eighteenth-century **Powerscourt Estate** gardens and waterfall (house and gardens daily 9.30am–5.30pm, €8; waterfall 9.30am–4/5.30/7pm, €5) are easily accessible.

A further 30km south of Enniskerry, the beautifully tranquil monastic site of **Glendalough** ("valley of the two lakes") and the surrounding valley forms one of the most dramatic landscapes in the country. The monastery was founded in the sixth century by St Kevin, and the 30m-high tapering round tower on the bank of the Lower Lake has epitomized mystical Ireland in tourist brochures for decades. The **visitor centre** (Lower Lake; daily 9.30am–5/6pm; €3) runs tours (daily 2pm) of the monastic site, and the **Wicklow Mountains National Park Information Centre** (Upper Lake; daily 10am–4/6pm) can provide information on walking routes. Several companies run day-tours to Glendalough from Dublin (recommended operators include Over the Top Tours, Ⓦwww.overthetoptours.com, and Wild Wicklow Tours, Ⓦwww.wildwicklowtours.com; both €25–28), but you can make your own way by taking the St. Kevin's bus (4 daily; €13 single/€20 return; Ⓦwww.glendaloughbus.com) from outside the Mansion House on Dawson St. *The Glendalough Hostel* is ideally located near the monastic settlement (Ⓣ0404/45342, Ⓦwww.glendaloughinternationalhostel.com; dorms €20, rooms €55), and has its own restaurant.

NEWGRANGE

One of the foremost visitor attractions in the country, **Brú na Bóinne** ("the palace of the Boyne") encompasses the three rotund mounds of earth rising above the Neolithic passage tombs of **Newgrange**, **Knowth** and **Dowth**, south of the River Boyne in County Meath. The extensive exhibition in the visitor centre (daily 9/9.30am–5.30/7pm; €3, €6 with entrance to Newgrange) includes information on the sites, how they were built and the artwork of enigmatic spirals carved into the stone walls. There is also a full-scale replica of the five-thousand-year-old chamber at Newgrange as well as a model of one of the smaller tombs at Knowth. The tombs themselves have been comprehensively excavated and reconstructed, and the **guided tour** of Newgrange (from the visitor centre) includes a simulation of the rising sun during the Winter Solstice, during which the rays of light enter through a strategically positioned slit above the entrance, casting first light on the burial chamber itself before spreading along the nineteen-metre length of the passage. To get to the site, take the Bus Eireann service #100 from the Busáras bus depot in Dublin city centre (see p.618) to Drogheda, from where a shuttle bus #163 connects to the visitor centre.

The southeast

The southeast is Ireland's sunniest and driest corner. The region's medieval and Anglo-Norman history is richly concentrated in **Kilkenny**, a bustling, quaint inland town, while to the west, at the heart of County Tipperary is the **Rock of Cashel**, a spectacular natural formation topped with Christian buildings from virtually every period. In the southwest, **Cork** is both relaxed and

spirited, the perfect place to ease you into the exhilarations of the west coast.

WEXFORD

WEXFORD is a convenient stop-off point if you're coming into Ireland from Rosslare. It's a fairly bustling town during the day, with the main concentration of shops and businesses on the long stretch, North and South Main Street. Its early Celtic and Nordic heritage is apparent in the town's narrow streets and old town walls.

Wexford can seem like a ghost town on weekday nights, but scratch the surface and you'll find there's a fair amount of *craic* to enjoy in the town's lively pubs and bars. October brings an injection of energy with the **Wexford Opera Festival** (ⓦwww.wexfordopera.com).

For nature and history lovers, the **Irish National Heritage Park** at Ferrycarrig (5km west of town off the N11; €8; ⓣ053/912 0733) is a worthwhile trip, taking you through nine thousand years of Irish history in the appropriate settings.

Arrival and information

Bus and train stations Located on Redmond Square at the north end of the quays.
Tourist information centre Crescent Quay (Mon–Sat 9am–5pm, Sun 11am–5pm, extended hours in summer; ⓣ053/912 3111, ⓔwexfordtouristoffice@failteireland.ie).

Accommodation

Kirwan House Hostel 3 Mary St ⓣ053/91208, ⓦwww.wexfordhostel.com. The only hostel in Wexford, in a pretty Georgian building with clean, bright rooms. Dorms €22, doubles €60.
St George's Guesthouse George St ⓣ05/914 3474, ⓦwww.stgeorgeguesthouse.com. Has fresh, pleasant decor, and can accommodate small groups at a discount. Bed and breakfast €30–50 per person.

Eating and drinking

The Centenary Stores Charlotte St. Has live traditional music on Sunday lunchtimes, rock bands on a Thursday night and nightclub every Thursday to Sunday. Food is served noon–6pm, with mains from €10.
Sky and the Ground 112 South Main St. Pub which hosts music most nights (both traditional and non-traditional bands), and serves good-quality pub food.

FERRIES

Ferries from Wales (Fishguard and Pembroke) and France (Cherbourg and Roscoff) arrive at **ROSSLARE HARBOUR**, on the southeastern corner of Ireland. Trains leave here for Waterford (1 daily; 1hr 20min), Wexford (5 daily; 25min) and Dublin (5 daily; 3hr), and there are also daily bus services to Dublin and the west.

LIMERICK

LIMERICK, which lies on the River Shannon, is at the heart of the midwest region of Ireland, equidistant between Galway to the north and Cork to the south. There is not much to see or do here, but it is an important **transport hub**, with major roads from Dublin, Galway, Killarney and Cork converging here. Limerick is steeped in history: its origins are Viking, and the impressive buildings of King John's Castle and St Mary's Cathedral bear witness to the city's Norman heritage. **Shannon airport** is only 24km northwest. Bus Éireann run direct services from Limerick to Dublin, Cork, Killarney, Tralee, Waterford, Ennis, Galway, Westport, Sligo and Derry. Irish Rail operate direct trains to Dublin, Cork and Ennis. The only **hostel** in Limerick is *Courtbrack Accommodation* on Courtbrack Avenue, South Circular Road, (ⓣ061/302 500; June 9–Sept 2; dorm €23, doubles €50), ten minutes' walk from the centre. For reasonable **food** in a pleasant setting, try *The Locke Bar and Bistro* (3 George's Quay; food served from 3pm; mains €5–12), where you can sit outside overlooking the river. Good **bars** include *Charlie Chaplin's*, on Chapel Street, which has a great atmosphere and a DJ every night.

KILKENNY

KILKENNY is Ireland's finest medieval city, its castle set above the broad sweep of the River Nore and its narrow streets laced with carefully maintained buildings. In 1641, the city became the virtual capital of Ireland, with the founding of a parliament known as the Confederation of Kilkenny. The power of this short-lived attempt to unite resistance to English persecution of Catholics had greatly diminished by the time Cromwell's wreckers arrived in 1650. Kilkenny never recovered its prosperity, but enough remains to indicate its former importance.

What to see and do

Left at the top of Rose Inn Street is the broad **Parade**, which leads up to the castle. To the right, the High Street passes the eighteenth-century **Tholsel**, once the city's financial centre and now the town hall. Beyond is **Parliament Street**, the main thoroughfare, where the **Rothe House** (April–Oct Mon–Sat 10.30am–5pm, Sun 3–5pm; Nov–March Mon–Sat 10.30am–4.30pm; €5) provides a unique example of an Irish Tudor merchant's home, comprising three separate houses linked by cobbled courtyards. The thirteenth-century **St Canice's Cathedral** (Mon–Sat 9/10am–1pm & 2–4/6pm, Sun 2–4/6pm; €4) has a fine array of sixteenth-century monuments, many in black Kilkenny limestone. The **round tower** next to the church (same hours; €3; combined ticket with cathedral €7) is the only remnant of a monastic settlement reputedly founded by St Canice in the sixth century; there are superb views from the top. It's the imposing twelfth-century **Castle**, though, which defines Kilkenny (tours daily: April–Sept 10/10.30am–5/7pm; Oct–March Tues–Sun 10.30am–12.45pm and 2–5pm; €6; ⓣ056/770 4100). Its library, drawing room, bedrooms and Long Gallery of family portraits are open for viewing, as is the **Butler Gallery** (daily April–Sept 9.30/10am–6/5pm; Oct–March 10.30am–12.45pm & 2–5pm; free), housing exhibitions of modern art.

Arrival and information

Train and bus Both stations are just north of the centre, off John St. Some services stop on Patrick St.
Tourist office Rose Inn St, in the sixteenth-century Shee Alms House (May–Sept Mon–Fri 9/9.30am–6/5.30pm, Sat 10am–6pm, July & Aug also Sun 11am–5pm; ⓣ056/775 1500).
Listings The weekly *Kilkenny People* (€1.80) and *Whazon?* (free publication available in hostels, pubs and restaurants; ⓦwww.whazon.com) has listings information. See also ⓦwww.kilkenny.ie and ⓦwww.southeastireland.com.
Festivals The town is renowned for The Cat Laughs comedy festival in June (ⓦwww.thecatlaughs.com) and its Arts Festival in August (ⓦwww.kilkennyarts.ie).

Accommodation

Advance booking is advisable in summer, especially during festivals in June and August.
Banville's 49 Walkin St ⓣ056/777 0182, ⓔmbanville@eircom.net. Very pleasant and friendly B&B, a 5min walk from the town centre. Doubles €60–70.
Kilkenny Tourist Hostel 35 Parliament St ⓣ056/776 3541, ⓔkilkennyhostel@eircom.net. An excellent budget option in a rambling Georgian building. Dorms €17–20, doubles €46.
MacGabhainn's Backpacker Hostel 24 Vicar St ⓣ056/777 0970, ⓔhostel-vicarstreet@hotmail.com. Colourful but basic hostel with two lovely dogs. Dorms €17.
Tree Grove camping Danville House, New Ross Rd ⓣ056/777 0302, ⓦwww.treegrovecamping.com. March–Nov 15. Campsite 1.5km south of the city on the R700. Bike rental available. €8.

Eating

Billy Byrne's 39 John St ⓣ056/772 1783. Fine pub lunches for €9.
Café Sol William St ⓣ056/776 4987. Award-winning café-restaurant particularly good for salads and light mains (from €8).
Gourmet Store 56 High St. Hummus, panini, bagels and wraps made to order at this little deli. From €3.

Kyteler's Inn St Kieran St. Decent food in medieval surroundings, accompanied by regular traditional-music sessions.

Shali 6 Dean St. Excellent Indian restaurant offering authentic dishes at very good prices. Mains from €8, three-course Sunday lunch €9.

Drinking and nightlife

Parliament St and Ormonde St are best for live traditional and rock music; John St has a more commercial feel with clubs and pop music.

Edward Langton's 69 John St. Huge, swanky bar with a popular club on Tues, Thurs and Sat from 10pm. Also serves good pub grub (mains €12).

The Pumphouse 26–28 Parliament St. Popular with young and old, locals and travellers alike. Music most nights, and there's also a pool table.

Ryans 62 Friary St. Intimate, candlelit bar with traditional music on Thurs and jazz, blues, rock and open-mic sessions other nights.

Tynan's 2 Horseleap Slip, St John's Bridge. Riverside bar with cosy Victorian interior and beer garden; there are still relics from its days as a pharmacy and grocery store.

Moving on

Train Dublin (6 daily; 1hr 40min–2hr).

Bus Cork (8 daily; 2hr 50min–5hr 20min); Dublin (7 daily; 2hr 15min–2hr 45min).

THE ROCK OF CASHEL

The extraordinary **ROCK OF CASHEL** (daily 9am–4.30/5.30pm; €6) appears as a mirage of crenellations rising bolt upright from the vast encircling plain and is where St Patrick reputedly used a shamrock to explain the doctrine of the Trinity. Walking from **Cashel** town, the first sight you'll encounter on the Rock is the fifteenth-century **Hall of the Vicars**, whose vaulted undercroft contains the original **St Patrick's Cross**. **Cormac's Chapel**, built in the 1130s, is the earliest and most beautiful of Ireland's Romanesque churches; both north and south doors feature intricate carving, while inside, the alleged sarcophagus of King Cormac has an exquisite design of interlacing serpents and ribbon decoration. The graceful limestone **Cathedral**, begun in the thirteenth century, is Anglo-Norman in conception, with its Gothic arches and lancet windows. The tapering **round tower** is the earliest building on the Rock, dating from the early twelfth century. The **Cashel Heritage Centre** (daily 9.30am–5.30pm; closed Sat & Sun Nov–Feb; free) on Main Street has a small exhibition that covers the history of the town, as well as tourist information.

Cashel is most often visited as a day-trip from Cork or Kilkenny; buses going towards Cork drop off and pick up outside *The Bakehouse* bakery, those towards Kilkenny and Dublin on the other side of the street. The *Cashel Lodge* (Dundrum Rd [R505]; ⓣ062/61003, ⓦwww.cashel-lodge.com; dorms €18, doubles €60, camping €8) is a beautifully renovated coach-house blessed with spectacular views and located close to the rock. *Ryan's* on Ladyswell St and *Davern's* on Main St are atmospheric traditional **pubs** which also serve food, and *The Bakehouse* on Main St is a cosy place for a light lunch.

CORK

Everywhere in **CORK** there's evidence of its history as a great mercantile centre, with grey stone quaysides, old warehouses, and elegant, quirky bridges spanning the River Lee to each side of the city's island core – but the lively atmosphere and large student population, combined with a vibrant social and cultural scene, are equally powerful draws. Massive stone walls built by invading Normans in the twelfth century were destroyed by William III's forces during the **Siege of Cork** in 1690, after which waterborne trade brought increasing prosperity, as witnessed by the city's fine eighteenth-century bow-fronted houses and ostentatious nineteenth-century churches.

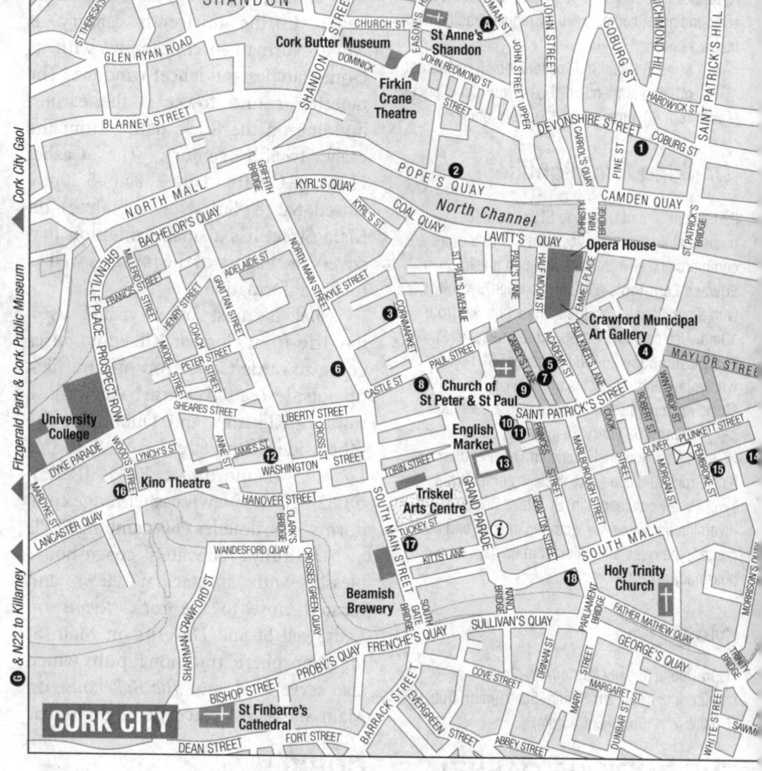

What to see and do

The graceful arc of **St Patrick's Street** – which with **Grand Parade** forms the commercial heart of the centre – is crammed with major chain stores. Just off here on Princes Street, the sumptuous **English Market** (Mon–Sat 9am–5.30pm) offers the chance to sample local delicacies like *drisheen* (a peppered sausage made from a sheep's stomach lining and blood). On the far side of St Patrick's Street, chic Paul Street is a gateway to the bijou environs of French Church Street and Carey's Lane. The west of the city is predominantly residential, though Fitzgerald Park is home to the **Cork Public Museum** (Mon–Sat 11am–1pm & 2.15–5/6pm, Sun 3–5pm; free), which focuses on Republican history.

Shandon area

North of the River Lee is the historic **Shandon area**, a reminder of Cork's eighteenth-century status as the most important port in Europe for dairy products. The striking **Cork Butter Exchange** survives, stout nineteenth-century Neoclassical buildings given over to craft workshops. At one corner of the old butter market is the **Cork Butter Museum** (O'Connell Square; 10am–5/6pm; €4), which exhibits, amongst other items, a keg of thousand-year-old butter. Behind the square is the pleasant Georgian church of **St Anne Shandon** (Mon–Sat 10am–3/5pm; €6), easily recognizable from all over the city by its weather vane – an eleven-foot salmon. The church tower gives excellent views over

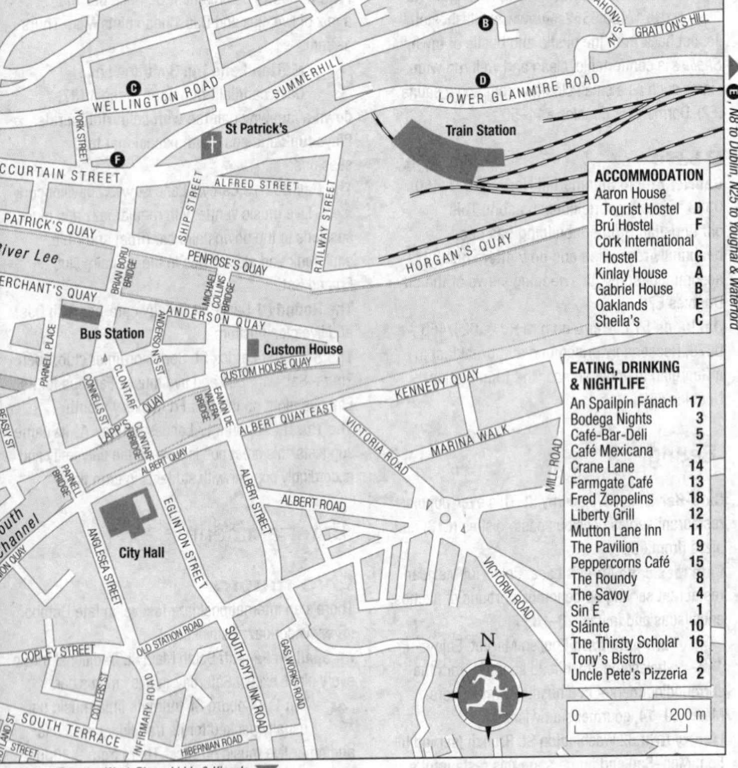

the city and an opportunity to ring the famous bells. Around 2km west along North Mall in the Sunday's Well area of the city, is the nineteenth-century **Cork City Gaol** (daily 9.30/10am–6/5pm; €7), with wax figures and an excellent audioguide focusing on social history.

Arrival and information

Train station About 1km east of the city centre on Lower Glanmire Rd.

Bus station On Parnell Place by Merchant's Quay.

Ferry Boats from Swansea and Roscoff arrive at Ringaskiddy, 13km from town. A shuttle bus runs regularly to the centre.

Tourist office Grand Parade (Mon–Sat 9/9.30am–6/4.45pm, July & Aug also Sun 10am–5pm; ⓣ021/425 5100, ⓦwww.corkkerry.ie).

Internet Internet Exchange, Wood St.

Accommodation

Hostels

Aaran House Tourist Hostel Lower Glanmire Rd ⓣ021/455 1566, ⓔtracy_flynn3@hotmail.com. Friendly and very convenient for train and bus stations. Dorms €10, triples €60.

Brú Hostel 57 McCurtain St ⓣ021/450 1074, ⓦwww.bruhostel.com. Modern facilities with a bar attached, where guests can claim a free pint. Dorms €12, doubles €50.

Cork International Hostel 1–2 Redclyffe, Western Rd ⓣ021/454 3289, ⓦwww.corkinternational hostel.com. Part of the An Óige group, housed in a big, red-brick building opposite the university. Take bus #8 (or walk 15min) from the centre. Dorms €16, doubles €52.

Kinlay House Bob & Joan's Walk, off Upper John St, Shandon ⓣ021/450 8966, ⓦwww .kinlayhousecork.ie. With great facilities, this large but friendly hostel is in a lovely part of town near St. Anne's Shandon. Dorms €15, doubles €44.

Sheila's 4 Belgrave Place, Wellington Rd ⓣ021/450 5562, ⓦwww.sheilashostel.ie. Set back from the hustle and bustle of town, *Sheila's* is comfortable, clean and well run with extras such as a small cinema room and a sauna (€2). Dorms €15, doubles €44–50.

B&Bs

Gabriel House Summerhill North ⓣ021/450 0333, ⓦwww.gabrielhousebb.com. This old Christian Brothers building has been beautifully renovated and now offers quality accommodation with sweeping views of the city. Doubles €70.

Oaklands 51 Lower Glanmire Rd ⓣ021/450 0578. Reasonably priced bed and breakfast in a Georgian townhouse near the train station. Doubles €68.

Eating

Café-Bar-Deli 18 Academy St. This ever-popular restaurant serves delicious pasta dishes (€13) and pizza (from €9).

Café Mexicana Carey's Lane. Colourful Mexican restaurant serving up generous portions of nachos, enchiladas and fajitas. €6–18.

Farmgate Café English Market. Enjoy wholesome, fresh food sourced from the surrounding market in a bustling atmosphere. Mains €9–14, gourmet sandwiches €7.

Liberty Grill 32 Washington St. Brunch (served till 5pm Mon–Sat) and burgers are this restaurant's specialities. Mains from €10.

Peppercorns Café 8 Pembroke St. All-day breakfast (€8) and cheap lunches, plus smoothies and coffee.

Tony's Bistro 69 North Main St. Cork's ultimate greasy spoon. The all-day breakfast is €7.

Uncle Pete's Pizzeria 31 Pope's Quay. Grab a €2 slice of thin-crust pizza to takeaway from this quality Italian place. Open late.

Nightlife

For listings, pick up the free *Whazon?* (ⓦwww.whazon.com) or the *Evening Echo*. *Totally Cork* also has listings, plus good reviews and articles.

Bodega Nights Cornmarket St, Coal Quay. Popular club with regular DJs and salsa on Wed. Open Wed–Sun.

Crane Lane Phoenix St (ⓦwww.cranelanetheatre.com). Billed as the "House of Jazz, Blues and Burlesque", this theatre has a late bar, regular shows and gigs, and is open daily.

Fred Zepelins 8 Parliament St. Rock bar with a mix of live gigs and DJs. Cheap pints Mon–Thurs 4–8pm.

Mutton Lane Inn 3 Mutton Lane. Cosy candlelit pub open since 1787, down a laneway painted with colourful murals. Plays funk and soul, with occasional trad sessions.

The Pavilion 13 Carey's Lane ⓦwww.pavilioncork.com. Live music venue with regular jazz and blues sessions in the downstairs bar (free) and r'n'b, soul, funk and electro DJs in the upstairs club on Fri and Sat.

The Roundy 1 Castle St. Trendy café-bar with DJs and live gigs upstairs.

The Savoy St Patrick St. Cork's premier club, open Thurs–Sat, with DJs and live music. Famous for its Eighties night on the first Fri of every month.

The Thirsty Scholar 17 Lancaster Quay. As its name suggests, this great pub is close to the university and accordingly popular with students in term time.

Entertainment

Live music

There's an international jazz festival in late October (ⓦwww.corkjazzfestival.com).

An Spailpín Fánach South Main St. Traditional music every night, except Saturday, in this famous bar.

Sin É 8 Coburg St. Intimate little music bar, usually packed for its traditional sessions and other live music on Tues–Thurs from 9.30pm and Fri and Sun at 6.30pm.

Sláinte Market Lane, off Patrick St. Traditional music Wed and Thurs nights, while on Fri local jazz, rock or funk sessions take place. On Sun there's a barbecue from 6pm.

Theatre and cinemas

The Kino Cinema Washington St ⓣ021/427 1571, ⓦwww.kinocinema.net. Screens independent films and co-hosts the excellent film festival in mid-October (ⓦwww.corkfilmfest.org).

Triskel Arts Centre Tobin Street ⓣ021/427 2022, ⓦwww.triskelart.com. A lively spot with cinema, exhibitions, readings and concerts.

Moving on

Train Dublin (15 daily, 10 on Sun; 2hr 35min–3hr 35min); Killarney (9 daily; 1hr 30min–2hr).

Bus Cashel (8 daily; 1hr 35min–1hr 50min); Dublin (6 daily; 4hr 25min); Galway (12 daily; 4hr 25min); Kilkenny (7 daily, only 2 direct; 3hr 10min–4hr 15min); Killarney (13 daily; 2hr).

The west coast

If you've come to Ireland for mountainous scenery, sea and remoteness, you'll hit the jackpot in County Kerry. By far the most visited areas are the town of **Killarney** and a scenic route around the perimeter of the Iveragh Peninsula known as the **Ring of Kerry**. County Clare's **Ennis** and the more tourist-ridden **Doolin** are marvellous spots for **traditional music**. **Galway** is an exceptionally enjoyable, free-spirited city, and a gathering point for young travellers. To its west lies **Connemara**, a magnificently wild coastal terrain, with the nearby, elementally beautiful **Aran Islands**, in the mouth of Galway Bay. Further up the coast, the landscape softens around the historic town of **Westport**, while further north, **Sligo** has many associations with the poet W.B.Yeats. In the far northwest, the 1134km of folded coastline in **County Donegal** is spectacular, the highlight being **Slieve League**'s awesome sea cliffs, the highest in Europe. There are plenty of international flights directly into the region (to Shannon and Knock airports).

KILLARNEY AND AROUND

KILLARNEY has been heavily commercialized and has little of architectural interest, but its location amid some of the best lakes, mountains and woodland in Ireland definitely compensates. **Cycling** is a great way of seeing the terrain, and makes good sense – local transport is sparse.

What to see and do

Around the town, three spectacular **lakes** – Lough Leane, Muckross Lake and the Upper Lake – form an appetizer for MacGillycuddy's Reeks, the highest mountains in Ireland.

Knockreer Estate

The entrance gates to the **Knockreer Estate**, part of the **Killarney National Park**, are just over the road from Killarney's cathedral. Tall wooded hills, the highest being **Carrantuohill** (1041m), form the backdrop to **Lough Leane**, and the main path through the estate leads to the restored fifteenth-century tower of **Ross Castle** (April to mid-Oct daily 9/9.30am–5/6.30pm; €6, gardens free), the last place in the area to succumb to Cromwell's forces in 1652.

Muckross Estate

Two kilometres south of Killarney is the **Muckross Estate**, where you should aim first for Muckross Abbey. Founded by the Franciscans in the mid-fifteenth century, it was suppressed by Henry VIII, and later, finally, by Cromwell. Back at the main road, signposts point to **Muckross House** (daily 9am–5.30/7pm; €7 or €12 joint ticket with farm), a nineteenth-century neo-Elizabethan mansion with wonderful gardens and a traditional working farm. The estate gives access to well-trodden paths along the shores of Muckross Lake where you can see one of Killarney's celebrated beauty spots, the **Meeting of the Waters**. Close by is the massive shoulder of Torc Mountain, shrugging off **Torc Waterfall**. The Upper Lake is beautiful, too, with the main road running along one side up to **Ladies' View**, from where the view is truly spectacular.

Gap of Dunloe and the Black Valley

West of Killarney lies the **Gap of Dunloe**, a natural defile formed by glacial overflow that cuts the mountains in two. **Kate Kearney's Cottage**, a pub located 10km from Killarney at the foot of the track leading up to the Gap, is the last fuelling stop before **Lord Brandon's Cottage**, a summer tearoom (June–Aug), 11km away on the other side of the valley. The track winds its way up

the desolate valley between high rock cliffs and waterfalls, past a chain of icy loughs and tarns to the top, to what feels like one of the most remote places in the world: the **Black Valley**, named after its entire population perished during the famine (1845–49). There's a wonderfully isolated *An Óige* **hostel** here too (Ⓣ064/34712, Ⓦwww.anoige.ie; dorms €17; March–Oct). The quickest way to Killarney from here is to carry on down to Lord Brandon's Cottage and take the boat back across the Upper Lake.

Arrival and information

Train and bus stations Next to each other on Park Rd, a short walk east of the centre.
Tourist office Beech Rd off New St (daily 9am–6/8pm; Ⓣ064/31633, Ⓦwww.corkkerry.ie).
Internet Leaders, 9 Beech Rd; Web-Talk, 53 High St.
Listings Check out *The Kerryman* (€1.80, from all newsagents).

Accommodation

Hostels

Killarney Railway Hostel Fair Hill Ⓣ064/663 5299, Ⓦwww.killarneyhostel.com. Clean and friendly and opposite the station. Dorms €15, doubles €44–50.
Neptune's Town Hostel Bishop's Lane, off New St Ⓣ064/663 5255, Ⓦwww.neptuneshostel.com. Large, welcoming hostel with colourful rooms and good facilities. Breakfast not included. Dorms €15, doubles €45.
Paddy's Palace Hostel 31 New St Ⓣ064/663 5382, Ⓦwww.paddyspalace.com. Small and basic with the cheapest accommodation in Killarney; dorms €11–18, doubles €37.
The Súgan Hostel Lewis Rd Ⓣ064/663 3104, Ⓦwww.killarneysuganhostel.com. Cosy family-run hostel with colourful decor. There's also bike rental, cheaper if you're a guest. Dorms €15, doubles €40.

Camping

Flesk Caravan and Camping Muckross Rd Ⓣ064/663 1704, Ⓦwww.killarneyfleskcamping.com. 1.5km south of the centre on the N71 Kenmare road. €8 per person.

Eating and drinking

The Country Kitchen 17 New St. Cheap, hearty food, including full Irish breakfast (€9).
Courtney's 24 Plunkett St. Huge but informal bar popular with young people for its mid-week trad sessions, live bands on Fri and DJ sets on Sat.
Cronin's Restaurant 9 College St. Busy, informal restaurant offering reasonably priced, filling dishes such as lasagne or fresh fish and chips for €12.
McSorley's 10 College St. There's traditional music in the main bar here every night in summer, followed by a live band. The upstairs club is the biggest in Killarney, open nightly.
O'Connor's Bar 7 High St. Old and intimate little pub with local Irish musicians on Thurs and Fri. You can also book Gap of Dunloe tours here (see p.629).

Moving on

Train Cork (9 daily; 1hr 20min–1hr 40min); Dublin (7 daily; 3hr 15–30min).
Bus Cork (13 daily; 1hr 35–50min); Dingle (2–5 daily; 2hr–2hr 40min); Dublin (10 daily; 6hr 10min–7hr 30min); Waterville (1 daily; 1hr 55min).

THE RING OF KERRY

Most tourists view the spectacular scenery of the 179km **Ring of Kerry**, west of Killarney, without ever leaving their tour coach or car; therefore, anyone straying from the road or waiting until the afternoon, will experience the slow twilights of the Atlantic seaboard in perfect seclusion. **Cycling** the Ring takes three days, and a bike provides access to mountain roads. **Buses** from Killarney circle the Ring in summer (May–Sept 2 daily; from €20 return). The public bus departs from the bus station and private tour operators (book through the tourist office) from their respective offices in town. For the rest of the year, buses travel only the largely deserted mountain roads, as far as Cahersiveen.

VALENTIA ISLAND

At **Kells Bay** (heading anticlockwise on the main N70 around the Ring of Kerry), the road veers inland towards **CAHERSIVEEN**, the main shopping centre for the western part of the peninsula. It has an independent **hostel**, *Sive*, 15 East End

(☎066/947 2717, ⓔinfo@sivehostel.ie; dorms €13, rooms €19). From the town, lanes lead out to **VALENTIA ISLAND**, Europe's most westerly harbour, its position on the Gulf Stream providing a mild, balmy climate. Access is by road bridge from Portmagee, or by **ferry** (April–Sept; single €1.50, return €2) which crosses from Reenard Point (4km from Cahersiveen) to **Knightstown** whose main street has a few shops, a post office and a couple of bars.

As the island is a mere 11km by 3km, the best way to explore it is to **walk**. The much-touted **Grotto**, tucked away inside the entrance to a gaping slate quarry, holds a crude statue of the Virgin perched two hundred feet up amid dripping icy water. More exciting is the spectacular cliff scenery to the northwest. Valentia Island's **accommodation** options are *Spring Acre* (March–Oct; ☎066/947 6141, ⓔspringacre@eircom.net; doubles €70) opposite the pier where the ferry docks, while *The Ring Lyne* (☎066/947 6103, ⓔtheringlyne@hotmail.com; dorms €13, doubles €30) provides **hostel** accommodation in Chapeltown, 6km west.

The stretch of coast south of Valentia is wild and almost deserted, apart from a scattering of farms and fishing villages such as Waterville and Ballinskelligs. Sweet-smelling, tussocky grass dotted with wild flowers is raked by Atlantic winds, ending in abrupt cliffs or sandy beaches.

DINGLE

The fishing village of **DINGLE**, little more than a few streets by the side of Dingle Bay, is the best base for exploring the stunning **Dingle Peninsula**. Signposts to Dingle use the Gaelic name, An Daingean.

What to see and do

Formerly Kerry's leading port in medieval times, then later a centre for smuggling, the town's main attractions nowadays are aquatic: the star of the show is undoubtedly **Fungi** the dolphin who's been visiting the town's natural harbour for some twenty years (a number of boats offer trips out to see him from around €15). Alternatively, there's **Oceanworld** on the waterfront (daily 10am–5pm), whose numerous aquaria include a touch pool and shark tank as well as a turtle exhibition.

Arrival and information

Arrival The nearest train stations are Killarney and Tralee. Bus Éireann provides a bus service between Dingle and Killarney (2 daily) and Tralee (4/6 daily). The bus stop is at the back of Supervalu on Strand St. By car, take the N86 from Tralee, or the R561 from Castlemaine to reach Dingle.

Bike rental Foxy John's on Main St (€10/50 per day/week).

Tourist office At the Quay (April–Oct Mon–Sat 10am–6pm; May–Sept also Sun; ☎066/915 1188). They can book accommodation.

Internet Dingle Internet Café, Main St.

Accommodation

Hideout Hostel Dykegate St ☎066/915 0559, ⓦwww.thehideouthostel.com. Friendly hostel in a renovated hotel building, offering small dorms and spacious private rooms, all en suite. There's a budget restaurant adjacent. Dorms €18, doubles €44.

Kirrary B&B Avodale St ☎066/915 1606, ⓔcollinskirrary@eircom.net. Homely and welcoming establishment offering excellent local knowledge and terrific breakfasts, including home-made scones. Doubles €70.

Rainbow Hostel 2km west of the centre in Miltown ☎066/915 1044, ⓦwww.rainbowhosteldingle.com. Family-run and very friendly, also has camping facilities. Free shuttle into town. Dorms €16, doubles €40, camping €9.

Eating and drinking

An Droichead Beag Main St. Nightly traditional music sessions in a brilliantly atmospheric pub.

Dick Mack's Green St. Many a celebrity has stopped for a drink in this friendly bar, formerly a cobbler's shop; check out the names on the pavement outside.

Goat Street Café Upper Main St. Extremely popular café offering delicious pancakes for breakfast, salads, fresh fish, curries and noodles for lunch and occasional dinners. Mains €11.

John Benny's Strand St. Popular pub offering quality fresh seafood at reasonable prices.

Novocento Gourmet Store Main St. Excellent takeaway pizza slices for just €2.

O'Flaherty's Bridge St. Traditional music sessions most nights in this big, colourful bar.

The Oven Doors Holyground. Serves everything from tea and scones to inexpensive pizzas. Open till 9pm.

DINGLE PENINSULA

The **Dingle Peninsula** is a place of intense, shifting beauty: spectacular mountains, long sandy beaches and splinter-slatted rocks. It defines the extraordinary coast at **Slea Head** and ensures that, remote though it is, it's firmly on the tourist trail. Here is one of the greatest concentrations of Celtic ruins in Ireland, and the now uninhabited Blasket Islands once generated a wealth of Irish literature.

Public transport in the west of the peninsula amounts to a very irregular **bus** from Dingle to Dunquin, making **cycling** the best way to explore (see p.631 for bike rentle).

The Irish-speaking area west of Dingle is rich in relics of the ancient Gaelic and early Christian cultures: there's the spectacular **Dún Beag** (daily 9am–6/7pm; €3), about 6km west of Ventry. A promontory fort, its defences include four earthen rings, with an underground escape route by the main entrance. West of the fort, the hillside above the road is studded with stone **beehive huts**, cave dwellings, forts, churches, standing stones and crosses – over five hundred in all. The beehive huts were built and used for storage up until the late nineteenth century, but standing among ancient buildings – such as the **Fahan group** – you're looking over a landscape that's remained essentially unchanged for centuries.

Slea Head

At **Slea Head** the view encompasses the desolate, splintered masses of the **Blasket Islands** (uninhabited since 1953, though there are some summer residents). In the summer, boats bound for **Great Blasket** depart daily from the pier just south of Dunquin (April–Oct hourly; €20 return; ⓣ066/915 6422). Great Blasket's delights are simple ones: tramping the footpaths that crisscross the island, sitting on the beaches watching the seals and dolphins, or savouring the stunning sunsets. Camping is free, and there's a café serving good, cheap vegetarian meals. At **DUNQUIN**, there's an An Óige **hostel** (ⓣ066/915 6121, ⓔmailbox @anoige.ie; dorms €14, doubles €40; Feb–Nov).

ENNIS

In daytime hours there's little of interest in County Clare's main town, **ENNIS**, but at night, you'll find a town buzzing with traditional music. Nightly pub sessions are the local music scene's lifeblood. The town hosts a couple of traditional music **festivals**: Fleadh Nua (ⓦwww.fleadhnua.com) in the last week of May, and the Ennis Trad Festival (ⓦwww.ennistradfestival.com) in mid-November.

Arrival and information

Train and bus stations Alongside one another, a 10min walk southeast of the town centre down Station Rd.

Tourist office Same building as the Clare Museum on Arthur's Row (June–Sept Mon–Sun 9.30am–5.30pm; Oct–May Tues–Sat 9.30am–1pm & 2–5pm; ⓣ065/682 8366, ⓦwww.shannonregiontourism.ie).

Bike rental Tierney's Cycles, 17 Abbey St.

Accommodation

The tourist office can help organize accommodation.

The Rowan Tree Harmony Row ⓣ065/686 8672, ⓦwww.rowantreehostel.ie. Ennis's only hostel offers top-quality accommodation, in a picturesque location on the bank of the River Fergus. There's also a licensed café-bar serving budget meals. Dorms €16–19, doubles €50–60.

Eating and drinking

All of the pubs below also offer decent pub grub for less than €10.

Numero Uno 3 Barrack St ⓣ065/684 1740. Cheery fast-food place with burgers and pizza to eat in or take away (€3–12).

Live music

Safe bets for high-standard sessions include:

Brogan's 24 O'Connell St. Cosy bar with an open fire, serving good pub-grub. Live trad sessions on Tues & Thurs.

The Copper Jug Court View. Popular place with pretty stained-glass windows and sessions every Friday.

Cruise's Abbey St. One of the most crowded pubs in Ennis, with nightly music sessions.

Moving on

Trains Dublin (8 daily; 3hr 5min–4hr 25min).

Bus Doolin (3 daily; 1hr 25min); Dublin (18 daily; 4hr 45min–6hr 15min).

DOOLIN AND AROUND

Some 40km northwest of Ennis is the tiny seaside village of **DOOLIN**, famed for a steady, year-round supply of **traditional music.**

The village is the perfect base from which to explore the mystically barren expanse of **The Burren**, a vast landscape of cracked limestone terraces stretching forth to the wild Atlantic Ocean. The area is dotted with well-preserved megalithic remains such as the **Poulnabrone Dolmen** (on the R480, 20min drive from Doolin), an imposing tomb constructed from three massive limestone slabs dating from 2500 BC. **The Cliffs of Moher**, 4km south of Doolin, constitutes the area's most famous tourist attraction, with their great bands of shale and sandstone rising 660 feet above the waves. The visitors' centre (daily 9am–5/6/7/8.30pm) can organize tours to O'Brien's Tower, built in 1835 as a viewing point for visitors.

A **ferry** (April–Sept) runs from Doolin pier to the **Aran Islands** (see p.635). **LAHINCH**, a small village 20km south of Doolin, lies on the edge of a sandy strand which attracts hoards of surfers for its famous beach break. *Lahinch Hostel* (Church St; ⓣ065/708 1040, ⓦhomepage.eircom.net/~patshostel/; dorms €17) provides decent dormitory accommodation, and you can rent boards from Lahinch Surf Shop (ⓣ065/708 1543, ⓦwww.lahinchsurfshop.com) or organize lessons at the Lahinch Surf School (ⓣ087/960 9667, ⓦwww.lahinchsurfschool.com).

Accommodation

Aille River Hostel ⓣ065/707 4260, ⓦwww.ailleriverhosteldoolin.ie. Renovated three-hundred-year-old cottage with camping facilities, beautifully located overlooking the Aille River in the centre of Doolin village. Dorms €16, rooms €23.

Doolin Hostel ⓣ065/707 4421, ⓦwww.doolinhostel.com. Doolin's oldest purpose-built hostel offering basic but comfortable accommodation. Dorms €16, doubles €36.

Half Door ⓣ065/707 5959, ⓦwww.halfdoordoolin.com. Luxury B&B decorated to the highest standards with sitting room and conservatory for guest use, offering gourmet breakfasts such as pancakes or goat's cheese omelettes instead of the usual greasy fry-up. Doubles €62–70.

Rainbow Hostel ⓣ065/707 4415, ⓦwww.rainbowhostel.net. A welcoming, family-run place offering bike rental (€8–12/day) and free guided walks of the area. Dorm €16, doubles €40–48.

Eating and drinking

All three of Doolin's pubs, *O'Connor's*, *McGann's* and *McDermott's*, have nightly award-winning traditional music sessions, and serve excellent food.

Doolin Café Head here for a lighter lunch of hearty home-made soups (€4) and salads (€8).

O'Connor's Particularly recommended for its fresh cod and giant portions of mussels.

GALWAY

Granted city status in 1484, **GALWAY** developed in the Middle Ages into a flourishing centre of trade with the continent, a period of prosperity that is evident in its most impressive architecture. After centuries of decline, Galway has undergone a revival in recent years,

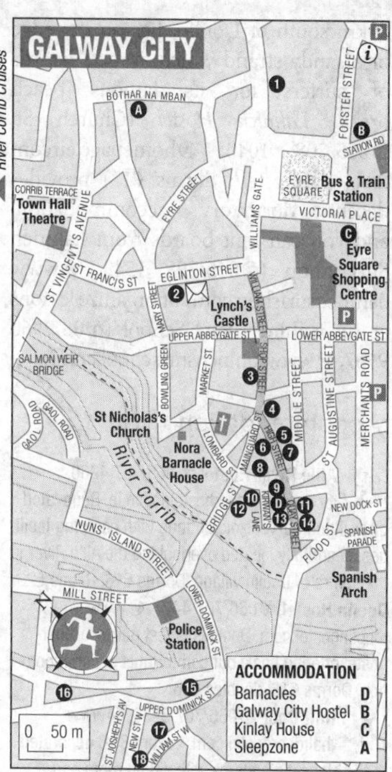

EATING, DRINKING & NIGHTLIFE

Blue Note	17	La Salsa	6
Busker Browne's	10	The Living Room	12
The Crane Bar	18	McCambridges	3
Cuba	1	McDonagh's	13
Da Tang Noodle House	7	Mustard	16
Fat Freddy's	14	Neachtain's	9
Front Door	8	The Quays	11
GPO	2	Róisín Dubh	15
The King's Head	5	Taaffe's	4

and its reputation as party capital of Ireland is well justified. University College Galway guarantees a high number of young people in term time, but the energy is most evident during Galway's **festivals**, especially the **Arts Festival** in the last two weeks of July (Ⓦ www.galwayartsfestival.com), and the Galway Races in the last week of July (Ⓦ www.galwayraces.com).

What to see and do

Maritime Galway's prosperity was expressed in the distinctive townhouses of the merchant class, some of which still stand, even though development has destroyed some of the city's character. Just about the finest medieval townhouse in Ireland is fifteenth-century **Lynch's Castle**, on Shop Street – along with Quay Street, the social hub of Galway. Now housing the Allied Irish Bank, it has a stone facade decorated with carved panels, gargoyles and a lion devouring its prey. Down by the River Corrib stands the **Spanish Arch**; more evocative in name than in reality, it's a sixteenth-century structure that was used to protect galleons unloading wine and rum. Across the river lies the **Claddagh** district, the old fishing village that once stood outside the city walls and gave the world the Claddagh ring as a symbol of love and fidelity. Past the Claddagh the river widens out into **Galway Bay**; for a pleasant sea walk follow the road until it reaches **Salthill**, the city's seaside resort. There are several beaches along the prom, though for the best head 5km from Salthill to **Silverstrand** on the Barna road.

Arrival and information

Train and bus stations Off Eyre Square, on the northeast edge of the city centre.
Tourist office Forster St (May–Sept daily 9am–5.45/7pm; Oct–April Mon–Sat 9am–5.45pm; kiosk in Eyre Square high summer Ⓣ 091/537 700, Ⓦ www.irelandwest.ie). Books B&B accommodation.
Internet *Café 4*, High St; Netaccess, Olde Malte Arcade, High St; E-2008, Forster St.

Accommodation

Barnacles 10 Quay St Ⓣ 091/568 644, Ⓦ www.barnacles.ie. Buzzing hostel conveniently located for the good pubs and cafés on Quay St; the larger dorms are a little crowded, but smaller ones are bright and comfortable. The pretty double overlooking the street is excellent value. Dorms €10–16, doubles €50–60.
Galway City Hostel Frenchville Lane, Station Rd Ⓣ 091/566 959, Ⓦ www.galwaycityhostel.com. Self-proclaimed as the "happiest little hostel in Galway" this is indeed a convivial place, opposite the train station. Dorms €15–20, doubles €55–65.

Kinlay House Merchant's Rd ⓣ091/565 244, ⓦwww.kinlaygalway.ie. Enormous, impersonal hostel just off Eyre Square. Day-tours to the Aran Islands, the Cliffs of Moher and Connemara depart right outside the door. Dorms €16–25, doubles €50–70.

Sleepzone Bóthar na mBan, Wood Quay ⓣ091/566 999, ⓦwww.sleepzone.ie. Ultra modern hostel with a mini-hotel feel, bright en-suite rooms, a huge communal kitchen and a free internet café. Dorms €15–20, doubles €50–60.

Camping

Salthill Caravan Park Ballyloughlane, Renmore ⓣ091/523 972, ⓦwww.salthillcaravanpark.com. Family-run park located right on the beach, less than 2km from the centre. April–Sept.

Eating

Busker Browne's Kirwans Lane. Reasonably priced bangers and mash, pastas and stews served at this trendy bar-restaurant. Mains from €10.

Da Tang Noodle House 2 Middle St. Excellent noodle dishes in pretty surroundings. Lunch €6–9, dinner €12–14.

Fat Freddy's The Halls, Quay St. Good pizzas, salads and antipasti at this fun, colourful bistro. Mains €10–15.

La Salsa 6 Mainguard St. Mexican takeaway offering giant burritos, nachos and burgers. €4–7.

McCambridges 38–39 Shop St. The queues run out the door every lunchtime at this gourmet deli renowned for their sandwiches, wraps and rolls. €2.50–5.

McDonagh's 22 Quay St. A must for the freshest seafood at any time of day, especially the fish and chips. The takeaway next door has a few informal tables and is much cheaper than the restaurant. Mains €8–34.

Mustard The Bridge Mills, Dominick St. Gourmet pizza and burger bar. Mains €7–14.

Drinking and nightlife

The Quay St area leading down to the river is known as the "Left Bank" due to the proliferation of popular pubs, restaurants and cafés. See the weekly *Galway Advertiser* (free; ⓦwww.advertiser.ie/galway) or *Galway City Tribune* (€1.60) for listings.

Bars

Blue Note 3 West William St. Atmospheric little pub with intimate booths and snugs, a heated smoking garden, and DJs most nights. Check out their "Hangover Brunch" on Sun.

Crane Bar 2 Sea Rd. Holds revered traditional music sessions nightly from 9pm.

Front Door Cross St. Big, light bar with great decor and DJs every weekend.

The King's Head 15 High St. Reputedly serves the best Guinness in town. Live music most nights.

The Living Room 5 Bridge St. Popular late-night bar on three levels with retro decor. DJ Thurs–Sun.

The Quays Quay St. One of the city's best-loved pubs, whose atmospheric interior was taken from a medieval French church. Serves good-value food around midday.

Neachtain's 17 Cross St. Old-fashioned pub that attracts an eccentric, arty crowd.

Róisín Dubh Dominick St. Popular music bar and venue which plays host to top-class Irish and international acts.

Taaffe's 19 Shop St. One of the best places to hear traditional music, where there are nightly sessions.

Clubs

Cuba Eyre Square ⓦwww.cuba.ie. Very popular club, on three floors. Comedy nights on Sunday.

GPO Eglinton St ⓦwww.gpo.ie. Different club nights every night of the week.

Moving on

Train Dublin (6 daily; 2hr 30min–3hr).

Bus Cork (12 daily; 4hr 25min); Doolin (4 daily; 1hr 40min–2hr 50min); Dublin (16 daily; 3hr 30–45min); Killarney (7 daily; 4hr 40min); Westport (8 daily; 1hr 35min–3hr 45min).

THE ARAN ISLANDS

The **Aran Islands** – **Inishmore**, **Inishmaan** and **Inisheer**, 50km out across the mouth of Galway Bay – make spectacular settings for a wealth of early remains and some of the finest archeological sites in Europe. The isolation of the Irish-speaking islands prolonged the continuation of a unique, ancient culture into the early twentieth century.

Inishmore

Although **Inishmore** is very tourist-orientated, it has such a wealth of dramatic ancient sites that its popularity is well justified. It's a long strip of an island, a great tilted plateau of limestone with a scattering of villages along the sheltered northerly coast, and land that

GETTING TO THE ISLANDS

There are daily **ferries** to Inishmore year-round (less frequent to the other islands), departing from Galway city, Rossaveal (30km west by bus) and Doolin in County Clare. A return trip starts at around €25, depending on the season, with some student reductions and good-value accommodation packages. Book tickets in Galway city through Aran Island Ferries, 4 Forster St (Ⓣ091/568 903, Ⓦwww.aranislandferries.com); Inismór Ferries, 29 Forster St (Ⓣ091/566 535, Ⓦwww.arandirect.com); or O'Brien Shipping (Ⓣ065/707 4455 or Ⓣ091/567 283, Ⓦwww.doolinferries.com) – all three companies have desks in the Galway tourist office. You can also **fly** with Aer Árann Islands (Ⓣ091/593 034, Ⓦwww.aerarannislands.ie) for around €45 return; book online or at Galway tourist office.

slants up to the southern edge, where dramatic cliffs rip along the entire shoreline. As far as the eye can see is a tremendous patterning of stone, some of it the bare pavements of grey rock split into bold diagonal grooves, latticed by dry-stone walls.

What to see and do

Most of Inishmore's sights are to the northwest of **KILRONAN**, the island's principal town. The first hamlet in this direction is Mainistir, from where it's a short signposted walk to the twelfth-century **Teampall Chiaráin** (Church of St Kieran), one of several ecclesiastical sites on Inishmore. Five kilometres or so down the main road is Kilmurvey, a fifteen-minute walk from the most spectacular of Aran's prehistoric sites, **Dún Aonghasa**, accessed via its **visitor centre** (daily 10am–4/6pm; €3). Nearby **Dún Eoghanachta** is a huge drum of a stone fort, set in a lonely field with the Connemara mountains as a backdrop. Access is via tiny lanes from Dún Aonghasa with a detailed map (the visitor centre sells Ordnance Survey maps); otherwise retrace your steps to Kilmurvey and follow the road west for 2km. At the **seven churches**, just east of Eoghannacht, there are ancient slabs commemorating seven Romans who died here, testifying to the far-reaching influence of Aran's monasteries.

Arrival and information

Bus Seasonal minibuses (€10) run tours up through the island's villages; you can walk back to the ferry dock from any point. Pony-and-trap tours are also available for a negotiable fee.

Ferry Boats dock at Kilronan.

Tourist office Just west of where the ferry docks at Kilronan (daily 10/11am–7/5pm; Ⓣ099/61263).

Bike rental Mullin's and BNN's near the pier (€10/day).

Accommodation

Accommodation can be booked through the Kilronan tourist office, or when you buy your ferry ticket.

Kilronan Hostel Kilronan Village Ⓣ099/61255, Ⓦwww.kilronanhostel.com. Cheery hostel with great facilities, including free internet and wi-fi. Very convenient for the ferry. Dorms €17, doubles €45.

Mainistir House Hostel Ⓣ099/61318, Ⓦwww.mainistirhousearan.com. A 20min walk west from the pier, this peaceful, nicely decorated hostel offers a renowned "all you can eat" buffet every night for €15. Dorms €18, doubles €50–70.

Eating and drinking

Seafood is the island's great speciality, with most of the popular restaurants located in Kilronan.

An tSean Ceibh (The Ould Pier). Simple and much cheaper than the *Pier House*, with a few outdoor tables in fine weather and serving fresh fish and chips and seafood chowder.

Joe Watty's Bar A great pub with traditional music most nights; serves good soups and stews, from €6.

Pier House Restaurant Spectacular setting with panoramic views and great food, but pricey, so go for a light lunch (from €7.50).

Inishmaan

In comparison with Inishmore, **Inishmaan** is lush, with stone walls forming a maze that chequers off tiny fields of grass and clover. The island's main sight is **Dún Chonchubhair**: built some time between the first and seventh centuries, its massive oval wall is almost intact and commands great views. Inishmaan's indifference to tourism means that amenities for visitors are minimal; if you arrive on spec, ask at the pub for information (Ⓣ099/73003) – it's a warm and friendly place that also serves snacks in summer. For **accommodation**, try the B&B *Ard Álainn* (April–Sept; Ⓣ099/73027, Ⓦwww.galway.net/pages/ard-alainn; doubles €50–65) or *An Dún* (Ⓣ099/73047; doubles €50–65), both near Dún Chonchubhair.

Inisheer

Inisheer, less than 3km across, is the smallest of the Aran Islands, and tourism plays a key role here. A great plug of rock dominates the island, its rough, pale-grey stone dripping with greenery, topped by the fifteenth-century **O'Brien's Castle**, standing inside an ancient ring fort. Set around it are low fields, a small community of pubs and houses, and windswept sand dunes. The **Inisheer Island Cooperative** hut by the pier (Mon–Thurs 9am–5pm, Fri 9am–4pm; Ⓣ099/75008) will give you a map and a list of **B&Bs**; *Radharc an Chláir*, by the castle (Ⓣ099/75019; doubles €70), is a good bet. There's also a **hostel**, *Brú Radharc na Mara* (Ⓣ099/75024, Ⓔmaire.searraigh@oceanfree.net; dorms €15, doubles €40; mid-March to Oct), and a **campsite** near the pier. Meals are available at the *Óstán Inis Oírr* hotel. For **music**, head for *Tigh Ned's* bar.

WESTPORT

Set on the shores of Clew Bay, **WESTPORT** is one of the west's liveliest spots. Planned by the eighteenth-century architect James Wyatt, its formal layout comes as quite a surprise in the midst of its rural surrounds. The craggy **Croagh Patrick** makes an imposing background to the town, standing at 764m above the bay – the climb is a strenuous one, but rewarded by spectacular views. St Patrick reputedly prayed on the mountain for forty days for the conversion of the Irish to Christianity, and on the last Sunday of July, known as "Reek Day", which coincides with the Celtic festival of Lughnasa, many tackle the pilgrimage to the summit barefoot.

Another attraction is **Westport House** (April–Sept daily 10am–4/5.30pm; March & Oct Sat & Sun only; €12), a couple of kilometres out of town towards the bay. The beautifully designed house dates from 1730 and is privately owned. Inside the house is a *Holy Family* by Rubens and an upstairs room with intricate Chinese wallpaper dating from 1780 – outside there's a giant water flume, train rides, boating and a bird and animal park. There is a well-serviced campsite in the grounds of the estate (Ⓣ098/27766; €15).

Arrival and information

Bus station On Mill St in the centre.
Train station Altamount St, 10min north of the centre.
Tourist office James St (Mon–Fri 9am–6pm, closed Sat pm Nov–Jan; Ⓣ098/25711, Ⓦwww.westporttourism.com).
Internet *Dunnings Cyberpub*, The Octagon, James St.

Accommodation

For more B&Bs ask at the tourist office.
Abbeywood House Newport Rd Ⓣ098/25496, Ⓦwww.abbeywoodhouse.com. Located 2min from the centre and within view of Croagh Patrick, this is a friendly and comfortable place with good facilities. Dorms €20, doubles €60.
The Old Mill James St Ⓣ098/27045, Ⓦwww.oldmillhostel.com. Situated in an old stone courtyard and extremely central. Dorms €19, doubles €48.

Radharc Na Mara Deer Park East, Newport Rd ⓣ098/28166. Good-value, friendly B&B a short walk from town. Doubles €64–70.

Eating

Antica Roma Bridge St. Offers a good selection of pizzas (from €8) and tasty fish-and-chips. Closed Mon.

The Quay Cottage The Quay. By the entrance to Westport House, this restaurant prides itself on its seafood dishes and serves plenty of vegetarian food. Lunch €9.50, dinner €12–25.

Sol Rio Bridge St ⓣ098/28944. This relaxed, Mediterranean-style restaurant serves a mix of continental and Irish food, and is a good lunch option. Lunch mains €5–10.

The Stuffed Sandwich Bridge St ⓣ098/27611. Makes every kind of sandwich you could think of, as well as smoothies and salads. €3–8.

Drinking and nightlife

Cozy Joe's Bridge St. Has a late bar with a DJ till 2am Thurs–Mon.

Matt Molloy's Bridge St. This bar is owned by the eponymous Chieftains' flute player, and occasionally features visiting celebrities.

Toby's Bar The Fairgreen. Small, cosy bar high above the river, perfect for a quiet drink or a chat with local old-timers.

Moving on

Train Dublin (3 daily; 3hr 30min–3hr 40min).

Bus Dublin (5 daily; 5hr); Galway (3 daily; 1hr 50min).

SLIGO

SLIGO is, after Derry, the biggest town in the northwest of Ireland. The legacy of **W.B. Yeats** – perhaps Ireland's best-loved poet – is still strongly felt here: the **Yeats Memorial Building** on Hyde Bridge (Mon–Fri 10am–5pm; free) features a photographic exhibition and film on his life, while the poet's Nobel Prize for Literature and other memorabilia are on show in the **Sligo County Museum** in the library on Stephen Street (Mon–Fri 10am–4.45pm). **The Model Arts Centre** on The Mall (Tues–Sat noon–6pm, Sun noon–4pm; free) houses works by the poet's brother, **Jack B. Yeats**, along with a broad collection of modern Irish art. Across the River Garavogue on Abbey Street stands the thirteenth-century **Dominican Friary** and visitor centre (April–Oct daily 10am–6pm; €3).

Arrival and information

Train station Union St, 5min west of the centre.

Bus station Near the train station, on Lord Edward St.

Tourist office Temple St (June–Aug daily 9/10am–6/7pm; Sept–May Mon–Fri 9am–5pm; ⓣ071/916 1201, ⓦwww.sligotourism.ie).

Bike rental Flanagan's, Market Yard.

Internet Café Online, Stephen St.

Listings Check the weekly *Sligo Champion* (€1.60).

Accommodation

Hostels and B&Bs

Harbour House Finisklin Rd ⓣ071/917 1547, ⓦwww.harbourhousehostel.com. Comfortable hostel 10min walk from the centre with spacious, bright rooms. Dorms €15, doubles €30–45.

Railway Hostel 1 Union Place. Small, homely hostel next to the train station. Dorms €16, doubles €40.

Tree Tops Cleveragh Rd ⓣ071/916 0160, ⓦwww.sligobandb.com. 1km southeast along Pearse Rd; very pleasant rooms, great breakfasts and friendly, knowledgeable hosts. Doubles €74.

Camping

Greenlands Caravan Park Rosses Point ⓣ071/917 7113. This park is 8km west of town (bus #473) on the seafront. April–Sept; €11.

Strandhill Caravan and Camping Park Strandhill ⓣ071/916 8111. Located 5km from town (bus #472). The beach here, while unsafe for swimming, attracts plenty of surfers. April–Sept.

Eating

Café Society 3 Teeling St. Eclectic menu of burgers, chickpea curry, jacket potatoes, soups and sandwiches served 8.30am–9pm at very reasonable prices. Mains €6–9.

The Loft 17–19 Lord Edward St. Extensive menu of world cuisine. The adjoining *Gateway Bar* does less-expensive bar food. Mains €10–18.

Pepper Alley Rockwood Parade. Spacious sandwich bar also offering full Irish breakfasts and a selection of hot dishes. €4–8.

Drinking and nightlife

Earley's Bridge St. One of the best pubs for traditional music (Thurs).

Furey's Bridge St. Traditional music sessions almost every night.

Shoot the Crows Gratton St. Long and narrow pub with diverse live music sessions to suit all tastes most nights of the week.

Velvet Kempten Promenade, off Bridge St ⓦwww.velvetroom.ie. Large, swanky club housed in an old brewery. Dress up.

Moving on

Train Dublin (5 daily; 3hr 5min).

Bus Derry (6 daily; 2hr 30min); Dublin (9 daily; 3hr 15–50min); Enniskillen (6 daily; 1hr 25–55min); Galway (5 daily; 2hr 35min).

DONEGAL TOWN

DONEGAL TOWN is a busy place focused around its old marketplace – The Diamond – and a fine base for exploring the stunning coastal countryside and inland hills and loughs from. Just about the only sight in the town itself is the well-preserved shell of **O'Donnell's Castle** on Tírchonaill Street by The Diamond (April–Oct daily 10am–6pm; Nov–March daily 9.30am–4.30pm; €4), a fine example of Jacobean architecture. On the left bank of the River Eske stand the few ruined remains of **Donegal Friary**, while on the opposite bank a woodland path known as Bank Walk offers wonderful views of **Donegal Bay** and the **Blue Stack Mountains**.

Arrival and information

Bus The stop for Bus Éireann departures and arrivals is outside the *Abbey Hotel* in the centre of town; private company Feda O'Donnell buses from Galway arrive outside the tourist office.

Tourist office The Quay (Mon–Sat 9am–5/8pm, July & Aug also Sun 9am–8pm; ⓣ074/972 1148, ⓦwww.irelandnorthwest.ie).

Accommodation

There are dozens of B&Bs in Donegal, but to avoid a lot of walking, call in to the tourist office.

Atlantic Guesthouse Main St ⓣ074/972 1187, ⓦwww.atlanticguesthouse.ie. Family-run establishment in the centre of town with bright and cheery rooms. Doubles €50–80.

Donegal Town Independent Hostel ⓣ074/972 2805, ⓔlincunn8@eircom.net. Just past the roundabout on the Killybegs road, a 5min walk from town, this peaceful and very friendly hostel also has camping (€9). Dorms €18, doubles €44.

Eating and drinking

The Blueberry Tea Room Castle St. Good-quality, reasonably priced food served in a very cosy atmosphere. It has an internet café upstairs. Mains up to €12.

Mama's Main St. Bar-restaurant offering good-value roasts, stews and lighter snacks. €7–10.

The Reel Inn Bridge St. A lively bar packed with local old-timers, even at midday. Traditional music every night.

Simple Simon The Diamond. Deli in an organic food store offering healthy take away lunches. €2–5.

Moving on

Bus Derry (3–7 daily; 1hr 30min); Dublin (9–10 daily; 3hr 30min–5hr 55min); Glencolmcille (2 daily; 1hr 25min); Sligo (8 daily; 1hr 5–55min).

TEELIN BAY AND SLIEVE LEAGUE

To the west of Donegal town lies one of the most stupendous landscapes in Ireland – the stark and beautiful **Teelin Bay** and the majestic **Slieve League cliffs**. An ideal **base** for exploring the region is the busy, but always welcoming, *Derrylahan Independent Hostel* (ⓣ074/973 8079, ⓔderrylahan@eircom.net; dorms €14–18, doubles €40–50, camping €8), a 2km walk from Kilcar along the coastal road to Carrick.

Nestled to the rear of the Slieve League and ringed by grassy hills rolling down to the sea, Teelin Bay is an unspoilt fishing port, where you can organize diving, dolphin-watching, charter sea-angling and sightseeing boat trips to the Slieve League (contact Paddy Byrne ⓣ074/973 9365).

There are two routes up to the ridge of **Slieve League**: a back way following the signpost to Baile Mór just before Teelin, and the road route from Teelin to Bunglass, a thousand sheer feet above the sea. The former path has you looking up continually at the ridge known as One Man's Pass (see below), on which walkers seem the size of pins, while the front approach swings you up to one of the most thrilling cliff scenes in the world, the **Amharc Mór**. On a good day you can see a third of Ireland from the summit.

GLENCOLMCILLE

Dangerous in windy weather, **One Man's Pass** is only a few feet wide in places and leads via Malinbeg – where there's the excellent *Malinbeg Hostel* (ⓣ074/9730006, ⓦwww.malinbeghostel.com; dorms €15, doubles €35–40) and the stunning Silver Strand beach, sheltered by vertiginous sea-cliffs – and Malinmore to **GLENCOLMCILLE**. Since the seventh century, following Columba's stay in the valley, it has been a place of pilgrimage: every June 9 at midnight the locals commence a three-hour barefoot itinerary of the cross-inscribed slabs that stud the valley basin, finishing up with Mass at 3am in the small church. If you want to attempt *Turas Cholmcille* ("Columba's Journey") yourself, get a map of the route from the Glencolmcille Hill Walkers Centre, which also has lovely modern budget accommodation (ⓣ074/973 0302, ⓦwww.ionadsuil.ie; rooms €25), or the **Folk Village Museum** (Easter–Sept Mon–Sat 10am–6pm, Sun noon–6pm; €3), a cluster of replica, period-furnished thatched cottages. A path up to the left from here leads to the wonderfully positioned *Dooey Hostel* (ⓣ074/973 0130, ⓦwww.dooeyhostel.com; dorms €15, doubles €30), while **B&Bs** include *Corner House* (ⓣ074/973 002; doubles €60; May–Sept), 400m down the Ardara road from *Biddy's Bar* in the village centre. *Roarty's* bar, at the other end of the village, is good for lively, traditional music sessions, particularly on a Friday. The best **food** on offer is at *An Cistin*, part of the Foras Cultúir Uladh complex.

Northern Ireland

Both the pace of political change and the uncertainty of its future continue to characterize Northern Ireland. In 1998, after thirty years of the Troubles, its people overwhelmingly voted in support of a political settlement and, it was hoped, an end to political and sectarian violence. For a time the political process gradually inched forwards, hampered by deep mistrust and suspicion on both sides. In recent years, however, considerable headway has been made in the peace process, with the resumption of devolved government in Northern Ireland, and a greater sense of hope evident on both sides of the community. **Belfast** and **Derry** are two lively and attractive cities, and the northern coastline – especially the bizarre geometry of the **Giant's Causeway** – is as spectacular as anything in Ireland. To the southwest is the huge lake complex **Lough Erne**, and **Enniskillen**, a town resonant with history.

BELFAST

A quarter of Northern Ireland's population lives in the capital, **BELFAST**. While the legacy of **the Troubles** is clearly visible in areas like West Belfast – peace walls, derelict buildings and political murals on every corner – security measures have been considerably eased, though there are certain flashpoints such as the Short Strand and the Ardoyne, which remain inadvisable to visit.

There's no doubt that the city is going from strength to strength with an arts

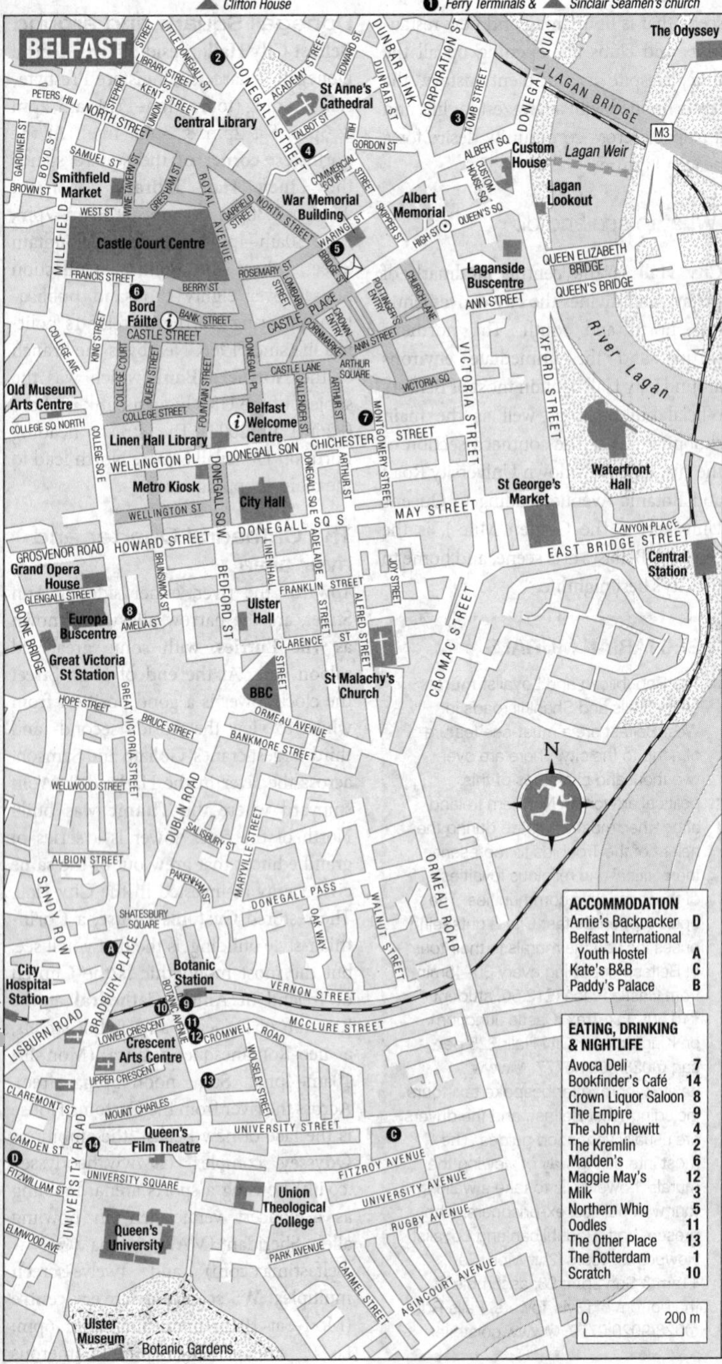
BELFAST
Clifton House
1, Ferry Terminals & Sinclair Seamen's church
The Odyssey
St Anne's Cathedral
Central Library
Custom House
Lagan Weir
Lagan Lookout
LAGAN BRIDGE
M3
Smithfield Market
War Memorial Building
Albert Memorial
Castle Court Centre
Laganside Buscentre
QUEEN ELIZABETH BRIDGE
QUEEN'S BRIDGE
River Lagan
Bord Fáilte
Old Museum Arts Centre
Belfast Welcome Centre
Linen Hall Library
Metro Kiosk
City Hall
Waterfront Hall
St George's Market
Grand Opera House
Europa Buscentre
Great Victoria St Station
Ulster Hall
Central Station
Stormont Estate
St Malachy's Church
BBC
City Hospital Station
Botanic Station
Crescent Arts Centre
Queen's Film Theatre
Union Theological College
Queen's University
Ulster Museum
Botanic Gardens
DONEGALL STREET
NORTH STREET
ROYAL AVENUE
CASTLE STREET
CHICHESTER STREET
VICTORIA STREET
OXFORD STREET
MAY STREET
HOWARD STREET
DONEGALL SQ S
EAST BRIDGE STREET
CROMAC STREET
ORMEAU AVENUE
ORMEAU ROAD
GREAT VICTORIA STREET
DUBLIN ROAD
DONEGALL PASS
SANDY ROW
BRADBURY PLACE
LISBURN ROAD
UNIVERSITY ROAD
BOTANIC AVENUE
VERNON STREET
MCCLURE STREET
UNIVERSITY STREET
UNIVERSITY AVENUE
FITZROY AVENUE
RUGBY AVENUE
AGINCOURT AVENUE
N
ACCOMMODATION
Arnie's Backpacker D
Belfast International Youth Hostel A
Kate's B&B C
Paddy's Palace B
EATING, DRINKING & NIGHTLIFE
Avoca Deli 7
Bookfinder's Café 14
Crown Liquor Saloon 8
The Empire 9
The John Hewitt 4
The Kremlin 2
Madden's 6
Maggie May's 12
Milk 3
Northern Whig 5
Oodles 11
The Other Place 13
The Rotterdam 1
Scratch 10
0 200 m

scene that is flourishing and new restaurants and clubs are opening up all the time. Despite its turbulent history, the city is imbued with a new zest for life, and a palpable cross-community desire for a peaceful future.

What to see and do

City Hall is the central landmark of Belfast, and divides the city conveniently into north and south. The northern section and the immediate environs around City Hall contain most of Belfast's official buildings, as well as the main shopping areas. The southern section of the city, especially down University Road and Botanic Avenue, leading to Queen's University ("The Golden Mile"), is the centre of Belfast's arts scene, and home to the city's best nightlife.

SECTARIAN MURALS

The Republican and Loyalist **murals** on the Falls and Shankill roads in West Belfast are a must-see feature of a trip to the city. There are over two thousand examples of this political artwork in Northern Ireland altogether, mostly painted during the height of the Troubles to represent the political and religious loyalties of the respective communities. The open-topped Belfast City Sightseeing buses include the murals in their tour of Belfast, departing every 30–45min from Castle Place (£12.50, student £10.50). Taxi Trax (Castle Junction on King St, near City Hall; £25 per car; ⓣ028/9031 5777, ⓦwww.taxitrax.com) offer bespoke taxi tours including West Belfast, and the drivers are usually very good guides. The most interesting way of viewing the murals, however, is to take a walking tour with political ex-prisoners, who present both Republican and Loyalist viewpoints. Tours (2hr; Mon–Sat 11am & Sun 2pm; £8; assemble at the bottom of Divis Towers, Falls Rd; ⓣ028/9020 0770, ⓦwww.coiste.ie).

Donegall Square and around

Belfast City Hall, presiding over central Donegall Square, is an austere Presbyterian building (tours Mon–Fri 11am, 2pm & 3pm, Sat 2pm & 3pm; free). At the northwest corner of the square stands the **Linen Hall Library** (Mon–Fri 9.30am–5.30pm, Thurs 9.30am–7pm, Sat 9.30am–4pm), entered on Fountain Street, where the Political Collection houses over eighty thousand publications covering Northern Ireland's political life since 1966. Nearby is the branch of the **Northern Bank** which was the subject of the UK's biggest bank robbery (£26m) in 2004. The streets heading north off Donegall Square North lead to the main shopping area.

The Cathedral Quarter and river area

Towards the river, either side of Ann Street, are the narrow alleyways known as **The Entries**, with some great old saloon bars. At the end of High Street the clock tower is a good position from which to view the world's second- and third-largest cranes, Goliath and Samson, across the river in the Harland & Wolff shipyard where the **Titanic** was built. North of the clock tower is a series of grand edifices that grew out of the same civic vanity as invested in the City Hall. The restored **Customs House**, a Corinthian-style building, is the first you'll see, but the most monolithic is the Church of Ireland **St Anne's Cathedral** at the junction of Donegall and Talbot streets, a neo-Romanesque basilica (Mon–Fri 10am–4pm, Sun noon–3pm; free). Across the river from the Customs House is the face of new Belfast, the ambitious **Odyssey** complex (ⓦwww.theodyssey.co.uk) housing a sports arena doubling as a concert venue, ten-pin bowling alley, Sheridan IMAX cinema (ⓦwww.belfastimax.com) and twelve-screen multiplex, **W5 science discovery centre** (Mon–Sat 10am–6pm, Sun noon–6pm; £6.80, student £5.40) and numerous

restaurants. Further along the waterside is the impressive Waterfront Hall concert venue (Ⓦwww.waterfront.co.uk).

Stormont Estate

Completed in 1938, parliament buildings in the **Stormont Estate**, four miles east of the centre (bus #4a from Donegall Square West), have housed the parliament of Northern Ireland and successive assemblies and conventions; since the Good Friday Agreement in 1998 they have been home to the Northern Irish Assembly and Power Sharing Executive. A mile-long processional avenue leads up to the magnificent, Neoclassical building, which stands in extensive parkland. The six frontal pillars represent the six counties of the North. The white facade was "painted" with manure during World War II to disguise it from the air, but the "paint" permanently stained the stone; on close inspection you can still see remnants of it. Although the building is closed to the public, the grounds are open (Mon–Sun 7am–7.30pm; free), offering woodland walks and spectacular views over the city and docklands.

The Golden Mile

The area of **South Belfast** known as "The Golden Mile" stretches from the **Grand Opera House**, on Great Victoria Street, down to the university, and has plenty of restaurants, pubs and bars at each end. Further south on University Road, **Queen's University** is the architectural centrepiece, flanked by the Georgian terrace, University Square. Just south of the university are the verdant **Botanic Gardens** whose Palm House (Mon–Fri 10am–4/5pm, Sat & Sun 1–5pm; free) was the first of its kind in the world.

Arrival and information

Air Belfast International Airport is 19 miles west of town (buses every 10–30min to Europa bus station; £7 single, £10 return; Ⓣ028/9448 4848, Ⓦwww.belfastairport.com); Belfast City Airport is 3 miles northeast (bus #600 every 20min to city centre 5.30am–10pm; £2.50 return; Ⓣ028/9093 9093, Ⓦwww.belfastcityairport.com).

Train Most trains call at the central Great Victoria St Station, though those from Dublin and Larne terminate at Central Station on East Bridge St.

Bus Buses from Derry, the Republic, the airports and ferry terminals arrive at Europa bus station beside Great Victoria St train station; buses from the north coast use Laganside Bus Centre in Queen's Square. A regular Centrelink bus connects all bus and train stations.

Boat Ferries from Stranraer dock at Corry Rd (taxi £7), and those from Liverpool further north on West Bank Rd (taxi £8); while ferries from Cairnryan dock 30km north at Larne (bus or train to centre).

Tourist office The Belfast Welcome Centre, 47 Donegall Place (Mon–Sat 9am–5.30/7pm, summer Sun 11am–4pm; Ⓣ028/9024 6609, Ⓦwww.gotobelfast.com). Bord Fáilte, for information about the Republic, is at 53 Castle St (Mon–Fri 9am–5pm; Ⓣ028/9026 5500).

City transport

Information on all buses and trains is available at Ⓣ028/9066 6630 or Ⓦwww.translink.co.uk.

Bus The city is served by Metro bus service. Day, tickets for the whole network cost £3.50 Mon–Sat; £2.70 after 10am Mon–Sat and all day Sun. Single tickets cost £1.20–1.80. The Metro kiosk in Donegall Square West provides free bus maps. Ulsterbus serves outlying areas.

Bike rental Lifecycles, Unit 35, Smithfield Market (£10/day, £16 for 2hr guided tour).

Accommodation

Hostels

Arnie's Backpackers 63 Fitzwilliam St Ⓣ028/9024 2867, Ⓦwww.arniesbackpackers.co.uk. Cheerful and relaxed independent hostel with a homely atmosphere and colourful garden, near the university. Dorms £10–12.

Belfast International Youth Hostel 22–32 Donegall Rd Ⓣ028/9031 5435. Large, well-equipped but characterless modern HINI hostel, just west of Shaftesbury Square. Dorms £10–15, doubles £35.

Paddy's Palace 68 Lisburn Rd Ⓣ028/9033 3367, Ⓦwww.paddyspalace.com. Convivial hostel in an old Georgian building, with a large garden and party atmosphere. Dorms £8–13, doubles £38.

B&Bs

Kate's B&B 127 University St Ⓣ028/9028 2091, Ⓔkatesbb127@hotmail.com. Chintzy but very popular and friendly B&B, offering an "all-you-can-eat" breakfast. £25.

Eating

Many of the best places to eat and the liveliest pubs are around Great Victoria St and in the university area.

Avoca Deli Arthur St. Gourmet deli counter in the centre of town offering quality soups, salads and mains to eat in or take away. £4–9.

Bookfinders Café 47 University Rd. Bohemian café at the back of a charmingly messy bookshop. Poetry nights on Fridays from 8pm. Lunch from £3.

Maggie May's 45 Botanic Ave. Huge, economically priced portions in this cosy café with lots of veggie choices, open for lunch and dinner. Sandwiches from £3, mains £5.

Oodles 43 Botanic Ave. Create your own menu and have noodles and crispy vegetables stir-fried in front of you. From £4.

The Other Place 78 Botanic Ave. Fine breakfasts, and plenty of pizzas, pastas and baked potatoes. £5–10.

Drinking and nightlife

Belfast's best entertainment is pub music, though there's also a vibrant club scene and plenty of DJ bars. For listings check *The Big List* (free; Ⓦwww.thebiglist.co.uk), available in pubs, record shops and hostels, and the *Belfast Evening Telegraph*.

Pubs

Crown Liquor Saloon 46 Great Victoria St. The city's most famous pub, decked out like a spa bath, with a good range of Ulster food, such as champ and colcannon (both potato dishes) and Strangford oysters in season.

The Empire 42 Botanic Ave. Music hall and cellar bar in a converted church, with nightly live music or comedy.

The John Hewitt 53 Donegall St. Owned by Belfast Unemployed Resource Centre, this popular bar has some of Belfast's best traditional music sessions on Tues, Wed and Sat evenings, blues on Thurs and jazz on Fri.

Madden's 52–74 Berry St. Unpretentious and atmospheric pub, with regular traditional music sessions (Fri & Sat).

The Rotterdam 54 Pilot St. Names big and small play in this docklands venue, plus traditional music on Thurs (9.30pm).

Clubs and bars

The Kremlin 90 Donegall St Ⓦwww.kremlin-belfast.com. Ireland's biggest gay venue with a host of events throughout the week.

Milk 10–14 Tomb St. Ever-popular and ever-packed club playing dance music for all tastes every night.

Northern Whig 2–10 Bridge St. Massive upmarket bar in the premises of the old newspaper, featuring pre-club DJs most nights.

Scratch 5–6 Lower Crescent. Belfast's flashiest club – two floors of pop music and pitchers of cocktails.

Shopping

High Street The main shopping area is the long stretch of Donegall Place and Royal Avenue, where you'll find big fashion and retail names. The big shopping centre Castle Court is on Royal Avenue.

Arcades and markets Away from main thoroughfare Royal Ave are more alternative and more locally inspired outlets. Haymarket Arcade houses some great film and music stores. East of City Hall off Oxford St is the Belfast institution that is St George's Market, which displays all sorts of delicacies (Fri & Sat).

Vintage/alternative Unsurprisingly, things get more alternative in the university area: The Rusty Zip, 28 Botanic Ave, is full of vintage gems, and No Alibis, 83 Botanic Ave, is a great bookstore which specializes in crime and often holds music events in the evening.

Directory

Exchange Thomas Cook, 10 Donegall Square West (Ⓣ0845/308 9139); and the Belfast Welcome Centre (see below).

Hospitals Belfast City Hospital, Lisburn Rd (Ⓣ028/9032 9241); Royal Victoria, Grosvenor Rd (Ⓣ028/9024 0503).

Internet Belfast Welcome Centre, 47 Donegall Place; *Friends Café*, 109–113 Royal Ave; ITXP, 175–177 Ormeau Rd; Revelations, 27 Shaftesbury Square.

Left luggage Belfast Welcome Centre, 47 Donegall Place.

Police North Queen St Ⓣ028/9065 0222.

Post office Castle Place.

THE MOURNE MOUNTAINS

If you're based in Belfast but fancy a day-trip out of the metropolis, the beautiful **Mourne Mountains** provide the perfect escape. The mountain range comprises twelve peaks, of which Slieve Donard, at 850m, is the highest in Northern Ireland. From Belfast, buses #20, #720 and #237 run from the Europa bus station to Newcastle (up to 15 daily; 1hr); from Newcastle, the Mourne Rambler service (July 2–Aug 2) tracks a loop through the area (£4.50 day-ticket; Ⓦwww.discovernorthernireland.com).

Moving on

Train Coleraine (9–10 daily; 1hr 20–45min); Derry (5–9 daily; 2hr 30min); Dublin (5–9 daily; 2hr 20min); Larne Harbour (9–25 daily; 1hr 10min).
Bus Derry (11–32 daily; 1hr 50min); Dublin (20 daily; 3hr); Enniskillen (5-16 daily; 2hr–2hr 20min).

THE GIANT'S CAUSEWAY

Since 1693, when the Royal Society publicized it as one of the great wonders of the natural world, the **Giant's Causeway**, 65 miles northwest of Belfast on the coast, has been a major tourist attraction. Consisting of an estimated 37,000 polygonal basalt columns, it's the result of a massive subterranean explosion some sixty million years ago which spewed out a huge mass of molten basalt onto the surface and, as it cooled, solidified into massive polygonal crystals. Taking the path down the cliffs from the **visitor centre** (daily 10am–4.30/5/6pm; free; car parking £6) or the shuttle bus (every 15min; £2 return) brings you to the most spectacular of the blocks where many people linger, but if you push on, you'll be rewarded with relative solitude and views of some of the more impressive formations high in the cliffs. One of these, **Chimney Point**, has an appearance so bizarre that the ships of the Spanish Armada opened fire on it, believing that they were attacking Dunluce Castle, a few miles further west. An alternative two-mile circuit follows the spectacular cliff-top path from the visitor centre, with views across to Scotland, to a flight of 162 steps leading down the cliff to a set of basalt columns known as the **Organ Pipes**, from where paths lead round to the shuttle-bus stop alongside the Causeway proper.

GETTING TO THE GIANT'S CAUSEWAY

Trains from Belfast go to Coleraine, where there's a regular connection to Portrush; from either, you can catch the "open-topper" bus (July & Aug 4 daily; £4.30) to the Causeway, or from Portrush there's bus #172, both running via Bushmills. A restored **narrow-gauge railway** runs between Bushmills and the Causeway (July–Aug 7 daily, plus some days in other months; 20min; single £5.25, return £6.75; ⓣ028/2073 2844). The **Antrim Coaster coach** (Goldline Express #252) runs from Larne direct to the Causeway (2 daily; Oct–June not Sun; 2hr 30min; £4.30) and on to Coleraine via Bushmills, Portrush and Portstewart, Antrim Glens and stunning seascapes en route.

Carrick-a-Rede

If you've developed an appetite for the stunning scenery and walks on this coast, a visit to the **Carrick-a-Rede Rope Bridge**, 13km east of the Causeway, is a must (March–Oct daily 10am–6/7pm, weather permitting; £3.30). For the past two hundred years, fishermen have reputedly erected a bridge from the mainland cliffs to Carrick-a-Rede island over a vast chasm, so as to check their salmon nets. Now, the National Trust is responsible. Venturing across the swaying rope bridge high above the water is an exhilarating experience, but not for the faint-hearted. Ulsterbus #402 runs between Bushmills and the rope bridge via the Causeway in summer months.

PORTSTEWART

PORTSTEWART, a pleasant coastal resort ten miles west of the Giant's Causeway, makes a good base: there's an IHH **hostel**, *Rick's Causeway Coast Independent Hostel*, at 4 Victoria Terrace (ⓣ028/7083 3789, ⓔrick@causewaycoasthostel.fsnet.co.uk; dorms £12, rooms £36) and several **B&B** options. The bus stop for the Giant's Causeway is 100m from the hostel.

There are some reasonable **bars**, including *Shenanigans* on the Promenade, which is open till 1am. If you're after a big night out, *Kelly's* (1 Bushmills Rd ⓦwww.kellysportrush.co.uk) is a

short taxi-ride away, and its **club** night, Lush! on Wednesdays and Saturdays is renowned. **Surfing** can be organized at Ocean Warriors (ⓣ028/7083 6500, ⓦwww.oceanwarriors.co.uk) on the Promenade.

DERRY

DERRY lies at the foot of Lough Foyle, less than three miles from the border with the Republic. The city presents a beguiling picture, its two hillsides terraced with pastel-shaded houses punctuated by stone spires, and, being seventy percent Catholic, has a very different atmosphere from Belfast.

However, from Partition in 1921 until the late 1980s, the Protestant minority maintained control of all important local institutions. The situation came to a head after the Protestant Apprentice Boys' March in August 1969, when the police attempted to storm the Catholic estates of the Bogside. In the ensuing tension, British troops were widely deployed for the first time in Northern Ireland. On January 31, 1972, the crisis deepened when British paratroopers opened fire on civilians, killing thirteen unarmed demonstrators in what became known as **Bloody Sunday**.

Derry is now greatly changed: tensions eased considerably here long before Belfast, thanks in part to a determinedly even-handed local council, although defiant murals remain and marching is still a contentious issue. The city centre has undergone much regeneration, and Derry has a justifiable reputation for innovation in the arts.

What to see and do

You can walk the entire mile-long circuit of Derry's seventeenth-century **city walls** – some of the best-preserved defences in Europe. Reinforced by bulwarks, bastions and an earth rampart with parapet, the walls encircle the original medieval street pattern with four gateways – Shipquay, Butcher, Bishop and Ferryquay – surviving from the first construction, in slightly revised form. City Tours offer informative walking tours of the walls (11 Carlisle Rd; daily 10am, noon & 2pm; £4; ⓣ0771/293 7997, ⓦwww.derrycitytours.com), which explore fifteen hundred years of history and an introduction to the Bogside murals. Taxi tours also available by arrangement (£25/hr for 4 people).

Guildhall Square and around

Guildhall Square, once the old quay, is where most of the city's cannons are lined up, between Shipquay and Magazine gates. A reconstruction of the medieval **O'Doherty Tower** houses splendid displays on the city's turbulent political history and an exhibition on the Spanish Armada (check with the tourist office for opening times). After you turn left at **Shipquay Gate**, the promenade doglegs at Water Bastion where the River Foyle once lapped the walls at high tide. Continue on to Newgate Bastion and **Ferryquay Gate**, where you can look out across the river to the Waterside area, once primarily Protestant, now almost half Catholic.

St Columb's Cathedral

Between Ferryquay and Bishop's Gate the major sight is the Protestant **St Columb's Cathedral** (Mon–Sat 9am–4/5pm; £1.50), just within the southern section of the walls; it overlooks **The Fountain**, the Protestant enclave immediately outside the same stretch of walls, and offers one of the best views of the city. The cathedral was used as a battery during a fifteen-week siege in 1688–89, and in the entrance porch you'll find the cannonball shot into the grounds by James II's besieging army with proposals for the city's surrender.

South wall sights and the Bogside

Back on the walls, pass the white sandstone **courthouse** next to Bishop's Gate and you'll see, downhill to the left, the only remaining tower of the old Derry jail. At the **Double Bastion** sits the Roaring Meg cannon, used during the siege, while down in the valley below are the streets of the Bogside. These were once the undisputed preserve of the IRA, and **Free Derry Corner** marks the site of the original barricades erected against the British army at the height of the Troubles. Nearby are the Bloody Sunday and Hunger Strikers' memorials. Further along the city wall is the **Royal Bastion**, former site of the Rev. George Walker statue which was blown up in 1973. It is in Walker's and their predecessors' memory that the Protestant Apprentice Boys march around the walls every August 12.

Arrival and information

Air City of Derry airport (Ⓣ028/7181 0784, Ⓦwww.cityofderryairport.com) is 7 miles northeast, connected to the centre by bus.

Train Trains from Belfast arrive on the east bank of the Foyle with a free connecting bus to the bus station.

Bus station Foyle St beside Guildhall Square.

Tourist office 44 Foyle St (July–Sept daily 9/10am–5/7pm; Oct–June Mon–Fri 9am–5pm, mid-March to June also Sat 10am–5pm; Ⓣ028/7126 7284, Ⓦwww.derryvisitor.com).

Internet Webcrawler Cyber Café, 52 Strand Rd.

Listings Check the bi weekly *Derry Journal* (£0.90).

Accommodation

Derry City Independent Hostel 44 Great James St Ⓣ028/7137 7989, Ⓦwww.derry-hostel.co.uk. A very friendly, bohemian hostel with furniture from around the world. Hosts regular barbecues in the summer. Dorms £12.

Dolce Vita 46 Great James St Ⓣ028/7137 7989. Run by the people at *Derry City* hostel, the adjacent building has private double and twin rooms in a similar style. Doubles £36.

The Saddler's House 36 Great James St Ⓣ028/7126 9691, Ⓦwww.thesaddlershouse.com. Beautifully decorated Georgian townhouse run by knowledgeable hosts and serving excellent breakfasts. This, together with its sister B&B *The Merchant House*, is a real treat. They also have two self-catering cottages available to rent. Late-night revellers not welcome. Doubles £50.

Eating

Badger's Bar 16 Orchard St. Good-value pub lunches.

Café del Mondo 4 Shipquay Place. Not-for-profit café serving excellent value stews, soups and salads from around the world. Mains £3.50–6.

The Exchange Exchange House, Queen's Quay. Upmarket restaurant and wine bar serving succulent steaks and a variety of fish and vegetarian dishes. Mains £10–16.

Halo Pantry and Grill New Market St. Housed in a former shirt factory, this excellent new restaurant on two floors serves top-quality food using locally sourced ingredients at very reasonable prices. *Pantry* mains £7, *Grill* mains £15.

Drinking and nightlife

Bound for Boston 27–31 Waterloo St. This live music venue has a great beer-garden and seven pool tables.

Earth Niteclub Above *Café Roc* and hugely popular for it's r'n'b nights on a Saturday.

Peadar O'Donnell's/The Gweedore Bar 59–63 Waterloo St. Traditional and contemporary music every night.

Pepe's Strand Rd. Gay pub and club (Fri & Sat) which plays a lot of cheese.

Sandino's Café Bar Water St. Intimate candlelit café-bar with a Che Guevara theme downstairs, and a live music venue upstairs. Trad sessions on Sun from 5pm.

Moving on

Train Belfast (4–9 daily; 2hr 30min); Coleraine (5–9 daily; 1hr).

Bus Donegal (3–7 daily; 1hr 25–45min); Dublin (7 daily; 4hr); Enniskillen (5–15 daily; 2hr–4hr 20min); Sligo (3–5 daily; 2hr 30min).

ENNISKILLEN

An attractive, conservative small town, **ENNISKILLEN** sits on a lake island, a narrow ribbon of water passing each side of the town between Lower and Upper **Lough Erne**. The water loops its way

around the core of the town, its glassy surface lending Enniskillen a sense of calm and reflecting the mini-turrets of **Enniskillen Castle**. Rebuilt by William Cole, to whom the British gave Enniskillen in 1609, the castle houses the **Fermanagh County Museum** and the **Regimental Museum of the Royal Inniskilling Fusiliers** in the keep (July & Aug Tues–Fri 10am–5pm, Sat–Mon 2–5pm; May, June & Sept closed Sun; Oct–April closed Sat & Sun; £2.95), a proud, polished display of paraphernalia of the town's historic regiments. A mile along the Belfast road stands **Castle Coole** (1–6pm: May–Aug daily except Thurs; April & Sept, Sun & bank holidays; £5). A perfect Palladian building of Portland stone, with an interior of fine plasterwork and superb furnishings, it sits in a beautiful landscaped garden (daily 10am–4/8pm; free).

Lough Erne

The earliest people to settle in this region lived on and around the two lakes of **Lough Erne**, which features many crannogs (artificial islands). The maze of waterways protected the settlers from invaders and created an enduring cultural isolation. Stone carvings suggest that Christianity was accepted far more slowly here than elsewhere, and several pagan idols have been found on Christian sites.

The easiest place to visit is **Devenish Island**, two miles northwest of Enniskillen. St Molaise founded a monastic settlement here in the sixth century and it remained an important religious centre until the early seventeenth century. It's a delightful setting and the considerable ruins span the entire medieval period. There are regular ferries (April–Sept daily 10am–6pm; £3) from Trory Point, three miles north of Enniskillen on the A32 road. Four miles further north along the Kesh road lies **Castle Archdale** forest park from whose marina ferries (Oct–March Sat & Sun 2–6pm; April–Sept Sat & Sun 10am–6pm; July & Aug daily 10am–6pm; £3) depart to **White Island**. The island's ruined abbey is known for its early Christian carvings that look eerily pagan: the most disconcerting is the lewd female figure known as a Sheila-na-Gig, with bulging cheeks, a big grin, open legs and arms pointing to her genitals.

Arrival and information

Bus The station is on Wellington Rd.
Tourist office Opposite the bus station (Mon–Fri 9am–5.30/7pm; Easter–Sept also Sat & Sun 10/11am–6/5pm; ⓣ028/6632 3110, ⓦwww.fermanagh-online.com).

Accommodation

The tourist office can help finding B&Bs, most of which are some distance from the town centre.
The Bridges Belmore St ⓣ028/6634 0110. Situated by the war memorial, this is a modern HINI hostel, complete with on-site restaurant. Dorms £15, doubles £38.

Eating and drinking

Blakes of the Hollow 6 Church St ⓣ028/6632 2143. This old pub has been run by the same family since 1887, and continues to pull the crowds. There's a smart bistro (*Café Merlot*) on the lower ground floor.
The Fort Lodge Hotel Forthill St ⓣ028/6632 3275. Live music and DJs at weekends, and good bar food throughout the day and a lunch carvery in their *Crannog Lounge*. Lunch £6.50.
Leslie's 10 Church St. Generously filled sandwiches to eat in or take away. From £2.
Pat's 1–5 Townhall St ⓣ028/6632 7462. Cosy pub with live music every weekend and a good selection of roasts, pies, burgers and stir-fries. Mains £6–9.

Moving on

Bus Belfast (8–10 daily; 2hr 20min); Derry (15 daily; 2hr 30min–4hr 30min); Dublin (7 daily; 2hr 20min–3hr).

Italy

HIGHLIGHTS

VENICE: catch a waterbus at night for some utterly romantic views

SIENA: attend the Palio, a frenetic and fiercely partisan horse race

ROME: see the spectacular Colosseum up close

NAPLES: eat pizza in its home town

POMPEII: explore the evocative remains of a city buried by ash

PALERMO: prepare to be dazzled by the Sicilian capital's unique architectural mix

ROUGH COSTS

DAILY BUDGET Basic €25/occasional treat €45

DRINK Wine €2.50/glass

FOOD Pizza €3–5

HOSTEL/BUDGET HOTEL €18–25/€30–60

TRAVEL Train: Rome–Naples (190km) 2hr, €20; bus: 2hr, €16

FACT FILE

POPULATION 58.7 million

AREA 301,230 sq km

LANGUAGE Italian

CURRENCY Euro (€)

CAPITAL Rome (population: 2.7 million)

INTERNATIONAL PHONE CODE ⓣ39

Introduction

Of all the countries in Europe, Italy is perhaps the hardest to classify. A modern industrialized nation and a harbinger of global style, its designers lead the way with each season's fashions. But it is also a Mediterranean country, with all that that implies. If there is a single national characteristic, it is to embrace life to the full, manifest in its numerous local festivals and in the importance placed on good food. There is also, of course, the country's enormous cultural legacy: Tuscany alone has more classified historical monuments than any country in the world, and every region holds its own treasures.

Italy wasn't unified until 1861, a fact that's borne out by the regional nature of the place today. In the northwest, the well-to-do cities of **Turin** and **Milan** epitomize the wealthy, industrial north; further south is **Genoa**, a bustling port with a long seafaring tradition. By far the biggest draw in the north is **Venice**, a unique and beautiful city – though you won't be alone in appreciating it. The centre of the country, specifically **Tuscany**, boasts classic, rolling countryside and the art-packed towns of Florence, Pisa and Siena, while neighbouring **Umbria** has a quieter appeal. **Rome**, the capital, harbours a dazzling array of ancient and Renaissance gems. South of here in Campania, **Naples**, a vibrant, unforgettable city, is the spiritual heart of the economically undeveloped Italian south, while close by are fine ancient sites and the spectacular **Amalfi Coast**. Puglia, the "heel" of Italy, has underrated pleasures – most notably Lecce, a Baroque gem of a city. **Sicily** is a law unto itself, with attractions ranging from Hellenic remains to the drama of Mount Etna, and the beguiling city of Palermo. **Sardinia**, too, feels far removed from the mainland, especially in its relatively undiscovered interior.

CHRONOLOGY

753 BC Rome founded by Romulus and Remus.
509 BC The city becomes a Republic.
49 BC Julius Caesar successfully wages war against members of the Senate and extends the Roman Empire across Europe.
80 AD Building of the Colosseum.
476 Last Roman Emperor Romulus Augustus overthrown by barbarians.
756 Papal States created after Frankish forces defeat the Lombards.
1173 Building of the Tower of Pisa begins.
1512 Michelangelo completes his frescoes in the Sistine Chapel, as the Italian Renaissance flourishes.
1804 Napoleon declares himself emperor of Italy.
1814 Following Napoleon's defeat, Italy is divided into various states.
1861 Unification of Italian states into a Kingdom by Giuseppe Garibaldi.
1898 First Italian football league established.
1915 Italy joins World War I on the side of the Allies.
1922 Fascist Benito Mussolini becomes Prime Minister.
1929 The Lateran Treaty declares Vatican City an independent state. It is the smallest state in the world.
1940 Italy enters World War II on the side of the Nazis.
1943 Allies capture Sicily and imprison Mussolini. Italy declares war on Germany.
1945 Mussolini is captured and executed by Italian communists.
1946 Republic replaces the monarchy.
1957 The Treaty of Rome establishes the European Economic Community.
2007 Silvio Berlusconi wins a third term as prime minister, amid persistent allegations of corruption.
2009 Earthquake in L'Aquila, around 100km east of Rome, kills over 260 people and leaves thousands homeless.

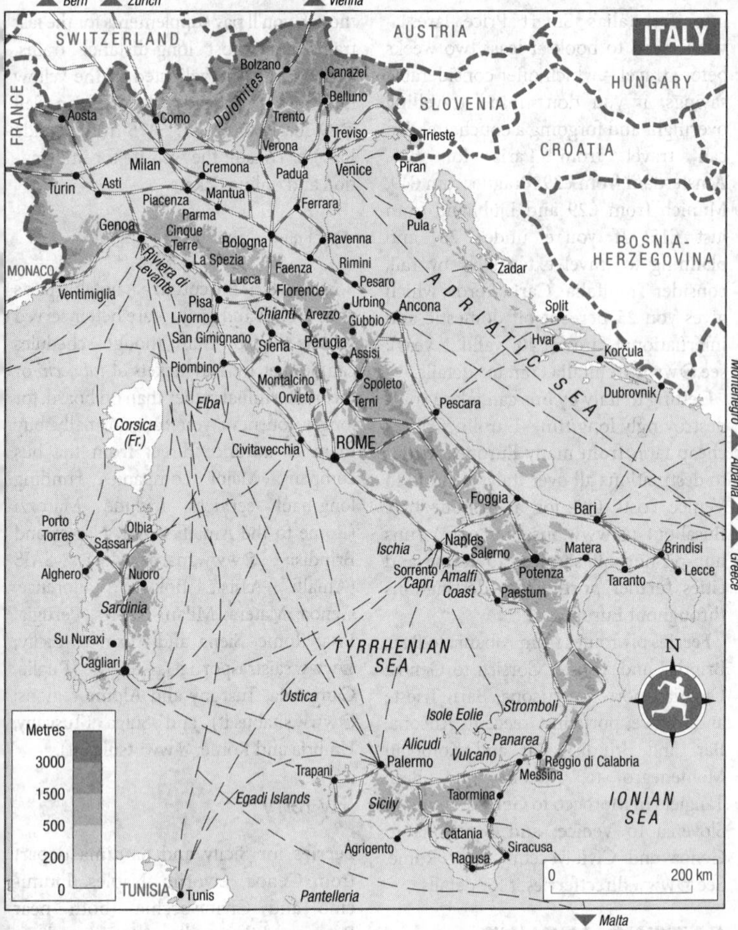

ARRIVAL

The majority of tourists arrive at the **airports** of Rome or Milan, although low-cost European airlines Ryanair and easyJet also offer services to Bari, Bologna, Brindisi, Genoa, Naples, Palermo, Parma, Perugia, Pisa, Rimini, Turin and Venice, plus destinations in Sardinia and Sicily. Budget Italian airline blu-express (Ⓦ www.blu-express.com) flies from Nice, Mykonos and Ibiza to Rome, as well from many Italian cities; Meridiana (Ⓦ www.meridiana.it) has routes between many European and Italian cities. From North America, national carrier Alitalia (Ⓦ www.alitalia.com) runs direct flights to Milan, Rome and Venice, with numerous connecting flights to other cities, although you can invariably find cheaper deals with US airlines such as Delta and American Airlines. Meridiana operates direct flights from New York to Rome, Naples and Palermo. The cheapest option, though, can be to fly to London and get a budget flight onward from there.

Train travel from the UK often works out more expensive, but there is a vast choice of routes, mostly arriving in Milan. From elsewhere in Europe, look

into Trenitalia's Smart Price fares – you'll need to book at least two weeks before travel – which offer considerable savings, if you don't mind travelling overnight and forgoing a couchette. You can travel from Paris for €25, Amsterdam from €29, Prague from €49, Munich from €29 and Ljubljana from just €15. If you're under 26, and planning to travel extensively by rail, consider Trenitalia's Carta Verde, which gives you 25 percent off domestic and international fares (E40; valid 1 year); see Ⓦwww.trenitalia.com for details.

Getting to Italy **by bus** can take a soul-destroyingly long time. Eurolines offers cheap fares from many European cities to destinations all over Italy; London to Venice costs €85 for a 30-hour trip. Busabout (Ⓦwww.busabout.com) runs hop-on-hop-off services to Rome and cities further north from destinations throughout Europe.

Ferries ply routes from Albania to Bari, Brindisi and Trieste; Corsica to Genoa; Croatian ports to Ancona, Bari, Trieste and Venice; ports in Greece to Ancona, Bari and Brindisi; Bar and Kotor in Montenegro to Ancona and Bari; Tangiers in Morocco to Genoa; Pirano in Slovenia to Venice; and Barcelona to Genoa and Civitavecchia, near Rome. See Ⓦwww.directferries.it for details.

GETTING AROUND

By train

Train tickets are cheap and the rail network extensive, though delays are common. **Trains** are operated by Italian State Railways (Ferrovie dello Stato or FS; Ⓦwww.ferroviedellostato.it). For most journeys you'll have a choice between Eurostar – the priciest and fastest trains, which require you to reserve a seat – the slower Intercity and the cheap, snail-paced Diretto, Interregionale and Regionale. **InterRail** and **Eurail** passes are valid on the whole FS network, though you'll pay supplements for the fast trains and most long-distance trains. **Tickets** must be validated in the yellow machines at the head of the platform. Call Ⓣ89.20.21 (Ⓣ06.6847.5475 from outside Italy) or consult the website for information and online tickets.

By bus

Some parts of the country – notably parts of the south and Sicily – are better served by **bus** than by train, though schedules can be sketchy. Buy tickets at *tabacchi* or the bus terminal rather than on board; for longer journeys you can normally buy them in advance direct from the bus company. Major companies running long-haul services include Marozzi (Rome to the Amalfi Coast, Naples and Brindisi; Ⓦwww.marozzivt.it), SAIS (Amalfi, Assisi, Bologna, Florence, Genoa, Matera, Milan, Naples, Perugia, Pisa, Rome, Siena and Turin to Sicily; Ⓦwww.saistrasporti.it), SITA (Puglia, Campania, Tuscany and Alpine regions; Ⓦwww.sitabus.it) and Sulga (Tuscany, Umbria and Rome; Ⓦwww.sulga.it).

By ferry

Ferries for Sicily and Sardinia depart from Genoa, Livorno, Naples, Fiumicino and Civitavecchia (both near Rome), while smaller islands such as Capri, plus towns in the Bay of Naples and along the Amalfi coast, are served by speedier **hydrofoils**. Book well **in advance** for the longer routes in high season to find the cheapest fares; for timetables, see Ⓦwww.directferries.it.

ACCOMMODATION

Book **hotels** in advance in the major cities and resorts, especially in summer. Rates vary greatly but on average you can expect to pay €60 for a double without private bathroom (*senza bagno*) in a one-star hotel, and a minimum of €80 for a double in a three-star. In very

busy places you might have to stay a minimum of three nights.

B&Bs and **agriturismi** (farmstays) can make a good-value alternative. They are often in spectacular locations and provide excellent Italian home cooking, though you may need a car to get to them: ask for a list from the local tourist office.

There are **hostels** in every major Italian city, charging €17–30 per person for a dorm bed, though for two people travelling together, this isn't much cheaper than a budget hotel room. You can see the full list of Italy's HI hostels on Ⓦwww.ostellionline.org. Alternatively, **student accommodation** is a popular budget option in university towns (July and August only), or ask the tourist board about local **case per ferie**, usually religious houses with rooms or beds to let. They can be better value than hostels but often have curfews.

There are plenty of **campsites** and in most cases you pay for location rather than facilities, which can vary enormously. Daily prices are around €7 per person, plus €10 for a two-person tent. See Ⓦwww.camping.it for information.

FOOD AND DRINK

There are few places in the world where you can eat and drink as well as in Italy. If you eat only pizza and panini, you'll be missing out on the distinctive **regional cuisines**; don't be afraid to ask what the *piatti tipici* (local dishes) are. Most Italians start their day in a bar, with a cappuccino and a *cornetto* (croissant), a **breakfast** that should cost around €2 if you stand at the counter – or at least double that if you take a seat. At **lunchtime**, bars sell *tramezzini*, sandwiches on white bread, and panini. Another stopgap are *arancini,* fried meat- or cheese-filled rice balls, particularly prevalent in the south. Italian ice cream (*gelato*) is justifiably famous; for the best choice go to a *gelateria*. **Markets** sell fresh, tasty produce for next to nothing, and work out much cheaper than supermarket shopping.

APERITIVO TIME

When you're strapped for cash but want to have a good time, it's worth remembering that between about 6pm and 9pm, most bars either bring you **snacks** or have an *aperitif* buffet if you buy a drink. These snacks are often substantial enough to fill you up, so you'll be able to save on buying dinner.

The ultimate budget option for sit-down food is pizza. Although trattorias or restaurants often offer a fixed-price *menu turistico*, it's generally not very good – food is cooked in huge batches to cater for the peak-time tourist droves, with unappetizing results. Traditionally, a trattoria is cheaper than a restaurant, offering *cucina casalinga* (home-style cooking). But in either, pasta dishes go for around €6–9; main fish or meat courses will normally be €9–15. Order vegetables (*contorni*) separately. Afterwards there's fruit (*frutta*) and desserts (*dolci*). As well as the cover charge (*coperto*), service (*servizio*) will often be added, generally about ten percent (if it isn't, it's customary to leave a tip of a couple of euros).

Drink

Bars are less social centres than functional places for a quick coffee or beer. You pay first at the cash desk (*la cassa*), present your receipt (*scontrino*) and give your order. Coffee comes small and black (*espresso*, or just *caffè*), with a dash of milk (*macchiato*) or cream (*con panna*), or there's the ever-popular *cappuccino*. Tea (*tè*) comes with lemon (*con limone*) unless you ask for milk (*con latte*); it's also served cold (*tè freddo*). A *spremuta* is a fresh fruit juice; crushed-ice fruit *granite* are a refreshing alternative.

Wine is invariably drunk with meals, and is very cheap. Go for the local stuff:

ask for *un mezzo* (a half-litre) or *un quarto* (a quarter). Bottles are pricier but still good value; expect to pay at least €12 a bottle in a restaurant. The cheapest and most common brands of **beer** (*birra*) are the Italian Peroni and Moretti. Draught beer (*alla spina*) is served in measures of a pint (*una media*) and half-pint (*una piccola*). A generous shot of spirits, or fiery grappa, made from grape pips and stalks, costs from €3. Amaro is a bitter liqueur drunk after meals to aid digestion. Drinking in pubs is pricey – around €5 for a beer and €5–9 for a cocktail – while drinking in clubs can be ruinous, although the entrance fee of €10–15 usually includes one drink.

Most places will be happy to serve you **tap water** (*acqua del rubinetto*), which is perfectly safe to drink. For bottled water, ask for *acqua naturale* (still) or *acqua frizzante* (sparkling).

CULTURE AND ETIQUETTE

Italy remains strongly **family-oriented**, with an emphasis on the traditions and rituals of the Catholic Church, and it's not unusual to find people living with their parents until their early thirties. While the north is cosmopolitan, the south can be rather provincial; women travelling on their own may attract unwanted attention in smaller areas. When entering churches, ensure that your knees and shoulders are covered. In towns and villages all over the country, life stops during the middle of the day for a long lunch.

Tipping is not a big deal in Italy; in restaurants – if a service charge is not included – it's acceptable to reward good service with a couple of euros. In bars, you may see some Italians leave a coin on the counter after finishing their coffee – a convenient way of ridding themselves of small change, but by no means expected of tourists. Likewise, taxi drivers will not expect a tip. **Smoking** is outlawed in all enclosed public places; you can be charged a hefty fine for lighting up.

SPORTS AND OUTDOOR ACTIVITIES

Spectator sports are popular here – Italians are particularly passionate about **football** (*calcio*), though cycling, motorcycling and motor racing are also high-profile sports. Going to a football match in Italy can be an exhilarating experience. The season runs from the end of August to June; ⓦwww.lega-calcio.it for details of matches; tickets cost from €15.

Campania, Sardinia and Sicily, with their pristine coastlines and clear waters, provide excellent conditions for **scuba diving** and **snorkelling**, while Rome, Milan, Turin, Venice and, at the other end of the country, Mount Etna in Sicily, are within easy reach of **ski resorts**. The same mountainous terrain is perfectly suited to summertime **hiking**; ask at local tourist offices for maps and itinerary information.

COMMUNICATIONS

Post office opening hours are Monday to Friday 8am to 6.30pm, with branches in larger towns sometimes also open on Saturdays. Stamps (*francobolli*) can also be bought at *tabacchi* – ask for *posta prioritaria* if you want letters to arrive

STUDENT AND YOUTH DISCOUNTS

Entrance to many of Italy's state-owned museums and archeological sites is free or reduced for EU citizens aged under 18. Students under 25 in full-time education are often eligible for discounts too; carry an ISIC card as proof of age. For one week each year, publicly owned museums and sites open their doors for free for the Settimana dei Beni Culturali (Cultural Heritage Week), usually in the spring.

Italian

	Italian	Pronunciation
Yes/No	*Sì/No*	See/Noh
Please	*Per favore*	Pear fah-vure-ay
You're welcome	*Prego*	Pray-goh
Thank you	*Grazie*	Grraat-see-ay
Hello/Good day/Hi	*Ciao/buongiorno/salve*	Chow/bon jaw-noh/salvay
Goodbye	*Ciao/arrivederci*	Chow/arriva-derchee
Excuse me	*Mi scusi*	Mee scoo-see
Good	*Buono*	Bwo-noh
Bad	*Cattivo*	Cat-ee-voh
Near	*Vicino*	Vih-chee-noh
Far	*Lontano*	Lont-ah-noh
Today	*Oggi*	Ojj-ee
Yesterday	*Ieri*	Ee-air-ee
Tomorrow	*Domani*	Doh-mahn-ee
How much is...?	*Quanto è…?*	Cwan-toe ay…?
What time is it?	*Che ore sono?*	Keh orr-ay son-noh
I don't understand	*Non ho capito*	Non oh kapee-toe
Do you speak English?	*Parla Inglese?*	Parr-la inglay-zay?
One	*Uno*	Oo-noh
Two	*Due*	Doo-ay
Three	*Tre*	Tray
Four	*Quattro*	Cwattr-oh
Five	*Cinque*	Chink-way
Six	*Sei*	Say
Seven	*Sette*	Set-tay
Eight	*Otto*	Ot-toe
Nine	*Nove*	Noh-vay
Ten	*Dieci*	Dee-ay-chee
Ticket	*Biglietto*	Bil-yettoh
Where is...?	*Dov'è…?*	Doh-vay…?
Entrance	*L'ingresso*	Lingress-oh
Exit	*L'uscita*	Loo-shee-tah
Platform	*Il binario*	Il bin-ah-ree-oh
Toilet	*Il bagno*	Il ban-yo
Ferry	*Il traghetto*	Il trag-ettow
Bus	*L'autobus*	Lout-o-boos
Plane	*L'aereo*	Lah-air-ay-oh
Train	*Il treno*	Il tray-no
I would like a...	*Vorrei…*	Vorr-ay…
Bed	*Letto*	Lett-oh
Single/double room	*Camera singola/doppia*	Cam-errah singolah/doppiah
Cheap	*Economico*	Eck-oh-no-micoh
Expensive	*Caro*	Car-oh
Open	*Aperto*	Apairt-oh
Closed	*Chiuso*	Queue-zoh
Breakfast	*Colazione*	Coll-ats-ioh-nay
Hotel	*L'hotel*	Lott-ell
Hostel	*L'ostello*	Lost-ellow

ITALY ON THE NET

ⓦ**www.enit.it** Official tourist board site.
ⓦ**www.paginegialle.it** Italian directory of phone numbers.
ⓦ**www.trenitalia.com** Italian rail timetables.

home before you do. Public **phones** are card-operated; get a phone card (*scheda telefonica*) from *tabacchi* and newsstands for €5/10. For landline calls – local and long-distance – dial all digits, including the area code. International directory enquiries (Ⓣ176) are pricey. Most towns have at least one place with **internet** access; hourly rates are around €2–4.

EMERGENCIES

Most of the **crime** you're likely to come across is small-time. You can minimize the risk of this by being discreet, not flashing anything of value and keeping a firm hand on your camera and bag, particularly on public transport. The police come in many forms: the *Vigili Urbani* deal with traffic offences and the *Carabinieri* with public order and drug control; report thefts to the *Polizia di Stato*. Italy treats soft and hard drugs offences with equal severity.

Pharmacies (*farmacie*) can give advice and dispense prescriptions; there's one open all night in towns and cities (find the address of the nearest on any pharmacy door). For serious ailments, go to the *Pronto Soccorso* (casualty) section of the nearest hospital (*ospedale*).

EMERGENCY NUMBERS

Police Ⓣ112 for all emergencies.

INFORMATION

Most towns, major train stations and airports have a **tourist office** (*ufficio turistico*), which will give out maps for free. As for maps, Studio FMB has excellent hiking maps covering the north of the country, as does Club Alpino Italiano, available throughout Italy.

MONEY AND BANKS

Italy's currency is the euro (€). You'll get the best rate of exchange at a **bank**; hours are Monday to Friday 8.30am to 1.30pm and 2.30 to 4pm. ATMs (*bancomat*) are widespread. The Italian way of life is cash-based, and many smaller restaurants and B&Bs will not accept credit cards.

OPENING HOURS AND HOLIDAYS

Most shops and businesses open Monday Saturday 8/9am to 1pm and 4–7/8pm, though in the north, offices work a 9am to 5pm day. Just about everything, with the exception of bars and restaurants, closes on Sunday. Most churches keep shop hours. Museums traditionally open Tuesday to Sunday 9am to 7pm. Most archeological sites open daily from 9am until an hour before sunset.

Many of Italy's inland towns close down almost entirely for the month of August, when Italians head for the coast. Everything closes for national holidays: January 1, January 6, Easter Monday, April 25, May 1, June 2, August 15, November 1, December 8, December 25 and 26.

Rome

Of all Italy's historic cities, **ROME** (Roma) exerts the most fascination. Its sheer weight of history is endlessly compelling, with eras crowding in on each other to a breathtaking degree. Classical features – the Colosseum, the Roman Forum, the spectacular Palatine Hill – stand alongside ancient basilicas containing relics from the early Christian period, while Baroque fountains and churches define the city centre. But it's not all history and brickwork: Rome has a vibrant, chaotic life of its own, its crowded streets thronged with traffic, locals, tourists and students.

What to see and do

Rome's city centre is divided neatly into distinct areas. The **centro storico** (historic centre) occupies a hook of land on the east bank of the River Tiber, bordered to the east by Via del Corso and to the north and south by water. The old Campus Martius of Roman times, it became the heart of the Renaissance city and is now an unruly knot of narrow streets holding some of the best of Rome's classical and Baroque heritage, as well as much of its nightlife.

From here, Rome's central core spreads east, across Via del Corso to the major shopping streets and alleys around the **Spanish Steps** and the main artery of Via Nazionale, and south to the **Roman Forum**, **Colosseum** and **Palatine Hill**. The west bank of the river is home to the **Vatican** and **St Peter's** and, to the south of these, **Trastevere** – even in ancient times a distinct entity from the city proper, and now a hub of the city's nightlife.

The Roman Forum

The best place to start a tour of the city is the Roman Forum (daily 8.30am–1hr before sunset; 2-day joint ticket with Colosseum and Palatine Hill €12), the bustling centre of the ancient city.

Running through the heart of the Forum, the **Via Sacra** was the best-known street of ancient Rome, lined with its most important buildings, such as the Curia in the Forum's northwestern corner – begun in 45 BC, this was the home of the Senate during the Republican period. Next to the Curia is the **Arch of Septimius Severus**, erected in the early third century AD to commemorate the emperor's tenth anniversary in power. The grassy, wide-open scatter of paving and beached columns in front of it was where most of the life of the city took place. In the centre of the Forum is the **House of the Vestal Virgins**, where the six women charged with keeping the sacred flame of Vesta alight lived. On the far side of the site, the towering **Basilica of Maxentius** is probably the Forum's most impressive relic. From the basilica, the Via Sacra climbs to the **Arch of Titus** on a low arm of the Palatine Hill, its reliefs showing the spoils of Jerusalem being carried off by eager Romans.

Palatine Hill

From the Forum, turn right at the Arch of Titus to reach the **Palatine Hill** (daily 8.30am–1hr before sunset; 2-day joint ticket with Colosseum and Forum €12), now a beautiful archeological garden. In the days of the Republic, the Palatine was the most desirable address in Rome. From the **Farnese Gardens**, on the right, a terrace looks back over the Forum, while the terrace at the opposite end looks down on the alleged centre of Rome's ancient beginning – an Iron Age hut, known as the **House of Romulus**, the best-preserved part of a ninth-century village.

Close by, steps lead down to the **Cryptoporticus**, a passage built by Nero to link the Palatine with his palace on the far side of the Colosseum, and decorated along part of its length with Roman stuccowork. A left turn leads to

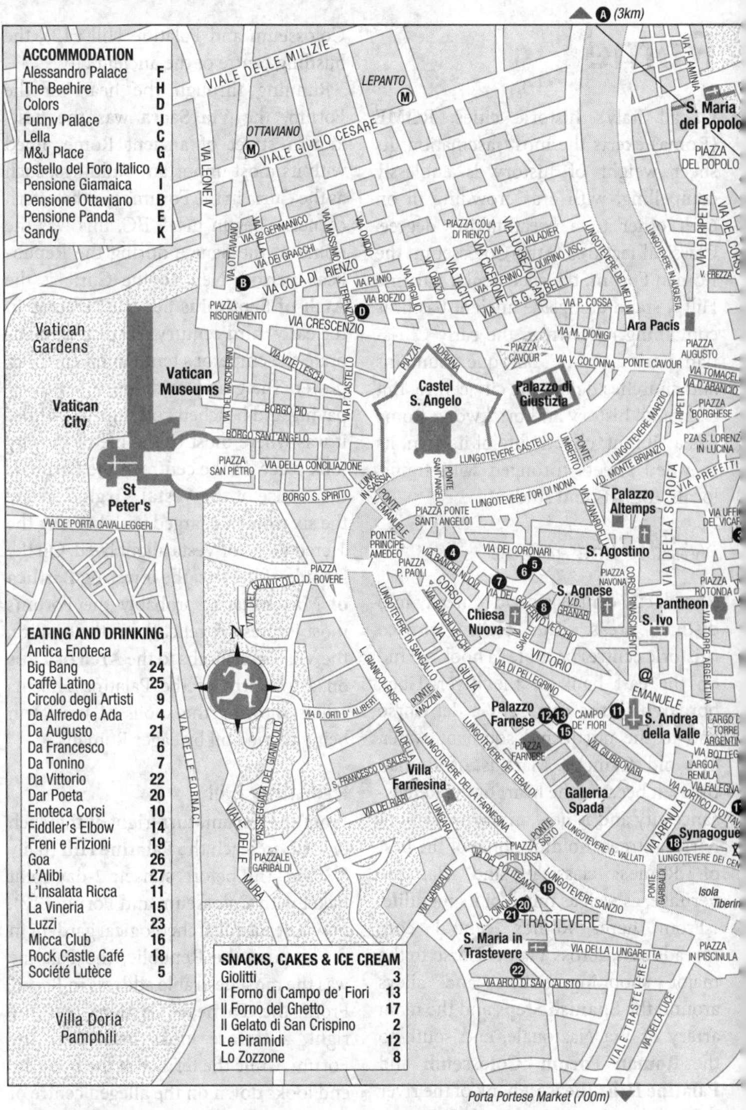

the newly renovated **House of Augustus** (Mon, Wed, Sat & Sun 11am–6pm), which holds beautiful frescoes in striking shades of blue, red and ochre, dating back to 30 BC and considered to be among the most magnificent examples of Roman wall paintings anywhere; even the builders' ancient graffiti has been meticulously preserved.

The Capitoline Hill

Formerly the spiritual and political centre of the Roman Empire, the Capitoline Hill lies behind the Neoclassical Vittoriano monument on traffic-choked Piazza Venezia. Atop the Capitoline is one of Rome's most elegant squares, **Piazza del Campidoglio**, designed by Michelangelo in the 1530s and flanked by the two wings

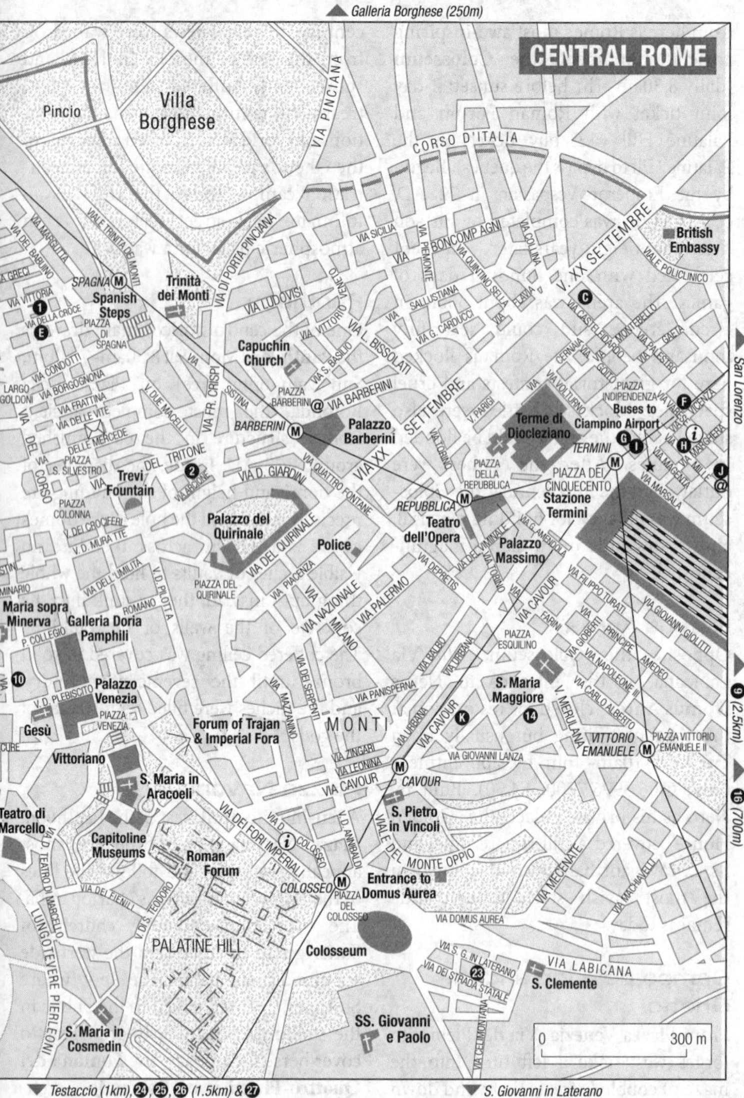

of one of the city's most important museums of ancient art – and the oldest public gallery in the world, dating back to 1471 – the **Capitoline Museums** (Tues–Sun 9am–8pm; €6.50). The Palazzo Nuovo, the museum's left-hand wing, contains some of the best of the city's Roman and Greek sculpture. Highlights of the Palazzo dei Conservatori opposite include various parts of the colossal statue of the Emperor Constantine which once stood in the Forum, and sixteenth-century frescoes.

Colosseum

Immediately outside the Forum, the fourth-century **Arch of Constantine** marks the end of the Via Sacra. Across

from here is Rome's most awe-inspiring ancient monument, the **Colosseum** (daily 8.30am–1hr before sunset; 2-day joint ticket with Roman Forum and Palatine Hill €12; buy tickets at the Palatine Hill to bypass the queues). Begun by the Emperor Vespasian in 72 AD, construction was completed by his son Titus about eight years later – an event celebrated with one hundred days of games. The arena was about 500m in circumference and could seat fifty thousand people; the Romans flocked here for gladiatorial contests and cruel spectacles. Mock sea battles were also staged here – the arena could be flooded in minutes. After the games were outlawed in the fifth century, the Colosseum was pillaged for building material, and is now little more than a magnificent shell.

Domus Aurea

Opposite the Colosseum, off Via Labicana, is the entrance to Nero's **Domus Aurea** (closed for restoration at the time of writing but usually open Tues–Fri 10am–4pm by appointment only; ⓣ06.3996.7700; €4.50). Built by Nero as his private palace, the "Golden House" covered a full square mile, and its extravagant halls were decorated in the most lavish style, though little remains today.

Campo de' Fiori and the Ghetto

From Piazza Venezia, Via del Plebiscito forges west; take a left turn into the maze of cobbled streets that wind down to pretty **Campo de' Fiori**, one-time heart of the medieval city, now home to a colourful produce market (Mon–Sat 6am–2pm). Surrounded by bars, it's a great spot to watch the *passeggiata* (early-evening stroll).

A short walk from here, east of Via Arenula, a warren of narrow streets make up the Ghetto. Having moved here from Trastevere in the thirteenth century, the city's Jews were walled off from the rest of the city in 1556, and subsequently suffered centuries of ill treatment, culminating in the deportations of World War II, when a quarter of the Ghetto's population died in concentration camps. Today, the area has an intimate, back-street feel, and is an atmospheric place for a wander.

Pantheon

One of the centro storico's main draws is the **Pantheon** (Mon–Sat 8.30am–7.30pm, Sun 9am–6pm; free) on Piazza della Rotonda, the most complete ancient Roman structure in the city, finished around 125 AD. Inside, the diameter of the dome and height of the building are precisely equal, and the hole in the dome's centre is a full 9m across; there are no visible arches or vaults to hold the whole thing up – instead, they're sunk into the concrete of the walls of the building. The coffered ceiling was covered in solid bronze until the seventeenth century, and the niches were filled with statues of the gods.

Piazza Navona

A ten-minute stroll west of the Pantheon, **Piazza Navona** is one of the city's most appealing squares, and follows the lines of the Emperor Domitian's chariot arena. The Borromini-designed church of **Sant'Agnese in Agone** on the west side supposedly stands on the spot where St Agnes, exposed naked to the public in the stadium, miraculously grew hair to cover herself. Opposite, the **Fontana dei Quattro Fiumi** is by Borromini's arch-rival, Bernini; each figure represents one of the four great rivers of the world – the Nile, Danube, Ganges and Plate – though only the horse, symbolizing the Danube, was actually carved by Bernini.

The Ara Pacis and around

Walking north along the Lungotevere (riverside drive) from here, you'll arrive at the striking **Ara Pacis** (Tues–Sun

9am–7pm; €6.50). Built in 13 BC to celebrate Augustus's victory over Spain and Gaul, the "altar of peace" is housed in a slick travertine and glass container designed by American architect Richard Meier in 2006. Inside, the altar supports a frieze showing Augustus and his family.

Via di Ripetta arrows north from here to harmonious **Piazza del Popolo**, where the church of **Santa Maria del Popolo** (daily 7am–noon & 4–7pm) holds some of the best Renaissance art of any Roman church. Two pictures by Caravaggio attract the most attention – the *Conversion of St Paul* and the *Crucifixion of St Peter*.

Villa Borghese

Leafy **Villa Borghese,** just a few minutes' stroll east of Piazza del Popolo, is a tranquil haven from the noise of the city. It harbours several fine museums (see Ⓦwww.villaborghese.it for details), not least the **Galleria Borghese** (Tues–Sun 9am–7pm; timed entry every 2hr; Ⓣ06.32.810; call to book at least a day in advance; €10.50), a dazzling collection of mainly Italian art and sculpture. Highlights include Canova's sculpted marble *Pauline*, the sister of Napoleon portrayed as a reclining Venus, in Room 1; spectacular sculptures by Bernini in rooms 2–4; and the six Caravaggios in Room 8. The picture gallery upstairs contains masterpieces by Antonello da Messina, Raphael, Rubens, Titian and many more.

The Spanish Steps and Trevi Fountain

The area immediately southeast of Piazza del Popolo is historically the artistic quarter of the city, with a distinctly cosmopolitan air. At the centre of the district, long, thin **Piazza di Spagna** features the distinctive boat-shaped Barcaccia fountain, the last work of Bernini's father. The **Spanish Steps** – a venue for international posing – sweep up from the piazza to the sixteenth-century church of **Trinità dei Monti**. From the top of the Spanish Steps, narrow Via Sistina winds down to Piazza Barberini, dominated by Bernini's Fontana del Tritone, its muscular Triton held up by four dolphins. West down Via del Tritone, hidden among a web of narrow streets, is one of Rome's more surprising sights – the **Trevi Fountain**, a deafening gush of water over Baroque statues and rocks built onto the back of a Renaissance palace, which can barely be seen for the crowds.

Trastevere

Over on the Tiber's west bank, picturesque **Trastevere**, once the city's shabby bohemian quarter, is now somewhat gentrified, and home to much of the city's most vibrant nightlife and some of its best restaurants. On Sunday morning, the sprawling **Porta Portese** flea market (5am–2pm; bus #H from Termini station) stretches down Via Portuense to Trastevere station in a congested medley of antiques, clothing and junk.

The hub of the area is **Piazza di Santa Maria in Trastevere**, and the magnificent twelfth-century church of the same name on the western side of the square. Held to be the first official church in Rome, built on a site where a fountain of oil is said to have sprung on the day of Christ's birth, it is resplendent with thirteenth-century mosaics.

Trastevere's other main sight is the church of **Santa Cecilia,** built on the site of the second-century home of the patron saint of music. Locked in the hot chamber of her baths for several days, she sang her way through the ordeal, securing her status as the patron saint of music, until her head was hacked half off with an axe.

St Peter's basilica

The **Vatican City**, a tiny territory north of Trastevere, is partly hemmed in by high walls, but opens its doors to the rest of the city in the form of Bernini's **Piazza San**

Pietro. **St Peter's** (daily 7am–6.30/7pm; free) was built to a plan initially conceived at the end of the fifteenth century by Bramante and finished off over a century later by Carlo Maderno, bridging the Renaissance and Baroque eras. The interior is full of Baroque features, although the first thing you see, on the right, is Michelangelo's *Pietà*, completed when he was just 24. On the right-hand side of the nave, the bronze statue of St Peter was cast in the thirteenth century by Arnolfo di Cambio. Bronze was also used in Bernini's imposing 28m-high *baldacchino*, the centrepiece of the sculptor's embellishment of the interior. To the right of the main doors, you can ascend by stairs or lift to the **roof**, from where there's a steep walk up 320 steps to the **dome** (daily 8am–5/6pm; €5, €7 with lift), well worth the effort for its glorious views over the city.

The Vatican Museums

A ten-minute walk from the northern side of Piazza San Pietro takes you to the **Vatican Museums** (Mon–Sat 9am–6pm; last admission 4pm; last Sun of each month 9am–2pm; last admission 12.30pm; €14, €8 students under 26; last Sun of the month free) – quite simply the largest, richest museum complex in the world, stuffed with treasures from every period of the city's history. The queues to get in can be daunting – go 2–3 hours before the museum closes to avoid the crush. If you're pushed for time, start off at the **Stanze di Raffaello**, at the opposite end of the building to the entrance, a set of rooms decorated for Pope Julius II by Raphael among others. Raphael's *School of Athens* fresco depicts his artistic contemporaries as classical figures: Leonardo is Plato and Michelangelo the serious-looking Heraclitus. Other highlights include the **Galleria Chiaramonte**, a superb collection of Roman statues, and the **Galleria delle Carte Geografiche**, with its incredibly precise, richly pigmented maps of Italy.

The **Sistine Chapel**, of course, is the main draw. Built for Pope Sixtus IV in 1481, it serves as the pope's private chapel and hosts the conclaves of cardinals for the election of each new pope. The paintings down each side wall depict scenes from the lives of Moses and Christ by Perugino, Botticelli and Ghirlandaio, among others. But it's Michelangelo's ceiling frescoes of the *Creation* that everyone comes to see, executed almost single-handedly over a period of about four years for Pope Julius II. The *Last Judgment*, on the west wall of the chapel, was painted by Michelangelo over twenty years later. The nudity caused controversy from the start, and the pope's zealous successor, Pius IV, insisted that loincloths be added – removed in a recent restoration.

Arrival

Air Rome has two airports. Leonardo da Vinci, better known as Fiumicino, handles all scheduled flights; Ciampino is for charter services and low-cost flights. Two train services link Fiumicino to Rome: the Leonardo Express to Termini (every 30min until 11.37pm; 30min; €11), and the FMI to Trastevere, Ostiense and Tiburtina stations (every 30min until 11.27pm; €5.50). Terravision coach services (Ⓦ www.lowcostcoach.com) travel to Termini station (1hr 10min; €7). From Ciampino, two operators make the 40min trip to Termini station: Terravision (€4) and SIT bus (€5). The cheapest way of getting into town is to take an Atral bus to Anagnina metro stop, then a metro to Termini station (€2.20), though this will take twice as long.
Bus Domestic bus services arrive at the bus terminal outside Stazione Tiburtina.
Train The main train station is Termini, meeting-point of the metro lines and city bus routes. Some long-distance services use Stazione Tiburtina, particularly at night. The two stations are connected by metro and bus.

Information

Tourist office The best place to go for information is Enjoy Rome (Mon–Fri 8.30/9am–6.30/7pm, Sat 8.30am–2pm; Via Marghera 8a Ⓣ 06.445.0734, Ⓦ www.enjoyrome.com), a friendly, independently-run tourist office, staffed by English-speakers, which

offers maps, advice and a free accommodation-finding service, and organizes walking tours. Near the Colosseum on Via dei Fori Imperiali, I Fori di Roma (daily 9.30am–6.30pm; ⓣ06.679.7702) is an information centre with plenty of maps and pamphlets. There's also a tourist information booth at Fiumicino airport (daily 8am–7pm; ⓣ06.6595.4471), and green tourist information kiosks (PIT) near every major sight (daily 9.30am–7.30pm). ⓦwww.060608.it is a council-run tourist website; you can also call ⓣ06.0608 (daily 9am–9pm).

Discount passes The Roma Pass (€23 for three days; ⓦwww.romapass.it) is well worth investing in – it gives you free access to all public transport within the city, as well as free entry to the first two sights you visit, plus many further discounts. Buy the pass from tourist information kiosks or from participating sights.

City transport

Public transport is cheap and reasonably reliable. A day-pass (BIG; €4), single ticket (BIT; valid for 75min on all public transport, including one trip on the metro; €1), 3-day pass (BTI; €11) or 1-week ticket (CIS; €16) for the metro and bus network can be bought from most newspaper stalls and *tabacchi*, from ticket machines in metro stations and on Piazza dei Cinquecento outside Termini station. Stamp tickets to validate them at the entrance gates to metros and on board buses.

Bus The bus network is extensive; useful routes include the #40 from Termini station, which passes through the centre en route to the Vatican, and #116 from the Barberini metro stop, which serves both Villa Borghese and the centro storico. A network of night buses (*bus notturni*) serves most parts of the city, running roughly hourly until about 5.30am. #N1 follows metro line A; #N2 calls at all stops along metro line B; and #N3 runs from Trastevere to Termini station.

Metro The quickest way to get around, with trains every 3–5min. The city's two metro lines, A and B, meet beneath Termini station and run 5.30am–11.30pm (Fri & Sat till 1.30am).

Taxi A costly way to get around, with the meter starting at €2.80. Depending on luggage and the time of travel, it should cost around €10 to get from Termini to the centre. You can hail one in the street, or try the ranks at Termini and Piazza Venezia.

Accommodation

In high season (April–July, Sept & major religious holidays) Rome is very crowded, so book accommodation as far in advance as possible. If you arrive without a booking, make straight for Enjoy Rome (see opposite). Many of the city's cheaper hotels are located close to Termini station, but it's pretty insalubrious; pay a bit more to stay in the centre if you can.

Hostels

Rome's vast HI hostel, Ostello del Foro Italico (Viale delle Olimpiadi 61 ⓣ06.323.6267, ⓦwww.hostelbooking.com; dorms €19) is way out of the centre and should be a last resort. All of the hostels below offer breakfast and free internet, except where indicated; none have a curfew.

Alessandro Palace Via Vicenza 42 ⓣ06.446.1958, ⓦwww.hostelalessandro.com. Buzzing hostel, with lively international staff, a kitchen and bar. Dorms €25–35, rooms €110.

The Beehive Via Marghera 8 ⓣ06.4470.4553, ⓦwww.the-beehive.com. Funky hotel with designer furnishings, spotless rooms, a café and a sunny garden. Dorms €25, shared-bath rooms €80, rooms in shared apartments nearby €70.

Colors Via Boezio 31 ⓣ06.687.4030, ⓦwww.colorshotel.com. Clean, airy and decorated in zingy colours, *Colors* has friendly, knowledgeable staff and guests have the use of the kitchen and terrace. Breakfast included for private rooms only. Dorms €23–29, private rooms €70.

Funny Palace Via Varese 33 ⓣ06.4470.3523, ⓦwww.funnyhostel.com. Spread over three buildings, this hostel may lack a lively common area but the 4-person dorms are comfortable, with parquet floors and decent beds. Dorms €25, rooms €100

M&J Place Via Solferino 9 ⓣ06.446.2802, ⓦwww.mejplacehostel.com. Quirky murals of Rome decorate the walls of this popular hostel, whose dorms sleep up to 10 people. It's conveniently located above the *Living Room* club. Dorms €20–32.50, shared-bath rooms €100.

Pensione Ottaviano Via Ottaviano 6 ⓣ06.3973.8138, ⓦwww.pensioneottaviano.com. The dorms are simply furnished and on the cramped side, but *Ottaviano* is a good place to meet other travellers, and there are views of St Peter's from the rooms. Dorms €19.90–27.90.

Sandy Via Cavour 136 ⓣ06.488.4585, ⓦwww.sandyhostel.com. Good-value, laid-back hostel near the Colosseum. Dorms €21–33.

Hotels

Lella Via Palestro 9 ⓣ06.484.940, ⓦwww.solomonhotels.com. Though its rates are comparable to the private rooms in Rome's hostels, *Lella*'s ensuites are of a much higher standard – spacious and warmly decorated. Some come with bathtubs, and some with a terrace. €80.

Pensione Giamaica Via Magenta 13 ⓣ06.490.121, ⓔmd0991@mclink.it. If you can look beyond the pea-green walls and old-fashioned decor, this family-run *pensione* with shared-bath rooms in a quiet street near Termini is a bargain. Breakfast is €5 extra, but there is a fridge for guests' use and plenty of bars nearby. €56.

Pensione Panda Via della Croce 35 ⓣ06.678.0179, ⓦwww.hotelpanda.it. Ideally placed near the Spanish Steps, and with neat shared-bath rooms with wood-beamed ceilings, this hotel is in high demand. No breakfast. €78.

Eating

All of Rome's neighbourhoods have at least one food market (generally Mon–Sat 7am–2pm); those at Campo de' Fiori and at Piazza Vittorio Emanuele near Termini have an abundance of stalls selling fresh Italian produce and, in the case of the latter, African fruits and Asian food too. Two central supermarkets are Dì per Dì (Via Poli 47), near the Trevi Fountain, and Conad, a 24hr supermarket in the mall underneath Termini station.

Snacks, cakes and ice cream

Giolitti Via degli Uffici del Vicario 40. Closed Mon. A Roman institution, with a choice of seventy ice cream flavours.

Il Forno di Campo de' Fiori Campo de' Fiori 22. This legendary take-away sells filling slices of pizza for about €1.50 to takeaway – try the potato and rosemary. The bakery next door serves large filled focaccia sandwiches for about €2.70. Closed Sun.

Il Forno del Ghetto Via del Portico d'Ottavia 1. Historic Jewish bakery with marvellous ricotta and dried fruit-filled cakes.

Il Gelato di San Crispino Via della Panetteria 42. Closed Tues. Close to the Trevi fountain and selling some of Rome's best ice cream; the fruit flavours – particularly pear and plum – are outstanding.

Le Piramidi Vicolo del Gallo 11. Closed Mon. Just off Campo de' Fiori, this Middle Eastern takeaway sells tasty falafel and kebabs for around €4.

Lo Zozzone Via del Teatro Pace 32. Tasty takeaway pizza *bianca* (without tomato) with a range of fillings costs around €3.50, or you can eat at one of the outdoor tables for a couple of euros extra.

Restaurants and pizzerias

The centro storico, Trastevere and Testaccio are full of small, family-run restaurants.

Da Alfredo e Ada Via dei Banchi Nuovi 14. Dinner only, Mon–Fri. Genuine home cooking at great prices, in a cosily wood-panelled dining room. Three courses cost less than €20.

Da Augusto Piazza de' Renzi 15. The service may be slapdash, but the setting (an enchanting cobbled piazza) and the food (hearty Roman staples) are what make this rowdy trattoria special. You can have a full meal for €12.

Da Francesco Piazza del Fico 29. This always-heaving trattoria near Piazza Navona serves pizzas (€7) and classic Roman mains such as roast lamb (from €10).

Dar Poeta Vicolo del Bologna 45. One of the best – and cheapest – pizzerias in Rome (try the house special, with courgettes and sausage), so expect to queue. An antipasto, a pizza and a drink will come to around €10.

Da Tonino Via del Governo Vecchio 18/19. Closed Sun. Excellent, unpretentious Roman cooking at low prices; packed at lunch and dinner. *Straccetti con rucola* (strips of beef with rocket) will set you back just €7.

Da Vittorio Via San Cosimato 14a. Closed Sun. Crispy Neapolitan pizza in the heart of Trastevere. Pizza €6.

Enoteca Corsi Via del Gesù 87. Lunch only, but hearty dishes in generous portions and good wines, with a well-stocked wine shop next door (open till 8pm). Pasta €7; mains such as roast veal and potatoes €10.

L'Insalata Ricca Largo dei Chiavari 85. If you can't face another pizza, this place has over thirty types of salad (around €7) on the menu – all freshly prepared and served in huge portions.

Luzzi Via Celimontana 1. Closed Wed. This neighbourhood favourite near the Colosseum, with plenty of outdoor tables, is a fun, raucous place to sample an extensive range of pizza and pasta dishes, plus mainly meaty mains (€6–9).

Drinking and nightlife

The two main areas to go for a drink are Trastevere and the centro storico, particularly around Campo de' Fiori. Bohemian Monti, near the Colosseum, and studenty San Lorenzo, east of Termini, are full of laid-back bars. There's a concentration of clubs in Testaccio, running the gamut from vast glittering palaces to more down-to-earth student places; the

WATER FOUNTAINS

All over Rome, there are small water fountains from which you can drink. The water is ice-cold, clean and free, so bring a water bottle and fill up.

door charge can be anything from €5 to €25. Some of the trendier venues operate a list-only policy; dress up.

Bars

Antica Enoteca Via della Croce 76. Though in the heart of the touristy Spanish Steps area, this atmospheric bar manages to preserve its old-world charm. A buzzy place for an after-dinner drink.
Fiddler's Elbow Via dell'Olmata 43. An Irish pub that's largely frequented by Italians, this tucked-away place is full of cosy, wood-panelled nooks, and the drinks are reasonably priced too.
Freni e Frizioni Via del Politeama 17. This ex-garage (the name means "Brakes and Clutches"), cluttered with vintage machinery, is a popular early-evening hangout, thanks to its generous *aperitivo* buffet – just buy a drink (from €5) and dig in.
La Vineria Campo de' Fiori 15. Closed Mon. Historic *vineria* that spills out onto the square during the summer; drink indoors at a third of the price. If it's packed, try the lively *Sloppy Sam's*, a couple of doors to the left.
Société Lutèce Piazza di Montevecchio 17. Closed Mon. A 10min walk from Piazza Navona in a picturesque piazza, this laid-back bar puts on a free *aperitivo* buffet from 6.30pm – get here early.

Clubs and music venues

Big Bang Via Monte Testaccio 22 ⓣ329.546.6296. Fri & Sat only. Popular venue for live acts and club nights, with a happy hour from 10pm till midnight. DJs play anything from rock to new wave to indie.
Caffè Latino Via Monte Testaccio 96 ⓣ06.5728.8556. Closed Mon & Tues. One of Testaccio's longest-established clubs – despite the name, the music is mainly funk, disco and chart.
Circolo degli Artisti Via Casilina Vecchia 42 ⓦwww.circoloartisti.it. Closed Mon. Huge bar, disco and garden with live indie-rock; cheap and fun. Bus #412 from Via del Tritone.
Goa Via Libetta 13 ⓣ06.574.8277. Closed Mon. One of Rome's historic clubs, with ethno-industrial decor and big-name DJs.
L'Alibi Via Monte Testaccio 40. Predominantly – but not exclusively – male venue that's one of Rome's best gay clubs. Downstairs cellar disco and upstairs open-air bar.
Micca Club Via Pietro Micca 7a ⓦwww.miccaclub.com. Closed Mon, Tues & June–Aug. DJ sets, live acts and monthly burlesque nights in a cool, brick-vaulted space.
Rock Castle Café Via B. Cenci 8 ⓣ06.6880.7999. This long-established "disco pub" consists of six medieval-style rooms. The music is mainly rock, hip-hop and pop, attracting a lively, studenty crowd.

Entertainment

Cinemas Those showing films in English include the Nuovo Olimpia (Via in Lucina 16G, off Via del Corso), and the Metropolitan at Via del Corso 7. *RomaC'è*, a comprehensive listings guide (out Wed, €1), contains a short English section.
Classical music The city's churches host a wide range of concerts, many of them free. International names appear at Rome's Auditorium in the northern suburbs (Viale P. de Coubertin; ⓣ06.808.2058, ⓦwww.auditorium.com; bus #M from Termini).
Opera The opera scene is concentrated on the Teatro dell'Opera, Piazza B. Gigli in winter (ⓣ06.4816.0255, ⓦwww.operaroma.it) and various outdoor venues in summer.

FESTIVALS

Festival delle Letterature ⓦwww.festivaldelleletterature.it. The floodlit Basilica of Maxentius provides a stunning backdrop to readings by international authors. June.
Estate Romana ⓦwww.estateromana.comune.roma.it. Events including concerts and cultural happenings – many of them free – in parks and piazzas around town. June–Sept.
La Festa di Noantri Piazza Santa Maria in Trastevere and around. Trastevere's traditional summer festival in honour of the Virgin, with street stalls selling snacks and trinkets, and a grand finale of fireworks. Last two weeks of July.
RomaEuropa Festival ⓦwww.romaeuropa.net. A cutting-edge performing arts festival, generally with some big-name acts, in locations around town. Mid-Sept to Nov.
Rome Film Festival ⓦwww.romacinemafest.it. A host of film stars descend on the city for its annual film festival, and there are enough screenings, retrospectives and events to keep film fans happy. Mid- to end Oct.

Shopping

Shops With the exception of the Galleria Alberto Sordi on Via del Corso, malls and department stores are few and far between. The boutiques around Piazza di Spagna are for big-spenders only, but nearby Via del Corso is lined with shops selling cheap-to-mid-range clothing, books and CDs. Other mainstream outlets can be found along Via Cola di Rienzo near the Vatican, and Via Nazionale, off Piazza della Repubblica. Via del Governo Vecchio off Piazza Navona has a string of great vintage stores, and the alleys off Campo de' Fiori harbour independent jewellery and clothing shops.
Markets Porta Portese flea market (see p.661) is the city's best known, but Via Sannio (Mon–Fri 8.30am–1.30pm, Sat 8.30am–6pm; metro San Giovanni) is also a great place to find vintage bargains.

Directory

Embassies Australia, Via Antonio Bosio 5 ⓣ06.852.721; Canada, Via Salaria 243 ⓣ06.85444.3937; New Zealand, Via Clitunno 44 ⓣ06.853.7501; UK, Via XX Settembre 80 ⓣ06.4220.0001; US, Via V. Veneto 119 ⓣ06.46.741.
Exchange Offices at Termini station operate out of banking hours; also Yex (see "Internet" below).
Hospitals Ambulance ⓣ118; central hospital: Policlinico Umberto I ⓣ06.49.971; International Medical Center ⓣ06.488.2371.
Internet Yex (Corso Vittorio Emanuele 106; daily 8am–2am; €2.90/30min) is a central option; Splashnet (see "Laundry") has lots of terminals too (€1/30min).
Laundry Splashnet at Via Varese 33; €3–5.20 per load (6–10kg).
Left luggage At Termini station (daily 6am–11.50pm; €4 for the first 5hr, then €0.60/hr).
Pharmacies PIRAM, Via Nazionale 228 (24hr), near Termini. Rota posted on pharmacy doors.
Police Emergencies ⓣ112; main police station (*questura*) at Via S. Vitale ⓣ06.46.861.
Post office Piazza San Silvestro 19 (Mon–Fri 8am–7pm, Sat 8am–1.15pm).

Moving on

Air Cagliari (1 daily; 1hr 10min).
Bus Agrigento (1 daily; 13hr 30min); Amalfi (summer 1–2 daily; 5hr); Lecce (4 daily; 7–9hr); Palermo (1daily; 12hr 30min); Perugia (4–5 daily; 3hr); Sorrento (2 daily; 4hr).
Train Bologna (every 15min; 2hr 40min–3hr 40min); Florence (every 15min; 1hr 30min–3hr); Milan (every 15min; 4hr–6hr 20min); Naples (every 30min; 1hr 20min–2hr 50min); Turin (8 daily; 5hr 40min–8hr 30min); Paris (7 daily; 12–16hr); Vienna (4 daily; 12hr 45min–13hr 30min); Zurich (9 daily; 7hr 30min–13hr).

Northwest Italy

The northwest of Italy is many people's first experience of the country, and while it often represents its least stereotypical "Italian" aspect, there are some iconic towns in the area. The vibrant city of **Turin** was the first capital of Italy after the Unification in 1860, and still holds many reminders of its past. **Milan**, the upbeat capital of the heavily industrial region of **Lombardy**, continues to be taken seriously for its business and fashion credentials, The region of **Liguria** to the south is home to the country's most spectacular stretch of coastline. The chief town of the province is the sprawling port of **Genoa**, while southeast, towards Tuscany, the **Cinque Terre**'s rugged stretch of coastline continues to wow travellers with its cliff-top villages and clear blue waters.

TURIN

Following the 2006 Winter Olympics, **TURIN** (Torino) – a virtual Fiat company town and the home of Martini and Lavazza coffee – has emerged resplendent with gracious avenues, opulent palaces and splendid galleries. It's a lively, bustling place with cafés, nightlife and contemporary art to rival any European city.

What to see and do

The grid plan of the Baroque centre makes finding your way around easy. **Via Roma** is the central spine, a grand affair lined with designer

shops and ritzy cafés and punctuated by the city's most elegant piazzas, notably **Piazza San Carlo**. Around the corner, the **Museo Egizio** (Tues–Sun 8.30am–7.30pm; €7.50) holds a superb collection of Egyptian antiquities. A ten-minute walk northwest brings you to the fifteenth-century **Duomo**, home of the Turin Shroud, which is kept under wraps and away from the public's eyes. This piece of cloth, imprinted with the image of a man's body, had long been claimed as the shroud in which Christ was wrapped after his crucifixion, although 1989 carbon-dating tests suggested that it was a medieval fake, made between 1260 and 1390.

The **Palazzo Madama**, looming over **Piazza Castello**, is architecturally stunning, and has a collection of Baroque, Gothic, Renaissance and decorative art on show (Tues–Sat 10am–6pm; Sun 10am–8pm; free). East of Via Roma, the **Mole Antonelliana**, which Turin residents proudly call the "Eiffel Tower of Turin", boasts great views over the city from the top of its panoramic lift (Mon–Fri & Sun 9am–8pm, Sat 9am–11pm; €4, €6 including museum).

SKIING THE MILKY WAY

The snow-capped peaks surrounding Turin are home to some of the best ski slopes in the region. Known collectively as the **Milky Way**, the five Italian resorts hosted the 2006 Winter Olympics. The resorts are Sestriere (2035m), Sauze d'Oulx (1509m), Sasicario (1700m) Cesana Torinses (1350m) and Claviere (1850m). Sestriere is the most sophisticated, while Sauze d'Oulx is great for its après-ski scene. All the towns are linked by ski lifts, and a daily ski pass costs an affordable €41. Getting to the slopes is reasonably straightforward, and involves a train from Turin to Oulx (hourly; 1hr 15min), and then a bus to your chosen destination. The tourist office in Torino can supply a full list of timetables and accommodation.

Museums

Turin has a good selection of modern art museums: the **Galleria Civica d'Arte Moderna e Contemporanea (GAM)**, on Via Magenta 31 (Tues–Sun 9am–7pm; €7.50), holds works dating from the eighteenth century to the present day, by artists such as Giorgio de Chirico and Lucio Fontana. For more contemporary art, the **Castello di Rivoli**, 20km outside Turin (Tues–Sun 10am–5pm; €6.50), is home to the most important collection of postwar art in Italy, with works by Jeff Koons, Carl Andre and Mario Merz. On weekdays, take bus #36 from Piazza Statuto and then walk for twenty minutes; at weekends, there's an (infrequent) direct shuttle bus from Piazza Castello.

Arrival and information

Air Take the train to Turino Dora (€5.50, every 30min). From here bus #52 goes to Porta Nuova. In July and August a train runs straight to Porta Nuova. Ask in the station for up-to-date timetables.
Train Turin's main train station is Porta Nuova.
Tourist office The main office is located in the Atrium at Piazza Solferino (Mon–Sun 9.30am–7pm; ⓣ011.535.181, ⓦwww.turismotorino.org). There is a smaller centre at Porta Nuova train station (Mon–Sat 9.30am–7pm, Sun 9.30am–3pm).
Discount passes Pick up a Torino Card (€15/two days, €17/three days) for travel on all buses, entrance to all museums and discounts on theatre and concert tickets.
Internet Internet Train, Via Carlo Alberto 18, or 28 Via delle Orfane, also has cheap international calls (internet €2/hr).
Post office Via San Domenico 19.

Accommodation

Many of Turin's budget hotels are off Via Nizza, just one block over from the train station. The streets opposite Porta Nuova, close to Piazza Carlo Felice, are more expensive but smarter.
Bella Vista Via Galliari 15 ⓣ011.669.9121. Top-floor hotel with big windows and comfortable beds, just a short walk from the station. €50.

Hotel Due Mondi 3 Via Saluzzo ⓣ011.650.5084, ⓦwww.hotelduemondi.it Large, comfortable rooms in a boutique-style hotel. Discounts are available. €50.
Open 011 Corso Venezia ⓣ011.250.535. Welcoming hostel with helpful staff and large, spotless rooms. Take the train to Torino Dora, or get bus #46 (Dora stop), #52 (Viba stop) or #10 from Porto Nuova station. Dorm bed €17.50.
Ostello Torino Via Alby 1 ⓣ011.660.2939. Inviting HI hostel with small rooms and internet access; 30min walk from Porta Nuova or take bus #52. Dorm bed €14.50.
Paradiso Via Berthollet 3 ⓣ011.669.8678. Clean one-star hotel close to the train station. €40.

Eating

Gran Bar Piazza Gran Madre di Dio 2. Cool wine and coffee bar, overlooking the river, with cheerful staff. Also serves delicious sandwiches. Mains from €5.
Il Bacardo Piazza della Consolata 1. A reasonably priced restaurant with lovely outdoor seating and known for its delicious cakes.
San Augusto Via San Quintino. Simply the best pizzeria in Turin. The menu includes local delicacies such the deliciously smelly *taleggio* cheese fondue (€8).
Urbani Via Saluzzo. Thronged with locals, this classy place serves cheap meals. Pizzas from €5.

Drinking and nightlife

The liveliest areas are Il Quadrilatero, a few minutes west of Piazza Castello, Via San Quintino, and the Murazzi on the edge of the River Po, where people congregate at outside tables. For what's on, look out for the pamphlet *Zero*, free from bars. The standard price for drinks is around €6 for cocktails and €3–5 for beers.
AEIOU Via Spanzotti 3 ⓣ011.385.8580. Big warehouse-style club for dancing all night; features rock, Cuban, jam sessions, art and theatre projects. Entrance usually free.
Arancia di Mexxarate Piazza Emanuele Filiberto. Buzzy place with tables crammed together outside. Serves drinks until 4am.
Fusion Café San Agostino 17. Cocktails and snacks, outdoor seating and atmospheric lighting.
Jam Club Arcate Murazzi del Po. An extensive club with a different DJ every night. Free entry for women until 12.30am, otherwise entrance €5; the busy bar opposite overlooks the river.

Moving on

Train Geneva (every 2hr; change at Milan; 6–7hr); Genoa (every 30min; 1hr 45min); La Spezia (frequent; 3hr); Lyon (twice daily; change at Chambery; 5hr); Milan (frequent; 1hr 50min); Nice (every hour; change at Ventimiglia; 4hr 45min); Paris (4 daily; 5hr 45min); Rome (frequent; 7hr); Venice (frequent; 4hr 30min).

MILAN

MILAN (Milano) is the capital of Italy's fashion and design industry, a fast-paced and somewhat unfriendly business city ruled by consumerism and the work ethic. The swanky shops and nightlife are a big draw, but it's a historic place, too – the Gothic cathedral has few peers in Italy, while Leonardo da Vinci's iconic fresco of *The Last Supper* is unmissable.

What to see and do

Piazza del Duomo

A good place to start a tour of Milan is **Piazza del Duomo**, the city's historic centre and home to the world's largest Gothic cathedral, begun in 1386 and not completed till almost five centuries later. The gloomy interior gives access to the cathedral's fourth-century **baptistery** (Tues–Sun 9.45am–12.45pm & 2–5.45pm; €1.50) and the **cathedral roof** (Tues–Sun 9am–5pm; €5.50 by elevator, €4 on foot), where you are surrounded by a forest of lacy Gothic carving and subjected to superb views of the city. The **Museo del Duomo** (daily 10am–1.15pm & 3–6pm; €6) displays casts of many of the three thousand or so statues and gargoyles that spike the cathedral. On the north side of the piazza, the opulent **Galleria Vittorio Emanuele II** is a cruciform glass-domed gallery designed in 1865 by Giuseppe Mengoni, who was killed when he fell from the roof a few days before the inaugural ceremony. The

Galleria leads through to the world-famous eighteenth-century **La Scala** opera house.

Pinacoteca di Brera

At the far end of Via Brera is Milan's most prestigious gallery, the awe-inspiring **Pinacoteca di Brera** (Tues–Sun 8.30am–7.30pm; €7.50), filled with works looted from the churches and aristocratic collections of French-occupied Italy.

Castello Sforzesco

To the west, the **Castello Sforzesco** rises imperiously from the mayhem of **Foro Buonaparte**, laid out by Napoleon as part of a grand plan for the city. The castle houses the **Museo d'Arte Antica** and **Pinacoteca** (both Tues–Sun 9am–5.30pm; €3) – the former contains Michelangelo's *Rondanini Pietà,* the latter paintings by Vincenzo Foppa, the leading Milanese artist before Leonardo da Vinci.

Santa Maria delle Grazie and the Last Supper

South of the Castello, the church of **Santa Maria delle Grazie** is Milan's main attraction. A Gothic pile, partially rebuilt by Bramante (who added the massive dome), it is famous for its fresco of *The Last Supper* by Leonardo da Vinci, which covers one wall of the refectory. Advance booking is essential (call ⓣ02.8942.1146; viewing Tues–Sun 8am–7pm; €8).

Arrival and information

Air Linate is Milan's closest airport, 7km from the city centre and connected by the airport bus to Stazione Centrale (every 30min, 6.05am–9.35pm; 20min; €2.50). Ordinary city buses (#73; €1) also run until around midnight from Linate to Piazza San Babila. Malpensa airport is 50km away towards Lago Maggiore and connected by train to Cadorna station (every 30min; €9) and by bus with Stazione Centrale (until 10.30pm; €5.50).

Bus Buses arrive at and depart from Piazza Castello, in front of the Castello Sforzesco.

Train Most international trains pull in at the Stazione Centrale, northeast of the centre on Piazza Duca d'Aosta (metro lines MM2 or MM3).

Tourist office The main tourist office is at Stazione Centrale (Mon–Sat 9am–6pm, Sun 9am–1pm & 2–5pm; ⓣ02.7252.4301/2/3, ⓦwww.provincia.milano.it) and is tricky to find – go up in the elevator to the second floor and it's on the right, through a neon-lit archway into what looks like a disused gallery. There's another at Via Marconi 1, off Piazza Duomo (daily 8.45am–1pm & 2–6pm; Sun 9am–1pm & 2–5pm; same number). Both have the ever-helpful free listings guide, *Milano Mese*, in Italian and English and the *Milan by Night* map, as well as the *Zero* listings guide.

City transport

Bus, metro and tram An efficient network of trams, buses and metro (stations denoted below as MM) runs 6am–midnight. There are interconnecting stations so you can change from metro onto overground and back.

Night bus These take over after the other options close, and run until 1am following the train routes, or until about 3am following alternative routes.

Tickets Tickets (normally valid 1hr 15min; €1) can be used for one journey only on the metro or as many bus and tram journeys as you can make in that time; alternatively buy a *blochetto* of ten tickets (€9.20), or a 24hr ticket (€3), valid on metro, tram and buses, from the Centrale or Duomo metro stations.

Accommodation

There are plenty of one-star hotels, mostly concentrated in the area around Stazione Centrale, and along Viale Vittorio Veneto and Corso Buenos Aires. When there is an "exposition" on (there are about 25 a year, lasting 2–3 days each) prices rocket.

ACISJF Corso Garibaldi 121 ⓣ02.2900.0164. Hostel run by nuns and open to women under 25 only. Accommodation is in four-bedded rooms. Dorm bed €18.

Ciao Bella 4 Via Balzaretti ⓣ02.2395.1135. A friendly, welcoming hostel with large en-suite rooms. There's a terrace and private garden for guests to relax in as well as wi-fi throughout. 25min walk from Stazione Centrale or take the metro three stops to Piola. Dorm bed €27.

Hotel Demidoff 2 Via Plinio, ⓦwww.hoteldemidoffmilan.com. Rooms are slightly on

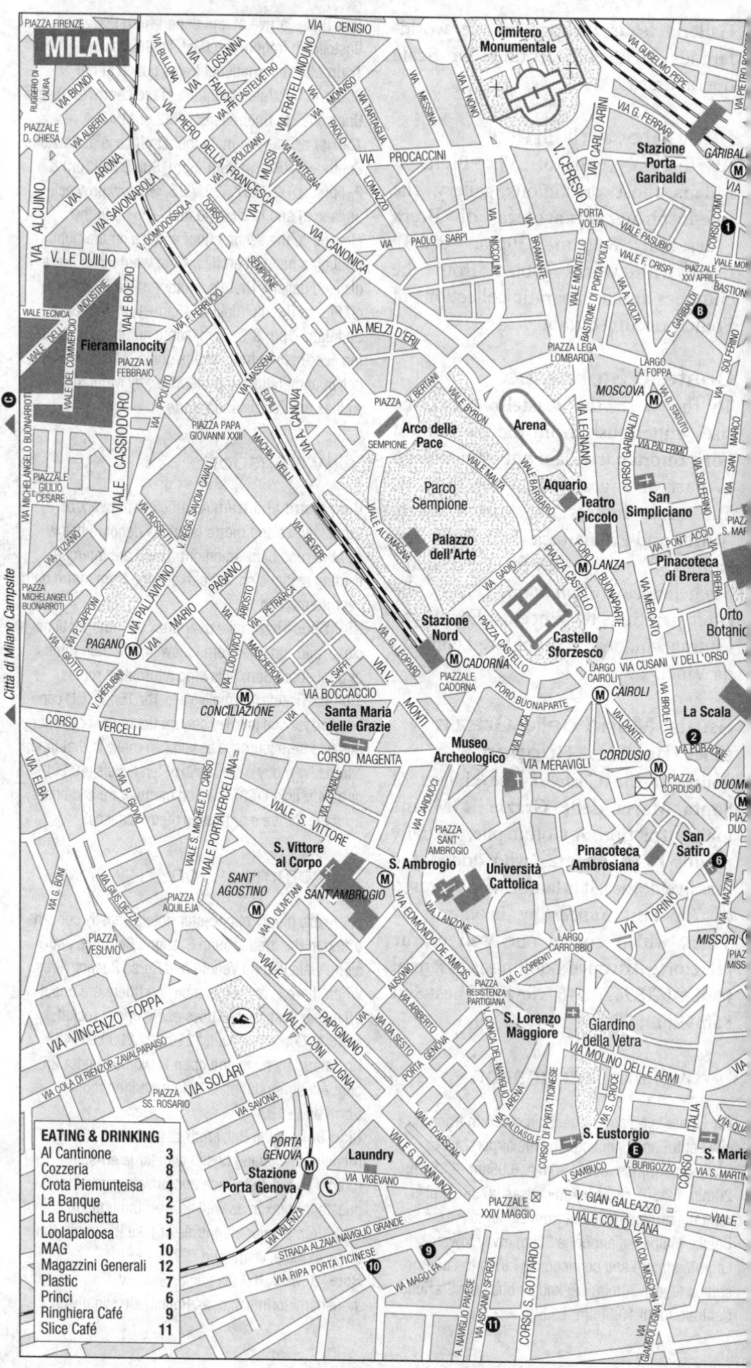
MILAN
EATING & DRINKING
Al Cantinone 3
Cozzeria 8
Crota Piemunteisa 4
La Banque 2
La Bruschetta 5
Loolapaloosa 1
MAG 10
Magazzini Generali 12
Plastic 7
Princi 6
Ringhiera Café 9
Slice Café 11
Città di Milano Campsite
Cimitero Monumentale
Stazione Porta Garibaldi
GARIBALDI
Fieramilanocity
Arco della Pace
Arena
Parco Sempione
Aquario
Teatro Piccolo
San Simpliciano
Palazzo dell'Arte
Pinacoteca di Brera
Orto Botanico
Stazione Nord
Castello Sforzesco
La Scala
Santa Maria delle Grazie
Museo Archeologico
S. Vittore al Corpo
S. Ambrogio
Università Cattolica
Pinacoteca Ambrosiana
San Satiro
S. Lorenzo Maggiore
Giardino della Vetra
S. Eustorgio
Laundry
Stazione Porta Genova
MOSCOVA
LANZA
CADORNA
CAIROLI
CORDUSIO
DUOMO
MISSORI
PAGANO
CONCILIAZIONE
SANT' AGOSTINO
SANT'AMBROGIO
PORTA GENOVA
VIA CENISIO
VIA PROCACCINI
VIA PAOLO SARPI
VIA CANONICA
VIA MELZI D'ERIL
CORSO SEMPIONE
VIA ALCUINO
V. LE DUILIO
VIALE CASSIODORO
VIA MARIO PAGANO
VIA BOCCACCIO
CORSO VERCELLI
CORSO MAGENTA
VIA MERAVIGLI
VIALE S. VITTORE
VIA TORINO
VIA MOLINO DELLE ARMI
VIA VINCENZO FOPPA
VIA SOLARI
VIALE CONI ZUGNA
VIA VIGEVANO
STRADA ALZAIA NAVIGLIO GRANDE
VIA RIPA PORTA TICINESE
VIALE COL DI LANA
V. GIAN GALEAZZO
PIAZZALE XXIV MAGGIO
CORSO S. GOTTARDO
CORSO DI PORTA TICINESE
CORSO ITALIA
VIALE G. D'ANNUNZIO
PIAZZALE CADORNA
FORO BUONAPARTE
PIAZZA CASTELLO
LARGO CAIROLI
VIA DANTE
VIA CUSANI
VIA BROLETTO
CORSO GARIBALDI
VIA LEGNANO
PORTA VOLTA
PIAZZA LEGA LOMBARDA
LARGO LA FOPPA
LARGO CARROBBIO
PIAZZA RESISTENZA PARTIGIANA
VIA EDMONDO DE AMICIS
PIAZZA SANT' AMBROGIO
PIAZZA AQUILEJA
PIAZZA VESUVIO
PIAZZA SS. ROSARIO
PIAZZA FIRENZE
PIAZZA VI FEBBRAIO
PIAZZA PAPA GIOVANNI XXIII
PIAZZALE GIULIO CESARE
PIAZZA MICHELANGELO BUONARROTI
VIA MICHELANGELO BUONARROTI

Stazione Centrale
Canadian Consulate
US Consulate
Giardini Pubblici
Museo Civico di Storia Naturale
PAC
Villa Reale
Exchange
Museo Bagatti Valsecchi
Museo Poldi Pezzoli
Palazzo Marino
UK Consulate
Australian Consulate
Galleria Vittorio Emanuele II
Duomo
Museo del Duomo
Palazzo Reale
Ospedale Maggiore (Università)
Palazzo di Giustizia
Torre Velasca
Giardino della Guastalla
Rotonda della Besana
S. Nazaro
Stazione Porta Vittoria
Linate Airport
ACCOMMODATION
ACISJF B
Ciao Bella D
Hotel Demidoff A
La Cordata Casa Scout E
Piero Rotta C
0 500 m

the small side, but it's very close to the main train station and the chic Corso Buenos Aires shops. €46.
La Cordata Casa Scout Via Burigozzo 11 ⓣ02.5831.4675, ⓔostello@lacordata.it. Well-equipped hostel superbly located for the canal area; free internet and no curfew. Dorm bed €18.
Piero Rotta HI Hostel Via Martino Bassi 2 ⓣ02.3926.7095, ⓦwww.ostellionline.org. This huge official HI hostel is relaxing and has comfortable beds. Although it's a little way from the centre and located in the red light area of Milan, it's a cheap option. No curfew, check-out 10am. Metro QT8 then a 7min walk down Via Salmoiraghi. Dorm bed €19.

Eating

Al Cantinone Via Agnello 19. Famous old trattoria and bar, with home-made pasta and some choice wines, frequented by city suits at lunchtime. Pastas €5, mains €6.
Cozzeria Via Lodovico Muratori 7. This is the place to head to if you're a fan of seafood. Mussels are sold by the kilo (a serving of mussels with chips €14).
Crota Piemunteisa Piazza Beccaria 10. A vast array of chunky sandwiches for around €4.40.
La Bruschetta Piazza Beccaria 12. One of the best-known city-centre pizzerias, though you'll have to wait for a table. Pizza €8.
MAG Ripa di Porta Ticinese 43. Trendy coffee and sandwich bar looking out over the canal.
Princi Via Speronari. Chain of bakeries selling fresh pastries and breads by the kilo. The delicious breads are baked in huge, on-site stone ovens. €1–2 per brioche.
Slice Café Via Ascanio Sforza 9. Funky bar with leopard-print sofas on the waterfront; 6–9.30pm all you can eat buffet (including pastas, pizzas and salads) with a drink for €7. Beware – after this, prices rise considerably.

Drinking and nightlife

Nightlife centres on the streets around the Brera gallery, the club-filled Corso Como, and the Navigli and Ticinese quarters, clustered around Milan's thirteenth-century canals. Drinks go for around €4 a beer and €7 for cocktails. Foreign students can often get free admission to clubs, especially on Tues: otherwise fees are €5–15.
La Banque Via Porrone 6. Formerly a bank, this chic bar is close to the cathedral.
Loolapaloosa Corso Como 15. Popular pub-style student hangout offering *aperitifs* (5–10pm) and solid tables to dance on to a mixture of pop, old-school favourites and Latin.

LA SCALA

The season at **La Scala** (ⓣ02.860.775, ⓦwww.teatroallascala.org), one of the world's most prestigious opera houses, runs from December to July. Although seats are expensive and can sell out months in advance, there is often a chance of picking up a seat in the gods (from €25) an hour or so before a performance, by heading to the box office.

Magazzini Generali Via Pietrasanta 14 ⓦwww.magazzinigenerali.it. Huge warehouse attracting a mixed crowd, playing dance, and occasionally live music by international indie bands
Plastic Viale Umbria 120. A gay-friendly venue playing house, electronic, pop and avant-garde music: Friday is Britpop night.
Ringhiera Caffe Ripa di P. La Ticinese 5. Lively pub with atmospheric interior. Happy hour 5.30–10pm. All cocktails are €5.

Shopping

The fashion streets of Milan are world famous for having some of the most expensive and exclusive shops in the world. For those with cash to flash, Corso Vittorio Emanuele, running between Piazza del Duomo and Piazza San Babila, has some of the top designer names in the industry. For those with less cash but just as much style, high-street stores are around Via Torino (off Piazza Duomo) and Corso Buenos Aires (running northeast from metro Porta Venezia). The boutiques in the Navigli area in the southwest of the city have a range of quirkier, affordable clothing (nearest station metro Porto Genova).

Directory

Consulates Australia, Via Borgogna 2 ⓣ02.7770.4217; Canada, Via V. Pisani 19 ⓣ02.67.581; UK, Via San Paolo 7 ⓣ02.723.001; US, Via Principe Amedeo 2/10 ⓣ02.290.351.
Exchange The office in Stazione Centrale is a good bet, or try Galleria del Corso, just off the Corso Venezia.
Hospitals Fatebenefratelli, Corso Porta Nuova 23 ⓣ02.63.631; Ospedale Maggiore Policlinico, Via Francesco Sforza 35 ⓣ02.55.031.
Internet Piazza d'Aosta 14 (Mon–Sat 9am–10pm; €5.60/hr); Metaverse Internet, Via Plinio 48 (€3.20/hr)

A DAY-TRIP TO LAKE COMO

Trains leave for Como San Giovanni every hour, and take 35 minutes. The lake itself is a ten-minute walk straight out of the station. You can take a boat trip, or enjoy a stroll around the relaxed, pretty town and surrounding area – maybe looking out for Como's best-known resident, George Clooney. To take a picnic to the waterside, try Como's well-stocked deli *Casa del Parmigiano* at Via Giuseppe Garibaldi 49.

Laundry Via Vigevano (10am–7pm; €4 per wash).
Police Via Montebello ⓣ02.62.261.
Post office Piazza Cordusio 2, or right outside the Stazione, in the middle of Piazza d'Aosta.

Moving on

Train Bologna (frequent; 1–2hr); Geneva (every 2hr; 4hr 30min); Lyon (4 daily – 1 direct; change at Chambery or Dijon; 6hr); Paris (4 daily; 7–8hr); Rome (frequent; 4hr); Venice (every 30min; 2hr 30min); Verona (every 30min; 1hr 20min); Vienna (3 daily; 11–14hr; change at Verona or Venice Mestre); Zagreb (1 daily; 10hr 15min; change at Venice Mestre); Zurich (hourly; 3hr 45min).

GENOA

GENOA (Genova) has retained its reputation as a tough, cosmopolitan port but combines the beauty of Renaissance palaces dotted along the small, winding streets. It was one of the five Italian maritime republics, and reached the height of its power in the fifteenth and sixteenth centuries. After a long period of economic decline, Genoa is gradually being cleaned up, and the city now offers an interesting mix of ultramodern architecture and amenities, and old-style streets and restaurants.

What to see and do

Genoa spreads outwards from its old town around the port in a confusion of tiny alleyways and old palaces. Its people speak a near-impenetrable dialect – a mixture of Neapolitan, Calabrese and Portuguese.

Palazzo Ducale

From 1384 to 1515, except for brief periods of foreign domination, the doges ruled the city from the ornate, stuccoed **Palazzo Ducale** in Piazza Matteotti (Tues–Sun 10am–7pm; €4). Decorated with elaborate frescoes, the rooms are a sight to behold. Walk up the tower to the palace's cramped prison cells, which still contain the shackles and scrawled graffiti of prisoners past. Various exhibitions are held in the palace throughout the year while there's also an indoor restaurant on the top floor.

Cattedrale di San Lorenzo

Close by, the Gothic **Cattedrale di San Lorenzo**, complete with Baroque chancel, is home to the Renaissance chapel of St John the Baptist, whose remains once rested in the thirteenth-century sarcophagus. After a particularly bad storm, priests carried his casket through the city to placate the sea, and a commemorative procession takes place each June 24 to honour him. His reliquary is in the **treasury** (tours Mon–Sat 9am–noon & 3–6pm; €5.50), along with a polished quartz plate on which, legend says, Salome received his severed head.

The waterfront

Sadly ruined by a hideous concrete overpass that divides the town from the sea, the waterfront area has undergone a massive restoration project, manifested most obviously in the huge **Aquarium** (Mon–Fri 9.30am–7.30pm, Sat & Sun 9.30am–8pm; €13). **Piazza Caricamento**, opposite the Aquarium, is a hive of activity, fringed by African and Middle Eastern cafés and market stalls.

Piazza Banchi and around

Behind Piazza Caricamento is a thriving commercial zone centred on **Piazza Banchi**, formerly the heart of the medieval city, off which the long **Via San Luca** leads north to the **Galleria Nazionale di Palazzo Spinola** (Tues–Sat 8.30am–7.30pm, Sun 1.30–7.30pm; €4), displaying work by the Sicilian master Antonello da Messina. North of here, **Via Garibaldi** is lined with frescoed and stuccoed Renaissance palaces, whose courtyards and buildings you can peek into. Two are now museums housing Genoese paintings: the **Palazzi Bianco and Rosso** (both Tues–Fri 9am–7pm, Sat & Sun 10am–7pm; joint ticket €7), adorned with fantastic chandeliers, mirrors, gilding and frescoed ceilings.

Arrival and information

Air Genoa's airport is only a 20min bus-ride from Stazione Principe, and buses run every 25min; tickets for the Volabus, a coach running to and from the airport, are €4 and are available from stations and *tabacchis*.

Bus Buses arrive at the main bus terminal outside Stazione Principe.

Ferry Ferries arrive at the Stazione Marittima, a 10min walk downhill from Stazione Principe.

Train Trains from Ventimiglia and points west arrive at Stazione Principe in Piazza Acquaverde, just above the port; trains from La Spezia, Rome and points south arrive at Stazione Brignole in Piazza Verdi, on the east side of the city centre; trains from Milan and Turin usually stop at both, but if you have to travel between the two, take bus #28 or #33 (tickets available from *tabacchi* or newspaper stands). You can easily get to the city centre on foot from either station.

GENOESE FESTIVALS

A lively and cosmopolitan city, Genoa holds innumerable **festivals** throughout the year. The summer is a particularly busy time, with a line-up including the Tango Festival, Film Festival, Tall Ships Races and Mediterranean Music Festival. Dates vary, so check out events at Ⓦwww.comune.genova.it.

Tourist office Stazione Principe Ⓣ010.246.2633, Ⓦwww.apt.genova.it (daily 9.30am–1pm & 2.30–6pm); Piazza delle Feste Ⓣ010.248.5710 (daily 10am–7pm); and at Piazza Mateotti Ⓣ010.868.7452, Ⓦwww.comune.genova.it (daily 9.30am–7.45pm). All give out the free listings guide *Passport*.

Discount passes The tourist office sells a Genova pass, which gets you access to several museums and tourist attractions (€29/three days – including free bus travel).

Internet Internet Oblo, Magazzini del Cotone 3 (daily 11am–midnight; €2/hr).

Accommodation

The best areas to stay are the roads bordering the old town, and Piazza Colombo and Via XX Settembre, near Stazione Brignole.

Astro Via XX Settembre 3/21 Ⓣ010.581.533. Friendly one-star hotel, clean, if somewhat ramshackle, and very close to Stazione Brignole. €40.

Barone Via XX Settembre 2/23 Ⓣ010.587.578. Small hotel with light rooms and welcoming owners, 200m from Stazione Brignole. €50.

Genova Passo Costanzi 10 Ⓣ010.242.2457. Friendly, clean and well-run HI hostel with great views over the port. Single-sex dorm beds and internet access. Take bus #40 or (evening) #640 from Stazione Brignole. From Stazione Principe take bus #35 to Via Napoli and change to bus #40. Dorm bed €16.

Villa Doria Via al Campeggio Villa Doria 15, Pegli Ⓣ010.696.9600, Ⓦwww.camping.it/liguria/villadoria. Leafy campsite 8km from Genoa. It's set in parkland, with its own café, shop and solarium: take a train to Pegli and then bus #93. Pitches €10.

Eating and drinking

For cheap lunches, snacks and picnic ingredients, try the covered *Mercato Orientale*, halfway down Via XX Settembre in the cloisters of an Augustinian monastery. There are lots of restaurants and bars down Via Ravecca, a few hundred metres southeast of the port. For late-night drinking, head to the bars around Piazza delle Erbe, just south of Palazzo Ducale.

Gloglo Piazza Lavagna 19r. *Aperitifs* come with tasty snacks at this relaxed place on a typically Italianate square. Staff are chatty and drinks are generous.

Il Clan Salita Pallavicini 16. Trendy bar packed to the rafters with the young and hip. Arrive early to bag one of the loft bed-seats.

La Focacceria di Teabaldo Via Balbi, opposite *Soglia Hotel*. This takeaway place does cheap yet

tasty baked treats by the slice (€2.50) – be sure to try the delicious Genovese *focaccia al pesto*.

Louisiana Jazz Club Via S. Sebastiano 36r ⓦwww.louisianajazzclub.com. Established jazz venue with live music, a bar and a restaurant.

Oltre Confine Café Opposite Piazza San Lorenzo. At the foot of Cattedrale di San Lorenzo, this bar is great for early evening *aperitivo* or for late-night salsa dancing (wine & *aperitivo* from €5).

Ostaja do Castello Salita Santa Maria di Castello 32r ⓣ010.246.8980. Open till 1am, closed Sun. Family-run trattoria, offering delicious seafood pasta dishes from €8.

Sa Pesta Via Giustiniani 16. Closed Sun & Mon. Extremely popular with locals, this place is well known for its good local cooking, including *farinata*, a thin chickpea-based pancake. Dishes from €9.

Trattoria da Maria Via Testadoro 14/b, just off Via XXV Aprile. No-nonsense, endearingly chaotic place which serves up simple Ligurian cooking at rock-bottom prices. Pasta €4.50.

Moving on

Ferry Bastia (weekly, daily during summer; 4hr 45min); Olbia (daily in summer; 10hr); Palermo (6 weekly; 20hr); Porto Torres (daily; 11hr).

Train Bologna (frequent; 1–2hr); Milan (every 30min; 1hr 30min); Naples (direct 2 daily; 8hr); Pisa (frequent; 2hr); Rome (frequent; 5–6hr).

THE RIVIERA DI LEVANTE

A superb stretch of lush green hills sheltering beautiful seaside resorts, the **RIVIERA DI LEVANTE** stretches eastwards from Genoa. The ports that once survived on navigation, fishing and coral diving are now well versed in the ways of tourism, and while the resorts are hectic during summer months, the towns are still charming enough to ensure they're worth visiting.

BOAT TRIPS

There are a wide range of **boat trips** available in Genova, from romantic 45min excursions around the port at night to full-day whale-watching expeditions. There's a kiosk at Via Sottoripa 7/8 ⓣ010.265.712; or check at: ⓦwww.whalewatchliguria.it and ⓦwww.battellierigenova.it.

The coastline is wild and beautiful in parts and a coastal path meanders over the cliff-tops to each of the resorts. All the towns can be reached by train.

Santa Margherita Ligure

Pretty **SANTA MARGHERITA LIGURE** is a small, palm tree-lined resort, with a minuscule pebble beach and concrete jetties to swim from. **Accommodation** options include the comfortable and friendly *Annabella*, Via Costasecca 10, just off Piazza Mazzini (ⓣ0185.286.531; €62). The very welcoming *Nuova Riviera*, Via Belvedere 10, is a hotel in Art Nouveau style with an annexe of cheaper rooms (ⓣ0185.287.403, ⓦwww.nuovariviera.com; €60; self-catering apartments €65). For good local **food**, try *Il Faro*, Via Merigliano (closed Tues), or the long-established *Da Pezzi*, at Via Cavour 21 (closed Sat), a canteen-like locals' hangout serving pasta, grills and takeaway snacks. For a more expensive but extremely tasty meal, try *Oca Bianca*, Via XXV Aprile 21, famed for its succulent grills (ⓣ0185.288.411, daily 7pm–2am). The **tourist office** is on Via XXV Aprile (daily 9.30am–12.30pm & 2/3–5/7.30pm; ⓣ0185.287.485, ⓦwww.apttigullio.liguria.it). **Scooters and bikes** are a fun way of getting around: go to Via XXV Aprile 11 (ⓣ0185.284.420, ⓦwww.gmrent.it).

Rapallo

RAPALLO is a lovely Riviera town, with brightly coloured beach huts lining the pebbled shore. A tangle of narrow lanes peppered with small trinket shops and delicious Italian restaurants looks onto the waterfront promenade. The **tourist office** is at Lungo Vittorio Veneto 7 (Mon–Sat 9.30am–12.30pm & 3–7.30pm, Sun 9.30am–12.30pm, 4.30–7.30pm; ⓣ0185.230.346). For decent **accommodation**, *Albergo Fernanda*, 9 Via Milite Ignoto (ⓣ0185.502.44, ⓦwww.hotelfernando.com; €55) is a 5 minutes walk from both the station and the beach.

There are a couple of **campsites** – try the large, grassy *Rapallo* at Via San Lazzaro 4 (Ⓣ0185.262.018, Ⓦwww.campingrapallo.it; €6.50 per person, plus €9 per tent). The best place to **eat** is the authentic *Bansin*, at Via Venezia 105 (closed Sun lunch) in the heart of the old town.

Cinque Terre

The **CINQUE TERRE** (Ⓦwww.cinqueterreonline.com) is a series of five beautiful villages – **Monterosso**, **Vernazza**, **Corniglia**, **Manarola** and **Riomaggiore** – perched on tiny cliff-bound inlets lapped by azure blue sea and linked by a coastal pathway. Trains from La Spezia in the south and Levanto in the north run three times an hour and stop at each of the villages. It's possible to visit all the villages in one day via the pathway, although it can get busy at peak seasons and you'll need sturdy shoes. Each village has a tourist office at its train station, with internet access. The **Cinque Terre Card** (validity available for 1 (€5), 2 (€8), 3 (€10) and 7 days (€20) is sold at the tourist offices. The card gives access to the paths and village lifts (where available). Other cards can include train (from €8.50, 1 day; €14.70, 2 days; €19.50, 3 days; €36.50, 7 days) and ferry travel (€19.50, 1 day only). There is also a hop-on boat that stops at each of the villages every hour for €16 per day. Monterosso is probably the liveliest place, though all of the villages have good restaurants and relaxed bars.

Accommodation tends to be expensive in summer months, at about €120 for a double room, or there are rental apartments that have to be taken for a week at a time. Manarola is the best of the villages for budget accommodation: the clean *Ostello Cinque Terre* on Via Riccobaldi 21 (Ⓣ0187.920.215, Ⓦwww.hostel5terre.com; €20) offers gorgeous views, delicious food and chilled-out communal spaces. To get there, head to the top of the town and turn left; it's the green building behind the church. Just down the road from here, at 110 Via Renato Birolli (the main street), *La Cantina dello Zio Bramante* is a small *bruschettieri* and *enoteca* worth a visit just for its delicious anchovy *crostini*.

Northeast Italy

Venice, the premier draw in Northeast Italy, is one of Europe's most stunning –and unmissable – cities. The region around it, the **Veneto**, still bears the imprint of Venetian rule and continues to prosper. Gorgeous, vibrant **Verona** plays on its Shakespeare connections and centres on a fairly intact Roman amphitheatre, while nearby Padua hums with student activity and has some artistic and architectural masterpieces. South, between Lombardy and Tuscany, **Emilia-Romagna** is the heartland of northern Italy, a patchwork of ducal territories formerly ruled by a handful of families, whose castles and fortresses still stand proudly in well-preserved medieval towns. **Parma** is a wealthy provincial town worth visiting for its easy-going ambience and delicious food as well as masterful paintings by Parmigianino and Correggio. The coast is less interesting but, just south of the Po delta, **Ravenna** boasts probably the finest set of Byzantine mosaics in the world.

VERONA

The magnificent city of **VERONA**, with its Roman sites and streets of pink-hued medieval buildings, stands midway between Milan and Venice. It reached its zenith as an independent city-state in the thirteenth century under the Scaligeri family, who were energetic

> **TREAT YOURSELF**
> Nowadays the Roman Arena is used as an **opera venue** for big summer productions. The sight of the stands lit up by the thousands of candles handed out to the audience is a pretty special one. The ticket office (☎045.800.5151, ⓦwww.arena.it) is outside the arena. Prices begin at €21.

patrons of the arts; many of Verona's finest buildings date from their rule.

What to see and do

The city centre nestles in a deep bend in the River Adige, and the main sight of its southern reaches is the central hub of **Piazza Bra** and its mighty **Roman Arena** (Mon 1.30–7.15pm, Tues–Sun 8.30am–7.15pm; July & Aug closes 3.30pm; €5). Dating from the first century AD, and originally holding seating for some twenty thousand (although now it's mainly taken over by a stage and seating for the outdoor summer theatre, see box above), this is the third-largest surviving Roman amphitheatre in the world, and offers a tremendous panorama from the topmost of the 44 marble tiers.

Historical centre

To the north of the Roman amphitheatre, **Via Mazzini**, a narrow traffic-free street lined with expensive shops, leads northwards to a group of squares, the most absorbing of which is the **Piazza dei Signori**, flanked by the medieval **Palazzo degli Scaligeri**. At right angles to this is the fifteenth-century **Loggia del Consiglio**, the former assembly hall of the city council and Verona's outstanding early Renaissance building while, close by, the twelfth-century **Torre dei Lamberti** (same hours as Arena; €3 by elevator, €2 on foot) gives dizzying views of the city. **Juliet's house** is situated in the heart of the old town, at Via Capello 23 (Mon 1.30pm–7.30pm; Tues–Sun 8.30am–7.30pm; €4.50) – even if you don't want to pay to go inside, you can see the famous balcony, rub the right breast of her statue (supposedly for good luck) and read some of the thousand love-notes posted on the walls (some with the aid of age-old chewing gum).

Arche Scaligere and the Duomo

Beyond the square, in front of the Romanesque church of **Santa Maria Antica**, the **Arche Scaligere** are the elaborate Gothic funerary monuments of Verona's first family, set in a wrought-iron palisade decorated with ladder motifs, the emblem of the Scaligeri. Verona's **Duomo** (Tues–Sat 10am–5.30pm, Sun 1.30–5.30pm; €5) lies just around the river's bend, a mixture of Romanesque and Gothic styles that houses an *Assumption* by Titian.

Roman theatre

The **Roman theatre**, on the north side of the river, is worth climbing up to for its gorgeous views. In July and August, a Shakespeare festival (in Italian, but it's still great to soak up the atmosphere) and a jazz festival make use of this amazing venue. Box office ☎899.199.057; ⓦwww.geticket.it. Ticket prices start at €8.

Basilica di San Zeno Maggiore

A kilometre or so northwest, the **Basilica di San Zeno Maggiore** (Mon–Sat 8.30am–6pm, Sun 1–6pm; €2.50) is one of the most significant Romanesque churches in northern Italy. Its rose window, representing the Wheel of Fortune, dates from the twelfth century, as does the magnificent portal.

Arrival and information

Train The train station is connected with Piazza Bra by bus #11, #12, #13 or #14. Alternatively, it's a straightforward 15min walk down Corso Porta Nuova.
Tourist office At the train station ☎045.800.0861, ⓦwww.tourism.verona.it (Mon–Sat 8am–7pm, Sun

9am–2pm; 3–5pm), and at Via degli Alpini 9 (Mon–Sat 9am–7pm, Sun 9am–3pm).

Discount passes The Verona Card (€8) covers all Verona's museums and churches and can be purchased at the tourist offices.

Exchange Via Cappello 3 (Mon–Sat 9am–8.30pm), or at the station (daily 7.30am–8.30pm).

Internet The Internet Train on Via Roma (Mon–Fri 10am–10pm, Sat & Sun 2–8pm; €3.50/hr) or *Square Café* (see below), with free access if you buy a drink.

Accommodation

Albergo Trento Corso Porto Nuova ⓣ045.596.037 ⓦwww.albergotrento.it Just over the road from the Roman Arena, this one-star place has small but comfortable rooms right in the heart of the action. €50.

Casa della Giovane Via Pigna 7 ⓣ045.596.880, ⓦwww.casadellagiovane.com. For women under 26 only, this simple, clean hostel is right in the old centre. The curfew is 11pm unless you're going to the opera. Take bus #73 from the station to Piazza Erbe, from where it's a 5min walk. Dorm bed €22.

HI Hostel Via Fontana del Ferro 15 ⓣ045.590.360. Hostel in a frescoed palazzo on the north side of the river, curfew 11.30pm, breakfast included. Take bus #72, #73 or #90 from the station. Dorm bed €20.

Eating and drinking

Antimo café Via Roma 4. Chilled-out bar in a quiet backstreet. Wine €2.20.

Osteria Casa Vino Vicolo Orette 8. Closed Tues. Romantic restaurant set down a cosy side street. Mains €10.

Retro Gusto 1-3 Via Berni Francesco. Popular with locals, this restaurant/deli serves wonderfully light yet filling home-made dishes, and has a fantastic wine list. Mains from €9.

Square Via Sottoriva 15. Modern bar oozing urban chic, and strong on cocktails. There's a DJ several evenings a week, magazines galore and free internet. Beer and wine €3. Open from 6pm, live jazz and *aperitivo* time with a generous free buffet which you can pick at as you drink.

Via Roma 33 Via Roma 33 ⓣ045.591.917. Super-chic restaurant with atmospheric outdoor tables full of young, well-dressed Veronese. Open until 2am weekends. Mains €11.

Moving on

Train Milan (frequent; 1hr 20min); Padua (frequent; 40min–1hr); Rome (hourly via Padua; 5hr); Venice (every 30min; 1hr–1hr30min).

PADUA

Extensively rebuilt after World War II bomb damage and hemmed in by industrial sprawl, **PADUA** (Padova) is not the most alluring city in northern Italy. However, it's a particularly ancient city with a sense of the real Italia and makes a good base for seeing Venice (35min away by frequent trains). Donatello and Mantegna both worked here, and in the seventeenth century Galileo researched at the university.

What to see and do

Cappella degli Scrovegni

Just outside the city centre, through a gap in the Renaissance walls off **Corso Garibaldi**, the stunning Giotto frescoes in the lapis-ceilinged **Cappella degli Scrovegni**, affectionately referred to as the "scrawny chapel" for its diminutive size (slots for a 20min viewing must be booked, but bookable on the day; €12; ⓣ049.201.0020), are the main reason for coming to Padua. Commissioned in 1303 by Enrico Scrovegni in atonement for his father's usury, the chapel's walls are covered with breathtakingly detailed and largely well-preserved illustrations of the life of Mary, Jesus and the story of the Passion. It's a bit of a rush to see forty masterpieces in twenty minutes, but well worth it.

Piazza del Santo

In the southwest of the city, down Via Zabarella from the *cappella*, is the starkly impressive Piazza del Santo. The main sight here is Donatello's **Monument to Gattamelata** of 1453, the earliest large bronze sculpture of the Renaissance. On one side of the square, the basilica of San Antonio, or **Il Santo**, was built to house the body of St Anthony; the **Cappella del Tesoro** (daily 9am–12.30pm & 2.30–5pm) houses the saint's tongue and chin in a head-shaped reliquary.

The university

From the basilica, **Via Umberto** leads back towards the university, established in 1221, and older than any other in Italy except Bologna. The main block is the **Palazzo del Bo**, where Galileo taught physics from 1592 to 1610. The major sight is the sixteenth-century **anatomy theatre** (March–Oct tours Mon, Wed & Fri at 3.15pm, 4.15pm & 5.15pm, Tues, Thurs & Sat at 9.15am, 10.15am & 11.15am; Nov–Feb tours Mon, Wed & Fri at 3.15pm & 4.15pm, Tues, Thurs & Sat at 10.15am & 11.15am; €5; ⓣ049.827.3047, booking possible only for groups of ten or more).

The Giardino dell'Arena

Situated in the north of the city and surrounding the *cappella*, this garden (Oct–March 8am–6pm, April–Sept 8am–8pm) is a lush, verdant place to chill out or picnic and has an open-air cinema on summer evenings (ask at the tourist office for details).

Arrival and information

Train Padua train station is at the far end of Corso del Popolo, a few minutes' walk north of the city walls or a short tram stop away.
Tourist office There is a branch at the station (Mon–Sat 9am–7pm, Sun 9am–noon), but the main office is in Galleria Pedrocchi, just off Via 8 Febbraio (Mon–Sat 9am–1.30pm & 3–7pm; ⓣ049.876.7927, ⓦwww.turismopadova.it).
Discount passes The tourist office sells the 48hr Padova Card (48hr/€15; 72hr/€20), which buys museum access, free bus travel and a parking space.

Accommodation

Albergo Verdi 7 Via Dondi dall'Orologio ⓣ049.836.4163, ⓔinfor@alberghoverdipadova.it. While it doesn't look much from the outside, *Albergo Verdi* has spacious rooms that are stylish and comfortable. There's a lovely terrace where breakfast is served. €40
Dante Via San Polo 5 ⓣ049.876.0408, ⓔhotel.dante@virgilio.it. An old-fashioned hotel with stone floors and antique wooden furniture. Rooms are on the small side but it's a stone's throw from the sights. €59
HI Hostel Via A. Aleardi 30 ⓣ049.875.2219. A large, somewhat soulless hostel, but the cheapest accommodation in town. 11pm curfew. Bus #3, #8, or #18 from the station. Dorm bed €19.
Sporting Center Via Roma 123 ⓣ049.793.400, ⓦwww.sportingcenter.it. Extremely well equipped, spacious campsite 15km away in Montegrotto Terme, with a reasonable two-star hotel on site (€64). Also a restaurant, large swimming pool and thermal spa. Served by frequent trains (15min). €6.30 per person, plus €8.50 per tent.

Eating and drinking

For eating on the go, there's a daily fruit market on, aptly, Piazza della Frutta, or a supermarket, Punto, at Via Incollo Tommaseo (Mon–Sat 9am–6pm). On summer evenings, the bars around Prato della Valle and Piazza delle Erbe are the best place to head for some lively drinks.
Da Emilio Green Point Via Boccalerie 7–9. Takeaway salad bar with delicious fresh fruit and veg. Closed Sun.
Il Bagatto Via Santa Lucia 79. Modern bar in a backstreet. Wine €3.50, *aperitif* buffet until 10pm.
Miniera Via S. Francesco 144. A fashionable, dimly lit late-night spot, largely frequented by students.
Osteria L'Anfora Via dei Soncin 13. *Osteria* that serves delicious fresh pasta (from €14) and has an extensive wine list.

Moving on

Train Bologna (frequent; 1hr 10min); Milan (hourly; 2hr 30min); Parma (frequent; 2–3hr; change at Bologna); Venice (every 10min; 30min); Verona (frequent; 40min–1hr 20min).

VENICE

The first-time visitor to **VENICE** (Venezia) arrives with a heavy burden of expectations, most of which won't be disappointed. It is an extraordinarily beautiful city, and the major sights are all they are cracked up to be. The downside is that Venice is expensive and deluged with tourists. Twenty million come here each year, most seduced by the famous motifs – Carnival time (see p.686), glass ornaments, singing gondoliers and the fabulously pricey cafés. To avoid the mêlée, stroll down one of the intriguing and peaceful side streets.

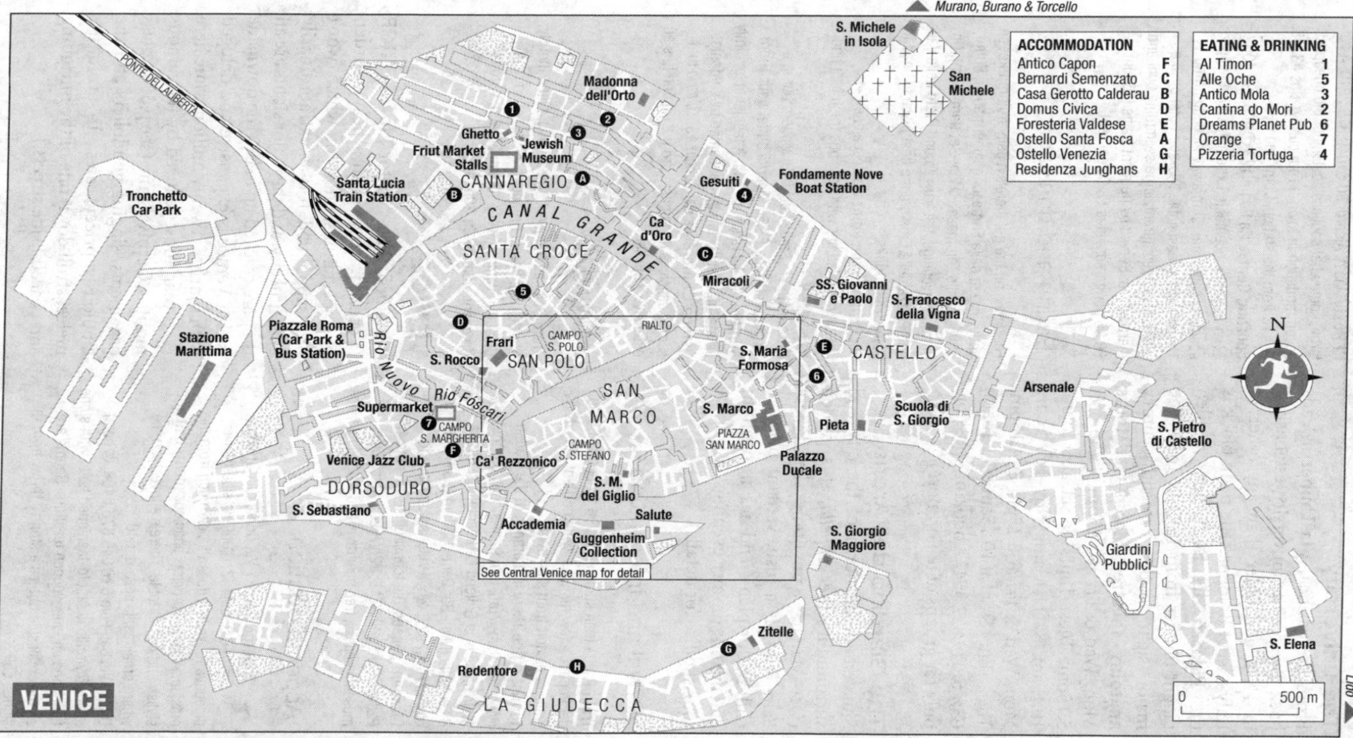
VENICE
Murano, Burano & Torcello
Lido
ACCOMMODATION
Antico Capon F
Bernardi Semenzato C
Casa Gerotto Calderau B
Domus Civica D
Foresteria Valdese E
Ostello Santa Fosca A
Ostello Venezia G
Residenza Junghans H
EATING & DRINKING
Al Timon 1
Alle Oche 5
Antico Mola 3
Cantina do Mori 2
Dreams Planet Pub 6
Orange 7
Pizzeria Tortuga 4
N
0 500 m
S. Michele in Isola
San Michele
Madonna dell'Orto
Ghetto
Jewish Museum
Friut Market Stalls
CANNAREGIO
Santa Lucia Train Station
PONTE DELLA LIBERTÀ
Tronchetto Car Park
CANAL GRANDE
Gesuiti
Fondamente Nove Boat Station
Ca d'Oro
SANTA CROCE
Miracoli
SS. Giovanni e Paolo
S. Francesco della Vigna
Piazzale Roma (Car Park & Bus Station)
Stazione Marittima
Rio Nuovo
Rio Fóscari
Frari
CAMPO S. POLO
RIALTO
SAN POLO
S. Rocco
S. Maria Formosa
CASTELLO
SAN MARCO
S. Marco
PIAZZA SAN MARCO
Arsenale
Supermarket
CAMPO S. MARGHERITA
CAMPO S. STEFANO
Pieta
Scuola di S. Giorgio
S. Pietro di Castello
Venice Jazz Club
Ca' Rezzonico
Palazzo Ducale
DORSODURO
S. M. del Giglio
S. Sebastiano
Salute
Accademia
Guggenheim Collection
S. Giorgio Maggiore
Giardini Pubblici
See Central Venice map for detail
Zitelle
S. Elena
Redentore
LA GIUDECCA

What to see and do

Piazza San Marco

Flanked by the Grand Canal, **Piazza San Marco** is probably the busiest square in the whole of Italy, let alone Venice. It's lined with some stunning architecture such as the dominating **Campanile** (Oct–March 9.45am–4pm, April–June 9.30am–5pm, July–Sept 9.45am–8pm; €6), which began life as a lighthouse in the ninth century, but is in fact a reconstruction: the original tower collapsed on July 14, 1902. It is the tallest structure in the city, and the 98m-high tower provides magnificent views of the neighbouring islands and lagoons, as well as the red clay rooftops of the city.

Basilica di San Marco

Across the piazza, the **Basilica di San Marco** (March–Oct Mon–Fri 9.45am–4.45pm, Sun 2–4.45pm; April–Sept Mon–Fri 9.45am–5pm, Sun 2–5pm; €2) is the most exotic of Europe's cathedrals, modelled on Constantinople's Church of the Twelve Apostles, finished in 1094 and embellished over the succeeding centuries with trophies brought back from abroad. Inside, a steep staircase leads from the church's main door up to the **Museo di San Marco** and the **Loggia dei Cavalli** (March–Oct 9.45am–4.45pm; April–Sept 9.45am–5pm; €4), where you can enjoy fine views of the city and the Gothic carvings along the apex of the facade. However, it's the **Sanctuary**, off the south transept (March–Oct Mon–Fri 9.45am–4.45pm, Sun 1–4.45pm; April–Sept Mon–Fri 9.45am–5pm, Sun 1–5pm; €2), that holds the most precious of San Marco's treasures, the **Pala d'Oro**, or golden altar panel, commissioned in 976 in Constantinople. This mind-blowingly intricate explosion of gold, enamel, pearls and gemstones is generally considered to be one of the greatest accomplishments of Byzantine craftsmanship. The **Treasury** (same times; €2) is a similarly dazzling warehouse of chalices, reliquaries and candelabra, while the tenth-century **Icon of the Madonna of Nicopeia** (in the chapel on the east side of the north transept) is the most revered religious image in Venice. Considered by Venetians to be the protector of the city after being brought here from Constantinople by Doge Enrico Dandolo in 1204, she was carried at the head of the Imperial Army in battles.

VENICE ORIENTATION

The 118 islands of central Venice are divided into six districts known as *sestieri*, with that of **San Marco** (enclosed by the lower loop of the Canal Grande) home to most of the essential sights. On the east it's bordered by **Castello**, to the north by **Cannaregio**. On the other side of the Canal Grande is **Dorsoduro**, which stretches from the fashionable quarter at the southern tip of the canal to the docks in the west. **Santa Croce** roughly follows the curve of the Canal Grande from Piazzale Roma to a point just short of the Rialto, where it joins the smartest of the districts on this bank, **San Polo**.

Palazzo Ducale

The **Palazzo Ducale** (daily: April–Oct 9am–7pm; Nov–March 9am–5pm; €17 combined ticket with Piazza San Marco museums, €11.50 with student card) was principally the residence of the doge. Like San Marco, it has been rebuilt many times since its foundation in the first years of the ninth century, but the earliest parts of the current structure date from 1340. As well as fabulous paintings and impressive administrative chambers, the Palazzo contains a maze of prison cells, reached by crossing the world-famous **Ponte dei Sospiri** (Bridge of Sighs).

Dorsoduro

In the Dorsoduro area west of San Marco, five minutes' walk from the impressive

European art collection in the **Galleria dell'Accademia** (Mon 8.15am–2pm, Tues–Sun 8.15am–7.15pm; €6.50), the unfinished Palazzo Venier dei Leoni is home of the **Guggenheim Collection** (daily except Tues 10am–6pm; €12). Peggy Guggenheim lived here for thirty years until her death in 1979. Her private collection is an eclectic mix of pieces from her favourite Modernist artists, with works by Brancusi, De Chirico, Max Ernst and Malevich.

San Polo

On the northeastern edge of **San Polo** is the former trading district of **Rialto**. It still hosts the lively Rialto market, which is located on the far side of the Rialto bridge and has stalls heaving with fresh fruit and vegetables and a shiny array of fish.

Fifteen minutes' walk west of here is the mountainous brick church **Santa Maria Gloriosa dei Frari** (Mon–Sat 9am–6pm, Sun 1–6pm; €3), the main reason people visit San Polo. The collection of artworks here includes a couple of rare paintings by Titian – most notably his radical *Assumption*, painted in 1518. Titian is also buried in the church. At the rear of the Frari is the **Scuola Grande di San Rocco** (daily 9am–7pm; €5.50), home to a cycle of more than fifty major paintings by Tintoretto.

Cannaregio

In the northernmost section of Venice, **Cannaregio**, you can walk from the bustle of the train station to some of the quietest and prettiest parts of the city in a matter of minutes. The district boasts one of the most beautiful *palazzi* in Venice, the **Ca D'Oro**, or Golden House (Mon 8.15am–2pm, Tues–Sun 8.15am–7.15pm; €5), whose facade once glowed with gold leaf, and what is arguably the finest Gothic church in Venice, the **Madonna dell'Orto** (Mon–Sat 10am–5pm; €2.50), which contains Tintoretto's tomb and two of his paintings. Cannaregio also has the dubious distinction of containing the world's first **ghetto:** in 1516, all the city's Jews were ordered to move to the island of the **Ghetto Nuovo**, an enclave that was sealed at night by Christian guards. Even now it looks quite different from the rest of Venice, its many high-rise buildings a result of restrictions on the growth of the area. The **Jewish Museum** (daily: Oct–May 10am–5.30pm; June–Sept 10am–7pm; €3) in Campo Ghetto Nuovo organizes interesting tours of the area (daily except Sat 10.30am–4.30pm; on the half hour; €8.50 including museum admission), and the Campo's **cafés** are worth visiting too.

Castello

Campo Santi Giovanni e Paolo is the most impressive open space in Venice after Piazza San Marco, dominated by the huge brick church of **Santi Giovanni e Paolo** (San Zanipolo), founded by the Dominicans in 1246 and best known for its funeral monuments to 25 doges. The other essential sight in this area is the **Scuola di San Giorgio degli Schiavoni** (Mon 2.45–6pm, Tues–Sat 9.15am–1pm & 2.45–6pm, Sun 9.15am–1pm; €3), to the east of San Marco, set up by Venice's Slav population in 1451. The building has a superb cycle by Vittore Carpaccio on the ground floor.

Venice's other islands

Immediately south of the Palazzo Ducale, Palladio's church of **San Giorgio Maggiore** stands on the island of the same name and has two pictures by Tintoretto in the chancel – *The Fall of Manna* and *The Last Supper*. On the left of the choir, a corridor leads to the Campanile (daily: Oct–April 9.30am–12.30pm & 2.30–4.30pm, May–Sept 9.30am–12.30pm & 2.30–6.30pm; €3), one of the best vantage points in the city. The long island of **La Giudecca**, to the west, was where the wealthiest

aristocrats of early Renaissance Venice built their villas. The main reason to come today is the Franciscan church of the **Redentore** (Mon–Sat 10am–5pm; €2.50), designed by Palladio in 1577 in thanks for Venice's deliverance from a plague that killed a third of the population.

Arrival and information

Air The city's Marco Polo airport is on the edge of the lagoon, linked to the city centre by ACTV bus #5 (€3.50) and ATVO bus (€5) across Ponte della Libertà, and the more expensive waterbus (from €10).
Bus All road traffic comes into the city at Piazzale Roma, at the head of the Canal Grande, from where waterbus services run to the San Marco area.
Train Santa Lucia train station is on the north side of the canal, to the west of the city centre. Waterbus services run to San Marco, and you can cross over the Ponte degli Scalzi bridge to reach San Polo or follow the canal along to get to Cannaregio.
Tourist office The main tourist office is at San Marco 71/f, a couple of minutes' walk east of the square (daily 9am–3.30pm; ⓣ041.529.8711, ⓦwww.turismovenezia.it). There are also desks at the train station and airport (daily 8am–6.30pm). All three hand out the free English-language listings magazine *Leo* or, for nightlife, the bilingual *Venezia da Vivere*.
Discount passes Tourist offices sell the Museum Pass (€18), which gives entry to most of the main civic museums (it does not include the Accademia or Guggenheim), the Museum Card (€16), which gets you into the museums on Piazza San Marco plus a few others, the Chorus Pass (€8), which gives entry to fourteen churches, and the Venezia Card (ⓦwww.venicecard.it; €54/80 for two/seven days), which covers the waterbuses, most museums and most churches.

City transport

Walking is the fastest way of getting around – you can cross the whole city in an hour.
Gondola The *traghetti* (ferries) that cross the Canal Grande (€0.50 a trip) are a cheap way of getting a ride on a gondola. These old gondolas, stripped of their finery and rowed by two oarsmen, cross from seven piers between the station and the Bacino San Marco (the stretch of water along San Marco), and are indicated by yellow signs along the Grand Canal. Otherwise, the boats are ludicrously expensive, though split between six people they become more affordable: the official tariff is €73 for 50min but you may be quoted up to €100 for 45min and an extra €100 for a singer.
Waterbus Tickets for the waterbus (*vaporetto*) are available from most landing stages. Flat-rate fares are €6 for any one continuous journey including the Canal Grande, or €3.50 excluding it. There are also one-day (€10.50) and three-day (€22) tickets available. Although the waterbuses vary in comfort and can get packed during peak seasons (school holiday times and summer in particular), they're an inexpensive and fun way to see the city and are worth riding on just for the experience.

Accommodation

Accommodation is the major expense in Venice and you should always book ahead – you might also consider staying in nearby Padua (30min away by train) or Trieste (2hr away by train). There are booking offices (all open daily 9am–8pm) at the station, the Tronchetto, Piazzale Roma, airport and at the *autostrada*'s Venice exit. The low season generally runs from November till the start of Carnival, but can vary from place to place. Prices are usually reduced by around twenty percent at this time.
Alex Rio Terra Frari San Polo 2606 ⓣ041.523.1341, ⓦwww.hotelalexinvenice.com. See map, pp.684–685. Cosy one-star option with bright sunny rooms, some with a small terrace which overlooks the canal. €60.
Antico Capon Campo S. Margherita, Dorsoduro 3004/B ⓣ041.528.5292, ⓦwww.anticocapon.com. Very basic, functional rooms in a friendly, family-run place. Breakfast is at one of the cafés on the square. Prices vary hugely so it's best to book in advance. €45.
Bernardi Semenzato Calle dell'Oca, Cannaregio 4366 ⓣ041.522.7257, ⓦwww.hotelbernardi.com. A wonderful choice in the Cannaregio area. Rooms vary from twins to large apartments which sleep up to six. All tastefully decorated, some rooms overlooking the canals. €55.
Casa Gerotto Calderan Calle S Marcuola, Cannaregio ⓣ041.716048. Welcoming place not far from the train station. Dorm beds sometimes available. €60, dorm bed €23.
Domus Civica Calle Campazzo, San Polo 3082 ⓣ041.721.103, ⓦwww.domuscivica.com. Mid-June to mid-Sept. Basic hostel in university accommodation just a 10min walk from Santa Lucia train station. Dorms are small (holding around three people) but it's one of the cheapest bets in Venice. Curfew 12.30am. Dorm bed €21.60.

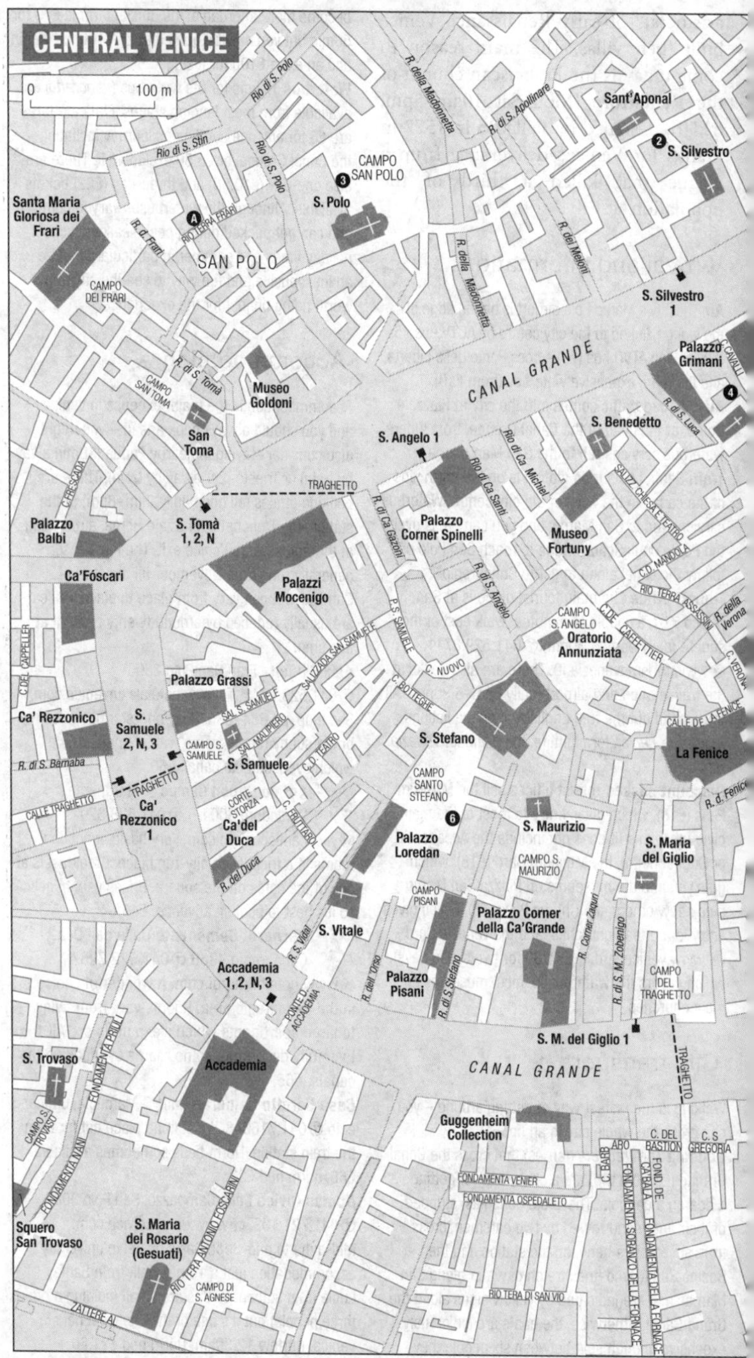
CENTRAL VENICE
0
100 m
Sant'Aponal
S. Silvestro
CAMPO SAN POLO
S. Polo
Santa Maria Gloriosa dei Frari
CAMPO DEI FRARI
SAN POLO
S. Silvestro 1
CANAL GRANDE
Palazzo Grimani
Museo Goldoni
CAMPO SAN TOMÀ
San Toma
S. Benedetto
S. Angelo 1
TRAGHETTO
Palazzo Balbi
S. Tomà 1, 2, N
Palazzo Corner Spinelli
Museo Fortuny
Ca'Fóscari
Palazzi Mocenigo
CAMPO S. ANGELO
Oratorio Annunziata
Palazzo Grassi
Ca' Rezzonico
S. Samuele 2, N, 3
CAMPO S. SAMUELE
S. Samuele
S. Stefano
La Fenice
Ca' Rezzonico 1
CAMPO SANTO STEFANO
S. Maurizio
Ca'del Duca
Palazzo Loredan
CAMPO S. MAURIZIO
S. Maria del Giglio
CAMPO PISANI
Palazzo Corner della Ca'Grande
S. Vitale
Accademia 1, 2, N, 3
Palazzo Pisani
CAMPO DEL TRAGHETTO
S. M. del Giglio 1
S. Trovaso
Accademia
CANAL GRANDE
Guggenheim Collection
Squero San Trovaso
S. Maria dei Rosario (Gesuati)
CAMPO DI S. AGNESE

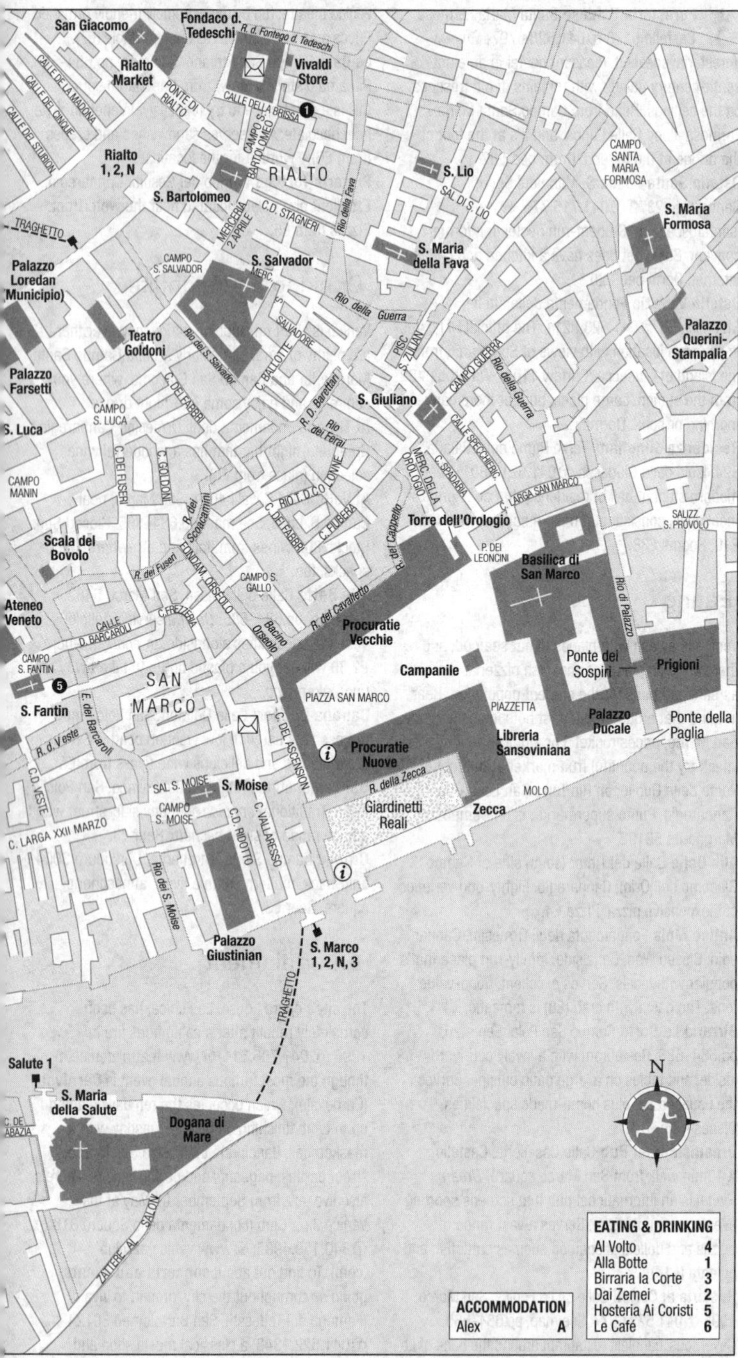
San Giacomo
Fondaco d. Tedeschi
R. d. Fontego d. Tedeschi
Vivaldi Store
Rialto Market
Ponte di Rialto
Calle della Brissa
Calle de la Madona
Calle del Cinque
Calle del Sturion
Campo S. Bartolomeo
Rialto 1, 2, N
RIALTO
S. Lio
Sal di S. Lio
Rio della Fava
Campo Santa Maria Formosa
S. Maria Formosa
S. Bartolomeo
Merceria 2 Aprile
C.D. Stagneri
Traghetto
S. Maria della Fava
Campo S. Salvador
S. Salvador
Palazzo Loredan (Municipio)
Rio della Guerra
Salvadore
Teatro Goldoni
Rio del S. Salvador
Palazzo Querini-Stampalia
Pisc S. Zulian
Campo Guerra
Rio della Guerra
Palazzo Farsetti
C. Ballotte
C. del Fabbri
R. D. Barettari
S. Giuliano
Campo S. Luca
Rio dei Ferai
Calle Specchieric.
S. Luca
C. dei Fuseri
C. Goldoni
Merc. della Orologio
C. Spadaria
Campo Manin
Lonne
Rio T. D.C.O
C. Larga San Marco
R. dei Scoacamini
C. dei Fabbri
C. Fiubera
R. del Cappello
Torre dell'Orologio
Salizz. S. Provolo
Scala del Bovolo
P. dei Leoncini
Basilica di San Marco
R. dei Fuseri
Fondam. Orseolo
Campo S. Gallo
Rio di Palazzo
Ateneo Veneto
C. Frezzeria
R. del Cavalletto
Procuratie Vecchie
Calle D. Barcaroli
Bacino Orseolo
Ponte dei Sospiri
Prigioni
Campo S. Fantin
Campanile
SAN MARCO
Piazza San Marco
Piazzetta
S. Fantin
E. dei Barcaroli
C. del Ascension
Palazzo Ducale
Ponte della Paglia
R. d. Veste
Procuratie Nuove
Libreria Sansoviniana
C.D. Veste
Sal S. Moise
S. Moise
R. della Zecca
Molo
Campo S. Moise
C. Vallaresso
Giardinetti Reali
Zecca
C. Larga XXII Marzo
C.D. Ridotto
Rio del S. Moise
Palazzo Giustinian
S. Marco 1, 2, N, 3
Traghetto
Salute 1
S. Maria della Salute
C. de Abazia
Dogana di Mare
Zattere al Salon
N
ACCOMMODATION
Alex A
EATING & DRINKING
Al Volto 4
Alla Botte 1
Birraria la Corte 3
Dai Zemei 2
Hosteria Ai Coristi 5
Le Café 6

Foresteria Valdese Santa Maria Formosa, Castello 5170 ⓣ041.528.6797, ⓦwww.foresteriavenezia.it. Pleasant hostel in an eighteenth-century palace with remains of old frescoes on the ceilings. Head from Campo Santa Maria Formosa along Calle Lunga, and it's at the foot of the bridge at the far end. Dorm bed €22.
Ostello Santa Fosca S. Maria dei Servi, Cannaregio 2372 ⓣ041.715.775, ⓦwww.santafosca.com. Student-run hostel in a former convent. Basic but does have a kitchen and cheap internet. Dorm bed €20.
Ostello Venezia Fondamenta delle Zitelle, Giudecca 86 ⓣ041.523.8211. The official HI hostel, in a superb location with views of San Marco from the island of Giudecca. Curfew 11pm. Waterbus #82 from the station. Large place, but get there early morning or book. Dorms €27.
Residenza Junghans Terzo Ramo della Palada 394, Isola della Giudecca ⓣ041.521.0801. Neat, modern student hall of residence that does great meal deals consisting of main meal and wine from €10. Rooms €38.

Eating

Venice is awash with places to eat seafood, and there are also plenty of cheapish pizzerias as well as bars and pubs for the student population. Bear in mind that around the tourist hotspots like Piazza San Marco, prices rocket. For a quick, healthy snack try the bountiful fruit market at the foot of Ponte delle Guglie, on Rio Terra San Leonardo in Cannaregio. Punto supermarket is on Campo di Margherita 5019B.
Alle Oche Calle del Tintor (south side of Campo S. Giacomo dell'Orio), Cannaregio. Eighty-odd varieties of inexpensive pizza. Pizza €4.
Antico Mola Fondamenta degli Ormesini, Cannaregio. Closed Wed. Canalside, family-run place that's popular with locals. Serves excellent, good-value food. The pasta with crab (€8) is fantastic.
Birraria La Corte Campo San Polo. See map, pp.684–685. Restaurant with a lovely courtyard inside, and tables on a large patio outside. Serves the usual pizzas plus home-made specialities. Dishes from €13.
Dreams Planet Pub Calle Casellerie, Castello. A 10min walk from San Marco square, *Dreams Planet* is an international pub that screens sporting events open until 2am. Serves a vast range of pizzas and delicious seafood such as cuttlefish and polenta (€14).
Hosteria ai Coristi Calle de La Fenice, San Marco 1995 ⓣ041.522.6677. See map, pp.684–685. Cavernous, candlelit restaurant around the back of La Fenice theatre, run by the extremely friendly Armando. Prices aren't low, but pizzas are affordable (€7).
Le Café Campo San Stefano. See map, pp.684–685. Situated a stone's throw from San Marco square, this is a great place to try (expensive) Venetian-style hot chocolate. Also serves sandwiches and crêpes (from €6) – worth it for the location.
Pizzeria Tortuga Campo dei Gesuiti, Cannaregio. Excellent pizza place located near the waterfront. Pizzas from €5.

Drinking and nightlife

Venice is short on clubbing action, however there are plenty of bars, particularly around Campo Santa Margherita and Campo San Giacomo, where you can relax and enjoy some late-night drinks.
Al Timon Fondamenta degli Ormesini, Cannaregio. Great late-night bar that has a wonderful wine selection (glass from €5).
Al Volto Calle Cavalli 4081, San Marco, near Campo S. Luca. See map, pp.684–685. Closed Sun. Stocks 800 wines from Italy and elsewhere; good snacks, too.
Alle Botte Calle della Bissa, San Marco 5482. See map, pp.684–685. *Osteria* serving delicious Venetian specialities alongside an *enoteca* where €2.80 will get you a plastic bottle to take away any undrunken *vino*.
Cantina Do Mori Calle Do Mori, San Polo. Snug, atmospheric bar with low wooden beams. Serves great nibbles and delicious wine (glass from €5).
Dai Zemei off the Rughetta del Ravano, San Polo 1045. Traditional *enoteca* on a tiny side-street with a huge range of great *cechetti*. Beer €3.
Orange Campo Santa Margherita, Dorsoduro 3054. Laid-back, modern bar in a lively, atmospheric square. Beer €3.

Entertainment

The city's opera house, La Fenice, has been completely rebuilt after a calamitous fire in 1996 (ⓣ041.786.511, ⓦwww.teatrolafenice.it), though the most famous annual event is **Carnival** (Carnevale), which occupies the ten days leading up to Lent, finishing on Shrove Tuesday with a masked ball, dancing in the Piazza San Marco, street parties, pageants and performances. There's also live jazz from September till May at the Venice Jazz Club (Fondamenta dello Squero 3102, ⓣ340.150.4985, ⓦwww.venicejazzclub.com). To find out about **concerts and events** going on throughout the city, drop in to Vivaldi (Fontego dei Tedeschi, San Bartolomeo 30124 ⓣ041.522.1343, a classical music shop and

ticket office. Alternatively, check out the website Ⓦwww.musicinvenice.com or Ⓦwww.veniceconcerts.com, which also has details of summertime Shakespeare performances at the Teatro Fondamenta Nuove.

Directory

Exchange Strada Nuova 4194 (daily 9am–6.30pm).
Hospital Ospedale Civili Riunti di Venezia, Campo Santi Giovanni e Paolo (Ⓣ041.523.0000).
Internet Calle delle Occa, Cannaregio 4426a (Mon–Sat 10am–10.30pm; €3/hr).
Laundry Calle Chioverette, Santa Croce (8kg wash €4; 9am–11pm).
Police Fondamenta di San Lorenzo (Ⓣ041.270.5511).
Post office Salizada del Fontego dei Tedeschi 5554, by the Rialto Bridge (Mon–Fri 8.30am–2pm, Sat 8.30am–1pm).

Moving on

Train Bologna (every 30min; 1hr 30min); Florence (hourly; 2hr 40min); Milan (every 30min; 2hr 30min–3hr 30min); Padua (every 20min; 30min); Verona (frequent; 1hr 30min); Trieste (hourly; 2hr).

BOLOGNA

BOLOGNA is the oldest university town in Europe (the institution dates back to the eleventh century) and teems with students and bookshops. Known for its left-wing politics, "Red Bologna" has long been the Italian Communist Party's spiritual home. It also boasts some of the richest food in Italy, a busy cultural life and a convivial café and bar scene.

What to see and do

The compact, colonnaded city centre has 38km of covered arcades, built to cover the horses brought to Bologna by the first university students, and is still startlingly medieval in plan.

Piazza Maggiore and around

Buzzing **Piazza Maggiore** is dominated by the basilica of **San Petronio,** which was originally intended to have been larger than St Peter's in Rome. On the piazza's western edge, the Palazzo D'Accursio holds the **Museo Morandi** (Tues–Fri 9am–6.30pm, Sat & Sun 10am–6.30pm; free), a rewarding museum dedicated to the works of one of Italy's most important twentieth-century painters. Just north of the square, in the centre of Piazza del Nettuno, is the marble and bronze **Fountain of Neptune**, a famous emblem of the city. Created by Giambologna in the late sixteenth century, it shows the sea-god lording it over an array of cherubs, mermaids and dolphins. There's an open-air **cinema** in Piazza Maggiore in the summer – ask at the tourist office for details.

Archiginnasio

Bologna's university – the **Archiginnasio** – was founded at more or less the same time as the Piazza Maggiore, though it didn't get a special building until 1565. The most interesting part is the **Teatro Anatomico** (Mon–Fri 9am–6.45pm, Sat 9am–1.45pm; free), the original medical faculty dissection theatre, whose tiers of seats surround a professor's chair, covered with a canopy supported by figures known as *gli spellati* – the skinned ones.

Piazza San Domenico

South, down Via Garibaldi, **Piazza San Domenico** is the site of the church of **San Domenico**, built in 1251 to house the relics of St Dominic. The angel and figures of saints Proculus and Petronius were the work of a very young Michelangelo.

Due Torri

At Piazza di Porta Ravegnana, the **Torre degli Asinelli** (daily 9am–5/6pm; €3) and perilously leaning **Torre Garisenda** are together known as the Due Torri, the only survivors of hundreds of towers that were scattered across the city during the Middle Ages, when possession of the towers determined the ranks of power within the city. Superstition holds that any student who enters these towers

before graduation won't graduate at all. The climb to the top of the Torre degli Asinelli up endless flights of narrow stairs takes about twenty minutes, but you'll be rewarded with spectacular views over Bologna's rooftops.

Arrival and information

Air Bologna's airport is northwest of the centre, linked by Aerobus (20min; €5) to the train station and Via dell' Indipendenza in the centre of town. Some low-cost companies such as WindJet use Forlí airport, 60km southeast of Bologna. The E-BUS runs from here into town (1hr 25min; €10).
Bus All long-distance buses terminate in Piazza XX Settembre, next to the train station.
Train The train station is on Piazza delle Medaglie d'Oro – about a 20min walk to the centre along Via dell'Indipendenza, or take bus #30 (€1).
Tourist office There are information booths at the airport (daily 9am–7pm) and the train station (Mon–Sat 9am–7pm; ⓣ051.251.947), and a main office at Piazza Maggiore 1E (daily 9am–7pm; ⓣ051.239.660): all provide the free English-language magazine *L'Ospite di Bologna*.
Internet Iperbole at Piazza Maggiore 6 (Mon–Fri 9.30am–6.30pm, Sat 9.30am–1.30pm & 3.30–6.30pm; free but booking necessary; ⓣ051.219.3184); or try Internet Point at Via San Vitale 27A (daily 9am–10pm; €1/hr).

City transport

Walking is the best way to see Bologna, as the centre is compact and can be walked across in under 30min. Alternatively, you can rent bikes at Autorimessa Pincio, Via dell' Indipendenza 71z (4min walk from the train station; €1.50/hr, €15/day).

Accommodation

Trade fairs happen several times a year (March–early May & Sept–Dec are peak times), during which prices can double – so it's best to book ahead. There's a free accommodation booking service in the tourist office at Piazza Maggiore 1E (ⓣ051.648.7607).
Albergo Pallone Via del Pallone 4 ⓣ051.421.0533, ⓦwww.albergopallone.it. Basic but clean place with a hostel feel and friendly staff. Buses #36 and #37 stop at Sferisterio at the end of Via del Pallone, 30m from the hotel. No breakfast. €50.
Hostel San Sisto-Due Torri Via Viadagola 5 and 14 ⓣ051.501.810. 15min bus ride from town (#93 from Via Irnerio until 8pm, then #21/B from outside the station until 12.44am; on Sun, #301 goes from the bus station). These rather characterless HI hostels are difficult to find but have personable staff. Dorms €16–17.50, rooms €38.
Panorama Via Livraghi 1 ⓣ051.221.802, ⓦwww.hotelpanoramabologna.it. Rooms at this pretty hotel near Piazza Maggiore are spacious and bright, and some have lovely views over the hills. €59.
Pensione Marconi Via Marconi 18 ⓣ051.262.832, ⓦwww.pensionemarconi.it. This one-star on the first floor of a modern block may not look particularly inviting, but the rooms inside are clean if basic (some with private bathrooms). Ask for a room at the back, as it's on a major road. €55.

Eating

There's a central supermarket at Via Garibaldi 1, 5min south of Piazza Maggiore, as well as some great food markets: the Mercato delle Erbe at Via Ugo Bassi 25 is a covered produce market, while the lively street markets that cram Via Drapperie and Via Orefici, just off Piazza Maggiore, are perfect for snacks and picnics.
AF Tamburini Via Drapperie 2. This renowned deli, its ceiling thick with hanging sausages and hams, sells no end of cheeses and picnic food, and also has a few tables – a plate of pasta costs about €5.
Altero Via dell' Indipendenza 33. Pizza by the slice (around €1.50–2) till 1am. The Nutella-topped version makes a satisfying late-night snack.
Il Doge Via Caldarese 5. Closed Mon. This backstreet pizzeria 50m from the Due Torri has pizzas for around €7, as well as regional specialities.
Osteria al 15 Via Mirasole 13. Closed Sun. A lovely old-fashioned trattoria with no menu (the waiter recites the day's specials), enormous portions and very fair prices. Full meal €15.

Drinking

The cheapest and liveliest area is the pub and bar-lined Via Zamboni, where the university students hang out.
Bar Calice Via Clavature 13/A. It's standing room only at this tiny bar in the evenings, thanks to its lavish free *aperitivo* buffet (about 7–9pm) – you can snack to your heart's content for the price of a drink.
English Empire Via Zamboni 24/A. A lively English-style pub; during happy hour (daily 7–9pm), the *aperitivo* buffet is sufficient to make up dinner. Beer €4. Open till 2am.
La Scuderia Piazza Verdi 2. Occupying a former stable block near Via Zamboni, this

huge bar is aimed squarely at students, with occasional live acts, cheap drinks and plenty of room to dance.

The Cluricaune Via Zamboni 18/B. This vast Irish pub is a popular student hangout, with cocktails at €5.50, cheap bar food and a daily happy hour (till 8.30pm). Open till 3am.

Moving on

Air Alghero (1 daily; 1hr 20min).

Bus Rome (1 daily; 5hr 30min); Siena (1 daily; 2hr 30min).

Train Ferrara (every 30min; 30min); Florence (every 30min; 1hr–1hr 30min); Genoa (3 daily; 3hr 30min); Milan (every 30min; 1hr–2hr 20min); Rimini (every 30min; 1hr 30min); Rome (every 30min; 2hr 40min–3hr); Turin (7 daily; 3hr 30min–4hr 10min); Venice (every 30min; 1hr 30min–2hr); Verona (hourly; 1hr–1hr 40min).

PARMA

PARMA is an extremely pleasant town, with dignified streets, large green spaces, a wide range of good restaurants and an appealing air of provincial affluence. There's also plenty to see, not least the works of two key late-Renaissance artists – Correggio and Parmigianino.

What to see and do

Piazza Garibaldi is the fulcrum of Parma, and its cafés and surrounding alleyways are liveliest at night. The mustard-coloured **Palazzo del Governatore** flanks the square, behind which stands the Renaissance church of **Madonna della Steccata**. Inside there are frescoes by a number of sixteenth-century painters, notably Parmigianino. It's also worth visiting the **Duomo**, on Piazza del Duomo in the northeast of the city centre, to see the octagonal **Baptistery** (Mon–Sun 9am–12.30pm & 3–6.45pm; €5), considered to be Benedetto Antelami's finest work, built in 1196. Frescoes by Correggio are in the **Camera di San Paolo** (Tues–Sun 8.30am–1.45pm; €2), in the former Benedictine convent off Via Melloni, a few minutes' walk north.

East of the cathedral square, it's hard to miss Parma's biggest monument, the **Palazzo della Pilotta**, begun for Alessandro Farnese in the sixteenth century and rebuilt after World War II bombing. It now houses the city's main art gallery, the **Galleria Nazionale** (Tues–Sun 8.30am–1.30pm; €6), whose extensive collection includes more works by Correggio and Parmigianino. If you've had enough of all things cultural and fancy checking out some shopping streets, stroll down the wide and laid-back **Strada della Repubblica**.

Arrival and information

Train Parma's train station is a 15min walk from Piazza Garibaldi and all the buses in the city pass through it.

Tourist office Via Melloni ⓣ0521.218.889, ⓦwww.turismo.comune.parma.it (Tues–Sat 9am–7pm; Mon 9am–1pm & 3pm–7pm; Sun 9am–1pm).

Internet Next door to the tourist office on Via Melloni – internet access from €4/hr. There's also a number of wireless hotspots around the town – ask the tourist office for a map.

Accommodation

Albergo Amorini Via Gramsci ⓣ0521.983.239. A walk through the lovely Parco Ducale brings you to the lively student area. *Albergo Amorini* is one of the cheapest options here and is well located for the best nightlife. €55.

Foresteria Edison Largo Otto Marzo 9a ⓣ0521.967.088, ⓔsolares@solaresonline.it. An arts foundation with comfortable dorms. To get here take bus #2 from the Teatro Regio to the *capolinea* (the end of the line) and head right – it's round the back of the building opposite the art cinema. €40, dorm bed €20.

La Pilotta Room & Breakfast Strada Garibaldi ⓣ0521. 281 415, ⓔinfo@lapilotta.it. Privately owned B&B right in the centre of Parma. Run by the jolly Clementina, rooms are large, comfortable and great for the price. March–Aug only. €40.

Ostello della Gioventù Via San Leonardo 86 ⓣ0521.191.7547, ⓦwww.ostelloparma.it. Large hostel with big rooms and helpful staff, shared hot showers and kitchen space. Take bus #2 or #13 from the train station to Centro Torri (a shopping centre with two prominent towers) – the hostel is opposite. Dorm bed €19.

Eating

There's a supermarket (Dimeglio) on Strada XXII Lugio 27c.

20 Settembre Via XX Settembre ⓣ0521.385.594, ⓦwww.ventisettembre.it. Cosy side-street restaurant with live music on Wed. Pasta €7.

Formaggi & Salumi 65b Strada Garibaldi. Brilliantly stocked-up deli, ideal for a picnic.

Il Gallo D'Oro Borgo Salina 3 (just off Via Farini). Closed Sun eve. Superb unfussy local fare, such as *torta fritta* (small triangles of fried dough served warm with a variety of the cold cuts Parma is known for), at inexpensive prices. Mains €8.

La Cantina di Tom Piazza del Carbone 9 ⓣ0521.030.815. Popular and fashionable place ideal for drinks and snacks (closed Sat, Sun lunch & Mon night). Pizza €4.

Sorelle Pichi Via Farini 28. Specialising in cured meats; does a particularly spectacular ravioli. Mains €9.

Drinking

In the evening, the best place to head to is lively Via Farini or Strada D'Azeglio, which has a buzzy, youthful atmosphere.

Bottiglia Azzura Borgo Felino 63. Charming *enoteca* also serving food.

Centrale del Rum Via Farini 54c. Chilled-out hideaway off the beaten track, serving 218 kinds of rum. Open till 1am. Rum €2.50.

Le Malve Café Via Farini 12b. Vivacious customers overflow into the streets from this popular student hangout. Beer €3.

Entertainment

Free summer concerts are held in the Parco Vero Pellegrini – see the tourist office for details. There's also an annual Verdi festival in May/June (see the tourist office for details), while the Teatro Regio on Via Garibaldi (ⓣ0521.039.300) is renowned for its opera. There are open-air films in the summer, usually beginning at 9.30pm ⓣ0521.218.889 for details.

Moving on

Train Bologna (every 30min; 50min); Florence (frequent; 2hr); La Spezia (frequent; 2hr); Milan (frequent; 1hr 15min–1hr 45min); Padua (frequent; 2hr 30min; change at Bologna); Torino (frequent; 3hr 30min; change at Milan); Venice (every 30min; 3–4hr; change at Bologna).

RAVENNA

RAVENNA's colourful sixth-century mosaics are one of the crowning achievements of Byzantine art – and pretty much the only reason for visiting the town. The mosaics are the legacy of a quirk of fate 1500 years ago, when Ravenna briefly became capital of the Roman Empire, and can be seen in a day. The **basilica of San Vitale**, ten minutes northwest of the centre, was completed in 548 AD. Its mosaics, showing scenes from the Old Testament and the life of Christ, are in the apse. Across from the basilica is the tiny **Mausoleo di Galla Placidia**, whose mosaics glow with a deep-blue lustre. Galla Placidia was the daughter, sister, wife and mother of various Roman emperors, and the interior of her fifth-century mausoleum, whose cupola is covered in tiny stars, is breathtaking. Next to San Vitale, the **National Museum of Antiquities** (Tues–Sun 8.30am–7pm; €4) displays a sixth-century statue of Hercules capturing a stag. East of here, on the **Via di Roma,** is the sixth-century basilica of **Sant'Apollinare Nuovo**. Mosaics run the length of the nave, depicting processions of martyrs bearing gifts. Five minutes' walk up Via di Roma, the **Arian Baptistery**, also known as the **Basilica dello Spirito Santo**, has a fine mosaic ceiling. A **combined ticket** (€9.50) covers most of Ravenna's sights; it's available from any of the participating museums, and is valid for a week. Opening times for all the sights are daily 9am–5pm.

There is a large HI **hostel**, *Hostel Dante*, on Via Aurelio Nicolodi (ⓣ0544.421.164 dorms €15), which has sparse rooms and a good, free breakfast. The hostel is a ten-minute walk out of town or take Metrobus Rosso from the opposite side of the station. For **eating**, there are small delis near the hostel, which sell good picnic food. Alternatively, head to Piazza del Popolo where there are a few bars and

restaurants including *Grand Italia* (Piazza del Popolo 9–10), which has outdoor seating and does a generous free buffet, as well as large pizzas.

Central Italy

The Italian heartland of **Tuscany** is one mass of picture-postcard landscapes made up of lovely, walled towns and rolling, vineyard-covered hills. **Florence** is the first port of call, home to a majestic Duomo, the extensive Uffizi gallery and the elegant Ponte Vecchio. **Siena**, one of the great medieval cities of Europe, is also the scene of Tuscany's one unmissable festival – the Palio – which sees bareback horseriders careering around the cobbled central square, while **Pisa**'s leaning tower, a feat of engineering against gravity, and intricately decorated cathedral justifiably attract hordes of tourists. To the east lies **Umbria** (Ⓦwww.regioneumbria.eu), a beautiful region of thick woodland and undulating hills; the capital, **Perugia**, is a buzzing and energetic town, while **Assisi** is famed for its gorgeous setting and extraordinary frescoes by Giotto.

FLORENCE

FLORENCE (Firenze) is undoubtedly the highlight of Tuscany. Its chapels, galleries and museums are works of art in themselves, and every corner brings you face to face with architectural splendour. Some of the most famous pieces in Western art are on display here, including Michelangelo's *David* in the Accademia and Botticelli's *Birth of Venus* in the Uffizi.

What to see and do

Florence's major sights are contained within an area that can be crossed on foot in a little over half an hour. From Santa Maria Novella train station, most visitors gravitate towards **Piazza del Duomo**, beckoned by the pinnacle of the dome. **Via dei Calzaiuoli**, which runs south from the Duomo, is the main catwalk of the Florentine *passeggiata*, a broad pedestrianized avenue lined with shops. It ends at Florence's other main square, the **Piazza della Signoria**, fringed on one side by the graceful late fourteenth-century **Loggia della Signoria** and dotted with statues, most famously a copy of Michelangelo's *David*.

The Duomo

The **Duomo** (Mon–Sat 10am–5pm) was built between the late thirteenth and mid-fifteenth centuries to an ambitious design. The fourth largest church in the world, its ambience is more that of a great assembly hall than of a devotional building. The seven stained-glass roundels, designed by Uccello, Ghiberti, Castagno and Donatello, are best inspected from a gallery that forms part of the route to the top of the dome (€6), from where the views are stupendous. Next door to the Duomo stands the **Campanile** (daily 8.30am–7pm; €6) begun by Giotto in 1334. As well as offering an impressive bird's-eye view of Florence, this contains several enormous bells and more than fifty intricately carved marble reliefs. Opposite, the **Baptistery** (Mon–Sat noon–7pm, Sun 8.30am–2pm; €3), generally thought to date from the sixth or seventh century, is the oldest building in the city. Its gilded bronze doors were cast in the early fifteenth century by Lorenzo Ghiberti, and described by Michelangelo as "so beautiful they are worthy to be the gates of Paradise". Inside, the Baptistery is equally stunning, with a thirteenth-century mosaic floor and ceiling and the tomb of Pope John XXIII, the work of Donatello and his pupil Michelozzo.

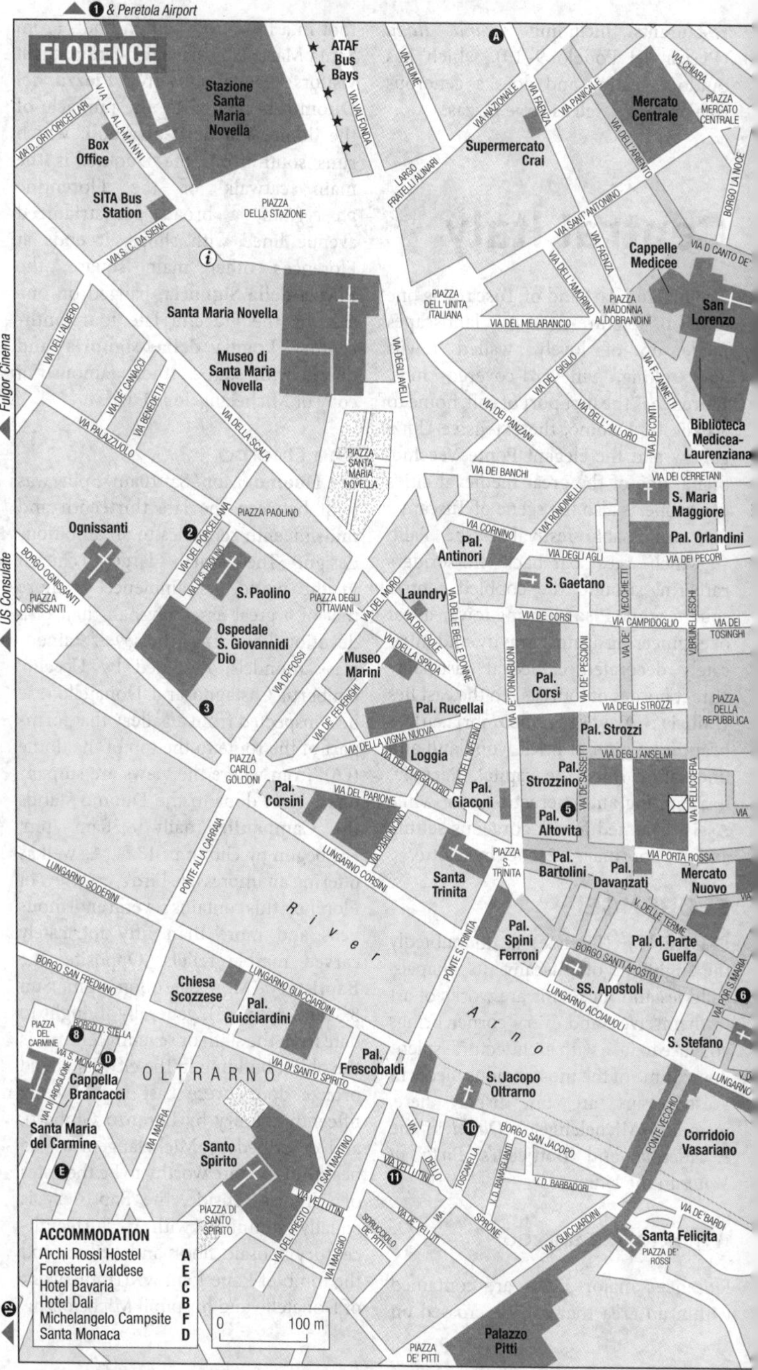

ACCOMMODATION

Archi Rossi Hostel	A
Foresteria Valdese	E
Hotel Bavaria	C
Hotel Dali	B
Michelangelo Campsite	F
Santa Monaca	D

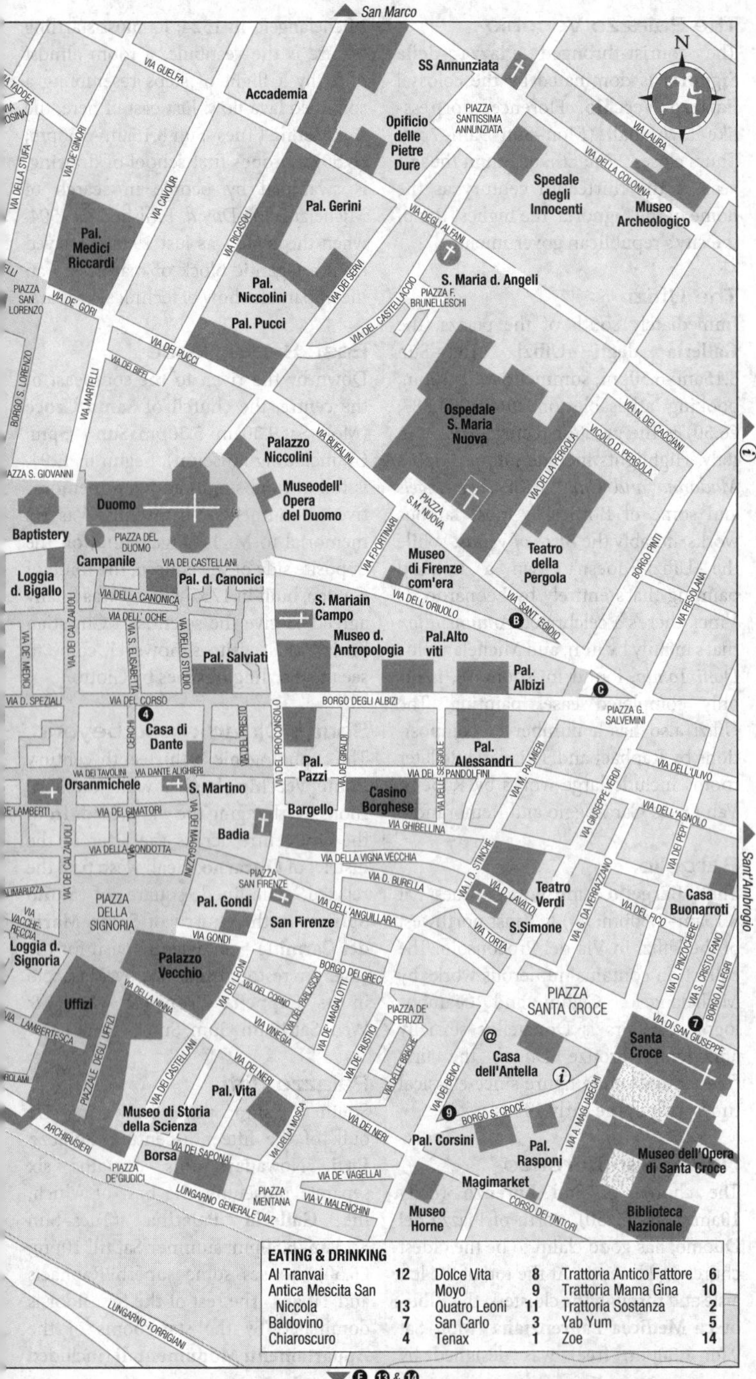
San Marco
N
SS Annunziata
Accademia
Opificio delle Pietre Dure
PIAZZA SANTISSIMA ANNUNZIATA
Spedale degli Innocenti
Museo Archeologico
Pal. Gerini
Pal. Medici Riccardi
Pal. Niccolini
Pal. Pucci
S. Maria d. Angeli
PIAZZA F. BRUNELLESCHI
Ospedale S. Maria Nuova
Palazzo Niccolini
Museodell' Opera del Duomo
Duomo
Baptistery
Campanile
PIAZZA DEL DUOMO
PIAZZA S. GIOVANNI
PIAZZA SAN LORENZO
Loggia d. Bigallo
Pal. d. Canonici
S. Mariain Campo
Museo d. Antropologia
Pal.Alto viti
Pal. Albizi
Museo di Firenze com'era
Teatro della Pergola
PIAZZA S.M. NUOVA
PIAZZA G. SALVEMINI
Pal. Salviati
Casa di Dante
Pal. Pazzi
Pal. Alessandri
Orsanmichele
S. Martino
Casino Borghese
Bargello
Badia
PIAZZA SAN FIRENZE
San Firenze
Pal. Gondi
Teatro Verdi
S.Simone
Casa Buonarroti
PIAZZA DELLA SIGNORIA
Loggia d. Signoria
Palazzo Vecchio
Uffizi
PIAZZA DE' PERUZZI
PIAZZA SANTA CROCE
Casa dell'Antella
Santa Croce
Pal. Vita
Museo di Storia della Scienza
Borsa
PIAZZA DE'GIUDICI
PIAZZA MENTANA
Pal. Corsini
Pal. Rasponi
Magimarket
Museo Horne
Museo dell'Opera di Santa Croce
Biblioteca Nazionale
Sant'Ambrogio
VIA GUELFA
VIA TADDEA
VIA DE' GINORI
VIA DELLA STUFA
VIA CAVOUR
VIA RICASOLI
VIA DEI SERVI
VIA DEGLI ALFANI
VIA LAURA
VIA DELLA COLONNA
VIA DEL CASTELLACCIO
VIA DE' GORI
VIA DEI PUCCI
VIA DEI BIFFI
VIA MARTELLI
BORGO S. LORENZO
VIA BUFALINI
VIA N. DEI CACCIANI
VICOLO D. PERGOLA
VIA DELLA PERGOLA
BORGO PINTI
VIA FIESOLANA
VIA F.PORTINARI
VIA DEI CASTELLANI
VIA DELLA CANONICA
VIA DELL' OCHE
VIA DELL'ORIUOLO
VIA SANT' EGIDIO
VIA DE' MEDICI
VIA DEI CALZAIUOLI
VIA S. ELISABETTA
VIA DELLO STUDIO
VIA D. SPEZIALI
VIA DEL CORSO
BORGO DEGLI ALBIZI
VIA DEL PROCONSOLO
VIA DEL PRESTO
VIA DEI GIRALDI
VIA DELLE SEGGIOLE
VIA M. PALMIERI
VIA GIUSEPPE VERDI
VIA DELL'ULIVO
VIA DEI TAVOLINI
VIA DANTE ALIGHIERI
VIA DEI PANDOLFINI
VIA DELL'AGNOLO
VIA DE'LAMBERTI
VIA DEI CIMATORI
VIA DEI MAGAZZINI
VIA GHIBELLINA
VIA DEI PEPI
VIA DELLA CONDOTTA
VIA DELLA VIGNA VECCHIA
VIA D. BURELLA
VIA I. D. STINCHE
VIA D. LAVATOI
VIA G. DA VERRAZZANO
VIA DEL FICO
VIA DELL 'ANGUILLARA
VIA TORTA
VIA GONDI
BORGO DEI GRECI
VIA DEI LEONI
VIA DEL CORNO
VIA DEL PARLASCIO
VIA DE' MAGALOTTI
VIA D. PINZOCHERE
VIA S. CRISTO FANO
BORGO ALLEGRI
VIA DI SAN GIUSEPPE
VIA DELLA NINNA
VIA LAMBERTESCA
PIAZZALE DEGLI UFFIZI
VIA VINEGIA
VIA DE' RUSTICI
VIA DELLE BRACHE
VIA DEI CASTELLANI
VIA DEI NERI
VIA DEI BENCI
BORGO S. CROCE
VIA A. MAGLIABECHI
ARCHIBUSIERI
VIA DEI SAPONAI
VIA DELLA MOSCA
VIA DE' VAGELLAI
LUNGARNO GENERALE DIAZ
VIA V. MALENCHINI
CORSO DEI TINTORI
LUNGARNO TORRIGIANI
EATING & DRINKING
Al Tranvai 12
Antica Mescita San Niccola 13
Baldovino 7
Chiaroscuro 4
Dolce Vita 8
Moyo 9
Quatro Leoni 11
San Carlo 3
Tenax 1
Trattoria Antico Fattore 6
Trattoria Mama Gina 10
Trattoria Sostanza 2
Yab Yum 5
Zoe 14
F, 13 & 14

The Palazzo Vecchio

The tourist-thronged **Piazza della Signoria** is dominated by the colossal **Palazzo Vecchio**, Florence's fortress-like town hall (Mon–Sun 9am–7pm, Thurs closes 2pm; €6), begun in the last year of the thirteenth century as the home of the Signoria, the highest tier of the city's republican government.

The Uffizi

Immediately south of the piazza, the **Galleria degli Uffizi** (Tues–Sun 8.15am–6.50pm; summer Sat till 10pm; booking advisable on ⓣ055.294.883; €6.50) is the greatest picture gallery in Italy. Highlights include Filippo Lippi's *Madonna and Child with Two Angels* and some of Botticelli's most famous works, notably the *Birth of Venus*. While the Uffizi doesn't own a finished painting that's entirely by Leonardo da Vinci, there's a celebrated *Annunciation* that's mainly by him, and Michelangelo's *Doni Tondo*, found in Room 18, is his only completed easel painting. The Uffizi also has a number of compositions by Raphael and Titian, while later rooms include large works by Rubens, Van Dyck, Caravaggio and Rembrandt.

Bargello

The **Bargello museum** (Tues–Sat 8.15am–1.50pm; €4) lies just northwest of the Uffizi in Via del Proconsolo. The collection contains numerous works by Michelangelo, Cellini and Giambologna. Upstairs is Donatello's sexually ambiguous bronze *David*, the first freestanding nude figure since classical times, cast in the early 1430s.

North: San Lorenzo

The church of **San Lorenzo** (daily 10am–5pm; €2.50), north of Piazza del Duomo, has good claim to be the oldest church in Florence. At the top of the left aisle and through the cloisters, the **Biblioteca Medicea-Laurenziana** (Mon–Sat 9am–1.30pm; free) was designed by Michelangelo in 1524; its most startling feature is the vestibule, a room almost filled by a flight of steps resembling a solidified lava flow. Just east of here, the **Accademia** (Tues–Sun 8.15am–6.50pm; €6.50), Europe's first school of drawing, is swamped by people in search of Michelangelo's *David*. Finished in 1504, when the artist was just 29, and carved from a gigantic block of marble, it's an incomparable show of technical bravura.

East: Santa Croce

Down by the river, to the southeast of the centre, the church of **Santa Croce** (Mon–Sat 9.30am–5.30pm, Sun 1–5pm; €4, including museum), begun in 1294, is full of tombstones and commemorative monuments, including Vasari's memorial to Michelangelo and, on the opposite side of the church, the tomb of Galileo, built in 1737 when it was finally agreed to give the scientist a Christian burial. Most visitors, however, come to see the dazzling frescoes by Giotto.

South: Oltrarno and beyond

The photogenic thirteenth-century **Ponte Vecchio**, loaded with jewellers' shops overhanging the water, leads from the city centre across the river to the district of **Oltrarno**. Head west, past the relaxed, café-lined square of **Santo Spirito**, to the church of **Santa Maria del Carmine** – an essential visit for the superbly restored frescoes by Masaccio in its **Cappella Brancacci** (Mon & Wed–Sat 10am–5pm, Sun 1–5pm; €4).

Palazzo Pitti

South of Santo Spirito is the massive bulk of the fifteenth-century **Palazzo Pitti**. Nowadays this contains six separate museums, the best of which, the **Galleria Palatina** (Tues–Sun 8.15am–6.50pm; summer Sat till 10pm; €6.50), houses some superb Raphaels and Titians. The rest of the first floor is dominated by the staterooms of the **Appartamenti Monumentali** (included

in the Galleria Palatina ticket). The Pitti's enormous formal garden, the delightful **Giardino di Boboli** (Tues–Sun 8.15am–4.30/7.30pm; €4), is also worth a visit. Beyond here, the multicoloured facade of **San Miniato al Monte** (daily 8am–12.30pm & 2.30–7pm) lures troupes of visitors up the hill. The interior is like no other in the city, and its form has changed little since the mid-eleventh century.

Arrival and information

Air Pisa's international airport is connected by a regular train service (1hr) with Florence's central Santa Maria Novella train station (on timetables as "Firenze SMN"). Alternatively, the Terravision bus goes to Pisa Airport from outside the train station (1hr; €8). Flights also come into Florence's tiny Peretola airport, 5km out of the city and connected by bus.

Bus The main bus station is located alongside Santa Maria Novella – the SITA buses are a quick, easy way to travel to nearby cities such as Siena and Pisa. ATAF runs the reliable local service.

Train The main train station is at Piazza Santa Maria Novella, in the northwest of the city centre, a 10min walk from the Piazza del Duomo.

Tourist office The main official tourist office at Via Manzoni 16 (Ⓣ055.233.20, Ⓦwww.firenzeturismo.it). There's also a small branch opposite the train station at 4 Piazza della Stazione, and another small office near Santa Croce at Borgo S. Croce 29 (Mon–Sat 8.30am–7pm; Sun 8.30am–1.30pm; Ⓣ055.212.245).

City transport

Bike rental Renting a bicycle is a great way to explore the side-streets and enjoy the river views; the council's *Mille e una bici* scheme (€1.50/hr, €8/day) makes it easy – there are numerous pick-up/drop-off points around town – including one at the train station.

Bus If you want to cover a long distance in a hurry, take one of the orange ATAF buses; tickets (€1) are valid for one hour and can be bought from *tabacchi*.

Accommodation

Florence's most affordable hotels are close to the station, in particular along and around Via Faenza, Via Fiume, Via della Scala and Piazza di Santa Maria Novella. Advance booking is advisable, or try the *Informazioni Turistiche Alberghiere* accommodation office at the train station (daily 8.45am–8pm; Ⓣ055.282.893), which can make last-minute reservations for a fee.

Archi Rossi Hostel Via Faenza 94r Ⓣ055.29.08.04, Ⓦwww.hostelarchirossi.com. Lively, arty hostel right by the station with free internet and a private garden. Also has free pizza and pasta nights. Dorms range from 3 to 12 beds. Dorm bed €20.25.

Foresteria Valdese Via dei Serragli 49 Ⓣ055.212.576, Ⓦwww.istitutogould.it/foresteria. A charming hostel in a beautiful old convent, where many of the generously proportioned rooms have en-suite bathrooms and large terraces – book early. Double €44.

Hotel Bavaria 26 Borgo degli Albizi Ⓣ055.234.0313, Ⓦwww.hotelbavariafirenze.it Simple one-star hotel with small rooms, all with shared bathrooms. Located just a block from the Duomo. €49.

Hotel Dali Via dello Oriulol Ⓣ055.234.0706 Ⓦwww.hoteldali.com. Set on a lovely cobbled street in a great central location. The rooms are traditionally decorated with old wooden furniture in light airy rooms. Some with private bathroom. €65.

Michelangelo Campsite Piazzale Michelangelo, Viale Michelangelo 80 Ⓣ055.681.197, Ⓦwww.camping.it/toscana/michelangelo. Centrally located campsite with great views. There's also a popular restaurant and a late night disco. Walking distance from city centre, or take bus #12 or #13. €10.60 per person plus €6.60 per tent.

Santa Monaca Via Santa Monaca 6, Oltrarno Ⓣ055.268.338, Ⓦwww.ostello.it. Very popular hostel in a converted fifteenth-century convent, with a 1am curfew. Located on the southern side of the Arno, it's a 15min walk from the train station. Has free internet and cooking facilities. Dorm bed €16.20.

Eating

The best place to find picnic food and snacks is the Mercato Centrale, just east of the train station. Otherwise, try a *vinaio*, a wine cellar/snack bar that serves *crostini* and other snacks. Supermarkets include Magimarket (Mon–Sat 8am–9pm, Sun 9am–9pm) Corso dei Tintori 18–24 and Supermercato Crai (daily 8am–9pm) on Via Faenza 48r.

Al Tranvai Piazza T. Tasso 14/r Ⓣ055.225.197. Closed Sun. Good, inexpensive Florentine specialities – arrive early to secure a table. Gnocchi €7.

Antica Mescita San Niccolú Via San Niccolú 60/r. Closed Sun. Delicatessen and *osteria* with an

unrivalled cheese and wine selection, plus superb Tuscan soups. Lunch buffet 12.30–2.30pm, €10.

Baldovino Via San Giuseppe 223 ⓣ055.241.773. Open until 1am, closed Mon. Charming trattoria just off the Piazza San Croce. Pizza €7.

Chiaroscuro Via del Corso 36r. Small, buzzy café and bar with generous *aperitif* buffet. Coffee €1.50, drink with buffet €8.

Quatro Leoni 1 Via dei Vellutini. Large restaurant with indoor and outdoor seating. The *gran fritto dell' aia* (fried chicken and rabbit) is a house speciality. Meals from €10.

Trattoria Antico Fattore 1/3 Via Lambertesca ⓣ055.288 975. Closed Sun. Fantastic food and cheap prices, located a couple of streets from the Uffizi. Great home-made pasta dishes from €8.

Trattoria Mama Gina 37 Borgo S.Jacopo. On the south side of the Arno, Mama Gina serves delicious regional dishes. The Tuscan fried chicken with garlic courgettes is a must (meals from €10).

Trattoria Sostanza 25 Via Porcellana. This is where the real Florentines go for the best *bisteca* (€22) in town. A simple, no-frills affair, with superlative food.

Drinking and nightlife

Mercato Generale, just east of the bus and train station, has some of Florence's cheapest bars.

Dolce Vita Piazza del Carmine. 5.30pm–1.30am, closed Sun. Trendy late-night hangout that also stages small-scale art exhibitions.

Moyo Via dei Benci 23r. Chilled-out café and bar with great cocktails, serving food until 5pm and drinks with buffet until 2am. Large beer/ cocktail €5.

San Carlo 32 Borgognissanti. Great cocktails and large choice of early evening *aperitivo*. First drink from €5.

Tenax Via Pratese 47. Fri & Sat from 10pm. The city's biggest club and one of its leading venues for new and established bands, playing an eclectic mix of indie, trance, modern pop and old classics. Bus #29 or #30.

Yab Yum Via de' Sassetti 5r. City-centre club, near the Duomo, playing new dance music. Mon–Sat from 8pm.

Zoe Daily 8am–3am. Atmospheric cocktail bar, with small-scale painting exhibitions, outdoor seating and snack food during the day. Cocktails €5.

Entertainment

For listings information, call in at Box Office, Via Alamanni 39 (ⓣ055.210.804), or consult *Firenze Spettacolo* and *Informa Città*. As for festivals, in May the Maggio Musicale (ⓦwww.maggiofiorentino.com) puts on concerts, gigs and other events throughout the city, while the Festa di San Giovanni (June 24) sees the city's saint honoured with a massive fireworks display. Free concerts and events take place around Florence throughout the summer – see the tourist office for details. There's a cinema, Fulgor, at 22 Via Maso Finguerra.

Directory

Consulates UK, Lungarno Corsini 2 ⓣ055.284.133; US, Lungarno Vespucci 38 ⓣ055.239.8276.

Exchange The city is full of ATMs and exchange bureaux; the one at the station is open 8am–7pm daily.

Hospitals Santa Maria Nuova, Piazza Santa Maria Nuova 1 ⓣ055.27.581. English-speaking doctors are on 24hr call at the Tourist Medical Service, Via Lorenzo il Magnifico 59 ⓣ055.475.411.

Internet Internet Train is at Via Guelfa 54/56, Via dell'Oriuolo 40r, and Borgo San Jacopo 30r (€3.20p/hr).

Laundry Wash & Dry (all daily 8am–10pm; €8/ load): Via della Scala 52–54r; Via Nazionale 129r; Via del Sole 29r.

Police Via Zara 2 ⓣ055.49.771.

Post office Via Pellicceria 3 (daily except Sun 8.30am–12.30pm & 3–6pm).

Moving on

Bus Siena (hourly; 1hr 30min).

Train Bologna (every 30min; 1hr); Genoa (hourly; 3hr 50min; change at Pisa); Milan (frequent; 2hr 10min); Naples (frequent; 3hr 15min); Nice (frequent; 8–9hr; change at Pisa); Paris (2 daily; 10–12hr; change at Milan); Perugia (hourly; 2hr); Pisa (every 20min; 1hr 10min); Rome (every 30min; 1hr 40min–2hr 30min); Venice (hourly; 2hr 40min); Verona (hourly; 3hr).

PISA

The Leaning Tower in **PISA** is an iconic image, yet its stunning beauty is often underrated, with its intricate carvings appearing as though they're icing details on a very large wedding cake. It's set alongside the **Duomo** and **Baptistery** on the manicured grass of the **Campo dei Miracoli**, whose buildings date from the twelfth and thirteenth centuries, when Pisa was one of the great

PISA'S FESTIVALS

Pisa is known for its **Gioco del Ponte**, held on the last Sunday in June, when teams from the north and south banks of the city stage a series of "battles", including pushing a seven-tonne carriage over the Ponte di Mezzo. But the town's most magical event is the **Luminara** on June 16, when buildings along the river are festooned with candles to celebrate San Ranieri, the city's patron saint.

Mediterranean powers. Beyond this pretty square, however, Pisa is somewhat dilapidated, and in the evenings the city takes on an eerie atmosphere.

What to see and do

Leaning Tower

Perhaps the strangest thing about the **Leaning Tower** (daily 8.30am–8.30pm; €15), begun in 1173, is that it has always tilted; subsidence disrupted the foundations when it had reached just three of its eight storeys. For the next 180 years a succession of architects were brought in to try to correct the tilt, until 1350 when the angle was accepted and the tower completed. Eight centuries after its construction, it was thought to be nearing its limit, and the tower, supported by steel wires, was closed to the public in the 1990s – though it's open for visits once again now that the tilt (and 5m overhang) has been successfully halted.

Duomo

The **Duomo** (Mon–Sat 10am–7.30pm, Sun 1–7.30pm; €2) was begun a century earlier than the Tower, its facade – a delicate balance of black and white marble, and tiers of arcades – setting the model for Pisa's highly distinctive brand of Romanesque. The interior continues this use of black and white marble. The third building of the Miracoli ensemble, the circular **Baptistery** (daily 8/9am–4.30/7.30pm; €5), is a slightly bizarre mix of Romanesque and Gothic, embellished with statues (now largely copies) by Giovanni Pisano and his father Nicola. The originals are displayed in the Opera del Duomo **museum** (March–Sept daily 8am–7.45pm; Oct–Feb daily 9am– 4.45pm; €5) to the east of the Piazza del Duomo.

Camposanto

Along the north side of the Campo is the **Camposanto** (same hours; €5), a cloistered cemetery built towards the end of the thirteenth century. Most of its frescoes were destroyed by Allied bombing in World War II, but two masterpieces survived relatively unscathed in the Cappella Ammanati – a fourteenth-century *Triumph of Death*, and *The Last Judgement*, a ruthless catalogue of horrors painted around the time of the Black Death.

Arrival and information

Train Pisa's train station is south of the centre on Piazza della Stazione, a 10min walk (or bus #3) from Campo dei Miracoli. Take bus LAM Rosso for the 10min journey to the Leaning Tower. From the airport, take the hourly Florence train for the 5min journey.

Tourist office 16 Piazza Vittorio Emanuele II (Mon–Fri 9am–7pm; Sat 9am–1.30pm, closed Sun; ⓣ050.42.291, ⓦwww.pisaturismo.it) and Piazza Arcivescovado 8, near the Tower (daily 10am–7pm). Both sell a tourist ticket (€10.50) giving admission to most of Pisa's museums, bar the Leaning Tower.

Internet 5 Via G Carducci at €3.50/hr.

Accommodation

Albergo Amalfitana 44 Via Roma ⓣ050.29.000. Located in the old part of town in the winding lanes near the tower, *Albergo Amalfitana* has somewhat chintzy but homely rooms, and a lovely outdoor courtyard. Doubles from €70.

Campeggio Torre Pendente Viale delle Cascine 86 ⓣ050.561.704, ⓦwww.campingtorrependente.it. Large, well-maintained campsite 1km west of Campo dei Miracoli, with a restaurant, shop and

large outdoor swimming pool. Closed Nov–March. Tent & car from €20.

HI Hostel Via Pietrasantina 15 ⓣ050.890.622. A large hostel with seemingly endless dorms. Not the most welcoming of places, but it's a cheap bed for the night. Take bus #3 from the station or Campo dei Miracoli. Dorm bed €18.

Pensione Helvetia Via G. Boschi 31, off the Piazza Arcivescovado ⓣ050.553.084. Basic, family-run *pensione* near the Leaning Tower, just behind the *Grand Hotel Duomo* on Via Santa Maria. Doubles from €60.

Eating

Avoid eating around the Tower if you can, as prices here are sky-high for tourists. The best area for restaurants is around the Piazza delle Vettovaglie, and there are fruit markets around Via D. Cavalca. Try the fresh fruit and veg stalls on Via Domenica Cavalca, although be careful, as prices can seem a little high for a couple of oranges.

Caffetteria delle Vettovaglie Piazza delle Vetto vaglie 33. Closed Sun. Trendy bar-restaurant with a different menu every day. Mains €8.

Jackson Pollock Piazza Vettovaglie 21 ⓣ050.570.178. Excellent home-cooked food in a charmingly ramshackle setting with friendly owners. Gnocchi with pesto €7.

La Bottega del Gelato Piazza delle Garibaldi. Great *gelato* and handily located for a pit-stop midway between the station and the Duomo.

Snack Café Miami Via Carlo Fedeli. On the way from the station to the tower, *Café Miami* does hearty sandwiches, pasta and pizza from €5.

Vineria di Piazza Piazza delle Vettovaglie 13. Good soups at decent prices. Soup and fresh bread €6.

Entertainment

Cinema Lumiere Vicolo del Tidi 6 ⓣ050.971.1532, ⓦwww.lumierecinema.it. Shows arthouse and some original language films.

Toscana in Tour Via S. Giuseppe 5 ⓣ333.260.2152, ⓦwww.toscanaintour.it. Bike rental with ridiculous-looking quadricycles.

Moving on

Bus Florence, from Pisa Airport (hourly; 1hr 10min; €8).

Train Florence (every 15min; 1hr); Lucca (every 15min; 20min); Siena (hourly; 1hr 45min).

SIENA

SIENA, 78km south of Florence, is the perfect antidote to its better-known neighbour. Self-contained behind excellently preserved medieval walls, its cityscape is a majestic Gothic attraction that you can roam around and enjoy without venturing into a single museum. It is also a lively university town, so there is no shortage of places to go in the evening. During the Middle Ages, Siena was one of the major cities of Europe – the size of Paris, it controlled most of southern Tuscany and developed a highly sophisticated civic life, with its own written constitution and a quasi-democratic government.

THE SIENA PALIO

The **Siena Palio** is the most spectacular festival in Italy, a minute-and-a-half-long bareback horse-race around the Campo contested twice a year (July 2 at 7.45pm and Aug 16 at 7pm) between the seventeen ancient wards – or *contrade* – of the city. Even now, a person's *contrada* frequently determines which churches they attend and where they socialize. There's a big build-up, with trials and processions for days before the big event, and traditionally all Sienese return to their *contrada* the night before the race; emotions run too high for rivals to be together, even if they're husband and wife. The Palio itself is a hectic spectacle whose rules haven't been rewritten since the race began – thus supposedly, everything is allowed except to gouge your opponents' eyes out. For the best view, you need to have found a position on the inner rail by 2pm and to keep it for the next seven hours. Beware that toilets, shade and refreshments are minimal, the swell of the crowd can be overwhelming, and you won't be able to leave the Campo for at least two hours after the race. If you haven't booked a hotel room, reckon on staying up all night.

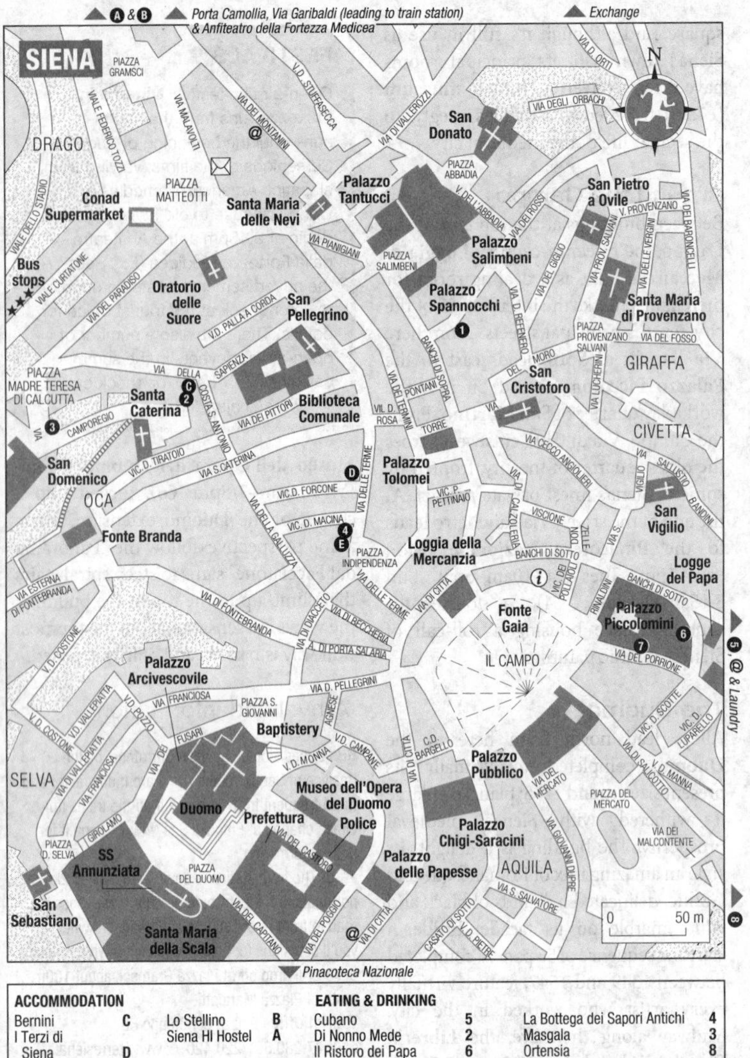

ACCOMMODATION				EATING & DRINKING			
Bernini	C	Lo Stellino	B	Cubano	5	La Bottega dei Sapori Antichi	4
I Terzi di Siena	D	Siena HI Hostel	A	Di Nonno Mede	2	Masgala	3
La Perla	E			Il Ristoro dei Papa	6	Ortensia	8
				Il Sasso	1	Osteria Le Logge	7

What to see and do

The **Campo** is the centre of Siena in every sense: the main streets lead into it, the Palio takes place around its café-lined perimeter, and it's the natural place to gravitate towards. It's been called the most beautiful square in the world, an assessment that seems pretty fair – taking a picnic onto the stones to watch the shadows move around the square is a good way to while away an afternoon.

The Palazzo Pubblico

The **Palazzo Pubblico** (daily 10am–6/7pm) – with its 107m-high bell-tower, the **Torre del Mangia** (€7) – occupies virtually the entire south side of the

square, and although it's still in use as Siena's town hall, its principal rooms have been converted into a **museum** (€7.50), frescoed with themes integral to the secular life of the medieval city.

Around the Campo

Between buildings at the top end of the Campo, the fifteenth-century **Loggia di Mercanzia**, built as a dealing room for merchants, marks the intersection of the city centre's principal streets. From here **Via Banchi di Sotto** leads east to the **Palazzo Piccolomini** and on into the workaday quarter of **San Martino**. From the Campo, Via di Città cuts west across the oldest quarter of the city, fronted by some of Siena's finest private *palazzi*. At the end of the street, Via San Pietro leads to the **Pinacoteca Nazionale** (Mon 9am–1pm, Tues–Sat 10am–6pm, Sun 8.15am–1.15pm; €4), a fourteenth-century palace housing a roll-call of Sienese Gothic painting.

The Duomo

Alleys lead north from here to the **Duomo**, completed to virtually its present size around 1215; plans to enlarge it withered with Siena's medieval prosperity. The building is a delight, its style an amazing mix of Romanesque and Gothic, delineated by bands of black and white marble on its facade. Inside, a startling sequence of 56 panels, completed between 1349 and 1547, feature virtually every artist who worked in the city. Midway along the nave, the **Libreria Piccolomini** (daily 10.30am–7.30pm; €6), signalled by Pinturicchio's brilliantly coloured fresco of the *Coronation of Pius II*, has superbly vivid frescoes.

Museums

Opposite the Duomo is the complex of **Santa Maria della Scala** (daily 10.30am–6.30pm; €6), the city's hospital for over eight hundred years and now a vast museum that includes the frescoed Sala del Pellegrinaio. The

FESTIVALS

Open-air film festival **Cinema in Fortezza** runs from the end of June until the beginning of August. Screenings of the films, varying from slapstick American comedies and world arthouse to old Italian classics, begin at 9.45pm at the Anfiteatro della Fortezza Medicea (€5). See the advertisements posted around town or check at the tourist office for details. There are also a number of open-air jazz events in the summer: call ⓣ0577.271.401, or check out ⓦwww.sienajazz.it.

Museo dell'Opera del Duomo (Mon–Fri 9.30am–7/8pm; €6), tucked into a corner of the Duomo extension, offers a fine perspective: follow the "Panorama dal Facciatone" signs to steep spiral stairs that climb up to the top of the building; the views are sensational but the topmost walkway is narrow and scarily exposed.

Arrival and information

Bus Buses stop along Viale Curtatone, by the Basilica of San Domenico, and are much faster and more frequent from Florence than the trains (for which change at Empoli). See ⓦwww.sena.it for more information.
Train The train station is down in the valley 2km northeast of the centre; to get into town, cross the road in front of the station and head left, where you'll see signs for a lift taking you down to the city buses. All drop off at Piazza Gramsci, about 100m north of Piazza Matteotti.
Tourist office Piazza del Campo 56 ⓣ0577.280.551/220.420, ⓦwww.terresiena.it (daily 9am–7pm).
Discount passes If you plan on doing a lot of sightseeing, the Biglietto Cumulativo includes entrance to most of Siena's museums (€12/14/17 valid for two/three/seven days), and can be bought at any of the participating museums.
Exchange Via del Moro 4 (Mon–Sat 10am–5pm).
Internet Internet Siena, Via Montanini 93 (daily 9am–11pm; €2/hr). Internet Train, 121 Via di Citta and 54 Via Pantaneto (Mon–Sat 10am–8pm; Sun 2–7pm; €4/hr)
Laundry Siena Laundromat, Via di Pantaneto 38 (daily 8am–10pm; €3/wash, €3/dry).

Post office Piazza Matteotti 37 (Mon–Sat 8.15–7pm; closed Sun).

Accommodation

In summer, Siena gets ridiculously booked up; it's worth phoning ahead for accommodation, or booking rooms at the Siena Hotels Promotion booth opposite San Domenico (Mon–Sat 9am–8pm; ⓣ0577.288.084, ⓦwww.hotelsiena.com).

Bernini Via della Sapienza 15 ⓣ0577.289.047, ⓦwww.albergobernini.com. Charming and old-fashioned one-star hotel run by a homely family; the views from the huge windows and open-air breakfast terrace are breathtaking. Midnight curfew. Rooms from €55.

I Terzi di Siena 13 Via dei Termini, ⓣ033.9669.9143, ⓦwww.terzidisiena.com. Owned by the lovely Elisabetta, this private apartment has large spacious rooms, a self-catering kitchen and a beautiful terrace overlooking the rolling countryside. €60.

La Perla 25 Via delle Terme ⓣ057.747.144. Small, one-star *pensione* but a great central location just minutes from the Duomo and Campo. €50.

Lo Stellino Via Fiorentina 95 ⓣ0577.588.926, ⓦwww.sienaholidays.com. Pretty hotel with beautifully decorated rooms, next to the *HI hostel*, with kitchen facilities and a garden. €60.

Siena HI Hostel Via Fiorentina 89 ⓣ0577.52.212. A friendly and comfortable hostel, with dorm beds two to a room. 2km northwest of the centre; take bus #10 from the train station or Piazza Gramsci, or bus #15 from Piazza Gramsci. If you're coming from Florence, ask the bus driver to let you off at "Lo Stellino". Midnight curfew. Dorm bed €14.30.

Eating

For good picnic supplies try Conad supermarket (Mon–Sat 8.30am–8.30pm, Sun 9am–1pm) on Piazza Matteotti, shopping arcade.

TREAT YOURSELF

Osteria Le Logge Via del Porrione 33. Extremely popular with tourists and locals alike, this restaurant specialises in simple, home-made dishes which taste exquisite. *Taglierini al Tartufo* is highly recommended for those who love the delicate taste of truffles (€25 main-course size). Worth booking in summer. Closed Sun.

FOOD AND FILMS

Markets take place in different piazzas every day from 9am to 1pm year round; in summer, there are also brilliantly performed **operas** in the Piazza del Duomo and an open-air **cinema** at the Parco di Montestaffoli. Ask at the tourist office for details.

Di Nonno Mede Via Camporegio 21 ⓣ0577.247.966. Popular pizzeria with stunning views out over the Duomo. Pizza €5.

Il Ristoro del Papa Logge del Papa 1, between Banchi di Sotto and Bia del Porrione ⓣ0577.284.062. Friendly, unpretentious pizzeria and restaurant with outdoor seating area and lively atmosphere. Pizza €6.

Il Sasso Via dei Rossi 2a ⓣ0577.247.049. Closed Sun. Chic, cosy restaurant down a small side street. Pizza €7.

La Bottega dei Sapori Antichi Via delle Terme 39/41. Extravagantly stocked deli with a fabulous wine selection.

Drinking and nightlife

The lively bars around the Campo, though a bit pricier than elsewhere, are open until late and drinks come with great snacks early in the evening.

Cubano Via San Martino 31. Lively Cuban-themed place.

Masgala 1 Camporegio. Great cocktails (especially the mojitos) and fantastic views over the Duomo. Beer €4.

Ortensia Via di Pantaneto 95. Student hangout with a friendly hippy owner. Lasagne €4, beer €1.50.

Moving on

Bus Florence (hourly; 90min); San Gimignano (hourly; 1hr; except Sun – involves a change at Poggibonsi).

Train Florence (hourly; 1hr 30min); Pisa (every 30min; 1hr 50min); Perugia (every 90min; 3hr); Rome (every 70min; 3hr 20min).

SAN GIMIGNANO

One of the best-known villages in Tuscany, **SAN GIMIGNANO**'s skyline of towers, framed against the classic rolling hills of the Tuscan countryside, has justifiably caught the tourist imagination, and in high season is extremely busy. The village was a force to be reckoned with in

the Middle Ages: it had a large population of fifteen thousand but was hit hard by the Black Death and never quite recovered – today there's half that number.

You can walk across the town in fifteen minutes, and around the walls in an hour. The main entrance gate, facing the bus terminal on the south side of town, is **Porta San Giovanni**, from where **Via San Giovanni** leads to the town's interlocking main squares, **Piazza della Cisterna** and **Piazza del Duomo**. The more austere Piazza Duomo, off to the left, is flanked by the **Collegiata Cathedral** (Mon–Sat 10.30am–5/7.00pm, Sun 12.30–5pm; €3.50), frescoed with Old and New Testament scenes. The **Palazzo del Popolo**, next door (daily 9.30/10am–5.30/7pm; €5), gives you the chance to climb the **Torre Grossa** (€4.10), the town's highest surviving tower. North from Piazza Duomo, **Via San Matteo** is one of the grandest and best preserved of the city streets, with quiet alleyways running down to the walls. The **Wine Museum**, at the Parco della Rocca, is free to enter and you can enjoy a glass of wine while admiring the spectacular view. There are wine-tasting evenings throughout the year (€5; ⓣ0577.941.267 for details).

A **combined museum ticket** (€7.50) is available at any of the participating sites.

Arrival and information

Bus is the best way to get here from Florence (hourly; 1hr 20min) or Siena (hourly; 1hr).
Train The nearest train station is Poggibonsi, on the Siena–Empoli line; buses run to San Gimignano every hour (€1.60).
Tourist office 1, Piazza del Duomo (daily 9am–1pm & 2/3–6pm; ⓣ0577.940.008, ⓦwww.sangimignano.com).
Internet Café just outside Porta San Mateo (€2/20min).

Accommodation

Accommodation is expensive, and it's advisable to book in advance. The tourist office has lists of private rooms (from €40 for a double), which are often available. The Associazione Extralberghiere, Piazza della Cisterna 6 (daily 10am–6pm, closed Thurs & Sun 1–2pm; ⓣ0577.943.190) or the Siena Hotels Promotion, Via San Giovanni 125 just inside Porta San Giovanni (Mon, Wed, Fri & Sat 9.30am–12.30pm & 2.30–7pm; Tues & Thurs 2.30–7pm; ⓣ0577.940.809) can also help.
Foresteria del Monastero S Girolamo Via Folgore 30 ⓣ0577.940.573, ⓔmonasterosangimignano@gmail.com. Basic accommodation but an excellent budget choice in a quiet monastery. Booking essential. Dorm €25.
Il Boschetto Loc. Santa Lucia 38c ⓣ0577.940.352, ⓦwww.boschettodipiemma.it. Well-equipped campsite 3km downhill in the village of Santa Lucia. Has a swimming pool, tennis courts and on-site restaurant Adult €10, tent €7.
Le Vecchie Mura 15 Via Piandornella ⓣ0577.940.270. The most fabulous restaurant in San Gimignano (see below) also rents out private rooms with a/c, satellite TV and dinner on your doorstep. €60.

Eating and drinking

Take a picnic up to the Parco di Montestaffoli and enjoy the views of the village and surrounding countryside. Try *Gustava Enoteca,* Vai S Matteo 2, an overflowing deli that also has a tiny sit-down area and an amazing range of wines.
Cum Quibus Via San Martino 17 ⓣ0577.943.199. Closed Tues. Welcoming restaurant with a small outdoor courtyard, serving interesting Tuscan specialities such as wild boar with polenta €14.
Di Vinorum Piazza Cisterna 30/Via degli Innocenti 5 ⓣ0577.907.192. Lovely spot for an early evening drink. The bar is built into the town wall and has a cool stone interior and leafy garden, not to mention some fantastic views. Wine from €3.
Gelateria di Piazza Piazza Cisterna 1. Great *gelateria* right on the piazza.
Le Vecchie Mura 13 Via Piandornella ⓣ0577.940270. Romantic restaurant with wonderful views of the Tuscan hillside. Serves delicate, tasty dishes such as sage and butter ravioli (€8) and great house wine.

PERUGIA

Lovely, hilltop **PERUGIA**, the Umbrian capital, is an attractive medieval university town full of young people of every nationality, many of them students at the Università per Stranieri (Foreigners' University). It's a great place to amble,

people-watch, and eat chocolate – Italy's best-known chocolate, Perugini, is made here.

What to see and do

Perugia hinges on a single street, **Corso Vannucci**, a broad pedestrian thoroughfare. At the far end, the austere **Piazza Quattro Novembre** is backed by the plain-faced **Duomo San Lorenzo** (daily 8am–noon & 4pm–sunset) and is interrupted by the thirteenth-century Fontana Maggiore. The lavishly decorated **Collegio di Cambio** (daily 9am–12.30pm & 2.30–5.30pm; €2.60) sits at Corso Vannucci 25. This is the town's medieval money exchange, frescoed by the famous architect Perugino and said to be the most beautiful bank in the world. The Palazzo dei Priori houses the **Galleria Nazionale di Umbria** (daily 8.30am–7.30pm; closed first Mon of each month; €6.50), one of central Italy's best galleries, whose collection includes statues by Cambio, frescoes by Bonfigli and works by Perugino. **Via dei Priori** is a lovely, winding, cobbled street which gently bends through the rambling white buildings. This leads down to Agostino di Duccio's colourful **Oratorio di San Bernardino**, whose richly embellished facade is by far the best piece of sculpture in the city. On the southern side of town, along Corso Cavour, the cloisters of the large church of **San Domenico** hold the **Museo Archeologico Nazionale dell'Umbria** (Mon 2.30–7.30pm, Tues–Sun 8.30am–7.30pm; €4), home of one of the most extensive Etruscan collections around.

THE UMBRIA JAZZ FESTIVAL

One of the most prestigious jazz events in Europe, the **Umbria Jazz Festival** has featured stars such as Dizzy Gillespie and Keith Jarrett. It takes place in July and while the main events tend to be in Perugia, there are offshoots – performances and workshops that often make use of stunning churches, courts and open-air spaces – in towns across the region. ⓦwww.umbriajazz.com.

Arrival and information

Bus Buses arrive at Piazza Partigiani. Follow the bank of escalators up to Piazza Italia. Spoletina are the biggest bus operators in southeastern Umbria – see ⓦwww.spoletina.com. Buses #1,# 6, #7 or #8 run from the bus terminal to the train station.

Train Trains arrive well away from the centre of Perugia on Piazza Vittorio Veneto; buses go from outside the station to Piazza Italia or Piazza Matteotti (15min). Tickets can be bought from the ticket stand for €1.

Tourist office On Piazza IV Novembre 3 (Mon–Sat 8.30am–1.30pm & 3.30–6.30pm, Sun 9am–1pm; ⓣ075.573.6458, ⓦwww.regioneumbria.eu) and Piazza Matteotti 18 (Mon–Sat 8.30am–1.30pm & 3.30–6.30pm, Sun 9am–1pm; ⓣ075.573.6458). Both provide the invaluable free *Little Blue What to Do* book of information on Perugia.

Internet Coffee Break at Via Danzetta 22 (daily 11am–1am; €1/hr).

Accommodation

Eden Via C Caporali 9 ⓣ075.572.8102, ⓦwww.hoteleden.perugia.it. A simply decorated two-star in the centre of town with a nice terrace and a lovely bar right downstairs that does great *aperitivo*. €80.

Hotel Rosalba Via del Circo 7 ⓣ075.572.0626, ⓦwww.hotelrosalba.com. Run by a warm and friendly owner, *Hotel Rosalba* has lovely, fresh rooms in a quiet but central location. €70.

Ostello Della Gioventù Via Bontempi 13 ⓣ075.572.2880, ⓦwww.ostello.perugia.it. Welcoming hostel 2min from the Duomo, with a 1am curfew. Closed between 9.30am and 4pm. Dorm bed €15.

Spagnoli Via Cortonese 4 ⓣ075.501.1366. Located near to the train station, this is a handy option to save the walk up the hill into town. Basic, large dorms with shared showers. Dorm bed €15.

Eating

Perugia is full of markets and delis friendly to the budget traveller's wallet and stomach. Co-op (daily

9am–8pm) supermarket is on Piazza Matteotti 15 while Mercato Coperto (Mon–Sat 9am–1pm) is a covered market off Piazza Matteotti, next to the information centre.

Antica Salumeria Granieri Amato Green stall on Piazza Matteotti selling sandwiches made from hot roast pork, an Umbrian speciality.

Del Soprammuro Piazza Matteotti 24. Excellent *pasticcherie* (the coffee is delicious and the pastries are fresh and flaky) with cosy upstairs seating and seats on the piazza, excellent for admiring the surrounding hills and revelling in the *dolce vita*.

Il Gufo 18 Via della Viola. Dishes made with deliciously fresh, seasonal ingredients. The grilled vegetables with black rice and baked brie are especially good (€9).

Mediterranea Piazza Piccinino 11/12 ⓣ075.572.1322. A vast selection of tasty, cheap pizzas. Get here early as it fills up fast. Pizza €5.

Drinking and nightlife

Frequented by both local and international students, Perugia's nightlife is varied and lively. ⓦwww.egeneration.pg.it, effectively Perugia's *Little Blue Book* online, is worth checking out for information on club nights and events.

Cocco pub Piazza Matteotti. A stall where locals buy drinks to sit out on the piazza steps. Belgian beer €3.

La Terraza Via Matteotti (next to tourist office). Outdoor bar with sweeping views. Cocktails from €5.

L'Officina Borgo XX Gingro 56 ⓣ075.572.1699. Tucked away so you hardly notice it, this modernist *enoteca*'s centrepiece is a glass-walled kitchen, while its walls are lined with dusty bottles. The staff are extremely friendly and the wine is fantastic. Glass of wine €3.

Punto di Vista Viale dell'Indipendenza 2. Extremely popular bar with beautiful views of the rolling countryside and snow-capped peaks in the distance. Open until 2.30am. Beer €4.

FESTIVALS

As well as its jazz festival, Perugia has a stream of eclectic events throughout the year that are well worth looking up in advance. In mid-October there's a **chocolate festival** that lasts for ten days, while the **Christmas market** is splendid in its scale and opulence. See the tourist office website (ⓦwww.regioneumbria.eu) for details.

Moving on

Bus Siena (11am & 9pm; 1hr 30min).
Train Assisi (hourly; 20min); Florence (hourly; 2hr); Rome (hourly; 2hr).

ASSISI

Just a twenty-minute train ride from Perugia, **ASSISI** is Umbria's best-known town thanks to St Francis, Italy's premier saint and founder of the Franciscan order. It has a medieval hill-town charm and is easy to navigate around in just a few hours.

The **Basilica di San Francesco**, now restored to its former glory after a devastating earthquake in 1997, is at the end of Via San Francesco (daily 8.30am–6pm). It houses one of the most overwhelming collections of art outside a gallery anywhere in the world. St Francis lies under the floor of the Lower Church, in a crypt only brought to light in 1818. The walls have been lavishly frescoed by artists such as Cimabue and Giotto, and the stained-glass windows cast a dim light that enhances the magical atmosphere. The Upper Church, built to a light and airy Gothic plan, is richly decorated too, with dazzling frescoes about the life of St Francis. A short trek up the steep Via di San Rufino leads to the thirteenth-century **Duomo**, which holds the font used to baptize St Francis.

From the train station, there are half-hourly buses into town. The **tourist office** is on Piazza del Comune 12 (Mon–Sat 8am–2pm & 3–6.30pm, Sun 10am–1pm & 2–5pm). There is a small **hostel**, *Ostello della Pace* (177 Via Di Valecchie; ⓣ075.816.767, ⓦwww.assisihostel.com; dorm bed €16), located on a beautiful hillside just below the town. For **lunch** or a snack, head to *Il Duomo* on Via Porta Perlici 11, which does tasty, stone-oven pizzas (€4). Alternatively, *Trattoria Pallotta*, 2 Via Volta Piana (closed Tues) has a great range of hearty dishes ranging from the usual fare of pasta to wild boar specialities (from €13).

SPOLETO

SPOLETO is a tiny hilltop town adorned with small and winding cobbled streets, beautiful Romanesque churches and the remains of an ancient amphitheatre. **Piazza della Libertà** is where you will find the **Museo Archeologico** (Mon–Sun 8.30am–7.30pm; €2), and where you can also glimpse the ancient arena. From here it's a short walk to the elegant **Duomo** (7.30am–12.30pm & 3–6pm). Inside, the superlative apse frescoes were painted by the fifteenth-century Florentine artist Fra Lippo Lippi – he died shortly after their completion amid rumours that he was poisoned for seducing the daughter of a local noble family. The **Ponte delle Torri**, a photo-favourite, is an astonishing piece of medieval engineering, best seen as part of a circular walk around the base of the **Rocca** – everyone's idea of a cartoon castle, with towers, crenellations and sheer walls. **Piazza del Mercato** is a great place to head for a spot of lunch, where there are numerous restaurants offering fixed-price lunch deals. The best is the *Mad Cow* restaurant, right on the corner of the square, unmissable for the large cow posters plastered over everything (€10 fixed menu), or *Pizzeria Zeppelin* at 81 Corso Giuseppe Mazzini, which does great slices of pizza for just €1.

There is a small **hotel**, *Villa Redenta* at 1 Via di Redenta (☎0743.224.936, Ⓦwww.villaredenta.com; €25) just a short walk from the station in the lower town. If you're looking for somewhere closer to the action, *Il Panciolle*, Via del Duomo 3 (☎0743.456.77; €65), is a reasonably priced two-star hotel with seven rooms. There's also a swish restaurant downstairs that specialises in grilled meat dishes.

URBINO

URBINO, one of the most prestigious courts in Europe in the fifteenth century, is today a pretty university town, notable for its gorgeous hilltop location and laid-back atmosphere. While there's not a huge amount here of interest, it's a good place to explore if you're looking for a more authentic Italian experience with a relaxed student vibe.

What to see and do

In the centre of town, the **Palazzo Ducale** is a fitting monument to Federico da Montefeltro, the fifteenth-century Duke of Urbino whose enthusiastic embrace of Renaissance culture defines the city to this day. It is now home to the **Galleria Nazionale delle Marche** (Mon 8.30am–2pm, Tues–Sun 8.30am–7.15pm; €4). Among the paintings in the Appartamento del Duca are Piero della Francesca's strange *Flagellation*, and the *Ideal City*, a famous perspective painting of a symmetrical and deserted cityscape. The most interesting and best preserved of the *palazzo*'s rooms is Federico's Studiolo, a triumph of illusory perspective.

The pleasant jumble of Renaissance and medieval houses making up the rest of Urbino is a welcome antidote to the rarefied atmosphere of the Palazzo Ducale, if also a somewhat tougher terrain up and down the hills. You can wind down and rest your calf muscles in one of the many bars and trattorias, or take a picnic up to the gardens within the **Fortezza Albornoz,** from where you'll get great views of the town and countryside.

Arrival and information

Bus Urbino isn't on a train line and can be difficult to reach. The best approach is by bus from Perugia (daily; 1hr 50min; €13) or from Pésaro (every 30min – last bus around 8pm; 1hr; €2.75). Buses stop in Borgo Mercatale, at the foot of the Palazzo Ducale, which is reached either by lift just to the left or by Francesco di Giorgio Martini's spiral staircase.

Tourist office The tourist office is at 3 Via Puccinotti ☎0722.2613 (Mon–Sat 9am–1pm & Tues–Fri 3–6pm) and Piazza Mercatale (6.30am–8.30pm) just by the lift.

Accommodation

For accommodation, the cheapest options are private rooms – lists are available from the tourist office, but be prepared to do the leg work yourself.

Albergo Italia Corso Garibaldi 32 ⓣ0722.2701, ⓦwww.albergo-italia-urbino.it. This business-style hotel is a short walk from the lift and stumbling distance from the bars of Palazzo Ducale. €80.

Hotel Rafaello 38/40 Via Santa Margherita ⓣ0722.4896. Once up the steep hill, the rooms in the *Rafaello* provide stunning views. Prices increase in line with the altitude. €90.

Pensione Fosca Via Rafaello 67 ⓣ0722.329.622. A pleasant family-run place right in the centre with white-washed walls and big windows. €60.

Eating and drinking

A picnic from one of the delis, or the Margherita Conad supermarket on Via Raffaello 37 (Mon–Sat 7.30am–2pm, 4.30–8pm), provides good self-catering alternatives.

Bar L'Isola Via dei Veterani 18. A friendly, low-key place with internet access.

Dolce Vita 1 Via Garibaldi. Great place for *aperitivo*, delicious wine and large bowls of pasta. They also have an extensive sushi menu if you fancy a change. Meals from €9.

El Piquero Via Domenico 1. Often packed student club with different music every night. Beer included in entry, €5.

FROM ITALY AND BEYOND

The main arrival and departure port on the eastern coast is the transit town of **Ancona**, with ferries taking you to Croatia, Albania, Greece and Turkey. Ferries leave from Stazione Marittima, a few kilometres north of the train station (take bus #1). All of the ferry companies have ticket offices dotted around the port, plus there are dozens of agencies around town if these happen to be closed. destination include: Corfu, Greece (weekly; 15hr); Durrësi, Albania (3 weekly in summer; 18hr); Igoumenítsa, Greece (daily; 15hr); Pátra, Greece (daily; 22hr); Split, Croatia (daily; 4hr 30min–9hr); Stari Grad, Croatia (July & August only; weekly; 9hr); Vis, Croatia (weekly; 9hr); Zadar, Croatia (daily; 9hr).

Il Ghiottore 10 Via Mazzini. Great pizza place. Slices from €1.80.

Il Cotegiano 13 Via Puccinoltti. Vast range of salads at around €8 to deal with your veggie cravings.

Pizzeria il Buco 1 Via Battisti. Popular with the student crowd, this takeaway pizza parlour does large, delicious slices from €1.40.

Moving on

Bus Perugia (daily; 1hr 50min); Pésaro (every 30min; 1hr).

Southern Italy

The Italian **south** or *mezzogiorno* offers quite a different experience from that of the north; indeed, few countries are more tangibly divided into two distinct, often antagonistic, regions. **Naples** is the obvious focus, an utterly compelling city just a couple of hours south of Rome. In the **Bay of Naples**, highlights are the resort of Sorrento and the island of **Capri**, crawling with tourists these days but still beautiful enough to be worth your time, while the ancient sites of **Pompeii** and **Herculaneum** are Italy's best-preserved Roman remains. South of Naples, the **Amalfi Coast** is a contender for Europe's most dramatic stretch of coastline. In the far south, **Matera**, jewel of the Basilicata region, harbours ancient cave dwellings dug into a steep ravine. Puglia – the long strip of land that makes up the "heel" of Italy – boasts the Baroque wonders of **Lecce,** and is also useful for ferries to Greece and Croatia.

NAPLES

Wherever else you travel south of Rome, the chances are that you'll wind up in **NAPLES** (Napoli). It's the kind of city people visit with preconceptions, and it rarely disappoints: it is filthy, large and overbearing; it is crime-infested; and it

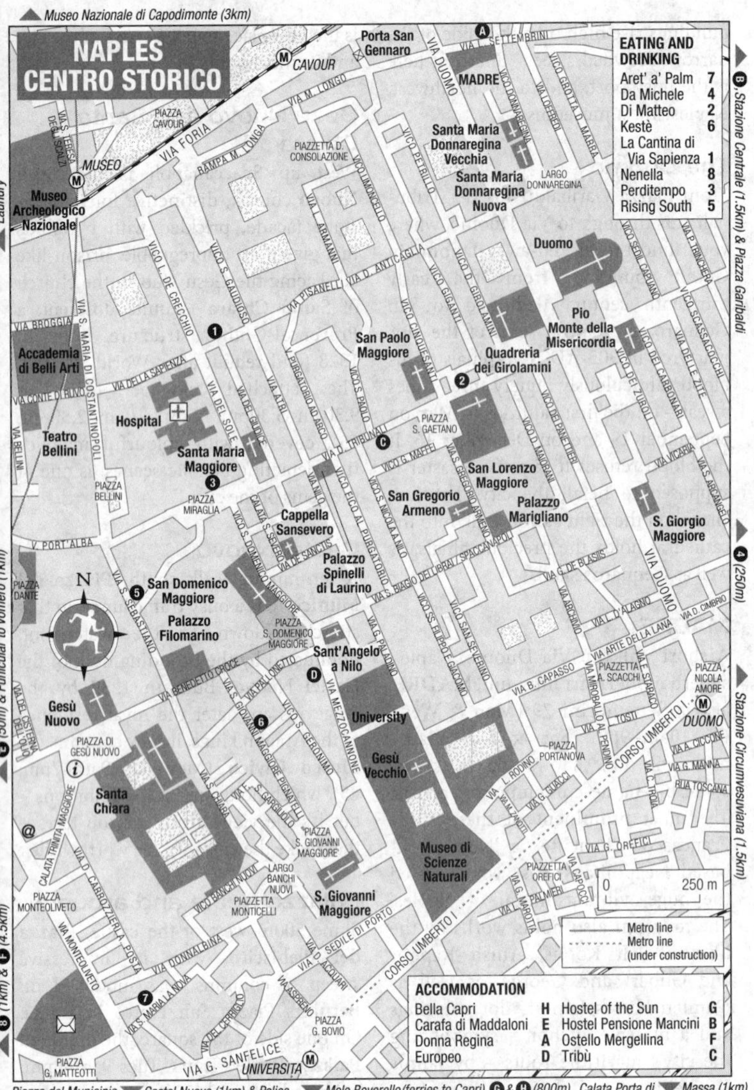

is most definitely like nowhere else in Italy – something the inhabitants will be keener than anyone to tell you. One thing, though, is certain: a couple of days here and you're likely to be as staunch a defender of the place as its most devoted inhabitants.

What to see and do

The area between the vast and busy Piazza Garibaldi, the city's transport hub, and Via Toledo, the main street a mile or so west, makes up the old part of the city – the **centro storico**, whose

buildings rise high on either side of the narrow, crowded streets. South of here is the busy port, and to the northwest, Naples' finest museums.

The Duomo

From Piazza Garibaldi, Via dei Tribunali cuts through to Via Duomo, where you'll find the tucked-away **Duomo**, a Gothic building from the early thirteenth century dedicated to San Gennaro, the patron saint of the city, martyred in 305 AD. Two phials of his blood miraculously liquefy three times a year – on the first Saturday in May, on September 19 and on December 16. If the blood refuses to liquefy, disaster is supposed to befall the city. The first chapel on the right as you walk into the cathedral holds the precious phials, as well as Gennaro's skull.

MADRE

A short walk up Via Duomo, Naples' superb modern art museum, **MADRE**, at Via Settembrini 79 (Mon & Wed–Fri 10am–9pm, Sat & Sun 10am–midnight; €7), shows off works by some big-name contemporary artists. The most prominent of these is by Francesco Clemente, a New York-based Neapolitan artist who created the huge, vibrant mural of Naples. The museum also holds works by the likes of Jeff Koons, Anish Kapoor and Gilbert and George, as well as Damien Hirst's famous dot paintings and a massive anchor – symbolizing the city's maritime roots – by Jannis Kounellis.

Spaccanapoli and around

On the other side of Via Duomo, busy Via dei Tribunali and its parallel, Via San Biagio dei Librai – commonly known as **Spaccanapoli** – make up the heart of the old city and Naples' busiest and architecturally richest quarter. A maelstrom of hurrying pedestrians, revving cars and buzzing scooters, this is the best place to get a sense of the city and its inhabitants.

Gesù Nuovo and Santa Chiara

West up Spaccanapoli is the **Gesù Nuovo** church, distinctive for its lava-stone facade, prickled with pyramids that give it an impregnable, prison-like air. Facing the Gesù Nuovo, the church of **Santa Chiara** is quite different, a Provencal-Gothic structure built in 1328 (and rebuilt after World War II). The attached **cloister** (Mon–Sat 9.30am–5.30pm, Sun 10am–2.30pm; €5), covered with colourful majolica tiles depicting bucolic scenes, is one of the gems of the city.

Castel Nuovo

A ten-minute walk south, **Piazza del Municipio** is a busy traffic junction that stretches down to the waterfront, dominated by the brooding hulk of the **Castel Nuovo**. Built in 1282 by the Angevins and later the royal residence of the Aragon kings, it now contains the **Museo Civico** (Mon–Sat 9am–7pm; €5), which holds periodic exhibitions – but it's the views from the top terrace that make the entrance fee worthwhile.

Palazzo Reale and around

Some 500m west of the castle, **Piazza del Plebiscito**, with its impressive sweep of columns, was modelled on Bernini's Piazza San Pietro in Rome. On one side of the square, the dignified **Palazzo Reale** (Thurs–Tues 9am–8pm; €4) was built in 1602 to accommodate a visit by Philip III of Spain. Upstairs, the first-floor rooms are sumptuously decorated with gilded furniture, *trompe-l'oeil* ceilings, and seventeenth- and eighteenth-century paintings.

Just beyond the castle, the opulent **Teatro San Carlo** (guided tours Thurs–Mon 9am–5.30pm, €5; booking required on ⓣ081.553.4565) is the largest opera house in Italy, and one of

the most distinguished in the world. The cheapest seats you can book are €25, but unsold tickets are available to students and under-30s for €15 an hour before the performance starts.

Museo Archeologico Nazionale

Arrowing north from the Piazza del Plebiscito, Via Toledo leads to the **Museo Archeologico Nazionale** (Wed–Mon 9am–7.30pm; €6.50), Naples' essential sight, home to the best of the finds from the nearby Roman sites of Pompeii and Herculaneum. The ground floor concentrates on sculpture, including the *Farnese Bull* and the *Farnese Hercules* from the Baths of Caracalla in Rome. The mezzanine houses the museum's collection of mosaics, while upstairs, wall paintings from the villas of Pompeii and Herculaneum are the museum's other major draw. Don't miss the "secret" room of erotic Roman pictures and sculptures, once thought to be a threat to public morality.

Museo Nazionale di Capodimonte

At the top of the hill is the city's other major museum, the **Museo Nazionale di Capodimonte** (Thurs–Tues 8.30am–7.30pm; €7.50; bus #R4 from Via Toledo or #178 from the Museo Archeologico), the former residence of the Bourbon King Charles III, built in 1738. This has a huge and superb collection of Renaissance and Flemish paintings, including a couple of Brueghels, canvases by Perugino and Pinturicchio, an elegant *Madonna and Child with Angels* by Botticelli and Lippi's soft, sensitive *Annunciation*.

Vomero

Vomero, the district topping the hill immediately above the old city, can be reached by funicular from Corso Vittorio Emanuele, west of the Gesù Nuovo, or Piazza Augusteo near the Teatro San Carlo. A five-minute stroll from the station, the star-shaped fortress of **Castel Sant'Elmo** (Wed–Mon 9am–6.30pm; €3) was built in the fourteenth century and hosts occasional exhibitions. Occupying Naples' highest point, its lovely views are only topped by those from the terraced gardens of the **Certosa e Museo di San Martino** (Thurs–Tues 8.30am–7.30pm; €6), a former Carthusian monastery. Now a museum, it contains seventeenth- and eighteenth-century Neapolitan painting and sculpture.

Arrival and information

Air Naples' Capodochino Airport is connected with Piazza Garibaldi by orange bus #3S (every 30min; journey time 30min; €1.10). The red-and-white official airport bus Alibus (every 20min; €3) runs to Piazza Garibaldi and then Piazza Municipio.

Bus Most long-distance, inter-regional buses and local buses use Piazza Garibaldi, but some (for Amalfi, Sorrento and Pompeii) use Piazza Immacolatella, in the port area.

Ferry Hydrofoils dock at Molo Beverello, a short bus ride or a 15min walk from the centre; ferries arrive at Calata Porta di Massa, connected with Molo Beverello by free shuttle bus.

Train Trains arrive at Piazza Garibaldi, the main hub of all transport services.

Tourist information There's tourist information at the train station (Mon–Sat 9am–7pm, Sun 9am–2pm) and airport (daily 9am–7pm), but the main tourist office is at Piazza del Gesù Nuovo (Mon–Sat 9am–7pm, Sun 9am–2pm; ⓣ081.551.2701, ⓦwww.inaples.it). Pick up the free listings booklet *Qui Napoli*, handy for events and transport times.

Discount cards If you are around for more than a day, invest in the Artecard (from €12; sold in the station, museums and online at ⓦwww.campaniaartecard.it), which is valid on various combinations of city transport, along with free museum entrance.

City transport

Tickets Buy tickets – valid on all city transport – from *tabacchi*. €1.10 tickets are valid for 1hr 30min, €3.10 ones for the day. A 24hr, €6 Unico Costiera ticket also allows you to travel on SITA buses (to Amalfi, for example) and Circumvesuviana trains (for Pompeii). Stamp tickets on board to validate them.

Bus and metro Walking is the best option in the centre, but an extensive bus and metro network is available for the footsore. Useful routes include #R2 between the port and the station and #E1 for the centro storico – Piazza del Gesù, Via Santa Chiara and Via Tribunale. Underground metros – indicated by a red M symbol – are fast but only run every 10min or so. Stops include Piazza Garibaldi, Piazza Cavour, Piazza Dante and Piazza Vanvitelli in Vomero.
Funicular Funicular railways run up to Vomero and the suburbs of Chiaia and Mergellina.

Accommodation

Many of the cheaper hotels are unappealingly sited around Piazza Garibaldi, near the station. If you can afford it, shell out a few extra euros to stay in one of the budget hotels in the historic centre instead. Breakfast is included in all options below, unless stated otherwise.

Hostels and hotels

Bella Capri Via Melisurgo 4 ⓣ081.552.9494, ⓦwww.bellacapri.it. Right by the port, with bright common areas and small, a/c dorms. It's also a hotel, with simple rooms overlooking the bay. Ten percent discount with this book. Dorms €20, rooms €80.
Europeo Via Mezzocannone 109/c ⓣ081.551.7254, ⓦwww.sea-hotels.com. Although cramped, rooms are central and great value. No breakfast, and you pay extra for a/c. €62.
Hostel of the Sun Via Melisurgo 15 ⓣ081.420.6393, ⓦwww.hostelnapoli.com. Colourful hostel next to the port. The friendly staff are full of advice on how to spend your time in the city and organize nightlife tours and pasta parties. Free internet. Dorms €18; ten percent discount on doubles (€60–70) with this book.
Hostel Pensione Mancini Via Mancini 33 ⓣ081.553.6731, ⓦwww.hostelpensionemancini.com. Small, very basic place right across from the station. Ten percent discount with this book. Dorms €18, rooms €55.
Ostello Mergellina Salita della Grotta 23 ⓣ081.761.2346, ⓔnapoli@ostellionline.org. Metro to Mergellina or bus #R3 from Piazza Municipio. HI hostel some way out of the centre with a view of the bay. Dorms €16, rooms (bunk beds only) €40

TREAT YOURSELF

If you're going to splurge on accommodation anywhere in Italy, Naples is the place: your money will go a lot further and the city's clutch of boutique B&Bs make memorable places to stay. Choose between arty **Tribù** (Via Tribunali 339; ⓣ081.454.793, ⓦwww.tribunapoli.com; €80), with a cool, designer feel; **Donna Regina** (Via Settembrini 80; ⓣ081.446.799, ⓦwww.discovernaples.net; €92), a beautifully restored ex-convent run by a family of artists; and **Carafa di Maddaloni** (Via Maddaloni 6; ⓣ081.551.3691, ⓦwww.bb-carafa.com; €120), with beautiful, frescoed rooms filled with antiques.

Camping

Vulcano Solfatara Via Solfatara 161, Pozzuoli ⓣ081.526.2341, ⓦwww.solfatara.it. Metro to Pozzuoli, then a 10min walk uphill. This well-equipped campsite, on the edge of a volcanic crater, has a swimming pool, mini-market and takeaway. Camping €9.60 per person, plus €5.20 per tent; 2-person bungalows €51

Eating

Spaccanapoli and Via Tribunali are full of grocery stores, which make up panini for a few euros, and there's a central supermarket, Fior do Cafè, near the university at Via Mezzocannone 99. Colourful produce markets are found all over the centre; one of the best (daily 8am–1pm) takes up the streets around Via Pignasecca, a few streets west of the Gesù Nuovo.
Da Michele Via Cesare Sersale 1–3. Closed Sun. One of Naples' most historic pizzerias, serving up enormous, tasty and cheap pizzas (from €2.50) since 1870.
Di Matteo Via Tribunali 94. Closed Sun. A strong contender for the title of Naples' best pizzeria, *Di Matteo* is famous for its deep-fried versions (around €5).
La Cantina di Via Sapienza Via Sapienza 40–41. Closed dinner & Sun. Proprietor Gaetano dishes up hearty home-cooked classics like *polpette fritte* (fried meatballs) for €5; full meals cost €10–12.
Nennella Vico Lungo Teatro Nuovo 103–105. Closed Sun. Authentic Neapolitan cuisine like *pasta e fagioli* (soup with pasta and beans) and sautéed *friarelli* (local chicory-like greens) are served up in this very basic trattoria, which is always heaving at lunchtime. Full meals €10–12.

Drinking and nightlife

Most clubs close in July and August and move to the beach; the Neapolitans who remain congregate for a beer in the studenty bars around Piazza del

Gesù Nuovo. The rest of the year, the bars and clubs along Via Cisterna dell'Olio, just off the piazza, are a good bet.

Aret' a' Palm Piazza Santa Maria La Nova 14. Easy to find thanks to the huge palm tree outside (the name means "behind the palm" in Neapolitan dialect), this is the most popular of the laid-back bars in the centre. It's open till 2.30am but is an ideal pre-club stop.

Kestè Largo San Giovanni Maggiore Pignatelli 26–27 ⓣ081.551.3984. A buzzy bar with DJs and live music. Go early for the *aperitivo* buffet and stay for the band or DJ set. Closed Aug.

Perditempo Via San Pietro a Maiella 8. Tiny bar with stacks of new and used CDs and LPs, live music and a cool crowd. Closed Sun & Aug.

Rising South Via S. Sebastiano 19 ⓣ335.879.428. Closed mid-May to Sept. The coolest club in Naples, with a velvet Baroque interior, great cocktails and loungey tunes. Call to be put on the list on Thurs, Fri & Sat.

Directory

Consulates UK, Via dei Mille 40 ⓣ081.423.8911; US, Piazza della Repubblica 2 ⓣ081.583.8111.

Exchange At Stazione Centrale (daily 8am–7.30pm).

Hospital Ambulance ⓣ118; the Guardia Medica Permanente in Palazzo Municipio is open 24hr.

Internet Navig@ndo (Via S. Anna dei Lombardi 28; Mon–Fri 9.30am–8pm, Sat 10am–2pm; €2/hr).

Laundry Bolle Blu, Corso Novara 62–64, near the station (Mon–Sat 8.30am–8pm).

Pharmacy At the train station (24hr).

Police ⓣ113. Main police station is at Via Medina 75 ⓣ081.551.5607.

Post office Piazza Matteotti Giacomo 2. Mon–Fri 8am–6.30pm, Sat 8am–12.30pm.

Moving on

Air Palermo (2 daily; 50min).

Bus Amalfi (6 daily; 2–3hr); Assisi (1 daily; 5hr); Atrani (4 daily; 1hr 50min); Lecce (3 daily; 5hr 30min); Perugia (1daily; 4hr 30min); Pompeii (hourly; 35min); Sorrento (2 daily; 1hr 20min).

Ferry Capri (8 daily; 1hr 20min); Palermo (2 daily; 8–10hr 30min).

Hydrofoil Capri (every 30min; 40min); Sorrento (8 daily; 50min).

Train Lecce (12 daily; 5hr 30min); Palermo (5 daily; 8–11hr); Pompeii (from Stazione Circumvesuviana; every 30min; 20min); Rome (every 10min; 1hr 20min–2hr 40min); Siracusa (7 daily; 8–10hr); Sorrento (every 20min; 55min).

THE BAY OF NAPLES

Of the islands that dot the bay, **Capri** is the best place to visit if you're here for a short time. **Sorrento**, the brooding presence of **Vesuvius** and the incomparable Roman sites of **Herculaneum** and **Pompeii** are further draws.

Herculaneum

The town of **Ercolano**, a half-hour hop on the train from Naples on the Circumvesuviana line (€1.80 one-way), is the modern offshoot of the ancient site of **HERCULANEUM** (daily: April–Oct 8.30am–7.30pm; Nov–March 8.30am–5pm; ticket office shuts 1hr 30min before; €11), situated at the seaward end of Ercolano's main street. A residential town destroyed by the eruption of Vesuvius on August 2, 79 AD, it's much smaller than Pompeii, and as such is a more manageable site – less architecturally impressive, but with better-preserved buildings. Because it wasn't a commercial town, there's no central open space, just streets of villas and shops, cut by two very straight main streets. Highlights include the **House of the Mosaic Atrium**, with its mosaic-laid courtyard, the large baths complex and the **Casa del Bel Cortile**, which contains a group of skeletons, poignantly lying in the pose they died in. Ercolano's tourist office is at Via IV Novembre 82 (ⓣ081.788.1243; Mon–Sat 8am–2pm & 4–6pm).

Vesuvius

Its most famous eruption, in 79 AD, buried the towns and inhabitants of Pompeii and Herculaneum, and **VESUVIUS** has long dominated the lives of those who live on the Bay of Naples. It's still an active volcano – the only one on mainland Europe – and there have been hundreds of (mostly minor) eruptions over the years. The people who live here fear its reawakening, and with good reason – scientists calculate it should erupt every thirty

years or so, and it hasn't done so since 1944. Vesuviana Mobiltá bus services from Naples' Piazza Garibaldi, as well as Herculaneum and Pompeii, run twice daily to a point 1000m up (E9 from Naples). Alternatively, buses run from Ercolano train station (last bus 12.45pm) to a car park and huddle of souvenir shops and cafés. The walk up to the **crater** from the bus stop takes about half an hour on marked-out paths. At the top (admission €6.50), the crater is a deep, wide, jagged ashtray of red rock emitting the odd plume of smoke. You can walk most of the way around, but take it easy – the fences are old and rickety. See Ⓦwww.vesuviopark.it for information on trails around the volcano.

Pompeii

The other Roman town destroyed by Vesuvius, **POMPEII** (daily: April–Oct 8.30am–7.30pm; Nov–March 8.30am–5pm; ticket office closes 1hr 30min earlier; €11) was one of Campania's most important commercial centres. Of a total population of twenty thousand, it's thought that two thousand perished, asphyxiated by the toxic fumes of the volcanic debris, their homes buried under several metres of ash and pumice. The full horror of their death is apparent in plaster casts made from the shapes their bodies left in the volcanic ash – gruesome, writhing figures, some with their hands covering their eyes.

Seeing the site will take you half a day at least. Entering from the Pompeii-Villa dei Misteri side, you come across the **Forum**, a slim open space surrounded by the ruins of some of the town's most important official buildings. North of here lies a small baths complex, and beyond, the **House of the Faun**, its "Ave" (Welcome) mosaic outside beckoning you in to view the atrium and the copy of a tiny bronze dancing faun. A few streets southwest, the **Lupanare** was Pompeii's only purpose-built brothel, worth a peek for its racy wall paintings. A short walk from the Porta Ercolano is the **Villa dei Misteri**, the best preserved of all Pompeii's palatial houses. It derives its name from a series of frescoes in one of its larger chambers, depicting the initiation rites of a young woman into the Dionysiac Mysteries, an orgiastic cult transplanted to Italy from Greece in the Republican era.

On the other side of the site, the **Grand Theatre** is still used for performances, as is the **Little Theatre** on its far left side. From here, it's a short walk to the **Amphitheatre**, one of Italy's most intact and also its oldest, dating from 80 BC.

SORRENTO

Topping the rocky cliffs close to the end of its peninsula, **SORRENTO**'s inspired location and pleasant climate has drawn travellers from all over Europe for two hundred years. Nowadays it caters mostly to the package-tour industry, but this bright, lively place manages to retain its southern Italian roots. Accommodation and food, though not exactly cheap, are much better value than most of the other resorts along the Amalfi Coast, making it a good base from which to explore the area. Sorrento's centre, **Piazza Tasso**, makes a lively focus for the evening *passeggiata*. The town isn't well provided with beaches: most people make do with the rocks and a tiny, crowded strip of sand at **Marina Grande** – fifteen minutes' walk or a short bus ride from Piazza Tasso.

Arrival and information

Bus Autolinee Curreri coaches from Naples Airport (6 daily; 1hr 15min; €10) stop at Via degli Aranci, near the train station; SITA buses (every 45min; 1hr 40min; €3.20) from Amalfi arrive at the station.

Ferry Metrò del Mare operates high-season connections from Naples (6 daily; 1hr; €6.50) to Sorrento's port, a short walk from the centre.

Train The station is a 5min walk from the centre.

Tourist office The office in the large yellow Circolo dei Foresteri building at Via de Maio 35, just off Piazza Sant'Antonino (Mon–Sat 8.45am–6.15pm; ⓣ081.807.4033, ⓦwww.sorrentotourism.com) can help with accommodation.

Accommodation

Camping Nube d'Argento Via del Capo 21 ⓣ081.878.1344, ⓦwww.nubedargento.com. Closed Nov–Feb. A 15min walk from Piazza Tasso towards Marina Grande, this campsite has a pool, restaurant and sea views. Camping €11 per person, plus €6 per tent, two-person bungalows €85.

Hostel Le Sirene Via degli Aranci 160 ⓣ081.807.2925, ⓦwww.hostellesirene.com. 200m from the station, this hostel is a little cramped, but there's a kitchen, and no curfew. Dorms €16–19, rooms €45–50.

Ulisse Via del Mare 22 ⓣ081.877.4753, ⓦwww.ulissedeluxe.com. A 5min walk from the centre and just 300m from the sea, this "deluxe hostel" has vast, distinctly un-hostelly a/c en suites (no dorms) with a modern, slightly corporate feel. €73.

Eating

There's a Standa supermarket at Corso Italia 223, and Ortofrutticola da Armando, near the station at Via degli Aranci 72, makes panini to order.

Da Franco Corso Italia 265. Wooden bench seating is overhung with racks of Parma ham at this no-frills local pizzeria. Pizzas from €5.50.

Giardiniello Via Accademia 7. Just off Corso Italia, this restaurant-pizzeria with a small garden specializes in fish and barbequed meats, and also does cheap pastas; try the gnocchi *alla sorrentina* for €5.

Mami Camilla Via Cocumella 4 ⓣ081.878.2067, ⓦwww.mamicamilla.com. Call before 6pm to book a four-course dinner at this cookery school for just €18.

Drinking and nightlife

In summer, all the clubbing action takes place at venues out of Sorrento, along the coast. Promoters distribute tickets from midnight onwards in Piazza Tasso; clubs are a 10min taxi ride from here.

Chaplin's Corso Italia 18. This Irish pub is a bit of a tourist magnet, but it's an appealingly raucous place to sink a skinful, and is open till 3am.

English Inn Corso Italia 55. Not as lively as *Chaplin's*, this pub is open all day, serves cheap burgers at lunchtimes and has an outside dancefloor.

Insolito Corso Italia 38E. A trendy, all-white space open day and night; sleek sister bar *li'ly* (Via Fuorimura 47) is also a disco.

Moving on

Bus Amalfi (every 40min–1hr; 1hr 30min); Naples (2 daily; 1hr 20min); Rome (1–2 daily; 3hr 45min).

Ferry Capri (8 daily; 25min).

Hydrofoil Amalfi (2 daily; 1hr 10min); Capri (every 30min; 20min); Naples (6 daily; 50min).

CAPRI

Rising from the sea off the far end of the Sorrentine peninsula, the island of **Capri** is the most sought-after destination in the Bay of Naples. During Roman times the emperor Tiberius retreated here to indulge in debauchery; more recently the Blue Grotto and the island's remarkable landscape have drawn tourists in their droves. Capri is a busy and expensive place, but it's easy enough to visit as a day-trip (and there's no budget accommodation on the island). In July and August, however, you may prefer to give it a miss rather than fight through the crowds.

What to see and do

CAPRI TOWN is a very pretty place, with winding alleyways converging on the tiny main square of Piazza Umberto. The Giardini di Augusto give tremendous views of the coast below and the towering jagged cliffs above. Opposite, take the hairpin path, Via Krupp, down to **MARINA PICCOLA**, a huddle of houses and restaurants around a few patches of pebble beach – pleasantly quiet out of season, though in summer it's heaving. You can also reach the ruins of Tiberius' villa, the **Villa Jovis**, from Capri town (daily 9am–1hr before sunset; €2), a steep thirty-minute trek east. The site is among Capri's most exhilarating, with incredible views.

ANACAPRI, the island's other main settlement, though less picturesque is the starting point for some worthwhile excursions: from here a chair-lift (daily: March–Oct 9.30am–4.30/5pm, Nov–Feb 9.30am–3.30pm; €8 return) carries you up 596m **Monte Solaro**, the island's highest point, where there's a pricey but

picturesquely sited café. The island's most famous attraction, the **Blue Grotto**, is an hour's trek down Via Lo Pozzo, or take a bus from the main square. At €10.50, with tip expected, it's a bit of a rip-off, with boatmen whisking visitors through the grotto in five minutes flat, but the intense, glowing blue of the cave is undeniably beautiful.

Arrival and information

Ferry Ferries and hydrofoils dock at Marina Grande, the waterside extension of Capri Town, which perches on the hill above, connected by funicular. Buses link the island's main centres – Marina Grande, Capri Town, Marina Piccola and Anacapri – every 15min (€1.40, or €6.90 for a day ticket).
Tourist office Piazza Umberto in Capri town ⓣ081.837.0686, ⓦwww.capritourism.com (April–Oct Mon–Sat 8.30am–8.30pm, Sun 8.30am–2.30pm; Nov–March 9am–1pm, 3.30–6.45pm).

Eating

Picnics are the only way to avoid paying Capri's inflated restaurant prices. Alimentari da Brioches (Via Fuorlovado 5, Capri Town) makes up panini to order for about €5.
Scialapopolo Via Le Botteghe 4, Capri Town. This good-value *tavola calda*'s €12 menu gets you pasta followed by a main meal such as roast pork. Snacky takeaway meals are also available.
Vini e Bibite Piazza Diaz, Anacapri. One of the island's cheapest sit-down options, with €10 deals (main course and drink) at lunch. The pizzeria opposite, *La Materita* (closed Tues) is run by the same management, and has pizzas from €6.

THE AMALFI COAST

Occupying the southern side of Sorrento's peninsula, the **Amalfi Coast** is perhaps Europe's most beautiful stretch of coast, its corniche road winding around the towering cliffs. There are no trains; buses from Sorrento and Naples take the coast road – a spectacular ride of hairpin bends with fantastic views of the undulating coastline.

Amalfi

In Byzantine times, **AMALFI** was an independent republic and a naval superpower, with a population of some seventy thousand. Vanquished by the Normans in 1131, it was then devastated by an earthquake in 1343. A few remnants of Amalfi's past glories survive, and its narrow alleyways and tucked-away piazzas make it fun to wander through. The **Duomo** dominates the main piazza, its gaudy facade topped by a glazed-tiled cupola. St Andrew is buried in its crypt, though the most appealing part of the building is the cloister (daily 9am–7.45pm, earlier in winter; €2.50) – Arabic in feel, with its whitewashed arches and palms. Close by at Piazza del Municipio 6, the **Museo Civico** (Mon, Wed, Fri 8am–2pm; Tues & Thurs 8am–2pm & 4.30–6.30pm; free) displays the Tavole Amalfitane – the book of maritime laws that governed the Republic, and the rest of the Mediterranean, until 1570. Beyond these, the focus is the busy seafront, where there's a crowded **beach**.

Arrival and information

Bus SITA buses from Sorrento and Naples and Marozzi buses from Rome (June–Sept 1 daily; 5hr 30min) arrive in Piazza Flavio Gioia, on the waterfront.
Ferry Ferries and hydrofoils from Naples, Capri and Sorrento arrive in the tiny harbour.
Train The nearest major train station is at Salerno, from where there are SITA buses and ferries to Amalfi.
Tourist office Corso delle Repubbliche Marinare 27 ⓣ089.871.107, ⓦwww.amalfitouristoffice.it (May–Sept Mon–Sat 8.30am–1pm & 3–6pm, Sun 9am–1pm; Oct–April Mon–Fri 8.30am–1pm & 3–6pm, Sat 9am–1pm).

Accommodation

Almost all the hotels in Amalfi are expensive; it makes sense to base yourself in a hostel in one of the nearby towns, such as Atrani or Positano, a short bus ride from Amalfi.
A' Scalinatella Piazza Umberto I 5–6, Atrani ⓣ089.871.492, ⓦwww.hostelscalinatella.com. SITA bus to Atrani. This popular, family-run hostel-cum-hotel has beds and rooms in buildings around Atrani, some overlooking the main square. Dorms €25, rooms €75.

Beata Solitudo Piazza G. Avitabile 4, Agerola ⓣ081.802.5048, ⓦwww.beatasolitudo.it. SITA bus to Agerola. This basic hostel 16km north of Amalfi has a small campsite attached, with 5- to 8-bed dorms and a few private en suites. Camping €5 per person, plus €3.30 per tent, dorms €11.50, rooms €80.

Sant'Andrea Via Costanza d'Avalos ⓣ089.871.145, ⓦwww.albergosantandrea.it. One of the cheaper options in town, this pretty hotel on the central square has views of the Duomo from most rooms. €70.

Eating

There's a Dogi supermarket at Piazza dei Dogi 29, a 2min walk from Piazza Duomo.

Da Memé Via Salita Marino Sebaste 8. A 5min walk from the Duomo but tucked away on a backstreet, this cheery restaurant has an extensive menu with mains from €8 and pizza from €4.

San Giuseppe Via Ruggiero 4. Closed Thurs. This very simple restaurant puts a few tables out on a tiny courtyard and serves pizza and pretty much everything else at low prices.

Moving on

Bus Ravello (every 30min; 30min); Sorrento (hourly; 1hr 40min).

Ferry Naples (2 daily; 2hr); Sorrento (5 daily; 50min).

Ravello

The best views of the coast are inland from Amalfi, in **RAVELLO**. For a time an independent republic, nowadays it's

BARI AND BRINDISI TRANSPORT

Numerous ferries arrive at the busy ports of **Bari** and **Brindisi** on a daily basis, and the two cities are also served by budget airlines Ryanair and easyJet.

Bari

Ferries arrive at the port from Albania (Durrës: hourly, 8hr); Croatia (Dubrovnik, Korčula and Hvar: up to 3 weekly, 9hr 30min–16hr 30min); Montenegro (Bar: 2–5 weekly, 8–9hr; Kotor: 1 weekly, 9hr); and Greece (Igoumenítsa: 2–3 daily, 8–10hr; Corfu: 1–2 daily, 5–6hr; Pátra: 1–2 daily, 15–16hr). The port is connected with the train station by bus #20 (every 40min; €1.50).

Trains to Naples (6 daily; 3hr 30min–5hr 30min) and Lecce (hourly; 1hr 30min) leave from the central station in Piazza Aldo Moro; trains to Matera (every 30min; 1hr 30min) use the private FAL line, leaving from the small station on the corner of the same piazza.

Buses Marinobus services to Naples also depart from the piazza (4 daily; 3hr 45min). From the **airport**, the Pugliarbus runs to Brindisi airport (3–4 daily; 1hr 40min) and to Matera (2 daily; 2hr 15min); bus #16 goes to the central station (every 40min–1hr; €0.80).

Tourist office Piazza Aldo Moro ⓣ0809.909.341 (Mon–Sat 9am–7pm & 3–6pm; Sun 10am–1pm).

Brindisi

Ferries The central Stazione Marittima, used by ferries from Albania (Valona: 6 weekly, 8hr 30min; Vlore: 1 daily, 8hr), is a 10min walk from the centre of town; ferries from Greece (Corfu: 1–2 daily, 6hr; Igoumenítsa: 2–3 daily, 7hr 30min; Pátra: 1 daily, 13hr 30min; Kefalloniá: 1 daily, 10hr 15min) dock at Costa Morena, 2km southeast of town but linked by shuttle bus.

Trains The station is a 20min walk west of the port, on Piazza Crispi.

Buses Miccolis buses to Lecce (3 daily; 35min) and Naples (3 daily; 6hr) and Marozzi buses to Rome (4 daily; 6hr 30min) all depart from Viale Togliatti in the new town. From the **airport**, buses (€3) meet arrivals and run into town via the port and train station. COTRAP buses run from the airport to Lecce (40min; €5).

Tourist office Lungomare Margherita 43/44 ⓣ0831.523.072 (April–Oct daily 9am–1pm & 3–11pm; Nov–March Mon–Fri 9am–1pm & 3–8pm, Sat 9am–1.30pm).

little more than a large village. What makes it more than worth the thirty-minute bus ride up from Amalfi's Piazza Flavio Gioia, however, is its unrivalled location, spread across the top of one of the coast's mountains. The **Duomo** (daily 8.30am–noon, 5.30–8pm) is a bright eleventh-century church with a richly-ornamented interior, but Ravello's real draws are its two villas: a two-minute walk from the Duomo are the gardens of the **Villa Rufolo** (9am–sunset; €5), the spectacular venue for a renowned arts festival in the summer (tickets from €10; ⓦwww.ravellofestival.com); a ten-minute walk south is the equally stunning **Villa Cimbrone** (daily 9am–sunset; €5).

Tourist information is at Via Roma 18 (daily: March–Oct, Dec & Jan 9am–8pm, Feb & Nov 9am–5pm; ⓣ089.857.096, ⓦwww.ravellotime.it).

MATERA

Tucked into the instep of Italy in the Basilicata region, **Matera** is one of the south's most fascinating cities. The main point of interest is its *sassi*, rock dwellings dug out of a ravine. During the 1950s and 1960s the residents were forcibly evicted, as the city had degenerated into one huge slum. New blocks were constructed just outside the town to house the population and the *sassi* were left empty, but in 1993 the area was declared a World Heritage Site and has since been slowly repopulated with hotels, restaurants and workshops.

The focus of the Sassi district, a warren of rock streets, is the **chiese rupestri** or rock-hewn churches (all open daily: April–Oct 9am–1pm & 3–7pm, Nov–March 9.30am–1.30pm & 2.30–4.30pm; €2.50 each, or €6 for all). The most spectacular is the **Madonna de Idris**, with frescoes dating from the fourteenth century. For an insight into what life was like for the *sassi*-dwellers, stop by the **Casa Grotta**, just below Madonna de Idris (daily: April–Oct 9.30am–8pm; Nov–March 9.30am–5pm; €1.50), or the **C'era una Volta** exhibition at Via Fiorentini 251 (daily: Easter–Oct 9am–7pm; Nov–Easter 9am–1pm & 3–6.30pm; E1.50), a *sassi* dwelling with its life-size inhabitants and their furniture sculpted out of the local tufa by generations of the same family.

Arrival and information

Air Matera is 60km southwest of Bari airport. Buses operated by Pugliairbus (2 daily; 2hr 15min; €5) run to Piazza Moro in Matera.

Bus Direct coach services from Rome (Mon–Sat 1 daily; 5hr 45min; run by Autolinee Liscio) and from Naples (2 daily; 5hr; run by Autolinee Marino) stop at the Matera Villa Longo station, a 20min walk out of town but connected by bus and the FAL rail line.

Train The train station, on Piazza Matteotti, is served by the private FAL rail line (ⓦwww.fal-srl.it) from Bari.

Tourist office Via de Viti de Marco 9, off Via Roma ⓣ0835.331.983, ⓦwww.aptbasilicata.it (Mon & Thurs 9am–1.30pm & 4–6.30pm, Tues, Wed & Fri 9am–1.30pm).

Accommodation

Casa Per Ferie Sacro Cuore Recinto Mario Pagano 11 ⓣ0835.336.451, ⓦwww.sacrocuoremt.it. Run by nuns and surrounded by lovely gardens, this makes a restful place to stay. The large rooms do have a rather institutional feel, however. €60.

Le Monacelle Via Riscatto 9/10 ⓣ0835.344.097, ⓦwww.lemonacelle.it. This ex-friary is now a smart hotel, with two dorm rooms available. They sleep 16, but different areas are partitioned off, and they are nicely decorated, with solid wooden bunks. Dorms €17.60.

Eating and drinking

There's a Sisa supermarket on Via de Viti de Marco, along from the tourist office.

TREAT YOURSELF

If you're going to splash out on one of the atmospheric new cave hotels, make it the **Antica Locanda San Martino** (Via San Martino 22; ⓣ0835.256.600, ⓦwww.locandadisanmartino.it): a cool, fragrant *sassi* conversion 100m from the city centre. Rooms €109.

Il Terrazzino Vico S. Giuseppe 7. Closed Tues. A *sassi* restaurant with great views and a cheap tourist menu; try the *orecchiette* pasta with sausage, tomato and mozzarella (€5), or if you can't decide from the many pizza options, go for the *Sorpresa*: a "surprise", with toppings chosen by the pizza-maker (€8).
La Gravina Via del Corso 80. This *tavola calda* is a good lunchtime option, with salads, pizzas and snacky mains (€3–5) to take away or eat in.

LECCE

LECCE, 40km south of Brindisi port, is often called the "Florence of the south". These alleys may be well-trodden, but a real sense of discovery still accompanies a visit to the city's vine-enveloped stonework. Carved from soft sandstone, these buildings were built for wealthy families, churchmen and merchants during the fifteenth to seventeenth centuries, and are among the most beautiful examples of the style; the most impressive were designed by Giuseppe Zimbalo, known as Lo Zingarello. A short walk from the central Piazza Sant'Oronzo is **Santa Croce** (daily 8am–1pm & 4.30–9pm, earlier in winter), the most famous of Lecce's churches, where delicate engravings soften the Baroque outline of the building. Inside, the excess continues with a riot of stars, flowers and foliage covering everything from the top of columns to chapel altarpieces. Lecce's other highlight is the **Piazza del Duomo**, an elegantly proportioned square surrounded by Baroque *palazzi*. The **Duomo** itself (daily 6.30am–noon & 5–7.30pm, earlier in winter) is an explosion of Baroque detail.

Arrival and information

Air Lecce is 40km from Brindisi Airport; from here, COTRAP buses (6 daily; 40min; €5) run to the centre.
Bus Buses arrive at the Porta Napoli, a 10min walk from the centre, and at the train station.
Train The train station is 1km south of the centre on Via Oronzo Quarta.
Tourist office Via Principe Umberto I 13 (daily 9am–1pm & 4.30–7pm; ⓣ0832.683.398, ⓦwww.turismo.provincia.le.it).

Accommodation

Centro Storico B&B Via Vignes 2b ⓣ0832.242.727, ⓦwww.bedandbreakfast.lecce.it. A lovely B&B in a sixteenth-century *palazzo* with beautifully decorated rooms and a sunny rooftop terrace. €60.
Namastè Via Novoli km 4.5 ⓣ0832.329.647, ⓦwww.ostellolecce.it. Bus #26 from the station. A small campsite and hostel set in a tranquil pine forest 6km out of Lecce. Camping €5 per person, plus €8 per tent; dorms €17, mini-apartments with kitchen €50.

Eating and drinking

Alle Due Corti Corte dei Giugni 1. Simple but expertly prepared dishes in a family restaurant with an appealingly homespun feel. Dishes around €10.
Caffè Letterario Via G. Paladini 46. Open from 7.30am till 2am, this café-bar organizes a wealth of arty events, including DJ sets and live music nights, usually on Wednesday or Friday.
Osteria degli Angeli Via Cavour 4. Closed Sun in summer & Tues in winter. A reliable central option for a no-frills meal; antipasto and pizza will set you back about €15.

Moving on

Train Bari (hourly; 2hr); Bologna (8 daily; 7–9hr); Brindisi (hourly; 35min); Naples (5 daily; 5–8hr); Rome (5 daily; 6–11hr);

Sicily

Perhaps the most captivating of Italy's islands, **SICILY** (Sicilia) feels socially and culturally separate from the rest of Italy. Occupying a strategically vital position, the largest island in the Mediterranean has a history and outlook that has less in common with its modern parent than with its erstwhile rulers – from the Greeks who first settled the east coast, in the eighth century BC, through a bewildering array of Romans, Arabs, Normans, French and Spanish, to the Bourbons, seen off by Garibaldi in 1860. Substantial relics remain, and temples,

theatres and churches are scattered across the island.

The capital, **Palermo**, is a bustling city with an unrivalled display of Norman art and architecture and Baroque churches. The most obvious other target is the chic eastern resort of **Taormina**. From here you can visit **Mount Etna**, or travel south to the ancient Greek centre of **Siracusa**. To the west, the greatest draw is the grouping of temples at **Agrigento**, the largest concentration of the island's Greek remains.

PALERMO

In its own wide bay beneath the limestone bulk of Monte Pellegrino, **PALERMO** is stupendously sited. Originally a Phoenician, then a Carthaginian colony, this remarkable city was long considered a prize worth capturing, and under Saracen and Norman rule in the ninth to twelfth centuries it became the greatest city in Europe, famed for the wealth of its court and peerless as a centre of learning. Nowadays it's a brash, exciting city, whose uniquely varied architecture and museums are the equal of anything on the mainland.

What to see and do

Around the Quattro Canti

The heart of the old city is the Baroque **Quattro Canti** crossroads, with **Piazza Pretoria** and its racy fountain just around the corner. In nearby Piazza Bellini, the church of **La Martorana** (Mon–Sat 8.30am–1pm & 3.30–7pm, earlier in winter, Sun 8.30am–1pm) is one of the finest survivors of the medieval city. Its slim twelfth-century campanile and spectacular mosaics make a marked contrast to the adjacent squat chapel of **San Cataldo** (Mon–Sat 9.30am–2pm & 3.30–7pm, Sun 9am–2pm; €1) with its little Saracenic red golfball domes.

Alberghiera

In the district of Alberghiera, a warren of narrow streets to the southwest, you'll find the deconsecrated church of **San Giovanni degli Eremiti** (Via dei Benedettini; closed for restoration at the time of writing), built in 1148. Built on the remains of a mosque, it's topped with five rosy domes and holds late thirteenth-century cloisters. From here it's a few paces north to the **Palazzo dei Normanni** (Mon, Tues & Thurs–Sat 8.30am–noon & 2–5pm, Sun 8.30am–12.30pm; entrance on Piazza Indipendenza; €6), the seat of the Sicilian regional parliament. It was originally built by the Saracens and was enlarged by the Normans, under whom it housed the most magnificent of medieval European courts. The beautiful **Cappella Palatina**, the private royal chapel of Roger II, is almost entirely covered in glorious twelfth-century mosaics.

The Cattedrale

The Norman **Cattedrale** (Mon–Sat: March–Oct 9.30am–5.30pm; Nov–Feb 9.30am–1.30pm; Sun 8am–1.30pm & 4.30–6pm) was much restored in the eighteenth century. Still, the triple-apsed eastern end and the lovely matching towers are all original, and the interior boasts a fine portal and tombs containing the remains of some of Sicily's most famous monarchs.

The Museo Archeologico Regionale, Vucciria and around

To the northeast, off Via Roma, the **Museo Archeologico Regionale** (Tues–Fri 8.30am–1.15pm, 3–6.15pm, Sat–Mon 8.30am–1.15pm; €6) is a magnificent collection of artefacts, mainly from the island's Greek and Roman sites. Two cloisters hold anchors, Bronze-Age pottery, coins and jewels retrieved from the sea off the Sicilian coast.

Southeast of here, be sure to walk through the **Vucciria market** area (daily

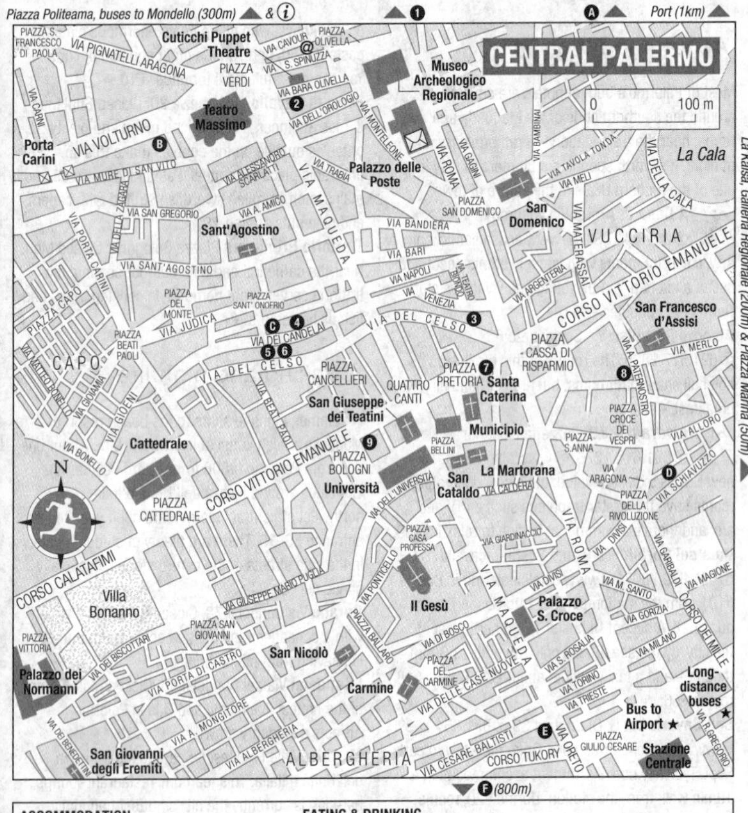

ACCOMMODATION				EATING & DRINKING					
A Casa di Amici	B	Baia del Corallo	A	Al Santa Caterina	7	Ferro di Cavallo	3	La Cuba	1
Albergo Paradiso	D	San Saverio	F	Antica Focacceria	8	Garage	6	Pub 88	5
Alvorada B&B	C	Vittoria	E	Basile	2	I Candelai	4	Trattoria Primavera	9

from 8am) – although not as lively as it once was, it still offers glimpses of old Palermo. You can cut through to Sicily's **Galleria Regionale** (closed for restoration at the time of writing), on Via Alloro, in the rough-and-ready La Kalsa district. It's a stunning art collection, with works from the eleventh to the seventeenth centuries.

Arrival and information

Air Prestia e Comandè buses meet arrivals and stop at the train station and Piazza Politeama (50min; €5.60). Trinacria Express run trains to the central station (every 30min; 45min; €5).

Ferry and hydrofoil Services from Naples dock just off Via Francesco Crispi, from where it's a 10min walk up Via E. Amari to Piazza Castelnuovo.

Train Trains arrive at Stazione Centrale, at the southern end of Via Roma – buses #101 and #102 run to the centre. Buy tickets (€1.20; valid for 1hr 30min) at *tabacchi* shops or the booth outside the station. Red line and yellow line buses start at the station and do circuits of the centre for €0.52/day. There's a left-luggage office at the station (daily 7am–10.30pm; €4/5hr).

Tourist office The main tourist office is at Piazza Castelnuovo 34 (Mon–Fri 8.30am–2pm & 2.30–6pm; ⓣ091.605.8351, ⓦwww.palermotourism.com). There's a smaller branch at the airport (Mon–Sat 8.30am–7.30pm).

Internet *Aboriginal Internet Café*, Via S. Spinuzza 51 (daily 9am–3am; €3.50/hr).

Accommodation

Most of Palermo's budget hotels are situated around the southern ends of Via Maqueda and Via Roma, near the train station – a rather sleazy area at night. It's worth spending a bit more to stay in one of the modern B&Bs in the centre of town.

A Casa di Amici Via Volturno 6 ⓣ091.584.884, ⓦwww.acasadiamici.com. Arty, colourful rooms with vaguely ethnic decor and use of a kitchen, run by young and vivacious staff. Dorms €25, doubles €56.

Albergo Paradiso Via Schiavuzzo 65 ⓣ091.617.2825. The rooms at this family-run hotel all share bathrooms, but are light and airy. No breakfast. €48.

Alvorada B&B Piazzetta delle Api ⓣ091.616.1276, ⓦwww.alvorada.it. This new B&B is excellent value: the nicely decorated rooms have three-star trappings such as TV and a/c, and there's a communal lounge to relax in. €69.

Baia del Corallo Via Plauto 27, Sferacavallo ⓣ091.679.7807, ⓦwww.ostellopalermo.it. Bus #101 from the station to Piazza De Gasperi, then bus #628. A decent HI hostel 12km northwest of the city, by the sea. Buses only run until 11.30pm though – and a taxi will cost about €35. Dorms €18, rooms €56.

San Saverio Via G. Di Cristina 39 ⓣ091.654.7099, ⓦwww.ostellopalermo.com. Open mid-July to early Sept. Typically no-frills student accommodation a 10min walk from the station. Dorms €20, rooms €40.

Vittoria Via Maqueda 8 ⓣ091.616.2437. This simple, family-run hotel near the station has been recently renovated; all rooms are now en suite. No breakfast. €50.

Eating

The city's markets are a great place to pick up a picnic; try Ballarò, between Piazza Carmine and Piazza Ballarò in the Alberghiera district. There's a GS supermarket in Piazza Marina.

Al Santa Caterina Corso Vittorio Emanuele 254. Closed Wed. Filling portions of pizza and pasta. Book one of the tiny balcony tables for a bird's-eye view of Palermo's busiest thoroughfare. Seafood spaghetti €7.

Antica Focacceria Via A. Paternostro 58. A feast of *panelle*, *arancini* (fried rice and meat balls), pizza and tasty sweet *cannoli* will set you back just €6 at this popular backstreet takeaway.

Basile Via Bara 76. Closed Sun. This lunch-only *tavola calda* is crammed with locals on weekdays, who fill up on its enormous plates of pasta (€2.50) and various meat and fish options. You can get a full meal for under €10.

Ferro di Cavallo Via Venezia 20. Closed Sun, Mon & Tues at dinner. A well-priced menu and plenty of tables outside on the cobbles make this an enjoyable place for a meal. Pasta dishes are €5 and mains such as rolled swordfish stuffed with capers and pine nuts around €8.

Trattoria Primavera Piazza Bologni 4. Closed Mon. Near the cathedral and with outdoor seating, this trattoria serves great home-style cooking. Meat and fish dishes start at €7.

Drinking and nightlife

In summer, nightlife shifts to the beach resort of Mondello, which is full of lively bars, a half-hour bus ride from Palermo (#806 from Teatro Politeama). The clubs around Piazza dell'Unità d'Italia, northwest of central Palermo, are open year-round; entrance €5–15. There are plenty of studenty bars in the side streets of the centro storico, especially on Via dei Candelai.

Garage Via Candelai 78. Closed Sun. This tiny bar with a dancefloor and cheap cocktails (around €3) is heaving from midnight on.

I Candelai Via dei Candelai 65. Closed Mon. Some of the hottest live music and DJs in Palermo. Attracts a studenty crowd.

La Cuba Viale Francesco Scaduto, near Piazza dell'Unità d'Italia. This tearoom-restaurant-lounge-bar-club is currently the city's hottest hangout, attracting a trendy clientele to match. Dress up.

Pub 88 Via dei Candelai 88. A perennial centro storico favourite among the city's university students, this is a good place for a drink before heading on elsewhere.

Moving on

Buses (services run by SAIS and Interbus) are quicker than trains in Sicily, taking scenic cross-country routes rather than lumbering round the coast. Buy bus tickets from the agencies in Via Balsamo, by the station.

Air Bologna (2 daily; 1hr 25min); Cagliari (1 daily; 1hr 15min); Florence (2 daily; 1hr 15min); Milan (7 daily; 1hr 30min); Rome (9 daily; 1hr).

Bus Agrigento (6–9 daily; 2hr); Florence (4 weekly; 17hr); Naples (1 daily; 12hr); Rome (1–2 daily; 17hr); Siracusa (2–4 daily; 3hr 15min); Taormina (change at Catania; 9–16 daily; 2hr 40min).

Ferry Genoa (18 daily; 20hr); Naples (2–3 daily; 8–10hr); Rome (Civitavecchia; 6 weekly; 12–14hr).

Train Agrigento (8 daily; 2hr); Siracusa (change at Messina; 10 daily; 5hr 45min–7hr); Taormina (change at Messina; 15 daily; 3hr 45min–5hr 30min).

TAORMINA

On Sicily's eastern coast, and dominating two grand sweeping bays, **TAORMINA** is the island's best-known resort. The outstanding remains of its classical theatre, with Mount Etna as an unparalleled backdrop, arrested passing travellers when Taormina was no more than a medieval hill village, though nowadays it's rather chi-chi, full of designer shops and pricey cafés. It still has plenty of charm, though, its main pedestrianized street, Corso Vittorio Emanuele, lined with fifteenth- to nineteenth-century *palazzi* interspersed with intimate piazzas. The **Teatro Greco** (daily 9am–1hr before sunset; €6) is the only real sight, founded by the Greeks in the third century BC, though most of what's left is a Roman rebuilding from the first century AD, when a deep trench was dug in the orchestra to accommodate animals and gladiators. In July and August it's the venue for an international arts festival (ⓦwww.taormina-arte.com).

The closest beach to Taormina is at **MAZZARÓ**, with its much-photographed islet, **Isola Bella**: it's a scenic thirty-minute descent on foot, or use the cable car (every 15min; €3 return) from Via Pirandello.

Arrival and information

Air Catania airport is 45km from Taormina; buses run from here to the centre of town.
Bus The bus terminal is in Via Pirandello, a 5min walk from the centre.
Train The train station, Taormina-Giardini Naxos, is way below town – it's a steep 30min walk up or a short bus ride to the centre (€1.50).
Tourist office The main office is on Palazzo Corvaja, Piazza Santa Caterina (Mon–Thurs 8.30am–2pm & 4–7pm, Fri 8.30am–2pm; ⓣ0942.23.243, ⓦwww.gate2taormina.com). Also at the train station (same hours).

Accommodation

Casa Grazia Via Lallia Bassia 20 ⓣ0942.24.776, ⓔcasagrazia@libero.it. Open March–Oct. A 5min walk from the Teatro Greco, this family-run hotel has neat rooms, some en suite, all with balcony. The top-floor room, with its private panoramic terrace, must be the town's best bargain at €65. No breakfast. €55.
Taormina's Odyssey Traversa A, Via G. Martino 2, off Via dei Cappuccini ⓣ0942.24.533, ⓦwww.taorminaodyssey.com. A pretty hostel with eight- to ten-person dorms, sea views, a terrace and a kitchen, 10min walk from Porta Messina. The hostel also has a 5-room guesthouse in the centre (Via Paterno di Biscari 13). Dorms €19, rooms €60.

Eating

There's a mini-market that can make up panini for a couple of euros at Via Bagnoli Croce 68; eat them over the road in the leafy Giardini Pubblici.
Rosticceria di Cateno Aucello Via Cappuccini 8. This takeaway with a few outdoor tables has a handful of tasty pasta dishes and mains such as chicken and chips (€4–7).
Vecchia Taormina Vico Ebrei 3. The best of the pizzerias, serving up light, crispy offerings from its wood-fired stove.

Drinking and nightlife

In town, the action takes place in picturesque but posey Piazza Paladini, off the Corso. Alternatively, the summer beach-bars of nearby Spisone are reachable by path from Taormina or by bus from Via Pirandello.
Morgana Scesa Morgana 4. With its sumptuous, candlelit interior and lounge music, *Morgana* attracts Taormina's beautiful people; dress up.
Re di Bastoni Corso Umberto 1. Closed Mon in winter. Grab one of the outdoor tables to watch the evening *passeggiata* along Taormina's main drag.

Moving on

Bus Palermo (via Catania; hourly; 3hr 40min).
Train Palermo (via Messina; 12 daily; 4hr 30min –5hr 40min); Siracusa (6 daily; 2hr–2hr 50min).

MOUNT ETNA

Mount Etna's massive bulk looms over much of the coastal route south of Taormina. If you don't have the time to

reach the summit, the **Circumetnea rail service** (€11 return; InterRail passes not valid) trundles around the base from **GIARRE-RIPOSTO**, thirty minutes by train or bus from Taormina; if you make the entire trip to Catania, allow four hours. Catania itself is an attractive place, dotted with lava-encrusted relics and splendid Baroque *palazzi*.

At 3340m, Etna is a substantial mountain and the **ascent** is a spectacular trip, worth every effort to make; the fact that it's also one of the world's biggest volcanoes (and still active) only adds to the draw. On **public transport**, you'll need to come via Catania, by bus (daily 8.15am, also mid-June to mid-Sept Mon–Fri 11.20am; 1hr) from Catania train station up to the huddle of souvenir shops and restaurants at the *Rifugio Sapienza* (Ⓣ095.915.321; Ⓦwww.rifugiosapienza.com; B&B €49 per person), a cosy, chalet-style hotel which marks the end of the drivable road up the south side of Etna. To get up Etna, you can either take the cable car (9am–sunset; €49.50 return), or walk (the trip up will take four hours, the return a little less). Take warm clothes, good shoes and glasses to keep the flying grit out of your eyes. The return bus to Catania leaves at 4.30pm, so if you want to walk all the way you'll have to stay the night in the *Rifugio*. If you're spending the night in Catania, the **tourist office** in the train station (Mon–Sat 8am–8pm; Ⓣ095.730.6255) can help with accommodation, though if you are travelling alone the cheapest option is the easy-going **hostel**, *Agora*, Piazza Currò 6, near the cathedral (Ⓣ095.723.3010; Ⓦwww.agorahostel.com; dorms €21, rooms €55).

SIRACUSA

Further down Sicily's eastern seaboard, **SIRACUSA** (ancient Syracuse) was first colonized by the Greeks in 733 BC and grew to become their main power base in Sicily. Today, the city boasts some of the best Greek archeological remains anywhere, and also has a strong Baroque character in its old town, squeezed onto the island of **Ortygia**, and connected to the new town by two bridges – a wonderful place for a wander.

What to see and do

Ortygia

Near the bridge that connects Ortygia to the mainland, the **Temple of Apollo**, built in the sixth century BC, is probably Sicily's most ancient Doric temple. Over the years, it was transformed into a Byzantine church, then an Arab mosque, and into a church again under the Normans. At the centre of the island, the most obvious attraction is the **Duomo** (daily 8am–6/7pm), set in a conch-shaped piazza studded with Baroque architecture, and itself incorporating twelve fluted columns from the fifth-century-BC temple that originally stood here. At the other end of the square, the church of **Santa Lucia** (Tues–Sun 11am–2pm & 5–7pm) harbours a Caravaggio painting, the *Burial of Santa Lucia*. Round the corner at Via Capodieci 16 is the severe thirteenth-century facade of the **Galleria Regionale di Palazzo Bellomo** (currently closed for restoration), an outstanding collection of medieval art, and paintings by Antonello da Messina.

The Archeological Museum and around

North of the train station, the city is mainly new, though the best of Siracusa's archeological sights are also here. It's a twenty-minute walk to Viale Teocrito (or take bus #12 from Riva Nazario Sauro), from where you walk east for the **Museo Archeologico Regionale** (Tues–Sat 9am–6pm, Sun 9am–3pm; €8), housing a wealth of material from the early Greek colonies; the collection's highlight is a headless marble *Venus*, sculpted rising from the sea.

Round the corner, the ruined **Basilica di San Giovanni** has interesting catacombs (daily 9.30am–12.30pm & 2.30–5.30pm; €6).

The Archeological Park

Siracusa's extensive **Parco Archeologico** (Tues–Sun 9am–2hr before sunset; €8) is a ten-minute walk west of the archeological museum. Here, the **Ara di Ierone II**, an enormous third-century-BC altar, is the first thing you see, though the main highlight is the **Teatro Greco**. Cut out of the rock and looking down towards the sea, it hosts a summer season of Greek plays (Ⓦwww.indafondazione.org). Nearby, the **Latomia del Paradiso**, a leafy quarry, is best known for the **Orecchio di Dionigi**, an S-shaped cave, 65m long and 20m high, that Dionysius is supposed to have used as a prison. The last section of the park contains the neglected-looking **Roman amphitheatre.**

Hourly buses make the 55min journey to the tumbledown town of **NOTO** – a good day-trip. The town's crumbling suburbs give way to a lovely Baroque centre that was named a UNESCO World Heritage Site in 2002. Also within easy reach of town are the sandy **beaches** of Fontane Bianche (bus #21 or #22 from Via Crispi; every 2hr; 25min).

Arrival and information

Air Interbus run services from Catania airport to Siracusa.

Bus Interbus services from Palermo, Rome, Pisa, Florence and Genoa stop in Corso Umberto, near the station.

Train Siracusa's train station is on Via Crispi, a 20min walk from Ortygia and connected with the island by free shuttle bus (every 30min until 9pm; 5min).

Tourist office Via Maestranza 33 ⓣ0931.464.256 (Mon–Thurs 8.15am–2pm & 2.45–5.30pm, Fri 8.15am–2pm).

Accommodation

Ares Via Mirabella 49 ⓣ0931.461.145, Ⓦwww.aresbedandbreakfast.it. The five rooms at this Ortygia B&B are cosily decorated. Owner Enzo knows everyone in town and is happy to show guests the sights. €80.

Casa Cristina Via Chindemi 8 ⓣ0931.62.205, Ⓦwww.casacristinasr.it. The lovely, airy rooms at this welcoming B&B are a bargain, with dead-ahead views of the Temple of Apollo; one has a lovely frescoed ceiling. €80.

Casa Mia Corso Umberto 112 ⓣ0931.463.349, Ⓦwww.bbcasamia.it. This B&B, in an old palazzo not far from Ortygia, has pleasant rooms, a sunny breakfast terrace and helpful owners. €75.

Lolhostel Via F. Crispi 92/96 ⓣ0931.465.088, Ⓦwww.lolhostel.com. Siracusa's only hostel, just a 10min walk from Ortygia, offers 4-person dorms and private en-suites.

Eating

There's a Conté supermarket in Via Giusto Monaco (closed Sun), as well as a colourful produce market in Via Benedictis (Mon–Sat 7am–2pm).

Castello Fiorentino Via del Crocifisso 6. This popular pizzeria serves up superb pizzas with inventive toppings; try the Bella Donna, with sausage, roast potato and rosemary (€7).

Da Seby Via Mirabella 21. Closed Sun. This hole-in-the-wall *tavola calda* with a handful of tables is great value, with a range of tasty hot meals such as swordfish with salad for €5. It's open till 8.30pm, but in the evening only pizza is available.

Osteria La Gazza Ladra Via Cavour 8. Closed Mon. Your dinner is prepared in front of you at this family-run trattoria, with the day's specials, such as pasta with courgettes and mint (€7.50) chalked up on a blackboard.

Drinking and nightlife

Nightlife centres on the lively Piazzetta San Rocco in Ortygia and the nearby Via delle Vergini and Via Roma. It's also worth exploring Ortygia's tucked-away alleys and courtyards – off Via Amalfitana an alley leads to a courtyard with three lively bars, one of which, *Il Sale*, puts on a free *aperitivo* buffet daily 7–9pm.

Enoteca Solaria Via Roma 86. Closed Sun. A laid-back *enoteca* with some 500 bottles lining the walls. Also serves food such as grilled tuna for around €10.

Il Sedano Allegro Via delle Vergini 5. Closed Tues. A bohemian bar with a cosy, cluttered interior and a lovely terrace out back. You can also order simple bar meals – *bruschette*, burgers and so on – for €2–8.

Moving on

Bus Agrigento (Via Catania; 4–16 daily; 4hr 30min); Palermo (2–4 daily; 3hr 15min).
Train Agrigento (3 daily; 5hr 45min–8hr); Palermo (5 daily; 5hr–7hr 45min).

AGRIGENTO

Halfway along Sicily's southern coast, **AGRIGENTO** is primarily of interest for the substantial remains of Greek poet Pindar's "most beautiful city of mortals", strung out along a ridge facing the sea a few kilometres below town. The series of Doric temples here, mostly dating from the fifth century BC, are the most evocative of Sicily's remains. They are also the focus of a constant procession of tour buses, so budget accommodation should be booked in advance (though Agrigento could be a day-trip from Palermo). A road winds down from the modern city to the **Valle dei Templi**; buses from the station drop off at a car park between the two separate zones of **archeological remains** (daily 8.30/9am–7pm; €8, joint ticket with museum €10). The eastern zone is home to the scattered remains of the oldest of the temples, the **Tempio di Ercole**, probably begun in the last decades of the sixth century BC, and the better-preserved **Tempio della Concordia**, dated to around 430 BC, with fine views of the city and sea.

The western zone, back along the path and beyond the car park, is less impressive but still worth wandering around. The mammoth construction that was the **Tempio di Giove**, the largest Doric temple ever known, was in fact never completed, left in ruins by the Carthaginians and further damaged by earthquakes; the small remnant that is standing is a nineteenth-century reconstruction. Via dei Templi leads back to the town from the car park via the excellent **Museo Archeologico Regionale** (Tues–Sat 9am–7pm, Sun 9am–1pm; €6, joint ticket with Valle dei Templi €10) – an extraordinarily rich collection devoted to local finds.

From June to mid-September the Valle dei Tempi opens at **night**: once the sun has set over the ruins, they're spectacularly illuminated by floodlights.

Arrival and information

Air SAIS buses run to Agrigento from Catania airport, and Sal buses from Palermo airport.
Bus SAIS buses from Rome and Naples arrive in Piazzale Rosselli, near the train station.
Train Trains arrive at Agrigento Centrale at the edge of the old town (don't get out at Agrigento Bassa). Buses #1, #2 and #3 from outside the station (€1 from *tabacchi*, or €1.50 on board) go to the temples.
Tourist office Via Empedocle 73 ⓣ800.236.837 (Mon, Tues, Thurs & Fri 8am–2pm, Wed 8am–2pm & 3.30–6pm).

Accommodation

Camere a Sud Via Ficani 6 ⓣ349.638.4424, ⓦwww.camereasud.it. In an excellent location just off Agrigento's main drag, this friendly B&B has bright, spacious rooms and a roof terrace. Free internet. Only three rooms, so book ahead. €70.
Internazionale San Leone Viale Emporium 192, San Leone ⓣ0922.416.121, ⓦwww.campingvalledeitempli.com. Bus #2 from outside the station (every 30min till 9pm). A basic campsite 5km out of town in the coastal resort of San Leone. Camping €7.50 per person, plus €6 per tent.
Letto e Latte Via Cannatello 101 ⓣ0922.651.945, ⓦwww.lettolatte.it. This tranquil B&B 1km from the Valle dei Templi (the bus stops just outside) has six clean, tastefully furnished en-suite rooms. €60.

Eating and drinking

Most of the cheap pizzerias are at Villagio Mosè, east of town, below the temples. In town, lively Via Atenea is the best place for a drink.
Ambasciata di Sicilia Via Giambertoni 2. Closed Mon. This folksy trattoria has lovely views from its terrace and reasonably priced dishes.
Atenea Via Ficani 32. Closed Sun. A family-run trattoria in a quiet courtyard just off Via Atenea. No-frills pasta and meat and fish mains for €6–8.
Le Cuspidi Piazza Cavour 19. The best ice creams in town, with unusual flavours such as fresh ricotta and almond, as well as the classics.

Sardinia

Just under 200km from the Italian mainland, **SARDINIA** (Sardegna) is often regarded as the epitome of Mediterranean Europe. Its blue seas, white sands and rolling hills are beautiful and its way of life relaxed. Sardinia also holds fascinating vestiges of the various powers – Roman, Carthaginian, Genoese and Pisan – that have passed through, alongside striking remnants of Sardinia's only significant native culture, known as the Nuraghic civilization, in the seven thousand tower-like *nuraghi* that litter the landscape. The capital, **Cagliari**, is worth exploring for its excellent museums and some of the island's best nightlife. From here, it's only a short trip to the renowned ruined city at **Nora**, and the quieter beaches at **Chia**. The other main ferry port and airport is Olbia, in the north, little more than a transit town for the exclusive resorts of the Costa Smeralda. There's a third airport at the resort of **Alghero** in the northwest.

CAGLIARI

Rising up from its port and crowned by an old citadel squeezed within a protective ring of fortifications, **CAGLIARI** has been Sardinia's capital since at least Roman times and is still the island's biggest town. Nonetheless, its centre is easily explored on foot, with almost all the wandering you will want to do encompassed by the citadel.

What to see and do

The citadel

The most evocative entry to the **citadel** is from the monumental **Bastione San Remy** on Piazza Costituzione. From here, you can potter in any direction to enter its intricate maze. The citadel has been altered little since the Middle Ages, though the tidy Romanesque facade on the mainly thirteenth-century **cathedral** (April–Oct 9am–noon & 5–7pm, Nov–March 9am–12.30pm & 4–6pm; Mass on Sun 9am, 10.30am, noon & 7pm) in Piazza Palazzo is in fact a fake, added in the twentieth century in the old Pisan style.

Piazza dell'Arsenale

At the opposite end of Piazza Palazzo, a road leads into the smaller **Piazza dell'Arsenale,** site of several museums including the **Museo Archeologico Nazionale** (Tues–Sun 9am–8pm; €4), great for anyone interested in Sardinia's past. In the same complex, the **Pinacoteca Nazionale** (same hours; €2 or €5 combined ticket with above) features some glowing fifteenth-century altarpieces, while the **Museo delle Cere** (Tues–Sun 9am–1pm & 4–7pm; €1.50) displays a series of beautiful anatomical waxworks executed by Clemente Susini for nineteenth-century medical students.

Towers

Off the piazza stands the **Torre San Pancrazio** (Tues–Sun April–Oct 9am–1pm & 3.30–7.30pm; Nov–March 9am–4.30pm; €2), from where it's only a short walk to the **Torre dell'Elefante** (hours and price as San Pancrazio), named after the small carving of an elephant on one side; climb to the top for stupendous views over the city and coast.

Anfiteatro Romano

Nearby, Viale Buon Cammino leads to the **Anfiteatro Romano** (Tues–Sat 9.30am–1.30pm, Sun 3.30–5.30pm (Sun 10am–4pm Nov–March; €3.30). Cut out of solid rock in the second century AD, the amphitheatre could hold the city's entire population of twenty thousand.

Beaches

To get to **Poetto Beach**, the long stretch connected to Cagliari, take bus #PF or #PQ from outside the train station and,

in the summer, #PN, and get off wherever a patch catches your fancy.

Arrival and information

Air The airport sits beside the Stagno di Cagliari, the city's largest lagoon, a 15min bus ride west of town.
Boat Cagliari's port lies in the heart of the town, opposite Via Roma.
Tourist office There are tourist offices at the port (Via Roma 145), and opposite the train and bus stations on Piazza Matteotti (April–Sept Mon–Sat 8.30am–7.30pm; Oct–March Mon–Fri 9am–1.30pm & 3–6pm, Sat 9am–2pm; ⓣ070.669.255, ⓦwww.comune.cagliari.it).
Internet *Lamari*, a pleasant café at Via Napoli 43. €3 p/hour, but discounted to €0.50 if you buy a drink.
Laundry Via Sicilia 23 (8am–10pm).

Accommodation

Booking is essential in summer.
Albergo Aurora Salita S. Chiar 19 ⓣ070.658.625. A slightly shabby but comfortable hotel in the centre of the city, just off Piazza Yenne. €60.
Hostel Marina 2 Piazza San Sepolcro ⓣ070.450.9709; ⓔcagliari@aighostels.com. Located in the heart of the old town and a short walk from the port and train station, this new hostel has cosy, freshly decorated dorms. Dorm bed €22.
La Perla Via Sardegna 18 ⓣ070.669.446. A no-frills, family-run place in the centre of the old town, with double and triple rooms. €39.
Palmas Via Sardegna 14 ⓣ070.651.679. A simple one-star option with camp-style beds in fairly bleak rooms. But it's a steal for the price. With shared bathroom, €19.

Eating

Piazza Yenne is full of outdoor cafés and has a great *gelateria, L'Isola del Gelato*. The best restaurants are around the streets surrounding Via Sardegna.
Antico Forno Via M. Sabotino 9. Good deli with local specialities, including the traditional *su coccoi* bread, which is made from semolina or fine flour and moulded into different shapes according to the region – here it has spikes.
Da Fabio Via Sardegna 90. Excellent home-made pasta. Try the *seadas*, a traditional Sardinian dessert pastry filled with sheep's cheese and honey. Pasta €6.50.
Degli Spiriti Via Canelles 34/San Lorenzo 10. Packed with the young and cool, this restaurant and bar serves great pizzas and cocktails and the views over the city are spectacular. Pizza €7. Open until 3am.
La Damigiana Corso Vittorio Emanuele 115. A simple trattoria with low prices. Mains €7.

Drinking and nightlife

Amparias Via Savoia 4. Has cheap pizzas, vibrant atmosphere and loud music.
De Candia Via Genovese 12/16. Lounge bar on the bastion with bed-style seating, chill-out tunes and arty photographic projections.
Mojito Salita Santa Chiara 25. Tiny, red-draped bar just off Piazza Yenne, with outdoor couches in the summer.

Moving on

Bus Chia (hourly; 1hr 15min); Pula (hourly; 50min). For more information on buses in Sardinia, see ⓦwww.arst.sardegna.it.
Ferry Civitavecchia (1 daily; 16hr 45min); Genoa (mid-July to Aug 2 weekly; 20hr); Livorno (1 weekly; 7hr); Naples (1–2 weekly; 16hr); Palermo (1 weekly; 13hr 30min); Trápani (1 weekly; 11hr). For more information about ferries, there's an office at Via Cugia 1(ⓣ070.342.341, ⓦwww.ferroviesardegna.it).
Train Alghero (4 daily via Sassari; 5hr); Olbia (4 daily; 4hr–4hr 40min).

NORA AND AROUND

The charming little town of **PULA**, an hour outside Cagliari, is a great base to explore **Nora** and the stunning southern beaches. *Hotel Quattro Mori*, a basic but clean hotel at Via Cagliari 10, is the cheapest **accommodation** option (ⓣ070.920.9124; €35) – otherwise, your best bet is to ask at the helpful tourist information centre, located right in the middle of the jolly Piazza del Popolo, the central piazza. The piazza is full of little cafés; one of the best is the cheap and cheerful *Mr Jingle's Café* at no. 5, which serves great local pastries flavoured with saffron. Outside of the summer months some establishments may be shut.

Nora Archeological Centre

To get to **NORA** from Pula, take an eight-minute ride on the Follesa bus from Piazza Giovanni XXIII, or follow the signs and walk the pleasant 25 minutes to get here. Nora is the site of an **ancient city** (daily 9am–sunset; ⓣ070.920.9138) thought to date from the eighth century BC. An administrative, religious and commercial centre for over 1000 years, it was abandoned around the seventh century AD when the Arab invasion forced the inhabitants to retreat inland. The monuments – a theatre, thermal baths (which made use of the natural springs to be found here), a forum, a temple, an aqueduct and noble houses – suggest a sophisticated people, and many of the intricate mosaics decorating the town remain intact.

Laguna di Nora

Next to the archeological centre is the **lagoon** (July & Aug daily 10am–5pm; June & Sept daily 10am–4pm; ⓣ070.920.9544; €8), originally a fish farm and now an environmental park where you can observe nesting birds and local wildlife, paddle around in a **canoe** (€25/3hr, including entry to the lagoon park), or take a **snorkelling** trip to see the Roman remains on the bed of the bay (€25/3hr). Nora beach itself, flanked by the **Torre del Coltellazzo** and the **Torre di Sant Efisio** (which you can climb up for a view over to the mountains of Santa Margherita), is a lovely, family-orientated place for a swim.

Chia

For more secluded beaches, take a bus from Pula's Via Lamarmora to **CHIA** (hourly; 25min); Chia beach is a five-minute walk from where the bus terminates. From here, white sands lapped by turquoise blue waters stretch along the west coast for about 4km. *Campeggio Torre Chia* is a large **campsite** just a stone's throw from the beach, and has a small on-site shop and restaurant; take a left off the main road from the Chia junction and head towards the sea (ⓣ070.923.0054; €10.50 per adult, plus €6.50 per tent).

ALGHERO

In the northwest of Sardinia, **ALGHERO** is a lively resort with a Catalan flavour. From the **Giardino Pubblico**, the **Porta Terra** is the first of Alghero's seven defensive towers, erected by the prosperous Jewish community before their expulsion in 1492. **Via Roma** runs down from here through the old town's puzzle of lanes to the pedestrianized **Via Carlo Alberto**, home to most of the bars and shops. Turn right to reach **Piazza Cìvica**, the old town's main square, at one end of which rises Alghero's mainly sixteenth-century **cattedrale** (guided tours Feb–Sept Mon–Fri 10am–1pm; free). The best excursions are west along the coast, past the long bay of **Porto Conte** to the point of **Capo Caccia**, where the spectacular sheer cliffs are riddled by deep marine caves. The most impressive of these is the Grotta di Nettuno, or **Neptune's Grotto** (April–Sept daily 9am–7pm; Oct daily 9am–5pm; Nov–March daily 9am–2pm; €10), a long snaking passage that delves far into the rock and is full of stalagmites and stalactites. The return boat trip from the port costs €11, or take the bus from the Giardino Pubblico to Capo Caccia (June–Sept 3 daily from 9am; Oct–May 1 daily).

Arrival and information

Air The airport is 30min out of town, and served by the AA bus, for which you can buy tickets in any *tabacchi*.

Bus Long-distance buses arrive in Via Catalogna, on the Giardino Pubblico.

Train Trains arrive 3km north of the centre and are connected to the port by regular local buses.

Tourist office 9 Piazza Porta Terra ⓣ079.979.054, ⓦwww.comune.alghero.ss.it (April–Sept Mon–Sat

8am–8pm, Sun 9am–1pm; Nov–March Mon–Sat 8am–2pm).

Accommodation

Alguer Via Parenzo 79 ⓣ079.930.478. HI hostel located in a fairly distant but tranquil spot 6km along the coast at Fertilia, reachable by hourly local bus from Alghero. Dorm bed €20.

La Mariposa ⓣ079.950.480, ⓦwww.lamariposa.it. Popular, well-equipped campsite 2km north of town, with direct access to the beach. April to mid-Oct. Adults from €12, plus tents from €6.

Mario & Giovanna's B&B 51 Via Canepa, ⓣ339.890.3563. A small, family-run B&B with just three rooms. A great choice and a handy 10min walk away from town and the beach. €55.

Eating and drinking

Alghero's restaurants are renowned for seafood, at its best in spring and winter. There's also a supermarket, Conad, at Via Mazzini 1a, and a great covered food market on Via Sassari.

Casablanca Via Umberto 76. Good, casual pizzeria. Pizza €4.

La Lepanto Via Carlo Alberto 135 ⓣ079.979.116, ⓦwww.lalepanto-ristorante.it. One of the finest fish restaurants in Alghero. Swordfish gnocchi €13.

L'Ormeggio Banchina Porto. Port-side bar, excellent for a sundown *aperitif*. Summer months only. Beer €4.

Poco Loco Via Gramsci 8. Pizzeria with live music and bowling. Try the testing metre-long pizza (€20, serves 4). Internet available from 5.30pm. Open until 1am.

Trattoria Maristella Via Kennedy 9. Tasty, reasonably-priced fish restaurant popular with locals. Seafood pasta €8.

Moving on

Train Cagliari (4 daily via Sassari; 5hr); Sassari (every 2hr; 40min).

Latvia

HIGHLIGHTS

JŪRMALA: join the Latvian summer beach party at this string of seaside resorts

SIGULDA: explore the castle ruins and hiking trails of the gorgeous Gauja Valley

RĪGA: view the exquisite Jugendstil architecture, and party in the lively capital's many bars

LIEPĀJA: stay in a former military prison in Latvia's premier music city

RUNDĀLE PALACE: visit this spectacular Baroque pile – the highlight of southern Latvia

ROUGH COSTS

DAILY BUDGET Basic €35/occasional treat €50

DRINK Aldaris beer €2.30

FOOD Pork with potatoes and sauerkraut €5

HOSTEL/BUDGET HOTEL €12/€28–40

TRAVEL Bus: Rīga–Liepāja 3hr 30min–4hr 30min €7.50; train: Rīga–Sigulda 1hr 10min €2.50

FACT FILE

POPULATION 2.2 million

AREA 64,589 sq km

LANGUAGE Latvian; Russian also widely spoken

CURRENCY Lats (Ls)

CAPITAL Rīga (population: 717,371)

INTERNATIONAL PHONE CODE ⓣ371

Introduction

Since becoming a member of the European Union in 2004, Latvia has enjoyed impressive economic growth, although the legacy of Soviet occupation, which left the country with a large Russian minority population, means it has entered the new era as a culturally divided country. Unlike their Baltic neighbours, Latvians are a minority in their country's larger cities; they are more withdrawn and harder to win over. Although visitors are most likely to be drawn to the lively capital of Rīga, to experience the true spirit of Latvia you'll need to head into the vast countryside, with its parks, lakes and forests.

The most obvious destination is the capital, **Rīga**. Its architectural treasures, lively nightlife and countless eating options make it a prime destination for budget travellers, and it's also popular with stag parties. Places within easy reach of the capital include the palace of **Rundāle**, while those wishing to combine trips to the beach with live music can head either to the nearby resort area of **Jūrmala** or to the port city of Liepāja. **Ķemeri National Park**, near Jūrmala, offers numerous nature trails, while in the scenic **Gauja Valley**, the attractive small towns of **Sigulda** and **Cēsis** can both be used as bases for hiking, biking, canoeing and other outdoor pursuits.

CHRONOLOGY

800s AD Vikings seize the areas around present-day Latvia.
1201 German traders found the city of Rīga.
1285 Rīga joins the Hanseatic League, bringing the Baltic region closer economic ties with the rest of Europe.
1330 Rīga Castle is built for the Livonian Knights (it now houses the President of Latvia).
1561 Southern Latvia is conquered by Poland; Catholicism is adopted.
1629 Parts of Latvia are conquered by Sweden.
1793 Latvian land is taken by Russia, following the partition of Poland.
1816 The system of serfdom is abolished.
Late 1800s Cultural and intellectual movements led by the "Young Latvians" increase Latvian national self-consciousness.
1905 Peasant revolt against the rich, land-owning German nobility in Latvia. Brutal repression follows.
1920 Latvia gains independence, despite German and Soviet military attempts to prevent it.
1940 Latvia is taken by the Soviets at the beginning of World War II, as well as by the Germans a year later. Both cause horrendous suffering for Latvians.
1945 By the end of the war Soviets are still in control, and Communism rules.
1991 Collapse of the Soviet Union brings about the Latvian restoration of independence.
1999 Vaira Vike-Freiberga, the first female President of Latvia, takes office.
2004 Latvia joins the EU.
2007 After centuries of disputes, Latvia's borders with Russia are set under a treaty signed by both countries.

ARRIVAL

Rīga International Airport (Lidosta Rīga) is served by numerous European airlines, including easyJet, Ryanair, Aer Lingus, Lufthansa, Air France, KLM, Turkish Airlines and Austrian Airlines, as well as Latvia's airBaltic (Ⓦwww.airbaltic.com). You can easily get to the city centre by taking bus #22 or a taxi, which should cost no more than 12Ls.

Options for cross-border **train** travel are fairly limited, with connections to Vilnius, Lithuania, and Moscow, Russia, but not to Tallinn, Estonia. Both Eurolines (Ⓦwww.eurolines.ee) and Ecolines (Ⓦwww.ecolines.net) offer frequent **bus services** linking Rīga with Tallinn, Vilnius and St Petersburg, among others. A **ferry** service runs

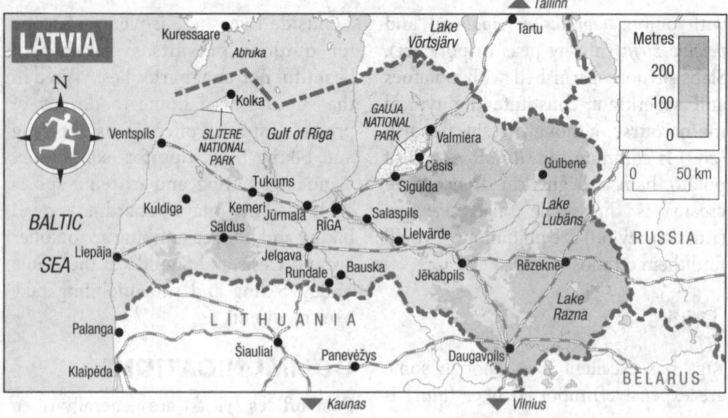

from the Rīga terminal to Stockholm, Sweden, daily and to Lübeck, Germany, four times a week.

GETTING AROUND

Buy **train** tickets in advance: stations have separate windows for long-distance (*starpilsetu*) and suburban (*pirpilsetu*) trains. Long-distance services are divided into "passenger" (*pasazieru vilciens*) and "fast" (*ātrs*) – both are quite slow but the latter, usually requiring a reservation, stops at fewer places. On timetable boards, look for *atiet* (departure) or *pienāk* (arrival). Check train timetables online at Ⓦwww.ldz.lv.

Buses are slightly quicker than trains, though marginally more expensive. Buy long-distance tickets in advance from the ticket counter and opt for an express (*ekspresis*) bus if possible.

Rīga has plentiful and cheap public transportation in the form of buses and trams. **Bicycles** are inexpensive to rent and a good way of getting around the resort areas and small towns.

ACCOMMODATION

Outside Rīga and Jūrmala accommodation is fairly limited. Even in tourist areas, towns will often only have a couple of hotels and a campsite. Budget travellers still have a limited choice but **hostel beds** in the centre of Rīga are easily obtained (check Ⓦwww.hostellinglatvia.com or Ⓦwww.hostels.com). A number of small-sized, good-value **hotels** and **guesthouses** are emerging, but rooms are often in short supply and advance reservations are required in summer. In Rīga and Jūrmala there are agencies offering well-priced **private rooms** of a reasonable standard. There's a handful of decently equipped **campsites** in Rīga, Jūrmala, Sigulda and Cēsis. Prices are normally quoted in Lats, though some are provided in euros.

FOOD AND DRINK

While meat or fish and potatoes remain the bedrock of Latvian cuisine, Rīga has something to suit every palate, with a lot of good international cuisine and vegetarian options. **Eating out**, particularly in the capital's classier joints, is fairly expensive, but there are plenty of self-service fast-food places, offering filling meals for around 3Ls. The numerous supermarkets and markets make **self-catering** a viable option.

Restaurants tend to be open from noon to midnight, with bars keeping similar hours (although some are open past 2am). Cafés typically open at 9 or 10am.

Popular national **starters** include cabbage soup (*kāpostu zupa*), sprats

with onions (*sprotes ar sīpoliem*) and *pelēkie zirņi* (mushy peas in pork fat). Slabs of pork garnished with potatoes and sauerkraut constitute the typical **main course**, although freshwater fish (*zivs*) is common too. *Rasols* (cubes of potato, ham and gherkin drenched in cream) is the staple salad. *Pelmeni* (Russian ravioli) are ubiquitous – you'll find them on most menus.

Drinks

Rīga has excellent **bars**, though some are expensive. Imported **beer** (*alus*) is widely available, but the local brews are fine and also cheaper – the most common brands are Aldaris and Cēsu. Worth trying once is *Rīga Melnais Balzāms* (Rīga Black Balsam), a kind of bitter liqueur (45 percent) made from a secret recipe of roots and herbs and supposed to cure all ailments.

Coffee (*kafija*) and tea (*tēja*) are usually served black – ask for milk (*piens*) and/or sugar (*cukurs*).

CULTURE AND ETIQUETTE

Latvians are rather reserved and tend to greet each other with solemn handshakes rather than effusive hugs. The distinctive Russian and Latvian communities do not mix much and some resent being mistaken for the other. In the workplace **women** still tend to fill more traditional roles, and the general attitude to women travelling alone tends to be mildly sexist, although there is little risk of harassment. A ten percent **tip** is appropriate for good service in a restaurant.

SPORTS AND ACTIVITIES

Ice hockey is the national sport, and the revered national team plays at the 12,500-seat Arena Rīga (Skanstes 21, ⓣ6738 8200, ⓦwww.arenariga.com: Latvian language only). You'll need to book in advance for important games.

Outside Rīga there is plenty of scope for **outdoor pursuits**; a number of beautiful **national parks**, best visited in the summer and home to dozens of protected species, offer extensive hiking and biking trails ripe for exploration. Canoeing, rafting and extreme sports such as mountain boarding, quad biking and bungee jumping are on offer around Cēsis and Sigulda in the Gauja Valley. Skiing and snowmobiling take over in winter.

COMMUNICATIONS

Post offices (*pasts*) are generally open from 8am to 8pm during the week and from 8am to 6pm on Saturdays. Poste restante is reasonably efficient. Modern **public phones** are operated with either credit cards or magnetic cards (*telekarte*), which come in 2 and 5Ls denominations, and are sold at post offices and most newsagents. Using mobile phones from other European countries is fairly inexpensive, but check roaming charges with your phone company. There are plenty of **internet cafés**, costing around 1.50Ls/hr in the capital and 1Ls elsewhere. Free **wi-fi** is available in most youth hostels and hotels, as well as many cafés and restaurants.

EMERGENCIES

Theft is the biggest hazard. If you're staying in a cheap hotel, don't leave

LATVIA ON THE NET

ⓦ**www.latviatourism.lv** General portal offering links to all manner of Latvia-related subjects.
ⓦ**www.virtualriga.com** Information on travel, entertainment and accommodation.
ⓦ**www.latviansonline.com** News and features in English.
ⓦ**www.rigathisweek.lv** Site run by *Riga This Week*, a free listings magazine.

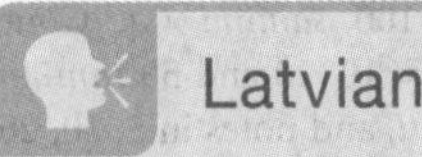

Latvian

In Latvian, the stress always falls on the first syllable of the word. The exception is the word for thank you *(paldies)*, which has the stress on the second.

	Latvian	Pronunciation
Yes	*Jā*	Jah
No	*Nē*	Neh
Please	*Lūdzu*	Loodzoo
Thank you	*Paldies*	Paldeeass
Hello/Good day	*Labdien*	Labdeean
Goodbye	*Uz redzēsanos*	Ooz redzehshanwas
Excuse me	*Atvainojiet*	Atvainoyet
Today	*Sodien*	Shwadien
Yesterday	*Vakar*	Vakar
Tomorrow	*Rīt*	Reet
What time is it?	*Cik ir pulkstenis?*	Tsik ir pulkstenis?
Open/Closed	*Atvērts/Slēgts*	Atvaerts/Slaegts
Good/Bad	*Labs/Slikts*	Labs/Slikts
Do you speak English?	*Vai jūs runājat angliski?*	Vai yoos roonahyat angliski?
I don't understand	*Es nesaprotu*	Es nesaprwatoo
How much is...?	*Cik tas maksā…?*	Tsik tas maksah…?
Cheap/Expensive	*Lēts/Dārgs*	Laets/Dahrgs
Student ticket	*Studentu biļeti*	Studentu bilyeti
Boat	*Kuģis*	Kugyis
Bus	*Auto*	Owto
Plane	*Lido*	Lidaw
Train	*Dzelzceļa*	Dzelzcelyuh
Where is the...?	*Kur atrodas…?*	Kur uhtrawduhs...?
Near/Far	*Tuvs/Tāls*	Tuvs/Taals
I'd like...	*Es vēlos…*	Es vaalaws…
I'm a vegetarian	*Es esmu veģetārietis/te(m/f)*	Es asmu vejyetahreatis/te
The bill, please	*Lūdzu rēķinu*	Loodzu rehkyinu
Toilet	*Tualete*	Tuuhlete
One	*Viens*	Viens
Two	*Divi*	Divi
Three	*Trīs*	Trees
Four	*Četri*	Chetri
Five	*Pieci*	Pietsi
Six	*Sesi*	Seshi
Seven	*Septiņi*	Septinyi
Eight	*Astoņi*	Astonyi
Nine	*Deviņi*	Devinyi
Ten	*Desmit*	Desmit

valuables in your room. Muggings and casual violence are not unknown in Rīga; avoid parks and back streets after dark. **Police** (*policija*), who are unlikely to speak much English, will penalize you if you're caught drinking in public – expect a stiff fine. Some strip clubs are notorious for ripping off drunk foreign males (see box, p.740).

Pharmacies (*aptieka*) are well-stocked with over-the-counter painkillers, first aid items, sanitary products and the like. In larger cities, they tend to be open from 8am until 7pm. There are

EMERGENCY NUMBERS

Police ⓣ02; Ambulance ⓣ03; Fire ⓣ01.

24-hour pharmacies in the capital, where, with some luck, you'll find an English speaker. **Emergency medical care** is free, but if you fall seriously ill head for home, as many Latvian medical facilities are still lagging behind those in Western Europe.

INFORMATION

Tourist offices run by the Latvian tourist board (ⓦwww.latviatourism.lv) are located at the centre of most major cities and well-touristed towns. Jāņa Sēta (Elizabetes iela 83–85, Rīga) is well stocked with guides, and publishes its own maps. *Rīga in your Pocket* (ⓦwww.inyourpocket.com; 2Ls) is an excellent English-language **listings** guide. *The Baltic Times* (ⓦwww.baltictimes.com) provides weekly updates on current affairs and events in English while *Rīga This Week* is a detailed listings guide.

MONEY AND BANKS

Latvia's currency is the *lats* (plural *lati*) – normally abbreviated to Ls – which is divided into 100 *santīmi* (s). Coins come in 1, 2, 5, 10, 20 and 50 *santīmi*, and 1 and 2 *lati*, and notes in 5, 10, 20, 50, 100 and 500 *lati*. **Bank** (*banka*) **hours** vary, but in Rīga many are open Monday to Friday from 9am to 5pm, and on Saturdays from 10am to 3pm. Outside the capital, many close at 1pm and most are closed on weekends. **Exchanging cash** is straightforward, even outside banking hours, as Rīga is full of currency exchange offices *(valktas apmaiņa)*; shop around to get the best rate. ATMs are plentiful nationwide and accept most international cash cards. At the time of writing, €1 was equal to 0.7Ls, $1 to 0.5Ls and £1 to 0.8Ls. Major banks such as the Hansa Banka, Rīgas Komercbanka and Unibanka will cash **traveller's cheques** (TravelEx Visa and American Express preferred) and some give advances on **credit cards**. In Rīga the bigger hotels will also cash traveller's cheques. Credit cards are accepted in an increasing number of establishments.

STUDENT AND YOUTH DISCOUNTS

ISIC cards will get you a fifty percent discount off entry to most museums and attractions, and even some eateries – look for the ISIC sign on doors. HI-affiliated hostels offer discounts for YHA card holders.

OPENING HOURS AND HOLIDAYS

Shops are usually open weekdays from either 8am or 10am to 6pm or 8pm, and on Saturdays from 10am to 7pm. Some food shops are open until 10pm and are also open on Sundays. In Rīga there are a few 24-hour shops, which sell food and alcohol. Most shops and all banks close on the following **public holidays**: 1 January, Good Friday, Easter Sunday, Easter Monday, May 1, the second Sunday in May, June 23 and 24, November 18, December 25, 26 and 31.

Rīga

RĪGA is the largest, liveliest and most cosmopolitan of the Baltic capitals, with a great selection of accommodation to suit any budget and a wide variety of world cuisine, ranging from cheap Eastern European buffets to the most exquisite sushi. A heady mixture of the medieval and the contemporary, the city has a good deal to offer architecture and history enthusiasts in the narrow cobbled streets of Old Rīga and the wide boulevards of the New Town.

The city also has all the trappings of a modern capital city, with efficient and affordable public transportation, along with excellent shopping to rival that of any Western city. Revellers coming to Rīga to sample its notorious nightlife will not be disappointed with the impressive variety of clubs, bars and live music venues.

What to see and do

Old Rīga (Vecrīga), centred around Cathedral Square (Doma laukums) and bisected from east to west by Kaļķu

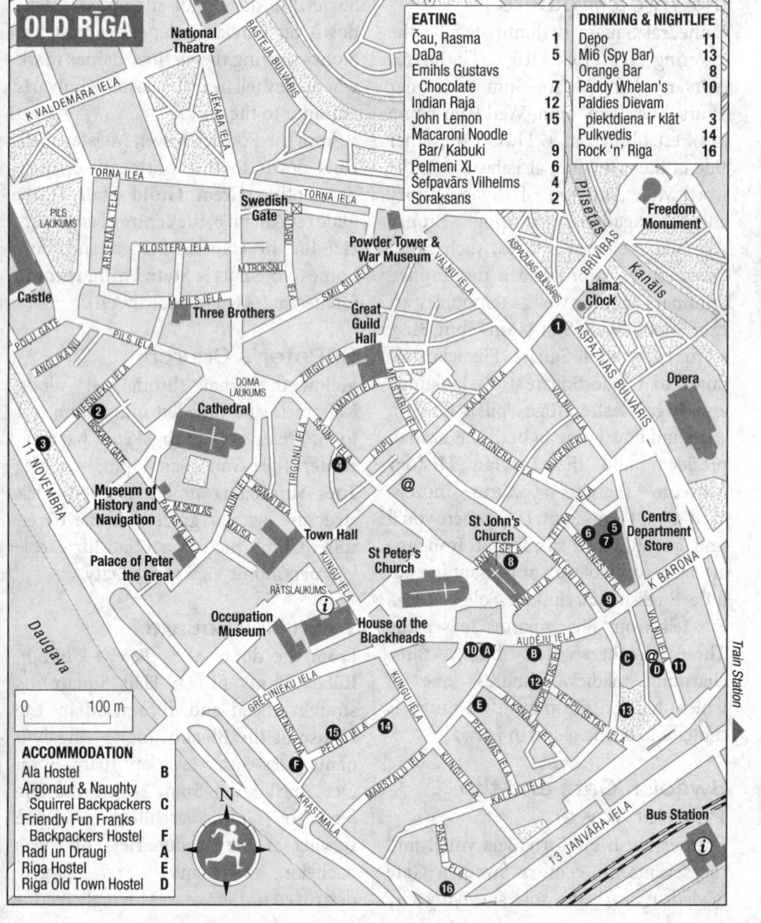

iela, forms the city's nucleus and is home to most of its historic buildings. With its cobbled streets, medieval buildings, narrow lanes and hidden courtyards, it gives the impression of stepping back in time. To the east, Old Rīga is bordered by Bastejkalns Park, beyond which lies the **New Town** (Milda). Built during rapid urban expansion between 1857 and 1914, its wide boulevards are lined with four- and five-storey apartment buildings, many decorated with extravagant Jugendstil motifs.

Rīga Cathedral, Castle and the Three Brothers

Cathedral Square is dominated by the towering red-brick **Rīga Cathedral** (winter daily 10am–5pm; summer Thurs–Tues 9am–6pm, Wed 9am–5pm; 2Ls), established in 1211. On the other side of the cathedral, at Palasta 4, is the worthwhile Museum of Rīga's History and Navigation, featuring Bronze Age and medieval articles, such as an executioner's sword and a mummified criminal's hand, as well as temporary art exhibitions (Wed–Sun 11am–5pm; 3Ls).

From Cathedral Square, Pils iela runs down to Castle Square (Pils laukums) and **Rīga Castle** (Rīgas pils), built in 1515 and now home to both the Latvian president and the **Latvian History Museum** (Latvijas vēstures muzejs; Wed–Sun: 11am–5pm; 1Ls), where you'll find an attractive display of Iron-Age artefacts and tableaux of peasant life but little English description. Follow Mazā Pils iela from Pils laukums to see the **Three Brothers** (Trīs brāli), three charming medieval houses, one of which, built in the fifteenth century, is thought to be the oldest in Latvia.

Swedish Gate and the Powder Tower

Further north on Torņa iela you'll find the seventeenth-century **Swedish Gate** (Zviedru vārti), the sole surviving city gate. At the end of Torņa iela is the Powder Tower *(Pulvertornis)*, a vast, fourteenth-century bastion, home to the **War Museum** (winter Wed–Sun 10am–5pm; summer Wed–Sun 10am–6pm; free), which gives a well-presented account of the country's turbulent history.

Bastion Hill and the Guild Hall

Bastion Hill (Bastejkalns) – the park that slopes down to the city canal at the end of Torna iela – is a reminder of the city's more recent history: on January 20, 1991, four people were killed by Soviet fire during an attempted crack-down on Latvia's independence drive. Stones bearing the victims' names mark where they fell near the Bastejas bulvāris entrance to the park.

From the Powder Tower, Meistaru iela runs down to the fourteenth-century neo-Gothic **Great Guild Hall** (Lielā ģilde) at Amatu 6, the centre of commercial life in Hanseatic Rīga and now home to the **Latvia State Philharmonic** Orchestra (ⓦwww.music.lv/en).

St Peter's Church

Follow the urban throng west along Kaļķu iela and turn left into Šķūņu iela to **St Peter's Church** (Pēter baznīca; winter Tues–Sun 10am–5pm; summer Tues–Sun 10am–6pm), a large red-brick structure with a graceful three-tiered spire. Climb the tower (2Ls) for excellent panoramic views of the city.

Town Hall Square

From the doors of St Peter's Church, **Rātslaukums** (Town Hall Square) is straight ahead and dominated by the **House of the Blackheads** *(Melngalvju* nams; Tues–Sun: May–Sept 10am–5pm; Oct–April 11am–5pm; 2Ls), a masterpiece of Gothic architecture. Once serving as the headquarters of Rīga's bachelor merchants, and largely destroyed in 1941, it was lovingly recon-

structed for the 800th anniversary of Rīga's foundation in 2001. Oozing opulence, with an excellent photo exhibition in the warren-like cellar, it is well worth a visit.

Next door, an imposing concrete structure accommodates the excellent **Occupation Museum** (Latvijas okupācijas muzejs; May–Sept daily 11am–5pm; Oct–April Tues–Sun 11am–5pm; donations welcomed), devoted to atrocities committed against Latvia's population by the Nazis and Soviets. Exhibits include reconstructed gulag barracks and letters to loved ones thrown from trains by Latvians forcibly removed to Siberia.

The Freedom Monument

The modernist **Freedom Monument** (Brīvības piemineklis) dominates the view along Brīvības bulvāris as it enters the **New Town**, holding aloft three stars symbolizing the three regions of Latvia. Incredibly, the monument survived the Soviet era, and nowadays two soldiers stand guard here in symbolic protection of Latvia's independence.

National Art Museum

Esplanade Park runs north from Brīvības bulvāris. At the far end of the park, the worthwhile **Latvian National Art Museum** (Valsts mākslas muzejs; Valdemāra iela 10; winter: daily except Tues 11am–5pm; summer: daily except Tues 11am–7pm; 1–4Ls; ⓦwww.vmm.lv), housed in a grandiose Neoclassical building, displays an impressive array of nineteenth- and twentieth-century Latvian paintings, sculptures and drawings, as well as changing modern art exhibitions.

Fin-de-Siècle residences and Jews in Latvia Museum

Rīga is home to some of the most beautiful examples of Art Nouveau

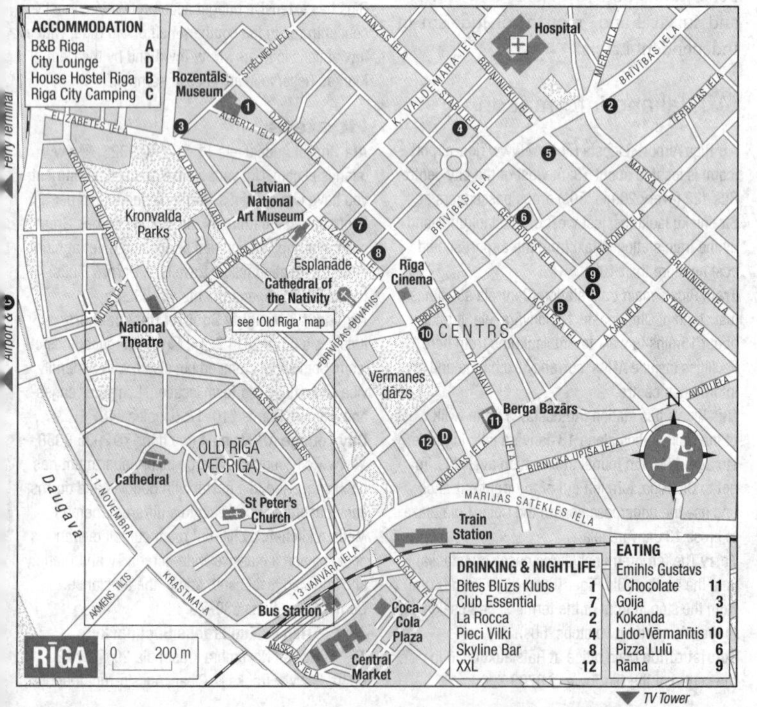

architecture in Europe, with over two hundred buildings having survived World War II. Inspired by Austrian and German styles, **Jugendstil architecture** embodies the ideal that "everything useful should be beautiful". Its motifs of mythological creatures and nymphs, which decorate the facades of many of the New Town's apartment buildings, have been described as "music in stone". A stroll along Strēlnieku iela and Alberta iela will take in some fine examples, many in the process of restoration. The beautiful facades of Elizabetes iela 10a and 10b were designed by the Russian-born architect Mikhail Eisenstein, whose own residence at Alberta iela 4 features majestic lions astride the turrets.

Branching off Elizabetes, at Skolas 6, you will find a small but gritty and informative **Jews in Latvia Museum** (Sun–Thurs noon–5pm; donation) on the history of Jewish life in Latvia from the eighteenth century onwards, including the persecution both by Nazis and Soviets, and survival and "rebirth" of Judaism in independent Latvia.

Arrival and information

Air Rīga Airport (Lidosta Rīga; ⓦwww.riga-airport.com) is located about 13km west of the city centre. Bus #22 (every 20min; 50s) drops passengers at Strēlnieku laukums, just west of Rātslaukums, and by the train station. A taxi from the airport should cost no more than 10Ls.
Train Rīga's main train station (Centrālā stacija) is just south of Old Rīga on 13 Janvāra iela; it takes about 15mins to walk to Rātslaukums from here. Facilities include ATMs, currency exchange and an information centre.
Bus Rīga's bus station (Autoosta) is 5min walk west of the train station along 13 Janvāra iela; luggage storage, ATM and tourist information available. To get to Old Rīga, turn left out of the front entrance and use the underpass next to the Coca-Cola Plaza to cross 13 Janvāra iela.
Ferry The ferry terminal (Jūras pasazieru stacija) is to the north of Old Rīga. Trams #5, #7 or #9 run from the stop in front of the terminal on Ausekļa iela to the city centre (two stops; 50s).
Tourist office Main office at Rātslaukums 6 in the centre of the Old Town ⓣ6703 7900, ⓦwww.rigatourism.com (daily 10am–7pm), with other branches at the bus station (daily 9am–7pm) and the train station (daily 10am–6.30pm). They have accommodation lists and sell copies of *Rīga In Your Pocket* as well as the Rīga Card (10/14/18Ls for 24/48/72hr; ⓦwww.rigacard.lv), which gives unlimited use of public transport plus museum discounts; check first that it saves money on your particular itinerary.

City transport

Public transport Both Old Rīga and the New Town are easily navigated on foot, and you can reach outlying attractions by frequent and efficient public transport, running between 5.30am and midnight. Buy flat-fare single-journey tickets from the conductor for 50s. For bus, tram and trolleybus routes and timetables go to ⓦwww.rigassatiksme.lv.
Taxis Short journeys shouldn't be more than 3Ls; insist that the meter is turned on. To avoid being swindled, it's best to book a taxi by phone; Smile Taxi (ⓣ2233 0330) and Lady Taxi (ⓣ2780 0900) are generally reliable.

Accommodation

Rīga has extensive budget accommodation, mostly concentrated in the southern half of Old Rīga, with a few options in nearby New Town and by the Central Market. Reserve in advance in summer.

Hostels

Ala Hostel Audēju iela 11 ⓣ2640 9323, ⓦwww.alahostel.com. Not your typical hostel environment; you have two spacious, wi-fi enabled rooms per floor sharing a bathroom and kitchen corner. Great choice for the location and peace and quiet at night, if not for meeting fellow travellers. Dorm 7.50Ls; rooms 21–25Ls; apartments 48–63Ls.
Argonaut & Naughty Squirrel Backpackers Kalēju iela 50 ⓣ2614 7214, ⓦwww.argonauthostel.com. Somewhat cramped but clean, with a friendly vibe and a good Old Town location. Luggage "cages" and internet. Dorms €10–17; doubles €40.
City Lounge A. Kalniņa 4 (top floor) ⓣ2935 8958, ⓦwww.citylounge.lv. A large luxury apartment has been converted to a hostel with doubles and dorms, each decorated according to a different theme. Modern kitchen, a chill-out room complete with hookahs and a massive wide-screen TV and friendly and knowledgeable staff add to the ambiance. Dorms €11; rooms €30–70.
Friendly Fun Franks Backpackers Hostel Novembra krastmala 29 ⓣ6722 0040, ⓦwww.franks.lv. Clean, Aussie-run, friendly

hostel in Old Rīga with 24hr bar, kitchen, wi-fi, and internet. Organizes nights out and trips to the AK-47 shooting range; free beer on arrival. Dorms €8–15; doubles €35–40.

House Hostel Riga Barona iela 44 (entrance from Lāčplēša iela) ⓣ6735 0227, ⓦwww.riga-hostels.com. Run by Riga Out There, an expat tour operator, this central hostel popular with adventurous backpackers has spacious dorms and rooms with shared facilities and wi-fi and offers a plethora of tours (see p.741); dorms €15–17 euros; doubles €50.

Riga Hostel Mārstaļu iela 12 ⓣ6722 4520, ⓦwww.riga-hostel.com.lv. Excellent Old Town location, bathroom in each dorm, kitchen, spacious common room, internet. Dorms €11; doubles €40.

Riga Old Town Hostel Valņu iela 43 ⓣ6722 3406, ⓦwww.rigaoldtownhostel.lv. Clean dorms and doubles, free internet, wi-fi, bed linen and sauna. Five minutes' walk from bus station. Reception doubles as a bar and quirky walking tours are on offer. Dorms 5–6Ls; singles 17Ls; doubles 30Ls.

Hotels

B&B Riga Ģertrūdes iela 43 ⓣ6727 8505, ⓦwww.bb-riga.lv. A friendly family-run guesthouse in Central Riga offering en-suite rooms equipped with cable TV, fridges and microwaves. Breakfast vouchers and airport transfers available. Single €49; double €64.

Radi un Draugi Mārstaļu iela 1/3 ⓣ6728 0200, ⓦwww.draugi.lv. One of the few affordable places in the Old Town, with an old-world charm but modern amenities, with wi-fi equipped en suites with cable TV. Very popular, so book well in advance. Singles €60; doubles €74.

Camping

Riga City Camping Behind the Ķīpsala exhibition centre at Ķīpsalas iela 8 (late May–mid-Sept only) ⓣ6706 5000, ⓦwww.rigacamping.lv. This large campsite is 2km northwest of Old Rīga and offers ample tent space; it's very popular with mobile homes. Tents for rent (5Ls); tennis court and internet use also available. Catch bus #5, #7 or #21 from Valdemāra iela; get off once you've crossed the river. Camping 3Ls per person.

Eating

Many bars and cafés do cheap and filling food and there are also plenty of reasonably priced restaurants serving international cuisine.

Cafés and snack bars

Emihls Gustavs Chocolate Marijas iela 13/VI (inside the Berga bazārs arcade). Chocolate heaven, from the exquisite truffles to the small cups of rich, flavoursome liquid chocolate (1.50Ls). Daily until 9pm. Second branch inside Galerija Centrs on Audēju iela.

Goija Strēlnieku iela 1a. A chilled-out Moroccan den, where you can lounge around with a hookah or sip one of their many teas while sampling delectable Arabic sweets.

John Lemon Peldu iela 21. Artsy, welcoming place to while away an afternoon with a coffee (1.30Ls) or a unique Bob Marley pizza (3.80Ls).

Pelmeni XL Kaļķu iela 7. Popular fast-food restaurant on Old Rīga's main street offering six types of *pelmeni* (Russian ravioli) filled with meat or cheese, plus soups and drinks. 1Ls/200g. Also at Audēju 16 (entrance from Valņu).

Pizza Lulū Ģertrūdes iela 27. Fashionable little pizzeria with pizza by the slice, ideal for lunch or late-night snacking. 2–3Ls.

Šefpavārs Vilhelms Šķūņu iela 6. Self-service, create-your-own-pancake place near Cathedral Square. 3Ls.

Restaurants

Čau, Rasma Aspazijas bulvaris 20. The decor in this unpretentious cellar restaurant is rather tacky, but you can't beat the large portions of hearty traditional Latvian cooking. Pigs' ears with crackling, blood sausage and grey peas with bacon are all on the menu here, as are local beers. Mains 3.50–6Ls.

DaDa Audēju iela 16 (Galerija Centrs). Trendy, informal restaurant with a Dadaist theme. Fill up a bowl with fresh meat, seafood, vegetables and noodles, pick a sauce and have it cooked in front of you. 5.50–8Ls.

Indian Raja Vecpilsētas iela 3. Authentic, flavourful Indian food in a cosy cellar setting – an expat favourite. Huge mains 5–7Ls.

Kokanda Bruņinieku 12. This is an excellent choice for inexpensive Central Asian cusine; try any of the grilled meats or the large, spicy dumplings. Weekday business lunch 3.50Ls.

Lido-Vērmanītis Elizabetes iela 65. All manner of tasty Baltic meat-and-potato dishes, plus salad and fruit bars on the ground floor, pizza and fast food in the cellar. Mains 3.50Ls.

Macaroni Noodle Bar/Kabuki Audēju 14. Extensive menu of excellent home-made pasta and noodle dishes, as well as sushi and sashimi platters, oriental gyoza dumplings and much more, in this stylish twin restaurant with minimalist decor. Mains 5–7Ls. Kabuki also does an excellent bento box weekday lunch special for 3.99Ls.

Rāma Barona iela 56. Hare-Krishna-run vegetarian place in the New Town, catering for vegans, with a tasty range of dirt-cheap Asian dishes. 2.50Ls.

Soraksans Miesnieku iela 12. Cook your own meal on the table (if you dare!) at this popular Korean spot, or choose one from the many inexpensive meat, fish and vegetarian mains. Mains 4–8Ls; cheap weekday lunch special 3Ls.

Drinking and nightlife

The Old Town offers innumerable opportunities for bar hopping, with a wide range of watering holes (many of which serve decent food) filling up with fun-seeking locals seven nights a week.

Bars

Mi6 (Spy Bar) Kalēju iela 52. The combination of strong cocktails, basement hookah-smoking, Bond films and slightly cheesy decor attracts an arty crowd. Mon–Thurs 5pm–1am, Fri & Sat 5pm–4am.

Orange Bar Jāņa sēta 5. Orange industrial decor, alternative music, a lively young crowd dancing on the furniture and cheap bar food. Packed on weekends. Sun–Thurs noon–midnight, Fri & Sat noon–2am.

Paddy Whelan's Grēcinieku iela 4. Big, lively Irish pub/sports bar, popular with locals and expats alike, offering 18 kinds of beer and cider on tap, as well as great curry from its Indian menu. Happy hour 5pm–7pm. Sun–Thurs 11am–1am, Fri & Sat 11am–3am.

Paldies Dievam piektdiena ir klāt Novembra krastmala 9. This bright, Caribbean-themed bar is a great place for a wide range of cocktails and for watching bikini-clad women dancing on the bar. Sun–Thurs 9am–midnight, Fri 9am–4am, Sat 10am–4am.

Pieci Vilki (Five Wolves) Stabu iela 6. Watering hole popular with locals. Warm decor, reasonably priced drinks and excellent food. Huge portions of chicken wings 4Ls.

Skyline Bar Elizabetes iela 55. Behold Rīga's splendour from a window seat on the 26th floor of the *Reval Hotel Latvija* while sipping a strawberry daiquiri.

Clubs

Club Essential Skolas iela 2 ⓦ www.essential.lv. Plays adventurous music with DJs from all over Europe and provides a funky chill-out zone. Dress well. Thurs & Sun 10pm–6am, Fri & Sat 10pm–8am; 3–5Ls.

Depo Vaļņu iela 32 ⓦ www.klubsdepo.lv. Post-industrial cellar space with alternative DJ nights and live garage bands. A laid-back café during the day. Thurs–Sat 8pm–5am; 3–5Ls.

La Rocca Brīvības iela 96 ⓦ www.larocca.lv. Mingle with the Russians, dance in a cage above the dance floor in Rīga's premier techno club, or check out the hip-hop room. Cocktails 3Ls. Fri & Sat 10pm–6am; 3–5Ls.

Pulkvedis (Nobody Writes to the Colonel) Peldu iela 26/28 ⓦ www.pulkvedis.lv. The hippest club in Rīga: edgy music on two levels, good DJs and an easy-going, fun-seeking local clientele. Closes 5am Fri & Sat; 3Ls.

XXL Kalniņa iela 4 ⓦ www.xxl.lv Popular gay club and restaurant attracting a mixed, dance-oriented crowd. Good food, male striptease and wild decor. Daily until 7am; cover charge 2–10Ls.

Entertainment

Live Music

Bites Blūzs Klubs Dzirnavu iela 34a. Laid-back, unpretentious blues pub festooned with photos of musicians; regular live acts.

Opera Aspazijas bulvāris 3 ⓦ www.opera.lv. Opera and ballet shows, sometimes featuring international artists. 4–40Ls, depending on event.

Rock 'n' Riga 13 janvāra 33. New bar festooned with Hendrix, ACDC and Jim Morrison memorabilia with live rock acts most nights and excellent Valmiermuiža microbrew (2.50Ls).

Cinemas

Forum Cinemas (Coca-Cola Plaza) 13 Janvāra iela 8 ⓦ www.forumcinemas.lv. Second-largest cinema in northern Europe with 14 screens. 2–4.50Ls.

Riga Cinema Elizabetes iela 61 ⓦ www.kino.riga.lv. Rīga's oldest cinema, showing foreign films as well as blockbusters. 3Ls.

GENTLEMEN BEWARE...

If you find yourself inebriated in a bar and being chatted up by an attractive Latvian girl, think twice before following her to a bar of her choice. A popular scam in Rīga involves mercenary beauties who seek out drunk foreign men and lure them into bars or clubs run by their unsavoury associates. They present the man with an extortionate bill for drinks consumed, and if he refuses to pay they beat him up until he divulges his credit card details. Places to avoid include: The Lord Pub, Roxy, Puzzle, Saxon, Mary and Cigar Bar. Should you encounter trouble, call the tourist hotline: ⓣ 2203 3000.

Shopping

Art Nouveau Riga Strēlnieku iela 9 ⓦwww.artnouveauriga.lv. Dedicated entirely to Art Nouveau merchandise, such as small plaster faces copied from the decorations on Rīga's facades. 8am–7pm.
Central Market (Centrāltirgus) A row of massive 1930s former Zeppelin hangars next to the bus station selling everything from half a cow to fake designer watches.
Dzintara Galerija Torņa iela 4. An extensive collection of amber jewellery and various amber-encrusted items.
Food and curio bazaar Elizabetes iela 83/85. Soviet kitsch, freshly-baked bread, organically grown produce and gourmet food samples. Second and last Saturday of each month.

Directory

Bike rental Gandrs, Kalnciema iela 28 ⓣ6761 4775.
Embassies Canada, Baznīcas iela 20/22 ⓣ6781 3945; Ireland, Alberta iela 13 ⓣ6703 9370; UK, Alunāna iela 5 ⓣ6777 4700; US, Raiņa bulvāris 7 ⓣ6703 6200.
Exchange Marika: Basteja iela 14, Brīvības bulvāris 30 (both 24hr).
Hospital ARS, Skolas iela 5 ⓣ6720 1007. Some English-speaking doctors.
Internet access Interneta Planeta Kafe, Vaļņu iela 41 (24hr); Internet Klubs, Kalku iela 10 (24hr).
Left luggage At the bus station (daily 6.30am–11pm), from 25–50s/hour, depending on weight, 20s each additional hour. Lockers at the left-luggage office (Rokas Bagāžas) in the train station basement (50s–1.50Ls per day, 4.30am–midnight).
Pharmacy Vecpilsētas aptieka, Audēju iela 20, ⓣ6721 3340 (24hr).
Post office Brīvības bulvāris 32 (Mon–Fri 7am–10pm, Sat & Sun 8am–8pm).
Tours Rīga Out There, at House Hostel Rīga (see p.739; ⓣ2938 9450, ⓦwww.rigaoutthere.com), organizes off-the-wall activities, such as AK-47 shooting in an underground bunker and bobsleighing, as well as excellent nightlife and sightseeing tours, all with an English-speaking guide.

Moving on

Train Cēsis (5 daily; 1hr 50min); Liepāja (1 daily; 3hr); Majori, Jūrmala (every 30min; 40min); Moscow, (2 daily; 16hr); St Petersburg, (1 daily; 12hr); Salaspils (at least one hourly; 15 min); Sigulda (12 daily; 1hr); Vilnius, (1 every other day – odd dates; 7hr).
Bus Bauska (every 30min; 1hr 10min–1hr 30min); Cēsis (at least 13 daily; 2hr); Kaunas (1 daily; 4hr 30min); Klaipēda (4 daily; 5hr); Liepāja (at least 12 daily, 3hr–4hr 30min); Moscow (1 daily, 17hr); Pärnu, (at least 10 daily; 3hr 30min); Sigulda (at least 8 daily; 1hr); St Petersburg, (2 daily; 12–14hr); Tallinn (at least 10 daily; 5hr 30min); Tartu (2 daily; 5hr); Vilnius (at least 9 daily; 4hr–4hr 30min).

The rest of Latvia

In summer, the whole of Latvia seems to head to the beach – be it **Jūrmala**, the lively string of seaside resorts near Rīga, or the picturesque port of **Liepāja**, with its unspoiled stretch of sand and its music festival. Nature lovers can either head to **Kemeri National Park** or inland to the picturesque little towns of **Cēsis** and **Sigulda**.

JŪRMALA

A 20-kilometre string of small seaside resorts lining the Baltic coast west of Rīga, **JŪRMALA** was originally favoured by the tsarist nobility and later drew tens of thousands of holiday-makers from all over the USSR; it continues to be a popular beach resort today. Its wide clean sandy **beach**, backed by dunes and pine woods and dotted with beer tents and climbing frames, is thronged with people in summer, especially during the week-long **music festival** in July.

Jomas iela, the pedestrianized main street running east from the station square, teems with people and has a number of excellent restaurants and cafés, as well as craft stalls and art exhibitions. A few paths lead to the beach from Jūras iela, north of Jomas iela.

Arrival and information

Trains Trains leave Rīga's station from platforms 3 and 4 (1.95Ls return). Majori is the main stop for Jūrmala, eleven stops from Rīga.
Minibuses Minibuses depart from the Central Minibus Station (opposite the train station; 70s one way) every 10min between 6am and midnight in the summer. Take either the Rīga–Sloka or the Rīga–Dubulti minibus and get off in front of the Majori train station.
Tourist office Lienes 5 ⓣ6714 7900, ⓦwww.jurmala.lv (Mon–Fri 9am–7pm, Sat 10am–5pm, Sun 10am–3pm). Helpful staff can fix you up with accommodation and provide information on regional excursions (ⓦwww.jurmalatour.lv).

Accommodation

Elina Lienes iela 43 ⓣ6776 1665, ⓦwww.elinahotel.lv. This perpetually popular guesthouse has clean rooms 5min walk from the beach. Singles 35–45Ls; doubles 40–60Ls; quads 50–65Ls; apartments 55–130Ls.
Kempings Nemo Atbalss iela 1, Vaivari ⓣ6773 2350, ⓦwww.nemo.lv. Large campsite popular with caravans and families in a pleasant middle-of-the-forest location just behind the beach, with cleanish facilities and a water park on site (3–5Ls). Tents 7Ls; cabins 9–35Ls.
Riga Beach Hostel Dzintaru prospects 50, Dzintari ⓣ2837 4185 ⓦwww.rigabeachhostel.lv. Spanking new HI-affiliated hostel a stone's throw from the beach, with spacious, clean dorms and internet access. Dorms 8–15Ls.

Eating and drinking

Café 53 Jomas iela 53. Nab a spot on the shaded outdoor terrace and pick from a wide range of inexpensive local dishes – from pickled herring to hearty portions of pork ribs, washed down with a local Užavas beer. Mains 3.50–5Ls.
Sue's Asia Jomas iela 74. Busy restaurant serving large portions of excellent Indian, Thai and Chinese cuisine. The *Tom yum kuung* is authentically spicy and flavoursome (5Ls). Closes midnight.
Zangezur Jomas iela 80. Popular Armenian restaurant specialising in grilled meats and other tasty dishes, such as aubergines with garlic and walnuts. Try the *hinkale* – large meat dumplings (3Ls).

Entertainment

Dzintari Concert Hall Turaidas iela 1, Dzintari ⓣ6776 2117 ⓦwww.dzk.lv. This open-air, 2000-capacity concert hall is located near the beach and hosts regular music events in the summer.

Moving on

Train Rīga (at least two hourly between 5.40am and 10.30pm; 30min); Ķemeri (15 daily between 6.20am and 00.10am; 35min).

ĶEMERI NATIONAL PARK

An extensive preserve west of Jūrmala, **Ķemeri National Park** is home to a wealth of protected ancient forests and wetlands, with 237 bird species nesting around the fourteen islets of Lake Kaņieris. The park's fauna includes moose, elk, deer, wolves and foxes, and this is the only place in Latvia where certain plant species can be found.

To get to the park, take the suburban train from Riga to the spa town of **Ķemeri** (20 stops, Tukums direction, 2Ls one-way), known for its sulphurous springs, and follow Tukuma iela from the train station until you reach **Ķemeru Park** and the landmark *Hotel Ķemeri.* Take the trail behind the hotel straight to the Ķemeri **tourist office** in the Meza Maja (Forest House) at Tūristu 18a (May & Sept Wed–Sun 10.30am–4pm, June–Aug: daily 10.30am–4pm; ⓣ6714 6824, ⓦwww.kemeri.gov.lv), which has information on hiking in the park, and bird- and animal-watching excursions, such as the excellent "Bat Night" in July. Though two of the walking trails are currently closed, there is an attractive 800m board-walk through the bog behind the Meza Maja, as well as a 3km trail in the vicinity of the nearby Lake Slokas, featuring some sulphur springs and a bird-watching tower. An easy 12km cycling trail starts by the lake and finishes in Ķemeri; there are three longer and more challenging trails by Lake Valgums.

SALASPILS

The concentration camp at **SALASPILS**, 14km southeast of Rīga, is where most of Rīga's Jewish population perished during World War II. One hundred thousand people died here, including prisoners of war and Jews from other countries, who were herded into the Rīga Ghetto after most of the indigenous Jewish population had been liquidated. The site is marked by monumental sculptures, with the former locations of the barracks outlined by white stones; look for the offering of toys by the children's barracks.

To get here take a **suburban train** from Rīga central station in the Ogre direction and alight at **Dārziņi** (70s one-way; at least one train hourly from Rīga) from where a clearly signposted path leads to the clearing, fifteen minutes' walk through the forest. The stop itself is not well signposted; it's the first one to be completely surrounded by pine forest.

RUNDĀLE PALACE

One of the architectural wonders of Latvia, Baroque **Rundāle Palace** (Rundāles Pils; daily May–Oct 10am–6pm; Nov–April 10am–5pm; combined ticket to the palace, exhibitions and gardens 6Ls; students 5Ls ⓦwww.rundale.net;) is 77km south of Rīga. Its 138 rooms were built in two phases during the 1730s and 1760s and designed by **Bartolomeo Rastrelli**, the architect responsible for the Winter Palace in St Petersburg. It was privately owned until 1920 when it fell into disrepair, but has largely been returned to its former glory through meticulous restoration. Each opulent room is decorated in a unique fashion and there are changing art exhibitions both inside the palace and in the vast landscaped gardens. There are frequent buses from Rīga to **Bauska** (every 30min between 7am–8pm; 1hr 30min; 1.70Ls); then take a local service to Pilsrundāle (5 buses daily to Bauska; 30 min; 50s). The palace is across the street from the bus stop.

SIGULDA

Dotted with parks and clustered above the southern bank of the River Gauja around 50km northeast of Rīga, **SIGULDA** is Gauja National Park's main centre and a good jumping-off point for exploring the rest of the **Gauja Valley**.

What to see and do

From the train station, Raiņa iela runs north into town, passing the bus station. After about 800m a right turn into Baznaca iela brings you to the impressive seven-hundred-year-old **Sigulda Church** (Siguldas baznīca). Sigulda is home to three castles: Krimulda Castle (Krimuldas pilsdrupas) and Sigulda Castle (Siguldas pilsdrupas), a former stronghold of the German Knights of the Sword, from which you can see Turaida Castle (Turaidas pils), the most impressive of the three.

If you head west from the train station along Ausekļa Iela, you will shortly come across the bobsleigh track where you can hurtle down a concrete half-tube at

TREAT YOURSELF

LEARN TO FLY!

To experience the sensation of skydiving without the hassle of parachutes or airplanes, head to **Aerodium** (Tues–Fri 4–8pm, Sat & Sun noon–8pm ⓣ2838 4400, ⓦwww.aerodium.lv (book online); 25Ls for two minutes; 5/6Ls per minute thereafter on weekdays/weekends), 5km outside Sigulda (take any Rīga-bound bus and ask to be dropped off at the Silciems stop; 60s). Don the floppy protective gear and experience the intense adrenaline rush of hovering atop an air current created by a giant fan. Beginners fly up to 5m above the fan, while professionals reach heights five times that.

80km/hr during the summer months (Sat & Sun noon–5pm; 7Ls per person per ride) or check out the view of the Gauja Valley from the top floor (daily; 40s) of the tower.

Turaida Castle

You can reach **Turaida Castle** by bus (for Turaida or Krimulda) from Sigulda bus station. Alternatively, take the cable car (18 daily, 10am–7.30pm; 2Ls) across the Gauja River to Krimulda Castle, descend the wooden staircase signposted "Gūtmaņis Cave", then follow the path past the cave – the setting for a legend of "star-crossed lovers". The path turns to the right before rejoining the main road just short of Turaida itself. Built on the site of an earlier stronghold by the bishop of Rīga in 1214, Turaida Castle was destroyed when lightning hit its gunpowder magazine in the eighteenth century. These days its cellar exhibitions chart the castle's history (daily 10am–5/7pm; 3Ls) and it's possible to climb up the main tower.

Information

Tourist office Valdemāra 1a, just west of the train and bus stations ⓣ6797 1335, ⓦwww.tourism.sigulda.lv (Mon–Fri 8am–7pm, Sat 9am–2pm). Helpful multilingual staff can book you into private rooms and provide information on exploring the Gauja Valley. They can also arrange bungee jumping from the cable car (Fri–Sun from 6.30pm until last customer; 25Ls per person) and hot-air ballooning (book in advance, ⓣ6761 1614, ⓦwww.altius.lv).

Gauja National Park Administration Baznīcas iela 7 ⓣ6780 0388, ⓦwww.gnp.gov.lv (May–Sept Mon & Wed–Fri 10am–5pm, Tues 8.30am–5pm; rest of the year Mon, Thurs & Fri 9am–1pm, Tues 1–7pm). North of the bus and train stations along Raiņa iela, this helpful office provides detailed information on hiking trails in the Gauja National Park, including the popular trail from Sigulda to the village of Ligatne. Detailed map 1.80Ls.

Accommodation

Hotel Pils Pils iela 4b ⓣ6770 9625 ⓦwww.hotelpils.lv. Centrally-located hotel by the bus station, with large, airy rooms equipped with cable TV and a/c. Breakfast included. Singles 33Ls; doubles 43Ls.

Makara Kempings Peldu iela 1 ⓣ2924 4948, ⓦwww.makars.lv. Large campsite (open May–Sept) in a shady riverside spot northwest and downhill from the town centre. Arranges canoeing and rafting trips. 6Ls.

Melnais Kaķis Pils iela 8 ⓣ6797 0272. Spotless (if somewhat small) rooms with a bar and canteen-style restaurant next door. The disco may keep you awake on Fridays and Saturdays. Rooms 25Ls.

Eating and drinking

Kaķu Māja Pils iela 8. The *Black Cat* café offers large helpings of inexpensive canteen-style food and a tempting range of cakes. Main and a drink 3.50Ls.

Pils Bars Pils iela 4b. Next to the bus station, this informal spot offers beer and basic meals.

Zalumnieku Piestātne Kafejnīca Pils iela 9. Another canteen-style place with a roomy, rustic interior serving large portions of Latvian food; pay by weight. Complete meal 3Ls. There's also a separate pizza restaurant; medium pizza 3.50Ls.

Moving on

Train Cēsis (5 daily; 45min); Rīga (13 daily; 1hr 15min).

Bus Cēsis (at least hourly; 50min); Rīga (at least hourly; 1hr 15min).

GAUJA NATIONAL PARK

Encompassing a diverse range of flora and fauna, **Gauja National Park** (ⓦwww.gnp.gv.lv) covers over 920 square kilometres of near-pristine forested wilderness, bisected by the 425-kilometre Gauja River. The valley is ideal for exploring by bike, as most of the hiking trails are accessible to cyclists. Numerous "wild" campsites are located along the river's banks, and major campsites in Sigulda, Cēsis and Valmiera, at the north end of the park, arrange overnight canoeing and rafting trips.

CĒSIS

The well-preserved little town of **CĒSIS**, 35km northeast of Sigulda, has a prewar atmosphere. From the **train** and **bus** stations walk down Raunas iela to

Vienības laukums, Cēsis's main square. The attractive, somewhat run-down wooden **Old Town** lies to the south of here, along Rīgas iela. Nearby, on Skolas iela, is the thirteenth-century **St John's Church** (Svēta Jāņa baznīca). East of the square are the impressive remains of **Cēsis Castle** (Cēsu pils; daily 10am–6pm; 2Ls; 3Ls for joint ticket with Exhibition Hall and History and Art Museum, both closed Mon) founded by the Knights of the Sword in 1209, where a toppled statue of Lenin lies anachronistically on the green. Explore the narrow winding staircases of the towers with a lantern, peer into the gloom of the dungeon, and see the working forge.

Information

Tourist office Pils 9 ⓣ412 1815, ⓦwww.tourism.cesis.lv (daily 10am–6pm). The helpful staff charge 2Ls to arrange accommodation and also provide information on cultural events, such as the Arts Festival (ⓦwww.cesufestivals.lv), and various outdoor activities, such as horseriding, quad biking, canoeing and cycling.

Accommodation

Kolonna Vienības iela 1 ⓣ412 0122, ⓦwww.hotelkolonna.com. Cēsis's grand hotel has free internet, decent breakfasts and surprisingly good-value, spacious rooms. Singles 50Ls; doubles 66Ls.
Province Niniera iela 6 ⓣ412 0849. Friendly, small guesthouse with five clean doubles. 32Ls.
Žagarkalns Mūrlejas iela 12 ⓣ2626 6266, ⓦwww.zagarkalns.lv. Campsite on the western side of Cēsis by the river with clean facilities; you can rent a tent and sleeping bag. Canoe, catamaran and rafting trips available, as well as bicycle rental. 2.50Ls per person.

Eating and drinking

Aroma Cafe Lenču iela 4. Popular, cheap and cheerful eatery; many items under 3Ls. Extensive selection of teas from 1.50Ls.
Bars Draugi Rigas iela 13. Café doubling as a sports bar; stop here for a quick meal or a beer.
Province Niniera iela 6. Inexpensive, well-prepared food in the restaurant of this welcoming guest-house. Try the soups or the *shashlik* (4.50Ls).

Moving on

Train Rīga (5 daily 5.50am–6.54pm, all stopping at Sigulda; 1hr 50min).
Bus Rīga via Sigulda (at least one hourly between 6am–8pm; 2hr); bear in mind that in Sigulda passengers are dropped off at the junction of A2 (Vidzemes šoseja) and Gāles iela, rather than the main bus station).

LIEPĀJA

A busy trading port, **LIEPĀJA**, 205km west of Rīga, is Latvia's third-biggest city with faded eighteenth- and nineteenth-century facades contrasting with crumbling military installations. The city draws visitors with one of Latvia's best beaches and the country's largest rock festival.

What to see and do

One of the city's main draws is the **Baltic Beach Party** (ⓦwww.balticbeachparty.lv) in late July, a carnivalesque weekend of fashion shows, live music and sporting events. In mid-August the country's largest rock festival, **Liepājas Dzintars**, takes place, and showcases Latvian rock. The centre of town is south of the Tirzniecības Canal and bisected north to south by Lielā iela. The long white beach stretches beyond the outdoor concert halls and beer gardens of the lush **Jūrmala Park** to the west of the centre. North of Tirdzniecības Canal and reachable by buses #4 and #7 and minibus #3, lies the suburb of **Karosta,** formerly a Russian naval fortress and now a conglomeration of wide, semi-abandoned boulevards lined with the crumbling remains of military barracks, imposing tsarist-era buildings and run-down concrete housing blocks, which are fascinating to explore.

Arrival and information

Bus and train station Both stations are in the same building 1500m north of the town centre and south of Karosta; there is no luggage storage or

ATM. To get to the centre catch a tram (30s) down Rīgas iela.

Tourist office Rožu laukums 5/6 ⓣ6348 0808, ⓦwww.liepaja.lv/turisms (Mon–Fri 9am–7pm, Sat 9am–6pm, Sun 10am–3pm). Friendly staff can arrange accommodation and provide free city maps.

Accommodation

Fontaine Jūras iela 24 ⓣ6342 0956, ⓦwww.fontaine.lv. This centrally located hotel with a funky red exterior has uniquely decorated rooms (think Elvis, Soviet kitsch) and a curio shop/reception in which to rummage for hidden treasures. Singles 15–25Ls; doubles 27Ls; family room 35Ls; apartment 65Ls.

Liepāja Travellers Hostel Republikas iela 25 ⓣ2869 0106, ⓦwww.liepajahostel.lv. Between the beach and the city centre, this friendly hostel offers clean dorms. Dorms 10–12Ls; rooms 36Ls.

Eating, drinking and entertainment

Fontaine Palace Dzirnavu iela 4 ⓦwww.sheriffontaine.lv. Right by Tirdzniecības Canal, this converted warehouse stages live concerts on weekends, and alternative music nightly, as well as the Fontaine Festival in July. 24hr fast food joint attached. Closes 4am Fri & Sat.

Kiss Me Lielā iela 13. Espresso bar with red love seats and a glass front serving a wide range of filling salads, soups, crepes and desserts. Great coffee for only 80s.

Latvia's 1st Rock Café Stendera iela 18/20, ⓦwww.pablo.lv. One of Liepāja's top spots – four floors of good, cheap food; live music nightly and rooftop beer garden. Closes 4am Fri & Sat.

TREAT YOURSELF

PRISONER FOR A NIGHT

For a taste of Soviet-style incarceration, book into **Karosta Prison** (Karosta Scientums, Invalīdu iela 4 ⓣ2636 9470, ⓦwww.karostascietums.lv; 8Ls) and spend the night in a creepy, musty cell. Clean bed linen is provided, which is more than the real inmates received, but aside from that, living conditions remain unchanged – you still have to use the same communal washing facilities and squatter toilets. Tours of the imposing red building are also available (May–Oct daily 10am–6pm; 2Ls), as well as "Behind Bars" role-playing, with groups of visitors subjected to mock interrogation by staff in period garb; arrange an English-speaking experience with the tourist office in advance. Take eastbound bus #4 just south of the bus station to reach the prison.

Moving on

Train Rīga (1 daily at 6am; 3hr).

Bus Klaipėda via Palanga (daily at 8.32pm; 2hr); Rīga (at least hourly between 3am and 7.30pm; 3hr–4hr 30min).

Lithuania

HIGHLIGHTS

PALANGA: Lithuania's premier beach resort; the place to hear live music and party all night

CURONIAN SPIT: a wild, beautiful National Park on the Baltic coast

DEVIL'S MUSEUM, KAUNAS: a fun and quirky collection of devil figures from around the world

GENOCIDE MUSEUM, VILNIUS: a haunting reminder of man's inhumanity

TRAKAI: a fairytale medieval castle sitting on its own little island

ROUGH COSTS

DAILY BUDGET Basic €35/occasional treat €50

DRINK Utenos beer €1.70

FOOD Cepelinai (potato and meat parcels) €4

HOSTEL/BUDGET HOTEL €12/€37

TRAVEL Train: Vilnius–Paneriai €0.60; Bus: Kaunas–Nida €18

FACT FILE

POPULATION 3.4 million

AREA 65,200 sq km

LANGUAGE Lithuanian; Russian widely spoken

CURRENCY Litas (Lt)

CAPITAL Vilnius (population: 550,000)

INTERNATIONAL PHONE CODE ⓣ370

Introduction

Lithuania is a vibrant and quirky country, which has undergone rapid modernization since becoming independent from the Soviet Union in 1990. You'll find a lively nightlife, both in Vilnius and on the coast, ample grounds for outdoor pursuits in the as yet unspoiled national parks, and a number of good beaches, as well as a stark contrast between slick, modern city life and rural poverty. Fiercely proud of their country, Lithuanians are more exuberant and welcoming than their Baltic neighbours and you are likely to encounter their hospitality everywhere.

Lithuania is predominantly rural – a gently undulating, densely forested landscape scattered with lakes, and fields dotted with ambling storks in the summer; travel is inexpensive, and even in well-trodden destinations the volume of visitors is low, leaving you with the feeling that there's still much to discover here. **Vilnius**, with its Baroque Old Town, is the most architecturally beautiful of the Baltic capitals, and boasts a boisterous nightlife, while the second city, **Kaunas**, also has an attractive centre and a couple of unique museums, along with a handful of surprisingly good restaurants and bars. The port city of **Klaipėda** is a convenient overnight point en route to the resorts of **Neringa** (the Curonian Spit), a unique sliver of sand dunes and forest that shields Lithuania from the Baltic Sea, or to **Palanga**, Lithuania's party town where everyone flocks in the summer for a good time.

CHRONOLOGY

2000 BC The ancestors of the Lithuanians settle in the Baltic region.
1009 AD First recorded mention of the name Lithuania in the Quedlinburg Annals.
1236 Grand Duke Mindaugas unites Lithuania to ward off German crusaders.
1252 Mindaugas is crowned King of Lithuania.
1386 After an arranged marriage between the King of Lithuania and the Queen of Poland, Lithuania officially converts to Christianity.
1410 The Polish-Lithuanian alliance defeats the Teutonic Knights, increasing their military influence in the Baltic region.
1547 First Lithuanian book, *The Simple Words of Catechism*, is published.
1795 Russia takes control of Lithuania.
1865 Growth of the Lithuanian liberation movement leads to violent repression by the Russians.
1900 Mass Lithuanian emigration across the world to escape Russian repression.
1920 Lithuania gains independence from Russia after heavy fighting.
1939 Lithuania is invaded by Nazi Germany.
1945 During both German and Soviet occupation, thousands of Lithuanian Jews are killed whilst thousands of other Lithuanians are deported.
1990 Following the success of the nationalist "Sajudis" movement, Lithuania is the first Soviet Republic to declare its independence from Moscow.
1991 Lithuanian independence is recognized by the USSR before its collapse.
2004 Lithuania joins the EU; thousands emigrate to work in Western Europe.
2006 Government collapses as the Labour Party leaves the ruling coalition.
2009 Lithuania's economy takes a downturn as a result of global economic recession.

ARRIVAL

Most tourists arrive by **air**; Vilnius airport is served by fourteen European airlines, though no budget airlines, while Kaunas handles daily Ryanair flights from London, Frankfurt, and Dublin. Lithuania has good **rail** connections with neighbouring countries, with direct trains arriving in Vilnius from Warsaw, Moscow and St Petersburg,

amongst others. Several **bus** companies, including Eurolines (ⓦwww.eurolines.ee), provide regular services to Vilnius's central bus station. There are also frequent **ferries** from Kiel, Germany, and Karlshamn, Sweden, to Klaipėda on Lithuania's Baltic coast (ⓦwww.krantas.lt).

GETTING AROUND

Buses are slightly quicker, more frequent and more expensive than trains. You should buy long-distance **train** tickets in advance – stations have separate windows for long-distance and suburban (*priemiestinis* or *vietinis*) trains. Long-distance services are divided into "passenger" (*keleivinis traukinys*) and "fast" (*greitas*); the latter usually require a reservation. On timetable boards, look for *isvyksta* (departure) or *atvyksta* (arrival).

It's best to buy long-distance **bus** tickets in advance, and opt for an express (*ekspresas*), to avoid frequent stops. You can also pay for your ticket on board, although this doesn't guarantee you a seat. On the Curonian Spit, buses may agree to stow your bicycle for an extra 5Lt. There are plenty of buses travelling to Lithuania's Baltic neighbours.

In Vilnius and Kaunas there is frequent and efficient public transport: buses, trolleybuses and route taxis cover most of the city. Smaller places, such as the Curonian Spit, are best explored by **bicycle**; bike rentals are inexpensive and plentiful.

ACCOMMODATION

A good way to keep accommodation costs down is by staying in **private rooms**. The most reliable agency is Litinterp, with offices and guesthouses in Vilnius, Kaunas and Klaipėda; the latter can book rooms in Palanga and on the Curonian Spit. Spartan double rooms in Soviet-era **budget hotels** cost as little as 80Lt. Smaller, smarter mid-range places charge 120–200Lt a double.

There are a few **hostels**, charging 35–40Lt per night. Space is limited and it's best to call in advance; in popular spots like Nida and Palanga, reservations are essential in summer. There are a lot of **campsites** in rural areas, charging around 10Lt per person, 10–15Lt per tent.

FOOD AND DRINK

Lithuanian **cuisine** is based on traditional peasant dishes. Typical starters include marinated mushrooms (*marinuoti grybai*), herring (*silkė*) and smoked sausage (*rukyta desra*) along with cold beetroot soup (*saltibarsčiai*). A popular **national dish** is *cepelinai*, or

zeppelins – cylindrical potato parcels stuffed with meat, mushrooms or cheese. Others include potato pancakes (*bulviniai blynai*), and *koldūnai* – boiled or fried dumplings with meat or mushroom filling. Popular **beer snacks** include deep-fried sticks of black bread with garlic (*kepta duona*) and smoked pigs' ears. Pancakes (*blynai*, *blyneliai* or *lietiniai*) come in a plethora of sweet and savoury varieties.

Most cafés and bars do reasonably priced food. Well-stocked supermarkets, such as Iki and Maxima, are found in Vilnius and elsewhere. Many restaurants are open between 11am and midnight daily, with cafés open from 7/8am and with bars closing at 2am at the earliest.

Beer (*alus*) is popular, local brands being Švyturus, Utenos and Kalnapilis, and so is **mead** (*midus*), Lithuania's former nobleman's drink. The leading local **firewaters** are Starka, Trejos devynerios and Medžiotojų – invigorating spirits flavoured with herbs. Many lively bars in Vilnius and Kaunas copy American or Irish models, although there are also plenty of folksy Lithuanian places, while cafés (*kavinė*) come in all shapes and sizes. Coffee (*kava*) and tea (*arbata*) are usually served black; ask for milk (*pienas*) and/or sugar (*cukrus*).

CULTURE AND ETIQUETTE

Urban Lithuania is rapidly becoming Westernized, with city dwellers enjoying a thoroughly modern lifestyle. There is a stark difference, however, between the cities and the far poorer rural Lithuania, where traditional culture remains firmly in place and where electronic communication has yet to make inroads. If eating with locals, it is rude to refuse second helpings of food; when toasting someone, always look them in the eye. Always give an odd number of flowers when visiting Lithuanians; even numbers are for the dead. Shaking hands across the threshold is bad luck. Family ties are strong, and extended family gatherings are common. Women tend to fill traditional roles. Only tip in restaurants to reward good service and it suffices to round up the bill by leaving behind spare change; ten percent is fair.

SPORTS AND ACTIVITIES

Lithuania's top sport is **basketball**, with the national team the reigning European champions, and locals religiously following the games on TV. Catch a game at Vilnius's Siemens Arena. Lithuania's **national parks**, as well as the Curonian Spit, offer various opportunities for **outdoor activities** such as hiking, biking and canoeing.

COMMUNICATIONS

In major towns, **post offices** (*pastas*) are open Monday to Friday 8am to 6pm and Saturday 8am to 3pm; in smaller places hours are more restricted. **Stamps** are also available at some kiosks and tourist offices. **Public phones** operate with cards (*telefono kortelė*) which you can purchase at post offices and kiosks. Getting a pre-paid SIM card for your mobile with either Bitė, Omnitel or Tele 2 (8Lt) is a good way of avoiding roaming charges, though using another European mobile in Lithuania is relatively inexpensive. To make a long-distance call, dial ⓣ8 before the area code. When calling

JUMP TO IT!

Active Holidays Rodunios kelias 8-102, Vilnius ⓣ6982 4795, ⓦwww.activeholidays.lt. If you want to try your hand at anything that involves jumping, diving, wheels, raucous nightlife, or even plain old sightseeing, these guys will find it for you, and organize transport and an English-speaking guide.

LITHUANIA ON THE NET

Ⓦwww.tourism.lt National tourist board site with useful information.
Ⓦwww.tourism.vilnius.lt Vilnius tourist information.
Ⓦwww.muziejai.lt Portal for Lithuanian museums.
Ⓦwww.lietuva.lt General information about the country.

Lithuania from abroad, omit the initial 8. For **international calls**, dial ⓣ8, wait for the tone, then dial ⓣ10, then the country code as usual. There's a good choice of **internet cafés** in Vilnius and a few in Kaunas; many cafés and restaurants also have **wi-fi**.

EMERGENCIES

You're unlikely to meet trouble in Lithuania; pickpocketing, car theft and late-night mugging are the most common crimes. You should be aware that a scam operates in Vilnius, whereby drunk foreign men are sought out by beautiful women who lure them into bars run by unsavoury characters, who then charge the men extortionate amounts for drinks and beat them up if they refuse to pay. The cash-starved **police** expect to be taken seriously, so be polite if you have dealings with them. A few of the younger ones may speak a little English. **Emergency health care** is free but if you get seriously ill, head home.

INFORMATION

Most major towns have **tourist offices** (Ⓦwww.tourism.lt), often offering accommodation listings and event calendars in English. The **In Your Pocket** guides to Vilnius, Kaunas and Klaipėda (available from bookshops, newsstands, tourist offices and some hotels; Ⓦwww.inyourpocket.com; 5–6Lt) are indispensable sources of practical information. Regional **maps** and detailed street plans of Vilnius are available in bookshops and kiosks.

EMERGENCY NUMBERS

Police ⓣ02; Ambulance ⓣ03; Fire ⓣ01.

MONEY AND BANKS

Lithuania's currency is the **Litas** (usually abbreviated to Lt), which is divided into 100 centai. Coins come as 1, 2, 5, 10, 20 and 50c, and 1, 2 and 5Lt, with notes of 10, 20, 50, 100 and 200Lt. The litas is pegged to the euro (€1 = 3.45Lt). **Bank** (*bankas*) opening hours vary, though branches of the Vilniaus Banks are usually open Monday to Friday 8am to 3/4pm. They generally give advances on Visa/MasterCard/AmEx cards and cash traveller's cheques (commission 2–3 percent). Outside banking hours, find an **exchange office** (*valiutos keitykla*). There are plentiful **ATMs** in all major towns as well as the Curonian Spit; **credit cards** are widely accepted.

OPENING HOURS AND PUBLIC HOLIDAYS

Opening hours for **shops** are 9/10am to 6/7pm. Outside Vilnius, some places take an hour off for lunch; most usually close on Sunday (though some food shops stay open). Most shops and all banks will be closed on the following **public holidays**: January 1, February 16, March 11, Easter Sunday, Easter Monday, May 1, July 6, August 15, November 1, December 25 & 26.

STUDENT AND YOUTH DISCOUNTS

An ISIC or an IYTC card will get you fifty percent discount on museums and sights, as well as on public transport and some long-distance trains during term-time. A YHA card gets discounts at HI-affiliated youth hostels, while ISIC/IYTC cards are accepted at any hostel.

Lithuanian

	Lithuanian	Pronunciation
Yes	*Taip*	Tape
No	*Ne*	Ne
Please	*Prašau*	Prashau
Thank you	*Ačiu*	Achoo
Hello/Good day	*Labas*	Labass
Goodbye	*Viso gero*	Viso gero
Excuse me	*Atsiprašau*	Atsiprashau
Sorry	*Atleiskite*	Ahtlayskita
Where?	*Kur?*	Kur?
Can you show me?	*Galėtumėt man parodyti?*	Gahlehtumet mahn pahrawdeeti?
Student ticket	*Bilietˇa studentas*	Bileahtah studantahs
Toilet	*Tualeto*	Tuahlataw
I'd like to try that	*Aš norėčiai išbandyti to*	Ahsh nawrehchow ishbahndeeti taw
I don't eat meat	*Aš nevalgau mėsiško*	Ahsh navahlgow mehsishkaw
Bill	*sˇaskaita*	sahskaitah
Good/Bad	*Geras/Blogas*	Gerass/Blogass
Near/Far	*Artimas/Tolimas*	Artimass/Tolimass
Cheap/Expensive	*Pigus/Brangus*	Piguss/Branguss
Open/Closed	*Atidarytas/Uždarytas*	Atidaritass/Uzhdaritass
Today	*Siandien*	Shyandyen
Yesterday	*Vakar*	Vakar
Tomorrow	*Rytdiena*	Ritdyena
How much is...?	*Kiek kainuoja...?*	Kyek kainwoya...?
What time is it?	*Kiek valandų?*	Kyek valandoo?
I don't understand	*Nesuprantu*	Nessuprantu
Do you speak English?	*Ar jųs kalbate angliškai?*	Ar yoos kalbate anglishkay?
One	*Vienas*	Vyenass
Two	*Du/dvi*	Du/Dvee
Three	*Trys*	Triss
Four	*Keturi*	Keturee
Five	*Penki*	Penkee
Six	*Šeši*	Sheshee
Seven	*Septyni*	Septinee
Eight	*Aštuoni*	Ashtuonee
Nine	*Devyni*	Devinee
Ten	*Dešimt*	Deshimt

Vilnius

VILNIUS is a cosmopolitan and thoroughly modern city that is relatively compact and easy to get to know, boasting a variety of inexpensive attractions and a lively nightlife. A vague undercurrent of menace from the city's recent brutal history mingles with an air of optimism and the poignant beauty of its medieval heart, its elaborate Baroque churches jostling for space amidst glitzy restaurants, strip bars and dilapidated old buildings that line its cobbled streets. Beguiling, and sometimes downright odd, the city draws you in like no other.

What to see and do

At the centre of Vilnius, poised between the medieval and nineteenth-century parts of the city, is **Cathedral Square** (Katedros aikštė). To the south of here along Pilies gatvė and Didžioji gatvė is the Old Town, containing perhaps the most impressive concentration of Baroque architecture in northern Europe. West of the square in the **New Town** is Gedimino prospektas, a nineteenth-century boulevard and the focus of the city's commercial and administrative life. The traditionally **Jewish areas** of Vilnius between the Old Town and Gedimino prospektas still retain some sights, such as the synagogue.

Cathedral Square

Cathedral Square is dominated by the Neoclassical **cathedral** (Arkikatedra bazilika; daily 7.30am–7:30pm), dating from the thirteenth century when a wooden church was built here on the site of a temple dedicated to Perkųnas, the god of thunder. The highlight of the airy, vaulted interior is the opulent **Chapel of St Casimir**, the patron saint of Lithuania. Next to the cathedral on the square is the white belfry, once part of the fortifications of the vanished Lower Castle. Between the Cathedral and the belfry lies a small coloured tile with *stebuklas* (miracle) written on it, marking the spot from where, in 1989, two million people formed a human chain that stretched all the way to Tallinn, Estonia, to protest against the Soviet occupation of the Baltic States.

Gediminas Hill and the Upper Castle Museum

Rising behind the cathedral is the tree-clad Gediminas Hill, its summit crowned by the red-brick **Gediminas Tower** – one of the city's best-known landmarks – founded by Grand Duke Gediminas, the Lithuanian ruler who consolidated the country's independence. The tower houses the worthwhile **Upper Castle Museum** (Aukstinės pilies muziejus; May–Sept daily 10am–7pm; Oct–April Tues–Sun 11am–5pm; 4Lt, free on Wed in winter), with displays of armour and models showing the former extent of Vilnius's medieval fortifications. The view of Old Town from the top is unparalleled. Take the funicular from the courtyard of the **Applied Art Museum** (2Lt, students 1Lt).

The Lithuanian National Museum

About 100m north of the cathedral is the **Lithuanian National Museum**, Arsenalo 1 (Lietuvos Nacionalinis Muziejus; Tues–Sat 10am–5pm, Sun 10am–3pm; 5Lt), tracing the history of Lithuania from prehistoric times to 1940 through an interesting collection of artefacts, paintings and photographs, though the labels are mostly in Lithuanian and Russian. A little further north on Arsenalo, a separate department houses the much snazzier **Prehistoric Lithuania Exhibition** (same hours), displaying flint, iron, bronze and silver artefacts and covering the history of Lithuanians up to the Middle Ages.

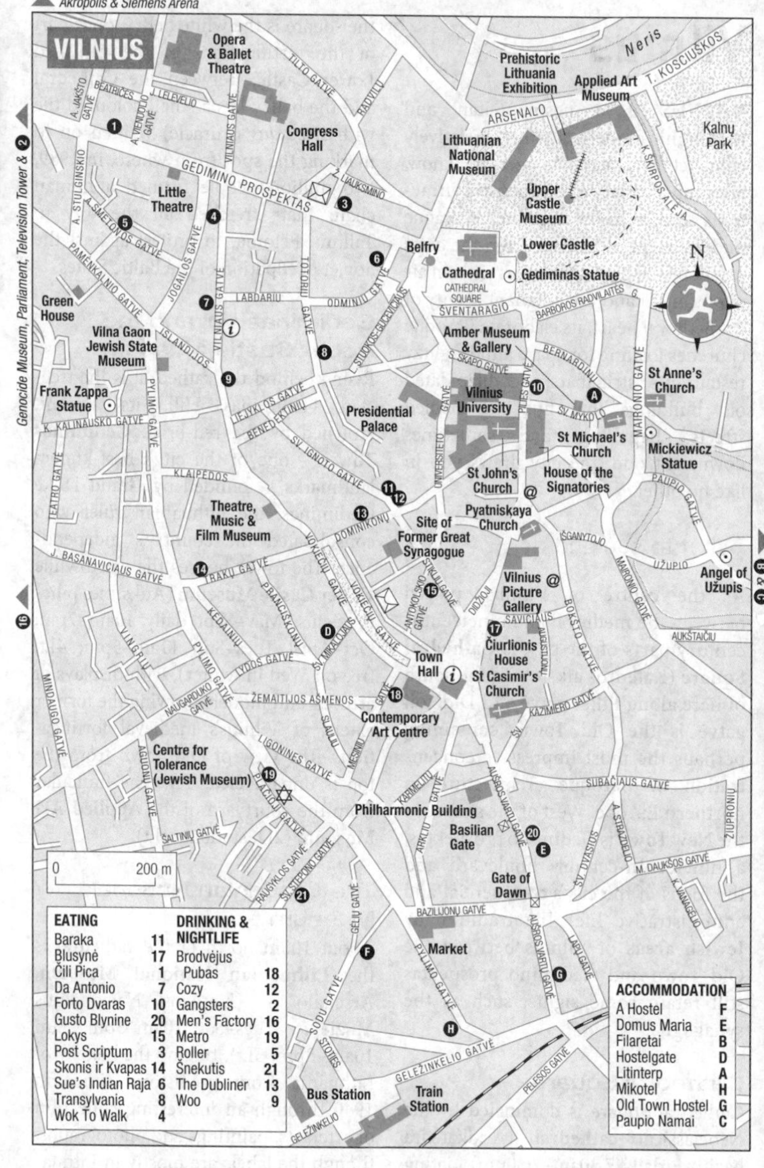

The Old Town

The **Old Town**, just south of Cathedral Square, is a network of narrow, often cobbled streets, that forms the Baroque heart of Vilnius, with the pedestrianized Pilies gatvė cutting into it from the south eastern corner of the square. To the west of this street is **Vilnius University**, constructed between the sixteenth and eighteenth centuries around nine linked courtyards that extend west to Universiteto gatvė. Within its precincts

is the beautiful Baroque **St John's Church** (Sv Jono baznyčia), founded during the fourteenth century, taken over by the Jesuits in 1561 and given to the university in 1737.

The Presidential Palace and St Anne's Church

The **Presidential Palace**, just west of the university on Daukanto aikštė, was originally built during the sixteenth century as a merchant's residence and remodelled into its present Neoclassical form at the end of the eighteenth century. Napoleon Bonaparte, who stayed here briefly during his ill-fated campaign against Russia in 1812, is said to have been so impressed by **St Anne's Church** (Šv. Onos Bažnyčia; May–Sept Tues–Sun 10am–6pm) on Maironio gatvė, to the east of Pilies gatvė, that he wanted to take it back to Paris on the palm of his hand. Studded with skeletal, finger-like towers, its facade overlaid with intricate brick traceries and fluting, this late sixteenth-century structure is the finest Gothic building in Vilnius.

Užupis and the Vilnius Picture Gallery

Just south of St Anne's a bridge over the river Vilnia forms the border of the self-declared independent republic of **Užupis**, home to a flourishing population of artists, bohemians and yuppies. Stroll up from *Užupio Café* across the bridge to see the psychedelic art gallery with weird and wonderful creations suspended above the river. Some of the buildings are in dire need of repair, but there is a young, up-and-coming feel to the area. West of Užupis, Pilies gatvė becomes Didžioji gatvė as it heads south, with the restored Baroque palace at no. 4 housing the **Vilnius Picture Gallery** (Vilniaus Paveikslų Galerija; Tues–Sat noon–6pm, Sun noon–5pm; 6Lt), with a marvellous collection of sixteenth- to nineteenth-century paintings and sculptures from around the country.

Town Hall Square and around

The colonnaded Neoclassical building at the end of Town Hall Square (Rotušės aikštė) is the **Town Hall**. The **Contemporary Art Centre** (Suolaikinio meno centras or SMC; Tues–Sun 11am–6.30pm; 5Lt) lies behind it, hosting fascinating modern art exhibitions with interactive elements. East of the square, lies the striking, newly renovated **St Casimir's Church** (Šv. Kazimiero Bažnyčia; Mon–Fri 10am–6.30pm, Sun 8am–1.30pm). This is the oldest Baroque church in the city, dating from 1604, and it has a beautiful interior. South of here, Didžioji becomes Aušros Vartų gatvė, leading to the **Gate of Dawn** (Aušros Vartų), the sole survivor of the nine city gates. A chapel above the gate houses the image of the Madonna of the Gates of Dawn, said to have miraculous powers and revered by Polish Catholics; open-air mass is held on Sundays.

The choral synagogue

Today, the Jewish population of Vilnius numbers only five thousand and, out of the 96 that once existed, the city has just one surviving **synagogue**, at Pylimo 39 (open for services Mon–Fri 8–9.30am & 7.30–8pm; Sat 10am–2pm; Sun 8.45–9.45am & 7.30–8pm; visiting hours 10am–2pm daily except Sat).

Jewish Museum

The **Vilna Gaon Jewish State Museum** (Valstybinis Vilniaus Gaono Žydų Muziejus) is housed in three separate branches; 5Lt entry. The **Jewish community offices** at Pylimo 4 (Mon–Fri 9am–5pm) have displays upstairs on Jewish partisan resistance, life in the Vilnius ghetto, and an exhibit on Lithuanians who risked their lives to save Jews during the Nazi occupation. The **Green House**, slightly uphill at Pamėnkalnio 12 (Mon–Thurs 9am–5pm, Sun 10am–4pm), contains a harrowing display on the fate of

JEWISH VILNIUS

Before World War II, Vilnius was one of the most important centres of Jewish life in eastern Europe. The Jews – first invited to settle in 1410 by Grand Duke Vytautas – made up around a third of the city's population, mainly concentrated in the eastern fringes of the Old Town around present-day Vokiečių gatvė, Zydų gatvė and Antokolskio gatvė. Massacres of the Jewish population began soon after the Germans occupied Vilnius on June 24, 1941, and those who survived the initial killings found themselves herded into two ghettos. The smaller of these ghettos centred around the streets of Zydų, Antokolskio, Stiklių and Gaono and was liquidated in October 1941, while the larger occupied an area between Pylimo, Vokiečių, Lydos, Mikalojaus, Karmelitų and Arklių streets and was liquidated in September 1943. Most of Vilnius's 80,000 Jewish residents perished in Paneriai forest on the southwestern edge of the city (see p.759).

Vilnius and Kaunas Jews during World War II, including eyewitness accounts, and many extremely disturbing photographs with some captioning in English. Guided museum tours in English can be arranged (30Lt), as well as "history of Jewish Vilnius" tours (☎5/262 0730). The Centre for Tolerance, at Naugarduko 10/2 (Mon–Thurs 10am–6pm, Sun 10am–4pm), inside a restored former Jewish theatre, houses some excellent twentieth-century Jewish artwork, as well as fine religious items and an excellent display in English on the second floor charting the history of Jews in Lithuania from the fourteenth century until the present day.

Frank Zappa statue

On Kalinausko street, the bronze head of rocker **Frank Zappa** is perched on a column against a backdrop of street art. Civil servant Saulis Paukstys founded the local Zappa fan club and, in 1992, commissioned the socialist-realist sculptor Konstantinas Bogdanas to create this unique sculpture.

Gedimino prospektas and the Genocide Museum

Gedimino prospektas, running west from Cathedral Square, remains the most important commercial street. On the southern side of **Lukiskių aikštė**, a square around 900m west of Cathedral Square, is Gedimino 40, Lithuania's former KGB headquarters. The building also served as Gestapo headquarters during the German occupation and, more recently, the Soviets incarcerated political prisoners in the basement. It's now the excellent **Genocide Museum** (Genocido aukų muziejus; entrance at Aukų 2a; Wed–Sat 10am–6pm, Sun 10am–5pm; 6Lt), its torture cells and execution courtyard making a grim impression. Well-labelled, detailed exhibits on Soviet occupation, deportation and Lithuanian partisan resistance are upstairs; the optional English-language cassette-tape commentary (8Lt) is worthwhile if you want a detailed prison tour.

Arrival and information

Train and bus The main train station is at Geležinkelio 16, with 24hr luggage storage in the basement, a 24hr currency exchange, ATMs, detailed timetables, information office and Maxima supermarket. The main bus station, just across the road, has luggage storage, and an ATM.

Tourist office The multilingual staff at the two main branches at Vilniaus 22 (☎5262 9660; Mon–Fri 9am–6pm;,žioji 31 (☎5262 6470, Ⓦwww.vilnius-tourism.lt; same hours) offer advice on accommodation, attractions and festivals (Ⓦwww.vilniusfestivals.lt). The best source of listings is the excellent *Vilnius in Your Pocket* city guide (6Lt).

City transport

Public transport Buses and trolleybuses cover most of the city. Tickets cost 2Lt from newspaper kiosks

or 2.50Lt from the driver. You can buy a one-, three-/ ten-day ticket from the kiosk just to the left of the train station near the trolleybus stop for 13/23/46Lt. Validate your ticket by punching it in the machine on board. Alternatively, hail a minibus at any bus stop in the direction you're going, pay the driver 3–4Lt and you'll be dropped off at the stop you require.

Taxi Prices are usually reasonable and fares should cost no more than around 2Lt per kilometre. Phoning ahead is one way of ensuring a fair rate; try Vilniaus Taksi Plius (Ⓣ5261 6161) or Ekipažas (Ⓣ5239 5539).

Accommodation

Hostels

A Hostel Sodų 17 Ⓣ5213 9994, Ⓦwww.ahostel.lt. Clean, bright Japanese-style sleeping cubicles, dorms and en-suite VIP rooms, popular with the backpacking set. Dorms can be noisy. Five minutes' walk from the train and bus stations and the Old Town. Dorms €9; rooms €25.

Filaretai Filaretų 17 Ⓣ5215 4627, Ⓦwww.filaretaihostel.lt. HI-affiliated hostel in the Užupio district, with large, clean dorm rooms and cheap laundry facilities, 15min walk east of the Old Town, or bus #34 from the train station. Dorms 34Lt; single/double/triple 70/50/40Lt per person.

Hostelgate Šv. Mikalojaus 3/1 Ⓣ6383 2818, Ⓦwww.hostelgate.lt. This bustling, friendly, central hostel run by outgoing, helpful staff, offers clean dorms, kitchen, lounge and wi-fi. Staff organize all manner of tours. Dorms 39Lt; double/triple/quad 110/150/188Lt.

Old Town Hostel Aušros Vartų 20–10 Ⓣ5262 5357, Ⓦwww.lithuanianhostels.org. Cramped, rowdy, but comfortable HI-affiliated hostel near the train and bus stations with dorms and doubles. Free internet; reservations essential in summer. Dorms 38Lt; rooms 150Lt.

Hotels and guesthouses

Domus Maria Aušros Vartų 12 Ⓣ5264 4880, Ⓦwww.domusmaria.lt. Central guesthouse in a beautiful former monastery. Some of the bright, comfortable en-suite rooms look out onto the Gate of Dawn. Single/double/triple/quad 119/269/329/369Lt.

Litinterp Bernardinų 7/2 Ⓣ5212 3850, Ⓦwww.litinterp.lt. Stay in this well-located central guesthouse with airy, comfortable rooms and shared bathrooms and kitchenettes, or ask the very helpful multilingual staff to book you a private room in the Old Town with a host family. Book in advance in summer. Single/double/triple 110/180/240Lt, with/without bathroom 90/160/210Lt.

Mikotel Pylimo 63 Ⓣ5260 9626, Ⓦwww.mikotel.lt. Small hotel a few steps away from the train and bus stations, with pristine, modern en suites and quirky decor. Single/double/triple 190/240/290Lt.

Paupio Namai Paupio 31a Ⓣ85210 2700, Ⓔhotel@paupio.lt. There's something for everyone in this friendly place just east of the Old Town, from basic dorms, to rooms with shared bathrooms and kitchen, to en-suite apartments. A decent breakfast is included in the price; not all staff speak English. Dorms 45Lt; single/double/triple 95/170/225Lt, with/without bath 80/140/150Lt.

Eating

There's a fast-growing range of eateries in Vilnius offering everything from Lithuanian to Indian cuisine. There's little difference between eating and drinking venues: bars and cafés serve both snacks and meals and often represent better value for money than restaurants.

Cafés and snack bars

Gusto Blynine Aušros Vartų 6. Substantial, tasty crepes with every imaginable sweet or savoury filling (6Lt).

Post Scriptum Gedimino 7. Popular café serving fresh juices, good cakes and cheap mains (10Lt).

Skonis ir Kvapas Trakų 8. The most beautiful vaulted interior in town. Big pots of tea, excellent coffee and an affordable range of hot meals. Drinks 7Lt; mains 10–15Lt.

Restaurants

Baraka Šv. Ignoto 12. Vegetarian restaurant serving inventive and inexpensive daily specials. Particularly popular at lunchtime. Mains 15–20Lt.

TREAT YOURSELF

AN UNPARALLELED DINING EXPERIENCE

DOMM R Didžioji 31 (Town Hall) Ⓣ6867 7707. This is a meal you will remember for the rest of your life. Not only is it the ultimate in modern luxurious dining, the presentation of the creative dishes goes above and beyond anything else Vilnius has to offer. Tuck into dishes that come with their own MP3 soundtrack or emerge from a cloud of smoke, as if in a magician's act. The duck is divine. 6pm–midnight; closed Sun. Mains around 80Lt.

Blusynė Saviclaus 5. Small, friendly place, with an inventive menu of well-prepared food; fish soup with absinthe 14Lt. Open from 3pm Mon–Wed, from 1pm Thurs–Sun.

Čili Pica Gedimino 23. Popular place for inexpensive thin-crust and deep-pan pizzas. Six more branches, including one at the Europa shopping mall. Medium pizza 15–18Lt.

Da Antonio Vilniaus 23. Smart but down-to-earth Italian restaurant, with prompt service and delicious home-made pasta. Pasta dishes 20–28Lt.

Forto Dvaras Pilies 16. An excellent place to try *cepelinai* (zeppelins; 10Lt) or stuffed potato pancakes (8.50Lt). Cheap, tasty and filling.

Lokys Stiklių 8/10. Cosy Lithuanian cellar restaurant specializing in creatures that roam the forests. The well-cooked game dishes are worth the splurge. Beaver stew 25Lt; bilberry dumplings 15Lt.

Sue's Indian Raja Odminių 3. One of the best restaurants in town, this place is popular with expats and locals alike. Gorge yourself on generous portions of excellent curry, and be warned that the vindaloo is not for the faint-hearted.

Transylvania Totorių 22. Tuck into hearty portions of good solid Romanian food – stews, grilled meats, dumplings – in a rustic restaurant-cum-pub. Lunchtime deals 12Lt.

Wok To Walk Vilniaus 19. A great little spot where you choose from an array of noodles, rice, vegetables and sauce and it's all wok-fried in front of you. Quick and tasty. Mains 20Lt.

Drinking and nightlife

Vilnius has a growing club scene well worth trying, though you may have just as good a time (and cheaper too) in some of the bars mentioned below.

Bars

Brodvėjus Pubas Mėsinių 4. Popular drinking/dancing venue with live bands (Thurs–Sun) and DJs, and a full menu of snacks and hot meals including lunchtime specials. Beer 6.50Lt; cover charge 5Lt.

Cozy Dominikonų 10. Cosy, chilled-out cellar bar with a choice of three rooms, DJ appearances, extensive drinks menu and a bargain two-course business lunch (15Lt).

The Dubliner Dominikonų 6. Friendly expat favourite complete with pub quiz. The Guinness is not cheap, but worth it, and the food is a cut above your average pub grub. Happy hour 4–7pm.

Šnekutis Šv. Stepono 8. An excellent place to sample traditional beers and ales from all over Lithuania. The rustic decor and traditional beer snacks are a nice touch.

Woo Vilniaus 22. Chic urban-style cellar with an Asian theme; DJs play a smooth grooves/alternative set.

Clubs

Gangsters Mečetės 4/5, Ⓦ www.gangsterclub.lt. Catering both to students and a slightly older crowd, this popular club alternates between R'n'B and various DJ sets. Check website for listings. Thurs–Sat 10pm–4am.

Men's Factory Ševčenkos 16 Ⓦ www.gayclub.lt. Flamboyantly decorated gay bar/club 20min walk west of the Old Town. Thurs 10pm–4am, Fri & Sat 10pm–6am; entry 20–40Lt.

Metro Pylimo 43 Ⓦ www.metroclub.lt. Subterranean club catering to a student crowd; local rock music most nights, decent DJs playing alternative sets on other nights. Mon–Thurs 10am–11pm, Fri 10am–6am, Sat 4pm–6am; entrance 15–30Lt.

Roller Smetonos 5. Attracting mostly a student crowd, this is the place to don your rollerskates and groove along to a disco set of whatever the local DJs throw together. Good fun and the occasional pile-up. Thurs 8pm–2am, Fri & Sat 10pm–5am; entrance 20–25Lt.

Entertainment

Cinemas

Forum Cinemas Akropolis Ozo 25 Ⓦ www.forumcinemas.lt. Modern, multi-screen cinemas in Vilnius's largest shopping mall, showing the latest blockbusters in original language, with subtitles. 18Lt.

Skalvija Goštauto 2/15 Ⓦ www.skalvija.lt. Foreign films are shown in this central venue by the river.

Live music

Opera & Ballet Theatre Vienuolio 1 Ⓣ 5262 0727, Ⓦ www.opera.lt. Stunning building featuring well-attended performances by local opera and ballet companies.

Siemens Arena Ozo 14 Ⓣ 5/1653. Top venue for sports and concerts featuring international stars.

Vilnius Congress Concert Hall Vilniaus 6/14 Ⓣ 5261 8828, Ⓦ www.lvso.lt. Chamber music, symphonic orchestra performances and ballet.

Shopping

Akropolis Ozo 25. Large shopping complex with a variety of clothing and jewellery shops, featuring an indoor ice rink and the Vichy Aqua Park with water slides and a wave pool (69Lt).

Amber Aušros Vartų 9. An extensive array of amber jewellery and handicrafts.
Lino kopos Krokuvos 6. Linen creations by cutting-edge designer Giedrius Šarkauskas. Closed Sun.

Directory

Embassies and consulates Australia, Vilniaus 23 ☎5212 3369; Canada, Jogailos 4 ☎5249 0950; Ireland, Gedimino 1 ☎5262 9460; UK, Antakalnio 2 ☎5/246 2900; US, Akmenų 6 ☎5266 5500.
Exchange Parex, outside the station at Geležinkelio 6 (24hr).
Hospital Vilnius University Emergency Hospital, Šiltnamių 29 ☎5260 8684.
Internet Collegium, Pilies 22; Netcafe, Antakalnio 36.
Left luggage Train station: 24hr luggage storage in the basement. Bus station: baggage room open 5.30am–9.45pm.
Pharmacy Eurovaistinė, Ukmergės 282 (Maxima), 24hr; Gedimino Vaistinė, Gedimino 27, Mon–Fri 7.30am–9.30pm, Sat 10am–5pm.
Police Jogailos 3 ☎5261 6208.
Post office Gedimino prospektas 7 (Mon–Fri 7am–9pm, Sat 9am–4pm).

Moving on

Train Kaunas (13–15 daily; 1hr 15min–2hr); Klaipėda (3 daily; 5hr); Moscow (2–3 daily; 16hr); Paneriai (19–24 daily; 20min); St Petersburg (1–2 daily; 14hr); Warsaw (1 daily; 9hr).
Bus Kaunas (every 20–30min between 6.30am and 8.15pm; 1hr 30min–2hr); Klaipėda (6–9 daily; 4hr); Palanga (7 daily, 5hr); Nida (1 daily at 7am; 5hr); Rīga (9–13 daily; 5hr–5hr 30min); Tallinn (1 daily at 9pm; 11hr 40min); Trakai (17–21 daily; Alytus-bound buses); Warsaw (4 weekly; 9hr).

PANERIAI

PANERIAI, the site where the Nazis and their Lithuanian accomplices murdered one hundred thousand people during World War II, most of whom were Jews, lies within the Vilnius city limits in a **forest** at the edge of a suburb, 10km southwest of the centre. To get there, take a train from Vilnius station (2Lt; over 20 daily) bound for either Kaunas, Trakai or Paneriai (one stop). From the station, turn right and follow the road into the woods for about ten minutes. The entrance to the site is marked by two stone slabs with Russian and Lithuanian inscriptions commemorating the murdered "Soviet citizens", flanking a more recent (1990) central slab with a Hebrew inscription commemorating "seventy thousand Jewish men, women and children". From the memorial a path leads to the small **Paneriai Museum**, Agrastų 15 (Sun–Thurs 9am–5pm; call ahead to check that it's open ☎6808 1278), which features some personal effects of the victims and a photographic record of the site. Paths lead to the pits in the woods where the Nazis burnt the bodies of their victims and to another eight-metre pit where the bones of the dead were crushed.

TRAKAI

Twenty-eight kilometres west of Vilnius lies the little town of **TRAKAI**, a mix of concrete Soviet-style buildings merging with the wooden cottages of the Karaite community. The former capital of the Grand Duchy of Lithuania, Trakai was founded during the fourteenth century and, standing on a peninsula jutting out between two lakes, it's the site of two impressive medieval castles.

What to see and do

Follow Vytauto gatvė from the train and bus stations and turn right down Kėstučio gatvė to reach the remains of the **Peninsula Castle**, now partially restored after having been destroyed by the Russians in 1655. Skirting the ruins along the lakeside path, you will see the spectacular **Island Castle** (Salos pilis), one of Lithuania's most famous monuments, reachable by two wooden drawbridges and preceded by souvenir and rowing-boat rental (15Lt) stalls. Built around 1400 AD by Grand Duke Vytautas, under whom Lithuania reached the pinnacle of its power during the fifteenth century, the castle fell into ruin from the seventeenth century until a 1960s restoration returned it to its

former glory (May–Sept 10am–7pm; Oct–April 10am–6pm; 12Lt, students 6Lt, permission to take photos 4Lt).

Trakai is home to three hundred Karaim, Lithuania's smallest ethnic minority – a Judaic sect of Turkish origin whose ancestors were brought here from the Crimea by Grand Duke Vytautas to serve as bodyguards. Witness their cultural contribution to Trakai at the **Karaite Ethnographic Exhibition** (22 Karaimų gatvė; Wed–Sun 10am–6pm; 4Lt, half-price with Island Castle ticket); or head to the nearby Kenesa – one of only two Karaim prayer houses in Lithuania, and similar in design to a synagogue.

You can sample *kibinai* (5–7Lt), the Karaite culinary speciality – a mince-meat pasty – served up at **cafés** such as *Senoji Kibininė*, Karaimų 65, and *Kybynlar*, Karaimų 29; wash it down with *gira*, a semi-alcoholic drink made from fermented bread. To get to Trakai, take a bus from Vilnius's main bus station (at least one hourly between 5.45am and 6.35pm; 6Lt; last bus from Trakai at 8.45pm) or a train (6–8 daily; 3.50Lt).

The rest of Lithuania

Lithuania is predominantly rural – a gently undulating, densely forested landscape scattered with lakes, and fields dotted with ambling storks in the summer. The major city of **Kaunas**, west of the capital, rivals Vilnius in terms of its historical importance. Further west, the main highlights of the coast are the **Curonian Spit**, whose dramatic dune-scapes are reachable by ferry and bus from **Klaipėda**, and **Palanga**, Lithuania's party town where everyone flocks in the summer for a good time.

KAUNAS

KAUNAS, 98km west of Vilnius and easily reached by bus or rail, is Lithuania's second city, seen by many Lithuanians as the true heart of their country; it served as provisional **capital** during the interwar period of 1920–1939. It is undergoing rapid modernization, with the mirror-like exteriors of new buildings reflecting parts of the medieval city wall. While much of Kaunas is a busy urban sprawl, visitors will invariably be drawn to the old heart of the city where the main attractions lie.

What to see and do

The most picturesque part of Kaunas is the **Old Town** (Senamiestis), centred around **Town Hall Square** (Rotušės aikštė), on a spur of land between the Neris and Nemunas rivers. The square is lined with fifteenth- and sixteenth-century merchants' houses in pastel stucco shades, but the overpowering

HILL OF CROSSES

Up on a hill, 10km north of the town of Šiauliai, lies the **Mecca of Lithuania**, an ever-growing, awe-inspiring collection of over 400,000 crosses. There are many myths surrounding the Hill's origin, but it is thought to have been built to commemorate warriors killed in a great battle. In pagan times, crosses were put up as offerings to the gods; in the Soviet era, they were planted by grieving families to commemorate killed and deported loved ones, and kept multiplying despite repeated bulldozing by the authorities. Today, crosses are often planted to give thanks for a happy event in a person's life.

To get here, take a train from Vilnius to Šiauliai (5–8 daily; 2hr 45min–3hr 30min) and then take a taxi or Riga-bound bus (8 daily; 15min), getting off at the large Kryžių Kalnas sign and walking the remaining 2km.

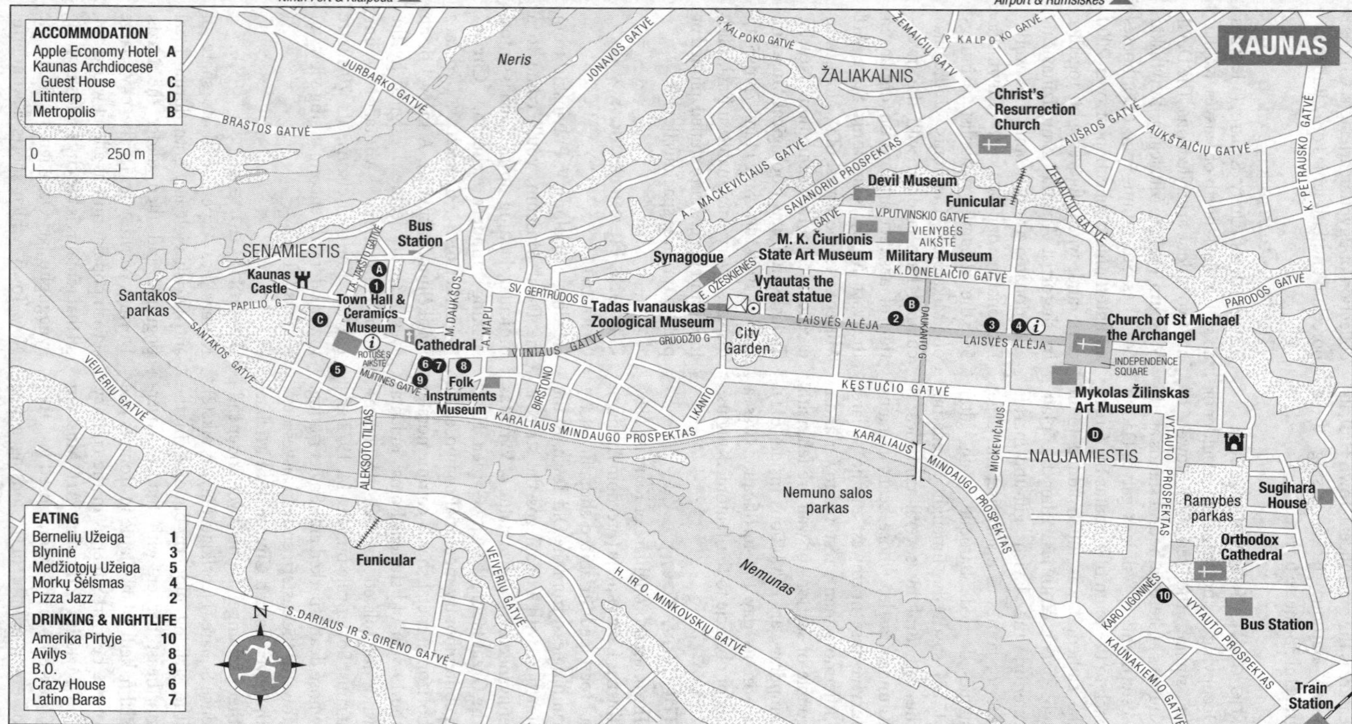
KAUNAS
ACCOMMODATION
Apple Economy Hotel A
Kaunas Archdiocese Guest House C
Litinterp D
Metropolis B
0 250 m
EATING
Bernelių Užeiga 1
Blyninė 3
Medžiotojų Užeiga 5
Morkų Šelsmas 4
Pizza Jazz 2
DRINKING & NIGHTLIFE
Amerika Pirtyje 10
Avilys 8
B.O. 9
Crazy House 6
Latino Baras 7
Ninth Fort & Klaipėda
Airport & Rumšiškės
Vilnius
Pažaislis Monastery
Botanical Gardens
Botanical Gardens
Neris
Nemunas
ŽALIAKALNIS
SENAMIESTIS
NAUJAMIESTIS
Christ's Resurrection Church
Devil Museum
Funicular
M. K. Čiurlionis State Art Museum
Military Museum
VIENYBĖS AIKŠTĖ
Synagogue
Vytautas the Great statue
Tadas Ivanauskas Zoological Museum
City Garden
Church of St Michael the Archangel
INDEPENDENCE SQUARE
Mykolas Žilinskas Art Museum
Sugihara House
Ramybės parkas
Orthodox Cathedral
Bus Station
Train Station
Bus Station
Kaunas Castle
Town Hall & Ceramics Museum
ROTUŠĖS AIKŠTĖ
Cathedral
Folk Instruments Museum
Santakos parkas
Nemuno salos parkas
Funicular
JURBARKO GATVĖ
BRASTOS GATVĖ
JONAVOS GATVĖ
P. KALPOKO GATVĖ
ŽEMAIČIŲ GATV
P. KALPOKO GATVĖ
AUŠROS GATVĖ
AUKŠTAIČIŲ GATVĖ
K. PETRAUSKO GATVĖ
A. MACKEVIČIAUS GATVĖ
SAVANORIŲ PROSPEKTAS
ŽEMAIČIŲ GATVĖ
V.PUTVINSKIO GATVĖ
GATVĖ
K.DONELAIČIO GATVĖ
PARODOS GATVĖ
E. OŽESKIENĖS
SV. GERTRŪDOS G
LAISVĖS ALĖJA
DAUKANTO G
GRUODŽIO G
VILNIAUS GATVĖ
PAPILIO G.
IA. JAKŠTO GATVĖ
M.DAUKŠOS
A.MAPU
MUITINĖS GATVĖ
SANTAKOS GATVĖ
VEIVERIŲ GATVĖ
ALEKSOTO TILTAS
BIRŠTONO
I.KANTO
KĘSTUČIO GATVĖ
MICKEVIČIAUS
VYTAUTO PROSPEKTAS
KARALIAUS MINDAUGO PROSPEKTAS
KARALIAUS MINDAUGO PROSPEKTAS
H. IR O. MINKOVSKIŲ GATVĖ
VEIVERIŲ GATVĖ
S.DARIAUS IR S.GIRENO GATVĖ
KARO LIGONINĖS
VYTAUTO PROSPEKTAS
KAUNAKIEMIO GATVĖ
N

feature is the magnificent **Town Hall**, its tiered Baroque facade rising to a graceful 53-metre tower.

The cathedral and castle

Occupying the northeastern shoulder of the square, the red-brick tower of Kaunas's austere **cathedral** stands at the western end of Vilniaus gatvė. Dating back to the reign of Vytautas the Great, the cathedral was much added to in subsequent centuries. After the plain exterior, the lavish gilt-and-marble interior comes as a surprise; the large, statue-adorned Baroque high altar (1775) steals the limelight. Predating the cathedral by several centuries is **Kaunas Castle**, whose scant remains survive just northwest of the square. Little more than a restored tower and a couple of sections of wall are left, with temporary art exhibitions inside (6Lt), but in its day the fortification was a major obstacle to the Teutonic Knights.

The New Town

The main thoroughfare of Kaunas's New Town is **Laisvės alėja** (Freedom Avenue), a broad, pedestrianized shopping street running east from the Old Town. At the junction with L. Sapiegos the street is enlivened by a bronze statue of **Vytautas the Great** facing the City Garden. Here, a contemporary memorial composed of horizontal metal shards commemorates the 19-year-old student Romas Kalanta, who immolated himself in protest against Soviet rule on May 14, 1972 and whose death sparked anti-Soviet rioting. Towards the eastern end of Laisvės alėja, the silver-domed **Church of St Michael the Archangel** looms over Independence Square (Nepriklausomybės aikštė). The striking modern building in the northeast corner, with the controversial naked "Man" statue in front, is one of the best art galleries in the country, the **Mykolas Žilinskas Art Museum** (Tues–Sun 11am–5pm; closed last Tues of every month; 6Lt), housing a fine collection of Egyptian artefacts, Chinese porcelain and Lithuania's only Rubens.

The museums

Just north of Unity Square (Vienybės aikštė), a block north of Laisvės, Kaunas has two unique art collections. The **Devil Museum** (Velnių Muziejus), Putvinskio 64 (Tues–Sun 11am–5pm; 6Lt), houses an entertaining collection of over 2000 devil and witch figures put together by the artist Antanas Žmuidzinavičius and donated from around the world. Diagonally opposite, at Putvinskio 55, the dreamy, symbolist paintings of Mikalojus Čiurlionis, Lithuania's cultural hero credited with the invention of abstract art, are on display in the vast **M. K. Čiurlionis State Art Museum** (same times; 6Lt), along with excellent temporary exhibitions. Nearby, **Tadas Ivanauskas Zoological Museum**, Laisvės 106 (Tues–Sun 11am–7pm; 5Lt), displays every imaginable animal, bird, insect and sea creature stuffed, pinned or pickled on three spacious floors.

Christ's Resurrection Church

Heading east along V. Putvinskio from the Devil Museum, you'll come to a funicular, leading up to Kaunas's most striking modern church, **Christ's Resurrection Church** (Kristaus Prisikėlimo Bažnyčia). A marvel or an eyesore? You decide. Designed by the man behind the city's Military Museum, Latvian Kārlos Reisons, its 70-metre tower offers all-encompassing views of Kaunas (5Lt).

Jewish Kaunas

Kaunas has experienced its share of anti-Jewish violence, both during local pogroms and then under the Nazis. During World War II, the city's large Jewish population was all but wiped out; all that remains is the city's sole surviving **synagogue** at Ožeškienės 13 in the New Town, which sports a wonderful

sky-blue interior (daily services 5.45–6.30pm, Sat 10am–noon) and a **memorial** to the 1700 children who perished at the Ninth Fort. The small and austere former Japanese consulate is now a **museum to Chiune Sugihara** (Vaižganto 30; Mon–Fri 10am–5pm, Sat & Sun 11am–4pm; 3Lt), the consul who saved thousands of Jewish lives during the war by issuing Japanese visas against orders to the contrary.

To reach the Ninth Fort, take any westbound inter-city bus from Kaunas bus station (every 10–30min) and get off at the IX Fortas stop. The **Ninth Fort Museum**, Žemaičių plentas 73 (daily except Tues 10am–6pm; 5Lt), is housed in the tsarist-era fortress where the Jews were kept by Nazis while awaiting execution in the killing field beyond; exhibits cover extermination of Jews and deportation of Lithuanians by the Soviets. A massive, jagged stone memorial crowns the site.

Arrival and information

Air Kaunas's international airport is located around 20km north of Kaunas. Bus #29 (2Lt) passes through the Old Town and stops at the main bus and train stations. Minibus #120 has more frequent departures for the airport from the minibus station at the north end of M. Valančiaus in the Old Town, but make it clear to the driver that the airport is your final destination (2.50Lt).

Train and bus Kaunas's train and bus stations are both along Vytauto at the southeastern end of the centre, a 10min walk from Laisvės alėja; take any trolleybus passing in front of the stations to the Old Town (2Lt). There is luggage storage at both, and an ATM out on the main street. Note that trains from Vilnius currently stop at Kaunas 1, as opposed to the main station; follow the track down the hill to the main road and catch bus #53 on the same side of the street to the Old Town (2.50Lt).

Tourist office Laisvės 36 ⓣ37/323 436, ⓦwww.kaunastic.lt (une–Aug Mon–Fri 9am–7pm, Sat 10am–6pm, Sun 10am–3pm, Sept–May Mon–Thurs 9am–6pm, Fri 9am–5pm). Provides English-language leaflets, free maps and copies of *Kaunas in Your Pocket* (ⓦwww.inyourpocket.com; 6Lt).

Internet Internet Copy 1, Kęstučio 54/7 (Mon–Fri 7.40am–6pm, Sat & Sun 9am–6pm; 4Lt/hr).

Accommodation

Apple Economy Hotel Valančiaus 19 ⓣ37/321 404, ⓦwww.applehotel.lt. Simple but comfy en suites in the Old Town – reliable and obtainable 365 days a year, just like the fruit it's named after. Single/double/family room 150/225/430Lt.

Kaunas Archdiocese Guest House Rotušės 21 ⓣ37/322 597, ⓦkaunas.lcn.lt/sveciunamai. With a location between two churches that's hard to beat, this charming place has clean doubles and free internet. Consumption of alcohol is forbidden on the premises. Single/double/quad 50/80/110Lt.

Litinterp Gedimino 28–7 ⓣ37/228 718, ⓦwww.litinterp.lt. Ever-reliable guesthouse option run by trilingual staff, offering basic, clean, en-suite rooms in Kaunas Old Town. They can also sort you out with rooms in private residences. Single/double/triple 160/160/180Lt.

Metropolis Just off Laisvės alėja at Daukanto 21 ⓣ37/205 992, ⓦwww.greenhillhotel.lt. Grand old Soviet hotel in a great location with inexpensive wi-fi-enabled en suites. A real bargain. Single/double/triple/quad 105/135/180/235 Lt.

Eating

Cafés and snack bars

Blyninė Laisvės 56. Cheapo Lithuanian restaurant serving good portions of traditional dishes such as the pancakes after which it's named and the ever-present *cepelinai*. Mains 8–12Lt.

Morkų Šėlsmas Laisvės 78b. Cosy café specialising in a variety of fresh fruit juices; also a good spot for a light meal. Open Mon–Fri 10am–6pm.

Restaurants

Bernelių Užeiga Valančiaus 9. Dine on huge portions of meaty Lithuanian staples in an attractive rustic interior. Mains 15–20Lt.

Medžiotojų Užeiga Rotušės 10. Carnivore heaven serving a range of game dishes – from deer to beaver. You can also enjoy a tasty and inexpensive set lunch on weekdays (20Lt).

Pizza Jazz Laisvės alėja 68. Delicious thin-crust pizzas to be had at this popular chain restaurant. Medium pizza 15Lt.

Drinking and nightlife

Bars

Avilys Vilniaus 34. Excellent microbrewery in a cosy cellar offering two types of beer, beer soup, beer ice cream, and a range of standard meat

dishes and beer snacks. Wash down a plate of smoked pigs' ears with a pint of grog (warmed honey beer with extra honey and lemon). 10Lt.

B.O. Muitinės 9. This friendly, popular and unpretentious bar is one of the best places to hook up with a young, arty crowd. Closes 3am Fri & Sat.

Crazy House Vilniaus 16. If you're into slapstick comedy, then the moving furniture and nets dropping from the ceiling will appeal to you; otherwise, avoid the cellar and have a cheap beer (5Lt) on the outdoor terrace.

Clubs

Amerika Pirtyje Vytauto 74 Ⓦwww.america.lt. Very popular with students and playing a pounding mix of pop music most nights as well as hosting some good DJs and the odd bit of live music. Wed & Sun 9pm–3am; Thurs 9pm–4am, Fri & Sat 9pm–5am, entry 10–30Lt.

Latino Baras Vilniaus 22. Small and bustling, with consistently good Latin music, this club is a great place to mingle and show off your dance moves. Dance lessons available. Fri & Sat 9pm–4am; entry 10–40Lt.

Moving on

Train Vilnius (13–15 daily; 1hr 15min–2hr).

Bus Klaipėda (7–9 daily; 3hr); Nida (1 daily on Fri & Sun at 7am; 4hr 30min); Palanga (7 daily; 3hr 45min); Rīga (9–14 daily; 4hr–4hr 30min); Tallinn (1 daily via Rīga at 9pm; 9hr); Vilnius (every 20–30min between 5.15am and 9.30pm; 1hr 30min–2hr); Warsaw (4 weekly; 7hr).

KLAIPĖDA

KLAIPĖDA, Lithuania's third largest city and most important port, lies on the Baltic coast, 275km northwest of Vilnius. Though it has a handful of sights, the city is of more interest as a staging post en route to the Curonian Spit, or the party town of Palanga.

The helpful **tourist office** in the Old Town at Turgaus 7 (July & Aug Mon–Fri 9am–7pm, Sat & Sun 10am–4pm; Sept–June Mon–Fri 9am–6pm; Ⓣ46/412 186, Ⓦwww.klaipedainfo.lt) has internet access (2Lt/30min) and stocks the excellent *Klaipėda in Your Pocket* (5Lt). From Turgaus turn right into Teatro gatvė and then left before the riverside park. The old ferry terminal with regular departures to Smiltynė, the gateway to the Curonian Spit, lies on the opposite side of Pilies gatvė.

There are several good **accommodation** options in town. Try the HI-affiliated *Klaipėda Traveller's Guesthouse*, Butkų Juzės 7–4 (Ⓣ46/211879, Ⓔguestplace@yahoo.com; 42Lt), a basic but friendly hostel right next to the bus station. It is a fifteen-minute walk west along S. Daukanto gatvė from the bus or train station to the *Litinterp Guest House* at Puodzių 17 (Mon–Fri 8.30am–5.30pm, Sat 9.30am–3pm; Ⓣ6561 8817, Ⓦwww.litinterp.lt; single/double/triple 80–90/80–90/70Lt per person), with clean, attractive rooms; it can also provide central private rooms.

Good **places to eat** include: *Čili Kaimas*, Manto 17, where you can feast on *cepelinai*, potato pancakes and other Lithuanian staples in a rustic-themed interior; and *Ararat*, an outstanding Armenian establishment on Liepų 48a, serving tender, delicately spiced grilled meats (25Lt) and excellent wine.

Moving on

Train Vilnius (3 daily; 5hr).

Bus Kaunas (13 daily; 3hr); Liepāja (3 daily; 2hr 30min); Nida (direct: 1–2 Fri–Sun; from Smiltynė: 8 daily; 50min); Palanga (11 daily; 30–45min; route taxis every half-hour); Rīga (4 daily; 4–5hr); Vilnius (13–15 daily; 4–5hr).

Ferry Smiltynė (Jun–Aug every 30 min, 5am–2am; 15min); rest of the year at least one hourly, 7am–10pm); 2.90Lt.

PALANGA

Twenty-five kilometres north of Klaipėda, **PALANGA** is Lithuania's top seaside resort – party central in the summer.

What to see and do

Palanga's biggest attraction is its 10km white sandy **beach**; throughout the summer months it hosts a number of

outdoor all-night music events. The wooden **pier**, jutting into the sea at the end of Basanavičiaus gatvė, is where families and couples gather to watch the sunset (around 10pm in July).

From the beach, head east along pedestrian **Basanavičiaus** with the rest of the human tide, past the street musicians and vendors, countless eateries, arcade games, amusement park rides and amber stalls. Get fired out of a bungee catapult (45Lt) or dance all night at one of the beachside clubs. Music venues are also located on Vytauto gatvė, the main street bisecting Palanga, and on S. Darius ir S. Girėno gatvė, running alongside the Botanical Garden.

The lush Botanical Garden (Botanikos Sodas) houses a fascinating **Amber Museum** (May–Sept Tues–Sat 10am–8pm, Sun 10am–7pm; Oct–April Mon–Sat 11am–5pm, Sun 11am–4pm; 7Lt) with around twenty-five thousand pieces of "Baltic Gold", many with insects and plants trapped inside. The **Anatanas Mončys House Museum** at S. Daukanto 16 (Tues noon–5pm, Wed–Sun 2–9pm; 5Lt) displays unique wooden sculptures, collages and masks made by the Lithuanian sculptor. Visitors are allowed to handle all the exhibits due to a clause in the sculptor's will specifying that others can touch his work.

Arrival and information

Bus The bus station on Kretingos gatvė is a couple of blocks away from Basanavičiaus gatvė, the main tourist street.

Tourist office Kretingos 1 ⓣ460/48811, ⓦwww.palangatic.lt. June–Aug daily 9am–6pm; rest of the year Mon 1–5pm, Tues–Fri 9am–5pm, Sat 10am–2pm. Multilingual and helpful staff can book accommodation and provide detailed information on events in and around town.

Accommodation

Due to the town's immense summertime popularity, advance bookings are essential. The cheapest option is to haggle with the locals holding up "Nuomojami kamberiai" (rooms for rent) signs as the bus enters Palanga, although the quality may vary considerably.

Alanga Nėries gatvė 14 ⓣ460/49215, ⓦwww.alanga.lt. This spotlessly clean hotel offers spacious en suites with balconies and wi-fi. Spa, sauna, gym and laundry service available. Doubles/suites/apartments 300/420/550Lt.

Ema Jurates gatvė 32 ⓣ460/48608, ⓦwww.ema.lt. This brightly painted guesthouse has cosy modern doubles and a creperie on site. Singles/doubles 27–33/40–60Lt.

Zyrdoji Liepsna Gintaro 36 ⓣ460/52441. Welcoming budget hotel a couple of blocks from the bus station, with simple, airy en-suite rooms. Singles/doubles/apartments 120/170/300Lt.

Eating, drinking and nightlife

Čagino restoranas Basanavičiaus 14. Come to this light, bright Russian restaurant for ample portions of hearty meat dishes, soups and pancakes. Mains 20Lt.

Čili Pica Basanavičiaus 45. The ubiquitous and ever-popular pizza chain by the pier serving a huge range of inexpensive pizzas. Medium pizza 35Lt. Closes 4am Fri & Sat.

Honolulu Night Club Nėries 39. Two-tiered entertainment: lively disco with kitschy decor upstairs (Mon–Thurs & Sun 7pm–3am, Fri & Sat 9pm–6am), and packed nightclub downstairs (daily 10pm–6am).

Kupeta Dariaus ir Girėno 13. Large, raucous and a bit peculiar; order a Kupeta cocktail to make the waiter dance. Lithuanian rock bands nightly. 9am–midnight.

Laukinių Vakarų Salūnas Basanavičiaus 24a. Packed with a young crowd and offering nightly karaoke, wet t-shirt competitions and the occasional live band. Sun–Thurs 9pm–5am, Fri & Sat 9pm–6am.

Žuvinė Basanavičiaus 37a. Fish restaurant with a library feel to it; the generous portions of well-prepared seafood dishes cannot be faulted. Mains 25–30Lt.

Moving on

Bus Kaunas (9 daily; 5hr); Klaipėda (at least one hourly between 7am and 9pm; 30–45min); Riga via Liepāja (1 daily; 4hr 30min); Vilnius (12 daily; 7hr).

NERINGA: THE CURONIAN SPIT

NERINGA, or the **Kursių Nerija**, is the Lithuanian section of the Curonian Spit, a 97-kilometre sliver of land characterized by vast sand dunes and pine forests. Some of the area can be seen as a day-trip from Klaipėda, though it really warrants a stay of several days to soak up the unique atmosphere. Ferries from the quayside towards the end of Žvejų gatvė in Klaipėda (2.90Lt return) sail to **Smiltynė** on the northern tip of the spit. From the landing stage, frequent **minibuses** (9Lt) run south towards more scenic parts of the spit, stopping at the villages of **Juodkrantė**, **Pervalka** and **Preila**, and terminating at **Nida**, 35km south.

Nida

NIDA is the most famous village on the spit – a small fishing community boasting several streets of attractive blue- and brown-painted wooden houses. Although there are plenty of visitors in the summertime it never feels crowded. There are several good **eateries** on Naglių gatvė and Lotmiškio gatvė, as well as along the waterfront. From the end of Naglių, a shore path runs to a flight of wooden steps leading up to the top of the **Parnidis dune** south of the village. From the summit you can gaze out across a Saharan sandscape stretching to Russia's Kaliningrad province. Retrace the trail along the waterfront to see elaborate **weathervanes** with unique designs – each village has its own. Stop by the **Nida History Museum** (Pamario 53; daily 10am–6pm; 3Lt), which traces the village's heritage through photos of crow-eating fishermen and fishing paraphernalia. Also along Pamario is the cemetery with traditional wooden **krikštas** – carved wooden boards instead of headstones – placed upright at the foot of the resting body. Nida's long, luxuriant **beach** is on the opposite side of the spit, a 30min walk through the forest from the village.

Arrival and information

Bus Buses from the mainland and from Smiltynė stop on Naglių 18e, Nida's main street. Everything in Nida is within walking distance.

Tourist office Taikos 4 ⓣ 6826 7448, ⓦ www.visitneringa.com (June–Aug Mon–Sat 10am–8pm, Sun 10am–3pm; Sept–May Mon–Thurs 9am–noon & 1–5pm, Fri 9am–noon & 1–4pm). The extremely helpful staff provide information on accommodation and events.

Accommodation

Nida has a few budget guesthouses, but as they tend to fill up in the summer, advance reservations are

CYCLING THE SPIT

The best way to explore the Curonian Spit is by **cycling** (bike rental 8Lt/hour, 30Lt/day) along well-marked biking trails that meander through pine forest and along the sand dunes. Early morning is a good time to catch a glimpse of elk, foxes, wild boar and roe deer, particularly near **Juodkrantė**, 29km away. Juodkrantė is also home to **Witches' Hill** (Raganos kalnas), a truly entertaining wooden sculpture trail in the woods with wonderfully macabre statues of devils, witches and folk legend heroes – try sliding down the devil's giant tongue. *Vila Flora*, along the waterfront, serves simple yet nicely cooked offerings of fresh fish (35Lt) and pancakes (10Lt). Heading back towards Nida, stop off at the side of the main road to catch a glimpse of the huge **heron and cormorant colony** in the trees. Take a dip in the bracing sea and graze on wild strawberries, blueberries and raspberries in the summer. Don't forget your mosquito repellent. When passing through **Preila**, look for the *rųkyta žuvis* signs and stop at a traditional smokery for some delicious smoked fish, which is considerably cheaper than in Nida.

ACTIVITIES AROUND NIDA

Nida offers a wide variety of activities for outdoor enthusiasts and adrenaline junkies alike during the summer months. *Irklakojis* (stall by the shore path; ⓣ6188 1957, ⓦwww.irklakojis.lt) arranges **hiking**, **biking** or **canoeing** trips in the area. Alternatively, try exhilarating **blokarting** (windsurfing on land) on the disused airstrip (65Lt per hour) or roll around on a **Segway**.

required. Private rooms (120–150Lt) are available through the tourist office. Litinterp in Klaipėda can book local B&B rooms (160–200Lt) in advance, for a slightly higher price; a minimum of three nights required.

Inkaro Kaimas Naglių 26 ⓣ469/52123, ⓦwww.inkarokaimas.lt. A beautifully decorated double, quad and a two-room apartment are on offer at this welcoming seaside guesthouse, presided over by the effusive Valentina. All are en suite, and have satellite TV and kitchenette. Doubles/apartments 200/250–280Lt.

Kambarių nuoma (rooms to rent) Lotmiškio 7 ⓣ469/52256, ⓔciciunas@takas.lt. Run by an English-speaking couple, this friendly guesthouse has a pristine kitchen, pleasant garden, airy rooms and is just 1min walk from the sea. Single/double 160/180Lt.

Misko Namas Pamario 11 ⓣ469/52290, ⓦwww.miskonamas.com. Colourful house with a range of en-suite rooms and apartments, communal kitchen, lovely private garden and a friendly hostess. Doubles 221–256Lt; apartments 290–338Lt.

Nidos Kempingas 2km southwest of town at Taikos 45a (take Taikos gatvė out of town and follow the signs) ⓣ469/52045, ⓦwww.kempingas.lt. This campsite has clean cooking and bathroom facilities, ample tent space and swanky self-catering apartments. Tent space for up to 4 people 17Lt; doubles 250Lt; 4- to 6-room apartments 330–450Lt.

Eating and drinking

Baras Bangomūša Naglių 5. Homely, informal place, popular with tourists and locals alike – one of the best spots in Nida to try the local smoked fish. *Koldūnaī* (12Lt) and other Lithuanian dishes available.

Čili Pica Naglių 16. Perpetually popular pizza spot by the harbour with large outdoor terrace (June–Aug 9am–3am). Medium pizza 20Lt.

In Vino Taikos 32. Enjoy the best views in Nida from the rooftop terrace of this popular hilltop wine bar while choosing your poison from the extensive drinks menu.

Nidos Seklyčia Lotmiškio 1. Upmarket restaurant by the sea offering traditional dishes such as *cepelinai*, as well as wonderfully fresh fish dishes (40Lt) and grilled meats (30Lt). You have to pay extra for the vegetables, though.

Moving on

Bus Kaunas (via Klaipėda; Fri & Sun 1 per day at 2.25pm; 4hr 30min); Smiltynė (8 daily; 1hr 30min; all stop at Juodkrantė; 3 daily stop at Preila and Pervalka); Vilnius (via Klaipėda; Fri & Sun 1 per day at 3.15pm; 7hr).

Macedonia

HIGHLIGHTS

SKOPJE: charming historic centre and beautifully ugly Yugoslav buildings

MAVROVO: national park with good skiing and hiking

SVETI JOVAN BIGORSKI: the best of Macedonia's many monasteries

OHRID: large, mountain-ringed lake with the country's most beautiful town on its shore

BITOLA: Macedonia's appealing second city

ROUGH COSTS

DAILY BUDGET Basic €25/occasional treat €35

DRINK Wine from €1.60 per bottle

FOOD Tavče gravče (bean casserole) €1.25

HOSTEL/BUDGET HOTEL €12/€25

TRAVEL Skopje–Ohrid (167km) €7.30 by bus; Skopje–Bitola (172km) €4 by train.

FACT FILE

POPULATION 2 million

AREA 25,738 sq km

LANGUAGE Macedonian

CURRENCY Denar (MKD)

CAPITAL Skopje (population 550,000)

INTERNATIONAL PHONE CODE ⓣ389

Introduction

It's easy to see why the French refer to a mixed salad as a macédoine: this hotchpotch of Ottoman rule, Yugoslav domination, Orthodox faith and Albanian influence represents one of Europe's most varied societies. While traditional tourist sights are thin on the ground, this land of vineyards and rolling fields is a grand place to kick back, and refreshingly places more emphasis on free time than profit margins. In few countries would you have your bus journey interrupted for a spot of apple-picking, or find yourself being cooked a mountaintop meal by a cabinet minister. This, however, is Macedonia.

The capital, **Skopje**, is something of a Yugoslav symphony in grey, though one whose brutal architecture is softened by friendly locals and an appealing old Ottoman centre. Most travellers prefer to base themselves around **Lake Ohrid**, a delightful, mountain-fringed expanse straddling the Albanian border. Between Skopje and Ohrid, a glut of immaculately painted **monasteries** compete for your attention; **Sveti Jovan Bigorski** is the most enjoyable, and lies within **Mavrovo**, a national park that provides great hiking opportunities, as well as skiing in the winter.

CHRONOLOGY

168 BC The Macedonian area absorbed by the Roman Empire.
395 AD The Roman Empire splits, Macedonia falling under Byzantine rule.
447 Attila the Hun rampages through the area.
1394 Beginning of five hundred years of Ottoman rule.
1878 Russian victory over the Ottoman Empire; Macedonia is ceded to Bulgaria, though soon returned at the instigation of Western powers.
1910 Gonxha Agnesë Bojaxhiu, now known to the world as Mother Teresa, is born in Skopje.
1912 The Turks are ousted in the Balkan Wars, Macedonia being shared between Serbia and Greece.
1918 The Serb-ruled area that comprises today's Macedonia is given to the Kingdom of Serbs, Croats and Slovenes.
1945 Macedonia becomes part of socialist Yugoslavia.
1963 Over one thousand killed by an earthquake in Skopje.
1991 Macedonia gains independence from Yugoslavia.
1993 Admitted to the UN as "Former Yugoslav Republic of Macedonia".
2001 Civil war between government and ethnic Albanian insurgents.
2005 Macedonia becomes an official candidate for EU membership.

ARRIVAL

Thessaloniki and Sofia are the closest **airports** for budget flights, though there

"THEN WHAT ARE WE? FYROMANIANS?"

As soon as Macedonia declared independence from Yugoslavia, a different kind of battle broke out along the Greek border, one regarding two matters integral to a new country: name and flag. Athens objected to the use of the name – the bulk of historical Macedonia now lies under Greek control – and also to a flag featuring the ancient kingdom's sixteen-pointed Vergina Sun. The new nation squeezed into the UN as the "former Yugoslav Republic of Macedonia", or FYROM for short, and later changed their flag to end a Greek economic blockade. Many nations now recognize the "Republic of Macedonia", but this battle of nomenclature remains locked in stalemate, and is unlikely to end anytime soon.

are a smattering of international flights to Skopje and even to Ohrid. Most, however, make their way to Macedonia overland. There are couple of daily **bus** services from Tirana in Albania (via Ohrid), but poor neighbourly relations mean that there are very few direct services from Greece. In summer you may be able to catch a minibus from Thessaloniki to Skopje, but better are the two daily **trains** that run the same route. Train is also the best form of attack from Belgrade and beyond: there are four daily trains via Niš, including one that makes its way from Ljubljana, via Zagreb. Note that citizens of some countries, notably South Africa, still need **visas** to enter Macedonia; check Ⓦwww.mfa.gov.mk for more information.

GETTING AROUND

Almost all travel in Macedonia is by **bus**. Services are punctual and reasonably frequent, and the vehicles themselves are really not that bad. Note that buses take one of two routes between Skopje and Ohrid, one through Bitola, and a more picturesque trip through Kičevo; schedules are available online at Ⓦwww.sas.com.mk. There is also a limited **train** network; though a good way to arrive from Greece, it suffers from slow and irregular services and is rarely used by travellers. The best domestic line is the thrice-daily run service between Skopje and Bitola, which passes through wonderful mountain scenery.

ACCOMMODATION

Accommodation is not terribly varied but generally quite affordable. Skopje's team of overpriced **hotels** are now supplemented by a few cut-price alternatives (from around €30), while in the hinterlands – including Ohrid – you'll be able to make use of **private rooms**, known as *sobi*; you'll often be met at bus stations by homeowners with rooms to spare. Prices vary wildly depending upon location and facilities, but generally expect to pay from €10 to €30 for a

double room. There are now a few **hostels** in Skopje and Ohrid, each costing around €10 for a dorm bed, while **campsites** can be found around the lakes of Ohrid and Prespa.

FOOD AND DRINK

The Macedonian diet is dominated by barbecued **meat** (*skara*), of which the most popular variety are sausage-shaped kebabs (*kebapči*), usually served with chopped onion and spongy, freshly baked bread. Other items to look out for on a regular menu are soups (*čorba*) and *tavče gravče*, beans cooked in sauce. The ubiquitous *burek* – a pastry filled with meat, cheese or spinach – is a good, cheap **breakfast** choice. **Vegetarians** can find solace in a number of excellent salads and *ajvar* – a meze-like starter made from red peppers – while pizzerias are everywhere and always have veggie toppings. You'll find baklava – syrupy Turkish **sweets** – all over the country.

Drink

The consumption of **coffee** (*kafa*) seems almost obligatory, and it's traditionally served Turkish-style (black, with grounds at the bottom), though espresso is now gaining currency. More local in nature is **boza**, a refreshing millet-based drink available in cake shops. There are some good domestic **beers**, or *pivo* (Skopsko is the most popular brand) but Macedonia is most famed for uniformly good **wines**. Vranec (red) and Smederevka (white) are two local grape varieties worth trying, while Tikveš is a reliable, easy-to-find label covering these and the typical international varieties. Note that after 7pm alcohol can only be bought in bars and licensed restaurants.

CULTURE AND ETIQUETTE

Macedonia is a real mishmash of cultures, and it's very important to make a few cultural notes. **Political and ethnic issues** still dominate – taking Greece's side in the country's naming dispute won't win you any friends, and neither will promoting Albanian or Macedonian nationalism to the "wrong" side. Only two-thirds of the population are Macedonians of Slav ethnicity – the vast majority of whom belong to the **Orthodox church** – while most of the remaining third are ethnic Albanian. Tensions still run high between the two groups – 2001 saw a civil war between the government and Albanian insurgents – though travellers are unlikely to notice.

You'll find yourself **smoking** a lot in Macedonia – either your own fumes or secondhand. While **tipping** at restaurants is generally a simple exercise in rounding up. Don't feel that you're being booted out if your waiter stomps over to ask for money mid-meal, as they're often required to settle accounts at the end of their shift.

SPORTS AND OUTDOOR ACTIVITIES

Activities in Macedonia centre around the mountains. The national parks of Mavrovo, Galičica and Pelister are excellent for **hiking** – Mavrovo and Pelister also offer good **skiing** opportunities – while the crystal waters of Lake Ohrid make it good for **diving**. The country's empty roads also make it ideal

MACEDONIA ON THE NET

www.exploringmacedonia.com National tourism portal.

www.culture.in.mk Information about music, film and performing arts.

www.culturalcornerstones.org Contains photos and pictures of Šutka's Roma music.

faq.macedonia.org Frequently asked questions, and some useful answers.

Macedonian

Macedonia uses the **Cyrillic alphabet**, which poses inevitable problems with street signs, train and bus timetables. For most of these there's no transliteration into Latin script, but many restaurants have dual-language menus, and a decent level of English is spoken across the country.

	Macedonian	Pronunciation
Yes	Да	Da
No	не	Ne
Please	молам	Molam
Thank you	благодарам	Blago-daram
Hello/Good day	здраво	Zdravoh
Goodbye	до гледање	Dog-led-anyeah
Excuse me	извинете	Eezvee-neteh
Where?	каде?	Ka-deh?
Good	добар	Dobar
Bad	лош	Losh
Near	блиску	Bleeskoo
Far	далеку	Dalekoo
Cheap	евтин	Evteen
Expensive	скап	Skal
Open	отворен	Otvoren
Closed	затворен	Zatvoren
Today	денес	Denes
Yesterday	вчера	Vchera
Tomorrow	утре	Ootre
How much is...?	колку чини тоа...	Kolkoo chinee toe-ah...?
What time is it?	колку е часот?	Kolkoo eh chasot?
I don't understand	не разбирам	Ne razbee-ram
Do you speak English?	зборувате ли англиски?	Zvo-roo-vateh lee Angliskee?
One	еден	Eh-den
Two	два	Dva
Three	три	Tree
Four	четири	Cheh-tee-ree
Five	пет	Pet
Six	шест	Shest
Seven	седум	Sedum
Eight	осум	Ossum
Nine	девет	Devet
Ten	десет	Deset

for **bike-riding**, but since there are precious few places to rent wheels it makes sense to bring your own.

COMMUNICATIONS

Most **post offices** (*pošta*) are open Monday to Friday 7am to 5pm, and sometimes also on Saturday mornings. These are the best places from which to make **phonecalls** or purchase phone cards. International calls are often best made from **internet** cafés, which are now easy to find in cities and larger towns; expect to pay around 40 MKD per hour.

EMERGENCIES

The crime rate is pretty low by European standards, even in Skopje. However, it's prudent to carry your

EMERGENCY NUMBERS

For police, ambulance or the fire department call ⓣ112.

passport, or a photocopy of the picture page, at all times. You'll find **pharmacies** (*apteka*) in all major towns and cities, and a surprising number have English-speaking staff; opening hours vary but some are 24hr. For more serious matters head to a **hospital**; outside Skopje taxis may be faster than ambulances.

INFORMATION

There are now a few **tourist information offices** dotted around the country, and though they're slowly starting to learn what travellers require, keeping regular hours is still a bit of a challenge.

STUDENT AND YOUTH DISCOUNTS

Many museums and galleries offer cut-price student tickets, while InterRail and Balkan Flexipass tickets are valid on Macedonian trains.

MONEY AND BANKS

The currency is the **denar** (usually abbreviated to MKD), comprising coins of 1, 2, 5, 10 and 50 MKD, and notes of 10, 50, 100, 500, 1000 and 5000 MKD. Exchange **rates** are currently around 60 MKD to the euro, 70 MKD to the pound, and 43 MKD to the US dollar.

Accommodation prices are usually quoted in euros, though you can also pay in denar. Money can be **exchanged** at an exchange office or bank; the latter are usually open Monday Friday 8am to 5pm. **ATMs** are easy to find in urban areas, though stock up on cash if you're heading into the sticks.

OPENING HOURS AND HOLIDAYS

Most **shops** stay open until 8pm on weekdays, and mid-afternoon on Saturdays. Sundays are still special in Macedonia – don't expect too much to be open, even in central Skopje. Things also grind to a halt on **public holidays**: January 1, 2 and 7, May 1 and 2, August 2, September 8 and October 11, as well as Orthodox Easter (usually April).

Skopje

Until recently, budget travellers used to treat **SKOPJE** (Скопје) as a transport hub, or a place to run errands before heading out into the hinterlands, but better budget accommodation and a fun-loving populace have given it a new lease of life. The city was ravaged by an earthquake in 1963, then fell victim to Yugoslav redesign at the worst possible time; the resulting experiment in **architectural brutality** can only count Minsk and Pyongyang as serious rivals. However, Skopje grows on its visitors – something like a bad joke you can't help but laugh at – and many find themselves sad to leave.

What to see and do

The **Čaršija** district north of the river contains the bulk of Skopje's sights, and is the obvious place from which to kick off a trip around the city.

Čaršija and the Kale

Turkish times linger on in the shape of several mosques – **Mustapha Pasha** is the largest and most intricately decorated – and two former bathhouses, the copper-domed **Daud Pasha** (daily except Mon 9am–3pm; 100 MKD) and the **Čifte Amam** (Mon–Sat: April–Sept 10am–9pm, Oct–March 10am–6pm; 50 MKD). These splendid structures are sadly long out of use as *hamams*, and both now used as repositories of contemporary art; those seeking history instead can head to the **Museum of Macedonia** (daily except Mon 9am–3pm, 100 MKD; Sun to 1pm, free), which is well worth an hour or two. All are outdone, however, by wonderful little **Sveti Spas** (Tues–Fri 9am–5pm, Sat & Sun 9am–3pm; 120 MKD), a secluded fourteenth-century monastery. Its church was built mostly underground – under Ottoman rule churches were not allowed to be higher than mosques – and its carved-walnut iconostasis is jaw-dropping.

West of Čaršija is the **Kale**, a fortress badly damaged during the earthquake. Most of what you see today originally dates from the tenth century. Tourists come here for the views, but the wise head further up the hill to the excellent **National Museum of Contemporary Art** (Tues–Sat 10am–5pm, Sun 9am–1pm; free), from where you can see the whole of Skopje. The art's not bad, either.

South of the Vardar

Cross the **Stone Bridge** (Kamen Most) and you'll find yourself in Skopje's main square, **Ploštad Makedonija**. To your left is a shopping area, while on your right are two of the most distinctively Yugoslav buildings in the city. The first is what appears to be a communist-era factory, dropped unceremoniously in the centre of town; it is in fact an office block used by a utilities company. Behind it is the **Central Post Office**, a bizarre concrete spaceship whose lavish interior counts as a Skopje must-see.

Marking the start of largely pedestrianized **Makedonija**, a crescent of elegant buildings – survivors of the

ŠUTKA

The Skopje district of Šuto Orizari, more commonly referred to as **Šutka**, is home to Europe's largest **Roma** community. The area is impoverished and dilapidated, but a visit can be quite fascinating – colourful buildings, litter-lined streets and a bustling daily market make it feel something like an Indian town transported to the Balkans. It's also one of Macedonia's foremost centres of song and dance, but events run to no schedule – sunny summer afternoons are your best bet. Buses #19 and #20 run here from the post office and train station respectively, or it's only 100 MKD by cab.

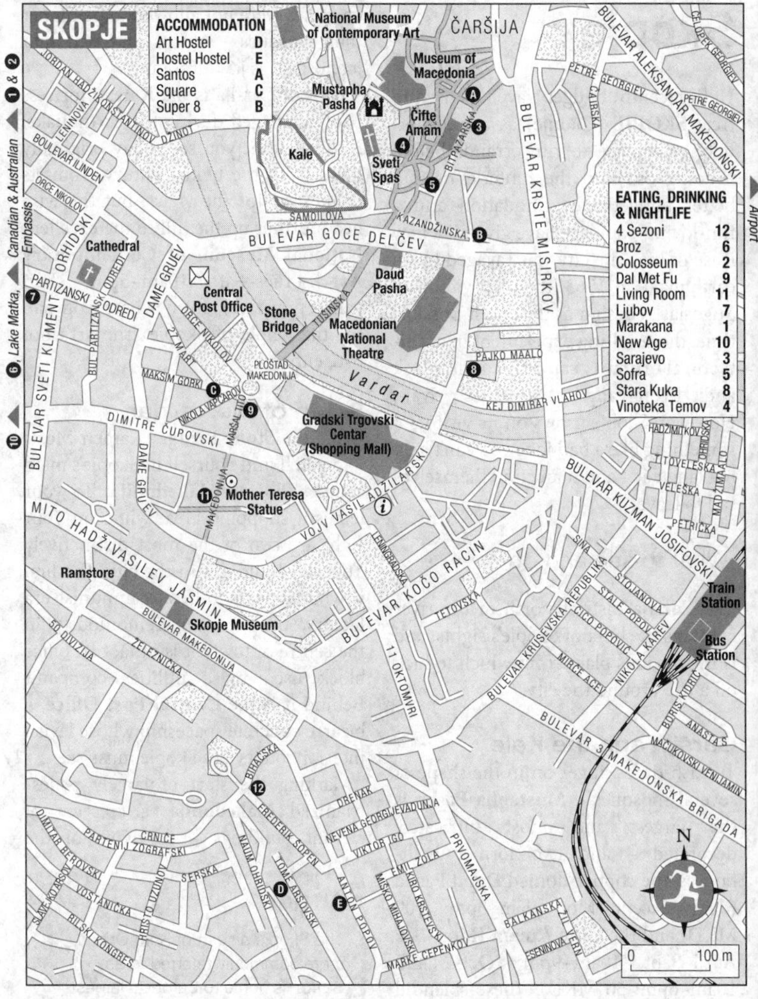

'quake – provides some much-needed respite, before the street-front dissolves into mini-tiled cubism. **Mother Teresa** was born further down the road, and a memorial hall, chapel and statue have been placed here in her honour. At the very end of the road, you'll see the imposing **Skopje Museum** (Tues–Sat 9am–5pm, Sun 9am–1pm; free); fronted by a large clock which stopped during the earthquake, it provides a constant reminder of the calamity.

Arrival and information

Air Skopje's somewhat provocatively renamed Alexander the Great airport – the Greeks were not amused – is 21km east of the city, though as there's no public transport a taxi is the only option. This should cost no more than €20, though aim for €15.

Train and bus The main train and bus stations – don't be too put off by the former – are located right next to each other, a 20min walk or 60 MKD taxi ride southeast of the centre.

Tourist office Moše Pijade (9am–5pm, closed Sun; ⓣ02/311 6854). Can hand out pamphlets and give practical advice.

City transport

Buses Tickets for central rides cost 20-30 MKD.
Taxis start at a very reasonable 50 MKD, and a city-centre trip will rarely cost more than 100 MKD. The normal way of getting around, even for locals.

Accommodation

Skopje now has two excellent hostels, both located in a quiet residential neighbourhood a 15min walk from the centre (60 MKD by taxi from the station).

Hostels

Art Hostel Tome Arsovski 14 ⓣ02/322 3789, ⓦwww.art-hostel.com.mk. Friendly, good-looking hostel whose large common area features free internet and a free pool table. Free breakfast and free coffee round out the picture. €12.
Hostel Hostel Ognjan Prica 18 ⓣ02/322 2321, ⓦwww.hostel.com.mk. More homely than funky, though its artistic owners stage occasional events and can point you to other ones. Huge breakfasts. €12.

Hotels

Santos Bitpazarska 125 ⓣ02/322 6963. Very central, and its cute little rooms represent excellent value. €30.
Square Nikola Vapcarov 2 ⓣ02/322 5090, ⓦwww.hotelsquare.com.mk. Stylish mini-hotel set atop a building with echoes of the communist era – the elevator ride up is a trip back in time. Has a great terrace with a river view. €60.
Super 8 Krste Misirkov 57 ⓣ02/321 2225, ⓦwww.hotelsuper8.com.mk. Drab location off a main road, but the modern rooms are super-cosy and all sport flatscreen TVs. Breakfast €2. €60.

Eating and drinking

The terms "café" and "bar" are somewhat fuzzy; what passes for the former during the day will generally morph into the latter by night.

Cafés and bars

Broz Crvena Voda 4. A bizarre communist-themed coffee-chain parody – Starbuckski? – whose walls are lined with subtle revolutionary pictures. Upstairs seats have good mountain views.
Living Room Makedonija 29. Plush place usually packed with coffee-guzzlers by day, and cocktail-drinkers by night. Weekends see DJs spin house and retro.

TREAT YOURSELF

Vinoteka Temov Gradište 1a ⓣ02/321 2779. Sophisticated yet rustic wine bar that puts on live traditional music most nights. A full range of local wines are available, from 500–3000 MKD per bottle. Booking advisable.

Ljubov Partizanski Odredi 5. Café-bar tucked into an ugly concrete building, but full of sofas and arty frills on the inside. Named after the local word for love, and accordingly full of preening, well-dressed types. Has DJ sets most nights.
New Age Kosta Šahov 9. A little hard to find, but worth the effort – dim lighting and floor cushions make this the kind of place to while away a whole rainy day. Coffee, cocktails and shakes abound, while the range of teas is immense.

Restaurants

4 Sezoni Frederik Šopen. Tiny joint that uses fresh dough and veg to bake your pizza (from 170 MKD) or sandwich (70 MKD) to order – well worth the wait. Those with less patience will find a cheaper alternative across the main road.
Dal Met Fu Makedonia. Without doubt the most popular place in town, and attractive for sure, though a little overpriced and prone to slow service. Take a pizza for 220 MKD and up, or something more interesting like breaded mozzarella with saffron.
Sarajevo Bitpazarska. Working-man's den with snack-style mains. Ten bite-size *kebapči* with bread and onions will set you back just 100 MKD, or try a *tavče gravče*.
Sofra *Kapan An*, Bitpazarska. On the second level of a former traders' hostel. Extensive and inventive local menu – try melon and cured ham in port, trout or oysters in curry sauce – all reasonably priced. Excellent salads, too.
Stara Kuka Pajko Maalo 14. Traditional restaurant serving hearty meals that are worth splashing out on; the casseroles are excellent. Walking distance from the centre, and taxi drivers know the name. Mains 200–600 MKD.

Nightlife

Colosseum Železnička 66. House venue that regularly ropes DJs in from overseas. Surprisingly polished, and you're almost obliged to pop some

moves. In summer they host outdoor events in Gradski Park. Admission 200 MKD.
Marakana Gradski Park. Youngish club near the stadium that features live jazz or cover bands almost every night. Admission 50–100 MKD.

Entertainment

Macedonian National Theatre Kej Dimitar Vlahov. One of Skopje's very best concrete monstrosities – quite a claim – plays host to ballet and operatic performances. TIcket office 1–8pm; tickets from 200 MKD.
Premium Cinema in the Ramstore shopping mall; tickets 150 MKD.

Shopping

The streets of Čaršija are a good place to hunt for souvenirs. For shopping malls you can choose between the Gradski Trgovski Centar (CIty Shopping Centre), a relic of years gone by just off the north end of Makedonija, and the shiny new Ramstore, at the end of Makedonija to the south.

Directory

Embassies and consulates Australia, Londonska 11b ⓣ02/306 1114; Canada, Bulevard Partizanski ⓣ02/322 5630; UK, Salvador Aljende ⓣ02/329 9299; US, Ilindenska ⓣ02/311-6180.
Money There are ATMs dotted around the city centre, and in the bus station, which also has exchange booths. Otherwise all banks should be able to exchange money.
Hospital Re-Medika, Makedonska Brigada 18 ⓣ02/260 3100.
Internet Gradski Trgovski Centar (9am–10pm; 120 MKD/hr).
Pharmacy Dimitri Čupovski 13; 24hr.
Post office Orce Nikolov (7am–7.30pm, Sun 8am–2pm).

Moving on

Train Belgrade (3 daily, 9hr); Bitola (3 daily; 3hr–3hr 50min); Thessaloniki (3 daily; 4hr).
Bus Belgrade (12 daily; 7hr); Bitola (12 daily; 2hr 40min); İstanbul (5 daily; 12hr); Mavrovi Anovi (7 daily; 1hr 45min); Ohrid (12 daily; 3–4hr); Sofia (5 daily; 8hr); Tirana (2 daily; 10hr).

SKOPJE'S FESTIVALS

Buskerfest Over a week of eclectic street performances; late May or early June.
Pivo-Lend ⓦwww.pivolend.com.mk. Beer festival held each September within the fortress walls.
Skopje Jazz Festival ⓦwww.skopjejazzfest.com.mk. Acclaimed event featuring musicians from around the world, spread over a week each October.
Skopje Film Festival ⓦwww.skopjefilmfestival.com.mk. Well worth checking out. Screenings in the Kultura cinema at Luj Paster 2.
Vino-Skop ⓦwww.vinoskop.com. Wine festival offering the opportunity to taste local produce, usually held in October.

LAKE MATKA

A mere half-hour drive from Skopje, pretty **Lake Matka** provides an easy break from – or alternative to – the grey of the capital. The artificial lake is surrounded by richly forested peaks, and its edges are dotted with cute restaurants, many of which can only be accessed by **boat**. You'll be approached by boat owners, who typically charge €10 for a short ride around, and a trip to either a restaurant or some nearby **caves**. It's also possible to stay by the lake in an easy-to-find mountaineering hut named *Matka* (ⓣ02/305 2655; dorms €7), highly recommended since certain evenings occasionally see the nearby slopes illuminated by firefly light. Unfortunately direct buses from Skopje had ceased at the time of writing; enquire locally for the latest details, or climb in a cab (350 MKD).

Western Macedonia

Travellers heading from Skopje to Ohrid have two bus routes to choose from. The first heads south through the major – for

Macedonia – city of **Bitola**, a pleasant place with some interesting nineteenth-century architecture. Heading west instead will bring you close to the national park of **Mavrovo**, good for hiking in summer and skiing in winter. This latter route also takes an hour less on the road. **Ohrid** itself is Macedonia's prime attraction, the name referring both to a large, mountain-ringed lake, and the beautiful old town that sits on its northern shore. Just to the east, and sitting next to another pristine lake, is charming **Pelister National Park**.

MAVROVO NATIONAL PARK

Mavrovo National Park (Ⓦwww.npmavrovo.org.mk) spreads its wings over one of Macedonia's most beautiful corners, a rich and rugged land where rushing streams tumble down slopes cloaked with pine and birch. There are a wealth of sights and activities to choose from – the wonderful monastery of **Sveti Jovan Bigorski** is a delight to visit, **camping** and **hiking** are possible most of the year, while winter snows make for some of the most affordable **skiing** and **snowboarding** in Europe. Also notable is **GALIČNIK**, a remote village which each July hosts a traditional wedding festival so popular that prospective couples have to apply by lottery.

Mavrovo

Most travellers base themselves in the little town of **MAVROVO** (Маврово). This cute resort sits next to a lake of the same name, but is sadly not accessible on public transport; to get here head by bus to **Mavrovi Anovi**, 8km away on the other side of the lake, from where it'll be a 150 MKD taxi-ride. *Hotel Bistra* (Ⓣ042/489002, Ⓦwww.bistra.com; €70) is right next to the ski slopes and good value for the price; they can also help to organize cheaper accommodation for impoverished backpackers.

SKIING IN MAVROVO

The **Zare Lazarevski** resort (Ⓦwww.zarelaz.com) is the place to head for wintertime fun. The season lasts from Nov 15 to mid-April, day-passes cost just 750 MKD, and skis can be rented for a similar price.

Sveti Jovan Bigorski

Macedonia has no shortage of wonderful monasteries, but **Sveti Jovan Bigorski** (Свети Јован Бигорски) takes the biscuit. Tucked away in delightfully bucolic countryside near the Albanian border, its whitewashed buildings are edged with dark wood, and should the fireflies come out to play in the evening it will feel like you've stepped into a Hayao Miyazaki *anime* – simply delightful. Better still, you'll almost always be able to stay for a nominal fee, and invited to attend the slightly haunting services at 7am and 7pm. Note that the monks have been known to curtail the visits of those who reply wrongly to the inevitable question of your religion – "Orthodox, of course!" is the correct answer. To get here, jump on any bus heading between Debar and Gostivar (both accessible from Skopje and Ohrid), and ask to be let off at the monastery.

BITOLA

Cute little **BITOLA** (Битола) is one of the only urban centres in Macedonia that can be termed "pretty"; you'll doubtless wonder if it can really be the second-largest city in the country. Its laid-back air also disguises some historical pedigree – in the Ottoman era, such was the importance of this trading hub that a string of **consulates** set up on the main thoroughfare. Amazingly, some remain: the Turkish one still functions because of Bitola's sizeable Turkish minority, while neither the British nor French ones will leave town before the other one does. All are housed in

splendid **nineteenth-century buildings**, more of which line the city's pedestrianized main road, Maršal Tito.

Bitola's **train** and **bus** stations sit side-by-side in contrasting states of disrepair, a fifteen-minute walk south of the centre. There's no real reason to overnight, but it makes a convenient break on the Skopje–Ohrid route. The most appealing **rooms** are the splendid collection on offer at the *Hotel De Niro* (Ⓣ047/229656, Ⓦwww.hotel-deniro.com; €52).

PELISTER NATIONAL PARK

A pristine national park between Bitola and Ohrid, **Pelister** (Националниот парк пелистер) overlooks **Lake Prespa**, a shimmering expanse that, while nowhere near as deep as Ohrid, boasts surrounding mountain scenery every bit as beautiful. On the northern side of the park sits a small **ski resort**, accessible from Bitola; take a bus to Turnovo and a taxi the rest of the way (€20 all in). From here a spine trail zigzags south to Malo Ezero, a picturesque lake at the park's centre. The lake can also be approached from the wonderfully unspoilt village of **BRAJČINO**, a great hiking base to the southwest. With its hand-stacked rock walls it shows almost no signs of the modern day. The only official accommodation in the village is at a motel known to locals as *Nikolina*'s (Ⓣ047/482222; €25), though it's quite easy to score a sobi room, especially in summer when you'll likely be met coming off the bus. Buses to Brajčino leave on the half-hour from Resen, a town on the main Ohrid–Bitola stretch. Just off this latter route is **MALOVIŠTE**, a gorgeous old village whose population has nosedived to almost nothing. Now being thrown funds to polish up and lure people back, it's well worth a visit to walk the cobbled streets, breathe some fresh air (buy some land, raise a family...) and admire this relic of a bygone age.

OHRID

Vast almost to the point of appearing sea-like, **Lake Ohrid** is Macedonia's major draw. A backdrop of **mountains** encircles the lake like a torn sky, looping through Albanian territory on the way back around. This is the only place in the country that can be described as touristy, but even in peak season the combination of genteel streets and gently lapping waves lends a relaxed air to proceedings. Locals are friendly and the nightlife surprisingly lively for a small town. Worth mentioning is a rivalry with the capital – Skopje folk joke that Albanians are lucky since they get the same lake without Ohrid's people – so a few choice words may get you a beer or two.

Lake Ohrid is not only one of the **deepest lakes** in Europe – almost 300m in places – but also one of the oldest. Appropriately, it has played host to lakeside communities since the **Neolithic period**, but it was not until Roman times that Ohrid (Охрид) developed as a town. Large basilicas were constructed from the fifth century, and Slavic tribes starting moving in shortly after that. Ohrid's importance as a religious centre was maintained under Ottoman rule, and the town became a popular tourist destination during the Yugoslav period.

What to see and do

Most sights are located within the walls of the **Old Town**, whose steep lanes are home to a glut of churches (usually 100 MKD to enter), museums and galleries. There are also a range of sights and activities around the **lake** itself.

The Old Town

The best place from which to commence a tour around the Old Town is the **Upper Gate**. In the area immediately to the south you'll find a fascinating **icon gallery** (no set hours; 100 MKD), home

to some of the best examples found in the Ohrid area. Staff here should also be able to open up the adjacent **Sveta Bogorodica**, a thirteenth-century church with wonderful interior frescoes.

West of the gate you've a choice of uphill paths; one heads to the **Fortress of Tsar Samoil** – usually closed off and in any case more interesting from the outside – while the other leads past an old **Roman amphitheatre** to **Sveti Kliment**, a large, modern church. This is built next to the ruins of the oldest church in Ohrid – dating from the fifth century, its foundations are on display under a rather ugly shelter.

From Sveti Kliment it's a hop and a skip down the slopes to **Sveti Jovan Kaneo**, whose lakeside setting makes it Ohrid's most appealing church. The walk east back into town is rather lovely, and passes the tranquil residential enclave of **Kaneo**. Back in the centre you'll find the **National Museum** (daily except Mon 10am–3pm; 100 MKD), an interesting place to while away an hour or two.

The lake

For all the Old Town's religious and historical significance, the timeless majesty of **Lake Ohrid** is still the main tourist magnet. Locals swear that the water remains clean enough to drink, and with visibilty of up to 20m they may well be right. Motorized "water-taxis" are available for €10 and up, though since they dilute both the clarity of the water and the beauty of the lake you may care to make use instead of the **rowing boats** available for hire at various lakeside points.

At the time of writing there were no boat services across the lake to Albania, but you can get within a walk of the border by heading to the monastery of **Sveti Naum**. Magical grounds surround the seventeenth-century building, whose interior is filled with vivid frescoes. In the summer you can get here by boat from Ohrid town, and buses run every couple of hours during the day, heading between the lake and **Galičica National Park** (Ⓦwww.galilica.org.mk), itself a great place for a hike.

DIVING IN OHRID

The best place from which to drop into Ohrid's crystal waters is **Gradište**, a village halfway between Ohrid town and Sveti Naum; cliffs tumble deep into the water, and you can peek at an **underwater Bronze Age village**. Its discoverer, Micho, organizes diving trips (from €50) and lessons from a base at the *Hotel Granit*, on the east of the lake; check out Ⓦwww.amfora.com.mk for details.

Arrival and information

Airport A 14km, 300 MKD taxi-ride from town.
Bus The station has been moved to a new, inconvenient location a 50–70 MKD cab ride north of the Old Town. Onward tickets can be bought from a Cyrillic-topped shack at the compound entrance.
Tourist office Located inside the bus terminal, but not much use even on the rare occasions that it chooses to open.

Accommodation

Most budget travellers end up staying at *sobi* (private rooms), especially when the hotels are booked up in summer months. You'll likely be met at the bus station by those with rooms to spare, though you can go hunting yourself in the Old Town. Camping is also possible at three sites along the lake between Ohrid and Sveti Naum.

Antonio's Guesthouse Dejan Vojvoda 94 Ⓣ070/736906. Clean dormitory accommodation in a family home, though inconveniently located to the north of the Old Town. Free tea, coffee and wi-fi access. €10.

Vila Forum Kuzman Kapidan 1 Ⓣ046/251340, Ⓦwww.villaforumohrid.com.mk. In an ideal location between the Roman amphitheatre and the city gate, the four rooms in this quality guesthouse are usually booked solid in summer, but drop to a bargain €30 off season. €45.

Vila Lucija Kosta Abraš 29 ⓣ046/265608, ⓔlucija@mt.net.mk. So close to the lake that you may wake to see your ceiling ashimmer with reflected sunlight. The spick-and-span rooms are excellent value, and come with almost painfully powerful showers. €30.

Vila Sveti Sofija Kosta Abraš 64 ⓣ046/254370, ⓦwww.vilasofija.com.mk. Well-equipped boutique rooms set in a beautiful, traditionally styled building. €60.

Eating and drinking

Ohrid's culinary scene is terribly uninspired for a place with such tourist appeal. There's a curl of identikit café-bars at the end of Kliment Ohridski.

Gladiator Local meals in a superb, easy-to-find location above the amphitheatre. Mains aren't the cheapest (300 MKD and up), but there are some bargains on the menu: 100 MKD will buy you a bowl of veal broth with bread, while a little more will get you a filling omelette.

Jazz Inn Kosta Abraš 80. At weekends this is the place to head for live music, though it's not always as mellow as the name might suggest. Sometimes stays open very, very late.

Kaneo Kaneo. This restaurant-cum-bar occupies a terrace next to the lapping waves in delightful Kaneo; grilled fish is the speciality. May–Oct only.

Liquid Kosta Abraš 52. Bar that's busy most nights with a young and fun-loving clientele – a good place to make new friends, get drunk with existing ones, or a mixture of the two.

Restorant Neim One of the only Old Town restaurants cheap enough to be popular with locals; the stuffed peppers (140 MKD) are recommended, as are the kebabs (120 MKD). A bottle of red will only set you back 300 MKD.

Taverna Kosta Abraš 1. Slightly pricey Macedonian dishes (mains from 600 MKD) served up overlooking the lake. Proud of their Ohrid trout, but since fishing for this endangered species is illegal think twice before ordering it.

Moving on

Bus Bitola (6 daily; 1h 30min); Resen (6 daily; 50min); Skopje (12 daily; 3–4hr).

Montenegro

HIGHLIGHTS

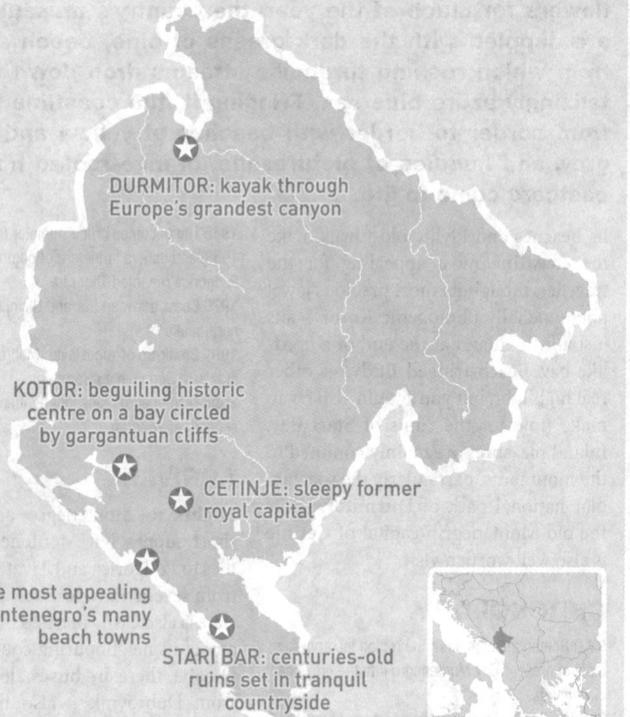
DURMITOR: kayak through Europe's grandest canyon
KOTOR: beguiling historic centre on a bay circled by gargantuan cliffs
CETINJE: sleepy former royal capital
BUDVA: the most appealing of Montenegro's many beach towns
STARI BAR: centuries-old ruins set in tranquil countryside

ROUGH COSTS

DAILY BUDGET basic €25/occasional treat €40

DRINK Nikšičko Tamno beer €1 (bottle from shop)

FOOD Sarma €2.50–4

GUESTHOUSE/BUDGET HOTEL €20/€40

TRAVEL Budva–Kotor (26km) €3 by bus; Podgorica–Virpazar (30km) €1.80 by train

FACT FILE

POPULATION 670,000

AREA 13,812 sq km

LANGUAGE Montenegrin

CURRENCY Euro (€)

CAPITAL Podgorica (population 200,000)

INTERNATIONAL PHONE CODE ⓣ382

Introduction

The tiny new state of Crna Gora is better known under its Italian name, Montenegro. When translated into English – "Black Mountain" – this may sound somewhat dull, but Montenegro is a land exploding with colour. Soaked with flowers for much of the year, the country's muscular peaks are dappled with the dark greens of pine, beech and birch from which rushing turquoise streams drop down to a tantalizingly azure blue sea. Fringing it, the coastline is dotted from border to border with beaches of yellow and volcanic grey, and huddles of picturesque, orange-roofed houses – a postcard come to life.

Its beaches and idyllic old towns make the **coastline** most appealing for the traveller, though its most precious jewel phenomenally photogenic **Kotor** – sits just a little inland at the end of a fjord-like bay. Beach-fringed **Budva** is other real highlight, but you should also try to make time for the ruins of **Stari Bar**. Inland pleasures are mainly confined to the mountains, particularly the spectacular national park of **Durmitor**, while the old Montenegrin capital of **Cetinje** is also well worth a visit.

CHRONOLOGY

9 AD Roman annexation of the region incorporates most of present-day Montenegro into the province of Dalmatia.
395 The Roman Empire splits into eastern and western halves, with Montenegro lying on the line of division.
990 Slav state of Duklja established.
1190 Successor state of Zeta annexed by Serbia.
1499 Much of Montenegrin interior falls to the Ottoman Empire; the Venetian Empire controls the coast.
1697 Ottomans defeated in Great Turkish War; Petrović clan assumes control.
1797 Venice falls to Napoleon, who transfers the Gulf of Kotor to Austrian rule.
1878 Montenegro granted independence following the Congress of Berlin.
1918 Kingdom of Serbs, Croats and Slovenes formed, incorporating Montenegro.
1929 Montenegro becomes part of the new Kingdom of Yugoslavia.
1945 Tito becomes prime minister (president from 1953) and ushers in the era of communist rule; Podgorica renamed Titograd.
1979 Coast between Bar and Ulcinj damaged by earthquake.
1991 Break-up of Yugoslavia; Montenegro votes to stay with Serbia in a referendum.
2006 Montenegro gains independence following a second referendum.

ARRIVAL

Flights to Montenegro are in pretty short supply, but Montenegro Airlines flies to Podgorica and Tivat (near Kotor) from several European destinations. The state is also easily reached overland from any of its neighbouring countries. From Croatia, there are **buses** along the coast from Dubrovnik – also home to the closest budget flights – and also a couple of services from Split; some of these will require a bus change after a short walk across the border. From Serbia, there are several daily buses between Belgrade and the Montenegrin coast, via Podgorica; daily **trains** – including a night service – also run from Belgrade to Bar along the same route. From Bosnia-Hercegovina there are direct buses to Podgorica from Trebinje and Sarajevo.

Perhaps the most romantic way to arrive in Montenegro is by **ferry** from Italy. Montenegro Lines (Ⓦwww.montenegrolines.net) runs between two and five weekly services to Bar from

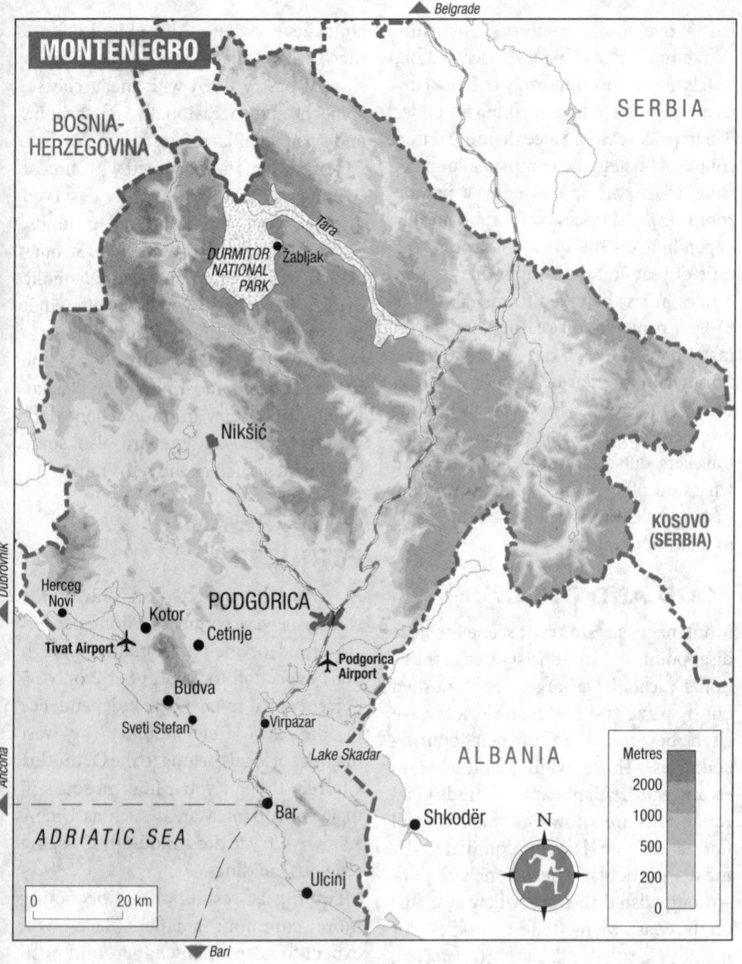

Bari, and summer-only services from Ancona.

Note that citizens of some countries, notably South Africa, still need **visas** to enter Montenegro. You may have to apply at a Serbian embassy, since not all Montenegrin ones are up and running yet.

GETTING AROUND

For a country with such a small population, the frequency of intercity **buses** is quite remarkable. In addition, Montenegro has poured substantial funds into the upgrading of its main travel arteries, and travel times are accordingly short. A **train** line heads to Bar from the Serbian border, and a freight-only spur from Podgorica to Niksič may soon reopen for passenger service. While services are infrequent, prices are dirt-cheap and almost every inch of track affords breathtaking views – catch one if you can.

ACCOMMODATION

The accommodation scene in Montenegro can be somewhat frustrating.

Partly due to the country's premature marketing as a "luxury" destination, **hotels** are almost uniformly overpriced – it can be tough to find anything for under €50 in peak season. Since there are only a couple of **hostels** and **campsites** country-wide, most end up staying at a **private room** (*sobe*). Prices vary dramatically depending on the quality of room, the time of year and the location in question – rates in less heralded towns dip below €10 per person in off-season, though you may pay three times more during summer in popular destinations such as Budva and Kotor. In warmer months, proprietors with rooms to spare wait for travellers outside the bus stations – see what's on offer before handing over any cash – while travel agencies are often able to make bookings.

FOOD AND DRINK

Montenegro's **restaurant** scene is a little disappointing. In tourist areas, traditional meals have largely been pushed out by pizza and pasta, and prices have risen beyond those of neighbouring countries. Those willing and able to escape said Italian staples – traditional restaurants are known as *konoba* – will find a cuisine largely dominated by **meat** – particularly beef, lamb and pork – though fish dishes are widely available on the coast. Menu items to look out for include grilled kebabs (*ćevapčići*), cabbage leaves stuffed with mincemeat (*sarma*), bean soup with flecks of meat (*pasulj*), gulaš (goulash), and the artery-clogging *karađorđe vasnicla*, a breaded veal cutlet roll stuffed with cheese. Vegetarians will struggle, but can take refuge in the hearty salads available almost everywhere. Also ubiquitous are the Turkish snack staples of *burek*, a slice of pastry filled with meat, cheese, spinach and occasionally mushroom, and syrupy baklava sweets.

Coffee (*kafa*) is consumed with almost religious fervour, usually served Turkish-style with unfiltered grounds, but also available espresso-style. Strong-as-hell **rakija** remains the alcoholic drink of choice – you'll be offered it constantly if visiting someone's home – but travellers usually subsist on some fine local beers, most notably Nikšićko, which also comes in an excellent dark variety (*tamno*). There are also some good **wines**, such as the red Vranac.

CULTURE AND ETIQUETTE

As might be expected in one of the world's newest countries, Montenegrins are proud of their **nationality**, though don't expect all to be anti-Serb: only 55 percent voted in favour of independence in the 2006 referendum. The vast majority of locals belong to the **Orthodox Church**, though you'll find mosques in majority-Albanian areas such as Ulcinj. As always, try to dress modestly if visiting religious buildings.

Tipping at restaurants is becoming more common; smaller places will expect to keep small change, and posh restaurants to receive up to ten percent of the bill. Note that despite an official **smoking** ban, Montenegrins still do much of their breathing through small, tobacco-filled cylinders: non-smokers may have a tough time avoiding the fumes.

MONTENEGRO ON THE NET

Ⓦ **www.montenegro.travel** Official tourist board site.
Ⓦ **www.themontenegrotimes.com** Homepage of an interesting English-language weekly.
Ⓦ **www.rivijera.net** Useful listings of coastal accommodation, often including pictures.

SPORTS AND OUTDOOR ACTIVITIES

Outdoor activities come in two main flavours: mountain and coastal. **Hiking** is a joy around the peaks of Montenegro's national parks, most notably Durmitor, which is also good for **kayaking**, and **skiing** in winter. On the beach it's a different story, with **watersports** including jetskiing, parasailing and zorbing available at various points along the coast – Budva is the prime spot, though kayaking around Kotor Bay is a delight.

COMMUNICATIONS

Most **post offices** (*pošta*) are open Monday to Friday 8am to 7pm, Saturday 8am to noon. These are also your best bet for **phonecalls** as public phones are in extremely short supply; local landlines are cheap to call, though calls to mobile phones are usually €1 per minute. Getting **online** can also be tricky as there are surprisingly few internet cafés; where they do exist, prices are generally €1–2 per hour.

EMERGENCIES

Montenegro has a pretty low crime rate as far as muggings and petty theft go, though of course it pays to be vigilant, especially around bus stations. The **police** (*policija*) are generally easygoing, and some speak basic English.

Pharmacies (*apoteka*) tend to follow shop hours, though you'll find emergency 24-hour telephone numbers posted in the windows. If they can't help, you'll be directed to a **hospital** (*bolnica*), most of which are pretty good.

EMERGENCY NUMBERS

Police ⓣ92; Ambulance ⓣ94; Fire ⓣ93.

STUDENT AND YOUTH DISCOUNTS

Quite a few sights and museums now offer discounted fares to students, and for what it's worth, InterRail tickets are valid on Montenegro's single line (which never costs more than a few euros anyway).

INFORMATION

Many towns and resorts now have a **tourist information office**, though hours can be infrequent and staff do not always speak English. It's also unlikely that they'll book rooms for you – head to a travel agent instead – but they can advise on local accommodation.

MONEY AND BANKS

Though not yet a member of the EU, Montenegro uses the **euro** (€). **Banks** are generally open Monday to Friday 9am to 6pm, Saturday 9am to noon, and **ATMs** are widespread.

OPENING HOURS AND HOLIDAYS

Most **shops** open Monday to Saturday 9am to 8pm – **banks** follow similar hours – and things slow down somewhat on Sundays. Museums are usually closed on Mondays, and all shops and banks shut down on **public holidays**: January 1, 7 and 8, April 27, May 1, 2 and 9, and November 29.

Montenegrin

Montenegrin is the official language, though it's essentially the same as Serbian (except that it uses the Roman alphabet rather than Cyrillic). You should be able to get by using Croatian (see p.257), with which it has strong similarities.

The coast

Blessed with sunshine, pristine beaches lapped by clear Adriatic waters, and appealing, whitewashed old towns, the **Montenegrin coast** has become one of Europe's hottest properties. Heading north–south from Croatia to the Albanian border, you'll first hit charming **Herceg Novi**, before the coast ducks inland to swallow up magnificent **Kotor** – without doubt the most picturesque town in the land. South of here, the littoral swings back out to the beaches of **Budva**, something of a party capital during the summer. It's then mountain-edged coast all the way to **Bar**, home to some terrific ruins, and Albanian-flavoured **Ulcinj**.

HERCEG NOVI

Developed as a coastal resort during eighteenth-century Austro-Hungarian rule, **HERCEG NOVI** is quite possibly the most likeable town in the country. Its steep maze of lanes is lined with stately, crumbling villas, and decades of international sailors have bequeathed unto it plants and flowers from around the world – with tropical notes hovering over the cobblestoned paths, it's a real holiday for your nose – while nearby **beaches** are good for a swim.

Arrival and information

Buses arrive at a small station on Jadranski put; turn right then walk downhill and you'll be in the Old Town in about 5min.

Information and tours The excellent Black Mountain agency (⊕031/321655, ⓦwww.montenegroholiday.com) can book private rooms, and also arrange great tours of the local area, as well as rafting trips to Durmitor (see box, p.796). They have an office at the bus station.

Internet There are a couple of cafés north in the Old Town's main square; €2/hr.

What to see and do

Most sights are concentrated within Herceg Novi's appealing, walled **Old Town**. At its centre you'll find the **Church of Archangel Michael**, just over a hundred years old but perhaps looking a few decades more than that. From here you can climb the steps to take in views from the "bloody tower" of **Kanli Kula** (€1). Downhill, the seafront **promenade** makes for a delightful walk. Head east for twenty minutes, then turn inland to find the elegant, seventeenth-century **Savina Monastery**.

Accommodation

There's a dearth of good-value accommodation in town, though the Black Mountain agency (see opposite) can book private rooms from €10 per person.

Autocamp Zelenika Sunčana obala ⊕067/678631. Campsite 3km east of town; open April–Oct.

Centar Sava Ilića ⊕031/332442. A short way west of the centre, with just about the cheapest rooms in town. Open April–Oct. €30.

Plaža Sava Kovačevića ⊕031/346151. The innards of this glass-fronted behemoth bring to mind a Yugoslav version of *The Shining*, and though too expensive for most it's worth popping by for coffee. €90.

Eating

Kafana Pod Lozom Trg Nikole Đurkovića. A 2min walk from the church (past the clock-tower and turn right), this restaurant cooks up cheap local specialities – you'll be able to fill up for €5. Try the *gulaš*, or the *sarma*.

Moving on

Note that when heading south, most buses cut out the Bay of Kotor loop with a quick ferry ride (no extra charge). Travelling via Kotor will increase the following journey times – excepting Kotor – by around 45min.

Bus Bar (6 daily; 2hr 30min); Budva (every 30min–1hr; 1hr 15min); Kotor (hourly; 45min); Podgorica (hourly; 2hr).

KOTOR

Perched on the edge of a majestic bay, the medieval Old Town of **KOTOR** is the undisputed jewel in Montenegro's crown. Though no longer Europe's best-kept secret, Kotor's sudden elevation to the tour-bus league has failed to dim the timeless delights of its maze of cobbled alleyways and secluded piazzas. Enclosing cafés and churches galore, the town **walls** are peered down upon by a series of hulking peaks. Down below, a harbour now bustling with sleek yachts marks the end of the **Bay of Kotor**, made fjord-like by the thousand-metre cliffs that rise almost vertically from the serene waters.

First colonized by the Greeks, Kotor came to prominence in the twelfth century, then passed through Serb, Austro-Hungarian and Bosnian hands before fifteenth-century Ottoman conquests forced it under the protective wing of Venice. Its period under Venetian rule ended in 1797, the shape of today's Kotor having been laid out in the intervening years.

What to see and do

Kotor's charms are best appreciated by heading to the **Old Town**, *sans* map, and getting lost in the maze of streets. You'll likely enter through the Sea Gate, next to the harbour, and emerge onto the main square, Trg od Oružja. Cafés spill out from glorious buildings, the most notable of which are the old **Rector's Palace**, and a leaning **clock tower**. Burrow through the streets and before long you'll end up at **St Tryphon's Cathedral**, backed by a wall of

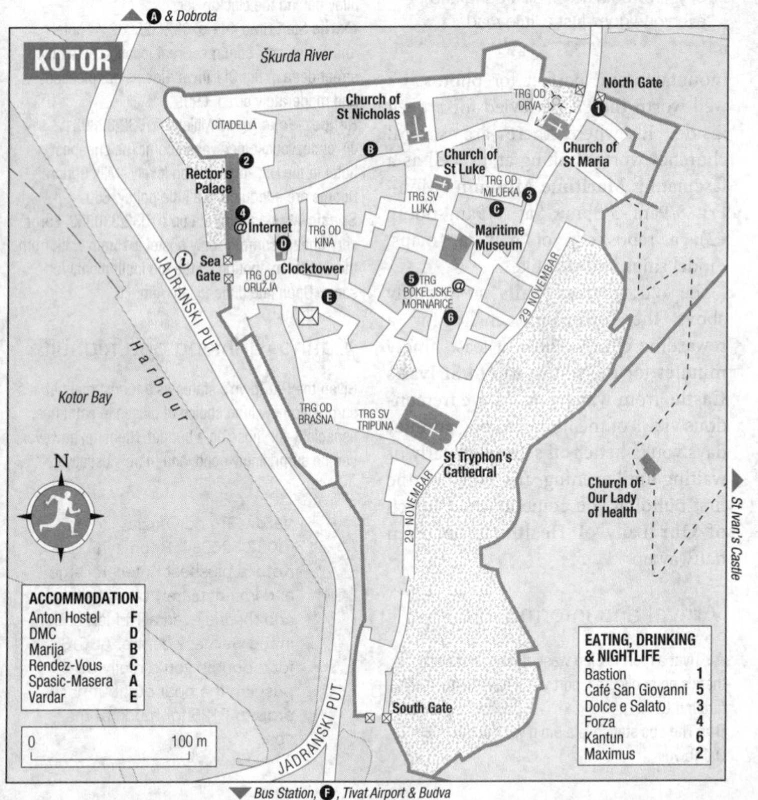

FESTIVALS IN AND AROUND KOTOR

Kotor's festival year kicks off in February, with folk dances and church music on the **day of St Tripun**; this is closely followed by the **Masked Ball**, a colourful event that sees masked processions head through the Old Town. In April there's the **Montenegrin Dance Festival**, which showcases pretty much every kind of dance, before theatrical and musical performances kick off the summer at the **International Summer Carnival** (ⓦwww.kotorkarneval.com), held in late July/early August. Around the same time is **Refresh** (ⓦwww.refreshfestival.com), a four-day music festival roping in some big-name DJs, but all pale in comparison to **Boka Nights** in August, when boats fill the bay, fireworks go off all around and everyone goes just a little mad.

mountains and perfect for photos; it's well worth the €2 fee levied for a peek inside. Elsewhere there are several churches worth looking at, as well as a fascinating **Maritime Museum** (Mon–Fri 8/9am–5/8pm; Sat 8/9am–noon; €2), a repository of nautical maps, model ships and suchlike.

The old **fortress walls** sit proudly above the town, and make for a rewarding climb. Allow at least ninety minutes for the round-trip to **St Ivan's Castle**, from which you'll have tremendous views of the fjord. On hot summer days you're better off setting off early or waiting until evening, and note that the first building you come to, the **Church of Our Lady of Health**, is not even halfway up.

Arrival and information

Air Tivat airport is 6km west of Kotor, but since there's no public transport you'll have to get a cab (around €20).

Bus The bus station is a 5min walk south of the Old Town.

Internet There are a few terminals in *Forza* café (€2/hr).

Tourist office Located just outside the main entrance to the Old Town (daily 8am–5pm, July & Aug to 9pm), and able to book accommodation.

Accommodation

At all times of year, you're likely to be approached by *sobe*-owners as you get off the bus. Alternatively, the tourist office can book rooms from €20 per person. Rooms are mainly grouped in two areas: Škaljari, uphill from the industrial mess abutting the bus station, and the more pleasant area of Dobrota, on the bayside just north of the Old Town.

Anton Hostel Mažina, Tivat ⓣ069/039751, ⓦwww.montenegrohostel.com. Stylish hostel located in Tivat, 8km from Kotor and convenient for touring the area. Facilities include internet access, home cooking and a swimming pool. Three-night minimum stay. €8.

DMC ⓣ032/323446, ⓦwww.tameridian.me. Not a hotel but a travel agency able to organize private rooms from around €15 per person. Located in the alley behind the clocktower.

Marija Stari Grad 449 ⓣ032/325062, ⓔhotel.maria.kotor@t-com.me. Great location on a quiet street deep in the Old Town. Rooms are pleasant and moderately sized. €90.

Rendez-Vous Trg od Mlijeka ⓣ032/323931, ⓔrendezvouskotor@yahoo.com. The cheapest hotel in the Old Town sits on lovely "Milk Square". Rooms are adequate, if a little pokey. €50.

Spasic-Masera Dobrota bb ⓣ032/330258. Large, very cheap, summer-only hostel a 15min walk from the Old Town, though a little too institutional for some. Open late June to late Aug. €6.

Eating, drinking and nightlife

Given the Old Town's status as a tourist magnet, it's surprising how little choice of places to eat it has, especially for those on a budget. Nightlife, however, can be surprisingly good, and there's usually live

TREAT YOURSELF

Vardar Trg od Oružja ⓣ032/326084. Rooms in Kotor's plushest hotel are large and immaculately designed, and there's even a Turkish bath in the wellness centre. At €185 for a double you'd really be pushing the boat out, but prices drop to €125 for much of the year.

music on weekends, which see the cobbled streets thumping until midnight.

Cafés

Forza Trg od Oružja. The best of a whole clutch of cafés on the main square, and a perfect place to watch Kotor strolling by. Also has internet access.

Restaurants

Bastion Trg od Drva. Seafood restaurant offering a more authentic Old Kotor atmosphere than you'll find elsewhere, and a great terrace. Squid filled with ham and cheese €12, fish salad €5.

Café San Giovanni Trg Bokeljske Mornarice. Just what the backpacker doctor ordered in a town of pricey restaurants – take-away slices of pizza for €1.

Dolce e Salato Trg od Mlijeka. Outdoor seats in this quiet square are a perfect place for breakfast – a slice of *burek*, a Turkish coffee and a piece of strudel will come to just €3.50.

Kantun Trg Bokeljske Mornarice. Perhaps the best of Kotor's glut of pizzerias, with the *calzone* particularly good. Pizzas from €7.

Club

Maximus Citadella. Take your pick from several music-themed floors at the biggest nightclub in the country, occasional host to big-name DJs. Entry €10–15.

Moving on

Bus Bar (6 daily; 1hr 45min); Budva (every 30min–1hr; 30min); Cetinje (hourly; 1hr); Podgorica (hourly; 1hr 30min).

BUDVA

Of Montenegro's seemingly never-ending chain of picturesque coastal towns, **BUDVA** is by far the most popular. Filled to the brim with bars, restaurants and limestone houses, its Old Town is almost as pretty as the one in nearby Kotor, and there's plenty of fun to be had on the buffet of beaches that dash up and down the coast, as well as at the seafront bars which pop up in the summer.

What to see and do

Budva's focal point is the **Old Town** – more of a place to stroll and sup coffee than sightsee – though most travellers are here for the **beaches**, and there are plenty to choose from.

The Old Town

The highlight of the Old Town is the area around the **Church of the Holy Trinity**, itself home to frescoes that, while far from ancient, are rather beautiful. Looming over this is the fifteenth-century **citadel** (April–Oct 9am–7pm; €2), which offers splendid views of the Adriatic waves pummelling in. Within easy walking distance are the **town museum** (Tues–Fri 8am–8pm, Sat & Sun 2–8pm; €2), which houses Greek and Roman booty from the ruins being unearthed beneath the citadel, and a **Museum of Modern Art** (Mon–Sat 8am–2pm & 4–7pm; free).

Beaches and islands

The main beach, **Slovenska Plaža**, curls a few pebbly kilometres east from the Old Town, but far nicer are the sandy **Mogren** beaches, west of the Old Town, which attract a more youthful crowd. Better still is the beach on uninhabited **Sveti Nikola Island**, which you'll see jutting up offshore; in summer, regular water taxis will shuttle you across for €2.50.

Sveti Stefan

A few kilometres south of Budva, and visible from the road if you're heading south to Bar, is the incredibly picturesque island of **Sveti Stefan**, an old fishing village fishscaled with orange

> **WATER ACTIVITIES IN BUDVA**
>
> The **Watersports Centre** on Slovenska Plaža, the main beach, is the place to head for all kinds of watery fun. Jetskis and parasailing are on offer for the adventurous (€60/hr), kayaks and pedaloes for the more peaceable (€3–5/hr), or give zorbing a try – walking like a hamster in an oversized beach ball.

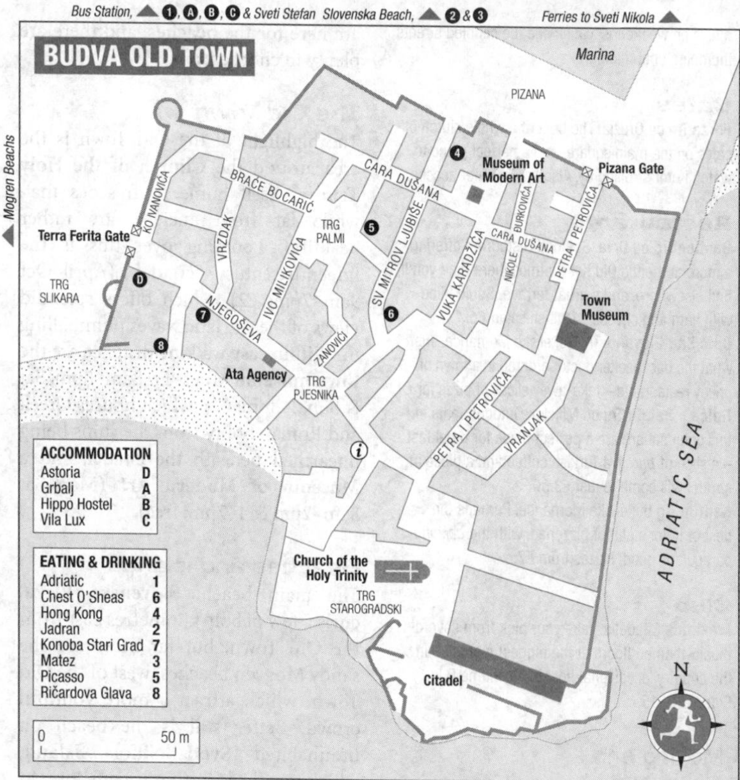

roofs, and the photo-darling of Montenegro's tourist literature. Its houses were converted in the 1950s to provide luxury accommodation – it was a favourite with movie stars – and since it has once again been cordoned off for the creation of a five-star resort, you're likely to have to pay for entry.

Arrival and information

Bus The station is a 15min walk from the Old Town, and a 10min walk from the main beach.

Tourist office Njegoševa 28 ⓣ033/402550. Unwilling to advise on accommodation, but not bad for maps and travel information.

Accommodation

If you're not met at the bus station – almost a certainty in summer – your best option for private rooms is to head to Ata (ⓣ033/452000, ⓦwww.budvatravelagency.com) in the Old Town who can make bookings for €15–35 per room.

Grbalj Trg Sunca ⓣ033/452300, ⓦwww.hotelgrbalj.com. Value-for-money hotel just down the road from the bus station. Rooms are cheery enough, and kept clean. €35.

Hippo Hostel Proletarska 37 ⓣ069/253631, ⓦwww.hippohostel.com. Despite its inconvenient location a 20min walk north of the seafront, this Irish-run hostel is worth tracking down, and its

TREAT YOURSELF

Astoria Njegoševa 4 ⓣ033/451110, ⓦwww.hotelastoria.co.me. Friendly boutique hotel just inside the Old Town walls, offering artistically designed rooms and wonderful views from a rooftop terrace. Doubles from €129, though off season you may get a suite for the same price.

common areas make it easy to hang out with fellow backpackers. Open April–Oct, two-night minimum July & Aug. €18.

Vila Lux Jadranski put bb ⓣ033/455950, ⓦwww.vilalux.com. The cheapest hotel in the centre, though you'd never guess it – rooms are just fine, and the free breakfasts will fill you up until lunchtime. Good discounts for single travellers. €52.

Eating, drinking and nightlife

Restaurants

Adriatic Mediteranska bb. No view whatsoever, but pizzas and pasta dishes go from just €3, and draught beer for €1 a glass. Just outside the Old Town on the way to the bus station.

Hong Kong Cara Dušana 17. The cheapest place to fill up in the Old Town, with rice and noodle dishes from just €3. More elaborate mains are available, though they're not terribly authentic.

Jadran Slovenska Obala 10. Hugely popular waterfront restaurant whose international menu includes schnitzels for €8 and mussels for €9.

Konoba Stari Grad Njegoševa. May look like nothing special from outside, but the seafood served here is excellent (if a little pricey), and there's a grand beach terrace out back.

Picasso Trg Palmi. Simple menu of pizzas, salads and suchlike, and a wonderful, tree-shaded outdoor courtyard in which to eat.

Cafés, bars and clubs

Chest O'Sheas Mitrov Ljubiše. Appealing Irish pub smack in the middle of the Old Town, with sports events on screen and Guinness on tap.

Matez This boat-shaped bar is the most distinctive of a line of open-air discos dotting the harbour road. Open May–Oct.

Ričardova Glava Njegoševa. Beachside tables and pounding waves make "Dick's Head" – the owners don't get the joke – the most atmospheric place for coffee.

Moving on

Bus Bar (hourly; 1hr); Cetinje (every 30min; 1hr); Kotor (every 30min–1hr; 30min); Podgorica (every 30min; 1hr 30min); Ulcinj (3 daily; 1hr 30min).

BAR

The pleasant town of **BAR** is literally the first port of call for many visitors to Montenegro, thanks to regular ferry connections with Italy. While the beach is rocky and there are no real attractions in the centre, it's worth at least an afternoon thanks to the magnificent ruins of **Stari Bar** (8am–8pm; €1) – *stari* means old – which sit 5km up the hill. The beauty of its setting is quite staggering – sheer cliffs surround this old town on all sides, and tiny farming communities dot the valleys below. Fragments of pottery found in the area date it as far back as 800 BC, though it wasn't until the **sixth century** that the Byzantine Empire created what you see today; the destruction also in evidence was caused during the Ottoman resistance battles of the 1870s. A trip to Stari Bar should set you back no more than €5 by taxi.

Accommodation

There are few *sobe* rooms in central Bar, so it's best to head to Šušanj, a pleasant district hanging over the almost unpronounceable beach of Zukotrlica. It's a 20min walk north along the seafront, or a €2 cab ride.

Sidro Obala ⓣ030/312200. The cheapest hotel in central Bar. Rooms are overpriced but perfectly adequate. €44.

Val Mila Damjanovića ⓣ067/206603. Block of comfy apartments located in the Šušanj district. €30.

Eating and drinking

Kaldrma Stari Bar. Adorable veggie restaurant – think cushions and rugs – near the entrance to the ruins.

Karađuzović Stari Bar. Small café near the ruins that's great for breakfast; €3 will buy you a slice of *burek*, a Turkish sweetie and an espresso.

Marina Vladimira Rolovića bb. Varied menu that's moderately priced considering the restaurant's location atop the ferry terminal – pasta meals from €6.

Pulena Vladimira Rolovića 11. Popular pizza-pub tucked into the fantastic Yugoslav-era Robna Kuka centre. Service ranges from slow to lightning-fast.

Moving on

Train Podgorica (7 daily; 1hr); Virpazar (7 daily; 25min).

Bus Budva (hourly; 1hr); Kotor (8 daily; 1hr 45min); Podgorica (7 daily; 1hr 45min); Ulcinj (7 daily; 40min).

ULCINJ

Montenegro's southernmost town, **ULCINJ** is worth visiting as a day-trip or for those on their way to Albania, and indeed you may well feel that you've already crossed the border – around 70 percent of the population here are ethnic eventy Albanian, a demographic best evidenced by a number of **mosques**. The **Old Town**, while crying out for renovation, is well worth a wander, and Montenegro's longest beach – **Velika Plaža** – lies just to the south (best accessed by taxi). This idyllic 12km-long curl of grey sand was, however, slated for development at the time of writing.

The interior

The mountains visible from the coast hint at the beauty of its interior, an area sadly bypassed by most travellers. Granted, the capital, **Podgorica**, is an uninteresting place with almost no budget accommodation, but **Cetinje**, the former capital, makes a delightful stopover. Best of all is the mountainous north, particularly **Durmitor**, a spectacular national park where you can hike though unspoilt pastureland, ski past 2000-metre-plus peaks, or raft through the colossal Tara Canyon.

CETINJE

Sleepy **CETINJE** sits just over the mountainous crest from Budva and Kotor, and is well placed for a visit if you're heading between coast and interior. Cetinje became Montenegro's **capital** on independence in 1878, and of the clutch of embassies that were established, many remain visible today as faded relics of the city's proud past. Though the status of capital has long been passed to Podgorica, many government offices – and, in fact, the presidential seat – remain in Cetinje.

What to see and do

Central Cetinje is small enough to walk around in an hour or two, and almost all sights are located on or near **Njegoševa**, a mostly pedestrianized central thoroughfare. The sights listed below are open 9am–5pm, and can be visited on a €8 combined ticket, or cost from €3 to €5 each.

Trg Dvorski and Trg Revolucije

The **Palace of King Nikola** sits at the southern end of Trg Dvorski. Prior to becoming king in 1910, Nikola was a military leader and poet (as well as a prince, of course), and his old palace is full of regal bric-à-brac. Opposite this is the **Ethnographic Museum**, which mainly features nineteenth-century costumes. Down the road in Trg Revolucie you'll find the **Biliarda**, once the residence of King Petar II, and named after a billiard table – still visible today – that he once had hauled here from Kotor. Like Nikola, his eventual successor, King Petar was a jack of many trades, this time a bishop, diplomat and poet. Near the Biliarda you'll find the **National Museum**, worth visiting for its first-floor art gallery, and nestled into the hillside across the square is **Cetinje Monastery**.

The embassies

Cetinje's former **embassies** are quite fascinating, and it's fun to track them down – basically, look for any oldish building sporting a crest. Nearest the bus station is the grey **French embassy**, covered with an assortment of lemon and blue tiles. Down on Trg Dvorski, the **Serbian embassy** contains the aforementioned ethnographic museum, the **Bulgarian** one is now a great café, and the **Belgian** is...nothing special. Further down the road, the crumbling **British embassy** is now a music academy; turn left for the **Turkish**

embassy, now home to the Faculty of Drama, and the pick of the bunch – the gorgeous, peach-coloured **Russian embassy**, which with a nicer roof would be quite at home in St Petersburg.

Accommodation

Grand ⓣ041/235047. Yugoslav-era beast at the end of Njegoševa, full of hairdressers, souvenir shops and the like, but the rooms are somewhat bare. €60.
Zicer ⓣ041/231177. Motel in the long building next to the bus station; rooms are fresher than you'd expect from the outside. €35.

Eating and drinking

Restoran Nacionale Njegoševa. Rich and varied menu of local specialities, including delicious *gulaš* and *sarma*. Mains €5–10.

Moving on

Bus Budva (every 30min; 1hr); Kotor (hourly; 1hr 15min); Podgorica (every 30min; 45min).

PODGORICA

Travellers tend to avoid **PODGORICA**, and with good reason: there's precious little to see in the Montenegrin capital, and its hotels – more used to businessmen than backpackers – are vastly overpriced. That said, it's not an unpleasant place, and may be worth a look if you have a few hours between trains or buses. The city centres on the canyon-like **Morača**, a fast-flowing turquoise river edged by parkland and spanned by a couple of pedestrian bridges. One of these, the Gazela, dives down below street level, where rarely will you find such peace at the centre of a European capital. You'll also find some interesting fortress remains at the confluence with the Morača's tributary, the **Ribnica**.

Arrival and information

Airport 11km south of the city. No public transport; taxis €15 (set fare) to the centre.
Train and bus The main train and bus stations are located adjacent to each other a 15min walk from the centre.
Tourist office Slobode 47 ⓣ020/667535, ⓦwww.podgorica.travel. Pretty good for information, and can advise on accommodation. Mon–Fri 8am–8pm, plus Sat (same hours) June–Oct.

Accommodation

Since it can be tough to find a double for under €100, it's important to remember that buses to cheaper towns – anywhere, in other words – run until fairly late, and trains to the coast even later.
Evropa Orahovačka 16 ⓣ020/623444, ⓦwww.hotelevropa.cg.yu. How convenient – Podgorica's cheapest hotel is located right next to the train and bus stations. Rooms are good and there's a restaurant downstairs. €70.
Steve's Place 19 Decembar 60 ⓣ067/372936, ⓦstevesplacehostel.com. Finally, a cheap place to stay…Steve is an affable American, and his place a well-located flat with just a few beds, so reserve online if at all possible. €10.

Eating and drinking

Restaurants in Podgorica are better value than the hotels, and *burek*-serving snack-bars are easy to find. For nightlife, the best place to head is Njegoševa and the surrounding area.
Duchovny Centar Njegoševa 27. Scoff down cheap, tasty local fare – mostly veggie – in this church-like restaurant; try the salty pancakes with cream. You can eat for under €5.
Karver Obala Ribnice. This characterful riverside café fills an old Turkish bath, is a cool hangout for evening drinks, and has a bookshop selling a few English-language cheapies... what more could you want? Latte €1.
Zabjelo 19 Decembar. Odd Rastafarian-themed joint in the north side of the football stadium, selling cheap, tasty *burek* – try the mushroom variety (€1.20).

Directory

Embassies and consulates UK, Bulevar Sveti Petra Cetinjskog 149 ⓣ020/205460; US, Ljubljanska ⓣ020/410500.
Hospital Podgorica Hospital, Ljubljanska 1 ⓣ020/225125.
Internet The ⓦwww.klub at Bokeška 4 has a few terminals, as does *Karver* café.
Post office Slobode 1 (Mon–Sat 8am–8pm). Has telephones for public use.

Moving on

Train Bar (10 daily; 1hr); Virpazar (10 daily; 35min). **Bus** Bar (7 daily; 1hr 45min); Budva (every 30min; 1hr 30min); Cetinje (every 30min; 30min); Herceg Novi (hourly; 2hr); Kotor (hourly, 1hr 30min).

LAKE SKADAR

Oozing over the Albanian border, beautiful **Skadar** is the largest lake in the Balkans, and also one of its most untouched. However, since it lies on the train line, it's easily accessible and can make a good stop-off on your way to or from the coast. The main jump-off point is **VIRPAZAR**, a cute little fishing village at the northern end of the lake, a kilometre back down the line to Podgorica from the station. From here it's a pleasant walk along the lake's western shore, and if you've brought along a bike you'll be in heaven – an hour's ride will bring into visible range a clutch of **offshore monasteries**. Accommodation is available in Virpazar at the *Pelikan* (☎020/711107, Ⓦwww.pelikan-zec.com; €58), which also has an excellent restaurant.

DURMITOR NATIONAL PARK

A land of jagged, pine-cloaked mountains and alpine pastureland, **Durmitor** is the most scenic place in inland Montenegro, and a hive of **outdoor activity** throughout the year. Dozens of 2000-metre-plus peaks drop down to the spectacular **Tara Canyon**, a kilometre-deep rip in the Earth bisected by a crashing river. You'll have guessed by now that Durmitor is a prime spot for skiing, hiking, camping, rafting and far more.

Durmitor is centred on the mountain town of **ŽABLJAK**, accessible by bus along a bumpy, winding road that can turn even the stomachs of the locals. There's plenty of **accommodation** here, though as elsewhere in the country the hotels are a little dear; best value are the *Enigma* (☎052/360130; €60) and the *Javor* (☎052/361337; €60). Better for budget travellers are private rooms – from €10 per person – which you'll be offered on exiting the bus. Durmitor is also a great place for **camping**, and there are a number of sites around the park.

ACTIVITIES IN DURMITOR

Durmitor is perhaps most famed for its **rafting**, which is among the best in Europe. This can be arranged though agencies on the coast or in Žabljak – try Summit (☎052/360082) or Žabljak Tourist (☎052/361115) – which charge around €50 per person for a half-day trip. **Hiking** is great from June to September, though since this is a wild area do come prepared if you're planning a multi–dayer, and be warned that the weather can change rapidly, even in summer. Wintertime opens up **skiing** possibilities, and **snowboarding** is on the rise too; the main slopes are accessible from Žabljak, with day passes costing €15, and ski hire almost the same.

Morocco

HIGHLIGHTS

CHEFCHAOUEN: beautiful little town in the Rif mountains, where the houses look like they're made of blue meringue

MEDINA, FES: an incredible labyrinth of alleys, sights and smells in the world's best-preserved medieval city

DJEMAA EL FNA, MARRAKESH: a spontaneous live circus in a large square in the middle of town, featuring everything from snake charmers to tooth pullers

ESSAOUIRA: arty, laid-back seaside and surfing resort where Jimi Hendrix once played impromptu concerts on the beach

ROUGH COSTS

DAILY BUDGET basic €20/occasional treat €30

FOOD Tagine €3–4

DRINK Pot of mint tea €0.50

HOSTEL/BUDGET HOTEL €10–15

TRAVEL Marrakesh–Casablanca train (3hr) €8–12; bus (3–4hr): €5–8

FACT FILE

POPULATION 34.3 million

AREA 446,550 sq km

LANGUAGES Arabic, Berber languages, French

CURRENCY Dirham (dh)

CAPITAL Rabat (population: 2 million)

INTERNATIONAL PHONE CODE ⓣ212

Introduction

Just an hour's ferry ride from Spain, Morocco seems very far from Europe, with a deeply traditional Islamic culture. Throughout the country, despite its 44 years of French and Spanish colonial rule, a more distant past constantly makes its presence felt. A visit here is a challenging, intense and rewarding experience.

Berbers, the indigenous population, make up over half of Morocco's population; only around ten percent of Moroccans claim to be "pure" **Arabs**. More obvious is the legacy of the **colonial** period: until independence in 1956, the country was divided into Spanish and French zones, the latter building **Villes Nouvelles** (new towns) alongside the long-standing **Medinas** (old towns) in all the country's main cities.

Many people come to Morocco on cheap flights, mainly to Marrakesh, but coming by boat from Europe, your most likely introduction to the country is **Tangier** in the north, still shaped by its heyday of "international" port status in the 1950s. To its south, in the Rif mountains, the town of **Chefchaouen** is a small-scale and enjoyably laid-back place, while inland lies the enthralling city of **Fes**, the greatest of the four imperial capitals (the others are Meknes, Rabat and Marrakesh). The sprawl of **Meknes**, with its ancient walls, makes an easy day-trip from Fes.

The power axis of the nation lies on the coast in **Rabat** and **Casablanca**. "Casa" looks a lot like Marseille, while the elegant, orderly capital, Rabat, has some gems of Moroccan architecture. Further south, **Marrakesh** is an enduring fantasy that won't disappoint. The country's loveliest resort, **Essaouira**, a charming walled seaside town, lies within easy reach of both Marrakesh and Casablanca.

CHRONOLOGY

42 AD Romans take control of the coastal regions of Morocco.
600s Arabs conquer Moroccan lands, introducing Islam.
1062 Marrakech is built by the Berber dynasty of Almoravids.
1195 Almoravids replaced by the Almohads, who conquer Southern Spain.
1269 The capital is moved to Fes.
1415 The Portugese capture the Moroccan port of Ceuta.
1492 Influx of Jews who have been expelled from Spain.
1860 Spanish wage war with Morocco, ultimately gaining land in Ceuta.
1904 France and Spain divide various areas of influence in Morocco.
1912 Under the terms of the Treaty of Fes, Morocco becomes a French protectorate.
1943 Moroccan Independence Party, Istiqlal, is founded.
1956 Morocco declares independence from France.
1963 First general elections.
1975 Clashes as Morocco forcefully takes back land in the Sahara from the Spanish.
2004 Earthquake along the Mediterranean coast kills over five hundred.
2006 Introduction of cheap flights to Marrakesh leads to a noticeable increase in tourism.
2007 Moroccan Government and Polisario Independence Movement remain unable to come to an agreement regarding the disputed land in the Western Sahara.

ARRIVAL

To reach Morocco from Europe you can either fly or take a ferry. The main **airports** are in Casablanca, Fes and Marrakesh, the last of which is served

regularly by budget airlines from UK and European airports. Ryanair (Ⓦwww.ryanair.com) and easyJet (Ⓦwww.easyjet.com) both sell cheap online tickets.

The ports of Ceuta and Tangier are both on the north coast of Morocco and **ferries** arrive from France (Sète), Italy (Genoa, one per week) and Spain (Algeciras, Tarifa). From Ceuta you can catch buses on to Chefchaouen and Tangier. From Tangier you can catch trains and buses to all of the major cities in Morocco. Boat tickets can be booked online (Ⓦwww.comanav.co.uk, www.euroferrys.com and www.nautasferry.com) or at the ports themselves.

GETTING AROUND

The **train** network is limited, but for travel between the major cities, trains are the best option. A table of direct and connecting services to any other station is available at any station ticket office or on the ONCF (national rail company) website (Ⓦwww.oncf.ma). Couchettes (160dh extra) are available on trains from Tangier to Marrakesh (9hr 30min), and are worth the money for extra comfort and security. Only direct trains are listed in this chapter.

Collective **grands taxis** are usually big Peugeots or Mercedes, plying set routes for a set fare and are much quicker than buses, though the drivers can be reckless. Make clear you only want *une place* (one seat), otherwise drivers may assume you want to charter the whole car. Expect to wait until all six places in the taxi are taken, though you can pay for the extra places if you are in a hurry. Within towns **petits taxis** do short trips, carrying up to three people. They queue in central locations and at stations and can be hailed on streets when they're empty. Payment – usually no more than 15dh – depends on distance travelled.

Buses are marginally cheaper than grands taxis, and cover longer distances, but are slower. CTM (the national company) is the most reliable. Supratours (Ⓦwww.oncf.ma) run express buses that connect to train services.

ACCOMMODATION

Accommodation is inexpensive, generally good value and usually pretty easy to find, although it's more difficult in main cities and resorts in the peak seasons: August, Christmas, and Aïd el Kebir (currently Nov). Cheap, unclassified **hotels** and *pensions* (charging about 100–200dh for a double) are mainly in each town's Medina (old town), while hotels with stars tend to concentrate in the Ville Nouvelle (new town). At their best, unclassified Medina hotels are beautiful, traditional houses with whitewashed rooms grouped around a central patio. The worst can be extremely dirty, with a poor water supply. Few have en-suite bathrooms, though a *hammam* (public Turkish bath) is usually close at hand. Except in Marrakesh, most hotels do not include breakfast in their room price. HI **hostels** (*auberges de jeunesse*), often bright, breezy and friendly, generally require you to be in by 10pm or 11pm and out by 10am daily. **Campsites** are usually well out of town and tend to charge around 15dh per person plus the same again for your tent.

FOOD AND DRINK

Moroccan cooking is wholesome and filling. The main dish is usually a **tajine** (casserole). Classic *tajines* include chicken with lemon and olives, and lamb with prunes and almonds. The most famous Moroccan dish is **couscous**, a huge bowl of steamed semolina piled with vegetables, mutton, chicken or fish. Restaurant **starters** include *salade marocaine*, a finely chopped salad of tomato and cucumber, or soup, most often the spicy, bean-based *harira*. **Dessert** will probably be fruit, yoghurt or a pastry. Breakfast is cheapest if you buy *msimmen, melaoui* (which taste like pancakes), *harsha* (a heavy gritty griddle bread) or pastries from street-side shops and eat them at cafes.

The best **budget meals** are at local diners, where *tajines* or roast chicken with chips and salad are usually under 50dh. Even cheaper are sandwiches and *shwarmas*, which cost 15–20dh from street-side vendors, however be careful about ordering *kefta* (minced meat) if you have a weak stomach. Fancier restaurants, definitely worth an occasional splurge, are mostly in the Ville Nouvelle and will often offer a bargain set menu at 65–150dh.

Vegetarianism is not widely understood and meat stock may be added even to vegetable dishes. If **invited to a home**, you're unlikely to use a knife and fork; copy your hosts and eat only with your right hand.

Drink

The national drink is **thé à la menthe** – green tea with a large bunch of mint and a massive amount of sugar. Coffee (*café* in French; *qahwa* in Arabic) is best in French-style cafés. Moroccans tend to take their coffee with half milk and half coffee (*nus-nus*) in a glass. Many cafés and street stalls sell fresh-squeezed orange juice, and **mineral water** is readily available. As an Islamic nation, Morocco gives alcohol a low profile, and it's generally impossible to buy in the Medinas; however bars are always around in the Ville Nouvelle. Moroccan **wines**, usually red, can be very drinkable, while the best-value **beer** is Flag Speciale. Most local **bars** are male domains; hotel bars, on the other hand, are more mixed and not much more expensive. The big supermarkets sell alcohol; ask a petit taxi to take you to the nearest Acima or Marjane.

CULTURE AND ETIQUETTE

Morocco is a Muslim country, and in rural areas particularly, people can be quite **conservative** about dress and displays of affection. It's not the done thing to kiss and cuddle in public, nor even for couples to hold hands. **Dress** is more conservative in rural areas, though even in the cities you can feel uncomfortable in sleeveless tops, short shorts or skirts above the knee. The heat can be oppressive so long, light, loose clothing is best. A shawl allows women to cover up whilst wearing sleeveless tops.

Be sensitive when **taking photographs**, and always ask permission. In certain places, particularly the Djemaa el Fna in Marrakesh, people may demand money from you just for happening to be in a shot you have taken. Also note that it is illegal to photograph anything considered strategic, such as an airport or a police station.

When invited into people's homes, remove footwear before entering the reception rooms. If invited for a meal, take a gift: a box of sweets from a posh patisserie usually goes down well.

It is acceptable (and a good idea) to try **bargaining** at every opportunity (see box below). If you do it with a smile, you can often get surprising reductions.

SPORTS AND ACTIVITIES

Casablanca and Essaouira cater to **surfers**: the former has better waves while the latter is excellent for **windsurfing**. Tangier and Rabat have decent beaches but with less developed services. Mohammedia, a thirty-minute ride from both Rabat and Casablanca, is a great destination for avid surfers. Anywhere on the Atlantic coast you should be aware of strong undertows.

The Moroccan mountain ranges offer great **hiking** opportunities. Good starting points include: Chefchaouen, in the Rif; Fes and Meknes near the Middle Atlas; and Marrakesh, two hours away from Mount Toubkal – the second highest mountain in Africa. Consult local tourist information offices or hotels for advice and details of the trails.

Horse riding is an expensive but increasingly popular way of seeing Morocco. *La Roseraie Hotel*, located in the High Atlas, 60km from Marrakesh, is a great place from which to hire horses and venture into the mountainous countryside. Prices depend on your itinerary but it's not cheap (ⓣ0524 439128, ⓦwww.laroseraiehotel.com).

Football is Morocco's most popular sport. You will see it being played in every conceivable open space. If you start up a game on a beach it won't be long before you are joined by some

SHOPPING

You can pick up bargains throughout Morocco, and you will kick yourself if you go home empty-handed. However, getting a price you can brag about in the hostel requires a willingness to enter into the spirit of **haggling**. The first price you will be given will often be at least three and up to ten times more than you should pay. Though quality makes a difference, we've included rough prices for some popular goods you could reasonably fit into a backpack. Fixed-price shops in the Ville Nouvelle also give a good approximation of what you should be paying in the medina.

- Small kilims (coarse rugs) 500–1500dh
- Leather bags (cheaper in Fes than Marrakesh) 150–300dh
- Leather baboush (slippers) 70–150dh
- Silk scarves 50–100dh
- Jelaba (Traditional Moroccan dress) 100–150dh

Moroccans; equally you'll usually be welcome in pick-up games. All the major cities have teams and money is being poured into new stadiums. For league tables see Ⓦwww.maroc.net/sports and for information on stadiums see Ⓦwww.maroc-football.com.

COMMUNICATIONS

Post offices (PTT) are open Monday to Friday 8am to 4.15pm; larger ones stay open until 6pm, and also open Saturday 8am to noon. You can also buy **stamps** at postcard shops and sometimes at tobacconists. Always post items at a post office. International **phone calls** are best made with a phonecard (from post offices and some tobacconists). Alternatively, there are privately run *téléboutiques*, open late. You must dial all ten digits of Moroccan phone numbers. **Internet** access is available pretty much everywhere, and at low rates: 5–10dh/hr is typical.

EMERGENCIES

Street **robbery** is rare but not unknown, especially in Tangier and Casablanca. Hotels are generally secure for depositing money; campsites less so. There are two main types of **police** – grey-clad gendarmes, with authority outside city limits; and the navy-clad sûreté in towns. There's sometimes a brigade of "tourist police" too. Moroccan **pharmacists** are well trained and dispense a wide range of drugs. In most cities there is a night pharmacy, often at the town hall, and a rota of *pharmacies de garde* that stay open till late and at weekends. You can get a list of English-speaking **doctors** in major cities from consulates. Steer clear of **marijuana** (*kif*) and hashish – it's illegal, and buying it leaves you vulnerable to scams, as well as potentially large fines and prison sentences.

MOROCCO ON THE NET

Ⓦwww.visitmorocco.com Moroccan tourist board's website.
Ⓦwww.geocities.com/thetropics/4896/morocco.html A selection of information for visitors.
Ⓦwww.morocco.com Huge collection of links to sites about every aspect of Morocco.

EMERGENCY NUMBERS

Police – Sûreté ⓣ19, Gendarmes ⓣ177, Fire and ambulance ⓣ15.

INFORMATION

There's a **tourist office** (Délégation du Tourisme) run by the Office National Marocain du Tourisme (**ONMT**) in every major city, and sometimes also a locally funded Syndicat d'Initiative. They stock a limited selection of leaflets and maps, and can put you in touch with official guides. Travel agencies tend to have a fuller range of brochures regarding local activities. There are scores of "**unofficial guides**", some of whom are genuine students, while others are out-and-out hustlers (though these have been clamped down on). If they do find you, be polite but firm. Note that it's illegal to harass tourists. Tourist offices are usually understocked and often can't give away maps; local bookshops and street-side kiosks are a better bet. The most functional are those in the *Rough Guide to Morocco*.

MONEY AND BANKS

The unit of currency is the **dirham** (dh), divided into 100 centimes; in markets, prices may well be in centimes rather than dirhams. There are coins of 10c, 20c, 50c, 1dh, 5dh and 10dh, and notes of 20dh, 50dh, 100dh and 200dh. You can get dirhams in Algeciras (Spain) and Gibraltar, and can usually change foreign notes on arrival at major sea- and airports. It can be

Moroccan Arabic

Moroccan Arabic is the country's official language, and there are three Berber languages, but much of the country is bilingual in **French**. For some useful French words and phrases see p.385.

	Moroccan Arabic
Yes	Eyeh
No	La
Please	Afek/Minfadlik
Thank you	Shukran
Hello	Assalam aleikum
Goodbye	Bissalama
Excuse me	Issmahli
Where?	Fayn?
Good	Mezziyen
Bad	Mish Mezziyen
Near (here)	Krayb (min hina)
Far	Baeed
Cheap	Rkhis
Expensive	Ghalee
Open	Mahlul
Closed	Masdud
Today	El Yoom
Yesterday	Imbarih
Tomorrow	Ghedda
How much is...?	Shahal...?
What time is it?	Shahal fisa'a?
I (m) don't understand	Ana mish fahim
I (f) don't understand	Ana mish fahma
Do you (m) speak English?	Takellem ingleezi?
Do you (f) speak English?	Takelma ingleezi?
One	Wahad
Two	Jooj
Three	Tlata
Four	Arba'a
Five	Khamsa
Six	Sitta
Seven	Seba'a
Eight	Temeniya
Nine	Tisaoud
Ten	Ashra

difficult to change traveller's cheques anywhere but a bank. For **exchange** purposes, the most useful and efficient chain of banks is the **BMCE** (Banque Marocaine du Commerce Extérieur). Post offices will also change cash, and there are bureaux de change in major cities and tourist resorts. Many banks give cash advances on credit cards, which can also be used in tourist hotels (but not cheap unclassified ones) and the **ATMs** of major banks. Banking hours are Monday to Friday 8.15am to 3.45pm (Mon–Fri 9.30am–2pm during the holy month of Ramadan). Morocco is inexpensive but poor, and **tips** can make a big difference; it's customary to tip café waiters a dirham or two. At the time of writing, £1 was equal to around 12.60dh, $1 to 8.80dh, €1 to 11.15.

STUDENT AND YOUTH DISCOUNTS

It is always worth pointing out that you are a student when you are bargaining. However, the informality of most transactions means that there are not many established student discounts. There are a few exceptions, though: ONCF, the train network, has a card for young people that can be purchased for 99dh, which gives you fifty percent reductions on sixteen trips. Student cards entitle you to cheaper entry at some museums and other sights, and a small discount on some ferry tickets. They're not worth going out of your way to get, but if you have one you might as well bring it along.

OPENING HOURS AND HOLIDAYS

Shops and stalls in the *souk* (bazaar) areas open roughly 9am to 1pm and 3 to 6pm. Ville Nouvelle shops are also likely to close for lunch, and also once a week, usually Sunday. Islamic **religious holidays** are calculated on the lunar calendar and change each year. In 2010 they fall (approximately) as follows: Feburary 26 is **Mouloud** (the birthday of Mohammed); **Ramadan** (when all Muslims fast from sunrise to sunset) roughly August 11 to September 10; the end of Ramadan is celebrated with **Aïd es Seghir** (aka Aïd el Fitr), a two-day holiday; November 16 is **Aïd el Kebir** (when Abraham offered to sacrifice his son for God); December 7 is the Muslim New Year. Non-Muslims are not expected to observe Ramadan, but should be sensitive about not breaking the fast in public. **Secular holidays** are considered less important, with most public services (except banks and offices) operating normally even during the two biggest ones – the Feast of the Throne (July 30), and Independence Day (Nov 18).

Northern Morocco

The northern tip of Morocco contains enough on its own to justify the short ferry ride over from Spain: in three days or so you could check out the delightfully seedy city of **Tangier** and the picturesque, laid-back little mountain town of **Chefchaouen** in the Rif mountains.

TANGIER

For the first half of the twentieth century **TANGIER** (Tanja in Arabic; Tanger in French) was an "International City" with its own laws and administration, attracting notoriety through its flamboyant expat community. With independence in 1956, this special status was removed and the expat colony dwindled. Its mixed colonial history and proximity to Spain means that Spanish is a preferred second language. Today Tangier is a grimy but energetic port, mixing modern nightclubs and seedy Moroccan bars with some fine colonial architecture.

What to see and do

The **Grand Socco**, or Zoco Grande – once the main market square (and, since Independence, officially Place du 9 avril 1947) – offers the most straightforward approach to the **Medina**. The arch at the northwest corner opens onto Rue d'Italie, which leads up to the Kasbah. To the right, Rue es Siaghin leads to the atmospheric but seedy **Petit Socco**, or Zoco Chico, the Medina's main square.

The Kasbah

To get to the Kasbah you can walk from the Petit Socco. Rue des Almohades (aka Rue des Chrétiens) and Rue Ben Raisouli leads to the lower gate. The **Kasbah** (citadel), walled off from the Medina on the highest rise of the coast, has been the palace and administrative quarter since Roman times. The main point of interest is the former Sultanate Palace, or **Dar el Makhzen** (Mon, Wed, Thurs, Sat & Sun 9am–4pm, Fri 9am–noon & 1.15–4pm; 10dh), now converted into a museum of crafts and antiquities, which gives you an excuse to look around, though the exhibits are rather sparse.

Beaches

Tangier's best **beach** is along the Route Malabata (east of the Medina, 15–20dh petit taxi from Grand Socco). The beach is long, relatively clean and sandy; the water suffers a bit from being next to a port though it is safe enough for a swim. Unfortunately there are few amenities and no watersports on offer at Tangier's beaches. In late July/August there are vendors selling refreshments, but outside this period bring enough water and food to last you the day, as there are no nearby shops.

Caves of Hercules

Perhaps the area's most popular tourist attraction is the **Caves of Hercules** (Grottes d'Hercule), where the sea has eroded the cave entrance to form the shape of Africa. Petits taxis cost around 120–150dh from Grand Socco for the round trip and waiting time, and the journey itself is worth it for the extraordinary views of Morocco's northern

ARRIVING IN MOROCCO

From Algeciras (Spain) you can arrive in Morocco either at Tangier or Ceuta. **Tangier** is the better option as it allows you to connect to all the major transport links, and is itself worth a visit. **Ceuta** is a dull Spanish enclave with Fnideq, a small but charming Moroccan border town, 3km away. From here you'll have limited transport options.

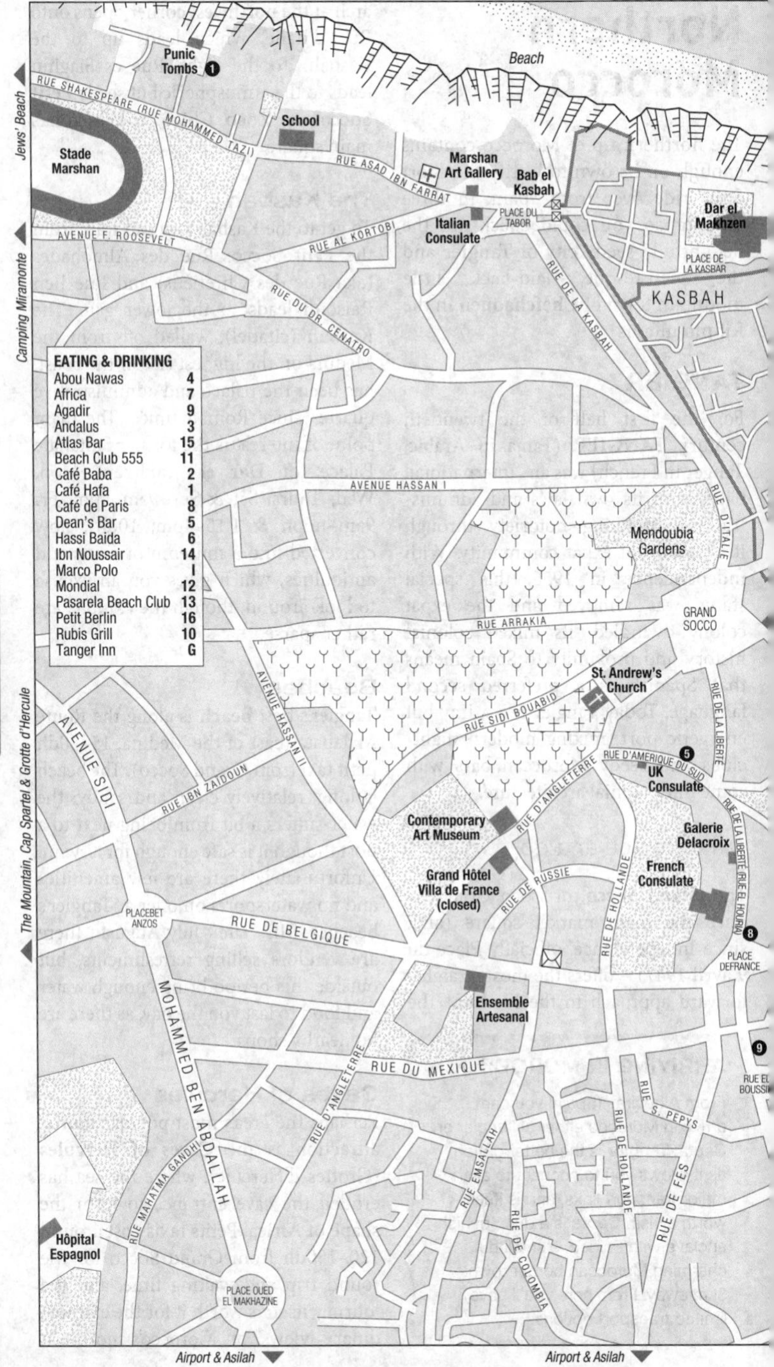

Punic Tombs
Beach
Jews' Beach
RUE SHAKESPEARE (RUE MOHAMMED TAZI)
School
Stade Marshan
RUE ASAD IBN FARRAT
Marshan Art Gallery
Bab el Kasbah
PLACE DU TABOR
Italian Consulate
Dar el Makhzen
PLACE DE LA KASBAR
KASBAH
AVENUE F. ROOSEVELT
RUE AL KORTOBI
Camping Miramonte
RUE DU DR. CENATRO
RUE DE LA KASBAH
EATING & DRINKING
Abou Nawas 4
Africa 7
Agadir 9
Andalus 3
Atlas Bar 15
Beach Club 555 11
Café Baba 2
Café Hafa 1
Café de Paris 8
Dean's Bar 5
Hassi Baida 6
Ibn Noussair 14
Marco Polo I
Mondial 12
Pasarela Beach Club 13
Petit Berlin 16
Rubis Grill 10
Tanger Inn G
AVENUE HASSAN I
Mendoubia Gardens
RUE D'ITALIE
GRAND SOCCO
RUE ARRAKIA
St. Andrew's Church
RUE SIDI BOUABID
AVENUE HASSAN II
RUE DE LA LIBERTE
RUE D'AMERIQUE DU SUD
UK Consulate
The Mountain, Cap Spartel & Grotte d'Hercule
AVENUE SIDI
RUE IBN ZAIDOUN
RUE D'ANGLETERRE
Contemporary Art Museum
Galerie Delacroix
Grand Hôtel Villa de France (closed)
RUE DE RUSSIE
RUE DE HOLLANDE
French Consulate
RUE DE LA LIBERTE (RUE EL HOURIA)
PLACEBET ANZOS
RUE DE BELGIQUE
PLACE DEFRANCE
Ensemble Artesanal
MOHAMMED BEN ABDALLAH
RUE DU MEXIQUE
RUE D'ANGLETERRE
RUE S. PEPYS
RUE EL BOUSSI
RUE EMSALLAH
RUE DE HOLLANDE
RUE DE FES
RUE MAHATMA GANDHI
Hôpital Espagnol
RUE DE COLOMBIA
PLACE OUED EL MAKHAZINE
Airport & Asilah
Airport & Asilah

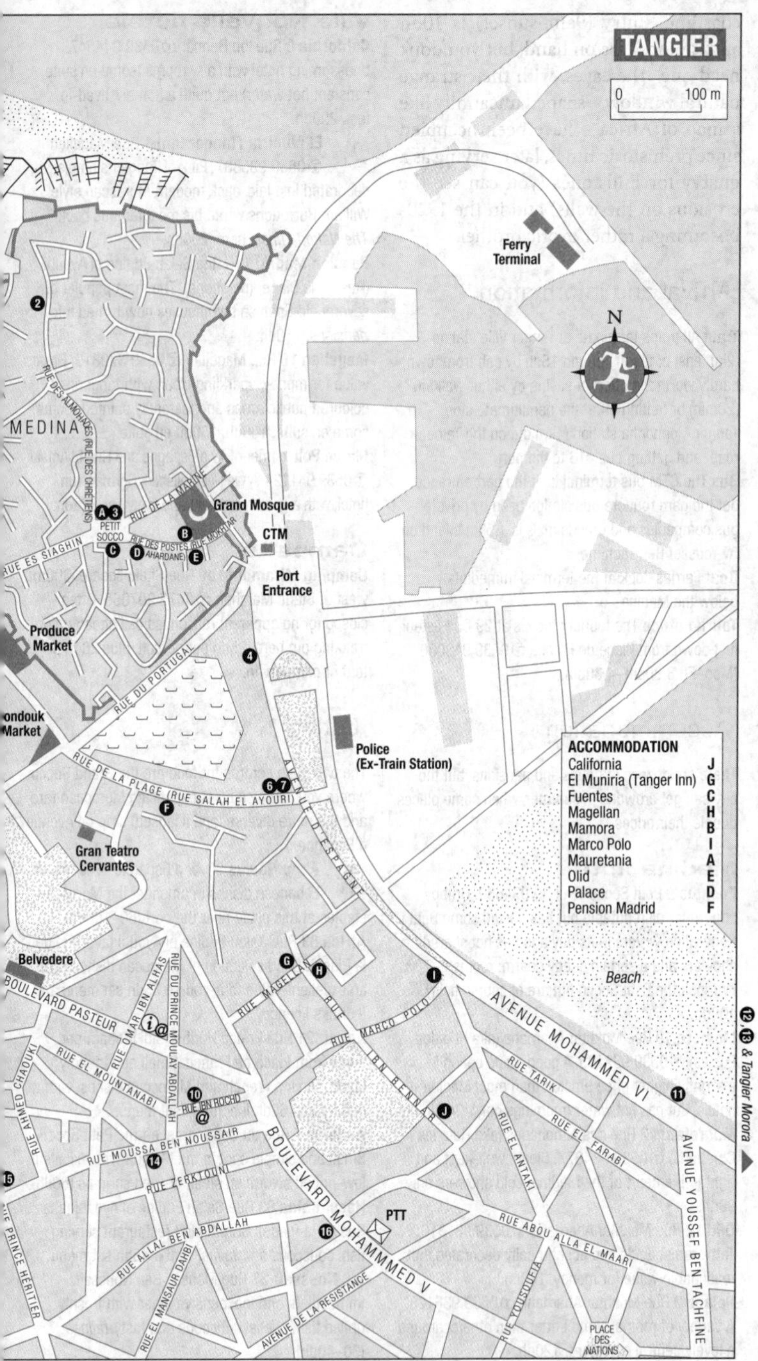
TANGIER
0 100 m
Ferry Terminal
N
MEDINA
RUE DES ALMOHADES (RUE DES CHRETIENS)
RUE DE LA MARINE
Grand Mosque
PETIT SOCCO
RUE DES POSTES (RUE MOKHTAR AHARDANE)
RUE ES SIAGHIN
CTM
Port Entrance
Produce Market
Fondouk Market
RUE DU PORTUGAL
Police (Ex-Train Station)
RUE DE LA PLAGE (RUE SALAH EL AYOURI)
AVENUE D'ESPAGNE
Gran Teatro Cervantes
Belvedere
BOULEVARD PASTEUR
RUE OMAR IBN ALHAS
RUE DU PRINCE MOULAY ABDALLAH
RUE MAGELLAN
RUE MARCO POLO
RUE IBN BENNAR
RUE EL MOUNTANABI
RUE AHMED CHAOUKI
RUE IBN ROCHD
RUE MOUSSA BEN NOUSSAIR
RUE ZERKTOUNI
BOULEVARD MOHAMMMED V
PTT
RUE ALLAL BEN ABDALLAH
RUE EL MANSOUR DAHBI
AVENUE DE LA RESISTANCE
RUE PRINCE HERITIER
AVENUE MOHAMMED VI
Beach
RUE TARIK
RUE EL FARABI
RUE EL ANTAKI
RUE ABOU ALLA EL MAARI
RUE YOUSSOUFIA
AVENUE YOUSSEF BEN TACHFINE
PLACE DES NATIONS
ACCOMMODATION
California J
El Muniria (Tanger Inn) G
Fuentes C
Magellan H
Mamora B
Marco Polo I
Mauretania A
Olid E
Palace D
Pension Madrid F
12, 13 & Tangier Morora
Cap Malabata, Tanger Ville Station, Bus Station, Place de la Ligue, Arabe & Tetouan

coastline. Entry (9am–sunset) is 10dh and "guides" are on hand, but you don't need one. The caves, with their strange natural window – shaped uncannily like a map of Africa – have been occupied since prehistoric times, later serving as a quarry for millstones (you can see the erosions on the walls) and in the 1920s becoming a rather exotic brothel.

Arrival and information

Train All trains terminate at Tanger Ville station (2km east of town), around 15dh by cab from town, hardly worth the effort of saving by either walking (20min) or getting off at the penultimate stop, Tanger Moghogha station (4km out on the Tetouan road) and getting bus #13 to the port.
Bus The CTM bus terminal is at the port entrance, but the gare routière bus station used by private bus companies and grands taxis is 1.5km inland on Av Youssef Ben Tachfine.
Boat Ferries dock at the terminal immediately below the Medina.
Tourist office The tourist office is at 29 Bd Pasteur, just down from Place de France ⓣ0539 948050 (Mon–Fri 8.30am–4.30pm).

Accommodation

There are dozens of hotels and pensions, but the city can get crowded in summer, when some places double their prices.

Medina hotels

Fuentes 9 Petit Socco ⓣ0539 934669. Grubby and rather disreputable but has hosted some Beat Generation writers in its day and has hot shared showers and a certain seedy charm; rooms 2–7 overlook the Petit Socco but are of course noisy. 100dh.
Mamora 19 Rue Mokhtar Ahardane (aka Rue des Postes) ⓣ0539 934105. A good-value option in a slightly higher price bracket than most Medina hotels, but has hot water (mornings only). 240dh dbl.
Mauretania 2 Rue des Almohades (aka Rue des Chrétiens) ⓣ0539 934677. Clean, well-kept and right in the heart of the Medina; cold showers only. 90dh.
Olid 12 Rue Mokhtar Ahardane ⓣ0539 931310. Tatty, ramshackle and eccentrically decorated, but reasonable value for money. 120dh.
Palace 2 Rue Mokhtar Ahardane ⓣ0539 936128. A variety of rooms, some better than others, around a lovely central courtyard. 120dh.

Ville Nouvelle hotels

California 8 Rue Ibn Bennar ⓣ0539 944547. Unassuming hotel with airy rooms (some en suite, constant hot water) but quite a homely, lived-in feel. 200dh.
El Muniria (Tanger Inn) 1 Rue Magellan ⓣ0539 935337. Pick of Tangier's hotels, decorated in a laid-back modern Moroccan style. William Burroughs wrote his most famous book, *The Naked Lunch*, here. 200dh.
Pension Madrid 140 Rue Salah Eddine el Ayoubi (Rue de la Plage) (no phone). The most popular of several old Spanish townhouses now turned into *pensions*. 150dh.
Magellan 16 Rue Magellan ⓣ0539 372319. Great value for money, sparkling clean with tangerine-coloured public areas and tastefully painted rooms, some en suite. 100dh, 150dh en suite.
Marco Polo corner of Av d'Espagne and Rue El Antaki ⓣ0539 941124. A well-established, German-run hotel, with a good restaurant and lively bar. 572dh.

Campsite

Camping Miramonte off Rue Shakespeare, 300m west of Stade Marshan ⓣ0672 207055. Often closed for no apparent reason, so call ahead before trekking out here. 25dh per person, plus 20dh per tent or campervan.

Eating

The two main centres for food are the Grand Socco, where you can pick up cheap, filling Moroccan fare and the more diverse (and licensed) strip on Avenue d'Espagne.
Abou Nawas 30 Av d'Espagne. A couple of Lebanese dishes in amongst the Moroccan staples at this place near the port (60–100dh).
Africa 83 Rue Salah Eddine el Ayoubi (aka Rue de la Plage). Good selection of Moroccan dishes, with an excellent-value four-course 55dh set menu and a drinks licence.
Agadir 21 Rue Prince Héritier Sidi Mohammed, uphill from Place de France. Small and friendly place, serving French and Moroccan dishes, with a good-value 60dh lunchtime set menu.
Andalus 7 Rue du Commerce, off the Petit Socco. Small and simple spot in the Medina with excellent, low-priced swordfish steak or fried shrimps (60dh).
Hassi Baida 83 Rue Salah Eddine el Ayoubi (aka Rue de la Plage). Bright, tiled restaurant serving fish, couscous and *tajine*, with a 45dh set menu.
Ibn Noussair 37 Rue Moussa Ben Noussair. Immaculate and inexpensive diner with freshly grilled fish, paella, couscous and tasty *tajines* (30–40dh).

TANGIER'S CAFÉ CULTURE

Tangier is best enjoyed from a café and the Petit Socco is packed with them, each offering the opportunity to relax and observe the hustle on the street. Two further-flung cafés should also not be missed: **Café Hafa** is cut into the cliff face and looks across the Mediterranean to Spain; **Café Baba** (take the street into the Dar el Makhzen and turn down the right hand fork at Place Amrah where it's signposted) has played host to various notables, from Mick Jagger to European royalty. Both cafés are very popular with locals and frequented by Ludo-playing Moroccans. For a more upmarket choice, head for Tangier's most famous and reputedly oldest cafe, the **Café de Paris** on Place de France.

Marco Polo corner of Av d'Espagne and Rue el Antaki. Generous servings at a fair price with snappy service and good views of the bay (50–90dh).
Petit Berlin 40 Av Mohammed V. *Tajines* at roadside prices but in an upmarket setting, with tapas bar upstairs, and a 50dh lunchtime set menu.
Rubis Grill 3 Rue Ibn Rochd, off Rue du Prince Moulay Abdallah. Well-prepared European-style food, intimate decor and exemplary service (70–90dh).

Drinking and nightlife

There are a number of big clubs along the seafront. Entrance is usually free for foreigners, and always free for women, but guys may have to pay 100dh.

Bars

Atlas Bar 30 Rue Prince Héritier, across the road from the *Hôtel Atlas*. Cosy tapas bar open since 1928.
Dean's Bar Rue d'Amérique du Sud. Close to the Medina and now popular with Moroccans, this bar had an illustrious artistic clientele in Tangier's heyday, including Francis Bacon and Ian Fleming. A good spot to soak up Tangier's former glories.
Tanger Inn 1 Rue Magellan. A colonial institution decorated with photos of the Beat Generation authors (Burroughs, Ginsberg and Kerouac) who stayed at the hotel, but quiet midweek off-season.

Clubs

Beach Club 555 Av Mohammed VI ⓣ0539 944950, ⓦwww.beachclub555.com. A long-time favourite with a swimming pool and bustling dance-floor, but has a reputation for prostitutes.
Pasarela Beach Club Av Mohammed VI ⓣ0539 945246. Chic interior with restaurant, swimming pool, and a friendly policy towards foreigners.
Mondial Av Mohammed VI ⓣ0663 536288. One of the classier clubs along the strip, with DJs and live acts.

Directory

Consulates UK, Trafalgar House, 9 Rue d'Amérique du Sud ⓣ0539 93 06939 or 40, ⓔuktanger2 @menara.ma.
Exchange BMCE, 19 Bd Pasteur has a bureau de change and ATM. Bureaux de change on Rue es Siaghin between the Grand and Petit Socco.
Internet Cybercafé Adam, 4 Rue Ibn Rochd (off Bd Pasteur); River-Net, 29 Bd Pasteur (on the corner of Rue du Prince Moulay Abdallah).
Pharmacies There are several English-speaking pharmacies on Place de France and Bd Pasteur.
Post office Main PTT, 33 Bd Mohammed V.
Police The Brigade Touristique are based at the former train station by the port ⓣ0539 931129.

Moving on

The overnight train from Tangier to Marrakesh allows you to venture south without losing time. If you want to go east (such as to Chefchaouen) take a bus.
Bus Casablanca (41 daily; 6hr); Chefchaouen (7 daily; 3hr 30min); Fes (17 daily; 5hr 45min); Fnideq (for Ceuta) (15 daily; 1hr); Marrakesh (11 daily; 10hr); Meknes (9 daily; 7hr); Rabat (39 daily; 5hr); Tetouan (50 daily; 1hr 30min).
Train Casablanca Voyageurs (4 daily; 5hr 45min–7hr 25min); Fes (1 daily, plus 4 connecting services; 4hr 40min); Marrakesh (1 daily, plus 3 connecting services; 11hr); Meknes (1 daily, plus 4 connecting services; 3hr 55min); Rabat (4 daily; 4hr 45min).
Ferry Algeciras, Spain (18–25 daily; 1hr–2hr 30min); Tarifa, Spain (8 daily; 35min); Genoa (1 weekly; 48hr), Gibraltar (1 weekly; 1hr 30min), Sète (1 every 4–5 days; 36hr).

CEUTA/FNIDEQ

Due to the fast ferry, the drab Spanish enclave of **CEUTA** is a popular entry point for travellers coming from Spain. On disembarking you have to catch a

taxi or local bus to the Moroccan border. Once across the border there are lots of grands taxis that will take you the 3km to the Moroccan town of **FNIDEQ** (3dh). It is advisable to arrive early to leave time for moving on.

Fnideq has some pleasant **hotels** along the one main road, Mohammad V; *Hotel Nador* at no.136 (150dh) is the cheapest option whilst *Hotel Fnideq* at no.172 (250dh) is far cleaner and more comfortable. If you're looking for a **restaurant**, try the moderately priced *La Costa* at 232 Mohammad V, one of the finest seafood restaurants in Northern Morocco.

Moving on

The bus station is signposted at the roundabout where the seafront and Av Mohammad V meet, marked by a fountain. Buses are infrequent, so it's often quicker and similarly priced to get a grand taxi to Tetouan or Tangier for better connections.
Bus Casablanca (6 daily; 8hr); Marrakesh (2 daily; 11hr); Meknes (1 daily; 7hr); Rabat (6 daily; 7hr); Tangier (15 daily; 1hr); Tetouan (8 daily; 30min).
Ferry Algeciras, mainland Spain (16–20 daily; 35min). Tickets can be booked at Ceuta port; it is advisable to arrive an hour early. Times to avoid are at the end of Easter week and the last week of August due to a huge increase in demand.
Taxis to Tetouan and Chefchaouen are at Fnideq bus station, while those for Tangier can be picked up by 280 Av Mohammed V.

TETOUAN

Coming from Ceuta, you usually need to pick up onward transport at **TETOUAN**, a town with a walled Medina and a reputation for having the worst hustlers in Morocco – but a grand taxi from Fnideq will leave you close enough to Tetouan's bus station to head straight out again. There are regular **buses** to Meknes, Fes and destinations nationwide. For Tangier, Chefchaouen or Ceuta it's easiest to travel by **grand taxi**. The ONCF office on Av 10 Mai, alongside Place Al Adala, sells **train** tickets that include a shuttle bus to the station at Tnine Sidi Lyamani (or sometimes to Tangier). If you're stuck in Tetouan, cheap hotels near the bus station include the friendly *Principe*, 20 Av Youssef Ibn Tachfine (☎0533 113128; 100dh), on the corner of Boulevard de Mouquaouama midway between the bus station and Place Moulay el Mehdi.

Moving on

Bus Casablanca (31 daily; 6hr); Chefchaouen (19 daily; 2hr); Fes (14 daily; 5hr 20min); Fnideq (for Ceuta) (8 daily; 1hr); Marrakesh (8 daily; 10hr); Meknes (6 daily; 6hr); Rabat (25 daily; 5hr); Tangier (50 daily; 1hr 30min).

CHEFCHAOUEN

Shut in by a fold of the Rif mountains, **CHEFCHAOUEN** (sometimes abbreviated to Chaouen or Xaouen) had, until the arrival of Spanish troops in 1920, been visited by just three Europeans. It's a town of extraordinary light and colour, its whitewash tinted with blue and edged by golden stone walls. *Pensions* are friendly and cheap and Chefchaouen is one of the best places to spend your first few days in Morocco.

The main entrance to the Medina is a tiny arched entrance, Bab el Ain, but the quickest way to negotiate your way to the centre is to get a petit taxi to Place el Makhzen (ask for the Kasbah), where you will find *Hotel Parador*, an expensive hotel, but a good place to pop into for a beer or a swim. From here it is only a two-minute walk to **Place Outa el Hammam.** This is where most of the town's evening life takes place. By day the town's focus is the **Kasbah** (Mon, Wed, Thurs, Sat & Sun 9am–1pm & 3–6.30pm, Fri 9am–noon & 3–6.30pm, Tues 3–6.30pm; 10dh), a quiet ruin with shady gardens and a small museum, which occupies one side of the square.

Chefchaouen is best enjoyed pottering around the Medina and relaxing at coffee shops or on your terrace. For the more adventurous there are **hiking** trails that start from the town. Or you

can catch a grand taxi from Place el Makhzen to go to the Oued Laou beach (250dh) or hike along rivers and waterfalls to God's Bridge (Pont de Dieu).

Arrival and information

Arrival Buses and grands taxis drop you outside the town walls.
Tourist office There is no tourist office in Chefchaouen, but your hotel should be able to help with general information.

Accommodation

Hostel

HI hostel Rue Sidi Abdelhamid ⓣ0666 865355, ⓔsarham03@live.fr. A very inexpensive but basic and inconveniently located hostel with adjoining campsite (dorms only; 30dh).

Hotels

Hotel Andaluz 1 Rue Sidi Salem ⓣ0539 986034. Basic *pension* just around the corner from *La Castellena* with a central courtyard, friendly staff, terrace and a very decent English language book collection. 100dh.
Hotel Ouarzazat Rue Alkharazine ⓣ0539 988990. Bright as a new pin, this good-value little hotel has small but fresh rooms done out in Chefchaouen blue and white, and constant hot water in the shared showers. 100dh.
Pension La Castellena 4 Sidi Ahmed El Bouhali ⓣ0539 986295. Follow the signs at the near end of the Place Outa el Hammam. Cheap and clean with a terrace, laid-back atmosphere and great central seating area. Very popular with travellers. 100dh.

Campsite

Camping Azilan Rue Sidi Abdelhamid ⓣ0539 986979, ⓦwww.campingchefchaouen.com. Located up on the hill above town, by the modern *Hôtel Asma*. Chefchaouen's campsite is inexpensive but can be crowded in summer. 20dh per person, plus 20dh per tent.

Eating and drinking

Restaurant Assada on a nameless street just opposite *Hotel Bab el Ain*. Cheap meals (35–40dh) enjoyed by both locals and tourists. Very welcoming staff and a terrace that overlooks the medina.
Casa Aladin Zenkat el Targui, off north end of Place Outa El Hammam. Two floors and a terrace, beautifully done out in *Arabian Nights* style, as its name suggests, serving great *tajines*, couscous (including vegetarian) and other staple fare (set menus 75dh & 100dh).
Café Restaurant Jebli Place Outa El Hammam. One of several cheap options on the square, serving decent Moroccan food (35–50dh). Has a well-furnished terrace overlooking the square.

Moving on

Buy tickets a day in advance for Fes and Meknes.
Bus Casablanca (4 daily; 9hr); Fes (7 daily; 5hr); Meknes (3 daily; 5hr 30min); Rabat (4 daily; 8hr); Tangier (7 daily; 3hr 30min); Tetouan (19 daily; 2hr).

Central Morocco

Between the mountain ranges of the Rif to the north and the Atlas to the south lie the cities that form Morocco's heart: the great imperial cities of **Meknes** and **Fes**, the modern capital, **Rabat**, and the country's largest city and commercial capital, **Casablanca**.

MEKNES

More than any other Moroccan town, **MEKNES** is associated with a single figure, the Sultan Moulay Ismail, during whose reign (1672–1727) the city went from provincial centre to spectacular capital showcasing over fifty palaces and fifteen miles of exterior walls. Today Meknes is slightly dull, but the Medina's palaces and monuments reward a day's exploration, and the ancient sites of Volubilis and Moulay Idriss are nearby.

What to see and do

Place El Hedim

Place El Hedim originally formed the western corner of the Medina, but Moulay Ismail had the houses here demolished to provide a grand approach to his palace quarter. The **Dar Jamaï**

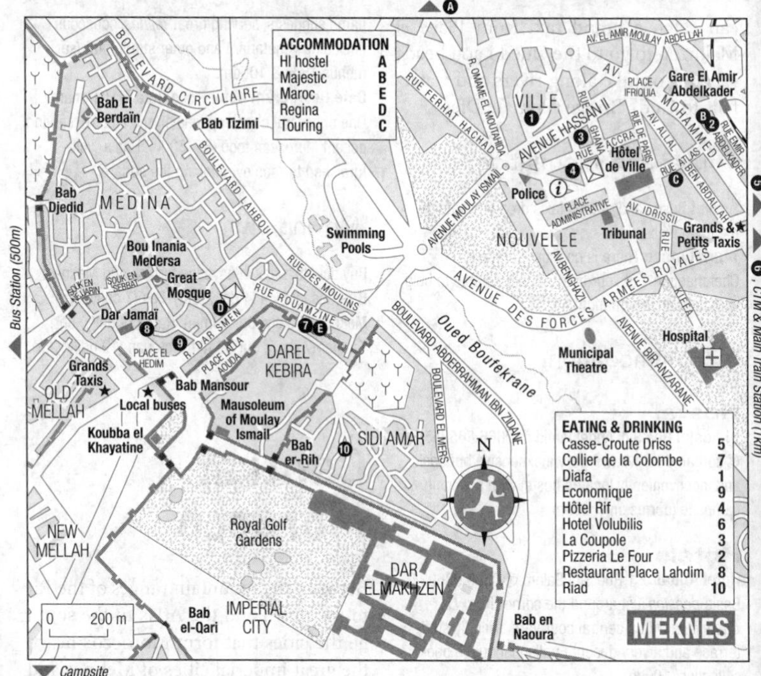

(daily except Tues 9am–5pm; 10dh), at the back of the square, is a great example of a nineteenth-century Moroccan palace, and the museum inside is one of the best in Morocco, with a fantastic display of Middle Atlas carpets. The lane immediately to the left of the Dar Jamaï takes you to the Medina's major market street: on your left is **Souk en Nejjarin**, the carpet souk; on your right, leading to the Great Mosque and Bou Inania Medersa, are the fancier goods offered in the **Souk es Sebbat**. The **Bou Inania Medersa** (daily 9am–5.30pm; 10dh), constructed around 1340–50, has an unusual ribbed dome over the entrance hall and from the roof you can look out to the tiled pyramids of the Great Mosque.

The Koubba el Khayatine and Moulay Ismail's Mausoleum

Behind the magnificent **Bab Mansour** (open for occasional exhibitions) is Place Lalla Aouda. Straight ahead bearing left, you come into another open square, on the right of which is the green-tiled dome of the **Koubba el Khayatine**, once a reception hall for ambassadors to the imperial court (daily 9am–5pm; 10dh). Below it, a stairway descends into a vast series of subterranean vaults, known as the **Prison of Christian Slaves**, though it was probably a storehouse or granary. Nearby is the entrance to **Moulay Ismail's Mausoleum** (daily except Fri 9am–noon & 3–5.30pm; 10dh donation expected), where you can approach the sanctuary.

Volubilis and Moulay Idriss

A short grand taxi ride from Meknes (300dh for round trip plus two hours waiting time) takes you to two of the most important sites in Morocco's history. **Volubilis** was once the Roman capital of the province; it is still possible to follow the outline of the old city and walk amongst some

well-preserved ruins. **Moulay Idriss** was established by the Prophet's great grandson who is credited with bringing Islam to Morocco. Today, it is a small but bustling town, which Moroccans treat with great respect. It is worth a trip for the views from the top of the town and for an insight into the religious heart of Morocco (particularly true in the festival that takes place in the second week of August). However, non-Muslims are barred from visiting the religious shrines of Moulay Idriss for which the town is famous.

Arrival and information

Train Meknes has two train stations, both in the Ville Nouvelle. All trains stop at Gare de Ville, but Gare El Amir Abdelkader (some services only) is more central.
Bus and taxi Private buses and most grands taxis arrive west of the Medina by Bab el Khemis; CTM buses arrive at their terminus on Av de Fès, near the Gare de Ville, and grands taxis from Fes will drop you in town on their way through.
Tourist office 27 Place Administrative (Mon–Fri 8.30am–4.30pm; ⓣ0535 524426).

Accommodation

Hostel

HI hostel Av Okba Ben Nafi ⓣ0535 524698. An easy 1.5km walk northwest of the city centre. Well-maintained and friendly with small dorms and some double rooms around a pleasant courtyard. Dorms 50dh. Breakfast included. 140dh.

Hotels

Majestic 19 Av Mohammed V, Ville Nouvelle ⓣ0535 522035, ⓕ0535 527427. A good one-star: old, but good-value, comfortable, friendly and handy for El Amir Abdelkader train station. 314dh.
Maroc 7 Rue Rouamzine, Medina ⓣ0535 530075. Pick of the Medina hotels, with plain but decent rooms around a shaded patio garden. Hot water 7am–noon & 7–11pm.160dh.
Regina 19 Rue Dar Smen ⓣ0535 530280. Best option of several cheap hotels on this street. Has central open area with sofas and terrace overlooking medina. 100dh.

Campsite

Camping Caravaning International (aka Camping Aguedal; no phone). A half-hour walk from Place el Hedim (or a 15dh petit taxi ride), situated opposite the Heri es Souani. Although a little pricey, this is one of the best campsites in Morocco with good facilities (hot water showers available for 7dh). 17dh per person plus 10dh per tent.

Eating and drinking

There are good places to eat in all price categories in Meknes, good cheap eats on Rue Rouamzine near Hôtel Maroc, and plenty of bars, several in Ville Nouvelle hotels, including the bar of the 1930s-style *Hôtel Volubilis* at 45 Av des FAR.
Casse-Croute Driss 34 Rue Emir Abdelkader, Ville Nouvelle. Fresh fried fish – cheap (15–20dh per portion) and tasty – but the restaurant is a bit cramped.
Collier de la Colombe 67 Rue Driba, Medina. Outstanding international cuisine at moderate prices in an ornate early twentieth-century Medina mansion (110–135dh).
Diafa 12 Rue Badr el Kobra (off Av Hassan II at its western end), Ville Nouvelle. Great home cooking with a multi-choice set menu (110dh), in what looks like a private house in a residential street.
Economique 123 Rue Dar Smen, opposite Bab Mansour, Medina. A popular café/restaurant serving straight Moroccan food at low prices (30–50dh).
Hôtel Rif Rue Omar Ben Chemssi, formerly Rue Accra. The bar is pleasant, has live music and is not overly expensive and if you want to cool down you can use the pool (75–100dh).
La Coupole corner of Av Hassan II and Rue Ghana, Ville Nouvelle. Reasonably priced Moroccan and European food. Has a bar and nightclub (70–140dh).
Pizzeria Le Four 1 Rue Atlas, Ville Nouvelle. Decent pizzas, pasta and other Italian dishes, though the interior is a bit on the gloomy side (50–70dh).
Restaurant Place Lahdim north corner of Place El Hedim. Decent Moroccan food that comes with a great view over the Medina (50–70dh).

TREAT YOURSELF

TREAT YOURSELF

Riad 79 Ksar Chaacha, Medina (follow the green signs from Dar el Kabira) ⓣ0535 530542, ⓦwww.riadmeknes.com. Refined traditional cuisine – the best in town, say locals – in beautifully restored salons or in the patio garden that's magic in the evening. Set menu 110–160dh. Daily 11am–3pm & 6.30–9.30pm. Booking ahead is wise but not vital.

Moving on

Train Casablanca Voyageurs (14 daily; 3hr 20min); Fes (15 daily; 35min); Marrakesh (8 daily; 6hr 30min); Rabat (14 daily; 2hr 20min); Tangier (1 daily; 5hr, plus 5 connecting services).
Bus Casablanca (20 daily; 4hr 30min); Chefchaouen (4 daily; 5hr 30min); Fes (roughly every 30min; 1hr); Marrakesh (6 daily; 9hr); Rabat (hourly; 3hr); Tangier (9 daily; 7hr); Tetouan (6 daily; 6hr).

FES (FEZ)

The most ancient of the imperial capitals, **FES** (Fez in English) stimulates the senses and seems to exist somewhere between the Middle Ages and the modern world. Some two hundred thousand of the city's half-million inhabitants (though actual figures are probably much higher than official ones) live in the oldest part of the Medina, **Fes el Bali.**

What to see and do

Getting lost is one of the great joys of the Fes Medina. However, if you want a more informed approach, pick up a small green book called "Fes" from the paper kiosks; this book corresponds to the tourist trails within the Medina that are marked out by coloured stars. Tour guides also can be employed at the Bab Boujeloud; the official ones wear medallions to identify themselves.

Talâa Kebira

Talâa Kebira, the Medina's main artery, is home to the most brilliant of Fes's monuments, the **Medersa Bou Inania** (daily 9am–5pm; closes 4pm during Ramadan; 10dh), which comes close to perfection in every aspect of its construction, with beautiful carved wood, stucco and *zellij* tilework. Continuing down Talâa Kebira you reach the entrance to the **Souk el Attarin** (Souk of the Spice Vendors), the formal heart of the city. To the right, a street leads past the charming **Souk el Henna** – a tree-shaded square where traditional cosmetics are sold – to Place Nejjarin (Carpenters' Square). Here, next to the geometric tilework of the **Nejjarin Fountain**, is the imposing eighteenth-century **Nejjarin Fondouk**, now a woodwork museum (daily 10am–5pm, closes 4pm during Ramadan; 20dh), though the building is rather more interesting than its exhibits. Immediately to the right of the fountain, Talâa Seghira is an alternative route back to Bab Boujeloud, while the alley to the right of that is the aromatic **carpenters' souk**, ripe with the scent of sawn cedar, and top on the list of great Medina smells.

FES ORIENTATION

Fes can be difficult to get to grips with, orientation-wise. The Medina in Fes is uniquely vast and beautiful, with two distinct parts: the newer section, **Fes el Djedid**, established in the thirteenth century, is mostly taken up by the Royal Palace; the older part, **Fes el Bali**, founded in the eighth century on the River Fes, was populated by refugees from Tunisia on one bank – the **Kairaouine quarter** – and from Spain on the other bank – the **Andalusian quarter**. In practice, almost everything you will want to see is in the Kairaouine quarter. There are several different gates through which you can enter the old city. **Bab Boujeloud** is the most popular and recognizable entry point and is a useful landmark. From here you can turn left at the *Restaurant La Kasbah* to get on to **Talâa Kabira**, the Medina's main thoroughfare. From the north, **Bab el Guissa** offers another port of entry. For **views** of the Medina have a drink at the *Hotel Palais Jamaï* (next to Bab Jamaï) or *Hotel les Merenides*. There's an impressive view from the Arms Museum in the fort above the bus station (daily except Mon 8.30am–6pm; 10dh).

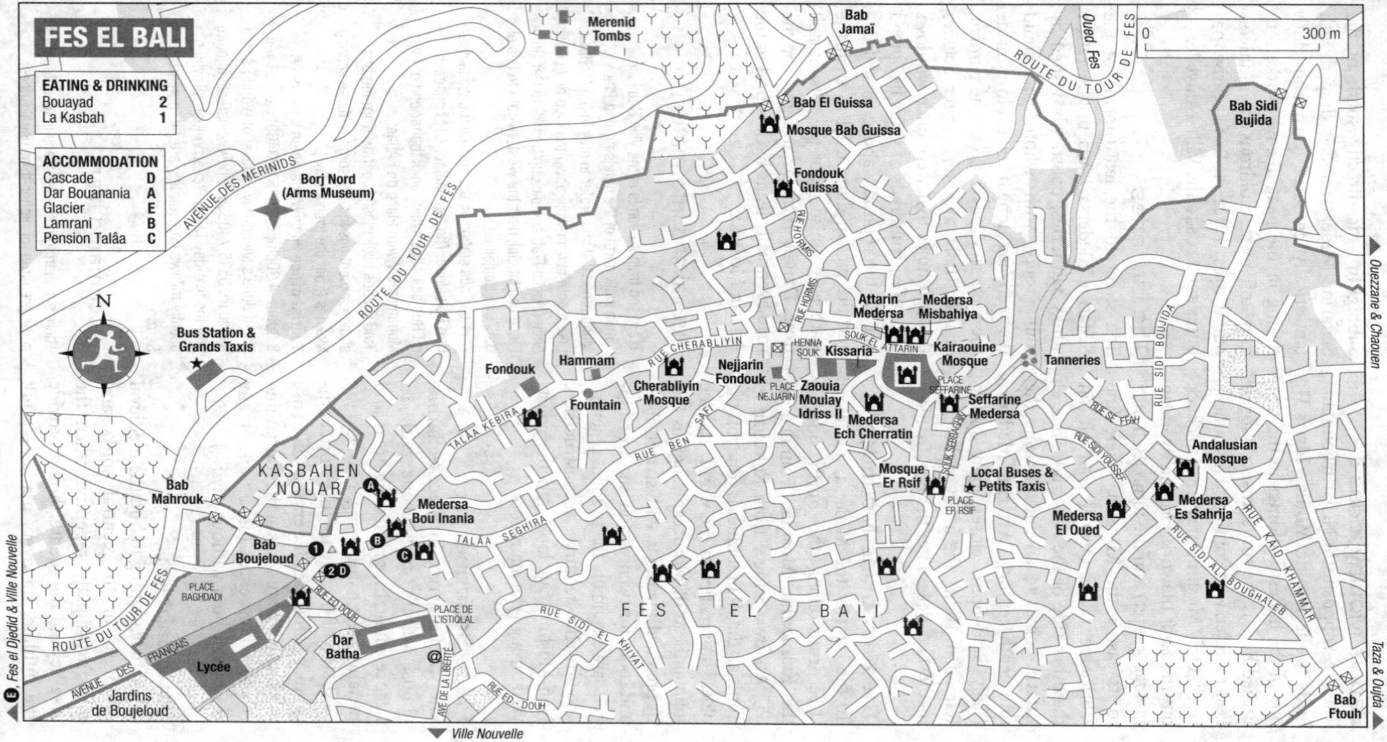

FES EL BALI

EATING & DRINKING

Bouayad	2
La Kasbah	1

ACCOMMODATION

Cascade	D
Dar Bouanania	A
Glacier	E
Lamrani	B
Pension Talâa	C

Merenid Tombs
Bab Jamaï
Bab El Guissa
Mosque Bab Guissa
Fondouk Guissa
Bab Sidi Bujida
Oued Fes
Route du Tour de Fes
Avenue des Merinids
Borj Nord (Arms Museum)
Bus Station & Grands Taxis
Rue Hormis
Attarin Medersa
Medersa Misbahiya
Souk el Attarin
Henna Souk
Kissaria
Kairaouine Mosque
Place Seffarine
Tanneries
Rue Sidi Boujida
Fondouk
Hammam
Rue Cherabliyin
Cherabliyin Mosque
Nejjarin Fondouk
Place Nejjarin
Zaouia Moulay Idriss II
Medersa Ech Cherratin
Seffarine Medersa
Fountain
Talâa Kebira
Rue Ben Safi
Rue Se Ffah
Rue Sidi Youssef
Andalusian Mosque
Souk Sebbaghine
Mosque Er Rsif
Place Er Rsif
Local Buses & Petits Taxis
Medersa Es Sahrija
Medersa El Oued
Rue Kaid Khammar
Rue Sidi Ali Boughaleb
Kasbahen Nouar
Bab Mahrouk
Medersa Bou Inania
Talâa Seghira
Bab Boujeloud
Place Baghdadi
Rue ed Douh
Place de l'Istiqlal
Fes el Bali
Rue Sidi el Khiyat
Dar Batha
Lycée
Avenue des Français
Jardins de Boujeloud
Ave de la Liberté
Rue Ed - Douh
Bab Ftouh
0 300 m
N
Ouezzane & Chaouen
Taza & Oujda
Ville Nouvelle
E, Fes el Djedid & Ville Nouvelle

Zaouia Moulay Idriss II

The street opposite the Nejjarin Fountain leads to the **Zaouia Moulay Idriss II**, one of the holiest buildings in the city. Buried here is the son and successor of Fes's founder, who continued his father's work. Only Muslims may enter to check out the *zellij* tilework, original wooden *minbar* (pulpit) and the tomb itself. Just to its east is the **Kissaria**, where fine fabrics are traded. Over to your left (on the other side of the Kissaria), Souk el Attarin comes to an end opposite the fourteenth-century **Attarin Medersa** (daily 9am–5pm; closes 4pm during Ramadan; 10dh), the finest of the city's medieval colleges after the Bou Inania.

The Kairaouine Mosque

To the right of the Medersa, a narrow street runs along the north side of the **Kairaouine Mosque**. Founded in 857 AD by a refugee from Kairouan in Tunisia, the Kairaouine is one of the oldest universities in the world, and the fountainhead of Moroccan religious life. Its present dimensions, with sixteen aisles and room for twenty thousand worshippers, are essentially the product of tenth- and twelfth-century reconstructions. Non-Muslims can look into the courtyard through the main door.

Place Seffarine

The street emerges in **Place Seffarine**, almost wilfully picturesque with its faience fountain, gnarled fig trees and metalworkers hammering away. On the west side of the square, the thirteenth-century **Seffarine Medersa** is still in use as a hostel for students at the Kairaouine (visitors may enter for a look at any reasonable hour without paying).

Souk Sabbighin

If you're beginning to find the medieval prettiness of the central *souks* and *medersas* slightly repetitive, then the area beyond the square should provide the antidote. The dyers' market – **Souk Sabbighin** – is directly south of the Seffarine Medersa, and is draped with fantastically coloured yarn and cloth drying in the heat. Below, workers in grey toil over cauldrons of multicoloured dyes. Place er Rsif, nearby, has buses and taxis to the Ville Nouvelle.

The tanneries

The street to the left (north) of the Seffarine Medersa leads to the rather stinky **tanneries**, constantly visited by tour groups with whom you could discreetly tag along if you get lost. Inside the tanneries (pay a tip to the *gardien*, usually 10dh, to enter), water deluges through holes that were once windows of houses. Hundreds of skins lie spread out on the rooftops, above vats of dye and the pigeon dung used to treat the leather, reminiscent of the pits of hell from Dante's *Inferno*. Straight on, the road eventually leads back round to the Attarin Medersa.

Arrival and information

Train The train station is in the Ville Nouvelle, 15min walk north of the hotels around Place Mohammed V. If you prefer to stay in the Medina, take a petit taxi, or walk down to Place de la Résistance (aka La Fiat) and pick up bus #9 to Dar Batha/ Place de l'Istiqlal, near the western gate to Fes el Bali, Bab Boujeloud.

Bus The bus station is just outside the walls near Bab Boujeloud. The terminal for CTM buses is off Rue de l'Atlas, which links the far end of Av Mohammed V with Place de l'Atlas.

Taxi Grands taxis mostly operate from the bus station; exceptions include some of those serving Meknes (from the train station).

Tourist office Place Mohammed V (Mon–Fri 8.30am–4.30pm; ⓣ0535 623460) can tell you about June's seven-day Festival of World Sacred Music (ⓣ0535 740535, ⓦwww.fesfestival.com) and the five-day Tadloui (cherry) festival which usually follows immediately after it in nearby Sefrou.

Accommodation

There's a shortage of hotel space in all categories, so be prepared for higher-than-usual prices;

Fes el Djedid & Fes el Bali ▲

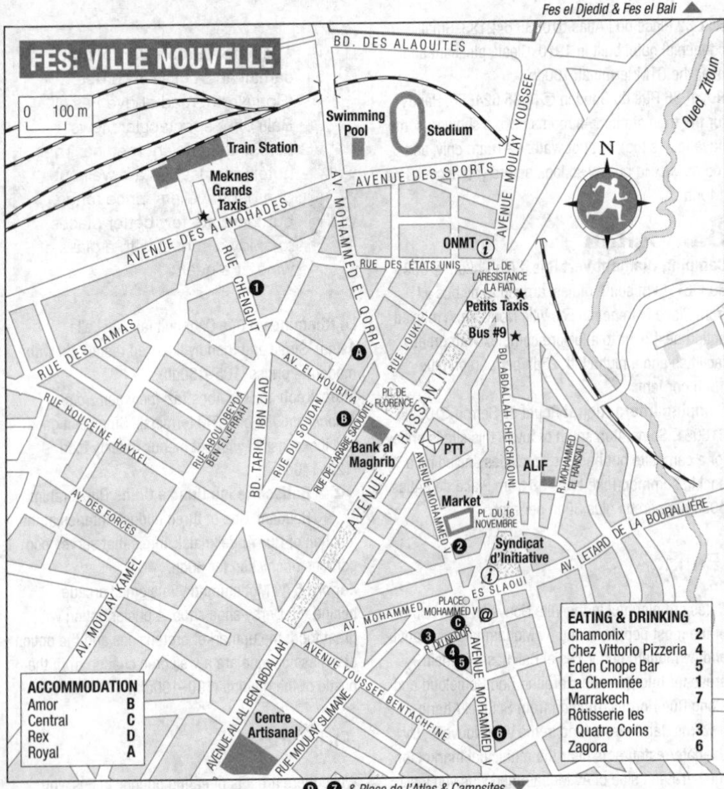

D, 7 & Place de l'Atlas & Campsites ▼

booking ahead is advisable. For atmosphere and character, the Medina is the place to be, though you'll need an easy-going attitude towards size and cleanliness. The less engaging Ville Nouvelle has a wider choice of hotels.

Hostel

HI hostel 18 Rue Abdeslam Seghrini ☎0535 624085. One of Morocco's best hostels – well kept, friendly and spotlessly clean. Dorms only; 55dh, breakfast included.

Medina hotels

Cascade Just inside Bab Boujeloud, Fes el-Bali ☎0535 638442. An old building, with a useful public *hammam* (bath house) behind. Small rooms, but clean and friendly. The fantastic view from the terrace, where you can drink if you bring your own, is the real draw. 150dh.

Dar Bouanania 21 Derb ben Salem (sign posted on Talâa Kebira) ☎0535 637282, Ⓔdarbouanania@gmail.com. Not quite a riad, but the budget equivalent, with spacious rooms and traditional decor for very reasonable prices. 300dh.

Glacier down an alley off Place des Alaouites, Fes el-Djedid ☎0535 626261. Best choice in Fes el Djedid, small rooms around an interior courtyard, shared hot showers. 80dh.

Lamrani Talâa Seghira, Fes el-Bali ☎0535 634411. Friendly with small but spotless rooms, mostly doubles, opposite a *hammam*. 150dh.

Pension Talâa 14 Talâa Seghira, Fes el Bali ☎0535 633359. A small place, slightly more comfortable than the other Medina cheapies. 150dh.

Ville Nouvelle hotels

Amor 31 Rue de l'Arabie Saoudite ☎0535 622724. One block from Av Hassan II, behind the Bank al-Maghrib. Comfortable though sombre rooms with good bathrooms but hot water evenings and early mornings only. 192dh.

Central 50 Rue Ibrahim Roudani ☎0535 622333. Clean and well furnished with inviting rooms and good prices – best in the Ville Nouvelle.180dh.

Rex 32 Place de l'Atlas ⓣ0535 642133. Small, congenial hotel built in 1910. Clean, pleasant and near the CTM terminal. 100dh.
Royal 36 Rue du Soudan ⓣ0535 624656. Handy for the train station. All rooms have a shower (some have toilets too), but hot water 6–10am only, and rooms vary in quality so look before you accept. 140dh.

Campsites

Camping Diamant Vert Rue d'Ain Chkeff ⓣ0535 608367. 6km south of Fes, arrived at by bus #17 from Place Florence in Fes Ville Nouvelle. A relaxed option next door to a leisure complex with great facilities and a nightclub. 25dh per person plus 15dh per tent.
Camping International Route de Sefrou ⓣ0535 618061. Some 4km south of town, this site is pricey for a campsite but has good facilities, including a pool in summer. Take bus #38 from Place de l'Atlas. 40dh per person plus 30dh per tent.

Eating

Cafés are plentiful in the Ville Nouvelle, with some of the most popular along Av Mohammed es Slaoui and Av Mohammed V. Fes el Bali has two main areas for budget eating: around Bab Boujeloud and along Rue Hormis (running from Souk el Attarin towards Bab Guissa), and in the Ville Nouvelle, try the café/restaurants near the municipal market, on the left-hand side of Av Mohammed V as you walk from the post office. Place Al Achabine, just south of Mosque Bab Guissa, is home to several good-quality, cheap Moroccan food stalls.

Fes el Bali

Bouayad inside Bab Boujeloud. Claims to be the oldest restaurant in the Medina. It serves decent meals at cheap prices (menu 70dh) with discounts if you are staying at *Hotel Cascade*.
La Kasbah inside Bab Boujeloud. Two terraces with views over Bab Boujeloud, not to mention great *pastilla* and delicious *tajines* (the prune and almond meat variety is particularly recommended). 55dh for main and drink, menu 77dh.

Ville Nouvelle

Chamonix 5 Rue Moukhtar Soussi, off Av Mohammed V. A reliable restaurant serving Moroccan and European dishes. Attracts a young crowd, and stays open late in summer (menu 65dh).
Chez Vittorio Pizzeria 21 Rue Ibrahim Roudani, nearly opposite *Hôtel Central*. Pizza and pasta; reliable and good value, but not very exciting (65–85dh).

TREAT YOURSELF

The hotels **Palais Jamaï** (Bab Jamaï) and **Les Merenides** (Borj North, road above Fes el Bali) offer spectacular views across the ancient medina. The hotels themselves are well out of most travellers' price range, but there are few better places to enjoy a sunset with a glass of wine or a beer.

La Cheminée 6 Rue Chenguit (aka Av Lalla Asma). Small and friendly licensed restaurant with moderate prices (105–130dh).
Marrakech 11 Rue Abes Tazi (between *Hôtel Mounia* and the old CTM terminal). Small, but good and inexpensive, with set menus of tasty food (120–140dh).
Rôtisserie les Quatre Coins Rue Ibrahim Roudani. One of three budget eateries at the junction of Rue Abdelkhalek Tomis that serve good portions of chicken for 60dh.
Zagora 5 Av Mohammed V in a small arcade, behind the Derby shoe shop. A pricier option with great food; the upmarket pretensions and the option of a glass of wine are a welcome change from the bustle of the medina (130–190dh).

Drinking

While there are lots of eating options in Fes, you have to look a little harder for bars. *Eden Chope Bar*, 55 Av Mohammed V, south of Place Mohammed V, with its 1930s mock-classical interior, does good bar snacks but is mainly male, or try the hotel bars.

Directory

Exchange BMCE, Place Mohammed V, Place de l'Atlas and Place Florence (all with ATMs).
Internet Cyber Club, corner of Av Mohammed V and Rue el Moujahid el Ayachi, opposite *Hôtel Central*; London Cyber and Cyber Didi, Place Batha nearly opposite the #9 bus stop.
Pharmacy Night pharmacy in the *baladiya* (town hall) on Av Moulay Yousef (daily 9.30pm–8.30am).
Police Commissariat Central is on Av Mohammed V behind the post office.
Post office Corner of avenues Mohammed V and Hassan II; also in Place Batha and Place des Alaouites.

Moving on

Train Casablanca Voyageurs (15 daily; 3hr 20min); Marrakesh (8 daily; 7hr 15min); Meknes (15 daily;

30min); Rabat (15 daily; 2hr 50min); Tangier (1 daily; 5hr 35min, plus 5 connecting services). **Bus** Casablanca (30 daily; 5hr 30min); Chefchaouen (7 daily; 5hr); Marrakesh (5 daily; 10hr); Meknes (approximately half-hourly; 1hr); Rabat (hourly; 4hr); Tangier (17 daily; 5hr 45min); Tetouan (14 daily; 5hr 20min).

RABAT

Often undervalued by tourists, Morocco's capital city, RABAT has a modern political centre (with elegant French architecture), several historical monuments, accessible bars and an ancient Kasbah overlooking a sandy beach. Though it should not take priority over Fes, Marrakesh or Chefchaouen, it is worth a visit if you have the time.

What to see and do

Rabat's compact **Medina** – the whole city until the French arrived in 1912 – is wedged on two sides by the sea and the river, on the others by the twelfth-century Almohad and fifteenth-century Andalusian walls. Laid out in a simple grid, its streets are very easy to navigate.

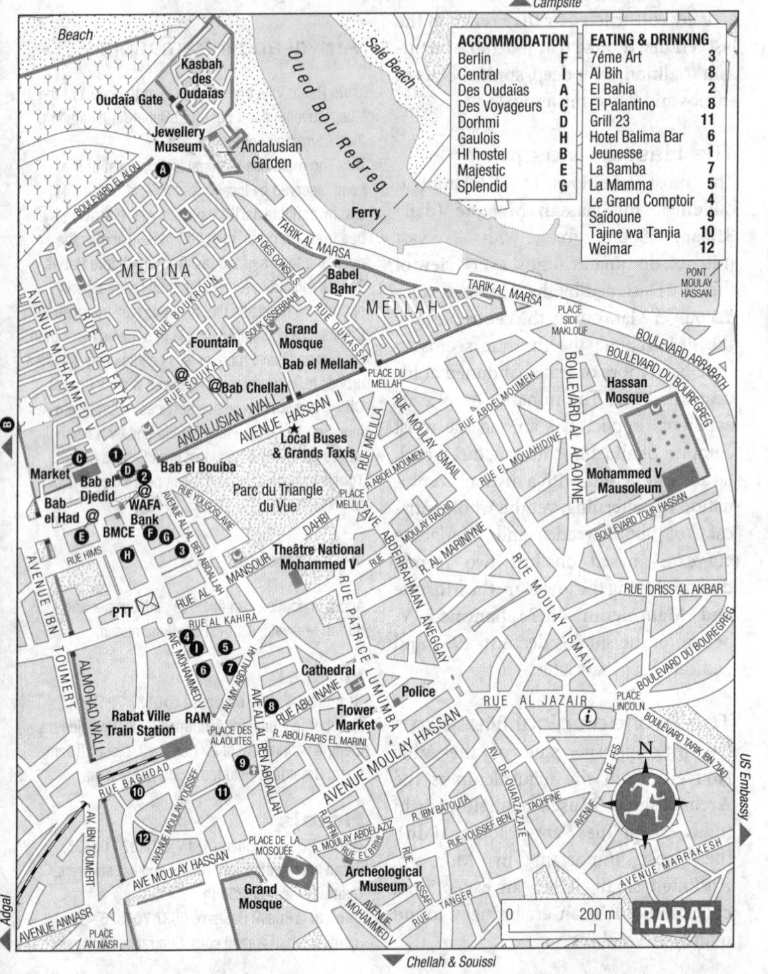

Kasbah des Oudaïas and around

North lies the **Kasbah des Oudaïas**, a charming and evocative quarter whose principal gateway – Bab el Kasbah or **Oudaïa Gate**, built around 1195 – is one of the most ornate in the Moorish world. Its interior is now used for art exhibitions. Down the steps outside the gate, a lower, horseshoe arch leads directly to **Moulay Ismail's Palace** (daily except Tues 9am–4pm; 10dh), which hosts quite an interesting Jewellery Museum. The adjoining **Andalusian Garden** – one of the most delightful spots in the city – was actually constructed by the French in the last century, though true to Arab Andalusian tradition, with deep, sunken beds of shrubs and flowering annuals.

The Hassan Mosque

The most ambitious of all Almohad buildings, the **Hassan Mosque** (daily 8.30am–6.30pm; free), with its vast minaret, dominates almost every view of the city. Designed by the Almohad ruler Yacoub el Mansour as the centrepiece of the new capital, the mosque seems to have been more or less abandoned at his death in 1199. The minaret, despite its apparent simplicity, is among the most complex of all Almohad structures: each facade is different, with a distinct combination of patterning, yet the whole intricacy of blind arcades and interlacing curves is based on just two formal designs. Facing the tower are the **Mosque and Mausoleum of Mohammed V**, begun on the sultan's death in 1961 and dedicated six years later.

The Archeological Museum

On the opposite side of the Ville Nouvelle from the mausoleum is the **Archeological Museum** on Rue Brihi (daily except Tues 9am–4.30pm; 10dh), the most important in Morocco. Although small, it has an exceptional collection of Roman-era bronzes, found mainly at Volubilis.

Chellah

The royal burial ground, called **Chellah** (daily 8am–6pm; 10dh), is a startling sight as you emerge from the long avenues of the Ville Nouvelle, with its circuit of fourteenth-century walls, legacy of **Abou el Hassan** (1331–51), the greatest of the Merenid rulers. Off to the left of the main gate are the partly excavated ruins of the Roman city that preceded the necropolis. A set of Islamic ruins are further down to the right, situated within a second inner sanctuary, approached along a broad path through half-wild gardens.

Arrival and information

Train Rabat Ville train station is at the heart of the Ville Nouvelle; don't get off at Rabat Agdal station, 2km from the centre.

Bus The main bus terminal is 3km west of the centre, served by local buses #17, #30 and #41, and by petits taxis. It's easier, if you're arriving by bus from the north, to get off in Salé across the river, and take a grand taxi from there into Rabat.

Taxi Grands taxis for most intercity destinations operate from outside the main bus station; those to Casablanca cost only a couple of dirhams more than the bus and leave more or less continuously. Meknes grands taxis run from Av Hassan II with Av Chellah.

City transport Local bus services radiate from Av Allal Ben Abdallah, Place Melilla and Av Hassan II, where petits taxis and local grands taxis gather.

Tourist office 22 Rue d'Alger, near Place Lincoln Ⓣ0537 660663.

Accommodation

Accommodation can fill up in midsummer and during festivals; it's best to phone ahead.

Hostel

HI hostel 43 Rue Marrassa Ⓣ0537 725769, Ⓔauberge.jeunes.rbt@hotmail.fr. Just outside the Medina walls north of Av Hassan II. Closed 10am–noon. Breakfast included. 65dh per person.

Hotels

Berlin 261 Av Mohammed V Ⓣ0537 703435. Small hotel with bright rooms and hot showers. Centrally located. 250dh.

Central 2 Rue Al Basra Ⓣ0537 707356, Ⓔhotel.central.rabat@gmail.com. Central position near

train station. A good budget choice and, with 34 rooms, likely to have space. 130dh.

Des Oudaïas 132 Bd el Alou ⓣ0537 264043. The closest hotel to the Kasbah, with comfortable and spacious rooms. The salon downstairs adds character. 200dh.

Des Voyageurs 8 Souk Semarine, near Bab Djedid (no phone). Inexpensive, popular and often full. Clean, airy rooms but no showers. 90dh

Dorhmi 313 Av Mohammed V, just inside Bab Djedid ⓣ0537 723898. Above *Café Essalem* and Banque Populaire. Well furnished and maintained. 130dh.

Gaulois 1 Rue Hims (corner of Av Mohammed V) ⓣ0537 723022. Two-star with grand entrance and decent rooms, some en suite. Pricier than other options if the cheap rooms have gone, but can be excellent value for money. 190dh.

Majestic 121 Av Hassan II ⓣ0537 722997, ⓦwww.hotel.majestic.ma. Popular and good value, with bright, spotless rooms, some overlooking the Medina. 348dh.

Splendid 8 Rue Ghazza ⓣ0537 723283. Nice place whose best rooms overlook a courtyard, but hot water evenings only. Café-restaurant *Ghazza* opposite is good for breakfast. 191dh.

Eating

Rabat has a wide range of good restaurants serving both Moroccan and international dishes. The cheapest ones are in the Medina.

7éme Art Av Allal Ben Abdallah. Cheap popular and trendy café serving hamburgers, salads and grilled meats in a garden area (30–60dh).

Al Bih 41 Av Ben Abdallah. Small and affordable restaurant, close to Ville station with decent Lebanese food (25–50dh).

El Bahia Av Hassan II, built into the Andalusian wall, near the junction with Av Mohammed V. Reasonably priced *tajines*, kebabs and salads, in a pleasant courtyard, upstairs or on the pavement outside, though service can be slow (70–90dh).

Grill 23 386 Av Mohammed V. Cheap but delicious *shwarma*, hamburgers and big salads. Convenient for a take-away to carry with you on a train journey (it's just up the street from the station), though there's a nice seating area too (35–50dh).

Jeunesse 305 Av Mohammed V, Medina. One of the city's best budget restaurants, with generous portions of couscous, and decent *tajines* (25–35dh).

La Bamba 3 Rue Tanta, behind the *Hôtel Balima*. European and Moroccan dishes, with good-value set menus (80dh European, 110dh Moroccan). Licensed.

TREAT YOURSELF

Le Grand Comptoir 279 Av Mohammed V ⓦwww.legrandcomptoir.ma. Very classy Parisian-style brasserie with wonderful 1920s-style decor and live music that ranges from jazz to traditional Moroccan. Serves excellent meat and seafood dishes and a decent selection of wines. A meal with wine will set you back 250–300dh.

La Mamma 6 Rue Tanta, behind the *Hôtel Balima*. Good pizzas and pasta dishes (50–65dh). *La Dolce Vita*, next door, is owned by the same patron and serves up luscious Italian-style ice cream for afters.

Saïdoune in the mall at 467 Av Mohammed V, opposite the *Hôtel Terminus*. A good Lebanese restaurant run by an Iraqi; licensed, but closed Friday lunchtime. Menu 55dh.

Tajine wa Tanjia 9 Rue Baghdad. A lovely little place with a wide range of excellent *tajines* and *tanjia* (jugged beef or lamb) for around 70–95dh.

Weimar 7 Rue Sana'a inside the Goethe Institute. Considered by some expats to serve the best food in Rabat; you can choose from a range of pastas, meats and salads accompanied by German wine and beer. Expect to spend around 120dh plus drinks.

Drinking and nightlife

Avenues Mohammed V and Allal Ben Abdallah have some good cafés, but the best bars are situated in Agdal, a bit of a trek from the centre. Late-night options include a string of disco-bars around Place de Melilla and on Rue Patrice Lumumba.

El Palantino Av Allal Ben Abdallah. Great, atmospheric Spanish-style bar with happy hour 6.30–7.30pm. Offers a range of meals, but the tapas (35–40dh, selection 115–135dh) are especially good value, filling and very tasty.

Hotel Balima Bar Av Mohammed V. This bar is conveniently located in the centre of town and has a terrace overlooking the Parliament but it closes at 10pm.

Directory

Embassies Australia represented by Canada; Canada, 13bis Rue Jaâfar as Sadiq, Agdal ⓣ0537 687400; New Zealand represented by the UK; UK, 28 Av SAR Sidi Mohammed, Souissi ⓣ0537 633333; USA, 2 Av Mohammed el Fassi

(Av Marrakech) ☎0537 762265. Irish citizens covered by their embassy in Lisbon (☎00-351-1/396 9440), but have an honorary consul in Casablanca (☎0522 660366).
Exchange Along Av Allal Ben Abdallah and Av Mohammed V. BMCE and Wafa Bank at the northern end of Av Mohammed V have bureaux de change open weekdays till 8pm and on Saturday mornings.
Internet Cheapest places are on or off Rue Souika in the Medina; others include sacar@.net, 83 Av Hassan II; Phobos, 113 Av Hassan II, by *Hôtel Majestic*.
Police Av Tripoli, near the Cathedral. Police post at Bab Djedid and north end of Rue des Consuls.
Post office Halfway down Av Mohammed V.

Moving on

Train Casablanca Port (half-hourly 6.30am–9pm; 1hr); Casablanca Voyageurs (14 daily; 1hr); Fes (15 daily; 3hr); Marrakesh (9 daily; 4hr 20min); Meknes (14 daily; 2hr); Tangier (4 daily; 4hr 40min).
Bus Casablanca (frequent; 1hr 20min); Essaouira (13 daily; 7hr 30min); Fes (hourly; 4hr); Marrakesh (hourly; 5hr 30min); Meknes (hourly; 3hr); Salé (frequent; 15min); Tangier (39 daily; 5hr).

CASABLANCA

Morocco's main city and economic capital, **CASABLANCA** (or "Casa") is

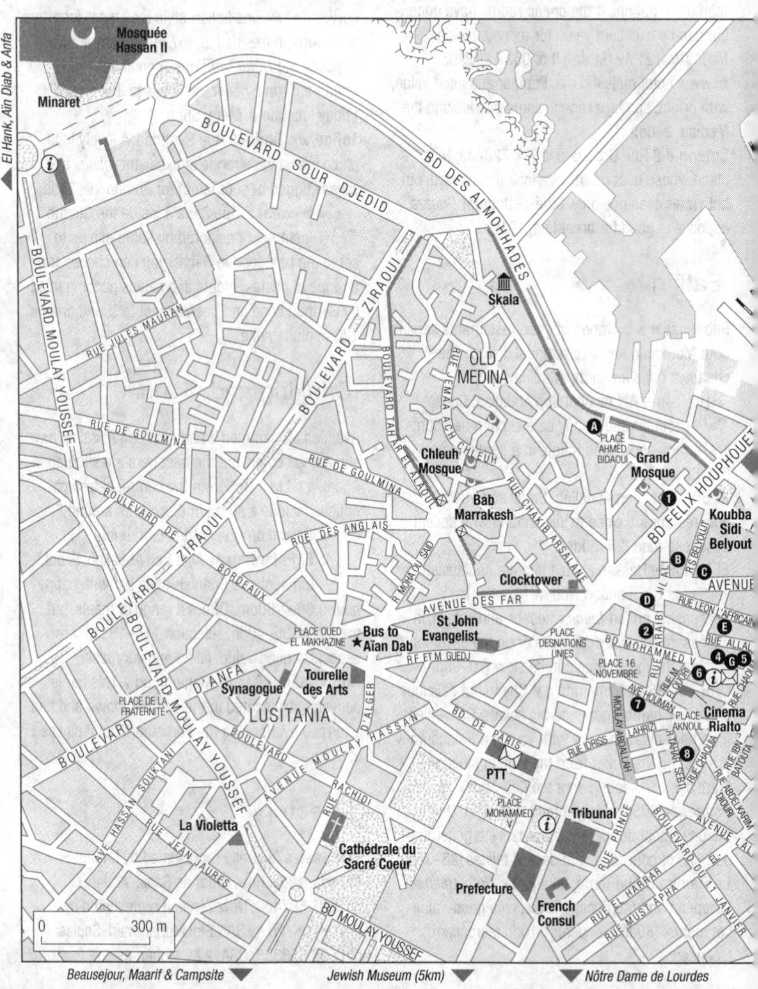

also North Africa's largest port. Casa's Westernized image does not fit with most travellers' stereotype of Morocco but the city offers good food, beaches and decent shopping.

What to see and do

Casablanca's **Medina**, above the port and recently gentrified, is largely the product of the late nineteenth century, when Casa began its modest growth as a commercial centre. Film buffs will be disappointed to learn that Bogart's *Casablanca* wasn't shot here (it was filmed entirely in Hollywood) – *Rick's Bar* (expensive) commemorates it as a gimmick at 248 Boulevard Sour Jedid.

Grande Mosquée Hassan II

The city's main monument, the **Grande Mosquée Hassan II** (tours daily except Fri 9am, 10am, 11am, & 2pm in winter, 2.30pm in summer, Fri 9am & 2pm/2.30pm; 120dh, students 60dh), opened in 1993, is the world's second

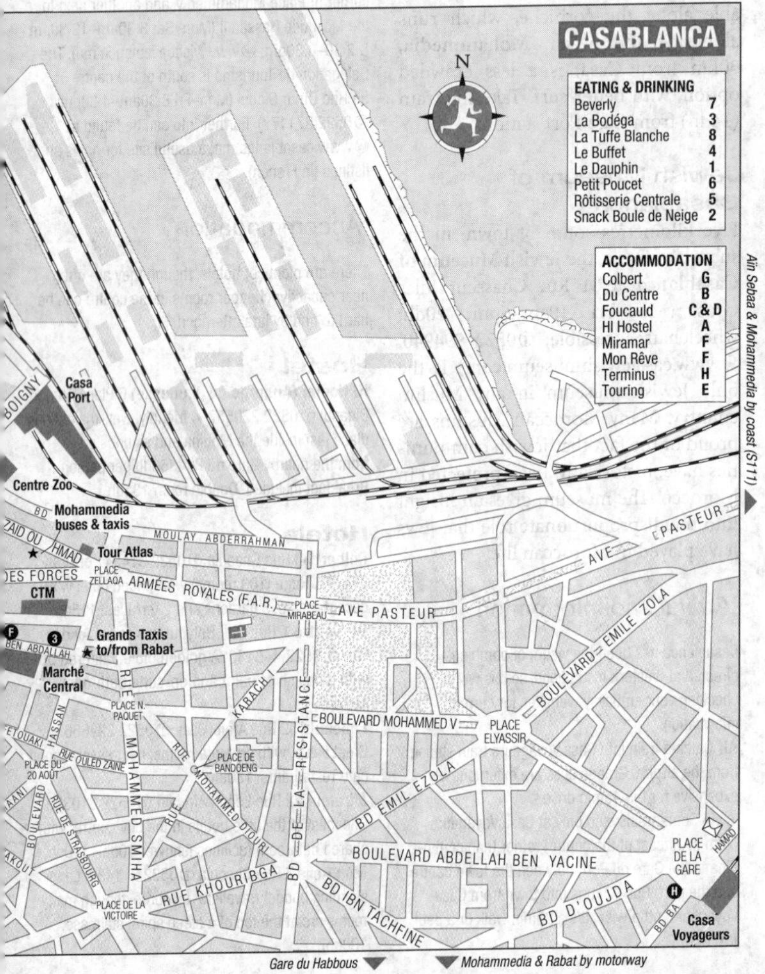

largest mosque, with space for one hundred thousand worshippers, and a minaret that soars to a record 200m. Commissioned by the last king, who named it after himself, it cost an estimated £320m/US$500m, raised by not wholly voluntary public subscription. It's a twenty-minute walk northwest from the centre.

The beaches

The **Ain Diab beach**, to the west of Mosque Hassan II, is one of Morocco's best easily accessible beaches. Surf lessons and equipment are readily available along the corniche, which runs alongside the beach. **Mohammedia**, 30km from Casa, is a less crowded option, with better surf. Take the train (14dh) from Casa Port station.

Jewish Museum of Casablanca

Five kilometres south of town, in the suburb of Oasis, the **Jewish Museum of Casablanca** at 81 Rue Chasseur Jules Gros (Mon–Fri 10am–6pm; 20dh; wheelchair accessible; ⓣ0522 994940, ⓦwww.casajewishmuseum.com) is the only Jewish museum in any Muslim country. Many Moroccan Muslims are proud of the fact that Jewish communities have, historically, been protected in Morocco. The museum gives an insight into the disproportionate role that Jews have played in Moroccan life.

Arrival and information

Casablanca has been the victim of bombings directed at Western institutions, so it is worth checking your embassy websites for current information.

Air Catch a train into Casa Voyageurs train station from the airport. Grands taxis are extortionately expensive for the 45min drive.

Train Some trains stop only at Casa Voyageurs (2km southeast of the centre) rather than continuing to the Gare du Port, between the town centre and the port. Bus #2 runs into town from Casa Voyageurs; otherwise, it's a 20min walk or a petit taxi ride.

Bus Take the CTM if possible as it drops you downtown on Rue Léon l'Africain, behind *Hôtel Safir* on Av des FAR; other buses arrive at the bus station (Gare du Habbous) southeast of town on Route des Ouled Ziane.

Taxi Most grands taxis arrive at the bus station; some from Rabat arrive a block east of the CTM terminal; those from Essaouira come into a station south of the centre on Bd Brahim Roudani in Maarif.

Tourist office The best information office is the Syndicat d'Initiative at 98 Bd Mohammed V (Mon–Fri 8.30am–4.30pm, Sat 8.30am–noon; ⓣ0522 221524), where you can also arrange a three-hour guided tour by car for 450dh. The Conseil Regional du Tourisme has a kiosk in the corner of Place Mohammed V, and another next to the Mosquée Hassan II (Mon–Sat 8.30am–12.30pm & 2.30–6.30pm; ⓦwww.visitcasablanca.ma). The Delegation de Tourisme is south of the centre at 55 Rue Omar Slaoui (Mon–Fri 8.30am–4.30pm; ⓣ0522 271177). Further info can be found at ⓦwww.casablanca.ma, a useful site for news and listings (in French).

Accommodation

There are plenty of hotels, though they are often near capacity; cheaper rooms in the centre can be hard to find by late afternoon.

Hostel

HI Hostel (Auberge de Jeunesse) 6 Place Ahmed Bidaoui ⓣ0522 220557. A friendly, well-maintained place just inside the Medina and signposted from the nearby Gare du Port (60dh per person). Breakfast included. Double room 135dh.

Hotels

Colbert 38 Rue Chaouia ⓣ0522 314241 or 0522 314711. Huge (103 rooms) well-priced hotel with decent rooms, 3 gardens and 2 terraces. 115dh.

Du Centre 1 Rue Sidi Belyout, corner of Av des FAR ⓣ0522 446180. A golden oldie, cheered up with a splash of paint and en-suite bathrooms. 194dh.

Foucauld 52 Rue Araibi Jilali ⓣ0522 222666. Great value, with en-suite rooms, near several good café/restaurants. 130dh.

Miramar 22 Rue León l'Africain ⓣ0522 310308. Cheapest of the little hotels in the city centre, with shared bathroom facilities (shower 10dh). 110dh.

Mon Rêve 7 Rue Chaouia ⓣ0522 311439. Long-standing budget travellers' favourite, though many rooms are at the top of a steep spiral staircase. 130dh].

Terminus 184 Bd Ba Hamad ⓣ0522 240025. Handy for Casa Voyageurs: clean, decent rooms with shared hot showers. 190dh.

Touring 87 Rue Allal Ben Abdallah ⓣ0522 310216. Refurbished old French hotel that's friendly and excellent value; the best option in an area of cheap hotels. 130dh.

Campsite

Camping Oasis Dar Bouazza, Route d'Azzour, 18km from town ⓣ0522 290767. A new campsite, run by the Syndicat d'Initiative, but rather a long way from town. 30dh per person and a tent.

Eating and drinking

Casa has the reputation of being the best place to eat in Morocco, and if you can afford the fancier restaurant prices, this is certainly true. For those on a budget, head for the smaller streets off Bd Mohammed V and in the central *marché*, where it is possible to bring fish for the outdoor restaurants to cook for you.

Beverly 6 Av Houman El Fetwaki. A cheap place to pick up filling food on the go; popular with locals (20–40dh).

La Bodéga 127 Rue Allal Ben Abdallah ⓣ0522 541842, ⓦwww.bodega.ma. Lively restaurant with a good selection of Spanish cuisine (70–100dh). The atmosphere is enhanced by a downstairs bar and dancefloor.

La Tuffe Blanche 57 Tahar Sebti. One of the few remaining Jewish eating places, serving kosher dishes and alcohol for about 80–120dh a head.

Le Buffet 99 Bd Mohammed V. Quick, bright and popular, with a reasonable 65dh *menu du jour*.

Le Dauphin 115 Bd Felix Houphouët Boigny ⓣ0522 221200. One of Casa's most famous and popular restaurants, with great seafood served in the restaurant and bonhomie dished up in the cramped bar. Worth queuing for; main dishes 45–95dh, menu 115dh.

Petit Poucet 86 Bd Mohammed V. 1920s-Parisian-style restaurant with a reasonably priced menu (70–100dh). Next door there is a much cheaper snack bar – one of the best places in town for serious drinking.

Rôtisserie Centrale 36 Rue Chaouia. Best of a bunch of cheap chicken-on-a-spit joints on this little stretch of road opposite the Marché Central. *Snack Amine Adam*, next door, is a good cheap fish option.

Snack Boule de Neige 72 Rue Araibi Jilali. Tasty, cheap dishes including chicken, liver, *shwarma*, and, on Fridays, couscous (30dh).

Shopping

There is an unusually large selection of high street stores in the Maarif quarter. While the old medina is a bit down at heel, it has some charm and is a great place to pick up practical and cheap Moroccan and Western goods. The Harbous area offers hassle-free shopping for Moroccan textiles and artisan work in beautifully fresh and well-proportioned arcades.

Moving on

Train (Port station) to: Rabat (half-hourly 6.30am–8.30pm; 1hr).

Train (Voyageurs station) to: Fes (15 daily; 3hr 55min); Marrakesh (9 daily; 3hr 15min); Meknes (14 daily; 3hr 15min); Mohammed V airport (hourly 6am–10pm; 35min); Rabat (19 daily; 1hr); Tangier (4 daily; 5hr 40min).

Bus to: Essaouira (26 daily; 6hr); Fes (28 daily; 5hr 30min); Marrakesh (every 30min; 4hr); Meknes (16 daily; 4hr); Rabat (frequent; 1hr 20min); Tangier (41 daily; 6hr); Tetouan (31 daily; 6hr 30min);

Southern Morocco

MARRAKESH

MARRAKESH (Marrakech in French) is a city of immense beauty, low, pink and tent-like before a great range of mountains. It's an immediately exciting place, especially its ancient Medina. Marrakesh's population is growing and it has a thriving industrial area; the city remains the most important market and administrative centre in southern Morocco.

What to see and do

The Djemaa el Fna is at the heart of the city, with most things of interest emanating from it. There are many cheap hotels and pensions nearby so it's worth going straight there. To the north

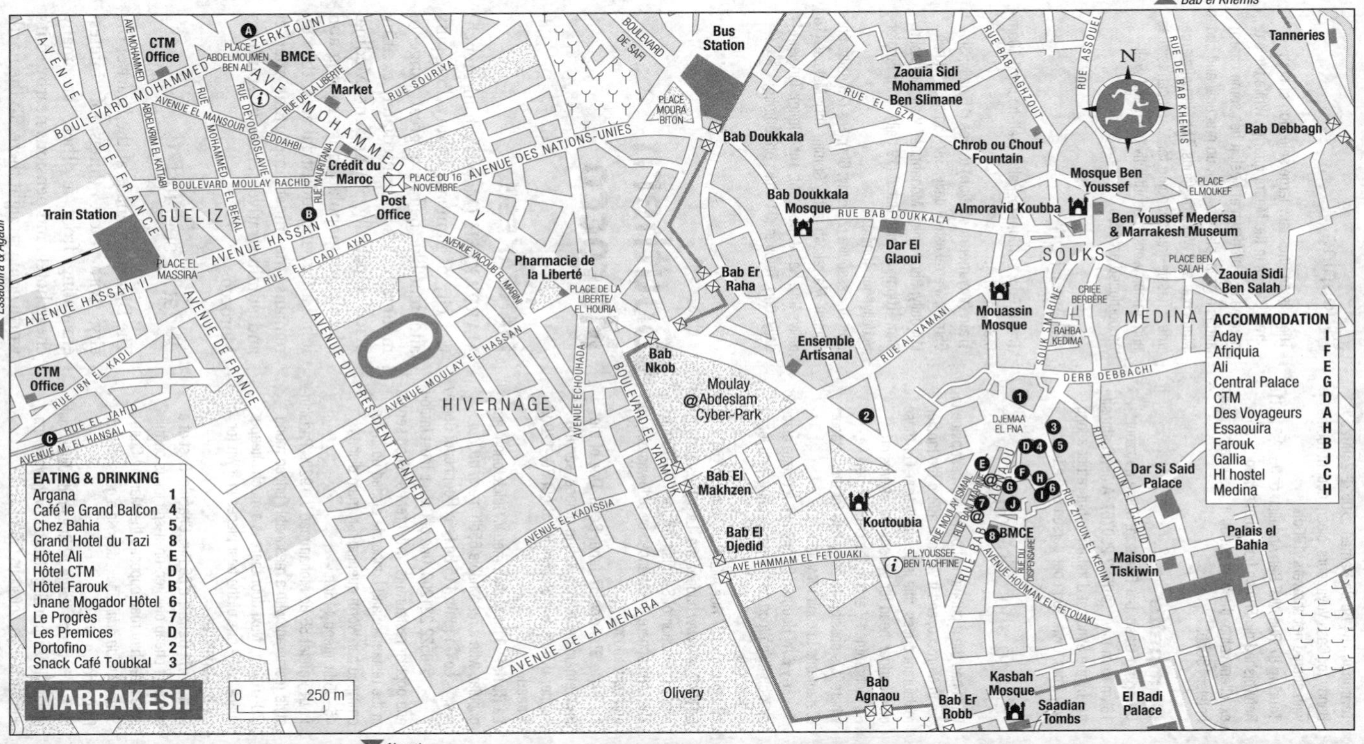
MARRAKESH
EATING & DRINKING
Argana 1
Café le Grand Balcon 4
Chez Bahia 5
Grand Hotel du Tazi 8
Hôtel Ali E
Hôtel CTM D
Hôtel Farouk B
Jnane Mogador Hôtel 6
Le Progrès 7
Les Premices D
Portofino 2
Snack Café Toubkal 3
ACCOMMODATION
Aday I
Afriquia F
Ali E
Central Palace G
CTM D
Des Voyageurs A
Essaouira H
Farouk B
Gallia J
HI hostel C
Medina H
0 250 m
Bab el Khemis
Essaouira & Agadir
Airport
GUELIZ
HIVERNAGE
MEDINA
SOUKS
Train Station
CTM Office
BMCE
Market
Crédit du Maroc
Post Office
Pharmacie de la Liberté
Bus Station
Bab Doukkala
Bab Doukkala Mosque
Bab Er Raha
Bab Nkob
Moulay @Abdeslam Cyber-Park
Bab El Makhzen
Bab El Djedid
Olivery
Bab Agnaou
Bab Er Robb
Kasbah Mosque
Saadian Tombs
El Badi Palace
Maison Tiskiwin
Palais el Bahia
Dar Si Said Palace
Koutoubia
Ensemble Artisanal
Dar El Glaoui
Mouassin Mosque
Zaouia Sidi Mohammed Ben Slimane
Chrob ou Chouf Fountain
Almoravid Koubba
Mosque Ben Youssef
Ben Youssef Medersa & Marrakesh Museum
Zaouia Sidi Ben Salah
Bab Debbagh
Tanneries
DJEMAA EL FNA
CRIEE BERBERE
RAHBA KEDIMA
PLACE ZERKTOUNI
PLACE ABDELMOUMEN BEN ALI
PLACE DU 16 NOVEMBRE
PLACE EL MASSIRA
PLACE DE LA LIBERTE/ EL HOURIA
PLACE MOURA BITON
PLACE ELMOUKEF
PLACE BEN SALAH
PL.YOUSSEF BEN TACHFINE
AVENUE DE FRANCE
BOULEVARD MOHAMMED V
AVE MOHAMMED V
AVE MOHAMMED ABDELKRIM EL KATTABI
AVENUE EL MANSOUR
RUE MOHAMMED EL BEKAL
RUE DEYOUGOSLAVIE
RUE DE LA LIBERTE
EDDAHBI
RUE MAURITANIA
BOULEVARD MOULAY RACHID
RUE SOURIYA
BOULEVARD DE SAFI
AVENUE DES NATIONS-UNIES
AVENUE HASSAN II
RUE EL CADI AYAD
AVENUE YACOUB EL MARINI
AVENUE MOULAY EL HASSAN
AVENUE DU PRESIDENT KENNEDY
RUE IBN EL KADI
RUE EL JAHID
AVENUE M. EL HANSALI
AVENUE ECHOUHADA
BOULEVARD EL YARMOUK
AVENUE EL KADISSIA
AVENUE DE LA MENARA
AVE HAMMAM EL FETOUAKI
RUE AL YAMANI
RUE BAB DOUKKALA
RUE EL GZA
RUE BAB TAGHZOUT
RUE ASSOUEL
RUE DE BAB KHEMIS
SOUK SMARINE
DERB DEBBACHI
RUE ZITOUN EL DJEDID
RUE ZITOUN EL KEDIM
RUE MOULAY ISMAIL
RUE BANI MARINE
RUE BAB AGNAOU
RUE DU DISPENSAIRE
AVENUE HOUMAN EL FETOUAKI
N

of the Djemaa are the famous souks of Marrakesh, where you can spend hours getting lost and picking up bargains. Just to the west is the great minaret of the Koutoubia mosque. This towers over the start of Avenue Mohammed V, which connects the Medina to Gueliz, where you can find the train station, CTM and tourist information as well as some modern cafés, supermarkets and bars. It's a fairly long walk between Gueliz and the Medina, but there are plenty of taxis and the regular buses #1 and #16 between the two. Further west of the Koutoubia, just past Bab Djedid, there is a district of opulent hotels with fantastic, if pricey, bars. For current information on Marrakesh visit Ⓦwww.ilove-marrakech.com.

Djemaa el Fna

There's nowhere in the world like the **Djemaa el Fna**: by day it's basically a market, with a few snake charmers and an occasional troupe of acrobats; in the late afternoon it becomes a whole carnival of musicians, storytellers and other entertainers; and in the evening dozens of stalls set up to dispense hot food to crowds of locals, while the musicians and performers continue. If you get tired of the spectacle, or if things slow down, you can move over to the rooftop terraces of the *Restaurant Argana* or the *Grand Balcon* to gaze at it all from above.

The Koutoubia

The absence of any architectural feature in the Djemaa serves to emphasize the drama of the **Koutoubia Minaret**. Nearly 70m high and visible for miles, it was begun shortly after the Almohad conquest of the city, around 1150, and displays many features that were to become widespread in Moroccan architecture – the wide band of ceramic inlay, the pyramid-shaped merlons, and the alternation of patterning on the facades.

The northern Medina

Just before the red ochre arch at its end, Souk Smarine (an important Medina thoroughfare) narrows and you get a glimpse through the passageways to its right of the **Rahba Kedima**, a small and fairly ramshackle square whose most interesting features are its apothecary stalls. At the end of Rahba Kedima, a passageway to the left gives access to another, smaller square – a bustling, carpet-draped area known as **La Criée Berbère**, which is where slave auctions used to be held.

Cutting back to **Souk el Kebir**, which by now has taken over from the Smarine, you emerge at the **kissarias**, the covered markets at the heart of the souks. Kissarias traditionally sell more expensive products, which today means a predominance of Western designs and imports. Off to their right is **Souk des Bijoutiers**, a modest jewellers' lane, while at the north end is a convoluted web of alleys comprising the **Souk Cherratin**, essentially a leatherworkers' market.

The Ben Youssef Medersa

If you bear left through this area and then turn right, you should arrive at the open space in front of the Ben Youssef Mosque. The originally fourteenth-century **Ben Youssef Medersa** (daily 9am–6pm; 50dh; combined ticket for this, the Marrakesh Museum and Almoravid Koubba 60dh) – the annexe for students taking courses in the mosque – stands off a side street just to the east. It was almost completely rebuilt in the sixteenth century under the Saadians, with a strong Andalusian influence. Parts have exact parallels in the Alhambra Palace in Granada, and it seems likely that Muslim Spanish architects were employed in its construction.

The Marrakesh Museum and Almoravid Koubba

Next door to the Medersa is the **Marrakesh Museum** (daily 9am–6.30pm;

40dh; combined ticket 60dh), which exhibits jewellery, art and sculpture, both old and new, in a beautifully restored nineteenth-century palace. Almost facing it, just south of the Ben Youssef Mosque, the small **Almoravid Koubba** (daily 9am–6pm; same ticket as Marrakesh Museum) is easy to pass by, but it is the only building in the whole of Morocco from the eleventh-century Almoravid dynasty still intact. The motifs you've just seen in the medersa – the pine cones, palms and acanthus leaves – were all carved here first.

If you're keen to buy items in the souks, you should study the more-or-less fixed prices of the range of crafts in the excellent **Ensemble Artisanal** (Mon–Sat 8.30am–7pm, Sun 9am–1pm), just inside the ramparts on Av Mohammed V.

The Saadian Tombs

Sealed up by Moulay Ismail after he had destroyed the adjoining El Badi Palace, the sixteenth-century **Saadian Tombs** (daily except Fri 8.30–11.45am & 2.30–5.45pm, Fri 8.30–11.30am & 2.45–5.45pm; 10dh), accessed by a narrow alley near the Kasbah Mosque, lay half-ruined and half-forgotten for centuries but are now restored to their full glory. There are two main mausoleums in the enclosure. The finer is on the left as you come in, a beautiful group of three rooms built to house El Mansour's own tomb and completed within his lifetime. The tombs of over a hundred more Saadian princes and royal household members are scattered around the garden and courtyard, their gravestones likewise brilliantly tiled and often elaborately inscribed.

El Badi Palace

Though substantially in ruins, enough remains of Ahmed el Mansour's **El Badi Palace** (daily 8.30–11.45am & 2.30–5.45pm; 10dh) to suggest that its name – "The Incomparable" – was not entirely immodest. It took a later ruler, Moulay Ismail, over ten years of systematic work to strip the palace of everything movable or of value and, even so, there's a lingering sense of luxury. What you see today is essentially the ceremonial part of the palace complex, planned for the reception of ambassadors. To the rear extends the central court, over 130m long and nearly as wide, and built on a substructure of vaults in order to allow the circulation of water through the pools and gardens. In the southwest corner of the complex is the original (and, in its day, much celebrated) *minbar* (pulpit) from the Koutoubia mosque (admission is an extra 10dh, payable at the main gate).

Rue Zitoun el Djedid

Heading north from El Badi Palace, **Rue Zitoun el Djedid** leads back to the Djemaa, flanked by various nineteenth-century mansions. Many of these have been converted into carpet shops or tourist restaurants, but one of them has been kept as a museum, the **Palais El Bahia** (daily except Fri 8.45–11.45am & 2.45–5.45pm, Fri 8.45–11.30am & 3–5.45pm; 10dh), former residence of a grand vizier. The name of the building means "The Brilliance", an exaggeration perhaps, but it's a beautiful old palace with two lovely patio gardens and some classic painted wooden ceilings. Also on this route is the **Dar Si Said** palace, which houses the **Museum of Moroccan Arts** (daily except Tues 9am–11.45pm & 2.30–5.45pm; 10dh). A further superb collection of Moroccan and Saharan artefacts is housed in the **Maison Tiskiwin** (daily 9.30am–12.30pm & 2.30–5.30pm; 20dh), which lies between the El Bahia and Dar Si Said palaces at 8 Rue de la Bahia.

Mount Toubkal

Imlil, the setting-off point for trekkers wanting to climb the second highest peak in Africa, is within 2–3 hours' grand taxi drive of Marrakesh (30dh for

a place, usually changing taxis at Asni; 180dh to charter the taxi one-way). Most trekkers set out early to mid-morning from Imlil to stay the night at the Toubkal refuge (5–6hr), which gets crowded in summer. It's best to start from here at first light the next morning in order to get the clearest possible panorama from Toubkal's heights (afternoons can be cloudy). The ascent is not difficult if you are fit, but it can be very cold.

Arrival and information

Air The airport, 4km southwest, is served by bus #19 (every half-hour) – petits taxis (80dh by day, 120dh by night) are a more convenient option.

Train From the train station, west of Gueliz, cross Avenue Hassan II and take bus #3/#4/#8/#10/#14/#66 or a petit taxi (10–15dh) for Place Foucauld by the Djemaa.

Bus The bus terminal is just outside the north-western walls of the Medina by Bab Doukkala; from here it's a 20 min walk to the Djemaa, or take bus #3/#4/#5/#8/#10/#14/#16/#17/#26/#66 (opposite Bab Doukkala), or a petit taxi (8–10dh). CTM buses take you to their office south of the train station.

Tourist office Place Abdelmoumen Ben Ali ((Mon–Fri 8.30am–4.30pm; ⓣ0524 436239) keeps current details of services you might need.

Accommodation

The Medina has the main concentration of cheap accommodation – most places quite pleasant – and, unusually, has a fair number of classified hotels too. Given the attractions of the Djemaa el Fna and the souks, this is the first choice. Booking in advance is advisable. All our recommendations are in the Medina unless stated otherwise.

Hostel

HI hostel Rue El Jahid, Gueliz ⓣ0524 447713. Immaculate, refurbished and close to the train station. Closed 10am–noon. Breakfast included. Dorm only; 70dh.

Hotels

Aday 111 Derb Sidi Bouloukat ⓣ0524 441920. A small hotel near the Djemaa; clean, friendly and well-kept. 110dh.

Afriquia 45 Sidi Bouloukate ⓣ0524 442403. Colourful hotel that's a favourite with backpackers; basic rooms and a lively terrace. 130dh.

Ali Rue Moulay Ismail ⓣ0524 444979. Popular with High Atlas trekkers (guides can be found here). Rooms have showers, and there's cheap dorm accommodation (70dh). Breakfast included. 300dh.

Central Palace 59 Sidi Bouloukate ⓣ0524 440235. Clean, simple rooms, some of which are stylish and have a/c. Good place to book tours to the Sahara. 155dh.

CTM Pl Djemaa el Fna ⓣ0524 442325. Well situated, right on the Djemaa, with a choice of rooms, including some (modernized and relatively expensive) overlooking the square. 150dh.

Des Voyageurs 40 Bd Mohammed Zerktouni ⓣ0524 447218. Pleasant, old-fashioned hotel with big, clean rooms and a nice little garden. 144dh.

Essaouira 3 Derb Sidi Bouloukat ⓣ0524 443805. Well-run cheapie, with laundry service, baggage deposit and rooftop café. 100dh.

Farouk 66 Av Hassan II, on the corner with Rue Mauretania, Gueliz ⓣ0524 431989, ⓔhotelfarouk@hotmail.com. Excellent hotel with en-suite rooms and a popular restaurant, within walking distance of the train station. Breakfast included. 210dh.

Medina 1 Derb Sidi Bouloukat ⓣ0524 442997. Clean, friendly and good value, with an English-speaking proprietor and breakfast on the roof terrace. 100dh.

Eating and drinking

The most atmospheric place to eat is the Djemaa el Fna, where foodstalls set up around sunset and serve up everything from *harira* soup and couscous to stewed snails and sheep's heads, all eaten at trestle tables. For tea with a view, the terrace cafés of the *Hôtel CTM* and neighbouring *Café le Grand Balcon* overlook the Djemaa el Fna, as do two relatively reasonable rooftop restaurants: *Argana* and *Les Prémices*. Cheap restaurants tend to gather in the Medina, with posher places uptown in Gueliz, along with French-style cafés and virtually all the city's bars.

TREAT YOURSELF

Gallia 30 Rue de la Recette ⓣ0524 445913 ⓔhotel.gallia@menara.ma. Beautifully kept hotel in a restored Medina mansion with immaculate en-suite rooms off two tiled courtyards, one with fountain, palm tree and caged birds. There's central heating in winter and a/c in summer. A real treat. Book ahead. 500dh dbl b&b.

SHOPPING IN THE SOUKS

Marrakesh is famous for its **souks**, where you can buy goods from all over Morocco. Prices are rarely fixed so before you set out, head to the supposedly fixed price Ensemble Artisanal (Mon–Sat 8.30am–7pm, Sun 8.30am–1pm), on Avenue Mohammed V, midway between the Koutoubia and the ramparts at Bab Nkob, and get an idea of how much things are worth. It pays to **bargain** hard as the first price you are told can easily be five or ten times the going rate, with the most obscene prices to be found around the edges of the souks. A lane opposite the *Café de France* on the Djemaa el Fna leads to a stuccowork arch that marks the beginning of the crowded **Souk Smarine**, an important thoroughfare traditionally dominated by **textiles**. At its end the street splits in two. If you take the left-hand fork you will pass a cashpoint, dyers, carpenters and end up at the **slipper** (*babouch*) souk. The right-hand fork leads immediately to Berber **carpet sellers** (on the right), **jewellers** and eventually to the **leather** souk.

Chez Bahia Rue Riad Zitoun el Kedim, 50m from Djemaa el Fna. Basic café/diner with decent *pastilla*, *tajine*, breakfast and snacks at low prices (mains 20–25dh).
Grand Hotel du Tazi corner of Av El Mouahidine and Rue Bab Agnaou (where the taxis drop you off for the Djemaa). Cheapest place in the Medina to enjoy a drink. The meals are good but on the pricey side (80–100dh).
Hotel Ali Rue Moulay Ismail. The eat-all-you-like buffet here, served 7–11pm, is justifiably popular and good value at 80dh. There are also lunchtime menus.
Hotel Farouk 66 Av Hassan II, Gueliz. Pizzas or an excellent-value set menu with soup or salad, then couscous, *tajine* or *brochettes*, followed by fruit or home-made yoghurt, for 60dh.
Jnane Mogador Hôtel Derb Sidi Bouloukat by 116 Rue Riad Zitoun el Kedim ⓣ0524 426323, ⓦwww.jnanemogador.com. This wonderful riad-style hotel provides a tranquil spot for a decently priced Moroccan meal overlooking the rooftops (menus 90–150dh).
Le Progrès 20 Rue Bani Marine. The best of several decent choices in a street of cheap eating places (40–60dh).
Portofino 279 Av Mohammed V. Some of the best Italian food in Morocco, with chic décor and very professional, friendly service (pizza or pasta 30–85dh).
Snack Café Toubkal in the southeast corner of Djemaa el Fna. Salads, *tajines* and couscous, set menus (45–50dh) and good-value breakfasts (18dh).

Directory

Exchange BMCE has branches with adjoining bureaux de change and ATMs in the Medina (Rue Moulay Ismail, facing Place Foucauld) and Gueliz (114 Av Mohammed V).
Internet Moulay Abdeslam Cyber-Park on Av Mohammed V opposite the Ensemble Artisanal; Super Cyber de la Place in an arcade off Rue Bani Marine by the *Hôtel Ichbilia*; Hanan Internet at the southern end of Rue Bab Agnaou.
Mountain trekking guides Ask at the *Hôtel Ali*.
Pharmacy and doctor Pharmacie du Progrès, Place Djemaa el Fna at the top of Rue Bab Agnaou; Pharmacie de la Liberté, just off Place de la Liberté (or Houria). If you're in need of a doctor try Dr Abdelmajid Ben Tbib, 171 Av Mohammed V ⓣ0524 431030.
Post office Place du 16 Novembre, midway along Av Mohammed V, and on the Djemaa el Fna.

Moving on

Train Casablanca Voyageurs (9 daily; 3hr 10min); Fes (8 daily; 7hr 10min); Meknes (8 daily; 6hr 35min); Rabat (9 daily; 4hr 15min); Tangier (1 daily; 10hr 25min).
Bus Casablanca (half-hourly 4am–9pm; 4hr); Essaouira (25 daily; 3hr 30min); Fes (8 daily; 10hr); Meknes (6 daily; 9hr); Rabat (hourly; 5hr 30min); Tangier (11 daily; 10hr).

ESSAOUIRA

ESSAOUIRA, the nearest beach resort to Marrakesh, is a lovely eighteenth-century walled seaside town. A favourite with the likes of Frank Zappa and Jimi Hendrix back in the 1960s, its tradition of hippy tourism has created a much more laid-back relationship between local residents and foreign visitors than you'll find in the rest of Morocco. Today Essaouira is a centre for arts and crafts

ESSAOUIRA ORIENTATION

Still largely contained within its ramparts, Essaouira is a simple place to get to grips with. At the northeast end of town is the **Bab Doukkala**; at the southwest is the town's pedestrianized main square, **Place Prince Moulay el Hassan**, and the fishing **harbour**. Between them run two main parallel streets: Av de l'Istiqlal/Av Mohammed Zerktouni and Rue Sidi Mohammed Ben Abdallah.

in addition to being the country's top windsurfing spot.

What to see and do

The ramparts

Essaouira is a great place in which to wander and the **ramparts** are the obvious place to start. Heading north along the lane at the end of Place Prince Moulay el Hassan, you can access the **Skala de la Ville**, the great sea bastion topped by a row of cannons, which runs along the northern cliffs. At the end is the circular **North Bastion**, with panoramic views (closes at sunset). Along the Rue de la Skala, built into the ramparts, are the **wood-carving workshops**, where artisans use thuja, a distinctive local hardwood. You can find another impressive bastion by the harbour, the **Skala du Port** (daily 9am–5.30pm; 10dh).

The souks

The town's **souks** spread around and to the south of two arcades, on either side of Rue Mohammed Zerktouni, and up towards the Mellah (former Jewish ghetto), in the northwest corner of the ramparts. Worth particular attention are the **Marché d'Épices** (spice market) and **Souk des Bijoutiers** (jewellers' market). Art studios and hippie-style clothing shops centre around Place Chefchaouni by the clocktower.

The beaches

The **southern beach** (the northern one is less attractive) extends for miles, past the Oued Ksob riverbed and the ruins of an old fort known as the **Bordj el Berod**. If you're after **watersports**, Magic Fun Afrika (Ⓣ0524 473856, Ⓦwww.magicfunafrika.com) is the closest beachside operator to the Medina, near the *Sofitel* hotel. They rent out wind- and kite-surfing gear and offer lessons in both.

Arrival and information

Bus The bus station is about 500m (10min walk) northeast of Bab Doukkala. Especially at night, it's worth taking a petit taxi (about 7dh).

Taxi Grands taxis also operate from the bus station, though they may drop arrivals at Bab Doukkala or Place Prince Moulay el Hassan.

Tourist office Av du Caire (Mon–Fri 9am–4.30pm; Ⓣ0524 783532).

Accommodation

Accommodation can be tight over Easter and in summer, when advance booking is recommended. Local residents may approach you with offers of rooms, and Jack's Kiosk (Ⓣ0524 475538), a newspaper shop on Place Prince Moulay el Hassan, displays ads for apartments.

Hotels

Central 5 Rue Dar Dheb, off Av Mohammed Ben Abdallah Ⓣ0524 783623, Ⓔsi2007@live.fr. Cheap and cheerful place with friendly staff. Basic rooms in a nice old house around a patio with a fig tree. 100dh,

Majestic 40 Rue Laâlouj, opposite the museum Ⓣ0524 474909. The former French colonial courthouse, with clean rooms, though a little cheerless. The terrace is one of the town's highest points. 130dh.

Sahara Av Okba Ibn Nafia Ⓣ0524 475292, Ⓕ0524 476198. Big rooms around a central well, all en suite. 250dh.

Smara 26 Rue Skala (near the North Bastion) Ⓣ0524 475655. Cheap and popular hotel, with decent rooms and a stunning view over the town and the Atlantic from its terrace. 104dh, 196dh with sea view.

Souiri 37 Rue Attarine Ⓣ0524 475339, Ⓦwww.hotelsouiri.com. Popular, colourful Medina hotel

with a range of rooms, the cheaper ones with shared bathroom facilities. 230dh.
Tafraout 7 Rue Marrakech ⓣ0524 476276. Recently renovated with friendly staff and comfortable rooms, some en suite, but not much character, and not all rooms have outside windows. 280dh.

Campsite

Camping Sidi Magdoul 1km south of town behind the lighthouse ⓣ0524 472196. Clean, friendly and well-managed, with hot showers, bungalows in spring and summer (120dh) and an area of soil and trees for pitching tents in. 12dh per person plus 15–25dh tent.

Eating and drinking

For an informal meal, you can do no better than eat at the line of grills down at the port. The official prices are on a board as you walk down to the port but haggle to get more for your money. Restaurants can be a bit expensive, but there are plenty of places to pick up cheap sandwiches.
Dar Baba 2 Rue de Marrakech (first floor), on the corner with Rue Sidi Mohammed Ben Abdallah. Italian dishes, including pizza, but best is their own fresh pasta (45–65dh).
Essalam 23 Place Moulay El Hassan. The cheapest set menus in town (30–65dh), and certainly value for money, though the choice is a little bit limited. Good for breakfast too.
Laayoune 4 bis Rue Hajjali. *Tajines* and other Moroccan staples (menus at 68–88dh) served in a relaxed setting with friendly service, but with back-breakingly low tables.
La Petite Perle 2 Rue el Hajjalli. A small place with low divan seating and generous servings of traditional Moroccan cooking (set menus for 60–95dh).
Les Chandeliers 14 Rue Laâlouj ⓣ0524 475827, ⓦwww.leschandeliers.net. A well-established restaurant and wine bar run by a French family and offering both Continental and Moroccan options. Dinner only (set menus 95–135dh).

Moving on

Bus Casablanca (26 daily; 6hr); Marrakesh (25 daily; 3hr 30min); Rabat (13 daily; 8hr 30min).

The Netherlands

AMSTERDAM: experience canals, coffeeshops and world-famous art

DELFT: enjoy wonderful apple cake in Vermeer's home town

ROTTERDAM: a buzzing port with great nightlife

HOGE VELUWE NATIONAL PARK: cycle through woods to the world's best collection of Van Goghs

MAASTRICHT: a cosmopolitan university town with a tranquil old quarter

ROUGH COSTS

DAILY BUDGET Basic €55/occasional treat €70

DRINK Beer €2

FOOD Pancake €7

HOSTEL/BUDGET HOTEL €20–32/€60–95

TRAVEL Train: Amsterdam–Maastricht €28.70; Bus: Amsterdam–Haarlem €4

FACT FILE

POPULATION 16.5 million

AREA 41,526 sq km

LANGUAGE Dutch

CURRENCY Euro (€)

CAPITAL Amsterdam (population 1 million)

INTERNATIONAL PHONE CODE ⓣ31

Introduction

Despite the popular reputation of its most celebrated city, Amsterdam, the Netherlands is not all sex and drugs (there's little rock'n'roll). Delve deeper and you will find a diminutive country packed with unique, iconic images: flat, fertile landscapes punctuated by tulips, windmills and church spires; ornately gabled terraces flanking peaceful canals; and mile upon mile of grassy dunes, backing onto stretches of pristine sandy beach.

Though most people travel only to atmospheric **Amsterdam**, nearby is a group of worthwhile towns known collectively as the **Randstad** (literally "rim town"), including **Haarlem** and **Delft** with their old canal-girded centres, and **Den Haag** (The Hague), a stately city with fine museums and easy beach access. The dynamic port city of **Rotterdam** is a canvas for noteworthy architecture and alternative art. Outside the Randstad, life moves more slowly. To the south, the landscape undulates into heathy moorland, best experienced in the **Hoge Veluwe National Park**. Further south lies the compelling city of **Maastricht**, squeezed between the German and Belgian borders.

CHRONOLOGY

58 BC Julius Caesar conquers the area of the present-day Netherlands.
1275 Amsterdam is founded by Count Floris V of Holland.
1477 The Austrian Habsburgs take control.
1500s Protestant Reformation spreads through the Netherlands, leading to wars against the Catholic Habsburg rulers based in Spain.
1579 The Union of Utrecht is signed by seven provinces to form the United Provinces against Spain, and declaring independence for the Netherlands in 1581, heralding a "Golden Age" of trade and colonial expansion.
1603 The Dutch East India Company establishes its first trading post in Indonesia, an area that it would gradually colonize.
1806 Napoleon annexes the Kingdom of Holland for France.
1813 The French are driven out and the Prince of Orange becomes sovereign of the United Netherlands.
1853 Vincent Van Gogh is born.
1914–18 The Netherlands remains neutral during World War I.
1940 Nazi Germany invades the Netherlands, forcing the deportation and murder of Dutch Jews including Anne Frank's family.
1945 Germany is expelled by Allied forces.
1947 Anne Frank's diary is published.
1975 Cannabis is decriminalized – tourism booms.
1992 The Maastricht Treaty is signed, transforming the European Community into the European Union.
1997 Treaty of Amsterdam clears the way for the introduction of a single European currency.
2003 The permanent International Criminal Court is established in The Hague to try war criminals.
2007 Controversial government plans to ban the burqa (Islamic dress for women) in public places gains Cabinet support.

ARRIVAL

Most tourists arrive at Amsterdam's Schiphol airport, one of Europe's busiest, which is served by over seventy budget airline routes and well connected by train to many Dutch cities. Some international flights also land at Rotterdam airport. There are good train links to the UK, France, Belgium and Germany. High-speed trains frequently travel to Amsterdam from Paris, Brussels and Frankfurt (Ⓦwww.nsinternational.nl), and InterRail passes (Ⓦwww.raileurope.co.uk) are accepted. The Dutchflyer (Ⓦwww.dutchflyer.co.uk) connects London with Amsterdam Centraal by train and boat, while Stenaline ferries

(Ⓦwww.stenaline.co.uk) travel between Harwich and the Hook of Holland. P&O ferries (Ⓦwww.poferries.com) leave from Hull and dock in Rotterdam.

GETTING AROUND

Trains (Ⓦwww.ns.nl) are fast and efficient, fares relatively low, and the network comprehensive. With any ticket, you're free to stop off en route and continue later that day. Various **passes** cut costs – ask at the station. The **Voordeelurenabonnement** costs €15, is valid for three months, and gives a forty percent discount to the card-holder and their travelling companions for off-peak travel.

Urban **buses** and **trams** are very efficient. You only need one kind of ticket: a **strippenkaart** (Ⓦwww.vbn-bv.nl/ovinfo). You can buy two- (€1.60) and three-strip (€2.40) *strippenkaarts* from bus drivers, or better-value fifteen-strip (€7.30) or 45-strip (€21.60) *strippenkaarts* in advance from train stations, tobacconists and public transport offices. One *strippenkaart* can be used by any number of people – you just cancel the requisite number of strips per person.

There's a nationwide system of **cycle** paths. You can rent bikes cheaply from main train stations and outlets in almost any town and village. Theft is rife: never leave your bike unlocked, and don't leave it on the street overnight – most stations have a storage area. For more information on cycling in the Netherlands, including maps, check out ⓦwww.holland.com/uk.

ACCOMMODATION

Accommodation can be pricey, especially in Amsterdam during peak season. Many of the smaller towns like Haarlem have few budget options, so it may be cheaper to stay in Den Haag or Rotterdam and make day-trips to the Randstad towns. Book ahead during the summer and over holiday periods, especially Easter. The cheapest one- or two-star **hotel** double rooms start at around €60; three-star hotel rooms begin around €80. Prices usually include a reasonable breakfast. There are thirty excellent, if similar, HI **hostels** nationwide (ⓦwww.stayokay.com), charging €20–28 per person including breakfast. If you use them extensively then it may be worth buying a **Stayokay Card** which costs €15 and gives a discount of €2.50 every night. Larger cities have independent hostels with lower prices, and these are often more lively. **Private rooms** can usually be arranged through the VVV office (see opposite) in town, and usually cost around €20–25 including breakfast. There are plenty of well-equipped **campsites**: expect to pay around €4 per person, plus €3–5 for a tent. Some sites also have **cabins** for up to four people, for around €35 a night.

FOOD AND DRINK

Dutch **food** tends to be plain but thanks to its colonial history, the Netherlands boasts the best **Indonesian cuisine** outside Indonesia. *Nasi goreng* and *bami goreng* (rice or noodles with meat) are good basic dishes; chicken or beef in peanut sauce (*sateh*) is always available. A *rijsttafel* is rice or noodles served with a huge range of tasty side-dishes.

Breakfast (*ontbijt*) is filling, and usually consists of rolls, cheese, ham, eggs, jam and honey, chocolate spread and sprinkles or peanut butter. **Snacks** include chips – *frites* or *patat* – smothered with mayonnaise, curry, satay or tomato sauce, *kroketten* (bite-size chunks of meat goulash coated in breadcrumbs and deep fried) and *fricandel* (a frankfurter-like sausage). **Fish** specialities sold from street kiosks include salted raw herrings, smoked eel (*gerookte paling*), mackerel in a roll (*broodje makreel*) and mussels. Other common snacks are kebab (*shoarma*) and falafel. Most bars serve toasties, sandwiches and rolls (*tosti*, *boterham* and *broodjes* – *stokbrood* if made with baguette) and, in winter, *erwtensoep*, a thick pea soup with smoked sausage, and *uitsmijter*: fried eggs on buttered bread, topped with ham or roast beef. In **restaurants**, the dish of the day (*dagschotel*) is the cheapest option. Many places have at least one meat-free item, and you'll find vegetarian restaurants in most towns.

Sampling the Dutch and Belgian **beers** in every region is a real pleasure, often done in a cosy brown café (*bruine kroeg*, named because of the colour of the tobacco-stained walls); the big brands Heineken, Amstel, Oranjeboom and Grolsch are just the tip of the iceberg. A standard, small glass is *een pils*; a bigger glass is *een vaasje*. You may also come across *proeflokalen* or tasting houses, small, old-fashioned bars that close around 8pm, and specialize in **jenever**, Dutch gin, drunk straight; *oud* (old) is smooth, *jong* (young) packs more of a punch. **Coffee** is normally good and strong, while **tea** generally comes with lemon. **Chocolate**

(*chocomel*) is also popular, served hot or cold.

DRUGS

Purchases of up to 5g of cannabis, and possession of up to 30g (the legal limit) are tolerated; in practice, many "**coffeeshops**" offer discounted bulk purchases of 50g with impunity. Coffeeshops in city centres – neon-lit dives pumping out mainstream rock, reggae or techno – are worth avoiding. Less touristy districts house more congenial, high-quality outlets. When you walk in, ask to see the **menu**, which lists the different hashes and grasses on offer. Take care with space-cakes (cakes or biscuits baked with hash), mainly because you can never be sure what's in them, and don't ever buy from street dealers. All other narcotics are illegal, and don't even entertain the notion of taking a "souvenir" home with you.

CULTURE AND ETIQUETTE

The Dutch are renowned for their liberal and laid-back attitude, so there isn't much in the way of etiquette to observe. Don't be embarrassed about speaking to locals in English – unlike many of their fellow Europeans, the Dutch are happy to converse in English and are generally helpful. A five to ten percent **tip** is generally expected in cafés and restaurants.

SPORTS AND ACTIVITIES

The Netherlands is a nation of **cyclists**, and you won't have any problems finding cycle paths or bikes for rent. With most of the country's major towns sat cheek by jowl in the Randstad, cycling from city to city is very easy. If you're looking for a more rural experience, the island of Texel and the Hoge Veluwe National Park near Arnhem are ideal, with the park even providing free bicycles for visitors. **Football** is also extremely popular, with the season running from September to May and matches held on Sunday at around 2.30pm, with occasional games on Wednesday too. The major teams are PSV Eindhoven, Feyenoord in Rotterdam, and Amsterdam's Ajax.

COMMUNICATIONS

Post offices are open Monday to Friday 9am to 5pm, Saturday 9am to noon. Post international items in the "Overige" slot. Most **public phones** take phonecards – available from post offices and VVVs (see below) – or credit cards. The operator is on ⓣ0800/0410 (free). Many cafés and public libraries offer **internet access**.

EMERGENCIES

As long as you're wary of pickpockets and badly lit streets at night, you're unlikely to come into contact with the police. **Pharmacies** (*apotheek*) are open Monday to Friday 8.30am to 5.30pm; if they are closed there'll be a note of the nearest open pharmacy on the door. Duty **doctors** at the Centrale Doktorsdienst (ⓣ0900/503 2042) offer advice; otherwise head for any hospital (*ziekenhuis*). If you need the emergency services, police, ambulance and fire are all on ⓣ112.

INFORMATION

VVV tourist offices are usually in town centres or by train stations and have information in English, including maps and accommodation lists; they will also book rooms for a small charge.

THE NETHERLANDS ON THE NET

ⓦ**www.holland.com** National tourist board.

ⓦ**www.ns.nl** Train information.

Dutch

	Dutch	Pronunciation
Yes	*Ja*	Yah
No	*Nee*	Nay
Please	*Alstublieft*	Alstooblee-eft
Thank you	*Dank u/Bedankt*	Dank yoo/Bedankt
Hello/Good day	*Hallo*	Halloh
Goodbye	*Dag/Tot ziens*	Dahg/Tot Zeens
Excuse me	*Pardon*	Pardon
Where?	*Waar?*	Waah?
Good	*Goed*	Gud
Bad	*Slecht*	Slecht
Near	*Dichtbij*	Dichtbye
Far	*Ver*	Vare
Cheap	*Goedkoop*	Gudkoop
Expensive	*Duur*	Dooer
Open	*Open*	Open
Closed	*Gesloten*	Gesloten
Push	*Duwen*	Doowen
Pull	*Trekken*	Trekken
Today	*Vandaag*	Vandahg
Yesterday	*Gisteren*	Histehren
Tomorrow	*Morgen*	Morgen
How much is...?	*Wat kost...?*	Wat kost...?
I don't understand	*Ik begrijp het niet*	Ick bechripe het neet
Do you speak English?	*Spreekt u Engels?*	Spraicht oo Engells?
One	*Een*	Ayn
Two	*Twee*	Tway
Three	*Drie*	Dree
Four	*Vier*	Veer
Five	*Vijf*	Vife
Six	*Zes*	Zess
Seven	*Zeven*	Zayven
Eight	*Acht*	Acht
Nine	*Negen*	Nehen
Ten	*Tien*	Teen

MONEY AND BANKS

The Dutch currency is the **euro** (€). **Banking hours** are Monday 1 to 4pm, Tuesday to Friday 9am to 4pm; in larger cities some banks also open Thursday 7 to 9pm and occasionally on Sat mornings. **GWK exchange offices** at train stations open late daily. You can also change money at most VVV tourist offices, post offices and bureaux de change, though rates are worse. **ATMs** are widespread. Smaller places (including B&Bs and restaurants) may not accept cards.

OPENING HOURS AND HOLIDAYS

Many **shops** stay closed on Monday morning, although markets open early. Otherwise, opening hours tend to be 9am to 5.30/6pm, with many shops closing late on Thursdays or Fridays. In major cities, night shops (*avondwinkels*) open 4pm to 1/2am.

STUDENT AND YOUTH DISCOUNTS

CJP is part of the European Youth Card Association and is a worthwhile investment. Costing €15, it offers countless discounts to under-26s for one year (Ⓦwww.cjp.nl). Buy it online at Ⓦwww.stayokay.com or Ⓦwww.euro26.org, or in person at Stayokay hostels or VVV offices. Discounts include most museums, galleries and tourist attractions throughout the country, as well as theatre, film and other leisure activities. If you are over 26, then the nationwide **Museum Card** (Museumkaart), costing €39.95 for one year, may be more suitable. It is readily available at museums, many of which offer free entry to card holders.

Museum times are generally Tuesday to Saturday 10am to 5pm, Sunday 1 to 5pm, although these vary widely. Shops and banks are closed, and museums adopt Sunday hours, on **public holidays**: January 1, Good Friday, Easter Sunday and Monday, April 30, May 5, Ascension Day, Whitsun and Monday, December 25 and December 26.

Amsterdam

AMSTERDAM is a charming capital, with a beguiling mix of the provincial and the cosmopolitan and an enduring appeal for backpackers. For many, its array of world-class museums and galleries – notably the **Rijksmuseum**, **Anne Frank House** and the **Van Gogh Museum** – are reason enough to visit.

The city started out as a fishing village at the mouth of the River Amstel, and subsequently grew as a major European trading centre. Amsterdam accommodated its expansion with the cobweb of **canals** that gives the city its distinctive and elegant shape today, and around which a *gezellig* café culture has been established.

Amsterdam emerged as the fashionable focus for the alternative movements of the 1960s, a reflection on the longstanding tolerant attitudes of the Dutch. This bestowed a unique character on the city, which still takes a progressive approach to social issues and culture, with a buzz of open-air summer events and intimate clubs and bars.

Uncertainty awaits for Amsterdam, as its government proceeds to shut its iconic coffeeshops and Red Light District windows. But with an ever-youthful atmosphere and a club scene that has recently come of age, Amsterdam won't stop rocking.

What to see and do

Amsterdam's compact centre contains most of the city's leading attractions, and it takes only about forty minutes to stroll from one end to the other. Centraal Station lies on the centre's northern edge, and from here the city fans south in a web of concentric canals, surrounded by expanding suburbs.

At the heart of the city is the **Old Centre**, an oval-shaped area with a jumble of streets and beautiful narrow canals. This is the unlikely setting for the infamous **Red Light District**. Forming a ring around it is the first of the major canals, the **Singel**, followed closely by the **Herengracht**, **Keizersgracht** and **Prinsengracht**, created during the city's expansion in the seventeenth century. Development was strictly controlled, resulting in the tall, very narrow residences with decorative gables. This is the Amsterdam you see in the brochures: still, dreamy canals, crisp reflections of seventeenth-century town houses and cobbled streets. For shops, bars and restaurants, you're better off exploring the crossing-streets that connect the canals.

To the south is the city's main square and energetic party venue, **Leidseplein**, with the leafy **Vondelpark** nearby. The **Jordaan** to the northwest features mazy streets and narrow canals, and offers perfect strolling territory. To the east is the **Old Jewish Quarter**.

Centraal Station and the Damrak

The medieval core fans south from the nineteenth-century **Centraal Station**, one of Amsterdam's most resonant landmarks. From here, the busy thoroughfare **Damrak** marches into the heart of the city, lined with overpriced restaurants and bobbing canal boats, and flanked on the left first by the Modernist stock exchange, the **Beurs** (now a concert hall), and then by the enormous De Bijenkorf department store. The **Sexmuseum**, Damrak 18 (daily: 9.30am–11.30pm; €3), presents the "art of loving" throughout the ages for your viewing pleasure.

The Red Light District

East of Damrak, the infamous **Red Light District**, stretching across two canals – Oudezijds Voorburgwal and Oudezijds Achterburgwal – is one of the real sights of the city. The atmosphere is undeniably sleazy, but it's

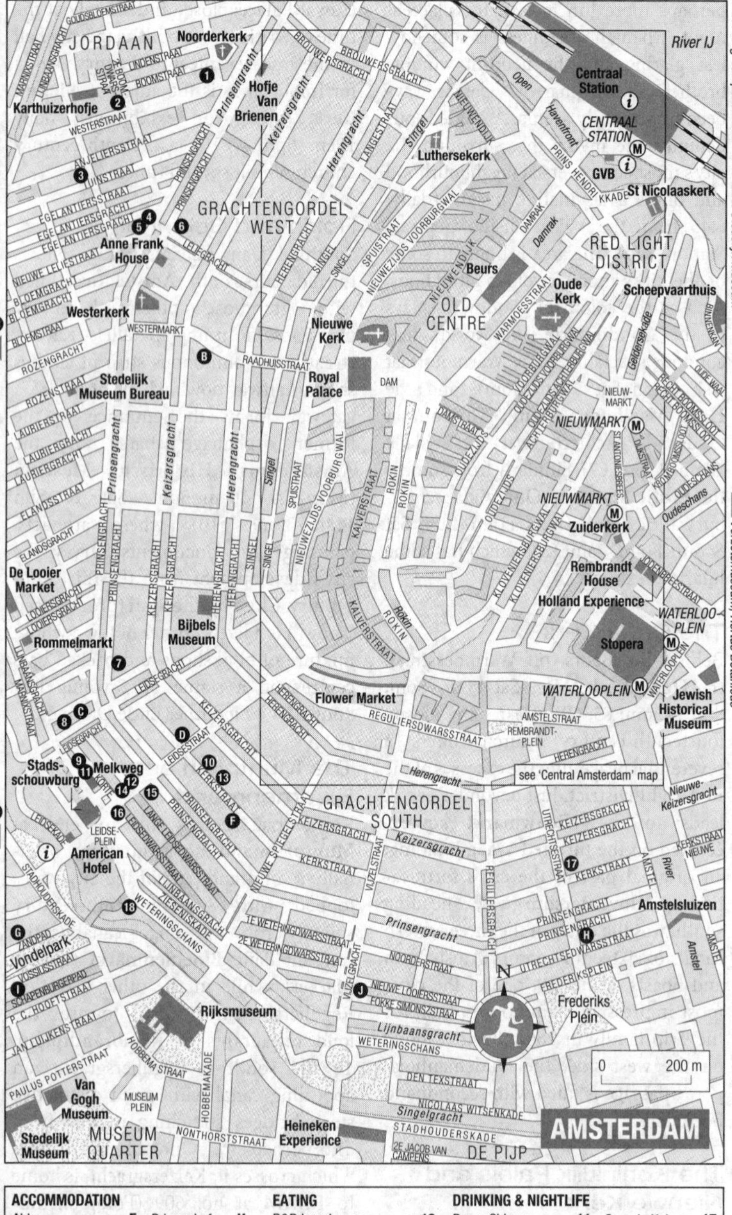

ACCOMMODATION

Abba	E	Prinsenhof	H
Clemens	B	The Shelter Jordaan	A
Euphemia	J	Stayokay Vondelpark	G
Flying Pig Uptown	I		
Golden Bear	D		
Hans Brinker	F		
International Budget Hostel	C		

EATING

B&B Lunchroom	12
De Blaffende Vis	2
De Eettuin	3
De Zotte Proeflokaal	8
Los Pilones	13
Royal Bagelsand Muffins	15
Winkel	1
Wok to Walk	14

DRINKING & NIGHTLIFE

Boom Chicago	11	Soenda Kelapa	17
The Bulldog	16	Spanjer & van Twist	6
De Prins	5	Sugar Factory	9
De Twee Zwaantjes	4		
Happy Feelings	10		
Het Molenpad	7		
Jimmy Woo	9		
Paradiso	18		

perhaps more fun to visit the place at night, when the seediness is somehow less glaring and the neon-lit window brothels down narrow passageways become strangely scenic. A guided tour debunks the myths that surround the city's most controversial neighbourhood and offers a fascinating insight (daily: 6:45 from the VVV outside Centraal Station; €10). The area is home to some of the city's more frivolous attractions, such as the colourful window displays of the **Condomerie**, the world's first condom speciality shop, Warmoestraat 141 (Mon–Sat 11am–6pm), and the **Hash Marihuana Hemp Museum** at Oudezijds Achterburwal 148 (daily 10am–11pm; €7). Similarly frolicsome is the **Erotic Museum**, Oudezijds Achterburwal 54 (Sun–Thurs 11am–1am, Sat & Sun 11am–2am; €5), which has some hilarious exhibits.

The Oude Kerk

Behind the Beurs, off Warmoesstraat, the **Oude Kerk** (Mon–Sat 11am–5pm, Sun 1–5pm; €5, CJP €4), a bare, mostly fourteenth-century church, offers a reverential peace after the excesses of the Red Light District. Just beyond, Zeedijk leads to the **Nieuwmarkt square**, centred on the turreted **Waag** building, an original part of the city's fortifications. **Kloveniersburgwal**, heading south, was the outer of the three eastern canals of sixteenth-century Amsterdam and boasts, at no. 29, one of the city's most impressive canal houses, built for the Trip family in 1662. Further along on the west side, the Oudemanhuispoort passage is filled with secondhand bookstalls.

The Koninklijk Paleis and Nieuwe Kerk

At the southern end of Damrak, the **Dam** (or Dam Square) is the centre of the city, its war memorial serving as a meeting place for tourists. On the western side, the **Koninklijk Paleis** (Royal Palace; closed indefinitely at the time of writing) was built as the city hall in the mid-seventeenth century. Vying for importance is the adjacent **Nieuwe Kerk** (open for exhibitions, daily 10am–6pm; €10), a fifteenth-century church rebuilt several times.

Rokin and Beginhof

South of Dam Square, **Rokin** follows the old course of the Amstel River, lined with grandiose nineteenth-century mansions. Running parallel, Kalverstraat is a monotonous strip of clothes shops, halfway down which, at no. 92, a gateway forms the entrance to the former orphanage that's now the **Amsterdams Historisch Museum** (Mon–Fri 10am–5pm, Sat & Sun 11am–5pm; €10), where artefacts, paintings and documents survey the city's development from the thirteenth century. Close by, the **Spui** (pronounced "spow") is a lively corner of town whose mixture of bookshops and packed bars centres on a statue of a young boy known as *'t Lieverdje* (Little Darling).

The Muntplein and Bloemenmarkt

Kalverstraat comes to an end at **Muntplein** and the Munttoren – originally a mint and part of the city walls, topped with a seventeenth-century spire. Across the Singel canal is the fragrant daily **Bloemenmarkt** (Flower Market), while in the other direction Reguliersbreestraat turns towards the loud restaurants of **Rembrandtplein**. To the south is Reguliersgracht, an appealing canal with seven distinctive steep bridges stretching in line from Thorbeckeplein. One of the canals which crosses it, Keizersgracht, is home to **FOAM** at no. 609 (Fotografiemuseum Amsterdam; daily: 10am–6pm, open until 9pm Thurs & Fri; €7.50, CJP €4; Ⓦ www.foam.nl), a hip, modern gallery which updates its diverse photographic exhibitions regularly.

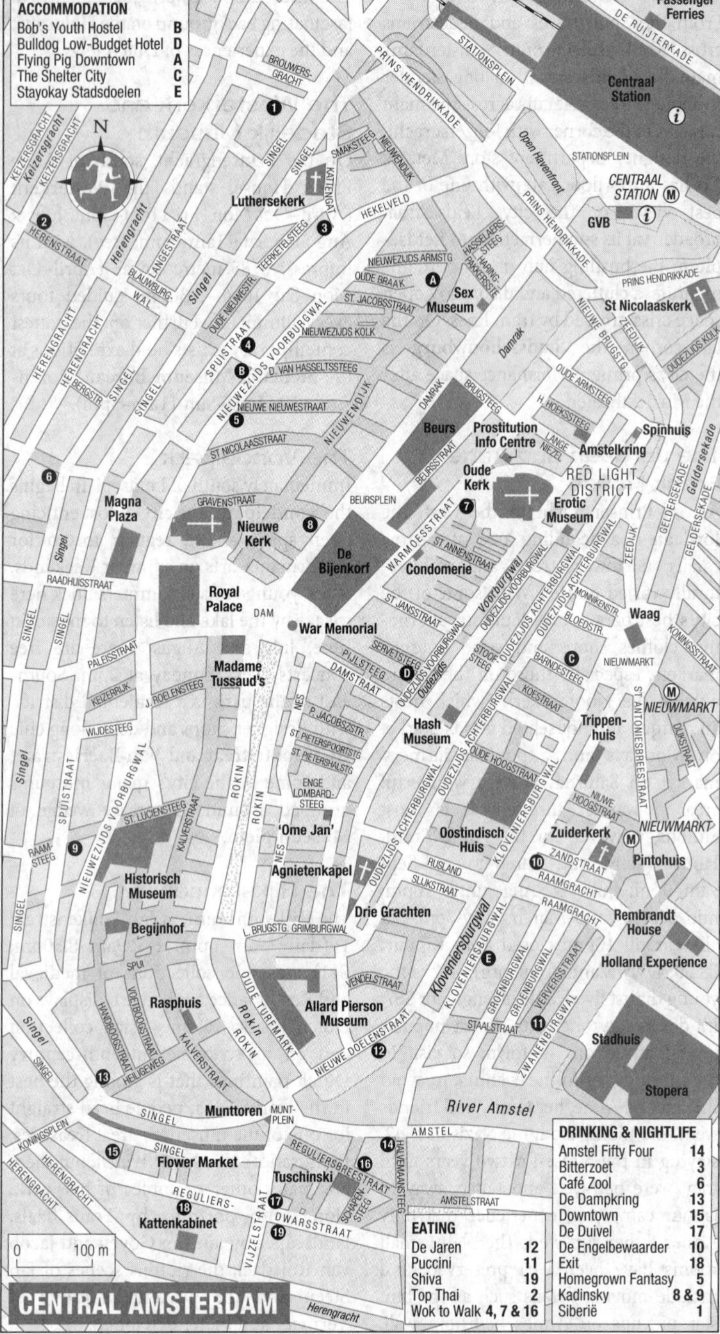
ACCOMMODATION
Bob's Youth Hostel B
Bulldog Low-Budget Hotel D
Flying Pig Downtown A
The Shelter City C
Stayokay Stadsdoelen E
N
Passenger Ferries
DE RUIJTERKADE
STATIONSPLEIN
Centraal Station
PRINS HENDRIKKADE
Open Havenfront
CENTRAAL STATION
GVB
BROUWERSGRACHT
SINGEL
KATTENGAT
Luthersekerk
HEKELVELD
NIEUWENDIJK
SMAKSTEEG
KEIZERSGRACHT
HERENSTRAAT
Herengracht
LANGESTRAAT
TEERKETELSTEEG
BLAUWBURGWAL
Singel
OUDE NIEUWESTR.
NIEUWEZIJDS ARMSTG
OUDE BRAAK
HASSELAERSSTEEG
HARINGPAKKERSSTEEG
Sex Museum
ST. JACOBSSTRAAT
NIEUWEZIJDS KOLK
NIEUWEZIJDS VOORBURGWAL
SPUISTRAAT
D. VAN HASSELTSSTEEG
Damrak
ZEEDIJK
NIEUWE BRUGSTG
St Nicolaaskerk
OUDEZIJDS KOLK
OUDE ARMSTEEG
HERENGRACHT
BERGSTR
NIEUWE NIEUWESTRAAT
BRUGSTEEG
H. HOEKSSTEEG
Spinhuis
Beurs
Prostitution Info Centre
Amstelkring
LANGE NIEZEL
ST NICOLAASSTRAAT
BEURSSTRAAT
Oude Kerk
RED LIGHT DISTRICT
Geldersekade
GRAVENSTRAAT
BEURSPLEIN
Magna Plaza
Nieuwe Kerk
Erotic Museum
De Bijenkorf
WARMOESSTRAAT
ST ANNENSTRAAT
Condomerie
Voorburgwal
OUDEZIJDS ACHTERBURGWAL
RAADHUISSTRAAT
Royal Palace
DAM
ST JANSSTRAAT
MONNIKENSTR.
Waag
BLOEDSTR.
KONINGSSTRAAT
War Memorial
SERVETSTEEG
STOOFSTEEG
BARNDESTEEG
NIEUWMARKT
PALEISSTRAAT
Madame Tussaud's
PIJLSTEEG
DAMSTRAAT
Oudezijds
KOESTRAAT
KEIZERRIJK
J. ROELENSTEEG
NES
ST ANTONIESBREESTRAAT
NIEUWMARKT
P. JACOBSZSTR.
Hash Museum
Trippenhuis
WIJDESTEEG
ST PIETERSPOORTSTG
ST PIETERSHALSTG
DIJKSTRAAT
ENGE LOMBARDSTEEG
OUDE HOOGSTRAAT
ROKIN
NIEUWE HOOGSTRAAT
ST. LUCIENSTEEG
KALVERSTRAAT
'Ome Jan'
Oostindisch Huis
KLOVENIERSBURGWAL
Zuiderkerk
NIEUWMARKT
RAAMSTEEG
ZANDSTRAAT
Pintohuis
Historisch Museum
Agnietenkapel
RUSLAND
RAAMGRACHT
SLIJKSTRAAT
Drie Grachten
Rembrandt House
Begijnhof
L. BRUGSTG. GRIMBURGWAL
Kloveniersburgwal
Holland Experience
SPUI
VENDELSTRAAT
GROENBURGWAL
VERVERSSTRAAT
Rasphuis
OUDE TURFMARKT
Allard Pierson Museum
Rokin
HANDBOOGSTRAAT
VOETBOOGSTRAAT
STAALSTRAAT
ZWANENBURGWAL
Stadhuis
HEILIGEWEG
NIEUWE DOELENSTRAAT
Stopera
River Amstel
Munttoren
MUNTPLEIN
KONINGSPLEIN
AMSTEL
Flower Market
REGULIERSBREESTRAAT
HALVEMAANSTEEG
Tuschinski
SCHAPENSTEEG
AMSTELSTRAAT
REGULIERSDWARSSTRAAT
Kattenkabinet
VIJZELSTRAAT
0 100 m
CENTRAL AMSTERDAM
Herengracht
DRINKING & NIGHTLIFE
Amstel Fifty Four 14
Bitterzoet 3
Café Zool 6
De Dampkring 13
Downtown 15
De Duivel 17
De Engelbewaarder 10
Exit 18
Homegrown Fantasy 5
Kadinsky 8 & 9
Siberië 1
EATING
De Jaren 12
Puccini 11
Shiva 19
Top Thai 2
Wok to Walk 4, 7 & 16

Around Leidseplein

From the Spui, trams and pedestrians cross Koningsplein onto Amsterdam's main drag, **Leidsestraat** – a long, slender shopping street that cuts across the main canals. On the corner with Keizersgracht, the designer department store Metz & Co has a top-floor café with one of the best views of the city. Leidsestraat broadens at its southern end into **Leidseplein**, the bustling hub of Amsterdam's nightlife, a cluttered and disorderly open space criss-crossed by tram lines. On the far corner, the **Stadsschouwburg** is the city's prime performance space after the Muziektheater.

The Jordaan and Anne Frank House

Across Prinsengracht to the west, the **Jordaan** is a beguiling area of narrow canals, narrower streets and architecturally varied houses. With some of the city's best bars and restaurants, alternative clothes shops and good outdoor markets, especially those on the square outside the Noorderkerk (which hosts an antique and household goods market on Mondays and a popular farmers' market on Saturdays), it's a wonderful area to wander through. It is most famous, however, for the **Anne Frank House** (daily: mid-March to mid-Sept 9am–9pm; July & Aug until 10pm; mid-Sept to mid-March 9am–7pm; Sat all year till 10pm; closed Yom Kippur; €8.50; Ⓦwww.annefrank.org), where the young diarist lived, at Prinsengracht 267. It's deservedly one of the most popular tourist attractions in town, so visit in the morning, or in the evening, to avoid the queues. Anne, her family and friends went into hiding from the Nazis in 1942, staying in the house for two years until they were betrayed and taken away to labour camps, an experience that only Anne's father survived. The plain, small rooms have been well preserved, and include moving details such as the film star pin-ups on Anne's bedroom wall. The museum also provides plenty of fascinating background on the Holocaust and the experiences of Dutch Jews.

The Westerkerk and Stedelijk Museum

On the Prinsengracht, south of Anne Frank House, stands the **Westerkerk** (April–Oct Mon–Fri 11am–3pm, July & Aug also Sat 11am–3pm; free), with its impressive 85-metre tower (April–Oct Mon–Sat 10am–5.30pm; guided tours every 30min; €5). Further on, the hottest contemporary artists hold exhibitions at the **Stedelijk Museum Bureau**, Rozenstraat 59 (Tues–Sun 11am–5pm).

The Vondelpark

Immediately south of Leidseplein begins the **Vondelpark**, the city's most enticing open space and a regular forum for performance arts on summer weekends, when young Amsterdammers flock here to laze by the lake and listen to music; in June, July and August there are free concerts every Sunday at 2pm. Southeast of the park is a residential district, with designer shops and delis along chic **P.C. Hooftstraat** and **Van Baerlestraat**, and some of the city's major museums grouped around the grassy wedge of **Museumplein**.

The Rijksmuseum

The **Rijksmuseum**, at Jan Luijkenstraat 1 (daily 9am–6pm, Fri 9am–8.30pm; €11), has fine collections of medieval and Renaissance applied art, displays on Dutch history, a fine Asian collection and an array of seventeenth-century Dutch paintings that is among the best in the world. Most people head straight for one of the museum's great treasures, Rembrandt's *The Night Watch*, but there are many other examples of his work, along with portraits by Frans Hals, landscapes by Jan van Goyen and Jacob van Ruisdael, the riotous scenes of Jan Steen and the peaceful interiors of Vermeer and Pieter de Hooch.

The Vincent Van Gogh Museum and Stedelijk Museum

For the popular **Vincent Van Gogh Museum** at Paulus Potterstraat 7 (Sat–Thurs 10am–6pm, Fri 10am–10pm; €15), it's best to arrive early in high season, as long queues can be a problem. The collection includes the early years in Holland, continuing to the brighter works he painted after moving to Paris and then Arles, where he produced vivid canvases like *The Yellow House* and the *Sunflowers* series. Along the street, at Paulus Potterstraat 13, the **Stedelijk Museum** of modern art (Ⓦwww.stedelijkindestad.nl) was closed for refurbishment at the time of writing, but should have reopend by the time you read this. Changing exhibitions remain on show at the Stedelijk Museum Bureau (see opposite).

The Heineken Experience and De Pijp

The rather disappointing **Heineken Experience** at Stadhouderskade 78, east from the Rijksmuseum (daily 11am–7pm, last entry 5.30pm; €15), provides an overview of Heineken's history and the brewing process, with a couple of free beers thrown in afterwards. South of here is the neighbourhood known as **De Pijp** (The Pipe) after its long, sombre canyons of brick tenements. This has always been one of the city's closest-knit communities, and one of its liveliest, with numerous inexpensive Surinamese and Turkish restaurants and a cheerful hub in the long slim thoroughfare of **Albert Cuypstraat**, whose food and clothes **market** (Mon–Sat 9.30am–5pm) is the largest in the city.

East of the centre

East of Rembrandtplein across the Amstel, the large, squat **Muziektheater** and **Stadhuis** flank **Waterlooplein**, home to the city's excellent **flea market** (Mon–Sat). Behind, Jodenbreestraat was once the main street of the Jewish quarter (emptied by the Nazis in the 1940s); no. 6 is **Het Rembrandthuis** (Rembrandt House; daily 10am–5pm; €8, CJP €5.50), which the painter bought at the height of his fame, living here for over twenty years. It displays a large number of the artist's engravings and paintings, plus a number of archeological findings from the site.

The Jewish Quarter

The excellent, award-winning **Joods Historisch Museum**, at Nieuwe Amstelstraat 1 (Jewish Historical Museum; daily 11am–5pm; closed Yom Kippur; €7.50, CJP €4.50), is cleverly housed in a complex of Ashkenazi synagogues dating from the late seventeenth century and gives an imaginative introduction to Jewish life and beliefs. Photographs and film footage give a vivid impression of Amsterdam's long-gone Jewish ghetto, while interactive pieces explain Jewish customs.

Down Muiderstraat, the prim **Hortus Botanicus**, at Plantage Middenlaan 2 (Mon–Fri 9am–5pm, Sat & Sun 10am–5pm; July & Aug until 7pm, Dec & Jan until 4pm; €7), is a pocket-sized botanical garden with eight thousand plant species; stop off for a relaxed coffee and cakes in the orangery. The eye-catching Plancius Building at Plantage Kerklaan 61 houses the excellent **Verzetsmuseum** (Dutch Resistance Museum; Tues–Fri 10am–5pm, Sat–Mon 11am–5pm; €6.50, CJP €3.50), where a variety of exhibits depict the ways in which the Dutch people opposed Nazi oppression.

Arrival and information

Air Schiphol airport is connected by train to Centraal Station (every 10min, hourly at night; 15min).

Train Centraal Station is the hub of all bus and tram routes and just 5min walk from central Dam square.

Bus International buses arrive at Amstel Station, 10min south of Centraal Station by metro.

Tourist office The main VVV is outside Centraal Station, at Stationsplein 10 (daily 9am–6pm; ⓣ0900/400 4040, ⓦwww.iamsterdam.nl); there's another inside the station on platform 2b (daily 11am–7pm); a smaller kiosk on Stadhouderskade (April–Sept daily 9.30am–6pm; Oct–March daily 10am–5.30pm) and an office in the airport arrivals hall (daily 7am–10pm).
Discount card The Iamsterdam Card from the VVV (€38/48/58 for 24/48/72hr; ⓦwww.iamsterdam.nl), gives free or reduced entry to major museums and attractions, unlimited public transport and selected restaurant discounts. The VVV also has a monthly listings guide, *Day by Day – Amsterdam* (€1.95).

City transport and tours

Public transport There's an excellent network of trams, buses and the metro (all daily 6/7am–midnight). The GVB public transport office in front of Centraal Station (Mon–Fri 7am–9pm, Sat & Sun 10am–6pm; ⓣ0900/8011, ⓦwww.gvb.nl) has free route maps and an English guide to the *strippenkaart* ticketing system (see p.835). After midnight, night buses take over, running roughly hourly from Centraal Station to most parts of the city (single ticket €3.50).
Bike rental From Centraal Station or from a number of firms around town: Bike City, Bloemgracht 70 ⓣ020/626 3721, ⓦwww.bikecity.nl; Damstraat Rent-a-Bike at Damstraat 20 ⓣ020/625 5029, ⓦwww.bikes.nl; or MacBike (ⓣ020/620 0985, ⓦwww.macbike.nl) at Mr Visserplein 2, Marnixstraat 220, Weteringschans 2, and Stationsplein 5. All charge around €12 a day, plus €50 deposit with ID.
Bike tours Yellow Bike, at Nieuwezijds Kolk 29 (ⓣ020/620 6940, ⓦwww.yellowbike.nl), organizes three-hour 'city' and 'countryside' tours, from €21.50 per person. Mike's Bike Tours, at Kerkstraat 134 (ⓣ020/622 7970, ⓦwww.mikesbiketoursamsterdam.com), offers similar tours at better rates, with student discounts.
Walking tours There are interesting free walking tours of the main sights (daily 11.15am & 1.15pm from the National Monument in Dam Square; 3hr; ⓦwww.neweuropetours.eu).

Accommodation

In high season, and weekends throughout the year, it's always worth booking ahead, or you'll find almost everywhere full.

Hostels

Bob's Youth Hostel Nieuwezijds Voorburgwal 92 ⓣ020/623 0063, ⓦwww.bobsyouthhostel.nl. Lively and smoky, this is an old backpackers' favourite. Also has apartments with kitchens. 10min walk southwest from Centraal Station. Dorms €22, doubles €80.
Bulldog Low-Budget Hotel Oudezijds Voorburgwal 220 ⓣ020/620 3822, ⓦwww.bulldog.nl. Part of the *Bulldog* coffeeshop chain, this super-smart hostel has a bar, DVD lounge, roof terrace and laundry facilities. There are dorms with TVs and showers, doubles and apartments. Dorms €32, doubles €95.
Flying Pig Downtown Nieuwendijk 100 ⓣ020/420 6822, ⓦwww.flyingpig.nl. Clean, large establishment run by ex-backpackers, with free kitchen, internet, an all-night bar and no curfew; not for faint-hearted non-smokers. 5min walk from Centraal Station. There's also the slightly quieter and recently refurbished *Flying Pig Uptown* by the Vondelpark at Vossiusstraat 46 (ⓣ020/400 4187; tram #1/#2/#5 to Leidseplein, then a 5min walk). Both dorms €30, doubles €80.
Hans Brinker Kerkstraat 136 ⓣ020/622 0687, ⓦwww.hans-brinker.com. Well-established and raucously popular cheapie with a bright café attached (meals €5–7). Tram #1/#2/#5 to Prinsengracht. Dorms €25, doubles €80.
International Budget Hostel Leidsegracht 76 ⓣ020/624 2784, ⓦwww.internationalbudgethostel.com. Excellent, homely budget option on a peaceful little canal in the heart of the city. Tram #1/#2/#5 to Prinsengracht. Dorms €32, doubles €80.
The Shelter Jordaan Bloemstraat 179 ⓣ020/624 4717, ⓦwww.shelter.nl. Easy-going Christian hostel tucked away in the Jordaan district. Single-sex dorms only. Café serves dinner and dessert for €5. Tram #13/#17 to Marnixstraat. There's a sister hostel in the Red Light District, *The Shelter City*, at Barndesteeg 21 (ⓣ020/625 3230), with a 2am curfew. Dorms €22.50.
Stayokay Stadsdoelen Kloveniersburgwal 97 ⓣ020/624 6832, ⓦwww.stayokay.com. The more accessible of the two HI hostels, with clean semi-private dorms. HI members have priority in high season. Tram #4/#9/#16/#24/#25 to Muntplein. Dorms €24, doubles €61.
Stayokay Vondelpark Zandpad 5 ⓣ020/589 8996, ⓦwww.stayokay.com. For facilities, this is the better of the two HI hostels, a huge place with bar, restaurant, TV lounge and bike rental; there's also a twice-daily shuttle to Schiphol. Secure lockers and a lift. Tram #1/#2/#5 to Leidseplein, then a 5min walk. Dorms €33.50, doubles €93.

Hotels

Abba Overtoom 118 ⓣ020/618 3058, ⓦwww.hotel-abba.nl. Conveniently located for the big art

museums and Leidseplein. All rooms have TVs, some are en suite, and those at the back of the hotel are quiet. Breakfast is included. Tram #1 to Constantijn Huygensstraat. Doubles €55.
Clemens Raadhuisstraat 39 ⓣ020/624 6089, ⓦwww.clemenshotel.com. Clean, neat and good value for money, with breakfast included. Ask for a quieter room at the back. Tram #13/#17 to Westermarkt. Doubles €80.
Euphemia Fokke Simonszstraat 1 ⓣ020/622 9045, ⓦwww.euphemiahotel.com. A likeable, laid-back atmosphere, and big, basic rooms at reasonable prices, which means it's usually full. Tram #16 or #24 to Weteringcircuit. Doubles €70.
Golden Bear Kerkstraat 37 ⓣ020/624 4785, ⓦwww.goldenbear.nl. The first gay hotel in the city, with clean and spacious rooms. Minimum stay of four nights if the weekend is included, April–Nov. Trams #1, #2 & #5 to Kerkstraat. Doubles €88.
Prinsenhof Prinsengracht 810 ⓣ020/623 1772, ⓦwww.hotelprinsenhof.com. Housed in an eighteenth-century canal house. Only two rooms are en suite, but a hearty breakfast is included and service couldn't be friendlier. Doubles €69.

Campsites

Vliegenbos Meeuwenlaan 138 ⓣ020/636 8855, ⓦwww.vliegenbos.com. In Amsterdam North, a 10min ride on bus #32, #33 or night bus #361 from Centraal Station. Closed Oct–March. €10.50.
Zeeburg Zuider IJdijk 20 ⓣ020/694 4430, ⓦwww.campingzeeburg.nl. Tram #26 from Centraal Station to Zuiderzeeweg or night bus #359 to Flevoweg. Open all year. €10.50, two-person cabin €40.

Eating

Amsterdam has an extensive supply of ethnic restaurants, especially Indonesian, Chinese and Thai, as well as *eetcafés* that serve decent, well-priced food in an unpretentious setting.

Cafés

B&B Lunchroom Leidsestraat 44. Serves a vast array of hot and cold sandwiches with hearty fillings. Giant muffins (€2.50) satisfy even the sweetest tooth.
Café Zool Oude Leliestraat 9. The service is slow, but this family-run café serves inexpensive yet delicious juices and pancakes. Pancakes €5–7.
De Jaren Nieuwe Doelenstraat 20–22, near Muntplein. Modern, grand café with a waterside terrace – a perfect place for people-watching and newspaper-browsing in the sun. *Appeltaart* €4.
Puccini Staalstraat 17–21, near Waterlooplein. Dreamy cakes, pastries and chocolates, all handmade. Sandwiches €9.
Royal Bagels and Muffins Prinsengracht 454, near Leidseplein. Great snack place, with big cups of coffee and half-price refills. Bagels €4.
Winkel Noordermarkt 43, opposite the Noorderkerk. Popular local hang-out on Saturday mornings during the farmers' market. Famously delicious apple cake. Mains €12.

Restaurants

De Blaffende Vis Westerstraat 118 ⓣ020/625 1721. Great bar/restaurant in the Jordaan. Popular with students and gets raucous at weekends. Mains €12.
De Eettuin 2e Tuindwarsstraat 10 ⓣ020/623 7706. Hefty portions of meaty Dutch food served with fries and unlimited salad. Mains €15.
Los Pilones Kerkstraat 63 ⓣ020/623 4633. A vibrant, authentic Mexican restaurant with free tortilla chips on arrival and an extensive tequila menu. Daily from 4pm. Beef fajitas €13.
Shiva Reguliersdwarsstraat 72 ⓣ020/624 8713. Outstanding Indian restaurant, with well-priced, expertly prepared food, and veggie options. Mains €15.
Soenda Kelapa Utrechtsestraat 89 ⓣ020/627 9416. A small Indonesian restaurant with no frills but generous portions of excellent food. Daily from 6pm. Set menu €14.
Top Thai Herenstraat 22 ⓣ020/623 4633. Some of the best-value authentic Thai food in Amsterdam. Popular and friendly. Daily from 4pm. Pad thai €10.
Wok to Walk Leidsestraat 96, Kolksteeg 8, Reguliersbreestraat 45, Warmoestraat 85. Your favourite noodle dish stir-fried to greasy perfection in minutes. Daily noon–midnight. Stir fry €7.

Drinking and nightlife

There is a distinction between bars and coffeeshops, where smoking dope is the primary pastime (ask to see the menu). You must be 18 or over to enter these, and don't expect alcohol to be served. Most are open 9am–1am (2/3am at weekends). Check out the widely available *Smokers Guide* (€6.50; ⓦwww.smokersguide.com) for advice. Most clubs open around 10pm–4am. Drinks cost around fifty percent more than in a bar, but entry prices are low and there's rarely any kind of door policy.

Bars

De Duivel Reguliersdwarsstraat 87. Amsterdam's only hip-hop café, with hip-hop and funk from midnight. Open daily 8pm–3/4am.

De Engelbewaarder Kloveniersburgwal 59. Relaxed and informal haunt of Amsterdam's bookish types, with live jazz on Sunday afternoons.
De Prins Prinsengracht 124. Roomy and welcoming *bruine kroeg*, also popular for its great-value food. Daily 10am–1/2am.
De Twee Zwaantjes Prinsengracht 114. Tiny oddball Jordaan bar where locals sing along raucously to accordion music – you'll either love it or hate it.
De Zotte Proeflokaal Raamstraat 29. Belgian hang-out just north of Leidseplein with food, liqueurs and hundreds of different kinds of beer. Daily 4pm–1am.
Het Molenpad Prinsengracht 653. One of the city's most atmospheric brown cafés, with excellent, if pricey, food. Fills with young professionals after 6pm.
Spanjer & van Twist Leliegracht 60. A popular place which is perfect for laid-back summer afternoons, with chairs overlooking the quietest canal in Jordaan. Also serves lunch and dinner.

Coffeeshops

The Bulldog Leidseplein 15–17 and other central outlets. More like a dodgy club than a coffeeshop, and certainly not the place for a thoughtful smoke. The dope is reliably good though, if expensive.
De Dampkring Handboogstraat 29. With colourful decor and a refined menu, this coffeeshop is known for its good-quality hash.
Happy Feelings Kerkstraat 51. Celebrated hippie hang-out with friendly staff.
Homegrown Fantasy Nieuwezijds Voorburgwal 87a. Part of the Dutch Passion seed company, selling the widest range of (mostly Dutch) marijuana in Amsterdam.
Kadinsky Zoutsteeg 9 & Rosmarijnsteeg 9, both in the old centre. Sensational chocolate chip cookies, scrupulously accurate deals and a background of jazz dance.
Siberië Brouwersgracht 11. Slightly off the beaten tourist track, very relaxed and friendly – worth a visit whether you want to smoke or not.

Clubs

Bitterzoet Spuistraat 2 Ⓦwww.bitterzoet.com. Club with an eclectic mix of nights, featuring live bands as well as DJs.
Jimmy Woo Korte Leidsedwarsstraat 16 Ⓦwww.jimmywoo.com. A chic, loungey club where East meets West. It's a favourite of stylish Amsterdammers, so dress well.
Paradiso Weteringschans 6–8 Ⓦwww.paradiso.nl. One of the principal venues in the city, which hosts an unmissable club night on Fridays, from midnight onwards.
Sugar Factory Lijnbaansgracht 238 Ⓦwww.sugarfactory.nl. A "night theatre" featuring everything from spoken word to cabaret, including straightforward club nights.

Entertainment

Amsterdam buzzes with places offering a wide and inventive range of entertainment. The best source of listings information is the *Uitburo*, or *AUB* (Ⓦwww.aub.nl). Wednesday's *Het Parool* newspaper has a good entertainment supplement, *Uit en Thuis*.

Cinemas and comedy

Boom Chicago Leidseplein 12 Ⓣ020/423 0101, Ⓦwww.boomchicago.nl. Amsterdam's popular, multi media comedy show combines sketches and rapid-fire improv. The show is energetically performed by Americans who delve deep into the Dutch, and indeed their own, psyche with hilarious results. Dinner is also available, and jugs of cocktails and pitchers of beer keep the laughter flowing throughout the night. Tickets are €20/24 for the weekday/weekend shows, but there are a few €10 tickets sold each day at noon for that night's show – be quick!
Cinecenter Lijnbaansgracht 236 Ⓣ020/788 2150, Ⓦwww.cinecenter.nl. Shows the big blockbusters alongside foreign-language films. Tickets €8.50, CJP €7.
De Uitkijk Prinsengracht 452 Ⓣ020/623 7460, Ⓦwww.uitkijk.nl. The oldest film theatre in Amsterdam, and one of the more intimate. Tickets €8, CJP €7.

Live music venues

Akhnaton Nieuwezijds Kolk 25 Ⓣ020/624 3396, Ⓦwww.akhnaton.nl. Specializes in African and Latin American music and dance parties.
Bimhuis Piet Heinkade 3 Ⓣ020/788 2188, Ⓦwww.bimhuis.nl. Premier jazz venue. Free improv sessions on Tues from 8pm. Take tram #25/#26 to stop Muziekgebouw/Bimhuis from Centraal Station. Discount of €2 per ticket for CJP holders.
Café Alto Korte Leidsedwarsstraat 115 Ⓦwww.jazz-cafe-alto.nl. Legendary jazz café-bar, with free live music every night from 10pm. Big on atmosphere, though not space. Daily 9pm–3/4am.
Melkweg Lijnbaansgracht 234 Ⓣ020/531 8181, Ⓦwww.melkweg.nl. Amsterdam's famous entertainment venue which combines music, theatre, photography, film and media arts under one roof. There are quality DJs playing at the weekend, a monthly film programme, theatre, gallery, bar and restaurant.

Classical music and opera

Beurs van Berlage Damrak 277 ⓣ020/530 4141, ⓦwww.beursvanberlage.nl. The splendid interior of the former stock exchange hosts a wide selection of music from the Dutch Philharmonic and Dutch Chamber orchestras.

Concertgebouw Concertgebouwplein 2–6 ⓣ020/671 8345, ⓦwww.concertgebouw.nl. Catch world-renowned orchestras playing amid wonderful acoustics. Summer concerts and free lunchtime performances on Wednesdays. There are CJP discounts, and "Sprint Seats" for under-27s sold 45min before the start of each concert for €10.

Gay Amsterdam

Amsterdam has one of the biggest and best-established gay scenes in Europe: attitudes are tolerant and facilities unequalled. The nationwide organization COC, at Rozenstraat 14 (ⓣ020/626 3087, ⓦwww.cocamsterdam.nl), can provide information, and has a café and popular club nights. For further advice contact the English-speaking Gay & Lesbian Switchboard (Mon–Fri noon–6pm, Sat & Sun 4–6pm; ⓣ020/623 6565, ⓦwww.switchboard.nl) or check ⓦwww.gayamsterdam.com. The gay and lesbian bookshop Vrolijk is just behind Dam Square at Paleisstraat 135 (Mon 11am–6pm, Tues–Thurs 10am–6pm, Fri 10am–7pm, Sat 10am–5pm, Sun 1–5pm; ⓦwww.vrolijk.nu).

Gay cafés and bars

Amstel Fifty Four Amstel 54. Perhaps the best-established bar, at its most vivacious in summer when the punters spill out onto the street.

Downtown Reguliersdwarsstraat 31, off Rembrandtplein. A favourite with visitors. Relaxed and friendly, with inexpensive meals. Daily 10am–8pm.

Exit Reguliersdwarsstraat 42, off Rembrandtplein. An established, popular gay nightclub with four bars, featuring dancers and DJs. Thurs & Fri midnight–4am, Sat midnight–5am.

Directory

Bookshop The American Book Center, Spui 12 (Mon 11am–7pm, Tues–Sat 10am–8pm, Sun 11am–6.30pm), is central and well stocked, including travel guides.

Embassies and consulates Note that most are in Den Haag, not Amsterdam. Australia, Carnegielaan 4, Den Haag ⓣ070/310 8200; Canada, Sophialaan 7, Den Haag ⓣ070/311 1600; Ireland, Dr Kuyperstraat 9, Den Haag ⓣ070/363 0993; New Zealand, Eisenhowerlaan 77N, Den Haag ⓣ070/346 9324; UK, Lange Voorhout 10, Den Haag ⓣ070/427 0427; US, Lange Voorhout 102, Den Haag ⓣ070/310 2209.

Exchange GWK in Centraal Station and Leidseplein; Thomas Cook at Dam 23, Damrak 1–5 and Leidseplein 31a; American Express at Damrak 66.

Hospital De Boelelaan 1117 ⓣ020/444 4444.

Laundry The Clean Brothers at Westerstraat 26 (daily 8am–8pm), or Powders at Kerkstraat 56.

Left luggage Centraal Station.

Police Elandsgracht 117 ⓣ0900/8844.

Post office Singel 250 (Mon–Fri 9am–5pm, Thurs until 8pm, Sat 10am–1.30pm).

Moving on

Train Arnhem (for Hoge Veluwe National Park; every 15min; 1hr 10min); Berlin (every 2hr; 6hr 30min); Brussels (hourly; 3hr); Den Haag HS (every 10min; 50min); Haarlem (every 10min; 15min); Leiden (every 15min; 45min); Maastricht (every 30min; 2hr 35min); Rotterdam (every 10min; 1hr); Schiphol airport (every 10min; 15min); Texel (via Den Helder; every 30min; 1hr 15min); Utrecht (every 15min; 30min).

The Randstad

The string of towns known as the **Randstad**, or "rim town", situated amid a typically Dutch landscape of flat fields cut by canals, forms the country's most populated region and still recalls the landscapes painted in the seventeenth-century heyday of the provinces. Much of the area can be visited as day-trips from Amsterdam, but it's easy and more rewarding to make a proper tour. **Haarlem** is worth a look, while to the south, the university centre of **Leiden** makes a pleasant detour before you reach the refined tranquillity of **Den Haag** (The Hague) and the busy urban centre of **Rotterdam**. Nearby **Delft** and **Gouda** repay visits too, the former with one of the best-preserved centres in the region.

HAARLEM

Just over fifteen minutes from Amsterdam by train, **HAARLEM** is a

handsome, mid-sized city that sees itself as a cut above its neighbours. It makes a good alternative base for exploring northern Holland, or even Amsterdam itself, especially if you can't find a bed in the city or would rather be somewhere less hectic.

What to see and do

The core of the city is **Grote Markt** and the adjoining Riviervischmarkt, flanked by the gabled, originally fourteenth-century **Stadhuis** and the impressive bulk of the **Grote Kerk** or **Sint Bavokerk** (entrance at no. 23; Mon–Sat 10am–4pm; €2). Inside, the mighty Christian Müller organ of 1738 is said to have been played by Handel and Mozart. The town's main attraction is the outstanding **Frans Hals Museum**, at Groot Heiligland 62 (Tues–Sat 11am–5pm, Sun noon–5pm; €10), a five-minute stroll from Grote Markt in the Oudemannhuis almshouse. It houses a number of his lifelike seventeenth-century portraits, including the *Civic Guard* series, which established his reputation.

Arrival and information

Train and bus The train station is north of the centre, about 10min walk from the Grote Markt; buses stop outside.

Tourist office In the Millennium Monument, Verwulft 11 (Mon–Fri 9.30am–5.30pm, Sat 10am–5pm, Sun 11am–3pm; ⓣ0900/616 1600, ⓦwww.vvvhaarlem.nl).

Accommodation

Amadeus Grote Markt 10 ⓣ023/532 4530, ⓦwww.amadeus-hotel.com. Pleasant, if slightly sparse rooms; make the most of the location by asking for one with a view of the Markt. Doubles €80.

Carillon Grote Markt 27 ⓣ023/531 0591, ⓦwww.hotelcarillon.com. A friendly hotel with decent rooms and a good bar downstairs, which serves a tasty breakfast. Excellent location on the Markt. Doubles €65.

Stayokay Haarlem Jan Gijzenpad 3 ⓣ023/537 3793, ⓦwww.stayokay.com. Inconveniently located out of town on a main road, but otherwise this HI hostel is of the usual high standard. From the station it's 15min on bus #2, direction Noord. Dorms €28, doubles €95.

Eating and drinking

Crackers Junction of Lange Veerstraat and Kleine Houtstraat. Dim, smoky bar with good music and beer by the pint.

Grand Café Fortuyn Grote Markt 21. Cosy café-bar whose 1930s decor creates an ambience of faded opulence. Atmospheric spot for a drink. Glass of wine €3.

In den Uiver Riviervischmarkt 13. A traditional "brown" café which serves up live jazz alongside their beer at the weekend.

Jacobus Pieck Warmoesstraat 18 ⓣ023/532 6144. Simple yet elegant bistro with steaks aplenty and better-value meals served at lunchtime. Closed Sun.

Restaurant La Plume Lange Veerstraat 1 ⓣ023/531 3202. Popular spot serving traditional Dutch dishes and pasta. Mains €16.

Moving on

Train Amsterdam CS (every 10min; 15min); Amsterdam Schiphol (every 10min; 30min); Delft (every 30min; 40min); Den Haag HS (every 30min; 30min); Den Helder (every 15min; 1hr 20min); Leiden (every 10min; 20min).

Bus Schiphol airport (every 10min; 45min; bus 300).

LEIDEN AND THE BULBFIELDS

The charm of **LEIDEN** lies in the peace and prettiness of its gabled streets and canals, though the town's museums are varied and comprehensive enough to merit a visit.

What to see and do

The most appealing quarter is **Rapenburg**, a peaceful area of narrow pedestrian streets and canals that is home to the country's principal archeological museum, the **Rijksmuseum Van Oudheden** (National Museum of Antiquities; Tues–Sun 10am–5pm; €8.50, CJP €7.50). Outside sits the first-century AD Temple of Teffeh, while inside are more Egyptian artefacts, along with

classical Greek and Roman sculptures and exhibits from prehistoric, Roman and medieval times. Across Rapenburg, a network of narrow streets converges on the Gothic **Pieterskerk**. East of here, Breestraat marks the start of a vigorous **market** (Wed & Sat), which sprawls right over the sequence of bridges into Haarlemmerstraat, the town's major shopping street. Close by, the **Burcht** (daily 10am–10pm; free) is a shell of a fort, whose battlements you can clamber up for views of the town centre. The **Molenmuseum de Valk**, on Molenwerf at 2e Binnenvestgracht 1 (Tues–Sat 10am–5pm, Sun 1–5pm; €2.50), displays the history of windmills.

The bulbfields

Along with Haarlem to the north, Leiden and Delft are the best bases for seeing the Dutch **bulbfields** that flourish here in spring. The view from the train as you travel from Haarlem to Leiden can be sufficient in itself as the line cuts directly through the main growing areas, the fields divided into stark geometric blocks of pure colour. Should you want to get closer, make a bee-line for **LISSE**, home to the **Keukenhof** (mid-March to mid-May daily 8am–7.30pm; €13.50; Ⓦwww.keukenhof.nl), the largest flower gardens in the world. Some six million blooms are on show for their full flowering period, complemented by five thousand square metres of greenhouses. Buses (every 30min; #54) run to the Keukenhof from Leiden bus station. Connexxion's combined bus and entry ticket costs €20 and can be bought at Ⓦwww.connexxion.nl/keukenhof or at the VVV.

Arrival and information

Train and bus stations Both no more than 10min walk north of the centre.

Tourist office A short walk from the stations at Stationsweg 41 (Mon 11am–5.30pm, Tues–Fri 9.30am–5.30pm, Sat 10am–4.30pm, Sun 11–3pm; Ⓣ071/527 8880, Ⓦwww.leiden.nl).

Accommodation

Flying Pig Beach Hostel Parallel Boulevard 208 Ⓣ071/362 2533, Ⓦwww.flyingpig.nl. A 30min bus ride from Leiden in the beach town of Noordwijk, this place is the antidote to the bland-but-comfortable hostels found all over the Netherlands and your best bet for visiting Leiden on a budget. The bar is a real traveller hang-out; you could be forgiven for thinking you were in South America. There's a free shuttle from the two *Flying Pig* hostels in Amsterdam, or take bus #40 or #42 from Leiden to the lighthouse square in Noordwijk. Dorms €25, doubles €80.

Nieuw Minerva Boommarkt 23 Ⓣ071/512 6358, Ⓦwww.nieuwminerva.nl. Cosy and central canalside hotel with some interesting Dutch-themed rooms, including "Delftware" and "Rembrandt". Doubles €116.

Eating and drinking

Barrera Rapenburg 56. Buzzy canalside café-bar with big sandwiches for €5. Daily 10am–1am.

Jazzcafé The Duke Oude Singel 2 Ⓦwww.jazzcafetheduke.com. Bar with live music most nights.

La Bota Herensteeg 9–11 by the Pieterskerk Ⓣ071/514 6340. Hidden studenty spot which serves great-value food and beers. Daily 5–10pm. Mains €8–13.

M'n Broer By the Pieterskerk at Kloksteeg 7. Slightly pricey Dutch menu in a traditional setting; open for evening meals only. Mains €14–18.

Moving on

Train Amsterdam CS (every 15min; 45min); Amsterdam Schiphol (every 10min; 20min); Delft (every 15min; 20min); Den Haag HS (every 10min; 15min); Haarlem (every 10min; 20min); Rotterdam (every 10min; 30min); Utrecht (every 30min; 1hr).

DEN HAAG

With its urbane atmosphere, **DEN HAAG (THE HAGUE)** is different from any other Dutch city. Since the sixteenth century it has been the Netherlands' political capital, though its older buildings are a rather subdued collection with little of Amsterdam's flamboyance. Diplomats and multinational businesses ensure that many of the city's hotels and

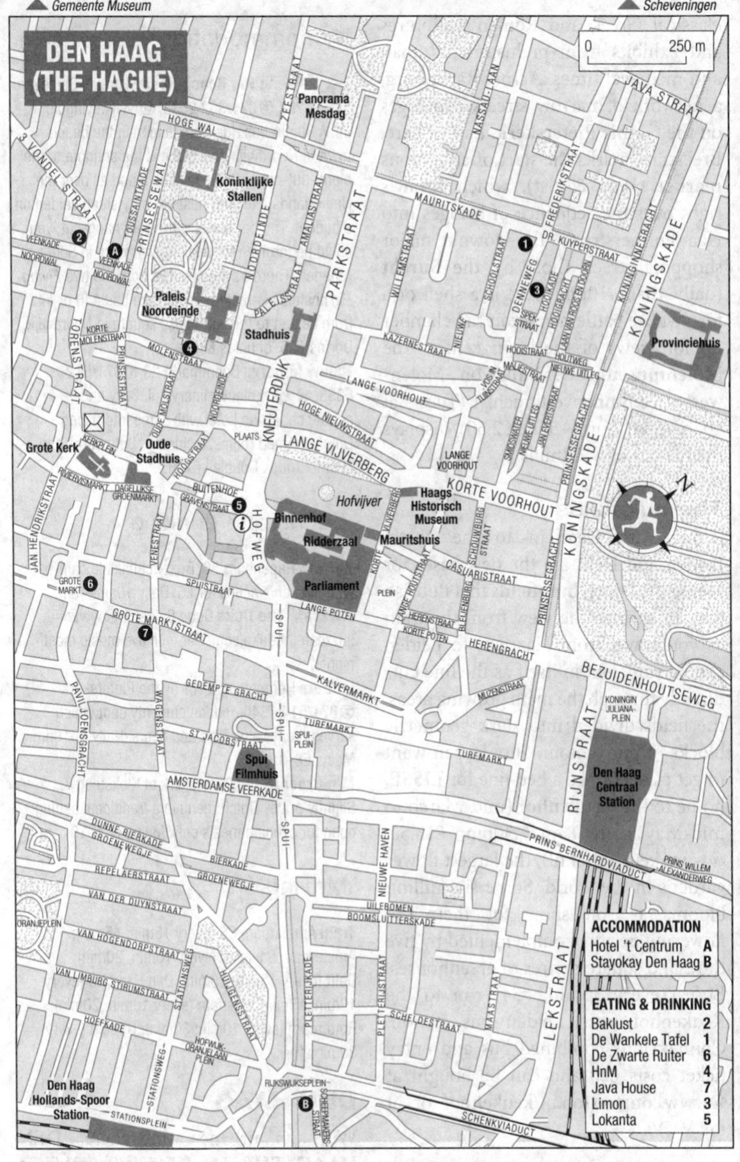

restaurants are in the expense-account category, and the nightlife is similarly packaged. But among all this, Den Haag does have cheaper and livelier bars and restaurants, as well as some excellent museums.

What to see and do

The modern and historical centres of the city interweave about a kilometre north of Den Haag HS station, with the main sights clustered together. More

attractions – including the seaside at **Scheveningen** – are further north, all of which are easily accessible on public transport.

The Binnenhof and Mauritshuis

Right in the centre, the **Binnenhof** is the home of the Dutch parliament and incorporates elements of the town's thirteenth-century castle. The present complex is a rather mundane affair, the small **Hof Vijver** lake mirroring the symmetry of the facade. Inside there's little to see except the **Ridderzaal**, a slender-turreted structure that can be viewed on regular guided tours from the information office at Binnenhof 8a (Mon–Sat 10am–4pm; €5). Immediately east of the Binnenhof, the **Mauritshuis picture gallery** at Korte Vijverberg 8 (Tues–Sat 10am–5pm, Sun 11am–5pm, plus April–Sept Mon 10am–5pm; €12, CJP €6.75), located in a magnificent seventeenth-century mansion, is of more interest, famous for its extensive range of Flemish and Dutch paintings including work by Vermeer, Rubens, Bruegel the Elder and Van Dyck.

Panorama Mesdag and the Gemeente-museum

About fifteen minutes' walk from the Mauritshuis, **Panorama Mesdag** at Zeestraat 65 (Mon–Sat 10am–5pm, Sun noon–5pm; €6) is an astonishing 360-degree painting of seaside scenes of Scheveningen from the 1880s. North, the **Gemeente-museum**, Stadhouderslaan 41 (Tues–Sun 11am–5pm; €9, CJP €5.50; bus #24/tram #17 from Centraal Station), contains superb collections of musical instruments and Islamic ceramics, and modern art, with the world's largest collection of Mondrian paintings.

Scheveningen

Just 4km from Den Haag and easily accessible by tram (#1 from Spui or outside the VVV), **Scheveningen** is one of the Netherlands' most popular beach resorts, and has all the usual attractions like a pier, casino and Sea Life Centre. For accommodation, ask at the VVV on the seafront at Gevers Deynootweg 1134 (Mon–Fri 9.30am–6pm, Sat 10am–5pm, Sun 10am–3pm; ⓣ0900/340 3505, ⓦwww.scheveningen.nl).

Arrival and information

Train The city has two train stations – Den Haag Hollands Spoor (HS) and, about 1km to the northeast, Den Haag Centraal Station (CS). Trains from the UK, France and Belgium stop at the former, whilst the latter is handy for local trains.

Tourist office Hofweg 1, close to the Binnenhof (Mon–Sat 10am–6pm, Sun noon–5pm; ⓣ0900/340 3505, ⓦwww.denhaag.com); offers a small stock of private rooms.

Accommodation

Hotel 't Centrum Veenkade 5 ⓣ070/346 3657, ⓦwww.hotelhetcentrum.nl. Simple, well-located, clean place near the Paleis Noordeinde. Tram #17 from Centraal Station or Holland Spoor to Noordwal. Doubles €95.

Stayokay Den Haag Scheepmakersstraat 27 ⓣ070/315 7878, ⓦwww.stayokay.com. HI hostel that's very handy for Hollands Spoor. Walk from HS station or take trams #1, #9, #12 or #16 to Rijswijkseplein from Centraal. Dorms €28, doubles €95.

Eating and drinking

Baklust Veenkade 19. Dainty crockery, wildflowers in vases and bright decor mirror the sugary sweetness of the delicious cakes. Also serves savoury snacks. Closed Mon. Cakes €2–4.

De Wankele Tafel Mauritskade 79. A great vegetarian option off the beaten track, with a choice of soup, daily special and dessert for €14.50. Mon–Sat 4.30–9.30pm.

De Zwarte Ruiter Grote Markt 27. Popular bar with good, cheap food served throughout the day and a youthful atmosphere. Mains €7–10.

HnM Molenstraat 21a. Variety abounds, with tasty Dutch, Indonesian, French and Italian specials in a fun part of town. Mains €10–12.

Java House Wagenstraat 33. A basic but economic canteen-style café serving filling Indonesian set meals (€5.50–7). Mon–Fri noon–7pm, Sat–Sun noon–6pm.

Limon Denneweg 39a. Friendly place, always full of people hungry for the superb tapas, in an area full of quality food joints. Dinner only, closed Sun. Tapas from €4.

Lokanta Buitenhof 4. Fun, bright restaurant serving Mediterranean food, including plenty of veggie options. Closed Mon. Mains €9–14.

Moving on

Trains from HS Amsterdam CS (every 10min; 50min); Amsterdam Schiphol (every 15min; 30min); Delft (every 10min; 10min); Gouda (every 15min; 40min); Haarlem (every 30min; 30min); Leiden (every 10min; 15min); Rotterdam (every 10min; 20min).

DELFT

DELFT, 2km inland from Den Haag, is perhaps best known for **Delftware**, the delicate blue and white ceramics to which the town gave its name in the seventeenth century, and as the home of the painter **Johannes Vermeer**. With its gabled red-roofed houses standing beside tree-lined canals, the town has a faded tranquillity – though one that can suffer beneath the tourist onslaught during summer.

What to see and do

A good starting point is to follow the Historic Walk around the old town with a map from the VVV (€2.20). A fifteen-minute walk south of the centre at Rotterdamsweg 196 is the **Koninklijke Porceleyne Fles**, a factory producing Delftware (daily 9am–5pm; Nov to mid-March closed Sun; €6.50). The **Markt** is also worth exploring for its collection of small speciality art shops and galleries, with a food market every Thursday. The **Nieuwe Kerk** (April–Oct Mon–Sat 9am–6pm; Nov–March Mon–Fri 11am–4pm, Sat 10am–5pm; €3.30, tower €3) and the Renaissance **Stadhuis** opposite frame the square. William the Silent – leader of the struggle for Dutch independence in the seventeenth century – is buried in this fine old church and you can climb the 370 steps of the tower for spectacular views. West of here, **Wynhaven**, an old canal, leads to Hippolytusbuurt and the Gothic **Oude Kerk** (same hours and ticket as Nieuwe Kerk), perhaps the town's finest building, with an unhealthily leaning tower. Vermeer fans should check out the **Vermeer Centrum**, Delft's newest attraction (daily 10am–5pm; €6) at Voldersgracht 21. Although there are no actual Vermeer paintings, only reproductions, the studio space explaining Vermeer's technique is worth a visit.

Arrival and information

Train From Delft's train station, aim for the big steeple you see on exit and it's a 10min walk north to the Markt.

Tourist office Delft's VVV, called TIP, is just north of the Markt at Hippolytusbuurt 4 (April–Sept Mon & Sun 10am–4pm, Tues–Fri 9am–6pm, Sat 10am–5pm; Oct–March Mon 11am–4pm, Tues–Sat 10am–4pm, Sun 10am–3pm; ⓣ0900/515 1555, ⓦwww.delft.com).

Accommodation

Delftse Hout Campsite Korftlaan 5 ⓣ015/213 0040, ⓦwww.delftsehout.nl. All kinds of accommodation, from chalets to grass huts and eco-homes. Take bus #64 from the station. Camping huts €42.50.

Oosteinde Oosteinde 156 ⓣ015/213 4238, ⓦwww.bb-oosteinde.nl. B&B with lovely rooms, right in the centre. Minimum stay two nights. Doubles €65.

The Soul Inn Willemstraat 55 ⓣ015/215 7246, ⓦwww.soulinn.nl. A small hotel, with imaginative, artistic decor and quirky rooms. Handy location for the station. Doubles €60.

Eating

Kleyweg's Stads-Koffyhuis Oude Delft 133 ⓣ015/212 4625. A bustling café which serves delicious sweet and savoury pancakes and has a canalside terrace. Pancakes €6–9.

Kobus Kuch Beestenmarkt 1 ⓣ015/212 4280. A gem of a café/restaurant – don't miss the famous *appeltart met slagroom* (apple cake with cream) dished up in cosy surroundings for €3.10.

Uit de Kunst Oude Delft 140, near Oude Kerk. Charming little café decorated with 1940s memorabilia and offering home-made cakes and cheap snacks. Closed Mon & Tues.

Drinking and nightlife

Bebop Jazz Café Kromstraat 33 Ⓦwww.jazzcafebebop.nl. Holds jam sessions every other Tuesday.

Locus Publicus Brabantse Turfmarkt 67. Popular local bar, serving a staggering array of beers as well as a good selection of cheap snacks. Sandwiches €3.

Speakers Burghwal 45–49 Ⓦwww.speakers.nl. The only club in town, with a variety of live acts featuring everything from DJs to comedians.

Moving on

Train Amsterdam (every 30min; 1hr); Den Haag HS (every 10min; 10min); Rotterdam (every 10min; 12min).

ROTTERDAM

Just south of Delft lies **ROTTERDAM**, at the heart of a maze of rivers and artificial waterways that together form the outlet of the rivers Rijn (Rhine) and Maas (Meuse). After devastating damage during World War II, Rotterdam has grown into a vibrant city dotted with premier cultural attractions and built around Europe's busiest port. Fortunately redevelopment hasn't obliterated the city's earthy character: its grittiness is part of its appeal, as are its boisterous bars and clubs.

What to see and do

You can get a feel for the city by walking from the station (or taking tram #7 from just outside) down to the Museumpark along Mauritsweg. More idiosyncratic attractions lie further east, whilst Delfshaven is a short, and rewarding, journey southwest.

The Museumpark and around

The enormous **Boijmans Van Beuningen Museum**, at Museumpark 18–20 (Tues–Sun 11am–5pm; €9, free on Wed; Ⓦwww.boijmans.nl), has a superb collection of works by Monet, Van Gogh, Picasso, Gauguin and Cézanne, while its earlier canvases include several by Bosch, Bruegel the Elder and Rembrandt. A stroll through the Museumpark brings you to the **Nattuurmuseum Kunsthal** (Tues–Sat 10am–5pm, Sun 11am–5pm; €9, CJP €5; Ⓦwww.kunsthal.nl) which showcases first-rate exhibitions of contemporary art, photography and design. Also in the park is the **Netherlands Architecture Institute** (same hours as Kunsthal; €5; Ⓦwww.nai.nl), with regularly changing exhibitions focusing on particular architects or areas. For alternative art, you can't do better than a wander along **Witte de Withstraat** with its tiny, inexpensive galleries (check Ⓦwww.tentrotterdam.nl, www.wdw.nl or www.showroommama.nl for current exhibitions).

The Maritiem Museum and Museum Het Schielandhuis

Near the Leuvehaven is the entertaining **Maritiem Museum** (Maritime Museum; Tues–Sat 10am–5pm, Sun 11am–5pm, also Mon 10am–5pm in July and August; €7.50, CJP €3). A short walk away is **Blaak**, a pocket-sized area that was levelled in World War II, but has since been rebuilt. The architectural highlight is a remarkable series of topsy-turvy, cube-shaped houses, the *kubuswoningen*, completed in 1984. At Overblaak 70 is the **Kijk-Kubus** (Show Cube; daily 11am–5pm; Jan & Feb Sat & Sun 11am–5pm; €2.50), which offers somewhat disorientating but compelling tours of the house. Nearby, the Binnenrote **market** (Tues & Sat) sells cheese, fish and flowers.

Delfshaven

If little in Rotterdam city centre can exactly be called picturesque, **DELFSHAVEN**, a couple of kilometres southwest of Centraal Station, makes up for it (tram #4 or #8 direction Schiedam to Spanjaardstraat or take the metro). Once the harbour that served Delft, it was from here that the Pilgrim Fathers set sail

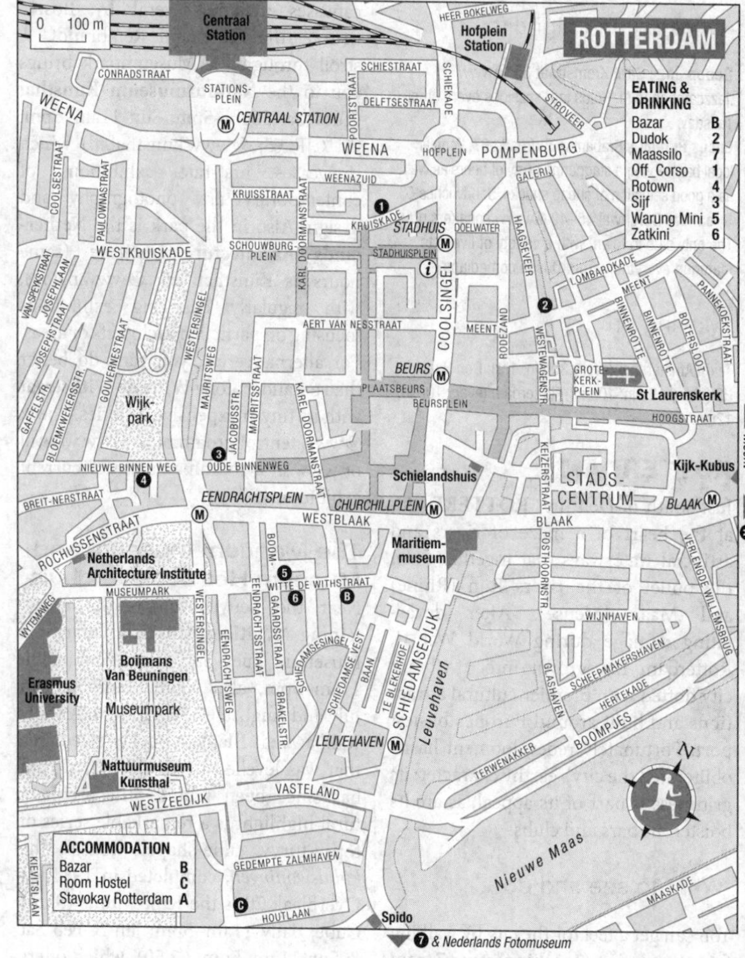

for the New World in 1620. Most of the buildings lining the district's two narrow canals are eighteenth- and nineteenth-century warehouses. Formerly a *jenever* distillery, the **Museum de Dubbelde Palmboom**, Voorhaven 12 (Tues–Fri 10am–5pm, Sat & Sun 11am–5pm; €3), is now a wide-ranging historical museum.

Arrival and information

Train Centraal Station is just north of the centre, and is the hub of a useful tram and metro system, though best avoided late at night.

Tourist office Main VVV at Coolsingel 5 (Mon–Thurs 9am–5.30pm, Fri 9am–9pm, Sat 9am–5.30pm, Sun 10am–5pm; ⓣ010/271 0120, ⓦwww.vvvrotterdam.nl). You can pick up the Rotterdam Welcome discount card for €5 (ⓦwww.rotterdam.info).

Use-It Schaatsbaan 41 (mid-May to mid-Sept Tues–Sun 9am–6pm, July & Aug also Mon 1–5pm; mid-Sept to mid-May Tues–Sat 9am–5pm; ⓣ010/240 9158, ⓦwww.jip.org/usecms). Very useful information centre for budget travellers located close to the station. Their free "Do-It-Yourself" tours are particularly handy.

BOAT TRIPS

A fun way to see the city is from the water. One possibility is to take an exhilarating trip in a **water taxi** from the Leuvehaven (€3.20; also from the Veerhaven for a much shorter journey for €2.50; ⓦwww.watertaxirotterdam.nl) to the splendid *Hotel New York*, which occupies the building where transatlantic cruise liners once docked. Close by is the **Nederlands Fotomuseum**, Wilhelminakade 332 (Tues–Fri 10am–5pm, Sat & Sun 11am–5pm; €6, CJP €3), where there's a small exhibition on Rotterdam photography as well as changing exhibitions. From here you can walk back to the centre over the futuristic bridge, the **Erasmusbrug**, an ideal spot for photos. There are also numerous **boat trips** from the Leuvehaven through the harbour (year-round; 1hr 15min; €9.50). In July and August, **day-trips** run to Dordrecht, Schoonhoven, the nineteen windmills at Kinderdijk, and the Delta Project, from €39–49 per person; contact the VVV or Spido for details (ⓣ010/275 9988, ⓦwww.spido.nl).

Accommmodation

Bazar Witte de Withstraat 16 ⓣ010/206 5151, ⓦwww.hotelbazar.nl. A superb hotel on one of the hippest streets in the city, with an excellent restaurant. Each floor is decorated in the style of a different continent – the rooms are unique so choose your favourite from the website before you book. Some have balconies, others hot tubs, but all have character in abundance. From the station take trams #7 or #20 to Museumpark or trams #8 to Churchillplein. Doubles €75.

Room Hostel Van Vollenhovenstraat 62 ⓣ010/282 7277, ⓦwww.roomrotterdam.nl. Very funky hostel in a better location than the HI option. Extremely helpful staff organize events for guests, and there's a vibrant bar and quieter lounge. From Centraal Station take tram #7 to Westerstraat or tram #8 to Vasteland. Dorms €20, doubles €55.

Stayokay Rotterdam Overblaak 85–87 ⓣ010/436 5763, ⓦwww.stayokay.com. HI hostel which promises all of the facilities expected from the Stayokay chain. Take the metro to Blaak station, then it's a short walk. Dorms €28, doubles €95.

Eating

The best places for cheap and tasty food are Oude and Nieuwe Binnenweg and Witte de Withstraat.

Bazar Witte de Withstraat 16 ⓣ010/206 5151. Popular bar/restaurant serving excellent Middle Eastern food with colourful surroundings and a lively atmosphere. Mains €10–15.

Dudok Meent 88 ⓣ010/433 3102. An expansive grand café with slick service and the city's most famous apple pie (€3.15).

Sijf Oude Binnenweg 115 ⓣ010/433 2610. One of the many agreeable pub-style places along this stretch. Mains are reasonable: €14.50, including unlimited fries and salad, or cheaper daily specials for €10–12.

Warung Mini Witte de Withstraat 47. A cheap and cheerful canteen dishing up hefty portions of decent Surinamese and Chinese. Open until 6am at the weekend to satisfy those late-night cravings. Mains €6–9.

Drinking and nightlife

Maassilo Maashaven Zuidzijde 1–2 ⓦwww.maassilo.com. Trendy club in a converted grain silo. Open Thurs–Sat. Metro Maashaven.

Off_Corso Kruiskade 22 ⓦwww.offcorso.nl. Arty club in an old cinema, specializing in electro and techno. Open Thurs–Sat. Metro Stadhuis.

Rotown Nieuwe Binnenweg 17–19 ⓦwww.rowtown.nl. A pre-party bar with gigs by up-and-coming bands. Also serves food, including cheap pasta dishes (€6.50) on Monday and Tuesday evenings; open till 2am.

Zatkini Witte de Withstraat 88. Lively Spanish bar on a great street. Serves food until 10pm.

Shopping

Rotterdam is famous for vintage clothing, and many of the best places are concentrated around Nieuwe Binnenweg: try Sister Moon at 89b, or Episode on nearby Oude Binnenweg at 144a. There are also plenty of vinyl shops round here, including Triple Vision (Nieuwe Binnenweg 131b; closed Sun–Tues) and Mid-Town Records (Nieuwe Binnenweg 79a).

Moving on

Train Amsterdam CS (every 10min; 1hr); Amsterdam Schiphol (every 10min; 50min); Delft (every 10min; 15min); Den Haag HS (every 10min; 20min); Gouda (every 10min; 20min); Leiden (every 10min; 30min); Utrecht (every 15min; 45min).

GOUDA

A pretty little place some 25km northeast of Rotterdam, **GOUDA** is almost everything you'd expect of a Dutch country town: a ring of quiet canals encircling ancient buildings and old quays.

What to see and do

The **Markt** is the largest in the Netherlands, a reminder of the town's prominence as a centre of the medieval cloth trade, and later of the manufacture of cheeses and clay pipes. A touristy **cheese market** is held here every Thursday morning from June to August. Slap bang in the middle, the elegant Gothic **Stadhuis** dates from 1450. On the north side is the **Waag**, a tidy seventeenth-century building whose top two floors house a cheese museum (April–Oct Tues, Wed & Fri–Sun 1–5pm, Thurs 10am–5pm; €2). South, off the Markt, the sixteenth-century **St Janskerk** (April–Oct Mon–Sat 9–5pm; Nov–March 10am–4pm; €2.75) is famous for its magnificent stained-glass windows depicting Biblical and secular scenes.

Arrival and information

Train and bus stations Both 10min north of the centre.

Tourist office VVV Markt 27 (Mon 1–5.30pm, Tues–Fri 9.30am–5.30pm, Sat 10am–4pm; June–Aug also Sun noon–3pm; ⓣ0900/468 32888, ⓦwww.vvvgouda.nl). Can also help arrange private rooms.

Accommodation

B&B Bij Van Briemen Lange Dwarsstraat 21 ⓣ018/251 1367, ⓦwww.bijvanbriemen.nl. Bed and breakfast in a very pleasant residential area close to the centre. Doubles €60.

De Utrechtsche Dom Geuzenstraat 6 ⓣ018/252 8833, ⓦwww.hotelgouda.nl. This quiet family hotel is situated right in the centre of town, 15min walk from the train station. Doubles €60.

Eating and drinking

Café Central Markt 23. A lively bar with an outdoor terrace.

Eetcafé Vidocq Koster Gijzensteeg 8 ⓣ018/252 2819. Atmospheric, popular bar off the Markt which also serves dinner. Mains €15.

Gewoon Gouds Markt 42. Varied menu with views of the Stadhuis. Serves tapas at dinner. *Broodjes* €4–6.

Kamphuisen Hoge Gouwe 19 ⓣ018/251 4163. Offers good-quality Dutch food at a reasonable price. Closed Mon. Mains €15.

Moving on

Train Amsterdam (every 30min; 50min); Den Haag HS (every 15min; 40min); Rotterdam (every 10min; 20 min); Utrecht (every 10min; 20min).

UTRECHT

"I groaned with the idea of living all winter in so shocking a place," wrote Boswell in 1763, and the university town of **UTRECHT**, surrounded by shopping centres and industrial developments, still promises little as you approach. But the centre, with its distinctive sunken canals – whose brick cellar warehouses have been converted into chic cafés and restaurants – is one of the country's most pleasant.

What to see and do

For a place of its size, there's surprisingly little in the way of sights and museums in Utrecht. The focal point is the **Dom Tower**, built between 1321 and 1382, which at over 110m is the highest church tower in the country. A guided tour (May–Sept Mon–Sat 10am–5pm, Sun noon–5pm; Oct–April Mon–Fri noon–4pm, Sat 11am–4pm, Sun noon–4pm; €7.50) takes you unnervingly close to the top, from where you can see Rotterdam and Amsterdam on a clear day. Below is the Gothic **Dom Kerk**; only the eastern part of the cathedral remains after the nave collapsed in 1674, but it's worth peering inside (May–Sept Mon–Fri 10am–5pm, Sat 10am–3.30pm, Sun 2–4pm; Oct–April Mon–Fri 11am–4pm, Sat 11am–3.30pm, Sun 2–4pm; free) and wandering through the Kloostergang,

the fourteenth-century cloisters that link the cathedral to the chapterhouse.

Arrival and information

Train and bus stations Both lead into the Hoog Catharijne shopping centre.
Tourist office Close to the Dom Tower at Domplein 9 (Mon noon–6pm, Tues–Fri 10am–6pm, Sat 10am–5pm, Sun noon–5pm; Ⓣ0900/128 8732, Ⓦwww.utrechtyourway.nl).

Accommodation

Stayokay Utrecht-Bunnik Rhijnauwenselaan 14 Ⓣ030/656 1277, Ⓦwww.stayokay.com. Peaceful, family-orientated HI hostel located a good 5km out of the centre in an old country manor house. Take bus #40 or #41 from the train station to Rhijnauwen. Dorms €28, doubles €80.
Strowis Boothstraat 8 Ⓣ030/238 0280, Ⓦwww.strowis.nl. A pleasant guesthouse with a fresh feel, a kitchen and free internet access in the relaxing lounge. Take a short ride on bus #3/#4/#8/#11 to the Janskerkhof stop. Dorms €15, doubles €60.

Eating and drinking

De Oude Muntkelder Oudegracht 112. A good option among the many cafés on this busy stretch by the canal; serves inexpensive pancakes for around €8.
De Soepterrine Zakkendragerssteeg 42 Ⓣ030/231 7005. An intimate, homely restaurant which serves hearty food including home-made soup and cheese fondue. Mains €11–15.
De Werfkring Oudegracht 123. Offers an affordable vegetarian menu: a good spot for a healthy lunch. Mon–Sat noon–8pm. Soup €4.
De Winkel van Sinkel Oudegracht 158. The hippest bar in town with regular dance nights and a chill-out room downstairs.
Studenten Café Neutje Neude 30. Low lighting and old-fashioned decor conceal a tiny but buzzing student hot-spot with a good selection of beers and cheap snacks. Open till 2am. Toasties €3.

Moving on

Train Amsterdam (every 15min; 30 min); Arnhem (every 15min; 35min); Gouda (every 10min 20min); Maastricht (every 30min; 2hr); Rotterdam (every 15min; 40min).

Beyond the Randstad

Outside the Randstad towns, the Netherlands is relatively unknown territory to visitors. To the north, there's superb cycling and hiking to be had through scenic **dune reserves** and delightful villages, with easy access to pristine beaches, while the island of **Texel** offers the country's most complete beach experience, and has plenty of birdlife. The **Hoge Veluwe National Park**, near Arnhem, boasts one of the country's best modern art museums and has cycle paths through a delightful landscape. Further south the landscape slowly fills out, moving into a rougher countryside of farmland and forests and eventually into the hills around **Maastricht**, a city with a vibrant, pan-European feel.

TEXEL

The largest of the islands off the north coast – and the easiest to get to (2hr from Amsterdam) – **TEXEL** (pronounced "tessel") offers diverse and pretty landscapes, and is one of Europe's most important bird-breeding grounds.

What to see and do

Texel's main settlement, **DEN BURG**, makes a convenient base and has bike rental outlets. On the coast 3km southeast of Den Burg is **OUDESCHILD**, home to the **Maritiem en Juttersmuseum** (Beachcombers' Museum; Tues–Sat 10am–5pm, Sun noon–5pm, July & Aug also Mon 10am–5pm; €6), a fascinating collection of marine junk from wrecks. In the opposite direction is **DE KOOG**, with a good sandy beach and the **EcoMare nature centre**, at Ruijslaan 92 (daily 9am–5pm; €8.50; Ⓦwww.ecomare.nl), a bird and seal sanctuary as well as natural history museum: from

here you can visit the **Wad**, the banks of sand and mud to the east of the island, where seals and birds gather.

Arrival and information

Boat Ferries from the town of Den Helder on the mainland (take bus #33 from the station to the port) depart every hour (20min; €3; coming from Amsterdam, ask for an all-in discounted *Waddenbiljet*). Once on Texel, various buses greet the ferry's arrival and depart for destinations across the island.
Tourist office Den Burg's VVV is at Emmalaan 66 (Mon–Fri 9am–5.30pm, Sat 9am–5pm; ⓣ022/231 4741, ⓦwww.texel.net) where you can pick up leaflets, maps and information on cycling routes.

Accommodation

Camping is the most popular option here, with good campsites dotted around the island.
De Koorn Aar Grensweg 388 ⓣ022/231 2931, ⓦwww.koorn-aar.nl. Small, well-run campsite (with chalets) close to Den Burg. Closed Nov–March. €28 for a tent for two people.
Kogerstrand Badweg 33 ⓣ022/231 7208, ⓦwww.texelcampings.nl. Campsite set among the beachside dunes in De Koog, the island's busiest resort. Closed Nov–March. €15.
Stayokay Texel Haffelderweg 29 ⓣ022/231 5441, ⓦwww.stayokay.com. HI hostel on the outskirts of Den Burg that's more suited to families and groups, although it has a big bar and terrace. Dorms €30, doubles €85.

Eating and drinking

De Pangkoekehuus Kikkertstraat 9, De Cocksdorp. Cosy place serving delicious filled pancakes for around €7.
Freya Gravenstraat 4 ⓣ022/232 1686. Be sure to book ahead for Den Burg's best restaurant, which serves a delicious three-course set menu each night for €24.50.

HOGE VELUWE NATIONAL PARK

Some 70km southeast of Amsterdam, and just north of the town of **ARNHEM**, is the huge and scenic **Hoge Veluwe National Park** (daily: Nov–March 9am–6pm; April 8am–8pm; May & Aug 8am–9pm; June & July 8am–10pm; Sept 9am–8pm; Oct 9am–7pm; €7 park only, €3.50 after 5pm, €14 with Kröller-Müller museum; ⓦwww.hogeveluwe.nl). Formerly the estate of wealthy local couple Anton and Helene Kröller-Müller, it has three entrances – one near the village of **Otterlo** on the northwest perimeter, another near **Hoenderloo** on the northeast edge, and a third to the south at **Rijzenburg**, near the village of Schaarsbergen. The easiest way to get here is by bus #2 from Arnhem's bus station (every 30min; €1.10) to Koningsweg stop, from where the Rijzenburg entrance is a five-minute walk. Here, you can pick up free white bicycles, by far the best way to explore the park.

What to see and do

Within the park is the **Museonder** (daily 9.30am–5/6pm), an underground natural-history museum, and the **St Hubertus Hunting Lodge** (guided tours only; €2), the former Art Deco home of the Kröller-Müllers. The park's unmissable highlight is the **Kröller-Müller Museum** (Tues–Sun 10am–5pm; €14 including park admission; ⓦwww.kmm.nl), a superb collection of fine art including nearly three hundred paintings by Van Gogh, plus works by Picasso, Seurat, Léger and Mondrian. Behind the museum is a lovely and imaginative **sculpture garden** (Tues–Sun 10am–4.30pm; same ticket).

Arrival and information

Train and bus From nearby Arnhem's train station, you can catch a bus to the park from the neighbouring bus station (see above).
Tourist office Arnhem's VVV office is near the station, at Stationsplein 13 (Mon–Fri 9.30am–5.30pm, Sat 9.30am–5pm; ⓣ0900/112 2344, ⓦwww.vvvarnhem.nl).

Accommodation

Hoge Veluwe Campsite ⓣ055/378 2232, ⓦwww.hogeveluwe.nl. Official campsite by the

park's northeastern Hoenderloo entrance. Closed Nov–March. €4.
Stayokay Arnhem Diepenbrocklaan 27 ⓣ 026/442 0114, ⓦ www.stayokay.com. Set in a no-man's-land north of town, this hostel provides good, cheap accommodation and also serves dinner. Take bus #3 to the Rijnstate hospital, from where it is a 5min walk. Dorms €28, doubles €80.

Moving on

Train Amsterdam (every 15min; 1hr 10min); Utrecht (every 30min; 40min).

MAASTRICHT

Squashed between the Belgian and German borders, **MAASTRICHT** is one of the most delightful cities in the Netherlands. A cosmopolitan place, where three languages happily coexist, it's also one of the oldest towns in the country.

What to see and do

The busiest of Maastricht's many squares is **Markt**, at its most crowded during the Wednesday and Friday morning **market**, with the mid-seventeenth-century **Stadhuis** (Mon–Fri 9am–12.30pm & 2–5pm; free) at its centre. Just west, **Vrijthof** is a grander open space flanked by a line of café terraces on one side and on the other by **St Servaaskerk** (daily 10am–4.30pm, Sun until 12.30pm; €3.70), a tenth-century church. Next door is **St Janskerk** (Easter–Oct Mon–Sat 11am–4pm; free), with its tall fifteenth-century Gothic tower (Mon–Sat 11am–4pm; €1.50). On the other side of the square lies the appealing district of **Stokstraat Kwartier**, with narrow streets winding out to the fast-flowing River Jeker and the **Helpoort** fortress gateway of 1229. South of here, the **casemates** in the **Waldeck Park** (guided tours: July–Sept daily 12.30pm & 2pm; Oct–June Sat & Sun 2pm; €4.25) are further evidence of Maastricht's once-impressive fortifications. Fifteen minutes' walk south is the 110m hill of **St Pietersberg**. Of the two ancient defensive tunnel systems under the hill, the **Zonneberg** is the better, situated on the far side of the hill at Casino Slavante (hourly guided tours: July–Sept daily 1.50pm; €4.90, €8.50 including fort).

Bonnefantenmuseum

On the east side of the river is the city's main art gallery, **Bonnefantenmuseum** at Avenue Céramique 250 (Tues–Sun 11am–5pm; €8). Designed by Aldo Rossi, it's situated in the newest part of Maastricht, **Céramique**, which offers a complete contrast to the feel of the historic city. The collection ranges from Old Masters to contemporary artists, but is less of an attraction than the building itself.

Arrival and information

Train and bus The centre of Maastricht is on the west bank of the river. You're likely to arrive, however, on the east bank, in the district Wijk, home to the train and bus stations and many of the city's hotels.
Tourist office The VVV, Kleine Straat 1, at the end of the main shopping street (May–Nov Mon–Sat 9am–6pm, Sun 11am–3pm; Nov–May Mon–Fri 9am–6pm, Sat 9am–5pm; ⓣ 043/325 2121, ⓦ www.vvvmaastricht.eu), has copies of a tourist guide (€4.95) with map and a list of private rooms.

Accommodation

Botel Maastricht Maasboulevard 95 ⓣ 043/321 9023, ⓦ www.botelmaastricht.nl. Moored on the river not far from the Helpoort, this is a fun place – there's a huge difference in cabin size for the same price, so ask for a larger one when you book. Doubles €44.
Camping De Bosrand Moerslag 4 ⓣ 043/409 1544, ⓦ www.campingdebosrand.nl. Campsite 25min south of town on bus #57. Closed Nov–March. €7.
La Cloche Bredestraat 4 ⓣ 043/321 2407, ⓦ www.lacloche.com. Pleasant and extremely central hotel with just eight rooms. Check-in is at *Café Cloche*, round the corner at Vrijthof 12. Doubles €80.
Stayokay Maastricht Maasboulevard 101 ⓣ 043/750 1790, ⓦ www.stayokay.com. HI hostel with a big riverside terrace done up in a funky retro

style, but it can feel soulless. A few minutes' walk from the centre and 15min from the station. Dorms €33, doubles €93.

Eating and drinking

Coffeelovers Dominican Sq 1. A stylish café within a bookshop in a beautiful converted church. The great coffee is a perfect accompaniment to browsing the books. Closed Sun.

DeliBelge Tongersestraat 44a. Good place to pick up a cheap snack if you're in the university quarter. Sandwich €3.

Lunch & Zo Sint Amorsplein 2 ⓣ043/326 4904. A hip and modern café. The decor is minimalist, but the coffee, served with sugary surprises, is far from it. Coffee €2, high tea €13.50.

Pizzeria Napoli Markt 71. Great pizzas which taste even better with a twenty percent student discount. The kitsch surroundings make for a cheap but cheerful atmosphere. Pizza €10.

Tribunal Tongersestraat 1. Happening brown café that's popular with students, with large, sociable tables. Beer €3.

Zondag Wijckerbrugstraat 42 ⓣ043/321 9300. A bustling and bright café-bar near the station, serving snacks, soups and salads until 10pm. Sandwiches €6.

TREAT YOURSELF

Mes Amis Tongersestraat 5 ⓣ043/325 7866, ⓦwww.mesamis.nl. Maastricht is renowned for its superb cuisine, and gastronomic titillation awaits at this laid-back restaurant. The four-course dinner menu for €31.50 ("Menu Des Amis") consists of exquisite, well-presented regional food, and can be accompanied by an impressive variety of wines by the glass. Or, if you're feeling flush, there is a specially selected glass of wine to accompany each course for an extra €18.50. Daily from 5pm, closed Tues.

Moving on

Train Amsterdam (every 30min; 2hr 35min); Liège (hourly; 30min); Utrecht (every 30min; 2hr).

Norway

HIGHLIGHTS

THE LOFOTEN ISLANDS: visit this Arctic archipelago in summer for gorgeous scenery, swimming and fishing

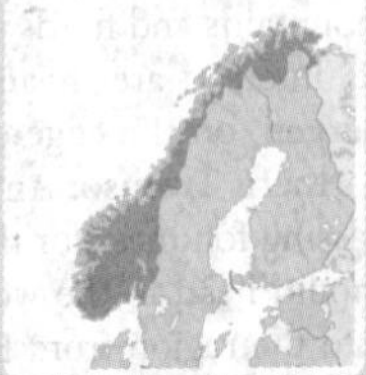

GEIRANGERFJORD: take the Trollstigen Highway to this glorious fjord for the quintessential Norwegian experience

GRUNERLØKKA: this former working class district of Oslo is now home to a buzzing collection of bars, clubs and boutique shops

STAVANGER: a little gem of a university town, with great bars and restaurants and sandy, surfable beaches nearby

ROUGH COSTS

DAILY BUDGET Basic €70/occasional treat €95

DRINK Beer €7

FOOD Fish soup €15

HOSTEL/BUDGET HOTEL €30–40/€70

TRAVEL Train: Oslo–Bergen €35–95 (7hr); Bus: Oslo–Trondheim €55 (8hr).

FACT FILE

POPULATION 4 million

AREA 324,220 sq km

LANGUAGE Norwegian

CURRENCY Norwegian krone (kr)

CAPITAL Oslo (population 500,000)

INTERNATIONAL PHONE CODE ⓣ47

Introduction

Norway's extraordinary landscape will lift your heart while high prices squeeze your wallet. The pay-off is the country's mix of likeable, easy-going cities and breathtaking wilderness – during summer, you can hike up a glacier in the morning and thaw out in an urban bar in the evening, watching the sun dip below the horizon for all of half an hour, if at all. Deeper into the countryside, you'll find vast stretches of distinctive glacier-formed landscapes. And because of Norway's low population density, it really is possible to travel for hours among all this natural grandeur without seeing a soul.

Beyond **Oslo** – a pretty, increasingly cosmopolitan capital surrounded by mountains and fjords – the major cities of interest are historic **Trondheim**, **Bergen**, on the edge of the fjords, and northern **Tromsø**. Anyone with even a passing fondness for the great outdoors should head to the **western fjords**: dip into the region from Bergen or **Åndalsnes**, or linger in one of the many quiet waterside towns and villages. Further north, deep in the Arctic Circle, the **Lofoten Islands** are well worth the effort for their calm atmosphere and sheer beauty. To the north of here, the tourist trail focuses on the long journey to **Nordkapp**, the northernmost accessible point in Europe; the route leads through **Finnmark**, one of the last strongholds of the Sami and their herds of reindeer. Tourism reaches its height from June to August when opening hours are long and activities plentiful; the rest of the year you'll find many establishments closed unless you're in major towns.

CHRONOLOGY

10,000–2000 BC Seal- and reindeer-hunting tribes move into present-day Norway.

800–1050 AD Norwegian Vikings become a dominant force in Europe, conducting successful raids across Britain and the continent.

900 King Harald becomes the first ruler of a united Norway.

1030 The Norwegians adopt Christianity.

1262 Norway increases her empire, forming unions with Greenland and Iceland.

1350 Almost two-thirds of the population die during the Black Death.

1396 The Kalmar Union unites Norway with Denmark and Sweden under a single ruler.

1536 Sweden leaves the Kalmar Union, leaving Norway under Danish control.

1814 Norwegian hopes of independence are dashed after Sweden invades and takes control.

1905 Parliament declares independence from Sweden. Haakon VII is crowned the first king of an independent Norway in 525 years.

1913 Norway becomes one of the first countries in the world to give women the vote.

1914 Norway remains neutral during World War I.

1939–1945 Norway initially declares neutrality during World War II but is invaded by the Nazis in 1940. Widespread acts of sabotage take place until liberation in May 1945.

1960s The discovery of oil and gas in the North Sea leads to greater economic prosperity.

1981 Gro Harlem Brundtland becomes Norway's first female prime minister.

2005 Prime Minister Kjell Bodevik is defeated in the general elections, and is replaced by Labour candidate Jens Stolenberg.

2007 Norway is rated as world's most peaceful country in the Global Peace Index survey.

ARRIVAL

Norway has dozens of **airports**, but the five busiest for budget travellers are Oslo, Bergen, Trondheim, Haugesund and Stavanger. The main low-cost carriers are Ryanair, which flies to Haugesund and Oslo, and Norwegian Air Shuttle (Ⓣ21 49 00 15, Ⓦwww.norwegian.no). SAS

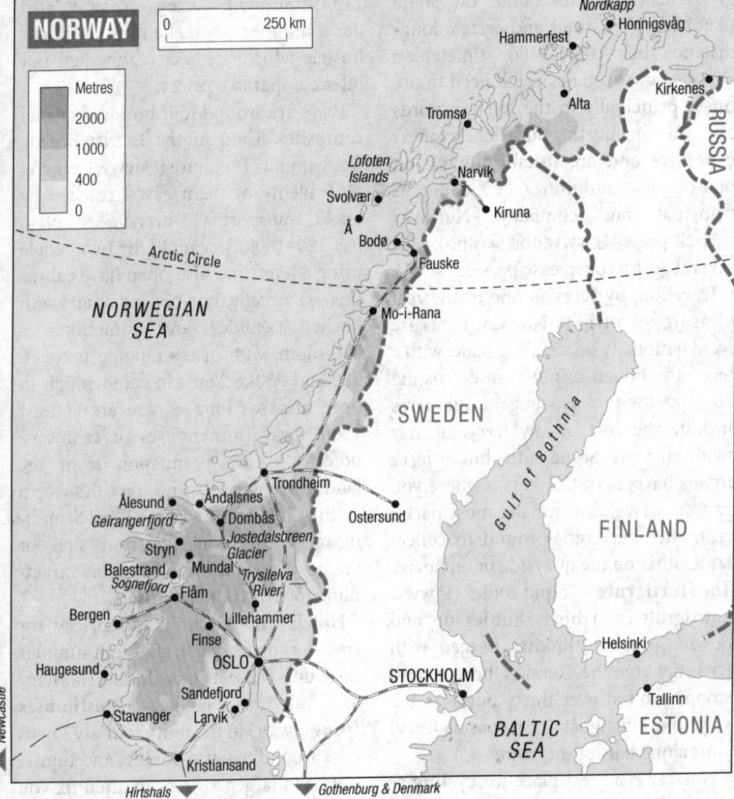

(ⓦwww.sas.no) also flies to most destinations in the country, with partner airline Widerøe (ⓦwww.wideroe.no) picking up the rest; if you buy in advance flights can be very reasonable and are certainly the fastest way to get around this vast country.

Norway's long coastline is served by a number of **ferry** companies; the biggest are DFDS Seaways (UK ⓣ0871 522 9955, ⓦwww.dfds.co.uk) and Color Line (ⓦwww.colorline.com), which ply routes between Newcastle in the UK and Copenhagen in Denmark and the major ports of Stavanger and Bergen. There are frequent international **trains** to Oslo from Stockholm and Gothenburg in Sweden, and international **buses**, run by Eurolines.

GETTING AROUND

Public transport is very reliable. In the winter (especially in the north), services can be cut back severely, but no part of the country is isolated for long. A synopsis of all the main air, train, bus and ferry services is given in the free *NRI Guide to Transport and Accommodation* brochure, available in advance from the Norwegian Tourist Board, and all local tourist offices have detailed regional public transport timetables.

There are four main **train** routes. These link Oslo to Stockholm in the east, to Kristiansand and Stavanger in the southwest, to Bergen in the west and to Trondheim and on to Fauske and Bodø in the north. InterRail and Eurail **rail passes** are valid in Norway, and also

give substantial discounts on some major ferry crossings and certain long-distance bus routes. For timetables, check Ⓦwww.nsb.no. You'll need to use **buses** principally in the western fjords and the far north. Bus tickets aren't expensive and are usually bought on board; in addition the country's principal bus company, Nor-Way Bussekspress (Ⓦwww.nor-way.no), sells several go-as-you-please passes.

Travelling by **ferry** is one of the real pleasures of a trip to Norway. Rates are fixed nationally on a sliding scale, with a ten- to fifteen-minute ride costing 20–30kr for foot passengers. Bus fares include the cost of any ferry journey made en route. Some of the busier ferry routes have a control kiosk, where you pay on arrival, but for the most part a crew member comes round to collect fares either on the quayside or on board. The **Hurtigrute** – "rapid route" (Ⓦwww.hurtigruten.no) boat shuttles up and down the coast, linking Bergen with Kirkenes, on the Russian border, and stopping off at over thirty ports on the way; the Hurtigbåt (fast coastal ferry) runs along part of this route.

Norway is a great place for **cycling** as much of the country is sparsely populated and scenic. Bike Norway (Ⓦwww.bike-norway.com) has all the information you could ever need.

ACCOMMODATION

For budget travellers as well as hikers, climbers and skiers, **hostels** provide the accommodation mainstay; there are about a hundred in total, spread right across the country and run by Norske Vandrerhjem (Ⓦwww.vandrerhjem.no). Prices vary greatly (200–300kr), and bed linen costs extra, although the more expensive hostels nearly always include breakfast in the price of the room. Most places also have a supply of doubles for 400–500kr. HI members get a 15 percent discount. Many HI hostels close 11am–4pm, and there's often an 11pm/midnight curfew. Norway also has a number of excellent independent hostels which are less regimented but offer comparable prices.

There are around four hundred official **campsites** listed in the tourist board's free camping brochure (Ⓦwww.camping.no), plenty of them easily reached by public transport. On average expect to pay 120–160kr per night for two people using a tent. Sites also often have **cabins** (*hytter*), usually four-bedded affairs with kitchen facilities and sometimes a bathroom, with prices ranging between 250 and 750kr. You can camp rough in open areas as long as you are at least 150m away from houses or cabins or otherwise have permission from the landowner, and leave no trace. It's worth getting hold of a Camping Card Scandinavia (CCS); available from sites or online (Ⓦwww.camping.no), it attracts numerous discounts for users.

Hotels are generally too pricey for travellers on a budget, although summer discounts can net you a double room for as little as 600kr. **Guesthouses** (*pensjonater*) in the more touristy towns cost around 550kr a double, and tourist offices in larger towns can often fix you up with a **private room** in someone's house for around 350–400kr a double. Finally, in coastal districts, especially the Lofoten Islands, **sjøhus** (literally "sea houses") and **rorbus** (converted fishermen's cabins) can be rented from about 500kr per cabin and sleep anywhere from 2–8 people.

FOOD AND DRINK

Norwegian **food** can be excellent: fish is plentiful, as are reindeer steak and elk. However, eating well on a tight budget can be difficult. Breakfast (*frokost*) – a self-service affair of bread, cheese, eggs, preserves, cold meat and fish, washed down with unlimited tea and coffee – is usually good at hostels, and very good in hotels. If it isn't included in the room rate, reckon on an extra 50–70kr.

Picnic food is the best stand-by during the day, although there are **fast-food** alternatives. The indigenous Norwegian variety, served up at street stalls (*gatekjøkken*), consists mainly of rather unappetizing hot dogs (*varme pølse*), pizza slices, and chicken and chips. A much better choice, and often no more expensive, is simply to get a *smørbrød*, a huge open sandwich heaped with a variety of garnishes. The best deals for sit-down food are at **lunchtime** (*lunsj*), when self-service *kafeteri* offer a limited range of daily specials (*dagens rett*) costing 80–100kr. These include a fish or meat dish with vegetables or salad, often a drink, sometimes bread, and occasionally coffee, too. In the larger towns, you'll also find more traditional cafés called *kaffistovas*, which serve high-quality Norwegian food at quite reasonable prices. **Dinner** (*middag*) at a restaurant will be out of the range of most budgets, but the seafood can be superb. Again, the best deals are at lunchtime, when some restaurants put out a *koldtbord* (the Norwegian *smörgåsbord*) – at these for a fixed price (100–200kr) you can eat as much as you like. Note that in contrast to southern Europe, Norwegians tend to eat dinner quite early – usually between 6.30 and 8.30pm.

Drink

Due to heavy regulation and taxing, alcohol prices are among the highest in Europe. Buying from the supermarkets and **Vinmonopolet** (the state-run off-licences) is often the only way you'll afford a tipple: in a bar, **beer** costs around 60kr for 500ml. It comes in three strengths: class I is light, class II is what you get in supermarkets and is the most widely served in pubs (what you get when you ask for "a beer"), while class III is the strongest and only available at Vinmonopolet. In the cities, bars stay open until at least 1am if not later; in the smaller towns, they tend to close at around 11pm. Everywhere, look out for *aquavit*, served ice-cold in little glasses; at forty percent ABV, it's real headache stuff. Outside bars and restaurants, **wines** and **spirits** can only be purchased from Vinmonopolet. There's generally one in each town, more in the cities; opening hours are usually Mon–Wed 10am–4/5pm, Thurs 10am–5/6pm, Fri 9am–4/6pm, Sat 9am–1/3pm. You have to be 18 to buy wine and beer, 20 to buy spirits.

CULTURE AND ETIQUETTE

Norwegian people are generally scrupulously polite, helpful and self-deprecating. The famous **Nordic reserve** is apparent, but usually evaporates under the influence of direct friendliness or, failing that, alcohol – which Norwegians consume in large quantities.

Table manners are conventionally European; there's no need to **tip**, as service staff are usually well paid. Almost everyone speaks excellent English, even in the most isolated towns.

SPORTS AND OUTDOOR ACTIVITIES

Every kind of snow-based sport is represented in Norway, but **skiing** is the national winter pastime and is taken very seriously indeed. In the north of the country, dogsledding and snowmobile trips can also help you make the most of the snow, while sailing and kayaking are great ways to enjoy the western fjord region. There are also plentiful hiking and climbing routes, with transport

NORWAY ON THE NET

ⓦ **www.visitnorway.com** Official Norwegian Tourist Board site.
ⓦ **www.use-it.no** Youth travel information site for Norway.

details and maps available from local tourist offices.

Despite the Norwegian national team's rather dismal international performance, **football** is hugely popular and there's always a good turnout to see local teams. The Norway Cup, held every summer, is the biggest youth football tournament in the world and packs out youth hostels and stadiums around the country.

COMMUNICATIONS

Many hotels have **internet** access, and most libraries offer free access for around 15min. **Post office** opening hours are usually Monday to Friday 8/8.30am to 4/5pm, Saturday 8/9am to 1pm. Stamps are available from post offices, snack and newspaper kiosks and some bookstores. Most public phones only accept **phonecards**, available in a variety of denominations from kiosks. There are no area codes. Directory enquiries is ⓣ1881 within Scandinavia, ⓣ1882 international. The international operator is on ⓣ115.

EMERGENCIES

Norway is well known for its lack of crime, and the **police** are amiable and can normally speak English. Most gozod hotels as well as pharmacies and tourist offices have lists of local **doctors** and dentists. Norway is not in the EU but reciprocal health agreements mean EU citizens get free hospital treatment with an EHIC card. If **pharmacies** (*apotek*) are closed they usually have a rota in the window advising of the nearest pharmacy that is open.

INFORMATION

Every town has a **tourist office**, usually with a stock of free maps and timetables. Many book private rooms and hotel beds, some rent out bikes and change money. During the high season – late June to August – they normally open daily for long hours, outside of these months they mostly adopt shop hours; many close down altogether in winter.

EMERGENCY NUMBERS

Police ⓣ112; Ambulance ⓣ113; Fire ⓣ110.

MONEY AND BANKS

Norway's currency is the **krone** (kr), divided into 100 øre. Coins come in 50 øre, 1kr, 5kr, 10kr and 20kr denominations; notes are in 50kr, 100kr, 200kr, 500kr and 1000kr denominations. At the time of writing, €1 was worth 8.57kr; £1 was 9.79kr; and US$1 was 5.98kr.

Banking hours are Monday to Friday 9am to 3.30pm, Thursday till 5pm, though many banks close thirty minutes earlier in summer. Most airports and some train stations have exchange offices, open evenings and weekends, and some tourist offices also change money, though at worse rates than banks and post offices. **ATMs** are commonplace even in the smaller towns.

OPENING HOURS AND HOLIDAYS

Opening hours are usually Monday to Wednesday and Friday 9am to 5pm, Thursday 9am to 6/8pm, Saturday 9am to 1/3pm. Almost everything – including supermarkets – is closed on Sunday, the main exceptions being newspaper and snack-food kiosks

STUDENT AND YOUTH DISCOUNTS

Like most of Europe, Norway offers discounts for students and under-26s. You'll nearly always get a discount on transportation on presentation of an ISIC card and equally tend to get about 30 percent off most sights and museums. The best rule of thumb is to always ask.

Norwegian

	Norwegian	Pronunciation
Yes	*Ja*	Ya
No	*Nei*	Nay
Please	*Vaersågod*	Varsaagod
Thank you	*Takk*	Takk
Hello/Good day	*Godmorgen/Goddag*	Godmorgan/Goddag
Goodbye	*Adjø*	Ad-yur
Excuse me	*Unnskyld*	Un-shy-ld
Where?	*Hvor?*	Vor?
Good	*God*	God
Bad	*Dårlig*	Door-lig
Near	*Inaerheten*	Eyenar-he-ten
Far	*Langt borte*	Langt borteh
Cheap	*Billig*	Billig
Expensive	*Dyrt*	Deert
Open	*Åpen*	Or-pen
Closed	*Stengt*	Stengt
Today	*I dag*	Ee-daag
Yesterday	*I går*	Ee-gaar
Tomorrow	*I morgen*	Ee morn
How much is...?	*Hvormyeer...?*	Vorm-yeer...?
What time is it?	*Hvor mangeer klokken?*	Vor mang-eer klock-en?
I don't understand	*Jeg forstår ikke*	Yeg forst-aar ik-ke
Do you speak English?	*Snakkerdu engelsk*	Snack-er du eng-elle-sk?
One	*En*	En
Two	*To*	To
Three	*Tre*	Tray
Four	*Fire*	Feer-eh
Five	*Fem*	Fem
Six	*Seks*	Seks
Seven	*Sju*	Shu
Eight	*Åtte*	Or-teh
Nine	*Ni*	Nee
Ten	*Ti*	Tee

(*narvesen*) and takeaway food stalls. Most businesses are closed on **public holidays**: January 1, Maundy Thursday, Good Friday, Easter Sunday and Monday, May 1, Ascension Day (mid-May), May 17 (Norway's National Day), Whit Sunday and Monday, December 25 and 26.

Oslo

Today's **OSLO** is largely the work of the late nineteenth and early twentieth centuries, an era reflected in the wide avenues, dignified parks and gardens, solid buildings and long, consciously classical vistas. The half a million inhabitants enjoy all the trappings of metropolitan life within easy reach of both dense forest and sandy beaches. For entertainment, the city is blessed with a clutch of first-rate museums, plentiful (if generally expensive) cafés and restaurants and a lively bar and clubbing scene, with everything from grunge rock warehouses to swanky chandeliered bijou bars. Norwegians love the outdoors and you'll find a tempting array of outdoor pursuits, from swimming to skiing, at close hand.

What to see and do

Oslo's main street, **Karl Johans gate**, leads west up the slope from Oslo S train station.

Domkirke and Stortinget

The **Domkirke** (Cathedral; daily 10am–5pm; free) is located just off Karl Johans gate but was closed at time of writing for structural renovations. Once reopened (set for May 2010), the elegant interior, its nave and transepts awash with maroon, green and gold

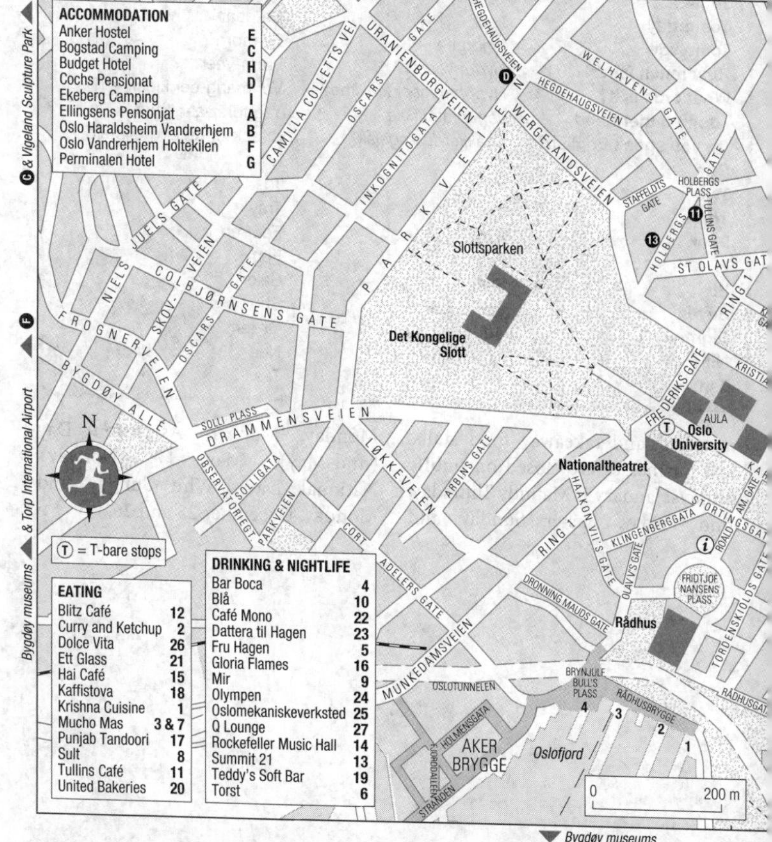

paintwork, will be worth a look. From here it's a brief stroll up Karl Johans gate to the **Stortinget**, the parliament building, an imposing chunk of neo-Romanesque architecture that was completed in 1866. In front of the parliament, a narrow park-piazza flanks Karl Johans gate; in summer it teems with promenading city folk, while in winter people flock to its floodlit open-air skating rinks.

Royal Palace

Det Kongelige Slott (Royal Palace) stands right at the top of Karl Johans gate, and its lovely grounds – **Slottsparken** – are open to the public. Try timing your visit to coincide with the daily changing of the guard (1.30pm) – an eccentric but good-humoured business. During the summer, guided tours of the palace run every 20 minutes (Mon–Thurs & Sat 11am–5pm, Fri & Sun 1–5pm; 95kr; buy tickets at the central post office).

The university and around

Located on Karl Johans gate, the very grand, nineteenth-century **university buildings** fit well into this monumental end of the city centre. The similarly handsome **Nationaltheatret** (National Theatre) is just opposite, while at Universitetsgata 13, you'll find the **Nasjonalgalleriet** (Tues, Wed & Fri 10am–6pm, Thurs 10am–7pm, Sat & Sun 11am–5pm;

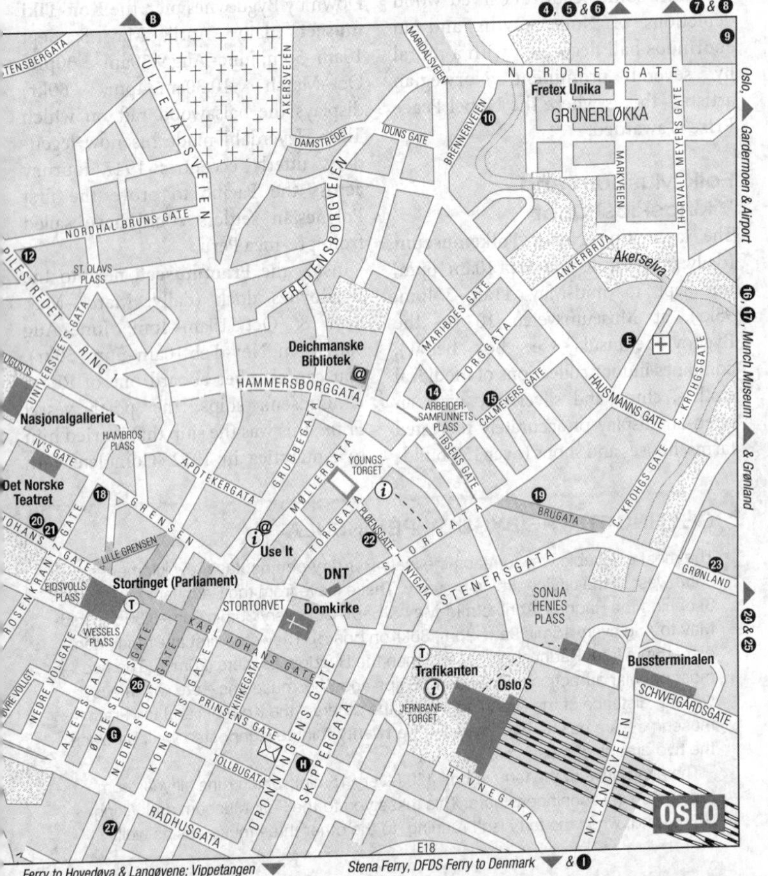

free; ⓦwww.nasjonalgalleriet.no), home to Norway's largest and best collection of fine art. Highlights include wonderfully romantic landscapes by Johan Christian Dahl and grim social commentary by sometime Edvard Munch mentor Christian Krohg. A room devoted to Munch features the original version of the famous *Scream*.

City Hall

Heading south from the university buildings, you can't miss the monolithic brickwork of the massive City Hall, the **Rådhus** (daily 9am–6pm; guided tours Mon & Wed at 10am, noon and 2pm; free), opened in 1950 to celebrate the city's 900th anniversary. Venture inside to admire some beautiful carved-wood depictions of Norse myths and an enormous hall decorated with a mural by several prominent Norwegian artists – this is where the Nobel Peace Prize is awarded.

Folk Museum and Vikingskipshuset

The fascinating **Norsk Folkemuseum** (daily: mid-May to mid-Sept 10am–6pm; mid-Sept to mid-May 11am–3/4pm; 95kr), at Museumsveien 10 on the Bygdøy peninsula (see box below), combines indoor collections of medieval clothes, china and silverware with an open-air display of accurately recreated farms, houses and shops (over 150 buildings in all) from different periods of Norwegian history.

Nearby, the **Vikingskipshuset** (Viking Ships Museum; daily; May–Sept 9am–6pm; Oct–April 11am–4pm; 50kr) houses a trio of ninth-century Viking ships, with viewing platforms to let you see inside the hulls. The three oak vessels were retrieved from ritual burial mounds in southern Norway towards the end of the nineteenth century, each embalmed in clay. The star exhibit, the **Oseberg ship**, is thought to have originally been used as a pleasure boat for short cruises.

Kon-Tiki museet and Frammuseet

Down by Bygdøynes pier, the **Kon-Tiki museet** (daily: April, May & Sept 10am–5pm; June–Aug 9.30am–5.30pm; Oct–March 10.30am–4pm; 60kr) displays the balsawood raft on which Thor Heyerdahl made his now legendary, utterly eccentric 1947 journey across the Pacific to prove the first Polynesian settlers could have sailed from pre-Inca Peru.

Inside the **Frammuseet**, next to the Bygdøynes dock (daily: March–May, Sept & Oct 10am–4pm; June–Aug 9am–6pm; Nov–Feb 10am–3pm; 50kr), you can clamber aboard one of Roald Amundsen's ships, the polar vessel *Fram*; this was the ship that carried him to Antarctica in 1912. Complete with

GETTING TO THE BYGDØY PENINSULA

The most enjoyable way to reach the leafy **Bygdøy peninsula**, a few kilometres southwest of the city centre, is by **ferry**. These leave from the Rådhusbrygge (pier 3) behind the Rådhus (April to mid-May & Sept–Oct every 30min 9am–6.30pm; mid-May to Aug every 15min 9am–9pm; 36kr on board). They stop first at Dronningen pier (15min from Rådhusbrygge) and then the Bygdøynes piers (20min). The two most popular attractions – the Viking Ships and Folk museums – are within easy walking distance of the Dronningen pier, the others – the Kon-Tiki and the Fram museums – are beside Bygdøynes. It's a twenty-minute signposted walk between the two groups of museums.

The alternative to the ferry is **bus #30** (every 15min), which runs all year from Kirkeristen in Dronningens gate. This takes you to the Folk Museum and Viking Ships, and, when the ferry isn't running, to the other three museums as well.

most of its original fittings, the interior gives a superb insight into the life and times of these early polar explorers.

Munch Museum

Just out of the centre but without question a major attraction, the **Munch-museet**, Tøyengata 53 (June–Aug daily 10am–6pm; Sept–May Tues–Fri 10am–4pm, Sat & Sun 11am–5pm; 75kr; ⓦwww.munch.museum.no), is reachable by T-bane (underground) or bus #20: get off at Tøyen/Munch-museet and it's a signposted five-minute walk. Born in 1863, **Edvard Munch** is Norway's most famous painter. His lithographs and woodcuts – gloom, fog, naked women – are on display here, as well as his early paintings and the great signature works of the 1890s. The museum owns one of two versions of *The Scream*, stolen in 2004 and returned to the museum about two years later in mysterious circumstances. Note that the museum is set to move to a new home near the Opera House in December 2013.

Vigeland Sculpture Park

On the other side of the city and reachable on tram #12 and #15 from the centre (get off at Vigelandsparken), Frogner Park holds one of Oslo's most striking cultural targets in the open-air **Vigeland Sculpture Park** (free access), which commemorates another modern Norwegian artist, Gustav Vigeland. Vigeland started on the sculptures in 1924 and was still working on them when he died in 1943. A long series of life-size figures frowning, fighting and posing lead up to the central fountain, an enormous bowl representing the burden of life, supported by straining, sinewy bronze Goliaths, while underneath water tumbles out around clusters of playing and standing figures.

The islands of the inner Oslofjord

The archipelago of low-lying, lightly forested **islands** in the **inner Oslofjord** is the city's summer playground. Although most of the islets are cluttered with summer homes, the least populated are favourite party venues for the city's youth. Ferries to the islands leave from the Vippetangen quay, at the foot of Akershusstranda – a twenty-minute walk south from Oslo S.

The nearest island, **Hovedøya**, reachable by ferries #92 and #93 (May–Sept every 30min–1hr 7.30am–7pm; Oct–April three daily; 10min), is also the most interesting, with the overgrown ruins of a twelfth-century Cistercian monastery, and rolling hills covered in farmland and deciduous woods. There are plenty of footpaths to wander, you can swim from the shingle beaches on the south shore, and there's a seasonal café opposite the monastery ruins. Camping is not permitted as Hovedøya is a protected area.

The pick of the other islands is wooded **Langøyene** (ferry #94; May–Sept hourly 9.30am–7pm; 30min), the most southerly of the archipelago and the one with the best beaches; at night the ferries are full of people armed with sleeping bags and bottles, on their way to join swimming parties. You can camp rough here for a maximum of one night.

Arrival

Air Oslo airport – Gardermoen – is located about 50km north of the city centre: the Airport Express train (every 10min; 20min; 170kr) and the SAS Airport bus (every 30min to the *Radisson SAS* hotel; 50min; 110kr, 170kr return) run into the city, but the ordinary NSB (Norwegian rail) train is less expensive and offers student discounts of up to about 30 percent (every 30min–1hr; 30min; 100kr). Ryanair flights land at the city's secondary airport, Torp, which is located 110km southwest. Express buses are timed to meet flight arrivals (1hr 30min; 180kr, 300kr return) and stop at the main bus terminal in the city.

Train All trains arrive at Oslo Sentralstasjon, known as Oslo S, at the eastern end of the city centre.

Bus The central bus terminal is a short walk northeast beneath the Galleriet shopping centre: it handles most long-distance buses, though some services terminate on the south side of Oslo S at the bus stands beside Havnegata.

Ferry Car ferries from Germany and Denmark arrive at either the Vippetangen quays, a 15min walk south of Oslo S (take bus #60 to the centre), or at Hjortneskaia, some 3km west of the city centre; bus #31 to the centre usually connects with the ferries' arrival.

Information

Tourist office The main tourist office is in the centre, behind the Rådhus at Fridtjof Nansens plass 5 (April, May & Sept Mon–Sat 9am–5pm; June–Aug daily 9am–7pm; Oct–March Mon–Fri 9am–4pm; Ⓦwww.visitoslo.com), with a second branch just outside Oslo S in the Trafikanten centre (Mon–Fri 7am–8pm, Sat & Sun 8am–6/8pm). Both issue free city maps, make reservations on guided tours, run a hotel and hostel booking service, and sell the useful Oslo Pass (220/320/410kr for one/two/three days), which gives free museum admission, limited discounts in shops and restaurants and free city transport.
Youth information There is also a youth information office, Use It, at Møllergata 3 (Ⓣ24 14 98 20, Ⓦwww.use-it.no) where under-27s can access free luggage storage and internet.
Hiking information The Norwegian hikers' association, Den Norske Turistforening (DNT), has an office in the centre at Youngstorget 1 (Ⓣ40 00 18 68, Ⓦwww.turistforeningen.no), selling hiking maps and giving general advice and information on route planning.
City listings All information offices provide *Streetwise* – a free budget guide to Oslo – as well as the excellent *Oslo Official Guide* and *What's On in Oslo*.

City transport

Transport information The city transport Trafikanten information office is on Jernbanetorget, the pedestrianized square outside Oslo S (Mon–Fri 7am–8pm, Sat 8am–6pm; Ⓣ177, Ⓦwww.trafikanten.no), and supplies a useful free transit map and comprehensive timetable booklet, *Rutebok for Oslo*.
Trams and buses The trams run on six lines, crossing the centre from east to west. Buses also criss cross the city; most routes converge at Oslo S and Carl Berners plass.
Underground The Tunnelbanen (T-bane) has six lines, all of which also run along the loop of track circling the centre from Majorstuen in the west to Tøyen in the east.
Ferry Numerous local ferries cross the Oslofjord to the south of the centre, connecting the city with its outlying districts and archipelagos.
Tickets Local transport tickets cost a flat-fare of 25kr; a 24hr travel pass, available from Trafikanten, costs 65kr. Night buses cost 50kr.

Accommodation

It's best to book in advance; failing that, you should at least call ahead to check on space. A good budget alternative to the hostels listed below is a private room (from 450kr), booked by the tourist office near Oslo S, though there's often a minimum two-night stay and you should book before 7pm.

Hostels

Anker Hostel Storgata 55 Ⓣ22 99 72 00, Ⓦwww.ankerhostel.no. Lively, clean and friendly hostel (despite the drab corridors) in the hip Grunerløkka district, less than 10min walk from Oslo S. Bed linen and breakfast at additional cost. Reservations necessary during winter. Dorms 205kr, rooms 540kr.
Oslo Haraldsheim Vandrerhjem Haraldsheimveien 4, Grefsen Ⓣ22 22 29 65, Ⓦwww.haraldsheim.no. Best of the HI hostels, 4km northeast of the centre, with about 70 rooms, mostly in four-bed dorms, many en suite. Take tram #15 or bus #31 from the bottom of Storgata to the Sinsenkrysset stop, from where it's a signposted 5–10min walk; the airport express bus also reaches the same stop. Advance booking necessary in summer. Breakfast included. Dorms 245kr, rooms 415kr.
Oslo Vandrerhjem Holtekilen Micheletsvei 55, 1368 Stabekk Ⓣ67 51 80 40, Ⓦwww.vandrerhjem.no. Located 8km west of the city centre, with both dorms and one- to four-bedded rooms, plus kitchen and laundry facilities. From the city centre, take bus #151, 153, 161, 162, 252 or 261 to the Kveldsroveien bus stop; the hostel is 100m away on the right. Breakfast included; bed linen 60kr. Dorms 245kr, rooms 470kr.

Hotels and guesthouses

Budget Hotel Prinsens gate 6 Ⓣ22 41 36 10, Ⓦwww.budgethotel.no. Brand-new budget hotel with a range of rooms conveniently located above shops near Oslo S. 490kr.
Cochs Pensjonat Parkveien 25 Ⓣ23 33 24 00, Ⓦwww.cochspensjonat.no. Reasonable guesthouse in a pleasant location just north of the royal palace, with good deals on triples and quads. The cheapest rooms have shared bathrooms. Triples and quads 300kr per person, rooms 460kr.
Ellingsens Pensonjat Holtegata Ⓣ25 22 60 03 59, Ⓦwww.ellingsenspensjonat.no. Lovely B&B in a nineteenth-century home, about 1km north of the

centre, with bright, high-ceilinged rooms. Shared bathrooms. 330kr.

Perminalen Hotel Øvre Slottsgate 2 ⓣ 23 09 30 81, ⓦ www.perminalen.no. Spick-and-span budget option near the fortress with close ties to the army. The majority of the rooms are spacious four-bed en-suite dorms. Breakfast included. Dorms 360kr, rooms 620kr.

Campsites

Bogstad Camping Ankeveien 117 ⓣ 22 51 08 00, ⓦ www.bogstadcamping.no. Large campsite in a good location by a lake, about 9km from the city centre. Take bus #32 from Oslo S. Camping 250kr, four-bed huts 1000kr.

Ekeberg Camping Ekebergveien 65 ⓣ 22 19 85 68, ⓦ www.ekebergcamping.no. Family-oriented campsite on a hill to the east of Oslo. Bus #34 or #46 from Oslo S. June–Aug only. 250kr.

Eating

Those carefully counting the kroner will find it easy to buy bread, fruit and snacks from stalls and shops across the city centre, while fast-food joints offering kebabs, pizza and hot dogs (*pølser*) are legion. For a picnic, buy a bag of freshly cooked, shell-on prawns from one of the fishing boats at the Rådhusbrygge pier, or head to the principal open-air market on Youngstorget (Mon–Sat 7am–2pm), a brief stroll north of the Domkirke along Torggata.

Blitz Café Pilestredet 30C. This alternative cultural centre, a legalized squat in a listed building, serves vegetarian lunches for around 30kr and has live music twice a month. Closed weekends and sometimes in summer.

Curry and Ketchup Kirkeveien 51. Fun, quirky and popular little gem of an Indian restaurant, a 10–15min walk from the palace, with low prices and huge portions – don't let the name put you off.

Dolce Vita Prinsens gate 22. This Italian café makes and sells the best ice cream in Oslo, along with proper food at decent prices.

Ett Glass Karl Johans gate 33, entrance round the corner on Rosenkrantz gate. Popular, candlelit café/bar. Inexpensive menu focuses on light meals.

Hai Café Calmeyers gate 6. Authentic Vietnamese food at low prices though the decor's not up to much.

Kaffistova Rosenkrantz gate 8. This self-service café feels a bit like a school cafeteria but serves traditional Norwegian dishes at very fair prices. There's usually a vegetarian option, too.

Krishna Cuisine Kirkeveien 59b & Colosseum Senter. The city's best vegetarian option – run by monks – has two branches in the north of the city. Closed Sun.

Mucho Mas Thorvalds Meyersgate 36 & Bogstadveien 8. Cute, relaxed bar/restaurant that does a roaring trade in good, reasonably priced Mexican food.

Punjab Tandoori Grønland 24. The best of Grønland's cheap curry restaurants, with main dishes from 65kr.

Sult Thorvald Meyersgate 26. The changing menu at this hip resto boasts seasonal, organic ingredients. Surprisingly low prices for what you get. The attached bar *Tørst* is popular too.

Tullins Café Tullins gate 2. Close to the Nasjonalgalleriet, this fashionable café serves light meals, snacks and coffee in the daytime and turns into a bar at night. Reasonably priced.

United Bakeries Karl Johans gate 37. Traditional, freshly baked Norwegian buns, cakes and doorstop sandwiches at pretty good prices right in the centre of town. Take a number for service.

Drinking

Oslo's hippest cafés and bars can be found in the former working-class area of Grünerløkka along Thorvald Meyersgate and Markveien in particular as well as in the immigrant district of Grønland. Downtown Oslo also has a vibrant bar scene, at its most frenetic on summer weekends. The busiest mainstream bars are concentrated in the side streets near the Rådhus and along the Aker Brygge, while similarly popular places clustered around Universitetsgata and on Rosenkrantz gate.

Bar Boca Thorvald Meyers gate 30. Tiny, friendly 1950s-retro bar in Grünerløkka, with great cocktails. Get there early.

Dattera til Hagen Grønland 10. This Grønland gem is a café by day and a lively bar at night, sometimes with a DJ on its small, upstairs dance-floor. Check out the massive beer garden and the great food.

Fru Hagen Thorvald Meyersgate 38. Faded-grandeur chic: battered upholstery, dark red walls plus good food. Open till 3am most nights.

TREAT YOURSELF

Summit 21, on the twenty-first floor of the *Radisson SAS Scandinavia* hotel at Holbergs gate 30, is a swish modern bar boasting glorious, panoramic views over Oslo – including from the men's toilets (the women's have a strange twist too). Sip a vertiginous cocktail (100kr) and admire the skyline.

Mir Toftesgate 69. Adorably oddball bar tucked away in a courtyard, complete with old aeroplane seats and candlelight. Live music three or four nights a week.

Olympen Grønlandsleiret 15. Chic, airy bar with chandeliers, leather banquettes, black-and-white-clad waiters – and the best beer selection in Oslo. The *Pigalle* club upstairs is open weekend nights for dancing.

Oslomekaniskeverksted Tøyenbekken 34. Probably the coolest bar in Oslo, housed in an old car-mechanic's warehouse. The mellow atmosphere is perfectly complemented by battered couches and an open fire – plus a brilliant beer garden for summer. No food but you can bring your own takeaway. Take a right off Grønland and it's two blocks down on the left, just around the back of the theatre.

Q Lounge Kongens gate 5. If the weather's good don't miss this uber-trendy rooftop bar atop *Grims Grenka* design hotel.

Teddy's Soft Bar Brugata 3. Genuine 1950s US dive bar, complete with a Wurlitzer jukebox and the best burgers in town.

Nightlife and entertainment

There are several generic clubs in the centre around Karl Johans gate, but if you want to party with the locals, head to Grønland, Grünerløkka, or the area around Youngstorget. Entry can set you back 50–100kr – though drinks prices are the same as anywhere else in Oslo. Nothing gets going much before 11pm; closing times are generally 3–4am. For entertainment listings check *Natt & Dag*, a monthly Norwegian-language broadsheet available free from cafés, bars and shops.

Blå Brenneriveien 9c ⓦwww.blaaoslo.no. Creative, cultural nightspot down a tiny side-street, featuring everything from live jazz and DJ nights to public debates and poetry readings. In summer, there's a pleasant riverside terrace, and the food is pretty good too. Open till 3.30am at weekends.

Café Mono Pløensgate 4 ⓦwww.cafemono.no. Popular bar/club just by Youngstorget. Decor and music are rock-themed, and you can often catch local and international bands here. Open till 3am.

Gloria Flames Grønland 18 ⓦwww.gloriaflames.no. An indie kid favourite, with a great roof terrace and DJ nights at the weekend.

Rockefeller Music Hall Torggata 16, entrance on Mariboes gate ⓦwww.rockefeller.no. This former bathhouse is now one of Oslo's major concert venues, hosting well-known and up-and-coming bands – mostly rock or alternative.

Shopping

For all the major chains head to Karl Johans gate; for vintage and trendy, Grünerløkka is the place to be.

Fretex Unika Markveien 51. Special branch of the national charity shop, with added cool – the clothes and furniture on sale here are hand picked, and there are some genuine secondhand treasures to be found.

Trabant Markveien 56. Pick up vintage and vintage-inspired fashions at this impeccably cool Grünerløkka boutique.

Tronsmo Kristian Augusts gate 19. Excellent independent bookshop, a cult among Oslo bookworms, with a basement full of comics and graphic novels.

Directory

Embassies and consulates Canada, Wergelandveien 7 ⓣ22 99 53 00; Ireland, Haakon VII's gate 1, 5th Floor ⓣ22 01 72 00; UK, Thomas Heftyes gate 8 ⓣ23 13 27 00; USA, Henrik Ibsens gate 48 ⓣ21 30 85 40.

Exchange There are bureaux de change in the central post office and Oslo S station.

Hospital Legevakten, Storgata 40 ⓣ22 93 22 93. Accident & emergency.

Internet Internet access is available free at the city library, Deichmanske Bibliotek, Arne Garborgs Plass 4 (Mon–Thurs 10am–7pm, Fri & Sat 10am–4pm).

Laundry A Snanvask, Thorvald Meyers gate 18 (Mon–Fri 10am–8pm, Sat 10am–3pm).

Left luggage Oslo S (daily 4.30am–1.10am) has luggage lockers, as does Use It (see p.874).

Pharmacy Jernbanetorgets Apotek, Jernbanetorget 4b, is a 24hr pharmacy near Oslo S ⓣ23 35 81 00.

Post office Dronningens gate 15 (Mon–Fri 8am–5pm, Sat 9am–2pm).

Moving on

Train Åndalsnes (2–3 daily; 5hr 30min–6hr 30min); Bergen (4–5 daily; 7–8hr); Gothenberg (3–5 daily; 4hr); Kristiansand (5 daily; 4hr 30min); Stavanger (3–5 daily; 7hr 30min); Trondheim (2–4 daily; 8–10hr).

Bus Bergen (4–5 daily; 10hr).

Southern Norway

Regular trains and buses run from Oslo to the lively harbour towns of **Kristiansand** and **Stavanger** on the south coast. The landscape in this half of the country may not be as dramatic as in the north, but there is still plenty to attract visitors in large numbers, particularly during the summer months. Attractive forests provide ample opportunity for camping and walking; watersports, sailing in particular, are popular on the many lakes and beaches; and both towns are fortunate to have vibrant bar and restaurant scenes.

KRISTIANSAND

The small summer seaside resort of **KRISTIANSAND** is diverting enough to merit a stopover on your way to Stavanger, with a few good museums, a well-preserved neighbourhood of eighteenth-century wooden houses and a clutch of lively cafés and restaurants.

What to see and do

The neo-Gothic **cathedral** (daily 11am–2pm) is right in the middle of town, just beside Wergelands Park, a landscaped square designed by prominent nineteenth-century poet/soldier General Wergeland. Nearby, the excellent **Art Museum** (Sørlandets Kunstmuseum; Tues–Fri 11am–4pm, Sat and Sun noon–4pm, opens & closes 1hr later in winter; free) on Skippergate showcases some interesting modern Norwegian artists – check out the contemporary sculpture gallery on the first floor.

Along the seafront, a walk along the promenade takes in the fantastic **fish market** (June–Aug Mon–Sat 7am–8pm; rest of year Mon–Fri 7am–5pm, Sat 7am–4pm) and accompanying fish restaurants (*Pieder Ro* is the favourite) at the southernmost end. There's also an artificial city **beach** at the northern end of the walkway.

Plunge back into town via Kronprinsensgate for a look at **Posebyen**, Kristiansand's picturesque old town. Less than 2km north of the town centre, the nature reserve of **Baneheia** includes some beautiful swimming and fishing spots, forest trails and a healthy wildlife population. If you're here for a few days check out the famous **zoo**, twenty minutes outside of town.

Arrival and information

Arrival The train and bus stations are right next to each other on Vestre Strandgate on the west side of town.

Tourist office Rådhusgaten 6 ⓣ 38 12 13 14, ⓦ www.sorlandet.com (mid-June to mid-Aug Mon–Fri 9am–6pm, Sat 10am–6pm, Sun noon–6pm; rest of year Mon–Fri 9am–3.30pm).

Accommodation

There is no hostel in Kristiansand.

123 Hotel Ostre Strandgate 25 ⓣ 38 70 15 66, ⓦ www.123-hotel.no. Comfortable, well-equipped hotel with self-service check-in. Good deals on quads. 590kr.

Frobusdalen Rom Frobusdalen 2 ⓣ 91 12 99 06, ⓦ www.gjestehus.no. This lovely B&B in an old sea-captain's mansion is the best place to stay in town. 400kr.

Eating and drinking

Drømmeplassen Corner of Skippergaten and Kirkegata. The best bread, buns and pastries in town plus coffee, tea and good-value lunch specials.

Frk. Larsen Markensgata 5. Mellow café/bar with great food at reasonable prices plus an impressive cocktail list.

Moving on

Train Oslo (5 daily; 4hr 30min); Stavanger (5 daily; 3hr 30min).

Bus Bergen (4 daily; 5hr).

STAVANGER

STAVANGER is a breezily charming seaside city that has grown sleek and prosperous as the hub of Norway's oil industry. The presence of a thriving university gives the town a real buzz, and there's a number of excellent but unpretentious bars that wouldn't be out of place in the capital.

What to see and do

The heart-shaped pond, **Breiavatnet**, in the compact town centre is a helpful reference point; the twelfth-century **Norman cathedral** (June–Aug daily 11am–7pm; Sept–May Tues–Sat 11am–4pm; free) is just north of here and the pretty harbour is visible from the cathedral steps.

Boats to the vertiginous **Pulpit Rock** (Preikestolen), the region's most famous attraction, leave regularly from the harbour and connect with an onward bus service (timetable and tickets available from the tourist office; about 1hr 30min in total) to the trailhead. The bus deposits you by the Preikestolen's youth hostel, from which it's a two-hour hike to the cliff top for a truly breathtaking view.

Stavanger's delightful **old town** is just northwest of the cathedral – stroll around the charming cobbled streets or drop into the entertaining **Norwegian Canning Museum** at Øvre Strandgate 88 (daily 11am–4pm; 60kr), showcasing traditional local industries such as herring canning. Further east along the harbour, the **Oil Museum** (daily June–Aug 10am–7pm, rest of year 10am–4/6pm; 80kr; ⓦwww.norskolje.museum.no) is a slick, well-designed space lovingly detailing the history of the oil industry in a series of fascinating interactive exhibits.

All over Stavanger, look out for the series of **Antony Gormley sculptures** – austere human figures staring out to sea, placed at regular intervals throughout the city.

STAVANGER'S BEACHES

The 70km of coastline curving south from Stavanger is famous for its sandy beaches, the best in Norway, where **surfers** congregate over the summer. Buses leave regularly from the town centre and timetables are available at the tourist office. The closest is **Solastranda**, but it's worth making the slightly longer journey to **Viste**, with its sculptural-looking rock formations, or to the surf at **Orre** or **Vaule**. Beware: even in high summer, the water is freezing.

Arrival and information

Air The airport, 15km south of the city, is connected to the bus station by regular *flybussen* (daily every 15–20min 5am–9pm, Sat till 4pm; 30min; 75kr). The airport bus from Haugesund airport (for Ryanair flights) costs 130kr.

Train and bus The train and bus stations are next door to each other on Jernbaneveien, facing Breiavatnet.

Ferry International ferries to Britain and Denmark arrive at the town's northernmost quay, by Sandvigå. Domestic ferries to Bergen and nearby towns leave from Jorenholmen on the eastern side of the harbour.

Tourist office Opposite the cathedral at Domkirkeplassen 3 ⓣ51 85 92 00, ⓦwww.regionstavanger.com (June–Aug daily 7am–8pm; Sept–May Mon–Fri 9am–4pm, Sat 9am–2pm).

Accommodation

Budget accommodation anywhere near the centre is hard to come by, and even in the outlying areas it is limited; be sure to book ahead.

Preikestolhytta Preikestolen ⓣ51 74 20 74, ⓦwww.preikestolhytta.no. Large, pleasant hostel at the foot of the hiking trail to Pulpit Rock, with gorgeous views and fishing and boating equipment for hire. The hostel's café/restaurant serves good meals or you can self-cater. Dorms 250kr, rooms 575kr.

Stavanger Bed and Breakfast Vikedalsgate 1a ⓣ51 56 25 00, ⓦwww.stavangerbedandbreakfast.no. The only budget option near the centre is this no-nonsense B&B. Prices include a cooked breakfast and an evening snack, which make up for the rather drab rooms. 690kr.

Stavanger Camping Mosvangen ⓣ 51 53 29 71, ⓦ www.mosvangencamping.no. Campsite by a lake, 25min walk from the centre (bus #4 and ask for directions). Open May–Oct. Camping 110kr, cabins 500–600kr for up to four people.

Stavanger Youth Hostel Mosvangen Henrik Ibsengate 19 ⓣ 51 54 36 36, ⓦ www.vandrerhjem.no. Basic but comfortable summer hostel, right next to *Stavanger Camping Mosvangen*. Open mid-June to late Aug only. Free internet, breakfast 50kr. Dorms 295kr; family room 980kr.

Eating and drinking

Stavanger has a disproportionate number of good, if expensive, restaurants, many of which line the pedestrianized harbour area north of the cathedral. Evening drinking options are plentiful, with some great bars on and around Nedre Strandgate and Øvre Holmegate; on a sunny evening head to Skagenkaien. Note that according to local laws, nightclubs cannot open before 10pm.

Bøker & Børst Øvre Holmegate 32 ⓦ www.bokerogborst.com. Relaxed, book-lined café/bar on a street of candy-coloured houses. There's a regular calendar of events with jazz nights, local folk-pop bands and DJs every Sat. Nice garden out back. Gay-friendly.

Charlottenlund Kongsgaten 45. Expensive-looking but serves affordable light lunches and snacks in the daytime. Dinner is pricey, but the lakeside terrace is a nice place to have a beer and watch the ducks.

Naree Thai Breigata 22. Cheap and cheerful Thai restaurant that's popular with the locals. Mains start around 130kr. Good selection.

Ostehuset Hospitalgaten 6. Deli and café near the cathedral with a huge range of sandwiches to eat at long tables or take away. Main fish and meat dishes too, plus make-your-own pizza.

Sting Valberget 3 ⓦ www.cafe-sting.no. This charming café/bar serves wine by weight as well as decently priced food. Live music, poetry readings, and jazz in the tiny downstairs club.

Nightlife

Cementen Nedre Strandgate ⓦ www.checkpoint.no. Friendly, likeable nightclub overlooking the harbour. DJs at weekends. Open daily 10pm–3.30am.

Checkpoint Charlie Larshertevigsgate 5. Eastern-bloc chic and loud indie music have made this a student favourite. DJs and live music several nights a week.

Gnu Nedre Strandgate 23. Friendly bar around the back of *Cementen* (see above) with a jukebox, a giant chandelier, soccer memorabilia, a disused stairlift and band photos on the walls. Happy hour before 9pm and all day Sun.

Kontoret Skagen 16. One of Stavanger's oldest drinking haunts, this eighteenth-century pub has a good selection of beers and a real old-man atmosphere.

Moving on

Train Kristiansand (5 daily; 3hr 30min); Oslo (5 daily; 8hr).

Bus Bergen (8 daily, 5hr 15min); Kristiansand (2–4 daily; 4hr 15min).

Hurtigbåt express boat Bergen (2–4 daily; 4hr).

Bergen and the fjords

The **fjords** are the most familiar and alluring image of Norway – huge clefts in the landscape which occur along the west coast right up to the Russian border, though the most beguiling portion lies between **Bergen** and **Ålesund**. Bergen is a handy springboard for the fjords, notably the **Flåm valley** and its inspiring mountain railway, which trundles down to the Aurlandsfjord, a tiny arm of the mighty **Sognefjord**, Norway's longest and deepest. North of the Sognefjord, **Nordfjord** is the smaller and less stimulating, though there's superb compensation in the **Jostedalsbreen** glacier (Europe's largest), which nudges the fjord from the east. The tiny S-shaped **Geirangerfjord**, further north again, is magnificent too – narrow, sheer and rugged.

BERGEN

BERGEN is the second biggest city in Norway but somehow doesn't feel like it, perhaps because of its air of old-world, well-fed calm. It's one of the rainiest places in rainy Norway, but benefits from a spectacular setting among seven hills and is altogether one of the country's most enjoyable cities. There's plenty to

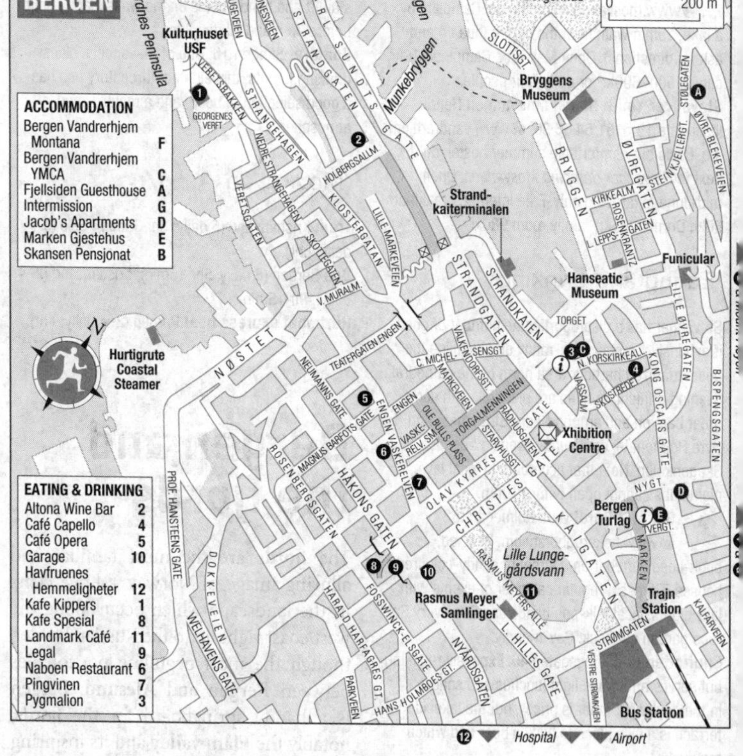

see, from fine old buildings to a series of good museums, and Bergen is also within easy reach of some of Norway's most spectacular scenic attractions, both around the city and further north.

Founded in 1070, the city was the largest and most important town in medieval Norway, a regular residence of the country's kings and queens. Later it became a Hanseatic port and religious centre, though precious little of that era survives today.

What to see and do

The city centre divides into two main parts: the wharf area, **Bryggen**, adjacent to the Bergenhus fortress – once the working centre of the Hanseatic merchants and now the oldest part of Bergen; and the **modern centre**, which stretches inland from the head of the harbour and takes in the best of Bergen's museums, cafés and bars.

Torget and Bryggen

The obvious place to start a visit is **Torget**, an appealing harbourside plaza that's home to a colourful fresh produce and fish market. From here, it's a short stroll round to **Bryggen**, where a string of distinctive wooden buildings (now a UNESCO protected site) line up along the waterfront. These once housed the city's merchants and now hold shops, restaurants and bars. Although none of these structures was actually built by the Hanseatic Germans – most of the originals were destroyed by fire in 1702 – they carefully follow the original building line. Among them, the **Hanseatic Museum** (mid-May to mid-Sept daily 9am–5pm;

rest of year Tues–Sat 11am–2pm, Sun 11am–4pm; 50kr) is the most diverting, an early eighteenth-century merchant's dwelling kitted out in late Hansa style.

Bryggens Museum

Also worth visiting is the **Bryggens Museum** (mid-May to Aug daily 10am–5pm; Sept to mid-May Mon–Fri 11am–3pm, Sat noon–3pm, Sun noon–4pm; 50kr), just along the harbourfront, where a series of imaginative exhibitions attempts a complete reassembly of local medieval life – from domestic implements, handicrafts and maritime objects through to trading items.

Mount Fløyen

Nearby you'll find the **Fløibanen**, a dinky funicular railway (every 15min: Mon–Fri 7.30am–11pm/midnight, Sat 8am–11pm/midnight, Sun 9am–11pm/midnight; return fare 70kr), which runs to the top of **Mount Fløyen** (320m), from where there are panoramic views over the city, and a network of forest walks.

Art museums

In the modern centre, Bergen's four main **art museums** are on the south side of an artificial lake. The pick of these is the **Rasmus Meyer Samlinger**, Rasmus Meyers Allé 7 (11am–5pm; closed Mon mid-Sept to mid-May; 50kr), which holds an extensive collection of Norwegian paintings from the eighteenth to early twentieth centuries, including several works by Edvard Munch.

Arrival

Air The airport, 20km south of the city, is connected to the bus station by regular *flybussen* (every 15–20min: 5am–9pm, Sat till 4pm; 45min; 75kr). The airport bus from Haugesund costs 180kr.
Train and bus The train and bus stations face Strømgaten, a 5min walk southeast of the head of the harbour.
Ferry International ferries and cruise ships arrive at Skoltegrunnskaien, the quay just beyond Bergenhus fortress, on the east side of the harbour; domestic ferries and catamarans line up on the opposite side of the harbour at the Strandkaiterminalen.
Hurtigrute The city is also the southern terminus of the Hurtigrute coastal steamer, which leaves from near Nøstebryggen.

Information

Tourist office Vågsallmenning 1, a few metres from the head of the harbour ⓣ55 55 20 00, ⓦwww.visitbergen.com (May & Sept daily 9am–8pm; June–Aug daily 8.30am–10pm; Oct–April Mon–Sat 9am–4pm). Issues maps and books private rooms.
Discount passes The tourist office sells the Bergen Card (190kr one day/250kr for two days), which allows travel on all the city's buses and free entrance to (or discounts for) most of the city's sights, including sightseeing trips.
Hiking information The DNT-affiliated Bergen Turlag, Tverrgaten 4–6 (Mon–Wed & Fri 10am–4pm, Thurs 10am–6pm, Sat 10am–2pm; ⓣ55 33 58 10), can advise on hiking trails in the region and sells hiking maps.

Accommodation

Accommodation is plentiful, but book ahead in summer, especially if you've got your heart set on staying in the town centre. Private rooms (from around 450kr) can be booked through the tourist office.

Hostels

Bergen Vandrerhjem Montana Johan Blyttsveie 30, Landås ⓣ55 20 80 70, ⓦwww.montana.no. This large, comfortable hostel is not so conveniently located in the hills 4km east of the centre, but almost always has beds available, as well as a nice view over the city. Dorms 200kr, rooms 780kr.
Bergen Vandrerhjem YMCA Nedre Korskirkeallmenningen 4 ⓣ55 60 60 55, ⓦwww.vandrerhjem.no. Close to Torget, a 5–10min walk from the train station. HI hostel with 160 beds, guest kitchen and laundry facilities – but fills quickly. Dorms 320kr, rooms 925kr.
Intermission Kalfarveien 8 ⓣ55 30 04 00, ⓦwww.intermissionhostel.no. Cheapest beds in town at this basic but sociable hostel close to the train station. Christian-run, but not overwhelmingly so. Mid-June to mid-Aug only. Dorms 150kr.
Jacob's Apartments Kong Oscars gate 44 ⓣ55 54 41 60, ⓦwww.apartments.no. Popular and very centrally located hostel with a first-class restaurant (with a wine list to die for) at the front that also serves as reception. Laid-back, fun, and a good place to meet other travellers. Book ahead in summer. Dorms 220kr, rooms 660kr.

Marken Gjestehus Kong Oscars gate 45 ⓣ55 31 44 04, ⓦwww.marken-gjestehus.com. Bright, modern decor and helpful staff make this 21-room hostel one of Bergen's best accommodation options. Dorms 175kr, rooms 450kr.

Hotels and guesthouses

Fjellsiden Guesthouse Øvre Blekeveien 16 ⓣ55 32 17 91, ⓦwww.harila.biz. Charming, simple guest-house with a homely feel. Dorms 450kr; rooms 700kr.

Skansen Pensjonat Vestrelidsallmenningen 29 ⓣ55 31 90 80, ⓦwww.skansen-pensjonat.no. Simple but cosy little place in a nineteenth-century stone house just above the Fløibanen terminus, near Torget. Doubles 650kr, 800kr for a four-person apartment.

Eating, drinking and nightlife

Bergen has a good supply of first-rate restaurants concentrated in the Bryggen, with local seafood the speciality. Less expensive – and more fashionable – are the city's café/restaurants, which often double up as lively bars. Several of the best are located to the southwest of Ole Bulls plass, the main pedestrianized square.

Café Capello Skostredet 14. Groovy little lunchtime café (1960s downstairs, 1970s upstairs) serving sinfully delicious pancakes plus huge *smørbrød* from 55kr.

Café Opera Engen 18. White wooden building near Ole Bulls plass, bustling with a fashionable crew drinking beer and good coffee. Tasty, filling dishes (from 100kr) include some good veggie options. Turns into a crowded club-like venue in the evening with DJs.

Garage Christies gate 14. Near-darkness and sticky floors in the club downstairs, friendly bar upstairs. Look out for the unusual door handles – they're trophies handed out in the Norwegian equivalent of the Grammies, donated by musicians.

Havfruenes Hemmeligheter Nygårdsgaten 53. Reasonably priced, unfussy fish restaurant – snack on fishcakes or try the sparklingly fresh fish, prepared in traditional Norwegian style.

Kafe Kippers Kulturhuset USF, Georgernes verft. Café/bar in a former herring factory converted into an arts centre, with inexpensive food (kitchen open till 11pm) and a prime seashore location; the terrace is the place to be on sunny summer days.

BERGEN'S FESTIVALS

In May/June, the annual **Bergen International Festival** (ⓦwww.festspillene.no) consists of twelve days of music, ballet, folklore and drama, supplemented by **Nattjazz** (ⓦwww.nattjazz.no), a prestigious international jazz festival.

TREAT YOURSELF

Altona Wine Bar Sundtsgate 22 or Strandgaten 81. This classy joint, in a maze of sixteenth-century rooms occupying the basement of the *Augustin* hotel, is the place to come for great – if expensive – wine. Choose from whatever's open (just divide the bottle price by five) or ask them to open something new for you.

Kafe Spesial Christies gate 13. Cheap food and quirky decor have made this bar/restaurant popular with students. Menu mainstays are pizza and pasta, with an average price around 75–80kr.

Landmark Café Rasmus Meyers Allé 5. Centre for the local art scene complete with minimalist decor and a weekly changing menu. Closed Mon.

Legal Christies gate 11. Intimate bar done up in fifties- and sixties-ish retro. Reasonably priced snacks and it's open late too.

Naboen Restaurant Sigunds gate 4. Excellent meals at manageable prices at this easy-going restaurant, which features Swedish specialities. Mains from 192kr.

Pingvinen Vaskerelven 14. Popular student place that does good, traditional Norwegian grub plus snacks at very fair prices well into the night.

Pygmalion Nedre Korskirkeallmenningen 5. Cosy organic café with art on the walls and a good choice of vegetarian dishes plus great burgers. Main dishes start at around 130kr; snacks from 60kr.

Directory

Exchange The main post office offers competitive exchange rates for foreign currency and traveller's cheques.

Hospital Haukeland Universitetssykehus, Jonas Liesvei 65.

Internet Free internet at the public library, Bergen Offentlige Bibliotek, Strømgaten 6 (Mon–Thurs 8.30am–8pm, Fri 8.30am–4.30pm, Sat 10am–4pm).

Laundry Jarlens Vaskoteque, Lille Øvregate 17, near the funicular (Mon, Tues & Fri 10am–6pm, Wed & Thurs 10am–8pm, Sat 10am–3pm).

Left luggage There are left-luggage lockers at the train station.

Pharmacy Apoteket Nordstjernen, at the bus station (Mon–Fri 8am–midnight, Sat 9.30am–midnight).

TRANSPORT IN THE FJORDS

Only Bergen, Flåm and Åndalsnes are accessible by rail – everything in between, including most of the Sognefjord, Nordfjord and the Jostedalsbreen glacier, is linked by a complicated but fully integrated system of **buses** and **ferries**. Bear in mind that there are often only 1–2 ferries a day so don't expect to move quickly, or if you do, pick up a timetable and plan carefully.

Post office 2nd floor, Xhibition shopping centre (Mon–Fri 8am–6pm, Sat 9am–3pm).

Moving on

Train Flåm (via Myrdal; 4 daily; 3hr).
Bus Ålesund (1–2 daily; 10hr 30min); Oslo (express 3 weekly, 9hr; otherwise 1–4 daily, 11hr); Stavanger (6 daily; 5hr); Trondheim (2 daily; 14hr).
Ferry Balestrand (1–2 daily; 4hr); Flåm (May–Sept only; 1–2 daily; 5hr 30min).

FLÅM VALLEY

If you're short of time, but want to sample a slice of fjord scenery, you can get a taste by taking the train from Bergen to **Myrdal**, where specially built trains squeak down a remarkable branch line that plummets 866m into the **Flåm valley** and the **Aurlandsfjord**. The track took four years to lay and is one of the steepest anywhere in the world, making a wondrously dramatic journey. Pick up transport timetables from the tourist office or at the train station before you set out.

Flåm

The village of **FLÅM**, the train's destination, lies alongside meadows and orchards on the Aurlandsfjord, a matchstick-thin branch of the Sognefjord. There are some excellent hiking trails: hikers can get off the train at **Berekvam** station, the halfway point, and stroll down from there, or else walk from Flåm to Berekvam and then hop on the train. Flåm itself is a tiny village that has been developed for tourism to within an inch of its life, but out of season – or on summer evenings, when the day-trippers have gone – it can be a pleasantly restful place.

Information

Tourist office At the ferry dock (daily: May & Sept 8.30–11.30am & noon–4pm; June–Aug 8.30am–8pm; ⓣ57 63 33 13, ⓦwww.visitflam.com), by the train station. Can book ferry tickets, accommodation and dispense information on local hikes.

Accommodation and eating

There's not much to Flåm, but if you do decide to stay overnight there's some decent accommodation. Food in Flåm is overpriced so your best bet for food is to get picnic supplies from the Coop supermarket behind the tourist office.

Flåm Camping ⓣ57 63 21 21, ⓦwww.flaam-camping.no. Excellent combined campsite and hostel, 200m from the train station. May–Sept only. Camping 195kr, dorms 190kr, rooms 470kr.

Gjørven Hytter ⓣ57 63 21 67. Simple, bucolic lodgings in cabins nestled in an orchard, 3km from the village. Four- to eight-person cabin 600–1400kr.

SOGNEFJORD AND JOSTEDALSBREEN

With the exception of Flåm, the southern shore of the **Sognefjord** remains sparsely populated and relatively inaccessible, whereas the north shore boasts a couple of very appealing resorts. Of these, pretty **Fjærland** makes an ideal base for the breathtaking **Jostedalsbreen glacier**.

Balestrand

Top-of-the-list **BALESTRAND** is the prettiest base, a tourist destination since the mid-nineteenth century when it was discovered by European travellers in search of cool, clear air and mountain scenery. The beauty of the fjord aside, there is little to see in town apart from the quaint little stave **church**, though Fjærland and Jostedalsbreen (see p.884) are within easy striking distance; daily excursions from Balestrand will take you

to the village, glacier museum and glacier itself for around 525kr.

Arrival and information

Buses (and express boats from Bergen and Flåm) arrive at Balestrand's minuscule harbourfront, near which you'll find the **tourist office** (Mon–Sat 10am–1pm & 3–5.30pm, later in summer; ⓣ57 69 12 55).

Accommodation and eating

Kringsjå Hotel 100m from the tourist office ⓣ57 69 13 03, ⓦwww.vandrerhjem.no. Comfortable and very appealing place incorporating the local HI hostel. Late June to mid-Aug only. Dorms 250kr, doubles 790kr.
Kviknes Hotel Right on the Balestrand harbourfront. Its rooms are well out of budget range but pop in for a drink or dinner at the bar.

Fjærland

The delightful village of **FJÆRLAND** (also known as Mundal) can be reached direct by ferry from Balestrand from May to early September (two daily; 1hr 30min; passengers 175kr), and by bus throughout the rest of the year (change at Sogndal; 2 daily; 1hr). Formerly one of the most isolated spots on the Sognefjord, Fjærland is now connected to the road system, but retains its old-fashioned atmosphere and appearance, with a string of handsome clapboard buildings in a wildly beautiful location.

Fjærland is also Norway's self-styled book town, packed with little shops selling musty paperbacks, while various **literature events** are held here in summer. The town's other attraction is its proximity to the southern edge of the Jostedalsbreen glacier.

Information

Tourist office in the centre of the village, about 10min walk from the ferry dock (May–Sept daily 10am–6pm; ⓣ57 69 32 33, ⓦwww.fjaerland.org). Organizes glacier walks on Jostedalsbreen.
Note that there's no ATM in town so bring plenty of cash along with you; if you're really stuck the glacier museum will let you withdraw money through their credit-card machine.

Accommodation

The tourist office can also book private rooms, from about 450kr.
Alma Haugen Guesthouse ⓣ57 69 32 43. Lovely little guesthouse with two quaint rooms for a very affordable 400kr.
Bøyum Camping ⓣ57 69 32 52. On the edge of the village, beside the glacier museum. They have four-berth huts (from 550kr per night) as well as dorms 150kr, rooms 270kr, cabins 710kr and space for camping 120–150kr.

Jostedalsbreen

The **Jostedalsbreen glacier** is a vast ice plateau that dominates the whole of the inner Nordfjord region. The glacier's 24 arms – or nodules – melt down into the nearby valleys, giving the local rivers and glacial lakes their distinctive blue-green colouring. The glacier is protected within the **Jostedalsbreen Nasjonalpark**, whose guides take organized **glacier walks** (June–Sept; from around 300kr) on its various arms, ranging from two-hour excursions to all-day, fully equipped hikes. Bookings can be arranged at Fjærland's tourist office, but you can also reach an arm of the glacier under your own steam by strolling north from Fjærland on Highway 5; about 10km north of the village, just before the tunnel, a signed side-road leads the 200m to the Bøyabreen glacier arm, though you're not allowed to walk on it – viewing only.

The diverting **Glacier Museum** (April, May, Sept & Oct 10am–4pm; June–Aug 9am–7pm; 110kr; ⓦwww.bre.museum.no), located between the village and the glacier arm, is worth a stop for its engaging mixture of interactive exhibits, multimedia presentations (don't miss the one on climate change) and very informative displays.

ÅNDALSNES

Travelling north from Oslo by train, the line forks at Dombås – the Dovre line continuing northwards over the fells to Trondheim (see p.886), the Rauma line beginning a thrilling, rollercoaster rattle

west down through the mountains to the **Isfjord** at Åndalsnes (1hr 30min). This is one of only two Norwegian fjords accessible by train, which explains the number of backpackers wandering its principal town of **ÅNDALSNES**, many people's first – sometimes only – contact with fjord country. Despite a wonderful setting between lofty peaks and looking-glass water, the town is unexciting, but it does make a convenient base for further explorations.

Arrival and information

Arrival The train and bus stations are in the north of town on Jernbanegata.
Tourist office At the train station (mid-June to mid-Aug Mon–Fri 9am–6pm, Sat & Sun 11am–6pm; mid-Aug to mid-June Mon–Fri 8am–3.30pm; ⓣ71 22 16 22, ⓦwww.visitandalsnes.com). Has a free and comprehensive guide to local hikes as well as bus, boat and train timetables.

Accommodation

Åndalsnes Camping og Motell ⓣ71 22 16 29, ⓦwww.andalsnes-camping.com. Riverside spot with space for camping, plus rooms and cabins. Also rowing boats and bikes for rent. It's a 25min walk from the train station – take the first left after the river on the road out to the hostel. Camping 150kr, rooms 375kr and cabins 450–550kr.
Åndalsnes Hostel Setnes, 1.5km outside of town ⓣ71 22 13 82, ⓦwww.aandalsnesvandrerhjem.no. Outstanding HI hostel occupying a group of charming wooden buildings in a rural setting 1.5km away from the town centre, towards Ålesund. Mid-May to Aug, plus open for advanced bookings the rest of the year. Dorms 270kr, rooms 690kr.

Moving on

Train Dombås (2–3 daily; 1hr 30min); Oslo (2–3 daily; 5hr 30min–6hr 30min).
Bus Ålesund (3–4 daily; 2hr 20min); Geiranger (mid-June to late Aug 2 daily; 3–4hr).

THE GEIRANGERFJORD

On the north side of the Jostedalsbreen glacier is the Nordfjord, though it lacks the scenic lustre of its more famous neighbours. You're much better off pressing on to the S-shaped **Geirangerfjord**, one of the region's smallest and most breathtaking fjords. A convoluted branch of the Storfjord, it cuts deep inland, marked by impressive waterfalls and with a village at either end of its snake-like profile.

You can reach the Geirangerfjord in dramatic style by bus from the north or south, but you'd do best to approach from the north if you can as the views are prettiest and the transportation more reliable. From Åndalsnes, the wonderful **Trollstigen Highway** climbs through some of the country's highest mountains before sweeping down to the tiny Norddalsfjord. From here, it's a quick ferry ride and dramatic journey along the Ørnevegen, the Eagle's Highway, for a first view of the Geirangerfjord and the village that bears its name glinting in the distance. There are few places as stunning anywhere in western Norway.

ÅLESUND

Some 120km west of Åndalsnes, the fishing and ferry port of **ÅLESUND** is immediately – and obviously – different from any other Norwegian town. In 1904, a disastrous fire left ten thousand people homeless and the town centre destroyed. A hectic reconstruction programme saw almost the entire area speedily rebuilt in a style that borrowed heavily from the German Jugendstil (Art Nouveau) movement. Kaiser Wilhelm II, who used to holiday hereabouts, gave assistance, and the architects ended up creating a strange but fetching hybrid of up-to-date foreign influences and folksy local elements, with dragons, faces, flowers and even a decorative pharaoh or two. The finest buildings are concentrated on the main street, **Kongensgate**, and around the slender, central harbour, the **Brosundet**. If you've got a bit of time and are feeling energetic tackle the 418 steps to the Kniven viewpoint right in the centre of town: take Lihauggata from Kongensgata and just keep climbing; the views are worth it.

Arrival and information

Air Ålesund's airport is located on an island just outside of town. Airport buses (100kr; 20min) are timed to correspond with flight arrivals and departures.
Bus The town's bus station is by the waterfront, a few metres south of the Brosundet.
Tourist office On the harbourside ⓣ70 15 76 00, ⓦwww.visitalesund.com (June–Aug daily 8.30am–6pm; Sept–May Mon–Fri 9am–4pm).

Accommodation

Ålesund Youth Hostel Parkgata 14 ⓣ70 11 58 30, ⓦwww.vandrerhjem.no. Official HI hostel in a creaky but clean old building. Dorms 200kr, rooms 650kr.

Eating and drinking

Lille Løvenvold Løvenvold gate 2. Cool but comfy red-walled café/bar with retro furniture, great coffee and cheap sandwiches to soak up the beer. Nice little garden out back and regular DJ nights.
Lyspunktet Kipervik gate 1. Modern café with a gastropub feel. Big slouchy sofas, internet access and burgers, pasta and sandwiches at low prices.
Sjøbua Fiskerestaurant Brunholmgata 1. One of the best fish restaurants in Norway, with a real old-world feel. Very expensive but first-rate seafood, plus you can meet your dinner in the lobster tank.
Ta Det Piano Kipervik gate 1b. Cool little alternative art café and gallery with graffiti-style art on the walls. Salads, sandwiches and burgers from around 100kr. Regular DJ nights.

Moving on

Air SAS operates 2 daily flights to Trondheim (40min) and at least 6 daily to Oslo (55min).
Bus Bergen (daily; 10hr); Trondheim (1–3 daily; 9hr).

TREAT YOURSELF

BROSUNDET GJESTEHUS

Apotekergata 8 ⓣ70 12 10 00, ⓦwww.brosundet.no. This super-cool boutique hotel, designed by the most celebrated architects in Norway, occupies a beautifully converted old wharfside warehouse. The in-house restaurant *Maki* is excellent if pricey. 1200kr and up.

Northern Norway

The long, thin counties of **Trøndelag** and **Nordland** mark the transition from pastoral southern to blustery northern Norway. The main town of Trøndelag, appealing **Trondheim**, is easily accessible from Oslo by train, but north of here travelling becomes more of a slog as the distances between places grow ever greater. In **Nordland** you reach the **Arctic Circle**, beyond which the land becomes ever more spectacular, not least on the exquisite, mountainous **Lofoten Islands**, whose idyllic fishing villages (and inexpensive accommodation) richly merit a stop. Further north still, the provinces of **Tromsø** and **Finnmark** are subtle in their appeal, and the travelling can be hard, with **Tromsø**, a lively urban centre and university town, making the obvious stopping point. As for Finnmark, most visitors head straight for **Nordkapp**, from where the midnight sun is visible between early May and the end of July.

TRONDHEIM

TRONDHEIM, a loveable and atmospheric city with much of its eighteenth-century centre still intact, has been an important Norwegian power base for centuries, its success guaranteed by the excellence of its harbour and its position at the head of a wide and fertile valley. The early Norse parliament, or **Ting**, met here, and the city was once a major pilgrimage centre. Trondheim also possesses a handful of low-key sights – the marvellous cathedral excepted – a clutch of good restaurants, a string of busy bars and some very good shopping.

What to see and do

The city centre, holding most of the main sights, occupies a small island at the mouth of the River Nid.

Domkirke

The colossal **Nidaros Domkirke** – Scandinavia's largest medieval building, gloriously restored following the ravages of the Reformation and several fires – remains the focal point of the city centre (May to mid-Sept Mon–Fri 9am–3/5.30pm, Sat 9am–2pm, Sun 1–4pm; mid-Sept to April Mon–Fri noon–2.30pm, Sat 11.30am–2pm, Sun 1–3pm; 50kr). Taking Trondheim's former name (Nidaros means "mouth of the River Nid"), the cathedral is dedicated to King Olav, Norway's first Christian ruler, who was buried here. Thereafter, it became the traditional burial place of Norwegian royalty and, since 1814, the monarch's place of coronation. Highlights of the interior are the Gothic choir and the gargoyles on the pointed arches, as well as the striking choir screen and font, both the work of the Norwegian sculptor Gustav Vigeland.

Army and Resistance Museum

Behind the Domkirke lies the heavily restored Archbishop's Palace, now housing the **Army and Resistance Museum** (Mon–Sat 10am–4pm, Sun noon–4pm; free). Its most interesting section is on the top floor and recalls the German occupation during World War II, dealing honestly with the sensitive issue of collaboration and resistance.

Torvet and the Stiftsgården

Near at hand is **Torvet**, the main city square, a spacious open area anchored by a statue of Olav Tryggvason, perched on a stone pillar like a medieval Nelson. The broad and pleasant avenues of Trondheim's centre that radiate out from here date from the late seventeenth century, when they doubled as fire breaks. They were originally flanked by long rows of wooden buildings, now mostly replaced by uninspiring modern structures, but one conspicuous survivor is the **Stiftsgården** (only visitable on hourly guided tours: June to late Aug Mon–Sat 10am–4pm, Sun noon–4pm; 60kr), the yellow creation just north of Torvet on Munkegata. Built in 1774–78 as the home of a provincial governor, it's now an official royal residence.

Munkholmen

If you have an extra day in Trondheim and the weather's fine, squeeze in a day-trip by ferry (every 15min: July & Aug 10am–4/6pm; 55kr) to the "Monk's Island" from the harbour. This lovely island has a rich history: it was originally the town's execution grounds, but later housed a monastery, which then became a prison and finally a customs house before becoming the simple parkland recreation spot it is today.

Arrival and information

Train and bus The combined bus and train terminal (Sentralstasjon) is just over the bridge from the town centre.

Hurtigrute Trondheim is the first major northbound stop of the Bergen–Kirkenes Hurtigrute coastal boat, which docks about 600m behind and to the north of Sentralstasjon.

Tourist office Bang in the middle of town on the main square ⓣ73 80 76 60, ⓦwww.trondheim.no (June–Aug Mon–Fri 8.30am–6/8pm, Sat & Sun 10am–4/6pm; rest of year Mon–Fri 9am–4pm, Sat & Sun 10am–2pm).

Accommodation

The tourist office runs a room reservation service and has a small supply of private rooms from 350kr.

Singsaker Sommerhotell Rogerts gate 1 ⓦsommerhotell.singsaker.no. Charming summer-only hotel/hostel with a nice courtyard a short walk from the centre. Dorms 240kr, rooms 665kr.

Trondheim Interrail Centre Elgeseter gate 1 ⓣ73 89 95 38, ⓦwww.tirc.no. Fantastic, thrown-together summer hostel in the Trondheim University student union – a cavernous network of bars, theatres and music venues – established and run by local students. Free internet and a great café/bar on the premises. Only open July to early Aug. Dorms 180kr.

Trondheim Youth Hostel Weidemannsvei 41 ⓣ73 87 44 50, ⓦwww.trondheim-vandrerhjem.no. Inconveniently located but cheap and cheerful official hostel,

a steep 20min hike east from the centre over the Bakkebru bridge. Dorms 245kr, rooms 390kr.

Eating and drinking

Baklandet Skydsstasion Øvre Bakklandet 33. Characterful café/resto/bar housed in an old coaching inn in the lovely Bakklandet area. Serves up tasty traditional dishes at very reasonable prices – try the *bacalao*.

Bari Munkegata 25. Slick, fashionable bar/restaurant with a good-value lunch menu (light meals from around 110kr).

Choco Olav Tryggvasons gate 29 (entry from Nordre gate) and Nedre Bakklandet. Both branches of this relaxed café have a sizeable local following. Good sandwiches and salads, at average prices and an undeniably cool yet laid-back attitude.

Den Gode Nabo Øvre Bakklandet 66. A huge selection of international beers and a glorious, floating beer garden make this one of Trondheim's best-loved pubs. The food's good too, with a daily fish dish supplied by sister restaurant *Chablis* just upstairs.

Dromedar Nedre Bakklandet 3, Nordre gate and Olav Tryggvasons gate 14. Great coffee, cakes and sandwiches during the week at this cosy indie coffeeshop, now with several outlets across the city. Cheap drinks and tapas in the evenings.

Frati Munkegata 25. Justifiably popular, friendly, family-run Italian. Pizza and pasta around 140kr; mains slightly more.

Godt Brod Thomas Angellsgata 16. Organic bakery and café serving delicious fresh pastries and sandwiches.

Mormors Stue Nedre Enkeltskillingsveita 2. Like your granny's house, but much cooler, with lace doily tablecloths in an old wooden home. Choose from a range of well-priced light meals, all-you-can-eat cake and coffee for 69kr (Sun only), dinner for 135kr – or just sip a cold beer.

Ørens Kro Munkegata 40. Dockside restaurant serving up generous traditional Norwegian meals for around 200kr in an old riverside warehouse. Live music twice a week.

Persilleriet Erling Skakkes gate 39. Good-value vegetarian meals at this hole-in-the-wall café. Lunch around 60kr, dinner 80–100kr.

Moving on

Train Bodø (2 daily; 10hr); Dombås (1–4 daily; 2hr 30min–3hr); Oslo (2–4 daily; 7–10hr).

Bus Ålesund (1–4 daily; 9hr); Bergen (2 daily; 14hr).

THE ARCTIC CIRCLE

North of Trondheim, it's a long, 730km haul up the coast to the next major place of interest, Bodø. The nine-hour train trip is a rattling good journey, though, with the scenery becoming wilder and bleaker the further north you go.

Considering the amount of effort it takes to get here, crossing the **Arctic Circle** – which you'll do en route – is something of an anticlimax. The bare, bleak landscape, uninhabited for the most part, is undeniably impressive, though rather disfigured by the gleaming **Polarsirkelsenteret** (Arctic Circle Centre; daily: May & Sept 10am–6pm; June–Aug 8/9am–8/10pm; ⓣ91 85 38 33, ⓦwww.polarsirkelsenteret.no), a giant Arctic-kitsch lampshade of a building by the highway and stuffed with every sort of tourist bauble imaginable.

BODØ

BODØ is literally the end of the line: this is where all trains and many long-distance buses terminate. It's also a stop on the Hurtigrute coastal boat route and the main port of departure for the Lofoten Islands (see box opposite). The **bus station** (Sentrumsterminalen) at Sjøgata 3 is also home to the **tourist office** (mid-May to Aug Mon–Fri 9am–8pm, Sat 10am–6pm, Sun noon–8pm; Sept to mid-May Mon–Fri 9am–3.30pm; ⓣ75 54 80 00, ⓦwww.visitbodo.com), which has a small supply of **private rooms** (around 350–500kr). Other budget accommodation options are in short supply – it's really best to move on – but if you're determined to stay, *Bodøsjøen Camping* (ⓣ75 56 36 80; 250kr) is about 3km southeast of the town centre. A good option for **food** is the traditional and inexpensive *Løvolds Kafeteria* (Mon–Fri 9am–6pm, Sat 9am–3pm), down by the quay at Tollbugata 9: its Norwegian menu features local ingredients, with cheap daily specials. You'll find a younger crowd at *Kafé Kafka*, Sandgata 5b, where the menu includes pasta, burgers and salads and there's free internet.

THE LOFOTEN ISLANDS

Stretched out in a skeletal curve across the Norwegian Sea, the **Lofoten Islands** are perfect for a few simple, uncluttered days. Life moves more slowly here (and transport links reflect this) so be prepared to kick back and switch to the slow lane. For somewhere so far north the weather is exceptionally mild, and there's plentiful **accommodation** (Ⓦwww.lofoten.info) in *rorbuer*. Originally fishermen's shacks, these are now more often well-equipped huts, sleeping from two to six (400–1000kr per hut per night). In addition, the islands have four hostels and plenty of campsites.

Austvågøy

The main town on **Austvågøy**, the largest and northernmost island of the group, is **SVOLVÆR**, a hub of island bus routes but otherwise not worth much of your time. **Passenger ferries** from Bodø (car ferries stop at Moskenes only) dock about 1km west of the town centre, whereas the Hurtigrute docks in the centre, a brief walk from the **bus station** and the busy **tourist office**. Here you can pick up island-wide information and bus schedules (late May to mid-June & late Aug Mon–Fri 9am–4pm & Sat noon–4pm; mid-June to mid-Aug Mon–Fri 9am–7pm, Sat & Sun noon–4pm; late Aug to mid-May Mon–Fri 9am–3.30pm; Ⓣ76 06 98 07, Ⓦwww.lofoten.info).

One of the most pleasant places **to stay** in Svolvær is the *Svolvær Sjøhuscamp*, by the seashore at the foot of Parkgata (Ⓣ76 07 03 36, Ⓦwww.svolver-sjohuscamp.no; from 440kr), five minutes' walk from the square. Alternatively, at the east end of the harbour, a causeway leads out to the slender islet of Svinøya, where accommodation at *Svinøya Rorbuer* (Ⓣ76 06 99 30, Ⓦwww.svinoya.no) consists of traditional *rorbuer* from 1000kr.

GETTING TO THE LOFOTEN ISLANDS

The **Hurtigrute coastal boat** calls at two ports, Stamsund and Svolvær (a five-and-a-half-hour journey from Bodø, while the southern Lofoten **ferry** leaves Bodø for Moskenes, Værøy and Røst. There are also **passenger express catamarans**, which work out slightly cheaper than the Hurtigrute, linking both Bodø and Narvik with Svolvær. By **bus** the main long-distance services from the mainland to the Lofoten are from Bodø to Svolvær via Fauske and from Narvik to Svolvær. Finally you can **fly** with Wideroe, which can actually work out cheaper if you buy far enough in advance. All in all, however, transport to and from the islands is slow and infrequent, so be prepared to take your time. Timings vary so you're best off checking with the transport offices in Bodø or your place of departure.

Vestvågøy

The next large island to the southwest, **Vestvågøy**, is the one that really captivates most travellers, due in no small part to the atmospheric village of **STAMSUND**, whose older buildings are strung along a rocky, fretted seashore. It's the first port of call for the **Hurtigrute coastal boat** as it heads north from Bodø. Getting here from Austvågøy is also reasonably easy with several **buses** making the trip daily (except Sun), though you'll have to change at Leknes, 16km west. The scenery on this island is truly spectacular and hikers will be well rewarded with stunning views.

In Stamsund, the first place to head for is the smashing HI **hostel** (Ⓣ76 08 93 34, Ⓦwww.vandrerhjem.no; dorms 120kr, rooms 400kr, cabins 500kr; closed mid-Oct to early March; self-catering only); friendly and very informal, it's made up of several cosy *rorbuer* perched over a pint-sized bay, about 1km up the road from the port and 150m from the nearest bus stop – ask the driver to tell you where to get off. **Fishing** around here is first-class: the hostel rents out rowing boats and lines; afterwards, you can cook

your catch on the hostel's wood-burning stoves. Bikes are also available for rent (120kr) – the friendly proprietor will suggest cycle routes. For great fish soup and other local dishes – and very friendly service – head to the *Skjaerbrygga* restaurant, right in the centre of town near the supermarket.

Flakstadøya and Moskenesøya

By any standard the next two Lofoten Islands, **Flakstadøya** and **Moskenesøya**, are extraordinarily beautiful. As the Lofoten archipelago tapers towards its southerly conclusion, rearing peaks crimp a sea-shredded coastline studded with a string of fishing villages. Remarkably, the €10 road travels along almost all of this dramatic shoreline, by way of tunnels and bridges, to **MOSKENES**, the **ferry port** midway between Bodø and the remote, southernmost bird islands of **Værøy** and **Røst**.

Some 6km further on, the road ends at the tersely named Å, one of the Lofotens' most delightful villages, its huddle of old buildings rambling over a foreshore that's wedged in tight between the grey-green mountains and the surging sea. There's an assortment of smart *rorbuer* (from 850kr) surrounding the dock, and a good HI **hostel** (dorms 180kr, rooms 360kr). Here you'll also find the pub and the only **restaurant** in town, which serves very good seafood. All accommodation can be reserved on ⓣ76 09 11 21, ⓦwww.lofoten-rorbu.com.

Local **buses** run the length of the E10 from Leknes to Å four or five times daily from late June to late August, less frequently the rest of the year. They don't, however, always coincide with sailings to and from Moskenes, so if you're heading from the ferry port to Å, you may have to walk or take a (prohibitively expensive) taxi.

TROMSØ

TROMSØ, the "gateway to the arctic", likes to think of itself as the capital of northern Norway, with two cathedrals, a clutch of interesting museums and lively (and affordable) nightlife, patronized by its high-profile student population. Certainly, as a base for this part of the country, it's hard to beat, set in magnificent landscape – dramatic mountains and craggy shoreline – and offering easy access to the plethora of winter and summer activities available in this part of the world. It's an easy-going, friendly city and a great place to spend a few days.

What to see and do

In the centre of town you can't miss the striking woodwork of the **Domkirke** (Tues–Fri noon–4pm). From the church, it's a short walk north along the

THE NORTHERN LIGHTS AND MIDNIGHT SUN

Tromsø's northerly location but relatively mild climate has made it a popular spot from which to view the **Northern Lights**, or Aurora Borealis, which occur here all year round but most frequently between November and April. Caused by solar winds as they hit the Earth's atmosphere, they light up the sky in shimmering waves of blue, yellow and green – a spectacle of celestial proportions.

In the summertime there's an entirely different Arctic phenomena to behold: the breathtaking **midnight sun**. In Tromsø you're so far north that the sun never actually dips beneath the horizon. Head for the highest hill between May 18 and July 25 around midnight and you'll see the sun, hovering over the horizon in the west, setting the sky spectacularly aglow. For a great view head for Fjellheisen, a cable car that runs to the top of **Mount Storsteinen** (take bus #26 and ask for a cable-car round-trip ticket; April to mid-May & late Sept 10am–5pm, mid-May to mid-Aug 10am–1am, mid-Aug to Sept 10am–10pm; 120kr).

harbourfront to the most diverting of the city's museums, the **Polar Museum** (daily: March to mid-June & mid-Aug to Sept 11am–5pm; mid-June to mid-Aug 10am–7pm; Oct–Feb 11am–4pm; 50kr; ⓦwww.polarmuseum.no), whose varied displays include skeletons retrieved from the permafrost of Svalbard and a detailed section on the polar explorer Roald Amundsen, as well as a bewildering quantity of stuffed animals – all crammed in to an old harbourside warehouse.

On the other side of the water, over the spindly Tromsø Bridge, the white and ultramodern **Arctic Cathedral** (bus #20, 24, 26 or 28 from city centre; June to mid-Aug Mon–Sat 9am–7pm, Sun 1–7pm; mid-Aug to May daily 3/4–6pm; all year Sun service 11am–noon; afternoon and midnight sun concerts in summer; 30kr) is spectacular, made up of eleven immense triangular concrete sections representing the eleven Apostles left after the betrayal.

Back in the centre, a ten-minute stroll south along the waterfront from the harbour brings you to **Polaria**, Hjalmar Johansengate 12 (daily: mid-May to mid-Aug 10am–7pm; mid-Aug to mid-May noon–5pm; 95kr), which combines polar exhibits and an aquarium – complete with walk-through seal tank – with displays about the region's fragile eco system.

Arrival and information

Boat The Hurtigrute coastal boat docks in the centre of town at the foot of Kirkegata.

Bus Long-distance buses arrive and leave from the adjacent car park.

Tourist office Kirkegate 2, near the Domkirke ⓣ77 61 00 00, ⓦwww.visittromso.no (mid-May to Aug Mon–Fri 9am–7pm, Sat & Sun 10am–5pm; Sept to mid-May Mon–Fri 9am–4pm, Sat 10am–4pm).

Accommodation

The tourist office has a small supply of private rooms from 300kr.

ABC Hotell Nord Parkgate 4 ⓣ77 66 83 00, ⓦwww.hotellnord.no. Basic but comfortable budget hotel 400m from the centre of town. Free wi-fi and student discounts available. 590kr.

AMI Hotell Skolegate 1 ⓣ77 62 10 00, ⓦwww.amihotel.no. Good-value hotel close to the centre of town, with free wi-fi, free tea and coffee, and discounts for longer stays and for students. 586kr.

Fjellheim Sommerhotell Mellanveien 96 ⓣ77 75 55 60, ⓦwww.fjellheimsommerhotell.no. A good budget option in a converted school 15min walk from the centre. Mid-June to early Aug only. Dorms 250kr, rooms 700kr.

Tromsø Camping ⓣ77 63 80 37, ⓦwww.tromsocamping.no. Pleasant campsite over the bridge on the mainland, about 1800m beyond the Arctic Cathedral. Camping 150kr, cabins 450kr.

Tromsø Youth Hostel Åsgårdsveien 9 ⓣ77 65 76 28, ⓦwww.vandrerhjem.no. Frugal, no-frills summer hostel some 2km west of the quay; hop on bus #26 from the centre. Mid-June to mid-Aug only. Dorms 225kr, rooms 510kr.

Eating

Aunegården Sjøgata 29. Bustling restaurant in a gorgeous old listed building serving traditional lunches, plus coffee and heavenly cakes fresh from the on-site bakery.

Helmessen Delikatesser Storgate 66. Fabulous upscale deli with everything from glorious cinnamon buns to gourmet sandwiches and great coffee. The best place in town for picnic items.

Kaffebønner Strandtorget 1 & Stortorget 3. Buzzing, modern café with lunchtime panini offers and excellent coffee.

Verdensteatret Storgata 93b. Popular café/bar housed in an old movie theatre that attracts an arty young crowd with its cheap lunch food, drinks and pumping DJ nights.

Drinking and nightlife

Åpenbar Grønnegata 81. Modern bar serving tapas by day and an eclectic mix of music in its three club rooms by night.

TREAT YOURSELF

Emma's Drømekjokken
Kirkegata 8. The best restaurant in town, "Emma's Dream Kitchen" serves sublime locally sourced fare from Arctic char to reindeer at prices to match. Go to the downstairs café, *Emma's Under*, and prices are slightly lower but the food just as delicious.

Blå Rock Café Strandgate 14/16 (just off Strandtorget) Ⓦwww.blarock.no. Much-loved bar with a jukebox and a rock'n'roll air.
Driv Tollbugata 3 Ⓦwww.driv.no. Cosy student café/bar in a waterfront warehouse near the polar museum where the food and beer is cheap and the company cheerful and welcoming.
Ølhallen Pub This welcoming, traditional pub is attached to the Mack Brewery (daily tours in summer) and serves its full range of microbrews. Daytime only: Mon–Sat from 9am.
Skarven Strandtorget 13. The place to go for summer drinks late into the polar evening. Also does good traditional food.
Tromsø Jernbanestasjon Strandgate 33. Quirky pub with a railway theme – half the seating is from old trains. This is the place to go if you're looking to watch the football.

Moving on

Bus All southbound buses go via Narvik (2–5 daily; 4hr 30min to Narvik); Nordkapp (late June to mid-Aug 2 daily except Sat; 14hr).

MAGERØYA AND NORDKAPP

Beyond Tromsø, the northern tip of Norway enjoys no less than two and a half months of permanent daylight on either side of the summer solstice. Here, the bleak and treeless island of **Magerøya** is connected to the northern edge of the mainland by an ambitious combination of tunnels and bridges.

Honningsvåg

The island's only significant settlement is the fishing village of **HONNINGSVÅG**, which makes a steady income from accommodating the hundreds of summertime tourists bent on visiting Nordkapp – the North Cape – just 34km away.

Long-distance **buses** arrive in the centre of the village. The summer-only *North Cape Guesthouse*, just behind the seafront at Elvebakken 5a, is the best budget **accommodation** option (Ⓣ92 82 33 71, Ⓦwww.northcapeguesthouse.com; dorms 250kr, rooms 600kr). Alternatively, there's *NAF Nordkapp Camping* (Ⓣ78 47 33 77; Ⓦwww.nordkappcamping.no; late May to mid-Sept; four-bed cabins 550kr, camping 110kr), 8km from Honningsvåg on the road to Nordkapp. For **food**, there are a couple of takeaway kiosks along Storgata and a very good seafood restaurant, the *Sjøhuset Restaurant & Bar*, at the *Honningsvåg Brygge Hotel*, though it's not cheap.

Nordkapp

Whilst the 307m-high cliff known as Nordkapp isn't actually the northernmost point of Europe (that honour belongs to Knivskjellodden, along an 18km signposted track from highway E69), it's officially as far north as you can get by public transport. It's a hassle to get here, but there *is* something exhilarating about this bleak, wind-battered promontory. Originally a Sami sacrificial site, it was named by the English explorer Richard Chancellor in 1553. These days the headland is occupied by **Nordkapphallen** (North Cape Hall; daily: early to mid-May & Sept to mid-Oct 11am–3pm; mid-May to Aug 11am–1am; mid-Oct to April 12.30–2pm; 195kr for 48hr, including parking), a flashy tourist centre that contains souvenir shops, cafés, restaurants, a panoramic movie, and huge windows from where you can survey the surging ocean below.

To reach Nordkapp, there's a limited bus from Honningsvåg (late June to mid-Aug 1–2 daily; 45min); when the buses aren't running, the only option is a taxi (at least 1000kr return), though the road is closed throughout the winter and often in spring too – check with the tourist office beforehand. For travellers northbound on the Hurtigrute coastal boat, a special coach is laid on to get from Honningsvåg to Nordkapp and back within the two-and-a-half-hour stop.

Poland

HIGHLIGHTS

SOPOT: relax on the vast stretch of white sand near Poland's lively summertime resort

NIGHT OUT IN WARSAW: live it up among the glass skyscrapers and abandoned factories of the country's dynamic capital

WROCŁAW: discover this elegant gem of a city, with gorgeous architecture unspoilt by tourist hordes

KAZIMIERZ, KRAKÓW: explore Poland's Jewish heritage in the ancient synagogues and winding alleyways of this now hip neighbourhood

TATRA MOUNTAINS: hike among jagged alpine peaks, swim in crystal-clear lakes and sample fresh trout in bustling mountain resorts

ROUGH COSTS

DAILY BUDGET Basic €22/occasional treat €35

DRINK Vodka (50ml shot) €1

FOOD Żurek soup €1–2

HOSTEL/BUDGET HOTEL €8/25

TRAVEL Train: Warsaw–Kraków (390km; 3hr) €22; bus: (6hr) €10

FACT FILE

POPULATION 38.5 million

AREA 312,685 sq km

LANGUAGE Polish

CURRENCY Złoty (zł/PLN)

CAPITAL Warsaw (population: 1.7 million)

INTERNATIONAL PHONE CODE ⓣ48

Introduction

Change is a constant in Poland these days. The transition to capitalism may have been difficult for some, but the past twenty years have witnessed such vigorous growth that even when Western markets collapsed in 2008, Poland's economy remained relatively solid. Visitors may be struck by how enthusiastically the Poles seem to have embraced consumer culture, but below the surface lies a society still firmly rooted in traditional values of family, community and the Catholic church.

Much of **Warsaw**, the capital, conforms to stereotypes of Eastern European greyness, but its historic centre, beautiful parks and vibrant nightlife are diverting enough. **Kraków**, the ancient royal capital in the south, is the real crowd-puller, rivalling the elegance of Prague and Vienna, while **Gdańsk** on the Baltic Sea offers an insight into Poland's dynamic politics as well as the golden beaches in the nearby resort of **Sopot**. In the west, stately **Wrocław** charms visitors with its architecture and vibrant student life, while quintessentially Polish **Poznań** is still revered as the independent heart of the nation. For outdoorsy types, the **Tatra Mountains** on the Slovak border offer unspoilt natural beauty and exhilarating hiking, plus skiing in the winter.

CHRONOLOGY

966 AD Mieszko I creates the Polish state.
1025 Bolesław I, Mieszko's son, is crowned the first King of Poland.
1300s Gdańsk and several other northern cities join the Hanseatic League, and trade prospers.
1385 The Union of Krewo unites the countries of Poland and Lithuania through an arranged marriage.
1410 United Polish and Lithuanian forces defeat the occupying military-religious order, the Teutonic Knights, at the Battle of Grunwald.
1500s The Renaissance sweeps through Poland, giving it significant cultural importance in Europe.
1569 The Lublin Union establishes the Polish–Lithuanian Commonwealth.
1700s Russia, Prussia and Austria divide Polish–Lithuanian land between them in the three Partitions.
1863 The January Uprising against Russian authority is brutally repressed.
1918 Independent Polish state created following the defeat of Germany, Russia and Austria-Hungary in World War I.
1926 Marshal Jozef Piłsudski stages a military coup, marking the failure of democracy.
1939 Poland is invaded by Nazi Germany, beginning World War II.
1945 By the end of the war more than six million Poles are dead. Soviets drive out the Nazis, and occupy large parts of Poland; the country's borders shift around 200km west.
1947 Poland becomes a communist state.
1978 Karol Wojtyła, Archbishop of Kraków, is elected to become pope, taking the name John Paul II.
1980 Workers' uprising at Gdańsk, led by Lech Wałęsa, sweeps through Poland. He forms the Solidarity Party, which becomes an important anti-communist movement.
1990 Wałęsa becomes the first popularly elected president of Poland.
2004 Poland accedes to the EU.
2007 Parliamentary elections overturn the conservative government led by the controversial Kaczyński twins. Moderate Donald Tusk becomes prime minister, although Lech Kaczyński remains president.

ARRIVAL

Several budget **airlines** fly into Warsaw and Kraków, Poland's two most popular cities, but there are also an increasing number of flights into numerous other airports, including Gdańsk, Wrocław and Poznań, from major Western European destinations.

Poland has fast **rail** connections with all its neighbouring countries. Several direct trains arrive daily in both

Kraków and Warsaw from Central Europe's backpacker hotspots – Prague, Budapest and Vienna. Poznań, Wrocław and Warsaw have regular connections to Germany.

Several Polish **bus** companies, including Polski Express (ⓣ022/843 3091, ⓦwww.polskiexpress.net) and Eurolines, provide services from all major European capitals to Warsaw. On the southern border, there are daily public buses to the mountain town of Zakopane from the Slovakian resort of Poprad.

GETTING AROUND

The primary means of transport for budget travellers in Poland is by train, and the PKP **railway** system runs three main types. Express services (*ekspresowy*), particularly IC (*intercity*) or EC (*eurocity*), stop at major cities only, and seat reservations (*miejscówka*, 5–10zł/€1.10–2.20) are compulsory. "Fast" trains (*pospieszny*) are less costly, but not necessarily slower. The cheapest services (*osobowy*) are less predictable – some are quick, while others stop at every haystack. Seats come in two classes, with first-class simply meaning a six-seat compartment rather than one for eight people; it's rarely worth the extra cost. You can buy tickets in advance at Orbis travel agencies (branches in all towns and cities). **InterRail passes** – including the "one-country" pass – are valid, though you'll still have to pay for seat reservations. The main city stations

are generally termed "główny"; departures (*odjazdy*) are printed on yellow posters; arrivals (*przyjazdy*) on white; "peron" means platform. You can check times and find the best ticket deals on the PKP timetable (ⓦrozklad-pkp.pl).

Intercity **buses** operated by PKS, the national bus company, are cheap but slow and often overcrowded; only in the southern mountain regions are buses generally faster than trains. Polski Express (ⓦwww.polskiexpress.net) offers pricier journeys in more comfortable and faster buses – particularly out of Warsaw.

With a predominantly flat landscape and accommodation never more than 50km away, Poland is a tempting place for **cyclists**. There are repair shops in many cities and you can take bikes on most trains. Note, however, that thanks to poor road surfaces and dangerous driving, Poland is one of Europe's leading nations for road fatalities.

ACCOMMODATION

Private hostels proliferate in Kraków and Warsaw and have cropped up in other cities as well. They generally offer excellent service, with internet access and laundry, for around 45zł per bed. During the Polish summer holidays (July & Aug), however, it is advisable to book ahead. Even the smallest towns have a **public hostel** (*schroniska młodzieżowe*), which costs around 30zł a head; for a complete list check ⓦwww.ptsm.org.pl. In large cities they're centrally located and open year-round, though usually with lockouts and curfews. Similarly priced to the private ones, **summer hostels** open to cope with the extra demand in July and August; the *Dizzy Daisy* chain (ⓣ012/422 3258, ⓦwww.dizzydaisy.pl) is best set up for foreign travellers. There is at least one **budget hotel** in every town, with 120zł normally enough to get you a Spartan but habitable room with communal toilet and shower; there are often excellent discounts for students. Tourist offices can also often find you cheap rooms in **private houses** (*kwatera prywatna*; 70–80zł).

Polish **campsites** are often a fair distance from town centres and are not always cheaper than a dorm bed in a hostel (30–60zł). Though some of these sites, especially in the national parks, have excellent facilities, you should generally expect to find a toilet and little else. For a list of campsites in Poland, check out ⓦwww.eurocampings.co.uk/en/europe/poland.

FOOD AND DRINK

Poles are passionate about their food, and meals of feast-like proportions will probably characterize your stay. The cuisine is an intriguing mix of European and Eastern influences and, whilst often wonderfully flavoursome and nutritious, it does live up to its reputation for heaviness. **Polish meals** generally start with soups, the most popular of which are *barszcz*, beetroot broth, and *Żurek*, a sour soup of fermented rye. The basis of most main courses is fried or grilled meat, such as *kotlet schabowy* (breaded pork chops). Two inexpensive specialities (8–12zł) you'll find everywhere are *bigos* (sauerkraut stewed with a variety of meats) and *pierogi*, dumplings stuffed with cottage cheese and onion (*ruskie*), meat (*z mięsem*), or cabbage and mushrooms (*z kapustą i grzybami*). The national snack is the *zapiekanka*, a baguette topped with mushrooms, melted cheese and tomato sauce. For **vegetarians** sick of cabbage and mushrooms, a few veggie cafés (such as the *Green Way* chain) have cropped up in recent years.

Restaurants are open until 9 or 10pm, later in city centres, and prices are lower than in Western Europe: in most places outside of Warsaw and Kraków you can have a two-course meal with a drink for 40zł. The cheapest option is the local **milk bar** (*bar mleczny*; usually open from breakfast until 6/7pm), which provides fast and filling daytime meals

for workers, while cake shops (*cukierna*) produce sweet pastries that rival any in Central Europe.

Drink

The Poles can't compete with their Czech neighbours when it comes to **beer** (*piwo*), but a range of microbreweries (*browars*) are supplementing the drinkable national brands. Even in Warsaw, you won't pay more than 12zł for a half-litre. Tea (*herbata*) and coffee (*kawa*) are both popular; the former often comes with lemon rather than milk. But it's **vodka** (*wódka*), ideally served neat and cold, which is the national drink. As well as the clear variety, it's well worth trying the flavoured types – king amongst Polish vodkas is the legendary Żubrówka, infused with the taste of bison grass.

CULTURE AND ETIQUETTE

As a nation in which over 75 percent of people are practising Roman Catholics, Poland maintains many conservative religious and social customs, especially in the countryside where men are often still seen as the breadwinners. Poland's young, urban population tend to be both more relaxed and wilder than their parents. Yet Poles of all ages are also warm, passionate people, fond of handshakes and of lively, informal conversation over a vodka. Table manners follow the Western norm and it is common to reward good service with a ten percent **tip**, though Poles will sometimes leave less.

SPORTS AND OUTDOOR ACTIVITIES

The most popular **sport** is soccer and the national and top league teams often attract sell-out crowds, but even local village matches or Western European games shown in the local bar invariably bring many fans. Since Poland and Ukraine were chosen to host Euro 2012, the country has been beset by a flurry of stadium construction. Despite lacking any international stars, the Poles also enjoy tennis and cycling whilst American sports – especially basketball – are starting to make an impact. For most **hikers**, the highlight of Poland is the Tatra Mountains in the south, though the country's 23 national parks offer many opportunities for beautiful secluded walks and horseriding. **Watersports** are concentrated around Sopot in the north whilst the **skiing** season (Nov–Feb) brings tourists flocking to southern mountain resorts like Zakopane.

COMMUNICATIONS

Internet cafés charging 4–6zł/hr are present in all towns. Main **post offices** (*Poczta*) usually open Monday to Saturday 8am to 8pm; branches close earlier. For **public phones** you'll need a card (*karta telefoniczna*), available at post offices and RUCH newsagent kiosks.

EMERGENCIES

Poland is a very safe country to travel in, though inevitably thefts from dorms and pickpocketing do occur. Safely store your valuables whenever possible and, on night trains, lock your compartment when you sleep. Polish **police** (*policja*) are courteous but unlikely to speak English. **Medical care** can be basic and most foreigners rely on the expensive private medical centres run

POLAND ON THE NET

ⓦ www.poland.travel The official tourist website with general details on Poland's major sights and visa information.
ⓦ www.thenews.pl Polish Radio's English-language service, focusing on national news and current events.
ⓦ www.culture.pl News and essays on Polish cultural events and history.

Polish

	Polish	Pronunciation
Yes	*Tak*	Tahk
No	*Nie*	Nyeh
Please	*Proszę*	Prosh-eh
Thank you	*Dziękuję*	Djen-ku-yeh
Hello/Good day	*Dzień dobry*	Djen doh-brih
Goodbye	*Do widzenia*	Doh veed-zen-yah
Excuse me/Sorry	*Przepraszam*	Psheh-pra-shahm
Today	*Dzisiaj*	Djyish-eye
Yesterday	*Wczoraj*	Vchor-eye
Tomorrow	*Jutro*	Yoo-troh
What time is it?	*Która godzina?*	Ktoo-rah go-djee-nah
I don't understand	*Nie rozumiem*	Nyeh roh-zoom-yem
How much is...?	*Ile kosztuje...?*	Ill-eh kosh-too-yeh...
Do you speak English?	*Pan/i/mówi po angielsku?*	Pahn/ee/movee poh ahn-gyel-skoo?
Where is the...?	*Gdzie jest...?*	G-djeh yest...?
entrance	*wejście*	vey-shche
exit	*wyjście*	viy-shche
toilet	*toaleta*	to-a-le-ta
hotel	*hotel*	ho-tel
hostel	*schronisko/hostel*	sro-nees-ko
church	*kościoł*	kosh-choow
What time does the... leave/arrive?	*O ktorej odchodzi/ przychodzi...?*	O ktoo-rey ot-ho-djee/ pshih-ho-djee...?
boat	*łódz*	woodj
bus	*autobus*	aw-tow-boos
plane	*samolot*	sa-mo-lot
train	*pociąg*	po-chonk
I would like a...	*Proprozę...*	Po-pro-she...
Bed	*Łóżko*	woosh-ko
Single room	*Pokoj jednoosobowy*	Po-koi yed-no-o-so-bo-vi
Double room	*Pokoj lózkiem*	Po-koi woosh-kyem
Cheap	*Tani*	Tah-nee
Expensive	*Drogi*	Droh-gee
Open	*Otwarty*	Ot-var-tih
Closed	*Zamknięty*	Zahmk-nee-yen-tih
One	*Jeden*	Yed-en
Two	*Dwa*	Dvah
Three	*Trzy*	Trshih
Four	*Cztery*	Chter-ih
Five	*Pięć*	Pyench
Six	*Sześć*	Sheshch
Seven	*Siedem*	Shedem
Eight	*Osiem*	Oshem
Nine	*Dziewięć*	Djyev-yench
Ten	*Dziesięć*	Djyesh-ench

EMERGENCY NUMBERS

Police ⓣ997 (ⓣ112 from mobile phones); fire service ⓣ998; ambulance ⓣ999.

by Medicover (ⓣ041/9596, ⓦwww.medicover.pl) For non-prescription medication, local pharmacists are helpful and often speak English.

INFORMATION

Most cities have a **tourist office** (*informacja turystyczna*, or IT), which is generally run by the local municipality though some are merely private agencies selling costly tours.

MONEY AND BANKS

Currency is the **złoty** (zł/PLN), divided into 100 groszy. Coins come in 1, 2, 5, 10, 20 and 50 groszy, and 1, 2 and 5 złoty denominations; notes as 10, 20, 50, 100 and 200 złoty. At the time of writing, €1=4.2zł, US$1=2.90zł and £1=4.8zł. **Banks** (usually open Mon–Fri 7.30am–5pm, Sat 7.30am–2pm) and exchange offices (Kantors) offer similar exchange rates. Major credit cards are widely accepted, and **ATMs** are common in cities. Euros are not widely accepted, even in Warsaw.

OPENING HOURS AND HOLIDAYS

Most shops open on weekdays from 10am to 6pm, and all but the largest close on Saturday at 2 or 3pm and all day Sunday. RUCH kiosks, selling public transport tickets (*bilety*), open at 6 or 7am. Most museums and historic monuments are closed once a week. Entrance tends to be inexpensive, and is often free one day of the week. **Public holidays** are: January 1, Easter Monday, May 1, May 3, Corpus Christi (May/June), August 15, November 1, November 11, December 25 and 26.

STUDENT AND YOUTH DISCOUNTS

The major cities all have **tourist cards** (available for one day or longer) that give discounts on transport and at the main sights. Your ISIC card can halve entry prices for museums and city transport, especially in Warsaw, and cut intercity train fares by a third. A Hostelling International card can earn you up to 25 percent off at public hostels.

Warsaw

Packed with a bizarre mix of gleaming office buildings and grey, communist-era apartment blocks, **WARSAW** (Warszawa) often bewilders backpackers. Yet if any city rewards exploration, it is the Polish capital. North of the lively centre are stunning Baroque palaces and the meticulously reconstructed Old Town; to the south are two of Central Europe's finest urban parks; and towards the east lie reminders of the rich Jewish heritage extinguished by the Nazis.

Warsaw became the capital in 1596 and initially flourished as one of Europe's most prosperous cities. In 1815, however, Poland's weak international position allowed the Russians to conquer the city and, despite a series of rebellions, it was not until the outbreak of World War I that this control collapsed. Warsaw again became the capital of an independent Poland in 1918, but the German invasion of 1939 ensured that this was to be tragically short-lived. Infuriated by the 1944 Warsaw Uprising, Hitler ordered the total destruction of the city, leaving 850,000 Varsovians dead and 85 percent of Warsaw in ruins. Rebuilding is an ongoing process.

What to see and do

The main sights are on the western bank of the Wisła (Vistula) river where you'll find the central business and shopping district, **Śródmieście**, grouped around Centralna station and the nearby Palace of Culture. The more picturesque and tourist-friendly **Old Town** (Stare Miasto) is just to the north.

The Old Town

The title **Old Town** (Stare Miasto) is, in some respects, a misnomer for the historic nucleus of Warsaw. After World War II the beautifully arranged Baroque streets were destroyed, only to be painstakingly reconstructed in the years afterwards. This area comes alive in the summer, as tourists, street performers, outdoor cafés and festivals take over the quaint squares and cobblestone streets. Plac Zamkowy (Castle Square), on the south side of the Old Town, is the obvious place to start a tour.

Royal Castle

On the east side of the square is the thirteenth-century **Royal Castle**, once home of the royal family and seat of the Polish parliament, now the Castle Museum (Tues–Sun 10/11am–4/6pm; 22zł, Sun free). Though the structure is a replica, many its furnishings are originals, having been hidden during the war. After passing the most lavish section of the castle – the Royal Apartments of King Stanisław August – you visit the Lanckoranski Gallery, which contains a fascinating range of aristocratic portraits including two paintings – *Girl in a Picture Frame* and *Scholar at His Desk* – by Rembrandt.

Old and New Town Squares

On ul. Świętojańska, north of the castle, stands St John's Cathedral, the oldest church in Warsaw. A few yards away, the **Old Town Square** (Rynek Starego Miasta) is one of the most remarkable bits of postwar reconstruction anywhere in Europe. Flattened during the Uprising, its three-storey merchants' houses have been rebuilt in near-flawless imitation of the Baroque originals. It's also home to the **Warsaw Historical Museum** (Tues & Thurs 11am–6pm, Wed & Fri 10am–3.30pm, Sat & Sun 10.30am–4.30pm; 6zł, free Sun), where you can watch an English-language film (Tues–Sun at noon; 6zł on Sun) showing poignant footage of both the vibrant, multicultural 1930s city and the ruins left in 1945. Crossing the ramparts heading north brings you to the **New Town Square** (Rynek Nowego

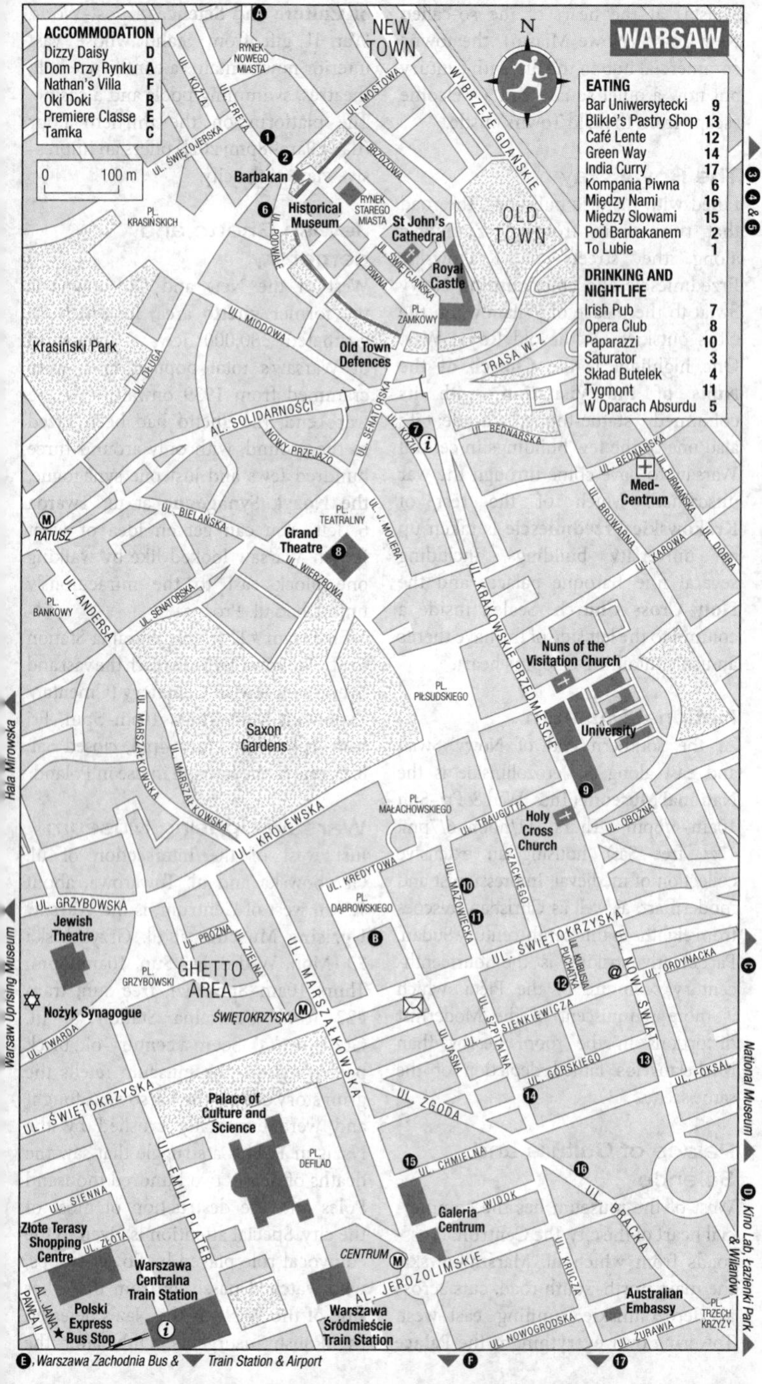

WARSAW

ACCOMMODATION

Dizzy Daisy	D
Dom Przy Rynku	A
Nathan's Villa	F
Oki Doki	B
Premiere Classe	E
Tamka	C

EATING

Bar Uniwersytecki	9
Blikle's Pastry Shop	13
Café Lente	12
Green Way	14
India Curry	17
Kompania Piwna	6
Między Nami	16
Między Slowami	15
Pod Barbakanem	2
To Lubie	1

DRINKING AND NIGHTLIFE

Irish Pub	7
Opera Club	8
Paparazzi	10
Saturator	3
Skład Butelek	4
Tygmont	11
W Oparach Absurdu	5

0 100 m

3, 4 & 5
Hala Mirowska
Warsaw Uprising Museum
C
National Museum
D, Kino Lab, Łazienki Park & Wilanów
E, Warszawa Zachodnia Bus & Train Station & Airport
F
17

Miasta) at the heart of the so-called New Town (Nowe Miasto), the town's commercial hub in the fifteenth century but now a quiet square and a welcome escape from the Old Town's bustle.

The Royal Way

Lined with historic buildings, the road that runs south from pl. Zamkowy along the streets of Krakowskie Przedmieście and chic, bustling Nowy Świat to the palace of Wilanów, on the city's outskirts, is the old **Royal Way**. One highlight is the **Church of the Nuns of the Visitation**, with its columned, statue-topped facade; it's also one of the few buildings in central Warsaw to have come through the war unscathed. Much of the rest of **Krakowskie Przedmieście** is taken up by university buildings, including several fine Baroque palaces and the **Holy Cross Church**. Sealed inside a column to the left side of the nave there's an urn containing Chopin's heart.

National Museum

At the southern end of Nowy Świat and east along al. Jerozolimskie is the **National Museum** (Tues, Wed & Fri–Sun 10am–4/6pm, Thurs 11/noon–6/7pm; 12zł, free Sat), housing an extensive collection of medieval, Impressionist and modern art, as well as Christian frescoes from eighth- to thirteenth-century Sudan. Particularly striking is the fourteenth-century sculpture of the Pietá, which is more reminiscent of the Modernist distortions in the room nearby than Michelangelo's famed depiction of the same scene.

Palace of Culture and Science

West of the museum lies the commercial heart of the city, the Centrum crossroads from which ul. Marszałkowska, the main north–south road, cuts across al. Jerozolimskie running east–west. Towering over everything is the **Palace of Culture and Science**, a post-World War II gift from Stalin whose vast interior now contains a conference hall, theatres, swimming pools and a casino. The platform on the thirtieth floor (daily 9am–8pm; 20zł) offers an impressive view of the city.

Jewish Ghetto and cemetery

West of the New and Old towns is the former **ghetto** area, in which an estimated 380,000 Jews – one-third of Warsaw's total population – were crammed from 1939 onwards. By the war's end, the ghetto had been razed to the ground, with only around three hundred Jews and just one synagogue, the **Nożyk Synagogue** at ul. Twarda 6, left. You can get an idea of what Jewish Warsaw looked like by walking one block east to the miraculously untouched ul. Próżna.

Take tram #22 from Centralna Station to ul. Okopowa 49/51 to reach the vast and overgrown **Jewish Cemetery** (Cmentarz Zydowski; Mon–Thurs 10am–5pm, Fri 9am–1pm, Sun 11am–4pm, closed Sat; 8zł), one of the few still in use in Poland.

Warsaw Uprising Museum

Just west of the intersection of ul. Grzybowska and ul. Towarowa, about 1.5km west of Centrum, is the **Warsaw Uprising Museum** at ul. Grzybowska 79 (Mon, Wed & Fri–Sun, 10am–6pm; Thurs 10am–8pm; 4zł, free Sun; tram #22 from Centralna Station to ul. Grzybowska). Set in a century-old brick power station, the museum retells the grim story of how the Varsovians fought and were eventually crushed by the Nazis in 1944 – a struggle that saw the deaths of nearly two hundred thousand Poles and the destruction of most of the city. Special attention is given to the equivocal role played by Soviet troops, who watched passively from the other side of the Wisła as the Nazis defeated the Polish insurgents. Only after the

city was a charred ruin did they move across to "liberate" its few remaining inhabitants.

Łazienki Park

About 2km south of the commercial district, on the eastern side of al. Ujazdowskie, is the much-loved **Łazienki Park** (bus #116, 180 or 195 from Nowy Świat). Once a hunting ground, the area was bought in the 1760s by King Stanisław August, who turned it into a park and built the Neoclassical **Łazienki Palace** (Tues–Sun 9am–4pm; 12zł) across the park lake. Most of the furnishings survived the war intact, but the park itself is the real attraction, with its oak-lined paths pleasantly cool in summer and alive with peacocks and red squirrels.

Wilanów Palace

The grandest of Warsaw's palaces, **Wilanów** (Wed–Mon 9.30/10.30am–4.30pm; mid-May to mid-Sept Wed till 6pm, Sun till 7pm; 16zł, free Sun), makes an easy excursion from the centre: take bus #180 south from Krakowskie Przedmieście or Nowy Świat to its terminus. Converted in the seventeenth century from a small manor house into the "Polish Versailles", the palace displays a vast range of decorative styles. The mix of English, Chinese and Italian designs is mirrored in the delightful palace **gardens** (daily 9am–sunset; 5zł, free Thurs) and lake, on which you can take a gondola cruise (May–Sept 9am–sunset; 5zł).

Arrival and information

Air Okęcie airport is 8km southwest of the Old Town: avoid the rip-off taxi drivers and take bus #175 (N32 at night) into town.

Train The main train station, Warszawa Centralna, in the modern centre is located just to the west of the Centrum crossroads, under the Palace of Culture and Science.

Bus The main bus station, Międzynarodowa Dworzec PKS, is located right next to the Warszawa Zachodnia train station, 3km west of Centralna station. To get into town from here catch eastbound buses #127, #130, #158 or #517. Polski Express intercity buses use the bus stop on al. Jana Pawła II, just outside the western entrance of Centralna train station.

Tourist office The best source of information is the helpful IT office at 65 Krakowskie Przedmieście (daily 9am–8pm; ⓣ022/9431, ⓦwww.warsawtour.pl), which has excellent free city maps and brochures. There are also IT offices at Centralna station and the Airport.

Travel agents STA Travel, ul. Krucza 41/43 (ⓣ022/529 3800) can reserve international or domestic flights and train tickets, and sells ISIC Cards.

City transport

Tickets for trams, buses and the metro (single trip 2.80zł; 1hr 4zł) are bought from green RUCH kiosks or from automatic ticket machines. Always punch your tickets in the machines on board, as Warsaw's zealous inspectors are extremely thorough. There are also good-value day/3-day/week passes available (9zł/16zł/32zł), which should be punched the first time you use them. Tickets for students (*ulgowy*) are half-price, but you need to show ID.

Bus Well-developed if busy system that runs until around 11pm; after that, night buses leave every 30min from behind the main train station.

Trams A crowded but efficient means of transport during rush hour. Run till 11pm.

Metro A small subway system running north–south through the centre of town is the fastest way to get around, though its route is very limited.

Taxis Generally cost 1.60–2.60zł per kilometre, with a minimum fare of 6zł, but only take taxis that have the company name, telephone number and price per kilometre clearly marked. English is spoken at Ele (ⓣ022/811 1111) and Glob (ⓣ9668).

Accommodation

Warsaw has many good private hostels, mainly in Śródmieście, as well as several less appealing public ones with curfews. All the hostels listed below offer free internet, breakfast and free/cheap laundry services unless otherwise stated. Most offer singles/doubles for 110/160zł. Hotels tend to be pricier than elsewhere in Poland.

Hostels

Dizzy Daisy ul. Górnośląska 14 ⓣ022/213 8630, ⓦwww.hostel.pl. A clean and friendly summer hostel near the Łazienki Park. Dorms 40zł.

Dom Przy Rynku Rynek Nowego Miasta 4 ⓣ609 260 625, ⓦwww.cityhostel.net. This small and friendly place has the most affordable rooms in the Nowe Miasto. Dorms 40zł.

Nathan's Villa ul. Piękna 24/6, off Marszałkowska, around 500m south of Centrum ⓣ022/622 2946, ⓦwww.nathansvilla.com. Here you'll find stylish rooms, nice bathrooms and smiling service. Dorms 45zł.

Oki Doki pl. Dąbrowskiego ⓣ022/826 5112, ⓦwww.okidoki.pl. With an eccentric communist-era interior and an accompanying bar (0.5lt beer 6zł), this hostel has by far the liveliest feel of any in town. Dorms 40–60zł.

Tamka ul. Tamka 30 ⓣ022/826 3095, ⓦwww.tamkahostel.pl. This place has colourful (if basic) dorms and a garden that's handy for a summer barbecue. Dorms 35–45zł.

Hotel

Premiere Classe ul. Towarowa 2 ⓣ022/624 0800, ⓦwww.premiereclasse.com.pl. The city's best budget hotel provides spacious rooms with satellite TV. Breakfast is not included (20zł). Rooms (for up to three people) 199zł.

Eating

Milk bars

Bar Uniwersytecki ul. Krakowskie Przedmiescie 20/22. A long-time favourite with cash-strapped university students. Mains 4–8zł.

Pod Barbakanem ul. Mostawa 27-9. Popular milk bar just outside the Old Town with wholesome grub. Mains 4–8zł.

Cafés

Blikle's Pastry Shop ul. Nowy Świat 35. Mouthwatering array of pastries, cakes and chocolates. Cake slices 3.50–6zł.

Café Lente ul. Kubusia Puchatka 8. Set back on a quiet side street, this friendly and cosy café is the perfect place to grab a light lunch or relax over coffee and a book. Salads 20zł.

Między Nami ul. Bracka 20. Inauspicious outside (look out for the unmarked grey awnings), but this cultured cafe is an excellent choice if you want a light meal, with some innovative vegetarian choices. Mains 20–30zł.

Między Slowami ul. Chimielna 30. Nicely set back from the busy street in a bright courtyard, this is a great chilling spot after a hard day's shopping. Sandwiches 13zł.

To Lubie ul. Freta 4/6. With a pleasant outdoor summer patio and invitingly warm interiors, this place has delicious cakes, making it a good choice for an afternoon break. Cakes 12zł.

Restaurants

Green Way ul. Szpitalna 6. Locals pack out this fun, inexpensive veggie canteen. Mains 10–13zł.

India Curry ul. Zurawia 22. The best choice if you're seeking something Indian is this curry house with a wide variety of tasty dishes from across the subcontinent (20–45zł).

Kompania Piwna ul. Podwale 25. This Bavarian-style restaurant near the Old Town Square is good value. Large beers and huge steaks are the standard fare, but also look out for the cheap, tasty fish dishes. Mains 20–35zł.

Drinking and nightlife

The bar scene in Warsaw has really taken off in the last few years, and the city now genuinely provides a great night out that rivals Prague and needn't blow your budget. Praga, across the river, is a formerly dangerous neighbourhood that now boasts a lively, bohemian bar scene – an interesting alternative to the more glitzy hangouts you'll find downtown.

Bars

Irish Pub ul. Miodowa 3. For those seeking a pint of the black stuff and live Irish folk and rock music (8–11pm on most nights). 1lt Guinness 30zł.

Paparazzi ul. Mazowiecka 12. One of the flashiest bars in town, featuring an after-work crowd and a truly impressive list of creative cocktails (22–25zł).

Skład Butelek ul. 11 Listopada 22. A wonderfully quirky gathering place for Warsaw's creative types, hidden away in the basement of an old factory. 0.5lt beer 9zł.

W Oparach Absurdu ul. Zabkowska 6. Chaotic, lively and decorated with all the haphazard charm of a flea market. Look for the giant plastic spider over the door. 0.5lt beer 8zł.

Clubs

Opera Club pl. Teatralny 1. Dancefloors and semi-private rooms are scattered through the caverns and dark chambers beneath the Grand Theatre, making for a novel night out. Cocktails 18–25zł.

Saturator ul. 11 Listopada 22. Pulling in hipsters from all over town with its three dancefloors and anything-goes attitude, this place grooves to electro-pop and Eighties hits well into the wee hours. Cocktails 12–18zł.

Tygmont ul. Mazowiecka 6. The best jazz club in town, with live bands Mon–Thurs (6pm–midnight) and Latino dance classes over the weekend from 7.30pm. Look smart as there's a strict dress code.

Entertainment

The city's festivals enhance the celebratory vibe, especially the Warsaw "Summer Jazz Days" Festival, a series of outdoor concerts held throughout the months of July and August. Check out the English-language *Warsaw Insider* (available in most hotels) for a monthly list of events.

Cinema

Films are often shown in English with Polish subtitles, though it's always best to ask regarding the popular Hollywood titles. Tickets range from 15–25zł.

Kinoteka pl. Defilad 1. Multiplex in the Palace of Culture and Science showing the latest blockbusters.

Kino.Lab ul. Ujazdowskie 6 Ⓦ www.kinolab.art.pl. This small cinema shows a wide range of avant-garde films.

Music

Live bands are apt to appear in the city bars without any warning; *Tygmont* and the *Irish Pub* are your best bets.

Grand Theatre (Teatr Wielki) pl. Teatralny 1 Ⓣ 022/692 0200, Ⓦ www.teatrwielki.pl. This is worth visiting just for its Neoclassical facade, but it also hosts the best of Poland's National Opera. 25–130zł depending on seats.

Theatre

Jewish Theatre (Teatr Żydowski) pl. Grzybowski Ⓣ 022/620 6281, Ⓦ www.teatr-zydowski.art.pl. The most striking of Warsaw's several small theatres, specializing in productions (often given in Yiddish) that depict the life of the Jews in Warsaw before the Holocaust. English translations via headphones are available.

Shopping

Malls For the flashiest boutiques and department stores, first explore the gleaming new Złote Terasy shopping mall (replete with such Western titles as H&M and Zara), opposite the Palace of Culture and Science on ul. Emilii Plater, before passing through to the mainly pedestrianized streets of ul. Chimielna and ul. Nowy Świat.

Markets The Hala Mirowska market on al. Jana Pawła II is the place to head for a strange collection of guns, clothes and Christian icons from both East and West (Sat & Sun; get there early for the best deals).

Directory

Embassies and consulates Australia, ul. Nowogrodzka 11 Ⓣ 022/521 3444; Canada, ul. Matejki 1/5 Ⓣ 022/584 3100; Ireland, ul. Mysia 5 Ⓣ 022/849 6633; New Zealand, al. Ujazdowskie 51 Ⓣ 022/521 0500; South Africa, ul. Koszykowa 54 Ⓣ 022/625 6228; UK, al. Róż 1 Ⓣ 022/311 0000; USA, ul. Ujazdowskie 29/31 Ⓣ 022/504 2000.

Exchange The Old Town has a host of Kantor stores willing to exchange foreign cash or travellers' cheques, though you will have to shop around for the best rates. Banks will change your travellers' cheques but they can be slow and rarely offer the best rates. Interchange Poland Ltd at ul. Chmielna 30 (Ⓣ 022/826 3169; 8am–10pm daily) is also a reliable option.

Hospitals The nearest public hospital to the centre is the Prasci, al. Solidarności 67 (Ⓣ 022/818 5061). In emergencies, many backpackers use the private Med-Centrum, ul. Bednarska 13 (Ⓣ 022/826 3886; Mon–Fri 8am–6pm).

Internet There is a 24hr internet cafe in the Centralna station, or try Eccoms Internet, Nowy Świat 53 (9am–11pm daily; 5zł/hr).

Laundry Most of the hostels have cheap laundry services available. There are no self-service laundrettes, but Alba (26 ul. Chmielna Ⓣ 022/827 4510) does run an expensive washing service (12–18zł per garment).

Left luggage There is a 24hr left luggage room and lockers with storage for up to ten days in the Centralna station.

Pharmacies APTEKA Pharmacy is open 24 hours a day in the Centralna Station. A more central chemist is at ul. Nowy Świat 18/20 (8am–9pm).

Post office ul. Świętokryszka 31/33 (24hr).

Moving on

Train Berlin (9 daily; 6hr); Budapest (1 daily; 11hr); Gdańsk (17 daily; 5hr); Kraków (24 daily; 4–6hr); Poznań (23 daily; 3hr 30min); Prague (2 daily; 10hr); Toruń (9 daily; 3hr); Vienna (3 daily; 8hr); Wrocław (15 daily; 6hr); Zakopane (8 daily; 6–8hr).

Bus PKS (Ⓦ www.pks.warszawa.pl) runs regular long-distance services to all the major Polish cities from the main terminal.

Northern Poland

Even in a country accustomed to shifting borders, **northern Poland** presents an unusually tortuous historical puzzle.

Successively the domain of the crusading Teutonic order, the Hansa merchants and the Prussians, it's only in the last sixty years that the region has become definitively Polish. The conurbation of **Gdańsk**, **Sopot** and Gdynia, known as the Tri-City, lines the Baltic coast with its dramatic shipyards and sandy beaches, while highlights inland include the medieval centres of **Malbork** and **Toruń**.

GDAŃSK

Both the starting point of World War II and the setting of the famous strikes against communist control, **GDAŃSK** has played more than a fleeting role on the world stage. Traces of its past can be seen in the steel skeletons of derelict shipyard cranes and the Hanseatic architecture of the beautifully restored old town. After all the social and political upheavals of the last century this lively city is now busy reinventing itself as a tourist hub.

What to see and do

With its medieval brick churches and narrow eighteenth-century merchants' houses, Gdansk certainly looks ancient. But its appearance is deceptive: by May 1945, the core of the city lay in ruins, and the present buildings are almost complete reconstructions.

The Main Town (Główne Miasto)

Huge stone gateways guard both entrances to ul. Długa, the main thoroughfare. Start from the sixteenth-century gate at the top, **Brama Wyżynna**, and you'll soon come across the huge tower of the Town Hall, which houses a **Historical Museum** (June–Sept Mon 10am–3pm, Tues–Sat 10am–6pm, Sun 11am–6pm; Oct–May Tues 10am–3pm, Wed–Sat 10am–4pm, Sun 11am–4pm; 10zł, free Mon June–Sept, Tues Oct–May) with shocking photos of the city's wartime destruction. Past the Town Hall, the street opens onto the wide expanse of ul. Długi Targ, where the ornate facade of Arthur's Court (same hours as Historical Museum; 10zł) stands out in a square filled with fine mansions.

The streets that run parallel are also worth exploring, especially ul. Mariacka, brimming with amber traders, and ul. Chlebnicka, adjacent to **St Mary's Basilica** (Mon–Sat 9am–6pm, Sun 1–6pm; free), the largest church in Poland.

The waterfront and shipyards

At the end of ul. Długi Targ the archways of the **Brama Zielona** open directly onto the waterfront. Halfway down is the fifteenth-century **Gdańsk Crane**, the biggest in medieval Europe, which is part of the vast **Central Maritime Museum** (Sept–June Tues–Sun 10am–4pm; July & Aug daily 10am–6pm; 10zł) that spreads out on both banks of the river. Highlights include an exhibition of primitive boats and maritime paintings; for an extra 8zł you can also tour the cargo ship SS *Soldek* docked just outside. Further north loom the cranes of the famous Gdańsk **shipyards**, crucible of the political strife of the 1980s. Poignantly set outside the rusting shipyard gates is the monument to the workers that formed the anti-communist Solidarity movement, many of whom were killed during the 1970s riots. It was here that frustrated workers began Poland's bloody struggle to topple communism, a story detailed in the **Roads to Freedom** exhibition, currently in the Solidarity offices at ul. Piastowskie 24 (Tues–Sun 9am–5pm; 6zł; 2zł on Wed), though scheduled to move in the next few years.

Arrival and information

Air Gdańsk Lech Wałęsa airport lies 8km out of the city centre. Buses B (3zł) take you to the railway

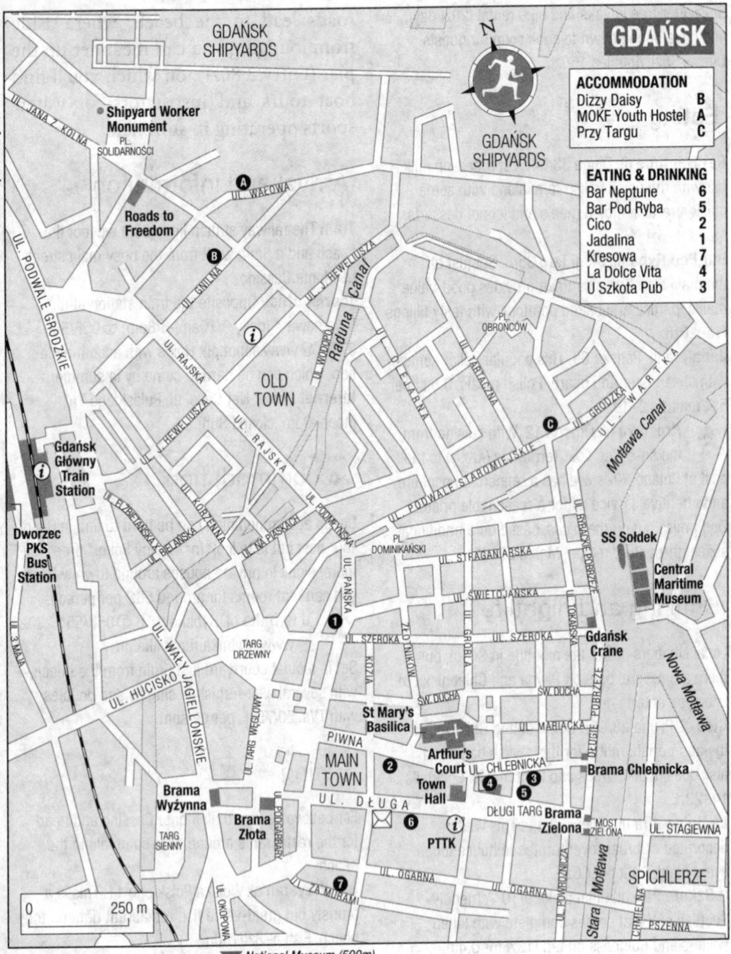

station and the Main, leaving about every 20min. Taxis are 60zł.

Train and bus Make sure to get off at the Główny (Central) Station, which is a 10min walk northwest of ul. Długa, at the heart of the Main Town. The bus station is just across the lines from the railway station, and can be reached by the underground tunnels.

Tourist information ul. Długa 45 ⓣ058/301 9151, ⓦwww.pttk-gdansk.pl (Mon–Fri 9am–6pm, Sat & Sun 10am–6pm). There are other offices at the airport terminal, the railway station (daily 9am–5pm), and on ul. Heweliusza 13/17 (daily 8am–6pm) where you can check your luggage in advance if you're heading to the airport.

Accommodation

Dizzy Daisy ul. Gnilna 3 ⓣ058/301 3919, ⓦwww.hostel.pl. The town's summer hostel is close to the railway station and comes with reasonable rooms and pleasant service. Open July & Aug. Dorms 45–55zł.

MOKF Youth Hostel ul. Walowa 21 ⓣ058/301 2313, ⓦwww.mokf.com.pl. Basic hostel in an old red-brick school building, recently renovated with new bathrooms and a new lick of paint. 5zł for sheets. Dorms 24zł.

Przy Targu ul. Grodzka 21 ⓣ058/301 5627, ⓦwww.gdanskhostel.com.pl. This hostel has a central location by the riverside in the Main Town.

Staff offer free kayaks and bike rental (20zł/day), and have been known to cook soup for guests. Dorms 55zł, doubles 150zł.

Eating

Bar Neptune ul. Długa 33/34. A spruced-up milk bar with the usual Polish fare, along with some quick, pre-assembled meals and lots of desserts. Mains 4–6zł.

Bar Pod Ryba ul. Długi Targ 35/8. Set just off the main street, this canteen provides good-value mains, particularly baked potatoes with tasty fillings (15–20zł).

Jadalina ul. Panska 69. This popular cellar comes with cheap beer and hearty Polish meals. 0.5lt beer 5zł; mains 12–19zł.

Kresowa ul. Ogarna 12. With cuisine from the so-called Lost Territories (*kresy*) to the east of Poland, *Kresowa* has a refined atmosphere and attentive service all for a reasonable price. Don't miss out on the *bigos*, based on a traditional sixteenth-century recipe. Mains 20–35zł.

Drinking and nightlife

Local clubbers prefer the nightlife in Sopot, but there are several bars on Piwna and Chlebnicka to keep you entertained.

Cico ul. Piwna 28/30. "Come in and Chill Out" is the appropriate motto for this stylish bar, which also does good coffees and light meals. Cocktails 14–22zł.

La Dolce Vita ul. Chlebnicka 2. This wildly decorated club/bar reverberates to house tunes every night. 0.5lt beer 6zł.

U Szkota Pub ul. Chlebnicka 9/10. A friendly Scottish pub that comes complete with kilted waiters and Guinness on tap (13zł for 0.4lt).

Moving on

Train. Kraków (11 daily; 9hr); Malbork (every 30min; 50min); Poznań (5 daily; 4–5hr); Sopot (every 20min; 25min); Toruń (6 daily; 3hr 30min); Warsaw (13 daily; 5hr); Wrocław (3 daily; 7hr).

SOPOT

Some 15km northwest of Gdańsk is Poland's trendiest coastal resort, which boasts Europe's longest wooden pier (512m) and a broad stretch of golden sand. With a vibrant nightlife, **Sopot** is a magnet for young party animals. All roads lead to the beach, where aside from lounging you can meander up the pier (entry 3.80zł), on which you'll find boat tours and instructors for water-sports operating in summer.

Arrival and information

Train The railway station lies 400m west of the beach and a 5min walk from the busy main street, ul. Monte Cassino.

Tourist office Opposite the train station at ul. Dworcowa 4 (daily 9/10am–6/8pm; ⓣ058/550 3783, ⓦwww.sopot.pl). Helps with accommodation, which can be hard to come by in summer.

Internet Cooler Net Cave, ul. Pułaskiego 7a (noon–9pm, closed Sun).

Accommodation

Cheap accommodation can be hard to find in Sopot. Your best bet is to look for "Wolny Pokoj" (free room) signs in private houses around town, where you can rent rooms for around 50zł per person.

U Rybaka pl. Rybakow 16 ⓣ058/551 2302, ⓦwww.urybaka.republika.pl.
Set in a quiet courtyard just 5min from the beach, with several well-furnished singles and doubles with TVs. 50/75zł per person.

Eating

For best value, avoid ul. Monte Cassino and head for the restaurants around 1km south along the beach.

Bar Przystan al. Wojska Polskiego 11. This is a touristy but great-value fish restaurant right on the beach. Fish 4–8zł/100g.

Dobra Kuchnia ul. Jagiełły 6/1. The best place for reasonably priced Polish classics in the centre. Mains 10–20zł.

Drinking and nightlife

Soho ul. Monte Cassino 61. Just along the main drag not far from the pier, *Soho* boasts colourful interiors that draw the punters in all night long.

Viva ul. Mamuzski 2.The self-styled "Top Club in the Tri-City" provides chart dance and hip-hop for lots of manic teenage clubbers.

MALBORK

The spectacular fortress of **MALBORK** was built as the headquarters of the

Teutonic Order in the fourteenth century and still casts a threatening shadow over what is otherwise a sleepy town. You enter over a moat and through the daunting main gate, before reaching an open courtyard. Brooding above is the **High Castle**, which harbours the centrepiece of the Knights' austere monasticism – the vast **Castle Church** with its faded chivalric paintings. The guided tours (3hr; Tues–Sun: mid-April to mid-Sept 9am–7pm, rest of year 10am–3pm; 25zł) are mandatory. There are three daily in English (11am, 1.30pm, 3.30pm), but only in the summer. The **railway** and **bus stations** are sited next to each other about ten minutes' walk south of the castle; there are trains every thirty minutes from Gdańsk (50min).

TORUŃ

Once one of the most beautiful medieval towns in Central Europe, **Toruń** was founded by the Teutonic Knights and is still rich with their architectural legacy. Now a friendly university city, with bars and cafés sprinkled throughout the compact streets, it combines lively nightlife with a status as a UNESCO World Heritage Site.

What to see and do

Highlight of historical Toruń is the mansion-lined Market Square (Rynek) and its fourteenth-century Town Hall, now the **Town Museum** (Tues–Sun 10am–4/6pm; 10zł), with a fine collection of nineteenth-century paintings and intricate wood carvings. South of the Rynek, at ul. Kopernika 15/17, is the **Copernicus Museum** (Tues–Sun 10am–4/6pm; 10zł), in the brick house where the great man was born, which contains a fascinating model collection of his original instruments. **St John's Cathedral** (Mon–Sat 10am–5pm, Sun 2–5.30pm; 2zł), lies at the eastern end of ul. Kopernika, and has a tower offering panoramic views over the city (4zł extra). Further to the northeast lies the **New Town** district, with its opulent commercial residences grouped around the Rynek Nowomiejski.

Arrival and information

Train Toruń Główny, the main railway station, is 2km away south of the river; buses #22, #25 and #27 (every 10min; 2.40zł) run from outside the station to pl. Rapackiego on the western edge of the Old Town, the first stop after crossing the river.

Bus From the bus station on ul. Dąbrowskiego it is a short walk south to the centre.

Tourist office Rynek Staromiejski 25 ⓣ056/621 0931, ⓦwww.it.torun.pl (Mon & Sat 9am–4pm, Tues–Fri 9am–6pm; May–Sept also Sun 9am–1pm).

Internet Ksero, ul. Franciszkanska 5 (Mon–Fri 8am–7pm, Sat 9am–4pm).

Accommodation

Dom Turisty PTTK ul. Legionów 24 ⓣ056/622 3855. Simple and clean public hostel 10min north of the Old Town; take bus #27 four stops from the main train station. Dorms 30zł, singles/doubles 65/80zł.

Orange ul. Prosta 19 ⓣ056/652 0033, ⓦwww.hostelorange.pl.The only central hostel, with friendly staff and a cosy atmosphere. Dorms 30zł, singles/doubles 50/90zł.

Eating

Kafe Katarynka ul. Prosta 13. A warm, inviting basement café in the New Town with a thick menu of coffees, teas and desserts, as well as the best beer in Toruń. Cakes 8zł.

Manekin ul. Wysoka 5, north of Rynek Nowomiejski. The perfect place for pancake lovers, specializing in innovative meat, veg, and sweet fillings (8–10zł).

Oberza ul. Rabiańska 9. A cosy restaurant near the Market Square that boasts a farmhouse interior and quick, traditional buffet meals. Mains 15zł.

Pod Arkadami ul. Rozana 1. Clean, bright milk bar on the Market Square with filling soups and potato dishes. Mains 5-8zł.

Drinking and nightlife

Bar Mockba Rynek Staromiejski 22. There's a fun mix of hip-hop and rock in this cellar club on the main square. Cocktails 15–23zł.

PIERNIKI

You can't leave Toruń without trying the local **pierniki**, or gingerbread, which has been made here since the town was founded. Pierniczek (Żeglarska 25) is a shop offering a mouth-watering if eccentric range.

Café Faijka ul. Małe Garbary 1. This chilled-out place, filled with cushions, offers a huge range of colourful cocktails and shishas that bubble milk or gin instead of water. Cocktails 12–20zł.

Moving on

Train Gdańsk (6 daily; 3hr 30min); Kraków (6 daily; 8hr); Poznań (7 daily; 2hr 30min); Warsaw (10 daily; 4hr); Wrocław (3 daily; 5hr 30min).

Southern Poland

Southern Poland garners more visitors than any other region in the country, and its attractions are clear from a glance at the map. The **Tatra Mountains** that form the border with Slovakia are the most spectacular in the country, snowcapped for much of the year and markedly alpine in feel. The former royal capital of **Kraków** is an architectural gem and the country's intellectual heart. Pope John Paul II was archbishop here until his election in 1978, but equally important are the city's Jewish roots: before the Holocaust, this was one of Europe's most vibrant Jewish centres. This multi-cultural past echoes in the old district of Kazimierz, and its culmination is starkly enshrined at the death camps of **Auschwitz-Birkenau**, 50km west of the city.

KRAKÓW

KRAKÓW was the only major city in Poland to come through World War II essentially undamaged, and its assembly of monuments has since been hailed as one of Europe's most compelling by UNESCO. The city's Old Town (Stare Miasto) swarms with visitors in summer, but retains an atmosphere of *fin-de-siècle* stateliness, its streets a cavalcade of churches and palaces. A university centre, Kraków has a tangible buzz of arty youthfulness and boasts a dynamic nightlife.

What to see and do

Kraków is bisected by the River Wisła, with virtually everything of interest on the north bank. At the heart of the **Old Town** is the Main Square (Rynek Główny), with the **Wawel** hill, ancient seat of Poland's kings and Church, and the rejuvenated **Kazimierz** lying to the south.

The Market Square

The largest square in medieval Europe, the Market Square (Rynek) is now a broad expanse with the vast **Cloth Hall** (Sukiennice) at its centre, ringed by magnificent houses and towering spires. Originally just a collection of outdoor market stalls, the Cloth Hall was first built in 1300 and reconstructed during the Renaissance. It still houses a bustling covered market. To its south is the tiny copper-domed **St Adalbert's**, the first church to be founded in Kraków. On the

THE HEJNAŁ

Legend has it that during one of the thirteenth-century Tatar raids, a guard watching from the tower of St Mary's Church saw the invaders approaching and blew his trumpet, only for his alarm to be cut short by an arrow through the throat. Every hour a local fireman now plays the sombre melody (*hejnał*) from the same tower, halting abruptly at the point when the guard is supposed to have been hit.

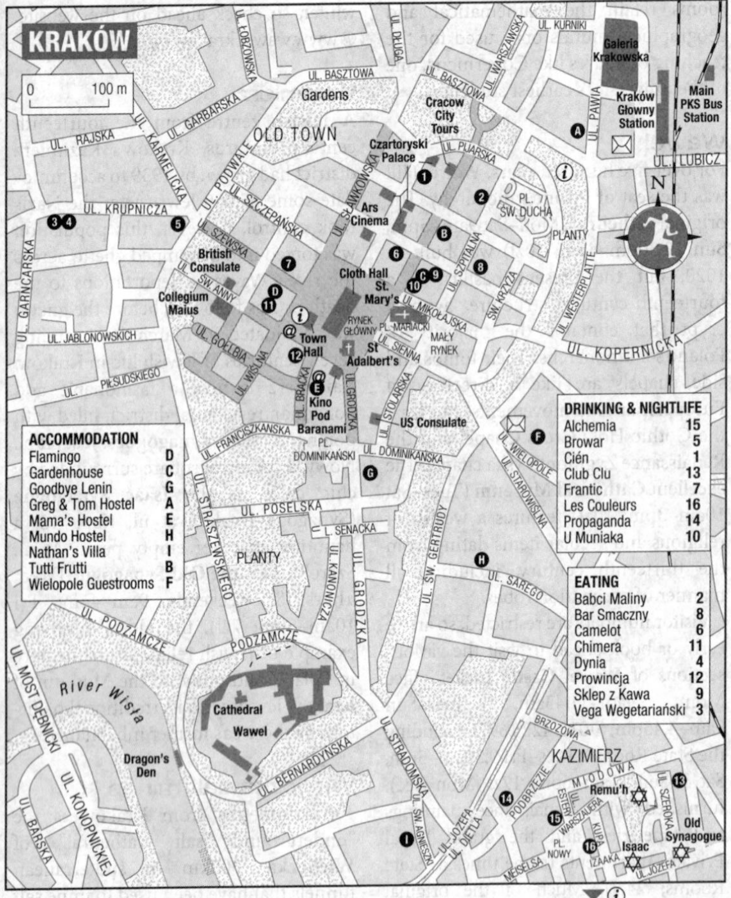

east side is the Gothic **St Mary's Church** (Mon–Sat 11.30am–6pm, Sun 2–6pm; 6zł), the taller of its two towers topped by an amazing ensemble of spires. Inside is the stunningly realistic triptych high altar (1477–89), an intricate woodcarving that depicts the Virgin Mary's Quietus among the apostles.

Czartoryski Palace

A few blocks north of the Rynek on ul. Pijarska is the **Czartoryski Palace**, which, though unimpressive on the outside, houses Kraków's finest art collection (Tues–Sat 10am–6pm, Sun 10am–4pm; 10zł). Highlights include Rembrandt's brooding *Landscape with Merciful Samaritan* and Leonardo da Vinci's *Lady with an Ermine*, as well as a striking Egyptian exhibition.

The university

West from the Rynek is the university area, whose first element was the fifteenth-century **Collegium Maius** building, at ul. Jagiellońska 15. Now it's the **University Museum** and is open for guided tours only (Mon, Wed & Fri 10am–3pm; Tues [free] 3–6pm; Thurs 10am–6pm; Sat 10am–2pm; 16zł; ☎012/422 0549) – book at least a day in advance. Inside, the ground-floor

rooms retain the mathematical and geographical murals once used for the teaching of figures like Copernicus, one of the university's earliest students.

Wawel

For over five hundred years, Wawel Hill was the seat of Poland's monarchy. The original **cathedral** (Mon–Sat 9am–5pm, Sun 12.30pm–4pm; 10zł) was built in 1020, but the present basilica is a fourteenth-century structure, with a crypt that contains the majority of Poland's 45 monarchs. Their tombs and side chapels are like a directory of European artistic movements, not least the Gothic Holy Cross Chapel and the Renaissance Zygmuntówska chapel. The excellent **Cathedral Museum** (Tues–Sat 10am–3pm; 10zł) features a wealth of religious and secular items dating from the thirteenth century, including all manner of coronation robes.

Visitor numbers are restricted, so arrive early or book ahead to visit the various sections of **Wawel Castle** (ticket office Mon 9am–11.45am, Tues–Sun 9am–4.45pm; ⓣ012/422 1697), including the State Rooms (Tues–Fri 9.30am–5pm, Sat & Sun 11am–6pm; 17zł, Mon free), furnished with Renaissance paintings and tapestries, and the grand Royal Private Apartments (same times as State Rooms; 24zł). Much of the original contents of the Royal Treasury and Armoury (Mon 9.30am–1pm [free]; Tues–Sun 9am–4.45pm; 17zł) were sold to pay off royal debts, but still feature some fine works, like the Szczerbiec, the country's original coronation sword. The castle's opening hours tend to change in winter, so check ahead on the website: ⓦwww.wawel.krakow.pl/en/.

Kazimierz

A **Jewish** centre from the fourteenth century onwards, Kraków's Kazimierz district had grown by 1939 to accommodate some 65,000 Jews. After the Nazis took control, however, this population was forced into a cramped ghetto across the river. Waves of deportations to the death camps followed, before the ghetto was liquidated in March 1943, ending seven centuries of Jewish life in Kraków. Kazimierz is now a fashionable and bohemian residential district, filled with poignantly silent **synagogues**. Just off pl. Nowy, a colourful square surrounded by chic cafés, is the **Isaac Synagogue** (Synagoga Izaaka), at ul. Kupa 18, a haunting space of empty pews. At ul. Szeroka 24 is the **Old Synagogue** (Wed, Thurs & weekends 9am–4pm; Fri 10am–5pm; 7zł), the oldest surviving example of Jewish religious architecture in Poland and home to the Museum of Kraków Jewry, with its traditional paintings by the area's former inhabitants.

Wieliczka salt mines

Ten kilometres from Kraków is the "underground salt cathedral" of **Wieliczka**, 300km of subterranean tunnels that have been used to mine salt since the thirteenth century. Tours pass by an underground lake and a number of impressive statues and edifices – including chandeliers – carved out of rock salt. To visit, catch bus #304 from ul. Kurniki next to the main train station (every 20min; 2.60zł).

SMOK – THE DRAGON OF KRAKÓW

On the western side of Wawel hill is the **Dragon's Den** (April–Oct daily 10am–5/6pm; 3zł), a cavern accessed by spiral staircase. This was reputedly once the home of Smok, a dragon whose rather objectionable diet included children, cattle and unsuccessful knights. Krak, the legendary founder of Kraków, tricked him into eating a sheep stuffed with sulphur; to quench the burning, Smok drank half the Wisła, causing him to explode. Despite his unfortunate end, the dragon is now the symbol of the city.

Arrival and information

Air Kraków airport is situated 15km to the west of the city centre. It's easiest to catch the free shuttle bus to the airport's railway station, which has trains twice an hour to Kraków Główny (15min; 4am–midnight; 6zł). The equivalent taxi ride is 70zł.

Train and bus Kraków Główny, the central train station, and the main PKS bus station just opposite, are 5min walk northeast from the city's historic centre.

Tourist office The main tourist office is in the Old Town Hall Tower, Rynek Główny 1 (ⓣ012/433 7310). There is also a smaller outlet between the railway station and the Old Town (ul. Szpitalna 25 ⓣ012/432 0110) as well as one in the Kazimierz district (ul. Jozefa 7 ⓣ012/422 0471). Their website (ⓦwww.krakow.pl) provides the latest information regarding festivals and accommodation.

Tours You'll be bombarded with tour offers for the city and surrounding sights, but these are often rushed and cost four times as much as public transport. If you do want a tour, try Cracow City Tours at ul. Floriańska 44 (daily 7.30am–11pm; ⓣ012/421 1327, ⓦwww.cracowcitytours.pl), which offers a wide range of itineraries and discounts for students.

Tourist card The Kraków Tourist Card (2/3 days, 45/65zł; ⓦwww.krakowcard.com) gains you free entrance to all the major museums, as well as discounts at some of the pricier restaurants, shops and tour providers in the city.

Accommodation

The number of hostels has mushroomed in the last few years, but it is still worth booking ahead if you want to stay in the most central spots. All hostels have free internet, breakfast and cheap laundry services.

Flamingo ul. Szewska 4 ⓣ012/422 0000, ⓦwww.flamingo-hostel.com. A clean, colourful place with a lively party crowd. Dorms 35/45, doubles 130–160zł.

Gardenhouse ul. Floriańska 5 ⓣ012/431 2824, ⓦwww.gardenhousehostel.com. A hostel made for those seeking a relaxed ambience, with airy dorm rooms and a quiet courtyard just off the Rynek. Dorms 40zł, doubles 140zł.

Goodbye Lenin ul. Grodzka 34 ⓣ012/430 3053, ⓦwww.goodbyelenin.pl. A funky, mural-adorned backpacker base with a full kitchen and bright, spacious rooms. Dorms 35–40zł, doubles 140–160zł.

TREAT YOURSELF

Wielopole Guestrooms, ul. Wielopole 3 ⓣ012/422 1475, ⓦwww.wielopole.pl. If you want a break from hostel parties and busy city streets, try this stylish hotel, ideally poised between the Old Town and Kazimierz. Here you'll find spacious but cosy apartments, satellite TV and free internet access. Singles/doubles with breakfast 249/349zł.

Greg & Tom Hostel ul. Pawia 12 ⓣ012/422 4100, www.gregtomhostel.com. A lively, youthful place right across from the train station, with single beds in all the dorms (no bunks) and nightly activities like vodka tasting and Polish dinners. Dorms 50–55zł, doubles 160–170zł.

Mama's Hostel ul. Bracka 4 ⓣ012/429 5940, ⓦwww.mamashostel.com.pl. This chilled-out hangout comes with friendly staff and has a great position above the Bracka café scene. Bring earplugs on account of the club downstairs. Dorms 40–50zł, doubles 180zł.

Mundo Hostel ul. Sarego 10 ⓣ012/422 6113, ⓦwww.mundohostel.eu. Probably the most beautiful hostel in Krakow, with each room decorated according to a different ethnic theme and great-value doubles. Dorms 50zl, doubles 80zl.

Nathan's Villa ul. Św. Agnieszki 1 ⓣ012/422 3545, ⓦwww.nathansvilla.com. The popular villa has a bar, cinema and handy location between the Old Town and Kazimierz. Dorms 40–60zł, doubles 160–180zł.

Tutti Frutti ul. Floriańska 29 ⓣ012/428 0028, ⓦwww.tuttifruttihostel.com. This welcoming hostel does the basics (especially breakfast) very well and also provides guides for guests seeking the best places to go out. Dorms 35–40zł, 3–4 bed apartments 150/200zł.

Eating

Kraków's centre is renowned for its bars, restaurants and cafés which offer much beyond the Polish culinary staples.

Milk bars

Babci Maliny ul. Szpitalna 38. This upmarket milk bar has a mountain hut interior and provides suitably wholesome Polish classics. Mains 7–16zł.

Bar Smaczny ul. Św. Tomasza 24. A cheap central canteen that specializes in quick, if unexciting meals. Mains 4–8zł.

Vega Wegetariański ul. Krupnicza 20. Inexpensive but innovative veggie dishes are on offer here; think tofu, beans and lots of greens. Mains 9–14zł.

Cafés and restaurants

Camelot ul. Św. Tomasza 15. A chic, artsy café with excellent desserts, including the best apple pie in town (9.50zł).

Chimera ul. Św. Anny 3. Popular salad bar that charges by the scoop (3.50–16zł). Around 30 salads are on offer, based on everything from couscous to cottage cheese and radish sprouts.

Dynia ul. Krupnicza 20. The city's most stylish student hangout has some delicious smoothies (6zł) and amazing breakfasts for those craving a taste of home (12–19zł).

Prowincja ul. Bracka 3. Homey, relaxed café with a wonderful wooden loft, thick hot chocolate and Krakow's best lattes. Drinks 8zł.

Sklep z Kawa ul. Św. Tomasza 21. Had enough of terrible coffees while on the road? Then head to this fabulously old-fashioned café, which has an array of exotic coffee-bean varieties. Drinks and cakes 5–13zł.

Drinking and nightlife

For best value head to Kazimierz or the student quarter to the west of the Old Town.

Bars

Alchemia ul. Estery 5. Murky, quirky and always packed, this candle-lit rabbit warren has live jazz on the weekends and a stuffed crocodile over the bar. 0.5lt beer 7zł.

Browar ul. Podwale 6. A German-style beer hall serving home-made *piwo*, including an intriguing ginger brew. 0.5lt beer 5–7zł.

Les Couleurs ul. Estery 10. A smoky and colourful Parisian-style café/bar serving light meals and alcoholic beverages of every description. Cocktails 10–16zł.

Propaganda ul. Miodowa 20. The People's Republic lives on in this popular hangout, cluttered with propaganda posters, old uniforms and antique radios. 0.5lt beer 7.50zł.

Clubs

Cién ul. Św. Jana 15. House music packs this place out with a lively late-teenage crowd. Cocktails 11–17zł.

Club Clu ul. Szeroka 10/2. Cellar club with chart dance tunes in the heart of Kazimierz. Cocktails 10–17zł.

Frantic ul. Szewska 5. With two dancefloors, there's plenty of space here for grooving to a mix of R'n'B and old school hits. Cocktails 15–20zł.

U Muniaka ul. Floriańska 3. The city's best live jazz from 9.30pm every night. 0.33lt beer 7zł.

Entertainment

Cinema tickets are 10–18zł throughout the city.

Ars ul. Św. Jana 6 Ⓦ www.ars.pl. Offers the latest blockbusters, though don't expect all of them to be in English.

Kino Pod Baranami Rynek Główny 27 Ⓦ www.kinopodbaranami.pl. Offers a range of Western, Polish and Bollywood titles.

Shopping

Arts and crafts Touristy Floriańska and the boutiques in the Rynek contain a few bargain art dealers amongst the overpriced souvenirs. Kazimierz is filled with reasonably priced galleries and secondhand shops and, on Sundays, pl. Nowy becomes a colourful flea market of cheap clothes and jewellery.

Clothes and food For a western "mall experience", head for Galeria Krakowska (Mon–Sat 8am–11pm, Sun 10am–9pm), just next to the railway station. It has all the fashionable Western brands that you could wish for, in addition to a large Carrefour Supermarket.

Directory

Consulates UK Św. Anny 9 ⓣ 012/421 7030; US Stolarska 9 ⓣ 012/424 5100.

Exchange To avoid the large commission charged at the banks, look around the Kantor exchanges that fill the streets around the Rynek for the best rates.

Hospital Krakówski Szpital Specjalistyczny, Pradnicka 80 ⓣ 012/614 2000.

KRAKÓW'S FESTIVALS

Hardly a month passes in Kraków without some cultural celebration taking over the streets. Highlights include the **Jewish Culture Festival** (June/July), which culminates in an open-air concert of international Jewish musicians on ul. Szeroka, and the lively **Summer Jazz Festival** (July/Aug).

Internet Cafés are common all over the centre and generally charge 5zł/hr. Two slightly cheaper places are: Pl@net, Rynek 24 (daily 10am–10pm; 4zł/hr), and Hetmanska, ul. Bracka 4 (24hr; 3zł/hr).
Left luggage The railway station has a left-luggage depot (7am–10pm, 4zł for 24hr).
Pharmacies Euro Apteka, ul. Krowoderska 31 (daily 8am–10pm; ⓣ012/430 0035).
Post office ul. Westerplatte 20.

Moving on

Train Berlin (2 daily; 10–12hr); Bratislava (1 daily; 7hr 30min); Budapest (2 daily; 10hr 30min); Gdańsk (15 daily; 9hr); Poznań (12 daily; 7hr); Oświęcim/Auschwitz (10 daily, 1hr 30min); Prague (2 daily; 7–9hr); Toruń (6 daily; 7hr 30min); Warsaw (25 daily; 3hr on Intercity, 4–6hr on others); Wrocław (12 daily; 5hr); Zakopane (19 daily; 3hr).
Bus Zakopane (every 20min; 2hr). Eurolines (ⓦwww.eurolines.pl) runs services to all major European capitals from near the main station at ul. Bosacka 18.

OŚWIĘCIM (AUSCHWITZ-BIRKENAU)

A visit to the Auschwitz camps provides a fascinating, if emotional, day-trip from Kraków. In 1940, **OŚWIĘCIM**, a small town 70km west of Kraków, became the site of the Oświęcim-Brzezinka concentration camp, better known by its German name of **Auschwitz-Birkenau**. Of the many camps built by the Nazis, this was the largest and most horrific: something approaching two million people, 85 percent of them Jews, died here. You can join a tour (4–5 daily in English in summer, 3 in winter; 39zł) but a detailed guidebook (4zł) is just as helpful.

GETTING TO AUSCHWITZ

You can catch one of the regular buses (15 daily; 1hr 40min; 11zł) to the main camp from Kraków's PKS Terminal. There's an hourly shuttle-bus service to the Birkenau section from the car park at Auschwitz from April to October. Taxis are also available; otherwise it's a 3km walk.

Auschwitz

Most of the Auschwitz buildings have been preserved as the **Museum of Martyrdom** (daily: March & Nov 8am–4pm; April & Oct 8am–5pm; May & Sept 8am–6pm; June–Aug 8am–7pm; Dec–Feb 8am–3pm; free; ⓦwww.auschwitz.org.pl). The bulk of the camp consists of the prison cell blocks, with the first section dedicated to "exhibits" found in the camp after liberation: rooms full of clothes and suitcases, toothbrushes, glasses, shoes and a gruesome mound of women's hair. Other barracks are given over to national memorials, and the blocks terminate with the gas chambers and the ovens where the bodies were incinerated.

Birkenau

The huge **Birkenau** camp (same hours) is less visited, though it was here that the majority of executions took place. Birkenau was designed purely as a death camp, and the huge gas chambers at the back of the camp were damaged but not destroyed by the fleeing Nazis in 1945. Victims arrived in closed trains on the platform, where those who were fit to work (around 25 percent) were separated from those who were driven straight to the gas chambers. The railway line is still there, just as the Nazis abandoned it. Allow 1–2 hours to fully explore the 175-hectare site.

ZAKOPANE AND THE TATRAS

Some 80km long, with peaks of up to 2500m, the **Tatras** are the most spectacular part of the mountain range extending along Poland's border with Slovakia. The main base for skiing and hiking on the Polish side is the popular resort of **ZAKOPANE**. There are good

road and rail links with Kraków 60km to the north, as well as several mountain resorts across the border in Slovakia.

What to see and do

Skiing here is cheap, with the premier slopes of Kasprowy Wierch just a few minutes out of town, and plenty of places in the centre to rent equipment. **Hikers** may want to avoid the 9km path to the lovely but busy Morskie Oko lake in high season, but there's no shortage of other, more secluded trails. Świat, at ul. Zamoyskiego 12 (Ⓣ018/201 3199, Ⓦwww.swiat.biz.pl), organizes **rafting** tours (with English-speaking guides) on the nearby Dunajec River. Zakopane's **market** at the bottom of ul. Krupówki sells a wide range of traditional local goods, including *oscypek* (smoked sheep's cheese) and small wood-carvings. This latter local tradition is intriguingly displayed in the whimsical wooden tombs of the nearby Old Cemetery (Stary Cementarz).

Arrival and information

Train and bus Both stations are a 10min walk east of the pedestrianized main street, ul. Krupówki.

Tourist office Just west of the stations at ul. Kościuszki 17 (8am–8pm; Ⓦwww.zakopane.pl). Helpful with accommodation.

Hiking information The Tatra National Park Information Centre, near the park entrance at ul. Chałubińskiego 44 (daily 7am–3pm; Ⓣ018/202 3300), provides good-quality maps and information on routes.

Internet Ksero, ul. Galicy 8 (daily 9am–11pm, 5zł/hr).

Accommodation

Finding a place to stay is rarely a problem in Zakopane as, in addition to the hostels, many homeowners in town offer private rooms.

Flamingo ul. Krupówki 24 Ⓣ018/200 0222, Ⓦwww.flamingo-hostel.com. Clean, modern hostel on the party strip for those who like to be in the thick of things. Dorms 40zł, doubles 150zł.

Goodbye Lenin ul. Chłabówka 44 Ⓣ018/200 1330, Ⓦwww.goodbyelenin.pl. Lying 3.5km out of town, this cosy house in the woods is the perfect place to focus on hiking and skiing. Call ahead for a ride from the bus station. Dorms 40zł, doubles 120–130zł.

Hotel Fian ul.Chałubińskiego 38 Ⓣ018/201 5071, Ⓦwww.fian.pl. With a sauna and jacuzzi to ease hiking aches, this place also prides itself on the "gastronomic experience" offered by its resident Polish chef. Singles/doubles with satellite TV and breakfast 105/205zł.

Stara Polona ul. Nowotarska 59 Ⓣ018/206 8902, Ⓦwww.starapolana.pl. A warm wood-panelled interior, satellite TV, and friendly service make this hostel excellent value. Dorms 30–50zł.

Eating and drinking

Head to the area around ul. Krupówki where you'll find no shortage of lively bars and restaurants.

Genesis pl. Niepodległości 1. The town's lager-and-lasers type club attracts Poland's top DJs at weekends. Daily 9pm–5am; 5zł cover on Fri & Sat.

Mala Szwajcarla ul. Zamoyskiego 11. A quiet, refined Swiss restaurant with delicious fondues for two. Fondues 45zł, other mains 20-40zł.

Owczarnia ul. Galicy 4. Giant grilled steaks, *kielbasa* (sausage) and local trout are the specialities in this lively grill-house. Mains 15–30zł.

Paparazzi ul. Galicy 8. This chic cocktail bar has some leafy outdoor seating and fruity drinks (17–21zł).

Moving on

Train Gdańsk (4 daily; 12hr); Kraków (19 daily; 3hr); Poznań (4 daily; 11hr); Warsaw (8 daily; 6hr).

Bus Kraków (about every 30min, 5am–9pm; 2hr; better-value than the train) leaves from the PKS Terminal.

INTO SLOVAKIA

There are 2 daily buses to **Poprad** (2hr, 20zł), a Slovakian skiing and hiking centre. In summer, you can also spend a day at the spa at **Oravice** (book tours at the tourist office; 100zł).

Western Poland

Tossed for centuries back and forth between the Poles, Germans and Czechs, Poland's southwestern province of Silesia is a fascinating blend of cultures, languages and architectural styles. Its main city, **Wrocław**, is the focus of Poland's new economic dynamism. Vibrant **Poznań** to the north, the heart of the original Polish nation, is one of the country's oldest cities and a key commercial link to Western Europe.

WROCŁAW

WROCŁAW (pronounced "vrots-waf") is a city used to rebuilding. For centuries – as Breslau – it was largely dominated by Germans, but this changed after the war, as thousands of displaced Poles flocked to the decimated city. The various influences are reflected in Wrocław's architecture, with its mammoth Germanic churches, Flemish-style mansions and Baroque palaces. The latest rebuilding came after a catastrophic flood in the early 1990s, which left most of the centre underwater. Fortunately, the reconstruction that followed has left the pretty Old Town rejuvenated and without the tourist mobs of Kraków. The city has also been actively reaching out to foreign investors in both technology and finance. This along, with a lively university scene, lends Wrocław a vigorous air of economic and cultural well-being.

What to see and do

Wrocław's centre is delineated by the River Odra to the north and the bow-shaped ul. Podwale – the latter following the former city walls, whose moat is now bordered by a shady park.

The Market Square

In the heart of the town is the vast **Market Square** (Rynek) and the thirteenth-century town hall, with its magnificently ornate facades. The hall is now the **Historical Museum** (Wed–Sat 10am–5pm, Sun 10am–6pm; 10zł). In the northwest corner of the square are two curious Baroque houses known as **Jaś i Małgosia** (Hansel and Gretel), linked by a gateway giving access to **St Elizabeth's**, the finest of Wrocław's churches. Its ninety-metre tower (Mon–Sat 10am–6pm, Sun 1–6pm; 5zł) is the city's most prominent landmark.

Jewish quarter

Southwest of the square lies the former **Jewish quarter**, whose inhabitants were driven from their tenements during the Third Reich. One of the largest synagogues in Poland, the **Synagoga pod Białym Bocianem** (Synagogue Under the White Stork), lies hidden in a courtyard at ul. Włodkowica 9. Visits can be arranged through the Jewish Information Centre (Mon–Thurs 9am–5pm, Fri 9am–3pm; 6zł; ☎071/787 3902).

The Racławice Panorama and the National Museum

To the east, a rotunda houses Wrocław's best-known sight, the **Panorama of the Battle of Racławice** (April–Sept daily 9am–5pm; Oct–March Tues–Sun 9am–4pm; shows every 30min but expect queues; 20zł, including entrance to the National Museum). This painting – 120m long and 15m high – was commissioned in 1894 for the centenary of the Russian army's defeat by Tadeusz Kościuszko's militia at Racławice, a village near Kraków. You can also visit the nearby **National Museum** (Wed–Sun 9/10am–4/6pm; 15zł, Sat free), with its fun and colourful exhibition of twentieth-century Polish installation artists like Jozef Szajna.

University quarter

North of the Market Square is the historic and buzzing **university quarter**, full of bargain eateries and tiny bookshops. At its centre is the huge Collegium Maximum, whose Aula Leopoldina assembly hall, upstairs at pl. Uniwersytecki 1 (daily except Wed 10am–3.30pm; 6zł), is one of the greatest secular interiors of the Baroque age.

Wyspa Piasek and Ostrów Tumski

Northeast from the Market Hall, the Piaskowy Bridge leads to the island of **Wyspa Piasek** and the fourteenth-century church of St Mary of the Sands, with its majestically vaulted ceiling. Two elegant little bridges connect Wyspa Piasek with **Ostrów Tumski**, the city's ecclesiastical heart. Ulica Katedralny leads past several Baroque palaces to the vast and gloomy Cathedral of St John the Baptist, which was rebuilt after the war.

Arrival and information

Air Take bus #406 to the railway station from the airport (30min, 2.40zł). The equivalent taxi ride costs more than 50-60zł.

Train The main train station, Wrocław Główny, faces the broad boulevard of ul. Piłsudskiego, a 15min walk south of the Market Square.

Bus The main station is just to the south of the railway station.

Tourist office Rynek 14 (daily: April–Oct 9am–9pm, Nov–March 9am–8pm; ⓣ071/344 3111, ⓦwww.wroclaw.pl). Books accommodation.

Internet Adan, ul. Ruska 60/61 (daily 9am–10pm, 6zł/hr).

Accommodation

Babel ul. Kołłątaja 16/3 ⓣ071/342 0250, ⓦwww.babelhostel.pl. Close to the train station, this small hostel has friendly staff and cheerful rooms. Dorms 40–45zł, doubles 120–150zł

Cinnamon ul. Kazimierza Wielkiego 67 ⓣ071/344 5858, ⓦwww.cinnamonhostel.com. Pleasant, airy rooms and friendly staff make this spice-themed hostel a winner. Dorms 40–45zł, doubles 125–135zł.

Mleczarnia ul. Wlodkowica 5 ⓣ071/787 7570, ⓦwww.mleczarniahostel.pl. Comfortable, bohemian hangout, situated above a candlelit coffee bar. Dorms 40–45zł; doubles/apartments 220/275zł.

Nathan's Villa ul. Świdnicka 13 ⓣ071/344 1095, ⓦwww.nathansvilla.com. This hostel has clean dorms and all the mod cons. Dorms 45–60zł, doubles 150–190zł.

Savoy pl. Kościuszki 19 ⓣ071/340 3219, ⓦwww.savoy.wroc.pl. With a TV and bathroom included, these are the best budget hotel rooms in town, though internet access and breakfast are extra. Singles/doubles 140/170zł.

Eating

Bazylia ul. Kuźnicza 42. Stylishly minimalist canteen, with a wonderful view onto the Collegium. Mains 5–7zł.

Kuchnia Marche ul. Świdnicka 53. Excellent range of international cuisine in a lively, family-friendly setting. Mains 10–25zł.

Mis ul. Kuźnicza 48. Milk bar that provides quick, filling grub for the student crowd. Mains 3–5zł.

Pod II Strusiem ul. Ruska 61. Set in a rejuvenated former lavatory, this place dishes out some tasty pizzas (7–17zł).

Drinking and nightlife

Bezsennosc ul. Ruska 51. Just 10min away from the Rynek, this graffiti-lined cellar resounds to a fun mix of electronic and reggae tunes. Cocktails 12–17zł.

PRL Rynek 10. Festooned with portraits of Lenin and Mao, this popular communist-themed bar also has a dancefloor downstairs. Cocktails 10–16zł.

TREAT YOURSELF

A meal at the renowned **JaDka restaurant** on ul. Rzeznicza 24/5 may not be cheap (though some classics like *pierogi* come in at only 20zł), but you can be assured of world-class Polish cuisine and excellent service.

Rej's Pub ul. Kotlarska 32a. This unassuming little student pub has the best-value beer in town at 0.5lt for 3–7zł.

Moving on

Train Berlin (2 daily; 6–8hr); Dresden (3 daily; 3hr 30min); Gdańsk (4 daily; 7–8hr); Kraków (12 daily; 5hr); Poznań (27 daily; 3hr); Prague (2 daily; 6hr 30min); Toruń (3 daily; 5hr); Warsaw (15 daily; 6hr).

POZNAŃ

Thanks to its position on the Berlin–Warsaw–Moscow rail line, **POZNAŃ** is many visitors' first taste of Poland. Long identified as the cradle of Polish nationhood, today it's an economically dynamic city with stunning architectural diversity.

What to see and do

The sixteenth-century **town hall** that dominates the **Old Town Square** (Stary Rynek) boasts a striking eastern facade which frames a frieze of notable Polish monarchs. Inside is the **Poznań Historical Museum** (Tues–Thurs 9am–3pm, Fri noon–9pm, Sat & Sun 11am–6pm; 5.50zł), worth visiting for the Renaissance Great Hall on the first floor. East of the Old Town Square, a bridge crosses to the quiet holy island of **Ostrów Tumski**, dominated by Poland's oldest cathedral, the **Cathedral of Sts Peter and Paul**. Most of the structure was reconstructed after the war. Poland's first two monarchs are buried in the crypt.

Arrival and information

Air Poznań's airport is 7km west of the Old Town and is served by bus #59 (30min; 3.60zł), which runs to the Rondo Kaponiera just north of the railway station, and by tram L to the station itself (4.20zł). The 10min taxi ride from the airport is 30zł.

Train The main railway station, Poznań Główny, is 2km southwest of the historic quarter; trams #5 & #8 run from the western exit on ul. Glogowska to the city centre.

Bus The PKS Terminal is a 15min walk south from the Old Town Square, at the intersection of ul. Ratajczaka and ul. Królowej Jadwigi.

Tourist information ul. Ratajczaka 44 (Mon–Fri 10am–7pm, Sat 10am–5pm). There is also a handy Provincial Tourist Office on the Old Town Square at no. 59/60 (May–Oct Mon–Fri 9am–8pm, Sat 10am–8pm, Sun 10am–6pm; Nov–April Mon–Fri 10am–8pm, Sat 10am–5pm).

Poznań Card (30zł/40zł/45zł for 1/2/3 days), available at the tourist offices. This handy card buys you free trips on the city's buses and trams, free entry into the major museums and discounts at several restaurants.

Public transport Poznań's public transport works on a timed basis; a 15min (2zł) ticket should be adequate for any travel within the centre.

Accommodation

The city's trade fairs, which take place throughout the year (July & Aug excepted), can cause hotel prices to double, so always book ahead.

Dizzy Daisy al. Niepodległości 26 ⓣ061/829 3902, ⓦwww.hostel.pl. The town's summer hostel offers dorms with standard facilities and a friendly atmosphere. July–Sept. Dorms 35zł.

Frolic Goats ul. Wrocławska 16/6 (entry at ul. Jaskolcza) ⓣ061/852 4411, ⓦwww.frolicgoatshostel.com. This unassuming central hostel has all the facilities a backpacker could need. Free Internet access and breakfast are included. Dorms 50zł, doubles 170zł.

Mini Hotelik al. Niepodległości 8a ⓣ061/633 1416, ⓦwww.trans-tor.poznan.pl. This little place not far from the train station may look a bit tattered, but its rooms are clean, cheerful and good value. The nicest look out onto a small park. Singles/doubles with TV 65/130zł.

Eating

Cafe Ptasie Radio ul. Kościuszki 74. A favourite with the arty elite, this sophisticated and cosy café provides cheesy pasta dishes and salads. Mains 14–19zł.

Pod Kuchcikiem Św. Marcin 75. This canteen provides classic milk bar grub alongside some nice salads and milkshakes. Mains 4–10zł.

Spaghetti Bar Piccolo ul. Rynkowa 1. The buffet here comprises simple but tasty spaghetti dishes that are ready as you enter. Mains 4–9zł.

Drinking and nightlife

Brovaria Stary Rynek 73. This bar in the Old Town Square may be predictably pricey, but the home-made *piwo* makes a trip irresistible. 0.5lt mulled honey beer 8zł.

SQ Klub Stary Browar, ul. Polwiejska 42. The most exclusive club in town (20zł admission) attracts international DJs and the more stylish local clubbers. 0.5lt beer 9zł.

Moving on

Train Berlin (7 daily; 3–5hr); Gdańsk (6 daily; 5hr); Kraków (10 daily; 7hr); Toruń (6 daily; 2hr 30min); Warsaw (24 daily; 3–4hr); Wrocląw (26 daily; 3hr).

Portugal

HIGHLIGHTS

PORT WINE LODGES, PORTO: numerous lodges here offer free tours and tastings

THE DOURO RAIL ROUTE: beautifully scenic line along the foot of the steep Douro river valley

QUIEMA DAS FITAS, COIMBRA: join in this university town's renowned end-of-term celebrations in May

A NIGHT OUT IN LISBON: check out the Bairro Alto and dance till dawn

THE ALGARVE BEACHES: the Ilha de Tavira has some of the best

ROUGH COSTS

DAILY BUDGET Basic €40/occasional treat €60

DRINK Vinho verde €8 a bottle

FOOD Grilled sardines €8

HOSTEL/BUDGET HOTEL €18/€40

TRAVEL train: Lisbon–Faro (297km; 3hr 15min–4hr) €18–19.50; bus: Porto–Lisbon (314km; 3hr 30min–4hr 30min) €17.50.

FACT FILE

POPULATION 10.6 million

AREA 92,391 sq km

LANGUAGE Portuguese

CURRENCY Euro (€)

CAPITAL Lisbon (population: 564,500)

INTERNATIONAL PHONE CODE ⓣ351

Introduction

Although Portugal is perhaps best known for the "fun in the sun" resorts of the Algarve, there's much more to the Iberian peninsula's lesser-visited country than beautiful beaches. Portugal is geographically diverse yet small enough to travel around easily, with lively cities, mountain ranges, rural villages and a stunning coastline all within rapid reach of each other. Another draw is the relaxed, laid-back pace of life, meaning that even in the biggest metropolises, stress and bustle is remarkably rare. And most importantly for the budget traveller, Portugal is still a relatively cheap country to visit.

Scenically, some of the most interesting parts of the country are in the north: the **Minho**, a verdant area home to Portugal's only national park; and the sensational gorge and valley of the **Douro**, followed along its course by the railway, off which antiquated branch lines edge into remote countryside. For contemporary Portugal, spend some time in **Lisbon** and **Porto**, the two major cities, both treasure-troves of cultural attractions with a vibrant nightlife to boot. And if it's monuments you're after, head to the centre of the country – above all, **Coimbra** and **Évora** – which retains a faded grandeur. The coast is virtually continuous beach, and apart from the **Algarve** and a few pockets around Lisbon and Porto, resorts remain low-key. Perhaps the loveliest are the wild, isolated beaches of the southern **Alentejo**.

CHRONOLOGY

219 BC The Romans capture the Iberian Peninsula from the Carthaginians, taking the settlement of "Portus Cale" in the process.

711 The Islamic Moors take control of large parts of present-day Portugal.

868 Establishment of the First County of Portugal, within the Kingdom of León.

1095 Crusaders help Portuguese to defeat the Moors.

1139 Afonso I, of the Burgundy dynasty, declares himself king of an independent Portugal.

1386 The Treaty of Windsor, the oldest diplomatic alliance in the world, is signed between England and Portugal securing mutual military support.

1500s Portugal builds up a large empire with colonies across the world including Mozambique, Goa and Brazil.

1580 During a succession crisis, Philip II of Spain invades and crowns himself Philip I of Portugal.

1703 The Methuen trade treaty with England, following which port wine becomes popular internationally.

1755 An enormous earthquake destroys much of the capital city Lisbon.

1822 Brazil declares independence from Portugal.

1916 Portugal joins World War I on the side of the Allies.

1926 Military coup, led by Antonio de Oliveira Salazar, sweeps control of the country; he remains in power until 1968.

1939 Portugal remains neutral during World War II.

1974 Government overthrown in a near bloodless coup.

1975 Independence is granted to all Portuguese African colonies.

1976 First free elections are held.

1986 Portugal joins the European Community.

2007 Mass demonstrations against the Portuguese government's economic reforms.

ARRIVAL

Portugal's three international **airports** are in Faro, Lisbon and Porto. Faro and Lisbon in particular are well linked to the rest of Europe by the budget airlines (notably easyJet), with services to and from Faro increasing during summer. **Bus** is the quickest and most convenient method of overland transport from Spain, particularly if you are arriving

from the south. Common daily routes include Sevilla–Faro, Sevilla–Lisbon and Madrid–Lisbon. **Trains** are a more costly but usually more comfortable option; the Madrid–Lisbon *trenhotel* runs nightly.

GETTING AROUND

CP (ⓦwww.cp.pt) operates Portugal's **trains**, which are generally reasonably priced – particularly in the case of suburban services from Porto and Lisbon. Those designated *Regionais* stop at most stations. *Intercidades* are twice as fast and twice as expensive, and must be reserved. The fastest and most luxurious are the *Rápidos* (known as "Alfa"), which speed between Lisbon, Coimbra and Porto. **InterRail passes** are valid, though supplements must be paid on *Intercidades* and *Rápidos*. You can check timetables online (select "Horários y preços") or call the information line on ⓣ808 208 208.

The **bus** network, made up of many regional companies, is more comprehensive and services are often faster, while for long journeys buses can also be cheaper than trains. On a number of major routes (particularly Lisbon–Algarve), express coaches can knock hours off standard multiple-stop bus

journeys; Rede Expressos (Ⓦwww.rede-expressos.pt) is the largest bus operator. Other key operators include Rodonorte in the north (Ⓦwww.rodonorte.pt), Rodotejo in the Ribatejo (Ⓦwww.rodotejo.pt), Rodoviária do Alentejo in the Alentejo (Ⓦwww.rodalentejo.pt) and EVA in the Algarve (Ⓦwww.eva-bus.com). For 24hr national bus information call Ⓣ707 22 33 44.

Cycling is popular, though there are few facilities and little respect from motorists. In the north and centre of the country the terrain is rather hilly, flattening out south of Lisbon. Bikes can be transported on any *Regional* train for €1.50–2.50 (free if the bike is dismantled) as long as there is space. Bus companies' policies vary so enquire before travelling.

ACCOMMODATION

There are over forty state-owned **youth hostels** (*Pousadas de Juventude*; Ⓦwww.pousadasjuventude.pt); most stay open all year and some impose a curfew. All require a valid HI card; for details see Ⓦwww.hihostels.com. Alternatively, hostels in Portugal can provide you with a guest card, which must be stamped every night that you stay (€2 per stamp); once you have five stamps you're a fully paid-up member of HI. A dormitory bed costs €9–18, depending on season and location; doubles in a hostel cost €22–45. There is also a growing number of **independent hostels**, particularly in Lisbon and Porto; they're a slightly pricier alternative to official youth hostels but tend to be more conveniently located, and are often well equipped, with kitchen facilities and internet access.

In almost any town you should be able to find a single room for under €30 and a double for under €50; cities are slightly more expensive. The main budget stand-bys are **pensions**, or *pensões* – hotels, often present only in larger towns and cities tend to be rather pricier. Seaside resorts invariably offer cheaper **rooms** (*quartos*) in private houses; tourist offices have lists. At the higher end of the scale are **pousadas** (Ⓦwww.pousadas.pt), often converted from old monasteries or castles, which charge at least four-star hotel prices. No matter what type of accommodation you select, **breakfast** will usually be included (exceptions are noted in this chapter).

Portugal has around two hundred **campsites**, most small, low-key and attractively located, and all remarkably inexpensive – you'll rarely pay more than €5 a person. You can get a map list from any tourist office, or find details online at Ⓦwww.roteiro-campista.pt. Camping rough is banned; beach areas are especially strict about this.

FOOD AND DRINK

Portuguese **food** is cheap and served in plentiful portions. Virtually all cafés dish up a basic meal for under €10, and for a little more you have the run of most of the country's restaurants. **Snacks** include *tosta mistas* (cheese and ham toasties); *pastéis de bacalhau* (codfish cakes); and *sandes* (sandwiches). In **restaurants** you can usually have a substantial meal by ordering a *meia dose* (half portion), or *uma dose* (one portion) between two. Most serve an *ementa turística* (set meal), which can be good value, particularly in *pensões* that serve meals, cheaper workers' cafés or *churrasqueiras* (grill restaurants serving meat and fish dishes). It's often worth opting for the *prato do dia* (dish of the day), usually the cheapest dish on the menu, and, if you're on the coast, going for fish and seafood.

Meals usually begin with uninvited appetizers (from bread, butter and olives to more elaborate entrées), which often carry a hefty price-tag; if in doubt ask, and don't be afraid to send these items back or ignore them. Typical **dishes** include *sopa de marisco*

(shellfish soup); *caldo verde* (finely shredded kale leaves in broth); and *bacalhau* (dried cod, cooked in myriad different ways). *Caldeirada* is a fish stew cooked with onions and tomatoes, *arroz marisco* a similar stew cooked with seafood and rice. *Cabrito assado* (roast kid) is common in the north of the country, while down south you're sure to see chicken piri-piri (chicken with chilli sauce) on the menu. **Puddings** include *arroz doce* (rice pudding), *salada da fruta* (fruit salad) and *pudím molotoff* (a kind of lightly toasted meringue drenched in caramel sauce). **Cakes** – *bolos* or *pastéis* – are often at their best in *pastelarias* (patisseries), though you'll also find them in cafés and *casas de chá* (tearooms). Among the best are custard tarts (*pastéis de nata*).

Drink

Portuguese **wines** (*tinto* for red, *branco* for white) are very inexpensive and of high quality. The fortified **port** (*vinho do Porto*; see p.947) and madeira (*vinho da Madeira*) wines are the best known. The light, slightly sparkling **vinhos verdes** are produced in the Minho, and are excellent served chilled. **Brandy** is available in two varieties, Macieiera and Constantino, while Lisbon specializes in the cherry brandy Ginjinha, which is served at tiny hole-in-the-wall bars throughout the city. The two most common Portuguese **beers** (*cervejas*) are Sagres and Super Bock.

CULTURE AND ETIQUETTE

Portugal is a **Catholic** country, so it's wise to show respect when visiting churches (bare shoulders should be covered up and short skirts may be frowned upon), and avoid visiting during services, which take place on Sundays and sometimes other days at around 9.30am. It's also a good idea to learn a few basic phrases in **Portuguese** (see p.927); it will certainly endear locals to you, and outside the main tourist areas English may not be widely understood. In restaurants, it is usual to **tip** five percent to ten percent if you're satisfied with the service.

Lone women travellers should face no problems, but might attract a bit of curiosity from locals.

SPORTS AND OUTDOOR ACTIVITIES

In Portugal, **football** isn't just a sport: it's a national passion. During all major matches, the country goes quiet as people flock to restaurants and bars to watch them on television. The three biggest and most successful football clubs are FC Porto, Sporting Lisbon and Benfica. **Surfing** is also popular (see box below). Portugal's **natural parks** (*parques naturais*) and its one **national park**, the Parque Nacional de Peneda-Gerês in the Minho, are a hikers' paradise. More information about the parks can be found at Ⓦwww.icn.pt, and tourist offices located near parks can provide maps and other details. In the

SURFING IN PORTUGAL

Portugal is a surfer's paradise, with some of Europe's best beaches for catching waves. Popular spots include **Peniche** in central Portugal, Guincho beach near **Cascais** in Lisbon, the **Alentejo coast**, and Lagos and the wilder waters of Sagres in the **Algarve**. First-timers should try a **surf school** such as Peniche Surf Camp (Ⓦwww.penichesurfcamp.com; €453 for a week in high season) or The Surf Experience in Lagos (Ⓦwww.surf-experience.com; €467 for a week); accommodation is usually included in courses. For those with a bit more experience, equipment is available for hire in all popular surfing spots (around €60 for a week's board hire).

PORTUGAL ON THE NET

ⓦ**www.visitportugal.com** Tourist board site, with information and advice.
ⓦ**www.portugalvirtual.pt** Comprehensive directory listings.
ⓦ**www.spottedbylocals.com/lisbon** Up-to-the minute recommendations from Lisbon residents.
ⓦ**www.algarveuncovered.com** Detailed site dedicated to the Algarve region.

Algarve, pick up a copy of the excellent *Trails in the Algarve* booklet, a guide to walking routes in the region, available for €5 from tourist offices.

COMMUNICATIONS

Internet cafés are common (€1.50–3/hr). **Post offices** (*correios*) are normally open Monday to Friday 9am to 6pm, Saturday 9am to noon. For **poste restante**, look for a counter marked *encomendas*. International **phone calls** can be made direct from any phone booth; phonecards cost €3, €6 or €9, from post offices, larger newsagents and tobacconists. The operator is on ⓣ118 (domestic), ⓣ098 (international).

EMERGENCIES

Lisbon and the larger tourist areas have seen increases in **petty crime**, such as street theft. Pilfering from dorms is relatively rare, but it's always wise to use the lockers provided or buy a padlock for your luggage. Travel on trains and buses is safe, with thefts a rarity. Portuguese **police** are stationed in most towns, and can be recognized by their dark blue uniforms. Lisbon and Porto have separate **tourist police** to deal with issues affecting visitors.

EMERGENCY NUMBERS

All emergencies ⓣ112.

For minor health complaints go to a **pharmacy** (*farmácia*); pharmacists are highly trained and can dispense many drugs without a prescription. Normal opening hours are Monday to Friday 9am to 1pm and 3 to 7pm, Saturday 9am to 1pm. A sign at each one will show the nearest 24hr pharmacy. You can get the address of an English-speaking doctor from a pharmacy or consular office.

INFORMATION

You'll find a **tourist office** (*turismo*) in almost every town. Staff can help you find a room, and provide local maps and leaflets.

MONEY AND BANKS

Currency is the euro (€). **Banks** are open Monday to Friday 8.30am to 3pm; in Lisbon and in some of the Algarve resorts, **exchange offices** may open in the evening to change money. ATMs can be found all over and credit cards are widely accepted; traveller's cheques are increasingly difficult to exchange outside tourist hotspots, and commission on them can be high.

OPENING HOURS AND HOLIDAYS

Shop **opening hours** are generally Monday to Friday 9am to 12.30/1pm and 2/2.30 to 6/6.30pm, Saturday 9am to 12.30/1pm. Larger supermarkets tend to stay open until 8pm, but most are closed on Sunday, with some

STUDENT AND YOUTH DISCOUNTS

If you're under 26 it's well worth investing in a Euro 26 card (ⓦwww.euro26.org), which often gives the holder sixty percent off admission costs, plus discounts on train and bus travel and accommodation in official youth hostels. Some sights offer a less significant discount on production of a valid university card.

Portuguese

	Portuguese	Pronunciation
Yes	*Sim*	Sing
No	*Não*	Now
Please	*Por favor*	Por favor
Thank you	*Obrigado* [said by men]/ *Obrigada* [said by women]	Obrigado/obrigada
Hello/Good day	*Olá*	Orla
Goodbye	*Adeus*	Adayoosh
Excuse me	*Desculpe*	Deskulp
Where?	*Onde?*	Ond?
Good	*Bom*	Bom
Bad	*Mau*	Maw
Near	*Perto*	Pertoo
Far	*Longe*	Lonje
Cheap	*Barato*	Baratoo
Expensive	*Caro*	Karoo
Open	*Aberto*	Abertoo
Closed	*Fechado*	Feshardoo
Today	*Hoje*	Oje
Yesterday	*Ontem*	Ontaygn
Tomorrow	*Amanhã*	Amanya
How much is...?	*Quanto é...?*	Kwantoo eh...?
What time is it?	*Que horas são?*	Kay orash sow?
I don't understand	*Não compreendo*	Now comprendoo
Do you speak English?	*Fala Inglés?*	Farla inglayz?
One	*Um/Uma*	Oom/ooma
Two	*Dois/Duas*	Doysh/dooash
Three	*Três*	Treysh
Four	*Quatro*	Kwatroo
Five	*Cinco*	Sinkoo
Six	*Seis*	Saysh
Seven	*Sete*	Set
Eight	*Oito*	Oytoo
Nine	*Nove*	Nove
Ten	*Dez*	Desh
Where is the station?	*Onde é a estação?*	Ond e a estasow?
On the left/right	*A esquerda/direita*	A eeshkerdah/deeraitah
A ticket to...	*Um bilhete para...*	Oom beelyet para...
What time is the train/ bus to...?	*A que horas é o comboio/ autocarro para...?*	A kay oras e o convoyo/ autocarro para...?
I would like a room (single/double)	*Queria um quarto individual/casal*	Kereea um kwarto individooal/cazal
May I see the room?	*Posso ver o quarto?*	Posso ver o kwarto?
At the restaurant		
A table for one/two	*Uma mesa para uma pessoa/duas pessoas*	Uma mehzah para ooma pessoa/duash pessoash
I'm a vegetarian	*Sou vegetariano/a*	So vejetarianoh/ah
A bottle of water/wine	*Uma garrafa de água/vinho*	Ooma garrafuh de aigua/vinyo

exceptions in the Algarve. Museums, churches and monuments open from around 10am to 6pm, with many state institutions free from 10am until 2pm on Sunday; almost all, however, close on Mondays and at Easter; smaller places often close for lunch.

The main **public holidays** are: January 1, Feburary carnival, Good Friday, April 25, May 1, Corpus Christi, June 10, June 13 (Lisbon only), August 15, October 5, November 1, December 1, December 8 and December 25.

Lisbon and around

There are few more immediately likeable European capitals than **LISBON** (Lisboa). A lively city, it remains in some ways curiously provincial, and rooted as much in the 1920s as the 2010s. Wooden trams clank up outrageous gradients, past mosaic pavements, Art Nouveau cafés and the medieval quarter of Alfama, which hangs below the São Jorge castle. The city invested heavily for Expo 98 and the 2004 European Football Championships, reclaiming rundown docks and improving communication links, and today it combines an easy-going pace and manageable scale with a vibrant, cosmopolitan identity.

Lisbon has a huge amount of historic interest. Though the **Great Earthquake** of 1755 (followed by a tidal wave and fire) destroyed most of the grandest buildings, several monuments from Portugal's sixteenth-century golden age survived the quake and frantic reconstruction led to many impressive new palaces and churches, as well as the street grid pattern spanning the city's seven hills.

What to see and do

Many of Lisbon's historical sights, such as the Sé (cathedral) and the Castelo de São Jorge, are located in the centre's eastern portion, best reached by following Rua de Conceição and its continuations as they wind away from the **Baixa**, the city's eighteenth-century core, towards the ancient district of **Alfama**. The city centre can be explored on foot, but a quick hop on a **tram** or **elevador** is definitely a less strenuous way of scaling Lisbon's seven hills. Public transport is also necessary to reach outlying sights such as those located in **Belém**, 6km west of the centre, and the **Fundação Calouste Gulbenkian**, north of the city's main artery, the Avenida da Liberdade. The Baixa is the city's principal shopping district, with more elegant and trendy boutiques located in **Chiado** and **Bairro Alto** respectively. Bairro Alto is also the area to head for food, *fado* and fun, as it is home to many of the city's bars and restaurants.

Baixa

The heart of the capital is the lower town – the **Baixa** – Europe's first great example of Neoclassical design and urban planning. It's an imposing quarter of rod-straight streets, some streaming with traffic, but most pedestrianized with mosaic cobbles where pavement artists and shoe-shiners ply their trade. The Baixa's northenmost boundary is **Rossio Square** (officially Praça dom Pedro IV), the area's hub, busy at almost all hours of the day and night and housing some old-style cafés and the grand Teatro Nacional, built in the 1840s. At the waterfront end of the Baixa lies the city's other main square, the beautiful arcaded Praça do Comércio.

The Sé

A couple of blocks east of the Baixa on the Largo da Sé stands the **Sé** or cathedral (Tues–Sat 9am–7pm; Sun & Mon 9am–5pm). The oldest church in Lisbon, it was founded in 1147 to commemorate the city's reconquest from the Moors, and occupies the site of the principal mosque of Moorish Lishbuna. Like so many of Portugal's cathedrals, it is Romanesque and extraordinarily restrained in both size and decoration. It was damaged in the 1755 earthquake, and was extensively restored in the 1930s.

Castelo de São Jorge

From the Sé, Rua Augusto Rosa and its continuations wind up towards the

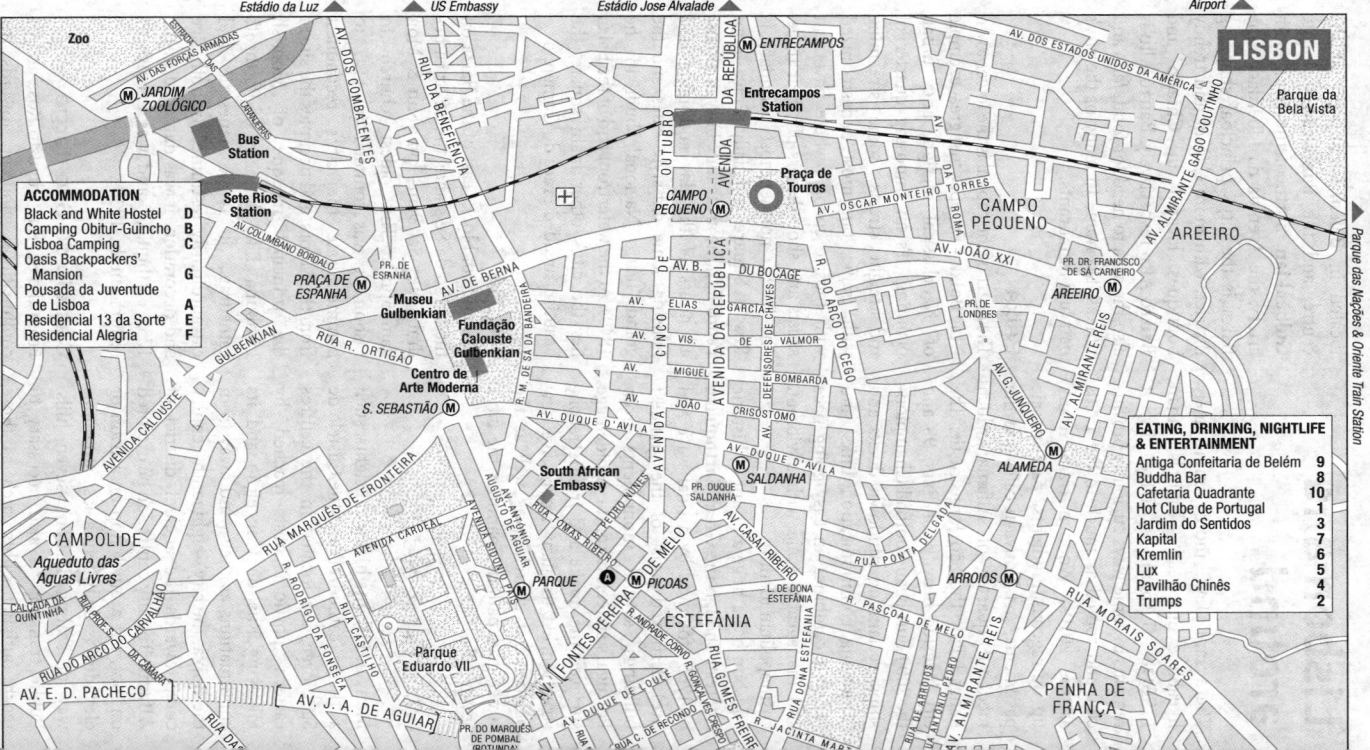

LISBON

ACCOMMODATION

Black and White Hostel	D
Camping Obitur-Guincho	B
Lisboa Camping	C
Oasis Backpackers' Mansion	G
Pousada da Juventude de Lisboa	A
Residencial 13 da Sorte	E
Residencial Alegria	F

EATING, DRINKING, NIGHTLIFE & ENTERTAINMENT

Antiga Confeitaria de Belém	9
Buddha Bar	8
Cafetaria Quadrante	10
Hot Clube de Portugal	1
Jardim do Sentidos	3
Kapital	7
Kremlin	6
Lux	5
Pavilhão Chinês	4
Trumps	2

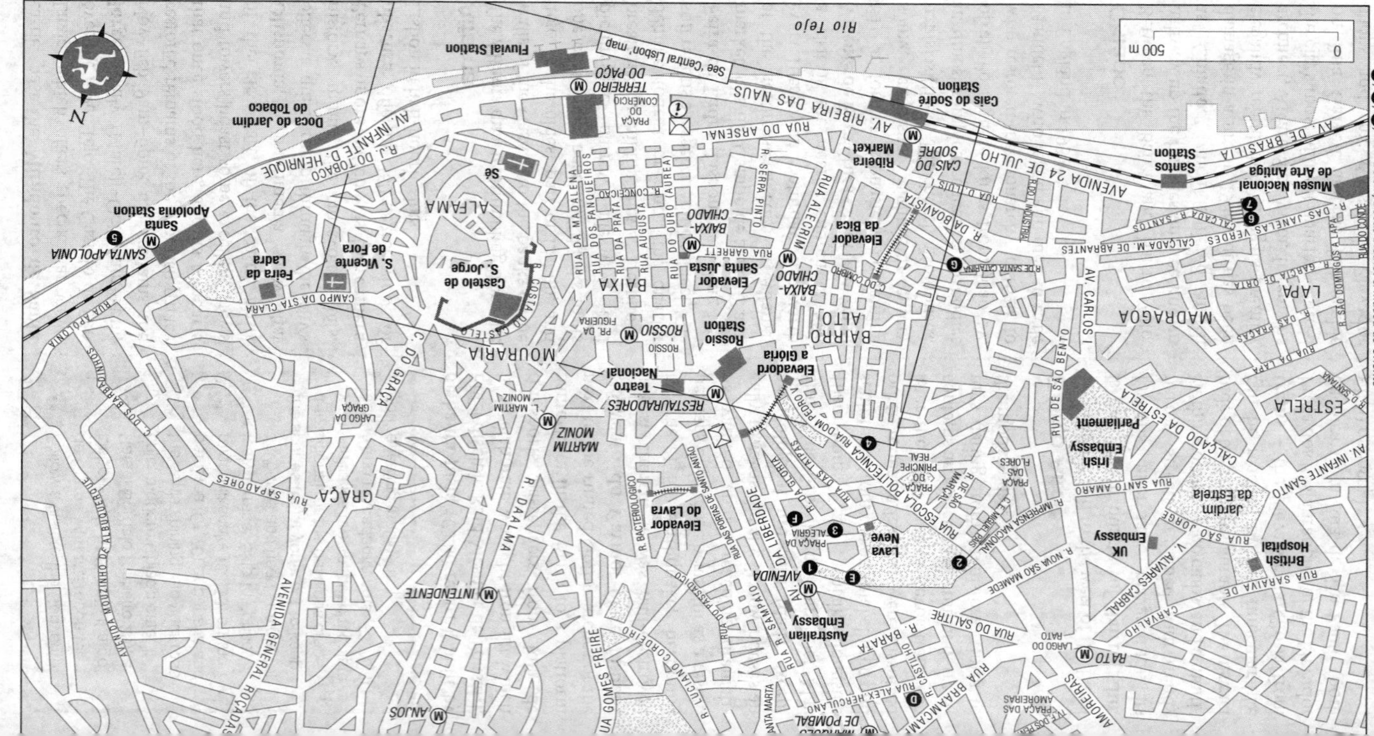
Rio Tejo
0
500 m
Fluvial Station
See 'Central Lisbon' map
TERREIRO DO PAÇO
PRAÇA DO COMÉRCIO
Cais do Sodré Station
Doca do Jardim do Tobaco
AV. INFANTE D. HENRIQUE
R.J. DO TOBACO
AV. RIBEIRA DAS NAUS
RUA DO ARSENAL
Santos Station
AV. DE BRASÍLIA
AVENIDA 24 DE JULHO
CAIS DO SODRÉ
Ribeira Market
Museu Nacional de Arte Antiga
Belém, Docas District & Museu do Oriente
Sé
ALFAMA
Santa Apolónia Station
SANTA APOLÓNIA
S. Vicente de Fora
Feira da Ladra
CAMPO DA STA CLARA
Castelo de S. Jorge
COSTA DO CASTELO
RUA DA MADALENA
RUA DOS FANQUEIROS
RUA DA PRATA
RUA AUGUSTA
R. CONCEIÇÃO
RUA DO OURO (AUREA)
BAIXA
BAIXA-CHIADO
Elevador Santa Justa
RUA GARRETT
R. SERPA PINTO
RUA ALECRIM
Elevador da Bica
R. DA BOAVISTA
RUA D. LUIS I
R. DO INDUSTRIAL
CALÇADA R. SANTOS
RUA DAS JANELAS VERDES
CALÇADA M. DE ABRANTES
R. DE SANTA CATARINA
C. DO COMBRO
BAIRRO ALTO
ROSSIO
PR. DA FIGUEIRA
Rossio Station
Elevadord a Glória
Teatro Nacional
RESTAURADORES
MOURARIA
L. MARTIM MONIZ
MARTIM MONIZ
LARGO DA GRAÇA
C. DO GRAÇA
RUA APOLÓNIA
C. DOS BARBADINHOS
RUA SAPADORES
GRAÇA
AVENIDA MOUZINHO DE ALBUQUERQUE
AVENIDA GENERAL ROÇADAS
R. DAALMA
INTENDENTE
ANJOS
UA GOMES FREIRE
R. LUCIANO CORDEIRO
R. BACTERIOLOGICO
Elevador do Lavra
RUA DAS PORTAS DE SANTO ANTÃO
RUA DO PASSADICO
AVENIDA DA LIBERDADE
AV. AVENIDA
RUA R. SAMPAIO
ANTA MARTA
R. DA GLÓRIA
RUA DAS TAIPAS
RUA DOM PEDRO V
RUA ESCOLA POLITECNICA
PRAÇA DO PRINCIPE REAL
PRAÇA DA ALEGRIA
Lava Neve
Australian Embassy
R. BARATA
RUA DO SALITRE
DE POMBAL
RUA ALEX. HERCULANO
R. CASTILHO
RUA BRAAMCAMP
PRAÇA DAS AMOREIRAS
AMOREIRAS
RATO
LARGO DO RATO
CARVALHO
V. ALVARES CABRAL
R. NOVA SAO MAMEDE
R. IMPRENSA NACIONAL
C.E. MIGUEL PAIS
R. DE SÃO MARÇAL
PRAÇA DAS FLORES
RUA SANTO AMARO
RUA DE SÃO BENTO
AV. CARLOS I
Irish Embassy
UK Embassy
Parliament
RUA SÃO JORGE
Jardim da Estrela
British Hospital
RUA SARAIVA DE
AV. INFANTE SANTO
CALÇADO DA ESTRELA
ESTRELA
MADRAGOA
LAPA
R. DA LAPA
R. DAS PRAÇAS
R. GARCIA DE ORTA
R. SÃO DOMINGOS A LAPA
RUA DO CONDE
R. D. SANTANA
N

castle, past the **Miradouro de Santa Luzia**, which offers spectacular views over the River Tejo. The **Castelo de São Jorge** (daily March–Oct 9am–9pm, Nov–Feb 9am–6pm; €5) contains the restored remains of the Moorish palace that once stood here, and its ramparts and towers boast some excellent views of the city. Part of the castle hosts **Olispónia**, a multimedia show that offers a quick romp through the city's history, minus the unsavoury bits. Perhaps more enticing is the **camera obscura**, offering 360-degree views of Lisbon in half-hourly slots.

Alfama

The **Alfama quarter**, tumbling from the walls of the Castelo to the banks of the Tejo, is the oldest part of Lisbon, and one of its most beautiful, thanks to its picturesque narrow alleyways and breathtaking hilltop views. Despite a definite tourist presence, the quarter still retains a largely traditional feel. The **Feira da Ladra**, Lisbon's rambling flea market, fills the Campo de Santa Clara, at the northeastern edge of Alfama, every Tuesday and Saturday. Also worth a visit is the nearby church of **São Vicente de Fora** (Tues–Sun 10am–6pm; €4), a former monastery containing some exquisite eighteenth-century *azulejos* (tiles). The church also houses, in almost complete sequence, the bodies of all Portuguese kings from João IV, who restored the monarchy in 1640, to Manuel II, who lost it and died in exile in England in 1932.

Chiado

Between the Baixa and Bairro Alto, halfway up the hill, lies an area known as **Chiado**, which suffered much damage in a fire in 1988 but has been elegantly rebuilt by Portugal's premier architect, Álvaro Siza Viera. It remains the city's most affluent quarter, centred on **Rua Garrett** and its fashionable shops and chic cafés. The **Elevador de Santa Justa** (€2.80 return), built by Eiffel disciple Raul Mésnier de Ponsard, is an elaborate wrought-iron lift which transports passengers from Rua de Santa Justa in the Baixa to a platform next to the ruined Gothic arches of the **Convento do Carmo**. Once Lisbon's largest church, it was half-destroyed by the 1755 earthquake, becoming perhaps even more beautiful as a result, its vaulted arches reaching dramatically towards the sky. It now houses an **archeological museum** (daily except Sun: June–Sept 10am–7pm, Oct–May 10am–6pm; €2.50) which, alongside sculptures from the original church and other monasteries that were dissolved after the 1834 Liberal Revolution, also contains an eclectic assortment of treasures dating from prehistoric times to the modern day.

TREAT YOURSELF

Follow a visit to the Convento de Carmo with afternoon tea Lisbon-style at **Royale** (Largo Rafael Bordalo Pinheiro 29), a chic, modern Chiado café. If the sun's shining, sip your rose petal tea (€1.70) or papaya and mint milkshake (€3.50) on the leafy terrace. Skip the pricey savouries and head straight for the scones (€4) if you want to keep it traditional, or the delicious crêpe with vanilla ice cream, hot chocolate sauce and macadamia nuts (€3.70) if you're feeling indulgent.

Bairro Alto

High above and to the west of the Baixa is the vibrant quarter of **Bairro Alto**, Lisbon's after-dark playground. Its narrow streets are lined with trendy clothing outlets, *fado* clubs, and a multitude of bars and restaurants. The district can be reached by two funicular-like **trams** – the Elevador da Glória from Praça dos Restauradores or the Elevador da Bica from Rua de São Paulo (both €1.40 one way).

The Fundação Calouste Gulbenkian

The **Fundação Calouste Gulbenkian** is a ten-minute walk north of Lisbon's main park, the Parque Eduardo VII – or take the metro to São Sebastião or Praça de Espanha. The Foundation, established by the oil magnate and prolific collector Calouste Gulbenkian, helps finance various aspects of Portugal's cultural life – including an orchestra, three concert halls and the two art galleries located here. The **Museu Calouste Gulbenkian** (Tues–Sun 10am–6pm; €4, free Sun 10am–2pm) is Portugal's greatest museum, divided into two distinct parts – the first devoted to Egyptian, Greco-Roman, Islamic and Oriental arts, the second to European, including paintings from all the major schools. There's also a stunning room full of Art Nouveau jewellery by René Lalique. Across the gardens, the **Centro de Arte Moderna** (same hours; €4, joint ticket €7) houses works by all the big names from the twentieth-century Portuguese scene, as well as some top British artists such as Anthony Gormley and David Hockney.

Museu Nacional de Arte Antiga

The **Museu Nacional de Arte Antiga** (Tues 2–6pm, Wed–Sun 10am–6pm; €3, free Sun 10am–2pm), another of Lisbon's top art museums, is situated near the riverfront to the west of the city at Rua das Janelas Verdes 95 (tram #15 from Praça do Comércio). Its core is formed by fifteenth- and sixteenth-century Portuguese works, the acknowledged masterpiece being Nuno Gonçalves' St Vincent Altarpiece, depicting Lisbon's patron receiving homage from all ranks of its citizens. There are also ceramics, textiles and furniture from Portugal on display, as well as decorative arts from Asia and Africa.

Museu do Oriente

Set in a converted *bacalhau* warehouse down on the docks en route to Belém, the vast new **Museu do Oriente** (Avenida Brasília, Doca de Alcântara Norte; daily except Tues 10am–6pm, Fri until 10pm; €4) is home to a wealth of artefacts from the Orient, with a particular emphasis on Portugal's former Asian colonies. Exhibits include aboriginal engravings, Chinese porcelain and figurines of a variety of Asian gods. To reach the museum, take tram #15 from Praça do Comércio.

Belém

Six kilometres west of the centre lies the suburb of **Belém**, from where, in 1497, Vasco da Gama set sail for India. Partly funded by a levy on all spices other than pepper, cinnamon and cloves, whose import had become the sole preserve of the Crown, the **Mosteiro dos Jerónimos** (Monastery of Jerónimos; Mon–Sat: May–Sept 10am–6.30pm; Oct–April 10am–5pm, free; cloisters same hours €6, free Sun 10am–2pm, joint ticket with Torre €8; tram #15 from Praça do Comércio) was begun in 1502 and is the most ambitious achievement in the flamboyant late Gothic style which thrived under Manuel I (1495–1521). Vaulted throughout and fantastically embellished, the cloister is one of the most original and beautiful pieces of architecture in Portugal, holding Gothic forms and Renaissance ornamentation in an exuberant balance.

Another monument from the Age of Discoveries is the turreted **Torre de Belém** (daily except Mon: May–Sept 10am–6.30pm; Oct–April 10am–5pm; €3, free Sun 10am–2pm), on the edge of the river around 500m from the monastery, built during the last five years of Dom Manuel's reign to guard the entrance to Lisbon's port. Step back into the present day at the **Centro Cultural de Belém**, which in addition to holding an exciting array of

concerts, exhibitions and events (see ⓦwww.ccb.pt), is home to the **Museu Colecçao Berardo** (daily 10am–7pm, until 10pm Fri; free), a captivating collection of modern and contemporary art which includes works by Andy Warhol, Paula Rego and Picasso.

Also of interest is the vast concrete **Padrão dos Descobrimentos** (Monument to the Discoveries; daily except Mon: May–Sept 10am–7pm; Oct–April 10am–6pm; €2.50) on the waterfront, built in 1960 to commemorate the 500th anniversary of the death of Henry the Navigator, King João I's son, who began Portugal's worldwide explorations; inside are changing exhibitions on the city's history. A lift takes you to the top for spectacular views.

Parque das Nações and the Oceanarium

Built on reclaimed docklands for Expo '98, the **Parque das Nações** (Park of Nations), 5km east of the centre, has become a popular entertainment park, containing concert venues, theatres, restaurants and a large shopping centre, Centro Vasco de Gama. The park occupies a traffic-free riverside zone punctuated by water features and some dazzling modern architecture. The main attraction is the **Oceanário de Lisboa** (daily 10am–7pm; €11; metro Oriente), Europe's second largest oceanarium, an awe-inspiring collection of fish and sea mammals based around a central tank the size of four Olympic swimming pools. The information kiosk opposite Centro Vasco da Gama supplies maps of the park.

Football stadiums

Lovers of the beautiful game will find Lisbon a paradise, with two top-ranking Portuguese clubs based in the city. Benfica are based at the impressive **Estádio da Luz** (Colegio Militar/Luz metro, zone 2), built for Euro 2004, which can be visited daily by guided tour at 10am, 11am, noon, 2.30pm, 3.30pm and 4.30pm (€10). Sporting's **Estádio Jose Alvalade** (Campo Grande metro) was also constructed for the same event, and is equally modern (tours Mon–Fri 11.30am, 2.30pm and 4.30pm; €8). If you're in town on a match day (the season runs from September to June; check ⓦwww.slbenfica.pt and ⓦwww.sporting.pt for fixtures), head to the stadium a few hours before kick-off to secure a ticket (from €20).

Arrival and information

Air From Portela airport, 7km northeast of the centre, the #91 Aerobus (every 20min 7.45am–9pm; 20min; €3) runs from outside arrivals to Praça dos Restauradores, Rossio, Praça do Comércio and Cais do Sodré; the ticket is then valid for transport on buses and trams for that day. Local buses #44 and #45 (€1.40) run from the road outside the airport to central stops including Rossio, but do not allow large suitcases on board during rush hours.

Train Trains from northern and central Portugal stop at Santa Apolónia Station, a 15min walk from Praça do Comércio or a quick hop on the metro (blue line). Trains from the Algarve terminate at Oriente station, at the end of the red metro line. Local trains from Sintra stop at Rossio station at the northwestern end of the square.

Bus The main Rede Expressos bus station is next to the Jardim Zoológico metro stop.

Tourist office The main tourist office is the Lisboa Welcome Centre, on the corner of Praça do Comércio and Rua do Arsenal (daily 9am–8pm; ⓣ210 312 700, ⓦwww.visitlisboa.com). There are also Ask Me Lisboa kiosks around the city, including one at the airport (daily 6am–midnight) and one at Santa Apolónia station. Note that Ask Me Lisboa is a private company so will only book rooms with its associated partner hotels.

City transport

Metro Lisbon's metro (ⓦwww.metrolisboa.pt) has four lines, blue (*azul*), green (*verde*), red (*vermelha*), and yellow (*amarela*); tickets cost €0.80/1.10 each (for central/all zones). The metro runs between 6.30am and 1am.

Tram and bus Trams and buses (ⓦwww.carris.pt) are the most enjoyable way of getting around. Tram #28, which runs from Martim Moniz through the Alfama to Prazeres, has become something of

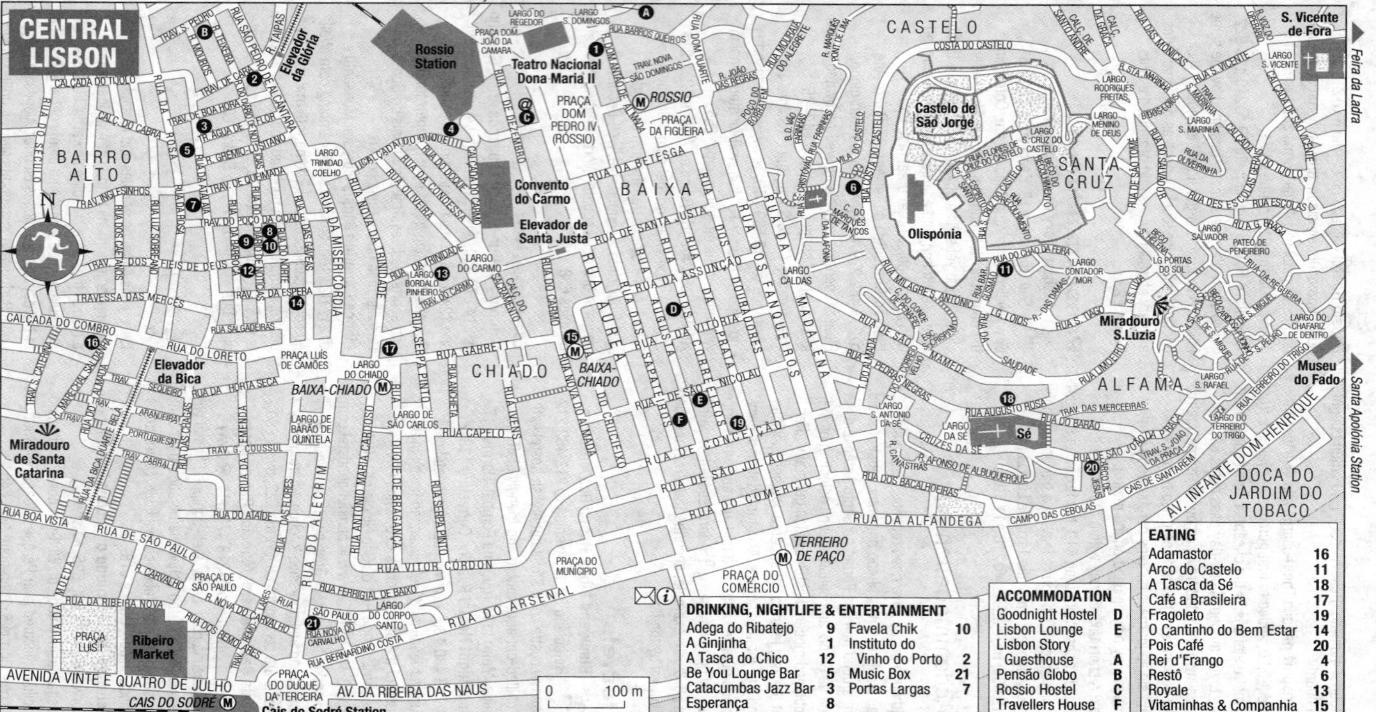

CENTRAL LISBON
Praça dos Restauradores & Avenida de Liberdade
Feira da Ladra
Santa Apolónia Station
CASTELO
BAIRRO ALTO
BAIXA
CHIADO
SANTA CRUZ
ALFAMA
DOCA DO JARDIM DO TOBACO
Rossio Station
Teatro Nacional Dona Maria II
PRAÇA DOM PEDRO IV (ROSSIO)
PRAÇA DA FIGUEIRA
ROSSIO
Convento do Carmo
Elevador de Santa Justa
Elevador da Glória
Elevador da Bica
Castelo de São Jorge
Olispónia
Miradouro S.Luzia
Miradouro de Santa Catarina
Museu do Fado
S. Vicente de Fora
Sé
BAIXA-CHIADO
TERREIRO DE PAÇO
PRAÇA DO COMÉRCIO
PRAÇA DO MUNICÍPIO
PRAÇA LUÍS DE CAMÕES
Ribeiro Market
PRAÇA LUÍS I
CAIS DO SODRÉ
Cais do Sodré Station
AVENIDA VINTE E QUATRO DE JULHO
AV. DA RIBEIRA DAS NAUS
AV. INFANTE DOM HENRIQUE
RUA DO ARSENAL
RUA DA ALFÂNDEGA
RUA DO COMÉRCIO
RUA AUGUSTA
RUA DA PRATA
RUA DOS FANQUEIROS
RUA DA MADALENA
RUA GARRETT
RUA DA MISERICÓRDIA
RUA DO ALECRIM
0 100 m
DRINKING, NIGHTLIFE & ENTERTAINMENT
Adega do Ribatejo 9
A Ginjinha 1
A Tasca do Chico 12
Be You Lounge Bar 5
Catacumbas Jazz Bar 3
Esperança 8
Favela Chik 10
Instituto do Vinho do Porto 2
Music Box 21
Portas Largas 7
ACCOMMODATION
Goodnight Hostel D
Lisbon Lounge E
Lisbon Story Guesthouse A
Pensão Globo B
Rossio Hostel C
Travellers House F
EATING
Adamastor 16
Arco do Castelo 11
A Tasca da Sé 18
Café a Brasileira 17
Fragoleto 19
O Cantinho do Bem Estar 14
Pois Café 20
Rei d'Frango 4
Restô 6
Royale 13
Vitaminhas & Companhia 15

a tourist must-do. Tickets cost €1.40 when bought on board.

Transport passes The rechargeable Viva Viagem card (€0.50, added to first purchase), available from all metro stations, is the cheapest, most convenient way to get around. A one-day pass costs €3.70 and allows unlimited travel on buses, trams, metro and *elevadores*. The cards can also be loaded with single journeys (singles purchased in a metro station may only be used on the metro).

Taxi A short taxi journey within the city centre shouldn't cost more than €10, but taxis can be hard to find at night – if you're leaving a bar or club book one by phone from Rádio Táxis de Lisboa (Ⓣ218 119 000) or Teletáxis (Ⓣ218 111 100).

Accommodation

Although prices have risen recently, Lisbon still has plenty of small, cheap pensions, most of which are around Rua das Portas de Santo Antão and Rua da Glória, and boasts a good selection of well-equipped modern hostels, which generally offer (at the very least) a lounge area, kitchen facilities and free internet access. Accommodation is easy to find outside Easter and midsummer, when prices rise by up to fifty percent. Addresses below written as 53-3°, for example, describe the street number followed by the floor.

Hostels

Black and White Hostel Rua Alexandre Herculano 39-1°, Avenida Ⓣ213 462 212, Ⓦwww.costta.com. Small but stylish hostel with a chilled-out atmosphere and friendly staff. Good value. Metro to Marquês de Pombal. Dorms €17.

Goodnight Hostel Rua dos Correeiros 113-2° Ⓣ213 430 139, Ⓦwww.goodnighthostel.com Funky, friendly and well-designed hostel in the heart of the Baixa. Dorms €20, twins €50.

Lisbon Lounge Rua de São Nicolau 41, Baixa Ⓣ213 462 061, Ⓦwww.lisbonloungehostel.com. Upmarket hostel near Rossio with spacious, airy dorms and an impressive kitchen where nightly meals are served for €8. Dorms €22, twins €60.

Oasis Backpackers' Mansion Rua de Santa Catarina 24, Chiado Ⓣ213 478 044, Ⓦwww.oasislisboa.com. Lively, well-equipped hostel with its own bar, located below the Miradouro de Santa Catarina. Laundry facilities available. Metro to Baixa-Chiado. Dorms €18.

Pousada de Juventude de Lisboa Rua Andrade Corvo 46 Ⓣ213 532 696, Ⓦwww.pousadasjuventude.pt. Well-run hostel with good facilities, located near Parque Eduardo VII. Metro to Picoas. Dorms €17, en-suite twin €45.

Rossio Hostel Calçada do Carmo 6 Ⓣ213 426 004. Immaculately clean, efficiently run and well-designed hostel with large dorms and excellent doubles. Dorms €23, doubles €64.

Travellers House Rua Augusta 89 Ⓣ210 115 922, Ⓦwww.travellershouse.com. Designed by the same folk as *Rossio*, this larger hostel is another slick operator, with nice touches such as personal safes, a library of travel guides and organized events. Dorms €23.

Pensions and hotels

Lisbon Story Guesthouse Largo de São Domingos 18, Baixa Ⓣ211 529 313, Ⓦwww.lisbonstoryguesthouse.com. Combining the best of hostel and hotel, *Lisbon Story* offers eight simple yet stylish private rooms with a Lisbon theme, a kitchen, and a large lounge well stocked with travel books. Great breakfast. €50.

Pensão Globo Rua do Teixeira 37, Bairro Alto Ⓣ213 462 279, Ⓦwww.cb2web.com/globo. Pleasant pension with clean, well-renovated rooms in a variety of shapes and sizes. €40–75.

Residencial 13 da Sorte Rua do Salitre 13, Liberdade Ⓣ213 539 746, Ⓦwww.trezedasorte.no.sapo.pt. "Lucky 13" is a well-located pension with good-value en-suite rooms. €55.

Residencial Alegria Praça da Alegria 12 Ⓣ213 220 670, Ⓦwww.alegrianet.com. Friendly new French owners have transformed a standard *residencial* into a comfortable, well-decorated haven in this quiet square. Worth treating yourself. Doubles €68.

Campsites

Camping Obitur-Guincho Lugar da Areia, Guincho Ⓣ214 870 450, Ⓦwww.orbitur.pt. A well-located site 12km out of the city in surfer's paradise Guincho, boasting a restaurant, supermarket, and sports facilities. Train from Cais do Sodré to Cascais, then bus to Guincho. €6.

Lisboa Camping Parque Florestal Monsanto Ⓣ217 623 100, Ⓦwww.lisboacamping.com. Well-equipped campsite in a large park 6km west of the centre, complete with pool and shops. The entrance is on Estrada da Circunvalação on the park's west side. Bus #43 from Cais do Sodré. €5.

Eating

Lisbon has some great cafés and restaurants serving large portions of food at reasonable prices, although these are creeping upwards. Lunch is particularly good value, with plenty of bargain dishes of the day and set menus on offer. Alongside the usual Portuguese restaurants serving grilled meat

and fish, there are a large number of seafood places (especially on Rua das Portas de Santo Antão), and inexpensive restaurants featuring food from Portugal's former colonies (including Angola, Goa and Macau). Many restaurants are closed on Sundays. The best food market is Mercado da Ribeira, Avda 24 de Julho, Cais do Sodré (Mon–Sat 10am–11pm).

Cafés

Antiga Confeitaria de Belém Rua de Belém 90, Belém. Historic tiled café famous for its delicious *pastéis de nata* (€0.90) – better than all the imitations.
Café a Brasileira Rua Garrett 120, Chiado. The most famous of Rua Garrett's old-style coffee houses, once frequented by Lisbon's literary set.
Cafetaria Quadrante Centro Cultural de Belém. The cultural complex's self-service café serves hearty salads by weight (€1.65 per 100g), with the bonus of a large terrace by the Tejo.
Fragoleto Rua da Prata 74, Baixa. Divine home-made ice cream to take away (from €1.90).
Pois Café Rua São João da Praça 93, Baixa. Eclectically furnished café with a relaxed atmosphere and plenty of international books and papers to peruse. Serves brunch, quiche (€6.50), sandwiches and daily specials (including vegetarian options). Closed Mon.
Vitaminhas & Companhia Cheap lunch stop next to Baixa-Chiado metro station, offering a variety of sandwiches, salads, soups and fresh juices. Pasta salad €3.

Restaurants

Adamastor Rua Marechal Saldanha 24. Cheerful place with some outdoor seats serving up cheap Portuguese dishes. Closed Sun. Roast chicken €6.
Arco do Castelo Rua do Chão da Feira 25. Tasty curries (from €8) are on the menu at this long-established Goan restaurant by the castle. Closed Sun.
A Tasca da Sé Rua Augusto Rosa 62. Good value little restaurant opposite the cathedral with particularly good fish dishes. Garlic prawns €9.
Esperança Rua do Norte 95, Bairro Alto. Trendy trattoria with an extensive and reasonably priced menu of pasta, pizza and risotto. Wine is also good value. Pizza from €7.50.
Jardim do Sentidos Rua da Mãe d'Agua 3. Classy vegetarian restaurant beyond Praça da Alegria with a shady garden and an appetizing menu of international dishes. Chilli €9.50.
O Cantinho do Bem Estar Rua do Norte 46, Bairro Alto. The service may be erratic, but this tiny place is great value for money – its portions feed two with ease. Cod cakes €12.50.
Rei d'Frango Calçada do Duque 5, Baixa. A bargain in the Baixa, this workers' café serves up plentiful portions of Portuguese dishes such as grilled sardines and chicken. Lunchtime dishes of the day are only €5. Closed Sun.
Restô Rua Costa do Castelo 7, Castelo. Two-in-one venue, with tapas and barbecued meat served in a buzzing courtyard, and more expensive international dishes on offer in the upstairs restaurant. Both have excellent river views. Dinner only. Steak €11.

Drinking and nightlife

The densest concentration of bars and clubs is in Bairro Alto. In summer, crowds spill out of bars and into the streets, creating a festive atmosphere. More expensive late-night action can be found in the Docas (Docklands) district, just east of the 25 de Abril bridge (train to Alcântara Mar from Cais do Sodré or tram #15), where the Doca de Alcântara and the Doca de Santo Amaro (further from the city) host waterfront bars, cafés and clubs in converted warehouses. Lisbon's gay scene centres around Praça do Príncipe Real in the north of Bairro Alto. Clubs don't really get going until at least 2am and tend to stay open till 6am. Admission fees range from €10 to €20 (usually including a drink).

Bars

A Ginjinha Largo de São Domingos 8, Baixa. The original *ginjinha* (cherry brandy) bar, this small stand-up place located in lively Largo de São Domingos is a great place to start a night out in Lisbon. *Ginjinha* €0.90.
Be You Lounge Bar Rua do Atalaia 145, Bairro Alto. The name might conjure up images of comfy sofas, but this bar is actually more of a bargain basement: grab a drink and head out to join the revellers in the street. Vodka and mixer €2.50.
Favela Chik Ruado Diário de Notícias 66, Bairro Alto. Funky and friendly little bar with great cocktails and a DJ spinning old-school tunes.
Instituto do Vinho do Porto Rua de São Pedro de Alcântara 45, Bairro Alto. Over 200 types of port, from €1 a glass. Closed Sun.
Pavilhão Chinês Rua Dom Pedro V 89, Bairro Alto. Ideal for a chic cocktail, this famous (and pricey) drinking den is decorated with a unique selection of kitsch artefacts.
Portas Largas Rua da Atalaia 105, Bairro Alto. "Big doors" is a popular spot for a pre-club *caipirinha* or two.

Clubs

Buddha Bar Rua Gare M Alcântara Ⓦwww.buddha.com.pt. The pick of the docklands nightspots, boasting a roof terrace with views of the 25 de Abril bridge.

Kapital Av 24 de Julho 68, opposite Santos station. Smart club popular with trendy (and wealthy) young Lisboetas.

Kremlin Escadinhas da Praia 5. Down on the docklands, this former clubbing destination remains the place to head for house tunes. Closed Sun.

Lux Ⓦ www.luxfragil.com. Av Infante Dom Henrique Armázem A, opposite Santa Apolónia station. The city's best and most fashionable club, often hosting top DJs. Closed Mon.

Trumps Rua da Imprensa Nacional 104b, Rato Ⓦ www.trumps.pt. The biggest gay venue in Lisbon. Closed Mon.

Entertainment

To hear some *fado* (see below), head for Bairro Alto, where many restaurants put on performances (from €15 upwards, including dinner). What's-on listings can be found in the monthly *Agenda Cultural*, available free at tourist offices, or at Ⓦ lisbon.angloinfo.com.

Fado and live music

Adega do Ribatejo Rua do Diário de Notícias 23, Bairro Alto. Small, atmospheric restaurant with nightly *fado* performances. Singers include a couple of professionals, the manager and even one of the cooks. Closed Sun. Minimum charge €15.

A Tasca do Chico Ruado Diário de Noticíias 39. Make like the locals and catch some amateur *fado* in this bar on Mon and Wed. Free entry.

Catacumbas Jazz Bar Travessa da Água da Flor 43, Bairro Alto. Popular little bar with jazz, blues and Brazilian beats concerts from Mon–Thurs.

Hot Clube de Portugal Praça da Alegria 39 Ⓦ www.hotclubedeportugal.org. Tiny basement jazz club, which hosts local and visiting artists. Closed Mon.

Music Box Rua Nova do Carvalho 24 Ⓦ www.musicboxlisboa.com. Live music venue near Cais do Sodré, with a schedule packed full of DJs and bands playing almost every musical style imaginable.

Shopping

The trendy Bairro Alto shops tend to open from early afternoon until midnight; elsewhere, opening hours are standard.

El Dorado Rua do Norte 23, Bairro Alto. Funky store with a great selection of vintage and new clothes and music.

Mercado da Ribeira Av 24 de Julho, Cais do Sodré. The city's main food market, which is also home to a variety of craft stores.

Outra Face da Lua Rua da Assunçao 22, Baixa. Vintage emporium stocking a mishmash of goodies, from clothing to toys. There's also an in-store café.

A Vida Portuguesa Rua Anchieta 11, Baixa. From tiles to sardines, if it's Portuguese, you'll find it here.

Directory

Embassies Australia, Av da Liberdade 198–2° Ⓣ 213 101 500; Canada, Av da Liberdade 196–200 Ⓣ 213 164 600; Ireland, Rua da Imprensa à Estrela 1–4° Ⓣ 213 929 440; South Africa, Av Luis Bívar 10 Ⓣ 213 535 713; UK, Rua de São Bernardo 33 Ⓣ 213 924 000; US, Av das Forças Armadas Ⓣ 217 273 300.

Exchange Main bank branches in the Baixa. Exchange office at the airport (24hr) and at Santa Apolónia station (daily 8.30am–3pm).

Hospital British Hospital, Rua Saraiva de Carvalho 46 Ⓣ 213 955 067.

Internet PT Comunicaçoes, Praça Dom Pedro IV 68, Baixa; Web C@fe, Rua do Diário de Notícias 126, Bairro Alto.

FADO

Difficult to classify but often described as falling somewhere between the blues and flamenco, the emotional and melodramatic musical genre of **fado** (literally "fate") is as typically Portuguese as sardines and Cristiano Ronaldo. *Fado* has its roots in early nineteenth-century Alfama, where it thrived until the early twentieth century, when it was subject to censorship. Despite the authorities' efforts, the genre continued to develop, and still features in the charts today thanks to a new generation of performers. Lisbon is the best place to hear *fado*, although Coimbra also has its own style (see p.943). To get the most out of a show, first visit the modern **Museu do Fado** at Largo do Chafariz de Dentro 1 (daily except Mon 10am–6pm; €3), which gives an excellent audio-guide introduction to the history of the genre and its brightest stars, including *grande dame* Amália Rodrigues and rising talent Joana Amendoeira.

Laundry Lava Neve, Rua de Alegría 37, Bairro Alto (closed Sat pm & Sun).
Left luggage Available at Oriente and Santa Apolónia stations.
Pharmacy Throughout the city, including Farmácia Estácio, Rossio Square.
Post office Praça do Comércio.
Tourist police Praça dos Restauradores.

Moving on

Train Braga (13 daily; 3hr 30min–6hr); Coimbra (hourly; 2–4hr); Évora (3 daily; 2hr 30min); Faro (6 daily; 3hr 15min–4hr); Madrid (nightly; 10hr 30min); Porto (hourly; 3hr 15min–4hr); Sintra (every 20min; 40min); Tavira (6 daily; 4hr 30min–5hr); Tomar (hourly; 2hr).
Bus Alcobaça (7 daily; 2hr); Coimbra (hourly; 2hr 20min); Évora (hourly; 1hr 30 min–2hr 30min); Faro (10 daily; 3hr 15min–4hr 30min); Lagos (7–10 daily; 4hr–4hr 30min); Madrid (4 daily; 7hr 30min); Porto (hourly; 3hr 30min–4hr); Porto Côvo (2–3 daily; 3hr 30min); Sevilla (6 weekly; 7hr); Tomar (2–4 daily; 1hr 45min–2hr); Vila Nova de Milfontes (3–7 daily; 3hr 30min–4hr).

BEACHES AROUND LISBON

The coast around Lisbon offers ample opportunities to escape from the summer heat of the capital. Half an hour south of Lisbon, dunes stretch along the **COSTA DA CAPARICA**, which the quirks of the River Tejo's currents have largely spared from pollution. Costa da Caparica is a thoroughly Portuguese resort, popular with surfers and crammed with restaurants and beach cafés, yet solitude is easy enough to find, thanks to the **transpraia** (mini-railway) that runs along the 8km of dunes in summer. The easiest way to get here is to take bus #153 from Praça de Espanha (every 20min; €2.50). Buses stop along Rua dos Pescadores by the beach, which leads to the main square, Praça da Liberdade.

Another popular seaside escape is the former fishing village of **CASCAIS**, forty minutes to the west of the city, which boasts three beaches and a campsite (see p.936). To get here, take the train from Cais do Sodré (every 20–30min; €1.70). Cascais has a particular appeal to surfers due to its proximity to Guincho beach (see box, p.925), reached by local bus, which has played host to World Surfing Championships.

SINTRA

The cool, hilltop woodland setting of **SINTRA** once attracted Moorish lords and the Portuguese kings from Lisbon during the hot summer months, and the palaces they constructed remain amongst Portugal's most spectacular attractions. Sintra is best seen on a day-trip from Lisbon, as its hotels and restaurants are pretty pricey. That said, there are certainly enough sights to keep you occupied for several days.

What to see and do

An amalgamation of three villages, Sintra can be confusing, but there are plenty of local buses connecting the sights.

Palácio Nacional

The **Palácio Nacional** (daily except Wed 10am–5.30pm; €5), about fifteen minutes' walk from the train station, is an obvious landmark, with its distinctive conical chimneys. The palace was probably in existence under the Moors, but takes its present form from the rebuilding commissioned by Dom João I and his successor, Dom Manuel, in the fourteenth and fifteenth centuries. Its style is a fusion of Gothic and the latter king's Manueline additions. The **chapel** and its adjoining chamber – its floor worn by the incessant pacing of the half-mad Afonso VI who was confined here for six years by his brother Pedro I – are well worth seeing, as is the curious Magpies Room, decorated with hundreds of paintings of the birds with the motto "Por Bem" ("For the good") in their beaks.

Quinta da Regaleira

Also within walking distance of the centre is another must-see site, the beautiful **Quinta da Regaleira** (daily: Feb, March & Oct 10am–6.30pm; April–Sept 10am–8pm; Nov–Jan 10am–5.30pm; €6, or €10 for guided visits booked in advance on ⓣ219 106 650). One of Sintra's most elaborate private estates, it lies ten minutes' walk west of the Palácio Nacional on the Seteais–Monserrate road. The house and its fantastic gardens were built at the beginning of the twentieth century by an Italian theatrical set designer for one of the richest industrialists in Portugal. One highlight is the **Initiation Well**, inspired by the initiation practices of the Knights Templar and Freemasons. The vast gardens are full of surprising delights, with chapels, follies and fountains at every turn; you could easily spend hours here.

Monserrate

Beyond Quinta da Regaleira, the road leads past a series of beautiful private estates to **Monserrate** (closed for renovation until 2010) – about an hour's walk – whose 30-hectare **garden**, filled with endless varieties of exotic trees and subtropical shrubs and plants, extends as far as the eye can see.

Moorish castle and Palácio de Pena

Two of Sintra's main sights can be reached on bus #434 – the €4.50 ticket allows you to get on and off as much as you like. Starting at the train station, the bus stops outside the Praça da República tourist office before proceeding to the ruined ramparts of the **Castelo dos Mouros** (Moorish castle; daily 9.30am–7pm; €3.50), from where the views over the town and surrounding countryside are extraordinary. Further on, the bus stops at both entrances to the immense **Pena Park**, at the top end of which rears the fabulous **Palácio de Pena** (Tues–Sun 10am–6pm; April–Sept €11, Oct–March €8), a wild, nineteenth-century fantasy of domes, towers and a drawbridge that doesn't draw. The cluttered, kitschy interior has been preserved as left by the royal family on their flight from Portugal in 1910.

Arrival and information

Train Trains run regularly to Sintra from Lisbon's Rossio station (40min).

Tourist office There's one tourist office at the station, and a larger one (daily 9am–7/8pm; ⓣ219 231 157) just off the central Praça da República.

Accommodation

Sintra's popularity keeps prices high; below are some of the cheaper options.

Piela's Av Desiderio Cambournac 1 ⓣ219 241 691. Pleasant pension in Estefania, above central Sintra. €55.

Vila Marques Rua Sotto Mayor 1 ⓣ219 030 027, ⓦwww.vilamarques.net. Old-fashioned but attractive and scrupulously clean rooms north of the Palacio Nacional. Shared bathroom €50, en-suite €60.

Eating

Adega das Caves Rua de Pendora 2. Cheap sandwiches and grilled fare just off the main square. Grilled squid €8.

Casa Piriquita Rua das Padarias 1. Cosy café just south of Praça da República, serving snacks and Sintra's famous *queijadas* (cheese cakes). Sandwiches from €3.

Estrada Velha Rua Consiglieri Pedroso 16. On the road to the Quinta da Regaleira, this good-value café serves sandwiches (from €1.50), crêpes and other snacks.

Central Portugal

The Beiras, Estremadura and Ribatejo regions that comprise central Portugal have played crucial roles in each phase of the nation's history – and the

monuments are here to prove it. The vast plains of the Beiras are dominated by **Coimbra**, an ancient university town and Portugal's former capital, perched high above the Beira Litoral. Below the Beiras lie Estremadura and Ribatejo, both comparatively small areas of fertile rolling hills, which boast an extraordinary concentration of vivid architecture and engaging towns. **Alcobaça** in Estremadura and **Tomar** in the wine-producing Ribatejo are two of the most striking, both housing famously grand religious monuments; while seaside **Nazaré** offers a relaxing escape from all that culture.

ALCOBAÇA

The pretty town of **ALCOBAÇA** is dominated by the vast, beautiful **Mosteiro de Santa Maria de Alcobaça** (daily: April–Sept 9am–6pm, Oct–March 9am–5pm; €5). From its foundation in 1147 until its dissolution in 1834, this Cistercian monastery was one of the greatest in the world. Its **church** (free) is one of the largest in Portugal, with a Baroque facade that conceals an interior stripped of most of its later adornments and restored to its original simplicity. The monastery's most precious treasures are the fourteenth-century **tombs** of Dom Pedro and Dona Inês de Castro, sculpted with phenomenal wealth of detail to illustrate the story of Pedro's love for Inês, the daughter of a Galician nobleman. Fearing Spanish influence over the Portuguese throne, Pedro's father, Afonso V, forbade their marriage, which nevertheless took place in secret. Afonso ordered his daughter-in-law's murder, after which Pedro waited for his succession to the throne in 1357 before exhuming Inês's corpse, and forcing the royal circle to acknowledge her as queen by kissing her decomposing hand. The tombs – inscribed with the motto "Até o Fim do Mundo" (Until the End of the World) – have been placed foot to foot so that on Judgement Day, the lovers may rise and immediately see one another. The monastery's most impressive room is the **kitchen**, featuring a gigantic conical chimney, and a stream tapped from the river to provide Alcobaça's famously gluttonous monks with a constant supply of fresh fish.

Arrival and information

Bus Alcobaça's bus station is 5min walk from the monastery in the centre of town, across the bridge.

Tourist office Opposite the monastery on Praça 25 de Abril (daily 10am–1pm & 2/3–6/7pm; ⓣ 262 582 377).

Accommodation and eating

Parque de Campismo Av Professor Vieira Natividade ⓣ 262 582 265. Small municipal site 10min north of the bus station. Closed Jan. €4.

Pensão Corações Unidos Rua Frei António Brandão 39 ⓣ 262 582 142. Neat, clean pension with modern bathrooms facing the monastery. The restaurant below the *pensão* serves good-value regional cooking. Double €40.

Ti Fininho Rua Frei António Brandão 34. Offers reasonably priced grilled fish and meats, omelettes, and wine by the jug.

Moving on

Bus Coimbra (1 daily; 1hr 30min); Nazaré (every 30min; 20min); Tomar (3 daily; 1hr 30min).

NAZARÉ

A curious combination of fishing village and beach resort, **NAZARÉ** retains considerable charm despite its success as a tourist hotspot. Womenfolk, often dressed in the local costume of a voluminous knee-length skirt and bright blouse topped with a headscarf, tour the streets advertising rooms for rent and selling handmade crafts and dried fruit, which adds to Nazaré's festive atmosphere. The town's main attraction is its long strip of sand, streaming away from a backdrop of craggy cliffs. Although frequent bus

connections with Alcobaça make visiting on a day-trip an easy option, Nazaré offers good-value **accommodation** in the form of private rooms (€40); the tourist office on Avenida da República (July & Aug 9am–9pm; Sept–June 9.30am–1pm & 2–6pm; ⓣ262 561 194) has a list. The village's plentiful **restaurants** dish up great seafood; head to *Cocinha da Nazaré* at Rua da Leiria 17d, a few minutes northeast of the tourist office, for some of the best (grilled squid €6).

TOMAR

Riverside **TOMAR** is famous for its spectacular headquarters of the Portuguese branch of the Knights Templar, which overlooks the town from a wooded hill. It's also an attractive town in its own right – especially during the lively **Festa dos Tabuleiros**, a week of music and dancing, with a procession of women wearing headdresses made of trays stacked high with bread or paper flowers, held the first week of July.

What to see and do

Built on a simple grid plan, Tomar's centre preserves its traditional charm, with whitewashed houses lining narrow cobbled streets. West of the central Praça da República is the former Jewish quarter, where at Rua Joaquim Jacinto 73 you'll find an excellently preserved fourteenth-century synagogue, now the **Museu Luso-Hebraicoa Abraham Zacuto** (daily 10am–1pm & 2–6pm; free), one of the few surviving synagogues in Portugal. A fifteen-minute walk uphill from the town centre, the **Convento de Cristo** (daily: June–Sept 9am–6pm; Oct–May 9am–5pm; €5) is set among pleasant gardens with excellent views of the surrounding woodland. Founded in 1162 by Gualdim Pais, first Master of the Knights Templar, it was the Order's headquarters. At the heart of the complex, surrounded by serene cloisters, is the **Charola**, the high-ceilinged, sixteen-sided temple from which the knights drew their moral conviction. The beautiful adjoining two-tiered **Principal Cloister** is one of the purest examples of the Renaissance style in Portugal.

Arrival and information

Bus and train The stations are located next to each other on Av dos Combatentes de Grande Guerra, 10min south of the town centre.
Tourist office At the top of Av Dr Cândido Madureira (April–Sept Mon–Fri 10am–7pm, Sat & Sun 10am–1pm & 2–6pm, Oct–March daily 10am–1pm & 2–6pm.

Accommodation and eating

Parque de Campismo ⓣ249 329 824. Tomar's campsite is a short walk east of Rua Marquês de Pombal. €4.
Residencial Luz Rua Serpa Pinto 144 ⓣ249 312 317, ⓦwww.residencialluz.com. Tomar's cheapest option may have seen better days, but it's centrally located with en-suite rooms. No breakfast. €32.50
Residencial União Rua Serpa Pinto 94 ⓣ249 323 161. A pleasant pension on the main street with comfortable, decent-sized rooms. €40.
Restaurante O Tabuleiro Rua Serpa Pinto 148. Friendly restaurant offering a daily menu of delicious regional and international dishes, served in large portions. *Arroz de peixe* €6.

Moving on

Bus Alcobaça (3 daily; 1hr 30min); Porto (1 daily; 4hr).
Train Coimbra (10 daily; 2hr–2hr 30min); Lisbon (15 daily; 2hr).

COIMBRA

COIMBRA was Portugal's capital from 1143 to 1255 and ranks behind only Lisbon and Porto in historic importance. Its university, founded in 1290, was the only one in Portugal until the beginning of the twentieth century. For a provincial town it has significant riches, and the many students provide Coimbra with a rather vivacious

atmosphere during term-time – especially in May, when they celebrate the end of the academic year with the **Queima das Fitas**, a symbolic tearing or burning of their gowns and faculty ribbons followed by some serious partying. This is when you're most likely to hear the Coimbra *fado*, distinguished from the Lisbon version by its mournful pace and complex lyrics. During the summer months, the atmosphere is rather more subdued.

What to see and do

Old Coimbra sits on a hill on the right bank of the River Mondego, with the university crowning its summit. The main buildings of the **Old University** (March–Oct daily 9am–7pm; Nov–Feb Mon–Fri 9am–5pm, Sat & Sun 10am–4pm; €6), dating from the sixteenth century, are set around a courtyard (entrance free) dominated by a Baroque clocktower and a statue of João III. The **chapel** is covered with *azulejos* and intricate decoration, but takes second place to the **library**, a Baroque fantasy with *trompe-l'oeil* ceilings presented to the faculty by João V in the early eighteenth century. Halfway down the hill towards the centre stands the **Sé Velha** (Old Cathedral; Mon–Thurs 10am–1pm & 2–6pm, Fri 10am–1pm, Sat 10am–5pm; free), a solid and simple construction that's one of Portugal's most important Romanesque buildings.

Restraint and simplicity certainly aren't the chief qualities of the flamboyant **Igreja de Santa Cruz** (Mon–Fri 7.30am–6.30pm, Sat 7.30am–12.30pm & 2–7.30pm, Sun 8.30am–12.30pm & 4–7.30pm; €2.50), at the bottom of the hill on Praça 8 de Maio. It houses the tombs of Portugal's first kings, Afonso Henriques and Sancho I, and an elaborately carved pulpit, works which hark back to Coimbra's time as the site of a major sculptural school in the sixteenth century.

For attractive views of the city, cross the river and climb upwards to the monastery of **Santa Clara-a-Nova**, in a serene hilltop spot. The church can be visited for free, while guided visits to the beautiful cloister and low choir cost €2 (cloister only €1.50). Built in 1650, the convent is now home to both the tomb of former king Dom Dinis's wife Isabel and, more surprisingly, an army barracks.

Other areas of interest include the epicentre of the students' social scene, **Praça da República**, a ten-minute walk from Praça 8 de Maio up Rua Olímpio Nicolau Rui Fernandes and its continuation, and the rambling **Botanic Garden** (Mon–Sat: April–Sept 9am–8pm; Oct–March 9am–5.30pm; €1.50) which sits in the shadow of the sixteenth-century **aqueduct** to the east of Praça da República.

Arrival and information

Train Intercity trains stop at Coimbra B, 3km north of the city, from where there are frequent connecting services to Coimbra A in the town centre.
Bus The main bus station is on Av Fernão de Magalhães, 15min walk from the centre – turn right out of the bus station and head down the main road.
City transport The main hub for Coimbra's local buses is Av Emídio Navarro near train station A. A single journey paid for on board costs €1.50; 3 tickets bought in advance at a newsstand cost €2. Buses 1, 3, 7, 8, 10 and 11 run from here to Praça da República.
Tourist office Opposite the bridge on Largo da Portagem (Mon–Fri 9.30am–1pm & 2–5.30pm, Sat & Sun 10am–1pm & 2.30–5.30pm; ⓣ 239 488 120, ⓦ www.turismodocentro.pt/coimbra).

Accommodation

Grande Hostel de Coimbra Rua Antero de Quental 196 ⓣ 239 108 212, ⓦ www.grandehostelcoimbra.com. Hippyish hostel near Praça da República, set in a big old house with a garden, lounge and kitchen. A good place to meet fellow travellers. Dorms €18, double €40.
Pousada de Juventude Rua Henrique Seco 14 ⓣ 239 822 955, ⓦ www.pousadasjuventude.pt. Basic but cheap hostel 10min north of Praça

da República. Buses #7 and #29 from Av Emídio Navarro pass close by. Dorms €12, twin €28.

Residencial Antunes Rua Castro Matoso 8 ⓣ239 854 720, ⓦresidencialantunes.planetaclix.pt. Old-fashioned rooms in a prime location near the aqueduct. €45.

Residencial Domus Rua Adelino Veiga 62 ⓣ239 828 584, ⓦwww.residencialdomus.com. Friendly place with clean but faded en-suite rooms. €40.

Eating, drinking and nightlife

Most of the town's restaurants can be found tucked away in the alleys between Largo da Portagem – the place to head for cafés – and Praça 8 de Maio.

Adega Paço do Conde Rua Paço do Conde 1. Atmospheric, locally renowned *churrasqueira* serving tasty barbecued meat and fish. Meat and vegetable skewer €5.

Associação Académica de Coimbra Praça da República. If you can befriend a student and tag along, you'll get access to the outdoor union bar, a lively place serving snacks and bargain drinks (first beer €0.60, €1 after that).

Café Tropical Praça da República. A favourite haunt of students, with outdoor tables and cheap drinks. Closed Sun.

Jardim da Manga Rua Olímpio Nicolau Rui Fernandes. Self-service café serving up good-value meals in a pretty spot.

Shots Bar Rua da Manutenção 30. Pint-sized place popular with international students specializing in – you've guessed it – shots (5 for €5).

Via Latina Rua Almeida Garrett 1. Popular club open Tues–Sat from midnight onwards.

Moving on

Train Lisbon (hourly; 2–3hr); Porto (hourly; 1hr 20min–2hr); Tomar (hourly; 2hr 30min).

Bus Alcobaça (2 daily; 1hr 30min); Lisbon (hourly; 2hr 20min); Porto (8–10 daily; 1hr 30min).

Northern Portugal

Porto, the country's second largest city, is an attractive and convenient centre from which to begin an exploration of the region. Magnificently set on a rocky cliff astride the River Douro, it is perhaps most famous for the port-producing suburb of **Vila Nova de Gaia**, supplied by vineyards further inland along the river. The **Douro Valley** is traced by a spectacular rail route, with branch lines following valleys north along the River Tâmega to **Amarante** and along the Corgo to the pretty town of **Vila Real** – a good base for exploration of the Parque Natural do Alvão, and the main centre for transport connections into the isolated rural region of **Trás-os-Montes** – literally "behind the mountains". In the north-west, the **Minho**, considered by many to be the most beautiful part of the country, is a lush wilderness of rolling mountain forests and rugged coastlines (the Costa Verde), with some of the most unspoilt beaches in Europe. A quietly conservative region, its towns have a special charm and beauty, amongst them the religious centre of **Braga**, and the self-proclaimed birthplace of the nation, **Guimarães**, both of which can be visited by day-trip from Porto, but also make good bases from which to explore the rest of the Minho.

PORTO

Capital of the north, **PORTO** (sometimes called Oporto in English) is very different from Lisbon – unpretentious and unashamedly commercial, yet extremely welcoming. As the local saying goes: "Coimbra sings; Braga prays; Lisbon shows off; and Porto works." Already possessing considerable appeal, the city received something of a makeover thanks to funding received for Euro 2004, and now boasts an efficient metro system, state-of-the-art football stadium and a top concert venue, the Casa da Música.

What to see and do

The waterfront Ribeira district is Porto's historic heart, with narrow,

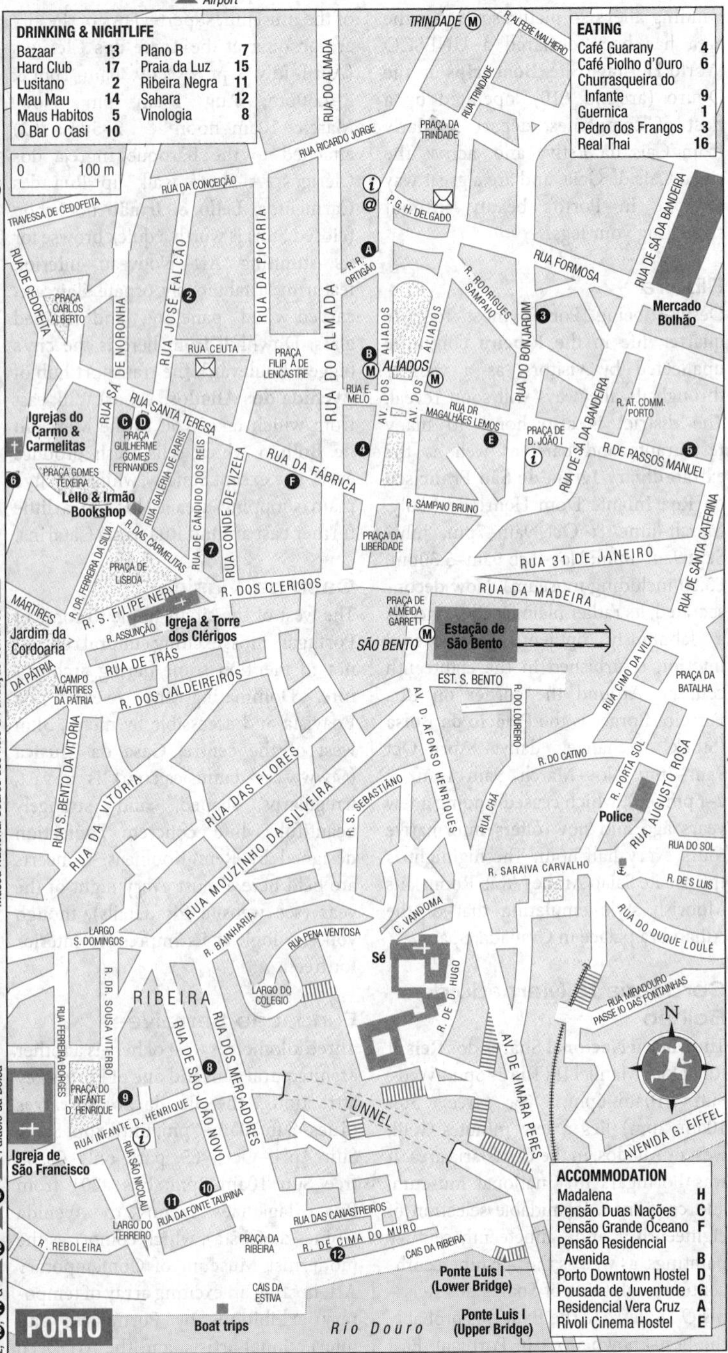

Airport
DRINKING & NIGHTLIFE
Bazaar 13
Hard Club 17
Lusitano 2
Mau Mau 14
Maus Habitos 5
O Bar O Casi 10
Plano B 7
Praia da Luz 15
Ribeira Negra 11
Sahara 12
Vinologia 8
EATING
Café Guarany 4
Café Piolho d'Ouro 6
Churrasqueira do Infante 9
Guernica 1
Pedro dos Frangos 3
Real Thai 16
ACCOMMODATION
Madalena H
Pensão Duas Nações C
Pensão Grande Oceano F
Pensão Residencial Avenida B
Porto Downtown Hostel D
Pousada de Juventude G
Residencial Vera Cruz A
Rivoli Cinema Hostel E
0 100 m
TRINDADE
ALIADOS
SÃO BENTO
Mercado Bolhão
Igrejas do Carmo & Carmelitas
Lello & Irmão Bookshop
Igreja & Torre dos Clérigos
Jardim da Cordoaria
Estação de São Bento
Police
Sé
RIBEIRA
Igreja de São Francisco
TUNNEL
Ponte Luís I (Lower Bridge)
Ponte Luis I (Upper Bridge)
Boat trips
Rio Douro
Bus Station
Estação de Campanhã
Port Lodges, 16 & 17
H & Vila Nova de Gaia
PORTO

winding alleys so picturesque that the area has been declared a UNESCO World Heritage Site. **Boat trips** up the Douro (around €10), operated by a host of companies, depart regularly from Cais da Estiva and, across the river, Cais de Gaia, and are a great way to take in Porto's beauty without stretching your legs.

Ribeira

Despite being Porto's most touristy quarter, life in the **Ribeira** continues unaffected by visitors, as a wander through its alleyways will soon reveal. The district is also home to many restaurants and bars, as well as the extraordinary **Igreja de São Francisco** on Rua Infante Dom Henrique (daily: March–June & Oct 9am–7pm; July–Sept 9am–8pm; Nov–Feb 9am–5.30pm; €3.50 including museum). Now deconsecrated, its rather plain facade conceals a fabulously opulent, gold-covered interior, refurbished in the eighteenth century. Around the corner on Rua Ferreira Borges is the **Palácio da Bolsa** (Stock Exchange; daily: April–Oct 9am–7pm Nov–March 9am–1pm & 2–6pm; €6), which ceased trading a few years ago and now offers informative tours every half-hour. The highlight is the ornate Salão Arabe (Arab Room), its Moorish style emulating that of the Alhambra palace in Granada, Spain.

Cordoaria to Mercado de Bolhão

The **Museu Nacional Soares dos Reis** at Rua Dom Manuel II (Tue 2–6pm, Wed–Sun 10am–6pm; €3, free Sun 10am–2pm) lies a few minutes' walk west of Aliados, in the Cordoaria area. It was Portugal's first national museum, and contains a formidable selection of eighteenth- and nineteenth-century paintings, as well as the late nineteenth-century sculptures of Soares dos Reis – his *O Desterro* ("The Exile") is probably the best-known work in Portugal. East of the museum, superb views of the city are on offer at the **Torre dos Clérigos** (April–July, Sept & Oct 9.30am–1pm & 2–7.30pm; Aug 10am–7pm; Nov–March 10am–noon & 2–5pm; €2) attached to the Baroque Ingreja dos Clérigos. A short walk up Rua das Carmelitos, **Lello & Irmão** bookshop (closed Sun) is worth a quick browse for its stunning Art Nouveau interior, featuring a fabulously ornate staircase, carved-wood panelling and stained glass. Downhill from here is the city's biggest boulevard, the transport hub of **Avenida dos Aliados**, a short walk east from which takes you to the **Mercado de Bolhão** which sells fresh produce every day except Sunday, while the city's main shopping area is located a little further east around Rua Santa Catarina.

Casa da Música

The west of the city is home to some of Portugal's most exciting cultural centres, not to mention some daring architecture. Dominating the Avenida da Boavista and accessible by metro, 3km west of the centre, **Casa da Música** (Ⓦwww.casadamusica.com) is a vast, irregularly shaped, and strangely beautiful white concrete confection designed by Rem Koolhaas. Concerts are held here almost every night of the year (see website for details), though you can look at its impressive interior for free.

Fundação Serralves

Three kilometres west of here is another architectural gem and one of Porto's key attractions, the **Fundação Serralves** (Tues–Sun 10am–7pm, until 8pm Sat & Sun April–Oct); €5, park only €2.50; free Sun 10am–2pm; bus #201 from Rua Magalhães Lemos to Avenida Gomes da Costa), which comprises the modernist Museum of Contemporary Art, hosting an exciting array of temporary exhibitions by Portuguese and international artists, and the Art Deco

Serralves Villa, set in a vast, beautiful park. The **park** too is worth visiting on a sunny day, encompassing everything from formal gardens to wild woods, and even a farm featuring species from northern Portugal.

Foz do Douro

The coastline at **Foz** makes an easy escape from the city, reached via bus #500 from outside São Bento station. For much of the year the Atlantic Ocean is too chilly for all but the most hardy swimmers, but the beaches fill up with sun-worshippers once summer rolls round. Foz is also home to a buzzing nightlife scene revolving around its numerous beach bars.

Vila Nova de Gaia

South of the river and essentially a city in its own right, **Vila Nova de Gaia** (often referred to as Gaia) is dominated by the port trade. From the Ribeira, the names of the various companies, spelled out in neon letters above the terracotta roofs of the wine lodges, leave you in no doubt as to what awaits you. You can walk to Gaia across the **Ponte Luís I**: the most direct route to the lodges is across the lower level from the Cais da Ribeira, but taking the metro across the top level to the Jardim do Morro stop has the bonus of breathtaking views. The lodges offer **tours**, which generally explain the histories of both the company and of port production, and end in a tasting. Companies such as Croft, Graham's and Taylor's offer free tours while others, such as Sandeman, charge up to €4. Tours conclude with tastings of one or two ports, with more expensive options such as vintage ports available for an extra fee. As a general rule, the lodges on the riverfront charge the most. The tourist information kiosk on Avenida Diogo Leite has the helpful *Caves do Vinho do Porto* leaflet, which outlines timetables and prices of tours. If all this sampling whets your appetite, head to *Vinologia* (see p.949) to learn and taste more.

Arrival and information

Air From the Francisco Sá Carneiro airport, 10km north of the city, take metro line E (€1.95, including purchase of rechargeable Andante card) to the centre. Services runs until 1am.

Train Most trains from the south stop at the distant Estação de Campanhã; you may need to change here for a connection to the central Estação de São Bento (5min). Metro line B will also take you into the centre from Campanhã.

Bus The main bus terminal (Rede-Expressos) is on Rua Alexandre Herculano, a short walk east of São Bento.

Tourist office The largest and most helpful of three central tourist offices is just north of Av dos Aliados on Rua Clube dos Fenianos 25 (summer daily 9am–7pm; winter Mon–Fri 9am–5.30pm, Sat & Sun 9am–4.30pm; ⓣ 222 393 472, ⓦ www.portoturismo.pt).

Tourist passes All tourism offices sell the Porto Card, which offers free public transport and free or discounted entry to most of the city's sights. Available in 1, 2, and 3-day versions (€8.50, €13.50 and €17.50 respectively).

PORT

If you thought port was just an after-dinner tipple reserved for formal occasions, think again. Port wine comes in a variety of types and ages, as you'll discover on an afternoon tour of Gaia's port lodges. The relatively little-known **white ports** are served as an aperitif, and can be dry or sweet; another refreshing option is Croft's new "Pink", one of the the first **rosé** ports on the market. After dinner come either tawny or ruby ports: nutty-tasting **tawnies** are made from a blend of different barrel-aged wines, while deep red **rubies** age in the bottle. Further varieties include Late Bottled Vintage (**LBV**), made from good-quality grapes gathered in a single harvest and aged for five years, and the crème de la crème, **Vintage** port, which uses only the best grapes from a particularly fine harvest.

Internet Onweb, Praça Humberto Delgado 291. Just off Av dos Aliados.
Tourist police Rua Clube dos Fenianos 11.

City transport

Tickets The Andante card covers metro, tram, the funicular from opposite the Ponte Luis I to Praça da Batalha, and most bus lines. It costs €0.50, added to the price of your first ticket, and is available at the airport, in all metro stations and in the main tourist office. Once purchased, it can be recharged with single journeys or 24hr passes. Cards must be validated for each trip.
Metro Porto's sleek, five-line metro system (daily 6.30am–1am) is cheap and efficient. The lines meet at Trindade station, which also houses an Andante shop. A single trip in the centre costs €0.95, and a 24hr pass, valid on all forms of transport, costs €3.35.
Bus Single bus tickets can be purchased onboard for €1.45, but the Andante scheme offers better value.
Taxis Taxis are cheap and plentiful; two useful ranks are located at Praça da Ribeira and the Rotonda da Boa Vista, near Casa da Música.

Accommodation

Well-located, good-value rooms are on offer in the streets to the east and west of Av dos Aliados. There are also some bargain rooms around lively Praça da Batalha, east of Estação de São Bento. In addition to *residenciais* and *pensões*, Porto now boasts a number of central, well-equipped backpacker hostels.

Hostels

Porto Downtown Hostel Praça Guilherme Gomes Fernandes 66, 1° ⓣ220 018 094, ⓦwww.portodowntownhostel.com. Friendly, spotlessly clean and central place with ten-bed dorms and three double rooms. There's also an inviting lounge, kitchen facilities and free internet. Dorms €19, doubles €40.
Pousada de Juventude Rua Paulo Gama 552 ⓣ226 177 257, ⓦwww.pousadasjuventude.pt. Large, clean and modern, with a great view of the mouth of the Douro. It's 20min from the centre: take bus #207 from São Bento or #500 from Casa da Música. Dorms €15, twin €35.
Rivoli Cinema Hostel Rua Dr Magalhães Lemos 83 ⓣ220 174 634, ⓦrivolicinemahostel.blogspot.com. Efficiently run cinema-themed hostel which offers dorms and spacious twin rooms. There's also a roof terrace, with plans for a swimming pool. Dorms €19, twins €42.

Pensions and hotels

Pensão Duas Nações Praça Guilherme Gomes Fernandes 59 ⓣ222 081 616, ⓦwww.duasnacoes.com.pt. A deservedly popular option, with bright, decently sized rooms, most of which are en suite. No breakfast. €25–32.
Pensão Grande Oceano Rua da Fábrica 45 ⓣ222 038 770, ⓦwww.pensaograndeoceano.com. The en-suite rooms may be a little more faded than other options, but the price and location make it a decent standby. One room sleeps up to five. No breakfast. €35.
Pensão Residencial Avenida Av dos Aliados 141 ⓣ222 009 551, ⓦpensaoavenida.planetaclix.pt. Sparklingly clean rooms with smart, modern bathrooms. €45.
Residencial Vera Cruz Rua Ramalho Ortigão 14 ⓣ223 323 396, ⓦwww.residencialveracruz.com. More like a small hotel than a *residencial*, this place is just off Aliados and offers smart, well-kept rooms and a great breakfast. Pay in cash to get the best rates. €45.

Campsite

Madalena Rua do Cerro ⓣ227 122 520, ⓦwww.orbitur.com. Located 10km from the centre of Gaia, this site is well shaded and close to the beach. Take bus #906 from São Bento. €6.

Eating

Porto's culinary speciality is the mighty *francesinha* – a gutbusting sandwich of steak, ham and *Linguiça* sausage, the whole covered in a layer of molten cheese and a spicy beer and tomato sauce; an acquired taste, *tripas* (tripe) is also strangely popular. Restaurants offer good value for money, particularly the workers' cafés, which usually offer a set menu at lunchtime (but close around 7.30pm and at weekends). Prime areas are Rua do Almada and Rua de São Bento da Vitória. For international options, head to the trendy riverside Cais de Gaia complex which offers Italian, Indian and other world cuisines.
Café Guarany Av dos Aliados 85–89. Historical café-restaurant with a classy atmosphere and regular live music. Coffee and cake €2.60.
Café Piolho D'Ouro Praça de Parada Letão. Near the university, this diner is popular with students and serves incredibly cheap food throughout the day, before morphing into a packed bar at night. Closed Sun. Burger €4.
Churrasqueira do Infante Praça Infante Dom Henrique. A wide selection of good-value grilled meat and fish makes this *churrasqueira* a great budget option in the Ribeira. Closed Sun. Grilled hake €8.

Guernica Rua de Miguel Bombarda 598. Classy, modern restaurant serving delicious and different international dishes, such as wild boar and seafood pasta (€12); take bus #201 to Jardim do Palácio do Cristal.

Pedro dos Frangos Rua do Bonjardim 219. Cheap and cheerful café serving spit-roasted chicken. Open until 7pm; closed Tues.

Real Thai Cais de Gaia 250. Delicious Thai food in a smart contemporary setting with beautiful views. Good for vegetarians. Vegetable red curry €9.50.

Drinking and nightlife

The Ribeira area offers a fairly laid-back drinking scene, while Cais de Gaia is a good option for sophisticated sipping. More lively late-night bars can be found around Rua de Cândido dos Reis, near Aliados. Most of the city's big clubs are in the outlying Matosinhos district or near Foz.

Bars

Lusitano Rua José Falcão 137. Fun and lively mixed gay/straight bar.

Maus Habitos Rua Passos Manuel 178. Soak up some culture as you drink at this multipurpose venue, with art exhibitions, live bands and DJs.

O Bar O Cais Rua da Fonte Taurina 2. Relaxed bar with a clientele as varied as the soundtrack. Serves a variety of foreign beers, and jugs of cheap sangria.

Plano B Rua de Cândido dos Reis 30. Trendy late-night spot with live DJs playing the latest electronica.

Praia da Luz Av do Brazil, Foz. Classy beachside bar strewn with outdoor sofas and sunloungers, ideal for a relaxed sunset cocktail.

Ribeira Negra Rua da Fonte Taurina 66. Lively, inexpensive bar popular with students.

Sahara Cais da Estiva 4. Cosy shisha bar serving a plethora of teas and cocktails.

Vinologia Rua de São João Nov. 46. Innovative bar offering port tastings with knowledgeable, friendly staff. Even an expert could learn a lot here.

Clubs

Porto's clubs are outside the city centre; catch the #500 to Foz or one of the night buses from Aliados or Casa da Música if you can't afford a taxi.

Bazaar Rua de Monchique 13. Out near Foz, this fashionable split-level club plays mostly house music.

Hard Club Cais de Gaia, Vila Nova de Gaia Ⓦwww.hard-club.com. Porto's main venue for international DJs. Check the website for details, as music varies from night to night.

Mau Mau Rua do Outeiro 4, Foz. Popular with locals, this club offers a mixture of house and R&B, with occasional guest DJs. Wed–Sat until 4am.

Moving on

Train Braga (1hr 15min–1hr 40min); Coimbra (hourly; 1hr 20min–2hr 30min); Guimarães (13 daily; 1hr 30min); Lisbon (hourly; 3hr–3hr 30min).

Bus Braga (hourly; 1hr 30min); Coimbra (8–10 daily; 1hr 30min); Guimarães (12 daily; 1hr 40 min); Lisbon (hourly; 3hr 30min).

BRAGA

Capital of the Minho, **BRAGA** is also Portugal's religious capital – the scene of spectacular **Easter celebrations** with torchlight processions. But it's not all pomp and ceremony; it's also a lively university town, with a compact and pretty historical centre.

What to see and do

Rua Andrade Corvo leads from the train station to the centre, entered via the sixteenth-century **Arco da Porta Nova**.

The City

Just beyond here lies the oldest cathedral in the country, the extraordinary **Sé** (daily 8am–6.30pm; free), which dates back to 1070 and encompasses Gothic, Renaissance and Baroque styles. The most impressive areas of the Sé, the Gothic chapels – most notably the Capela dos Reis (Kings' Chapel), built to house the tombs of Henry of Burgundy and his wife Theresa, the cathedral's founders – may only be visited by guided tour (9am–noon & 2–6.30pm; €2 including museum). Near the cathedral is the **Archbishop's Palace** (Mon–Fri 9am–12.30pm & 2–6pm; free), a great fortress-like building which now houses university offices and a library. Just behind the palace lies the lovely **Jardim de Santa Bárbara**, an oasis of topiary and rose gardens. Braga's main square, the buzzing, café-lined **Praça da República**, is a short walk northwest of the garden.

Bom Jesus do Monte

Braga's real gem is **Bom Jesus do Monte**, set on a wooded hillside 3km above the city – its glorious ornamental stairway is one of Portugal's best-known images. A monumental place of pilgrimage, Bom Jesus was created by Braga's archbishop in the early eighteenth century. The #2 bus runs from in front of the Cristal Farmácia on Avenida da Liberdade in Braga to a car park next to the stairway twice every hour (€1.20). Turn left out of the car park to ascend the wide, tree-lined staircases and watch Bom Jesus's simple allegory unfold. Each landing holds a small fountain and a chapel containing tableau depictions of the life of Christ, leading up to the Crucifixion scene on the altar of the Neoclassical church which sits atop the staircase. The first fountain symbolizes the Wounds of Christ, the next five the Senses, and the final three represent the Virtues. Beyond the church are wooded gardens, grottoes and a number of hotels and restaurants.

Arrival and information

Train Braga's train station is almost 1km from the centre, down Rua Andrade Corvo.

Bus The bus station, a regional hub, is east of the centre on Av General Norton de Matos.

Tourist office At the corner of Praça da República and Av da Liberdade (Mon–Fri 9am–6.30pm, Sat & Sun 9am–12.30pm & 2–5.30pm; ⓣ 253 262 550, ⓦ www.cm-braga.pt).

Accommodation

Albergaria Senhora a Branca Largo da Senhora a Branca 58 ⓣ 253 269 938, ⓦ www.albergariasrabranca.pt. Smart, well-kept option close to the town centre. €50.

Campismo Parque da Ponte ⓣ 253 273 355. Cheap, basic campsite 2km south of central Braga. Bus #9, #18 or #56 from Av da Liberdade. €4.

Pousada de Juventude Rua de Santa Margarida 6 ⓣ 253 616 163, ⓦ www.pousadasjuventude.pt. Fairly basic but good value, with eight-bed dorms and en-suite twins. Dorms €15, twin €25.

Residencial Dora Largo da Senhora a Branca 92–94 ⓣ 253 200 180, ⓦ www.residencialdora.com. Close to Praça da República, this excellent-value option has a dozen sunny en-suite rooms, with breakfast provided by the owners' next-door bakery. Double €35.

Eating and drinking

A Brasileira Largo Barão de São Marinho. Bustling café with pavement tables serving drinks and light meals. Sandwich €3.

Churrasqueira da Sé Rua dom Paio Mendes 25. Popular little grill restaurant dishing up Portuguese classics such as sardines (€6.50).

Gosto Superior Praça Mousinho de Albuquerque 29. Northeast of Praça da República, this popular vegetarian restaurant dishes up delicious, cheap daily specials and home-made desserts in a trendy but relaxed environment. Lunch only on Sun. Lunch €5.50 including drink.

Moving on

Bus Guimarães (hourly; 30min–1hr); Porto (hourly; 1hr 20min); Vila do Gerês (Mon–Fri hourly, Sat & Sun 6 daily; 1hr 30min).

Train Lisbon (13 daily; 3hr 30min–4hr 30min); Porto (hourly; 1hr 15min–1hr 40min).

GUIMARÃES

The first capital of Portugal, **GUIMARÃES** remains an atmospheric and beautiful university town. The town's

PARQUE NACIONAL DA PENEDA-GERÊS

Encompassing mountains, valleys and moors, Portugal's only designated national park is a heaven for nature lovers, with ample opportunities for hiking, as well as more extreme sports. The main bases for exploration are the spa town of **Vila do Gerês** and **Ponte da Barca**, where the park's Regional Development Association, Adere-PG, is located. It's worth visiting them at Largo da Misericordia 10 (Mon–Fri 9am–12.30pm & 2.30–6pm) or online at ⓦ www.adere-pg.pt for information on walking routes and accommodation, including a booking service. Vila do Gerês is easily reached by bus from Braga, though to get to Ponte da Barca you'll need your own transport.

chief attraction is the hilltop **castle** (daily 9.30am–12.30pm & 2–5.30pm; free), whose square keep and seven towers are an enduring symbol of the emergent Portuguese nation. Built by the Countess of Mumadona and extended by Henry of Burgundy, it became the stronghold of his son, Afonso Henriques, Portugal's first independent king. Afonso launched the Reconquest from Guimarães, which was replaced by Coimbra as the capital city in 1143.

Other key sights include the **Archbishop's Palace** (daily except Mon 9.30am–12.30pm & 2–5.30pm; €3, free Sun 10am–2pm) near the castle, a fifteenth-century building which was perfectly restored and used as a presidential residence for Salazar, Portugal's former dictator; and the **Igreja de Nossa Senhora da Oliveira** on Largo da Oliveira (7.15am–noon & 3.30–7.30pm; free), a beautiful convent church founded by Countess Mumadona, in the picturesque medieval centre. The pretty **Praça de Santiago** is a popular spot for an alfresco coffee during the day, and comes alive again at night as its bars (such as *Tunel* at no. 29) fill with students.

Arrival and information

Bus Guimarães's bus station is 15min walk west of town in a vast shopping centre. Follow Av Conde de Margaride to reach the town centre.
Train The train station is south of town, connected to the centre by Av D. Afonso Henriques.
Tourist office On the corner of Av D. Afonso Henriques and Alameda de São Damaso (Mon–Fri 9.30am–6.30pm, Sat 10am–6pm, Sun 10am–1pm; ⓣ 253 412 450, ⓦ www.guimaraesturismo.com); plus in Praça de Santiago (Mon–Fri 9.30am–6.30pm, Sat 10am–6pm, Sun 10am–1pm; ⓣ 253 518 790).

Accommodation and eating

Cozinha Regional Santiago Praça de Santiago. Lovely little restaurant offering regional specialities at fair prices, set in a pretty square.
Pousada de Juventude Largo da Cidade ⓣ 253 421 380, ⓦ www.pousadasjuventude.pt. Stylish new hostel with excellent facilities: the best-value accommodation in town. Dorms €13, twin €34.
Residencial das Trinas Rua das Trinas 29 ⓣ 253 517 358, ⓦ www.residencialtrinas.com. Another good option in the town centre, with clean, comfortable en-suite rooms. Double €30, twin €35.

Moving on

Train Porto (hourly; 1hr 30min).
Bus Braga (hourly; 30min–1hr); Coimbra (2–6 daily; 2hr).

THE DOURO RAIL ROUTE

The Douro Valley, a narrow, winding gorge for the majority of its route, offers some of the most spectacular scenery in Portugal. The **Douro Rail Route**, which joins the river about 60km inland and then sticks to it across the country, is one of those journeys that needs no justification other than the trip itself.

Porto is a good place to begin a trip, though there are also regular connections along the line as far as **Peso da Régua**; beyond Régua, there are less frequent connections to **Tua** and **Pocinho**, which marks the end of the line. The trip from Porto to Pocinho takes 3hr 15min (€10.75), but the best way to experience the rail route is to take one of the branch lines which lead away from the main track at **Livração**, Regua and Tua.

Amarante

At **Livração**, about an hour from Porto, the Tâmega line cuts off for the lovely mountain town of **AMARANTE**. The journey is spectacular, the single-carriage train struggling uphill through pine woods and vineyards, with the river visible like a piece of lapis lazuli far below. Amarante is a pleasant place to stop, with much of its history revolving around the thirteenth-century hermit **Gonçalo**, the Portuguese equivalent of St Valentine, who is credited with founding just about everything in town. Although it has a nice church and unusual modernist museum, the main attraction is the riverside setting, the peaceful atmosphere and picturesque old streets.

Note that there are just two **trains** a day from Porto to Amarante in high season. The **tourist office** (July–Sept 9am–7pm; Oct–June 9am–12.30pm & 2–5.30pm) is on Alameda Teixeira de Pascoaes. Good, cheap **rooms** can be found at *Residencial A Raposeira*, Largo António Cândido 53 (ⓣ255 432 221; €35); for **food**, try the locally renowned *Adega A Quelha* on Rua de Olivença.

Vila Real

Shortly after Livração, the main line finally reaches the Douro and heads upstream to **Peso da Régua**, the depot through which all port wine must pass on its way to Porto. From here, the narrow-gauge Corgo train line branches off through the mountains destined for **VILA REAL**. The gateway to Trás-os-Montes – and the closest this rural province gets to a city – Vila Real is a lively little spot with an invitingly laid-back atmosphere and some surprisingly sophisticated shopping. It also makes a great base for exploration of the nearby **Parque Natural do Alvão**, a mountainous park containing an impressive variety of flora and fauna given its petite size (only 72 sq km). Also close to Vila Real, reached by bus #1 from Rua Gonçalo Cristóvão (direction UTAD; ask driver where to get off), is the **Palacio de Mateus** (March–May & Oct 9am–1pm & 2–6pm; June–Sept 9am–7pm; Nov–Feb 10am–1pm & 2–5pm; house and gardens €7.50, gardens only €4.50), instantly recognizable as the house depicted on labels of Mateus Rosé wine. This palatial baroque residence can be visited by guided tour, and is set in a well-tended formal garden.

Vila Real's **tourist office** (June–Sept Mon–Fri 9.30am–7pm, Sat & Sun 9.30am–12.30pm & 2–6pm; Oct–May Mon–Sat 9.30am–12.30pm & 2–6pm) is at Av Carvalho Araújo 94. The best-value **accommodation** in the centre of Vila Real is the charming, well-kept *Residencial Real* at Rua Central 5 (ⓣ259 325 879; €40), with the bonus of breakfast in the downstairs *pastelaria*. Other options are the campsite, fifteen minutes northeast of the centre up Av 1 de Maio (ⓣ259 324 724), and the *Pousada de Juventude* 1km northeast of town on Rua Dr Manuel Cardona (ⓣ259 373 193, ⓦwww.pousadasjuventude.pt; dorms €10, twins €22–25). The bulk of the town's **restaurants** are on Rua Teixeira de Sousa; a good budget option is *Churrasqueira Real* at no. 14 (half a roast chicken €4.50).

Southern Portugal

The huge, sparsely populated plains of the **Alentejo**, southeast of Lisbon, are overwhelmingly agricultural, dominated by vast cork plantations. This impoverished province is divided into large estates that provide nearly half of the world's cork but only a meagre living for its rural inhabitants. Visitors to the Alentejo often head for **Évora**, the province's dominant and most historic city. But the **Alentejo coast**, the Costa Azul, is a breath of fresh air after the stifling plains of the inland landscape, and offers a low-key alternative to the busy Algarve.

With its long, sandy beaches and picturesque rocky coves, the southern coast of the **Algarve** is the most visited region in the country. West of **Faro**, the region's capital, you'll find the classic postcard images of the Algarve – a series of tiny bays and coves, broken up by rocky outcrops and fantastic grottoes, which reach their most spectacular around the resort of **Lagos**. To the east of Faro lie the less-developed sandy offshore islets, **the Ilhas** – which front the coastline for some 25 miles – and the lower-key towns of **Olhão** and **Tavira**. In summer it is wise to book accommodation in advance, as the Algarve is a popular package holiday destination.

ÉVORA

ÉVORA, a UNESCO World Heritage Site, is one of the most attractive towns in Portugal. The Romans were in occupation for four centuries and the Moors, who settled for just as long, left their stamp in the tangle of narrow alleys that rise steeply among the whitewashed houses. Most of the monuments, however, date from the fourteenth to the sixteenth centuries, when, with royal encouragement, the city was one of the leading centres of Portuguese art and architecture.

What to see and do

The **Templo Romano** in the central square is the best-preserved Roman temple in Portugal, its stark remains consisting of a small platform supporting more than a dozen granite columns with a marble entablature. Next to the temple lies the church of the **Convento dos Lóios**. The convent is now a luxury *pousada*, but the church (Tues–Sun 9.30am–12.30pm & 2–5pm; €3), dedicated to São João Evangelista, contains beautiful *azulejos* and an ossuary under the floor. Nearby, the Romanesque **cathedral** (daily 9am–12.30pm & 2–5pm, cloisters and museum €3; museum closed Mon), was begun in 1186, about twenty years after the reconquest of Évora from the Moors. The most memorable sight in town is the **Capela dos Ossos** (daily 9am–1pm & 2.30–5.30pm; €1.50) in the church of **São Francisco**, just south of Praça do Giraldo. A gruesome reminder of mortality, the walls and pillars of this chilling chamber are covered with the bones of more than five thousand monks; an inscription over the door reads, *Nós ossos que aqui estamos, Pelos vossos esperamos* – "We bones here are waiting for your bones". Just below the church lies a beautiful, shady park with a duck pond and a small café.

Arrival and information

Bus and train Évora's bus and train stations are 1km west of the old town, a 20min walk from the central Praça do Giraldo.

Tourist office Praça do Giraldo (May–Sept Mon–Fri 9am–7pm, Sat & Sun 9.30am–12.30pm & 2–5.30pm; Oct–April 9.30am–12.30pm; ⓣ 266 730 030).

Accommodation

Évora's tourist appeal pushes accommodation prices over the norm. In addition to the places listed below, there are also some attractive *turismo rural* properties in the nearby countryside; the tourist office has details.

Parque de Campismo Estrada de Alcáçovas ⓣ 266 705 190. This well-equipped campsite is 2km out of town on the Alcáçovas road; take the hourly buses #5 and #8 from Praça 1 de Maio. €4.

Pensão Giraldo Rua dos Mercadores 27 ⓣ 266 705 833. Clean, comfortable rooms; those with en-suite (€60) are more spacious. Prices rise in Aug and Sept. €48.

Pousada de Juventude Rua Miguel Bombarda 40 ⓣ 217 232 100, ⓦ www.pousadasjuventude.pt. Recently re-opened after extensive renovations, this central hostel is an excellent budget option. Dorms €16, twin €40.

Residencial Policarpo Rua Freiria de Baixo 16 ⓣ 266 702 424, ⓦ www.pensaopolicarpo.com. Beautiful, rambling old place full of rustic charm. Also has rooms sleeping three or four. €40–57.

Eating and drinking

O Antão Rua João de Deus 5. The place to come for regional specialities such as rabbit. Closed Wed. *Alentejana* €14.

O Aqueducto Rua do Cano 13a. Prize-winning restaurant serving imaginative dishes. Closed Sun eve and all Mon. Daily special €12.

Bar Oficin@ Rua da Moeda 27. Friendly, laid-back bar open until 2am. Closed Sun.

Casa dos Sabores Rua Miguel Bombarda 50. Pleasant café offering inexpensive sandwiches, salads and pastries. Sandwich €2.50.

Moving on

Bus Lagos (1 or 2 daily; 4hr–4hr 30min); Lisbon (14 daily; 1hr 30min).

Train Faro (2 daily; 4hr 30min–5hr 30min); Lisbon (3 daily; 2hr 30 min–2hr 45min).

THE ALENTEJO COAST

Starting south of Lisbon, the **Alentejo coast** features towns and beaches as inviting as those of the Algarve. Some of

the most attractive are pretty **Porto Côvo**, the bustling resort of **Vila Nova de Milfontes**, and the small surfers' haven of **Zambujeira do Mar**, at the southern point of the coastline stretch. Though exposed to the winds and waves of the Atlantic, with colder waters, the Alentejo coast is fine for summer swimming and far quieter than the Algarve. Outside the summer season, the area is blissfully quiet.

Local **bus** services and roughly three express buses daily from Lisbon take you within easy reach of the whole coastline, stopping at Porto Côvo (3hr–3hr 30min), Vila Nova de Milfontes (4hr), and Zambujeira do Mar (4hr 15min). **Accommodation** is plentiful in these resorts, especially Vila Nova de Milfontes, but it's wise to book ahead during the summer months. **Surfing** is popular along the Alentejo coast; first-timers can have lessons at Surf Milfontes in Vila Nova de Milfontes (ⓣ919 922 193, ⓦwww.surfmilfontes.com).

Porto Côvo

The first appealing coastal town below Lisbon is **PORTO CÔVO**, a popular Portuguese resort which boasts some beautiful beaches. The sleepy old town is little more than a few cobbled streets, but you won't be stuck for places to stay if you feel the urge to spend a night or two here. Cliff-top paths lead to **Praia do Somouqueira**, an impressive stretch of golden sand.

There's an attractive **campsite** (ⓣ269 905 136, ⓔcamping-portocovo@gmail.com; €5) with its own restaurant and shop just outside town on the road to Vila Nova de Milfontes. A good choice for **rooms** in town is *Maresia*, at Rua Cândido do Silva 57 (ⓣ269 905 449; €55) and above the **restaurant** of the same name, which serves delicious seafood.

Vila Nova de Milfontes

The larger (but still attractively low-key) resort of **VILA NOVA DE MILFONTES** lies south of Porto Côvo on the estuary of the River Mira, whose sandy banks merge into the coastline. This is the most popular and one of the most beautiful resorts in the region, its streets lined with houses and hotels painted in the typical Alentejan white and blue. Adding to the charm is a handsome little castle and an ancient port, reputed to have harboured Hannibal and his Carthaginians during a storm.

Regular **buses** connect Vila Nova de Milfontes with Porto Côvo (30min). **Dorm** beds, attractive en-suite rooms and a guest kitchen can be found at backpackers' favourite *Casa Amarela* on Rua Dom Luis Castro e Almeida (ⓣ283 996 632, ⓦwww.casaamarelamilfontes.com; dorms €20, twin/double €45), and there are a couple of large **campsites** to the north of town: the well-equipped *Parque de Campismo Milfontes* (ⓣ283 996 140, ⓔparquemilfontes@netc.pt; €6) and the more modest *Campifèrias* (ⓣ283 996 409, ⓔnovafeiras@oninet.pt; €5). **Bars and restaurants** largely lie between the castle and Largo de Rossio, with smart new *Pica Tapa* on Travessa de Sociedade serving up delicious Portuguese cuisine with a twist either à la carte or on set menus priced from €15. Opposite lies *Pacific Bar*, a key fixture of the town's nightlife.

Zambujeira do Mar

Southwest of Odemira southern Alentejo's main inland town, is the tiny village of **ZAMBUJEIRA DO MAR**, where a large

TREAT YOURSELF

Step back in time into a world of baronial elegance at the **Castelo de Milfontes** (ⓣ283 998 231, ⓔcastelo.milfontes@mail.telepac.pt; from €100), the town's oldest building and its premier lodgings. Complete with drawbridge, the ivy-clad castle/fort offers characterful, wood-panelled rooms with unbeatable views across the bay.

cliff provides a dramatic backdrop to the beach, which is prime **surfing** territory. Zambujeira do Mar certainly livens up in summer, with a music festival featuring mostly Portuguese bands held every August, but it's still quieter than Vila Nova de Milfontes. There are only a few small **pensions**, such as the well-run *Mar-e-Sol* (☎283 961 171; €50), a few private rooms to rent and a pleasant **campsite** (☎283 961 172, ⓦwww.campingzambujeira.com.sapo.pt), about 1km from the cliffs. Restaurants are concentrated around Rua Miramar; *O Martinho* is a decent choice.

There are no direct **transport** connections between Zambujeira and the Algarve; the best way to get there is to take a local bus to Odemira (40min), then a bus to Faro (2hr). However, these connections can be erratic; check ⓦwww.rodalentejo.pt for details.

FARO

FARO is the capital of the Algarve, with excellent beaches within easy reach, and – thanks to its university – a laid-back nightlife scene. While its suburbs may be modern, Faro retains an attractive historic centre south of the marina.

What to see and do

The **Cidade Velha**, or Old Town, is a semi-walled quarter entered through the eighteenth-century town gate, the **Arco da Vila**. Here you'll find the majestic **Sé** (Mon–Sat 10am–6pm; €3 including cathedral museum and outdoor bones chapel), which offers superb views – and a home for several nesting storks – from its bell tower. The nearby **Museu Municipal** (opening hours vary, check with tourist office; €2) is housed in a sixteenth-century convent on Largo Dom Alfonso III; the most striking exhibit is a third-century Roman mosaic of Neptune and the four winds, unearthed near Faro train station. Faro's most curious sight is the Baroque **Igreja do Carmo** (Mon–Fri 10am–1pm & 3–5pm, Sat 10am–1pm) near the central post office on Largo do Carmo. A door to the right of the altar leads to a macabre **Capela dos Ossos** (€1), its walls decorated with bones disinterred from the adjacent cemetery. The nearby **beach** (Praia de Faro) can be reached by bus from the Avenida stop opposite the bus station, or by boat from the harbour. Five boats a day also go to the more tranquil **Ilha do Farol**; the tourist information office has timetables.

Arrival and information

Air Taxis from the airport, 6km west of town, to the centre cost around €10, or take bus #16 or #14 (up to 24 daily; 7am–9.40pm; €1.30), a 20min journey to town. To get to the airport, catch the bus from the stop opposite the bus station.

Train A few minutes beyond the central bus station, up Av da República.

Bus Right in the centre, behind the *Hotel Eva*, north of the marina.

Tourist office The main office is near the harbour at Rua da Misericórdia 8 (Mon–Fri 9.30am–5.30/7pm, Sat & Sun 9.30am–12.30pm & 2–5.30/7pm; ☎289 803 604, ⓦwww.rtalgarve.pt); there's also a branch at the airport.

Accommodation

Pousada de Juventude Rua da Polícia de Segurança Pública 1 ☎289 826 521, ⓦwww.pousadasjuventude.pt. Basic but friendly hostel a 10min walk east of the centre; some rooms have en suite (€40). Dorms €17, twin €32.

Pensão São Filipe Rua Infante Dom Henrique 55 ☎289 824 182, ⓦwww.guesthouse-saofilipe.com. The recently renovated rooms are on the small side, but are immaculately clean. No breakfast. €55.

Residencial Adelaide Rua Cruz dos Mestres 7 ☎289 802 383, ⓦwww.adelaideresidencial.com. Smart, comfortable air-conditioned rooms. €60.

Residencial Oceano Rua Ivens 21 ☎289 823 349. A pleasant, good-value choice in the town centre. €50.

Eating and drinking

Adega Nova Rua Francisco Barreto 24. A good-value restaurant which is always crammed with locals. Pork chops €7.50.

Café do Coreto Jardim Manuel Bívar. Right next to the marina, this café is open all day serving sandwiches, pizza and drinks. Pizza from €8.
Columbus Rua Dr Francisco Gomes. Late-night disco bar with a relaxed, friendly atmosphere.
Mesa dos Mouros Largo da Sé 10 Lovely spot by the cathedral with a touch of class; mains include delicious seafood dishes (around €14).
Upa Upa Café Bar Rua Conselheiro de Bívar 51. Chilled-out spot perfect for a drink before hitting the bars and clubs around nearby Rua do Prior.

Moving on

Train Lagos (7 daily; 1hr 40min); Lisbon (4 daily; 5hr 30min–6hr); Olhão (16 daily; 10min); Tavira (12–17 daily; 35–45min).
Bus Évora (3–5 daily; 4hr–4hr 30min); Lagos (8 daily; 2hr 15min); Lisbon (7–9 daily; 4hr–4hr 30min); Olhão (every 15min–1hr; 20min); Sevilla, Spain (2 daily; 4hr 40min); Tavira (7–11 daily; 1hr).

LAGOS

The seaside town of **LAGOS** is one of the Algarve's most popular destinations and attracts large numbers of visitors each summer, drawn by its beautiful beaches and lively nightlife. Lagos was also favoured by Henry the Navigator, who used it as a base for African trade. Europe's first slave market was built here in 1441 in the arches of the Customs House, which still stands in the Praça da República near the waterfront.

What to see and do

On the waterfront and to the rear of the town are the remains of Lagos's once impregnable fortifications, devastated by the Great Earthquake. One rare and beautiful church which did survive was the **Igreja de Santo António**; decorated around 1715, its gilt and carved interior is wildly obsessive, every inch filled with a private fantasy of cherubic youths struggling with animals and fish. The church forms part of a visit to the adjacent **Museu Municipal** (daily except Mon 9.30am–12.30pm & 2–5pm; €2), housing an extraordinarily eclectic collection of artefacts including Roman busts and deformed animal foetuses.

Lagos's main attraction, however, is its splendid beaches, the most secluded of which lie below extravagantly eroded cliff faces south of town. **Praia de Dona Ana** is considered the most picturesque, though its crowds make the smaller coves of **Praia do Pinhão**, down a track just opposite the fire station, and **Praia Camilo**, a little further along, more appealing. Over the river east of Lagos is a splendid sweep of sand – **Meia Praia** – where there's space even at the height of summer. Meia Praia is an ideal destination for **watersports** enthusiasts, as various companies based here offer water-skiing and sailboard lessons, and it's also popular with surfers. Those who like to keep their feet dry might prefer an excursion to the extraordinary rock formations around **Ponta da Piedade**, a headland that can be viewed by boat (around €10) from the harbour.

Arrival and information

Train The train station is across the river,15min walk from the centre via a swing bridge in the marina.
Bus The bus station is slightly closer to the town centre, just off the main Av dos Descobrimentos.
Tourist office On Largo Marquês de Pombal in the central pedestrian zone (April & May Mon–Fri 10am–6pm & Sat 10am–2pm; June & Sept Mon–Sat 10am–6pm; July & Aug daily 10am–8pm; ⓣ 282 764 111).

Accommodation

Angela Guesthouse Loteamento da Ameijeira, Rua Teixeira Gomes Bloco AN1-2 ⓣ 962 616 552, ⓔ angelaguesthouse@hotmail.com. Pleasant, comfortable rooms with shared bathroom in a private apartment. €40.
Campismo da Trindade Rossio da Trindade ⓣ 282 763 893. Small, busy campsite close to the sea. To reach it, follow the main road 200m beyond the fort. €8.
Gold Coast Hostel Rua Gil Vicente 48 ⓣ 916 594 225, ⓔ goldcoast_hostel@yahoo.com. Friendly, relaxed hostel with a shared kitchen and outdoor terrace. Dorms €22.

Pensão Caravela Rua 25 de Abril 16 ⓣ 282 763 361. Well-kept rooms right in the centre of town. €55.

Pousada de Juventude Rua Lançarote de Freitas 50 ⓣ 282 761 970, ⓦ www.pousadasjuventude.pt. Busy, well-equipped hostel in a central location. Dorms €17, twin from €37.

Rising Cock Hostel Travessa do Forno 14 ⓣ 968 758 785, ⓦ www.risingcock.com. Tackily named but popular party hostel. Dorms €27.

Eating, drinking and nightlife

Bon Vivant Rua 25 de Abril 105. Multistorey bar-club with a "tropical" roof terrace.

Casa Rosa Rua do Ferrador 22. Popular with travellers, this café serves good-value international dishes. Chilli con carne €5.

Eddie's Bar Rua 25 de Abril 99. Friendly bar with loud music and cheap drinks.

Mullens Bar Rua Cândido dos Reis 86#. Atmospheric bar-restaurant with lively music until 2am.

Néctar Enoteca Rua Silva Lopes 19. Smart wine bar with an extensive tapas menu. Closed Tues. Octopus salad €5.

No Patio Rua Lançarote de Freitas 46 ⓣ 282 763 777. Run by a British expat chef, *No Patio* ("on the patio") offers beautifully prepared fusion cuisine at a reasonable price. Thai-style monkfish and prawns €15. Reservations recommended.

Moving on

Train Faro (7 daily; 1hr 40min); Lisbon (4 daily; 5hr 15min).

Bus Faro (5 daily; 2hr 15min); Porto Côvo (1 daily; 3hr); Sevilla, Spain (2 daily; 6hr 30min); Vila Nova de Milfontes (1 daily; 1hr 45min).

OLHÃO AND THE ISLANDS

OLHÃO, 8km east of Faro, is the largest fishing port in the Algarve and an excellent base for visiting the local sandbank islands. The pedestrianized centre, close to the seafront, is pretty yet free of tourist hordes, and ensures Olhão retains an unspoilt traditional charm.

What to see and do

Although Olhão has no sights to speak of, its café-strewn centre is worth a wander, and there's a bustling market on Av 5 de Outubro. The town's main attraction, however, is its close proximity to and good connections with two of the sandbank islands which comprise the **Ria Formosa Natural Park**. The islands of Armona and Culatra boast some superb, spacious beaches, so expansive that they still feel uncrowded even at the height of summer. Ferries to the islands operate year-round, and depart regularly from the jetty to the left of the municipal gardens. The service to **Armona** (30min; €3.10 return) drops you off at a long strip of holiday chalets and huts that stretches right across the island on either side of the main path. On the ocean side, the beach disappears into the distance and a short walk will take you to totally deserted stretches of sand. Boats to **Culatra** (30min; €3.10 return) call first at Praia da Culatra, a vast expanse of sand stretching away from Culatra town. The same service then makes its way to **Praia do Farol** (1hr; €3.70 return), considered to be one of the most beautiful beaches on the sandbank islands. Heading east, away from the holiday homes, the beach becomes quieter, and eventually leads to the peaceful Praia dos Hangares.

Arrival and information

Train and bus The train station is east of Av da República northeast of town, while the bus station is nearby, to the west of the Avenida.

Tourist office Largo Sebastião Martins Mestre (May–Sept Mon–Fri 9.30am–7pm; Oct–April Mon–Fri 9.30am–noon & 1–5.30pm; ⓣ 289 713 936).

Accommodation and eating

Camping Olhão ⓣ 289 700 300, ⓦ www.sbsi.pt. Large, well-equipped campsite 2km east of town. In summer a bus runs from near the municipal garden. €4.

Pensão Bela Vista Rua Teófilo Braga 65 ⓣ 289 702 538. Offers neat and tidy en-suite rooms with air conditioning; the restaurant beneath offers excellent local dishes (grilled cod €8). €50.

Pensão Bicuar Rua Vasco da Gama 5 ⓣ 289 714 816, ⓦ www.pension-bicuar.net. Friendly guesthouse with a kitchen, roof terrace, and pleasant rooms with shower and sink which sleep up to four. €45.

Ria Formosa Av 5 de Outubro 14. Popular restaurant with tasty seafood and rice dishes. *Arroz marisco* €8.

TAVIRA

TAVIRA is a good-looking little town made up of cobbled streets, and split into two pretty halves by the River Gilão. The Romans and Moors who once ruled Tavira left behind monuments that contribute to the town's appeal, but the main tourist attractions, the superb island beaches of the **Ilha de Tavira**, actually lie offshore. Boats to the island depart from the quayside on Rua do Cais from July to mid-September (12 daily; 20min; €2 return), with year-round boats from Quatro Águas (up to 12 daily; 5min; €1.50 return), 2km east of town. The beach is backed by dunes and stretches west almost as far as Fuzeta, 14km away. Despite some development – a small chalet settlement, a **campsite,** and a handful of bars and restaurants facing the sea – it's still easy to find your own peaceful patch of sand. Back in central Tavira, it's worth wandering up to the remains of the **Moorish castle** (Mon–Fri 8am–5pm, Sat & Sun 9am–7pm; free), perched high above the town, with its walls enclosing a pretty garden that affords splendid views. Close to the castle, at Calçada da Galeria 12, a former water tower has been converted into a **camera obscura**, offering views of the town (Mon–Sat 10am–5pm; €3.50).

Arrival and information

Train 1km from the centre of town, at the end of Rua da Liberdade.
Bus Buses pull up at the terminal by the river, a 2min walk from the central square, Praça da República.
Tourist office Rua da Galeria 9, southwest of Praça da República (July & Aug Mon–Fri 9am–7pm, Sept–June Mon–Fri 9.30am–1pm & 2–5.30pm; ⓣ 281 322 511).

Accommodation

Camping Tavira Ilha de Tavira ⓣ 281 324 455, ⓦ www.campingtavira.com. Busy campsite with a great location on the Ilha de Tavira; follow the path opposite the ferry dock to reach it. Open April–Sept. €5.
Pousada de Juventude Rua Miguel Bombarda 36 ⓣ 217 232 100, ⓦ www.pousadasjuventude.pt. Brand-new hostel with excellent facilities. Dorms €17, twin €30, en-suite twin €35.
Residencial Princesa do Gilão Rua Borda d'Agua de Aguiar 10 ⓣ 281 325 171, ⓔ residencial-gilao@hotmail.com. Modern, a/c rooms with an unbeatable location on the far side of the river. €55.

TREAT YOURSELF

A Ver Tavira Calçada da Galeria 13 ⓣ 281 381 363. Tavira's finest restaurant is situated next to the castle, with superb views over town from its smart dining room. The menu boasts a delicious fusion of local ingredients and international recipes, and the price is reasonable given the quality of the food and beauty of the setting. Open year-round for lunch and dinner, except in July and August when it's open for dinner only. Garlic shrimp with starfruit €17.50.

Eating and drinking

Arco Rua Almirante Cândido dos Reis 67. Friendly, laid-back bar on the far side of the river, which attracts both locals and visitors. Closed Mon.
Beira Rio Rua Borda da Àgua de Assêca 44–46. Serves decent pasta, pizza and salads. Spaghetti carbonara €9.
Restaurante Imperial Rua Dr José Pires Padinha 22. Riverside restaurant serving cheap and cheerful meat and fish dishes. Grilled squid €7.
Tavira Romano Praça da República. Bustling café with outdoor tables serving delicious ice cream and cakes.
UBI Rua Vale Caranguejo. Tavira's only club is a warehouse-like space reached by following Rua Almirante Cândido dos Reis to the outskirts of town. Closed Mon in summer, open Fri & Sat only in winter.

Romania

HIGHLIGHTS ✪

THE CARPATHIANS: stunning mountain scenery, under two hours from the capital

SIGHIŞOARA: beautiful medieval citadel in the heart of Transylvania, with authentic Dracula connections

MUZEUL ASTRA, SIBIU: a fascinating open-air museum of Romanian village architecture, set in a scenic landscape

BUCHAREST: hectic traffic, Stalinist architecture, pretty residential streets and good dining and nightlife

ROUGH COSTS

DAILY BUDGET Basic €25/occasional treat €35

DRINK Beer €1–2; bottle of Romanian wine €5

FOOD Two-course meal with wine €9

HOSTEL/BUDGET HOTEL €10–15/€40

TRAVEL Bucharest–Sibiu by train (210km; 3hr) €13.50; by bus (260km; 5hr) €8.50

FACT FILE

POPULATION 22,215 million

AREA 237,500 sq km

LANGUAGE Romanian

CURRENCY New leu (RON); plural: lei

CAPITAL Bucharest (population: 2 million)

INTERNATIONAL PHONE CODE ⓣ40

Introduction

Nowhere in Eastern Europe defies preconceptions quite like Romania. The country suffers from a poor image, but don't be put off – outstanding landscapes, a surprisingly efficient train system, a huge diversity of wildlife and a bizarre mix of cultures and people await you if you seek them out.

Romanians trace their ancestry back to the Romans, and they like to stress their Latin roots, although they have Balkan traits too. They see their future as firmly within the Euro-Atlantic family and were delighted to join NATO and then, on January 1, 2007, the European Union.

The capital, **Bucharest**, is perhaps daunting for the first-time visitor – its savage history is only too evident – but parts of this once-beautiful city retain a voyeuristic appeal. More attractive by far, and easily accessible on public transport, is **Transylvania**, a region steeped in history, offering some of the most beautiful mountain scenery in Europe as well as a uniquely multi-ethnic character. Its chief cities, such as Braşov, Sibiu and Sighişoara, were built by Saxon (German) colonists, and there are also strong Hungarian and Roma (Gypsy) presences here. In the border region of the **Banat**, also highly multi-ethnic, Timişoara is Romania's most Western-looking city and famed as the birthplace of the 1989 revolution.

CHRONOLOGY

513 BC The Dacian tribe inhabit the area of present-day Romania.
106 AD The Roman emperor Trajan conquers the Dacian tribe.
271 Following attacks from the Goths, the Romans withdraw from the area.
1000s Hungary conquers and occupies parts of present-day Romania.
1200s Division of Romanian population into different principalities including Wallachia, Moldavia and Transylvania.
1400s Principalities of Moldavia, Transylvania and Wallachia come under attack from the Turkish Ottomans but remain independent.
1448 Vlad "the Impaler" becomes Prince of Wallachia; he is later credited as the inspiration for the character of Dracula.
1700s The Austrian Habsburgs take control of large parts of the Romanian principalities after military successes over the Ottomans.
1862 After battling for independence, Wallachia and Moldavia unite to form Romania. Bucharest is declared the capital.
1878 Romania's claim to independence is formalized by the Treaty of Berlin.
1881 Carol I is named the first King of Romania.
1918 After invasion by the central powers during World War I, Romania is freed and her borders increased.
1939–1945 Romania sides with Germany at start of World War II, but changes allegiance to the Allies towards the end. Soviets take large parts of Romanian territory.
1947 Soviet influence remains and the Communist Party comes into power in Romania.
1965 Nicolae Ceauşescu becomes Communist Party leader and adopts a foreign-policy stance independent of the Soviets.
1989 Revolution leads to the overthrow of the Communist regime.
2004 Romania joins NATO.
2007 Romania joins the European Union.
2008 NATO's largest ever summit is held at Bucharest's colossal Palace of Parliament.

ARRIVAL

Arriving by **air**, most airlines serve Bucharest's Otopeni (Henri Coanda) airport, but there are half a dozen regional airports (of which Timişoara is the most important), served by Austrian Airlines (ⓦwww.aua.com) and a growing number of budget airlines such as Wizzair (ⓦwww.wizzair.com) and Carpatair (ⓦwww.carpatair.com). An option worth considering for visits to Transylvania is to get a budget flight to Budapest and then travel to Romania

by land, which is a relatively straightforward option, usually crossing from Békéscaba in Hungary to Vârsand in Romania.

Travelling to Romania by **train** is also fairly simple, via Paris, Vienna and Budapest, and there are also through trains from Prague, Belgrade, Sofia and Kiev. This will usually cost as much as flying into the country, but works well as part of a larger Europe-wide trip using either an InterRail pass (for European residents) or a Eurail pass (for non-European residents). Rail Europe (Ⓦwww.raileurope.co.uk), International Rail (Ⓦwww.international-rail.com) and Trainseurope (Ⓦwww.trainseurope.co.uk) all have numerous rail pass and point-to-point ticket options. The international operator **Eurolines** has details on bus journeys to Romania and you can book both one-way and return tickets (with an open-ended option) through them (Ⓦwww.eurolines.co.uk).

GETTING AROUND

InterCity **trains** are the most comfortable; they're followed by Rapid and Accelerat services, which stop more often. Personal trains stop everywhere and are generally grubby and crowded. Some overnight trains have **sleeping carriages** (*vagon de dormit*) and **couchettes** (*cuşet*) for a modest surcharge. Seat reservations are required for all fast trains, and are automatically included with locally purchased tickets. You'll also need a reservation for **international trains** even if you do not require one before entering Romania, so be sure to book a seat before departure or face a fine. The best place to **buy tickets** and book seats is at the local Agenţia SNCFR (Ⓦwww.cfr.ro; generally open Mon–Fri 7.30am–7.30pm, Sat 8am–noon); at the station tickets are slightly cheaper but available only one hour in advance. Wasteels, a Europe-wide youth rail travel agency (Ⓦwww.wasteelstravel.ro), available in some major

stations, offers discounts for under-26s. Both **InterRail** and **Eurail** are valid.

Trains are complemented by an ever-improving rural **bus** (*autobuz*) network, usually from beside the train station. On busy routes there are also **minibus** (*maxitaxi*) services, usually fast and frequent, even if the driving can be manic. Maxitaxis also make quite a few surprisingly long inter-city journeys; expect to pay the same as the Accelerat train fare or a bit more. **Taxis** are cheap and an attractive alternative to crowded public transport. Most are honest, but be sure to choose a taxi with a clearly marked company name, and check that the meter is working.

ACCOMMODATION

Apart from a growing number of four- and five-star hotels offering Western comforts (and prices), standards tend to be fairly low. Cheaper **hotels** cost 210–240 lei per person per night, for a basic room and shared shower; breakfast is normally an extra 13–21 lei. An alternative is to take a **private room** (*cazare la persoane particulare*), which will probably be the only option in smaller towns and villages. In season you may come across people offering accommodation at the train or bus station; expect to pay around 50 lei. **Hostels** (Ⓦwww.hihostels-romania.ro) are becoming less rare, and university towns have student accommodation (*caminul de studenţi*) from late June to August, for around 30 lei per night. **Campsites** are usually very basic. Expect to pay around 20 lei per night for tent space, with little more than a tap and dirty toilet. Outside national parks, most officials will turn a blind eye if you are discreet about camping wild.

FOOD AND DRINK

Breakfast (*micul dejun*) is typically a light meal, featuring rolls and butter (*chifle cu unt*) and an *omleta* washed down with a coffee (*cafea*) or tea (*ceai*).

The most common **snacks** are flaky pastries (*pateuri*) filled with cheese (*cu brânză*) or meat (*cu carne*), and a variety of spicy grilled sausages and meatballs such as *mici* and *chiftele*. Menus in most **restaurants** concentrate on grilled meats, or *friptura*. *Cotlet de porc* is the common pork chop, while *muşchi de vacă* is fillet of beef.

Traditional **Romanian dishes** can be delicious. The best-known of these is *sarmale* – pickled cabbage stuffed with rice, meat and herbs, usually served with sour cream. Stews (*tocană*) and other dishes often feature a combination of meat and dairy products. **Vegetarians** could try asking for *caşcaval pane* (hard cheese fried in breadcrumbs); *ghiveci* (mixed fried veg); *ardei umpluţii* (stuffed peppers); or vegetables and salads. Establishments called **cofetărie** serve coffee and cakes, and sometimes beer and ice cream. Coffee, whether *cafea naturală* (finely ground and brewed Turkish-style), *filtru* (filtered) or *nes* (instant), is usually drunk black and sweet; ask for it *cu lapte* or *fără zahăr* if you prefer it with milk or without sugar. **Cakes** and **desserts** are sweet and sticky, as throughout the Balkans. Romanians also enjoy pancakes (*clătite*) and pies (*plăcintă*) with various fillings.

Evening **drinking** takes place in outdoor beer gardens, *cramas* (beer cellars), restaurants (where boozers often

ROMANIA ON THE NET

Ⓦ**www.romaniatourism.com** and Ⓦ**www.romaniatravel.com** Official tourism sites.
Ⓦ**www.mountainguide.ro** Hiking information and links.
Ⓦ**www.eco-romania.ro** Association of ecotourism operators.
Ⓦ**www.inyourpocket.com** Online guide to Bucharest.
Ⓦ**www.sapteseri.ro** Online listings guide for most large cities.

outnumber the diners), and in a growing number of Western-style cafés and bars. Try **țuică**, a powerful plum brandy taken neat; in rural areas, it is homemade and often twice distilled to yield fearsomely strong *palincă*. Most **beer** (*bere*) is German-style lager. Romania's best **wines** are Grasa and Feteasca Neagră, and the sweet dessert wines of Murfatlar. Expect to pay 40–90 lei for a good-quality bottle.

CULTURE AND ETIQUETTE

Generally speaking, Romanians tend to be very open and friendly people. They will think nothing of striking up a conversation on buses and trains, even if they don't speak much English, and will try their best to communicate through any language barrier.

When speaking to older people, it is respectful to address them using either *Domnul* (Mr) or *Doamnă* (Mrs), while shaking someone's hand is the most common and familiar way of **greeting** – although bear in mind that a Romanian man may well kiss a woman's hand on introduction. The welcoming attitude of the Romanians may mean you are **invited to someone's home**; it is considered polite to bring a small gift with you, which you should also wrap. A bottle of wine, chocolates or flowers are all appropriate – although if you do bring flowers you should ensure an odd number of blooms, as even-numbered bouquets are strictly for funerals.

Tipping in restaurants is not necessary, although it will be appreciated.

SPORTS AND OUTDOOR ACTIVITIES

Romania's landscape is dominated by the spectacular Carpathian Mountains. A continuation of the Alps, they encircle Transylvania and provide the country with a rocky backbone perfect for activities ranging from hiking and skiing to caving and mountain biking.

The main mountain ranges, the Bucegi, the Făgăraş, the Apuseni and the Retezat, provide the best-known destinations for **hiking**. There are numerous well-marked trails allowing day-trips or longer expeditions, sleeping in a mountain refuge or *cabana* – these are usually very friendly and sociable places, and make good bases for hiking, caving or climbing. All of the trails are marked on the excellent Hartă Turistica maps, which can be found in hiking shops and bookshops in most major towns. Some *cabanas* also sell maps. Spring and summer are the best seasons to explore the mountains, and a large number of trails should only be attempted in warmer weather.

Romania also offers some of Europe's cheapest **skiing** and **snowboarding** between November and April (Ⓦwww.ski-in-romania.com). There are several major ski and snowboarding resorts in Romania, the most popular of which is Poiana Braşov, near Braşov. Other resorts include Sinaia, Buşteni and Predeal, all on the main road north from Bucharest, Păltiniş near Sibiu, Borşa to the north in Maramureş, and Ceahlău and Durău on the border of Moldavia. Although Borşa is arguably the best resort for beginners, the larger resorts all have a number of easy and medium pistes and one or more black run.

COMMUNICATIONS

Post offices (*poşta*) in major cities are open Monday to Friday 7am to 8pm, Saturday 8am to 1pm; in smaller places they may close an hour or two earlier. You can **phone** from the orange cardphones or post offices. Phonecards (10 or 15 lei – get the latter for international calls) are available from post offices and news kiosks. Rates are lower from 11pm to 7am. **Internet** access is available in most towns.

Romanian

	Romanian	Pronunciation
Yes	*Da*	Da
No	*Nu*	Noo
Please	*Vă rog*	Ve rog
Thank you	*Mulţumesc*	Mult-sumesk
Hello/Good day	*Salut/bună ziua*	Saloot/boona zhewa
Goodbye	*La revedere*	La re-ve-dairy
Excuse me	*Permiteţi-mi*	Per-mi-tets-may
Where?	*Unde?*	Oun-day?
Good	*Bun/bine*	Boon/Bee-ne
Bad	*Rău*	Rau
Near	*Apropriat*	A-prope-reeat
Far	*Departe*	D'par-tay
Cheap	*Ieftin*	Yeftin
Expensive	*Scump*	Scoomp
Open	*Închis*	Un-keez
Closed	*Deschis*	Des-keez
Today	*Azi*	Az
Yesterday	*Ieri*	Ee-airy
Tomorrow	*Mâine*	Mwee-ne
How much is...?	*Cât costa…?*	Cuut costa…?
What time is it?	*Ce ora este?*	Che ora est?
I don't understand	*Nu înţeleg*	Noo unts-eledge
Do you speak English?	*Vorbiţi Englezeste?*	Vor-beetz eng-lay-zeste?
One	*Un, una*	Oon, oona
Two	*Doi, doua*	Doy, doo-a
Three	*Trei*	Tray
Four	*Patru*	Pat-ru
Five	*Cinci*	Chinch
Six	*Şase*	Shass-er
Seven	*Şapte*	Shap-tay
Eight	*Opt*	Opt
Nine	*Nouă*	No-ar
Ten	*Zece*	Zay-chay

EMERGENCIES

Watch out for pickpockets in crowded buses and trams. Do not believe anyone claiming to be a policeman and asking to see your passport and/or the contents of your wallet. Make sure you have health insurance. Bucharest's central emergency **hospital** is up to western standards, while Medicover Unirii, 64–66 Marasesti Blvd (ⓣ021/310 1599, ⓦwww.medicover.com), also offers Western-standard care, with English-speaking doctors. **Pharmacies** (*farmacie*) are open Mon–Sat 9am–6pm.

EMERGENCY NUMBER

In all emergencies call ⓣ112.

INFORMATION

Local authorities are now obliged to have **tourist offices**, but you're best off going to privately run **tourist agencies**, many of which have English-speaking staff.

MONEY AND BANKS

Romania's currency is the new (or "heavy") **leu** (plural lei, international

code RON). Despite being introduced as long ago as 2005, some shops and restaurants still list prices in old lei – if you're told that something costs a hundred thousand lei, for instance, you should knock off four zeroes to get the actual price. Hotels, rental agencies and other services quote prices in euros. There are plenty of **ATMs** in towns. **Changing money** is best done at private exchange offices (*casa de schimb*) and traveller's cheques can be changed at most major city banks. Never change money on the streets. **Credit cards** are generally accepted at hotels and upmarket shops. At the time of writing 1 leu = €0.24, €1 = 4.23 lei.

OPENING HOURS AND HOLIDAYS

Shop **opening hours** are Monday to Friday 9am to 6pm, Saturday 9am to 1pm, with many food shops open until 10pm (or even 24hr), including weekends. Museums and castles also open roughly 9am to 6pm (though most are closed on Mon or Tues); **admission charges** are minimal, so they are only quoted in this chapter unless they are above the norm. **National holidays** are: January 1 and 2, Easter Monday, May 1, December 1, December 25 and 26.

Bucharest

Arriving in **BUCHAREST** (Bucureşti), most tourists want to leave as quickly as possible, but to do so would mean missing the heart of Romania. Bucharest does have its charm and elegance – it just needs digging for. Among the ruptured roads and disintegrating buildings you'll find leafy squares, beautiful, if crumbling, eclectic architecture and dressed-up young Romanians adding a touch of glamour to the surroundings. What's more, it's a dynamic city, changing faster than any other in Romania as new office-towers sprout and shops and bars appear all over.

Head south of the centre into the Centru Civic and you'll come across unfinished projects from Ceauşescu's reign, such as the abandoned cultural

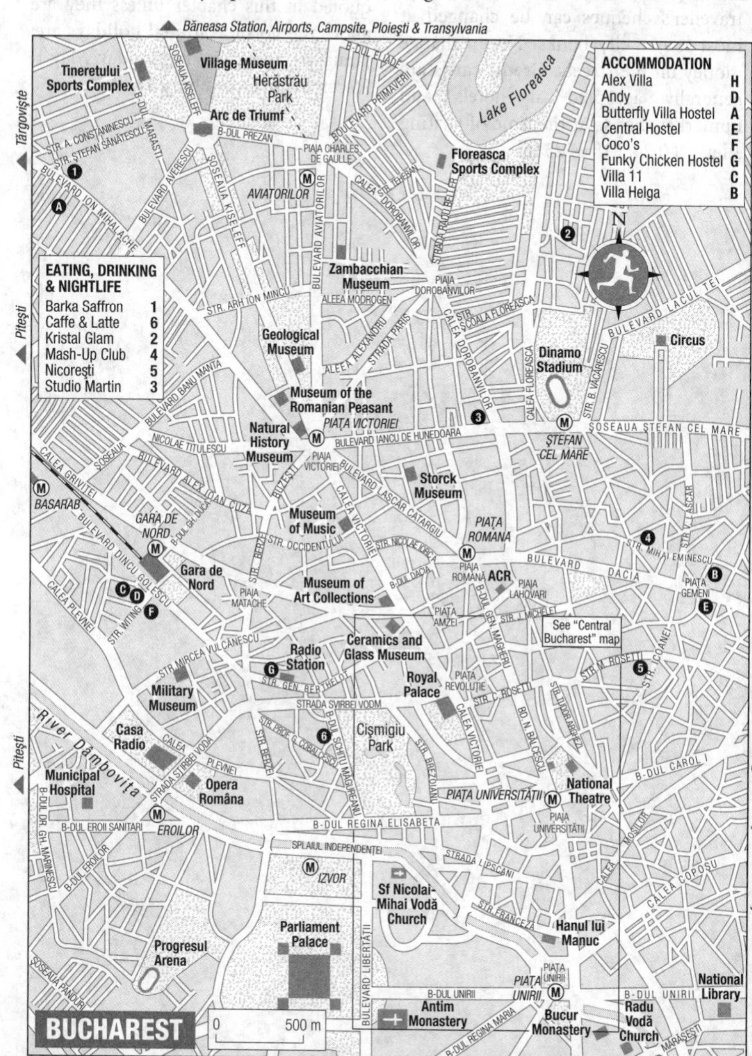

centre known to locals as "Hiroshima". Seeing the true scale of what a dictatorship can do is something you won't forget, and reason enough to spend a day or two in the capital.

What to see and do

The heart of the city lies to the north of the Dâmbovița river, between two north–south avenues; it's a jumble of modern hotels, ancient Orthodox churches, and decaying apartment blocks, relieved by some attractive parks. Freezing in winter and hot and dusty in the summer, the northern outskirts are cooled by woodlands and a girdle of lakes.

Piața Revoluției

Most inner-city sights are within walking distance of Calea Victoriei, an avenue of vivid contrasts, scattered with vestiges of *ancien régime* elegance interspersed with apartment blocks, glass and steel facades and cake shops. Fulcrum of the avenue is **Piața Revoluției**, created during the 1930s on Carol II's orders to ensure a field of fire around the Royal Palace.

On the north side of the square is the **Athénée Palace Hotel** (now a Hilton), famous for its role as an "intelligence factory" from the 1930s until the 1980s, with its bugged rooms, tapped phones and informer prostitutes. To its east are the grand **Romanian Atheneum**, the city's main concert hall, and the **University Library**, torched, allegedly by the Securitate, in the confusion of the 1989 revolution, but since rebuilt and reopened.

To the southeast of the square is the former Communist Party HQ, now the **Senate**, where Nicolae Ceaușescu made his last speech from a low balcony on December 21. His speech drowned out by booing, the dictator's disbelief was broadcast to the nation just before the TV screens went blank. He and his wife Elena fled by helicopter from the roof, but were captured and executed on Christmas Day.

The Royal Palace

The **Royal Palace**, on the western side of Piața Revoluției, now contains the excellent **National Art Museum** (Wed–Sun 10/11am–6/7pm; 15 lei, free on first Wed of month), with fantastic works by El Greco, Rembrandt, Brueghel and the great modern Romanian sculptor Brâncuși, plus a huge and marvellous collection of medieval and modern Romanian art.

The Crețulescu Church and Cişmigiu Park

Standing opposite the Senate, the restored eighteenth-century **Crețulescu Church** fronts a tangle of streets wending west towards **Cişmigiu Park**, Bucharest's oldest, containing a boating lake, playgrounds, summer terrace cafés and animated chess-players.

The historic centre

At the southern end of B-dul Brătianu is Bucharest's **historic centre**: a maze of dusty cobblestone streets with decrepit houses and tiny shops, centred on the pedestrianized Strada Lipscani. The whole area is currently in the midst of a major EU-funded renovation project, urgently necessary to save what's left, even if it causes the area to lose some of its authenticity.

The Stavropoleos Church

Just southwest of Strada Lipscani stands the small **Stavropoleos Church**; built in the 1720s, it has gorgeous, almost arabesque, patterns decorating its facade, and an elegant columned portico.

The Old Court and around

Even further south of the centre, just beyond the Stavropoleos Church, are the modest remains of the **Curtea Veche** (Old Court; daily 10am–4pm),

Vlad the Impaler's fifteenth-century citadel. Dating from 1559, the adjacent Old Court Church is Bucharest's oldest church. Inside the large white building opposite the church you'll find the lush courtyard of the **Hanul lui Manuc Inn**, home to a hotel and restaurant (closed for renovation at the time of writing). The inn's southern wall forms one side of Piața Unirii, which is where the old Bucharest makes way for the new.

The Centru Civic

The infamous **Centru Civic** was Ceaușescu's pet urban project. After an earthquake in 1977 damaged much of the city, Ceaușescu took the opportunity to remodel the entire southern portion of central Bucharest as a monument to Communism. By the early 1980s bulldozers had moved in to clear the way for the Victory of Socialism Boulevard (now Bulevardul Unirii), taking with them thousands of architecturally significant houses, churches and monuments. Now colossal apartment blocks line Bulevardul Unirii, at 4km long and 120m wide slightly larger – intentionally so – than the Champs-Elysées on which it was modelled. The eastern end of the boulevard is now a banking district, while the other end is dominated by the Palatul Parlamentului (Parliament Palace).

Palatul Parlamentului

The **Palatul Parlamentului** (Parliament Palace) is supposedly the second-largest administration building in the world. Started in 1984 – but still not complete despite the toil of 100,000 workers – the building contains 1100 rooms and a nuclear shelter, and now houses the Romanian Parliament and a conference centre. Guided tours in English (daily 10am–4pm; 15 lei, plus 30 lei for the use of cameras) start to the left of the entrance as you face the building.

Piața Universității

You're bound to pass through busy **Piața Universității**, overshadowed by the *Hotel Intercontinental* on B-dul Carol I. This is where students pitched their post-revolution City of Peace encampment, which was violently overrun, together with the illusion of true democracy, by the miners that President Iliescu had called in to "restore order" in June 1990. The miners returned to Bucharest in 1991, this time in protest against the government rather than to protect it.

The National Theatre and Bucharest University

Just to the east of Piața Universității rises Elena Ceaușescu's **National Theatre** (Teatrul National), resembling an Islamicized reworking of the Colosseum. Across the boulevard, **Bucharest University** is surrounded by students, snack stands and book vendors. The bulbous domes of the Students' Church, originally a Russian church, appear through a gap in the grand buildings to its south.

Museum of the Romanian Peasant

Stretching north from Piața Victoriei, Șoseaua Kiseleff leads into the more pleasant, leafy suburbs. At no. 3, the **Muzeul Țăranului Român** (Museum of the Romanian Peasant; Tues–Sun 10am–6pm, last entry 5pm; 6 lei) is a must-see, giving an insight into the country's varied rural traditions, with exhibits on everything from costume and textiles to wood and glass painted icons; to the rear there's a beautiful wooden church of the type found in Maramureș, as well as an excellent souvenir shop. The unexceptional Natural History and Geological museums are adjacent.

Herăstrău Park and the Village Museum

Just to the north of the museums, traffic heading for the airports and Transylvania swings around a familiar-looking

SCAMS

Despite Bucharest's reputation for **scams**, it's safer than it was. Still, never pay for anything in advance, never change money without knowing the exchange rate, and never hand your passport or wallet to anyone claiming to be a policeman.

Arc de Triumf, commemorating Romania's participation on the side of the Allied victors in World War I. To the right, in **Herăstrău Park**, the city's largest, is the **Muzeul Satului** (Village Museum; daily 9am–6pm; 6 lei), a fabulous ensemble of wooden houses, churches, windmills and other structures from various regions of the country.

Arrival and information

Air Otopeni (Henri Coandă) airport is 18km north of the centre; the only reliable taxis are marked Fly Taxi (outside International Arrivals or ⓣ9440), charging around 70 lei to the centre; alternatively, head for the #783 bus stop just outside – buy your two-ride ticket (6 lei) from the RATB kiosk. Aurel Vlaicu (Băneasa) airport is 8km north of the centre. Buses #131, #335 and #780 leave from outside the airport. Reputable taxi firms such as Fly Taxi (ⓣ9440) and Cristaxi (ⓣ9461) charge around 25 lei to the centre. An hourly rail service connects both airports with Gara de Nord station (45min).

Train Virtually all trains terminate at the Gara de Nord, from where it's a 30min walk into the centre, or a short ride on the metro (change lines at Piața Victoriei to reach Piața Universității). There are taxis outside the main entrance beyond the Wasteels ticket office.

Tourist information Bucharest has no tourist office; pick up a copy of the English-language listings magazine *Bucharest in Your Pocket* (ⓦwww.inyourpocket.com; 12 lei at newsstands or from the Gara de Nord's Wasteels office, or free in hotels).

City transport

Public transport, although crowded, is efficient and very cheap. The most useful lines of the metro system are the M2 (north–south) and M3 (a near-circle). There's also an array of trams, buses and trolleybuses.

Tickets must be bought from kiosks located near the bus stops, and validated in the machine on board.

Taxi After 11.30pm, you'll have to depend on taxis, which remain cheap, at about 2 lei/km; the most reputable companies are Cristaxi (ⓣ9461), Cobalcescu (ⓣ9451) or Meridian (ⓣ9444) – make sure the meter is running.

Accommodation

Private apartments are often more spacious than hotel rooms – try ⓦwww.bucharest-accommodation.ro) or Professional Realty (ⓣ021/2320406, ⓦwww.accommodation.com.ro), both of which have centrally located rooms and apartments from around 250 lei per day.

Hostels

Alex Villa Str Avram Iancu 5 ⓣ021/313 3198, ⓦwww.alexvilla.ro. This bright and lively HI hostel has a/c rooms sleeping 2–8, free internet and a common room with cable TV. Take trolleybus #85 from Piața Universității east to the Calea Moșilor stop, and continue on foot past the roundabout, turning right at the Greek church. Dorms 40 lei, rooms 100 lei.

Butterfly Villa Hostel Str Dumitru Zosima 82 ⓣ021/224 1918, ⓦwww.butterfly-villa.com. Friendly hostel just outside the city centre, with large a/c rooms, lockers, free internet, breakfast, laundry and a barbeque in the garden during summer. From Gara de Nord take tram #24 or bus #282 to Piața Domenii; Str Dumitru Zosima is just across the street. Dorms 50 lei, rooms 135 lei.

Central Hostel Str Salcamilor 2 ⓣ021/610 2214, ⓦwww.centralhostel.ro. Clean and simple with free breakfast, laundry (6 lei) and internet access (first 15min free). Take bus #79, #86 or #133 from Gara de Nord to Piața Gemeni, two stops after Piața Romană; then take the first right off B-dul Dacia into Str Viitorului. Dorms 55–70 lei, rooms 160 lei.

Funky Chicken Hostel Str Gen. Berthelot 63 ⓣ021/312 1425, ⓦwww.funkychickenhostel.com. This cheap and cheerful place offers free cigarettes to all guests but no breakfast. No reservations, but guaranteed accommodation for everyone who turns up. From Gara de Nord, follow B-dul Golescu, cross Str Berzei and enter the street next to the pharmacy. Dorms 34 lei.

Villa 11 Str Institutul Medico-Militar 11 ⓣ0722/495 900, ⓔvila11bb@hotmail.com. Friendly and quiet hostel just 5min walk from Gara de Nord. Facilities include laundry (10 lei) and bikes (free for local use, 45 lei per day outside Bucharest). Dorms 64 lei, rooms 135 lei.

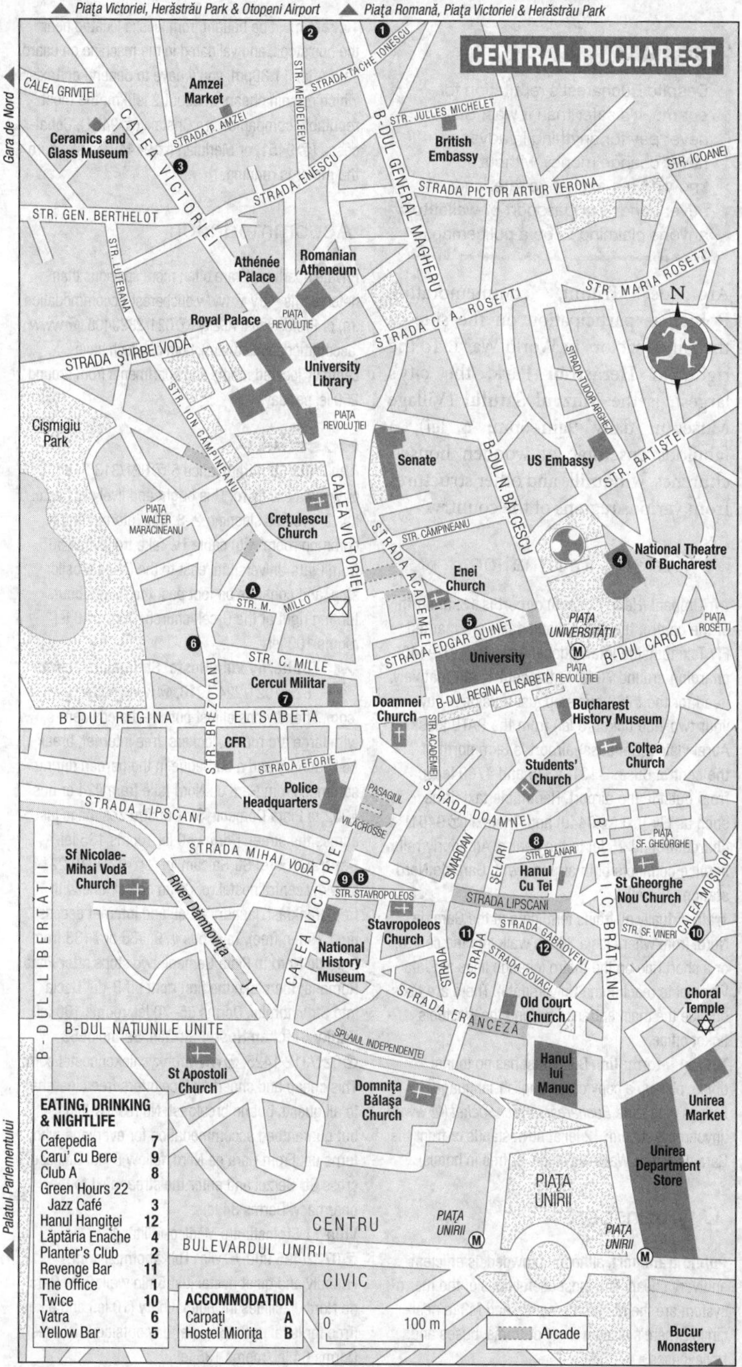
Piaţa Victoriei, Herăstrău Park & Otopeni Airport
Piaţa Română, Piaţa Victoriei & Herăstrău Park
CENTRAL BUCHAREST
Gara de Nord
Palatul Parlementului
Amzei Market
Ceramics and Glass Museum
British Embassy
Athénée Palace
Romanian Atheneum
Royal Palace
University Library
Cişmigiu Park
Senate
US Embassy
Creţulescu Church
National Theatre of Bucharest
Enei Church
University
Cercul Militar
Doamnei Church
Bucharest History Museum
CFR
Police Headquarters
Colţea Church
Students' Church
Sf Nicolae-Mihai Vodă Church
Hanul Cu Tei
St Gheorghe Nou Church
Stavropoleos Church
National History Museum
Old Court Church
Choral Temple
St Apostoli Church
Domniţa Bălaşa Church
Hanul lui Manuc
Unirea Market
Unirea Department Store
PIAŢA UNIRII
CENTRU CIVIC
Bucur Monastery
EATING, DRINKING & NIGHTLIFE
Cafepedia 7
Caru' cu Bere 9
Club A 8
Green Hours 22 Jazz Café 3
Hanul Hangiţei 12
Lăptăria Enache 4
Planter's Club 2
Revenge Bar 11
The Office 1
Twice 10
Vatra 6
Yellow Bar 5
ACCOMMODATION
Carpaţi A
Hostel Mioriţa B
0 100 m
Arcade

Villa Helga Str Mihai Eminescu 184 ⓣ021/212 0828, ⓦwww.villahelga.com. This popular HI hostel is still one of the best, with breakfast included and discounts available for groups of more than five or with a youth hostel card. There's a TV room, a clean kitchen and a sunny courtyard where guests have been known to pitch tents. Dorms 60 lei, rooms 144 lei.

Hotels

Andy Str Witing 2 ⓣ021/300 3050, ⓦwww .andyhotel.ro. Conveniently placed hotel with its own restaurant, in a high-rise building opposite the station. Fairly small rooms with bath, TV and breakfast included. 420 lei.
Carpăti Str Matei Millo 16 ⓣ021/315 0140, ⓦwww.hotelcarpatibucuresti.ro. Near Cişmigiu Park, quiet and with helpful staff. Singles and doubles available, some with shared showers or toilet and some en suite, all with TV. 210 lei.
Coco's B-dul Golescu 29 ⓣ021/311 0535, ⓦwww.cernahotel.ro. Situated opposite the *Andy* and formerly known as the *Cerna, Coco's* offers clean, light rooms with flatscreen TVs and modern furnishings. Some rooms have small concrete balconies. Breakfast included. 210 lei.
Hostel Mioriţa Str Lipscani 12 ⓣ021/312 0361. A hotel rather than a hostel, the *Mioriţa* has a great central location, spacious rooms (and beds) and cable TV. Breakfast included. 230 lei.

Eating

Bucharest's restaurant scene has improved dramatically in recent years, and there's now a wide selection of ethnic cuisines to choose from, as well as the traditional Romanian fare. Beware, though, that a few restaurants still have the nasty habit of charging food by weight – if the menu shows the cost per 100 grams, check the real price with the waiter.

Cafés and restaurants

Barka Saffron Str Av Sănătescu 1. Just west of the Arc de Triumf, this is a relaxed, charmingly decorated establishment with first-class international, Indian and vegetarian food. They also do freshly squeezed fruit juices. Daily noon–11.30pm. Mains 15–25 lei.
Cafepedia B-dul Elisabeta 11–13. This sophisticated new coffeehouse is one of Bucharest's best and is a great place to relax with a coffee, cocktail, book or laptop. A few light dishes and salads are available.
Caffe and Latte B-dul Schitu Măgureanu 35. Small, colourful café opposite Cişmigiu Park serving a fabulous range of coffees, shakes, sandwiches and cakes (till 10pm). They sell alcoholic drinks too. Cakes 5–10 lei, coffee 8–15 lei.
Caru' cu bere Str Stavropoleos 5. Superb restaurant housed in a spectacular nineteenth-century beer-house replete with carved wooden balconies, stained-glass windows and uniformed waiters. The menu features a broad range of Romanian dishes (15–50 lei), and beer is still brewed on the premises.
Hanul Hangiţei Str Gabroveni 16. A neighbourhood restaurant serving good Romanian cuisine – busy at lunchtime. A number of traditional dishes are available, including *escalop de mistreţ* (escalope of wild boar). Daily noon till midnight. Mains 16–25 lei.
Nicoreşti Str Maria Rosetti 40. Traditional Romanian dishes at rock-bottom prices with accompanying live music. Few vegetarian options. Mains 15–20 lei.
Vatra Str Brezoianu 23. Very central, very affordable, with great Romanian dishes such as *ciorba* (soup; 8 lei).

Drinking and nightlife

In the historic centre, the area around Strada Gabroveni attracts the crowds, while in summer, the clubs and restaurants around the lake in Herăstrău Park are popular. The weekly Romanian-language *Şapte Seri* magazine (ⓦwww.sapteseri.ro), free in bars, has events and cinema listings.

Bars

Green Hours 22 Jazz Cafe Calea Victoriei 120 ⓦwww.green-hours.ro. Cramped cellar-bar with frequent live music and arty theatre shows that attract a lively alternative crowd. Open 24 hours.
Lăptăria Enache 4th floor of the National Theatre, Piaţa Universităţii ⓣ021/315 8508. One of Bucharest's most popular bars, with live music in winter, and free films on the rooftop terrace in summer. Entrance near the *Intercontinental* hotel near the *Café Deko* sign. Daily noon–2am (Fri & Sat till 4am).
Planter's Club Str Stirbei Voda 68. Immensely popular bar-cum-club with a small dancefloor and pricey drinks. Daily 10am–5am.
Revenge Bar Str Selari 9–11. Atmospheric cellar-bar with vaulted brick ceilings and an eclectic mixture of music played at deafening levels. Daily 5pm–7am.
Yellow Bar Str E. Quinet 10, near Piaţa Universităţii. Trendy cellar-lounge bar with comfortable sofas, lots of beautiful people and a good cocktail list. Mon–Fri 10am–2am, Sat & Sun 5pm–5am.

Clubs

Club A Str Blănari 14 ⓦwww.cluba.ro. Catering to a studenty crowd, this good-time party place is the

city's most established club. Mon–Wed 10pm–5am, Thurs–Sun 9pm–5am.

Kristal Glam Str. J.S. Bach 2 Ⓦ www.clubkristal.ro. The only real choice for serious clubbers, this imposing, all-action club regularly plays host to some of Europe's star DJs (Seb Fontaine, Pete Tong and Steve Mac, to name just a few). Thurs–Sun 10pm–5am.

Mash-Up Club Str. Mihail Eminescu 89 Ⓣ 0728/330 565. Unpretentious new club frequented by laid-back 20-somethings that plays the latest dubstep, funk, breakbeat and electronica. Fri & Sat 11pm–5am.

Studio Martin B-dul Iancu de Hunedoara 61, near Piața Victoriei Ⓦ www.studiomartin.ro. Brings in the ravers with its international guest DJs (playing techno and house) and gay-friendly atmosphere. Fri & Sat 10pm–5am.

The Office Str Tache Ionescu 2 Ⓦ www.theoffice.ro. Fashionable club, with a hip crowd and great dance/disco music, but pricey and posey. Thurs–Sat 9.30pm–5am, Sun 10pm–2am.

Twice Str Sf. Vineri 4. Banging techno tunes at Bucharest's biggest club; heaving and very popular. Wed–Sat 9pm–5am.

Shopping

Unirea department store Piața Unirii 1. Dauntingly large but a good place to find familar labels. Mon–Sat 9am–9pm, Sun 9am–3pm.

Bucuresti Mall Calea Vitan 55–59. Daily 10am–10pm. Good for mid-range shops.

Hanul cu Tei bazaar Between Str. Lipscani 63–65 and Str. Blănari 5. Romanian antiques and souvenirs. Mon–Sat 10am–6pm.

Târgul Vitan flea market Calea Vitan. Sun only.

Unirii Market Just behind the Unirea department store (see above), with trinkets, souvenirs and fresh foods. Open daily.

Directory

Embassies and consulates Australia, 5th floor, Str Buzesti 14–18 Ⓣ 021/316 7558; Canada, Str Tuberozelor 1–3 Ⓣ 021/307 5000; UK, Str J. Michelet 24 Ⓣ 021/210 7300; US, Str T. Arghezi 7–9 Ⓣ 021/200 3300.

Exchange Traveller's cheques can be changed at most major banks – try the BCR at B-dul Regina Elisabeta 5 or Banc Post at Calea Vitan 6.

Gay and lesbian For information, contact Accept Ⓣ 021/252 9000, Ⓦ www.accept-romania.ro.

Hospital Spitalul Clinic de Urgența, Calea Floreasca 8 Ⓣ 021/599 2300. Medicover Unirii, 64–66 Marasesti Blvd Ⓣ 021/310 1599, Ⓦ www.medicover.com.

Internet *Pizza Hut* and *KFC* offer free wi-fi, as do most hotels and upmarket cafés. There is an internet point above *Green Hours 22 Jazz Cafe* at Calea Victorei 120. PC-Net have internet cafés at Calea Victoriei 136 and B-dul Regina Elisabeta 25.

Laundry Immaculate Cleaners, Str. Polonă 76 (Mon–Fri 7.30am–8.30pm, Sat 9am–5pm); Nufărul, Calea Moșilor 276 (Mon–Fri 7am–8pm, Sat 9am–1pm).

Left luggage *Bagaj de mână* (10 lei; open 24hr) at the Gara de Nord, opposite platforms 4 and 5.

Pharmacy Sensiblu has pharmacies throughout the city. Its 24hr branches are at B-dul Ion Mihalache 106 and Str Radu Beller 6. Helpnet has 24hr pharmacies at B-dul Ion Mihalache 92 and B-dul Unirii 2.

Post office Str M. Millo 10 (Mon–Fri 7.30am–8pm, Sat 8am–2pm).

Moving on

Train Brașov (every 45min–1hr; 2hr 30min–4hr 45min); Sibiu (3 daily; 4hr 45min–5hr 50min); Sighișoara (9 daily; 4hr–7hr 30min); Timișoara (9 daily; 7hr 30min–10hr 30min).

Bus Brașov (every 30min; 2hr 45min); Sibiu (4 daily; 4hr 30min).

Transylvania

From Bucharest, trains carve their way north through the spectacular **Carpathian mountain range** into the heart of **Transylvania**. The Carpathians offer Europe's cheapest skiing in winter and wonderful hiking during the summer (see p.963), along with caves, alpine meadows, dense forests sheltering bears, and lowland valleys with quaint villages.

The population is a mix of Romanians, Magyars, Germans, Roma and others, thanks to centuries of migration and colonization. The Trianon Treaty of 1920 placed Transylvania within the Romanian state, but the character of many towns still reflects past patterns of settlement. Most striking are the former seats of Saxon power with their defensive towers and fortified churches. Sighișoara is the most picturesque but

THE FORTIFIED CHURCHES OF TRANSYLVANIA

Transylvania's Saxon legacy is clearly apparent in the fortified churches erected throughout the region's villages following the migration of the Saxons to Romania under King Géza II in 1150. There are over a hundred fortified churches scattered across rural Transylvania, and seven have been listed as UNESCO World Heritage sites. The Mioritics Association, in conjuction with UNESCO, is dedicated to preserving the fortified churches and developing tourism around them (ⓦwww.fortified-churches.com). Despite this, most are not well known and there is little information available. However, most are accessible with their original gate-key, which is usually kept by one of the elder villagers for safekeeping. Simply ask in the village for the key-holder, who should be able to open up the church and show you around. It is normal to pay them a small amount (about 5 lei) for their trouble.

could be the Saxons' cenotaph: they have left their houses and churches but their living culture has evaporated, as it threatens to do in Braşov and Sibiu.

BRAŞOV

With an eye for trade and invasion routes, the medieval Saxons sited their largest settlements near Transylvania's mountain passes. **BRAŞOV**, which they called Kronstadt, grew prosperous as a result, and Saxon dominance lasted until the Communist government brought thousands of Moldavian villagers to work in the new factories. As a result, there are two parts to Braşov: the Gothic and Baroque centre beneath Mount Tâmpa, which looks great, and the surrounding sprawl of flats, which doesn't. The central square, surrounded by restored merchants' houses, is now the heart of a buzzing city with many new bars and restaurants.

What to see and do

Buses from the station will leave you near the central square, **Piaţa Sfatului**. Leading northeast from the square the pedestrianized **Strada Republicii** is the hub of Braşov's social and commercial life.

Piaţa Sfatului

Piaţa Sfatului is overshadowed by the Gothic pinnacles of the city's most famous landmark, the **Black Church** (Mon–Sat 10am–5pm), which stab upwards like a series of daggers. An endearingly monstrous hall-church that took almost a century to complete (1383–1477), it is so called for its soot-blackened walls, the result of being torched by the Austrian army in 1689. Inside, by contrast, the church is startlingly white, with oriental carpets creating splashes of colour along the walls of the nave. In summer (June–Sept Tues, Thurs & Sat at 6pm), the church's 4000-pipe organ is used for concerts.

The fifteenth-century council house (Casa Sfatului) in the centre of Piăta Sfatului now houses the **History Museum**, which has a small exhibition dedicated to the Saxon guilds that dominated Braşov in medieval times (Tues–Sun 10am–5pm).

Mount Tâmpa

A length of fortress wall runs along the foot of **Mount Tâmpa**, behind which a **cable car** (Tues–Sun 9.30am–9pm; 8 lei) whisks tourists up to the summit. However, the trails to the top offer a challenging walk and some fantastic views.

Museum of the Bârsa Land Fortifications

Of the original seven bastions (towers maintained by the city's trade guilds), the best preserved is that of the weavers, on Str Coşbuc. This complex of wooden galleries and bolt holes now contains the

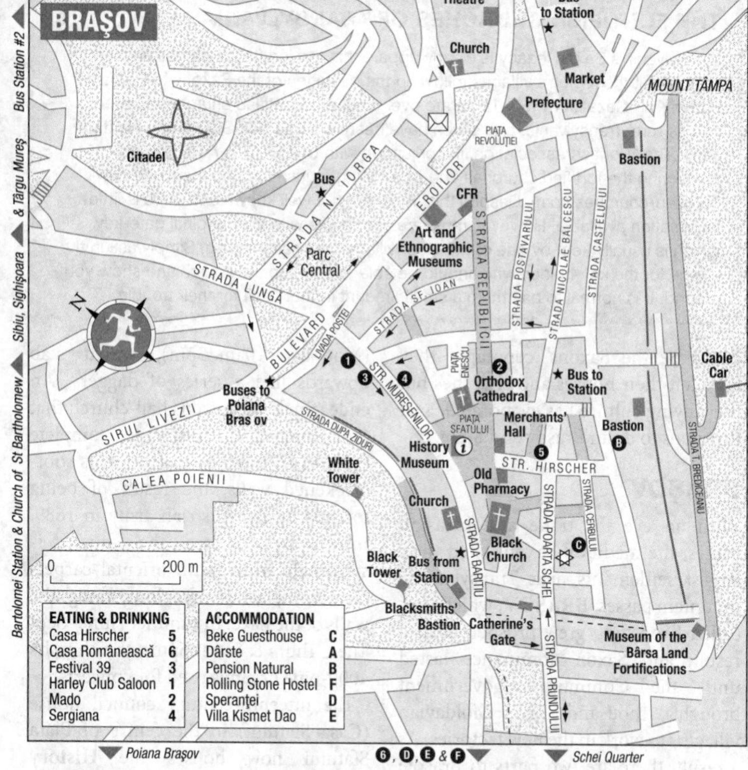

Museum of the Bârsa Land Fortifications (Tues–Sun 10am–4pm). Inside are models and weaponry recalling the bad old days when the region was repeatedly attacked by Tatars, Turks and by Vlad the Impaler, who left hundreds of captives on sharp stakes to terrorize the townsfolk. The Saxons' widely publicized stories of Vlad's cruelty unwittingly contributed to Transylvania's dark image and eventually caught Bram Stoker's attention as he conceived *Dracula*.

Arrival and information

Train Braşov's train station is northeast of the old town, 2km from the centre – take bus #4 into town or spend around 5 lei on a taxi.

Tourist office In the History Museum, Piaţa Sfatului 30 (☎0268/419078, Ⓦwww.brasovtourism.eu). Daily 9am–5pm.

Internet Cyber Café, Str Republicii 58 (daily 11am–9pm); Internet Café, Str Michael Weiss 11; and on the mezzanine floor of the train station.

Accommodation

Beke Guesthouse Str Cerbului 32 ☎0723/511 997. Basic and quiet guesthouse, and the spotless rooms have a traditional Romanian feel. Guests are provided with their own key. 80–100 lei.

Dârste 6km southeast of Braşov at Calea Bucureşti 285 ☎0268/339 967, Ⓦwww.campingdirste.ro. Modern campsite with cabins; it's best reached by taxi. Camping 13 lei, double cabins 55–120 lei.

Pension Natural Str Castelului 58 ☎0744/321 273, Ⓦwww.pensiuneanatural.ro. Immaculate family-run pension with a tranquil garden beside the city walls. Rooms 185 lei, apartment 250 lei.

Rolling Stone Hostel Str Piatra Mare 2a ☎0268/311 962 or 0744/816970 (mob), Ⓦwww.rollingstone.ro. Friendly and very sociable hostel

in the historic Schei district (near the Piața Unirii terminal of bus #4). Helpful staff provide maps and information as well as a drink on arrival. Dorms and rooms are clean and attractive, but check that the apartments aren't too far from the centre. Free breakfast, barbecue in the garden and wi-fi. Dorms 42 lei, rooms 150 lei, apartments 150–250 lei.

Speranței Str Piatra Mare 101 ⓣ0268/472 415, ⓦwww.hospice.ro. At this hospice with accommodation for the general public, close to *Rolling Stone*, your payment helps towards treatment for cancer victims. 140 lei.

Villa Kismet Dao Str Democrației 2b ⓣ0268/514 296, ⓦwww.kismetdao.com. Busy, popular hostel with no lockout, curfew or checkout time. Breakfast is included and there is a large kitchen with balcony and a barbecue in the garden. Free perks include internet access, laundry and a large TV room with over 100 DVDs. Just up the hill from Piața Unirii – bus #4 from the train station or use the hostel's cut-price pick-up service. Dorms 42 lei, rooms 150 lei.

Eating and drinking

Casa Hirscher Piața Sfatului 12–14. This lovely restaurant housed in an atmospheric seventeenth-century building serves quality Romanian and international specialities. Mains 20–40 lei.

Casa Românească Piața Unirii 15. Friendly and cheap restaurant just around the corner from *Rolling Stone*, with a courtyard offering views of the *piața*. Traditional Romanian fare, and good-sized portions. Open 11am–midnight. Mains 9–25 lei.

Festival 39 Str Mureșenilor 23. A great place to drink, this bar is full of the strangest things – from badly stuffed animals to plastic trophies.

Harley Club Saloon Str Mureșenilor 13. A few doors up the street from *Festival 39*, this American-themed pub has plenty of seating and serves a decent range of bar food.

Mado Str Republicii 10. A popular restaurant on the main street, with outdoor seating and a spacious interior. The dishes – in large portions – include traditional Romanian and Turkish specialities; you can also try some Romanian wines, such as the hearty and spicy hot wine favoured in rural Transylvania during winter. Home-made cakes too. Mains 15–30 lei.

Sergiana Str Mureșenilor 22. Serves good Romanian food in the atmospheric cellars. Open 11am–midnight. Mains 12–30 lei.

Moving on

Train Bucharest (every 45min–1hr; 2hr 30min–4hr 45min); Sibiu (8 daily; 2hr 15min–3hr 55min); Sighișoara (10 daily; 1hr 40min–3hr); Timișoara (2 daily; 8hr 45min).

Bus Bran (every 30min 7am–6pm Mon–Fri, hourly Sat & Sun; 45min); Bucharest (hourly; 2hr 45min); Zărnești (hourly Mon–Fri, 8 Sat, 2 Sun; 1hr).

BRAN

Cosy little **BRAN**, 28km southwest of Brașov, is situated at the foot of the stunning Bucegi Mountains. Despite what you may hear, its **castle** (Tues–Sun 9am–5pm) has only tenuous associations with Dracula, aka Vlad the Impaler, who may have attacked it in 1460. Hyperbole is forgivable, though, as Bran really does look like a vampire count's residence. The castle was built in 1377 by the Saxons of Brașov to safeguard what used to be the main route into Wallachia, and it rises in tiers of towers and ramparts from amongst the woods, against a glorious mountain background. A warren of stairs, nooks and chambers around a small courtyard, the interior is filled with elaborately carved four-poster beds, throne-like chairs and portraits of grim-faced boyars.

Arrival

Bus Services from Brașov to Bran and Zărnești leave from bus station 2, 3km north of central Brașov at the end of Str Lungă; take bus #12 from the centre of Brașov or bus #10 from the train station, and get off opposite the stadium.

Accommodation

Private rooms *Ovi-Tours* (Str Bologa 16 ⓣ0268/236 666) have some clean and rustic-style rooms. 80 lei.

Jo's Villa B-dul Alexandru Vlahuta 21 ⓣ0268 316836, ⓦwww.guesthouse.ro. A comfortable alternative run by an affable British expat, set in a large garden, with kitchen facilities and immaculate en-suite doubles. 140 lei.

Moving on

Bus Brașov (every 30min 7am–6pm Mon–Fri, hourly Sat & Sun; 45min); Zărnești (8 daily; 30min).

RÂŞNOV AND ZĂRNEŞTI

For a more authentic experience than Bran, jump off the Braşov bus in nearby **RÂŞNOV**, where the hilltop fortress and the views are stunning. North of Bran is **ZĂRNEŞTI**, a charming small town that is the perfect jumping-off point for trips into the Făgăraş Mountains. You can stay at the *Pensiunea Mosorel*, Str Dr Senchea 162 (ⓣ0268/222 774, ⓦwww.pensiuneamosorel.go.ro; 200 lei). For a near-medieval mountain escape, spend a night at *Cabana Montana* (ⓣ0744/801 094; 120 lei), in the picturesque hamlet of **MAGURĂ**, on the flanks of the Piatra Craiului Mountains just south of Zărneşti. Phone ahead and they'll pick you up from Zărneşti's bus station.

SIGHIŞOARA

A forbidding silhouette of battlements and needle spires looms over the citadel of **SIGHIŞOARA**, perched on a hill overlooking the Târnave Mare valley; it seems fitting that this was the birthplace of Vlad Ţepeş, the man known to posterity as **Dracula**. Look out for the Medieval Arts and the Inter-ethnic Cultural **festivals** held annually in July and August, when Sighişoara may be overrun by thousands of beer-swillers.

What to see and do

The route from the train station to the centre passes the **Romanian Orthodox Cathedral**, its gleaming white, multi-faceted facade a striking contrast to the dark interior. Across the **Târnave Mare** river, the **citadel** dominates the town from a hill whose slopes support a jumble of ancient houses. Steps lead up from the lower town's main square, Piaţa Hermann Oberth, to the main gateway, above which rises the mighty **clock tower**. This was built in the fourteenth century when Sighişoara became a free town controlled by craft guilds – each of which had to finance the construction of a bastion and defend it in wartime.

Sighişoara grew rich on the proceeds of trade with Moldavia and Wallachia, as attested by the regalia and strongboxes in the tower's **museum** (Mon, Sat & Sun 9am–4.30pm, Tues–Fri 9am–6.30pm). The ticket also gives access to the seventeenth-century **torture chamber** and the **Museum of Armaments** next door, with its small and poorly presented Dracula Exhibition.

In 1431 or thereabouts, the child later known as Dracula was born at Str Muzeului 6 near the clock tower. At the time his father – Vlad Dracul – was commander of the mountain passes into Wallachia, but the younger Vlad's privileged childhood ended eight years later, when he and his brother Radu were sent to Anatolia as hostages to the Turks. There Vlad observed the Turks' use of terror, which he would later turn

WOLF AND BEAR TRACKING IN THE CARPATHIANS

Romania has the largest **wolf** and **brown bear** populations in Europe. Transylvanian Wolf (ⓣ0744/319 708, ⓦwww.transylvanianwolf.ro) is an organization offering guided walks (around 300 lei for up to 5 people, 65 lei for each extra person) tracking wolves, bears, red deer and lynx under the eagle eye of Dan Marin, an experienced tracker who has been voted one of the top three guides in the world by readers of *Wanderlust* magazine and who works closely with conservation organizations and the new Piatra Craiului National Park.

In winter there's also the chance to see some spectacular snow-covered landscapes, and take part in sleigh rides and cross-country skiing. If you really want to treat yourself, you can also stay in the Marins' spectacular family guesthouse (Str. I. Metianu nr. 108, Zărneşti; 360 lei), where all meals (breakfast, dinner and packed lunch) are home-cooked and included in the price.

against them, earning the nickname of "The Impaler". Nowadays, Vlad's birthplace is a mediocre tourist restaurant.

Arrival and information

Train Sighişoara's train station is on the northern edge of town, on Str Libertății.
Tourist office There's tourist information at the *International Café*, Piaţa Cetăţii 8.

Accommodation

Private rooms Backpackers are met at the station by runners for the town's many excellent private rooms; the best are with the Faur family in the citadel at Str Cojocarilor 1 (Ⓣ0744/119 211, Ⓔkristinafaur2003@yahoo.com); guests have use of a kitchen. 100 lei.
Burg Hostel Str Bastionului 4–6 Ⓣ0265/778 489, Ⓦwww.burghostel.ro. Centrally located with clean dorms, doubles and triples. There is a bar in the cellar, internet access (3.50 lei per hour) and free wi-fi. Breakfast isn't included, but there is a good-value restaurant in the courtyard. Dorms 35 lei, rooms 90 lei.
Nathan's Villa Str Libertății 8 Ⓣ0265/772 546, Ⓦwww.nathansvilla.com/sighisoara.html. Friendly, popular hostel with no curfew and no checkout time. Bright, airy dorms, all with ten beds, and one private double with en-suite bath. Other perks include free breakfast and laundry. Dorms 40 lei, double 110 lei.

Eating and drinking

Casa cu Cerb Str Şcolii 1 Ⓣ0265/774 625, Ⓦwww.casacucerb.ro. In the hotel of the same name on Piaţa Cetăţii, with a sunny and pleasant outdoor seating area. One of the best restaurants in the citadel, with good breakfasts, light meals and more expensive dinners. Daily 9am–10pm. Mains 15–35 lei.

TREAT YOURSELF

Casa cu Cerb Str Şcolii 1 Ⓣ0265/774 625, Ⓦwww.casacucerb.ro. A good choice for romantics, as the bathtubs fit two and the most expensive rooms have four-poster double beds. The contents of the minibar are also included in the price along with breakfast. 220 lei.

Casa Vlad Dracul Str Cositorarilor 5. This cavernous, Dracula-themed restaurant is tucked away in a fifteenth-century building thought to have been the birthplace of Vlad Dracul. International menu, with mains around 25 lei.
International Café Piaţa Cetăţii 8. A cosy café serving delicious and filling sandwiches and cakes, and just about the only quiche in Transylvania. Mon–Sat 8am–9pm in summer, 10am–6pm in winter. Sandwiches and quiche 8 lei.
La Strada Str Morii 7. Good pizzas and outdoor seating. Mon–Thurs & Sun 10am–midnight, Fri & Sat 10am–1am. Mains 10–120 lei.
Rustica Str 1 Decembrie 1918 no. 5. Fairly good Romanian food in nice surroundings and a popular bar at night. Good breakfast menu. Mains 15–25 lei.
The Music Pub In the basement of the *Burg Hostel*, with some live rock/pop music, mainly weekend evenings.

Moving on

Train Braşov (10 daily; 1hr 45min–2hr 45min); Bucharest (8 daily; 4hr 15min–5hr); Sibiu (change at Copşa Mică or Mediaş; 15 daily; 2hr 5min–2hr 45min).

SIBIU

The narrow streets and old gabled houses of **SIBIU**'s older quarters seem to have come straight off the page of a fairytale. Like Braşov, Sibiu was founded by Germans invited by Hungary's King Géza II to colonize strategic regions of Transylvania in 1143. Its inhabitants dominated trade in Transylvania and Wallachia, but their citadels were no protection against the tide of history, which eroded their influence after the eighteenth century. Within the last decades almost the entire Saxon community has left Romania. Sibiu still has stronger and more lucrative links with Germany than any Transylvanian town, and its stint as European Capital of Culture in 2007 left its buildings handsomely refurbished.

What to see and do

To reach the old town cross the square from the train station and follow Str Gen. Magheru to **Piaţa Mare** – one of

three conjoined squares that form the centre.

Piața Mare

On the western side of Piața Mare stands the **Muzeul Brukenthal** (Tues–Sun 10am–6pm), one of the finest Museum in Romania with an evocative collection of works by Transylvanian painters. The city's **Muzeul de Istorie** (History Museum; Tues–Sun 10am–6pm) is nearby in the impressive Old City Hall. On the northern side of Piața Mare, the huge Catholic church stands next to the **Council Tower** (daily 10am–6pm), which offers fine views to the Carpathians.

The cathedral

Just beyond the Council Tower, on Piața Huet, the **Evangelical Cathedral** (9am–6pm, Sun from 10am) is a massive hall-church raised during the fourteenth and fifteenth centuries. Climb the tower (Mon–Sat noon–4pm), or descend to the crypt, which contains impressive tombstones of local notables as well as of Mihnea the Bad, the Impaler's son, stabbed to death outside here in 1510.

Muzeul Astra

Set aside most of a day to explore Sibiu's wonderful open-air **Muzeul Astra** (Tues–Sun 10am–6pm) on Calea Rășinari, south of the centre; take trolleybus #1 to the end of the line. Set against a mountain backdrop, the museum offers a fantastic insight into rural life, with authentically furnished wooden houses, churches and mills; there's also a traditional inn serving local food and drink.

Arrival and information

Train and bus Sibiu's train and bus stations are next to each other on Piața 1 Decembrie 1918, 400m northeast of the main square.
Tourist office Sibiu's excellent tourist office, inside the City Hall at Str Samual Brukenthal 2 (Ⓣ0269/208 913, Ⓦwww.sibiu.ro; Mon–Sat 9am–5pm & Sun 9am–1pm), also sells maps and hands out the *Sibiu Live* and *Șapte Seri* listings magazines.

Accommodation

Ela Str Nouă 43 Ⓣ0269/215 197. A friendly, family-run hotel, with a pleasant garden, eight spotless en-suite rooms and guest kitchen. Breakfast is extra (15 lei). From the train station take Str 9 Mai, turn right onto Str Rebreanu, then first left onto Str Nouă. 120 lei.
Evangelisches Pfarrhaus Piața Huet 1 Ⓣ0269/211 203, Ⓦwww.evang.ro/hermannstadt. Next to the cathedral, the Lutheran parish house (daily 8am–3pm, or call in advance so a key can be left for you) has a hostel with simple rooms sleeping two to four. Dorms 40 lei.
Old Town Hostel Piața Mică 26 Ⓣ0269/216 445, Ⓦwww.hostelsibiu.ro. Located above a historic pharmacy in a 450-year-old building, the hostel has three large, airy dorms and also offers en-suite doubles at a different location. Breakfast is included and there's a kitchen, plus free tea and coffee. Internet access is free, and the hostel can also arrange bike hire (35 lei per day); laundry costs 10 lei for 5kg. Dorms 45 lei, rooms 180 lei.
Pensiune and Camping Sălișteanca at Str. Băii 13, Săliște Ⓣ0269/553 121, Ⓦwww.salisteanca.com. A fantastic choice in summer, when the town's hostels are packed, this riverside campsite is also a lovely place to stay in its own right, with clean, modern facilities. There are also a few large en-suite rooms available, furnished in traditional Transylvanian style. Breakfast 12 lei; dinner is available in the *pensiune* on request. Campsite 12 lei per person and 34 lei per tent, rooms 85 lei.
Podul Minciunilor Str Azilului 1 Ⓣ0269/217 259. A small, family-run guesthouse, with five doubles and one triple. No breakfast, but will do laundry on request (20 lei). 110 lei.

Eating and drinking

Art Café Str Filarmonicii 2 Ⓦwww.galeria-artvo.ro. In the cellars of an atmospheric building, this stays open from 8am until 2am or later. Drinks are cheap and there are occasional jazz gigs.
The Chill Out Club Piața Mică 23 Ⓦwww.chilloutsibiu.ro. Sibiu is quiet after 9pm; however, there are a few options if you want to stay out later. This club plays mostly house music, and holds out till 6am.
Crama Sibiu Vechi Str Ilarian 3. This cellar restaurant decorated in local style is the best place for something typically Romanian, complete with live

folk music and staff dressed in traditional costume. They also have cheap wine on tap. Daily noon–11.30pm. Mains 12–30 lei.

La Turn Piața Mare 1. In a good central location next to the Council Tower, this place has a range of grilled and barbecued dishes. Daily 10.30am–11pm. Mains 11–36 lei.

Mara Str Bălcescu 21. Excellent local food is served up here, and they have a large selection of wines, including Romanian varieties. Daily 10am–midnight. Mains 14–40 lei.

Moving on

Train Brașov (7 daily; 2hr 10min–3hr 50min); Bucharest (3 daily; 5hr 25min); Sighișoara (change at Copșa Mică or Mediaș; 16 daily; 2hr 15min–3hr); Timișoara (2 daily; 5hr 10min–6hr).

Bus Bucharest (4 daily; 4hr 30min).

The Banat

Once a much larger territory that now lies between Romania and neighbouring Hungary and Serbia, the featureless plains of **Banat** were ruled from **Timişoara** until the Turks conquered it in 1552; they governed until 1716 when they were ousted by the Habsburgs. The region's current frontiers were drawn up during the Versailles conference of 1918–20. Today, Romanian Banat is still home to a diverse population that for centuries has included Slovaks, Bulgarians, Ukrainians and Germans living alongside Serbians, Romanians and Hungarians.

TIMIŞOARA

The engaging city of **TIMIŞOARA**, 250km west of Sibiu near the Serbian border and the rail junction at Arad, is Romania's most Westward-oriented city, its good location and multilingual inhabitants attracting much foreign investment. The city's fame abroad rests on its crucial role in the overthrow of the Ceauşescu regime. A Calvinist minister, Lászlo Tökes, stood up for the rights of the Hungarian community, and when the police came to evict him on December 16, 1989, his parishioners barred their way. The riots that ensued inspired the people of Bucharest to follow, so that Timişoara sees itself as the guardian of the revolution.

What to see and do

Approaching from the train station, you'll enter the centre at the attractive pedestrianized Piaţa Victoriei, with fountains and flowerbeds strewn along its length. North of here, antique trams trundle past the Baroque **Town Hall** on the central Piaţa Libertăţii, while two blocks further north is the vast Piaţa Unirii.

Piaţa Victoriei

The focal point of Piaţa Victoriei is the huge **Romanian Orthodox Cathedral**, completed in 1946 with a blend of neo-Byzantine and Moldavian architectural elements. At the opposite end, the unattractive Opera House stands near the **castle**, which now houses the **Museum of the Banat**'s broad collection of archeological and historical artefacts. (Mon–Sat 10am–4pm).

Piaţa Unirii

Piaţa Unirii is dominated by the monumental **Roman Catholic and Serbian Orthodox cathedrals**. Built between 1736 and 1773, the former (to the east) is a fine example of Viennese Baroque; the latter is roughly contemporaneous and almost as impressive.

The Ethnographic Museum

In 1868, the municipality demolished most of the redundant citadel, leaving two bastions to the east and west of Piaţa Unirii. The eastern one is occupied by the **Ethnographic Museum** (Tues–Sun 10am–5pm; entrance at Str Popa Şapcă 4). Varied folk costumes, painted glass icons and furnished rooms

illustrate the region's ethnic diversity, but don't provide a comprehensive history – for example, there's no mention of the thousands of Serbs deported in 1951 when the Party fell out with Tito's neighbouring Yugoslavia.

Arrival and information

Train Timișoara Nord train station is a 15min walk west of the centre along B-dul Republicii.
Tourist office The tourist office (Mon–Fri 9am–8pm, Sat 9am–5pm; ⓣ 0256/437 973, ⓦ www.primariatm.ro), on the ground floor of the opera building at Str Alba Julia 2, has maps and copies of the free English-language listings magazine *Timișoara What Where When*.
Internet There's cheap internet access at Savoya 22, south of Piața Unirii.

Accommodation

Camping International 4km west of town on Aleea Pădurea Verde ⓣ 0256/208 925, ⓦ www.campinginternational.ro. Open all year, the well-kept campsite also has huts sleeping two to four people. Take trolleybus #11 from the train station or centre. Campsite 10 lei, huts 60 lei.
Hotel Nord B-dul Gen, Dragalina 47 ⓣ 0256/497 504, ⓦ www.hotelnord.ro. The hotel is conveniently located opposite the train station, but can get a bit noisy outside at night. Inside it is bright and clean with en-suite rooms. Breakfast is included. 100–200 lei.
Hotel Timisoara Str. Marasesti 1–3 ⓣ 0256/498 862, ⓦ www.hoteltimisoara.ro. Despite its plain appearance, the hotel is clean and modern and benefits from a central location. 220 lei.

Eating, drinking and nightlife

There's a useful 24hr supermarket, Stil, on Str Mărășești (at Str Lazăr), a short walk northwest of Piața Libertății. Party animals should head for the canalside bars behind the cathedral such as the *Bănăteana* (Parcul Justiției 1), or the *Terasa Boss* (Str V. Pârvan 1). Find out what's going on in the weekly *Șapte Seri* (ⓦ www.sapteseri.ro), found free at most bars.
Baroque Piața Unirii 14. This place lives up to its name, with wrought-iron tables and chairs outside and a decadent array of teas, coffees, milkshakes and hot chocolate – both alcoholic and non alcoholic. Breakfasts for around 15 lei, hot drinks from 5 lei. Daily 8am–1am.
Club 3 Piața Victoriei 7 ⓦ www.club30.ro. In the Cinema Timiș, this has good jazz, often live. Daily 6pm–3am.
Club XXI Piața Victoriei 2. Serves large, hearty meals, including some traditional dishes from the Banat region. Daily 10am–midnight. Mains 15–23 lei.
Harold's Aleea Studenților 17. Simple, understated and surprisingly classy restaurant, with a wide selection of international and vegetarian options, including the large "Harold's Vegetarian Plate" – to share for 52 lei. Daily 11.30am–midnight. Most mains about 20 lei.
Java Coffee House Str Rodnei 6. Open 24 hours a day (in theory), this dark bar on the southeastern corner of Piața Unirii is a good place for a coffee or something stronger. Drinks range from the classic to the more inventive, including their "ice cream chocolate coffee". Drinks 7–18 lei.
Piranha Cocktail Bar Str Savoya 5. A popular drinking den with a range of cocktails and truly eye-catching surroundings, complete with fish tanks, live lizards and snakes. Open around the clock (in theory), it's also a pleasant place for morning coffee.
Pizza Rustica Piata Unirii, Str Pavel Chinezu 6. Pleasant pizzeria serving a good range of pizzas and pasta dishes (15–30 lei).

Moving on

Train Brașov (1 daily; 9hr); Bucharest (6 daily; 7hr 30min–8hr 45min); Sibiu (1 daily; 5hr 5min–6hr 30min).

Russia

HIGHLIGHTS

THE HERMITAGE: view thousands of priceless treasures at Russia's premier museum

KUNSTKAMMER: don't miss Peter the Great's eighteenth-century collection of curiosities

PETER AND PAUL FORTRESS: caper along the battlements in period costume and take a dip in the Neva River

BANYA: purge your pores in style at Moscow's Sandunovsky baths

THE KREMLIN: see the Orlov Diamond, the world's largest cannons and stunning churches at the historical and political heart of Russia

ROUGH COSTS

DAILY BUDGET Basic €50/occasional treat €75

DRINK Beer (pivo) €2.50

FOOD Pancake (blini) €1.50

HOSTEL/BUDGET HOTEL €15–28/€45

TRAVEL Train: Moscow–St Petersburg (7–9hr) €40–75

FACT FILE

POPULATION 142 million

AREA 17,075,400 sq km (including six thousand islands)

LANGUAGE Russian

CURRENCY Ruble (R)

CAPITAL Moscow (population 10.5 million)

INTERNATIONAL PHONE CODE ☎7

Introduction

European Russia stretches from the borders of Belarus and Ukraine to the Ural mountains, over 1000km east of Moscow; even without the rest of the vast Russian Federation, it constitutes by far the largest country in Europe. Formerly a powerful tsarist empire and a Communist superpower, Russia continues to be a source of fascination for travellers. While access is still made relatively difficult by lingering Soviet-style bureaucracy – visas are obligatory and accommodation usually has to be booked in advance – independent travel is increasing every year, and visitors are doubly rewarded by the cultural riches of the country and the warmth of the Russian people.

Moscow, Russia's bustling capital, combines the frenetic energy of an Eastern city with the cosmopolitan feel of a Western one. With its show-stopping architecture – from the tsarist palaces of the Kremlin and the onion domes of St Basil's Cathedral, through the monumental relics of the Communist years, to the massive building projects of today – and the impersonal human tide that packs its streets and subways, the metropolis can feel rather overwhelming. By contrast, **St Petersburg**, Russia's second city, is Europe at its most gracious, an attempt by the eighteenth-century tsar Peter the Great to emulate the best of Western European elegance in what was then a far-flung outpost. Its people are more relaxed and friendly, and its position in the delta of the River Neva is unparalleled, giving it endless watery vistas. Visible – often ostentatious – but uneven wealth creation in both cities has made them twin figureheads for Russia's recent high-speed renaissance.

CHRONOLOGY

862 AD A Scandinavian warrior, Rurik, founds the state of "Russ".
989 Grand Duke Vladimir I adopts Orthodox Christianity.
1552 Ivan the Terrible conquers the Tatars and builds the famous domed St Basil's Cathedral in Red Square, Moscow.
1613 Michael Romanov is elected as Tsar of Russia, ushering in 300 years of Romanov rule.
1725 Peter the Great builds the new capital of St Petersburg after defeating Sweden in the Great Northern War.
1751 First recorded reference to "vodka" is made in a decree made by Empress Elizabeth.
1812 Napoleon invades Russia but is defeated.
1869 Tolstoy writes *War and Peace*.
1892 Tchaikovsky composes the famous ballet, *The Nutcracker*.
1905 Revolution leads to the masses gaining both a constitution and a parliament.
1914 Russia enters World War I on behalf of the Allies.
1917 The October Revolution witnesses the Communist Bolsheviks, led by Lenin, overthrowing the monarchy and government.
1924 Joseph Stalin takes control of the Soviet Union.
1941 The Nazis invade Russian territory; after intense fighting and victory at Stalingrad, the Red Army repel the Germans from Russia.
1961 Yuri Gagarin becomes the first human to travel into space aboard the *Vostok*.
1962 The Cuban Missile Crisis heightens tensions with the US during the Cold War.
1991 The Soviet Union collapses; many former Soviet countries declare independence. Boris Yeltsin is elected President.
1999 Yeltsin resigns and is replaced by Vladimir Putin.
2007 Russian relations with the US deteriorate over their plans to install anti-missile launchers around Russia's borders.
2008 Russia goes to war with Georgia over Georgia's offensive against Southern Ossetia.
2009 President Medvedev announces Russia's rearmament plan, which includes nuclear force.

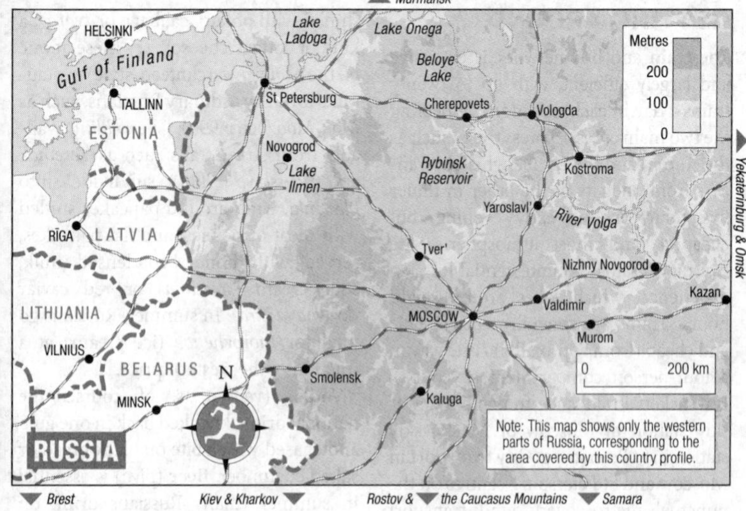

ARRIVAL AND VISAS

Moscow's Sheremetyevo and Domodedovo airports and St Petersburg's Pulkovo Airport are all served by numerous international flights. All **airports** are connected with their respective cities by regular and efficient public transport. Besides being the main hub for all domestic **trains**, including the trans-Siberian ones, Moscow is served by trains from Rīga, Tallinn, Warsaw, Berlin and Budapest, while European train routes into St Petersburg include arrivals from Helsinki, Rīga and Vilnius. Train stations in both Moscow and St Petersburg are well connected to the metro; all Moscow's "vokzals" link to a stop on the (brown) circle line. The most convenient way to come to St Petersburg for travellers coming from the Baltic States may be by **bus**, as they are more frequent than trains. **Ferries** into St Petersburg from Helsinki and Tallinn arrive at the Vasilyevskiy Island ferry terminal.

Anyone travelling on a **tourist visa** to Russia must (nominally) have **accommodation** arranged before arrival. If you book a hostel in advance you can request visa support before you go. If you haven't yet decided where to stay when you get your visa, tourist agents in your home country are often prepared to arrange visa "invitations" in which they state that you will be staying at a randomly selected hotel. There is no obligation to actually do so once in Russia. If you book your hostel on arrival, request visa assistance – hostels can direct you to a visa registration agency. Note that it's important to **register your visa** within three working days of your arrival. On arrival you fill out an immigration card: you will be given back the bottom half which you must keep and present on departure.

VISA CONTACTS

www.russianembassy.net Russian embassies and consulates.
www.scottstours.co.uk Visa service, handy for travellers combining Russia with Ukraine, Belarus, the Baltics or Central Asia.
www.trans-siberian.co.uk The Russia Experience organizes trips to Moscow and St Petersburg and across the world's largest country on board the iconic trains. Personalized trip packages available.
www.visatorussia.com Outstanding visa service.

GETTING AROUND

The **train** and **bus** network is extensive and largely efficient, with up to twenty trains a day in each direction connecting the two main cities. Express trains such as the *Aurora* and the Er-200 whisk passengers from one city to the other in under five hours in the early evening, but cheapest, and most atmospheric, are overnight trains, a quintessential Russian experience, which takes around eight hours. Trains are generally safe, reliable and cheap (from approx R800 one way in a four-person compartment or coupé). Buy tickets in advance from Leningradskiy station in Moscow or Moskovskiy station in St Petersburg. **City transport** in Moscow and St Petersburg centres on the punctual metro; overground transport includes buses, trams, trolleybuses and minibuses (*marshrútki*). Official taxis can be very expensive, whereas unofficial ones are not necessarily safe. **Bike** hire in St Petersburg offers a pleasant way to see the city's quieter outer corners, but cycle around Moscow at your peril.

ACCOMMODATION

Hostels tend to be safer, cleaner and more pleasant than cheap **hotels**, many of which have "economy" rooms unaltered since Soviet times. The standard rate is around R700–800 a night; aim to reserve three to four weeks in advance in the summer. Booking ahead by phone or with Ⓦwww.hostels.com will guarantee you a bed for the night. See p.983 for more on accommodation.

FOOD AND DRINK

Moscow and St Petersburg are bursting at the seams with cafés and restaurants covering everything from budget blowouts to *elitni* (elite) extravagance. Japanese is the cuisine *du jour*, so sushi abounds, but traditional Russian fare is still at the heart of many locals' everyday diets. **National dishes** worth tasting include *borshch* (beetroot soup), *shchi* (cabbage soup) and *pirogi* (small pies stuffed with potato, cabbage or *tvorog*, a kind of cottage cheese). Try these at one of the *stolovaya* (canteen-style) restaurants loved by ordinary Russians, such as *Moo-Moo* (see p.994). Cheap *blini*, available from street stalls such as *Teremok* and *Russkiye Blini*, subdivide into *blinchiki*, wrap-around pancakes stuffed with meat or berries, and flat pancakes, served with honey, condensed milk, sour cream (*smetana*) or red caviar (*krasnaya ikra*). In summer, Russians go mad for *morozhenoe* (ice cream) at a fraction of the western price.

Vodka (*vódka*) is, of course, the national drink, knocked back in one gulp and chased with a bite on black bread or salted cucumber. **Beer** (*pivo*) is essential in summer (many Russians drink on their way to work); try Baltika, rated in strength from 3 to 9, Stariy Melnik or Nevskoe. Refined palates may prefer excellent semi-sweet Georgian **wines** (Khvanchkara was Stalin's favourite). For cheap eating and drinking, you could do a lot worse than to stock up at a *produkti* (product store), or at *rynki* (markets), scattered across both cities, though concentrated in the suburbs. These sell the full range of Russian dairy delights (try *kefir* – sour milk), salami, sausages and cheap fresh fruit and veg. Traditionally, breakfast is eaten at 8am and "dinner" at 3pm; evening meals out tend to be eaten around 9pm.

CULTURE AND ETIQUETTE

Though the Western practise of eating out is now widespread, Russians love to entertain at home, and if you're invited over always bring a small present, be it a bottle of vodka or some chocolates. **Tipping** is in vogue only at high-end eating and drinking establishments, and five to ten percent should cover it. In **churches**, women should cover their head and shoulders, and men in shorts may be refused entry; you'll also notice that Russians avoid turning their back

to the iconostasis that screens the altar. Russians are rather superstitious; you'll see people rubbing the noses of the dog statues at the Metro Ploshad' Revolutsii for good luck. Old-fashioned chivalry is alive and well, with men opening doors for women and offering to help with heavy lifting. You'll notice young people giving up their seats to the elderly on public transport; follow their example before being told to.

SPORTS AND ACTIVITIES

Spectator sports centre on **football**, with Moscow's biggest teams being Dinamo (Leningradskiy prospect 36 ⓣ095/612 7172, ⓦwww.fcdynamo.ru; Metro Dinamo) and Spartak (Spartak stadium, 3rd Grazhdanskaya ul. 47a ⓣ095/105 0562, ⓦwww.spartak.com; Metro Preobrazhenskaya Ploshchad), while Petersburgers support Zenit (Petrovskiy stadium, 2nd Petrovskiy Island ⓦwww.fc-zenit.ru; Metro Sportivnaya).

Skating rinks include Moscow's year-round covered rink at Gorky Park, Krymskiy Val ul. 9, Metro Park Kultury, and Iskra at Selskokhozyaytvennaya ul. 26, Metro Botanichesky Sad. Winter **sledging** in Moscow benefits from good verticals on the Sparrow Hills (Vorobyovye gory; Metro Universitet), where you can overlook Moscow State University, the largest of the "seven sisters", the city's collection of 1950s Stalinist-Gothic skyscrapers. Summer or winter, **swim** in the open air at Chayka, Tuchaninov per. 1/3, Metro Park Kultury, or Luzhniki, Luzhnetskaya nab. 24, Metro Vorobyevy Gory. Cycling enthusiasts can see St Petersburg year-round with a **bike tour** (Skatprokat Rent a Bike, Goncharnaya ul. 7, Metro Pl. Vosstaniya) or **walking tour** (Peter's Walking Tours, through International Youth Hostel, ⓦwww.peterswalk.com; R600 for 4–5hr).

COMMUNICATIONS

Most **post offices** are open Monday to Saturday 8am to 7pm, and blue postboxes are affixed to walls across both cities. However, local mail is slow and not particularly reliable, so for urgent letters use **express companies** such as WestPost, which let you obtain a Finnish PO address, then receive your post in Russia as poste restante, or DHL. **Internet cafés** are abundant and cheap; most hostels offer internet access on a limited number of screens for free or for R1 per minute. For **international calls** get a pre-paid international phone card such as the Zebra Telecom card or Evroset' card, usable from any phone. Ask at a bank or telecoms kiosk for a *telefonnaya karta*. ⓦwww.waytorussia.net lets you buy a card pin online, which you can use to make instant international calls. Non-Russian **mobiles** work on roaming via local providers, but you'll pay an arm and a leg. Get a local SIM card for R200–400 (bring your passport with you to buy one), or stick to SMS.

EMERGENCIES

Beware of **petty crime**, particularly pickpockets in the metro and in bus and train stations during rush hour. Don't leave valuables in your hotel room, and lock the door before going to sleep. If you have a dark complexion exercise extra caution, especially at night, as racist attacks are not unknown. Your embassy will be able to advise you on what to do if you get robbed. The **police** (*militsia*) wear blue-grey uniforms; always make sure you have photocopies of your passport and visa on you, as they do stop people at random and often look for an excuse to fine you. When

EMERGENCY NUMBERS

Police ⓣ02; Ambulance ⓣ03; Fire ⓣ01. Moscow rescue service (for help with any incidents while holidaying in Moscow) ⓣ095/937 9911. You'll be connected to an English-speaking operator.

Russian

	Russian	Pronunciation
Yes	да	Da
No	нет	Nyet
Please	пожалуйста	Pazháaloosta
Thank you	спасибо	Spaséeba
Hello/Good day	здравствуйте	Zdrávstweetye
Goodbye	до свидания	Da svidáaneya
Excuse me	извините	Izvinéetye
Sorry	простите	Prostitye
Where?	где?	Gdye?
Good/Bad	хороший/плохой	Khoróshee/Plokhóy
Near/Far	близко далеко	Bléezki/Dalyekó
Cheap/Expensive	дешевый/дорогой	Deshóvy/Daragóy
Open/Closed	открыто/закрыто	Otkryto/Zakryto
Today	сегодня	Sevódnya
Yesterday	вчера	Vcherá
Tomorrow	завтра	Závtra
How much is...?	сколько стоит...?	Skólka stóyit...?
What time is it?	Который час?	Katóree chass?
I don't understand	я не понимаю	Ya ne ponimáyou
Do you speak English?	вы говорите по-английски?	Vwee gavoréetye po angliyski?
Where are the toilets?	где туалеты?	Gdye tualyéty?
My name is...	меня зовут...	Menyá zavóot...
What is your name?	как вас зовут?	Kak vas zavóot?
I don't speak Russian	я не говорю по-русски	Ya nye gavaryóo pa-róosski
Can I have....	можно...	Mózhna...
Tea	чай	Chay
Beer	пиво	Péeva
Juice	сок	Sok
I am a vegetarian	я вегетарианец	Ya vegetariyánets
The bill, please	счет пожалуйста	Shchyot, pazháloosta
Men's toilet (often seen as M)	мужчины	moózhshini
Women's toilet (often seen as Z)	женщины	zhénshini
Breakfast	завтрак	Závtrak
One	один	Adéen
Two	два	Dva
Three	три	Tree
Four	четыре	Chetéeri
Five	пять	Pyat
Six	шесть	Shest
Seven	семь	Syeem
Eight	восемь	Vósyem
Nine	девять	Dáyvyat
Ten	десять	Dáysyat

traversing busy roads, look for an underground crossing – переход (*perekhod*) – as many drivers do not honour zebra crossings. High-street **pharmacies** (*aptéka*) offer many familiar medicines over the counter. Foreigners tend to rely on expensive **private clinics** for treatment, so travel insurance is essential. St Petersburg **water** contains the giardia parasite,

which can cause severe diarrhoea – metranidazol is the cure. Moscow's tap water is safe to drink.

INFORMATION

Tourist offices are few and far between. Moscow's official tourist office (Gostiniy Dvor, Ilyichna ulitsa, Metro Kitai Gorod) has some English-language info, mostly on excursions out of town. Much better is St Petersburg's Tourist Information Office (Sadovaya ulitsa 14/52, Metro Gostiny Dvor); pick up the excellent *In Your Pocket* guide and a bite-size *Yellow Pages*. Hostel and hotel receptions carry leaflets and maps, and you can get up-to-date bar, restaurant and entertainment listings and reviews from **English-language papers**. The *Moscow Times* and the more ponderously pro-Kremlin *Moscow News* are well-established; *Element* is directed at young city-dwellers (Ⓦwww.element moscow.ru), and there's also the tongue-in-cheek expat mag *The Exile* (Ⓦwww .exiledonline.ru) and *Where Moscow* magazine (Ⓦwww.wheremoscow.spn .ru). **Maps** in English are cheap and readily available at bookstores such as Moskva (Tverskaya ul. 8/7, Moscow) and Dom Inostrannoi Knigi (Kuznetsky Most 18/7, Metro Kuznetsky Most, Moscow).

MONEY AND BANKS

Russia's currency is the **ruble**, divided into 100 kopeks. There are coins of 1, 5, 10, 20 and 50 kopeks and 1, 2 and 5 rubles, and notes of 5, 10, 50, 100, 500 and 1000 rubles. Everything is paid for in rubles, although some hostels make a habit of citing prices in either euros or dollars. At the time of writing €1=R44. Only **change money** in an official bank or currency exchange. Most **exchange offices** are open Monday to Saturday 10am to 8pm or later, and **ATMs** are plentiful. In general, prices in both cities range from "new Russian" prices (Moscow was recently named the most expensive city in the world) down to what the average Russian salary will cover, making many shops, bars and cafés highly affordable for the budget-conscious traveller.

RUSSIA ON THE NET

Ⓦ**www.go-magazine.ru** The *Moscow Times*'s online guide to the capital.
Ⓦ**www.sptimesrussia.com** English-language online newspaper, with useful tourist information and current listings.
Ⓦ**www.moscowcity.com** Official Moscow city guide.
Ⓦ**www.city-guide.spb.ru** Official St Petersburg city guide.
Ⓦ**www.waytorussia.com** Outstanding, detailed practical advice.

STUDENT AND YOUTH DISCOUNTS

"Foreigner prices" at museums and galleries are often steeper than for Russian citizens, though most museums offer tickets for foreign **students** which cost half or two-thirds of the full price. An ISIC card is your best bet, though other student cards often work too. Ask for *adeen studyencheskiy bilyet* (one student ticket) in your most authentic accent.

OPENING HOURS AND HOLIDAYS

Most **shops** are open Monday to Saturday 8am to 7pm or later; Sunday hours are slightly shorter. **Museums** tend to open 9am–5pm, with last ticket sales an hour before closing time, and they are invariably closed one day a week, with one day a month put aside as a "cleaning day". **Churches** are accessible from 8am until the end of evening service. **Clubs** open late – many until 6am – or don't close at all, morphing into early-morning cafés. Russian **public holidays** fall on January 1, 6, 7 and 19, Feburary 23 (Defender of the Motherland Day), March 8 (Women's Day), May 1 and 2 (Labour Day), May 9 (Victory Day), June 12 (Russia Day), and November 4 (Day of Popular Unity).

Moscow

To Westerners, **MOSCOW** (Москва) may look European, but its chaotic spirit is never far beneath the surface. Far removed from its beginnings as a humble wooden town in 1147, today Moscow is Russia's New York City – its residents brash and opinionated, and its glitzy, cosmopolitan heart catering to a well-heeled elite, with the odd pocket of extreme urban poverty. Like its American counterpart, the city never sleeps; you can get anything you want around the clock. Above all, Moscow is an assault on all the senses: a relentless crush of people on the subway, cliquey nightspots, designer shops, any cuisine you can think of, heavy traffic, endless queuing, golden-domed churches and historical treasures.

What to see and do

Moscow's general **layout** is a series of concentric circles and radial lines emanating from Red Square and the Kremlin, and the centre is compact enough to explore on foot. Moscow's sights can also be mapped as strata of its history: the old Muscovy that Russians are eager to show; the now retro-chic Soviet-era sites such as VDHKh, Lenin's Mausoleum and the Sculpture Park; and the exclusive restaurants and shopping malls that mark out the new Russia.

TREAT YOURSELF

Get the city grit out of your skin at the exquisitely elaborate **Sandunovsky baths** (Neglinnaya ul. 14/ 3–7 ⓦwww.sanduny.ru; Metro Teatralnaya), patronized by Muscovites since 1896. Join Russian businessmen and socialites in the *banya*, a wooden hut heated with a furnace, where you are invited to sweat out impurities, get beaten energetically with birch twigs, and finally plunge into ice-cold water. Respite comes from the obligatory follow-up: beer with dried fish. Men's and women's baths are separate, with the women's section more like a modern spa. A two-hour session costs R800; on weekdays there's 50 percent off between 8am and 2pm.

Red Square

Every visitor to Moscow is irresistibly drawn to **Red Square**, the historic and spiritual heart of the city. The name (*Krasnaya ploshchad*) derives from *krasniy,* the old Russian word for beautiful. The Lenin Mausoleum squats beneath the ramparts of the Kremlin and, facing it, sprawls **GUM** – the State Department Store in Soviet times – and now devoted to costly fashion outlets. At the southwest end stands the incomparable St Basil's Cathedral. Opposite it you'll find the Historical Museum, directly behind which a golden circle on the ground marks Moscow's Kilometre Zero. In front of St Basil's Cathedral is the fenced-off Lobnoe Mesto (Place of Executions) where Ivan the Terrible and Peter the Great presided over public beheadings and hangings during their respective reigns.

The Lenin Mausoleum and Kremlin wall

In post-Communist Russia, the **Lenin Mausoleum**, which houses Vladimir Ilyich Ulianov's embalmed corpse (Tues, Thurs, Sat & Sun 10am–1pm; free; queue at the Alexander Gardens entrance to Red Square), can be seen as either an awkward reminder of the old days or a cherished relic. Descend past stony-faced guards into the dimly lit chasm where the leader's body lies. Stopping or giggling will earn you stern rebukes. Behind the Mausoleum, the **Kremlin wall** – 19m high and 6.5m thick – contains a **mass grave** of Bolsheviks who perished during the battle for Moscow in 1917. The ashes of an array of luminaries, including writer Maxim Gorky and the first man in space, Yuri

Gagarin, are here too. Beyond lie the graves of a select group of Soviet leaders, each with his own bust; Stalin still gets the most flowers.

St Basil's Cathedral

No description can do justice to **St Basil's Cathedral** (Mon & Wed–Sat 10am–5pm, Sun 11am–7pm; closed Tues; free) – perhaps the most famous symbol of Russia – its multicoloured onion domes silhouetted against the skyline where Red Square slopes down towards the Moskva River. The exterior is far more impressive than the interior, which consists of a stone warren of small chapels and souvenir stalls. Built in 1561 to celebrate Ivan the Terrible's capture of the Tatar stronghold of Kazan in 1552, its name commemorates St Basil the Blessed, a "holy fool" who foretold the fire that swept Moscow in 1547.

The Kremlin

Brooding and glittering in the heart of the capital, the **Kremlin** (Aleksandrovsky Sad; 10am–5pm, closed Thurs; R350; ⓦwww.kreml.ru; Metro Borovitskaya) is both the heart of historical Moscow and home to its present-day parliament, the Duma. Its founding is attributed to Prince Yuriy Dolgorukiy, who built a wooden fort here in about 1147. Look out for the **Tsar Cannon**, cast in 1586. One of the largest cannons ever made, this was intended to defend the Saviour Gate, but has never been fired. Close by looms the earthbound, broken **Tsar Bell**, the largest bell in the world, cast in 1655. **Cathedral Square** is the historic heart of the Kremlin, dominated by the magnificent, white **Ivan the Great Bell Tower**. Of the square's four key churches, the most important is the **Cathedral of the Assumption**, with a spacious, light and echoing interior, walls and pillars smothered with icons and frescoes, and temporary exhibitions housed in its belfry. The **Cathedral of the Archangel** houses the tombs of Russia's rulers from Grand Duke Ivan I to Tsar Ivan V, while the golden-domed **Cathedral of the Annunciation** (closed for renovations at time of writing) hides some of Russia's finest icons, including works by Theophanes the Greek and Andrey Rublev.

Inside the Kremlin: the Armoury Palace

The unmissable **Armoury Palace** (ticketed entry at 10am, 11.15am, 1.30pm and 2.45pm; R700, students R200) boasts a staggering array of treasures – among them the tsars' coronation robes, jewellery and armour. A separate part of the Armoury Palace houses the Diamond Fund (daily sessions 10am and noon; buy tickets at the Kremlin entrance) – a priceless collection of jewels, including the 190-karat Orlov Diamond, which belonged to Catherine the Great, and the world's largest sapphire.

The Museum of Modern History

Formerly the Museum of the Revolution, the **Museum of Modern History** at Tverskaya ul. 21 (Tues–Sat 10am–6pm, Sun 10am–5pm, closed last Fri of the month; R150; Metro Tverskaya) brings the Communist past alive with striking displays of Soviet propaganda posters, photographs and state gifts, although there's a frustrating lack of English translation.

KREMLIN ETIQUETTE

You may only purchase **tickets** for the set entry times to the Armoury and the Diamond Fund an hour before the session; Soviet-style bureaucracy prevents you from purchasing a ticket in advance. Even if you are in possession of a ticket, you will still have to queue for both attractions separately and watch tour groups and people with connections being ushered in before you. It's all part of the experience...

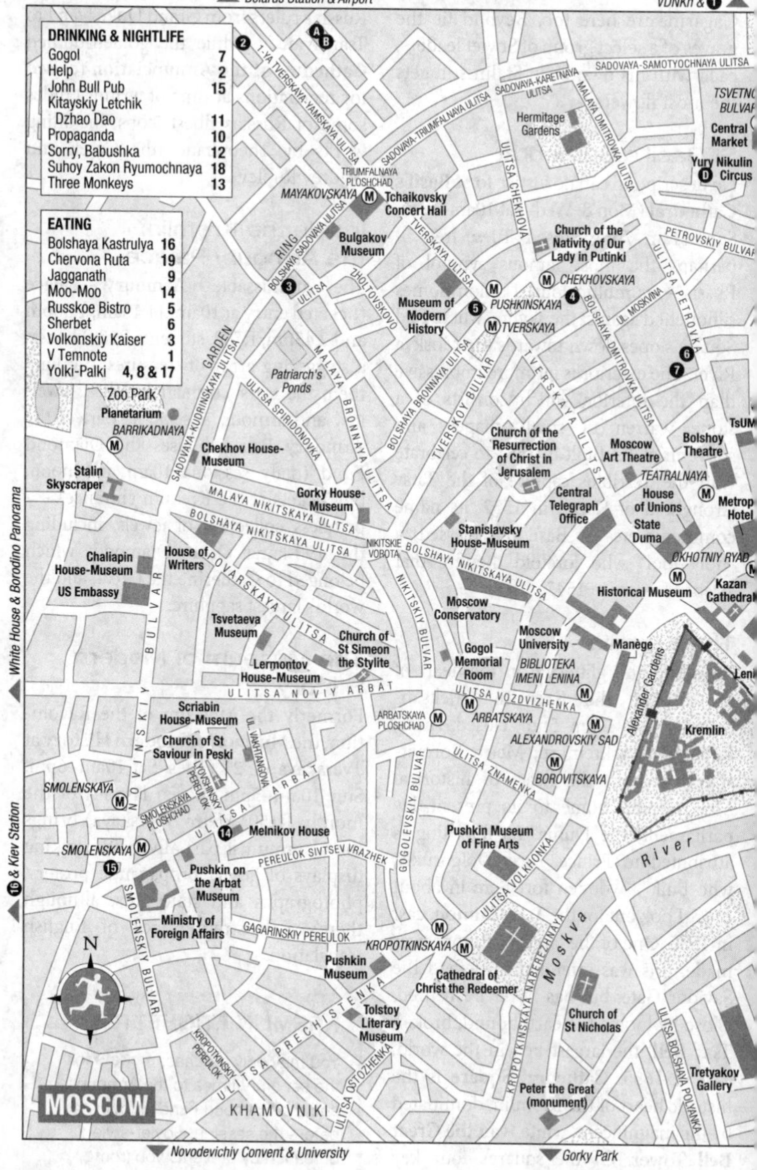

The Pushkin Museum of Fine Arts

Founded in 1898 in honour of the famous Russian poet, the **Pushkin Museum of Fine Arts** at Volkhonka ul. 12 (Tues–Sun 10am–7pm; R150–300, separate fee for Impressionist wing; Metro Kropotkinskaya) holds a hefty collection of **European paintings**, from Italian High Renaissance works to Rembrandt, and an outstanding display of Impressionist works.

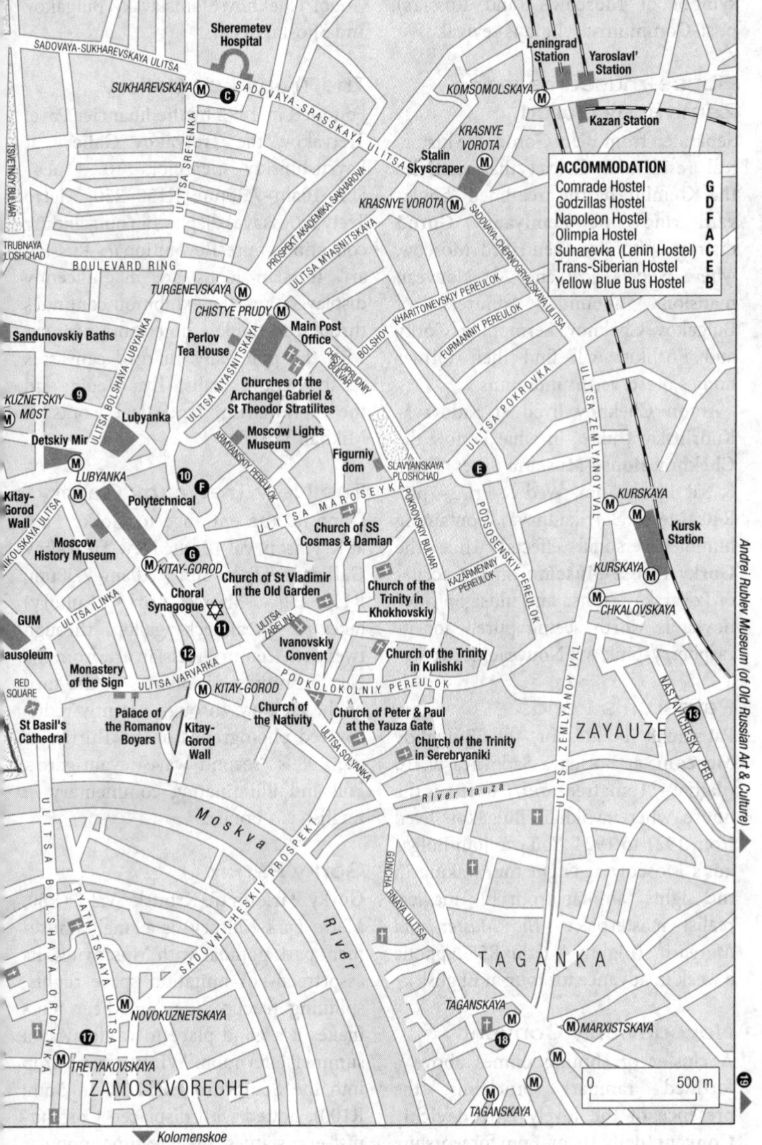

Cathedral of Christ the Redeemer

Demolished and turned into a swimming pool in 1934, the **Cathedral of Christ the Redeemer** (daily 10am–6pm; free), opposite the Pushkin Museum of Fine Arts at Volkhonka ul. 15, was reconstructed thanks to the efforts of Moscow Mayor Yury Mikhaylovich Luzhkov, who began rebuilding it in 1994. Now this strident, even garish, building is a

symbol of Moscow's (and Russia's) post-Communist religious revival.

House-museums in the Zemlyanoy Gorod

Separated from Beliy Gorod, the historical residential district that encircles the Kremlin, by the tree-lined "boulevard ring", the **Zemlyanoy Gorod** district epitomizes gentrified Moscow, where Neoclassical and Art Nouveau mansions abound. Admirers of Bulgakov, Chekhov, Lermontov, Gorky and Pushkin will find their former homes preserved as museums.

Anton Chekhov lived at Sadovaya-Kudrinskaya ul. 6, in what is now the **Chekhov House-Museum** (Tues, Thurs & Sat 11am–5pm, Wed & Fri 2–7pm; R40; Metro Barrikadnaya), containing humble personal effects, while the **Gorky House-Museum** on the corner of Povarskaya ulitsa and ulitsa Spiridonovka is worth seeing purely for its raspberry-pink Art Nouveau decor.

Patriarch's Ponds

Patriarch's Ponds, or the **Bulgakov Museum**, at Bolshaya Sadovaya ul. 10 (daily 1–11pm; free; ⓣ970 0619), is the house where Mikhail Bulgakov lived from 1921 to 1924. You can join Bulgakov's Moscow at Night tour, taking in the sights familiar from his magical realist masterpiece, *The Master and Margarita* (nightly 1–6am; R550; phone a week in advance for tour in English).

Novodevichiy Convent

A cluster of shining domes above a fortified rampart proclaims the presence of the lovely **Novodevichiy Convent** (daily 10am–6pm for worship; museum 10am–5pm; closed Wed & last Mon of month; R100; Metro Sportivnaya), founded by Ivan the Terrible in 1524. At its heart stands the white Cathedral of the Virgin of Smolensk. In its **cemetery** lie numerous famous writers, musicians and artists, including Gogol, Chekhov, Stanislavsky, Bulgakov and Shostakovich.

The Tretyakov Gallery

Founded in 1892 by the financier Pavel Tretyakov, the **Tretyakov Gallery** at Lavrushinskiy pereulok 10 (Tues–Sun 10am–7.30pm; R150–250; Metro Tretyakovskaya) displays an outstanding collection of pre-Revolutionary Russian art. Russian icons are magnificently displayed, and the exhibition continues through to the late nineteenth century, with the politically charged canvasses of the iconic realist Ilya Repin and the nightmarish, fantastical works of Mikhail Vrubel.

The New Tretyakov Gallery

Opposite the entrance to Gorky Park at Krymskiy val 10, the **New Tretyakov Gallery** (Tues–Sun 10am–7.30pm; R150–250; Metro Park Kultury) takes a breakneck gallop through twentieth-century Russian art, from the Neo-primitivist visionaries of the turn of the century, through recently rediscovered photographs of the Thirties to the 1980s "second wave" avant-garde. Full and illuminating commentary in English is a bonus.

Gorky Park

Gorky Park on ul. Krimsky Val 7 (R50; Metro Park Kultury) is a small amusement park popular with Muscovites. Its assortment of imitation space flights, spinning teacup rides and beer tents makes it a good place to while away a summer afternoon. Whilst there, drop into the **Sculpture Park** (10am–5pm; R100), dotted with displaced Communist-era statues of one-time popular heroes, including a young Lenin.

VDNKh

Visit the Exhibition of Economic Achievements, or **VDNKh** (Prospekt Mira; Metro VDNKh/Prospekt Mira), an enormous statue park, to see Soviet

triumphalism rampant in the form of statue upon statue of ordinary workers in heroic poses. Glance at the permanent trade-fair-cum-shopping-centre housed in the grandiose Stalinist architecture of the All-Union Agricultural Exhibition of 1939, check out the People's Friendship Fountain, flanked by Soviet maidens, each symbolizing a Soviet republic, then gape at one of the most hubristic Soviet monuments ever built, the **Space Obelisk**, which bears witness to Soviet designs on the stratosphere. A rocket blasts nearly 100m into the sky on a stylized plume of energy clad in shining titanium, unveiled in 1964, three years after Gagarin orbited the earth. Moscow's giant Ferris wheel, small amusement park and numerous food vendors help to create a fairground-like atmosphere. For a fantastic view over the VDNKh, take the lift to the 25th floor of *Hotel Cosmos* across Prospect Mira.

Arrival and information

Air Flights from Western Europe arrive either at Sheremyetevo, or the newer, more efficient, Domodedovo. From Sheremetyevo you can take the Aeroexpress train to Metro Savyolovsky station on the grey line (hourly between 5.45am and 11pm; R250). Minibus (*marshrutka*) #48 runs to Metro Rechnoy Vokzal (R20). From Domodedovo, frequent Aeroexpress trains run to Metro Paveletskaya (6am–midnight; R200); otherwise take a bright blue Scania bus (every 15min; R60) or bus #405 to Metro Domodedovskaya (R40).
Train All stations are conveniently located by a metro station. Trains from Berlin, Vilnius and Warsaw arrive at Belorusskiy station (Belorusskiy vokzal, Tverskaya Zastava ploshchad' 7; Metro Belorusskaya) while Rizhsky station (Rizhsky vokzal, Rizhskaya ploshchad' 79/3; Metro Rizhskaya) serves Latvian destinations such as Rīga. Leningradsky station (Leningradsky vokzal, Komsomolskaya ploshchad' 3; Metro Komsomolskaya) is the departure point for frequent trains to St Petersburg; Kievsky station (Kievsky vokzal, Kievskogo vokzala ploshchad' 2; Metro Kievskaya) is the final destination for trains from Kiev and Odessa, while Yaraslavlsky station (Yaraslavlsky vokzal, Komsomolskaya ploshchad' 5; Metro Komsomolskaya) is the starting point for trans-Siberian adventures.
Bus Ecolines buses from Germany and the Baltic States terminate at Aerovokzal on Leningradskoe shosse (near Metro Komsomolskaya). Eurolines runs from European destinations including Berlin, Rīga, Tallinn and Helsinki to both St Petersburg and Moscow. Moscow's main bus station with intercity departures is at Uralskaya ulitsa 2; Metro Shcholkovskaya.
Tourist office 4 Ilyinka Street, Gostiny Dvor ⓣ095/232 5657, ⓦwww.moscowcity-ru.
Good guides include the official Moscow guide from the tourist information office and the *Moscow Multilingual Guide*, available at ⓦwww.streetbystreet.ru.

City transport

Buses Bus stops are marked with yellow signs.
Metro With its Soviet mosaics, murals and statuary, Moscow's Metro (5.30am–1am) is deservedly world-famous. Stations are marked with a large "M" and you can plan your journey on ⓦwww.metroway.ru. Single fare costs R22; buy a card for 10 or 20 journeys (ask at the *kassa* for *dyéssiyet/dvátset póezdok*).
Minibuses *Marshrutkas* are cheap (around R25 a journey). They wait to fill up with passengers, then take the route advertised on the side. You can ask to get out at any point. Pay the driver on board.
Trams and trolleybuses Often the best way to tackle a big road like a section of Tverskaya ulitsa or the Garden Ring. Trolleybus stops have blue-and-white signs. Most routes operate from 5am to 1am; fares cost R22 or ten for R165 from small kiosks; R25 on board; same tickets are used for buses.

Accommodation

Hostels

Comrade Hostel Maroseyka ul. 11, 3rd floor ⓣ095/628 3126, ⓦwww.comradehostel.com. Clean, spacious, inexpensive dorms right near Moscow's lively nightlife. Kitchen, common room and wi-fi included, plus a helpful owner. Metro Kitai Gorod. Dorms R700.
Godzillas Hostel Bolshoi Karetniy 6, flat 5 (first floor) ⓣ095/699 4223, ⓦwww.godzillashostel.com. Relaxed, popular hostel, consisting of rooms in two large, fully equipped apartments a short walk from the centre. Helpful staff provide lots of Moscow information. Metro Tsvetnoy Bulvar/Tverskaya. Dorms $25–28, doubles $70.
Napoleon Hostel Maly Zaloutinskiy pereulok 2, 4th floor ⓣ095/628 6695, ⓦwww.napoleonhostel.ru.

Fun, friendly hostel with dorms named after Russian cities. In the best possible location for sampling the Moscow nightlife. DVD/widescreen TV; beers for R30 during happy hour (6–8pm). Metro Kitay Gorod. Dorms R900–1000.

Olimpia Hostel 4th Tverskaya-Yamskaya 6/12, apt 57 ⓣ926/668 9029, ⓦolimpia-hostel.com. Well-located, clean, lively hostel with English-speaking staff who make you feel at home. Mod cons, such as wi-fi and TV/DVD lounge, and some of the cheapest rates in Moscow. Second branch nearby with similar amenities. Metro Tverskaya. Dorms R519–649, doubles R1499 per person.

Suharevka (Lenin Hostel) Bolshaya Sukharevskaya Square 16/18, flat 5, entrance 1, on 4th floor ⓣ095/241 1446, ⓦwww.suharevkahotel.ru. HI-affiliated hostel situated right on the Garden Ring, with staggeringly cool interiors, knowledgeable staff, a large common room, wi-fi and a great atmosphere. Backpacker favourite. Metro Sukharevsky. Dorms R449–750, doubles R1200 per person.

Trans-Siberian Hostel Barashevsky pereulok 12 ⓣ095/916 2030, ⓦwww.transsiberianhostel.com. Quiet, intimate hostel with friendly, English-speaking staff, guest lockers, kitchen, common room and a resident cat. Metro Kurskaya. Dorms $20–22, doubles $50.

Yellow Blue Bus Hostel 4th Tverskaya-Yamskaya ul. 5, flat 8 ⓣ095/250 1364. Small, friendly hostel, with cosy dorms, large kitchen, internet and wi-fi. Large private rooms in a separate building. Make sure you know how to get in, as staff are not always on site. Metro Mayakovskaya. Dorms R670–835, doubles R1200 per person.

Eating

For cheap eats, go for "canteens", a café/restaurant format favoured by locals where you compile a tray of dishes smorgasbord-style. Many small restaurants offer business lunches for around R160.

Canteens and cafés

Jagganath Kuznetskiy Most ul. 11 This veggie café-cum-health food store is an unlikely but much-loved Moscow institution. Curries, light cakes and fresh salads will delight those tiring of unrelenting carb and dairy dishes. Minuscule prices, and ethical without being too earnest. Internet points. *Pirogi* from R35; home-made ginger beer R25. Metro Kuznetskiy Most.

Moo-Moo ul. Arbat 45/24. Inexpensive soups, salads, *pelmeni*, grilled meats and desserts. Just point at what you want. Pork *shashlik* R150. Metro Smolenskaya or ul Myanitskaya 14.

Russkoe Bistro Tverskaya ul. 16; other branches around the city. Super-cheap snack-size pies and pancakes from chain popular with locals. Grab a quick *pirog* for R30. Metro Pushkinskaya.

Volkonskiy Kaiser Bolshaya Sadovaya ul. 2/46, Metro Mayakovskaya and ul. Maroseika 4/2, Metro Kitai Gorod. Sit nursing a hot chocolate on a chilly day or pick up teatime goodies to go, at this lovely French patisserie. Cakes from R45.

Yolki-Palki Neglinnaya 8/10; Bolshaya Dmitrovka ul. 23/8; Klimentovskiy per. 14/1, and other branches. Russian/Ukrainian/Mongolian food at rock-bottom prices, even if the interior design is a tad tacky. Russian salads, grills and *blini* (R150).

Restaurants

Bolshaya Kastrulya pl. Evropy 1. Welcome to *pelmeni* heaven, with a huge variety of dumplings – from the traditional meat variety, to unusual squid and vegetarian options. Large portions, and great views of the Moskva River from the second floor. Mains R200. Metro Kievskaya.

Chervona Ruta 3-ya Krutitskii per. 2. Traditionally decorated Ukrainian restaurant with a large selection of hearty, delicious dishes. Try the *golubtsy* (cabbage rolls stuffed with meat); R250. The portion of *dryaniki* (fried potato pancakes) is big enough for two; wash it down with a blueberry compote drink. Metro Proletarskaya.

Sherbet ul. Petrovska 15; also ul. Stretenka 32. Elegant, wildly popular lunch spot with generous Uzbek and Arabic dishes, as well as scented hookahs. *Plov* (spiced rice with lamb, onion and carrot), R220. Metro Teatralnaya.

V Temnote (In The Dark) ul. Oktyabrskaya 2/4. Follow your waitress to your table in complete darkness and savour your meal with all your senses bar sight. The food is a mix of Russian and international influences. Mains R300. Metro Novoslobodskaya.

Drinking

Moscow's famous nightlife is marred by the practice of "face control", excluding the not-so-beautiful people from *elitni* clubs. The venues listed here are largely accessible.

Bars

Gogol Stoleshnikov per. 11. Stylish 24hr bar-club-café with *fin-de-siècle* decor, al fresco dining in summer and a free ice-rink in winter. The "Soviet menu" is excellent value, and cocktails are R160–300. Metro Kuznetskiy Most.

Help 1-ya Tverskaya Yamskaya ultisa, 27/1. Macho, pub-like bar serving award-winning cocktails

(R250), with deals including 2-for-1s after midnight and free desserts on Wednesdays. Open 24 hours. Metro Belorusskaya.

John Bull Pub Smolenskaya pl. 1. This well-located split-level British pub is where expats and Russians flock for excellent house beers, an intimate and relaxed environment and good pub grub with a Russian twist. Metro Smolenskaya.

Suhoy Zakon Ryumochnaya Taganskaya pl. 88, bld. 1. This lively watering hole is dedicated to serving different types of vodka. Beer lovers will enjoy the 4.2-litre kegs on offer, and staff are efficient and pleasant. Metro Taganskaya.

Clubs

Kitayskiy Letchik Dzhao Dao Lubyanskiy proezd 25/1 Ⓦwww.jao-da.ru. Descend to the artfully scuffed-up basement labyrinth, host to outstanding alternative bands on weekends. Beers from R70–90; entry R300. Metro Kitay Gorod.

Propaganda Bolshoy Zlatoustinskiy per. 7. Try your luck with the "face control" at this perennially popular club. Drum 'n' bass nights on Fridays; international DJs regularly. If you'd rather not know if your face passes muster, go early for drinks or dinner. 2 for 1 after midnight Mon–Wed. Metro Kitay Gorod.

Sorry, Babushka Slavyanskaya pl. Ⓦwww.sorrybabushka.ru. Relaxed and unpretentious club with prices that won't drain your wallet, playing anything from trance to R'n'B to hip-hop. Open until 6am; R500. Metro Kitay Gorod.

Three Monkeys Nastavnichesky per. 11, bld. 1. Three-level gay club featuring a raucous transvestite show. In the karaoke room people take singing battles very seriously. Open until 7am. Metro Chkalovskaya.

Entertainment

Theatre, classical music and ballet all have superb vintages in Russia, and can be surprisingly cheap, provided you ask for the cheapest ticket available (*samiy deshoviy bilyet*).

Cinema

Dome Cinema 18/1 Olimpiyskiy pr. English-language films. Metro Prospekt Mira/Kievskaya.

Music

B2 Bolshaya Sadovaya ul. 8/1. A staple venue on the live music scene. Men pay R300 after 10pm Fri/Sat. Metro Mayakovskaya.

Tchaikovsky concert hall Triumfalnaya ploshad 4/31 Ⓦwww.meloman.ru. Pick a night when Russian music heads the bill and admire the view; the hall is festooned with red stars. Tickets start at just R100. Metro Mayakovskaya.

Theatre

Bolshoy Theatre Teatralnaya pl. 1 Ⓣ095/250 7317, Ⓦwww.bolshoi.ru. The world's most famous ballet. Metro Teatralnaya.

Shopping

Get hold of Soviet paraphernalia and memorabilia including coins, medals, uniforms and postcards at the Museum of Modern History shop, from R50. Kristall (Pokrovka ul. 19) does a great selection of vodkas, from Yuri Dolgoruki costing R500 to Kristallnaya for R120. Stalls inside churches are worth a browse for small icons, delicate chains and crosses, or "holy" honey, from around R40.

Directory

Embassies Australia: 13 Kropotkinskiy pereulok, Metro Park Kultury Ⓣ095/956 6070; Canada: 23 Starokonuyushenniy pereulok, Metro Kropotkinskaya Ⓣ095/105 6000; Ireland: Grokholskiy pereulok 5 Ⓣ095/937 5911; New Zealand: 44 Povarskaya ulitsa, Metro Barrikadnaya, Ⓣ095/956 3579; UK: 10 Smolenskaya naberezhnaya, Metro Smolenskaya Ⓣ095/956 7200; USA: 19 Novinskiy bulvar, Metro Smolenskaya Ⓣ095/728 5000.

Internet Cafemax, ul. Pyatnitskaya 25/1, Metro Novokuznetskaya; Netcity, Kamergersky per. 5/6, Teatralnaya metro; IMAGE.RU, Novoslodbodskaya ul. 16a, Metro Novoslobodskaya; Time Online, Okhotni Ryad shopping centre, basement level to the right of the escalators, Metro Okhotni Ryad.

Laundry California Cleaners, Maliy Gnezdnikovskiy pereulok 12.

Left luggage Most train stations have lockers and/or a 24hr left-luggage office.

Medical European Medical Center, Spiridonovskiy pereulok 1, Metro Pushkinskaya Ⓣ095/933 6655, Ⓦwww.emcmos.ru; International SOS Clinic, 31 Grokholskiy pereulok 31, 10th floor, Metro Prospekt Mira, Ⓣ095/937 5760, Ⓦwww.sosclinic.ru. Both recognized by international insurance companies.

Pharmacy Stariy Arbat, Arbatskaya ul. 25; Multifarma, Turistkaya ul. 27; 24hr pharmacy at pr. Mira 71.

Post office Central Telegraph Office, Tverskaya ul. 7; Main Post Office, Myasnitskaya ul. 26/2, 9am–6pm. Express postal services via Westpost, Ⓦwww.westpost.ru; Courier Service, Bolshaya Sadovaya 10; Metro Mayakovskaya. DHL: 1st Tverskaya Yamskaya ul. 11, Metro Belorusskaya.

Moving on

Train Berlin (1 daily except Wed; 25hr); Budapest (1 daily; 37hr); Helsinki (1 daily; 12hr); Rīga (1 daily; 15hr 30min); St Petersburg (12 daily; 4hr 30min–8hr); Tallinn (1 daily; 15hr); Vilnius (1 daily; 14hr); Warsaw (1 daily; 18hr).
Bus Rīga (2 daily; 20hr); St Petersburg (1 daily; 13hr); Tallinn (1 daily; 18hr 30min).

St Petersburg

ST PETERSBURG (Санкт-Петербург), Petrograd, Leningrad and St Petersburg again – the city's succession of names mirrors Russia's turbulent history. Founded in 1703 by **Peter the Great** as a "window in the West", three hundred years on St Petersburg, a self-assured and future-focused city, still retains more of a Western European feel than Moscow. A sophisticated capital of the tsarist empire, the cradle of the Communist Revolution of 1917, and a symbol of Russian stoicism due to the city's heroic endurance of a three-year Nazi siege during World War II, present-day St Petersburg has eased into modernity without sacrificing any of its old-world magnificence and charm, its shopping malls and nightclubs sitting alongside its opulent palaces. The city is easy to navigate and the pace of life is relaxed. The best **time to visit** is during the midsummer White Nights (mid-June to mid-July), when darkness never falls. From May to October all bridges across the Neva are raised from 1am to 5am – a beautiful sight, best seen from a boat.

What to see and do

St Petersburg's centre lies on the south bank of the River Neva, with the curving River Fontanka marking its southern boundary. The area within the Fontanka is riven by a series of avenues fanning out from the golden spire of the Admiralty, on the Neva's south bank. Many of the city's top sights are located on and around **Nevskiy prospekt**, the backbone and heart of the city for the last three centuries, stretching from the Alexander Nevskiy Monastery to Palace Square. Across the Neva is **Vasilevskiy Island**, with the Strelka at its eastern tip, and the Petrograd Side, home to the Peter and Paul Fortress. Beyond the River Fontanka lies **Smolniy**, where the Bolsheviks fomented revolution in 1917.

The Winter Palace

The two-hundred-metre-long Baroque **Winter Palace** at the westernmost end of Nevskiy prospekt is the city's largest, most opulent palace, which was the official residence of the tsars, their court and 1500 servants. The main building was finished in 1762 and the Small and Large Hermitages were added by Catherine the Great, while the New Hermitage was launched as Russia's first public art museum in 1852.

The Hermitage

The **Hermitage** collection (Tues–Sat 10.30am–6pm, Sun 10.30am–5pm; R350, free to students, free admission first Thurs of every month) embraces over three million treasures and works of art, from ancient Scythian gold and giant malachite urns to Cubist pieces, making it one of the world's greatest museums. After the elaborately decorated state rooms and the Gold Collection, the most popular section covers modern European art from the nineteenth and twentieth centuries, with an array of works by Picasso, Gauguin, Van Gogh, Rodin, Monet and Renoir.

Kazan Cathedral

Curving **Kazan Cathedral** (10am–6pm; free entry; Metro Nevskiy prospekt), built between 1801 and 1811, was modelled on St Peter's in the Vatican and is unique in die-straight St Petersburg. The cathedral was built to house a

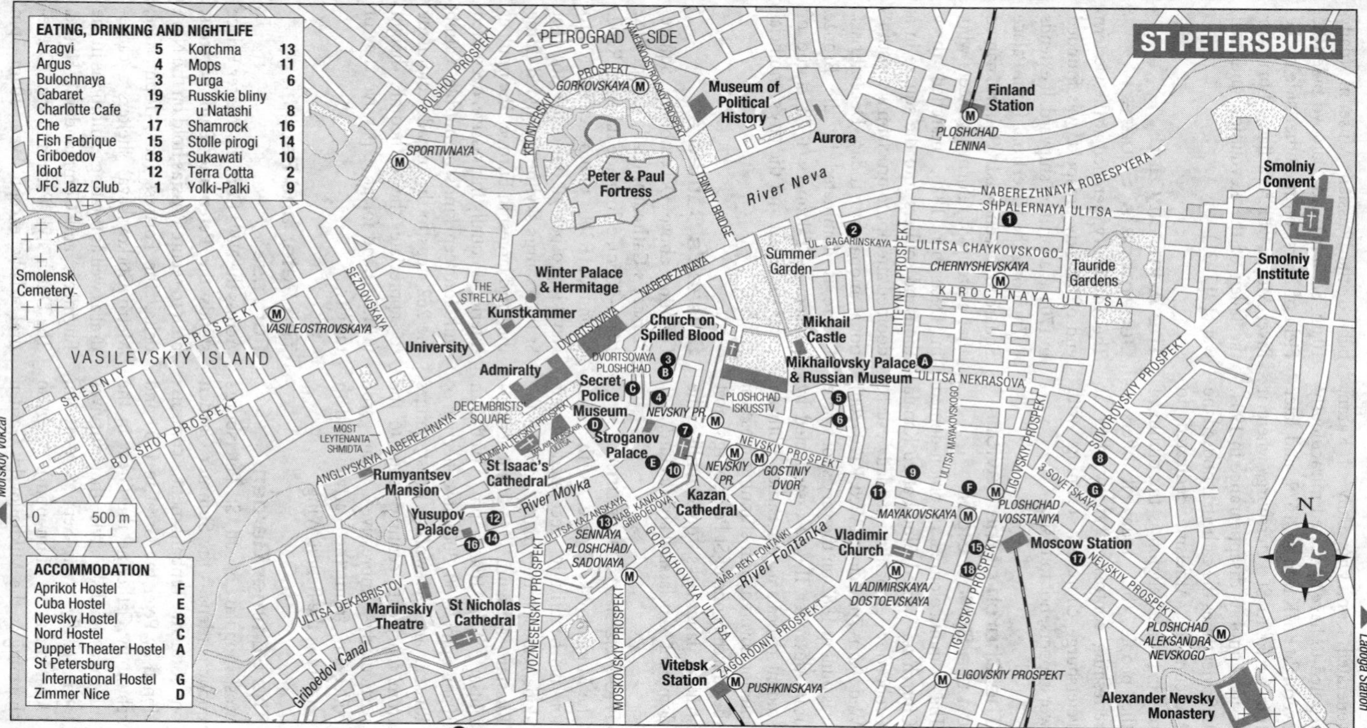
ST PETERSBURG
EATING, DRINKING AND NIGHTLIFE
Aragvi 5
Argus 4
Bulochnaya 3
Cabaret 19
Charlotte Cafe 7
Che 17
Fish Fabrique 15
Griboedov 18
Idiot 12
JFC Jazz Club 1
Korchma 13
Mops 11
Purga 6
Russkie bliny u Natashi 8
Shamrock 16
Stolle pirogi 14
Sukawati 10
Terra Cotta 2
Yolki-Palki 9
ACCOMMODATION
Aprikot Hostel F
Cuba Hostel E
Nevsky Hostel B
Nord Hostel C
Puppet Theater Hostel A
St Petersburg International Hostel G
Zimmer Nice D
0 500 m
PETROGRAD SIDE
BOLSHOY PROSPEKT
KAMENNOOSTROVSKIY PROSPEKT
GORKOVSKAYA
KRONVERSKIY
SPORTIVNAYA
Museum of Political History
Aurora
Finland Station
PLOSHCHAD LENINA
Peter & Paul Fortress
TRINITY BRIDGE
River Neva
NABEREZHNAYA ROBESPYERA
SHPALERNAYA ULITSA
Smolniy Convent
Smolniy Institute
UL. GAGARINSKAYA
LITEYNIY PROSPEKT
ULITSA CHAYKOVSKOGO
CHERNYSHEVSKAYA
Tauride Gardens
KIROCHNAYA ULITSA
Summer Garden
Smolensk Cemetery
SEZDOVSKAYA
THE STRELKA
Winter Palace & Hermitage
Kunstkammer
DVORTSOVAYA NABEREZHNAYA
VASILEOSTROVSKAYA
Church on Spilled Blood
Mikhail Castle
University
VASILEVSKIY ISLAND
SREDNIY PROSPEKT
Admiralty
DVORTSOVAYA PLOSHCHAD
Mikhailovsky Palace & Russian Museum
ULITSA NEKRASOVA
Secret Police Museum
PLOSHCHAD ISKUSSTV
NEVSKIY PR.
DECEMBRISTS' SQUARE
MOST LEYTENANTA SHMIDTA
ANGLIYSKAYA NABEREZHNAYA
BOLSHOY PROSPEKT
ADMIRALTEYSKIY PROSPEKT
MALAYA MORSKAYA ULITSA
Stroganov Palace
NEVSKIY PROSPEKT
GOSTINIY DVOR
ULITSA MAYAKOVSKOGO
LIGOVSKIY PROSPEKT
SUVOROVSKIY PROSPEKT
3 SOVETSKAYA
Rumyantsev Mansion
St Isaac's Cathedral
River Moyka
Kazan Cathedral
MAYAKOVSKAYA
PLOSHCHAD VOSSTANIYA
Yusupov Palace
ULITSA KAZANSKAYA
NAB. KANALA GRIBOEDOVA
SENNAYA PLOSHCHAD/ SADOVAYA
GOROKHOVAYA ULITSA
NAB. REKI FONTANKI
River Fontanka
Vladimir Church
Moscow Station
VOZNESENSKIY PROSPEKT
MOSKOVSKIY PROSPEKT
VLADIMIRSKAYA/ DOSTOEVSKAYA
ULITSA DEKABRISTOV
Mariinskiy Theatre
St Nicholas Cathedral
ZAGORODNIY PROSPEKT
Griboedov Canal
Vitebsk Station
PUSHKINSKAYA
LIGOVSKIY PROSPEKT
PLOSHCHAD ALEKSANDRA NEVSKOGO
Alexander Nevsky Monastery
N
Morskoy Vokzal
Ladoga Station

venerated icon, Our Lady of Kazan, reputed to have appeared miraculously overnight in Kazan in 1579, and later transferred to St Petersburg, where it resided until its disappearance in 1904. In Soviet times the cathedral housed the Museum of Atheism, dedicated to proving that "religion is the opium of the people", but today it offers a refreshing contrast to many other St Petersburg churches, teeming with worshippers, not tourists.

The Church of the Saviour on the Spilled Blood

The multicoloured, onion-domed **Church on Spilled Blood** at 26 Kanala Groboedova embankment (daily except Wed 10am–7pm, closed Wed; R170–300) was built in 1882 on the very spot where Tsar Alexander II was assassinated by student radicals a year earlier. With an interior covered with stunning mosaics, the church is one of St Petersburg's most striking landmarks, quite unlike the dominant Neoclassical architecture.

The Russian Museum

The Mikhailovsky Palace, worth a visit for its beautifully decorated rooms alone, houses the main part of the **Russian Museum** (4 Inzhenernaya Ulitsa; Mon 10am–5pm, Wed–Sun 10am–6pm; R150–300). Its collection of Russian art, the world's finest, ranges from fourteenth-century icons to the particularly impressive avant-garde collection from the early twentieth century in the Benois Wing.

The Summer Garden

Most popular of all St Petersburg's public gardens is the **Summer Garden** on Kutuzov Embankment, commissioned by Peter the Great in 1704 and rebuilt by Catherine the Great in the informal English style that survives today (daily: May–Sept 8am–10pm; Oct–March 11am–6pm). Also charming is the Mikhailovsky Garden behind the Russian Museum (daily 10am–8/10pm) and Marsovo pole (the Field of Mars) on the other side of the River Moyka where a flame burns for the fallen of the Revolution and civil war (1917–21).

The Admiralty and Decembrists' Square

The **Admiralty**, perched at the western end of Nevskiy prospekt, was founded in 1704 as a fortified shipyard. It extends 407m along the waterfront from Palace Square to **Decembrists' Square**, named after a group of reformist officers who, in December 1825, marched three thousand soldiers into the square in a doomed attempt to proclaim a constitutional monarchy. Today, Decembrists' Square is dominated by the Bronze Horseman, Falconet's 1778 statue of Peter the Great and the city's unofficial symbol.

St Isaac's Cathedral

Looming above Decembrists' Square, **St Isaac's Cathedral** (daily except Wed 10am–10pm, colonnade till 4pm; R300, colonnade R300, photos extra; Metro Nevskiy prospekt) is one of the glories of St Petersburg's skyline, its gilded dome the third largest in Europe. The opulent interior is equally impressive, decorated with fourteen kinds of marble. Climb the 262 steps to the outside colonnade to appreciate the cathedral's height (101.5m) and for an expansive view of the city.

The Peter and Paul Fortress

Across the Neva from the Winter Palace stands the **Peter and Paul Fortress**, built to secure Russia's hold on the Neva delta. The Fortress (6am–10pm; free; Metro Gorkovskaya) shelters a cathedral as well as rotating exhibitions in the Engineers' and Commandant's House. The Dutch-style Peter and Paul Cathedral (daily except Wed 10am–7pm

R70–280; ticket valid for 10-day re-entry to the cathedral and all museums, though not the private exhibitions), completed in 1733, remained the tallest structure in the city until the 1960s. Sited around the nave are the tombs of **Romanov monarchs** from Peter the Great onwards, excluding Peter II, Ivan VI and Nicholas II. The Nevskaya panorama roof walk (10am–8pm) gives an excellent view of the Winter Palace, and you can spot sunbathers by the Neva Curtain Wall from March onwards. Inside the fortress, period dress is available for rent by the hour for those interested in some costumed capering.

Cruiser Aurora

Anchored a short walk along the Neva from the Peter and Paul fortress is the **Cruiser Aurora** (Petrogradskaya naberezhnaya, Tues–Thus, Sat & Sun 10.30am–4pm, free), the famous battle ship that fired the opening shot of the revolution of 1917.

Kunstkammer

Not to be missed is the **Kunstkammer** at Universitetskaya nab. 3, Vasilevsky Island (11am–6pm, closed Mon and last Tues of the month; R200; Metro Vasileostrovskaya), Russia's oldest public museum, founded by Peter the Great in 1714. Its name (meaning "art chamber" in German) dignified Peter's fascination for curiosities and freaks: he offered rewards for "human monsters" and unknown animals, which were preserved in vinegar or vodka. The result is a grisly but strangely compelling exhibition, with excellent commentary on all exhibits.

Museum of Russian Political History

The lively **Museum of Political History** at Kuibysheva ulitsa 2/4 (daily except Thus 10am–6pm, R180; free entry on public holidays; Metro Gorkovskaya) gives in-depth insights into Soviet-era political and social life, displaying children's textbooks reworked to demonize the *kulaks* (moneyed peasants), appalling photographic evidence of Stalin's purges, and film footage recalling how Western culture enthralled Soviet youngsters in the 1960s and 1970s. Helpful attendants can provide English-language booklets.

Secret Police Museum

The **Secret Police Museum**'s intriguing exhibition on the History of the Political Police (Admiralteysky prospect 6, Mon–Fri; 10am–6pm R100; Metro Nevskiy Prospect) at an annexe of the Museum of Political History includes previously classified police reports on individuals suspected of subversive activity from the dying days of the late Tsarist regime to the present. Look out for Okhrana (Tsarist secret police) reports on Lenin from 1909, photos of undercover KGB officers at meetings between US presidents and Soviet leaders, and painfully recent testimonies from Russian federal agents operating in Grozny, Chechnya. Limited English translations are available.

Smolniy Convent and Institute

Smolniy Convent (3/1 Rastrelli Square, daily except Wed 10am–6/8pm R200; Metro Chernyshevskaya), a peerless ice-blue Rastrelli Baroque creation, is the focal point of the Smolniy district, now a concert and exhibition hall (concerts R100–600; exhibitions R70–200). The neighbouring **Smolniy Institute** (pl. Proletarskoy diktaturi 3) is now the headquarters of St Petersburg's Governor, but was built between 1806 and 1808 to house the Institute for Young Noblewomen; Lenin orchestrated the October Revolution of 1917 from here, and changed the course of history. A statue of the man himself still stands in front of the building, and as you enter the Institute's grounds look out for the now

familiar Communist slogan: "Workers of the World, Unite!" (Пролетарии всех стран, соединяйтесь!).

Alexander Nevsky Monastery

At the eastern end of Nevskiy prospekt lies the **Alexander Nevsky Monastery** (June–Aug 10am–8pm; rest of the year 11am–5pm; free; Metro Ploshchad' Aleksandra Nevskogo), founded in 1713 by Peter the Great and one of only four monasteries in the Russian Empire with the rank of *lavra*, the highest in Orthodox monasticism. Two famous **cemeteries** lie in the monastery grounds: the Necropolis for Masters of the Arts, where Dostoyevsky, Rimsky-Korsakov, Tchaikovsky and Glinka lie, and, directly opposite, the Lazarus Cemetery, the oldest in the city with elaborately decorated tombs. Tickets are required for entry to both (April–Oct 9.30am–8pm; Nov–March 9.30am–4pm, closed Thurs; R150/R70 students).

Rumyantsev Mansion

Further west along the Neva embankment, the focal point of the **Rumyantsev Mansion** (Angliyskaya naberezhnaya 44, daily except Wed 11am–5pm, R60–110; Metro Sadovaya) is the exhibition on Leningrad during the Great Patriotic War, which details the horrors of life in a desperate city, besieged by the Nazis between 1941 and 1944. The most harrowing exhibit is the diary of 11-year old Tanya Savicheva, who continued going to school as, one by one, her entire family died of starvation.

Yusupov Palace

Purchased by the aristocratic Yusupov family in 1830, the elaborately decorated **Yusupov Palace** on the Naberezhnaya Reki Moiky 94 (daily 11am–5pm; R200–500 including audio guide; Metro Nevsky Prospect) was the scene of the murder of the sinister monk, Rasputin, deemed to have had undue influence over the royal family. In 1916, Felix Yusupov and his associates poisoned Rasputin in the cellar (where you can see a wax likeness of the man). When the poison failed to take effect, they shot him, rolled him up in a carpet and threw him in the river; he finally died from drowning, having clawed his way through much of the ice.

Arrival and information

Air International flights arrive at Pulkovo Airport, Terminal 2. Have some rubles on you when you arrive as the ATM is not always working. Take a bus (#13, #113 or #213) or a commercial minibus, both departing around every 15min, to the end of the metro line (Moskovskaya), or get the Pulkovo Express Bus, which runs 24/7, to Pushkinskaya metro.

Train Services from Helsinki arrive at Finland station (Findlyanskiy vokzal), at Ploshchad' Lenina 6, Metro Ploshchad' Lenina. Trains from Rīga and Vilnius terminate at Vitebsk station (Vitebskiy vokzal), Metro Pushkinskaya. Trains from Moscow (up to 14 daily) draw into Moscow station (Moskovskiy vokzal), Metro Ploshchad Vosstaniya.

Bus Most buses arrive at the Central Bus Station, Obvodnovo kanal 36, 15min walk from Metro Ligovskiy Prospekt. Buses from the Baltic States also stop at St Petersburg's Baltiyskiy station at Obvodnogo kanal 120, Metro Baltiskaya. See timetables at Ⓦ www.eurolines.eu.

Ferry In the summer months (ie when the ice melts) there are ferries from Tallinn, Helsinki and Rostock, operated by Silja Line (Ⓦ www.silja.com) and Estonian operator Tallink (Ⓦ www.tallink.ee). They arrive at the Morskoy vokzal, Prospect Morskoy Slavy 1, Metro Vasilieostrovskaya, at the western end of Vasilevskiy Island (bus or minibus to the centre).

Tourist office The helpful main centre at Sadovaya ul. 14/52 (Ⓣ 812/310 8262, Ⓦ www.visit-petersburg.com; Metro Nevskiy prospekt) has a wealth of material in English. For listings and events pick up the quarterly freebie *Where St Petersburg*, the Friday *St Petersburg Times* and the monthly *Pulse* from hotels and shops.

City transport

Metro The St Petersburg metro, the deepest in the world, runs from 5.30am to midnight. Small numbers of journeys (R20 a journey) are sold using tokens (*zhetoni*), which you feed into ticket

machines. For 10 or more rides to be used over a fixed number of days, buy a plastic card.

Buses and trolleybuses Often the best way to tackle a big road like Nevskiy prospekt, overground transport is more useful in the city centre than the metro. Buy tickets from the driver on embarking (R18).

Minibuses *Marshrutkas* (yellow in St Petersburg) are cheap (around R20–25 a journey) and cheerful. The K-147 goes from Moskovskiy vokzal right to the upper end of Nevskiy prospekt.

Boat One of the best ways to see the city is by boat (May–Oct) – either a private motorboat from any bridge on Nevskiy prospekt (from R1800/hr per boat), or a large tour boat by the Anichkov Bridge (R250 per person). AngloTourismo offer guided tours in English from the pier on Fontanka 64, by Lomonosova Bridge; ⓣ921/989 47 22. Try the excellent "St Petersburg by Night" boat tour; it takes in the more spectacular of the city's bridges, all lit up, as they are raised for the night.

Accommodation

Hostels

Aprikot Hostel Nevskiy Prospekt 106, apt 7 ⓣ812/273 8626, ⓔmail@economhotel.ru. Excellent central location, bright, spacious dorms with shared facilities, large kitchen, high-speed internet and helpful owners. Bed linen R70 extra. Metro Mayakovskaya. Dorms R800–850, doubles R1100–1500.

Cuba Hostel Kazanskaya ul. 5, 4th floor ⓣ812/921 7115, ⓦwww.cubahostel.ru. Lively, vibrantly decorated hostel in an excellent location behind Kazan Cathedral. Free tea, coffee, pasta and rice in the kitchen, plus free internet. Bikes to rent from R150 for 2 hours. Metro Nevskiy Prospekt. Mixed dorms/single-sex R550/800, doubles R1250 per person.

Nevsky Hostel Bolshaya Konushennaya ul. 11 ⓣ812/611 1183, ⓦwww.nevskyhostels.com. Spacious, modern dorms with shared facilities and safes, a short walk from the city's main attractions. Wi-fi enabled; excellent buffet breakfast at *Nevsky Hotel* R260. Metro Nevskiy Prospekt. Dorms R950–1050.

Nord Hostel Bolshaya Morskaya ul. 10 ⓣ812/571 0342, ⓦwww.nordhostel.com. It couldn't be more central, but the kitchen/communal area closes at 10pm. Comfortable dorms with shared facilities; internet access. Breakfast included. Metro Gostiniy Dvor. Dorms €24, doubles €65–82.

Puppet Theater Hostel Nekrasova ul. 12 ⓣ812/272 5401, ⓦwww.hostel-puppet.ru. HI-affiliated, professional if slightly subdued outfit with two single-sex dorms and a spacious double. There's internet access, but no kitchen, and the parrot may strain your nerves. Metro Mayakovskaya. Dorms R700, doubles R900 per person.

St Petersburg International Hostel 3-ya Sovetskaya ul. 28. ⓣ812/329 8018, ⓦwww.ryh.ru. Popular, with spacious dorms and doubles, so book well ahead. Continental breakfast with attendant babushkas' bullying is an integral part of the experience. Bike rental available. Metro Pl. Vosstaniya. Dorms R770, doubles R910 per person.

Zimmer Nice Malaya Morskaya ul. 8, apt. 7 ⓣ812/315 5489, ⓦwww.zimmer.ru. Intimate, centrally located, quiet hostel with private singles, doubles and triples. Shared facilities, including a modern kitchen and internet access. Metro Sadovaya. Singles R1440–2430 per person, doubles R1260–1800 per person, triples R1080 per person.

Eating

Canteens and cafés

Bulochnaya Bolshaya Konyushennaya 15. An authentic Russian bakery. Delicious pies and cakes, attentive service, decent coffee and 50ml shots of berry liqueurs for an alluring R20 make this an essential mid-afternoon fuelling point. Slab of cheesecake R45. Metro Nevskiy Prospekt.

Charlotte Cafe ul. Kazanskaya 2. An attractive café/deli serving tasty salads and freshly made sandwiches with imaginative fillings. Light meal R300. Metro Nevskiy Prospekt.

Russkie bliny u Natashi 5-ya Sovetskaya ul. 24. Pig out on the city's most outstanding pancakes at the cheapest prices. *Blini* with red caviar R90.

Stolle pirogi ul. Dekabristov 19. Quality pies in chic environs. Buy a section of a thick plait or decorated square of pie; specialities include seasonal berries and salmon. Pies from R55.

Yolki-Palki Nevsky pr. 88. Popular with locals and tourists alike, this all-you-can-eat buffet amidst cheesy decor is a great spot for inexpensive salads, grilled meats, Russian soups and calorie-laden desserts. R200. Metro Mayakovskaya.

Restaurants

Aragvi Nab. Reki Fontanky 9. One of the most popular Georgian restaurants in the city, and deservedly so. Their selection of *lobio* starters is superb; the *khachapuri*, oozing cheese, is enough for two; and the generous mains include delicately spiced grilled meats, and baked sheeps'

brains with coriander for the more adventurous. Mains R350. Metro Gostiny Dvor.

Idiot Nab. reki Moyki 82. Unchallenging vegetarian restaurant teeming with foreigners. Free vodka shot on arrival. Farmers' cheesecake with honey R180. Metro Sadovaya.

Korchma Nab. Kan. Griboedova 69/18. Russian tavern with a welcoming atmosphere and generous portions of superb, hearty soups, and a huge range of meat dishes. Live entertainment on weekends. Metro Sadovaya.

Sukawati Ul. Kazanskaya 8. Behind the Kazan Cathedral, this trendy restaurant is a great place to gorge yourself on Indonesian food; go for the *ryaistafel* (taster menu) and then retreat to the chic cellar bar for cocktails. Mains R350. Metro Nevskiy Prospekt.

Drinking

Bars

Argus Bolshaya Konyushennaya ul. 15. Noisy, central, British-style bar, with its own small brewery. Bar snacks such as grilled cheese on toast for R140. Metro Nevskiy Prospekt.

Che Poltavskaya ul. 3. This cocktail-focused bar/café fancies itself something rotten, but it's open 24hr and has great bands on late. Expensive though, with mojitos at R285. Metro Moskovskiy Vokzal.

Shamrock ul. Dekabristov 27. Perpetually popular with expats and Russians alike, this cosy Irish pub offers 13 types of beer and excellent pub grub, as well as live bands. Packed when premiership football is on. Metro Sadovaya.

Terra Cotta ul. Gagarinskaya 6/1. Fantastic international menu, extensive (and quite expensive) bar and a lively dancefloor – all in keeping with the city's dine, drink and dance trend. Open until 3am Fri & Sat. Metro Chernyshevskaya.

Clubs

Cabaret Nab. Obvodnogo Kanala 181. Gay club housed in the old Soviet Culture Palace, with extravagant transvestite shows at 2.30am and a friendly atmosphere. Fri–Sun 11pm–6am; R100–400. Metro Baltiyskaya.

Fish Fabrique Ligovskiy pr. 53. This grungy place, which once launched St Petersburg's hippest bands, is now a slackers' haven at the heart of the city's famous artists' colony. Rich honey beer (*medovúkha*) R90; gig admission R150–250; open until 6am. Metro Mayakovskovo.

Griboedov Voronezhskaya ul. 2a. Cool, if self-conscious, club in a former bomb shelter, hosting decent DJs and alternative bands. 9pm–6am; DJs from midnight; admission R100–400. Metro Ligovskiy Prospekt.

Purga Nab. Reki Fontanky 11. You'll either love or hate the two *Purga* clubs; *Purga* I hosts New Year's celebrations nightly, complete with address by Soviet leader, while next door, *Purga* II is the place to go with your other half for a mock wedding. Rowdy fun. 4pm–6am; R100/300 Fri & Sat. Metro Mayakovskaya.

TREAT YOURSELF

Mops Rubinsteina ul. 12 ⓣ812/572 3834, ⓦwww.mopscafe.ru; Metro Dostoevskaya. This Thai-restaurant-cum-cocktail-bar embodies moneyed St Petersburg's flawless, if studied, chic. Secure a seat on the summer veranda if you can. Mains start from a steep R260, but permit yourself a cocktail, if nothing else. Exquisite spring rolls, soups and imaginatively executed mains make this dining experience a real treat.

Entertainment

Beware: theatres tend to close for the summer until mid-September. For details of what's on, check the listings papers (see p.1000).

Classical, opera and ballet

Mariinskiy Theatre (formerly Kirov Theatre) Teatralnaya pl. 1 ⓣ812/326 4242, ⓦwww.mariinsky.ru. Tickets €8–120. Performances at 7pm, matinees at noon.

Philharmonia Mikhaylovskaya ul. 2 ⓣ812/110 4290. Draws international classical musicians as well as Russia's finest. Performances at 7pm. Metro Nevskiy Prospekt.

Live music

JFC Jazz Club Shpalernaya ul. 33. The city's most exciting, intimate jazz club, tucked away in a courtyard; nightly performances from experimental jazz to blues. The Annual Spring Festival draws international musicians. Music 7–11pm. Admission R200–700. Metro Chernyshevskaya.

Shopping

Kuznechniy market 3 Kuznechniy Pereulok. Shop for Russian speciality foods here, such as mouth

watering displays of sweets and cakes, salted cucumbers, sausages, plaited cheese rinds and caviar. Daily 8am–8pm, Sun 8am–7pm. Metro Vladimirskaya.

Nevsky Souvenir Nevsky Prospekt 3. Pick up high-quality (though not cheap) Russian souvenirs here, as well as the obligatory matrioshka dolls. There's also stunning amber jewellery by local artists, as well as Fabergé-style eggs made from real eggs. Metro Nevsky Prospekt.

Udelnaya market Those interested in Soviet kitsch may wish to rummage around at this giant jumble sale presided over by a small army of babushkas. Turn right out of the metro then right after crossing the railway tracks. Sat & Sun 10am–5pm. Metro Udelnaya.

Directory

Consulates Australia: Italyanskaya ul. 1, Metro Nevskiy Prospekt ⓣ812/325 7333; Canada: Malodetskoselskiy pr. 32, Metro Frunzenskaya ⓣ812/325 8448; UK: pl. Proletarskoy diktatury 5 ⓣ812/320 3245; US: Furshtadtskaya ul. 15, Metro Chernyshavskaya ⓣ812/331 2600.

Internet Quo Vadis, Nevskiy prospect 76, 9am–11pm, Metro Mayakovskaya; Cafemax at the Hermitage, in the Rastrelli Gallery, 10.30am–6pm; Free Time, Lomonosova ul. 2 (24hr), Metro Nevskiy Prospekt.

Left luggage Main stations have lockers and/or a 24hr left-luggage office.

Laundry May, Reki Moiky 42, Metro Nevskiy Prospekt; 11am–7pm.

Medical MEDEM International Clinic & Hospital, Ul. Marata 6, Metro Mayakovskaya ⓣ812/336 3333; American Medical Clinic, Naberezhnaya Reki Moyky 78, Metro Sadovaya ⓣ812/740 2090.

Pharmacy Petropharm, at Nevskiy pr. 22–24 (24hr).

Post office Main office at Pochtamskaya ul. 9, Metro Nevskiy Prospekt (24hr).

Express letter post: Westpost, Nevskiy pr. 86, ⓦwww.westpost.ru. DHL: Nevskiy pr. 10, ⓦwww.dhl.ru.

Moving on

Train Helsinki (1 daily; 6hr, 3hr from 2011); Moscow (2 express trains, 4hr 30min–5hr, and 10 others; 7–9hr); Rīga (1 daily; 8hr); Vilnius (1 daily; 12hr).

Bus Helsinki (2 daily; 6hr 30min); Rīga (1 daily; 10hr); Tallinn (6 daily; 7hr); Tartu (1 daily; 8hr 30min); Warsaw (Tues–Fri & Sun 1 daily; 22hr).

DAY-TRIPS FROM ST PETERSBURG

The Imperial palaces of **Peterhof** and **Tsarskoe Selo**, half an hour to an hour outside the city, are both splendid. Although entering the palaces is increasingly expensive, you can slip away from the crowds into the surrounding parks, which are a joy in themselves. As you leave St Petersburg on the bus, look out for the awe-inspiring war monument to Leningrad's World War II sacrifice, and Lenin "hailing a taxi" near Finland station.

The Peterhof

Most visitors with time for just one day-trip opt for **Peterhof** (park 9am–7pm, R150–300; palace 10.30am–6pm, closed Mon and last Tues of month, R500), 29km west of St Petersburg, known as the "Russian Versailles" and famed for the marvellous fountains and impressive cascades at the Great Palace. Though originally built between 1709 and 1724 for Peter the Great, each of the subsequent rulers made their mark on the grounds. Travel by hydrofoil in summer (at least one hourly 10am–6pm; R200 each way; 30–40min) from outside the Winter Palace or take minibus #224 or #424 from Avtovo metro station (R30). Trains also run from Baltiyskiy station in the capital to Noviy Peterhof station; alternatively, take bus #350, #351, #352 or #356 from in front of the station.

Tsarskoe Selo and Pavlovsk

Tsarskoe Selo (also known as Pushkin, after the "Russian Shakespeare" who was schooled at the neighbouring Lyceum school), 17km southeast of St Petersburg, centres on the **Catherine Palace** (10am–5pm, closed Tues and last Mon of the month; R550/280 students, park only R180/R90 students). The ostentatious blue-and-white Baroque structure built by Catherine the Great is surrounded by a richly landscaped park.

Scottish architect Charles Cameron's elegant Neoclassical Gallery stretches high above it.

To get to Pushkin, take one of the frequent minibuses (R30) from outside Moskovskaya metro station; #286, #299, #342 and #545 ply the route; alternatively, take a train to Detskoe selo from Vitebsky station or bus #371 or #382. Minibuses #286 and #299 will take you to the more intimate Pavlovsk Palace, its magnificent Neoclassical interior set amidst luxurious 1500-acre grounds at **Pavlovsk** (10am–5pm, closed Fri and first Mon of the month; palace R400/250 students, park R150/80 students).

Serbia

HIGHLIGHTS

SUBOTICA: enjoy the city's unspoilt feel and fantastical Secessionist architecture

NOVI SAD: admire the view from Petrovaradin, the hilltop fortress that hosts the EXIT Festival every summer

BELGRADE: explore the nightlife and café culture of Serbia's hectic, hedonistic capital city

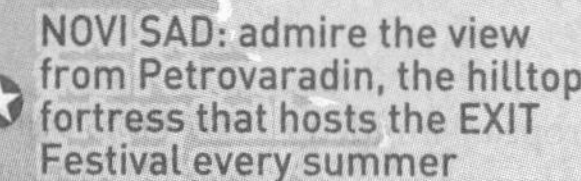

STUDENICA MONASTERY: the finest of Serbia's fresco-laden, medieval monastic churches

ROUGH COSTS

DAILY BUDGET basic €25/occasional treat €35

DRINK Beer (half-litre) €1

FOOD Pljeskavica (hamburger) €1–2

HOSTEL/BUDGET HOTEL €15/€35

TRAVEL Belgrade–Novi Sad (74km) €5 by bus; Belgrade–Niš (235km) €6 by train.

FACT FILE

POPULATION 7.5 million (excluding Kosovo)

AREA 88,361 sq km

LANGUAGE Serbian

CURRENCY Dinar (din)

CAPITAL Belgrade (population 1.6 million)

INTERNATIONAL PHONE CODE ⓣ381

Introduction

Serbia is a buzzy and boisterous country, compact enough for visitors to sample both Belgrade's urban hedonism and the gentler pace of the smaller towns or national parks within a few days – and it's one of Europe's most affordable destinations to boot. Grittier than its blue-eyed neighbour Croatia, it is nevertheless an integral part of any backpacker's Balkan tour: at the heart of the region, it gives easy access to the cluster of cultures and histories crammed into this small corner of Europe.

Serbia's young, European-minded population brings a bubbling energy to its bars, cafés and clubs, producing an adrenalin-charged nightlife unmatched anywhere else in the Balkans. The general determination to have a good time confounds the expectations of many a traveller, arriving with memories of the 1990s, when Serbia's name was not often off war reporters' lips. Today, it's just as likely to attract headlines for its crop of top-notch tennis players or the annual EXIT festival in Novi Sad.

Serbia's capital, **Belgrade**, is a sociable, hectic city that energizes and exhausts by turns. Northwest of the city on the iron-flat Vojvodina plain sits lovely **Novi Sad**, window to the **Fruška Gora** hills, while further north – a stone's throw from the border with Hungary – enchanting **Subotica** is sprinkled with early twentieth-century Secessionist architecture. Deep in the mountainous tract of land to the south of Belgrade are three key struts of Serbia's religio-cultural heritage – Žiča, Studenica and Sopoćani **monasteries**. East of here, **Niš** is a pleasant small town to pause in en route to or from Bulgaria or Macedonia.

CHRONOLOGY

168 BC The Romans defeat the Illyrian tribe and establish their rule of the area of present-day Serbia.

630 AD Serbs settle in the region.

1166 Stefan Nemanja, leader of the Serbs, declares independence from Byzantine rule.

1219 The Serbian Orthodox Church is established.

1389 The Ottomans defeat the Serbs in the Battle of Kosovo, ushering in four centuries of direct rule.

1804 National hero Karađorđe ("Black George") begins the First Serbian Uprising against the Ottomans.

1913 The Ottomans lose their remaining authority in Serbia during the Balkan wars.

1918 Following World War I the Kingdom of Serbs, Croats and Slovenes is formed.

1929 The Kingdom is renamed Yugoslavia.

1945 Following World War II, Serbia is absorbed into Socialist Yugoslavia.

1989 Slobodan Milošević, a Serbian communist, becomes President of Serbia.

1992 The wars of the disintegration of Yugoslavia begin. Fighting ends three years later.

1993 The International Criminal Tribunal for the former Yugoslavia is set up in The Hague to try those accused of war crimes.

1998 Serbia launches a violent campaign against the ethnic Albanian community in Kosovo, costing thousands of lives.

1999 NATO's "Operation Merciful Angel" – a ten-week war from the air to end Milošević's ethnic cleansing campaign – drives Yugoslav National Army forces out of Kosovo.

2000 Mass protests lead to the resignation of Milošević.

2003 Serbian prime minister, Zoran Đinđić, is assassinated in Belgrade.

2006 Milošević dies in prison, awaiting trial at the International Criminal Tribunal for the former Yugoslavia on charges of genocide.

2006 Montenegro peacefully gains independence from Serbia.

2007 Serbia wins the Eurovision Song Contest.

2008 Kosovo declares independence from Serbia after nine years under UN administration. Serbia does not recognize Kosovo as an independent state.

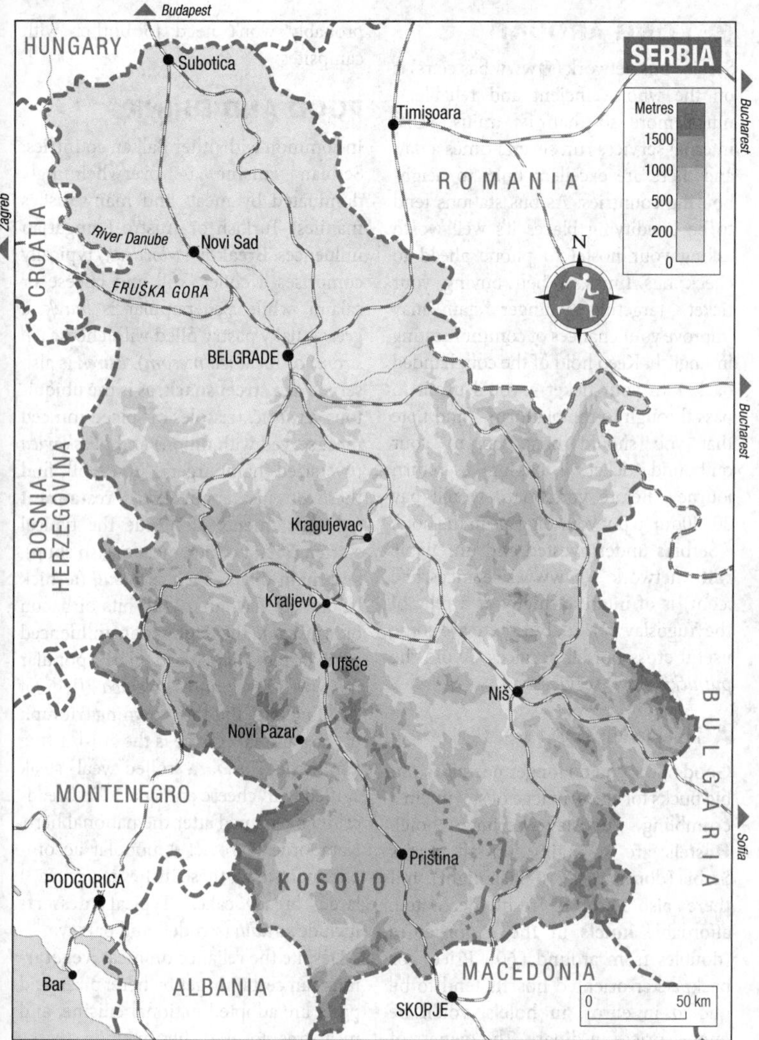

ARRIVAL

At the heart of the Balkans, Serbia is easily accessed by **bus** or **train** from Bulgaria (via Niš), Hungary (via Subotica), and other neighbouring Balkan countries including Croatia, Macedonia, Montenegro, Bosnia-Herzegovina, Albania and Romania. **Flight** operators from the UK include British Airways and the Yugoslav national airline JAT (ⓦwww.jat.com), inherited by Serbia – the air hostesses' mandatory blue eyeshadow and severe manner evoke times gone by. The nearest airports servicing budget airline flights from London are Budapest (8hr by train) and Zagreb (5–6hr by bus). No visas are needed for nationals of the US, Canada, Australia, New Zealand, UK, Republic of Ireland, or any EU country staying in Serbia for up to ninety days.

GETTING AROUND

Serbia's **bus** network (Ⓦwww.bas.co.rs) is on the whole efficient and reliable – much more so than its trains. Most internal services run several times a day, and there are excellent links to neighbouring countries. As bus stations tend to be unedifying places it's well worth asking your hostel to phone ahead to check bus times. When buying your ticket, targeting younger staff may improve your chances of communicating in English. Keep hold of the coin handed back with your ticket – you'll use it to pass through to the platform – and note that you should hang on to your outbound ticket if taking a return journey. Before you board, you'll pay 30–40din to put your luggage in the hold.

Serbia's underinvested and unreliable **rail** network (Ⓦwww.zeleznicesrbije.com) is of interest chiefly as a relic of the Yugoslav period, but there are some useful cross-border services. Avoid the *putnički* (slow) services.

ACCOMMODATION

Good news: you no longer need fork out big bucks for the privilege of staying in a crumbling Yugoslav heritage hotel. **Hostels** are springing up all across Serbia (dorms cost €10–20 a night), and there's also a crop of freshly decorated, affordable **hotels** in the major cities (doubles from around €60). Prices for backpacker-oriented hostels tend to be quoted in euros; in hotels, you'll be quoted prices in dinars. The owners of leading hostels across southeastern Europe have formed a new consortium, Balkans Best Hostels, which gives serial hostellers a five percent discount: see Ⓦwww.balkansbesthostels.com. **Rooms** in people's homes (*sobe*) are less commonly offered than in Croatia or Bosnia-Herzegovina, but **apartmani** (furnished individual rooms or suites) are available, with doubles starting at around €40. Given the range of cheap hostel accommodation available, you probably won't need to bother with campsites.

FOOD AND DRINK

In common with other Balkan countries, Serbian **cuisine** is overwhelmingly dominated by meat, and many dishes manifest Turkish or Austro-Hungarian influences. **Breakfast** *(doručak)* typically comprises a coffee, roll and cheese or salami, while also popular is *burek*, a greasy, flaky pastry filled with cheese (*sa sirom*) or meat (*sa mesom*). *Burek* is also served as a **street snack**, as is the ubiquitous *ćevapčići* (rissoles of spiced minced meat served with onion) and *pljeskavica* (oversized hamburger). You will find these on just about every **restaurant** (*restoran*) menu, alongside the typical starter, *čorba* (a thick meat or fish soup), and **main dishes** such as *pasulj (*a thick bean soup flavoured with bits of bacon or sausage), the Hungarian-influenced paprika-red *gulaš,* particularly popular in Vojvodina, and *kolenica* (leg of suckling pig). But the crowning triumph of the national cuisine is the gut-busting *karađorđe šnicla*, a rolled veal steak stuffed with cheese and coated in breadcrumbs – named after the national hero, Karađorđe Petrović. A popular accompaniment to all these dishes is *pogača*, a large bread cake. Typical **desserts** include *strudla* (strudel) and baklava.

Despite the reliance on meat, **vegetarians** can certainly get by here: pizza and pasta are adopted national cuisine, and meat-free local dishes include *srpska salata* (tomato, cucumber, and raw onion), *šopska salata* (as *srpska*, but topped with grated *kashkaval* white cheese), and *burek*.

Drink

You will not want for **coffee** (*kafa*) in Serbia, but sadly the traditional Turkish kind (thick, black, with grounds in) can be hard to come by, as many youngsters prefer to drink the

Western variants. Balkan **beer** (*pivo*) brands like Lav, Jelen and Montenegrin Nikšićko are very palatable. On the whole **wine** tends to be disproportionately pricey on restaurant menus, but Montenegrin Vranac and Macedonian Tikveš are more affordable. Everyone should sample *slijvovica* – plum *rakija* – but pace yourself to avoid waking up with a shocked head and raw throat.

CULTURE AND ETIQUETTE

Even though tourists are quite a rarity in some parts, part of the charm of travel in Serbia is a sense of "live and let live" – you are unlikely to be quizzed intrusively or pestered to buy wares. Serbian culture as a whole is far from conservative – a fact you'll quickly grasp from the fashion choices youngsters make. You should cover arms and legs in Orthodox churches, however. **Tipping** in restaurants is not essential, but in the nicer places you should leave ten percent.

SPORTS AND OUTDOOR ACTIVITIES

Serbia's countryside is beautiful, varied and never more than a short bus ride away. In the summer, **hike** or walk in the Fruška Gora National Park (Ⓦwww.npfruskagora.co.rs); in winter hit the slopes with Balkan daredevils at Kopaonik National Park (Ⓦwww.npkopaonik.com) The locals are passionate about **football**, and a derby between Belgrade's Red Star (Ⓦwww.redstarbelgrade.com) and FK Partizan (Ⓦwww.partizan.rs) can become extremely heated. If you're keen to watch a match but don't want to risk the pyrotechnics (burning the stands of the stadium is a favourite way of venting post-defeat disappointment), you might prefer to choose another fixture: one featuring Novi Sad's FK Vojvodina (Ⓦwww.fkvojvodina.com), for example.

EMERGENCY NUMBERS

Police Ⓣ92; Ambulance Ⓣ94; Fire Ⓣ93; Road assistance Ⓣ987.

COMMUNICATIONS

Internet cafés are widespread in Serbia's cities; expect to pay around 100din/hr; **wi-fi** is widely available in cafés. **Public phones** use Halo cards, sold with 300din and 600din credit at post offices, kiosks and tobacconists. Most **post offices** (*pošta*) are open Monday to Friday 8am to 7pm. **Stamps** (*markice*) can also be bought at newsstands.

EMERGENCIES

The **crime** rate, even in Belgrade, is low by European standards, though the usual precautions apply. **Identity checks** are not uncommon, so carry a photocopy of your passport.

Pharmacies (*apoteka*) tend to follow shop hours of around Monday to Friday 8am to 8pm, Saturday 8am to 3pm.

SERBIA ON THE NET

Ⓦwww.belgraded.com Entertaining blog by a young Belgrader, with his tips on what to do in the city.
Ⓦwww.belgradeeye.com Excellent English-language site aimed at younger visitors; includes information on a fast-changing club scene.
Ⓦwww.birn.eu.com Excellent news site with news and views from across the Balkans.
Ⓦyankee-in-belgrade.blogspot.com Observations on Belgrade's oddities noted down by an American expat.
Ⓦwww.serbia-tourism.org Official tourist board site.

Serbian

Serbia uses the **Cyrillic alphabet** as well as the Latin one. Many street signs (see opposite) and bus and train timetables are in Cyrillic only, so it's worth being able to decode at least the first few letters of a word. Serbian, like Bosnian, is very closely related to Croatian (see p.257) and all three languages will be understood in all three countries.

INFORMATION

All the towns covered in this chapter have a **tourist information office** (*turističke informacije*) with materials in English. These are a good place to start in the smaller towns, for example if you want to hire a car.

MONEY AND BANKS

The currency is the **dinar** (usually abbreviated to din), comprising coins of 1, 2, 5, 10 and 20din (and also 50 para coins – 100 para equals 1din), and notes of 10, 20, 50, 100, 200, 1000 and 5000din. Exchange rates are currently around 90din to €1, 110din to £1, and 65din to US$1. You'll see *menjačnica* (exchange office) signs everywhere; euros are by far the easiest foreign currency to exchange, while ATMs are also widely available in towns. Debit/credit cards are accepted in most hotels and restaurants.

STUDENT AND YOUTH DISCOUNTS

Euro<26 student cards (see p.52) are valid in Serbia, as is the Balkan Flexipass (see p.35). Some museums lop around a third off the entry fee for students.

OPENING HOURS AND HOLIDAYS

Most **shops** open Monday to Friday 8am to 7/8pm (sometimes with a break for lunch), plus Saturday 8am to 2pm, and sometimes later in Belgrade. Most **museums** are closed on Mondays. Shops and banks close on **public holidays**: January 1, 2 and 7, Febuary 15, and May 1 and 2. The Orthodox Church celebrates Easter between one and five weeks later than the other churches.

Belgrade

BELGRADE (Београд; Beograd) is a hectic, sociable city, where throughout spring and summer all ages throng the streets at all hours. With a seemingly endless supply of bars and clubs, its nightlife is one of the unexpected high points on any European itinerary.

The city sits at a strategic point on the junction of the Danube and Sava rivers – something that has proved a source of weakness as well as strength over the ages: Belgrade has been captured as many as sixty times by Celts, Romans, Huns, Avars and more. The onslaught continued right through the twentieth century, when the city suffered heavy shelling during World War II and in 1999 withstood 78 days of airstrikes.

All that considered, contemporary Belgrade is pretty picturesque. The mingling and merging of styles can be off-putting, particularly when a row of beautiful older frontages is interrupted by a postwar interloper, but the grand nineteenth-century buildings and delicate Art Nouveau facades still stand alongside the Yugoslav experimentation, eloquent witnesses of the city's time under the Ottoman and Austro-Hungarian empires.

What to see and do

The city's most attention-grabbing attraction is the **Kalemegdan Fortress**, poised atop a peak overlooking a curve of the mighty Danube: it's literally unmissable. Just outside the park boundary is the **Old City**, whose dense lattice of streets conceals Belgrade's most interesting sights. South of here is Belgrade's central square, **Trg Republike**, and the old bohemian quarter of **Skadarlija**, beyond which lie several more sights worth seeing, including one of the world's largest Orthodox churches. For a spot of rest and recuperation, head west across the Sava to the verdant suburb of **Zemun**, in New Belgrade, or further south towards the island of **Ada Ciganija**, Belgrade's own miniature beach resort.

BELGRADE STREET NAMES

Трг Републике	Trg Republike
Трг Слободе	Trg Slobode
Краља Петра	Kralja Petra
Краља Милана	Kralja Milana
Кнез Михаилова	Knez Mihailova
Француска	Francuska
Добрачина	Dobračina
Змај Јовина	Zmaj Jovina

Kalemegdan Fortress

Splendidly sited on an exposed nub of land overlooking the confluence of the Sava and Danube rivers is **Kalemegdan Park**, dominated by the **fortress** of the same name. The whole complex is a paean to Serbian heroism, topped with the proud Victory Monument of 1912. Originally built by the Celts in the third century BC, before expansion by the Romans, the fortress has survived successive invasions; most of what remains is the result of a short-lived Austrian occupation in the early eighteenth century. The grounds contain several museums, sports facilities and cafés; they are also uniquely popular with canoodling teenage couples. The best of the attractions is the **Military Museum** (Tues–Sun 10am–5pm; 100din), where a history thick with conflict is divertingly presented and told in a clear, unsanitized manner. Note the display cases of weapons and illuminated manuscripts, and depictions of the particularly gruesome methods of torture the Turks used on the nationalist rebel Hajduks.

The Orthodox Cathedral and museum

Leaving the park and crossing Pariska, you'll find yourself in the oldest part of

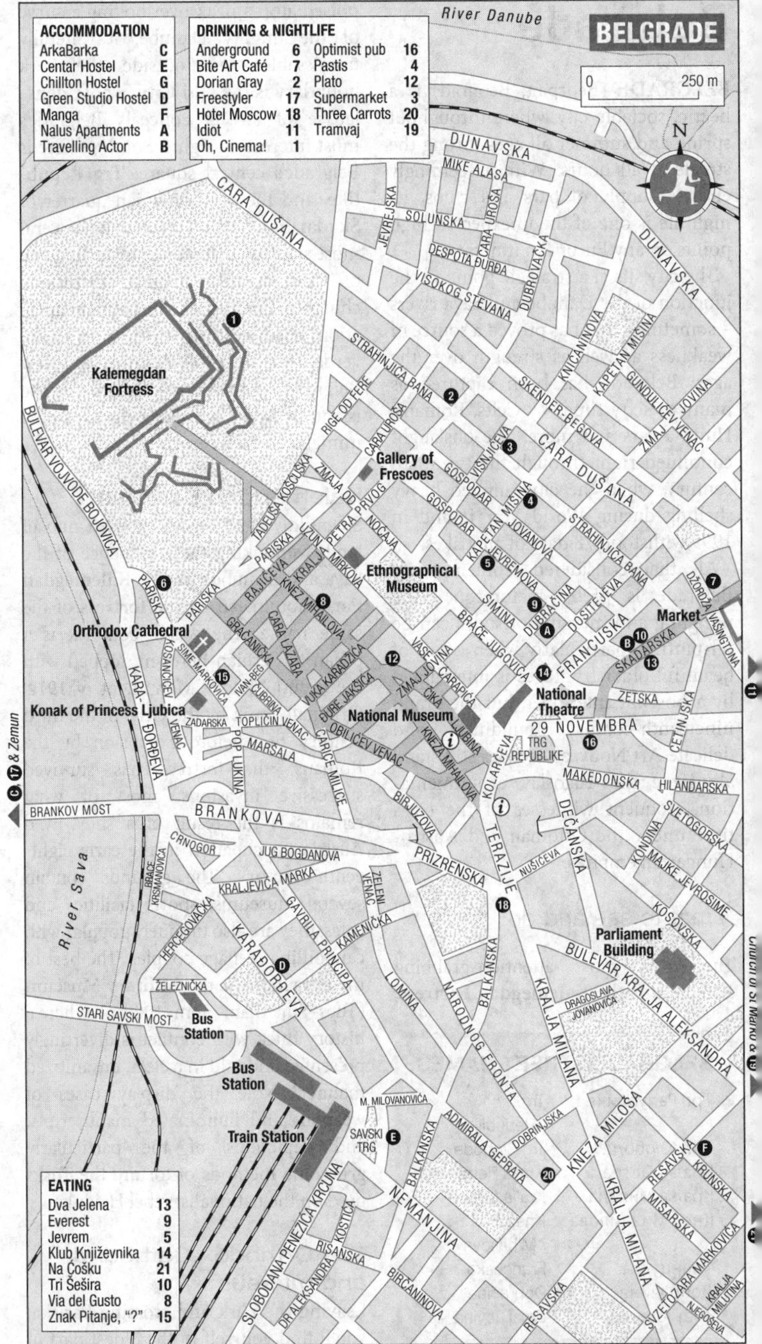

Tito's Mausoleum & Ada Ciganlija
Church of St Sava & G

the city. At Kralja Petra 7 is the **Orthodox Cathedral**, a rather stark Neoclassical edifice built in 1840 featuring a fine Baroque tower. Built around the same time is the **"?" café**, or *Znak Pitanje* (see p.1016), whose noncommittal name was originally adopted as an interim solution after a spat with church officials over its first choice, *Café at the Cathedral*. Opposite, at Kralja Petra 5, stands the **Museum of the Serbian Orthodox Church** (Mon–Fri 8am–3pm, Sat 9am–noon, Sun 11am–1pm; 50din), where a small collection of heavily jewelled Bibles and other gorgeously decorated paraphernalia is housed in the HQ of the Patriarchate. With long-haired, black-cloaked monks striding the corridors, you get an instant flavour of the Orthodox church on stepping inside.

Konak of Princess Ljubica

Just around the corner at Sime Markovića 8 is the **Konak of Princess Ljubica** (Tues–Sat 10am–5pm, Thurs until 8pm, Sun 10am–2pm; 100din), the abode of a nineteenth-century noblewoman which underlines the Balkans' position as a cultural crossroads: a Napoleon III-themed room sits alongside a Turkish-style room with a Koran stand. It seems nineteenth-century Belgraders loved socializing too: there's a big semicircular sofa for chatting guests in nearly every room.

The Ethnographical Museum and Gallery of Frescoes

A short walk northeast lie two more interesting museums. At Studentski trg 13, the **Ethnographical Museum** (Tues–Sat 10am–5pm, Sun 9am–2pm; 150din) is a lively people's history of crafts and clothes in the Balkans. It's hard to imagine Serbian girls today submitting to the heavy woollen dresses weighed down with coins worn a century ago. Beyond here, at Cara Uroša 20, the **Gallery of Frescoes** (Tues–Sat 10am–5pm, Thurs noon–8pm, Sun 10am–2pm; 100din) houses replicas of 1200 of the country's most feted medieval frescoes – a must if you don't have the opportunity to visit the originals at the monasteries of southern Serbia, Macedonia and Kosovo. The style is fresh and colourful – lots of puce and blue.

Trg Republike and around

The main street leading south from Kalemegdan is Kneza Mihailova, a pedestrianized *korzo* (promenade) with narrow, pretty fronts. It becomes more commercialized and hulkish at its southern end as it approaches **Trg Republike** (Republic Square), the main square where hordes of young people gather before a big night out. An irregularly shaped space, it's dominated by the imperious National Museum on its north side (closed for more than seven years and still awaiting renovation), and the National Theatre.

East of Trg Republike is **Skadarlija**, the former bohemian district that centres on charming, cobbled Skadarska. South of Trg Republike is the wide swathe of **Terazije**, which slices through the commercial and business hub of the city.

Parliament Building

A left turn part way down Terazije brings you to the **Parliament Building** (Skupština), a building that has seen its fair share of drama. In October 2000, after Milošević tried to claw back the presidential election he'd lost, hundreds of demonstrators forced their way into the parliament building and threw fake ballot papers out of the windows as the building blazed inside. The Parliament was again the scene of protests after Kosovo's declaration of independence in 2008.

Church of St Marko

Around five minutes' walk along Kralja Aleksandra beyond the Parliament

Building is the **Church of St Marko**, a grandiose, five-domed neo-Byzantine structure modelled on the revered monastery of Gračanica in Kosovo. It holds the tomb of the Serbian Emperor, Tsar Dušan, protected by muscled stone guards.

Church of St Sava

Dominating the skyline south of Terazije is the magnificent gilded dome of the **Church of St Sava**, at Svetosavski trg in the Vračar district. Built on the spot where the Turks supposedly burnt the bones of the founder of the Serbian Orthodox Church in 1594, it is a perfect example of the way religious and national identities fuse here: banner-sized Serbian flags hang from the roof. It also stakes a fair claim to be one of the largest Orthodox churches in the world, with a cavernous interior that has been under stop-start construction for over a hundred years. The church is a twenty-minute walk south of Trg Republike.

Tito's Mausoleum

Another outlying site well worth the trip is **Tito's Mausoleum** (Tues–Sun 9am–2pm; free; bus #40 or #41 from Kneza Miloša), located around 1.5km south of the centre on Botićeva 6. There is a whole "memorial complex" here, but the former Yugoslav leader's tomb lies in the House of Flowers (Kuća cveća), designed in 1975 as his winter garden. In the adjoining **museum**, check out the display of gifts from foreign dignitaries – just imagine Tito's delight at receiving that Bolivian witch-doctor's costume.

Ada Cignalija

In the summer months Belgraders flock to **Ada Ciganlija** (literally, "gypsy island"), a stretch of wooded park along the bank of the Sava just south of the centre. The island's sandy beaches have earned it the local nickname "Belgrade's seaside", and city-dwellers enjoy its giant water slides, water-skiing and naturist area; the more adventurous can even try bungee-jumping from a crane. To get here, take bus #53 or #56 from Zeleni Venac.

Zemun

For a spot of rest and recuperation, head across the Sava River to the New Belgrade and the west bank suburb of **Zemun**, a jumble of low-slung houses and narrow winding streets centred around the hilly waterside district of Gardoš, which holds the Baroque **Nikolajevska Church**, the city's oldest Orthodox church. To get here take bus #15 from Zeleni Venac, or bus #83 from outside the train station, and alight on Glavna, the main street.

South of Gardoš is the vast park, **Ušće**, where Belgraders keep in shape running, biking and rollerblading. By night the river waters here tremble to the beats emanating from the *splavovi* (see p.1016). You can even stay on board one (see opposite). In the grounds of Ušće sits the **Museum of Contemporary Art** on Ušće bb (daily except Tues 10am–5pm; 80din; Ⓦwww.msub.org.rs), an excellent gallery purpose-built for modern art in 1958, with exhibitions of impressionism, Tito-era work, photography and film.

Arrival and information

Air Belgrade's Nikola Tesla airport is 18km northwest of the city in Surčin, and connected to the centre by regular JAT buses (hourly 7am–10pm; 200din), which drop off at the train station and Trg Slavija. Alternatively, take bus #72 (5.15am–midnight; 60din), which terminates at the Zeleni Venac market. A taxi should cost no more than 1000din but avoid the sharks in the arrivals hall.
Train and bus The main train station (*železnička stanica*) and bus station (*autobuska stanica*) are adjacent to each other on Savski trg and Železnička, 15min walk southwest of the centre.
Tourist office The main information centre is on Makedonska 5 (Mon–Fri 9am–8pm, Sat 9am–5pm, Sun 10am–4pm; Ⓣ11/334 3460, Ⓦwww.tob.co.rs/eng), with another branch in

arrivals at the airport, and a third in the subway under Terazije. They offer city maps, leaflets for hostels and advice on onward travel, as well as the *Visit Serbia* brochure, at the back of which are coupons attracting discounts at Belgrade museums and bars. Maps of cities in Serbia and across the Balkans are sold at Belgrade's Plato bookshop and stalls on Knez Mikhailova.

City transport

Public transport Buses, trolleybuses and trams operate throughout the city. Night buses operate between midnight and 4am (65din).

Tickets can be bought from a kiosk or newsstand (30din) or on board (40din) – either way, they must be validated in the machine on board.

Taxis are affordable and frankly the easiest way to get to the few places that are too far to walk from the centre, like New Belgrade. Flag fall is 120din, after which it's around 50din/km. Aim to catch a taxi from the street or small rank; sharks operate around bus or train stations and at the airport.

Accommodation

Belgrade's hostel scene has grown exponentially over the last couple of years; there are now more than thirty to choose from.

Hostels

ArkaBarka Bulevar Nikole Tesle bb ⓣ64/200-4445, ⓦwww.arkabarka.net. This floating hostel is a cool concept exactingly executed, with snug cabin-like rooms, on-board entertainment (playlists on the laptop), and drinks on deck (the small balcony edging the raft). Great views back down the Sava to the fortress. To reach it, head towards the river through Ušće park. Dorms €15, doubles €38, triples €50.

Centar Hostel Gavrila Principa 46a ⓣ11/761-9686, ⓦwww.hostelcentar.com. The emphasis here is on functionality rather than flair – you get new sheets daily, your own water-cup, breakfast and a welcome pack containing a pan scourer. Near the bus station, it's well located for a stopover. Dorms €9–17; doubles €44.

Chillton Hostel Katanićeva 7 ⓣ11/344-1826, ⓦwww.chilltonhostel.com. A garret plastered with posters from visiting bands, *Chillton*'s well-stocked kitchen is ideal for swapping travellers' tales. A 15min walk south of Trg Republike, near St Sava's (bus #83 from the train station). Dorms of 4–10 beds €13–19.

Green Studio Hostel Karađorđeva 69/42 ⓣ11/263-3626, ⓔgreenhostelstudio.gmail.com. Airy loft with convivial communal space and free beers. Close to the bus station. Dorms €15–19.

Manga Resavska 7 ⓣ11/324-3877, ⓦwww.mangahostel.com. Opened in 2008 by enthusiastic couch-surfers, *Manga* occupies a small chalet of its own, including a cosy exposed-brick cellar where guests share dinner with the sparky staff. Free *rakija* on arrival. Dorms €12–25; single room €23.

Furnished rooms and apartments

Nalus Apartments Dobračina 18a ⓣ11/328-3938, ⓦwww.nalus-apartmani.com. A set of modern, trendy doubles, located squarely between Trg Republike and Strahinjića Bana. Shared bathroom. Double 4200din.

Travelling Actor (Serbian: Putujući Glamac) Gospodar Jevremova 65 (corner of Skadarska) ⓣ11/323-4156, ⓦwww.travellingactor.rs. If you're starting to tire of life on the road, a couple of nights here will set you straight: soft beds, spanking new bathrooms and an outstanding location. Twins €88, doubles €60.

Eating

For serious nights out, you need serious fuel, and the best place to eat Serbian is Skadarska, where live music and open-air dining are the perfect accompaniments to traditional fare.

Dva Jelena Skadarska 32. With singers belting out classic local tearjerkers in its grand salon, *Dva Jelena* combines old-world charm with authenticity. *Jagnjece pecenje* (roast lamb) 750din.

Everest Gospodar Jevremova 47a (corner with Dobraćina). This soothing veggie café is an ideal antidote to hedonistic Belgrade. Mains include salads bursting with fresh veg and macrobiotic meals (boiled grains and algae); desserts include home-made cheesecake and apple pie. Home-made samosa 60din.

Jevrem Gospodar Jevremova 36. True romance: dine on the terrace of a nineteenth-century townhouse heaped with geraniums. Music Fri & Sat. Barbecued pork (*leskovačka mućkalica*) 590din. Closed Sun.

Na Ćošku Beogradska 37 (at the corner with Krunska). The sophisticated light menu and Art Nouveau surroundings might seduce you into accompanying lunch with a glass or two of wine. Prawn and truffle chowder 320din. Closed Sun.

Tri Šešira Skadarska 29. Skadarlija's oldest restaurant is a great place to be introduced to the rough charms of Serbian dining: the mixed grill includes no less than six types of meat. Energetic live folk music 8pm–1am. Grilled pork 620din.

TREAT YOURSELF

Klub Književnika Francuska 7 ⓣ11/262 7931. With delicious food, fine wines and impeccable service, an evening at the "Writers' Club", a one-time haunt of the Yugoslav literati, passes in a pleasurable blur. Consider booking ahead. Karađorđević schnitzel 820din. Until 1am.

Via del Gusto Knez Mihailova 48. Grab a tasty Italian bite on Belgrade's Piccadilly. Filled pies 130din.
Znak Pitanje, or **"?"** Kralja Petra 6. A characterful inn with low wooden tables that serves solid Serbian fare (see also p.1013). Smederevo cutlet 400din.

Drinking and nightlife

There are a staggering number of places to drink and dance, with heavy concentrations along posers' paradise Strahinjića bana ("Silicon Valley"), Obilićev venac (a peaceful square perfect for sundowners) and Njegoševa. No two venues are the same, with owners competing to stand out from the crowd with funky design and long cocktail lists. In summer, it's all aboard the *splavovi* – floating bars and clubs – to dance the night away. Most are concentrated on the bank of the Danube behind the *Hotel Jugoslavija* – a conspicuous block on the main road towards Zemun – and along the Sava around the Brankov Bridge.

Bars and cafés

Dorian Gray Kralja Petra 87–89. Patrons sip champagne cocktails under a spidery iron awning in this grown-up, glamorous bar.
Hotel Moscow Balkanska 1. Enjoy the ambience of the city's top hotel over an afternoon coffee; each one comes with a tasting miniature of the sumptuous cream cakes on offer.
Optimist pub 29 Novembra 22. Optimism was probably at a premium in 1999, when this bar was founded. Laid-back and affordable.
Pastis Strahinjića Bana 52b. Sophisticos huddle round wooden tables in this French-style bistro bar. Decorative baguettes and a mini *bicyclette* complete the look. Until 2am.
Plato Akademski Plato 1. Serbs are a literary lot, and this bookstore-cum-café by the philosophy faculty is a Belgrade institution. Live jazz at night (when it's open until 2am).
Supermarket Corner of Strahinjića Bana and Višnjića. If Belgrade hasn't already sharpened your sense of the surreal, check out this vast "concept store", a warehouse with a futuristic aesthetic. Freshly squeezed juices 150din. Until 2am.
Three Carrots Kneza Miloša 16. The city's inevitable Irish bar is tastefully decorated in dark wood, but not particularly cheap. Until 2am.

Clubs and live music

Anderground Pariska 1. A warren of vast rooms under the fortress pounding out house, hip-hop and techno. Until 4am.
Bitef Art Café Skver Mire Trailović 1 ⓦwww.bitef.rs. Energetic live funk and jazz in a converted Evangelical church. 200din entry fee. Until 4am.
Freestyler Brodarska bb, New Belgrade, ⓦwww.splavfree.rs. All-night party *splav* with scantily clad dancers. Closed Mon.
Idiot Dalmatinska 13, 1km southeast of Džordža Vašingtona, off Ruzveltova. Students swarm into this small basement club by the Botanic Gardens. Until 2am.
Oh, Cinema! Gračanička 18. Views of the Danube and live music draw crowds on summer weekends, when the club stays open till dawn.
Tramvaj Ruzveltova 2. Fuggy hideaway more than public catwalk, this grungy watering hole has live bands playing every night. Until 4am.

Entertainment

Tickets for events at major arts venues are on sale at the Bilet Servis ticket agency at Trg Republike 5 (Mon–Fri 9am–8pm, Sat 9am–3pm).
Kolarac Concert Hall Studentski trg 5, ⓦwww.kolarac.rs. Hosts many of the concerts of the Beogradska Filharmonija. Box office 10am–2pm & 2.30–7.30pm; tickets 200–500din.
National Theatre Trg Republike 1 ⓦwww.narodnopozoriste.co.rs. Tickets to opera, ballet and plays are a snip at 100–800din. Box office 10am–2pm & 5pm till performance.

Shopping

Big Bull Vase Čarapića 9. If only meat-based gifts will bring the memories flooding back, make for this flagship store of a nationwide chain of butchers, not far from *Plato* café.
Kalenić Pijaca Maksima Gorkog bb. Belgrade's biggest open-air market, a 20min walk southeast of Trg Republike in the Vračar district (just east of St Sava's). You can stock up on edible souvenirs or essentials for hostel cooking: smallholders sell enormous fresh veg, honey and *ajvar* (pepper-aubergine puree).

Directory

Embassies and consulates Australia, Čika Ljubina 13 ⓣ11/330-3400; Canada, Kneza Miloša 75 ⓣ11/306-3000; Ireland, Fruškogorska 1/II ⓣ11/218-3581; UK, Resavska 46 ⓣ11/264-5055; US, Kneza Miloša 50 ⓣ11/361-9344.
Exchange You can hardly move without seeing a "Menjačnica" sign; there are several along Knez Mihailova.
Hospitals Emergency Centre, Pasterova 2 ⓣ11/361-8444 (24hr).
Internet Cyber Shark, Tržni Centar on Trg Republike (one floor up; 100din/hr).
Laundry Veseraj, Kralja Milana 23.
Left luggage (пртљаг – *prtlag*). At train station (around 200din/day).
Pharmacy Prvi Maj, Kralja Milana 9 ⓣ11/324-1349; Sveti Sava, Nemanjina 2 ⓣ11/264-3170. Both 24hr.
Police Savski trg 2 ⓣ11/645-764.
Post office Zmaj Jovina 17 (Mon–Sat 8am–7pm).

Moving on

Train Budapest (2 daily; 8hr); Kraljevo (2 daily; 4hr); Ljubljana (4 daily; 10hr); Niš (10 daily; 4hr); Novi Sad (10 daily; 1hr 30min); Skopje (2 daily; 8hr 30min); Split (3 night trains; 9hr); Ušče (2 daily; 5hr); Zagreb (5 daily; 7hr).
Bus Budva (10 daily; 11hr); Dubrovnik (1 daily; 14hr); Kraljevo (every 1hr–1hr 30min; 2hr); Mostar (2 daily; 11hr); Niš (every 20min; 3hr); Novi Sad (every 20–40min; 1hr 20min); Novi Pazar (every 1hr–1hr 30min; 3hr); Sarajevo (9 daily; 7hr); Subotica (every 40min; 3hr 30min); Zagreb (5 daily; 5–6hr).

Northern Serbia

North of Belgrade, stretching up towards the Hungarian border and spanning the southern part of the fertile Pannonian Plain, is **Vojvodina**, one of Serbia's most ethnically eclectic regions, with a large Hungarian minority. The region's capital, **Novi Sad**, is a charming spot that's a feasible day-trip from the capital or a handy springboard north to Subotica and Hungary. It's also an ideal base for forays into **Fruška Gora**, the gently undulating hills to the south peppered with medieval Orthodox monasteries.

NOVI SAD AND AROUND

Situated on the main road and rail routes towards Budapest some 75km northwest of Belgrade, **NOVI SAD** (Нови Сад) has long charmed visitors with its comely buildings – remnants of Austro-Hungarian rule. But today it's an emphatically young town – especially in the summer, when thousands of international revellers swarm to Petrovaradin Fortress for the four-day EXIT festival.

What to see and do

Novi Sad developed in tandem with the huge **Petrovaradin Fortress** (open access) on the Danube's south bank. The fortress rises picturesquely from rolls of green hillside, its delicate lemon-yellow buildings set inside sturdy fortifications. It took its present shape in the eighteenth century when the Austrians tried to create an invincible barrier against the Turks. Unfortunately its defences quickly became outdated, and the authorities decided to imprison independent-minded troublemakers here instead – including Karađorđe and, a century later, a young Tito.

As you approach from town, look out for the **plaque** on the right of the bridge commemorating those killed during the NATO bombing – Novi Sad was one of the cities hardest hit in the spring of 1999, losing all its bridges. Once on the south bank, go on a little further and climb the steps to the right of the church; you'll arrive just under the **clock tower**. The functional twentieth-century architecture of Novi Sad itself looks less alluring than the fortress does from the opposite bank, but the views of the surrounding countryside are magnificent.

Across the river, the hub of the city is **Trg Slobode** (Freedom Square), a

THE EXIT FESTIVAL

For four days at the beginning of July each year the grounds of Petrovaradin Fortress are overrun by **EXIT Festival** revellers (ⓦwww.exitfest.org). Established as the premier music event in southeastern Europe, EXIT now attracts some of the biggest names in pop, techno and hip-hop (the 2009 line-up included Lily Allen, Arctic Monkeys and Madness). Buy tickets and camping passes via the website. You can rent rooms in Novi Sad for the duration: check ⓦwww.exittrip.org, which helps with booking accommodation and transport.

spacious plaza bounded on either side by the neo-Gothic **Catholic Church of the Virgin Mary** and the neo-Renaissance town hall. Running east from here is bustling Zmaj Jovina which, together with the adjoining bar-filled alleyway Laze Telečkog and wide, pedestrianized Dunavska, forms the town's central nexus of streets for eating, drinking and socializing. At the bottom end of Dunavska (nos 35–37) is the excellent **Museum of Vojvodina** (Tues–Sun 9am–5pm; 100din), spread across two buildings. It delves first into Serbia's archeology and ethnography, then comes closer to home with the traumas of two world wars.

Finally, sun-lovers should head for the **Štrand** (May–Sept; 35din), a sandy beach on the Danube's north bank, opposite the fortress, which has bars, cafés and a "school's out" vibe.

Sremski Karlovci

On the eastern fringes of the Fruška Gora National Park, the enchanting small town of **SREMSKI KARLOVCI** (Сремски Карловци) is highly recommended for a short trip out of Novi Sad. Its main square, Branka Radičevića, with the Orthodox and Catholic churches side by side and the Four Lions fountain, is highly picturesque, but Sremski Karlovci's status as a national treasure comes courtesy of its speciality wine, **Bermet**, made exclusively here since 1770. Drunk with desserts or as an aperitif, Bermet was popular in the Austro-Hungarian court and served on board the *Titanic*'s maiden voyage. The tourist information office on the main square can point you to the delightful **wine cellar** owned by the Živanović family at Metropolita Stratimirovića 86b (daily 10am–7pm), where you can buy your own supplies – swing open the side-gate to enter their orchard; there's also a quaint beekeeping museum. Alternatively, relax with a glass or two on the civilized outdoor decking of the hotel of the same name on the main square.

Sremski Karlovci is a ten-minute taxi ride from Novi Sad (around 400din); catch a cab from the rank on Ilije Ognjanovića.

Arrival and information

Train and bus The adjacent bus and train stations are 1km north of the centre on Bulevar Jaše Tomića. The easiest way into town is to hop in a taxi (around 250din) or take bus #4 (30din) from in front of the train station. Walking takes about 30min; head straight down Bulevar Oslobođenja and turn left into Jevrejska at the market.

Tourist office Mihaila Pupina 9 and Modena 1 (Mon–Fri 7.30am–8pm, Sat 7.30am-2pm; ⓣ21/421-811, ⓔticns@nadlanu.com).

Accommodation

Fontana Nikole Pašićeva 27 ⓣ21/661-2760, ⓦwww.restoranfontana.com. The rooms above this "ethno" restaurant are decorated in a traditional Serbian style. Doubles 3500din.

Hotel Mediteraneo Ilije Ognjanovića 10 ⓣ21/427-135, ⓦwww.hotelmediteraneo.rs. Bright, fresh, nautical-themed hotel that punches well above its two-star rating. Doubles €80, 3-person apartments €100.

Sova Hostel Ilije Ognjanovica 26 ⓣ21/527-566, ⓦwww.hostelsova.com. The communal space is like stepping into someone's living room, with

slightly faded decor and a tiny kitchen, but the bedrooms are funky. The 2–4 person room is excellent value at €15 per person. Dorms also €15.

Eating

Alla Lanterna Dunavska 27. The decor is a tad faux-rustic but the big plates of pasta and pizza are scrumptious. Pasta 450din.

Arhiv Ilije Ognjanovića 16. Stylish basement restaurant serving imaginative international cooking. Chicken with pears and almonds in red wine 400din.

Foody Modena 1–3. Committed costcutters will warm to this functional canteen. *Kotleti* 200din.

Pekara Perec Laze Telečkog 9. Mouthwatering breakfast goodies at this street bakery include *perec* (doughy pretzels; 25din) and croissants with Eurokrem chocolate spread, 40din.

Drinking

Divan Dušan Laze Telečkog 6. This tiny, original café/bar is crammed with eye-catching art and antiques; it's rather like drinking cocktails in a toy-box. Soya caramel macchiato 115din; Opal Martini 230din. Open 9am–midnight.

Jelisavetin Bastion Petrovaradinska tvrđava. International DJs draw the crowds at this massive, multi-room club in the fortress's underground chambers. Open until 5am Fri & Sat.

Moving on

Train Belgrade (every 2hr; 2hr); Budapest (2 daily; 6hr); Subotica (10 daily; 2hr).

Bus Belgrade (hourly; 1hr 20min); Subotica (20 daily; 1hr 30min).

SUBOTICA

Some 175km north of Belgrade, Vojvodina's second city, **SUBOTICA** (Суботица; Hungarian: Szabadka), is a wonderful counterpoint to the capital, its Secessionist buildings, green spaces, wide pavements and burghers riding around on old-fashioned bicycles all contributing to its unspoilt, wholesome air. Just a stone's throw from Hungary, Subotica feels tangibly more like its northern neighbour. Historically, the ties are close: Subotica reached its apotheosis in the years of the Austro-Hungarian Empire, when it was granted the status of a Royal Free Town.

What to see and do

The city's central square, **Trg Slobode**, is the gleaming heart of the town; its bold red city hall, built in 1912, is almost too gaudy to look at in full sunlight. In front, the inscrutable Tsar Jovan Nenad surveys the brilliant blue fountain added in 2001. Just behind the tsar's back runs the Korzo, a sweet pedestrianized street featuring the fairytale **Piraeus Bank** building, with its door and windows straight out of a medieval

MONASTERIES AROUND NOVI SAD

Shadowing the city to the south are the low rolling hills of the **Fruška Gora**, once an island in the now evaporated Pannonian Sea. These days, its orchards and vineyards comprise a national park carved up by a web of simple hiking trails. The hills – known among devotees as the Holy Mountain – also house more than fifteen monasteries (there were once 35).

About 15km south of Novi Sad, just off the main road before the village of Irig, is **Novo Hopovo**, where a Byzantine church is housed within a picturesque monastery. Not far off are two more sixteenth-century monastic churches: elegant white **Krušedol** and **Vrdnik-Ravanica**, which has Tsar Lazar's collarbone on display.

Hiring a car is the most practical way to access the monasteries, which are all within 50km of town. With a European or international driver's licence you can hire a vehicle from Hertz (Jevrejska 23; ⓣ21/529-719, ⓦwww.hertz.com) or Autotehna (Balkanova 29; ⓣ21/474-516, ⓦwww.autotehna.com) in Novi Sad. Alternatively, contact the tourist office in Sremski Karlovci (see opposite), who can, with some warning, organize group sightseeing tours of the main monasteries (1200din) or arrange for a driver (around 2000din for 3hr).

castle, created by architects Dezsó Jakab and Marcell Komor at the start of the twentieth century. Branching off the Korzo, more of the pair's work is on show on multicoloured Matije Korvina (also known as Engelsova).

Passing through the short passageway by *Boss Pizzeria*, you'll come out onto Rajhlov park square; at no. 5, the **Likovni Susret Contemporary Art Gallery** (daily except Sat 8am–1pm; 50din) occupying the 1904 mansion of architect Ferenc Raichle, exhibits work by local artists. The real draw however is the attention-seeking interior decor, from the cutesy hearts at the entranceway to the bulbous alcoves upstairs.

Further out, northwest of the city centre is yet another Jakab/Komor collaboration: the dignified but now deserted 1902 **synagogue**, where a moving plaque remembers the "4000 Jewish citizens with whom we lived and built Subotica".

Back in the centre, reached by walking west from spacious Trg Republike (adjoining Trg Slobode) to Trg Kathedrale, is the 1779 Catholic **Cathedral of St Theresa**. The cathedral is starting to show its age – the dramatic crack down the centre makes it looks as if it's about to cleave into two great stone halves – and a curiously moving place; in the surrounding square, the scattered statues are a poignant mix of classical piety (the two hands clasped in prayer) and postwar brutalism (the enormous monument to the "victims of fascism" who died during World War II).

Lake Palić

Eight kilometres north of town and easily accessed by #6 bus from Maksima Gorkog, **Lake Palić** (Ⓦwww.palic.rs) makes an excellent day-trip in summer. It has something for everyone: sunbathing on the men's and women's lidos for the gilded youth; popcorn and pedaloes for the kids – all set against a fantastical Art Nouveau background, once again the work of the irrepressible Jakab and Komor. There are plenty of cafés here for ice creams and coffees, but for anything more substantial your cheapest option may be to stock up for a picnic at the supermarket on your left when you get off the bus from town.

Arrival and information

Bus Subotica's bus station is located on Marksov Put, an easy 15min walk from the centre on the road to Belgrade.
Train The train station dominates one side of the square by Rajhlov Park.
Tourist office Trg Slobode 1 Ⓣ24/670-350, Ⓦwww.visitsubotica.rs (Mon–Fri 7.30am–7pm, Sat 9am–1pm). The excellent staff can provide glossy tourist information brochures and maps.

Accommodation

Hotel Patria Đure Đakovića bb Ⓣ24/554-500, Ⓦwww.hotelpatria.rs. This budget four-star hotel proves you get more bang for your buck outside Belgrade; the fully redecorated rooms have modern bathrooms and satellite TV. Doubles 5800din
Incognito Huga Badalića 3, left off Maksim Gorkog Ⓣ62/666-674, Ⓦwww.hostel-subotica.com. This new hostel, with 47 beds, is just a 3min walk from the central square, with basic but clean rooms. Dorms €10; apartment for 2–4 people €20.

Eating and drinking

Boss Matije Korvina 7–8. A statue-strewn courtyard at the back of the Likovni Susret mansion – this pizzeria and bar is the place where people come to be seen.
Népkör Žarka Zrenjanina 11. Outstanding Hungarian food in a spacious townhouse. Someone's had fun with the menu (fancy "a pageant of local cheeses" or "concealed brains"?). *Gulaš* to share 150din; set menu 300din.
Pekara Fidelnika Trg Republike 18. Elegant and appetizing Austrian-style bakery on the main square. 7am–9pm. Pastries 90din.
Stara Picerija Matije Korvina 5. This busy pizzeria excels at delivering simple pleasures: first-class food alfresco, in a cute cobbled alleyway, with cheerful feel-good classics on the stereo. Large pizza 440din.
Trubadur Rajhlov Park 11. Atmospheric alternative bar lit by soft Victorian-style street lamps in the shadow of a Gothic mansion.

Moving on

Train Belgrade (6 daily; 3hr 30min–5hr); Budapest (2 daily; 2hr 30min); Novi Sad (10 daily; 2hr).
Bus Belgrade (20 daily; 3hr 30min); Niš (5 daily; 6hr); Novi Sad (20 daily; 1hr 30min); Szeged, Hungary (every 2hr; 1hr 30min).

Southern Serbia

South of Belgrade, the softly rolling hillsides studded with low red-roofed houses are the setting for three of the country's most precious medieval monasteries: **Žiča**, **Studenica** and **Sopoćani**. Elsewhere, the south's main city, **Niš**, conveniently straddles major road and rail routes to Bulgaria and Macedonia, and is an attractive small town to stop in with some fascinating sights.

ŽIČA, STUDENICA AND SOPOĆANI MONASTERIES

In the hilly stretch from Kraljevo, itself some 170km south of Belgrade, south to Novi Pazar lie some of Serbia's most impressive monasteries. **Žiča**, just 4km southeast of Kraljevo, was a thirteenth-century creation of St Sava – Serbia's patron saint and the first archbishop of the independent Serbian Church – with a vivid red exterior that evokes the red Serbs use to paint eggs at Easter.

Set against the wild, roaming slopes some 12km (and accessible by bus) from the village of Ušće is **Studenica**. The first and greatest of the Serbian monasteries, it was established in 1190 by Stefan Nemanja, founder of the Nemanjić dynasty, whose marble tomb lies in the Church of the Virgin Mary. Studenica's **superb frescoes** were the work of an innovative but still anonymous Greek painter who created *trompe-l'oeil* frescoes to resemble mosaics.

Around 16km from Novi Pazar is **Sopoćani**, a thirteenth-century construction that once stretched across a whole complex but of which only the Holy Trinity Church remains. The *Assumption of Virgin Mary* is the most famous of its unusually large Byzantine frescoes; the bright colours and expressive faces are said to prefigure the Italian Renaissance.

NIŠ

The pleasant university town of **NIŠ** (Ниш), 235km southeast of Belgrade, is a useful stopover point between Belgrade and Sofia or Skopje. Its inhabitants have a definite small-town pride, as well they might: this is the birthplace of Constantine, the Roman emperor responsible for the conversion of the whole empire to Christianity. Its collection of intriguing – if macabre – sights is a gritty reminder of the darker sides to Serbia's history, but the focus in the cafés and bars crammed with students is all on having a good time.

What to see and do

The city's centrepiece is its main square, **Trg Kralja Milana**, which sits across the Nišava from **Niš Fortress**. A Roman

VISITING THE MONASTERIES

While Žiča is easily accessible by bus from Kraljevo (every 30–45min; 35din), you'll probably need a car if you want to see more than one monastery in a day. Try Inter Rent-A-Car in Niš (ask hostel staff to call ⓣ63/467-447 or 63/775-6741 for you; ⓦwww.rentacarnis.rs) or Autotehna in Kraljevo (Karađorđeva 12/1; ⓣ36/319-944, ⓦwww.autotehna.com); prices should start at around €40–50 per day. If you have more time, you could try public buses: on the Kraljevo–Novi Pazar route, you can get off at Ušće, from which there are 2–3 daily buses to Studenica.

fortress once stood here – a circle of Roman tombstones remains inside – but the current fortifications date from the beginning of the eighteenth century. Enter from the main Istanbul Gate facing the bridge; inside, the town authorities have put real effort into making this a place residents can enjoy, with the beautiful **mosque of Bali Beg** converted into an exhibition space and the row of cafés in the shadow of the fortress's inner wall a cool spot to unwind. Each August the whole fortress is given over to the Nišville jazz festival (ⓦwww.nisville.com).

The fortress apart, Niš does suffer from a surfeit of rather grim sights. The first, to your right as you leave the fortress, is the miniature blue-domed **memorial chapel** perched on the lawn, which commemorates the local people killed in the NATO bombings. East of the centre on Brače Taskoviča, **Ćele Kula** (the Tower of Skulls; Mon–Sat 9am–4pm, Sun 10am–2pm; 100din; take any bus towards Niška Banja or a return taxi – 400din) is more gruesome still. It dates from 1809, when Stevan Sinđelić, commander of a nationalist uprising, found his men surrounded by the Turkish army on nearby Čegar Hill and took drastic action against his adversaries, firing into his gunpowder supplies and blowing up most of the Turks and all the Serbs around him. Following the battle, to deter future rebellion the ruling Pasha ordered that the heads of the Serbian soldiers killed in the battle be stuffed and mounted on the tower; 952 went into the making of this macabre totem pole, though today only 58 remain.

Even more evocative is the derelict **Crveni Krst** (Red Cross) concentration camp, a ten-minute walk down busy Bulevar 12 Februar from the bus station (Tues–Sun 8am–4pm; 100din), where the hand-painted German signs for the washroom, messroom and kitchen make it all seem very recent. The barbed-wire fences and watchtowers, so familiar from camps in Poland and Germany, are a reminder that the displacement and genocide of millions was a truly pan-European operation.

Arrival and information

Bus The bus station is a 5min walk from town, west of the citadel on Bulevar Februar 12.
Train The train station is 2km west of town on Dimitrija Tucovica.
Tourist office Voždova Karađorđa 7 ⓣ18/523-118, ⓦwww.nistourism.org.rs (Mon–Fri 7.30am–7pm, Sat 9am–1pm). Provides useful information and maps.

Accommodation

Hostel Niš Dobrička 3a ⓣ18/513-703, ⓦwww.hostelnis.rs. Make this spotless hostel with engaging owners your first port of call; it's a few minutes' walk west from the fortress entrance. If it's full, staff can help you find a room in nearby spa town Niška Banja. Dorms 1000–1500din.
Hotel Ambasador Trg Kralja Milana ⓣ18/501-800, ⓦwww.srbijaturist.com. This Yugoslav-era hotel is a decent alternative to the *Hostel Niš* – excellently located on the main square, albeit in an unsightly high-rise. Double rooms €35.

Eating and drinking

Cobbled Kazandžijsko Sokače (Tinker's Alley), just south of Trg Kralja Milana, is the town's social hub, thronging with café-bars.
Flocafé Kazandžijsko Sokače. Bright young cocktail bar with seats facing out into the street for people-watching.
Hamam Tvrđava bb. Grills and fish in the old Turkish bath just inside the fort entrance. Mains 400din.
Mamma Pizza Nade Tomić 10. The wood-fired pizzas are a great option for veggies, as long as you steer clear of the house pizza – which comes topped with five types of meat. Pizzas 500din.
Sinđelić Nikole Pašića 25. Named after the kamikaze general behind the Tower of Skulls episode, *Sinđelić* excels at simple, hearty Serbian food. Mains 500–700din.

Moving on

Train Belgrade (7 daily; 4-5hr); Kraljevo (4 daily; 3hr 45min); Skopje (4 daily; 5–6hr); Sofia (2 daily; 5hr).
Bus Belgrade (every 20min; 3hr); Kraljevo (6 daily; 3hr); Skopje (6 daily; 5–6hr); Sofia (2 daily; 2hr 30min).

Slovakia

HIGHLIGHTS

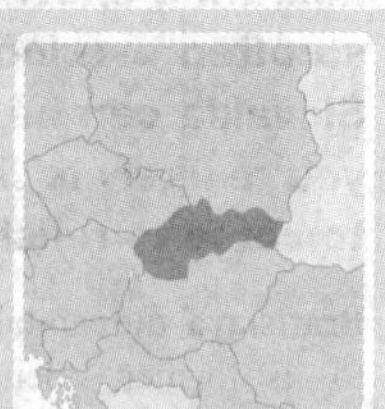

HIGH TATRAS: admire the majesty of Slovakia's highest peaks

LEVOČA: explore the crumbling backstreets of this beautiful walled town

KOŠICE: join Slovakia's second city as it gradually comes to life

BRATISLAVA: indulge in the capital's fantastic gastroculture

DANUBE: cruise between Europe's closest capitals

ROUGH COSTS

DAILY BUDGET Basic €25/occasional treat €30

DRINK Beer €1.40

FOOD Potato dumplings €2

HOSTEL/BUDGET HOTEL €10/20

TRAVEL Train: Bansk Štiavnice–Poprad (247km) €9

FACT FILE

POPULATION 5.4 million

AREA 49,037 sq km

LANGUAGE Slovak

CURRENCY Euro (€)

CAPITAL Bratislava (population: 450,000)

INTERNATIONAL PHONE CODE ⓣ421

Introduction

Long, narrow Slovakia boasts beautiful, varied scenery, from the lusciously fertile plains of the Danube basin and the rolling hills of the Low Tatras, studded by jewel-like lakes, to the exhilarating snow-capped peaks of the High Tatras. Landlocked, so often overlooked by sun-and-sea-seeking summer tourists, Slovakia can be difficult to break into – but with a bit of effort, you're likely to find the people friendly under their shyness, and to come to relish the rural, slightly old-fashioned way of life.

Bratislava, the capital, has been restored to its former splendour in the past couple of decades and now boasts a perfect, tiny city centre with a maze of cobbled streets lined by cafés, museums, bars and concert halls. In the Low Tatras, the old mining town of **Banská Štiavnica**, now a UNESCO heritage Site, is a gem surrounded by mountains and lakes and ideal for some relaxed walking, and further east, settlements such as **Starý Smokovec** provide a cosy base for skiing or trekking through the impressive craggy heights of the High Tatras. **Košice**, Slovakia's second city, still has interesting relics of the communist way of life.

The republic has a diverse population, with over half a million ethnic **Hungarians** in the south, as well as thousands of **Romanies** (Gypsies) and several thousand **Ruthenians** (Rusyns) in the east.

CHRONOLOGY

450 BC Celts inhabit the area known as present-day Slovakia.

623 AD Samo becomes King of the Slavs after defeating the Avarians near Bratislava.

828 First Christian church consecrated in Slovakia.

862 First Slavic alphabet written in Greater Moravia by apostles Cyril and Methodius of the Byzantine Empire.

997 The Nitrian Principality, or present-day Slovakia, is absorbed into the Hungarian Empire.

1241 Mongol invasion of Slovakia results in heavy losses.

1526 Defeat in the Battle of the Mohacs leads the Habsburgs to move their capital to Bratislava.

1800s Growth in Slovak nationalism.

1895 Czech and Slovak peoples partake in mutual co operation against their Hungarian oppressors.

1918 The independent republic of Czechoslovakia is established upon the defeat of Austria-Hungary in World War I.

1939 Germany takes the Sudetenland in Czechoslovakia, before occupying the rest of the country.

1945 Slovak National Uprising against German occupation is successful, but thousands of Slovakian Jews have already been sent to concentration camps.

1948 The Communist Party comes into power in Czechoslovakia.

1991 The collapse of Soviet Communism leads the way for political independence in Czechoslovakia.

1993 Slovakia gains full independence after Czechoslovakia splits peacefully.

2004 Slovakia joins NATO and the EU.

2007 Slovakian troops withdraw from Iraq.

January 2009 The euro replaces the Slovak koruna as the national currency.

ARRIVAL

Most international visitors will fly into **Bratislava** or **Vienna** airports. The two capitals are only 60km apart, cheap flights to Vienna are often more readily available, and it has easy connections into Bratislava. There is also an international airport in **Košice**, which receives flights from Prague, Vienna, London and Dublin, as well as domestic flights.

Slovakia has good **rail connections** with Austria, Hungary, Poland and the Czech Republic. Most international trains terminate in Bratislava, but trains from Budapest, Krakov and Prague also run to Košice.

Buses from Europe run frequently to Bratislava, run mainly by Eurolines (ⓦwww.eurolines.sk). The Student Agency (ⓦwww.studentagencybus.com) runs domestic and international coaches that are cheap, comfortable and offer direct routes between cities. There are offices in Bratislava (Obchodná 48; ⓣ0800 121 121) and Košice (Mlynská 11; ⓣ055/729 4024).

You can also take the **hydrofoil** from Budapest or Vienna to Bratislava. These arrive at Razusovo Nabrezie Embankment or Fajnorova Nabrezie Embankment, in the heart of the city, and are operated by Mahart (ⓦwww.mahartpassnave.hu).

GETTING AROUND

Train services are slow, but some journeys are worth it for the scenery alone. Slovak Railways (Železnice Slovenskej republiky or ŽSR) runs fast *rýchlik* trains that stop at major towns; the *osobn ý vlak*, or local train, stops everywhere. You can buy **tickets** (*lístok*) for domestic journeys at the station (*stanica*) before or on the day of departure. Supplements are payable on all EuroCity (EC) trains, and occasionally for InterCity (IC) and Express (Ex) trains. ŽSR runs reasonably priced sleepers (*lužkový vozeň*) and couchettes (*ležadlový vozeň*) – book in advance, no later than six hours before departure. **InterRail** is valid; **Eurail** requires supplements. Search train timetables online at ⓦwww.zsr.sk.

Buses (*autobus*) are quicker and cover a more extensive network. The state bus company is Slovenská automobilová doprava or SAD. Buy your **ticket** from the driver, or book in advance if you're travelling at the weekend or early in the morning on one of the main routes.

Although much of Slovakia is mountainous and therefore not an ideal option for **cyclists**, the countryside around Bratislava has easy and well-maintained bike paths that run into Austria and Hungary. More demanding rides can take you into the Little Carpathians. Most trains allow bikes.

ACCOMMODATION

Arrange **accommodation** as far in advance as possible and, if you can, get hold of an ISIC (International Student Identity Card) Card, as this will exempt you from the tax slapped onto

accommodation. The best options in university towns (which many of the major tourist destinations are) are cheap **student accommodation**. This is available through CKM, the student travel agency (Ⓦwww.ckm.sk) or the local tourist office. Otherwise, **private rooms** are a good bet – keep your eyes peeled for *Zimmer frei* or *Priváty* signs or book through the local tourist office. Prices start at around €10 per person per night. New **hotels** and pensions are opening up all over Slovakia – these are usually more expensive than private rooms, but tend to be clean and comfortable and offer breakfast.

There is no real network of **hostels,** though a few are affiliated to HI (see Ⓦwww.hihostels.com) and others come under CKM. Bratislava has some private hostels, although these aren't particularly cheap. In the High Tatras, you can find a fair number of chalet-style **refuges** (*chata*) scattered about the hillsides, with basic dorm beds from €8/bed. **Campsites** are plentiful, and many feature simple **bungalows** (*chata* again), often available for upwards of €7.50/bed.

FOOD AND DRINK

Slovak **food** is no-nonsense and filling; traces of Hungarian, Polish and Ukrainian influences can be found in different regions. Although it's undeniably tasty, it can get pretty heavy on the stomach after a while (a speciality is fried ham wrapped in fried cheese), particularly as fresh salads or green vegetables are still a rarity in local restaurants – although a delicious garlic soup (*cesnaková*) might feature. Most menus start with **soup** (*polievka*). Main courses are usually pork, beef or chicken, and are served with potatoes (*zemiaky*) or dumplings. Typical **desserts** include apple or cottage-cheese strudel, and *palačinky* (cold pancakes) filled with chocolate, fruit and cream.

A classic mid-morning **snack** at the *bufet* (stand-up canteen) is **párek**, a hot frankfurter dipped in mustard or horseradish and served inside a white roll. *Bryndzovè halušky* is the national dish – dumplings with a thick sheep's cheese sauce and crumbled, grilled bacon – but Hungarian goulash is also very popular, as are **langoše** – deep-fried dough smothered in a variety of toppings.

In outlying regions **closing time** will still be 9 or 10pm; the bigger cities have restaurants open till 11pm or later. The **cake shop** (*cukráreň*) is an important part of social life, particularly on Sunday mornings when it's often the only place that's open in town. Whatever the season, you'll see everyone, from sober-looking businessmen to tough guys in leather jackets, licking dainty ice-cream cones (*zmrzlina*), available at *cukráreň* or dispensed from little window-kiosks in the sides of buildings.

Drink

Coffee (*káva*) is usually drunk black, but coffee chains inspired by *Starbucks* and the like are beginning to open up in bigger cities.

Vineyards in the south of Slovakia produce some pretty good white **wines** – one of the most distinctive is the sweet wine, Tokaj. The most famous local firewaters are *slivovice*, a plum **brandy** available just about everywhere, and *borovička*, made with juniper berries. Another popular drink is Kofola, a Coke-like soft drink with a strong aniseed taste drunk by the pint. Slovaks love draught **beer**, and you'll find *pivnica (*beer halls) in most towns, as well as wine bars (*vináreň*), which usually have slightly later opening hours and often double as nightclubs.

CULTURE AND ETIQUETTE

It's worth bearing in mind that Slovakia is one of the most **Catholic** countries in Europe, and when visiting churches, it's

important to cover up or you won't be let in.

Outside of Bratislava, people don't generally speak much English (although some do speak German), and this, combined with their natural shyness, means they aren't massively forthcoming or friendly. A bit of effort with some Slovak words makes a massive difference – *Dobrý deń* (hello), *Dovidenia* (goodbye), *Prosim* (please) and *D'akujem* (thank you) will take you far, and you'll often find that once you can break through a somewhat unwelcoming exterior, people are actually far more willing to help you than you thought.

For **tipping**, ten percent is usual.

SPORTS AND OUTDOOR ACTIVITIES

Slovaks are fanatical about **ice hockey**, which you can see live on screens in bars across the Republic – or you can go to games in stadiums from September to April (Ⓦwww.hcslovan.sk). Tickets cost between €13 and €50 and can be bought from the arena on match days. Bratislava is due to host the ice-hockey world cup in 2011.

Naturally, there's plenty of **hiking**, **skiing** and **mountaineering** to be done in the High Tatras (Ⓦwww.tatry.sk is an excellent guide) and caving in the Slovak Karst in east Slovakia (Ⓦwww.saske.sk/cave).

SLOVAKIA ON THE NET

Ⓦ**www.slovakia.org** Political, historical, cultural and economic information.
Ⓦ**www.slovakia.travel** Tourist information in a variety of languages with travel tips and event information.
Ⓦ**www.slovakspectator.sk** English-language weekly, with news and listings.
Ⓦ**www.whatsonslovakia.com** Website of the English-language publication, detailing events and attractions for the coming month.

COMMUNICATIONS

Most **post offices** (*po ta*) open Monday to Friday 8am to 5pm. You can also buy stamps (*známky*) from some tobacconists (*tabák*) and street kiosks. Cheap local calls can be made from any **phone**, but for international calls it's best to use a card phone; buy a card (*telefonná karta*) from a tobacconist or post office. Internet cafés have appeared in the larger towns; expect to pay €5–7/hr.

EMERGENCIES

The **state police** (*polícia*) wear khaki-green uniforms, and the local municipal or *mestsk· polícia* wear a variety of outfits. Theft from cars and hotel rooms is your biggest worry, though pickpocketing is also common in the larger towns. You should carry your passport with you at all times, though you're most unlikely to get stopped. Minor ailments can be easily dealt with by the **pharmacist** (*lekáreň*), but language is likely to be a problem. If the pharmacy can't help, they'll direct you to a **hospital** (*nemocnica*).

INFORMATION

Just about every town has some kind of **tourist office** (*informačnè centrum*), most with English speakers. In summer they're generally open Monday to Friday 9am to 6pm, Saturday and Sunday 9am to 2pm; in winter they tend to close an hour earlier and all day Sun (sometimes also Sat). **Maps** are available from bookshops and some hotels (a town plan is *plán mesta* or *orientačná mapa*).

MONEY AND BANKS

The euro was introduced in Slovakia in January 2009. It can still take a while for

EMERGENCY NUMBERS

Police Ⓣ158; Ambulance Ⓣ155; Fire Ⓣ150.

Slovak

	Slovak	Pronunciation
Yes	*Áno*	Uh-no
No	*Nie*	Nyeh
Please	*Prosím*	Pro-seem
Thank you	*D'akujem vam*	Dya-koo-yem vam
Hello/Good day	*Dobrý deň/Ahoj*	Dob-rie den[y]/a-hoy
Goodbye	*Dovidenia*	Do-vid-en-ya
Excuse me	*Prepáčte*	Pre-patch-teh
Where	*Kde*	Gde
Good	*Dobrý*	Dob-rie
Bad	*Zle*	Zleh
Near	*Blízko*	Bli-sko
Far	*D'aleko*	D[y]a-lek-o
Cheap	*Lacný*	Lats-nie
Expensive	*Drahý*	Dra-hie
Open	*Otvorený*	Ot-vor-eh-nie
Closed	*Zatvorený*	Zat-vor-eh-nie
Today	*Dnes*	Dnes
Yesterday	*Včera*	Ftch-er-a
Tomorrow	*Zajtra*	Zuyt-ra
How much is...?	*Kol'ko stát'...?*	Kol-ko stat[y]...?
What time is it?	*Kol'ko je hodín?*	Kol-ko ye hod-in?
I don't understand	*Nerozumiem*	Ne-ro-zoom-yem
Do you speak English?	*Hovoríte po Anglicky?*	Hov-or-i-te po ang-lits-ky?
Entrance	*Vchod*	FHod
Exit	*Východ*	VeeHot
Ticket	*Lístok*	Leestok
Hotel	*Hotel*	Hotel
Toilet	*Záchod*	ZaHod
Square	*Námestie*	Nahmestee
Station	*Stanica*	Stani-tza
Do you have a...?	*Máte...?*	Ma-teÖ...?
Single room	*jednopostel'ovú izbu*	yed-no-pos-tye-lyo-voo iz-bu
Open	*Otvorené*	Otvor-en-air
Closed	*Zatvorené*	Zatvor-en-air
Cheap	*Lacné*	Luhts-nair
One	*Jeden*	Yed-en
Two	*Dva*	Dva
Three	*Tri*	Tri
Four	*Štyri*	Shtir-i
Five	*Pät'*	Pyat[y]
Six	*Šest'*	Shest[y]
Seven	*Sedem*	Sed-em
Eight	*Osem*	Oss-em
Nine	*Devät'*	Dev-yat[y]
Ten	*Desat'*	Dess-at[y]

STUDENT AND YOUTH DISCOUNTS

To get up to fifty percent off entry into some attractions you will need an ISIC card, as many places will not accept individual university cards.

people to calculate conversions from the old Slovakian koruna, particularly in rural areas. **Credit** and **debit cards** are accepted in most upmarket hotels and restaurants and some shops, and there are plenty of **ATMs** in all the larger towns. **Exchange offices** (*zmenáren*) can be found in all major hotels, travel agencies and department stores.

OPENING HOURS AND HOLIDAYS

Opening hours for shops are Monday to Friday 9am to 6pm, Saturday 8am to noon, with some shops and most supermarkets staying open later, and supermarkets in large towns opening on a Sunday too. Smaller shops take an hour or so for lunch between noon and 2pm.

The basic opening hours for **castles** and **attractions** are Tuesday to Sunday 9am to 5pm. Out of the season, hours are often restricted to weekends and holidays. Most castles are closed in winter. When visiting a sight, ask for an *anglický* text. **Admission** rarely costs more than €4. **Public holidays** include January 1, January 6, Good Friday, Easter Monday, May 1, May 8, July 5, August 29, September 1, September 15, November 1, December 24, 25 and 26.

Bratislava

Although you can walk across the lovely old town centre of **BRATISLAVA** in about four minutes, the number of restaurants, bars, shops, galleries, pretty courtyards and churches that cram together here is incredible. The large student population makes for a lively after-dark atmosphere, and while the concrete communist monstrosities to the south of the river are admittedly fairly hideous, the contrast between this and the sophistication of the old town is part of the fascination. To top it off, Bratislavans tend to be friendly and welcoming, so all in all the capital is a great place to spend a relaxed couple of days exploring.

What to see and do

The **Starè Mesto** – where you'll spend most of your time – lies on the north side of the Danube; on the rocky hill to the west is the **castle**. Northeast of the old town are the residential blocks of the **Nove Mesto**, which give way to sprawling suburbs.

The Old Town

Opposite the mass of the **Kostol trinitárov**, one of the city's finest churches, a footbridge lined with stall-holders and musicians crosses a small section of what used to be a moat towards the city's last remaining double gateway. The tower above the gateway's second arch, the **Michalská veža** (or St Michael's Tower; Tues–Fri 9.30/10am–4.30/5pm, Sat & Sun 11am–6pm, €1.50), provides an impressive, ornate entrance to the old town.

Michalská and Ventúrska, which run into each other, are lined with some of Bratislava's finest **Baroque palaces** alongside the university library, so there are usually plenty of students milling about amongst the shoppers enjoying coffees and lunches in one of the innumerable cafés.

A little northeast of here are the adjoining main squares of the **old town** – Hlavnè námestie and Františkánske námestie. Up Františkánska, you'll find the **Mirbach Palace** (Tues–Sun 11am–6pm; €2.25), one of the best preserved of Bratislava's Rococo buildings.

Primate's Palace

The Neoclassical **Primate's Palace** (Primacálny palác; Tues–Sun 10am–5pm; €2) has as its main claim to fame the Hall of Mirrors, where Napoleon and the Austrian emperor signed the Peace of Pressburg (as Bratislava was then called) in 1805. The beautifully restored rooms are adorned with attractive "English tapestries" and portraits of Maria Theresa and Josef II.

Nový most (Most SNP)

The most insensitive of Bratislava's postwar developments took place on the west side of the old town, when, following the annihilation of the city's Jewish population by the Nazis, the Communist authorities tore down

ACTIVITIES IN AND AROUND BRATISLAVA

Bratislava and Vienna are the world's closest capitals, and you can take a day-trip to Vienna by **hydrofoil** from Bratislava's Razusovo Nabrezie Embankment (up to 3 daily; 1hr 15min; €15–27; ⓦwww.twincityliner.com). **Cycling** and **roller-blading** along the Danube, to Austria upstream or Hungary downstream, is also extremely popular. The Small Carpathian mountains surrounding Bratislava are beautiful and make for a lovely day's cycling or walking (see ⓦwww.bratislavasightseeing.com or call ⓣ09/0768 3112 for suggested routes and guided tours). Bicycles can be rented from Luka Tours in the courtyard of the Slovak National Gallery (€12/4hr; €18/day).

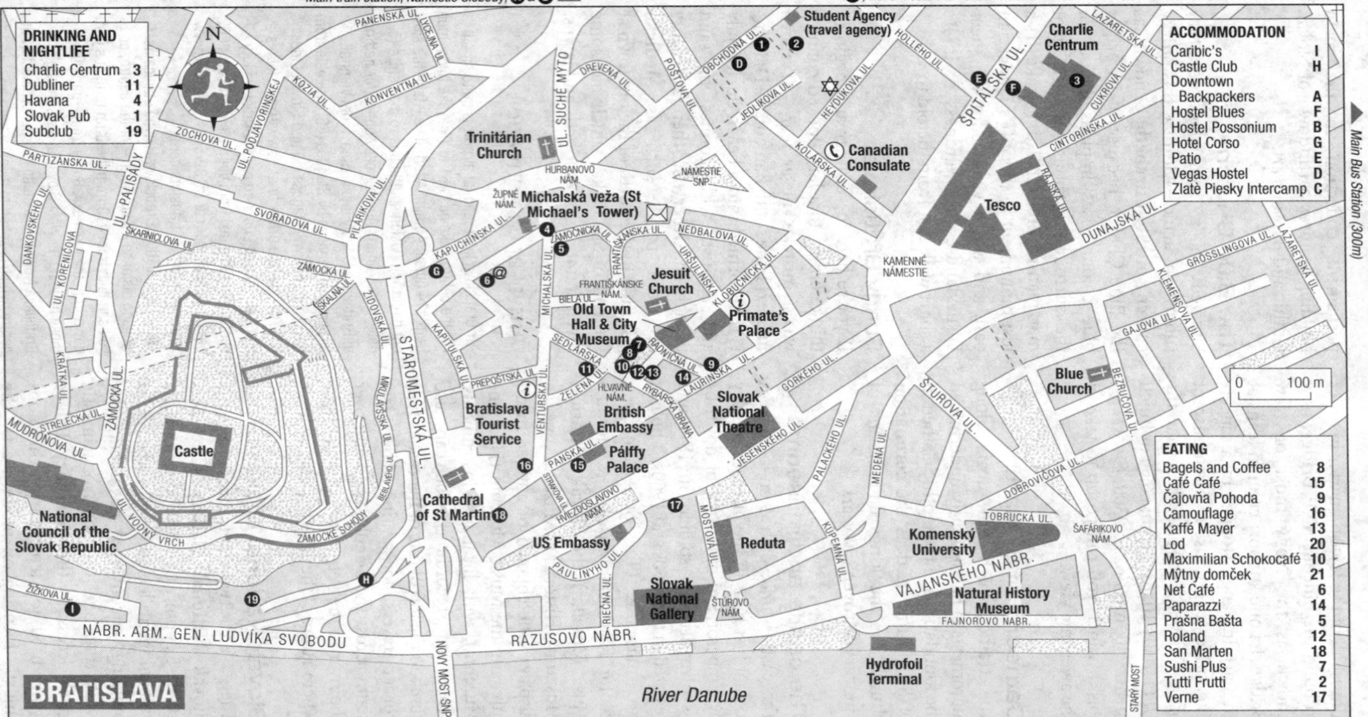
BRATISLAVA
DRINKING AND NIGHTLIFE
Charlie Centrum 3
Dubliner 11
Havana 4
Slovak Pub 1
Subclub 19
ACCOMMODATION
Caribic's I
Castle Club H
Downtown Backpackers A
Hostel Blues F
Hostel Possonium B
Hotel Corso G
Patio E
Vegas Hostel D
Zlatè Piesky Intercamp C
EATING
Bagels and Coffee 8
Café Café 15
Čajovňa Pohoda 9
Camouflage 16
Kaffé Mayer 13
Lod 20
Maximilian Schokocafé 10
Mýtny domček 21
Net Café 6
Paparazzi 14
Prašna Bašta 5
Roland 12
San Marten 18
Sushi Plus 7
Tutti Frutti 2
Verne 17
Main Bus Station (300m)
Petržalka, 20 & 21
0 100 m
Castle
National Council of the Slovak Republic
Trinitárian Church
Michalská veža (St Michael's Tower)
Jesuit Church
Old Town Hall & City Museum
Primate's Palace
Student Agency (travel agency)
Canadian Consulate
Charlie Centrum
Tesco
Blue Church
Slovak National Theatre
British Embassy
Pálffy Palace
Bratislava Tourist Service
Cathedral of St Martin
US Embassy
Reduta
Slovak National Gallery
Komenský University
Natural History Museum
Hydrofoil Terminal
River Danube
STAROMESTSKÁ UL.
NÁBR. ARM. GEN. LUDVÍKA SVOBODU
RÁZUSOVO NÁBR.
VAJANSKÉHO NÁBR.
FAJNOROVO NÁBR.
NOVY MOST SNP
STARÝ MOST
ŠPITÁLSKA UL.
DUNAJSKÁ UL.
ŠTÚROVA UL.
KAMENNÉ NÁMESTIE
HURBANOVO NÁM.
ŽUPNÉ NÁM.
NÁMESTIE SNP
FRANTIŠKÁNSKE NÁM.
HLAVNÉ NÁM.
HVIEZDOSLAVOVO NÁM.
ŠTÚROVO NÁM.
ŠAFÁRIKOVO NÁM.
UL. PALISÁDY
ZÁMOCKÁ UL.
ZÁMOCKÉ SCHODY
UL. VODNÝ VRCH
MUDROŇOVA UL.
PANENSKÁ UL.
LYCEJNA UL.
KONVENTNÁ UL.
KOZIA UL.
ZOCHOVA UL.
UL. PODJAVORINSKEJ
PARTIZÁNSKA UL.
SVORADOVA UL.
ŠKARNICLOVA UL.
PILÁRIKOVA UL.
KAPUCHÍNSKA UL.
ZÁMOČNÍCKA UL.
MICHALSKÁ UL.
VENTÚRSKA UL.
SEDLÁRSKA
ZELENÁ UL.
RADNIČNÁ UL.
LAURINSKÁ
RYBÁRSKA BRÁNA
PANSKÁ UL.
PREPOŠTSKÁ UL.
KAPITULSKÁ UL.
ŽIDOVSKÁ UL.
MIKULÁŠSKA UL.
BEBLAVÉHO UL.
SKALNÁ UL.
UL. KORENIČOVA
DANKOVSKÉHO UL.
KRÁTKA UL.
STRELECKÁ UL.
ŽIŽKOVA UL.
PAULINYHO UL.
RIEČNA UL.
MOSTOVÁ UL.
KÚPEMNÁ UL.
PALACKÉHO UL.
MEDENÁ UL.
JESENSKÉHO UL.
GORKÉHO UL.
DOBROVIČOVA UL.
TOBRUCKÁ UL.
BEZRUČOVA UL.
GAJOVA UL.
KLEMENSOVA UL.
GROSSLINGOVA UL.
LAZARETSKÁ UL.
CINTORÍNSKA UL.
CUKROVÁ UL.
RAJSKÁ UL.
HOLLÉHO UL.
HEYDUKOVA UL.
KOLÁRSKA UL.
JEDLIKOVA UL.
OBCHODNÁ UL.
POŠTOVÁ UL.
DREVENÁ UL.
UL. SUCHÉ MÝTO
NEDBALOVA UL.
URŠULÍNSKA
KLOBUČNÍCKA UL.
FRANTIŠKÁNSKA UL.
BIELA UL.
STRAKOVA UL.

almost all of the Jewish quarter in order to build the hideous **SNP Bridge**, now known as the **Nový most** or New Bridge. Its one support column leans at an alarming angle, topped by a saucer-like, pricey penthouse café reminiscent of the *Starship Enterprise*, known as the *UFO* (daily 10am–11pm; €6.50 or lunch menu €30; ⓣ02/6252 0300, ⓦwww.u-f-o.sk), which you can go up to take in the awesome view.

Cathedral of St Martin

The traffic which now tears along Staromestská has seriously undermined the foundations of the Gothic Cathedral of St Martin, used as the **coronation church** for the kings and queens of Hungary for over 250 years.

The castle and museums

The **castle** (*hrad*; daily 9am–6/8pm) is a giant box built in the fifteenth century by Emperor Sigismund, burnt down by its own drunken soldiers in 1811 and restored in the 1950s and 1960s. It houses two museums (Tues–Sun 9am–5pm; €4 for Historical Museum, €2 for the Music Museum): the **Slovak Historical Museum** (Historické Múzeum), which displays a hotchpotch of antique furniture, and the Music Museum (Hudobnè Múzeum), with local folk instruments, scores and recordings. You can also climb to the top of one of the castle's four corner towers, for an incredible **view** south across the Danube plain and over the river to the Petr alka housing estate, where a third of the city's population lives.

Slovak National Gallery

There are two entrances to the **Slovak National Gallery** (Tues–Sun 10am–5.30pm; €4): the one on the embankment lets you into the main building, a converted naval barracks, while the one on Stúrovo námestie gives access to the **Esterházy Palace** wing, used for temporary exhibitions (mostly focusing on modern art). The permanent collection in the main building features a rundown of Slovak Gothic and Baroque art.

The Blue Church

Situated in a somewhat desultory suburb on Sienkie wiczova, this quirky church of **St Elizabeth**, known as the Blue Church because of its bright blue colour, rises implausibly out of the surrounding houses like a giant marzipan-covered Christmas cake. It's a lost monument to this city's Hungarian past, and worth visiting for the sheer Disneyland-esque weirdness of it. It's a short walk east from the old town.

Sunny Bratislava

If you're here in summer and begin to think coming to a land-locked country was a mistake, never fear – **Tyršovo nábrežie**, the south bank of the Danube, is transformed into a beach during July and August, with tonnes of sand brought in. Otherwise, there are plenty of green parks, such as **Medická Záhrada** in the north of the old town at the end of Spitaltska, which has some lovely fountains, flower beds and lawns.

Arrival and information

Air Bratislava International airport is quite small. For the centre, take bus #61 to Trnavske Myto, then tram #14 (about 45min). Alternatively take the slow but direct Terravision shuttle bus to the centre (5 daily; €10; 70min). Another easy option for getting to Bratislava is to fly into Vienna. From Vienna airport, bus services by Blaguss (€6, available from the driver; ⓦwww.blaguss.sk) and Slovak Lines (€7.70, from the driver or at ⓦwww.slovaklines.sk) take around 90min to reach Bratislava city centre. A shuttle taxi from Vienna airport costs €62 per four-passenger car (ⓣ02/5441 1240, ⓦwww.bratislava-airport-transfers.com).

Train Main station, Bratislava-Hlavná stanica, is walking distance – 1km north – of the centre, or you can take tram #13 from the tram terminus just down from the main exit. Some trains, particularly those heading for west Slovakia, pass through Bratislava Nové Mesto station, 4km northeast of the centre, which is linked to town by tram #6.

Bus The main bus station is Bratislava autobusová stanica, on Mlynské nivy, 14min walk east of the centre. Trolleybuses #206 and #208 serve the centre, Hodžovo námestie.

Tourist office BKIS, Klobucnícká 2 (June–Sept Mon–Fri 8.30am–7pm, Sat 9am–5pm, Sun 10am–5pm; Oct–May Mon–Fri 8.30am–6pm, Sat 9am–4pm, Sun 10am–3pm; ⓣ 02/5443 3715, ⓦ www.bkis.sk, ⓦ www.bratislava.sk).

Discount card The Bratislava City Card is available from BKIS tourist offices: it's available for up to three days (costing up to €12) and gets you a twenty percent discount on a variety of tours and attractions, as well as free transport.

City transport

Walking is the only way to see the mainly pedestrianized Staré Mesto (old town).

Trams Outside the old town, trams are the easiest way to travel. Buy your ticket before you board and validate it in one of the yellow machines inside – inspectors target routes going to the airport and bus and train terminals; fines are €40. Buy single tickets from machines at the tram terminus and newsagents: €0.50/15min; €0.70/up to 60min. A day pass costs €3.50 and a three-day pass €7; you can buy these from-Bratislava Transport (Obchodna 14, ⓦ www.dpb.sk), and at the booth to the left of the train station's main exit. You also need a half-fare ticket for any bulky luggage.

Buses The bus network serves the town both sides of the river; trams and trolleybuses only run north of the river. Buy bus tickets from the driver when you get on. Single tickets €0.75 , or you can use a day-pass (see above).

Bike rental See ⓦ www.bratislava.info/trips/bike for information but there are no special bike paths in Bratislava's streets, and motorists can be erratic.

Taxis Taxis are equipped with a meter, but even so, it's quite normal to bargain the price in advance. To order a taxi, call ⓣ 02/16 186.

Accommodation

Accommodation is expensive, and the cheapest options are dorms in hostels (although these tend to be very noisy). You can book centrally located private rooms through the tourist office, which can be a good budget option if there are a few of you. If you have a valid ISIC card, you can get tax knocked off your accommodation price.

Hostels

Downtown Backpacker's Panenská 31 ⓣ 02/5464 1191, ⓦ www.backpackers.sk. Friendly HI-affiliated place on the edge of the old town, with 24hr check in, internet access, a busy bar, common room and kitchen facilities. Dorms €14–18, doubles €60, without bathrooms.

Hostel Blues Špitalska 2 ⓣ 09/0520 4020, ⓦ www.hostelblues.sk. Exceptionally friendly and helpful staff run a clean, vibrant hostel with a cosy common room and kitchen, and a lively bar. Each room is named after a European capital. Occasional live music nights as well. Dorms €12–19, doubles from €62.

Hostel Possonium Šancová 20 ⓣ 02/2072 0007, ⓦ www.possonium.sk. Small hostel run by super-friendly staff, with mad, brightly coloured decor, garden, laundry, internet and bar. Short walk from the station (down the road straight out of the station, on the left). Dorms €13, doubles €55.

Patio Špitálska 35 ⓣ 02/5292 5797, ⓦ www .patiohostel.com. 5min walk from the city centre, this refurbished hostel has 24hr reception, a laundry, basic kitchen and internet access. On the down side, its slightly institutional walls are paper thin. Go through the car-park alley and turn left to get there. Dorms €16, doubles €60.

Vegas Hostel Obchodná 48 ⓣ 02/5262 2777, ⓦ www.vegashostel.sk. Run by the friendly Lucas, this is a clean, bright hostel with internet, breakfast and laundry. Great location. Dorms €16, double €46.

Hotels and pensions

Caribic's Žižkova 1a ⓣ 02/5441 8334, ⓦ www .caribics.com. Pleasant, comfortably furnished rooms in an old fisherman's lodge, a few minutes' walk from the old town. A little noisy due to passing trams. Excellent restaurant downstairs. Double €65.

Castle Club Zámocké Schody 4, entrance on Beblaveko 14 ⓣ 091/0328 2330. Small family house in the shadow of the castle, run by a reticent Scotsman. Gorgeous airy rooms with wonderful views. Doubles €75, quads €100, with breakfast.

Hotel Corso Kapucinska 7 ⓣ 02/5441 6450, ⓦ www.bratislavahotel.sk. Brightly decorated business-hotel-style rooms a stone's throw from the city centre. Doubles €80.

Gremium Gorkého 11 ⓣ 02/5413 1026. Decent, inexpensive option in the old town. Clean and not unfriendly, with basic en-suite bathrooms, above a sports bar. Doubles €60.

Campsites

Zlaté Piesky Intercamp ⓣ 02/4425 7373, ⓦ www.intercamp.sk. 8km northeast of the city centre. Take tram #2 from the main train station or #4 from town. Swimming lake with lifeguard services and a pleasant beach, as well as two restaurants on-site. Tent camping May to mid-Oct.

€3.50 per person camping, or €20 for a basic bungalow sleeping up to three.

Eating

Trznica Market at Námestie SNP 25 is an excellent indoor market, selling local herbs, fruits and vegetables – perfect for a healthy snack.

Cafés

Traditional Viennese-style cafés compete for space and status on the main square of the old town. They're all excellent in their different ways: *Maximilian Schokocafé* boasts the best hot chocolates and a chocolate fountain inside, while *Roland* is more of a formal restaurant, with an impressive Art Deco interior. *Kaffé Mayer* has been there for almost a century, and boasts the most impressive selection of cakes.

Bagels and coffee Hlavné Námesti 6. Great breakfasts, especially when you can sit outside and soak up the rays.

Café café Panská. Alfresco dining on director's chairs, with refreshing salads and light bites at reasonable prices. Salads and snacks €4.

Čajovňa Pohoda Radnicá 1. Hip teahouse with a huge range of herbal teas served in kitsch teapots and cups.

Net café Baštová. A smoky, quirky café run by the Austrian Institute, with internet available.

Tutti Frutti Obchodna UL. A jolly little stall located at the back of the mall selling costume jewellery and electronics, offering delicious fresh fruit juice from €1.15.

Restaurants

Lod Tyršovo nábrežie. "The Boat", on the southern side of the river, boasts great views over the Danube towards the castle. It also has a theatre with concerts as well as plays and serves standard, but decent, Slovak dishes.

TREAT YOURSELF

Camouflage Ventúrska 1 ⓣ02/2092 2711. A cool, chic restaurant with original pictures by Andy Warhol from the *Camouflage* series, phenomenal international cuisine and impeccable service. The two-course lunch menu is a not unreasonable €16, and includes mouth watering specialities such as smoked eel with wasabi seasoned artichoke puree. Otherwise mains are between €12 and €20.

Mýtny domček Starý Most petržalská strana. Perfect for a super cheap, delicious traditional Slovakian meal. The garlic soup, and fried ham and cheese (yes, that does constitute a meal) is delicious. Just over the Old Bridge, on the south side of the river. Mains €4–5.

Prašná Bašta Zámočnícka 11. Situated in a lovely courtyard by Michalská gate, this is an arty restaurant with live classical and jazz music and delicious international food. Mains €8.

San Marten Panská 33 ⓣ0911 340 341. A cosy red restaurant and bar a little removed from the hustle and bustle of the main square, in the shadow of St Martin's Cathedral. The Italian food is top notch and the atmosphere buzzing.

Sushi PLUS Hlavné Námesti 8. Eager-to-please staff serve good sushi and tempura in a pleasantly calming wood-and-paper interior.

Verne Jesenského 9. Quirky underground restaurant and pub full of pouffy armchairs and cosy little nooks, generally populated by students who come here for the cheap, tasty food. Mains from €4.

Drinking and nightlife

There are few purely dance clubs, but you'll find plenty of late-opening pubs and bars helping to fill the gap. In the summer, people spill out onto the streets of the old town, chatting and drinking until the early hours.

Charlie Centrum Špitálska 4. Bratislava's longest-serving nightspot, with a multiscreen arthouse cinema and a late-night bar/club in the basement.

Dubliner Sedlárska 6. Very popular, stereotypical Irish bar, with live sports events on screens and occasional live music.

Havana Bar Michalská 26. Enjoy hot, lively evenings full of mojitos and Cuban music spilling out onto the streets.

Slovak Pub Obchodná 62. This large pub manages to be popular with both backpackers and local students. Something of an institution.

Subclub Nábrežie arm. Gen. L. Svobodu ⓦwww.subclub.sk. Situated in an old atomic bunker in the base of the castle, *Subclub* is populated by Bratislava's young and hip. Entry €6–10; open until 3am.

Entertainment

The tourist office stocks *Kam do mesta* (free) and the English-language *What's on Bratislava & Slovakia* (€1.50; ⓦwww.whatsonslovakia.com). The weekly *Slovak Spectator*, available from kiosks and hotels, has news and some listings.

Opera and ballet Slovak National Theatre, Historical Building, Hviezdoslavovo námestie. Tickets

can be bought here 1hr before the performance (€8–30). Some of the less well known performances in the studio cost as little as €3, and you can also attend public rehearsals for €1.60. See Ⓦwww.snd.sk.
Classical music The Reduta concert hall, Hviezdoslavovo námestie, is home to the Slovak Philharmonic Orchestra. See Ⓦwww.filharm.sk. There are also open-air concerts in summer in courtyards and spaces across the city, such as outside the Jesuit church by Michalská. Ask at the tourist office for details.
Cinema The Istropolis complex on Trnavské myto, Vajorská 100 (tram #2 from the station; tram #4 or #6 from the centre) shows a range of international current films. See Ⓦwww.istropoliscinema.sk.

Shopping

Michalská and Ventúrska are good places for general souvenir shopping; there are also plenty of souvenir stalls lining the main square.
Aupark Shopping Centre Einsteinova 18. Big shopping centre in the new town full of brand names.
Bookshops Oxford Bookshop, Rajská 10 (Mon–Sat 9am–1pm & 2–6pm, Sun 9am–noon; Ⓣ02/5262 2029, Ⓦwww.oxfordbookshop.sk). Good selection of English-language books.

Directory

Embassies and consulates Australia, Ventúrska 10 Ⓣ02/5443 2985; Canada, Mostová 2 Ⓣ02/5920 4031; UK, Panská 16 Ⓣ02/5441 9632; USA, Hviedoslavovo námestie 5 Ⓣ02/5443 3338.
Festivals The prestigious Bratislava Music Festival (Ⓦwww.hc.sk) is held in October, and in summer, there's the brilliant Summer Culture Festival (Ⓦwww.bkis.sk).
Hospital Poliklinika Rúzinov on Ruzinovská 10 (trams #8, #9, #14 and #50; Ⓣ02/4827 9257).
Internet Net café Baštová; 8am–10pm, €0.60/10min.
Laundry Vydavatelstvo Perfekt, Karpatska 7.
Left luggage Train stations daily 5.30am–midnight; bus station Mon–Fri 6am–10pm, Sat & Sun 6am–6pm.
Pharmacy Lekáreň Pokrok, Račianske Mýto 1; 24hr; Ⓣ02/4445 5291.
Post office POFIS, Námestie Slobody 27.
Travel agencies Student Agency Travel, Obchodná 48 Ⓣ0800 121 121, Ⓦwww.studentagencybus.com. Best agency for cheap flights, and comfortable coaches.

Moving on

Bus Bánska Štiavnica (3–4 daily; 3hr 10min–4hr 30min); Poprad-Tatry (every 15min; 5hr 35min–7hr 45min); Košice (hourly; 6hr 50min–8hr).
Train Brno (8 daily; 1hr 30min–2hr); Košice (10 daily; 5hr 20min–7hr 10min); Prague (7 daily; 4hr 20min–6hr 30min); Poprad-Tatry (7 daily; 4hr 12min–5hr).

Slovakia's mountain regions

One of the great attractions of Slovakia is its **mountains**, particularly the **High Tatras**, which reach Alpine heights and have a stunning, austere beauty. By far the country's most popular destination, they are, in fact, the least typical of Slovakia's mountains, which are otherwise predominantly densely forested, round-topped limestone ranges. In the heart of the mountains lie **small towns** originally settled by German miners in the thirteenth century, and still redolent of those times. Rail lines, where they exist, make for some of the most scenic **train journeys** in the country.

BANSKÁ ŠTIAVNICA

Set in stunning countryside in the Low Tatras, the UNESCO-protected town of **BANSKÁ ŠTIAVNICA** is a previously German mining town, whose cobbled, winding streets and pretty buildings make it a highly recommended stop in a tour of Slovakia. It's extremely picturesque, and its inhabitants are relaxed and friendly.

What to see and do

The principal sights are in the historic core of the town, whose nucleus is the pretty main square, **Námestie sv**

Trojice, housing the red marble Holy Trinity column and some lovely burgher houses.

The Old Castle

Starý zámok, the sober **Old Castle** (May–Oct daily 9am–5pm; Nov–April Mon–Fri 8am–4pm; €2.40), which was begun in the thirteenth century, currently houses exhibits of **Baroque sculptures** and medieval blacksmiths' work and boasts gorgeous views of the countryside.

Klopačka

The seventeenth-century Klopačka or **Clapper Tower**, up on Sládkoviča, houses a wooden clapper that stems from the tradition of raising miners out of bed at 5am. Nowadays it claps for the amusement (or massive eventual irritation) of tourists and tower staff.

Arrival and information

Train and bus Both stations are at the bottom of a steep hill leading to the old town.
Tourist office Námestie sv Trojice 3 (May–Sept Mon–Sat 8am–5.30pm; Oct–April Mon–Fri 8am–4pm, Sat 8am–2pm; ⓣ045/694 9653, ⓦwww.banskastiavnica.sk, ⓦwww.banskastiavnica.org). Go in through the gate and turn right – the staff are extremely helpful.
Internet Allcom shop, Radničné Námestie 11/1 (Mon–Sat 9am–5pm).

WALKS

By far the most enjoyable activity in Banská Štiavnica is to set out in the direction of the hills and keep going till cold or hunger brings you back. The rolling hills and dappled forests are idyllic in good weather and impressively austere when it's grey. There are several lakes, made from mining pits filled with water, that are brilliant fun to jump into if you're hard (or foolish) enough to brave the cold. The paths are easy to follow, and you can get maps at your hotel or the tourist office.

Accommodation

Penzion Kachelman Kammerhofská 18 ⓣ045/692 23 19, ⓦwww.kachelman.sk. Comfortable, cosy rooms in a chalet-style building decked out with antlers on the walls, with a good restaurant beneath. Jacuzzi and sauna €13/hr. Doubles €29.
Penzion Tomino Akademicá 9 ⓣ045/692 1307, ⓦwww.penziontomino.sk. Excellent price for its central location, and small, cheerful rooms. Doubles €25.

Eating and drinking

Art Café Akademicá 2. Cheerful local hang-out with occasional live musicians and plenty of buzz.
Kaviareň Divná pani Andreja Kmeťa 8. Whether you're after somewhere to spend an afternoon reading or an evening spot for a cosy drink, this arty café-bar, with decor that looks like the brainchild of a ship captain and his florally minded wife, is the perfect hang-out.
U Mateja Akademicá 4. Friendly restaurant with delicious hearty food and a lovely terrace. Mains from €4.
Vodka Bar Banský Dom Radničné Nám. A raucous local's pub built in an old stable, where you're likely to get pulled into a good-natured table football tournament.

Moving on

Train Bratislava (every 2hr; 3hr 30min–4hr 20min).
Bus Bratislava (every 30min–1hr 30min; 3hr 30min–4hr 15min); Poprad (every 1hr–1hr 30min; 3hr 30min–4hr 10min).

THE HIGH TATRAS

Rising like a giant granite reef above the patchwork Poprad plain, the **High Tatras** are the main reason for venturing this far into Slovakia. They're an inspirational sight, with cascading waterfalls and lush green forests below and stunning snow-capped peaks above. The sheer number of visitors (enthusiastic walkers in summer and skiers in winter) lower down can be a little off-putting, but if you walk just a little further above the tree line, you leave the crowds behind and find snow under foot, scree slopes looming over you and

ZDIAR: THE GINGER MONKEY

If you fancy really getting away from it all, the **Ginger Monkey** hostel is set in the rarely visited mountain town of Zdiar, near the Slovakia–Poland border. It's a brilliant place to enjoy a couple of days off the beaten track and take in the stunning scenery, either from the comfort of the terrace, or trekking or skiing through it. The hostel is a traveller's paradise – friendly and laid-back, with a chill-out room full of sagging comfy sofas and breakfast included. To get there, take a bus from Poprad (hourly) in the direction of Lysa Polana, and Zdiar is about 40min away. Dorms €14, twin €34. ⓣ0421 524498084, ⓦwww.gingermonkey.eu.

breathtaking views all around. Sadly, a huge storm in 2004 uprooted much of the pine forest here, but the surrounding peaks are still sufficiently impressive.

To make the most of your visit, use the severely unprepossessing **POPRAD** as the transport hub, but go straight on to one of the mountain resorts. The best base in the mountains by far is the scattered settlement of **STARÝ SMOKOVEC.**

Arrival and information

Train The mainline train station for the Tatras is Poprad-Tatry in Poprad. From there, tiny red tram-like trains (TEZ; hourly; 25min to Starý Smokovec; €2.40) trundle across the fields, linking Poprad with the string of resorts and spas halfway up the Tatras within the Tatra National Park.

Tourist office In Poprad: at the western end of námestie sv Egidia (Mon–Fri 9am–5pm, Sat 9am–noon; July & Aug Mon–Fri 8am–6pm, Sat 9am–1pm, Sun 1–4pm; ⓣ052/16 186, ⓦwww.poprad.sk). In Starý Smokovec: down the road to your right as you face the *Grand Hotel* (Mon–Fri 9am–5pm; in summer also Sat & Sun 8am–2pm; ⓣ052/442 34 40, ⓦwww.tatry.sk).

Accommodation

The tourist office at Starý Smokovec can help with accommodation.

Eurocamp FICC Just south of Tatranská Lomnica ⓣ052/446 77413, ⓦwww.eurocamp-ficc.sk. Bungalows with hot showers, and a restaurant and café on site. The campsite has its own train station: either take the ordinary train from Poprad-Tatry via Studený Potok or the TEZ, changing at Starý Smokovec and Tatranská Lomnica. Tent and person €4, double bungalow €12.

Pension Gerlach Nový Smokovec 22, Starý Smokovec ⓣ090/535 0448. Run by the same couple who run *Villa Kunerad*, this pension is simple but clean and homely. To the left of the *Grand Hotel*, towards the station. Doubles €35.

Pension Tatra Starý Smokovec 42 ⓣ090 365 0802, ⓦwww.tatraski.sk. Airy, brightly lit rooms in a sweet wooden chalet-style building. There's internet access and a cosy lounge downstairs. Doubles €40.

Villa Kunerad Nový Smokovec 40, Starý Smokovec ⓣ090/535 0448, ⓦwww.penziongerlach.sk. Spacious, comfortably furnished rooms in a large chalet. It's the bright yellow building to the right behind the *Grand Hotel*. Double €35.

Eating and drinking

Starý Smokovec can look positively dead of an evening but take heart, if you know where to go, plenty of people are out and about. For supplies for mountain walks, head to Potravinў supermarket next to *Cafe Michalka*.

Cafe Hoepfner First floor of *Hotel Smokovec*, Starý Smokovec 25. Hearty plates of escalopes with piles of potatoes, and good coffee during the day. With occasional live jazz.

Cafe Michalka Starý Smokovec. Go down the main street with the *Grand Hotel* on your left, and it's at the bottom end on the left. A nice terrace, tasty food, and internet access.

TREAT YOURSELF

If you're planning to spend all your energy on mountain activities, you might want to pamper yourself by staying in one of the luxurious rooms at the plush **Grand Hotel** (Starý Smokovec; ⓣ052/4780 000, ⓦwww.grandhotel.sk). Access to the jacuzzis and sauna is €18 for non-guests, and €5 to use their swish round swimming pool, enclosed in a glass dome. Doubles €85.

HIKING IN THE TATRAS

Although your walk might begin like an over crowded shopping trip, accompanied by families and ice-cream vans, a hike in the Tatras invariably culminates in spectacular scenery from exhilarating heights. You'll be contending with heat and sun as well as lots of snow and seriously steep paths, and the mountains are covered in avalanche warnings, so make sure you have everything you need: sunscreen, sunglasses, a hat, gloves, waterproofs, a whistle, a torch, good hiking boots and enough water.

Hiking is best from July to September, when the views are wonderfully clear. Many paths are open year-round, though high-level paths, above the mountain huts, are open mid-June to October only.

The most straightforward and rewarding climb **from Starý Smokovec** is to follow the blue-marked path that leads from behind the *Grand Hotel* to the summit of Slavkovský št (2452m), a return journey of nine hours. For a shorter walk, take the **narrow-gauge funicular**, starting from behind the *Grand Hotel* (daily 7.30am–7pm, closed May & Nov; €5.70 up, €2 down, €6.40 return), 250m to Hrebienok. From here, follow the red trail for about an hour to the beautiful (but predictably over-popular) **Obrov waterfalls**. For details of other trails and accommodation in mountain huts, check out Ⓦwww.tatry.sk.

Don't go without the green 1:25 000 *Vysoké Tatry* hiking map (available from the tourist office). For daily weather reports and more information on hiking go to the Horská služba (mountain rescue), just uphill from Starý Smokovec station (Ⓣ052/442 28 20, Ⓦwww.hzs.sk, or Ⓣ052/776 55 51, Ⓦwww.shmu.sk).

Cable car

If you don't have the time or inclination to hike, you can still enjoy fabulous views by taking a series of **cable cars** (daily 8.30am–3.50/5.50pm; closed May & Nov; €8 up, €6.40 down, €13 return) from Tatranská Lomnica to the summit of Lomnick štít (2632m), the Tatras' second-highest peak.

Tatry Pub Starý Smokovec 21. Recognizable by the flashing red and blue PUB sign outside it, this is great for a cosy beer in the evening and turns into an implausibly lively disco playing cheesy tunes and dance anthems at the weekends.

Activities

Climbing To climb here, you have to be a member of a recognized climbing club with a valid membership card or you must hire a guide – available at Spolok horských vodcov (Ⓣ052/442 20 66, Ⓦwww.tatraguide.sk).

Skiing The ski season runs from December to March and there are plenty of places in Starý Smokovec to rent equipment. Check Ⓦwww.tatry.sk or Ⓦwww.vt.sk for details. Štrbské Pleso hosts national and international skiing events, Ⓦwww.parksnow.sk.

Moving on (from Poprad)

Train Bratislava (4–5 daily; 2hr 50min–3hr 40min); Košice (hourly; 1hr 7min–1hr 55min).

Bus Levoča (twice hourly; 15–45min); Prešov (hourly; 1hr 05min–2hr).

East Slovakia

Stretching from the High Tatras east to the Ukrainian border, the landscape of **East Slovakia** is decidedly different from the rest of the country. It has a far bleaker atmosphere than elsewhere, with communist blocks encroaching onto even the prettiest of city squares. Ethnically, this is probably the most diverse region in the country, although sadly, racism is still prevalent. The majority of the country's Romanies live here, mostly on the edge of Slovak villages, often in shantytowns; and in the ribbon-villages of the north and east, the Rusyn minority struggle to preserve their culture and religion. The land that stretches northeast up the Poprad Valley to the Polish border and east along the River Hornád towards Prešov is known as the **Spiš** region, for

centuries a semi-autonomous province within the Hungarian kingdom.

LEVOČA

Some 25km east of Poprad, across a broad sweep of undulating Spiš countryside, sits the medieval walled town of **LEVOČA**, declared the capital of the Spiš region in 1271. Although it's famous for its beauty across Slovakia, it attracts a limited number of visitors and has a contemplative, solitary feel to it.

What to see and do

Inside the walls of the historic town, the crumbling streets lead up to **Námestie Majstra Pavla**, the main square and heart of the town. The backstreets are easy to explore, set out on a grid system, with most streets leading to the city walls.

SV Jakub

The Catholic church of **SV Jakub** (Mon 11/11.30am–4/5pm, Tues–Sat 8.30/9am–4/5pm, Sun 1–4/5pm; Nov–Easter closed Sun & Mon) is crammed with **religious art**, the star attraction being the magnificent sixteenth-century wooden altarpiece by the renowned Gothic sculptor Master Pavol of Levoča. The church can be visited only with a guide, and tours (every 30min, hourly in winter; €2.50) leave from the ticket office opposite the main entrance. A small **museum** (daily 9am–5pm; €1.50) dedicated to Master Pavol stands opposite the church on the eastern side of the square.

Lutheran church and the Cage of Shame

The last building in the centre of the square is the oddly squat **Lutheran church**, built in an uncompromisingly Neoclassical style: its contrast with the lavish Catholic church is striking.

Set just between the two churches is the **Cage of Shame**, where transgressors were imprisoned as an example to the rest of the town. It's described on its plaque as a cage for "punishing the moral delicts of the women". Charming.

Arrival and information

Bus The bus station is a 10min walk southeast of the old town. If you're coming from the east get off one stop earlier at the Košice gate.
Tourist office Námestie Majstra Pavla 58, in the northwest corner of the main square (Mon–Fri 9am–noon & 12.30–4pm, Sat 9am–noon; ⓣ053/451 37 63, ⓦwww.levoca.sk).
Internet Internet café on Nová 38. Daily 9am–5pm.

Accommodation

There is an abundance of private rooms, which the tourist office can help organize.
Faix Probstnerová cesta 6 ⓣ053/451 1111. A comfortable hotel set in a cheerful yellow corner building in the centre of town. Doubles €40.
Oaža Nová 65 ⓣ053/451 4511 ⓦwww.ubytovanieoaza.sk. Simply decorated, clean, bright rooms in a friendly house with kitchen and garden (with a nice hillside view). Doubles €20.
Penzion Gabi Železničný Riadok 16 ⓣ0910 985 548. A family-run establishment with clean, homely rooms and breakfast. €12 per person.

Eating

There's a good convenience store, Milk Agro, at Vzsoké 30.
Penzion Arkáda Námestie Majstra Parla 26. A relatively formal restaurant attached to the hotel, with a wine cellar which might just be a godsend if you have to spend a whole night in Levoča. Mains €6–7.
Bagetka Námestie Majstra Pavla 43. Lunchtime baguettes for €2. Don't be put off by the fact it looks like a dusty knick-knack shop.
Reštaurácia Slovenka Námestie Majstra Pavla 62. Slovak specialities such as meat-filled potato pancakes for around €5 a plate. The friendly owner Josef speaks perfect English.

PREŠOV

Capital of the Slovak Šariš region and a cultural centre for the Rusyn (Ruthenian) minority, **PREŠOV** is a relatively vibrant student town.

What to see and do

Most attractions lie along the pretty main square, the Hlavná ulica; the wide, sweeping main street that runs alongside it is Hlavná.

Hlavná ulica

At the tip of Hlavná ulica, the main square flanked by creamy eighteenth-century facades, is the **Greek Catholic cathedral**, decked out in grand Rococo style. On the other side of the square, at the widest point, the Gothic Roman Catholic and Protestant churches vie with each other: the fourteenth-century Catholic church of **sv Mikuláš** has the edge, not least for its modern Moravian stained-glass windows. Behind sv Mikuláš is the much plainer **Lutheran church**, built in the mid-seventeenth century.

Expozìcia Judaìk Zozbierky E. Barkanyho

The Orthodox Jewish synagogue, **Expozìcia Judaìk Zozbierky E. Barkanyho**, on a side street just off the main square, was built in 1898, and is Moorish in design, covered in intricate, brightly coloured patterns. It's now home to the **Museum of Jewish Culture** (Sun–Fri 9am–1pm & 2–4pm, free), with interesting exhibits on the chequered history of Jews in Slovakia. The main reason to visit, however, is to admire the synagogue's painted interior.

Arrival and information

Train and bus The bus and train stations are opposite each other about 1km south of the main square; buses and trolleybuses into town stop at Na Hlavnej.

Tourist office Hlavná 67, 100m from the town hall (Mon–Fri 9am–6pm, Sat 9am–1pm; ⓣ 051/324 8877, ⓦ www.presov.sk or www.micpresov.sk).

Internet Internet Ruz, Hlavná 140. At the northern end of Hlavná, upstairs in the bright yellow building (daily 8am–9pm).

Accommodation

The friendly tourist office staff have limited English, but can help with accommodation.

Pension Alex Slovenská 80 ⓣ 051/77 234 44, ⓦ www.alexpension.sk. Very clean and airy rooms with modern furnishings and cheerful proprietors. Doubles €46.

Pension Atrium Floriánová 4 ⓣ 051/75 821 95. Pleasantly decorated rooms in a lovely side street filled with cafés. Doubles €58 with breakfast.

DM SPSS, Domov mládeže Alexandra Duchnoviča Sabinovská 2 ⓣ 051/771 85 47. Superb-value accommodation in student halls, where you can get a spacious en-suite double room with a balcony for €20. No cooking facilities.

Eating and nightlife

It's a bit of a mystery what people do of an evening in Prešov, as the night-time streets are eerily deserted.

Babylon Wine Pub Hlavná. The alfresco area in front of the Protestant church is permanently packed, and the adjoining cosy cellar restaurant offers good-value pizzas (€3).

Bageta Cukrárèn Hlavná 38. A branch of the Slovak answer to *Subway*, serving fresh, cheap baguettes.

Christiana Hlavná 105. An enchanting semi-covered terrace with a piano and pots of flowers, where you can chill with a coffee and a paper, or a beer by candlelight. There's an attached basement bar with live music, comfy sofas, and an arty bookshop.

Wave Klub Hlavná 121. You're likely to be the only customers in this friendly but weird bar unless it's a Saturday night (when DJs play until 1am). There are S&M mannequins in the corner. An experience.

Moving on

Train Košice (daily; 1hr); Spišska Nová Ves (up to 7 daily; 1hr. From here you can take a bus to Levoča – this is a good way to travel if you'd like to take in some of the Spiš scenery from the train).

Bus Levoča (daily; 1hr–1hr 20min).

KOŠICE

KOŠICE is unappealing at first glance, with the communist-era blocks rising up around it, but the city boasts some pretty buildings and a lovely square in its centre. Just 21km north of the Hungarian

border, Košice also acts as a magnet for the Hungarian community – to whom the city is known as Kassa – and the Romanies of the surrounding region.

What to see and do

Hlavné Námestie is the main square and the nucleus of city life, where every teenager in town can be found canoodling on a park bench and in the grass. The singing fountain by the state theatre in its centre is a popular spot for meeting and people-watching.

Cathedral of St Elizabeth

The fine **Gothic cathedral** on the main square is dedicated to St Elizabeth of Hungary; there are scenes from her life on the right-hand side of the altar. One of its two contorted towers serves as a vantage point (Mon–Fri 9.30am–4.30pm, Sat 9am–1.30pm).

East Slovak Museum

Follow Hlavná north out of the main square to reach the bulky nineteenth-century **East Slovak Museum** (Tues–Sat 9am–5pm, Sun 9am–1pm), filled with medieval and Baroque religious art.

Arrival and information

Air There's a small international airport in Košice, where airlines such as Sky Europe, a rickety outfit of dubious reliability, fly. From the airport turn right on your exit to the bus stop and take any bus to the centre of town. The fares are timed, and a 30min ticket (30min základný, €0.55) will get you into town.

Train and bus The train and bus stations are opposite each other. Walk west through the Municipal Park towards the old town; it's a 10min walk.

Tourist office Štúrova 1, in the spectacularly musty Dargov department store (Mon–Fri 8am–7pm, Sat 8am–1pm; ⓣ055/16186) at the southern end of the main square. They provide *Best in Košice*, a free booklet with listings for hotels, restaurants, nightlife and attractions.

Internet Internet Café, Hlavná 9 (€1.66/hr).

Accommodation

Hostels

The tourist office can help with finding rooms.

Domov Mládeže Medická 2 ⓣ055/643 56 88, ⓦwww.dmmed.kecom.sk. Outside of the city centre, *Domov Mládeže* is a big block of a hostel, with basic but comfortable rooms. Dorms €10, doubles €23.

Metropol Sturova 28 ⓣ055/24872. Clean and friendly student hostel with a wooden, ski-chalet like interior, a few minutes' walk from the centre. Doubles €26.80.

Penzion Slovakia Orlia 6 ⓣ055/728 98 20, ⓦwww.penzionslovakia.sk. Attached to the popular *Rosto Steakhouse*, this guesthouse is cool and quiet with comfortable, clean rooms. Doubles €55.

Campsite

A T C Salaš Barca ⓣ055/623 33 97. Thirty pitches and with a swimming pool. Open May–Oct. €8 per person.

Eating

There´s a Tesco supermarket at the northern end of the main square.

Ajvega Orlia 10. A vegetarian place with a summer terrace, serving soya versions of standard Slovak dishes, signposted by a wall painting of a semi-clad blonde. Mains €3–6.

Bageteria 104 Hlavná. Take away baguettes – a godsend in a place where otherwise people don't seem to eat lunch at all.

Bluebell Hlavnú 22. Off Hlavná, in the courtyard behind the pink building opposite the cathedral. A cheerful café with a lovely terrace.

Cavearia Theatru Hlavná 78. Where the cool youth of Košice hang out over champagne and lattes.

Drinking and nightlife

Košice can seem dead at night, but if you find the more popular bars, you're in for a buzzing, if really quite random, evening. For big-name gigs, check out Košice Steel Arena (Nerudova 12; ⓣ055/622 35 25, ⓦwww2.steelarena.sk) which hosts quite a few.

Cactus Pub Zamocnicka. A dingy downstairs pub with good music, attracting a friendly crowd.

Cult Retro Club 49 Kováčska. A mirrored, flashing cheese-fest boasting 400ft of optic cable and 25 disco balls.

Jazz Club Kováčska 39. Cosy ambience, with a café in front and large, leafy bar in the back and live jazz.

Krasne Vina Masiarska 24. Let the lovely Peter recommend a series of delicious wines either in his cosy wine cellar, or the dreamy, bird-filled garden attached. 100ml tasters of wine from €0.50 and snacks €3.25.

Moving on

Train Bratislava (daily; 5–9hr); Prešov (11 daily; 20–50min).

Bus The Student Agency has an office at Mlynská 11 (Ⓣ055/729 4024, Ⓦwww.studentagencybus.com) – good for domestic and international connections. Poprad (every 1–2hr; 2hr 15min–2hr 45min).

Slovenia

HIGHLIGHTS

PTUJ: Slovenia's oldest settlement is also its most endearing

SŎCA VALLEY: stunningly scenic location for hiking, rafting and skiing.

OLD TOWN, LJUBLJANA: stunning architecture a hilltop castle and leafy riverside cafés

ŠKOCJAN CAVES: magnificent underground canyon

PIRAN: historic coastal town strewn with gorgeous Venetian Gothic architecture and pretty squares

ROUGH COSTS

DAILY BUDGET Basic €40/occasional treat €60

DRINK Pivo (beer) €2.50 for half a litre

FOOD Pizza €5–7

HOSTEL/BUDGET HOTEL €15–20/€60–80

TRAVEL Ljubljana–Maribor (130km) €9 by train; Ljubljana–Bled (65km) €7 by bus

FACT FILE

POPULATION 2 million

AREA 20,273 sq km

LANGUAGE Slovenian

CURRENCY Euro (€)

CAPITAL Ljubljana (population 250,000)

INTERNATIONAL PHONE CODE ⓣ386

Introduction

Stable, prosperous and welcoming, Slovenia is a charming and comfortable place to travel, with architecturally grand, arty cities, and lush pine-forested countryside, perfect for hiking and biking in summer and skiing in winter. The country managed to avoid much of the strife that plagued other nations during the messy disintegration of the Yugoslav Republic, and has integrated quickly with Western Europe, joining the euro zone at the start of 2007. Administered by German-speaking overlords until 1918, Slovenes absorbed the culture of their rulers while managing to retain a strong sense of ethnic identity through their Slavic language.

Slovenia's sophisticated capital, **Ljubljana**, is manageably small and cluttered with Baroque and Habsburg buildings. Elsewhere, the Julian Alps provide stunning mountain scenery, most accessible at **Lake Bled** and **Lake Bohinj**, and most memorable along the **Soča Valley**. Further south are spectacular caves, including those at **Postojna** and **Škocjan**, while the short stretch of Slovenian coast is punctuated by two starkly different towns: **Piran** and **Portorož**. In the eastern, wine-making reaches, **Ptuj** is Slovenia's oldest and best-preserved town, while the country's second city, **Maribor**, is a worthwhile stopover point on the way to Austria.

CHRONOLOGY

181 BC The Romans conquer the area of present day Slovenia.
550 AD Slavs begin to inhabit the area.
600s The first Slovenian state, the Duchy of Carantania, is established.
745 The Frankish Empire takes over Carantania, and converts the Slavs to Christianity.
1335 The Habsburgs take control of Slovenian regions through marriage.
1550 First book is published in the Slovenian language.
1867 Slovenia is brought under the direct control of Austria.
Late 1800s Growth of Slovenian nationalism.
1918 Following the collapse of the Austro-Hungarian Empire after World War I, Slovenia is incorporated into the Kingdom of the Serbs, Croats and Slovenes.
1929 The Kingdom is renamed Yugoslavia.
1945 After being occupied by the Germans during World War II, a liberation force led by Slovenian General Tito incorporates Slovenia into the Republic of Socialist Yugoslavia.
1950s The industrialization of Slovenia leads to rapid economic development.
1980 General Tito dies; disintegration of Yugoslavia begins.
1990 Slovenians vote for independence in a referendum.
1991 Slovenia declares its independence from Socialist Yugoslavia, leading to a ten-day war with the Yugoslav army. The Slovenians win.
2003 The oldest wooden wheel in the world, thought to be 5000 years old, is discovered in Slovenia.
2004 Slovenia joins NATO as well as the EU.
2007 Slovenia is the first former communist state to adopt the European single currency.

ARRIVAL

Direct **flights** to Slovenia from the UK are increasing in number, with low-cost carrier easyJet (Ⓦwww.easyjet.com) flying daily to Ljubljana. Slovenia's location – wedged between Austria, Croatia, Hungary and Italy – makes it easily approachable by **road** or **rail**; Ljubljana is well connected by bus and train with major cities in all four countries. Access to the Slovene coast is also straightforward: buses arrive daily from Trieste (Italy) and Pula (Croatia), and you can also enter the country via a ferry from Venice.

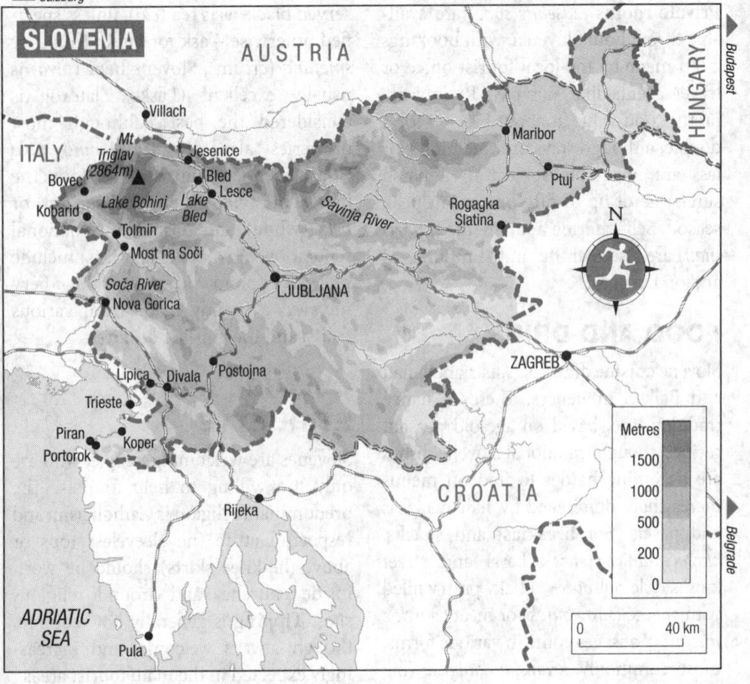

GETTING AROUND

Slovene Railways (Slovenske železnice; ⓦwww.slo-zeleznice.si) is smooth and efficient. **Trains** (*vlaki*) are divided into slow (LP), and Intercity (IC) express trains, as well as the fast Inter City Slovenia trains (ICS) between Ljubljana and Maribor. Reservations (*rezervacije*) are obligatory, but free, on ICS trains, and there is a €5 booking fee for international trains to Italy. Most timetables have English notes; "departures" is *odhodi*, "arrivals" is *prihodi*. Eurail and InterRail passes are valid.

The **bus** network consists of an array of local companies offering a reliable service. Towns such as Ljubljana, Maribor and Koper have big bus stations, where you can buy your tickets in advance – recommended if you're travelling between Ljubljana and the coast in high season. Elsewhere, simply pay the driver or conductor. You'll be charged extra for cumbersome items of baggage.

All public transport services are significantly reduced on Sundays.

ACCOMMODATION

Accommodation is universally clean and good quality. **Hostels** are growing in number, and there's a smattering of student dorms (*dijaški dom*) that significantly boost capacity during the summer, though facilities are extremely basic. Expect to pay about €15–20 per person per night (€10 in student dorms). **Campsites** are numerous and generally have good facilities, restaurants and shops. Two people travelling with a tent can expect to pay €20–30. The majority of campsites are open from May to September. Camping rough without permission is punishable by a fine.

In the capital, doubles at a two-star **hotel** start around €55. Family-run **pensions** in rural areas, especially the mountains, offer the same facilities as hotels but usually at a lower price.

Private rooms (*zasebne sobe*) are available throughout Slovenia, with bookings often made by the local tourist office or travel agents like Kompas. Rooms are pretty good value at about €35–50 for a double, although stays of three nights or less are invariably subject to a harsh surcharge of up to fifty percent in peak season. Self-catering **apartments** (*apartmaji*) are also plentiful in the mountains and on the coast.

FOOD AND DRINK

Slovene **cuisine** draws on Austrian, Italian and Balkan influences. There's a native tradition, too, based on age-old peasant recipes, though traditional Slovene dishes are becoming harder to find on menus increasingly dominated by Italian pizzas and pastas. For **breakfast** and **snacks**, *okrepčevalnice* (snack bars) and street kiosks dole out *burek*, a flaky pastry filled with cheese (*sirov burek*) or meat (*burek z mesom*). Sausages come in various forms, most commonly *kranjska klobasa* (big spicy sausages). **Menus** in a *restavracija* (restaurant) or *gostilna* (inn) will usually include roast meats (*pečenka*) and schnitzels (*zrezek*). Goulash (*golaž*) is also common. Two traditional dishes are *žlikrofi*, ravioli filled with potato, onion and bacon; and *žganci*, once the staple diet of rural Slovenes, a buckwheat or maize porridge often served with sauerkraut. Few local dishes are suitable for **vegetarians**, though international restaurants will usually offer something veggie. On the coast you'll find plenty of fish (*riba*), mussels (*školjke*) and squid (*kalamari*). Typical **desserts** include strudel filled with apple or rhubarb; *žtruklji*, dumplings with fruit filling; and *prekmurska gibanica*, a delicious local cheesecake.

Drinking

Daytime **drinking** takes place in small café-bars, or in a *kavarna*, where a range of cakes, pastries and ice cream is usually on offer. **Coffee** (*kava*) is generally served black, as is **tea** (*čaj*), unless specified otherwise – ask for *mleko* (milk) or *smetana* (cream). Slovene **beer** (*pivo*) is usually excellent (Laško Zlatorog is considered the best), although most breweries also produce *temno pivo* ("dark beer"), a Guinness-like stout. The local **wine** (*vino*) is either *črno* (red) or *belo* (white) and has an international reputation. Favourite aperitifs include *slivovka* (plum brandy), the fiery *sadjevec*, a brandy made from various fruits, and the gin-like *brinovec*.

CULTURE AND ETIQUETTE

Slovenes are welcoming people, who are only too willing to help tourists. The predominant religion is Catholicism, and respectful attire (no sleeveless tops or above-the-knee skirts) should be worn inside churches and around religious sites. **Tipping** is generally not required, though always welcome, and increasingly expected in the main tourist areas.

SPORTS AND OUTDOOR ACTIVITIES

Slovenia's dramatic and varied landscape provides ample opportunities for any number of sporting activities, be it **hiking**, **cycling** and **rafting** in summer, or **skiing** in winter. Most places cater well for adventure-seekers, especially in the mountains, with healthy competition generally keeping prices fair. Local tourist offices have comprehensive information on activities and sporting agencies. For more information, see the boxes on p.1056 and p.1059.

COMMUNICATIONS

Most **post offices** (*pošta*) are open Monday to Friday 8am to 6/7pm and Saturday 8am to noon. Stamps (*znamke*) can also be bought at newsstands. Public **phones** use cards (*telekartice*; €3, €4, €7, €14.5), available from post offices, kiosks and tobacconists. Make long-distance

Slovene

	Slovene	Pronunciation
Yes	*Ja*	Ya
No	*Ne*	Ne
Please	*Prosim*	Proseem
Thank you	*Hvala*	Huala
Hello/Good day	*Živijo/dober dan*	Jeeveeyo/dober dan
Goodbye	*Nasvidenje*	Nasveedenye
Excuse me	*Oprostite*	Oprosteete
Where?	*Kje?*	Kye?
Good	*Dobro*	Dobro
Bad	*Slabo*	Slabo
Near	*Blizu*	Bleezoo
Far	*Daleč*	Daalech
Cheap	*Poceni*	Potzenee
Expensive	*Drago*	Drago
Open	*Odprto*	Odpurto
Closed	*Zaprto*	Zapurto
Today	*Danes*	Danes
Yesterday	*Včeraj*	Ucheray
Tomorrow	*Jutri*	Yutree
How much is...?	*Koliko stane…?*	Koleeko stane…?
What time is it?	*Koliko je ura?*	Koleeko ye oora?
I don't understand	*Ne razumem*	Ne razoomem
Do you speak English?	*Ali govorite angleško?*	Alee govoreete angleshko?
One	*Ena*	Ena
Two	*Dve*	Dve
Three	*Tri*	Tree
Four	*Štiri*	Shteeree
Five	*Pet*	Pet
Six	*Šest*	Shest
Seven	*Sedem*	Sedem
Eight	*Osem*	Osem
Nine	*Devet*	Devet
Ten	*Deset*	Deset

and international calls at a post office, where you're assigned to a cabin and given the bill afterwards. **Internet** access is widespread (€2–4/hr).

EMERGENCIES

The **police** (*policija*) are generally easygoing and likely to speak some English. **Pharmacies** (*lekarna*) follow shop hours, and a rota system covers night-time opening; details are in the window of each pharmacy.

EMERGENCY NUMBERS

Police ☎113; Ambulance & Fire ☎112.

INFORMATION

Most towns and resorts have a **tourist information office**, most of which can arrange accommodation. A very high standard of English is spoken almost everywhere.

MONEY AND BANKS

Slovenia adopted the euro in January 2007. **Banks** (*banka*) generally open

SLOVENIA ON THE NET

Ⓦ **www.slovenia.info** Official tourist board site.
Ⓦ **www.ljubljana.si** Detailed information on sights and events in the capital.
Ⓦ **www.burger.si** Superb interactive maps and panoramic photos.

Monday to Friday 8.30am to 12.30pm and 2 to 5pm, Saturday 8.30am to 11am/noon. You can also change money in tourist offices, post offices, travel agencies and exchange bureaux (*menjalnica*). **Credit cards** are accepted in a large number of hotels and restaurants, and **ATMs** are widespread.

OPENING HOURS AND HOLIDAYS

Most **shops** open Monday to Friday 8am to 7pm and Saturday 8am to 1pm; an increasing number open on Sun. Museum times vary, but many close on Mondays. All shops and banks are closed on the following **public holidays**: January 1 and 2, Febuary 8, Easter Monday, April 27, May 1 and 2, June 25, August 15, October 31, November 1, December 25 and 26.

STUDENT & YOUTH DISCOUNTS

The EURO<26 card (€14) is valid in Slovenia, and can be used to get discounts of up to 50 percent on many attractions. You can also purchase the affiliated SŽ-EURO<26 (€18; from most train stations) to get an additional 30 percent off train fares within Slovenia, and 25 percent off international rail travel.

Ljubljana

The Slovene capital **LJUBLJANA** curls under its castle-topped hill, an old centre marooned in the shapeless modernity that stretches out across the plain, a vital and fast-growing capital. The city's sights are only part of the picture; first and foremost Ljubljana is a place to meet people and enjoy the nightlife.

What to see and do

Ljubljana's main point of reference is **Slovenska cesta**, a busy north–south thoroughfare that slices the city down the middle. Most of the sights are within easy walking distance of here, with the **Old Town** straddling the River Ljubljanica to the south and east and the nineteenth-century quarter to the west, where the principal museums and galleries are.

The Old Town

From the bus and train stations head south down Miklošičeva cesta for ten minutes and you'll reach **Prešernov trg**, the hub around which everything in Ljubljana's delightful **Old Town** revolves. Overlooking the bustling square and the River Ljubljanica, the Baroque seventeenth-century **Church of the Annunciation** (daily 9am–noon & 3–7pm), blushes a sandy red; it's worth a look inside for Francesco Robba's marble high-altar, richly adorned with spiral columns and plastic figurines. Robba, an Italian architect and sculptor, was brought in to remodel the city in its eighteenth-century heyday. His best piece, a beautifully sculpted **fountain** that symbolizes the meeting of the rivers Sava, Krka and Ljubljanica, lies across the river, in front of the town hall on Mestni trg. To get there cross the elegant **Tromostovje** (Triple Bridge), one of many innovative creations by Jože Plečnik in Ljubljana, his birthplace. A local darling, Plečnik made his mark on the city between the two world wars with his classically inspired designs, and in doing so brought Ljubljana into Europe's architectural elite.

St Nicholas' Cathedral and the market

A little east of Mestni trg, on Ciril-Metodov trg, **St Nicholas' Cathedral** (daily 6am–noon & 3–6pm; free) is the most sumptuous and overblown of Ljubljana's Baroque statements. Smothered with fabulous frescoes, this is the best preserved of the city's ecclesiastical buildings. Along the riverside, you can't fail to miss Plečnik's **colonnaded market** (closed Sun). Just beyond the market, also take a look at the beautiful **Dragon Bridge**, each corner pylon topped with spitting dragons – the city's symbol.

The castle

Opposite the market, Študentovska ulica winds up the thickly wooded hillside to the **castle** (daily 9/10am–9/11pm), originally a twelfth-century construction whose present appearance dates from the sixteenth century, following an earthquake in 1511. Climb the **clock tower** (daily 9/10am–6/9pm; €5 including entrance to the Virtual Museum) for a superlative view of the Old Town below and the magnificent Kamniške Alps to the north. A **funicular railway** (€3 return) provides an easier way up and down the castle hill.

South of Prešernov trg

Back on the western side of the river, further south on Slovenska cesta, the park-like expanse of Kongresni trg slopes away from the early eighteenth-century **Ursuline Church**, whose looming Baroque coffee-cake exterior is one of the city's most impressive. Vegova Ulica leads south from Kongresni trg towards Trg francoske revolucije, passing on the way the chequered pink,

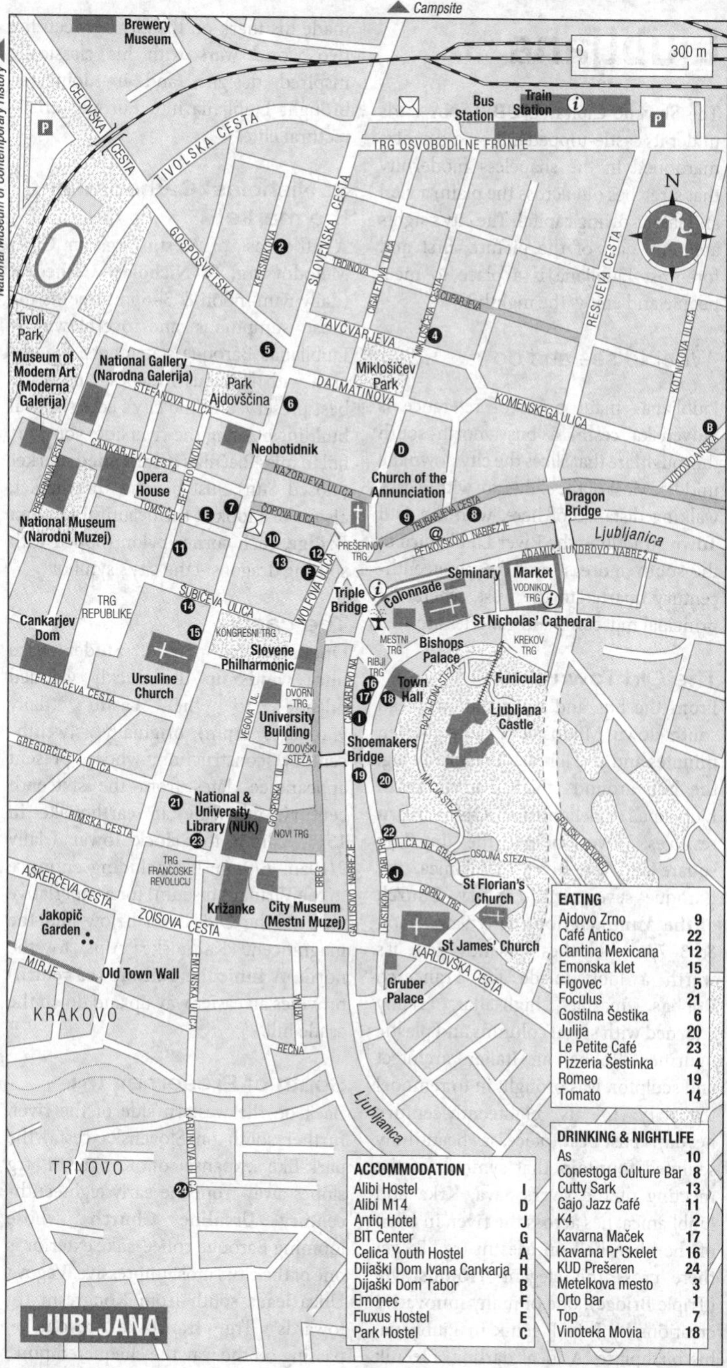
Campsite
National Museum of Contemporary History
Brewery Museum
0
300 m
CELOVŠKA CESTA
TIVOLSKA CESTA
Bus Station
Train Station
TRG OSVOBODILNE FRONTE
GOSPOSVETSKA
KERSNIKOVA
SLOVENSKA CESTA
TRDINOVA
CIGALETOVA ULICA
MIKLOŠIČEVA CESTA
CUFARJEVA
RESLJEVA CESTA
KOTNIKOVA ULICA
TAVČARJEVA
Tivoli Park
Museum of Modern Art (Moderna Galerija)
National Gallery (Narodna Galerija)
Park Ajdovščina
Miklošičev Park
DALMATINOVA
KOMENSKEGA ULICA
VIDOVDANSKA
ŠTEFANOVA ULICA
Neobotidnik
CANKARJEVA CESTA
PREŠERNOVA CESTA
BEETHOVNOVA
Opera House
NAZORJEVA ULICA
Church of the Annunciation
Dragon Bridge
TOMSIČEVA
ČOPOVA ULICA
TRUBARJEVA CESTA
PETKOVŠKOVO NABREŽJE
Ljubljanica
ADAMIČ-LUNDROVO NABREŽJE
National Museum (Narodni Muzej)
PREŠERNOV TRG
WOLFOVA ULICA
Seminary
Market
VODNIKOV TRG
Triple Bridge
Colonnade
TRG REPUBLIKE
ŠUBIČEVA ULICA
St Nicholas' Cathedral
Cankarjev Dom
KONGRESNI TRG
MESTNI TRG
Bishops Palace
KREKOV TRG
Slovene Philharmonic
RIBJI TRG
CANKARJEVO NABREŽJE
Town Hall
RAZGLEDNA STEZA
Funicular
ERJAVČEVA CESTA
Ursuline Church
VEGOVA UL.
DVORNI TRG
University Building
Ljubljana Castle
GREGORČIČEVA ULICA
ŽIDOVSKI STEZA
Shoemakers Bridge
MAČJA STEZA
National & University Library (NUK)
GOSPOSKA UL.
RIMSKA CESTA
NOVI TRG
GRAJSKI DREVORED
ULICA NA GRAD
OSOJNA STEZA
TRG FRANCOSKE REVOLUCIJE
GALLUSOVO NABREŽJE
BREG
STARI TRG
LEVSTIKOV TRG
GORNJI TRG
AŠKERČEVA CESTA
St Florian's Church
Križanke
City Museum (Mestni Muzej)
Jakopič Garden
ZOISOVA CESTA
St James' Church
KARLOVŠKA CESTA
MIRJE
Old Town Wall
EMONSKA ULICA
VRTNA
Gruber Palace
KRAKOVO
REČNA
Ljubljanica
TRNOVO
KARUNOVA ULICA
LJUBLJANA
EATING
Ajdovo Zrno 9
Café Antico 22
Cantina Mexicana 12
Emonska klet 15
Figovec 5
Foculus 21
Gostilna Šestika 6
Julija 20
Le Petite Café 23
Pizzeria Šestinka 4
Romeo 19
Tomato 14
DRINKING & NIGHTLIFE
As 10
Conestoga Culture Bar 8
Cutty Sark 13
Gajo Jazz Café 11
K4 2
Kavarna Maček 17
Kavarna Pr'Skelet 16
KUD Prešeren 24
Metelkova mesto 3
Orto Bar 1
Top 7
Vinoteka Movia 18
ACCOMMODATION
Alibi Hostel I
Alibi M14 D
Antiq Hotel J
BIT Center G
Celica Youth Hostel A
Dijaški Dom Ivana Cankarja H
Dijaški Dom Tabor B
Emonec F
Fluxus Hostel E
Park Hostel C

green and grey brickwork of the **National University Library**, arguably Plečnik's greatest work. The **Illyrian Monument** on Trg Francoske revolucije was erected in 1930 in belated recognition of Napoleon's short-lived attempt to create a fiefdom of the same name centred on Ljubljana. Virtually next door is the seventeenth-century monastery complex of **Križanke**, originally the seat of a thirteenth-century order of Teutonic Knights.

Museums west of Slovenska

The town's cultural quarter boasts a neat collection of museums and galleries. The grand **National Museum** (daily 10am–6pm, Thurs till 8pm; €5; Ⓦwww.narmuz-lj.si), at Prešernova cesta 20, features a comprehensive archeological display and interesting temporary exhibitions. The building also houses the **Natural History Museum** (same hours and ticket), notable for having the only complete mammoth skeleton found in Europe. **The National Gallery** at Prešernova cesta 24 (Tues–Sun 10am–6pm; €7) is rich in local medieval Gothic work, although most visitors gravitate towards the halls devoted to the Slovene Impressionists, and in particular the outstanding works by Ivan Grohar and Rihard Jakopič. Diagonally across from here the **Museum of Modern Art** at Cankarjeva cesta 15 (Tues–Sun 10am–6pm; Ⓦwww.mg-lj.si) flaunts the more experimental styles of the twentieth century.

Tivoli Park

Beyond the galleries lies **Tivoli Park**, an expanse of lawns and tree-lined walkways backed by dense woodland, perfect for a short ramble. A villa above the centre contains the most enjoyable of Ljubljana's museums, the **National Museum of Contemporary History** (Tues–Sun 10am–6pm; €3.50) with dioramas, video screens and period music combining to produce an evocative journey through Slovenia's conflict-riddled twentieth-century history, including both world wars and the struggle for independence in 1991.

Arrival and information

Air Brnik airport is 23km north of the city, and connected by hourly buses (40min; €5). Taxis should cost around €35–40; ask for a meter.

Train and bus stations Both located side-by-side on Trg Osvobodilne fronte, a short walk north of the centre.

Tourist office The Slovenian Tourist Information Centre (STIC) is at Krekov trg 10 (daily 8am–7/9pm; Ⓣ01/306-4575), with the main Ljubljana Tourist Information Office (TIC) in the Old Town on Adamič Lundrovo Nabrežje 2, next to the Triple Bridge (daily 8am–7/9pm; Ⓣ01/306-1215, Ⓦwww.visitljubljana.si); there's another branch at the train station (daily 8/10am–7/10pm; Ⓣ01/433-9475).

Discount passes The Ljubljana Tourist Card (€12.52), available from all the above tourist offices, entitles you to three days' unlimited travel on the city's public bus network, and discounted entrance fees to selected museums, galleries and restaurants.

Walking Tours The Ljubljana Tourist Information Office organizes a range of pleasant walking tours (April–Sept; €10) around the Old Town.

City transport

City transport Ljubljana's buses are cheap and frequent; you pay on the bus – put your money in a box next to the driver (€1.25 per journey) – or buy tokens (*žetoni*; €0.80) in advance from post offices and most newspaper kiosks.

Bikes A delightful way to see the city on warmer days; rent them from the STIC for €5/day.

Accommodation

Early reservations are advised in the summer. Student residences are available in July and August only.

Hostels

Alibi Hostel Cankarjevo Nabrežje 27 Ⓣ01/251-1244, Ⓦwww.alibi.si. Large, youthful place right in the heart of the old town, with graffiti art on the walls and large communal spaces. Dorms €12, double from €15.

Alibi M14 Miklosiceva 14 Ⓣ01/232-2770, Ⓦwww.alibi.si. The smaller sister hostel to *Alibi*

Hostel is ideally located with lovely, modern double rooms. Dorms €12–20, doubles €15–30.

Celica Youth Hostel Metelkova 9 ⓣ01/430-1890, ⓦwww.hostelcelica.com. Brilliantly original hostel in a refurbished former military prison in the centre of Metelkova (the city's artistic hub), with bright dorms and two/three-bed "cells", each designed by a different architect or artist. Dorms €20, doubles €54.

Dijaški Dom Ivana Cankarja Poljanska cesta 26 ⓣ01/474-8600, ⓦwww.dic.si. The city's cheapest option – basic student dorms 10min walk east of Krekov trg. Dorms €9.

Dijaški Dom Tabor Vidovdanska 7 ⓣ01/234-8840, ⓔddtaborlj@guest.arnes.si. Busy student hostel, with adequate rooms and helpful staff. Dorms €10.

Fluxus Hostel Tomšičeva 4 ⓣ01/251-5760, ⓦwww.fluxus-hostel.com. Clean and bright hostel in a beautiful old building, with a friendly host and a more homely feel than most. Dorms €21.

Park Hostel Tabor 9 ⓣ01/300-2500, ⓦwww.hotelpark.si. Rather characterless hostel on the top floor of the drab high-rise hotel of the same name, though the views over the city are pretty special. Dorms €21, hotel doubles €130.

Hotels

Antiq Hotel Gornji trg 3 ⓣ01/421-3560, ⓦwww.antiqhotel.si. Charming, centrally located hotel decorated with period furniture. The budget rooms offer excellent value. Doubles €77–170.

BIT Center Litijska 57 ⓣ01/548-0055, ⓦwww.bit-center.net. Modern, functional rooms (€46) in a sports centre 2km east of the centre. Dorm beds also available (€15) and guests get a 50 percent discount on sports facilities. Buses #5, #9 and #13.

Emonec Wolfova 12 ⓣ01/200-1520, ⓦwww.hotel-emonec.com. In the heart of town, with immaculate, minimalist rooms (doubles €70) and an apartment sleeping 4 (€105).

Campsite

Ježica Dunajska 270 ⓣ01/568-3913, ⓦwww.ljubljanaresort.si. Pleasant site 5km north of the centre, which also has a few bungalows. Buses #6 or #8 from Slovenska cesta. €17 per person.

Eating

Ljubljana's Old Town boasts a tight concentration of restaurants to suit all budgets. The best choice for snacks are the many kiosks and stands near the stations and scattered elsewhere throughout town, selling *burek*, hot dogs and the local *gorenjska* sausages. There's a lively food market on Vodnikov trg. On summer evenings the cafés and bars of Ljubljana's Old Town spill out onto the streets, and a wander along the riverbanks will yield one enticing place after another.

Cafés

Café Antico Stari trg 27. Lovely Old Town hangout with a pleasantly dated ambience.

Le Petite Café Trg Francoske revolucije 4. Parisian-style café, ideal for a coffee and croissant during the day or a glass of wine in the evening.

Tomato Šubičeva ulica 2. Snazzy diner-café, serving cheap sandwiches and snacks. €2–8.

Restaurants

Ajdovo Zrno Trubarjeva 7. Excellent vegetarian canteen in a pleasant courtyard, with a self-service salad bar and daily specials like cannelloni, risotto or curry. 3-course lunch €6.

Cantina Mexicana Knafljev prehod. On a lively alleyway between Slovenska cesta and Wolfova ulica, this colourful restaurant serves reasonable Mexican dishes and fancy cocktails. Fajitas €10.

Emonska klet Plečnikov trg 1. The food at this capacious cellar (formerly the halls of the Ursuline convent) is often secondary to live music and a cracking bar. Just off Slovenska cesta. 3-course lunch €6.

Figovec Gosposvetska 1. Charmingly rustic restaurant specializing in horseflesh steaks and traditional Slovene standards. More expensive than most, but with good reason. €15.

Foculus Gregorčičeva 3. Warm colours and leaf prints create an autumnal backdrop to the cheap pizza and salad options. €5–7.

Gostilna Šestika Slovenska cesta 40. Highly recommended for its generous portions of traditional Slovenian home-style cooking. Plenty of sausages, schnitzels and fish. Mains from €7.

Julija Stari trg 9. First-rate place with a simple Mediterranean menu and a lovely Old Town location. €8–10.

Pizzeria Šestinka Miklošičeva cesta 22. Giant slices of thin-crust pizza to eat in or take away for just €1.50. Open 9am–midnight.

Romeo Stari trg 6. Standing obediently opposite *Julija*, this stylish place serves up Mexican burritos, salads and stirfries until late. €5–9

Drinking and nightlife

The informative free English-language magazine *Ljubljana Life* (ⓦwww.ljubljanalife.com), available

from the tourist offices, contains bar and club listings.

Bars

Conestoga Culture Bar Trubarjeva 43. Arty little café-bar with great breakfasts, board games for lazy afternoons, and good music in the evenings, including electro DJs, live rock bands and open-mic sessions.

Cutty Sark Knafljev prehod 1. English pub with draught beers and a raucous atmosphere.

Kavarna Maček Krojaška 5. Lively and laid-back riverside café-bar with large outdoor terrace.

Kavarna Pr'Skelet Ključavničarska ulica 5. Cavernous themed bar with swinging skeletons and doors hidden in bookcases. 2-for-1 cocktails all night make the outdoor terrace the best value on the riverfront.

Vinoteka Movia Mestni trg 1. Cosy little bar that's the best place in the city to sample Slovenia's exceptional wines.

Clubs and venues

As Čopova 5 (entrance on Knafljev prehod). Resident DJs turn the cellar below this upmarket restaurant into a bouncing dancefloor on weekends.

Gajo Jazz Club Beethovnova 8. Suitably refined and atmospheric venue for the genre, with quality live offerings.

K4 Kersnikova 4. Stalwart of Ljubljana's alternative scene, offering varied music, and gay nights every Sun.

KUD Prešeren Karunova 14. Superb gig venue that also hosts regular literary events, workshops and art exhibitions.

Metelkova mesto Metelkova cesta Ⓦwww.metelkova.org. Ljubljana's alternative cultural mecca, consisting of a cosmopolitan cluster of clubs and bars, is located in the former army barracks next to the *Celica* youth hostel.

Orto Bar Grablovičeva 1. Loud and groovy bar-cum-club east of the train station with pumping disco tunes and frequent live-rock evenings.

Top Slovenska cesta (top of the Nama department store). Take a glass elevator up to this fashionable rooftop disco with excellent views of the Old Town.

Entertainment

The free monthly pamphlet, available from tourist offices, has complete listings.

Cankarjev Dom Prešernova cesta 10 Ⓣ01/241-7300, Ⓦwww.cd-cc.si. The city's cultural headquarters, hosting major orchestral and theatrical events, as well as folk and jazz concerts.

International Summer Festival Ⓣ01/241-6026, Ⓦwww.festival-lj.si, July to mid-Sept. Features orchestral concerts at major venues.

National Opera and Ballet Theatre Župančičeva 1 Ⓣ01/241-1740, Ⓦwww.opera.si. The impressive nineteenth-century neo-Renaissance building stages contemporary and classical works.

Shopping

BTC City Šmartinska 152. Massive shopping centre on the northeastern fringes of the capital. Buses #2, #7 and #12.

Flea Market Cankarjevo Nabrežje. Local handicraft stalls along the eastern riverbank (Sun 8am–1pm).

Kod & Kam Trg Francoske revolucije 4. Best place to go for maps, including specialist hiking and sailing prints.

Directory

Embassies and consulates Australia, Dunajska cesta 50 Ⓣ01/425-4252; Canada, TRG Republike 3 Ⓣ01/252-4444; Ireland, Palaca Kapitelj, Poljanski nasip 6 Ⓣ01/300-8970; UK, Trg Republike 3 Ⓣ01/200-3910; US, Prešernova 31 Ⓣ01/200-5500.

Exchange At the train station and *Menjalnica* on Pogaršarjev trg.

Hospital Bohoričeva 4 Ⓣ01/232-3060.

Internet Cybercafe Xplorer, Petkovškovo Nabrežje 23 (daily 10am/2pm–10pm); Cyber Café, Slovenska 10 (Mon–Sat 7/11am–11pm/midnight); Slovenian Tourist Information Centre, Krekov trg 10 (daily 8am–7/9pm).

Laundry Chemo-express, Wolfova 12 (Mon–Fri 7am–6pm).

Left luggage At the train station (€2/day).

Pharmacy Prisojne 7 Ⓣ01/230-6230 (24hr).

Post office Slovenska 32 and Trg Osvobodilne fronte 5.

Moving on

Train Divača (hourly; 1hr 30min); Koper (3 daily; 2hr 30min); Maribor (hourly; 1hr 45min–2hr 30min); Postojna (hourly; 1hr); Ptuj (3 daily; 2hr 30min).

Bus Bled (hourly; 1hr 15min); Bohinj (hourly; 2hr); Bovec (4 daily; 4hr 15min); Divača (8 daily; 1hr 30min); Kobarid (3 daily; 3hr 30min); Koper (8 daily; 2hr); Maribor (7 daily; 3hr 45min); Piran (8 daily; 2hr 40min); Portorož (8 daily; 2hr 30 min); Postojna (hourly; 1hr).

Southwest Slovenia

Not to be missed while you're in Ljubljana is a visit to either the **Postojna** or **Škocjan caves** – both spectacular, and both easily manageable either as a day-trip from the capital or en route south to Slovene Istria, to Croatia or to Italy. A trip easily combined with the caves is to **Predjama Castle**, near Postojna, an atmospherically sombre castle craftily etched into the karst landscape. On the small stretch of Adriatic coastline are a number of charismatic towns, heavily influenced by a legacy of Venetian rule. Of these, **Piran** is by far the most rewarding, its fishing-village charm and gorgeous architecture contrasting starkly with the brash modernity of neighbouring **Portorož**.

POSTOJNA

Hourly trains run the 65km route from Ljubljana to **POSTOJNA**, but as the walk to the caves is shorter from the bus stop, most people opt for this mode of transport. Once in the town, signs direct you to the **caves** (May–Sept daily 9am–5/6pm; Oct-April daily 10am–3/4pm; tours every 1–2hr; €20). Inside, a railway whizzes you through a host of preliminary systems before the guided 1.5km walking tour starts. The vast and fantastic jungles of rock formations are quite breathtaking, while the 40m high "concert hall" makes for a suitably climactic finale. Consider bringing a jacket and appropriate footwear; the air inside the caves is decidedly chilly. Private rooms in Postojna town can be arranged by Kompas, Titov trg 2a (Mon–Fri 8am–7pm, Sat 9am–1pm; ⓣ05/721-1480, ⓦwww.kompas-postojna.si; from €20 per person). *Hostel Proteus* (Trzaska Cesta 36, ⓣ05/726-1336) has basic dorms (€13).

PREDJAMA CASTLE

7km northwest of the caves, but not served by public transport, is **Predjama Castle** (daily 9/10am–4/6pm; tours every 1–2hrs; €8). Pushed up high against a cave entrance in the midst of the dramatic karst landscape, this sixteenth-century castle is an impressive sight and affords excellent views of the surrounding countryside. Its damp and rather melancholy interior is less rewarding, though there are a few interesting exhibits from this and an earlier castle that stood nearby. The easiest way to get here is to rent bikes from the *Hotel Sport* at Kolodvorska 1 in Postojna (€10 per day).

ŠKOCJAN CAVES

Much less visited (but arguably more enchanting) than Postojna, the **Škocjan Caves** are a stunning system of echoing chambers, secret passages and collapsed valleys carved out by the Reka River, which begins its journey some 50km south near the Croatian border. Daily **tours** (June–Sept hourly, 10am–5pm; Oct–May 2–3 daily, 10am–3pm; €14) take you through several stalactite-infested chambers and halls, before you reach the breathtaking **Murmuring Cave**, reputedly the world's largest subterranean canyon. To get here, take one of the two daily shuttle-buses from Divača train station (free with valid train tickets, check ⓦwww.slo-zeleznice.si for timetable information). If you need to stay, try the rooms in *Gostilna Malovec* (Kraška cesta 30a; ⓣ05/763-1225; doubles €40), in Divača.

PORTOROŽ

Easily reached by bus from the train terminus in Koper, **PORTOROŽ** ("Port of Roses") sprawls at the beginning of a long, tapering peninsula that projects like a lizard's tail north into the Adriatic. Popular since the end of the nineteenth century for its mild climate and the health-inducing properties of its salty

mud baths, the resort is now a vibrant strip of high-rise hotels and glitzy casinos. The main "beach" is in fact just a continuation of the concrete promenade, and there's not a great deal of culture here, though the town's modernity and buzzing nightlife are unrivalled on this stretch of the coast.

The **tourist office** (daily: July & Aug 9am–9pm; Sept–June 9/10am–5/7pm; ⓣ05/674-2220, ⓦwww.portoroz.si) is on the main coastal strip, Obala Maršala Tita, just down from the bus terminal. The *Panorama Residence* is a new **hostel** located halfway between Portorož and Piran with lovely views of the Istrian coast (Šentjane 25, ⓣ04/075-2660, dorms €14, rooms €23). Tourist Service Portorož (ⓣ05/674-0360), near the bus station, offers good-value private rooms (from €20 per person), or there's the three-star *Camp Lucija* (ⓣ05/690-6000 ⓦwww.metropol-resort.com, €16; April–Sept) just beyond the Marina to the south of Portorož.

Restaurants in Portorož can be pricey; *Kakadu* on Obala Maršala Tita is the best budget option, offering pizza, pasta and fish dishes for €7. The bamboo-clad *Alayah* on the main beachfront is a popular, laid-back spot for a drink; try the *Paprika* club on the same strip for cocktails and late-night dancing.

PIRAN

PIRAN, at the tip of the peninsula, 4km from Portorož, couldn't be more different. Its web of arched alleys, tightly packed ranks of houses and little Italianate squares is delightful. The centre, 200m around the harbour from the bus station, is **Tartinijev trg**, named after the eighteenth-century Italian violinist and composer Giuseppe Tartini, who was born in a house on the square (you can visit during irregular opening hours, ask at the Tourinform office) and is commemorated by a weather-beaten bronze statue in the centre. With its striking oval-shape, it's one of the loveliest squares on this coast, fringed by a mix of Venetian palaces and a grand-looking Austrian town hall. From the square's eastern edge, follow Rozmanova ulica all the way up to the barn-like Baroque **Church of Sv Jurij**, crowning a commanding spot on the far side of Piran's peninsula.

TREAT YOURSELF

Exploit Portorož's historical reputation as a healing centre to the full with a trip to the extravagant **Terme & Wellness Palace**, Obala 33 (ⓣ05/692-9001, ⓦwww.lifeclass.net). Four hours in the 1000-square-metre sauna park (daily 2–9pm) – complete with ice cave – costs €20–25, while there's also an exhaustive selection of pricey spa treatments to choose from.

Arrival and information

Bus station. On Cankarjevo nabrežje, a 5min seafront walk from the main square, Tartinijev trg.
Tourist office Tartinijev trg ⓣ05/673-0220. July & Aug daily 9am–1.30pm & 3–9pm; Sept–June Mon–Fri 9am–5pm & Sat 10am–2pm.

Accommodation

Private rooms can be booked through Maona, at Cankarjevo nabrežje 7, between the bus station and the square (ⓣ05/673-4520, ⓦwww.maona.si; €20–60).
Alibi Hostels Bonifacijeva 11 & 14, & Trubarjeva 60 ⓣ03/136-3666, ⓦwww.alibi.si. Three old houses, each room decorated with a theme from a different region, town or attraction in Slovenia. Dorms €15, rooms €25.
Fiesa Camping Fiesa 57b ⓣ05/674-6230. Decent site 1km past the church. €10 per person.
Hostel Val Gregorčičeva 38a ⓣ05/673-2555, ⓦwww.hostel-val.com. Friendly and well-run, with a guesthouse feel and a delightful restaurant. Rooms €20–25.

Eating and drinking

Though a pleasant drinking spot, things quieten down fairly early in Piran. For a big night out, head

over to Portorož, where the beachside discos stay open until dawn.

Batana Kidričevo nabrežje. A simple pizzeria with pleasant terrace. Pizza €6.

Café Teater St Jenkova 1. Sophisticated cocktail bar overlooking the harbour.

Da Noi Prešernovo nabrežje. Popular, cellar-like bar on the seafront; open later than most.

Riva Gregorčičeva 35. One of the more romantic seafront restaurants, serving tasty meat and fresh fish dishes. €7–20.

Moving on

Bus Ljubljana (7–10 daily; 2hr 40min); Portorož/Koper (every 20min; 10/40min); Trieste (Mon–Sat 5 daily; 1hr).

Northwest Slovenia

Within easy reach of Ljubljana are the stunning mountain lakes of **Bled** and **Bohinj**. The magnificent **Soča valley**, on the western side of the Slovene Alps, is much less touristed, and small towns like **Kobarid** and **Bovec** make excellent bases for hiking and adventure sports.

GETTING TO THE LAKES

Buses are the easiest way to get to the lakes (hourly from Ljubljana; 1hr 15min to Bled, 2hr to Bohinj). Direct **train** access to the region is via the main northbound line from Ljubljana (hourly; 40min–1hr; €4), which calls at Bled-Lesce, from where regular buses run to the lake. Trains on the Jesenice-Nova Gorica branch call at both Bled Jezero (5min walk from the northwest corner of Bled) and Bohinjska Bistrica (7 daily). An old-fashioned steam train also sporadically plies the same route, providing a wonderful scenic option as it chugs steadily through the mountains towards Italy (see Ⓦwww.slo-zeleznice.si; €10).

HIKING

The tourist offices in Bled and Ribčev Laz can advise about hiking routes around the lakes, and recommend guides for climbing **Mount Triglav**. The hike to the summit (Slovenia's tallest peak at 2863m) and back takes two to three days and can be daunting, particularly if weather conditions deteriorate, but the views are magnificent.

BLED

The lake resort of **BLED** has all the right ingredients for a memorable visit – a placid mirror lake with a romantic island, a medieval cliff-top castle and a backdrop of snow-capped mountains. In summer, the lake forms the setting for a whole host of watersports – including major rowing contests – and in winter the surface becomes a giant fairy-tale skating rink. Perhaps the most visited place outside of the capital, Bled manages to retain a magical calm despite the hordes of tourists.

What to see and do

A constant relay of stretched gondolas leaves from below the *Park Hotel*, the *Pension Mlino*, and the bathing resort below the castle, ferrying tourists back and forth to Bled's picturesque **island** (€12 return). With an early start (and by renting your own rowing boat from the Castle Boat House for about €10 per hour) you can beat them to it. Crowning the island, the Baroque **Church of Sv Marika Božja** is the last in a line of churches on a spot that's long held religious significance: under the present building lie remains of a pre-Roman temple. From the north shore a couple of crooked paths run uphill to **Bled Castle** (daily 8am–6/8pm; €7), originally an eleventh-century fortification whose present appearance dates from the seventeenth; the museum, containing local artefacts, is pretty dull, but the

lovely courtyard affords magnificent views across the lake and towards the Alps. Bikes can be rented cheaply from most guesthouses and tour agencies, providing an excellent way to see the surrounding area; the circumference of the lake can be cycled in thirty minutes. There are bathing areas in the southwest and northeast corners of the lake, both with grassy expanses for sunbathing.

Vintgar Gorge

The main attraction in the outlying hills is the **Vintgar Gorge** (May–Oct daily 8am–7pm; €4), 4km north of town, an impressive defile accessed via a series of wooden walkways and bridges suspended from the rock face. To get here, take the morning bus (10am) to the village of Zasip, climb to the hilltop chapel of **Sv Katarina** and pick up a path through the forest to the gorge entrance.

Arrival and information

Train Trains from Ljubljana stop at Bled-Lesce, 4km southeast of Bled itself and connected to the town by regular buses. Trains from Soča Valley arrive in Bled Jezero, 5 mins walk from the western shore.
Bus station 5 mins walk northeast of the lake on Grajska cesta.
Tourist office Cesta svobode 10, opposite the *Park Hotel* ⓣ 04/574-1122, ⓦ www.bled.si. Mon–Sat 8am–6/9pm, Sun 9/11am–1/5pm.

Accommodation

Private rooms are available through Kompas in the shopping centre at Ljubljanska 4 (ⓣ 04/572-7501, ⓦ www.kompas-bled.si).
Bled campsite Kidričeva 10 ⓣ 04/575-2000, ⓦ www.camping-bled.com. Beautifully located amid the pines at the western end of the lake, this family-friendly campsite features first-rate facilities. €12.50 per person.
Pension Bledec Grajska 17 ⓣ 04/574-5250, ⓦ www.youth-hostel-bledec.si. This hostel offers spacious and homely dorms and double rooms, decked out with traditional furniture. Free bike rental. Dorms €19, rooms €25.
Travellers Haven Riklijeva cesta 1 ⓣ 04/139-6545, ⓦ www.travellers-haven.com. The friendliest hostel in Bled, with tastefully furnished dorms, a homely kitchen-cum-common area, and free bike rental and laundry facilities. Dorms €20.

Eating and drinking

The best places for eating are in the hillside area between Bled's bus station and castle, though most pensions on the lake's perimeter offer decent food too. Bizarrely, the shopping centre on Ljubljanska is home to a few popular bars.
George Best Bar Grajska 21. Laid-back pub with a pleasant terrace, just past the Pension Bledec.
Gostilna Pri Planincu Grajska 8. Serves up solid Slovene home cooking, plus plenty of pizzas and pasta. Mains €10.
Jasmin Cesta svobode. Next door to the tourist office, this sophisticated café has a good range of specialist teas, cakes and cocktails for after dark.

LAKE BOHINJ

From Bled hourly buses make the 25km trip through the verdant, mist-laden Sava Bohinjka Valley to **Lake Bohinj**. In appearance and character Lake Bohinj is utterly different from Bled: the lake crooks a narrow finger under the wild mountains, evergreen woods slope gently down to the water, and in the relative absence of visitors compared to Bled, a lazy stillness hangs over all.

Ribčev Laz

RIBČEV LAZ (referred to as Jezero on bus timetables), at the eastern end of the lake, is where most facilities are based. **Walking trails** lead round both sides of the lake (the 12km circumference can be walked in 3 hours), or north onto the eastern shoulders of the Triglav range. One route leads north from Stara Fužina into the Voje valley, passing through the dramatic **Mostnica Gorge**, a popular local beauty spot.

Ukanc, Mount Vogel and the Valley of the Seven Lakes

About 5km from Ribčev Laz at the western end of the lake is the hamlet of **UKANC** (sometimes referred to as Zlatorog), where a **cable car** (daily 7am–6pm, every 30min; closed Nov; €13

return) whizzes you up to the summit of **Mount Vogel** (1540m) in no time – if the Alps look dramatic from the lakeside, from Vogel's summit they're breathtaking. Ukanc is also the starting point for a 45-minute walk north to the photogenic **Savica Waterfalls** (April–Oct 8am–8pm; €2.40). From here, the serious hiking can commence, either as a day-trip to the **Valley of the Seven Lakes** – an area strewn with eerie boulders and hardy firs – or as an expedition to scale Mount Triglav itself (see p.1056).

Arrival and information

Train Trains on the Jesenice-Nova Gorica line call at Bohinjska Bistrica (4km from Bohinj lake, connected by two morning shuttle buses; June–Oct).

Bus Buses from Ljubljana and Bled stop outside the tourist office in Ribčev Laz, terminating in Ukanc on the southwestern corner of the lake.

Tourist information Ribčev Laz 48 Ⓣ04/574-6010, Ⓦwww.bohinj.si. The excellent centre is 50m from the lake, next to the Mercator supermarket. July & Aug daily 8am–8pm; Sept–June Mon–Sat 8am–6pm, Sun 9am–3pm.

Accommodation

The tourist office offers a plentiful choice of private rooms and apartments (Ⓦwww.bohinj-info.com) around Ribčev Laz and in the idyllic villages of Stara Fužina and Studor, 1km and 2.5km north respectively.

Backpackers Hostel Studor 13, Srednja vas Ⓣ03/146-6707. Housed in a 200 year-old renovated building in the centre of Triglav National Park, offering photography courses and horseriding amongst other activities. Free pick-up from Bohinj. Dorms €25, Doubles €50.

Hostel Pod Voglom Ribčev Laz Ⓣ04/572-3461 Ⓦwww.hostel-podvoglom.com. Part of the PAC adventure sports complex, this hostel has basic facilities, located right on the lake; organizes winter and summer activities. Dorms €17.

Zlatorog Ukanc 2 Ⓣ04/572-3482. Pleasant campsite on the western tip of the lake; a good base for trips up the mountains. €11 per person.

Eating and drinking

Center Next to the tourist office, this place is better than most of the standard pizzerias by the lake at Ribčev Laz. Pizza €5–7.

POD Outdoor bar-restaurant 5 mins' walk east of town along Ribčev Laz, offering grilled meats and pizzas. Mains €7.

THE SOČA VALLEY

On the other, less touristy side of the mountains from Bohinj, the **River Soča** slices through the western spur of the Julian Alps, running parallel with the Italian border. During World War I, the Soča marked the front line between the Italian and Austro-Hungarian armies; now memorial chapels and abandoned fortifications are nestled incongruously amidst awesome Alpine scenery. The valley is also a major centre for activity-based tourism, with the foaming, emerald river providing ideal **rafting** and **kayaking** conditions throughout the spring and summer, and the mountain slopes perfect for **skiing** and **snowboarding** in winter. The main tourist centres are **Kobarid** and **Bovec**, both small towns boasting a range of walking possibilities. The 1:50,000 *Zgornje Posočje* **map** covers trails in the region.

Kobarid

It was at the little Alpine town of **KOBARID** that German and Austrian troops finally broke through Italian lines in 1917, almost knocking Italy out of World War I in the process. The **Kobarid Museum**, Gregorčičeva 10

GETTING TO THE SOČA VALLEY

Four daily buses (3hr) travel from Ljubljana. Approaching the Soča valley from the Bled-Bohinj area involves catching one of ten daily trains from Bohinjska Bistrica to **Most na Soči** (40min; €2), where five buses daily run onwards up the valley. Getting here from the coast is an arduous task: from Koper, several bus changes are required to reach Kobarid, and expect a journey of 5–7hr.

(daily 9/10am–5/6/7pm; €5), presents a thoughtful account of the 29 months of fighting in the region through a collection of photographs, maps and mementoes. On Kobarid's main square, a processional way leads up to a three-tiered **Italian War Memorial**, opened by Benito Mussolini in 1938, from where you can enjoy views of the surrounding Alps. This also marks the start of the Kobarid historical trail, a five-kilometre loop where remote woodland paths are punctuated by forgotten wartime landmarks. Maps of the trail are available from the tourist office on Trg Svobode 16 (daily 9am–7pm, closed weekends in winter; ⓣ05/380-0490). At the trail's farthest point from town bubbles the **Kozjak waterfall** (40min walk), less impressive for its height than for the cavern-like space that it has carved out of the surrounding rock.

The tourist office can find **private rooms** (from €20) in Kobarid and surrounding villages, and there are two well-equipped **campsites**: the *Koren* (ⓣ05/389-1311, ⓦwww.kamp-koren.si; €10); and the *Lazar* (ⓣ05/388-5333, ⓦwww.lazar-sp.si; €11) – located on opposite banks of the River Soča, 500m out of town near the trail. Kobarid's excellent restaurants attract visitors across the border from Italy; *Kotlar* (Trg svobode 11) and *Topli Val* (Trg svbode 1) are generally regarded amongst the country's top **restaurants**, though if you're on a tight budget, try the pizzas at *Fedrig* on Volaričeva 11.

Moving on

Bus Bovec (5 daily; 40min); Ljubljana (3–4 daily; 4hr); Nova Gorica (3 daily; 1hr 15min).

Bovec

25km up the valley from Kobarid, the village of **BOVEC** straggles between imperious mountain ridges. Thanks to its status as a winter ski resort, it has a greater range of accommodation options and sporting agencies than Kobarid, and as a result, a more vibrant atmosphere. The quickest route into the mountains from here is provided by the **gondola** that departs on the hour 1km south of the village (June–Sept 8am–3pm; €11.50 return), which ascends to the pasture-cloaked Mount Kanin over to the west.

The **tourist office** is around the corner from the bus stop at Trg Golobarskih žrtev 8 (July & Aug daily 8.30am–8.30pm; Sept–June Mon–Fri 9am–5pm, Sat & Sun 9am–noon; ⓣ05/389-6444, ⓦwww.bovec.si), and can help with renting private **rooms**. Europe's first sustainable outdoor **hostel**, *Eco Camp Adrenaline* (12km from Bovec, free pickup; ⓣ04/138-3662, ⓦwww.adrenaline-check.com; camping & dorms €15) offers double tents sheltered under individual wooden constructions right on the river. They also have a 10-bed dorm, host nightly BBQs and can organize all forms of adventure sports. The best place to **eat** around the main square is *Stari Kovai*, at Rupa 3, with a long list of inexpensive pizzas alongside the usual schnitzels.

ADVENTURE SPORTS

In Kobarid the main **rafting** company is X-Point (ⓣ05/388-5308, ⓦwww.xpoint.si), just north of Trg svobode at Stresova 1; they also organize paragliding and kayaking. Rafting trips cost €37. Popular outfits in Bovec include Bovec Rafting Team (ⓣ05/388-6128, ⓦwww.bovec-rafting-team.com), located in a small hut a few minutes' walk from the main square, and Soča Rafting (ⓣ05/389-6200, ⓦwww.socarafting.si), opposite the tourist office at Trg Golobarskih zrtev 14.

Eastern Slovenia

The lush landscapes to the east of Ljubljana – where many of the country's most reputable vineyards are concentrated – have generally been less explored by travellers. But as host to Slovenia's second city, **Maribor**, and oldest settlement, **Ptuj**, which lie on the main routes to Austria and Hungary respectively, the region can reward the passing visitor with its rich historical heritage, traditional culture and passion for fine wine.

MARIBOR

Located 130km northeast of Ljubljana, **MARIBOR** is perched snugly on the Drava river between hillside vineyards and the Pohorje mountain range. Though beset by war and occupation, the old town's beautiful architecture preserves myriad historical and cultural influences, and the nightlife is unrivalled outside of Ljubljana.

What to see and do

Maribor's main attractions are condensed in a pedestrianized centre. Looming over Trg Svobode, the imposing, late nineteenth-century red-bricked **St Mary's Franciscan church** (daily 6am–noon & 3–7.45pm) catches the eye first. Opposite the church, **Maribor Castle** houses the regional museum (Tues–Sat 9am–4pm, Sun 9am–2pm; ⓣ02/228-3551; €3). Nearby you can foray into the labyrinth of underground catacombs that make up the **Vinag Wine Cellar** (open by prior arrangement only; ⓣ02/220-8114), stopping to sample some of the acclaimed vintages. On the western fringe of the pedestrianized zone sits the photogenic **Slomškov trg**, a serene, leafy opening surrounded by a few landmarks, including the university building and **National Theatre** (ⓣ02/250-6100). Opposite the university, and mimicking its distinct yellow colour, is the sixteenth-century gothic **Cathedral Church**, with a bell tower that offers fantastic views to the edges of the city and beyond (daily 7am–6pm; free). South of Slomškov, another charming square, **Glavni trg**, epitomizes the hopscotch architectural styles of the city. Its centrepiece is the mournful **Plague Memorial**, erected after the deadly disease wiped out around a fifth of the town's population in the seventeenth century.

WINE TASTING

Maribor is one of the Podrevje region's six wine-producing areas, and a tasting trip along any of the three wine roads surrounding the city makes for a very pleasant afternoon; the tourist office rents bikes for €5 per day and provides excellent cycling maps with the routes and wineries clearly marked.

Lent

Between Glavni and the river, the streets become narrow and uneven, as you enter the oldest part of town, **Lent**, which hosts a myriad of open-air events during the Lent festival at the end of June each year, comprising two entertaining weeks of street theatre, dance performances and jazz, rock and classical concerts. It is here that the world's oldest productive vine, a protected national monument, grows majestically outside the **Old Vine House** (Tues–Sun 10am–6pm; free). Inside, a small exhibition complements the range of top-quality, reasonably priced vintages from the area.

Pohorje

Just a short bus ride (#6; €1) or cycle southwest from the centre is the sprawling **Pohorje** mountain range.

Take the hourly cable car (€7 return) up the slope, where – depending on the season – you can hike, mountain bike, horseride and ski, or simply sit and admire the glorious views of Maribor and the countryside surrounding it.

Arrival and information

Train station Partizanska cesta 50. Turn left out of the exit and the road curves directly into the town centre.
Bus station Mlinska ulica 1 (just off Partizanska cesta).
Tourist office Partizanska cesta 6a, opposite the Franciscan church ⓣ02/234-6611, ⓦwww.maribor-pohorje.si. Daily 9am–6/7pm.

Accommodation

The tourist office can help with booking private accommodation (from €20 per person).
Alibi C2 Cafova 2 ⓣ05/166-3555 ⓦwww.alibi.si. Another branch of the popular Ljubljana-based chain, in a large renovated villa near the train station. Dorms €18, doubles €45.
Camp Pohorje Pot k Mlinu 57 ⓣ02/614-0950. Open all year round, this well-equipped site also organizes a range of sporting activities on the nearby Pohorje Mountain. €6.70 per person.
Lollipop Hostel Maistrova ulica 17 ⓣ04/024-3160, ⓔlollipophostel@yahoo.com. Small, clean and friendly hostel 5 mins' walk from the centre with kitchen facilities and a homely common room. Free city tours given by the English owner. Dorms €20.
Hostel Uni Volkmerjev prehod 7 ⓣ02/250-6700, ⓦwww.termemb.si. Somewhat characterless but comfortable hotel right in the centre. All rooms have cable TV. Doubles €54.

Eating and drinking

The best bars are located in Lent, on the banks of the Drava.
Ancora Jurčičeva 7. This atmospheric bar-restaurant serves up giant portions of decent and affordable Mediterranean dishes. Mains €4–8.
KGB Vojašniški trg 5. The most popular joint in Maribor, this lively underground cellar bar attracts all ages, with live music most evenings.
Satchmo Jazz Club Strossmayerjeva ulica 6. Hosts high-calibre jazz and rock sessions; see ⓦwww.jazz-klub.si for programme.
Takos Mesarski prehod 3. Tucked away on a narrow alley, this colourful restaurant has all the usual Mexican staples, and a comprehensive cocktail list; transforms into a club on Fri & Sat.

Moving on

Train Ljubljana (10–12 daily; 2hr); Ptuj (8 daily; 1hr); Vienna (2 daily; 3hr 40min).
Bus Ljubljana (4–5 daily; 2hr 30min); Ptuj (every 30min; 40min).

PTUJ

PTUJ is arguably Slovenia's most attractive town, rising up from the Drava valley in a flutter of red roofs, and topped by a charming castle. The streets themselves are the main attraction, with scaled-down mansions standing shoulder-to-shoulder on scaled-down boulevards, medieval fantasies crumbling next to Baroque extravagances.

What to see and do

Ptuj's main street is **Prešernova ulica**, an attractive thoroughfare which snakes along the base of the castle-topped hill. At its eastern end is **Slovenski Trg**, home to a fine-looking sixteenth-century bell tower and the **Church of St George**, a building of twelfth-century origin festooned with numerous exceptional frescoes. From here Prešernova leads to the **Archeological Museum** (mid-April to Dec daily 10am–5/6pm; €4), housed in what was once a Dominican monastery, gutted in the eighteenth century and now hung with spidery decoration, and worth a look for the carvings and statuary around its likeably dishevelled cloisters. At either end of Prešernova, cobbled paths wind up to the **castle**. An agglomeration of styles from the fourteenth to the eighteenth centuries, the castle was home to a succession of noble families, the most prominent of which were the Herbersteins, Austro–Slovene aristocrats who made their fortune in the Habsburg Empire's wars against the Turks.

Arrival and information

Train and bus stations Both on Osojnikova cesta, 5min walk northeast of town.

Tourist office Slovenski trg 5 ⓣ02/779-6011, ⓦwww.ptuj-tourism.si (daily 9am–6/8pm). The Centre for Free Time Activities (CID), near the bus station at Osojnikova 9 (Mon–Fri 9am–6pm, Sat 10am–1pm; ⓣ02/780-5540, ⓦwww.cid.si), can also provide friendly assistance, and free internet access.

Accommodation

Eva Jadranska ulica 20 ⓣ02/771-2441, ⓦwww.bikeek.si. Modern facilities and a spacious communal area make this place very good value. Reception is in an adjacent bike shop (bike rental €11 per day). Dorms €12, doubles €30.

Kurent Osojnikova cesta 9 ⓣ02/771-0814, ⓔyhptuj@csod.si. Large youth hostel offering tidy, four- and six-bed dorms with private bathrooms. €18.

Terme Ptuj Pot v Toplice ⓣ02/749-4580, ⓦwww.terme-ptuj.si. Across the river, 2km west of town, guests at this fabulous campsite can also use the Thermal Park pools and saunas. Camping €16 per person; four-person cottages €110.

Eating and drinking

Café Evropa Mestni trg. The liveliest venue for a drink, by day or night.

Kitajski Vrt Dravska ulica. Plush Chinese restaurant serving up giant sizzling plates of noodles, meat and vegetarian dishes. Mains €6.

Perutnina Ptuj (*Gostilna PP*) Novi trg 2. Cheap and cheerful, with a sunny terrace and filling daily specials for €5.

Ribič Dravska ulica 9. The exceptional seafood at this riverside restaurant justifies the slightly higher price tag. From €10.

Moving on

Train Budapest (2 daily; 6hr 15min); Ljubljana (2 daily; 2hr 30min); Maribor (7 daily; 1hr).

Bus Maribor (every 30min; 40min).

Spain

HIGHLIGHTS

MUSEO GUGGENHEIM, BILBAO: the building is as big an attraction as the art it houses
SAN SEBASTIÁN: stunning beaches and mouth-watering cuisine - the perfect pit stop
SANTIAGO DE COMPOSTELA: the end-point of Europe's most famous pilgrim trail
BARCELONA: perhaps Europe's most alluring city
PLAZA MAYOR, SALAMANCA: the finest square in a beautiful university city
MADRID: world-class museums and legendary nightlife
ALHAMBRA, GRANADA: evocative Moorish palace atop this charming Andalucian city

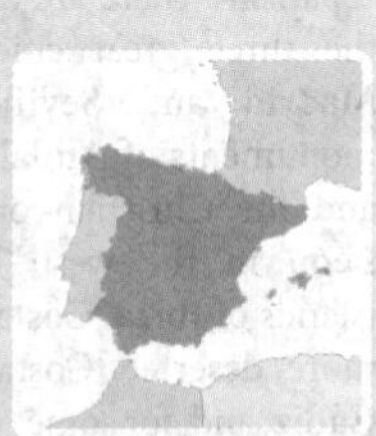

ROUGH COSTS

DAILY BUDGET Basic €50/occasional treat €70

DRINK €1.50–2.20 per caña (small beer)

FOOD Three-course menú del día €10

HOSTEL/BUDGET HOTEL €12–24/€20–45

TRAVEL Madrid–Barcelona (505km): bus €37–60, train €55–110

FACT FILE

POPULATION 46.7 million

AREA 504,030 sq km

LANGUAGE Spanish, Catalan

CURRENCY Euro (€)

CAPITAL Madrid

INTERNATIONAL PHONE CODE ⓣ34

Introduction

Spain has so much more to offer than the tourist brochure cliché of bullfights, crowded beaches, paella and flamenco. You don't have to travel for very long, or very far, to discover ancient castles, world-class museums, idyllic whitewashed villages, isolated coves and beaches, and a wealth of art and architecture. The separate kingdoms that made up the original Spanish nation remain very much in evidence and the sheer variety impresses, in a diversity of language, culture and tradition.

Of the regions, **Catalunya** in the northeast is vibrant and go-ahead; **Galicia** in the northwest a verdant rural idyll; the **Basque country** around Bilbao a remarkable contrast between post-industrial depression and unbridled optimism; and **Castilla y León** and the **south** still, somehow, quintessentially "Spanish". There are definite highlights: the three great cities of **Barcelona**, **Madrid** and **Seville**; the Moorish monuments of **Andalucía** in the south and the Christian ones of **Castilla y León** in the west; beachlife on the islands of **Ibiza**, **Costa del Sol** or on the more deserted Costa de la Luz near **Cádiz**; and, for some of the best trekking in Europe, the **Pyrenees**. The neighbouring independent state of **Andorra**, famed for its winter sports and duty-free shopping, is also covered in this chapter.

Spain can be visited all year round, depending on the destination, though Madrid and parts of Andalucía get unbearably hot in the summer as their residents flee for the coast. Depending on what you're after, you can party at numerous quirky local festivals, engage in all manner of outdoor pursuits, sample the seasonal and regional specialities, take in the splendid and varied architecture that traces Spain's multicultural heritage and partake in some of Europe's best nightlife.

CHRONOLOGY

1000 BC Phoenicians colonize the Iberian Peninsula, establishing the cities of Cádiz and Málaga.

400s BC Carthaginians exert power over large parts of present-day Spain.

200s BC The Romans capture "Hispania" during the Punic Wars.

711 AD The Islamic Moors conquer Spain, and Moorish culture flourishes.

1085 With the capture of Toledo, Spanish Christians begin to diminish the influence of the Moors in Spain.

1480 The Spanish Inquisition persecutes non-Christians, leading to mass conversions of Jews.

1492 Christopher Columbus discovers lands in the Americas for the Spanish Crown.

1605 The world's first "novel", *Don Quixote* by Cervantes, is published.

1714 The British capture Gibraltar.

1800s Spanish colonies in the Americas gain their independence.

1931 Surrealist artist Salvador Dalí completes his most famous painting, *The Persistence of Memory*.

1936 The Spanish Civil War breaks out as Nationalist forces led by General Franco defeat Republican forces.

1939 Spain remains neutral at the outbreak of World War II.

1975 Franco dies and is replaced by King Juan Carlos.

1977 First free elections are held in almost four decades.

2004 Bombs detonated on busy Madrid trains leave 191 people dead. An Islamic group takes responsibility.

2007 The government's struggle with Basque separatists, ETA, continues as the group end their ceasefire.

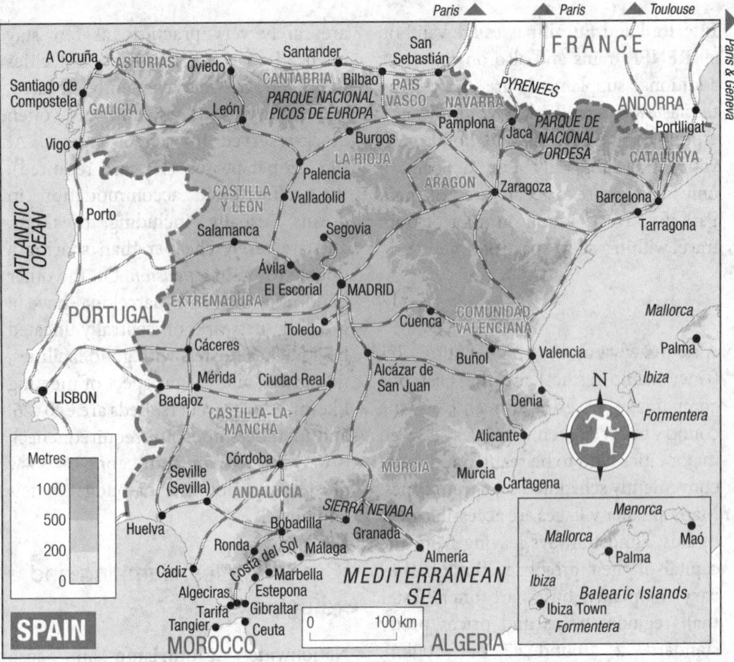

ARRIVAL

Getting to Spain is very straightforward. The quickest – and cheapest – way is on one of the budget-airline **flights** (try Iberia subsidiary Clickair as well as easyJet and Ryanair). All the major airlines serve Barcelona and Madrid. Other major airports include Alicante, Málaga, Valencia, Seville, the Balearic Islands and Gibraltar. **Trains** from France serve San Sebastían (from Biarritz), Barcelona (from Toulouse and Perpignan) and Girona (from Perpignan); while **trains** from Portugal run from Lisbon to Madrid via Cáceres and from Porto to Santiago de Compostela. **Ferries** also arrive in Bilbao and Santander from the UK, and regular ferries from Morocco serve the ports of Algeciras and Tarifa, among others.

GETTING AROUND

Spain's public transport is backpacker friendly, offering safe and efficient travel options. Whilst the high-speed trains are often more comfortable for longer journeys, they are also more expensive than buses.

By train

RENFE (Ⓦwww.renfe.es) operates three types of train: *cercanías* (red) are local commuter trains that service major cities; *media distancia* (orange) run between cities, and are equivalent to buses in speed and cost, while *larga distancia* express trains (long-distance; grey) include the private high-speed trains such as the *AVE* (Madrid–Zaragoza and Madrid–Seville), *Alaris* (Madrid–Valencia), *Altaria* (Madrid–Alicante) and *Euromed* (Barcelona–Alicante). To avoid queuing at the station, buy tickets from travel agents that display the RENFE sign, or online from the RENFE website and print the ticket out at the station using the code given. Return fares (*ida y vuelta*) often get a ten to twenty percent discount.

InterRail and **Eurail** passes are valid on all RENFE trains and also on *Euromed*; additional supplements are charged on the fastest trains. Book well in advance, especially at weekends and holidays. If you're travelling only around Spain, it only makes sense to get an Interrail Spain Pass if you're planning on a lot of train travel within a short space of time.

By bus

Alsa (Ⓦwww.alsa.es) and Auto Res (Ⓦwww.auto-res.net) are the best **bus** companies, covering much of the country between them. Services between major cities tend to be regular and more conveniently scheduled than train times. Many smaller villages are accessible only by bus, almost always leaving from the capital of their province. Though they vary in quality, buses are often faster than regional trains and prices pretty standard at around €7 per 100km. Frequency is drastically reduced on Sundays and holidays.

ACCOMMODATION

Simple, reasonably priced rooms (*habitaciones*) or beds (*camas*) are widely available in rural Spain, advertised in private houses or above bars, often with the phrase "*camas y comidas*" ("beds and meals"). In most towns, you'll be able to get a double for around €40, a single for €20 or so. Prices in popular areas often drop in low season.

Hotels and hostels

Hotels go by various names. Budget travellers are best sticking to *casas de huéspedes* (*CH*) and *pensiones* (*P*) – simple accommodation without breakfast. Slightly more expensive are **hostales** (*H*) and *hostal-residencias* (*HsR*), categorized from one to three stars; both are budget hotels and not to be confused with hostels. Youth **hostels** (*albergues juveniles*; Ⓦwww.reaj.com) are rarely very practical, as few stay open all year and in towns and cities they can be inconveniently located, suffer from curfews and are often block-reserved by school groups. At €12–25 per person (HI card required), they offer basic accommodation in dorms, usually including breakfast, and are rarely cheaper than sharing a double room in a *pensión*. On the other hand, Madrid and Barcelona have a growing network of centrally located **backpacker hostels** with good facilities, no curfew, and the prospect of meeting like-minded travellers. Beds are €20–26, and membership is not required: check Ⓦwww.hostelspain.com or Ⓦwww.hostels.com for lists of budget hotels and hostels.

Casas rurales, camping and refugios

Nationwide, **agroturismo** and **casa rural** programmes offer excellent cheap accommodation in rural areas. Tourist offices have full lists. There are hundreds of **campsites** throughout Spain, charging about €4 per person plus the same for a tent. The National Tourist Board has the free *Mapa de Campings* and the complete *Guía de Campings* (€6); also see Ⓦwww.vayacamping.net. In popular mountain areas you'll find *refugios* (mountain shelters) which comprise dorm-style accommodation and are on a first-come, first-served basis, typically costing €10–15 per night. Bring your own bedding and cooking equipment.

FOOD AND DRINK

Bars and cafés are best for **breakfast**, which can consist of *churros con chocolate* (long tubular doughnuts with thick drinking chocolate), *tostadas* (toast) *con aceite* (with oil) or *con mantequilla y mermelada* (butter and jam), or *tortilla* (omelette). **Coffee** and **pastries** are available at the many excellent

pastelerías and *confiterías*, while *bocadillos* (sandwiches filled with sliced meats, cheese or *tortilla*), are available everywhere. *Tabernas, tascas, bodegas, cervecerías* and bars all serve **tapas** or *pintxos*: mini portions of meat, fish, *tortilla* or salad for €1.30–3.50 a plate. Their big brothers, **raciones** (€5–12), make a sufficient meal in themselves. Good-value two- or three-course main meals (*cubierto, menú del día* or *menú de la casa*) with wine are served at **comedores** or **cafeterías** (€7–10). *Cafeterías* serve rather bland *platos combinados* such as egg and fries or *calamares* and salad, with bread and a drink included (€6–9). Most restaurants also offer a weekday lunchtime *menú del día* (€10–12), while on weekends the prices start from around €13. **Fish** and **seafood** are fresh and excellent, particularly regional specialities such as Galician fish stews (*zarzuelas*) and Valencian paellas (which may also contain meat). Restaurants serving exclusively fish and seafood are called **marisquerías**. The big cities, notably Madrid, Barcelona and Seville, are great for **vegetarians**, with scores of veggie restaurants, plus fusion cuisine and Asian specialities widely available.

Drink

Wine (**vino**), either *tinto* (red), *blanco* (white) or *rosado/clarete* (rosé), is usually very good. The best red is Rioja, and Catalunya produces the best whites, especially Penedès or Peralada; alternatively, try the refreshing Galician Albariño or the more economical Ribeiro. Vino de Jerez, Andalucían **sherry**, is served chilled and either *fino/jerez seco* (dry), *amontillado* (medium), or *oloroso/jerez dulce* (sweet). *Cerveza*, lager-type **beer**, is more expensive than wine but also good; good beers include San Miguel, Cruz Campo, Alhambra and Estrella del Galicia. A shandy is a *corto con limón* (with fizzy lemon) or a *butano* (with fizzy orange). **Sangría**, a red wine-and-fruit punch, and **sidra**, a dry farmhouse cider most typical in Asturia and the Basque Country, are worth sampling. Spaniards often take a *copa* of liqueur with their coffee; the best are *anís* (like Pernod) or *coñac*, local vanilla-flavoured brandy; order spirits by brand name. There are cheaper Spanish equivalents (*nacional*) of most spirits. **Coffee** is invariably espresso, unless you specify *cortado* (with a drop of milk), *con leche* (a more generous dollop) or *americano* (weaker black coffee). **Tea** is drunk black. If you want milk, ask afterwards: ordering *té con leche* might get you a glass of milk with a teabag floating on top.

CULTURE AND ETIQUETTE

The main cultural difference between Spain and other European countries is its **daily schedule**. Lunch is usually eaten from 2pm and dinner from 8pm. In the largest Spanish cities, a lot of shops, tourist offices and restaurants stay open all day, without a siesta break. However, in smaller towns and especially villages, don't expect much to be open between the hours of 2 and 5pm. In terms of **tipping**, ten percent in restaurants is the norm, although not everyone does tip – and nor do all waiters expect it. When paying by credit/debit card in shops, you will always need photo ID, so make sure you carry some with you at all times.

SPORTS AND ACTIVITIES

The beaches on the south coast are the best for **swimming**, while the north coast is ideal for watersports such as **windsurfing** and **surfing**: Playa de Zurriola in San Sebastián is a popular choice, as is Santander's Sardinero beach. Tarifa, at the southernmost tip of Spain, is a year-round paradise for kitesurfers and windsurfers. The Mediterranean waters of Costa Brava and Costa del Sol, as well as the Balearic Islands,

offer numerous good scuba diving and snorkelling spots. Whitewater junkies can head to Catalunya's Noguera Pallaresa river, or Cantabria's Carasa river for kayaking, hydrospeed and rafting. There are numerous great paragliding destinations along the Mediterranean coast and in Aragón. The Aragonese Pyrenees, Picos de Europa and the Sierra Nevada, in Andalucía, are excellent in winter for **skiing** and equally good for **hiking** in summer. Outside the main cities, Spain is also a cycle-friendly country, with numerous scenic and challenging options throughout the country.

Spectator sports

Spain has some great sporting events for spectators. A match at Real Madrid's Estadio Santiago Bernabéu is a must for any **football** fan (tickets €20–90; ⓣ913 984 300, ⓦwww.realmadrid.es), as is a game at the Camp Nou, FC Barcelona's 100,000-seater stadium (tickets €25–190; ⓣ902 189 900, ⓦwww.fcbarcelona.com). If you're lucky enough to get hold of a ticket for a match between the two, you'll witness an unforgettable atmosphere. For something a bit different, the Basque **jai alai** (or *pelota vasca*) is a fast-paced game where teams volley a ball within a three-walled court using wicker *cestas*; match details on ⓦwww.fipv.net. Another activity to witness from the safety of the sidelines is the **bull runnings** (or *encierros*), the most famous of which take place every July in Pamplona during the Fiesta de San Fermín (see p.1133). Every morning for a week, man and bull run together along the narrow city streets in an electrifying, unmissable spectacle.

COMMUNICATIONS

Post offices (*correos*) open Monday to Friday 8.30am to 2pm, Saturday 9am to noon; big branches in cities open until 8pm. You can make international calls from almost any public **phone**. The prepaid phonecards (*tarjetas telefónicas*) for domestic and overseas calls are the cheapest way to pay (available from tobacconists, newspaper kiosks and internet cafés); in larger cities, discount call centres (*locutorios)* abound. The operator is ⓣ1009 domestic, ⓣ1008 for calls to Europe and ⓣ1005 for the rest of the world. Within Spain, dial all nine digits. **Internet** access is widely available, and wi-fi is becoming a standard service in many youth hostels.

EMERGENCIES

Violent crime is rare, but there are multiple scams practised in larger cities, guaranteed to relieve you of

BULLFIGHTING

Bullfighting, or **la corrida**, is synonymous with Spanish culture, though in recent years its popularity has been in decline among the younger generation of Spaniards, who deem it a cruel practice. It is a unique spectacle: half-dance, half gladiatorial combat, with six bulls fought by three matadors, two each, one after the other. The matador's support team consists of two *picaderos* on horseback and three *banderilleros* on foot. First, the *picaderos* pierce the muscles on the bull's neck with long lances; then, the *banderilleros* take turns running at the bull, plunging pairs of sharp darts between its shoulders. Finally, the matador, armed with a red cape, performs the dance of death with the weakened bull, judged on his bravery and the elegance of his performance by the crowd before killing the bull with a single thrust to the heart. The audience waves white handkerchiefs to express approval; a bull's ear is awarded for a good performance: two for an excellent one, and both ears and a tail for an utterly exceptional spectacle, though that has not been seen since the 1970s.

> ### EMERGENCY NUMBERS
> All emergencies ⓣ112; Ambulance ⓣ061; Policía Nacionál ⓣ091.

your wallet. Petty thieves tend to work in groups and rely on distraction techniques; be particularly vigilant around market areas and during fiestas, and be discreet with your valuables. Report robberies to the **Policía Nacionál**; to avoid queuing at the police station (*comisaría*), you can report your loss by phone (ⓣ902 102112) or online under *Denuncias* at ⓦwww.policia.es. For minor **health** complaints, go to a pharmacy (*farmacía*), which you'll find in almost any town. In more serious cases, head to *Urgencias* at the nearest **hospital**, or get the address of an English-speaking doctor from the nearest consulate, *farmacía*, local police or tourist office.

INFORMATION

The **Spanish National Tourist Office** (*Información* or *Oficina de Turismo*) has a branch in virtually every major town, giving away detailed city maps and accommodation lists. There are also provincial or regional *Turismos*, which have information on the entire province, rather than just the city. Both types are usually open Monday to Friday 9/10am to 1pm and 4pm to 7/8pm, Saturday 9am to 1/2pm.

> ### SPAIN ON THE NET
> ⓦ**www.tourspain.co.uk** Comprehensive website of the Spanish tourist board.
> ⓦ**www.spain.info** Information on almost every aspect of Spain.
> ⓦ**www.guiadelocio.com** Nationwide restaurant and entertainment listings, updated weekly (in Spanish only).
> ⓦ**www.gospain.org** Useful links directory.

MONEY AND BANKS

Currency is the euro (€). **Banks** and *cajas de ahorro* have branches in all but the smallest towns, open Monday to Friday 8.30am to 2pm; some are also open Saturday 9am to 1pm. You can usually change cash at larger hotels (bad rates, but low commission), at travel agents, and at most El Corte Inglés department stores. In tourist areas, you'll also find **casas de cambio**, with more convenient hours, but worse exchange rates. **ATMs** (**cajeros automáticos**) are widespread and all major credit cards (particularly Visa and MasterCard) are widely accepted in many shops, restaurants and hotels, especially in larger cities.

OPENING HOURS, HOLIDAYS AND FESTIVALS

In general, shops **open** Monday to Saturday 9am to 8pm and closed (or open for a shorter time) on Sunday. Smaller towns take a **siesta** between 1pm and 4pm, although many shops in cities such as Madrid and Barcelona will stay open all day. Shops and banks are closed on the following public holidays: January 1 and 6, the week before Easter Monday, May 1, August 15, October 12, November 1, December 6, 8 and 24. In addition, each town and city will celebrate their own annual **fiesta** in honour of their patron saint – check the town/regional tourist offices for dates. Local communities put an extraordinary amount of effort into their fiestas; don't miss include: Fiesta de **San Fermín** in Pamplona (second week of July), – the famous running of the bulls; **La Tomatina** in Buñol, near Valencia (second-last or last Wed in Aug) – messy fun with tomatoes; **Semana Santa** in Seville, Málaga and Córdoba (week leading up to Easter Sunday) – spectacular processions, feasting and fireworks, followed by Seville's **Feria de Abril** (late April); the decadent **Carnaval** in Cádiz (Feb/March); Valencia's **Las Fallas** (March 15–19) – processions, fireworks and carousing around the clock.

Spanish

	Spanish	Pronunciation
Yes	*Si*	See
No	*No*	Noh
Please	*Por favor*	Por fahvor
Thank you	*Gracias*	Grath-yass
Hello/Good day	*Hola*	Ola
Goodbye	*Adiós*	Ad-yoss
Excuse me	*Con permiso*	Con pairmeeso
Sorry (strong)	*Lo siento*	Loh see-en-toh
Sorry (mild)	*Perdón*	Pear-don
Where?	*¿Donde?*	¿Donday?
Good	*Bueno*	Bwaynoh
Bad	*Malo*	Maloh
Near	*Próximo*	Prox-eemo
Far	*Lejos*	Layhoss
Cheap	*Barato*	Bar-ahto
Expensive	*Caro*	Cahro
Open	*Abierto*	Ahb-yairto
Closed	*Cerrado*	Thairrado
Today	*Hoy*	Oy
Yesterday	*Ayer*	A-yair
Tomorrow	*Mañana*	Man-yana
Toilet	*Aseo/baño*	Ahseyoh/ bahnio
I don't eat meat	*No como carne*	Noh cohmoh carnay
The bill	*La cuenta*	Lah kwentah
How much is...?	*¿Cuánto cuesta…?*	¿Kwanto kwesta…?
What time is it?	*¿Tiene la hora?*	¿Tee-eynay-la ora?
Do you speak English?	*¿Habla inglas?*	¿Ahblah eenglays?
Where is...?	*¿Dónde está…?*	¿Don-des-ta…?
I don't understand	*No entiendo*	Noh ent-yendo
I would like...	*Quisiera…*	Ki-si-yeah-ra…
One	*Un/Uno*	Oon/Oon-oh
Two	*Dos*	Doss
Three	*Tres*	Tress
Four	*Cuatro*	Kwatro
Five	*Cinco*	Theenko
Six	*Seis*	Say-eess
Seven	*Siete*	See-ettay
Eight	*Ocho*	Oh-cho
Nine	*Nueve*	Nwa-vay
Ten	*Diez*	Dee-yeth

Madrid

When Philip II moved the seat of government to **MADRID** in 1561 his aim was to create a symbol of Spanish unification and centralization. Given its lack of natural advantages, such as a sea port, and extreme temperatures in winter and summer, it was only the determination of successive rulers to promote a strong central capital that ensured its success. Today, Madrid's streets are a beguiling mix of old and new, with narrow, atmospheric alleys and wide, open boulevards. It is also home to some of Spain's best artworks, from the Museo del Prado's world-renowned classical collection, to the impressive modern works at the Reina Sofía. Galleries and sights aside, much of Madrid's charm comes from immersing yourself in the daily life of the city and tapping into its frenetic energy: hanging out in the traditional cafés and *chocolaterías* or the summer *terrazas*, packing the lanes of the Sunday Rastro flea market, or playing very hard and very late in a thousand bars, clubs, and discos.

What to see and do

Central **Puerta del Sol** is officially the centre of the nation: a stone slab in the pavement outside the main building on the south side marks **Kilómetro Zero**, from where six of Spain's *Rutas Nacionales* (National Routes) begin. The city's emblem, a statue of a bear pawing a *madroño* bush, lies on the north side. To the west, c/Arenal heads directly towards the Teatro Real and Palacio Real, but there's more of interest along **c/Mayor**, one of Madrid's oldest thoroughfares, which runs southwest through the heart of the medieval city.

Plaza Mayor

Plaza Mayor is the most important architectural and historical landmark in Madrid and the centrepiece of Madrileño life for centuries. In this beautiful seventeenth-century square, *autos-da-fé* (trials of faith) and executions were held by the Inquisition, kings were crowned, demonstrations, festivals, and bullfights staged. These events were watched by up to 50,000 spectators and by royalty from the frescoed **Real Casa de la Panadería** (Royal Bakery). Today, the plaza is a pleasant place to sip a drink in an outdoor café or sprawl on the cobbles with young Madrileños. In summer, it's an outdoor theatre and music stage, in autumn, a book fair, and a Christmas market in mid-December.

Plaza de la Villa

About two-thirds of the way along c/Mayor is the **Plaza de la Villa**, almost a casebook of Spanish architectural development. The oldest survivor here is the **Torre de los Lujanes**, a fifteenth-century building in Mudéjar style where King Francis I of France was held prisoner by Carlos I after defeat in battle. Next in age is the **Casa de Cisneros**, built in 1537 by a nephew of Cardinal Cisneros in Plateresque style; and to complete the picture is the **Ayuntamiento** (Town Hall), begun in the seventeenth century, but later remodelled in Baroque mode.

Palacio Real

Palacio Real, or Royal Palace, on Calle de Bailén (Mon–Sat 9.30am–5/6pm, Sun 9am–3pm; €8, students €3.50, free Wed to EU citizens; Metro Ópera), built after the earlier Muslim Alcázar burned down on Christmas Day 1734, was the principal royal residence until Alfonso XIII went into exile in 1931. The present royal family inhabits a more modest residence on the western outskirts of the city, using the Palacio Real only on state occasions. The building claims more rooms than any other European palace; a **library** with one of the biggest collections of books, manuscripts, maps

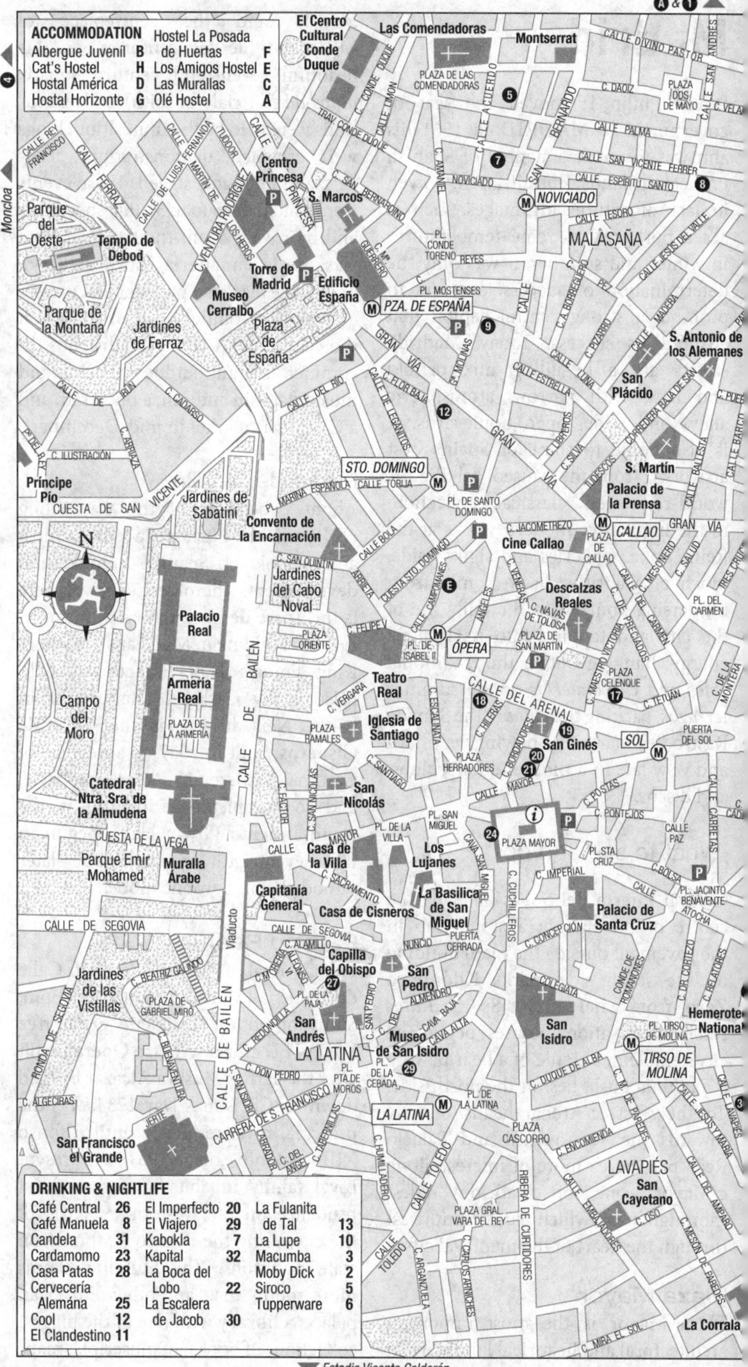
ACCOMMODATION
Albergue Juveníl B
Cat's Hostel H
Hostal América D
Hostal Horizonte G
Hostel La Posada de Huertas F
Los Amigos Hostel E
Las Murallas C
Olé Hostel A
DRINKING & NIGHTLIFE
Café Central 26
Café Manuela 8
Candela 31
Cardamomo 23
Casa Patas 28
Cervecería Alemána 25
Cool 12
El Clandestino 11
El Imperfecto 20
El Viajero 29
Kabokla 7
Kapital 32
La Boca del Lobo 22
La Escalera de Jacob 30
La Fulanita de Tal 13
La Lupe 10
Macumba 3
Moby Dick 2
Siroco 5
Tupperware 6
A & 1
4
Moncloa
Estadio Vicente Calderón
El Centro Cultural Conde Duque
Las Comendadoras
Montserrat
PLAZA DE LAS COMENDADORAS
PLAZA DOS DE MAYO
CALLE DIVINO PASTOR
C. DAOIZ
CALLE PALMA
CALLE SAN VICENTE FERRER
CALLE ESPIRITU SANTO
CALLE TESORO
NOVICIADO
MALASAÑA
Centro Princesa
S. Marcos
Parque del Oeste
Templo de Debod
Torre de Madrid
Edificio España
Museo Cerralbo
Plaza de España
PZA. DE ESPAÑA
PL. MOSTENSES
PL. CONDE TORENO
Parque de la Montaña
Jardines de Ferraz
GRAN VÍA
S. Antonio de los Alemanes
San Plácido
S. Martín
Palacio de la Prensa
STO. DOMINGO
PL. DE SANTO DOMINGO
Príncipe Pío
CUESTA DE SAN VICENTE
Jardines de Sabatini
Convento de la Encarnación
Cine Callao
PLAZA DE CALLAO
CALLAO
Jardines del Cabo Noval
Descalzas Reales
PLAZA DE SAN MARTÍN
PL. DEL CARMEN
Palacio Real
PLAZA ORIENTE
PL. DE ISABEL II
ÓPERA
Teatro Real
CALLE DEL ARENAL
PLAZA CELENQUE
Armería Real
PLAZA DE LA ARMERÍA
Campo del Moro
Iglesia de Santiago
PLAZA RAMALES
San Ginés
PUERTA DEL SOL
SOL
PLAZA HERRADORES
Catedral Ntra. Sra. de la Almudena
San Nicolás
PL. DE LA VILLA
PL. SAN MIGUEL
PLAZA MAYOR
CUESTA DE LA VEGA
Parque Emir Mohamed
Muralla Árabe
Casa de la Villa
Los Lujanes
Capitanía General
Casa de Cisneros
La Basilica de San Miguel
Palacio de Santa Cruz
PL. JACINTO BENAVENTE
CALLE DE SEGOVIA
Viaducto
Jardines de las Vistillas
PLAZA DE GABRIEL MIRÓ
Capilla del Obispo
San Pedro
San Andrés
LA LATINA
Museo de San Isidro
San Isidro
Hemeroteca Nacional
PL. TIRSO DE MOLINA
TIRSO DE MOLINA
CALLE DE BAILÉN
CARRERA DE S. FRANCISCO
San Francisco el Grande
PL. PTA. DE MOROS
PL. DE LA CEBADA
PL. DE LA LATINA
PLAZA CASCORRO
CALLE TOLEDO
RIBERA DE CURTIDORES
PLAZA GRAL VARA DEL REY
LAVAPIÉS
San Cayetano
La Corrala
RONDA DE SEGOVIA

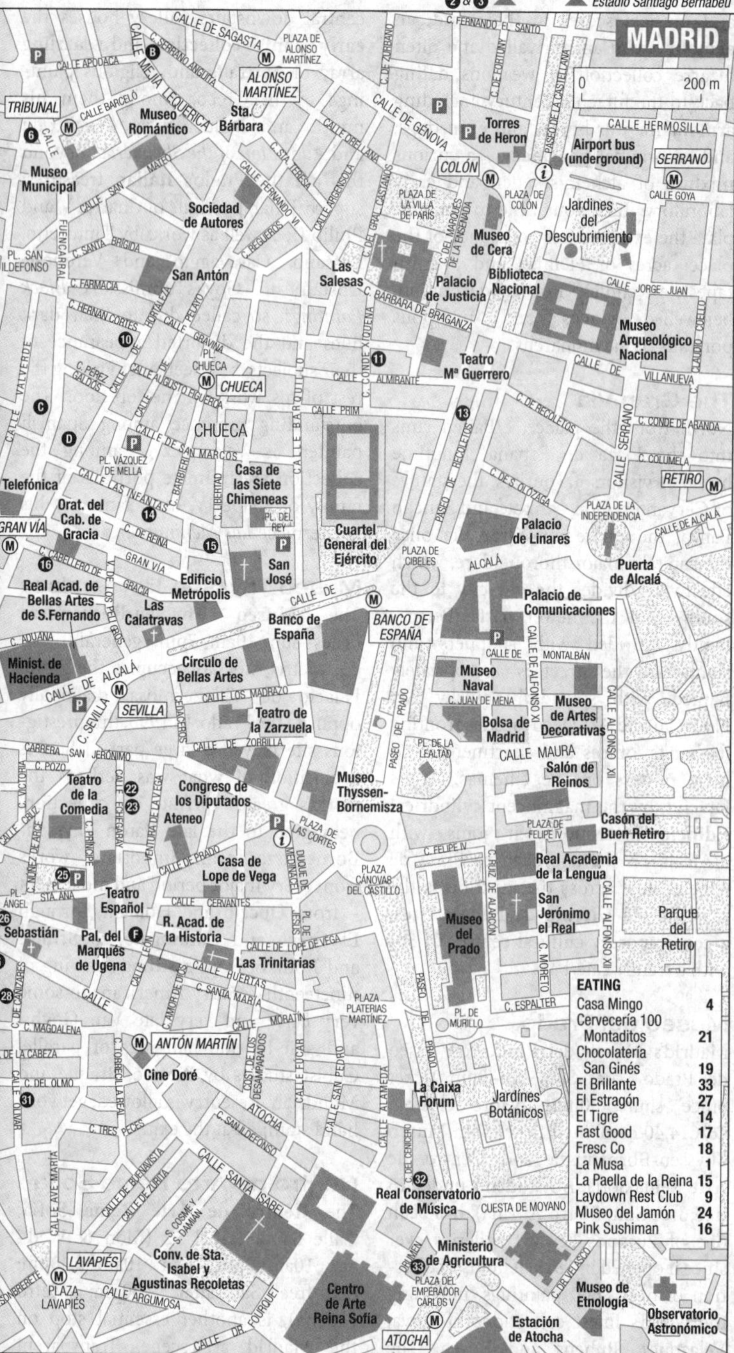

SPAIN

MADRID

www.roughguides.com

and musical scores in the world; an **armoury** with an unrivalled and often bizarre collection of weapons dating back to the fifteenth century, including armour for war horses and even dogs; and an original **pharmacy** – a curious mixture of alchemist's den and early laboratory. Take your time to contemplate the extraordinary opulence of the place: acres of Flemish and Spanish tapestries, endless Rococo decoration, bejewelled clocks and pompous portraits of the monarchs.

The Gran Vía

North from the palace, c/Bailén runs into the Plaza de España, longtime home of visitors' favourites, the statues of Cervantes, Don Quixote and Sancho Panza. The square joins **Gran Vía**, once the capital's major thoroughfare, which effectively divides the old city to the south from the newer parts. Permanently crowded with shoppers and sightseers, the street is appropriately named, with splendidly quirky Art Nouveau and Art Deco facades fronting its banks, offices and apartments, and huge posters on the cinemas. At its far end, by the magnificent cylindrical **Edificio Metropolis**, it joins with c/Alcalá on the approach to Plaza de Cibeles. Just across the junction is the majestic old **Círculo de Bellas Artes**, a contemporary cultural centre (€1.50) with a trendy café/bar.

Museo del Prado

Madrid's **Museo del Prado**, on Paseo del Prado (Tues–Sun 9am–8pm, ticket office shuts 30min before closing; €6/€14.40 combined ticket with Museo Thyssen-Bornemisza and Centro de Arte Reina Sofía; EU students under 25 free; free Sun; Metro Atocha), has been one of Europe's key art galleries ever since it opened in 1819. It holds a collection of over 8600 paintings, including the world's finest collections of Goya, Velázquez, Rubens and Bosch. The central downstairs gallery houses the **early Spanish collection**, and a dazzling array of portraits and religious paintings by El Greco, among them his mystic and hallucinatory *Crucifixion* and *Adoration of the Shepherds*. Beyond this are the Prado's **Italian** treasures: superb Titian portraits of Charles V and Philip II, as well as works by Tintoretto, Bassano, Caravaggio and Veronese. Upstairs are Goya's unmissable *Black Paintings*, so called due to their dark hues and the distorted appearance of their subjects, best seen after visiting the rest of his work on the top floor. The outstanding presence among Spanish painters is Velázquez – among the collection are intimate portraits of the family of Felipe IV, most famously his masterpiece *Las Meninas*.

Museo Thyssen-Bornemisza

The **Museo Thyssen-Bornemisza** (Tues–Sun 10am–7pm; general ticket €6; Metro Atocha) occupies the grand Palacio de Villahermosa, diagonally opposite the Prado. In 1993, this prestigious site played a large part in Spain's acquisition of what was perhaps the world's greatest private art collection, belonging to the late Baron Thyssen-Bornemisza, with important works from every major period and movement – from Duccio and Holbein, through El Greco and Caravaggio, to Schiele and Rothko; from a strong showing of nineteenth-century Americans to some very early and very late Van Goghs; and side-by-side hangings of parallel Cubist studies by Picasso, Braque and Mondrian. Re-entry is allowed; get your hand stamped at the exit.

Centro de Arte Reina Sofía

The **Centro de Arte Reina Sofía**, Calle Santa Isabel 52 (Mon & Wed–Sat 10am–9pm, Sun 10am–2.30pm; €6, free Sat after 2.30pm; Metro Atocha), is another essential stop on the Madrid art scene. Transparent

lifts shuttle visitors up the outside of the building. As well as the exhibition halls (top floor) and collection of twentieth-century art (second floor), the centre features a cinema, excellent art and design bookshops, a print, music and photographic library and a restaurant, bar and café. However, it is **Picasso's Guernica** – his signature Cubism piece – that most visitors come to see, and rightly so. Superbly displayed along with its preliminary studies, this icon of twentieth-century Spanish art and politics – a response to the Fascist bombing of the Basque town of Guernica in the Spanish Civil War – carries a shock that defies all familiarity. Other halls are devoted to **Dalí** and Surrealism, early twentieth-century Spanish artists including **Miró** and post-World War II figurative art, mapping the beginning of abstraction through to Pop and avant-garde.

The Rastro

The **Rastro** flea market (Sun & public hols 10am–3pm) is as much a part of Madrid's weekend ritual as a Mass or a *paseo*. The stalls sprawl south from Metro La Latina to the Ronda de Toledo, getting particularly busy along c/Ribera de Curtidores, the road leading south from Plaza de Cascorro. Expect a great atmosphere, but you'll have to search hard for bargains among the junk. Keep a tight grip on your possessions. Afterwards, while away the afternoon in the bars and *terrazas* around Puerta de Moros.

Parque del Buen Retiro and Parque del Oeste

The most central and most popular of Madrid's parks in which to while away an afternoon is the **Parque del Buen Retiro** (Metro Retiro) behind the Prado, a stunning mix of formal gardens and wilder spaces. You can row a boat, picnic, check out a travelling art exhibition at the beautiful **Palacio de Velázquez** and the nearby **Palacio de Cristal** and, above all, promenade. On Sunday afternoons, half of Madrid turns up for a *paseo*, whilst listening to groups of musicians enjoying impromptu jamming sessions by the lake. You can also visit the newly built "Hill of the Absents" – a mound constructed in memory of those who died in the Madrid bombing of 2004. Although charming by day, Retiro is best avoided at night. The **Parque del Oeste** on the city's western edge (Metro Ventura Rodríguez) is worth visiting for its spectacular views around sunset; it also boasts a genuine Egyptian temple – Templo de Debod, donated to Spain by Egyptian president Nasser in 1968 as a gesture of thanks to Spanish archeologists who saved it from the rising waters of Lake Nasser.

Arrival and information

Air Busy Barajas airport (Ⓦwww.aena.es), 12km from the centre, is served by all major airlines from Europe, North and Latin America. Line #8 runs to Nuevos Ministerios metro station (6am–2am; 12min; €1; additional €1 supplement from Terminal 4). Bus #200 leaves terminals 1 and 2 (5.20am–11.30pm; weekdays every 10min; weekends & public hols every 20min; €1) for the Avenida de America interchange, where you can get the metro into the centre. AeroCITY minibuses (24hr; Ⓣ917 477 570, Ⓦwww.aerocity.com) drop passengers off door-to-door for €5–17, depending on number of passengers (seven maximum).

Train Trains from the north and Portugal arrive at the Estación de Chamartín, in the north of the city, connected to the centre via metro line #10. Estación de Atocha serves the south, east and west of Spain. Local trains use the Estación de Príncipe Pío (Estación del Norte).

Bus Terminals are scattered throughout the city, but the largest – used by all international services – is the Estación del Sur (Metro Méndez Alvaro) on c/Méndez Alvaro, south of Estación de Atocha.

Tourist office Run by helpful staff, the main Centro de Turismo de Madrid, Plaza Mayor 27, Metro Sol (daily 9.30am–8.30pm; Ⓣ915 881 636, Ⓦwww.esmadrid.com), offers access to its excellent website and city database. Branches at Plaza de Colón, Metro Colón and Terminal 4 at the airport (same hours). What's-on listings are detailed in free

English-language monthly *InMadrid* (Ⓦwww.in-madrid.com), *esMADRID* magazine (Ⓦwww.esmadrid.com), *Guía del Ocio* (Ⓦwww.guiadelocio.com), and *Metropolis*, which comes free with *El Mundo* on a Friday.

City transport

The centre is comfortably walkable, but Madrid also has efficient buses and metro system.

Bus The urban bus network (Ⓦwww.emtmadrid.es) is extensive. Buses run from 6am to 11.30pm; there are also 26 night-bus *búhos* (owls) in the centre, from Plaza de Cibeles and Puerta del Sol (midnight–6am; every 15min).

Metro Ⓦwww.metromadrid.es. Runs 6.05am–2am; flat fare €1, €6.70 for a ten-journey ticket, also valid on buses.

Tour bus Hop-on hop-off Madrid Visión (Ⓦwww.madridvision.es) tour buses stop at all the major sights (June 21–Sept 20 9.30am–midnight; shorter hours rest of the year; 1 day €16, 2 days €20.50).

Accommodation

The best budget accommodation is in the area surrounding the buzzing, pedestrianized Plaza Santa Ana. Other promising areas include Gran Vía and along noisy c/Fuencarral towards Chueca and Malsaña.

Hostels

Albergue Juveníl c/Mejia Lequerica 21 Ⓣ915 939 688, Ⓦwww.ajmadrid.es. This government-run hostel is a gem. The stylish decor mixes ultra-modern furnishings and graffiti murals. Facilities include a gym, free internet, TV/DVD/games room and laundry. Breakfast buffet, sheets and lockers included. Metro Alonso Martínez or Tribunal. Dorms: under-26s €19–20, over-26s €25.

Cat's Hostel c/Cañizares 6 Ⓣ913 692 807, Ⓦwww.catshostel.com. Huge backpackers' haven in a converted eighteenth-century palace with beautiful central patio. Rooms are a bit cramped but there's a lively cellar bar, nightly tapas bar crawls, free internet and wi-fi. Metro Antón Martín. Dorms €19–21, doubles €80.

Hostal América c/de Hortaleza 19, 5th floor Ⓣ915 226 448, Ⓦwww.hostalamerica.net. Welcoming hostel with spacious, airy rooms centred around a quiet patio, run by a mother and son (and a dog called Ronnie). You can chill out on the terrace and use the free wi-fi. Metro Gran Vía. Singles €36, doubles €48, triples €67, quads €78.

Hostel La Posada de Huertas c/de las Huertas 21 Ⓣ914 295 526, Ⓦwww.posadadehuertas.com. Spacious, secure, colourful dorms with lockers in the heart of Madrid's nightlife draw international backpackers. Helpful staff, nightly tapas-bar tours, free breakfast, internet and kitchen facilities are just some of the perks. Metro Antón Martín. Dorms €18–20, doubles €80.

Los Amigos Hostel Campomanes 6-4° Ⓣ915 471 707, Ⓦwww.losamigoshostel.com. Very popular and friendly hostel with bright dorms, lockers, kitchen and internet, on a quiet street near the Palacio Real. Metro Ópera. Separate branch at c/Arenal 26–24 Ⓣ915 592 472. Dorms €21–24, doubles €80.

Olé Hostel c/Manuela Malasaña 23–1° Ⓣ914 465 165, Ⓦwww.olehostel.com. Right in the centre of Madrid's trendiest nightlife, this dorm accommodation has all the standard facilities you'll need, from internet to laundry and kitchen. Metro Bilbao/San Bernardo. Dorms €16.

Hotels

Hostal Horizonte c/Atocha 28 Ⓣ913 690 996, Ⓦwww.hostalhorizonte.com. Well-maintained and attractive rooms near the Plaza Santa Ana, though it can be noisy. Metro Antón Martín. Singles €29–40, doubles €44–55.

Las Murallas c/Fuencarral 23-4° Ⓣ915 321 063, Ⓦwww.hostalmurallas.com. Accommodation with private bathrooms and balconies overlooking one of Madrid's best shopping streets. Metro Gran Vía. Singles €22, doubles €42, triples €54.

Eating

Madrid has an incredible variety of restaurants, and it's easy to dine out on a tight budget. In summer, all areas of the city have pavement café/bars, where you can sip coffee by day and drink pretty much all night.

Cafés and tapas

Cervecería 100 Montaditos c/Mayor 22. This chain is popular country-wide thanks to, as the name implies, its choice of a hundred sandwiches, at just €1.20 a pop. Good for a quick snack: simply fill in a menu form, pay at the counter and wait for your food. Metro Sol.

Chocolatería San Ginés Pasadizo de San Ginés 5. Possibly the most popular post-night-out/ breakfast spot for *chocolate con churros*. A local institution. Metro Sol.

El Brillante Glorieta del Emperador Carlos V 8. Renowned for its squid *bocadillos* and super-efficient staff. Metro Atocha.

El Tigre c/de las Infantas 30. This great bar is deservedly popular; if you're willing to elbow your way through the crowds, it is the best in the capital for free tapas – every *caña* (€1.50) comes with a heaped plate. Metro Gran Vía.
Museo del Jamón c/Mayor 7. Extraordinary place where hundreds of hams hang from the ceiling, and even the *cañas* (€1.20) come with a free tapa. Plate of *jamón* €2.50–16, depending on the quality. Numerous other branches. Metro Sol.

Restaurants

Casa Mingo Paseo de la Florida 34. Asturian cider house with several cheap and simple specialities. If the roast chicken doesn't grab you, go for the *chorizo a la sidra*. Metro Príncipe Pío.
El Estragón Pl de la Paja 10. Terracotta tiles, gingham tablecloths and delicious vegetarian food: try the Cuban-style rice with salsa and fried plantain. Economical *menú del día*, and internet access. Metro La Latina.
Fast Good c/de Tetuán 2, Metro Sol. Like fast food, only good for you, this is an excellent spot for a fresh hamburger, tasty sandwiches and even healthy French fries. Also at c/de Juan Bravo 3, Metro Núñez de Balboa.
Fresc Co c/Las Fuentes 12. All-you-can-eat buffet for under €10 at this popular chain restaurant. Metro Ópera.
La Musa c/Manuela Malasaña 18. Always heaving with a young clientele, the food here is sensational. Try the *bombas* (stuffed potatoes) or fried green tomatoes. *Menú del día* €11. Metro Bilbao.
La Paella de la Reina c/de la Reina 39. This is where Madrileños head to sate their rice-related cravings. Like any good *arrocería*, this place only cooks a variety of paellas for two people or more, so bring a friend. *Arroz negro* (€14 per person) is delicious. Metro Gran Vía.
Pink Sushiman c/ de Caballero de Gracia 8. Sidle up to the conveyer belt and grab the dishes you fancy as they pass by in this Japanese tapas bar. Plates are colour-coded and on weekdays, any five go for a bargain €10. Metro Gran Vía.

Drinking and nightlife

Most bars in Madrid only really get going around 10.30pm. The drinking culture is very laid-back, with most Madrileños having a drink and a tapa in one bar before moving on to another; most tapas bars are known for a particular speciality. Madrid parties late, with clubs open from 1am until well beyond dawn. For diving in and out of clubs, the best areas are the student haunt of Malasaña, focused on Plaza del Dos de Mayo, gay-area Chueca and multi cultural Lavapiés/Anton Martín.

Bars

Café Manuela c/San Vincent Ferrer 29. Beautiful decor and a large selection of board games. Good for coffee or jugs of fruity sangría. Closed Aug. Metro Tribunal.
Cervecería Alemána Plaza Santa Ana 6. One of Hemingway's favourite haunts and consequently full of Americans; good traditional atmosphere and excellent German beers. Pricey but worth it. Closed Aug. Metro Sol.
El Clandestino c/de Barquillo 34. Immensely popular bar serving great mojitos to an accompaniment of indie/rock music, sometimes live. Metro Chueca.
El Imperfecto c/Coloreros 5. Far from being imperfect, this is an excellent bar for cocktails – sip on their great mojitos whilst admiring the topsy-turvy interior, and listening to live jazz on Tuesdays. Metro Sol.
El Viajero Plaza de la Cebada 11. Essential spot for a beer on a warm night, when you can watch the world pass by from the open-air rooftop *terraza*. Metro La Latina.

Clubs

Cool c/Isabel La Católica 6. Disco and house dominate the dancefloor at this chic club filled with beautiful people. Entry price varies depending on event; things get lively after 3am. Metro Santo Domingo.
Kapital c/Atocha 125. A biggie, worth mentioning simply for the seven levels of different dancefloors – everything from hip-hop to salsa to r'n'b. The €20 admission includes one drink. Dress well. Metro Atocha.

TREAT YOURSELF

Get dressed-up and loosen the purse strings at **Laydown Rest Club** (Plaza Mostenses 9 ⓣ915 487 937, ⓦwww.laydown.es; Metro Plaza de España). No tables and chairs here – kick your shoes off, climb onto one of the large white beds and enjoy a meal, Roman-style, served by waiters in togas. The food is innovative Mediterranean and their Sunday brunch and *menú del día* deals are particularly good. To find it, head east along c/de General Mitre from Plaza Mostenses and take the first lane on the right.

La Fulanita de Tal c/del Conde de Xiquena 2 ⓦwww.fulanitadetal.com. Anything-goes lively lesbian club where everyone is welcome. The crowd packs the dancefloor to pop and r'n'b. Metro Chueca.
La Lupe c/de Hortaleza 51. Extremely popular dance spot attracting a mixed straight/gay crowd with its repertoire of catchy mainstream pop tunes. Metro Chueca.
Macumba Above Estación Chamartín. Weekend favourite for hardcore clubbers, where the likes of Ministry of Sound hit the decks until 9am. Entry price varies. Metro Chamartín.
Siroco c/San Dimas 3. Very popular late-night music venue with up-and-coming local bands playing everything from pop and rock to hip-hop, acid jazz and funk. Metro Noviciado.
Tupperware Corredora Alta de San Pueblo 26. This club is fun through-and-through, from its über-kitsch decor to its eclectic playlist – soul, indie and Sixties and Seventies classics. Free entry. Open until 3.30am daily. Metro Tribunal.

Entertainment

Big rock concerts are usually held at Palacio Vistalegre, Utebo 1 (Metro Oporto), and La Peineta stadium, Avenida Arcentales (Metro Las Musas). Flamenco is at its best in the summer, especially at the Cumbre Flamenco, a week of free concerts held in a metro station in September. In July and August, the city council sponsors a Veranos de la Villa programme of concerts and free cinema in some attractive outside venues.

Cinema

Cine Doré c/Santa Isabel 3. Offers a bargain (€2) programme of classic films, a pleasant bar and, in summer, an outdoor cine-terraza; home to the Filmoteca Nacional (national film library).
La Enana Marrón Travesía de San Mateo 8; €4. Artsy and independent Spanish-language films. Metro Alonso Martínez.
Renoir c/Martín de los Héroes 14 and 12. English-language films remain un-dubbed; student discounts offered. Metro Plaza de España.

Bullfights

Plaza de Toros c/de Alcalá 237. Hosts some of the year's most prestigious events, especially during the May/June San Isidro festivities; ticket prices start from around €5 for standing *sol* (sun) tickets, with *sombra* (shade) tickets costing upwards from €10 and the most expensive ringside seats selling for around €100. Tickets for all but the biggest events are available at the box office (ⓣ913 562 200, ⓦwww.las-ventas.com). Metro Ventas.

Live music

Café Central Plaza del Angel 10 ⓦwww.cafecentralmadrid.com. One of the best places in the world to hear live jazz; attracts big international musicians. Open from noon for drinks, with music nightly from 10.30pm; get here before 9pm to secure weekend tickets. Metro Sol.
Kabokla c/de San Vicente Ferrer 55 ⓦwww.kabokla.es. Lively Brazilian venue with live samba and percussion bands most nights. Hosts samba and capoeira classes as well. Metro Noviciado.
La Boca del Lobo c/Echegaray 11 ⓦwww.labocadellobo.com. Dark, atmospheric venue with a reputation for showcasing new rock and alternative acts. Live music from 10.30pm, followed by DJs. Metro Sevilla or Sol.
La Escalera de Jacob c/de Lavapiés 11 ⓦwww.laescaleradejacob.es. Intimate, multi faceted venue with fusion, soul, jazz, funk and indie nights, a loyal local following and some great live performances. Metro Antón Martín.
Moby Dick c/Avda. de Brasil 5 ⓦwww.mobydickclub.com. Popular, nautically themed venue attracting live rock bands, both local and international. Metro Santiago Bernabéu.

Flamenco

Candela c/Olmo 2. Legendary bar frequented by foreign visitors, with formal flamenco upstairs and spontaneous performances in the bar downstairs. Daily 10.30pm–late; best after 1am. Metro Antón Martín.
Cardamomo c/Echegaray 15. This dark, smoky flamenco bar attracts a young, spirited local crowd and on Tuesdays and Wednesdays puts on a live flamenco jamming session that's not to be missed. Free entry. Daily 9pm–3.30am. Metro Sevilla.
Casa Patas c/Cañizares 10. Classic flamenco club with bar and restaurant, and incredible performances. Best nights Thurs & Fri; can get rather crowded. Entrance €15, or €30–35 with dinner. Metro Antón Martín.

Shopping

Alternative shops Chueca and also c/Fuencarral and c/Hortaleza (off Gran Vía). There are several great places to find that quirky something, but particularly worth visiting is Mercado de Fuencarral, c/Fuencarral 45 (Mon–Sat 10am–9pm), a three-storey mall with over forty shops and stalls selling outlandish clothes, accessories and more.
Bookshops Casa del Libro, Gran Vía 29 (Metro Gran Vía), is a huge bookshop with a large selection in English. Petra's International Bookshop, c/de Compomanes 13 (Metro Ópera), lets you swap

your old books for other secondhand ones. Pasajes Librería Internacional, c/de Génova 3 (Metro Alonso Martínez), is one of the better shops, with an extensive English section.
Designers All the big names that will probably blow your budget span several streets of the Salamanca district, principally Paseo Castellana, c/Goya, c/Velázquez and c/Serrano.
High street For friendlier prices, shop for popular names on Gran Vía and the streets radiating from Sol.
Traditional handicrafts The area from Plaza Mayor to Puerta de Toledo is filled with shops selling everything from religious icons to embroidered shawls – great for browsing and picking up the odd authentic souvenir, but often quite expensive.

Directory

Embassies Australia, Plaza Descubridor Diego de Ordás 3 ☎913 536 600; Canada, c/Nuñez de Balboa 35 ☎914 233 250; Ireland, Paseo de la Castellana 46, 4th floor ☎914 364 093; New Zealand, c/ de Pinar 7 ☎915 230 226; UK, c/Fernando el Santo 16 ☎915 249 700; US, c/Serrano 75 ☎915 872 200.
Exchange Large branches of most major banks on c/Alcalá and Gran Vía. Round-the-clock currency exchange at the airport; Banco Central is best for AmEx traveller's cheques.
Hospitals Anglo-American Medical Unit (Unidad Médica), c/del Conde de Aranda 1, Metro Retiro ☎914 351 823; Hospital General Gregorio Marañón, c/del Doctor Esquerdo 46, Metro Sainz de Baranda ☎915 868 000.
Laundry Ondablu, c/León 3, also has internet (Metro Antón Martín); Onda Luna, c/Estrella 10 (Metro Gran Vía).
Left luggage Estación de Atocha has lockers (daily 6am–10pm); Estación de Chamartín also has lockers (daily 7am–11pm). There is also a *consigna* at the Estación Sur de Autobuses (6.30am–midnight). There are also 24hr *consignas* at the airport terminals 1, 3 and 4.
Pharmacies Farmacia Atocha, c/Atocha 114 ☎915 273 415; Farmacia del Globo, c/Atocha 46 ☎913 692 000; Farmacia Velásquez, c/Velásquez 70 ☎915 756 028 (24hr). All have a list of night pharmacies posted outside.
Post office Palacio de Comunicaciones, Plaza de Cibeles, Metro Banco de España.

Moving on

Train Barcelona (25 daily; 2hr 40min–3hr 30min); Bilbao (2 daily; 5hr); Cáceres (5 daily; 3hr 30min–4hr 30min); Cádiz (2 daily; 4hr 30min); Córdoba (every 30min between 6.30am–10pm; 1hr 40min–2hr); Granada (2 daily; 4hr 30min); León (8 daily; 3hr 30min–4hr 30min); Málaga (12 daily; 2hr 40min–3hr); Mérida (5 daily; 4hr 20min–6hr 40min); Oviedo (4 daily; 4hr 30min–5hr 30min); Pamplona (4 daily; 3hr); Salamanca (7 daily; 2hr 30min); San Sebastián (2 daily; 5hr 20min); Santiago de Compostela (2 daily; 7–9hr); Segovia (13 daily; 30min–1hr 30min); Seville (22 daily; 2hr 30min); Toledo (11 daily; 30min); Valencia (13 daily; 3hr 45min).
Bus Alicante (5–10 daily; 5hr); Almería (5 daily; 7hr); Barcelona (20 daily; 7hr 30min–8hr); Bilbao (6 daily; 4hr 45min); Cáceres (7 daily; 4hr–4hr 30min); Cádiz (6 daily; 7hr); Córdoba (6 daily; 4hr 45min); El Escorial (hourly; 1hr); Granada (14 daily; 4hr 30min–5hr); León (12 daily; 4hr 15min); Málaga (4–8 daily; 6hr); Mérida (9 daily; 4–5hr); Oviedo (12 daily; 5hr); Pamplona (6 daily; 5hr); Salamanca (23 daily; 2hr 30min); San Sebastián (9 daily; 6hr); Santander (8 daily; 5hr 45min); Santiago de Compostela (5 daily; 8–9hr); Segovia (10am–11pm every 30min; 1hr 30min); Seville (8 daily; 6hr); Toledo (6.30am–10pm every 30min; 1hr 15min); Valencia (16 daily; 4hr); Zaragoza (20 daily; 3hr 45min).

Day-trips from Madrid

Surrounding the capital are some of Spain's most fascinating cities, all an easy day-trip from Madrid or a convenient stop-off on the main routes out. From **Toledo** you can turn south to Andalucía or strike west towards Extremadura. To the northwest the roads lead past **El Escorial**, from where a bus runs to Franco's tomb at **El Valle de los Caídos**, and through the dramatic scenery of the Sierra de Guadarrama to **Segovia**.

TOLEDO

Capital of medieval Spain until 1560, UNESCO World Heritage Site **TOLEDO** is the spiritual heart of Catholic Spain and a city redolent of past glories. Set in a desolate landscape, it rests on a rocky mound isolated on three sides by a looping gorge of the Río Tajo.

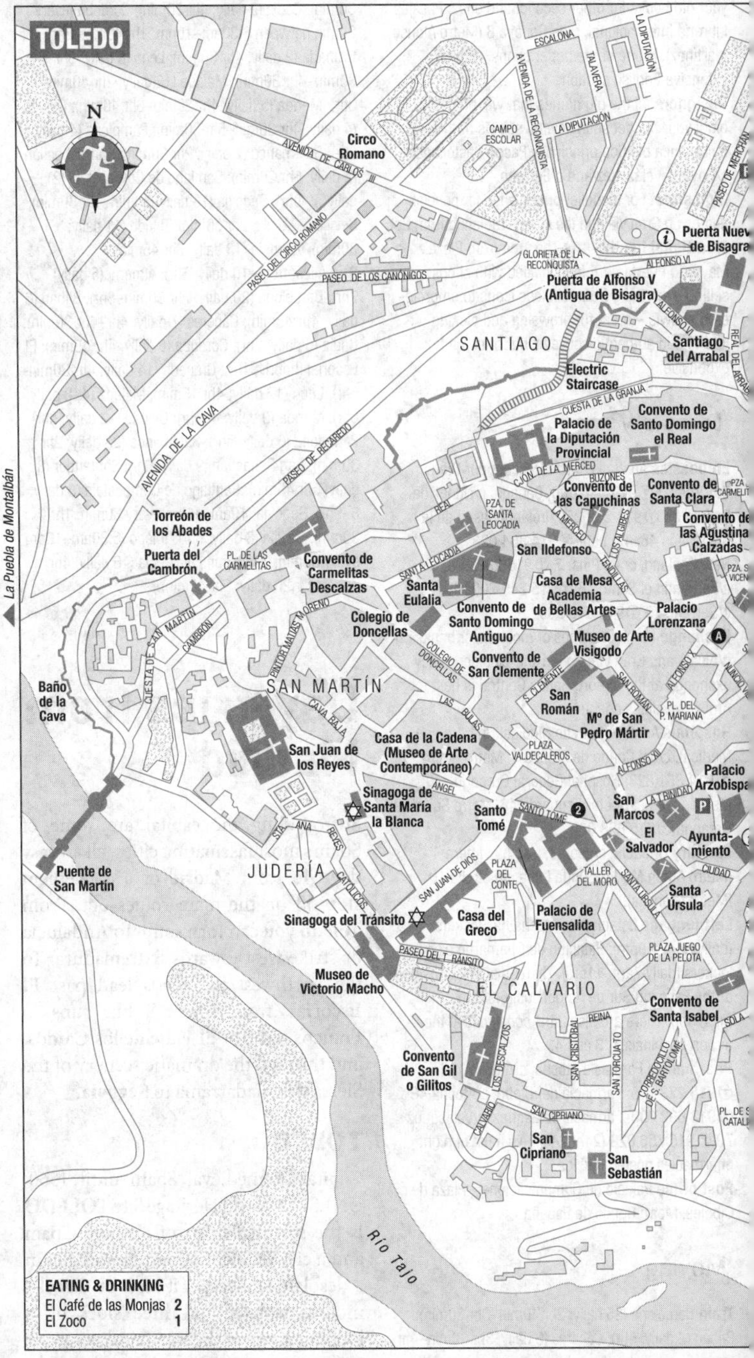
Ávila
TOLEDO
N
Circo Romano
AVENIDA DE CARLOS III
PASEO DEL CIRCO ROMANO
PASEO DE LOS CANÓNIGOS
ESCALONA
TALAVERA
LA DIPUTACIÓN
AVENIDA DE LA RECONQUISTA
CAMPO ESCOLAR
PASEO DE MERCHÁN
Puerta Nueva de Bisagra
GLORIETA DE LA RECONQUISTA
ALFONSO VI
Puerta de Alfonso VI (Antigua de Bisagra)
Santiago del Arrabal
REAL DEL ARRABAL
SANTIAGO
Electric Staircase
CUESTA DE LA GRANJA
Palacio de la Diputación Provincial
Convento de Santo Domingo el Real
CJÓN. DE LA MERCED
BUZONES
Convento de las Capuchinas
Convento de Santa Clara
PZA. CARMELITAS
Convento de las Agustinas Calzadas
AVENIDA DE LA CAVA
PASEO DE RECAREDO
Torreón de los Abades
Puerta del Cambrón
PL. DE LAS CARMELITAS
Convento de Carmelitas Descalzas
REAL
PZA. DE SANTA LEOCADIA
LA MERCED
LOS ALJIBES
TENDILLAS
San Ildefonso
SANTA LEOCADIA
Santa Eulalia
Casa de Mesa Academia de Bellas Artes
Palacio Lorenzana
PZA. S. VICENTE
Colegio de Doncellas
Convento de Santo Domingo Antiguo
Museo de Arte Visigodo
A
PINTOR MATÍAS MORENO
COLEGIO DE DONCELLAS
Convento de San Clemente
CUESTA DE SAN MARTÍN
CAMBRÓN
SAN MARTÍN
S. CLEMENTE
SAN ROMÁN
ALFONSO X
San Román
Mº de San Pedro Mártir
PL. DEL P. MARIANA
Baño de la Cava
CAVA BAJA
LAS BULAS
Casa de la Cadena (Museo de Arte Contemporáneo)
PLAZA VALDECALEROS
ALFONSO XII
San Juan de los Reyes
Palacio Arzobispal
Sinagoga de Santa María la Blanca
ÁNGEL
Santo Tomé
SANTO TOMÉ
2
San Marcos
LA TRINIDAD
P
STA. ANA
REYES
El Salvador
Ayuntamiento
CIUDAD
Puente de San Martín
JUDERÍA
CATÓLICOS
SAN JUAN DE DIOS
PLAZA DEL CONDE
TALLER DEL MORO
SANTA ÚRSULA
Santa Úrsula
Sinagoga del Tránsito
Casa del Greco
Palacio de Fuensalida
PLAZA JUEGO DE LA PELOTA
PASEO DEL TRÁNSITO
Museo de Victorio Macho
EL CALVARIO
REINA
Convento de Santa Isabel
SOLA
Convento de San Gil o Gilitos
LOS DESCALZOS
SAN CRISTÓBAL
SAN TORCUATO
CORREDORCILLO DE S. BARTOLOMÉ
PL. DE S. CATALINA
CALVARIO
SAN CIPRIANO
San Cipriano
San Sebastián
Río Tajo
La Puebla de Montalbán
EATING & DRINKING
El Café de las Monjas 2
El Zoco 1

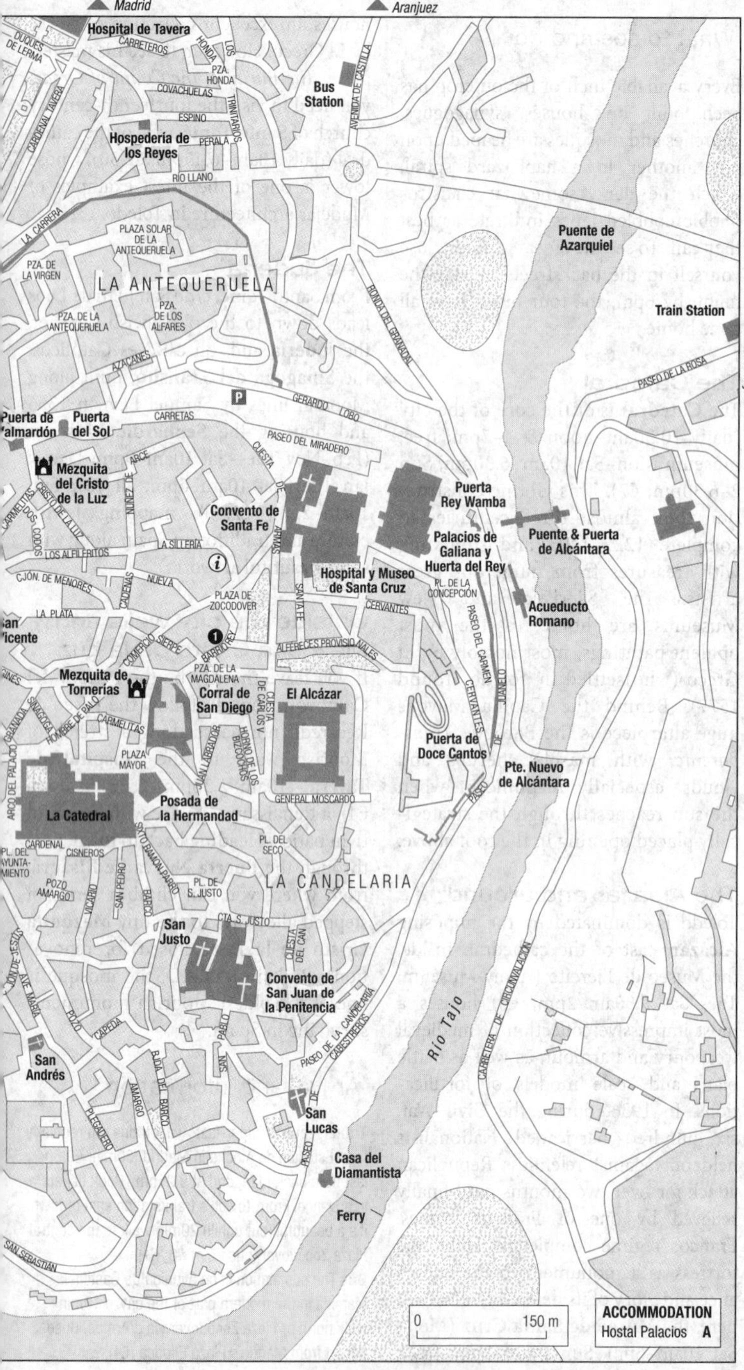

SPAIN

DAY-TRIPS FROM MADRID

www.roughguides.com

What to see and do

Every available inch of the outcrop has been built on: houses, synagogues, churches and mosques are heaped upon one another in a haphazard spiral, which the dark, somewhat claustrophobic cobbled lanes infiltrate as best they can. To see the city at its finest, lose yourself in the backstreets or stay the night; by 6pm, the tour buses have all gone home.

The Catedral

The **Catedral** is at the core of the city (daily 10.30am–noon & 4–7pm; free; museum Mon–Sat 10am–6.30pm, Sun 2–6.30pm; €7). This Gothic construction took almost three centuries to complete (1227–1493) and is bursting with treasures from numerous great artists. The Sacristía and New Museums are home to the most opulent paintings, most notably by El Greco (who settled in Toledo around 1577). Behind the Capilla Mayor's huge altarpiece is the Baroque *Transparente*, with marble cherubs and clouds, especially magnificent when the sun reaches through the strategically placed opening in the roof above.

The Alcázar and around

Toledo is dominated by the imposing **Alcázar**, east of the cathedral. Inside, the Museo de Ejército (Army Museum; Tues–Sat 9.30am–2pm; €8) houses a most impressive collection of medieval weaponry and armour, as well as battle plans and scale models of fortifications. In 1936, during the Civil War, six hundred barricaded Nationalists held out against relentless Republican attack for over two months until finally relieved by one of Franco's armies. Franco's regime completely rebuilt the fortress as a monument to the endurance and glory of its defenders. North of here, the **Museo de Santa Cruz** (Mon–Sat 10am–6pm, Sun 10am–2pm; free), houses an excellent collection of works by El Greco. However, to see his masterpiece, *The Burial of the Count of Orgaz*, you need to visit the fourteenth-century church of **Santo Tomé**, west of the cathedral (daily 10am–6.45pm; €2.30), whose tower is one of the finest examples of Mudéjar architecture in Toledo.

The Judería

From Santo Tomé, c/de San Juan de Dios leads down to the old Jewish Quarter, the **Judería** and, on c/Reyes Católicos, the **Sinagoga del Tránsito**, built along Moorish lines by Samuel Levi in 1366 and housing the **Sephardic Museum** (Feb–Nov Tues–Sat 10am–9pm; Dec & Jan Tues–Sat 10am–6pm; all year Sun 10am–2pm; €2.40), mapping Jewish culture and tradition in Spain along with some beautiful artwork.

Outside the city walls and Mezquita Cristo de la Luz

If you leave the city by the **Puerta del Cambrón**, you can follow the Paseo de Recaredo northeast along a stretch of Moorish walls to the **Hospital de Tavera** (10am–1.30pm & 3–5.30pm; €4), a Renaissance palace with beautiful twin patios. Heading back to town, pass through the **Puerta Nueva de Bisagra**, from where you can climb a series of stepped alleyways to the tiny **Mezquita Cristo de la Luz** (closed for renovation). Built in 999 AD, the mosque is one of the oldest Moorish monuments surviving in Spain.

Arrival and information

Train Frequent, super-fast *Avant* trains run regularly from Estación de Atocha in Madrid (30min; €9.50; last train back to Madrid at 9.25pm). Book tickets in advance. From Toledo's train station east of town, it's a beautiful (but uphill) 20min walk to the central Plaza Zocódover (bus #5 or #6; €1).

Bus The bus station is on Avenida de Castilla la Mancha in the modern part of the city, a 10min walk north of Plaza Zocódover via c/Armas. Buses depart from Madrid's Plaza Elíptica (€4), with

the last bus back to the capital at 10.30pm (Sun 11.30pm).

Tourist office Opposite the Puerta Nueva de Bisagra (Mon–Sat 9am–7pm, winter Mon–Fri 9am–5pm; Sun 9am–3pm; ⓣ925 220 843, ⓦwww.turismocastilla lamancha.com); you can book all manner of walking tours here (ⓦwww.toledopaisajes.com), including the excellent night walks.

Accommmodation

Hostal Palacios c/Alfonso X El Sabio 3 ⓣ925 280 083, ⓦwww.hostalpalacios.net. Spacious rooms with a/c, and a popular restaurant/tapas bar downstairs serving regional specialities. Single €30, double €50.

Eating and drinking

Toledo boasts that its marzipan is the world's finest. Try a selection from its numerous shops and make up your own mind.

El Café de las Monjas c/Santo Tomé 2. Choose from the wide selection of fresh fruit juices or enjoy excellent *chocolate con churros* at this popular café. Juices €3.50; hot chocolate €2.50.

El Zoco Plaza Barrio Rey 7. Just off the touristy Plaza de Zocódover, *El Zoco* offers better value than the restaurants on its neighbouring square. *Menú del día* from €10. Serves the local speciality, *perdiz* (partridge).

EL ESCORIAL

Fifty kilometres northwest of Madrid, nestled in the foothills of the Sierra de Guadarrama, are **SAN LORENZO DEL ESCORIAL** and the monastery of **El Escorial** (Tues–Sun: April–Sept 10am–6pm; Oct–March 10am–5pm; €8; with 1hr guided tour €10; €8.50 combined with El Valle de los Caídos; free Wed for EU citizens). The city grew around this enormous, severe-looking building, which resembles a jail rather than a palace. Start at the monastery's west gateway, which leads into the **Patio de los Reyes** and the impressive Basilica. Move on to the **Salas Capitulares**, outside and around to the left, to see works by El Greco, Velázquez and Ribera. Nearby, the staircase next to the Sacristía leads down to the **Panteón de los Reyes**, the final resting place of virtually all Spanish monarchs since Charles V, where they lie in gilded tombs (guided/audioguide visits only). You'll pass the **Pruderia**, where corpses are left to rot for twenty years prior, and the **Panteón de los Infantes**, for the younger royal corpses – the sheer number of tiny marble coffins makes an eerie exhibit. The **Palace** itself, with the spartan Habsburg Apartments inhabited by Philip II, are fascinating, housing the chair that supported his gouty leg and the deathbed from which he looked down into the church. The Bourbon Apartments were remodelled by Charles III and display collections of tapestries and eighteenth-century fashion (€3.60 extra; join a guided tour in advance; ⓣ918 905 903).

Arrival and information

Train From Madrid's Estación de Atocha to El Escorial (hourly; 1hr; €6.50 return), then a connecting local bus up to the town centre (€1.15); otherwise it's a 20min uphill walk.

Bus Routes #661 and #664 leaving from the Moncloa area, Madrid (every 15min weekdays, hourly on weekends; 50min), take you right to the monastery.

VALLE DE LOS CAÍDOS

If time permits, take a trip to the **Valle de los Caídos (Valley of the Fallen)**, 15km from El Escorial – a monument no less impressive than the monastery itself. A giant basilica carved into the heart of the mountain is topped with allegedly the world's tallest cross, 150m high. The austere, grandiose interior is decorated in black marble, watched over by archangels with swords; though it was said to be a monument to all those who died during the Spanish Civil War, the basilica was built by Franco's prisoners of war, and it is Franco whose tomb is behind the altar. A bus runs from El Escorial's bus station (Tues–Sun 3.15pm, returning 5.30pm; entrance & bus €7.50, with monastery as well €8.50).

Tourist office c/Grimaldi 4 (Mon–Fri 10am–6pm, Sat & Sun 10am–7pm; ⓣ918 905 313, ⓦwww.sanlorenzoturismo.org).

Eating and drinking

Bar Monasterio c/Grimaldi, opposite the tourist office. Small bar with arched brick ceiling. A convenient spot for snacks and drinks.

Restaurante Alaska Plaza San Lorenzo 4. Carnivores will enjoy this informal restaurant specializing in local meat dishes. The *menu del día* is a very reasonable €12.

SEGOVIA

Located 87km northwest of Madrid, **SEGOVIA** has a remarkable number of architectural achievements for a small city. Known to locals as the "stone ship", from a bird's-eye view the city resembles a boat, with its three most celebrated attractions at the stern, bow and mast: the Alcázar, Aqueduct and cathedral, respectively.

What to see and do

The **Aqueduct**, a magnificent structure that dominates the Plaza del Azoguejo, stretches over 800m and towers 30m high. And as if these dimensions weren't impressive enough, the entire structure stands up without a drop of mortar. No one knows exactly when it was built, but it was probably around the end of the first century AD under the Emperor Trajan. Dominating the Plaza Mayor in the heart of the old city, the **cathedral** (daily 9.30am–6.30pm; until 5.30pm in winter) was the last major Gothic building constructed in Spain and it takes that style to its logical extreme, with pinnacles and flying buttresses tacked on at every conceivable point. Beside the cathedral, c/Daoiz leads on to a small park in front of the **Alcázar** (daily: April–Sept 10am–7pm; Oct–March 10am–6pm; €4, free for EU citizens third Tues of every month; tower access €2). This extraordinary castle with narrow towers and turrets is said to have inspired Walt Disney's design for Sleeping Beauty's castle. And indeed, it isn't entirely authentic – after the fifteenth-century original was destroyed by fire in 1862, an imitation model was built in its place.

Segovia is an excellent city for walking, with some beautiful churches just outside the boundaries. The most impressive is **Vera Cruz** (Tues–Sun 10.30am–1.30pm & 4–7pm; closed Nov; €1.75), a remarkable twelve-sided building in the valley facing the Alcázar, erected by the Knights Templar in the early thirteenth century. Climb the tower for a highly photogenic vista of the city.

Arrival and information

Train *Cercanía* snail-trains run to Segovia from Madrid's Estación de Atocha or Chamartín (2hr); the train station is a 15min walk out of town – turn right out of the station and follow the left-hand fork to the central Plaza Mayor. The much faster AVE train (35min) from Chamartín drops you off at the Segovia-Guiomar station, 5km from town; take bus #11 to the Aqueduct (every 15min).

Bus Frequent buses from Madrid's Paseo de Florida bus station (Metro Príncipe Pío) take only 30min. The entrance to the old city is a 10min walk up the Avenida de Fernández Ladreda.

Tourist office Plaza del Azoguejo 1 (Sun–Fri 10am–7pm, Sat 10am–8pm; ⓣ921 466 720, ⓦwww.turismodesegovia.com); regional tourist office at Plaza Mayor 10 (July–Sept daily 9am–8pm, Fri & Sat until 9pm; rest of year 9am–2pm & 5–8pm; ⓣ921 460 334, ⓦwww.turismocastillayleon.com).

Accommodation

Hostal Aragón Plaza Mayor 4 ⓣ921 460 914. This simple, family-run *hostal* is hidden between two restaurants on the main square. Rooms have shared bathrooms and are slightly weathered but spacious – and the location can't be beat. €20.

Eating and drinking

Casa Duque c/Cervantes 12. Traditional restaurant specializing in the local delicacy of *cochinillo asado* (suckling pig) since the 1890s; it's well worth splurging on the *menú gastronómico*, which includes both suckling pig and the famed *ponche*

segoviano dessert (€39.50). Or raid the informal tapas "cave" for meaty delights and inexpensive *cazuelas* (stews).

La Cueva de San Esteban Plaza San Esteban. Tavern with chunky wooden tables and a brilliant atmosphere. Perfect for sharing *raciones* of local meats.

Extremadura

The harsh environment of **Extremadura**, west of Madrid, is known as the "cradle of the conquistadors". Remote before and forgotten since, the area enjoyed a brief golden age when the heroes returned with their gold to live in a flourish of splendour. **Cáceres** preserves an entire town built with conquistador wealth, the streets crowded with the ornate mansions of returning empire-builders, as does Trujillo, the birthplace of Pizarro. An even more ancient past becomes tangible in the wonders of **Mérida**, the most completely preserved Roman city in Spain. The province attracts fewer tourists in June and July, as temperatures get unbearably hot.

CÁCERES

Old **CÁCERES**, 295km southwest of Madrid, was built largely on the plunders of the New World and is home to the University of Extremadura. The Ciudad Monumental – a maze of tiny, winding streets, lined with immaculate historical buildings – is enclosed by medieval stone walls, with storks nesting on every rooftop.

What to see and do

Almost every building in the central **Plaza Mayor** is magnificent, featuring ancient walls pierced by the low **Arco de la Estrella**, the **Torre del Horno**, one of the best-preserved Moorish mud-brick structures in Spain, and the **Torre del Bujaco** – whose foundations date back to Roman times and which you can climb for a great view of the city (Mon–Sat 10am–2pm & 4–7.30pm; €2.50). Another highlight, through the Estrella gate, is the **Casa de Toledo-Montezuma** to which a follower of Cortés brought back one of the New World's more exotic prizes – a daughter of the Aztec emperor as his bride. Near the Plaza de San Jorge, on c/Cuesta del Marqués 4, you'll find the entertaining **Casa Museo Árabe**, a traditionally decorated Moorish house (Tues–Sun 10.30am–2pm & 4.30–7.30pm; €1.50) complete with a harem and an original water cistern. On the Plaza de las Veletas is the **Museo Provincial** (April–Sept Tues–Sat 9am–2.30pm & 5–8.15pm, Sun 10.15am–2.30pm; rest of the year closes 1hr earlier; EU citizens free, non-EU €1.20 or free on Sun), whose highlight is the *aljibe* (cistern) of the original Moorish Alcázar, with rooms of wonderful horseshoe arches.

Arrival and information

Train and bus The stations face each other across the Carretera Sevilla, 3km out of town; bus #1 runs every 15min to Plaza de San Juan (€0.80), a square near the centre, with signs leading on towards the Plaza Mayor.

Tourist office Regional tourist office, Plaza Mayor 10 (June–Sept Mon–Fri 8am–3pm, Sat & Sun 10am–2pm; Oct–May Mon–Fri 9am–2pm & 4–6pm; ⓣ927 010 834, ⓦwww.turismocaceres.org, and ⓦwww.turismoextremadura.com). For arts and entertainment listings, pick up *La Guía Ocio*.

TREAT YOURSELF

The streets of Cáceres are blisteringly hot during the summer months, and the Arab baths at **El Aljibe de Cáceres** on c/Peña (ⓣ927 223 256, ⓦwww.hammamcaceres.com) are the perfect remedy with the traditional warm, hot, then cold pools. Sessions are at 10am, noon, 4pm, 6pm and 8pm; extra session at 10pm Fri & Sat; €15/€13 students. Reservations are essential.

Accommodation

Albergue Las Veletas c/Margallo 36 ☎927 211 210. Bright, spacious dorms and rooms all have modern furnishings and a/c. Spotless bathrooms and very friendly staff make it popular with young Spaniards. Breakfast in on-site cafeteria for an additional €3. Dorms €18, doubles €40.
Pensión Carretero Plaza Mayor 22 ☎927 247 482. The large rooms with shared bathrooms are distinctly no-frills and can be noisy at night, but the location is as central as it gets, at a rock-bottom price. €20.

Eating and drinking

Arabia Riad Plaza Mayor s/n. Lavishly decorated Arabic-style teahouse. Linger here over a wide selection of exotic teas or smoke a leisurely hookah. Teas €2.50–3.50.
El Extremeño Plaza del Duque 10. Bar popular with local students, and rightly so: the half-gallon tubes of beer are very reasonably priced (€5.50).
Mesón Ibérico Plaza San Juan 10. Traditional restaurant serving local specialities. Try the selection of excellent hams and cheeses, *migas* (chorizo-fried breadcrumbs), the *conejo al ajillo* (rabbit in garlic sauce) or the tasty *técula mécula* dessert. *Menú del día* €12.

Moving on

Train Madrid (5 daily, 4hr); Mérida (5 daily; 1hr).
Bus Madrid (8 daily; 4hr); Mérida (5 daily; 4hr 30min); Salamanca (4 daily; 3hr 30min); Seville (8 daily; 4hr); Trujillo (8 daily; 45min).

MÉRIDA

MÉRIDA, 70km south of Cáceres, contains one of Europe's most remarkable concentrations of Roman monuments, including two impressive aqueducts.

What to see and do

A **combined ticket** (€10) gives access to all the archeological sites (daily 9.30am–2pm & 5–7.30pm, 6.30pm in winter). The beautiful **Teatro Romano and Anfiteatro** were presents to the city from Marcus Agrippa in around 15 BC. The stage is in a particularly good state of repair, and in July and August it's the scene for a season of classical plays (tickets from €10). In its day, up to fifteen thousand people would gather in the adjacent amphitheatre to watch gladiatorial combats and fights with wild animals. By the theatre's entrance, you'll find the vast, red-brick bulk of the **Museo Nacional de Arte Romano** (March–Nov Tues–Sat 10am–2pm & 4–9pm, Sun 10am–2pm; Dec–Feb closes at 6pm; €2.50, free Sat pm & Sun am). This high-ceilinged building does full justice to its superior collection, including portrait statues of Augustus, Tiberius and Drusus, some glorious mosaics, coins, and other Roman artefacts. Further south, behind the Plaza de Toros, is the Casa de Mitreo – the remains of a Roman villa with an impressive mosaic. To the east of town you'll find the outline of the Circo Romano, which accommodated up to 30,000 people during chariot races. Also worth seeing is the magnificent **Puente Romano**, the pedestrian Roman bridge across the islet-strewn Guadiana on the city's west side – sixty arches long, and defended by an enormous Moorish **Alcazaba fortress.**

Arrival and information

Train station A 5min walk along c/Mártir Santa Eulalia from the main Plaza de la Villa and the tourist information office.
Bus station On Avenida de la Libertad, a 15min walk across the Lusitania bridge or a short bus ride (bus #4 or #6) to the city centre.
Tourist office c/Santa Eulalia 64 (daily 9.30am–2pm & 5–9pm; ☎924 330 722, Ⓦwww.merida.es). Pick up Extremadura's monthly entertainment listings guide, *Guíate*, with some pages in English.

Accommodation

Hostal El Alfarero c/Sagasta 40 ☎924 303 183, Ⓦwww.hostalelalfarero.com. The pick of the budget options in the centre, this *hostal* offers simple, tastefully decorated en suites with TV and a/c. You can also enjoy good-quality local cuisine at the *Mesón El Alfarero* next door. Doubles €50, triples €65, quads €80.

Hostal Nueva España Avda. Extremadura 6 ☎924 313 356. Characterless yet clean rooms with TV and private bath, just a short walk from the train station. €30.

Eating and drinking

There are several popular restaurants directly in front of the Museo Nacional de Arte Romano, all offering a bargain *menú del día* for €10, and numerous bars around Plaza de la Constitución.

Cervecería 100 Montaditos c/Felix Valverde Lillo 3. The ever-popular casual bar with a hundred different tiny sandwiches on offer; tick your selections and hand your form in at the bar. *Motaditos* €1–2.50.

Mesón El Yantar Avda José Álvarez Saez de Buruaga 12. Snack here on the best hams of the region, sample local *extremeño* dishes, or raid the shop for gourmet meats and cheeses to take home.

Moving on

Train Barcelona (1 daily at 7.56am; 13hr); Cáceres (5 daily; 1hr); Madrid (5 daily, 5hr); Seville (2 daily; 4hr 30min).

Bus Cáceres (7 daily; 1hr); Madrid (8–9 daily; 4hr 20min); Salamanca (5 daily; 4hr); Seville (6 daily; 3hr 15min); Trujillo (4 daily; 2hr).

TRUJILLO

Nicknamed the "Cradle of the Conquistadors", little **TRUJILLO** is the birthplace of key figures who shaped the fate of the New World, much of the town's wealth a direct result of the conquerors' plunders.

What to see and do

The town, a charming maze of russet-coloured houses and mansions, has at its heart the large, pedestrianized Plaza Mayor, just beneath the fortress walls of the Old Town – the well-preserved historical sector. In the southwestern corner of the Plaza stands the **Palacio de la Conquista** (closed for renovations), the most elaborate mansion in town, built for Hernando Pizarro, the brother of Francisco Pizarro – the swineherd turned conqueror of Peru – and his wife, the daughter of Francisco's union with Inés, his Incan consort. Across the plaza is the **Iglesia de San Martín** (Mon–Sat 10am–2pm & 4.30–6.30pm, Sun 10am–12.30pm; €1.40), which contains the family tombs of Francisco de Orellana, the first European to sail down the Amazon. West of the plaza is the **Palacio de Orellana-Pizarro**, decorated with the coats of arms of the town's two most powerful families. In the Old Town uphill, encased within the crumbling medieval walls, head for the Gothic **Iglesia Santa María Mayor** (Mon–Sat 10am–2pm & 4–7pm; €1.25); from its Romanesque tower, you get all-encompassing views of the town, surrounded by arid plains. An even better view is the one from the restored tenth-century Moorish **castle** (daily 10am–2pm & 4–7pm; summer 5–8pm; €1.40).

Arrival and information

Bus station In the Lower Town, 5min walk from the Plaza Mayor, and served by regular daily buses from Madrid and Cáceres, as well as several from Mérida.

Tourist office Plaza Mayor (daily 11am–2pm & 4–7pm; ☎927 322 677, Ⓦwww.trujillo.es); sells discounted combined tickets to various attractions.

Accommodation

Hostal Trujillo c/Francisco Pizarro 4–6 ☎927 322 274, Ⓦwww.hostaltrujillo.com. A short walk from the Plaza Mayor, this simple guesthouse offers clean, a/c rooms. Good restaurant on-site. Singles €40, doubles €50, triples €70, quads €90.

Pensión Boni c/Domingo de Ramos 11 ☎927 321 604. Basic rooms with shared facilities, superbly located just off the Plaza Mayor. €30.

Eating and drinking

El Burladero Plaza Mayor 7. A large selection of tapas, including some excellent cured meats, is the draw at this popular bar. Wash it down with some great local wines.

Mesón La Troya Plaza Mayor 10. A local favourite, Trujillo's best-known restaurant serves up large portions of *extremeño* specialities, such as *migas* (breadcrumbs fried with chorizo) and hearty stews. If you go for the *menú del día* (€15), you better be ravenous, as the portions are huge.

Castilla y León

The foundations of modern Spain were laid in the kingdom of **Castilla y León**, west and north of Madrid. A land of frontier fortresses – the *castillos* from which it takes its name – it became the most powerful and centralizing force of the Reconquest. The monarchs of this triumphant and expansionist age were enthusiastic patrons of the arts, endowing their cities with superlative monuments above which, quite literally, tower the great Gothic cathedrals of **Salamanca** and **León**.

SALAMANCA

SALAMANCA is probably the most graceful city in Spain, home to arguably the oldest and what was once the most prestigious university in Europe. It's a small place, but with many golden sandstone monuments and an attractive Plaza Mayor. As if that weren't enough, Salamanca's student population ensure their town is lively at night during term time.

What to see and do

For a postcard-worthy view of Salamanca, go to the extreme south of the city and cross its oldest surviving monument, the much-restored, four-hundred-metre-long **Puente Romano** (Roman Bridge). To explore Salamanca from close-up make for the grand **Plaza Mayor**, its bare central expanse enclosed by a four-storey refined Baroque building decorated with iron balconies and medallion portraits, the restrained elegance of the designs heightened by the changing strength and angle of the sun. It is particularly rewarding to wander Salamanca's streets by night, when the glorious architecture is subtly lit up by street lights, giving it an almost magical feel; for the best views, take a stroll along the pedestrian Calle de la Compañía.

Casa de las Conchas and Patio de las Escuelas Menores

From the south side of Plaza Mayor, Rúa Mayor leads to the celebrated fifteenth-century **Casa de las Conchas**, or House of Shells, so called because its facades are decorated with rows of carved scallop shells, symbol of the pilgrimage to Santiago de Compostela. It now houses the university library. From here, c/Libreros leads to the **Patio de las Escuelas Menores** and the Renaissance entrance to the **Universidad** (currently closed for renovation). The ultimate achievement of Plateresque art, a Spanish style characterized by ornate decoration, this reflects the tremendous reputation of Salamanca in the early sixteenth century, when it was Europe's greatest university with the most important astronomy department in the world, consulted by Columbus before he set off on his sea voyage. Spotting the legendary "*rana de suerte*" (lucky frog) on its intricately sculpted facade allegedly brings you a year of good luck (if you don't want help, read no further; otherwise, look closely at the skulls).

The cathedrals

A further declaration of Salamanca's prestige, the late-Gothic **Catedral Nueva** (daily 9am–8pm; free) was begun in 1512, and acted as a buttress for the Catedral Vieja, which was in danger of collapsing. Entry to the **Catedral Vieja** (daily 10am–7.30pm; €4.50) is inside the Catedral Nueva. Tiny by comparison and a stylistic hotch-potch of Romanesque and Gothic, its most striking feature is the fifteenth-century Renaissance altarpiece, its 54 tablets depicting the life of Christ. As you look at the Catedral Nueva from the Plaza de Anaya, try to spot the ice-cream cone and the astronaut, carved into the Puerta de Ramos during the last restoration. For a unique glimpse of the cathedrals' interiors from

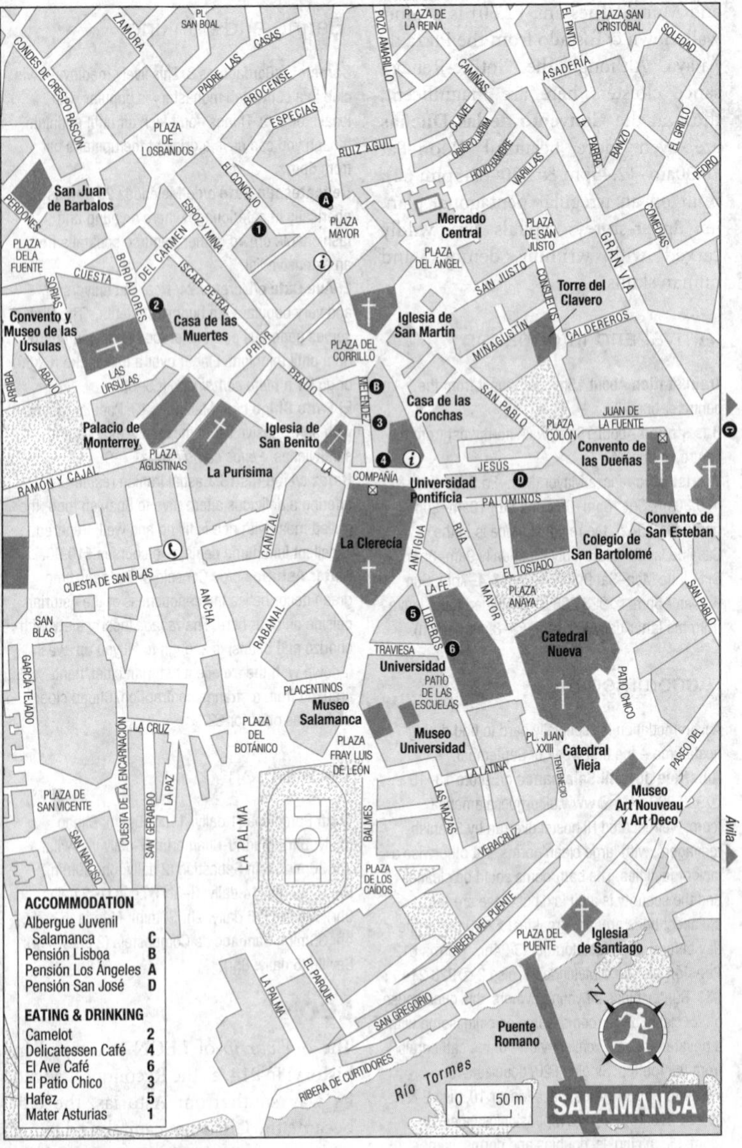

up high, plus several history and art exhibitions hidden in a maze of little rooms, as well as excellent views over Old Salamanca, check out the **Ieronimus exhibition** (entrance from the Plaza de Juan XXIII, at the southwestern corner of the Catedral Nueva; daily 10am–7.15pm; €3).

The convents

The **Convento de San Esteban** (daily 10am–1pm & 4–8pm, closed Sun pm

and Mon & Tues am; €2.50) is a short walk down c/Tostado from the Plaza de Anaya. Although the Gothic-Renaissance cloisters here are magnificent, those at the **Convento de las Dueñas** are even more beautiful (Mon–Sat 10.30am–12.45pm & 4.30–6.45pm; €2). Built on an irregular pentagonal plan, its upper-storey capitals are wildly carved with writhing demons and human skulls.

Arrival and information

Train station About 15min northeast from the centre or bus #2.
Bus station About 15min walk northwest from the centre, or bus #4.
Tourist office Plaza Mayor (Mon–Fri 9am–2pm & 4–6.30pm, Sat 10am–6.30pm, Sun 10am–2pm; ⓣ923 218 342); the regional office is in the Casa de las Conchas (July–Sept daily 9am–8pm; Oct–June Mon–Sat 9.30am–2pm & 4–7pm, Sun 9.30am–5pm; ⓣ923 268 571). Guided tours leave from the latter daily at 11am (€7–8 per person).

Accommodation

Accommodation is especially hard to find during fiesta time – the first week of September.
Albergue Juvenil Salamanca c/Escoto 13–15 ⓣ923 269 141, ⓦwww.alberguesalamanca.com. Well-located HI hostel overrun by Spanish teenagers, with large clean dorms, but otherwise a lack of facilities. The bathrooms could be cleaner and the security is a bit lax, but these are the cheapest beds around. Breakfast €2.40 (order the day before); luggage storage €3/24hr. Dorms €12.
Pensión Lisboa c/Meléndez 1, piso 2 ⓣ923 214 333. Run by pleasant young owners, this guesthouse offers clean, basic rooms, some en suite, some with a private terrace. Excellent views of the cathedrals from the rooftop. Singles €20, doubles €45.
Pensión Los Ángeles Plaza Mayor 10, piso 2 & 3 ⓣ923 218 166, ⓦwww.pensionlosangeles.com. Clean singles, doubles and dorms, some with private bath, as central as you can get, though some lack windows. Particular bargain for groups. Singles €15–25, doubles €25–60, triples €45–80.
Pensión San José c/Jesús 24 ⓣ923 265 461. Spotless, airy singles, doubles and triples, some en suite, located right near the cathedrals on a quiet street; the owners are friendly and helpful. Singles €20, doubles €35, triples €55.

Eating and drinking

Camelot c/Bordadores 3. This lively medieval-style club in a converted monastery is popular with local students. Things don't kick off until midnight, though you can have a drink at the upstairs bar from 6pm.
Delicatessen Café c/de Meléndez 25. Atmospherically lit café/lounge where a young and fashionable crowd gather to nurse cocktails from an extensive list.
El Ave Café c/Libreros 24. Near the university and very popular with hungry students, "The Bird" serves generous portions of food to fill you up from 8am until midnight. Linger over a milkshake (€2.50) or go for a *plato combinado* (€5–8).
El Patio Chico c/de Meléndez 13. Popular tavern with an extensive list of inexpensive tapas and sandwiches. *Platos combinados* €7–9.
Hafez c/Libreros 18. Casual Iranian restaurant offering a delicious alternative to Spanish food; the grilled meat with rice is filling and well prepared. Excellent lunchtime deals; two courses €10.90.
Mater Asturias c/de Consejo 3. The zany lime-green decor belies the seriousness of the Asturian cuisine on offer here. The *fabada* (hearty stew with chorizo and beans) is enough to fill you up; wash it down with the excellent Asturian cider, hand-cranked from a strange contraption. Cheap cider-and-tapas offer for €2.

Moving on

Train Barcelona (1 daily; 11hr 15min); Bilbao (daily; 6hr); Madrid-Chamartín (7 daily via Ávila; 2hr 30min); San Sebastián (2 daily; 6hr 30min).
Bus Cáceres (14 daily; 3–5hr); León (1–2 daily; 3hr); Madrid (16 daily; 2hr 30min); Mérida (5 daily; 4hr 30min); Santiago de Compostela (2 daily; 7hr); Seville (5 daily; 8hr).

LEÓN

The old *barrio* of **LEÓN** is steeped in history: in 914, as the Reconquest edged its way south from Asturias, the city became the Christian capital, and along with its territories it grew so rapidly that by 1035 the county of Castile had matured into a fully fledged kingdom. For the next two centuries, Castilla y León jointly spearheaded the war against the Moors, but by the thirteenth century Castilla's power had eclipsed that of even her mother territory.

What to see and do

Historic sights aside – most notably in its monumental Catedral – León also has an attractive and enjoyable modern quarter and its Barrio Húmedo is where you'd head for a lively spot of tapas bar hopping.

The Catedral

León's enormous Gothic **Catedral** (July–Sept Mon–Sat 8.30am–1.30pm & 4–8pm, Sun 8.30am–2.30pm & 5–8pm; Oct–June closes 1hr earlier) dominates the Old Town by day and night; dating back to the city's final years of greatness, it is perhaps the most beautiful of Spanish Gothic cathedrals. The kaleidoscopic stained-glass windows, which cover an amazing 19,375 square feet, present one of the most magical and harmonious spectacles in Spain, best appreciated from the inside.

Real Basílica de San Isidoro

The city's other great attraction is the **Real Basílica de San Isidoro**, in its namesake plaza, a few minutes' walk west from the Catedral. It was commissioned by Ferdinand I, who united the two kingdoms in 1037, as a shrine for the bones of St Isidoro, and royal mausoleum. Its Panteón Real (July & Aug Mon–Sat 9am–8pm, Sun 9am–2pm; Sept–June Mon–Sat 10am–1.30pm & 4–6.30pm, Sun 10am–1.30pm; €4, free Thurs pm), a pair of twelfth-century, small crypt-like chambers, features some of the most imaginative and impressive paintings of Romanesque art. It once contained the bones of eleven kings and twelve queens, but now lies empty, the French troops having destroyed the graves during the Napoleonic wars.

Monasterio de San Marcos

The opulent **Monasterio de San Marcos**, on the Plaza de San Marcos far west of the city's old pedestrianized quarter by the Río Bernesga (daily 10am–2pm & 4–7pm) was built in 1168 for the Knights of Santiago, one of several chivalric orders founded in the twelfth century to lead the Reconquest. It served as a resting point for weary pilgrims on their way to Santiago de Compostela. The church's sacristy houses the small Museo de León (Tues–Sat 10am–2pm & 4–7pm, Sun 10am–2pm; €1.20; free on weekends), containing some beautiful statuary and church treasures.

Museo de Arte Contemporaneo (MUSAC)

A short walk north of the Monasterio San Marcos along Avenida de los Reyes Leóneses, is the award-winning **Museo de Arte Contemporaneo** (Tues–Fri 10am–3pm & 5–8pm, Sat & Sun 11am–3pm & 5–9pm; free), its exterior covered with 37 shades of glass. It's known for its excellent temporary exhibitions of modern art by contemporary Spanish artists, which include collages, photographic exhibitions, sculpture and video installation.

Arrival and information

Train and bus stations Both just south of the river: the train station at the end of Avenida de Palencia, the bridge into town, and the bus station on Paseo Ingeniero Saenz de Miera – from here, turn left onto the Paseo to reach the bridge. Casco Antiguo (the old city) is a 10min walk or a short bus ride (#7; €1) along Avenida de Ordoño II.

Tourist office Plaza de la Regla 3 (July & Aug daily 9am–8pm, Fri & Sat until 9pm; Sept–June Mon–Fri 9am–2pm & 5–8pm, Sat & Sun 10am–2pm & 5–8pm; ⓣ902 203 030, ⓦwww.turismocastillayleon.com).

Accommodation

Hostal San Martín Plaza Torres de Omaña 1, 2° ⓣ987 815 187, ⓦwww.sanmartinhostales.com. Plain, bright rooms and spick-and-span bathrooms presided over by a friendly owner. Wi-fi available and Barrio Húmedo is a 5min walk away. Singles €22–30, doubles €42, triples €54.

Pensión La Torre de San Isídoro c/La Torre 3, 1° ⓣ987 225 594, ⓦwww.lahiguera.net/torresanisidoro. Spacious, excellent quality rooms with private bathrooms. Friendly owner offers laundry service and free wi-fi. Singles €25, doubles €45.
Pensión Puerta Sol c/Puerta del Sol 1, 2° ⓣ987 211 966. Basic accommodation overlooking the Plaza Mayor. It doesn't get any more central than this, but don't expect to get a lot of sleep. €12–18.

Eating and drinking

Free tapas is the name of the game in León, particularly in the Barrio Húmedo around Plaza San Martín.
El Llar Plaza San Martín 9. Authentic Leónese bar with dark wood interior and terracotta walls. The *patatas allioli* (potatoes with garlic mayonnaise) – free with every drink – are brilliant.
Estrella de Golizna c/de Ancha 22. Bustling café/bar with hearty daily specials on offer; the *garbanzos con bacalao* (butter bean and cod stew) is excellent. Dish of the day €3.95.
La Bicha Plaza Tiendas s/n. Great place for all sorts of meaty tapas. Try the delicious house special, *morcilla* (black pudding).
Restaurante Artesanos c/Juan de Arfe 2. Excellent upmarket restaurant serving imaginative Leónese dishes. The fish in particular is fresh, tender and expertly prepared; try the *merluza*. *Menú del día* €20.

Moving on

Train Barcelona (4 daily; 10hr–11hr 40min); Bilbao (daily at 3.07pm; 5hr); Madrid (9 daily; 3hr–4hr 30min); San Sebastián (daily at 3.07pm; 5hr); Santiago de Compostela (daily at 2.03pm; 6hr).
Bus Barcelona (3 daily; 10hr); Bilbao (1–2 daily except Sat; 4–6hr); Cáceres (3 daily; 6hr); Madrid (10 daily; 3hr 30min–4hr); Santander (7 daily; 3hr 30min–7hr); San Sebastián (6 weekly; 6hr 40min); Seville (3 daily; 10hr 30min).

Andalucía

The southern region of **Andalucía** is likely to both meet and defy your preconceptions of Spain. It is the parched, passionate home of **flamenco** and the **bullfight**, tradition and fierce pride. But it's also much more than the cliché. Evidence of the **Moors**' sophistication remains visible to this day in **Córdoba**, in **Seville**, and, particularly, in **Granada's Alhambra**. Extending to either side of **Málaga** is the **Costa del Sol**, Europe's most developed resort area, but you can find unspoiled beaches even there, and along the **Costa de la Luz**, on the way to **Cádiz**, one of Spain's oldest cities. Andalucía is also where Europe stops and Africa begins: from **Tarifa**, the kite-surfer and windsurfer capital on the most southerly tip of Europe, the mountains of that great continent appear almost close enough to touch.

GRANADA

If you see only one town in Spain, it should be **GRANADA**, with its wonderful backdrop of the **Sierra Nevada mountains**. Here stands Spain's most visited monument, the **Alhambra**. Granada was established as an independent kingdom in 1238 by **Ibn Ahmar**, a prince of the Arab Nasrid tribe. The Moors of Granada maintained their autonomy for two and a half centuries, but by 1490 only the city itself remained in Muslim hands. On January 2, 1492, Granada fell to the army of Ferdinand and Isabella following a seven-month siege and the Christian Reconquest of Spain was complete, followed by the expulsion of Jews from Spain and the persecutions of its Muslim population. Today Granada is a vibrant city, combining modern infrastructure with grand Moorish architecture and an exuberant nightlife.

What to see and do

The main attraction of the town is without doubt the **Alhambra**, the stunning Moorish palace complex set up on a hill overlooking the city. However, Granada's centre has some fine architecture of its own, including the **cathedral** and the **Capilla Real**. On

A hot tip is to buy a **bono turístico Granada** (tourist voucher; €30/33 if you buy it in advance over the phone; ⓣ902 100 095, ⓦgranadamap.com/bono) from the audioguide kiosk in Plaza Nueva, which lets you jump the lengthy queues and gets you into a range of museums and sights throughout the city, as well as allowing ten bus trips.

an adjacent hill to the Alhambra lies the **Albaicín**, offering the opportunity to wander through atmospheric cobbled streets and whitewashed houses with Moorish touches still in evidence. In fact, Granada retains much of its North African legacy, from the *teterías* offering shisha and sweet pastries to the Arabic doorways of its houses, and traditional Arabic baths.

The Alhambra: the Alcazaba and the Palacios Nazaríes

The standard approach to the **Alhambra** is along the Cuesta de Gomérez that climbs uphill from Plaza Nueva, either on foot or by taking the Alhambrabus from Plaza Nueva (every 10min; €1). Start your visit with the earliest, most ruined, part of the fortress – the **Alcazaba**. It was this building's distinctive hue that gave the complex its name, as "al-Hambra" means "red" in Arabic. At the summit is the **Torre de la Vela**, from where there's a fine view of the whitewashed houses clustered on the hillsides below.

The buildings in the **Palacios Nazaríes** – undoubtedly the Alhambra's gem – show a brilliant use of light and space with ornamental stucco decoration, in rhythmic repetitions of supreme beauty. Elegant Arabic inscriptions from the Koran cover the palace walls. The sultans used the **Palacio del Mexuar**, the first series of rooms, for business and judicial purposes. In the **Serallo**, beyond, they received distinguished guests: here is the royal throne room, known as the **Hall of the Ambassadors**, the largest room of the palace. The last section, the **Harem**, formed their private living quarters. These are the most beautiful rooms of the palace, and include the **Patio de los Leones**, which has become the archetypal image of Granada. Try to come back to the Palacios Nazaríes at night, just to see the serene reflection in the perfectly proportioned pool of the Patio de los Arrayanes.

The Alhambra: the Palacio de Carlos V and the Generalife

Next to the Palacios Nazaríes is the **Palacio de Carlos V**, an ostentatious piece of Renaissance architecture, with a circular courtyard where bullfights once took place, which was built by its namesake Charles V, the grandson of Ferdinand and Isabella. A wing of the Palacios Nazaríes was demolished to make way for it. The palace's lower floor is home to Museo de la Alhambra

ALHAMBRA PRACTICALITIES

Tickets for the Alhambra (daily: March–Oct 8.30am–2pm & 2–8pm; Nov–Feb 8.30am–2pm & 2–6pm; €12) are limited, so buy in advance by phone or online (lines open 8am–midnight, €1 booking fee; ⓣ902 888 00, ⓦwww.alhambra-tickets.es), and then collect them from the Alhambra ticket office; bring the credit card used to purchase the ticket and your passport. If there are no tickets available online, get to the ticket office for 7am on the day you want to visit and queue up for the limited tickets sold on the day. Tickets are timed for the **Palacios Nazaríes**; you are given a 30min slot to make your way around, make sure not to miss it. The extremely worthwhile nocturnal visits to the Palacios Nazaríes (March–Oct Tues–Sat 10–11.30pm; Nov–Feb Fri & Sat 8–9.30pm; €12) also need to be booked in advance.

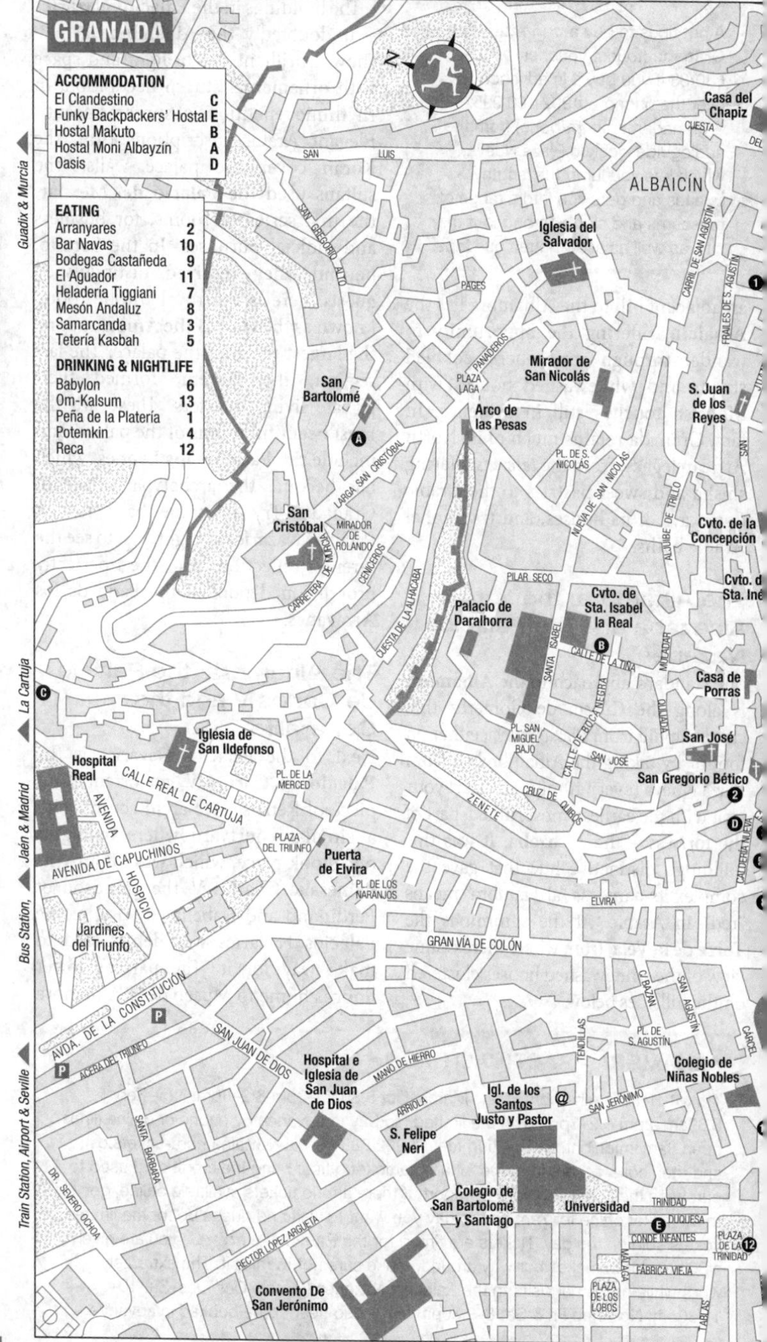
GRANADA
ACCOMMODATION
El Clandestino C
Funky Backpackers' Hostal E
Hostal Makuto B
Hostal Moni Albayzín A
Oasis D
EATING
Arranyares 2
Bar Navas 10
Bodegas Castañeda 9
El Aguador 11
Heladería Tiggiani 7
Mesón Andaluz 8
Samarcanda 3
Tetería Kasbah 5
DRINKING & NIGHTLIFE
Babylon 6
Om-Kalsum 13
Peña de la Platería 1
Potemkin 4
Reca 12
Guadix & Murcia
La Cartuja
Bus Station, Jaén & Madrid
Train Station, Airport & Seville
Antequera & Málaga
ALBAICÍN
Casa del Chapiz
Iglesia del Salvador
Mirador de San Nicolás
S. Juan de los Reyes
San Bartolomé
Arco de las Pesas
San Cristóbal
Mirador de Rolando
Cvto. de la Concepción
Palacio de Daralhorra
Cvto. de Sta. Isabel la Real
Casa de Porras
San José
San Gregorio Bético
Iglesia de San Ildefonso
Hospital Real
Puerta de Elvira
Jardines del Triunfo
Hospital e Iglesia de San Juan de Dios
Igl. de los Santos Justo y Pastor
S. Felipe Neri
Colegio de San Bartolomé y Santiago
Universidad
Colegio de Niñas Nobles
Convento De San Jerónimo
SAN LUIS
SAN GREGORIO ALTO
PAGES
PANADEROS
PLAZA LAGA
PL. DE S. NICOLÁS
NUEVA DE SAN NICOLÁS
CARRIL DE SAN AGUSTÍN
FRAILES DE S. AGUSTÍN
ALJIBE DE TRILLO
LARGA SAN CRISTÓBAL
CARRETERA DE MURCIA
CENICEROS
CUESTA DE LA ALHACABA
PILAR SECO
SANTA ISABEL
CALLE DE LA TIÑA
MULADAR
CALLE DE BOCA NEGRA
OLIVIDA
PL. SAN MIGUEL BAJO
SAN JOSÉ
CRUZ DE QUIRÓS
ZENETE
CALDERÍA NUEVA
PL. DE LA MERCED
CALLE REAL DE CARTUJA
AVENIDA
PLAZA DEL TRIUNFO
PL. DE LOS NARANJOS
AVENIDA DE CAPUCHINOS
HOSPICIO
ELVIRA
GRAN VÍA DE COLÓN
AVDA. DE LA CONSTITUCIÓN
ACERA DEL TRIUNFO
SAN JUAN DE DIOS
MANO DE HIERRO
ARRIOLA
C/ BAZAN
SAN AGUSTÍN
PL. DE S. AGUSTÍN
TENDILLAS
SAN JERÓNIMO
CÁRCEL
SANTA BÁRBARA
DR. SEVERO OCHOA
RECTOR LÓPEZ ARGUETA
TRINIDAD
DUQUESA
CONDE INFANTES
PLAZA DE LA TRINIDAD
MÁLAGA
FÁBRICA VIEJA
PLAZA DE LOS LOBOS
TABLAS

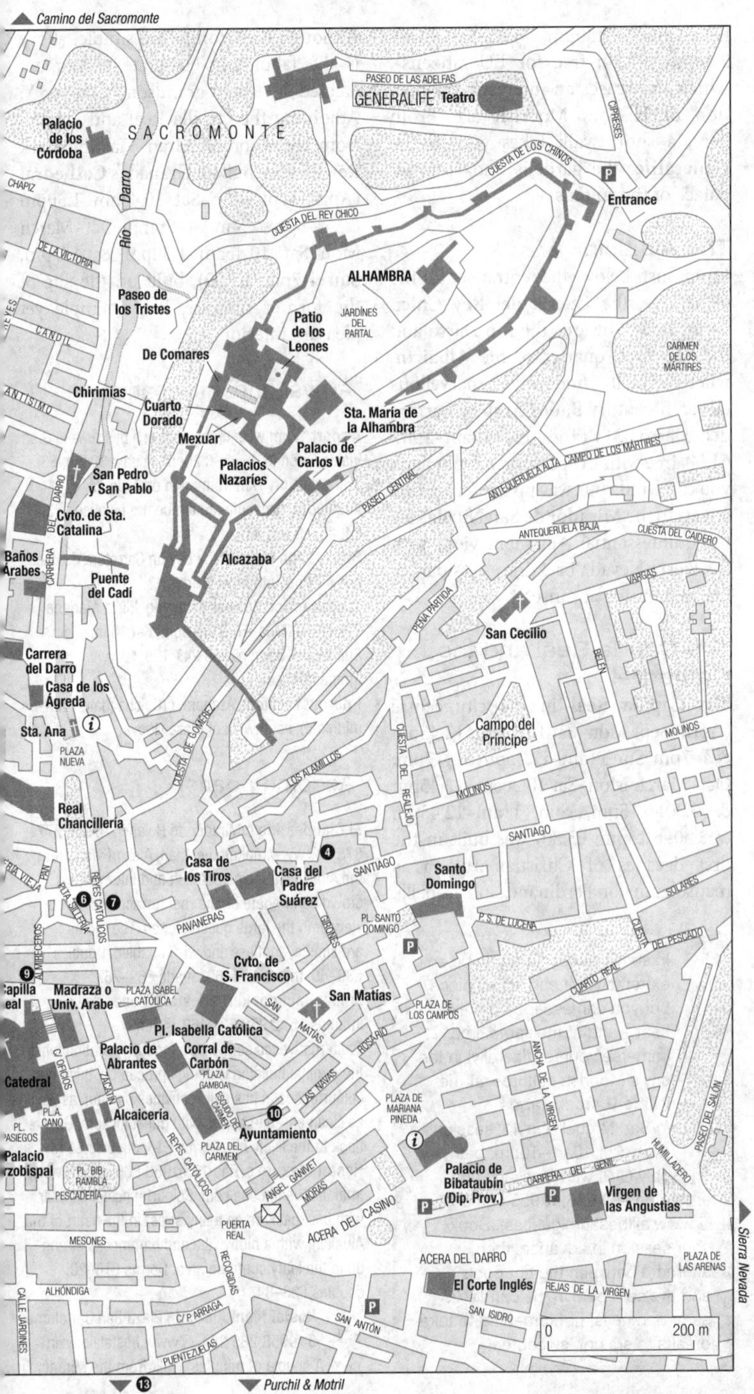

Camino del Sacromonte
PASEO DE LAS ADELFAS
GENERALIFE
Teatro
CIPRESES
Palacio de los Córdoba
SACROMONTE
CUESTA DE LOS CHINOS
Entrance
CHAPIZ
Río Darro
CUESTA DEL REY CHICO
DE LA VICTORIA
ALHAMBRA
Paseo de los Tristes
Patio de los Leones
JARDÍNES DEL PARTAL
REYES
CANDIL
CARMEN DE LOS MÁRTIRES
De Comares
Chirimías
ANTISIMO
Cuarto Dorado
Sta. María de la Alhambra
Mexuar
Palacio de Carlos V
Palacios Nazaríes
San Pedro y San Pablo
ANTEQUERUELA ALTA
CAMPO DE LOS MÁRTIRES
PASEO CENTRAL
DARRO
Cvto. de Sta. Catalina
ANTEQUERUELA BAJA
CUESTA DEL CAIDERO
Baños Árabes
CARRERA DEL
Alcazaba
Puente del Cadí
VARGAS
PEÑA PARTIDA
San Cecilio
Carrera del Darro
BELÉN
Casa de los Ágreda
Sta. Ana
Campo del Príncipe
CUESTA DE GOMEREZ
CUESTA DEL REALEJO
MOLINOS
PLAZA NUEVA
LOS ALAMILLOS
MOLINOS
Real Chancillería
SANTIAGO
Casa de los Tiros
Casa del Padre Suárez
SANTIAGO
Santo Domingo
SOLARES
PAN
RÍA VIEJA
PLTA. SILLERÍA
REYES CATÓLICOS
PAVANERAS
PL. SANTO DOMINGO
GIBONES
P. S. DE LUCENA
CUESTA DEL PESCADO
ALMIRECEROS
Cvto. de S. Francisco
Capilla Real
Madraza o Univ. Arabe
PLAZA ISABEL CATÓLICA
SAN MATÍAS
San Matías
PLAZA DE LOS CAMPOS
CUARTO REAL
Pl. Isabella Católica
ROSARIO
Palacio de Abrantes
Corral de Carbón
C/ OFICIOS
ANCHA DE LA VIRGEN
Catedral
ZACATÍN
PLAZA GAMBOA
ESCUDO DEL CARMEN
LAS NAVAS
PLAZA DE MARIANA PINEDA
PASEO DEL SALÓN
PL.A CANO
Alcaicería
PL. PASIEGOS
Ayuntamiento
PLAZA DEL CARMEN
HUMILLADERO
Palacio Arzobispal
PL. BIB-RAMBLA
REYES CATÓLICOS
ÁNGEL GANIVET
MORAS
Palacio de Bibataubín (Dip. Prov.)
CARRERA DEL GENIL
Virgen de las Angustias
PESCADERÍA
PUERTA REAL
ACERA DEL CASINO
Sierra Nevada
MESONES
RECOGIDAS
ACERA DEL DARRO
PLAZA DE LAS ARENAS
ALHÓNDIGA
El Corte Inglés
REJAS DE LA VIRGEN
CALLE JARDINES
C/ P ARRAGA
SAN ANTÓN
SAN ISIDRO
0
200 m
PUENTEZUELAS
13
Purchil & Motril

(Tues noon–2.30pm, Wed–Sat 9am–2.30pm; €1.50; free for EU citizens), which showcases an interesting collection of Hispano-Moorish art. From here, a short walk takes you to the **Generalife**, the gardens and summer palace of the sultans.

The Albaicín

From just below the entrance to the Generalife, the **Cuesta del Rey Chico** winds down towards the Río Darro and the old Arab quarter of the **Albaicín**, where you'll find the marvellous eleventh-century **Baños Árabes**, Carrera del Darro 31 (Tues–Fri 10am–2pm; €1.50, free with EU passport). From here, you can wind your way up the serpentine streets to the **Mirador de San Nicolás** for the quintessential Alhambra view, with the Sierra Nevada backdrop – it's particularly stunning at sunset.

The Capilla Real and the Cathedral

The **Capilla Real** in the city centre (April–Sept Mon–Sat 10.30am–12.45pm & 4–7pm, Sun 11am–12.45pm & 4–7pm; Oct–March Mon–Sat 10.30am–12.45pm & 3.30–6.15pm, Sun 11am–12.45pm & 3.30–6.15pm; €3.50) was built in the first decades of Christian rule as a mausoleum for Ferdinand and Isabella. Although their tombs are simple, above is the fabulously elaborate monument erected by their grandson, Charles V. Adjoining the Capilla Real and entered from the door on Gran Vía, the stark Renaissance bulk of Granada's **Cathedral** (April–Sept Mon–Sat 10.45am–1.30pm & 4–8pm, Sun 4–8pm; Oct–March Mon–Sat 10.45am–1.30pm & 4–7pm, Sun 4–7pm; €3.50), built on the site of the former mosque, has a simple yet pleasant interior.

TREAT YOURSELF

In summer, Granada can be an extremely hot and sticky place, but you can escape from the heat – and at the same time immerse yourself (literally) in the city's Moorish culture – at the **Aljibe Baños Árabes** (c/San Miguel Alta 41; sessions every 2hr 10am–10pm; bath only €19, with massage and aromatherapy €26; ⓣ958 522 867, ⓦwww.aljibesanmiguel.es). Book your session in advance, then alternate between the hot pools and the cold pool in the candle-lit semi-darkness, not forgetting to take breaks to sip hot, sweet tea.

Arrival and information

Airport 17km west of the centre; a bus runs to Gran Vía de Colón (6.40am–8.25pm, hourly; 30min; €3).

Train station 1km from town on Avda de Andaluces, connected to the centre by buses #3, #4, #6, #9 and #11.

Bus station North of the city on Carretera de Jaén; bus #3 runs into town (15min).

Tourist office Several, including: Plaza Mariana Pineda 10 (Mon–Fri 9am–8pm, Sat 10am–7pm, Sun 10am–3pm; ⓣ958 247 128, ⓦwww.granadatur.com).

Internet Locutorio Azahara, c/Colcha (daily 9am–midnight), southwest of Plaza Nueva.

Accommodation

El Clandestino c/Miradór de Rolando ⓣ958 277 875, ⓦwww.makuto.net/clan. A short walk from the Albaicín, a mixed Spanish and international crowd congregate on the roof terrace with a fab view or in the large guest kitchen. The rooms are simple, spotless and wi-fi enabled. Doubles €36–45, triples €54–60, quads €69–75.

Funky Backpackers' Hostal c/Conde de Las Infantas 15 ⓣ958 221 462, ⓔfunky@alternativeacc.com. In a temporary location while the original building is being spruced up, this bright, colourful hostel has daily activities on offer, as well as clean en-suite dorms with guest lockers. Guests flock to the lively bar. Dorms €18, doubles €44.

Hostal Makuto c/Tiña 18 ⓣ958 805 876, ⓦwww.makutoguesthouse.com. Colourful hostel popular with backpackers on a tiny street in the heart of the Albaicín, with a hippy vibe and hammocks strung up in the leafy common area. Dorms €18–20, doubles €28–34.

Hostal Moni Albayzín Plaza San Bartolomé 5 ⓣ958 285 284, ⓦwww.hostalalbayzin.com. A couple of minutes' walk from the Miradór

San Nicolas, this budget guesthouse offers stunning views of the Alhambra from its own rooftop terrace, as well as clean en-suite rooms with a/c. Doubles €50–60.
Oasis Placeta Correo Viejo 3 ⓣ958 215 848, ⓦwww.hosteloasis.com. Firm backpacker favourite, with spotless en-suite dorms arranged around a leafy central courtyard. All the guest amenities you can think of, including a chillout zone on the roof, and as an extra bonus, the young, energetic staff do free tapas bar crawls several night a week. Dorms €20.

Eating

Granada has some good, cheap restaurants, but your best bet is to head to a tapas bar, which often serve free tapas with every drink. The best areas for eating are Calle Elvira, the labyrinth of Albaicín, Plaza Trinidad and around and Calle Las Navas, off Plaza del Carmen.
Arranyares c/Cuesta Marañas 4. Very popular Moroccan restaurant just off the main tourist drag; the couscous dishes are excellent. Mains €6–10. No alcohol.
Bar Navas c/Navas 14. Try the great selection of *bocadillos* while people-watching from the outdoor seating; *boquerones* (fresh anchovies) and cheese with honey are particularly tasty. Follow it with a jug of sangría. Selection of *bocadillos* €5.50.
Bodegas Castañeda c/Almireceros 1. The oldest tapas bar in town, with rustic features and festooned with hams. Go for the generous portions of home-made pâté or a selection of tasty *montaditos* (tiny sandwiches). Tapas €2–4.
El Aguador Plaza de la Romanilla 12. Informal restaurant with extensive outdoor seating, with a good *menú del día* (€10) featuring decent gazpacho, paella, and other Spanish classics.
Heladería Tiggiani Plaza Nueva and c/Cuchilleros. The place for superb, originally flavoured ice cream; two scoops €1.80.
Mesón Andaluz c/Cetti Meriem 6. Friendly restaurant specializing in Andalucian cuisine, including the excellent *fritura mixta* (fried fish platter), large enough for two people. Good *menú del día* €12.
Samarcanda c/Caldería Vieja 3. Vegetarians rejoice, for this great Lebanese spot has something for everyone. The falafel is excellent.
Tetería Kasbah Caldería Nueva 4. The Moroccan food here is overpriced and rather insipid, but this is a good spot to savour *pasteles árabes* (Arabic sweets) accompanied by one of the many teas.

Drinking and nightlife

Nightlife is focused on Calle Elvira, with its large number of bars. Another good area is around the university, on c/Gran Capitán and c/Pedro Antonio de Alarcón. In term time, students also gather in pubs near the bus station around the Campo del Príncipe, a square on the southern slopes of the Alhambra.
Babylon c/Silleria, between Plaza Nueva and Gran Vía. Heaving reggae club popular with foreign students.
Om-Kalsum c/Jardines 17. Friendly and popular bar serving delicious tapas with an Arabic twist. The little chicken kebabs are great, though it's hard to fault any of the dishes. Tapas €1.90–3.
Peña de la Platería Plazolete de Toqueros 7 ⓦwww.laplateria.org.es. Serious flamenco club hidden within the Albaicín for those with a genuine interest in the art. Excellent performances Thursdays at 10.30pm; entry €8 with drink.
Potemkin Plaza Hospicio Viejo s/n. Tiny, lively watering-hole run by a former drummer with Johnny Rotten. Tapas are imaginatively prepared and you get one with every drink. Drinks €1.50.
Reca c/Alhondiga. Smart little bar with outside seating on Plaza Trinidad, perpetually filled with locals. Try some of the *jamón* with your drink.

Moving on

Train Almería (4 daily; 2hr 15min); Barcelona (2 daily; 12hr); Madrid (2 daily; 4hr 50min); Málaga (5 daily; 1hr 50min); Ronda (3 daily; 2hr 30min); Seville (4 daily; 3hr); Valencia (2 daily; 7hr).
Bus Almería (6 daily; 2hr 15min); Cádiz (4 daily; 5hr 30min); Córdoba (8 daily; 2hr 45min); Madrid (13 daily; 5hr); Málaga (20 daily; 1hr 45min); Ronda (2 daily; 3hr 45min); Seville (6–7 daily; 3hr).

CÓRDOBA

Now a minor provincial capital, **CÓRDOBA** was once the largest city of Roman Spain, and for three centuries the heart of the great medieval caliphate of the Moors. It's an engaging, atmospheric city, easily explored on foot.

What to see and do

For visitors, Córdoba's main attraction is a single building: **La Mezquita** – the grandest and most beautiful mosque ever constructed by the Moors in Spain.

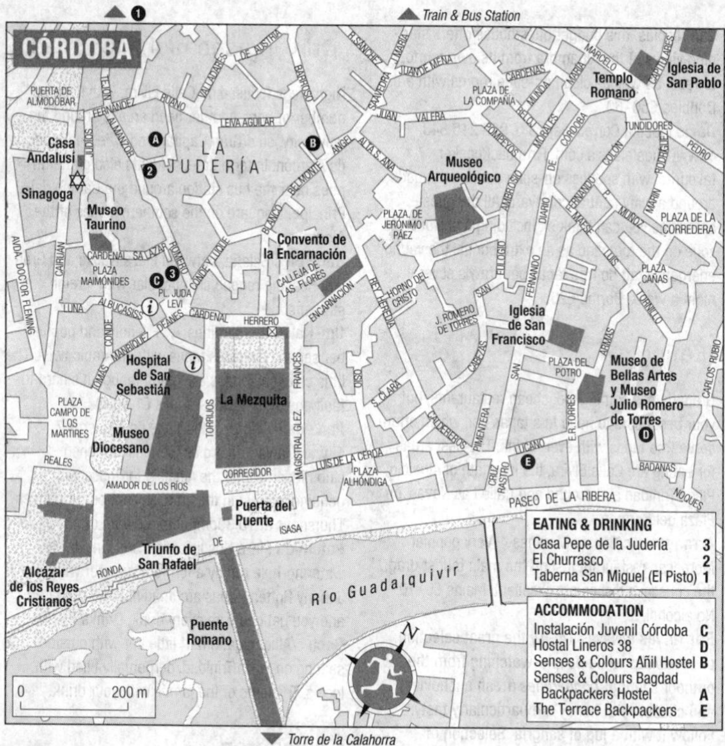

This stands right in the centre of the city, surrounded by the labyrinth of old Jewish and Moorish quarters, and is a building of extraordinary mystical and aesthetic power.

La Mezquita

Córdoba's domination of Moorish Spain began thirty years after the conquest, in 756 AD, when the city was placed under **Abd ar-Rahman I**, who established control over all but the north of Spain. It was he who began the building of the Great Mosque – in Spanish, **La Mezquita** (Mon–Sat 10am–7pm, Sun: Mass at 11am & 1pm, open 2–7pm; €8) – which is approached through the **Patio de los Naranjos**, a classic Islamic court preserving both its orange trees and fountains for ritual purification before prayer. Inside, a thicket of nearly a thousand twin-layered red and white archways combine to mesmerizing effect, the harmony culminating only at the foot of the beautiful **mihrab** (prayer niche). In the centre of the mosque, you'll find a Renaissance cathedral, built in 1523, though it's the mihrab that commands most of the attention.

La Judería and around

North of La Mezquita lies **La Judería**, Córdoba's old Jewish quarter, a fascinating network of atmospheric lanes. Near the heart of the quarter, at c/Maimonides 18, is a tiny **synagogue** with fine stuccowork (Tues–Sat 9.30am–2pm & 3.30–5.30pm, Sun 9.30am–1.30pm; €0.30, free for EU citizens), one of only three in Spain that survived the Jewish expulsion of 1492. East of La Judería, the **Museo Arqueológico** (Tues 2.30–8.30pm, Wed–Sat 9am–8.30pm, Sun 9am–2.30pm; €1.50,

free for EU citizens) occupies a small Renaissance mansion in which Roman foundations have been incorporated into an imaginative display.

Torre de la Calahorra

Behind the Mezquita, across the attractive pedestrianized Roman Bridge (Puente Romano) stands the medieval **Torre de la Calahorra** (daily 10am–6pm; €4.50), housing an entertaining high-tech museum; don the headphones and tap into the talking dioramas, which bring the history of Córdoba and the Moorish irrigation systems to life. There's a great view of the Mezquita from the top of the tower, and also from across the bridge at night.

Arrival and information

Bus and train Combined station is 1km northwest of the old town. Bus #3 goes to La Judería, whilst #4 heads slightly further north to Plaza Tendillas.
Tourist office Palacio de Congresos y Exposiciones, c/Torrijos 10 (Mon–Fri 9am–7.30pm, Sat & Sun 9am–3pm; ⓣ957 355 179, ⓦwww.turismodecordoba.org).
Internet Ch@t, c/Claudio Marcelo 15 (Mon–Sat 10am–2pm & 5–9.30pm).

Accommodation

Hostal Lineros 38 c/Lineros 38 ⓣ957 482 517, ⓦwww.hostallineros38.com. Well-located guesthouse decorated in Moorish style, whose plush doubles feature spacious bathrooms, a/c and wi-fi access. €30–45 per person.
Instalación Juvenil Córdoba Plaza Juda Levi s/n ⓣ957 355 040, ⓦwww.inturjoven.com. The town's only HI youth hostel, very centrally located, with en-suite and wi-fi equipped doubles, triples and quads. There's also a cheap café on-site. €18, over-26s €24.
Senses & Colours Añil Hostel c/Barroso 4 ⓣ957 491 544, ⓦwww.sensesandcolours.com. Quiet, brightly decorated hostel in the heart of the Judería with an attractive roof terrace. En-suite dorms have a/c and small luggage lockers; lack of guest kitchen is the only real drawback. Other hostel branch at c/Fernández Ruano 11. Dorms €14, doubles €34.
The Terrace Backpackers c/Lucano 12 ⓣ957 492 966. Extremely popular backpacker haunt with bright, cosy en-suite dorms and doubles, guest kitchen, wi-fi, and a chill-out rooftop terrace. 5min walk to the Mezquita. Dorms €16, doubles €38.

Eating and drinking

Avoid the touristy places around La Mezquita; the best bars and restaurants are in La Judería and the old quarters off to the east, above Paseo de la Ribera.
Casa Pepe de la Judería c/Romero 1. The tapas bar at this excellent Sephardic (Spanish-Jewish) restaurant serves excellent regional specialities; their *salmorejo* (a thicker, more savoury *gazpacho*) and *berenjenas con miel* (aubergines with honey) are delectable.
El Churrasco c/Romero 16. Popular with the locals and tourists alike, this restaurant is named after the massive pork chops with spicy sauce that it does so well. Excellent selection of generously portioned tapas. Mains €8–10; tapas €1.50–3.50. If you fancy splashing out, try the *menú de degustación* (€30).
Taberna San Miguel (El Pisto) Pl. San Miguel 1. Over a hundred years old, this Córdoba institution serves excellent Montilla wine, accompanied by regional tapas; try the *rabo de toro* (oxtail) or the *callos en salsa picante* (tripe in spicy sauce). Closed Sun and August.

Moving on

Train Cádiz (2 daily; 3hr); Granada (2 daily; 2hr 45min); Madrid (19 daily; 1hr 40min–4hr 30min); Málaga (13 daily; 1hr–1hr 20min); Seville (22 daily; 45min–1hr 15min).
Bus Granada (9 daily; 3hr 30min); Madrid (7 daily; 4hr 50min); Málaga (7 daily; 2hr); Seville (7 daily; 2hr).

SEVILLE (SEVILLA)

SEVILLE (Sevilla) is the great city of the Spanish south, one of the earliest Moorish conquests (in 712 AD) and, as part of the Caliphate of Córdoba, the second city of al-Andalus. Under the Almohad dynasty, Seville became the capital of the last real Moorish empire in Spain from 1170 until 1212 before being conquered by Fernando III in 1248. With a monopoly on trade with the New World, the city grew in wealth and influence and, centuries on, still remains one of the most prosperous and beautiful of Spain's cities. Illustrious history aside, it is the city's life that

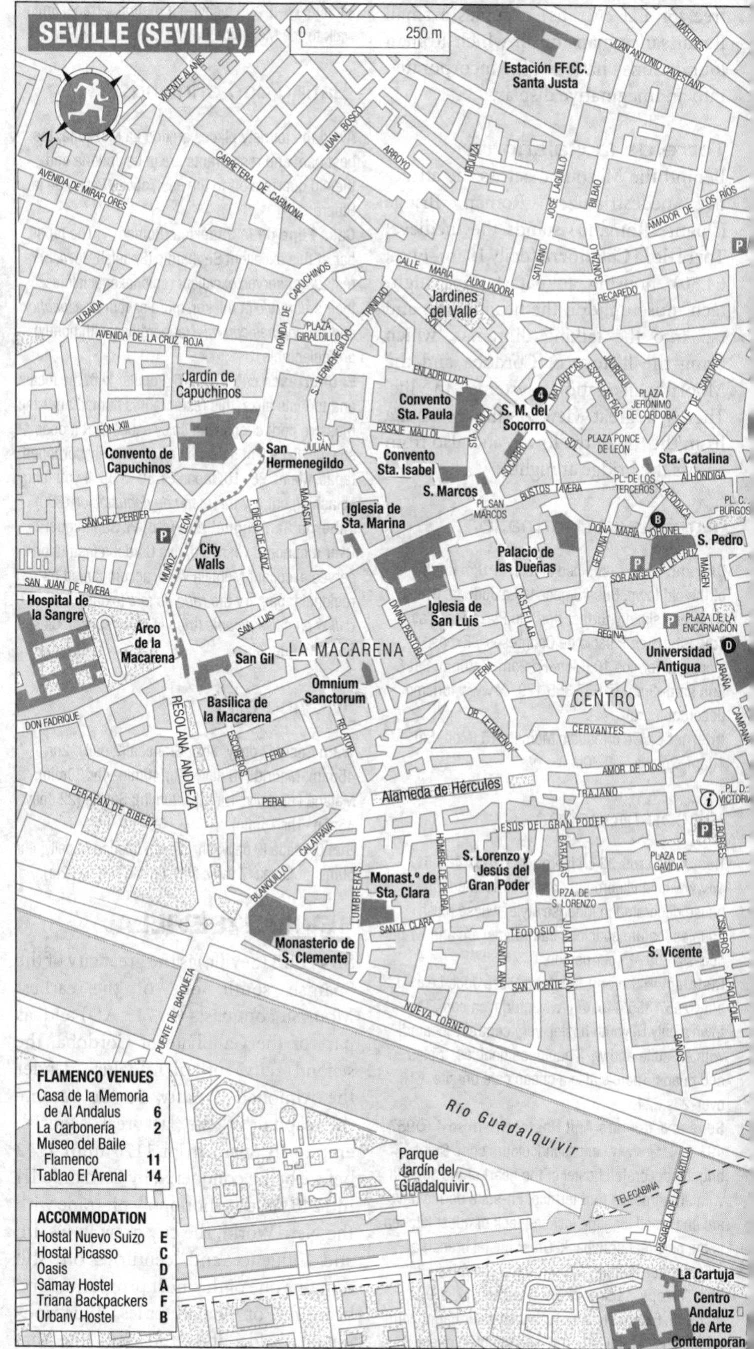
SEVILLE (SEVILLA)
0
250 m
N
Estación FF.CC.
Santa Justa
MARTIRES
JUAN ANTONIO CAVESTANY
VICENTE ALANIS
JUAN BOSCO
ARROYO
CARRETERA DE CARMONA
AVENIDA DE MIRAFLORES
URQUIZA
JOSE LAGUILLO
BILBAO
AMADOR DE LOS RÍOS
SATURNO
GONZALO
RECAREDO
CALLE MARÍA AUXILIADORA
RONDA DE CAPUCHINOS
TRINIDAD
SOL
Jardines
del Valle
ALBAIDA
AVENIDA DE LA CRUZ ROJA
PLAZA
GIRALDILLO
S. HERMENEGILDO
ENLADRILLADA
Jardín de
Capuchinos
Convento
Sta. Paula
S. M. del
Socorro
MATAHACAS
ESCUELAS PÍAS
JAUREGUI
PLAZA
JERÓNIMO
DE CÓRDOBA
CALLE DE SANTIAGO
LEÓN XIII
PASAJE MALLOL
STA. PAULA
PLAZA PONCE
DE LEÓN
Convento de
Capuchinos
San
Hermenegildo
S.
JULIÁN
Convento
Sta. Isabel
SOCORRO
Sta. Catalina
ALHÓNDIGA
S. Marcos
PL. SAN
MARCOS
BUSTOS TAVERA
PL. DE LOS
TERCEROS
APODACA
PL. C.
BURGOS
SÁNCHEZ PERRIER
MUÑOZ LEÓN
F. DIEGO DE CÁDIZ
MACASTA
Iglesia de
Sta. Marina
DOÑA MARÍA CORONEL
S. Pedro
City
Walls
Palacio de
las Dueñas
GERONA
SOR ANGELA DE LA CRUZ
IMAGEN
SAN JUAN DE RIVERA
Hospital de
la Sangre
Iglesia de
San Luis
CASTELLAR
PLAZA DE LA
ENCARNACIÓN
Arco
de la
Macarena
SAN LUIS
DIVINA PASTORA
REGINA
Universidad
Antigua
San Gil
LA MACARENA
FERIA
LARAÑA
Omnium
Sanctorum
CENTRO
CAMPANA
DON FADRIQUE
RESOLANA
ANDUEZA
Basílica de
la Macarena
ESCOBEROS
FERIA
RELATOR
DR. LETAMENDI
CERVANTES
AMOR DE DIOS
PERAFÁN DE RIBERA
PERAL
Alameda de Hércules
TRAJANO
PL. D.
VICTORIA
JESÚS DEL GRAN PODER
CALATRAVA
S. Lorenzo y
Jesús del
Gran Poder
BARAJAS
PLAZA DE
GAVIDIA
BORGES
BLANQUILLO
LUMBRERAS
Monast.º de
Sta. Clara
HOMBRE DE PIEDRA
PZA. DE
S. LORENZO
SANTA CLARA
TEODOSIO
JUAN RABADÁN
CISNEROS
Monasterio de
S. Clemente
SANTA ANA
S. Vicente
SAN VICENTE
ALFAQUEQUE
NUEVA TORNEO
PUENTE DEL BARQUETA
BAÑOS
Río Guadalquivir
Parque
Jardín del
Guadalquivir
TELECABINA
PASARELA DE LA CARTUJA
La Cartuja
Centro
Andaluz
de Arte
Contemporan
FLAMENCO VENUES
Casa de la Memoria de Al Andalus 6
La Carbonería 2
Museo del Baile Flamenco 11
Tablao El Arenal 14
ACCOMMODATION
Hostal Nuevo Suizo E
Hostal Picasso C
Oasis D
Samay Hostel A
Triana Backpackers F
Urbany Hostel B

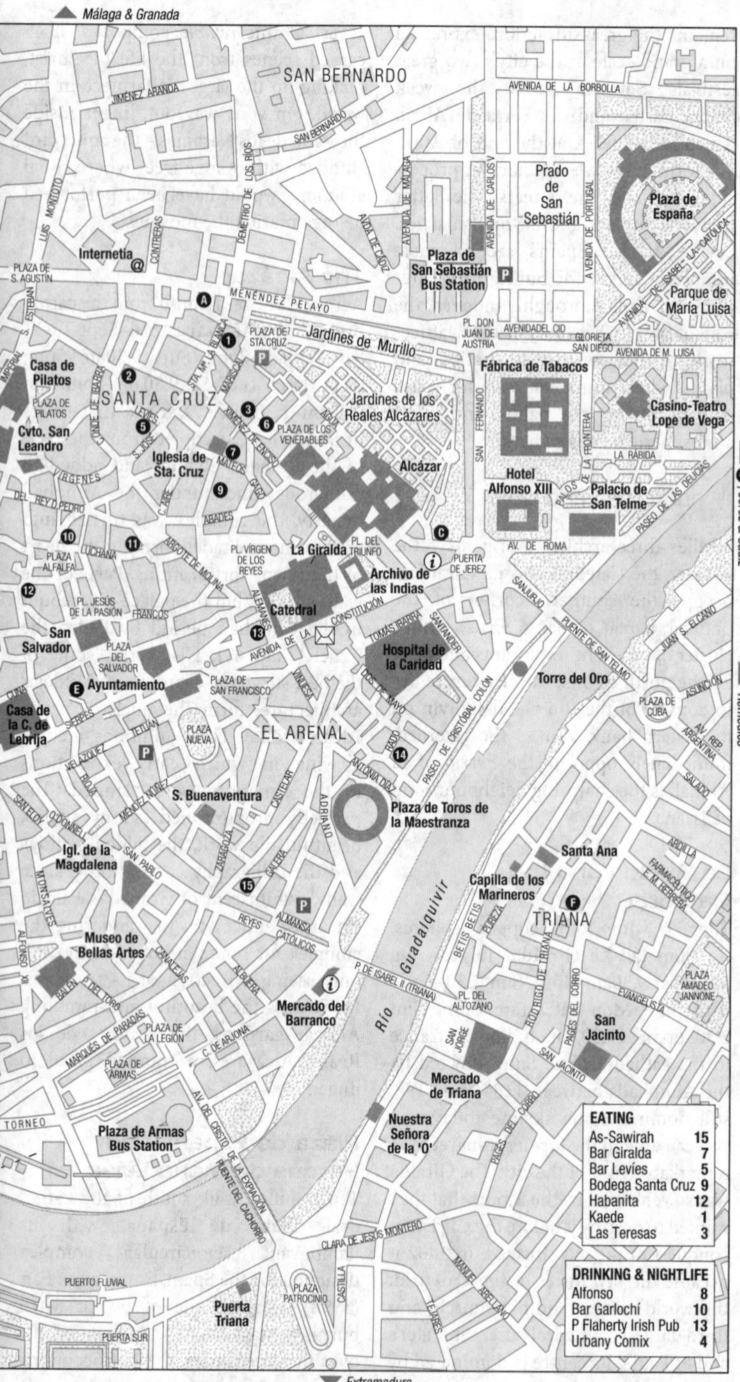
Málaga & Granada
SAN BERNARDO
JIMÉNEZ ARANDA
SAN BERNARDO
AVENIDA DE LA BORBOLLA
Prado de San Sebastián
Plaza de España
AVENIDA DE MÁLAGA
AVENIDA DE CARLOS V
AVENIDA DE PORTUGAL
AVDA DE CÁDIZ
DEMETRIO DE LOS RÍOS
LUIS MONTOTO
CONTRERAS
Internetia
PLAZA DE S. AGUSTÍN
Plaza de San Sebastián Bus Station
AVENIDA DE ISABEL LA CATÓLICA
Parque de María Luisa
MENÉNDEZ PELAYO
PLAZA DE STA.CRUZ
Jardines de Murillo
PL. DON JUAN DE AUSTRIA
AVENIDA DEL CID
GLORIETA SAN DIEGO
AVENIDA DE M. LUISA
Casa de Pilatos
PLAZA DE PILATOS
SANTA CRUZ
STA. Mª LA BLANCA
MARISCAL
Fábrica de Tabacos
Jardines de los Reales Alcázares
Casino-Teatro Lope de Vega
Cvto. San Leandro
LEVÍES
S. JOSÉ
CONDE DE IBARRA
XIMÉNEZ DE ENCISO
PLAZA DE LOS VENERABLES
AGUA
SAN FERNANDO
LA FRONTERA
LA RÁBIDA
Iglesia de Sta. Cruz
MATEOS GAGO
Alcázar
Hotel Alfonso XIII
Palacio de San Telmo
PALOS DE LA FRONTERA
PASEO DE LAS DELICIAS
8, Jeréz & Cádiz
VÍRGENES
DEL REY D. PEDRO
C. AIRE
ABADES
PLAZA ALFALFA
LUCHANA
ARGOTE DE MOLINA
PL. VIRGEN DE LOS REYES
La Giralda
PL. DEL TRIUNFO
PUERTA DE JEREZ
AV. DE ROMA
Archivo de las Indias
SANJURJO
PL. JESÚS DE LA PASIÓN
FRANCOS
ALEMANES
Catedral
AVENIDA DE LA CONSTITUCIÓN
TOMÁS IBARRA
SANTANDER
Hospital de la Caridad
PUENTE DE SAN TELMO
JUAN S. ELCANO
San Salvador
PLAZA DEL SALVADOR
Ayuntamiento
PLAZA DE SAN FRANCISCO
VINUESA
DOS DE MAYO
PASEO DE CRISTÓBAL COLÓN
Torre del Oro
PLAZA DE CUBA
ASUNCIÓN
Remedios
CUNA
Casa de la C. de Lebrija
SIERPES
TETUÁN
PLAZA NUEVA
EL ARENAL
AV. REP. ARGENTINA
VELÁZQUEZ
RIOJA
MÉNDEZ NÚÑEZ
ADRIANO
ANTONIA DÍAZ
S. Buenaventura
CASTELAR
Plaza de Toros de la Maestranza
SALADO
SAN ELOY
O'DONNELL
ZARAGOZA
Igl. de la Magdalena
SAN PABLO
GALERA
Santa Ana
ARDILLA
FARMACÉUTICO E.M. HERRERA
MONSALVES
Capilla de los Marineros
BETIS
PUREZA
TRIANA
Río Guadalquivir
REYES CATÓLICOS
ALMANSA
Museo de Bellas Artes
ALFONSO XII
CANALEJAS
ALBUERA
BAILÉN
P. DEL TORO
P. DE ISABEL II (TRIANA)
PL. DEL ALTOZANO
RODRIGO DE TRIANA
PAGÉS DEL CORRO
PLAZA AMADEO JANNONE
EVANGELISTA
Mercado del Barranco
MARQUÉS DE PARADAS
PLAZA DE LA LEGIÓN
C. DE ARJONA
SAN JORGE
San Jacinto
SAN JACINTO
PLAZA DE ARMAS
Mercado de Triana
TORNEO
Plaza de Armas Bus Station
AV. DEL CRISTO DE LA EXPIACIÓN
PUENTE DEL CACHORRO
Nuestra Señora de la 'O'
PAGÉS DEL CORRO
CLARA DE JESÚS MONTERO
MANUEL ARELLANO
PUERTO FLUVIAL
PLAZA PATROCINIO
CASTILLA
TEJARES
Puerta Triana
PUERTA SUR
Extremadura
EATING
As-Sawirah 15
Bar Giralda 7
Bar Levíes 5
Bodega Santa Cruz 9
Habanita 12
Kaede 1
Las Teresas 3
DRINKING & NIGHTLIFE
Alfonso 8
Bar Garlochí 10
P Flaherty Irish Pub 13
Urbany Comix 4

remains the great attraction, expressed on a grand scale at the city's two great festivals: **Semana Santa**, the week before Easter, and the **Feria de Abril**, which lasts a week at the end of April. The former involves spectacular processions through the streets; the latter firework displays and all-night parties. Seville is also Spain's second most important centre for **bullfighting** after Madrid. While thoroughly modern, the soul of the city lies in its historic latticework of narrow streets, patios and plazas, where minarets jostle for space among cupolas and palms, and in its atmospheric flamenco bars.

What to see and do

Seville's three architectural gems – the Alcázar, the Catedral and La Giralda – occupy the southern corner of the popular *barrio* of Santa Cruz, with a cluster of excellent restaurants and bars. To the north of this, the city centre lies in a curve of the Río Guadalquivir, on its eastern bank. Across the riverbed, immediately opposite the *barrio* of El Arenal, is the charming neighbourhood of Triana.

La Giralda and the Catedral

Topped with four copper spheres, the 90m tall **La Giralda** (July & Aug Mon–Sat 9.30am–4pm, Sun 2.30–6pm; Sept–June Mon–Sat 11am–5pm, Sun 2.30–6pm; €7.50, including entrance to the cathedral, free Sun), erected by the Almohads between 1184 and 1198, still dominates the skyline today and you can ascend the former minaret for a remarkable view of the city. The Giralda was so venerated by the Moors that they wanted to destroy it before the Christian conquest of the city. Instead, in 1402 it became the bell tower of the **Catedral**, the world's largest Gothic church, and third largest cathedral after St Peter's and St Paul's. Its centre is dominated by a vast Gothic *retablo* composed of 45 carved scenes from the life of Christ, making up the largest altarpiece in the world. On your way out, linger inside the Patio de los Naranjas – the courtyard studded with orange trees where ritual ablutions would have been performed before entering the mosque.

The Alcázar

Across Plaza del Triunfo from the cathedral lies the **Alcázar** (April–Sept Tues–Sat 9.30am–7pm, Sun 9.30am–5pm; Oct–March Tues–Sat 9.30am–5pm, Sun 9.30am–1.30pm; €7), a site that rulers of Seville have occupied from the time of the Romans. Rebuilt and added to numerous times, under the Almohad dynasty, the complex was turned into an enormous citadel, forming the heart of the town's fortifications. Parts of the walls survive, but the palace was rebuilt in the Christian period by Pedro the Cruel (1350–69). His works, some of the best surviving examples of Mudéjar architecture, form the nucleus of the Alcázar today. Later additions include a wing in which early expeditions to the Americas were planned. The perfectly proportioned, sunny patios, beautiful tile work, the gilded ceilings and the calligraphy carved into palace walls, reminiscent of Granada's Palacio Nazaríes, entice you to wandering the complex for hours at your leisure, still only seeing a fraction of its treasures. Don't miss the beautiful and rambling Alcázar **gardens**, the Jardines de los Reales Alcázares, a tranquil place to linger.

Plaza de España and Parque de María Luisa

Ten minutes' walk south of the cathedral, **Plaza de España**, with its flamboyant semicircular complex designed for the Spanish Americas Fair (1992), was the site of public witch burnings staged by the Inquisition for over three centuries, the last occurring

in 1781. The adjoining beautiful Parque de María Luisa, with over 3500 trees, features several grand pavilions which house several worthwhile **museums**.

Torre del Oro and Hospital de la Caridad

By the river, west of the Catedral, stands the twelve-sided **Torre del Oro** (Tues–Fri 10am–2pm, Sat & Sun 11am–2pm; €1, free with EU passport) built in 1220 as part of the Alcázar fortifications and named after the gold brought back to Seville from the Americas and stored here. Across from here is the **Hospital de la Caridad** (Mon–Sat 9am–1.30pm & 3.30–7.30pm, Sun 9am–1pm; €5) founded in 1676 by Don Miguel de Manara, the alleged inspiration for Byron's Don Juan, who repented his youthful excesses and set up this hospital for the relief of the dying and destitute. There are some magnificent paintings by Murillo and Valdés Leal inside – the latter's meditations on death are particularly haunting.

The Museo de Bellas Artes

There's more superb art at the **Museo de Bellas Artes** on Plaza del Museo (Tues 2.30–8.30pm, Wed–Sat 9am–8.30pm, Sun 9am–2.30pm; €1.50, free for EU citizens), housed in a beautiful former convent. Highlights include paintings by Murillo, as well as Zurbarán's *Carthusian Monks at Supper* and El Greco's portrait of his son.

Triana

Across the river lies the **Triana** *barrio* that was once home to the city's gypsy community and is still a lively and atmospheric place. At Triana's northern edge is **La Cartuja** (Oct–March Mon–Fri 10am–8pm, Sat 11am–8pm, Sun 10am–3pm; April–Sept Tues–Fri 10am–9pm, Sat 11am–9pm; €3 including museum), a fourteenth-century former Carthusian monastery, where Columbus allegedly planned his early voyages – home to the **Museo del Arte Contemporáneo**, which hosts excellent photographic exhibitions by international names as well as work by local artists.

Isla Mágica

Just north of the Triana, lies the **Isla Mágica** (mid-April to mid-June Sat & Sun 11am–10pm, plus select days 11am–7pm; mid-June to mid-Sept daily until 11pm; check low-season days online; closed Feb to mid-April €27, evening tickets €19; ⓦ www.islamagica.es), a compact amusement park with a New World theme. Summer evenings are a good time to check out its selection of adrenalin-charged rides; highlights include the "Anaconda", the "Wet'n'Wild" ride with almost vertical drops and the "Jaguar" – the stomach-churning roller-coaster with 360-degree turns.

Arrival and information

Air Amarillos shuttle bus runs every 30min from the airport to the Avda del Cid and train station (5.45am–12.45am; 30min; €2.10).

Train Estación Santa Justa is north of the centre, on Avda Kansas City; bus #C1 (€1) connects it to the centre and to the San Sebastián bus station, #32 goes to Plaza de la Encarnación.

Bus The main bus station is at Plaza de Armas, beside the river by the Puente del Cachorro, but buses for destinations within Andalucía (plus Barcelona, Alicante and Valencia) leave from the more central terminal at Plaza de San Sebastián. Bus #C3 connects the two.

Tourist office The municipal tourist office at Plaza San Francisco 19 (Mon–Fri 9am–7.30pm, Sat & Sun 10am–2pm; ⓣ 954 590 188, ⓦ www.turismo.sevilla.org) has regional and city information while the Avda de la Constitución 21 branch (Mon–Fri 9am–7.30pm, Sat 10am–3.30pm; ⓣ 954 787 578, ⓦ www.andalucia.org) provides free copies of monthly listings *El Giraldillo* (ⓦ www.elgiraldillo.es). You can pick up a SevillaCard (24hr/€28) next door at Iconos, which is useful for high-octane sightseeing in a short period of time.

Accommodation

The most attractive – and pricey – area to stay is the maze-like barrio Santa Cruz, near the Catedral.

Cheaper options are available in c/Farnesio, on the periphery of the *barrio*, or slightly further out beyond Plaza Nueva, towards the river. During Easter Week and the Feria de Abril, prices double; book several months in advance.

Hostal Nuevo Suizo c/Azofaifo 7 ⓣ954 229 147, ⓦwww.nuevosuizo.com. Popular with international travellers, this is more like a hotel than a hostel, with a lovely terrace, free teas and coffees, and trips to flamenco shows organized by the supremely friendly staff. Dorms €17–23, doubles €29–33.

Hostal Picasso c/San Gregorio 1 ⓣ954 210 864, ⓦwww.sevillebackpacker.com. Great central location, en-suite dorms with a/c, safes and bicycles for rent all available at this bustling backpacker haunt. Dorms €18.

Oasis Plaza Encarnación 29 ⓣ954 293 777, ⓦwww.hosteloasis.com. Fantastic backpacker favourite, with helpful staff, clean dorms on several floors festooned with greenery, with all modern amenities and breakfast included. Great for nightly tapas bar crawls. Dorms €21–23.

Samay Hostel Av. Menéndez Pelayo 13 ⓣ955 100 160, ⓦwww.samayhostels.com. Top backpacker choice favoured by young international travellers. In a modern, marble-floored building with light, spacious, secure en-suite dorms, breakfast, wi-fi and a large roof terrace. Ask for a dorm facing away from the busy main street. Dorms €18–23, doubles €56–60.

Triana Backpackers c/Rodrigo de Triana 69 ⓣ954 459 960, ⓦwww.trianabackpackers.com. Friendly and sociable place in the Triana, whose staff organize lots of guest events, such as a tapas night. Plain but a/c dorms inside a lovely building with all mod cons. Dorms €17–22, doubles €52.

Urbany Hostel c/Doña Maria Coronel 12 ⓣ954 227 949, ⓦwww.sevillaurbany.com. Funky, bright hostel, with excellent showers, secure dorms with key-card access, lockers and all-you-can-eat breakfast buffet. The common room is perpetually lively. Dorms €17–22, doubles €50.

Eating

Seville is packed with lively bars and restaurants, with ample choices in the Barrio Santa Cruz, the streets around Plaza Nueva and Triana.

As-Sawirah c/Galera 5. Excellent Moroccan restaurant near Triana serving light, fluffy couscous dishes and particularly good *tagines*. *Menú del día* €12.

Bar Giralda c/Mateos Gago 1. *Frituras* (fried fish platters) and *cazuela Tío Pepe* (meat stew with sherry) are among the specials at this top tapas bar, set in a former *hammam*.

Bar Levíes c/San José 15. Packed at night, this informal bar serves large portions of tapas. Try the *salmorejo* (thick, savoury gazpacho) or the *solomillo al whisky* (steak cooked in whisky). Tapas €1.80–2.50.

Bodega Santa Cruz c/Rodrigo Caro 1. Popular bar serving cheap tapas (€1.90–2.50). Try the *pringá*, a meaty sandwich and local speciality.

Habanita c/Golfo s/n, off c/Pérez Galdos. Informal Caribbean-style restaurant with good vegetarian options. Try anything with aubergines or the sweet potatoes with spicy sauce. Mains €7.

Kaede c/San José 32. Popular, elegant Japanese restaurant serving first-rate sashimi and lunchtime bento box specials. *Menú del día* €15, but worth it.

Las Teresas c/Santa Teresa 2. Atmospheric hole-in-the-wall with bullfighting paraphernalia adorning the walls and hams hanging from the ceiling. Sample the *jamón jabugo* – the house special – with a glass of *fino*.

Drinking and nightlife

There are bars all over Seville, but the Plaza Alfalfa area, north of the Catedral, is particularly lively at night. The other main area for nightlife, popular with tourists and Seville's gay population, is just across the river in Triana, on Calle Betis.

Alfonso Paseo de las Delicias at Avda de la Palmera. This chilled-out terrace bar in the middle of Parque de María Luisa is a great spot for a leisurely evening drink or three. Open until 5am.

Bar Garlochí c/Boteros 4. Weird and wonderful bar popular with *Sevillanos*, with a mock-religious theme and a sacrilegious house special – the Sangre de Cristo cocktail.

P Flaherty Irish Pub c/Alemanes 7. Lively expat haunt next to the Catedral, with Guinness on tap, a wide selection of beers, good pub grub and sports on TV nightly.

Urbano Comix c/Matahacas 5. Dress down to enter this student den, with a punk and rock music soundtrack. Varied live bands most nights; open until the wee hours.

TREAT YOURSELF

Unleash your latin passion at the **Museo del Baile Flamenco** (c/Manuel Rojas Marcos 3 ⓣ954 340 311, ⓦwww.museoflamenco.com). It offers one-week intensive flamenco courses for €330, which, though pricey, is a unique experience.

Flamenco

Flamenco – or more accurately Sevillanas – music and dance can be seen at dozens of places in the city. To avoid the tacky and expensive ones, head to one of the following bars, or go to c/Rodrigo de Triana, the home of a handful of flamenco academies, to check out the students in action.

Casa de la Memoria de Al Andalus c/Ximénez de Enciso 28 ⓣ954 560 670. Fantastic daily performances at this cultural centre, at 7.30pm/9pm/10.30pm depending on season. Book tickets in advance (€16).

La Carbonería c/Levíes 18. Tapas bar in an old coal merchant's building, packed to the rafters with locals and a few lucky tourists, with excellent spontaneous flamenco performances most nights. Thursdays are best.

Tablao El Arenal c/Rodo 7 ⓣ954 216 492. One of the best dinner-and-flamenco venues run by a former dancer, with nightly performances 8–9.30pm & 10–11.30pm; €36/70 with drink/ dinner.

Bullfighting

The season starts with the Feria de Abril and continues until October, with most *corridas* held on Sun evenings. Tickets from the Plaza de Toros de la Maestranza, Paseo de Colón 12 (ⓣ902 5223 506), which also houses a *taurino* museum, from as little as €12.

Directory

Consulates Australia, Federico Rubio 14 ⓣ954 220 971; Ireland, Plaza de Santa Cruz 6 ⓣ954 216 361; US, Plaza Nueva 8 ⓣ954 218 751.

Exchange Banks and *cambios* in the tourist office on Avda de la Constitución.

Hospital Hospital Universitario Virgen Macarena, c/Dr Marañon s/n (ⓣ950 080 000) has English-speaking doctors. For emergencies, call ⓣ061.

Internet Correos Avda de la Constitución 32 (Mon–Fri 8.30am–10pm, Sat 9.30am–10pm, Sun noon–10pm).

Laundry Lavandería Roma, c/Castelar 4.

Left luggage Coin-operated lockers at the train station. *Consignas* at both bus stations.

Pharmacies Throughout the town centre; check the notice in the window for the nearest pharmacy open after hours.

Police c/Arenal 1 (ⓣ954 590 558) and c/Credito 11 (ⓣ954 378 496).

Post office Avda de la Constitución 32.

Moving on

Train Almería (4 daily; 3hr 20min–5hr 20min); Cádiz (10 daily; 2hr); Córdoba (14 daily; 40min); Granada (4 daily; 3hr–3hr 20min); Madrid (every 30min between 6.15am and 9.45pm; 2hr 30min); Málaga (12 daily; 2hr 30min); Valencia (daily at 8.20am; 8hr 30min).

Bus Almería (3 daily; 5hr 45min); Cádiz (10 daily; 1hr 45min–2hr); Córdoba (13 daily; 1hr 45min); Granada (8 daily; 3hr); Madrid (8 daily; 6–8hr); Málaga (9 daily; 2hr 30min); Ronda (6 daily; 2hr); Tarifa (4 daily; 3hr 30min).

CÁDIZ

CÁDIZ is among the oldest settlements in Spain, founded about 1100 BC by the Phoenicans, and has long been one of the country's principal ports. In the eighteenth century it enjoyed a virtual monopoly on the Spanish-American trade in gold and silver. Central Cádiz, built on a peninsula island, entices with its grand open squares, narrow alleyways and high, turreted houses. It's also the spiritual home of flamenco, and has a tremendous atmosphere – slightly seedy, definitely in decline, but still full of mystique. Cádiz's big party time is its annual **Carnaval**, complete with frenzied costumed revelry, normally held in February and early March.

What to see and do

With its blind alleys, backstreets and cafés, Cádiz is fascinating to wander around; you're drawn more by the atmosphere than by any particular sight. For sweeping views of the city, climb the **Torre Tavira**, Marqués del Real Tesoro 10 (daily: June–Sept 10am–8pm; Oct–May 10am–6pm; €4), tallest of the 160 lookout towers in the city, with a fascinating *cámara oscura*, a device that uses mirrors to zoom in on any part of the city and project a live image on to a flat surface in the tower with the aid of pulleys (guided shows hourly). The huge white sea-facing **Catedral Nueva** (Tues–Fri 10am–8pm, Sat 10am–2pm, Sun

11am–1pm; €5 including museum, free Tues–Fri 7–8pm & Sun) is a blend of High Baroque and Neoclassical styles as a result of it taking 116 years to build, decorated entirely in stone. You can then take a stroll along the oceanfront, taking in two beautiful parks – the Alameda Apodaca, running along the Bay of Cádiz, with its fabulous views and enormous bulbous trees, and the large, sculpted Parque Genovés – home to numerous exotic plants. Cádiz also has two main **beaches**: the often-crowded little crescent Playa de la Caleta at its western end, and the far nicer Playa de la Victoria, near the old town (take bus #1 from Plaza de España).

Arrival and information

Train The station is at the southeastern end of the old town, a 5min walk to the Plaza de San Juan de Dios.

Bus Arriving by bus, you'll be dropped a few blocks north of the Plaza de San Juan de Dios, along the waterfront.

Tourist office Turismo municipal office, Paseo de Canalejas (Mon–Fri 8.30am–6pm, Sat & Sun 10am–1.30pm & 4–7pm; ⓣ956 241 001); turismo regional, Avda Ramón de Carranza 1 (Mon–Fri 9am–7.30pm, Sat & Sun 9am–5pm; ⓣ956 203 191), with plenty of useful maps of the region.

Accommodation

Casa Caracol c/Suárez de Salazar 4 ⓣ956 261 166, ⓦwww.caracolcasa.com. The only backpacker hostel in town, this place has a chilled-out vibe, laid-back staff, open-plan dorms and perpetually lively common room. You won't get much sleep, but you'll never lack for company and can take part in rooftop parties. Dorms €19.

Pensión Fantoni c/Flamenco 5 ⓣ956 282 704, ⓦwww.hostalfantoni.es. Small hotel with simple en-suite rooms, an attractive courtyard and roof terrace, centrally located down a quiet street. Singles €60, doubles €70–75.

Eating and drinking

For a drink, or tapas, head to the Barrio de la Viña, just east of Playa de la Caleta, where there are plenty of gems along the tiny streets, or go to Plaza de Las Flores.

Freiduría Las Flores Plaza Las Flores s/n. A Cádiz institution, this *freiduría* (fry shop) serves up large, cheap portions of all kinds of fish. Try the excellent *cazón adobo* (marinated shark) or the *tortilla de camarónes* (shrimp patty). Tapas €1.30–2.90.

Malagueño c/Mesón 5. Excellent little hole-in-the-wall place with an extensive tapas list. The *jamón* and the *boquerones en vinagre* (marinated fresh anchovies) are truly scrumptious. Closed Sun.

Taberna Plaza Tío de la Tiza s/n. *Bodega* with outdoor seating serving up excellent gazpacho, *salmorejo* (thicker, more savoury gazpacho with bacon) and cooked *gambas* (large prawns) by the pound.

Moving on

Bus to: Almería (1 daily at 3pm; 7hr); Granada (4 daily; 5hr); Málaga (6 daily; 4hr); Ronda (2–3daily; 3hr); Seville (8–10 daily; 2hr); Tarifa (5 daily; 2hr).

Train to: Córdoba (4 daily; 2hr 30min); Madrid (2 daily; 4hr 30min); Seville (7 daily; 1hr 45min).

TARIFA

If there is one thing that defines **TARIFA**, it is the prevailing, massively powerful wind, which has made the most southerly point in mainland Europe one of the world's most popular wind- and kite-surfing destinations. The elements aside, there's a good feel to the place – with its funky, laid-back atmosphere and maze of narrow streets. Africa feels very close, too, with the Rif mountains clearly visible – and easily accessible, via the ferry that runs to Tangier in Morocco.

What to see and do

The ten-kilometre white, sandy **beaches, Playa de los Lances** and **Playa Valdevaqueros**, are the places to head for wind- and kite-surfing, whilst just to the east of town are the dramatic rocky coves of **La Caleta**. If you're keen to try kite-surfing or other aquatic sports, you can book a course or rent equipment from a number of outfitters on c/Batalla del Salado, including Art of Surfing at no. 47 (ⓣ605 031 880, ⓦwww.artofsurfing.com) and the better Wave Bandits Kite School out of town, on

the N-340 at Km 82.7 (Ⓣ619 471 735, Ⓦwww.wavebandits.com); most charge similar prices, with a four-hour kite-surfing taster course costing €115. Alternatively, you can go on a **whale-watching trip**; try Whale Watch, Avda de la Constitución 6 (€30–42; Ⓣ956 627 013, Ⓦwww.whalewatchtarifa.net), to see the local population of pilot whales and dolphins; in July and August, killer whales can also be seen.

Arrival and information

Bus Buses drop off passengers at the stop on the main road, Batalla del Salado; the town centre is a 10min walk south along the road.
Tourist office Paseo de la Alameda (Mon–Fri 10am–2pm & 4–6pm, Sat & Sun 10am–2pm; Ⓣ956 680 993, Ⓦwww.aytotarifa.com).

Accommodation

In the summer, book accommodation in advance. There are a few campsites near the main windsurfing beaches: *Tarifa* (Ⓣ956 684 778), *Paloma* (Ⓣ956 684 203) and *Torre de la Peña* (Ⓣ956 684 903), all of which are fully equipped and have their own pools.
Melting Pot Hostel c/Turriano Gracil 5 Ⓣ956 682 906, Ⓦwww.meltingpothostels.com. Backpacker/kite-surfer haven with fully equipped kitchen, cosy lounge/bar with wi-fi and helpful staff. En-suite dorms are fairly small, but the ambience is great and kite-surfing courses can be arranged through the hostel. Dorms €22–25, doubles €54.
Pensión Correo c/Colonel Moscardo 8 Ⓣ956 680 206, Ⓦwww.pensioncorreo.com. Attractive little hotel in a tiny street in the old town with light and clean wi-fi-equipped rooms, some en suite, and even a small book-exchange. Singles €30, doubles €60–80, triple €90.

Eating and drinking

Bamboo c/Paseo Alameda 2 Ⓣ956 627 304. Bob Marley on the stereo, deep sofas and fantastic breakfasts, smoothies and fresh juices. Turns into a hip bar after dark. Daily 10am–2am.
Chilimosa c/Peso 6. Fabulous vegetarian restaurant/takeaway serving up healthy food with an eastern twist. Falafel with salad €3.40.
Trattoria Paseo de la Alameda s/n. Lively Italian restaurant offering generous portions of decent pizza and pasta. Mains €5–9.

Moving on

Ferry Tangier, Morocco (summer 3–5 daily; winter 5 weekly; 30–45min; €35 one way).
Bus Algeciras (5–7 daily; 30min); Cádiz (5–7 daily; 1–2hr); La Línea de la Concepción (7 daily; 1hr 30min–2hr); Málaga (2 daily; 2hr); Seville (4 daily; 3hr).

MÁLAGA

MÁLAGA is the second city of the south after Seville, one of the oldest in Spain, and also the main city on the Costa del Sol, the richest resort area in the Mediterranean.

What to see and do

While the clusters of high-rises look pretty grim as you approach, the historic centre (Old Town) has plenty of charm. The most popular beach in town is the Playa de la Malagueta, ten minutes' walk from the Old Town, while the old fishing villages of El Palo and Pedregalejo, 4km east of the centre, boast a series of attractive small **beaches** and a promenade lined with some of the best fish and **seafood restaurants** in the province; to get there, catch bus #11 along Paseo del Parque. Just east of the Old Town rises Mount Gibralfaro where, above the ruins of a Roman theatre, tower the Moorish citadels of **Alcazaba** (Tues–Sun: April–Oct 9.30am–8pm; Nov–March 8.30am–7pm; €2.10), built in 1057, and **Castillo de Gibralfaro** (daily: April–Oct 9am–8pm; Nov–March 9am–6pm; €2.10; joint ticket with Alcazaba €3.45), rebuilt in the fourteenth and fifteenth centuries. The ruins offer spectacular views of the town and the glittering Mediterranean beyond.

Málaga's most famous native son, born here in 1881, is honoured in the excellent **Museo Picasso**, c/San Agustín 8 (Tues–Thurs & Sun 10am–8pm, Fri & Sat 10am–9pm; €6), which displays an intimate collection of works spanning Picasso's entire career, donated by the artist's daughter-in-law and grandson.

Arrival and information

Air Hundreds of charter and budget flights arrive at Málaga Airport, the hub of the south, every week. From the airport, catch the electric train (every 30min; €1.25) to the main train station, or continue another stop to Málaga Centro: Alameda for the city centre. The airport bus (#19) leaves every 20–30min to the centre, via the main bus station (€1).

Train and bus The stations are across the road from each other, a 15min walk to Old Town; alternatively, take buses #3 and #4 from the train station, or buses #4 and #12 from the bus station along the Alameda Principal. There are ATMs and luggage storage at both.

Tourist office Plaza de la Marina (Mon–Fri 9am–7.30pm, Sat 10am–7pm, Sun 10am–2pm; ⓣ952 122 020, ⓦwww.malagaturismo.com).

Accommodation

Casa Babylon c/Pedro de Quejana 3 ⓣ952 267 228, ⓦwww.casababylonhostel.com. Colourful, sociable and full of character, this is the place to meet fellow travellers. The staff are great, all mod cons are included, and it's located a short walk from Málaga's historical centre. A winner. Dorms €14–16.

Picasso's Corner c/San Juan de Letrán 9 ⓣ952 212 287, ⓦwww.picassoscorner.com. Friendly, helpful hostel with good breakfast, bike rental, and a chilled-out vibe. The dorms are on the small side, though, and it can be noisy at night. Dorms €17–19.

Eating and drinking

Málaga specialities – *fritura malagueña* (battered and fried small fish and squid) and sweet Málaga wine – can be enjoyed at a vast choice of tapas bars and restaurants. You'll find plenty of them in the area between Plaza de la Merced and Plaza de los Mártires, which is buzzing till late at the weekend. On the beach, don't miss out on *espeto* – fresh sardines grilled on spears over an olive-wood fire.

Clandestino c/Niño de Guevara 3. Chilled-out and popular restaurant serving inexpensive meat dishes and pastas with imaginative sauces. Mains €7–10.

Mesón Lo Güeno c/Marín Garcia 9. Over 75 different tapas (€2.50–4.50) to choose from in this little rustic bar – a Málaga institution for over thirty years.

Moving on

Train Barcelona (1 daily at 7.10am; 13hr); Córdoba (10 daily; 2hr 10min–3hr 30min); Madrid (10 daily; 4–7hr); Seville (8 daily; 2hr 30min).

Bus Almería (3 daily; 3hr–4hr 30min); Córdoba (2–5 daily; 2hr 30min–3hr 30min); Granada (14 daily; 2hr); Madrid (9 daily; 6hr); Ronda (9 daily; 2hr 45min); Seville (9 daily; 2hr 30min).

RONDA

Built on an isolated ridge of the sierra, and ringed by dark, angular mountains, the spectacular *pueblo blanco* of **RONDA**, a large cluster of attractive whitewashed houses, is split in two by a gaping river **gorge** with a sheer drop, spanned by an incredible eighteenth-century arched bridge, from which hundreds of people were thrown to their deaths during the Civil War.

What to see and do

Most sights of interest lie in the tiny, atmospheric old quarter on the eastern side of the gorge. These include the distinctive **Baños Árabes** (daily 10am–7pm, Sat & Sun 10am–3pm; €3) and the delightful tiled garden of the **Casa Don Bosco** (daily 9am–2pm & 2.30–6pm; €1.50) at Calle San Juan de Lefran 20. Behind the town church is the **Palacio de Mondragón** (Mon–Fri 10am–7pm, Sat & Sun 10am–3pm; €3), probably once the palace of the Moorish kings and now home to the **Museo Municipal** (same hours, included in the price). The principal gate of the town, through which the Christian conquerors passed, stands beside the **Alcázar**, destroyed by the French in 1809. In the modern Mercadillo quarter is Spain's oldest Plaza de Toros (**bullring**) where three generations of the Romero family shaped the rules of bullfighting into what they are today (daily 10am–8pm; €6 including the interesting museum of *corrida* memorabilia). Nearby, the **Jardínes de Forestier** ascend the gorge in a series of stepped terraces, offering superb views of the river, the bridge and the remarkable stairway of the **Casa del Rey Moro** (daily 10am–7pm), an early eighteenth-century mansion on the opposite side of the gorge.

Arrival and information

Bus and train stations Both are located a short walk northeast of the bullring. The bus station is by Plaza Redondo, while the train station is several blocks north, along Avenida Andalucía.

Tourist office Opposite the entrance to the bullring at Plaza de Toros (Mon–Fri 10am–7pm, Sat 10am–2pm & 3–5pm, Sun 10am–2.30pm; ⓣ952 187 119, ⓦwww.turismoderonda.es).

Accommodation

Hostal Andalucía c/Martínez Astein 19 ⓣ952 875 450. Clean, spacious rooms with sinks, directly across the street from the train station. €20.

Hotel Águilar c/Naranja 28 ⓣ952 871 994. Friendly family-run guesthouse with clean rooms, some en suite. €20–22.

Eating and drinking

Bodega La Valencia c/Pedro Romero 9. Popular tapas bar serving regional specialities such as *rabo de toro* (oxtail) and the excellent *morcilla con arroz*. Tapas €1.50.

Restaurante del Escudero Paseo de Blas Infante 1, behind the Plaza de Toros. Treat yourself here to some of the best Andalucian cuisine in the region while looking over the Tajo gorge. The meat dishes are superb and the *menú de degustación* is around €18. Closed Sun eve.

Soul Arte Pizzería c/Santa Cecilia at c/María Cabrera-Prim. Excellent little pizzeria with a wide range of thin-crust pizzas. Mains €5.

Moving on

Bus Cádiz (3–4 daily; 2hr 30min); Granada (twice daily; 3hr 30min); Málaga (7–10 daily; 3hr 30min); Seville (3–5 daily; 2hr 30min).

Train Algeciras (6 daily; 1hr 45min); Córdoba (twice daily; 2hr); Granada (3daily; 2hr 30min); Madrid (2daily; 4hr); Málaga (daily at 7.12am; 1hr 50min).

ALGECIRAS

The main reason to visit the gritty, busy port of **ALGECIRAS**, a bus ride along the coast from Cádiz, is for the **ferry to Tangier** in Morocco or the Spanish enclave of **Ceuta**. The best place to buy tickets is at the **port**, directly from the ferry companies, as many travel agents will only offer tickets from their client companies – though wait till Tangier before buying any Moroccan currency. Cheap **accommodation** is plentiful; if you have to stay in Algeciras overnight, try the family-run *Hostal Fez* at c/Río 7 (ⓣ956 099 088; €20), with its simple, clean rooms around a tiled courtyard and free wi-fi. For an all-you-can-eat lunchtime buffet (€7), head to the first floor of the *Hotel Al-Mar* on Avda de la Marina, or try one of the numerous kebab places that abound in the streets closest to the port.

Moving on

Ferry Ceuta (10–12 daily; fast ferry 35min; €40); Tangier (hourly; 1hr–2hr 30min; €38–40 one way).

Train Granada (3 daily; 4hr); Madrid (2 daily; 6hr); Ronda (5 daily; 1hr 40min).

Bus Córdoba (2 daily; 6hr); Granada (6 daily; 3hr 45min–5hr 30min); La Línea (every 30min; 30min); Málaga (every 30min; 1hr 45min–3hr).

GIBRALTAR

Long coveted for its strategic position at the entrance to the Mediterranean, the British territory of **GIBRALTAR**, at the southern tip of Spain, has been the source of tension between the two countries for nearly three hundred years since it was ceded to **Britain** under the Treaty of Utrecht. It is now a small slice of Britain perched next to the Spanish mainland, complete with red post-boxes, chippies and, of course, the pound. Its **tax-free status** makes it an excellent place to shop; pay in pounds sterling rather than euros, as the exchange rate is dire.

What to see and do

The town is dominated by the huge **Rock of Gibraltar**, the area's main attraction and thought, in antiquity, to be a pillar of Hercules. Take the cable car running from Red Sands Road (daily 9.30am–5.15pm, £6.50/8 one way/round trip) to the top of the rock for spectacular views of the coastline and the distant African continent. Signs from

the cable-car exit will lead you to the **nature reserve** (daily 9.30am–7.15pm; £8) on the Rock, which includes the immense **St Michael's Cave**, the **Great Siege Tunnels**, constructed in 1782–83, and the **Apes' Den** – the home of the peninsula's famous simian residents. The Barbary macaques are not afraid of humans, and may jump on you; remain calm and don't try to pet or feed them.

Arrival and information

Arrival Bus to La Línea de la Concepción, then to get to Gibraltar, simply walk across the border and follow Winston Churchill Avenue into town (10min).
Tourist office Bilingual on Casemates Square (Mon–Fri 9am–5.30pm, Sat & Sun 10am–3pm; ⓣ 350 507 62).

Accommodation

Emile Youth Hostel Montagu Bastion, Line Wall Rd ⓣ 350 51106, ⓔ emilhostel@yahoo.co.uk. The only budget place in Gibraltar, with clean dorms and rooms, breakfast included, and an annoying lockout policy 10.30am–4.30pm. Dorms £15.

Eating

The Horseshoe 193 Main St. One of the better places to eat, serving hearty pub lunches.
Marrakech Restaurant 9 Governor's Parade. Serves tasty couscous and other Moroccan dishes.

Moving on

Bus La Línea de la Concepción to: Algeciras (every 30–45min; 30min); Cádiz (4 daily; 2hr 30min); Málaga (3–5 daily; 2hr 30min); Seville (4 daily; 5hr).

ALMERÍA

Founded by the Phoenicans, and having risen to prominence as the main port of Moorish Córdoba, **ALMERÍA** is an attractive, prosperous city sandwiched in between the Mediterranean and the barren mountain looming behind it.

What to see and do

The town is dominated by the grand, crumbling, tenth-century **Alcazaba** (Tues–Sun 9am–8.30pm; closes 6.30pm Nov–March; €1.50/free with EU passport), which was built by the Córdoba Caliph Abd-ar Rahman III. During its heyday, the fortress complex held up to 20,000 people and was said to rival Granada's Alhambra with the beauty of its palaces and sculpted gardens, though now little remains. The fabulous views of the coast are still well worth the climb, though. What looks like another fortress on Plaza de Catedral is, in fact, Almería's **cathedral** (Mon–Fri 10am–2pm & 4–5.30pm, Sat 10am–2pm; €2), built in 1524, and fortified to withstand the frequent pirate raids from North Africa and Turkey in the sixteenth century; it even used to have its own cannons. Behind the cathedral, on c/Pintor Díaz Molina 9, the excellent **Centro Andaluz de la Fotografía** (11am–2pm & 5.30–9.30pm; free) houses temporary photography exhibitions by top international names.

Arrival and information

Train and bus Both buses and trains pull in at the combined Estación Intermodal on Carretera La

MINI HOLLYWOOD

Between the 1950s and the 1980s, the desert landscape around Almería was used as the set for such Hollywood classics as *Lawrence of Arabia* and *Indiana Jones and the Last Crusade*, as well as numerous "spaghetti westerns"; Clint Eastwood's career was launched here in *A Fistful of Dollars.* Visit the three Wild West sets and watch the spirited re-enaction of the capture of Jesse James (daily noon & 5pm) at Oasys, aka **Mini Hollywood** (June–Oct daily 10am–9pm; rest of year Sat & Sun only; €19), 25km inland from Almería. To get there, take a Tabernas-bound bus which can drop you off by the entrance; getting back can be trickier (walk back to the main road and flag down a bus).

Ronda, 10min walk from the city centre. No luggage storage available.
Tourist office c/Parque de Nicolás Salmarón at Martínez Campos (Mon–Fri 9am–7.30pm, Sat & Sun 9.30am–3pm; ⓣ950 175 220, ⓦwww.almeria-turismo.org).

Accommodation

Hostal Americano Avda. de la Estación 4 ⓣ950 258 011. Friendly guesthouse located between Old Town and the bus/train station offering clean singles and doubles; en suite €2 extra. €20–22.
Hostal Nixar c/Antonio Vico 24 ⓣ950 237 255. Centrally located cheapie with tidy basic rooms, some en suite; airier rooms are upstairs. €20.

Eating and drinking

Baños Árabes y Tetería c/Perea 99. Pick from a great selection of teas, gorge yourself on baklava, smoke a hookah (€5) or indulge in a relaxing bathing session. Book in advance for the baths (ⓣ950 231 010).
Bodega Las Botas c/Fructuoso Pérez 3. This popular tapas bar festooned with hams is a great place to try the local speciality of oxtail stew, washed down with a glass of *tinto de verano*. Tapas €1.50.
La Encina c/Marín 16. Even if you don't splurge on a delectable *menú degustación* (€33) at Almería's top restaurant, stop by for the imaginative tapas (€1.30); *arroz negro* and the home-made pâté are delicious. Closed Sun night & Mon.

Moving on

Train Barcelona (1 daily; 13hr); Granada (4 daily; 2hr 15min); Madrid (2 daily; 6hr 45min–10hr); Seville (4 daily; 5hr 30min).
Bus Granada (12 daily; 2hr 15min–4hr); Madrid (6 daily; 7hr); Málaga (8 daily; 3hr 30min–6hr); Seville (3 daily; 5hr 45min – 9hr); Tabernas (2–7 daily; 40min); Valencia (5 daily; 8hr 30min).

Valencia and Alicante

Much of the coast around **Valencia** and further south on the **Costa Blanca** has been insensitively overdeveloped, suffering from mass package-tourism and its associated ills. The main cities, however – vibrant **Valencia** and relaxed **Alicante** – are appealing and worth a stop for anyone travelling down the east coast.

VALENCIA

VALENCIA has been working hard to shed its provincial reputation in recent years and is emerging as an exciting, cosmopolitan city to rival Madrid and Barcelona. The City of Arts and Sciences complex is the best example of this but Valencia's exuberance is also evident in its diverse nightlife. The city can also take pride in some good museums, a reasonable beach, and, of course, its festivals: the world-famous **Las Fallas**, international music festival **Benicassim** and the riotous **Tomatina**, held in nearby Buñol.

What to see and do

The Plaza del Ayuntamiento, a few blocks north of the train station, marks the centre of town with most of Valencia's key sights a short walk from here. However, the most interesting area for wandering is undoubtedly the maze-like **Barrio del Carmen**, with its arty, bohemian atmosphere. Stretching north of the Mercado Central up to the riverbed of the Río Turia, it's full of historic buildings being renovated and stylish cafés opening up next to crumbling townhouses.

The town centre

The **Palacio del Marqués de Dos Aguas** is an excellent example of traditional Valencian architecture. Hipólito Rovira, who designed its extraordinarily detailed alabaster doorway, died insane in 1740, which should come as no surprise to anyone who's seen it. On the **Plaza Patriarca** stands the Neoclassical former university, with beautiful cloisters. From here, up c/de la Paz, is the **Plaza de la Reina**, home to the

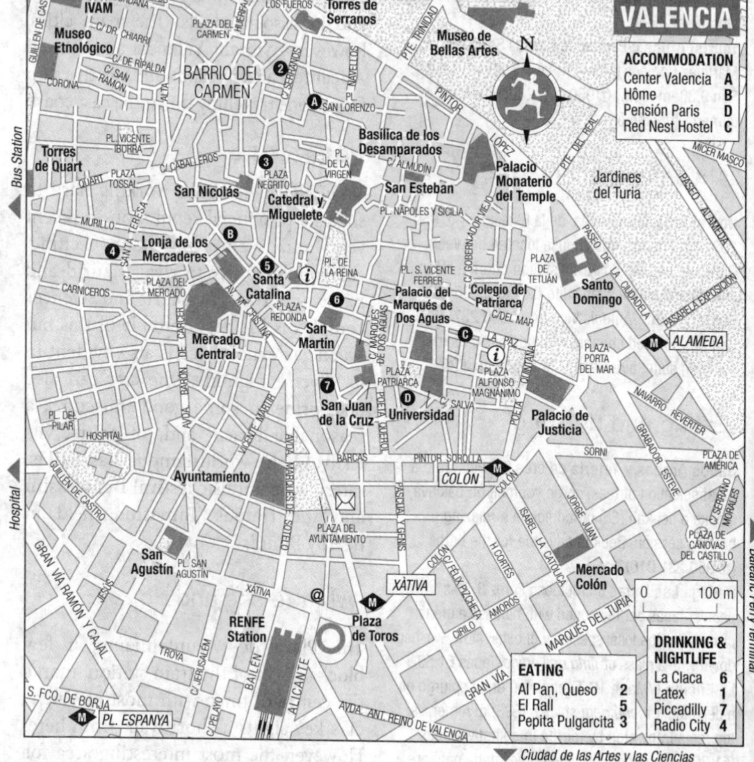

impressive thirteenth-century **Catedral**, whose bell tower, the **Miguelete** (daily 10am–7.30pm; €2), gives stunning city views. Just southwest of the cathedral lies the enormous **Mercado Central**, a huge iron and glass structure housing over one thousand stalls selling local fruit, vegetables and seafood until 2pm (closed Sun).

The museums

Art lovers will find **IVAM**, the modern art museum at c/Guillém de Castro 118 (Tues–Sun 10am–8pm; €2, free Sun) a treat, but the real highlight of the city's museums is the **Ciudad de las Artes y las Ciencias** (City of Arts and Sciences; Mon–Thurs 10.30am–7pm, Fri & Sun 10.30am–8pm, Sat 10.30am–9pm; July daily until 9pm, Aug until 10pm; €31.60 for three-day full-access pass; ⓣ902 100 031, ⓦwww.cac.es). Sitting in a huge landscaped park that was built in the old riverbed of the Río Turia, this breathtaking collection of futuristic concrete, steel and glass architecture comprises five main buildings, four of which were designed by local architect Santiago Calatrava. The complex includes an eyeball-shaped IMAX **cinema**, a vast **science museum**, a huge **oceanographic park** (with beluga whales, sharks and turtles) and a dramatic pistachio nut-shaped **arts centre**. Take bus #19, #35, #95 or #40 from the city centre.

Arrival and information

Train station Centrally located: cross the busy c/Xàtiva ring road and up Avda Marqués de Sotelo for the Plaza del Ayuntamiento, continuing north for the Barrio del Carmen.

Bus station To the northwest, on the far bank of the Río Turia riverbed; take local bus #8, the metro to Turia, or a 30min walk.
Boat Bus #19 connects the Balearic Ferry Terminal with the central Plaza del Ayuntamiento.
Tourist office Regional tourist office at c/Paz 48 (Mon–Fri 9am–8pm, Sat 10am–8pm, Sun 10am–2pm; ⓣ963 986 422, ⓦwww.comunitatvalenciana.com); municipal office on Plaza de la Reina 19 (Mon–Sat 9am–7pm, Sun 10am–2pm; ⓣ963 153 931, ⓦwww.turisvalencia.es). Both hand out the free English-language listings guides *24-7 Valencia* and *Hello Valencia*.

City transport

Bus and metro Most of Valencia's key sights are walkable from the town centre, but the public transport system is efficient and easy to use. Bus journeys cost €1.20, the metro €1.30 for journeys within the central zone A.
Discount cards The Valencia Tourist Card (€10/16/20 for 1/2/3 days) gives you unlimited travel on buses and metro and discounts in some museums, shops and restaurants. Available at tourist offices.

Accommodation

Although prices given here are for high season, many hostels put prices up even further for the Las Fallas festival.
Center Valencia c/Samaniego 18 ⓣ963 914 915, ⓦwww.center-valencia.com. Clean, basic dorms with good facilities, including free internet, roof terrace, laundry service and breakfast. Dorm bed €22.50.
Hôme c/La Lonja 4 T963 916 229, ⓦwww.likeathome.net. One of three *Hôme* hostels in the city. Comfortable, relaxed accommodation, with kitchen, free internet and TV room, in a great central location. Book ahead in summer. €23 in four-bed dorm.
Pensión Paris c/Salvá 12 ⓣ963 526 766, ⓦwww.pensionparis.com. Bright, clean, spacious rooms at budget prices, in a central location. Metro Colón. Doubles €32 with shared bath, €40 private bath.
Red Nest Hostel c/La Paz 36 ⓣ963 427 168, ⓦwww.rednesthostel.com. Bright, fun decor and lots of communal space, with pool table and table football. Metro Colón. Dorms €23–27.

Eating

There are plenty of decent options near the Mercado Central and in the Barrio del Carmen but avoid touristy places too near the plazas de la Reina and de la Virgen.
Al Pan, Queso c/Serranos 19. A Brazilian café offering tapas-style snacks and exotic fruit juices. *Menú del día* €6.50. Mon–Fri 9am–midnight, Sat & Sun 10am–midnight.
El Rall c/Tundidores 2 ⓣ963 922 090. In an attractive square in the heart of Barrio del Carmen, this local favourite specializes in rice dishes, including the famous Valencian paella (€12). Daily 1.30–3.30pm & 8–11.30pm.
Pepita Pulgarcita c/Caballeros 19. Tapas (from €4.50 for one or €6.50 to share) and light meals are available in this stylish, yet unpretentious restaurant. Mon 7pm–1.30am, Tues–Sun 1pm–1.30am.

Drinking and nightlife

Valencia can seem dead at night, but only because the action is widely dispersed. The best of the city-centre nightlife is in the Barrio del Carmen (c/Caballeros, c/Quart and c/Alta). For salsa, head to the bars on c/Juan Llorens. The best gay bars and clubs are in and around c/Quart.
La Claca c/San Vicente Martir 3. A laid-back spot to mingle with the locals, DJs play retro-pop most nights and there's occasional live music.
Latex Avda Constitución 29. Popular, alternative club with electronica and house DJs playing on two floors. Fri & Sat 2am–7.30am; €12 entry includes free drink.

FESTIVALS

The famous **Las Fallas** are held annually from March 15 to 19, when hundreds of papier-mache caricatures are installed and then burnt in the streets of Valencia amidst a riot of fireworks in a tribute to St Joseph, the patron saint of carpenters. Summer heralds a host of festivals in and around Valencia: you can rock-on at the **Festival Internacional de Benicassim** (ⓦwww.fiberfib.com), a four-day music festival in the beach town of Benicassim, between Barcelona and Valencia, featuring well-known indie, pop and electronic acts; or indulge in some childhood fantasies at **La Tomatina** (ⓦwww.latomatina.es), essentially an enormous public tomato fight that takes place on the last Wednesday in August, in the tiny town of Buñol, one hour to the west of the city.

Piccadilly c/Embajador Vich 7. The range of theme nights and music, from electronica to retro Eighties and Nineties, make this one of the most eclectic clubs in town. €12 with a free drink, free before 2.30am. Wed–Sat 12.30–7.30am, Sun 9pm–5am.
Radio City c/Santa Teresa 19 Ⓦ www.radiocityvalencia.com. Lively and popular bar with exhibitions, theatre, dance and music performances. Free entry; see website for programme.

Directory

Banks Main branches of most banks are around Pl del Ayuntamiento or along c/Játiva 24. Outside banking hours, try Caja de Ahorros, c/Játiva 14, to the left as you come out of the train station.
Consulates UK, c/Colon 22 Ⓣ 963 520 710; US, c/Dr Romagosa 1 Ⓣ 963 516 973.
Hospital Avda Cid, at the Tres Cruces junction Ⓣ 963 862 900.
Internet Locutorio Internet, c/Pie de la Cruz 16; Workcenter, c/Xátiva 19.
Laundry The L@undry Stop, c/Baja 17 (daily 8am–10pm).
Left luggage At the bus station (€3.50/24hr).
Pharmacies Farmacia Baviera, c/Don Juan de Austria (24hr; Ⓣ 963 512 459).
Police Gran Vía Ramón y Cajal 40 (Ⓣ 963 539 539).
Post office c/San Vicente Mártir 23.

Moving on

Train Alicante (12 daily; 1hr 30min–2hr 15min); Barcelona (14 daily; 3–5hr); Granada (twice daily; 9hr); Madrid (10–14 daily; 3hr 30min–4hr 30min).
Bus Alicante (15–20 daily; 2hr 30min–3hr 30min); Barcelona (17–19 daily; 4–5hr); Denia (10 daily; 1hr 45min); Madrid (16–19 daily; 4hr); Seville (3 daily; 11hr).
Ferry Ibiza (1–6 weekly; 3–7hr); Palma (6–13 weekly; 9hr).

ALICANTE

ALICANTE is a thoroughly Spanish city, despite its proximity to a strip of package-holiday resorts. With good beaches nearby, lively nightlife and plenty of cheap hotels and restaurants, it's worth a day or two's stopover.

What to see and do

Wide esplanades give the town an elegant air, and around the Plaza de Luceros and along the seafront *paseo* you can relax beneath palm trees at terrace cafés. If you can, time your visit to coincide with the **Hogueres fiesta** of processions, fire and fireworks, which culminates in an orgy of burning on the night of June 23/24. The towering fortress **Castillo de Santa Bárbara** (daily 10am–10pm; €2.40 for the lift), on the bare rock behind the town beach, is Alicante's only real sight, with pleasant park areas and a tremendous view from the top. Access to it is from Playa Postiguet via a tunnel, then a lift shaft cut straight up through the rock. For the best local **beaches**, head for **Playa San Juan**, ten minutes from the town, on the tram towards Costa Blanca (hourly).

Arrival and information

Air The airport is 12km south of town. Buses (Line C6, 6.30am–10.20pm; every 40min; €2.50) stop opposite the bus station on c/Portugal.
Train The main train station is on Avda Salamanca, but trains on the private FGV line to Benidorm and Denia leave from the small station at the far end of the Playa Postiguet.
Bus Local and long-distance services arrive at the bus station on c/Portugal, a 15min walk from the town centre.
Regional tourist office Avda Rambla Méndez Nuñez 23 (Mon–Fri 9am–8pm, Sat 10am–8pm, Sun 10am–2pm; Ⓣ 965 200 000, Ⓦ www.comunitatvalenciana.com)
Municipal tourist office Esplanada de España 1 (Mon–Fri 10am–7pm, Sat 10am–2pm, closed Sun; Ⓣ 965 143 452, Ⓦ www.alicanteturismo.com). There are also offices inside the train and bus stations, and at the airport.

Accommodation

Outside July and August, you shouldn't have too much trouble finding accommodation, with the bulk of the options concentrated at the lower end of the old town, above the Esplanada de España – especially on c/San Fernando, c/Jorge Juan and c/Castaño.
Albergue Juvenil La Florida Avda de Orihuela 59 Ⓣ 965 918 250. Pretty institutional HI hostel, with café and laundry facilities. From October to June many spaces are reserved for students, so booking ahead is essential. Full board for under-25s €15.25.

Camping Costa Blanca c/Convento 143, El Campello ⓣ965 630 670, ⓦwww.campingcostablanca.com. In a small town, Campello, 10km to the north of Alicante, and close to the beach. Easily accessible by tram or bus (Línea 21). €5.89 for one person, €5.89 one tent.

Hostal Les Monges Palace c/San Agustín 4 ⓣ965 215 046, ⓦwww.lesmonges.es. Elegant rooms, stylishly decorated with excellent facilities for the price. Great central location too. En-suite double with TV €50.

Hostal Ventura c/San Fernando 10 ⓣ965 208 337. Fifth-floor hotel with tidy, en-suite rooms but rather small bathrooms. Doubles €39.25.

Eating and drinking

Known locally as El Barrio, the concentration of streets stretching north from the main Rambla to the castle contains an impressive 119 bars and is without a doubt the best place for eating, drinking and merry-making, with the crisscross of streets around c/Virgen de Belén and c/d'els Sants Metges probably best.

Desdén c/Labradores 22. A more sophisticated option than *La Banca*, this bar plays dance, jazz and funk music to an attractive crowd. Several similar options along the same strip.

El Cisne de Oro c/César Elguezábal 23. Popular tapas bar full to the brim with locals sampling delicious Alicante specialities, such as *pulpo* and *pastel de tortilla*.

La Banca c/d'els Sants Metges 1. Fun bar with cheap drinks that gets livelier in the small hours. Mojitos €3, draught beer €0.50.

La Matanza Castellana c/Bailén 13. One of the few, if not the only, places in town to offer free tapas with every drink. Closed Mon.

Directory

Consulate UK, Plaza Calvo Sotelo 1–2 ⓣ965 216 022.

Internet Cyber Café, c/San Vicente 46. Daily 9am–midnight, until 3am in summer.

Post office Junction of c/Alemania and c/Arzobispo Loaces (Mon–Fri 8am–8.30pm, Sat 9.30am–1pm).

Moving on

Train Barcelona (8 daily; 5–6hr); Madrid (9 daily; 3hr 30min–4hr); Valencia (10 daily; 2hr).

Bus Barcelona (11 daily; 8hr); Granada (6 daily; 5hr); Madrid (8 daily; 6hr); Málaga (6 daily; 8hr); Valencia (15–20 daily; 2hr 30min–3hr 30min).

The Balearic islands

The chief **Balearic islands** – Ibiza, Mallorca and Menorca – each maintain a character that is distinct from the mainland and from each other. **Ibiza**, firmly established among Europe's hippest resorts, has a floating summer population drawn from every corner of Europe, and beyond. **Mallorca**, the largest of the Balearics, still battles with its mass-market image, though in reality you'll find the worst clichés are crammed along the Bay of Palma and are easy to avoid. Away from these there are soaring pine-forested mountains, traditional villages, lively fishing ports, some beautiful coves and the Balearics' one real city, **Palma**. The farthest island from the mainland, **Menorca**, is relatively tranquil by comparison, where limited nightlife is compensated for by an abundance of unspoilt coves bathed by waters turquoise enough to rival the Caribbean. Prices on all the Balearic islands are considerably above the mainland, and from mid-June to mid-September budget **rooms** are in extremely short supply, so book in advance.

Getting there

Ferries from mainland Spain and inter-island connections are overpriced considering the distances involved and special **flight** deals mean it can be cheaper, as well as quicker, to fly. The three main ferry companies are **Acciona Transmediterranea** (ⓦwww.southernferries.co.uk), **Balearia** (ⓦwww.balearia.com) and **Iscomar** (ⓦwww.iscomar.com) and they operate from Barcelona, Valencia and Denia (just south of Valencia) on the mainland and have connections to and between Ibiza, Palma, Port d'Alcúdia, Maó and Ciutadella on the islands. Ferry timetables and

prices vary hugely and some services, particularly the fast boats, only run in summer. By way of example: a single journey for an under 25-year old foot passenger with Acciona Transmediterranea from Barcelona to Palma (8hr) costs €79; a single from Dénia to Ibiza with Balearia costs €89 and takes 4hr 15min; and the 2hr 30min journey from Port d'Alcúdia on Mallorca to Ciutadella on Menorca costs €39 if booked more than seven days in advance. For the latest fares and schedules, see Ⓦwww.aferryto.com, a useful one-stop-shop (in English) for all routes and services.

IBIZA

IBIZA (Eivissa in Catalan) is an island of excess. Internationally heralded as one of the world's top clubbing destinations, each summer Europe's best DJs play at its clubs, attracting large numbers of people looking to party 24/7. Yet it also has a quieter side, particularly in the north, with beautiful beaches and a bohemian vibe, a legacy from the 1960s when the island was a hippy hang-out.

What to see and do

In physical as well as atmospheric terms, **IBIZA TOWN** is the most attractive place on the island. Set around a dazzling natural harbour, it's one of the Mediterranean's most cosmopolitan small capitals. The old city walls enclose the ancient quarter of **Dalt Vila**, whilst the port area is a maze of small, whitewashed houses, market stalls and expensive boutiques specializing in boho fashions. Most **beaches** are easily accessible from the town – the best include **Las Salinas**, a long strip of sand surrounded by forests (bus #11; hourly 9.30am–7.30pm), and **Cala Bassa**, a cove on the easterly side of the island 20km northeast of Ibiza Town and roughly 9km west of the island's second clubbing town of **SANT ANTONI**; take bus #3 from Ibiza Town to Sant Antoni (every 30min; 7.30am–midnight), then bus #7 (every hour; 9.30am–6.30pm, except 1.30–2.30pm) from Sant Antoni to Cala Bassa. For celebrity spotting, head to the tiny **Platja de Benirràs**, near San Miguel, a favourite of the Euro jet-set.

Arrival and information

Air The airport is 7.5km out of town; there are regular shuttle buses (daily 6.50am–11.50pm; €1.70), or you can take a taxi (€16).

Boat The terminal on Passeig des Moll serves ferries to and from the mainland and Mallorca; boats from Formentera arrive at the terminal on Avenguida Santa Eularia.

Tourist office Opposite the ferry building, at c/Antoni Riquer 2 (May–Oct Mon–Fri 8am–8pm, Sat 9.30am–7.30pm; Nov–April Mon–Fri 8am–3pm, Sat 9.30am–1pm; Ⓣ971 191 951). For a list of all tourist offices in Ibiza and a wealth of information about the island see Ⓦwww.ibiza.travel. Alternatively, check out Ⓦwww.ibiza-spotlight.com for excellent up-to-date information.

Accommodation

Camping Cala Nova Platja Cala Nova Ⓣ971 33 17 74, Ⓦwww.campingcalanova.com. Located 20km north of Ibiza Town – but only 50m from the beach. €7.20 per tent plus €7.10 per person.

Camping La Playa Cala Martina, Es Canar Ⓣ971 33 85 25, Ⓦwww.camping-laplaya-ibiza.com. East-coast camping among pine trees with direct access to the beach. €12 per tent plus €10 per person.

Casa de Huéspedes Vara de Rey Vara de Rey 7 Ⓣ971 301 376, Ⓦwww.hibiza.com. Pleasant, artistically furnished rooms with shared toilets and showers. Just 5min from the port. Open all year. Doubles €60.

Hostal Bimbi c/Ramón Muntaner Ⓣ971 305 396, Ⓦwww.hostalbimbi.com. Comfortable, well-located hotel, a block from Figueretes beach and a 10min walk from Ibiza Town. Closed Nov–April. Doubles €46.

Hostal Sol y Brisa Avgda Bartomeu Vicent Ramon 15 Ⓣ971 310 818. Clean and friendly. Doubles €50.

Eating and drinking

Base Bar c/Garijo 15–16. Pumping music and a raucous crowd, next to the *Rock Bar*. Closed Nov–April.

Bon Profit Pl del Parque 5. Popular, reasonably priced Spanish restaurant with mains under €10. Kitchen closes at 10pm. Closed Sun and Jan.
Can Pou Bar c/Lluis Tur i Palau 19. Affordable, popular bar on the waterfront.
Comidas Bar San Juan c/Arturo Mari Ribas 5. Family-run, small place, with a great Spanish menu. Arrive early to avoid queuing. Closed Sun and Feb.
Lo Cura c/Antonio Mari Ribas 4. Tiny little bar near the port, with cheap drinks and DJ.
Rock Bar c/Garijo 14. One of the cheaper portside bars, attracting many English-speakers and top DJs. A good place to meet fellow partygoers pre-clubbing.
Sunset Café Pl del Parque 9. Despite the name, this is really a funky bar on the popular Plaza del Parque.

Clubs

Ibiza's formidable club scene needs little introduction. The season is short, however (mid-June to Sept), with August being particularly busy. Most of the main venues don't close until well past dawn. The handy Discobus links these clubs with the centre of town and runs through the night (€2.10 one way). Be prepared to spend a lot of money, though, with entrance fees upwards of €35 and astronomical bar prices. Look out for touts selling discounted tickets around the port bars each night, and for club promoters handing out free invites on the beaches. Alternatively, head to Playa d'Embossa to party day and night at the famous beach bar *Bora Bora* (free entry).
Amnesia Ibiza Town–Sant Antoni road, km6 ⓦwww.amnesia.es. A good mix of music across various nights. On Wednesdays, the island's most popular gay night, La Troya, is held here.
El Divino Port d'Eivissa ⓦwww.eldivino-ibiza.com. Only a short walk from central Ibiza Town, has a seated terrace, great views over the harbour and a mix of popular music.
Pacha Avgda 8 d'Agost ⓦwww.pacha.com. A more commercial scene than some other Ibizan clubs, with a capacity of over three thousand. Playing a variety of music, including Spanish pop, jazzy house, soul and funk, but predominantly house – in different rooms.
Privilege Ibiza Town–Sant Antoni road, km7 ⓦwww.privilegeibiza.com. One of the biggest clubs in the world, with a capacity for 10,000 – and hosting extravagant club nights every day of the week.
Space Platja d'en Bossa ⓦwww.space-ibiza.es. Day-venue with legendary terrace. Sunday sessions are a favourite.

Gay bars and clubs

Ibiza has one of the best gay scenes in Europe (ⓦwww.gayibiza.net), with a lot of the action centred in the port and another cluster of bars on c/d'Alfonso XII. Many mainstream Ibizan clubs hold a weekly gay night.
Anfora c/San Carlos 7, Dalt Vila ⓦwww.disco-anfora.com. Ibiza's only dedicated gay club. May to mid-Oct 11pm–6am; closed mid-Oct to April.
Angelo c/Alfonso XII 11. Another trendy bar, tucked away below *Soap*. Easter–Oct daily 10pm–4am; Nov–Easter weekends only.

MALLORCA

MALLORCA has a split identity. There are sections of its coast where the concrete curtain of high-rise hotels and shopping centres is continuous, but the spread of development tends to be isolated, sectioned off into ugly ghettos that are easy to avoid. Elsewhere the island is as appealing as it gets in the Mediterranean, particularly in the northwest where several stunning coves and pretty villages are framed by the dramatic backdrop of the Tramuntana mountains.

Palma

PALMA is an attractive, historic and cosmopolitan city filled with quaint streets, stylish boutiques and lively bars and restaurants. The main sight is the **cathedral** (April–May & Oct Mon–Fri 10am–5.15pm, Sat 10am–2.15pm; June–Sept Mon–Fri 10am–6pm, Sat 10am–2.15pm; Nov–March Mon–Fri 10am–3.15pm, Sat 10am–2.15pm; €4), which was built in recognition of the Christian Reconquest of Mallorca, and later worked on by Gaudí. Nearby, within the old "Portela" quarter, are the **Arab baths** (daily: April–Nov 9am–7.30pm; Dec–March 9am–6pm; €1.50), whilst up the hill overlooking the bay lies the **Castell Bellver** (April–Sept Mon–Sat 8.30am–8.30pm, Sun 10am–6.30pm; Oct–March Mon–Sat 8.30am–6.45pm, Sun 10am–4.30pm; €2.10), offering spectacular views from its high point over the city.

Several decent **beaches** are a bus ride away from the city centre. Bus #3 departs from the top of Plaça Rei Joan Carlos 1, outside C&A, and goes all the way to the attractive beach of Illetes, stopping off en route at the beaches at Cala Major and Portal Nous.

Arrival and information

Air Palma airport, 8km east of the city, is served by bus #1 (every 15min; €2) to the Passeig Mallorca.
Boat The large ferry port is 3.5km west of the city centre, connected to Palma by bus #1.
Tourist office Plaça de la Reina 2 (Mon–Fri 9am–8pm, Sat 9am–2pm; ⓣ 971 173 992, ⓦ www.infomallorca.net).
Internet Azul Computer Group, c/Soledad 4, just off the Plaça de la Reina; €2.90/hr.

Accommodation

The best areas to look for accommodation are around the Passeig Mallorca, on c/Apuntadores or c/Sant Feliu running west from Passeig d'es Born.
Hostal Apuntadores c/Apuntadores 8 ⓣ 971 713 491, ⓦ www.palma-hostales.com. Not as much character as the *Ritzi* next door, but the rooms are quieter and more comfortable. Private rooms April–Sept €55, with bath €70; dorms only the rest of the year €20–22.
Hostal Brondo c/Ca'n Brondo 1 ⓣ 971 719 043, ⓦ www.hostalbrondo.net. Stylish hotel, tastefully decorated in traditional Mallorcan style. Rooms are comfortable and quieter than the options on c/Apuntadores. Double with bath €70, without €55.
Hostal Ritzi c/Apuntadores 6 ⓣ 971 714 610, ⓦ www.hostalritzi.com. Ramshackle Palma institution in a great location at the heart of La Lonja. Rooms are basic, and with no lift the rooms on the fourth floor are quite a climb. Breakfast included. Doubles with shared bath €55.

> **TREAT YOURSELF**
> Hidden amid the tourist trappings of La Lonja, behind a large wooden door, **Abaci** (c/Sant Joan 1, just off c/Apuntadores) is one of Palma's most decadent treats. The bar is dripping in excess, with fruit draped over the elegant staircase, copious flowers, and even caged birds. Unsurprisingly the drinks aren't cheap but then the opulent surrounds are probably worth a €15 mojito.

Eating and drinking

The best place to go strolling in search of food is the largely pedestrianized La Lonja.
Bar Dia c/Apuntadores 18. Cheap, delicious and popular with locals – always a good sign. Specializing in tapas, from tortilla for €2.50 to prawns in garlic for €12.
La Bóveda c/Boteria 3. Hugely popular, elegant bar-restaurant in the heart of La Lonja, serving an excellent array of original tapas from €3.50. The more interesting choices, such as dates wrapped in bacon, are around the €6/7 mark. Always busy.
Vecchio Giovani c/Sant Joan 3. A good-value option for lunch; three-course *menú del día* comes in at €11 (Mon–Fri only).

Nightlife

Most of the major clubs are along the Paseo Marítimo. The larger, more famous venues charge entry, but this includes a free drink.
Abraxas Paseo Marítimo 42. Waterfront venue with guest DJs from Ibiza and the UK. Cover charge around €12.
Tito's Plaça Gomila 3. Arranged over three floors and with fantastic views across the bay of Palma. Cover charge €20.

Sóller

Set beneath the dramatic Tramuntana mountains, where the air is scented by orange and lemon groves, the beautiful town of **SÓLLER** is one of Mallorca's highlights. The town also makes a great base from which to explore the stunning northwest coast, including excursions to the nearby villages of **Fornalutx**, **Deia** and **Valdemossa**. You can also take the tram on to **Port Sóller** (every 30min in summer; €4 one way), a little coastal town with plenty of character and a small, sandy cove that's good for bathing. The best way to get to Sóller from Palma is by train (see box opposite).

Information

Tourist office Located in a converted train carriage next to the train terminal (Mon–Fri 9.30am–2pm

PALMA–SÓLLER TRAIN RIDE

The **train ride from Palma to Sóller** (7 daily; €10 one way, €17 return) is definitely worth the trip. Built in 1912 to carry fruit to Palma, the line rattles and rolls in wooden carriages through the dusty outskirts of the capital before a cross-country climb up mountain passes and through tunnels, passing almond groves, unruffled lakes and craggy peaks topping a thousand metres.

& 3–5pm, Sat 9.15am–1pm; ⓣ971 638 008, ⓦwww.sollernet.com).

Internet Internet sin Café, c/de la Luna 30.

Accommodation

Casa Margarita c/Reial 3 ⓣ971 634 214. The only budget option in town, with pleasant, basic rooms. Delightful Margarita, the owner, is a mine of information on the local area. Doubles with shared bath €34.

Eating and drinking

Mon c/de la Luna 5. Pizzeria (pizzas from €4.70) and takeaway that also serves baguettes and hamburgers. A cheaper option than the tourist-geared restaurants on Plaça Espanya.

Sa Fabrica de Gelats c/Romaguera 12. Gelateria serving a wide range of delicious flavours, including orange cream, made with home-grown Mallorcan oranges. Two scoops €2.40.

MENORCA

In 1993 **MENORCA** was declared a biosphere reserve and as such the island has largely avoided the ugly development seen elsewhere in the Balearics. Instead, idyllic coves and tranquil bays abound. It's possible to get to some of the coastal resorts with local transport from the main towns of **Maó** or **Ciutadella**, but you'll need your own wheels if you want to discover the more isolated beauty spots. Cycling is a great option as the roads are flat and quiet. Unlike its larger neighbours, however, Menorca is not for those in search of a party – out of season, nightlife on the island is virtually non existent.

Maó

As most visitors stay in resorts along the coast, the Menorcan capital of **MAÓ** is relatively free from tourists and so retains an authentic feel and is a great place to stay. It has an impressive port, some lovely old streets and enough picturesque squares in which to while away a lazy afternoon or two. Local buses provide access to nearby attractions, such as the lunar landscape of the **Cap de Favaritx**, the lively town of **Fornells**, or the beach resorts in the southeast, such as **Cala en Porter**.

Arrival and information

Air Menorca's international airport is 5km southwest of Maó. Buses (€1.60) run every 30min from 6am to midnight to Maó's central bus station.

Boat Ferries from Palma and Barcelona arrive at Maó harbour, a short walk from the town centre.

Bicycle and motorbike rental Autos Menorsur, Moll de Llevant 35.

Tourist office Moll de Llevant 2 (Mon–Fri 8am–8pm, Sat 8am–1pm; ⓣ971 355 952, ⓦwww.menorca.es). Hands out copies of *Menorca Weekly*, the island's weekly listings guide.

Internet Locutorio Call Point II, c/Sant Elies 54.

Accommodation

Camping Son Bou Crta San Jaime ⓣ971 372 727, ⓦwww.campingsonbou.com. Located south of Alaior, a 30min bus ride from Maó. €7.75 per person; tent €4.40.

Hostal La Isla c/Santa Caterina 4 ⓣ971 366 492. More expensive than *Orsi*, but a few extra euros gets you a more comfortable room, a TV and private bath. Very friendly owner and decent bar downstairs. En-suite double €48.

Posada Orsi c/Infanta 19 ⓣ971 364 751. Brightly coloured rooms, sociable atmosphere and roof terrace make this a popular choice, but the colours can't quite hide the slightly institutional feel. Doubles with shared bath €42.

Eating and drinking

The best place for eating and drinking is down by the Port, where there are plenty of

TREAT YOURSELF

A wonderful exception to Menorca's limited nightlife is the fabulously located club, **Cova d'en Xoroi** in Cala en Porter (www.covadenxoroi.com). Set in a large cave carved out of the cliff face, it's lit up to dramatic effect at night. The terraces give stunning views out to sea, especially at sunset or even sunrise (the club is open until dawn). Resident and top guest DJs match the ambient music to the tranquil setting. Open Fri & Sat from 11pm; entrance €20, including one drink.

bars and restaurants – open mainly in July and August.

Elefante Moll de Llevant 106. One of several bars along this strip, with a bohemian vibe and occasional live music. The tapas, such as *habas con chorizo* (€3.50), are a cut above the norm. The café-bar turns into a bar-club with DJs after midnight. Definitely the coolest little spot along the Port.

L'Antic Plaça de la Conquesta 5. Café-bar with the ideal location on a pretty square. A great spot for breakfast, with a good range of teas, interesting *bocadillos* from €4, and crêpes from €4.50. Good atmosphere at night too, with occasional live music.

Mirador Café Plaça Espanya 2. Café-bar with the usual range of drinks and tapas, but it's the great views across the harbour from the terrace that makes it such a popular choice.

Ciutadella and around

Well-preserved **CIUTADELLA** has a lovely old quarter and harbour and is Menorca's prettiest town. Nearby are some of the most beautiful and secluded virgin beaches in the Mediterranean, such as **Cala Turqueta** and **Macarella** – both have soft white sand and turquoise waters and are about a twenty-minute drive from Ciutadella (also reachable by bike). There are no facilities at Turqueta, so bring your own lunch, while at Macarella, *Bar Susy* serves simple meals (pizzas from €8, tapas from €4) and has toilets and showers. A short walk from Macarella over the white stone gorge takes you to the even more picturesque bay of **Macarelleta**.

Arrival and information

Bus Buses arrive at Plaça dels Pins, a few minutes' walk from the centre of town.

Boat Ferries from Alucudia in Mallorca arrive on the north side of the harbour, a 10min walk from town.

Bicycle and motorbike rental Velos Joan, Sant Isidre 78.

Tourist office Plaça Catedral 5 (Mon–Fri 9.30am–8.30pm, Sat 9am–1pm; ⓣ971 382 693, www.menorca.es).

Internet Locutori Rupit 18.Net, c/Castell Rupit 18.

Accommodation

Camping S'Atalaia Ctra Cala Galdana, Ferreries, ⓣ971 374 232, www.campingsatalaia.com. Between the town of Ferreries and the resorts of Santa Galdana. €6.90 person, €3.80 tent.

Pensión Oasis c/Sant Isidre 33 ⓣ971 382 197. Comfortable, spacious rooms set back from a pretty courtyard and restaurant. Double with private bath €35.

Eating and drinking

The charming market (Plaça Francesc Netto and Plaça Llibertat, Mon–Sat mornings) is a good place to pick up provisions for a picnic (there are no facilities at most of the isolated beaches). The best restaurants are off the side street of Plaça d'es Born. For nightlife, it's best to start the evening at the bars and cafés of the old town, then from midnight head down to the Port, where the bars and clubs (in high season) stay open until 6am.

Ca'n Nito c/Plaça d'es Born 11. A lively bar on the main square, popular for drinks and tapas. *Platos combinados*, such as chicken and chips (€8.50), also available.

Gabanna Plaça de Sant Joan 3. An attractive, bohemian bar that becomes a club later in the evening, with alternative jazz, world and house music. Open till 4am.

La Guitarra c/Nostra Senyora dels Dolors 1. Family-run restaurant serving traditional Menorcan specialities, such as *caldereta de llagosta* (lobster stew), in an atmospheric cellar. Mains from €14.

Catalunya

With its own language, culture and, to a degree, government, **Catalunya** has a unique identity. **Barcelona**, the capital, is very much the main event, one of the most vibrant and exciting cities in Europe. Inland, the monastery of **Montserrat**, Catalunya's premier sight, is perched on one of the most unusual rock formations in Spain and makes for a great day-trip. To the north, the rugged **Costa Brava** is slowly shedding its erstwhile unfortunate touristy image and boasts the best beaches in the region, along with some appropriately wacky and wonderful homages to surrealist artist Salvador Dalí.

BARCELONA

BARCELONA, the self-confident and progressive capital of Catalunya, is a tremendous place to be. A thriving port and the most prosperous commercial centre in Spain, it has a sophistication and cultural dynamism way ahead of the rest of the country. But Barcelona has also evolved an individual and eclectic cultural identity, most perfectly and eccentrically expressed in the architecture of **Antoni Gaudí**, but also evident in the diversity of cultural events.

What to see and do

Though it boasts outstanding **Gothic** and **Art Nouveau** buildings, and some great museums – most notably those dedicated to Picasso, Miró and Catalan art – Barcelona's main appeal lies in getting lost in the narrow side-streets of the **Barri Gòtic** (Gothic Quarter); rising, eating and drinking late; hitting the beach or lazing in the parks; and generally soaking up the atmosphere. As in any large city, keep an eye on your valuables.

Las Ramblas

One of the most popular avenues in Europe, **Las Ramblas** has been overtaken by sightseers, tourist bars, postcard stalls and human statues; it's largely avoided by locals. However, as it bisects the city, Las Ramblas remains a useful point of reference, so it's worth strolling down to orient yourself before getting lost in the more interesting maze of side streets in the Barri Gòtic to the east or El Raval to the west. If you are walking down Las Ramblas towards the sea, just off to your right is the glorious **La Boqueria**, the city's main food market (Mon–Sat 8am–8.30pm), a splendid gallery of sights and smells. A little further on, by the metro station, stands the **Liceu**, Barcelona's celebrated opera house (daily 11.30am–1pm, €4; daily guided tours of the interior at 10am, €8.70; and behind the scenes at 9.15am, €10; booking required: Ⓣ934 859 914, Ⓦwww.liceubarcelona.com). Further down still, positioned to the left off Las Ramblas, further into the Barri Gòtic, is the elegant but seedy nineteenth-century **Plaça Reial**. Decorated with tall palm trees and iron lamps, it's the haunt of bohemians, eccentrics and hundreds of alfresco diners and drinkers. Right at the harbour end of Las Ramblas, Columbus stands perilously perched atop a tall, grandiose column, the **Mirador de Colón** (daily: May & Oct 9am–8pm; June–Sept 9am–8.30pm; Nov–April 10am–6.30pm; €2.30). Take the lift to his head for a fine view of the city.

El Raval

The once-notorious red-light district of **El Raval** lies on the west side of Las Ramblas. With its two universities and numerous bars, clubs and arts centres, it is now one of the most exciting and authentic areas of the city. For a taste of the area's regeneration, walk up the **Rambla de Raval** – a boulevard with pavement cafés and bars – on your way to the **Museu d'Art Contemporani de Barcelona** or **MACBA**, a stunning white-walled and glass edifice (Mon & Wed–Fri 11am–8pm, Sat 10am–8pm,

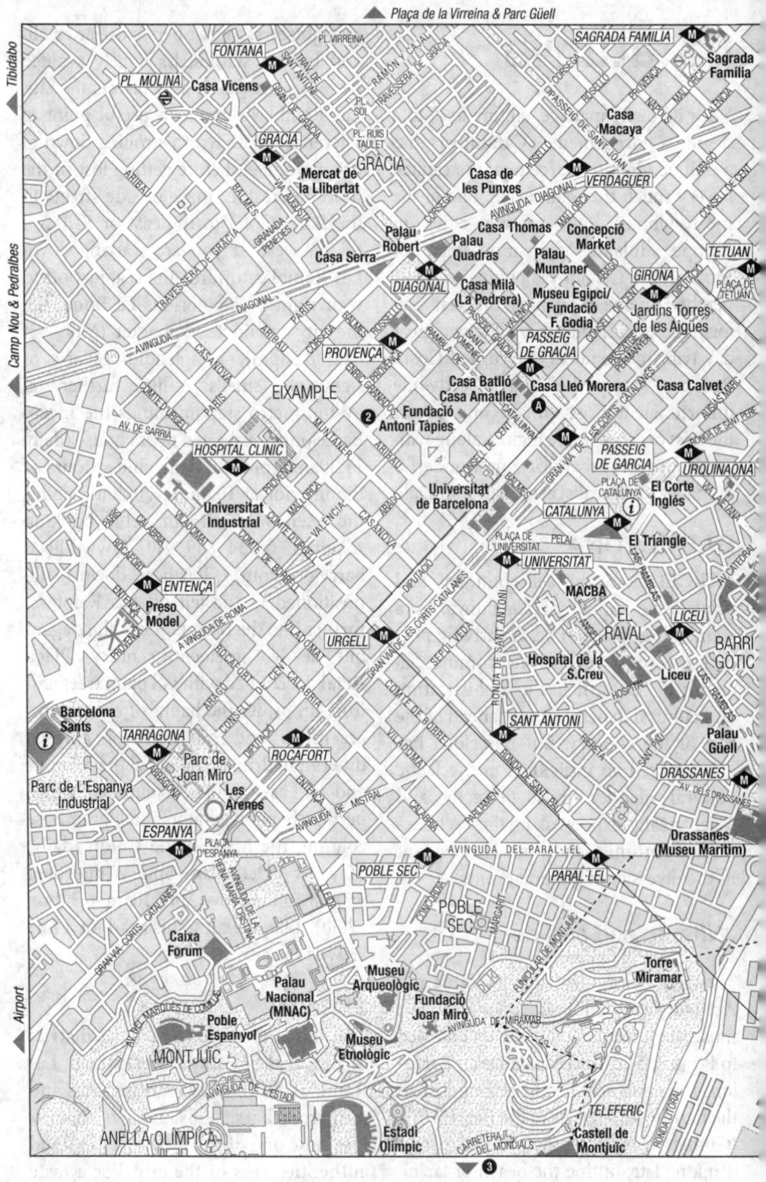

Sun 10am–3pm, open till midnight Thurs & Fri in summer; €7.50 to visit the whole museum, individual exhibitions less; ⓣ934 12 08 10, ⓦwww.macba.cat), which houses displays by international and national artists.

Next door is the more urban and experimental **Centre de Cultura Contemporània de Barcelona** or **CCCB** (Tues–Sun 11am–8pm, Thurs till 10pm; €4.50 one exhibition, €6.50 two or more; ⓣ933 06 41 00,

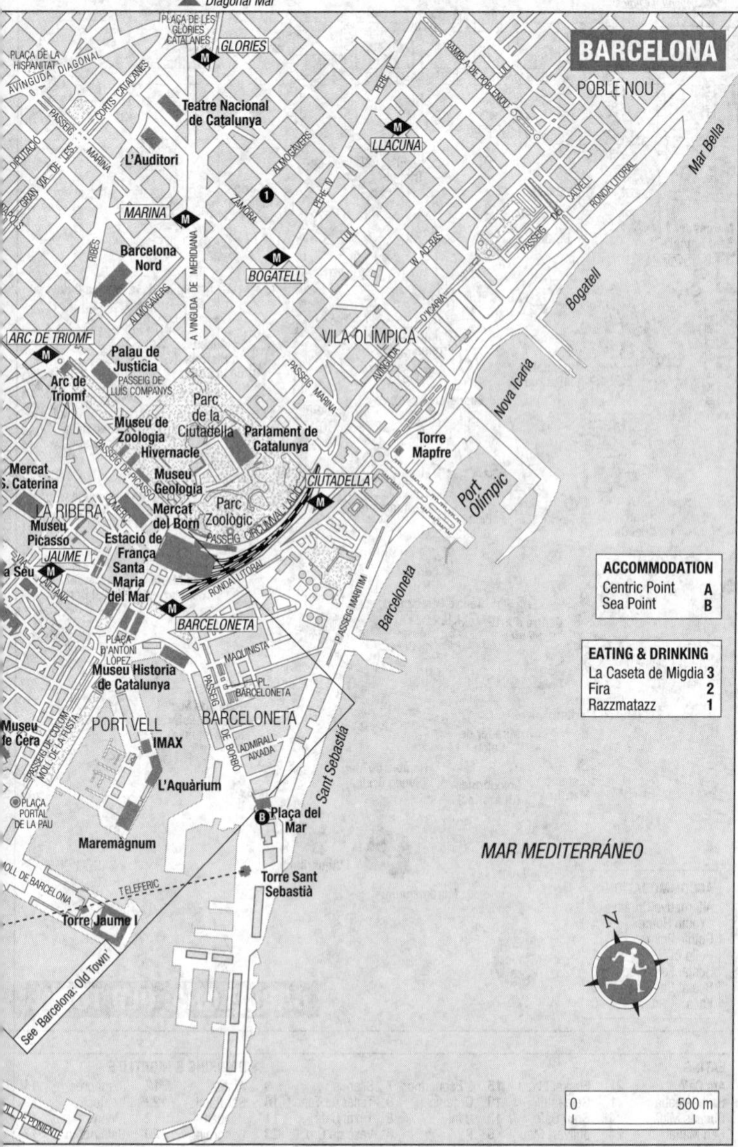

Ⓦwww.cccb.org). Firmly on the cutting edge of contemporary culture, there's always something interesting happening here (including Sónar; see box, on p.1129). There's also a great bookshop and café-bar with terrace, the perfect place to exercise your critical faculties post-exhibition.

Barri Gòtic

The **Barri Gòtic** dates principally from the fourteenth and fifteenth centuries,

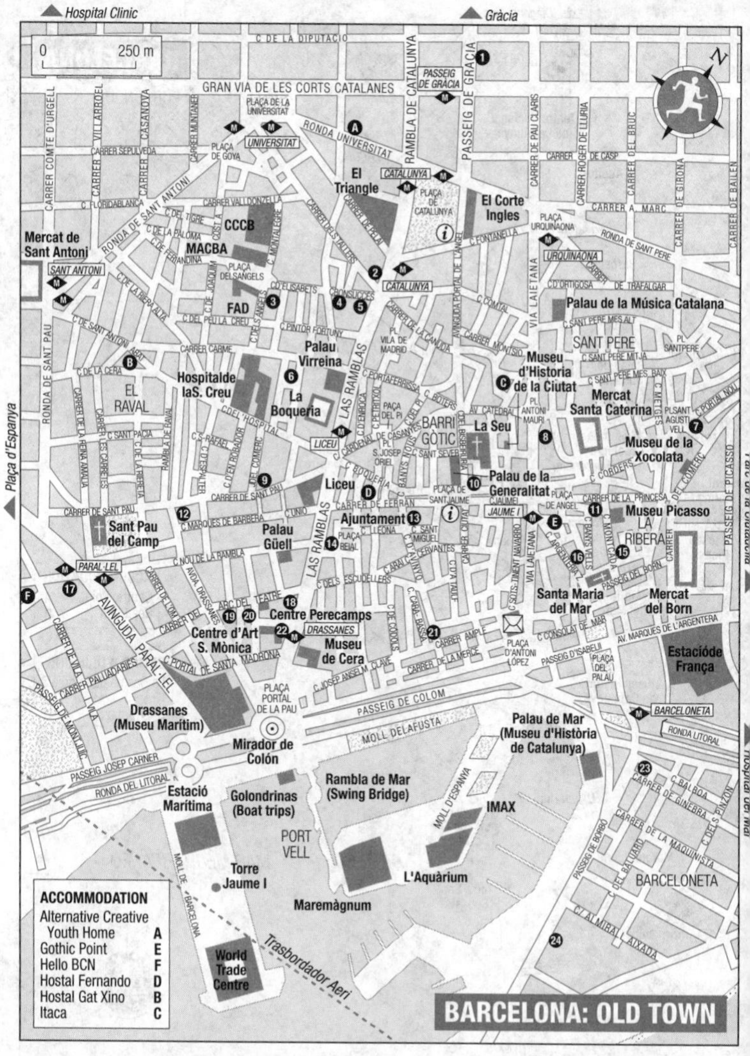

when Catalunya reached the height of its commercial prosperity. The quarter is centred on **Plaça de Sant Jaume**, just behind which lies **La Seu**, Barcelona's cathedral (daily 8am–12.45pm & 5.15–7.30pm, free; 1–5pm €5), one of Spain's great Gothic buildings. Barcelona's finest Roman remains were uncovered nearby, beneath the beautiful **Plaça del Rei**, and now form part of the **Museu d'Història de la Ciutat** (April–Sept Tues–Sat 10am–8pm,

Sun 10am–3pm; Oct–March Tues–Sat 10am–2pm & 4–7pm, Sun 10am–3pm; €5, students €2.50). You'll also be able to see the interiors of the Plaça del Rei's finest buildings – including the famous **Saló del Tinell**, on whose steps Ferdinand and Isabella stood to receive Columbus on his triumphant return from his famous voyage of 1492.

La Ribera and Parc de la Ciutadella

Heading east from Plaça de Sant Jaume, you cross Vía Laietana into **La Ribera** and reach the **Carrer de Montcada**, crowded with beautifully restored old buildings. One of these houses the **Museu Picasso** (Tues–Sun 10am–8pm; €9.50, free Sun from 3pm, free guided tours in English Thurs & Fri at 4pm; ⓣ932 56 30 22, ⓦwww.museupicasso.bcn.es), one of the world's most important collections of Picasso's work. Continue down the street and at its end you'll find yourself opposite the stunning basilica of **Santa Maria del Mar** (daily 9am–1.30pm & 4.30–8pm; Sun choral Mass at 12.30pm), built on what was the seashore in the fourteenth century. The elongated square leading from the church to the old Mercat del Born is the **Passeig del Born**, heart of the trendy **El Born** neighbourhood, a pleasant area for wandering. A few minutes' walk from here is the green and peaceful **Parc de la Ciutadella**, whose attractions include the meeting place of the Catalan parliament, a lake, Gaudí's monumental fountain and the interesting city **zoo** (daily 10am–5pm, until 7pm in summer; €16).

Port Vell, Barceloneta and Port Olímpic

The attractive **Port Vell** area, centred on the Maremàgnum complex, features an upmarket shopping mall, an overpriced aquarium, cinema, IMAX theatre and a multitude of bars and pricey restaurants. The other side of the port, past the marina, the **Barceloneta** district, in contrast, is one of the few remaining *barris* harbouring genuine local Catalan life: here, you'll find cleaned-up **beaches**, and the city's most famous **seafood** restaurants. A **cable car**, the **Trasbordador Aeri**, runs from the tip of Barceloneta to Montjuïc (daily: Jan, Feb & mid-Oct to Dec 10.30am–5.45pm; March to mid-June & mid-Sept to mid-Oct 10.45am–7pm, mid-June to mid-Sept 11am–8pm; €9.50 one way, €12.50 return). Walk 1km north along the beach promenade and you'll find **Port Olímpic** with its myriad bars and restaurants. At night, the tables are stacked up, dancefloors emerge and the area hosts one of the city's liveliest (and brashest) bar and club scenes.

Sagrada Família

Barcelona offers – above all through the work of **Antoni Gaudí** (1852–1926) – some of the most fantastic and exciting modern architecture anywhere in the world. Without doubt his most famous creation is the incomplete **Temple Expiatori de la Sagrada Família** (daily April–Sept 9am–8pm; Oct–March 9am–6pm; €11; metro Sagrada Família), in the northeastern sector of the Eixample district. With construction still ongoing, the interior is a giant building site, but it's fascinating to watch Gaudí's last-known plans being slowly realized. The size alone is startling, with eight spires rising to over 100m. Take the lift, or climb up one of the towers, and you can enjoy a dizzy view down over the whole complex and clamber still further round the walls and into the towers.

Gràcia and Parc Güell

The residential neighbourhood of **Gràcia**, north of the centre, has a bohemian, village-like feel, and is a good place for an authentic night out. Popular with arty student types, the bars are best stumbled upon by chance – try your

luck around the Plaça de la Virreina. Close by is the Verdi cinema, c/Verdi 32, which shows non-mainstream films in English. Take the L3 line to Fontana and head east along c/Asturies.

In the eastern part of Gràcia, **Parc Güell** (daily 10am–sunset; free) is Gaudí's most ambitious project after the Sagrada Família – and shouldn't be missed. This almost hallucinatory experience, with giant decorative lizards and a vast Hall of Columns, contains a small **museum** (daily: April–Sept 10am–7.45pm; Oct–March 10am–5.45pm; €4) with some of the furniture Gaudí designed. To get here, take the metro to Vallcarça or Lesseps (15min walk from either) or bus #24 from Plaça de Catalunya to the eastern side gate.

Montjuïc

The hill of **Montjuïc** features the varied attractions of half a dozen museums, gardens, the Poble Espanyol, a superbly sited castle and spectacular views of the sprawling city below. The most obvious approach is to take the metro to **Plaça d'Espanya** and walk from there up the imposing Avda de la Reina María Cristina. If you'd rather start with the castle, take the **Funicular de Montjuïc** (daily: April–Sept 9am–10pm; Oct–March 9am–8pm; every 10min; €1.35 single), which runs from Paral.lel metro station to the start of the **Telefèric de Montjuïc** (daily: April, May & Oct 10am–7pm; June–Sept 10am–9pm; Nov–March 10am–6pm; €6, €8.30 return), which in turn leads to the **Castell de Montjuïc** (grounds open daily 7am–8pm). This eighteenth-century fortress offers magnificent views across the city, has an outdoor café within its ramparts and a panoramic pathway into the surrounding woods. The alternative option to reach Montjuïc is to take bus #50 from Plaça Universitat along Gran Vía to Montjuïc.

MNAC, the Poble Espanyol and the Fundació Joan Miró

The **Palau Nacional**, set at the back of **Montjuïc**, is the imposing peach-coloured home to one of Spain's great museums, the **Museu Nacional d'Art de Catalunya** or **MNAC** (Tues–Sat 10am–7pm, Sun 10am–2.30pm; €8.50, free first Sun of month). Its enormous bounty includes a Romanesque collection that is the best of its kind in the world and a substantial number of Gothic, Baroque and Renaissance works. Nearby is the **Fundació Joan Miró** (Oct–June Tues–Sat 10am–7pm, Sun 10am–2.30pm; July–Sept Tues–Sat 10am–8pm, Thurs till 9.30pm, Sun 10am–2.30pm; €8), devoted to one of the greatest Catalan artists and the most adventurous of Barcelona's art museums. Downhill and to the west of MNAC is the **Poble Espanyol** or "Spanish Village" (Mon 9am–8pm, Tues–Thurs 9am–2am, Fri 9am–4am, Sat 9am–5am, Sun 9am–midnight; €8.50; Ⓦ www.poble-espanyol.com), consisting of replicas of famous or characteristic buildings from all over Spain, and with a lively club scene at night.

Arrival and information

Air The airport is 18km southwest of the city centre and is linked by train to the main train station,

DAY-TRIP: MONTSERRAT

The weird and bulbous mountains of **Montserrat**, 60km northwest of Barcelona, make for an interesting day-trip out of the city. As well as some short hikes (1–3hr) through the national park's unusual rock formations, the main attraction is the Benedictine monastery, with its well-preserved sixteenth-century basilica housing a twelfth-century image of La Moroneta, patron saint of Catalunya. To get here, take the train from Plaça Espanya (every hour at 36min past; 90min) to Monserrat Aeri (for the cable car), or to Monistrol de Monserrat (for the rack railway to the town).

Barcelona Sants (daily 6.08am–11.38pm, every 30min; €2.80), from where you can take the metro to the city centre (line #3 to Liceu for Las Ramblas). Some trains from the airport also run on to Plaça de Catalunya, a more direct way of reaching the Barri Gòtic. The Aerobús (6am–1am, every 8min; €4.05) runs to Plaça d'Espanya, Gran Vía de les Corts Catalanes and Plaça de Catalunya.

A taxi to the centre will cost around €24.

Train Barcelona Sants (metro Sants) is the city's main train station, for national and some international arrivals – many national buses also stop here. Estació de França (metro Barceloneta), near Parc de la Ciutadella, is the terminal for long-distance Spanish and European express and intercity trains.

Bus The main bus terminal for international and long-distance services is the Estació del Nord (three blocks north of Parc de la Ciutadella; metro Arc de Triomf).

Ferry Balearics ferries dock at the Estació Marítima (metro Drassanes) at the bottom of Las Ramblas.

Tourist office Plaça de Catalunya (daily 9am–9pm; ⓣ932 853 834, ⓦwww.barcelonaturisme.com; metro Catalunya).

City transport

Metro and bus The quickest way of getting around is by metro (Mon–Thurs & Sun 5am–midnight, Fri till 2am, all night Sat) as bus routes (5am–10.30pm, plus night-bus network) are far more complicated – though every bus stop does display a comprehensive route map. There's more information on ⓦwww.tmb.net, or pick up a free transport map at TMB customer service centres at Barcelona Sants or Universitat and Diagonal metro stations.

Tickets and discount cards Ticket prices for bus and metro are: zone 1 single (covers all major sights) €1.35; ten-ride *targeta* (a "T10") €7.70; one-day pass (T-Dia) €5.80; thirty-day (€47.90). The Barcelona Card, available from any tourist office (two days €26, five days €42; ten percent discount online), covers transport to and from the airport, all city transport, plus discounts at museums, shops and restaurants. The Articket (€20, available at ticket offices; ⓦwww.articketbcn.org) covers entry to seven of the city's main art galleries. Note that student ticket prices in museums and galleries are often only available to those who are both a student and under 25.

Bus Turistic Links Barcelona's major sights, at which you can hop off and on at your leisure (€21 for one day, €27 for two days); tickets are available at tourist offices or on the bus itself.

Bicycles Many hostels rent out bikes, or try Barcelona Rent a Bike, c/Tallers 45 (€6/2hr up to €15/24hr; ⓦwww.barcelonarentabike.com).

Taxis Black-and-yellow taxis are plentiful and very useful late at night. There's a minimum charge of €1.15, €1.30 after 10pm and at weekends, with an average cross-town journey costing €6–7.

Accommodation

Accommodation in Barcelona is among the most expensive in Spain, and in summer you'll be hard pushed to find a hostel bed for under €20, or a double room for under €60. You're also strongly advised to book ahead, at least for the first couple of nights. Most of the cheapest accommodation is in the side streets off and around Las Ramblas and in El Raval. The tourist office at Plaça de Catalunya can help find rooms (though not hostel space), or you can use Barcelona Online (ⓣ933 437 993, ⓦwww.barcelona-on-line.es) or the hostel and budget-hotel reservation service ⓦwww.hostelbarcelona.com. There are hundreds of campsites on the coast in either direction, but none less than 11km from the city.

Hostels

Albergue Mare de Déu de Montserrat Pg Mare de Déu del Coll 41–51, Horta ⓣ932 105 151, ⓦwww.tujuca.com. A lovely HI mansion hostel with gardens and views, around 30min from the centre. Five-night maximum stay. Metro Vallcarça. Dorms from €21.50.

Alternative Creative Youth Home Ronda de la Universitat 17 ⓣ635 669 021, ⓦwww.alternative-barcelona.com. Self-consciously cool, but no less enjoyable for it, this well-organized hostel attracts the arty crowd its name suggests, with shared kitchen, wi-fi and helpful, informed staff. Metro Catalunya. Dorms €18.70–36.70.

Centric Point c/Passeig de Gràcia 33, Eixample ⓣ932 156 538, ⓦwww.equity-point.com. A beautiful, old mansion conversion in the smart Passeig de Gràcia. The smaller dorm rooms have en-suite bathrooms. Free wi-fi and shared kitchen. Book ahead, especially in summer. Metro Passeig de Gràcia. Dorms €23, breakfast included.

Gothic Point c/Vigatans 5–9, La Ribera ⓣ932 687 808, ⓦwww.equity-point.com. Excellent location, featuring a sunny patio with deckchairs, plus bike rental, wi-fi and organized social events. Almost always full, so book ahead. Metro Jaume I. Dorms €23; breakfast included.

Hello BCN c/Lafont 8–10 ⓣ934 428 392, ⓦwww.hellobcnhostel.com. A busy hostel 10min from Las Ramblas. Crowded dorms but great atmosphere; also has gym, kitchen, free internet and bar. Metro Paral.lel. Dorms €24, doubles with bathroom €65.

Itaca c/Ripoll 21, Barri Gòtic ⓣ933 019 751, ⓦwww.itacahostel.com. Funky little hostel near La Seu, with spacious mixed dorms (women-only dorm also available), plus plenty of communal spaces and a kitchen. Metro Jaume I. No smoking and curfew 4–6am. Dorms €25, doubles for around €60 also available. Breakfast not included.

Sea Point Pl. del Mar 1–4, Barceloneta ⓣ932 247 075, ⓦwww.equity-point.com. Not so hot on facilities but the excellent beachside location is popular with the surfers. En-suite dorms, but no kitchen. The organized social activities join up with sister hostels *Gothic* and *Central*. Metro Barceloneta. Dorms €25, breakfast included.

Hotels

Hostal Fernando c/de Ferran 31, Barri Gòtic ⓣ933 017 993, ⓦwww.hfernando.com. Well-kept *hostal* a cut above the norm, plus top-floor dorm accommodation. Metro Liceu. Dorms €19–25, rooms €60–75.

Hostal Gat Xino c/Hospital 155, El Raval ⓣ933 248 833, ⓦwww.gatrooms.com. Rooms are small but stylish and comfortable, with double glazing, wi-fi access, a/c and TV. The attractive roof terrace opens in summer for drinks and music. Breakfast included. Metro Sant Antoni. Doubles with private bath €70–90.

Eating

Barcelona is a reasonably expensive place to eat out. Awash as it is with trendy new restaurants, the best bet for a cheap meal is to take advantage of the lunchtime *menú del día* many places offer from Monday to Friday – you can get three courses with wine and bread for as little as €10. For picnics, head for La Boqueria market off Las Ramblas, or stop in at one of the many bakeries. Tapas is another option, and there are hundreds of excellent bars in the old town, although these can end up being costly, depending on the portion size.

TREAT YOURSELF

For a night away from the hubbub and hordes of downtown Barcelona, head to sea. **Willowmoon**, a sailing boat moored in Marina Port Vell, close to the city centre, offers unique B&B accommodation in its cosy en-suite cabin. With only one set of guests allowed at a time, the deck is all yours, a secluded spot to catch some rays or watch the sun set. €60 per person per night; see ⓦwww.willowmoon.uk.com for details.

Cafés

Buenas Migas Pl. Bonsuccés 6, El Raval. Small café with outside seating in the heart of arty Raval, serving delicious pizza or quiche slices for under €5. Pasta of the day €3.90. Metro Liceu.

Silenus c/Angels 8, El Raval. The set lunch isn't cheap (€14) but it's worth stopping here for at least a coffee to enjoy the shabby-chic decor. Free wi-fi. Metro Liceu.

Téxtil Café c/Montcada 12, La Ribera. In the atmospheric medieval courtyard of the textile museum, with braziers in winter. Closed Mon. Metro Jaume I.

Tapas bars

Ba-ba-reeba Pg. de Gràcia 28, Eixample. Delicious range of tapas, all at reasonable prices (€3–8.50). Open until 1.30am. Metro Passeig de Gràcia.

Euskal Etxea Pl. Montcada 1–3, La Ribera. Specializing in mouthwatering *pinchos* (Basque tapas) from €1.80 each. Closed Mon. Metro Jaume I.

Taller de Tapas c/de l'Argenteria 51. One of several city-centre branches of this popular chain of tapas bars/restaurants offering simple, quality food in elegant, relaxed surroundings. Tapas €3–12. Highly recommended. Metro Jaume I.

Vaso de Oro c/de Balboa 6. A tiny but lively bar, packed with locals, noise and character. Excellent tapas, at around €4–5. Closed Sept. Metro Barceloneta.

Restaurants

Arc Café c/Carabassa 19, Barri Gòtic. Bohemian brasserie-bar with attractive split-level interior. Set lunch €9.60. Popular Thai food nights on Thurs and Fri with curries from €5–10. Metro Drassanes.

Can Manel Pg. Joan de Borbó 60, Barceloneta. Probably the best-value place by the harbour, with a weekday €10.50 *menú del día*. Closed Mon. Metro Barceloneta.

Gelaaati! c/Llibreteria 7. Home-made Italian ice creams, in an array of delicious – and sometimes unusual – flavours. Two scoops €2.50, three scoops €3. Metro Jaume I.

Gran Café c/Avinyó 9, Barri Gòtic. Elegant Barcelona institution offering exceptional service and good Catalan/French food. Weekday *menú del día* €13. Metro Jaume I.

Julivert Meu c/ Bonsuccés 7, El Raval ⓣ933 180 343. Excellent selection of traditional Catalan dishes. Eat well for €10–15. Metro Liceu.

L'Economic Pl. Sant Agustí Vell 13, La Ribera ⓣ933 196 494. The beautiful tiled dining room is the backdrop for one of the city's bargains – an excellent three-course lunch for under €10, wine included. Closed weekends. Metro Jaume I.

Organic c/Junta de Comerc 11. Funky, organic vegetarian restaurant with a hippy vibe. Three courses with as much soup and salad as you can eat for €15. There's another branch inside La Boqueria market that does takeaways. Metro Liceu.

Ovni c/Via Laietana 32. Stylish, good-value restaurant serving all-you-can eat buffet for €8.95 or €10.60 at weekends. Free internet access for 30min. Metro Jaume I.

Ra Pl. Gardunya 34, behind La Boqueria market. Outdoor café by day, serving an excellent €10.99 three-course lunch menu; trendy bar/restaurant by night. One of several similar establishments on the same strip. Metro Liceu.

Drinking and nightlife

Barcelona's nightlife is some of Europe's best, though it's not cheap. The high-tech theme palaces are concentrated mainly in the Eixample, especially around c/Ganduxer, Avda Diagonal and Vía Augusta. Laid-back and/or alternative places can be found in the streets of El Raval, while the waterfront Port Olímpic area is a more mainstream summer-night playground, where big, brash identikit clubs lure in large groups of fun-seeking tourists and hen parties with cheap two-for-one drinks deals. Music bars close at 3am, the clubs at 4 or 5am, though later at weekends. For listings, pick up a copy of *Butaxaca*, a free weekly guide available in most bars and clubs, or buy the weekly *Guía del Ocio* from any newsstand (ⓦwww.guiadelociobcn.com). The thriving gay scene in Barcelona (ⓦwww.gaybarcelona.net) is prevalent in the so-called Gaixample, a few square blocks northwest of the main university: *SexTienda*, at c/Rauric 11 (near Plaça Reial), supplies free maps of gay Barcelona with a list of bars, clubs and contacts.

SÓNAR

If electronica is your thing, make sure you're in town for **Sónar** (ⓦwww.sonar.es), an internationally recognized multimedia art and progressive music festival, held every June in Barcelona. Day-tickets cost €30, night-tickets €48, whilst a three-day, two-night pass will set you back €140.

Bars

Ambar Rambla del Raval. Retro lamps, shabby sofas and quirky artwork make this café-bar a stylish place to while away an afternoon/evening. Open till 3am with DJs at weekends. Cocktails from €6.50. Metro Paral.lel or Liceu.

Bar Pastis c/ Santa Mònica 4, El Raval. Opened in 1946 to cater to French sailors and judging by the Gallic music and weary oil paintings, it hasn't changed much since. A small gem (but perhaps not for non-smokers). Open till 3am Fri & Sat. Metro Drassanes.

Boadas c/de Tallers 1. A popular old-fashioned cocktail bar just off Las Ramblas. Mon–Thurs noon–midnight, Fri & Sat noon–3am. Metro Liceu.

Cangrejo c/Monserrat 7, El Raval. Fun bar playing Spanish music; becomes a lively club later in the evening. Open till 3am Fri & Sat. Metro Drassanes.

Fira c/Provença 171, Eixample. Only in Barcelona – fairground rides and circus paraphernalia adorn this long-standing theme bar. Tues–Sat from 11pm till late. Metro Provença.

La Caseta del Migdia Mirador de Migdia, Passeig de Migdia ⓦwww.lacaseta.org. Deckchairs, DJs and alfresco drinking make this the perfect place in Barcelona to watch the sun set. Open till 2.30am Thurs–Sat in summer. Check website for programme. Bus or funicular to Montjuïc (see p.1126).

Clubs

Jamboree Pl. Reial 17, Barri Gòtic. Cavernous (and smoky) basement club with an international crowd dancing to hip-hop or funky jazz. Cover charge €9. Metro Liceu.

Moog c/Arc del Teatre 3, El Raval. From disco to drum'n'bass with regular appearances from top UK and Euro DJs. Despite the large, industrial setting the atmosphere is relaxed and both gay and straight friendly. See ⓦwww.masimas.com/moog for line-up. Open midnight–5am. Cover charge €9. Metro Drassanes.

Razzmatazz Club c/Amogàvers 122, Poble Nou. Well worth the taxi or metro ride out of town – Barcelona's music scene happens here. Five rooms, each dedicated to a different sound. Open Fri & Sat 1–6am. Cover charge €15, includes drink. Metro Marina.

Sala Apolo/Club Nitsa c/Nou de la Rambla 113, Poble Sec. Regular live gigs by biggish names and burgeoning stars from the worlds of alternative electronica, rock and techno – *Nitsa* club night rules the roost at weekends. Cover charge varies. Metro Paral.lel.

Shopping

Barcelona has a well-deserved reputation for great shopping. The big names of the fashion industry occupy the smart Passeig de Gràcia, but if this breaks your budget head to the oceanic shopping centre Maremagnum which has many high-street brands under one roof. For more unusual purchases, the crooked passages of La Ribera and El Born are home to dozens of little boutiques, whilst in El Raval, numerous funky vintage shops lie along the Carrer de la Riera Baixa. There are also a number of excellent speciality food retailers in the city, and chocolate shops are scattered throughout the Ciutat Vella. Note that all prices are fixed, with the exception of Els Encants flea market.

La Botifarrería de Santa María c/Santa María 4, El Born. Sells fabulous speciality hams, cheeses and their famous *botifarras* (sausages).

Papabubble c/Ample 28, Barri Gòtic. Sweet-smelling candy store, where you can watch confectionery taking shape before your eyes. Closed Aug.

Produit National Brut c/Avinyó 29, Barri Gòtic. Vintage and customized clothes for men and women, plus retro sunglasses.

Xocoa c/Princesa 10, La Ribera. *Chocolatier* selling handmade chocolates and funky chocolate bars sealed in retro-style wrapping.

Directory

Consulates Australia, Pl. Gala Placidia 1°3, Gràcia ⓣ934 909 013; Canada, c/Elisenda de Pinós 10, Sàrria ⓣ932 042 700; Ireland, Gran Vía Carles III 94, Les Corts ⓣ934 915 021; New Zealand, Trav. de Gràcia 64, Gràcia ⓣ932 090 399; UK, Avda. Diagonal 477, Eixample ⓣ933 666 200; US, Passeig de la Reina Elisenda 23, Sàrria ⓣ932 802 227.

Emergency numbers Hospital ⓣ061; Police ⓣ112.

Exchange Most banks are located in Pl. de Catalunya and Pg. de Gràcia. ATMs and money exchange available at the airport; Barcelona Sants; the tourist office at Pl. Catalunya; and at *casas de cambio* throughout the centre.

Hospitals 24hr accident and emergency centres at: Centre Perecamps, Avda Drassanes 13, El Raval ⓣ934 410 600; Hospital Clinic, c/Villaroel 170, Eixample ⓣ932 275 400; Hospital del Mar, Pg. Marítim 25, Vila Olímpica ⓣ932 483 000.

Internet Internet centres abound in Barcelona. Try easyEverything, Ronda de l'Universitat 35, Eixample, or at Ramblas 31, Barri Gòtic; Internet Gallery Café, Barra de Ferro 3.

Language classes Group conversation classes in Spanish or Catalan available free at libraries. See ⓦwww.bcn.cat/joventut for more details.

Laundry Lavomatic, Pl. Joaquim Xirau 1, Barri Gòtic, and c/Consolat del Mar 43, La Ribera.

Left luggage Lockers at all the stations; €3–4.50 per day.

Lost property Oficina de Troballes, Pl. Carles Pi I Sunyer 8, Barri Gòtic.

Pharmacies At least one *farmacia* (marked with a green cross) in each neighbourhood is open 24hr – look in the window of any pharmacy for addresses.

Police Guàrdia Urbana (City Police), Ramblas 43, ⓣ932 562 430; open 24hr.

Post office Correus, Pl. d'Antoni López (Mon–Fri 8.30am–9.30pm, Sat 8.30am–2pm).

Moving on

Bus Alicante (4 daily; 9hr); Madrid (7–15 daily; 7hr 30min); Valencia (14–17 daily; 5hr); Zaragoza (15–25 daily; 3hr 30min–5hr).

Train Girona (hourly; 1hr 15min–1hr 30min); Tarragona (every 30min; 1hr); Valencia (16 daily; 3–5hr); Zaragoza (15 daily; 3hr 40min–5hr 30min).

Ferry Acciona Transmediterranea (ⓦwww.southernferries.co.uk) is the main ferry company with regular services operating from Barcelona to Palma on Mallorca, Máo on Menorca and Ibiza Town. Journey times and frequencies vary hugely depending on routing and the time of year. For the latest schedules and prices, see ⓦwww.aferryto.com.

THE COSTA BRAVA

Stretching for 145km from the French border to the town of Blanes, the **Costa Brava** (Rugged Coast) boasts wooded coves, high cliffs, pretty beaches and deep blue water. The more rugged northern part, dominated by the spectacular **Cap de Creus** headland and park, and the bohemian town of **Cadaqués**, is the most attractive yet least crowded, with a natural appeal all its own. Inland are the twin hubs of **Girona**, the beautiful medieval capital of the region, and **Figueres**, Dalí's birthplace and home to his outrageous **museum**. **Buses** in the region are almost all operated by SARFA (ⓣ902 30 20 25, ⓦwww.sarfa.es), with an office in every town. To visit the smaller and more picturesque coves, a car or bike is useful, or you could walk the fabulous

Camí de Ronda necklace of footpaths running along the coastline.

Figueres

The northernmost parts of the Costa Brava are reached via **FIGUERES**, a provincial Catalan town with a lively *rambla* and plenty of cheap food and accommodation. The place would pass almost unnoticed, however, were it not for the most visited museum in Spain after El Prado, the surreal **Teatre-Museu Dalí** (March–June & Oct 9.30am–5.45pm; July–Sept 9am–7.45pm; Nov–Feb 10.30am–5.45pm, Oct–May closed Mon; €11). Born in Figueres, Dalí also died here and the museum plays host to some of his most eccentric work. The extraordinary pink facade, topped with enormous eggs and bronze mannequins, sets the tone for the exhibitions inside, which include collages, sculptures and mechanical contraptions requiring audience participation, as well as more conventional art.

Arrival and information

Train To make your way into the centre of town, simply follow the "Museu Dali" signs from the train station.

Tourist office In front of the post office building by the Plaça del Sol (July–Sept Mon–Sat 9am–8pm, Sun 10am–3pm; Oct–June 9am–2pm & 3–7pm; ⓣ972 503 155, ⓦwww.figueresciutat.com). It runs English-language guided walks of the town in summer.

Accommodation

Hostal Androl Cra. Nacional 2, km 8.5 ⓣ972 675 496. Offers more expensive rooms but also has year-round camping (€25 high season for two people, including a tent) and a restaurant/bar. Doubles €44.

Pensión San Mar c/Rec Arnau 31 ⓣ972 509 813. Good option for a comfortable room. Doubles €34.

Eating

There's a gaggle of cheap tourist restaurants in the narrow streets around the Museu Dalí and some nice, but pricier, pavement cafés lining the *rambla*.

> **FESTIVAL CASTELL DE PERALADA**
>
> Every July and August, the **Festival Castell de Peralada** (ⓦwww.festivalperalada.com) attracts internationally acclaimed musicians and artists, to perform within the gardens of this medieval castle just outside of Figueres. Tickets cost €25–35.

Creperie Bretonne Annaick c/Cap de Creus. Continuing the absurdist theme, this restaurant is worth a visit for the decor alone, though their wide range of stuffed crêpes and salads (set lunch menu from €8.80) is equally enticing.

Moving on

Bus Barcelona (3–8 daily; 1hr 30min); Cadaqués (3 daily; 1hr 15min); Girona (3–8 daily; 1hr).

Train Barcelona (every 30min; 2hr); Girona (every 30min; 30min); Madrid (daily; 11hr).

Cadaqués

The beautiful fishing village of **CADAQUÉS**, an hour by regular SARFA bus from Figueres, was Dalí's home from 1930 until his death, and has attracted an arty crowd ever since. The stunning **Casa-Museu Dalí** (daily: mid-June to mid-Sept 9.30am–9pm; mid-Sept to Jan & mid-March to mid-June 10.30am–6pm; €10; booking required ⓣ972 251 015), the museum set up in his jumble of a home, lies 1km northeast in the tiny Portlligat cove and offers an enthralling glimpse into his private life. Cadaqués itself is a picture-postcard, whitewashed village with tiny beaches and narrow cobbled streets straddling a hill topped by an imposing church. **Accommodation** is expensive; the cheapest options are at the *Pensión Marina*, La Riera 3 (ⓣ972 159 091; double €50), and at the campsite on Ctra Port-Lligat 17 (ⓣ972 258 126; €7.50 per person, €9.50 per tent; April–Sept). For a **drink** or a **meal**, the areas around c/Miguel Rosset and below the church are the liveliest. To visit some

of the surrounding coast, rent a **bike** or **scooter** from Rent@Bit on Avda Caritat Serinyana 9 (scooter €45/day; bike €20/day) – internet access also available.

Girona

GIRONA, 37km south of Figueres and 100km from Barcelona, is one of Spain's loveliest unsung cities, with alleyways winding around its compact old town, the **Barri Vell**, through the atmospheric streets of **El Call**, the beautifully preserved medieval Jewish quarter. The city was fought over every century since the Romans first set foot here, and is dominated by its towering **cathedral** (daily: April–Oct 10am–8pm; Nov–March 10am–7pm; €5, free Sun; services Sat from 4.30pm, Sun 10am–2pm, at which time only part of the cathedral can be visited). Girona's eclectic past is tangible in its **medieval walls**, which provide a great afternoon's walk.

Girona is also popular with hikers and cyclists who use the city as a base for the many great routes in the area, details of which are available at the tourist office.

Arrival and information

Bus and train The bus and train stations, located next to one another off the Crta. Barcelona, are a 20min walk southwest from the centre.

Tourist office On the *rambla* (Mon–Fri 8am–8pm, Sat 8am–2pm & 4–8pm, Sun 9am–2pm; ⓣ972 226 575, ⓦwww.ajuntament.gi/turisme). There's also an information stand at the train station.

Accommodation

Alberg Ceverí de Girona C/dels Ciutadans 9 ⓣ934 838 363. HI hostel with good, central accommodation. Dorms for under-25s €20.20 with a HI card.

Pensió Margarit c/Ultònia 1 ⓣ972 20 10 66, ⓦwww.hotelmargarit.com. A good option slightly out of the centre but not far from the station. Doubles and twins €40.

Pensión Massó Plaça Sant Pere 12 ⓣ972 207 1750. In a quiet location on the other side of town to the train station. Doubles €35.

SPRING AND SUMMER IN GIRONA

For a fortnight from the second Saturday in May each year, Girona decks itself out in its floral finest to celebrate the **Tems de Flors**. Many houses in the historic centre, elaborately wreathed in fragrant blooms, open to the public.

From the end of June until mid-September, open-air bars set up shop in the **Parc de la Devesa** to the north of the city centre, quenching the thirst of young people who flock there to enjoy live music and the long summer evenings.

Eating and drinking

For evening drinking it's best to go into the Barri Vell or the area around Plaça Independència, where most of the bars and clubs are.

Alberg Ceverí de Girona C/dels Ciutadans 9. During term time the hostel offers a great set-lunch menu for €6.20, a real bargain compared to what's on offer elsewhere.

La Terra c/Ballesteries 23. An attractive tiled café-bar by day – serving good-value quiches, salads and burgers – and a trendy, buzzing bar by night. Open till 3am on weekends.

Moving on

Bus Barcelona (3–7 daily; 1hr 30min); Figueres (3–8 daily; 1hr).

Train Barcelona (every 30min; 1hr 30min); Figueres (every 30min; 30min); Madrid (1 daily; 10hr 45min).

The Pyrenees

With the singular exception of **Pamplona** at the time of its bull-running fiesta, the area around the Spanish Pyrenees is little visited – the majority of people who come here at all travel straight through. In doing so they miss out on some of the most wonderful scenery in Spain, and some of the country's most attractive trekking. Also

striking is the slower pace of life, especially in **Navarra** in the west, a partly Basque region, and **Aragón** in the centre. There are few cities here – Pamplona itself and **Zaragoza**, with its fine Moorish architecture, are the only large centres – but there are plenty of attractive small towns and, of course, the mountains themselves, with several beautiful **national parks** as a focus for exploration.

PAMPLONA

PAMPLONA (Iruña) has been the capital of Navarra since the ninth century, and long before that was a powerful fortress town defending the northern approaches to Spain. Even now it has something of the appearance of a garrison city, with its hefty walls and elaborate pentagonal citadel.

What to see and do

The compact and lively streets of the old town offer plenty to look at: the elaborately restored **cathedral** with its magnificent cloister and interesting **Museo Diocesano** (June–Sept Mon–Sat 10am–7pm; Oct–May Mon–Fri 10am–2pm & 4–7pm, Sat 10am–2pm; €4.40); the colossal **city walls** and **citadel**; the display of regional archeology, history and art in the **Museo de Navarra** (Tues–Sat 9.30am–2pm & 5–7pm, Sun 11am–2pm; €2, free Sat pm & all Sun; Ⓦwww.cfnavarra.es/cultura/museo), and much more – but most visitors come here for just one thing: the thrilling week of the Fiestas de San Fermín (see box below).

Arrival and information

Train station 2.5km from the old part of town; bus #9 runs every 15min to the end of Paseo de Sarasate, a few minutes' walk from the central Plaza del Castillo – there is a RENFE ticket office at c/Estella 8.
Bus station c/Conde Oliveto in front of the citadel.
Tourist office c/Eslava 1, on Plaza San Francisco (summer Mon–Fri 9am–8pm, Sat 10am–8pm, Sun 10am–2pm; winter Mon–Sat 10am–2pm & 4–7pm, Sun 10am–2pm; Ⓣ848 420 420, Ⓦwww.turismo.navarra.es). Pick up pocket-sized monthly *El Bolo Feroz* for detailed events listings.
Internet Kuria.net, c/Curia 15 (Mon–Sat 10am–2.30pm & 5–10pm).

Accommodation

Rooms are in short supply during summer, and at fiesta time you've virtually no chance of a place without booking. Most hotels double their prices during San Fermín, so you're better off staying nearby (San Sebastián is a viable option) and travelling to Pamplona to enjoy the night-long festivities and early morning running of the bulls. If you end up sleeping rough, remember that there is safety in numbers – head for one of the many parks such as Vuelta del Castillo or Media Luna and bring a sleeping bag, as the nights are cool. For a hot shower or bath, there are public baths at c/Eslava 9

SAN FERMÍN: THE RUNNING OF THE BULLS

From midday on July 6 until midnight on July 14, Pamplona embraces the riotous non stop celebration of the **Fiestas de San Fermín**. The focus is the **encierro**, or running of the bulls – in which the animals decisively have the upper hand. Six bulls are released each day at 8am to run from their corral near the Plaza San Domingo to the bullring. In front, around and occasionally under them scramble the hundreds of locals and tourists who are foolish or drunk enough to test their daring against the horns. To watch the *encierro* it's essential to arrive early – crowds form an hour before it starts. The best vantage points are near the start or on the wall leading into the bullring. The event has two parts: first the bull runnings; then bullocks with padded horns are let loose on the crowd inside the bullring. If you watch the actual running, you won't be able to get into the bullring, so go on two separate mornings to see both. At midnight on July 14, there's a mournful candlelit procession, the **Pobre De Mi**, to wind up the festivities. See Ⓦwww.sanfermin.com for more details.

(Tues–Sat 8.30am–8pm, Sun 9am–1pm; shower €1, towel and soap €0.80). All prices below are high season, outside of fiesta time.

Ezcaba Camping ⓣ948 330 315, ⓦwww.campingezcaba.com. Located 7km out of town, on the road to France, reached by bus #7. Fills up several days before the fiesta. €5.20 per person, €5.60 per tent.

Pensión Escaray Lozano c/Nueva 24-1° ⓣ948 227 825, ⓔjescaray@pnte.cfnavarra.es. Good enough, rooms with wooden floors and high ceilings in a recently renovated building. Doubles €40, singles €20.

Pensión Eslava c/Hilarión Eslava 13-1° ⓣ948 221 558. Don't let the building's peeling facade put you off, the rooms inside (albeit weathered) are clean enough with bright tartan bedspreads. Doubles €20, singles €10.

Pensión Otano c/San Nicolás 5 ⓣ948 227 036/948 225 095, ⓦwww.casaotano.com. This bar-cum-*pensión* is in a great location and the rooms are comfortable. Doubles €48, singles €38, but much higher during the festival.

Eating and drinking

Pamplona has a number of great little restaurants, but the cheapest food is available at the Caprabo supermarket (daily 9am–9pm), inside the Mercado de Santo Domingo, the town's main food market (Tues–Sat 9.30am–2pm & 5–7pm), worth a browse in its own right. The best areas for nightlife are the Casco Antiguo and San Juan.

Dom Lluis c/San Nicolás 1. Good selection of Castilian dishes, and the €12 set menu has a lot of choice.

Erburu c/San Lorenzo 19. Something of a local institution, this bar serves €4–5 sandwiches during the day, and on weekends is open until 3am for dancing and drinks.

Otano c/San Nicolás 5. Popular bar, and deservedly so. Excellent *pinchos* from around €2.30 and *raciones* from €7.

Sarasate c/San Nicolás 19. An excellent vegetarian restaurant that could convert even the most committed carnivores. There's a weekday €10.50 set menu (€16.50 at weekends). Daily 1–4pm, also open Fri & Sat eve from 8.30pm.

Moving on

Train Madrid (4 daily; 3hr 30min); San Sebastián (3 daily; 1hr 40min–2hr 10min).

Bus Santander (twice daily; 3hr 30min); San Sebastián (6 daily; 1–3hr); Zaragoza (2–3 daily; 4hr).

ZARAGOZA

ZARAGOZA is the capital of Aragón, and easily its largest and liveliest city, with over half the province's one million people and the majority of its industry. There are some excellent bars and restaurants tucked in among its remarkable monuments, and it's also a handy transport centre, with good connections into the Pyrenees and east towards Barcelona.

What to see and do

Many places of interest are clustered around the rectangular Plaza del Pilar, near the Río Ebro. Other beautiful medieval monuments are a short walk away. Try and be in town for **Semana Santa** – the week before Easter – for the spectacular street processions.

Aljafería

Zaragoza's highlight, the **Aljafería** (Mon–Wed & Sat 10am–2pm & 4.30–8pm, Fri 4.30–8pm, Sun 10am–2pm; €3), was built in the eleventh century by the independent dynasty of Beni Kassim, and is the city's only surviving legacy from Moorish times. After Zaragoza was re-conquered in 1118, the palace was Christianized and used by the *reconquista* kings of Aragón. From the original design, the foremost relic is a tiny and beautiful mosque adjacent to the ticket office. Further on is an intricately decorated court, the **Patio de Santa Isabella**. Across from here, the **Grand Staircase** (added in 1492) leads to a succession of rooms remarkable chiefly for their carved ceilings.

Basílica de Nuestra Señora del Pilar

The most imposing of the city's churches, majestically fronting the Río Ebro, is the **Basílica de Nuestra Señora del Pilar** (daily: summer 6.45am–9.30pm; winter 6.45am–8.30pm), one of Zaragoza's two cathedrals. It takes its name from the

column that the Virgin is said to have brought from Jerusalem during her lifetime to found the first Marian chapel in Christendom. Topped by a diminutive image of the Virgin, the pillar forms the centrepiece of the Holy Chapel and is the focal point for pilgrims, who line up to kiss an exposed section encased in a silver sheath.

San Salvador

In terms of beauty, the basilica can't compare with the nearby Gothic-Mudéjar old cathedral, **San Salvador**, or **La Seo** (summer Tues–Fri 10am–6.30pm, Sat & Sun 10am–12.30pm & 3–6.30pm; winter Tues–Fri 10am–2pm & 4–6.30pm, Sat & Sun 10am–noon & 4–6.30pm; €2), at the far end of the pigeon-thronged Plaza del Pilar.

Roman remains

The city has recently been bringing to light its Roman past in several underground excavations: the **Forum** and **River Port** (just off the Plaza del Pilar), and the **Roman Baths** (all Tues–Sat 10am–2pm & 5–9pm, Sun 10am–2pm; €2.50) and the **amphitheatre** on c/San Jorge (Tues–Sat 10am–9pm, Sun 10am–2pm; €3.50). You can visit all of them with a combined ticket (€7). Following the semicircle of c/Coso and c/Cesar Augusto, the **Roman walls** are steadily being excavated; the best place to view them is at c/Echegaray at the junction with c/Coso, where remains of towers and ramparts can be seen.

Arrival and information

Train and bus Zaragoza's stunning modern station, Intermodal Delicias, serves all train and bus destinations. It's on Avda Navarra, about a 30min walk from the centre and connected by bus #51 (every 10min).

Tourist office Plaza del Pilar (daily: summer 10am–9pm; winter 10am–8pm; ⓣ976 72 12 82, ⓦwww.zaragozaturismo.es); and Torreón de la Zuda (Mon–Sat 10am–2pm & 4.30pm–8pm, Sun 10am–2pm; ⓣ976 201 200). There's an English information line on ⓣ902 142 008. The Zaragoza Card, available at the tourist office (24hr €15/48hr €20; ⓦwww.zaragozacard.com), includes entrance to all the city's museums and monuments, unlimited travel on the tourist bus and various discounts in hotels, bars and restaurants.

Internet Conecta-T, c/Murallas Romanas 4, next to the Mercado Central. Mon–Fri 10am–11pm, Sat & Sun 11am–11pm.

Accommodation

Albergue Juvenil Baltasar Gracián c/Franco y López 4 ⓣ902 088 905, ⓔbalta@aragob.es. Standard youth hostel 30min walk from the centre. HI card necessary, and you'll need to make a reservation five days in advance. Breakfast included. Under-26s €11.68, otherwise €15.86.

Hostal Descanso c/San Lorenzo 2 ⓣ976 291 741. Light, bright and cheerful rooms, each with sink and some overlooking the attractive Plaza de San Pedro below. Shared bathroom. Doubles €30, singles €20.

Pensión Iglesias c/Verónica 14-2° ⓣ976 293 161. In a great location with some rooms overlooking the Roman amphitheatre. Rooms have TVs and a sink and shower behind glass partitions; loos and bathrooms separate. Doubles €40, singles €20.

Eating and drinking

El Tubo, the name given to the streets around c/Estébanes and c/Libertad, is the best place for bar-hopping and tapas, while the bars around the church of Santa María de Magdalena have a more bohemian and alternative vibe. The districts of El Casco, La Paz and Bohemia are best for late-night bars and dancing. Those on a self-catering budget can try Zaragoza's main fresh-food market, Mercado Central, on c/Caesar Agosto (daily until 2pm).

Bodegas Almau c/Estébanes 10. Fill your boots during happy hour (daily 7–8pm) when sixty items are just €0.60 each – including beer, wine and tapas. Right in the heart of El Tubo, this deservedly popular joint has been feeding the crowds since 1870.

Café Tertulia Actual c/Don Jaime I 28. Great lunchtime menu for €7.90 (€11.90 on weekends), and art exhibitions inside. Also open until late for drinks.

Fantoba c/Don Jaime I 21. A beautiful bakery dating back to 1856 and specializing in Aragonese *dulces*. Each sugary treat is small but perfectly turned out. Pay by weight.

Gran Café Zaragozano c/Coso 35. A lively place for breakfast or drinks throughout the afternoon

and evening. Quirky decor, from barbers' chairs to transparent flooring.

Lai Lai c/Don Jaime 34 ⓣ976 200 651. This elaborately decorated Chinese restaurant (complete with fountain) provides a good four-course lunch for €7.65 Mon–Fri, more on weekends.

Mejillonera c/Moneva 3. *Mejillones* (mussels) are the speciality here. Get them *a la marinera* (in white wine and garlic) for €2.40 a tapa, or try the *calamares fritos* (fried squid) for €3.40.

Moving on

Train Barcelona (14–16 daily; 2–5hr); Bilbao (4 daily; 4hr 55min–7hr 40min); Madrid (13 daily; 1hr 45min–4hr 30min); Pamplona (7 daily; 2–3hr).
Bus Barcelona (15–25 daily; 3hr 30min–5hr); Madrid (19 daily; 3hr 45min); Pamplona (7–8 daily; 2hr–2hr 45min).

PARQUE NACIONAL DE ORDESA

For summertime walking, there's no better destination than the **Parque Nacional de Ordesa**, focused on a vast, trough-like valley flanked by imposingly striated limestone palisades. From Zaragoza's Estación Central you'll need to take an 8.30am bus to reach the town of **Sabiñánigo** in time to connect with the 11am service (July & Aug Mon–Sat also at 7pm; Sept–June Fri & Sun also at 5pm) to **Torla,** the best base for the park. Note that bus services between Torla and Sabiñánigo are very limited, so plan your journey well: see ⓦwww.alosa.es more details. At Torla, a regular shuttle bus takes you to and from the park (the park is not accessible by car) but trekkers should opt instead for the lovely trail (1hr 30min) on the far side of the river, well marked as the GR15.2. Further **treks** can be as gentle or as strenuous as you like, the most popular outing being an all-day trip to the **Circo de Soaso** waterfalls. For detailed information on the park, contact either Torla's tourist office (summer only Mon–Fri 10am–1pm & 6–8pm, Sat & Sun 9.30am–1.30pm & 5–8.30pm; ⓣ974 486 184) or the park's **Centro de Visitantes**, 3km north of the Puente de los Navarros (ⓣ974 486 472, ⓦwww.ordesa.net).

Accommodation

Reserve well in advance for accommodation in July and August; even the three campsites, *San Antón* (ⓣ974 486 063), *Río Ara* (ⓣ974 486 248), and *Valle de Bujaruelo* (ⓣ974 486 348), strung out between 1km and 3km north, often fill up.

Refugio Lucien Briet c/A'rruata ⓣ974 486 221, ⓦwww.ordesa.net/refugio-lucienbriet. Simple *refugio* in the middle of Torla offering good-value meals. Dorms €10, double with private bath €40.

Andorra

A tiny country nestled in the Pyrenees, Andorra is one of the oldest nations in Europe. Set up by Charlemagne in the eighth century as a buffer between France and the Islamic Moors, it became an independent, democratic principality in 1993. It's the only country in the world with Catalan as its official language, although Spanish is also widely spoken, as is basic English in some touristy places.

The capital, **Andorra la Vella**, offers a few sights and some good shopping, while next-door **Escaldes-Engordany** lays claim to the biggest thermal spa in Europe. Duty-free shopping, winter sports and summer hiking are the main attractions of this picturesque alpine nation: to the northwest is the popular ski resort of **Pal-Arinsal**, while the hills around **Ordino** boast excellent trails and breathtaking valley views. East of Ordino, a road weaves through jaw-dropping mountainscapes to **Canillo**, home to a captivating Romanesque chapel, and near the French border are sleepy **Soldeu** and the busy ski slopes of **Grandvalira**.

ARRIVAL

Andorra doesn't have an airport, but regular buses link the tiny nation to the nearest international ones three to four hours' drive away, in Barcelona (225km) and Toulouse (180km). Alsina Graells (ⓣ920 42 22 42, ⓦwww.alsa.es) has several daily services from Barcelona (€24), as does Nadal Autocars (ⓣ805 151, ⓦwww.autocarsnadal.com), from €25.50, while Novatel (ⓣ804 010, ⓦwww.andorrabybus.com) does airport transfers from both Barcelona and Toulouse (from €31). Alternatively, you can travel by rail from Barcelona to La Tour de Carol, on the Franco-Hispanic border, or l'Hospitalet, a French town whose SNCF train station connects to Perpignan and beyond, and then take a local bus for a few euros to various Andorran towns. The international phone code is ⓣ376 and the currency is the euro.

ENTRY REQUIREMENTS

Passports are required to cross the Andorran border. If entering by bus, you may not be inspected, but you'll

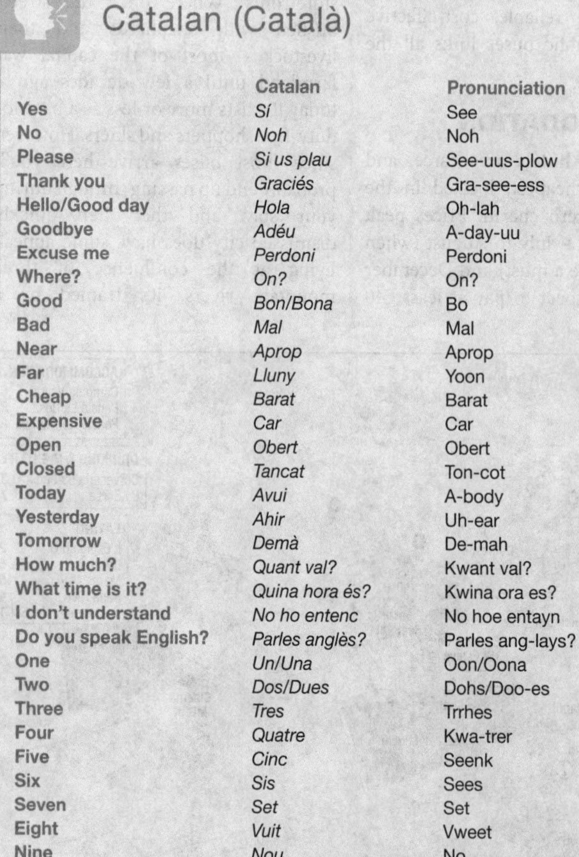

Catalan (Català)

	Catalan	Pronunciation
Yes	*Sí*	See
No	*Noh*	Noh
Please	*Si us plau*	See-uus-plow
Thank you	*Graciés*	Gra-see-ess
Hello/Good day	*Hola*	Oh-lah
Goodbye	*Adéu*	A-day-uu
Excuse me	*Perdoni*	Perdoni
Where?	*On?*	On?
Good	*Bon/Bona*	Bo
Bad	*Mal*	Mal
Near	*Aprop*	Aprop
Far	*Lluny*	Yoon
Cheap	*Barat*	Barat
Expensive	*Car*	Car
Open	*Obert*	Obert
Closed	*Tancat*	Ton-cot
Today	*Avui*	A-body
Yesterday	*Ahir*	Uh-ear
Tomorrow	*Demà*	De-mah
How much?	*Quant val?*	Kwant val?
What time is it?	*Quina hora és?*	Kwina ora es?
I don't understand	*No ho entenc*	No hoe entayn
Do you speak English?	*Parles anglès?*	Parles ang-lays?
One	*Un/Una*	Oon/Oona
Two	*Dos/Dues*	Dohs/Doo-es
Three	*Tres*	Trrhes
Four	*Quatre*	Kwa-trer
Five	*Cinc*	Seenk
Six	*Sis*	Sees
Seven	*Set*	Set
Eight	*Vuit*	Vweet
Nine	*Nou*	No
Ten	*Deu*	Deoo

> **EMERGENCY NUMBERS**
>
> Police ⓣ110; Ambulance and Fire ⓣ118; Medical ⓣ116; Mountain Rescue ⓣ112.

probably have to present your passport when buying your bus ticket.

GETTING AROUND

Its small size makes Andorra easy to get around – most places can be visited as day-trips. Touring on foot takes advantage of the wonderful hiking trails, while the cheap fuel makes renting a car in the capital a good option for the less energetic. The reliable, cost-effective network of public buses links all the main towns.

ACCOMMODATION

Good **budget hotels** are scarce, and most of the cheapest, located in the capital, have zero charm. Prices peak in high season – July to August (when reservations are a must) and December to March – expect to pay at least €40 for a double room. On the other end of the scale, there are many low-priced, well-equipped **campsites** throughout Andorra, and in summer you can stay for free in one of the 26 state-run **refugis** – simple mountain cabins; – information is available at tourist offices. Camping in the wild is illegal except around *refugis*.

ANDORRA LA VELLA

The name of the national capital **ANDORRA LA VELLA** is a bit of a misnomer: "Old Andorra" is for the most part a collection of neon-lit, soulless tourist restaurants and ageing storefronts. Where once the streets bustled with shepherds and their livestock – most of the capital was farmland until a few decades ago – today it exists more or less as a base for duty-free shoppers and skiers. However, since most buses arrive here you'll probably end up passing through during your stay, and the often quickly dismissed city does have some appeal. Lying at the confluence of three mountain rivers, it's framed by a

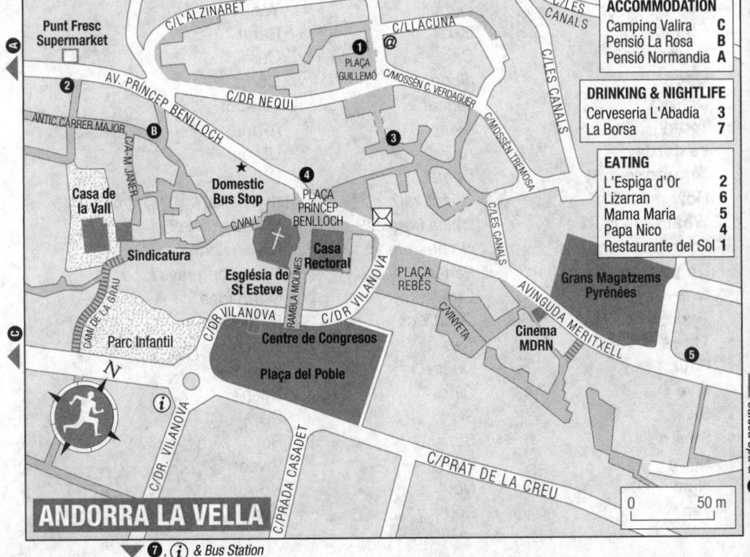

stunning backdrop of towering mountains. As well as a few lively bars it holds enough sights to while away an agreeable afternoon – and enough bargain hunting to while away a few lifetimes.

What to see and do

The capital is bisected by the Avinguda del Príncep Benlloch, which further east becomes the shop-filled Avinguda de Meritxell and then, on towards neighbouring Escaldes-Engordany, Avinguda de Carlemany. The old quarter lies just south of Príncep Benlloch.

Barri Antic and the Casa de la Vall

Towards the western end of town, **Barri Antic** is the capital's old quarter and, with its cobbled streets and quiet *plaças*, a great escape from the shopping mall that is the rest of the city. In the centre is one of the oldest parliaments in Europe – and certainly the smallest – the **Casa de la Vall** (Mon–Sat 9.30am–1.30pm & 3–7pm, Sun 10am–2pm; Nov–April closed Sun; free guided tours; bookings required on ⓣ829 129). Built in 1580 and complete with towers, battlements and steel-barred windows, it provides an appropriately historical base for the courts and the Sindic, Andorra's representative house. South of here, Plaça del Poble makes a great hang-out in the evenings and houses the **Centre de Congresos**, one of the country's only theatre and music venues; see ⓦwww.andorralavella.ad for more details.

Grans Magatzems Pyrénées

Avinguda Meritxell and the streets around have the highest concentration of shops, including Andorra's largest department store, the **Grans Magatzems Pyrénées**, at no. 11 (Mon–Fri 9.30am–8pm, Sat 9.30am–9pm, Sun 9.30am–7pm; Aug weeknights until 9pm), which also houses several cafeteria-style restaurants on the top floor.

Arrival and information

Buses International buses arrive at the Central d'Autobusos, located just southeast of the small Parc Central, 5min south of the city centre. Domestic buses leave from just west of pl. Benlloch.
National tourist office c/Dr Vilanova 13 (July & Aug Mon–Sat 9am–1pm & 3–7pm, Sun 10am–1pm; Sept–June Mon–Sat 10am–1.30pm & 3–7pm, closed Sun; ⓣ820 214, ⓦwww.andorra.ad).
Municipal tourist office Pl. de la Rotonda (July & Aug Mon–Sat 9am–9pm, Sun 9am–7pm; Sept–June 9.30am–1.30pm & 3.30–7.30pm; ⓣ873 103).

Accommodation

Camping Valira Av. de Salou ⓣ722 384, ⓦwww.campvalira.com. 10min from the city centre; the not-quite-in-the-wild camping facilities are good and there is a pool and restaurant. Open all year round. €5.75 one adult, €5.75 tent, bungalows €75 for two people.
Pensió La Rosa Antic Carrer Major 18 ⓣ821 810, ⓔpensiolarosa@andorra.ad. Just inside the gates of the old quarter, the 24 simply styled rooms are excellent value. Doubles €29, singles €19.
Pensió Normandia Av. Príncep Benlloch 49, ⓣ820 125, ⓔnicoleas@andorra.ad. Centrally located, and a step above *La Rosa*. Doubles €50, singles €25.

TREAT YOURSELF

The **Caldea Spa** (daily 9am–midnight; closed most of Nov and three weeks in May; €33 for 3hr, €25 for 2hr evening session; ⓣ800 999, ⓦwww.caldea.com), 1km east of Casa de la Vall, in Escaldes-Engordany, is the largest health centre on the continent, pumping in water from the nearby thermal springs to offer everything from Turkish baths to exfoliating hydro-massages. Particularly spectacular are the mountain views from the outdoor lagoon. The thermal water is rich in sodium, silica and sulphur and is reputed to have considerable therapeutic effects for skin and respiratory ailments. Even if the spa is not your cup of tea, the eleventh-floor bar offers some nice views.

Eating

The cheapest eats in town are from Punt Fresc, a budget supermarket with a large range of products, at Príncep Benlloch 22 – it's a great place to stock up before a day's hike.

L'Espiga d'Or Av. Príncep Benlloch, opposite Punt Fresc supermarket. This pleasant bakery has a wide selection of sweet treats to take away or to eat in their small café at the back.

Lizarran Av. Meritxell 86. Set just off the shopping thoroughfare, this popular, traditional restaurant-bar has a terrace and serves a large selection of tapas and sandwiches for €1.30 a pop, main plates €6.

Mama Maria Av. Meritxell 25 ⓣ869 996. Large, attractive tapas restaurant serving Catalan-style dishes from €3.95. Or try one of their large pizzas for €9.90. Daily until 11pm.

Papa Nico Av. Príncep Benlloch 4 ⓣ867 333. Busy, bustling bar-restaurant serving good range of tapas from around €3.25 and *platos combinados* from €10. Similar to *Mama Maria* but with more atmosphere.

Restaurante del Sol Plaça Guillemó. The cheapest – and most popular – option on a square full of dining possibilities. *Menú del día* €8.50.

Drinking and nightlife

Party animals be warned, nightlife in the capital leaves much to be desired, especially out of ski season.

Cerveseria L'Abadia Cap del Carrer 2. Up the stairs from the Pl. Guillemó, this popular local pub has Leffe and Hoegaarden on draught. Daily till 3am.

La Borsa Av. Tarragona 36. Just around the corner from the bus station, a happening club in-season, but social rigor mortis otherwise.

Directory

Car rental Avis, c/Príncep Benlloch 89 ⓣ866 860.

Cinema MDRN Cinemes, av Meritxell 26. Offers good discounts weekday afternoons with tickets at €3.30. All films in Spanish.

Embassies The British consulate is in La Massana, 5km north of town, at Casa Jacint Ponts 3/2, Av. Sant Antoni (ⓣ839 840). The closest US, Canadian, Australian and New Zealand representatives are in Barcelona.

First aid centre c/La Lacuna on the corner with c/Mossè Enric Marfany (Mon–Fri 8.30am–8.30pm, Sat, Sun and public holidays 9–11am & 6–7pm).

Hospital Hospital Nostra Senyora de Meritxell, just next to Caldea spa (ⓣ871 000).

Internet Future@point, c/de la Sardana 6; E-Café, c/l'Alziranet 5 (pl. Guillemó).

Pharmacy Les Tres Creus, c/Canals 5 (ⓣ820 212, ⓦwww.farmacialestrescreus.com), usually has someone who speaks English.

Post offices Spanish Post at C. Joan Maragall 10; French La Poste at rue Pere d'Urg 1 (Mon–Fri 8.30am–2.30pm, Sat 9.30am–1pm).

Moving on

Domestic bus services connect the capital to all of the main towns listed in this chapter (7am–9pm; €1.20–4.60). Check with the tourist office for schedules, but don't expect the buses to follow them.

Buses Barcelona (9–12 daily; 3hr 30min–4hr 30min); Madrid (daily; 9hr); Toulouse (2–6 daily Mon, Wed, Fri & Sun; 2hr 30min); Valencia (3 weekly; 8hr 30min).

LA MASSANA

Ascending northwest out of Andorra la Vella, the CG3 follows the Valira del Nord through a verdant valley, arriving at **LA MASSANA** 5km or so on. The town itself, presided over by a modern church clock-tower, has little to detain you and the real joy is in the hiking or skiing – check with the helpful tourist office for specifics.

Information

Tourist office c/Avinguda Sant Antoni 1, Plaça de les Fontetes, (Mon–Sat 9am–1pm & 3–7pm, Sun 9am–1pm & 3–6pm when the ski station is open; ⓣ835 693). The book *36 Interesting Itineraries of Ordino and La Massana*, which covers all the walks in great detail, is available at the tourist office (€2).

Internet Porquets' Si, Avinguda Els Traves, Els Plats 4 (€1.50/30min; €3/hr).

Accommodation

Borda Jovell Hostel Av. Jovell 18 ⓣ836 520, ⓦwww.andornet.ad/bordajovell. Up the steep hill in Sispony, this basic hostel has a hundred cheap bunks – even less if you bring your own sleeping bag. Dorm bed with breakfast €17.

Camping Xixerella Carretera de Pal ⓣ836 613, ⓦwww.campingxixerella.com. Campsite with great facilities, and activities from mini-golf to volleyball. €6.30 one adult, €6.30 one tent.

Eating

Versio Original Carrer Josep Rossell. This trendy establishment has great Pop Art decor and comfortable seats. The menu comprises fresh, modern cuisine, from salads to risottos. Set lunches available.

PAL AND ARINSAL

At the western end of the La Massana commune lies **PAL**, one of the best-preserved villages in Andorra, hugging the slopes that veer up to Pal-Arinsal, part of the popular Vallnord ski complex (Ⓦwww.vallnord.com). Pal is also a great base for summer time activities – ask at the tourist office in Massana for details. Head back down to La Massana to take the road up to **ARINSAL**, 2km north-west, much bigger than Pal, also a great base for summer treks and known for its lively **nightlife**. *El Surf* (next to the cable-car station), the most popular place in town, is an Argentinian steakhouse until 11.30pm before becoming a raucus bar/club until 4am during the ski season. Or try *El Cau* at c/d'Arinsal 5, a popular restaurant, bar and club with themed nights such as "beach party" and "Seventies disco" (open till 3am). For accommodation try *Hostal Pobladó*, c/d'Arinsal 10 next to the cabin lift (Ⓣ835 122, Ⓦwww.hotpoblado.com; doubles without bath €40, with €60), which also has a cheap restaurant attached with pizzas from €8 and *platos combinados* €7.

ORDINO

The peaceful town of **ORDINO** makes a great base for getting out to explore Andorra's northern peaks and valleys. All the usual winter sports are available at Ordino's ski station, Arcalís (see Ⓦwww.vallnord.com), and the helpful tourist office has information on the many summer activities offered, from canyoning and bungee jumping to rambling and high mountain fishing. On the town's *peatonal*, the pedestrian walkway, the **Casa Areny-Plandolit** (Tues–Sat 9.30am–1.30pm & 3–6.30pm, Sun 10am–2pm; €2.40) is a luxurious mansion and one-time residence of the eponymous Don Guillem d'Areny-Plandolit, a wealthy and powerful nineteenth-century baron who served as president of Andorra.

Information

Tourist office Located next to the sports centre on Travessia d'Ordino in Ordino (July & Aug Mon–Sat 8.30am–6pm, Sun 9am–1pm; Sept–June Mon–Sat 8.30am–1pm & 3–7.30pm, Sun 9am–1pm; Ⓣ878 173, Ⓦwww.ordino.ad).

Accommodation

Camping Borda d'Ansalonga Ctra. De Serrat, 2km north along CG3 Ⓣ850 374, Ⓦwww.campingansalonga.com. Spectacular riverside camping with great facilities including a pool, restaurant and bar. Open mid-June to mid-Sept for camping and all year for caravans. One person €6.40, tent €4.50.

Hotel Santa Barbara Plaça d'Ordino 1 Ⓣ738 100, Ⓔsantabarbara@andorra.ad. An attractive building in the village centre, located on the main pedestrianized street. Many of the nicely done-up and spacious rooms have views onto the main *plaça*. Doubles with bath €70, breakfast not included.

Eating

Most restaurants are on the *peatonal*.

5 Sentits Just outside of town at Ctra. General 3. Quite out of the way but very trendy compared to other Ordino bars and restaurants. Relax on a comfy leather sofa, leaf through a magazine and enjoy a wide range of drinks.

Bar Quim Pl. Mayor 10. This restaurant fills up around lunchtime, when the clientele tucks into the €7.50 (basic) or €9.90 (full) set menu.

Topic c/General d'Ordino. Located at the top of the *peatonal*, this bar-restaurant boasts a terrace with great views over the valley, snowy peaks just visible in the background. Good lunchtime deals, soup, main dish and coffee for €7.75, pizzas from €8.50.

CANILLO

The countryside around **CANILLO** offers great opportunities for hiking, biking and canyoning – the tourist office can provide full details, though the town

itself is not particularly attractive or interesting.

Information

Tourist office In the centre on the main Avinguda Sant Joan de Caselles (Mon–Sat 9am–1pm & 3–7pm, Sun 8am–4pm; ⓣ753 600, ⓦwww.vdc.ad). It hands out *Valls de Canillo*, an excellent free pocket-sized brochure with details of local walks in the hills. If planning a trip to Soldeu get information here, as Soldeu's tourist office is only open for a limited period during the summer.

Accommodation

Camping Casal Ctra. General ⓣ851 451, ⓦwww.campingcasal.com. Given the lack of budget accommodation in Canillo, your best bet is probably camping. *Casal* is just a few hundred metres west from the tourist office and open all year round. One adult €3.50, tent €3.50.
Camping Pla Prat de l'Areny de Moixa ⓣ851 333, ⓦwww.campingpla.cyberandorra.com. Not far from *Camping Casal*, *Pla* also offers standard campsite facilities. One adult €3.50, tent €3.30.
Pensió Comerç Ctra. General ⓣ851 020. Central but basic accommodation. Doubles €32.

Eating

Burger Roc Opposite the tourist office, this takeaway place does great burgers from €3.10 for those after a junk-food fix.
La Relliscada Ctra. General Canillo. Popular with locals, this bar-restaurant does a great *menú del día* for €13 and good-value *platos combinados* from €6.50.
Taverna de l'Iguana Opposite the tourist office. Serves filling crêpes from €7.50 that are highly recommended, plus baguettes and paninis from €4. Internet access also available.

GRANDVALIRA

Considered the best in the Pyrenees, the slopes of the **Grandvalira ski resort** loom east, blanketed by plenty of snowfall in the winter and verdant green after May. Grandvalira is the largest ski resort in Andorra, stretching from Canillo to Pas de La Casa, and, as such, can accommodate a range of abilities, from beginners to experts, with five black (very difficult) runs; for more information, see ⓦwww.grandvalira.com. In summer, walkers can **hike** across sixteen trails of varying difficulty, while the resort also converts into a **mountain-bike park** (July 6–Sept 9 daily 10am–5pm), accessed by the cable car from Canillo or Soldeu. A €20 day-pass gives unlimited use of a freestyle bike park, eleven freeride and cross-country tracks (covering a total of 70km), plus the cable-car ride. Bikes can be rented from shops in both towns.

SOLDEU

East of Canillo, the mountainous landscape is sliced through by a river with the Vall d'Incles beyond, which opens up at **SOLDEU**. A tiny, serene place, it has the vague air of a Seventies' ski village. There's little going on, but check with the tourist office in Canillo for tips on hiking routes from here.

Accommodation

Hotel Bruxelles c/General ⓣ851 010 & 852 099. Right in the centre of Soldeu, the *Bruxelles* has some nice rooms and also serves good, cheap meals, set lunch €12.80. Double room with bath around €40 to €50 in summer, and €71 during ski season (Dec to early April).

Eating and drinking

Fat Albert's Also along from the town church. *Slim Jim's* bigger brother, this watering hole stays open later in the evenings and also offers live music Wed & Fri.
Slim Jim's Just up from Soldeu's church. This friendly, English-run café dishes up baguettes and burgers from €5.

The north coast

Spain's **north coast** veers wildly from the typical conception of the country, with a rocky, indented coastline full of cove beaches and fjord-like *rías*. It's an immensely beautiful region – mountainous, green and thickly forested, with frequent rains often shrouding the countryside in a fine mist. In the east, butting against France, is **Euskadi**, or the País Vasco – the **Basque Country** – which, despite some of the heaviest industrialization on the peninsula, remains remarkably unspoiled. **San Sebastián** is the big seaside attraction, a major resort with superb but crowded beaches, but there are any number of lesser-known, equally attractive coastal villages all the way to **Bilbao** and beyond. Note that the Basque language, Euskera, bears almost no relation to Spanish (we've given the alternative Basque names where popularly used) – it's perhaps the most obvious sign of Spain's strongest separatist movement. To the west lies **Cantabria**, centred on the port of **Santander**, with more good beaches and superb trekking in the mountains of the **Picos de Europa**. In the far west, **Galicia** is green and lush but, despite its fertile appearance, has a history of famine and poverty. This province also treasures its independence, and Gallego is still spoken by around 85 percent of the population. For travellers, the obvious highlight here is the world-class city of **Santiago de Compostela**, the greatest goal for pilgrims in medieval Europe.

SAN SEBASTIÁN

The undisputed queen of Basque resorts, **SAN SEBASTIÁN** (Donostia) has excellent beaches and is acknowledged by Spaniards as an unrivalled gastronomic centre. Along with Santander, San Sebastián has always been a fashionable place to escape the heat of the southern summers, and in July and August it's packed with well-to-do families. Its summer **festivals** include annual rowing races between the villages along the coast, and an International Jazz Festival (late July; ⓦwww.jazzaldia.com) that attracts top performers to play in different locations around town.

What to see and do

San Sebastián is beautifully situated around the deep, still bay of **La Concha**. The **Parte Vieja** (old quarter) sits on the eastern promontory, while newer development has spread inland along the banks of the River Urumea and around the edge of the bay to the foot of **Monte Igeldo**.

Parte Vieja

The **Parte Vieja**'s cramped and noisy streets are where crowds congregate in the evenings to wander among the small bars and shops or sample the shellfish from the traders down by the fishing harbour. Here, too, are the town's chief sights: the gaudy Baroque facade of the church of **Santa María** and the more elegantly, restrained, sixteenth-century **San Vicente**. The centre of the old town is the Plaza de la Constitución, known locally as "La Consti"; the numbers on the balconies of the buildings around the square date back to the days when it was used as a bullring. Behind La Consti, winding footpaths criss cross up to the top of **Monte Urgull**. From the mammoth figure of Christ on its summit, there are great views out to sea and back across the bay to town.

Monte Igeldo

For still better views across the bay head to the top of **Monte Igeldo**: take bus #16 or walk around the coastline to its base, from where a **funicular**

(daily: April–June 10am–9pm; July–Sept 10am–10pm; Oct–March 11am–6pm; closed all of Jan & Wed in winter; €2.50 return) will carry you to the summit.

City beaches

La Concha beach is the most central and most celebrated, a wide crescent of yellow sand stretching round the inlet from the town. Out in La Concha bay is a small island, **Isla de Santa Clara,** which makes a good spot for picnics; a boat leaves from the Paseo Mollaberria (June–Sept 10am–8.30pm; every 30min; €3.40).

Ondarreta, considered the best beach in San Sebastián for swimming, lies beyond the rocky outcrop that supports the **Palacio Miramar** (gardens open 9am–sunset; free), once a summer home of Spain's royal family. The beach's facilities are good (showers €0.80, towels €0.90 and lockers €1.20) but the atmosphere here is more staid – it's known as La Diplomática for the number of Madrid's "best" families who holiday here. Far less crowded, and popular with surfers, **Playa de Zurriola** and the adjacent **Playa de Gros** have breakwaters to shield them from dangerous currents.

Arrival and information

Train The mainline train station is across the Río Urumea on Paseo de Francia, although local lines to Hendaye and Bilbao (rail passes not valid) have their terminus on c/Easo.

Bus National buses arrive at Plaza Pío XII, 20min walk or a bus journey (#28) from the Parte Vieja. The terminal isn't very user-friendly – some *taquillas* close at lunch and there are no luggage lockers. Buy tickets from the appropriate *taquilla* along Paseo de Bizkaia or Avda de Sancho El Sabio at least 30min before boarding.

Tourist office Alameda del Boulevard 8 (summer Mon–Sat 8.30am–8pm, Sun 10am–7pm; winter Mon–Thurs 9am–1.30pm & 3.30pm–7pm, Fri & Sat 9.30am–8pm, Sun 10am–2pm; ⓣ943 481 166, ⓦwww.sansebastianturismo.com). Also has an online reservations service at ⓦwww .sansebastianreservas.com.

Listings guide The free, detailed *Donostiaisia* is in Spanish, available at tourist offices.

Accommodation

During busy July and August prices are inflated. High season extends to September when the popular cinema festival takes place.

La Sirena Hostel Paseo de Igüeldo 25 ⓣ943 310 268, ⓦwww.donostialbergues.org. Fantastic location, just 200m from Ondarreta beach, in a great Swiss-cottage-style building. Kitchen facilities, free internet access and laundry available. Book in advance, especially in summer. HI card required. Dorms under-26s €17, over 26 €18.85.

Pensión Amaiur c/31º de Agosto 44 ⓣ943 429 654, ⓦwww.pensionamaiur.com. Incredible attention to detail marks out the *Amaiur*: the charming owners have thought of everything, from lending beach towels to organizing book-exchanges. All rooms – especially the kitchens – are well equipped and stylish. Internet and wi-fi access. Doubles €50, singles €39.

Pensión Arsuaga c/Narrica 3-3º ⓣ943 420 681. Colourful rooms, some with balconies and each cheerfully decorated with paintings, books and plants. Not as slick as *Amaiur* or *Larrea*, but a good budget option. Doubles €43, singles €20

Pensión Larrea c/Narrica 21-1º ⓣ943 422 694, ⓦwww.pensionlarrea.com. The owner, Amparo, is probably the friendliest person you'll meet on your travels. The rooms are also excellent, and bathrooms have powerful, spacious showers. Every room has balcony, soundproof windows and wi-fi access. Doubles €50–60.

Eating and drinking

Food in the Basque country is generally considered the best in Spain and it's easy to see why in San

TREAT YOURSELF

Bodegón Alejandro c/Fermín Calbetón 4 ⓣ943 427 158, ⓦwww.bodegonalejandro .com. This is the most affordable of the three great restaurants established in San Sebastián by the Michelin-starred chef, Martín Berasategui. The set menu, at €33.50, is a not-to-be-missed chance to sample world-class food. Closed Sun night, Mon and Tues.

Sebastián. The Parte Vieja, especially along c/Fermín Calbetón, is crammed with bars serving gourmet *pinchos* and tapas. Don't forget to sample the excellent Rioja.

Bidebide c/31 de Agosto. Minimalist, sleek furnishings, chill-out music and great food that isn't as expensive as you'd expect. Burgers from €4.75, salads from €5.90 and *platos combinados* from €7.25.

Bocado Plaza Carlos Blasco de Imaz. Located above the aquarium, this bar/restaurant serves overpriced food, but it's a great spot to have a drink (and a *pincho*) and take in the magnificent views across the bay. Come here for sunset.

Fuego Negro c/31° Agosto 31. A couple of doors up from *Gandarias*, serving more modern and experimental *pinchos* from €2 to €3.20.

Gandarias c/31 de Agosto 23. Traditional bar and restaurant, serving excellent *pinchos* at great prices, starting from €1.50.

Nightlife

Etxekalte c/Mari Kalea 11. Jazz, urban soul and hip-hop in a relaxed, low-key bar. DJs Thurs–Sat from 12.30am. Open 6pm–4am in winter, 5am in summer. Free entry.

Tas-Tas c/Fermín Calbetón 35. The happy hour (8pm–1am), drinks promotions and group discounts make this a popular backpacker choice. Great for a fun night. Free entry. Daily until 3am.

Zibbibo's Plaza Sarriegi 8. This mini-club plays dance music, serves good sangria and has happy hours and themed nights, attracting an international crowd. Free entry.

Directory

Internet Locutorio Puerto, c/Puerto 39, and Zarr @net, c/San Lorenzo 6, are open till late.

Laundry c/Iparragirre 6 ⓣ943 293 150. Drop-off service available. Daily 8am–10pm.

Pharmacy c/Legazpi 7 ⓣ943 424 826. Any pharmacy will be able to tell you which branch is open 24hr; it changes daily.

Post office c/Urdaneta 7 ⓣ902 197 197.

Moving on

Train Bilbao (7–9 daily; 2hr 30min); Madrid (3 daily; 6hr 30min); Pamplona (2–3 daily; 1hr 45min); Salamanca (2 daily; 6–7hr); Zaragoza (2–3 daily; 3–4hr).

Bus Bilbao (1–2 hourly; 1hr 10min); Madrid (8–9 daily; 6hr 30min); Pamplona (13 daily; 2hr).

BILBAO

Although traditionally an industrial city, **BILBAO** (Bilbo) has given itself a makeover and is now a priority destination on any Spanish tour. A state-of-the-art metro, designed by British architect Norman Foster, links the city's widely spread attractions: the breathtaking Museo Guggenheim by Frank Gehry – along with Jeff Koons' puppy sculpture in flowers – is a major draw; the airport and one of the many dramatic river bridges are Calatrava-designed; and there are various bids to further develop the riverfront with university buildings and public parks. The city's vibrant, friendly atmosphere, elegant green spaces and some of the best cafés, restaurants and bars in Euskadi, combine to make Bilbao an appealing destination. From the first Saturday after August 15, the whole city goes totally wild during the annual bullfighting extravaganza, **La Semana Grande**, with scores of open-air bars, live music and impromptu dancing.

What to see and do

The **Casco Viejo**, the old quarter on the east bank of the river, is focused on the beautiful **Teatro Arriaga**, the elegantly arcaded **Plaza Nueva** and the fourteenth-century Gothic **Catedral**

FEVE RAIL LINE

If you're not in a great hurry, you may want to make use of the independent **FEVE rail line** (ⓣ902 100 818, ⓦwww.feve.es; rail passes not valid). The 650-kilometre track begins at Bilbao and follows the coast west, with inland branches to Oviedo and León, all the way to El Ferrol in Galicia. Despite recent major repairs and upgrading, it's still slow but it's cheap and a terrific journey, skirting beaches, crossing rivers and snaking through a succession of limestone gorges.

de Santiago (Tues–Sat 10am–1.30pm & 4–7pm, Sun 10.30am–1.30pm; free). However, it is along the Río Nervión that a whole number of exciting new buildings have appeared.

Museo Guggenheim

A good route leads from the Casco Viejo down the river past the Campo Volantín footbridge and the more imposing Puente Zubizuri to the sensual, billowing titanium curves of the **Museo Guggenheim** (daily 10am–8pm; Sept–June closed Mon; €11, ticket office shuts 30min before closing; ⓦ www.guggenheim-bilbao.es), described as "the greatest building of our time" by architect Philip Johnson. The building and exterior sculptures are arguably more of an attraction than most of the art inside: the permanent collection, which includes works by Kandinsky, Klee, Mondrian, Picasso, Chagall and Warhol, to name a few, is housed in traditional galleries; temporary exhibitions and individual artists' collections are displayed in the huge sculpted spaces nearer the river.

Museo de Bellas Artes

Further along from the Guggenheim, on the edge of the Parque de Doña Casilda de Hurriza, is the **Museo de Bellas Artes** (Tues–Sun 10am–8pm; €6, combined ticket with the Guggenheim €12.50, free on Wed), which houses works by Goya and El Greco and some fine temporary exhibitions.

Arrival and information

Air From the airport (ⓣ 902 404 704), the Bizkaibus runs to Plaza Moyúa in the centre (daily 6.15am–midnight; every 20–30min; €1).
Train The FEVE and RENFE train stations are located just over the river from the Casco Viejo.
Bus Most buses arrive some way out of the centre at Estación Termibús in San Mamés – from here to the centre is a 20min walk.
Ferry P&O ferries from Portsmouth arrive at Santurtzi, 14km north of the city centre and connected by regular buses and trains.
Tourist office c/Plaza Ensanche 11 (Mon–Fri 9am–2pm & 4–7.30pm; ⓣ 944 795 760, ⓦ www.bilbao.net), with branches in the basement of the theatre at Plaza Arriaga 1 and at Abandoibarra etorbidea 2, near the Guggenheim. All provide a good listings guide called *Bilbao*. There's also a central reservations system (ⓣ 902 877 298, ⓦ www.bilbaohotels.com) for all bookings, from rooms to restaurants.

City transport

Metro €1.35 for a single journey, €3 for a day-pass.
Tram Offering better views than the metro, the swish overground tram (also known as tranvía/Euskotran) costs €1.10 for a single, €3 for a day-pass. Make sure you validate your ticket in the platform's machine before boarding the tram, or you could face a hefty fine.
Bilbaocard Good value if you're planning on covering the city in a short space of time, as it can be used on all transport systems in the city (1 day €6, €10 for 2, €12 for 3). It also provides discounts on some museums – check at the tourist office for details.
Bike rental For a healthier option, the council offers free bike rental; Arriaga tourist office is a popular pick-up/drop-off point, but there are several others around the city (ⓣ 645 006 635).

Accommodation

In summer and at weekends, booking ahead is advisable.
Albergue Bilbao Ctra. Basurto-Kastrexana Errep 70 ⓣ 944 270 054, ⓦ albergue.bilbao.net. Ten minutes from the city centre, connected by #58 and #80 bus, this eight-storey building has a TV room, internet and laundry. HI card required. Dorms €16–€22.
Pensión de la Fuente c/Sombrereria 2-2º ⓣ 944 169 989. Good-value *pensión* in a beautifully renovated building. Communal sitting area, and laundry service for €6. Doubles with bath €45, without €34.
Pensión Mendez c/Santa María 13-4º ⓣ 944 160 364, ⓦ www.pensionmendez.com. Attractive rooms, all with balcony. Be warned, the *pensión* is on the fourth floor – and there's no lift. Popular so book ahead. Doubles without bath €35, with €45.
Pensión Serantes c/Somera 14-2º ⓣ 944 151 557. Owned by friendly people, the *Serantes* enjoys a great location. The hall is painted fluorescent, but the rooms themselves are spacious and tranquil. Doubles without bath €25, with €35.
Residencia Manoli c/Libertad 2-4º ⓣ 944 155 636, ⓦ www.pensionmanoli.com. Don't let the

slightly musty interior put you off, the rooms are clean enough. All come with bathroom, balcony and wi-fi. Doubles without bath €30.

Eating and drinking

Bar Bizitza c/Torre 1. Quirky, alternative bar with a great vibe and cool music. Open plan but with an intimate feel. Daily 5pm–1.30am.

Café Iruña c/Jardines de Albia & corner of Colón de Larreategui. Dating back to 1903, this atmospheric, buzzing café has separate smoking and non-smoking areas, both decorated with ornate tiles and murals. *Pinchos* from €2.30, *menú del día* €13.25.

Gatz c/Sta Maria 10. Lively bar known for its award-winning "fusion" tapas. Sample the creative *pinchos* for €1.60 a pop and wash them down with *txakoli* (Basque wine) for €1.50.

Rio-Oja c/Perro 4. Highly recommended Basque restaurant, specializing in grilled meats (€7–15), fish (€12) and stews (from €7). Portions are filling and good value.

Directory

Consulate UK, Alameda Urquijo 2-8º ⓣ944 157 600.
Currency exchange Available in all main bank branches (general opening hours are Mon–Sat 8.30am–2pm). Bureau de change in the basement of El Corte Inglés, Gran Vía 7–9.
First aid clinic Alameda Urquijo 65 ⓣ944 434 792.
Hospital Santa María, Ctra. Santa María 41 ⓣ944 006 900.
Internet Laser, c/Sendaja 31.
Lost property Luis Briñas 14 ⓣ944 204 981.
Pharmacy Farmacia Zaballa, Gran Vía 56 (daily 9am–10pm; ⓣ944 411 796).
Post office Alameda Urquijo 19 ⓣ902 197 197; open Mon–Fri 8.30am–8.30pm.

Moving on

Bus San Sebastián (hourly; 1hr 10min); Santiago de Compostela (3 daily; 11–12hr); Santander (30 daily; 1hr 30min).
Train Barcelona (2 daily; 9–11hr); Madrid (1–2 daily; 5hr 10min–8hr 30min); San Sebastián (6–7 daily; 2hr 30min); Santander (3 daily; 3hr).

SANTANDER

Long a favourite summer resort of Madrileños, **SANTANDER** has an elegant, reserved, almost French feel. Some people find it a clean, restful base for a short stay; for others, it is dull and snobbish. On a brief visit, the balance is tipped in its favour by its excellent beaches and the sheer style of its setting. Be aware that some establishments close after the summer season (mid-June to mid-September).

What to see and do

The narrow **Bahía de Santander** is dramatic, with the city and port on one side, in clear view of open countryside, and high mountains on the other; it's a great first view of Spain if you're arriving on the ferry from England. Santander was severely damaged by fire in 1941 and what's left of the city divides into two parts: the **town and port**, clumsily reconstructed on the old grid around a mundane cathedral; and the beach suburb of **El Sardinero**, a twenty-minute walk (or bus #7 or #9; €1) from the centre. There are few real sights to distract you, and it's for the glorious beaches that most people come. The first of these, **Playa de la Magdalena**, begins on the near side of the wooded headland of the same name. This beautiful yellow strand, sheltered by cliffs and flanked by a summer windsurfing school, is deservedly popular. If you find these beaches too crowded, head for **Somo** (which has a surf school, boards to rent and a summer campsite) or **Pedreña**; jump on a *lancha*, a cheap taxi-ferry (every 15min; €3.70 return) from the central Puerto Chico dock.

Arrival and information

Ferry Ferries from Plymouth dock in the middle of the Bahía de Santander, right opposite the Jardines de Pereda and the tourist office (see ⓦwww.brittany-ferries.co.uk for more information).
Train and bus The RENFE and FEVE train and bus stations are centrally located, side by side near the waterfront at Plaza de las Estaciones.
Bike rental The local council offers free bikes for loan – check the tourist office for details.
Tourist office The best is in the Jardines de Pereda (daily: mid-June to mid-Sept 9am–9pm; mid-Sept

to mid-June Mon–Fri 9am–7pm, Sat 10am–2pm; ⓣ942 203 000/01, ⓦwww.santander.es).

Accommmodation

Some places shut down outside the peak summer season of mid-June to mid-September.

Club Náutico La Horadada Avda de la Reina Victoria s/n, Playa Magdalena ⓣ942 280 402, ⓦwww.horadada.es. Santander's only hostel enjoys a prime location on Magdalena beach. The attached nautical club offers sailing, canoeing and windsurfing. Open all year but book ahead in summer. Dorms €12.

Pensión La Corza c/Hernán Cortés 25 ⓣ942 212 950. Great central location – modern, spacious rooms, all with TV – in a friendly house. Doubles with bath €55, without €42.

Pension La Soledad Avda de los Castros 17 ⓣ942 270 936. In a great location for El Sardinero beach, and worth checking out if the *Luisito* is full. July & Aug only. Doubles €47.

Pensión Luisito Avda de los Castros 11 ⓣ942 271 971. A sound option just minutes away from El Sardinero beach, with a very welcoming owner. All rooms have views overlooking the pleasant front lawn or the neighbour's vegetable garden. Closed Oct–June. Doubles €47.

Eating and drinking

Bodega Cigaleña c/Daoiz y Velarde 19. Traditional, atmospheric *bodega*. The straightforward *pinchos*, such as regional cheeses for €1.75, or dried hams for €2.25, are very popular with locals.

Bodega la Conveniente c/Gómez Oreña 9. Curious yet successful mix of traditional *bodega* and chic piano-bar. Elegant, spacious interior and great food too. Definitely worth the inevitable wait for a table (no reservations).

California Café c/Casimiro Sainz 3, just off the sea front. Baguettes and burgers from €3, *platos combinados* from €7. Not much atmosphere, but good for cheap, filling food.

Canela Plaza de Cañadío. One of several lively and popular bars on the Plaza de Cañadío. Do as locals do and come here after a few *pinchos*, before heading on to the late-night bars, such as *Rocambole*.

El Solecito c/Bonifaz 19. Fun decor, and excellent pizzas from around €8.

La Rana Verde c/Daoiz y Velarde 30. Famed for its many varieties of *patatas bravas* ranging from the mild to the "nuclear" (portion €2.70). Sandwiches and *bocadillos* from €2.20.

Rocambole c/Hernán Cortes 35. Very popular late-night subterranean bar, with live music on Thursdays. Start your evening elsewhere but make sure you end it here. Open till 5am, 6am on weekends and every day in summer. Free entry.

Directory

Consulate UK, Paseo de Pereda 27 ⓣ942 220 000.
Currency exchange Banco Santander, Avenida Calvo Sotelo, 19, across from the post office.
Internet Café Nubero, Francisco de Quevedo 13, daily 10am–midnight.

Moving on

Ferry Plymouth, UK (twice weekly; 24hr); Portsmouth, UK (twice weekly; 22hr).
Train Madrid (3 daily; 6hr 10min–8hr 30min); see also the Feve Train Line box on p.1145.
Bus Bilbao (hourly; 1hr 45min); Santiago de Compostela (2–3 daily; 8hr–10hr 10min).

PARQUE NACIONAL PICOS DE EUROPA

The **Picos de Europa** (ⓦwww.picosdeeuropa.com) offer some of the finest hiking, canoeing and other mountain activities in Spain. The densely forested national park boasts two glacial lakes, a series of peaks over 2400m high, and wildlife including otters and bears. From Santander, about 80km to the east, the park is reached by car by passing through San Vicente de la Barquera, Unquera and Cares; alternative access is from Oviedo in the south, a spectacular drive of 80km along winding, narrow roads. **CANGAS DE ONÍS**, a major gateway to the park, has a helpful **tourist office** (June–Sept daily 10am–9pm; Oct–May Mon–Sat 10am–2pm & 4–7pm, Sun 10am–2pm; ⓣ985 848 005, ⓦwww.cangasdeonis.com/turismo) and **accommodation**, at *Hospedaje Torreón* (ⓣ985 848 211, ⓦwww.galeon.com/calidadtotal/pensiontorreon; July & Aug €50, rest of year €35). There's also a private hostel, *Albergue La Posada del Monasterio* (ⓣ985 848 553, ⓦwww.posadadelmonasterio.com; dorms €15) in an atmospheric old monastery in La Vega-Villanueva,

2km northwest of Cangas de Onís; the management organizes canoeing, hiking and other activities in the park. Alternatively, you can stay at **COVADONGA** in the park at the *Hospedería del Peregrino* (☎985 846 047; €39.50).

SANTIAGO DE COMPOSTELA

SANTIAGO DE COMPOSTELA, built in a warm golden granite, is one of the most beautiful of all Spanish cities and has been declared a national monument. The **pilgrimage to Santiago** (see box below) captured the imagination of medieval Christian Europe on an unprecedented scale, peaking at half a million pilgrims each year during the eleventh and twelfth centuries. The route continues to be well trodden by the faithful, with around 100,000 visitors claiming their Compostela (offical certificate) annually. Santiago retains some of its ancient political and cultural importance – it's the seat of Galicia's regional government, and home to a great contemporary art gallery as well as a large student population and buzzing nightlife.

What to see and do

Manageable in size, with many pedestrianized areas, Santiago is ideal to discover on foot. Most sights are grouped near each other in the historic **old town**; make your way down narrow, winding streets to visit the impressive cathedral and other religious attractions and monuments, such as the Monastery of San Martín Pinario and the Centro Galego art gallery. Santiago's **university** is another sight worth seeing – parts of the eighteenth-century faculty of geography and history are open to the public. The large **Parque de Alameda** separates the old centre from the modern new town, which boasts many bars and cafés.

Catedral de Santiago

All roads lead to the **cathedral** (daily 7.30am–9pm, visits allowed outside Mass), whose sheer grandeur you first appreciate upon venturing into Praza do Obradoiro. The fantastic granite pyramid adorned with statues of St James was built in the mid-eighteenth century by an obscure Santiago-born architect, Fernando Casas y Novoa. Just inside this facade is the building's original west front: the **Pórtico de Gloria**. So many millions have pressed their fingers into the roots of its sacred Tree of Jesse that five deep holes have been worn into the solid marble. Behind, the **High Altar** symbolizes the spiritual climax of the pilgrimage. Visitors climb steps behind the altar, embrace the *Most Sacred Image of Santiago*, kiss his

THE CAMINO DE SANTIAGO

The most famous Christian pilgrimage in the world, the **Camino de Santiago** – or Way of St James – traces a route through France and Spain to Santiago de Compostela (Saint James of the Field of Stars), the supposed burial place of St James the Apostle and the third-holiest site in Christendom after Jerusalem and Rome. Pilgrims identify themselves by attaching a large scallop shell to their backpack. Many carry a "pilgrim passport" that permits overnight stay in some mountain refuges, and collect stamps along the way in order to receive a Compostela (certificate of completion) from the Church authorities. To be eligible, you must walk at least 100km or cycle 200km. Aside from those motivated by faith, people are drawn by the physical challenge of the long hike, the stunning countryside, and the spiritual benefits of a temporary retreat from hectic urban life. Begin from your own doorstep, or from one of the popular starting points in France and Spain. For more details, see Ⓦwww.xacobeo.es.

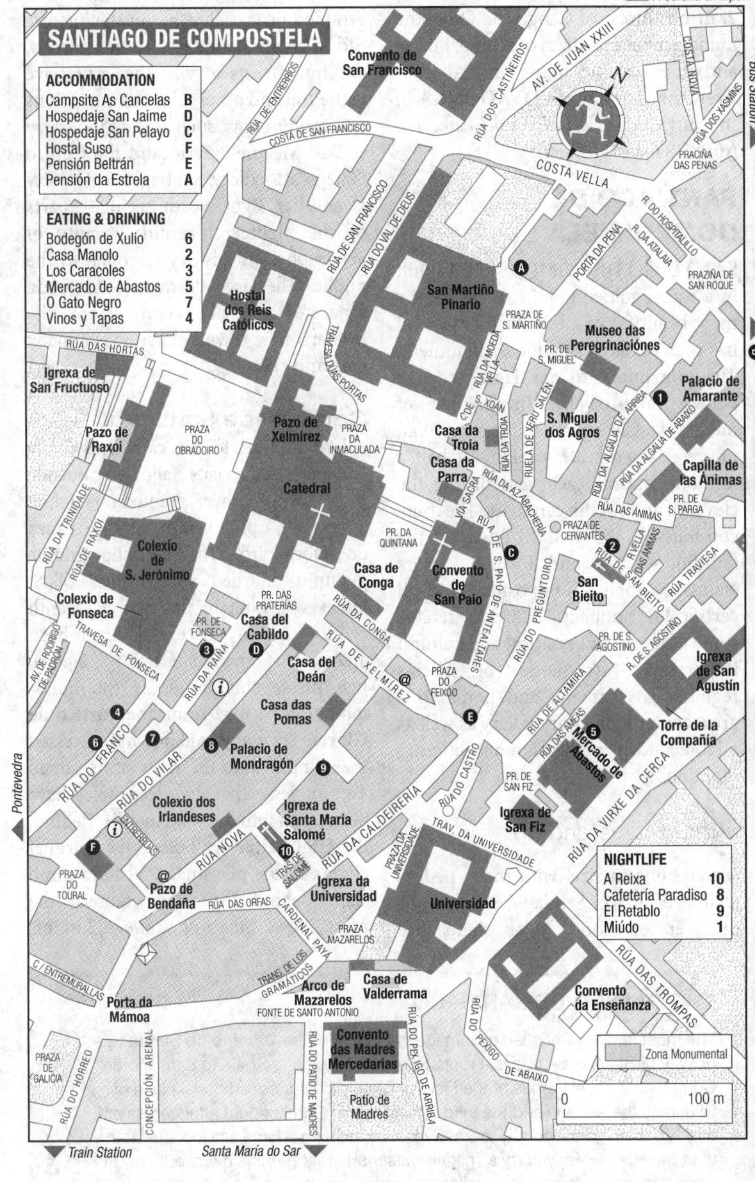

bejewelled cape, and receive a Latin certificate called a Compostela – a procedure that's seven centuries old. The elaborate pulley system in front of the altar is for moving the immense incense-burner – **El Botafumeiro** – which, operated by eight priests, is swung in a vast ceiling-to-ceiling arc across the transept. It is stunning to watch, but takes place only during certain festival services – check with the tourist office. You can also visit the treasury, archeological museum,

cloisters and crypt (Mon–Sat 10.30am–2pm & 4–8pm; closed Aug; €5).

San Martín Pinario monastery and around

The enormous Benedictine **San Martín Pinario monastery** stands close to the cathedral, the vast altarpiece in its church depicting its patron riding alongside St James. Nearby is the **Convento de San Francisco**, reputedly founded by the saint himself during his pilgrimage to Santiago. In the north of the city are Baroque **Convento de Santa Clara**, with a unique curving facade, and a little southwards, **Convento de Santo Domingo de Bonaval**. This last is perhaps the most interesting of the buildings, featuring a magnificent seventeenth-century triple stairway, each spiral leading to a different storey of a single tower. The adjacent **Museo do Pobo Gallego** is a fascinating museum of Galician culture (Tues–Sat 10am–2pm & 4–8pm, Sun 11am–2pm; free). Just next door is the **Centro Galego de Arte Contemporánea** (Tues–Sun 11am–8pm; free), a beautiful gallery designed by Portuguese architect Álvaro Siza and host to changing exhibition cycles.

Arrival and information

Air The airport, 1km northeast of town (Ⓣ981 547 501, Ⓦwww.aena.es), is linked to the centre by hourly buses (€1.80).

Train station A walkable distance south of the plaza along Rúa do Horreo.

Bus station 1km or so north of the town centre; bus #5 runs every 20–30min to Praza Galicia at the city's southern edge.

Tourist office Rúa do Vilar 63 (daily: Semana Santa and June 9am–9pm; rest of year 9am–2pm & 4–7pm; Ⓣ981 555 129, Ⓦwww.santiagoturismo.com); it has an accommodation booking system (Ⓣ902 190 160, Ⓦwww.santiagoreservas.com) and a branch at the airport. Spanish guided tours leave from Plaza de Platerías daily at noon (April to mid-Oct also at 6pm; €8).

Listings guide *Culturall* is a very comprehensive monthly guide. Available at tourist offices.

Accommodation

You should have no difficulty finding inexpensive accommodation; note that *pensiones* here are often called *hospedajes*.

Campsite As Cancelas Rúa do 25 de Xulio 35 Ⓣ981 580 266, Ⓦwww.campingascancelas.com. 2km northeast of the cathedral; take city bus #4 or #6. Located in a tranquil green zone, this camping offers good facilities, including an outdoor swimming pool. One person €5.90, tent €6.15.

Hospedaje San Jaime Rúa do Vilar 12-2º Ⓣ981 583 134. Decent, central budget accommodation. Rooms are basic but spacious and clean. Ask for one with a balcony and great views of the cathedral. Doubles €25.

Hospedaje San Pelayo c/San Paio 2 Ⓣ981 565 016. Basic, standard *pensión* rooms with a couple of extras thrown in: free laundry service and kitchen access. Just 3min from the cathedral. Doubles without bath €30, with €40.

Hostal Suso Rúa do Vilar 65 Ⓣ981 583 134. Clean, modern rooms with new bathrooms and free wi-fi access. The café below does a great breakfast – *churros* cost just €0.80, *platos combinados* from €5. Doubles €40.

Pensión Beltrán c/Preguntoiro 36-2º Ⓣ981 582 225. Beautiful *pensión*, set in an old converted palace with stunning views and at absolute bargain rates. Rooms have modern furnishings but the large *salón* maintains gorgeous antiques. The very friendly owner will make you feel at home. July–Sept only. Doubles €20, singles €14.

Pensión da Estrela Plazuela de San Martín Pinario 5-2º Ⓣ981 576 924, Ⓦwww.pensiondaestrela.com. Spotless, inviting rooms with warm-coloured decor. All have private bathrooms. Stunning views of the square below. Doubles €55.

Eating and drinking

Thanks, perhaps, to the students, there are plenty of cheap restaurants and excellent bars. For tapas and *pinchos* it's best to wander the lively streets of the historic centre, particularly Rúa do Franco and Rúa da Raíña.

Bodegón de Xulio Rúa do Franco 24. Good choice for fish on a street that's full of seafood restaurants. Portion of *pulpo a la Gallego*, the Galician octopus speciality, €8.95.

Casa Manolo Praza de Cervantes 25 Ⓣ981 582 950. The modern, elegant interior and central location make it seem more expensive than it actually is – the excellent set menu is just €8.50. Daily 1–4pm & 8–11.30pm, closed Sun evening.

Los Caracoles c/Raíña 14 ⓣ981 561 498. Cosy interior with low-hanging lamps and stone brick walls. Try their snail speciality. Also serves a hearty three-course lunch menu for €9.80. Daily 11am–4.30pm & 7.30pm–1am for dinner, till 2am for drinks.

Mercado de Abastos Plaza de Abastos. Well-maintained food market built around an attractive granite structure. Quality fresh, local produce at cheap prices. Mon–Sat 8am–2pm.

O Gato Negro c/Raíña s/n. Very basic decor means this bar easily goes unnoticed. It shouldn't – its traditional Galician food is first class.

Vinos y Tapas Rúa do Franco 10. Wide range of cheap, tasty *pinchos* on display, starting from €1. A great place to start the evening before heading off to one of the late night bars. Glass of *cava* €1.75, jug of *sangría* €10.

Nightlife

A Reixa Tras de Salomé 3. Basement bar with low lighting and a chilled-out vibe. The huge CD collection behind the bar means an eclectic play list. Can get quite smoky. Daily till 2.30am.

Cafetería Paradiso Rúa do Vilar 29. This gorgeous green-tiled, mirrored bar is a good place to start the night. *Raciones*, such as the fiery *pimientos de padrón*, from €3; set lunch menu €12.

El Retablo Rúa Nova 13 ⓣ981 564 851. Very large bar with dancefloor and €5 *copas*. Warms up after midnight.

Miúdo c/Truques 3 ⓣ617 082 447. Same smoky, laid-back vibe as *A Reixa*. Interesting prints adorn the stone walls; cool, relaxed clientele populate the bar. Open until 3am on weekends.

Directory

Internet Cibernova, Rúa Nova 5 (daily 10am–midnight); Rúa de Xelmírez 19 (daily 9.30am–11.30pm).

Laundry Lobato, c/Santiago de Chile 7 ⓣ981 599 954 – self-service. España, c/Xeneral Pardiñas 38 ⓣ981 592 410 – drop-off service.

Lost property Rúa da Trindade ⓣ981 542 323.

Pharmacy Cantón do Toural 1; Praza do Toural 11 (both 24hr).

Post office Rúa das Orfas s/n. Mon–Fri 8.30am–8.30pm, Sat 9am–2pm.

Moving on

Bus Bilbao (2–3 daily; 9hr 15min–11hr 15min); Madrid (3–6 daily; 9hr), Porto (4 weekly; 2hr 30min); Santander (2–3 daily; 8hr–10hr 10min).

Train A Coruña (14 daily; 45min); Bilbao (daily; 10hr 45min); León (daily; 6hr); Madrid (2 daily; 8–9hr).

Sweden

HIGHLIGHTS

THE ICE HOTEL: the original and best - a chilly treat worth breaking the budget for

INLANDSBANAN: whistle past virgin forest and crystal-clear streams en route to Lapland

STOCKHOLM: edgy fashion, cool cafés and perhaps the most beautiful setting of any European capital

GOTHENBURG: hop on a tram and explore Sweden's second city

GOTLAND: join the summer exodus to Sweden's party island

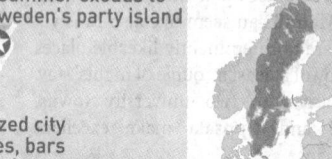

MALMÖ: fun-sized city offering beaches, bars and a towering skyscraper

ROUGH COSTS

DAILY BUDGET Basic €35/occasional treat €50

DRINK Akvavit (schnapps) €5

FOOD Tunnbrodsrulle (Swedish kebab) €4

HOSTEL/BUDGET HOTEL €18/€50

TRAVEL Train: Stockholm–Gothenburg €60 (3hr); Bus: Stockholm–Gothenburg €25 (7hr)

FACT FILE

POPULATION 9 million

AREA 449,964 sq km

LANGUAGE Swedish

CURRENCY Swedish krona (kr)

CAPITAL Stockholm (population: 815,000)

INTERNATIONAL PHONE CODE ☏46

Introduction

Sweden combines stylish, sophisticated cities and a vast wilderness of dense forests and crystal-clear mountain lakes. Quality of life is high, almost everyone speaks fluent English, and even a short visit here leaves you with the impression that the Swedes have somehow got things "right". While the country is not entirely populated by blonde, blue-eyed sauna-loving eco-warriors, you'll find plenty to reinforce the stereotype.

As with the rest of Scandinavia, Sweden can prove a challenge for the budget traveller. However, a recent dip in the value of the krona has seen it drop behind Norway and Denmark in terms of travel costs. If you stick to hostels, eat out only at lunch and resist the temptation to buy a round of drinks you can still manage to explore beyond a flying visit.

First on the list for almost any traveller is **Stockholm**. One of Europe's most beautiful capital cities, it's a bundle of islands hosting a picture-postcard old town, fine museums and the country's most active nightlife. After Stockholm, Sweden's other main cities **Gothenburg** and **Malmö** can seem like also-rans yet they are both eminently likeable places worthy of at least a couple of nights' stay. Similarly, the two university towns, **Lund** and **Uppsala** make excellent day-trips.

During summer Sweden's interior beckons with the opening of the 1300-kilometre **Inlandsbanan** rail line running along the spine of the country through lakeland and bear country as far as the **Arctic Circle**. Summer is also the time to join the rush to **Gotland**, Sweden's Baltic island escape. If you're here in winter you shouldn't miss a trip to Swedish Lapland and consider taking a splurge on a night at the *Icehotel* near **Kiruna** in the far north.

CHRONOLOGY

98 AD Tacitus refers to a Scandinavian tribe known as the "Suiones".

800s The Swedish Vikings become a powerful force in Europe over the following few centuries.

1255 City of Stockholm founded.

1397 The Kalmar Union unites Sweden with Denmark and Norway through a marriage arrangement.

1520 Hundreds of nobles are killed by Danish forces during the "Stockholm Bloodbath". A counter attack is led by Swede Gustav Vasa.

1523 Gustav is crowned King Gustav I and leads the Protestant Reformation of Sweden.

1536 Sweden leaves the Kalmar Union, asserting independence.

1628 The *Vasa* battleship sinks in Stockholm harbour – a national embarrassment now turned into a money-spinning tourist attraction.

1721 Sweden is defeated by a coalition led by Russia in the Great Northern War, ending the success of the Swedish Empire.

1814 Sweden invades and conquers Norway.

1901 First Nobel Prize ceremony held, as part of the will of Swedish inventor Alfred Nobel.

1905 Sweden peacefully concedes Norwegian independence.

1914 Sweden remains neutral during World War I.

1939 Sweden declares neutrality during World War II, and is one of only five countries to maintain it.

1943 The first IKEA store is opened by founder Ingvar Kamprad.

1974 ABBA top the charts after winning the Eurovision Song Contest with "Waterloo".

1986 Prime Minister Olof Palme is assassinated in Stockholm; the crime is still unresolved.

1995 Sweden joins the EU after a closely fought referendum.

2003 Swedish voters reject the adoption of the euro.

2006 After seventy years of rule, the Social Democrats finally lose an election to the centre-right Alliance for Sweden.

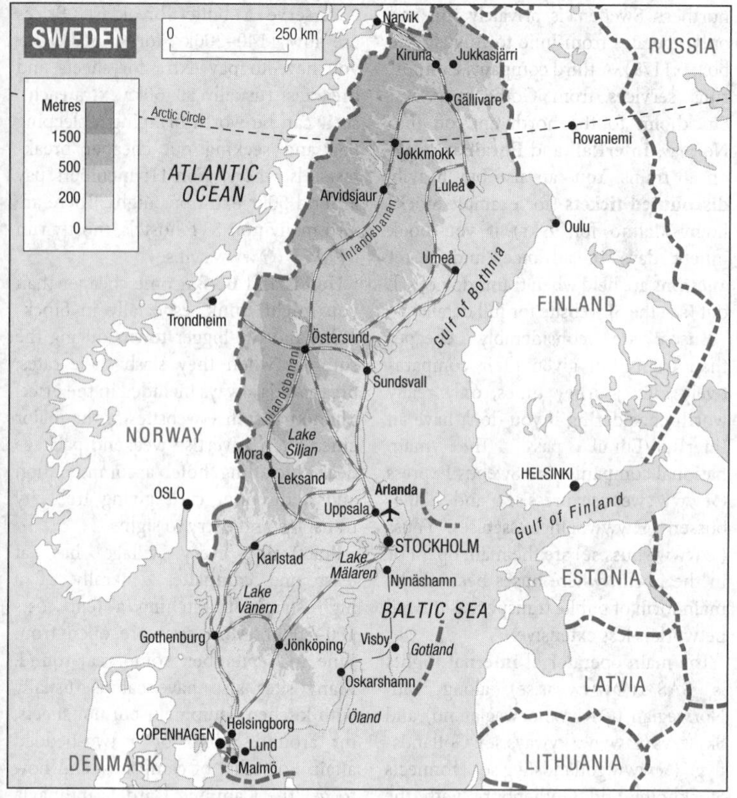

ARRIVAL

Most travellers arrive at one of Stockholm's three international **airports**. The largest and most convenient, Arlanda, is served by the big international carriers including Sweden's SAS as well as a few budget airlines such as easyJet and Norwegian (although neither fly here from the UK). Ryanair uses Skavsta and Västerås airports, both a long way from Stockholm (around 90km); they also fly into Gothenburg although if you are heading to southern Sweden bear in mind that there is a wider choice of budget routes to Copenhagen Aiport, just twenty minutes by train from Malmö.

International **trains** arrive in Stockholm, Malmö and Gothenburg from Norway, Denmark and Germany; in the north, Kiruna is the first stop in Sweden for visitors arriving from northern Norway.

International **ferry routes** include: Stockholm–Tallinn (Estonia), Stockholm–Helsinki and Turku (Finland); Helsingborg–Helsingør (Denmark) and Oslo (Norway); Gothenburg–Kiel (Germany) and Newcastle (UK).

GETTING AROUND

The best way to explore Sweden is by train. **Swedish State Railways**' extensive network (SJ; ⓦwww.sj.se) runs as far north as Östersund and, on the east coast, Sundsvall. The famous **Inlandsbanan** line (ⓦwww.inlandsbanan.se), which travels through central and

northern Sweden, is privately run and only operates from June to August (see box, p.1179). A third company, **Connex**, runs services from Gothenburg and Stockholm to the north and on into Norway. **InterRail** and **Eurail** are valid on all trains. You can also buy heavily **discounted tickets** (for example Stockholm–Malmö for 99kr) if you book ninety days in advance, and **ticket auctions** are held when trains do not sell out (see the SJ website for full details).

Buses are considerably cheaper than trains but given their comparatively long journey times, only really worth considering if you don't have an InterRail/Eurail pass. The main national companies are Swebus Express (Ⓦwww.swebusexpress.se) and Säfflebussen (Ⓦwww.safflebussen.se). Ybuss (Ⓦwww.ybuss.se) are the main operator in the north, where buses become the main form of public transport as the rail network is less extensive.

The main operator of **internal flights** is SAS (Ⓦwww.sas.se) along with Norwegian (Ⓦwww.norwegian.no) and Skyways (Ⓦwww.skyways.se). Gotlandsflyg (Ⓦwww.gotlandsflyg.se) connects Stockholm and Gothenburg with the island of Gotland. As an example price you can fly from Stockholm to Kiruna with Norwegian for around 550kr.

Ferries are an essential mode of transport given Sweden's long coastline and thousands of islands. Information on accessing the islands of Stockholm's archipelago and Gotland is given in the chapter.

ACCOMMODATION

Sweden has an excellent network of **hostels** (*vandrarhem*) mostly operated by the STF (Ⓦwww.svenskaturistforeningen.se). They are found all over the country, often in incongruous surroundings, such as prisons or ships. Double rooms are usually available as well as dorms, and virtually all hostels have self-catering kitchens and serve a buffet breakfast. Prices are low (140–200kr for a bed), but you have to pay extra for sheets and breakfast (usually 50–60kr extra each), so it can be worth bringing a sleeping bag and seeking out cheaper breakfasts elsewhere. Non-HI members pay around 50kr extra per night. There are also many non-STF hostels, mostly run by SVIF (Ⓦwww.svif.se).

Hotels and **B&Bs** come cheaper than you might think, especially in Stockholm and the bigger towns during the summer when they slash their rates; breakfast is always included in the price. The tourist-office websites of the major cities often advertise weekend package deals including hotel accommodation and a discount card giving free city transport and entry to sights.

Practically every village has at least one **campsite**, generally of a high standard. Pitching a tent costs 100–200kr. Most sites are open from June to September, some year-round. Many sites also have cabins, usually with kitchen equipment but not sheets, for around 500kr for a two-bedded affair. For a list of campsites, and how to get the Camping Card Scandinavia (125kr), which you need to pitch a tent, see Ⓦwww.camping.se.

FOOD AND DRINK

Thanks in part to IKEA cafés invariably dishing them up, Swedish meatballs (*köttbullar*) are familiar across the world. However there is rather more to the national cuisine than this. **Seafood** is particularly good with marinated salmon (*gravlax*) and herring (*strömming*), the latter pickled, smoked and even fermented, served everywhere; you'll often find them offered as part of a classic **smörgåsbord** buffet with potato salad, rye bread, cheeses and fruit. Other specialities include reindeer and elk – both surprisingly tasty – and sweet cloud berries (delicious with ice cream).

Breakfast (*frukost*) is invariably a help-yourself buffet of juice, cereals, bread, boiled eggs, jams, salami and coffee or tea. For **snacks**, a *gatukök* (street kitchen) or *korvstånd* (hot-dog stall) will serve hot dogs, burgers, chips and the like for around 40kr. Coffee shops always display a range of freshly baked pastries (coffee and cake for 40–60kr), and also serve *smörgåsar* – open sandwiches piled high with toppings (40–60kr) – and usually a good range of salads.

Lunch (*lunch*; usually served around noon) is the main meal of the day for many Swedes. Restaurants tend to be great value at lunchtime, with most places offering a **set meal** (*dagens rätt*) of a main dish with bread, salad and coffee at 70–90kr. Otherwise meals in restaurants, especially at **dinner** (*middag*), can be expensive: 200–250kr for two courses, plus drinks. Better value are pizzerias and Thai restaurants. Note that Swedes tend to eat early, tucking into dinner from around 6pm.

Drinking

Although the costs have come down in recent years, Sweden remains one of the most expensive places in Europe to **drink**. In a bar or pub you'll pay around 50kr for half a litre of one of the main national brands, Spendrups or Falcon. Unless you specify, it will be *starköl*, the strongest beer, or the slightly weaker *mellanöl*; *folköl* is the cheaper and weaker brew; cheapest (around half the price) is *lättöl*, a concoction that is virtually non alcoholic. With the exception of the latter, the only outlets where you can buy alcohol outside of bars and restaurants are the government-run **Systembolaget** (known informally as System) shops, where alcohol costs around a third of what you'll pay in a bar. There are at least one or two branches in even the smallest towns. A glass of **wine** in a bar or restaurant costs around 60kr, while you can buy a whole bottle for a little more at Systembolaget.

CULTURE AND ETIQUETTE

Swedes are a mix of apparent contradictions: fiercely patriotic yet globally minded, confident yet self-deprecating, orderly yet creative. Throughout the country you'll find the small ritual of *fika* – a verb that means something like "to have a coffee and a bun and a chat with a friend or two" – is a common pastime, along with singalongs and complaining about winter. **Traditional festivities** like Midsummer's Day and Easter inspire enormous enthusiasm, and on holidays young and old alike head for the countryside to celebrate. The vast majority of Swedes speak some **English** and most speak it with disarming fluency, so Anglophone travellers will have no problem striking up conversations.

SPORTS AND OUTDOOR ACTIVITIES

Football is Sweden's national sport and IFK Gothenburg the biggest and most successful domestic side. Naturally enough, winter sports are where the

SWEDEN ON THE NET

ⓦ www.cityguide.se Up-to-date events listings in the main Swedish cities.
ⓦ www.thelocal.se English-language news, views, listings and blogs on life in Sweden.
ⓦ www.stockholmtown.com Everything you ever wanted to know about the Swedish capital.
ⓦ www.svenskaturistforeningen.se Tips and ideas on where to visit in Sweden, courtesy of STF (the Swedish Youth Hostel Association).
ⓦ www.visit-sweden.com Slick tourist-office site with plenty of themed ideas and itineraries.

Swedes excel on the world stage and skiing, snowboarding and ice hockey are all very popular. The best ski resorts are in Åre, Kittelfjäll, Riksgränsen and Ramundberget. In summer, everyone flocks to Sweden's exquisite, unpolluted lakes and to Stockholm's archipelago for **swimming**, **kayaking** and **sailing**. Sweden is a fantastic place for **hiking**, with some of Europe's most unspoilt wildernesses to explore. The most trekked path is the 500-kilometre Kungsleden (King's Trail; see p.1182).

COMMUNICATIONS

The Swedish **postal service** scrapped normal post offices in 2001. Instead, you can send and receive mail and buy stamps at supermarkets, newsagents and tobacconists (look for the blue postal sign). **Public phones** usually only take prepaid cards (*telefonkort*), available from newsagents and kiosks. Directory enquiries is on ⓣ118 118 (domestic), ⓣ118 119 (international). **Internet** cafés and gaming centres are relatively common in larger towns (40–60kr/hr). Access is free in local libraries, many of which offer wi-fi.

EMERGENCIES

The **police** are courteous and fluent in English. Hospital treatment is free for anyone with a European Health Insurance Card (EHIC). **Pharmacies** (*Apoteket*) operate normal shop opening hours with a rota system for late opening. Stockholm has a 24-hour pharmacy (see p.1167).

INFORMATION

Almost all towns have a **tourist office**, giving out good-quality maps and timetables; they are also usually able to book accommodation, rent out bikes and change money. You're only likely to buy a map if you are going hiking – if so try ⓦwww.kartbutiken.se, which stocks a wide range.

EMERGENCY NUMBERS

All emergencies ⓣ112.

STUDENT AND YOUTH DISCOUNTS

The main cities all have **tourist cards** or passes, which offer either free or discounted entry to museums, unlimited use of local transport (often including ferries), and sometimes other goodies, such as discounts in cafés and restaurants. An **ISIC card** can halve the price of museums, and attract variable discounts on accommodation, shops, restaurants and transport (for example 20 percent of Swebuss and 30 percent of SJ trains).

MONEY AND BANKS

Sweden's currency is the **krona** (abbreviated to kr; plural: kronor), made up of 100 öre. There are coins of 50 öre, 1kr, 5kr and 10kr, and notes of 20kr, 50kr, 100kr, 500kr and 1000kr. At the time of writing €1 was worth 10.5kr, US$1 was 7.5kr, and £1 was 12kr. **Banks** are open Monday to Friday 9.30am to 3pm, and on Thursday also 4 to 5.30pm. Outside these hours you can **change money** at airports and ferry terminals, as well as at Forex offices, which usually offer the best rates (minimum 30kr commission). **ATMs** are plentiful and **credit cards** are accepted just about everywhere.

OPENING HOURS AND HOLIDAYS

Shops open Monday to Friday 9am to 6pm, and on Saturday from 9am to 1/4pm. Some larger stores stay open until 8/10pm, and may open on Sunday (noon–4pm). Banks, offices and shops close on **public holidays** (Jan 1, Jan 6, Good Fri, Easter Sun & Mon, May 1, Ascension, Whit Sun & Mon, June 20 & 21, Nov 1, Dec 24–26 & 31). They may also close early the preceding day.

Swedish

	Swedish	Pronunciation
Yes	*Ja*	Ya
No	*Nej*	Nay
Please	*Var så god*	Vaa-show-go
Thank you	*Tack*	Tak
Hello/Good day	*Hej*	Hay
Goodbye	*Hejdå*	Hay-doe
Excuse me	*Ursäkta*	Urh-shekta
Where?	*Var?*	Vaar?
Good	*Bra*	Braa
Bad	*Dålig*	Doo-ah-lig
Near	*Nära*	Nera
Far	*Avlägsen*	Arv-lessen
Cheap	*Billig*	Billi
Expensive	*Dyr*	Deyur
Open	*Öppen*	Upp-en
Closed	*Stängd*	Stengd
Today	*I dag*	Ee daa
Yesterday	*I går*	Ee gor
Tomorrow	*I morgon*	Ee morron
How much is...?	*Vad kostar det...?*	Vaa kostar day...?
What time is it?	*Hur mycket är klockan?*	Hoor mucker er clockan?
I don't understand	*Jag förstår inte*	Yaa fur-stor int-eh
Do you speak English?	*Talar du engelska?*	Taalar doo eng-ul-ska?
One	*Ett*	Ett
Two	*Två*	Tvo
Three	*Tre*	Tray
Four	*Fyra*	Feera
Five	*Fem*	Fem
Six	*Sex*	Sex
Seven	*Sju*	Shoo
Eight	*Åtta*	Otta
Nine	*Nio*	Nee-o
Ten	*Tio*	Tee-o

Stockholm

With the air of a grand European capital yet on a small, Scandinavian scale, **Stockholm** is a vibrant and instantly likeable city. Built on fourteen islands, water and green space dominate the landscape, but there are still plenty of distinctly urban attractions to fill your days from elegant museums and royal palaces to achingly cool bars and clubs. In fact, given its huge range of appeal you may well find yourself booking an extra night or two to do the place justice.

What to see and do

Taking a **boat tour** is the classic way to see Stockholm. Once you've checked into your accommodation, head straight to the harbour fronting the *Grand Hotel* from where you can pick one up from any number of operators (see p.1164). Once you have a fix on the city's layout you will cover most ground on foot or take the T-bana metro for cross-city trips.

The key **sights** to tick off are the Gamla Stan (old town), Vasa Museum, the National and Modern art museums as well as Sodermalm's SoFo neighbourhood. Aside from these it's best, in summer at least, to stroll around the parks and gardens (especially Djurgården) and take a trip to the Stockholm archipelago. In winter the city's ice rinks and cosy coffee-houses come into their own.

Central Station and the Stadshuset

The first impression of Stockholm for most people is the vast yet elegant **Central Station**, the transport hub for the city with the bus terminal next door and metro underneath. A short walk south across the bridge to Kungsholmen is one of the city's main attractions: the **Stadshuset** (Town Hall) at Hantverkargatan 1 (guided tours daily 10am, noon & 2pm; June–Aug also 11am & 3pm; 60kr; T-Centralen). Climbing its gently tapering 106-metre-high red-brick **tower** (May–Sept daily 10am–4pm; 20kr) is well worth the effort for the unrivalled views of the city.

Gamla Stan

Just a 200-metre walk south from the Central Station across Vasabron Bridge is Stockholm's old town, **Gamla Stan**. One of the best-preserved medieval towns in Europe, there are plenty of worthy sights to explore but its main appeal is simply strolling around, particularly in the evening after the tourists depart and the lamp-lit streets become more intimate.

Stortorget, the main square, is surrounded by beautiful terracotta and saffron-coloured eighteenth-century buildings – look out for no. 7 where you'll see a cannon ball lodged into the wall, supposedly fired during the Stockholm Bloodbath of 1520. The surrounding narrow streets are clogged with arts and craft shops, restaurants and bars. The excellent **Nobel Museum** on Stortorget (daily 10am–5pm, closes 8pm Tues; 60kr) showcases the work of various Nobel Prize winners.

Gamla Stan: Kungliga Slottet

Stockholm's most distinctive monumental building, the **Kungliga Slottet** (Royal Palace; T-Gamla Stan), is a beautiful Renaissance successor to Stockholm's original castle. The Swedish Royals don't actually live here, having relocated to the Drottningsholms Slot 10km west of the city, but no one seems to have told the royal guards who put on a display of pomp, pageantry and shouting at the daily changing of the guard (Mon–Sat 12.15pm, Sun 1.15pm). Inside are the royal **apartments** (mid-May to mid-Sept daily 10am–4/5pm; mid-Sept to mid-May Tues–Sun noon–3pm; 90kr), a dazzling collection of regal furniture, tapestries

and Rococo decoration, while the **Treasury** (same times as apartments; 90kr) displays ranks of regalia, including jewel-studded crowns and a sword belonging to Gustav Vasa.

Gamla Stan: Storkyrkan

Close to the royal palace, Stockholm's cathedral, the **Storkyrkan** (daily 9am–4/6pm; 30kr, free in winter), was consecrated in 1306 and is where the monarchs of Sweden are married and crowned. Look out inside for the animated fifteenth-century sculpture of *St George and the Dragon*, which incorporated elk horns into the design, and for the royal pews – more like golden billowing thrones.

Gamla Stan: Riddarholmen

Across the bridge from Gamla Stan, Riddarholmen or "Nobles Island" is often less crowded but just as pretty. It's also home to a Stockholm landmark, the thirteenth-century **Riddarholmskyrkan** (daily 10am–4pm; 30kr), with its iron latticework spire. Originally a thirteenth-century monastery, the church is now the burial place of Swedish monarchs.

The National Art Museum

The **National Art Museum** (Tues 11am–8pm, Wed–Sun 11am–5pm; 100kr; T-Kungsträdgården), next to the *Grand Hotel*, houses an impressive collection of paintings, from Rembrandts to Renoirs as well as a large dollop of local talent like Swedish artists Carl Larsson, Ernst Josephson and C.F. Hill. Perhaps less expected is the eclectic applied-arts collection which includes beds slept in by kings, Art Nouveau coffee pots, examples of Swedish furniture design and even a 1950s Italian Vespa, displayed next to fine examples of European sculpture.

STOCKHOLM BY KAYAK

Seeing Stockholm by boat is one thing but getting right down to water level on a kayak gives you a terrific sense of freedom – you can stop off just about anywhere – and a unique vantage point on the city. The best place to rent kayaks is the **Djurgärdsbrons Sjöcafé** at Galärvarvsvägen 2 on Djurgärden (from 70kr per hour).

TREAT YOURSELF

Summer or winter, a trip to Stockholm's glorious Art Nouveau spa, the **Centralbadet** (88 Drottninggatan 88 ⓦwww.centralbadet.se; Mon–Fri 6am–8pm, Sat 8am–8pm, Sun 8am–5pm; 130kr, Fri after 3pm & Sat 170kr) should not be missed. A quiet oasis off busy Drottninggatan, the spa has a stunning oval-shaped pool set within a stained-glass atrium, three saunas – both dry and steam – as well as bubbling spa baths and an elegant café.

Moderna Muséet

Stockholm's answer to London's Tate Modern or Bilbao's Guggenheim, the **Moderna Muséet** (Tues 10am–8pm, Wed–Sun 10am–6pm; 80kr) on Skeppsholmen certainly keeps up with its rivals in terms of grand modernist architecture though the art collection plays second fiddle in some respects. Connoisseurs will appreciate the large selection of cubist painting as well as lesser-known works by Picasso and Dalí, plus a peppering of American pop art. In summer, there's a great café with outdoor seating.

Norrmalm and Östermalm

Modern Stockholm lies immediately north of Gamla Stan. It's split into two distinct sections: the central **Norrmalm** and the classier, residential streets of Östermalm to the east. Norrmalm was redeveloped in the 1970s and is dominated by high-rises and the huge public-square-cum-roundabout, Sergels

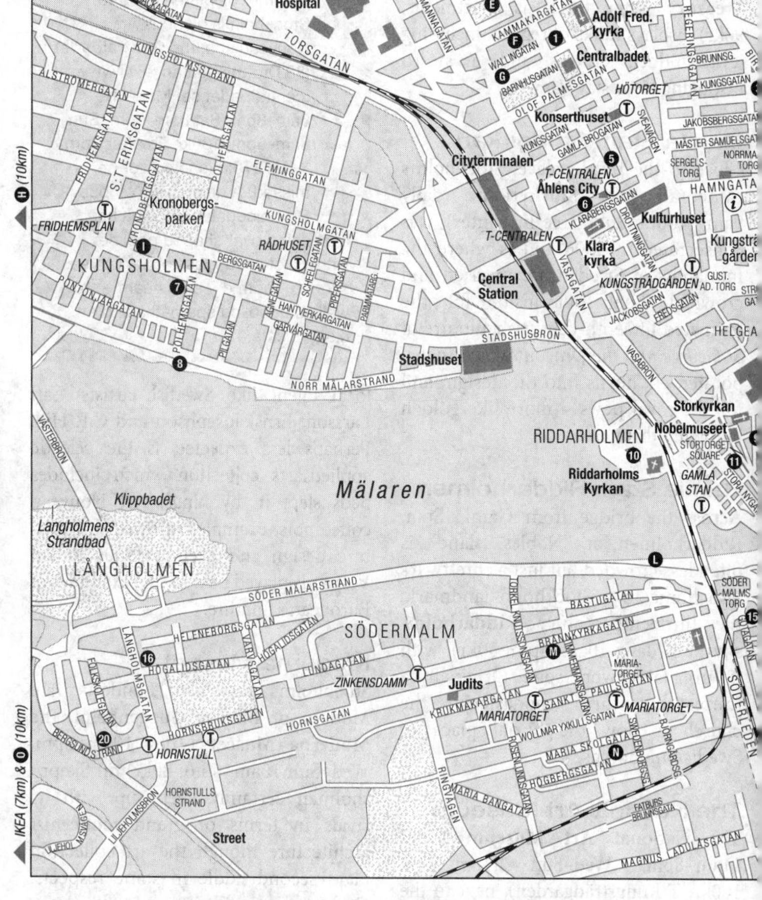

Torg. Taking up most of the east side of the square is the **Kulturhuset** (Tues–Fri 11am–9pm, Sat & Sun 11am–5pm), an interesting mix of exhibition space/art gallery/cinema/theatre and meeting place. Norrmalm is also home to Stockholm's biggest department stores, Åhlens and NK, as well as H&M's flagship store on Hamngatan. The eastern boundary is marked by **Kungsträdgården**, the most central of the city's numerous parks

Ostermalm, west of Norrmalm, is the address of choice for upmarket Stockholmers. It also hosts the city's most exclusive nightlife – particularly on Stureplan, where you'll find legions of fake-tanned designer-clad revellers queuing round the block for top night-clubs. The main attractions during the day are the Östermalms Saluhall food market (see p.1165) and the **Historiska Muséet** (May–Sept daily 10am–5pm, Oct–April same hours but closed Mon; 60kr; T-Karlaplan). Highlights here include a Stone Age household and a mass of Viking weapons, boats and most interestingly gold, over 52kg of the stuff.

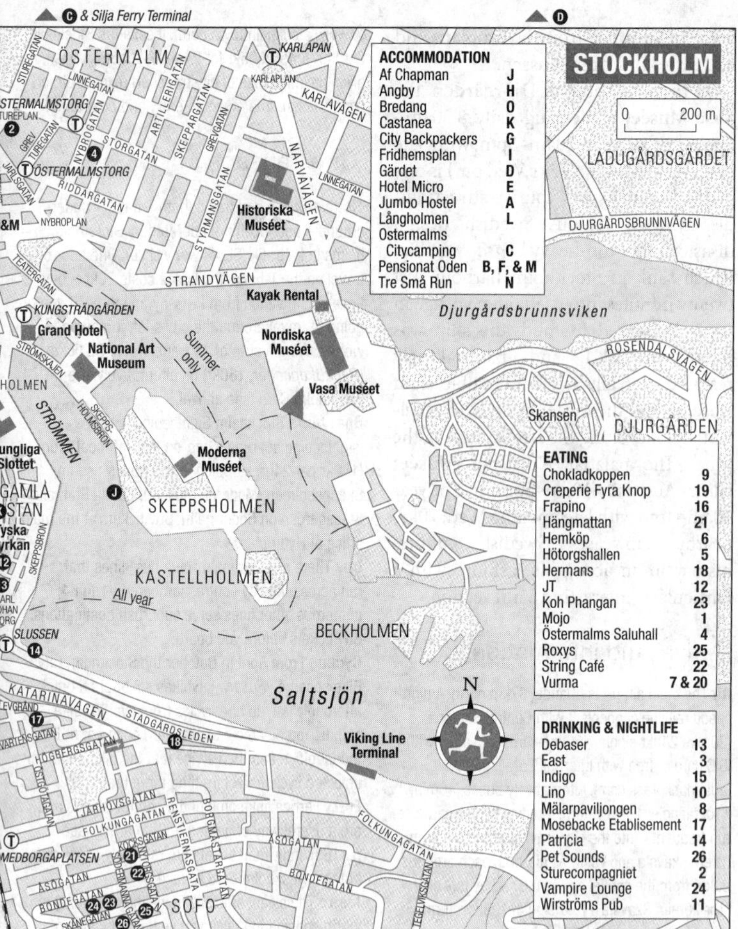

Södermalm and Långholmen

Stockholm's hippest island has to be **Södermalm**, just south of Gamla Stan. Head south from the traffic hub of Slussen along Götgatan, past Medborgarplatsen, lined with shops and bars, to arrive at the central district of **SoFo** (South of Folkungagatan), which bristles with cool bars, clubs and boutiques. To the west of Södermalm, **Hornstull** is SoFo's quieter cousin, with a cluster of bars and restaurants along Hornsgatan and around Bergsundstrand. It's a short walk from here to the lovely, uninhabited island of **Långholmen**, perfect for picnics or summertime beach-lazing at the small stretch of sand on the north shore.

Djurgården

A former royal hunting ground, **Djurgården** is the nearest large expanse of park to the city centre and home to several interesting museums. You could walk to the park from Central Station, but it's quite a hike: it's quicker to take a bus or ferry instead. Bus #44 makes the journey from Karlaplan, while the #47 and #69 run from Nybroplan. Ferries

leave in summer from Nybroplan, and all year round from Slussen.

On the west shore of **Djurgården**, the **Vasa Muséet** (June–Aug daily 8.30am–6pm; rest of year 10am–5pm with late opening Wed; 95kr, 75kr Wed pm) is one of the country's top tourist attractions, displaying a famous Swedish design disaster: the top-heavy *Vasa* warship, which sank in Stockholm harbour just twenty minutes into its maiden voyage in 1628. Preserved in mud, the ship was raised in 1961 and painstakingly restored. It really is an incredible sight close up and the museum does an excellent job of evoking the atmosphere of the time. The palatial **Nordiska Muséet** (June–Aug daily 10am–5pm; rest of year 10am–4pm with late opening Wed; 70kr) nearby showcases Swedish cultural history in an accessible fashion, with a particularly interesting Sámi section.

Arrival and information

Air The main airport is Arlanda, 37km north. A high-speed rail line connects it with Central Station (20min; 240kr single, 460kr return; half-price with ISIC card or free with InterRail/Eurail; Ⓦwww.arlandaexpress.com). Alternatively buses (40min; 110kr single; 199kr return; Ⓦwww.flygbussarna.se) run frequently into the city arriving at the Cityterminalen. Skavsta and Västerås airports, each around 90km from the capital are connected by bus only (1hr 20min; Skavsta 110kr single, 199kr return; Västerås 99kr single, 189kr return).

Bus Cityterminalen, adjacent to Central Station, handles all bus services, both domestic and international.

Ferry Viking Line ferries arrive at Tegelvikshamnen in Södermalm, in the south of the city. The terminal is a 30min walk from the centre, or connected by bus to Slussen T-bana station. The Silja Line terminal is in the northeastern reaches of the city, a short walk from Gärdet or Ropsten T-bana stations.

Train By train, you arrive at Central Station, a cavernous structure on Vasagatan in Norrmalm. All branches of the Tunnelbana, Stockholm's metro, meet at T-Centralen, the station directly below Central Station.

Tourist office The tourist office is at Hamngatan 27 in Norrmalm (April–Sept Mon–Fri 9am–7pm, Sat 10–5pm, Sun 10am–4pm, Oct–March same times but closes 5pm Mon–Fri; Ⓣ08/508 28 508, Ⓦwww.stockholmtown.com). It sells the Stockholm Card (375/495/595kr for 24/48/72 hours), which gives unlimited use of city transport (except airport connections), free museum entry and boat tours.

City transport

Tickets Buses and trains (both T-bana – underground – and local) are operated by Storstockholms Lokaltrafik (SL; Ⓦwww.sl.se). One hour of travel on the T-bana and buses costs 20kr – buy tickets in advance from Pressbyrån stores. If you're going to travel around the city a lot, it may be worth buying a strip of 16 transferable SL tickets (*Rabattkuponger*, 160kr) or, alternatively, the Stockholm Card (see above).

Boat tours Stockholm Sightseeing (Ⓦwww.sightseeing.se) runs a hop-on, hop-off boat tour (100kr per 24hr) stopping at the Vasa Museum, Skeppsholmen (Moderna Museet), Gamla Stan and Stadsgården on Södermalm. Buy tickets at the main office at Nybroplan.

Bus There are four main "blue bus" lines that run across the city centre, numbered #1 to #4; numerous other lines serve suburban destinations. Buy tickets before you board.

Cycling From April to October the Stockholm City Bike scheme (Ⓦwww.citybikes.se) offers a quick, affordable way to hire cycles from over 70 bike stands. You buy the city bike card online or at the tourist office and then swipe it at the bike stand to unlock a cycle (max hire time three hrs)

Ferry Ferries link some of the central islands and are a useful way of getting to Djurgården (see p.1163). Individual tickets are relatively expensive but the Stockholm Card is valid.

Metro The clean, efficient Tunnelbana (T-bana) is worth considering once you've tired of walking. There are three lines (red, green and blue) and trains run Sun–Thurs 5am–midnight, Fri & Sat 24hr.

Taxi Taxis are expensive (the meter starts at 45kr) and only worth considering if you are in a group. You can hail taxis in the street or try Stockholm Taxi (Ⓣ08/15 00 00) or Taxi (Ⓣ08/020 93 93 00).

Accommodation

Af Chapman Flaggmansvägen 8, Skeppsholmen Ⓣ08/463 22 66, Ⓦwww.stfchapman.com. A Stockholm landmark, the *Af Chapman* is a tall sailing ship converted into probably the world's most elegant hostel. If you can't get a bed on board there are more rooms on dry land in the hostel building, which houses the reception and a breakfast room plus a decent café. Dorms 185kr, rooms 530kr.

THE HOSTEL WITH WINGS

Taking the prize for Sweden's quirkiest place to stay, the **Jumbo Hostel** (ⓦwww.jumbohostel.com; dorm bed 350kr) at Arlanda Airport is a full-sized Boeing 747, transformed into a youth hostel in 2008. Instead of rows of seats there are 25 dorm rooms decorated with a nod to the jet's 1970s Pan-Am days. The cockpit, still with knobs and switches to play with, has been converted into a luxurious "suite" (3300kr per night) with a tiny private bathroom.

Castanea Kindstugatan 1, Gamla Stan ⓣ08/22 35 51, ⓦwww.castaneahostel.com. The Old Town location of this quiet, non-STF hostel takes some beating while inside are clean and brightly decorated dorms. Dorms 220kr, rooms 650kr.
City Backpackers Upplandsgatan 2a, Norra Bantorget ⓣ08/20 69 20, ⓦwww.citybackpackers.se. Fun, sociable non-STF hostel with four-bed rooms and cheaper eight-bed dorms. Free pasta, internet, bike rental, and, this being Sweden, free sauna. Dorms 230kr, rooms 650kr.
Fridhemsplan Zinkens väg 20, Södermalm ⓣ08/616 81 00, ⓦwww.zinkensdamm.com. Huge official hostel, with "hotel style" beds (no bunks) and flat-screen TVs in every dorm. It's a little anonymous but professionally run and the location is good for downtown shopping, though a fair walk from Central Station. Fridhemsplan T-bana. Dorms 225kr, rooms 500kr.
Gärdet Sandhamnsgatan 59 ⓣ08/463 22 99, ⓦwww.stfturist.se/gardet. Newly renovated, modernist-style hostel set in quiet parkland northeast of the centre and within walking distance of Djurgården and the Vasa Museum. Dorms 280kr, rooms 540kr.
Långholmen Kronohäktet, Långholmen ⓣ08/720 85 00, ⓦwww.langholmen.com. Stockholm's grandest official hostel is located within an old prison on leafy Långholmen island. Spend the night in a converted cell: there are dorms with shared bathroom as well as en-suite doubles. To reach it take the T-bana to Hornstull, turn left and follow the signs. Dorms 230kr, rooms 570kr.

Hotels and pensions

Hotel Micro Tegnerlunden 8 (near Drottninggatan) ⓣ08/545 455 41, ⓦwww.hotelmicro.se. Bargain prices for central Stockholm. The rooms are windowless cabin-style affairs but pleasant enough and there are clean men's and women's bathrooms along each corridor. 495kr.
Pensionat Oden Kammakargatan 62, Hornsgatan 66b & Odengatan 38 ⓣ08/796 96 00, ⓦwww.pensionat.nu. Mini-chain with three branches all offering medium-sized en-suite rooms. The Oden City branch is the nicest with bright, airy rooms and close to the action in Norrmalm. 895kr.
Tre Små Rum Högbergsgatan 81 ⓣ08/641 23 71, ⓦwww.tresmarum.se. The name means "three small rooms" but there are now seven at this good-value hotel in the heart of Södermalm. Delicious buffet breakfast is served in the lovely kitchen area and there are cycles for hire for 150kr per day. Mariatorget T-bana. 795kr.

Campsites

Ängby Blackebergsvägen 25 ⓣ08/37 04 20, ⓦwww.angbycamping.se. Pretty, well-organized site west of the city on Lake Mälaren and near the beach. T-bana to Ängbyplan, then a 300-metre walk. Open all year. 100kr (2-person tent).
Bredäng Stora Sällskapets Väg ⓣ08/97 70 71, ⓦwww.bredangcamping.se. Pricey place with a hostel and restaurant on site, 10km southwest of the centre by Lake Mälaren. Take T-bana to Bredäng from where it's a 700m walk. April–Oct only. Camping 250kr, dorm bed 200kr, room 520kr.
Östermalms Citycamping Fiskartorpsvägen 2 ⓣ08/10 29 03. Surrounded by woodland, this is Stockholm's only centrally located campsite, at the Östermalm sports ground, a 30min walk from the centre. Late June to late Aug only. 155kr.

Eating

Food courts and markets

Hemköp Below Åhléns, Klarabergsgatan 50. Convenient supermarket with an excellent deli counter and in-house bakery. Mon–Fri 8am–9pm, Sat & Sun 10am–9pm.
Hötorgshallen Hötorget. A cheap and varied indoor market, awash with small cafés and ethnic snacks. To the north is the Kungshallen food court. Mon–Fri 10am–6pm, Sat 10am–3pm.
Östermalms Saluhall Östermalmstorg. Pig out in style at this elegant indoor market packed with discerning foodie types. Wine bars and restaurants surround the stalls. Mon–Thurs 9.30am–6pm, Fri 9.30–6.30pm, Sat 9.30–4pm.

Cafés

Chokladkoppen Stortoget 20, Gamla Stan. It may be bang in the middle of touristy Stortoget but this Old Town café is popular with locals and visitors

alike, not least for tasty sandwiches and thick, delicious hot chocolate.

Hängmattan Södermannag. 10, Södermalm, opposite Mariatorget T-bana. A fun, wholefood vegetarian café down a quiet Soder side-street; often hosts acoustic sets come evening.

Mojo Adolf Fredriks Kyrkogata 12, Norrmalm. Excellent coffee and the best carrot cake in town in a great location close to the shops of Norrmalm.

String Café Nytorgsgatan 38, Södermalm. Laid-back retro café. Like the furniture? You can buy it. Good coffee, plus muffins, brownies and the like.

Vurma Polhemsgatan 15, Kungsholmen, & Bergsundstrand 31, Södermalm. Kitsch and cosy café that doubles as a bakery. It's become something of a Stockholm institution with a second branch opening on Södermalm.

Restaurants

Creperie Fyra Knop Svartensgatan 4, Södermalm. Good-value crêpes are served in this dark, evocative restaurant which is fashionably tatty and often packed.

Frapino Långholmsgatan 3, Hornstull. Fantastic pick'n'mix salads and good-value lunch deals.

Hermans Fjällgatan 23b. Join the locals for a guilt-free feast at this veggie restaurant which also boasts some of the best views of Stockholm. You may need a taxi back after the all-you-can-eat lunch buffet (98kr).

JT Järntorget 78/Västerlånggatan 78, Gamla Stan. Refined yet affordable food in the heart of the old town – one of the best places to try Swedish classics such as meatballs and lingonberries (lunch menu 90kr).

Koh Phangan Skånegatan 57, Södermalm. Thai restaurant/bar with an interior resembling a tropical forest strewn with fairy lights. The food – green curries, pad thai and the like – struggles to compare with the decor but it's competently put together.

Roxys Nytorget 6. The place to come for some Med sunshine on a plate – flawless tapas and more adventurous dishes such as tuna with mango; there's a classy bar to boot.

Drinking and nightlife

Bars and pubs

East Stureplan 13, Östermalmstorg. Lively, busy bar/restaurant with a heated outdoor area, always packed at weekends when DJs play late into the night.

Indigo Götgatan 19. The steep hill of Götgatan, which runs south from Slussen is packed with bars and this is one of the most stylish – all coloured neon lights and trendy furniture with even trendier locals sitting on it.

Pet Sounds Skånegatan 80, Södermalm. Cool bar-restaurant that plays host to a mixed crowd of indie kids and older SoFo regulars. DJs play sets in the basement area and you can buy what you hear at the Pet Sounds music shop across the road.

Vampire Lounge Östgötagatan 41, Södermalm. Subterranean cocktail bar – comfy red sofas, bare stone walls and hip clientele. Try the Vlad the Impaler if you want to kick-start your evening.

Wirströms Pub Stora Nygatan 13, Gamla Stan. Popular expat hangout where you can watch the footie/rugby/cricket over a Guinness. Quiz nights and live music are held in its cellar bar.

Live music and clubs

Debaser Karl Johans Torg 1 ⓦ www.debaser.se. Legendary live music and DJ venue, attracting great local and international bands and packing in hundreds of energetic clubbers. T-bana Slussen/Gamla Stan.

Mosebacke Etablisement Mosebacke Torg 3 ⓦ www.mosebacke.se. This gig venue/club/bar has an incredibly varied music programme from jazz to electro. The sprawling terrace is one of the best places in town to hang out in summer, with barbecues and live music. T-bana Slussen.

Sturecompagniet Sturegatan 4 ⓦ www.sturecompagniet.se. Stockholm's largest club boasts a terrific light-show with house and techno sounds blaring on three floors of bars. Dress to impress and start queuing early. T-bana Östermalmstorg.

Gay Stockholm

Lino Södra Riddarholmshamnen 19, Riddarholmen ⓦ www.linoclub.com. Currently the hippest gay club in Stockholm, playing house and eighties/nineties hits. Sat till 3am.

Mälarpaviljongen Norr Mälarstrand 62 ⓦ www.malarpvailjongen.se. Open-air bar-restaurant down by the water with great views of Gamla Stan. It attracts a mixed gay/straight crowd and puts on events during the annual Stockholm Pride.

Patricia Stadsgårdshamnen, Slussen ⓦ www.patricia.st. Drag shows, dancing and comedy on what was the British Queen Mother's royal yacht. Also an excellent restaurant on the upper deck. Gay on Sun only. Slussen T-bana.

Shopping

Åhlens City Klarabergsgatan 50, T-Centralen. Stockholm's biggest department store – the place

to stock up on Bjorn Borg underkecks or, if you can fit into them, ultra-hip Acne jeans.

H&M Hamngatan 37. The main Stockholm branch of one of Sweden's biggest retail success stories; floor to ceiling cut-price fashion.

IKEA Modulvägen 1, Skärholmen (7km southwest of Stockholm). If you're dying to see the world's largest IKEA then hop on one of the free shuttle buses leaving from the southeast entrance of the Gallerian shopping mall, Regeringsgatan (Mon–Fri on the hour 10am–7pm).

Judits Hornsgatan 75. Truly fantastic second hand clothes emporium with a wealth of great shoes and accessories at affordable prices. The menswear equivalent is just up the road.

Street Hornstulls Strand 4. Inspired by London's Camden Market, Street has transformed a run-down area of Stockholm into a vibrant weekend meeting and browsing spot (April–Sept only) packed with arty and design types.

Directory

Embassies Australia, Sergels Torg 12 ⓣ08/613 29 00; Canada, Tegelbacken 4 ⓣ08/453 30 00; Ireland, Östermalmsgatan 97 ⓣ08/661 80 05; UK, Skarpögatan 6–8 ⓣ08/671 30 00; US, Dag Hammarskjöldsväg 31 ⓣ08/783 53 00.

Hospital Medical Care Information ⓣ08/672 24 00.

Internet Best value (19kr per hour) at Sidewalk Express (ⓦwww.sidewalkexpress.com) with branches at Arlanda Aiport, Central Station, City Terminalen and Kulturhuset.

Laundry Tvättsmaten, Västmannagatan 61 ⓣ08/34 64 80.

Left luggage Lockers in Central Station (50kr per 24hr).

Pharmacy C.W. Scheele, Klarabergsgatan 64 ⓣ08/454 81 30 (24hr).

Post office There's no central post office, but you can send packages from Posten counters in branches of Åhlens and ICA.

Moving on

Ferry Helsinki (Helsingsfors) (2 daily; 15hr); Tallinn, (3–4 weekly; 15hr); Turku (Åbo) (4 daily; 13hr).

Train Copenhagen (5 daily; 5hr 10min); Gothenburg (hourly; 3hr by X2000, 5hr by Intercity); Helsingborg (hourly, change at Lund; 5hr); Kiruna (1 nightly; 15hr 30min); Lund (hourly; 4hr 10min); Malmö (hourly; 4hr 30min); Oslo (1 daily; 6hr); Östersund (4 daily; 5hr 20min); Uppsala (every 30min; 40min).

Around Stockholm

One of the key excursions from Stockholm is to the royal palace of Drottningholm, on the shores of Lake Mälaren, west of the capital. In summer the pine-clad islands of Stockholm's **archipelago** make an enticing escape from the city while history buffs should head to the elegant town of **Uppsala**, a short train ride away.

DROTTNINGHOLM PALACE

Just 10km west of Stockholm, the **Drottningholm Palace** (May–Aug daily 10am–4.30pm; Sept daily noon–3pm; Oct–April Sat & Sun noon–3.30pm; 80kr; ⓦwww.royalcourt.se) is a Versailles-like monument to excess dating from the mid-seventeenth century. The Swedish royal family made it their permanent residence in 1981, and, while you're unlikely to spot any of them, you are free to wander through sections of the palace on guided tours and visit the manicured gardens. The best way to get here is one of the ferries which leave from the quay near the Stadthus (90kr one way), although you can also reach it on the less regal combination of T-bana to Brommaplan followed by the #77 bus.

THE STOCKHOLM ARCHIPELAGO

For 80km east of the capital stretches the **Stockholm archipelago**, made up of 30,000 islands, most of which are little more than lumps of rock rising up from the sea. In summer, the area bristles with tourists, day-trippers, sailing boats and locals making use of their summer homes. Boats to the islands leave from Strömkajen near Slussen and are run by Waxholmbolaget (ⓣ08/614 64 50,

Ⓦwww.waxholmsbolaget.se). If you're sticking around for a while, invest in a Båtluffakortet (Island Hopping Card; 340kr), a **pass** that entitles you to five days of unlimited transport; it's available at the tourist office, where you can also pick up a boat timetable. Alternatively, single tickets start at 75kr one way.

Vaxholm

Just an hour's scenic boat-ride from Stockholm and also connected by road, **Vaxholm** is the most easily accessible of the archipelago islands, which means it can be swamped with visitors in summer. However, it's still a charming spot, only two miles long, and boasts an elegant harbourside packed with restaurants, cafés and shops. Throughout July and August there are frequent concerts and outdoor events held here.

The **tourist office** is in the quaint Rådhuset (Ⓣ08/541 314 80). If you decide to **stay** overnight on the island there's a peaceful STF hostel (Ⓣ08/541 750 60, Ⓔinfo@bogesundsslottsvandrarhem.se; dorms 185kr) at Per Brahesväg 1, about 3km from the harbour.

Grinda

After Vaxholm, the blissfully quiet island of **Grinda** comes as a relief. It's also very popular in summer but you can usually escape the crowds and find a secluded stretch of sand; there are plenty of great swimming spots too. The main sight on the island is the **Grinda Wärdhus**, an Art Nouveau summerhouse dating from 1908. It's now a hotel with an award-winning restaurant. More affordable **accommodation** is available at the island's STF youth hostel (Ⓣ08/542 49072, Ⓔinfo@grindawardshus.se; dorms 200kr; May–Oct), right by the beach on the south side of the island. Direct ferries from Stockholm to Grinda take 1hr 30min and cost 90kr.

Siaröfortet

Locals rave about this cute little island, an hour's ferry ride north of Vaxholm (2hr 10min from Stockholm). It's known as **Siaröfortet** after its small naval fort, built during World War I. The fort has been turned into a museum but the real attraction is the island's indented coastline perfect for kayaking and swimming. There's also a lovely STF **youth hostel** with a sauna (Ⓣ08/243 090; double rooms from 225kr, dorm beds from 180kr; May to mid-Oct only).

UPPSALA

Forty minutes' train ride north of Stockholm, the pretty university town of **UPPSALA** makes an excellent day-trip. Just north of the restaurant- and bar-lined River Fyris, which bisects the town, you'll find the vast Gothic **Domkyrkan** (daily 8am–6pm; free), Scandinavia's largest cathedral. Poke around and you'll find the tombs of Reformation rebel monarch Gustav Vasa and his son Johan III, as well as local hero Carl Linnaeus, the famous botanist.

The other key sights to see are the remarkable royal burial mounds at **Gamla (Old) Uppsala**. Thought to have been created by the Svea tribe some 1500 years ago they were once the site of gruesome human sacrifices – with unfortunate victims strung up from a tree. The place where this took place is marked by the **Gamla Uppsala Kyrka** (daily 9am–4/6pm), a church built when the Swedish kings first took baptism in the new faith. The worthwhile **Gamla Uppsala Museum** (Feb–April & Sept–Nov Wed, Sat & Sun noon–3pm; May–Aug daily 11am–5pm; 50kr) fills you in on all the background.

Uppsala's **train** and **bus stations** are a couple of blocks east of the river. Signs indicate the way to the cathedral and **tourist office** (Mon–Fri 10am–6pm, Sat 10am–3pm; mid-June to mid-Aug also Sun noon–4pm; Ⓣ018/727 48 00, Ⓦwww.uppland.nu). For cheap **eats** try the huge takeaway salads at *Cupido* inside Forum Gallerian across from the

station. Further south, near the tourist office at Drottninggatan 5, *Ekocaféet* does a nice line in organic ales and veggie mains. The most convenient and best-value **place to stay** is the *Uppsala Vandrarhem City Hostel* (☎018/10 00 08, Ⓦwww.uppsalacityhostel.se; dorms 170kr, rooms 350kr; no breakfast) at St Persgatan 16, four blocks north of the station along Kungsgatan.

Southern Sweden

Southern Sweden is dominated by endless expanses of farmland while its coastline is famous for its superb beaches. Local dialects are strong and cause much mirth among metropolitan Stockholmers. Yet to portray the area as a rural backwater would do it a disservice. Here you'll find the grand port city of **Gothenburg**, well deserving exploration. South of here, **Helsingborg**, a stone's throw from Denmark, and **Malmö**, still sixteenth-century at its core, are both worth a day or two, while **Lund**, a medieval cathedral and university town is an essential day-trip from Malmö. Lying 90km off the southern coast in the Baltic Sea is the attractive island of **Gotland**, whose beaches and bars are awash with visitors over the summer.

GOTHENBURG

Sweden's second city, **GOTHENBURG** (Göteborg, pronounced *Yuh-teh-borr*) is Scandinavia's largest seaport and home to some of Sweden's biggest brands including Volvo and Ericsson. Beyond the industrial gloom of its shipyards you'll find an attractive and distinctly continental city with broad avenues, beautiful parks and several outstanding museums and galleries. With students making up an eighth of the population it's also a fun, youthful city with plenty of good hostels and a renowned nightlife scene.

What to see and do

Exploring Gothenburg by tram is one of the great pleasures of the city although most of its sights can be covered on foot. The main streets to orientate towards are Avenyn and Linnégatan along which you'll find many of the key sights such as the Konstmuseum and the modern Universeum science centre. It's also worth taking a **boat tour** of the canals and spending an afternoon lazing in Slottskogen, the city's most attractive swathe of green space.

Maritima Centrum and the Opera House

A short walk north from the station, the **Maritima Centrum** (March–Oct daily 10am–4/6pm; 75kr) offers you the chance to clamber aboard a destroyer and submarine moored at the quayside. It's worth coming down here just to look at the shipyards beyond, like a rusting Meccano set put into sharp perspective by the striking **Opera House** (daily noon–6pm), a graceful and imaginative ship-like structure.

Avenyn and the Röhsska Museet

Running south from the central area around the station, Kungsportsavenyn

THE FULL PACKAGE

Gothenburg can be an affordable place to book a hotel room thanks to the **Gothenburg Package** (from 550kr/person), run by the city tourist board. This deal gets you a double room in a central hotel, with breakfast and a free Gothenburg Pass worth 245kr – book a minimum of four days ahead at Ⓦwww.goteborg.com.

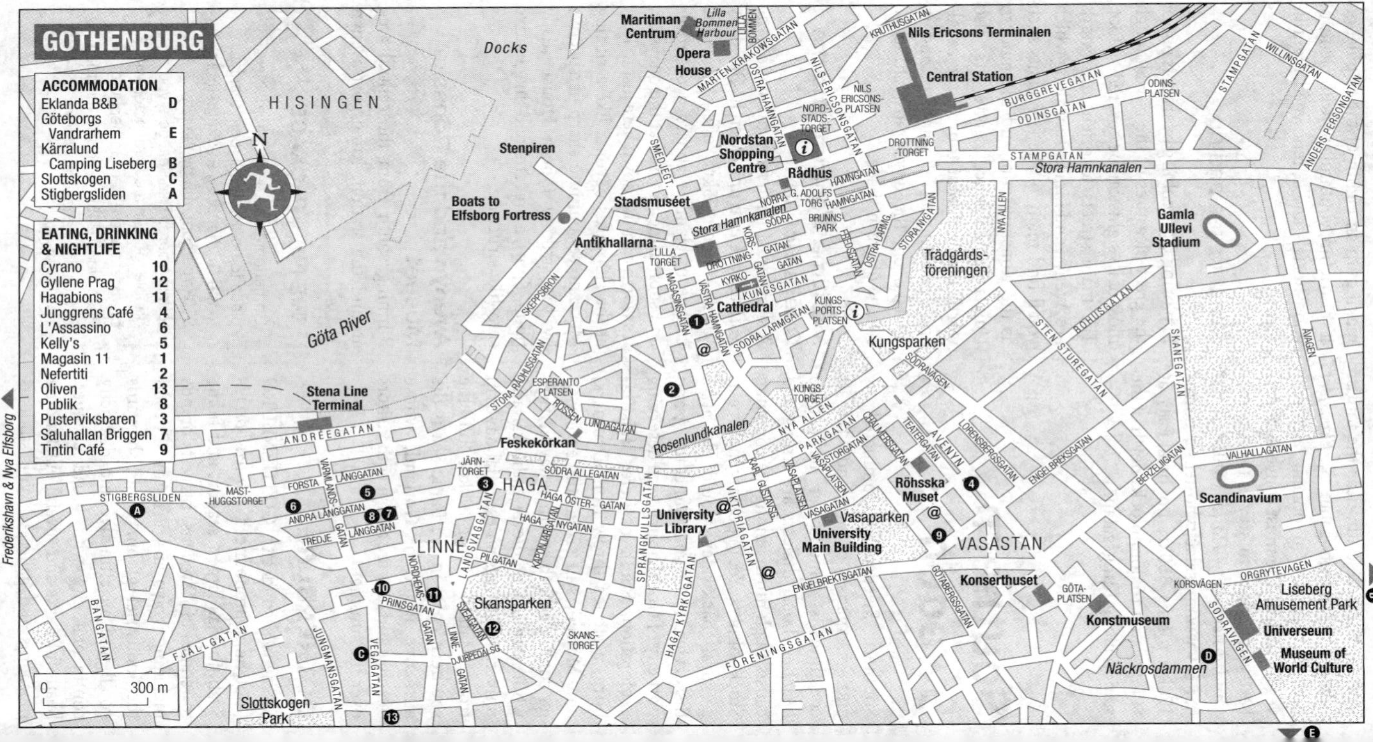
GOTHENBURG
ACCOMMODATION
Eklanda B&B D
Göteborgs Vandrarhem E
Kärralund Camping Liseberg B
Slottskogen C
Stigbergsliden A
EATING, DRINKING & NIGHTLIFE
Cyrano 10
Gyllene Prag 12
Hagabions 11
Junggrens Café 4
L'Assassino 6
Kelly's 5
Magasin 11 1
Nefertiti 2
Oliven 13
Publik 8
Pusterviksbaren 3
Saluhallan Briggen 7
Tintin Café 9
HISINGEN
Docks
Göta River
Stenpiren
Boats to Elfsborg Fortress
Stena Line Terminal
Maritiman Centrum
Lilla Bommen Harbour
Opera House
Nils Ericsons Terminalen
Central Station
Nordstan Shopping Centre
Rådhus
Stadsmuséet
Antikhallarna
Cathedral
Stora Hamnkanalen
Trädgårds-föreningen
Kungsparken
Gamla Ullevi Stadium
Scandinavium
Liseberg Amusement Park
Universeum
Museum of World Culture
Näckrosdammen
Konstmuseum
Konserthuset
VASASTAN
Röhsska Museet
Vasaparken
University Main Building
University Library
Rosenlundkanalen
Feskekörkan
HAGA
LINNÉ
Skansparken
Slottskogen Park
Frederikshavn & Nya Elfsborg
0 300 m

is Gothenburg's showiest thoroughfare. Known simply as **Avenyn**, this wide strip was once flanked by private houses fronted by gardens and is now lined with overpriced yet popular pavement restaurants and brasseries. About halfway down, the excellent **Röhsska Museet** at Vasagatan 37–39 (Tues noon–8pm, Wed–Fri noon–5pm, Sat & Sun 11am–5pm; 40kr; Ⓦwww.designmuseum.se) traces the history of design from 1850 to the present day as well as hosting regular fashion shows by young designers from Gothenburg University.

The Konstmuseum

At the end of Avenyn is Gothenburg's museum of art, the **Konstmuseum** (daily except Mon 11am–5/6pm, Wed till 9pm; 40kr, free for under-20s), a unique collection of Nordic and international works. Among the highlights are paintings by Edvard Munch, P.S. Krøyer and Carl Larsson as well as big hitters such as Picasso, Chagall and Rembrandt. The square outside the museum, **Götaplatsen**, is home to a city icon – Carl Milles' seven-metre-high bronze statue of *Poseidon* in all his naked glory.

Liseberg Amusement Park

Five minutes' walk southeast of Götaplatsen is **Liseberg**, a surprisingly attractive amusement park (late April to early Oct; opening times vary; Åkpass 290kr for unlimited rides all day; Ⓦwww.liseberg.com) with adrenaline-pumping rides and acres of gardens, restaurants and fast-food outlets.

Universeum and the Museum of World Culture

Across the street from Liseberg is the **Universeum** (daily: June–mid-Aug 9am–8pm; rest of year 10am–6pm; Ⓦwww.universeum.se; 169kr), a fun yet expensive science museum (it's worth getting a Gothenburg Pass just to visit here). The main attraction is a huge, climate-controlled tropical forest packed with butterflies, monkeys, tree frogs and brightly coloured birds. There's also a large seawater aquarium where you come face to face with sharks, moray eels and giant rays.

Adjacent to the Universeum, the **Museum of World Culture** (Tues–Sun noon–5pm, late opening Wed & Thurs; Ⓦwww.varldskulturmuseet.se; free) features imaginative exhibits on global issues such as HIV/Aids, human trafficking and fair trade as well as more upbeat topics such as Bollywood and hip-hop.

Haga and Linnégatan

Just a few minutes' walk west of Avenyn, the old working-class district of **Haga** is now a picturesque area of cobbled streets lined with plenty of daytime cafés and boutiques. A few steps further, **Linnégatan** is a more charismatic and cosmopolitan version of Avenyn, with a better range of places to eat and drink and edged with impressive Dutch-inspired architecture.

Slottskogen Park

South of Linnégatan, the **Slottskogen Park** (tram #13 or #2 to Linnéplatsen) is the city's largest park, a lovely expanse of woodland, lakes and wide avenues perfect for joggers and cyclists. Several vantage points offer sweeping views over the city and there's also a small zoo with a flamingo house and a seal pond, and a natural history museum, though the latter is distinctly missable.

Arrival and information

Air The main airport, Gothenburg Landvetter, is 25km east of the city; buses (every 15–20min; 30min; 80kr; Ⓦwww.flygbussarna.se) connect to the Nils Ericson terminal next to Central Station. Gothenburg City airport, used by budget airlines Ryanair and Air Berlin among others, is a corrugated steel shack 17km north of the city; bus departures are synchronized with flight arrivals (30min; 60kr).

Bus Buses from all destinations use the Nils Ericson bus terminal, which adjoins Central Station.
Ferry Stena Line ferries from Frederikshavn in Denmark and Kiel in Germany dock within 20min walk of the centre. Trams #3 and #9 run past to the centre.
Train Trains arrive at Central Station on Drottningtorget, just north of the centre; an underground walkway leads into Nordstan, the city's biggest shopping mall.
Information Gothenburg has two tourist offices: a kiosk (Mon–Fri 10am–6pm, Sat 10am–5pm, Sun noon–5pm) in Nordstan, the shopping centre next to Central Station, and a main office on the canal front at Kungsportsplatsen 2 (June–Aug daily 9.30am–6/8pm; rest of year Mon–Sat 9.30am–2/5pm; ⓣ031/61 25 00, ⓦwww.goteborg.com).
Discount passes The tourist office sells the Gothenburg Pass (245/340kr for 24/48hr), giving unlimited bus and tram travel, free or half-price museum entry, free Paddan boat tours and a fifty-percent discount on a day-trip to Frederikshavn in Denmark.
Internet Sidewalk Express (19kr per hour) have branches at Central Station and Vasaplatsen. Otherwise try Game Net, at Viktoriagatan 22.

City transport

Trams Gothenburg's tram network dates back to the 1870s and is the most atmospheric way to get around. There are 12 colour-coded routes – pick up a map from the tourist office. Tickets (25kr or free with Gothenburg Pass) can be bought from the on-board vending machines.
Boat tours Paddan boats (ⓦwww.stromma.se) offer open-topped boat tours (April–Oct; 130kr) along the city's canal network as well as trips out to the Gothenburg archipelago. Boats depart from Kungsportsplatsen.
Cycling The city is packed with cycle paths and bike racks are found at most attractions. You can rent bikes (120kr per day) from Cykelkungen at Chalmersgatran 19 (ⓦwww.cykelkungen.se).

Accommodation

Eklanda B&B Eklandagatan Nr 3 E. Larsson ⓣ031/43 50 55, ⓦwww.vandrarhem.com. Quiet "home from home" B&B in a great location close to Universeum and Liseberg. Apartments also available to rent. Take tram #14 to Korsvägen. Cash only. Rooms from 325kr.
Göteborgs Vandrarhem Mölndalsvägen 23 ⓦwww.goteborgsvandrarhem.se. Though it's pricier than the rest, this brisk, well-equipped hostel is Gothenburg's most central; take tram #4, direction towards Mölndal (stop: Getebergsäng). Dorms 250kr, rooms 550kr.

CHEAP BEER, GOOD TIMES

A rather unprepossessing street between Linnégatan and the ferry docks, **Andra Långgattan** comes alive at night when its bars and restaurants open for business. Competition keeps prices down – it's one of the few places in Sweden you can buy a beer for under 40kr and there are plenty of cheap Indian and Thai restaurants. *Publik* and *Kelly's* (see opposite) both make good starting points for a bar crawl.

Kärralund Camping Liseberg Olbergsgatan. ⓦwww.liseberg.se. Busy campsite 4km from the centre aimed mostly at families visiting the Liseberg Amusement Park. There is also a youth hostel (dorms only) on site. From the city centre, hop on tram #5 to Welandergatan (direction: Torp). Tents 150kr, dorms 210kr.
Slottskogen Vegagatan 21 ⓣ031/42 65 20, ⓦwww.sov.nu. Large, well-appointed and sociable hostel in a lively part of town. Two minutes' walk from Linnégatan; take tram #1 or #6 to Olivedalsgatan. Dorms 135kr, rooms 295kr.
Stigbergsliden Stigbergsliden 10 ⓣ031/24 16 20, ⓦwww.hostel-gothenburg.com. Comfortable hostel in a charming old sailor's mission, close to Linné and the Stena ferry terminal. Tram lines #3, #9 and #11 from the city centre. Dorms 165kr, rooms 400kr.

Eating

Shops and markets

Oliven corner of Olivedalsgatan 11/Vegagatan. Old-fashioned corner deli selling everything you'd need for a picnic in the nearby Slottskogen park.
Saluhallan Briggen Nordhemsgatan near Linnégatan. Indoor food market with plenty of cheap ethnic stalls as well as high-quality deli counters.

Cafés

Hagabions Linnégatan 21. Sample some imaginative vegetarian food (vegan lasagne anyone?) at this lovely café before catching a film in the attached arthouse cinema.
Junggrens Café Avenyn 37. This old-school, traditional café has been a Gothenburg favourite for

years, and the prices are surprisingly low for this part of town.
Magasin 11 Magasingatan 11. Funky Americana-themed coffee shop which does the best espresso in town as well as delicious milkshakes.

Restaurants

Cyrano Prinsgatan 7. An authentic Provençal bistro that also does great-value pizza, this is a cracking local restaurant with a convivial atmosphere.
Gyllene Prag Sveagatan 2. Czech restaurant with a good range of beers and hearty main dishes such as *pilsner schnitzel* (pork in a beer batter).
L'Assassino Andra Långgatan 35. Cool bistro/bar with photo exhibits on the walls and a good-value menu of filling salads and mains such as *moules mariniere* (99kr). Half-price menu on Mon/Tues.
Tintin Café Engelbrektsgatan 22, off Avenyn. This 24-hour, Tintin-themed diner is popular among students and late-night drinkers. A fun experience at 4am on a Saturday.

Drinking and nightlife

Kelly's Andra Långgatan 20. Not the most stylish bar in town but wildly popular with students, attracted by cheap beer and vegan food.
Nefertiti Hvitfeldtsplatsen 6 Ⓦ www.nefertiti.se. The best place to see live jazz and world music, with impressive acts visiting from overseas as well as local bands.
Publik Andra Långgatan 28. Stripped-down decor and an underground feel. There's live music and poetry readings on occasion, plus the kitchen turns out some good, cheap dishes.
Pusterviksbaren Järntorgsgatan 14. Currently Gothenburg's hippest bar/club, with live music or DJs most nights and a friendly, unpretentious feel.

Moving on

Ferry Frederikshavn, Denmark (4–8 daily; 3hr 15min); Kiel, Germany (1 daily; 14hr).
Train Copenhagen (10 daily; 3hr 35min); Helsingborg (10 daily; 2hr 10min); Lund (10 daily; 3hr); Malmö (10 daily; 3hr); Oslo (3 daily; 4hr); Stockholm (hourly; 3hr by X2000, 5hr by Intercity).

HELSINGBORG

At **HELSINGBORG** only a narrow sound separates Sweden from Denmark; indeed, Helsingborg was Danish for most of the Middle Ages, with its castle controlling the southern regions of what is now Sweden. Fought over for centuries, the Swedes finally took it back for good in 1710. While most visitors arrive by ferry and then get straight on a train to somewhere else, it is worth a couple of hours of exploration, particularly the dramatically redeveloped harbour area which has breathed new life into the town.

What to see and do

Helsingborg's standout sight is the strikingly modern **Henry Dunkers Kulturehus** (daily except Mon 10am–5pm, till 8pm on Thurs; 70kr), an arts centre/exhibition space and history museum housed in a prize-winning white building by Danish architect, Kim Utzon. Just to the north is a strip of harbourside café-bars.

The town's **kärnan** or keep (June–Aug daily 11am–7pm; Sept–May daily except Mon 9/11am–3/4pm; 20kr) can't really compete with Denmark's Elsinore castle just across the water. Much of it has fallen into ruin, with a fourteenth-century brick tower, the only survivor from the original castle. The views from the top are worth the entrance fee however. Off Stortorget, the town's main square, and along **Norra Storgatan** are Helsingborg's oldest buildings, attractive seventeenth- and eighteenth-century merchants' houses with quiet courtyards.

Arrival and information

Arrival Apart from the HH Ferries passenger ferry from Helsingør (Denmark), which pulls up across an arm of the docks, and the Acelink ferries, which arrive on Hamntorget, all ferries, trains and buses arrive at Knutpunkten, the harbourside central terminal.
Tourist office It's just a couple of minutes' walk from the central terminal to the tourist office inside the town hall at the corner of Stortorget and Järnvägsgatan (Mon–Fri 9/10am–6/8pm, Sat 9/10am–2/5pm; mid-June to Aug also Sun 10am–3pm; Ⓣ 042/10 43 50, Ⓦ www.helsingborg.se), which has free city maps and masses of brochures.

Accommodation

Helsingborgs Vandrarhem Järnvägsgatan 39 ⓣ042/14 58 50, ⓦwww.hbgturist.com. Cheap, central and very comfortable youth hostel. Dorms 195kr, rooms 359kr.

Råå Vallar Camping Kustgatan, Råå Vallar ⓣ042/10 76 80, ⓦwww.camping.se. Pretty waterfront site 5km south of Helsingborg. Take bus #1 from outside the Rådhus. 200kr.

Eating and drinking

Bara Vara Nedre Långvinkelsgatan 15. Great decor, fun atmosphere and a good selection of cocktails too. Open summer only Thurs–Sat only.

Bishops Arms Södra Storgatan 2. English-style pub that's a firm favourite with locals after work. Fullers and Sam Adams beers available.

Café Annorledes Södra Storgatan 15. The loopily traditional decor includes mannequins dressed in vintage clothes. Coffee, cakes and sandwiches at low prices.

Moving on

Ferry Helsingør, Denmark (3 hourly; 25min).

Train Gothenburg (10 daily; 2hr 10min); Lund (hourly; 40min); Malmö (hourly; 45min).

MALMÖ

Linked to continental Europe by the impressive Öresund bridge, **MALMÖ** is Sweden's most cosmopolitan city. More than a hundred languages are spoken on its streets and you'll find Turkish and Thai food as popular as meatballs and herring. In fact, Malmö didn't even become Swedish until 1658 having been Denmark's second city for generations. Today it's the country's third largest town, an attractive mix of chocolate-box medieval squares and striking modern architecture, most notably the Turning Torso skyscraper, Scandinavia's tallest building.

What to see and do

Mostly flat and home to an extensive cycle network, Malmö is the perfect place to hire a bike and explore at leisure. Most of the sights are squeezed into the compact medieval centre although the **beaches** and modern **docklands** to the north make a tempting excursion. South of the old centre is the bohemian district of **Möllevångstorget**, where you'll find many of the best places to eat and drink.

Stortorget

The city's main square, **Stortorget** is as impressive today as it must have been when it was first laid out in the sixteenth century. It's flanked on one side by the imposing **Rådhus**, built in 1546 and covered with statuary and spiky accoutrements. To its rear stands the fine Gothic **St Petri Kyrka** (daily 10am–6pm; free) while to the south runs **Södergatan**, Malmö's main pedestrianized shopping street.

Lilla Torg

A late sixteenth-century spin-off from Stortorget, **Lilla Torg** is everyone's favourite part of the city – indeed, it's been voted the most popular square in Sweden. Lined with cafés and restaurants, it's usually pretty crowded at night, with drinkers kept warm under patio heaters and bars handing out free blankets. On the south side of the square, through an archway, is the **Form/Design Centre** (Tues–Fri 11am–5pm, Sat & Sun noon–5pm, ⓦwww.formdesigncenter.com; free) a showcase for painfully trendy Swedish furniture, textiles and lighting with a pleasant "literary café" upstairs.

Malmöhus

A ten-minute walk west of Lilla Torg lies the **Malmöhus** (June–Aug 10am–4pm; Sept–May noon–4pm; 40kr), a low fortified castle defended by a wide moat and two circular keeps. Built by Danish king Christian III in 1536, the castle was later used for a time as a prison, but it now houses the **Malmö Museums**, a rather disparate collection

Turning Torso, beaches & Öresund Bridge

MALMÖ

EATING, DRINKING & NIGHTLIFE

Bageri Café	2	Hai	3
Barista Fair Trade Coffee	4	Mello Yello	1
Debaser	5	Moccasin	8
Green Mango	6	Möllan	7
		Red Dog	9

ACCOMMODATION

Cityroom and Apartments	B
Malmö Camping and Feriecenter	A
Malmö City Hostel	C
Malmö STF Vandrarhem	D

Folketspark, Möllevångstorget, 5, 6 & 7

Konsthall & D

of exhibitions on everything from geology to photography – and an aquarium, too. The pleasant grounds, the **Kungsparken**, are peppered with small lakes and an old windmill.

The Turning Torso and Öresund Bridge

A good twenty-minute walk or five-minute cycle ride north of the station is Malmö's most iconic sight, the 190-metre-high **Towering Torso** skyscraper. A spiralling helix of glass and steel, the structure was completed in 2005 and now lords it over the sea towards Denmark. A small museum next door shows a short film on the tower and its architect, Santiago Calatreva. Surrounding the tower are lots of modern apartments and cycle pathways. Heading coastwards takes you to a viewpoint of the **Öresund Bridge**, the seventeen-kilometre engineering marvel that links the city with Copenhagen, a journey of just 20min by train.

The beach

A pleasant bike ride or longish walk west of the Turning Torso brings you to **Ribersborg** or "Ribban", Malmö's artificial sandy beach created in the 1920s. A long access path, busy in summer with rollerbladers and cyclists, leads down to the sections of beach, each indicated by a jetty.

Möllevångstorget

Known as **Möllan** to the locals, this giant cobbled square was once the heart of working-class Malmö. By day it hosts a busy market with everything from cassava to Arabic sweets on sale while by night it becomes "alternative"

hang-out of choice for the city's young and impoverished.

Arrival and information

Air Copenhagen/Kastrup Airport (see p.320) is just 20min by train from Malmö's Central Station; trains leave round the clock and cost 78kr. Malmö's own airport Sturup, is used mostly by Swedish charter airlines flying to the Med and the odd Wizzair service to Poland. It's 30km southeast of the city; buses to the centre are timed to coincide with arrivals (40min; 99kr; Ⓦ www.flygbussarna.se).
Bus The main bus terminal is outside Central Station, in Centralplan.
Train All trains currently terminate at Central Station, including the local Pågatåg services that run from Helsingborg and Lund (rail passes are valid). A new underground station linking with the Öresund bridge is set to open in December 2010.
Tourist office Inside the station (Mon–Fri 9am–5/6/7pm, Sat 9/10am–2/3/5pm; May–Sept also Sun 10am–3/5pm; Ⓣ 040/34 12 00, Ⓦ www.malmö.se/turist). They sell the Malmö Card.
Discount passes The Malmö Card (130kr/160kr/190kr for one/two/three days) gives free museum entry, free travel on city buses, a free bus tour by bus and ten percent off the airport bus.
Internet Surfer's Paradise, Amiralsgatan 14, or Cyber Space, Engelbrektsgatan 13a.

City transport

Bus City buses are run by Ⓦ www.skanetrafiken.se; tickets start at 15kr and route maps are available at the tourist office.
Cycle rental Fridhems Cykelaffär, Tessins vag 13. Cycles from 75kr per day (50kr with Malmö Card). They're located about two blocks along Tessins vag which runs west from the castle.

Accommodation

Cityroom and Apartments Amiralsgatan 12 Ⓣ 040/795 94, Ⓦ www.cityroom.se. Bargain-priced double rooms (shared bathroom) and en-suite studios for rent in this classy apartment complex just south of the old centre. 495kr.
Malmö Camping and Feriecenter Strandgatan 101 Ⓣ 040/15 51 65, Ⓦ www.malmö.se/malmö-camping. Idyllic beachside campsite with views of the Öresund bridge. Bus #12B from Central Station. 150kr.
Malmö City Hostel Rönngatan 1 Ⓣ 040/611 62 20. Bright, comfortable and well-equipped STF hostel 1km south of the centre in a great location for nightlife and shops; take buses #2, #5, #7 or #8 to Davidshall. Dorms 180, rooms 360.
Malmö STF Vandrarhem Backavägen 18 Ⓣ 040/822 20. The city's second STF is really a fall-back option if everything else is booked up – it has all the facilities you'd expect but is inconveniently located, about 4km from the centre of town – take bus #21 from Central Station. Dorms 150kr, rooms 345kr.

Eating

Bageri Café Saluhallen, off Lilla Torg. Stop off here at lunchtime to buy filled baguettes and bagels.
Barista Fair Trade Coffee Södra Förstadsg 24. Chow down on lactose-free vegan muffins and drink certified organic espresso at this do-gooding café chain, now expanding nationwide.
Green Mango Ystadsgatan 10. Reliable Thai mains (from 69kr) and salads served in a pleasant setting off Möllevångstorget. If you're feeling brave try one of three-chilli dishes on the menu.
Hai Davidshallstorg 5. The best sushi in town (portions start at 40kr) is served in this buzzing restaurant on elegant Davidshallstorg.
Red Dog Södra Förstadsgatan 84a. Cheap and cheerful, studenty café with sandwiches from 35kr and wireless internet.

Drinking and nightlife

Debaser Norra Parkgatan 2 Ⓦ www.debaser.se. The Malmö branch of the popular Stockholm club/venue. Live music, DJ nights, dancing and drinking until late.
Mello Yello Lilla Torg 1. The best of Lilla Torg's many bar/restaurants, though there's not so much to choose between them.
Moccasin Fersensvägen 14. Loungey hang-out just south of the centre with comfy sofas and friendly staff; drinks are pricey but there's free finger-food at the bar.
Möllan Bergsgatan 37. Somewhere halfway between a pub and a bar, with outdoor seating and good, reasonably priced food.

Moving on

Train Copenhagen (every 20min; airport 21min, city 35min); Gothenburg (10 daily; 3hr); Helsingborg (at least hourly; 50min); Lund (at least hourly; 15min); Oslo (1 daily; 7hr 30min), Stockholm (hourly; 4hr 30min).

LUND

Just a short hop inland from Malmö, the university town of **LUND** makes for a pleasant afternoon wander. A recent survey named it the best place to live in Sweden and it's not hard to see why with its quaint cobbled streets, relaxed pace of life and mix of well-heeled residents and students from across the world. The main sight in town is the impressive, twin-towered **cathedral** (Mon–Fri 8am–6pm, Sat & Sun 9.30am), one of Scandinavia's finest medieval buildings. Inside is a quirky attraction: a fifteenth-century astronomical clock from which two mechanical knights pop out and clash swords as the clock strikes (daily Mon–Sat noon & 3pm, Sun 1pm & 3pm).

Surrounding the cathedral are several grand nineteenth-century buildings belonging to the university. Also nearby is the entrance to the vast **Kulturen** open-air museum (May–Aug daily 11am–6pm; Sept–April Tues–Sun noon–4pm; 70kr), a village in itself full of perfectly preserved cottages and permanent exhibitions covering everything from Viking weapons to Modernist design.

The **train station** is on the west edge of town, an easy walk from the centre. The **tourist office** (summer Mon–Fri 10am–6pm, Sat & Sun 10am–2pm; winter Mon–Fri 10am–5pm; ⓣ046/35 50 40, ⓦwww.lund.se) is opposite the cathedral at Kyrkogatan. The cheapest option for food is to put together a picnic at the Saluhallen on Mårtenstorget. Otherwise there are plenty of **cafés** around the old centre including the historic *Conditori Lundagård* at Kyrkogatan 17. Rail buffs may be enticed to spend the night on board the *Taget*, a 1940s train converted in inimitable Swedish style into a **youth hostel** (ⓣ046/14 28 20, ⓦwww.trainhostel.com; dorms 160kr, room 320kr). Located just behind the station, the sleeper carriages are a little pokey but a lot of fun.

GOTLAND

Sweden's largest island, **GOTLAND** is packed with historical intrigue, lined with great beaches, and, in summer at least, full of partying students. The star attraction is the beautifully preserved medieval town of **Visby** though the rest of the island is also well worth exploring, especially by bike.

What to see and do

Once the main trading centre of the Baltic, **VISBY** is an unspoilt gem of a town full of elegantly ruined churches and cute half-timbered houses. The best approach is to simply get lost in its warren of cobbled alleyways, using the thirteenth-century walls circling the town as a reference point. After a while you'll find your way to the main open space, Stora Torget, lined with bars and restaurants.

Visby's museums

You can learn everything you need to know about the island's past from the **Gotlands Fornsal** (May to mid-Sept daily 10am–5pm; mid-Sept to April daily except Mon noon–4pm; 75kr), a well-presented series of exhibitions covering everything from Viking rune stones and gold to the recent macabre discovery of shallow graves holding the bones of executed townsfolk from the Middle Ages.

Just opposite the museum is Visby's art gallery or **Konstmuseum** (Tues–Sun noon–4pm; 50kr), mostly focused on paintings depicting the island by residents themselves.

Visby cathedral and church ruins

Visby's graceful **cathedral**, St Maria (daily 8am–6.30/9pm; free), is a short walk west of Stora Torget. Its three towers, two octagonal and one square, can be seen for kilometres around. Of the town's ruined churches, the most

impressive and photogenic are **St Hans** on **St Hansgatan** and St Katarina on the east side of Stora Torget.

The rest of the island

The best beach near Visby is **Tofta Strand**, 20km south (take bus #10 or consider cycling; see below). There are plenty of others though, particularly on the east side of the island, and it can be worth hiring a car (see below) to explore at leisure. With your own wheels it's worth taking a trip up to **Fårö**, Gotland's tiny sister island, where you'll find the beach resort of Suder-sandsviken, and the mysterious-looking sea stacks known as Langhammers on the wind-battered north coast.

Arrival and information

Air The airport is 5km north of Visby. An infrequent bus service runs into the centre of town; taxis should cost 120–150kr.

Ferry Ferries arrive at the harbour, a 10min walk west of Visby.

Tourist office Skeppsbron 4–6, near the ferry terminal (mid-June to mid-Aug daily 8am–7pm; mid-Aug to mid-June Mon–Fri 8am–5pm, Sat & Sun 10am–4pm; ⓣ0498/20 17 00, ⓦwww.gotland.info).

Internet Gamecenter, Hamngatan 4 (summer only). Free wi-fi available at the university café (see opposite).

Island transport

Bus The main bus terminal is beyond the town wall to the southeast, on Kung Magnus väg.

Cycle hire Gotlands Cykeluthyrning, just behind the tourist office (ⓣ0498/21 41 33, ⓦwww.gotlandscykeluthyrning; from 75kr per day).

Car hire Mickes Biluthyrning (ⓣ0498/26 62 62, ⓦwww.mickesbiluthyrning.se; 250kr per day). Good selection of old VWs and the like at bargain prices.

Accommodation

STF Hostel Visby/Rävhagen ⓣ498/24 04 50. Quiet, woodland-cabin-style hostel, a couple of kilometres from t.he town walls. Dorms 175kr, rooms 400kr

Visby Logi St Hansgatan 31/Hästgatan 1430 ⓣ070/752 20 55, ⓦwww.visbylogi.se. Two beautiful historic homes in the heart of Visby converted into double and single rooms (shared bathroom), all decorated in tasteful greys and whites. No breakfast but kitchen facilities available. Doubles 650kr.

Visby Prison Hostel Skeppsbron 1 ⓣ0498/20 50 60, ⓦwww.gotland.net/visbyfangelse. Striking but shabby youth hostel in a converted prison. The dorms face onto a courtyard and the showers are just across – not great in bad weather. Dorms 170kr, rooms 350kr.

Visby Strandby & Snäcks Camping Holiday houses and a pleasant campsite just beside Snäck-viken beach, about 4km from the town centre. 26kr.

Eating, drinking and nightlife

Black Sheep Arms St Hansgatan 51. English-style pub serving up tasty fish and chips and a wide selection of beers; a favourite with locals and tourists alike.

Gutekällaren Stora Torget ⓦwww.gutekallaren.com. Housed in a historic building, this club/bar complex is heaving with bronzed, dressed-up twenty-somethings in summer and attracts Sweden's top DJ talent. Wed–Sun only.

GETTING TO GOTLAND

Visby is accessible by **ferry** from the mainland ports of **Nynäshamn**, a one-hour train ride south of Stockholm (change at Västerhaninge), and **Oskarhamn**, five hours by train from Gothenburg. Both crossings take around three hours and are run by Destination Gotland (ⓣ0771/22 33 00, ⓦwww.destinationgotland.se). For the cheapest fares (one-way tickets start at 149kr for students or 186kr for non-students), book 21 days in advance; regular fares cost around 25 percent more.

Two **airlines**, Gotlandsflyg (ⓦwww.gotlandsflyg.se) and Skyways (ⓦwww.skyways.se) fly to Gotland, with services all year round from Stockholm (Bromma, Arlanda and Skavsta airports) and summer flights from Gothenburg and cities as far afield as Oslo and Hamburg. From Stockholm you're looking at a minimum of 450kr one way, slightly cheaper outside June–Aug.

Munkkallaren Stora Torget Ⓦwww.munkkallaren.se. Visby nightlife stalwart with live bands (usually leather-clad Metallica clones) as well as house music later in the evening. Closed Sun.
University Café Cramérgatan. Part of the Gotland University campus just south of the old centre, this light, airy café offers the cheapest lunch deal in town with a choice of mains, coffee and drink for 70kr; non-students welcome. Mon–Fri lunch only.
Strykjärnet Wallersplats 3 Ⓦwww.creperielogi.se. Quality crêpes (around 85kr) served in a narrow iron-shaped building on the corner of Adelgatan and Hästgatan. There's a lovely terrace out back and a rather chic double room (1500kr) for hire upstairs (ask if you can have a nose around).

Central Sweden

The rural Sweden of most visitors' imaginations begins in the central areas of the interior: vast tracts of forest, peaceful lakes and log cabins. Deep-blue **Lake Siljan**, at the heart of the province of Dalarna, is a major draw, particularly in midsummer when it's a focus of festivities celebrating the long days and warm weather. From here one of Europe's classic rail journeys, the Inlandsbanan, begins its slow route north to the Arctic Circle via the towns of Orsa and Östersund.

LAKE SILJAN

Lake Siljan (Ⓦwww.siljan.se) holds a special, misty-eyed place in the Swedish heart. Thousands head here in summer to stay at its iconic red lakeside cabins, potter around in canoes and kayaks and hike in the surrounding countryside. If you happen to be here around Midsummer's Night, head to the town of **Leksand** at the south end of the lake, which holds a huge festival with maypole dances and longboat races.

Mora, at the north end of Siljan, has more facilities and is the starting point for the Inlandsbanan rail route (see box below). The **tourist office** (Mon–Fri 10am–5pm, Sat 10am–2pm, closed Sun; Ⓣ0250/59 20 20) at the train station gives out information on activities around the lake, and the central HI **hostel** is at Fredsgatan 6 (Ⓣ0250/381 96, Ⓔinfo@maalkullann.se; dorms 190kr, rooms 350kr).

ORSA

The Inlandsbanan, having begun in Mora (see above), makes its first stop at **ORSA**, fifteen minutes up the line, where the nearby **Grönklitt Bear Park** (mid-May to mid-Sept daily 10am–3/6pm; 160kr; Ⓦwww.orsagronklitt.se; bus #118) provides the best chance to see the brown bears that roam over large swathes of central Sweden. The STF **hostel** at the park (Ⓣ0250/462 00; dorm beds 240kr) has good facilities.

ÖSTERSUND

ÖSTERSUND, halfway point on the Inlandsbanan, is a very provincial but

THE INLANDSBANAN

The **Inlandsbanan** (Inland Railway), which cuts a route through 1300km of Sweden's best-looking scenery, ranks amongst the most enthralling of European train journeys. The quaint, toy-like line links central Sweden with Gällivare in the north, a two-day trip if attempted without a break. The railway (Ⓣ0771/53 53 53, Ⓦwww.inlandsbanan.se) operates from June to the end of August only.
Ticket fares are calculated per kilometre – for example, Mora to Östersund costs 395kr, Östersund to Gällivare is 918kr; reserving a seat costs 50kr.
Discounts and rail cards InterRail and Eurail pass holders travel for free apart from seat reservation fees. Students receive a 25 percent discount. The Inlandsbanan Card (1450kr) offers unlimited travel on the line for fourteen days.

welcoming town on the shores of **Lake Storsjön** (Great Lake). It's most famous for the Loch Ness-style monster, the Storsjöodjur, said to inhabit the lake. More prosaically the town is also a major inland rail junction: as well as the Inlandsbanan, routes head west to Stockholm and east to Trondheim in Norway.

What to see and do

Apart from monster-spotting (there are eight "observation points" along the lakeshore), the main thing to do is visit **Jamtli** (11am–5pm; closed Mon Sept–May; 90kr), an impressive, partly open-air **museum**, fifteen minutes' walk north from the centre along Rådhusgatan. The key exhibits are the ninth-century **Överhogdal Viking tapestries**, whose simple hand-woven patterns of horses, dogs and other beasts are quite breathtaking.

From the **harbour** you can take the bridge over the lake to the rather idyllic **Frösön** island, site of the original Viking settlement here.

Arrival and information

Bus The main bus station is on Gustavs III Torg, off Rådhusgatan.
Train It's a 5min walk north into the centre from Ostersund Central train station.
Tourist office Rådhusgatan 44 (Mon–Fri 9am–5pm; June–Aug until 7/8pm and also Sat & Sun 10am–3/7pm; ⓣ063/14 40 01, ⓦwww.turist.ostersund.se). They sell the Östersundskortet, valid for three days (June–Aug; 270kr), giving free access to the town's sights, free bike rental and other discounts.
Internet Free internet in the municipal library on Rådhusgatan, opposite the bus station.

Accommodation

Frösö Camping ⓣ063/432 54. The most picturesque of Östersund's campsites. June to early Aug only; bus #3 or #4 from the centre. 120kr.
Frösötonets Häbäge ⓣ063/51 57 67, ⓦwww.frosotornet.se. Over on Frösön island this hostel is made up of wooden, turf-roofed cabins; surprisingly comfortable. Dorms 150kr.
Jamtli Hostel ⓣ063/12 20 60, ⓦwww.jamtli.com. Quaint, appealing hostel in the grounds of Jamtli museum. Booking ahead is essential in summer. 175kr.

Eating and drinking

Captain Cook Hamngatan 9. Wood-panelled drinking haunt and restaurant – mains around 100kr – with a jumble of memorabilia on the walls. Live music on Wed.
News Samuel Permansgatan 9. Possibly Östersund's nicest hang-out, this breezy, attractively designed bar serves decent food and fills up at the weekend with a young crowd.
Wedermarks Café Prästgatan 27. Popular, congenial, traditional café with a cosy downstairs lunch bar and an elegant upstairs seating area.

Moving on

Train Stockholm (5 daily; 6hr); Trondheim (2 daily; 4hr) Uppsala (3 daily; 4hr 30min).

Northern Sweden

Northern Sweden – Swedish Lapland – is the wildest, strangest part of the country, worlds away from the busy and cosmopolitan south. The region is famous for the northern lights and midnight sun as well as the Sámi people – reindeer herders who were once the sole inhabitants here. The Sámi are still visible, especially in the small town of **Jokkmokk**, which almost straddles the Arctic Circle. A couple of hundred kilometres further north, **Kiruna** is the access point for the celebrated **IceHotel**, a fascinating if chilly sight, or even a once-in-a-lifetime stay if you're feeling rich.

The most atmospheric way to reach the far north of the country is the Inlandsbanan rail line (see box, p.1179) although you can also get here via regular rail services from Stockholm and by air to Kiruna.

THE ARCTIC CIRCLE AND JOKKMOKK

After a brief stop at Arvidsjaur, the Inlandsbanan finally crosses the **Artic Circle** at a point 7km south of Jokkmokk. Painted white rocks indicate this latitudinal milestone making it an essential photo stop; killjoys will point out that the real Arctic Circle (66°33) has shifted a further kilometre north owing to changes in the earth's orbit but no one seems to care. **JOKKMOKK** itself is a welcome oasis after hours on a tiny train. The town is a renowned handicraft centre, with a Sámi educational college keeping the language and culture alive and a vibrant winter market.

What to see and do

The **Ájtte Museum** (Mon–Fri 9/10–4/6pm, Sat & Sun 9am/noon–4/6pm; Oct–April closed Sat; 50kr) on Kyrkgatan is the place to bone up on Samí culture. Have a glance, too, at the so-called **Lapp Kyrka**, enclosed by a wide wooden fence, in which corpses were interred during winter, waiting for the thaw when the Sámi could go out and dig graves.

Jokkmokk's **Great Winter Market** (first Thurs, Fri & Sat of Feb) is the best and busiest time to visit; you'll need to book accommodation a good six months in advance. A smaller, less traditional autumn fair at the end of August is an easier option.

Arrival and information

Tourist office Stortorget 4 (mid-June to mid-Aug daily 9am–6pm; mid-Aug to mid-June Mon–Fri 8.30am–4pm; ⓣ0971/222 50, ⓦwww.turism .jokkmokk.se).

Accommodation

Jokkmokk Camping Center ⓣ0971/123 70, ⓦwww.jokkmokkcampingcenter. Family-friendly site with cabins and heated swimming pools in a lakeside location 3km east of Jokkmokk. Camping 120kr, cabins 500kr.

STF Åsgård Vandrarhem Åsgatan 20 ⓣ0971/559 77, ⓦ www.jokkmokkhostel.com. Just opposite the tourist office, Jokkmokk's youth hostel is housed in a rather grand 1920s house with a sauna in the basement. Dorms 150kr, rooms 305kr.

KIRUNA

With its nearby airport, rail connections to Norway and proximity to the *IceHotel* (see box below), **KIRUNA**, 145km north of the Arctic Circle has become the unlikely tourist hub for Swedish Lapland. The town is dominated by its iron ore mine, the world's largest, and became a focus during World War II, when the supply of iron was fought over by the Germans and Allies. Kiruna has lately achieved modest international fame after it was announced that portions of the town would have to be moved 4km northwest, to avoid them collapsing into the **mine** beneath.

What to see and do

Guided tours of the **mine** (daily 11am & 3pm; book at the tourist office; 280kr),

THE ICEHOTEL

If you've made it this far north, a visit to Sweden's world-famous **IceHotel** (ⓦwww.icehotel.com; bus #501) 17km west of Kiruna in the small village of Jukkasjärvi, is a tempting prospect. Although the hotel operates year-round, the obvious time to come is December to April when the fairytale-like ice structure is in place; one-hour tours (295kr) allow visitors a look inside the rooms.

If you can stump up around 2000kr per person you could consider spending a night in its igloo-like conditions; temperatures hover around –5°C to –8°C although you'll be toasty warm, wrapped up tight in an army sleeping bag and lying on reindeer skins. You can also stay in the hotel's regular, heated chalets (winter prices start at 1350kr per person per night with large discounts in summer).

run by LKAB, the mining company, are truly fascinating and slightly spooky.

Another unusual day-trip from Kiruna is to **Esrange**, a civilian space centre that launches and monitors satellites (tours in English Tues & Thurs 9.15am; book at the tourist office; 390kr). Anyone who had even the most passing childhood interest in astronauts and spaceships will enjoy this glimpse into a genuine scientific workplace.

Arrival and information

Air Kiruna airport is 10km from the city. An airport bus (40kr) runs during the summer; otherwise take a shared taxi (125kr/person).

Train The train station is at the western edge of town, on Bangårdsvägen. It's a 10min uphill walk into the centre from here.

Bus The bus station is at the top of Skolgatan.

Tourist office Right in the town centre, on the main square at Lars Janssonsgatan 17 (Mon–Fri 8.30am–5/6/8pm, Sat till 3/6pm, open Sun till 5pm mid-June to mid-Aug; ⓣ0980/188 80, ⓦwww.lappland.se).

Accommodation

Camp Ripan Campingvägen 5 ⓣ0980/630 00, ⓦwww.ripan.se/en. Family-oriented campsite with an on-site restaurant and swimming pool. Between December and April you can even hire an igloo for the night. Camping 205kr, cabins 1200kr.

Kiruna Youth Hostel Bergmästaregatan 7 ⓣ0980/171 95, ⓦkirunahostel.com. Sociable and well-equipped STF hostel just round the corner from the bus station, with TV, sauna and kitchen facilities. Dorms 160kr, rooms 390kr.

Yellow House Hantverkaregatan 25 ⓣ0980/137 50, ⓦwww.yellowhouse.nu. Popular independent hostel across not one but two yellow houses. Advance booking recommended. Dorms 170kr, rooms 440kr.

Eating and drinking

Momma's Steakhouse Lars Janssonsgatan 15. Rowdy bar/restaurant in the *Scandic Hotel* with live music on Wed. Drinks are pricier than you'd expect.

O'Leary's Föreningsgatan 11. This uninspiring chain pub/restaurant is one of the liveliest nightlife choices in Kiruna, with friendly staff and a good if greasy food menu.

Safari Attractive, cosy café serving buns, coffee and sandwiches, near the bus station. Outdoor terrace in summer. Closed Sun.

Moving on

Train Narvik, Norway (2 daily; 3hr); Stockholm (2 daily; 17hr).

THE KUNGSLEDDEN TRAIL

Sweden's premier trek, the **Kungsledden** (Kings Trail) winds through 500km of wilderness from Abisko, 98km west of Kiruna, south to Hemavan. Mountain huts are spaced every 10–20km along the route to allow for a day's walk between them. The northern section of the trail between Abisko and Kebnekaise (86km) is the most popular and well worth tackling if you have around a week to spare. **Absiko** is just an hour and twenty minutes by train from Kiruna on the Narvik line and is the location of the *Abisko Mountain Lodge* (ⓦwww.abiskomountainlodge.se; dorms 230kr, rooms 750kr), starting point for the trail. For more information on each section of the trail visit ⓦwww.stfturist.se.

Switzerland

HIGHLIGHTS

ZÜRICH: trendy bars, cutting-edge clubs and a beautiful medieval old town

LAUSANNE: lively and extremely hilly town in a beautiful setting on Lake Geneva

JUNGFRAU REGION: breathtaking scenery plus unlimited hiking and adventure sports

WORLD'S HIGHEST BUNGEE JUMP: a death-defying 220m off the Verzasca Dam

THE MATTERHORN: towering, world-famous mountain peak, with guaranteed skiing and snowboarding year-round

ROUGH COSTS

DAILY BUDGET basic €45/occasional treat €70

DRINK Beer €4

FOOD Fondue €16

HOSTEL/BUDGET HOTEL €20/€70

TRAVEL Train: Geneva–Zürich (2hr 45min) €47; bus: Luzern–Interlaken Ost (1hr 50min) €28

FACT FILE

POPULATION 7.5 million

AREA 41,293 sq km

LANGUAGE German, French, Italian, Romansch

CURRENCY Swiss Franc (Fr.)

CAPITAL Bern (population: 128,041)

INTERNATIONAL PHONE CODE ⓣ41

Introduction

All the quaint stereotypes are true – cheese, chocolate, clocks, obsessive punctuality – but there's much more to Switzerland than this. The major cities are cosmopolitan and vibrant, transport links are excellent, and the scenery will take your breath away. Switzerland is diverse and multilingual – almost everyone speaks some English along with at least one of the official languages (German, French, Italian and, in the south-east, Romansch).

The most visited Alpine area is the picturesque **Bernese Oberland**, but the loftiest Alps are further south, where the Toblerone-peaked **Matterhorn** looms above **Zermatt**. In the southeast, forested mountain slopes surround chic **St Moritz**. Of the northern German-speaking cities, **Zürich** has tons of sightseeing and nightlife and provides easy access to the tiny principality of **Liechtenstein** on the Rhine. **Basel** and the capital, **Bern**, are quieter, each with an attractive historic core, while **Luzern** lies in an appealing setting of lakes and mountains. In the French-speaking west, the cities of **Lake Geneva** – notably **Geneva** and **Lausanne** – make up the heart of Suisse-Romande. South of the Alps, Italian-speaking Ticino can seem a world apart, particularly the palm-fringed lakeside resorts of **Lugano** and **Locarno**. Wherever you head to there is something for budget travellers, whether it's losing yourself in the streets of the old towns, taking in the breath-taking scenery or joining the locals for *rösti* in the beerhalls.

CHRONOLOGY

800–58 BC The Helvetian Celtic tribe inhabit the area of present day Switzerland.
58 BC Julius Caesar conquers the Helvetians.
1291 AD Three valleys unite against Habsburg rule with some success; they form the basis of the Swiss Confederation.
1388 The Swiss Confederation defeats the Habsburgs.
1536 Protestant Reformation in Switzerland led by Calvin.
1719 Liechtenstein becomes an independent principality of the Holy Roman Empire.
1803 The Swiss start to produce chocolate.
1864 Red Cross founded in Geneva.
1866 Liechtenstein gains full independence.
1914 Switzerland remains neutral during WWI.
1920 The League of Nations headquarters are based in Geneva.
1921 Liechtenstein adopts Swiss currency.
1939–1945 Switzerland remains neutral during WWII. Neutrality tainted by the acceptance of Nazi plunder by Swiss banks.
1959 A political agreement known as the "magic formula" is established between four parties in order to share power.
1971 Swiss women are among the last in Europe to gain the vote.
1993 Liechtenstein elects Europe's youngest leader, Mario Frick, at the tender age of 28.
1998 Swiss banks agree to pay $1.25 billion in compensation to Holocaust survivors and families.
2006 Referendum backs plan to make Swiss asylum laws the toughest in Europe. Liechtenstein remeasures its borders discovering it has grown in size by 50 hectares.
2009 Swiss tennis number one, Roger Federer, enters the record books having won fifteen Grand Slam titles.

ARRIVAL

Switzerland's main **airports** are Geneva International Airport (ⓦwww.gva.ch) and Zürich Airport (ⓦwww.zurich-airport.com). Of the no-frills budget airlines, easyJet, based in the UK, flies to Geneva and Basel, whilst Air Berlin flies into Zürich. Travelling to Switzerland from the continent, it's most likely you'll arrive by **train**. Geneva is the terminus for trains from Toulouse,

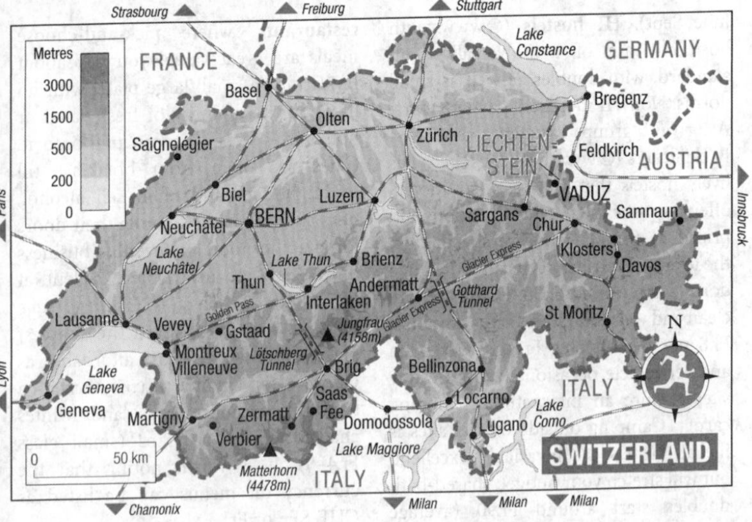

Lyon and the south of France. Services from Paris also arrive at Lausanne and Bern. Travelling via Strasbourg, or heading south from Germany, you're most likely to arrive at one of Basel's international stations. Zürich is the major rail hub for services arriving from Austria and Eastern Europe; overnight trains from both Prague and Vienna terminate here; there's also a direct line from Milan. Undoubtedly the most scenic way to cross the border is by **ferry**; crossing the beautiful Lake Maggiore, from one of the Italian resorts such as Stresa, to arrive in Locarno. Similarly, boats arrive in the far northeast of Switzerland from the German side of Lake Constance.

GETTING AROUND

Public transport is comprehensive. Main stations keep a public copy of the national timetable, which covers all rail, bus, boat and cable-car services. Travelling by **train** is comfortable, hassle-free and extremely scenic, with many mountain routes an attraction in their own right. The main network, run by SBB-CFF-FFS, covers much of the country, but many routes, especially Alpine lines, are operated by smaller companies. **Buses** take over where train track runs out – generally yellow postbuses, which depart from train station forecourts. InterRail and Eurail are valid on SBB and most smaller lines, but the discounts they bring are patchy on boats, cable cars and mountain railways (specified in the text as "IR" for InterRail and "ER" for Eurail). Postbuses are free with all Swiss passes (specified as "SP") – although Alpine routes command a Fr.8–15 supplement, along with seat reservation – but not to Eurail and Inter-Rail pass-holders. Most lake **ferries** run only in summer (June–Sept), and sometimes duplicate routes which can be covered more cheaply and quickly by rail.

ACCOMMODATION

Accommodation isn't as expensive as you might think, and is nearly always excellent. Tourist offices can often book rooms for free in their area; some have display-boards (with a courtesy phone) on the street or at the train station, giving details of every hotel. When you check in, ask for a **guest card**, which can give substantial discounts on local attractions and transport. A **hostel** (Jugendherberge; Auberge de Jeunesse; Albergo/Ostello per la Gioventù) represents great value for money (always book ahead

June–Sept). **HI hostels** (Ⓦwww.youthhostel.ch) are of a universally high standard, with doubles as well as small dorms. Non-HI members pay Fr.6 extra. A rival group known as Swiss Backpackers (Ⓦwww.backpacker.ch) has lively hostels that are less institutional, often in prime town-centre locations and priced to compete; they're specified in the text as SB hostels. Typically a bed in a dorm costs around Fr.30. **Campsites** are clean and well equipped. Prices are about Fr.8 per person plus Fr.8–12 per pitch and per vehicle, occasionally more. Many sites require an international camping carnet. Camping outside official sites is illegal. **Hotels** are invariably excellent, but will stretch your budget; shared-bath doubles start around Fr.90 (average Fr.110), en suites around Fr.135.

FOOD AND DRINK

Eating out in Switzerland can punch a hole in your wallet. Burgers, pizza slices, kebabs and falafel are universal **snack** standbys, as are pork *bratwürst* sausages. Dairy products find their way into most Swiss dishes. Cheese **fondue** – a pot of wine-laced molten cheese into which you dip cubes of bread or potato – is the national dish. Another speciality is **raclette** – piquant molten cheese spread on a plate and scooped up with bread or potato. A Swiss-German staple is **rösti**, grated potatoes topped with cheese, chopped ham or a fried egg. Almost everywhere offers vegetarian alternatives. **Cafés** and **restaurants** usually serve meals at set times (noon–2pm & 6–10pm), with only snacks available in between. To get the best value, make lunch your main meal, and always opt for the dish of the day (*Tagesmenu, Tagesteller, Tageshit*; *plat/assiette du jour*; *piatto del giorno*) – substantial nosh for around Fr.18 or less. The same meal in the evening, or choosing *à la* carte anytime, can cost double. The main department stores, Manor and Globus, both have excellent **self-service restaurants**, where pick-and-choose meals are great value: you pay about Fr.7/13 for a small/large plate, with no limit on the quantity of fresh salad or hot daily special you can pile onto it. Cafés are open from breakfast till midnight/1am and often sell alcohol; **bars** and **pubs** tend to open their doors for late-afternoon and evening business only. **Beers** are invariably excellent, at Fr.5-8 for a glass (*e'Schtange, une pression, una birra*). Even the simplest places have **wine**, most affordably as *Offene Wein, vin ouvert, vino aperto* – a handful of house reds and whites chalked up on a board (small glass Fr.4–5). It is worth noting that the currency on menus can be listed as CHF, SFr. or Fr.

CULTURE AND ETIQUETTE

It's not customary to **tip;** restaurant prices are calculated to include service. If you're impressed by the service you could copy the locals and round up your bill to the nearest franc.

SPORTS AND ACTIVITIES

Spectacular Alpine scenery and an excellent transport infrastructure combine to make Switzerland one of Europe's top destinations for skiing, hiking and climbing. For **skiers and snowboarders**, the choice of prestigious resorts is overwhelming. Verbier is renowned for its challenging on and off-piste skiing, as is Zermatt. The quaint picturesque **resorts** of the Jungfrau region – Grindelwald, Mürren and Wengen – cater better for intermediates; whilst those of the Graubünden – Davos, Klosters and St Moritz–are magnets for the rich and famous. Lift passes vary in price between resorts – typically you should expect to pay Fr.55–65 for a day pass or Fr.265 upwards for six days. Glaciers at Saas Fee and Zermatt stay open for summer

ADVENTURE SPORTS IN SWITZERLAND

With its landscape of mountains, glaciers, deep gorges and fast-flowing rivers, Switzerland is ideal territory for **adventure sports**. Dozens of companies, based in all the main resorts, offer activities through the summer, such as **canyoning** (Fr.110/half-day), **river-rafting** (Fr.110/half-day), **bungee-jumping** (Fr.85 from 100m; Fr.230 from 180m), **zorbing** (where you're strapped inside a giant plastic sphere and rolled down a mountainside; Fr.50), **house-running** (where you hook a rope round yourself and run full-tilt down the side of a tall building; Fr.75), and **flying fox** (where you glide down a vertical cliff on a rope; Fr.80). **Hang-gliding** (Fr.180), **paragliding** (Fr.160) and **skydiving** from 4000m (Fr.430) can all be done alone or in tandem with an instructor. Tourist offices and Ⓦwww.myswitzerland.com have full details.

skiing (Fr.64 for a day lift pass at both). **Hiking** is a major summer sport in Switzerland and with over 65,000km of marked trails, most revealing stunning Alpine vistas, it's not hard to see why. The Jungfrau region is particularly popular as a base for hiking; whilst proximity to the Matterhorn makes Zermatt popular with hikers, as well as more serious climbers. Hiking trails are clearly signed in yellow; more challenging mountain trails in red and white. Ask at the local tourist office for further information or consult Ⓦwww.myswitzerland.com for routes and tips.

COMMUNICATIONS

Main **post offices** tend to open Monday to Friday 7.30am to noon and 1.30 to 6.30pm, Saturday 8 to 11am. Most **public phones** take phonecards (*taxcards*), available from post offices and news kiosks, as well as credit cards; some take Swiss and euro coins. Kiosks also sell good-value discount cards for calling internationally. The expensive **operator** is on Ⓣ111 (domestic) or Ⓣ1141 (international). **Internet access** is widespread, available at cafés (Fr.4–12/hr) or free at many hotels and hostels.

SWITZERLAND AND LIECHTENSTEIN ON THE NET

Ⓦwww.myswitzerland.com Tourist office site – vast, detailed and authoritative.
Ⓦwww.postbus.ch Details of the postbus network, including Alpine routes.
Ⓦwww.museums.ch Information on museums nationwide.
Ⓦwww.swissinfo.org News database in English, with good links.
Ⓦwww.tourismus.li The Liechtenstein tourist board.

EMERGENCIES

Swiss **police** – who may not speak English – are courteous enough. You'll have to pay **hospital** (*Spital, hôpital, ospedale*) bills up-front and claim expenses back later. Every district has one local **pharmacy** (*Apotheke, pharmacie, farmacia*) open outside normal hours; each pharmacy has a sign telling you where the nearest open one is.

INFORMATION

All towns have a **tourist office** (*Verkehrsverein* or *Tourismus*; *Office du Tourisme*; *Ente Turistico*), invariably located near the train station and always extremely useful. Most staff speak English, but **opening hours** in smaller towns allow for a long lunch and can be limited at weekends and in the off-season. All have accommodation and transport lists, and

EMERGENCY NUMBERS

Police Ⓣ117; Fire Ⓣ118; Ambulance Ⓣ144.

STUDENT AND YOUTH DISCOUNTS

If you have an ISIC card, you can take advantage of student discounts at almost all **museums** and galleries (sometimes admission is discounted by as much as fifty percent). Although there is no student discount available for cable-car tickets, during the winter season many resorts offer a youth discount on **lift passes** for under 20s.

maps. *Swiss Backpacker News* (ⓦwww.backpacker.ch) is an excellent free paper, widely available.

MONEY AND BANKS

Both Switzerland and Liechtenstein use the **Swiss franc** (CHF or Fr.), divided into 100 Rappen (Rp), centimes or centisimi (c). There are coins of 5c, 10c, 20c, 50c, Fr.1, Fr.2 and Fr.5, and notes of Fr.10, Fr.20, Fr.50, Fr.100, Fr.200 and Fr.1000. Train stations are the best places for **changing money**. **Banks** usually open Monday to Friday 8.30am to 4.30pm; some in cities and resorts also open Saturday 9am to 4pm. **Post offices** give a similar exchange rate to banks, and **ATMs** are everywhere. Many shops and services, especially in tourist hubs, accept euros. At the time of writing, €1 was roughly equal to Fr.1.50, US$1 to Fr.1.06 and £1 to Fr.1.72.

OPENING HOURS AND HOLIDAYS

Shop hours are Monday to Friday 9am to 6.30pm, Saturday 8.30am to 4pm, sometimes with a lunch break and earlier closing in smaller towns. **Museums** and attractions generally close on Monday. Almost everything is closed on **public holidays**: January 1, Good Friday and Easter Monday, Ascension Day, Whit Monday, December 25 and 26. In Switzerland, shops and banks close for all or part of the national holiday (Aug 1) and on a range of local holidays. Liechtenstein keeps May 1 as a public holiday, and August 15 as the national holiday.

Lake Geneva

French-speaking Switzerland, or Suisse Romande, occupies the western third of the country, comprising the shores of **Lake Geneva** (Lac Léman) and the hills and lakes leading north almost to Basel. The ambience here is thoroughly Gallic: historical animosity between Geneva and France has nowadays given way to a yearning on the part of most francophone Swiss to abandon their bumpkin compatriots in the east and embrace the EU. **Geneva**, at the southwestern tip of the lake, was once a haven for free thinkers from all over Europe; now it's a city of diplomats and big business, but head to the lake on a warm day to experience its more relaxed side. Halfway around the lake, **Lausanne** is full of young people; it's a cultured, energetic town acclaimed as the skateboarding capital of Europe. Further east, **Vevey** is an excellent base to explore the lake's shore, its vineyards and the stunning medieval **Château de Chillon**, which drew Byron and the Romantic poets. **Mont Blanc**, Western Europe's highest mountain (4807m), is visible from Geneva city centre, while Vevey and neighbouring **Montreux** have breathtaking views across the water to the French Alps. On a sunny day, the train ride around the beautiful northern shore is memorably scenic, but the lake's excellent boat service (IR no discount; ER & SP free; Ⓦwww.cgn.ch) helps bring home the full grandeur of the setting.

GENEVA

The Puritanism of **GENEVA** (Genève) is inextricably linked with the city's struggle for independence. By the time the city's independence from the dukes of Savoy was won in 1602, its religious zeal had painted it as the "Protestant Rome". Geneva remained outside the Swiss Confederation until 1815, and acquired a reputation for joylessness which it still struggles to shake off. Today, while sharply focused on its prominent role in international diplomacy and big business there is still plenty for budget travellers, with its many galleries and beautiful Old Town.

What to see and do

The **Rive Gauche**, on the south bank, takes in a grid of waterfront streets which comprise the main shopping and business districts and the adjacent high ground of the Old Town. Further south lies **Carouge**, characterized by artisans' shops and picturesque Italianate architecture. Behind the grand hotels lining the northern **Rive Droite** waterfront is the main station and the cosmopolitan (and in places sleazy) **Les Pâquis** district, filled with cheap restaurants. Further north are the offices of the dozens of international organizations headquartered in Geneva, including the UN.

Jet d'Eau and the Old Town

On the Rive Gauche, beyond the ornamental flowerbeds of the Jardin Anglais, erupts the roaring 140-metre-high plume of Geneva's trademark **Jet d'Eau**. Nearby is the main thoroughfare of the **Old Town**, the cobbled, steeply ascending Grande Rue. Here, among the numerous jewellery shops and galleries, you'll find the atmospheric seventeenth-century **Hôtel de Ville** and the arcaded armoury, backed by a lovely terrace with the longest wooden bench in the world (126m). A block away is the huge late-Romanesque **Cathédrale St-Pierre** (Mon–Sat 9.30am–5/6.30pm, Sun noon–6.30pm; free), with an incongruous eighteenth-century portal and a plain, soaring interior. Tucked behind the Cathedral, the excellent **Musée Internationale de la Réforme** (Tues–Sun 10am–5pm; Fr.10; Ⓦwww.musee-reforme.ch), housed in the eighteenth-century Maison Mallet,

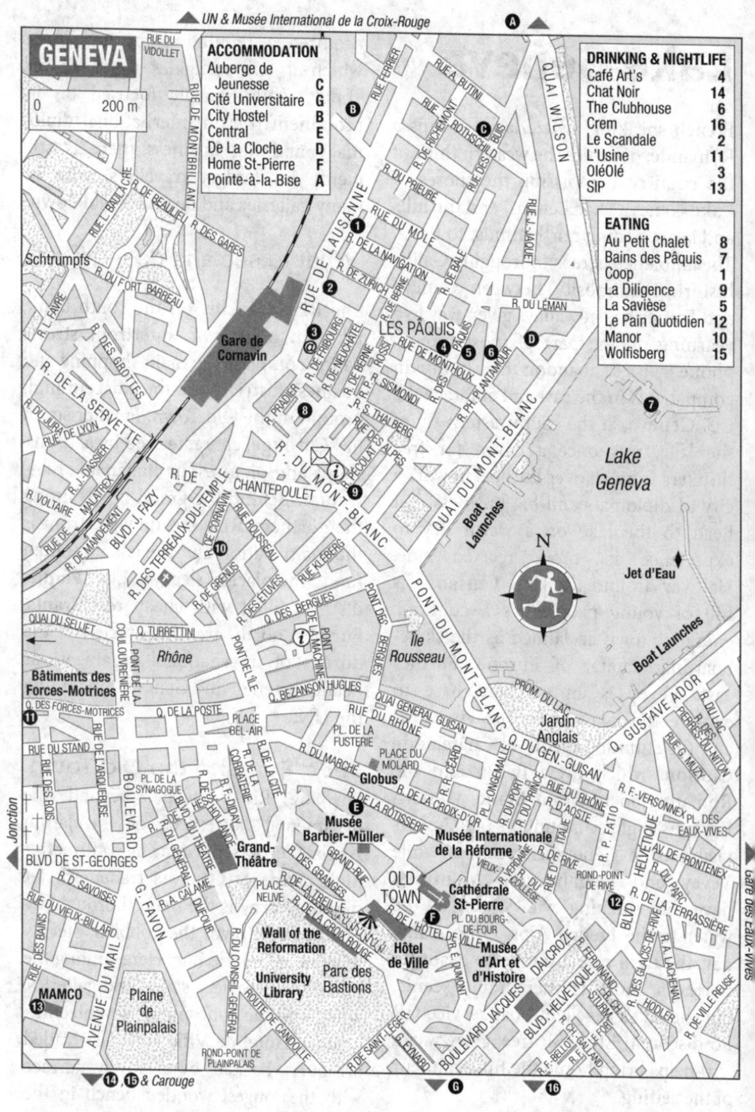

documents Geneva's contribution to the Reformation. Round the corner is the hub of the Old Town, **place du Bourg-de-Four**, a picturesque split-level square perched on the hillside and ringed by cafés. Alleys wind down from here to the university park and its austere **Wall of the Reformation** (1909–17) alongside busy place Neuve where you will also find giant chess and draughts boards to while away an hour or so.

The Musée d'Art et d'Histoire

A stroll east of the Old Town is the gigantic **Musée d'Art et d'Histoire**, 2 rue Charles Galland (Tues–Sun 10am–5pm, Ⓦwww.ville-ge.ch/mah; free). The fine art collection includes

pieces by Rodin, Renoir and Modigliani; the highlight, however, is Konrad Witz's famous altarpiece, made for the cathedral in 1444, showing Christ and the fishermen transposed onto Lake Geneva. The basement holds a massive archeological collection, including Egyptian mummies and Greek and Roman statuary.

MAMCO

Make time, if possible, for **MAMCO**, a top-quality museum of modern and contemporary art housed in a spacious factory west of the Old Town at 10 rue des Vieux-Grenadiers (Tues–Fri noon–6pm, Wed till 9pm, Sat & Sun 11am–6pm; first Sunday of month free; Fr.8/students Fr.6; Ⓦ www.mamco.ch).

Museé International de la Croix-Rouge

About 1km north of the station is the thought-provoking **Musée International de la Croix-Rouge** (Mon & Wed–Sun 10am–5pm; Fr.10/5; Ⓦ www.micr.ch; bus #8 or #F to Appia), which documents the origins and achievements of the Red Cross through carefully chosen audiovisual material. Quietly dramatic exhibits – such as the 34 footprints in a tiny cell space where a delegate found seventeen people crammed together – leave a powerful impression.

Palais des Nations

Across the road stands the imposing UN complex (tram #13 or #15 to Nations). Guided tours of the **Palais des Nations** (April–Oct daily 10am–noon & 2–4pm, July & Aug 10am–5pm, Nov–March Mon–Fri only; Fr.10/student Fr.8; passport required; Ⓦ www.unog.ch) start in the new wing and take you through to the original Palais des Nations, built to house the League of Nations between 1929 and 1936. The highlight is the Council Chamber, with allegorical ceiling murals by José-Maria Sert. Don't expect to see debates in session though; the tour is didactic in tone, aiming to enlighten visitors as to the workings and structure of the UN.

Carouge

Twenty minutes south of the centre by tram #12 or #13 lies the late-Baroque suburb of **Carouge**, built by the king of Sardinia in the eighteenth century as a separate town. Its low Italianate houses and leafy streets are now largely occupied by fashion designers and small galleries, and the area's reputation as an outpost of tolerance and hedonism lives on in its numerous cafés and music bars.

Arrival and information

Air From the airport, 5km northwest, trains and bus #10 run into the city.
Train The main station, Gare de Cornavin, lies at the head of rue du Mont-Blanc in the city centre. Expresses from Paris, Lyon and Grenoble arrive in a separate French section (passport control), while local French trains from Annecy/Chamonix terminate at Gare des Eaux-Vives on the east side of town (tram #12 or #16 into the centre).
Bus The international bus station (Gare Routière) is on place Dorcière in the centre.
Ferry Boats dock at several central quays.
Tourist office In the main post office at 18 rue du Mont-Blanc Ⓣ 022 909 70 00, Ⓦ www.genevatourism.ch (Mon–Sat 9/10am–6pm, Sun 10am–4pm). Staff will reserve rooms for a Fr.5 fee. There's also a desk within the municipality's information office, on the Pont de la Machine (Mon noon–6pm, Tues–Fri 9am–6pm, Sat 10am–5pm; Ⓣ 022 418 20 00, Ⓦ www.ville-ge.ch). Both have stacks of material in English, including information on budget accommodation options.

Accommodation

Make sure you pick up a Geneva transport card when checking into a hostel – this entitles you to free public transport for the duration of your stay.

Hostels

Auberge de Jeunesse (HI) 30 rue Rothschild Ⓣ 022 732 62 60, Ⓦ www.youthhostel.ch and www.yh-geneva.ch. Big, bustling, well-maintained 360-bed hostel in a central location. No kitchens but breakfast included. Dorms Fr.29, doubles Fr.85.

Cité Universitaire 46 av Miremont ⓣ 022 839 22 22, ⓦ www.unige.ch/cite-uni. Huge place 3km south of the centre (bus #3), with dorms and rooms available July–Sept. Breakfast extra. Dorms Fr.23, rooms Fr.60.

City Hostel (SB) 2 rue Ferrier ⓣ 022 901 15 00, ⓦ www.cityhostel.ch. Friendly 100-bed backpacker place near the HI hostel; an excellent budget option. Each corridor shares a kitchen. No breakfast. Three- or four-bed dorms Fr.32, two-bed dorms Fr.36.50, doubles Fr.87.

Home St-Pierre 4 Cour St-Pierre ⓣ 022 310 37 07, ⓦ www.homestpierre.ch. In the heart of the Old Town opposite the cathedral, with two dorms plus single and double rooms (all women-only), a large kitchen, roof terrace and wi-fi. Breakfast is extra. Dorms Fr.29, rooms Fr.34.

Hotels

Central 2 rue de la Rôtisserie ⓣ 022 818 81 00, ⓦ www.hotelcentral.ch. Quiet, good-value top-floor rooms just south of the Old Town, all with balcony. Rooms from Fr.115.

De la Cloche 6 rue de la Cloche ⓣ 022 732 94 81, ⓦ www.geneva-hotel.ch/cloche. Eight high-ceilinged rooms in a quiet area of the Pâquis, 50m from the lake. Regularly full. Rooms Fr.155.

Campsite

Pointe-à-la-Bise ⓣ 022 752 12 96, ⓦ www.tcs.ch. Good-quality site 7km to the northeast in Vésanaz; bus #E. April–Sept. Fr.7 per person, tents Fr.12.40.

Eating

Cafés and snack options

Bains des Pâquis 30 quai du Mont-Blanc. Popular café-bar attached to the lake front & swimming area. Great spot to soak up some sunshine. *Plat du jour* Fr.14.

Coop 39 rue de Lausanne. Budget supermarket with plenty of choice for self-catering and picnics.

Manor 6 rue Cornavin. Supermarket on the ground floor of this department store, with deli counters selling good take-away paninis and ciabattas (Fr.6.50), pizza slices (Fr.4) and curries (Fr.4). Closed Sun.

Wolfisberg 5 place du Temple, La Carouge. Busy café with outdoor seating, takeaway paninis for Fr.5 and huge weekend brunch menu 9am–3pm for Fr.30.

Restaurants

Au Petit Chalet 17 rue de Berne. Unpretentious place for Swiss fondues and rösti (Fr.18); also serves good pizzas for Fr.21. Closed Mon.

TREAT YOURSELF

La Savièse 20 rue des Pâquis. You can choose from lasagne and vegetarian dishes for Fr.22, but the speciality here is the fantastic fondues at Fr.25. There's also an all-you-can-eat raclette main for Fr.33. The friendly staff will show you the ropes if you are new to fondue and this is a great restaurant to visit in a group; book for weekend nights. Mon–Fri all day, Sat and Sun pm only.

La Diligence 2 rue Pécolat. Mexican restaurant just off the rue du Mont-Blanc. Nachos for Fr.15, enchiladas and burritos Fr.24 (vegetarian) and Fr.26 (meat).

Le Pain Quotidien 21 Boulevard Helvétique. Homely café with delicious pastries (Fr.3.50), a wide selection of newspapers and a lavish weekend brunch menu (Fr.28–32).

Drinking and nightlife

Bars

Café Art's 17 rue des Pâquis. Café-bar with a relaxed bohemian feel. Beer Fr.8, wine Fr.5, cocktails Fr.15.

Chat Noir 13 rue Vautier, La Carouge ⓦ www.chatnoir.ch. Bar and cellar venue with live music (anything from folk to metal). Wed–Sat until 5am.

The Clubhouse 25 rue Philippe Plantamour ⓦ www.theclubhouse.ch. Lively sports bar with super friendly staff. Live music and DJs at weekends; great atmosphere for watching sporting events. Sun–Thurs until 1am, Fri & Sat until 2am. Lunch deals during the week for Fr.20, brunch deals Fr.25.

Le Scandale 24 rue Lausanne ⓦ www.lescandale.ch. Funky bar with different DJs each night, comfy armchairs and a giant glitter ball, all adding to the eclectic atmosphere. Drinks from Fr.5. Tues–Fri 11am–2am, Sat 5pm–2am.

Ole Ole 11 rue de Fribourg. Tapas bar with personality, offering cocktails at Fr.15, glasses of wine at Fr.5 and bottles of beer at Fr.8. Chalk boards on the walls list burgers for Fr.25 and a host of tapas dishes for Fr.10. Open until 2am.

Clubs

crem 10 Bd Helvétique ⓦ www.lacrem.ch. One of Geneva's trendiest bar-clubs, where DJs spin music till 5am (Thurs–Sat).

SIP 10 rue des Vieux Grenadiers ⓦ www.lasip.ch. Former factory with modern, hip interior and wide-ranging programme; open Thurs–Sat till 4/5am.

L'Usine 4 place des Volontaires ⓦ www.usine.ch. Converted factory hosting a plethora of arts and live-music events. Zoo (ⓦ www.lezoo.ch) run club nights here (hip-hop, breakbeat, electronica) for urban night owls.

Entertainment

Cinema During July and Aug films are screened by the lakeside on the quai Gustave-Ador (Fr. 17; ⓦ www.orangecinema.ch). Two Pathé cinema complexes, Rialto on rue de Lausanne and Rex in the city centre, show recent blockbusters for Fr.18.

Shopping

Designer stores The rue du Rhône and the Rive Gauche are lined with the glass-fronted facades of expensive jewellers and big-name designers.
Carouge A better bet for more affordable and whimsical shopping; it's crammed with cute boutiques and hosts a colourful market (Wed & Sat).
Flea market At Plainpalais near Geneva's Old Town pick up anything from old records and retro kitchenware to gemstones (Wed & Sat).
Globus 48 rue du Rhône. One of Geneva's largest department stores.
Off the Shelf 15 bd Georges Favon (upstairs) ⓦ www.offtheshelf.ch. Friendly English bookshop, stocking an impressive selection of novels, non-fiction and travel guides.

Directory

Consulates Australia, 2 chemin des Fins ⓣ 022 799 91 00; Canada, 5 av. de l'Ariana ⓣ 022 919 92 00; New Zealand, 2 chemin des Fins ⓣ 022 929 03 50; UK, 37 rue de Vermont ⓣ 022 918 24 00; USA, 7 rue Versonnex ⓣ 022 840 51 60. Embassies are in Bern.
Exchange At the train station (Mon–Sat 7am–7.40pm, Sun 9.15am–5.50pm). Cash points all the way down rue du Mont-Blanc.
Hospital Hôpital Cantonal, 24 rue Micheli-du-Crest ⓣ 022 372 33 11.
Left luggage At the train station (4.30am–12.45am; Fr.4/7).
Laundry Lavseul, 29 rue de Monthoux (7am–midnight).
Post office 18 rue du Mont-Blanc.
Internet Charly's Checkpoint, 7 rue de Fribourg; 15mins Fr.1. (Mon–Sat 9am–midnight, Sunday 1–11pm).
Pharmacy Amavita, at the train station.

Moving on

Train Barcelona (1 daily; 9hr 30min); Basel (hourly; 2hr 45min); Bern (every 30min; 1hr 45min); Lausanne (every 15min; 35min); Lyon (10 daily; 1hr 40min); Montreux (every 30min; 1hr 10min); Vevey (every 30min; 1hr 5min); Zürich (every 30min–1hr; 2hr 45min).
Ferry (May–Sept) Lausanne (2 daily; 3hr 30min); Vevey (2 daily; 4hr 30min).

LAUSANNE

Geneva's neighbour **LAUSANNE** is attractive, vibrant and has something for everyone. It's tiered above the lake on a succession of south-facing terraces, with the Old Town at the top, the train station and commercial districts in the middle, and the one-time fishing village of Ouchy, now prime territory for waterfront café-lounging and strolling, at the bottom. The hills are incredibly steep; copy the locals and catch a bus into the Joret forests above the city, and then blade or **skateboard** your way down to **Ouchy**: aficionados have been clocked doing 90kph through the streets. Switzerland's biggest university makes this a lively, fun city to visit. For chilled-out bars, head for the converted warehouses of the trendy Flon district.

What to see and do

To get to the central **place St-François** from the train station, walk up the steep **rue du Petit-Chêne**, or take the metro to **Flon**; from the metro platforms, lifts shuttle you up to the level of the giant Grand Pont, between **place Bel-Air** on the left and St François on the right. From here, rue St-François drops down into the valley and up the other side to the cobbled **place de la Palud**, an ancient, fountained square flanked by the arcades of the Renaissance town hall.

The Cathedral and around

From place de la Palud the medieval Escaliers du Marché lead up to the

Cathedral (Mon–Fri 7am–7pm, Sat & Sun 8am–7pm), a fine Romanesque-Gothic jumble. Opposite, in the former bishop's palace, is the **Musée Historique** (Tues–Sun 11am–5/6pm, also Mon Jul & Aug; Fr.8/students free; Ⓦwww.lausanne.ch/mhl). Next door is the **MUDAC Musée de Design et d'Arts Appliqués Contemporains** (same hours as Musée Historique; Fr.10/students Fr.5; Ⓦwww.mudac.ch). A permanent collection of contemporary glass art is on the second floor while temporary exhibitions are displayed on the ground and first floor. Lausanne suffered many medieval fires, and is the last city in Europe to keep alive the tradition of the **nightwatch**: every night, on the hour (10pm–2am), a sonorous-voiced civil servant calls out from the cathedral tower "C'est le guet; il a sonné l'heure" ("This is the nightwatch; the hour has struck").

Collection de l'Art Brut

Ten minutes' walk northwest of Riponne on Avenue. Vinet (or bus #2 or #3 to Jomini) is the fascinating **Collection de l'Art Brut**, 11 av. des Bergières (Tues–Sun 11am–6pm; July & Aug also Mon same hours; Fr.10/students Fr.5; Ⓦwww.artbrut.ch). This unique gallery is devoted to "outsider art", the creative output of ordinary people with no artistic training at all – often loners, psychotics or the criminally insane. It's utterly absorbing.

Ouchy, the Olympic Museum and Museé de l'Elysée

Ouchy's waterfront hosts regular free music events all summer, and people come down here to do a spot of café sunbathing or blading (rent blades or skates from beside Ouchy metro). In a park on the waterfront sits Lausanne's **Olympic Museum** (daily 9am–6pm; Nov–March closed Mon; Fr.15/students Fr.10; Ⓦwww.olympic.org), a vacuous place that trumpets the Olympic ideal through snippets of archive footage, stirring music and Cathy Freeman's old running shoes. Bypass it for the **Musée de l'Elysée**, an excellent museum of photography in the same park (Tues–Sun 11am–6pm; Fr.8/students Fr.4, free on first Sat of month).

LAUSANNE FESTIVALS

Lausanne's big party is the **Festival de la Cité** in early July (Ⓦwww.festivaldelacite.ch), featuring music, dance and drama on several open-air stages in the Old Town. Also check out July's big-name **Paleo Rock Festival** in nearby Nyon (Ⓦwww.paleo.ch).

Arrival and information

Boats from Lake Geneva arrive on the quayside at Ouchy.
Train Lausanne's train station is below the Old Town; from place de la Gare, head up rue du Petit-Chêne.
Tourist office Lausanne has two tourist offices (Ⓣ021 613 73 92, Ⓦwww.lausanne-tourisme.ch): one in the train station (daily 9am–7pm), the other beside Ouchy metro station (daily 9am–7pm; Oct–March closes 6pm; Ⓣ021 013 73 01).

Accommodation

Hostels

Jeunotel (HI) 36 chemin du Bois-de-Vaux Ⓣ021 626 02 22, Ⓦwww.youthhostel.ch. Huge place beside Vidy campsite with four-bed dorms and rooms, plus cheap meals on request (Fr.13.40). Dorms Fr.36, doubles Fr.93.

Lausanne Guest House (SB) 4 Epinettes Ⓣ021 601 80 00, Ⓦwww.lausanne-guesthouse.ch. Fabulous, friendly hostel with lake views, kitchen, wi-fi, four-bed dorms and rooms. Dorms Fr.33, rooms Fr.95.

Hotels and guesthouses

Old Inn 11 av de la Gare Ⓣ021 323 62 21, Ⓦwww.oldinn.ch. Quiet, spartan little *pension* with 11 twin rooms and a shared kitchen. Room Fr.120.
Pension Bienvenue 2 rue du Simplon Ⓣ021 616 29 86, Ⓦwww.pension-bienvenue.ch. Respectable, women-only guesthouse behind the station. Long stays available. Rooms Fr.55.

Campsite

Camping Vidy ⓣ 021 622 50 00, ⓦ www.campinglausannevidy.ch. Bus #1 to Maladière and walk 5min to get to this decent lakeside campsite with restaurant and supermarket. Bungalows available to rent Fr.56. Fr.7.50 per person, tents Fr.12.

Eating

Café Romand place St-François (under *Le Dynasty*). Bustling, heartwarming place with cosy alcoves for beer, coffee or heavy Swiss fare. Mains Fr.17–27. Closed Sun.
Café Saint Francois place St-François. Soak up the sun at this café by the church. Ever-changing lunch menus Fr.17 and Fr.19, takeaway pastries for Fr.4.
Coop City rue St Laurent and av du Théâtre. There are supermarkets in the basements of both of these department stores. Mon–Fri 8.30am–7pm, Sat 8am–6pm.
Laxmi 5 Escaliers du Marché. Indian restaurant. All-you-can-eat buffet lunches are Fr.19 (Fr.16 for vegetarian dishes); evening mains cost a little more. Closed Mon lunch & Sun.
Le Barbare 27 Escaliers du Marché. Perfect little café amongst the rooftops of the Old Town. There's a sun-trap terrace for summer and it's cosy inside in winter. Pizza Fr.15, sandwich Fr.6.
Manora 17 place St-François. Branch of the self-service cafeteria chain; wide range of hot and cold food for Fr.13 or under.
Namaste 6 rue Curtat. Small but great Nepalese place with cosy inside space. Your best bet is to get takeaway and find a spot on the grass opposite. Meat and veg dish with rice Fr.10 to take-away, Fr.12 to eat in.

Drinking and nightlife

Bars

Au Château 1 place du Tunnel. Bar with funky music and some flavoursome home-brewed beers.
Bleu Lézard 10 rue Penni Enning ⓦ www.bluelezard.ch. Fashionable, lively café-bar with regular live music sets downstairs. Mon–Fri until 1am, Sat 2am.
Nomade place de L'Europe 9 ⓦ www.restaurantnomade.ch. Relaxed wine and tapas bar on the edge of the Flon. Glass of wine from Fr.8, tapas Fr.10. Closed Sun.

Clubs

D! place Centrale. Happening basement club playing house and drum 'n' bass. Thurs–Sat.
Le Loft 1 Escaliers Bel-Air. Bar and club with a mixed programme, including popular electro nights. Free entry for women before midnight. Wed–Sat.
MAD (Moulin à Danse) 23 rue de Genève ⓦ www.mad.ch. Cutting-edge dance club with adjoining theatre, art galleries and alternative-style café; hub of the trendy Flon district. Attracts well-known DJs.
VO Le Music Club 11 place. du Tunnel. Unpretentious café-bar and live venue with regular DJ nights.

Moving on

Train Basel (every 30min; 2hr 10min); Bern (every 30min; 1hr 10min); Geneva (every 15min; 35min); Montreux (every 15min; 20min); Vevey (every 15min; 15min); Zürich (every 30min; 2hr 10min).
Ferry (May–Sept) Geneva (3 daily; 3hr 30min); Montreux (5 daily; 1hr 30min); Vevey (5 daily; 1hr).

VEVEY

East of Lausanne, trains meander through steep vineyards to **VEVEY**, a small market town looking over the French Alps. It holds a Street Artists' Festival in late August with jugglers, acrobats and mime artists performing at the lakeside (ⓦ www.artistesderue.ch). Vevey's charm centres on the huge Grande Place, a few minutes' walk southeast of the station – known also as **place du Marché** and packed with market stalls (Tues & Sat) – and the narrow streets which lead off into the Old Town to the east. The excellent fine art museum, **Musée Jenisch** on rue de la Gare (Tues–Sun 11am–5.30pm; Fr.12), puts on high-quality exhibitions drawing on its extensive graphic collections (it has one of Europe's largest collections of Rembrandt lithographs). A vast collection of cameras is on display at the Camera Museum on the place du Marché (Tues–Sun 11am–5.30pm; Fr.8/students Fr.6; ⓦ www.cameramuseum.ch). East of the square on the waterfront is a statue of Charlie Chaplin, who moved to Vevey from the US in the 1950s to escape McCarthyism. Chaplin looks out to the lake and a giant statue of an eight-metre fork, previously a temporary exhibit but now part of the permanent landscape. To head on to

Montreux and Chillon, ditch the train in favour of bus #1 (direction Villeneuve), which plies the coast road every 10min. If you have time, walk the floral lakeside path.

Arrival and information

Train From the train station it's a 5min walk to the Grande Place and the lake.
Tourist office In the pillared Grenette building on Grande Place ⓣ0848 868 484, ⓦwww.montreux-vevey.com (June–Sept Mon–Fri 9am–6pm & Sat 8.30am–12.30pm; Oct–May Mon–Fri 9am–noon & 1pm–5.30pm, Sat 9am–noon). Vevey and Montreux tourist offices have the same information. Be sure to get a "Riviera card" when checking in at your hostel or hotel; this entitles you to free public transport during your stay, in addition to discounts at local museums.

Accommodation

La Pichette campsite ⓣ021 921 09 97 Lakeside campsite 2km west of Vevey. April–Sept. Fr.5 per person, tents Fr.4.
Les Négociants 27 rue du Conseil ⓣ021 922 70 11, ⓦwww.hotelnegociants.ch. Simple, cosy rooms with TV and en-suite bathrooms. Fr.143 for two in a double.
Riviera Lodge 5 Grande Place ⓣ021 923 80 40, ⓦwww.rivieralodge.ch. Excellent hostel near the lake with 8-bed dorms, large shared kitchen and modern chill-out areas. Dorms Fr.35, rooms Fr.90.

Eating and drinking

Charly's Café 45 rue du Lac. Great café-restaurant with covered roof terrace; open until midnight, food served until 9pm. Club sandwich and chips Fr.21.
Les Négociants 27 rue du Conseil. Hotel brasserie serving good Swiss fare. Rösti Fr.21.
Manora St Antoine mall, opposite the train station (second floor). Large branch of the self-service chain, serving inexpensive hot and cold dishes for Fr.13 and under.

MONTREUX JAZZ FESTIVAL

The sleepy town of Montreux livens up during its star-studded **Montreux Jazz Festival** (ⓦwww.montreuxjazz.com), held in early July. The festival's been running for over forty years, and although it's pulled in the likes of Miles Davies and Ray Charles in the past, "jazz" is now something of a misnomer; these days the festival features big-name acts from all types of popular music. Check online for tickets (Fr.50–150), or just join the street parties and free entertainment around the lake.

Moving on

Train Geneva (every 30min; 1hr); Lausanne (every 15min; 15min); Montreux (3 hourly; 5min).
Bus Montreux (#1; every 10 min).

CHÂTEAU DE CHILLON

The highlight of a journey around Lake Geneva is the spectacular thirteenth-century **Château de Chillon** (daily 9/10am–4/6pm; Fr.12/students Fr.10; ⓦwww.chillon.ch), one of the best-preserved medieval castles in Europe. It's a 45-minute walk east from Montreux, or a short ride on bus #1. Your first glimpse of the castle, jutting out into the water and framed by craggy mountains, is simply unforgettable. On entering, you receive a pamphlet directing you to the atmospheric stone dungeons, where François Bonivard, a Genevan priest, was imprisoned from 1530 to 1536; the story captured the imagination of Lord Byron, who composed his poem *The Prisoner of Chillon* after a sailing trip here with Shelley in 1816. Upstairs you'll find grand knights' halls, lavish bedchambers and dreamy views of the lake.

The Swiss heartland

The Mittelland – the populated countryside between Lake Geneva and Zürich, flanked by the Jura range to the north and the high Alps to the south – is a region of gentle hills, lakes and some high peaks. There's a wealth of cultural and historical interest in the German-speaking cities of **Basel**, **Luzern** and the federal capital, **Bern**. Wherever you base yourself, the mountains are never more than a couple of hours away by train.

BASEL

Situated on the Rhine, where Switzerland, France and Germany touch, **BASEL** (Bâle in French) is a logical staging post en-route north. Despite its pan-European location, the city has gained a reputation for insularity. Certainly, Basel feels like a working city; it's neither as picturesque as Bern or Luzern, nor as vibrant as Zürich. Yet it's a wealthy place and, thanks to longstanding patronage of the arts, boasts a smattering of first-rate museums and galleries, in addition to some superb contemporary architecture. It's also holds a massive three-day **carnival** in February (ⓦwww.fasnacht.ch), beginning at 4am on the Monday after Mardi Gras.

> **TREAT YOURSELF**
>
> **Au Violon** Im Lohnhof 4 ⓣ061 269 87 11, ⓦwww.au-violon.com. Comfortable, stylish Old Town hotel (a converted former prison), next to St Leonhard's Church. There are fourteen converted "cell rooms" (all en suite) or you can opt for the grandeur of a former "police office" with great views over the Old Town to the Munster. There is also a garden terrace, weather permitting. Fr.160.

What to see and do

The River Rhine curves through the centre of Basel, flowing from east to north. On the south/west bank (1km north of the main station) is the historic Old Town, which is centred on the hectic, higgledy-piggledy main square, **Barfüsserplatz**. Across the river, on the north bank lies **Kleinbasel**; historically scorned by the city's prosperous merchants as a working-class quarter. Look out for the Lällekönig bust facing towards the **Mittlere Brücke**, sticking its tongue out at the Kleinbaslers. Nowadays, the steps down to the Rhine are a popular place to sit and catch the sun.

Historisches Museum

The city's cultural pre-eminence in the fifteenth and sixteenth centuries is amply demonstrated in the **Barfüsserkirche**, now home to the **Historisches Museum** (Tues–Sun 10am–5pm; Fr.7/students Fr.5); don't miss the sumptuous medieval tapestries hidden behind protective blinds.

The Münster

Sixteenth-century lanes lead up behind the Historisches Museum to Basel's cathedral, the **Münster** (daily 10/11am–4/4.30/5pm). Inside, in the north aisle, is the tomb of the Renaissance humanist Erasmus, and behind the church is the Pfalz terrace, a fine spot for a picnic. From Barfüsserplatz, shop-lined Gerbergasse and Freiestrasse run north to Marktplatz, dominated by the elaborate scarlet facade of the sixteenth-century **Rathaus**.

Kunstmuseum and Museum für Gegenwartskunst

Back at Barfüsserplatz, Steinenberg climbs east to meet St Alban-Graben. Here, at no. 16, you'll find Basel's **Kunstmuseum** (Tues–Sun 10am–5pm; Fr.12 includes entry to Museum für Gegenwartskunst; free on 1st Sun of

month), which has a dazzling array of twentieth-century art, in addition to an outstanding medieval collection, including a large number of works by the Holbein family. Set in a tranquil spot down by the river, the **Museum für Gegenwartskunst** (Tues–Sun 11am–5pm; joint admission with Kunstmuseum) contains installations by Frank Stella and Joseph Beuys.

Museum Jean Tinguely

A walk away on the north bank, in Solitude Park, is the beautifully designed **Museum Jean Tinguely** (Tues–Sun 11am–7pm; Fr.15/students Fr.10; ⓦwww.tinguely.ch), dedicated to one of Switzerland's best-loved artists. Tinguely used scrap metal, plastic and bits of everyday junk to create room-sized Monty-Pythonesque machines that – with the touch of a button – judder into life, clanking and squeaking. Sculptures veer between the grotesque and the comical.

Fondation Beyeler

Basel's finest gallery – **Fondation Beyeler** (daily 10am–6pm, Wed until 8pm; Fr.23/students Fr.12; tram #6; ⓦwww.beyeler.com) is out in the suburbs; but it's certainly worth the trip. Sympathetically designed by Renzo Piano, architect of Paris's Pompidou Centre, the gallery contains a small but exceptionally high-quality collection, featuring some of the most impressive works by Picasso, Giacometti, Rothko, Rodin, Bacon, Miró and others. Sink into a huge white sofa opposite a giant Monet and indulge in dreamy contemplation of the water lilies in front of you and the watery gardens outside.

Arrival and information

Train Basel has two train stations straddling three countries. Basel SBB is the main one, most of it in Switzerland; at one end, past passport control, is a section in French territory entitled Bâle SNCF which handles trains from Paris and Strasbourg. Trams #8 and #11 shuttle to Barfüsserplatz. Some trains from Germany terminate at Basel Badischer Bahnhof (Basel Bad. for short), in a German enclave on the north side of the river (passport control), from where tram #6 runs to Barfüsserplatz.

Tourist office In a side entrance of the Stadt Casino on Barfüsserplatz ⓣ061 268 68 68, ⓦwww.basel.com (Mon–Fri 8.30am–6.30pm, Sat 9am–5pm, Sun 10am–4pm), with a branch office inside the main SBB train station (Mon–Fri 8.30am–6.30pm, Sat 9am–5pm & Sun 9am–4pm). A full list of Basel's museums and galleries is available here. If you stay overnight you're entitled to a Mobility Card, giving free city transport; pick it up from your hotel at check-in. The Basel Card (Fr.20/27/35 for 24/48/72 hours) grants free museum entry, free city tours, plus discounts at restaurants, bars and clubs.

Accommodation

Hostels

Basel Backpack (SB) Dornacherstr. 192 ⓣ061 333 00 37, ⓦwww.baselbackpack.com. Good hostel in a funky renovated factory/arts complex behind the station. Colour-coded dorms, bar, kitchen and industrial-style bathrooms. Tram #15 or #16 to Tell Platz. Dorms Fr.32, rooms Fr.49.

Jugendherberge City (HI) Pfeffingerstr. 8 ⓣ061 365 99 60, ⓦwww.youthhostel.ch/basel. Comfortable hostel on a quiet street behind the station, with internet and garden area. 4-bed rooms Fr.32, doubles Fr.41.

Jugendherberge St Alban (HI) St Alban-Kirchrain 10 ⓣ061 272 05 72, ⓦwww.youthhostel.ch. Quiet hostel on the river due to open spring 2010. Dorms Fr.41.

Eating

Manora Greifengasse 22. Excellent-value self-service hot meals, salads and snacks for Fr.13 or under.

Mr Wong Steinenvorstadt 3. Popular Asian fast-food joint just off Barfüsserplatz with noodle dishes from Fr.11.

Parterre Klybeckstr. 1. Lively Kleinbasel hangout, with busy outside terrace and a creative, vegetarian-friendly menu; mains Fr.22–34. Closed Sun.

Zum Roten Engel Andreasplatz. Busy little café in a dinky cobbled square, attracting a studenty clientele.

Drinking and nightlife

Bars

Eoipso Dornachstr. 192. Trendy, spacious industrial bar in a buzzing factory complex behind the train station.

Fischerstube Rheingasse 45. Atmospheric Kleinbasel beerhall with an older clientele.

Nightclubs and live music

Atlantis Klosterberg 10 ⓦwww.atlan-tis.ch. Club-bar with regular music and dancing; club nights Fri and Sat till 4am.
Bird's Eye Kohlenberg 20 ⓦwww.birdseye.ch. Basel's main jazz venue. Entrance prices vary, but generally hover around Fr.10. Open Tues–Sat from 8pm.
Kaserne Klybeckstr. 1b ⓦwww.kaserne-basel.ch. Alternative hangout with varied live music, theatre and dance programme. Mutates on Tues into Basel's premier gay/lesbian meeting-point.

Moving on

Train Geneva (hourly; 2hr 45min); Interlaken Ost (every 30min; 2hr 10min); Lausanne (every 30min; 2hr 5min); Lugano (every 2 hours; 3hr 50min); Luzern (hourly; 1hr 10min); Zürich (2 hourly; 1hr).

LUZERN (LUCERNE)

An hour south of Basel is beautiful **LUZERN** (Lucerne), offering captivating mountain views, lake cruises and a picturesque medieval quarter. The **train station** and **tourist office** (Mon–Fri 8.30am–6.30/7.30pm, Sat & Sun 9am–6.30/7.30pm; winter closed Sun afternoon and an hour earlier other days; ⓣ041 227 17 17, ⓦwww.luzern.org) is south of the river where you'll be greeted by the striking concert hall KKL. Busy Pilatusstrasse heads southwest, where 100m along is the **Sammlung Rosengart gallery** (daily 10/11am–5/6pm; Fr.18) with a superb collection of twentieth-century art. The alleyways of the Old Town span both riverbanks, linked by the fourteenth-century **Kapellbrücke**, a covered wooden bridge which, after a disastrous fire in 1993, has been reconstructed and the medieval paintings fixed to its roof beams replaced by facsimiles. Northeast of the Old Town is **Löwenplatz**, dominated by the absorbing **Bourbaki Panorama** (Tues–Sun 9/10am–5/6pm; Fr.8/students Fr.7), a 110m-by-10m circular mural, depicting the flight of General Bourbaki's 87,000 strong army into Switzerland during the Franco-Prussian War. Just off the square is the **Löwendenkmal**, a dying lion hewn out of a cliff-face to commemorate seven hundred Swiss mercenaries killed by French revolutionaries in 1792.

A pleasant 2km stroll east along the lakeside (or bus #6 or #8) lies the **Verkehrshaus** (daily 10am–5/6pm; Fr.24/students Fr.22, or Fr.32 including IMAX cinema, Fr.16 if arriving after 4pm; ⓦwww.verkehrshaus.ch). This is the transport museum, a vast complex containing original space capsules, railway locomotives, cable cars and a planetarium. An incongruous highlight is the museum dedicated to whimsical contemporary Swiss artist **Hans Erni** (daily 10am–5/6pm; Fr.12 without Verkehrshaus; ⓦwww.hansernimuseum.ch). A ten-minute walk along the lake from the train station is the friendly *Backpackers Lucerne* (ⓣ041 360 04 20, ⓦwww.backpackerslucerne.ch; with kitchen facilities, dorms Fr.31, doubles Fr.38) while across the lake is the central *Tourist Hotel* (ⓣ041 410 24 74, ⓦwww.touristhotel.ch; dorms Fr.38, doubles Fr.90). Coop at the station can supply picnic bits and the *World Café* in the KKL building has daily hot specials with a global twist from Fr.18.

Lake Luzern

You shouldn't leave Luzern without taking a trip on the **lake** (ferry routings at ⓦwww.lakelucerne.ch; ER & SP free, IR half-price; tourist info at ⓦwww.lakeluzern.ch), Switzerland's most beautiful and dramatic by far, the thickly wooded slopes rising sheer from the water.

Engelberg

An hour on the train takes you to the picturesque Alpine resort of **ENGELBERG**, from where a four-stage cable car serves the snowbound summit of Mount Titlis (3239m), the highest point

in Central Switzerland (ⓦwww.titlis.ch). Here you can hit the snow year round and countless offers are available for snowboarders to take advantage of, as well as rental deals for mountain bikes, scooters and DevilBikes.

BERN

Of all Swiss cities, **BERN** is the most immediately charming. Crammed onto a steep-sided peninsula in a crook of the fast-flowing River Aare, the city's quiet, cobbled lanes, lined with sandstone arcaded buildings, have changed little in five hundred years. It's sometimes hard to remember that this quiet, attractive town of just 130,000 people is the nation's capital.

What to see and do

Bern's compact old centre is best explored from the focal east–west **Spitalgasse**. As it leads away from the Bahnhofplatz, Spitalgasse becomes **Marktgasse**, Kramgasse and then Gerechtigkeitsgasse, before taking you across the river Aare to the **Bärengraben** (or bear pits). Many of Bern's larger museums are clustered around Helvetiaplatz, on the south bank of the river, across the Kirchenfeldbrücke.

The Old Town and the Münster

Marktgasse, lined with attractive seventeenth- and eighteenth-century buildings and arcaded boutiques, leads you past a number of historic landmarks, such as the sixteenth-century Zytglogge; a distinctively top-heavy clock tower, converted from a medieval town gate. To the left in Kornhausplatz, the most notorious of Bern's fountains, the horrific **Kindlifresserbrunnen**, depicts an ogre devouring a baby. Münstergasse, one block south, takes you to the fifteenth-century Gothic **Münster** (Mon–Sat 10am–5pm, Sun 11.30am–4pm), noted for the magnificently gilded high-relief *Last Judgement* above the main entrance. Its 254-stepped tower (closes 30min earlier; Fr.4), the tallest in Switzerland, offers terrific views.

The Bärengraben

At the eastern end of the centre, the Nydeggbrücke crosses the river to the **Bärengraben** (open access), Bern's famed bear-pits, which have housed generations of morose shaggies since the early sixteenth century. Legend has it that the town's founder, Berchtold V of Zähringen, named Bern after killing one of the beasts during a hunt. Since an overhaul in 2009 the new layout features the bear-pits as the centrepiece of a much larger park-like enclosure with three bears.

The Kunstmuseum

Bern's **Kunstmuseum**, near the station at Hodlerstrasse 8–12 (Tues 10am–9pm, Wed–Sun 10am–5pm; Fr.7, more for temporary exhibitions; ⓦwww.kunstmuseumbern.ch), is especially strong on twentieth-century art, with works by Matisse, Kandinsky, Braque and Picasso.

The Historisches Museum and around

The vast **Historisches Museum** (Tues–Sun 10am–5pm; Fr.13; ⓦwww.bhm.ch), on Helvetiaplatz, south of the river, is home to the superb **Einstein Museum** (same hours, Fr.18), which documents the physicist's eventful family life and his chequered early career. Exhibits include examples of the young Einstein's schoolwork, complete with scathing marginalia.

Zentrum Paul Klee

East of the centre at Ostring, the **Zentrum Paul Klee** (Tues–Sun 10am–5pm; Fr.18; ⓦwww.paulkleezentrum.ch; bus #12) has the world's largest collection of works by the artist, who spent much of his life in Bern. The building is a stunning, triple-arched design by the star Italian architect Renzo Piano.

Arrival and information

Train To the west of the Old Town; the main entrance is on Bahnhofplatz.
Tourist office In the train station ⓣ031 328 12 12, ⓦwww.berninfo.com (June–Sept Mon–Sun 9am–8.30pm; Oct–May Mon–Sat 9am–6.30pm & Sun 10am–5pm). Staff sell the Bern Card (Fr.20/31/38 for 24/48/72 hours), which entitles you to free public transport and discounts.

City transport

Bern's Old Town is compact and can easily be covered on foot.
Bikes Bern rollt, Hirschengraben ⓦwww.bernrollt.ch. (daily 7.30am–9.30pm). Rental is free for the first 4 hours, but you need photo ID and Fr.20 deposit and must return bikes the same day.
Bus #12 runs from the train station, through the Old Town to the Bärengraben and then to the Zentrum Paul Klee.

Accommodation

Hostels

Bern Backpackers/Hotel Glocke (SB) Rathausgasse 75 ⓣ031 311 37 71, ⓦwww.bernbackpackers.com. Very central hostel (if a little noisy) with a large common room and kitchen area. Dorms Fr.33, rooms Fr.140.
HI Hostel Weihergasse 4 ⓣ031 311 63 16, ⓦwww.youthhostel.ch/bern. Good hostel in a quiet location beside the river, just below the Bundeshaus. Breakfast included. Dorms Fr.33, doubles Fr.51.
Landhaus (SB) Altenbergstr. 4 ⓣ031 331 41 66, ⓦwww.landhausbern.ch. Excellent hostel in an old house near the Bärengraben. Full of character, with wonky wooden floors and a lively downstairs bar. Dorms have neat 2-bed cubicles. Dorms Fr.33, doubles Fr.160.

Campsite

Eichholz campsite Strandweg 49 ⓣ031 961 26 02, ⓦwww.campingeichholz.ch; take tram #9 to Wabern. Good-value campsite. April–Sept. Fr.7.50 per person, tents Fr.7.

Eating and drinking

For cheap and easy supplies, Migros supermarket at the train station is open until 9pm.
Altes Tramdepot Gr Muristalden 6 ⓦwww.altestramdepot.ch. Microbrewery with fantastic views across the river to the Old Town. The restaurant here serves Swiss cuisine; rösti Fr.18, pretzels (Fr.10).
Le Lötschberg Zeughaugasse 16, ⓦwww.loetschberg-aoc.ch. Relaxed, trendy wine bar and deli serving a range of cheese platters and substantial salads for Fr.9–15. Closed Sun.
Markthalle Bubenbergplatz 9. Huge building offering different world foods. Pick up a pizza slice for Fr.8 or stick around for tacos or noodles from Fr.15.
Sous Le Pont Neubrückstrasse 8 ⓦwww.souslepont.ch. Café-bar in the Reitschule, a huge graffitied house on Bollwerk run by a collective. Tues–Thus 11.30am–2.30pm & 6pm–midnight, Fri 7pm–2am, Sat 7pm–2am.
Tibits Bahnhofplatz 10 ⓦwww.tibits.ch. Excellent vegetarian self-service place, with a great selection of salads and hot dishes. Pay by weight.

Nightlife and live music

Bern hosts a huge open-air rock event (ⓦwww.gurtenfestival.ch) in July.
Dampfzentrale Marzilistr. 47 ⓣ031 310 05 40, ⓦwww.dampfenzentrale.ch. Bern's premier venue for live music, hosting a range of acts.
Reitschule Neubrückstrasse 8 ⓦwww.reitschule.ch. Cultural and political arts squat at the heart of the alternative clubbing scene.

Shopping

Kramgrasse and Rathausgasse are lined with quirky boutiques. Waisenhausplatz market sells everything from crafts to clothes and CDs (May–Oct, Tues 8am–7pm & Sat 8am–5pm). There's a produce market in Bärenplatz (Tues & Sat 7am–noon), and on the first Saturday of each month, Munsterplattform hosts a craft market. Brand new Westside (bus #14 and trains every 15mins) is a modern shopping complex housing everything from H&M to Tommy Hilfiger, with a food hall, water park and spa (ⓦwww.bernaqua.ch). A good place to while away a rainy day.

Directory

Embassies Australia, embassy in Berlin ⓣ0049 (0)30 88 00 88 0, consulate in Geneva ⓣ022 799 91 00; Canada, Kirchenfeldstr. 88, Bern ⓣ031 357 32 00; Ireland, Kirchenfeldstr. 68, Bern ⓣ031 352 14 42; New Zealand, embassy in Berlin ⓣ0049 (0)30 20 62 10, consulate in Geneva ⓣ022 929 03 50; UK, Thunstr. 50, Bern ⓣ031 359 77 00; USA, Jubiläumstr. 93, Bern ⓣ031 357 70 11.

Hospital Inselspital, Freiburgstr. ☎031 632 24 64.
Internet Weblane, Kramgrasse, 47. Self-service internet (daily 9am–11pm, Fr.4 for 30min).
Laundry Jet Wash, Dammweg 43.
Left Luggage in the station (6am–midnight; Fr.5/6/8 for different-sized lockers).
Pharmacy Bahnhof Apotheke, in the station.
Post office Schanzenstr., behind the station.

Moving on

Train Basel (every 30min; 55min); Geneva (every 30min; 1hr 45min); Interlaken Ost (every 30min; 55min); Lausanne (every 30min; 1hr 10min); Luzern (every 30min; 1hr 20min); Zürich (every 30min; 1hr–1hr 25min).

The Swiss Alps

South of Bern and Luzern, and east of Montreux, lies the grand Alpine heart of Switzerland, a massively impressive region of classic Swiss scenery – high peaks, sheer valleys and cool lakes – that makes for great summer hiking and world-class winter sports. The Bernese Oberland, centred on the **Jungfrau Region**, is the most accessible and touristed area, but beyond this first great wall of peaks is another even more daunting range in which the **Matterhorn**, marking the Italian border, is the star attraction. Note that very little happens in the mountains in the **off-seasons** (April, May, Oct & Nov); shops and hotels may be shut at these times, cable cars closed for renovations, and smaller resorts virtually deserted.

THE JUNGFRAU REGION

The spectacular **Jungfrau Region** is named after a grand triple-peaked ridge – the Eiger, Mönch and Jungfrau – which crests 4000m. Endlessly touted hereabouts is the rack-railway excursion up to the **Jungfraujoch**, the highest train station in Europe at 3454m. The cable-car ride up the **Schilthorn** (2970m) gets second billing, but is in fact quicker, cheaper, offers a more scenic ride up, and has better views from the top. A return trip from Interlaken takes six hours to the Jungfraujoch, or four hours to the Schilthorn (both including an hour at the summit). Setting off on the first train of the day (6.30am) brings discounts on both routes. The most beautiful part of the region's countryside is the **Lauterbrunnen valley**, overlooked by the resort of **Mürren**, which provides an excellent base for winter skiing and summer hiking, as does **Grindelwald**, in its own valley slightly east. **Interlaken** is the main transport hub for the region, but the sheer volume of tourist traffic passing through the town can make it a less than restful place to stay.

TO THE JUNGFRAUJOCH

Switzerland's most popular **mountain railway** trundles south from Interlaken before coiling up across mountain pastures, and tunnelling clean through the Eiger to emerge at the **Jungfraujoch** (3454m), an icy, windswept col just beneath the Jungfrau summit. Touted relentlessly as the "Top of Europe" – the journey is scenic in parts, but very long (2hr 20min from Interlaken) and prohibitively expensive; it's only worthwhile on a clear day, when you gain spectacular **panoramic views** from the Sphinx Terrace (3571m) to Germany's Black Forest in one direction and across a gleaming wasteland to the Italian Alps in the other. Don't forget your sunglasses.

INTERLAKEN

INTERLAKEN is centred on its long main street, Höheweg, which is lined with cafés and hotels and has a train station at each end, though the best way to arrive is by boat. The town lies on a neck of land between two of Switzerland's most attractive lakes, and it exists chiefly to amuse the trippers passing through on

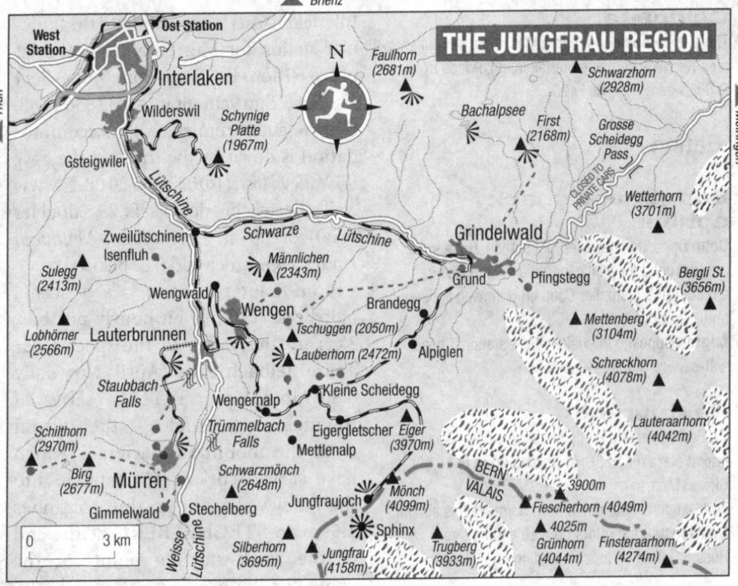

their way to the mountains. Interlaken Ost station is the mainline terminus and the departure point for trains into the mountains (see box opposite); coming from Luzern, you could get out at Brienz and do the last stretch to Interlaken Ost by boat. Trains from the Bern/Zürich direction pass first through Interlaken West (docking point for boats from Thun).

Arrival and information

Train Interlaken West is located close to Bahnhofstrasse, which becomes the main street, Höheweg, at the far eastern end of which is Interlaken Ost station.

Tourist office Beneath the town's tallest building at Höheweg 37 ⓣ033 826 53 00, ⓦwww.interlaken.ch (summer Mon–Fri 8am–7pm & Sat 8am–5pm; July & Aug also Sun 10am–noon & 5–7pm; winter Mon–Fri 8am–noon, 1.30–6pm and Sat 9am–noon).

> **TREAT YOURSELF**
>
> Interlaken is a real hub for extreme sports; paragliders spiral above the town, dominating the skyline. If you decide to splash out on an adventure, **Alpin Raft** (Hauptstrasse 7; ⓣ033 823 41 00, ⓦwww.alpinraft.ch) is the most popular, arranging everything from tandem skydiving (Fr.380) to canyon jumping (Fr.129), and bookable direct or through hostels.

Accommodation

Accommodation fills up quickly in the high seasons, so it really is essential to book ahead. There are hotel lists and courtesy phones at both stations.

Hostels

Backpackers Villa Sonnenhof (SB) Alpenstr. 16 ⓣ033 826 71 71, ⓦwww.villa.ch. Excellent hostel; quieter than *Balmer's*, but well-equipped and friendly. Dorms Fr.35, doubles Fr.59.

Balmer's Herberge (SB) Hauptstr. 23-33 ⓣ033 822 19 61, ⓦwww.balmers.com. Sociable hostel 15min south of town, its DJ bar and summer beer garden the hub of Interlaken's lively backpacker scene. Dorms Fr.27, rooms Fr.37.

Happy Inn (SB) Rosenstr. 17 ⓣ033 822 32 25, ⓦwww.happy-inn.com. Reasonable back-up option if *Balmer's* and *Sonnenhof* are full. Dorms Fr.24, rooms Fr.32.

Campsite

There are a number of campsites in the Interlaken area (Ⓦ www.campinginterlaken.ch). Prices from Fr.8 per person, tents Fr.20.

Eating

Budget and snack options

Coop Opposite Interlaken Ost station. Huge supermarket, good for picnic ingredients and also has a restaurant; a smaller Coop on Höheweg is open until 10.30pm.
Migros Opposite Interlaken West station. Cheap self-service staples. Closed Sun.

Restaurants

PizPaz Centralstr. Large place serving reasonably priced pizza (Fr.16.50) and pasta (from Fr.14.40). Closed Mon.
Tell Hauptstr. Just down from *Balmer's* this simple Swiss restaurant offers up rösti and fondue. Rösti Fr.18. Open lunch and dinner.

Drinking and nightlife

Most backpackers congregate at one of the busier hostel bars: *Balmer's* is the most popular and has cheap beer; *Funny Farm Hauptstrasse* is a maverick hostel attracting party-goers; and *Happy Inn* has a lively downstairs bar.
Positiv Einfach Centralstr. 11. A hip music bar, good for a change from the backpacker scene.

Moving on

Train Bern (every 30min; 55min); Grindelwald (every 30min; 35min); Jungfraujoch (every 30min; 2hr 20min – change at Grindelwald or Lauterbrunnen, then Kleine Scheidegg); Lauterbrunnen (every 30min; 20min); Luzern (hourly; 1hr 55min); Zürich (every 2hr; 2hr 5min).

LAUTERBRUNNEN

It's hard to overstate just how stunning the **Lauterbrunnen valley** is. An immense U-shaped cleft with bluffs on either side rising 1000m sheer, doused by some 72 waterfalls, it is utterly spectacular. The **Staubbach falls** – the highest in Switzerland at nearly 300m – tumble just beyond the village of **LAUTERBRUNNEN** at the valley entrance, whose train station (served by trains from Interlaken Ost) is opposite both the funicular station for Mürren and the **tourist office** (Mon–Fri 9am–6pm; June–Sept also Sat & Sun 9am–6pm; Ⓣ 033 856 85 68, Ⓦ www.lauterbrunnen.ch). **Accommodation** is down by the tracks at the cosy *SB Valley Hostel* (Ⓣ 033 855 20 08, Ⓦ www.valleyhostel.ch; dorms Fr.25, doubles Fr.30) or up at the excellent *Mountain Hostel* in Gimmelwald (see below).

From Lauterbrunnen, it's a scenic half-hour walk, or an hourly postbus, 3km up the valley to the spectacular **Trümmelbach falls** (April–Nov daily 8.30/9am–5/6pm; Fr.11), a series of thunderous waterfalls – the run-off from the mountain glaciers – which have carved corkscrew channels into the valley walls. The postbus continues 1.5km to **STECHELBERG** at the end of the road, starting point for the **cable-car ride** up to Gimmelwald, Mürren and the Schilthorn; the huge base station complex is 1km before the hamlet.

MÜRREN AND UP TO THE SCHILTHORN

The cable car from Stechelberg leaps the valley's west wall to reach the quiet hamlet of **GIMMELWALD**, a little-visited spot with the superb self-catering *Mountain Hostel* (Ⓣ 033 855 17 04, Ⓦ www.mountainhostel.com; April–Nov Fr.25). Further up is the car-free village of **MÜRREN**. It's worth the journey for the views: from here, the valley floor is 800m straight down, and the panorama of snowy peaks filling the sky is dazzling. Mürren is also accessible from Lauterbrunnen on the BLM Bergbahn, comprising a steep funicular to Grütschalp (single Fr.8.20/return Fr.16.40) and a spectacular little cliff-edge train from there (IR no discount; ER twenty-five percent discount; SP free). It's easy to do a return trip by cable-car and train. The cable car continues from Mürren on a breathtaking ride (20min) up to the 2970m summit of the **Schilthorn**

(Ⓦwww.schilthorn.ch), where you can enjoy exceptional panoramic views and sip cocktails in the revolving *Piz Gloria* summit restaurant. Schilthornbahn **prices**, compared to the Jungfraujoch ride, are a **bargain**. From Stechelberg to the top is Fr.91.80 return trip, from Mürren Fr.71.40 (IR no discount; ER twenty-five percent discount; SP free to Mürren, then fifty percent off). Going up before 8.40am or after 3.10pm knocks the ticket price down to Fr.69.

GRINDELWALD

Valley-floor trains from Interlaken Ost also run to the more popular holiday centre of **GRINDELWALD**, nestling under the craggy trio of the Wetterhorn, Mettenberg and Eiger. Numerous trails around **Pfingstegg** and especially **First** – both at the end of gondola lines from Grindelwald – provide excellent hiking. The **tourist office** (daily 8/9am–noon & 1.30–5/6pm; shorter hours in April & Nov; Ⓣ033 854 12 12, Ⓦwww.grindelwald.com) is 200m east of the station. A steep fifteen-minute walk will get you to Terrassenweg, a quiet lane running above the village, where there's an excellent **HI hostel** (Ⓣ033 853 10 09, Ⓦwww.youthhostel.ch; dorms Fr.33, doubles Fr.57) and the friendly *Naturfreundehaus* (Ⓣ033 853 13 33; dorms Fr.31, rooms Fr. 36). The well-run *SB Mountain Hostel* (Ⓣ033 853 3838, Ⓦwww.mountainhostel.ch; dorms Fr.37, rooms Fr.51) is on the valley floor beside Grindelwald-Grund station (trains from Grindelwald pass through Grund on their way up to Kleine Scheidegg).

Mountain transport

Trains There are two routes to the top of the Jungfrau from Interlaken, travelling either via Lauterbrunnen or Grindelwald. All trains terminate at the spectacularly located hamlet of Kleine Scheidegg, where you must change for the final pull to Jungfraujoch; the popular practice is to go up one way and down the other.

Fares and tickets The adult return-trip fare from Interlaken to the Jungfraujoch is a budget-crunching Fr.181 (IR no discount; ER Fr.130; SP free to Grindelwald, then fifty percent off to Kleine Scheidegg and 25 percent off to the top) – but the discounted "Good Morning ticket", valid if you travel up on the first or second trains of the day (which start from Interlaken Ost at 6.30am & 7.20am) is Fr.157 from Interlaken, and Fr. 137 from Lauterbrunnen and Grindelwald.

Walking Hiking some sections, up or down, is perfectly feasible in summer, and can help save a great deal on train tickets. Excellent transport networks and vista-rich footpaths linking all stations mean that with a hiking map and timetable you can see and do a great deal in a day.

ZERMATT AND THE MATTERHORN

The shark's-tooth **Matterhorn** (4478m) is the most famous of Switzerland's mountains; in most people's minds, the Matterhorn stands for Switzerland like the Eiffel Tower stands for France. One reason it's so famous is that it stands alone, its impossibly pointy shape sticking up from an otherwise uncrowded horizon above **ZERMATT** village; another is that the quintessential Swiss chocolate, Toblerone, was modelled on it.

What to see and do

Zermatt's main street is thronged year-round with an odd mixture of professional climbers, tour groups, backpackers and fur-clad socialites. No cars are allowed in the village; electric minibuses ferry people between the train station at the northern end of the village and the cable-car terminus 1km south. Opposite the station, GGB Gornergrat-Bahn trains (ER 25 percent discount, IR half-price, SP free) climb above the village, giving spectacular Matterhorn views (sit on the right). They take you all the way up to the **Gornergrat**, a vantage point with a magnificent Alpine panorama including Switzerland's highest peak, the **Dufourspitze** (4634m). In summer, GGB trains leave Zermatt once-weekly

at dawn to arrive in time for a breathtaking Alpine sunrise. At the south end of Zermatt village a cable car heads up via Furi to the **Schwarzsee** (2583m), the most popular point from which to view the peak and, in summer, the trailhead for a zigzag walk (2hr) to the *Berghaus Matterhorn* inn (3260m), right below the mountain. All of Zermatt's cable cars and trains bring you to trailheads and spectacular views, while lifts to **Trockener Steg** give access to 21km of ski runs and a snowboard halfpipe that are open all summer long (day pass Fr.64).

Arrival and information

Train The only way to reach Zermatt is on the spectacular narrow-gauge MGB train line (ER no discount, IR half-price, SP free; ⓦwww.mgbahn.ch). Coming from Bern, Zürich or Milan change at Brig (Briga in Italian); coming from Geneva, Lausanne or Paris change at Visp. The most celebrated way to arrive is on the long east–west St Moritz-to-Zermatt Glacier Express, a day-long journey by panoramic train (reserve at any train station; ER twenty-five percent discount, SP free; IR half-price; ⓦwww.glacierexpress.ch).

Tourist office Outside the station (Mon–Sat 8.30am–6pm; June–Sept & Dec–April also Sun 9.30am–noon & 4–6pm). There's a hotel list courtesy phone here.

Alpin centre Bahnhofstr. 58 ⓣ027 966 24 60; ⓦwww.alpincenter-zermatt.ch (daily 8.30am–noon & 3–7pm). Runs fixed rope courses for Fr.135 and ice climbing for Fr.190.

Ski and Snowboard School In the Alpin Centre ⓣ027 966 24 64 (Mon–Fri 8am–noon & 3–7pm, Sat & Sun 5am–9pm).

Accommodation

Hotel Tannenhof To the east of the Kirchplatz ⓣ027 967 3188, ⓦwww.tannenhof.zermatt.info. Good-value hotel, popular with climbers. Cosy doubles, available with or without a private bathroom. Doubles Fr.90/Fr.110 with bathroom.

Matterhorn campsite Bahnhofstr. ⓣ027 967 39 21, ⓔmatterhorn@campings.ch. Very close to the village; just north of the train station. June–Sept. Rooms Fr.11.

Matterhorn Hostel (SB) Schulmattstr. ⓣ027 968 19 19, ⓦwww.matterhornhostel.com. Friendly staff, but rather cramped and in need of a re-vamp. Dorms Fr.34, doubles Fr.66.

Zermatt Youth Hostel Winkelmatten, Staldenweg 5 ⓣ027 967 23 20, ⓦwww.youthhostel.ch. Excellent hostel on the east side of the village. Half-board only. Dorms Fr.50, doubles Fr.110.

Eating and drinking.

Brown Cow Bahnhofstr. In the *Hotel Post*. Popular pub, serving reasonably priced snacks; sandwiches (Fr.9) and burgers (Fr.12).

Cafe du Pont Bahnhofstr. Simple restaurant with wooden interior, popular with both locals and tourists. Serves up traditional Swiss fare (rösti Fr.15, fondue Fr.23) as well as burgers and sandwiches.

North Wall Steinmattstr. Lively British-run bar across the river.

Papperla Pub Steinmattstr. 34 ⓦwww.papperlapub.ch. Zermatt's busiest après-ski spot.

Moving on

Train Brig (hourly; 1hr 20min); Visp (hourly; 1hr 10min); St Moritz (1–2 daily; 7hr 50min)

ZÜRICH

A beautiful city, set astride a river and turned towards a crystal-clear lake and distant snowy peaks, **ZÜRICH** has plenty to recommend it. The steep, cobbled alleys of the Old Town are great to wander around, with an engaging café culture and a wealth of nightlife, whereas to the northwest of the centre the city's former industrial quarter, known as "Züri-West", has become home to many of the city's trendiest clubs. Whether wandering the streets of the Old Town, window shopping in Bahnhofstrasse or day-tripping to the Rhine Falls, you may end up spending longer here than originally planned.

What to see and do

Across the River Limmat from the station, the narrow lanes of the medieval **Niederdorf** district stretch south, quiet during the day and bustling after dark. The waterfront is lined with fine Baroque *Zunfthäuser* (guildhalls), arcaded lower

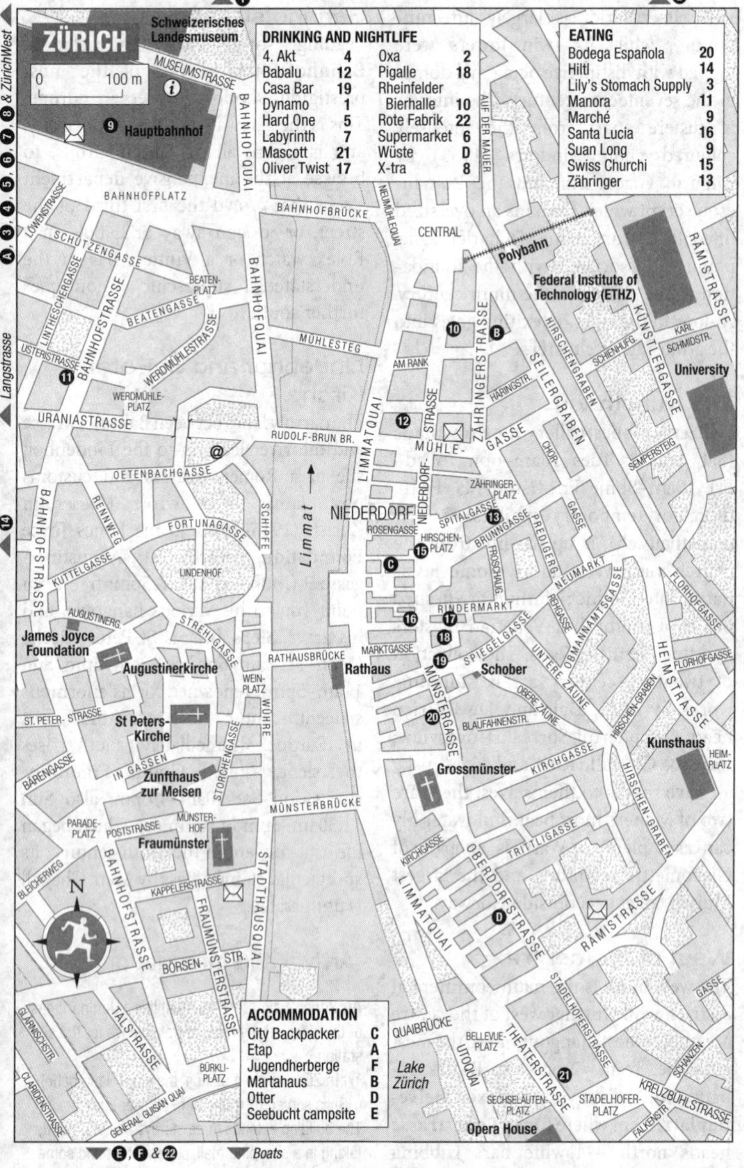

storeys fronting the quayside, now mostly upmarket restaurants. One block in is **Niederdorfstrasse**, initially tacky, but offering plenty of opportunities to explore atmospheric cobbled side alleys and secluded courtyards: Lenin lived at Spiegelgasse 14 in 1917 (pre-Revolution). Just south is Zürich's trademark **Grossmünster** (Great Minster; Mon–Sun 9/10am–5/6pm), where Huldrych Zwingli, father of Swiss Protestantism, began preaching the Reformation in

1519. Its exterior is largely fifteenth-century, while its twin towers were topped with distinctive octagonal domes in the seventeenth century. The interior is austere apart from the intensely coloured choir windows (1933) by Augusto Giacometti and the Romanesque crypt which contains an oversized fifteenth-century statue of Charlemagne, popularly associated with the foundation of the church in the ninth century. A door to the right on exiting gives into the atmospheric **cloister**.

The Kunsthaus

Switzerland's best gallery, the **Kunsthaus** (Sat, Sun & Tues 10am–6pm, Wed–Fri 10am–8pm; Fr.14/students Fr.10, more for temporary exhibits; Ⓦwww.kunsthaus.ch), is up the hill from the church via several alleys. Some fascinating late-Gothic paintings are fleshed out by a roomful of Venetian masters and fine Flemish pieces. The collection of twentieth-century art is stunning: works by Miró, Dalí and De Chirico head a wonderful Surrealist overview; Picasso, Chagall, Klee and Kandinsky all have rooms to themselves; there are two of Monet's most beautiful water lily canvases, plenty of Warhols, an array of Giacometti's sculpture, and the largest Munch collection outside Norway.

West of the centre

The **west bank** is the main commercial district, while further west of the centre are the coolest hangouts and the best streetlife. Tram #2 or #3 to Bezirksgebäude will deliver you to relaxed **Helvetiaplatz**, from where funky **Langstrasse** heads north – lowlife bars rubbing shoulders with avant-garde galleries, the smells of kebabs and pizza mixing with the aroma of marijuana. This fascinating street is a mixture of styles and cultures – Swiss-German blending with French-African, Turkish, Balkan, East Asian and Latin American.

Bahnhofstrasse

Leading south from the station, **Bahnhofstrasse** is one of the most prestigious shopping streets in Europe. This is the gateway into the modern city, and is where all of Zürich strolls, to browse at the inexpensive department stores that crowd the first third of the street, or to sign away Fr.25,000 on a Rolex watch or a Vuitton bag at the understated super-chic boutiques further south.

Lindenhof and St Peter Kirche

The narrow lanes between Bahnhofstrasse and the river lead up to the Lindenhof, site of a Roman fortress and customs post. James Joyce wrote *Ulysses* in Zürich (1915–19), and the James **Joyce Foundation**, nearby at Augustinergasse 9 (Mon–Fri 10am–5pm; free), can point you to his various hangouts, and his grave. Steps away is **St Peter Kirche** (Mon–Fri 8am–6pm, Sat 8am–4pm, Sun 11am–5pm), renowned for its enormous sixteenth-century clock face – the largest in Europe. Immediately south rises the slender-spired Gothic **Fraumünster** (Mon–Sat 10am–4/6pm; also Sun 11.30am–6pm in summer), which began life as a convent in the ninth century; its spectacular stained glass by Marc Chagall is unmissable.

Arrival and information

Air Zürich's airport (Flughafen) lies 11km northeast of the city centre. Frequent trains leave for the city station.

Train Zürich's main station, the giant Hauptbahnhof (HB), is served by trains from all over Europe. The building extends three storeys below ground, taking in a shopping mall, supermarket and some good eateries; the main concourse is the haunt of pickpockets and bag-snatchers, so keep your valuables safe.

Bus The international bus station is 50m north on Sihlquai.

Tourist office On the station concourse Ⓣ044 215 40 00, Ⓦwww.zuerich.com (Mon–Sat 8/8.30am–7/8.30pm, Sun 8.30/9am–6/6.30pm).

Staff will book rooms for free, and sell the Zürich Card (Fr.19/38 one/three days), which entitles you to free rides on public transport and free entry to museums.

City transport

Bike rental Passes available for one day/week for a bargain cost of Fr.2/7 (with photo ID & Fr.20 deposit) from Velogate, next to platform 18 of the station (May–Oct, Mon-Fri 6.30am–11pm, Sat & Sun 8am-11pm).
Tram and bus Although most sites can be covered on foot, the tram and bus system is easy to use (ⓦwww.vbz.ch), with all tickets valid on trams, buses, some boats and local "S-Bahn" city trains.
Tickets Buy tickets from machines at every stop: choose between the green button (24hr; Fr.8); blue button (1hr; Fr.4); or yellow button (short one-way hop; Fr.2.40). You'll need a multizone ticket to get to or from the airport.
Taxis Alpha Taxi ⓣ044 777 77 77; Züritaxi ⓣ044 222 22 22.

Accommodation

Hostels

City Backpacker (SB) Niederdorfstr. 5 ⓣ044 251 90 15, ⓦwww.city-backpacker.ch. Good atmosphere and central location, plus kitchen use, laundry and internet (Fr.20 key deposit). Can be a little cramped when full. No check-in after 10pm. Dorms Fr.35, rooms Fr.110.
Jugendherberge (HI) Mutschellenstr. 114 ⓣ043 399 78 00, ⓦwww.youthhostel.ch. Rather institutional hostel, out in a southwestern suburb. Tram #7 (direction Wollishofen) to Morgental, then 5min walk. Breakfast included. 4-bed dorms Fr.41.50, rooms Fr.66.

TREAT YOURSELF

Otter Oberdorfstr. 7 ⓣ044 251 22 07, ⓦwww.wueste.ch. Friendly staff make this quirky Old Town hotel stand out from the crowd. Rooms are decorated thematically and there's also a dreamy top-floor apartment. Breakfast included; bathrooms are shared. The downstairs bar means you are only ever a few steps away from a good night out. Pay more for a balcony room with stunning views of the Old Town. Double Fr.150.

Hotels

Etap Technoparkstr. 2 ⓣ044 276 20 00, ⓦwww.etaphotel.com. Generic, functional hotel out west in the old industrial quarter, behind the trendy Schiffbau arts centre. Fr.99.
Martahaus Zähringerstr. 36 ⓣ044 251 45 50, ⓦwww.martahaus.ch. Clean Old Town budget hotel with cabin dorms and doubles, plus a café, internet and laundry. Dorms Fr.40, doubles Fr.150.

Campsite

Seebucht Seestr. 559 ⓣ044 482 16 12, ⓦwww.camping-zurich.ch. Well-serviced site on the lakeside, 2km south of the centre. Bus #161 or #165 from Bürkliplatz to Stadtgrenze. Closed Oct–April. Fr.8 per person, tents Fr.12.

Eating

A wander through the Niederdorf district will turn up dozens of eating options – sausage, noodle and french-fry stands, plus beer halls serving daily specials for about Fr.13.

Snack options

Manora 5th floor of Manor store, Bahnhofstr. 75. Good, varied, self-service fare for under Fr.13.
Marché Train station lower level. Good-value main courses for Fr.16, pizzas and paninis Fr.6. Open 6.30am–11pm.
Suan Long Train station lower level. Cheap, filling stir-fries – meat and vegetarian meals Fr.15.

Cafés and restaurants

Bodega Española Münstergasse 15. Atmospheric tapas bar and paella restaurant. Tapas from Fr.10.
Hiltl Sihlstr. 28 ⓦwww.hiltl.ch. Top-quality vegetarian buffet, with budget prices for takeaway. Daily specials Fr.16.50. Mutates into a trendy cocktail bar at night.
Lily's Stomach Supply Langstr. 197. Bustling pan-Asian noodle-bar, serving enormous bowls of noodles and wok dishes from Fr.15. Eat in or take out.
Santa Lucia Marktgasse 21. Popular local chain, serving a wide selection of good-value pasta and pizza dishes from Fr.17. Open late.
Swiss Churchi in *Hotel Adler*, Rosengasse 10. Fantastic people-watching opportunities from this restaurant in the summer when tables spill out onto the Hirschenplatz. Huge portions of Swiss fondue or raclette for Fr.25.
Zähringer Zähringerplatz 11. Co-operative-run café-bar with an alternative-minded clientele and a simple, substantial daily menu (Fr.20).

Drinking and nightlife

Supplementing its lively music venues, Zürich's club scene has skyrocketed recently, and you'll find dance floors heaving. The hip quarter around Langstrasse, west of the centre, is full of DJ bars, and the industrial quarter to the northwest is where the best clubs hide themselves. August sees the Street Parade (Ⓦwww.street-parade.ch), a hedonistic weekend of techno street dancing. *ZüriTipp* (Ⓦwww.zueritipp.ch) magazine has listings and is available at the tourist office.

Bars

4. Akt Heinrichstrasse 22. Lively Züri-west bar, packed with a young crowd.
Babalu Schmidgasse 6. Tiny, chic DJ-bar on an Old Town side street.
Casa Bar Münstergasse 20. Live jazz and blues nightly in the Old Town.
Hard One Hardstrasse 260. Stylish, dimly lit fifth-floor lounge bar with views over the industrial quarter.
Oliver Twist Rindermarkt 6. Homely English pub on an Old Town lane with British and Irish beers.
Pigalle Marktgasse 14. Gay bar filled with the elegantly wasted. Open till 4am Fri and Sat.
Rheinfelder Bierhalle Niederdorfstr. 76. Best of the beerhalls, filled with locals and serving cheap daily specials. Closed Sun.
Wüste In *Hotel Otter*, Oberdorfstr. 7. Mellow, relaxed bar near the Grossmünster. Open till 2am at the weekend.

Clubs

Dynamo Wasserwerkstr. 21. Alternative, punkish bands and dance nights for a young crowd.
Labyrinth Pfingstweidstr. 70. Hard house at this mixed gay/straight venue.
Mascott Theaterstrasse 10 Ⓦwww.mascotte.ch. Most popular of the Old Town clubs. Renowned for its Tuesday rock/metal "Karaoke from Hell" night.
Oxa Andreasstr. 70. Techno and house music, plus famed after-hours parties (Sun 5am–noon).
Rote Fabrik Seestr. 395 Ⓦwww.rotefabrick.ch. Alternative bands, big-name DJs, cheap food and a great riverside bar.
Supermarket Geroldstrasse 17 Ⓦwww.supermarket.li. Popular Züri-West club, attracting international DJs Thurs–Sat.
X-tra Limmatstr. 118 Ⓦwww.x-tra.ch. Spacious modern bar, with popular upstairs DJ club.

Shopping

Bahnhofstrasse is the place to find designer and high-street stores.
Flea market Bürkliplatz (May–Oct Sat 8am–4pm).
Jelmoli Seidengasse 1. Zürich's largest department store.
Kirchgasse has a high concentration of second-hand bookshops, antiques shops and galleries.
Niederdorfstrasse is crammed with boutiques from grungy indie fashions to fabulous jewellery.
Schober Napfgasse 4. Good option for chocolate and cakes.
Travel Book Shop Rindermarkt 20. Good selection of maps and travel guides. Closed Sun and Mon am.

Directory

Consulates Ireland, Claridenstr. 25 Ⓣ044 289 25 15; UK, Hegibachstr. 47 Ⓣ044 383 65 60; USA, Dufourstr. 101 Ⓣ044 422 25 66. Embassies are in Bern.
Exchange/bank UBS Bahnhofstrasse 45 (Mon–Fri 8.15am–4.15pm); or try the station.
Hospital Permanence Medical Centre, Bahnhofplatz 15 Ⓣ044 215 44 44.
Internet Urania, Uraniastrasse 3 (Mon–Sat 7/8am–11pm & Sun 10am–10pm).
Laundry Available at *Martahaus* and City Backpacker.
Left luggage In the station.
Pharmacy Bellevue, Theaterstrasse 14 (24hr) Ⓣ044 266 62 22.
Post office Kasernenstrasse, beside the station.

Moving on

Train Basel (2 hourly; 1hr); Bern (every 30min; 1hr–1hr 25min); Geneva (every 30min–1hr; 2hr 45min); Innsbruck (5 daily; 3hr 20min); Interlaken Ost (every 2hr; 2hr 5min); Lausanne (every 30min; 2hr 10min); Lugano (hourly; 3hr); Luzern (every 30min; 45min); Milan (hourly; 4hr 25min); Prague (1 daily; 13hr); Sargans (every 30min; 1hr); St Moritz (hourly; 3hr 20min – change at Chur); Vienna (3 daily; 9hr).

THE RHINE FALLS

A great fine-weather excursion from Zürich is the half-day trip north to the **Rhine Falls** (Ⓦwww.rhinefalls.com), Europe's largest waterfalls, which tumble 3km west of **SCHAFFHAUSEN**. They are magnificent, not so much for their height (a mere 23m) as for their impressive breadth (150m) and the sheer drama of the place, with spray rising in a cloud of rainbows above the

forested banks. The turreted castle **Schloss Laufen** on the south bank completes the spectacle. Be here on August 1, Switzerland's national holiday, for the famous fireworks display. At the time of writing the observation deck was under renovation and will open in spring 2010. In summer, the best views are from daredevil boats, which scurry about in the spray (Fr.6.50–11). Take a **train** from Zürich either to Winterthur – from where hourly trains serve Schloss Laufen's own little station (April–Oct only) – or to Schaffhausen, from where you can walk (20min) or take bus #1 or #6 to Neuhausen Zentrum, 5min from the falls.

Ticino

The Italian-speaking region of **Ticino** (*Tessin* in German and French) occupies the balmy, lake-laced southern foothills of the Alps. It's a little pocket of Italy in Switzerland and radically different in almost every way: culture, food, architecture, attitude and driving style owe more to Milan than Zürich. Switzerland has controlled the area since the early 1500s, when it defeated the Duke of Milan's army. The main attractions are the beautiful lakeside resorts of **Locarno** and **Lugano**, where mountain scenery merges with the subtropical flora encouraged by the warm climate. The best way to enjoy these chic lakeside towns is to join the locals in wandering through the alleys with an ice cream.

Unless you approach from Italy, there's only one train line in – through the 16km **Gotthard Tunnel**. The track's spiralling contortions on the approach climb are famous: trains pass the onion-domed church at Wassen three times, first far above you, then on a level, and finally far below, before entering the subalpine tunnel.

LOCARNO

Mainline trains speed south to Lugano and Milan, while a branch line heads west from Bellinzona to **LOCARNO**. It's an old town with lots of character on a broad sweeping bay in **Lake Maggiore**, its piazzas overlooked by subtropical gardens of palm trees, camellias and bougainvillea. It can get overrun with the rich and wannabe-famous on summer weekends yet manages to retain its sun-drenched cool.

What to see and do

The town's focus is the **Piazza Grande**, just off the lake front, where exquisitely groomed locals parade to and fro on warm summer nights. The Renaissance Old Town is ranged on gently rising ground behind the piazza.

The church of **Madonna del Sasso** (daily 6.30am–6.45pm), consecrated in 1487, is an impressive ochre vision floating above the town on a wooded crag. The walk up (or down) through a wooded ravine and past decaying shrines is glorious; or take the funicular (Fr.6.60 return) from just west of the station to Ticino's greatest photo-op, looking down on the church and lake.

From the top station, an ear-poppingly steep cable car climbs to **Cardada**, set amidst fragrant pine woods, with walking routes and a spectacular, silent chairlift whisking you up to **Cimetta**, where the restaurant terrace offers a view you won't forget in a hurry.

LOCARNO INTERNATIONAL FILM FESTIVAL

Early August's Locarno International Film Festival (Ⓦwww.pardo.ch) is catching up with Cannes in terms of star appeal; catch nightly offerings on Europe's largest movie screen, set up in Piazza Grande.

A short bus ride east of Locarno is **Valle Verzasca**, where braver travellers can re-enact the opening scene of the James Bond film *Goldeneye*, by **bungee-jumping** a world-record 220m off the Verzasca Dam (April–Oct daily; Fr.255; book on ⓣ091 780 78 00, ⓦwww.trekking.ch) – in July & August, you can jump by moonlight; see website for details.

Arrival and information

Train Locarno's train station is 150m northeast of Piazza Grande.

Boat The landing stage is between the train station and Piazza Grande; summer boats run to nearby Swiss lakeside resorts such as Ascona, and south to Italian ones such as Stresa (on the main line to Milan).

Tourist office In the Casino complex opposite the landing stage ⓣ091 791 00 91, ⓦwww.maggiore.ch (Mon–Fri 9am–6pm; April–Oct also Sat 10am–6pm, Sun 10am–1.30pm & 2.30–5pm). Really helpful staff.

Accommodation

Delta campsite ⓣ091 751 60 81, ⓦwww.campingdelta.com; March–Oct. Expensive but well-equipped campsite 20min walk south along the lakeshore (just past the lido). You can pay extra for a lakeside pitch. Rooms Fr.26.

HI hostel "Palagiovani" Via Varenna 18 ⓣ091 756 15 00, ⓦwww.youthhostel.ch; bus #31/36 to Cinque Vie. Friendly hostel 10min walk from the centre of town with four- or six-bed dorms Fr.39 and doubles Fr.64.

Eating and drinking

Cantina Canetti Little place just off the Piazza Grande with plain local cooking (from Fr.14) and live accordion on weekend nights.

TREAT YOURSELF

Garni du Lac Via Ramogna 3 ⓣ091 751 29 21, ⓦwww.du-lac-locarno.ch. In a great location by the lake, this fabulous hotel offers a buffet breakfast on its roof terrace, weather permitting, and en-suite rooms with balconies overlooking either the Piazza Grande or the lake. Doubles Fr.160.

Manora Branch of the self-service chain by the train station, with a wide range of good, cheap meals for Fr.13 or under. Open late and Sun.

Migros Gustibus Piazza Grande. Takeaway spot offering paninis for Fr.5 and pizza slices for Fr.2.50.

Moving on

Train Basel (every 2hr; 4hr 10min); Bellinzona – change for Lugano (every 30min; 25min); Zürich (hourly; 3hr 10min).

LUGANO

With its cluster of piazzas and tree-lined promenades, **LUGANO** is the most alluring of Ticino's lake resorts, less touristy than Locarno but with twice the chic factor.

What to see and do

The centre of town is **Piazza della Riforma**, a huge café-lined square just by the exceptionally beautiful **Lago di Lugano**. Through the maze of steep lanes northwest of Riforma, Via Cattedrale dog-legs up to the **Cattedrale San Lorenzo**, characterized by a fine Renaissance portal, fragments of interior frescoes and spectacular views from its terrace. Also from Riforma, narrow Via Nassa – home of big-name designer boutiques – heads southwest to the medieval church of **Santa Maria degli Angioli**, containing a stunning wall-sized fresco of the Crucifixion. A little further south is the **Museo d'Arte Moderna**, Riva Caccia 5 (Tues–Sun 10am–6pm; Fr. 12/students Fr.8; ⓦwww.mdam.ch), with world-class exhibitions; a little further still is the modestly named district of **Paradiso**, from where a funicular rises to **San Salvatore**, a rugged rock pinnacle offering fine views of the lake and surrounding countryside.

The best of the lake is behind (south of) San Salvatore on the Ceresio peninsula, accessed by boats or postbuses. The jewel of this area is **Morcote** on the southern tip of the peninsula; tranquil

stepped lanes lead up to its photogenic church of **Santa Maria del Sasso**, and several walks explore the woods, including a trail back to San Salvatore (2hr 30min).

Arrival and information

Train Lugano's train station overlooks the town from the west, linked to the centre by a short funicular or by steps down to Via Cattedrale.
Tourist office Palazzo Civico, off Riforma ⓣ091 913 32 32, ⓦwww.lugano-tourism.ch (Mon–Fri 9am–5.30/7pm; April–Oct also Sat 9am–6pm, Sun 10am–6pm). Boats around the lake (IR & ER no discount, SP free) depart from directly opposite.

Accommodation

HI hostel Via Cantonale 13, Savosa ⓣ091 966 27 28, ⓦwww.youthhostel.ch. Take bus #5 to Crocifisso from the stop 200m from the train station (March–Oct). Excellent, quiet hostel with a large garden area and swimming pool. Dorms Fr. 26, doubles Fr.48.
Hotel Pestalozzi Piazza Indipendenza ⓣ091 921 46 46, ⓦwww.pestalozzi-lugarno.ch. More central (150m from the lake) with a great restaurant and friendly staff. Single room Fr.66 and double Fr.112.
La Piodella campsite ⓣ091 994 77 88, ⓦwww.campingtcs.ch. One of several lakeside campsites in Agno, 3km west of the town. Take the train from the FLP station (direction Ponte Tresa). Fr.8.40 per person, tents Fr.14.40.

Eating and drinking

Coop Via Nassa. Fantastic rooftop terrace with self-service.
La Tinèra off Via dei Gorini, behind Riforma. Good place for pasta and tasty Ticinese chicken stews (Fr.18). Closed Sun and Mon.
Manora Piazza Cioccaro. Inexpensive self-service staples for under Fr.13. There's an outside terrace at this branch.

Moving on

Train Luzern (every 2hr; 2hr 45min); Zürich (hourly; 3hr).
Bus St Moritz (mid-June to mid-Oct daily, otherwise 3 weekly; 3hr 45min); book at the train station.

Liechtenstein

Only slightly larger than Manhattan island, **Liechtenstein** is the world's sixth-smallest country. It's an unassuming place squashed between Switzerland and Austria, ruled over by His Serene Highness Prince Hans Adam II, and has made a mint from nursing some Fr.90 billion in its numbered bank accounts. The main reason to visit is for the novelty value – an easy day-trip from Zürich, less than two hours away on a train you can see the whole country in a day. Swiss francs are legal tender, but the phone system is separate (country code ⓣ423).

VADUZ

From Sargans train station on the Zürich–Chur line, regular bus #1 shuttles over the Rhine (no border controls) in half an hour to the capital **VADUZ**, a tiny town bulging with glass-plated **banks** and squadrons of aimless visitors. The central hub is the post office, where all buses stop, midway between the two parallel main streets, Äulestrasse and pedestrianized Städtle. Facing it is the sleek **Kunstmuseum** (Tues–Sun 10am–5pm, Thurs till 8pm; Fr.12/students Fr.8), displaying temporary art exhibitions, some of which draw on the private collection inherited – and added to – by the prince. Perched on the forested hillside above is the prince's restored sixteenth-century **castle** (no public access).

Postbuses from Vaduz serve all points in Liechtenstein – if you have time to spare, catch bus #10 to the mountain resort of **MALBUN**, at 1602m. Buses also serve Feldkirch just across the border in Austria (passport needed), from where trains run on to Bregenz, Innsbruck and Vienna.

Arrival and information

Arrival Buses from Sargans stop on Vaduz's main street, by the post office.

Tourist office Städtle 37 ⓣ 00423 239 63 00, ⓦ www.tourismus.li (daily 9am–5pm; Nov–April closed Sat & Sun). They can bang a stamp into your passport as a memento (Fr.2).

Accommodation

HI hostel Schaan-Vaduz Untere Rüttigasse 6 ⓣ 232 50 22 (March–Oct). Quiet rural location, looking out over fields and mountains. 5min walk from the Mühleholz bus stop in Schaan (2km north of Vaduz). Dorms Fr.32.50, doubles Fr.56.50.
Mittagsspitze campsite ⓣ 392 36 77, ⓦ www.campingtriesen.li. Tranquil campsite with swimming pool, 5km south in the countryside near Triesen. Fr.8.50 per person, tents Fr.8.

Eating and drinking

Café Wolf Städtle 29. Pavement café with daily two-course set lunch menu (Swiss/Italian fare) for Fr.18/22.
Pizza Bar Potenza Herrengasse 9. Tiny bar serving up crispy thin-crust pizzas (from Fr.12.50) to bankers, locals and tourists.

Moving on

Bus Malbun (hourly; 30min).

Turkey

HIGHLIGHTS

COVERED BAZAAR, İSTANBUL: the world's largest covered market with over 3000 stalls

CAPPADOCIA: a lunar landscape, complete with eerie caves and underground cities

EPHESUS: one of the world's best-preserved ancient cities

ANTALYA: enjoy an operetta in the atmospheric open air theatre of Aspendos

KAŞ: a great base for beaches, ancient sites, and adventure sports

ROUGH COSTS

DAILY BUDGET Basic €25/occasional treat €40

DRINK Raki €3

FOOD Kebab with side order €6

HOSTEL/BUDGET HOTEL €15/€15–25

TRAVEL Bus: Ankara–Nevşehir (250km) €13

FACT FILE

POPULATION 72 million

AREA 780,580 sq km

LANGUAGE Turkish

CURRENCY Turkish lira (TL)

CAPITAL Ankara (population: 4.3 million)

INTERNATIONAL PHONE CODE ⓣ90

Introduction

Turkey has multiple identities. Poised between East and West, mosques coexist with churches, and Roman remnants crumble alongside ancient Hittite sites. The country is politically secular, though the majority of its people are Muslim, and is an immensely rewarding place to travel, not least because of the people, whose reputation for friendliness and hospitality is richly deserved.

Much of the country's delights are inexpensive pleasures. Whether it's indulging in tasty *börek* pastries or dancing in back-street bars, there are plenty of activities to consume your time but not your budget.

Most visitors begin their trip in **İstanbul**, a heady mixture of European shopping districts, Ottoman architecture and Anatolian cultural influences. South from here, small country towns are swathed in olive groves, while the area is littered with ancient sites, most notable of all **Ephesus**. Beyond the functional city of **İzmir**, the **Aegean coast** is Turkey at its most developed, with large numbers drawn to hedonistic party resorts such as **Bodrum** and **Marmaris**. Beyond here, the aptly named Turquoise Coast is home to resorts famous for their fabulous water- and adventure-sports facilities such as **Fethiye** and **Kaş**. Inland from here is the spectacular **Cappadocia**, with its famous rock churches, subterranean cities and landscape studded with cave dwellings. Further north, **Ankara**, Turkey's capital, is a planned city whose contrived Western feel gives some indication of the priorities of the modern Turkish Republic.

CHRONOLOGY

1250 BC According to Homer's *Iliad* Troy is cleverly taken by the Greeks who sneak into the city in a wooden horse.

334 BC Alexander the Great marches through Anatolia, present-day Turkey.

129 BC Romans conquer Anatolia.

47 AD St Paul brings Christianity to Anatolia.

330 Emperor Constantine founds Constantinople, calling it the new Rome and establishing the Byzantine Empire.

1288 The Islamic Ottoman Empire starts to expand across present-day Turkey.

1526 The Ottomans defeat the Habsburgs taking large areas of Europe.

1832 Following heavy fighting, the Greeks gain independence from Ottoman Turkey.

1918 The Ottomans enter World War I on the side of the Germans and are defeated by the Allies.

1923 After its War of Independence, Turkey is declared a Republic led by President Kemal Atatürk.

1928 The Turkish constitution declares Turkey to be a secular state.

1945 Turkey remains neutral during World War II, lending nominal assistance to the Nazis whilst outwardly supporting the Allies.

1960 Army takes power in a coup that encounters minimal resistance, dismissing the ruling Democrat Party and hanging its leaders.

1980 Once more the army overthrows government and takes control. Governance is given back to civilians a couple of years later.

1993 Tansu Cillar becomes Turkey's first female Prime Minister.

2005 Talks about Turkish accession to the EU are held, but a decision remains elusive.

2007 Tens of thousands of secularists protest in Ankara against Islamist Prime Minister Erdogan's proposed run for president.

2009 Rare meeting between Prime Minister Erdogan and Ahmet Türk, leader of the pro-Kurdish Democratic Society Party.

ARRIVAL AND VISAS

Tourist **visas** (€10–45 depending on nationality) are required for individuals from most countries and can be obtained upon arrival. These usually last for three months and enable visitors to

travel between Turkey and neighbouring countries. Contact your local Turkish embassy for more information.

The most common point of **arrival** is İstanbul with overland travellers arriving at the *otogar (*bus station) or Sirkeci train station located near the pier in Eminönü. International air arrivals fly into İstanbul's Atatürk **airport**, where connecting flights can be caught to other popular destinations such as İzmir and Ankara. For travellers heading to Turkey's Turquoise Coast, Antalya's international airport is a good bet for the region's many resorts. If you're travelling to Turkey by sea you're likely to arrive at either Kuşadasi or Marmaris where ferries connect Turkey with the Greek islands.

GETTING AROUND

The **train** system, run by TCDD (Ⓦwww.tcdd.gov.tr) is limited. The most useful services are the express routes between İstanbul and Ankara, and other long-distance links to main provincial cities such as Edirne, Konya, Denizli and İzmir. Cheap sleeper cabins are available on overnight services. Reservations are only necessary at weekends or on national holidays. An ISIC card gets a twenty percent discount. InterRail passes are valid, Eurail aren't.

Long-distance buses are more reliable. Most routes are covered by several competing firms, which all have ticket booths at the bus station (*otogar* or terminal) from which they operate, as well as an office in the town centre. **Fares** vary only slightly between companies: expect to pay about 10TL/100km. For short hops you're most likely to use a **dolmuş**, a **car** or **minibus** that follows a set route, picking up and dropping off along the way. Sometimes the destination will be posted on a sign at the kerbside, and sometimes within the *dolmuş* itself, though you'll generally have to ask. Fares are very low.

Nearly all **ferries** are run by Türkiye Denizcilik Işletmesi (TDI), who operate

everything from inner-city shuttles and inter-island lines to international routes. Overnight services are popular, and you should buy **tickets** in advance through authorized TDI agents. A third-class double cabin from İstanbul to İzmir costs about 100TL per person. Students get a thirty percent discount with an ISIC card.

ACCOMMODATION

Finding **accommodation** is generally no problem, except in high season at the busier coastal resorts and in the larger towns. A double room in a one-star hotel costs 30–55TL in season depending on the location, with breakfast sometimes included. Basic ungraded **hotels** or **pansiyons** (pensions) offer fairly spartan rooms, with or without bathroom, for as low as 20TL. There's also a well-established network of **backpacker hotels**. Most rooms tend to be sparse but clean, at 7–20TL for a dorm bed, 25–50TL for an en-suite double. Many resort-based places close in winter, so it's wise to call ahead. **Campsites** are common only on the coast and in national parks. Per-person charges are around 5–20TL, plus 5–7TL per tent. Campsites often rent out tents or provide chalet accommodation for 20–40TL.

FOOD AND DRINK

At its finest, Turkish food is one of the world's great cuisines, yet prices are on the whole affordable. **Breakfast** (*kahvaltı*) served at hotels and *pansiyons* is usually a buffet (approximately 5TL though often included in the price), offering bread with butter, cheese, jam, honey, olives and tea or coffee. Many workers start the morning with a *börek* (1.50TL) or a *poça*, pastries filled with meat, cheese or potato that are sold at a tiny *büfe* (stall/café) or at street carts. Others make do with a simple *simit* (sesame-seed bread ring). Snack vendors hawk *lahmacun*, small "pizzas" with meat-based toppings, and, in coastal cities, *midye dolma* (stuffed mussels). Another option is *pide*, or Turkish pizza – flat bread with various toppings.

Meat dishes in **restaurants** include several variations on the kebab (*kebap*). Fish and seafood are good, if usually pricey. **Mezes** – an extensive array of cold appetizers – come in all shapes and sizes, the most common being *dolma* (peppers or vine leaves stuffed with rice), *patlícan salata* (aubergine in tomato sauce), and *acılı* (a mixture of tomato paste, onion, chilli and parsley). Most budget restaurants are alcohol-free; some places marked *içk ili* (licensed) may be more expensive.

For **dessert**, there's every imaginable concoction at a *pastane* (sweet shop): best are the honey-soaked baklava, and a variety of milk puddings, most commonly *sütlaç*. Other sweets include *aşure* (Noah's pudding), a sort of rosewater jelly laced with pulses, raisins and nuts: and *lokum* or Turkish delight.

NARGILES

Any visitor to Turkey will soon observe the nation's love affair with smoking. Smoke-free zones in restaurants and other public places are virtually nonexistent. Instead, a variety of bars exist specializing in **nargile** (waterpipe) smoking. *Nargiles* use special flavoured tobacco with varieties ranging from chocolate to strawberry. In touristy cafés smoking a *nargile* can cost about 16TL compared with 7TL in a locals' joint.

Drinks

Tea (*çay*) is the national drink, with sugar on the side but no milk. **Turkish coffee** (*kahve*) is served in tiny cups. Instant coffee is losing ground to fresh filter coffee in trendier cafés. **Fruit juices** (*meyva suyu*) can be excellent but are usually sweetened. You'll also come across **ayran**, watered-down yoghurt, which makes a refreshing drink. The

main locally brewed brands of **beer** (*bira*) are Efes Pilsen and Tuborg. The national aperitif is anis-flavoured *rakí* – a strong spirit consisting of 45 percent alcohol. It's usually topped up with water and enjoyed with mezes or a *nargile* (see box opposite).

CULTURE AND ETIQUETTE

Turkey's unspoken codes of conduct can catch the first-time visitor off guard. Away from the main cities you should **dress modestly** and avoid shorts and revealing attire – this is particularly important the further east you travel. If you are a female traveller, it is essential to wear a headscarf or shawl if you plan on visiting a mosque.

In almost every sphere of social interaction, **tea drinking** plays an important role. You'll notice shop salesmen commonly invite you to peruse their goods over tea.

Although interaction between Turkish men and women is quite formalized, single female travellers may experience some harassment. Note also that while many young Turkish women visit bars and clubs few of them go out unaccompanied at night and you should observe this rule away from tourist areas.

SPORTS AND ACTIVITIES

Most tour operators in the established resorts have information about both summer and winter adventure sports. For **scuba diving**, check out Ⓦwww.meddiving.com. Undoubtedly the most popular sport enjoyed by locals is **football**, with Galatasaray, Beşiktaş and Fenerbahçe (all from İstanbul) being three of the nation's favourite teams. Major stadiums for national games include 19 Mayıs stadium, located in Ankara. To find out about games and buy tickets, visit Ⓦwww.biletix.com.

HAGGLING

Shopping in Turkey requires more than just money. In bazaars, market stalls and independent shops, you should try **haggling** – the original price quoted can be three times the price of the item's actual value.

Avoid displaying too much enthusiasm over your desired item and if the price quoted sounds expensive, inform the shopkeeper that you would like to shop around for a better deal – this might result in a better offer.

COMMUNICATIONS

Most **post offices** (PTT) open Monday to Saturday 8.30am to 5.30pm, with main branches open till 7/8pm and also on Sun. Use the yurtdışı (overseas) slot on postboxes. **Phone calls** can be made from Turk Telecom booths and the PTT. Post offices and kiosks sell phonecards (30, 60 and 100 units) and also have metered phones. Some payphones accept credit cards. Numerous private phone shops (Köntürlü telefon) offer metered calls at dubious, unofficial rates. The international operator is on Ⓣ115. There are **internet** cafés in most towns, charging 1.50TL–3.50TL/hr.

INFORMATION

Most towns of any size have a **tourist office** (Turizm Danışma Bürosu)

TURKEY ON THE NET

Ⓦ**www.about-turkey.com** Tourist information.
Ⓦ**www.hitit.co.uk** Alternative tourism.
Ⓦ**www.istanbulcityguide.com** Good city listings.
Ⓦ**www.mymerhaba.com** Information site aimed at ex pats.
Ⓦ**www.turkishdailynews.com** Main local English newspaper.
Ⓦ**www.turkeytravelplanner.com** Turkey expert's personal guide to the country.

generally open Monday to Friday 8.30am to 12.30pm and 1.30 to 5.30pm. Staff may not speak English, but they often have good brochures and maps, and should be able to help you with accommodation. City tourist offices normally stock reasonable street plans.

MONEY AND BANKS

Currency is the **Turkish lira** (TL), divided into 100 kuruş. There are coins of 1, 5, 10, 25, 50 kuruş, and 1TL, and notes of 1, 5, 10, 20, 50, 100TL. Exchange rates for foreign currency are always better inside Turkey. Many pensions

Turkish

Turkish		Pronunciation
Yes	*Evet*	Evet
No	*Hayır/yok*	Hi-uhr/yok
Please	*Lütfen*	Lewtfen
Thank you	*Teşekkürler/mersi/sağol*	Teshekkewrler/sa-ol
Hello/Good day	*Merhaba*	Merhabuh
Goodbye	*Hoşçakalın*	Hosh-cha kaluhn
Excuse me	*Pardon*	Pardon
Where?	*Nerede?*	Neredeh?
Good	*İyi*	Eeyee
Bad	*Kötü*	Kurtew
Near	*Yakın*	Yakuhn
Far	*Uzak*	Oozak
Cheap	*Ucuz*	Oojooz
Expensive	*Pahalı*	Pahaluh
Open	*Açık*	Achuhk
Closed	*Kapalı*	Kapaluh
Today	*Bugün*	Boogewn
Yesterday	*Dün*	Dewn
Tomorrow	*Yarın*	Yaruhn
How much is...?	*Ne kadar...?*	Ne kadar...?
What time is it?	*Saatiniz var mı?*	Saatiniz var muh?
I don't understand	*Anlamıyorum*	Anlamuh-yoroom
Do you speak English?	*İngilizce biliyor musunuz?*	Eengeeleezjeh beeleeyor moosoonooz
Sorry	*Özür dilerim*	Erzer delereem
Do you have...?	*...var mı?*	...va mur?
I would like...	*...istiyorum*	...e-stee-yo-rum
What is your name?	*Adınız ne?*	A-denurz nay?
Can you stop here?	*burada durabilir misiniz ?*	
I'd like the bill	*Hesabı Istiyorum*	hes-ab ee-stee-yo-rum
One	*Bir*	Bir
Two	*İki*	Iki
Three	*Üç*	Ewch
Four	*Dört*	Durt
Five	*Beş*	Besh
Six	*Altı*	Altuh
Seven	*Yedi*	Yedi
Eight	*Sekiz*	Sekiz
Nine	*Dokuz*	Dokuz
Ten	*On*	On

STUDENT AND YOUTH DISCOUNTS

Finding places that consistently offer **student discounts** in Turkey is a task in itself. Despite the presence of a large student population in many of the major cities, few shops or bars offer student discounts. Nevertheless, an ISIC card can get you a small discount on bus travel with some of the major firms such as Kamil Koç, Pamukkale, Uludag and Varan. It's also worth asking about student discounts before you book into a hotel, as many may be willing to offer a discount but reluctant to publicize the fact.

and hotels, particularly in the popular destinations, also quote prices in **euros**, particularly for more expensive options, and you can usually pay in either euros or Turkish lira. The current exchange rate is 2.60TL to £1; 1.60TL to US$1; and 2.20TL to €1.

Banks open Monday to Friday 8.30am to noon and 1.30 to 5pm; some, notably Garanti Bankasi, are open at lunchtimes and on Saturday. Some of the **exchange booths** run by banks in coastal resorts, airports and ferry docks charge a small commission. Private exchange offices have competitive rates and no commission. Almost all banks have ATMs. **Post offices** in sizeable towns also sometimes change cash and cheques, for a one-percent commission.

OPENING HOURS AND HOLIDAYS

Shops are generally open Monday to Saturday 9am to 7/8pm, and possibly Sunday, depending on the owner. There are two **religious holidays**. Kurban Bayram (the Feast of the Sacrifice) falls on November 16 to 19 in 2010, November 6 to 9 in 2011, and October 26 to 29 in 2012. Şeker Bayram (Sugar Holiday), which marks the end of the Muslim fasting month of Ramadan falls September 9 to 11 in 2010, and August 30 to September 1 in 2011. If either falls midweek, the government may choose to extend the holiday period to as much as nine days. Many shops and restaurants close as their owners return to their home towns for the holiday. Banks and public offices are also closed on the **secular holidays**: January 1, April 23, May 19, August 30, October 29.

EMERGENCIES

Street **crime** is uncommon and theft is rare. Police wear dark blue uniforms with baseball caps, with their division – *trafik*, *narkotik*, etc – clearly marked. In rural areas, you'll find the camouflage-clad Jandarma, a division of the regular army. For minor **health** complaints, head for the nearest pharmacy (*eczane*). Night-duty pharmacists are known as *nöbetçi*; the current rota is posted in every pharmacy's front window. For more serious ailments, go to a hospital (*klinik*) – either public (Devlet Hastane or SSK Hastanesi), or the much higher quality and cleaner private (Özel Hastane).

EMERGENCY NUMBERS

Police ☎155; Ambulance ☎112; Fire ☎110.

İstanbul

Arriving in **İSTANBUL** can result in sensory overload: backstreets teem with traders pushing handcarts, the smell of grilled food from roadside vendors lingers in the air whilst the sales patter of hawkers reverberates through the streets. Yet this is merely one aspect of modern İstanbul. With its trendy bars and pavement cafés, a distinctly Continental influence also pervades throughout.

İstanbul is the only city in the world to have played capital to consecutive Christian and Islamic empires, and retains features of both. Named **Byzantium** after the Greek Colonists Byzas, the city was an important trading centre. In the fourth century it was renamed **Constantinople** when Constantine chose it as the new capital of the Roman Empire. The city later became an independent empire, adopting the Greek language and Christianity as its religion. The region gradually became ruled by the Islamic **Ottomans** and in 1453 the city was captured by the Ottoman Conqueror Mehmet. By the nineteenth century, the glory days of Ottoman domination were over. After the War of Independence, the territorial boundaries of modern day Turkey were set and the country's leader, Atatürk, created a new capital in Ankara.

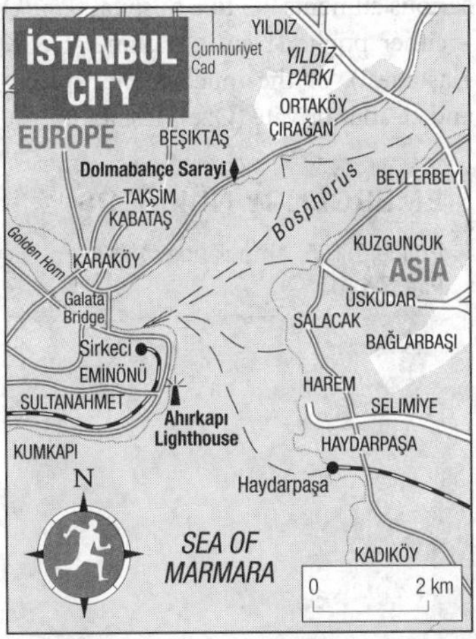

What to see and do

The city is divided in two by the **Bosphorus**, a stretch of water that runs between the Black Sea and the Sea of Marmara, dividing Europe from Asia. At right angles to it, the inlet of the **Golden Horn** cuts the European side in two. It is this European section where most visitors spend their time, wandering around the cobbled streets and tourist sites in **Sultanahmet** or exploring the fast-paced district of **Beyoğlu**. Sandwiched between the two is **Eminönü** and the old Levantine area of Galata, now **Karaköy**, home to one of the city's most famous landmarks, the Galata Tower. An exploration on foot of each of these areas can easily be done. Navigation between and beyond these areas, however, requires the use of public transport.

Aya Sofya

The former Byzantine cathedral of **Aya Sofya** (Tues–Sun 9.15am–4.30/6pm; 20TL), readily visible thanks to its massive domed structure, is perhaps the single most compelling sight in the city. Commissioned in the sixth century by the Emperor Justinian, it was converted to a mosque in 1453, after which the minarets were added; it's been a museum since 1934. For centuries this was the largest enclosed space in the world, and the interior – filled with shafts of light from the high windows around the dome – is still profoundly impressive. There are a few features left over from its time as a mosque – a mihrab (niche indicating the direction of Mecca), a mimber (pulpit) and the enormous wooden plaques which bear sacred names of God, the prophet Muhammad and the first four Caliphs. There are also remains of abstract and figurative mosaics.

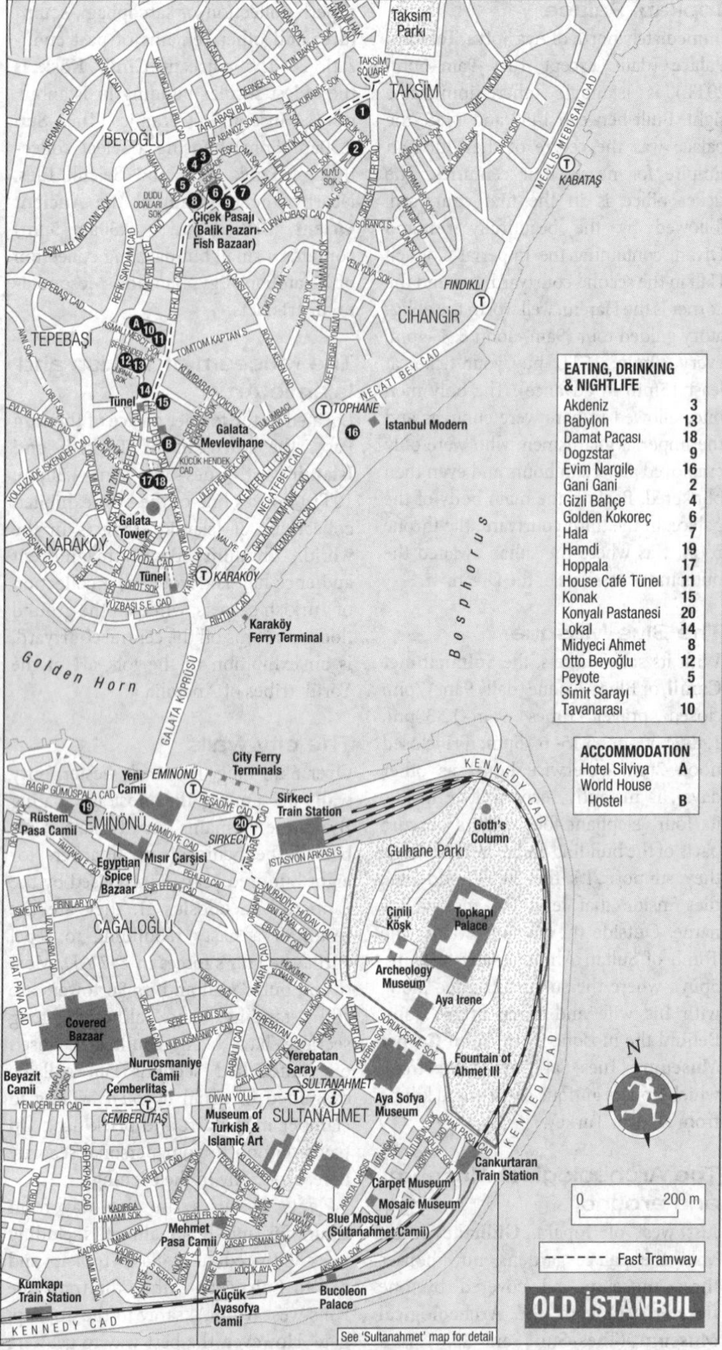
OLD İSTANBUL
Beşiktaş
Kadiköy
City Walls, Kariye Camii & Esenler Bus Station
Taksim Parkı
TAKSIM SQUARE
TAKSIM
BEYOĞLU
KABATAŞ
FINDIKLI
CIHANGIR
TEPEBAŞI
TOPHANE
İstanbul Modern
Çiçek Pasajı (Balik Pazarı-Fish Bazaar)
Tünel
Galata Mevlevihane
Galata Tower
KARAKÖY
Karaköy Ferry Terminal
Bosphorus
Golden Horn
GALATA KÖPRÜSÜ
City Ferry Terminals
Yeni Camii
EMİNÖNÜ
Rüstem Pasa Camii
Egyptian Spice Bazaar
Mısır Çarşisi
SIRKECI
Sirkeci Train Station
Goth's Column
Gulhane Parkı
CAĞALOĞLU
Çinili Köşk
Topkapı Palace
Archeology Museum
Aya Irene
Covered Bazaar
Beyazit Camii
Nuruosmaniye Camii
Çemberlitaş
ÇEMBERLITAŞ
Yerebatan Saray
SULTANAHMET
Fountain of Ahmet III
Aya Sofya Museum
Museum of Turkish & Islamic Art
Hippodrome
Carpet Museum
Mosaic Museum
Cankurtaran Train Station
Blue Mosque (Sultanahmet Camii)
Mehmet Pasa Camii
Küçük Ayasofya Camii
Bucoleon Palace
Kumkapı Train Station
KENNEDY CAD
See 'Sultanahmet' map for detail
0 200 m
Fast Tramway
EATING, DRINKING & NIGHTLIFE
Akdeniz 3
Babylon 13
Damat Paçası 18
Dogzstar 9
Evim Nargile 16
Gani Gani 2
Gizli Bahçe 4
Golden Kokoreç 6
Hala 7
Hamdi 19
Hoppala 17
House Café Tünel 11
Konak 15
Konyalı Pastanesi 20
Lokal 14
Midyeci Ahmet 8
Otto Beyoğlu 12
Peyote 5
Simit Sarayı 1
Tavanarası 10
ACCOMMODATION
Hotel Silviya A
World House Hostel B

Topkapı Palace

Immediately north of Aya Sofya, **Topkapı Palace** (daily except Tues 9am–5pm; 20TL) is İstanbul's other unmissable sight. Built between 1459 and 1465, the palace was the centre of the Ottoman Empire for nearly four centuries. The ticket office is in the first courtyard, followed by the beautifully restored Divan, containing the Imperial Council Hall in the second courtyard. Around the corner is the Harem, well worth the obligatory guided tour (9am–noon & 1–4pm, every 30min; 15TL; buy your ticket at least 15min in advance). The only men once allowed in here were eunuchs and the imperial guardsmen, who were only employed at certain hours and even then blinkered. Back in the main body of the palace, in the third courtyard, the throne room was where the sultan awaited the outcome of sessions of the Divan.

The Blue Mosque

With its six minarets, the **Sultanahmet Camii**, or Blue Mosque (daily 9am–7pm; closed prayer times 9am–12.30pm, 1.45–4.30pm, 5.15–6.15pm; Fri closed noon–2pm, otherwise hours as other days), is instantly recognizable; inside, its four "elephant foot" pillars obscure parts of the building and dwarf the dome they support. It's the 20,000-odd blue tiles inside that lend the mosque its name. Outside the precinct wall is the Tomb of Sultan Ahmet (daily 8.30am–5pm), where the sultan is buried along with his wife and three of his sons. Behind the mosque is the **Vakıf Carpet Museum** (Tues–Sat 9am–4pm; free), which houses antique carpets and kilims from all over Turkey.

The Archeological Museum and around

Just west of Topakı, **Gülhane Parkı**, once the palace gardens, now houses three museums all covered by one ticket (10TL). In the **Archeological Museum** (Tues–Sun 9am–5pm) is a superb collection of sarcophagi, sculptures and other remains of past civilizations. The adjacent **Çinili Köşk** is the oldest secular building in İstanbul, now a Museum of Ceramics (Tues–Sun 9.30am–5pm) housing a select collection of İznık ware and Selçuk tiles. Nearby, the **Museum of the Ancient Orient** (Wed–Sun 9:30am–5pm) contains a small but dazzling collection of Anatolian, Egyptian and Mesopotamian artefacts.

The Museum of Turkish and Islamic Art

Located in the former palace of Ibrahim Paşa, the **Museum of Turkish and Islamic Art** (Tues–Sun 9am–4.30pm; 10TL) houses one of the best-exhibited collections of Islamic artefacts in the world. Ibrahim Paşa's magnificent audience hall is devoted to a collection of Turkish carpets, while on the ground floor, in rooms off the central courtyard, is an exhibition of the folk art of the Yörük tribes of Anatolia.

The city walls

Over 6km long, İstanbul's western **city walls** are among the most fascinating Byzantine remains in Turkey; they barred the peninsula to attackers for eight hundred years. First raised by the Emperor Theodosius II, they are the result of a hasty rebuilding to repel Attila the Hun's forces in 447 AD. Most of the outer wall and its 96 towers are still standing, and although long sections have been rebuilt and closed off, untouched sections can still be examined in detail if you're willing to clamber in the dirt and brick dust. Do pay attention to your personal security here, especially in the evening.

Plenty of buses run this way from Eminönü and Sultanahmet, including bus #80 to Yedikule, #84 to Topkapı and #86 to Edirnekapı, while the tram line runs west from Aksaray to the Topkapı gate. However, the best way to get here

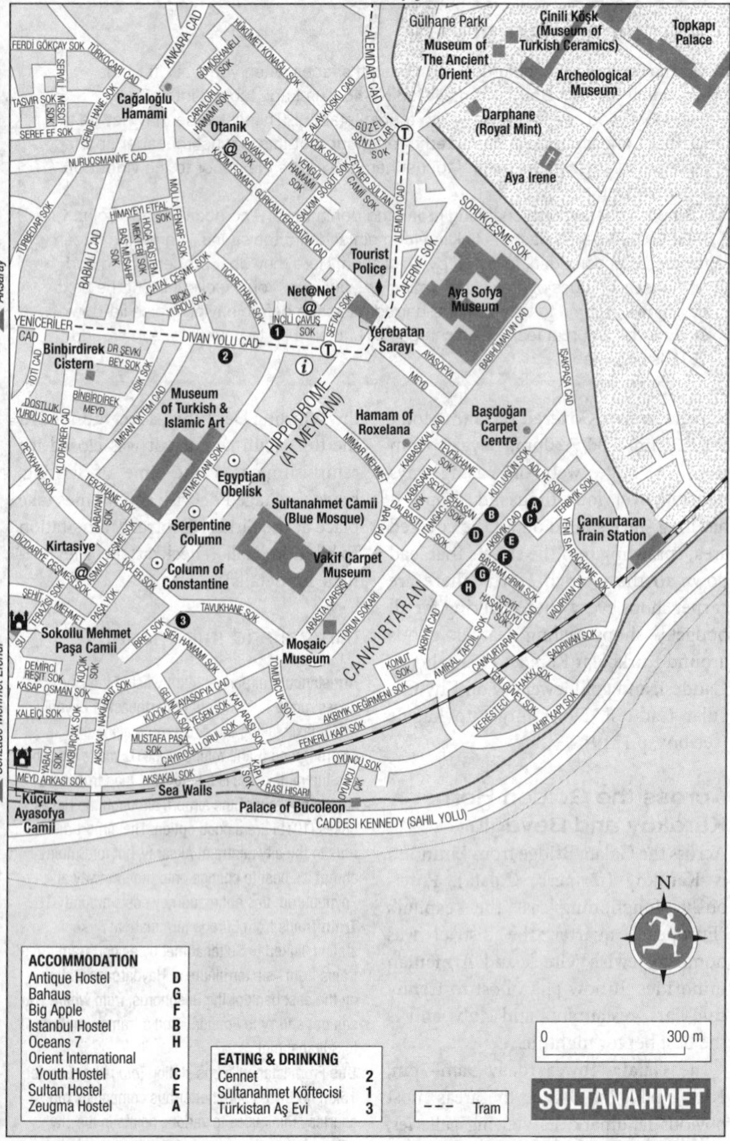

is to take the scenic train ride along the coast from Eminönü to Yedikûle, a district lying at the southern end of the walls in the attractive former Greek quarter of Samatya. This also has a few reasonable restaurants and cafés where you can stop before setting off on your exploration of the walls.

The Covered Bazaar

Off the main street of Divan Yolu lies the district of Beyazıt, centred on the

HISTORICAL NIŞANCI BATH

You may notice fleeting surprise on the staff's faces when you walk in to the **Historical Nişancı Bath** at Türkeli Cad No 45 Kumkapı, tucked into a busy neighbourhood street far away from tourist İstanbul. The welcome may not be the warmest, and smoking is permitted throughout, but this is much cheaper and far more authentic than the central tourist hamams, from the decor to the vigour of the treatment.

Strip in your personal changing room and don a towel – no nudity at any point. Next you will be led past the tinkling fountain and into the sauna. A gruelling fifteen minutes is encouraged, followed by exfoliation. Here they do it properly, hard and no-nonsense, tubes of grey skin forming on your skin. You'll feel sunburnt the next day. Finally, submit to the no-holds-barred massage before having a nice lie-down (and maybe a cup of tea). Basic charge 25TL, then a tip to your masseur: around 10TL is acceptable.

Kapalı Çarşı or **Covered Bazaar** (Mon–Sat 8.30am–6.30/7.30pm; Beyazıt tram stop), a huge web of passageways housing over four thousand shops. It has long since spilled out of the covered area, sprawling into the streets that lead down to the Golden Horn. There are carpet shops everywhere catering for all budgets, shops selling leather goods around Kurkçular Kapı and Perdahçılar Caddesi, and gold jewellery on Kuyumcular Caddesi. Don't forget to haggle (see box, p.1219).

Across the Golden Horn: Karaköy and Beyoğlu

Across the Galata Bridge from Eminönü is **Karaköy** (formerly Galata). Previously functioning as the capital's "European" quarter, the district was home to Jewish, Greek and Armenian minorities. It now plays host to trendy café-bars, restaurants and clubs and is the best bet for nightlife.

The **Galata Tower** (daily 9am–7pm; 10TL), built in 1348, is the area's most obvious landmark; its viewing galleries, café (Turkish coffee 5TL, beer 8TL) and ridiculously expensive restaurant offer the best panoramas of the city. Up towards Istiklâl Caddesi, **Beyoğlu**'s main boulevard, an unassuming doorway leads to the courtyard of the **Galata Mevlevihane** (9am–4.30pm, closed Wed; 5TL), a former monastery and ceremonial hall of the Whirling Dervishes, a sect founded in the thirteenth century. It was closed for refurbishment at the time of writing, however. Staged dervish ceremonies take place at the Sirkeci Central Train Station Exhibition Hall (check at the Mevlevihane for details).

Arrival and information

Air İstanbul's airport is 24km west of the city. Buses run to Taksim Square northeast of Beyoğlu (7TL). Taxis taking the direct route along the seafront road (Sahil Yolu) cost 30TL; make sure they use the meter. This is a better bet than trusting a shuttle bus tout at the airport, although the Havaş buses (10TL) are a good option. The airport metro runs to the city centre at Aksaray, but for Sultanahmet it's best to change onto the tramway at Zeytinburnu; this entire journey costs around 3TL.
Train Trains from Europe terminate at Sirkeci station, linked to Sultanahmet by a short tram ride; trains from Asia terminate at Haydarpaşa station on the east bank of the Bosphorus, from where you can get a ferry to Eminönü and a tram from there to Sultanahmet.
Bus From İstanbul's bus station (*otogar*) at Esenler, 15km northwest, the better bus companies run courtesy minibuses to various points in the city, although if you're heading for Sultanahmet it's often quicker to take the metro (actually an express tramway; 2.60TL). Some buses also stop at the Harem bus station on the Asian side, from where there are regular *dolmuşes* to Haydarpaşa station. Taxis to Sultanahmet cost approximately 20TL from the main *otogar*. Watch out for drivers who offer their services near to the departure area. These are usually unlicensed and do not operate a meter.

Tourist office The most central office (although not particularly helpful) is in Sultanahmet, near the Hippodrome on Divanyolu Cad (daily 9am–5pm; ⓣ0212/518 8754). Smaller branches are at the airport (24hr) and the two train stations. The branch at Sirkeci is especially helpful.

City transport

Bus Two bus services operate on the same city routes, either the private Halk Otobus service (pay conductor on entry; 1.40TL) or the more common municipality buses (marked IETT), for which you have to buy tickets (1.40TL) in advance from bus stations, newspaper kiosks or fast-food booths; some longer routes, usually served by double-deckers, require two advance tickets (look for the sign *iki bilet geçerlidin*). There are route maps at main bus stops.

Tram The European side has two tram lines, one running from Kabataş through Sultanahmet to Topkapı and outlying suburbs, the other running along Istiklâl Caddesi from Beyoğlu to Taksim using an antique tram; buy tokens (*jetons*; 1.40TL) from a booth before you enter the platform. The funicular from Tünel in Beyoğlu to Karaköy requires a 0.90TL *jeton.*

Train There's a municipal train network running along the Marmara shore – west from Sirkeci station on the European side, and east from Haydarpaşa on the Asian (allow at least 1hr to get to the Asian station from the centre). On the European side you buy a token (1.40TL) to let you through the turnstile onto the platform, while on the Asian side you buy a ticket (same price).

Dolmuş *Dolmuşes* have their point of departure and destination displayed somewhere about the windscreen.

Boat Ferries run between Eminönü and Karaköy on the European side, and Üsküdar, Kadiköy and Haydarpaşa in Asia; buy your ticket (1.40TL) from the dockside kiosks. There are also sightseeing hop-on-and-off boats which cruise the Bosphorus. These leave from the Boğaz Iskelesi terminal near the Eminönü tram stop and stop at either Anadolu Hisarı or Anadolu Kavaği. The trip on a government-run boat costs between 6 and 10TL, whereas private boat tours can cost up to 45TL (including hotel pick-up and guided tour). The cruise takes approximately 1hr 45min each way and the last return boat from Anadolu Kavaği in summer is at 5pm, after which you'll need to take a bus or *dolmuş*.

Travel passes The handy Akbil travel pass (from kiosks at most bus, tram, train and metro stations; deposit 6TL – get a receipt so you can claim the money back; then charge it with as much as you like), once charged with money, provides travellers with a marginal discount (approx 10 percent) on travel and makes it easier to hop on and off the metro, tram and bus. It looks like a large watch battery on a small piece of plastic that can be attached to a key ring. Any changes between modes of transport made within 45min of your first touch-in will not be charged, whereas if you were using *jetons* (1.40TL) then you would need one each time. To use it, touch it to the small button, usually marked, on turnstiles at stations or next to the driver on buses. In March 2009 the *Istanbulkart* was launched with a view to phasing out the Akbil. Eventually the *Istanbulkart* will be used to pay for everything from transport to cinema visits. At present, the Akbil is more reliable, until the *Istanbulkart* is fully connected to the transport network.

Accommodation

Some of the city's best small hotels and *pansiyons* are situated in Sultanahmet, particularly around Yerebatan Caddesi and the backstreets between the Blue Mosque and the sea. Taksim is also a convenient base, and comes into its own at night as a centre of cultural and culinary activity; take bus #T4 from Sultanahmet, which runs via Karaköy. From Eminönü and Aksaray, many buses pass through either Karaköy or Taksim, or both. Most hotels include breakfast in the price and some have a/c, cable TV and free internet access.

Sultanahmet

Antique Hostel Kutlugün Sok 51 ⓣ0212/638 1637, ⓦwww.antiquehostel.com. The rooms are a little stuffy but good looking nonetheless. The sea-view terrace is perched atop the city like an eyrie with an island bar and decent food available (mains 12–15TL). Wi-fi and breakfast included. Dorms €13–14, singles €35, doubles €60.

Bauhaus Akbıyık Cad, Bayram Fırını Sok 11–13 ⓣ0212/638 6534. Plenty of decent dorm beds and consequently lots of backpackers. The eight-bed dorm is inferior to the other two. Breakfast included. Great view from the roof terrace and a ten percent student discount. Dorms €12–15, double with shared bathroom €40, en-suite double €50, single with shared bathroom €25.

Big Apple Akbıyık Cad Bayram Fırını Sok No 12 ⓣ0212/517 7931, ⓦwww.hostelbigapple.com. The place as a whole has a slightly sombre feel but the dorms are clean and bright. Breakfast included. Dorms €13, doubles €60, singles €50.

İstanbul Hostel Kutlugün Sok 35 ⓣ0212/516 9380, ⓦwww.istanbulhostel.net. Friendly long-running hostel, with internet access, terrace and

bar. Ground-floor rooms are noisy. Dorms €12, doubles €171.

Oceans 7 Akbıyık Cad 47 ⓣ 0212/458 8668, ⓦwww.oceans7guesthouse.com. Includes one very nice six-bed dorm that looks like a private. Breakfast included and served in the adjacent, smart restaurant. Dorms €11, doubles €50, singles €40.

Orient International Youth Hostel Akbıyık Cad 13 ⓣ0212/518 0789, ⓦwww.orienthostel.com. Not exactly spotless but there's a good atmosphere and the 48 dorm beds keep the bar ticking over nicely. Dorms €10–15.

Sultan Hostel Akbıyık Cad 21 ⓣ0212/516 9260, ⓦwww.sultanhostel.com. The friendly bar-restaurant is a social focal point on this, the main hostel street, with dorm beds empty until the early hours. Despite the attempt at sound-proofing the music makes it through from the bar. Fine views from the terrace and decent food with mains around 8–10TL. Breakfast included. Dorms €18–20, doubles €42.

Zeugma Hotel Akbıyık Cad 35 ⓣ0212/517 4040, ⓦwww.zeugmahotel.com. One of the cheapest dorms in town, with twenty beds divided into four sections. But be warned that it is below ground and can get pretty hot. No breakfast but use of kitchen possible. Free internet. The private rooms are pricey. Dorms €10, doubles €60–80.

Beyoğlu and Taksim

Hotel Silviya Asmalı Mescid Sok 24/A ⓣ0212/292 7749, ⓦhotelsilviyaistanbul.com. An excellently priced hotel in the Beyoğlu area, just down the road from the *Tavanarası* restaurant. It is not plush by any means but a great choice if you fancy a change from hostels. Breakfast included. Singles 50TL, doubles 80TL.

World House Hostel Galipdede Cad No 85, Beyoğlu ⓣ0212/293 5520, ⓦwww.worldhouseistanbul.com. Just round the corner from Galata Tower, a nice alternative to the Sultanahmet hostels. The best dorm is at the top with great views of the tower. Wi-fi available and breakfast included. The mosque next door means there is no bar, but booze can be brought in. Dorms 25–30TL, doubles €42.

Eating

Sultanahmet has some decent restaurants, although the principal concentrations are in Beyoğlu and Taksim. The Balık Pazarı, particularly, behind the Çiçek Pasajı (off Istiklâl Cad), is a great area for mezes, kebabs and fish. Snacks include *kokoreç* (skeins of sheep's innards) sold from street stalls and delicious corn on the cob sold everywhere. The Beşiktaş neighbourhood is also worth a visit, not least for the wonderful "cream and honey" café. It has a different atmosphere to Sultanahmet and Beyoğlu, full of locals just going about their business.

Cafés

Beşiktaş Kaymakçı Köyiçi Meydanı Sok, Beşiktaş. Tiny, lovely breakfast café run by a sweet old lady. White tiles and chipped wood painted sky blue. Delicious home-made *kaymak* – a kind of Turkish clotted cream – served with rich honey and bread. Bustling even on weekdays, this is truly a Beşiktaş institution. Take the tram to Kabataş then it is a further 2km walk along the waterfront in the same direction or hop on a bus marked "Beşiktaş". From the waterfront bus station head northwest – about 5min walk – and you will come upon the market and shopping area, known as Beşiktaş Çarşışı. It is well known so ask to be pointed towards "Kaymaklı Pando" (Pando is the owner).

Damat Paçası Tımarcı Sok No 1/A, Beyoğlu. Cutesy little café just off "music street" (Galipdede Cad) to the right as you head towards the tower.

Evim Nargile In front of İstanbul Modern (the city's principal modern art gallery at Mecli-i Mebusan Cad in Tophane) you will find a kind of *nargile* bazaar – a string of eye-poppingly colourful cafés merging into one other. This is just one of them, sporting PVC beanbags.

Konyalı Pastanesi Ankara Cad, by the tram stop near Sirkeci train station. This place goes back to 1897 and they have their Turkish coffee down to a T. Couple it with the rich sesame *çörek*.

Simit Sarayı Istiklâl Cad, Taksim Square end. Chain with several branches, and fairly characterless, but they offer the famous chicken dessert – *tavuk göğsü* – and it is worth popping in for that alone.

Street snacks

Golden Kokoreç Balık Pazarı, Beyoğlu. The uniforms worn by the staff evoke your typical bland fast-food chain. But here they are serving up *kokoreç*, sheep innard skeins gathered into a doner kebab-like block then chopped up into little morsels with cleavers and served in a kind of baguette with hot sauce – totally delicious, especially late at night. This is also one of the best places to be fed *midye dolma* from the ice tray, one by one.

Restaurants

Cennet Divanyolu Cad No 31/A, Sultanahmet. It is a little surprising that acclaimed London restaurant *Moro* cited this as the inspiration for their own

gözleme (similar to a crêpe) as it is a rather tacky affair. But it is unashamedly so and consequently kind of charming, with staff in wonky fezzes encouraging customers to clap to live music – you get the idea. No booze. *Gözleme* 3–6TL, disappointing meze.

Gani Gani Kuyu Sok 13, Beyoğlu. The decor evokes rural Anatolia and the food, similarly traditional, is prepared with the respect it deserves. Try the Naumpasha Special – cheese-filled *pide*-style bread with yoghurt and pistachio nuts.

Hala Istiklâl Cad 211, near Turnacıbaşı Cad, Beyoğlu. If you don't want to go wandering too far from the main Beyoğlu thoroughfare then this is the most authentic purveyor of *mantı* and *gözleme* nearby. You'll see the women making the pancakes in the window – maybe it is auntie, which is what "hala" means. *Gözleme* 4.50–6TL.

Hamdi Tahmis Cad Kalçin Sok 17 ⓣ 0212/528 0390. Third-floor restaurant next to the spice bazaar. Fresh mezes and *köfte* are all served to a high standard. Highly popular and touristy but the views of the Golden Horn are irresistible. Reservations advised. Mains 12–18TL.

Hoppala Küçük Hendek Cad No 16C, Beyoğlu. *Mantı* specialists. With just three tables this tiny place on a side street goes for minimalist cool, with a carriage clock and a few vintage mirrors on the walls. Try the *mantı* with the spicy walnut topping (6TL) and the Turkish coffee with home-made liqueur (5TL).

Karadeniz Beşiktaş Çarşı, Beşiktaş. A tiny place bulging with office workers every lunchtime. Unfortunately for its long-suffering waiters the delicious *dürüm* mean that trend is set to continue.

Konak Istiklâl Cad, near Tünel. Very fresh salads and light, scorchingly hot flatbread accompany the excellent food such as *beyti kebap* for 10TL and *lahmacun* for just 2TL – surprising prices for such a smart place.

Midyeci Ahmet Dudu Odaları Sok No 40, Balık Pazarı, Beyoğlu. Owned by a man who started out selling *midye dolmas* on the street, he understands what rumbling Beyoğlu bellies want after a night on the *rakı*. Great atmosphere in amongst the late-night hustle and bustle. Fried squid 8TL.

Sultanahmet Köftecisi Divan Yolu Cad 12/A, Sultanahmet. Busy, basic restaurant; good for tasty traditional Turkish dishes. Mains 7–9YTL.

Tavanarası Asmalı Mescıt Sok 26/11 Kat 6, Beyoğlu. Easily missed on the street, high up on the sixth floor of an anonymous building, the lift doors open and you will be startled to find yourself stepping immediately into the traffic of a very small dark restaurant. An atmospheric treat, even if the food does not excel. Try the "G. Orhan Baba Köfte" (9TL) – meatballs and potato casserole topped with béchamel.

Türkistan Aş Evi Tavukhane Sok 36, Sultanahmet. A restored Ottoman house restaurant serving set three-course meals of Turkish dishes. Try the "Harput Marriage Feast Soup" of meat, chickpeas, potatoes, yoghurt and saffron for 7TL. Live music at night. Mains 15TL.

Drinking and nightlife

Backpackers, especially Antipodeans, tend to gather in the bars on Akbıyık Caddesi in Sultanahmet, but Beyoğlu is a much better choice, especially around Nevizade Sok.

Bars

Akdeniz Nevizade Sok 25, Beyoğlu. Rambling, multistorey student bar, with rock music and cheap drinks. A nice one for aimless sitting around.

Gizli Bahçe Nevizade Sok 27, Beyoğlu. Cutting-edge dance music in a dilapidated Ottoman town-house bar. Probably looks like a squat in daylight. This is hipster İstanbul, with languidly cool staff. No sign on the door, but the street is tiny and anybody will point you to it.

House Café Tünel Asmalı Mescit 9/1-2. If you are not hipstered-out and stony broke then you might squeeze in one more cocktail outside this café-bar.

Lokal 4 Tünel Meydanı. Formerly *Kaffeehaus*, this place has turned to the drink, and its new persona suits it very well. With high ceilings and a raucous atmosphere, its location means new faces are constantly arriving. Beers 10TL.

Otto Beyoğlu Şehbender Sok 5 ⓦ www.ottoistanbul.com. The thick graffiti in the main room is a kind of testament to its huge popularity. It has a vibrant and edgy atmosphere. Perhaps the delicious hazelnut vodka is the secret of its success. Towards midnight it turns clubby. Its sister bar *Otto Sofyalı* is just round the corner.

Clubs

Babylon Şehbender Sok 3, Asmalı Mescıt Tünel, Beyoğlu ⓦ www.babylon.com.tr. More of a gig and performance venue than a club, it attracts the most exciting, alternative Turkish and international acts.

Dogzstar Kartal Sok 3, Kat 3 ⓦ www.dogzstar.com. A pioneering club on the city's music scene, which seeks out innovative, genre-bending musicians and bands. There is currently a trend for electronic rock. Sometimes charges a small entrance fee.

Peyote Sahne Sok 24, Beyoğlu. Sweaty folk cool off on the godsend of a roof terrace before delving back into this deep/hard house hothouse.

Shopping

Bazaars

Arasta Bazaar Mimar Mehmet Ağa Cad 14, Sultanahmet. Good for handmade crafts and carpets.

Mısır Çarşısı (Egyptian Spice Bazaar). Çiçek Pazarı Sok, 5min southwest of Eminönü tram stop. Everything from spices to jewellery, natural apple tea and aphrodisiacs including chewy sweet-like blocks of Viagra.

Clothes

By Retro Istiklâl Cad 166/C, Suriye Pasajı. In a mini shopping arcade near Gönül Sok you will find this basement full of rails of vintage clothing.

Eymen Halcilik Arasta Çarşışı 107, Sultanahmet. Handmade traditional clothing for both men and women.

Mavi Jeans Istiklâl Cad 195. Kind of a Turkish Topshop.

Neofly Asmali Mescit Sok No 3/A, Beyoğlu. Men's generic streetwear – trainers, bright slogan t-shirts, jeans.

Second Hand Kuçuk Hendek Sok No 8. No sign on the huge window. A trove of trinkets such as vintage photo frames and old photos to go in them.

Ünal Istiklâl Cad 328. Eclectic mix of colourful traditional clothing made from rich textiles.

Bookshops

Pandora Kitap Evi Istiklâl Cad, Büyükparmakkapı Sok 8 ⓣ0212/243 3503.

Robinson Crusoe Kitabevi Istiklâl Cad 389. A good selection of maps as well as books including other titles from the Rough Guides series.

Entertainment

For listings pick up monthly *Time Out İstanbul* (5TL) from newsstands, bookshops, hotels and hostels. Also worth checking out is ⓦwww.beyogluin.com.

Atatürk Cultural Centre Taksim Square, Beyoğlu. Concert and exhibition venue. Principal centre for events during the International Music Festival (June–July).

Emek Cinema Yeşilçam Sok 5, Istiklâl Cad. Popular cinema regularly screening international releases. Student discount available.

Nardis Jazz Club Galata Kulesi Sok. Small, dimly lit jazz club where music rather than conversation takes centre stage. Performances by international artists during the İstanbul Jazz Festival (July).

Directory

Consulates Australia, 16 Floor Süzer Plaza, Elmadag Askerocagi Cad 15, Şişli 34367 ⓣ0212/243 1333; Ireland, Ali Rıza Gürcan Cad, Meridyen İş Merkezi Kat:4 No 417, Merter ⓣ0212/482 1862; New Zealand, İnönü Cad No 48/3, Taksim 80090 ⓣ0212/244 0272; USA, Kaplıcalar Mevkii Sok 2, Istinye 34460 ⓣ0212/335 9000.

Hospitals American Hospital, Güzelbahçe Sok 20, Nişantaşı ⓣ0212/231 4050; International Hospital, İstanbul Cad 82, Yeşilköy ⓣ0212/663 3000.

Internet Blue Internet Café, Yerbatan Cad 54; Seycom, Divan Yolu Cad 54/4, Sultanahmet; Net A Net, Divan Yolu Cad İncili Çavuş Sok 33, Sultanahmet; A Çayevi, Ebussuud Cad 37, Sirkeci.

Laundry Amfora, Binbirdirek Mah. Peykhane Cad 53/1; Ulya, Akbayık Cad, next to *Oceans* 7 hostel.

Left luggage Sirkeci and Haydarpaşa train stations.

Police Tourist Police, Yerebatan Cad, Sultanahmet ⓣ0212/527 4503.

Post office Yeni Posthane Cad, Sirkeci.

Telephone International Cheap Call, Dr Eminpaşa Sok 2, Divan Yolu Cad, Sultanahmet, or Net A Net, Divan Yolu Cad İncili Çavuş Sok 33, Sultanahmet.

Travel agents Road Runner Travel Agency (Alemdar Cad 2/B, Sultanahmet ⓦwww.roadrunnertravel.net) is a well-run company offering tours in İstanbul and the rest of the country. Fez Bus (Akbıyık Cad 15, Sultanahmet ⓦwww.feztravel.com) runs a hop-on-and-off bus system aimed at travellers who wish to visit several destinations in western Turkey. Passes cost €205–235. New Deal Travel Agency (Mimar Mehmetağa Sok) runs Atatürk Airport transfer buses, one every two hours until 8.50pm (€4).

Moving on

Train Ankara (6 daily; 8–9hr 30min); Budapest, Hungary (26hr); Edirne (1 daily; 5hr 30min); İzmir (1 daily; 7hr 30min); Konya (1 daily; 12hr); Sofía, Bulgaria (15hr).

Bus/dolmuş Alanya (hourly; 14hr); Ankara (hourly; 6hr); Antalya (4 daily; 12hr); Bodrum (5 daily; 12hr); Bursa (hourly; 5hr); Çanakkale (hourly; 5hr 30min); Datça (1 daily; 17hr); Denizli (hourly; 15hr); Edirne (hourly; 3hr); Fethiye (hourly; 15hr); İzmir (hourly; 10hr); İznık (Orhangazi; hourly; 5hr); Göreme (5 daily; 12hr 30min); Kaş (2 daily; 12hr); Konya (7 daily; 11hr); Kuşadası (3 daily; 11hr); Marmaris (4 daily; 13hr); Nevşehir (3 daily; 12hr); Sofía, Bulgaria (12hr); Ürgüp (5 daily; 12hr 30min).

Ferry Yalova (for Bursa or İznık, 8 daily; 1hr 30min).

Around the Sea of Marmara

Despite their proximity to İstanbul, the shores and hinterland of the Sea of Marmara are relatively neglected by foreign travellers – but there are good reasons to come: not least the border town of **Edirne** which was once the Ottoman capital, while nearby **Bursa**, the first Ottoman capital, has some of the finest monuments in the Balkans. Many visitors also stop off at the extensive World War I battlefields and cemeteries of the **Gelibolu** peninsula (Gallipoli), using either the port of **Eceabat** as a base, or, more commonly, **Çanakkale**.

EDIRNE

EDIRNE boasts an impressive number of elegant monuments and makes for an easily digestible introduction to Turkey. Bordering both Greece and Bulgaria, it's a small sleepy town where few of the locals speak English. The city springs to life for the week-long oil-wrestling festival of Kırkpınar (end of June).

What to see and do

You can see the sights on foot in a day. The best starting point is the **Eski Camii** bang in the centre, the oldest mosque in town, begun in 1403. Just across the way, the **Bedesten** was Edirne's first covered market. The name of the beautiful **Üç Şerefeli Camii**, dating from 1447, means "three-balconied", derived from the presence of three galleries for the muezzin on the tallest of the four idiosyncratic minarets.

A little way east, the masterly **Selimiye Camii** was designed by Minar Sinan. Its four slender minarets, among the tallest in the world, also have three balconies; the interior is most impressive, its dome planned to surpass that of Aya Sofya in İstanbul.

The main **Archeological Museum** (Tues–Sun 9am–5pm; 5TL), just northeast of the mosque, contains an assortment of Greco-Roman fragments and some Neolithic finds.

Arrival and information

Bus The bus station is 8km southeast of the centre. Upon arrival, walk through the terminal to the car park on the other side. Here you'll find *dolmuşes* which go to the centre of town (0.50TL). Get off either near the main shopping area or the Eski Camii mosque.
Train The train station is 5km southeast of the centre. *Dolmuşes* run into town from here (0.50TL).
Tourist office Talat Paşa Cad (daily 8.30am–5.30pm; ⓣ0284/213 9208).
Internet Eska Internet Café, Ilk Kapalıhan Cad 5.

Accommodation

Edirne Saray Hotel Eski İstanbul Cad 28 ⓣ0284/212 1457, ⓦwww.sarayhotel.com.tr. Very nice for the price with bright a/c rooms and smart bathrooms. Breakfast included. 40TL with bathroom, 35TL without.
Efe Hotel Maarif Cad 13 Kaleiçi ⓣ0284/213 6166, ⓦwww.efehotel.com. A most peculiar lobby but the rooms are impressive. Not cheap but if there are three of you the 135TL triple is worth haggling for. Singles 85TL, doubles 125TL, triple 135TL.
Hotel Aksaray Alipaşa Ortakapı Cad ⓣ0284/212 6035. Friendly welcome but there is smoke drifting everywhere and the rooms are scruffy. Breakfast not included. En suite 30TL.
Tuna Hotel Maarif Cad 17 ⓣ0284/214 3340, ⓦwww.edirnetunahotel.net. This place has a smart, new feel. Buffet breakfast included. Singles 50TL, doubles 70TL.

Eating and drinking

Imren Kahvaltı Salonu 1985 Saraçlar Cad 49. The focus is on breakfast and the locals share tables, quietly munching and looking drowsily out the big windows. Turkish breakfast 5TL, cream and honey 3.50TL.
Meşhur Edirne Ciğercisi Balıkpazarı Osmaniye Cad 43. You can have anything you want as long as it's liver, freshly floured and quickly deep-fried. Proper fast food, served with lots of onion and salad. An Edirne delicacy.

CROSSING TO BULGARIA

Edirne is a popular base for travellers crossing the border into **Bulgaria**. Regular buses leave from Edirne to Plovdiv and tickets cost 30–35TL. If visiting Edirne for the day, bring your passport along even if you don't intend to cross the border. When departing, officials at the bus station may ask to see your passport in order to verify that you haven't crossed over the border from Bulgaria illegally.

Pena Cafe Pub Alipaşa Ortakapı Cad 6. Sash windows usher cool breezes into this café-bar (beers 3.50TL, filter coffee 4.50TL) made up of small rooms with wooden floorboards and paneling. A young atmosphere in a middle-aged-feeling town.

Polat Lokantası Tahmis Çarşısı 8. The friendly English-speaking owner keeps his simple place spotless and smoke free – a rare thing in Turkey. Offers a fine variety of desserts (try the *kabak tatlısı*). Lentil soup 2TL, mains 5/6TL, meze 3.50TL.

Moving on

Bus/dolmuş Ankara (10pm & 11am; 10hr); Çanakkale (4 daily; 4hr 30min); İstanbul (hourly; 4hr 30min); İzmir (4 daily; 10hr); Plovdiv (take Sofía bus, get off at Plovdiv 7hr); Selcuk (one bus at 11.30pm; 7hr).

Train İstanbul only at 7.35am and 3.50pm (5hr).

ÇANAKKALE

Although celebrated for its setting on the Dardanelles, **ÇANAKKALE** has little to detain you. However, it is a popular base for visiting the Gelibolu (Gallipoli). Almost everything of interest in town – park, **Naval Museum** (Tues, Wed & Fri–Sun 9am–noon & 1.30–5pm; 3TL) and **Archeological Museum** (daily 8am–noon & 1–5.30pm; 5TL) – is within walking distance of the ferry docks, close to the start of the main Demircioğlu Caddesi.

Arrival and information

Bus station On the coastal highway, Atatürk Caddesi, a 15min walk from the waterfront; if you're arriving on the bus from İstanbul, get off at the ferry rather than going out to the bus station.

Ferry Ferries run every 30min between Çanakkale and Eceabat (hourly out of season). Tickets can be bought at the ferry terminal for 2TL.

Tourist office Beside the ferry docks (daily 8.30am—5.30/7pm depending on season; ⓣ0286/217 1187).

Accommodation

Except for a crowded couple of weeks during the Çanakkale/Troy Festival (mid-Aug), or on ANZAC Day (April 25), when the town is inundated with Antipodeans, you'll have little trouble finding budget accommodation.

Anzac House Cumhuriyet Meydanı 61 ⓣ0286/213 5969, ⓦwww.anzachouse.com. Clean, good-sized rooms with shared bathrooms. Dorm 16TL, singles with shared bathroom 28TL, doubles 42TL.

Crowded House Hostel İsmetpaşa Mah Hüseyin Avni Sok 4, Eceabat ⓣ0286/814 1565, ⓦwww.crowdedhousegallipoli.com. A 30min ferry ride from Çanakkale in Eceabat (on the Gallipoli peninsula) is this hostel, fresh faced and keen to please. Attractive natural light and crisp linen in the bedroom, LCD TVs and a buffet breakfast (included) make it a winner. Ten percent discount with ISIC card. En-suite dorm 20TL, singles 35TL, doubles 50TL, triples 60TL.

Yellow Rose Yeni Sok 5 ⓣ0286/217 3343, ⓦwww.yellowrose.4mg.com. Pretty bland, but good prices and you can economize further by using the kitchen. Breakfast is included and can be taken in the attractive garden. Dorms 16TL, doubles 20TL per person, 25TL with bathroom, singles 30TL with bathroom.

Eating and drinking

You will find stuffed mussels – *midye dolma* – sold on the streets. Do not combine with *rakı*. Be sure also to seek out the *peynir helvası* – Çanakkale's famous cheese dessert.

TREAT YOURSELF

Kervansaray Hotel Fetvane Sok No 13 ⓣ0286/217 7777, ⓦwww.otelkervansaray.com. The former home of an Ottoman judge: you'll find big plush rooms, a pretty garden and a quality buffet breakfast waiting in the morning. Be sure to get a room in the main, old building, as the annexe at the back of the garden has far less character. Singles €30–35, doubles €45–50.

Bade 24 Matbaa Sok (off Fetvane Sok). Tiny café popular with students. A huge mixed portion of their fine pre-made dishes with rice and a soft drink is just 6TL.

Kavala Balık Lokantası Kayserili Ahmetpaşa Cad 5. You won't find a menu in this smart, maritime-themed place but the English-speaking staff will explain what's on or even take you to the kitchen to see for yourself. Truly delicious grilled squid is well worth 13TL while the fabulous mixed meze is just 10TL.

Özel Çorba Salonu Saat Kulesi Meydanı. A nice airy place on a corner near the clock tower with big windows and a fine mosaic. They know their soup here so it may be the place to try their *kokteyl* of tripe, brain and trotter (5TL).

Secret Benzin Station Eski Balıkhane Sok 11. A long Antipodean-influenced bar, stacked with tables of people gazing into laptops (wi-fi access). Pizzas 8–11TL, filter coffee 5TL and cocktails 8–10TL.

Yalı Hanı no dot 1889' beri Fetvane Sokak 26. A peaceful and atmospheric little courtyard, home to a bookshop, café and gig venue (less peaceful during gigs).

Moving on

Bus İstanbul (6 daily; 5hr); İzmir (4 daily; 6hr); Selçuk (4 daily; 7hr).

Ferry Eceabat (hourly winter, every 30min in summer; 30min).

THE GELIBOLU (GALLIPOLI) PENINSULA

Though endowed with splendid scenery and beaches, the slender **Gelibolu** (Gallipoli) peninsula, which forms the northwest side of the Dardanelles, is known chiefly for its grim military history. In April 1915 it was the site of a plan, devised by Winston Churchill, to land Allied troops, many of them Australian and New Zealand units, with a view to putting Turkey out of the war. It failed miserably, with massive casualties. Nevertheless, this was the first time Australians and New Zealanders had seen action under their own commanders; the date of the first landings, April 25, is celebrated as ANZAC Day.

BATTLEFIELD TOURS

Various local companies offer **battlefield tours**. The best include those operated by the *Crowded House Hostel* in Eceabat (see opposite 50–60TL including lunch) and the Hassle Free Travel Agency in Çanakkale (located in *Anzac House*, see opposite; 60–70TL including lunch).

What to see and do

The World War I battlefields and Allied cemeteries are by turns moving and numbing in the sheer multiplicity of graves, memorials and obelisks. The first stop on most tours is the **Kabatepe Orientation Centre and Museum** (daily 8am–6pm; 3TL), beyond which are the **Beach, Shrapnel Valley** and **Shell Green** cemeteries, followed by **Anzac Cove** and **Arıburnu**, site of the ANZAC landing. Most tourists then bear right for **Büyük Anafartalar** village and **Çonkbayırı Hill**, where there's a massive New Zealand memorial and a Turkish memorial detailing Atatürk's words and deeds. Working your way back down towards the orientation centre, you pass **The Nek**, **Walker's Ridge** and **Quinn's Post**, where the trenches of the opposing forces lay within a few metres of each other: the modern road corresponds to no-man's-land.

BURSA

Draped along the leafy lower slopes of Uludağ, which towers more than 2000m above, **BURSA** – first capital of the Ottoman Empire and the burial place of several sultans – does more justice to its setting than any other Turkish city besides İstanbul. Gathered here are some of the finest early Ottoman monuments in Turkey, in a tidy and appealing city centre.

What to see and do

Flanked by the busy Atatürk Caddesi, the compact **Koza Parkı**, with its

fountains, benches and cafés, is the real heart of Bursa. On the far side looms the fourteenth-century **Ulu Camii**, whose interior is dominated by a huge *şadırvan* pool for ritual ablutions. A little way north is Bursa's covered market, the **Bedesten**, given over to the sale of jewellery and precious metals, and the **Koza Hanı**, flanking the park, still entirely occupied by silk and brocade merchants.

Yeşil Camii, Yeşil Türbe and the Museum of Turkish and Islamic Art

Across the river to the east, the **Yeşil Camii** (daily 8am–8.30pm) is easily the most spectacular of Bursa's imperial mosques. The nearby hexagonal **Yeşil Türbe** (daily 8am–noon & 1–7pm) contains the sarcophagus of Çelebi Mehmet I and assorted offspring. Just north of Yeşil Türbe is the **Museum of Turkish and Islamic Art** (Tues–Sun 8.30am–noon & 1–5.30pm; 3TL), with Çanakkale ceramics, glass items and a mock-up of an Ottoman circumcision chamber.

The Hisar and around

West of the centre, the **Hisar** ("citadel") district was Bursa's original nucleus. Narrow lanes wind up past dilapidated Ottoman houses, while walkways clinging to the rock face offer fabulous views. The best-preserved dwellings are a little way west in medieval **Muradiye**, where the Muradiye Külliyesi mosque and *medrese* complex was begun in 1424. This is the last imperial foundation in Bursa, although it's most famous for its tombs, set in lovingly tended gardens. Out beyond the Kültür Parkı, the **Yeni Kaplıca** (daily 9am–11pm; 16TL) are the nearest of Bursa's baths, a faded reminder of the days when the town was patronized as a spa.

Arrival and information

Bus station 5km north on the main road to İstanbul, from where bus #38 (every 15min) runs to Koza Parkı.
Tourist office Corner of Koza Parkı (Mon–Fri 8.30am–5.30pm; ⓣ0224/220 1848).

Accommodation

Hotel Çeşmeli Gümüşçeken Cad 6 ⓣ0224/224 1511. Female-run place with a handy location that makes up for its old-fashioned look. Singles 60TL with self-service breakfast, doubles 100TL.
Hotel Güneş İnebey Cad 75 ⓣ0224/222 1404. Cheap, clean and friendly. Single 30TL, double 45TL.

Eating and drinking

Arap Şükrü Sakarya Cad 6. Great for fish and other Turkish cuisine. Reasonably priced. Mains 15TL.
Çiçek Izgara Belediye Cad 15. Elegant restaurant with a decent take on Ottoman dishes. Try the *köfte* and *sütlü tel kadayıfı*. Mains 9TL.
İskender Atatürk Cad 60. A great choice for trying Bursa's speciality, the İskender kebap (similar to a döner but made of whole pieces of meat, rather than ground; 15TL).
Resimli Bar Ünlü Cd. American-style bar with frequent live music, often hard/alt rock.

Moving on

Bus Çanakkale (hourly; 5hr); İstanbul (hourly; 5hr); İznık (hourly; 2hr).

THE EVIL EYE

Take a short stroll around any Turkish town and it won't be long until you spot one of the ubiquitous evil eye symbols. This circular blue and white emblem with a dot in the middle is a good luck charm designed to ward off evil spirits. As well as being proudly displayed in homes and businesses, the symbol is also printed on pendants, bracelets and broaches.

The Aegean coast

The **Aegean coast** is, in many ways, Turkey's most enticing destination, home to some of the best of its Classical antiquities and the most appealing resorts. The city of **İzmir** serves as a base for day-trips to nearby sights and beaches. Visitors continuing south will be spoilt for sightseeing choices as the territory is rich in Classical, Hellenistic and Roman ruins, notably **Ephesus** and the remains inland at **Hierapolis** – sitting atop the famous pools and mineral formations of **Pamukkale**. The coast itself is better down south, too, and although the larger resorts, including **Kuşadası** and **Marmaris**, have been marred by the developers, **Bodrum** still has a certain charm.

İZMIR

İZMIR – ancient Smyrna – was mostly burned down in the Turkish–Greek war of 1922, and was built pretty much from scratch afterwards. Nowadays it is a booming, cosmopolitan and relentlessly modern city, home to nearly three million people. Orientation can be confusing – many streets are unmarked – but most points of interest lie near each other and walking is the most enjoyable way of exploring.

What to see and do

İzmir cannot be said to have a single centre, although **Konak**, the busy park, city bus terminal and shopping centre on the waterfront, is where visitors spend most time. It's marked by the ornate **Saat Kulesi** (clock tower), the city's official symbol. Head north and you'll reach the **Kültur Parkı**, a large park with regular outdoor entertainment particularly in the summer. Continue in the same direction and you'll soon reach the district of **Alsançak** – the hub of evening entertainment with alfresco bars and restaurants.

Archeological Museum

Southwest of the Konak Camii is İzmir's **Archeological Museum** (Tues–Sun 8.30am–5.30pm; 8TL). The collection consists of finds from all over İzmir province, including some stunning marble statues and sarcophagi.

Kemeraltı

Immediately east of Konak is **Kemeraltı**, İzmir's bazaar. The main drag, Anafartalar Caddesi, is lined with clothing, jewellery and shoe shops; Fevzipaşa Bulvarı and the alleys just south are strong on leather garments. A pleasant, relaxed alternative to the bazaar is the street market at the northernmost end of Sevgi Yolu, where you can browse jewellery, scarves, leather bracelets and lots of books, including English ones.

Kadifekale

A symbol of İzmir's historic past, the castle ruins of **Kadifekale** (always open; free) provide great views of İzmir's metropolitan expanse. To get to the castle, take a red-and-white city bus #33 from Konak and get off shortly after you see the national flag flying from the top of the hill. Buses back to Konak can be caught from the bus shelter at the corner of the road approaching the castle.

Arrival and information

Air İzmir's Adnan Menderes airport is approximately 15km outside of the city. A taxi from the airport to Çankaya is about 50TL. A cheaper alternative is to catch a Havaş shuttle bus (30min; 10TL). The Havaş service to the airport runs hourly 3.30am–11.30pm every day from the northern end of Gaziosmanpaşa Bulvari.

Train Intercity trains pull in at Basmane station, 1km from the seafront at the eastern end of Fevzipaşa Bulvarı.

Bus The bus station is way out on the east side of the city, from where buses #64 and #54 run to Basmane station and Konak. Buses to and from

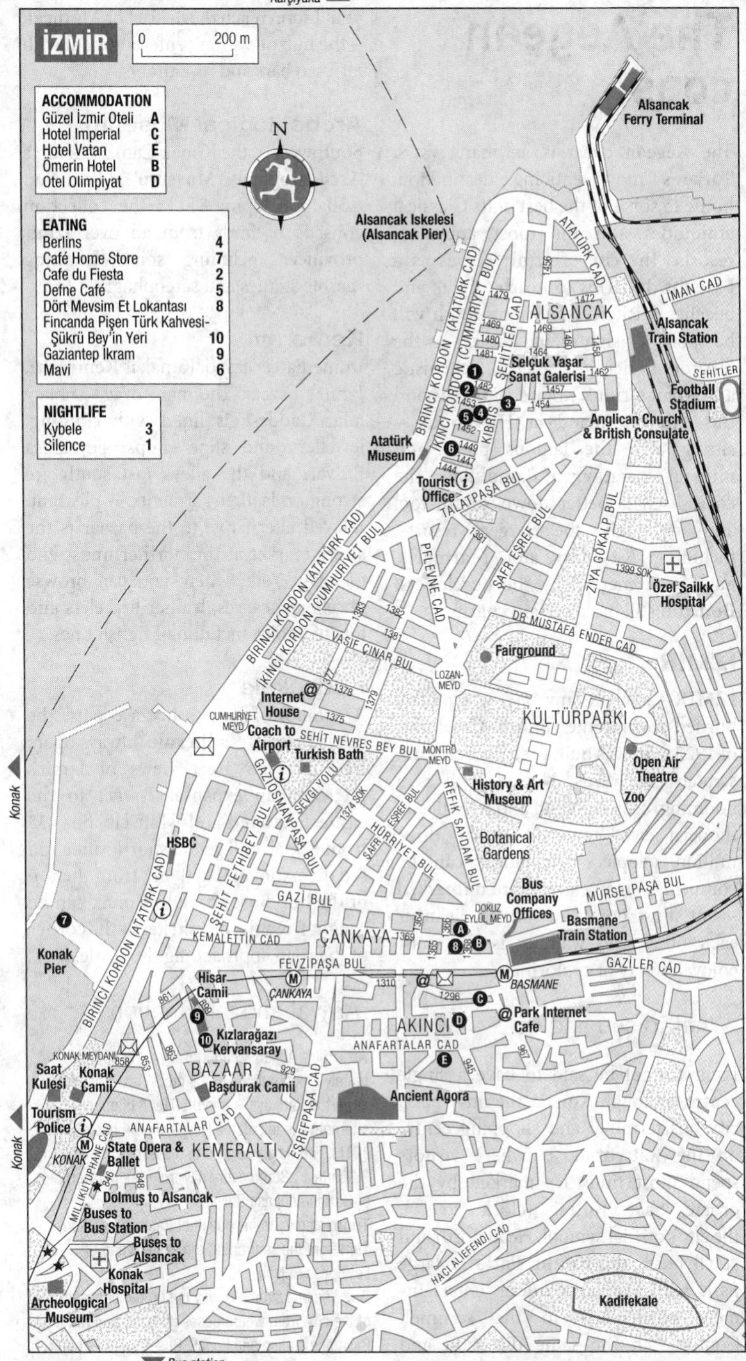
İZMİR
0 200 m
ACCOMMODATION
Güzel İzmir Oteli A
Hotel Imperial C
Hotel Vatan E
Ömerin Hotel B
Otel Olimpiyat D
EATING
Berlins 4
Café Home Store 7
Cafe du Fiesta 2
Defne Café 5
Dört Mevsim Et Lokantası 8
Fincanda Pişen Türk Kahvesi-Şükrü Bey'in Yeri 10
Gaziantep İkram 9
Mavi 6
NIGHTLIFE
Kybele 3
Silence 1
Karşiyaka
Alsancak Ferry Terminal
Alsancak Iskelesi (Alsancak Pier)
ALSANCAK
Alsancak Train Station
Selçuk Yaşar Sanat Galerisi
Football Stadium
Anglican Church & British Consulate
Atatürk Museum
Tourist Office
Özel Sailkk Hospital
Fairground
KÜLTÜRPARKI
Internet House
Coach to Airport
Turkish Bath
Open Air Theatre
Zoo
History & Art Museum
Botanical Gardens
Konak
HSBC
Bus Company Offices
Basmane Train Station
ÇANKAYA
Konak Pier
Hisar Camii
Park Internet Cafe
AKINCI
Kızlarağazı Kervansaray
BAZAAR
Başdurak Camii
Ancient Agora
Saat Kulesi
Konak Camii
Tourism Police
KEMERALTI
State Opera & Ballet
Dolmuş to Alsancak
Buses to Bus Station
Buses to Alsancak
Konak Hospital
Archeological Museum
Kadifekale
Bus station

Çeşme depart from the Uçkuyular bus station: bus #169 from Konak.

Tourist office Ali Çetinkaya Bulvarı 31/32, Alsancak. Housed on the sixth floor of a narrow, nondescript building next to *Sevinç Pastanesi*. Look for the tourist board sign high up at the top of the building. English will not necessarily be spoken and they may well not have maps of the city, unbelievably (daily 8am—7pm; ⓣ0232/463 97 91).

Internet Internet House, 1378 Sok 26B.

Post office The PTT near Cumhuriyet Med; open for postal services Mon–Sat 8am–8pm, Sun 8.30am–5pm; for money services including exchange, daily 8.30am–5pm.

City transport

Bus Intercity bus tickets can be bought from the bus ticket offices near the Basmane Gar (Basmane train station), and a free shuttle bus to the main bus terminal leaves from outside the offices. To get to Alsancak from Konak (2TL) take the #169, #554 or #8 all from the same bus stop on the opposite side of the road from Atatürk Kültur Merkezi (Mithatpaşa Cad). To get to the otogar from Konak you need the #54 or #64. Take them from the bus stop sandwiched between the Atatürk Kültür Merkezi and the flyover.

Dolmuş The city's *dolmuşes* (silver or white cars that gather alongside taxis and have their destination in the windscreen) cost 2TL per ride. Find one to head down to Konak from the Alsancak area on Talatpaşa Bulvarı north of the junction with 1407 Sok. Heading in the opposite direction pick one up just south of the Devlet Opera Balesi/State Opera and Ballet.

Metro The handy metro system (2TL) links Basmane station (the metro is located at the bottom of the escalators behind the station), Çankaya (the hotel district) and Konak. Ticket office 7am–9.30pm.

Accommodation

Although İzmir is one of Turkey's major cities, its tourism industry is only just developing. Consequently, good-quality budget hotels are hard to come by and *pansiyons* within the centre are nonexistent.

Güzel İzmir Oteli 1368 Sok 8 ⓣ0232/483 5069, ⓦwww.guzelizmirhotel.com. Very bright and airy rooms with none of the staleness that other, similar-looking hotels around here suffer from. Friendly welcome and professional attitude. Singles 35TL, doubles 65TL.

Hotel Imperial 1296 Sok 54 ⓣ0232/425 6883. A museum piece from the 1970s. The rooms are mournful but well looked after. Singles 30TL.

Hotel Vatan Anafartalar Cad 626 ⓣ0232/425 3461, 483 0637 & 484 5681, ⓦwww.vatanotel.com. Clearly aimed for sleek and modern but ended up with an interior design calamity. The owner is ever-so-slightly overbearing but endearing with it. Comfortable and good value. Breakfast included. Singles 40TL, doubles 80TL.

Ömerin Hotel 1368 Sok ⓣ0232/445 9898, ⓦwww.grandzeybekhotel.com. Nice big rooms and friendly staff. Some of the double rooms are suite-like. A fantastic 1970s lobby with a bubble telephone booth. Breakfast included. Singles 50TL, doubles 90TL, includes breakfast.

Otel Olimpiyat 945 Sok 2 ⓣ0232/483 0974. Like *Hotel Imperial*, it strains to rise above the dives around it. Friendly, a welcome change from the dour characters hereabouts. Doubles 52TL, singles 25TL.

Eating and drinking

Head to Sok numbers 1482, 1453 and 1452 in Alsancak for a night out. 1482 and 1453 have a certain grunginess about them, whilst narrow 1452 is a little smarter, though still young.

Berlins Sok 1453. Combatting the pervading scruffiness with bling, reggae and r'n'b.

Cafe du Fiesta Sok 1482 . A café that feels like it is squatting this 150-year-old mansion, packed out with teenagers, students and musicians. Nab the one-table balcony. Americano 4TL and cheeseburger 4TL.

Café Home Store Konak Pier. A lovely setting on a breezy terrace at the far end of the pier. Take a look and weigh up whether the view merits the 6–8TL coffee.

Defne Café 1452 Sok. It looks cute but its offer of two beers and twenty *midye dolma* for 15TL shows it has a naughty side.

Dört Mevsim Et Lokantası 1369 Sok 51A. A *lokanta* par excellence with mains running 10–17TL.

Fincanda Pişen Türk Kahvesi – Şükrü Bey'in Yeri Where Sok 905 meets Bazaar entrance "876 Sok 62". Come for Turkish coffee while relaxing on carpet-covered seating in the beating heart of the bazaar.

Gaziantep İkram near Hisar Camii. At the heart of the bazaar, this is an atmospheric place where market-fresh rocket accompanies standards of *lahmacun*, *pide* and *patlican kebap*. A touch overpriced with *pide* around 8TL.

Mavi Cumhuriyet Bulvarı 206, Alsançak. Music venue in an atmospheric old building. People head here around 10pm for live music – jazz on Mondays, general rock cover bands rest of the week.

Clubs

Kybele 1453 Sok. Live music and alt rock club with a tiny stage and super-speedy bar staff. Entrance is 15TL, which includes one drink. Beers thereafter run 10TL.
Silence 1482 Sok. Slightly cheaper music and alt rock club: entrance is 10TL with one free drink, then beers are 6TL after that.

Entertainment

Bostanlı Karşıyaka Açıkhava Tiyatrosu Saat Taşer Tiyatrosu, İzmir. Large concert hall hosting regular pop concerts in Konak Pier. Daily 10.30am–9.30pm.
Cinebonus Konak Pier, İzmir. Cinema with recent Hollywood releases. Student discount available.
State Opera and Ballet Milli Kütüphane Cad, Konak ☎0232/484 3692. A diverse programme of concerts ranging from classical to jazz and pop.

Moving on

Train Basmane station to: Denizli (3 daily; 5hr); İstanbul by way of a ferry from Bandirma (2 daily; 8hr); Selçuk (5 daily; 1hr 30min).
Bus/dolmuş Ankara (every 30min; 8hr); Bergama (hourly; 2hr); Bodrum (hourly; 4hr); Bursa (6 daily; 6hr); Çanakkale (8 daily; 5hr); Datça (hourly; 7hr); Denizli (hourly; 4hr); Fethiye (12–18 daily; 7hr); İstanbul (hourly; 9hr); Konya (1 daily; 8hr); Kuşadası (every 30min; 1hr 40min); Marmaris (hourly; 5hr); Nevşehir (1 daily; 12hr); Selçuk (every 40min; 1hr).

KUŞADASI

KUŞADASI is Turkey's most bloated resort, yet the old town has its charms even when the town centre is heaving with football shirts. Ferry services link it with the Greek island of Sámos, while the resort is a port of call for Aegean cruise ships, which disgorge vast numbers in summer.

What to see and do

Liman Caddesi runs from the ferry port up to Atatürk Bulvarı, the main harbour esplanade, from which pedestrianized Barbaros Hayrettin Bulvarı ascends the hill. To the left of here, the **Kale** district, huddled inside the town walls, is the oldest and most appealing part of town, with a mosque and some fine traditional houses. Kuşadası's most famous beach, **Kadınlar Denizi**, 3km southwest of town, is a popular strand, usually too crowded for its own good in season. For the closest sandy beach, head 500m further south, just before **Yılancı Burnu**, or alternatively try **Tusan beach**, 7km north of town, served by all Kuşadası–Selçuk *dolmuşes*, as well as more frequent ones labelled Şehir Içi. Much the best beach in the area is **Pamucak**, at the mouth of the Kücük Menderes river, 15km north, an exposed 4km stretch of sand that is as yet little developed; in season it's served by regular *dolmuşes* from both Kuşadası and Selçuk.

Arrival and information

Bus The combined *dolmuş* and long-distance bus station is about 2km out, past the end of Kahramanlar Caddesi on the ring road to Söke, while the *dolmuş* stop is closer to the centre on Adnan Menderes Bulvarı.
Tourist office (Mon–Fri 8am–5.30pm; summer also Sat & Sun; ☎0256/614 1103) is right by the ferry port.
Internet Available at m@ilhouse, opposite the Kale Camii on Barbaros Bul.

Accommodation

(Mr Happy's) Liman Hotel Mahmut Esat Bozkurt Cad (formerly Liman Cad) ☎0256/614 7770, Ⓦwww.limanhotel.com. The owner, Hasan ("Mr Happy"), is justifiably proud of his spotlessly clean rooms and hosts big barbecues on the roof terrace overlooking the harbour. Breakfast included. Doubles 70TL, more basic rooms 20TL.
Otel Şato Dağ Mah Çetin Sok 3 ☎0256/614 1123. More a bedsit than a hostel and though a little smoky and shabby the rooms are at least bright. Some have views of the *kervansaray*. 20TL per person.
Panorama (formerly Sammy's Place) Kıbrıs Cad 14 ☎0256/614 6619, Ⓦwww.otelpanorama.com. All rooms are en suite and the price includes breakfast on the roof terrace. A family room doubles as a dorm. Wi-fi is available. Singles 40TL, doubles 60TL.
Sezgin Hotel and Guesthouse Arsanlar Cad 68 ☎0256/614 4225, Ⓦwww.sezginhotel.com. Plush in a low-key way with a lovely garden and swimming pool. Singles 40TL, doubles 55TL.

FERRIES TO GREECE

Every day in high season a morning and evening ferry leaves from Kuşadası to the Greek island of **Sámos** (€30 one way, €35 day return, €50 open return; 1hr 15min). Meander on Kıbrıs Cad (☎0256/614 3859, Ⓦwww.meandertravel.com) runs up to two boats daily in summer. From Sámos, a popular follow-on destination is the party island **Íos** (see p.561). Tickets from Sámos to Íos can be bought from ITSA or By Ship travel agents located near the pier.

Eating and drinking

Adı Meyhane In old Kuşadası. Turkish live music and much *rakı* drinking. Locals may think you got lost. Try the *açılı ezme*, a spicy tomato dip.
Avlu Cephane Sok 15/A. Serves a wide range of kebabs, stews, steamed vegetables and mezes in an outdoor courtyard. Has upheld its excellent reputation for years. Mains 7TL.
Brodjes Yedieylul Sok. *Brodjes* is Flemish for "little breads", used to indicate sandwich – a friend suggested the name to the owner. Their superior kebabs come in lovely puffy bread.
Yuvam Restaurant Ev Yemekleri Yedieylul Sok (first right after *Oz Urfa* before *Avlu*). *Yuvam* means "home" and it certainly feels a little like you have wandered into one, especially when they have made a batch of their fabulous *mantı*, a ravioli-like dumpling filled with ground meat and served with a yoghurt-based sauce (7TL).

Moving on

Bus/dolmuş Bodrum (3 daily; 3hr); Fethiye (2 daily; 4hr 30min); Pamukkale (12 daily; 3hr 30min, 1 direct at 9.15am); Selçuk (every 15min; 20min).

SELÇUK

SELÇUK has been catapulted into the limelight of premier-league tourism by its proximity to the ruins of Ephesus. Pleasant Pamucak beach (see opposite) is easily accessible by a short *dolmuş* ride.

What to see and do

Ayasoluk hill (daily 8.30am–5.30pm; 5TL), the traditional burial place of St John the Evangelist, who died here around 100 AD, boasts the remains of a basilica built by Justinian that was one of the largest Byzantine churches in existence. Just behind the tourist office, the **Efes Archeological Museum** (Tues–Sun 8.30am–5.30pm; 5TL) has galleries of finds from Ephesus, while beyond the museum, 600m along the road towards Ephesus, are the scanty remains of the **Artemision** or sanctuary of Artemis.

Some 9km southwest of Selçuk lies **Meryemana** (daily dawn–dusk; 10TL), a tiny Greek chapel (Mass, summer daily 7.15am, Sun also 10.30am) where some Orthodox theologians believe the Virgin Mary passed her last years.

Arrival and information

Train and bus The train station lies a little east of the aquaduct. The bus and *dolmuş* terminal is a few minutes' walk south from the very centre of town.
Tourist office Opposite the bus terminal (daily 8.30am–noon & 1–5.30pm; winter closed Sat & Sun; ☎0232/892 6945).
Internet Cheap internet facilities are at NetHouse, Sieburg Cad 4/B.

Accommodation

ANZ Guesthouse 1064 Sok 12 ☎0232/892 6050, Ⓦwww.anzguesthouse.com. Popular backpacker choice with free use of (clapped-out) bikes. Check rooms as some are better than others. Doubles 30TL, dorm 18TL (shared bathroom), singles 25TL.
Atilla's Getaway Acarlar Köyü ☎0232/892 3847, Ⓦwww.atillasgetaway.com. They know how to throw a party here but the setting – peaceful, almost rural – is conducive to sloth-like relaxation too. A little out of town but the management shuttle to and from Selçuk centre four times daily. En-suite dorms €8, en-suite single €15, single with shared bathroom €12, en-suite doubles €22, camping €4.
Homeros Pansiyon Atatürk Mah Asmalı/1048 Sok 17 ☎0232/892 3995, Ⓦwww.homerospension.com. There are some really beautiful, richly decorated

rooms available here, though no dorm. Breakfast (included) served in a cosy room full of knick-knacks. Free home-made wine served at 7pm every day. Free pick up from bus station. Rooms 30TL per person.

Jimmy's Place Atatürk Mah, 1016 Sok 19 ⓣ0232/892 1982, ⓦwww.jimmysplaceephesus.com. A big welcoming place with very nice rooms, all en suite, and a decent dorm. There is a carpet shop tucked away in the building, which may or may not be a welcome addition. A good-quality breakfast is included. Standard rooms 45TL per person, dorm 20TL.

Wallabies Hostel Cengiz Topel Cad 2 ⓣ0232/892 3204, ⓦwww.wallabieshostel.com. A family affair, headed up by Mehmet (aka Geoff). Some rooms afford views of the Roman aqueduct and nesting storks (the best is room 305). Singles 20TL, doubles 40TL.

Eating and drinking

Mosaik Atatürk Mah 1005 Sok 6/B. Low tables and kilim conducive to a *nargile* session. *Nargile* 10TL, beer 4TL.

Old House Opposite *Mosaik*. Carefully prepared mains between 7 and 12TL served up in a shady little garden courtyard.

Selçuk Köftecisi Şahabettin Dede Cad. Easily overlooked because of its basic, rather bland appearance but, with forty years' experience behind it, this place is all about the food. Smoky bread cooked in a wood oven, known as Şirince bread, accompanies mains. Soups 4–5TL, meaty mains 6–9TL.

Moving on

Dolmuş Kuşadası (regular until 8/9pm; 30min); Pamucak beach (hourly; 15min); Şirince (every 45min until 7pm).

Bus Bodrum (3/4 direct daily; 3hr); Marmaris (one direct daily; 4 hr).

Train Denizli (5 daily; 4hr) İzmir (6 daily 1hr 30min).

EPHESUS

With the exception of Pompeii, **EPHESUS** (Efes in Turkish) is the largest and best-preserved ancient city around the Mediterranean. You'll need at least three partly shady hours, and a water bottle. Your best hope of avoiding the crowds is to visit early morning.

Originally situated close to a temple devoted to the goddess Artemis, Ephesus' location by a fine harbour was the secret of its success in ancient times, eventually making it the wealthy capital of Roman Asia, ornamented with magnificent public buildings.

What to see and do

Approaching **from Kuşadası**, get the *dolmuş* to drop you at the *Tusan Motel* junction, 1km from the gate. **From Selçuk**, it's a 3km walk (although most hotels and hostels offer free rides). In the centre of the site (daily 8am–5.30pm; 20TL; additional 15TL for entrance into the Terrace House) is the **Arcadian Way**, which was once lined with hundreds of shops and illuminated at night. The nearby theatre has been partly restored to allow its use for open-air concerts and occasional summer festivals; it's worth the climb to the top for the views of the surrounding countryside. About halfway along Marble Street is a footprint, a female head and a heart etched into the rock – an alleged signpost for a brothel. Across the intersection looms the elegant **Library of Celsus**, erected by the consul Gaius Julius Aquila between 110 and 135 AD. Just uphill, a Byzantine fountain looks across the Street of the Curetes to the public latrines, a favourite with visitors.

BODRUM

In the eyes of its devotees, **BODRUM** – ancient Halicarnassos – with its whitewashed houses and subtropical gardens, is the most attractive Turkish resort, a quality outfit in comparison to its upstart Aegean rivals.

What to see and do

The town's centrepiece is the **Castle of St Peter** (Tues–Sun 9am–noon & 1–5pm; summer open until 7pm; 10TL), built by the Knights of St John over a Selçuk fortress between 1437 and 1522. Inside,

the various towers house a **Museum of Underwater Archeology**, which includes coin and jewellery rooms, Classical and Hellenistic statuary, and Byzantine relics retrieved from two wrecks. The **Carian Princess Hall** (Tues–Fri 10am–noon & 2–4pm; 5TL extra) displays the skeleton and sarcophagus of a fourth-century BC noblewoman unearthed in 1989. There is also the **Glass Wreck Hall** (Tues–Fri 10am–noon & 2–4pm; 5TL extra) containing the wreck and cargo of an ancient Byzantine ship, which sank near Marmaris. Immediately north of the castle lies the bazaar, from where you can stroll up Türkkuyusu Caddesi to the **Mausoleum** (Tues–Sun 8.30am–5.30pm; 8TL), the burial place of Mausolus, ruler of Halicarnassos and the origin of the word mausoleum. Note that some of these displays may be closed without warning, though you can always bank on enjoying the fantastic views of the water from various vantage points in the castle.

Arrival and information

Bus The bus station is 500m up Cevat Şakir Caddesi, which divides the town roughly in two.
Ferry Ferries dock at the jetty west of the castle.
Tourist office Close to the jetty on Iskele Meydanı (Mon–Fri 8.30am–5.30pm; summer daily 8.30am–6.30pm).
Internet Hakim's Internet on Atatürk Caddesi.

Accommodation

Bodrum Backpackers Atatürk Cad 31/B ⓣ0252/313 2762, ⓦwww.bodrumbackpackers.net. Lively and friendly backpackers' hotel regularly hosting both budget travellers and the English party crowd. It is possible to sleep on the terrace for 10TL. Dorms 15TL, singles 20TL.
Hotel Güleç Üç Kuyular Cad 22 ⓣ0252/316 5222, ⓦwww.hotelgulec.com. Lovely garden and cool, wood-trimmed bedrooms demanding that you take a post-beach afternoon nap. Breakfast included. Singles €28, doubles €34.
Hotel Kalender Cevat Şakir Mah İnönü Cad Bitez Sok 15 ⓣ0252/319 5229, ⓦwww.hotelkalender.com. In the Gumbet neighbourhood, a little way out, but free pick-up from the bus station is offered. Bright, simple rooms with chairs and tables set outside around a central swimming pool. Singles €20, doubles €35.
Merhaba Otel Kumbahçe Mah Akasya Sok 11 ⓣ0252/316 3978, ⓦwww.merhabaotel.com. Near *Halikarnas* nightclub but double glazing manages to limit the sound levels. *Mavi* – perhaps the best bar in town – is your local. Backpacker prices are negotiable as there is no dorm. Free pick-up from the *otogar*, and offers 20TL daily boat trips. Rooms 15–25TL.

Eating and drinking

Berk Balık Cumhuriyet Cad 167. An excellent fish and meze restaurant at the far end of the bar strip. Try the 10TL mixed meze on the shady first-floor sea-facing terrace. Mains 10–18TL.
Halikarnas Far end of bar strip, near *Mavi* and *Berk Balık*. Fancies itself as the biggest nightclub in Europe. It'll cost you 30TL and pricy drinks to party like it's 1999, but if you're in the mood then the laser show, loved-up atmosphere and superb view of the bay can make it worth the money.
Mavi Cumhuriyet Cad 175. Tiny little bar with an outdoor terrace and live music every day. A cut above the rest in town.
Otantik Ocabaşı Atatürk Cad Çarşı Mah 46. Decent prices considering the location (opposite *Bodrum Backpackers*) probably thanks to the very high turnover. Its wood-burning oven assures succulence.

Moving on

Bus/dolmuş Denizli (1 daily; 5hr); Fethiye (6 daily; 4hr 30min); İzmir (hourly; 4hr); Kaş (3 daily; 6hr); Kuşadası (3 daily; 3hr); Marmaris (14 daily; 3hr 15min); Selçuk (hourly; 3hr).
Domestic ferry Datça (April–Oct 1 or 2 daily; 1hr 30min).
International ferry Bodrum Ferryboat Association (ⓣ0252/316 0882, ⓦwww.bodrumferryboat.com) runs ferries to Kos, as well as domestic services to Datça, while Bodrum Express Lines (ⓣ0252/316 1087, ⓦwww.bodrumexpresslines.com) handles hydrofoils to Kos, Rhodes and domestic services to Marmaris. Check websites for current prices.

PAMUKKALE

The rock formations of **PAMUKKALE** (literally "Cotton Castle"), 140km northeast of Marmaris, are the most-visited attraction in this part of Turkey, a series of white terraces saturated with dissolved calcium bicarbonate, bubbling

up from the feet of the Çal Dağı mountains beyond. The spring emerges in what was once the ancient city of **Hierapolis**, the ruins of which would merit a stop even if they weren't coupled with the natural phenomenon. Access to the travertine terraces is 5TL whilst up on the plateau is what is spuriously billed as the sacred pool of the ancients, (daily 8am–6.30pm; 23TL) open for bathing in the 35°C mineral water.

Hierapolis

The archeological zone of **HIERAPOLIS** lies behind the Pamukkale terraces and is admissible by the same entrance fee. Its main features include a **Temple of Apollo** and the infamous, albeit inconspicuous, **plutonium cavern**, where a toxic mixture of sulphur dioxide and carbon dioxide brews. The site has been firmly sealed off following the deaths of two German tourists. Perhaps the most interesting part of the city is the colonnaded street which once extended for almost 1km, terminating in monumental portals a few paces outside the walls – of which only the most northerly, a triple arch, still stands.

Moving on

Buses and dolmuş Buses run directly from Pamukkale village to Selçuk, Fethiye and Bodrum. Otherwise head to Denizli and change there. *Dolmuşes* run every 20min until 7pm then less regularly until 10pm.

Mediterranean coast

The first stretch of Turkey's Mediterranean coast, dominated by the Akdağ and Bey mountain ranges of the Taurus chain and known as the "Turquoise Coast", is its most popular, famed for its pine-studded shore, minor ruins and beautiful scenery. In the west, **Fethiye** is a perfect base for visits to **Ölüdeniz**, **Kaya Köyü** and **Butterfly Valley**. The scenery becomes increasingly spectacular as you head towards the site of **Olympos**, and **Kaş**, which offers great scuba-diving, before reaching the port and major city of **Antalya**.

FETHIYE

FETHIYE is well sited for access to some of the region's ancient sites, many of which date from the time when this area was the independent kingdom of Lycia. The best beaches, around the Ölüdeniz lagoon, are now much too crowded for comfort, but Fethiye is still a market town and has been able to spread to accommodate increased tourist traffic.

What to see and do

Fethiye itself occupies the site of the Lycian city of Telmessos, little of which remains other than the impressive ancient theatre, and a number of Lycian rock tombs on the hillside. You can also visit the remains of the medieval fortress behind the harbour area of town. In the centre of town the small **museum** (Tues–Sun 8.30am–5.30pm; 5TL) has some fascinating exhibits from local sites and a good ethnographic section.

Kaya Köyü and Ölüdeniz

One of the most dramatic sights in the area is the ghost village of **KAYA KÖYÜ** (Levissi), 7km out of town, served by *dolmuşes* from the old bus station. The village was abandoned in 1923, when its Anatolian-Greek population was relocated, and all you see now is a hillside covered with more than two thousand ruined cottages and an attractive basilica. **Ölüdeniz** is about two hours on foot from Kaya Köyü or a *dolmuş* ride from Fethiye. The warm waters of this lagoon make for pleasant swimming although the crowds can reach saturation level in high season –

in which case the nearby beaches of Belceğiz and Kidrak are better bets.

Arrival and information

Bus Fethiye's bus station is 2km east of the centre; *dolmuşes* to and from Ölüdeniz, Çalış Beach and Kaya Köyü leave from near the mosque (Yeni Camii) which is beyond the town hall and the PTT on Atatürk Cad.
Tourist office Close to the theatre, near the harbour at Iskele Meydanı 1 (daily 8.30am–5.30/7.30pm; ⓣ0252/612 1527).
Tours Daily boat tours generally run 35–55TL, lasting from 10.30am to 6.30pm. Tickets can be bought through your accommodation.
Internet Trend, Kayaiş Hani 6.

Accommodation

Ceylin Pansiyon Fevzi Çakmak Cad ⓣ0252/614 0031. No English spoken but a warm welcome nonetheless. The rooms are basic but clean and well presented. Breakfast included. 5min walk from the centre of town. 30TL per person.
Duygu Pension 2.Karagözler Ordu Cad 54 ⓣ0252/614 3563, ⓦwww.duygupension.com. Twelve rooms, some with amazing views of the bay, kept in great condition. Swimming pool and free bus station pick-up. May not be open off-season so call ahead. Singles 35TL, doubles 50TL.
Ferah Pension (Monica's Place) 2.Karagözler Orta Yol 21 ⓣ0252/614 2816, ⓦwww.ferahpension.com. Waking up to a view of the bay and one of Monica's excellent breakfasts is a rare treat. The upstairs dorm has a huge sea-facing window. Free transfer from the bus station. Private rooms 50TL, dorms 20TL.
Irem Pansiyon Fevzi Çakmak Cad 61 ⓣ0252/614 3985, ⓦwww.irempansiyon.com. A rather hotel-like *pansiyon*, the rooms bland but fine, with a/c and en suite. 25TL per person.

Eating and drinking

The town's main roads, Atatürk Cad and Cumhuriyet Cad, are minutes away from the harbour and are the focus for most of the town's amenities, bars and restaurants.
Meğri Lokantasi Carşı Cad near the duck pond. This *lokanta*, a humbler version of *Meğri Restaurant* round the corner, has a nice setting by the duck pond and delivers good traditional Turkish grub. Mains 8–13TL.
Mercan Balık Restaurant Hal ve Balık Pazarı, Zabıta Bürosu Yanı. One of numerous restaurants surrounding the little fish market which will cook the fish you buy for a paltry 5–6TL and give you salad and bread into the bargain.
Şamdan Restaurant Tütün Sok 9. A big canteen of a place on a backstreet near the fish market. Its little outdoor seating area is on the opposite side of the road – a nice quirk.
Sobe Tapas and Drinks Fevzi Çakmak Cad 19. A fancy little place with excellent views worth an expensive cocktail. Very pricey tapas – a mix of six comes in at 39TL.

Moving on

Bus Kaş (hourly; 4hr); Marmaris (every 30min; 3hr); Patara (10 daily; 1hr 30min).
Dolmuş Leave from near the mosque (Yeni Camii) which is beyond the town hall and the PTT

BUTTERFLY VALLEY

A simple set up where a steep-walled valley ends at a horseshoe bay, the whole of ★ **Butterfly Valley** (Kelebek Vadisi) is run by a single team who oversee your accommodation and transportation by boat to and from the beach at Ölüdeniz. The list of possible activities is satisfyingly brief, and the days become a nice cycle of sleeping, eating, swimming and night-time campfires. A waterfall that's home to the eponymous butterflies is twenty minutes' walk inland, and a few classes of yoga are sometimes laid on, usually for free. Accommodation is in tents on the beach (25–35TL per day including communal breakfast and dinner) or in bungalows (45/35TL), and just a few showers are shared by up to three hundred people in high season. Eating is communal and hearty under a shady trellis next to the beach. One downside is that in high season yachts of day-trippers anchor in the bay – the best time to come is in spring.

To book, contact the management via their blog (ⓦthebutterflyvalley.blogspot.com). There are three return trips daily: from the valley at 9am, 1pm and 5pm, and from Ölüdeniz at 11am, 2pm and 6pm. The valley is open March to October normally, but check when booking.

on Atatürk Cad to: Saklıkent (every 15min; 1hr); Kaya Köyü (30min; hourly) and Ölüdeniz (hourly; 30min).

KAŞ

KAŞ sprang to prominence after about 1850, when it established itself as a Greek fishing and timber port. It is beautifully located, nestled in a small curving bay below rocky cliffs. But what was once a sleepy fishing village is fast becoming an **adventure-sports centre** for backpackers, with nightlife to match, and provides a handy base for paragliding, mountain biking and some of the cheapest and best scuba-diving in Turkey. Many of the *pansiyons* listed can organize such activities, or try one of the numerous operators in town, such as the professionally run Bougainville (Ⓣ0242/836 3737, Ⓦwww.bougainville-turkey.com) or Sun Diving (Ⓣ0242/836 2637). Scattered around the streets and to the west are the remains of ancient **Antiphellos**, one of the few Lycian cities to bear a Greek name, small in number but nevertheless impressive. Five hundred metres west of town lies an almost complete **Hellenistic theatre**, behind which is a unique Doric tomb named Kesme Mezar, again almost completely intact. Kaş is also well situated for the nearby ruins of Kekova and Patara. On Fridays there is a big market behind the bus station.

Arrival and information

Bus All buses and *dolmuşes* arrive at the small bus station (*otogar*) just north of the town at the top of Elmalı Caddesi.
Tourist office In the town square at Cumhuriyet Maydanı 5 (April–Oct Mon–Fri 8.30am–7pm, Sat & Sun 10am–7pm; Ⓣ0242/836 1238).

Accommodation

Most *pansiyons* are located in the streets close to the bus station, particularly around Recep Bilgin Cad and immediately beyond.
Ateş Yeni Cami Sok 3 Ⓣ0242/836 1393, Ⓦwww.atespension.com. Meals can be taken on the pleasant rooftop terrace, with up to fifteen meze on offer in summer. Check the rooms – prices are negotiable on the less pleasant ones. You can use the pool at the *Hideaway Hotel* across the road (also worth checking out though a notch up price-wise). Doubles 40–50TL, dorms 15TL plus breakfast.
Hilal Pension Süleyman Yıldırım Cad Ⓣ0242 836 1207, Ⓦwww.korsan-kas.com. The really helpful owner here can orchestrate all manner of excursions and activities. The rooms are decent and you can often feast on reasonably priced fish from the barbecue come evening. Breakfast included. Singles 40TL, doubles 60TL.
Meltem Atatürk Buluari Meltem Sok Ⓣ0242/836 18 55, Ⓦwww.kasmeltempansion.com. Very nice, airy bedrooms, with cooling tiled floors. Ten out of the fourteen have balconies. Buffet breakfast included. Call for pick-up from the bus station. Singles 30TL, doubles 40TL.
Santosa Pension Recep Bilgin Cad 4 Ⓣ0242/836 1714. Family-run pension, quiet come evening, with great views from the communal rooftop. Bright and pleasant rooms, tiled floors. Singles 30TL, doubles 40TL.

Eating and drinking

Bar Celona Uzunçarşı Gürsoy Sok 2/A. The beer flows endlessly here and the nice little outdoor seating area on a small side street makes it difficult not to partake.
Bi Lokma (Mama's Kitchen) Hükümet Cad 2. A charming little place with nice views of the harbour from the terrace and a reassuringly brief menu. The highlight is probably Mama's home-made *mantı* for 8TL.
Mavi Cumhuriyet Medanı. A well-loved bar on the square that rivals *Bar Celona* for its drunk-making properties.

PARAGLIDING

Paragliding is perfect for thrill seekers or those craving a novel way of viewing the landscape. Flights last approximately twenty minutes, cost €100 and can be booked either through your *pansiyon* or the Naturablue office on Likya Cad 1/A (Ⓦwww.naturablue.com) or Bougainville (see above). If you're a paragliding novice you'll fly in tandem with an instructor – so all you need to do is hold on.

Smiley's Yat Limanı Girişi. Smiley is the twinkly-eyed owner. She makes fresh meze every day and has fostered an atmosphere conducive to both splurging and eating frugally. A good fish soup can be had for 7TL or go for delicious sea bream for around 20TL.
Sultan Garden Hükümet Cad. Marvelously atmospheric spot and excellent meze.

OLYMPOS AND ÇIRALI

The Lycian site of **OLYMPOS**, 50km before Antalya, is located on a beautiful sandy bay and the banks of a largely dry river. It's an idyllic location with a small village that is now firmly on the backpacker circuit. The site itself (3TL when someone is manning the ticket office) features some recently excavated tombs, the walls of a Byzantine church and a theatre, most of whose seats have gone. On the north side of the river are more striking ruins, including a well-preserved marble temple entrance. Beyond is a Byzantine bathhouse, with mosaic floors, and a Byzantine canal which would have carried water to the heart of the city. A pleasant 1.5km walk away is the holiday village of **ÇIRALI**. About an hour's well-marked stroll above the village's citrus groves flickers the dramatic **Chimaera** (open 24hr; 3TL), a series of eternal flames issuing from cracks in the bare rock. The fire has been burning since antiquity, and inspired the Lycians to worship the god Hephaestos (or Vulcan to the Romans). The mountain was associated with a fire-breathing monster, also known as the Chimaera, with a lion's head, a goat's rear and a snake for a tail.

Arrival and information

Bus Catch any Kaş–Antalya bus to the minibus stop on the main highway, 8km up from the shore; in season there are hourly minibuses from here to Olympos. There are also one or two minibuses a day from Antalya to Çıralı in season.
Money Note that there are no banks or ATMs in Olympos or Çıralı, so make sure you have enough cash before arriving. Many of the *pansiyons* can accept card payment for accommodation.

Accommodation

With few road names around Olympos – where all the following accommodation is – it's best to ask at the bus station ticket office for directions or arrange pick-ups.
Bayram's ⓣ 0242/892 1243, ⓦ www.bayrams.com. Accommodation ranges from bungalow shacks to tree-house dormitory rooms. Excellent facilities include laundry service and internet access. Tree-house dorm 30TL, bungalows 40–50TL.
Kadir's ⓣ 0242/892 1250, ⓦ www.kadirstreehouses.com. Good facilities including an alfresco nightclub. Organizes trips to Chimaera. Bungalows for 2/3 people 40TL, dorms 20TL.
Orange ⓣ 0242/892 1317, ⓦ www.olymposorangepension.com. Professionally run and good wholesome grub. Bungalows 35–40TL.
Şaban ⓣ 0242/892 1265, ⓦ www.sabanpansion.com. Treehouse-style *pansiyon* with excellent home-made food and a friendly, relaxed atmosphere. Dorms 20–30TL, cabin 35–40TL.

Eating and drinking

Be sure to ask for a menu with prices, as seafood can be very expensive.
Çirali Gözleme Çıralı village between the Orange Market and Olympos Rent A Car, close to the *Orange Motel*. For the most succulent specimens of *gözleme* hereabouts.
Orange Nestled amongst the rocks in a small side valley. A beach-restaurant and the best of the three bars in the area.
Yörükoğlu On the Çıralı end of the beach right next to the *Olympos Lodge Hotel*. Fine meze and a friendly owner.

ANTALYA

ANTALYA is blessed with an ideal climate and a stunning setting, and, despite the grim appearance of its concrete sprawl, it's an agreeable place – although the main area of interest for visitors is confined to the relatively small old quarter; its beaches don't rate much consideration. A short bus-ride away are the charming **Düden** falls where tourists and locals flock on hot summer days. Antalya's principal attraction, however, is situated on the outskirts of the city – **Aspendos**, a Roman theatre which still holds live performances.

What to see and do

Antalya is dominated by the **Yivli Minare** or "Fluted Minaret", erected in the thirteenth century. Downhill from here is the old **harbour**, recently restored and site of the evening promenade. North is the **bazaar**, while south, beyond the Saat Kalesi (clock tower), lies Kaleiçi or the **old town**, with every house now a carpet shop, café or *pansiyon*. On the far side, on Atatürk Caddesi, the triple-arched **Hadrian's Gate** recalls a visit by the emperor in 130 AD; Hesapçı Sokak leads south past the Kesik Minare to a number of tea gardens.

The Antalya Museum

The one thing you shouldn't miss is the **Antalya Museum** (Tues–Sun 9am–6.30pm; 15TL), one of the top five archeological collections in the country; it's on the western edge of town at the far end of Kenan Evren Bulvarı, easily reachable by a tram that departs from the clock tower in Kaleiçi.

Düden falls

A small but nonetheless enchanting waterfall, **Düden falls** attracts a large number of visitors. The upper falls provide the best visual spectacle and are situated in the midst of a park. There is even a precarious walkway carved out to enable visitors to walk behind the falls. To get to the falls from Kaleiçi, get a #14 bus from the *dolmuş otogar* (25min; 2TL). Ask the driver for Düden falls and you'll be dropped near the entrance.

Arrival and information

Air The airport is 12km northeast; Havaş buses into town depart from the domestic terminal, 5min walk from the international terminal, while city-centre-bound *dolmuşes* pass nearby.
Bus Antalya's main bus station is 7km north of town. From the bus station take bus #93 to Hadrian's Gate (*Üçkapılar*) then walk into the old town.
Tourist office A 15min walk west from the clock tower on Cumhuriyet Cad (daily 8am–6/7pm; ⓣ0242/241 1747).
Internet *Moonlight Café* on 1291 Sok opposite Hadrian's Gate.

City transport

Bus Buses and *dolmuşes* can be caught throughout the city though the system is currently in flux. *Sabah Pansiyon* produce their own leaflet detailing the city transport system and it is worth picking one up.
Tram The tram runs along Atatürk Cad, ending its route at the Museum. Tickets can be bought at the turnstile booths.

Accommodation

Most budget accommodation is in the area sandwiched between Hadrian's Gate and the back of the bazaar.
Blue Sea Garden Hotel Kılçarslan Mah Hesapçı Sok 65 ⓣ0242/248 8213, ⓦwww.hotelblueseagarden.com. The rooms are not exactly a knockout but most guests spend their time in the hotel's garden anyway, which has a pool and a small restaurant area. Price includes breakfast. Singles 40TL, doubles 60TL.
Dedekonak Kılınçaslan Mah Hıdırlık Sok 13 ⓣ0242/248 5264, ⓦwww.dedekonakpansiyon.com. Ottoman restoration, with massive windows in the faded yet impressive rooms. Freshly cooked meals served in the atmospheric garden. Singles 30TL, doubles 50TL.
Sabah Pansiyon Hesapçı Sok 60/A ⓣ0242/247 5345, ⓦwww.sabahpansiyon.8m.com. Backpacker-friendly place with decent rooms and a nicely sleepy courtyard. Price includes breakfast. Dorm 20TL, room with shared bathroom 30TL, en suite 40–50TL.
White Garden Kaleiçi Kılıçaslan Hesapçı Geçidi 9 ⓣ0242/241 9115. Charming Ottoman restoration; fifteen immaculate rooms with large en suites. Buffet Turkish breakfasts included. Singles 35TL, doubles 55TL.

Eating and drinking

Annem Zeynep'in Mutfağı Atatürk Cad 1304 Sok 4/1. Get in before the lunch rush and take your pick of perfectly prepared meze. Wonderful family atmosphere and a few outdoor tables on a dusty side street. Shady awning in French colours. Portions of meze 7TL.

Parlak Restaurant Kazım Özalp Cad Zincirlihan 7. So popular the waiters look a little apprehensive pre-service. Try the slow-roasted chicken – lipsmacking. Lovely fresh meze thanks to the high turnover. Meze 6–8TL, mains 12–25TL.

Topçu Kebap 1885 Kazım Özalp Cad 21. They have been honing their kebabs since 1885, and hordes descend every lunchtime to enjoy them. Near the square by the tram stop.

Fast-food stand outside football stadium The place to try *yengen* – a grilled sandwich with sliced *sucuk*, cheese and spicy tomato sauce (the secret ingredient that elevates it above mere *tost*) – the fans' match-day fuel.

Moving on

Bus/dolmuş Antalya (3 daily; 12hr); Denizli (6 daily; 5hr 30min); Fethiye, by inland route (6 daily; 4hr); İstanbul (4 daily; 12hr); İzmir (6 daily; 9hr 30min); Kaş (6 daily; 5hr); Konya (6 daily; 5hr 30min); Side (3 hourly; 1hr 15min); Nevşehir (1 daily; 11hr); Olympos (every 30min; 2hr).

Central Turkey

When the first Turkish nomads arrived in Anatolia during the tenth and eleventh centuries, the landscape must have been strongly reminiscent of their Central Asian homeland. **Ankara** grew as a result of immigration from the Anatolian villages to become the metropolis it is now. The south-central part of the country draws more visitors, not least for **Cappadocia** in the far east of the region, where water and wind have created a land of fantastic forms from the soft tufa rock, including forests of cones, table mountains and canyon-like valleys. Further south still, **Konya** is best known as the birthplace of the mystical Sufi sect and is a good place to stop over between Cappadocia and the coast.

ANKARA

Modern **ANKARA** is really two cities, a double identity that is due to the breakneck pace at which it has developed since being declared capital of the Turkish Republic in 1923. Until then Ankara – known as Angora – had been a small provincial city, famous chiefly for the production of soft goat's wool. This city still exists, in and around the old citadel that was the site of the original settlement. The other Ankara is the modern metropolis that has grown up around a carefully planned attempt to create a seat of government worthy of a modern, Western-looking state.

What to see and do

The city is bisected north–south by **Atatürk Bulvarı**, and everything you need is in easy reach of this broad and busy street. At the northern end, **Ulus Meydanı**, a large square and an important traffic intersection marked by a huge equestrian Atatürk statue, is the best jumping-off point for the old part of the city – a village of narrow cobbled streets and ramshackle wooden houses centring on the **Hisar**, Ankara's old fortress and citadel. To the south, the modern shopping district of **Kızılay** sees Turkish students congregate on its streets and aspiring authors sell and sign their books on street corners. At night, the area is awash with entertainment, bars and restaurants, as are the neighbouring districts of **Kavaklidere** and **Çankaya**.

The Museum of Anatolian Civilizations

Located in Ulus, at the end of Kadife Sokak, is the **Museum of Anatolian Civilizations** (Tues–Sun 9am–5.30pm; 15TL) which boasts an incomparable collection of archeological objects housed in a restored Ottoman *bedesten*, or covered market. Hittite carving and relief work form the most compelling section of the museum, mostly taken from Carchemish, near the present Syrian border. There are also Neolithic finds from Çatal Höyük, the site of one of Anatolia's oldest settlements and widely regarded as the world's first "city".

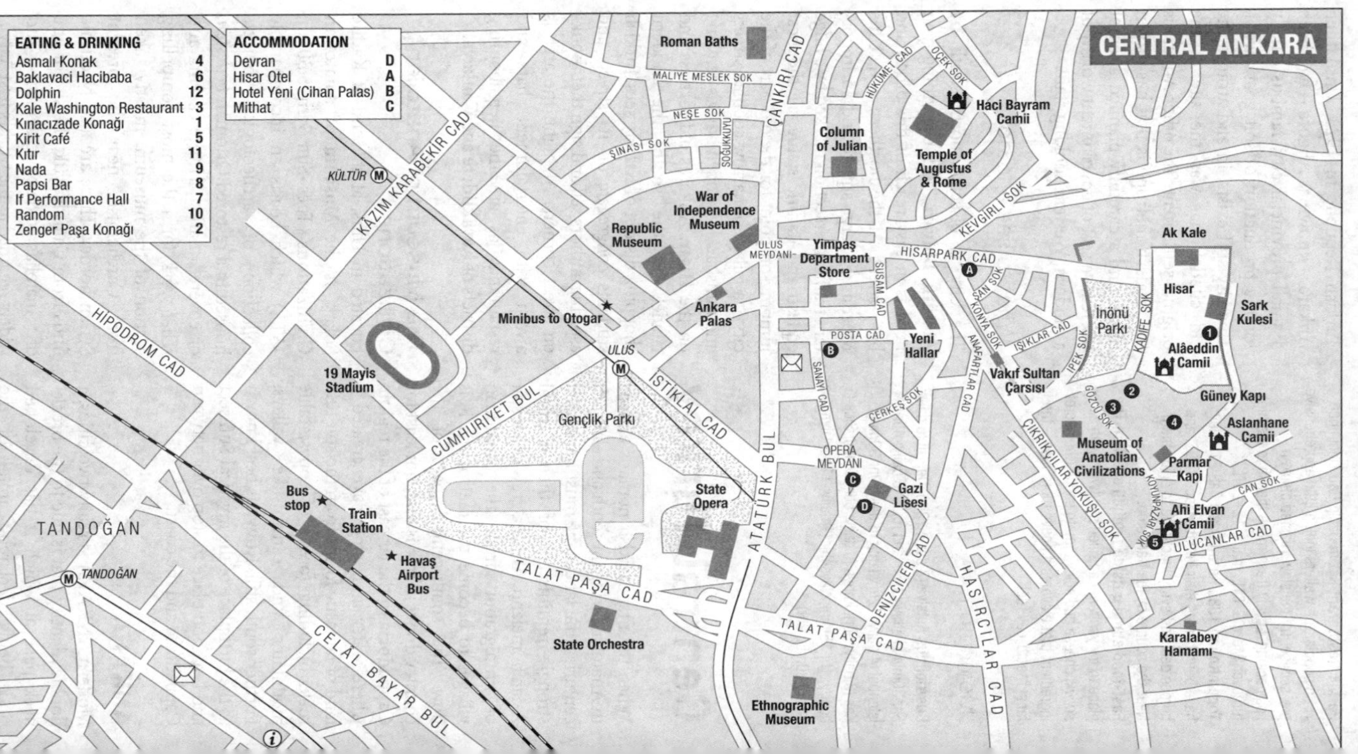
CENTRAL ANKARA
EATING & DRINKING
Asmalı Konak 4
Baklavaci Hacibaba 6
Dolphin 12
Kale Washington Restaurant 3
Kınacızade Konağı 1
Kirit Café 5
Kıtır 11
Nada 9
Papsi Bar 8
If Performance Hall 7
Random 10
Zenger Paşa Konağı 2
ACCOMMODATION
Devran D
Hisar Otel A
Hotel Yeni (Cihan Palas) B
Mithat C
Roman Baths
Column of Julian
Haci Bayram Camii
Temple of Augustus & Rome
Ak Kale
Hisar
Sark Kulesi
Alâeddin Camii
Güney Kapı
Aslanhane Camii
Parmar Kapi
Ahi Elvan Camii
Karalabey Hamamı
İnönü Parkı
Vakıf Sultan Çarsısı
Museum of Anatolian Civilizations
Yeni Hallar
Gazi Lisesi
Yimpaş Department Store
War of Independence Museum
Republic Museum
Ankara Palas
Minibus to Otogar
19 Mayis Stadium
Gençlik Parkı
State Opera
State Orchestra
Ethnographic Museum
Bus stop
Train Station
Havaş Airport Bus
TANDOĞAN
KÜLTÜR
ULUS
ULUS MEYDANI
OPERA MEYDANI
KÂZIM KARABEKIR CAD
HIPODROM CAD
CUMHURIYET BUL
ISTIKLAL CAD
ATATÜRK BUL
TALAT PAŞA CAD
CELÂL BAYAR BUL
ÇANKIRI CAD
MALIYE MESLEK SOK
NEŞE SOK
ŞINASI SOK
SOĞUKKUYU
HÜKÜMET CAD
OÇEK SOK
KEVGIRLI SOK
HISARPARK CAD
SUSAM CAD
POSTA CAD
SANAYI CAD
ÇERKEŞ SOK
DENIZCILER CAD
HASIRCILAR CAD
ANAFARTLAR CAD
KONYA SOK
SAN SOK
IŞIKLAR CAD
IPEK SOK
KADIFE SOK
GÖZCÜ SOK
ÇIKRIKÇILAR YOKUŞU SOK
KOYUNPAZARI SOK
CAN SOK
ULUCANLAR CAD

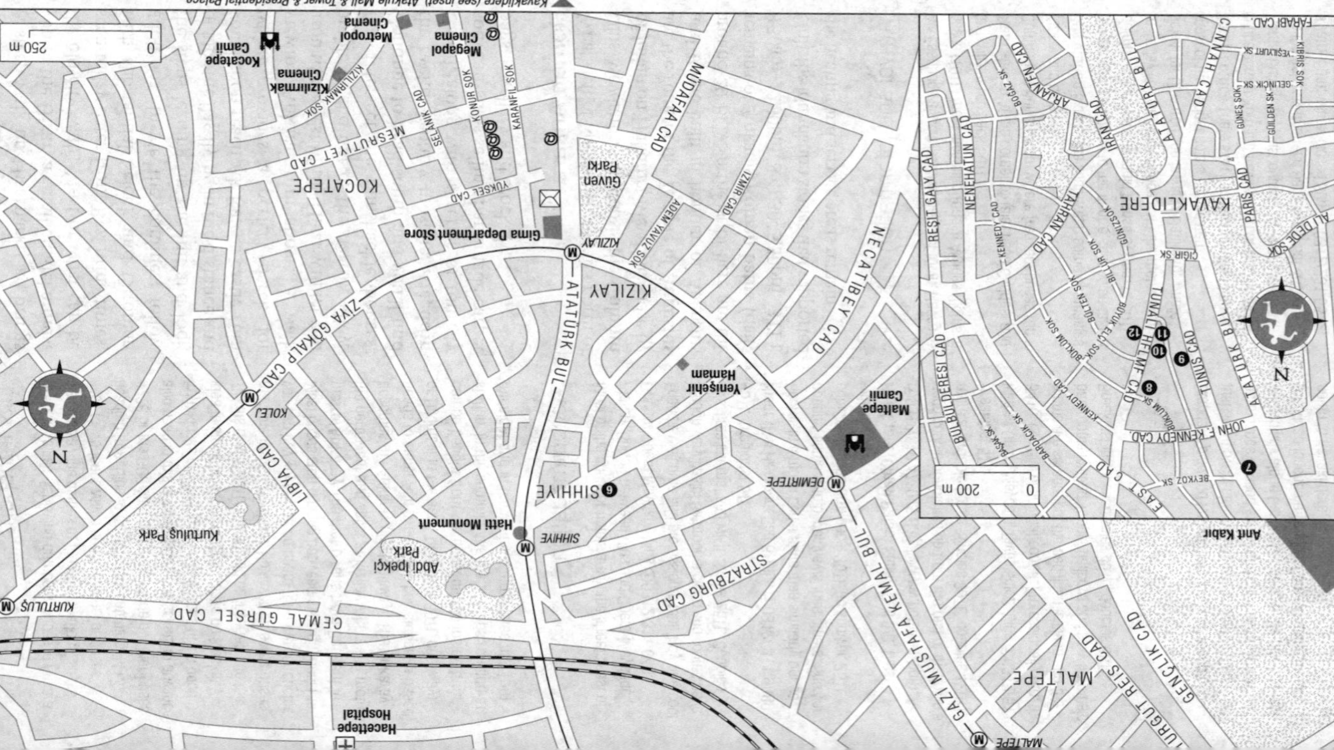
Kavaklidere (see inset), Atakule Mall & Tower & Presidential Palace
0 250 m
Kocatepe Camii
Metropol Cinema
Megapol Cinema
Kizilirmak Cinema
KIZILIRMAK SOK
SELANIK CAD
KONUR SOK
KARANFIL SOK
MESRUTIYET CAD
KOCATEPE
YÜKSEL CAD
Güven Parkı
MUDAFAA CAD
Gima Department Store
KIZILAY
ADEM YAVUZ SOK
IZMIR CAD
NECATIBEY CAD
ZIYA GÖKALP CAD
ATATÜRK BUL
KOLEJ
Yenişehir Hamam
Maltepe Camii
LIBYA CAD
SIHHIYE
DEMIRTEPE
Hatti Monument
Kurtuluş Park
Abdi Ipekçi Park
STRAZBURG CAD
KURTULUŞ
CEMAL GÜRSEL CAD
GAZI MUSTAFA KEMAL BUL
Hacettepe Hospital
MALTEPE
TURGUT REIS CAD
GENÇLIK CAD
Anıt Kabir
FARABI CAD.
CINNAH CAD
KIBRIS SOK
YESILYURT SK
GELINCIK SK
GÜNES SOK
GÜLDEN SK
ATATÜRK BUL
IRAN CAD.
ARJANTIN CAD
BOĞAZ SK
NENEHATUN CAD
REŞIT GALY CAD
KENNEDY CAD
TAHRAN CAD
GÜNIZSOK
KAVAKLIDERE
PARIS CAD
ALI DEDE SOK
ÇIĞIR SK
BILLUR SOK
BÜYÜK ELÇI SOK
BÜLTEN SOK
BÜKLÜM SOK
TUNALI HILMI CAD
TUNUS CAD
BULBULDERESI CAD
BAŞAK SK
BARDACIK SK
JOHN F. KENNEDY CAD.
EAST CAD
BEYKOZ SK
0 200 m
N

Hisar

A steep walk up Hisarpark Cad brings you to the **Hisar**, a small citadel amidst the old city walls. Most of what can be seen today dates from Byzantine times, with substantial Selçuk and Ottoman additions. Inside the confines, follow the steps leading up the hill and look out for the flag flying in the distance and you'll soon reach Ak Kale, a castle ruin which provides a perfect perch for viewing Ankara from above. A walk around the rest of the Hisar will let you amble in and out of the narrow alleys that intersect the ramshackle houses. Continue to head south and you'll find the twelfth-century mosque, **Alâeddin Camii**, along with a series of touristy souvenir stalls selling handmade carpet bags, jewellery and crockery.

Roman Ankara

What's left of Roman Ankara lies north of Ulus Meydanı. First stop is the **Column of Julian** on Hükümet Meydanı. Close by are the ruins of the **Temple of Augustus and Rome** built in honour of Augustus around 20 BC. Northeast of here are the remains of Ankara's **Roman baths** (daily 8.30am–12.30pm & 1.30–5.30pm; 3TL). Only the foundation stones that supported the heating and service areas remain.

Arrival and information

Air Esenboğa airport is 33km north of town. Havaş buses (10TL) meet incoming Turkish Airlines flights; a taxi will set you back 50TL.

Train station At the corner of Talat Paşa Caddesi and Cumhuriyet Bulvarı, from where frequent buses run to Kızılay and Ulus.

Bus station 5km to the southwest; some companies run service minibuses to the centre, otherwise take a *dolmuş* or the Ankaray rapid transit system (2.50TL) to Kızılay (10min) and change onto the metro (same ticket) for Ulus (red line towards Batıkent), where most of the budget hotels are located.

Tourist office There's an incredibly helpful tourist office across from the train station at Gazi Mustafa Kemal Bulvarı 121, just outside Maletepe station on the Ankaray (Mon–Fri 9am–5pm, Sat & Sun 10am–5pm; winter closed Sun; ☎0312/231 5572).

City transport

Bus As well as displaying numbers, buses in Ankara also display the names of their destinations, so it's easy to work out which one to catch. For buses heading from Ulus to Çankaya try catching #413, #228 or the GOP although a multitude of other buses also head in this direction. Buy bus tickets in advance from kiosks next to the main bus stops (it's a good idea to stock up, as some areas have no kiosks). Tickets cost 1.30TL and should be inserted into the machine next to the driver. However, on some buses you can buy your ticket on board from the conductor. Most buses stop running between midnight and 1am.

Metro/Ankaray The metro runs from Batıkent in the northwest and splits at Kızılay where the metro becomes the Ankaray (light railway). The Ankaray heads to either Aşti (where the bus station is based) or Dikimevi in the east. Tickets (1.30TL one way) can be bought from the ticket offices inside the station. In the summer, the metro stops running at midnight and in the winter it terminates at 11pm.

Accommodation

Most of the cheaper hotels are in the streets east of Atatürk Bulvarı between Ulus and Opera Meydanı.

Devran Opera Meydanı, Ulus ☎0312/311 0485. Friendly welcome and professional feel. Tidy and cool though very basic. Bathrooms clean and rooms have TVs. Free internet and wi-fi. Single 25TL, doubles 45TL, breakfast 5TL.

Hisar Otel Hisarpark Cad 6, Ulus ☎0312/ 311 9889. Rooms in a much better state than similarly priced options, some with better views than others. Shower cubicles, TV and firm beds. 20TL no shower, 25TL with shower.

Hotel Yeni (Cihan Palas) Sanayi Cad 5/B, Ulus ☎0312/310 4720 (5 Hat), ⓦwww.hotelyeni.com. A good couple of notches up from the rest of the town's more affordable hotels. Singles 80TL, doubles 120TL. Breakfast 5TL.

Mithat Opera Meydanı, Tavus Sok 2, Ulus ☎0312/311 5410, ⓦwww.otelmithat.com.tr. Professionally run, the rooms are sombre but the bed linen is clean and the bathrooms inviting. Proper bellboys and sexy lift music. Breakfast included. Singles 45TL, doubles 68TL.

Eating

Standard *pide* and kebab places can be found on just about every street in Ankara and there's an abundance of good sweet and cake shops. Ulus, particularly along Çankırı Caddesi, is the place to look for cheap lunchtime venues. Come evening, head south to Kavaklıdere.

Asmalı Konak Kalekapısı Sok 14, Hisar. Great range of fresh meze (5TL) in an atmospheric old building. Affable owner Osman is a big belly-dancing fan and organizes regular shows.
Kale Washington Restaurant Hisar. Impeccably smart place in Hisar. Worth getting your nice clothes out from the bottom of the backpack. Mains 15–25TL.
Kınacızade Konağı Hisar. A nice down-to-earth and warm atmosphere, with a cute two-table balcony and a fine range of breakfast choices. One room is a kind of mini-museum/shrine to the Ottoman period. Mains 10–12TL.
Kirit Café Koyunpazarı Sok 60, Samanpazarı (Jewish Quarter). A lovely new place near the citadel. Features a hundred-year-old Ottoman dress framed on the wall and a good vintage coffee machine. *Kirit* meatballs 9TL – grilled meatballs wrapped in a tortilla served with fries.
Zenger Paşa Konağı Hisar. Just climbing up to the restaurant is a treat. On the way up you will see women sitting by a fire making breads. Reasonable prices considering the wonderful views. *Pide* – Saturdays only – 8–9TL, meze 6TL; grills around 16TL. All served with freshly made bread.

Drinking

Dolphin Tunalı Hilmi Cad 99, Kavaklıdere. Long and narrow, low-lit drinking joint, with the atmosphere of a classic American bar.
If Performance Hall Tunus Caddesi 14/A, Kavaklıdere ⓣ0312/418 9506, ⓦwww.ifperformance.com. Opened 2002 and still maintain their policy of having bands on every night. A stalwart of the Ankara music scene. The beers are 8TL though.
Kıtır Tunalı Hilmi Cad 114/24, Kavaklıdere. Small, buzzy pub with a little fast-food window at the entrance – outdoor seating, too.
Nada Tunus Cad 85/A, Kavaklıdere ⓦwww.nada.com.tr. A place to look like you just happened to throw on your best outfit. Smart and sleek but nevertheless friendly.
Papsi Bar Tunalı Hilmi Cad 68/C, Kavaklıdere. Lively outdoor spot with an accordion player serenading drinkers.
Random Tunalı Hilmi Cad 114, Kavaklıdere (below *Kıtır*). Busy, intimate bar flooded with a young crowd.

Entertainment

Anadolu Gösteri Kongre Merkezi Türkocağl Cad Balgat. Large performance hall for theatre or music concerts. See ⓦwww.biletix.com for tickets.

Shopping

Ada Turan Güneş Bulvarı 44/B, Çankaya. National chain bookstore with a small selection of books in English and other languages.
Dünya Aktüel Tunalı Hilmi Cad 114/17, Kavaklıdere. Established seller of international books with a good travel section.
Neofly Bahçelievler 7 Cad No 2/7. Generic women's streetwear – colourful t-shirts, jeans, trainers etc.
Shades Tunalı Hilmi Pasaji 95/37. Quirky, vintage music store with an eclectic range from Turkish folk classics to rock and blues.

Directory

Embassies Australia, Nenehatun Cad 83, Gaziosmanpaşa ⓣ0312/459 9500; Canada, Cinnah Cad 58, Çankaya ⓣ0312/409 2700; New Zealand, Iran Cad 13/4, Kavaklıdere ⓣ0312/467 9054; UK, Şehit Ersan Cad 46/A, Çankaya ⓣ0312/468 6230; US, Atatürk Bul 110, Kavaklıdere ⓣ0312/455 5555.
Hamam Karacabey Hamami, Talat Paşa Bul 101 (men 6am–11pm; women 7am–7pm; from 15TL).
Hospital Hacettepe University Medical Faculty, west of Hasırcılar Sok, Sıhhıye ⓣ0312/305 5000.
Internet Intek Internet Café, Karanfil Sok 47/A, Kızılay; Internet Café, next to PTT, Maltepe.
Left luggage At the bus and train stations.
Post office Merkez Postahane, on Atatürk Bulvarı, Ulus.

Moving on

Train İstanbul (3 high-speed daily, changing at Eskisehir, 5hr 30min; 1 sleeper daily 10.30pm, 9hr 30min); İzmir (2 daily; 10hr).
Bus/dolmuş Antalya (12 daily; 10hr); Bodrum (10 daily; 10hr); Bursa (hourly; 7hr); Fethiye (2 daily; 12hr); İstanbul (every 30min; 7hr); İzmir (hourly; 8hr); Konya (14 daily; 3hr 30min); Marmaris (14 daily; 13hr); Nevşehir (12 daily; 4hr 30min).

CAPPADOCIA

A land created by the complex interaction of natural and human forces over vast spans of time, **CAPPADOCIA**, around 150km southeast of Ankara, is a unique visual experience. Its weird formations of soft, dusty rock have been adapted into caves and even underground cities over centuries by many cultures. Cappadocia scores highly on

value for money thanks to the wide selection of competitively priced accommodation, restaurants and activities on offer. The small town of Göreme is the favourite base for most visitors.

Göreme

The small town of **GÖREME** is the best known of the few remaining Cappadocian villages whose rock-cut houses and fairy chimneys are still inhabited. Despite the number of tourists milling around in high season there is a pleasant village feel here. A trip to the **Ihlara Valley** is highly recommended and is often included on the tour itineraries offered by the hostels.

What to see and do

About 2km outside the village, the **Göreme Open-Air Museum** (daily 8am–5/6pm; 15TL) is the site of over thirty churches, mainly dating from the ninth to the end of the eleventh century and containing some of the best of all the frescoes in Cappadocia.

Arrival and information

Bus When buying your bus ticket to Göreme be sure to check the end destination. Direct services arrive at the Göreme bus station, located in front of Müze Cad, in the centre of town. However, some firms will drop you off in Nevşehir, from where you'll have to continue by local bus or *dolmuş* (the last of which leaves Nevşehir at about 6pm). *Dolmuş* to Nevşehir runs hourly on Sundays, half-hourly otherwise.

Tourist office In the bus station (daily 5am–9pm). Has a useful accommodation list and maps of the local area.

Tours Nomad Travel offer good-value day-long trips including a southern Cappadocia option that takes in the Ihlara Valley, one of the region's real beauty spots. Their one-hour ballooning trips are €110, €130 high season. Cappadocia Balloons' (ⓣ0384/271 2442, ⓦwww.turkeyballoon.com) equivalent is €175. This extra cost is down to their greater experience, which is not to be sniffed at.

Accommodation

Cave hotels are the most popular form of accommodation in Göreme. Some of them can be tricky to find, though none are more than a 10min walk from the bus station, and the accommodation office there will arrange free pick-ups.

Kookaburra Motel & Pansiyon ⓣ0384/271 2549, ⓔkookagoreme@hotmail.com. Magnificent view of the chimneys from the terrace. The dorm is the nicest in town. 25TL per person for a double, singles 30TL, dorms 15TL, all including breakfast.

Köse Pansion ⓣ0384/271 2294, ⓔdawn@kosepension.com. Large, homely *pansiyon* with swimming pool. The mattress-strewn dorm is in a large, atmospheric wooden hall on the rooftop. Dorms 12.50TL, private double €30.

Rock Valley Hostel ⓣ0384/271 2153, ⓦwww.rockvalleycappadocia.com. Nice wooden dorm with heating chimney for snugness. Big pool with the valley looming up all around – very atmospheric. A pleasant, low-key option. Dorm 10TL, doubles 50–60TL.

Shoestring ⓣ0384/271 2450, ⓦwww.shoestringcave.com. A warm, sociable atmosphere. Quality beds and bedding make these cave rooms very cosy indeed. Privates with shared bathroom 30–40TL, en suite 40–60TL, dorms 15–20TL.

Eating and drinking

Several restaurants and bars can be found on Müze Cad, behind the bus station.

Anatolia Kitchen Müze Cad 1. Offers local wine as well as beer. A quality mixed meze with pizza-like bread is 10TL, vegetable kebab of mushrooms, aubergine, tomato and peppers 12TL and *pide* 5–10TL. A nice shady terrace in the middle of town, a minute or two from the bus station.

Dibek Hakkı Paşa Meydanı. It won't take long for someone to tell you about this place's *testi kebab* but it takes the restaurant a long time to cook it – you need to order it at least three hours in advance.

Flintstones Bar Müze Caddesi. Local hub for low-key nocturnal entertainment. Plays good old-time and rock'n'roll. Beer 5TL, spirits 10TL.

Göreme Restaurant With kilim and cushions on the floor this place has a warm feel (welcome in sometimes chilly Göreme). Slightly slow service – the waiters also play live music, which makes getting the bill a bit tricky. Nice sun-dried tomato and pomegranate molasses starter 5TL. *Kuzu şiş* with a herby salad 12TL.

Moving on

Bus/dolmuş Ankara (daily; 6 hr); Konya (4 daily; 3hr); Nevşehir (Sun every hour, Mon–Sat every 30min; 30min) .

Derinkuyu and Kayamaklı

Among the most extraordinary phenomena of the Cappadocia region are the remains of a number of underground settlements, some of them large enough to have accommodated up to 30,000 people. The cities are thought to date back to Hittite times, though the complexes were later enlarged by Christian communities. Most thoroughly excavated is **DERINKUYU** (daily 8am–5.30pm; 15TL), 29km from Nevşehir and accessible by *dolmuş*. The city is well lit, and the original ventilation system still functions remarkably well, though some of the passages are small and cramped. The excavated area (only a quarter of the total) consists of eight floors and includes stables, wine presses and a dining hall or schoolroom with two long, rock-cut tables, plus a cruciform church and dungeon. Some 10km north of Derinkuyu is **KAYMAKLI** (daily 8am–5.30pm; 15TL), where only five of its underground levels have been excavated to date.

KONYA

Roughly midway between Antalya and Nevşehir, **KONYA** is a place of pilgrimage for the Muslim world – the home of Celalledin Rumi or the Mevlâna ("Our Master"), the mystic who founded the Mevlevî or Whirling Dervish sect, and the centre of Sufic mystical practice and teaching.

The Mevlâna Museum

The **Mevlâna Museum** (daily 9am–5pm, Mon 10am–5pm; 3TL) is housed in the first lodge (*tekke*) of the Mevlevî dervish sect, at the eastern end of Mevlâna Bulvarı, recognizable by its distinctive fluted turquoise dome. The main building of the museum holds the mausoleum containing the tombs of the Mevlâna, his father and other notables. The original *semahane* (ceremonial hall) exhibits some of the musical instruments of the first dervishes, the original illuminated poetical work of the Mevlâna, and a 500-year-old silk carpet from Selçuk Persia that is supposedly the finest ever woven. In the adjoining room, a casket containing hairs from the beard of the Prophet Muhammad is displayed alongside illuminated medieval Korans.

Karatay Tile Museum

Built by Emir Celaleddin Karatay in the thirteenth century, the interior of the **Karatay Tile Museum** (Alaaddin Bulvarı; daily 8am–noon & 1–5pm; 3TL) is equally as fascinating as the ceramics on show, with a beautifully decorated domed central ceiling and ornamental green tiles.

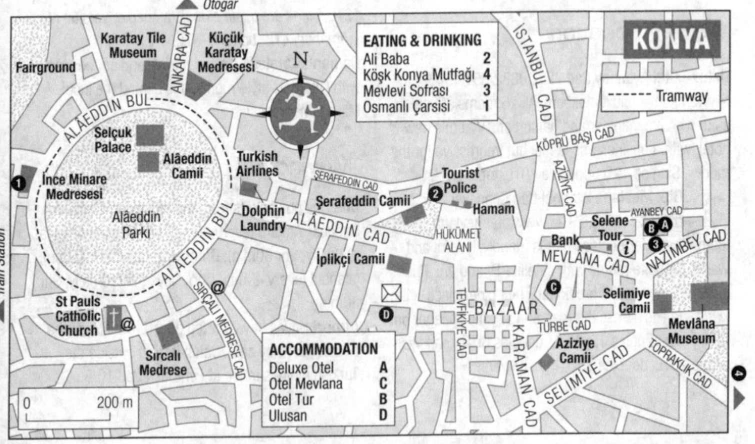

WHIRLING DERVISH CEREMONY

This meditational ceremony, where worshippers spin around to draw closer to God, is held at the Mevlâna Cultural Centre close to the museum. The ceremony is free and takes place every Saturday night. Tickets can be booked through most hotels or the tourist information office. Alternatively, Selene Travel Agency organizes private viewings of the ceremony from June to August. Performances take place on Monday, Wednesday and Friday at 8.30pm and cost 25TL but the performance only takes place if there are enough bookings.

Arrival and information

Bus station 10km out of town, from where the *otogar dolmuş* and tramway connects with the town centre.
Train station 2km out of the centre at the far end of Istasyon Caddesi, connected to the centre by regular *dolmuş*.
Tourist office Mevlâna Cad No 73 (May–Sept Mon–Sat 8.30am–5.30pm; Oct–April Mon–Fri 8am–5pm; ⓣ0332/353 4021 extension 115). Lots of useful information and free mystical music CDs.
Travel agent Selene Tours (Avanbey Sok 22 T02332/353 6745, ⓦwww.selene.com.tr) specialize in trips to Beyşehir, known for its natural beauty and Hittite monuments.
Internet Internet cafés are around Alaaddin Hill, next to the *McDonalds* or Ince Minare Medresesi.

Accommodation

Deluxe Otel Ayanbey Cad 22 ⓣ0332/351 1546, ⓦwww.konyadeluxeotel.com. All 25 rooms are en suite with a/c, minibar and flatscreen TV at this new hotel, with a business-style feel but impressive for the money. Singles 40TL, doubles 70TL, triple 90TL.
Otel Mevlana İstanbul Cad Cengaver Sok 2 ⓣ0332/352 0029, ⓦwww.otelmevlana.com. Characterful place that is friendly, helpful and warm. En-suite rooms with satellite TV and a/c. Price includes open buffet breakfast. Their older place – the *pansiyon* – is across the road and slightly cheaper but far inferior. Singles 35–40TL, doubles 60TL, *pansiyon* single 20TL, doubles 30TL (no showers).
Otel Tur Mevlana Cad Esarizade Sok 13 ⓣ0332/351 9825. A warm, modest affair, tended with care. Large rooms and decent bathrooms. Breakfast included. Singles 40TL, double 60TL, triple 80TL.
Ulusan Off Alaadin Cad on side road behind the PTT ⓣ0332/351 5004, ⓦsite.mynet.com/ulusanhotel. Kind of a smoky, sterile atmosphere but a solid choice nonetheless. Unusual breakfast area – a tiny impromptu lounge on an upper-floor landing. Singles 40TL, doubles 60TL.

Eating and drinking

There is a limited selection of restaurants and no reputable bars or pubs. The nightlife scene is underground and few women venture out at night alone. The area around Alaadin Parkı is where younger people hang out.
Ali Baba Eski Avukatlar Sok 5/A. Everything is about the *konya firin kebap*, lamb cooked for hours in a wood-fired oven, eaten with bread and a plateful of raw onion to cut through the richness. Near the Şerafettin mosque. A bit tricky to find but locally well known, so ask.
Köşk Konya Mutfağı Mengüç Cad 66. A fantastic place that looms up, a 10min walk from the town centre. The dining rooms scattered throughout the house are smart yet a nice ramshackle feel endures. Really good prices – barely anything exceeds 10TL – and excellent, traditional food. Try the *patlican orta* and, for dessert, the *höşmerim helvası*. To find it head down Topraklık Cad then bear right down Sokullu Mehmet Paşa Sok. You should spot it at the end of this road. Locals can direct you.
Mevlevi Sofrası Nazimbey Cad 1/A. Smart, spacious terrace with sweeping views of the museum garden. *Adana kebap* 7.50TL, *karışık ızgara* – mixed grill 12TL, *bıçak arasi, etli ekmek* (a crispier version of *lahmacun*) 4TL, *börek* 4–5TL.
Osmanlı Çarsisi A classic *nargile* and coffee place with Ottoman-style rooms. It is behind the Ince Minare Medresesi.

Moving on

Bus Buy bus tickets from the offices on Mevlâna Caddesi. Ankara (every 20min; 3hr 20min); Antalya (25 daily; 5hr 30min); Göreme (5 daily; 3hr 45min); İstanbul (every 40min; 9hr); Nevşehir (10 daily; 3hr 30min).
Airport Havaş have started an 8TL transfer to the airport (35TL by cab). Catch it from outside the Turkish Airlines office at Feritpaşa Cad 10/B.

Travel store

ROUGH GUIDES World Coverage

Travel

Andorra The Pyrenees, Pyrenees & Andorra Map, Spain
Antigua The Caribbean
Argentina Argentina, Argentina Map, Buenos Aires, South America on a Budget
Aruba The Caribbean
Australia Australia, Australia Map, East Coast Australia, Melbourne, Sydney, Tasmania
Austria Austria, Europe on a Budget, Vienna
Bahamas The Bahamas, The Caribbean
Barbados Barbados DIR, The Caribbean
Belgium Belgium & Luxembourg, Bruges DIR, Brussels, Brussels Map, Europe on a Budget
Belize Belize, Central America on a Budget, Guatemala & Belize Map
Benin West Africa
Bolivia Bolivia, South America on a Budget
Brazil Brazil, Rio, South America on a Budget
British Virgin Islands The Caribbean
Brunei Malaysia, Singapore & Brunei [1 title], Southeast Asia on a Budget
Bulgaria Bulgaria, Europe on a Budget
Burkina Faso West Africa
Cambodia Cambodia, Southeast Asia on a Budget, Vietnam, Laos & Cambodia Map [1 Map]
Cameroon West Africa
Canada Canada, Pacific Northwest, Toronto, Toronto Map, Vancouver
Cape Verde West Africa
Cayman Islands The Caribbean
Chile Chile, Chile Map, South America on a Budget
China Beijing, China, Hong Kong & Macau, Hong Kong & Macau DIR, Shanghai
Colombia South America on a Budget
Costa Rica Central America on a Budget, Costa Rica, Costa Rica & Panama Map
Croatia Croatia, Croatia Map, Europe on a Budget
Cuba Cuba, Cuba Map, The Caribbean, Havana
Cyprus Cyprus, Cyprus Map
Czech Republic The Czech Republic, Czech & Slovak Republics, Europe on a Budget, Prague, Prague DIR, Prague Map
Denmark Copenhagen, Denmark, Europe on a Budget, Scandinavia
Dominica The Caribbean
Dominican Republic Dominican Republic, The Caribbean
Ecuador Ecuador, South America on a Budget
Egypt Egypt, Egypt Map
El Salvador Central America on a Budget
England Britain, Camping in Britain, Devon & Cornwall, Dorset, Hampshire and The Isle of Wight [1 title], England, Europe on a Budget, The Lake District, London, London DIR, London Map, London Mini Guide, Walks In London & Southeast England
Estonia The Baltic States, Europe on a Budget
Fiji Fiji
Finland Europe on a Budget, Finland, Scandinavia
France Brittany & Normandy, Corsica, Corsica Map, The Dordogne & the Lot, Europe on a Budget, France, France Map, Languedoc & Roussillon, The Loire, Paris, Paris DIR, Paris Map, Paris Mini Guide, Provence & the Côte d'Azur, The Pyrenees, Pyrenees & Andorra Map
French Guiana South America on a Budget
Gambia The Gambia, West Africa
Germany Berlin, Berlin Map, Europe on a Budget, Germany, Germany Map
Ghana West Africa
Gibraltar Spain
Greece Athens Map, Crete, Crete Map, Europe on a Budget, Greece, Greece Map, Greek Islands, Ionian Islands
Guadeloupe The Caribbean
Guatemala Central America on a Budget, Guatemala, Guatemala & Belize Map
Guinea West Africa
Guinea-Bissau West Africa
Guyana South America on a Budget
Holland see The Netherlands
Honduras Central America on a Budget
Hungary Budapest, Europe on a Budget, Hungary
Iceland Iceland, Iceland Map
India Goa, India, India Map, Kerala, Rajasthan, Delhi & Agra [1 title], South India, South India Map
Indonesia Bali & Lombok, Southeast Asia on a Budget
Ireland Dublin DIR, Dublin Map, Europe on a Budget, Ireland, Ireland Map
Israel Jerusalem
Italy Europe on a Budget, Florence DIR, Florence & Siena Map, Florence & the best of Tuscany, Italy, The Italian Lakes, Naples & the Amalfi Coast, Rome, Rome DIR, Rome Map, Sardinia, Sicily, Sicily Map, Tuscany & Umbria, Tuscany Map, Venice, Venice DIR, Venice Map
Jamaica Jamaica, The Caribbean
Japan Japan, Tokyo
Jordan Jordan
Kenya Kenya, Kenya Map
Korea Korea
Laos Laos, Southeast Asia on a Budget, Vietnam, Laos & Cambodia Map [1 Map]
Latvia The Baltic States, Europe on a Budget
Lithuania The Baltic States, Europe on a Budget
Luxembourg Belgium & Luxembourg, Europe on a Budget
Malaysia Malaysia Map, Malaysia, Singapore & Brunei [1 title], Southeast Asia on a Budget
Mali West Africa
Malta Malta & Gozo DIR
Martinique The Caribbean
Mauritania West Africa
Mexico Baja California, Baja California, Cancún & Cozumel DIR, Mexico, Mexico Map, Yucatán, Yucatán Peninsula Map
Monaco France, Provence & the Côte d'Azur
Montenegro Montenegro
Morocco Europe on a Budget, Marrakesh DIR, Marrakesh Map, Morocco, Morocco Map,
Nepal Nepal
Netherlands Amsterdam, Amsterdam DIR, Amsterdam Map, Europe on a Budget, The Netherlands
Netherlands Antilles The Caribbean
New Zealand New Zealand, New Zealand Map

DIR: Rough Guide **DIRECTIONS** for short breaks

Available from all good bookstores

InterRail
FREE TO EXPLORE EUROP

"The most accurate maps in the world"

CITY MAPS 24 titles
Amsterdam · Athens · Barcelona · Berlin · Boston · Brussels Chicago · Dublin · Florence & Siena · Frankfurt · Lisbon · London Los Angeles · Madrid · Marrakesh · Miami · New York City · Paris Prague · Rome · San Francisco · Toronto · Venice · Washington DC
US$8.99 Can$13.99 £4.99

COUNTRY & REGIONAL MAPS 50 titles
Algarve · Andalucía · Argentina · Australia · Baja California Brittany · Crete · Croatia · Cuba · Cyprus · Czech Republic Dominican Republic · Dubai · Egypt · Greece · Guatemala & Belize Iceland · Ireland · India · Kenya · Mexico · Morocco · New Zealand Northern Spain · Peru · Portugal · Sicily · South Africa · South India Sri Lanka · Tenerife · Thailand · Trinidad & Tobago · Turkey Tuscany · Yucatán Peninsula and more.
US$9.99 Can$13.99 £5.99

WATERPROOF • RIP-PROOF • AMAZING VALUE

Make the most of your time on Earth™

Book Aid International
www.bookaid.org

Books change lives

Poverty and illiteracy go hand in hand. But in sub-Saharan Africa, books are a luxury few can afford.

Book Aid International knows that books change lives.

Every year we send over half a million books to partners in 12 countries in sub-Saharan Africa, to stock libraries in schools, refugee camps, prisons, universities and communities.

Join our Reverse Book Club and with every £2 you donate, we can send another book to some of the poorest countries in the world.

Go to **www.bookaid.org** and click on donate or call us on 020 7733 3577

Book Aid International is a charity and a limited company registered in England and Wales.
Charity No. 313869 Company No. 880754
39-41 Coldharbour Lane, Camberwell, London SE5 9NR
T +44 (0)20 7733 3577 F +44 (0)20 7978 8006
E info@bookaid.org www.bookaid.org

NOTES

NOTES

NOTES

Small print and

Index

A Rough Guide to Rough Guides

Published in 1982, the first Rough Guide – to Greece – was a student scheme that became a publishing phenomenon. Mark Ellingham, a recent graduate in English from Bristol University, had been travelling in Greece the previous summer and couldn't find the right guidebook. With a small group of friends he wrote his own guide, combining a highly contemporary, journalistic style with a thoroughly practical approach to travellers' needs.

The immediate success of the book spawned a series that rapidly covered dozens of destinations. And, in addition to impecunious backpackers, Rough Guides soon acquired a much broader and older readership that relished the guides' wit and inquisitiveness as much as their enthusiastic, critical approach and value-for-money ethos.

These days, Rough Guides include recommendations from shoestring to luxury and cover more than 200 destinations around the globe, including almost every country in the Americas and Europe, more than half of Africa and most of Asia and Australasia. Our ever-growing team of authors and photographers is spread all over the world, particularly in Europe, the US and Australia.

In the early 1990s, Rough Guides branched out of travel, with the publication of Rough Guides to World Music, Classical Music and the Internet. All three have become benchmark titles in their fields, spearheading the publication of a wide range of books under the Rough Guide name.

Including the travel series, Rough Guides now number more than 350 titles, covering: phrasebooks, waterproof maps, music guides from Opera to Heavy Metal, reference works as diverse as Conspiracy Theories and Shakespeare, and popular culture books from iPods to Poker. Rough Guides also produce a series of more than 120 World Music CDs in partnership with World Music Network.

Visit www.roughguides.com to see our latest publications.

Rough Guide travel images are available for commercial licensing at www.roughguidespictures.com

Rough Guide credits

Text editors: Edward Aves, Natasha Foges, Lara Kavanagh, Jo Kirby, Alice Park and Lucy White
Layout: Ajay Verma
Cartography: Rajesh Mishra and Maxine Repath
Picture editor: Nicole Newman
Production: Rebecca Short
Proofreaders: Diane Margolis and Stewart Wild
Editorial: Ruth Blackmore, Andy Turner, Keith Drew, James Smart, Róisín Cameron, James Rice, Emma Traynor, Emma Gibbs, Kathryn Lane, Monica Woods, Mani Ramaswamy, Harry Wilson, Lucy Cowie, Alison Roberts, Joe Staines, Peter Buckley, Matthew Milton, Tracy Hopkins, Ruth Tidball; **Delhi** Madhavi Singh, Karen D'Souza, Lubna Shaheen
Design & Pictures: **London** Scott Stickland, Dan May, Diana Jarvis, Mark Thomas, Sarah Cummins, Emily Taylor; **Delhi** Umesh Aggarwal, Jessica Subramanian, Ankur Guha, Pradeep Thapliyal, Sachin Tanwar, Anita Singh, Nikhil Agarwal, Sachin Gupta.
Production: Liz Cherry
Cartography: **London** Ed Wright, Katie Lloyd-Jones; **Delhi** Rajesh Chhibber, Ashutosh Bharti, Animesh Pathak, Jasbir Sandhu, Karobi Gogoi, Alakananda Bhattacharya, Swati Handoo, Deshpal Dabas
Online: **London** Faye Hellon, Jeanette Angell, Fergus Day, Justine Bright, Clare Bryson, Aine Fearon, Adrian Low, Ezgi Celebi; **Delhi** Amit Verma, Rahul Kumar, Narender Kumar, Ravi Yadav, Debojit Borah, Rakesh Kumar, Ganesh Sharma, Shisir Basumatari
Marketing & Publicity: **London** Liz Statham, Louise Maher, Jess Carter, Vanessa Godden, Vivienne Watton, Anna Paynton, Rachel Sprackett, Laura Vipond; **New York** Katy Ball, Judi Powers; **Delhi** Ragini Govind
Reference Director: Andrew Lockett
Operations Assistant: Becky Doyle
Operations Manager: Helen Atkinson
Publishing Director (Travel): Clare Currie
Commercial Manager: Gino Magnotta
Managing Director: John Duhigg

Publishing information

This second edition published February 2010 by
Rough Guides Ltd,
80 Strand, London WC2R 0RL
14 Local Shopping Centre, Panchsheel Park, New Delhi 110017, India
Distributed by the Penguin Group
Penguin Books Ltd,
80 Strand, London WC2R 0RL
Penguin Group (USA)
375 Hudson Street, NY 10014, USA
Penguin Group (Australia)
250 Camberwell Road, Camberwell, Victoria 3124, Australia
Penguin Group (Canada)
195 Harry Walker Parkway N, Newmarket, ON, L3Y 7B3 Canada
Penguin Group (NZ)
67 Apollo Drive, Mairangi Bay, Auckland 1310, New Zealand
Cover concept by Peter Dyer.

Typeset in Bembo and Helvetica to an original design by Henry Iles.
Printed in Italy by L.E.G.O. S.p.A, Lavis (TN)

1280pp includes index
A catalogue record for this book is available from the British Library
ISBN: 978-1-84836-458-5
The publishers and authors have done their best to ensure the accuracy and currency of all the information in **The Rough Guide to Europe on a Budget**, however, they can accept no responsibility for any loss, injury, or inconvenience sustained by any traveller as a result of information or advice contained in the guide.
3 5 7 9 8 6 4 2

Help us update

We've gone to a lot of effort to ensure that the 2nd edition of **The Rough Guide to Europe on a Budget** is accurate and up-to-date. However, things change – places get "discovered", opening hours are notoriously fickle, restaurants and rooms raise prices or lower standards. If you feel we've got it wrong or left something out, we'd like to know, and if you can remember the address, the price, the hours, the phone number, so much the better.

Please send your comments with the subject line "**Rough Guide to Europe on a Budget Update**" to ⓔ mail@roughguides.com. We'll credit all contributions and send a copy of the next edition (or any other Rough Guide if you prefer) for the very best emails.

Have your questions answered and tell others about your trip at ⓦ www.roughguides.com

Acknowledgements

Edward Aves would like to thank the following contributors for all their hard work in updating this edition: Laura Bennitt (northern England and Scotland); Sarah Cummins (Switzerland); Ella Davies (southern England and Wales); Michelle Doran (northern France, northern Italy, Corsica and Sardinia); Sarah Eno (Basics and Norway); Natasha Foges (southern Italy and Croatia); Emma Gibbs (Paris and southern France); Alex Gladwell (Greece); Hilary Heuler (Poland); Dan Jacobs (Morocco); Ciara Kenny (Ireland, Hungary and Slovenia); Anna Khmelnitski (Estonia, Latvia, Lithuania, Russia, central and southern Spain); Joanna Kirby (northern Spain, the Balearics, and Andorra); Neil McQuillian (Turkey); Sophie Middlemiss (Serbia); Roger Norum (Finland); Emily Paine (Czech and Slovak Republics); Alice Park (northern and eastern Germany); James Rice (Denmark); Kate Tolley (Netherlands); Andy Turner (Sweden, Itineraries and general odd jobs); Kate Turner (Portugal); Steven Vickers (Introduction); Christian Williams (Austria, central and southern Germany); Matt Willis (Romania and Bulgaria); and Martin Zatko for contributing the four brand-new chapters on Albania, Bosnia-Herzegovina, Macedonia and Montenegro.

He'd also like to thank Róisín Cameron for the gargantuan achievement of setting the book up in the first place; all his colleagues on the Europe team for helping out with editing when they'd much rather have been doing XML; and Ajay Verma for first-class typesetting.

Photo credits

All photos © Rough Guides except the following:

Cover
Top front cover image: Girls dancing Sevillanas, Seville © Ruth Tomlinson/Getty
Bottom front cover image: Ponte Pietra, Verona © SIME/Renier Stefano/4corners

Introduction
Early morning mist at Glastonbury Festival © Tom Oldham /photolibrary

Art and culture
Comic art in Brussels © Yvan Travert/photolibrary
Michelangelo's *The Creation of Adam*, Sistine Chapel, The Vatican © Christa Knijff/ photolibrary
Coriolanus at The Globe, London © Robbie Jack/ Corbis
Guggenheim Museum © Romain Cintract/corbis

Outdoor activities
Snowboarding in Chamonix, France © Julian Love/photolibrary
Bodyboarders, Praia do Amado, Algarve © Cro Magnon/Alamy
Sailing, Kós © Nicholas Pitt/Alamy
Walking in the Polish Tatras © Ken Gillham/ photolibrary

Festivals and events
Juggler at the Edinburgh Fringe © Grant Pritchard/photolibrary
EXIT Festival, Serbia © Marko Djurica/corbis

Full page
Lofoten Islands, Norway © Glyn Thomas/ photolibrary

Index

Map entries are in colour.

C

D

E

I

J

K

L

N

O

P

R

S

T

Map symbols

maps are listed in the full index using coloured text

- International boundary
- Province boundary
- Railway
- Funicular
- Cable car
- Motorway
- Tolled motorway
- Road
- Pedestrianized street
- Steps
- Path
- Ferry route
- Waterway
- Wall
- Mountains
- Peak
- Hill
- Rocks
- Ruins
- Cave
- Waterfall
- Fountain
- Viewpoint
- Lighthouse
- Point of interest
- Museum
- Stately home
- Monastery
- Church (regional)
- Synagogue
- Mosque
- Hospital
- Post office
- Tourist information
- Telephone office
- Internet access
- Bus stop
- Metro station
- RER station
- S-Bahn
- Tram stop
- U-Bahn
- London Underground Station
- FGC station
- Parking
- Gate
- Swimming pool
- Statue
- Building
- Church (town)
- Stadium
- Park/forest
- Christian cemetery
- Muslim cemetery
- Jewish cemetery
- Beach
- Glacier

CHAPTER 1

"I WILL NOW inspect your aft cargo bay," Worf informed her.

The Sattar woman squinted up at him. "I told you all of the cargo bays were searched last night by station security. In fact, they went over the entire ship with a portable particle sweeper! I don't know what else you expect to find poking around like this with a tricorder."

"I am aware the *Reaper* has been cleared, Senior Mate Cali." Worf knew that if he did not stop her, the Sattar would keep complaining and he would never get done. She had made it clear that the transport was on a tight turnaround, but that was none of his concern. "As Strategic Operations Officer, it is within my jurisdiction to inspect any vessel allied with the Klingon Empire."

"How nice for you." She wrinkled her fuzzy nose at him. "But you're wasting your time. We haven't contracted with any Klingons for months . . . and we aren't likely to if I can help it," she added bitterly.

Since the Sattar were not known for their honesty, Worf discounted her statement. The Sattar Collective had been reluctant members of the empire since their world had been conquered over one hundred years ago, yet when they were not operating on the narrow border between Federation trade laws and the Ferengi Alliance, many Sattar cooperated with Klingons to their own advantage.

Worf had watched the *Reaper* since her arrival the night before, timing his inspection just prior to their departure in order to catch them off guard. Cali, the senior mate assigned to accompany him, was typical of the Sattar he had encountered in the past. She was a small humanoid, covered with tawny fur that had been smoothed into decorative swirls on her face and chest. But her impetuous temper was reflected in the disheveled curls hanging over her forehead and the tangled mass of reddish-brown mane running down the back of her head and neck.

"The aft cargo bay," Worf prompted.

Cali snorted, but she turned on her heel. "It's right here, as if you didn't know."

As they entered the cargo bay, Worf's hand lingered on the curved support beam. It felt odd to be inside a Klingon vessel again, so right, and yet not—

"This isn't a bird of prey," Cali spoke up behind him, surprising him out of his reverie. Her arms were crossed. "It isn't even a cruiser. It's an old transport ship, in case you haven't noticed. I suppose we should be flattered we're worth this much effort."

Worf ignored her caustic remarks, proceeding with his investigation. The recent termination of the peace treaty between the Federation and the Klingon Empire made it imperative that he pursue every scrap of information. Odo's team had picked up traces of solotine in their particle sweep. It was a catalyst often used in Klingon explosive devices such as bombs and mines. But the *Reaper*'s cargo bay was empty except for stacked containers and anti-grav pallets.

"Open this panel." He gestured at random to one of the vents in the bulkhead. If this vessel had transported solotine, there would be a breakdown residue of nitrogen-dexitrin left in the atmospheric intake vents.

Cali shrugged and made an elaborate show of undoing the panel. Worf waited until she stepped aside, knowing how touchy Sattar were about physical contact. While Cali had simply bent over to reach the panel, Worf was forced to kneel down, leaning in to bring his tricorder close to the junction node of the vent. There were no immediate indicators of solotine contamination—

"Arrgh!" he exclaimed as a burst of white-hot steam erupted in his face.

Protecting his eyes, he jumped back, unbalanced by

his awkward position. He bumped into Cali and they both went down.

Worf's shoulder hit the deck, and he could feel Cali entangled in his legs. She was fighting to get away as he glared back at the plasma leak. The lethal stuff was merrily hissing into the air. Only his quick reflexes had kept him from getting a nasty plasma burn in his eyes. As it was, he had to restrain himself from rubbing his eyes, blinking to clear his vision.

Instinctively he edged toward the nearest bulkhead, protecting his back in case of an attack. But Cali was swearing in Klingon as she limped toward the door to hit the comm. "Plasma leak in the aft cargo bay," she drawled. "Get someone down here, will you?"

Worf did not appreciate the situation, or the smile on the Sattar's face when she turned around. He considered the possibility that she had somehow planned the accident. Aiming his tricorder at the plasma leak, he detected several other weak spots on the conduit, but no obvious signs of tampering.

Another Sattar appeared, this one with dun-colored fur shaved to a nub except for his stiff ridge of mane. The technician crawled under the leak to examine the conduit. "Shouldn't have opened the panel," he muttered. "These are delicate systems we've got here."

Cali ignored the technician's complaint. "Have you seen enough?" she asked Worf. "Or would you like to damage a few more conduits?"

Worf checked his tricorder readings. Normally he would prefer a few more samples, but he had adequate data for further analysis with the station's computer.

He closed the tricorder. "I . . . appreciate your co-operation," he muttered grudgingly.

"You mean the search is over? You found nothing to seize?" she countered in mock amazement. "Are you sure you did a thorough job?"

Ignoring her, Worf left the cargo bay and returned to the docking port. Though the Sattar crew had altered the interior of the transport, the Klingon infrastructure was intact. He knew exactly which way to turn to get back to the airlock, even though he could barely see through his burning eyes. He had to blink constantly to keep them from watering.

Cali jogged along behind him. "We'll have to do a rush check in order to make our rotation slot through the wormhole."

Worf refused to slow down or glance back at the Sattar. "You may inform Captain Ari that the *Reaper* remains cleared for departure."

"Ohhh . . . aren't we in a generous mood today!" When Worf did not respond, she caught up, running right on his heels. "Don't think I'm going to be grateful! You Klingons are all alike. If you can't keep it, you kill it. And you don't care who you destroy as long as you can call yourselves warriors." Her voice rose. "Hey, I'm talking to *you,* Klingon!"

Worf stopped and looked down at this feisty little Sattar, ready to make war with the entire Klingon Empire right here, right now. He wondered if she was any good with a bat'leth.

The spark of admiration in his gaze seemed to infuriate her even more. "You're dying to know what's going on, aren't you?" she taunted. "I don't know who you're gathering information for, the Klingons or the Federation—" She waved off his dark look. "Sure, you wear a Starfleet uniform. But you don't have to prove anything to me. I'm just telling you. You know nothing about this part of space."

"Your assessment would be informative," he said raising his tricorder. "Have you encountered recent Klingon activity in the nearby sectors?"

"Oh, sure! We'll have a nice long chat, right after our weekly game of ba'zon." She was smiling in that smug way again. "You've been on this station how long? Three weeks, maybe four?"

Her accuracy was unnerving. He could also tell he would get nothing more from Senior Mate Cali, and he was therefore unwilling to enter into a personal argument with her.

He remained silent until they reached the airlock and then he adhered strictly to protocol. "Does your captain plan to record your logs before departure?"

Cali laughed right in his face. Wisps of hair shook in a faint aureole around her head. "*Blimenny*. You do try to control everything, don't you?"

"It is for your own protection—"

"Spare me the hypocrisy." Cali deliberately turned away. "All Klingons are alike."

Before Worf could say anything, his comm badge signaled and Dax's voice asked, "Commander Worf?"

"Worf here," he immediately replied.

"Please report to upper pylon three."

That meant a large vessel was docking. "On my way," Worf confirmed.

Cali was still sneering as she let him through the airlock. "Explain all you want, but it's still the same old Klingon game. Glory! You'd think a bunch of idiots who are that violent and self-serving would have killed themselves off a long time ago."

As he left, Worf felt compelled to comment, "You must be an expert at self-defense. I can think of no other reason for your continued survival in the Klingon Empire."

Her eyes flashed. "I guess there's no such thing as justice in this universe, is there?"

The airlock slammed behind him, as Worf realized that was the very question he had been considering since he had transferred to the station. He knew that if he had anything to do with it, there would be justice served in this part of the universe. And he would do everything in his power to preserve the Federation's tentative balance with the Klingon Empire, and to prevent their conflict from escalating into war.

Worf ignored the pain that throbbed in his eyes, proceeding directly to the lower pylon. When he reached the viewport at the base of the pylon, there was no ship in dock. With practiced self-control, he resisted speculating on the incoming vessel.

Nodding to the Bajoran technician at the docking control station, Worf activated the viewer to Ops. "Commander Worf at lower pylon docking control."

Dax's face appeared, filling the small round screen.

"Worf, we've finally heard from the scoutship *Ceres.* Captain Iis reports they are being towed in by the Bajoran tug, *Hum'bernt."*

"The *Ceres* was damaged?"

"They suffered a hit-and-run attack while they were at full stop, shields down. They lost warp drive, navigation, sensors, and communications . . ." Dax looked grim. "Five crew members were killed, and the rest are ill with radiation poisoning from the nearby plasma storm. They were on thrusters when the *Hum'bernt* found them."

"Who attacked them?" Worf growled, already certain of the answer.

But Dax shook her head. "Their identity is unconfirmed. The *Ceres* was able to get only minimal readings, enough to know it was a single ship."

Worf glanced at the technician, who uneasily edged away. Another example of the lax security on this station. Now it was too late to try to classify this information. "When did it happen?"

"Yesterday, about this time."

He clenched his jaw. The attackers could be anywhere by now. "And they have no information on the vessel?"

"The scout was on the edge of the plasma storm, Worf, investigating some unusual readings. The radiation was interfering with their sensors when they were attacked." She glanced over her shoulder, toward Captain Sisko's office. "You're to get a report from Captain Iis. Most of the crew will be beamed directly to the infirmary for radiation treatment once the *Ceres* is within range."

Worf nodded curtly. "Have two security teams report to me here."

"Aye, Commander." As Worf reached out to terminate the transmission, Dax added, "Better make sure someone good is on the docking tractors. Remember the Andorian freighter that tug brought in last week?"

"Thank you, Commander," he said dryly. Now the Bajoran technician was looking worried. Maybe Dax's warning was just another example of her bizarre humor, but Worf could never be sure with the Trill.

Accessing the main viewer, Worf was able to watch the tug tow in the comparatively huge Starfleet scoutship. Dax had probably offered to assist with the station's tractor beams once they were within range, but Worf had seen for himself that nothing was that easy on the station. He had overheard far too much discussion lately among Kira, the Bajoran government, and the local version of the scavengers' union, arguing incessantly over towing regulations and whether tugs were required to bring a vessel into dock in order to receive payment. Worf thought it was nonsense, like many of the other convoluted procedures in this sector that seemed specifically designed to frustrate real, decisive action.

He did not believe he would ever become accustomed to this sort of delay, yet he didn't move a muscle in spite of his most fervent wish to get hold of the *Ceres*. A security team arrived and waited at one side with their portable equipment, and he ordered another team to go below to prepare one-man pods for an external examination of the scoutship. There were always clues left behind by weapons, clues that could be used to determine the exact course of a battle as well as the identity of the attacking vessel.

His personal contacts had reported considerable Klingon activity in the area, with vessels en route between the conquered Cardassian planets and the Klingon Empire. It was likely the *Ceres* had been attacked by Klingons. Or perhaps by a Sattar transport smuggling supplies to the Klingon outposts in Cardassian territory.

Yet Worf did not discount the possibility of a Maquis ambush. Tactically it made sense for them to take advantage of the situation to make a preemptive strike against Starfleet. Or it could have been a Jem'Hadar attack. Many of the officers on the station would agree with that hypothesis; there had been growing rumors of Jem'Hadar infiltration using cloaking devices captured during the failed Romulan-Cardassian invasion of the Dominion home world. But privately Worf considered that an unlikely possibility at this juncture.

Magnifying the image of the *Ceres,* Worf focused first on the imploded warp nacelle, then the punctured bulkheads in the body of the ship, particularly around the dish-shaped navigational array. The targeting had been precise, taking out the major weapons and sensor systems in two, perhaps three, sweeps. With that much damage and a crew complement of almost one hundred fifty, they were lucky there were only five deaths.

Worf switched to the pylon sensors to watch the docking. The *Hum'bernt* seemed to strain as it swung the *Ceres* around, then slowly backed her in. There were a few breathless moments as the scoutship neared the station when it seemed to speed up as the gap closed. Worf instinctively held his breath, though he knew it was an optical illusion from the adjustment of his eyes to the real space-time view.

The Bajoran technician suddenly became iron cool, smoothly catching the *Ceres* with the tractors and slowing her approach. The round port eased up to the station, an alignment of two microscopic points. They met at precisely the moment the *Ceres* stopped. The last few centimeters closed with a whisperlike shudder of contact through the pylon.

"Good work," Worf told the technician.

"Thank you, sir." She lifted her chin, as if determined to never again show trepidation about a docking maneuver.

There was a somber urgency to the preparations for opening the airlock, while communications were relayed regarding the transport of the most seriously injured to the infirmary. Captain Iis was waiting on the other side of the port, but she remained on board the *Ceres* as a long line of crew members with minor injuries filed onto the station. Medical technicians arrived to assist.

Despite the various degrees of shock that showed on the faces of the crew Worf's gaze kept returning to

Captain Iis. Her face was creased with lines of stress, but her pride shone through the sweat and smudges earned during their effort to return to safety. She offered a few words here and there, occasionally clasping an arm or giving a nod of reassurance. Worf had heard rumors about the crews under Captain Iis, of the bond they felt for one another. It couldn't match what he had experienced on the *Enterprise* . . . yet he admired their determination to be strong, to prove they weren't beaten, to be a credit to their captain.

Worf entered the docking port and came to attention in front of Captain Iis. "Commander Worf, requesting permission to board the *Ceres.*"

"Permission granted, Commander." Iis seemed to appreciate his adherence to protocol. "This is the last of the injured. I have a skeleton crew in place locking down the systems."

"The security team can assist as they begin the investigation," Worf offered. At the captain's tired nod, he called security inside and deployed them to their stations.

Distracted by the sight of her departing crew members, Iis told Worf, "I've sent one of my ensigns to fetch the data on the plasma storm. You'll need to plot the trajectory to make sure it's not coming this way."

"I am concerned about the attack on the *Ceres,*" Worf informed her, wondering at her choice of priorities at this moment.

"I don't have much to add to my initial report. We were at full stop, scanning the plasma storm . . .

defenseless. There was no provocation, no reason for it . . ." The captain seemed to shake herself, returning to the facts. "Perhaps the other ship was also skirting the plasma storm and couldn't read us through the emission waves. Then when they stumbled on us, they fired."

"It will be necessary to analyze your sensor logs."

"Of course, though I warn you, we didn't get enough data to be able to make a positive identification." Iis hesitated, then added, "But one of my lieutenants did catch a glimpse of the ship through a porthole, and she said it looked Klingon."

"A bird of prey?" Worf demanded.

"No, something different, a design she wasn't familiar with. By the way, this is all hearsay. Another one of my officers informed me of her sighting."

Worf seized on the clue. "I must speak with the lieutenant immediately."

Captain Iis grimaced. "That's impossible. She suffered a blow to the head. The doctor says she's in a coma and he's been unable to help her regain consciousness."

Worf's disappointment was sharp, reminding him that a good investigator did not get personally involved in a case. It could distort his interpretation of the evidence. Yet he had to admit satisfaction at even the most tentative confirmation that Klingons were involved. It was just as he suspected.

"I noticed that there's a Klingon vessel docked here," Captain Iis said quietly. "When did it get in?"

"The *Reaper* is a transport belonging to the Sattar

Collective." He didn't have to check his tricorder for the docking information. "They arrived yesterday at fourteen hundred hours."

"Do they have the legs to get here that fast?"

More to the point, Worf was not certain the *Reaper*'s weapons systems were capable of inflicting this much damage. But he intended to find out. "I have not yet completed my investigation. I will inform you as soon as I have analyzed the information."

An ensign rushed up to Captain Iis, offering her a padd. "Good," Iis said in relief, checking the data. "Commander, you had better get this to your science officer right away. I hope that storm isn't headed in this direction. The radiation caused almost as much damage to my crew as the attack did."

Worf took the padd, bracing the captain for a moment as she lost her balance. "You should go to the infirmary," he told her. The ensign chimed in, concerned but too respectful to do more than offer to support her captain.

Iis demurred, glancing up in concern at the ceiling of her bridge.

"There is nothing more for you to do," Worf said bluntly. Yet he felt a great deal of sympathy for Captain Iis, surveying the remnants of her command. "Repair crews are currently assessing the damage, and you will receive a report shortly on the condition of your ship."

Captain Iis nodded agreement, but she remained at her post until the last of her crew members had departed. Then she handed over command to a senior officer and prepared to follow the others through the airlock.

"Wait, Captain," Worf said. He signaled Ops for the transporter to take Iis to the infirmary. She could hardly stand up straight and her lips trembled from the effort. After everything else she had been through, it was not necessary for her to drag herself through the mile-long corridors to the infirmary in the core.

But as the captain dematerialized, Worf was not thinking of the buckled hull of the *Ceres.* Instead he saw the saucer section of the *Enterprise* buried in the ground, with that long scar stretching into the distance behind it. And the cracked glass of the bridge dome forming a jagged frame for the blue sky. . . . He hoped the *Ceres* could be repaired. He swore to himself that if the Sattar were responsible, he would discover the truth and make them pay for it. Perhaps this was the reason Senior Mate Cali was in such a hurry to leave DS9.

"Transporter, one to beam to Ops." Captain Iis had stressed urgency about the storm data, and he also wanted to watch the *Reaper* to see if the Sattar decided to depart now that the *Ceres* had been brought in. Their actions during the next hour could be very enlightening.

As Worf materialized in Ops, he felt the floor shake beneath his feet. "What was that?" he demanded, looking from Dax to O'Brien.

"I'm not sure," the chief admitted, examining his panel.

Visions of a Klingon offensive flashed through

Worf's mind, and he had time to regret that both Captain Sisko and Major Kira were off duty.

Dax offered, "I think it's the effects of that plasma storm. I've been tracking the emission waves. They're very strong. It must be one big mother of a storm."

"I'll increase power to the stabilizers," O'Brien agreed, "and I'll see what I can do about adjusting the shields. We don't want any radiation leakage."

"Captain Iis claims that the storm is dangerous." Worf handed Dax the padd with the *Ceres* sensor information before going to the tactical station. He quickly confirmed that there were no signs of unusual vessel activity on long-range sensors.

Then he accessed star charts of the neighboring sector, where the *Ceres* had been scanning the storm. Perhaps the attacker had been protecting the secrecy of a Klingon post just outside Bajoran space. Tactically it would be the ideal spot for a supply base. The flight plan of the *Reaper* indicated they had come from the opposite direction, however they could easily have falsified that information. He downloaded his tricorder data into the computer for a full analysis of the *Reaper*'s engines, weapons, and recent cargo.

"Interesting," Dax murmured, absorbed in the readings on the storm from the *Ceres*. "I'm going to send out a long-range probe."

Worf accessed docking control and canceled the Sattar's clearance, sealing the docking clamps with a security order. What with the interference of the emission waves, he could not risk the *Reaper*'s escaping before he had time to complete his analysis.

He noted the order in his log, then began to gather the preliminary reports from his security teams working on the *Ceres.* It was comforting to watch the data flow into his console. Soon he would know.

"Ready, Chief?" Dax asked.

"Fire away," O'Brien cheerfully confirmed, deep in his own calculations on the shield's EM dispersal and band-width rates.

Silence fell over them as each worked on his or her own problem. It reminded Worf of the best days on the *Enterprise.*

"Wow!" Dax softly exclaimed, reacting to the first readings as they came in. "I've never seen anything like this outside a particle accelerator. Unusually dense blackbody . . . hmmm . . . and high levels of complex oscillations." She continued to murmur her surprise, with Worf idly listening, until a new note crept in.

"Wait, what's this?" she muttered. "Escalating bursts. The data's being scrambled."

"Need more power?" O'Brien asked.

"Maybe. I'm going to tie the probe into long-range sensors for redundancy." Dax frowned over her panel as she quickly made the link. Worf found her technique interesting—not Starfleet standard, but then almost nothing on this station was Starfleet standard.

"I'm getting feedback," Dax told them. "Better isolate your systems."

Worf had already seen the spikes, and took the tactical station off line from the main sensor array. O'Brien was right behind him.

"Just for a moment," Dax assured them. "Until I get this fluctuation under control—"

A surge ran through the power relays, ringing alarms in the secondary stations. Dax tried to compensate, hitting the touch pads with frantic fingers.

"Cut power!" she called out.

O'Brien was wide eyed as he tried to comply. A spark shot up from the main circuit indicator on the science station. Dax jerked back, then tried to shut everything down as a burst of smoke rose from the console, followed by a shower of white-hot sparks.

Worf was already running toward Dax, and he grabbed her arms to pull her away. "Move!" he ordered.

A stasis beam shot down from the overhead array, attempting to contain the smoke. O'Brien leaped over the railing to retrieve a portable stasis unit, betraying his lack of confidence in the onboard systems.

"Apparently the storm is stronger than I thought," Dax admitted, coughing and warily watching her burning console. Worf made sure she was uninjured before helping her stand up.

"Worf to Captain Sisko," he announced, straightening his uniform.

A brief pause reminded him that Sisko hadn't had a day off in over a week. Yet the captain's voice betrayed no irritation. "Sisko here."

Worf eyed O'Brien's attempts to extinguish the fire. "Sir, you are needed in Ops. We have a slight . . . problem."

CHAPTER 2

THE CATWALK SHUDDERED as Keiko reached the door to the holosuite. She couldn't help bumping into a young Bajoran woman who had paused to check the numbers.

Keiko caught her by the arm to steady them both. "That was a strong one."

The Bajoran's eyes were round, but she was smiling. "I've never felt the station shake like this before."

Keiko let go of her. "I have. It's probably nothing serious."

The young woman dug into what Keiko had at first taken to be a bundle of costuming for a holoprogram. Instead, a baby peeked up through the folds, smiling up in a tiny echo of her mother's pert ridged nose and rosebud mouth.

"What a precious baby!" Keiko exclaimed.

"Yes, she is," the mother artlessly agreed. "I'm Betenn Catrin."

Keiko responded to her smile. "Hi, Catrin. I'm Keiko O'Brien."

Catrin joggled her baby. "I don't think I've met you before. Are you related to Miles O'Brien, chief of operations?"

Keiko nodded. "We're married." She reached out to tickle the baby's chin. "We have a daughter of our own. Molly is six now."

"Oh, I heard about that," Catrin said. "I thought you were both living on Bajor."

"The winter storms are severe this year in the Bernice Province," Keiko explained, resisting a tug of frustration at the thought. "We had to close down the science survey for a week or so." And she had just been getting somewhere with those hybrid Bernitii-Serran grains . . .

"I had a cousin who moved to Bernice." Catrin adjusted the baby. "I'm from Shakaar's province, but my mate got a posting to the station a few months ago and we couldn't pass up the opportunity. I'll never forget the trip here! I was out to here," she said, holding out one hand as far as she could in front of her stomach.

"Sounds familiar," Keiko replied. "It must be tough for you living on the station with an infant."

Catrin smoothed her hand over the little head. "Oh, I don't know . . . babies aren't easy no matter where you are. I sometimes think about the labor camp where I grew up and this seems like heaven. I can even work half-day shifts at Transient Registration so I get to see all the different people who come to the station."

Keiko didn't want to admit that she still found the constant stream of transients unnerving. She liked meeting new people as much as anyone, but the never-ending influx of strangers was sometimes overwhelming. And though the view of the wormhole was amazing, Keiko never developed a taste for the Cardassian structure of the station. She couldn't help it, the elongated curves and shadowy niches felt creepy to her. She was more at home with the sleek lines of the Starfleet temporary quarters that traveled with the survey team on Bajor.

But Catrin didn't notice Keiko's lack of enthusiasm. "Usually Brucen is home by now, but the docking crew is taking care of that Starfleet ship that just came in. I'm lucky the holosuite is available or Krystal would be coming with me to work."

"It *will* be available," Keiko told her, "as soon as I get my daughter out of there." She gave Catrin a frustrated look. "I hate leaving her here alone, even though I know it's safe. But I had to. Everyone responded when they called for volunteers to help with those injured crewmembers."

"It's awful, isn't it?" Catrin agreed. "Everyone's talking about it."

Keiko keyed her access code in the locking device on the door. She never took chances in this place. She had asked Miles to make one of his custom security seals so she could lock Molly inside the holosuite if she ever had to leave her alone.

"Which program is she doing?" Catrin asked.

"Level one riding lessons," Keiko said, as the door opened. "That's all she's talked about since she tried it on our last visit. Ponies!"

At the far end of the room, Molly was perched on a fat white pony. It was plodding in a circle around the paddock, stoically ignoring her kicking heels and the jostling of the reins. A holographic instructor was patiently indicating the finer points of horsemanship on the small image of an English rider floating incongruously above the pony's nose. Beyond the whitewashed fence were the images of other horses and riders going through their paces.

Molly pulled her pony to a halt, laughing as she almost lost her balance. "Whoa!" she ordered in a deep voice. Keiko wondered where she had picked up that tone of command.

"Hello, Molly," Catrin said as she removed Krystal from her bundles. "Your daughter is so sweet," she whispered to Keiko.

Keiko wanted to tell her that appearances could be deceiving, but she bit her tongue. "How was your ride today, Molly?"

"We jumped four fences and two *big* rivers." Molly appealed to the instructor. "Weren't they big? They were *huge.*"

"You're letting her jump?" Keiko panicked, reaching for Molly. She was only half convinced that riding was a good idea at her age, but Miles had encouraged her enthusiasm by bringing her to the holosuite for her first ride.

"The pupil has jumped only in the holo-image," the instructor assured Keiko, apparently programed to deal with nervous parents. "Molly has nearly completed the requisite maneuvers for the first level. In the second level she will learn how to interact with a real animal."

Molly's face lit up in glee. "I want more pony rides! Can I do more, Mommy?"

"Not today, sweetheart." Keiko exchanged a smile with Catrin that only mothers could understand. Then she lifted Molly from the pony, ordering, "End simulation." When Molly started to whine, she chided, "It's this little girl's turn. We can't keep her waiting."

"Begin infant nursery program," Catrin meekly requested. A white-clad nurse and a large sunny nursery appeared around them. "Oh, Krystal! Look at the bunnies!" Catrin guided the tiny hand to the fur. "Isn't it soft?"

Keiko quickly carried Molly outside before she could get hooked on the rabbits. Ponies were bad enough. Molly must have decided to be a good girl. She held her mother's hand without trying to squirm away as they carefully walked down the spiral stairs. But she kept insisting she wanted "better pony rides" next time. Rather than argue with her, Keiko asked how she got the pony to turn around and what made it go?

Absently listening to her daughter's prattle, Keiko

was surprised to feel somewhat wistful over her fervent joy. It wasn't that she was unhappy with her life, but it felt as if she was barely keeping up, as if nothing was settled. It was worse when she saw someone like Catrin. The woman had given up her entire way of life and left everyone she knew to live on the station just because her mate had gotten a good job. Yet she was happy with this situation in a way that went beyond a cheerful disposition. Her smile seemed to resonate deeper than other people's, as if she was fundamentally satisfied in a way that eluded Keiko.

"Come on, Molly. It's time for your nap." She picked up her daughter to carry her through the bar, hating the fact that the only holosuites were in Quark's. Molly couldn't even have a pony ride without having to hear shouts of "Dabbo!" and the laughter of intoxicated patrons. But Keiko tried not to rush, knowing that Molly would sense her dislike of the place and be more bothered by that than anything she might see, such as the Dabbo girl's large breasts spilling out of her tight bodice.

Keiko tried to sneak past, but Leeta's eyes lit up when she noticed them. "Keiko, you're back! And Molly, too!" Leeta brushed a finger across the girl's cheek. "Isn't she just the cutest little thing?"

It bothered Keiko that she wanted to pull Molly away, but she couldn't help thinking that Quark's would somehow contaminate her daughter. And even though Leeta was a close friend of Dax and Dr. Bashir, Keiko had only spoken to her a few times.

"Remember me?" Leeta was asking Molly. "I met you with your daddy the last time you went pony riding."

"I want to ride the pony," Molly demanded.

"You already had your lesson," Keiko reminded her, hoping she wouldn't chose this moment to throw a tantrum. Molly certainly would if she thought she could get Leeta's sympathy. "We'll come back another day."

"No, now," Molly insisted.

Leeta grinned at her. "I like to see a girl who knows her own mind."

"Oh, Molly knows exactly what she wants. And she usually wants it right now."

"Why not?" Leeta asked. "You're only wasting your life when you put things off. Right, Molly?" Then she smiled at Keiko. "I know Chief O'Brien would agree. He can't stand waiting for you both to come home. I bet you'll be glad when this survey is over and you can get back to a normal life."

"The survey will probably last for another few months," Keiko automatically replied, balking at the idea of a normal life on DS9. Somehow it seemed contradictory.

"You'll be gone that long?" Leeta asked. "Well, we've been hearing about this visit for weeks. He really misses you when you're both away."

"I know—"

"Welcome back!" Quark exclaimed, suddenly right next to Keiko. She edged away, shifting Molly to her other hip, but that didn't stop the Ferengi. "It's so nice of you to drop by Quark's! I can't tell you the satisfaction it gives me to offer quality holo-programs at a reasonable price to my Starfleet patrons—"

"Not today, Quark," Keiko told him. With a final nod to Leeta, she started toward the exit. She didn't have the energy for a chat with the annoying bar owner.

"Wait!" Quark called after her, following them between the tables. "I have a demo-program I'd like you to try. It's the Delanian baths, including the masseuse and private rock grotto. You can do it—" He grabbed her arm, whispering, "No charge! Just talk it up among your friends—"

Keiko shook him off with a disgusted look. "No thanks." She glanced at the blinking, battered dart board as she passed by. It was hard to imagine that this was where Miles spent most of his off time while she was on Bajor.

Quark warded her off with raised hands. "I was just trying to offer you some top-of-the-line entertainment. It's not like you have anything else to do while you're here."

Keiko glared at him, but thankfully Molly didn't seem upset. She was looking around with interest from her high vantage point. "Let's stay here, Mommy."

Quark's approving glance acknowledged the girl for the first time. "Maybe the O'Brien family should move in to Quark's. That is, since you all seem to like it here so much."

"Thank you," Molly replied solemnly, just as her mother had taught her. "Can I ride the pony?"

Quark gave Keiko a sly grin. "I don't see why not."

Keiko rolled her eyes as she turned away. Why did she ever try to talk sense to Quark? It never worked.

Abruptly the floor jolted to one side. Keiko managed to avoid Quark, stumbling into a table where she could support Molly. A few people let out frightened cries, then there was an instant of silence before the babbling surged up again.

"Something's not right," Quark muttered, glancing at Keiko. "Only the computer answers when I call Ops. Hey, maybe O'Brien will talk to you. You can call from my com . . ."

Keiko left Quark's without another word. She had no intention of calling Miles, either here or in their quarters. But she also wasn't going to sit here in the dark while the station shook itself apart around her. Hitching Molly more securely against her hip, she headed for home.

But Quark wasn't satisfied until he called out from the doorway, "Tell O'Brien to fix the stabilizers. This isn't good for business!"

Dax was busy with her own problems, but there was no way she could miss it when Sisko asked for Kasidy's call to be transferred to his office.

Since Kasidy had been on the station barely a week, Dax was highly interested in the effect her presence would have on Benjamin. She watched him through the glass doors and could almost hear his calm tone as he explained about the plasma storm. Actually, it made sense for Kasidy to check on the situation. Sisko had been called away in the middle of preparing his Bajoran sailship for their afternoon cruise.

Then Dax had to laugh when she heard O'Brien pause in the middle of his muttered curses over the feedback damage to her console. The engineer dashed off suddenly; apparently he remembered he should call Keiko. He seemed surprised when his wife wasn't home.

"There's some kind of big plasma storm out there," he said, keeping his voice low as he left a message. "You and Molly had better stay in our quarters until we get everything settled." He checked to see if anyone was listening. Dax pretended to be absorbed in the data she was retrieving from her damaged console. "I won't make it home for lunch, but I'll see you soon. I love you both."

O'Brien probably didn't realize he had let out a sigh as he ended the transmission. Then he was instantly back to giving orders and wrestling with the temperamental power systems.

Dax finished her data retrival, then joined Kira at the central Ops console. Kira had appeared in Ops not long after Sisko had arrived, even though it was her day off as well.

As Sisko returned from his office, Dax said, "I'd like to go down to the science lab and coordinate our analysis of the storm. The science station here won't be much use for a while."

Sisko came down the steps. "What's our current status?"

Dax accessed the information from the *Ceres,* putting the star chart of the nearby sectors on the tabletop display so both Kira and Sisko could see. The swirling edge of the storm was rendered in broken, shifting color lines according to the frequency and wavelengths of the emissions.

"The plasma nearly covers the neighboring sector." Dax pointed to the mass of the storm that blocked the starfield. "And it's moving extremely fast, causing the high level Alfven waves, both electromagnetic and radiation emissions, that are shaking the station. These shock fronts are also distorting our sensors, so it's difficult to track the trajectory and intensity of the storm."

"According to this, the storm is projected to pass through the far corner of the Bajoran sector," Sisko said. "That shouldn't be too bad."

"It's a big storm, Benjamin."

"We already have reports from vessels in the area," Kira confirmed. "The shock waves are interfering with navigation. I've recommended a docking alert for the Bajoran colonies."

Sisko glanced at Dax. "Perhaps we should do the same."

"It's probably a good idea," Dax admitted. "The shock waves will only get stronger as the storm passes."

Kira made a sound as if that was an understatement. "Remember that plasma storm last year? Everything was vibrating for days."

Sisko nodded to Kira. "Issue a general alert on all hailing frequencies. Warn vessels to dock or evacuate the sector. Include the coordinates and estimated trajectory of the storm."

"It's going to get pretty crowded around here," Kira warned.

"Coordinate with Bajoran Flight Control to route vessels to the nearest satellites or colony bases." Sisko frowned. "We can also open up those auxiliary docks and use the runabout landing pads if we need to."

"I'll shuffle some of the smaller vessels," Kira agreed. Sisko turned to Dax. "I know Dr. Bashir is busy with the injured crew of the *Ceres,* but include his report on the radiation damage in your assessment of the storm."

"The shields of the *Ceres* were down during their exposure," Dax reminded him.

O'Brien quickly put in, "We'll have no trouble with our shields, sir. I've got both generators operating at peak levels. The worst we'll have to deal with are these tremors." As if on cue, the deck shuddered. "Our stabilizers are compensating, but I'm working on a way to tie in the long-range sensors for a faster reaction time."

"Good," Sisko told the chief. "I'm sure that would make everyone on the station feel much better." O'Brien looked as if he fully understood. He was probably thinking about Keiko and Molly.

"Sir?" Kira asked. "I have Captain Ari of the

Reaper demanding to speak with you. I've put him off a half dozen times but he won't let me re-dock his vessel unless you talk to him first."

Worf went rigid with attention. "Sir, Captain Ari is the commander of the *Reaper,* a Sattar transport. I am currently completing the analysis of my latest inspection."

"Latest?" Sisko asked, as Dax leaned closer to see the display. Worf had already replied to Captain Ari's official complaint by posting the storm warning for ships to dock or evacuate the area. Sisko pointed out, "They have clearance to evacuate through the wormhole. Why have you sealed their docking clamps?"

Worf hesitated. "I suspect the *Reaper* may be involved in the attack on the *Ceres.* However my investigation is not yet completed."

"You'll have to formally charge them to hold them here, Commander," Kira warned.

Worf shook his head, indicating he didn't have enough evidence for that.

"No wonder the captain wishes to speak to me," Sisko murmured.

Dax knew this was important to Worf. He had completely ignored the flurry over the storm, concentrating on his investigation of the *Ceres* and the *Reaper.* Not since their fight with the Klingons had she seen him so absorbed and invigorated by his duties.

"Captain," she offered, drawing everyone's attention. "I had intended to suggest that the wormhole be closed to traffic."

Sisko raised one brow. "Why?"

"Alfven shock waves are penetrating the wormhole every time a ship goes through. We're already picking up elevated levels of ion compensation, among other things."

Sisko didn't miss the timeliness of her suggestion. Yet it was clear from Worf's reaction that he hadn't expected her assistance.

Sisko told Kira, "Along with that storm warning, include notification that the wormhole is temporarily closed."

"But, sir," Kira protested. "Most of the ships were planning to leave the sector through the wormhole."

Dax held firm. "I don't want to risk destabilizing it any further."

Sisko agreed. "Give me your preliminary report within the hour, Commander. Oh, and Major, send the new notification to the Sattar ship. Inform them that I am currently engaged with emergency duties."

"Aye, sir," Kira replied.

Dax followed Sisko up the steps as if heading for the turbolift to the science lab. But she quietly slipped into his office after him. "May I join you for a moment?"

As soon as the door closed behind them, Sisko asked, "What's wrong, Old Man?"

Dax almost smiled. "That *was* a Curzon maneuver, wasn't it?"

"You're even better at it than he was." Sisko leaned against his desk. "Out with it."

"I'm not sure yet, but the plasma storm appears to be veering off its original course."

"You mean it might pass directly through this system?" Sisko guessed.

"I'll know more within the hour," Dax assured him. "Some of the *Ceres* information has certainly been distorted by the emission waves. But if the bulk of it is correct, the storm has made a significant change in course and is heading directly toward us."

"What caused it to do that?" Sisko asked.

Dax shrugged. "I've never seen a storm like this before. But I'm afraid the wormhole might be a factor. We've seen the accelerator effect it has on electromagnetic waves. It could be drawing the storm in our direction."

"I see. That's why you recommended we close the wormhole. Will that cause the storm to shift course again?"

"It might. Then again, we haven't completely closed the wormhole. There's still the partial opening of the subspace relay to the Gamma Quadrant."

"You aren't suggesting we close the relay?" Sisko asked.

"I'm not sure if we *could* close it. It was practically burned into the subspace fabric by those comet fragments."

"And if we deactivated the relay, we would have no warning of what the Jem'Hadar and the Dominion are doing." Sisko shook his head. "No, the relay has to stay open."

Dax nodded. "This is all speculation, anyway. The *Ceres* data is definitely distorted . . ." She tried to give him a reassuring smile, but couldn't quite pull it off.

"Do your best," Sisko told her.

Then Dax had to face everyone in Ops. Like Sisko, they knew her well enough to realize there was something going on. But she didn't want to worry everyone needlessly. Besides, if her hunch was correct, they would hear the bad news soon enough.

CHAPTER 3

ODO PAUSED AT the railing overlooking the Promenade. He had made a general announcement to the public areas of the station regarding the emergency docking order. He thought it would calm everyone to know that the tremors were caused by emissions from the plasma storm, yet the level of excitement continued to heighten along with the influx of evacuees from the newly arriving vessels.

The activity on the Promenade reminded him of a Bajoran festival day, right down to the singing and dancing, as streams of people entered the temple. Not only were there more Bajorans, but there was a sampling of every other sort of humanoid race, especially in Quark's Bar. Odo had stopped by the bar for a moment but he couldn't stand Quark's jubilant pleasure in the face of the emergency. The tight Ferengi wasn't even complaining much about broken serving ware or spills, so you knew it had to be a profitable day.

Odo surveyed the throngs, mystified by the humanoid tendency to react to a crisis by throwing off all self-restraint. It was as if they were compelled to mirror chaos with chaos, when, by rights, they should be extra cautious during times of uncertainty. Many seemed to be indulging in a sensory abandonment comparable to his liquid state, yet he would no more start sliding down the banister right now than he would enter an open airlock with a Cardassian at his back. Didn't humanoids know how fragile they were?

Take Jake—there he was, leaning too far over the railing, trying to see everything happening down below on the Promenade.

Odo casually strolled past. "Back up there," he warned the young man. "You wouldn't want one of these shock waves to send you over the rail."

Jake straightened up, undaunted by Odo's tone. "Hi there, Constable. Isn't this great?"

"I'm not sure what is so 'great' about an emergency docking order," Odo replied, clasping his hands behind his back. "The station has already reached maximum capacity, and several more ships are waiting to dock."

"It's not really dangerous, is it?" Jake asked, more concerned.

"No, not really," Odo assured him. "But whenever

this many people are gathered in a confined area, there's bound to be trouble. Not to mention accidents. Why isn't everyone more careful?"

Jake shook his head in amusement. "You've just got to see it as a surprise holiday. A lot of these crews weren't expecting to get shore leave for weeks."

"Hmmm . . . I'm not sure your father would like you to be wandering around in all of this."

"My father is the one who keeps telling me to experience life. He'll probably want a blow-by-blow report when he gets home tonight."

Odo made a disapproving sound, but he let the matter drop. "I would suggest you stock up on food supplies. I hear there's a run on the replicators."

That hit Jake in a vital spot. He instantly started for his quarters. "Thanks for the tip! See you around."

"I'm sure," Odo murmured to himself. He had recommended a curfew for nonessential personnel, but Sisko had vetoed his suggestion. As the shock waves grew worse, perhaps the captain would reconsider.

One of his security staff signaled. "Sir, Starfleet security say they're having some trouble at the airlock to the *Ceres.* A Sattar is there looking for Commander Worf."

Odo had flagged any unusual activity among the Sattar for his immediate attention. He had noticed that Commander Worf had established surveillance on the *Reaper* shortly after it arrived, and Odo was interested in anything that caught Worf's attention. "Where is the Sattar now?"

"They're holding her at the airlock."

"Send two security personnel there. I'm on my way." He intended to handle this personally. The Sattar were the best covert transports available, with the captains controlling the "members" with a combination of familial and dictatorial authority. Then again, the Sattar had learned their trade while dodging the iron fist of the Klingons.

Odo unobtrusively made his way to the back of the Promenade, into one of the crossover bridges. With the slowdown in turbolift service, he decided to allow himself the luxury of traveling through the maintenance corridors.

Checking to make sure no one was watching, he slipped into the shadowed bulkhead. Unlocking the access door, he poured himself through the crack. Using the gravity of the station, he streamed down the ladder of the lower pylon, curving around power conduits and passing effortlessly through grillwork.

He had to reform to clear the security checks, but it was quicker than any other route. Besides, he usually excused his liquid forays through the station since they enabled him to become familiar with every nook and cranny. If shapeshifters were actively moving around DS9, they would be doing it this way.

Odo reformed before leaving the maintenance corridor. With the current alert regarding Dominion infiltration, he didn't want to take the chance of anyone seeing him re-solidify. If he ever got shot, he would wake up in a puddle in front of Captain Sisko, and his pride wouldn't allow that.

He smoothed his uniform, though he was certain it was in place. It was as much a part of him as his eyes or his hands. But his time with the Dominion had taught him that in every gesture lay the essence of the life-form. Since his primary form was a Bajoran male, he tried to *be* a Bajoran male, even if he wasn't very good at it.

Odo strode into the docking bay, a narrow, echoing space that doubled as a cargo hold. Ensign Mooh was the only Starfleet security guard on duty outside the closed airlock to the *Ceres.*

A small, huddled Sattar leaped up from a blue packing container at Odo's approach. She barely reached his chest, but she was threatening in her intensity, her dark red mane standing on end. "I know who you are. You're that shapeshifter!"

The security guard edged forward, ready to draw her phaser.

"I am Odo, chief of security for this station," he said, though he wasn't surprised that the Sattar knew exactly who he was. It was their mission in life to gather useful bits of information. "And who might you be?"

"Cali, senior mate of the *Reaper,* Sattar Collective," she retorted, lifting her chin.

"I see." Odo listened to Ensign Mooh report that Senior Mate Cali had tried to force her way into the *Ceres,* and had to be physically removed from the airlock. Odo had dealt with members of the Sattar Collective before, but it was apparently a new experience for Mooh.

"Cali, senior mate, you are charged with creating a disturbance," Odo informed her. "And for attempted trespass."

"I only wanted to see that Klingon. You know, the one in Starfleet. That Commander." She said the word like a curse. "He's done this to us, kept us here, missing our contract deadline in the Gamma Quadrant. He's got to pay for it!"

"The entire sector has been shut down due to the plasma storm," Odo assured her. "The *Reaper* isn't the only ship that has been prevented from going through the wormhole."

"We would have been gone long before the alert if that Commander hadn't canceled our clearance."

Odo had already noted the security hold on the *Reaper* in his latest report on Sattar activity. "Nevertheless that doesn't explain your presence here," he told her. "Commander Worf is stationed in Ops."

"I couldn't get into Ops," she grumbled. "But then some yellow-shirts said there's lots of security action in this pylon, something to do with the Klingon." She glared at the guard and the phaser on her hip. "This one wouldn't let me get half a word out before she called for security backup." She leaned toward Mooh. "You always this twitchy?"

The guard simply looked at Odo, exactly as she should. That was one of the nicer perks of working with trained Starfleet personnel: they always appealed to a higher rank.

"This is a secured area," Odo told the Sattar. "No unauthorized personnel are allowed to enter."

"I don't see why not. The turbolift brought me."

"It shouldn't have," Odo said grimly. Mooh quietly agreed. "She must have done something to it, but there's no sign of tampering. The lock-outs are still in place."

"Hey, I didn't do anything," Cali protested. "Is it my fault if the thing brings me here?"

Odo thought Cali's innocent expression was rather overdone. Then two of his Bajoran security officers arrived.

Cali lifted her hands into the air. "How many people does it take to kick one warm body out of a docking bay? Don't you all have anything better to do?"

"Take her to the brig," Odo told the security team. Then to the Sattar, he added, "I'll inform the *Reaper* that a senior officer must come for you. Perhaps waiting in a holding cell will show you that your actions have consequences."

Cali bristled even more, shaking tufts of hair in her fury. "I only wanted to talk to him! You interfering pack of *vetlhpu'.*"

Security hustled her off, silencing her objections. Odo moved to the console, activating the viewer. Mooh thoughtfully removed herself to the vicinity of the airlock.

Worf's face appeared on the screen. "Yes, Chief?"

"Commander, the *Ceres* was just visited by a rather irate Sattar. She was demanding to see you."

"Sattar!" Worf muttered, sounding remarkably like Cali when she had said commander.

"It was one of the senior mates of the *Reaper,* name of Cali. Would you like me to hold her?" Odo asked.

"No, you need not detain her on my behalf." Worf consulted his console as if ready to deactivate their communication.

Meanwhile Odo accessed recent security activity. "I suppose you have to agree it's a strange place for the prime suspect to appear, right on the doorstep of the *Ceres.* Yet I see that you no longer have the *Reaper* under surveillance. I gather the Sattar had no part in the attack on the *Ceres.*"

Worf was taken aback, but he quickly replied, "The *Reaper* is incapable of inflicting the damage done to the *Ceres.*" Then he recited a list of statistics concerning firepower and shields, making it clear that the only way the *Reaper* could attack the *Ceres* was by ramming her at full speed, and even then they would probably bounce off the duranium hull.

"Good," Odo agreed. "I will attempt to quell the rumor mill. It's likely the Sattar became aware of your suspicions, provoking this little display."

"Perhaps." Worf looked uncomfortable, and abruptly changed the subject. "Captain Sisko will shortly be making a general announcement regarding the storm."

"Oh? I hadn't heard of any new developments."

Worf didn't rise to the bait. "You are to report to Ops for a storm briefing at fifteen hundred hours."

"Very well, Commander." Odo thoughtfully deactivated the viewer. He would prefer to know all the information when it concerned the station. Yet Worf had made it clear that this lay under his jurisdiction.

Odo could certainly understand the need for security, yet Worf's manner was far more curt and dismissive than most of the other Starfleet personnel. Frankly, it reminded him of Cardassian behavior—their arrogance and pride, confident that they knew how to do everything better than everyone else. Watching Worf the past few weeks had made him realize just how much his own mannerisms had been subconsciously based on those of his former Cardassian commanders. He was beginning to wonder if it was necessary to distance himself so much from other people. It didn't seem to be doing any good for Commander Worf.

Nodding to Mooh, Odo entered the turbolift to go back up the pylon. Experienced shapeshifters were capable of ascending as easily as descending, but he wasn't adept enough to scale such heights.

He exited on the habitat ring, intending to have a walk around before returning to the Promenade. There were a few minor things to take care of, but he discovered a bigger problem when he ordered a Marlkin family to clear the main corridor. They informed him that the transient quarters were full.

"You can't block this exit," Odo told them, considering the station's limited options for additional housing. "If you will please wait in the Promenade, we will soon have temporary quarters arranged for you."

The Marlkins grumbled as they gathered up their neat campsite, complete with tenting covers and walls of storage containers. They finally moved along, reluctantly dragging the containers as the youngest child cried at being woken up. Odo waited nearby until they left. Marlkins were basically law-abiding citizens, but they had a tendency to be stubborn.

Odo was just leaving when O'Brien dashed around the corner. Without thinking, Odo curved away from him so they wouldn't touch. He wasn't sure if O'Brien noticed.

"Sorry, Constable!" O'Brien exclaimed. He hardly paused. "Got to get to Keiko before Sisko's announcement."

"Chief," Odo called out, trying to make him stop. "We need to establish temporary quarters. Apparently some of the indigent—"

"We're already on it! We're turning cargo bays fourteen, sixteen, and eighteen into housing. I'll meet you at your office with the plans. But right now I've got to go . . ."

O'Brien gave him a wry, what-else-can-I-do shrug as he hurried off.

The first thing O'Brien heard when he came through the door was the sound of crying in the other room.

"What's wrong with Molly?" he asked.

"She's throwing a tantrum. Just ignore her." Keiko brushed it off irritably. "What's happening with this storm?"

O'Brien braced himself against another tremor. "You two better stay inside. The station is getting more ships than we bargained for now that the wormhole is closed."

"I got your message," she reminded him. "Why can't I access the trajectory of the storm?"

"I think Dax is still working on it. But I'm sure everything will be fine. We've got the station in tip-top order. That is, as tip-top as this place ever gets."

Keiko frowned. "Miles, you're not talking to Molly. I don't need you to come in here and give me a pep talk. I want to know what's going on."

O'Brien made himself go to the replicator and order some coffee before he answered. He had come all the way down here in the middle of that mess in Ops, and Keiko still wasn't satisfied. He wanted to throw his hands into the air and give up. What else could he do?

The replicator indicated that it would take thirty minutes for his coffee to arrive. "Damn!" he muttered.

Now Molly was practically screaming in her room, calling out, "Daddy! Daddy! I want my Daddy!"

"Maybe I should go in there," he suggested, trying to peek through the half-open door. "She sounds upset."

"Let her be upset," Keiko said. "I told her she has to wait until tomorrow for another pony ride. She doesn't know how lucky she is that I'm willing to take her into Quark's again."

Keiko threw herself down on the couch, thumbing through some readings on the data clip. He recognized it as the one she used for her Bajor hybrid-grain project.

"I could take her in tomorrow if you'd like," he offered. "What did the instructor say?"

"He says she's almost ready for the second level pony program, but I think she should wait another half year."

"That's my little horsewoman," Miles said proudly. "And to think she's only been riding a few times! Maybe we'll both do a program tomorrow. There's some country in County Cork I'd like to show her on horseback."

Keiko threw the clip aside. "That's just like you, Miles! Can't you take my word for it, just this once? She's not ready for a real pony."

He felt the sting of her unjust accusation, but his voice was quiet. "I don't get much time with her, but I try to be involved with my daughter while she *is* here."

Keiko met his eyes, instantly showing how much she regretted her remark. "Oh, I'm sorry, Miles. I'm just going nuts here with nothing to do except deal with Molly."

O'Brien pushed aside his irritation and sat down on the couch next to his wife, though he was fully aware that fifteen different people were waiting for his orders. Picking up the clip, he said, "I thought you were cataloging your samples."

"This time I caught up on the way here. At least that twenty-hour delay at the moon station was good for something . . ." He winced in sympathy at her expression. He had only traveled once or twice with Molly, and it was not something he would soon forget. Glumly she added, "There's nothing more I can do now without a botany lab."

"Maybe after the storm blows over you can use the science lab." O'Brien wanted to forge on, but it was difficult to have a pleasant conversation with their daughter screaming in the next room. And he still hadn't gotten to the reason for his visit. He had to tell Keiko before she heard it from Sisko. "Speaking of the storm, you better stock up on food and water. It's starting to look as though it's going to pass through this sector, maybe even this system."

"I thought that might be the reason why the trajectory was classified!" Keiko exclaimed. "The plasma mass is optically thick, and there's not much information from inside blackbody sources. Dax must be going wild over this."

O'Brien had expected her to be worried. Instead she was thrilled. He would never be able to figure her out. "How do you know so much about plasma storms?"

Keiko gave him that sneaky grin he liked so much. "I used your computer to tap into some of the sensor data. But the science lab has restricted most of it."

"Maybe I can do something about that." O'Brien patted her leg as he got up, glad there was finally something he could do for her. "I can use my clearance to get you the same sensor information as the science lab, along with access to their analysis."

She jumped up and reached the console ahead of him. "Oh, Miles! I didn't want to ask. I know it's not strictly protocol, but I'd like to find out more about it."

"I don't see why you can't watch the storm from here." With a few keystrokes and a voice command, he accessed the data being processed by the science lab. "There you are."

Keiko hardly waited for him to finish before sliding her chair closer. "There were some unusual readings I wanted to check out. There's often a wide range of plasma types within fields and moving masses, and the catalyst reactions are fascinating."

"Good." O'Brien watched her for a moment, feeling pleased with himself. Molly was still crying in the other room, but at least she wasn't screaming anymore. Maybe he should go in and talk to her, try to cheer her up as well.

"What's this?" Keiko asked, then sat back with a sigh. The station's general intercom signal was replaced by the image of Captain Sisko, looking quite calm.

"As many of you are aware," Sisko began, "we have issued an emergency docking alert due to the approaching plasma storm. According to our reports, the storm will last at least another twenty-four hours. In addition, the tremors will increase in severity before they lessen." He paused to let the seriousness of his statement sink in. "Those of you who are unable to find lodgings may report to cargo bays fourteen, sixteen, and eighteen." His gentle smile indicated he understood the difficulty of the situation. "At least it's a bed, folks. I know we're all a little cramped, but it's only for one night. Captain Sisko, out."

"Sounds like a warning and a pat on the head at the same time," Keiko muttered, instantly returning to the science data.

"Just be glad we have our own quarters," O'Brien told her. "I'm going to help set up cots in the cargo bays."

"Have fun, dear." She smiled at him in sudden understanding. She even got up to kiss him.

O'Brien squeezed her waist with his hand, hesitating to go. There was only a muffled sob or two coming from Molly's room, and he considered looking in on her, but he was afraid that would only get her started again. She still wasn't clear on the concept of "tomorrow" versus "now." Besides, how would he have the heart to refuse those dark, teary eyes if she begged for a ride on the pony?

Keiko returned to the console, hardly bothering to glance up as the door opened. But at least she was feeling better. If only it was always as easy as a few keystrokes.

CHAPTER 4

WORF WAS SUPERVISING the pod inspection of the warp nacelles of the *Ceres* when he received an urgent summons to meet Commander Dax in the science lab. When he entered, both Bajoran and Starfleet scientists were busy at every post in the lab.

Dax detached herself from a group at one side, saving him the trouble of finding her. "Worf, I'm glad you could get here before the staff briefing."

"I do not have much time," he reminded her. "I must complete the preliminary report on the *Ceres* investigation."

"I think you'll want to see this." Dax seated herself at one of the main consoles. "And I'm sure Captain Sisko will want your opinion on it."

She brought up the standard chart of the neighboring sectors. A large portion of the starfield was blacked out by the plasma storm, with radiating lines indicating the various levels of the emission waves. The symbol of DS9 blinked in the bottom corner.

"See this?" Dax magnified an area in front of the approaching storm. "The ion readings are distorted by the emission waves, but even that isn't strong enough to completely scatter the trail."

"It is a ship," Worf realized.

"Yeah, but what is it doing there?" Dax asked. "They're being bombarded by radiation. Navigation and sensors must barely be working. It makes no sense."

Worf examined her data. "They are accelerating away from the storm front."

"They're going awfully slow if they're trying to get away." Dax glanced at him. "If the emission waves were at any other angle, I wouldn't have been able to detect them."

"The vessel is attempting to hide." Worf was certain of that. Their trajectory held them within the densest region of turbulence for exactly the reason he had been unable to detect their presence on his tactical sensors. It would take an in-depth analysis of wave bending, such as what Dax was doing, in order to spot the vessel. Even with that, they were lucky it was approaching the station dead on.

"According to the deflection ratio," she added, "it's not very large. Twenty-five thousand tons, at most."

Worf frowned. That was about the size of a family

space-yacht. How could it be the ship that had caused the damage to the *Ceres?*

"Thank you, Commander," he formally acknowledged. "Please continue tracking this vessel, and relay your information to the tactical station in Ops."

"Then you'll prepare a report for Sisko?" At his nod, she added, "If you decide to go after it, let me know. I'm dying to get closer to that storm before it gets closer to us." Then she unnerved him by adding, "I'm sorry the communications relay is down. You're going to miss Alexander's weekly call."

Worf drew back. "How do you know about that?"

"Dr. Bashir told me."

His voice rose. "How did the doctor know?"

"Didn't you tell him?" Dax shrugged it off. "Maybe it was Lieutenant Lau in communications. They have lunch together sometimes."

Worf could think of nothing to say to that. One simply didn't trade stories about the personal habits of one's superior officers. At least, not so openly.

Dax laughed, as if she knew exactly what he was thinking.

"Commander," Worf said stiffly in farewell. It was the correct response, but it sounded faintly absurd even to him. Maybe it was because Dax was still laughing as he left the lab.

As usual, when he arrived at Ops his duties absorbed any trifling personal considerations he might have had. The detection of the covert ship was of vital importance.

After feeding Dax's data into his tactical console,

he quickly checked the reports from his security teams. Most were assisting Odo with station patrols, but the best Starfleet investigators were attending to the *Ceres*. Tactically, it had been a perfect attack, leaving relatively few indicators of the source. But disruptor damage was obvious even to the naked eye, and most Klingon vessels used disruptors in their weapons systems.

He accessed the trajectory of the unidentified vessel. It was currently gaining position and holding remarkably steady in the boiling waves of the storm front. Valiant ship, with power enough to hold its own despite the adverse conditions.

The briefing was scheduled to begin within moments. Odo had already arrived, and the rest of the senior staff began to gather around the central console. Worf finished the download of his analysis on the covert ship, then, out of habit, he quickly checked his personal code. Since he had arrived at the station, he had received only one or two messages.

But this time an unexpected face appeared on the viewer. It was the Sattar who had escorted him through the *Reaper*, the one Odo had taken into custody. According to the last security report, she had been released on the recognizance of her captain.

Cali's face twisted as she spat out, *"Qu'vath!"* Worf tensed at the Klingon oath. She hardly took a breath as a stream of vile, broadly accented Klingon flowed out, accusing him of dishonor, deceit, and generally low behavior. Worf endured the brief tirade, noting that Cali did not ask for anything. She merely seemed to be venting about the damage that he, Worf, had personally done to their trade agreements. He resisted a twinge of guilt, regretting that it had not been more immediately apparent that the *Reaper* was incapable of inflicting damage to the *Ceres.* As they had with most Sattar vessels, the Klingons had removed the more advanced equipment, particularly weapons and power systems.

Cali's nostrils flared as she let out a final frustrated exclamation, comparing him to a form of slime found in the swamps of Qo'noS. On that note, the message terminated.

"Is there a problem, Commander?"

Worf realized Sisko was standing on the upper deck while the rest of the senior staff were watching him. They had obviously heard the angry Sattar, so it was necessary to give them an explanation. "It is not important, sir. I believe one of the senior mates of the *Reaper* has taken a personal dislike to me."

"I'm certain you can handle it." Sisko rested both hands on the console. "Now, if you could join us, we have plenty of other problems to deal with."

As Worf approached, he said, "Captain, there is an urgent matter we must discuss."

Sisko nodded permission, so Worf accessed the data for display on the main console. "Commander Dax found this ion trail during her analysis of the storm. It appears to be a small vessel. The shock waves prevented my tactical sensors from detecting it."

"Did you try to hail them?" Sisko asked.

"No, sir. I believe they are attempting to hide." Worf paused, noting that Sisko was not impressed. "It did not seem advisable to alert them that we are aware of their presence."

"But they could be damaged," Kira protested. "Or maybe their sensors are jammed and they don't know where they are."

"Request permission to take the *Defiant* to investigate." Sisko looked expectantly in Worf's direction. "Sir," the Klingon added quickly.

Sisko considered the starfield on the main viewer. "I don't believe that's necessary. They're almost in the system now." He turned to Kira. "Try hailing them."

"Aye, sir. We're having some trouble with communications, but they should get something . . ." She concentrated over her touchpads as Worf fought back his disappointment. Why was no one else concerned about the Klingon's aggressive campaign? They often talked of the possibility of Dominion infiltration, but what had the Dominion done compared to the Klingon invasion of Cardassia?

"I'm getting something on audio," Kira said.

Through the static came the question, "DS9? Is that . . ." then, ". . . in this sector. Location?"

"Distortion is pretty bad," Kira admitted. "I'm sending our coordinates and the storm warning via the burst signal." After a moment she looked up. "It's the Klingon yacht *Katon,* under Captain Alons of the House of Napos."

Worf's fist softly hit the edge of the console. Klingons! He was right. Napos was a minor house, but one that fully supported Gowron's policies, presumably including the attack on Cardassia and the current hostilities against the Federation.

He returned to the tactical station. He had not been ordered to power up weapons, but he was prepared for anything.

"The *Katon* has not altered course," he announced. "However it has increased speed considerably."

It took a moment for Kira to piece together a visual communication. Though it was distorted by the electromagnetic interference, they could see Captain Alons reclining back in the captain's chair. He was a barrel-chested, older Klingon with a languorous, sneering manner. As usual his brother, Sebas, hovered nearby. Worf did not recognize the other young Klingon who was grinning directly, insolently at him.

Worf tried to ignore the other one as Alons offered his greetings. "We weren't aware that we were in the Bajoran Sector, Captain Sisko. Now that we have our bearings we will be on our way."

"We have issued an emergency docking alert due to the storm," Sisko informed Alons. "The conditions make it unsafe for navigation."

"Thank you for your . . . concern." Alons cleared his throat with a pointedly disgusting sound. "I assure you that the *Katon* has gotten us through worse storms than this."

"You almost ran us over before you realized we

were here," Sisko reminded the Klingon. "You didn't even know you were in the Bajoran Sector, much less the system."

Alons stretched his lips in imitation of a smile. "All the more reason for us to leave."

"I must insist that you dock at DS9," Sisko repeated. "For your own safety—"

The young Klingon barked out a laugh, cutting him off. "How can you listen to this *pugh?"* he demanded to Alons. "When that shapeshifter stands beside him? And I won't even mention that *DenIb Qatlh!"*

Worf hardly flinched. He had heard it all before, the first time he had accepted disgrace and expulsion from the High Council. This stripling knew nothing of his sacrifices for the Klingon Empire.

"This is Ton," Alons briefly informed Sisko. "Eldest son of the House of Maang."

Sisko wasn't amused. "My officers are none of your concern."

"It only serves to show your lack of judgment!" taunted Ton of Maang. "Only scum would stand by *O'web*—"

"Silence!" Alons ordered. "The House of Mogh is no more."

Ton showed his brown-stained teeth. "But the Cybriss valley has flourished since the House of Maang took over the farms. The name of Mogh has been struck from every record, and the wine is all the sweeter for our trouble."

A growl of surprise rose in Worf's throat. He had

heard that Gowron had given away his family's lands and holdings, but he had not been able to gather more specific information. His brother Kurn had not answered his messages for over a month. Worf could dimly remember tales of his father's hunting lodge in the Cybriss valley, and vaguely remembered a summer his family had spent there when he was young. The thought of this hulking, slobbering idiot striding across even one acre of the lands belonging to his family's house . . .

Worf snarled, oblivious to everything else. Even through the broken image it was clear that Ton was laughing at him, laughing at his loss.

"Commander," Sisko said with a hint of warning in his voice.

The captain's quiet order reminded Worf of his duty. With difficulty he broke eye contact with Ton, nodding briefly to Sisko. He prepared the tractor beams, intending to power up and lock on as soon as the *Katon* was within range. Assuming they remained on course. The *Katon* could easily gain a long lead while the *Defiant* was prepared for departure. Worf was counting on the fact that the Klingons were unaware of the extensions he and Chief O'Brien had added to the station's tractor beams. The addition seemed like a prudent idea at the time, but he had not anticipated that his foresight would be so quickly rewarded.

Worf signaled the main console that he was ready with tractor beams, providing a countdown of when the *Katon* would be in range.

"Captain Alons, let's discuss this situation reasonably," Sisko requested.

Alons shook his head. "There is no reasoning with cowards!" He snapped an order to his helmsman.

"The *Katon* is changing course," Worf informed Sisko. "New heading two four seven, mark five point one."

"You can't simply fly through Bajoran space," Sisko told Alons.

"Why not?" Alons raised his hands, letting out loud guffaws as Sebas and Ton joined in.

Despite the change in course the *Katon* was curving into range. Worf was ready when the indicator blinked, and at Sisko's nod he locked on to the vessel.

"All vessels in this sector must dock for the duration of the storm alert," Sisko politely informed them. "That includes you."

For a split second Alons was the perfect vision of Klingon outrage. Then his image disappeared. The main viewer showed the *Katon* swerving in the grip of the tractor beams. Worf was busy compensating as the yacht attempted to form a warp field.

"The *Katon* has cut off communications," Kira announced. "No response."

Worf refrained from reporting until he had the situation under control. But he never doubted the outcome for an instant. "We have the *Katon,* sir. Tractors are holding."

"Bring them into the main dock in lower pylon

one," Sisko ordered. "I want them as far away from the habitat ring as possible."

"You'll have to give me a minute to transfer some ships around," Kira said quickly.

"Understood," Worf confirmed. It would give him time to conduct a thorough scan while the *Katon* was trying to break free.

But before he could calibrate the sensors to filter out the distortion of the emission waves, the *Katon* brought her engines to full stop. Only their shields continued to hold at maximum power, impenetrable to the station's sensors.

"The *Katon* has powered down her engines," Worf informed Sisko.

The captain raised one brow. "Perhaps they've decided to cooperate."

"You can bring them in now, Commander," Kira told him, adding, "Still no answer to our hails."

Dax shrugged. "You can only expect so much cooperation from Klingons these days."

Odo crossed his arms, speaking up for the first time. "That's certainly true."

"Sir, I believe they do not want us to scan their power systems," Worf said darkly.

"Your reasoning?" Sisko asked.

Worf automatically went to attention. "The *Katon* could be the vessel responsible for the damage to the *Ceres.*"

"That's an awfully small ship," O'Brien protested.

But Odo shook his head. "I've seen even smaller

vessels do worse damage for the Resistance." Kira smiled briefly in Odo's direction, agreeing, "That was one of our best tricks—packing engines into hulls the Cardassians wouldn't consider worth their trouble to destroy."

Worf shifted tractor control to the docking chief in the lower pylon, but he maintained a secondary beam on the *Katon* in case Alons tried to escape again. "Sensors indicate the *Katon* conforms to standard designs of the vessel's class. However, their shields are superior to specifications, and they could be concealing auxiliary enhancement systems."

"Suggestions?" Sisko asked.

"Request permission to board the *Katon,*" Worf instantly replied. "An internal inspection will reveal their weapons capability."

Sisko considered Worf for a moment. "Granted." He held up a quick finger. "But please, Commander, try not to antagonize them. I won't let this incident escalate into an open battle."

"Aye, Captain," Worf acknowledged, checking his console. "The *Katon* has docked. May I proceed?"

Sisko gave him a wry smile. "Very well, Commander. Though you won't be able to convince me you didn't plan this in order to get out of a briefing session."

"No, sir," Worf said, for lack of anything better to say. But as he headed for the turbolift, he was relieved that he wouldn't have to endure the endless minor details of securing the station against the storm.

As the turbolift descended, he grimly thought that it was a good thing Starfleet Headquarters had the foresight to post a Strategic Operations Officer to DS9, if only to have someone whose main duty was to protect the most valuable piece of territory within a hundred light years.

Captain Ari stood in front of a portal in the senior mates' lounge of the *Reaper,* watching as the immense tractors dragged the Klingon yacht the last few meters to the docking pylon. Cali entered and approached to a discreet distance, waiting to be recognized.

"Come see this, Cali," Ari said graciously. He enjoyed granting her permission to do things. It pleasantly reminded him of the years when Cali's mother had been the one ordering everyone about. "It must be the ship Commander Worf was looking for."

"We're lucky that Starfleet ship showed up in time," Cali commented, casting a disinterested eye on the *Katon.* "I can't believe I insulted that Klingon to his face and he still said he would grant our clearance for departure."

"Worf is an unusual Klingon," Ari said absently, not really concerned with teaching Cali the finer points of character study. Her raw energy was far too useful to blunt with systems of logical analysis.

"Did you send your message?" Ari asked her.

Cali grinned. "I even called him a *ghargh!* I taped it if you want to hear. I know I'm going to listen to it again and again."

"I'm sure it was a great pleasure for you," Ari agreed. "Did you remember to point out his dishonor in canceling our clearance without following proper procedure?"

"I wouldn't forget your part of the deal," she protested in a wounded tone of voice. "I wish I could do the whole thing over again. It's not every day you get to insult a Klingon. Or spray plasma in his eyes!"

Ari ignored the senior mate's cackling and moved on to more practical matters. "Now that we've gained another day, our members must take care to secure a good contract."

"You should see the opportunities waiting out there," Cali agreed.

"Make sure it's a one-way contract, one that takes us far from this sector." Ari thought that Starfleet's treatment of the Klingon yacht was quite revealing. When such a tiny ship rated an entire docking pylon, you knew there were problems. "You stay away from the Klingons. I'll put Shorci on that."

"You think the *Katon* did it?" Cali asked, looking from the sleek yacht to the discolored hull of the *Ceres.*

"That doesn't concern you." Ari impatiently waved Cali off. He was tired of her. "Send everyone out according to the deal roster. Cause minimal damage. Make sure Theosi understands that."

"As you will, Captain." Cali bounced on her toes, eager to get started. "To the members!" she pledged as she left.

Ari smiled to himself. One day she might figure out that the chains she struggled against were what actually bound her to the Collective. If she didn't die first, at some point she would acquire that wisdom. All Sattar did eventually, they simply required a firm hand until then.

CHAPTER 5

MOLLY WAS COLORING a tubba with her crayons when Keiko went in to check on her. As she washed the girl's tear-stained cheeks (all that was left of her tantrum) Molly asked about her friend's tubba, the Bajoran cat-like creature that belonged to one of the other children of the survey scientists.

"Tubba went on vacation, too," Keiko told her daughter. She knew it was only a matter of time before the subject of a pet came up. Keiko dreaded that day. It was difficult enough living this gypsy life with a child. How could she do it with a pet?

Miles certainly wouldn't be much help. He could hardly keep a house plant alive. If she hadn't put the bonsai on an automatic drip, it would be dead by now. She considered taking it back with her to Bajor, but she had grown the damn tree for Miles in the first place. The peat was in fair condition, but the shaggy trunk and branches of the tiny cypress were going to have to be brushed for days until the excess bark was shed.

Keiko knew she was obsessing again, so she tried to put the bonsai out of her mind. She had no control over anything else, why did she think she could train a tree she hardly ever saw?

She had just started reading Molly a story when the computer finally beeped, announcing that her biometric analysis was completed. It was turning out to be a complex problem for the lab to analyze the storm data, so she had used some of the species models she recently developed to do statistical comparisons of unfamiliar Bajoran organisms.

"Insufficient data," was flashing on the viewer. Molly trailed after her with the book as Keiko sat down. She keyed in an order to find correlations as low as sixty percent. When that didn't work, she kept lowering the percentage until she hit ten percent. While the computer still didn't consider that to be sufficient, it found several biological models that could be loosely applied to the pattern of emission waves from the plasma storm. There were even unmistakable signs of oscillations affecting one another and responding to outside stimuli.

Keiko felt a rush of elation that her efforts had finally yielded some results, even if they were on the modest side. Her analysis had sorted the data, but there was barely enough information to make rudimentary graphs of the plasma action. She needed more data before she could set up an experimental model, perhaps even incorporating the matrix of electrodynamic fields within nebulas along with the biological statistics.

"Computer," she said out loud. "Where is Commander Dax?"

"Dax is currently in Ops."

Keiko hesitated, then chided herself for doubting the importance of her discovery. From everything she had seen this afternoon, Dax was having a difficult time predicting the reactions of this plasma storm.

"Keiko O'Brien to Commander Dax."

Dax acknowledged, though she sounded rather perplexed. "What can I do for you, Keiko?"

"Actually I thought I might be able to help you," Keiko told her. "I've been running a biometric analysis of the plasma storm and I thought you might be interested in seeing the results."

There was a distinct pause, and Keiko could only imagine the dubious expression on Dax's face. "We've already tried comparative analysis using ecosystem structures and hydrofluid reaction dynamics."

"Yes, I know. But I've conducted a statistical survey, comparing the emissions to the EM matrix of an individual organism."

Dax sounded thoughtful. "I'd like to see what you have. Can you meet me in the science lab on level four?"

"Give me a few minutes to settle things here," Keiko said, distracted by Molly. The girl was skipping around the room, making noises as if she were riding a horse.

Keiko pulled a loose coverall over her unitard. "Molly, I'm going to call Ensign Kij and have her come over to sit with you for a while. That is, if she's not on duty."

The floor shifted to one side, and Keiko braced herself against the chair. Molly went down on her knees rather hard.

"Are you okay?" she asked, almost holding her breath. She didn't have time for anything dramatic.

Molly gravely examined her reddened knees, brushing the carpet fibers from her skin. She must have decided it was nothing. "Kij left, Mommy."

"She did?" Keiko stared at the girl. "How do you know?"

"I called her." Molly trotted over to point to the touchpad. "With that button."

"Good for you, Molly." She realized she shouldn't be surprised at her daughter's resourcefulness. She was learning how to take care of herself faster than other children her age, but then again her life wasn't exactly typical.

Molly nodded solemnly. "The nice lady said Kij left. Mommy, where is Wizen-on-Kost?"

"Far, far away. Kij will be happy there," Keiko said absently. Now how could she replace the kindhearted ensign who used to watch over Molly? She thought about that young Bajoran mother she had met at Quark's, but Catrin was undoubtedly still working.

Keiko had already realized she knew almost no one

on the station when she had been forced to leave Molly alone in the holosuite. There wasn't anybody here she would even consider a friend. It was ironic that Molly had more people she wanted to call than her mother did.

"Come on, Molly. We're going to the science lab."

"On Bajor?" Molly's expression said she wasn't ready for another interplanetary journey.

Keiko couldn't blame her. "No, the one here on the station. Go get your bag." The bag was packed with small games, story padds, and snacks, plenty to keep a six-year-old busy whenever Keiko had to take her somewhere. By the time she had left a message for Miles in case he happened to return, Molly emerged from her room with her jacket on and her bag firmly over her shoulder.

"You won't need your coat," Keiko reminded her. "We're on the station, and it's always warm here."

Molly thought about that until Keiko was ready to give in and go help her take the jacket off. But she slowly removed it, dropping it on the floor. "Mommy, why is it always warm?"

Keiko sighed, and as she ushered Molly from their quarters, she tried to explain the life-support systems of DS9 and planetary weather. Where was Miles when she really needed him?

Captain Sisko sighed as he ordered O'Brien to go deal with the latest malfunction in the overloaded replicator system. Kira and Odo were quietly talking about something near her console, not paying any attention. This briefing wasn't accomplishing much, anyway. *How can it when my senior staff is trickling away one by one?* he thought.

"Captain?" Dax asked, starting to edge after O'Brien. "I'd like to go hear what Keiko has found."

Sisko glared at her without thinking, then apologetically rubbed his eyes with one hand. He hadn't realized how much he had been looking forward to taking Kasidy out in the sailship until he couldn't. "This has turned into some day off," he murmured to himself.

"I'm sorry, Benjamin," Dax told him.

"It's not your fault." He straightened up. "Can't you tell me anything concrete about the effect the storm will have on the station?"

"Not with the data we have to work with," Dax said flatly. "This isn't the typical plasma storm blowing in from the Badlands. This one came from beyond Klingon territory, and it's moving faster than any storm documented in Starfleet records."

"You said that Dr. Bashir gave you his report on the radiation poisoning among the *Ceres* crew. Surely that can provide some clues to the composition of the plasma field."

"Plasma particles are notoriously hard to differentiate." Dax reminded him. "The same sort of radiation poisoning can be caused by different kinds of particles and/or energy waves. We're only guessing until we penetrate the blackbody mass itself."

"Unless Keiko has come up with something," Sisko said thoughtfully. "Sisko to Keiko O'Brien."

There was a longer hesitation than usual, then a flustered voice answered, "Yes, Captain?"

"Would you please bring your analysis up to Ops?" Sisko got Dax's nod as she moved to her science console. Sometime in the past few hours O'Brien had found time to repair it.

Odo moved forward. "If the briefing is over, sir, I'd like to get back to my post."

"Certainly, Constable." Sisko managed a slight smile. "I know a curfew might be the ideal solution, but I'm afraid that's impossible in this situation. However you may issue a public safety recommendation for everyone to stay in their quarters, either on their ships or here on the station."

Kira put in, "I've already advised the off-duty service personnel to remain in their quarters."

"Do the same for Starfleet officers," Sisko ordered.

Odo nodded. Sisko noted that he looked grudgingly pleased that his advice had been taken seriously, even if it was not entirely implemented. The chief hesitated as he started past the major, but Kira turned away to tell Sisko, "Commander Worf has relayed a message that the Klingons are refusing to open their airlock."

Sisko gestured to Odo. "Constable, see if you can assist Mister Worf. I don't want those Klingons to come out fighting."

"Understood, Captain."

Dax grinned at Odo as he went to the turbolift. "While you're at it, why don't you ask for their sensor logs on the plasma storm? I bet the *Katon* got a good look inside."

Kira rolled her eyes. "As if the Klingons would ever tell us."

Dax agreed. "Worf will be lucky if he can convince them to open the airlock."

"Before we condemn them, let's first give them a chance to cooperate," Sisko said lightly.

Both Kira and Dax looked down at their consoles, shamefaced. Sisko was determined to keep a check on the paranoia among his senior staff. Assumptions could inspire a deadly reaction in the current galactic-political climate.

He braced his chin in his hand, considering their limited options. But his calculations of energy output to shield intensity were lost as he started to wonder what Jake was doing. Perhaps he should call and tell Jake to stay inside tonight. Things were bound to get wild with all the crews stranded on the station.

"Let me know when Keiko arrives," he told Dax, going into his office.

He sat down and signaled his quarters, drumming his fingers on the desk when Jake didn't answer. "Computer, where is Jake?"

"Jake Sisko is in the habitat ring, level fifteen."

"Tell him to contact me in Ops." Sisko turned the viewer to a better angle, waiting for Jake to answer via the station's intercom.

Jake was panting when he came on, and his face bobbed out of the frame as he looked behind him. "Just a minute!" he called to someone. "I'll be right there—"

"Jake, what are you doing?" Sisko didn't want to sound irritated, but he also didn't have time for this.

"I'm hanging out with some friends." Jake seemed surprised he asked. "I told you earlier. I met these students from the University at Betazed and, boy, are they—" He paused to yell off screen, "All right, I'm coming!" He turned back to his dad. "They're a lot of fun."

Jake had mentioned the Betazoids when Sisko called to say he and Kasidy wouldn't be going out on the sailship. The students had been en route to the Gamma Quadrant to conduct an inter-species empathic survey when the emergency alert had forced their ship to dock at the station.

"Jake, I think it would be best if you stayed home tonight."

"Why?" Jake's smile faltered. "What's wrong, Dad?"

"Nothing, except that the station is overcrowded, and anything could happen."

Jake leaned closer so the others couldn't hear. "Think about what you just said, Dad. I'm not going to stay home because 'anything could happen.'" He widened his eyes in exasperation, then gave his dad a reassuring grin. "I've got to go now. They're waiting for me."

Sisko nodded, trying to give in gracefully. He couldn't squash Jake's excitement, not when he was so pleased that the young adults had accepted him on their own level.

As the transmission terminated, Sisko was left wondering what had prompted him to caution Jake like that. Jake could take care of himself. And if he couldn't, then the station was the best place for him to learn, while his father was nearby to lend a helping hand if he needed it. Jake would be much more on his own when he went to study on Earth.

"Captain?" Dax called through the intercom. "Keiko is here."

Sisko noticed the changed dynamic in Ops as soon as the door opened. Everyone was watching Keiko as she bent over her little girl. Molly was laughing and pointing up to something in the ceiling of Ops, chattering brightly. The crew were smiling in response, and for a moment, everyone was relaxed.

That changed as soon as Sisko spoke. "Thank you for coming, Keiko."

She handed Molly the toy, straightening up. "Sorry I had to bring her, Captain. I couldn't get a sitter."

"That's quite all right." Sisko glanced down at Molly. The girl put her finger in her mouth and stared up at him, suddenly as solemn as his crew. "Welcome back to the station, Molly."

"Remember Captain Sisko, honey?" Keiko reminded her daughter.

Molly nodded. "Can I ride the pony?"

"First, let me speak to your mother for a moment." Sisko turned back to Keiko. "I didn't know you were interested in plasma physics."

"I'm not." Keiko shifted her eyes from him to Dax.

"If this had been your basic hydrogen-complex plasma storm, I wouldn't have spent all afternoon examining the emissions."

Dax asked, "You said you ran the data against a biometric model?"

"Yes, because of the complexity of wave reactions. Everything from rapid Doppler shifts and magneto-optical effects, not to mention the wide number of magnetic fields being produced."

Dax was taking her seriously. "Come show me what you've got."

She moved over to make room for Keiko at the science station. Keiko input her data clip and concentrated on the program display. "The best match was against a plankton biomodel."

"Plankton?" Sisko repeated doubtfully.

"Yes, you know, algae, bacteria, phylum, and non-motile organisms that float in water."

"I know what plankton is," Sisko told her. "But what does plankton have in common with plasma?"

"Well, nothing, really," Keiko admitted. "That's why biometric analysis works when you don't have much data. It's used to compare organisms of different species, even plants and animals. My analysis indicates that the biometric behavior of plankton fits some of the same statistical curves as the sensor readings of the plasma storm."

Sisko thought Dax's reaction was revealing. "I've never heard of anyone trying that."

"I only found a ten percent correlation," Keiko

quickly pointed out. "What I need is more information on the internal conditions, the particle content, and rates of energy fluctuation."

Dax shook her head. "We've sent in probes, but we aren't receiving telemetry from within the blackbody." She gestured to one spiked pattern. "I've studied biometric analysis before, but the way these coefficients are graphed is confusing. Is that curve the response to external stimulation?"

"Yes, you can see some of the structured continuum, relating the past behavior to future reactions. That's movement." Keiko pointed to the indicators on the graph overlay. "I'd say it's changed course sometime during the past six hours."

Dax looked up at Sisko. "Her trajectory confirms it. The storm has been drawn off course by the wormhole."

Sisko looked back at Keiko. "What effect do you think the storm will have on the station?"

She was taken aback. "I don't know, sir. We need more data on the internal conditions, but once we have that, we could use the biometric models to break it down mathematically. Then the variables, such as phase lengths and radiation dynamics, could be predicted."

"O'Brien could use that information to adjust the shields for maximum coverage," Dax agreed. "Also, if we took a runabout inside, we'd be able to test the turbulence of the magneto-hydrodynamic systems inside the storm. That would help us shape the structural integrity field to protect the areas of the hull that would incur maximum stress."

"Very well," Sisko finally agreed. "But if you must go into the storm for your tests, why not use the *Defiant?*"

Dax pursed her lips in thought. "I'm not sure I can create an electrostatic field around something as big as the *Defiant.* And the runabout has much shorter shield harmonics, creating less mass interference within the waves. We need to distort our readings as little as possible."

"Of course. Then a runabout it is," Sisko agreed. "Use the *Rubicon*—have O'Brien help you with the alterations to the shields. That's a priority." He glanced at Keiko, who was whispering to Molly to wait just a minute more. Sisko tried not to think about Jake. "And Dax, take an experienced pilot with you. You'll need the help."

"Captain?" Keiko asked, still holding Molly's hand. "I'd like to go with Dax. There are a number of special techniques for sampling and identification when you're using biometric models." She must have seen his hesitation, because she quickly added, "I'm also fully qualified to pilot a runabout."

Sisko tried to soften his refusal. "I'm sorry, but I can't allow noncommissioned personnel to go into such a dangerous situation."

"But I'm a member of the survey team to Bajor, technically a member of Starfleet." Keiko ignored the pleading of Molly who was pulling on her hand for attention. "You won't find another scientist on this station with more knowledge of biometric analysis. And I'm already familiar with the plasma storm."

Sisko leaned over and tapped the access code that had appeared along with Keiko's data. "Yes, I see you that you are. I didn't mention how you acquired your data, but now that you bring it up, what will Chief O'Brien say to your going?"

Keiko gave him a look without batting an eye.

Sisko had never been so smoothly corrected. He turned to Dax. "What do you think, Commander?"

Dax tensed, recognizing a critical situation. "I could use Keiko's help," she admitted. "Biophysics isn't my strongest suit."

Molly was still tugging on Keiko's hand, her voice rising as she asked to see the console "where Daddy worked."

"What about Molly?" Sisko asked in a low voice.

"I'm doing this for Molly," Keiko replied.

"But who will take care of her? You said you couldn't find anyone."

Keiko's expression was pinched, as if she didn't want to discuss it. "I can leave her with the holonanny until Miles is done with work."

"Very well," he agreed. "I'll pass an order along to Quark to make one of his holosuites available for you."

"Thank you, Captain." But Keiko didn't smile.

Sisko returned to his office, feeling as if he had handled that rather badly. He had never questioned any other crew member's ability to go on a mission because of a lack of a sitter. Then again, Keiko was not a member of his crew.

Yet she was his responsibility because she was on DS9. Just like Kasidy . . .

He realized that it was Kasidy who was doing this to him. He was acting like a mother hen because of her. While he was handing out warnings to everyone else, what he really wanted to do was call Kasidy and make sure she was okay. But things had been tricky for them the past couple of weeks since she had moved to the station. He was being careful not to make any more assumptions, never forgetting that one time when it had almost ended their relationship.

Besides, Kasidy had made it very clear that she could take care of herself. She was probably in one of the cargo bays, assisting in setting up temporary housing. They had already spoken once today, so why did he have such a strong urge to call her, to see her face, to tell her he was thinking about her . . .

"Captain Sisko?" Kira asked over the intercom. "We have the captain of that sightseeing liner. He's protesting the fact that he can't close his airlock to keep the passengers out."

"Put it through," Sisko sighed. As usual, work called him away from Kasidy.

CHAPTER 6

WORF TOLD HIMSELF to be patient as Odo repeated into the comm, "All vessels that dock at DS9 must be inspected. According to section eight, article four—"

"We did not ask to dock here," Sebas interrupted. "You dragged us to this *He'So'pIgh!*"

"There is an emergency storm alert in effect," Odo calmly replied. "If the *Katon* does not comply with our regulations, we will be forced to notify the Klingon authorities."

"Ha!" the Klingon spat. "The High Council will hear of this, of *that* you can be sure!"

Standing behind Odo, Worf folded his arms across his chest, having resolved to remain silent until the security chief exhausted the diplomatic and regulatory methods of extracting the Klingons from the

Katon. Worf was pleased that he was not forced to perform this charade, though it probably would have ended much sooner had it been up to him.

Sebas was apparently enjoying sparring with Odo, though in Worf's opinion, the younger son of the House of Napos wasn't very quick with his retorts. Worf yawned broadly, a sign of contempt that he allowed Sebas to see.

The Klingon's hands clenched. "I will not speak with *Chap'on!*"

"You just did," Worf pointed out.

Sebas reached out as if to cut the transmission.

Worf warned him, "Perhaps you will change your mind when a laser welder cuts through your hull."

"You would not dare," Sebas sneered. "Not the warrior who runs from battle!"

Worf stared at him without moving a muscle. Sebas hesitated and Worf slightly bared his teeth at the novice.

"Please, gentlemen," Odo interrupted. "We can be civil with one another. If you and your captain will join us on the station, we can discuss this matter—"

"Enough talk!" Sebas held up a thick finger, the combat wristband shining a warning. "The *Katon* will wait out the storm, then we continue on our way." He snarled as if his words were final. He was young and arrogant, secure in his House and his father's alliance with Gowron. Worf almost envied the young upstart.

Odo glanced over his shoulder as the transmission ended. "So much for that. A waste of time, if you ask me."

Worf settled for saying, "I agree."

"Did you get anything with the point-blank scans?" Odo asked.

"Nothing unusual. However, essential systems are off line." He shook his head at the report from the security pods. "Some of the readings are distorted, perhaps indicating localized shielding."

Odo examined the data. "That could be caused by the emission waves."

Worf frowned. "I have not ruled out that possibility."

"You don't have enough here to convince Sisko that forced entry is necessary," Odo pointed out.

"I am aware of that fact."

Odo glanced toward the airlock. "On the other hand, Bajoran regulations give me some latitude with regard to the methods that constitute forced entry. Perhaps we can use a remote manipulator to trigger the automatic opening sequence of their airlock."

Worf was unsettled. "You have done this before?"

Odo gave him a hard look. "When the alternative is letting a Cardassian crew explode a Bajoran Resistance smuggler, you learn how to bypass automatic systems."

"I see. Of course, I welcome your assistance."

Odo inclined his head. "I'll call for the equipment."

"Commander Worf?" One of the security guards was motioning to a Starfleet officer waiting near the turbolift. "It's Captain Iis of the *Ceres,* here to see you."

Iis came forward without waiting for Worf's permission, slowly approaching the viewport showing the *Katon.* She was looking much better, as if she had washed, rested, and eaten. Now Worf could see that she moved with the grace of a lifelong athlete. As with many older humans, her face had fallen into comfortable, serene lines, and she defied vanity with her close-cropped silver hair.

Iis turned to Worf. "Is this the ship that attacked us?"

"We have insufficient data on their weapons systems," Worf reluctantly informed her. "They will not open the airlock."

Iis kept her eyes on the *Katon.* "I tried to speak to the lieutenant about what she might have seen, but she couldn't understand me. Dr. Bashir says she'll have to be sent back to Andoria for intensive brain treatment."

Worf was unsure if she was making a deliberate effort to suppress her emotions, or if the doctor had given her a sedative. Probably the latter.

"I will discover the truth," Worf told the captain.

"Ah, yes, the truth." She kept staring through the viewport. "Please tell me when you do. I'm sure there are plenty of people who want to know the truth."

Worf decided to stick with the safest answer. "Yes, sir."

Captain Iis looked at him intently. "Thank you for being so valiant, Commander. I do want to know if this ship was responsible. Yet even if it was, does that explain why this happened?"

"The Klingons have broken the peace treaty with

the Federation," Worf declared. "That is reason enough for them to attack a Starfleet vessel."

"Then you believe the Klingon Empire is prepared to engage us in a full-scale war?"

"Yes."

Iis sighed, her hands lightly clasped in front of her, watching as Odo opened the panel to the locking terminals. "Why?"

Worf began to list the statistical increases in Klingon traffic and weapons manufacture, when Iis cut him off. "What I meant is, why will the Klingons fight us? They've got more territory than they can possibly handle right now, and they're stretched to the limit with the Cardassians. What do they hope to gain by fighting Starfleet?"

Worf briefly clenched his jaw. "Klingons want to live as warriors."

"So you're saying it's part of their character to make war," Iis said thoughtfully. Then she almost smiled. "I've never believed in theories of species-determined behavior. If I did, then I would have to believe that you, Commander, were as ruthlessly violent as these Klingons appear to be. And I would have to believe that your security chief," she added, nodding to Odo, "is a devious shapeshifter intent on the genocide of all humanoid lifeforms."

Worf exchanged a look with Odo, wondering if the chief felt as exposed as he did. He also remembered Cali's taunt that Klingons were all alike, then tried to put it from his mind.

"No, Commander Worf," Iis finished with a sad

smile. "I don't believe in blaming genetics. We must examine our own actions to determine how we reached this terrible impasse with people who were once our friends."

"Perhaps," Worf felt compelled to agree. "Yet the hostilities appear to be escalating. We can only protect ourselves."

Iis shrugged as if she was too weary to argue the philosophy of peace. Meanwhile Odo's security team arrived, and the chief moved to the airlock, much to his apparent relief.

Worf knew he couldn't fight his own personal demons with the captain. "I have arranged living quarters for you," he offered by way of apology. "Starfleet personnel have volunteered to share their quarters with your crew for the duration of the storm."

"Thank you, Commander. That is most kind."

Worf glanced over at Odo, but the amount of equipment the team was unpacking revealed that it would be a while before any progress was made with the remote manipulators. "Allow me to escort you to Commander Dax's quarters. She recently departed to investigate the storm."

"No. Give the quarters to my wounded so they can leave the infirmary. I've ordered my senior staff to remain on board the *Ceres* during the repairs." She shook her head at his protest. "I know we may have to close decks, but I'd like to make every effort not to abandon ship. That is a matter of pride to my crew."

Worf admired the sentiment. "Very well, Captain."

Captain Iis was starting to leave when the red alert klaxons went off. Her alarm indicated that she was stretched to nearly the breaking point. Worf immediately accessed Ops.

"Commander!" Kira exclaimed as if relieved to see him. "We have a problem at dock eight. Those two freighters that are tethered to the passenger liner—we're losing one of them."

"On viewscreen," Worf ordered.

A cross view image appeared of a bulbous passenger liner, its slender nose tucked into the docking ring. The transport freighter next to it was moving, swinging away from the liner toward the docking ring. As it collided with the hull, he could feel the impact vibrate down the docking pylon.

"Tractors—" he started to say.

"Wrong angle! The docking ring is in the way."

"Prepare a runabout for emergency takeoff," Worf ordered.

"You can put a tractor on it from out there," Kira agreed, keying in the command to prepare the runabout. "Pad two will be ready when you get there. O'Brien is trying to secure the freighter from inside the docking ring."

Odo approached the console. "I'll assist Chief O'Brien. It will take some time to get through the shielding of the *Katon*'s hull."

Worf nodded, casting a longing look at the portal. "Keep me informed."

Kira's impatience was clear. "If that freighter breaks loose, it could hit the habitat ring—"

"On my way," Worf acknowledged. He didn't need anyone to remind him of his duty.

Cali crouched against the curving side of the maintenance corridor, prepared to slip under the narrow service crawlway if the technicians climbed to her level. But the scraping sounds continued past in a starboard direction toward the section where most of the work was being done to secure the Bajoran freighter.

She was the last of her team to leave the area, and she had been cut off when she turned back to reactivate the security sensors in the maintenance access junction. There would always be talk of possible sabotage, but she preferred to leave no evidence behind. Not when her members were in place, ready to take over the contract from the damaged freighter. That had been the trick—cutting one of the stasis lines during a shock wave so the freighter would snap like a whip. From the double impact, she figured the port warp nacelle had been crushed.

Now she needed to get out of this section before she was discovered.

"It shouldn't be long now." The male voice echoed strangely through the corridor. "Worf's holding it steady with the tractors."

Cali had heard that voice ever since her members had severed the stasis line. The technical response had been much faster than they had expected, yet she was the only one who hadn't gotten out in time. And she didn't intend to let these bumbling techies beat her at her own game.

"I see you're using your ingenuity, Mister O'Brien. I've never heard of a ship being secured in quite this manner," another voice commented.

Her hair rose in prickles up her spine as she recognized that voice. Odo, chief of security. The nosy shapechanger who had locked her in the brig for no good reason.

Still, she had been working on Captain Ari's deal, agitating the Klingon Commander, so she had been well compensated. And that hour in the brig had paid off with the lead on this sweet deal. One of her cell mates had been the purser of the now-damaged freighter, and he had barely needed any coaxing to give her the details of their next run. And *blimenny,* was it a creampuff! Carrying raw bulk chemicals to the Rw'arez Sector. You couldn't get much further away from the wormhole in one straight run, and from there they could go almost anywhere.

"We're still assessing the damage to the docking ring," O'Brien was saying. "I'm going to have someone check the main supports in this section. But from the looks of things, the freighter got the worst of it."

"Tell me, Chief," Odo said seriously. "Have you ever seen a stasis line snap like that?"

"No, can't say that I have."

Cali held her breath.

"Neither have I," Odo agreed.

O'Brien sounded concerned. "What did you find on the passenger liner?"

"No one noticed anything unusual before or during the time the stasis broke," Odo admitted. "And there are no internal sensor logs."

Cali was leaning so far forward that she risked being seen through the open hatchway.

"You're the detective," O'Brien tossed off. "But I think anything's possible when there's this much turbulence. Stasis lines do have tolerance limits. And Major Kira says that a few vessels are reporting problems with their airlock seals."

"Hmmm . . . perhaps you're right," Odo conceded.

Cali sat back grinning to herself.

"Now that you bring it up, I am worried about the other ships that are tethered by stasis lines," O'Brien added. "There were seven people injured inside the freighter, and they were lucky they all weren't killed. We're adding more lines to the other ships, but who knows what could happen once the storm hits."

"Perhaps we should recommend that the ships be evacuated."

"Some of them are docked safely," O'Brien protested, "but we probably should warn the vessels that are at higher risk. After all, you don't want to flood the station with a complete evacuation . . ."

Cali strained to hear as the voices faded. "We might have to find a way," Odo was saying. "If that storm is as bad as they . . ."

Cali listened for a moment longer, then took a chance and slipped down the ladder, dropping into a crouch in the main corridor of the docking ring. Looking both ways, she stayed low as she ran in the opposite direction from Odo and O'Brien.

After the overwhelming response of the repair crews, Cali was expecting it to be a real challenge to get out of the section. But she easily ran the security blockade, hardly needing the help of Theosi, who was loyally positioned nearby. The diversion required that only one of their members was detected by security, and he was released with a slap on the wrist.

Cali deployed her members ahead and behind, running tandem with Theosi through the docking ring. After all the deals she had pulled, there were probably a dozen unofficial contracts out on her, and any one of these stranded crew members could be looking for just that sort of latinum. She would have preferred to move through the service tunnels, but that was one thing the shapeshifter was good at—you could get in, but you couldn't travel between the sections. Then again, it made sense for them to lock the station down fairly tight. They were sitting on top of the wormhole, like a nice, big, fat target. At least, that's how Captain Ari put it.

At the airlock to the *Reaper,* Cali got word that her negotiation team had signed the contract for the chemical transport. She was pleased. This deal had gone smoothly from start to finish.

She was allowed into the captain's lounge without being announced. Not every senior mate could claim that privilege.

Despite her excitement, Cali slowed as she entered,

according the place the reverence it deserved. There was nothing Klingon about the captain's lounge, with its rounded walls and clear blue lighting—even the smell of polflowers on a warm afternoon.

Ari stayed seated, folding his data clip. He peered up at her for a moment, then smiled. "So you've done it again?"

Cali answered with a laugh. "It worked exactly as I planned."

Ari's expression was both admiring and pleased, without a trace of surprise, as if Cali's success was nothing more than he expected. The other seniors sometimes tried to advise her in her methods, as if any of them had completed a fraction of her deals! But Ari seldom presumed to offer advice. She had her high position among the crew partly because it was her inheritance, but also because the captain recognized her abilities. Ari encouraged her to push herself, agreeing that it was not her fault she was not talented at the administrative details of the vessel. But what did that matter, when her brilliant deals were beginning to be talked about among the other members of the Sattar Collective?

"Name your bonus," Ari told her. "With a contract this large, I presume you want a tithe."

Cali shook her head. "I'll take an option on a deal of my own."

Ari was immediately intrigued. "Do you have anything in mind?"

"Not yet, but there's plenty of action around here. We'll leave the terms open."

"Short-term option," Ari countered.

Cali shrugged. If she couldn't find anything of her own before they left then she didn't deserve a longer option. "Now I have a bonus for you," she told her captain. "I heard the chief of operations talking about the freighter. They believe it broke loose in the storm. We'll probably get a warning to evacuate our ship."

"Under galactic shipping codes, only the captain can order the evacuation of his crew. That is, unless the ship is improperly docked."

"Well, that's what they said," Cali insisted. "You know Starfleet. Out to save the galaxy from itself."

Ari pushed himself from the anti-grav chair and paced to the port window, considering the information. "Even if it's only a recommendation, it may be enough . . ."

Cali caught the scent of a deal in the air. She eagerly watched the captain, waiting for him to indicate whether he would ask her to join.

When Ari turned, she knew the news would be good.

"I think it's time we visited Commander Worf," Ari told her. "He has a debt of honor to repay to the Sattar Collective."

CHAPTER 7

DAX BELIEVED THAT one of the best ways to get to know somebody was to go on a long shuttle trip with them. She had figured that out while she was a cadet at Starfleet Academy, where she had been introduced to the concept of the two-person team.

During the past few months, since she had resolved things with Curzon, she was better able to appreciate the fact that she had attended the academy simply as Jadzia. After being kicked out of the Symbiont Institute on Trill, where the focus had been on generating competition among the initiates, it was a joy learning how to cooperate with others.

"Nearing the storm front at ten thousand kilometers," Dax announced. "How bad is that graviton interference?"

"It's holding steady now that the bleed has been boosted," Keiko confirmed.

Dax could already tell that Keiko was an competent technician, their first flurry of stabilizer adjustments had proved that, and her meticulous handling of Ops indicated that she was a perfectionist. But Keiko herself was still a mystery, not only to Dax but to a lot of people on DS9. Maybe even to Chief O'Brien.

"Leeta says you're going to be on the survey for another few months," Dax commented. "How is it going?"

"Oh, we're making progress." When Dax made it clear she was waiting for more, Keiko added, "Actually we're working so well together that Starfleet expanded the survey to include the archipelago of the southern continent. We're finding some rich calcium-complex vegetation that grows in the wet climate along the coast."

"So you like being on Bajor."

Keiko smiled at the non-question. "It's tough moving around with the survey team, never in the same place for more than a few weeks. But the work itself is fascinating." Then she sighed. "I guess you can't have everything . . ."

"Why not?" Dax asked.

Keiko looked at her. "For one thing, it's physically impossible to be on the station and Bajor at the same time."

Dax concentrated on the helm, letting Keiko's answer fall lightly into silence. She sympathized with Keiko's dilemma.

"Was Molly all right when you left her?" Dax asked.

"She'll be fine." Keiko acted as if leaving her was perfectly natural, though Dax knew that mother and daughter were seldom apart. "I activated the pony program, even though I swore I'd make her wait until tomorrow." She checked the chronometer. "It'll be over soon, and then the nanny program can deal with her. Miles doesn't know how lucky he is."

"He didn't look so happy standing on the service pad."

Keiko shrugged. "You have to admit it happened awfully fast. He was surprised, that's all."

Dax grinned. "I'd say it was fast! He was still trying to ask about radiation levels when you shut the hatch in his face."

Keiko looked uncomfortable, as if her mask had slipped. Dax remembered the way she had stared at the image of O'Brien on the viewscreen as the *Rubicon* rose to the launch padd. The chief kept waving until they were out of sight. Only then had Keiko taken a deep breath and returned to the launch sequence.

"I wonder how they're doing with that freighter," Keiko said.

Dax checked the station logs. "It's been secured. But Captain Sisko has issued an evacuation recommendation to all vessels below class two, due to the turbulence."

Keiko's eyes widened. "I thought there were no more quarters available on the station."

"There aren't." Dax frowned over the sensor data, as the runabout shook from the emission waves. "If the shock waves are this bad out here, what about the turbulence within the storm?"

Keiko glanced at the viewscreen. The pure, velvety black mass blocked out most of the starfield, but the leading edge was defined by veins of flashing energy discharge, marking the point where the plasma encountered normal space matter.

"Slowing to half impulse," Dax said. "The shock waves are getting stronger."

"Sensors are calibrated," Keiko confirmed. "The link to the biometric program is engaged. We're getting additional data on a wide range of Doppler shifts."

Dax prepared a burst transmission to send the new data back to the station. Communications would probably be lost once they were inside the storm.

"This close," Dax said thoughtfully. "I thought we would encounter line and recombination radiation. Even with a reflection level as low as one percent we should be getting *something* on the interior of the storm."

"There are those energy discharges along the edge," Keiko indicated. "The filaments are being spectrally recorded, but we have no background comparison with the main body of the plasma mass."

"So we can't tell if particles are being excited or emitted."

"It's an ideal blackbody," Keiko agreed. "Rates of

absorption and emission are the same. I wonder what's happening inside."

"My guess is that it's rotating on its own axis," Dax told her.

Keiko widened her eyes. "I didn't think plasma did that in a natural vacuum."

"Why else can't we get a fix on the wavelength angles?" Dax had finally thrown out Planck's law after wrestling with that impossible variable for most of the afternoon, trying to phase the momentum with value of energy release. "This isn't getting us anywhere. The spectroscopic analysis is giving us the same readings on the emissions that we got on the station: helium, carbon, nitrogen, oxygen, sulfur, calcium."

"It's the bulk of the interior elements we need to determine," Keiko agreed.

"All right, here we go," Dax announced. "Electrostatic field engaged."

"Spectral index is well within parameters," Keiko confirmed. "Both waves and particles are being polarized away from the runabout."

"Prepare to enter the plasma field."

Dax maneuvered the runabout in a vector that would sharply intersect the edge of the storm. She didn't want to risk deflection, unsure what effect that impact would have on the hull. She was also concerned about what might be concealed within the plasma. An ideal blackbody was theoretically impossible without a source of stabilized electric discharge. There was a distinct possibility that a comet-like pulsar or neutron star was at the heart of the storm, and if so, then the gravitational forces could easily overpower the runabout once they entered.

Dax glanced at Keiko, wondering if she should share that nasty piece of information. She had included it in the burst transmission to DS9 because the station needed to be warned of the possibility. But it was too late for them to turn back now.

"Sensors at maximum sensitivity," Keiko announced. "Prepared for entry."

"You know," Dax said, "there is a chance the hull could be crushed by the internal turbulence."

Keiko held her gaze. "If the storm is that strong, then the station won't be able to withstand the pressure either. We need to find out."

"You're right about that. I'm taking us in." Dax hit the thrusters and held on.

But the runabout penetrated the storm without a shudder. Helm control remained steady, while navigational orientation began to swing aimlessly around the chart, as if searching for some verifiable indicator to establish their position. Sensors were unable to penetrate the border of the storm.

Keiko switched the viewscreen to spectral-visual. "Look at that . . ."

Inside the blackbody, the plasma was alive. Constant re-ionization released photoconductive electrons, creating spectral colors within, and even beyond, humanoid sight. Other complex optical effects produced brilliant fluorescent streaks and luminescent flickers of light that twisted and swirled together in the hydrodynamic currents.

Dax slowed the runabout and released a dye marker to give their sensors a ground point. At first she was unsure if they were moving, then she realized the marker was cruising along at about the same speed they were.

She altered their course, concerned about the power spikes as particles and waves struck their electrostatic shields. She reminded herself to watch the relays to make sure the circuits didn't overload.

"I've narrowed the range on the sensors," Keiko announced. "But the interference is still too great to get anything beyond the most rudimentary readings."

"That's plasma for you," Dax said philosophically. "We need to isolate our targets."

Using the molecular beam, she released gas particles into the plasma. The computer would track the progress of their collisions and decomposition into charged electrons and photons.

"Keep an eye on the ternary collisions," Dax told Keiko, indicating the correct equation sequence. "Let me know if the cluster integrals get any larger."

"They already have," Keiko immediately replied.

"That fast?" Dax asked, having a look for herself. "This is some plasma storm."

She carefully recorded the thruster action against the movement of the released particles. They revealed an approximate reading of both longitudinal and transverse waves within the plasma, though the splitting of Alfven waves was recorded to the detriment of other variables, filling their data banks with random frequencies.

"Well, according to the gas particles, the plasma is rotating as a mass." Dax was glad to finally confirm one of her hunches about the storm. "It must be releasing huge amounts of rotational energy, approximately ten to the sixty-seventh power ergs per second. That's what supplies the relativistic particles and magnetic fields to sustain the storm."

"It's building on itself," Keiko realized.

"That's right, it's picking up particles through inverse Compton scattering. That keeps it moving in a steady vector." Dax returned to her readings. "I'll see if I can determine the oscillation distribution of the waves. That might give us a base frequency we can work with, but we'll need to isolate a sample of the plasma."

"How do you do that with charged particles that are in a constant state of flux?" Keiko asked.

"Usually we'd use the EGD converter. But the plasma is so dense that our power systems can't create a high enough electric field to contain the stuff." Dax grimly shook her head. "Maybe we should have brought the *Defiant* after all."

"Is there any other way to get a sample?" Keiko asked.

"Well, we could try a plasma trap," Dax decided.

She spent some time attempting to draw a sample of the plasma into a ring-shaped magnetic field. Despite the high temperatures of the trap, containment of the dense plasma was limited to fractions of microseconds. A bulge kept forming along the lateral surface, instantaneously extending tongues of plasma within the trap and disappearing on contact with the container walls.

"It's too unstable," Dax said. "Maybe I can create an open trap using two magnetic mirrors. That might contain the plasma long enough to get a sensor scan on it."

"Anything I can do?" Keiko asked.

"In a minute," Dax told her. "Let me just set this up."

Keiko got up to pace in the back of the runabout until Dax called her to return to the sensors.

"I'm establishing the trap in a vacuum field just outside the starboard hull. Look for patterns," Dax told her, ready to grasp at any straw. "Check number densities, temperatures, electric, and magnetic field strengths. We mainly need to determine the trajectory of relative particles."

"The ratio of negative and positive charges per unit volume are fairly equal," Keiko offered. "Though the numbers keep shifting."

"That's typical in high-density plasmas." Dax was preoccupied with the phase ratios. "That's why we get macroscopic readings rather than the motion of individual particles."

Keiko sighed and sat back in her chair. "Maybe I shouldn't have tried so hard to convince Captain Sisko to let me come. I'm not being much help."

"This isn't your part of the mission," Dax pointed

out. "It's mine, and I haven't been very successful. You're here because you're the most qualified person to analyze the data once I've gotten it."

Keiko let out an exasperated sound. "Then why did I have to fight so hard to get the captain's permission?"

"Benjamin was just worried about Molly," Dax tried to explain.

"Oh, I don't blame him for asking about Molly. How could he ignore her when she was practically jumping up and down on his feet?" Keiko turned to Dax. "But what does Miles have to do with it? I mean, really. Does anyone call and ask me how I feel every time he crawls into a fusion generator?"

"No . . ." Dax hesitated, but it needed to be said. "Try to look at it from Captain Sisko's perspective. After all, he did lose his wife during a mission."

Keiko returned to her console. "That's true. Don't mind me, I've been like this ever since I left Bajor. I hate to be interrupted when I'm in the middle of a project."

"Well, then, let's get on with this one," Dax said, smoothing things over. "I'm taking us in deeper."

She engaged thrusters. Temperatures rose as the plasma became denser.

"Here's something," Keiko said. "Helix patterns."

"Where?" Dax demanded. She examined the readings. "Magnetic lines of force. That's consistent with synchronic radiation but . . ."

"But what?"

"Look at the total heat flux. And the thermal energy

transported within the unit area. It's building, as if there's some other factor acting on the—"

The *Rubicon* lurched and a blinding flash of light shorted the viewscreen. Dax squeezed her eyes shut, covering her face with her hands.

Even when the emergency lights came on, she could barely see through the red spots in her vision.

"Computer is off line!" Keiko exclaimed.

Dax didn't breathe until the indicator signaled that the computer core was powering up again.

"Electrostatic field remains intact," Keiko added breathlessly.

That was exactly what Dax wanted to hear. The interior support systems came back on as indicators returned to normal—except for the viewscreen. She would have to replace the circuit buffer first and increase the repulsion of the electrostatic guard to keep the same thing from happening again.

"What was *that?*" Keiko asked.

"I'm not sure. But look. The sensors recorded the entire electromagnetic frequency range for the duration of the burst."

"Finally!" Keiko exclaimed. "That gives us the data we need to run a comparison against the biometric models."

Dax wasn't as pleased as Keiko. She wanted to know exactly what had happened. She slowed the sensor logs and saw what she had been dreading: fifty nanoseconds before the burst of light, a faint luminous current on the order of several hundred thousand amperes had created a stepped leader between the runabout and the plasma. The runabout acted as the ground, releasing an outward discharge, short-circuiting the plasma that was in magnetic flux around them. The white flash had been just one of the secondary results.

"There was a direct energy discharge between the plasma and the runabout," she told Keiko.

"I thought the electrostatic field would prevent that."

"Apparently the magnetic currents are strong enough to override our power systems." Dax considered the readings. "In fact, there's no way we can compensate for the reaction unless we completely shut off the shields. And the radiation levels make that impossible."

"If the runabout can destabilize the plasma, what will the station do to it?" Keiko asked. "Will the shields hold?"

"It's not just the station. What about the wormhole?" Dax countered.

"They might both act as electrodes," Keiko realized. "That would mean—"

"A plasma arc as big as Bajor."

"With everything in between instantly ionized." A flicker of her eyes betrayed her immediate thought of Molly. "We have to get back to the station to warn them. Everyone should be evacuated."

Dax was already activating the helm. "Impact with the magnetic currents could burn out the wormhole permanently. Or the plasma could be caught in its gravitational flux, which means the entire system would be covered by a self-generating plasma storm for the next few centuries."

"Bajor," Keiko whispered.

Dax couldn't understand the navigational sequence that she was getting. "We must have been thrown some distance by the discharge."

Keiko could tell something was wrong. Dax couldn't find the dye marker, and the angle of the transverse waves had altered.

"That wasn't just a magnetic field we ran into," Dax finally concluded. "The currents are being twisted into loops by the cyclonic turbulence. We've been transported deep inside the storm. I'm not even sure where we are."

"We couldn't have gone far," Keiko protested. "It lasted less than a second."

"I don't know. A reaction like that, involving high-intensity heat conduction and Coriolis forces from the rotation—it could have produced space-time variances within the magnetic loop."

Keiko was also checking the rudimentary readings of the sensors. "Particle and wave density are much higher in this area. And there's no sign of the dye marker or the gas particles we released."

"From the number of magnetic currents, I'd say we were much closer to the center of the storm."

"That can't be true!" Keiko insisted. "That would be faster than light—"

"Theory of relativity? You might as well forget

about that. Our time scale depends on our frame of reference. Inside the blackbody, our only reference is this highly charged, high-temperature energy matter."

"But the storm covers nearly half a sector!" Keiko looked as though she didn't know which way to turn. "It could take us a week to cross it at impulse."

"*If* we could figure out which way to go." Dax watched the particles perform their colored dance, flashing as if they were laughing at the runabout.

"What are we going to do?" Keiko finally asked.

"We're going to have to find a quicker way out of here. Unless you're willing to let a plasma storm get the better of us?"

Keiko's eyes flashed in return. "Never!"

Dax took a deep breath. "Then let's get to work."

CHAPTER 8

AFTER THE FREIGHTER was secured and Worf returned the runabout to the service pad, he made his way to his quarters. Even when the door shut on the evacuees who filled the corridor, he continued to feel stifled by the invasive grip of the station. He had been content while piloting the runabout, despite the adverse conditions, yet he did not realize it until he returned . . . here. He could hardly call it *home.*

As soon as he entered, he sat down at the computer. "Worf to Odo. What is your status?" During the tediously long time it had taken to secure the freighter, he had received regular reports from the technicians on their lack of success in deactivating the *Katon*'s airlock system.

Odo replied by audio only. "Things are proceeding

normally, Commander. The initial security bypass systems have been accessed."

"When will the airlock be opened?"

"We aren't changing an air filter, Commander. These are complex mechanical and security overrides. I remember one time it took more than twenty-two hours." Odo paused to make himself clear. "But you can rest assured. That lock will open."

"Understood."

"Good. Then let me get back to my business."

Worf did not bother to reply, cutting the transmission at Odo's request. He saw it as yet another example of everyone's lack of concern about the Klingon aggression. He was the only one who realized that time was running out.

He signaled the *Katon.* When they were slow to respond, he signaled them again.

While he waited for a response, he put in a replicator order. The computer indicated that there would be a delay before the food would be delivered. He had considered stopping by the replimat sometime during the afternoon, but he loathed the place. Its generic decor and nameless hordes were almost as bad as Quark's Bar.

Digging through transport containers that were piled in his closet, he finally found a bottle of *Hum'taS.* It was a favorite Klingon drink, a sticky, honey-based liquid that imparted a boost of energy. Deanna had brought it for him when she had returned from a week-long diplomatic junket on one of the Empire colonies. He wasn't sure if the gift had been meant as a joke, but to be prudent he had refrained from telling her that the stuff put his teeth on edge.

Now he was glad to have it. He took a long swig directly from the narrow neck, shuddering as he swallowed.

He went to the sink and splashed some water on his tender eyes, and managed to get down half the bottle by the time the *Katon* finally responded. He almost choked in his haste, but he made it to his desk without spitting the *Hum'taS* down the front of his uniform. Despite his wash, it felt like the stuff was stuck to his *loch,* and somehow his sash had slipped askew.

But Captain Alons looked even worse. In fact, the change was alarming. His heavy uniform was unhooked and swinging open—unthinkable for a Klingon seated in the command chair. His eyes were tiny red slits and his brow ridges were running with sweat. It took a lot to make a Klingon sweat.

Alons was slumped and looking off to one side as if unaware that he had activated visuals. "What is it?" he demanded impatiently.

"This is to inform you that the turbulence from the storm is making it hazardous for your crew to remain on board."

"Yes, yes. We received the warning. What of it?"

Worf offered, "Temporary quarters for you and your crew—"

Alons suddenly realized exactly who he was speaking to. He leaned forward, unsteady in his focus on the viewer. "You! You can do nothing for me."

Worf was compelled to maintain an attitude of

civility and cooperation, much as he wanted to reach through the viewer and grab Alons by the throat to choke some of the arrogance out of him.

"Captain Alons, you appear to be ill," Worf said reasonably. "Perhaps you are unable to judge the seriousness of this warning."

"Enough!" Alons slammed his hand on the arm of the chair. His head was shaking with the effort. "I will not listen to the lies of *Qu'vatlh!*"

The viewer returned to the blue Starfleet symbol. Worf restrained himself from hailing the *Katon* again. Alons would never cooperate with him, that much was clear.

Worf sent a copy of the conversation to Dr. Bashir, requesting his medical opinion on Alons's condition. Perhaps the captain had simply been called away in the middle of a *bat'leth* match, and yet, if Alons was unfit, Worf might be able to use that to get permission to board the *Katon*.

He was pulling off his uniform when the door signaled. He paused, the sash over his head. "Who is it?"

"Captain Ari, of the *Reaper,*" was the courteous reply.

Worf pulled his sash back on, settling it before saying, "Come in."

The door opened, letting in two Sattar. Cali returned his dubious look while Captain Ari introduced himself. The captain was short even for a Sattar, and only the darkened fuzz around his nose and eyes indicated his age.

"We apologize for disturbing you in your quarters," Captain Ari said. His voice was surprisingly sonorous for such a small creature.

Worf grunted an acknowledgement, distracted by his effort to keep Cali in view as she began roaming around the room, frankly examining the few possessions he had unpacked.

Captain Ari ignored his senior mate. "I felt it was high time we met, Commander Worf. This situation has remained unresolved for long enough."

Worf shifted as Cali moved behind him. She paused next to the replicator, and pointedly met his eyes.

"The replicator is malfunctioning," Worf said. When she glanced at the open bottle on his desk, he grudgingly told the captain, "However I can offer you *Hum'taS.*"

"Thank you," Ari accepted, taking a seat in the best chair. That is, Worf assumed it was the best chair since the senior Sattar had chosen it. He had not spent enough time in his new quarters to determine that for himself.

He grabbed the bottle, then glanced around, realizing that he had no containers for the liquid. He usually ordered serviceware from the replicator.

"There are no cups," he admitted.

Cali's short laugh was insulting. His lip curled as he stared her down.

Ari simply held out his hand for the bottle. "I'll join you, Commander. That is, if you don't mind."

Worf gave it to him, astonished. He never expected a Sattar to be so familiar with a Klingon.

Ari lifted the bottle and took a hefty swig, respectable even for a Klingon. Cali watched the captain with an expression of fascinated repulsion, while Worf reassessed the elder Sattar. *This one is not bound by the conceits of his own people.*

Ari's eyes flashed back at Worf, an unexpected moment of accord. "Join me for a moment, Commander."

Worf hesitated to sit down while Cali was searching his quarters. Without a word, Ari understood. He motioned with his head and Cali returned to lean on the back of his chair. She was facing away, as if uninterested in what they had to say. But Worf noticed that she kept a cautious eye on him as he sat down across from Ari.

The captain didn't waste words. "You have placed us in a terrible bind, Commander Worf. By delaying our clearance, you have caused us to lose our contract in the Gamma Quadrant."

Worf was not going to discuss his investigation of the attack on the *Ceres*. Not when the *Katon* situation remained unresolved. "The delay was unavoidable."

"Perhaps we differ on that point." Ari raised one hand as if to stop Worf from arguing. Worf noticed there were tiny swirls of fur even on the Sattar's palm. "I will say no more about it," Ari continued. "However I would like to ask you to do us a favor."

Worf immediately stiffened. "Is that . . . blackmail?"

"Commander Worf!" Ari protested, laughing. "Please don't misunderstand me. I simply came here to ask you for a personal favor. Your captain has sent us a warning to evacuate my crew to the station, yet I find I'm in the unenviable position of having nowhere to go."

"Major Kira is supervising the arrangements for temporary quarters."

Ari wrinkled his nose. "Please, Commander. Those cargo bays are fine for my members, but you must take into account the ways of the Sattar Collective. A captain's status is maintained through a strict hierarchy. You examined my ship, you saw the levels of accommodations. For me to be thrown together with not only my members, but among others, the lowest crews of alien vessels . . . well, it just wouldn't do."

"I see." But Worf did not see what this had to do with him.

"Breaking our social codes could disrupt the entire fabric of my command. And I'm sure Starfleet didn't intend to violate our cultural dictates with their evacuation order."

"Of course not," Worf said. "The evacuation warning is not mandatory. You may remain on board your vessel if you wish."

Captain Ari leaned back, glancing up at Cali. She was glaring at Worf as if resenting the suggestion.

"I believe you once thought my transport was capable of great feats," Ari said quietly. "But if any vessel is likely to buckle under the forces of the plasma storm, I'm afraid it's the *Reaper*. No, Commander, I do not wish to stay on board while that happens."

"No, of course not," Worf repeated, at a loss. "However I do not know how I can assist you."

"This will do quite well," Ari said, as if satisfied.

"What will?" Worf asked.

"This." Ari gestured to the room. "Your quarters. If you allow me to remain here tonight, I would be most appreciative."

Worf drew back. "Here? You want to stay here?"

"I believe most of the personnel on the station are sharing their quarters with evacuees, is that not correct?"

"Yes." Worf blinked for a moment. "That is—Yes, you may stay here."

He thoroughly disliked it, but he saw no other option. He should have offered his quarters to the crew of the *Ceres,* except he had difficultly thinking of these Cardassian rooms as *his.* He almost longed for the bare cell in the monastery on Boreth.

The replicator chimed and a thick slice of rokeg blood pie appeared.

"Malfunctioning, huh?" Cali smoldered, as if she disliked the situation as much as he did.

"Yes." His visions of a relaxing meal disappeared. He wondered if Cali was staying here tonight as well. Awkwardly, he stood up, unsure of what to do next.

Captain Ari smiled and waved a dismissive hand at him. "Don't mind us, Commander. Just go about your business."

"Yes." Worf wished he could think of something better to say.

"We *would* like something to eat," Cali said pointedly.

Worf was saved from answering by the flashing yellow alert. Since he was not summoned, he knew it had nothing to do with security.

Nevertheless, he used his clearance code to access Ops, shifting to block the viewer when Cali tried to see what was happening. There was a power conduit failure in the lower core and O'Brien had ordered an emergency shutdown of the aft generator.

That would leave only one generator to create power for the station. "Worf to O'Brien."

"I could use your help, Worf," O'Brien replied shortly, sounding as if he was running. "Can you meet me in the lower core?"

Worf acknowledged. He stood up, then hesitated, ordering, "Computer, allow Captain Ari access to my quarters."

As the computer confirmed the order, Ari gave Worf a quizzical look. "Thank you, Commander."

Worf did not care about anything in his quarters, or about the place itself, for that matter. But as he reached the door, he did glance back at the tempting slice of blood pie.

Cali noticed and immediately returned to the replicator. *"Ro'gegh'Iwchab!* How thoughtful of you."

She picked up the plate, smiling.

Worf left. He had the distinct feeling that she had gotten the better of him.

* * *

When O'Brien reached the main grid of the power plant, he knew he had a bigger problem than he had first thought.

His technicians were taking the aft fusion reactor off line and being extremely cautious, to boot. The containment of the silicon-sodium reaction was always difficult at the best of times.

But the real problem now was the power conduit leading to crossover bridge two. The wave guides had been disrupted from their alignment, and the power bleed was wedging open the distribution amplifier.

"We aren't going to be able to shut down the power stream until that amplifier outlet is closed," O'Brien reminded the technicians.

Lieutenant Kelly replied for both the Bajoran supernumeraries and Starfleet personnel. "We're trying to reroute the bleed by closing an upper junction node."

"Keep me informed," O'Brien ordered. They had all been working since morning and were more than ready for the shift change, yet he didn't hear a grumble among them.

He was reading the grid as he said, "O'Brien to Sisko."

"Sisko, here. What's your status, Chief?"

"Once the reactor is down, it won't take more than a couple of hours to recalibrate the wave guides in conduit two."

"Will one reactor provide enough power during that time?" Sisko asked.

"Well, we're running shields at maximum. I recommend we cut power to nonessential systems. We don't know how much we'll need once the storm hits."

"Very well," Sisko said.

O'Brien resisted the temptation to ask if they had heard from the *Rubicon.* "Oh, and you better shut the airlocks to the connecting tunnel. There's a jammed power bleed that could be leaking free radicals."

Kira suddenly spoke up, "We have reports that there are evacuees camped in all three crossover bridges—"

"You mean there are people in there? Just *sitting* in there?" O'Brien clutched his hair with one hand. "You've got to get them out!"

Worf approached the power grid. "May I assist, Chief?"

"Yes! Quick—clear everyone out of the second tunnel," O'Brien ordered. "And wear stasis belts. There's radiation leakage. And seal the airlocks!" he called after Worf, as the Klingon rapidly strode toward the turbolift, giving orders through his comm badge.

O'Brien reached for a tool kit as he hit his own badge. "Kira, transport me to the main junction node. If I don't get that amplifier shut, those people will be fried."

"Ready to energize," Kira confirmed.

The power plant dissolved into a golden glow as he was caught in the familiar grip of the transporter beam. At the last second he panicked, afraid that the transporter buffers weren't any better shielded than the power conduit. If there was significant interference from the emission waves, he could end up as *part* of the storm.

But he rematerialized safely on the narrow platform outside the maintenance tunnel. He rapidly tapped in his code, but the door didn't budge. The emergency shutdown sequence for the reactor had sealed the access because of excessive radiation leakage.

Out of habit, O'Brien glanced up. "Kira, I want you to find Rom. Tell him I need him here *now*. You can transport him to my signal—"

"Quark is answering," Kira interrupted.

"You tell him that if he doesn't send Rom down here now, I'll have him up on charges of murder."

"Understood," Kira acknowledged.

O'Brien took one breath and then another. "Come on, come on," he muttered.

The distortion of a transporter beam appeared next to him. Rom materialized, hunched over and looking worried. O'Brien could only imagine what Quark had been saying to his brother as he dematerialized.

"Hi there, Chief—" Rom started to say.

"Open this door! You have ten seconds." O'Brien ripped off the top of the access panel to the sealed door.

"What?" Slack jawed, Rom looked from him to the exposed circuitry. "Why don't you use your security bypass?"

"That would take two minutes. And you only have five seconds left."

Rom leaped for the panel, grabbing an isolinear

manipulator from O'Brien in mid air. When he bent over the circuitry he was a changed man, with every meticulous motion steady.

Since he seemed to work well under pressure, O'Brien warned him, "Three seconds."

He never imagined that Rom could do it. He had just been babbling off the top of his head to get the Ferengi moving, but as the word "one" hit his lips, the door slid open.

Rom was panting, his mouth hanging open.

O'Brien stared at him in shock. "You did it!"

"You said you wanted it open," Rom reminded him.

"Amazing! And you don't even know it." O'Brien pushed past Rom, ducking to enter the low maintenance tunnel.

But he immediately bumped into a hanging obstacle. Trying to see, he realized an entire Temmorian pod had slung their hammocks in the tunnel between him and the manual seal.

"What are you doing in here! Get out of here, you understand? Out!" He started crawling under them, wincing at the squeals of surprise as they jumped from their hammocks, getting in his way even more.

"Move it!" he roared. "This is an emergency!"

They obligingly tried to get out of his way, but O'Brien kept bumping into them, even stepping on them, and he was afraid he'd killed a few by the time he reached the amplifier. He groaned as he tried to turn the wheel. Throwing his entire weight into it, he felt something strain in his back as it finally shifted.

The amplifier made horrible creaking and screeching noises as he manually tightened the valve. Then he gave it an extra tug to make sure it was clamped shut.

Falling back against the curved wall, he tapped his comm badge. "Manual seal is in place. You can take the reactor off line."

"Confirmed," Lieutenant Kelly answered. "Conduit two is sealed."

O'Brien drew back from a sleepy Temmorian who peered close into his face. They didn't have the best eyesight.

"You have to leave the serviceway," he told the closest ones. An entire pod, babies and all, sleeping in the maintenance tunnel leading to the fusion generator. *Bloody Hell. Don't people know how to take care of their kids—*

"Good God—Molly!" he exclaimed.

Several Temmorians flinched, but he starting pushing his way back through them. If power was shut down to nonessential systems that meant Quark's holosuites would be turned off. That meant Molly was locked in a tiny room with gridded walls, probably crying her eyes out.

"Make way!" he yelled, speeding up.

He catapulted through the access door, barely breaking stride as he ran over Rom. "Get them out of there!" he ordered over his shoulder as he bolted toward the turbolift.

"Aye, aye, sir!" Rom sang out, obviously quite pleased to be given the responsibility.

Later, O'Brien had time to wonder exactly how long

it had taken him to reach Quark's from the lower core. He was sure he would never be able to beat his time, but while it was happening it felt like an eternity was passing as he shoved his way through the evacuees, ordering everyone to stand aside, yelling out that it was an emergency.

Quark's was even more crowded than the Promenade, and O'Brien had the odd sensation that his own living room had suddenly been overrun by strangers. Quark's always had its fair share of transient business, but this was entirely different. The chief didn't recognize anyone except for the harried staff.

Then he caught sight of Morn, precariously perched on a stool in the corner below the stairs and looking very unhappy. Apparently loyalty to your regular customers wasn't high on the list of the Ferengi Rules of Acquisition.

When he keyed open the lock on the holosuite, Molly was crying just as he had expected.

"Why, Daddy? Why?" she kept asking.

He picked her up, trying to explain. "We needed the power for lights and food."

"But why, Daddy? Why didn't you come? I called and called." She was crying as if she would never stop. "I want my mommy!"

"Hey, Molly, honey, I'm here now. It's okay." He held her and rocked her and tried to soothe her. "I did come for you."

"I called and called," she insisted.

He felt inordinately guilty, and directly responsible. After all, it had been his order to cut nonessential power. But Molly relaxed, letting her head fall on his shoulder. She was still crying, but the frantic edge was gone.

Not that anyone in Quark's would notice a crying baby. O'Brien carried Molly down from the mezzanine and started pushing through the crowd. You'd think people would see the child and move aside for him, but they were obviously having too much fun to actually open their eyes and look around.

"Hey! Back off there, buddy!" O'Brien ordered a particularly wobbly Bajoran.

From out of nowhere Quark appeared. "Stop pushing my customers around, O'Brien. And where's that brother of mine? You have to send him back, I need him here."

"Doesn't this place have a capacity rating?" O'Brien shot back. "This many people can't be safe."

Quark looked smug. "If I'm right, this entire station is over its capacity. Starfleet can't point any fingers at me." He sighed. "Business has never been better."

"I've heard what you're doing," O'Brien told him. "You're charging three times the regular price for everything."

"Supply and demand," Quark said, holding out his hands as if he didn't make the rules. "I charge what the market can bear."

"You mean you fleece the customers for all they're worth."

"Whatever." Quark leaned in conspiratorially. "See what you can do about getting the power to the holosuites back on. I'm losing latinum as we speak." He gestured with his chin to Molly. "I'll let you keep using one of them for the kid."

O'Brien wouldn't compromise the safety of the power grid, even for Molly. "Is Leeta here? I want her to watch Molly for me."

"She's here and *here* she stays," Quark retorted. "You can get away with that 'life or death' excuse to take one of my employees, but you can't take two. That would kill *me.*"

"But she's the only one I can trust who isn't on duty," O'Brien protested, keeping his voice low, trying to keep from disturbing Molly. She was limp and had finally stopped crying.

"Leeta *is* on duty." Quark pointed. "See, she's spinning the wheel for my customers, while lots of other customers are waiting their turn. I need more help around here, O'Brien, not less."

"Fine! Now what am I supposed to do?" O'Brien patted Molly's back, trying to think.

"Leave her on the bar," Quark shrugged. "Somebody's bound to look after her."

A passing Risan woman overheard and she lurched in closer, exclaiming over Molly. "How sweet! If you're giving her away, I'll take care of her."

A man tugged at the Risan's arm, stopping to give Molly a cursory glance. "Take her if you want. Only let's get back to the tables."

Molly chose that moment to raise her head. "I'm Mol-ee. What's your name?"

"Oooo," the Risan cooed. "I *love* her."

"There you go," Quark said, as if that settled it. "But you better get those holosuites back on."

O'Brien turned, pulling Molly away from the reaching hands of the Risan. "Thanks so much, but we have to go now."

"Please," the woman wheedled with practiced charm. "Just for a minute. I only want to hold her."

"No, sorry, we're very late. Thank you. Good-bye." O'Brien got away from her as fast as he could, pushing through the crowd as she gave a halfhearted pursuit.

The security office was just across the Promenade. O'Brien joined the streaming crowds, plotting a course that would get him there with a minimum of fuss. Every piece of floor space was taken, with only narrow aisles left between the people who were sitting, lying down, piled together, all watching each other. Up above, the mezzanine was lined with a mixed assortment of humanoids, each staking out territory in his own way. Several Marlkins were even perched on the railing, kicking their heels as O'Brien passed underneath.

Molly cringed at the echoing noise, covering her ears. It was terrible even with full baffles engaged, and he could tell the air quality was high on carbon dioxide. He reminded himself to adjust the exchange rate as soon as he got back to Ops.

He hugged Molly closer, protecting her from the jostling, until he finally reached security.

Odo's office was busy with security teams, both

Bajoran and Starfleet. O'Brien was glad to see that Odo was there, apparently unflustered by the activity. He set Molly down on the chair in front of the desk, ignoring the constable's sharp look.

"You curl up here, honey," he told Molly. "I'll be back soon to take you home."

"Excuse me?" Odo asked.

"I want to go with you," Molly protested.

"Be a good girl for Daddy," he told his daughter, hoping Odo would get the message. "I've got to run around and do a few more things before we can both go home. Will you promise to stay right here?"

Molly wrinkled her tiny brow, considering him, then Odo.

"Odo's a good friend of mine," O'Brien added. "You'll have fun waiting here, and I'll be back soon."

Molly finally gave a short, decisive nod, but she asked, "Where's Mommy?"

O'Brien hesitated, glancing up at Odo. "Any word from the *Rubicon?*"

Odo briefly shook his head. "The interference is too strong. We didn't expect to have contact while they were inside the storm."

O'Brien knew they were both thinking about the checkpoint that the runabout had just missed. But he assured Molly, "She'll be back before you know it. Why don't you play with one of the games in your bag? That's my girl."

When he stood up, O'Brien was surprised to see that Odo wasn't glaring at him. "I'm sorry, Odo, but I have nowhere else to put her. And I can't drag her along as I recalibrate the wave guides in the power conduit."

Odo glanced at Molly. She obediently pulled a game padd from her travel bag, though she was watching her father and Odo.

"It appears she'll be no problem," Odo said.

"Thanks," O'Brien said gratefully. "You're a cut above the rest, Constable. Oh, and if you hear anything—"

"I'll let you know," Odo assured him.

O'Brien let out a sigh of relief as he left. He didn't want to imagine what Keiko would say when she found out he had left their daughter with the security chief. Heaven only knew what kind of people would be drifting in and out of his office while she was there. Still, all in all, O'Brien was rather pleased with how he had worked everything out.

CHAPTER 9

"WHY WON'T THIS *be'el* thing work?" Cali demanded, punching the keypad of the replicator with her fist.

Captain Ari found her behavior quite amusing. "Have patience," he mildly chided. "The Klingon said it was malfunctioning."

Cali picked up the plate with the rokeg blood pie and considered it once more. But Ari knew she wouldn't be able to bring herself to eat Klingon food even if she were starving.

Ari tucked away his tiny grooming comb, deciding that a suitable amount of time had passed since the commander had left. He deliberately walked over and seated himself at the computer console.

"I want a four-minute warning before he returns,"

he ordered, confident that Cali would set up an airtight perimeter.

The senior mate mumbled into her comm, continuing with her thorough search of Worf's quarters. Ari was willing to bet the *Reaper* that Worf wouldn't be able to detect that his possessions had been touched. "Make a list of what you find," he added, intending to personally decipher this Klingon's psyche.

"You've got it," Cali confirmed.

As Ari logged on to the computer, he took full advantage of the technical data the members had been steadily gathering since they arrived at the station. Rather than directly accessing the files, he downloaded the recent memory storage into a data-clip that played on his microprocessor. A practically undetectable method of obtaining information.

Of all the tidbits he gathered, the conversation between Commander Worf and Captain Alons of the *Katon* was most enlightening. Now he only needed to decide how to use it.

"He doesn't have much stuff. But look at this." Cali waved a *bat'leth* trophy, the traditional ball and curved blade of First Place. "He probably sleeps with it at night so he can pretend he's a real warrior. Just like the rest of those beasts."

Ari declined to reply, but that didn't mean he agreed with her simplistic assessment. Perhaps the trophy had sentimental value. It was not polished and set out on display as ego would dictate, but tucked in a cabinet by itself, in a secret place of honor.

"Would you like to find out more about this Klingon?" Ari asked. "His personal logs and files are right here."

Cali hesitated, despite the eager glint in her eye. "Won't he detect our entry?"

"Yes. He'll know you tampered with his logs out of pure spite."

Cali grinned, coming towards the desk. "You have a deal in mind, don't you?"

Ari decided to make her wait, expertly entering the access code for the docking ring. The members had been specifically instructed to locate the emergency release for the docking clamps, just in case the *Reaper* needed to bypass official procedures in order to depart. At one point, it had looked as if they wouldn't have enough capital to pay their docking fees at the station, much less take on supplies for their next run. They had badly needed the new transport contract, and it was fitting that Cali had made the deal since it had been her fault that their last contract had been lost. She had given a hasty order, jettisoning half their cargo and bringing the *Reaper* to the edge of insolvency.

Yet there was a bright side to the ship's financial crisis. Cali's actions had cut short the growing respect for her among the senior members. Her deal-making skills made her popular, but after that last run, everyone down to the mewing infants knew that Cali couldn't be trusted with the captain's seat. No, Ari wouldn't be bothered for a long time by whispers in her ears to take advantage of the rights her lineage gave her.

Cali was eagerly gazing at him, waiting to be let in on the deal. She was completely in his hands.

"The Klingon yacht interests me," Ari told her, feeling magnanimous. "It's a shame to let a situation with such potential slip away."

"Do you think it attacked the *Ceres?*"

He waved one hand as if that was a given. "The Klingons won't come out, and security has not yet broken in. All we need is some leverage and we control the situation."

"You're going to help the Klingons?" Cali asked, wrinkling her nose at the very idea.

"I'm going to arrange a deal with the Klingons that will give us a small fortune."

She stared at the screen for a few moments, then shook her head. "You can't contact them. Starfleet will be all over us like a swarm of vacuum mites."

"The deal will be contracted later." Ari slipped a chip into the computer to record the entire process, including the communication between Alons and Worf, and the security reports that a free-lance technician had just arrived and was making progress in remote-triggering the *Katon*'s locking sequence. Ari also input a false identity and station code, pleased that both were finally proving useful.

He set up an order that would blow the clamps on the *Katon,* releasing it from the station. On the docking end, it would look as if the Klingons had broken into the computer and were trying to escape. The decoy and false identity would be detected under a diagnostic exam, but that suited his purposes perfectly.

Then he set up a chain reaction that would partially cover and scatter his entry and retreat, forming a trail back to Worf's personal logs. Using a covert universal program, he slipped into the memory block at the byte level. It took only a moment to find the entry for Worf's conversation with Alons. He had counted on the reknowned Starfleet fail safes that had left a few free bytes between the communiqué and the order to relay the transmission to Dr. Bashir. In the free space, Ari laid down a byte-sized switch, linking in a phantom loop. From the loop, he re-entered the log files and hooked up with the trail he had left behind.

Once the Klingon decoy had been discovered, it wouldn't take long before the trail and the attempt to hide it were also found, making it appear that Worf had planted a delayed program to blow open the clamping seals of the *Katon.*

Ari triggered the sequence. "The *Katon* has been jettisoned."

Cali ran to the port window, pressing her face against the glass to see out. "Are you sure? I don't—" she broke off. "Oh, there it goes."

Ari removed the data chip and joined her, watching as the *Katon* spun away from the station. Apparently the engines were off line, and the ship was at the mercy of the turbulent cosmic rays.

"I have a log of the entire transaction, including the cover-up as it was done from this console," Ari said quietly.

"You'll sell it to the Klingons," Cali guessed. "They can use it to prove that Worf set them up."

"Any Klingon would agree that's quite a bargaining chip to use against the Federation."

Cali was practically prancing, she was so excited. "It's brilliant! I can't believe that with only a few keystrokes you come up with a deal like that."

Ari gestured back to the computer. "Would you like to rummage around? The more you access the logs and cover up, the more you will help obscure the real path of entry."

"I'd like nothing better." Cali headed back to the vacated seat. "I'll plant something just nasty enough to make him think that's why I was inside. He'll be angry, but he may not throw me in the brig."

"Even that could be useful," Ari murmured, knowing that Cali could care less where she was, as long as she was in on a big deal.

He stayed at the portal until the *Katon* spun out of sight, wondering how long it would take Starfleet to recapture the yacht.

Worf had intended to go straight to the *Katon* once his team had cleared the evacuees from the connecting tunnel. But when he called ahead to inform Odo, the computer replied that the chief was in his security office.

Worf stormed through the Promenade, hardly breaking stride as he burst through the doors of Odo's office. "Why did you leave the *Katon?*"

Odo stopped bobbing up and down. A young human was hanging onto his back, yelling, "Gi-yup! Ya!"

Somehow Odo retained his dignity. "Commander Worf, this is Molly. Chief O'Brien's girl."

Worf stared at her kicking heels, remembering his first sight of Molly—as she was being born. He briefly closed his eyes. "We have met before."

"I want the saddle again!" Molly demanded.

Worf's mental image was instantly replaced by an equally distressing one of Odo turning into a riding animal for small children. He tried to banish both from his mind.

Odo swung Molly off his back. Worf could not tell how he did it so smoothly. "You can have another ride later," he assured her.

"Now," she insisted.

"No, you have to let your steeds rest occasionally."

"Why?"

Odo hardly missed a beat. "Because otherwise they die."

"Oh." Molly's mouth made a perfect "O" as she sat back in the cushioned chair.

"Nice child," Worf said doubtfully.

Odo impatiently sat down behind his desk. "What is it you wanted, Commander?"

"Yes." Worf remembered his anger. "Why have you left the *Katon?*"

"I thought that's what you said." Odo was looking at his viewer. "Commander, that airlock is not my only concern. In fact, it isn't even a high priority. Though I know that you disagree."

Worf tightened his lips. "What is the status of the remote accessing?"

"Things have been progressing more than satisfactorily. Particularly since Chief O'Brien sent Rom down to assist."

"Rom? Not the Ferengi!" Worf protested.

"You should appreciate that Ferengi, Commander. In fact, I was about to notify you to meet me in the lower pylon." Odo acted as if he couldn't help adding, "But your impatience—"

The red klaxons flashed in the corners of the security office as the computer announced, "Warning! Docking breech!"

Odo accessed the com, just as Kira announced on his badge, "Senior crew, report to the *Defiant*. A vessel has broken loose from the station."

Worf immediately headed for the door, but Odo called after him, "Commander, it's the *Katon!*"

Worf gave him a startled nod of thanks, and broke into a run. The *Katon* was not going to escape him now, not when he was this close.

In the turbolift, he signaled Kira in Ops. "How did the *Katon* get away?"

"It was jettisoned," Kira said briefly. "And now it's spinning. You'll get your own chance to try to lock onto it with tractors."

"On my way to the *Defiant,*" he acknowledged.

He felt justified in his foresight for insisting that the *Defiant* be put on standby alert. Because of that, the *Katon* was hardly a light year away by the time the crew was in place and ready to depart.

"Disengage docking clamps," Captain Sisko ordered.

"Aye, sir," replied Ensign DeGroodt at the helm—usually Dax's post.

Sisko was shaking his head at the distorted viewer. "How did it happen? Turbulence?"

Worf was already assessing that. "According to sensor logs, the docking clamps were blown."

"By the Klingons?" Sisko asked.

"Perhaps." Worf uneasily remembered that Rom had been working on the remote accessing. "However it is possible that our attempts to access the airlock systems triggered the reaction."

Sisko gave him a dark look. "I want a complete report."

"Aye, sir."

Worf was irritated by Dr. Bashir's worried expression and the way he stood so close to the captain, listening and watching everything. Meanwhile, Lieutenant Kelly at the engineering station gave him a sympathetic grin. Worf pointedly turned away but Kelly did not seem to mind.

It was a minor incident but one that would never have happened on the *Enterprise*. In his next tactical report, he would include his opinion that the lack of a tight, seasoned crew for the *Defiant* could be a significant detriment during their encounters with Klingon vessels.

He would soon have a chance to test that theory, while proving whether or not the *Katon* had the guns to destroy the *Ceres*. He had been looking forward to just such a challenge. Yet as they neared the yacht, he had to inform the captain, "The *Katon* has not powered up their engines or weapons systems."

"What about shields?" Sisko asked.

"Shields are holding," he replied. "The ship's status has not changed from its docking state."

Sisko narrowed his eyes. "Why do they continue to let it spin?"

"Perhaps they were injured in the explosion," Dr. Bashir quietly suggested.

As the *Defiant* came within range, Worf discovered that Kira was correct. It was nearly impossible to keep a tractor lock on the *Katon* while they were spinning in the emission waves. The frequencies kept shifting, flinging off the tractor beams.

"Perhaps the spin is not accidental," Worf finally ventured. "Tractors are unable to lock onto the *Katon.*"

"If it's a tactical decision," Sisko commented, "then it's not a very good one. At some point the ship will have to stop."

Kelly agreed, "And they must be losing their gravity field—"

"Captain," Worf interrupted. "Their engines are powering up!"

"A warp field is beginning to form," Ensign DeGroodt confirmed.

"Don't let them get away," Sisko ordered.

Worf boosted the tractors on the *Katon* as their spin slowed, catching it in the microsecond before the field could engage. "Tractors locked on, Captain. Warp field has been disrupted."

"Very good, Mister Worf." Sisko sat back. "Hail them."

It took a while for the link to be established, and when it was, so much static ran through the image that it was difficult to distinguish what they were seeing. It was an extreme close-up of Alons. The captain had one arm draped over the console, letting it support him as he leaned his face into view. One enormous eye blinked askew, and his spittle-covered lips and brown teeth were unpleasantly prominent. His swollen, mottled tongue shoved out and licked up a trickle of bloodsweat from his cheek.

"Captain, you're injured!" Sisko exclaimed, standing up.

Alons managed to groan and glare at the same time. "You will never take us alive!"

Sisko moved closer to the screen. "Captain Alons, let us beam you to our ship. We have a doctor—"

"TammoH!" Alons rasped. "You think you have beaten me. But you—you are the ones who are defeated. The glory is ours! Victory to the Empire!"

Worf realized what was happening even through the massive shielding. "Captain, their warp core is overloading. It will reach critical levels in approximately thirty seconds."

"Can we board the *Katon?"* Sisko demanded, ignoring the image of Alons.

"Negative," Worf replied. "Not until they lower their shields."

"Never!" Alons shouted from the main viewer. "I will die with my ship!"

Sisko appealed to the Klingon captain. "You have six crew members on board. Will you kill them as well?"

"My crew will follow me until I die." Alons managed to draw back and hold his head steady for a moment. Then he had to blink and rub his eyes because of the sweat, and the motion threw him off balance. "We have already won. Nothing can stop us now."

"He's delusional," Bashir said in a low voice.

"Alons, please lower your shields!" Sisko insisted. "Time is running out." Over his shoulder he asked Worf, "Isn't there some way you can get a transporter lock on them?"

Worf briefly shook his head, concentrating on the panel. "Not yet. Warp core is reaching critical. Ten-second countdown."

"Release tractor beam," Sisko ordered.

Worf complied, knowing the captain hoped to avert the destruction of the *Katon.* He fully agreed. He would rather see the Klingons try to run than allow them to destroy the only evidence of their crimes against the *Ceres.*

"Get some distance from that ship," Sisko ordered. "Half impulse."

"You conspired against us from the start," Alons sneered into the screen. "*You,* you traitorous *puj'O,* betraying your brothers."

Worf dimly realized that Alons was talking to him, but he concentrated on one last chance to lock onto them.

"The sight of you disgusts me!" Alons spit. "You are nothing more than a filthy Ferengi in Klingon hide. Selling yourself to the enemy. You're no warrior—"

Worf alerted security to report to the transporter room. "Locking on, Captain."

Alons was caught in mid sentence as the image further distorted, then automatically switched to an exterior view of the *Katon.* Worf tried to get a sensor reading as the shields failed from the power drain, but the *Katon* instantly exploded.

Inertial dampers weren't enough to buffer the shock wave. The *Defiant* lurched, then steadied.

"Five Klingons have been beamed on board," Worf reported. "One pattern was lost, however the others are alive."

The doctor immediately left for the transporter room, calling for medical assistance through his badge.

Sisko stared at the starfield for a moment, watching the last sparkles of the atomized yacht. His thoughtful frown made it clear that he was not quite satisfied with the outcome. "Take us back to the station."

Worf liked it even less than the captain. He analyzed the sensor readings of the explosion, but warp core breaches were basically all the same. He did not believe they would be able to determine the power capacity of the *Katon* even with in-depth analysis. The interference from the plasma emissions had destroyed that possibility.

As they neared the station, the security team reported that the doctor had sedated the Klingons and they had been transported to *Defiant*'s sick bay. Soon after, Dr. Bashir signaled the bridge.

Worf almost protested for security reasons when Sisko ordered Bashir to be put on the main viewer. But after only a few weeks under Sisko's command, he knew the captain would override him.

"What's wrong with the Klingons, Doctor?" Sisko asked.

"The crew of the *Katon* are suffering from severe radiation poisoning." Bashir glanced at Worf. "Commander Worf alerted me not more than an hour ago that Alons seemed to be in a . . . stressed condition. But his deterioration has advanced at an extraordinarily rapid rate. It's severe irradiation, the likes of which I've never seen before."

"The plasma storm," Sisko murmured.

"Perhaps," the doctor agreed doubtfully. "Or it could have been exposure to unstable chemicals, such as solotine. Finding the root cause will be difficult because it's not just their cellular membranes breaking down." Again Bashir glanced at Worf. "Their molecular structure is decomposing. Perhaps that's why we couldn't get a lock on the sixth man. I suggest we move them manually to the infirmary."

Worf would not let that pass. "Captain, I recommend that the Klingons be held in the *Defiant*'s sick bay."

Sisko considered the suggestion. "It might be wise. Do you have the facilities you need here, Doctor?"

Bashir reluctantly nodded. "I suppose the *Ceres* crew might not appreciate having Klingons in the same recovery room."

Worf stiffened. "I am concerned with security, Doctor."

"Of course, Commander," Bashir replied, making it clear that the rebuff had been noted.

"We *will* have a security problem if those Klingons get out of sick bay," Sisko pointed out to both of them. "The last thing we need is for the *Defiant* to fall into their hands."

"Aye, sir," Worf replied, confident he could secure them with these systems. If only the rest of the station were like the *Defiant*. "Permission to proceed?"

Sisko nodded, but Bashir was glumly shaking his head. "Don't worry about your prisoners, Commander. They're not going anywhere for a while."

The image of the docking pylon returned to the main viewer as Worf left the bridge. By his count, he had managed to offend every member of the senior staff today. Except perhaps Dax . . .

Gruffly he shrugged it off. He could not help it as long as *they* were continually offending him.

CHAPTER 10

"WHY DON'T YOU go rest for a while?" Dax suggested. "That bench is more comfortable than it looks."

Keiko shook her head. She already felt like dead weight on this mission, she certainly wasn't going to start napping on top of it. "I think we should consider going through a few more of those magnetic loops."

"The radiation levels went off the scale," Dax reminded her. "Who knows how many random particles penetrated the electrostatic field? There could be all kinds of dangerous free radicals being produced in here and in the components of the runabout. Not to mention in us."

Keiko didn't need to be told about the affects of irradiation on biological tissue. She had been keeping track of the interior particle count since they left the station. She had always intended to have another baby—she knew Miles would love to have a son—but the time had never seemed right. Now Molly was six years old and it was looking as if they might never have another child. But Keiko wanted that to be her choice rather than an accidental by-product of this mission.

Yet they weren't getting anywhere sitting here. "I've gotten only one good reading," she told Dax. "And that was during the flash. If we can get a few more samples, I can at least run the data against the biometric analysis."

Dax was obviously growing impatient, having exhausted their other options to communicate and/or navigate through the storm. But Keiko had been reluctant to insist on getting more data by going through the unstable loops. She kept fighting an unreasonable feeling that she was here by mistake. In fact, the whole mission felt like a terrible mistake—the kind you paid for with your life. If only the station wasn't going to pay for it as well, along with her husband and her baby . . .

"We have to get back to warn them," Keiko insisted.

"Going through the loops may take us further away. We could even end up in the heart of the storm, where the plasma density would probably disintegrate the molecular structure of the runabout."

"I'm willing to take that risk," Keiko retorted. "And so are you. You've been recalibrating the shields, haven't you?"

"Yes. We should be able to go through another loop without losing our internal systems."

Keiko waited, very much aware of who was in command. If Dax was hesitating, she must have good reasons. But Keiko didn't see what other choice they had.

Dax must have agreed. She adjusted their course, bringing them closer to a magnetic current. "I'll hold us in a constant vector in the direction of the strongest particle flow."

"Releasing dye marker," Keiko confirmed. Now they had two blips on their sensors, this one and the marker she had dropped soon after they had been deposited here. Sensors were still unable to detect the first marker left where they had entered the storm. Either it was too far away or else it had already degraded to charged particles.

"We're entering a current," Dax announced, frowning briefly. "Frequencies oscillating—"

Keiko dimmed the resolution on the viewscreen to keep the flash from blinding them. Yet when it came, it was so bright that everything appeared in negative exposure for a few moments afterward.

"Releasing dye marker," Keiko said automatically, her finger ready on the command key. As they had with the last loop, they appeared to be drifting in a relatively calm area of plasma, while around them other magnetic currents were forming.

Keiko started scrolling through the data that the sensors had gathered during the burst. "This is fantastic! Density rates, velocity, units of charge, molecule sequences . . ."

She glanced over at Dax, who was sitting bolt upright, staring at the viewscreen. Keiko checked the viewer but there was nothing unusual about the sparkling plasma.

"Dax? Is something wrong?"

Dax continued to stare, but as Keiko reached out to touch her, she suddenly shook her head. "Holding constant vector," she announced.

"What happened?" Keiko asked.

"We went through the magnetic loop." Dax gave her a quizzical glance.

"I think you were dazed," Keiko told her. "You couldn't hear me. Then you snapped out of it."

Dax instantly ordered, "Medical database, scan me for any unusual readings."

"Mental processes are undergoing heightened arousal," the computer replied blandly. "There is no biophysical damage."

Dax seemed relieved. "I think the electrical stimulation of the radiation acted like sensory overload. You better take the helm for the next loop, just in case it happens again."

Keiko nodded, but she asked, "Are you sure you want to go through another one?"

"You need at least three for a proper test sample, don't you?"

"Yes," Keiko admitted. "Four would be better."

"Then we'll do a few more. Don't worry about me.

Joined Trill are especially sensitive to radiation exposure because of the neural links to the symbiont." Dax patted her stomach fondly. "Our skull bones filter random particles, but there's not much protection down here."

Keiko ordered the computer to put a constant medical scan on Dax, just to be sure. "One more time may be enough."

"Then get ready, we're entering a current now."

"This area seems to be more active," Keiko agreed.

"Let's hope the next place is less active."

Keiko accepted the helm as the magnetic current grew stronger and their trajectory swung into line with the strongest particle flow. She tried to watch Dax and the sensors at the same time, as Dax recalibrated the plasma trap, attempting to capture the higher frequency ranges.

Keiko barely had time to nod her thanks. "Stepped leader forming."

The flash was muted to an acceptable level so this time she could see Dax briefly shake her head as if her ears were ringing. Then she froze, staring.

"Computer, analyze Dax's condition," Keiko ordered.

"There is a disturbance in mental processes caused by a paroxysmal malfunction of cerebral nerve cells."

"Is it dangerous?" Keiko asked.

"The seizure is not life threatening," the computer responded.

Dax blinked her eyes, coming out of it. She automatically tried to input helm orders and was confused. "Helm is not responding!"

"You gave helm control to me before we entered the loop," Keiko reminded her.

"I did?" Dax seemed disoriented.

"You shook your head after the flash, as if something hurt. Then you blanked out for—how long, computer?"

"The seizure lasted for ten point three seconds," the computer responded.

"How am I now?" Dax asked, to both Keiko and the computer.

"Elevated neural activity is currently within acceptable limits," the computer replied.

"That's three samples," Keiko said. "Let's try to hold position here until I get some of this data analyzed."

"I can agree with that." Dax rubbed her temples and was still frowning as she set the helm to track the slow drift of the most recent dye marker. The turbulence gave it an erratic path, and Keiko kept getting distracted by the sight of the bobbing marker. It seemed to dance and pirouette like a Pied Piper leading them off the edge of a cliff.

"You want something to drink?" Dax asked, getting up and stretching. When the uniform got in her way, she opened the jacket and shrugged it off, leaving only her black undershirt.

"Hot vanilla milk," she said, standing at the small replicator. "Are you hungry?" she asked Keiko.

"Just some tea right now." She couldn't help asking, "What is hot vanilla milk?"

"You've never had it?" Dax said. "I'm used to the dairy products of Trill, but the chemical structure is basically the same. The replicators make a pretty good mix."

"I've never heard of it," Keiko said.

"Julian says this is the Earth version." Dax set the teacup on the lower console. "My mother gave it to me when I was young, and even though it isn't the same, it has a similar effect."

"What kind of effect?"

Dax smiled into her cup. "Oh, comfort, I suppose. It's one of those things I drank when I was sick or feeling bad."

Keiko relaxed somewhat, reminded that Dax was biologically the same age as herself. She usually seemed much older.

Keiko raised her teacup in return. "Tea, for me, is also a comfort food." She sipped the hot fragrant blend. "My grandmother taught me how to make tea. Not just how to blend the leaves, but the experience of making tea. The setting, the motions, the flow and ebb of the experience."

They sipped companionably in silence, watching their consoles. Keiko's biometric program had accepted the data as adequate and the systematic comparison was under way. Dax was looking much better, as if she had recovered from the disorientation of the seizures. For a brief moment, Keiko was at peace, not thinking of their situation, but only about now.

She sighed. "I haven't had the chance to make tea for Miles since I got back."

"Is that something you always do?"

Keiko nodded. "It's . . . important."

"It sounds lovely," Dax said.

"It is." Keiko felt a pang of guilt that she hadn't tried harder to prepare tea for Miles this time. She hadn't even thought about it. She hoped that wasn't a sign of something emotionally larger and much worse waiting in the wings for them. As a couple, they had already suffered plenty to last for the rest of their lives.

"The chief must like it that you go to such an effort," Dax said.

"Yes . . ." Keiko knew Dax's curiosity was personal. After all, she was good friends with her husband. That's why she answered honestly. "But even after all these years, I don't think Miles understands."

"It's not exactly a game of darts," Dax agreed.

"I used to play darts with him once in a while, but lately—" Keiko was distracted by the program sequence. "We have insufficient data for a complete analysis, but the computer found three biometric programs that correlated as high as sixty-four percent. Two bacteria groups and a species of airborne fungi from Tantrus Two."

"Bacteria and fungi." Dax considered that. "Organisms that transform organic materials into inorganic chemicals. That makes sense since the plasma state is inherently destructive, causing matter to lose internal cohesion, transforming into random chains of excited particles."

"Yes, but there are some differences." Keiko indicated the flashing portions of the graphs and equations. "Some of the pattern sequences match up when they're reversed. See where the blue-green algae fixes molecular nitrogen from water, forming ammonia. Here the plasma is also undergoing nitrogen fixation, but the sequences that remain are organic catalytic patterns."

"These are carbon sequences," Dax agreed. "Do you think they're some sort of enzyme?"

"Actually it's more fundamental than that. These sequences are for plasmalogens. Naturally occurring phosphoglycerides, which, under certain conditions, release aldehyde, an organic compound. It's similar to the fatty acids found in eggs and red blood cells."

"And brain tissue," Dax agreed, following the biology. "According to these readings, the plasmalogens are mostly restricted to the magnetic currents."

"Exactly like bioacids in carbon-based life-forms, conducting nerve impulses and transporting nutrients between tissues and organs." She was literally on the edge of her seat. "Don't you see? Despite the extreme ionization—or maybe because of it—inorganic material is re-forming into particle chains of neural lipids. That's the basis of carbon-organic matter."

"But this is plasma, not an organism."

"This plasma exhibits all of the biochemical processes of life." Keiko could tell Dax didn't understand the magnitude of their discovery. "It's also in accordance with Yano's theory, which holds that the key to the transition from inorganic to organic activity lies in plasma. He did one study that recorded panspermia on a planet that had been sterile until a plasma storm swept through the system."

Dax sat forward. "It sounds as if you're saying the plasma is a life-form."

"Yes. I think it could be an organism in its own right."

"That's a big jump, Keiko, from plasmalogens to life-form."

"Look at the data. The biometric analysis proves the plasma mass is creating life-sustaining patterns and has an internal organization. Perhaps when this much matter becomes highly charged, a sort of massive protoorganism is formed."

"It would take extremely heavy matter to sustain itself," Dax said. "But if the plasma was blown off during the supernova of a neutron star, the carbon particles would have started out superdense and superheated, and it would have the extra energy of the pulsar propelling it away."

"Perhaps there's some way we can affect it," Keiko said. "Maybe make it change course."

"From inside?" Dax asked, making it clear what she thought of that suggestion.

Keiko sighed. There was nothing more she could accomplish drifting here.

Dax must have come to the same conclusion. "Let's

see if we can confirm your theory. If this is an organism, a few more bursts will help fill in those gaps."

Keiko accepted the helm, though she knew the radiation was harming Dax. "Why don't you put on a stasis belt? It will reduce the level of your exposure."

"I agree. And you should wear one, too." Dax got up to fetch the belts from a compartment. "It looks as if we're going to be in here for a while."

Keiko accepted the device as Dax wrapped one around her waist, switching it on. Keiko usually didn't like the tingling feeling that ran over her skin as the stasis was activated, but this time it was reassuring to be reminded she was protected. Why had she waited so long to get pregnant again? But what other choice did she have?

It was Dax who gave Keiko a grin of encouragement as they intersected another magnetic current. As usual, their vector veered into the angle of its directional flow.

At the flash, Keiko held her breath, watching Dax. She shook her head a few times, but she didn't black out. "I'll take helm now."

"Transferring helm," Keiko said automatically. "I guess that—"

"—stasis belt helped," Dax finished. "I knew you were going to say that."

Keiko was busy with the readings. "Sensors have detected the first dye marker! The others are almost out of range."

Dax compared the marker map with starcharts of the sector. "The markers are moving. It's impossible to tell whether we're near the middle again, or maybe towards the back."

"I wonder . . . ," Keiko started. "If we had more than four reference points, maybe we could plot the internal patterns of magnetic currents."

"Then we could figure out the quickest way out of here," Dax agreed.

"We'd need to drop a lot more markers," Keiko warned. "That means going through more loops. Are you sure you feel up to it?"

"Of course." Dax didn't seem bothered by the idea of additional radiation exposure.

Keiko hesitated. "Computer, what is Dax's current mental state?"

"Neural arousal is subsiding from the upper levels of acceptable parameters," the computer replied.

"I'm fine," Dax insisted. "Keiko, if you don't want to expose yourself, just say so."

"It's not that—"

"I've known all along that the loops are our only way out," Dax added.

"A few minutes ago you were resisting the idea," Keiko protested.

"Well, we've run out of other options. We know the station can't survive the energy surges inside this storm." Dax gazed at the plasma field on the viewer. "I'm sure the answer lies in those loops. It feels familiar somehow."

Now Keiko was really worried. "That doesn't sound like scientific reasoning to me."

"Do I have to make it an order?" Dax was suddenly very much in command.

Keiko stared at her, but all she could think about was Molly. "No. Let's start plotting markers."

CHAPTER 11

MOLLY POKED HER finger into Odo's side, then watched the hole fill in when she removed it. She kept testing different spots, as if trying to catch him in a place where it wasn't soft. Odo wondered if the feeling was comparable to being tickled. It certainly seemed to give Molly pleasure.

She giggled and darted out of reach as he made a halfhearted attempt to catch her. Then she ran up and gave him a particularly hard poke, sinking her finger into the knuckle.

"Ouch," Odo said mildly. Molly quickly pulled her finger back, looking up at him in concern. He clapped his hand over the spot as if he were mortally wounded. "You got me."

He said it rather flatly, but Molly laughed in delight. She had been saying, "You got me!" ever since she started playing a game in which she was the criminal and he had to capture her. In reality, Molly played while Odo attempted to corral her in the area behind his desk for safety's sake. He wondered when she would go to sleep.

When he had time, he accessed data on child rearing, finding some helpful advice on kindergarten-age children. The word meant children's garden in an old Earth tongue, and the basic principle was to encourage children towards self-understanding through play activities and freedom rather than the imposition of adult ideas.

After he read that, Odo let Molly go all the way to the doors so she could look through the glass. The constant shadowy flickers showed people hurrying past, and all sorts of loud noises echoed inside. It was enough to keep anybody awake, much less a confused child.

Since Molly seemed anxious whenever he wasn't near her, he remained at his desk while one of his lieutenants performed the hourly inspection of the brig. He knew what it was like to want constant reassurance, remembering how he had been left alone night after night during those early, confusing months after he had been found.

Yet humanoids had given him far more than his own people ever had. He felt he had a right to be bitter when he reflected on the differences between humanoid child care, which emphasized parental aid and a secure environment, and the Founder's habit of sending their infant shapeshifters to the other end of the galaxy. Theoretically the infants were supposed to make their way back home with the information they acquired along the way, but for a long time Odo had been wondering how large a percentage of their children were lost forever.

If Molly was an example, then loving attention was a far better solution. The girl was rambunctious but her innocent reliance on him had sprung forth with hardly any effort on his part.

As he organized the guard details, he still found time to fondly watch her play with her fruit cocktail. After reading that nutrition was vital for a child her age, he had been vigilant in plying her with the recommended foods. But she was more interested in splattering him with the juice than in eating, and he was fairly certain it was because she liked to watch the drops fall through him. He tried, but he couldn't block his instinctive reaction to shapeshift around foreign substances, especially when he kept getting distracted by work.

Yet when he received a call from O'Brien's quarters, he was vaguely disappointed at the thought of the chief coming for Molly.

But when Odo answered, Captain Iis appeared on the viewer instead of O'Brien. Odo hadn't met the captain personally, but he recognized her from the Starfleet records he had accessed when the *Ceres* was towed in.

"Security Chief Odo, here," he said courteously. "Is there something I can do for you, Captain Iis?"

"I've been informed that the Klingon yacht has left DS9." She was composed, but the weary droop of her eyes and slight swaying indicated that she had been awakened with the bad news.

"Yes, I regret to inform you that the *Katon* has been destroyed." Odo saw her sit back. "The locking clamps were blown and before they could be recaptured, Captain Alons initiated a warp breach. The Klingon crew were beamed aboard the *Defiant* and are currently in—"

"Sick bay," she finished. "On the *Defiant.* So I've heard. And my crew has heard. You know, many of them blame the *Katon* for the attack on the *Ceres."*

"I believe Commander Worf has not yet finished his investigation." Odo was distracted for a moment by Molly, as she crawled under the desk. He didn't like the idea of letting her sit on the floor, but it was better than fetching her away from the door every time it opened. "Commander Worf is on the *Defiant* if you would like to contact him."

"Perhaps I will," the captain said. "I don't want my crew getting in the way of his investigation. Tempers are running high, and there were terrible . . . losses."

Odo considered going down to the *Defiant* himself but Molly bumping around on his feet reminded him that he had to remain here. "Perhaps you should order your crew members to stay away from the *Defiant."*

Captain Iis actually started to smile. "Chief, you don't know my crew. I didn't mean to imply that they would cause trouble. I expect quite the contrary. They may feel it's prudent to act as back-up to your security, in order to assist you."

"I understand." Odo no longer felt sorry for Captain Iis. Even without a functioning starship, she still had her command and her crew. "I will inform Commander Worf."

"Thank you," Iis said simply. Then she yawned, a perfect expression of humanoid abandonment, something Odo treasured almost as much as a sneeze. "Excuse me," she added. "I'm going to find a flat spot and get back to sleep. Please contact me with any new developments."

"Yes, Captain." It wasn't until she signed off that he remembered he hadn't asked about O'Brien. "Computer, where is the location of chief . . . of operations?" he asked, not wanting to say his name in front of Molly.

"The chief is currently in command of Ops."

Apparently he was going to have custody of Molly for a while longer. She peeked up between his legs, giving him a sunny grin. He couldn't help thinking that it wouldn't be so bad.

The viewscreen signaled again. "Kira to Odo."

Odo instantly reached out to activate visuals. Kira was in Ops, and had been since midday, despite the fact that this was supposed to be her day off. Yet she still looked as energetic as when he had seen her at the staff briefing.

"What can I do for you, Major?" he asked formally.

"I'm arranging the quarters-sharing for the evacuees, and I noticed that you gave up your place to that

Marlkin family-crew. Where were you planning to sleep tonight?"

"Oh, any corner will do for me," he said offhandedly.

"Come on, Odo. It's Kira you're talking to." She gave him a wry grin. "I know how much you like your privacy."

"The Marlkins were in need. And I told them that quarters would be found for them."

"I think it's typical of you, though no one else would know it. I also think you should stay in my quarters tonight." She lifted her eyes to the heavens. "I've given my bedroom to those Bajoran diplomats who got stuck here, but you can always take the plant out of your bucket and bring it over to my place."

For a moment Odo was tempted. "That won't be necessary, Major."

"I'm offering because you're my friend, Odo. Not because I'm in charge of making sure everyone, including you, has a place to sleep."

His eyes lingered on the small closet where he had stashed his bucket earlier. "I've already arranged to stay here, just in case there's an emergency."

Part of him expected her to continue urging him until he accepted, but she was abruptly summoned away by O'Brien. "I've got to go now. If you change your mind, come on by."

"Thank you—" he started to say. But she ended the transmission.

He stared at the viewer for a few moments. Why had he hesitated to accept her invitation? He would like nothing better than to be near Kira, yet the idea of desolidifying for the night in front of anyone, even her, was discomforting, almost terrifying in its intimacy.

Yet he wanted to.

Molly held up a data clip. "What's this?"

Odo recognized a security report he had lost last week. So that's what had happened to it. He had hated his sneaking suspicions that Worf had somehow gotten hold of it. "It's a report for Captain Sisko on proper delegation of standard security procedures. May I have it back?"

She nodded, placing it on his knee.

"Are you tired, Molly?"

She happily shook her head. "I go to bed when Mommy reads me a story."

Odo had been avoiding mommy questions all evening. "I can read you a story."

She considered that. "Daddy does my stories at the spider."

"Spider? You mean an insect?" he asked, wondering if he should try to get her out from under his desk. It felt odd conversing through his knees with her.

"Mommy and I go to the spider." Molly was sitting cross-legged, and she grabbed onto his shoes, onto *him,* as she rocked back and forth. "It's shiny, and the stars are alllll around us."

"That's the station," Odo told her. "Deep Space Nine. You're on the station."

"No," she said seriously. "Mommy and I go to the spider to see Daddy."

"Don't you remember?" he asked. "Your father is here. He brought you to me."

She wasn't rocking any more, and she started to frown. "Where's Mommy?"

"She's away on a mission. She went to look at the storm." Molly didn't seem to understand, so he added, "Usually you go with your mother when she's on a mission. Like when you go to Bajor."

"Mommy went without me?" Molly asked, her voice rising in sudden understanding. "She's gone?"

"No, it's not like that. She didn't go to Bajor. She's not far away." Odo knew he would be sweating if that were possible. "You'll see her soon."

Molly seemed to draw into herself, peeking up at him. "Did my mommy go away because I was bad?"

"Of course not." Odo leaned forward, realizing the girl had tears in her eyes. He pushed the chair away and got down on the floor next to her. "Your mother didn't leave because you were bad. In fact, I bet your mother wishes she were here with you right now."

She sniffled, looking as if she wanted to believe him.

A voice carefully asked, "Chief?" and Odo realized that the door was open.

Odo stood up with as much composure as he could muster. "Yes, Zeischner?"

Security Guard Zeischner and his partner Larah were ushering in a group of young humanoids. Odo counted eight in all. Then he saw Jake, standing behind the rest, ducking his head.

He contented himself with a hard look at Sisko's son, then turned to hear Zeischner's report. "We found them chasing a Sattar through the habitat ring. Apparently there was a 'deal' that went sour. The Sattar got away, but I've got a good description."

Odo called Jake forward. "What happened?"

Jake glanced nervously back at the others. But when Odo didn't budge, he seemed resigned to confessing everything. "Col and Nesser wanted to play a joke on their friends. They're with the students' survey tour from University at Betazed. I didn't think—It was only a joke."

Odo examined the group of apparently bright young people who were looking rather ashamed of themselves. But one woman flung her white-blond hair over her shoulder, glaring at the others. "Do you have something to add?" Odo asked her.

"Yes, I do," she said, instantly stepping forward. "I'm Drennela Fort, and I must say we wouldn't be here if these *children* had tried to control themselves. I'm sick of their tricks and constant baiting—"

"Give it a rest, Dren!" another girl interrupted. "You don't get it worse than anyone else." Others also chimed in, dismissing Drennela's complaint.

The tallest young man, the one Jake had called Col, told Odo, "We're supposed to test one another. It's a part of gaining control of our empathic abilities. Only *some* people are too stuck up to—"

"Shut up!" the other girl interrupted. "That won't help anything."

"I suppose you know exactly what to do," Col retorted sarcastically. "How many times have you been arrested, Ransi?"

Odo broke in, "Perhaps I should ask all of you that question."

Security Guard Zeischner smiled at Larah without letting the youngsters see him. Jake had the grace to look contrite, giving Odo an apologetic shrug. "It was only a joke."

"You've said that three times," Odo reminded him. "Exactly what happened?"

"Meln and Ransi pulled something on Col and Nesser earlier." Jake glanced over his shoulder and must have thought better of beginning so far back. "Anyway, they decided to get even by turning over their cots."

"I see." It sounded like the same thing as Dax disarranging his quarters. "I have never understood the desire to interfere with other people's personal belongings."

The Betazoids exchanged glances among themselves as if they had never thought of it that way.

Ransi simply repeated, "We train our shields by testing each other."

"We're in an emergency situation," Drennela reminded them. "This is not the time for petty training exercises."

Odo tended to agree, but their arguing was serving no useful purpose. "And the Sattar?" he prodded. "How did he get involved in your training exercise?"

"It wouldn't be any good if Ransi could just ask the computer which one of us came into the room," Jake explained. "So we found this Sattar, a kid who was hanging around. He went in and turned the cots over."

"You let a Sattar into your quarters?" Odo slowly asked.

Jake quickly assured him, "Col and I stood in the door to watch. He turned over the ones we told him to, and . . . well . . ."

"Go on," Odo ordered.

"He suggested that we take something and hide it. Col said—"

Col spoke up for himself. "I told him to take Drennela's tricorder. But that was it! Ask Jake. I don't know what happened to the other things."

Jake was nodding agreement. "I didn't see him take anything else."

"You told him to take my tricorder?" Drennela demanded. "How could you? It's the only one I've got."

"I meant to get it back," Col insisted. "I was reaching for it as he came outside. But then, those other people were coming, and the three of you were right behind them. We were hiding around the corner."

"I only turned away for a second," Jake chimed in.

"And he was gone," Odo finished for them. "Jake, what possessed you to have anything to do with a Sattar? You of all people should know better."

"I know," he agreed. "But it didn't seem like a deal. I mean, we only paid him a few replicator rations for doing it."

"A nice haul," Odo commented. "Give Zeischner a list of the missing items and we'll try to locate this Sattar. We may be able to catch him when he uses those replicator rations." Odo sat down, noticing that Molly was lying on the blanket he had found for her. She was nearly asleep. He realized he had completely forgotten about her, and it gave him a frightening jolt.

Drennela stepped forward. "Will I get my tricorder back?"

Odo didn't think it was likely, but she was looking at him with such plaintive hope in her eyes. "Perhaps. Though usually in cases such as this, the items are immediately sold. Even if we catch the thief, he probably no longer has your tricorder."

Drennela stepped back without a word, but her pout was distinctly reproachful, as if he should be able to do something about it. Odo didn't even have to look at Jake for him to offer, "I'll buy you another one." Col was nearby, and he also agreed to help replace the tricorder.

"I had data on it," Drennela said to no one in particular. "Most of it was on chips, thank the stars! But I did lose everything from today's work."

Jake apologized to the young woman, but she didn't seem interested in hearing it.

She was first in line to report her losses, while Jake hesitated in front of Odo's desk. "I'm sorry, Odo. He was just a kid and I thought I had everything under control."

"You were dealing with a professional," Odo reminded him. "These others could file charges against you and Col for aiding and abetting burglary."

Now Jake really looked nervous. But the Betazoids didn't even consider the suggestion. They were obviously annoyed but they blamed themselves and Col more than Jake.

"I'll pay for everything that was stolen," Jake recklessly vowed to the rest.

Security Guard Zeischner raised one corner of his mouth, tapping the tricorder. "You're talking about quite a sum here, young man."

"I don't care. It's my fault," Jake insisted. "I should have known better." Odo was glad to see that Col was a steady lad, as he also pledged to replace the stolen items. Yet his forehead creased on hearing the approximate total, and Ransi compassionately rubbed his arm, whispering assurances to him.

"I'll have to put this incident on report," Odo told them. "Both your university guide and Captain Sisko will be informed." Jake sagged slightly at the news, but he didn't protest. "For now, I will trust you on your own recognizance. However, no more 'training exercises' on this station. Do you understand?"

The students were nodding in absolute agreement, eager to get away. Odo held out one hand to stop Jake. "As for you, I strongly suggest you return to your own quarters."

"That's exactly what I had in mind," Jake agreed with a sigh.

Odo glanced down at Molly, almost asking Jake to

take the girl with him so she could be put to bed properly. But that was out of the question. He couldn't tell O'Brien that his daughter had been sent off with Jake after he was brought in as an accessory to burglary.

"Go home," Odo told him.

Molly opened her eyes. "Is it time to go home?"

"Not yet. You go back to sleep."

Jake look startled and leaned forward to see over the edge of the desk.

"It's Molly O'Brien," Odo explained.

Jake's eyes widened. "Dax and Keiko aren't back yet?"

Odo sharply shook his head, motioning obliquely to the girl. Molly popped her head out, blinking at Jake.

"Hi," Jake said. "Remember me?"

She barely nodded as she crawled from under the desk and started to climb onto Odo's lap.

At first Odo tried to stop her, but she wiggled half way up and then he had to help her the rest of the way so she wouldn't fall.

"Is she okay here?" Jake asked. "If you want, I can take her home with me."

"No, she seems to be settling down here."

"Yeah, she does seem comfortable. Funny, I never imagined you as a dad before." Jake hesitated as he turned away. "Thanks, Odo."

Odo didn't quite know what to do as the girl squirmed around, trying to get comfortable on his lap. "For what?"

Jake smiled. "You didn't make me feel any more like an idiot than I deserved."

"Humph!" Odo glanced away. "Maybe I should be tougher on you. Then things like this wouldn't happen."

"Nah. Wait 'til I'm getting arrested every week." He cast his eyes down. "At least you know *this* won't happen again."

Odo nodded, making it clear by the way he watched Jake leave that he would have to prove himself. Yet to give the boy credit, he had never been much of a nuisance even when Nog was around to help him get in trouble.

Molly finally found a position she liked, tucked into the curve of his arm. Her head leaned against his chest and he could only see her profile—the upturned nose and chin, with her small mouth slightly open and moistly pink.

He gently stroked a hand against her long dark hair, held back in a thick braid. It was so silky that he could feel each strand against his palm. Then he brushed her rounded cheek with his knuckle. She shifted but kept her eyes closed, lying with complete trust in his arms.

He didn't want to disturb her, so he merely nodded to Zeischner and Larah as they left the office to return to their post. He was grateful they pretended to ignore the girl sleeping on his lap.

When Chief O'Brien finally appeared, Odo was relieved that he would finally be able to move again.

But it happened too fast. The chief burst through the door with apologies and explanations, rushing across the room to take Molly. Odo handed her over and felt as if some part of himself had accidently left with her. He didn't realize how warm she was until she was gone.

"I mean that, Odo," O'Brien was repeating. "You're the best. I don't know what I would have done without you."

Molly didn't even wake up. Her head was lying on O'Brien's shoulder, the dark braid swinging free.

"It was no bother," Odo said shortly, sitting back down in his chair.

"If I were you," O'Brien said. "I'd get some sleep. The storm is scheduled to hit sometime tomorrow morning."

Odo nodded. "Of course." He pretended to be absorbed in his monitor until O'Brien left. But he watched the father and daughter through the windows, heading towards the habitat ring. Then he glanced lower, where the glass was smudged with tiny fingerprints, each one as distinct as the little girl herself.

"Get some sleep," Odo murmured, repeating O'Brien's advice to himself. How naturally it had rolled off the chief's tongue, as if he expected Odo to lie down in a bed rather than pour himself into a bucket. And for some reason, the slip didn't annoy him.

It reminded him of Kira's offer. Much as he wanted

to accept, he decided that it would be more prudent to stay here where he could be summoned at a moment's notice.

Odo shook himself and called his relief. O'Brien was right, he was tired, and there was a big storm coming.

CHAPTER 12

O'BRIEN KNEW HE must be tired from how heavy Molly felt. He gripped his wrists, supporting her more firmly. She couldn't have gained weight in the past few hours.

She briefly woke and murmured, "Daddy," then she was asleep again.

She was a good girl. "No bother at all," Odo had said.

O'Brien knew this must be hard on his daughter. She was used to being with caregivers, both real and holographic, but not at night or for such long stretches of time. Besides, Odo hardly qualified as a caregiver, though Molly seemed none the worse for her stay with him. At least she was sleeping.

He just hoped Keiko got home before Molly woke

up. They still hadn't heard from the *Rubicon,* and it was hours past the checkpoint. As soon as Sisko had returned to Ops, O'Brien had demanded to know when they were going to search for the survey team. Sisko had responded by relieving him of duty and sending him home to get some rest.

O'Brien had no choice but to fetch Molly, but he couldn't take her home. Captain Iis had vacated the *Ceres* only after O'Brien gave her the stress evaluation report indicating that the damaged vessel was particularly vulnerable to shock waves. He had offered his own quarters for the use of Captain Iis and her senior staff, pointing out how dangerous it would be if the scout broke loose from its moorings. Even the repair crews had been recalled until after the storm was past.

Somehow he had found time between the various disasters to fetch a few things for himself and Molly. He picked up the bundle from a maintenance panel inside the habitat ring, and headed toward their temporary quarters. Major Kira had put them in with Commander Worf.

He had to ring the bell twice. "Hello, Worf? It's Chief O'Brien."

Finally he heard, "Enter."

The door opened, but the brooding tension in the darkened room made him hesitate to carry Molly inside. The front of Worf's uniform was partly open, and the knot on his ponytail had loosened. O'Brien hastily looked away from something disgusting that quivered on the plate in his hand.

That's when he saw the Sattar. She bristled, baring

her teeth, indicating she was prepared to protect the other Sattar. By contrast, the older one was reclining back in a chair, carefully positioned to have a view of the entire room.

"Kira assigned us to these quarters," O'Brien explained. Cautiously he entered, wondering how many were here. There were always more Sattar around than you could see. His hand securely held Molly's back just in case he needed to do some quick maneuvering. "The major said you were the only one still alone."

Worf made a noise of disgust. "I apologize. I neglected to notify Ops that Captain Ari and his senior mate were staying here."

"Great!" O'Brien exclaimed. "Now what are we going to do? Captain Iis and her staff are already in my quarters."

"Stay here," Worf told him. "You and the child may use my bed."

O'Brien's irritation vanished. "We can't kick you out of your own bed. Just give me some blankets and I'll settle her down out here—"

"This is where we're sleeping," the female Sattar interrupted. "We weren't offered the bed."

"The child may have it, Cali," the other Sattar chided.

Worf ignored them both, telling O'Brien, "I intend to return to the *Defiant* tonight."

O'Brien knew him well enough to recognize that tone, cautioning for silence in front of the Sattar. He had followed the disaster with the *Katon* from Ops, and he could understand why Worf preferred to remain near the Klingon prisoners.

"Are you sure?" he asked out of pure form.

Worf nodded shortly, sitting down at the table to finish his meal.

O'Brien didn't like the idea of rooming with a pack of Sattar, but at least he had his tool kit with the locking seals.

He carried Molly into the bedroom, and gently removed the clothes from her limp body. He had brought her favorite nightgown and the stuffed hippo she liked to sleep with. At least, it used to be her favorite. Things changed so quickly with his daughter, and he hadn't seen her in a couple of months.

As he pulled the covers over her, making sure she was far enough away from the edge, he wished he had taken better care of her today. He couldn't remember the last time he had her all to himself. Why couldn't it happen when he had time to enjoy it?

He checked the room with his tricorder to make sure there were no Sattar lurking in the vents. Outside, he could hear Cali's voice rising, ". . . and you're out to get them! Just the way you trapped us here when you thought the *Reaper* attacked the *Ceres.*"

As he closed the door behind him, O'Brien made sure Molly wasn't disturbed by the noise. But she hardly moved, clutching the hippo close to her chest.

Worf briefly glanced up as O'Brien returned. He was slightly hunched over the plate, steadily eating as he tried to ignore the Sattar.

"The only reason you let us go," Cali insisted, "is because now you have the Klingons."

"Cali, please," the elder Sattar admonished.

"He's the one who should be afraid," Cali snapped over her shoulder. "He destroyed their yacht! We're lucky he didn't have time to blow up the *Reaper* first."

Since Worf wasn't taking her seriously, O'Brien decided it was none of his concern. Just another crazy evacuee. He had seen plenty of them today, and this Sattar was not the worst by a long shot. He went to the replicator to call up some mutton stew. A hot shower was high on his list but when there was a contest involving his stomach, food always won out.

Despite Worf's lack of interest—or maybe because of it—Cali wouldn't back down. She took a few steps toward the table, physically confronting him. "I can prove you canceled the departure clearance for the *Reaper.* You wanted a Klingon suspect, so you planted evidence on our transport. But when the *Katon* arrived, you decided they were a better target."

"That is absurd." Worf was finally provoked into pushing away his plate.

"I saw it with my own eyes," she insisted. "You ordered traces of photons from massive disruptor discharges to be found on our hull so you could prove we attacked the *Ceres."*

Worf's hand smacked the table. "You lie!"

"I saw it in your files," she told him, smugly satisfied with herself.

"You accessed my files?" Worf's voice changed as he swiftly went to his computer console. From the way he struggled with the commands, O'Brien figured that somebody had disrupted his personal system.

Worf started to rise, his fingers splayed as if to grab the Sattar and shake the sass out of her. The replicator chimed, and O'Brien took his bowl of stew, leaning against the wall where he could keep one eye on the bedroom door and the other on the action. He hadn't seen anything so entertaining since Leeta had cut down the fast and insistent advances of the King of Aruth, a "moon-sized planet in the dead end of space," as she had put it. Among other things. The king had slunk out of Quark's never to return.

But Worf wasn't as good at controlling his rage. "You had no right to access my files!"

Cali tossed her mane. "You broke faith with us first."

Captain Ari sighed as he wearily stood up. "On behalf of my crew, Commander, I apologize for the intrusion. I did not realize what Cali had done until I woke from my nap."

Worf returned to his files, trying to determine the extent of damage that had been done. "I did not file this report on photon traces. You planted this! And you accuse me of treachery."

Cali started to laugh. She turned away, collapsing on the couch and holding her sides. Worf awkwardly stood there.

"Look at you!" she cried out as she rolled. "The big, bad Klingon! Don't like the taste of your own medicine, do you?"

"Cali!" Ari exclaimed sadly. "Commander Worf

was generous enough to lend us his quarters. Why repay his trust and tarnish the name of the *Reaper* with this idiotic stunt?"

"It's no big thing," she denied. "Besides, I couldn't help it. He's been such a mew-face over everything." She propped her head up to give Worf a self-righteous look. "I think it's because he's lost everything. What the Klingons didn't take, he gave away to that couple on Earth, including his son. Have you ever heard of anything so vile?"

"Enough!" Worf reached the couch in two strides.

"Just like a Klingon," she sneered up at him. "First try threats, then turn belligerent."

Worf seemed to clench up. "Do not provoke me."

"I'm stating a fact." She looked him over. "And you're undoubtedly the most Klingon Klingon I've ever met. Belligerent to the core." Her finger pointed at him. "You're so belligerent, you're fighting all the other Klingons, your own people! You can't even make peace with *one* other Klingon, can you? I call that—"

"Silence!"

Worf must have realized he had shouted. Nobody said a word. Captain Ari sighed again as he sat back down, resigned to facing the consequences. O'Brien ate a few bites of his stew, figuring it was best for him to stay out of it.

Cali waved a hand at Worf, turning to her captain. "I knew he was too much of a *Spo'noS* to do anything about it."

Worf stepped forward, as if that was too much. He

took hold of her arm to pull her off the couch. "Get up, Sattar. I could charge you with trespassing—"

"You let go of me!" she sneered, tensing.

"You will do as I—" Worf choked as Cali slammed her foot into his stomach.

O'Brien spit out a mouthful of stew, as the Sattar sprang to the back of the couch. She spun on one leg, landing a vicious kick to Worf's jaw.

Worf staggered sideways at the unexpected blow, even though he was also folded in over his stomach from the first well-aimed kick.

O'Brien flung his bowl away and grabbed the Sattar from behind. He was careful to use a security hold. She might be small, but she sure packed a mean bite.

"I don't like being pawed by Klingons," Cali spit out with a bitter laugh.

O'Brien was relieved when she didn't resist him. Once he was sure she was secure, he remembered to swallow what was left of the stew in his mouth.

Worf could not breathe. His world shrank to the constricted opening in his throat as he tried to force air into his lungs. He bent over as far as he could without falling. Dimly he could hear her laughter. He would rather drop dead than let that *veglargh* bring him to his knees.

Desperately wheezing, he staggered to the desk.

"Should I call . . . security?" O'Brien asked. It sounded as if he had been about to say "sick bay."

"I will take her. To the brig," Worf managed to rasp out. He removed a pair of stasis restraints from a drawer and tossed them to O'Brien. Then he sat down, propping himself up on the desk as he watched the chief attach the restraints around the Sattar's wrists. She was actually smiling, as if she was putting up with this because she thought it was funny.

"This is one of your senior mates?" O'Brien asked the captain. Ari was holding one hand over his eyes as if he were disgusted by what had happened. "I'd hate to see what the rest of your crew is like."

"A lot you know!" Cali taunted.

It only took one look from Captain Ari to make Cali shut up. It reminded Worf of Captain Picard's expression on those rare occasions when he was thoroughly disappointed in him. "Cali, you should consider your position if I do not find it in my best interests to defend you in this crime."

"It was nothing," Cali protested, suddenly sounding much more worried. "I just wanted to let some light into that vacuum he's been living in."

Captain Ari deliberately turned away as if distancing himself from both her and her actions. "Again, you have my deepest apologies, Commander."

Worf had had enough of this. He grunted, pushing himself to his feet. "Cali, senior mate, you are under arrest for assaulting a commanding officer of this station."

Cali cast a longing look at her captain, but she could only see the back of his mane. Worf took Cali from O'Brien. She twisted once in protest, then stopped, watching Ari the entire time.

O'Brien sighed as he went to pick up the bowl,

scraping some of the splattered stew off the rug. "I'm going to bed. This has been too exciting for me. It's so kind of you to let us stay, Worf."

But when Worf dragged a subdued Cali to the door, O'Brien added, "Let me know if Sisko decides to take the *Defiant* out. I'd like to go look for the *Rubicon.*"

Worf glanced back. The chief had served as an unexpected support, refraining from calling security and allowing him to recover himself. "I will inform the captain."

He forced himself to stand straight, ignoring the shooting pains in his stomach as he led Cali down the corridor. He would not allow her to think she had injured him in any way. Now that Captain Ari was out of sight, she was not acting nearly apologetic enough.

At least his mind was clearing. As they entered the turbolift, he could not resisting asking, "Why did you attack me?"

Cali shrugged. "I don't know."

Worf waited, but she had nothing more to say for herself. "Perhaps you are stupid after all."

Her nostrils flared. "You know, Klingons always grab Sattar the way you did, over the shoulder, pressing your fingers into our necks, moving us around as if we were pets. With less respect, because you know we don't dare bite you. A Klingon crushed my shoulder bone the day they took my mother away." She shrugged, pressing her lips together for a moment to hide the sudden trembling. "I don't know. Ever since then I can't stand to be shoved around."

Defiantly she raised her eyes.

"I was not aware of that," he told her.

Cali sniffed, tossing off her own words. "You are a soft one, aren't you? But I think there's fire under all that mush. I bet if you could have gotten off a return, it would have been a good one."

She grinned up at him in a completely infuriating way. He clenched his teeth together, wincing at the pain. She had really clipped his jaw.

He could not wait to get rid of her. He shoved her along faster, though taking care to touch only her wrists. He had a sneaking desire to belt her, just to make things even. After all, as Riker would say, she had cold-cocked him. But he relegated his fury into plans to use her image in his next combat program.

Zeischner was seated at the security desk. "We were looking for a male Sattar, Commander."

"I know nothing about that," Worf told the guard. "Book Cali, senior mate of the *Reaper,* for assaulting a commanding officer of this station."

"Who's pressing charges?" Zeischner asked as he came around the desk to take custody of Cali.

"I am." Worf ignored the man's surprise.

"I'll put her in with a Risan couple," Zeischner said as he handed Cali off to another guard. "She ought to have fun with that."

Cali glared back at Worf as the guard led her away. "This isn't over yet, Klingon!"

Larah pulled her along. "Yeah, yeah, they all say that, sugar drop. You know, you're pretty small to have such a big mouth on you."

Zeischner grinned at Worf. "Shall I get the chief? He's staying nearby in case of emergencies."

Worf glanced around, unwilling to ask.

Zeischner gestured to the door of the small storage room. "He locked himself in there. But I can signal him to wake up."

Worf was already shaking his head, picturing a bucket inside the closet with Odo sloshing around inside. "That will not be necessary."

"Aye, sir," Zeischner replied, apparently quite at ease with his superior's strange sleeping habits.

The computer signaled, and Dr. Bashir asked, "Security? I'm looking for Commander Worf."

"Worf here."

"We need you on the *Defiant,* Commander." Bashir sounded harassed. "We might have to transfer these Klingons to the brig."

"On my way," Worf assured the doctor.

"Don't bring any more guards," Bashir hastily added. "There are more than enough here already."

Worf acknowledged, as Zeischner confirmed, "Odo prepared a holding cell in case it was needed for the Klingons."

"I will inform you before the transfer begins," Worf told the guard. "Alert the patrols to take up position along the route from the docking ring."

Zeischner started to move toward the storage closet, but Worf stopped him. "There is no need to bother the security chief."

"Aye, sir," Zeischner replied. But there was a

hesitance in his voice, as if he would have preferred to inform Odo of the move.

Worf noted the guard's reaction, but he refused to rescind a direct order when it concerned the Klingons.

CHAPTER 13

It was late, but that shouldn't have been enough to distract Sisko from his usual end-of-the-day inspection of the station. But there were so many people on the station that they blurred into one nameless, milling mass. Most of them were so determined to enjoy themselves that it reminded him of Kasidy's "quarters warming" party last week. Her crew and most of his senior staff, as well as a revolving group of Bajoran docking technicians and customs inspectors, had joined the impromptu celebration of her move to the station. Even some of her neighbors had joined in, mostly Promenade employees, and the laughter and music had spilled into the corridor, lasting until early morning.

Sisko paused near a portal on the mezzanine of the

Promenade. What with the crowded conditions, he was able to walk around the station without attracting much attention, an unusual sensation for him. The two humanoids curled underneath the portal ignored him though he was only inches away. But then again, so was everyone else.

He gazed into the growing dark mass of the storm. It seemed to blot out the stars like a warning, and he couldn't blame Kasidy one bit if she was starting to regret her move. It had hardly been a week, and already a plasma storm was threatening to rip the station out of the fabric of space.

Yet Kasidy was a captain in her own right, and knew all about the dangers of living among the stars. Perhaps he kept thinking about her because she had been mentioned in so many of the reports today. Kira had praised Kasidy as one of their most staunch volunteers since the initial storm warning had been issued. He had never met a woman with more energy, or a stronger determination to do the right thing. He couldn't understand why she had remained a transport captain when she could obviously do anything, even attend Starfleet Academy, if she wished. But every time he tried to ask her about that, she had laughed off his questions. In general, she tended to be vague about her future plans.

Sisko would have liked nothing better than to track her down and talk about everything she had seen and done today. But she was probably asleep, and that was why he was wasting his time like this.

He turned away from the storm, knowing that he would have to face it down soon enough. Quickly finishing his tour of the mezzanine, he proceeded to the *Defiant* to get Bashir's final report before he made his decision.

The corridor outside the docking port for the *Defiant* looked like a war zone. There were more security guards here, both Starfleet and Bajoran, than he had seen on his entire tour of the upper core. There were also some guards in ship's security uniforms gathered near the turbolift. One lieutenant nodded as Sisko passed, and he recognized her as an officer from the *Ceres.*

As he entered the airlock, he could hear bellows of anger and yelled curses echoing through the corridors of the *Defiant.*

Sisko found Dr. Bashir and his assistant outside sick bay. "Problem with the Klingons, Doctor?"

Bashir looked as if he hadn't sat down all day. "They don't appreciate the regeneration treatment."

"Apparently not," Sisko said. "Can't you sedate them?"

"That interferes with the stimulation of regeneration, and I've given them the limit of neural blockers." Bashir had to raise his voice to be heard. "Regeneration is a highly invasive procedure, both on the cellular and chromosomal level. Their neural network has to be left intact to coordinate the repair."

Sisko looked through the door. Security guards were posted in the back corners of the room, flinching as the five Klingons struggled against the restraints of the med-beds. Their enraged faces were in stark contrast to their pale blue jumpers, which looked like children's footed pajamas. A portable regeneration unit was belted around the waist of each one.

Alons saw Sisko and started sputtering incoherently in Klingon. It sounded as if he was accusing him of cowardice and sadistic brutality. Sisko's Klingon didn't quite cover this sort of situation.

He turned away. "They seem to be recovering nicely. It's time they were moved to the brig."

Bashir sighed. "I thought you'd agree. I've already notified Worf."

In one sense, Sisko was relieved to see the Klingons looking so vigorous. "Then their radiation exposure was not as serious as you believed?"

"No, it's quite severe," Bashir gravely contradicted. "They'll have to undergo intensive treatment for at least a week, and two of them may never be able to reproduce."

Sisko prepared himself. "Was it caused by the storm emissions?"

"Even if they were near the storm for days, they had adequate shielding to protect them. However, Captain Alons informed me they were inside the blackbody itself. The *Ceres* crew didn't show a fraction of their exposure level, but they never entered the storm."

"How long were the Klingons inside the storm?"

"Hours at most. Less than a day."

"The runabout has been inside for nearly eight

hours," Sisko reminded him. "Will Dax's electrostatic guard protect them?"

"We have no way to know without data on the interior conditions. According to Worf's investigation, the *Katon* had superior shielding."

Sisko clenched his fist. His decision was made for him. He only wished he hadn't allowed Dax to take a runabout when this was obviously a task suited to the *Defiant.*

Worf appeared at the end of the corridor, followed by a phalanx of guards. "Captain," he said, acknowledging Sisko. "We are prepared for prisoner transfer."

"I'm ready whenever you are," Bashir agreed, wincing at the noise from the inner room.

Sisko nodded. "Commander, after you secure the Klingons in the brig, please notify the secondary crew that the *Defiant* will depart immediately."

"Sir?" Worf asked. "The secondary crew?"

"Yes. The senior officers will remain on the station while I investigate the storm."

Bashir suddenly revived. "Captain, request permission to come along. I have experience with biometric analysis, as well as the medical data on the Klingons' radiation degeneration. I would be able to assist you."

"You've been on duty since the beginning of the first shift," Sisko reminded him.

"With all due respect, sir, so have you."

Sisko didn't want to risk more of his top people in this storm, and yet he didn't have the scientific background to make informed decisions. Bashir did.

"Very well." Sisko stood next to Worf as the guards

placed the Klingons under stasis and transferred them to antigrav pallets. The shouts became blessedly muffled.

"Sir—" Worf started.

Sisko interrupted, "No, Commander, you're needed here."

"I agree." Worf lowered his voice. "However, Chief O'Brien requested to be informed if you decided to search for the *Rubicon.*"

Sisko knew he would have to deal with O'Brien at some point. "Thank you for reminding me, Commander."

Sisko couldn't keep a faint note of impatience from his voice, and Worf heard it, instantly drawing back into himself. Sisko knew why he felt defensive about the family members of his crew, but he didn't want to explain it to everyone. He wouldn't have told Kasidy, except for that desperate moment when he realized he was losing her. That alone had forced him to confess the truth.

Yet he wasn't satisfied as he followed Worf and the guards off the *Defiant.* Worf had never before indicated that he had any personal concern for another member of the crew. Sisko felt as if he had stomped on Worf when he was most in need of encouragement.

He followed the transport detail through the docking ring, approving of the way Worf dispersed the guards into a nonthreatening yet visible presence. Though the Klingons could barely move, they shouted their threats loud enough to penetrate the stasis fields. Refugees cringed back against the walls as they passed, overwhelmed and confused by the curses brought down on Starfleet, the Federation, Bajorans, Sisko, and Worf, not necessarily in that order of vehemence. Sisko decided that the Klingon prisoners were the least of his worries, and he turned into the habitat ring.

As the door to his quarters opened, he was immediately aware of the difference inside. The blue light was off, leaving the room dark. Then he saw the lumped shadows on the couches, and bit off his command for lights. He had almost forgotten about Kira's arrangements for some of the crew of the *Ceres* to stay with him and Jake.

He quietly made his way to his desk and activated the console. It made a good excuse to simply type in messages for Jake and Chief O'Brien, letting them know that the *Defiant* had left in search of the *Rubicon* and would return before the end of the third shift.

He sent O'Brien's message, noting that it had been routed to Worf's quarters. *Perhaps this overcrowding isn't all bad if it can get Worf to sympathize with his fellow officers.*

Then he saved the message to Jake, tagging it with an alert flash. Glancing at his son's closed door, he decided it would be better to let him sleep. According to the latest security report that had been waiting for him in Ops, Jake had already had a busy night with his Betazoid friends.

Sisko headed into his room for a quick refresher and a change of clothing, the next best thing to sleep and a good meal. But when the door opened he saw that Jake was asleep in his bed. He paused to look at his son's relaxed face, glad that he could at least say good-bye this way.

He hardly made a sound as he changed and freshened up, but the hiss of the door as he started to leave must have been the last straw.

"Dad?" Jake asked sleepily.

"Yes, Jake."

He rolled over. "You're home."

Sisko waited, wondering if his son would fall back asleep. But Jake said, "It must be late. I got in late."

"It is." Sisko gave in, letting the door close. He sat down on the edge of the bed, within the diminished starglow cast through the window.

Jake took one look and pushed himself up on his elbows. "You're mad at me. I know, I should have known better. That's what I told Odo, but I'm real sorry, and I'll pay for everything—" He broke off, sitting up so he could lean his head in his hands. "I don't blame you for being mad at me."

Sisko suddenly wanted to hug his son—his precious, honorable son—but that would only confuse him. And the last thing he wanted to do was hurt Jake.

So he restrained himself, asking, "Do you have enough credit to reimburse everyone?"

Jake ducked his head. "Almost, with Col paying half. If I could borrow some from you . . ."

"Once the replicators are back on line, I'm sure we'll be able to take care of it," Sisko assured him.

A ghost of Jake's smile appeared. "Thanks, Dad."

"I know what it's like," Sisko told him. "Strange things can happen to your judgment when your normal life is disrupted. It's different when you're on a mission. You expect unusual things to happen. But when you wake up in the morning, you don't expect that night you'll be sharing your quarters with five other people."

"Six," Jake corrected. "Kasidy was going to have to sleep on Leeta's floor, so I gave her my bed. I told her you wouldn't mind if I bunked in with you."

"Kasidy's here?"

"I thought you'd want that," Jake said.

"Yes." Sisko realized he was glad she was here, safe, and he was pleased at how easy Jake had made it for him. He would have offered Kasidy his own bed, but that might have offended her pride.

Jake yawned. "Why don't you come to bed?"

Sisko tried to smile. "Not yet. I'm taking the *Defiant* out to look for the runabout. So you won't have to put up with my snoring tonight."

Jake ignored his light tone. "You think something's wrong with them?"

"That's what we have to find out." Sisko didn't mention the fact that they also needed data on the interior radiation of the plasma storm.

"I saw Molly a few hours ago," Jake said. "I hope Keiko and Dax are all right."

"We'll make sure they are," Sisko told him, preferring that Jake concentrate on that than on the danger to the station. "I have to go now."

As Sisko got up, Jake blurted out, "You weren't going to wake me, were you?"

"I left you a message, but this is much better."

His son nodded. "Remember that next time you go searching after people who have disappeared. Please let me know first, even if you have to drag me out of a date, okay?"

"Okay," Sisko agreed, feeling his throat tighten.

Jake kept smiling until the door closed behind him. Sisko appreciated his effort.

He almost crossed the room to the other door. He wanted to look in on Kasidy, to see her sleeping, but he knew he couldn't without waking her. And he was already disturbing the *Ceres* crew. He heard coughing from the other side of the table, and two others were whispering near the couch.

He went to the console and recalled his message to Jake. He liked the casual intimacy and warmth in the words, so he simply changed the name to Kasidy and flagged it for her attention.

He was congratulating himself on navigating the personal bumps of the storm rather well when he reached the docking ring. O'Brien was waiting for him.

"I got your message," O'Brien said, even before Sisko stepped off the turbolift. "Worf says only the secondary crew is going along. He won't even let me on board!"

Sisko headed for the airlock where two of the security guards were still posted. "My orders were for the senior staff to remain here."

"But Bashir's on board," O'Brien insisted. "You have to let me go, too, sir. What if there are problems with the shielding? Or the power relays?"

"Then you better hope you've trained Kelly well," Sisko said sharply. "Because *he'll* have to take care of it."

"Captain, have a heart!" O'Brien clutched his arm with one hand. "I can't stay here when she's out there somewhere in trouble."

Sisko stopped, keeping his voice low so the docking technicians wouldn't overhear. "Request denied."

O'Brien's hand tightened. "It's not a request!"

"Mister, you should be glad I consider it a request." Sisko glanced down at his wrinkled uniform. "Do I have to order you to let go?"

"What? Oh—" O'Brien backed off when he realized what he was doing. "Sir, I didn't mean to—"

"Get some sleep, Chief. When I return, I'll need you to prepare the shields for storm impact."

O'Brien hesitated. "You will find them, sir? You won't come back without them?"

Sisko tensed at the direct plea. "I'll do whatever it takes to protect the station. You are dismissed, Chief O'Brien."

He turned away on his harsh order, resisting the urge to glance back from the airlock. He knew

O'Brien was watching him. And he knew what the chief would see: the same expression that Jennifer had on her face that last time he rushed off for the bridge, preparing to fight the Borg, a look that was somehow hopeful and frustrated at the same time, relying on him to save them all.

CHAPTER 14

"I'M FINE," DAX automatically replied. After listening to Keiko's worried inquires about her health for the past few hours, Dax had stopped paying much attention. Since she couldn't remember the blackouts it had soon stopped bothering her.

But she knew Keiko was right to be concerned. She had upped the critical levels in the medical data base, bypassing the preliminary warnings as per Starfleet regulations when the mission was of extreme urgency. As long as her neural activity returned to acceptable levels, she was determined to keep going through the magnetic loops.

"You were out for almost four minutes that time," Keiko told her.

"Never mind about me. We're starting to get some patterns here between the angle of transverse waves to the current and the location of the exit point." Dax didn't like the way they kept losing touch with their markers. Distance did not seem to be the determining factor, adding yet another random variable to their analysis. "I wish I could boost the sensors just a little more."

"You've already taken too much power from the shields," Keiko protested. She kept checking the readings on both their stasis belts.

"It won't matter how much we're exposed," Dax reminded her, "if we don't get back to the station. I say we should try a new vector."

They were near the periphery, toward the rear of the storm. Despite Keiko's worry over the radiation, she hadn't suggested leaving the plasma mass via the short route. They both knew the storm would hit the station before they could circle around.

"This layer of plasma seems occupied with gathering in new matter," Keiko commented. "It's filtering it deeper as it degrades the atoms into charged particles."

"No sign of organic carbon chains out here," Dax pointed out.

"That's because there aren't many magnetic currents," Keiko agreed. "The catalyst recombination must take place in the very heart of the plasma mass. Then the carbon sequences are distributed via the currents."

"I hope we don't find out what it's like in the

center," Dax said seriously. "Tobin, one of my past hosts, took part in a plasma research project for a power facility. There were obscure indicators that an inversion reaction was possible at maximum densities, but he was old at the time, and I can't remember the equation series. Isn't that typical?"

Keiko rolled her eyes. "I can't believe how much you do remember. All those lifetimes of experience."

"It comes in handy sometimes," Dax agreed with a gleeful grin.

Keiko hesitated, but Dax had laid the groundwork for her to feel comfortable enough to ask, "Don't you find it intimidating at times? I mean, I would feel as if someone were always looking over my shoulder, knowing that the next hosts will have access to all of my memories."

"It's true that most initiates have a strong streak of the exhibitionist in them." Dax laughed at Keiko's sudden blush. "That's why politicians and artists are usually willing to be the first hosts for young symbionts. I know I've always had a passion for holoprograms, even before I wanted to be joined."

"Just like Miles," Keiko said wistfully. "He loves role playing. I'd rather direct a performance than be in one."

"I didn't know you liked the theater."

Keiko smiled to herself. "A friend and I staged a few Noh dramas on the *Enterprise.* It's the classical Japanese form of storytelling, with the performers using their appearance and movements to suggest the essence of a tale."

"I'd like to see one of your plays."

"I think you'd like Noh," Keiko agreed.

"Did Chief O'Brien perform, too?"

Keiko wrinkled her nose. "No. He tried, but he hated practicing the speeches and movement patterns. And the masks drove him crazy. Not that I was surprised. He isn't fond of understatement or contemplation in any form."

"I always thought Chief O'Brien had quite a poetic streak in him," Dax protested. "He knows more ballads than anyone I've ever met. In another age, he probably would have been a wandering minstrel."

"That might have been nomadic enough for him," Keiko agreed dryly.

Dax almost pointed out that it was Keiko who kept leaving the station, not O'Brien. But the helm signaled, saving her from too terrible a breach of politeness. "Finally, we're entering a magnetic current."

They were silent for a few moments, but there was an uneasy tension in the air, as if something had been left unfinished.

Keiko sighed, admitting, "I hate this. It's like everything else in my life. We are jumping blindly through hoops, not knowing where we'll end up or when it will ever stop."

"You've already proven that the plasma is an organism. With each jump we're seeing how well the mass is integrated."

"That doesn't mean we're getting anywhere."

"It's all in how you look at it," Dax said philosophically.

Keiko bit her lip. "I suppose, but do you remember the Bajoran Gratitude Festival last year?"

"You bet I do." Dax usually tried not to think about the way she had felt that night, about how much she wanted Benjamin.

Keiko didn't notice her confusion. "That night Miles offered to leave the station and move to Bajor, but I told him we should keep doing this. Now, I'm wondering if maybe I made a mistake putting our lives on hold."

"Is that what you did?" Dax asked, trying to push the thought of Sisko away again.

But before Keiko could answer, the sensors signaled that a magnetic loop was forming. Dax transferred the helm to Keiko. The length and intensity of her seizures had varied with each location, but she wasn't taking any chances.

As Dax braced herself, the flash brightened the interior and seemed to freeze. She exchanged a look with Keiko at the appearance of the white viewscreen.

"I can't find any of our dye markers," Keiko announced.

Dax took the helm and slowed the thrusters. They had lost every one of their navigational points. "We're in a complete void: no EM radiation, no particles, no gravity pressure. A perfect vacuum."

"Maybe this is the heart of the storm," Keiko suggested.

"I doubt it. Of all the hypothetical conditions of the center of the storm, this is not one of them." Dax gave the uncooperative panels a sweeping glare. The void outside was so white it could have been of infinite depth or absolute flatness, squeezing them into two dimensionality. "Perhaps this is another consequence of the time-space inversion."

Keiko sagged to one side, as if she were losing consciousness. Before Dax could touch her, she disappeared.

"Keiko!" she cried out, grabbing the empty seat.

Keiko appeared on the viewscreen, standing in the field of white. She was looking around as if she couldn't see the runabout.

Before Dax could think of a way to signal her, Keiko turned and ran away. She was waving as if she were trying to get someone's attention. Dax maneuvered the thrusters to follow. Her eyes told her that another person was out there along with Keiko, but the sensors still weren't reading anything.

Then she realized it was Chief O'Brien. When he saw Keiko, he greeted her as if nothing unusual were happening. Keiko hugged him as if she would never let go, but just as Dax was maneuvering in with the runabout, Keiko abruptly pushed her husband away and started running.

Dax considered staying with O'Brien, but the chief headed after his wife. By the time they found Keiko again, she was standing among a few dozen Klingons. They were drinking and singing, floating in nothingness, toasting with empty hands. Keiko shifted among them when she saw O'Brien approaching. Though the chief tried to reach her, Keiko deftly avoided him while chatting and laughing with the Klingons. The warriors seemed oblivious to O'Brien's presence, yet they inadvertently kept him from getting to Keiko.

O'Brien was obviously frustrated, but that was nothing compared to Keiko's agonized expression every time she looked his way. As if she had no other choice but this.

Dax covered her face, unable to watch their struggle any longer.

"Are you all right?" Keiko asked.

Dax jerked up her head. Keiko was sitting next to her and the sparkling plasma field back was on the viewscreen.

"What happened?" Dax asked.

"You were unconscious for almost ten minutes this time," Keiko said. "I got dizzy myself on that one."

Thinking back, Dax asked, "Do you remember being in the void?"

Keiko frowned. "What void?"

Dax tried to get her bearings.

Keiko didn't give her time. "We're in an area of concentrated currents. We could enter one any second. Should I hold position to let you recover?"

"No, I feel fine," Dax said automatically.

"The computer said your neutral activity was the highest it's been so far. But it kept bobbing back down to acceptable levels."

Dax had never experienced anything like this before. "I saw you and Chief O'Brien in a white void. There were Klingons—"

Keiko's eyes were wide. "Klingons? You must have been hallucinating."

"No, it seemed to mean something," Dax told her.

"I don't know how you came up with Klingons, but we were talking about Miles as we went through that last loop."

Dax wrinkled her forehead. "We were?"

"You mean you don't remember?" Keiko asked. "I think we should stop. This can't be good for you."

"Temporary amnesia isn't uncommon following seizures," Dax told her. "I remember now that it's happened before. Besides, I don't care if I have convulsions. Plotting the currents is the only chance we have to get back in time."

Keiko checked the helm. "We're entering another magnetic current."

Dax braced herself again. "I'm wondering if the vision could be some sort of message from the plasma mass."

Keiko didn't look as if she was in the mood to listen. "I said this was an organism. I seriously doubt that it's sentient."

"That's not what I meant. It's conceivable that my mind is detecting and interpreting the wave patterns in much the same way the sensors do."

Keiko looked at her as if she were crazy. "Are Trill known for their telepathic ability?"

"Not really." Dax grinned as the energy built in the current. "But if we go through enough loops, maybe you'll start seeing O'Brien, too."

"No, thanks. I can wait," Keiko blurted out, as the stepped leader set off the formation of another loop.

This flash was more painful than usual. Dax

squeezed her eyes shut behind her hand, but she could swear she felt the photons penetrating her flesh and bone, striking her sore optic nerves.

"Where are we?" Keiko whispered, and Dax could hear the echo of Molly's high voice in her ear.

Blinking to clear her vision, what Dax heard was impossible—people, the wheels of vehicles, activity on the streets, even the breeze of a sunny afternoon.

She realized they were lurching along in a cart driven by an old Bajoran man. The rows of two-story structures indicated it was a suburb, and when she turned she saw the spires of the temple in the capital city. It was a beautiful spring day on Bajor.

"What's happening?" Keiko asked frantically, clutching the edge of the board that served as a seat.

"Maybe the plasma mass is trying to tell us something," Dax suggested. "Just try to relax. It doesn't look as if we're in any danger."

"What happened to the *Rubicon?"* Keiko asked.

"We're probably still in it." Dax examined the Bajorans on the streets—children mostly, along with their parents. The houses were joined by small fenced yards lining the walkway. In the door of one up ahead, she recognized a familiar face. "There's Chief O'Brien again!"

Keiko's mouth fell open when she saw her husband. He kissed a young girl good-bye, then a bouncing preschool boy. They ran to the fence to wave after him.

"Stop and let us off," Dax told the old man. When the cart pulled up, she motioned to Keiko. "Come on, it'll be faster on foot."

But by the time they reached the yard in front of the townhouse, the children had returned to their playing and O'Brien had disappeared. Keiko was staring at the girl. "Molly? Is that you?"

"Hi, Mom!" Molly sang out, absorbed in reassembling her bike. Apparently she had just added another gear. "Dad said you were going to meet him at the station."

The little boy ran to the fence, jumping up and down. "Mommy, Mommy, look what I made!"

Keiko reached out as if in a dream, taking the grubby yellow figurine. Her eyes never left the boy's face, full-cheeked and freckled like his father's, but with dancing almond eyes like her own.

Dax cleared her throat, reminding Keiko, "We need to determine how to get out of the storm."

Keiko was shaken out of her reverie. "This can't be real!"

"No, but anything you can tell me may help."

She looked at the house. "This is the Denarii quarter, where some of the Bajoran scientists live. I guess I would have chosen to move here if Miles had left the station and come to Bajor."

"Then perhaps this is an alternate time line."

Molly tightened the bolt and was finally able to give her mother her full attention. "Aren't you going with Dad?"

"Where?" Keiko asked.

"To the moon place," Molly said patiently, obviously mimicking Keiko's motherly inflections. "You know, you do it every year."

"It's our anniversary?" Keiko looked in the direction that O'Brien had gone. "He must have taken the public transport to the station. Maybe we can catch him before it leaves."

Dax followed Keiko into bustling streets, watching her signals for how to cut through the pedestrians. Keiko seemed stunned, but at least she was working with her on this.

But when they reached the platform, the transport had just left for the ground-to-space station. The ticketmaster recognized Keiko and called her over to give her a message padd that O'Brien had left behind.

Dax shamelessly looked over Keiko's shoulder, reading, "I'm not surprised you didn't come home today. Maybe you were right last night when you said you should have called it off on our wedding day instead of giving in to everyone. I should have listened to you then. I'm going to the moon chalet, but if you don't come I'll understand why. You've never really been happy with me."

Keiko clutched the padd tightly, insisting on handling the arrangements to get them to the station as fast as they could. Dax ended up with her in a hired cart, hanging on for dear life as it swerved around corners and between larger electronic transports. The city was a blur, and Dax knew she would never be able to retrace their path through the maze of entrances and tunnels that took them through the sprawling ground-to-space complex.

Then Keiko led her on a bewildering race through the station, across ramps and along elevated walkways. It was a strange hybrid, with the ponderous Cardassian structures enlarged and embellished by the highly ornamental Bajoran architecture. But even Bajorans were unable to impose harmony on the disorder of a major port of call.

They were stopped at an imposing gate by a uniformed official. "Tickets?"

"We don't have tickets," Keiko told her. "I'm trying to reach my husband before he leaves—"

"You must have a ticket to proceed beyond this point." The official gestured back down the long hall, from where they had come. "You may purchase your tickets at any one of our commercial counters, or you may apply for space assistance from your corporate sponsor."

"I'm not going anywhere. I just need to talk to him," Keiko insisted. "It's the next moon shuttle, and it's about to leave!"

The official checked her chronometer, then hesitated at Keiko's pleading eyes. Dax had hope. Bajorans were better than most when it came to sympathizing with each other. Maybe living through an occupation made it easier for people to understand each other's pain.

"I'll try to notify the shuttle docking port," the official told Keiko. "If you'll please stand aside."

The other official continued to allow passengers through the gate, while the first murmured into her comm device. Keiko slumped against the stone wall, her chin nearly touching her chest. A strand of hair had pulled loose and was hanging against her cheek.

"They'll tell O'Brien you're here," Dax tried to assure her.

Keiko sighed. "Maybe. Then again, maybe we'll have to go beg for a couple of tickets and fly to the moon. And maybe by the time we get there, he'll have given up and left for good."

"Don't be such a pessimist," Dax told her. "We're doing the best we can."

Keiko finally looked up. "Don't you understand? Miles and I have always done the best we could, but it always ends like this, with me chasing after him and neither of us knowing where we're going."

Dax asked, "What is it you want?"

"I want harmony. I want peace."

Suddenly they were sitting in the runabout again, staring up at the white void on the viewscreen.

Dax didn't know what else to say. "Maybe you picked the wrong guy."

Keiko looked at the void as if she couldn't believe her eyes. "Maybe you're right."

CHAPTER 15

"WHERE'S MOMMY?" MOLLY repeated sleepily.

O'Brien avoided her eyes, reminded of how he had stood in the portal and watched the *Defiant* go into the storm without him. After he had returned to Worf's quarters, he was able to sleep only fitfully, finally getting up to check some shield computations that were hammering at his head.

Molly hadn't gotten nearly enough sleep when he woke her up and got her dressed. He had managed to brush out the tangles in her long hair, but she had squirmed and whined the entire time, and she had done nothing but ask for Keiko.

He could make excuses for the little girl, knowing that her circadian rhythm was still messed up from leaving Bajor. He wondered if he should have let her continue sleeping, but he hated the idea of leaving her locked in the bedroom alone. What if she woke up again?

She was holding a granola bar in one hand, her elbow propped on the table as if she had forgotten it was there. He had dialed for some fruit and granola last night so he could be sure something would be waiting when she woke up.

"Eat up," he urged. "We have to get to work."

Molly gave the stale bar a dubious look then threw it against the wall. It shattered on impact, spraying nuts and rolled oats in every direction.

Moll-y!" he exclaimed reproachfully. She started to cry.

O'Brien decided that he had maintained enough continuity in his daughter's daily habits. He picked her up to leave, wondering again where Captain Ari had gone. He was sure Worf hadn't returned to his quarters after the *Defiant* had departed.

He waited a while for a turbolift, but one never showed up even after he keyed in his priority code. Molly fell back to sleep as he carried her through the habitat ring, but when they reached the Promenade the noise was loud enough to disturb her. She was yawning and pouting when they reached Odo's office.

Odo sighed when O'Brien brought Molly in.

"Where else can I take her?" he demanded in a rush, letting her down. "You don't expect me to leave her with strangers, do you?"

"No. She can stay with me." Odo leaned over. "Will you keep me company for a while?"

O'Brien expected the girl to pitch an absolute fit. By rights, she deserved one. But apparently she had gotten used to Odo's grim features. O'Brien had seen grown humanoids tremble under that gaze, but Molly simply exclaimed, "Let's play pony!"

"That's a good girl." O'Brien tried to give her a kiss good-bye, but she twisted away from his hands. She ran to the desk, hiding behind Odo's chair.

"Molly!" O'Brien felt helpless. When had his child become such a stranger? "Molly, come here and say good-bye," he insisted, walking towards her. "Daddy will come back for you soon."

"No!" she shouted, holding on to the chair as if for dear life.

O'Brien hesitated, then circled the desk. He only wanted to give her a kiss.

"Go away!" she shrieked, hiding her face. "No!"

"Come on, Molly," O'Brien coaxed. "I know you just miss your mommy."

"No, no, no! I want pony rides!" She dashed past him, clutching at Odo's leg. "Pony! I want my pony!"

"Hush, Molly!" But O'Brien wasn't sure she heard him.

Odo stood there stiffly, as if he didn't know what to do.

O'Brien took her arm, ordering, "Behave yourself! Stop it right now."

Her shrieks raised another few decibel levels. Even he pulled back. "I hate you! Go away! I want my po-nee!"

Odo sighed, and with an apologetic glance at

O'Brien, he swung the girl onto his back. He bobbed up and down slightly, a token gesture at horse-like movements.

"Ya! Gi'up!" Molly exclaimed. She was breathing hard and tears were shining on her face, but she wasn't screaming anymore. She completely ignored her father.

"Only once around the paddock," Odo told her. "Then your horse has to rest."

Solemnly she nodded. "Gi'up!"

Odo gravely began walking the perimeter of his office. O'Brien watched with sullen resentment. He knew Molly didn't hate him, but he didn't like her saying so in front of Odo. *He* could have played horsey with Molly only she hadn't asked him. Then again, he hadn't seen her awake for two minutes since she got to the station. Could he really blame her for attaching herself to Odo? Shouldn't he be grateful that there was *someone* she liked to be with?

"Not now!" Odo snapped as a guard tried to ask him a question. By the time he returned to his desk, there were three of them waiting to speak to him. O'Brien dreaded the scene Molly would make when Odo tried to stop.

But Molly didn't utter a word when Odo let her descend to the chair. She contented herself with slipping under the desk, disappearing from his sight.

"Thanks, Constable," O'Brien said, rather shame-faced. Apparently the shapeshifter made a better parent than he did.

"Think nothing of it, Chief," Odo demurred. He

seemed more interested in dispatching the guard details than talking about Molly, so O'Brien contented himself with one more nod of thanks, craning his head to try to see his little girl. "Bye, Molly. I'll be back for you soon."

She solemnly gazed up as if not recognizing him. Then she went back to work, busily making a tent out of a blanket using the drawers of the desk and the chair.

O'Brien left, feeling about as low as they came. As if things weren't bad enough already, he ran into Worf in the doorway.

O'Brien shoved past him, making Worf stumble into the side of the door. There were so many people staggering around from the shock fronts that no one paid much attention, that is, except for Worf.

"Sorry," O'Brien drawled sarcastically. "I could be helping out on the *Defiant,* but no, you made sure I was left hanging around here getting in everyone's way."

Worf's eyes darkened. "I could not allow you to board the *Defiant.*"

"Oh, you couldn't, could you?" O'Brien asked in a low voice. "Wouldn't you have done anything to save the mother of *your* child?"

Worf glared at the mention of Kay'lar. "How dare you speak of that!"

"Maybe I'm out of line," O'Brien agreed, "but you could have helped an old friend last night. Sisko was half convinced to take me along, and if I'd been on the bridge, he would have said yes."

"I was following orders."

"You follow orders only when it suits you." O'Brien leaned in closer. "There are times when you have to follow a deeper law."

Worf stared at him, caught by the truth of the accusation. Then he shook it off, not so much backing down as dismissing O'Brien from serious consideration. But his parting glare said that it wasn't over between them.

O'Brien couldn't stop him from going through the door, but as it closed, he swung around and slammed his fist into the plassteel window. It rang out, vibrating in its frame. He could see the startled faces of everyone inside looking out at him.

Shaking his fist, he stepped away from the window before painfully leaning over, clutching his wrist. Good thing he hit the plassteel rather than the titanium beam. Maybe he could get away with not going to the infirmary—if the throbbing ever let up.

"I'm glad I moved out of the way," someone said right behind him. "A blow like that could have crushed me."

O'Brien looked back, then down at Captain Ari. "Pardon me! I didn't see you there."

"So I gathered." The Sattar didn't seem disturbed. He leaned back against the beam. "I've been waiting to visit my wayward senior mate. Commander Worf agreed to allow me inside. That other one, that shifty creature, he was most uncooperative."

O'Brien politely nodded, examining his hand. It was stiffening up and the second knuckle was swelling in a bad way. He would need the full use of his hand today in order to strengthen the shields. The main power conduits would have to be linked into the secondary generators to cover bit losses in microwave transmission. Maybe he could go snag Rom again . . .

"You were arguing with the Klingon," Ari commented. "I thought you were friends. Last night you assisted him."

"We've known each other for almost seven years," O'Brien admitted. "Seven years!"

"You've been on other posts with him?"

O'Brien grinned in spite of himself. "On the *Enterprise.* Back before I became the glorified custodian of this station."

"That was when you were a warrior," Ari said, as if he understood. "And now, your friend has injured you in some way?"

O'Brien shrugged, irritated by that casual reference, as if now he was an ex-warrior.

"It is difficult to deal with Klingons," Ari acknowledged. "Their sense of honor serves their own needs. You must accommodate yourself to their codes rather than asking them to understand your own."

"I suppose," O'Brien agreed. "But isn't everyone that way?"

The Sattar smiled. "Of course. Then you understand what I'm suggesting. If you want something from the Klingon, put it in his own terms. Make it a matter of *his* honor, and he will do whatever it takes to salvage his pride."

"I don't want anything from Worf," O'Brien denied, remembering this was a Sattar he was talking to. Their small size and fluffy, innocent appearance was what lulled people into thinking they were harmless. "In fact," O'Brien finished. "The commander is probably right. I should get back to work."

O'Brien turned on his heel, shaking off Ari's insinuations against Worf. First he had to go to the infirmary to get his hand fixed, then stop by Quark's for Rom before rounding up his crew. They only had the rest of the morning before the storm would hit.

Worf did not appreciate being shoved around by O'Brien, especially after he had relayed the chief's message to Sisko and gotten subtly rebuked for his efforts. And he still had not gotten over Cali's infiltration of his logs. He clenched up every time he thought of her reading his personal meditations on Alexander, on the Klingon situation, on Deanna. It was intolerable!

Silently fuming, he waited until Odo had completed his orders to the guards and dismissed them to their posts. Then he handed over the data clip. "This is my report on perimeter patrol, as of oh six hundred hours."

"How industrious of you," Odo told him. "I usually rely on my guards to report on the status of the station."

"These are emergency conditions."

Odo held the clip in two fingers. "And did you find anything that needs my attention?"

"Yes, I found several questionable situations, such

as the continued presence of evacuees in the connecting tunnels."

"I'm aware of that, Commander. Guards have already been dispatched to remove those people to transient quarters." Odo tossed the clip onto his desk, but he did not sit down. Molly had appropriated his chair, but Worf believed Odo was trying to make a point.

"Commander," Odo began, making it clear his request was formal. "I would prefer to be notified whenever there is a prisoner transfer to my brig."

Worf almost sighed. "Zeischner is a competent officer. It was not necessary to disturb you."

"Nevertheless, in the future I would like to be informed. It is part of my duties as security chief on this station."

"Agreed." Worf would have agreed to anything at that moment to get on with it. "What is the status of the Klingon prisoners?"

"They are packed in fairly tightly, but at least they can bounce off one another. Apparently even Klingons have a threshold of pain."

Worf could have sworn there was a trace of satisfaction in Odo's voice. "I would like an hourly log of their conversations."

"You're going to listen to everything?" Odo asked incredulously. "I'm already running a pattern recognition program, and there's been nothing of significance so far."

"There are Klingon codes and words that you may not know," Worf told him.

"If you find any," Odo agreed, "please inform me."

Worf nodded shortly. "And the Sattar?"

"The senior mate of the *Reaper,*" Odo said thoughtfully. "She is in holding cell three along with a Risan couple caught picking pockets in Quark's. I believe Quark was taking a cut until they lifted latinum from the Dabbo table."

Worf thought Cali should feel right at home with them. "Captain Ari is waiting outside to see his officer. I believe he will not fight the charges."

"But you're considering dropping them," Odo guessed.

Worf wondered how he could tell. "Cali should pay for her crimes. She assaulted me and she broke into my private files."

Odo consulted his console. "You have the rest of this shift to decide. Then the charges will be recorded with the proper authorities. There are both civil and criminal accusations, so it could take several days to sort out."

"I will let you know my decision," Worf agreed. "First, I would like to hear what she has to say to Captain Ari."

"As would I," Odo murmured. "It's hard to believe a Sattar would act without her captain's express approval. But what have they to gain by her incarceration?"

Worf shook his head as he went to get Captain Ari. He had been wondering that himself. He had even woken, after a nervous half sleep on the floor of Sisko's office in Ops, dreaming of Captain Alons and

Sebas drinking from the bottle of *Hum'tas* in his quarters and rifling through his computer files. A childish dream, but a disturbing one.

When Captain Ari entered, he immediately said, "I must apologize again to both of you. My senior mate has been under a great deal of stress. Recently she was the cause of a cargo loss through her own negligence, and I'm afraid the other seniors are realizing their folly in promoting one so young to such a position of authority. And yet, her mother was a superb leader."

Worf remembered what Cali had said last night about the Klingons taking her mother away. It had also been a Klingon betrayal that had killed his own parents while they were living in the Kitomer colony.

Ari shook his head sadly. "If her behavior has been erratic lately, perhaps we have forgiven her too much, indulged her too often in her whims."

"If you'll excuse me for saying so," Odo retorted dryly, "her behavior has escalated beyond erratic and has now reached criminal proportions."

The captain lifted one hand as if there was nothing he could say to refute it. The proud Sattar almost looked humbled, and he turned away to hide his discomfort. "Despite the trouble she causes, she is a valuable member. I would not like to leave her behind."

Worf refrained from answering, accompanying Captain Ari into the brig. Odo ordered one of the guards to watch Molly so he could follow.

Cali rushed forward when she saw her captain,

managing to greet him with grateful delight while glaring past him at Worf and Odo.

From the corner of his eye, Worf could tell that the Klingons had seen him enter. Though no sounds penetrated the force field, every ritual gesture of disrespect and disgust was aimed in his direction.

But first, the Sattar. "When can I get out?" Cali asked Ari. "I'm going crazy in here with these two." She gestured to the Risan couple.

Ari glanced back at Worf. "You've been charged with assault and trespassing. You could be here for quite a while."

"If the assault is proved to be premeditated," Odo put in helpfully, "she could be sentenced to time in a penal colony."

"Don't I get some privacy to consult with my legal advisor?" Cali asked. "Or does Starfleet deny that too?"

"This is a favor," Odo informed her. "You'll get your consultation after the official charges are recorded."

Cali appealed to the Risan couple slumped against each other on the bed. "Aren't they keeping us here in unsafe conditions? Not enough food, only one bed for three people—"

"Everyone on the station is overcrowded," Worf interrupted, tired of this nonsense. "I offered you better quarters, but you attacked me."

Cali appealed to Ari. "See? He's been out to get me since he couldn't find anything on the *Reaper*. Just look what he's done to those Klingons!"

They automatically followed her dramatic gesture. The Klingons quickly realized they had somehow caught everyone's attention. Alons struck a righteous pose, crossing his arms across his chest. The others followed his example.

"See?" Cali cried out. "He's keeping them locked up in there. They can't speak to anyone. What is he trying to hide?"

"I would lower the baffles," Odo replied, "if they would stop shouting."

Worf ended further discussion by marching over to the damping field and shutting it off. "You will be silent," he ordered.

"The *loD'web* speaks," Ton sneered. "But we do not hear—"

Alons cut him off, "You think you can get away with destroying my ship? The Klingon Empire will not stand for this insult!"

"I did not wish to destroy the *Katon,*" Worf reminded him. "The self-destruct was initiated by you."

"You left me no choice," Alons sneered, leaning closer to the force field. "And now you will die!"

But his threat was ruined as he scratched impatiently at his neck, twisting his entire body as if unable to endure the prickling sensation of the regeneration.

"I know the *Katon* attacked the *Ceres.*" Worf raked a disgusted glance over Ton. "Your tricks will not stop me from proving your guilt, and then you will wish you had died along with your ship."

"You are dead to your own people!" Alons retorted, crossing his arms and turning his back on Worf. The others followed, relishing their show of contempt. Ton's self-satisfied expression was the worst. To know that such a Klingon—weak, prideful, undeserving—now possessed lands that rightfully belonged to the House of Mogh . . .

Worf strode through the brig. He saw no one, staring straight ahead as he entered the outer office. He wanted to keep going, through the Promenade, across the tunnel to the docking ring, where he could keep on going.

Instead, he stopped by Odo's desk and pretended to concentrate on the list of guard details that the chief had compiled. He was a true Klingon, a son of the Klingon Empire. He could let his anger course through his veins without shirking his duty.

When Odo ushered Captain Ari out of the brig, Ari again tried to apologize. But Worf was in no mood for equivocations. "We all suffer, Captain. That does not allow us to act like dishonorable barbarians."

"You may find it hard to believe, Commander, but I agree with you. Without honor among ourselves, we are no longer a family but a pack of scheming individuals. I see that happening to my members. The Sattar are a thing of contempt in the galaxy, are they not?"

Worf narrowed his eyes.

"Yes, a thing of contempt," Ari repeated. "Yet where is the hope I can offer my young members? We have nothing but what we can wrest from everyone else, and little chance of anything better. The Klingon government won't allow inter-ship alliances among the Sattar, so we will never be able to obtain good contracts, only bits and pieces left over by the organized shipping lines."

"Perhaps you could apply to the Klingon High Council."

"The Sattar who go to *Qo'noS* never return." Ari gave him a bleak smile. "I am not brave enough for that, Commander."

"I, too, have had my dealings with the council," Worf admitted. "There is much that has gone astray within my people. But I am not to blame for your misfortunes, and yet she attacked me!"

"Are you not to blame, perhaps more than anyone?" Ari asked in a deceptively mild voice. "You are a member of Starfleet, supporting a Federation of people who pride themselves on their honor and justice to all. Yet the Federation formed an alliance with the Klingons while they hold my world and others in virtual slavery. Why does the Federation support this infamy, turning a blind eye to the plight of the Sattar?"

Worf couldn't answer that. Everyone knew about the Sattar.

Ari pressed, "Perhaps Starfleet allows it for the sake of a 'larger' peace. If so, then tell me, Commander, what right do you have to decide that my people will suffer for your peace? Is that honorable?"

Worf could only stare at the Sattar. Thankfully, Odo broke in and urged the captain on his way. At the door, the security chief told the captain, "You will be notified by this evening about what will be done next with your senior mate."

Ari pulled away with the dignity of a senior Sattar. Nodding solemnly to Worf, then Odo, he declined further assistance to the door.

Worf felt something and looked down. Molly was standing right next to him. "Nice pony," she told him, patting his knee. "Good pony."

Worf carefully put down the clip and left without a word. Some things were too much for anyone to expect him to accept. He would be fine once he had a brisk walk around the docking ring.

CHAPTER 16

THE *DEFIANT*'S MAIN viewer showed the speckled plasma field, complete with flares and clusters and rippling diffractions of every scientific description.

Dr. Bashir could have watched it for hours, mesmerized by the shifting mosaic of colored lights. It was ironic that within this so-called blackbody, there was such a display of pure energy constantly colliding, combining, and deconstructing in vividly instantaneous reactions.

But Bashir didn't have much time to look at the viewer. He was at the main tactical station, and though he was unfamiliar with the primary readout for the sensors, he trusted in Dax's console to alert him to the important things. He also linked in the medical data base, running a diagnostic on the potential bio-effects of the infinite combinations of waves and subatomic particles within the plasma.

"Still no sign of the radiation that poisoned the Klingons," he informed the captain.

Sisko was also examining the sensor data. "Odd. Only the most cursory of readings, despite the photo-conductive activity."

Bashir agreed, "Too many random oscillations are distorting the base frequencies—"

The *Defiant* lurched without warning. Bashir barely caught the console while Ensign DeGroodt was flung from the helm into the side railing. When Bashir saw that she immediately began to push herself up, he stayed at his station, letting Lieutenant Clan'cee from the secondary tactical console assist her. He was glad that Clan'cee was along. He was one of the best physicists assigned to DS9. Bashir knew he would need all the help he could get to decipher the readings on this storm.

"I'm sorry, sir," DeGroodt apologized.

Bashir added, "I think sensors got something that time."

"What's causing it, Doctor?" Sisko was as irritated as the rest of them by the unpredictable course changes.

Bashir checked Clan'cee's notations as he reported, "It seems to occur whenever the density of a magnetic current reaches a certain threshold point. Since the waves are moving faster than light, there is a significant delay in the reaction of our inertial dampers."

"Can't we avoid the currents?" Sisko asked DeGroodt.

She was settling back into helm control. "I'm trying, Captain. But we get caught up and swept along before I can pull free. We're between two currents now, and if they converge . . . but it looks as though the port current will dissipate before that happens."

Clan'cee agreed. "The currents form and dissipate so rapidly that it's difficult to track a path through them."

Sisko glanced over at Bashir. "The incidents seem to be increasing as we penetrate deeper into the plasma."

"I suggest we hold position here," he replied. "Clan'cee and I have prepared a probe to release into one of the magnetic currents. That should give us more information on what causes the subspace disruptions."

"Proceed." Sisko frowned at the viewer as if he were determined to subdue the storm singlehandedly if it came down to that.

Bashir coordinated the probe launch with Clan'cee and DeGroodt as they skirted the current and maneuvered away before being drawn into the turbulence. The probe shot off, accelerating much faster than the sensors had recorded the velocity of the electromagnetic waves within the current.

Before Bashir could question the anomaly, a brilliant flash brightened the main viewer.

"Report!" Sisko ordered.

Bashir couldn't see his readings. "That exceeded the photoelectric threshold."

"I'm getting a high incidence of scattering," Clan'cee called out. "EM readings from the probe went off the scale."

Bashir was finally able to see to confirm, "We've lost telemetry with the probe."

The viewer had returned to normal brightness. "The current is gone as well," Sisko said, seeing the difference in the particle motion.

"I believe the probe's sensors set up a feedback loop, pushing the particles in the magnetic current to maximum ionization," Bashir explained. "That flash was a sort of rip in subspace, transferring the energy radically away from the particle flow."

"Transferring it where?" Sisko asked.

"That's impossible to tell," Bashir admitted. "The *Defiant* must be too large to penetrate the rips. When one forms, it deflects the *Defiant* away, causing our change in course."

"What about the runabout? Is it small enough to get through?"

Bashir reluctantly nodded. "I believe so. The Klingons kept raving about being caught in a maze that they couldn't get out of. That would make sense if their yacht was transported through the subspace rips."

"This storm is half a sector long." Sisko's jaw clenched. "The *Rubicon* could be anywhere."

Bashir realized that Clan'cee was looking in his

direction, waiting for him to inform the captain of the meaning of the probe's readings. Bashir considered taking Sisko into the lounge to tell him, but if Clan'cee knew, then the others would soon find out.

"Captain, according to the data from the probe, the station is in danger." He rushed to get it out all at once. "The plasma energy is comparable to that of a dwarf star. The atmosphere of Bajor may protect the inhabitants, but I doubt there will be anything left of the station or the wormhole. This storm is a natural cleansing agent, ionizing every particle in its path."

"Can't we stop it somehow?" Sisko demanded. "Or try to shift its course?"

"I don't even know what keeps it going." At the sudden hush, Bashir added, "Maybe with more data and using the biometric analysis . . . maybe we can come up with something. We have plenty of probes to get samples of the cascade bursts that precipitate the rip in subspace."

The tension on the bridge was already running high, but Bashir's analysis seemed to cast a pall over everyone. Except for the beeping of the computers, there was absolute silence as the captain considered the situation.

DeGroodt turned to offer, "Sir, I can try to hold us closer to the probes if that would cut down on interference."

Bashir immediately shook his head, picking up his medical tricorder to analyze the atmosphere of the bridge. "I recommend we position the *Defiant* much further away. The cascade burst appears to be the source of the dangerous alpha radiation."

Sisko stood up. "Why hasn't the medical alert warned us of excessive radiation exposure?"

"Because the contaminated molecules are currently in a metastable state. They disassociate after several minutes, and the effect is slow enough to be recorded as within acceptable levels." He scanned himself and compared the result with his normal cellular readings. As he glanced up, he caught a worried glance from one of the ensigns as she hurried off the bridge with a clip in hand.

"What is it, Doctor?" Sisko asked.

"Tertiary ionization is already occurring within our bodies. At this point I'm unable to determine the progress of the chemical transformations."

"Can you adjust shields to block the alpha radiation?" Sisko asked.

Lieutenant Kelly shifted uneasily at the engineering station, looking as if he wanted to crawl out of his own skin. "I can cover that frequency range, but the oscillations rebound all over the board."

"I'm not sure we can shield against this sort of radiation," Bashir agreed. "It's practically designed to penetrate and disintegrate matter. The shields may even be accelerating the process."

Sisko swept a glance at the bridge crew. "Then we had better work fast."

"Aye, sir," Bashir agreed, along with the others.

"Attach a subspace beacon to every probe," Sisko

ordered. "And send burst communiqués into the magnetic currents. Maybe one of them will get through to the *Rubicon.*"

Sisko sat back down, letting the rest stay unspoken. There was no telling what damage had already been done to Dax and Keiko. Or what additional exposure would do to the crew of the *Defiant.*

Sisko rested his chin in his hand. At that moment Bashir was sincerely glad that he was a doctor and not the captain of this ship. It was hard enough dealing with life and death on an individual basis. He wouldn't want to make that decision for forty people at one time, much less the thousands of people waiting back on the station.

We're going to die, Keiko thought. *I pushed my way on to this mission, and now we're going to die because of it.*

She had realized it was impossible to plot an internal map of the currents. They formed and dissipated so rapidly that the computer couldn't calculate the shifts in the patterns, not with the meager fifty or sixty markers the sensors could detect at any one time. And Dax couldn't take much more of—

"This way!" Dax cried out, making Keiko jump. The helm was locked from her control, but she started to input commands, acting as if she were flying the runabout. "Don't worry. We'll get there before the chief leaves this time."

"Dax," Keiko said soothingly. "It's all right. You can relax."

Dax glanced at her as if trying to remember something. Then she stared back up at the viewscreen, apparently seeing much more than Keiko could in the beautiful plasma particles.

"If we don't catch him, then we'll know for sure," Dax insisted. "But we have to get past the Klingons first!"

She went into a flurry of activity, trying to prevent some imagined catastrophe. Keiko had rerouted the computer relays to her station, but just to be certain Dax didn't somehow gain access, she had manually disconnected the main power node in the junction under her console.

Yet Keiko kept an eye on what Dax did, recognizing the command to cut power to the warp engines, which weren't on line in the first place. Keiko had already tried to engage warp drive, hoping the field could repell the particles. But the plasma disrupted the continuity of the field before it could form.

Then Dax tried to fire the torpedoes. Keiko hadn't tried that, but she wasn't willing to use brute force even at this point.

She moved to the rear of the runabout to ask, "Computer, is it possible for me to sedate Commander Dax?"

"Neurological activity indicates sedation would be unadvisable at this time."

"What is her current condition?" Keiko asked.

"Levels of tertiary radiation have risen above acceptable limits."

"You've already told me that," Keiko sighed.

"What do I do about it? And don't tell me to evacuate the vicinity. That's impossible."

"Continued proximity to alpha radiation will accelerate tissue irradiation," the computer responded.

Keiko turned to the small viewscreen, activating it. "Display on graph." The upward arc of alpha radiation poisoning was erratic but unmistakable. Deadly.

As if one look at Dax didn't make that perfectly clear.

Keiko asked, "Computer, is it possible that Dax's hallucinations are some sort of communication with the storm?"

"Insufficient data," it replied with maddening unconcern.

"No. Extrapolate," Keiko urged. "Could a plasma-based being communicate via EM waves directly to the brain of a Trill?"

"Insufficient data," it repeated.

"You want data, just scan Dax!" Keiko glared around the runabout, wishing there were a focus for her frustration.

"Commander Dax is suffering from sporadic electromagnetic stimulation of the neural tissue, causing spontaneous dissociative experiences."

"You mean hallucinations." She hadn't really believed Dax's wild theory, but part of her had been desperately hoping that Dax was accomplishing something toward their escape.

She returned to stand by her station, entering the command to maneuver the *Rubicon* from the magnetic current, letting them drift. There was no use going through more loops. It only made Dax worse, and it would take weeks for them to plot the interior of this complex organism. She was certain now that the plasma mass was an organism. Nothing else could be this integrated or intricately patterned while maintaining its rapid motion.

Next to her, Dax started hitting her touchpads as if realizing she was locked out. Keiko quickly slid into her seat before Dax could try to switch stations.

"We've stopped," Dax said, looking at the swirling plasma patterns. "How can we get out if you keep doing everything for him?"

Carefully, Keiko assured her, "We'll get moving in a minute. Just give me a chance to plot the shortest direction out of here."

"I know how to get out," Dax replied, her eyes wide and dazed. "I'm not sure how to get in."

Keiko input the coordinates of the nearest storm edge and held onto manual control in order to maneuver around the magnetic currents that formed. "You should rest for a while," she suggested. "You've been working for hours without a break."

"Have I?" Dax stiffly stood up, stretching her arms to the ceiling. "I believe it."

"Why don't you lie down on the bench?"

"What for?" Dax asked. "You aren't trying to pull something, are you?"

"I just said you should lie down and get some rest."

"You're not going to leave me out here." Dax was looking at her suspiciously. "Not after we've come all this way together."

"I'd never do that!"

Dax narrowed her eyes. "You wouldn't believe what I've seen some people do when they're desperate."

"I would believe anything right now," Keiko said faintly. Even without the influence of radiation-induced hallucinations, she had managed to come up with more than a dozen gruesome scenarios for what would happen in the next few hours. Top on the list was the image of a two-billion-volt plasma arc sparking between the station and the wormhole.

"You need me," Dax reminded her.

"I know. I don't know what I'd do without you."

Dax seemed satisfied with that, but Keiko felt even worse. She had really meant it, but in every sense of the word, Dax was no longer here.

All of her paranoid talk was making Keiko edgy, as if she weren't already numb enough from lack of sleep, and sick to her stomach from the surges of adrenaline that kept insisting she was about to die. She had partly turned while piloting, to make sure Dax didn't do anything unusual, but out of the corner of her eye she caught the blip on the sensors.

It looked like an indicator for a subspace transmission, but when she did a sensor sweep, nothing was there. Then she played back the sensor log, and saw that she hadn't imagined it.

Changing course, she retraced their route back toward the last magnetic current they had passed. Sensors picked up traces of a transmission signal that had degraded to the point that the computer didn't recognize it as decryptable codes. It could be another strange by-product of this highly unusual plasma storm, but then again . . .

Impulsively Keiko turned the runabout and traced the magnetic current upstream until she reached a point where the sensors recorded the highest incident of fragments.

Taking the runabout directly into the current, she plowed through the turbulence against the directional flow, trying to reach the center where the fragments were most densely clustered.

Radiation readings shot off the scale as the engines fought the surge of the current. The disruption started to cause the formation of another loop right behind the runabout.

Keiko routed maximum power to the engines, but it was too late. The runabout was sucked backward through the loop.

After the burst of light had faded, sensors picked up a much clearer indication of the transmission fragments in this area. She traced them toward another dissipating magnetic current, but she hesitated to take the runabout into it. What if the fragments were only an echo of their own attempts to hail the station?

She almost regretted her impulsive action. The rough navigational map of the plasma storm indicated that the *Rubicon* was further away from the periphery than before. Now she would have to plot a new course to get them out of the plasma, unless she followed the fragments through another loop.

Dax was huddled on the bench in the back, muttering orders as she stared at the blinking display on the transporter console. Keiko hoped she wasn't getting any ideas about leaving, and she quickly entered a command to route transporter control to her console.

If she kept going through loops, she would surely kill Dax. Yet they would both die if they didn't get out of the plasma mass. Everything kept twisting back on itself until Keiko didn't know what to trust. A familiar feeling, especially during the past few years. She felt cramped into her own existence, like a bonsai, dwarfed and twisted while struggling to grow. She knew what it was like to be windblown, gnarled, and stunted by adverse conditions, forced to bend to unrelenting forces. Yet bonsai were exquisite creations. Tiny miracles, the same way that Molly's smile was a tiny miracle every day.

"You have to stop!" Dax demanded behind her. "You were right, Keiko, it's not working. You have to walk away, it's the only chance we have to get out of here."

Dax tried to stand, but she collapsed back on the bunk, her hand reaching out imploringly.

"Is something wrong?" Keiko asked.

"You have to give him up," Dax whispered. "You almost did once before. The day you got married."

Keiko's mouth opened. "How did you know about that?"

Dax struggled to concentrate, to keep her eyes focused, as if to prove she knew what she was saying. "You have to leave him. Or everyone will die."

Keiko didn't even have to think about it. Every part

of her being rejected the idea. She and Miles belonged together.

"I'm not walking away from anything," she told Dax.

She changed vector to intersect the current where the transmission fragments were rapidly dissolving. The engines strained as they fought the electromagnetic waves, but Keiko held the helm steady. She was ready this time and when the loop formed behind them, she let the runabout go through.

Her head was swimming when the flash dissipated, and the medical alert was sounding a new alarm. Before Keiko could ask the computer what was happening, Dax rolled off the bench. Her arms and legs were twitching.

"Computer, what can I do for Dax?" She ran to her side.

"One cc of monocloride may inhibit the seizure."

Keiko ordered the helm to stop so they wouldn't run into the new current forming in front of them. She grabbed the med-kit on her way back, fumbling with the hypo. But once it was injected into Dax's neck, the distressing shaking began to ease off.

Keiko checked her pulse—rapid but strong. She was tossing her head, so Keiko stroked her hair, trying to soothe her exactly as she would for Molly. Dax looked much younger when she was unconscious.

Trying to be gentle, she pulled Dax back up on the bench. It wasn't easy, but she finally got the commander secured with the straps. If she had any doubts before, now she knew: the loops were definitely killing Dax.

Back at the helm, the dye marker map showed that the runabout had moved quite some distance to the rear on that last trip, but sensors were picking up even more traces of transmission signals behind her. She tracked them down until the computer was finally able to identify them as part of the routine hail used by Starfleet.

Keiko wondered if she were unduly twisted and hardened, but she already knew what she was going to do. She would kill both of them to save the station, and watching Dax die in pieces would be the hardest part. But she wouldn't give up.

Her teeth clenched as she swung the runabout into the nearest current. It was one of the strongest ones they had encountered. The engines strained but they weren't able to hold position. A stepped leader formed right behind them, and Keiko transferred power from the shields so they wouldn't slip past before the loop appeared. Shields fell to fifty-three percent.

As the runabout went through the loop, she felt herself losing consciousness.

"Welcome back, *Rubicon.*"

She was hearing things. She shook her head at the viewscreen as the image of a ship appeared, then was gone in the midst of the plasma. She was afraid she was starting to hallucinate, like Dax. At least she wasn't convulsing—

Her eyes blurred and, like a three-dimensional

mirage, a vessel shifted into view among the dancing particles.

"It's the *Defiant,"* Keiko whispered.

"Rubicon, can you read us?"

She had left the communications channel open to track the transmission fragments. "Yes! *Defiant,* we're here!"

As the *Defiant* maneuvered closer, Keiko checked the map of the markers. They had returned to the leading edge of the storm.

"Yes," Keiko repeated, just for herself. "We're here."

CHAPTER 17

". . . AND ADJUST THE regeneration to include . . ."

". . . will perhaps counteract the affects of tertiary radiation . . ."

Dax heard the voices and realized she was no longer on the *Rubicon.* It sounded like the infirmary on the station, and she had to wonder if this was yet another installment in the epic O'Brien romance. She already felt as if she had followed them through the system and back without accomplishing anything.

Somewhere above and behind her, Bashir was saying, "There seems to be a low spontaneous reversion to normal composition."

"What if the thresholds are crossed?" someone asked.

Bashir said quietly, "I won't let that happen."

Dax swallowed and had trouble moving her dry lips. "Did she do it?" she whispered.

"She's trying to say something," someone said.

It was hard to get the words out. "Did she give him up?"

"Dax, it's Julian. Can you hear me?"

Dax tried to focus. "Of course I can hear you."

His hand pressed down on her shoulder, but she hardly felt it for the burning, tearing pain that flashed through her entire body. "What's wrong with me?" she asked through clenched teeth.

"Trill are particularly susceptible to the tertiary radiation produced by alpha electromagnetic waves."

Her muscles spasmed, and her back arched under the strain. She tried to breathe through the terrible sensation of her insides squeezing out through her pores.

"According to the medical logs," Bashir said. "You've been suffering from electrochemical neural stimulation."

"Oh, really?" Dax panted. "I thought I was talking to the plasma gods. Are you telling me I made it all up?"

"Delirium can be a strange thing," Bashir agreed.

"Glad I'm all better now."

Bashir made a point of wiping the sweat from her brow. Dax didn't bother to thank him.

"Regeneration is a complex process," he explained. "Each of the DNA nucleotides containing radioactive phosphorus must be traced and the frequency analyzed. Then they're physically matched to the nearest 'neighbor' that wasn't degraded by the tertiary radiation. Only after that process can the damaged DNA chains be relinked."

"It sounds charming." Dax was unable to suppress a groan. "Are we almost done?"

Bashir was completely sympathetic, but then he could afford to be. He didn't feel the same way she did. "I'm sorry to say, Jadzia, but you'll be undergoing regeneration for the next five days."

"Days?" She stared at him. "Five days? Of this! You can't be serious."

"You're very lucky," he assured her, calling on his most doctorly manner. "You'll survive. It only feels as if you're turning into liquid mush."

"Five days?" she repeated incredulously. Dax suddenly looked around. "Where's Keiko? She isn't—"

"She's fine. I was able to put her on a portable unit. She went up to Ops for a debriefing on your mission."

Dax changed the subject abruptly. "Does the captain know about the magnetic currents in the storm? A plasma arc could be sparked between the station and the wormhole—"

"Yes, Keiko told us." Bashir concentrated on the blinking lights of the diagnostic hood. "Since it's too late to evacuate the station, I believe Sisko intends to close the wormhole."

"How?"

"With decompression explosives."

Dax stared at him. "That will close it permanently."

"Do you have another suggestion?" Bashir asked.

"I bet I can come up with one!" She struggled to her elbows. "Can't I have a portable unit so I can get out of here, too?"

"Dax, your irradiation activity is barely holding below threshold levels. If ionization continues to increase, I'll have to put you in stasis until we can get you to a med lab with a regeneration chamber. Starbase Fifteen is the closest one, and that's three weeks away."

"But you let Keiko leave," Dax protested, "and she was exposed for as long as I was."

"People react differently to radiation. Your chemical structure is more vulnerable to the free radicals that were produced. Do you want to be sterile for the rest of your life?"

Dax tried to slip out from under the diagnostic hood. "Getting out of bed isn't going to accelerate the ionization process."

Honestly he admitted, "No, but I doubt if you can get up."

That was exactly what she needed to hear. "Shove this thing aside and I'll show you."

He obligingly rolled the unit to the bottom of the bed, leaning against it to watch. She moaned as her feet swung over the edge, unprepared for the sudden lurch in her stomach.

"Feeling queasy?" Bashir asked solicitously.

"Not at all." She was breathless already. "No problem. Just get the portable unit, and I'll be on my way."

He hesitated, hearing the effort in her voice. "I strongly advise against this, Jadzia."

Dax stood up, hanging onto the bed. "I'm an old pro at this. You don't think I use Klingon exercise programs just to keep trim, do you?"

"No, you use them for teasing Worf."

She glared at him, refusing to rise to the bait. "Would you rather see everyone else in the same condition? Because that's what's going to happen if we can't protect the station."

Bashir shook his head, and kept on shaking it the entire time he retrieved a portable regenerator and adjusted the programming.

"Thanks," she said breezily as he adjusted it around her waist. "I owe you one."

"You owe me at least a dozen," he grimly reminded her. "And you're not fit to be walking around. If you suffer a systemic shock, it could kill you."

"I won't be the only dead body on your hands if that plasma storm hits the station."

Bashir frowned but he took her arm, supporting her. "I'll go with you." At her dubious look, he slung a med-kit over his shoulder. "I won't order you to bed, but I will insist on medical supervision."

"Thanks, Julian," Dax said, gratefully leaning on him.

* * *

O'Brien didn't like the way Keiko looked, sweating and blinking as if she could hardly stay conscious. She shouldn't be in Ops, she should be flat on her back in bed. He had found her in the *Defiant's* sick bay under a diagnostic hood not more than an hour ago, looking so pale and drawn that he was afraid she might die. But Bashir had assured them both that she was well under the threshold levels of irradiation.

He went to Keiko's chair and knelt down, checking the readouts of the portable regeneration unit at her waist. The whites of her eyes were completely bloodshot, and her eyelids were swollen and red. She coughed slightly with every few breaths.

He wished he could make it all go away. "You'll be fine, Keiko."

She stroked his hair with a lingering touch, as if she had thought about doing it and was glad she finally could. He leaned his cheek into her palm, then kissed it. He didn't care that Captain Sisko was sitting five feet away, examining the data on the plasma storm that Keiko had compiled.

Sisko put the clip down on his desk, bringing the tips of his fingers together. "According to the summary of your findings, the plasma storm is a living organism."

"Yes, it is," Keiko said simply.

O'Brien squeezed her hand and returned to his seat, knowing she would prefer it that way during her report.

"I agree that organic carbon compounds are being

produced," Sisko told her. "But how can plasma be alive?"

"Life is energy in motion." Her voice was rough, but that was how it usually sounded when she was exhausted. "This plasma mass consumes particles and maintains an internal rhythm and structure involving the magnetic currents. It also appears to be capable of propagating offspring when it passes suitable planets or moons."

Sisko didn't like what he was hearing. "If the plasma is an organism, then we are duty bound not to cause damage to it."

"In my professional opinion," Keiko said firmly. "The plasma mass is a living entity. It possesses an active, adaptive structure that utilizes its surroundings in order to survive."

"The latest science report suggests that we detonate nucleonic charges to scatter the storm, forming an alley of safety for the station."

"I don't think that's possible," she replied. "You would damage the internal patterns that maintain the organism, and it would almost certainly react to protect itself."

Sisko lifted one hand in frustration. "If you can determine that it *is* an organism, then you must know some way we can affect it."

"I'm not a nuclear physicist," Keiko reminded him. O'Brien admired her cool in the face of Sisko's pressure. "This is an energy life-form, not a biological one."

O'Brien wanted to support her. "That's true. We need—"

"Dax!" Sisko exclaimed as the door opened.

O'Brien turned as Dax came into the office, supported by Dr. Bashir. He quickly got up to offer her the chair, glad of the excuse to go stand next to Keiko. His hand cupped his wife's shoulder. He thought she would want him to let go, but she put her hand over his, keeping it there.

Dax had always impressed O'Brien with her tall, imposing presence, but now she folded herself into the seat with deceptive fragility. She looked even worse than Keiko, as if she had been starved for weeks. Her flesh was drawn tight to the bones of her face, and her skin had a sickly, ashen color. The spots were hardly visible.

Dax was also having difficulty breathing. "Captain, if you close the wormhole with decompression, we may never get it open again."

Bashir nodded. "And that won't solve the problem of how to protect everyone from the alpha radiation. It will take at least twenty-four hours for the plasma storm to pass through this sector."

Sisko looked from Dax to Keiko and turned to O'Brien. "You examined the effect on the *Rubicon*'s shields, Chief. Do you have any suggestions?"

"The alpha waves aren't dangerous until they pass through the shields. The automatic systems tried to screen for them, but the oscillations were too random for them to compensate."

"And we must have wide coverage," Bashir agreed, "to protect everyone against the radiation from the other cosmic rays."

O'Brien knew Sisko was waiting for a solution. "We could try to layer the shields, using different oscillation frequencies to catch the different angles of the scattering."

"That won't work," Dax said, examining the operations report on O'Brien's tricorder. "Our systems still can't compensate rapidly enough to stop electrons as they spontaneously bond and dissociate."

O'Brien nodded glumly. "I was also worried about the risk of pairing the charged particles. That could set off an energy discharge through the power relays."

In the silence, Keiko gave a loud sigh. "I don't know, but maybe we're going about this the wrong way. We can't fight each individual particle and wave. Plasma dynamics, like those of an organism, react as a whole. Why don't we use that?"

"You're talking field mechanics," O'Brien pointed out. "We've already tried deflection models, but the magnetic field of the plasma varies too much. The focus has to be tight—hardly wider than the station—and we still get leakage."

"But we wouldn't have to affect the entire EM spectrum," Dax said thoughtfully. "Only the direction of the propagation of the leading particle waves."

"We still won't be able to protect an area of space large enough to include the wormhole," O'Brien insisted.

"But don't you see? We won't have to if we can deflect the storm," Dax said. "A wave field sent into the storm front could act as a magnetic mirror, repelling the charged particles back along the path of their approach."

O'Brien looked down at Keiko. "I thought you said it might damage the plasma to change its internal patterns?"

Dax was already shaking her head. "This isn't matter we're dealing with, it's plasma. A liquid of charged particles following the waves in a helical motion. The direction of propagation can be reversed without affecting any of the other variables like frequency or temperature or energy dispersion. That's why magnetic mirrors are so useful in containing plasma for scientific study."

Sisko put his hands flat on the desk. "Dax, this is a big storm with a lot of momentum behind it. It would take a lot of energy to change its direction."

"We'll use its energy to our advantage," she told him. "Direction of propagation is a cascade reaction. If we can influence one particle, it will influence others. We can target the leading field lines and the organism should react as a whole, turning on itself."

"Leaving the sector the way it came," Keiko agreed.

"Can it be done?" Sisko asked O'Brien.

"You've got me," he admitted, taking his tricorder back from Dax to input the equations. "It's a good thing we upped the power amplitude this morning. That Rom is a godsend. He was able to link the outer shield wall to the deflector towers. Now we can absorb the energy directly from the cosmic rays and deflect it back at the storm."

Sisko glanced around, seeing they were in agreement. "It looks as if we have a plan, people. Let's make it work."

CHAPTER 18

KEIKO FELT MILES squeeze her hand as they entered Ops. She smiled in return as he headed for his station, then she hesitated at Kira's glare, thinking it was meant for her.

"Captain, you can't close the wormhole!" Kira protested as soon as Sisko appeared. Keiko realized that the major wasn't angry, but harried almost beyond endurance.

At the tactical station, Worf curtly reported, "Decompression explosives have been prepared, and torpedoes are ready to launch."

Keiko was about to object, but Dr. Bashir did it for her. "That could kill the aliens living inside the wormhole."

"The charge has been calibrated to affect only the periphery of the subspace fibers," Worf replied.

"Only the periphery!" Kira repeated sarcastically. "That will detach it from this quadrant, destroying the Celestial Temple of the Prophets."

"I'm not going to destroy anything," Sisko said flatly, cutting off the discussion. "We think we have another solution. We're going to repel the plasma mass back on itself."

Worf was examining his sensors. "Sir, our attempts to deflect the storm have proved ineffective."

"And we barely have enough power to keep the shields intact," Kira added. "We're already getting random radiation penetration."

"That's because we're trying to block the wave emissions." Dax had to stop because of her coughing. Keiko finished for her.

"A deflection field aimed at the plasma itself will reverse the direction of the particles."

Bashir was helping Dax down the steps. "She should be in the infirmary."

She shook her head. "Let's set up the deflector program. Then I'll route the data to the center console so I can sit down."

Keiko felt as bad as Dax looked, but she went to the science console to assist her. Accessing the patterns of her latest biometric analysis, she included the data that both the *Defiant* and the station had gathered while they were gone.

Kira checked her readings. "Impact with the station is estimated in two hours."

"We have enough time," Keiko said quietly.

"But you can't expect to match the variables of every wave," Kira protested. "That's impossible."

"We'll target the particle waves in the magnetic currents," Keiko told her. "That's the dominant internal rhythm according to the biometric analysis. We gathered enough data on their directional flow and internal oscillations to be able to accurately target those wave patterns."

Miles backed her up, saying, "The leakage won't matter as long as we can affect more than eighty percent of the area in contact with the deflection cone."

Sisko took a stance at the head of the main console. "Let me know when you can begin."

Dax was sagging as Keiko ran the final confirmation pattern against her biometric analysis. But she had to be ruthless. If the angle of oscillation was not correct, the power would be expended for nothing.

"Sorry," she murmured to Dax. "Another minute . . ."

Dax shrugged, wincing in lieu of a smile.

Keiko knew it wasn't the appropriate time, but she quietly added, "I knew the loops were killing you, but I kept going through. I'm sorry about that, too."

Dax quickly looked up, then nodded. "I would have done the same thing. We make a good team, you and I."

"Yes," Keiko agreed. "Just don't tell anyone about your hallucinations." She glanced around, making sure no one else could hear. "Miles can be sensitive about that kind of stuff. You know, superstitious."

"It had nothing to do with you," Dax admitted. "I guess I got you two confused with something else. I think it was because of what you said about the Gratitude Festival last year."

Keiko remembered the way Dax had acted that night, wrapping her arms around Sisko and practically climbing up his body. "Oh! I see."

"You and O'Brien make a good couple," Dax said. "Like Benjamin and Kasidy. Sometimes you can tell just by watching two people together."

"I know," Keiko agreed, realizing how much trust Dax was placing in her. "Then we'll keep the details between ourselves."

Dax nodded, but she was also swaying as if ready to pass out.

"Analysis completed," Keiko announced loud enough so everyone would know they were making progress.

Dax took one look at the figures and graphs of the biometric analysis and told O'Brien, "Good thing you increased the power output. We have the pitch angle of the frequency, but it needs to be oscillated in a rather complex pattern."

Dax made a few minor adjustments to the deflection program, then relayed the matrix to him. "I see what you mean," he muttered. "Irregular patterns."

Dax routed the science data to the center console as Miles reported, "Deflectors will be ready in a moment, sir."

Bashir helped Dax to a stool at the center console. "You've done enough."

"Not yet," Dax retorted with forced lightness.

Keiko leaned against the science console. She was locked out of control and could only monitor what was happening. Then she realized Miles was giving her a concerned look, and he motioned to her regeneration unit. She checked it to make him happy, and gave him a thumbs-up signal. Poor Miles looked as if he hadn't slept last night either, and she remembered how his hand had trembled when he touched her shoulder. Suddenly she didn't feel like the weak link around here, knowing everyone else was suffering, too. It was an awful thought, but she knew self-survival tended to bring out the baser instincts of biology.

"Deflectors on line," Miles announced.

Dax confirmed, "Matrix program tied in with the guidance systems."

Keiko carefully watched the indicator recording the rate of leakage against the error factor. If she had to, she would recalibrate her data.

"Activate deflectors," Sisko ordered.

It took a moment for the magnetic mirror to stabilize. "Narrow the density focus," Keiko murmured as Dax tried to compensate for the interference of the emission waves.

Miles frowned as he realized what she was doing. "We don't want to get intrabeam collisions."

"We've got room," Dax said. "I'll tell you where."

"Field lines focused," O'Brien confirmed. "Power holding steady."

The readings indicated that forty percent of the particles within the deflection beam were being reversed.

"It's not strong enough," Keiko said. "There must be something else we can do."

Dax lifted her head. "It's too steady. Every other variable has an irregular pattern."

Keiko knew what she meant. "What if we pulse the deflectors—"

"And target different areas to maximize our contact load," Dax agreed. "Then we can turn the tide."

"Hold on there!" O'Brien protested. "You want me to pulse the beam? That's much harder on the emitters. And the possibility of feedback overload increases by seventy percent."

"It's the only way we can have an effect on the plasma," Dax insisted.

Sisko nodded. "Do it."

Keiko went to Miles's station to access the biometric matrix and determine the optimal timing of the pulses. "It's complicated by the internal motion. The intervals will have to vary according to the location of contact."

Miles seemed amazed by what she was doing. "It's theoretically possible. But I don't know how the emitters will hold up."

Keiko knew that tone of voice. "I knew you could do it. Here's the pulse pattern sequence."

She stepped aside so he could enter the program. "New pattern entered," he announced. "Engaging deflectors."

Gasps rose at the sight on the main viewer. With each burst of the deflector beam, brilliant flashes rippled against the blackbody, twisting into the plasma itself and curling around the intricate folds and crinkles of a pattern more convoluted than brain tissue. It was like a living form of a mathematical equation, illuminated by hairline fractures of light.

Miles put an arm around Keiko's shoulder, drawing her closer. "Deflection rate at seventy-six percent and rising."

"I knew it would work," Keiko whispered, staring at the plasma mass. She could almost see it churning back on itself. Then she looked up at him. "Miles, I think we should have another baby."

His eyes widened. "Is *now* the time to talk about something like that?"

"Can you think of a better time?" she asked, wanting to laugh.

He started to smile, tightening his arm around her. "Sure! I think it's a great idea. We always said we would—"

"It's working!" Dax exclaimed. "Benjamin, we've done it. Cascade reversal is spreading and the forward movement has significantly slowed." She glanced up at Bashir. "I think I'll go back to the infirmary now."

"Finally!" the doctor exclaimed.

Miles swept Keiko up in a real hug as exclamations and sighs of relief rose in Ops. "I knew it," Keiko whispered, for Miles as well as herself. "I knew we could make it work!"

CHAPTER 19

After Sisko made the announcement that the storm had been deflected from the system, Odo knew that his time as a nanny was almost over. But he didn't expect the O'Briens to come for Molly so soon after the storm alert was rescinded.

Almost before they were through the door, O'Brien was saying, "Thanks so much, Odo. I don't know what we would have done without you."

Keiko looked as if she was barely able to keep standing, even with her husband's support, but her smile radiated warmth and gratitude. "Miles told me how wonderful you've been with Molly."

Molly looked over the edge of the desk. "Mommy?"

"I'm home, Molly." Keiko held out her arms. "How's my girl?"

Odo was ready to urge her towards her mother, afraid of the same sort of incident that had happened this morning with O'Brien. But Molly skipped out to meet her parents, letting Keiko kiss her and lifting her hands so her father would pick her up. She was babbling about her pony rides.

Keiko beamed at Odo. "She enjoyed herself, I can tell."

"Yeah," O'Brien agreed wryly. "Molly likes Odo."

Odo inclined his head. "And I like Molly."

Keiko wrinkled her nose up at her daughter, secure in her father's arms. "I guess you don't need your old parents so much, do you? But what would we do without you?"

Odo silently agreed.

"We can't thank you enough," O'Brien told him, reaching out for his hand.

Odo hesitated, but he shook hands with the chief. Usually he avoided it, perhaps because other people often didn't extend him the courtesy, as if they were afraid they could be absorbed by a mere touch. But the firm clasp was a seal of something they had shared—Molly.

"I don't mind watching her," Odo said gruffly. "If you need to go to the infirmary, I have some time to spare."

Keiko was coughing, glancing at the portable medical unit around her waist, but O'Brien assured him, "She'll be fine. Right now, the best thing for us is to go home and have a nice, long nap."

Molly waved good-bye to Odo. "Can I have more pony rides?"

"I would be glad to. Drop by anytime," Odo told her, meaning it. To Keiko, he added, "She already had her lunch. Corn chowder and a cheese sandwich, though she didn't like the tomatoes—"

Odo broke off, realizing how he must sound. Keiko hesitated, then gently put her hand on his arm. "Thank you, Odo. We'll both come see you, probably more often than you would like."

Odo nodded, sitting down and turning his chair away. He couldn't bear to watch them leave. But he could hear Molly's bright chatter as she talked about the games and funny things she had seen in the security office.

The door closed, then there was silence again. He turned to gaze at the chair where Molly had curled up to nap this morning. The same chair where Major Kira sat every Tuesday as they went over the weekly security report. He realized he was beginning to hope that someday the door would close and love and laughter would stay inside with him instead of always walking away.

He signaled Ops.

Kira answered, "Hi, Odo. Something I can help you with?"

It was on the tip of his tongue to ask to see her this evening, but what would he say? "Have dinner with me?" It was absurd. He didn't even eat.

"It was nothing," he muttered, shifting uneasily. "My hand slipped, is all."

Kira rewarded him with a smile. "Always glad to see you, Constable."

Odo stiffly nodded, ending the transmission. Then he sat there, comforting himself with the memory of her velvety brown eyes fondly gazing at him. Maybe it wasn't too much to ask—someday.

Sisko nodded to the O'Brien family as they passed him in the habitat ring. The chief was carrying Molly, so he figured they were finally heading back to their quarters. They certainly deserved it. Keiko had served above and beyond the call of duty after Dax had slipped into radiation-induced hallucinations. He intended to request a citation for her work.

Sisko waved as he turned the other way, toward the permanent resident section. The corridors were no longer lined with restless, bored evacuees surrounded by their piles of possessions. It was still overcrowded, but everyone was dashing about, intent on returning to their ships for departure. They were fortunate that the emission waves had diminished almost as soon as the plasma mass turned on itself. It wouldn't be long before the first vessels would receive clearance to go through the wormhole.

Kira was still in Ops coordinating the departure sequence. Sisko had promised to relieve her after he took a break for an hour or so. There was something he wanted to do first.

"Benjamin!" Kasidy exclaimed as the door opened. "I thought it was one of the *Ceres* people. They left some of their things—" She broke off, grinning at him. "Don't stand out there, Ben. You'll get run over."

"Thanks." Sisko walked inside. He couldn't take his eyes off her. It was remarkable the way she glowed, like a steady, burning flame. He wanted to hold his hands out to her, soaking up the soothing warmth.

She turned a complete circle in the center of the room, spreading her arms wide at the piles of blankets and dirty dishes. "I was going to roll around in Bacchanalian abandon, then take a long, hot shower."

"I'd like to see that." He went closer.

Kasidy smiled up at him. "I always celebrate after a life or death experience."

"So do I."

She hesitated, as if this were too good to be true. "You're stopping by for only a second, aren't you? To make sure I'm all right."

"Wrong." He was enjoying this. "Jake and I are going to use some of my Captain's prerogative and replicate a tricorder and a picnic lunch. I thought you might like to join us on the observation deck of the upper pylon. It's sure to be quite a sight, watching all of these vessels pull out."

She cocked her head. "Then you aren't mad about what I said to Jake?"

He hesitated, trying to remember. "What did you say to Jake?"

"Didn't he tell you? Last night after that freighter broke loose, he tracked me down." She shrugged slightly. "He was acting so worried, wanting to make sure my ship was secured and volunteering to help set up the temporary housing. I told him to go have some fun with those new friends of his. Actually, I insisted."

"Oh, you did?" He raised one brow in mock severity. "Did you know that I told him to stay in our quarters last night?"

"Yes."

"You did?" he asked in surprise. "And you still told him to go out?"

"Yes. I said you both needed to lighten up." Kasidy laughed outright at his expression. "Oh, I know he almost ended up getting arrested, but I'd do it all over again. When I left this morning he was in your room, furiously writing away. I think he wishes he'd been put in the brig, if only for a few minutes."

Sisko shook his head. "Captain, sometimes you're too much for me."

"I know I am." She gave him an arch look. "But you know I'm right."

"It's beginning to be a pattern," he agreed.

Kasidy put her arms around his neck. "You know, Ben, I think we've weathered our first storm together rather well."

"Yes, we have." He liked the way she felt in his arms, and he was glad that she hadn't been able to read his mind during the past twenty-four hours.

She laughed, as if she knew exactly what he was thinking. "I'd love to go on a picnic, but don't you have a million things to do?"

"Nothing more important than this."

Kasidy caught her breath. "You know, Ben, sometimes you say just the right things."

"Good." He kissed her, savoring her soft lips.

As they finally drew apart, she somehow managed to slip out of his grasp. "Come on, let's not miss anything."

He could never seem to hold onto her for very long. "Jake said he would meet us at the replimat."

But as they left, Sisko captured her hand, refusing to let go. He felt better than he had in a long, long time.

CHAPTER 20

WHEN WORF RETURNED to his quarters, he paced around for a few moments, noting the stains and general disarray that had been left behind by his guests. But beyond that, there was something fundamentally wrong. He knew that these rooms would never feel like home to him, not like his quarters on the *Enterprise*. He didn't belong here, and yet, where else did he belong?

Worf sat down at his console. This Klingon-Federation conflict could help determine where he belonged, but in the end, it was up to him to make a place for himself. Then he could make a home that included Alexander and all of the other people he cared about.

He activated the com. "Worf to *Reaper*, requesting to speak to Captain Ari."

Ari quickly came on the line, and his grave expression indicated he had been waiting for Worf's decision. "Yes, Commander?"

"Your senior mate has been released from the brig, Captain. Charges will not be filed against her."

"Thank you, Commander! I am most appreciative. If there is anything—"

Worf shook his head. "Do not thank me." For some reason, he added, "I did it for her."

"Oh." Ari hesitated. "Why, if I may ask?"

Worf briefly pressed his lips together. "I understand the way she feels."

"That is very . . . generous of you, Commander." Ari's voice gave the impression that it was highly dubious, as well.

Worf remembered Odo had not been as diplomatic when he had ordered him to release Cali. "You should prosecute her just to make an example for the rest of the Sattar," the chief had insisted. But Worf had already made up his mind.

He did not care what any of them thought. "Is the *Reaper* prepared to depart?"

"We could be. That is, once Cali returns."

Worf input the proper docking commands. "You have clearance to disembark within the next hour. I recommend that you do so immediately."

Ari leaned forward. "Are you in a rush to see us leave, Commander?"

This was why Worf had waited until he was in his quarters to make the call rather than doing it from Ops. "The Klingons will be released from the brig after sixteen hundred hours. Due to the termination of the peace treaty, they will be asked to leave immediately."

"I understand." Ari's voice grew hushed at the implications.

Worf was well aware that the Klingons would have no compunctions about ordering the Sattar to take them back to *Qo'noS*, even if it caused them to lose their transport contract. And without a ship, Alons could very well commandeer the *Reaper* for his own use.

Ari apparently thought about all that and more, because he kept staring at Worf as if he didn't understand, yet he didn't want to tip his hand. "Why are you telling me this?"

"You were correct this morning. I do not believe it is right that the Klingon government can interfere with what rightfully belongs to you." Worf tightened his fist. "They took away my lands, just as they would take your ship from your people. I cannot allow that to continue."

"You can't?" Ari asked.

"No."

Worf transmitted the documents he had filed with the High Council of the Federation of Planets requesting an inquiry into the condition and status of the Sattar Collective under the Klingon Empire.

Ari read the documents, considering them carefully. "This has already been received and docketed by the Federation Council. Can you cancel your request?"

"No. It will be processed until a ruling is reached," Worf told him. "The Sattar Collective will be investigated, along with your history involving the Klingon Empire. You can testify as to your current conditions, and the Klingon High Council will be asked to respond."

"But the peace treaty has been broken," Ari protested. "Why should the Klingons cooperate?"

"It will undoubtedly delay a ruling from the Federation Council. However, a new peace treaty must include discussions of your status within the Klingon Empire. In order for you to receive full protection from Starfleet, the Sattar Collective must apply to join the Federation."

Ari was slowly shaking his head. "I didn't think you had it in you, Commander, but you can strike a good deal when you put your mind to it. What is it you want?"

"This is not a deal," Worf denied. "I desire nothing for requesting the inquiry."

"But surely you must know how valuable this is to the Sattar?"

"It is done."

Ari hesitated. "Then there are no hidden strings, nothing we have to do for you?"

Worf drew back at the suggestion. "You have until sixteen hundred hours to leave, Captain Ari. Good luck."

He reached over to disengage, but Ari stopped him. "Thank you, Commander. You'll never know the depth of the gratitude of the Sattar."

Worf signed off, vaguely wondering why he heard a threat implied in those words.

He sighed as he stood up, glancing around the repellant rooms. He had been forced to agree with Captain Sisko on the release of Alons and his crew. The *Katon* had never fired on the station or the *Defiant,* and the destruction of the yacht had eliminated any evidence of their attack on the *Ceres.* Their tampering with the docking clamps had been ill conceived, and it was reason enough to hold them in the brig and give them an armed escort to a departing vessel. But it would only serve to antagonize the Klingon High Council to hold Alons here any longer.

Worf went to the window, wishing he could see the *Defiant* from here. From the first time he saw that ship, he knew she was worthy of a warrior, worthy of the war that was to come. Yet he suddenly felt his conviction falter. Perhaps everyone else was correct, and the Klingons knew they could not win in a fight against the Federation. Perhaps he had become so desperate to resolve his own private dilemma with his people that he was seeing conspiracies and incursions where there were none.

His fists tightened as he glared at the departing ships, at the busy image of prosperity on the station. Could he be wrong about the Klingon Empire?

* * *

After Cali had returned to the *Reaper* and talked to Captain Ari, she ran the entire way through the ring to Worf's quarters. She had been calculating her percentage of the Klingon deal, which she had initiated from inside the brig, when Ari told her it had been canceled. She had protested, not only because the contract points had been arranged, but because her bonus would enable her to redeem her debt to the rest of the members.

But then Ari explained what Worf had done for them, requesting a Federation inquiry into the Sattar situation. Cali didn't have to be told it was in their best interests to play along with Starfleet. If they were sucked into the Klingon offensive they would be nothing more than service drones for the duration of the hostilities. And knowing the Klingons, that could last for generations.

Cali signaled the door, hoping Worf was here. She didn't have much time left. The captain had tried to prevent her from leaving the *Reaper,* intending for them to be far away from the station by the time the Klingons were released. But Cali had called in the terms of her private deal, and Ari had been forced to allow her to go. But he had warned her that the *Reaper* would depart on schedule whether or not she returned.

"Enter!"

Cali went in, knowing that for once she had not carefully planned and prepared what she was going to say. So she stood just inside the door as Worf turned from the portal.

"What do you want?" He looked displeased and unhappy, as if he was thoroughly frustrated by everything that had happened.

"I don't know why I came," she admitted.

"You do not intend to thank me." He gazed out the window again.

"No. Like everyone else, I'm sure you have your reasons for what you do."

"Do you know many honorable people?" he countered.

"Do you?" she retorted.

"Yes."

She still thought that he must have gained something from helping them. But if he had found out about the Klingon deal, he would have exposed their involvement rather than give them the best hope the Sattar Collective had had in centuries.

"You will find honorable people in the Federation," Worf told her. "Perhaps they can help you if you deal with them honestly."

"Why would the Federation help us?" Cali demanded. "They don't care about us."

"The Federation has more reason to be prejudiced against me," Worf reminded her. "Yet only the Federation has supported my personal rights."

"Perhaps they have more to offer than we thought," Cali said slowly. The same impulse that had driven her here to discover the truth behind Worf's actions impelled her to make good on this deal. "Commander, you should watch your back for Klingons. All of you should."

"What do you mean?" he demanded, taking three strides to reach her. "Do you know about the *Ceres?"*

"No, no, you have far bigger worries than the *Ceres,"* she said, waving away his comment impatiently. "We've seen a thousand things that add up to an impending Klingon offensive. The *Reaper* is one of the last Sattar vessels in this area. The Collective has resolved to migrate deeper into Federation territory to avoid the coming hostilities."

"Is this true?" Worf demanded.

"You can check the movements of Sattar ships," Cali pointed out. "It's easy enough, except who watches things like that? By the way, I'm breaking ranks telling you this. It's not strictly dealable information until the area is vacated. But you could always find it on your own."

"Yes!" His eyes lit up with triumph. "Cali, you have been . . . most helpful."

"Just making square on the deal," she told him. "That's the only justice I've ever found in this galaxy."

"Perhaps," Worf agreed, finally returning her smile.

Cali turned to leave, but over her shoulder she couldn't resist a parting shot. "Oh, and Commander Worf, are you sure you don't want to inspect my aft cargo bay one more time?"